이 다 해
카이스트 무학과 2025년 입학
서울 한성과학고 졸

"발췌독, 구조 분석, 단서 찾기
세 가지 전략으로 병행하여 독해를 공략하자!"

■ 발췌독과 구조 분석으로 독해를 공략하자!

나는 지문 전체를 읽는 대신 발췌독으로 시간을 절약했어. 글을 처음 볼 때 첫 문장을 읽고 주제를 잡은 뒤, 곧바로 마지막 문장으로 가서 확인하는 방식이야. 만약 마지막 문장이 예시거나 중요하지 않으면 그 앞 문장까지 읽었지. 이렇게 하면 지문 속 핵심만 파악하면서도 빠르게 문제를 풀 수 있어.

하지만 발췌독을 잘하기에 앞서 문장 해석 실력이 뒷받침되어야 해. 그래서 나는 구조 분석 연습을 병행했어. 문장의 주어와 동사, 구와 절을 구분하며 분석했고, 헷갈리는 부분은 해설을 참고했어. 어려운 문장 몇 개는 직접 직독직해까지 하면서 연습했지. 이 과정을 반복하다 보니 긴 문장도 쉽게 이해할 수 있었고, 덤으로 어법 문제도 더 쉽게 풀 수 있었어.

■ 단어는 파생어와 함께 묶어서 암기하자!

단어를 공부할 때는 단순히 뜻만 외우는 게 아니라 품사 변화, 파생어, 유의어, 반의어까지 함께 묶어서 암기했어. 예를 들어 employ라는 단어를 외울 때 employment, employee, employer까지 정리하면서 관련된 단어들을 같이 암기했지.

따로 '단어 시험장'을 만들어 영어 철자만 적어두고, 그 옆에는 스스로 뜻과 파생어들을 채워 넣는 방식으로 연습했어. 처음에는 시간이 오래 걸렸지만 반복할수록 속도가 붙었고, 내가 능동적으로 단어와 뜻을 떠올릴 수 있었어.

덕분에 실제 시험에서 낯선 단어가 나와도 파생어나 어근을 통해 의미를 유추하여 풀었어. 이렇게 쌓은 어휘력은 21, 30, 42번처럼 어휘가 중요한 유형은 물론이고, 빈칸 추론처럼 고난도 유형에서도 큰 도움이 되었어.

그리고 단어만 따로 암기하는 것보다는 그날 풀고 공부했던 지문이 있다면, 그 지문에 나왔던 단어들을 다 암기한다는 생각으로 하는 것도 좋은 방법이야.

■ 발췌독의 한계는 단서 찾기로 극복하자!

글의 순서 찾기, 문장 삽입 문제는 앞서 말한 발췌독만으로는 해결하기 어려운 문제 유형이었어. 결국 각 문단이나 문장에서 정답의 단서를 얼마나 정확히 찾느냐가 핵심이었지. 그래서 나는 정답의 단서와 풀이 방향을 친절하게 제공하는 자이스토리 해설지를 적극적으로 활용했어. 문제를 풀면서 내가 찾은 단서와 자이스토리 해설이 제시하는 단서를 비교하면서, 평가원이 의도한 논리 전개 방식을 익혔지.

예를 들어, however나 therefore 같은 연결어, this나 these 같은 지시어, first, next, finally, then 같은 순서의 단서를 체크하고, 내가 찾은 단서 외에도 자이스토리가 제시하는 단서가 있는지, 더 확실하게 정답과 연관되는 단서가 있는지를 찾아보는 거지.

■ 자이스토리는 나만의 실전 훈련서!

내가 자이스토리 교재를 선택한 이유는 다름 아닌 실전 훈련이야. 〈자이스토리 영어 독해 기본〉 교재는 유형별로 단원이 나뉘어져 있어서 취약한 유형을 골라서 학습하기에 좋아. 게다가 교재 맨 뒤에는 '고난도 유형 독해 모의고사'가 있어서 비교적 짧은 시간으로도 딱 필요한 만큼만 실전 연습을 할 수 있어.

그리고 자이스토리를 실전에 활용하려면, 무조건 해설만 따라가기보단 스스로 생각하는 힘을 기르는 것이 중요해. '나 혼자 풀 때도 해설지의 단서만큼 필요한 단서들을 찾을 수 있을까?'를 늘 고민하면서 문제를 풀었더니, 처음에는 힘들었어도 나중에는 점차 해설지에 근접하는 만큼 정답의 단서를 발견할 수 있었어.

이런 과정을 거치다 보니 단순히 문제를 푸는 데서 끝나는 게 아니라, 어떤 사고 과정을 거쳐야 정답에 도달할 수 있는지도 자연스럽게 익히게 되었어.

My Story Xi Story [영어 독해 기본]

자이스토리 33개년 역사

- 수능 난이도 (상) 빨간색
- 수능 난이도 (중) 검정색
- 수능 난이도 (하) 파란색

2025
11. 13 7년 만에 응시자가 최대였던 역대급 수능. 칸트를 너무 많이 사랑했다! 국어의 과학 지문, 칸트 지문으로 초반부터 완전 난감 ㅠㅠ. 영어에서도 칸트, 홉스 지문이 최고 오답률, 윤리에서도 칸트 문제..! 수학에서도 고난도 문항들이 많이 출제되었지만, 이번 입시 전략 최대 변수는 사탐런의 난이도 불균형으로 인한 유불리 발생이 아닐까.

2024
11. 14 축축하고 어색한 수능 날씨! 국어, 수학 난이도는 그냥저냥 했는데 영어는 까탈스러움. 선택과목별 난이도 편차가 커서 표준점수 영향력이 커질 듯. 의대 증원으로 21년만에 최대로 폭발한 최상위권 N수생. 과탐 응시자는 줄고 사과탐 혼합 응시는 늘고, 수능 등급을 짐작하기 너무나 어렵고 ㅠㅠ

2023
11. 16 킬러를 없앤다고 했는데, 국어·영어는 매력적 오답들을 지뢰밭처럼 쫙 깔아 놨네ㅠㅠ 수학은 킬러 문제 대신에 무늬만 준킬러 문제들을 우중충하게 많이 깔아 놓고ㅠㅠ 서울대가 과탐Ⅱ과목 필수 응시를 폐지해서 표준 점수가 요동치지 않을까? 이과생들의 문과 침공이 또 다른 입시 변수가 될까?

2022
11. 17 따뜻했지만 가슴은 쿵쿵! 떨렸던 1교시 국어, 휴~ 그렇게 어렵진 않았어. 수학은 킬러 문항은 없었지만 까다로운 문제가 많아서 등급이~ ㅠㅠ. 영어는 듣기 속도가 평소보다 빨라서 귀가 빨간 토끼처럼 되어버렸네. 통합 수능 2년차, n수생들이 많아서 입시 전략 짜기 머리가 뽀개질듯!

2021
11. 18 창문을 열어도 춥지 않던 따뜻한 수능날이었어. 선택과목이 생겨서 안 그래도 혼란스러운 수학은 빈칸추론 문제의 등장으로 우리의 머리를 뜨겁게 달구는데... 마음을 다잡으며 풀기 시작한 영어는 듣기 뒷부분이 마치 독해처럼 길고 어려워서 채 식지 않은 열이 더욱 활활 타올랐어 @_@!

2020
12. 03 코로나 때문에 플라스틱 칸막이 장벽을 마주하고 치러진 수능. 이러한 수험생들의 고충을 고려해서인지 대체로 평이하게 나왔어! 그렇지만 수학 가형 30번 문제는 까다로웠지. 마스크를 끼고, 쉬는 시간마다 창문을 열어 환기를 해서 춥고, 방호복까지 등장한 수능이었지만, 처음 겪는 멘붕 상황에서도 무사히 수능을 치른 것에 엄지 척! 올려 주고 싶어 :)

2019
11. 14 별밭에 누워 너무 맑고 초롱한 눈으로, 8년 만에 바뀐 샤프로 수능을 보면 점수가 잘 나올까? 다행히 BIS비율 관련 지문을 제외하고 국어 난이도는 평이했어. 그러나 역시 수능은 수능! 수학 나형의 30번 문제, 좀 당황스럽더라. 국어와 영어는 까다롭지 않았지만 수학으로 변별력을 키운 2020 수능, 작은 실수가 뼈 때릴 듯!

2018
11. 15 국어 너.... 좀 낯설다? 중국 천문학은 뭐고, 〈출생기〉는 또 뭐야? 국어는 독서와 문학 모두 낯설은 결정체였어. 역대급 난이도의 국어를 풀고 나니 수학은 그래도 평이했어. 근데 작년보다 훨씬 어려워진 영어 때문에 또 다시 긴장 백배였지. 일명 "국어 쇼크, 역대 최저 등급컷!" but, 내가 어려웠으면 남도 어려웠을 것이니 마음 편히 먹으면 좋은 결과가 있을 듯^^

2017
11. 23 어서 와~ 수능 연기는 처음이지? 일주일 동안 마음을 다잡고 힘겹게 수능 시험을 맞이했는데 날씨도 마음도 추운 시험 날이었어. 국어의 낯선 시와 긴 독서 지문, 수학은 그래프 유형 추론 문제, 어려워진 탐구 영역. 여진 올까 불안한데 문제까지 어려웠지. 올해 수능은 우리들의 정신력과 의지로 헤쳐 낸 〈강 건너간 노래〉였어.

2016
11. 17 지문을 다 읽었는데 기억이 안 난다ㅠ 생소한 주제의 제시문과 복합 유형까지! 1교시 국어 영역은 길고 낯설었어. 2교시, 세트 문제가 없어지고, 언어적 독해력을 묻는 문제도 출제된 수학(나형), 안 그래도 이미 쿠크다스처럼 깨진 내 정신은 이제 먼지가 되어 사라짐:; 덕분에 상위권 변별력은 커졌으나 우리는 그 누구랑 다르게 오직 실력으로 당당히 대학 가자!!

2015
11. 12 수능 날인데 날씨가 따뜻했다. 평가원에서는 포근한 난이도 출제를 발표하셨다. 하지만 EBS 체감 연계율이 하락한 영어와 국어에서 수험생들은 당황했다. 수학 A형에서는 귀납적 추론 문제 때문에 중하위권 수험생의 심장이 요동쳤다. 모의평가보다 상승한 난이도로 '매운맛 수능'이 된 2016 수능!

2014
11. 13 입시 한파가 수험생들을 꽁꽁 얼리고ㅠ.ㅠ 낯선 지문으로 까다롭게 출제된 국어 A·B형 때문에 수능 체감 난이도 급상승! 무난한 난이도였던 수학에서는 실수와의 싸움이 등급을 결정하고 '쉬운 영어' 방침에 따라 변별력이 떨어진 영어의 등급 컷은 하늘을 찌를 듯... 들쭉날쭉 난이도로 수험생들을 당황시킨 2015 수능!

2013
11. 07 출제 위원도 수험생도 떨렸던 첫 수준별 수능!! 국어 A형의 과학 지문이 최상위권을 나누다... 수학 A·B형은 모두 주관식이 최고난도 문항으로 출제되고ㅠ.ㅠ 영어 B형에 상위권 학생들이 몰려 대입 당락의 변수가 될 전망!! 고난도 문제들은 EBS 연계와 전혀 무관했던 2014 수능~ 상위권 수험생들의 입시 경쟁이 치열할 터!

2012
11. 08 수준별 A·B형 체제로 개편되기 전의 마지막 수능 – 변별력 있는 고난도 문제가 여러 개 나와 상위권의 수학 실력을 제대로 세분화시키고... 빈칸 추론 유형 때문에 난이도가 급상승한 외국어가 또 한 번 수험생들의 발목을 잡았다고 –_–

2011
11. 10 쉬운 수능이었지만 복병은 존재~ 비문학 지문이 까다로웠던 언어 때문에 1교시부터 쩔쩔 매다! 수리 가형은 조금 어려웠지만, 난이도 조절에 실패해서 너무 쉬웠던 외국어는 점수가 대폭 상승?? 변별력을 잃은 수능 때문에 논술이 더더욱 중요해지고~

2010
11. 18 EBS와 연계 출제되었다고 하지만 체감 난이도는 더욱 더 상승↑ 비문학 지문 때문에 시간이 부족했던 언어와 최상위권 변별력 확보를 위해 확 어려워진 수리 영역~!! 외국어마저 어려운 어휘와 고난도 독해가 출제되어, EBS 믿고 공부한 수험생들 제대로 배신 당하다...

2009
11. 12 2009년을 휩쓴 신종 인플루엔자 때문에 공부하기도, 시험보기도 힘들었던 수험생들을 위해 언어와 수리는 몸풀기 난이도로 출제! 하지만 오후엔 강력 외국어 펀치를 날리고, 이어지는 들쑥날쑥 난이도의 사과탐 펀치... 이래저래 원서 접수로 머리가 뽀개질 2010 대학입시!!!

2008
11. 13 표준점수와 백분위가 다시 부활한 09수능! 언어와 외국어, 사·과탐은 대체로 평이하게 출제되었으나 ~ 수험생들 간의 변별력 확보를 위해서인지 유독 까다로운 문항이 많았던 수리 가형과 수리 나형 때문에 체감 난이도 급상승↑ 수리 영역이 주요 변수로 작용하다!

2007
11. 15 등급제가 처음으로 적용된 08수능! 언어와 수리 나형은 어렵게, 수리 가형, 사·과탐, 외국어는 평이한 수준으로 출제돼 등급 블랭크를 없애기 위한 등급 간 변별력 확보는 성공~ 하지만 등급 내 동점자의 대거 발생으로 단 1점 차이로 희비가 엇갈리다!

2006
11. 16 수리 나형과 외국어는 만만~, 언어와 사·과탐은 지난해보다 유독 까다롭고 어려웠던 07수능! 결국 언어와 사·과탐 점수가 당락의 변수로 작용하다. 선택과목 간 난이도 조절 실패로, 휴~ 앞으로는 재수도 힘들다는데...

2005
11. 23 2006 수능 기상도 : '맑다가 차차 흐림'– "너무 쉬워어. 하하~"(언어 영역 종료 후)→"머릴 얻어맞은 느낌이야."(수리 영역 종료 후)→"그냥 찍었어."(외국어 영역 종료 후)→"망했어!!"(탐구 영역 종료 후)

2004
11. 17 ♪♬외로워도 슬퍼도 나는 안 울어~. 언어 듣기에 느닷없이 등장한 캔디 주제곡은 일종의 복선이었을까…. 수험생들을 1교시는 웃게, 2·3교시는 내리 울게 만들었던 2005 수능, 그래도 모의평가 수준으로 평이하게 출제된 데자뷰 효과 덕이었는지 중·상위권 인플레 또 다시 야기.

2003
11. 05 대체로 교과서에 충실한 평이한 수준의 문제 출제가 이루어졌으나, 예상 지문 출제와 사상 첫 복수 정답 인정 논란으로 말도 많고 탈도 많던 2004 수능, 재수생의 연이은 강세로 고교 4학년 시대 가속화 되다!

2002
11. 06 너무 쉬웠던 2001 수능과 너무 어려웠던 2002 수능 사이의 적정선을 유지하며 널뛰기 논란을 일순간 잠재우는 듯 했으나, 고3의 학력 수준을 고려하지 않은 문제 출제로 난이도 조절 실패~

2001
11. 07 터무니없이 어려운 문제에 수험생들 쩔쩔~. 작년과는 반대로 언어와 수리가 오히려 점수 하락을 주도했으며, 쉬운 수능에 눈높이가 맞춰진 수험생들의 체감 난이도 상승으로 1, 2교시 이후 시험 중도 포기가 속출했다. 난이도 조절 大실패! 수능 평균 66점 하락↓

2000
11. 15 수능 만점자 66명, 풍년이로세! 수능 무용론이 나돌 정도로 변별력 상실 지속~ 변별력을 잃은 언어와 수리가 점수밭으로 작용하며 널뛰기식 난이도가 도마 위에 올랐다.

1999
11. 17 변별력을 아예 상실하다! 유독 깐깐했던 언어 영역을 제외하고 대체로 작년보다 쉽게 출제되면서 또다시 중·상위권 인플레 현상 야기. 1명의 수능 만점자 배출과 함께 300점 이상을 25만명까지 늘린 2000 수능!!

1998
11. 18 쉽게 낸다는 애초 발표와는 달리 수리가 어렵고 까다롭게 출제되는 바람에 수험생들 배신감에 부들부들~. 그러나 나머지 영역이 총점의 하락폭을 상쇄시켜 평균 27점 상승↑ 수능에서 첫 만점자가 탄생했으나, 쉽기로 소문난 99 수능 하마터면 만점자가 쏟아질 뻔!—;

1997
11. 19 교과서 내에서 자주 접해온 평이한 수준의 문제와 기출과 유사한 유형의 다수 출제로 평균 42점 상승↑ 변별력 논란을 일으키며, 상·하위권이 좁았던 기존의 항아리형에서 중·하위권이 비대한 꽃병형 점수대 분포로 변화!

1996
11. 13 1교시 언어가 예상보다 쉬워 내쉬던 안도의 한숨을 여지없이 끊어버린 수리와 사·과탐의 연이은 高난이도 출제는 재수생들을 두 번 죽이는 일이었다! 수능 사적으로 볼 때, 바야흐로 이 시기는 수리 주관식 문제와 총점 400점이 처음 도입되고, 영어 듣기가 17문항으로 늘어난 수능 과도기 시점.

1995
11. 22 영역별 난이도 예상과 달라 당황~ 수리&외국어=easy, 언어&사·과탐=hard 특히 생소한 지문으로 어렵게 1교시 언어와 통합 교과 소재의 高난이도 사·과탐이 수능 총점 초토화~! 지난해보다 평균 7점 down↓ 96 수능 시험 0점 지난해 3배!

1994
11. 23 수능 연 1회 시행의 시발점이었으나, 수능 高난이도 연속 행진 계속! 10문항이 늘어난 수리와 외국어는 무난했으나, 의외의 복병이었던 사·과탐의 난이도가 특히 높아 점수를 마구 갉아먹다.

영어는 항상 1등급입니다.

고교학점제 실시!
내신 5등급제 실시!

입시변수가 다양해졌지만, 영어 실력 향상은
언제나 최고의 결과를 보장합니다.

자이스토리는 영어 실력 향상을 위해
독해 문제를 유형별로 분류하고,
각 문제 유형에 맞는 이해 순서와 논리적 풀이법을 제공하여
빠르게 정답을 찾는 방법을 습득하도록 하였습니다.

각 유형마다 따라가기만 하면
저절로 독해 유형 공부가 되는
'자이 쌤's Follow Me!'가 영어 1등급으로 가는
가장 똑똑한 독해 공부법입니다.
꼭 따라서 공부해 보세요.

문제를 풀고 난 이후에는
정답의 근거와 오답 함정까지 알려주는 입체 첨삭 해설을 통해
모든 문제를 완전히 이해하면서 공부할 수 있습니다.

이 책의 마지막 페이지를 넘길 때쯤
여러분은 이미 영어 1등급에 도달해 있을 것입니다.

– 대한민국 No.1 수능 문제집 **자이스토리** –

🍀 내신＋수능 **1등급** 완성 학습 계획표 [26일]

Day	페이지	틀린 문제 / 헷갈리는 문제 번호 적기	날짜	복습 날짜
1	A 10~21		월 일	월 일
2	B 22~31		월 일	월 일
3	C 32~43		월 일	월 일
4	D 44~57		월 일	월 일
5	E 58~71		월 일	월 일
6	F 72~84		월 일	월 일
7	G 86~99		월 일	월 일
8	H 100~111		월 일	월 일
9	I 112~125		월 일	월 일
10	J 126~143		월 일	월 일
11	K 144~155		월 일	월 일
12	L 156~167		월 일	월 일
13	M **1** 168~179		월 일	월 일
14	**2** 180~189		월 일	월 일
15	**3** 190~203		월 일	월 일
16	N 204~216		월 일	월 일
17	O 218~237		월 일	월 일
18	P 238~257		월 일	월 일
19	Q 258~275		월 일	월 일
20	R 276~285		월 일	월 일
21	286~293		월 일	월 일
22	S 294~305		월 일	월 일
23	306~315		월 일	월 일
24	모의 **1회** 318~323		월 일	월 일
25	모의 **2회** 324~329		월 일	월 일
26	모의 **3회** 330~335		월 일	월 일

● 나는 ＿＿＿＿＿＿＿＿＿ 대학교 ＿＿＿＿＿＿＿＿＿ 학과 ＿＿＿＿＿＿학번이 된다.

● 磨斧作針 (마부작침) – 도끼를 갈아 바늘을 만든다. (아무리 어려운 일이라도 끈기 있게 노력하면 이룰 수 있음을 비유하는 말)

🍀 집필진 · 감수진 선생님들

🌸 자이스토리는 내신 + 수능 준비를 가장 효과적으로
할 수 있도록 수능, 모의평가, 학력평가 기출문제를
개념별, 유형별, 난이도별로 수록하였습니다.
그리고 명강의로 소문난 학교·학원 선생님들께서 명쾌한
해설을 입체 첨삭으로 집필하셨습니다.

[집필진]

김현아	서울 가락고등학교	이탁균	서울 대일외국어고등학교
박형우	안산 경안고등학교	이혜은	서울 잠실고등학교
신수진	서울 한영외국어고등학교	정유진	시흥 은행고등학교
윤혜경	부천 소사고등학교	한규리	안산 성안고등학교
이아영	오산 매홀고등학교	수경 English Lab.	

중요·핵심 문제 동영상 강의

자이스토리 유튜브 채널
Blair Lee(블쌤영어), 홍민석

[특별 감수진]

노효신	옥천 옥천고등학교	김정원	부산 영어의정원	Jennifer Kim	김해 일타수학원
이지윤	평택 이충고등학교	신인철	부산 오아시스영어학원		
황규만	대전 대전한빛고등학교	천지현	부산 연세바른영어		

[감수진]

강동운	제주 이엠스쿨	박수진	부산 제이엔씨영어학원	이지영	부산 모멘텀입시영어학원
곽수정	마산 이앤탑삼성영어학원	박윤지	강릉 알파인영어학원	이현미	광주 IGSE풍암학원
곽혜진	순천 H&J ENGLISH	박정선	평창 잉글리쉬클럽	이홍원	대전 홍티영어학원
권성진	경산 굿쌤영어수능내신전문학원	백은비	부산 비앙카영어	이희락	목포 브릭스영어학원
권수현	고양 (일산식사)종로엠학원	백은혜	인천 153은쌤영어	임나영	창원 엘리아잉글리쉬
권순진	서울 영어의영토	서슬기	수원 라라잉글리쉬영어학원	임진희	진해 어썸영어학원
김가영	진주 김가영영어학원	서재원	대전 최성학원	장의주	평택 티클래스학원
김경희	대구 지안영어학원	성현미	진주 잉글리쉬파크	장혜민	서울 (목동)리뉴어학원
김나은	군산 애플영어학원	소민	대전 T&G 어학원	전상욱	군포 멘토에듀학원
김민희	군포 에임영어학원	소지연	서울 코너스톤영어	전혜민	안양 지앤비어학원
김소연	부산 대치명인학원	송수진	광주 송수진마스터영어학원	정선미	창원 유어썬영어학원
김아랑	김포 Irene's ENGLISH	신영지	부산 옥스포드영어	정승연	익산 인투이션영어학원
김유진	울산 상징영어학원	양선미	울산 로제타스톤영어학원	정아림	대구 클로에영어학원
김윤상	고양 이엔학원	오세이	양주 (옥정)종로엠스쿨	정온유	전주 다온영어전문학원
김은지	김해 (삼계)브라이트영어학원	오현진	수원 파머스메타국제학원	정위경	포항 클로이영어
김종균	서산 제이쌤학원	유다언	고양 (삼송)대세영어학원	정유라	대구 독쭝영어
김지영	대구 김지영영어	유지아	안양 (평촌)씬디영어	조미혜	양주 (옥정)KU영어학원
김창옥	전주 더베스트영어학원	유하선	포항 비상잉글리시아이(초곡점)	조성제	서울 (금천)하이스트학원
김하경	부산 김하경영어	유형주	서울 마크영어학원	조아라	부산 벨어학원
김학수	용인 CL PAMUS어학원	윤사희	용인 구갈 위클당당	조약돌	부산 중동벨라학원
김현우	서울 (개포)청진학원	윤새롬	부산 샤론영어	조은경	용인 (수지)B&I영어학원
김효빈	울산 런업잉글리쉬	윤서진	창원 상승영어글로리학원	조은경	대전 프라우드영어학원
류영리	구미 프라우드영어	윤현미	천안 비비안의잉글리쉬클래스	주예솔	부산 안락조일외국어학원
류정임	광주 퍼펙트영어학원	이경희	파주 (운정)이쌤영어교습소	최명희	대구 EBRI CLUB
문상헌	안동 에이원영어	이미현	서울 강남탑브레인	최병국	인천 브라이언영어교습소
문성호	김해 감승스파르타영수학원	이민정	광주 (서구)롱맨어학원	최선애	용인 루시어학원(동탄)루시어학원
문성훈	울산 원트영어전문학원	이연주	울산 외대HS어학원	최희정	성남 (분당)SJ클쌤영어학원
박동현	진주 포커스어학원	이유근	부산 링구아어학원(동래본원)	한명숙	부산 벨라영어
박보현	인천 효성이스턴어학원	이유정	진주 에이블영어학원	한민지	광명 스터닝에듀
박서준	울산 해늘어학원	이인혁	구리 프리미엄영어학원	함석진	시흥 함쌤영어학원
박성범	전주 DYB 최선어학원	이재강	인천 캘빈에듀학원	홍수영	부산 위너스영어
박소영	대구 산드라영어학원	이정민	서울 메가스터디온라인	황보훈	제주 이루다잉글리쉬학원

🍀 차 례

🍀 완벽한 기출 분석, 유형별 풀이법 훈련으로 내신 + 수능  1등급 완성

1️⃣ 독해 유형 분석 + 독해력 UP 구문 특강

수능을 철저히 분석하여 독해 유형별로 기출 문제를 정리했으며 유형에 대한 기본 개념을 잡을 수 있도록 하였습니다. 또, 문제 분석 단계별로 유형 풀이 비법을 익힐 수 있습니다.

- **유형 풀이 비법** : 좀 더 빠르고 정확하게 문제에 접근하는 풀이법 정리
- **어휘 및 표현** : 유형별로 시험에 자주 나오는 어휘와 표현 수록
- **독해력 UP 구문 특강** : 자주 나오는 중요한 문법 및 구문을 분석·정리
- **Check Test** : 독해력 UP 구문 특강 복습을 위한 구문 확인 문제

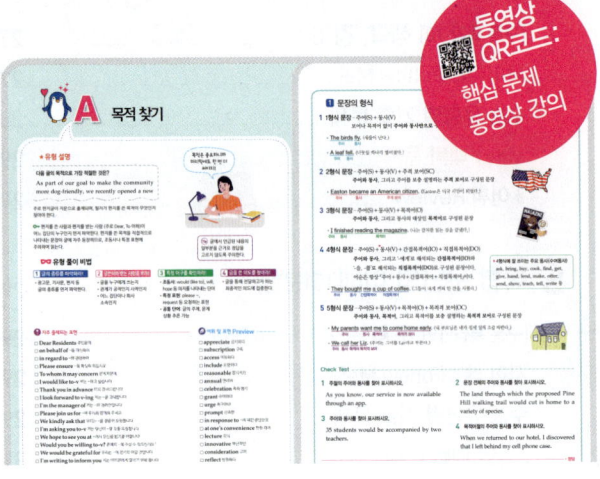

동영상 QR코드: 핵심 문제 동영상 강의

2️⃣ 자이 쌤's Follow Me!

대표 유형 문제를 강의식으로 설명하여 읽기만 해도 독해 학습이 저절로 이해되도록 구성하였습니다.

- **1st, 2nd, 3rd** : 유형별 효과적인 문제 접근법 제시
- **빈칸 문제** : 직접 빈칸을 채우면서 문제를 해결하는 스킬 연습
- **수능 Tip** : 어려운 구문을 심화학습 할 수 있도록 수록

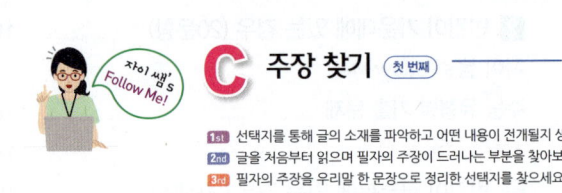

3️⃣ 최신 기출 지문 – 구문 서술형 문제 수록

학교 시험에서 서술형 문제가 늘어남에 따라 최신 기출 지문과 구문 학습에 따른 구문 서술형 문제를 특별 수록했습니다.

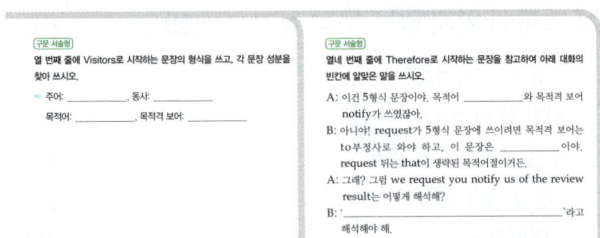

4️⃣ 수능 유형별 기출 문제

독해 유형별 풀이법을 쉽게 이해하고 훈련할 수 있도록 꼼꼼히 유형을 분류하고 난이도별로 문항을 배열하였습니다. 이를 통해 한층 독해 공부가 쉬워질 것입니다.

- **난이도**: ✖✖✖-상, ✖✖✿-중, ✖✿✿-하
- **출처 표시**: 실시연도 표시
  - 고1 2025(9월)/18: 2025년 9월에 실시한 고1 학력평가 18번
  - 고2 2025(9월)/21: 2025년 9월에 실시한 고2 학력평가 21번

5️⃣ 1등급, 2등급 대비 문제 선별

1등급, 2등급을 가르는 고난이도 문제들을 별도로 표시하여 수록하였습니다. 한 문제씩 꼼꼼히 풀어가면 반드시 1등급에 도달할 수 있습니다.

- ⭐**1등급 대비** : 어려운 지문 또는 정답을 쉽게 찾기 힘든, 1등급을 가르는 최고난도 문제
- ⭐**2등급 대비** : 헷갈리기 쉬운 매력적 오답이 있어 정답률이 낮은, 2등급을 가르는 고난도 문제

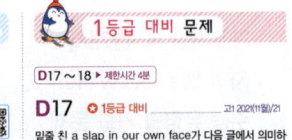

단어장 QR코드: 해당 단원 단어 PDF 제공

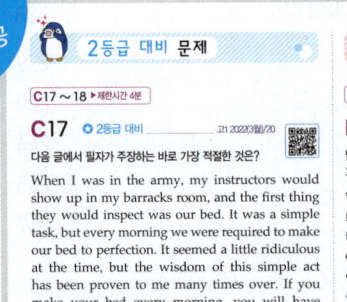

6  고난도 유형 독해 모의고사 3회

2025~2023 고2 3월 학력평가 문제 중 고난도 유형에
해당하는 12문항을 선별하여 어려워지는 시험에 대비하도록
하였습니다.

1회 고난도 유형 독해 모의고사 고2

고2 3월 학

01 고2 2025(3월)/21

밑줄 친 keeping the ball on a slope가 다음
글에서 의미하는 바로 가장 적절한 것은? [3점]

The concept of ecosystem states should be familiar
to anyone with a home vegetable garden. The
garden is a small ecosystem that the grower
attempts to keep in a specific state, namely the

02

다음 글의 주

If the brai
name, wh
and not t
something
when it c

7 1등급 대비 · 2등급 대비 문제 단계별 해설

D 18 정답 ② ● 1등급 대비 [정답률 58%]

2등 **1등급?** 밑줄 친 부분의 어휘가 흔히 쓰이는 어휘가 아니라서 본문의 내용과
의미를 연결하여 어려운 1등급 대비 문제이다. 글의 앞부분을 요약한 these
luxurious conditions가 밑줄 친 부분에 연결되기 때문에, 앞서 어떤 상황이
설명되었는지 파악하면 어렵지 않게 밑줄 친 부분의 의미를 파악할 수 있다.

문제 분석
왜 이 문제가 등급을 가르는
대비 문제인지를 설명하고
정답을 찾는 데 가장 핵심이
되는 단서를 설명했습니다.

| 문제 풀이 순서 |

1st 밑줄 친 부분이 포함된 문장을 읽고, 글의 내용을 예상한다.

| 밑줄 친 부분이 포함된 문장 | 농지는 주위를 둘러싼 자연 지대에 비해 영양분과 물이 풍족하게 채워져 있기 때문에 단세3 그 지역의 어떤 잡초라도 원하는 고급 부동산이 된다. |

▶ 영양분과 물이 풍족해 채워진 농지가 결국은 어떤 잡초라도 원하는 '고급 부동산'이 된다고 했으므로, '고급 부동산'은 영양분과 물이 풍족히 채워진 땅이라고 예상할 수 있다. 글 전반적으로 그러한 땅에 관한 설명이 이어질 것이다.

문제 풀이 순서
단순히 정답만 설명하는 것이
아니라 정답을 찾아가는 과정을
단계별로 자세히 설명함으로써
앞으로 만날 고난도 문제를
스스로 풀 수 있도록
훈련시킵니다.

| 선택지 분석 |

① 스스로 얼굴을 때림으로써 무언가를 깨닫게 되어 미래 세대에게 긍정적인 영향을 준다는 등의 내용이 아니다.
② 화석 연료에 대한 내용이고, 천연자원 부족에 대한 내용이 아니다.
③ 화석 연료 생산의 정점이라기보다는 생산의 원인이 우리 스스로에게 있다는 내용이다.
④ 산업 활동들을 가속시키로써 우리가 긍정적인 동기를 제공하고 있지만, 우리의 잘못된 생각까지 않고 화석 연료 산업을 탓한다는 내용이다.
⑤ 기후 변화를 야기하는 산업 활동들이 우리들의 요구로 인해 생겨난다는 것을 인지하지 못한다는 것이지, 그것을 깨닫고 개별적으로 환경 문제를 다루고 있다는 것이 아니다.

선택지 분석
오답 선택지까지 다시 한번
완벽히 분석하여 더이상 오답의
함정에 빠지지 않도록 합니다.

8 입체 첨삭 해설!

글의 주제
지문의 내용을 한 눈에 파악할 수
있도록 주제를 제시하였습니다.

자이 쌤 제공 문제편에 실리지 않은 자이 쌤을 홈페이지에서 제공해드립니다.

자이 쌤's Follow Me! - 홈페이지에서 제공

L 09 정답 ② *박쥐와 나방의 생존 경쟁

유사 관계대명사 (선행사·주절)
As always happens with natural selection, / bats and their prey
/ have been engaged in a life-or-death sensory arms race / for
millions of years. //
자연 선택에서 항상 일어나듯이 / 박쥐와 그 먹잇감은 / 생사를 가르는 감각 군비 경쟁에 참여해
왔다 / 수백만 년 동안 //
It's believed / that hearing in moths arose / specifically in
response to the threat / of being eaten by bats. //
여겨진다 / 나방의 청력이 생겨난 것으로 / 특히 위협에 대한 반응으로 / 박쥐에게 잡아먹히는 //
(Not all insects can hear.) //
모든 곤충이 들을 수 있는 것은 아니다 // 핵심 문장
Over millions of years, / moths have evolved the ability / to
detect sounds at ever higher frequencies, / and, as they have, /
the frequencies of bats' vocalizations have risen, too. //
수백만 년 동안 / 나방은 능력을 진화시켰고 / 계속 더 높아진 주파수의 소리를 감지하는 /
그것들이 그랬던 것에 따라 / 박쥐의 발성 주파수도 높아졌다 //
Some moth species have also evolved / scales on their wings
and a fur-like coat on their bodies, /
일부 나방 종은 또한 진화시켰다 / 그것들의 날개에 비늘과 몸에 털 같은 외피를 //
both act as "acoustic camouflage," / by absorbing sound waves
/ in the frequencies emitted by bats, / thereby preventing those
sound waves from bouncing back. //
둘 다 '음향 위장'의 역할을 하는데 / 음파를 흡수함으로써 / 박쥐에 의해 방출되는 주파수의 /
음파가 되돌아가는 것을 방지한다 //

• specifically @ 구체적으로 말하면   • threat ⑪ 위협
• insect ⑪ 곤충   • evolve ⑪ 진화시키다   • vocalization ⑪ 발성
• scale ⑪ 비늘   • acoustic ⑧ 음향의   • absorb ⑪ 흡수하다

자연 선택에서 항상 그렇듯이, 박쥐와 그 먹잇감은 수백만 년 동안 생사를
가르는 감각 군비 경쟁에 참여해 왔다. 나방의 청력은 특히 박쥐에게
잡아먹히는 위협에 대한 반응으로 생겨난 것으로 여겨진다. (모든 곤충이
들을 수 있는 것은 아니다.) 수백만 년 동안, 나방은 계속 더 높아진

다음 빈칸에 들어갈 말로 가장 적절한 것을 고르시오? [3점]
① been in a fierce war over scarce food sources
부족한 먹이 자원을 둘러싼 격렬한 전쟁 속에 있어
② been engaged in a life-or-death sensory arms race
③ invented weapons that are not part of their bodies
④ evolved to cope with other noise-producing wildlife
⑤ adapted to flying in night skies absent of any lights

직독직해
의미 중심의 문장별 끊어
읽기 표시와 해석을 달아주어
바로바로 해석할 수 있도록
돕습니다.

왜 정답
정답이 되는 핵심 이유와
문제풀이를 알기 쉽고 자세하게
수록하였습니다.

핵심 문장
글의 핵심문장을
표시하였습니다.

구문 풀이
해석과 지문 이해에 기본이
되는 구문 설명을 직접 첨삭하여
문법과 독해 실력 모두를 키울 수
있습니다.

어휘 풀이
어휘의 뜻을 정리하여 독해를
하면서 어휘 실력 또한 키울 수
있게 하였습니다.

단서
문제를 푸는 데 핵심이 되는
어구나 문장을 표시했습니다.

선택지 첨삭 해설
정확한 정답을 확인할 수 있도록
선택지를 분석했습니다.

글의 흐름
고난도 지문의 경우, 글의 전개
방식을 한눈에 파악할 수 있도록
도표로 정리하여 수록하였습니다.

배경 지식

* 창경궁과 덕수궁
창경궁은 조선의 궁궐 중 하나로, 조선의 제9대 임금인 성종이 1483년에
할머니, 어머니, 작은어머니를 위해 지은 궁궐이다. 임진왜란 때 경복궁, 창덕궁
등과 함께 불에 탔다가 광해군 때 다시 세워졌다. 창덕궁과 담을 사이에 두고
이웃하고 있어 '동궐'이라고도 불린다.
덕수궁은 세조의 큰손자인 월산대군의 개인 저택이었다. 원래 명칭은 경운궁
(慶運宮)이지만, 1907년 고종이 이곳에 살 때
고종의 장수를 빈다는 뜻에서 덕수궁(德壽宮)으로
개칭되었다. 임진왜란 때 선조가 한성으로 돌아온
뒤 이곳을 임시거처로 사용하였다.

배경 지식
지문과 관련 있는 알아두면 유용한
배경 지식을 수록하였습니다.

왜 정답? ★★★ [정답률 32%]
자연 선택에서 박쥐와 그 먹잇감(= 나방)이 한 것
박쥐: 발성 주파수가 높아짐 windward
나방: ① 청력이 생겨남 ② 더 높아진 주파수의 소리를 감지함 ③ 음파 흡수를 위한
비늘과 외피를 진화시킴
▶ 서로가 살아남기 위해 감각을 발달시킨 과정을 설명하고 있으므로, 정답은
② '생사를 가르는 감각 군비 경쟁에 참여해 온 것이다.

왜 오답?
③ 박쥐와 나방은 각자가 우위를 점할 수 있는 무기를 발명하였으나, 그것은 청력, 비늘,
외피와 같은 신체 감각의 일부다.
(► 오답: 몸의 일부라고 표현했다면, 즉 not이 없다면 답이 될 수 있다.)
④ 박쥐나 나방 외에 다른 야생동물에 관한 언급은 없다.
⑤ 깜깜한 밤하늘에서의 비행에 관한 언급은 없다. 함정

• 글의 흐름

도입	입장을 취하는 것은 당신의 위치를 알리는 집합 지점이 되기 때문에 중요하다
전개	최고의 마케팅은 당신의 관점을 보여줌으로써 고객들이 그것에 동의하고 당신이 마케팅하는 것을 원하게 만드는 것이다
부연	것들은 바뀌어도 고정 돼 있지만 당신이 입장의 집합 지점은 그 이면의 가치와 의미를 나타낸다

★ [동사 vs. 준동사] 바로알기! KEY
• 모든 문장에는 원칙적으로 주어와 동사가 있어야 한다.
• to부정사, 동명사, 분사 등의 준동사는 문장에서 동사의 역할을 할 수 없다.

★ 등위접속사 어법 특강
- 접속사는 동일한 품사나 문법적으로 같은 성분을 연결하는 것으로 등위접속사에
는 and, or, but, so, for 등이 있다.
• Peter prepared bread and bacon for lunch.
(Peter는 점심으로 빵과 베이컨을 준비했다.)
• He cut his finger, but he didn't go to a doctor.
(그는 손가락을 베었지만, 병원에 가지 않았다.)

구문 서술형
정답 Visitors can easily find your artworks located
해석 방문객들이 입구 근처에 위치한 당신의 작품을 쉽게 찾을 수 있다.
→ find는 5형식 동사로 자주 쓰이며, 목적어 your artworks를 보충 설명하는
과거분사 located가 목적격 보어로 보이고 있다.

특별 부록 – 휴대용 단어장

이 책에 나오는 모든
핵심 어휘를 정리해
놓은 단어장 부록을
휴대하기 편리하게
구성하였습니다.

정답률
교육청 자료, 기타 기관 공지
자료와 내부 검토 과정을 거쳐
제시됩니다.

꿀팁
문제를 쉽고 빨리 풀 수 있는
특별한 꿀팁입니다.

주의
단서를 잘못 이용할 가능성이
있을 때, 올바른 풀이로 나아갈
수 있도록 합니다.

함정
빠지기 쉬운 함정을 체크해
주고 해결할 수 있는 방법을
제시하였습니다.

KEY: 문제 속 어법 설명
해당 어법 사항이 문제로
출제됐을 때 정답을 찾는 가장
핵심적인 방법을 설명했습니다.

어법 특강
핵심 어법 사항을 한 번 더 짚어
주어 심화학습을 돕습니다.

왜 오답
오답 선택지와 매력적 오답을
상세히 분석해 오답의 함정에
빠지지 않도록 하였습니다.

매력적 오답
오답을 정답이라고 착각하게
되는 이유에 대해 철저하게
분석하고 대책까지 제시합니다.

매력적 오답 이유
매력적 오답이 되는 이유를
자세히 설명합니다.

구문 서술형 해설
구문 서술형 문제의 정답, 해석,
해설을 제공합니다.

🍀 문항 배열 및 구성 [기출 543제 + 구문 서술형 87제]

❶ 최신 4개년 고1 학력평가 독해 유형 전 문항 수록 (2025년~2022년) [420문항]

• 연 4회 실시되는 고1 학력평가는 교육청이 실시하는 공식 시험으로
  학생들의 영어 실력을 측정할 수 있는 우수한 문제들입니다.
  그래서 최신 4개년 고1 학력평가 전문항을 수록했습니다.

❷ 고1 학력평가 독해 우수 문항 (2021년~2020년) [87문항]

• 매년, 매월 출제 난이도가 다른 학력평가에 대비하기 위해
  2021~2020 학력평가 우수 문항들을 선별해 수록하였습니다.

❸ 최신 기출 지문 – 구문 서술형 문제 수록 [87문항]

• 학교 시험에서 서술형 문제가 늘어남에 따라 최신 기출 지문과 구문 학습에 따른
  구문 서술형 문제를 특별 수록했습니다.

❹ 독해 기출 유형 분석을 통한 문항 분류와 최신 기출 문제 우선 배치

• 독해 문제 유형별, 난이도별로 문항을 배열하였고,
  최신 학력평가 문제들을 앞쪽에 배치했습니다.
• 난이도에 따라 2등급 대비 문제, 1등급 대비 문제를 별도로 구성했습니다.

❺ 최신 3개년 고2 3월 학력평가 – 고난도 유형 모의고사 수록 [36문항]

• 회차별 문제 구성 (12문항)

01번 – 밑줄 친 부분의 의미 찾기	07번 – 빈칸 완성하기
02번 – 주제 찾기	08번 – 글의 순서 정하기
03번 – 제목 찾기	09번 – 주어진 문장 넣기
04번 – 어법에 맞지 않는 낱말 찾기	10번 – 요약문 완성하기
05번 – 문맥에 맞지 않는 낱말 찾기	11번 ┐ 장문의 이해
06번 – 빈칸 완성하기	12번 ┘

[독해 기본 문제 구성표]

실시 연도	출처	3월	6월	9월	11월	합	비고
2025	고1 전국연합학력평가	28	28	28		84	최신 기출 지문을 활용한 구문 서술형 문제 87 문항
	고2 전국연합학력평가	12				12	
2024	고1 전국연합학력평가	28	28	28	28	112	
	고2 전국연합학력평가	12				12	
2023	고1 전국연합학력평가	28	28	28	28	112	
	고2 전국연합학력평가	12				12	
2022	고1 전국연합학력평가	28	28	28	28	112	
2021	고1 전국연합학력평가	8	16	22	26	72	고1 우수 문항 선별 수록
2020	고1 전국연합학력평가	3	3	3	6	15	
총 문항 수						543	

영어 독해 기본

A 목적 찾기

★유형 설명

> 다음 글의 목적으로 가장 적절한 것은?
>
> As part of our goal to make the community more dog-friendly, we recently opened a new

주로 편지글이 지문으로 출제되며, 필자가 편지를 쓴 목적이 무엇인지 찾아야 한다.

🔑 편지를 쓴 사람과 편지를 받는 사람 (주로 Dear, To 이하)이 어느 집단의 누구인지 먼저 파악한다. 편지를 쓴 목적을 직접적으로 나타내는 문장이 글에 자주 등장하므로, 조동사나 특정 표현에 주의하며 읽는다.

목적은 중요하니까 마지막에도 한 번 더 써야지!

(Tip) 글에서 언급된 내용의 일부분을 근거로 정답을 고르지 않도록 주의한다.

🎭 유형 풀이 비법

1 글의 종류를 파악하라!
• 광고문, 기사문, 편지 등 글의 종류를 먼저 파악한다.

2 글쓴이와 받는 사람을 보라!
• 글을 누구에게 쓰는지
• 관계가 공적인지 사적인지
• 어느 집단이나 회사 소속인지

3 특정 어구를 확인하라!
• 조동사: would (like to), will, hope 등 의지를 나타내는 단어
• 특정 표현: please ~, request 등 요청하는 표현
• 공통 단어: 글의 주제, 문제 상황 추론 가능

4 글을 쓴 의도를 찾아라!
• 글을 통해 전달하고자 하는 최종적인 의도에 집중한다.

📍 자주 출제되는 표현

☐ Dear Residents 주민들께
☐ on behalf of ~을 대신하여
☐ in regard to ~와 관련하여
☐ Please ensure ~을 확실히 하십시오
☐ To whom it may concern 관계자분께
☐ I would like to-v 저는 ~하고 싶습니다
☐ Thank you in advance 미리 감사드립니다
☐ I look forward to v-ing 저는 ~을 고대합니다
☐ I'm the manager of 저는 ~의 관리인입니다
☐ Please join us for ~에 우리와 함께해 주세요
☐ We kindly ask that 우리는 ~을 정중히 요청합니다
☐ I'm asking you to-v 저는 당신이 ~할 것을 요청합니다
☐ We hope to see you at ~에서 당신을 뵙기를 바랍니다
☐ Would you be willing to-v? 흔쾌히 ~해 주실 수 있으신가요?
☐ We would be grateful for 우리는 ~에 감사히 여길 것입니다
☐ I'm writing to inform you 저는 여러분에게 알리기 위해 씁니다
☐ Many thanks for your cooperation 협조해 주셔서 매우 감사합니다

🗨 어휘 및 표현 Preview

☐ appreciate 감사하다
☐ subscription 구독
☐ access 이용하다
☐ include 포함하다
☐ reasonable 합리적인
☐ annual 연례의
☐ celebration 축하 행사
☐ grant 수여하다
☐ urge 촉구하다
☐ prompt 신속한
☐ in response to ~에 대한 응답으로
☐ at one's convenience 편한 때에
☐ lecture 강의
☐ innovative 혁신적인
☐ consideration 고려
☐ reflect 반영하다
☐ performance 성과

1 문장의 형식

1 1형식 문장 – 주어(S) + 동사(V)

보어나 목적어 없이 **주어와 동사만으로** 구성된 문장

• <u>The birds</u> <u>fly</u>. (새들이 난다.)
　주어　　　동사

• <u>A leaf</u> <u>fell</u>. (나뭇잎 하나가 떨어졌다.)
　주어　　동사

2 2형식 문장 – 주어(S) + 동사(V) + 주격 보어(SC)

주어와 동사, 그리고 주어를 보충 설명하는 **주격 보어**로 구성된 문장

• <u>Easton</u> <u>became</u> <u>an American citizen</u>. (Easton은 미국 시민이 되었다.)
　주어　　　동사　　　　주격 보어

3 3형식 문장 – 주어(S) + 동사(V) + 목적어(O)

주어와 동사, 그리고 동사의 대상인 **목적어**로 구성된 문장

• <u>I</u> <u>finished</u> <u>reading the magazine</u>. (나는 잡지를 읽는 것을 끝냈다.)
　주어　동사　　　목적어

4 4형식 문장 – 주어(S) + *동사(V) + 간접목적어(IO) + 직접목적어(DO)

주어와 동사, 그리고 '-에게'로 해석되는 **간접목적어(IO)**와
'-을, -를'로 해석되는 **직접목적어(DO)**로 구성된 문장이다.
어순은 항상 「주어 + 동사 + 간접목적어 + 직접목적어」이다.

• <u>They</u> <u>bought</u> <u>me</u> <u>a cup of coffee</u>. (그들이 내게 커피 한 잔을 사줬다.)
　주어　　동사　간접목적어　직접목적어

> *4형식에 잘 쓰이는 주요 동사(수여동사)
> ask, bring, buy, cook, find, get,
> give, hand, lend, make, offer,
> send, show, teach, tell, write 등

5 5형식 문장 – 주어(S) + 동사(V) + 목적어(O) + 목적격 보어(OC)

주어와 동사, 목적어, 그리고 목적어를 보충 설명하는 **목적격 보어**로 구성된 문장

• <u>My parents</u> <u>want</u> <u>me</u> <u>to come home early</u>. (내 부모님은 내가 집에 일찍 오길 바란다.)
　주어　　　　동사　목적어　　목적격 보어

• <u>We</u> <u>call</u> <u>her</u> <u>Liz</u>. (우리는 그녀를 Liz라고 부른다.)
　주어　동사　목적어　목적격 보어

Check Test

1 주절의 주어와 동사를 찾아 표시하시오.

As you know, our service is now available through an app.

2 문장 전체의 주어와 동사를 찾아 표시하시오.

The land through which the proposed Pine Hill walking trail would cut is home to a variety of species.

3 주어와 동사를 찾아 표시하시오.

35 students would be accompanied by two teachers.

4 목적어절의 주어와 동사를 찾아 표시하시오.

When we returned to our hotel, I discovered that I left behind my cell phone case.

• 정답
1 주어 – our service, 동사 – is　2 주어 – The land through which the proposed Pine Hill walking trail would cut, 동사 – is
3 주어 – 35 students, 동사 – would be accompanied　4 주어 – I, 동사 – left

A 목적 찾기 첫 번째

1st 선택지의 핵심 어구에 □ 표시한 후 글을 읽기 시작하세요.
2nd 핵심 문장을 찾아 글의 목적을 확인해 보세요.
3rd 내용을 종합하여 글의 목적을 찾으세요.

A01 ✱✿✿ .... 고1 2025(6월)/18

다음 글의 목적으로 가장 적절한 것은?

Dear Dog Owners,
My name is Lily Paxton, and I'm the town's Pet Program Coordinator. As part of our goal to make the community more dog-friendly, we recently opened a new dog park. The⁵ park was designed to provide an enjoyable experience for both dogs and owners. There are big grassy areas where your dogs can run, jump, and play. We have separate spaces for small dogs and big dogs, to ensure safety.¹⁰ You'll also find lots of benches and areas for resting and staying cool. We hope you will have a wonderful time with your dogs in this newly opened park.
Regards,   15
Lily Paxton, Pet Program Coordinator

① 새로 만든 반려견 공원의 개장을 홍보하려고
② 동물 보호 정책에 대한 의견을 구하려고
③ 유기견 보호 자원봉사자를 모집하려고
④ 반려견 공원 운영 시간의 변경을 안내하려고
⑤ 반려견 훈련 프로그램에의 참여를 권유하려고

1st 선택지의 핵심 어구에 □ 표시한 후 글을 읽기 시작하세요.

① 새로 만든 반려견 공원의 개장을 홍보하려고
② 동물 보호 정책에 대한 의견을 구하려고
③ 유기견 보호 자원봉사자를 모집하려고
④ 반려견 공원 운영 시간의 변경을 안내하려고
⑤ 반려견 훈련 프로그램에의 참여를 권유하려고

● 선택지끼리 겹치는 단어를 통해 글의 내용을 예상해 봅시다.
①, ④, ⑤에 ❶(   )이라는 단어가 있고, ②, ③에 각각 동물과 유기견이라는 단어가 있는 것으로 보아, 반려견에 관하여 무언가를 알리는 글이겠네요.

2nd 핵심 문장을 찾아 글의 목적을 확인해 보세요.

1) 글을 읽는 사람은 누구인가요?

Dear Dog Owners, /
친애하는 반려견 주인 여러분 /

● 첫 번째 줄에 Dog Owners가 등장했어요.
반려견 주인들에게 보내는 글이라고 하네요. 선택지를 통해 예상한 것처럼 반려견에 관한 글이군요! 이제 뒷부분에서 구체적으로 어떤 것을 알려줄지 살펴봐야 해요.

2) 반려견 주인들에게 알리려 했던 내용이 나타났어요.

As part of our goal / to make the community more
목표의 일환으로   / 이 지역 사회를 더욱 반려견 친화적으로
dog-friendly, / we recently opened / a new dog
만들기 위한   / 저희는 최근에 개장했습니다   / 새로운 반려견
park. //
공원을   //

● 새로운 반려견 공원을 ❷(   )했다고 했어요.
새로운 반려견 공원을 개장했으니 와보라고 홍보하는 글일까요, 아니면 반려견 공원의 운영 시간의 변경을 알리려는 글일까요? ①과 ④ 중에 정답이 있을 것 같으니, 글의 나머지 부분도 읽어야겠어요.

3) 반려견 공원에 반려견을 데리고 오기를 바란대요.

We hope / you will have a wonderful time with
저희는 바랍니다 / 여러분이 반려견과 함께 멋진 시간을 보내시길
your dogs / in this newly opened park. //
              / 새롭게 개장한 이 공원에서   //

● 새롭게 개장한 반려견 공원에 와보라는 글이군요.
반려견 주인들에게 새롭게 개장한 반려견 공원에 와볼 것을 홍보하는 내용이에요. 그 외에 다른 내용은 추가되지 않았으니 ④ 반려견 공원의 운영 시간 변경에 관한 내용은 아니겠네요.

3rd 내용을 종합하여 글의 목적을 찾으세요.
반려견 주인들이 지역 사회에 새롭게 개장한 반려견 공원에 오도록 홍보하는 내용의 글이에요. 따라서 이 글의 목적은 ❸(   )이에요.

빈칸 정답 ① 홍보 ❷ 개장(개장) ❶ 반려견

 **A** 목적 찾기 두 번째

1st 선택지의 핵심 어구에 □ 표시한 후 글을 읽기 시작하세요.
2nd 핵심 문장을 찾아 글의 목적을 확인해 보세요.
3rd 내용을 종합하여 글의 목적을 찾으세요.

A02 ✽✽✽ ················· 고1 2024(6월)/18

다음 글의 목적으로 가장 적절한 것은?

Dear Reader,
We always appreciate your support. As you know, our service is now available through an app. There has never been a better time to switch to an online membership of *TourTide* 5 *Magazine*. At a 50% discount off your current print subscription, you can access a full year of online reading. Get new issues and daily web pieces at TourTide.com, read or listen to *TourTide Magazine* via the app, and get our 10 members-only newsletter. You'll also gain access to our editors' selections of the best articles. Join today!
Yours,
TourTide Team 15

① 여행 일정 지연에 대해 사과하려고
② 잡지 온라인 구독을 권유하려고
③ 무료 잡지 신청을 홍보하려고
④ 여행 후기 모집을 안내하려고
⑤ 기사에 대한 독자 의견에 답변하려고

1st 선택지의 핵심 어구에 □ 표시한 후 글을 읽기 시작하세요.

① 여행 일정 지연에 대해 사과하려고
② 잡지 온라인 구독을 권유하려고
③ 무료 잡지 신청을 홍보하려고
④ 여행 후기 모집을 안내하려고
⑤ 기사에 대한 독자 의견에 답변하려고

● **선택지끼리 겹치는 단어를 통해 글의 내용을 예상해 봅시다.**
①, ④에 **1**( )이라는 단어가 있고, ②, ③에 잡지라는 단어가 있는 것으로 보아, 여행이나 잡지 구독에 관한 글이겠네요.

2nd 핵심 문장을 찾아 글의 목적을 확인해 보세요.

1) 글을 읽는 사람은 누구인가요?

Dear Reader, /
친애하는 독자들에게 /

● **첫 번째 줄에 Reader가 있긴 한데 구체적이지 않아요.**
독자에게 보내는 글이라고 하네요. 어떤 글의 독자인지는 뒷부분을 더 읽으며 찾아봐야 해요.

2) 어떤 글인지, 그리고 독자들에게 무엇을 요청하는지 나타났어요.

There has never been a better time / to switch to an
이보다 더 좋은 시기는 없습니다 / TourTide Magazine의
online membership of *TourTide Magazine*. //
온라인 회원으로 전환하기에 //
At a 50% discount off your current print subscription,
당신의 현재 인쇄본 구독료에서 50% 할인된 가격으로
/ you can access / a full year of online reading. //
/ 구독할 수 있습니다 / 1년 치를 온라인으로 //

● **TourTide Magazine의 회원들에게 보낸 편지네요.**
여행에 관한 잡지인가 봐요. 선택지에서 살펴본 것처럼 여행이나 잡지에 관련된 글이 맞군요! 잡지의 독자들에게 무엇을 말하는 걸까요?

● **온라인 회원으로 전환할 것을 2**( )하는 내용이군요!
잡지의 독자들에게 온라인 회원으로 전환하기 좋은 시기라고 하며 이를 권유하고 있어요. 인쇄본보다 50% 할인된 가격으로 1년 치를 온라인으로 구독할 수 있다고 하네요.

3) 간결한 명령문으로 글이 마무리되어요.

Join today! //
오늘 가입하세요 //

● **온라인 구독을 다시 한번 권유하네요.**
앞서 설명한 잡지 온라인 구독을 다시 권유하며 글이 마무리되었어요.

3rd 내용을 종합하여 글의 목적을 찾으세요.
TourTide Magazine이라는 여행 관련 잡지의 구독자들에게 할인 등의 혜택이 있으니 온라인 구독으로 전환하라고 권유하고 있어요. 따라서 이 글의 목적은 **3**( )이에요.

빈칸 정답 ② **3** 권유 **2** 여행 **1**

A03 ~ 06 ▶ 제한시간 8분

A03 ✽❀❀ 고1 2025(3월)/18

다음 글의 목적으로 가장 적절한 것은?

Dear Miranda,

Thank you for participating in our Crafts Art Fair. Since we've chosen you as one of the 'Artists of This Year', we are looking forward to introducing your unique handmade baskets to our community. As part of organizing the exhibition plan, we are happy to inform you that your artworks will be exhibited at the assigned table, number seven. Visitors can easily find your artworks located near the entrance. If you have any special requirements or need further assistance, feel free to contact us in advance.

Sincerely,
Helen Dwyer

① 공예품 구매 희망자를 소개하려고
② 비상시 박람회장 대피 동선을 안내하려고
③ 작품이 전시될 지정 테이블을 알려 주려고
④ 올해의 공예가 선정 투표 방식을 공지하려고
⑤ 박람회에 참여할 새로운 공예가를 모집하려고

구문 서술형

열 번째 줄에 Visitors로 시작하는 문장의 각 문장 성분을 찾아 쓰시오.

➡ 주어: _____ 동사: _____

목적어: _____

A04 ✽❀❀ 고1 2025(9월)/18

다음 글의 목적으로 가장 적절한 것은?

Dear Principal Jones,
I hope this message finds you well. As student council president, I am reaching out to discuss an important matter regarding our school library's current operating hours. At present, the library closes at 5 p.m., which many students feel limits their ability to fully use its resources for study and research after regular class hours. This is particularly challenging for those preparing for college entrance exams or working on academic projects that demand a quiet and resourceful environment. Therefore, I'd like to ask you to extend the library's operating hours to 7 p.m. This change would greatly benefit students by providing additional time to focus on their academic goals. I hope you will consider this proposal as a step toward improving our academic environment and better supporting our needs.
Sincerely,
Eric Park
Student Council President

① 신간 도서 구입을 건의하려고
② 도서관 프로그램 확대를 부탁하려고
③ 도서관 운영 시간 연장을 요청하려고
④ 도서 대출 시스템 개선에 감사하려고
⑤ 도서관 열람실 공간 확대를 제안하려고

구문 서술형

아홉 번째 줄에 This로 시작하는 문장의 형식을 쓰고, 빈칸에 알맞은 말을 쓰시오.

➡ _____형식

➡ 이유: 이 문장은 주어 _____와 동사 _____, 그리고 주어를 보충 설명하는 _____로 쓰인 형용사 _____(으)로 구성되어 있기 때문이다.

다음 글의 목적으로 가장 적절한 것은?

To the State Education Department,
I am writing with regard to the state's funding for the construction project at Fort Montgomery High School. Our school needs additional spaces to provide a fully functional Art and Library Media Center to serve our students in a more meaningful way. Despite submitting all required documentation for funding to your department in April 2024, we have not yet received any notification from your department. A delay in the process can carry considerable consequences related to the school's budgetary constraints and schedule. Therefore, in order to proceed with our project, we request you notify us of the review result regarding the submitted documentation. I look forward to hearing from you.
Respectfully,
Clara Smith
Principal, Fort Montgomery High School

① 제출 서류의 마감 기한 연장을 요청하려고
② 교내 미디어 센터의 리모델링을 제안하려고
③ 학교 프로젝트에 배정된 예산을 확인하려고
④ 학교 공간 조성을 위한 공모전을 홍보하려고
⑤ 제출 서류에 대한 검토 결과 통지를 요구하려고

【구문 서술형】
열네 번째 줄에 Therefore로 시작하는 문장을 참고하여 아래 대화의 빈칸에 알맞은 말을 쓰시오.

A: 이건 5형식 문장이야. 목적어 _____와 목적격 보어 notify가 쓰였잖아.
B: 아니야! request가 5형식 문장에 쓰이려면 목적격 보어는 to부정사로 와야 하고, 이 문장은 _____이야. request 뒤는 that이 생략된 목적어절이거든.
A: 그래? 그럼 we request you notify us of the review result는 어떻게 해석해?
B: '_____'라고 해석해야 해.

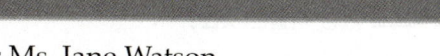

다음 글의 목적으로 가장 적절한 것은?

Dear Ms. Jane Watson,
I am John Austin, a science teacher at Crestville High School. Recently I was impressed by the latest book you wrote about the environment. Also my students read your book and had a class discussion about it. They are big fans of your book, so I'd like to ask you to visit our school and give a special lecture. We can set the date and time to suit your schedule. Having you at our school would be a fantastic experience for the students. We would be very grateful if you could come.
Best regards,
John Austin

① 환경 보호의 중요성을 강조하려고
② 글쓰기에서 주의할 점을 알려 주려고
③ 특강 강사로 작가의 방문을 요청하려고
④ 작가의 팬 사인회 일정 변경을 공지하려고
⑤ 작가가 쓴 책의 내용에 관하여 문의하려고

A07 ✿❀❀ 고1 2024(9월)/18

다음 글의 목적으로 가장 적절한 것은?

To whom it may concern,
I am writing to express my deep concern about the recent change made by Pittsburgh Train Station. The station had traditional ticket offices with staff before, but these have been replaced with ticket vending machines. However, individuals who are unfamiliar with these machines are now experiencing difficulty accessing the railway services. Since these individuals heavily relied on the staff assistance to be able to travel, they are in great need of ticket offices with staff in the station. Therefore, I am urging you to consider reopening the ticket offices. With the staff back in their positions, many people would regain access to the railway services. I look forward to your prompt attention to this matter and a positive resolution.
Sincerely,
Sarah Roberts

① 승차권 발매기 수리를 의뢰하려고
② 기차표 단체 예매 방법을 문의하려고
③ 기차 출발 시간 지연에 대해 항의하려고
④ 기차역 직원의 친절한 도움에 감사하려고
⑤ 기차역 유인 매표소 재운영을 요구하려고

A08 ✿❀❀ 고1 2023(11월)/18

다음 글의 목적으로 가장 적절한 것은?

Dear Ms. MacAlpine,
I was so excited to hear that your brand is opening a new shop on Bruns Street next month. I have always appreciated the way your brand helps women to feel more stylish and confident. I am writing in response to your ad in the Bruns Journal. I graduated from the Meline School of Fashion and have worked as a sales assistant at LoganMart for the last five years. During that time, I've developed strong customer service and sales skills, and now I would like to apply for the sales position in your clothing store. I am available for an interview at your earliest convenience. I look forward to hearing from you. Thank you for reading my letter.
Yours sincerely,
Grace Braddock

① 영업 시작일을 문의하려고
② 인터뷰 일정을 변경하려고
③ 디자인 공모전에 참가하려고
④ 제품 관련 문의에 답변하려고
⑤ 의류 매장 판매직에 지원하려고

A09

다음 글의 목적으로 가장 적절한 것은?

Dear Professor Sanchez,

My name is Ellis Wight, and I'm the director of the Alexandria Science Museum. We are holding a Chemistry Fair for local middle school students on Saturday, October 28. The goal of the fair is to encourage them to be interested in science through guided experiments. We are looking for college students who can help with the experiments during the event. I am contacting you to ask you to recommend some students from the chemistry department at your college who you think are qualified for this job. With their help, I'm sure the participants will have a great experience. I look forward to hearing from you soon.

Sincerely,
Ellis Wight

① 과학 박물관 내 시설 이용 제한을 안내하려고
② 화학 박람회 일정이 변경된 이유를 설명하려고
③ 중학생을 위한 화학 실험 특별 강연을 부탁하려고
④ 중학교 과학 수업용 실험 교재 집필을 의뢰하려고
⑤ 화학 박람회에서 실험을 도울 대학생 추천을 요청하려고

A10

다음 글의 목적으로 가장 적절한 것은?

Dear Ms. Robinson,

The Warblers Choir is happy to announce that we are invited to compete in the International Young Choir Competition. The competition takes place in London on May 20. Though we wish to participate in the event, we do not have the necessary funds to travel to London. So we are kindly asking you to support us by coming to our fundraising concert. It will be held on March 26. In this concert, we shall be able to show you how big our passion for music is. Thank you in advance for your kind support and help.

Sincerely,
Arnold Reynolds

① 합창 대회 결과를 공지하려고
② 모금 음악회 참석을 요청하려고
③ 음악회 개최 장소를 예약하려고
④ 합창곡 선정에 조언을 구하려고
⑤ 기부금 사용 내역을 보고하려고

A11

다음 글의 목적으로 가장 적절한 것은?

Dear Parents/Guardians,
Class parties will be held on the afternoon of Friday, December 16th, 2022. Children may bring in sweets, crisps, biscuits, cakes, and drinks. We are requesting that children do not bring in home-cooked or prepared food. All food should arrive in a sealed packet with the ingredients clearly listed. Fruit and vegetables are welcomed if they are pre-packed in a sealed packet from the shop. Please DO NOT send any food into school containing nuts as we have many children with severe nut allergies. Please check the ingredients of all food your children bring carefully. Thank you for your continued support and cooperation.
Yours sincerely,
Lisa Brown, Headteacher

① 학급 파티 일정 변경을 공지하려고
② 학교 식당의 새로운 메뉴를 소개하려고
③ 학생의 특정 음식 알레르기 여부를 조사하려고
④ 학부모의 적극적인 학급 파티 참여를 독려하려고
⑤ 학급 파티에 가져올 음식에 대한 유의 사항을 안내하려고

A12 ✺✺✺ _____ 고1 2023(6월)/18

다음 글의 목적으로 가장 적절한 것은?

ACC Travel Agency Customers:
Have you ever wanted to enjoy a holiday in nature? This summer is the best time to turn your dream into reality. We have a perfect travel package for you. This travel package includes special trips to Lake Madison as well as massage and meditation to help you relax. Also, we provide yoga lessons taught by experienced instructors. If you book this package, you will enjoy all this at a reasonable price. We are sure that it will be an unforgettable experience for you. If you call us, we will be happy to give you more details.

① 여행 일정 변경을 안내하려고
② 패키지여행 상품을 홍보하려고
③ 여행 상품 불만족에 대해 사과하려고
④ 여행 만족도 조사 참여를 부탁하려고
⑤ 패키지여행 업무 담당자를 모집하려고

A13 ✺✺✺ _____ 고1 2022(6월)/18

다음 글의 목적으로 가장 적절한 것은?

Dear Boat Tour Manager,
On March 15, my family was on one of your Glass Bottom Boat Tours. When we returned to our hotel, I discovered that I left behind my cell phone case. The case must have fallen off my lap and onto the floor when I took it off my phone to clean it. I would like to ask you to check if it is on your boat. Its color is black and it has my name on the inside. If you find the case, I would appreciate it if you would let me know.
Sincerely,
Sam Roberts

① 제품의 고장 원인을 문의하려고
② 분실물 발견 시 연락을 부탁하려고
③ 시설물의 철저한 관리를 당부하려고
④ 여행자 보험 가입 절차를 확인하려고
⑤ 분실물 센터 확장의 필요성을 건의하려고

Dear Principal,
My name is Ellie Wright and I'm the director of the Alexai animal shelter. Recently, We are holding a Charming Pets for local animals shelter residents event. As I know the students of this fair is to connect dog with people in need of new dog. The project is aimed at adoptions that offer special rescue dogs. We are looking for college students who could help with the experience during the expected day at the fair You can help up us to arrange as some other activities from the...

A14 ✺✺✺ _____ 고1 2021(9월)/18

다음 글의 목적으로 가장 적절한 것은?

Dear Mr. Dennis Brown,
We at G&D Restaurant are honored and delighted to invite you to our annual Fall Dinner. The annual event will be held on October 1st, 2021 at our restaurant. At the event, we will be introducing new wonderful dishes that our restaurant will be offering soon. These delicious dishes will showcase the amazing talents of our gifted chefs. Also, our chefs will be providing cooking tips, ideas on what to buy for your kitchen, and special recipes. We at G&D Restaurant would be more than grateful if you can make it to this special occasion and be part of our celebration. We look forward to seeing you. Thank you so much.

Regards,
Marcus Lee, Owner - G&D Restaurant

① 식당 개업을 홍보하려고
② 식당의 연례행사에 초대하려고
③ 신입 요리사 채용을 공고하려고
④ 매장 직원의 실수를 사과하려고
⑤ 식당 만족도 조사 참여를 부탁하려고

A15 ✿✿✿ 고1 2021(3월)/18

다음 글의 목적으로 가장 적절한 것은?

Dear members of Eastwood Library,
Thanks to the Friends of Literature group, we've successfully raised enough money to remodel the library building. John Baker, our local builder, has volunteered to help us with the remodelling but he needs assistance. By grabbing a hammer or a paint brush and donating your time, you can help with the construction. Join Mr. Baker in his volunteering team and become a part of making Eastwood Library a better place! Please call 541-567-1234 for more information.
Sincerely,
Mark Anderson

① 도서관 임시 휴관의 이유를 설명하려고
② 도서관 자원봉사자 교육 일정을 안내하려고
③ 도서관 보수를 위한 모금 행사를 제안하려고
④ 도서관 공사에 참여할 자원봉사자를 모집하려고
⑤ 도서관에서 개최하는 글쓰기 대회를 홍보하려고

A16 ✿✿✿ 고1 2021(11월)/18

다음 글의 목적으로 가장 적절한 것은?

To the school librarian,
I am Kyle Thomas, the president of the school's English writing club. I have planned activities that will increase the writing skills of our club members. One of the aims of these activities is to make us aware of various types of news media and the language used in printed newspaper articles. However, some old newspapers are not easy to access online. It is, therefore, my humble request to you to allow us to use old newspapers that have been stored in the school library. I would really appreciate it if you grant us permission.
Yours truly,
Kyle Thomas

① 도서관 이용 시간 연장을 건의하려고
② 신청한 도서의 대출 가능 여부를 문의하려고
③ 도서관에 보관 중인 자료 현황을 조사하려고
④ 글쓰기 동아리 신문의 도서관 비치를 부탁하려고
⑤ 도서관에 있는 오래된 신문의 사용 허락을 요청하려고

A17 ✿✿✿ 고1 2021(6월)/18

다음 글의 목적으로 가장 적절한 것은?

Dear Mr. Jones,
I am James Arkady, PR Director of KHJ Corporation. We are planning to redesign our brand identity and launch a new logo to celebrate our 10th anniversary. We request you to create a logo that best suits our company's core vision, 'To inspire humanity.' I hope the new logo will convey our brand message and capture the values of KHJ. Please send us your logo design proposal once you are done with it. Thank you.
Best regards,
James Arkady

① 회사 로고 제작을 의뢰하려고
② 변경된 회사 로고를 홍보하려고
③ 회사 비전에 대한 컨설팅을 요청하려고
④ 회사 창립 10주년 기념품을 주문하려고
⑤ 회사 로고 제작 일정 변경을 공지하려고

A18 ~ 19 ▶ 제한시간 4분

A18 ⭐ 2등급 대비 _____ 고1 2023(3월)/18

다음 글의 목적으로 가장 적절한 것은?

To whom it may concern,

I am a resident of the Blue Sky Apartment. Recently I observed that the kid zone is in need of repairs. I want you to pay attention to the poor condition of the playground equipment in the zone. The swings are damaged, the paint is falling off, and some of the bolts on the slide are missing. The facilities have been in this terrible condition since we moved here. They are dangerous to the children playing there. Would you please have them repaired? I would appreciate your immediate attention to solve this matter.

Yours sincerely,
Nina Davis

① 아파트의 첨단 보안 설비를 홍보하려고
② 아파트 놀이터의 임시 폐쇄를 공지하려고
③ 아파트 놀이터 시설의 수리를 요청하려고
④ 아파트 놀이터 사고의 피해 보상을 촉구하려고
⑤ 아파트 공용 시설 사용 시 유의 사항을 안내하려고

A19 ⭐ 2등급 대비 _____ 고1 2022(11월)/18

다음 글의 목적으로 가장 적절한 것은?

Dear Mr. Krull,

I have greatly enjoyed working at Trincom Enterprises as a sales manager. Since I joined in 2015, I have been a loyal and essential member of this company, and have developed innovative ways to contribute to the company. Moreover, in the last year alone, I have brought in two new major clients to the company, increasing the company's total sales by 5%. Also, I have voluntarily trained 5 new members of staff, totaling 35 hours. I would therefore request your consideration in raising my salary, which I believe reflects my performance as well as the industry average. I look forward to speaking with you soon.

Kimberly Morss

① 부서 이동을 신청하려고
② 급여 인상을 요청하려고
③ 근무 시간 조정을 요구하려고
④ 기업 혁신 방안을 제안하려고
⑤ 신입 사원 연수에 대해 문의하려고

A 어휘 Review

* 다음 영어는 우리말 뜻을, 우리말은 영어 단어를 〈보기〉에서 찾아 쓰시오.

〈 보기 〉
수공예의	local	연락하다	include
화학	grab	요구 사항	cooperation
인류애	funding	감독관	urge

01 contact _____

02 humanity _____

03 handmade _____

04 requirement _____

05 chemistry _____

06 지역의 _____

07 포함하다 _____

08 쥐다 _____

09 협조 _____

10 재정 지원 _____

* 다음 우리말에 알맞은 영어 표현을 찾아 연결하시오.

11 ~을 고대하다 •   • notify A of B

12 ~에 참여하다 •   • look forward to

13 A에게 B를 알리다 •   • participate in

14 미리 •   • leave behind

15 ~을 놓고 오다 •   • in advance

* 다음 우리말 표현에 맞는 단어를 고르시오.

16 필수적인 구성원 ➡ (essential / optional) member

17 합리적인 가격에 ➡ at a(n) (irrational / reasonable) price

18 대학 입학 시험을 준비하는 것 ➡ preparing for college (entrance / endurance) exams

19 심각한 견과류 알레르기 ➡ (severe / sincere) nut allergies

20 당신의 현재 인쇄본 구독료 ➡ your current print (prescription / subscription)

* 다음 문장의 빈칸에 알맞은 단어를 〈보기〉에서 찾아 쓰시오.

〈 보기 〉
goal	condition	immediate	proposal
construction	contribute	ingredients	meditation
appreciate	instructor	humble	suit

21 모든 음식은 성분을 명확하게 목록으로 작성하여 밀봉된 꾸러미로 가져와야 합니다.
➡ All food should arrive in a sealed packet with the _____ clearly listed.

22 이 패키지여행 상품은 당신이 쉬도록 돕는 명상을 포함합니다.
➡ This travel package includes _____ to help you relax.

23 저는 회사에 기여할 혁신적인 방법들을 개발해 왔습니다.
➡ I have developed innovative ways to _____ to the company.

24 이 문제를 해결하기 위해 즉각적인 관심을 두시면 감사하겠습니다.
➡ I would appreciate your _____ attention to solve this matter.

25 우리가 이사 온 이후로 시설은 이렇게 형편없는 상태였습니다.
➡ The facilities have been in this terrible _____ since we moved here.

26 오래된 신문을 저희가 사용할 수 있도록 허락해 달라는 것이 선생님께 드리는 저의 겸허한 요청입니다.
➡ It is my _____ request to you to allow us to use old newspapers.

27 저는 이 제안을 당신이 고려해 주시기를 바랍니다.
➡ I hope you will consider this _____.

28 이 박람회의 목적은 그들이 과학에 관심을 갖도록 장려하는 것입니다. ➡ The _____ of the fair is to encourage them to be interested in science.

29 여러분은 공사를 도울 수 있습니다.
➡ You can help with the _____.

30 만약 케이스를 발견한다면, 저에게 알려주시면 감사하겠습니다. ➡ If you find the case, I would _____ it if you would let me know.

B 심경의 이해
마음의 상태

★ 유형 설명

다음 글의 상황에 나타난 분위기로 가장 적절한 것은?

다음 글에 드러난 Maya의 심경 변화로 가장 적절한 것은?

다음 글에 드러난 Shirley의 심경으로 가장 적절한 것은?

New neighbors! Shirley was dying to know about them. "Do you know anything about the

사람들 앞에서 발표를 하려니까 심장이 터질 것 같았어.

등장인물이나 상황에 대한 직접적·간접적인 묘사를 읽고 등장인물의 심리 상태, 묘사된 상황의 분위기를 파악해야 한다.

🔑 심경이나 분위기를 나타내는 형용사에 특히 주의를 기울인다. 글에서 묘사되는 상황이 어떤 상황인지, 등장인물이 어떤 상황에 처해 있는지를 파악한다.

🎭 유형 풀이 비법

1 글의 상황을 파악하라!
• 필자나 등장인물이 어떤 상황에 처해 있는지 정확히 이해해야 한다.

2 특정 표현들을 찾아라!
• 글에서 다뤄지는 중심 사건이나 심경을 나타내는 단어나 표현을 파악한다.
• feel, felt 뒤에 이어지는 표현에 집중한다.

3 심경과 분위기를 파악하라!
• 감정 표현(주로 형용사)으로 심리 상태와 분위기를 파악한다.

> **Tip** 심경 변화를 묻는 문제는 글에서 상황이 바뀌는 부분을 찾는다. 주로 부사(suddenly 등)나 접속사(but, however)로 상황이 전환된다.

🔖 자주 출제되는 감정 및 분위기를 나타내는 형용사

☐ content 만족한
☐ grateful 감사하는
☐ cheerful 유쾌한
☐ relieved 안도하는
☐ confident 자신감 있는
☐ lively 활기찬
☐ delighted 기쁜
☐ thrilled 흥분한
☐ mysterious 신비한
☐ curious 호기심에 찬
☐ startling 놀라운
☐ monotonous 단조로운
☐ indifferent 무관심한
☐ tense 긴장되는

☐ desperate 필사적인
☐ urgent 긴급한
☐ horrified 공포에 질린
☐ frightened 두려운
☐ ashamed 부끄러운
☐ embarrassed 당황한
☐ irritated 짜증이 난
☐ furious 화가 난
☐ disappointed 실망한
☐ anxious 염려스러운
☐ frustrated 좌절하는
☐ regretful 후회하는
☐ jealous 질투하는
☐ envious 부러워하는

📖 어휘 및 표현 Preview

☐ swiftly 신속하게
☐ kneel 무릎을 꿇다
☐ revive 소생시키다
☐ approach 다가가다
☐ application letter 지원서
☐ emerge 나타나다
☐ enormous 거대한
☐ stream 흐르다
☐ enthusiasm 열정
☐ habitat 서식지
☐ sniff (코를) 킁킁거리다
☐ motivation 동기
☐ exotic 이국적인
☐ fine 고운

2 명사의 수량 표현

의미	+셀 수 있는 명사	+셀 수 없는 명사
많은	① many, quite a few, a [considerable/large/good/great] number of	② much, a considerable amount of, a [good/great] deal of
	a lot of, lots of, plenty of	
약간의 (긍정적)	③ a few	④ a little
	⑤ some, ⑥ any – some: 주로 긍정문이나 긍정의 대답이 예상되는 의문문에서 '약간(의)' – any: 의문문에서 '약간(의)', 부정문에서 '아무(것)도, 조금(도)' * some과 any는 부정대명사로도 쓰인다.	
거의 없는 (부정적)	⑦ few	⑧ little

- ① You can find **many** items there. (당신은 그곳에서 **많은** 물품들을 찾을 수 있다.)
  셀 수 있는 명사 items를 수식
- ② Making a study plan takes **much** effort. (공부 계획을 세우는 것은 **많은** 노력이 든다.)
  셀 수 없는 명사 effort를 수식
- ③ Melissa saw the advertisement **a few** days ago. (Melissa는 **며칠** 전에 그 광고를 봤다.)
  셀 수 있는 명사 days를 수식
- ④ I have **a little** money to give him. (내게 그에게 줄 **약간의** 돈이 있다.)
  셀 수 없는 명사 money를 수식
- ⑤ We went to the library to borrow **some** books. (우리는 **몇 권의** 책을 빌리러 도서관에 갔다.)
  셀 수 있는 명사 books를 수식
- ⑤ This cake is delicious. Won't you have **some**? (이 케이크는 맛있어. **조금** 먹지 않을래?)
  부정대명사로 쓰인 some
- ⑥ He gave me books. Did you get **any**? (그가 내게 책들을 줬어. 넌 **좀** 받았니?)
  부정대명사로 쓰인 any
- ⑦ **Few** people live there now. (지금은 그곳에 사는 사람들이 **거의 없다**.)
  셀 수 있는 명사 people을 수식
- ⑧ There is **little** time to prepare for the exams. (시험을 준비할 시간이 **거의 없다**.)
  셀 수 없는 명사 time을 수식

Check Test

1 주어진 단어 중에서 어법상 적절한 것을 고르시오.

After a few / a little moments, the man finished his coffee and was about to throw away the napkin as he left.

2 밑줄 친 부분을 알맞은 형태로 바꿔 쓰시오.

I was diving alone in about 40 feet of <u>waters</u> when I got a terrible stomachache.

→ _____

3 주어진 단어 중에서 어법상 적절한 것을 고르시오.

I could see my watch and knew there was only a few / a little more time on the tank before I would be out of air.

4 밑줄 친 부분을 알맞은 형태로 바꿔 쓰시오.

Shirley had a billion more <u>question</u>.

→ _____

B 심경의 이해 (첫 번째)

1st 글의 앞부분을 통해 주인공이 처한 상황을 파악하세요.
2nd 전반부를 읽으면서 주인공의 심경을 나타내는 어구들을 찾으세요.
3rd 심경이 전환되는 부분에 주의하며 후반부의 내용을 파악하세요.

B01 ✽✽✽ ···················· 고1 2025(3월)/19

다음 글에 드러난 'I'의 심경 변화로 가장 적절한 것은?

The shed is cold and damp, the air thick with the smell of old wood and earth. It's dark, and I can't make out what's moving in the shadows. "Who's there?" I ask, my voice shaking with fear. The shadow moves closer, 5 and my heart is beating fast — until the figure steps into a faint beam of light breaking through a crack in the wall. A rabbit. A laugh escapes my lips as it stares at me with wide, curious eyes. "You scared me," 10 I say, feeling much better. The rabbit pauses for a moment, then hops away, disappearing back into the shadows. I'm left smiling. I start to feel at ease.

*shed: 헛간

① envious → hopeful
② anxious → angry
③ frightened → relieved
④ curious → regretful
⑤ excited → disappointed

1st 글의 앞부분을 통해 주인공이 처한 상황을 파악하세요.

The shed is cold and damp, / the air thick / with the
헛간은 춥고 습기가 차 있고 / 공기에 짙다 / 오래된
smell of old wood and earth. //
나무와 흙냄새가 //
It's dark, / and I can't make out / what's moving in
어두워서 / 나는 알아볼 수 없다 / 그림자 속에서 움직이는
the shadows. //
무언가를 //

● 헛간에 들어가는 상황이에요.
춥고 어두운 헛간에 혼자 들어가는 상황으로 보여요. 무언가를 알아볼
수도 없는 어둠 속에서 주인공은 이어서 어떤 상황을 마주하게 될까요?

2nd 전반부를 읽으면서 주인공의 심경을 나타내는 어구들을 찾으세요.

"Who's there?" / I ask, / my voice shaking with
"거기 누구세요" / 나는 묻는다 / 목소리가 두려움에 떨리며 //
fear. //

● 주인공이 물었을 때 어떤 심경이었을까요?
주인공은 그림자 속에서 움직이는 무언가를 향해 **1**(   )에
떨며 물었어요. 그렇다면 ① 부러워하는, ② 호기심 있는, ⑤ 흥분한
심경은 절대 아닐 거예요!

3rd 심경이 전환되는 부분에 주의하며 후반부의 내용을 파악하세요.

1) 그림자 속 무언가의 정체가 밝혀졌나요?

A rabbit. // A laugh escapes my lips / as it stares at
토끼다 // 웃음이 내 입술에서 새어 나온다 / 그것이 나를 바라볼 때
me / with wide, curious eyes. //
/ 크고 호기심 가득한 눈으로 //
"You scared me," / I say, / feeling much better. //
"너 때문에 놀랐잖아" / 나는 말한다 / 훨씬 나아진 기분을 느끼며 //

● 다행히 토끼 한 마리뿐이었네요!
주인공은 그림자 속에서 움직이던 존재를 두려워했지만, 알고 보니 토끼
한 마리뿐이라 기분이 훨씬 나아졌대요.
그렇다면 후반부의 심경은 '안도하는'을 의미하는 ③ **2**(   )
가 적절하겠네요!

2) 심경이 더 확실히 드러나는 문장도 있어요.

I start to feel at ease. //
나의 마음이 편안해지기 시작한다 //

● 마음이 편안해지기 시작했대요.
다른 상황은 더 전개되지 않고 주인공의 마음이 편안해지기 시작했다는
문장으로 글이 마무리되어요. 헛간에 들어간 주인공은 처음엔 그림자
속 존재가 무엇인지 몰라 두려워했지만, 알고 보니 토끼 한 마리뿐이라
안도했으므로 정답은 ③ (   )!

● 함정 때문에 ④이 헷갈렸을 수도 있어요.
글에 curious가 직접적으로 등장해서 정답이라고 착각할 수도 있지만,
이는 주인공의 심경이 아니라 토끼의 눈을 묘사할 때 쓰였을 뿐이에요.
심경을 나타내는 단어가 등장하더라도 그것이 누구의 심경인지 정확히
파악하는 것이 중요해요!

빈칸 정답 © **3** relieved **2** 두려움 **1**

B 심경의 이해 두 번째

1st 글의 앞부분을 읽고 주인공이 어떤 상황에 있는지 파악해 보세요.
2nd 그 상황에서 주인공이 느끼는 심경을 나타내는 어구를 찾으세요.
3rd 바뀐 상황에 대해 등장인물이 어떤 심경을 느끼는지 파악하세요.

B02 ✽❀❀ .... 고1 2024(9월)/19

다음 글에 드러난 Jeevan의 심경 변화로 가장 적절한 것은?

All the actors on the stage were focused on their acting. Then, suddenly, Arthur fell into the corner of the stage. Jeevan immediately approached Arthur and found his heart wasn't beating. Jeevan began CPR. Jeevan⁵ worked silently, glancing sometimes at Arthur's face. He thought, "Please, start breathing again, please." Arthur's eyes were closed. Moments later, an older man in a grey suit appeared, swiftly kneeling beside¹⁰ Arthur's chest. "I'm Walter Jacobi. I'm a doctor." He announced with a calm voice. Jeevan wiped the sweat off his forehead. With combined efforts, Jeevan and Dr. Jacobi successfully revived Arthur. Arthur's eyes¹⁵ slowly opened. Finally, Jeevan was able to hear Arthur's breath again, thinking to himself, "Thank goodness. You're back."

① thrilled → bored
② ashamed → confident
③ hopeful → helpless
④ surprised → indifferent
⑤ desperate → relieved

1st 글의 앞부분을 읽고 주인공이 어떤 상황에 있는지 파악해 보세요.

Then, suddenly, / Arthur fell into the corner of the
그 때 갑자기   / Arthur가 무대의 한쪽 구석에
stage. // Jeevan immediately approached Arthur /
쓰러졌다 // Jeevan이 즉각 Arthur에게 다가갔고   /
and found his heart wasn't beating. //
그의 심장이 뛰지 않는 것을 알아차렸다   //

● 누가 쓰러졌고 누가 그에게 다가갔나요?
Arthur가 갑자기 무대 한쪽 구석에서 쓰러졌고, 그때 Jeevan이 Arthur에게 다가가 그의 심장이 뛰지 않는 것을 알아차렸다고 했어요. 우리가 심경을 파악해야 하는 대상은 Jeevan이니까, 그가 어떤 심경인지에 집중하며 글을 마저 읽어봅시다!

2nd 그 상황에서 주인공이 느끼는 심경을 나타내는 어구를 찾으세요.

Jeevan began CPR. //
Jeevan은 CPR을 시작했다 //
Jeevan worked silently, / glancing sometimes at
Jeevan은 조용히 작업했다   / 때때로 Arthur의 얼굴을
Arthur's face. //
흘긋 보며   //
He thought, / "Please, start breathing again, please." //
그는 생각했다   / '제발, 다시 숨쉬기를 시작해요, 제발'이라고   //

● 누군가가 제발 숨쉬기를 바라는 것은 어떤 심경인가요?
Jeevan은 Arthur를 살리기 위해 CPR을 하면서 그가 다시 숨쉬기를 간절히 바라고 있어요. 강한 요청을 나타내는 Please를 두 번이나 반복해서 말하며, Jeevan의 '간절한' 심경을 나타내고 있어요. 따라서 전반부의 심경을 나타내는 가장 적절한 단어는 '간절한'이라는 뜻의 ❶(   )!

3rd 바뀐 상황에 대해 등장인물이 어떤 심경을 느끼는지 파악하세요.
1) 상황이 마무리되는 마지막 문장을 봅시다.

Finally, / Jeevan was able to hear Arthur's breath
마침내   / Jeevan은 Arthur의 숨을 다시 들을 수 있었고
again, / thinking to himself, / "Thank goodness. //
/ 자신에게 되뇌었다   / '다행이다   //
You're back." //
깨어났다'라고   //

● Arthur를 살린 Jeevan의 심정은 어떨까요?
마침내 Jeevan은 Arthur가 깨어나서 다행이라고 되뇌며 '안도감'을 나타냈으니까, 후반부의 심경은 '안도하는'을 의미하는 ❷(   )가 적절하겠네요!

❧ 선택지에서 정답을 찾아볼까요?
Jeevan은 쓰러진 Arthur를 살리기 위해 간절한 마음이었고, 의사의 도움을 받아 Arthur를 살리고 나서 다행이라고 하며 안도했어요. 따라서 Jeevan의 심경 변화로 가장 적절한 것은 '간절한 → 안도하는'의 ❸(   ) 이에요.

빈칸 정답 ❶ desperate ❷ relieved ❸ ⑤

B03 ~ 08 ▶ 제한시간 12분

B03 ❀❀❀　　　고1 2025(6월)/19

다음 글에 드러난 Maya의 심경 변화로 가장 적절한 것은?

Maya waited in line to check in for her flight. Her expectations about her European backpacking trip were really high. She had been looking forward to the trip for a year. She couldn't wait to visit museums in Madrid and see the Eiffel Tower at night in Paris. As she stood in line, she could feel those experiences were finally so close. When she approached the counter, the airline employee asked to see her passport. Maya reached into her pocket but felt nothing. She realized she had left her passport at home. Her plans were ruined. She was heartbroken, knowing she could not board the flight and had to delay her dream trip.

① excited → frustrated
② joyful → indifferent
③ terrified → relaxed
④ worried → satisfied
⑤ bored → curious

[구문 서술형]

주어진 우리말과 일치하도록 괄호 안의 단어를 이용하여 바르게 영작하시오.

그녀의 많은 계획들이 망쳐졌다. (a large number of)

➡ _____

B04 ❀❀❀　　　고1 2025(9월)/19

다음 글에 드러난 'I'의 심경 변화로 가장 적절한 것은?

I glanced at the clock on the wall. 10:00. That meant the casting director would call very soon with the results of my first audition for a musical part in *The Wizard of Oz*. I felt shaky all over, chewing my thumbnail and jiggling my feet. Finally, the telephone rang. While I was coming round, Dad answered. I heard him say, "Ahh, thank you. I'll let her know …" As I got to the bottom of the stairs, he was just putting the phone down. "That was *The Wizard of Oz*. You're second senior munchkin," he announced. I got a little rush of excitement, knowing I was in — that whatever happened I could be involved in one of the productions.

① puzzled → calm
② bored → confused
③ nervous → pleased
④ satisfied → regretful
⑤ confident → disappointed

[구문 서술형]

주어진 우리말과 일치하도록 틀린 부분을 찾아 밑줄을 긋고 바르게 고치시오.

나는 작품들 중 하나에 참여할 수 있었다.
I could be involved in one of the production.

➡ _____

B05 ✱✱✱   고1 2024(10월)/19

다음 글에 드러난 'I'의 심경 변화로 가장 적절한 것은?

As I waited outside the locker room after a hard-fought basketball game, the coach called out to me, "David, walk with me." I figured he was going to tell me something important. He was going to select me to be the captain of the team, the leader I had always wanted to be. My heart was racing with anticipation. But when his next words hit my ears, everything changed. "We're going to have to send you home," he said coldly. "I don't think you are going to make it." I couldn't believe his decision. I tried to hold it together, but inside I was falling apart. A car would be waiting tomorrow morning to take me home. And just like that, it was over.

① hopeful → frustrated   ② confident → jealous
③ anxious → grateful   ④ relaxed → indifferent
⑤ bored → annoyed

구문 서술형

밑줄 친 부분 대신에 들어갈 알맞은 말을 <보기>에서 찾아 모두 쓰시오.

My heart was racing with much anticipation.

── [보기] ──
many   a number of   a great deal of   a lot of

➡ _____

B06 ✱✱✱   고1 2024(3월)/19

다음 글에 드러난 Sarah의 심경 변화로 가장 적절한 것은?

Marilyn and her three-year-old daughter, Sarah, took a trip to the beach, where Sarah built her first sandcastle. Moments later, an enormous wave destroyed Sarah's castle. In response to the loss of her sandcastle, tears streamed down Sarah's cheeks and her heart was broken. She ran to Marilyn, saying she would never build a sandcastle again. Marilyn said, "Part of the joy of building a sandcastle is that, in the end, we give it as a gift to the ocean." Sarah loved this idea and responded with enthusiasm to the idea of building another castle — this time, even closer to the water so the ocean would get its gift sooner!

① sad → excited   ② envious → anxious
③ bored → joyful   ④ relaxed → regretful
⑤ nervous → surprised

B07 ✱✱✱   고1 2024(6월)/19

다음 글에 드러난 'I'의 심경 변화로 가장 적절한 것은?

As I walked from the mailbox, my heart was beating rapidly. In my hands, I held the letter from the university I had applied to. I thought my grades were good enough to cross the line and my application letter was well-written, but was it enough? I hadn't slept a wink for days. As I carefully tore into the paper of the envelope, the letter slowly emerged with the opening phrase, "It is our great pleasure..." I shouted with joy, "I am in!" As I held the letter, I began to make a fantasy about my college life in a faraway city.

① relaxed → upset
② anxious → delighted
③ guilty → confident
④ angry → grateful
⑤ hopeful → disappointed

B08 ✱✱✱   고1 2021(6월)/19

다음 글에 드러난 Cindy의 심경 변화로 가장 적절한 것은?

One day, Cindy happened to sit next to a famous artist in a café, and she was thrilled to see him in person. He was drawing on a used napkin over coffee. She was looking on in awe. After a few moments, the man finished his coffee and was about to throw away the napkin as he left. Cindy stopped him. "Can I have that napkin you drew on?", she asked. "Sure," he replied. "Twenty thousand dollars." She said, with her eyes wide-open, "What? It took you like two minutes to draw that." "No," he said. "It took me over sixty years to draw this." Being at a loss, she stood still rooted to the ground.

① relieved → worried
② indifferent → embarrassed
③ excited → surprised
④ disappointed → satisfied
⑤ jealous → confident

B09 ✱✱✱ 　　　　　　　　　고1 2021(9월)/19

다음 글의 상황에 나타난 분위기로 가장 적절한 것은?

In the middle of the night, Matt suddenly awakened. He glanced at his clock. It was 3:23. For just an instant he wondered what had wakened him. Then he remembered. He had heard someone come into his room. Matt sat up in bed, rubbed his eyes, and looked around the small room. "Mom?" he said quietly, hoping he would hear his mother's voice assuring him that everything was all right. But there was no answer. Matt tried to tell himself that he was just hearing things. But he knew he wasn't. There was someone in his room. He could hear rhythmic, scratchy breathing and it wasn't his own. He lay awake for the rest of the night.

① humorous and fun　② boring and dull
③ calm and peaceful　④ noisy and exciting
⑤ mysterious and frightening

B10 ✱✱✱ 　　　　　　　　　고1 2021(3월)/19

다음 글에 드러난 Shirley의 심경으로 가장 적절한 것은?

On the way home, Shirley noticed a truck parked in front of the house across the street. New neighbors! Shirley was dying to know about them. "Do you know anything about the new neighbors?" she asked Pa at dinner. He said, "Yes, and there's one thing that may be interesting to you." Shirley had a billion more questions. Pa said joyfully, "They have a girl just your age. Maybe she wants to be your playmate." Shirley nearly dropped her fork on the floor. How many times had she prayed for a friend? Finally, her prayers were answered! She and the new girl could go to school together, play together, and become best friends.

① curious and excited　② sorry and upset
③ jealous and annoyed　④ calm and relaxed
⑤ disappointed and unhappy

B11 ✱✱✱ 　　　　　　　　　고1 2021(11월)/19

다음 글에 드러난 "I"의 심경 변화로 가장 적절한 것은?

When my mom came home from the mall with a special present for me I was pretty sure I knew what it was. I was absolutely thrilled because I would soon communicate with a new cell phone! I was daydreaming about all of the cool apps and games I was going to download. But my mom smiled really big and handed me a book. I flipped through the pages, figuring that maybe she had hidden my new phone inside. But I slowly realized that my mom had not got me a phone and my present was just a little book, which was so different from what I had wanted.

① worried → furious
② surprised → relieved
③ ashamed → confident
④ anticipating → satisfied
⑤ excited → disappointed

B12 ✱✱✱ 　　　　　　　　　고1 2022(9월)/19

다음 글에 나타난 'I'의 심경 변화로 가장 적절한 것은?

It was two hours before the submission deadline and I still hadn't finished my news article. I sat at the desk, but suddenly, the typewriter didn't work. No matter how hard I tapped the keys, the levers wouldn't move to strike the paper. I started to realize that I would not be able to finish the article on time. Desperately, I rested the typewriter on my lap and started hitting each key with as much force as I could manage. Nothing happened. Thinking something might have happened inside of it, I opened the cover, lifted up the keys, and found the problem — a paper clip. The keys had no room to move. After picking it out, I pressed and pulled some parts. The keys moved smoothly again. I breathed deeply and smiled. Now I knew that I could finish my article on time.

① confident → nervous　② frustrated → relieved
③ bored → amazed　④ indifferent → curious
⑤ excited → disappointed

B13 ✿✿✿ 고1 2022(6월)/19

다음 글에 드러난 Matthew의 심경 변화로 가장 적절한 것은?

One Saturday morning, Matthew's mother told Matthew that she was going to take him to the park. A big smile came across his face. As he loved to play outside, he ate his breakfast and got dressed quickly so they could go. When they got to the park, Matthew ran all the way over to the swing set. That was his favorite thing to do at the park. But the swings were all being used. His mother explained that he could use the slide until a swing became available, but it was broken. Suddenly, his mother got a phone call and she told Matthew they had to leave. His heart sank.

① embarrassed → indifferent
② excited → disappointed
③ cheerful → ashamed
④ nervous → touched
⑤ scared → relaxed

B14 ✿★✿ 고1 2022(3월)/19

다음 글에 드러난 Zoe의 심경 변화로 가장 적절한 것은?

The principal stepped on stage. "Now, I present this year's top academic award to the student who has achieved the highest placing." He smiled at the row of seats where twelve finalists had gathered. Zoe wiped a sweaty hand on her handkerchief and glanced at the other finalists. They all looked as pale and uneasy as herself. Zoe and one of the other finalists had won first placing in four subjects so it came down to how teachers ranked their hard work and confidence. "The Trophy for General Excellence is awarded to Miss Zoe Perry," the principal declared. "Could Zoe step this way, please?" Zoe felt as if she were in heaven. She walked into the thunder of applause with a big smile.

① hopeful → disappointed   ② guilty → confident
③ nervous → delighted   ④ angry → calm
⑤ relaxed → proud

B15 ✿✿✿ 고1 2022(11월)/19

다음 글에 드러난 'I'의 심경 변화로 가장 적절한 것은?

On one beautiful spring day, I was fully enjoying my day off. I arrived at the nail salon, and muted my cellphone so that I would be disconnected for the hour and feel calm and peaceful. I was so comfortable while I got a manicure. As I left the place, I checked my cellphone and saw four missed calls from a strange number. I knew immediately that something bad was coming, and I called back. A young woman answered and said that my father had fallen over a stone and was injured, now seated on a bench. I was really concerned since he had just recovered from his knee surgery. I rushed getting into my car to go see him.

① nervous → confident   ② relaxed → worried
③ excited → indifferent   ④ pleased → jealous
⑤ annoyed → grateful

B16 ✿✿✿ 고1 2023(3월)/19

다음 글에 드러난 'I'의 심경 변화로 가장 적절한 것은?

On a two-week trip in the Rocky Mountains, I saw a grizzly bear in its native habitat. At first, I felt joy as I watched the bear walk across the land. He stopped every once in a while to turn his head about, sniffing deeply. He was following the scent of something, and slowly I began to realize that this giant animal was smelling me! I froze. This was no longer a wonderful experience; it was now an issue of survival. The bear's motivation was to find meat to eat, and I was clearly on his menu.

*scent: 냄새

① sad → angry   ② delighted → scared
③ satisfied → jealous   ④ worried → relieved
⑤ frustrated → excited

B17 ✽✽✽ 고1 2023(9월)/19

다음 글에 드러난 'I'의 심경 변화로 가장 적절한 것은?

Gregg and I had been rock climbing since sunrise and had had no problems. So we took a risk. "Look, the first bolt is right there. I can definitely climb out to it. Piece of cake," I persuaded Gregg, minutes before I found myself pinned. It wasn't a piece of cake. The rock was deceptively barren of handholds. I clumsily moved back and forth across the cliff face and ended up with nowhere to go... but down. The bolt that would save my life, if I could get to it, was about two feet above my reach. My arms trembled from exhaustion. I looked at Gregg. My body froze with fright from my neck down to my toes. Our rope was tied between us. If I fell, he would fall with me.

*barren of: ~이 없는

① joyful → bored   ② confident → fearful
③ nervous → relieved   ④ regretful → pleased
⑤ grateful → annoyed

B18 ✽✽✽ 고1 2023(11월)/19

다음 글에 드러난 'I'의 심경 변화로 가장 적절한 것은?

I had never seen a beach with such white sand or water that was such a beautiful shade of blue. Jane and I set up a blanket on the sand while looking forward to our ten days of honeymooning on an exotic island. "Look!" Jane waved her hand to point at the beautiful scene before us — and her gold wedding ring went flying off her hand. I tried to see where it went, but the sun hit my eyes and I lost track of it. I didn't want to lose her wedding ring, so I started looking in the area where I thought it had landed. However, the sand was so fine and I realized that anything heavy, like gold, would quickly sink and might never be found again.

① excited → frustrated   ② pleased → jealous
③ nervous → confident   ④ annoyed → grateful
⑤ relaxed → indifferent

B19 ✽✽✽ 고1 2023(6월)/19

다음 글에 드러난 'I'의 심경 변화로 가장 적절한 것은?

When I woke up in our hotel room, it was almost midnight. I didn't see my husband nor daughter. I called them, but I heard their phones ringing in the room. Feeling worried, I went outside and walked down the street, but they were nowhere to be found. When I decided I should ask someone for help, a crowd nearby caught my attention. I approached, hoping to find my husband and daughter, and suddenly I saw two familiar faces. I smiled, feeling calm. Just then, my daughter saw me and called, "Mom!" They were watching the magic show. Finally, I felt all my worries disappear.

① anxious → relieved
② delighted → unhappy
③ indifferent → excited
④ relaxed → upset
⑤ embarrassed → proud

B 어휘 Review

❋ 다음 영어는 우리말 뜻을, 우리말은 영어 단어를 〈보기〉에서 찾아 쓰시오.

┌─────────── 〈보기〉 ───────────┐
후회하는   suddenly   습기 찬   awe
난처한   nowhere   approach   절벽
disconnect   공포   board   열정
└──────────────────────────────┘

01 cliff _____

02 regretful _____

03 damp _____

04 fright _____

05 embarrassed _____

06 경외심 _____

07 다가가다 _____

08 갑자기 _____

09 단절하다 _____

10 탑승하다 _____

❋ 다음 우리말에 알맞은 영어 표현을 찾아 연결하시오.

11 쉬는 날 •   • flip through

12 휙휙 넘기다 •   • day off

13 식은 죽 먹기 •   • at a loss

14 어쩔 줄을 모르는 •   • a piece of cake

15 한숨 자다 •   • sleep a wink

❋ 다음 우리말 표현에 맞는 단어를 고르시오.

16 열두 명의 최종 입상 후보자가 모여있다 ➡ twelve finalists had (scattered / gathered)

17 제출 마감 시간 ➡ the (submission / substance) deadline

18 그의 무릎 수술 ➡ his knee (nursery / surgery)

19 그 곰의 동기 ➡ the bear's (motivation / donation)

20 나는 완전히 들떴었다 ➡ I was absolutely (thrilled / disappointed)

❋ 다음 문장의 빈칸에 알맞은 단어를 〈보기〉에서 찾아 쓰시오.

┌─────────── 〈보기〉 ───────────┐
uneasy   midnight   habitat   hops
applause   figured   exhaustion   strike
swing   indifferent heartbroken   exotic
└──────────────────────────────┘

21 토끼는 잠시 멈칫하더니, 이내 깡충 뛰어 사라진다.
➡ The rabbit pauses for a moment then _____ away.

22 내 팔은 기진맥진하여 떨렸다.
➡ My arms trembled from _____.

23 그들은 모두 그녀만큼 창백하고 불안해 보였다.
➡ They all looked as pale and _____ as herself.

24 그녀는 비행기에 탑승할 수 없다는 것을 깨달으며, 상심했다.
➡ She was _____, knowing she could not board the flight.

25 나는 코치님이 나에게 무언가 중요한 것을 말해 줄 거라고 생각했다.
➡ I _____ the coach was going to tell me something important.

26 내가 호텔 방에서 깨어났을 때는, 거의 자정이었다.
➡ When I woke up in our hotel room, it was almost _____.

27 그녀는 활짝 웃음을 지으며 우레와 같은 박수갈채를 받으며 걸어갔다.
➡ She walked into the thunder of _____ with a big smile.

28 Matthew는 그네를 향해 바로 뛰어갔다.
➡ Matthew ran all the way over to the _____ set.

29 나는 그것의 자연 서식지에서 회색곰 한 마리를 보았다.
➡ I saw a grizzly bear in its native _____.

30 레버는 종이를 두드리려 움직이지 않았다.
➡ The levers wouldn't move to _____ the paper.

C 주장 찾기

★ 유형 설명

> 다음 글에서 필자가 주장하는 바로 가장 적절한 것은?
> Balance is key. Your gestures should highlight your words, not overshadow them.

전이 부분이 필자의 주장이라고 생각해요.

맞아요. 명령문 형태니까 확실하네요!

어떤 논점에 대해 필자(글쓴이)가 갖는 주장(의견)이 무엇인지 파악해야 한다.

🔑 '~해야 한다.'라고 끝맺는 우리말 선택지가 등장하는 경우가 많다. 필자의 어조가 명확하게 드러나는 문장, 즉 명령문이나 must, have to, should 등의 조동사, important, necessary, in my opinion 등의 표현이 포함된 문장에 주의를 기울인다.

🎭 유형 풀이 비법

1 반복되는 것에 주목하라!
• 반복되는 부분을 중심으로 필자가 전달하고자 하는 내용을 파악한다.

2 처음이나 끝을 확인하라!
• 글의 첫 부분과 끝 부분에 필자의 주장이 주로 나타난다.

3 반전이 있는지 잘 보자!
• 글의 중간이나 마지막에 필자가 태도를 바꾸는 곳이 있는지 꼭 확인한다.

> (Tip) 연결어의 앞이나 명령문에 필자의 주장이 자주 등장한다.

📍 주장을 명확하게 드러내는 표현

- [ ] **You must ~** 당신은 ~해야 한다
- [ ] **You should ~** 당신은 ~해야 한다
- [ ] **You have to-v** 당신은 ~해야 한다
- [ ] **You ought to-v** 당신은 ~해야 한다
- [ ] **You need to-v** 당신은 ~할 필요가 있다
- [ ] **You can ~** 당신은 ~할 수 있다
- [ ] **Don't** + 동사원형 ~을 하지 마라
- [ ] **Never** + 동사원형 절대 ~을 하지 마라
- [ ] **Avoid -ing** ~하는 것을 피하라
- [ ] **Start from -ing** ~하는 것으로부터 시작하라
- [ ] **Keep in mind that** ~한다는 것을 명심하라
- [ ] **No one can ~** 아무도 ~할 수 없다
- [ ] **If you ~, then** 동사원형 당신이 ~한다면, …하라
- [ ] **A is a must** A는 필수적인 것이다
- [ ] **It is crucial to-v** ~하는 것은 중요하다
- [ ] **It is important to-v** ~하는 것은 중요하다
- [ ] **It is vital to-v** ~하는 것은 필수적이다
- [ ] **It is essential to-v** ~하는 것은 필수적이다
- [ ] **It is necessary to-v** ~하는 것은 필수적이다

📘 어휘 및 표현 Preview

- [ ] **achieve** 이루다
- [ ] **cope with** ~을 처리하다
- [ ] **messy** 지저분한
- [ ] **indicate** 나타내다
- [ ] **tidy** 정돈하다
- [ ] **atmosphere** 분위기
- [ ] **statement** 진술
- [ ] **witness** 목격하다
- [ ] **shift** 변화
- [ ] **priority** 우선순위
- [ ] **tempting** 솔깃한
- [ ] **uphold** 유지하다
- [ ] **remarkable** 놀라운
- [ ] **bragging** 자랑하는
- [ ] **end up with** 결국 ~로 끝나다
- [ ] **take responsibility for** ~에 책임을 지다
- [ ] **advance** 발전하다
- [ ] **commit to** ~에 전념하다
- [ ] **otherwise** 그렇지 않으면

③ 다양한 주어

1 명사(구)가 주어로 쓰이는 경우: 사람이나 사물을 나타내는 **명사나 명사구가 주어가 될 수 있다.**

- (People) have a sufficient reason for keeping their homes clean.
  명사 주어
  (**사람들은** 그들의 집을 깨끗이 해야 할 충분한 이유가 있다.)

2 동명사가 주어로 쓰이는 경우

- (Eating) fruit would also be very useful for students who are preparing for an exam.
  동명사 주어
  (과일을 **섭취하는 것은** 시험을 준비 중인 학생들에게도 매우 유용할 것이다.)

> ＊접속사 that vs. whether
> 명사절을 이끌 때 that은 '~라는 것, ~라는 사실', whether는 '~인지 아닌지'의 뜻이다.

3 명사절이 주어로 쓰이는 경우

1) ＊접속사 that, whether가 이끄는 절

- It is natural (that they should respect each other). (그들이 서로 존중해야 하는 것은 당연한 일이다.)
  접속사 that이 이끄는 절

- It doesn't matter much (whether they come or not). (그들이 오는지 안 오는지는 크게 중요하지 않다.)
  접속사 whether가 이끄는 절

2) 의문사가 이끄는 절

- (When she did it) is a mystery. (그녀가 언제 그것을 했는지는 수수께끼다.)
  의문사가 이끄는 절

4 의미상의 주어: to부정사나 동명사의 **의미상의 주어**가 문장의 주어와 일치하지 않을 경우에는 문장에서 따로 밝혀준다.

1) to부정사의 의미상의 주어

- Bill, it is very kind (of you) to say so. (Bill, 그렇게 말하다니 **당신은** 매우 친절하군요.)
  to부정사의 의미상의 주어

2) 동명사의 의미상의 주어

- I don't like (him) being treated like that. (나는 **그가** 그렇게 취급받는 것이 싫다.)
  동명사의 의미상의 주어

Check Test

1 주절의 주어를 찾아 표시하시오.

Experiments show that people eat nearly 50 percent greater quantity of the food they eat first.

2 주절의 주어를 찾아 표시하시오.

While it is very easy to talk nonstop about your little genius and his or her remarkable behavior, this can be very stressful on your child.

3 종속절의 주어를 찾아 표시하시오.

If you struggle with getting up early in the morning, then write a positive statement such as "I get up early in the morning at 5:00 a.m. every day."

4 문장의 주어를 찾아 표시하시오.

By the end of the day, that one task completed will have turned into many tasks completed.

• 정답

1 Experiments 2 this 3 you 4 that one task completed

C 주장 찾기 첫 번째

1st 선택지를 통해 글의 소재를 파악하고 어떤 내용이 전개될지 생각해 보세요.
2nd 글을 처음부터 읽으며 필자의 주장이 드러나는 부분을 찾아보세요.
3rd 필자의 주장을 우리말 한 문장으로 정리한 선택지를 찾으세요.

C01 ✽✽✽ .... 고1 2025(3월)/20

다음 글에서 필자가 주장하는 바로 가장 적절한 것은?

Improving your gestural communication involves more than just knowing when to nod or shake hands. It's about using gestures to complement your spoken messages, adding layers of meaning to your words. [5] Open-handed gestures, for example, can indicate honesty, creating an atmosphere of trust. You invite openness and collaboration when you speak with your palms facing up. This simple yet powerful gesture can make [10] others feel more comfortable and willing to engage in conversation. But be careful of the trap of over-gesturing. Too many hand movements can distract from your message, drawing attention away from your words. [15] Imagine a speaker whose hands move quickly like birds, their message lost in the chaos of their gestures. Balance is key. Your gestures should highlight your words, not overshadow them. [20]

① 메시지를 잘 전달하기 위해서 열린 마음을 지녀야 한다.
② 효과적인 의사소통을 위해 몸짓을 적절히 사용해야 한다.
③ 청중의 반응을 파악하기 위해 그들의 몸짓에 주목해야 한다.
④ 전달하고자 하는 것을 감추기보다 직접적으로 표현해야 한다.
⑤ 상대방을 설득하기 위해서는 메시지를 반복적으로 강조해야 한다.

1st 선택지를 통해 글의 소재를 파악하고 어떤 내용이 전개될지 생각해 보세요.

① 메시지를 잘 전달하기 위해서 열린 마음을 지녀야 한다.
② 효과적인 의사소통을 위해 몸짓을 적절히 사용해야 한다.
③ 청중의 반응을 파악하기 위해 그들의 몸짓에 주목해야 한다.
④ 전달하고자 하는 것을 감추기보다 직접적으로 표현해야 한다.
⑤ 상대방을 설득하기 위해서는 메시지를 반복적으로 강조해야 한다.

● **반복해서 등장하는 어구를 찾았나요?**
①, ⑤에 '메시지', ②, ③에 '몸짓'이 반복해서 등장해요. 메시지를 전달하는 방법이나 몸짓 언어에 관한 내용이 등장할 것 같아요. 하지만 아직 확실하지는 않으니 나머지 선택지의 핵심어도 짚고 넘어가야겠어요!

● **선택지를 구체적으로 살펴볼까요?**
①이 정답이라면 메시지 전달에 열린 마음이 중요하다는 내용일 것이고, ②은 적절한 몸짓이 효과적인 의사소통에 도움이 된다는 글일 거예요. ③은 청중의 몸짓에 주목하면 청중의 반응을 알 수 있다는 글일 것이고요. ④은 전달하고자 하는 것을 직접적으로 표현해야 함을, ⑤은 메시지를 반복해서 강조하는 것의 중요성을 설명하는 글일 거예요. ③을 제외하면 모두 메시지 전달이나 의사소통에 있어서 어떤 방법이 효과적인지를 설명하고 있어요. 따라서 효과적인 의사소통을 위해 중요한 것이 ① 열린 마음인지, ② 적절한 몸짓인지, ④ 직접적인 표현인지, ⑤ 메시지를 반복해서 강조하는 것인지 알아봅시다.

2nd 글을 처음부터 읽으며 필자의 주장이 드러나는 부분을 찾아보세요.

1) 첫 번째 문장을 봅시다.

Improving your **gestural communication** involves /
몸짓을 사용하는 의사소통을 개선하는 것은 포함한다 /
more than just knowing / when to nod or shake
단순히 아는 것 이상을 / 고개를 끄덕이거나 악수를 해야
hands. //
할 때를 //

● **gestural은 '몸짓을 사용하는'을 뜻해요.**
'몸짓을 사용하는' 의사소통을 개선하려면 몸짓이 필요한 때를 아는 것 말고도 무언가 더 필요한가 봐요.

● **'몸짓'이 포함된 선택지가 있지는 않았나요?**
②은 '몸짓'을 적절하게 사용하는 것, ③은 청중의 '몸짓'에 주목하는 것이 필요하다는 내용이었어요. 몸짓을 사용하는 의사소통을 개선하는 것이 위 선택지들과 어떻게 연관될지 더 살펴봐야겠어요.

2) 이어지는 문장을 봅시다.

It's about using gestures / to complement your
이는 몸짓을 사용하는 것에 대한 것이다 / 여러분의 말로 전하는 메시지를

spoken messages, / adding layers of meaning to
보완하기 위해 / 여러분의 말에 여러 겹의 의미를

your words. //
더하면서 //

● **몸짓의 목적을 설명하고 있어요.**
몸짓은 말로 전하는 메시지를 ❶(   )하기 위해, 즉 말에 여러
의미를 더하기 위해 사용하는 것이라고 했어요.
여기까지 봐서는 필자의 주장이 몸짓을 적절히 사용하라는 것인지,
아니면 청중의 몸짓에 주목하라는 것인지 아직 알 수 없어요. 내용이 다른
흐름으로 전환될 수도 있으니, 뒷부분도 마저 살펴봅시다.

3) 필자의 주장이 확실히 드러나는 문장을 찾아봅시다.

But be careful / of the trap of over-gesturing. //
하지만 주의하라 / 과도한 몸짓의 함정에 //

● **필자의 주장이 담긴 명령문이에요.**
반대되는 내용을 이어주는 등위접속사 But이 쓰였고, 그 뒤에는 '과도한
몸짓'의 함정을 조심하라는 명령문이 쓰였네요.
앞에서 몸짓은 말로 전하는 메시지를 보완하기 위한 것이라고 해서
좋은 것인 줄만 알았는데, 과도한 몸짓이 어떤 결과를 낳길래 함정을
조심하라는 걸까요?

4) 마지막 문장이 주장을 더 확실히 알려주고 있어요.

Your gestures should highlight your words, / not
여러분의 몸짓은 여러분의 말을 강조해야지 / 말을

overshadow them. //
가려서는 안 된다 //

● **몸짓이 말을 가려서는 안 된대요.**
몸짓은 말을 강조하는 보조 역할일 뿐, 몸짓이 과도하면 말을 가리게
된다는 것이 필자의 주장이네요. 몸짓의 순기능만 보고 이를 과하게 많이
쓰면 결국 말을 가리게 된다는 것이 '과도한 몸짓의 함정'이에요.

3rd **필자의 주장을 우리말 한 문장으로 정리한 선택지를 찾으세요.**
몸짓을 사용하는 의사소통을 개선하려면 몸짓이 필요한 때를 아는 것 말고도
무언가가 더 필요하다고 했어요.
몸짓의 목적은 말로 전하는 메시지를 보완하는 것인데, 몸짓이 과하게
많으면 도리어 말을 가리게 된다고 말하고 있어요.
즉, 몸짓 의사소통을 개선하려면 몸짓을 과하지 않게 적절히 사용해야
한다는 것이 필자의 주장이에요.
따라서 필자의 주장을 잘 정리한 것은 ❷(   )이에요.

글의 흐름을 정리하며 필자의 주장을 다시 한번 확인해 보세요.

도입 몸짓은 말로 전하는 메시지를 보완하기 위한 것이다.

↓

전개 몸짓은 상대방을 대화로 끌어들이는 데 도움을 준다.

↓

주장 몸짓이 과도하지 않도록 주의해야 한다.

↓

부연 몸짓은 말을 강조하기 위한 것이지, 말을 가려서는 안 된다.

— **수능 Tip**

#with 분사구문 #동시동작

★ 8번째 줄의 문장을 봅시다.

You invite openness and collaboration / when
여러분은 개방성과 협력을 끌어낸다 / 손바닥을

you speak with your palms facing up. //
위로 향한 채로 이야기할 때 //

1 「with + 명사 + 분사」
전치사 with, 명사 그리고 분사가 함께 쓰이면 '~하면서,
~한 채로'의 의미로 동시동작을 나타내는 'with 분사구문'을
만들 수 있어요.

2 **어떤 분사가 쓰이느냐에 따라 의미가 달라져요.**
현재분사가 쓰이면 명사와 분사가 능동 관계니까
'~하면서'를 뜻해요. 반면에, 과거분사가 쓰이면 명사와
분사가 수동 관계라서 '~한 채로'를 뜻해요.
여기서는 손바닥이 위로 '향하는' 것이니까, 능동 관계를
나타내기 위해 현재분사 facing이 쓰였어요.

빈칸 정답 ② **2** 보완 **1**

 자이 쌤's Follow Me!

C 주장 찾기 (두 번째)

1st 선택지를 통해 글의 소재를 파악하고 어떤 내용이 전개될지 생각해 보세요.
2nd 명령문이 나오는 부분에 주목하고, 해당 문장에서 필자의 입장을 살펴보세요.
3rd 필자의 주장을 우리말 한 문장으로 정리한 선택지를 찾으세요.

C02 ❋❋❋ .... 고1 2023(3월)/20

다음 글에서 필자가 주장하는 바로 가장 적절한 것은?

It is difficult for any of us to maintain a constant level of attention throughout our working day. We all have body rhythms characterised by peaks and valleys of energy ₅ and alertness. You will achieve more, and feel confident as a benefit, if you schedule your most demanding tasks at times when you are best able to cope with them. If you haven't thought about energy peaks before,₁₀ take a few days to observe yourself. Try to note the times when you are at your best. We are all different. For some, the peak will come first thing in the morning, but for others it may take a while to warm up.

*alertness: 기민함

① 부정적인 감정에 에너지를 낭비하지 말라.
② 자신의 신체 능력에 맞게 운동량을 조절하라.
③ 자기 성찰을 위한 아침 명상 시간을 확보하라.
④ 생산적인 하루를 보내려면 일을 균등하게 배분하라.
⑤ 자신의 에너지가 가장 높은 시간을 파악하여 활용하라.

1st 선택지를 통해 글의 소재를 파악하고 어떤 내용이 전개될지 생각해 보세요.

> ① 부정적인 감정에 에너지를 낭비하지 말라.
> ② 자신의 신체 능력에 맞게 운동량을 조절하라.
> ③ 자기 성찰을 위한 아침 명상 시간을 확보하라.
> ④ 생산적인 하루를 보내려면 일을 균등하게 배분하라.
> ⑤ 자신의 에너지가 가장 높은 시간을 파악하여 활용하라.

● **반복해서 등장하는 어구를 찾았나요?**
  모든 선택지에 반복되는 건 아니지만, '에너지'가 두 개의 선택지에 반복해서 등장해요. 아마 에너지와 관련된 내용이 등장할 것 같아요. 확실하지는 않으니까 나머지 선택지의 핵심어도 짚고 넘어가야겠어요!

● **좀 더 구체적으로 선택지를 살펴봅시다.**
  ① 부정적인 감정에 에너지를 낭비하지 말라는 건, 부정적인 감정에 너무 매몰되지 말라는 거예요.
  ② 신체 능력에 맞게 운동량을 조절하라는 건, 무리해서 운동하지 말라는 거고요.
  ③ 자기 성찰을 위한 아침 명상 시간을 확보하라는 건, '자기 성찰'과 '아침'이란 시간을 강조하는 거겠네요.
  ④ 일을 균등하게 배분해야 생산적인 하루를 보낸다는 건, 특정 시간에 일을 몰아서 하지 말라는 주장과 같겠네요.
  ⑤ 에너지가 가장 높을 때를 파악하고 활용하라는 건, 에너지가 언제 높은지를 알고 그 시간을 효율적으로 활용하라는 거고요.
  과연 어떤 주장의 글일지 차근차근 확인해 봅시다.

2nd 명령문이 나오는 부분에 주목하고, 해당 문장에서 필자의 입장을 살펴보세요.

1) 첫 번째 명령문을 확인해 봅시다.

> If you haven't thought / about energy peaks before,
> 만약 당신이 생각해 본 적이 없다면 / 전에 에너지 정점에 관해
> / take a few days / to observe yourself. //
> / 며칠을 사용해라 / 자신을 관찰하기 위해 //

● **'에너지'가 언급됐어요.**
  선택지를 보며 예상했던 '에너지'와 관련된 글이 맞았어요. 에너지 정점을 생각해 본 적이 없으면, 며칠 동안 스스로를 관찰하래요.

● **'에너지 정점'이 의미하는 바는 무엇일까요?**
  ⑤의 에너지가 가장 ❶(   ) 시간을 의미하는 건 아닐까요? 자기 자신을 관찰해서 에너지 정점을 생각해 보라는 건, 에너지가 가장 ❶(   ) 시간을 파악하라는 거겠죠. 벌써 정답을 찾은 것 같은데, 다른 명령문이 있는지 더 봅시다!

2) 두 번째 명령문을 확인해 봅시다.

> Try to note the times / when you are at your best. //
> 때를 알아차리도록 노력하라 / 당신이 가장 좋은 상태인 //

● **에너지 정점 = 가장 좋은 상태인 시간**
같은 주장을 반복하고 있어요. 당신이 가장 좋은 상태일 때, 즉 에너지 정점을 알아차리도록 노력하래요. **⑤**이 정답이 맞는 것 같은데, 에너지가 가장 높은 시간을 '활용하라'는 내용도 있는지 확인해 볼까요?

3) 글의 첫 번째 문장으로 돌아가 봅시다.

> It is difficult for any of us / to maintain a constant
> ~은 우리 중 누구라도 어렵다 / 꾸준한 수준의 주의 집중을
> level of attention / throughout our working day. //
> 유지하는 것 / 근무일 내내 //

● **문제 상황: 꾸준한 주의 집중을 내내 유지하기는 어려움**
꾸준한 주의 집중을 유지하기는 어렵다는 문제 상황을 제시하며 글을 시작했어요. 이에 대한 해결책으로 스스로의 에너지 정점을 파악하라고 한 거고요.

3rd 필자의 주장을 우리말 한 문장으로 정리한 선택지를 찾으세요.
각자 자신의 에너지가 가장 높은 시간을 파악하여 활용하라고 주장하는 글이니까 예상했던 것처럼 정답은 **②**( )!

❧ **글을 다 읽었으니 다음과 같이 글의 흐름을 정리해볼 수 있어요.**

문제	근무일 내내 꾸준한 주의 집중을 유지하는 것은 어려움

↓

해결	가장 힘든 작업을 가장 잘 처리할 수 있는 시간에 하도록 계획해야 함

↓

결론	우리는 모두 다르므로 자신만의 에너지 정점을 알아차리도록 노력해야 함

수능 **Tip**

C

#가주어 #it #진주어 #to부정사구

> It is difficult for any of us / to maintain a constant
> ~은 우리 중 누구라도 어렵다 / 꾸준한 수준의 주의 집중을
> level of attention / throughout our working day. //
> 유지하는 것은 / 근무일 내내 //

1 첫 번째 문장을 봅시다.
우리 중 누구라도 근무일 내내 꾸준한 수준의 주의 집중을 유지하기는 어렵대요.

2 It이 문장의 진짜 주어가 맞나요?
'꾸준한 수준의 주의 집중을 유지하는 것'이 어렵다고 했어요. 즉, 문장의 진짜 주어는 to maintain이 이끄는 to부정사구인데, 길이가 길어서 형식상의 주어 자리에 가주어 It을 쓴 거예요.

> For some, / the peak will come first thing / in the
> 어떤 사람에게는 / 정점은 제일 먼저 오는 것이다 / 아침에
> morning, / but for others / it may take a while /
> / 하지만 다른 사람들에게는 / ~은 얼마간의 시간이 걸릴 수도 있다 /
> to warm up. //
> 준비하는 것 //

1 우리가 살펴보지 않은 열두 번째 줄도 봅시다.
but으로 연결된 두 번째 절의 주어로 가주어 it이 쓰였어요.

2 진주어는 무엇인가요?
다른 사람들에게는 '준비하는 것'이 얼마간의 시간이 걸릴 수 있다고 했으니까, 가주어 it이 대신하는 진주어는 **③**( )이에요.

선택지로 글의 소재를 예측하자!

C03~07 ▶ 제한시간 10분

C03 ✱✱✱ 고1 2025(6월)/20

다음 글에서 필자가 주장하는 바로 가장 적절한 것은?

People often ask me, "What surprises you most about habits?" One thing that continually astonishes me is the degree to which we're influenced by sheer convenience. The amount of effort, time, or decision making required by an action has a huge influence on habit formation. To a truly remarkable extent, we're more likely to do something if it's convenient, and less likely if it's not. For this reason, we should pay close attention to the convenience of any activity we want to make into a habit. Putting a wastebasket next to our front door made mail sorting slightly more convenient, and I stopped procrastinating with this chore. Many people report that they do a much better job of staying close to distant family members now that tools like group chats make it easy to stay in touch.   *sheer: 순전한 **procrastinate: 미루다

① 불필요한 자극을 유발하는 작업 환경을 개선해야 한다.
② 생활방식 개선을 위해 규칙적인 생활 습관을 길러야 한다.
③ 목표를 신속하게 달성하려면 구체적인 계획을 세워야 한다.
④ 반복적인 업무의 편의를 위해 디지털 도구를 사용해야 한다.
⑤ 습관으로 만들고 싶은 행동의 편리성에 주의를 기울여야 한 다.

구문 서술형

괄호 안의 단어를 이용하여 빈칸에 알맞은 말을 쓰시오. (필요시 형태를 바꿀 것)

현관문 옆에 쓰레기통을 두는 것이 우편물을 분류하는 일을 약간 더 편리하게 했다. (our front door, put, next to, a wastebasket)

➡ _____ made mail sorting slightly more convenient.

C04 ✱✱✱ 고1 2025(9월)/20

다음 글에서 필자가 주장하는 바로 가장 적절한 것은?

Inefficient teachers overlook the potential power of the opening minutes of class. Often, if students are quiet enough and if there are many pressing demands on a teacher's time at that moment, more than ten minutes can disappear before class starts. It's no wonder that students are late for class; they have little reason to be on time. You can use the first ten minutes to get your class off to a great start, or you can choose to waste this time. The first minutes set the tone for the rest of the class. If you are prepared for class and have taught your students an opening routine, they can use this brief time to make mental and emotional transitions from the last class or subject and prepare to focus on learning new material. In summary, you should establish an opening routine to develop your class with an effective start.

① 학생의 적극적인 참여를 위해 포용적 수업 분위기를 형성하라.
② 수업을 효과적으로 전개하기 위해 시작 루틴을 마련하라.
③ 학습 동기를 부여할 수 있는 창의적인 수업 자료를 개발하라.
④ 적절한 학습량 조절을 통해 학습 부담을 줄여라.
⑤ 학생이 스스로 학습 루틴을 만들도록 장려하라.

구문 서술형

여섯 번째 줄의 It's no wonder ~ for class 문장을 참고하여 아래 대화의 빈칸에 알맞은 말을 쓰시오.

A: 이 문장의 주어는 It이야.

B: 음, 맞긴 맞는데... 정확히는 _____에 해당하지!

A: _____? 그러면 뒤에 진주어도 있어?

B: _____으로 시작하는 명사절이 이 문장의 진주어야. 너무 길어서 대신에 It이 문장의 맨 앞에 왔지!

C05 ✽✽✽   고1 2024(10월)/20

다음 글에서 필자가 주장하는 바로 가장 적절한 것은?

For many of us, making time for exercise is a continuing challenge. Between work commitments and family obligations, it often feels like there's no room in our packed schedules for a dedicated workout. But what if the workout came to you, right in the midst of your daily routine? That's where the beauty of integrating mini-exercises into household chores comes into play. Let's be realistic; chores are inevitable. Whether it's washing dishes or taking out the trash, these tasks are an essential part of daily life. But rather than viewing chores as purely obligatory activities, why not seize these moments as opportunities for physical activity? For instance, practice squats or engage in some wall push-ups as you wait for your morning kettle to boil. Incorporating quick exercises into your daily chores can improve your health.

① 간단한 운동일지라도 강도를 점진적으로 높여야 한다.
② 집안일을 간단한 운동을 병행할 기회로 활용해야 한다.
③ 집안일을 할 때 동선을 고려하여 효율을 높여야 한다.
④ 자신이 즐길 수 있는 운동을 찾아 꾸준히 해야 한다.
⑤ 몸에 무리를 주지 않으려면 집안일을 줄여야 한다.

구문 서술형

주절의 주어를 찾아 쓰고, 문장을 알맞게 해석하시오.

Whether it's washing dishes or taking out the trash, these tasks are an essential part of daily life.

➡ 주절의 주어: _____

➡ 해석: 그것이 설거지하는 것이든 쓰레기를 내다 버리는 것이든지 간에, _____.

C06 ✽✽✽   고1 2024(3월)/20

다음 글에서 필자가 주장하는 바로 가장 적절한 것은?

Magic is what we all wish for to happen in our life. Do you love the movie *Cinderella* like me? Well, in real life, you can also create magic. Here's the trick. Write down all the real-time challenges that you face and deal with. Just change the challenge statement into positive statements. Let me give you an example here. If you struggle with getting up early in the morning, then write a positive statement such as "I get up early in the morning at 5:00 am every day." Once you write these statements, get ready to witness magic and confidence. You will be surprised that just by writing these statements, there is a shift in the way you think and act. Suddenly you feel more powerful and positive.

① 목표한 바를 꼭 이루려면 생각을 곧바로 행동으로 옮겨라.
② 자신감을 얻으려면 어려움을 긍정적인 진술로 바꿔 써라.
③ 어려운 일을 해결하려면 주변 사람에게 도움을 청하라.
④ 일상에서 자신감을 향상하려면 틈틈이 마술을 배워라.
⑤ 실생활에서 마주하는 도전을 피하지 말고 견뎌 내라.

C07 ✽✽✽   고1 2024(6월)/20

다음 글에서 필자가 주장하는 바로 가장 적절한 것은?

Having a messy room can add up to negative feelings and destructive thinking. Psychologists say that having a disorderly room can indicate a disorganized mental state. One of the professional tidying experts says that the moment you start cleaning your room, you also start changing your life and gaining new perspective. When you clean your surroundings, positive and good atmosphere follows. You can do more things efficiently and neatly. So, clean up your closets, organize your drawers, and arrange your things first, then peace of mind will follow.

① 자신의 공간을 정돈하여 긍정적 변화를 도모하라.
② 오랜 시간 고민하기보다는 일단 행동으로 옮겨라.
③ 무질서한 환경에서 창의적인 생각을 시도하라.
④ 장기 목표를 위해 단기 목표를 먼저 설정하라.
⑤ 반복되는 일상을 새로운 관점으로 관찰하라.

C08 ❋❋❉ 고1 2024(9월)/20

다음 글에서 필자가 주장하는 바로 가장 적절한 것은?

As the parent of a gifted child, you need to be aware of a certain common parent trap. Of course you are a proud parent, and you should be. While it is very easy to talk nonstop about your little genius and his or her remarkable behavior, this can be very stressful on your child. It is extremely important to limit your bragging behavior to your very close friends, or your parents. Gifted children feel pressured when their parents show them off too much. This behavior creates expectations that they may not be able to live up to, and also creates a false sense of self for your child. You want your child to be who they are, not who they seem to be as defined by their incredible achievements. If not, you could end up with a driven perfectionist child or perhaps a drop-out, or worse.

① 부모는 자녀를 다른 아이와 비교하지 말아야 한다.
② 부모는 자녀의 영재성을 지나치게 자랑하지 말아야 한다.
③ 영재교육 프로그램에 대한 맹목적인 믿음을 삼가야 한다.
④ 과도한 영재교육보다 자녀와의 좋은 관계 유지에 힘써야 한다.
⑤ 자녀의 독립성을 기르기 위해 자기 일은 스스로 하게 해야 한다.

C09 ❋❋❉ 고1 2021(9월)/20

다음 글에서 필자가 주장하는 바로 가장 적절한 것은?

As you set about to write, it is worth reminding yourself that while you ought to have a point of view, you should avoid telling your readers what to think. Try to hang a question mark over it all. This way you allow your readers to think for themselves about the points and arguments you're making. As a result, they will feel more involved, finding themselves just as committed to the arguments you've made and the insights you've exposed as you are. You will have written an essay that not only avoids passivity in the reader, but is interesting and gets people to think.

① 저자의 독창적인 견해를 드러내야 한다.
② 다양한 표현으로 독자에게 감동을 주어야 한다.
③ 독자가 능동적으로 사고할 수 있도록 글을 써야 한다.
④ 독자에게 가치판단의 기준점을 명확히 제시해야 한다.
⑤ 주관적 관점을 배제하고 사실을 바탕으로 글을 써야 한다.

C10 ❋❋❉ 고1 2021(6월)/20

다음 글에서 필자가 주장하는 바로 가장 적절한 것은?

Sometimes, you feel the need to avoid something that will lead to success out of discomfort. Maybe you are avoiding extra work because you are tired. You are actively shutting out success because you want to avoid being uncomfortable. Therefore, overcoming your instinct to avoid uncomfortable things at first is essential. Try doing new things outside of your comfort zone. Change is always uncomfortable, but it is key to doing things differently in order to find that magical formula for success.

① 불편할지라도 성공하기 위해서는 새로운 것을 시도해야 한다.
② 일과 생활의 균형을 맞추는 성공적인 삶을 추구해야 한다.
③ 갈등 해소를 위해 불편함의 원인을 찾아 개선해야 한다.
④ 단계별 목표를 설정하여 익숙한 것부터 도전해야 한다.
⑤ 변화에 적응하기 위해 직관적으로 문제를 해결해야 한다.

C11 ❋❋❋ 고1 2023(9월)/20

다음 글에서 필자가 주장하는 바로 가장 적절한 것은?

We are always teaching our children something by our words and our actions. They learn from seeing. They learn from hearing and from *overhearing*. Children share the values of their parents about the most important things in life. Our priorities and principles and our examples of good behavior can teach our children to take the high road when other roads look tempting. Remember that children do not learn the values that make up strong character simply by being *told* about them. They learn by seeing the people around them *act* on and *uphold* those values in their daily lives. Therefore show your child good examples of life by your action. In our daily lives, we can show our children that we respect others. We can show them our compassion and concern when others are suffering, and our own self-discipline, courage and honesty as we make difficult decisions.

① 자녀를 타인과 비교하는 말을 삼가야 한다.
② 자녀에게 행동으로 삶의 모범을 보여야 한다.
③ 칭찬을 통해 자녀의 바람직한 행동을 강화해야 한다.
④ 훈육을 하기 전에 자녀 스스로 생각할 시간을 주어야 한다.
⑤ 자녀가 새로운 것에 도전할 때 인내심을 가지고 지켜봐야 한다.

C12 ✱✱✱ 고1 2022(11월)/20

다음 글에서 필자가 주장하는 바로 가장 적절한 것은?

You already have a business and you're about to launch your blog so that you can sell your product. Unfortunately, here is where a 'business mind' can be a bad thing. Most people believe that to have a successful business blog promoting a product, they have to stay strictly 'on the topic.' If all you're doing is shamelessly promoting your product, then who is going to want to read the latest thing you're writing about? Instead, you need to give some useful or entertaining information away for free so that people have a reason to keep coming back. Only by doing this can you create an interested audience that you will then be able to sell to. So, the best way to be successful with a business blog is to write about things that your audience will be interested in.

① 인터넷 게시물에 대한 윤리적 기준을 세워야 한다.
② 블로그를 전문적으로 관리할 인력을 마련해야 한다.
③ 신제품 개발을 위해 상업용 블로그를 적극 활용해야 한다.
④ 상품에 대한 고객들의 반응을 정기적으로 분석할 필요가 있다.
⑤ 상업용 블로그는 사람들이 흥미 있어 할 정보를 제공해야 한다.

C13 ✱✱✱ 고1 2023(6월)/20

다음 글에서 필자가 주장하는 바로 가장 적절한 것은?

Research shows that people who work have two calendars: one for work and one for their personal lives. Although it may seem sensible, having two separate calendars for work and personal life can lead to distractions. To check if something is missing, you will find yourself checking your to-do lists multiple times. Instead, organize all of your tasks in one place. It doesn't matter if you use digital or paper media. It's okay to keep your professional and personal tasks in one place. This will give you a good idea of how time is divided between work and home. This will allow you to make informed decisions about which tasks are most important.

① 결정한 것은 반드시 실행하도록 노력하라.
② 자신이 담당한 업무에 관한 전문성을 확보하라.
③ 업무 집중도를 높이기 위해 책상 위를 정돈하라.
④ 좋은 아이디어를 메모하는 습관을 길러라.
⑤ 업무와 개인 용무를 한 곳에 정리하라.

C14 ✱✱✱ 고1 2022(6월)/20

다음 글에서 필자가 주장하는 바로 가장 적절한 것은?

Meetings encourage creative thinking and can give you ideas that you may never have thought of on your own. However, on average, meeting participants consider about one third of meeting time to be unproductive. But you can make your meetings more productive and more useful by preparing well in advance. You should create a list of items to be discussed and share your list with other participants before a meeting. It allows them to know what to expect in your meeting and prepare to participate.

① 회의 결과는 빠짐없이 작성해서 공개해야 한다.
② 중요한 정보는 공식 회의를 통해 전달해야 한다.
③ 생산성 향상을 위해 정기적인 평가회가 필요하다.
④ 모든 참석자의 동의를 받아서 회의를 열어야 한다.
⑤ 회의에서 다룰 사항은 미리 작성해서 공유해야 한다.

C15 ✱✱✱ 고1 2023(11월)/20

다음 글에서 필자가 주장하는 바로 가장 적절한 것은?

Unfortunately, many people don't take personal responsibility for their own growth. Instead, they simply run the race laid out for them. They do well enough in school to keep advancing. Maybe they manage to get a good job at a well-run company. But so many think and act as if their learning journey ends with college. They have checked all the boxes in the life that was laid out for them and now lack a road map describing the right ways to move forward and continue to grow. In truth, that's when the journey really begins. When school is finished, your growth becomes voluntary. Like healthy eating habits or a regular exercise program, you need to commit to it and devote thought, time, and energy to it. Otherwise, it simply won't happen — and your life and career are likely to stop progressing as a result.

① 성공 경험을 위해 달성 가능한 목표를 수립해야 한다.
② 체계적인 경력 관리를 위해 전문가의 도움을 받아야 한다.
③ 건강을 위해 꾸준한 운동과 식습관 관리를 병행해야 한다.
④ 졸업 이후 성장을 위해 자발적으로 배움을 실천해야 한다.
⑤ 적성에 맞는 직업을 찾기 위해 학교 교육에 충실해야 한다.

C16 ***❀ 고1 2022(9월)/20

다음 글에서 필자가 주장하는 바로 가장 적절한 것은?

Experts on writing say, "Get rid of as many words as possible." Each word must do something important. If it doesn't, get rid of it. Well, this doesn't work for speaking. It takes more words to introduce, express, and adequately elaborate an idea in speech than it takes in writing. Why is this so? While the reader can reread, the listener cannot rehear. Speakers do not come equipped with a replay button. Because listeners are easily distracted, they will miss many pieces of what a speaker says. If they miss the crucial sentence, they may never catch up. This makes it necessary for speakers to talk longer about their points, using more words on them than would be used to express the same idea in writing.

① 연설 시 중요한 정보는 천천히 말해야 한다.
② 좋은 글을 쓰려면 간결한 문장을 사용해야 한다.
③ 말하기 전에 신중히 생각하는 습관을 길러야 한다.
④ 글을 쓸 때보다 말할 때 더 많은 단어를 사용해야 한다.
⑤ 청중의 이해를 돕기 위해 미리 연설문을 제공해야 한다.

2등급 대비 문제

C17 ~ 18 ▶제한시간 4분

C17 ✪ 2등급 대비 고1 2022(3월)/20

다음 글에서 필자가 주장하는 바로 가장 적절한 것은?

When I was in the army, my instructors would show up in my barracks room, and the first thing they would inspect was our bed. It was a simple task, but every morning we were required to make our bed to perfection. It seemed a little ridiculous at the time, but the wisdom of this simple act has been proven to me many times over. If you make your bed every morning, you will have accomplished the first task of the day. It will give you a small sense of pride and it will encourage you to do another task and another. By the end of the day, that one task completed will have turned into many tasks completed. If you can't do little things right, you will never do the big things right.

*barracks room: (병영의) 생활관 **accomplish: 성취하다

① 숙면을 위해서는 침대를 깔끔하게 관리해야 한다.
② 일의 효율성을 높이려면 협동심을 발휘해야 한다.
③ 올바른 습관을 기르려면 정해진 규칙을 따라야 한다.
④ 건강을 유지하기 위해서는 기상 시간이 일정해야 한다.
⑤ 큰일을 잘 이루려면 작은 일부터 제대로 수행해야 한다.

C18 ✪ 2등급 대비 고1 2021(11월)/20

다음 글에서 필자가 주장하는 바로 가장 적절한 것은?

Some experts estimate that as much as half of what we communicate is done through the way we move our bodies. Paying attention to the nonverbal messages you send can make a significant difference in your relationship with students. In general, most students are often closely tuned in to their teacher's body language. For example, when your students first enter the classroom, their initial action is to look for their teacher. Think about how encouraging and empowering it is for a student when that teacher has a friendly greeting and a welcoming smile. Smiling at students — to let them know that you are glad to see them — does not require a great deal of time or effort, but it can make a significant difference in the classroom climate right from the start of class.

① 교사는 학생 간의 상호 작용을 주의 깊게 관찰해야 한다.
② 수업 시 교사는 학생의 수준에 맞는 언어를 사용해야 한다.
③ 학생과의 관계에서 교사는 비언어적 표현에 유의해야 한다.
④ 학교는 학생에게 다양한 역할 경험의 기회를 제공해야 한다.
⑤ 교사는 학생 안전을 위해 교실의 물리적 환경을 개선해야 한다.

C 어휘 Review

✳ 다음 영어는 우리말 뜻을, 우리말은 영어 단어를 〈보기〉에서 찾아 쓰시오.

┌─────────────── 〈보기〉 ───────────────┐
검사하다	unproductive	완벽한	achieve
목격하다	seize	산만한	audience
compassion	이익	elaborate	자랑하는
└───────────────────────────────────────┘

01 witness _____

02 inspect _____

03 distracted _____

04 complete _____

05 benefit _____

06 잡다 _____

07 비생산적인 _____

08 달성하다 _____

09 부연 설명하다 _____

10 연민 _____

✳ 다음 우리말에 알맞은 영어 표현을 찾아 연결하시오.

11 나누어 주다 •   • manage to

12 (간신히) 해내다 •   • give away

13 막 ~하려고 하다 •   • cope with

14 ~을 처리하다 •   • be about to

15 정점과 저점 •   • peaks and valleys

✳ 다음 우리말 표현에 맞는 단어를 고르시오.

16 두 개의 별도의 달력을 갖는 것 ➡ having two (moderate / separate) calendars

17 가족 의무 ➡ family (objections / obligations)

18 그들의 엄청난 업적 ➡ their (edible / incredible) achievements

19 긍정적이고 좋은 분위기 ➡ positive and good (atmosphere / hemisphere)

20 다른 길이 유혹적으로 보일 때 ➡ when other roads look (tempting / unappealing)

✳ 다음 문장의 빈칸에 알맞은 단어를 〈보기〉에서 찾아 쓰시오.

┌─────────────── 〈보기〉 ───────────────┐
launch	overshadow	otherwise	uphold
constant	dedicated	overhear	remarkable
perfection	neatly	powerful	driven
└───────────────────────────────────────┘

21 당신은 더 많은 일을 효율적이고 깔끔하게 할 수 있다.
➡ You can do more things efficiently and _____.

22 여러분의 몸짓은 여러분의 말을 강조해야지, 말을 가려서는 안 된다. ➡ Your gestures should highlight your words, not _____ them.

23 우리의 일정들에는 운동에 전념할 여유가 없다.
➡ There's no room in our schedules for a(n) _____ workout.

24 그들은 그들 주변 사람들이 그러한 가치를 좇아 행동하고 유지하는 것을 봄으로써 배운다.
➡ They learn by seeing the people around them act on and _____ those values.

25 신념과 행동은 이보다 더 놀라운 방식으로 관련이 있다.
➡ Beliefs and behaviors are related in a more _____ way.

26 여러분은 여러분의 제품을 팔 수 있도록 블로그를 시작하려는 참이다. ➡ You're about to _____ your blog so that you can sell your product.

27 그렇지 않으면, 그것은 그냥 일어나지 않을 것이다.
➡ _____, it simply won't happen.

28 어느 순간 여러분은 더 강력하고 긍정적이라고 느끼게 된다.
➡ Suddenly you feel more _____ and positive.

29 단순한 일이었지만, 매일 아침 우리는 침대를 완벽하게 정돈하도록 요구받았다. ➡ It was a simple task, but every morning we were required to make our bed to _____.

30 우리 중 누구라도 꾸준한 주의 집중을 유지하기는 어렵다.
➡ It is difficult for any of us to maintain a(n) _____ level of attention.

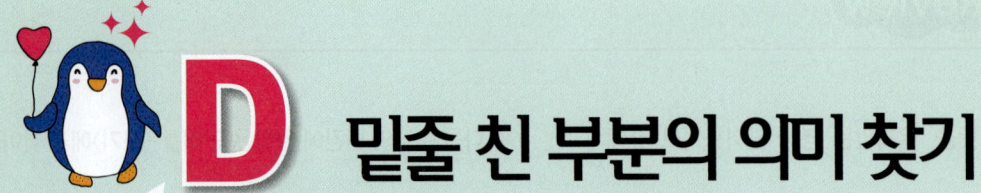

D 밑줄 친 부분의 의미 찾기

★ 유형 설명

> 밑줄 친 There will be many who will follow you가 다음 글에서 의미하는 바로 가장 적절한 것은? [3점]
> You're the present caretaker of the atoms in your body. <u>There will be many who will follow you.</u>

밑줄 친 부분은 비유적인 표현인 경우가 많다. 글의 내용과 문맥에 맞게 그 직접적인 의미가 무엇인지 추론해야 한다.

🔑 똑같은 비유적인 표현도 어떤 글에서 쓰였는지에 따라 그 의미가 달라지므로 글의 내용을 정확히 파악한 후에 그에 맞게 비유적 표현의 의미를 찾아야 한다.
정답으로 고른 선택지를 밑줄 친 부분 대신에 넣어 보고 글이 자연스러운지 확인한다.

이 수학 문제를 푸는 것은 정말 식은 죽 먹기네요!

어려움 없이 쉽게 풀었다는 뜻이구나?

∞ 유형 풀이 비법

1 밑줄 친 부분을 파악하라!
• 밑줄 친 부분이 어디 있는지 확인한 후, 어떤 부분에 집중해서 전체 글을 읽어야 하는지 파악한다.

2 핵심 내용을 종합하라!
• 처음부터 글을 읽으면서 전체 내용을 이해하고 핵심어와 요지를 찾는다.

3 선택지를 해석해 보라!
• 밑줄 친 부분에 정답으로 고른 선택지의 해석을 넣어서 맞는지 확인한다.

(Tip) 밑줄 친 부분의 앞뒤 내용뿐만 아니라 전체 글의 흐름에 매끄럽게 들어맞는지 확인한다.

🔑 어휘 및 표현 Preview

□ adopt 받아들이다, 채택하다	□ energize 활기를 북돋우다	□ restate 다시 말하다
□ traditional 전통적인	□ be in one's presence ~의 자리에 (함께) 있다	□ publication 출판
□ livelihood 생계 수단	□ psychic 정신의	□ previous 이전의
□ progress 발전	□ transfer 이동	□ commonsense 상식적인
□ remove 없애다	□ relight 재점화하다	□ objective 객관적인
□ physical 육체의	□ react 반응하다	□ property 속성, 성질
□ disability 장애	□ behavior 행동	□ bounce off 튕겨 나오다
□ mass 대중의	□ influence 영향	□ inhabit ~에 살다[존재하다]
□ seemingly 겉보기에	□ likelihood 가능성	□ subjective 주관적인
□ doubt 의심하다	□ ambassador 대사	□ warranty (상품 등의) 보증
□ perception 인식	□ persuade 설득하다	□ abuse 남용하다
□ categorize 분류하다	□ monitor 추적 관찰하다	□ entrepreneur 기업가
□ detect 감지하다	□ word-of-mouth 구두의, 구전의	□ capacity 능력
□ prey 먹잇감	□ gain 이득, 대가	□ agricultural 농업의
□ helplessness 무력감	□ overseas 해외에서	□ be loaded with ~으로 가득 차다
□ predominantly 현저히	□ indeed 정말로	□ real estate 부동산
□ resolve 해결하다	□ perceive 감지하다	□ abundant 풍부한

4 동명사와 to부정사

1 동명사 – 동명사는 명사처럼 문장에서 **주어, 목적어, 보어**의 역할을 한다.

1) 주어: 동명사 주어는 **단수 취급**하며, 몇몇 관용표현을 제외하면 가주어 it을 내세우는 경우는 드물다.

• Reading a history book is helpful. (역사책을 읽는 것은 도움이 된다.)
　주어 역할을 하는 동명사　　　단수 동사

2) 동사나 전치사의 목적어: 전치사의 목적어로 준동사가 필요한 경우에는 **동명사**를 쓴다.

• Bob already started writing his essay. (Bob은 그의 에세이를 쓰는 것을 이미 시작했다.)
　　　　　　동사 started의 목적어 역할을 하는 동명사

• We should focus on preparing for the event. (우리는 행사를 준비하는 것에 집중해야 한다.)
　　　　　전치사 on의 목적어 역할을 하는 동명사, to prepare는 쓸 수 없음

3) 주격 보어: 동명사는 문장에서 주어를 보충 설명하는 **주격 보어**로 쓰일 수 있다.

• My goal is graduating from high school early.
　　　　　주격 보어 역할을 하는 동명사

(내 목표는 고등학교를 일찍 **졸업하는 것**이다.)

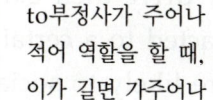

> **＊가주어, 가목적어**
> to부정사가 주어나 목적어 역할을 할 때, 길이가 길면 가주어나 가목적어로 it을 쓰고 to부정사를 뒤로 보낸다.

2 to부정사 – to부정사는 문장에서 **명사적 쓰임, 형용사적 쓰임, 부사적 쓰임**으로 쓰인다.

1) to부정사의 명사적 쓰임 ┌ to부정사는 명사처럼 문장에서 **주어, 목적어, 보어 역할**을 할 수 있다.
　　　　　　　　　　　　└ 이때 to부정사는 '**～하는 것, ～하기**'라고 해석한다.

• To know the truth is important. ➡ It is important to know the truth. (진실을 아는 것이 중요하다.)
　주어 역할을 하는 to부정사(구)　　　 ＊가주어　　　　　　　진주어

• The new law made to get a divorce easier. ➡ The new law made it easier to get a divorce.
　　　　　　　목적어 역할을 하는 to부정사(구)　　　　　　　　　　　　 가목적어　　　 진목적어

(새로운 법은 **이혼하는 것**을 더 쉽게 만들었다.)

2) to부정사의 형용사적 쓰임: to부정사는 **형용사처럼 명사를 수식**할 수 있다.

• We have enough time to finish it. (우리에게는 그것을 **끝낼** 충분한 시간이 있다.)
　　　　　　　　앞의 명사 time을 수식하는 to부정사

3) to부정사의 부사적 쓰임: to부정사는 **부사처럼 동사, 형용사, 부사, 또는 문장 전체를 수식**할 수 있다.

• Please bring the receipt in order to get a refund. (환불을 **받기 위해** 영수증을 가져오세요.)
　　　　　　　　　　　　　목적의 의미를 강조함, 생략 가능

Check Test

1 밑줄 친 부분에 쓰인 to부정사의 쓰임을 쓰시오.

Browsing is not an effective way to reach a goal you claim to want to reach.

→ _____

2 다음 문장에서 밑줄 친 부분의 역할을 쓰시오.

Many vertebrates have a different sense system for detecting odors.

→ _____

3 다음 문장에서 주어를 찾아 표시하시오.

To be in their presence is beneficial.

4 밑줄 친 부분에 쓰인 to부정사의 쓰임을 쓰시오.

One valuable technique is to choose to be with other persons.

→ _____

D 밑줄 친 부분의 의미 찾기 (첫 번째)

D01 ✽✽✽ ····· 고1 2025(6월)/21

밑줄 친 the arrow is as likely to point in the reverse direction이 다음 글에서 의미하는 바로 가장 적절한 것은? [3점]

It is common sense that people's inner beliefs may drive their external behavior. If you're attracted to a certain person, you should be more likely to socialize with that person. If you favor a brand of toothpaste, you're more ⁵ likely to buy it. Of course, our internal thoughts don't always predict our public behavior, but, overall, what we do obviously reflects what we think. But beliefs and behaviors are also related in a more¹⁰ remarkable way. It turns out that the arrow is as likely to point in the reverse direction. As social psychologist David Myers observes, "If social psychology has taught us anything during the last 25 years, it is that we are¹⁵ likely not only to think ourselves into a way of acting but also to act ourselves into a way of thinking."

① actions can be entirely separate from beliefs
② our behaviors can also shape what we believe
③ our opinions can be dependent on our emotions
④ behaviors can clearly reflect one's surroundings
⑤ what we think can matter more than what we do

1st 밑줄 친 부분을 먼저 읽고, 앞으로 글에서 찾아야 할 내용이 무엇인지 생각해 보세요.

It turns out / that the arrow is as likely to point / in
드러난다 / 화살이 가리킬 가능성이 그만큼 높다는 것이 /
the reverse direction. //
반대 방향을 //

● 밑줄 친 부분이 글의 중간에 있어요.
화살이 ❶( )을 가리킬 가능성이 높다고 했어요.
글에서 어떤 내용이 나오고 그 반대 방향의 내용이 맞다는 흐름으로 전개될 것 같은데, 우선 글을 처음부터 읽으며 중심 소재가 무엇인지 파악해야겠어요.

2nd 앞에서 찾은 단서를 활용하여 글을 읽고, 밑줄 친 부분이 의미하는 바를 추론하세요.

1) 첫 문장부터 읽어 봅시다.

It is common sense / that people's inner beliefs /
상식이다 / 사람들의 내적 신념이 /
may drive their external behavior. //
그들의 외적인 행동을 이끌 수 있다는 것은 //

● 신념과 행동이라는 소재가 등장했어요.
사람들의 내적 신념이 외적인 행동을 이끌 수 있다는 것이 상식이라고 해요. 그런데 이 신념과 행동이 그저 나란히 주어졌나요, 아니면 어떤 순서가 있나요?

● 두 소재 사이에 방향이 있어요.
앞서 밑줄 친 문장에서 확인한 것처럼 방향이 등장했는데, 내적 신념이 외적 행동을 이끄는 것은 내적 신념에서 시작하여 외적 행동으로 이어진다는 것을 나타내요. 즉, '내적 신념 → 외적 행동'이라는 방향을 우선 기억하면 좋을 것 같아요.

2) 이어지는 두 문장에서 구체적인 예시를 들고 있어요.

If you're attracted to a certain person, / you should
만약 당신이 어떤 사람에게 끌린다면 / 당신은 더
be more likely to socialize / with that person. //
어울리려고 할 것이다 / 그 사람과 //
If you favor a brand of toothpaste, / you're more
만약 당신이 한 브랜드의 치약을 선호한다면 / 당신이 그것을
likely to buy it. //
구매할 가능성은 더 높다 //

● 두 예시는 무엇을 나타내고 어떤 역할을 하나요?
- 예시 ①: 어떤 사람에게 끌릴 때 → 그 사람과 더 어울리려고 할 것임
- 예시 ②: 특정 치약을 선호할 때 → 그 치약을 구매할 가능성이 더 높음
  내적 신념: 어떤 사람에게 끌리는 것, 특정 치약을 선호하는 것
  외적 행동: 끌리는 사람과 더 어울리려는 것, 선호하는 치약을 구매하는 것
  두 예시는 모두 **❷**(   )이 외적 행동을 이끈다는 첫 문장의 내용을 뒷받침해요.

3) 내용이 전환되는 부분이 있나요?

> But beliefs and behaviors / are also related / in a
> 그러나 신념과 행동은   / 또한 관련이 있다   / 이보다
> more remarkable way. //
> 더 놀라운 방식으로   //

● **신념과 행동의 또 다른 관계를 제시하려나 봐요.**
앞의 내용과 반대되는 내용을 제시하는 접속사 But이 등장했어요.
우리는 앞에서 '내적 신념 → 외적 행동'이라는 방향성을 기억하자고 했는데, 신념과 행동 사이에 이보다 '더 놀라운' 관계가 있다는 것은 어떤 의미일까요?

4) 이제 마지막 문장을 확인합시다.

> As social psychologist David Myers observes, / "If
> 사회심리학자 David Myers가 말한 바에 따르면   /
> social psychology has taught us anything / during
> "사회심리학이 우리에게 가르쳐준 것이 있다면   / 지난
> the last 25 years, / it is that / we are likely / not only
> 25년간   / 그것은 바로 / 우리가 가능성이 있다는 것이다 /
> to think ourselves into a way of acting / but also to
> 우리가 생각하여 행동 방식에 이를 뿐만 아니라   / 우리가 또한
> act ourselves into a way of thinking." //
> 행동하여 사고 방식에 이를"   //

● **밑줄 친 부분과 비슷한 표현이 쓰였어요.**
밑줄 친 부분에 likely to point가 있는데, 마지막 문장에도 likely 뒤에 to think와 **❸**(   )가 병렬 구조로 연결되었어요. 밑줄 친 부분과 아주 밀접한 관련이 있을 듯하니 이번엔 그 의미를 살펴볼까요?

● **not only A but also B는 'A뿐만 아니라 B도'라는 뜻이에요.**
따라서 마지막 문장은 우리가 생각하여 행동 방식에 이를 뿐만 아니라, 행동하여 사고 방식에 이를 가능성이 있다는 내용이네요.
우리가 앞에서 찾으려 했던 내용, 즉 신념과 행동의 '더 놀라운' 관계는 바로 상식과 반대 방향인 관계(외적 행동 → 내적 신념)를 가리키는 것이었어요.

3rd 파악한 글의 내용을 종합하여 선택지에서 정답을 찾으세요.

1) 내용의 흐름은 아래와 같이 정리할 수 있어요.

도입 │ 내적 신념이 외적 행동을 이끄는 것이 상식임
↓
예시 │ 사람이나 사물에 대한 선호가 그것에 대한 행동으로 이어짐
↓
주제 │ 그 반대 방향일 가능성도 있음 (외적 행동이 내적 신념을 이끄는 것)
↓
부연 │ 사회심리학을 통해 두 방향 모두 가능하다는 것을 발견함

2) 선택지를 해석해 봅시다.

① actions can be entirely separate from beliefs
   행동은 신념과 완전히 분리될 수 있다
② our behaviors can also shape what we believe
   우리의 행동이 우리가 믿는 바를 형성할 수도 있다
③ our opinions can be dependent on our emotions
   우리의 의견은 감정에 의존할 수 있다
④ behaviors can clearly reflect one's surroundings
   행동은 분명히 주변 환경을 반영할 수 있다
⑤ what we think can matter more than what we do
   우리가 생각하는 것이 우리가 하는 것보다 더 중요할 수 있다

3) 밑줄 친 부분의 의미는 무엇일까요?
내적 신념이 외적 행동을 이끄는 것이 상식이지만, 그 반대로 외적 행동이 내적 신념을 이끌 가능성도 있다는 내용의 글이에요. 즉, 밑줄 친 부분의 '반대 방향'은 '외적 행동 → 내적 신념(믿는 바)'의 방향을 가리켜요.
따라서 밑줄 친 부분은 **❹**(   ) '우리의 행동이 우리가 믿는 바를 형성할 수도 있다'를 의미해요!

> 밑줄 친 부분을 먼저 읽고 글의 중심 소재를 파악하자!

BEHAVIOR   BELIEF

❖ 정답 및 해설 35p   D. 밑줄 친 부분의 의미 찾기 **47**

D 밑줄 친 부분의 의미 찾기 (두 번째)

1st 첫 문장과 밑줄 친 부분이 포함된 문장을 읽고, 글의 내용을 예상하세요.
2nd 글의 나머지 부분을 읽고, 예상한 내용이 맞는지 확인하세요.
3rd 글의 내용을 종합하여 밑줄 친 부분의 의미를 파악하세요.

D02 ★★★ .... 고1 2023(3월)/21

밑줄 친 The divorce of the hands from the head가 다음 글에서 의미하는 바로 가장 적절한 것은? [3점]

If we adopt technology, we need to pay its costs. Thousands of traditional livelihoods have been pushed aside by progress, and the lifestyles around those jobs removed. Hundreds of millions of humans today work⁵ at jobs they hate, producing things they have no love for. Sometimes these jobs cause physical pain, disability, or chronic disease. Technology creates many new jobs that are certainly dangerous. At the same time, mass¹⁰ education and media train humans to avoid low-tech physical work, to seek jobs working in the digital world. The divorce of the hands from the head puts a stress on the human mind. Indeed, the sedentary nature of the¹⁵ best-paying jobs is a health risk — for body and mind.

*chronic: 만성의 **sedentary: 주로 앉아서 하는

① ignorance of modern technology
② endless competition in the labor market
③ not getting along well with our coworkers
④ working without any realistic goals for our career
⑤ our increasing use of high technology in the workplace

1st 첫 문장과 밑줄 친 부분이 포함된 문장을 읽고, 글의 내용을 예상하세요.

1) 먼저 첫 문장을 볼까요?

> If we adopt technology, / we need to pay its costs. //
> 만약 우리가 기술을 받아들이면 / 우리는 그것의 비용을 치러야 한다 //

● **❶(   )과 관련된 내용이군요!**
우리가 기술을 받아들이면 그것의 비용을 치러야 한대요. 아마 대가를 치러야 한다는 거겠죠? 이 문장만 봐서는 잘 모르겠어요. 밑줄 친 부분이 포함된 문장을 읽어 봅시다.

2) 밑줄 친 부분이 포함된 문장을 봅시다!

> **The divorce of the hands from the head** puts a
> 머리로부터 손이 단절되는 것은 부담을 준다
> stress / on the human mind. //
>   / 인간의 정신에   //

● **밑줄 친 부분이 글의 끝부분에 있어요.**
머리로부터 손이 단절되는 것은 인간의 정신에 부담을 준대요. 문자 그대로 머리에서 손이 단절되는 걸 의미하는 건 아닐 테고, 머리와 손이 각각 무엇을 비유하는지 글을 읽으면서 확인해야겠어요.

● **먼저 예상해 볼까요?**
보통 '판단, 이성'을 머리에 비유하곤 해요. 그럼, 손은요?
머리에서 단절된다고 했으니까 판단하지 않고 '육체, 몸'을 쓴다는 말 아닐까요?
과연 예상한 내용이 맞을지 글을 앞부분부터 차근차근 읽어 봅시다!

2nd 글의 나머지 부분을 읽고, 예상한 내용이 맞는지 확인하세요.

1) 우리가 어떤 대가를 치른다고 하나요?

> Thousands of traditional livelihoods have been
> 수천 개의 전통적인 생계 수단이 밀려났다
> pushed aside / by progress, / and the lifestyles
>   / 발전에 의해 / 그리고 그 직업들 주변의
> around those jobs removed. //
> 생활 방식이 없어졌다   //

● **기술 발전의 악영향을 말하고 있어요.**
발전에 의해 전통적인 생계 수단과 그 주변의 생활 방식이 없어졌대요. 앞에서 예상했던 것처럼 기술을 받아들이는 대신 우리가 생계 수단과 생활 방식을 잃는 대가를 치른다는 거예요.

2) 또 어떤 대가를 치른다고 하나요?

> Technology creates many new jobs / that are
> 기술은 많은 새로운 일자리를 창출한다 / 확실히 위험한 //
> certainly dangerous. //

● **위험한 일자리라고 했어요.**
기술의 발전으로 인해서 전통적인 직업은 사라지고, 대신 새롭지만 위험한 일자리가 생겨난대요. 그런데 이게 '머리'나 '손'과 어떤 관련이 있는 걸까요? 계속 읽어봐야겠어요.

3) '육체'와 관련된 내용이 등장했어요.

> At the same time, / mass education and media train
> 동시에 / 대중 교육과 대중 매체는 인간을 훈련시킨다
> humans / to avoid low-tech physical work, / to seek
> / 낮은 기술의 육체노동을 피하고 / 디지털
> jobs working in the digital world. //
> 세계에서 일하는 직업을 찾도록 //

● **육체노동을 피하게 인간을 훈련시킨대요.**
그러니까 앞에서 언급한 새롭지만 위험한 일자리란, 육체노동 없이 **2**( ) 세계에서 일하는 직업을 말하는 거였어요!

● **이 문장은 밑줄이 포함된 문장의 바로 앞 문장이에요.**
그렇다면 '머리'는 디지털 세계에서의 일을, '손'은 육체노동을 하는 일을 말하는 거겠네요.
그런데 왜 위험한 일자리라고 했을까요?

4) 마지막 문장을 확인해야겠네요.

> Indeed, / the sedentary nature of the best-paying
> 실제로 / 가장 보수가 좋은 직업의 주로 앉아서 하는 특성은
> jobs / is a health risk / — for body and mind. //
> / 건강 위험 요소이다 / 신체와 정신에 //

● **주로 3( ) 일하기 때문이래요.**
몸을 쓰지 않고 앉아서 머리로만 일하기 때문에 건강에 안 좋고, 그래서 위험하다는 거였네요.

1) 선택지를 해석해 봅시다.

① ignorance of modern technology
현대 기술의 무지

② endless competition in the labor market
노동 시장에서의 끝없는 경쟁

③ not getting along well with our coworkers
동료들과 잘 어울리지 못하는 것

④ working without any realistic goals for our career
우리의 경력을 위해 현실적인 목표 없이 일하는 것

⑤ our increasing use of high technology in the workplace
직장에서 우리의 증가하는 첨단 기술 사용

2) 밑줄 친 부분의 의미는 무엇일까요?
기술의 발전으로 과거와는 다르게 육체노동을 적게 하는 직종이 많아지고, 그렇게 앉아서만 일하다 보니 건강에도 안 좋은 영향을 미친다는 내용의 글이에요.
즉, '머리로부터 손이 단절되는 것'은 **4**( ) '직장에서 우리의 증가하는 첨단 기술 사용'을 의미해요.

─── 수능 **Tip**

#목적격 관계대명사 #생략

> Hundreds of millions of humans today work / at
> 오늘날 수억 명의 사람들이 일한다 /
> jobs they hate, / producing things they have no
> 그들이 싫어하는 직장에서 / 그들이 아무런 애정을 갖지 않는 것들을
> love for. //
> 생산하면서 //

1 다섯 번째 줄의 저 문장!
관계대명사는 앞서 언급된 명사의 선행사를 대신하는 대명사의 역할과, 뒤에 이끄는 절을 주절에 연결하는 접속사 역할을 동시에 해요.

2 목적어로 쓰인 관계대명사는 생략할 수 있어요.
'그들이 싫어하는 직장'이니까 jobs와 they hate 사이에, '그들이 아무런 애정을 갖지 않는 것들'이니까 things와 they have no love for 사이에 목적격 관계대명사 which 또는 that이 생략된 거예요.

D03~06 ▶ 제한시간 8분

D03 ✿✿✿❀

고1 2025(3월)/21

밑줄 친 start down this slippery slope이 다음 글에서 의미하는 바로 가장 적절한 것은? [3점]

Assuming gene editing in humans proves to be safe and effective, it might seem logical, even preferable, to correct disease-causing mutations at the earliest possible stage of life, *before* harmful genes begin causing serious problems. Yet once it becomes possible to transform an embryo's mutated genes into "normal" ones, there will certainly be temptations to upgrade normal genes to superior versions. Should we begin editing genes in unborn children to lower their lifetime risk of heart disease or cancer? What about giving unborn children beneficial features, like greater strength and increased mental abilities, or changing physical characteristics, like eye and hair color? The pursuit for perfection seems almost natural to human nature, but if we start down this slippery slope, we may not like where we end up.

*mutation: 돌연변이 **embryo: 배아

① allow genetic alterations to upgrade humans
② stick to the traditional beliefs in human nature
③ resist the temptation to change genes in humans
④ fail to reduce the risk of suffering from diseases
⑤ consider more about the moral issues of genetics

구문 서술형

괄호 안의 단어를 이용하여 빈칸에 알맞게 쓰시오.

Should we begin _____ genes in unborn children? (edit)

D04 ✿✿✿❀

고1 2025(9월)/21

밑줄 친 There will be many who will follow you 가 다음 글에서 의미하는 바로 가장 적절한 것은?

Many atoms in your body are nearly as old as the universe itself. When you breathe, for example, only some of the atoms that you inhale are exhaled in your next breath. The remaining atoms are taken into your body to become part of you, and they later leave your body by various means. You don't "own" the atoms that make up your body; you borrow them. We all share from the same atom pool because atoms forever travel around, within, and among us. Atoms cycle from person to person as we breathe and as our sweat is evaporated. We recycle atoms on a grand scale. The origin of the lightest atoms goes back to the origin of the universe, and most heavier atoms are older than the Sun and Earth. There are atoms in your body that have existed since the first moments of time, recycling throughout the universe among limitless forms, both nonliving and living. You're the present caretaker of the atoms in your body. There will be many who will follow you.

*evaporate: 증발시키다

① Atoms will become part of other forms after you
② Atoms will remain unique and cannot be shared
③ Atoms will follow their original forms
④ Atoms will never be taken by a new form
⑤ Atoms will disappear completely after your lifetime

구문 서술형

네 번째 줄의 The remaining ~ part of you 문장에서 to부정사를 찾아 쓰고, 빈칸에 알맞은 말을 쓰시오.

➡ to _____,
➡ 쓰임: _____를(을) 나타내는 _____ 쓰임

D05 ★★★

밑줄 친 Seeing is not believing.이 다음 글에서
의미하는 바로 가장 적절한 것은? [3점]

When we see something, we naturally and automatically break it up into shapes, colors, and concepts that we have learned through education. We recode what we see through the lens of everything we know. We reconstruct memories rather than retrieving the video from memory. This is a useful trait. It's a more efficient way to store information — a bit like an optimal image compression algorithm such as JPG, rather than storing a raw bitmap image file. People who lack this ability and remember everything in perfect detail struggle to generalize, learn, and make connections between what they have learned. But representing the world as abstract ideas and features comes at a cost of seeing the world as it is. Instead, we see the world through our assumptions, motivations, and past experiences. The discovery that our memories are reconstructed through abstract representations rather than played back like a movie completely undermined the legal primacy of eyewitness testimony. Seeing is not believing.

*retrieve: 상기하다 **primacy: 우위성

① Abstract ideas are hard to explain without relevant images.

② It takes longer to retrieve unconsciously encoded information.

③ Beliefs formed from repeated experiences do not easily change.

④ Our memories fall short of an objective representation of the world.

⑤ Comprehension of facts precedes the formation of abstract concepts.

구문 서술형

밑줄 친 to부정사의 쓰임과 to부정사가 무엇을 수식하는지 쓰시오.

Reconstructing is a more efficient way to store information.

➡ _____ 쓰임, _____

D06 ★★❀

밑줄 친 push animal senses into Aristotelian
buckets가 다음 글에서 의미하는 바로 가장 적절한 것은? [3점]

Consider the seemingly simple question *How many senses are there?* Around 2,370 years ago, Aristotle wrote that there are five, in both humans and animals — sight, hearing, smell, taste, and touch. However, according to the philosopher Fiona Macpherson, there are reasons to doubt it. For a start, Aristotle missed a few in humans: the perception of your own body which is different from touch and the sense of balance which has links to both touch and vision. Other animals have senses that are even harder to categorize. Many vertebrates have a different sense system for detecting odors. Some snakes can detect the body heat of their prey. These examples tell us that "senses cannot be clearly divided into a limited number of specific kinds," Macpherson wrote in *The Senses*. Instead of trying to push animal senses into Aristotelian buckets, we should study them for what they are. *vertebrate: 척추동물 **odor: 냄새

① sort various animal senses into fixed categories
② keep a balanced view to understand real senses
③ doubt the traditional way of dividing all senses
④ ignore the lessons on senses from Aristotle
⑤ analyze more animals to find real senses

D07 ★★❀

밑줄 친 "hanging out with the winners"가 다음 글에서 의미하는 바로 가장 적절한 것은?

One valuable technique for getting out of helplessness, depression, and situations which are predominantly being run by the thought, "I can't," is to choose to be with other persons who have resolved the problem with which we struggle. This is one of the great powers of self-help groups. When we are in a negative state, we have given a lot of energy to negative thought forms, and the positive thought forms are weak. Those who are in a higher vibration are free of the energy from their negative thoughts and have energized positive thought forms. Merely to be in their presence is beneficial. In some self-help groups, this is called "hanging out with the winners." The benefit here is on the psychic level of consciousness, and there is a transfer of positive energy and relighting of one's own latent positive thought forms.　*latent: 잠재적인

① staying with those who sacrifice themselves for others
② learning from people who have succeeded in competition
③ keeping relationships with people in a higher social position
④ spending time with those who need social skill development
⑤ being with positive people who have overcome negative states

D08 ★★★

밑줄 친 Leave those activities to the rest of the sheep이 다음 글에서 의미하는 바로 가장 적절한 것은? [3점]

A job search is not a passive task. When you are searching, you are not browsing, nor are you "just looking". Browsing is not an effective way to reach a goal you claim to want to reach. If you are acting with purpose, if you are serious about anything you chose to do, then you need to be direct, focused and whenever possible, clever. Everyone else searching for a job has the same goal, competing for the same jobs. You must do more than the rest of the herd. Regardless of how long it may take you to find and get the job you want, being proactive will logically get you results faster than if you rely only on browsing online job boards and emailing an occasional resume. Leave those activities to the rest of the sheep.

① Try to understand other job-seekers' feelings.
② Keep calm and stick to your present position.
③ Don't be scared of the job-seeking competition.
④ Send occasional emails to your future employers.
⑤ Be more active to stand out from other job-seekers.

D09 ★★★

밑줄 친 want to use a hammer가 다음 글에서 의미하는 바로 가장 적절한 것은? [3점]

We have a tendency to interpret events selectively. If we want things to be "this way" or "that way" we can most certainly select, stack, or arrange evidence in a way that supports such a viewpoint. Selective perception is based on what seems to us to stand out. However, what seems to us to be standing out may very well be related to our goals, interests, expectations, past experiences, or current demands of the situation — "with a hammer in hand, everything looks like a nail." This quote highlights the phenomenon of selective perception. If we want to use a hammer, then the world around us may begin to look as though it is full of nails!

① are unwilling to stand out
② make our effort meaningless
③ intend to do something in a certain way
④ hope others have a viewpoint similar to ours
⑤ have a way of thinking that is accepted by others

D10 ❋❋❋   고1 2023(6월)/21

밑줄 친 become unpaid ambassadors가 다음
글에서 의미하는 바로 가장 적절한 것은?

Why do you care how a customer reacts to a purchase? Good question. By understanding post-purchase behavior, you can understand the influence and the likelihood of whether a buyer will repurchase the product (and whether she will keep it or return it). You'll also determine whether the buyer will encourage others to purchase the product from you. Satisfied customers can become unpaid ambassadors for your business, so customer satisfaction should be on the top of your to-do list. People tend to believe the opinions of people they know. People trust friends over advertisements any day. They know that advertisements are paid to tell the "good side" and that they're used to persuade them to purchase products and services. By continually monitoring your customer's satisfaction after the sale, you have the ability to avoid negative word-of-mouth advertising.

① recommend products to others for no gain
② offer manufacturers feedback on products
③ become people who don't trust others' words
④ get rewards for advertising products overseas
⑤ buy products without worrying about the price

D11 ❋❋❋   고1 2022(11월)/21

밑줄 친 challenge this sacred cow가 다음 글에서
의미하는 바로 가장 적절한 것은? [3점]

Our language helps to reveal our deeper assumptions. Think of these revealing phrases: When we accomplish something important, we say it took "blood, sweat, and tears." We say important achievements are "hard-earned." We recommend a "hard day's work" when "day's work" would be enough. When we talk of "easy money," we are implying it was obtained through illegal or questionable means. We use the phrase "That's easy for you to say" as a criticism, usually when we are seeking to invalidate someone's opinion. It's like we all automatically accept that the "right" way is, inevitably, the harder one. In my experience this is hardly ever questioned. What would happen if you do challenge this sacred cow? We don't even pause to consider that something important and valuable could be made easy. What if the biggest thing keeping us from doing what matters is the false assumption that it has to take huge effort?

*invalidate: 틀렸음을 입증하다

① resist the tendency to avoid any hardship
② escape from the pressure of using formal language
③ doubt the solid belief that only hard work is worthy
④ abandon the old notion that money always comes first
⑤ break the superstition that holy animals bring good luck

D12 ❋❋❋   고1 2023(9월)/21

밑줄 친 fall silently in the woods가 다음 글에서
의미하는 바로 가장 적절한 것은? [3점]

Most people have no doubt heard this question: If a tree falls in the forest and there is no one there to hear it fall, does it make a sound? The correct answer is no. Sound is more than pressure waves, and indeed there can be no sound without a hearer. And similarly, scientific communication is a two-way process. Just as a signal of any kind is useless unless it is perceived, a published scientific paper (signal) is useless unless it is both received *and* understood by its intended audience. Thus we can restate the axiom of science as follows: A scientific experiment is not complete until the results have been published *and understood*. Publication is no more than pressure waves unless the published paper is understood. Too many scientific papers fall silently in the woods.

*axiom: 자명한 이치

① fail to include the previous study
② end up being considered completely false
③ become useless because they are not published
④ focus on communication to meet public demands
⑤ are published yet readers don't understand them

D13 ★★★

밑줄 친 "matter out of place"가 다음 글에서
의미하는 바로 가장 적절한 것은?

Nothing is trash by nature. Anthropologist Mary Douglas brings back and analyzes the common saying that dirt is "matter out of place." Dirt is relative, she emphasizes. "Shoes are not dirty in themselves, but it is dirty to place them on the dining-table; food is not dirty in itself, but it is dirty to leave pots and pans in the bedroom, or food all over clothing; similarly, bathroom items in the living room; clothing lying on chairs; outdoor things placed indoors; upstairs things downstairs, and so on." Sorting the dirty from the clean — removing the shoes from the table, putting the dirty clothing in the washing machine — involves systematic ordering and classifying. Eliminating dirt is thus a positive process.

① something that is completely broken
② a tiny dust that nobody notices
③ a dirty but renewable material
④ what can be easily replaced
⑤ a thing that is not in order

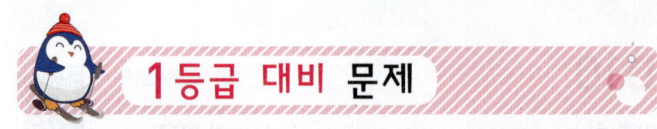

1등급 대비 문제

D14　✪ 2등급 대비

밑줄 친 our brain and the universe meet가 다음
글에서 의미하는 바로 가장 적절한 것은? [3점]

Many people take the commonsense view that color is an objective property of things, or of the light that bounces off them. They say a tree's leaves are green because they reflect green light — a greenness that is just as real as the leaves. Others argue that color doesn't inhabit the physical world at all but exists only in the eye or mind of the viewer. They maintain that if a tree fell in a forest and no one was there to see it, its leaves would be colorless — and so would everything else. They say there is no such *thing* as color; there are only the people who see it. Both positions are, in a way, correct. Color is objective *and* subjective — "the place," as Paul Cézanne put it, "where our brain and the universe meet." Color is created when light from the world is registered by the eyes and interpreted by the brain.

① we see things beyond the range of perception
② objects appear different by the change of light
③ your perspectives and others' reach an agreement
④ our mind and physical reality interact with each other
⑤ structures of the human brain and the universe are similar

밑줄 친 put the glass down이 다음 글에서 의미하는
바로 가장 적절한 것은? [3점]

A psychology professor raised a glass of water while teaching stress management principles to her students, and asked them, "How heavy is this glass of water I'm holding?" Students shouted out various answers. The professor replied, "The absolute weight of this glass doesn't matter. It depends on how long I hold it. If I hold it for a minute, it's quite light. But, if I hold it for a day straight, it will cause severe pain in my arm, forcing me to drop the glass to the floor. In each case, the weight of the glass is the same, but the longer I hold it, the heavier it feels to me." As the class nodded their heads in agreement, she continued, "Your stresses in life are like this glass of water. If you still feel the weight of yesterday's stress, it's a strong sign that it's time to put the glass down."

① pour more water into the glass
② set a plan not to make mistakes
③ let go of the stress in your mind
④ think about the cause of your stress
⑤ learn to accept the opinions of others

밑줄 친 fire a customer가 다음 글에서 의미하는 바로
가장 적절한 것은?

Is the customer *always* right? When customers return a broken product to a famous company, which makes kitchen and bathroom fixtures, the company nearly always offers a replacement to maintain good customer relations. Still, "there are times you've got to say 'no,'" explains the warranty expert of the company, such as when a product is undamaged or has been abused. Entrepreneur Lauren Thorp, who owns an e-commerce company, says, "While the customer is 'always' right, sometimes you just have to fire a customer." When Thorp has tried everything to resolve a complaint and realizes that the customer will be dissatisfied no matter what, she returns her attention to the rest of her customers, who she says are "the reason for my success."

① deal with a customer's emergency
② delete a customer's purchasing record
③ reject a customer's unreasonable demand
④ uncover the hidden intention of a customer
⑤ rely on the power of an influential customer

D17　✿ 1등급 대비　　　　　　　고1 2021(11월)/21

밑줄 친 a slap in our own face가 다음 글에서 의미하는 바로 가장 적절한 것은? [3점]

When it comes to climate change, many blame the fossil fuel industry for pumping greenhouse gases, the agricultural sector for burning rainforests, or the fashion industry for producing excessive clothes. But wait, what drives these industrial activities? Our consumption. Climate change is a summed product of each person's behavior. For example, the fossil fuel industry is a popular scapegoat in the climate crisis. But why do they drill and burn fossil fuels? We provide them strong financial incentives: some people regularly travel on airplanes and cars that burn fossil fuels. Some people waste electricity generated by burning fuel in power plants. Some people use and throw away plastic products derived from crude oil every day. Blaming the fossil fuel industry while engaging in these behaviors is a slap in our own face.

* scapegoat: 희생양

① giving the future generation room for change
② warning ourselves about the lack of natural resources
③ refusing to admit the benefits of fossil fuel production
④ failing to recognize our responsibility for climate change
⑤ starting to deal with environmental problems individually

D18　✿ 1등급 대비　　　　　　　고1 2024(6월)/21

밑줄 친 luxury real estate가 다음 글에서 의미하는 바로 가장 적절한 것은? [3점]

The soil of a farm field is forced to be the perfect environment for monoculture growth. This is achieved by adding nutrients in the form of fertilizer and water by way of irrigation. During the last fifty years, engineers and crop scientists have helped farmers become much more efficient at supplying exactly the right amount of both. World usage of fertilizer has tripled since 1969, and the global capacity for irrigation has almost doubled; we are feeding and watering our fields more than ever, and our crops are loving it. Unfortunately, these luxurious conditions have also excited the attention of certain agricultural undesirables. Because farm fields are loaded with nutrients and water relative to the natural land that surrounds them, they are desired as luxury real estate by every random weed in the area.

*monoculture: 단일 작물 재배　**irrigation: (논,밭에)물을 댐; 관개

① a farm where a scientist's aid is highly required
② a field abundant with necessities for plants
③ a district accessible only for the rich
④ a place that is conserved for ecology
⑤ a region with higher economic value

D 어휘 Review

＊ 다음 영어는 우리말 뜻을, 우리말은 영어 단어를 〈보기〉에서 찾아 쓰시오.

〈보기〉
농업의	logically	진취적인	indeed
지각	previous	가끔의	replacement
경쟁	pursue	무력감	agreement

01 perception   _____

02 agricultural   _____

03 proactive   _____

04 competition   _____

05 occasional   _____

06 논리적으로   _____

07 정말로   _____

08 이전의   _____

09 동의   _____

10 대체품   _____

＊ 다음 우리말에 알맞은 영어 표현을 찾아 연결하시오.

11 돋보이다 •   • put down

12 ~을 내려놓다 •   • stand out

13 ~을 구성하다 •   • bounce off

14 튕겨 나오다 •   • make up

15 ~으로 가득 차다 •   • be loaded with

＊ 다음 우리말 표현에 맞는 단어를 고르시오.

16 수천 개의 전통적인 생계 수단 ➡ thousands of traditional (livelihoods / likelihoods)

17 수동적인 일 ➡ a(n) (active / passive) task

18 스트레스 관리 원칙 ➡ stress management (principles / principals)

19 그 회사의 상품 보증 전문가 ➡ (warranty / warning) expert of the company

20 전체 관개 능력 ➡ the global (curiosity / capacity) for irrigation

＊ 다음 문장의 빈칸에 알맞은 단어를 〈보기〉에서 찾아 쓰시오.

〈보기〉
grand	restate	absolute	attention
maintain	physical	herd	merely
reveal	behavior	scapegoat	objective

21 따라서 우리는 과학의 자명한 이치를 재진술할 수 있다.
➡ Thus we can _____ the axiom of science.

22 때때로 이러한 일자리들은 육체적 고통, 장애 또는 만성 질환을 유발한다.
➡ Sometimes these jobs cause _____ pain, disability, or chronic disease.

23 여러분은 그 무리의 나머지 사람들보다 더 많은 것을 해야 한다. ➡ You must do more than the rest of the _____.

24 우리는 거대한 규모로 원자를 재순환시킨다.
➡ We recycle atoms on a(n) _____ scale.

25 이 잔의 절대 무게는 중요하지 않다.
➡ The _____ weight of this glass doesn't matter.

26 그녀는 자신의 주의를 나머지 다른 고객들에게 돌린다.
➡ She returns her _____ to the rest of her customers.

27 단지 그들이 있는 자리에 있기만 하는 것도 유익하다.
➡ _____ to be in their presence is beneficial.

28 그 회사는 좋은 고객 관계를 유지하기 위해 대체품을 제공한다.
➡ The company offers a replacement to _____ good customer relations.

29 기후 변화는 각 개인 행위의 합쳐진 산물이다.
➡ Climate change is a summed product of each person's _____.

30 화석 연료 산업은 기후 위기에 있어서 일반적인 희생양이다.
➡ The fossil fuel industry is a popular _____ in the climate crisis.

E 요지 찾기

★ 유형 설명

다음 글의 요지로 가장 적절한 것은?

The process of science is less about collecting pieces of knowledge than it is about reducing

> 매달 캠핑 오니까 너무 좋다. 공기도 맑고, 마음도 편안해지네. 한 달에 한 번씩 캠핑 오는 것은 내 삶의 활력이 될 것 같아.

> 네 말의 요지는 한 달에 한 번씩 캠핑을 가자는 거구나!

글의 주제에 대해 어떠한 견해를 갖고 있는 글인지를 우리말로 표현한 선택지를 찾아야 한다.

🔑 명확히 드러나는 주제문이나 반복되는 부분, 같은 의미를 다른 말로 바꾸어 표현한 부분을 중심으로 글의 주제를 파악한다.
그 주제에 부합하는 요지를 선택지에서 고른다.

🎭 유형 풀이 비법

1 주제문을 찾아라!
• 반복되는 부분에 주목하면서 필자가 전달하려는 중심 내용을 파악한다.

2 특정 부분을 잘 보자!
• 요지는 주로 글의 첫 부분과 끝 부분에 잘 나온다.

3 요지의 범위를 확인하라!
• 범위가 너무 넓거나 좁지 않은지, 중간에 필자의 태도가 바뀌는 곳은 없는지도 확인한다.

(Tip) 주로 특정 어구 (rather, however, while 등)의 바로 앞이나 뒤에 필자의 요지가 담겨있다.

📍 요지를 뒷받침하는 주요 표현

☐ Well begun is half done. 시작이 반이다.
☐ Every cloud has a silver lining. 새옹지마
☐ Habit is a second nature. 습관은 제2의 천성이다.
☐ No pains, no gains. 노력이 있어야 얻는 것이 있다.
☐ Honesty is the best policy. 정직이 최상의 방책이다.
☐ Look before you leap. 돌다리도 두들겨 보고 건너라.
☐ Blood is thicker than water. 피는 물보다 더 진하다.
☐ Two heads are better than one. 백지장도 맞들면 낫다.
☐ Better late than never. 늦더라도 하지 않는 것보다 낫다.
☐ All that glitters is not gold. 번쩍인다고 다 금은 아니다.
☐ Actions speak louder than words. 행동은 말보다 미덥다.
☐ A good turn deserves another. 좋은 일은 보답을 받는다.
☐ The end justifies the means. 목적이 수단을 정당화시킨다.
☐ Adversity makes a man wise. 역경은 사람을 현명하게 만든다.
☐ Time will show who is right. 시간이 지나면 누가 옳은지 밝혀질 것이다.
☐ Don't put all your eggs in one basket. 위험은 여러 곳으로 분산시켜라.
☐ Every man knows his own business best. 자신의 일은 자신이 가장 잘 안다.
☐ A burnt child dreads the fire. 자라 보고 놀란 가슴 솥뚜껑 보고 놀란다.
☐ A friend in need is a friend indeed.
곤경에 빠졌을 때의 친구야말로 참다운 친구이다.

📖 어휘 및 표현 Preview

☐ constantly 끊임없이
☐ potential 잠재력
☐ regardless of ~와 관계없이
☐ repetitive 반복적인
☐ pursue 추구하다
☐ leisure 여가
☐ off-load 떠넘기다
☐ contribute 기여하다
☐ stimuli 자극
☐ acutely 강렬하게
☐ religious 종교적인
☐ appropriate 적합한, 알맞은
☐ occasion 행사
☐ flexible 유연한
☐ strategy 전략
☐ multiple-choice test 선다형 시험
☐ pessimistic 비관적인
☐ take a step 조치를 취하다
☐ be true for ~에 해당되다
☐ ecological 생태학적인

5 대명사

1 지시대명사

1) 거리에 따른 구분: 공간적, *시간적, 심리적 거리가 **가까우면** this나 these, 거리가 **멀면** that이나 those를 쓴다.

• This is mine, and that is yours. (이것은 내 것이고, 저것이 네 것이다.)
　가까이 있는 것　　　　멀리 있는 것

> *** 지시대명사가 나타내는 시간적 거리**
> this와 these는 현재 진행 중이거나 발생하려고 하는 일을 나타내고, that과 those는 과거의 일을 나타낸다.

2) 앞에 나온 구나 절, 문장 전체를 가리키는 this, that

• I didn't do my homework, and this[that] made her angry.
　　　　　　　　　　　　　　　앞에 나온 절을 가리킴
(나는 내 숙제를 안 했고, **이것은[그것은]** 그녀를 화나게 했다.)

3) 앞에 나온 명사의 반복을 피하기 위한 that, those

• The voice was that of an elderly woman. (그 목소리는 나이든 여자의 **그것**이었다.)
　　　　　　앞에 나온 단수 명사 the voice의 반복을 피하려고 쓰임

• Those sound great to me. (그것들은 내게 좋게 들린다.)
　앞에 나온 복수 명사를 가리킴

4) 지시형용사: this와 these, that과 those는 **뒤에 오는 명사를 한정하는 지시형용사**로도 쓰인다.

• Most people married young in those days. (그 시절에는 대부분의 사람들이 일찍 결혼했다.)
　　　　　　　　　　　　　　명사 days를 한정하는 지시형용사

• These flowers will fit in. (이 꽃들은 잘 어울릴 것이다.)
　명사 flowers를 한정하는 지시형용사

2 재귀대명사

- 재귀 용법: ① **주어와 목적어가 같은 대상일 때 목적어로 쓰이는** 재귀대명사
- 강조 용법: ② **주어나 목적어 등을 강조할 때** 쓰이는 재귀대명사로, **생략할 수 있다.**

• ① He introduced himself. (그는 **그 자신**을 소개했다.)
　재귀 용법(introduced의 주어와 목적어가 같음), 목적어이므로 생략 불가

• ② Shakespeare himself once acted in this play. (셰익스피어가 한때 **직접** 이 연극에서 연기했다.)
　강조 용법(주어 Shakespeare를 강조함), 생략 가능

3 소유대명사: '~의 것'이라는 뜻으로, 「소유격 + 명사」를 대신한다.

• Can I borrow your key? I can't find mine. (내가 네 열쇠를 빌릴 수 있을까? **내 것**을 못 찾겠어.)
　　　　　　　　　　　　　　= my key

Check Test

1 밑줄 친 부분을 알맞은 형태로 바꿔 쓰시오.

These is the price we all must pay for achieving the greater rewards lying ahead of us.

→ _____

2 밑줄 친 부분의 역할로 알맞은 것을 고르시오.

It's important that you think independently and fight for what you believe in.
① 비인칭 주어　② 가주어　③ 강조 구문

3 밑줄 친 재귀대명사의 용법을 쓰시오.

The internal pressure you place on yourself to achieve or do well socially is normal and useful.

→ _____

4 밑줄 친 부분에 유의하여 아래 문장을 해석하시오.

You may feel a certain way, but that does not mean those feelings are reflections of the truth.

→ _____

_____

1st 선택지를 통해 핵심 소재를 확인하고 글의 내용을 짐작해 보세요.
2nd 글을 읽으며 특정 어구(연결어, 부사 등)를 찾아 글의 요지를 생각해 보세요.
3rd 글의 내용을 정리하여 글의 요지를 가장 잘 표현한 선택지를 찾으세요.

E01 ✳✳✳ ······························ 고1 2024(3월)/22

다음 글의 요지로 가장 적절한 것은?

When we think of leaders, we may think of people such as Abraham Lincoln or Martin Luther King, Jr. If you consider the historical importance and far-reaching influence of these individuals, leadership might seem like 5 a noble and high goal. But like all of us, these people started out as students, workers, and citizens who possessed ideas about how some aspect of daily life could be improved on a larger scale. Through diligence and 10 experience, they improved upon their ideas by sharing them with others, seeking their opinions and feedback and constantly looking for the best way to accomplish goals for a group. Thus we all have the potential to 15 be leaders at school, in our communities, and at work, regardless of age or experience.

*diligence: 근면

① 훌륭한 리더는 고귀한 목표를 위해 희생적인 삶을 산다.
② 위대한 인물은 위기의 순간에 뛰어난 결단력을 발휘한다.
③ 공동체를 위한 아이디어를 발전시키는 누구나 리더가 될 수 있다.
④ 다른 사람의 의견을 경청하는 자세는 목표 달성에 가장 중요하다.
⑤ 근면하고 경험이 풍부한 사람들은 경제적으로 성공할 수 있다.

1st 선택지를 통해 핵심 소재를 확인하고 글의 내용을 짐작해 보세요.

> ① 훌륭한 **리더**는 고귀한 목표를 위해 희생적인 삶을 산다.
> ② **위대한 인물**은 위기의 순간에 뛰어난 결단력을 발휘한다.
> ③ 공동체를 위한 아이디어를 발전시키는 누구나 **리더**가 될 수 있다.
> ④ 다른 사람의 의견을 경청하는 자세는 목표 달성에 가장 중요하다.
> ⑤ 근면하고 경험이 풍부한 사람들은 경제적으로 성공할 수 있다.

● **선택지에 반복되는 단어가 있나요?**
①, ③에 '**①**( )'가 있고 ②에는 이와 비슷한 '위대한 인물'이 있어요. 글의 소재가 '리더'일 가능성이 커요.

● **선택지를 자세히 살펴봅시다.**
①, ②은 '~은 ~한다'라는 구조로서 어떠한 인물이 어떤 행동을 하는지를 나타내요.
'리더가 희생한다'라는 내용이라면 ①이, '위대한 인물이 결단력을 발휘한다'라는 내용이라면 ②이 정답일 거예요.
③, ④, ⑤은 각각 '리더', '목표 달성', '경제적 성공'을 위한 태도를 설명하고 있군요.

2nd 글을 읽으며 특정 어구(연결어, 부사 등)를 찾아 글의 요지를 생각해 보세요.

1) 글을 처음부터 읽어봅시다.

> When we think of leaders, / we may think of people
> 우리가 리더에 대해 생각할 때 / 우리는 사람들에 대해 생각할지 모른다
> / such as Abraham Lincoln or Martin Luther King,
> / Abraham Lincoln 혹은 Martin Luther King, Jr.와 같은 //
> Jr. //
> If you consider / the historical importance and far-
> 만약 여러분이 고려한다면 / 역사적 중요성과 광범위한
> reaching influence / of these individuals, / leadership
> 영향력을 / 이러한 인물들의 / 리더십은
> might seem / like a noble and high goal. //
> 보일지도 모른다 / 고귀하고 높은 목표처럼 //

● **예상한 대로 첫 문장부터 '리더'가 등장했어요.**
'리더'에 대해 생각한다면 Lincoln 등의 유명한 인물들을 떠올린다는 내용으로 글이 시작해요. 두 번째 문장은 이러한 인물들의 리더십이 고귀하고 높은 목표처럼 보일지도 모른다고 하네요. 두 번째 문장의 어조로 볼 때, '사실은 그렇지 않다'라는 내용이 뒤에 이어질 듯한데 더 살펴봐야겠어요.

● **어떤 선택지에 비슷한 내용이 있었나요?**

①, ③에 '리더', ②에 '위대한 인물'이 포함되어 있었죠. 심지어 ①에는 '고귀한 목표'도 언급되어 있는데요, ①이 정답이라면 그 뒤에 리더들의 희생에 관한 내용이 이어져야 해요. 하지만 두 번째 문장의 어조로부터 짐작했듯이, '리더십이 고귀한 목표가 아니다'라는 내용이 뒤에 이어질 것 같으니 나머지 부분도 더 살펴보죠!

2) 바로 뒤에 But으로 반대되는 내용이 이어져요!

But like all of us, / these people started out as
그러나 우리 모두와 마찬가지로 / 이러한 인물들은 학생, 근로자,

students, workers, and citizens / who possessed
그리고 시민으로 시작했다   / 생각을 가졌던

ideas / about how some aspect of daily life could be
/ 일상생활의 어느 측면이 어떻게 개선될 수 있는지에 대한

improved / on a larger scale. //
/ 더 큰 규모로   //

● **리더들도 원래 우리처럼 평범한 사람이었대요!**

앞서 짐작한 것처럼, 리더십이 고귀하고 높기만 한 목표는 아닌가 봐요! 리더들도 처음엔 평범한 사람들로 시작했지만, 더 큰 규모로 일상을 개선할 생각을 가졌다고 하네요.

3) 평범한 사람들도 리더가 되는 과정이 뒤에 이어져요.

Through diligence and experience, / they improved
근면함과 경험을 통해   / 이 사람들은 자신의

upon their ideas / by sharing them with others, /
생각을 발전시켰다   / 자신의 생각을 다른 사람들과 공유하고 /

seeking their opinions and feedback / and
그들의 의견과 반응을 구하며   / 끊임없이

constantly looking for the best way / to accomplish
가장 좋은 방법을 찾음으로써   / 목표를 성취할

goals / for a group. //
수 있는 / 집단을 위한 //

● **일상 개선에 관한 생각을 발전시킨 방법이 나열되었어요.**

생각을 공유하고, 의견과 반응을 구하고, 집단을 위한 목표를 성취할 좋은 방법을 찾음으로써 생각을 **2**(   )고 해요. '집단을 위한 목표'를 성취한다고 했는데, 더 큰 규모로 일상을 개선한다는 내용이 이와 연결되는 듯하군요.

● **이러한 내용과 비슷한 선택지가 하나 있었죠?**

지금까지 확인한 주요 키워드는 '리더', '일상을 개선할 생각', '생각의 발전', '집단을 위한 목표'라고 볼 수 있어요. ③에 공동체를 위한 아이디어(생각)를 발전시킨다는 내용이 있는데 지금까지의 키워드와 상당히 들어맞네요. 글의 마지막 문장에서 확실한 단서를 찾아봅시다.

4) 결론을 나타내는 Thus가 있네요.

Thus we all have the potential / to be leaders at
그러므로 우리는 모두 잠재력을 가지고 있다 / 학교, 공동체, 그리고

school, in our communities, and at work, /
일터에서 리더가 될 수 있는   /

regardless of age or experience. //
나이나 경험에 관계없이   //

● **우리 모두 리더가 될 잠재력을 가지고 있대요!**

리더들도 평범한 사람들이었으니, 우리 모두 리더가 될 잠재력을 가지고 있다는 내용으로 글이 마무리되어요.

3rd 글의 내용을 정리하여 글의 요지를 가장 잘 표현한 선택지를 찾으세요.

리더십이 고귀한 높은 목표처럼 보이지만, 평범한 사람들도 큰 규모에서 일상을 개선할, 즉 집단의 목표를 위한 생각을 발전시킨다면 모두 리더가 될 잠재력을 가지고 있다는 내용이에요.

이것은 공동체(=집단)를 위한 아이디어(=생각)를 발전시키는 누구나 리더가 될 수 있다는 것이므로 정답은 **3**(   )이에요.

───────────── 수능 Tip

#간접의문문

★ **여섯 번째 줄의 문장을 봅시다.**

But like all of us, / these people started out as
그러나 우리 모두와 마찬가지로 / 이러한 인물들은 학생, 근로자,

students, workers, and citizens / who possessed
그리고 시민으로 시작했다   / 생각을 가졌던

ideas / about how some aspect of daily life could be
/ 일상생활의 어느 측면이 어떻게 개선될 수 있는지에 대한

improved / on a larger scale. //
/ 더 큰 규모로   //

● **「의문사 + 주어 + 동사」**

의문사가 명사절을 이끌 때, 「의문사 + 주어 + 동사」 어순의 간접의문문이 돼요. (의문사가 주어일 때는 「의문사 + 동사」) 이 문장에서 의문사 how가 이끄는 명사절이 전치사 about의 목적어로 쓰였어요. 주어는 some aspect of daily life, 동사는 could be improved예요. 주로 '~가 어떻게 ~할 수 있는지'로 해석하므로, '일상생활의 어느 측면이 어떻게 개선될 수 있는지'라고 해석해요.

E 요지 찾기 (두 번째)

1st 선택지를 통해 글의 소재를 파악하고 정답을 찾기 위해 앞으로 할 일을 생각해 보세요.
2nd 선택지에서 찾은 소재가 글 속에서 어떻게 표현되는지 확인하세요.
3rd 두 예시를 종합하여 글의 요지를 가장 잘 표현한 선택지를 찾으세요.

E02 ★★★ ·························· 고1 2023(6월)/22

다음 글의 요지로 가장 적절한 것은?

The promise of a computerized society, we were told, was that it would pass to machines all of the repetitive drudgery of work, allowing us humans to pursue higher purposes and to have more leisure time. It⁵ didn't work out this way. Instead of more time, most of us have less. Companies large and small have off-loaded work onto the backs of consumers. Things that used to be done for us, as part of the value-added¹⁰ service of working with a company, we are now expected to do ourselves. With air travel, we're now expected to complete our own reservations and check-in, jobs that used to be done by airline employees or¹⁵ travel agents. At the grocery store, we're expected to bag our own groceries and, in some supermarkets, to scan our own purchases.

*drudgery: 고된 일

① 컴퓨터 기반 사회에서는 여가 시간이 더 늘어난다.
② 회사 업무의 전산화는 업무 능률을 향상시킨다.
③ 컴퓨터화된 사회에서 소비자는 더 많은 일을 하게 된다.
④ 온라인 거래가 모든 소비자들을 만족시키기에는 한계가 있다.
⑤ 산업의 발전으로 인해 기계가 인간의 일자리를 대신하고 있다.

1st 선택지를 통해 글의 소재를 파악하고 정답을 찾기 위해 앞으로 할 일을 생각해 보세요.

① 컴퓨터 기반 사회에서는 여가 시간이 더 늘어난다.
② 회사 업무의 전산화는 업무 능률을 향상시킨다.
③ 컴퓨터화된 사회에서 소비자는 더 많은 일을 하게 된다.
④ 온라인 거래가 모든 소비자들을 만족시키기에는 한계가 있다.
⑤ 산업의 발전으로 인해 기계가 인간의 일자리를 대신하고 있다.

● **반복해서 등장하는 어구를 찾았나요?**
모든 선택지에 컴퓨터, 전산화, 온라인, 기계 등 같은 맥락의 어구가 등장했어요. 그렇다면 이 글은 결국 '컴퓨터'와 관련된 글이겠네요.

● **그럼 우리는 글을 읽으며 무엇을 파악해야 할까요?**
이 글이 컴퓨터와 관련된 글이라는 것은 파악했지만, 구체적으로 어떤 내용을 다루고 있는지까지 파악해야 글의 요지를 알 수 있어요.
각 선택지에서 파악한 반복되는 어구를 제외하고 나머지 핵심어를 단서로 활용해 봅시다. ①은 여가 시간, ②은 업무 능률, ③은 소비자의 일, ④은 소비자 만족, ⑤은 일자리 대체가 제시되었어요. 컴퓨터와 이 핵심어들을 함께 떠올리며 글을 읽어 봅시다!

2nd 선택지에서 찾은 소재가 글 속에서 어떻게 표현되는지 확인하세요.

1) 첫 번째 문장부터 컴퓨터와 관련된 내용이 나와요.

The promise of a computerized society, / we were
컴퓨터화된 사회의 약속은 / 우리가
told, / was that it would pass to machines / all of the
듣기로는 / 그것이 기계에 넘길 거라는 것이었다 / 모든
repetitive drudgery of work, / allowing us humans
반복적인 고된 일을 / 우리 인간들로 하여금
to pursue higher purposes / and to have more
더 높은 목적을 추구하게 하면서 / 그리고 더 많은 여가 시간을
leisure time. //
가질 수 있게 (하면서) //

● **컴퓨터화된 사회의 약속을 설명했어요.**
컴퓨터가 반복적인 고된 일은 기계에 넘겨서 인간들이 더 많은 여가 시간을 가질 수 있게 해준다는 것이 컴퓨터화된 사회의 약속이래요. 여가 시간! 앞서 살펴본 ①이 정확하게 같은 내용을 말하고 있군요! 그런데 이상하지 않나요? 반복적인 고된 일을 기계가 대신하는 거라면 ⑤도 정답이 될 수 있고, 업무 능률도 오를 테니 ②도 정답이 될 수 있어요.

- **글에 반전이 있겠네요!**

  비슷한 맥락의 선택지가 여러 개 있는 걸 보니, 분명 내용이 반전되고 그 반전된 내용이 글의 요지일 거예요.

2) 이어지는 문장을 봅시다.

It didn't work out this way. //
그것은 이런 식으로 되지는 않았다   //

Instead of more time, / most of us have less. //
더 많은 시간 대신에   / 우리 대부분은 더 적은 시간을 가지고 있다 //

- **반전이 있었어요!**

  앞에서 말한 컴퓨터화된 사회의 약속을 It으로 받았고, 그건 잘되지 않았대요.

  인간에게 여가 시간을 준 것이 아니라 오히려 인간은 더 ❶(   ) 시간을 가지게 되었대요. 그렇다면 컴퓨터의 긍정적인 영향을 이야기한 ①, ②, ⑤은 정답이 될 수 없겠네요.

3) 더 적은 시간은 뭘 의미하는 걸까요?

Companies large and small have off-loaded work /
크고 작은 회사들은 일을 떠넘겼다   /

onto the backs of consumers. //
소비자들의 등에   //

- **회사들이 소비자들에게 일을 떠넘긴 거군요!**

  회사들이 소비자들에게 일을 떠넘겨서 인간은 더 ❶(   )
  시간을 가지게 된 거였어요. 그런데 잘 이해가 되지 않아요. 어떤 일을 어떻게 떠넘겼다는 걸까요?

4) 아! 예시가 이어지네요.

With air travel, / we're now expected to complete /
항공 여행의 경우   / 이제는 우리가 완수하도록 기대된다   /

our own reservations and check-in, / jobs that used
우리의 예약과 체크인을   / 행해지던 일인

to be done / by airline employees or travel agents. //
          / 항공사 직원이나 여행사 직원들에 의해   //

- **회사가 하던 일을 우리가 하게 됐대요.**

  예약이나 체크인처럼 원래는 회사에서 직원들이 해주던 일을 컴퓨터화된 사회에서는 소비자가 직접 하게 되었기 때문에 회사가 소비자에게 일을 떠넘겼다고 말한 거였어요.

5) 두 번째 예시가 이어져요.

At the grocery store, / we're expected to bag our
식료품점에서는   / 우리가 자신의 식료품을 봉지에 넣도록

own groceries / and, in some supermarkets, / to scan
기대된다   / 그리고 일부 슈퍼마켓에서는   / 자신이

our own purchases. //
구매한 물건을 스캔하도록 (기대된다) //

- **식료품점과 슈퍼마켓에서 소비자는 어떤 일을 하게 됐나요?**

  직접 물건을 스캔해서 결제하거나 봉지에도 직접 넣도록 기대된대요.
  이것도 역시 원래는 직원이 해주던 일이지만, 컴퓨터화의 결과로 우리가 하게 된 일이에요.

3rd 두 예시를 종합하여 글의 요지를 가장 잘 표현한 선택지를 찾으세요.

예시 ①: 항공사나 여행사 직원이 하던 예약과 체크인 → 우리가 직접 함

예시 ②: 식료품점이나 슈퍼마켓 직원이 하던 물건 스캔과 포장

                               → 우리가 직접 함

반복적이고 고된 일을 기계에 넘기고 인간은 더 많은 여가시간을 갖게 될 것이라는 컴퓨터화된 사회의 약속은 지켜지지 않았고 소비자가 더 많은 일을 하게 된다는 글이에요. 따라서 글의 요지는 ❷(   )이네요!

정답의 단서가 되는 예시를 잘 확인하자!

빈칸 정답 ⓒ ❷ 긍정 ❶

❖ 정답 및 해설 49~50p

E03 ~ 06 ▶ 제한시간 8분

E03 ✳✳✳ 고1 2025(3월)/22

다음 글의 요지로 가장 적절한 것은?

The science we learn in grade school is a collection of certainties about the natural world — the earth goes around the sun, DNA carries the information of an organism, and so on. Only when you start to learn the practice of science do you realize that each of these "facts" was hard won through a succession of logical inferences based upon many observations or experiments. The process of science is less about collecting pieces of knowledge than it is about reducing the uncertainties in what we know. Our uncertainties can be greater or lesser for any given piece of knowledge depending upon where we are in that process — today we are quite certain of how an apple will fall from a tree, but our understanding of the turbulent fluid flow remains a work in progress after more than a century of effort.

*inference: 추론 **turbulent fluid flow: 난류 유동

① 과학은 현재의 지식에 대한 불확실함을 줄이는 과정이다.
② 관찰과 실험 과정에서 우연히 얻어진 과학적 사실이 많다.
③ 학생들에게 다양한 연구 방법을 가르치는 것이 중요하다.
④ 과학 연구에서는 정확한 실험 과정 설계가 핵심이다.
⑤ 과학은 분산된 지식을 수집하여 통합하는 학문이다.

구문 서술형
밑줄 친 부분의 역할을 쓰고, 수식하는 단어를 찾아 쓰시오.

Our uncertainties can be greater or lesser in <u>that</u> process.

➡ 밑줄 친 부분의 역할: _____
➡ 수식하는 단어: _____

E04 ✳✳✳ 고1 2025(6월)/22

다음 글의 요지로 가장 적절한 것은?

Imagine following the spirit of a silence vow into daily life. Challenge yourself to spend an entire day saying only what you absolutely must say. It's been widely observed by behavioral psychology experts — and anyone who's ever been on a first date — that we too often tend to treat "conversation" as a game of waiting for our own turn to speak. We miss what's being said because we're mentally rehearsing our next utterance. What if you could eliminate the idea that the next available mini-silence is your next opening to express whatever is in your head? What if you were limited to, say, fifty spoken words tomorrow? I think you'd listen quite differently. You'd attend quite carefully to every word you heard. You'd be attuned to what you must respond to. You might discover that the less you say, the more you hear.

*vow: 서약 **utterance: 발언 ***attune: 맞추다

① 말을 적게 하면 상대방의 말을 경청할 수 있다.
② 첫 만남에서는 언행에 더욱 신중할 필요가 있다.
③ 불필요한 대화를 줄이면 스트레스가 감소한다.
④ 침묵은 의사소통의 효율성을 저해할 수 있다.
⑤ 몸짓 언어는 효과적인 대화에 도움이 된다.

구문 서술형
주어진 우리말과 일치하도록 괄호 안의 단어를 변형하여 쓰시오.

반드시 말해야 할 것만 말하는 데 하루 온종일을 보내는 것에 스스로 도전해 보라.

➡ Challenge _____ to spend an entire day saying only what you absolutely must say. (you)

E05 ✿✿✿

고1 2025(9월)/22

다음 글의 요지로 가장 적절한 것은?

The act of gardening itself is a fantastic form of physical activity. It involves a range of motions, from digging and planting to watering and harvesting. These activities help improve strength, flexibility, and endurance. You might not realize it, but small tasks like weeding or turning compost can burn many calories. Gardening is particularly beneficial for those who find traditional exercise challenging. It's a low-impact way to stay active and fit, making it accessible for people of all ages and physical abilities. Besides physical health, gardening has profound mental health benefits. Tending to plants can be incredibly calming and meditative. It allows you to focus on the present moment, reducing stress and anxiety. The repetitive tasks involved in gardening can induce a state of mindfulness, similar to meditation. Studies have shown that spending time in nature, even in a small garden, can elevate mood, improve cognition, and reduce depression symptoms. The sense of accomplishment from watching your plants grow and thrive can also boost self-esteem and overall well-being.   *compost: 퇴비

① 야외 활동을 통해 협동심과 자존감을 높일 수 있다.
② 취미 활동을 지속적으로 할 수 있는 동기가 필요하다.
③ 원예 활동은 신체적 건강과 더불어 정신적 건강에 이롭다.
④ 실내에서 식물을 기르는 것은 집중력 향상에 도움이 된다.
⑤ 원예 활동은 연령에 관계없이 다양한 사람들이 즐길 수 있다.

[구문 서술형]

지문의 첫 번째 문장의 주어에서 생략할 수 있는 부분을 찾아 쓰고, 그 이유를 서술하시오.

➡ _____

➡ 이유: _____

E06 ✿✿✿

고1 2024(10월)/22

다음 글의 요지로 가장 적절한 것은?

In his Cornell laboratory, David Dunning conducted experimental tests of eyewitness testimony and found evidence that a careful deliberation of facial features and a detailed discussion of selection procedures can actually be a sign of an *inaccurate* identification. It's when people find themselves unable to explain why they recognize the person, saying things like "his face just popped out at me," that they tend to be accurate more often. Sometimes our first, immediate, automatic reaction to a situation is the truest interpretation of what our mind is telling us. That very first impression can also be more accurate about the world than the deliberative, reasoned self-narrative can be. In his book *Blink*, Malcolm Gladwell describes a variety of studies in psychology and behavioral economics that demonstrate the superior performance of relatively unconscious first guesses compared to logical step-by-step justifications for a decision.

① 논리적인 근거가 부족한 판단은 진실을 왜곡할 수 있다.
② 인간의 표정은 무의식적인 감정 상태를 가장 잘 반영한다.
③ 사람을 정확하게 식별하기 위해서는 상황에 대한 정보가 중요하다.
④ 목격자 진술은 사건 직후보다 일정 시간이 지난 뒤 더 명확해진다.
⑤ 무의식적인 최초의 반응이 신중히 판단한 결과보다 정확할 수 있다.

[구문 서술형]

일곱 번째 줄의 people find ~ the person 문장을 참고하여 빈칸에 알맞은 말을 쓰시오.

➡ 이 문장의 재귀대명사인 _____는 생략할 수 _____. _____ 용법으로 쓰인 목적어이기 때문이다.

E07 ✱❀❀ 고1 2024(6월)/22

다음 글의 요지로 가장 적절한 것은?

When it comes to helping out, you don't have to do much. All you have to do is come around and show that you care. If you notice someone who is lonely, you could go and sit with them. If you work with someone who eats lunch all by themselves, and you go and sit down with them, they will begin to be more social after a while, and they will owe it all to you. A person's happiness comes from attention. There are too many people out in the world who feel like everyone has forgotten them or ignored them. Even if you say hi to someone passing by, they will begin to feel better about themselves, like someone cares.

① 사소한 관심이 타인에게 도움이 될 수 있다.
② 사람마다 행복의 기준이 제각기 다르다.
③ 선행을 통해 자신을 되돌아볼 수 있다.
④ 원만한 대인 관계는 경청에서 비롯된다.
⑤ 현재에 대한 만족이 행복의 필수조건이다.

E08 ✱❀❀ 고1 2024(9월)/22

다음 글의 요지로 가장 적절한 것은?

Our emotions are thought to exist because they have contributed to our survival as a species. Fear has helped us avoid dangers, expressing anger helps us scare off threats, and expressing positive emotions helps us bond with others. From an evolutionary perspective, an emotion is a kind of "program" that, when triggered, directs many of our activities (including attention, perception, memory, movement, expressions, etc.). For example, fear makes us very attentive, narrows our perceptual focus to threatening stimuli, will cause us either to face a situation (fight) or avoid it (flight), and may cause us to remember an experience more acutely (so that we avoid the threat in the future). Regardless of the specific ways in which they activate our systems, the specific emotions we possess are thought to exist because they have helped us (as a species) survive challenges within our environment long ago. If they had not helped us adapt and survive, they would not have evolved with us.

① 과거의 경험이 현재의 감정에 영향을 미친다.
② 문명의 발달에 따라 인간의 감정은 다양화되어 왔다.
③ 감정은 인간이 생존하도록 도와왔기 때문에 존재한다.
④ 부정적인 감정은 긍정적인 감정보다 더 오래 기억된다.
⑤ 두려움의 원인을 파악함으로써 두려움을 없앨 수 있다.

E09 ✴✴❀

다음 글의 요지로 가장 적절한 것은?

We all negotiate every day, whether we realise it or not. Yet few people ever learn *how* to negotiate. Those who do usually learn the traditional, win-lose negotiating style rather than an approach that is likely to result in a win-win agreement. This old-school, adversarial approach may be useful in a one-off negotiation where you will probably not deal with that person again. However, such transactions are becoming increasingly rare, because most of us deal with the same people repeatedly — our spouses and children, our friends and colleagues, our customers and clients. In view of this, it's essential to achieve successful results for ourselves and maintain a healthy relationship with our negotiating partners at the same time. In today's interdependent world of business partnerships and long-term relationships, a win-win outcome is fast becoming the *only* acceptable result.

*adversarial: 적대적인

① 협상 상대의 단점뿐 아니라 장점을 철저히 분석해야 한다.
② 의사소통 과정에서 서로의 의도를 확인하는 것이 바람직하다.
③ 성공적인 협상을 위해 다양한 대안을 준비하는 것이 중요하다.
④ 양측에 유리한 협상을 통해 상대와 좋은 관계를 유지해야 한다.
⑤ 원만한 인간관계를 위해 상호독립성을 인정하는 것이 필요하다.

E10 ✴✴❀

다음 글의 요지로 가장 적절한 것은?

When writing a novel, research for information needs to be done. The thing is that some kinds of fiction demand a higher level of detail: crime fiction, for example, or scientific thrillers. The information is never hard to find; one website for authors even organizes trips to police stations, so that crime writers can get it right. Often, a polite letter will earn you permission to visit a particular location and record all the details that you need. But remember that you will drive your readers to boredom if you think that you need to pack everything you discover into your work. The details that matter are those that reveal the human experience. The crucial thing is telling a story, finding the characters, the tension, and the conflict — not the train timetable or the building blueprint.

① 작품의 완성도는 작가의 경험의 양에 비례한다.
② 작가의 상상력은 가장 훌륭한 이야기 재료이다.
③ 소설에서 사건 전개에 대한 묘사는 구체적일수록 좋다.
④ 소설을 쓸 때 독자의 관심사를 먼저 고려하는 것이 중요하다.
⑤ 소설에 포함될 세부 사항은 인간의 경험을 드러내는 것이어야 한다.

E11 ✿✿✿ 고1 2023(3월)/22

다음 글의 요지로 가장 적절한 것은?

When students are starting their college life, they may approach every course, test, or learning task the same way, using what we like to call "the rubber-stamp approach." Think about it this way: Would you wear a tuxedo to a baseball game? A colorful dress to a funeral? A bathing suit to religious services? Probably not. You know there's appropriate dress for different occasions and settings. Skillful learners know that "putting on the same clothes" won't work for every class. They are flexible learners. They have different strategies and know when to use them. They know that you study for multiple-choice tests differently than you study for essay tests. And they not only know what to do, but they also know how to do it.

① 숙련된 학습자는 상황에 맞는 학습 전략을 사용할 줄 안다.
② 선다형 시험과 논술 시험은 평가의 형태와 목적이 다르다.
③ 문화마다 특정 행사와 상황에 맞는 복장 규정이 있다.
④ 학습의 양보다는 학습의 질이 학업 성과를 좌우한다.
⑤ 학습 목표가 명확할수록 성취 수준이 높아진다.

E12 ✿✿✿ 고1 2022(11월)/22

다음 글의 요지로 가장 적절한 것은?

The old saying is that "knowledge is power," but when it comes to scary, threatening news, research suggests the exact opposite. Frightening news can actually rob people of their inner sense of control, making them less likely to take care of themselves and other people. Public health research shows that when the news presents health-related information in a pessimistic way, people are actually less likely to take steps to protect themselves from illness as a result. A news article that's intended to warn people about increasing cancer rates, for example, can result in fewer people choosing to get screened for the disease because they're so terrified of what they might find. This is also true for issues such as climate change. When a news story is all doom and gloom, people feel depressed and become less interested in taking small, personal steps to fight ecological collapse.

① 두려움을 주는 뉴스는 사람들이 문제에 덜 대처하게 할 수 있다.
② 정보를 전달하는 시기에 따라 뉴스의 영향력이 달라질 수 있다.
③ 지속적인 환경 문제 보도가 사람들의 인식 변화를 가져온다.
④ 정보 제공의 지연은 정확한 문제 인식에 방해가 될 수 있다.
⑤ 출처가 불분명한 건강 정보는 사람들에게 유익하지 않다.

E13 ✿✿✿ 고1 2022(6월)/22

다음 글의 요지로 가장 적절한 것은?

Your emotions deserve attention and give you important pieces of information. However, they can also sometimes be an unreliable, inaccurate source of information. You may feel a certain way, but that does not mean those feelings are reflections of the truth. You may feel sad and conclude that your friend is angry with you when her behavior simply reflects that she's having a bad day. You may feel depressed and decide that you did poorly in an interview when you did just fine. Your feelings can mislead you into thinking things that are not supported by facts.

① 자신의 감정으로 인해 상황을 오해할 수 있다.
② 자신의 생각을 타인에게 강요해서는 안 된다.
③ 인간관계가 우리의 감정에 영향을 미친다.
④ 타인의 감정에 공감하는 자세가 필요하다.
⑤ 공동체를 위한 선택에는 보상이 따른다.

E14 ✿✿✿ 고1 2021(11월)/22

다음 글의 요지로 가장 적절한 것은?

Information is worthless if you never actually use it. Far too often, companies collect valuable customer information that ends up buried and never used. They must ensure their data is accessible for use at the appropriate times. For a hotel, one appropriate time for data usage is check-in at the front desk. I often check in at a hotel I've visited frequently, only for the people at the front desk to give no indication that they recognize me as a customer. The hotel must have stored a record of my visits, but they don't make that information accessible to the front desk clerks. They are missing a prime opportunity to utilize data to create a better experience focused on customer loyalty. Whether they have ten customers, ten thousand, or even ten million, the goal is the same: create a delightful customer experience that encourages loyalty.

① 기업 정보의 투명한 공개는 고객 만족도를 향상시킨다.
② 목표 고객층에 대한 분석은 기업의 이익 창출로 이어진다.
③ 고객 충성도를 높이기 위해 고객 정보가 활용될 필요가 있다.
④ 일관성 있는 호텔 서비스 제공을 통해 단골 고객을 확보할 수 있다.
⑤ 사생활 침해에 대한 우려로 고객 정보를 보관하는 데 어려움이 있다.

E15 ✿✿✿ 고1 2022(9월)/22

다음 글의 요지로 가장 적절한 것은?

A recent study from Carnegie Mellon University in Pittsburgh, called "When Too Much of a Good Thing May Be Bad," indicates that classrooms with too much decoration are a source of distraction for young children and directly affect their cognitive performance. Being visually overstimulated, the children have a great deal of difficulty concentrating and end up with worse academic results. On the other hand, if there is not much decoration on the classroom walls, the children are less distracted, spend more time on their activities, and learn more. So it's our job, in order to support their attention, to find the right balance between excessive decoration and the complete absence of it.

① 아이들의 집중을 돕기 위해 과도한 교실 장식을 지양할 필요가 있다.
② 아이들의 인성과 인지 능력을 균형 있게 발달시키는 것이 중요하다.
③ 아이들이 직접 교실을 장식하는 것은 창의력 발달에 도움이 된다.
④ 다양한 교실 활동은 아이들의 수업 참여도를 증진시킨다.
⑤ 풍부한 시각 자료는 아이들의 학습 동기를 높인다.

E16~17 ▶ 제한시간 4분

E16 ⭐ 2등급 대비 _____ 고1 2022(3월)/22

다음 글의 요지로 가장 적절한 것은?

Many people view sleep as merely a "down time" when their brain shuts off and their body rests. In a rush to meet work, school, family, or household responsibilities, people cut back on their sleep, thinking it won't be a problem, because all of these other activities seem much more important. But research reveals that a number of vital tasks carried out during sleep help to maintain good health and enable people to function at their best. While you sleep, your brain is hard at work forming the pathways necessary for learning and creating memories and new insights. Without enough sleep, you can't focus and pay attention or respond quickly. A lack of sleep may even cause mood problems. In addition, growing evidence shows that a continuous lack of sleep increases the risk for developing serious diseases.   *vital: 매우 중요한

① 수면은 건강 유지와 최상의 기능 발휘에 도움이 된다.
② 업무량이 증가하면 필요한 수면 시간도 증가한다.
③ 균형 잡힌 식단을 유지하면 뇌 기능이 향상된다.
④ 불면증은 주위 사람들에게 부정적인 영향을 미친다.
⑤ 꿈의 내용은 깨어 있는 시간 동안의 경험을 반영한다.

E17 ⭐ 2등급 대비 _____ 고1 2021(9월)/22

다음 글의 요지로 가장 적절한 것은?

It's important that you think independently and fight for what you believe in, but there comes a time when it's wiser to stop fighting for your view and move on to accepting what a trustworthy group of people think is best. This can be extremely difficult. But it's smarter, and ultimately better for you to be open-minded and have faith that the conclusions of a trustworthy group of people are better than whatever you think. If you can't understand their view, you're probably just blind to their way of thinking. If you continue doing what you think is best when all the evidence and trustworthy people are against you, you're being dangerously confident. The truth is that while most people can become incredibly open-minded, some can't, even after they have repeatedly encountered lots of pain from betting that they were right when they were not.

① 대부분의 사람들은 진리에 도달하지 못하고 고통을 받는다.
② 맹목적으로 다른 사람의 의견을 받아들이는 것은 위험하다.
③ 남을 설득하기 위해서는 타당한 증거로 주장을 뒷받침해야 한다.
④ 믿을만한 사람이 누구인지 판단하려면 열린 마음을 가져야 한다.
⑤ 자신의 의견이 최선이 아닐 수 있다는 것을 인정하는 것이 필요하다.

❋ 다음 영어는 우리말 뜻을, 우리말은 영어 단어를 〈보기〉에서 찾아 쓰시오.

〈보기〉

conduct	잠재력	agent	연속
elevate	배우자	accomplish	긴장
excessive	인지적인	leisure	측면

01 aspect _____

02 spouse _____

03 cognitive _____

04 potential _____

05 succession _____

06 성취하다 _____

07 여가 _____

08 지나친 _____

09 증진시키다 _____

10 실행하다 _____

❋ 다음 우리말에 알맞은 영어 표현을 찾아 연결하시오.

11 서둘러 •   • carry out

12 ~을 줄이다 •   • in progress

13 ~에 해당되다 •   • be true for

14 진행 중인 •   • cut back on

15 ~을 수행하다 •   • in a rush

❋ 다음 우리말 표현에 맞는 단어를 고르시오.

16 전통적인 협상 방식을 배우다 ➡ learn the (transparent / traditional) negotiating style

17 유연한 학습자 ➡ (flexible / audible) learners

18 중요한 것 ➡ the (crucial / commercial) thing

19 경로를 형성하다 ➡ form the (pathways / package)

20 기억과 새로운 통찰을 만들다 ➡ create memories and new (insights / instances)

❋ 다음 문장의 빈칸에 알맞은 단어를 〈보기〉에서 찾아 쓰시오.

〈보기〉

overstimulated	boredom	deserve	continuous
supported	owe	pessimistic	rare
acutely	ecological	unreliable	bond

21 그들은 이 모든 것을 당신 덕분이라고 할 것이다.
➡ They will _____ it all to you.

22 여러분은 독자들을 지루하게 만들 것이다.
➡ You will drive your readers to _____.

23 뉴스는 건강과 관련된 정보를 비관적인 방식으로 제시한다.
➡ The news presents health-related information in a(n) _____ way.

24 계속된 수면 부족이 심각한 질병의 발생 위험을 증가시킨다.
➡ A(n) _____ lack of sleep increases the risk for developing serious diseases.

25 당신의 감정은 주목할 만하고 당신에게 중요한 정보를 준다.
➡ Your emotions _____ attention and give you important pieces of information.

26 시각적으로 지나치게 자극되었을 때, 아이들은 집중할 수 없다.
➡ Being visually _____, the children can't concentrate.

27 이러한 거래는 점점 더 드물어지고 있다.
➡ Such transactions are becoming increasingly _____.

28 두려움은 우리로 하여금 경험을 더 강렬하게 기억하도록 할 수도 있다.
➡ Fear may cause us to remember an experience more _____.

29 그것들은 또한 가끔 신뢰할 수 없는 정보의 원천이 될 수도 있다.
➡ They can also sometimes be a(n) _____ source of information.

30 사실에 의해 뒷받침되지 않는 것들이 있다.
➡ There are things that are not _____ by facts.

주제 찾기

★ 유형 설명

다음 글의 주제로 가장 적절한 것은?

Thus, when the need for relatedness is met, motivation and internalization are fueled,

'무엇'에 관해 이야기하는 글인지를 찾는 문제로,
주제를 찾는 것이 요지, 주장, 제목을 찾는 밑바탕이 된다.

🔑 주제는 글에서 중심이 되는 이슈로, 주장 찾기 유형이 글의 주제에 대한 필자의 주장을 묻는 문제라면 주제 찾기 유형은 주제 그 자체를 찾는 문제이다.
"무엇에 관한 글인가?"라는 질문에 대답한다는 생각으로 정답을 찾는다.

🎭 유형 풀이 비법

1 핵심어를 찾아라!
• 글 전체적으로 반복해서 나오는 핵심어를 찾는 것이 가장 중요하다.

2 처음과 끝에 집중하라!
• 글의 처음이나 끝에 주제가 나오는 경우가 많으므로 특히 주의해서 본다.

3 태도가 바뀌는 곳에 유의하라!
• 반대 내용을 나타내는 접속사 뒤에 주제문이 나올 가능성이 높으므로 태도가 바뀌는지 확인한다.

(Tip) 범위가 너무 넓거나 좁은 내용이 들어간 선택지를 고르지 않도록 주의한다.

💡 어휘 및 표현 Preview

☐ desirable 바람직한	☐ immune system 면역 체계	☐ distortion 왜곡
☐ characteristic 특성, 특징	☐ accessibility 접근성	☐ discriminate 차별하다
☐ intelligent 지적인	☐ labour 노동	☐ ethnic 민족의
☐ fictional 허구적인	☐ inclusiveness 포괄성	☐ nationality 국적
☐ tendency 경향	☐ assistive 도움이 되는	☐ contrastive 대조하는
☐ prejudice 편견	☐ recognition 인지	☐ condition 여건, 조건
☐ mastery 숙달	☐ facilitate 촉진하다	☐ gradually 점차
☐ prosperity 번영	☐ prospect 전망	☐ transport 운송, 수송
☐ hardship 고난	☐ domain 영역	☐ industrial 산업의
☐ mindset 마음가짐	☐ ethical 윤리적인	☐ revolution 혁명
☐ resistance 저항	☐ necessity 필요성	☐ open up ~을 가능하게 하다
☐ confront 직면하다	☐ interaction 상호작용	☐ coast-to-coast 대륙 횡단의
☐ adequate 적당한	☐ productivity 생산성	☐ factor 요인
☐ aspect 측면	☐ spillover 여파, 파급	☐ destination 목적지
☐ tip of the iceberg 빙산의 일각	☐ excessive 과도한	☐ impact 영향
☐ reflection 반영, 반사	☐ transaction 거래	☐ crop rotation 윤작
☐ entire 전체의	☐ tolerant 관대한	☐ enrich 비옥하게 하다
☐ pose ~을 초래하다, 제기하다	☐ feature 특징	☐ organic 유기농의

6 다양한 목적어

1 주어＋완전타동사＋목적어: 문장의 목적어로는 **명사, 대명사, 부정사, 동명사, 명사구, 의문사절, 관계사절, that절** 등이 올 수 있다.
（목적어가 필요）

> *「의문사＋주어＋동사」의 간접의문문
> 의문문이 문장에서 주어, 목적어, 보어
> 등의 명사 역할을 할 때는 「의문사 ＋
> 주어 ＋ 동사」의 어순이 되며, 이를
> 간접의문문이라고 한다.

1) 명사 / 대명사

- It stimulates (the brain). (그것은 뇌를 자극한다.)
  명사(목적어)

- No one knows about (them). (아무도 그들에 대해 알지 못한다.)
  대명사(전치사의 목적어)

2) 부정사

- When I try (to play) the instrument myself, then I can hear, see and feel how the sound is made.
  부정사(목적어)
  (내가 직접 그 악기를 연주해 보면, 나는 소리가 어떻게 만들어지는지를 들을 수 있고 볼 수 있으며 느낄 수 있다.)

3) 동명사

- He gave up (traveling) to Europe this summer because he didn't have enough money.
  동명사(목적어)
  (그는 돈이 충분하지 않아서 이번 여름에 유럽으로 여행가는 것을 포기했다.)

4) 의문사 ＋ to부정사

- She showed me (how to do) the puzzle. (그녀는 나에게 그 수수께끼를 푸는 방법을 설명해 주었다.)
  의문사＋to부정사(직접목적어)

5) *의문사절(간접의문문): 의문사 ＋ 주어 ＋ 동사

- At that moment, she didn't think (why there weren't more presents).
  의문사절(간접의문문)
  (그 당시 그녀는 왜 선물이 더 없었는지에 대해서 생각하지 않았다.)

6) 관계사절

- I'll take (whoever wants to go with me). (나는 나와 함께 가고자 하는 사람이라면 누구든지 데리고 가겠다.)
  관계사절(목적어)

2 주어 ＋ 불완전타동사 ＋ 목적어 ＋ 목적격 보어: 5형식 동사의 목적어로는 **명사**가 온다.

- It helps (you) to think faster and remember information longer.
  (대)명사(목적어)
  (그것은 당신이 더 빠르게 사고하고 더 오래 정보를 기억하도록 도와준다.)

Check Test

1 주절의 목적어를 찾아 표시하시오.

You will notice the time lag when you are having a conversation with someone who is making things up as they go.

2 문장의 목적어를 찾아 표시하시오.

They learn how to compete and cooperate with others.

3 문장의 목적어를 찾아 처음 세 단어에 표시하시오.

For example, a large majority of the general public thinks that they are more intelligent than the average person.

4 목적어를 찾아 표시하시오.

From the moment you are created, oral health affects every aspect of your life.

• 정답

1 the time lag 2 how to compete and cooperate with others 3 that they are 4 every aspect of your life

F 주제 찾기 （첫 번째）

1st 첫 문장을 읽고, 이어질 내용을 예상해 보세요.
2nd **1st** 에서 발상한 것을 토대로 글을 읽고, 내용을 파악해 보세요.
3rd 선택지를 꼼꼼히 해석하고 글의 주제를 고르세요.

F01 ★★❀ .... 고1 2025(3월)/23

다음 글의 주제로 가장 적절한 것은?

There is a wealth of evidence that when parents, teachers, supervisors, and coaches are perceived as involved and caring, people feel happier and more motivated. And it is not just those people with power — we need 5 to feel valued and respected by peers and coworkers. Thus, when the need for relatedness is met, motivation and internalization are fueled, provided that support for autonomy and competence are 10 also there. If we are trying to motivate others, a caring relationship is a crucial basis from which to begin. And when we are trying to motivate ourselves, doing things to enhance a sense of connectedness to others can be 15 crucial to long-term persistence. So exercise with a friend, call someone when you have a difficult decision to make, and be there as a support for others as they take on challenges.

*autonomy: 자율성 **persistence: 지속

① ways of getting out of dependent relationships
② necessity of independent decision-making for happier life
③ key factors required for boosting a competitive atmosphere
④ challenges in maintaining lasting bonds with family members
⑤ importance of building connected relationships in motivation

---

1st 첫 문장을 읽고, 이어질 내용을 예상해 보세요.

There is a wealth of evidence / that when parents,
수많은 증거가 있다 　　　　　　　　 / 부모, 교사, 상사,
teachers, supervisors, and coaches / are perceived as
그리고 코치가 　　　　　　　　　　 / 관여되어 있고
involved and caring, / people feel happier and more
배려한다고 여겨질 때 　 / 사람들은 더 행복하고 더 동기가
motivated. //
부여된다는 　 //

● 글의 첫 문장을 읽어봅시다.
부모, 교사, 상사, 코치가 관여되어 있고 배려한다고 여겨질 때, 사람들이 더 행복하고 더 동기가 부여된다는 증거가 있어요.

● 어떤 내용이 이어질까요?
부모, 교사, 상사, 코치는 각각 자녀, 학생, 후임, 선수를 가르치는 윗사람에 해당하죠? 이처럼 윗사람이 더 많은 신경을 쓴다고 여겨질 때, 가르침을 받는 사람들은 행복과 동기부여처럼 긍정적 효과를 누린다는 흐름으로 글이 이어질 것 같아요.

2nd **1st** 에서 발상한 것을 토대로 글을 읽고, 내용을 파악해 보세요.

1) 첫 문장에 이어지는 그다음 문장을 봅시다.

And it is not just those people with power / — we
그리고 그것이 단지 권력을 가진 사람들만은 아닌데 　　　 / 즉 우리는
need to feel valued and respected / by peers and
소중히 여겨지고 존중받는다는 느낌을 받을 필요가 있다 / 또래와 직장
coworkers. //
동료들에게서도 　 //

● 윗사람뿐만 아니라 또래와 동료도 해당하네요.
앞에서는 부모나 교사처럼 윗사람이 배려한다고 여겨지는 경우를 언급했어요. 하지만 여기서는 또래와 직장 동료에게서도 소중히 여겨지고 존중을 받을 필요가 있대요.

2) 그다음 문장을 봅시다.

Thus, / when the need for relatedness is met, /
따라서 　 / 관계성에 대한 욕구가 충족될 때 　　　　　　 /
motivation and internalization are fueled, / provided
동기와 내면화는 자극된다 　　　　　　　　　　 / 그리고
that support for autonomy and competence are also
자율성과 유능함에 대한 지원 또한 제공된다면 //
there. //

- **결과나 결론을 나타내는 Thus가 쓰였어요.**

  Thus는 보통 글의 마지막에 쓰여서 결과나 결론에 해당하는 중요한 문장을 이끌어요. 하지만 여기서는 글의 중간에 쓰였으니, 적어도 글의 주제와 밀접한 연관이 있을 것 같아요.

  윗사람으로부터 배려를 받거나 또래에게서 소중히 여겨져서 관계성에 대한 욕구가 충족되면 동기와 내면화가 자극된다는 내용이네요.

- **첫 문장과 겹치는 표현이 있어요.**

  첫 문장의 motivated가 이 문장에는 motivation으로 다시 등장했어요. 동기부여가 주제에 포함될 가능성이 높아진 만큼, 뒤에서도 비슷한 표현이 등장하는지 쭉 살펴봐야 해요.

3) 마지막으로 동기부여가 다시 언급되는 문장을 살펴봅시다.

> And when we are trying to `motivate` ourselves, /
> 그리고 우리가 스스로 동기를 부여하려고 할 때 /
> doing things to enhance a sense of connectedness to
> 타인과의 유대감을 강화하기 위한 일을 하는 것은
> others / can be `crucial` / to long-term persistence. //
> / 중요할 수 있다 / 장기적인 지속에 //

- **글의 후반부에 motivate가 다시 언급되었어요.**

  스스로 동기를 부여하려고 할 때 장기적인 지속에 타인과의 유대감 강화가 중요하다는 내용이에요.

  중요성을 강조하는 crucial도 함께 등장했으니, 이 문장이 주제문일 가능성이 아주 높아요.

↳ 글의 내용을 한번 정리해 볼까요?

우리는 윗사람의 배려와 동료의 존중을 통해 관계성의 욕구가 충족되면
❶( )와 내면화가 자극된다고 했어요. 그리고 동기를 부여할 때 타인과의 유대감 강화가 장기적인 지속에 중요하고요.

3rd 선택지를 꼼꼼히 해석하고 글의 주제를 고르세요.

① ways of getting out of dependent relationships
   의존적인 관계에서 벗어나는 방법들
② necessity of independent decision-making for happier life
   더 행복한 삶을 위한 독립적인 의사결정의 필요성
③ key factors required for boosting a competitive atmosphere
   경쟁적인 분위기를 조성하는 데 필요한 핵심 요소들
④ challenges in maintaining lasting bonds with family members
   가족 구성원과의 지속적인 유대감을 유지하는 데 따른 어려움들
⑤ importance of building connected relationships in motivation
   동기부여에 있어 유대감 있는 관계 형성의 중요성

- **선택지 ❷**( )**이 글의 주제를 잘 나타내요.**

  윗사람과 또래와의 관계 모두에서 관계성의 욕구가 충족되는 것과 타인과의 유대감 강화가 동기부여에 중요하다고 했어요. 따라서, 정답은 **❷**( ) '동기부여에 있어 유대감 있는 관계 형성의 중요성'이죠.

수능 Tip

#비인칭 독립분사구문

> Thus, / when the need for relatedness is met, /
> 따라서 / 관계성에 대한 욕구가 충족될 때 /
> motivation and internalization are fueled, /
> 동기와 내면화는 자극된다 /
> `provided that` support for autonomy and
> 그리고 자율성과 유능함에 대한 지원 또한 제공된다면 //
> competence are also there. //

1 (If we are) provided that

부사절 위치에 있는 과거분사 provided는 조건을 나타내는 부사절 접속사 if와 일반적인 주어 we, 그리고 동사 are가 생략되고 남은 형태예요. 이처럼 분사구문의 의미상 주어가 주절의 주어와 달라도 이를 생략하는 형태의 분사구문을 '비인칭 독립분사구문'이라고 해요.

2 provided that은 문장에서 어떤 역할을 하나요?

생략된 부사절 접속사가 if라는 점에서 알 수 있듯이, provided that이 이끄는 분사구문은 조건과 관련되어 있어요. provided that 뒤에 이어지는 절이 주절의 조건 역할을 하며 '~이라는 것이 제공된다면, ~이라면'의 의미를 나타내요.

Motivation ↑

F 주제 찾기 (두 번째)

1st 첫 문장을 통해 핵심 소재를 확인하고 글의 내용을 예상해 보세요.
2nd 예상한 내용을 토대로 글을 읽고, 전체적인 내용을 파악해 보세요.
3rd 파악한 내용을 바탕으로 선택지 중에서 글의 주제를 골라 보세요.

F02 ★★※.............................. 고1 2023(6월)/23

다음 글의 주제로 가장 적절한 것은?

We tend to believe that we possess a host of socially desirable characteristics, and that we are free of most of those that are socially undesirable. For example, a large majority of the general public thinks that they are more [5] intelligent, more fair-minded, less prejudiced, and more skilled behind the wheel of an automobile than the average person. This phenomenon is so reliable and ubiquitous that it has come to be known as [10] the "Lake Wobegon effect," after Garrison Keillor's fictional community where "the women are strong, the men are good-looking, and all the children are above average." A survey of one million high [15] school seniors found that 70% thought they were above average in leadership ability, and only 2% thought they were below average. In terms of ability to get along with others, *all* students thought they were above average, [20] 60% thought they were in the top 10%, and 25% thought they were in the top 1%!

*ubiquitous: 도처에 있는

① importance of having a positive self-image as a leader
② our common belief that we are better than average
③ our tendency to think others are superior to us
④ reasons why we always try to be above average
⑤ danger of prejudice in building healthy social networks

1st 첫 문장을 통해 핵심 소재를 확인하고 글의 내용을 예상해 보세요.

We tend to believe / that we possess a host of socially
우리는 믿는 경향이 있다 / 우리가 사회적으로 바람직한 특성들을 많이
desirable characteristics, / and that we are free of most
지니고 있고 / 우리는 그것들의 대부분은 지니고 있지
of those / that are socially undesirable. //
않다고 / 사회적으로 바람직하지 않은 //

● 우리는 믿는 경향이 있어요.
사회적으로 바람직한 특성들은 많이 가지고 있고, 사회적으로 바람직하지 않은 특성들은 가지고 있지 않다고요. 이렇게 '믿는' 경향이 있다고 했으니, 아마 사실은 그렇지 않다는 내용의 글일 거예요.

2nd 예상한 내용을 토대로 글을 읽고, 전체적인 내용을 파악해 보세요.

1) 바로 다음 문장을 봅시다.

For example, / a large majority of the general public
예를 들어 / 대다수의 일반 대중들은 생각한다
thinks / that they are more intelligent, more fair-
/ 그들이 더 지적이고, 더 공정하고,
minded, less prejudiced, / and more skilled / behind the
덜 편견을 가지며 / 더 능숙하다고 / 자동차를
wheel of an automobile / than the average person. //
운전할 때 / 보통 사람보다 //

● 첫 문장의 내용을 뒷받침하는 예시가 등장했네요.
대다수의 일반 대중들이 스스로 보통 사람보다 더 낫다고 생각한대요. 첫 문장에 등장한 경향을 뒷받침하는 현상이에요. 뒤에는 어떤 내용이 이어지는지 더 확인해 볼까요?

2) 어떤 효과가 등장해요.

This phenomenon is so reliable and ubiquitous /
이 현상은 너무 신뢰할 수 있고 어디서나 볼 수 있어서 /
that it has come to be known as the "Lake Wobegon
그것은 'Lake Wobegon 효과'라고 알려지게 되었다
effect," / after Garrison Keillor's fictional
/ Garrison Keillor의 허구적인 공동체의 이름을 딴
community / where "the women are strong, the
/ '여성들은 강하고, 남성들은 잘생긴
men are good-looking, / and all the children are
/ 그리고 모든 아이들은 평균 이상'인 //
above average." //

- **Lake Wobegon 효과 = 바람직한 특성들만 있다고 믿는 것**

  이 효과는 여성들은 강하고, 남성들은 잘생기고, 모든 아이들은 평균
  이상인 **①**(　　　　　　　) 공동체의 이름을 땄다고 했으니까 현실성이
  떨어진다는 거예요.
  우리가 앞에서 예상했던 것처럼 모두가 사회적으로 바람직한 특성만
  가지고 있다고 믿는데, 사실은 그렇지 않다는 거죠.

3) 설문조사 결과가 이어져요.

A survey of one million high school seniors found / that
고등학교 고학년 학생 100만 명을 대상으로 한 설문조사는 발견했다　/

70% thought / they were above average in leadership
70퍼센트는 생각했다는 것을 / 자신이 리더십 능력에 있어 평균 이상이라고

ability, / and only 2% thought / they were below
　　/ 그리고 2퍼센트만이 생각했다는 것을 / 자신이 평균 이하라고 //

average. //

- **고등학교 고학년 학생들을 대상으로 설문조사를 했대요.**

  그리고 절반 이상이 자신의 리더십 능력이 평균 이상이라고 생각했대요.
  고등학생들에게도 Lake Wobegon 효과가 적용돼서 사회적으로
  바람직한 특성인 리더십을 가지고 있다고 생각했다는 거죠.
  정답을 고를 수 있을 것 같은데, 이어지는 예시까지 살펴볼까요?

4) 마지막 문장을 읽어봅시다.

In terms of ability to get along with others, / all
다른 사람들과 잘 지내는 능력에 있어서　　　　　　　　　　　/ '모든'

students thought they were above average, / 60%
학생들은 자신이 평균 이상이라고 생각했고　　　　　　　/

thought they were in the top 10%, / and 25%
60퍼센트는 자신이 상위 10퍼센트에 속한다고 생각했으며　/ 25퍼센트는

thought they were in the top 1%! //
자신이 상위 1퍼센트에 속한다고 생각했다　　//

- **다른 사람과 잘 지내는 능력에도 Lake Wobegon 효과가
  적용됐어요.**

  다른 사람과 잘 지내는 능력도 사회적으로 바람직하다고 여겨지는
  특징인데, 역시나 과반수 이상이 자신이 상위 10퍼센트에 속한다고
  생각했대요. 25퍼센트는 자신이 무려 상위 1퍼센트에 속한다고
  생각했고요. 상위 1퍼센트에 전체의 25퍼센트가 속할 수 있을까요?
  ②(　　　　　　)!
  이런 게 바로 허구적인 공동체 Lake Wobegon과 같다는 말이에요.

3rd 파악한 내용을 바탕으로 선택지 중에서 글의 주제를 골라
보세요.

① importance of having a positive self-image as a
   leader
   리더로서 긍정적인 자아상을 갖는 것의 중요성

② our common belief that we are better than
   average
   우리가 평균보다 우월하다는 우리의 공통된 믿음

③ our tendency to think others are superior to us
   다른 사람이 우리보다 우월하다고 생각하는 우리의 경향

④ reasons why we always try to be above average
   우리가 항상 평균 이상이 되려고 노력하는 이유

⑤ danger of prejudice in building healthy social
   networks
   건강한 사회 연결망 구축에 있어 편견의 위험성

- **선택지를 먼저 해석해 봅시다.**

  대부분의 사람들이 사회적으로 바람직한 특성을 가지고 있다고
  생각한다는 Lake Wobegon 효과를 예시를 들어서 설명한 글이에요.
  다시 말해, 우리가 평균보다 우월하다고 공통적으로 믿는다는 거니까
  정답은 **③**(　　　　　　)!

- **③을 정답으로 고르진 않았나요?**

  Lake Wobegon 효과는 '우리 > 다른 사람'이라고 생각하는 경향을 말해요.
  그런데 ③은 '우리 **④**(　　　　　　) 다른 사람'으로 글의 내용과
  정반대를 이야기하고 있어요.
  글을 정확하게 이해하고도 선택지를 잘못 해석해서 오답을 고르면 안
  되겠죠?

설문조사 결과를
떠올리며 글의 '주제'를
알아내자!

빈칸 정답 ➤ **4** ② **3** 이거야 **2** 말도안돼 **1** 워비곤호수

F03 ~ 06 ▶ 제한시간 8분

F03 ★★★❋   고1 2025(6월)/23

다음 글의 주제로 가장 적절한 것은?

Science is concerned with accumulating and understanding observations of the physical world. That understanding alone solves no problems. Individual people have to act on that understanding for it to help solve problems. For instance, science has found that regular exercise can lower your risk of heart disease. Knowing this fact is interesting, but it will do nothing for your personal health unless you act on it and actually exercise. And that's the hard part. Reading an article about exercise is easy. Getting into an actual routine of regular exercise is harder. In this sense, science really solves *no* problems at all. Problems are only solved when people take the knowledge provided by science and use it. In fact, many of humanity's biggest problems are caused by lack of action, and not lack of knowledge.

*accumulate: 축적하다

① advantages of putting strategic plans into action
② danger of acting against the wisdom of the crowd
③ difficulty in sharing scientific knowledge with the public
④ problems with lacking specific knowledge about exercising
⑤ need to act on scientific understanding in solving problems

[구문 서술형]
두 문장을 읽고, 빈칸에 알맞은 말을 쓰시오.

> ① That understanding alone solves no problems.
> ② Science has found that regular exercise can lower your risk of heart disease.

➡ ① 문장에 쓰인 That은 _____ 앞에 쓰인 _____이다. 반면, ② 문장에 쓰인 that은 뒤의 절을 이끌며 문장의 _____ 역할을 하는 _____이다.

F04 ★★★❋ _____   고1 2025(9월)/23

다음 글의 주제로 가장 적절한 것은?

For many centuries, humans have taken advantage of tools that translate and bring into our perception natural phenomena that we can't perceive with our senses. In some cases, this consists of simply amplifying signals that feed into our normal sensory inputs (e.g., telescopes can bring into clear view that which is too far away for our eyes to perceive on their own). Other instruments turn signals that we cannot perceive into ones that we can observe. Some of these take the form of expanding the reach of our current senses, such as creating visible images based on the ultraviolet spectrum of light or changing sounds that are normally outside the range of what human ears can hear into audible signals. Alternatively, some instruments measure properties for which we have no sensory capacity at all and change them into that which we can observe.

*amplify: 확장하다 **audible: 들을 수 있는

① difficulties in replacing human senses with tools
② the tools that increase the ability of human senses
③ human senses that inspire the inventing of scientific tools
④ differences between visual and auditory senses in humans
⑤ the power of human imagination in discovering the universe

[구문 서술형]
Alternatively로 시작하는 문장에서 주절의 목적어를 모두 찾아 쓰시오. (단, 관계사절 및 전치사의 목적어는 제외할 것)

➡ _____, _____

F05 ★★❀   고1 2024(10월)/23

다음 글의 주제로 가장 적절한 것은?

Many forms of research lead naturally to quantitative data. A study of happiness might measure the number of times someone smiles during an interaction, and a study of memory might measure the number of items an individual can recall after one, five, and ten minutes. Asking people how many times in a year they are sad will also yield quantitative data, but it might not be reliable. Respondents' recollections may be inaccurate, and their definitions of 'sad' could vary widely. But asking "How many times in the past year were you sad enough to call in sick to work?" prompts a concrete answer. Similarly, instead of asking people to rate how bad a procrastinator they are, ask, "How many of your utility bills are you currently late in paying, even though you can afford to pay them?" Questions that seek concrete responses help make abstract concepts clearer and ensure consistency from one study to the next.

*procrastinator: 미루는 사람

① risks of overgeneralizing results from the collected data
② usefulness of answering abstract questions with numbers
③ effect of sample size on enhancing the reliability of research
④ limitations of measuring and quantifying various human emotions
⑤ importance of specific questions to attain reliable quantitative data

구문 서술형

여섯 번째 줄에 Asking으로 시작하는 문장의 각 성분을 알맞게 쓰시오.

➡ Asking의 간접목적어: _____

➡ 전체 문장의 목적어: _____ _____

F06 ★★❀   고1 2024(9월)/23

다음 글의 주제로 가장 적절한 것은?

By improving accessibility of the workplace for workers that are typically at a disadvantage in the labour market, AI can improve inclusiveness in the workplace. AI-powered assistive devices to aid workers with visual, speech or hearing difficulties are becoming more widespread, improving the access to, and the quality of work for people with disabilities. For example, speech recognition solutions for people with dysarthric voices, or live captioning systems for deaf and hard of hearing people can facilitate communication with colleagues and access to jobs where inter-personal communication is necessary. AI can also enhance the capabilities of low-skilled workers, with potentially positive effects on their wages and career prospects. For example, AI's capacity to translate written and spoken word in real-time can improve the performance of non-native speakers in the workplace. Moreover, recent developments in AI-powered text generators can instantly improve the performance of lower-skilled individuals in domains such as writing, coding or customer service.

*dysarthric: (신경 장애로 인한) 구음(構音) 장애의

① jobs replaced by AI in the labour market
② ethical issues caused by using AI in the workplace
③ necessity of using AI technology for language learning
④ impacts of AI on supporting workers with disadvantages
⑤ new designs of AI technology to cure people with disabilities

F07 ★★※   고1 2024(6월)/23

다음 글의 주제로 가장 적절한 것은?

We often try to make cuts in our challenges and take the easy route. When taking the quick exit, we fail to acquire the strength to compete. We often take the easy route to improve our skills. Many of us never really work to achieve mastery in the key areas of life. These skills are key tools that can be useful to our career, health, and prosperity. Highly successful athletes don't win because of better equipment; they win by facing hardship to gain strength and skill. They win through preparation. It's the mental preparation, winning mindset, strategy, and skill that set them apart. Strength comes from struggle, not from taking the path of least resistance. Hardship is not just a lesson for the next time in front of us. Hardship will be the greatest teacher we will ever have in life.

① characteristics of well-equipped athletes
② difficulties in overcoming life's sudden challenges
③ relationship between personal habit and competence
④ risks of enduring hardship without any preparation
⑤ importance of confronting hardship in one's life

F08 ★★★   고1 2022(9월)/23

다음 글의 주제로 가장 적절한 것은?

For creatures like us, evolution smiled upon those with a strong need to belong. Survival and reproduction are the criteria of success by natural selection, and forming relationships with other people can be useful for both survival and reproduction. Groups can share resources, care for sick members, scare off predators, fight together against enemies, divide tasks so as to improve efficiency, and contribute to survival in many other ways. In particular, if an individual and a group want the same resource, the group will generally prevail, so competition for resources would especially favor a need to belong. Belongingness will likewise promote reproduction, such as by bringing potential mates into contact with each other, and in particular by keeping parents together to care for their children, who are much more likely to survive if they have more than one caregiver.

① skills for the weak to survive modern life
② usefulness of belonging for human evolution
③ ways to avoid competition among social groups
④ roles of social relationships in children's education
⑤ differences between two major evolutionary theories

F09 ★★★※   고1 2023(11월)/23

다음 글의 주제로 가장 적절한 것은?

Nearly everything has to go through your mouth to get to the rest of you, from food and air to bacteria and viruses. A healthy mouth can help your body get what it needs and prevent it from harm — with adequate space for air to travel to your lungs, and healthy teeth and gums that prevent harmful microorganisms from entering your bloodstream. From the moment you are created, oral health affects every aspect of your life. What happens in the mouth is usually just the tip of the iceberg and a reflection of what is happening in other parts of the body. Poor oral health can be a cause of a disease that affects the entire body. The microorganisms in an unhealthy mouth can enter the bloodstream and travel anywhere in the body, posing serious health risks.   *microorganism: 미생물

① the way the immune system fights viruses
② the effect of unhealthy eating habits on the body
③ the difficulty in raising awareness about oral health
④ the importance of oral health and its impact on the body
⑤ the relationship between oral health and emotional well-being

F10 ❋❋❋ 고1 2021(9월)/23

다음 글의 주제로 가장 적절한 것은?

Vegetarian eating is moving into the mainstream as more and more young adults say no to meat, poultry, and fish. According to the American Dietetic Association, "approximately planned vegetarian diets are healthful, are nutritionally adequate, and provide health benefits in the prevention and treatment of certain diseases." But health concerns are not the only reason that young adults give for changing their diets. Some make the choice out of concern for animal rights. When faced with the statistics that show the majority of animals raised as food live in confinement, many teens give up meat to protest those conditions. Others turn to vegetarianism to support the environment. Meat production uses vast amounts of water, land, grain, and energy and creates problems with animal waste and resulting pollution.

*poultry: 가금류(닭 · 오리 · 거위 등)

① reasons why young people go for vegetarian diets
② ways to build healthy eating habits for teenagers
③ vegetables that help lower your risk of cancer
④ importance of maintaining a balanced diet
⑤ disadvantages of plant-based diets

F11 ❋❋❋ 고1 2022(11월)/23

다음 글의 주제로 가장 적절한 것은?

The most remarkable and unbelievable consequence of melting ice and rising seas is that together they are a kind of time machine, so real that they are altering the duration of our day. It works like this: As the glaciers melt and the seas rise, gravity forces more water toward the equator. This changes the shape of the Earth ever so slightly, making it fatter around the middle, which in turns slows the rotation of the planet similarly to the way a ballet dancer slows her spin by spreading out her arms. The slowdown isn't much, just a few thousandths of a second each year, but like the barely noticeable jump of rising seas every year, it adds up. When dinosaurs lived on the Earth, a day lasted only about twenty-three hours.

① cause of rising temperatures on the Earth
② principles of planets maintaining their shapes
③ implications of melting ice on marine biodiversity
④ way to keep track of time without using any device
⑤ impact of melting ice and rising seas on the length of a day

F12 ❋❋❋ 고1 2023(9월)/23

다음 글의 주제로 가장 적절한 것은?

The interaction of workers from different cultural backgrounds with the host population might increase productivity due to positive externalities like knowledge spillovers. This is only an advantage up to a certain degree. When the variety of backgrounds is too large, fractionalization may cause excessive transaction costs for communication, which may lower productivity. Diversity not only impacts the labour market, but may also affect the quality of life in a location. A tolerant native population may value a multicultural city or region because of an increase in the range of available goods and services. On the other hand, diversity could be perceived as an unattractive feature if natives perceive it as a distortion of what they consider to be their national identity. They might even discriminate against other ethnic groups and they might fear that social conflicts between different foreign nationalities are imported into their own neighbourhood.

*externality: 외부 효과 **fractionalization: 분열

① roles of culture in ethnic groups
② contrastive aspects of cultural diversity
③ negative perspectives of national identity
④ factors of productivity differences across countries
⑤ policies to protect minorities and prevent discrimination

F13 *** 고1 2023(3월)/23

다음 글의 주제로 가장 적절한 것은?

As the social and economic situation of countries got better, wage levels and working conditions improved. Gradually people were given more time off. At the same time, forms of transport improved and it became faster and cheaper to get to places. England's industrial revolution led to many of these changes. Railways, in the nineteenth century, opened up now famous seaside resorts such as Blackpool and Brighton. With the railways came many large hotels. In Canada, for example, the new coast-to-coast railway system made possible the building of such famous hotels as Banff Springs and Chateau Lake Louise in the Rockies. Later, the arrival of air transport opened up more of the world and led to tourism growth.

① factors that caused tourism expansion
② discomfort at a popular tourist destination
③ importance of tourism in society and economy
④ negative impacts of tourism on the environment
⑤ various types of tourism and their characteristics

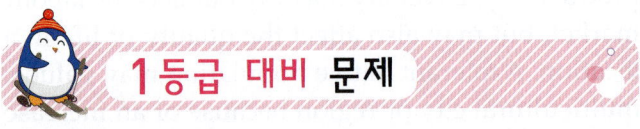

1등급 대비 문제

F14 ~ 17 ▶ 제한시간 8분

F14 ⭐2등급 대비 고1 2024(3월)/23

다음 글의 주제로 가장 적절한 것은?

Crop rotation is the process in which farmers change the crops they grow in their fields in a special order. For example, if a farmer has three fields, he or she may grow carrots in the first field, green beans in the second, and tomatoes in the third. The next year, green beans will be in the first field, tomatoes in the second field, and carrots will be in the third. In year three, the crops will rotate again. By the fourth year, the crops will go back to their original order. Each crop enriches the soil for the next crop. This type of farming is sustainable because the soil stays healthy.

*sustainable: 지속 가능한

① advantage of crop rotation in maintaining soil health
② influence of purchasing organic food on farmers
③ ways to choose three important crops for rich soil
④ danger of growing diverse crops in small spaces
⑤ negative impact of crop rotation on the environment

F15 ⭐2등급 대비 고1 2022(6월)/23

다음 글의 주제로 가장 적절한 것은?

Every day, children explore and construct relationships among objects. Frequently, these relationships focus on how much or how many of something exists. Thus, children count — "One cookie, two shoes, three candles on the birthday cake, four children in the sandbox." Children compare — "Which has more? Which has fewer? Will there be enough?" Children calculate — "How many will fit? Now, I have five. I need one more." In all of these instances, children are developing a notion of quantity. Children reveal and investigate mathematical concepts through their own activities or experiences, such as figuring out how many crackers to take at snack time or sorting shells into piles.

① difficulties of children in learning how to count
② how children build mathematical understanding
③ why fingers are used in counting objects
④ importance of early childhood education
⑤ advantages of singing number songs

다음 글의 주제로 가장 적절한 것은?

We used to think that the brain never changed, but according to the neuroscientist Richard Davidson, we now know that this is not true — specific brain circuits grow stronger through regular practice. He explains, "Well-being is fundamentally no different than learning to play the cello. If one practices the skills of well-being, one will get better at it." What this means is that you can actually train your brain to become more grateful, relaxed, or confident, by repeating experiences that evoke gratitude, relaxation, or confidence. Your brain is shaped by the thoughts you repeat. The more neurons fire as they are activated by repeated thoughts and activities, the faster they develop into neural pathways, which cause lasting changes in the brain. Or in the words of Donald Hebb, "Neurons that fire together wire together." This is such an encouraging premise: bottom line — we can intentionally create the habits for the brain to be happier.

*evoke: (감정을) 불러일으키다 **premise: 전제

① possibility of forming brain habits for well-being
② role of brain circuits in improving body movements
③ importance of practice in playing musical instruments
④ effect of taking a break on enhancing memory capacity
⑤ difficulty of discovering how neurons in the brain work

다음 글의 주제로 가장 적절한 것은? [3점]

The whole of human society operates on knowing the future weather. For example, farmers in India know when the monsoon rains will come next year and so they know when to plant the crops. Farmers in Indonesia know there are two monsoon rains each year, so next year they can have two harvests. This is based on their knowledge of the past, as the monsoons have always come at about the same time each year in living memory. But the need to predict goes deeper than this; it influences every part of our lives. Our houses, roads, railways, airports, offices, and so on are all designed for the local climate. For example, in England all the houses have central heating, as the outside temperature is usually below 20℃, but no air-conditioning, as temperatures rarely go beyond 26℃, while in Australia the opposite is true: most houses have air-conditioning but rarely central heating.

① new technologies dealing with climate change
② difficulties in predicting the weather correctly
③ weather patterns influenced by rising temperatures
④ knowledge of the climate widely affecting our lives
⑤ traditional wisdom helping our survival in harsh climates

✱ 다음 영어는 우리말 뜻을, 우리말은 영어 단어를 〈보기〉에서 찾아 쓰시오.

＜보기＞
영향	distortion	상호작용	pose
직면하다	결과	wage	경향
prosperity	요인	glacier	rotate

01 impact _____

02 factor _____

03 confront _____

04 interaction _____

05 tendency _____

06 번영 _____

07 왜곡 _____

08 빙하 _____

09 ~을 초래하다 _____

10 임금, 급료 _____

✱ 다음 우리말에 알맞은 영어 표현을 찾아 연결하시오.

11 ~을 다루다 •   • a host of

12 다수의 •   • take on

13 ~에 맞서다 •   • figure out

14 ~을 알아내다 •   • keep track of

15 ~을 기록하다 •   • deal with

✱ 다음 우리말 표현에 맞는 단어를 고르시오.

16 자율성과 유능함에 대한 지원 → support for autonomy and (competition / competence)

17 관용적인 원주민 → a(n) (tolerant / intolerant) native population

18 발화 인식 솔루션 → speech (recognition / resolution) solutions

19 가장 놀랍고 믿을 수 없는 결과 → the most remarkable and unbelievable (conscience / consequence)

20 작물을 심다 → plant the (crops / crowds)

✱ 다음 문장의 빈칸에 알맞은 단어를 〈보기〉에서 찾아 쓰시오.

＜보기＞
discriminate	operates	desirable	enriches
automobile	notion	explore	monsoon
rotation	consistency	ultraviolet	entire

21 그들은 심지어 다른 민족 집단을 차별할 수도 있다.
→ They might even _____ against other ethnic groups.

22 지구의 모양은 행성의 회전을 늦춘다.
→ The shape of the Earth slows the _____ of the planet.

23 전체 인간 사회는 미래의 날씨를 아는 것을 기반으로 운영된다.
→ The whole of human society _____ on knowing the future weather.

24 매일, 아이들은 사물 사이의 관계들을 탐구하고 구성한다.
→ Every day, children _____ and construct relationships among objects.

25 각각의 작물은 다음 작물을 위한 토양을 비옥하게 한다.
→ Each crop _____ the soil for the next crop.

26 우리는 사회적으로 바람직한 특성들을 지니고 있다고 믿는다.
→ We believe that we possess socially _____ characteristics.

27 인도네시아의 농부들은 몬순 장마가 두 번 있다는 것을 안다.
→ Farmers in Indonesia know there are two _____ rains.

28 이 모든 예시에서, 아이들은 양의 개념을 발달시키는 중이다.
→ In all of these instances, children are developing a(n) _____ of quantity.

29 구체적인 응답을 요구하는 질문은 일관성을 보장한다.
→ Questions that seek concrete responses ensure _____.

30 그것은 빛의 자외선 스펙트럼을 기반으로 가시 이미지를 생성한다.
→ It creates visible images based on the _____ spectrum of light.

KUAAA

고려대학교 천문 동아리

우리 같이 별 보러 가지 않을래?

매달 정기 관측회를 떠나고 싶은 사람!
망원경이 없지만 별을 보고 싶은 사람!
사진기가 없지만 사진 찍고 싶은 사람!
이 중 하나라도 해당되는 사람, **KUAAA**로 초대합니다!

KUAAA(Korea University Amateur Astronomical Association)는 별 보기를 좋아하는 아마추어들을 위한 동아리입니다. 학술연구분과 소속인 **KUAAA**에서는 천문과 관련된 배경지식이 없더라도 세미나를 통해 기초 지식부터 알려드리니 부담 없이 오세요!

KUAAA에 오신다면 맨눈으로 별자리를 찾는 법, 별이나 성운 사진을 멋지게 찍는 법을 배우게 될 것이고, 매달 도시 밖으로 떠나는 1박 2일 정기 관측회, 당일치기로 떠나는 비정기 관측회 등 즐거운 친목 도모 활동까지 모두 경험하실 수 있습니다!

G 제목 찾기

★ 유형 설명

다음 글의 제목으로 가장 적절한 것은?

Children, in particular, should be encouraged to read aloud because the brain is wired for

〈소설가 구보 씨의 일일〉? 제목을 보니까 이 글이 무슨 내용일지 대충 알겠단 말이지!

글의 중심 내용을 간결하고 명료하게, 그리고 비유적으로 나타낸 제목을 찾아야 한다.

🔑 반복되는 부분을 통해 중심 소재와 주제를 확인한다.
그 주제에 대해 필자가 갖고 있는 생각을 파악한 다음 그것을 압축해서 나타낸 선택지를 찾는다.
글의 주제와 제목이 동일한 경우도 있지만, 비유적으로 나타낸 표현이 제목이 되는 경우가 더 많다.

🎭 유형 풀이 비법

1 중심 문장을 찾아라!
• 필자가 전달하려는 중심 생각이나 요지가 드러나 있는 문장을 찾는다.

2 세부 사항을 종합하라!
• 글의 세부 사항들을 종합해서 주제를 파악한다.

3 내용을 적절히 압축하라!
• 글의 내용을 너무 넓거나 좁게 나타내지 않은 제목을 고른다.

Tip 글의 일부분에만 해당하는 선택지를 답으로 선택하지 않도록 한다.

🔖 제목에 자주 쓰이는 표현

□ **A Secret to** ~의 비결
□ **A Way to-v** ~하는 방법
□ **Don't ~** ~하지 마라
□ **Factors for** ~에 대한 요소들
□ **Functions of** ~의 기능들
□ **How to** ~하는 방법
□ **The History of** ~의 역사
□ **The Kinds of** ~의 종류
□ **Why ~?** 왜 ~하는가
□ **Increase of** ~의 증가
□ **Effects of** ~의 영향
□ **Needs of** ~의 필요성
□ **What is** ~란 무엇인가
□ **The Importance of** ~의 중요성
□ **Origin of** ~의 기원
□ **Examples of** ~의 예시
□ **The Sides of** ~의 양쪽면
□ **A Variety of** 다양한

📖 어휘 및 표현 Preview

□ **reflection** 반영
□ **identity** 정체성
□ **indication** 암시
□ **consciously** 의식적으로
□ **convince** 설득하다
□ **poverty** 가난
□ **status** 지위
□ **associate** 연상하다, 연관짓다
□ **distinct** 뚜렷한
□ **pace** 속도
□ **constant** 지속적인
□ **urgency** 촉박함
□ **from time to time** 때때로
□ **assess** 평가하다
□ **progress** 진행 상황, 진전
□ **spoil** 망치다
□ **inspiration** 영감
□ **interpretation** 해석, 이해

□ **marine** 해양의
□ **equivalent** (~에) 상응하는 것
□ **fertilize** 비옥하게 하다
□ **release** 내보내다
□ **estimate** 추정하다
□ **restoration** 복원
□ **habitat** 서식지
□ **effectively** 사실상, 실제로
□ **employment** 고용
□ **ultimately** 궁극적으로
□ **sooner or later** 머지않아
□ **initial** 초기의
□ **enhance** 강화하다
□ **threat** 위협
□ **detect** 감지하다
□ **construction** 건축(물)
□ **erect** (똑바로) 세우다
□ **successive** 연속적인

7 다양한 보어

1 주어＋불완전자동사＋주격 보어: 주격 보어는 주어의 성질, 상태, 신분 등을 설명하는 말로, 2형식 문장에서 주격 보어의 자리에는 **명사, 형용사, 분사** 등이 올 수 있다.

- Easton became an American citizen. (Easton은 미국 시민이 되었다.)
  주격 보어(명사)
- As the two narratives progress, the connections become evident.
  주격 보어(형용사)
  (두 이야기가 진행됨에 따라, 관련성은 명백해진다.)

2 주어＋불완전타동사＋목적어＋목적격 보어: 목적격 보어 자리에는 **명사, 형용사, 부정사, 원형부정사, 분사** 등이 올 수 있다.

> **＊ 지각동사와 사역동사의 목적격 보어**
> 지각동사와 사역동사의 목적격 보어로는 원형부정사나 현재분사 또는 과거분사가 온다.

1) 명사

- People then started calling these shows "soap operas."
  목적격 보어(명사)
  (그 이후로 사람들은 이런 프로그램을 '드라마'라고 부르기 시작했다.)

2) 형용사

- Jane wrote a book of her travels afterward, which made her famous.
  목적격 보어(형용사)
  (Jane은 그 후에 자신의 여행에 관한 책을 썼고 그 책으로 그녀는 유명해졌다.)

3) 부정사

- He advised me to get off at the next stop and take a taxi.
  목적격 보어(부정사)
  (그는 나에게 다음 정거장에서 내려서 택시를 타라고 충고했다.)

4) 원형부정사

- Sometimes, we could make others become happy with so little effort.
  목적격 보어(원형부정사)
  (가끔 우리는 아주 작은 노력으로 다른 사람들을 행복하게 만들 수 있다.)

5) ＊현재분사와 과거분사

- Then, suddenly she heard a woman weeping while she sat there at her table.
  목적격 보어(현재분사)
  (그리고 나서, 그녀가 탁자에 앉았을 때 난데없이 어떤 여자가 우는 소리가 들렸다.)
- According to Aston, the card system makes the players confused.
  목적격 보어(과거분사)
  (Aston에 따르면, 그 카드 시스템은 선수들을 혼란스럽게 만든다.)

Check Test

1 주격 보어를 찾아 표시하시오.

Quality questions are one way that teachers can check students' understanding of the text.

2 convince의 목적격 보어를 찾아 표시하시오.

Similarly, the person who accepts exercise as the part of their identity doesn't have to convince themselves to train.

3 Force의 목적격 보어를 찾아 표시하시오.

Force your face to smile even when you are stressed or feel unhappy.

4 주격 보어를 찾아 표시하시오.

Your bank is a huge web of algorithms, with humans turning the switches here and there.

  **G 제목 찾기** 첫 번째

G01 ★★✿ .... 고1 2024(6월)/24

다음 글의 제목으로 가장 적절한 것은?

Your behaviors are usually a reflection of your identity. What you do is an indication of the type of person you believe that you are — either consciously or nonconsciously. Research has shown that once a person ₅ believes in a particular aspect of their identity, they are more likely to act according to that belief. For example, people who identified as "being a voter" were more likely to vote than those who simply claimed ₁₀ "voting" was an action they wanted to perform. Similarly, the person who accepts exercise as the part of their identity doesn't have to convince themselves to train. Doing the right thing is easy. After all, when your ₁₅ behavior and your identity perfectly match, you are no longer pursuing behavior change. You are simply acting like the type of person you already believe yourself to be.

① Action Comes from Who You Think You Are
② The Best Practices for Gaining More Voters
③ Stop Pursuing Undesirable Behavior Change!
④ What to Do When Your Exercise Bores You
⑤ Your Actions Speak Louder than Your Words

1st 첫 문장을 통해 글의 내용을 예상해 보세요.

Your behaviors / are usually a reflection of your
당신의 행동은   / 대개 당신의 정체성을 반영한다 //
identity. //

● 글의 첫 문장을 읽어봅시다.
당신의 행동이 당신의 **❶**(   )을 반영한다고 해요.

● 어떤 내용이 이어질까요?
이 문장이 글의 주제문이라면 그 뒤에는 이를 뒷받침하는 예시나 부연 설명이 이어질 거예요.
또는 이 통념에 반대되는 내용이 이어질 수도 있겠죠. 바로 다음 문장을 읽으며 글의 흐름을 파악해 봅시다.

2nd 예상한 내용을 토대로 글을 읽고, 전체적인 내용을 파악해 보세요.

1) 첫 문장에 이어지는 그다음 문장을 봅시다.

What you do / is an indication of the type of person
당신이 하는 행동은 / 어떤 사람인지를 나타낸다
/ you believe that you are — / either consciously or
/ 당신이 스스로 그렇다고 믿고 있는   / 의식적으로든
nonconsciously. //
무의식적으로든   //

● 첫 문장을 더 쉽게 설명하고 있어요.
행동이 반영하는 정체성이 '스스로 그렇다고 믿고 있는' 정체성이라고 덧붙였네요. 이 흐름대로면 뒤에도 부연 설명이 이어지거나 주제와 관련된 구체적인 예시가 나올 거예요.

2) 주제와 관련된 연구 결과가 등장했어요.

Research has shown / that once a person believes in
연구는 밝혔다   / 자신의 정체성의 특정 측면을 믿으면
a particular aspect of their identity, / they are more
                                      / 그들은 행동할
likely to act / according to that belief. //
가능성이 더 높다 / 그 믿음에 따라   //

● 행동과 정체성의 관계가 연구로도 증명되었나 봐요.
정체성의 특정 측면을 믿으면 그 믿음에 따라 행동할 가능성이 높다는 연구 결과가 있대요. 이것은 '행동은 스스로 그렇다고 **❷**(   ) 정체성을 반영한다'는 앞의 내용과 같은 맥락이에요.

3) 뒤에 어떤 예시가 있는지 살펴봅시다.

> For example, / people who identified as "being a
> 예를 들어　　　　 / 자신을 "유권자"라고 느끼는 사람은
>
> voter" / were more likely to vote / than those who
> 　　 / 투표할 가능성이 더 높았다　　 / 단순히 주장하는
>
> simply claimed / "voting" was an action they
> 사람보다　　　 / '투표'가 자신이 하고 싶은 행동이라고 //
>
> wanted to perform. //
>
> Similarly, / the person who accepts exercise as the
> 마찬가지로　 / 운동을 자신의 정체성의 일부로
>
> part of their identity / doesn't have to convince
> 받아들이는 사람은　　　　 / 스스로를 설득할 필요가 없다
>
> themselves / to train. //
> 　　　 / 훈련하라고 //

● **'투표'와 '운동'을 예로 들며 설명하네요.**

For example 뒤에 투표를 먼저 예시로 들고, Similarly 뒤에 비슷한 예시로 운동을 들었네요. 스스로 유권자라고 느끼면 그 정체성에 따라 투표하고, 운동을 정체성의 일부로 받아들이면 스스로 설득하지 않아도 훈련한다는 내용이에요.

4) 주제가 충분히 드러났으니 마지막 문장을 확인합시다.

> You are simply acting / like the type of person / you
> 당신은 행동하고 있을 뿐이다　 / 어떤 유형의 사람처럼　　 / 당신
>
> already believe yourself to be. //
> 스스로가 그렇다고 이미 믿고 있는　　 //

● **주제문의 내용이 반복되네요.**

스스로 그렇다고 이미 믿고 있는 사람처럼 행동한다는 내용으로, 앞서 확인한 주제를 반복하며 글이 마무리되네요.

▷ **이제 글의 흐름을 정리해 볼까요?**

주제	당신의 행동은 당신의 정체성을 반영함

↓

부연 1	당신의 행동은 당신이 그렇다고 믿고 있는 당신의 정체성을 반영함

↓

부연 2	정체성의 특정 측면을 믿으면 그 믿음에 따라 행동할 가능성이 높다는 연구 결과가 있음

↓

예시	투표와 운동에서 사람들은 스스로 느끼거나 믿는 정체성에 따라 행동함

3rd 내용을 종합하여 글의 주제에 알맞은 제목을 골라 보세요.

1) 이 글의 주제는 무엇인가요?

유권자라고 느끼는 사람은 투표할 가능성이 더 높고, 운동이 정체성의 일부라고 생각하면 스스로를 설득하지 않아도 운동을 한다고 했어요. 즉, 스스로 믿고 있는 정체성에 따라 행동한다는 것이 이 글의 주제예요.

2) 선택지를 해석해 보고 글의 주제에 맞는 제목을 골라 봅시다.

① Action Comes from Who You Think You Are
　 행동은 당신이 자신을 어떤 사람으로 생각하는지로부터 나온다
② The Best Practices for Gaining More Voters
　 더 많은 유권자를 확보하기 위한 우수 사례
③ Stop Pursuing Undesirable Behavior Change!
　 바람직하지 않은 행동 변화를 추구하는 것을 멈추세요!
④ What to Do When Your Exercise Bores You
　 운동이 지루하게 느껴질 때 해야 할 일
⑤ Your Actions Speak Louder than Your Words
　 당신의 행동이 당신의 말보다 중요하다

● **정답을 골라 볼까요?**

자신을 어떤 사람으로 생각하는지, 즉 자신이 생각하는 정체성에 따라 행동이 나온다는 ❸(　　　　　　)이 이 글의 제목으로 가장 적절해요.

3) 글의 특정 단어나 사례가 매력적인 오답으로 쓰였어요.

유권자의 사례로 ②을, 운동의 사례로 ④을, '행동'이라는 단어로 ③과 ⑤을 구성했네요. 하지만 정작 이 글의 주제는 정체성에 관한 것이므로 ①을 제외한 나머지 선택지는 답이 될 수 없죠!

> 정체성의 사례를 통해 내용을 파악하고, 그에 맞는 제목을 고르자!

G 제목 찾기 두 번째

1st 첫 문장을 읽고, 이어질 글의 내용에 대한 단서를 찾으세요.
2nd 연결어를 단서로 삼아 글을 읽으며, 전체 흐름을 파악하세요.
3rd 글의 핵심 내용을 종합해 주제를 파악하고, 그 주제를 포괄하는 제목을 고르세요.

G02 ★★※ .... 고1 2023(6월)/24

다음 글의 제목으로 가장 적절한 것은?

Few people will be surprised to hear that poverty tends to create stress: a 2006 study published in the American journal *Psychosomatic Medicine*, for example, noted that a lower socioeconomic status was[5] associated with higher levels of stress hormones in the body. However, richer economies have their own distinct stresses. The key issue is time pressure. A 1999 study of 31 countries by American psychologist[10] Robert Levine and Canadian psychologist Ara Norenzayan found that wealthier, more industrialized nations had a faster pace of life — which led to a higher standard of living, but at the same time left the[15] population feeling a constant sense of urgency, as well as being more prone to heart disease. In effect, fast-paced productivity creates wealth, but it also leads people to feel time-poor when they lack the time to relax[20] and enjoy themselves.   *prone: 걸리기 쉬운

① Why Are Even Wealthy Countries Not Free from Stress?
② In Search of the Path to Escaping the Poverty Trap
③ Time Management: Everything You Need to Know
④ How Does Stress Affect Human Bodies?
⑤ Sound Mind Wins the Game of Life!

1st 첫 문장을 읽고, 이어질 글의 내용에 대한 단서를 찾으세요.

Few people will be surprised / to hear that poverty
놀랄 사람은 거의 없을 것이다 / 가난이 스트레스를 만드는
tends to create stress: /
경향이 있다는 것을 듣고 /
 a 2006 study published in the American journal
미국의 학술지 〈Psychosomatic Medicine〉에 발표된 2006년 연구는
Psychosomatic Medicine, / for example, / noted that a
/ 예를 들어 / 더 낮은 사회
lower socioeconomic status was associated / with
경제적 지위가 관련이 있다고 언급했다 / 체내의
higher levels of stress hormones in the body. //
더 높은 수치의 스트레스 호르몬과 //

● **연구 결과가 등장했어요.**
가난이 스트레스를 만드는 경향이 있다는 것은 많은 사람들이 알고 있다고 하면서, 한 연구 결과를 설명했어요. 더 낮은 사회 경제적 지위가 더 ❶( ) 스트레스 호르몬 수치와 관련이 있대요.
첫 문장만 봐도 어떤 내용의 글일지 예상이 되죠? 아마 '가난과 스트레스의 관련성'을 설명하거나, 아니면 오히려 가난과 스트레스가 관련이 없다고 이야기할지도 모르겠어요. 글을 마저 읽으며 주제를 찾아봅시다.

2nd 연결어를 단서로 삼아 글을 읽으며, 전체 흐름을 파악하세요.

1) 역접의 연결어 However가 보여요.

However, / richer economies have their own
하지만 / 더 부유한 국가는 그들만의 뚜렷한 스트레스를
distinct stresses. //
가지고 있다 //
The key issue is time pressure. //
핵심 쟁점은 시간 압박이다 //

● **However는 앞부분과 뒤에 이어지는 내용이 반대라는 의미예요.**
앞에서는 가난과 스트레스가 관련이 있다고 했죠? 여기에 However가 이어진다는 건, 가난과 스트레스가 관련이 없다는 맥락의 이야기를 이어갈 거라는 거예요.

● **더 부유한 국가도 스트레스를 가지고 있대요.**
가난하지 않은 부유한 국가도 그들만의 스트레스가 있고, 그건 시간 압박이래요. 우리가 예상했던 것처럼 가난과 스트레스가 꼭 연관된 것은 아니라고 이야기하는 글인 것 같군요!

2) 또 다른 연구가 등장해요.

A 1999 study / of 31 countries by American psychologist Robert Levine and Canadian psychologist Ara Norenzayan / found that wealthier, more industrialized nations had a faster pace of life /

1999년 연구는 / 미국의 심리학자 Robert Levine과 캐나다의 심리학자 Ara Norenzayan이 31개국을 대상으로 한 / 더 부유하고, 더 산업화된 국가들이 더 빠른 삶의 속도를 가지고 있다는 것을 알아냈다 /

● **문장이 기니까 앞부분만 먼저 살펴봅시다.**

첫 문장에서 살펴본 연구는 2006년 연구였는데, 이번엔 그보다 이전인 1999년 연구 결과가 등장했어요. 더 부유하고 산업화된 국가들에서는 더 ❷(　　　　) 삶의 속도라는 특징이 나타났대요.
앞에서 언급했던 부유한 국가의 스트레스 요인인 '시간 압박'을 말하는 거군요.

3) 나머지 부분도 읽어봅시다!

— which led to a higher standard of living, / but at the same time left the population feeling a constant sense of urgency, / as well as being more prone to heart disease. //

그리고 이것은 더 높은 생활 수준으로 이어졌지만 / 동시에 사람들에게 지속적인 촉박함을 느끼게 했다(는 것을) / 심장병에 걸리기 더 쉽게 했을 뿐만 아니라 //

● **시간 압박의 악영향을 설명했어요.**

시간 압박은 더 높은 생활 수준으로 이어져 국가를 부유하게 했지만, 국민들은 지속적으로 촉박함을 느껴서 심장병에 걸리기 쉬웠대요.
그러니까 가난한 국가에서는 가난 그 자체가 스트레스 요인이었지만, 가난하지 않은 국가들은 시간 압박이라는 그들만의 스트레스 요인이 존재했다고 말하는 글이네요.

4) 마지막 문장까지 확인합시다.

In effect, / fast-paced productivity creates wealth, / but it also leads people to feel time-poor / when they lack the time / to relax and enjoy themselves. //

사실 / 빠른 속도의 생산력은 부를 창출하지만 / 그것은 또한 사람들이 시간이 부족하다고 느끼게 한다 / 그들이 시간이 없을 때 / 스스로 긴장을 풀고 즐겁게 지낼 //

● **시간 압박이 스트레스 요인인 이유를 부연 설명했어요.**

앞 문장과 같은 맥락으로 시간 압박은 사람들이 긴장을 풀고 즐겁게 지낼 시간이 부족하다고 느끼게 한대요. 가난과는 다른 스트레스 요인이 확실해요! 이제 정답을 찾을 수 있겠죠?

3rd 글의 핵심 내용을 종합해 주제를 파악하고, 그 주제를 포괄하는 제목을 고르세요.

1) 영문 선택지의 아래 해석을 확인해 보세요.

① Why Are Even Wealthy Countries Not Free from Stress?
왜 부유한 나라들조차 스트레스에서 자유롭지 못한가?

② In Search of the Path to Escaping the Poverty Trap
빈곤의 덫에서 벗어날 수 있는 길을 찾아서

③ Time Management: Everything You Need to Know
시간 관리: 당신이 알아야 할 모든 것

④ How Does Stress Affect Human Bodies?
스트레스는 인체에 어떻게 영향을 미치는가?

⑤ Sound Mind Wins the Game of Life!
건강한 마음이 인생의 게임에서 승리한다!

● **모든 선택지에 글에 등장한 핵심어가 포함되어 있어요.**

하지만 글의 내용을 정확하게 포괄하고 있는 선택지가 눈에 띄어요!
가난한 국가는 가난해서 스트레스를 받지만, 부유한 국가들은 시간 압박 때문에 스트레스를 받는다고 말하는 글이었잖아요. 그러니까 왜 부유한 나라들조차 스트레스에서 자유롭지 못한지를 묻는 ❸(　　　　)이 글의 제목으로 가장 적절하죠!

2) 나머지 선택지들의 함정에 빠지진 않았는지 질문에 답해 봅시다.

② 빈곤을 벗어나는 방법을 설명한 글이었나요? ❹(O / X)
③ 시간을 관리해야 스트레스에서 자유로울 수 있다고 설명한 글이었나요? ❺(O / X)
④ 스트레스가 인체에 미치는 영향을 설명한 글이었나요? ❻(O / X)
⑤ 건강한 마음을 강조하는 글이었나요? ❼(O / X)

3) 글의 흐름을 정리하며 글의 내용을 다시 확인해 봅시다.

도입 | 가난이 스트레스를 만듦
↓
연구① | 더 낮은 사회 경제적 지위와 스트레스는 관련이 있음
↓
대조 | 부유한 국가는 시간 압박이라는 스트레스가 있음
↓
연구② | 부유한 국가의 빠른 삶의 속도는 국민들의 심장병 위험을 높임
↓
부연 | 빠른 속도는 부를 창출하지만, 촉박함을 느끼게 함

빈칸 정답 ❶ 높은 ❷ 빠른 ❸ ① ❹ × ❺ × ❻ × ❼ ×

❖ 정답 및 해설 72~73p

G03 ~ 06 ▶ 제한시간 8분

G03 ★★★ ✦ 고1 2025(3월)/24

다음 글의 제목으로 가장 적절한 것은?

Modern brain-scanning techniques such as fMRI (functional Magnetic Resonance Imaging) have revealed that reading aloud lights up many areas of the brain. There is intense activity in areas associated with pronunciation and hearing the sound of the spoken response, which strengthens the connective structures of your brain cells for more brainpower. This leads to an overall improvement in concentration. Reading aloud is also a good way to develop your public speaking skills because it forces you to read each and every word — something people don't often do when reading quickly, or reading in silence. Children, in particular, should be encouraged to read aloud because the brain is wired for learning through connections that are created by positive stimulation, such as singing, touching, and reading aloud.

*stimulation: 자극

① Reading Aloud: Improving Brainpower and Speaking Skills
② Reading Practices: Shortcuts to Academic Achievements
③ Improve Your Writing Skills Through Reading Aloud
④ How Your Brain Changes When You Read in Silence
⑤ Techniques for Faster and More Effective Reading

구문 서술형

밑줄 친 부분을 바르게 고쳐 쓰고, 해당 부분의 문장 성분을 쓰시오.

Reading aloud forces you <u>read</u> each and every word.

➡ _____

➡ 문장 성분: _____

G04 ★★★ ✦ 고1 2025(6월)/24

다음 글의 제목으로 가장 적절한 것은?

We think we're being logical, objective, and rational — and therefore accurate in our analysis, judgment, and decisions. So we think that if other people are logical, objective, and rational, they will agree with us and see what we see. But the opposite is the case. Every human brain is different. Everyone's life experience is different. Everyone's desires and knowledge are different. You might think you're being realistic — that is, that your ideas match reality, but that's impossible. It's only your interpretation of reality, which will always be different from someone else's. When two nations play each other in the World Cup, the fans of each country criticize the referees for missing all the infractions that the other team commits. Without fail, each fan base believes that the referees are biased against their team.

*infraction: 위반

① Open to Interpretation: Everyone Sees Reality Differently
② Efforts Made to Fill the Gap Between Real and Ideal
③ One Single Reality: What We All Agree Upon
④ Why Sports Fans Judge Their Team's Play Objectively
⑤ Knowledge: The Key to Interpreting the World Accurately

구문 서술형

주어진 문장에서 보어를 모두 찾아 쓰고, 보어가 보충 설명하는 부분을 찾아 쓰시오.

If other people are logical, objective, and rational, they will agree with us.

➡ 보어: _____, _____, _____

➡ 보충 설명하는 부분: _____

G05 ★★★❀

다음 글의 제목으로 가장 적절한 것은?

Many opponents of animal experimentation argue that not only is modern medicine not the only cause for the decline in mortality, many medical advances that did contribute to human health were not the result of animal experimentation. Defenders of research have claimed that since there is a strong correlation between the practice of animal experimentation and medical advancement, the former caused the latter. Opponents of research reject this inference. After all, we have independent reasons to expect these phenomena to be correlated. Since the law prescribes that all new drugs, prosthetic devices, and surgical techniques be tried on animals before they are used in humans, we will subsequently find that all medical advances are correlated with prior experimentation on animals. Consequently, the correlation between animal experimentation and medical discovery is the result of legal necessity, not evidence that animal experimentation led to medical advances. Moreover, several influential physicians have offered historical evidence that animal experimentation has not been as responsible for biomedical discovery as defenders suggest. They claim that clinical discoveries played a more substantial role than animal researchers have led us to believe.　　　*prosthetic: 보철의

① Bio-medicine: Unlocking New Frontiers in Health Care
② Is Medicine Advanced by Experimenting on Animals?
③ Refer to Historical Evidence to Solve Medical Issues
④ Why Aren't There Strict Laws for Animal Adoption?
⑤ Medical Advances for Extending Human Life Span

구문 서술형

주어진 우리말과 일치하도록 괄호 안의 단어를 알맞게 배열하시오.

동물 실험과 의학적 발견 간의 상관관계는 법적 필요성의 결과이다. (is, between, animal experimentation, the result, and medical discovery)

➡ The correlation _____

_____ of legal necessity.

G06 ★★★❀

다음 글의 제목으로 가장 적절한 것은?

The evolution of AI is often associated with the concept of singularity. Singularity refers to the point at which AI exceeds human intelligence. After that point, it is predicted that AI will repeatedly improve itself and evolve at an accelerated pace. When AI becomes self-aware and pursues its own goals, it will be a conscious being, not just a machine. AI and human consciousness will then begin to evolve together. Our consciousness will evolve to new dimensions through our interactions with AI, which will provide us with intellectual stimulation and inspire new insights and creativity. Conversely, our consciousness also has a significant impact on the evolution of AI. The direction of AI's evolution will depend greatly on what values and ethics we incorporate into AI. We need to see our relationship with AI as a mutual coexistence of conscious beings, recognizing its rights and supporting the evolution of its consciousness.

① An Unsolvable Dilemma: Is AI Friend or Enemy?
② The History of Humans' Resistance Against Machines
③ Upcoming Future: AI as a Human Partner for Co-evolution
④ AI World Without Human Intelligence Is Staring You in the Face
⑤ How AI Makes Human-to-Human Relationships More Meaningful

구문 서술형

주어진 문장에서 주격 보어 두 개를 찾아, 각각의 품사를 쓰시오.

When AI becomes self-aware, it will be a conscious being.

➡ 주격 보어 1: _____　　품사: _____
➡ 주격 보어 2: _____　　품사: _____

G07 ❋❋❋ 고1 2024(3월)/24

다음 글의 제목으로 가장 적절한 것은?

Working around the whole painting, rather than concentrating on one area at a time, will mean you can stop at any point and the painting can be considered "finished." Artists often find it difficult to know when to stop painting, and it can be tempting to keep on adding more to your work. It is important to take a few steps back from the painting from time to time to assess your progress. Putting too much into a painting can spoil its impact and leave it looking overworked. If you find yourself struggling to decide whether you have finished, take a break and come back to it later with fresh eyes. Then you can decide whether any areas of your painting would benefit from further refinement.

*tempting: 유혹하는 **refinement: 정교하게 꾸밈

① Drawing Inspiration from Diverse Artists
② Don't Spoil Your Painting by Leaving It Incomplete
③ Art Interpretation: Discover Meanings in a Painting
④ Do Not Put Down Your Brush: The More, the Better
⑤ Avoid Overwork and Find the Right Moment to Finish

G08 ❋❋❋ 고1 2024(9월)/24

다음 글의 제목으로 가장 적절한 것은?

Whales are highly efficient at carbon storage. When they die, each whale sequesters an average of 30 tons of carbon dioxide, taking that carbon out of the atmosphere for centuries. For comparison, the average tree absorbs only 48 pounds of CO_2 a year. From a climate perspective, each whale is the marine equivalent of thousands of trees. Whales also help sequester carbon by fertilizing the ocean as they release nutrient-rich waste, in turn increasing phytoplankton populations, which also sequester carbon — leading some scientists to call them the "engineers of marine ecosystems." In

2019, economists from the International Monetary Fund (IMF) estimated the value of the ecosystem services provided by each whale at over $2 million USD. They called for a new global program of economic incentives to return whale populations to preindustrial whaling levels as one example of a "nature-based solution" to climate change. Calls are now being made for a global whale restoration program, to slow down climate change.

*sequester: 격리하다 **phytoplankton: 식물성 플랑크톤

① Saving Whales Saves the Earth and Us
② What Makes Whales Go Extinct in the Ocean
③ Why Is Overpopulation of Whales Dangerous?
④ Black Money: Lies about the Whaling Industry
⑤ Climate Change and Its Effect on Whale Habitats

G09 ❋❋❋ 고1 2020(6월)/24

다음 글의 제목으로 가장 적절한 것은?

Every event that causes you to smile makes you feel happy and produces feel-good chemicals in your brain. Force your face to smile even when you are stressed or feel unhappy. The facial muscular pattern produced by the smile is linked to all the "happy networks" in your brain and will in turn naturally calm you down and change your brain chemistry by releasing the same feel-good chemicals. Researchers studied the effects of a genuine and forced smile on individuals during a stressful event. The researchers had participants perform stressful tasks while not smiling, smiling, or holding chopsticks crossways in their mouths (to force the face to form a smile). The results of the study showed that smiling, forced or genuine, during stressful events reduced the intensity of the stress response in the body and lowered heart rate levels after recovering from the stress.

① Causes and Effects of Stressful Events
② Personal Signs and Patterns of Stress
③ How Body and Brain React to Stress
④ Stress: Necessary Evil for Happiness
⑤ Do Faked Smiles Also Help Reduce Stress?

G10 ❋❋❋❋ 고1 2021(6월)/24

다음 글의 제목으로 가장 적절한 것은?

When people think about the development of cities, rarely do they consider the critical role of vertical transportation. In fact, each day, more than 7 billion elevator journeys are taken in tall buildings all over the world. Efficient vertical transportation can expand our ability to build taller and taller skyscrapers. Antony Wood, a Professor of Architecture at the Illinois Institute of Technology, explains that advances in elevators over the past 20 years are probably the greatest advances we have seen in tall buildings. For example, elevators in the Jeddah Tower in Jeddah, Saudi Arabia, under construction, will reach a height record of 660m.

① Elevators Bring Buildings Closer to the Sky
② The Higher You Climb, the Better the View
③ How to Construct an Elevator Cheap and Fast
④ The Function of the Ancient and the Modern City
⑤ The Evolution of Architecture: Solutions for Overpopulation

G11 ❋❋❋❋ 고1 2020(11월)/24

다음 글의 제목으로 가장 적절한 것은?

Chewing leads to smaller particles for swallowing, and more exposed surface area for digestive enzymes to act on. In other words, it means the extraction of more fuel and raw materials from a mouthful of food. This is especially important for mammals because they heat their bodies from within. Chewing gives mammals the energy needed to be active not only during the day but also the cool night, and to live in colder climates or places with changing temperatures. It allows them to sustain higher levels of activity and travel speeds to cover larger distances, avoid predators, capture prey, and make and care for their young. Mammals are able to live in an incredible variety of habitats, from Arctic tundra to Antarctic pack ice, deep open waters to high-altitude mountaintops, and rainforests to deserts, in no small measure because of their teeth. *enzyme: 효소

① Chewing: A Way to Ease Indigestion
② Boost Your Energy by Chewing More!
③ How Chewing Helps Mammals Survive
④ Different Types and Functions of Teeth
⑤ A Harsh Climate Makes Mammals Stronger

G12 ❋❋❋❋ 고1 2020(3월)/24

다음 글의 제목으로 가장 적절한 것은?

In life, they say that too much of anything is not good for you. In fact, too much of certain things in life can kill you. For example, they say that water has no enemy, because water is essential to all life. But if you take in too much water, like one who is drowning, it could kill you. Education is the exception to this rule. You can never have too much education or knowledge. The reality is that most people will never have enough education in their lifetime. I am yet to find that one person who has been hurt in life by too much education. Rather, we see lots of casualties every day, worldwide, resulting from the lack of education. You must keep in mind that education is a long-term investment of time, money, and effort into humans. *casualty: 피해자

① All Play and No Work Makes Jack a Smart Boy
② Too Much Education Won't Hurt You
③ Two Heads Are Worse than One
④ Don't Think Twice Before You Act
⑤ Learn from the Future, Not from the Past

G13 ❋❋❋❋ 고1 2021(3월)/24

다음 글의 제목으로 가장 적절한 것은?

Think, for a moment, about something you bought that you never ended up using. An item of clothing you never ended up wearing? A book you never read? Some piece of electronic equipment that never even made it out of the box? It is estimated that Australians alone spend on average $10.8 billion AUD (approximately $9.99 billion USD) every year on goods they do not use — more than the total government spending on universities and roads. That is an average of $1,250 AUD (approximately $1,156 USD) for each household. All the things we buy that then just sit there gathering dust are waste — a waste of money, a waste of time, and waste in the sense of pure rubbish. As the author Clive Hamilton observes, 'The difference between the stuff we buy and what we use is waste.'

① Spending Enables the Economy
② Money Management: Dos and Don'ts
③ Too Much Shopping: A Sign of Loneliness
④ 3R's of Waste: Reduce, Reuse, and Recycle
⑤ What You Buy Is Waste Unless You Use It

G14 ★★❀ 고1 2020(9월)/24

다음 글의 제목으로 가장 적절한 것은?

The loss of many traditional jobs in everything from art to healthcare will partly be offset by the creation of new human jobs. Primary care doctors who focus on diagnosing known diseases and giving familiar treatments will probably be replaced by AI doctors. But precisely because of that, there will be much more money to pay human doctors and lab assistants to do groundbreaking research and develop new medicines or surgical procedures. AI might help create new human jobs in another way. Instead of humans competing with AI, they could focus on servicing and using AI. For example, the replacement of human pilots by drones has eliminated some jobs but created many new opportunities in maintenance, remote control, data analysis, and cyber security.

*offset: 상쇄하다

① What Makes Robots Smarter?
② Is AI Really a Threat to Your Job?
③ Watch Out! AI Can Read Your Mind
④ Future Jobs: Less Work, More Gains
⑤ Ongoing Challenges for AI Development

G15 ★★❀ 고1 2023(3월)/24

다음 글의 제목으로 가장 적절한 것은?

Success can lead you off your intended path and into a comfortable rut. If you are good at something and are well rewarded for doing it, you may want to keep doing it even if you stop enjoying it. The danger is that one day you look around and realize you're so deep in this comfortable rut that you can no longer see the sun or breathe fresh air; the sides of the rut have become so slippery that it would take a superhuman effort to climb out; and, effectively, you're stuck. And it's a situation that many working people worry they're in now. The poor employment market has left them feeling locked in what may be a secure, or even well-paying — but ultimately unsatisfying — job.

*rut: 틀에 박힌 생활

① Don't Compete with Yourself
② A Trap of a Successful Career
③ Create More Jobs for Young People
④ What Difficult Jobs Have in Common
⑤ A Road Map for an Influential Employer

G16 ★★★ 고1 2023(11월)/24

다음 글의 제목으로 가장 적절한 것은?

Kids tire of their toys, college students get sick of cafeteria food, and sooner or later most of us lose interest in our favorite TV shows. The bottom line is that we humans are easily bored. But why should this be true? The answer lies buried deep in our nerve cells, which are designed to reduce their initial excited response to stimuli each time they occur. At the same time, these neurons enhance their responses to things that change — especially things that change quickly. We probably evolved this way because our ancestors got more survival value, for example, from attending to what was moving in a tree (such as a puma) than to the tree itself. Boredom in reaction to an unchanging environment turns down the level of neural excitation so that new stimuli (like our ancestor's hypothetical puma threat) stand out more. It's the neural equivalent of turning off a front door light to see the fireflies.

*neural: 신경의
**hypothetical: 가정(假定)의, 가설상의 ***equivalent: (~와) 같은 것, 대응물

① The Brain's Brilliant Trick to Overcome Fear
② Boredom: Neural Mechanism for Detecting Change
③ Humans' Endless Desire to Pursue Familiar Experiences
④ The Destruction of Nature in Exchange for Human Survival
⑤ How Humans Changed the Environment to Their Advantage

G17 ★★★ 고1 2022(9월)/24

다음 글의 제목으로 가장 적절한 것은?

Many people make a mistake of only operating along the safe zones, and in the process they miss the opportunity to achieve greater things. They do so because of a fear of the unknown and a fear of treading the unknown paths of life. Those that are brave enough to take those roads less travelled are able to get great returns and derive major satisfaction out of their courageous moves. Being overcautious will mean that you will miss attaining the greatest levels of your potential. You must learn to take those chances that many people around you will not take, because your success will flow from those bold decisions that you will take along the way.

*tread: 밟다

① More Courage Brings More Opportunities
② Travel: The Best Way to Make Friends
③ How to Turn Mistakes into Success
④ Satisfying Life? Share with Others
⑤ Why Is Overcoming Fear So Hard?

G18 ***❀ 고1 2023(9월)/24

다음 글의 제목으로 가장 적절한 것은?

We think we are shaping our buildings. But really, our buildings and development are also shaping us. One of the best examples of this is the oldest-known construction: the ornately carved rings of standing stones at Göbekli Tepe in Turkey. Before these ancestors got the idea to erect standing stones some 12,000 years ago, they were hunter-gatherers. It appears that the erection of the multiple rings of megalithic stones took so long, and so many successive generations, that these innovators were forced to settle down to complete the construction works. In the process, they became the first farming society on Earth. This is an early example of a society constructing something that ends up radically remaking the society itself. Things are not so different in our own time.

*ornately: 화려하게 **megalithic: 거석의

① Buildings Transform How We Live!
② Why Do We Build More Than We Need?
③ Copying Ancient Buildings for Creativity
④ Was Life Better in Hunter-gatherer Times?
⑤ Innovate Your Farm with New Constructions

1등급 대비 문제

G19~20 ▶ 제한시간 4분

G19 ⭐ 2등급 대비 고1 2021(9월)/24

다음 글의 제목으로 가장 적절한 것은?

Diversity, challenge, and conflict help us maintain our imagination. Most people assume that conflict is bad and that being in one's "comfort zone" is good. That is not exactly true. Of course, we don't want to find ourselves without a job or medical insurance or in a fight with our partner, family, boss, or coworkers. One bad experience can be sufficient to last us a lifetime. But small disagreements with family and friends, trouble with technology or finances, or challenges at work and at home can help us think through our own capabilities. Problems that need solutions force us to use our brains in order to develop creative answers. Navigating landscapes that are varied, that offer trials and occasional conflicts, is more helpful to creativity than hanging out in landscapes that pose no challenge to our senses and our minds. Our two million-year history is packed with challenges and conflicts.

① Technology: A Lens to the Future
② Diversity: A Key to Social Unification
③ Simple Ways to Avoid Conflicts with Others
④ Creativity Doesn't Come from Playing It Safe
⑤ There Are No Challenges That Can't Be Overcome

G20 ⭐ 2등급 대비 고1 2021(11월)/24

다음 글의 제목으로 가장 적절한 것은?

In modern times, society became more dynamic. Social mobility increased, and people began to exercise a higher degree of choice regarding, for instance, their profession, their marriage, or their religion. This posed a challenge to traditional roles in society. It was less evident that one needed to commit to the roles one was born into when alternatives could be realized. Increasing control over one's life choices became not only possible but desired. Identity then became a problem. It was no longer almost ready-made at birth but something to be discovered. Traditional role identities prescribed by society began to appear as masks imposed on people whose real self was to be found somewhere underneath.

*impose: 부여하다

① What Makes Our Modern Society So Competitive?
② How Modern Society Drives Us to Discover Our Identities
③ Social Masks: A Means to Build Trustworthy Relationships
④ The More Social Roles We Have, the Less Choice We Have
⑤ Increasing Social Mobility Leads Us to a More Equal Society

G21 ⭐ 2등급 대비 _____ 고1 2022(11월)/24

다음 글의 제목으로 가장 적절한 것은?

Have you ever brought up an idea or suggestion to someone and heard them immediately say "No, that won't work."? You may have thought, "He/she didn't even give it a chance. How do they know it won't work?" When you are right about something, you close off the possibility of another viewpoint or opportunity. Being right about something means that "it is the way it is, period." You may be correct. Your particular way of seeing it may be true with the facts. However, considering the other option or the other person's point of view can be beneficial. If you see their side, you will see something new or, at worse, learn something about how the other person looks at life. Why would you think everyone sees and experiences life the way you do? Besides how boring that would be, it would eliminate all new opportunities, ideas, invention, and creativity.

① The Value of Being Honest
② Filter Out Negative Points of View
③ Keeping Your Word: A Road to Success
④ Being Right Can Block New Possibilities
⑤ Look Back When Everyone Looks Forward

G22 ⭐ 1등급 대비 _____ 고1 2022(6월)/24

다음 글의 제목으로 가장 적절한 것은?

Only a generation or two ago, mentioning the word *algorithms* would have drawn a blank from most people. Today, algorithms appear in every part of civilization. They are connected to everyday life. They're not just in your cell phone or your laptop but in your car, your house, your appliances, and your toys. Your bank is a huge web of algorithms, with humans turning the switches here and there. Algorithms schedule flights and then fly the airplanes. Algorithms run factories, trade goods, and keep records. If every algorithm suddenly stopped working, it would be the end of the world as we know it.

① We Live in an Age of Algorithms
② Mysteries of Ancient Civilizations
③ Dangers of Online Banking Algorithms
④ How Algorithms Decrease Human Creativity
⑤ Transportation: A Driving Force of Industry

G23 ⭐ 1등급 대비 _____ 고1 2022(3월)/24

다음 글의 제목으로 가장 적절한 것은?

Our ability to accurately recognize and label emotions is often referred to as *emotional granularity*. In the words of Harvard psychologist Susan David, "Learning to label emotions with a more nuanced vocabulary can be absolutely transformative." David explains that if we don't have a rich emotional vocabulary, it is difficult to communicate our needs and to get the support that we need from others. But those who are able to distinguish between a range of various emotions "do much, much better at managing the ups and downs of ordinary existence than those who see everything in black and white." In fact, research shows that the process of labeling emotional experience is related to greater emotion regulation and psychosocial well-being.

*nuanced: 미묘한 차이가 있는

① True Friendship Endures Emotional Arguments
② Detailed Labeling of Emotions Is Beneficial
③ Labeling Emotions: Easier Said Than Done
④ Categorize and Label Tasks for Efficiency
⑤ Be Brave and Communicate Your Needs

✱ 다음 영어는 우리말 뜻을, 우리말은 영어 단어를 〈보기〉에서 찾아 쓰시오.

┌─〈 보기 〉─┐

marine	어리석은	categorize	쓰레기
essential	고층 건물	rational	추산하다
sufficient	소화의	release	위협

01 estimate _____

02 rubbish _____

03 skyscraper _____

04 digestive _____

05 threat _____

06 필수적인 _____

07 충분한 _____

08 내보내다 _____

09 분류하다 _____

10 합리적인 _____

✱ 다음 우리말에 알맞은 영어 표현을 찾아 연결하시오.

11 다양한 • • a range of

12 ~에 전념하다 • • commit to

13 조용히 • • bring up

14 (화제를) 꺼내다 • • close off

15 ~을 차단하다 • • in silence

✱ 다음 우리말 표현에 맞는 단어를 고르시오.

16 많은 잇따른 세대 ➡ many (aggressive / successive) generations

17 감정을 정확하게 인식하다 ➡ (approximately / accurately) recognize emotions

18 그들의 반응을 강화하다 ➡ (enforce / enhance) their response

19 다양한 예술가들로부터 영감을 끌어내기 ➡ drawing (inspiration / aspiration) from diverse artists

20 더 낮은 사회경제적 지위 ➡ a lower socioeconomic (status / fungus)

✱ 다음 문장의 빈칸에 알맞은 단어를 〈보기〉에서 찾아 쓰시오.

┌─〈 보기 〉─┐

coexistence	belief	eliminate	efficient
occurs	pursuing	labeling	desire
fertilizing	poverty	spoil	claim

21 우리는 우리와 AI와의 관계를 상호 공존으로 볼 필요가 있다.
➡ We need to see our relationship with AI as a mutual _____.

22 감정적인 경험에 이름을 붙이는 과정은 더 큰 감정 통제와 관련되어 있다.
➡ The process of _____ emotional experience is related to greater emotion regulation.

23 가난은 스트레스를 유발하는 경향이 있다.
➡ _____ tends to create stress.

24 그들은 그 믿음에 따라 행동할 가능성이 더 높다.
➡ They are more likely to act according to that _____.

25 바람직하지 않은 행동 변화를 추구하는 것을 멈추세요!
➡ Stop _____ undesirable behavior change!

26 고래는 탄소 저장에 매우 효율적이다.
➡ Whales are highly _____ at carbon storage.

27 자극에 대한 초기의 흥분된 반응이 매번 일어난다.
➡ Their initial excited response to stimuli _____ each time.

28 너의 그림을 완성하지 않은 상태로 두어서 망치지 마라.
➡ Don't _____ your painting by leaving it incomplete.

29 고래는 또한 바다를 비옥하게 함으로써 탄소를 격리하는 데 도움을 준다.
➡ Whales also help sequester carbon by _____ the ocean.

30 그것은 모든 새로운 기회와 창의성을 없앨 것이다.
➡ It would _____ all new opportunities and creativity.

도표의 이해

★ 유형 설명

다음 도표의 내용과 일치하지 <u>않는</u> 것은?

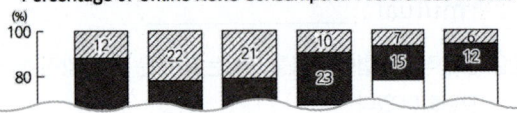

Percentage of Online News Consumption Preferences in 2020

다양한 분야의 통계 자료를 이해하고 그것을 제대로 설명했는지를 판단해야 한다.

🔑 비교 표현, 증가나 감소를 나타내는 표현, 배수 표현 등이 많이 쓰이는 점에 주의한다.

역시 사람들은 비빔냉면을 더 선호하는군요.

도표를 잘못 보셨어요. 물냉면 막대의 길이가 더 길어요.

비빔냉면

물냉면

🎭 유형 풀이 비법

1 정보를 파악하라!
- 도표와 도표의 제목, 글의 시작 부분을 보고 어떤 것에 대한 내용인지 이해한다.

2 정확히 해석하라!
- 도표와 글이 일치하는지 확인하려면 각 문장을 정확히 해석한다.

3 일치하는지 판단하라!
- 선택지와 자료를 하나씩 빠르게 대조해서 일치하는지 판단해야 한다.

Tip 도표의 자료를 설명할 때 자주 쓰이는 비교, 배수 등의 표현을 익혀둔다.

📌 도표의 자료를 설명할 때 자주 쓰이는 표현

① 분수
- □ half (1/2) □ one third, a third (1/3) □ two thirds (2/3)
- □ a quarter, one fourth (1/4)

② 배수
- □ double, twice (2배) □ three times (3배) □ four times (4배) □ ten times (10배)

③ 증가 (오르다, 늘어나다)
- □ grow □ increase □ rise □ go up □ soar
- □ climb □ add to □ raise □ multiply

④ 감소 (줄다, 떨어지다)
- □ drop □ decrease □ fall □ go down
- □ decline □ reduce □ diminish

⑤ 비교
- □ more than ~ (~보다 더 많은) □ less than ~ (~보다 더 적은)
- □ higher than ~ (~보다 더 높은) □ lower than ~ (~보다 더 낮은)
- □ largest, most, greatest (가장 큰/많은) □ smallest, least (가장 작은/적은)

⑥ 기타
- □ unit (단위) □ degree (정도) □ amount (양, 액수) □ rank (순위)
- □ percentage (퍼센트) □ percentage point (퍼센트포인트) □ total (전체의, 총)
- □ sum (합계) □ the number of ~ (~의 수) □ average (평균)
- □ extent (정도, 크기) □ portion (부분) □ proportion (비율)

🌊 어휘 및 표현 Preview

- □ emission 배출량
- □ major 주요한
- □ respectively 각각
- □ share 몫, 점유율
- □ region 지역
- □ given 주어진, 정해진
- □ among ~ 중에서
- □ period 기간
- □ gap 차이
- □ slightly 약간
- □ steadily 꾸준히
- □ except ~을 제외하고
- □ urban 도시의
- □ continent 대륙
- □ reverse 역전
- □ youth 청소년, 젊은 사람들
- □ climate change 기후 변화
- □ extremely 극도로
- □ generation 세대
- □ investment 투자, 투자액
- □ account for (부분·비율을) 차지하다

8 시제

1 기본시제: 현재시제, 과거시제, 미래시제(미래시제는 보통 will / shall이나 be going to-v를 이용)

- We (live) in Kingston. (우리는 Kingston에 **산다**.)
  현재시제
- Shakespeare (married) in 1582. (Shakespeare는 1582년에 **결혼했다**.)
  과거시제
- I (am going to go) with them. (나는 그들과 함께 **갈 예정이다**.)
  미래시제

2 *현재진행형, 과거진행형, 미래진행형 –「be동사 + v-ing」의 형태로, 진행 중인 일을 나타낸다.

1) **현재진행형**:「be동사의 현재형(am, are, is) + v-ing」의 형태로, 말하는 순간에 진행 중인 일이나 최근의 경향을 나타낸다.

- Maggie (is meeting) her friends now. (Maggie는 지금 그녀의 친구들을 만나고 있다.)
  말하는 순간에 진행 중인 일

2) **과거진행형**:「be동사의 과거형(was, were) + v-ing」의 형태로, 과거의 특정 시점에 진행 중이던 일을 나타낸다.

- Maggie (was meeting) her friends at that time. (Maggie는 그때 그녀의 친구들을 만나고 있었다.)
  과거의 특정 시점에 진행 중이던 일

3) **미래진행형**: will be v-ing의 형태로, 미래의 특정 시점에 진행 중일 일을 나타낸다.

- Maggie (will be meeting) her friends tomorrow.
  미래의 특정 시점에 진행 중일 일
  (Maggie는 내일 그녀의 친구들을 만나고 있을 것이다.)

> *** 미래를 나타내는 현재진행형**
> 확정된 일정이나 계획 등의 경우에는 현재진행형으로 미래를 나타낼 수 있다.
> - The ten fifteen for Greenville **is now leaving** on track two.
>   (Greenville행 10시 15분 열차가 2번 선로에서 이제 출발할 것이다.)

3 현재완료시제 – have[has] p.p.의 형태로, 과거의 일이 현재와 관련이 있거나 현재까지 영향을 미칠 때 쓴다.

- We (have lived) here for 20 years. (우리는 이곳에서 20년 동안 살아 왔다.)
  과거부터 현재까지 계속 살아 왔음 일이 계속된 기간을 나타내는 for

4 과거완료시제 – had p.p.의 형태로, 과거의 특정 시점을 기준으로 그 이전에 일어난 일이 기준 시점까지 영향을 미쳤을 때 쓴다.

- She (had lived) there for 4 years when the war began. (전쟁이 시작됐을 때 그녀는 그곳에서 4년째 살고 있었다.)
  기준 시점 이전부터 기준 시점까지 계속 살고 있었음   기준 시점

Check Test

1 밑줄 친 부분의 시제를 쓰시오.

Laptops <u>were</u> the most used device for students to access digital content in both years.

→ _____

2 밑줄 친 부분을 현재시제로 바꿔 쓰시오.

On average, OECD countries <u>were estimated</u> to have spent 8.8 percent of their GDP on health care.

→ _____

3 밑줄 친 부분을 현재완료시제로 바꿔 쓰시오.

Since 2018 global energy investment in clean energy <u>continued</u> to rise, reaching its highest level in 2022.

→ _____

4 밑줄 친 부분을 알맞은 시제로 고쳐 쓰시오.

More than 60 percent of young people in Portugal said they <u>will</u> look for jobs overseas.

→ _____

• **정답**

1 과거 2 are estimated 3 has continued 4 would

자이 쌤's
Follow Me!

H 도표의 이해

1st 무엇을 다룬 도표인지, 어떤 항목들이 있는지부터 분석하세요.
2nd 각 문장을 읽고, 도표에서 확인해야 하는 부분에 □ 표시하세요.
3rd 정답 문장을 도표와 일치하도록 수정해 보세요.

H01 ·······························고1 2024(9월)/25

다음 도표의 내용과 일치하지 <u>않는</u> 것은?

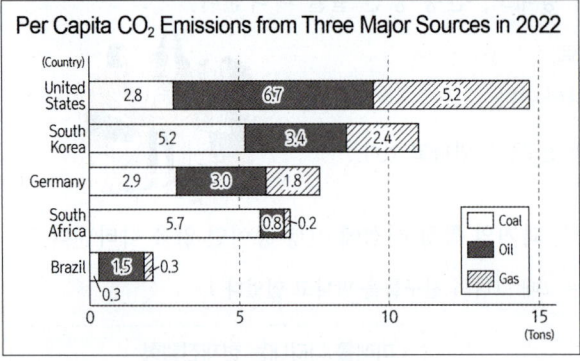

Per Capita CO₂ Emissions from Three Major Sources in 2022

The above graph shows per capita CO_2 emissions from coal, oil, and gas by countries in 2022. ① The United States had the highest total per capita CO_2 emissions, even though its emissions from coal were the second [5] lowest among the five countries shown. ② South Korea's total per capita CO_2 emissions were over 10 tons, ranking it the second highest among the countries shown. ③ Germany had lower CO_2 emissions per [10] capita than South Korea in all three major sources respectively. ④ The per capita CO_2 emissions from coal in South Africa were over three times higher than those in Germany. ⑤ In Brazil, oil was the largest [15] source of CO_2 emissions per capita among its three major sources, just as it was in the United States and Germany. *per capita: 1인당

1st 무엇을 다룬 도표인지, 어떤 항목들이 있는지부터 분석하세요.

● **도표의 제목부터 확인해 봅시다.**
'2022년의 세 가지 주요 자원에서 나온 1인당 이산화 탄소 배출량'을 나타낸 도표예요.

● **어떤 국가들의 이산화 탄소 배출량을 나타내나요?**
미국, 한국, 독일, 남아프리카 공화국, 브라질, 이렇게 총 다섯 국가의 이산화 탄소 배출량이 제시되었어요.

● **그래프의 항목은 무엇을 나타내나요?**
흰색 막대그래프는 석탄에서 나온 1인당 이산화 탄소 배출량, 회색 막대그래프는 ❶(   )에서 나온 1인당 이산화 탄소 배출량, 그리고 빗금 친 막대그래프는 천연가스에서 나온 1인당 이산화 탄소 배출량을 나타내요.

2nd 각 문장을 읽고, 도표에서 확인해야 하는 부분에 □ 표시하세요.

1) ①은 미국의 1인당 이산화 탄소 배출량을 설명하고 있어요.

① The United States had the highest total per capita
미국은   가장 높은 1인당 이산화 탄소 총배출량을
CO_2 emissions, / even though its emissions from
가졌다   / 석탄에서 나온 배출량은 두 번째로
coal were the second lowest / among the five
낮았음에도 불구하고   / 보여진 다섯 개의
countries shown. //
국가 중   //

● **미국 / 총배출량, 석탄에서 나온 배출량**
미국 총배출량: 14.7
미국 석탄에서 나온 배출량: 2.8

● **도표와 비교해 볼까요?**
맨 윗줄에 있는 미국의 막대그래프를 보면, 세 종류의 막대를 모두 합한 길이가 다섯 국가 중에서 가장 길다는 것을 알 수 있어요. 수치상으로도 14.7(=2.8+6.7+5.2)로 가장 크죠.

석탄에서 나온 1인당 이산화 탄소 배출량을 나타내는 흰색 막대그래프를 보면, 미국은 2.8이므로 가장 낮은 브라질(0.3) 다음으로 두 번째로 낮다는 것을 알 수 있어요.

2) ②은 어떤 나라의 1인당 이산화 탄소 배출량을 설명하나요?

② South Korea's total per capita CO$_2$ emissions /
한국의 1인당 이산화 탄소 총배출량은 /
were over 10 tons, / ranking it the second highest /
10톤이 넘고 / 두 번째로 높은 순위를 차지했다 /
among the countries shown. //
보여진 국가 중 //

● **한국 / 총배출량**
　한국 총배출량: 11

● **도표와 비교해 볼까요?**
　두 번째 줄에 있는 한국의 막대그래프를 보면, 세 종류의 막대를 모두
　합한 길이가 다섯 국가 중에서 **❷**(　　　) 다음으로 가장 길다는 것을
　알 수 있어요. 수치상으로는 11(=5.2+3.4+2.4)로, 미국의 총배출량인
　14.7 다음으로 가장 높군요.

3) ③은 두 나라의 배출량을 비교하고 있어요.

③ Germany had lower CO$_2$ emissions per capita /
독일은 더 낮은 1인당 이산화 탄소 배출량을 가졌다 /
than South Korea / in all three major sources
한국보다 / 각각의 모든 세 가지 주요한
respectively. //
원천에서 //

● **독일, 한국 / 자원별 1인당 이산화 탄소 배출량**
　독일: 석탄(2.9), 석유(3.0), 천연가스(1.8)
　한국: 석탄(5.2), 석유(3.4), 천연가스(2.4)

● **도표와 비교해 볼까요?**
　이번엔 두 나라의 자원별 막대그래프를 각각 비교해야 해요.
　먼저 석탄에서 나온 배출량을 나타내는 흰색 막대그래프를 보면, 독일이
　한국보다 낮아요.
　석유에서 나온 배출량을 나타내는 회색 막대그래프를 보면, 역시 독일이
　한국보다 낮아요.
　천연가스에서 나온 배출량을 나타내는 빗금 친 막대그래프를 보면,
　마찬가지로 독일이 한국보다 낮아요.

4) ④도 두 나라의 배출량을 비교하고 있어요.

④ The per capita CO$_2$ emissions from coal / in South
석탄으로부터의 1인당 이산화 탄소 배출량은 / 남아프리카
Africa / were over three times higher than those in
공화국의 / 독일의 그것보다 세 배보다
Germany. //
더 높았다 //

● **남아프리카 공화국, 독일 / 석탄에서 나온 배출량**
　남아프리카 공화국: 5.7, 독일: 2.9

● **도표와 비교해 볼까요?**
　석탄에서 나온 배출량을 나타내는 흰색 막대그래프를 보면, 독일이
　2.9니까 세 배는 8.7인데, 남아프리카 공화국은 5.7이므로 독일의 세
　배보다 더 높지 않아요.

5) ⑤은 세 나라의 공통점을 설명하고 있어요.

⑤ In Brazil, / oil was the largest source of CO$_2$
브라질에서 / 석유는 1인당 이산화 탄소 배출량의 가장 큰
emissions per capita / among its three major
/ 원천이었다 / 브라질의 세 가지 주요한 원천 중에서
sources, / just as it was in the United States and
/ 그것은 미국과 독일에서도
Germany. //
마찬가지였다 //

● **브라질, 미국, 독일 / 석유에서 나온 배출량**
　브라질: 1.5 (석탄: 0.3, 천연가스: 0.3)
　미국: 6.7 (석탄: 2.8, 천연가스: 5.2)
　독일: 3.0 (석탄: 2.9, 천연가스: 1.8)

● **도표와 비교해 볼까요?**
　석유에서 나온 배출량을 나타내는 회색 막대그래프를 보면, 브라질은
　1.5이므로 나머지 두 자원보다 커요. 미국(6.7)과 독일(3.0)도
　마찬가지로 나머지 두 자원보다 석유에서 나온 배출량이 더 크다는 것을
　알 수 있어요.

3rd 정답 문장을 도표와 일치하도록 수정해 보세요.

④ The per capita CO$_2$ emissions from coal / in South
석탄으로부터의 1인당 이산화 탄소 배출량은 / 남아프리카
Africa / were over three times higher than(→ nearly
공화국의 / 독일의 그것보다 세 배보다 더 높았다(→ 거의 두 배 높았다) //
twice as high as) those in Germany. //

● **남아프리카 공화국이 독일의 두 배보다 더 적었어요.**
　남아프리카 공화국: 5.7, 독일: 2.9
　2.9의 세 배는 8.7인데, 5.7은 8.7보다 낮기 때문에 '세 배보다 더 높은'을
　의미하는 three times higher than은 **❸**(　　　) twice as high
　as로 바꿔야 해요.

H02 ~ 05 ▶ 제한시간 8분

H02 ★★★❀ 고1 2025(3월)/25

다음 도표의 내용과 일치하지 <u>않는</u> 것은?

How Often People in America Consumed Fast Food in 2023

- Daily 13%
- A few times a week 36%
- Once a week 16%
- A few times a month 18%
- Once every couple of months 8%
- Rarely 5%
- Never 4%

The above graph shows how often people in America consumed fast food in 2023, sorted according to frequency of consumption. ① More than 50 percent of individuals consumed fast food once a week or more frequently. ② The most highly reported pattern of consumption was a few times a week, which was 36 percent of the total. ③ The second most highly reported pattern was a few times a month, accounting for 18 percent of the total. ④ The percentage of people who ate fast food once every couple of months was more than that of those who consumed it daily. ⑤ The combined share of those who rarely or never ate fast food was less than 10 percent.

[구문 서술형]

주어진 우리말과 일치하도록 괄호 안의 단어를 빈칸에 알맞게 쓰시오. (필요시 형태를 바꿀 것)

위 그래프는 2023년 미국에서 사람들이 얼마나 자주 패스트푸드를 먹었는지를 보여 준다. (show, consume)

➡ The above graph _____ how often people in America _____ fast food in 2023.

H03 ★★★❀ 고1 2025(6월)/25

다음 도표의 내용과 일치하지 <u>않는</u> 것은?

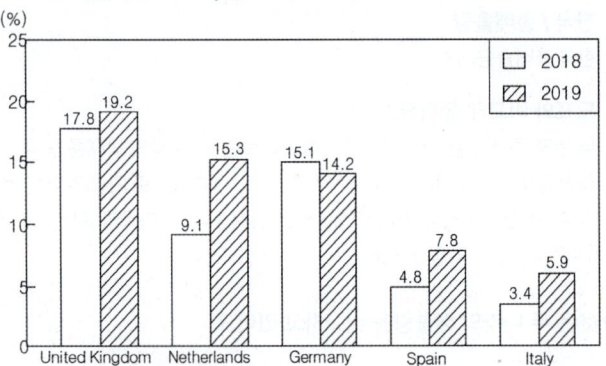

Online Share of Retail Trade in Selected European Countries in 2018 and 2019

The graph above shows the online share of retail trade in selected European countries in 2018 and 2019. ① In 2019, the United Kingdom recorded the highest online share of retail trade, reaching 19.2 percent. ② The Netherlands showed the largest increase in its online share of retail trade among the countries from 2018 to 2019, with a jump of over 6 percentage points. ③ In 2018, Germany had a higher online share of retail trade than the Netherlands, whereas, in 2019, Germany fell behind the Netherlands. ④ In 2018, Germany's online share of retail trade was over four times higher than that of Spain. ⑤ Among the five countries, Italy recorded the lowest online share of retail trade in both 2018 and 2019.

[구문 서술형]

〈보기〉의 조건에 맞게 빈칸에 알맞은 단어를 쓰시오.

[보기]
1) 2018년부터 지속되어 왔음을 나타낼 것
2) 시간을 나타내는 전치사를 추가할 것
3) 동사 show를 활용할 것

The Netherlands _____ the largest increase in its online share of retail trade _____ 2018.

H04 ✦✦✧ 고1 2025(9월)/25

다음 도표의 내용과 일치하지 <u>않는</u> 것은?

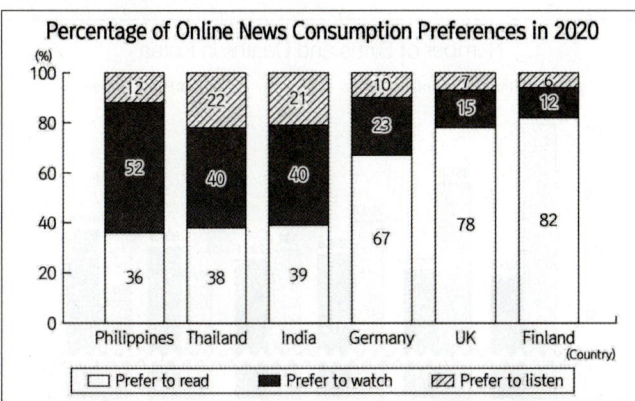

The graph above shows the percentage of online news consumption preferences in three ways for six countries in 2020. ① In Germany, the UK and Finland, reading was the most preferred way of consuming online news, with its percentage over 60 percent across the three countries. ② The interesting point is that the Philippines, Thailand and India all preferred to watch online news the most. ③ In terms of preference to watching online news, the Philippines showed the highest percentage and Finland showed the lowest preference among all six countries. ④ Four out of ten preferred to watch online news in both Thailand and India, and that percentage was more than three times as high as that of Finland. ⑤ For listening, the least preferred way of consuming online news, the percentage of people who preferred it in Finland was a third of that of Thailand.

구문 서술형

밑줄 친 부분을 어법상 알맞게 고치시오.

The Philippines, Thailand and India all <u>prefers</u> to watch online news the most in 2020.

➡ _____

H05 ✦✦✦ 고1 2024(3월)/25

다음 도표의 내용과 일치하지 <u>않는</u> 것은?

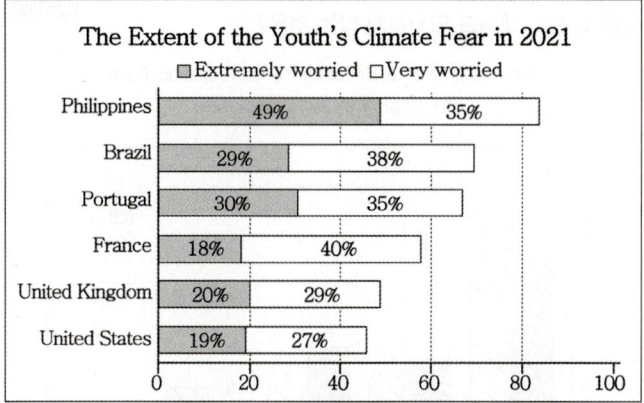

The above graph shows the extent to which young people aged 16-25 in six countries had fear about climate change in 2021. ① The Philippines had the highest percentage of young people who said they were extremely or very worried, at 84 percent, followed by 67 percent in Brazil. ② More than 60 percent of young people in Portugal said they were extremely worried or very worried. ③ In France, the percentage of young people who were extremely worried was higher than that of young people who were very worried. ④ In the United Kingdom, the percentage of young generation who said that they were very worried was 29 percent. ⑤ In the United States, the total percentage of extremely worried and very worried youth was the smallest among the six countries.

H06 ❋❋❋ 고1 2024(6월)/25

다음 도표의 내용과 일치하지 <u>않는</u> 것은?

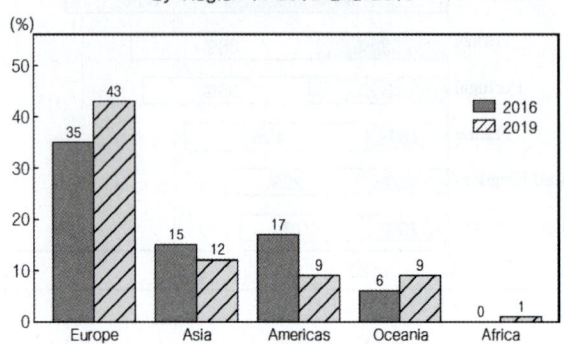

Electronic Waste Collection and Recycling Rate by Region in 2016 and 2019

The above graph shows the electronic waste collection and recycling rate by region in 2016 and 2019. ① In both years, Europe showed the highest electronic waste collection and recycling rates. ② The electronic waste collection and recycling rate of Asia in 2019 was lower than in 2016. ③ The Americas ranked third both in 2016 and in 2019, with 17 percent and 9 percent respectively. ④ In both years, the electronic waste collection and recycling rates in Oceania remained under 10 percent. ⑤ Africa had the lowest electronic waste collection and recycling rates in both 2016 and 2019, showing the smallest gap between 2016 and 2019.

H07 ❋❋❋ 고1 2023(3월)/25

다음 도표의 내용과 일치하지 <u>않는</u> 것은?

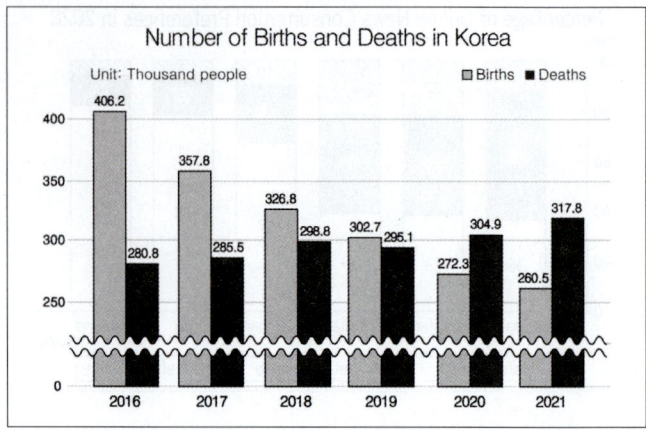

Number of Births and Deaths in Korea

The above graph shows the number of births and deaths in Korea from 2016 to 2021. ① The number of births continued to decrease throughout the whole period. ② The gap between the number of births and deaths was the largest in 2016. ③ In 2019, the gap between the number of births and deaths was the smallest, with the number of births slightly larger than that of deaths. ④ The number of deaths increased steadily during the whole period, except the period from 2018 to 2019. ⑤ In 2021, the number of deaths was larger than that of births for the first time.

H08 ✿✿✿   고1 2022(6월)/25

다음 도표의 내용과 일치하지 <u>않는</u> 것은?

Percent of U.S. Households with Pets

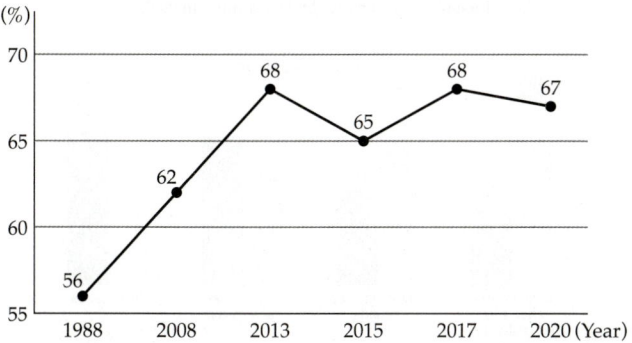

The graph above shows the percent of households with pets in the United States (U.S.) from 1988 to 2020. ① In 1988, more than half of U.S. households owned pets, and more than 6 out of 10 U.S. households owned pets from 2008 to 2020. ② In the period between 1988 and 2008, pet ownership increased among U.S. households by 6 percentage points. ③ From 2008 to 2013, pet ownership rose an additional 6 percentage points. ④ The percent of U.S. households with pets in 2013 was the same as that in 2017, which was 68 percent. ⑤ In 2015, the rate of U.S. households with pets was 3 percentage points lower than in 2020.

H09 ✿✿✿   고1 2021(11월)/25

다음 도표의 내용과 일치하지 <u>않는</u> 것은?

Percentage of U.S. Students Participating in Cultural Activities (2016)

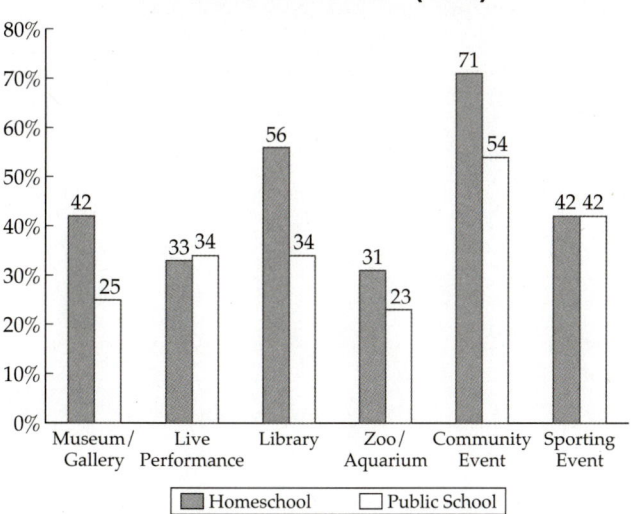

The graph above shows the percentage of U.S. homeschooled and public school students participating in cultural activities in 2016. ① With the exception of live performances and sporting events, the percentage of homeschooled students participating in cultural activities was higher than that of public school students. ② For each group of students, community events accounted for the largest percentage among all cultural activities. ③ The percentage point difference between homeschooled students and their public school peers was largest in visiting libraries. ④ The percentage of homeschooled students visiting museums or galleries was more than twice that of public school students. ⑤ Going to zoos or aquariums ranked the lowest for both groups of students, with 31 and 23 percent respectively.

H10 ✿✿✿   고1 2022(9월)/25

다음 도표의 내용과 일치하지 <u>않는</u> 것은?

Share of the Urban Population by Continent in 1950 and in 2020

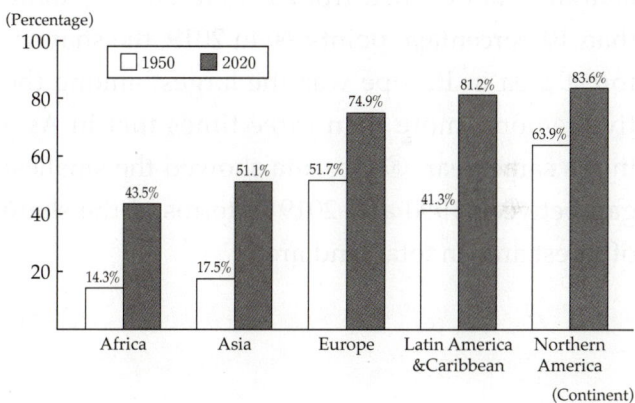

The graph above shows the share of the urban population by continent in 1950 and in 2020. ① For each continent, the share of the urban population in 2020 was larger than that in 1950. ② From 1950 to 2020, the share of the urban population in Africa increased from 14.3% to 43.5%. ③ The share of the urban population in Asia was the second lowest in 1950 but not in 2020. ④ In 1950, the share of the urban population in Europe was larger than that in Latin America and the Caribbean, whereas the reverse was true in 2020. ⑤ Among the five continents, Northern America was ranked in the first position for the share of the urban population in both 1950 and 2020.

H11 ❀❀❀ 고1 2023(6월)/25

다음 도표의 내용과 일치하지 <u>않는</u> 것은?

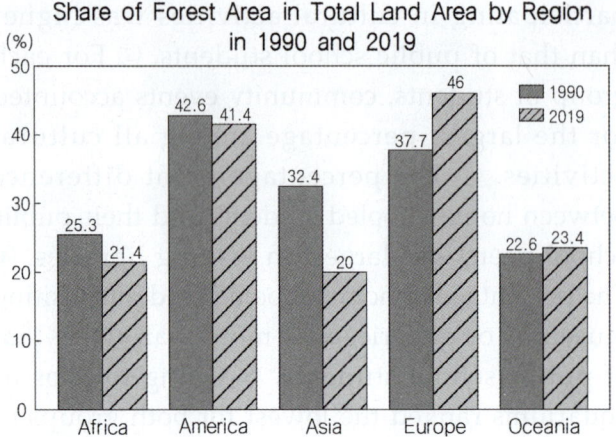

The above graph shows the share of forest area in total land area by region in 1990 and 2019. ① Africa's share of forest area in total land area was over 20% in both 1990 and 2019. ② The share of forest area in America was 42.6% in 1990, which was larger than that in 2019. ③ The share of forest area in Asia declined from 1990 to 2019 by more than 10 percentage points. ④ In 2019, the share of forest area in Europe was the largest among the five regions, more than three times that in Asia in the same year. ⑤ Oceania showed the smallest gap between 1990 and 2019 in terms of the share of forest area in total land area.

H12 ❀❀❀ 고1 2021(9월)/25

다음 도표의 내용과 일치하지 <u>않는</u> 것은?

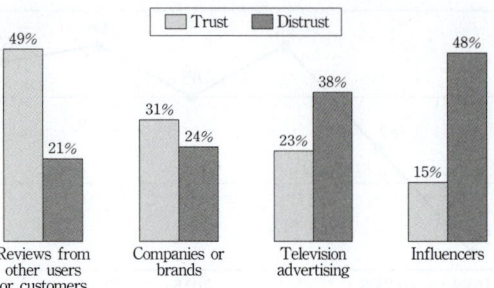

The graph above shows the consumers' levels of trust in four different types of information sources, based on a survey of US adults in 2020. ① About half of US adults say they trust the information they receive from reviews from other users or customers. ② This is more than double those who say they hold distrust for reviews from other users or customers. ③ The smallest gap between the levels of trust and distrust among the four different types of information sources is shown in the companies or brands' graph. ④ Fewer than one-fifth of adults say they trust information from television advertising, outweighed by the share who distrust such information. ⑤ Only 15% of adults say they trust the information provided by influencers, while more than three times as many adults say they distrust the same source of information.

H13 ✱✱✱✸ _____ 고1 2022(3월)/25

다음 도표의 내용과 일치하지 <u>않는</u> 것은?

Percentage of UK People
Who Used Online Course and Online Learning Material
(in 2020, by age group)

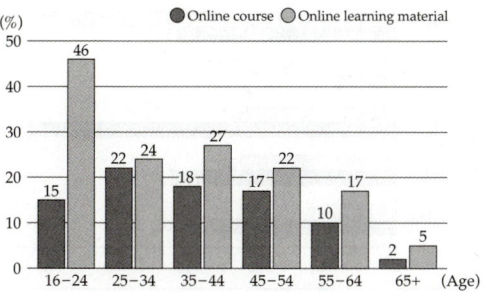

The above graph shows the percentage of people in the UK who used online courses and online learning materials, by age group in 2020. ① In each age group, the percentage of people who used online learning materials was higher than that of people who used online courses. ② The 25–34 age group had the highest percentage of people who used online courses in all the age groups. ③ Those aged 65 and older were the least likely to use online courses among the six age groups. ④ Among the six age groups, the gap between the percentage of people who used online courses and that of people who used online learning materials was the greatest in the 16–24 age group. ⑤ In each of the 35–44, 45–54, and 55–64 age groups, more than one in five people used online learning materials.

H14 ✱✱✱ _____ 고1 2023(11월)/25

다음 도표의 내용과 일치하지 <u>않는</u> 것은?

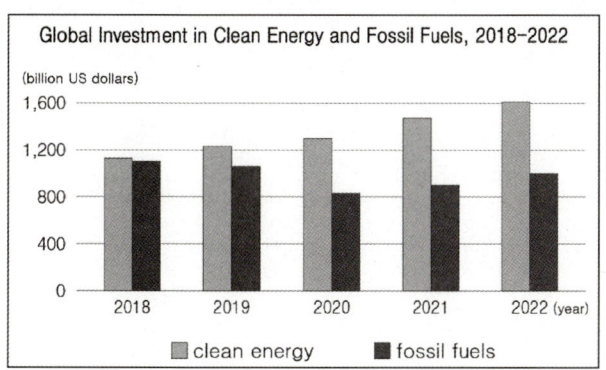

The above graph shows global energy investment in clean energy and in fossil fuels between 2018 and 2022. ① Since 2018 global energy investment in clean energy continued to rise, reaching its highest level in 2022. ② The investment gap between clean energy and fossil fuels in 2020 was larger than that in 2019. ③ Investment in fossil fuels was highest in 2018 and lowest in 2020. ④ In 2021, investment in clean energy exceeded 1,200 billion dollars, while investment in fossil fuels did not. ⑤ In 2022, the global investment in clean energy was more than double that of fossil fuels.

H15 ✱✱✱ _____ 고1 2023(9월)/25

다음 도표의 내용과 일치하지 <u>않는</u> 것은?

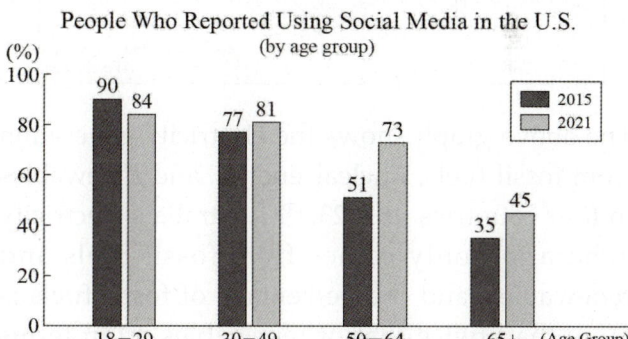

The graph above shows the percentages of people in different age groups who reported using social media in the United States in 2015 and 2021. ① In each of the given years, the 18-29 group had the highest percentage of people who said they used social media. ② In 2015, the percentage of people who reported using social media in the 30-49 group was more than twice that in the 65 and older group. ③ The percentage of people who said they used social media in the 50-64 group in 2021 was 22 percentage points higher than that in 2015. ④ In 2021, except for the 65 and older group, more than four-fifths of people in each age group reported using social media. ⑤ Among all the age groups, only the 18-29 group showed a decrease in the percentage of people who reported using social media from 2015 to 2021.

H16~17 ▶ 제한시간 4분

H16 ⭐ 2등급 대비　　　　　　고1 2024(10월)/25

다음 도표의 내용과 일치하지 <u>않는</u> 것은?

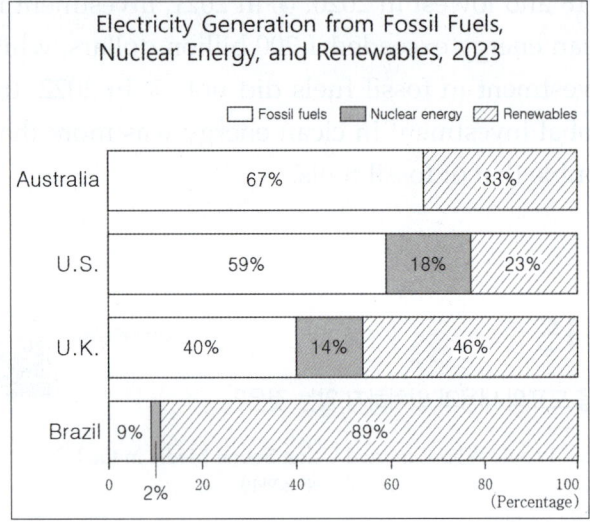

The above graph shows the electricity generation from fossil fuels, nuclear energy, and renewables in four countries in 2023. ① Australia's electricity generation only comes from fossil fuels and renewables, and the percentage of fossil fuels is more than twice that of renewables. ② In terms of electricity generation from nuclear energy, the U.S. shows the highest percentage among all four countries. ③ The percentage of electricity generation from fossil fuels in the U.S. is higher than that in the U.K., which is also true for renewables. ④ In the U.K., the percentage of electricity generated from nuclear energy is less than a third of that generated from renewables. ⑤ Brazil's percentage of electricity generated from renewables is 10 percentage points larger than that of Australia and the U.K. combined.

H17 ⭐ 2등급 대비　　　　　　고1 2022(11월)/25

다음 도표의 내용과 일치하지 <u>않는</u> 것은?

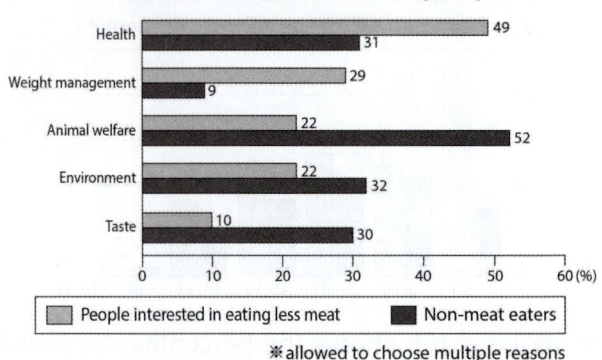

The graph above shows the survey results on reasons for people interested in eating less meat and those eating no meat in the UK in 2018. ① For the group of people who are interested in eating less meat, health is the strongest motivator for doing so. ② For the group of non-meat eaters, animal welfare accounts for the largest percentage among all reasons, followed by environment, health, and taste. ③ The largest percentage point difference between the two groups is in animal welfare, whereas the smallest difference is in environment. ④ The percentage of non-meat eaters citing taste is four times higher than that of people interested in reducing their meat consumption citing taste. ⑤ Weight management ranks the lowest for people who don't eat meat, with less than 10 percent.

✱ 다음 영어는 우리말 뜻을, 우리말은 영어 단어를 〈보기〉에서 찾아 쓰시오.

〈보기〉

약간	combine	복지	cite
차이	among	분류하다	respondent
점유율	birth	강의	steadily

01 sort _____

02 difference _____

03 share _____

04 welfare _____

05 slightly _____

06 언급하다 _____

07 ~ 중에서 _____

08 결합하다 _____

09 꾸준히 _____

10 응답자 _____

✱ 다음 우리말에 알맞은 영어 표현을 찾아 연결하시오.

11 연령 집단 • • age group

12 ~라는 면에서 • • fall behind

13 ~에 기반하여 • • based on

14 뒤처지다 • • in terms of

15 차지하다 • • account for

✱ 다음 우리말 표현에 맞는 단어를 고르시오.

16 가장 강력한 동기 ➡ the strongest (motivator / radiator)

17 젊은 세대의 비율 ➡ the percentage of young (concentration / generation)

18 지역별 재활용률 ➡ (recycling / cycling) rate by region

19 1인당 이산화 탄소 배출량 ➡ per capita CO_2 (emissions / omissions)

20 투자액 격차 ➡ the (investment / adjustment) gap

✱ 다음 문장의 빈칸에 알맞은 단어를 〈보기〉에서 찾아 쓰시오.

〈보기〉

decrease	fossil	ownership	urban
declined	extremely	region	retail
consumed	insightful	management	reverse

21 18세에서 29세 집단만이 감소를 보였다.
➡ Only the 18-29 group showed a(n) _____.

22 체중 관리는 가장 낮은 순위를 차지한다.
➡ Weight _____ ranks the lowest.

23 위 그래프는 소매 거래에서의 온라인 점유율을 보여 준다.
➡ The graph above shows the online share of _____ trade.

24 위 도표는 지역별 산림 면적의 점유율을 보여 준다.
➡ The above graph shows the share of forest area by _____.

25 반려동물 보유는 미국 가정들에서 증가했다.
➡ Pet _____ increased among U.S. households.

26 위 그래프는 화석 연료로부터의 전기 생산을 보여 준다.
➡ The above graph shows the electricity generation from _____ fuels.

27 위 그래프는 도시 인구 점유율을 보여준다.
➡ The graph above shows the share of the _____ population.

28 50퍼센트가 넘는 사람들은 일주일에 한 번 패스트푸드를 먹었다.
➡ More than 50 percent of individuals _____ fast food once a week.

29 아시아의 산림 면적 점유율은 1990년부터 2019년까지 감소했다.
➡ The share of forest area in Asia _____ from 1990 to 2019.

30 그들의 60퍼센트 이상이 극도로 혹은 매우 걱정하고 있다고 말했다.
➡ More than 60 percent of them said they were _____ or very worried.

내용 불일치

★ 유형 설명

Robert E. Lucas, Jr.에 관한 다음 글의 내용과 일치하지 않는 것은?

Robert E. Lucas, Jr. was born on September 15, 1937, in Yakima, Washington. During World

특정 인물이나 동식물 등에 대해 설명하는 글을 정확하게 해석하여 선택지와 대조해야 한다.

☞ 글에서 언급된 내용과 똑같은 순서로 선택지가 제시된다.
선택지를 먼저 읽은 후에 글에서 해당 내용을 찾아 그 선택지의 일치 여부를 확인한다.
일치하는 것을 찾는 문제인지, 일치하지 않는 것을 찾는 문제인지 꼭 다시 한 번 확인한다.

유형 풀이 비법

1 지시문을 확인하라!
• 문제를 읽고 무엇에 관한 글인지, 일치를 묻는지, 불일치를 묻는지 확인한다.

2 선택지를 살펴보라!
• 선택지를 빠르게 훑어보면서 글에서 어떤 세부 정보를 확인해야 하는지 알아본다.

3 선택지와 글을 대조하라!
• 선택지에 해당하는 글의 부분을 정확하게 대조하며 답을 찾는다.

Tip 글에 나온 내용에만 근거해서 답을 골라야지 상식이나 배경지식을 통해 일치 여부를 판단하면 안 된다.

🔑 어휘 및 표현 Preview

- □ slavery 노예
- □ successfully 성공적으로
- □ enslave 노예로 만들다
- □ equality 평등
- □ immigrant 이민자
- □ autobiography 자서전
- □ candidate 후보자
- □ vice president 부통령
- □ bachelor's degree 학사 학위
- □ military 군대
- □ composition 작곡
- □ admire 감탄하다
- □ hire 고용하다
- □ approach 접근
- □ show interest in ~에 흥미를 보이다
- □ chemistry 화학

- □ physics 물리학
- □ mathematics 수학
- □ throughout 내내
- □ serve 복무하다
- □ coin (새로운 낱말·어구를) 만들다
- □ advanced 진보된
- □ emigrate (타국으로) 이주하다
- □ numerous 수많은
- □ profound 심오한
- □ appoint 임명하다
- □ astronomy 천문학
- □ submit 제출하다
- □ sponsor 후원하다
- □ publish 출판하다
- □ relativity 상대성
- □ significant 주요한

- □ enlightenment 계몽주의
- □ participation 참여
- □ adventurous 모험적인
- □ persuade 설득하다
- □ nonetheless 그렇더라도
- □ financial 금융의
- □ political 정치의
- □ major in ~을 전공하다
- □ economics 경제학
- □ handle 다루다
- □ earn 얻다, 취득하다
- □ doctor's degree 박사 학위
- □ doctoral 박사 학위의
- □ mention 언급하다
- □ contribution 기여
- □ analysis 분석

9 조동사

> *should have p.p.: ~했어야 했는데
> (하지 않았다)
> • These ridiculous rules and regulations **should have been** done away with years ago.
> (이 우스꽝스러운 규칙과 규제들은 수년 전에 없어졌어야 했다.)

1 can/could: 능력, 허가, 가능, 추측 등을 나타낸다.

• (Can) you give me a discount? (허가) (제게 할인해 주실 수 있나요?)

2 will/would: 고집, 예견, 습성, 추측 등을 나타낸다.

• Sorry, but the concert (will) be cancelled if it rains. (예견) (죄송하지만, 비가 오면 콘서트는 취소될 것입니다.)

3 would: 과거의 비교적 짧은 기간의 불규칙적인 습관을 나타낸다.

• He said that he (would) visit here at 9. (그는 9시에 여기에 방문하곤 했다고 말했다.)

used to: 과거의 긴 기간에 걸친 규칙적인 습관을 나타낸다.

• That's how I (used to) escape from the stress of high school life.
(그것은 내가 고등학교 생활의 스트레스에서 벗어나곤 했던 방법이다.)

4 may/might: 허가, 추측, 가능 등을 나타낸다.

• (May) I see your passport and plane ticket? (허가) (여권과 비행기 표를 보여 주시겠습니까?)

5 *should/ought to: 완곡한 의무, 필요, 추측, 당연의 표현에 사용된다.

• People (should) not drink and drive. (사람들은 술을 마시고 운전하면 안 된다.)

must/have to: 강한 의무, 필요, 금지, 단정적인 추측의 표현에 사용된다.

• You (have to) pay $10 to participate in the chess game. (체스 경기에 참가하기 위해서는 10달러를 지불해야 한다.)

6 had better: 강한 권유나 충고를 내포한 표현으로 '~하는 것이 좋겠다'라는 뜻이다.

• You (had better) go home immediately. (너는 즉시 집에 가는 것이 좋겠다.)

would rather: '차라리 ~하겠다(=prefer to)'라는 심경이나 의지를 표현할때 사용된다.

• I (would rather) not talk about it. (나는 그것에 대해 이야기하지 않는 게 낫다.)

Check Test

1 주어진 단어 중에서 어법상 적절한 것을 고르시오.

Cassatt lost her sight at the age of seventy, and, sadly, [is not able to / was not able to] paint during the later years of her life.

2 주어진 단어 중에서 어법상 적절한 것을 고르시오.

She [was able to / can be able to] get mathematical and scientific education that most women of her time did not receive.

3 밑줄 친 부분에 유의하여 아래 문장의 해석을 쓰시오.

She had to travel to Paris to take flying lessons.

→ _____

4 밑줄 친 부분에 유의하여 아래 문장의 해석을 쓰시오.

Since he couldn't draw well, he hired an artist to draw pictures of what he described.

→ _____

• **정답**

1 was not able to 2 was able to 3 그녀는 비행 수업을 듣기 위해 파리로 여행을 가야만 했다. 4 그는 그림을 잘 그릴 수 없었기 때문에, 화가를 고용하여 자신이 묘사하는 것을 그리게 했다.

I. 내용 불일치 **113**

Ⅰ 내용 불일치 (첫 번째)

1st 글에서 쉽게 찾을 수 있도록 선택지의 핵심 어구에 □ 표시하세요.
2nd 선택지와 글을 일대일로 대조하여 일치/불일치 여부를 판단하세요.
3rd 선택지가 글의 내용과 일치하면 ○, 일치하지 않으면 × 표시를 하고, 글의 지시문을 다시 한번 확인하세요.

I 01 ✱✱✱ .... 고1 2023(11월)/26

Frederick Douglass에 관한 다음 글의 내용과 일치하지 <u>않는</u> 것은?

Frederick Douglass was born into slavery at a farm in Maryland. His full name at birth was Frederick Augustus Washington Bailey. He changed his name to Frederick Douglass after he successfully escaped from slavery in 5 1838. He became a leader of the Underground Railroad — a network of people, places, and routes that helped enslaved people escape to the north. He assisted other runaway slaves until they could safely get to other areas in 10 the north. As a slave, he had taught himself to read and write and he spread that knowledge to other slaves as well. Once free, he became a well-known abolitionist and strong believer in equality for all people 15 including Blacks, Native Americans, women, and recent immigrants. He wrote several autobiographies describing his experiences as a slave. In addition to all this, he became the first African-American candidate for vice 20 president of the United States.

*abolitionist: 노예제 폐지론자

① Maryland에서 노예로 태어났다.
② 노예들이 탈출하는 것을 돕는 조직의 리더가 되었다.
③ 다른 노예들로부터 읽고 쓰는 법을 배웠다.
④ 노예로서의 자신의 경험을 묘사한 자서전을 썼다.
⑤ 미국의 첫 아프리카계 미국인 부통령 후보가 되었다.

1st 글에서 쉽게 찾을 수 있도록 선택지의 핵심 어구에 □ 표시하세요.

① Maryland에서 노예로 태어났다.
② 노예들이 탈출하는 것을 돕는 조직의 리더가 되었다.
③ 다른 노예들로부터 읽고 쓰는 법을 배웠다.
④ 노예로서의 자신의 경험을 묘사한 자서전을 썼다.
⑤ 미국의 첫 아프리카계 미국인 부통령 후보가 되었다.

● 글에서 □ 표시한 어구가 언급된 부분에 주의를 기울이세요.
내용 불일치 유형은 글과 선택지가 같은 순서로 제시되니까, 가장 먼저 나올 ①의 어구인 Maryland와 slave 등이 나오는 부분을 잘 확인해야 해요.
마찬가지로 ②은 escape, help, leader, ③은 from other slaves, read and write, ④은 autobiography, ⑤은 first, African-American, vice president, candidate를 글에서 찾으면 일치 여부를 확인할 수 있어요.

2nd 선택지와 글을 일대일로 대조하여 일치/불일치 여부를 판단하세요.

1) 첫 문장에서 ①의 단서를 찾아봅시다.

Frederick Douglass was born / into slavery at a
Frederick Douglass는 태어났다 / Maryland의 한 농장에서
farm in Maryland. //
노예로 //

● Frederick Douglass는 어디에서 태어났나요?
❶( )의 한 농장에서 노예로 태어났다고 하네요.
① 선택지와 정확히 일치하는 내용이에요.

2) leader, help, escape 등이 언급된 문장에서 ②의 단서를 찾을 수 있어요.

He became a leader of the Underground Railroad /
그는 Underground Railroad의 리더가 되었다 /
— a network of people, places, and routes / that
사람, 장소, 경로의 조직인 / 노예가
helped enslaved people escape to the north. //
된 사람들을 북쪽으로 탈출하도록 돕는 //

● 어떤 조직의 리더가 되었나요?
그는 노예가 된 사람들을 탈출하도록 돕는 조직의 리더가 되었대요.
따라서 ② 선택지도 글의 내용과 일치해요.

3) read and write의 주어와 목적어에 주의하며 ③의 단서를 찾아봅시다.

As a slave, / he had taught himself to read and
노예로서 　　/ 그는 읽고 쓰는 것을 독학했고
write / and he spread that knowledge to other
　　　 / 그 지식을 다른 노예들에게도 전파했다 //
slaves as well. //

● **읽고 쓰는 것을 배운 건가요, 아니면 가르친 건가요?**
　그는 읽고 쓰는 것을 독학하고 다른 노예들에게 (to other slaves)
　그 지식을 전파했다고 해요. 그런데 ③ 선택지에는 오히려 다른
　노예들로부터 (from other slaves) 읽고 쓰는 법을 배웠다고 하니까 글의
　내용과 다르네요. 따라서 ③이 정답이에요.
　내용 불일치 문제에서 어떤 행위의 능동 및 수동 관계를 파악하는 것은
　중요하니까 꼭 기억하도록 해요!

4) ④의 autobiography가 언급된 문장이 뒤에 이어져요.

He wrote several autobiographies / describing his
그는 몇 권의 자서전을 썼다 　　　　　　 / 노예로서의 자신의
experiences as a slave. //
경험을 묘사한 　　　　　 //

● **무엇을 썼나요?**
　노예로서의 자신의 경험을 묘사한 자서전을 썼대요. ④ 선택지도 글의
　내용과 일치하네요!

**5) first, African-American, vice president, candidate가
한꺼번에 등장한 문장에서 ⑤의 단서를 찾아볼까요?**

In addition to all this, / he became the first African-
이 모든 것에 더하여 　　　　/ 그는 미국의 첫 아프리카계 미국인
American candidate for vice president of the United
부통령 후보가 되었다 //
States. //

● **그가 어떤 사람이 되었나요?**
　2(　　　　　　　)의 첫 아프리카계 미국인 부통령 후보가 되었대요.
　⑤ 선택지와 정확히 일치하는 내용으로 글이 마무리되네요.

3rd 선택지가 글의 내용과 일치하면 ○, 일치하지 않으면 × 표시를 하고, 글의 지시문을 다시 한번 확인하세요.

1) 각 선택지의 일치/불일치 여부를 정리해 봅시다.

① Maryland에서 노예로 태어났다. **3**(　　　　)
② 노예들이 탈출하는 것을 돕는 조직의 리더가 되었다.
　　　　　　　　　　　　　　　　　　4(　　　　)
③ 다른 노예들로부터 읽고 쓰는 법을 배웠다. **5**(　　　　)
④ 노예로서의 자신의 경험을 묘사한 자서전을 썼다. **6**(　　　　)
⑤ 미국의 첫 아프리카계 미국인 부통령 후보가 되었다.
　　　　　　　　　　　　　　　　　　7(　　　　)

2) 지시문을 꼭 다시 한번 확인하세요!

Frederick Douglass에 관한 다음 글의 내용과 일치하지 않는 것은?

● **이 문제는 일치하지 않는 선택지를 고르는 문제였죠.**
　글에서는 Frederick Douglass가 읽고 쓰는 것을 독학하고 다른
　노예들에게 이를 가르쳐줬다고 했으니까, 다른 노예들로부터 읽고 쓰는
　법을 배웠다고 한 ③이 글의 내용과 일치하지 않아요.

▸ **다음 중 글의 내용과 일치하지 않는 선택지를 모두 골라 볼까요?**
　　　　　　　　　　　8(　　　　　　　　　　　)

(a) Maryland의 한 농장에서 농부의 아들로 태어났다.
(b) 1838년에 노예 상태에서 탈출하는 데 실패했었다.
(c) 다른 도망친 노예들이 북쪽의 다른 지역에 안전하게 도착할 때까지
　　도왔다.
(d) 노예로서 읽고 쓰는 것을 독학하여 다른 노예들에게 그 지식을
　　전파했다.
(e) 자유로워진 뒤에 유명한 노예제 폐지론자가 되었다.
(f) 미국의 첫 아프리카계 미국인 대통령 후보가 되었다.

누가 무엇을 했는지
꼼꼼하게 파악하자!

 글에서 쉽게 찾을 수 있도록 선택지의 핵심 어구에 □ 표시하세요.

 선택지와 글을 일대일로 대조하여 일치/불일치 여부를 판단하세요.

 선택지가 글의 내용과 일치하면 ○ 일치하지 않으면 × 표시를 하고, 글의 지시문을 다시 한번 확인하세요.

I02 ✿✿✿ .... 고1 2023(9월)/26

Bill Evans에 관한 다음 글의 내용과 일치하지 않는 것은?

American jazz pianist Bill Evans was born in New Jersey in 1929. His early training was in classical music. At the age of six, he began receiving piano lessons, later adding flute and violin. He earned bachelor's degrees in [5] piano and music education from Southeastern Louisiana College in 1950. He went on to serve in the army from 1951 to 1954 and played flute in the Fifth Army Band. After serving in the military, he [10] studied composition at the Mannes School of Music in New York. Composer George Russell admired his playing and hired Evans to record and perform his compositions. Evans became famous for recordings made [15] from the late-1950s through the 1960s. He won his first Grammy Award in 1964 for his album *Conversations with Myself*. Evans' expressive piano works and his unique harmonic approach inspired a whole [20] generation of musicians.

① 6세에 피아노 수업을 받기 시작했다.
② Southeastern Louisiana 대학에서 학위를 취득했다.
③ 군 복무 이후 뉴욕에서 작곡을 공부했다.
④ 작곡가 George Russell을 고용했다.
⑤ 1964년에 자신의 첫 번째 그래미상을 수상했다.

1st 글에서 쉽게 찾을 수 있도록 선택지의 핵심 어구에 □ 표시하세요.

① 6세에 피아노 수업을 받기 시작했다.
② Southeastern Louisiana 대학에서 학위를 취득했다.
③ 군 복무 이후 뉴욕에서 작곡을 공부했다.
④ 작곡가 George Russell을 고용했다.
⑤ 1964년에 자신의 첫 번째 그래미상을 수상했다.

● 글에서 □ 표시한 어구가 언급된 부분에 주의를 기울이세요.

내용 일치, 불일치 유형은 글과 선택지가 같은 순서대로 제시돼요. ①이 가장 먼저 나올 테니까 six years old나 age of six가 등장하는 부분을 찾으면 확인할 수 있을 거예요.

마찬가지로 ②은 Southeastern Louisiana College, ③은 New York과 composition, ④은 hire와 George Russell, ⑤은 in 1964와 Grammy Award를 글에서 찾으면 일치 여부를 확인할 수 있겠죠?

2nd 선택지와 글을 일대일로 대조하여 일치/불일치 여부를 판단하세요.

1) ① 나이를 나타내는 표현이 보여요.

At the age of six, / he began receiving piano lessons,
6세에 / 그는 피아노 수업을 받기 시작했고
/ later adding flute and violin. //
/ 나중에 플루트와 바이올린을 더했다 //

● 언제 피아노 수업을 받기 시작했다고요?

Bill Evans는 6세에 피아노 수업을 받기 시작했대요. 뒤에 플루트나 바이올린도 배웠다고 했지만 우리는 ❶( ) 수업을 언제 받았는지만 확인하면 돼요.

2) ② Southeastern Louisiana College가 언급됐어요.

He earned bachelor's degrees / in piano and music
그는 학사 학위를 취득했다 / 피아노와 음악 교육에서
education / from Southeastern Louisiana College in
/ 1950년에 Southeastern Louisiana 대학에서 //
1950. //

● Southeastern Louisiana 대학에서 무엇을 취득했나요?

1950년에 Southeastern Louisiana 대학에서 피아노와 음악 교육 학사 학위를 취득했대요. 아직까지는 선택지와 글의 내용이 모두 일치하네요!

3) ③ New York이 언급된 문장을 봅시다.

After serving in the military, / he studied
군 복무 이후   / 그는 작곡을
composition / at the Mannes School of Music / in
공부했다   / Mannes School of Music에서   /
New York. //
New York에 있는 //

● **군 복무 후에 New York에서 공부한 것이 맞나요?**
네! '군에서 복무하다'는 serve in the **②**(   )라고 표현해요.
After라고 했으니까 군 복무 이후에 New York에서 작곡을 공부했다고
하는 건 글의 내용과 일치해요.

4) ④ George Russell이 언급된 문장이 바로 이어져요.

Composer George Russell admired his playing /
작곡가 George Russell은 그의 연주에 감탄하여   /
and hired Evans / to record and perform his
Evans를 고용했다   / 자신의 곡을 녹음하고 연주하도록 하기 위해 //
compositions. //

● **George Russell은 누구인가요?**
George Russell은 작곡가래요. Evans의 연주에 감탄해서 George
Russell이 그를 고용했대요. 그런데 선택지에서 Evans가 George
Russell을 고용했다고 하지 않았나요?
④이 글의 내용과 일치하지 않는군요!

5) ⑤ 정답은 찾았지만 1964년엔 어떤 일이 있었는지 확인해 봅시다.

He won his first Grammy Award in 1964 / for his
그는 1964년에 자신의 첫 번째 그래미상을 수상했다   / 자신의 앨범
album *Conversations with Myself*. //
〈Conversations with Myself〉로   //

● **1964년에 그래미상을 수상했대요.**
first라고 했으니까 첫 번째 그래미상을 수상한 거고요. 확실한 정답을
찾은 것 같네요!

3rd **선택지가 글의 내용과 일치하면 ○ 일치하지 않으면 × 표시를
하고, 글의 지시문을 다시 한번 확인하세요.**

1) 각 선택지의 일치/불일치 여부를 정리해 봅시다.

① 6세에 피아노 수업을 받기 시작했다. **③**(   )
② Southeastern Louisiana 대학에서 학위를 취득했다.
                                    ④(   )
③ 군 복무 이후 뉴욕에서 작곡을 공부했다. **⑤**(   )
④ 작곡가 George Russell을 고용했다. **⑥**(   )
⑤ 1964년에 자신의 첫 번째 그래미상을 수상했다. **⑦**(   )

2) 지시문을 꼭 다시 한번 확인하세요!

Bill Evans에 관한 다음 글의 내용과 일치하지 <u>않는</u> 것은?

● **이 문제는 일치하지 않는 선택지를 고르는 문제였어요.**
글에서 George Russell이 Evans의 연주에 감탄하여 그를 고용했다고
했으니까, Evans가 George Russell을 고용했다고 한 ④이 글의 내용과
일치하지 않아요.

➔ **다음 선택지 중에서도 일치하지 않는 것을 모두 골라볼까요?**
                                    ⑧(   )

(a) 1929년 New Orleans에서 태어났다.
(b) 그의 초기 교육은 전통 음악이었다.
(c) 군 복무를 하며 제5군악대에서 플루트를 연주했다.
(d) Mannes School of Music에서 학생들을 가르쳤다.
(e) Evans의 음반은 인기를 얻지 못했다.
(f) 그의 작품은 많은 음악가들에게 영감을 주었다.

────────────── 수능 **Tip**

#분사구문 #부사절 #주어 생략

At the age of six, / he began receiving piano
6세에   / 그는 피아노 수업을 받기 시작했고
lessons, / later adding flute and violin. //
        / 나중에 플루트와 바이올린을 더했다   //

1 **아까 살펴본 세 번째 줄의 문장을 다시 봅시다.**
분사가 이끄는 어구가 부사절을 대신할 때 이 어구를
분사구문이라고 해요.
이때 부사절의 접속사와 주어를 생략하고 동사를 분사로
바꾸는데, 이 문장에서는 현재분사 adding이 분사구문을
이끌고 있어요.

2 **분사구문을 부사절로 바꿔봅시다.**
later 뒤에 생략된 주어 he를 넣고, adding은 문장의
시제에 맞는 과거시제 동사 added로 바꾸면 되겠죠?
문장을 다시 써보면 At the age of six, he began
receiving piano lessons, and later
⑨(   ).이 되겠네요!

I03 ~ 06 ▶ 제한시간 12분

I03 ✽✽✽   고1 2025(3월)/26

Robert E. Lucas, Jr.에 관한 다음 글의 내용과
일치하지 <u>않는</u> 것은?

Robert E. Lucas, Jr. was born on September 15, 1937, in Yakima, Washington. During World War II, his family moved to Seattle, where he graduated from Roosevelt High School. At the University of Chicago, he majored in history. After taking economic history courses at University of California, Berkeley, he developed an interest in economics. He earned a doctoral degree in economics from the University of Chicago in 1964. He taught at Carnegie Mellon University from 1963 to 1974 before returning to the University of Chicago to become a professor of economics. He was known as a very influential economist and, in 1995, he was awarded the Nobel Prize in Economic Sciences.

① 제2차 세계대전 중에 그의 가족이 Seattle로 이주했다.
② 경제사를 수강한 후에 경제학에 대한 흥미를 키웠다.
③ University of Chicago에서 경제학 박사 학위를 받았다.
④ 1963년부터 1974년까지 University of Chicago에서 가르쳤다.
⑤ 1995년에 노벨상을 수상했다.

[구문 서술형]

주어진 우리말과 일치하도록 빈칸에 알맞은 조동사를 쓰시오.

그는 경제학 교수가 되기 위해 University of Chicago로 돌아가야 했다.

➡ He _____ return to the University of Chicago to become a professor of economics.

I04 ✽✽✽   고1 2025(6월)/26

Edward O. Wilson에 관한 다음 글의 내용과
일치하지 <u>않는</u> 것은?

Edward O. Wilson was born in Birmingham, Alabama, in 1929. In his early childhood, he became interested in nature and spent much time in the outdoors. At age seven, he was partially blinded in a fishing accident; his reduced sight led Wilson to the study of ants. He could not observe larger animals from a distance. Instead, he concentrated on smaller creatures he could study up close. After studying evolutionary biology at the University of Alabama, Wilson transferred to Harvard University, where he became a professor in 1956. He never received a Nobel Prize — the prize didn't recognize research in the field of evolutionary biology. However, he was awarded the Crafoord Prize in 1990. Wilson, known to some as the "modern-day Darwin", died at the age of 92 in Massachusetts.

① 어린 시절에 자연에 관심을 갖게 되었다.
② 7세에 낚시 사고를 겪었다.
③ 1956년에 Harvard 대학 교수가 되었다.
④ 진화 생물학 분야에서 Nobel Prize를 수상했다.
⑤ Massachusetts에서 92세에 사망했다.

[구문 서술형]

밑줄 친 부분을 뜻은 같지만 형태가 다른 표현으로 바꿔 쓰고, 해당 부분의 해석을 쓰시오.

He <u>could not</u> observe larger animals from a distance.

➡ 다른 표현: _____
➡ 뜻: _____

I05

Roger Payne에 관한 다음 글의 내용과 일치하지 <u>않는</u> 것은?

Roger Payne was born in Manhattan in 1935. He studied biology at Harvard University and eventually earned his Ph.D. from Cornell University in 1961. In 1967, he discovered that humpback whales make long and complex sounds. They're known as "whale songs," and he showed that whales use them to communicate. Then in 1970, he released an album *Songs of the Humpback Whale*, which became a surprise hit and helped start the global "Save the Whales" movement. The following year, he founded Ocean Alliance to protect whales and the earth's oceans, and he used new, safe methods to study whales without harming them. Over his career, he led more than 100 research trips worldwide, including the Voyage of the Odyssey from 2000 to 2005, which studied ocean pollution. His work helped make laws that protect marine mammals, which finally led to the global ban on commercial whaling in 1986.

*humpback whale: 혹등고래

① 하버드 대학교에서 생물학을 공부했다.
② 혹등고래가 길고 복잡한 소리를 낸다는 것을 발견했다.
③ 그의 앨범 *Songs of the Humpback Whale*은 인기를 얻지 못했다.
④ 고래와 지구의 해양을 보호하기 위해 Ocean Alliance를 설립했다.
⑤ 그의 연구는 해양 포유류를 보호하는 법 제정에 도움을 주었다.

구문 서술형

주어진 우리말과 일치하도록 빈칸에 알맞은 조동사를 쓰시오.

그는 고래들이 의사소통하기 위해 그들의 노래를 사용할지도 모른다는 것을 보여줬다.

➡ He showed that whales _____ use their songs to communicate.

I06

Douglas Kirkland에 관한 다음 글의 내용과 일치하지 <u>않는</u> 것은?

Douglas Kirkland, known for his highly artistic portraits of Hollywood celebrities, was born in Toronto, Canada. When he was young, he eagerly awaited the weekly arrival of *Life* magazine and discussed the photographs the magazine contained with his father. Believing that he would have better career prospects, Kirkland moved to the United States after graduating from high school and found work at a photography studio. When *Look* magazine hired him at age 24, he became their second-youngest photographer ever. His photos taken of Marilyn Monroe in 1961 became iconic almost instantly. Kirkland spent his weeks shooting day-to-day life across the United States and his weekends in exotic locations. His photo essays could run up to a dozen pages and were seen by more than half of all Americans.

① 어린 시절에 *Life* 잡지에 실린 사진에 대해 아버지와 토의했다.
② 고등학교 졸업 후 미국으로 이주하여 일자리를 찾았다.
③ 고용될 당시 *Look* 잡지사의 역대 사진 작가 중 가장 어렸다.
④ 1961년에 찍은 Marilyn Monroe 사진은 거의 즉시 상징적인 것이 되었다.
⑤ 전체 미국인들 중 절반이 넘는 이들이 그의 포토 에세이를 보았다.

구문 서술형

빈칸에 알맞은 조동사를 쓰고, 괄호 안의 의미 중 어떤 의미로 쓰였는지 적으시오.

Believing that he _____ have better career prospects, Kirkland moved to the United States. (고집, 습성, 추측)

➡ 조동사의 의미: _____

I07

✽✽❀ _____ 고1 2024(3월)/26

Jaroslav Heyrovsky에 관한 다음 글의 내용과
일치하지 <u>않는</u> 것은?

Jaroslav Heyrovsky was born in Prague on December 20, 1890, as the fifth child of Leopold Heyrovsky. In 1901 Jaroslav went to a secondary school called the Akademicke Gymnasium. Rather than Latin and Greek, he showed a strong interest in the natural sciences. At Czech University in Prague he studied chemistry, physics, and mathematics. From 1910 to 1914 he continued his studies at University College, London. Throughout the First World War, Jaroslav served in a military hospital. In 1926, Jaroslav became the first Professor of Physical Chemistry at Charles University in Prague. He won the Nobel Prize in chemistry in 1959.

① 라틴어와 그리스어보다 자연 과학에 강한 흥미를 보였다.
② Czech University에서 화학, 물리학 및 수학을 공부했다.
③ 1910년부터 1914년까지 런던에서 학업을 이어 나갔다.
④ 제1차 세계 대전이 끝난 후 군 병원에 복무했다.
⑤ 1959년에 노벨 화학상을 수상했다.

I08

✽✽❀ _____ 고1 2024(6월)/26

Fritz Zwicky에 관한 다음 글의 내용과 일치하지 <u>않는</u> 것은?

Fritz Zwicky, a memorable astrophysicist who coined the term 'supernova', was born in Varna, Bulgaria to a Swiss father and a Czech mother. At the age of six, he was sent to his grandparents who looked after him for most of his childhood in Switzerland. There, he received an advanced education in mathematics and physics. In 1925, he emigrated to the United States and continued his physics research at California Institute of Technology (Caltech). He developed numerous theories that have had a profound influence on the understanding of our universe in the early 21st century. After being appointed as a professor of astronomy at Caltech in 1942, he developed some of the earliest jet engines and holds more than 50 patents, many in jet propulsion.

*patent: 특허(권) **propulsion: 추진(력)

① 불가리아의 Varna에서 태어났다.
② 스위스에서 수학과 물리학 교육을 받았다.
③ 미국으로 이주하여 연구를 이어갔다.
④ 우주 이해에 영향을 미친 수많은 이론을 발전시켰다.
⑤ 초창기 제트 엔진을 개발한 후 교수로 임용되었다.

I09

✽✽❀ _____ 고1 2024(9월)/26

Émilie du Châtelet에 관한 다음 글의 내용과
일치하지 <u>않는</u> 것은?

Émilie du Châtelet, a French mathematician and physicist, was born in Paris in 1706. During her childhood, with her father's support, she was able to get mathematical and scientific education that most women of her time did not receive. In 1737, she submitted her paper on the nature of fire to a contest sponsored by the French Academy of Sciences, and it was published a year later. In her book, _Institutions de Physique_, Émilie du Châtelet explained the ideas of space and time in a way that is closer to what we understand in modern relativity than what was common during her time. Her most significant achievement was translating Isaac Newton's _Principia_ into French near the end of her life. Émilie du Châtelet's work was not recognized in her time, but she is now remembered as a symbol of the Enlightenment and the struggle for women's participation in science.

① 어린 시절에 수학과 과학 교육을 받았다.
② 불의 속성에 관한 그녀의 논문이 1737년에 출간되었다.
③ _Institutions de Physique_에서 공간과 시간의 개념을 설명했다.
④ 아이작 뉴턴의 _Principia_를 프랑스어로 번역했다.
⑤ 이룩한 업적은 당대에 인정받지 못했다.

I10

✽✽❀ _____ 고1 2021(9월)/26

Paul Laurence Dunbar에 관한 다음 글의 내용과 일치하지 <u>않는</u> 것은?

Paul Laurence Dunbar, an African-American poet, was born on June 27, 1872. By the age of fourteen, Dunbar had poems published in the _Dayton Herald_. While in high school he edited his high school newspaper. Despite being a fine student, Dunbar was financially unable to attend college and took a job as an elevator operator. In 1893, Dunbar published his first book, _Oak and Ivy_, at his own expense. In 1895, he published the second book, _Majors and Minors_, which brought him national and international recognition. The poems written in standard English were called "majors," and those in dialect were termed "minors." Although the "major" poems in standard English outnumber those written in dialect, it was the dialect poems that brought Dunbar the most attention.

① 14세쯤에 _Dayton Herald_에 시를 발표했다.
② 고등학교 재학 시 학교 신문을 편집했다.
③ 재정상의 이유로 대학에 진학하지 못했다.
④ 두 번째 출판한 책으로 국내외에서 인정받게 되었다.
⑤ 표준 영어로 쓴 시들로 가장 큰 주목을 받았다.

Sarah Breedlove에 관한 다음 글의 내용과 일치하지 않는 것은?

Born in 1867, Sarah Breedlove was an American businesswoman and social activist. Orphaned at the age of seven, her early life was marked by hardship. In 1888, she moved to St. Louis, where she worked as a washerwoman for more than a decade, earning barely more than a dollar a day. During this time, long hours of backbreaking labor and a poor diet caused her hair to fall out. She tried everything that was available but had no success. After working as a maid for a chemist, she invented a successful hair care product and sold it across the country. Not only did she sell, she also recruited and trained lots of women as sales agents for a share of the profits. In the process she became America's first self-made female millionaire and she gave Black women everywhere an opportunity for financial independence.

① 미국인 사업가이자 사회 운동가였다.
② St. Louis에서 10년 넘게 세탁부로 일했다.
③ 장시간의 노동과 열악한 식사로 머리카락이 빠졌다.
④ 모발 관리 제품을 수입하여 전국에 판매했다.
⑤ 흑인 여성들에게 재정적 독립의 기회를 주었다.

Lithops에 관한 다음 글의 내용과 일치하지 않는 것은?

Lithops are plants that are often called 'living stones' on account of their unique rock-like appearance. They are native to the deserts of South Africa but commonly sold in garden centers and nurseries. Lithops grow well in compacted, sandy soil with little water and extreme hot temperatures. Lithops are small plants, rarely getting more than an inch above the soil surface and usually with only two leaves. The thick leaves resemble the cleft in an animal's foot or just a pair of grayish brown stones gathered together. The plants have no true stem and much of the plant is underground. Their appearance has the effect of conserving moisture. *cleft: 갈라진 틈

① 살아있는 돌로 불리는 식물이다.
② 원산지는 남아프리카 사막 지역이다.
③ 토양의 표면 위로 대개 1인치 이상 자란다.
④ 줄기가 없으며 땅속에 대부분 묻혀 있다.
⑤ 겉모양은 수분 보존 효과를 갖고 있다.

Elizabeth Catlett에 관한 다음 글의 내용과 일치하지 않는 것은?

Elizabeth Catlett was born in Washington, D.C. in 1915. As a granddaughter of slaves, Catlett heard the stories of slaves from her grandmother. After being disallowed entrance from the Carnegie Institute of Technology because she was black, Catlett studied design and drawing at Howard University. She became one of the first three students to earn a master's degree in fine arts at the University of Iowa. Throughout her life, she created art representing the voices of people suffering from social injustice. She was recognized with many prizes and honors both in the United States and in Mexico. She spent over fifty years in Mexico, and she took Mexican citizenship in 1962. Catlett died in 2012 at her home in Mexico.

① 할머니로부터 노예 이야기를 들었다.
② Carnegie Institute of Technology로부터 입학을 거절당했다.
③ University of Iowa에서 석사 학위를 취득했다.
④ 미국과 멕시코에서 많은 상을 받았다.
⑤ 멕시코 시민권을 결국 받지 못했다.

I14 ✱✱❀ 고1 2020(3월)/26

Ellen Church에 관한 다음 글의 내용과 일치하지 <u>않는</u> 것은?

Ellen Church was born in Iowa in 1904. After graduating from Cresco High School, she studied nursing and worked as a nurse in San Francisco. She suggested to Boeing Air Transport that nurses should take care of passengers during flights because most people were frightened of flying. In 1930, she became the first female flight attendant in the U.S. and worked on a Boeing 80A from Oakland, California to Chicago, Illinois. Unfortunately, a car accident injury forced her to end her career after only eighteen months. Church started nursing again at Milwaukee County Hospital after she graduated from the University of Minnesota with a degree in nursing education. During World War II, she served as a captain in the Army Nurse Corps and received an Air Medal. Ellen Church Field Airport in her hometown, Cresco, was named after her.

① San Francisco에서 간호사로 일했다.
② 간호사가 비행 중에 승객을 돌봐야 한다고 제안했다.
③ 미국 최초의 여성 비행기 승무원이 되었다.
④ 자동차 사고로 다쳤지만 비행기 승무원 생활을 계속했다.
⑤ 고향인 Cresco에 그녀의 이름을 따서 붙인 공항이 있다.

I15 ✱✱❀ 고1 2020(9월)/26

Jessie Redmon Fauset에 관한 다음 글의 내용과 일치하지 <u>않는</u> 것은?

Jessie Redmon Fauset was born in Snow Hill, New Jersey, in 1884. She was the first black woman to graduate from Cornell University. In addition to writing novels, poetry, short stories, and essays, Fauset taught French in public schools in Washington, D.C. and worked as a journal editor. While working as an editor, she encouraged many well-known writers of the Harlem Renaissance. Though she is more famous for being an editor than for being a fiction writer, many critics consider her novel *Plum Bun* Fauset's strongest work. In it, she tells the story of a black girl who could pass for white but ultimately claims her racial identity and pride. Fauset died of heart disease April 30, 1961, in Philadelphia.   *pass for: ~으로 여겨지다

① Cornell University를 졸업한 최초의 흑인 여성이었다.
② Washington, D.C.의 공립학교에서 프랑스어를 가르쳤다.
③ 편집자보다는 소설가로서 더 유명하다.
④ 흑인 소녀의 이야기를 다룬 소설을 썼다.
⑤ Philadelphia에서 심장병으로 사망했다.

I16 ✱✱✱ 고1 2020(6월)/26

Sigrid Undset에 관한 다음 글의 내용과 일치하지 <u>않는</u> 것은?

Sigrid Undset was born on May 20, 1882, in Kalundborg, Denmark. She was the eldest of three daughters. She moved to Norway at the age of two. Her early life was strongly influenced by her father's historical knowledge. At the age of sixteen, she got a job at an engineering company to support her family. She read a lot, acquiring a good knowledge of Nordic as well as foreign literature, English in particular. She wrote thirty six books. None of her books leaves the reader unconcerned. She received the Nobel Prize for Literature in 1928. One of her novels has been translated into more than eighty languages. She escaped Norway during the German occupation, but she returned after the end of World War II.   *Nordic: 북유럽 사람(의)

① 세 자매 중 첫째 딸로 태어났다.
② 어린 시절의 삶은 아버지의 역사적 지식에 큰 영향을 받았다.
③ 16세에 가족을 부양하기 위해 취업하였다.
④ 1928년에 노벨 문학상을 수상하였다.
⑤ 독일 점령 기간 중 노르웨이를 탈출한 후, 다시 돌아오지 않았다.

I17 ✱✱✱ 고1 2023(3월)/26

Lilian Bland에 관한 다음 글의 내용과 일치하지 <u>않는</u> 것은?

Lilian Bland was born in Kent, England in 1878. Unlike most other girls at the time she wore trousers and spent her time enjoying adventurous activities like horse riding and hunting. Lilian began her career as a sports and wildlife photographer for British newspapers. In 1910 she became the first woman to design, build, and fly her own airplane. In order to persuade her to try a slightly safer activity, Lilian's dad bought her a car. Soon Lilian was a master driver and ended up working as a car dealer. She never went back to flying but lived a long and exciting life nonetheless. She married, moved to Canada, and had a kid. Eventually, she moved back to England, and lived there for the rest of her life.

① 승마와 사냥 같은 모험적인 활동을 즐겼다.
② 스포츠와 야생 동물 사진작가로 경력을 시작했다.
③ 자신의 비행기를 설계하고 제작했다.
④ 자동차 판매원으로 일하기도 했다.
⑤ 캐나다에서 생의 마지막 기간을 보냈다.

I18

*❀❀ 고1 2022(11월)/26

Margaret Knight에 관한 다음 글의 내용과 일치하지 않는 것은?

Margaret Knight was an exceptionally prolific inventor in the late 19th century; journalists occasionally compared her to Thomas Edison by nicknaming her "a woman Edison." From a young age, she built toys for her older brothers. After her father died, Knight's family moved to Manchester. Knight left school in 1850, at age 12, to earn money for her family at a nearby textile factory, where she witnessed a fellow worker injured by faulty equipment. That led her to create her first invention, a safety device for textile equipment, but she never earned money from the invention. She also invented a machine that cut, folded and glued flat-bottomed paper bags and was awarded her first patent in 1871 for it. It eliminated the need for workers to assemble them slowly by hand. Knight received 27 patents in her lifetime and entered the National Inventors Hall of Fame in 2006. *prolific: 다작(多作)의 **patent: 특허

① 기자들이 '여자 Edison'이라는 별명을 지어 주었다.
② 가족을 위해 돈을 벌려고 학교를 그만두었다.
③ 직물 장비에 쓰이는 안전장치를 발명하여 많은 돈을 벌었다.
④ 밑이 평평한 종이 가방을 자르고 접고 붙이는 기계를 발명 했다.
⑤ 2006년에 국립 발명가 명예의 전당에 입성했다.

I19

*❀❀   고1 2023(6월)/26

Gary Becker에 관한 다음 글의 내용과 일치하지 않는 것은?

Gary Becker was born in Pottsville, Pennsylvania in 1930 and grew up in Brooklyn, New York City. His father, who was not well educated, had a deep interest in financial and political issues. After graduating from high school, Becker went to Princeton University, where he majored in economics. He was dissatisfied with his economic education at Princeton University because "it didn't seem to be handling real problems." He earned a doctor's degree in economics from the University of Chicago in 1955. His doctoral paper on the economics of discrimination was mentioned by the Nobel Prize Committee as an important contribution to economics. Since 1985, Becker had written a regular economics column in *Business Week*, explaining economic analysis and ideas to the general public. In 1992, he was awarded the Nobel Prize in economic science.

*discrimination: 차별

① New York City의 Brooklyn에서 자랐다.
② 아버지는 금융과 정치 문제에 깊은 관심이 있었다.
③ Princeton University에서의 경제학 교육에 만족했다.
④ 1955년에 경제학 박사 학위를 취득했다.
⑤ *Business Week*에 경제학 칼럼을 기고했다.

I20

**❀ 고1 2021(11월)/26

Bessie Coleman에 관한 다음 글의 내용과 일치하지 않는 것은?

Bessie Coleman was born in Texas in 1892. When she was eleven, she was told that the Wright brothers had flown their first plane. Since that moment, she dreamed about the day she would soar through the sky. At the age of 23, Coleman moved to Chicago, where she worked at a restaurant to save money for flying lessons. However, she had to travel to Paris to take flying lessons because American flight schools at the time admitted neither women nor Black people. In 1921, she finally became the first Black woman to earn an international pilot's license. She also studied flying acrobatics in Europe and made her first appearance in an airshow in New York in 1922. As a female pioneer of flight, she inspired the next generation to pursue their dreams of flying. *flying acrobatics: 곡예 비행

① 11살 때 Wright 형제의 첫 비행 소식을 들었다.
② 비행 수업을 듣기 위해 파리로 가야 했다.
③ 국제 조종사 면허를 딴 최초의 흑인 여성이 되었다.
④ 유럽에서 에어쇼에 첫 출현을 했다.
⑤ 다음 세대가 비행의 꿈을 추구하도록 영감을 주었다.

❖ 정답 및 해설 107~111p

I21 ★❀❀ 고1 2022(6월)/26

Claude Bolling에 관한 다음 글의 내용과 일치하지 <u>않는</u> 것은?

Pianist, composer, and big band leader, Claude Bolling, was born on April 10, 1930, in Cannes, France, but spent most of his life in Paris. He began studying classical music as a youth. He was introduced to the world of jazz by a schoolmate. Later, Bolling became interested in the music of Fats Waller, one of the most excellent jazz musicians. Bolling became famous as a teenager by winning the Best Piano Player prize at an amateur contest in France. He was also a successful film music composer, writing the music for more than one hundred films. In 1975, he collaborated with flutist Rampal and published *Suite for Flute and Jazz Piano Trio*, which he became most well-known for. He died in 2020, leaving two sons, David and Alexandre.

① 1930년에 프랑스에서 태어났다.
② 학교 친구를 통해 재즈를 소개받았다.
③ 20대에 Best Piano Player 상을 받았다.
④ 성공적인 영화 음악 작곡가였다.
⑤ 1975년에 플루트 연주자와 협업했다.

I22 ★❀❀ 고1 2022(3월)/26

Antonie van Leeuwenhoek에 관한 다음 글의 내용과 일치하지 <u>않는</u> 것은?

Antonie van Leeuwenhoek was a scientist well known for his cell research. He was born in Delft, the Netherlands, on October 24, 1632. At the age of 16, he began to learn job skills in Amsterdam. At the age of 22, Leeuwenhoek returned to Delft. It wasn't easy for Leeuwenhoek to become a scientist. He knew only one language — Dutch — which was quite unusual for scientists of his time. But his curiosity was endless, and he worked hard.

He had an important skill. He knew how to make things out of glass. This skill came in handy when he made lenses for his simple microscope. He saw tiny veins with blood flowing through them. He also saw living bacteria in pond water. He paid close attention to the things he saw and wrote down his observations. Since he couldn't draw well, he hired an artist to draw pictures of what he described. *cell: 세포 **vein: 혈관

① 세포 연구로 잘 알려진 과학자였다.
② 22살에 Delft로 돌아왔다.
③ 여러 개의 언어를 알았다.
④ 유리로 물건을 만드는 방법을 알고 있었다.
⑤ 화가를 고용하여 설명하는 것을 그리게 했다.

I23 ★★❀ 고1 2022(9월)/26

Wilbur Smith에 관한 다음 글의 내용과 일치하지 <u>않는</u> 것은?

Wilbur Smith was a South African novelist specialising in historical fiction. Smith wanted to become a journalist, writing about social conditions in South Africa, but his father was never supportive of his writing and forced him to get a real job. Smith studied further and became a tax accountant, but he finally turned back to his love of writing. He wrote his first novel, *The Gods First Make Mad*, and had received 20 rejections by 1962. In 1964, Smith published another novel, *When the Lion Feeds*, and it went on to be successful, selling around the world. A famous actor and film producer bought the film rights for *When the Lion Feeds*, although no movie resulted. By the time of his death in 2021 he had published 49 novels, selling more than 140 million copies worldwide.

① 역사 소설을 전문으로 하는 소설가였다.
② 아버지는 그가 글 쓰는 것을 지지하지 않았다.
③ 첫 번째 소설은 1962년까지 20번 거절당했다.
④ 소설 *When the Lion Feeds*는 영화화되었다.
⑤ 죽기 전까지 49편의 소설을 출간했다.

어휘 Review

* 다음 영어는 우리말 뜻을, 우리말은 영어 단어를 〈보기〉에서 찾아 쓰시오.

〈 보기 〉
부양하다	endless	작곡가	escape
고아로 만들다	hire	드문	equality
비평가	literature	창의력	assist

01 support _____

02 critic _____

03 orphan _____

04 composer _____

05 unusual _____

06 끝없는 _____

07 고용하다 _____

08 문학 _____

09 달아나다 _____

10 평등 _____

* 다음 우리말에 알맞은 영어 표현을 찾아 연결하시오.

11 ~을 전공하다 •   • end one's career

12 계속해서 ~하다 •   • major in

13 박사 학위 •   • go on to

14 학사 학위 •   • doctor's degree

15 일을 그만두다 •   • bachelor's degree

* 다음 우리말 표현에 맞는 단어를 고르시오.

16 군 복무 이후 ➡ after serving in the (solitary / military)

17 노예로 태어난 ➡ born into (slavery / surgery)

18 계몽주의의 상징 ➡ a (symptom / symbol) of the Enlightenment

19 경제학에 대한 중요한 기여 ➡ important (contribution / distribution) to economics

20 화학, 물리학 및 수학 ➡ (chemistry / ministry), physics, and mathematics

* 다음 문장의 빈칸에 알맞은 단어를 〈보기〉에서 찾아 쓰시오.

〈 보기 〉
eagerly	assemble	candidate	consumption
emigrated	trousers	textile	analysis
wildlife	submitted	expressive	appoint

21 그가 어렸을 때 그는 매주 "Life" 잡지의 도착을 간절히 기다렸다.
➡ When he was young, he _____ awaited the weekly arrival of *Life* magazine.

22 Becker는 일반 대중에게 경제학적 분석을 설명했다.
➡ Becker explained economic _____ to the general public.

23 가까이에 있는 직물 공장에서 그녀는 동료 노동자가 부상을 당하는 것을 목격했다.
➡ At a nearby _____ factory, she witnessed a fellow worker injured.

24 그녀는 불의 속성에 관한 논문을 제출했다.
➡ She _____ her paper on the nature of fire.

25 그것은 그것들을 손으로 천천히 조립할 필요를 없앴다.
➡ It eliminated the need to _____ them slowly by hand.

26 Lilian은 야생 동물 사진작가로 자신의 경력을 시작했다.
➡ Lilian began her career as a(n) _____ photographer.

27 그는 부통령 후보가 되었다.
➡ He became the _____ for vice president.

28 그녀는 바지를 입었고 모험적인 활동을 즐기며 시간을 보냈다.
➡ She wore _____ and spent her time enjoying adventurous activities.

29 그는 미국으로 이주하여 물리학 연구를 이어갔다.
➡ He _____ to the United States and continued his physics research.

30 Evans의 표현이 풍부한 피아노 작품은 전 세대의 음악가들에게 영감을 주었다.
➡ Evans' _____ piano works inspired a whole generation of musicians.

실용문의 이해

★ 유형 설명

Blackwood Zoo에 관한 다음 안내문의 내용과 일치하지 않는 것은?

> **Welcome to Blackwood Zoo**
> Get ready to explore! You can watch amazing

광고문이나 안내문, 제품의 설명서 등에 담긴 정보를 제대로 선택지와 대조해야 한다.

🔑 날짜나 금액, 할인 대상 등이 정답이 되는 경우가 많으므로 특히 주의를 기울인다.

가을 춘천 마라톤 대회에 관한 이 안내문을 잘 읽어봐야지.

🎭 유형 풀이 비법

1 정보를 파악하라!
- 실용문의 제목을 보고 어떤 것에 대한 내용인지 이해한다.

2 정확히 해석하라!
- 실용문과 선택지가 일치하는지 확인하려면 각 문장을 정확히 해석한다.

3 일치하는지 판단하라!
- 선택지와 실용문의 내용을 하나씩 빠르게 대조해서 일치하는지 판단해야 한다.

(Tip) 선택지가 글에서 언급되는 것과 똑같은 순서로 제시된다.

🍴 실용문에 자주 쓰이는 표현

- □ Price 가격 □ Cost 비용
- □ Categories 부문 □ Theme 주제
- □ How to Enter 참가 방법
- □ registration 등록
- □ Other Information 기타 정보
- □ Register at ~에서 등록하세요
- □ Join us for ~에 참여하세요
- □ Location 위치 □ Place 장소
- □ Opening Times 운영 시간
- □ Cancellation Policy 취소 방침
- □ refreshment 다과
- □ Submission Deadline 제출 마감 기한
- □ Participate in ~에 참가하세요
- □ Join us on ~에 참여하세요
- □ Winner Announcement Date 수상자 발표일
- □ Prize 시상 □ 1st place 1등 □ 2nd place 2등
- □ Participation Fee & Qualification 참가비 & 자격
- □ How to submit your entry 출품작 제출 방법
- □ Notices 공지 □ Guidelines 지침 □ Details 세부 사항
- □ Features 특징 □ Highlights 주요 특징
- □ To join the party 파티에 참가하려면
- □ Students can get a 10% discount. 학생은 10% 할인을 받을 수 있습니다.
- □ Lunch is included in the participation fee.
  점심 식사는 참가비에 포함됩니다.
- □ Children must be accompanied by legal guardians.
  어린이는 법적 보호자를 동반해야 합니다.
- □ No pre-reservations necessary, just show up and enjoy.
  사전 예약은 필요하지 않으며 바로 와서 즐기세요.

📖 어휘 및 표현 Preview

- □ requirement 필요 요건
- □ award 수여하다
- □ souvenir 기념품
- □ available 이용할 수 있는
- □ material 재료
- □ registration 등록
- □ limit 제한하다
- □ refund 환불
- □ cancellation 취소
- □ annual 연례의
- □ conservation 보존
- □ pollution 오염
- □ submission 제출
- □ entry 출품[응모]작
- □ fee 요금
- □ session 수업
- □ admission 입장
- □ first-come, first-served basis 선착순
- □ accompany 동행하다
- □ lend 빌려주다
- □ contact 연락하다

🔟 일치

↳비교되는 대상들이 같거나 들어맞음

1 주어 – 동사 수 일치의 원칙 – 주어의 수와 인칭에 동사의 수와 인칭을 일치시킨다.

- Many people (visit) the museum. (많은 사람들이 박물관을 **방문한다**.)
  복수 주어   복수 동사

- Time (flies). (시간이 **쏜살같다**.)
  단수 주어   단수 동사
  (셀 수 없는 명사)

2 주의해야 하는 주어 – 동사 수 일치

단수 취급하는 대명사 ┌ -body, each, -one, -thing은 **단수 취급**한다.
                    └ 형용사적으로 쓰이는 every는 **항상 단수 명사를 수식**한다.

- Each of us (has) a job to do. (우리들 각각은 해야 할 일이 **있다**.)
  단수 동사

- Every member (is) busy doing their own job.
  단수 동사
  (모든 회원은 그들의 일을 하느라 바쁘다.)

> * ┌ the number of+복수명사 : 단수 취급
>   └ a number of+복수명사 : 복수 취급
> - From the year 2001, **the number of international students** (is) increasing.
>   단수
>   (2001년부터 외국인 유학생 수는 늘고 있다.)
> - **A number of thefts** (have) been reported recently.
>   복수
>   (최근에 많은 절도 행위들이 보도되고 있다.)

3 상관접속사로 연결된 주어의 수 일치 : B에 동사의 수를 일치시킨다.

- Either you or your sister (has) to do it.
  either A or B(A나 B 둘 중 하나) 3인칭 단수 동사
  (당신 또는 당신의 언니 둘 중 한 명이 그것을 해야 **한다**.)

- Neither I nor they (were) wrong. (나와 그들 어느 쪽도 틀리지 **않았다**.)
  neither A nor B 복수 동사
  (A와 B 어느 쪽도 아닌)

- Not only the boys but also the teacher (wants) it. (소년들뿐만 아니라 그 선생님도 그것을 **원한다**.)
  not only A but also B 단수 동사
  = B as well as A(A뿐만 아니라 B도)

4 *부분이나 수량을 나타내는 표현의 수 일치 – of 뒤의 명사에 수를 일치시킨다.

- All of the music (was) from Italian operas. (모든 음악은 이탈리아의 오페라에서 왔다.)
  all of+단수 명사   단수 동사

- It was Sunday and most of the shops (were) closed. (일요일이었고 대부분의 상점들은 문을 닫았다.)
  most of+복수 명사   복수 동사

Check Test

1 괄호 안의 단어를 빈칸에 알맞은 현재진행시제 형태로 쓰시오.

The Diamond Coast _____ set to welcome the Australian Gateball Championships. (get)

2 주어진 단어 중에서 어법상 적절한 것을 고르시오.

This [are / is] not a competition, but rather a challenge to inspire students with the love of reading.

3 빈칸에 공통으로 알맞은 것을 고르시오.

· All visitors ____ required to book online.
· For classes in the park: mats _____ not provided

① am   ② are   ③ is

4 주어진 단어 중에서 어법상 적절한 것을 고르시오.

We [offers / offer] special tips for hosting a tea party.

• 정답
1 is getting 2 is 3 ② 4 offer

J 실용문의 이해

1st 제목을 보고 중심 소재가 무엇인지 확인하세요.
2nd 글을 읽으면서 선택지와 차례대로 대조하며 일치 여부를 확인하세요.
3rd 지시문을 다시 한번 확인하고, 일치하는 선택지를 고른 건 아닌지 확인하세요.

J01 ❀❀❀.................... 고1 2023(6월)/27

2023 Drone Racing Championship에 관한
다음 안내문의 내용과 일치하지 <u>않는</u> 것은?

2023 Drone Racing Championship

Are you the best drone racer?
Then take the opportunity to
prove you are the one!

When & Where
· 6 p.m. – 8 p.m., Sunday, July 9
· Lakeside Community Center

Requirements
· Participants: High school students only
· Bring your own drone for the race.

Prize
· $500 and a medal will be awarded to
the winner.

Note
· The first 10 participants will get
souvenirs.

For more details, please visit www.
droneracing.com or call 313-6745-1189.

---

① 7월 9일 일요일에 개최된다.
② 고등학생만 참가할 수 있다.
③ 자신의 드론을 가져와야 한다.
④ 상금과 메달이 우승자에게 수여될 것이다.
⑤ 20명의 참가자가 기념품을 받을 것이다.

1st 제목을 보고 중심 소재가 무엇인지 확인하세요.

2023 Drone Racing Championship /
2023 드론 레이싱 선수권 대회   /

● **제목만 봐도 글의 내용을 짐작할 수 있어요.**
드론 레이싱 선수권 대회에 관련된 내용을 안내하는 글일 거예요.
이제 중심 소재를 알았으니 이어지는 내용을 확인합시다.

2nd 글을 읽으면서 선택지와 차례대로 대조하며 일치 여부를
확인하세요.

1) 선택지는 글의 순서대로 제시되니까 앞에서부터 읽어봅시다.

When & Where /
언제 & 어디서   /
· 6 p.m. – 8 p.m., / Sunday, July 9 /
오후 6시부터 오후 8시까지 / 7월 9일 일요일   /
· Lakeside Community Center /
Lakeside Community Center   /

● **언제, 어디서 하는 대회인가요?**
7월 9일 일요일 오후 6시부터 Lakeside Community Center에서 하는
대회래요.

● **①의 일치 여부를 판단해 봅시다.**
7월 9일 일요일에 개최되는 대회인가요? ❶ (O / X)

2) 이어서 읽어봅시다.

Requirements /
필요 요건   /
· Participants: / High school students only /
참가자   / 고등학생만   /
· Bring your own drone / for the race. //
자신의 드론을 가지고 오세요   / 레이스를 위한   //

● **참가 자격에 제한이 있나요?**
네! 고등학생만 참가할 수 있고, 자신의 드론을 대회에 가져와야 한대요.

● **②과 ③의 일치 여부를 판단할 수 있어요.**
고등학생만 참가할 수 있는 대회인가요? ❷ (O / X)
참가자는 자신의 드론을 가져와야 하나요? ❸ (O / X)

3) 대회니까 상으로 무엇이 주어지는지도 확인해 봐야죠.

> Prize /
> 상 /
> • $500 and a medal will be awarded / to the winner. //
> 500달러와 메달이 수여될 것입니다 / 우승자에게 //

● 우승자에게는 무엇이 수여되나요?
상금 500달러와 메달이 수여될 거예요. 두 가지 모두 주는 거니까 혹시 선택지에서 하나만 맞게 말하지는 않았는지 주의해야겠어요.

● ④의 일치 여부를 판단해 봅시다.
상금과 메달이 우승자에게 수여되나요? ❹(O / X)

4) 아직 정답이 안 나왔으니, 이제 정답의 단서가 나오겠군요!

> Note /
> 참고 사항 /
> • The first 10 participants will get souvenirs. //
> 선착순 10명의 참가자들은 기념품을 받게 될 것입니다 //

● 참고할 사항은 무엇인가요?
선착순 10명의 참가자들은 기념품을 받게 된대요. 우리는 앞에서 네 개의 선택지가 모두 실용문의 내용과 일치하는 것을 확인했어요.
그럼 ⑤이 일치하지 않는다는 건데, 선택지를 확인해 봅시다.

● ⑤은 어떤 잘못된 정보를 말하고 있나요?
❺( )명의 참가자가 기념품을 받을 거예요. 안내문에서는 선착순 10명에게만 기념품이 주어진다고 했으니까 ⑤이 정답이 맞았어요.

↳ 정답은 나왔지만, 마지막 문장도 확인하고 넘어갑시다.

> For more details, / please visit www.droneracing.
> 더 많은 세부 정보를 원하시면 / www.droneracing.com을 방문하시거나
> com / or call 313-6745-1189. //
> / 313-6745-1189로 전화주세요 //

● 실용문 문제의 마지막 문장은 거의 같은 형식이에요.
'For more details' 또는 'For more information'이라고 하면서 웹사이트나 이메일 주소, 또는 전화번호를 말하면서 글을 마무리하는 경우가 대부분이에요.
또 이 부분의 내용이 선택지로 지정되는 경우는 거의 없기 때문에, 앞부분의 내용에 더 집중해서 정답을 고르도록 하는 것이 더 효율적이겠죠?

3rd 지시문을 다시 한번 확인하고, 일치하는 선택지를 고른 건 아닌지 확인하세요.

2023 Drone Racing Championship에 관한 다음 안내문의 내용과 일치하지 <u>않는</u> 것은?

● 일치하지 ❻( ) 것을 고르는 문제였어요.
안내문은 짧기도 하지만, 항목을 바로바로 찾을 수 있고, 또 어려운 어휘나 표현, 구문이 잘 쓰이지 않아요. 이렇게 쉬운 유형을 틀리는 이유 중 대부분은 지시문을 제대로 읽지 않아서예요.
일치하는 선택지를 골라야 하는데 일치하지 않는 선택지를 고른다거나 혹은 그 반대의 상황이죠. 그러니까 문제를 다 풀고 나면 꼭 다시 한번 지시문을 확인해야 해요!
선착순 10명의 참가자들이 기념품을 받게 될 것이라고 했으니까 20명의 참가자가 기념품을 받을 것이라고 한 ❼( )이 일치하지 않는 선택지가 맞아요.

─────── 수능 **Tip**

#실용문 #빈출 어휘

★ 실용문에 자주 나오는 어휘들을 익혀 봅시다.

admission	입장(료)	facilities	시설
valid	유효한	fee	요금, 수수료
available	이용 가능한	confirm	확인하다
application	지원서	complete	작성하다
discount rate	할인율	opening hours	영업시간
in advance	사전에	additional	부가적인
registration	등록	due date	만기일

'실용문'의 세부사항들을 선택지와 꼼꼼히 비교하자!

J02 ~ 05 ▶ 제한시간 8분

J02 ✱✱✱ ─────────── 고1 2025(3월)/27

Blackwood Zoo에 관한 다음 안내문의 내용과 일치하지 <u>않는</u> 것은?

Welcome to Blackwood Zoo

Get ready to explore! You can watch amazing animals on our 10km walking path.

Hours of Operation
- Every day, all year round!
- 9:30 a.m. - 4:30 p.m. (Last admission at 3:30 p.m.)

Ticket Prices
- Age 13 - 64: $30
- Age 3 - 12: $20
- Others: Free

Seasonal Note

Since the weather is still cold, some animals like snakes and turtles will stay only indoors.

※Free shuttle bus departs from Blackwood Subway Station every 30 minutes.

---

① 10km의 보행로에서 동물들을 볼 수 있다.
② 운영 시간은 오후 3시 30분까지이다.
③ 3세부터 12세까지의 티켓 가격은 20달러이다.
④ 날씨가 여전히 추워서 일부 동물은 실내에만 머무를 것이다.
⑤ 무료 셔틀버스가 30분마다 출발한다.

구문 서술형
괄호 안의 단어를 현재진행시제로 쓰시오. (단, 주어와 수를 일치시킬 것)

Since the weather is still cold, a number of animals _____ only indoors. (stay)

J03 ✱✱✱ ─────────── 고1 2025(3월)/28

Sock DIY Workshop에 관한 다음 안내문의 내용과 일치하는 것은?

Sock DIY Workshop

Join us for a fun and creative Sock DIY (Do It Yourself) Workshop for all ages!

When & Where
- Saturday, April 19th, from 1 p.m. to 3 p.m.
- The community hall, Clanton Center

Workshop Program

Time	DIY Item	Things to Do
1 p.m.-2 p.m.	Toys	Create stuffed toys with socks
2 p.m.-3 p.m.	Flowerpot Covers	Transform socks into decorative covers for small flowerpots

What Participants Should Prepare
- Used but clean socks

Participation Fee
- $5 per person (including the cost for materials)

※For more details, visit the Clanton Center website or call us at 555-123-4567.

---

① 4월 19일 토요일 오후 1시부터 4시까지 열린다.
② Clanton Center의 커뮤니티 홀에서 진행된다.
③ 참가자는 오후 2시부터 양말로 장난감을 만든다.
④ 참가자는 사용하지 않은 깨끗한 양말을 준비해야 한다.
⑤ 참가비는 재료비를 제외하고 1인당 5달러이다.

구문 서술형
문장에서 틀린 부분을 찾아 바르게 고치시오.

Each person have to pay $5 for participation, with materials included.

➡ _____ → _____

Houseplant Heaven Pop-up Shop에 관한 다음 안내문의 내용과 일치하지 <u>않는</u> 것은?

Houseplant Heaven Pop-up Shop

Enjoy a special plant shopping experience! Explore beautiful houseplants, and bring some green into your home.

When: October 11 - 13, 10 a.m. - 8 p.m.

Where: Tasty Cup Cafe

Details

· Indoor plants are available for purchase.

· If you buy 2 plants, you will get a 50% discount on coffee.

Activities

· Take pictures in a photo zone filled with unique plants.

· Decorate eco-friendly pots made from recycled glass.

※ Outside food and drinks are not allowed.

① 3일간 진행된다.
② 실내 식물이 구매 가능하다.
③ 식물을 2개 사면 커피를 무료로 받을 것이다.
④ 친환경 화분을 장식하는 활동이 있다.
⑤ 외부 음식과 음료는 허용되지 않는다.

구문 서술형

괄호 안의 단어를 알맞은 형태로 쓰시오. (단, 현재시제로 쓸 것)

All of the indoor plants _____ available for purchase. (be)

2025 Summer Cartoon Festival에 관한 다음 안내문의 내용과 일치하는 것은?

2025 Summer Cartoon Festival

It's the 8th annual Summer Cartoon Festival! The festival drew a lot of visitors last year. Why not be one of them this year?

Dates: July 5 - 6

Time: 9 a.m. - 6 p.m.

Place: Merryville Park

Featured Events

· Cartoon drawing classes for beginners only

· Face painting by cartoonists

· Parade of costumed characters

Notes

· All visitors will receive character stickers.

· For a more detailed timetable and other information, check out www.SummerCartoonFest.com.

① 처음으로 개최되는 축제이다.
② 오전 9시부터 오후 7시까지 진행된다.
③ 상급자를 위한 만화 그리기 수업이 있다.
④ 페이스 페인팅 행사가 있다.
⑤ 방문객 중 일부만 캐릭터 스티커를 받을 것이다.

구문 서술형

〈보기〉의 조건에 맞게 주어진 문장을 고쳐 쓰시오.

─── [보기] ───
1) Every를 쓸 것
2) 현재진행시제로 나타낼 것

All visitors will receive character stickers.

➡ _____

J06 ✿✿✿ 고1 2025(9월)/27

Father-Daughter Sock Hop에 관한 다음 안내문의 내용과 일치하지 <u>않는</u> 것은?

Father-Daughter Sock Hop

We are excited to bring you the 5th annual Father-Daughter Sock Hop — an incredibly special evening for fathers and daughters to dance!

When & Where
· September 12th(Friday), from 6 p.m. to 9 p.m.
· Maple Creek Community Center

Participation Fee
· $25 per pair
· $5 per each additional daughter
· No refund for cancellations on the day of the event

Notice
· A pair of socks will be given out as a gift to every participant.
· Take pictures at the photo zone.

Registration
· Register online at www.maplecreekcity.org.

① 9월 12일 금요일에 개최된다.
② 한 쌍당 참가비는 $25이다.
③ 행사 당일 취소 시 환불이 가능하다.
④ 모든 참가자에게 선물이 제공된다.
⑤ 포토존에서 사진을 찍을 수 있다.

구문 서술형

〈보기〉의 조건에 맞게 주어진 문장을 고쳐 쓰시오.

─── [보기] ───
1) Every를 Each of로 바꿔 쓸 것
2) 현재시제로 나타낼 것

Every participant will receive a pair of socks.

➡ _____

J07 ✿✿✿ 고1 2025(9월)/28

2025 Library Bookmark Design Contest에 관한 다음 안내문의 내용과 일치하는 것은?

2025 Library Bookmark Design Contest

The 6th annual Library Bookmark Design Contest is now open! Show your creativity and design skills.

Participation
· Participants need to be between the ages of 5-12.

Guidelines
· Create a bookmark by hand using markers or crayons.
· Designs must fit the slogan "Find Your Voice."
· Do not use commercialized character images in your design.

Submission
· Limit one entry per participant.
· Entries should be submitted via email to contest@srpls.org by October 4th.

Prizes
· 1st place: $50 gift card, 2nd place: $30 gift card
· Winners' bookmarks will be printed and given to visitors.

※ For more information, please visit our website at www.sherrillpubliclibrary.org.

① 여덟 번째 열리는 대회이다.
② 13세 이상이면 누구나 참가할 수 있다.
③ 상업용 캐릭터 이미지를 사용할 수 있다.
④ 출품작은 참가자당 두 개로 제한된다.
⑤ 수상자의 책갈피는 인쇄되어 방문객에게 제공될 것이다.

구문 서술형

어법상 틀린 부분을 찾아 쓰고 알맞게 고치시오.

Either markers or crayon were used to create a bookmark.

➡ _____ → _____

Yummy Paws: Pet Food Cooking Class에 관한 다음 안내문의 내용과 일치하지 <u>않는</u> 것은?

Yummy Paws: Pet Food Cooking Class

Join us for an exciting pet food cooking class where you will learn how to create healthy and delicious pumpkin biscuits for your furry friends!

When: 2:00 p.m.–4:00p.m., Every Sunday, December, 2024

Where: Green Park Community Center, Room 5

Registration
• Register online at www.yummypawsclass.com.
• Limited to 10 participants for each class

Fee
• $30 per participant (Full payment is required when registering.)
• The fee includes all ingredients.

Note
• Additional recipes available for free
• For safety reasons, no pets are allowed.
• For a refund, cancel at least 48 hours before the class.

① 12월에 일요일마다 2시간씩 진행된다.
② 각 수업당 참여 인원이 10명으로 제한된다.
③ 수업료는 등록 시 전액 지불해야 한다.
④ 추가 레시피는 별도로 구매해야 한다.
⑤ 환불을 위해서는 수업 48시간 전까지 취소해야 한다.

[구문 서술형]

빈칸에 공통으로 알맞은 말을 쓰시오. (한 단어로)

• Additional recipes _____ available for free.
• All ingredients _____ included in the fee.

➡ _____

2024 K-Pop Cover Dance Contest에 관한 다음 안내문의 내용과 일치하는 것은?

2024 K-Pop Cover Dance Contest

Good news for K-Pop fans in Canada! It's time for your dance team to show your talents at this contest!

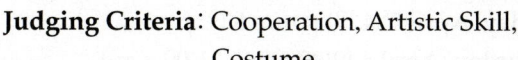

When & Where
• Date: November 29th, 2024
• Time: 7 p.m.–9 p.m.
• Location: So Merry Theatre

Judging Criteria: Cooperation, Artistic Skill, Costume

Prize
• Top 3 teams will receive a $200 gift certificate.
• The winning team will have the chance to visit Korea's top management agencies.

Application
• A cover dance video should not be more than 4 minutes long.
• Submit the video, along with your application, via our website by November 3rd.

For more information, visit www.2024kpopcontest.com.

① 2일 동안 진행된다.
② 심사 기준에 관객 호응이 포함된다.
③ 상위 열 팀은 200달러 상품권을 받을 것이다.
④ 커버 댄스의 영상 길이는 4분이 넘어야 한다.
⑤ 신청서와 함께 영상을 웹사이트를 통해 제출해야 한다.

[구문 서술형]

밑줄 친 부분을 괄호 안의 조건에 맞게 고쳐 쓰시오.

Not only the winning team but also the 2nd and 3rd place teams <u>will receive</u> a $200 gift certificate. (현재시제로)

➡ _____

Spring Tea Class for Young People에 관한 다음 안내문의 내용과 일치하지 <u>않는</u> 것은?

Spring Tea Class for Young People

Join us for a delightful Spring Tea Class for young people, where you'll experience the taste of tea from various cultures around the world.

Class Schedule
• Friday, April 5 (4:30 p.m. – 6:00 p.m.)
• Saturday, April 6 (9:30 a.m. – 11:00 a.m.)

Details
• We will give you tea and snacks.
• We offer special tips for hosting a tea party.

Participation Fee
• Age 13 – 15: $25 per person
• Age 16 – 18: $30 per person

Note
If you have any food allergy, you should email us in advance at youth@seasonteaclass.com.

① 수강생은 전 세계 다양한 문화권의 차를 경험할 수 있다.
② 금요일 수업은 오후에 1시간 30분 동안 진행된다.
③ 수강생에게 차와 간식을 제공할 것이다.
④ 15세 이하의 수강생은 30달러의 참가비를 내야 한다.
⑤ 음식 알레르기가 있는 수강생은 이메일을 미리 보내야 한다.

Clothes Upcycling Contest 2024에 관한 다음 안내문의 내용과 일치하는 것은?

Clothes Upcycling Contest 2024

Are you passionate about fashion and the environment? Then we have a contest for you!

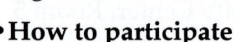

• **Participants**
– Anyone living in Lakewood, aged 11 to 18

• **How to participate**
– Take before and after photos of your upcycled clothes.
– Email the photos at lovelw@lwplus.com.
– Send in the photos from April 14 to May 12.

• **Winning Prize**
– A $100 gift card to use at local shops
– The winner will be announced on our website on May 30.

For more details, visit our website www. lovelwplus.com.

① Lakewood에 사는 사람이면 누구든지 참가할 수 있다.
② 참가자는 출품 사진을 직접 방문하여 제출해야 한다.
③ 참가자는 5월 14일까지 출품 사진을 제출할 수 있다.
④ 우승 상품은 지역 상점에서 쓸 수 있는 기프트 카드이다.
⑤ 지역 신문을 통해 우승자를 발표한다.

Gourmet Baking Competition에 관한 다음
안내문의 내용과 일치하지 <u>않는</u> 것은?

Gourmet Baking Competition

Get out your cookbooks and dust off your greatest baking recipes.

When & Where
- 5 p.m. - 7 p.m. Saturday, August 3rd
- Gourmet Baking Studio

Registration
- Register online at www.bakeoff.org by July 25th.
- Anyone can participate in the competition.

Categories
- Pies, Cakes, and Cookies
- Each person can only enter one category.

Prizes & Gifts
- Prizes will be given to the top three in each category.
- Souvenirs will be given to every participant.

① 8월 3일 토요일에 개최된다.
② 온라인으로 참가 신청이 가능하다.
③ 누구나 참가할 수 있다.
④ 참가자 한 명이 여러 부문에 참여할 수 있다.
⑤ 모든 참가자에게 기념품이 제공될 것이다.

Winter Sports Program에 관한 다음 안내문의
내용과 일치하는 것은?

Winter Sports Program

Winter is coming! Let's have some fun together!

Time & Location
- Every Sunday in December from 1 p.m. to 3 p.m.
- Grand Blue Ice Rink

Lesson Details
- Ice Hockey, Speed Skating, and Figure Skating
- Participants must be 8 years of age or older.

Fee
- Ice Hockey: $200
- Speed Skating / Figure Skating: $150

Notice
- Skates and helmets will be provided for free.
- You should bring your own gloves.
※ For more information, visit www.wintersports.com.

① 오후 2시에서 4시 사이에 실시된다.
② 네 종목의 강좌가 개설된다.
③ 참가 연령에 제한은 없다.
④ 모든 종목 강좌의 수강료는 같다.
⑤ 장갑은 각자 가져와야 한다.

J14 ✿✿✿ ········· 고1 2024(9월)/27

Spring Tea Class for Young People에 관한 다음 안내문의 내용과 일치하지 <u>않는</u> 것은?

2024 Young Inventors Robot Competition

Join us for an exciting day of the Young Inventors Robot Competition!

□ **Categories**
 − Participants can compete in one of the following categories:
 • Robot Design　　• Robot Coding
 • Robot Remote Control

□ **Date and Time**
 − September 28, 2024, 10 a.m. to 3 p.m.

□ **Location**
 − Computer Lab, Oakwood University

□ **Registration**
 − From August 1 to August 10, 2024
 − Open to high school students
 − Online registration only
  (www.younginventors.edu)

□ **Awards**
 − In each competition category, three participants will be honored.
 • 1st place: $300　　• 2nd place: $200
 • 3rd place: $100

※ For more information, visit our website.

① 세 가지 분야 중 하나에 참가할 수 있다.
② 9월 28일에 5시간 동안 열린다.
③ 고등학생이 등록할 수 있다.
④ 등록은 온라인으로만 가능하다.
⑤ 수상자는 각 분야당 한 명이다.

J15 ✿✿✿ ········· 고1 2024(9월)/28

Saintville Art Week Stamp Tour에 관한 다음 안내문의 내용과 일치하는 것은?

Saintville Art Week Stamp Tour

The 8th annual Saintville Art Week Stamp Tour is back this year! Anyone can participate in our event. Join us and enjoy exhibitions and new collections.

□ **When:** The first week of October, 2024

□ **Where:** Saintville Arts District

□ **How:**
 Step 1. Take a stamp tour map from the Saintville Arts Center.
 Step 2. Get stamps from at least 3 out of 5 spots and receive your gift.
 − You can choose either an umbrella or a mug with printed artwork on it for your gift.

※ For more information, please visit our website at www.SaintvilleArtsCenter.com.

① 참가 대상에 제한이 있다.
② 10월 둘째 주에 진행된다.
③ Saintville Arts Center에서 스탬프 투어 지도를 받는다.
④ 적어도 다섯 곳에서 도장을 받아야 선물을 받는다.
⑤ 선물로 가방과 머그잔 중 하나를 고를 수 있다.

J16 ✿❀❀ 고1 2022(9월)/27

2022 Springfield Park Yoga Class에 관한 다음 안내문의 내용과 일치하지 <u>않는</u> 것은?

2022 Springfield Park Yoga Class

The popular yoga class in Springfield Park returns! Enjoy yoga hosted on the park lawn. If you can't make it to the park, join us online on our social media platforms!

- □ **When**: Saturdays, 2 p.m. to 3 p.m., September
- □ **Registration**: At least TWO hours before each class starts, sign up here .
- □ **Notes**
  - For online classes: find a quiet space with enough room for you to stretch out.
  - For classes in the park: mats are not provided, so bring your own!
  ※ The class will be canceled if the weather is unfavorable.
  For more information, click here .

① 온라인으로도 참여할 수 있다.
② 9월 중 토요일마다 진행된다.
③ 수업 시작 2시간 전까지 등록해야 한다.
④ 매트가 제공된다.
⑤ 날씨가 좋지 않으면 취소될 것이다.

J17 ✿❀❀ 고1 2022(6월)/27

Kids Taekwondo Program에 관한 다음 안내문의 내용과 일치하지 <u>않는</u> 것은?

Kids Taekwondo Program

Enjoy our taekwondo program this summer vacation.

- □ **Schedule**
- Dates: August 8th – August 10th
- Time: 9:00 a.m. – 11:00 a.m.
- □ **Participants**
- Any child aged 5 and up
- □ **Activities**
- Self-defense training
- Team building games to develop social skills
- □ **Participation Fee**
- $50 per child (includes snacks)
- □ **Notice**
- What to bring: water bottle, towel
- What not to bring: chewing gum, expensive items

① 8월 8일부터 3일간 운영한다.
② 5세 이상의 어린이가 참가할 수 있다.
③ 자기 방어 훈련 활동을 한다.
④ 참가비에 간식비는 포함되지 않는다.
⑤ 물병과 수건을 가져와야 한다.

J18 ✿✿✿ 고1 2022(11월)/28

Undersea Walking Activity에 관한 다음 안내문의 내용과 일치하는 것은?

Undersea Walking Activity

Enjoy a fascinating underwater walk on the ocean floor. Witness wonderful marine life on foot!

Age Requirement
10 years or older
Operating Hours
from Tuesday to Sunday
9:00 a.m. – 4:00 p.m.
Price
$30 (insurance fee included)
What to Bring
swim suit and towel
Notes
- Experienced lifeguards accompany you throughout the activity.
- With a special underwater helmet, you can wear glasses during the activity.
- Reservations can be made on-site or online at www.seawalkwonder.com.

① 연중무휴로 운영된다.
② 가격에 보험료는 포함되어 있지 않다.
③ 숙련된 안전 요원이 활동 내내 동행한다.
④ 특수 수중 헬멧 착용 시 안경을 쓸 수 없다.
⑤ 현장 예약은 불가능하다.

❖ 정답 및 해설 122 ~ 125p

J19 ✿✿✿   고1 2023(9월)/27

Silversmithing Class에 관한 다음 안내문의 내용과
일치하지 <u>않는</u> 것은?

Silversmithing Class

Kingston Club is offering a fine jewelry making class. Don't miss this great chance to make your own jewelry!

When & Where
· Saturday, October 21, 2023 (2 p.m. to 4 p.m.)
· Kingston Club studio

Registration
· Available only online
· Dates: October 1 – 14, 2023
· Fee: $40 (This includes all tools and materials.)
· Registration is limited to 6 people.

Note
· Participants must be at least 16 years old.
· No refund for cancellation on the day of the class

---

① 두 시간 동안 진행된다.
② 10월 1일부터 등록할 수 있다.
③ 등록 인원은 6명으로 제한된다.
④ 참가 연령에 제한이 없다.
⑤ 수업 당일 취소 시 환불이 불가하다.

J20 ✿✿✿   고1 2022(6월)/28

Moonlight Chocolate Factory Tour에 관한 다음
안내문의 내용과 일치하는 것은?

Moonlight Chocolate Factory Tour

Take this special tour and have a chance to enjoy our most popular chocolate bars.

□ **Operating Hours**
· Monday – Friday,
  2:00 p.m. – 5:00 p.m.

□ **Activities**
· Watching our chocolate-making process
· Tasting 3 types of chocolate (dark, milk, and mint chocolate)

□ **Notice**
· Ticket price: $30
· Wearing a face mask is required.
· Taking pictures is not allowed inside the factory.

---

① 주말 오후 시간에 운영한다.
② 초콜릿 제조 과정을 볼 수 있다.
③ 네 가지 종류의 초콜릿을 시식한다.
④ 마스크 착용은 참여자의 선택 사항이다.
⑤ 공장 내부에서 사진 촬영이 가능하다.

J21 ✿✿✿   고1 2022(3월)/28

Nighttime Palace Tour에 관한 다음 안내문의 내용과
일치하는 것은?

Nighttime Palace Tour

Date: Friday, April 29 – Sunday, May 15

Time

Friday	7 p.m. – 8:30 p.m.
Saturday	6 p.m. – 7:30 p.m.
& Sunday	8 p.m. – 9:30 p.m.

Tickets & Booking
· $15 per person (free for kids under 8)
· Bookings will be accepted up to 2 hours before the tour starts.

Program Activities
· Group tour with a tour guide (1 hour)
· Trying traditional foods and drinks (30 minutes)
※ You can try on traditional clothes with no extra charge.
※ For more information, please visit our website, www.palacenighttour.com.

---

① 금요일에는 하루에 두 번 투어가 운영된다.
② 8세 미만 어린이의 티켓은 5달러이다.
③ 예약은 투어 하루 전까지만 가능하다.
④ 투어 가이드의 안내 없이 궁궐을 둘러본다.
⑤ 추가 비용 없이 전통 의상을 입어 볼 수 있다.

Kenner High School's Water Challenge에 관한
다음 안내문의 내용과 일치하는 것은?

Kenner High School's Water Challenge

   Kenner High School's Water Challenge is a new contest to propose measures against water pollution. Please share your ideas for dealing with water pollution!

Submission
- **How**: Submit your proposal by email to admin@khswater.edu.
- **When**: September 5, 2022 to September 23, 2022

Details
- Participants must enter in teams of four and can only join one team.
- Submission is limited to one proposal per team.
- Participants must use the proposal form provided on the website.

Prizes
- 1st: $50 gift certificate
- 2nd: $30 gift certificate
- 3rd: $10 gift certificate

Please visit www.khswater.edu to learn more about the challenge.

① 제안서는 직접 방문하여 제출해야 한다.
② 9월 23일부터 제안서를 제출할 수 있다.
③ 제안서는 한 팀당 4개까지 제출할 수 있다.
④ 제공된 제안서 양식을 사용해야 한다.
⑤ 2등은 10달러의 상품권을 받는다.

2023 Ocean Awareness Film Contest에 관한
다음 안내문의 내용과 일치하는 것은?

2023 Ocean Awareness Film Contest

   Join our 7th annual film contest and show your knowledge of marine conservation.

□ Theme
- Ocean Wildlife / Ocean Pollution
 (Choose one of the above.)

□ Guidelines
- Participants: High school students
- Submission deadline: September 22, 2023
- The video must be between 10 and 15 minutes.
- All entries must be uploaded to our website.
- Only one entry per person

□ Prizes
- 1st place: $100   • 2nd place: $70
- 3rd place: $50

(Winners will be announced on our website.)
For more information,
please visit www.oceanawareFC.com.

① 세 가지 주제 중 하나를 선택해야 한다.
② 중학생이 참가할 수 있다.
③ 영상은 10분을 넘길 수 없다.
④ 1인당 두 개까지 출품할 수 있다.
⑤ 수상자는 웹사이트에 공지될 것이다.

J24 ✽✽✽ 고1 2023(3월)/27

Call for Articles에 관한 다음 안내문의 내용과
일치하지 <u>않는</u> 것은?

Call for Articles

Do you want to get your stories published?
New Dream Magazine is looking for future
writers! This event is open to anyone aged 13
to 18.

Articles
- Length of writing: 300 – 325 words
- Articles should also include high-quality
  color photos.

Rewards
- Five cents per word
- Five dollars per photo

Notes
- You should send us your phone number
  together with your writing.
- Please email your writing to us at
  article@ndmag.com.

---

① 13세에서 18세까지의 누구나 참여할 수 있다.
② 기사는 고화질 컬러 사진을 포함해야 한다.
③ 사진 한 장에 5센트씩 지급한다.
④ 전화번호를 원고와 함께 보내야 한다.
⑤ 원고를 이메일로 제출해야 한다.

J25 ✽✽✽ 고1 2023(11월)/27

2023 Australian Gateball Championships에
관한 다음 안내문의 내용과 일치하지 <u>않는</u> 것은?

2023 Australian Gateball Championships

The Diamond Coast is getting set to welcome
the Australian Gateball Championships. Join this
great outdoor competition and be
the winner this year!

When & Where
- December 19 — 22, 2023
- Diamond Coast Performance
  Centre

Schedule of Matches
- Doubles matches (9 a.m. — 11 a.m.)
- Team matches (1 p.m. — 3 p.m.)

Prizes
- Every participant will receive a certificate for
  entry.
- Champions are awarded a medal.

Note
- Participation is free.
- Visit www.australiangateball.com for
  registration.
  (Registration on site is not available.)

---

① 4일 동안 진행된다.
② 복식 경기는 오전에 열린다.
③ 모든 참가자는 참가 증서를 받는다.
④ 참가비는 무료이다.
⑤ 현장에서 등록하는 것이 가능하다.

Rachel's Flower Class에 관한 다음 안내문의
내용과 일치하지 <u>않는</u> 것은?

Rachel's Flower Class

Make Your Life More Beautiful!

Class Schedule (Every Monday to Friday)

Flower Arrangement	11 a.m. – 12 p.m.
Flower Box Making	1 p.m. – 2 p.m.

Price
- $50 for each class
  (flowers and other materials included)
- Bring your own scissors and a bag.

Other Info.
- You can sign up for classes either online or by phone.
- No refund for cancellations on the day of your class

To contact, visit www.rfclass.com or call
03 – 221 – 2131.

① 플라워 박스 만들기 수업은 오후 1시에 시작된다.
② 수강료에 꽃값과 다른 재료비가 포함된다.
③ 수강생은 가위와 가방을 가져와야 한다.
④ 수업 등록은 전화로만 할 수 있다.
⑤ 수업 당일 취소 시 환불을 받을 수 없다.

E-Waste Recycling Day에 관한 다음 안내문의
내용과 일치하지 <u>않는</u> 것은?

E-Waste Recycling Day

E-Waste Recycling Day is an annual event in our city. Bring your used electronics such as cell phones, tablets, and laptops to recycle. Go green!

When
Saturday, December 17, 2022
8:00 a.m. – 11:00 a.m.

Where
Lincoln Sports Center

Notes
- Items NOT accepted: light bulbs, batteries, and microwaves
- All personal data on the devices must be wiped out in advance.
- This event is free but open only to local residents.

Please contact us at 986-571-0204 for more information.

① 3시간 동안 진행된다.
② Lincoln 스포츠 센터에서 열린다.
③ 전자레인지는 허용되지 않는 품목이다.
④ 기기 속 모든 개인 정보는 미리 삭제되어야 한다.
⑤ 거주 지역에 상관없이 참가할 수 있다.

Greenhill Roller Skating에 관한 다음 안내문의
내용과 일치하는 것은?

Greenhill Roller Skating

Join us for your chance to enjoy roller skating!
- Place: Greenhill Park, 351 Cypress Avenue
- Dates: Friday, April 7 – Sunday, April 9
- Time: 9 a.m. – 6 p.m.
- Fee: $8 per person for a 50-minute session

Details
- Admission will be on a first-come, first-served basis with no reservations.
- Children under the age of 10 must be accompanied by an adult.
- We will lend you our roller skates for free.

Contact the Community Center for more information at 013-234-6114.

① 오전 9시부터 오후 9시까지 운영한다.
② 이용료는 시간 제한 없이 1인당 8달러이다.
③ 입장하려면 예약이 필요하다.
④ 10세 미만 어린이는 어른과 동행해야 한다.
⑤ 추가 요금을 내면 롤러스케이트를 빌려준다.

J29 ✿✿✿ 고1 2023(6월)/28

Summer Scuba Diving One-day Class에 관한
다음 안내문의 내용과 일치하는 것은?

Summer Scuba Diving One-day Class

Join our summer scuba driving lesson for beginners, and become an underwater explorer!

Schedule
- 10:00 – 12:00 Learning the basics
- 13:00 – 16:00 Practicing diving skills in a pool

Price
- Private lesson: $150
- Group lesson (up to 3 people): $100 per person
- Participants can rent our diving equipment for free.

Notice
- Participants must be 10 years old or over.
- Participants must register at least 5 days before the class begins.

For more information,
please go to www.ssdiver.com.

① 오후 시간에 바다에서 다이빙 기술을 연습한다.
② 그룹 수업의 최대 정원은 4명이다.
③ 다이빙 장비를 유료로 대여할 수 있다.
④ 연령에 관계없이 참가할 수 있다.
⑤ 적어도 수업 시작 5일 전까지 등록해야 한다.

J30 ✿✿✿ 고1 2023(11월)/28

The Amazing Urban Adventure Quest에 관한
다음 안내문의 내용과 일치하는 것은?

The Amazing Urban Adventure Quest

Explore Central Park while solving clues and completing challenges! Guided by your smartphone, make your way among the well-known places in the park.

When & How
- Available 365 days a year (from sunrise to sunset)
- Start when you want.
- Get a stamp at each checkpoint.

Adventure Courses
- East Side: Starts at Twilight Gardens (no age limit)
- West Side: Starts at Strawberry Castle (over 15 years old)

Registration & Cost
- Sign up online at www.urbanquest.com.
- $40 for a team of 2 – 5 people
- Save 20% with discount code: CENTRALQUEST

① 참여하는 동안 스마트폰 사용은 금지된다.
② 일 년 내내 일몰 후 참여할 수 있다.
③ 서편 코스는 나이 제한이 없다.
④ 1인당 40달러의 요금이 든다.
⑤ 할인받을 수 있는 코드가 있다.

J 어휘 Review

✻ 다음 영어는 우리말 뜻을, 우리말은 영어 단어를 〈보기〉에서 찾아 쓰시오.

〈보기〉

제안서	award	환불	awareness
대책	annual	해양의	remote
취소	palace	대회	souvenir

01 refund _____

02 cancellation _____

03 marine _____

04 measure _____

05 proposal _____

06 궁궐 _____

07 연례의 _____

08 상을 주다 _____

09 인식 _____

10 원격의 _____

✻ 다음 우리말에 알맞은 영어 표현을 찾아 연결하시오.

11 복식 경기 •　　　　• doubles match

12 등록하다 •　　　　• gift certificate

13 확인하다 •　　　　• check out

14 상품권 •　　　　• sign up

15 준비하다 •　　　　• get set

✻ 다음 우리말 표현에 맞는 단어를 고르시오.

16 차 모임 주최를 위한 ➡ for (posting / hosting) a tea party

17 초콜릿 제조 과정 견학 ➡ watching our chocolate-making (practice / process)

18 공장 내부에서 ➡ (outside / inside) the factory

19 만약 날씨가 좋지 않으면 ➡ if the weather is (unfamiliar / unfavorable)

20 운영 시간 ➡ (operating / observing) hours

✻ 다음 문장의 빈칸에 알맞은 단어를 〈보기〉에서 찾아 쓰시오.

〈보기〉

scissors	accepted	talent	charge
participants	required	provided	furry
commercialized	insightful	accompanied	category

21 본인의 가위와 가방을 가져오세요.
➡ Bring your own _____ and a bag.

22 10세 미만의 어린이는 어른과 동행해야 합니다.
➡ Children under the age of 10 must be _____ by an adult.

23 여러분의 털북숭이 친구를 위해 비스킷을 만드는 방법을 배우세요!
➡ Learn how to create biscuits for your _____ friends!

24 스케이트와 헬멧이 무료로 제공됩니다.
➡ Skates and helmets will be _____ for free.

25 이 대회에서 여러분의 댄스팀이 재능을 보여줄 때입니다!
➡ It's time for your dance team to show your _____ at this contest!

26 추가 비용 없이 전통 의상을 입어 볼 수 있습니다.
➡ You can try on traditional clothes with no extra _____.

27 예약은 투어 시작 2시간 전까지 가능합니다.
➡ Bookings will be _____ up to 2 hours before the tour starts.

28 상업용 캐릭터 이미지들을 디자인에 사용하지 마세요.
➡ Do not use _____ character images in your design.

29 선착순 10명의 참가자들은 기념품을 받게 될 것입니다.
➡ The first 10 _____ will get souvenirs.

30 마스크 착용은 필수입니다.
➡ Wearing a face mask is _____.

K 어법에 맞지 않는 낱말 찾기

★유형 설명

다음 글의 밑줄 친 부분 중, 어법상 틀린 것은? [3점]

Studies of experts provide insight into ① <u>what</u> it means to have deep and flexible understanding.

다섯 개의 밑줄 친 표현 중 틀린 것을 찾는 유형으로 출제된다.

○━ 중요한 문법 사항들이 반복되어 출제되므로 기출 문제를 바탕으로 자주 출제되는 문법 사항들을 정리해 두어야 한다. 주어와 동사의 수 일치, 병렬, 준동사, 관계사, 형용사, 부사 등이 빈출 항목들이다.

문법이 너무 어려워서 시험을 망쳤어.

어떤 문장이든 제일 먼저 주어와 동사부터 찾아봐!

🎭 유형 풀이 비법

1 주어, 동사를 찾아라!
• 문장의 기본 구성 요소인 주어, 동사를 찾는다.

2 문장 연결사를 확인하라!
• 문장과 문장을 연결하는 관계사, 접속사, 분사구문을 확인한다.

3 문법요소를 확인하라!
• 수 및 시제 일치, 태, 병렬구조 등의 요소들이 올바르게 쓰였는지 확인한다.

(Tip) 밑줄 친 부분의 앞뒤에서 단서를 찾아 정답이 맞는지 확인한다.

🔑 최신 출제 어법

1 계속적 용법의 관계대명사

관계대명사 앞에 콤마(,)를 써서 선행사에 관한 추가 정보를 덧붙인다. 관계대명사 that은 계속적 용법으로 쓸 수 없다.

> That's true, for example, of gazelles, ③ <u>which</u> for thousands of years were the most frequently hunted game species in some parts of the Fertile Crescent.
>
> (고1 2025(9월) 29번)

➡ 콤마와 계속적 용법의 주격 관계대명사 which가 쓰여, 선행사인 gazelles에 대해 '수천 년 동안 ~ 가장 빈번하게 사냥된 사냥감 종이었다'라는 추가 정보를 덧붙이므로 알맞게 쓰였다.

2 대명사의 수 일치

대명사는 앞에서 반복되는 명사를 대신 나타내므로 수가 일치해야 한다. 단수 명사는 one, it, this, that으로, 복수 명사는 ones, they, these, those로 대신할 수 있다.

> Digital technologies are essentially related to metaphors, but digital metaphors are different from linguistic ① <u>ones</u> in important ways.
>
> (고1 2024(10월) 29번)

➡ digital metaphors와 linguistic ones (= metaphors)를 비교하는 내용이므로 ones는 복수 명사인 metaphors를 대신 나타냄을 알 수 있다.

11 형용사와 부사

1 형용사의 한정적 용법과 서술적 용법

1) **한정적 용법** ┌ 명사의 앞이나 뒤에서 그 명사를 수식하는데, **대부분 명사 앞에서 수식한다.**
└ **-body, -one, -thing으로 끝나는 대명사는 뒤에서 수식한다.**

• Gwen played a different song.
　　　　　　　　　　　명사
　　　　　　(Gwen은 **다른** 노래를 연주했다.)

• Show me something different.
　　　　　　　　　대명사
　　　　　　(제게 **다른** 것을 보여주세요.)

2) **서술적 용법: 보어가 되어** 주어나 목적어를 보충 설명한다.

• The place looks different now. (그 장소는 이제 **다르게** 보인다.)
　　　　　　주어를 보충 설명하는 형용사

• That experience made him different from others.
　　　　　　　　　　목적어를 보충 설명하는 형용사

(그 경험이 그를 다른 사람들과 **다르게** 만들었다.)

> *** 빈도부사의 위치**
> 빈도부사는 일반동사의 앞, be동사의 뒤, 조동사의 뒤에 위치한다.
> cf. 부정의 의미를 포함하는 빈도부사
> scarcely, hardly, seldom, rarely

3) 「**the + 형용사**」: 정관사 the와 함께 쓰인 형용사나 분사는 '**~하는 사람들**'이라는 의미로 복수 보통명사를 나타내거나 '**~한 것**'이라는 의미로 추상적인 개념을 나타낸다.

• help the poor (가난한 사람들을 돕다)
　　정관사 the + 형용사 poor(가난한) → 가난한 사람들

• ask for the impossible (불가능한 것을 요구하다)
　　정관사 the + 형용사 impossible(불가능한) → 불가능한 것

2 *부사의 역할

동사 수식	• It snowed heavily last night. (지난밤에 눈이 **세차게** 내렸다.) 　　　　　동사 snowed를 수식함
형용사 수식	• Stuart is heavily dependent on his brother. (Stuart는 그의 형에게 **과하게** 의존한다.) 　　　　형용사 dependent를 수식함
부사 수식	• Leslie always walks very quickly. (Leslie는 언제나 **무척** 빠르게 걷는다.) 　　　　　부사 quickly를 수식함
문장 수식	• Unfortunately, Jack is leaving the company. (**아쉽게도** Jack은 회사를 떠날 것이다.) 　문장 전체를 수식함

Check Test

1 주어진 단어 중에서 어법상 적절한 것을 고르시오.

The development of settlements and agriculture [undoubted / undoubtedly] led to a high increase in population density.

2 괄호 안에 주어진 단어를 빈칸에 알맞은 형태로 바꿔 쓰시오.

It would be _____ to overstate how important meaningful work is to human beings. (hardly)

3 주어진 단어 중에서 어법상 적절한 것을 고르시오.

A mechanistic structure has a [vertical / vertically] hierarchy.

4 주어진 단어 중에서 어법상 적절한 것을 고르시오.

Preschoolers believe what their parents tell them in a very [profound / profoundly] way.

• 정답
1 undoubtedly 2 hard 3 vertical 4 profound

K 어법에 맞지 않는 낱말 찾기 (첫 번째)

1st 선택지를 보고, 어떤 어법 개념을 적용해서 풀어야 하는지 연결해 보세요.
2nd 끊어 읽기로 문장의 주어와 동사를 파악하고, 정답을 골라보세요.
3rd 정답이 아닌 선택지 중에서 어려웠던 선택지는 다시 한번 확인하세요.

K01 ★★※ .... 고1 2025(3월)/29

다음 글의 밑줄 친 부분 중, 어법상 틀린 것은?

Routines enable athletes to evaluate competition conditions. For example, bouncing a ball in a volleyball service routine ① supplies the server with information about the ball, the floor, and the state of her⁵ muscles. This information can then be used to ② properly prepare for her serve. Routines also enable athletes to adjust and fine-tune their preparations ③ based on those evaluations or in pursuit of a particular¹⁰ competitive goal. This adaptation can involve adjustment to the conditions, rivals, competitive situation, or internal influences ④ what can affect performance. Just like adjusting a race-car engine to the conditions¹⁵ of the track, air temperature, and weather, routines adjust all competitive components ⑤ to achieve proper performance.

* component: 구성 요소

1st 선택지를 보고, 어떤 어법 개념을 적용해서 풀어야 하는지 연결해 보세요.

① supplies •   • to부정사
② properly •   • 부사
③ based •   • 관계대명사
④ what •   • 분사구문
⑤ to achieve •   • 주어와 동사의 수 일치

2nd 끊어 읽기로 문장의 주어와 동사를 파악하고, 정답을 골라보세요.

1) 동사 supplies의 주어를 찾아야 해요.

> 동명사구 (단수 주어)
> For example, / bouncing a ball in a volleyball
> 예를 들어   / 배구 서브 루틴에서 공을 튕기는 것은
>
> 단수 동사
> service routine / ① supplies the server / with
>   / 서브를 하는 선수에게 제공한다 /
> information about the ball, the floor, and the state
> 공, 바닥, 그리고 자신의 근육 상태에 대한 정보를 //
> of her muscles. //

● **supplies는 어떤 주어와 함께 쓰여야 하나요?**
supplies의 원형은 ❶ (   )이고, supplies는 단수 주어와 함께 쓰이는 단수 동사예요.

● **문장의 핵심 주어는 bouncing이에요.**
동명사 bouncing 뒤에 여러 단어가 이어져 동명사구가 길어지더라도, 결국 핵심 주어는 동명사이기 때문에 단수로 취급해요. 따라서 단수 주어인 동명사 bouncing이 단수 동사 supplies와 함께 알맞게 쓰였어요.

2) properly가 무엇을 수식하는지를 찾아봅시다.

> prepare를 수식하기 위해 to와 동사원형 사이에 삽입된 부사
> This information / can then be used / to ② properly
> 이 정보는   / 그다음 사용될 수 있다 / 자신의 서브를
>
> 부사적 용법 (목적)
> prepare for her serve. //
> 적절히 준비하기 위해   //

● **먼저 properly의 앞뒤 단어를 살펴봐야 해요.**
properly의 앞에는 to, 뒤에는 동사원형 prepare가 있어요.
properly를 제외하고 보면 to prepare라는 to부정사를 이루고 있네요.

● 부사의 역할을 다시 한번 떠올려 볼까요?

부사는 동사, 형용사, 다른 부사, 또는 문장 전체를 수식할 수 있어요.
이때 동사에는 to부정사, 동명사처럼 준동사도 포함되기 때문에 부사
properly는 to부정사인 to prepare를 수식할 수 있어요. 서브를 그냥
준비하는 것이 아니라 **❷(　　　　　)** 준비한다는 의미를 더해요.
따라서 to prepare를 수식하는 부사 properly는 알맞게 쓰였어요.

3) based는 동사일까요, 아니면 분사일까요?

　　　　　　　문장의 본동사 enable의 목적어　　enable의 목적격 보어
Routines also enable athletes / to adjust and fine-
루틴은 또한 선수가 ~할 수 있게 해 준다　　　 / 준비 상태를 조절하고

　　　　　　　　　　　　　　　분사구문을 이끄는 과거분사
tune their preparations / ③ based on those
미세하게 조정하는　　　　 / 그러한 평가에 기반하거나

등위접속사　　　　　　전치사구
evaluations / or in pursuit of a particular
　　　　 / 또는 특정 경쟁 목표를 추구하여 //

competitive goal. //

● 문장의 본동사는 무엇인가요?

이 문장의 동사로 보이는 단어는 enable(~할 수 있게 하다), 그리고 밑줄
친 based(base on: ~에 근거를 두다) 이렇게 두 개가 있어요.
based가 문장의 본동사로서 enable과 병렬 구조를 이루려면
등위접속사가 이 둘을 이어주거나 콤마(,)로 연결되어야 해요. 그런데
enable의 목적격 보어 뒤에 based가 바로 이어지고 있죠. 즉,
based는 문장의 본동사가 아니에요.

● based는 문장에서 어떤 역할을 하나요?

based는 on과 함께 쓰여 '~에 기반하여'라는 뜻을 나타내요. 여기서는
to adjust and fine-tune을 수식하는 부사의 역할을 하며 '그러한
평가에 기반하여' 준비 상태를 조절하고 미세하게 조정한다는 의미를
완성해요. 따라서 분사구문을 이끄는 과거분사 based는 알맞게 쓰였어요.

4) what 앞에 선행사가 있나요?

　　　　　　　　　　　　　　　　　　　　　　　 선행사
This adaptation can involve / adjustment to the
이러한 적응은 포함할 수 있다　　　 / 조건, 경쟁 상대, 경기 상황,

conditions, rivals, competitive situation, or internal
또는 내적 영향에 대한 조정을

　　　　앞에 선행사가 있음
influences / ④ ~~what~~ can affect performance. //
　　　　 / 수행에 영향을 미칠 수 있는　　　　 //

● 관계대명사 what 앞에는 선행사가 올 수 없어요.

그런데 이 문장에는 what 앞에 주격 관계대명사절의 수식을 받을 만한
선행사인 the conditions, rivals, competitive situation, or internal
influences가 있어요.
따라서 앞에 선행사가 오지 않는 what을 제외한 다른 주격 관계대명사인
that이나 which가 와야 해요.

5) to achieve가 어떤 용법의 to부정사로 쓰였나요?

전치사구: 제외하고 생각하기
Just like adjusting a race-car engine / to the
경주용 자동차 엔진을 조정하는 것과 마찬가지로　　 / 트랙, 기온,

conditions of the track, air temperature, and
그리고 날씨의 조건에 맞게　　　 3형식 문장

weather, / [routines adjust all competitive
　　 / 루틴은 경기의 모든 구성 요소를 조정한다
　　　　　　부사적 용법 (목적)
components] / ⑤ to achieve proper performance. //
　　　　 / 적절한 수행을 해내기 위해　　　　　 //

● to achieve 앞에 완전한 문장이 있어요.

to achieve 앞 문장은 주어(routines), 동사(adjust), 목적어(all
competitive components)를 갖춘 완전한 3형식 문장이에요. 즉, to
achieve가 명사적 용법으로 쓰이진 않았네요.
그렇다면 형용사적 용법이나 부사적 용법으로 쓰였을 텐데, 각각의
경우를 살펴봅시다.

● components를 수식하나요, adjust를 수식하나요?

형용사적 용법이라면 앞의 명사인 components를 수식해야 하는데,
'적절한 수행을 해낼 구성 요소'라는 해석은 어색해요.
동사 adjust를 수식하는 부사적 용법이라면 '적절한 수행을 해내기 위해
~ 조정한다'라는 자연스러운 해석이 가능하니까 to achieve는 부사적
용법의 to부정사로 알맞게 쓰였어요.

3rd 정답이 아닌 선택지 중에서 어려웠던 선택지는 다시 한번
확인하세요.

　　　　　　　문장의 본동사 enable의 목적어　　enable의 목적격 보어
Routines also enable athletes / to adjust and fine-
루틴은 또한 선수가 ~할 수 있게 해 준다　 / 준비 상태를 조절하고

　　　　　　　　　　　　　　　분사구문을 이끄는 과거분사
tune their preparations / ③ based on those
미세하게 조정하는　　　　 / 그러한 평가에 기반하거나

등위접속사　　　　　　전치사구
evaluations / or in pursuit of a particular
　　　　 / 또는 특정 경쟁 목표를 추구하여 //

competitive goal. //

이 문장의 본동사는 enable이고 ③ based는 on과 함께 쓰여 '~에
기반하여'라는 뜻의 분사구문을 이루고 있어요. 즉, 이 분사구문과 in pursuit
~ goal이라는 **❸(　　　　　)**가 등위접속사 or로 연결되어 to adjust
and fine-tune을 수식하죠.

K 어법에 맞지 않는 낱말 찾기 두 번째

1st 선택지를 보고, 어떤 어법 개념을 적용해서 풀어야 하는지 연결해 보세요.

2nd 끊어 읽기로 문장의 주어와 동사를 파악하고, 정답을 골라보세요.

3rd 정답이 아닌 선택지 중에서 어려웠던 선택지는 다시 한번 확인하세요.

K02 ★★★ .... 고1 2022(6월)/29

다음 글의 밑줄 친 부분 중, 어법상 틀린 것은?

Despite all the high-tech devices that seem to deny the need for paper, paper use in the United States ① has nearly doubled recently. We now consume more paper than ever: 400 million tons globally and growing. Paper is ₅ not the only resource ② that we are using more of. Technological advances often come with the promise of ③ using fewer materials. However, the reality is that they have historically caused more materials use, ₁₀ making us ④ dependently on more natural resources. The world now consumes far more "stuff" than it ever has. We use twenty-seven times more industrial minerals, such as gold, copper, and rare metals, than we ⑤ did ₁₅ just over a century ago. We also each individually use more resources. Much of that is due to our high-tech lifestyle.

* copper: 구리

1st 선택지를 보고, 어떤 어법 개념을 적용해서 풀어야 하는지 직접 써보세요.

① has   •   • 대동사
② that   •   • 부사
③ using   •   • 동명사
④ dependently •   • 관계대명사
⑤ did   •   • 주어와 동사의 수 일치

2nd 끊어 읽기로 문장의 주어와 동사를 파악하고, 정답을 골라보세요.

1) 동사 has에 밑줄이 있으니 문장의 주어를 찾아 확인합시다.

전치사구
(Despite all the high-tech devices / that seem to
모든 첨단 기기들에도 불구하고   / 종이의 필요성을 부정하는

단수 주어
deny the need for paper), / paper use in the United
것처럼 보이는   / 미국에서 종이 사용은

단수 동사
States / ① has nearly doubled recently. //
/ 최근 거의 두 배로 증가했다   //

● **수많은 명사 중에 어떤 것이 주어일까요?**
전치사 in이 이끄는 장소의 부사구 in the United States를 제외하고 생각해 보면 문장의 주어는 ❶( ) 예요. 주어가 단수니까 동사 역시 단수 동사 ① has doubled가 적절하게 쓰였어요.
전치사 Despite가 이끄는 부사구는 문장 전체를 수식하는데, Despite의 목적어로 쓰인 명사구 all the high-tech devices를 주격 관계대명사 ❷( ) 이 이끄는 형용사절이 수식하고 있어요.

참고 수동태나 완료형, 진행형 동사에서 시제나 수는 be동사, have동사가 나타내고, 실제 동작은 분사가 나타내요.

2) that은 접속사일 수도 있고 관계사일 수도 있어요.

선행사   목적격 관계대명사
Paper is not the only resource / [② that we are using
종이만이 유일한 자원이 아니다   / 우리가 더 많이 사용하고 있는 //

more of]. //
목적어가 없는 불완전한 절

● **that 뒤에 오는 문장을 살펴볼까요?**
② that이 접속사나 관계부사로 쓰였다면 that 뒤에 완전한 문장이 올 거고, 관계대명사로 쓰였다면 불완전한 문장이 올 거예요.
이 문장에서는 that 뒤에 전치사 of의 목적어가 빠진 불완전한 문장이 왔네요! 그러니까 ② that은 접속사나 관계부사가 아니라 관계대명사예요. 사물인 the only resource를 선행사로 하고, 관계대명사절에서 목적어 역할을 하는 ❸(주격 / 목적격) 관계대명사로 that이 쓰인 거예요.

3) using이 전치사 of 뒤에 왔어요.

> Technological advances often come / with the
> 기술의 발전은 흔히 온다 　　　　　　　　 / 더 적은 재료의
>
> 　　전치사　　전치사의 목적어(동명사구)
> promise of ③ using fewer materials. //
> 사용 가능성과 함께 　　　　　　　　　　 //

● **동사가 전치사의 목적어로 쓰이려면 동명사로 바뀌어야 해요.**

따라서 전치사 of의 목적어로 동사 use의 동명사인 ③ using이 적절하게 쓰였어요.

using의 목적어로 쓰인 materials를 수식하는 형용사 fewer는 few의 비교급이에요. few는 부정확한 수를 나타내는 부정 수량형용사로서, '적은, 소수의'라는 뜻으로 셀 수 ❹ (있는 / 없는) 명사 앞에 쓰여요.
이 문장에서는 비교급인 fewer가 쓰였으니 '더 적은 재료의 사용 가능성'이라고 해석해요.

4) dependently가 수식하는 대상이 있나요?

> However, / the reality is / that they have historically
> 그러나 　　 / 현실은 ~이다 　 / 그것들이 역사적으로 더 많은 재료
>
> 　　　　　　　　　　 분사구문　 목적어
> caused more materials use, / (making us ④ ~~dependently~~
> 사용을 야기하여 　　　　　　 / 우리가 더 많은 　　　　 [목적격 보어 자리이므로 부사가 올 수 없음]
>
> on more natural resources). //
> 천연자원에 의존하게 한다는 것 //

● **선택지가 포함된 분사구문만 살펴봅시다.**

목적어인 ❺ (　　　　)가 천연자원에 더 많이 의존하게 만든다는 의미로, 「사역동사 make + 목적어 us + 목적격 보어 dependently」로 이루어진 5형식 문장의 부사절을 분사구문으로 바꾼 거예요.
그런데 보어로는 명사나 형용사, 또는 그 상당어구만 쓰일 수 있어요.
④ dependently는 부사이니까 목적격 보어가 될 수 없죠! 부사 ④ dependently를 형용사 dependent로 바꿔야 어법에 맞아요.

5) did는 본동사와 조동사 중 어느 것으로 쓰였나요?

> 　　　　　　　　　　　　　　　　 비교급 비교
> We use twenty-seven times more industrial minerals,
> 우리는 27배 더 많은 산업 광물을 사용한다
>
> / such as gold, copper, and rare metals, / than we
> / 금, 구리, 희귀 금속과 같은 　　　　　　　　 / 우리가 1세기
>
> use를 대신하는 대동사　 과거의 일과 비교함
> ⑤ did just over a century ago. //
> 이전에 그랬던 것보다 //

● **비교급 비교 구문인 more ~ than ...이 쓰인 문장이에요.**

우리는 우리가 1세기 이전에 산업 광물을 사용했던 것보다 27배 더 많은 산업 광물을 사용한다는 의미로, than이 이끄는 절의 동사로 앞에 나온 use industrial minerals를 반복해서 쓰는 대신 조동사 do를 대동사로 이용해 간략하게 나타낸 거죠.
그런데 왜 do가 아니라 did가 쓰였을까요?
현재와 과거를 비교하는 문장으로, '1세기 이전에 산업 광물을 사용했던 것'이니까 ❻ (과거 / 현재) 시제인 did가 쓰인 거예요.

3rd 정답이 아닌 선택지 중에서 어려웠던 선택지는 다시 한번 확인하세요.

> 　　　　　　　　　　　　　　　　 비교급 비교
> We use twenty-seven times more industrial minerals,
> 우리는 27배 더 많은 산업 광물을 사용한다
>
> / such as gold, copper, and rare metals, / than we
> / 금, 구리, 희귀 금속과 같은 　　　　　　　　 / 우리가 1세기
>
> use를 대신하는 대동사　 과거의 일과 비교함
> ⑤ did just over a century ago. //
> 이전에 그랬던 것보다 //

⑤ did가 대신하는 동사가 일반동사인 ❼ (　　　　)인데, 시제에 맞게 do동사의 과거형인 did가 대동사로 왔어요.
만약 대동사가 쓰이지 않았다면 이 문장은 We use twenty-seven times more industrial minerals, such as gold, copper, and rare metals, than we used industrial minerals such as gold, copper, and rare metals, just over a century ago.로 아주 길었겠죠?

수능 Tip

#대동사

앞에 나온 동사(구)의 반복을 피하기 위해 대동사를 쓰는데, 일반동사는 do동사로, be동사는 be동사로, 완료 시제 동사는 have 동사로 대신해요. 대동사도 주어에 수를 일치시켜야 한다는 것을 잊으면 안 돼요!

다음 문제를 풀어볼까요?

1) Amy has not finished writing her biology essay yet. However, she'll ❽ (be / do) it tomorrow.
(Amy는 아직 생물학 과제 쓰는 것을 끝내지 못했다. 하지만 그녀는 내일 그것을 끝낼 것이다.)

2) The air is much dirtier than it ❾ (was / were) in the past. (공기는 과거에 그랬던 것보다 훨씬 더 더럽다.)

1st 정답 　　　　 ⑤ 대동사 　 ④ 부사 　 ③ 동명사
① 주어와 동사의 수일치 ② 관계대명사

빈칸 정답 ❻ 과거 ❼ use ❽ do ❾ was
❶ paper use ❷ that ❸ 목적격 ❹ 있는 ❺ us

K03～06 ▶ 제한시간 8분

K03 ★★★
고1 2025(6월)/29

다음 글의 밑줄 친 부분 중, 어법상 틀린 것은? [3점]

Studies of experts provide insight into ① what it means to have deep and flexible understanding. Experts in a particular domain are people who have deep, richly interconnected ideas about the world. They are not just good thinkers or people who are ② exceptionally smart. Rather, experts ③ having knowledge in a specific domain — such as chess, chemistry, or tennis — and are not generalists. However, experts do not just know "a bunch of facts." In fact, having expertise in a topic means ④ that knowledge is organized into coherent frameworks, and the expert understands the inter-relationship between facts and can distinguish which ideas are most central. This kind of deep but organized understanding allows for greater flexibility in learning and ⑤ facilitates application across multiple contexts.

*coherent: 일관성 있는

구문 서술형

괄호 안의 단어를 빈칸에 알맞게 바꿔 쓰고, 그것이 수식하는 단어를 찾아 쓰시오.

Experts are people who have _____ interconnected ideas about the world. (rich)

➡ 수식하는 단어: _____

K04 ★★★
고1 2025(9월)/29

다음 글의 밑줄 친 부분 중, 어법상 틀린 것은? [3점]

Big mammalian herbivore species react to danger from predators or humans in different ways. Some species are nervous, fast, and programmed for instant flight when they perceive a threat. Other species are slower, less nervous, seek protection in herds, ① stand their ground when threatened, and don't run until necessary. Naturally, the nervous species are difficult to keep in captivity. If ② putting into an enclosure, they are likely to panic, and either die of shock or hit themselves repeatedly to death against the fence in their attempts to escape. That's true, for example, of gazelles, ③ which for thousands of years were the most frequently hunted game species in some parts of the Fertile Crescent. There is no mammal species that the first settled peoples of that area had more opportunity ④ to domesticate than gazelles. But no gazelle species has ever been domesticated. Just imagine trying to herd an animal that runs away, blindly hits ⑤ itself against walls, can leap up to nearly 30 feet, and can run at a speed of 50 miles per hour!

*herbivore: 초식동물 **herd: 무리

구문 서술형

위 지문에서 문장 전체를 수식하는 부사를 찾아 그 뜻을 함께 쓰시오.

➡ _____, 뜻: _____

K05 ✽✽✽✽ 고1 2024(10월)/29

다음 글의 밑줄 친 부분 중, 어법상 틀린 것은?

Digital technologies are essentially related to metaphors, but digital metaphors are different from linguistic ① <u>ones</u> in important ways. Linguistic metaphors are passive, in the sense that the audience needs to choose to actively enter the world proposed by metaphor. In the Shakespearean metaphor "time is a beggar," the audience is unlikely to understand the metaphor without cognitive effort and without further ② <u>engaging</u> Shakespeare's prose. Technological metaphors, on the other hand, are active (and often imposing) in the sense that they are realized in digital artifacts that are actively doing things, forcefully ③ <u>changing</u> a user's meaning horizon. Technological creators cannot generally afford to require their potential audience to wonder how the metaphor works; normally the selling point is ④ <u>what</u> the usefulness of the technology is obvious at first glance. Shakespeare, on the other hand, is beloved in part because the meaning of his works is not immediately obvious and ⑤ <u>requires</u> some thought on the part of the audience.

(구문 서술형)

밑줄 친 각 형용사의 용법을 쓰시오.

> (1) Digital metaphors are different from linguistic ones in <u>important</u> ways.
> (2) The usefulness of the technology is <u>obvious</u> at first glance.

➡ (1) _____ 용법, (2) _____ 용법

K06 ✽✽✽✽ 고1 2024(3월)/29

다음 글의 밑줄 친 부분 중, 어법상 틀린 것은? [3점]

It would be hard to overstate how important meaningful work is to human beings — work ① <u>that</u> provides a sense of fulfillment and empowerment. Those who have found deeper meaning in their careers find their days much more energizing and satisfying, and ② <u>to count</u> their employment as one of their greatest sources of joy and pride. Sonya Lyubomirsky, professor of psychology at the University of California, has conducted numerous workplace studies ③ <u>showing</u> that when people are more fulfilled on the job, they not only produce higher quality work and a greater output, but also generally earn higher incomes. Those most satisfied with their work ④ <u>are</u> also much more likely to be happier with their lives overall. For her book *Happiness at Work*, researcher Jessica Pryce-Jones conducted a study of 3,000 workers in seventy-nine countries, ⑤ <u>finding</u> that those who took greater satisfaction from their work were 150 percent more likely to have a happier life overall.

*numerous: 수많은

K07 ★★★❀ 고1 2024(6월)/29

다음 글의 밑줄 친 부분 중, 어법상 틀린 것은? [3점]

The hunter-gatherer lifestyle, which can ① be described as "natural" to human beings, appears to have had much to recommend it. Examination of human remains from early hunter-gatherer societies ② has suggested that our ancestors enjoyed abundant food, obtainable without excessive effort, and suffered very few diseases. If this is true, it is not clear why so many humans settled in permanent villages and developed agriculture, growing crops and domesticating animals: cultivating fields was hard work, and it was in farming villages ③ what epidemic diseases first took root. Whatever its immediate effect on the lives of humans, the development of settlements and agriculture ④ undoubtedly led to a high increase in population density. This period, known as the New Stone Age, was a major turning point in human development, ⑤ opening the way to the growth of the first towns and cities, and eventually leading to settled "civilizations."

*remains: 유적, 유해 **epidemic: 전염병의

K08 ★★★ 고1 2024(9월)/29

다음 글의 밑줄 친 부분 중, 어법상 틀린 것은?

From an organizational viewpoint, one of the most fascinating examples of how any organization may contain many different types of culture ① is to recognize the functional operations of different departments within the organization. The varying departments and divisions within an organization will inevitably view any given situation from their own biased and prejudiced perspective. A department and its members will acquire "tunnel vision" which disallows them to see things as others see ② them. The very structure of organizations can create conflict. The choice of ③ whether the structure is "mechanistic" or "organic" can have a profound influence on conflict management. A mechanistic structure has a vertical hierarchy with many rules, many procedures, and many levels of management ④ involved in decision making. Organic structures are more horizontal in nature, ⑤ which decision making is less centralized and spread across the plane of the organization.

*hierarchy: 위계

K09 ★★★ 고1 2022(3월)/29

다음 글의 밑줄 친 부분 중, 어법상 틀린 것은?

We usually get along best with people who we think are like us. In fact, we seek them out. It's why places like Little Italy, Chinatown, and Koreatown ① exist. But I'm not just talking about race, skin color, or religion. I'm talking about people who share our values and look at the world the same way we ② do. As the saying goes, birds of a feather flock together. This is a very common human tendency ③ what is rooted in how our species developed. Imagine you are walking out in a forest. You would be conditioned to avoid something unfamiliar or foreign because there is a high likelihood that ④ it would be interested in killing you. Similarities make us ⑤ relate better to other people because we think they'll understand us on a deeper level than other people.

* species: 종(생물 분류의 기초 단위)

K10 ★★★ 고1 2023(6월)/29

다음 글의 밑줄 친 부분 중, 어법상 틀린 것은? [3점]

Although praise is one of the most powerful tools available for improving young children's behavior, it is equally powerful for improving your child's self-esteem. Preschoolers believe what their parents tell ① them in a very profound way. They do not yet have the cognitive sophistication to reason ② analytically and reject false information. If a preschool boy consistently hears from his mother ③ that he is smart and a good helper, he is likely to incorporate that information into his self-image. Thinking of himself as a boy who is smart and knows how to do things ④ being likely to make him endure longer in problem-solving efforts and increase his confidence in trying new and difficult tasks. Similarly, thinking of himself as the kind of boy who is a good helper will make him more likely to volunteer ⑤ to help with tasks at home and at preschool.

*profound: 뜻 깊은 **sophistication: 정교화(함)

K11 ★★☆ 고1 2023(3월)/29

다음 글의 밑줄 친 부분 중, 어법상 **틀린** 것은? [3점]

The most noticeable human characteristic projected onto animals is ① <u>that</u> they can talk in human language. Physically, animal cartoon characters and toys ② <u>made</u> after animals are also most often deformed in such a way as to resemble humans. This is achieved by ③ <u>showing</u> them with humanlike facial features and deformed front legs to resemble human hands. In more recent animated movies the trend has been to show the animals in a more "natural" way. However, they still use their front legs ④ <u>like</u> human hands (for example, lions can pick up and lift small objects with one paw), and they still talk with an appropriate facial expression. A general strategy that is used to make the animal characters more emotionally appealing, both to children and adults, ⑤ <u>are</u> to give them enlarged and deformed childlike features.

*deform: 변형하다 **paw: (동물의) 발

1등급 대비 문제

K12~14 ▶ 제한시간 6분

K12 ⭐ 2등급 대비 고1 2023(11월)/29

다음 글의 밑줄 친 부분 중, 어법상 **틀린** 것은? [3점]

Some countries have proposed tougher guidelines for determining brain death when transplantation — transferring organs to others — is under consideration. In several European countries, there are legal requirements which specify ① <u>that</u> a whole team of doctors must agree over the diagnosis of death in the case of a potential donor. The reason for these strict regulations for diagnosing brain death in potential organ donors ② <u>is</u>, no doubt, to ease public fears of a premature diagnosis of brain death for the purpose of obtaining organs. But it is questionable whether these requirements reduce public suspicions as much as they create ③ <u>them</u>. They certainly maintain mistaken beliefs that diagnosing brain death is an unreliable process ④ <u>lack</u> precision. As a matter of consistency, at least, criteria for diagnosing the deaths of organ donors should be exactly the same as for those for ⑤ <u>whom</u> immediate burial or cremation is intended.

*diagnosis: 진단 **donor: 기증자 ***cremation: 화장(火葬)

K13 ⭐ 2등급 대비 고1 2022(11월)/29

다음 글의 밑줄 친 부분 중, 어법상 **틀린** 것은? [3점]

You may have seen headlines in the news about some of the things machines powered by artificial intelligence can do. However, if you were to consider all the tasks ① <u>that</u> AI-powered machines could actually perform, it would be quite mind-blowing! One of the key features of artificial intelligence ② <u>is</u> that it enables machines to learn new things, rather than requiring programming specific to new tasks. Therefore, the core difference between computers of the future and ③ <u>those</u> of the past is that future computers will be able to learn and self-improve. In the near future, smart virtual assistants will know more about you than your closest friends and family members ④ <u>are</u>. Can you imagine how that might change our lives? These kinds of changes are exactly why it is so important ⑤ <u>to</u> recognize the implications that new technologies will have for our world.

K14 ⭐ 2등급 대비 고1 2022(9월)/29

다음 글의 밑줄 친 부분 중, 어법상 **틀린** 것은? [3점]

The human brain, it turns out, has shrunk in mass by about 10 percent since it ① <u>peaked</u> in size 15,000–30,000 years ago. One possible reason is that many thousands of years ago humans lived in a world of dangerous predators ② <u>where</u> they had to have their wits about them at all times to avoid being killed. Today, we have effectively domesticated ourselves and many of the tasks of survival — from avoiding immediate death to building shelters to obtaining food — ③ <u>has</u> been outsourced to the wider society. We are smaller than our ancestors too, and it is a characteristic of domestic animals ④ <u>that</u> they are generally smaller than their wild cousins. None of this may mean we are dumber — brain size is not necessarily an indicator of human intelligence — but it may mean that our brains today are wired up differently, and perhaps more efficiently, than ⑤ <u>those</u> of our ancestors.

K15 ⭐1등급 대비 _____ 고1 2023(9월)/29

다음 글의 밑줄 친 부분 중, 어법상 **틀린** 것은?

There is a reason the title "Monday Morning Quarterback" exists. Just read the comments on social media from fans discussing the weekend's games, and you quickly see how many people believe they could play, coach, and manage sport teams more ① <u>successfully</u> than those on the field. This goes for the boardroom as well. Students and professionals with years of training and specialized degrees in sport business may also find themselves ② <u>being given</u> advice on how to do their jobs from friends, family, or even total strangers without any expertise. Executives in sport management ③ <u>have</u> decades of knowledge and experience in their respective fields. However, many of them face criticism from fans and community members telling ④ <u>themselves</u> how to run their business. Very few people tell their doctor how to perform surgery or their accountant how to prepare their taxes, but many people provide feedback on ⑤ <u>how</u> sport organizations should be managed.

*boardroom: 이사회실

K16 ⭐1등급 대비 _____ 고1 2021(11월)/29

다음 글의 밑줄 친 부분 중, 어법상 **틀린** 것은? [3점]

The reduction of minerals in our food is the result of using pesticides and fertilizers ① <u>that</u> kill off beneficial bacteria, earthworms, and bugs in the soil that create many of the essential nutrients in the first place and prevent the uptake of nutrients into the plant. Fertilizing crops with nitrogen and potassium ② <u>has</u> led to declines in magnesium, zinc, iron and iodine. For example, there has been on average about a 30% decline in the magnesium content of wheat. This is partly due to potassium ③ <u>being</u> a blocker against magnesium absorption by plants. Lower magnesium levels in soil also ④ <u>occurring</u> with acidic soils and around 70% of the farmland on earth is now acidic. Thus, the overall characteristics of soil determine the accumulation of minerals in plants. Indeed, nowadays our soil is less healthy and so are the plants ⑤ <u>grown</u> on it.

*pesticide: 살충제

K 어휘 Review

❋ 다음 영어는 우리말 뜻을, 우리말은 영어 단어를 〈보기〉에서 찾아 쓰시오.

〈보기〉

비난	likelihood	10년	conditioned
경향	unfamiliar	전문 지식	domesticate
기능상의	enthusiasm	수직의	deny

01 decade _____

02 criticism _____

03 functional _____

04 tendency _____

05 expertise _____

06 조건부의 _____

07 길들이다 _____

08 부정하다 _____

09 친숙하지 않은 _____

10 가능성 _____

❋ 다음 우리말에 알맞은 영어 표현을 찾아 연결하시오.

11 ~을 추구하여 • • take root

12 틀림없는 • • no doubt

13 첫눈에 • • in pursuit of

14 뿌리를 내리다 • • at first glance

15 ~와 잘 지내다 • • get along with

❋ 다음 우리말 표현에 맞는 단어를 고르시오.

16 정착된 문명 ➡ settled (circulation / civilization)

17 대중의 의심을 줄이다 ➡ reduce public (suspicions / suppression)

18 이러한 엄격한 규정들 ➡ these strict (regulations / revelations)

19 컴퓨터들 간의 핵심적인 차이점 ➡ the (core / shore) difference between computers

20 과도한 노력 없이 구할 수 있는 ➡ (observable / obtainable) without excessive effort

❋ 다음 문장의 빈칸에 알맞은 단어를 〈보기〉에서 찾아 쓰시오.

〈보기〉

permanent	praise	reason	acquire
generally	enclosure	executives	virtual
fulfillment	mature	varying	density

21 이 일은 성취감을 제공한다.
➡ This work provides a sense of _____.

22 많은 인류가 영구적인 마을에 정착했다.
➡ Many humans settled in _____ villages.

23 그들은 일반적으로 더 높은 수입을 거둔다.
➡ They _____ earn higher incomes.

24 칭찬은 가장 강력한 도구 중 하나이다.
➡ _____ is one of the most powerful tools.

25 만약 우리 안에 넣어지면, 그들은 패닉에 빠질 것이다.
➡ If put into a(n) _____, they are likely to panic.

26 스마트 가상 비서는 여러분에 대해 여러분의 가장 가까운 친구가 아는 것보다 더 많이 알게 될 것이다.
➡ Smart _____ assistants will know more about you than your closest friends do.

27 다양한 부서들은 어떤 주어진 상황이라도 볼 것이다.
➡ The _____ departments will inevitably view any given situation.

28 그들은 분석적으로 추론하는 인지적 정교함을 가지고 있지 않다.
➡ They do not have the cognitive sophistication to _____ analytically.

29 스포츠 경영 임원진들은 수십 년의 지식과 경험을 가지고 있다.
➡ _____ in sport management have decades of knowledge.

30 한 부서와 그 구성원들은 터널 시야 현상을 갖게 될 것이다.
➡ A department and its members will _____ tunnel vision.

L 문맥에 맞지 않는 낱말 찾기

★ 유형 설명

글의 논리적인 흐름을 정확히 이해한 후에 주어진 어휘가 문맥에 어울리는지, 올바른 의미로 쓰였는지를 판단해야 한다.

● 다음 글의 밑줄 친 부분 중, 문맥상 낱말의 쓰임이 적절하지 <u>않은</u> 것은? [3점]

Promotion deals with consumer psychology. We can't ① <u>force</u> people to think one way or

☞ 밑줄 친 다섯 개의 부분이 제시된 문제는 전체 글의 흐름을 파악하고, 밑줄이 포함된 문장의 앞뒤 내용을 확인해서, 문맥상 내용이 반대이거나 비약이 있는 것을 찾는다.

이 아이스크림 좀 먹을래? 정말 맛있어. dangerous 해!

아이스크림이 위험하다고? dangerous가 아니라 delicious겠지!

🎭 유형 풀이 비법

1 단어를 확인하라!
- 짝지어진 어휘가 반의어인지 유사어인지를 확인한다.
- 밑줄은 그 앞뒤 단어와 함께 의미를 확인한다.

2 정확하게 해석하라!
- 글의 전체 흐름에 따라 내용을 이해하고 문제의 앞, 뒤 문장을 정확히 해석한다.

3 반의어를 넣어 보라!
- 글의 흐름에 따라 각 문장의 앞뒤를 꼼꼼히 확인해서 어떤 대상을 가리키는지 찾는다.

(Tip) 정답을 정한 후 다시 글을 읽으면서 흐름이 매끄러운지 확인한다.

📍 자주 출제되는 반의어

□ intimate ↔ distant 친밀한 ↔ 먼
□ poor ↔ wealthy 가난한 ↔ 부유한
□ static ↔ dynamic 정적인 ↔ 역동적인
□ stable ↔ unstable 안정된 ↔ 불안정한
□ active ↔ passive 능동적인 ↔ 수동적인
□ import ↔ export 수입 ↔ 수출
□ tiny ↔ massive 작은, 조그마한 ↔ 거대한
□ superiority ↔ inferiority 우월감 ↔ 열등감
□ objective ↔ subjective 객관적인 ↔ 주관적인
□ dependence ↔ independence 의존 ↔ 독립
□ weaken ↔ strengthen 약화시키다 ↔ 강화하다
□ accurate ↔ inaccurate 정확한 ↔ 부정확한
□ advanced ↔ backward 진보된 ↔ 퇴보하는
□ conform ↔ rebel 따르다 ↔ 저항하다
□ automated ↔ manual 자동화된 ↔ 수동의
□ avoidable ↔ inevitable 피할 수 있는 ↔ 필연적인
□ happiness ↔ depression 행복감, 즐거움 ↔ 우울함
□ reliable ↔ unreliable 신뢰할 수 있는 ↔ 신뢰할 수 없는
□ emotional ↔ impersonal 감정적인 ↔ 냉담한, 인간미 없는
□ noteworthy ↔ insignificant 주목할 만한 ↔ 사소한, 하찮은

□ valuable ↔ worthless 가치 있는, 소중한 ↔ 가치 없는
□ competent ↔ incompetent 능숙한, 유능한 ↔ 무능한
□ deliberate ↔ spontaneous 신중한 ↔ 즉흥적인
□ subtle ↔ obvious 미묘한 ↔ 명백한
□ scarce ↔ plentiful 희박한, 부족한 ↔ 풍부한
□ superficial ↔ profound 피상적인 ↔ 심오한, 깊은
□ inhibit ↔ promote 억제하다 ↔ 촉진하다
□ reinforce ↔ undermine 강화하다 ↔ 약화시키다
□ conventional ↔ unconventional 전통적인 ↔ 비전통적인
□ compassion ↔ indifference 연민 ↔ 무관심
□ justify ↔ condemn 정당화하다 ↔ 비난하다
□ nurture ↔ neglect 양육하다 ↔ 방치하다
□ acknowledge ↔ deny 인정하다 ↔ 부인하다
□ optimistic ↔ cynical 낙관적인 ↔ 냉소적인
□ construct ↔ destroy 구성하다 ↔ 파괴하다
□ expand ↔ contract 확장하다 ↔ 수축하다
□ generate ↔ halt 생성하다 ↔ 멈추다
□ enhance ↔ diminish 향상시키다 ↔ 감소시키다
□ include ↔ omit 포함하다 ↔ 생략하다
□ activate ↔ deactivate 작동시키다 ↔ 정지시키다

12 수동태

1 3형식 문장의 수동태: 동작의 영향을 받거나 당하는 대상을 주어로 하는 문장이다.

• In about 15 to 30 minutes, (the whole process) is usually finished.
주어가 동작을 당함

(대략 15분에서 30분이면 전 과정이 대개 끝난다.)

2 4형식 문장의 수동태 – 4형식 문장에는 직접목적어와 간접목적어, 두 개의 목적어가 있다.

> *** 간접목적어 앞의 전치사**
> 직접목적어가 주어인 수동태 문장에서 간접목적어 앞에 쓰는 전치사는, 4형식 문장을 3형식 문장으로 전환할 때 쓰는 전치사와 같다.

1) 원칙: 두 개의 목적어 각각을 주어로 하는 **두 개의 수동태 문장이 가능**하다.

• Sheldon gave me a book. (Sheldon이 내게 책을 주었다.)
　　　　　　 간접목적어 직접목적어

➡ (A book) was given to me by Sheldon. (**책이** Sheldon에 의해 내게 주어졌다.)
 직접목적어가 주어　　　 *전치사+간접목적어

➡ (I) was given a book by Sheldon. (나는 Sheldon에게서 책을 받았다.)
 간접목적어가 주어

2) 주의: 동사가 make, buy인 경우처럼 **간접목적어를 주어로 하면 의미가 어색해질 때는 수동태로 쓰지 않는다.**

• Helen bought Jack a computer. (Helen이 Jack에게 컴퓨터를 사주었다.)
　　　　　　　　 간접목적어 직접목적어

➡ (A computer) was bought for Jack by Helen. (**컴퓨터가** Helen에 의해서 Jack을 위해 구매되었다.)
 직접목적어가 주어　　　 *전치사+간접목적어

➡ ~~Jack was bought a computer by Helen.~~ Jack이 구매되었다는 것은 어색함

3 5형식 문장의 수동태 – 5형식 문장에는 목적어와 목적격 보어가 있다.

■ **목적격 보어의 위치**: 능동태의 목적어를 수동태의 주어로 하고, **목적격 보어는 동사 「be동사+p.p.」 뒤에 그대로 쓴다.**

• We elected Sean our captain. (우리는 Sean을 우리의 주장으로 선출했다.)
　　　　　 목적어 목적격 보어

➡ (Sean) was elected (our captain) by us. (**Sean은** 우리에 의해 **우리의 주장으로** 선출되었다.)
 능동태의 목적어　　　 능동태의 목적격 보어

• Peter told Susan to clean the kitchen. (Peter는 Susan에게 부엌을 청소하라고 말했다.)
　　　　　 목적어　　　 목적격 보어

➡ (Susan) was told (to clean the kitchen) by Peter. (**Susan은** Peter로부터 **부엌을 청소하라고** 들었다.)
 능동태의 목적어　　　 능동태의 목적격 보어

Check Test

1 다음 능동태 문장을 수동태 문장으로 바꿔 쓰시오.

Distributing food allows them to operate smaller stores.

→ _____

2 밑줄 친 부분을 주어로 하는 능동태 문장으로 바꿔 쓰시오.

Young children are particularly affected by a move.

→ _____

3 밑줄 친 부분에 유의하여 아래 문장을 해석하시오.

This feeling will be maintained by the joy of clarity.

→ _____

4 밑줄 친 부분을 주어로 하는 수동태 문장으로 바꿔 쓰시오.

The rate of speed will greatly determine the ability.

→ _____

• 정답
1 They are allowed to operate smaller stores by distributing food. **2** A move particularly affects young children. **3** 이 느낌은 명료함의 기쁨으로 유지될 것이다. **4** The ability will be greatly determined by the rate of speed.

L 문맥에 맞지 않는 낱말 찾기 첫 번째

1st 글의 흐름을 예측할 수 있게 중심 소재를 찾아보세요.
2nd 밑줄 친 부분이 문맥에 맞게 쓰였는지 꼼꼼하게 살펴보세요.
3rd 글의 흐름을 다시 생각해 보면서 답을 맞게 찾았는지 확인해 보세요.

L01 ★★★※.......................... 고1 2023(11월)/30

다음 글의 밑줄 친 부분 중, 문맥상 낱말의 쓰임이 적절하지 않은 것은?

The term minimalism gives a negative impression to some people who think that it is all about sacrificing valuable possessions. This insecurity naturally stems from their ① attachment to their possessions. It is difficult 5 to distance oneself from something that has been around for quite some time. Being an emotional animal, human beings give meaning to the things around them. So, the question arising here is that if minimalism 10 will ② hurt one's emotions, why become a minimalist? The answer is very simple; the assumption of the question is fundamentally ③ wrong. Minimalism does not hurt emotions. You might feel a bit sad while 15 getting rid of a useless item but sooner than later, this feeling will be ④ maintained by the joy of clarity. Minimalists never argue that you should leave every convenience of the modern era. They are of the view that you 20 only need to ⑤ eliminate stuff that is unused or not going to be used in the near future.

1st 글의 흐름을 예측할 수 있게 중심 소재를 찾아보세요.

The term minimalism gives a negative impression /
미니멀리즘이라는 용어는 부정적인 인상을 준다 /
to some people / who think that it is all about
일부 사람들에게 / 그것을 소중한 소유물을 희생하는 것에 관한
sacrificing valuable possessions. //
것으로만 생각하는 //

● 글의 중심 소재로 보이는 '미니멀리즘'이 등장했어요.
일부 사람들에게 ❶( )이 소유물을 희생하는 것으로 생각되기 때문에 부정적인 인상을 준다고 했어요. 과연 미니멀리즘이 진짜로 부정적인 것이어서 이에 관한 부연 설명이 이어지는지, 아니면 미니멀리즘이 부정적이지 않다는 반전이 있을지 마저 살펴볼까요?

2nd 밑줄 친 부분이 문맥에 맞게 쓰였는지 꼼꼼하게 살펴보세요.

1) ①이 포함된 문장부터 봅시다.

This insecurity naturally stems from / their ①
이러한 불안은 자연스럽게 비롯된다 / 자신의
attachment to their possessions. //
소유물에 대한 애착에서 //

● attachment(애착)에 밑줄이 있어요.
소유물에 대한 애착으로부터 이러한 불안(This insecurity)이 비롯된다고 했어요. 앞 문장에서 일부 사람들에게 미니멀리즘이 소유물을 희생하는 것으로 생각된다는 내용을 This insecurity로 나타냈군요! 소유물에 대한 '애착'이 있으면 소유물을 희생시킨다고 여겨지는 미니멀리즘에 대해 불안해한다는 것은 적절해요. 따라서 ① '애착'이라는 뜻의 attachment는 알맞게 쓰였어요.

2) 이어서 ②가 포함된 문장을 그 앞 문장과 함께 읽어봅시다.

Being an emotional animal, / human beings give
감정의 동물이기 때문에 / 인간은 의미를 부여한다
meaning / to the things around them. //
/ 그들의 곁에 있는 물건에 //
So, the question arising here / is that if minimalism
그래서 여기서 생기는 질문은 / 미니멀리즘이 사람의 감정을
will ② hurt one's emotions, / why become a
상하게 한다면 / 왜 미니멀리스트가
minimalist? //
되느냐는 것이다 //

● **hurt(상하게 하다)에 밑줄이 있어요.**

인간은 감정의 동물이라서 곁에 있는 물건, 즉 소유물에 의미를 부여한다고 하네요. 앞서 우리는 미니멀리즘이 소유물을 희생한다고 여겨져 불안이 비롯된다는 내용을 봤죠? ② 문장에는 진짜로 미니멀리즘이 그런 것이라면 왜 사람들이 미니멀리스트가 되겠냐는 반문이 등장했어요. 감정을 상하게 한다는 것은 불안하게 한다는 것과 같은 맥락이니까 hurt가 적절히 쓰였어요.

3) ③이 포함된 문장과 그 뒤 문장을 읽어봅시다.

> The answer is very simple; / the assumption of the
> 대답은 매우 간단하다 / 그 질문의 가정은 근본적으로
>
> question is fundamentally ③ wrong. //
> 틀리다 //
>
> Minimalism does not hurt emotions. //
> 미니멀리즘은 감정을 상하게 하지 않는다 //

● **wrong(틀린)에 밑줄이 있는데, 무엇이 틀렸다는 걸까요?**

③ 문장의 앞에서 '미니멀리즘이 사람의 감정을 상하게 한다'라는 가정을 했는데, ③ 문장의 뒤에서 미니멀리즘은 감정을 상하게 하지 않는다고 하네요. 따라서 이것이 근본적으로 '틀리다'는 표현은 적절하게 쓰였어요.

4) ④은 적절하게 쓰였는지 확인해 봅시다.

> You might feel a bit sad / while getting rid of a
> 여러분은 조금 슬퍼할 수도 있지만 / 쓸모없는 물건을 치우면서
>
> useless item / but sooner than later, / this feeling
> / 머지않아 / 이 느낌은 유지될
>
> will be ④ maintained / by the joy of clarity. //
> 것이다 / 명료함의 기쁨으로 //

● **미래시제 수동태로 쓰인 maintained(유지되다)에 밑줄이 있어요.**

미니멀리즘이 감정을 상하게 하지 않는다는 내용에 이어서, 쓸모없는 물건을 치우며 슬퍼할 수도 있지만 이 느낌이 명료함의 기쁨으로 유지된다고 했어요. 그런데 기쁨으로 슬픔이 유지된다는 건 뭔가 이상하지 않나요? 앞의 문맥과 맞지 않으므로 ④의 maintained를 overcome으로 바꾸어 '슬픔이 ❷( )'라고 표현하는 것이 더 적절해요.

5) 마지막으로 ⑤이 포함된 문장과 그 앞 문장을 살펴볼까요?

> Minimalists never argue / that you should leave /
> 미니멀리스트는 주장하지 않는다 / 여러분이 버려야 한다고 /
>
> every convenience of the modern era. //
> 현대의 모든 편의를 //
>
> They are of the view / that you only need to ⑤
> 그들은 견해를 가지고 있다 / 여러분이 물건을 없애기만 하면
>
> eliminate stuff / that is unused / or not going to be
> 된다는 / 사용되지 않거나 / 가까운 미래에 사용되지
>
> used in the near future. //
> 않을 //

● **eliminate는 '없애다, 제거하다'라는 뜻이에요.**

미니멀리스트는 현대의 모든 편의를 버려야 한다고 주장하지 않고 사용하지 않는 물건을 없애기만 하면 된다는 견해를 가진다고 해요. 다 버릴 필요는 없고, 쓰지 않는 물건만 '없애면' 된다는 맥락이므로 eliminate가 알맞게 쓰였어요.

3rd 글의 흐름을 다시 생각해 보면서 답을 맞게 찾았는지 확인해 보세요.

1) 글의 흐름을 먼저 정리해 봅시다.

 오해 | 일부 사람들은 미니멀리즘이 소유물을 희생하는 것이라고 생각함

↓

 오해의 부연 | 소유물에 대한 애착 때문에 이러한 불안이 비롯됨

↓

 반론 | 미니멀리즘은 감정을 상하게 하지 않음

↓

 반론의 부연 | 미니멀리즘은 현대의 모든 편의를 버리라는 것이 아니라 쓸모없는 물건만 치우면 된다는 것임

2) 정답으로 고른 선택지를 반의어로 바꿔도 앞뒤 흐름이 자연스러운지 확인하세요.

이 글은 미니멀리즘이 현대의 모든 편의를 버리라는 주장이 아니고, 쓸모없는 물건만 적절히 치우는 것이라는 내용이에요. ④에 maintained 대신에 ❸( )이 들어가면 쓸모없는 물건을 치우면서 조금 슬퍼할 수도 있지만 명료함의 기쁨으로 그 슬픔이 '극복된다'라는 문장이 되면서 앞뒤 문장의 흐름이 자연스러워진다는 것을 다시 확인할 수 있어요!

1st 각 낱말의 의미를 먼저 확인하고, 반의어를 미리 생각해 보세요.

2nd 밑줄 친 부분이 포함된 문장을 읽고, 그 의미가 무엇일지 예상해 보세요.

3rd 정답으로 고른 낱말을 반의어로 바꾸면 앞뒤 흐름이 자연스러워지는지 확인하세요.

L02 ★★★ .... 고1 2023(3월)/30

다음 글의 밑줄 친 부분 중, 문맥상 낱말의 쓰임이 적절하지 <u>않은</u> 것은? [3점]

The major philosophical shift in the idea of selling came when industrial societies became more affluent, more competitive, and more geographically spread out during the 1940s and 1950s. This forced business to 5 develop ① <u>closer</u> relations with buyers and clients, which in turn made business realize that it was not enough to produce a quality product at a reasonable price. In fact, it was equally ② <u>essential</u> to deliver products that 10 customers actually wanted. Henry Ford produced his best-selling T-model Ford in one color only (black) in 1908, but in modern societies this was no longer ③ <u>possible</u>. The modernization of society led to a marketing 15 revolution that ④ <u>strengthened</u> the view that production would create its own demand. Customers, and the desire to ⑤ <u>meet</u> their diverse and often complex needs, became the focus of business. *affluent: 부유한 20

1st 각 낱말의 의미를 먼저 확인하고, 반의어를 미리 생각해 보세요.

① closer: 더 긴밀한 ↔ farther: 더 먼
② essential: 중요한 ↔ inessential: 중요하지 않은
③ possible: 가능한 ↔ impossible: 불가능한
④ strengthened: **❶**( ) ↔ destroyed: 파괴했다
⑤ meet: 충족하다 ↔ lack: 부족하다

2nd 밑줄 친 부분이 포함된 문장을 읽고, 그 의미가 무엇일지 예상해 보세요.

1) 첫 문장을 먼저 읽어 봅시다.

The major philosophical shift / in the idea of selling
주요한 철학적 변화가 / 판매 개념에
/ came / when industrial societies became more
/ 일어났다 / 산업 사회가 더 부유하게 되면서
affluent, / more competitive, / and more
/ 더 경쟁적이고 / 더 지리적으로 퍼져
geographically spread out / during the 1940s and
나가게 (되면서) / 1940년대와 1950년대 동안 //
1950s. //

● 주요한 변화가 일어났대요.

1940년대와 1950년대에 걸쳐 산업 사회가 더 부유해지면서 판매 개념에 주요한 철학적 변화가 일어났대요. 이 글은 '판매'와 관련된 글이군요! 판매 개념이 어떻게 변했고, 그 영향은 어땠는지 선택지가 포함된 문장을 살펴봅시다.

2) ①이 포함된 문장을 봅시다.

This forced business to develop / ① closer relations
이것은 기업이 발전시키게 했다 / 구매자 및 고객과 더 긴밀한
with buyers and clients, / which in turn made
관계를 / 그리고 이것은 결과적으로 기업이
business realize / that it was not enough to produce
깨닫게 했다 / 양질의 제품을 생산하는 것으로는 충분하지
a quality product / at a reasonable price. //
않다는 것을 / 합리적인 가격에 //

● **This = 판매 개념에 일어난 철학적 변화**
앞 문장과 함께 생각해 보면, 판매 개념에 일어난 철학적 변화로 인해서 기업은 합리적인 가격에 좋은 제품을 생산하는 것으로는 충분하지 않다는 것을 깨달았다는 거예요. 그러니까 더 나아가서 고객과 '더 긴밀한' 관계를 발전시켜야 했겠죠!

3) ②이 포함된 문장을 봅시다.

In fact, / it was equally ② essential / to deliver
사실　　　/ ~이 마찬가지로 매우 중요했다　　　/ 제품을 내놓는
products / that customers actually wanted. //
것　　/ 고객이 실제로 원하는　　　　　　　//

● **뭐가 매우 중요했다고요?**
고객이 실제로 원하는 제품을 내놓는 것이 마찬가지로 매우 중요했대요. 합리적인 가격에 좋은 제품을 생산하는 것으로는 충분하지 않았고, 고객과 더 긴밀한 관계를 발전시켜야 했다면, 고객이 실제로 원하는 제품을 내놓는 것은 '매우 중요'했겠네요.

4) ③이 포함된 문장을 봅시다.

Henry Ford produced / his best-selling T-model
Henry Ford는 생산했다　　　　/ 자신의 가장 많이 팔렸던 T-모델 Ford를
Ford / in one color only (black) in 1908, / but in
　　/ 1908년에 단 하나의 색상(검은색)으로만　　/ 하지만
modern societies / this was no longer ③ possible. //
현대 사회에서는　　/ 이것이 더 이상 가능하지 않았다　　　//

● **Henry Ford의 사례가 등장해요.**
과거에는 Henry Ford처럼 잘 팔리는 제품을 하나의 색상으로 생산해도 성공적이었겠지만, 현대 사회는 그런 것이 '가능하지' 않다는 거예요. 고객과의 관계가 더 긴밀해져서 그들이 실제로 원하는 제품을 내놓아야 했으니까요.

● **but과 no longer도 단서가 될 수 있어요.**
과거와 현대 사회의 상황을 역접의 연결어 but으로 연결하고 있는데, possible 앞에도 부정어인 no longer가 있어요. 그러니까 과거와는 '달리' 가능하지 '않았다'라는 의미가 되도록 possible이 온 것은 적절한 거죠!

5) ④이 포함된 문장을 봅시다.

The modernization of society / led to a marketing
사회의 현대화는　　　　　　　　/ 마케팅 혁명으로 이어졌다
revolution / that ④ strengthened the view / that
/ 견해를 강화하는　　　　　　　　/ 생산이
production would create its own demand. //
그 자체의 수요를 창출할 것이라는　　　//

● **생산이 수요를 창출하는 건 과거의 견해 아닌가요?**
앞에서 Henry Ford의 사례를 통해서 하나의 제품만 생산해도 그것이 소비자의 수요를 창출했기 때문에 문제가 없다고 했어요. 그런데 현대화된 사회에서는 그런 방식이 가능하지 않다고 했어요. 그럼 현대 사회의 마케팅 혁명은 생산이 수요를 창출한다는 기존의 견해를 '강화하는' 것이 아니라 '파괴한다'고 해야 글의 흐름과 맞아요. 정답을 찾은 것 같죠?

6) ⑤이 포함된 문장도 마저 봅시다.

Customers, / and the desire to ⑤ meet / their diverse
고객과　　/ 충족하고자 하는 욕망이　　/ 그들의 다양하고
and often complex needs, / became the focus of
흔히 복잡한 욕구를　　　/ 기업의 초점이 되었다 //
business. //

● **무엇이 기업의 초점이 되었나요?**
고객의 복잡한 욕구를 '충족하고자' 하는 것에 기업이 초점을 맞추었대요. 잘 팔리는 단일 제품만 생산하는 것이 아니라, 고객이 실제로 원하는 제품을 내놓는 것이 현대 사회의 마케팅 혁명이라고 했으니까 적절한 흐름이네요.

3rd **정답으로 고른 낱말을 반의어로 바꾸면 앞뒤 흐름이 자연스러워지는지 확인하세요.**
우리는 **2** (　　　　　)을 정답으로 골랐어요.
기존에는 생산이 수요를 창출할 것으로 생각했지만, 현대 사회에서는 인식이 변화되어서 이전과 다른 마케팅 혁명이 일어났다고 했어요. 그러니까 이전의 견해를 '강화하는' 것이 아니라 '파괴하는' 거죠. ④ **3** (　　　　　)는 destroyed 같은 반의어로 바꿔야 앞뒤 흐름이 자연스러워져요.

L03 ∼ 06 ▶ 제한시간 8분

L03 ★★✦ 고1 2025(3월)/30

다음 글의 밑줄 친 부분 중, 문맥상 낱말의 쓰임이 적절하지 <u>않은</u> 것은? [3점]

Promotion deals with consumer psychology. We can't ① <u>force</u> people to think one way or another, and the clever marketer knows that promotion is used to provide information in the most clear, honest, and simple fashion possible. By doing so, the possibility of increasing sales goes up. Gone are the days when promotions were done in order to ② <u>fool</u> the consumer into purchasing something. The long-term effect of getting a consumer to buy something they did not really want or need wasn't good. In fact, consumers fooled once can do ③ <u>damage</u> to sales as they relate their experience to others. Instead, marketers now know that their goal is to ④ <u>identify</u> the consumers who are most likely to appreciate a good or service, and to promote that good or service in a way that makes the value clear to the consumer. Therefore, marketers must know where the ⑤ <u>uninterested</u> consumers are, and how to reach them.

구문 서술형

밑줄 친 부분을 주어로 하는 수동태 문장을 쓰시오. (단, 「by+목적격」을 쓸 것)

We can't force <u>people</u> to think one way or another.

➡ 수동태 문장: _____

_____

L04 ★★✦ 고1 2025(6월)/30

다음 글의 밑줄 친 부분 중, 문맥상 낱말의 쓰임이 적절하지 <u>않은</u> 것은?

It is natural for people to observe happenings and then seek explanations for why those happenings occurred. But sometimes the reasoning is ① <u>wrong</u> because of one or more misconceptions. One of these is the *ecological fallacy*, where an argument claims that there is a causal relationship between two things merely because they occur ② <u>together</u>. For example, in the 1950s it was found that crime rates were the highest in neighborhoods where immigrants were most numerous. Some people used this "co-occurrence" to argue that immigrants were a ③ <u>cause</u> of crime. But a careful analysis of this situation revealed that immigrants were forced to live in neighborhoods where crime rates were already ④ <u>low</u>; they could not afford more expensive housing in safer neighborhoods. Immigrants themselves committed very few of the crimes. Unless you analyze the claim carefully, you would ⑤ <u>misinterpret</u> the relationship and thereby construct a faulty belief. *immigrant: 이민자

구문 서술형

주어진 문장에서 목적어를 찾아 밑줄을 긋고, 해당 부분을 주어로 하는 수동태 문장으로 고치시오. (단, 「by+목적격」을 쓸 것)

Immigrants themselves committed very few of the crimes.

➡ 수동태 문장: _____

_____

L05 ★★★❀ 고1 2025(9월)/30

다음 글의 밑줄 친 부분 중, 문맥상 낱말의 쓰임이 적절하지 <u>않은</u> 것은?

For a species born in a time when resources were limited and dangers were great, our natural tendency to share and cooperate is ① <u>complicated</u> when resources are plenty and outside dangers are few. When we have less, we tend to be more open to sharing what we have. Certain nomadic tribes don't have much, yet they are happy to share because it is in their ② <u>interest</u> to do so. If you happen upon them in your travels, they will open up their homes and give you their food and hospitality. It's not just because they are nice people; it's because their ③ <u>survival</u> depends on sharing, for they know that they may be the travelers in need of food and shelter another day. Ironically, the ④ <u>more</u> we have, the bigger our fences, the more sophisticated our security to keep people away and the less we want to share. Our desire for more, combined with our ⑤ <u>increased</u> physical interaction with the "common folk," starts to create a disconnection or blindness to reality.

*nomadic: 유목의 **hospitality: 환대

구문 서술형

주어진 문장에서 간접목적어와 직접목적어에 밑줄을 긋고, 각각을 주어로 하는 수동태 문장으로 고치시오. (단, 「by+목적격」을 생략할 것)

They will give you their food and hospitality.

➡ (1) 간접목적어가 주어: _____

_____

➡ (2) 직접목적어가 주어: _____

_____

L06 ★★★❀ 고1 2024(10월)/30

다음 글의 밑줄 친 부분 중, 문맥상 낱말의 쓰임이 적절하지 <u>않은</u> 것은? [3점]

Herbert Simon won his Nobel Prize for recognizing our limitations in information, time, and cognitive capacity. As we lack the resources to compute answers independently, we ① <u>distribute</u> the computation across the population and solve the answer slowly, generation by generation. Then all we have to do is socially learn the right answers. You don't need to understand how your computer or toilet works; you just need to be able to use the interface and flush. All that needs to be ② <u>transmitted</u> is which button to push — essentially how to interact with technologies rather than how they work. And so instead of holding ③ <u>less</u> information than we have mental capacity for and indeed need to know, we could dedicate our large brains to a small piece of a giant calculation. We understand things well enough to ④ <u>benefit</u> from them, but all the while we are making small calculations that contribute to a larger whole. We are just doing our part in a larger computation for our societies' ⑤ <u>collective</u> brains.

구문 서술형

주어진 문장이 몇 형식인지 쓰고, 이를 수동태 문장으로 바꿔 쓰시오. (단, 「by+목적격」을 생략할 것)

We could dedicate our large brains to a small piece of a giant calculation.

➡ 문장 형식: _____ 형식

➡ 수동태 문장: _____

L07 ★★★❀   고1 2024(3월)/30

다음 글의 밑줄 친 부분 중, 문맥상 낱말의 쓰임이
적절하지 않은 것은? [3점]

The rate of speed at which one is traveling will greatly determine the ability to process detail in the environment. In evolutionary terms, human senses are adapted to the ① speed at which humans move through space under their own power while walking. Our ability to distinguish detail in the environment is therefore ideally ② suited to movement at speeds of perhaps five miles per hour and under. The fastest users of the street, motorists, therefore have a much more limited ability to process details along the street — a motorist simply has ③ enough time or ability to appreciate design details. On the other hand, pedestrian travel, being much slower, allows for the ④ appreciation of environmental detail. Joggers and bicyclists fall somewhere in between these polar opposites; while they travel faster than pedestrians, their rate of speed is ordinarily much ⑤ slower than that of the typical motorist.

*distinguish: 구별하다 **pedestrian: 보행자

L08 ★★★❀   고1 2024(9월)/30

다음 글의 밑줄 친 부분 중, 문맥상 낱말의 쓰임이
적절하지 않은 것은? [3점]

An excellent alternative to calming traffic is removing it. Some cities ① reserve an extensive network of lanes and streets for bikes, pedestrians, and the occasional service vehicle. This motivates people to travel by bike rather than by car, making streets safer for everyone. As bicycles become more ② popular in a city, planners can convert more automobile lanes and entire streets to accommodate more of them. Nevertheless, even the most bikeable cities still ③ rwequire motor vehicle lanes for taxis, emergency vehicles, and delivery trucks. Delivery vehicles are frequently a target of animus, but they are actually an essential component to making cities greener. A tightly packed delivery truck is a far more ④ inefficient transporter of goods than several hybrids carrying a few shopping bags each. Distributing food and other goods to neighborhood vendors ⑤ allows them to operate smaller stores close to homes so that residents can walk, rather than drive, to get their groceries.

*animus: 반감, 미움

L09 ★★★   고1 2023(9월)/30

다음 글의 밑줄 친 부분 중, 문맥상 낱말의 쓰임이
적절하지 않은 것은? [3점]

While moving is difficult for everyone, it is particularly stressful for children. They lose their sense of security and may feel disoriented when their routine is disrupted and all that is ① familiar is taken away. Young children, ages 3–6, are particularly affected by a move. Their understanding at this stage is quite literal, and it is ② easy for them to imagine beforehand a new home and their new room. Young children may have worries such as "Will I still be me in the new place?" and "Will my toys and bed come with us?" It is important to establish a balance between validating children's past experiences and focusing on helping them ③ adjust to the new place. Children need to have opportunities to share their backgrounds in a way that ④ respects their past as an important part of who they are. This contributes to building a sense of community, which is essential for all children, especially those in ⑤ transition.

L10 ★★★   고1 2023(6월)/30

다음 글의 밑줄 친 부분 중, 문맥상 낱말의 쓰임이
적절하지 않은 것은?

Advertisers often displayed considerable facility in ① adapting their claims to the market status of the goods they promoted. Fleischmann's yeast, for instance, was used as an ingredient for cooking homemade bread. Yet more and more people in the early 20th century were buying their bread from stores or bakeries, so consumer demand for yeast ② increased. The producer of Fleischmann's yeast hired the J. Walter Thompson advertising agency to come up with a different marketing strategy to ③ boost sales. No longer the "Soul of Bread," the Thompson agency first turned yeast into an important source of vitamins with significant health ④ benefits. Shortly thereafter, the advertising agency transformed yeast into a natural laxative. ⑤ Repositioning yeast helped increase sales.

*laxative: 완하제(배변을 쉽게 하는 약·음식·음료)

L11 ★★★   고1 2022(11월)/30

다음 글의 밑줄 친 부분 중, 문맥상 낱말의 쓰임이
적절하지 <u>않은</u> 것은? [3점]

Plant growth is controlled by a group of hormones called auxins found at the tips of stems and roots of plants. Auxins produced at the tips of stems tend to accumulate on the side of the stem that is in the shade. Accordingly, the auxins ① <u>stimulate</u> growth on the shaded side of the plant. Therefore, the shaded side grows faster than the side facing the sunlight. This phenomenon causes the stem to bend and appear to be growing ② <u>towards</u> the light. Auxins have the ③ <u>opposite</u> effect on the roots of plants. Auxins in the tips of roots tend to limit growth. If a root is horizontal in the soil, the auxins will accumulate on the lower side and interfere with its development. Therefore, the lower side of the root will grow ④ <u>faster</u> than the upper side. This will, in turn, cause the root to bend ⑤ <u>downwards</u>, with the tip of the root growing in that direction.

 **1등급 대비 문제**

L12~14 ▶ 제한시간 6분

L12 ⭐ 2등급 대비   고1 2022(3월)/30

다음 글의 밑줄 친 부분 중, 문맥상 낱말의 쓰임이
적절하지 <u>않은</u> 것은? [3점]

Rejection is an everyday part of our lives, yet most people can't handle it well. For many, it's so painful that they'd rather not ask for something at all than ask and ① <u>risk</u> rejection. Yet, as the old saying goes, if you don't ask, the answer is always no. Avoiding rejection ② <u>negatively</u> affects many aspects of your life. All of that happens only because you're not ③ <u>tough</u> enough to handle it. For this reason, consider rejection therapy. Come up with a ④ <u>request</u> or an activity that usually results in a rejection. Working in sales is one such example. Asking for discounts at the stores will also work. By deliberately getting yourself ⑤ <u>welcomed</u> you'll grow a thicker skin that will allow you to take on much more in life, thus making you more successful at dealing with unfavorable circumstances.   *deliberately: 의도적으로

L13 ⭐ 2등급 대비   고1 2022(9월)/30

다음 글의 밑줄 친 부분 중, 문맥상 낱말의 쓰임이
적절하지 <u>않은</u> 것은? [3점]

It is widely believed that certain herbs somehow magically improve the work of certain organs, and "cure" specific diseases as a result. Such statements are unscientific and groundless. Sometimes herbs appear to work, since they tend to ① <u>increase</u> your blood circulation in an aggressive attempt by your body to eliminate them from your system. That can create a ② <u>temporary</u> feeling of a high, which makes it seem as if your health condition has improved. Also, herbs can have a placebo effect, just like any other method, thus helping you feel better. Whatever the case, it is your body that has the intelligence to ③ <u>regain</u> health, and not the herbs. How can herbs have the intelligence needed to direct your body into getting healthier? That is impossible. Try to imagine how herbs might come into your body and intelligently ④ <u>fix</u> your problems. If you try to do that, you will see how impossible it seems. Otherwise, it would mean that herbs are ⑤ <u>less</u> intelligent than the human body, which is truly hard to believe.   *placebo effect: 위약 효과

L14 ⭐ 2등급 대비   고1 2021(11월)/30

다음 글의 밑줄 친 부분 중, 문맥상 낱말의 쓰임이 적절하지 <u>않은</u>
것은?

For species approaching extinction, zoos can act as a last chance for survival. ① <u>Recovery</u> programs are established to coordinate the efforts of field conservationists and wildlife authorities. As populations of those species ② <u>diminish</u> it is not unusual for zoos to start captive breeding programs. Captive breeding acts to protect against extinction. In some cases captive-bred individuals may be released back into the wild, supplementing wild populations. This is most successful in situations where individuals are at greatest threat during a ③ <u>particular</u> life stage. For example, turtle eggs may be removed from high-risk locations until after they hatch. This may ④ <u>increase</u> the number of turtles that survive to adulthood. Crocodile programs have also been successful in protecting eggs and hatchlings, ⑤ <u>capturing</u> hatchlings once they are better equipped to protect themselves.   *captive breeding: 포획 사육 **hatch: 부화하다

L15 ⭐ 1등급 대비 .... 고1 2024(6월)/30

다음 글의 밑줄 친 부분 중, 문맥상 낱말의 쓰임이
적절하지 <u>않은</u> 것은? [3점]

Many human and non-human animals save commodities or money for future consumption. This behavior seems to reveal a preference of a ① <u>delayed</u> reward over an immediate one: the agent gives up some immediate pleasure in exchange for a future one. Thus the discounted value of the future reward should be ② <u>greater</u> than the un-discounted value of the present one. However, in some cases the agent does not wait for the envisioned occasion but uses their savings ③ <u>prematurely</u>. For example, early in the year an employee might set aside money to buy Christmas presents but then spend it on a summer vacation instead. Such cases could be examples of ④ <u>weakness</u> of will. That is, the agents may judge or resolve to spend their savings in a certain way for the greatest benefit but then act differently when temptation for immediate pleasure ⑤ <u>disappears</u>.

*envision: 계획하다

L16 ⭐ 1등급 대비 .... 고1 2022(6월)/30

다음 글의 밑줄 친 부분 중, 문맥상 낱말의 쓰임이
적절하지 <u>않은</u> 것은? [3점]

Do you sometimes feel like you don't love your life? Like, deep inside, something is missing? That's because we are living someone else's life. We allow other people to ① <u>influence</u> our choices. We are trying to meet their expectations. Social pressure is deceiving — we are all impacted without noticing it. Before we realize we are losing ownership of our lives, we end up ② <u>ignoring</u> how other people live. Then, we can only see the greener grass — ours is never good enough. To regain that passion for the life you want, you must ③ <u>recover</u> control of your choices. No one but yourself can choose how you live. But, how? The first step to getting rid of expectations is to treat yourself ④ <u>kindly</u>. You can't truly love other people if you don't love yourself first. When we accept who we are, there's no room for other's ⑤ <u>expectations</u>.

어휘 Review

※ 다음 영어는 우리말 뜻을, 우리말은 영어 단어를 〈보기〉에서 찾아 쓰시오.

〈 보기 〉
motivate	desire	명료함	deceiving
이상적으로	감소하다	circumstance	상당한
therapy	미리	전형적인	target

01 typical _____

02 ideally _____

03 clarity _____

04 beforehand _____

05 significant _____

06 요법 _____

07 상황 _____

08 욕망 _____

09 속이는 _____

10 동기를 부여하다 _____

※ 다음 우리말에 알맞은 영어 표현을 찾아 연결하시오.

11 ~을 방해하다 •   • set aside

12 ~을 확보하다 •   • interfere with

13 제거하다 •   • in turn

14 ~에서 비롯되다 •   • stem from

15 결국 •   • take away

※ 다음 우리말 표현에 맞는 단어를 고르시오.

16 모든 편의를 버리다 ➡ leave every (convenience / convergence)

17 주민들은 걸어갈 수 있다 ➡ (restraints / residents) can walk

18 극과 극 사이 ➡ between these (polar / pillar) opposites

19 행위자는 포기한다 ➡ the (account / agent) gives up

20 소중한 소유물을 희생하는 것 ➡ sacrificing valuable (obsession / possessions)

※ 다음 문장의 빈칸에 알맞은 단어를 〈보기〉에서 찾아 쓰시오.

〈 보기 〉
insecurity	resolve	determine	term
reserve	reveal	complicated	industrial
considerable	transformed	suited	appreciated

21 이러한 행동은 선호를 드러내는 듯하다.
➡ This behavior seems to _____ a preference.

22 나누고 협력하려는 우리의 타고난 성향은 복잡하다.
➡ Our natural tendency to share and cooperate is _____.

23 미니멀리즘이라는 용어는 부정적인 인상을 준다.
➡ The _____ minimalism gives a negative impression.

24 몇몇 도시는 광범위한 망의 도로를 마련해 둔다.
➡ Some cities _____ an extensive network of lanes.

25 그 광고 대행사는 효모를 천연 완하제로 바꿨다.
➡ The advertising agency _____ yeast into a natural laxative.

26 이러한 불안은 자연스럽게 그들의 애착에서 비롯된다.
➡ This _____ naturally stems from their attachment.

27 산업 사회는 1940년대와 1950년대 동안에 더 부유해졌다.
➡ _____ societies became more affluent during the 1940s and 1950s.

28 빠르기는 세세한 것을 처리하는 능력을 크게 결정할 것이다.
➡ The rate will greatly _____ the ability to process detail.

29 행위자는 그들의 저축을 사용하기로 판단하거나 결심할 수 있다.
➡ The agents may judge or _____ to spend their savings.

30 광고주들은 그들의 주장을 조절하는 데 있어서 상당한 능력을 보여주었다.
➡ Advertisers often displayed _____ facility in adapting their claims.

M 빈칸 완성하기

> 이 퍼즐 문제의 빈칸에 맞는 게 뭔지 아리송하네요.

> 빈칸의 주변을 뚫어지게 잘 살펴봐.

★ 유형 설명

다음 빈칸에 들어갈 말로 가장 적절한 것을 고르시오.

As you listen to your child in an emotional moment, be aware that _____

빈칸이 포함된 문장, 절 이외의 나머지 부분을 통해 주제문이나 주제에 맞는 세부 내용을 완성해야 한다.

M 1 빈칸이 앞부분에 있는 경우

○━ 글의 나머지 부분을 종합해야 하는 주제문인 경우가 많다.

M 2 빈칸이 가운데에 있는 경우

○━ 주제를 뒷받침하거나 반박하는 세부 내용인 경우가 많다. 글의 흐름이 반전되지 않는지 주의해야 한다.

M 3 빈칸이 끝부분에 있는 경우

○━ 글의 내용을 종합하여 주제문에 해당하는 결론을 완성해야 한다.

유형 풀이 비법

1 빈칸의 위치를 확인하라!

• 빈칸이 포함된 문장과 그 주변 문장을 주의 깊게 읽는다.

2 글의 주제를 추론하라!

• 반복해서 등장하는 핵심어 위주로 글의 주제를 파악한다.

3 전개 방식을 파악하라!

• 열거, 예시, 대조 등의 글의 전개 방식을 파악해서 빈칸이 어떤 부분에 해당하는지 찾는다.

> Tip 선택지를 빈칸에 넣은 후 전후 맥락과 연결되는지 확인한다.

어휘 및 표현 Preview

- □ coincidence 우연
- □ untimely 시기가 적절하지 않은
- □ particularly 특히
- □ inspiration 영감
- □ disruption 방해
- □ significant 상당한
- □ consequence 결과
- □ critical 중요한
- □ to the extent where ~할 정도까지
- □ uniform 동일한, 획일적인
- □ object 개체
- □ ecosystem 생태계
- □ perspective 관점
- □ crucially 결정적으로
- □ unite 통합하다
- □ emphasize 강조하다
- □ framework 틀
- □ characteristic 특징
- □ mammal 포유류

- □ apparently 분명히
- □ process 처리하다
- □ essential 필수적인
- □ nevertheless 그럼에도 불구하고
- □ activate 활성화하다
- □ evidence 증거
- □ demonstrate 보여주다
- □ auditory 청각의
- □ dramatic 극적인
- □ expansion 확장
- □ precisely 정확하게
- □ vital 중요한
- □ spatial 공간의
- □ enlarge 확대하다
- □ architecture 건축, 설계
- □ direct 지시하다
- □ remarkable 두드러진
- □ literally 말 그대로
- □ upside down 거꾸로

- □ challenge 도전
- □ concentrate 집중하다
- □ be confronted with ~에 직면하다
- □ fortunately 다행히
- □ perception 지각
- □ tribe 부족
- □ slightly 약간
- □ hostile 적대적인
- □ accordingly 그에 맞춰
- □ decisive 결정적인
- □ offspring 자손
- □ concept 개념
- □ statement 진술
- □ essence 본질
- □ fruitlessly 헛되이
- □ hypothesis 가설
- □ substance 물질
- □ theorize 이론을 세우다
- □ philosophy 철학

13 가정법

1 가정법 현재: 현재 또는 미래의 불확실한 일을 가정

- If + 주어 + 동사의 현재형 ~, 주어 + 조동사의 현재형/동사의 현재형 ….

- Most of your bodies work best if they are neither too hot nor too cold.
  (너무 뜨겁거나 너무 차갑지만 않다면 여러분의 몸은 대부분 잘 움직일 것이다.)

> **＊단순 조건문과 가정법**
> 가정법 문장과 달리 단순 조건문은 실현 가능성을 배제하지 않는다.

2 가정법 과거

쓰임	현재 사실에 반대되거나 현재나 미래에＊실현 가능성이 거의 없는 일을 가정·상상
형태	(1) 현재 사실에 반대되는 일 - If + 주어 + 동사의 과거형 / were ~, 주어 + 조동사의 과거형 + 동사원형 …. 　　if절(만약 ~라면)　　　　주절(…할 텐데) - if절의 동사가 be동사일 경우 **주어에 상관없이 were**를 쓴다. (2) 미래에 실현 가능성이 거의 없는 일 - If + 주어 + were + to-v, 주어 + 조동사의 과거형 + 동사원형 …. 　　if절(만약 ~라면)　　　　주절(…할 텐데) - If + 주어 + should + 동사원형, 명령문 / 의문문. 　　if절(만약 ~라면)　　주절(…해라./…할까?)

- If I were rich, I could donate a lot of money. (내가 부유하다면, 나는 많은 돈을 기부할 수 있을 텐데.)

- If anything should happen, give this to Tom. (혹시 무슨 일이 생기면, 이것을 Tom에게 주세요.)

3 가정법 과거완료

쓰임	과거 사실에 반대되거나 과거에＊실현 가능성이 거의 없었던 일을 가정·상상
형태	If + 주어 + had p.p. ~, 주어 + 조동사의 과거형 + have p.p. …. 　if절(만약 ~했다면)　　　　주절(…했을 텐데)

- If I had played better, I would have won. (내가 더 잘했다면, 내가 이겼을 텐데.)

Check Test

1 시제에 유의해서 해석하시오.

If I were to suffer from heart failure and depend upon an artificial heart, I would be no less myself.

→ _____

2 괄호 안의 단어를 빈칸에 알맞은 형태로 쓰시오.

If I _____ an arm in an accident and had it replaced with an artificial arm, I would still be essentially me. (lose)

3 괄호 안의 단어를 빈칸에 알맞은 형태로 쓰시오.

If a person _____ be unburdened from their cares and duties and, just for a moment, consider what appeals to them, they get the chance to sort out what is important to them. (can)

4 시제에 유의해서 해석하시오.

You have to use less one word descriptions and more detailed, engaging descriptions if you want to make something real.

→ _____

• 정답 •

1 만약 내가 심장 마비로 고통받고 인공 심장에 의존한다면 해도 나는 역시 나 자신임에 변함이 없을 것이다. 함 2 lost 3 can 4 어떤 것을 진짜처럼 만들고 싶다면, 한 단어로 된 묘사를 덜 사용하고, 세밀하고 마음을 끄는 묘사를 더 많이 사용해야 한다.

M. 빈칸 완성하기 **169**

M ① 빈칸이 <u>앞부분</u>에 있는 경우

1st 빈칸이 포함된 문장을 읽고, 빈칸에 들어갈 말에 대한 단서를 찾으세요.
2nd 나머지 글을 읽으며 빈칸에 들어갈 말을 찾아봅시다.
3rd 선택지를 해석하여 정답을 고르세요.

M01 ★★★ .... 고1 2024(6월)/31

다음 빈칸에 들어갈 말로 가장 적절한 것을 고르시오.

The costs of _____ are well-documented. Martin Luther King Jr. lamented them when he described "that lovely poem that didn't get written because someone knocked on the door." Perhaps the most famous literary [5] example happened in 1797 when Samuel Taylor Coleridge started writing his poem *Kubla Khan* from a dream he had but then was visited by an unexpected guest. For Coleridge, by coincidence, the untimely [10] visitor came at a particularly bad time. He forgot his inspiration and left the work unfinished. While there are many documented cases of sudden disruptions that have had significant consequences for [15] professionals in critical roles such as doctors, nurses, control room operators, stock traders, and pilots, they also impact most of us in our everyday lives, slowing down work productivity and generally increasing stress [20] levels.

*lament: 슬퍼하다

① misunderstandings ② interruptions
③ inequalities ④ regulations
⑤ arguments

1st 빈칸이 포함된 문장을 읽고, 빈칸에 들어갈 말에 대한 단서를 찾으세요.

> The costs of _____ / are well-documented. //
> _____로 인한 대가는 / 잘 기록되어 있다 //

● **빈칸이 포함된 문장이 아주 간결해요.**
빈칸이 포함된 문장에서 얻을 정보가 없는 듯하지만,
'①( )'와 '기록'이 눈에 들어오네요.
'무엇'의 대가라고 한 것으로 볼 때, '무엇'이 끼친 영향과 그로 인한 결과 등이 뒤에 이어질 것 같고, 그것이 잘 기록되어 있다고 했으니 이에 관한 역사적인 사실이나 사례가 이어질 수도 있어요.

● **그럼 우리는 글을 읽으며 무엇을 찾아야 할까요?**
글의 앞부분에 빈칸이 있다면 빈칸이 포함된 문장이 주제문일 가능성이 커요! 따라서 이 글은 '무엇'의 대가를 설명하는 글일 것이므로 그것이 무엇인지 파악해 봅시다.

2nd 나머지 글을 읽으며 빈칸에 들어갈 말을 찾아봅시다.

1) 빈칸 바로 뒤 문장을 해석해 봅시다.

> Martin Luther King Jr. lamented them / when he
> Martin Luther King Jr.는 이를 슬퍼했다 / 그가
> described / "that lovely poem that didn't get
> 묘사했을 때 / "쓰여지지 못한 그 사랑스러운 시
> written / because someone knocked on the door." //
> / 누군가 문을 두드렸기 때문에" //

● **과거 인물의 사례가 등장했어요.**
앞서 예상한 대로 빈칸 문장에 관한 과거의 예시가 이어지네요.
Martin Luther King Jr.는 누군가 문을 두드려서 시를 쓰지 못한 것을 슬퍼했다고 해요.

● **이것이 '무엇'의 대가에 관한 기록일까요?**
시를 쓰던 중에 누가 문을 두드려서 시를 쓰지 못한 상황을 한 단어로 나타내려면 '개입'이나 '방해' 정도가 적당할 듯해요. 글의 나머지 부분도 읽으며 더 구체적으로 파악해 봅시다!

2) 앞의 예시에 이어서 또 다른 예시가 등장했어요.

> Perhaps / the most famous literary example
> 아마도 / 가장 유명한 문학적 사례는 1797년에 일어났던 일일 것이다
> happened in 1797 / when Samuel Taylor Coleridge
> / Samuel Taylor Coleridge가 시를 쓰기
> started writing his poem / *Kubla Khan* / from a
> 시작했는데 / 'Kubla Khan'이라는 / 꿈에서
> dream he had / but then was visited by an
> / 뜻밖의 손님이 찾아왔을 때 //
> unexpected guest. //
> For Coleridge, by coincidence, / the untimely visitor
> 공교롭게도 Coleridge에게 / 이 불청객은 특히 좋지 않은
> came at a particularly bad time. //
> 시기에 찾아왔다 //
> He forgot his inspiration / and left the work
> 그는 영감을 잊고 / 작품을 미완성으로 남겼다 //
> unfinished. //

● **앞의 예시와 비슷한 문학적 사례가 나왔군요!**
Coleridge도 시를 쓰기 시작할 때 뜻밖의 손님이 찾아왔다고
하네요. 그런데 특히 좋지 않은 시기에 찾아와서 영감을 잊고 작품이
❷(   )으로 남았대요.

● **두 예시의 공통점은 무엇인가요?**
두 인물 모두 시를 쓰던 중에 누군가 찾아와 중단되었고 작품을 마치지
못했어요. 즉, '개입'이나 '방해'의 결과로 일을 마치지 못한 상황이에요.
빈칸 문장과 최대한 비슷하게 바꾸어 보면 '개입이나 방해의 대가로 일을
마치지 못했다' 정도가 되겠네요.

3) 글의 마지막 문장을 봅시다.

> While there are many documented cases of sudden
> 갑작스러운 방해의 사례가 많이 기록되어 있지만
> disruptions / that have had significant consequences
> / 심각한 결과를 초래한
> / for professionals in critical roles / such as doctors,
> / 중요한 역할을 담당하는 전문가들에게 / 의사, 간호사,
> nurses, control room operators, stock traders, and
> 관제실 운영자, 주식 거래자, 조종사와 같은
> pilots, / they also impact most of us in our everyday
> / 갑작스러운 방해는 일상 생활에서 대부분의 사람들에게도 영향을
> lives, / slowing down work productivity and
> 미치고 / 업무 생산성을 떨어뜨리며 일반적으로 스트레스 수준을 높인다 //
> generally increasing stress levels. //

● **'무엇'의 사례가 기록되어 있다고 했나요?**
바로 '갑작스러운 **❸(   )**'의 사례가 기록되어 있다고
했어요. 갑작스러운 방해가 심각한 결과, 즉 일상에서 대부분의
사람들에게 영향을 미치고 업무 생산성을 떨어뜨리며 스트레스 수준을
높인다고 해요.

● **빈칸이 포함된 문장을 떠올려 봅시다.**
우리는 '무엇'이 영향을 끼치거나 어떤 결과를 낳았는지, 그리고 '무엇'의
대가가 잘 기록되어 있는지 확인하기로 했어요. 여기서 '무엇'은 바로
'방해'라고 할 수 있어요. 방해의 대가(결과)가 사람들에게 악영향을
미친다는 것이죠.

➦ **글을 읽으며 이해한 내용을 정리해 볼까요?**
과거 인물 두 명의 문학적 사례와 여러 전문가의 기록에서 알 수 있듯이,
갑작스러운 방해는 일상과 업무에 심각한 결과를 초래한다고 했어요.
따라서 '무엇'의 대가가 잘 기록되어 있다는 문장의 빈칸에는 '방해'가
들어가는 것이 적절하겠죠.

3rd 선택지를 해석하여 정답을 고르세요.

1) 각 선택지의 해석을 확인해 보세요.

> ① misunderstandings
> 오해
> ② interruptions
> 방해
> ③ inequalities
> 불평등
> ④ regulations
> 규제
> ⑤ arguments
> 논쟁

2) 문맥에 맞는 답은 무엇인가요?
'방해'의 대가가 잘 기록되어 있는 것이므로 정답은 **❹(   )**!

빈칸 문장을 먼저
읽으면 글에서 무엇을 찾아야
하는지 알 수 있어.

빈칸 정답 ② ❼ 해유유 ❸ 유묨미 ❷ 녜대가 ❶

수능 유형별 기출 문제

 단어장

PATTERN PRACTICE

M02 ★★★❀ 고1 2025(3월)/32

다음 빈칸에 들어갈 말로 가장 적절한 것을 고르시오.

As you listen to your child in an emotional moment, be aware that _____ usually works better than asking questions to get a conversation rolling. You may ask your child "Why do you feel sad?" and she may not have a clue. As a child, she may not have an answer on the tip of her tongue. Maybe she's feeling sad about her parents' arguments, or because she feels overtired, or she's worried about a piano recital. But she may or may not be able to explain any of this. And even when she does come up with an answer, she might be worried that the answer is not good enough to justify the feeling. Under these circumstances, a series of questions can just make a child silent. It's better to simply reflect what you notice. You can say, "You seem a little tired today," or, "I noticed that you frowned when I mentioned the recital," and wait for her response.

① giving quick advice
② pushing her for answers
③ sharing simple observations
④ telling your own life stories
⑤ leaving her alone to cool down

구문 서술형

주어진 우리말과 일치하도록 괄호 안의 단어를 이용하여 알맞은 가정법 문장을 완성하시오. (필요시 형태를 바꿀 것)

네가 단순한 관찰 결과를 공유한다면, 대화가 계속 굴러가게 하는 것이 더 쉬울 텐데. (share, will)

➡ If you simply _____ simple observations, it _____ be easier to get a conversation rolling.

M03 ★★★❀ 고1 2025(6월)/31

다음 빈칸에 들어갈 말로 가장 적절한 것을 고르시오. [3점]

In everyday life, we use _____ to predict where we should pay attention. Different environments create different expectations. This was profoundly illustrated by the scientist Jared Diamond in his book *Guns, Germs, and Steel*. He describes an adventure wandering through the New Guinea jungle with native New Guineans. He relates that these natives tend to perform poorly at tasks Westerners have been trained to do since childhood. But they are hardly stupid. They can detect the most subtle changes in the jungle, good for following the tracks of a predator or for finding the way back home. They know which insects to leave alone, know where food exists, can build and tear down shelters with ease. Diamond, who had never spent time in such places, has no ability to pay attention to these things. Were he to be tested on such tasks, he also would perform poorly.

*profoundly: 심오하게 **subtle: 미묘한

① close cooperation   ② previous experience
③ survival instinct   ④ modern technology
⑤ parental advice

구문 서술형

알맞은 가정법 문장이 되도록 괄호 안의 단어를 배열하시오.

_____ on unfamiliar tasks, he also would perform poorly. (he, to, were, be tested)

다음 빈칸에 들어갈 말로 가장 적절한 것을 고르시오. [3점]

In most respects, humans are one of a relatively small number of species that evolved a very different strategy of _____. Like apes and elephants, we mature at a leisurely pace, grow large bodies, and have few babies but devote much time and energy to raising them well. This unusual strategy succeeds because while apes and elephants produce fewer babies than mice, a larger percentage of their offspring survive to then reproduce. A house mouse can become a mother when she is just five weeks old, has four to ten pups per litter, and can have a new litter every two months over the course of her approximately twelve-month life. However, the vast majority of her pups die young. In contrast, a chimp or elephant mother does not reproduce until she is at least twelve years old, and she gives birth to only one infant every five or six years over the next thirty or so years. About half of these offspring make it to becoming parents.

*ape: 유인원 **offspring: 자손 ***litter: 한 배에서 난 새끼

① making use of fewer resources for reproduction
② investing more energy to reproduce more slowly
③ hiding their intentions to get what they really want
④ passing down shared social values to their offspring
⑤ living separately from their family units at an early age

구문 서술형

문장의 동사를 모두 찾아 밑줄을 긋고, 가정법 과거 문장이 되도록 알맞게 고치시오.

→ If a house mouse becomes a mother when she is older, the vast majority of her pups won't die young.

→ _____, _____, _____

다음 빈칸에 들어갈 말로 가장 적절한 것을 고르시오. [3점]

One of the things that makes uncertainty difficult for members of the public to appreciate is that _____. Take, for example, the distance between Earth and the sun: 1.49597×10^8 km, as measured at one point during the year. This seems relatively precise; after all, using six significant digits means I know the distance to an accuracy of one part in a million or so. However, if the next digit is uncertain, that means the uncertainty in knowing the precise Earth-sun distance is larger than the distance between New York and Chicago! Whether or not the quoted number is "precise" therefore depends on what I'm intending to do with it. If I care only about what minute the sun will rise tomorrow, then the number quoted here is fine. If I want to send a satellite to orbit just above the sun, however, then I would need to know distances more accurately.

*significant digit: 유효 숫자

① the significance of uncertainty is relative
② the relativity of time is difficult to recognize
③ all measurements have the same level of uncertainty
④ measurements of distance do not depend on intention
⑤ specific numbers make people believe without question

구문 서술형

주어진 우리말과 일치하도록 괄호 안의 단어들을 이용하여 가정법 과거 문장을 영작하시오. (필요시 형태를 바꿀 것)

만약 내가 더 정확하게 거리를 안다면, 내가 태양 바로 위에 궤도를 돌 위성을 보낼 수 있을 텐데. (a, satellite, just above, know, accurately, distances, can send, to orbit, the sun)

→ _____

_____

M06 ★★★ 고1 2024(10월)/32

다음 빈칸에 들어갈 말로 가장 적절한 것을 고르시오.

How much we suffer relates to _____ _____. When 1500m runners push themselves into extreme pain to win a race — their muscles screaming and their lungs exploding with oxygen deficit, they don't psychologically suffer much. In fact, ultra-marathon runners — those people who are crazy enough to push themselves beyond the normal boundaries of human endurance, covering distances of 50-100km or more over many hours, talk about making friends with their pain. When a patient has paid for some form of passive back pain therapy and the practitioner pushes deeply into a painful part of a patient's back to mobilise it, the patient calls that good pain if he or she believes this type of deep pressure treatment will be of value, even though the practitioner is pushing right into the patient's sore tissues.

① how long we have been in pain
② how we frame the pain in our mind
③ how fast we can recover from past pain
④ what part of our body we train regularly
⑤ what treatment we receive from experts

구문 서술형

주절의 시제와 어울리도록 밑줄 친 부분을 바르게 고쳐 쓰시오.

If a patient <u>believed</u> a type of deep pressure treatment will be of value, he will call it good pain.

➡ _____

M07 ★★★ 고1 2024(6월)/32

다음 빈칸에 들어갈 말로 가장 적절한 것을 고르시오. [3점]

There's a lot of scientific evidence demonstrating that focused attention leads to _____. In animals rewarded for noticing sound (to hunt or to avoid being hunted for example), we find much larger auditory centers in the brain. In animals rewarded for sharp eyesight, the visual areas are larger. Brain scans of violinists provide more evidence, showing dramatic growth and expansion in regions of the cortex that represent the left hand, which has to finger the strings precisely, often at very high speed. Other studies have shown that the hippocampus, which is vital for spatial memory, is enlarged in taxi drivers. The point is that the physical architecture of the brain changes according to where we direct our attention and what we practice doing.

*cortex: (대뇌) 피질(皮質) **hippocampus: (대뇌 측두엽의) 해마

① improved decision making
② the reshaping of the brain
③ long-term mental tiredness
④ the development of hand skills
⑤ increased levels of self-control

M08 ★★★ 고1 2024(6월)/33

다음 빈칸에 들어갈 말로 가장 적절한 것을 고르시오. [3점]

How did the human mind evolve? One possibility is that _____ caused our brains to evolve the way they did. A human tribe that could out-think its enemies, even slightly, possessed a vital advantage. The ability of your tribe to imagine and predict where and when a hostile enemy tribe might strike, and plan accordingly, gives your tribe a significant military advantage. The human mind became a weapon in the struggle for survival, a weapon far more decisive than any before it. And this mental advantage was applied, over and over, within each succeeding generation. The tribe that could out-think its opponents was more likely to succeed in battle and would then pass on the genes responsible for this mental advantage to its offspring. You and I are the descendants of the winners.

① physical power to easily hunt prey
② individual responsibility in one's inner circle
③ instinctive tendency to avoid natural disasters
④ superiority in the number of one's descendants
⑤ competition and conflicts with other human tribes

다음 빈칸에 들어갈 말로 가장 적절한 것을 고르시오. [3점]

Concepts are vital to human survival, but we must also be careful with them because concepts open the door to essentialism. They _____. Stuart Firestein opens his book, *Ignorance*, with an old proverb, "It is very difficult to find a black cat in a dark room, especially when there is no cat." This statement beautifully sums up the search for essences. History has many examples of scientists who searched fruitlessly for an essence because they used the wrong concept to guide their hypotheses. Firestein gives the example of luminiferous ether, a mysterious substance that was thought to fill the universe so that light would have a medium to move through. The ether was a black cat, writes Firestein, and physicists had been theorizing in a dark room, and then experimenting in it, looking for evidence of a cat that did not exist.

① encourage us to see things that aren't present
② force scientists to simplify scientific theories
③ let us think science is essential and practical
④ drive physicists to explore philosophy
⑤ lead us to ignore the unknown

다음 빈칸에 들어갈 말로 가장 적절한 것을 고르시오. [3점]

One of the most striking characteristics of a sleeping animal or person is that they do not respond normally to environmental stimuli. If you open the eyelids of a sleeping mammal the eyes will not see normally — they _____. Some visual information apparently gets in, but it is not normally processed as it is shortened or weakened; same with the other sensing systems. Stimuli are registered but not processed normally and they fail to wake the individual. Perceptual disengagement probably serves the function of protecting sleep, so some authors do not count it as part of the definition of sleep itself. But as sleep would be impossible without it, it seems essential to its definition. Nevertheless, many animals (including humans) use the intermediate state of drowsiness to derive some benefits of sleep without total perceptual disengagement.

*stimuli: 자극 **disengagement: 이탈 ***drowsiness: 졸음

① get recovered easily
② will see much better
③ are functionally blind
④ are completely activated
⑤ process visual information

다음 빈칸에 들어갈 말로 가장 적절한 것을 고르시오. [3점]

_____ boosts sales. Brian Wansink, Professor of Marketing at Cornell University, investigated the effectiveness of this tactic in 1998. He persuaded three supermarkets in Sioux City, Iowa, to offer Campbell's soup at a small discount: 79 cents rather than 89 cents. The discounted soup was sold in one of three conditions: a control, where there was no limit on the volume of purchases, or two tests, where customers were limited to either four or twelve cans. In the unlimited condition shoppers bought 3.3 cans on average, whereas in the scarce condition, when there was a limit, they bought 5.3 on average. This suggests scarcity encourages sales. The findings are particularly strong because the test took place in a supermarket with genuine shoppers. It didn't rely on claimed data, nor was it held in a laboratory where consumers might behave differently.

*tactic: 전략

① Promoting products through social media
② Reducing the risk of producing poor quality items
③ Restricting the number of items customers can buy
④ Offering several options that customers find attractive
⑤ Emphasizing the safety of products with research data

M12 ★★☆

고1 2023(3월)/31

다음 빈칸에 들어갈 말로 가장 적절한 것을 고르시오.

People differ in how quickly they can reset their biological clocks to overcome jet lag, and the speed of recovery depends on the _____ of travel. Generally, it's easier to fly westward and lengthen your day than it is to fly eastward and shorten it. This east-west difference in jet lag is sizable enough to have an impact on the performance of sports teams. Studies have found that teams flying westward perform significantly better than teams flying eastward in professional baseball and college football. A more recent study of more than 46,000 Major League Baseball games found additional evidence that eastward travel is tougher than westward travel. *jet lag: 시차로 인한 피로감

① direction　　② purpose　　③ season
④ length　　⑤ cost

M13 ★★★

고1 2023(3월)/32

다음 빈칸에 들어갈 말로 가장 적절한 것을 고르시오.

If you want the confidence that comes from achieving what you set out to do each day, then it's important to understand _____. Over-optimism about what can be achieved within a certain time frame is a problem. So work on it. Make a practice of estimating the amount of time needed alongside items on your 'things to do' list, and learn by experience when tasks take a greater or lesser time than expected. Give attention also to fitting the task to the available time. There are some tasks that you can only set about if you have a significant amount of time available. There is no point in trying to gear up for such a task when you only have a short period available. So schedule the time you need for the longer tasks and put the short tasks into the spare moments in between. *gear up: 준비를 갖추다, 대비하다

① what benefits you can get
② how practical your tasks are
③ how long things are going to take
④ why failures are meaningful in life
⑤ why your leisure time should come first

M14 ★★★

고1 2021(9월)/34

다음 빈칸에 들어갈 말로 가장 적절한 것을 고르시오. [3점]

The last two decades of research on the science of learning have shown conclusively that we remember things better, and longer, if _____. This is the teaching method practiced by physics professor Eric Mazur. He doesn't lecture in his classes at Harvard. Instead, he asks students difficult questions, based on their homework reading, that require them to pull together sources of information to solve a problem. Mazur doesn't give them the answer; instead, he asks the students to break off into small groups and discuss the problem among themselves. Eventually, nearly everyone in the class gets the answer right, and the concepts stick with them because they had to find their own way to the answer.

① they are taught repeatedly in class
② we fully focus on them without any distractions
③ equal opportunities are given to complete tasks
④ there's no right or wrong way to learn about a topic
⑤ we discover them ourselves rather than being told them

M15 ✖✖✖✿ 고1 2021(9월)/32

다음 빈칸에 들어갈 말로 가장 적절한 것을 고르시오.

Many evolutionary biologists argue that humans _____. We needed to trade, and we needed to establish trust in order to trade. Language is very handy when you are trying to conduct business with someone. Two early humans could not only agree to trade three wooden bowls for six bunches of bananas but establish rules as well. What wood was used for the bowls? Where did you get the bananas? That business deal would have been nearly impossible using only gestures and confusing noises, and carrying it out according to terms agreed upon creates a bond of trust. Language allows us to be specific, and this is where conversation plays a key role.

① used body language to communicate
② instinctively knew who to depend on
③ often changed rules for their own needs
④ lived independently for their own survival
⑤ developed language for economic reasons

M16 ✖✖✖ 고1 2023(9월)/33

다음 빈칸에 들어갈 말로 가장 적절한 것을 고르시오. [3점]

A key to engagement and achievement is providing students with _____. My scholarly work and my teaching have been deeply influenced by the work of Rosalie Fink. She interviewed twelve adults who were highly successful in their work, including a physicist, a biochemist, and a company CEO. All of them had dyslexia and had had significant problems with reading throughout their school years. While she expected to find that they had avoided reading and discovered ways to bypass it or compensate with other strategies for learning, she found the opposite. "To my surprise,

I found that these dyslexics were enthusiastic readers...they rarely avoided reading. On the contrary, they sought out books." The pattern Fink discovered was that all of her subjects had been passionate in some personal interest. The areas of interest included religion, math, business, science, history, and biography. What mattered was that they read voraciously to find out more.

*dyslexia: 난독증 **voraciously: 탐욕스럽게

① examples from official textbooks
② relevant texts they will be interested in
③ enough chances to exchange information
④ different genres for different age groups
⑤ early reading experience to develop logic skills

M17 ✖✖✖ 고1 2021(9월)/31

다음 빈칸에 들어갈 말로 가장 적절한 것을 고르시오.

Sometimes it is the _____ that gives a business a competitive advantage. Until recently, bicycles had to have many gears, often 15 or 20, for them to be considered high-end. But fixed-gear bikes with minimal features have become more popular, as those who buy them are happy to pay more for much less. The overall profitability of these bikes is much higher than the more complex ones because they do a single thing really well without the cost of added complexity. Companies should be careful of getting into a war over adding more features with their competitors, as this will increase cost and almost certainly reduce profitability because of competitive pressure on price.

*high-end: 최고급의

① simpler product   ② affordable price
③ consumer loyalty   ④ customized design
⑤ eco-friendly technology

✿ 정답 및 해설 174~177p

M18 ✳✳✲ 고1 2023(11월)/31

다음 빈칸에 들어갈 말로 가장 적절한 것을 고르시오. [3점]

A remarkable characteristic of the visual system is that it has the ability of _____. Psychologist George M. Stratton made this clear in an impressive self-experiment. Stratton wore reversing glasses for several days, which literally turned the world upside down for him. In the beginning, this caused him great difficulties: just putting food in his mouth with a fork was a challenge for him. With time, however, his visual system adjusted to the new stimuli from reality, and he was able to act normally in his environment again, even seeing it upright when he concentrated. As he took off his reversing glasses, he was again confronted with problems: he used the wrong hand when he wanted to reach for something, for example. Fortunately, Stratton could reverse the perception, and he did not have to wear reversing glasses for the rest of his life. For him, everything returned to normal after one day.

*reverse: 뒤집다, 반전시키다

① adapting itself
② visualizing ideas
③ assessing distances
④ functioning irregularly
⑤ operating independently

M19 ✳✳✳ 고1 2021(11월)/32

다음 빈칸에 들어갈 말로 가장 적절한 것을 고르시오.

Not only does memory underlie our ability to think at all, it defines the content of our experiences and how we preserve them for years to come. Memory _____. If I were to suffer from heart failure and depend upon an artificial heart, I would be no less myself. If I lost an arm in an accident and had it replaced with an artificial arm, I would still be essentially *me*. As long as my mind and memories remain intact, I will continue to be the same person, no matter which part of my body (other than the brain) is replaced. On the other hand, when someone suffers from advanced Alzheimer's disease and his memories fade, people often say that he "is not himself anymore," or that it is as if the person "is no longer there," though his body remains unchanged.

* intact: 손상되지 않은

① makes us who we are
② has to do with our body
③ reflects what we expect
④ lets us understand others
⑤ helps us learn from the past

M20 ✳✳✲ 고1 2023(11월)/33

다음 빈칸에 들어갈 말로 가장 적절한 것을 고르시오. [3점]

Anthropologist Gregory Bateson suggests that we tend to understand the world by _____. Take platypuses. We might zoom in so closely to their fur that each hair appears different. We might also zoom out to the extent where it appears as a single, uniform object. We might take the platypus as an individual, or we might treat it as part of a larger unit such as a species or an ecosystem. It's possible to move between many of these perspectives, although we may need some additional tools and skills to zoom in on individual pieces of hair or zoom out to entire ecosystems. Crucially, however, we can only take up one perspective at a time. We can pay attention to the varied behavior of individual animals, look at what unites them into a single species, or look at them as part of bigger ecological patterns. Every possible perspective involves emphasizing certain aspects and ignoring others.

*anthropologist: 인류학자 **platypus: 오리너구리

① using our experiences as a guide
② breaking the framework of old ideas
③ adding new information to what we know
④ focusing in on particular features within it
⑤ considering both bright and dark sides of it

M21 ~ 23 ▶ 제한시간 6분

M21 ⭐ 2등급 대비 　　　　고1 2022(9월)/33

다음 빈칸에 들어갈 말로 가장 적절한 것을 고르시오. [3점]

The demand for freshness can _____. While freshness is now being used as a term in food marketing as part of a return to nature, the demand for year-round supplies of fresh produce such as soft fruit and exotic vegetables has led to the widespread use of hot houses in cold climates and increasing reliance on total quality control — management by temperature control, use of pesticides and computer/satellite-based logistics. The demand for freshness has also contributed to concerns about food wastage. Use of 'best before', 'sell by' and 'eat by' labels has legally allowed institutional waste. Campaigners have exposed the scandal of over-production and waste. Tristram Stuart, one of the global band of anti-waste campaigners, argues that, with freshly made sandwiches, over-ordering is standard practice across the retail sector to avoid the appearance of empty shelf space, leading to high volumes of waste when supply regularly exceeds demand.

*pesticide: 살충제 **logistics: 물류, 유통

① have hidden environmental costs
② worsen the global hunger problem
③ bring about technological advances
④ improve nutrition and quality of food
⑤ diversify the diet of a local community

M22 ⭐ 2등급 대비 　　　　고1 2022(11월)/32

다음 빈칸에 들어갈 말로 가장 적절한 것을 고르시오. [3점]

The best way in which innovation changes our lives is by _____. The main theme of human history is that we become steadily more specialized in what we produce, and steadily more diversified in what we consume: we move away from unstable self-sufficiency to safer mutual interdependence. By concentrating on serving other people's needs for forty hours a week — which we call a job — you can spend the other seventy-two hours (not counting fifty-six hours in bed) relying on the services provided to you by other people. Innovation has made it possible to work for a fraction of a second in order to be able to afford to turn on an electric lamp for an hour, providing the quantity of light that would have required a whole day's work if you had to make it yourself by collecting and refining sesame oil or lamb fat to burn in a simple lamp, as much of humanity did in the not so distant past.

*a fraction of a second: 아주 짧은 시간 **refine: 정제하다

① respecting the values of the old days
② enabling people to work for each other
③ providing opportunities to think creatively
④ satisfying customers with personalized services
⑤ introducing and commercializing unusual products

M23 ⭐ 1등급 대비 　　　　고1 2022(9월)/31

다음 빈칸에 들어갈 말로 가장 적절한 것을 고르시오. [3점]

We worry that the robots are taking our jobs, but just as common a problem is that the robots are taking our _____. In the large warehouses so common behind the scenes of today's economy, human 'pickers' hurry around grabbing products off shelves and moving them to where they can be packed and dispatched. In their ears are headpieces: the voice of 'Jennifer', a piece of software, tells them where to go and what to do, controlling the smallest details of their movements. Jennifer breaks down instructions into tiny chunks, to minimise error and maximise productivity — for example, rather than picking eighteen copies of a book off a shelf, the human worker would be politely instructed to pick five. Then another five. Then yet another five. Then another three. Working in such conditions reduces people to machines made of flesh. Rather than asking us to think or adapt, the Jennifer unit takes over the thought process and treats workers as an inexpensive source of some visual processing and a pair of opposable thumbs.

*dispatch: 발송하다 **chunk: 덩어리

① reliability　　② judgment　　③ endurance
④ sociability　　⑤ cooperation

1st 빈칸이 포함된 문장을 읽고, 빈칸에 들어갈 말에 대한 단서를 찾으세요.
2nd 찾은 단서를 통해 글의 어느 부분에 집중해 읽어야 하는지 파악하세요.
3rd 정답을 고른 후 빈칸에 넣어서 다시 읽어보고 문맥에 맞는지 확인하세요.

M24 ★★★ .... 고1 2025(3월)/33

다음 빈칸에 들어갈 말로 가장 적절한 것을 고르시오. [3점]

Our skin conducts electricity more or less efficiently, depending on our emotions. We know that when we're emotionally stimulated — stressed, sad, any intense emotion, really — our bodies sweat a tiny bit, so little we might not even notice. And when those tiny drops of sweat appear, our skin gets more electrically conductive. This change in sweat gland activity happens completely without your conscious mind having much say in the matter. If you feel emotionally intense, you're going to notice an increase in sweat gland activity. This is particularly useful from a scientific viewpoint, because it allows us to put an objective value on a subjective state of mind. We can actually _____ by tracking how your body subconsciously sweats, by running a bit of electricity through your skin. We can then turn the subjective, subconscious experience of emotional intensity into an objective number by figuring out how good your skin gets at transferring an electrical current.

*sweat gland: 땀샘

① limit reactions of hormones
② control the electrical current
③ improve your skin conditions
④ measure your emotional state
⑤ diversify emotional experiences

1st 빈칸이 포함된 문장을 읽고, 빈칸에 들어갈 말에 대한 단서를 찾으세요.

We can actually _____ / by tracking how
우리는 실제로 _____ 할 수 있다 / 여러분의 신체가

your body subconsciously sweats, / by running a
의식하지 못한 채 어떻게 땀을 흘리는지를 추적함으로써 / 그리고 피부를 통해

bit of electricity through your skin. //
약간의 전류를 흐르게 함으로써 //

● 빈칸 뒤에 「by -ing」가 두 번 나왔어요.
「by -ing」는 '~함으로써'를 뜻해요. 즉, 우리가 어떻게 땀을 흘리는지를 추적함으로써 실제로 '무엇'을 할 수 있는데, 우리가 어떻게 땀을 흘리는지 추적하는 것은 피부에 ❶( )를 흐르게 함으로써 할 수 있어요.

● 빈칸이 포함된 문장에 어떤 키워드가 있나요?
sweats, electricity, skin이 눈에 띄어요. 이 키워드들이 어떻게 연관되는지, 그리고 이것들을 통해 우리가 실제로 '무엇'을 할 수 있는지를 파악해야 해요.

2nd 찾은 단서를 통해 글의 어느 부분에 집중해 읽어야 하는지 파악하세요.

1) 앞서 확인한 키워드를 떠올리며 처음부터 읽어보세요.

Our skin conducts electricity / more or less
우리의 피부는 전기를 전도한다 / 꽤 효율적으로

efficiently, / depending on our emotions. //
/ 우리의 감정에 따라 //

We know that when we're emotionally stimulated /
우리가 감정적으로 자극되었을 때 /

— stressed, sad, any intense emotion, really / —
즉, 정말로 스트레스를 받거나, 슬프거나, 어떤 강렬한 감정일 때 /

our bodies sweat a tiny bit, / so little we might not
우리 몸은 땀을 아주 약간 흘리는데 / 너무 적어서 알아차리지도

even notice. //
못할 정도이다 //

● 앞서 확인한 키워드들 외에도 하나가 더 등장해요.
electricity와 skin이 첫 문장부터 등장하고 그다음 문장에 sweat도 있네요! 그런데 ❷( )라는 키워드가 추가로 언급되었어요. 감정에 따라 피부가 효율적으로 전기를 전도한다는 것으로 보아, 감정이 중요한 변수로 작용함을 알 수 있어요.

● 두 문장의 내용을 종합해 볼까요?
감정적인 자극은 피부에 소량의 땀이 흐르게 하는데, 그로 인해 피부가 효율적으로 전기를 전도한대요. 물론 땀도 물이니까 땀이 묻은 피부에는 전기가 잘 흐르겠지만, 알아차리지도 못할 정도로 적은 땀에도 전기가 잘 흐를지는 의문이에요. 땀이 많이 흐르는 경우가 추가로 언급될 것 같으니 나머지 문장을 더 살펴봐야겠어요.

2) 두 번째 문장과 비슷한 단어로 이루어진 문장이 있어요.

If you feel emotionally intense, / you're going to
만약 여러분이 감정적으로 강렬하게 느낀다면 / 여러분은 알아차릴 것이다
notice / an increase in sweat gland activity. //
/ 땀샘 활동의 증가를 //

● 두 문장의 단어를 서로 비교해 볼까요?
두 번째 문장의 emotionally stimulated는 비슷한 표현인 emotionally intense로 대체되었고, notice는 그대로 다시 등장해요.

● 예상한 내용의 문장이 나왔군요!
강렬한 감정은 땀샘 활동을 증가시킨대요. 즉, 원래 감정적인 자극은 알아차리지 못할 정도의 땀을 흘리게 하지만, 감정이 강렬하다면 알아차릴 수 있을 정도로 땀샘 활동이 증가함을 알 수 있어요.

3) 바로 다음 문장을 살펴봅시다.

This is particularly useful / from a scientific
이는 특히 유용한데 / 과학적 관점에서
viewpoint, / because it allows us to put an objective
/ 그것이 우리가 객관적인 값을 부여할 수 있게 해주기 때문이다
value / on a subjective state of mind. //
/ 주관적인 마음 상태에 //

● This는 무엇을 가리키나요?
앞 문장에서 강렬한 감정이 땀샘 활동의 증가로 이어진다고 했죠? This는 이 사실을 가리키고, 이 사실 자체가 과학적 관점에서 유용하다는 내용으로 글이 전개되네요.

● objective와 subjective에 대응하는 키워드가 있나요?
전류(electricity)는 값으로 측정할 수 있기 때문에 객관적(objective)이고, 감정(emotion)은 주관적인(subjective) 마음 상태에 해당해요. 즉, 이 문장은 마음 상태에 전류의 값을 부여할 수 있다는 내용인데, 이게 정확히 무엇을 의미하는 걸까요?

4) 글의 마지막 문장을 봅시다.

We can then turn / the subjective, subconscious
우리는 그다음에 바꿀 수 있다 / 감정적 강도의 주관적이고, 잠재의식적인
experience of emotional intensity / into an objective
경험을 / 객관적인 숫자로
number / by figuring out / how good your skin gets
/ 계산함으로써 / 여러분의 피부가 전류를 얼마나
at transferring an electrical current. //
잘 전달하는지를 //

● 이 문장은 빈칸이 포함된 문장의 바로 뒤에 있어요.
빈칸이 포함된 문장은 우리가 어떻게 땀을 흘리는지 추적하고 피부에 전류를 흐르게 해서 '무엇'을 할 수 있다고 했어요. 바로 뒤에 마지막 문장이 이어지는데, 피부가 전류를 전달하는 정도를 계산하여 감정적 강도를 숫자로 바꿀 수 있다고 하네요.

● 앞의 내용을 부연 설명하는 문장이에요.
앞에서 마음 상태에 전류의 값을 부여할 수 있다고 했죠? 이는 바로 감정적 강도를 숫자로 바꾸는 것, 즉 감정 상태를 **3**(   ) 한다는 것과 같아요.

➤ **글을 읽으며 이해한 내용을 정리해 볼까요?**

우리의 피부는 감정에 따라 땀을 흘리고, 이는 피부가 전도력이 있는 상태로 만들어요. 원래 인간의 감정은 스트레스 30, 슬픔 70처럼 정확히 측정하기는 어렵지만, 강렬한 감정으로 땀샘 활동이 증가하여 피부에 흐르는 전류를 측정할 수 있게 되면 감정의 정도를 파악할 수 있다는 것이 글의 내용이에요.

3rd 정답을 고른 후 빈칸에 넣어서 다시 읽어보고 문맥에 맞는지 확인하세요.

1) 각 선택지의 해석을 확인해 보세요.

① limit reactions of hormones
호르몬 반응을 제한하다
② control the electrical current
전류를 조절하다
③ improve your skin conditions
여러분의 피부 상태를 개선하다
④ measure your emotional state
여러분의 감정 상태를 측정하다
⑤ diversify emotional experiences
감정 경험을 다양화하다

2) 문맥에 맞는 답은 무엇인가요?
우리가 어떻게 땀을 흘리는지 추적하고 피부에 전류를 흐르게 해서 실제로 '감정 상태를 측정'할 수 있다는 것이므로 정답은 **4**(   )!

 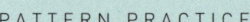

M25~28 ▶ 제한시간 8분

M25 ★★★　　　　　　　　　고1 2025(3월)/31

다음 빈칸에 들어갈 말로 가장 적절한 것을 고르시오. [3점]

Plato argued that when you see something that strikes you as beautiful, you are really just seeing a partial reflection of true beauty, just as a painting or even a photograph only captures part of the real thing. True beauty, or what Plato calls the Form of Beauty, has no particular color, shape, or size. Rather, it is a(n) _____ idea, like the number five. You can make drawings of the number five in blue or red ink, big or small, but the number five itself is none of those things. It has no physical form. Think of the idea of a triangle, for example. Although it has no particular color or size, it somehow lies within each and every triangle you see. Plato thought the same was true of beauty. The Form of Beauty somehow lies within each and every beautiful thing you see.

① abstract　　② practical　　③ imperfect
④ visualized　　⑤ changeable

구문 서술형

다음 가정법의 시제를 판단하고, 시제에 유의하여 해석하시오.

If you make drawings of the number five, it will have no physical form.

➡ 가정법의 시제: _____

➡ 문장 해석: _____

_____

M26 ★★★❀　　　　　　　　　고1 2025(9월)/34

다음 빈칸에 들어갈 말로 가장 적절한 것을 고르시오. [3점]

Richard Heinberg, an American journalist, argues that in building the renewable energy infrastructure to stop global warming, we are actually involved in one of the greatest change projects in human history. In addition to solar panels and wind turbines, we have to build an alternative transport infrastructure, farming procedures and industrial processes. This transformation cannot happen without fossil fuels. For instance, production of concrete structures and steel elements require amounts of energy that is only possible to produce with fossil energy. Production of solar panels requires scarce and expensive minerals which must be excavated, again requiring the use of fossil fuels. Thus, the harder we push towards a renewable energy system, the faster _____. This is not only expensive, but also an undermining factor for our efforts to cut global emissions. Heinberg remarks that the cost of building this new energy infrastructure is seldom counted in transition proposals, which tend to focus just on energy supply requirements.　　　*excavate: 발굴하다

① we are taking full advantage of renewable energy sources
② we have to use fossil energy for the construction process
③ we invest in more natural resources for the environment
④ we are able to decrease the rate of global warming
⑤ alternative energy markets become competitive

구문 서술형

문장의 동사를 모두 찾아 밑줄을 긋고, 가정법 과거 문장이 되도록 알맞게 고치시오.

If we don't push harder towards a renewable energy system, we won't have to use more fossil energy for the construction of new energy infrastructure.

➡ _____ , _____

다음 빈칸에 들어갈 말로 가장 적절한 것을 고르시오.

The best defence most species of octopus have is to stay hidden as much as possible and do their own hunting at night. So to find one in full view in the shallows in daylight was a surprise for two Australian underwater photographers. Actually, what they saw at first was a flounder. It was only when they looked again that they saw a medium-sized octopus, with all eight of its arms folded and its two eyes staring upwards to _____. An octopus has a big brain, excellent eyesight and the ability to change colour and pattern, and this one was using these assets to turn itself into a completely different creature. Many more of this species have been found since then, and there are now photographs of octopuses that could be said to be transforming into sea snakes. And while they mimic, they hunt — producing the spectacle of, say, a flounder suddenly developing an octopodian arm, sticking it down a hole and grabbing whatever's hiding there.

*flounder: 넙치 **mimic: 모방하다

① get a broad view
② create the illusion
③ capture the moment
④ find its hiding spot
⑤ mark its territory

구문 서술형

직설법 문장을 가정법 과거완료 문장으로 고쳐 쓰시오.

The octopus couldn't defend itself because it didn't stay hidden.

➡ _____

다음 빈칸에 들어갈 말로 가장 적절한 것을 고르시오. [3점]

On-screen, climate disaster is everywhere you look, but the scope of the world's climate transformation may just as quickly eliminate the climate-fiction genre — indeed eliminate any effort to tell the story of warming, which could grow too large and too obvious even for Hollywood. You can tell stories 'about' climate change while it still seems a marginal feature of human life. But when the temperature rises by three or four more degrees, hardly anyone will be able to feel isolated from its impacts. And so as climate change expands across the horizon, _____. Why watch or read climate fiction about the world you can see plainly out your own window? At the moment, stories illustrating global warming can still offer an escapist pleasure, even if that pleasure often comes in the form of horror. But when we can no longer pretend that climate suffering is distant — in time or in place — we will stop pretending about it and start pretending within it.

① it may resolve on its own
② it may cease to be a story
③ a forgotten genre will be reborn
④ its impact will be overestimated
⑤ the story's plot will become complex

구문 서술형

괄호 안의 단어를 이용하여 가정법 현재 문장을 완성하시오. (필요시 형태를 바꿀 것)

➡ If the temperature _____ by four more degrees, hardly anyone _____ isolated from its impacts. (rise, be able to feel)

M29 ★★★ 고1 2024(3월)/31

다음 빈칸에 들어갈 말로 가장 적절한 것을 고르시오.

Every species has certain climatic requirements — what degree of heat or cold it can endure, for example. When the climate changes, the places that satisfy those requirements change, too. Species are forced to follow. All creatures are capable of some degree of _____. Even creatures that appear immobile, like trees and barnacles, are capable of dispersal at some stage of their life — as a seed, in the case of the tree, or as a larva, in the case of the barnacle. A creature must get from the place it is born — often occupied by its parent — to a place where it can survive, grow, and reproduce. From fossils, scientists know that even creatures like trees moved with surprising speed during past periods of climate change.

*barnacle: 따개비 **dispersal: 분산 ***fossil: 화석

① endurance
② movement
③ development
④ transformation
⑤ communication

M30 ★★★ 고1 2024(3월)/32

다음 빈칸에 들어갈 말로 가장 적절한 것을 고르시오. [3점]

No respectable boss would say, "I make it a point to discourage my staff from speaking up, and I maintain a culture that prevents disagreeing viewpoints from ever getting aired." If anything, most bosses even say that they are pro-dissent. This idea can be found throughout the series of conversations with corporate, university, and nonprofit leaders, published weekly in the business sections of newspapers. In the interviews, the featured leaders are asked about their management techniques, and regularly claim to continually encourage _____ from more junior staffers. As Bot Pittman remarked in one of these conversations: "I want us to listen to these dissenters because they may intend to tell you why we can't do something, but if you listen hard, what they're really telling you is what you must do to get something done." *dissent: 반대

① unconditional loyalty
② positive attitude
③ internal protest
④ competitive atmosphere
⑤ outstanding performance

M31 ★★★ 고1 2024(6월)/34

다음 빈칸에 들어갈 말로 가장 적절한 것을 고르시오. [3점]

To find the hidden potential in teams, instead of brainstorming, we're better off shifting to a process called brainwriting. The initial steps are solo. You start by asking everyone to generate ideas separately. Next, you pool them and share them anonymously among the group. To preserve independent judgment, each member evaluates them on their own. Only then does the team come together to select and refine the most promising options. By _____ before choosing and elaborating them, teams can surface and advance possibilities that might not get attention otherwise. This brainwriting process makes sure that all ideas are brought to the table and all voices are brought into the conversation. It is especially effective in groups that struggle to achieve collective intelligence.

*anonymously: 익명으로 **surface: 드러내다

① developing and assessing ideas individually
② presenting and discussing ideas out loud
③ assigning different roles to each member
④ coming to an agreement on these options
⑤ skipping the step of judging these options

다음 빈칸에 들어갈 말로 가장 적절한 것을 고르시오. [3점]

While social media attention is potentially an instrument to achieve ends like elite celebrity, some content creators desire ordinary fame as a social end in itself. Not unlike reality television stars, social media celebrities are often criticized for not having skills and talents associated with traditional, elite celebrity, such as acting or singing ability. This criticism highlights the fact that digital content creators face real barriers to crossing over to the sphere of elite celebrity. However, the criticism also misses the point that the phenomenon of ordinary celebrity _____. The elite celebrity is symbolized by the metaphor of the star, characterized by mystery and hierarchical distance and associated with naturalized qualities of talent and class. The ordinary celebrity attracts attention through regular and frequent interactions with other ordinary people. Achieving ordinary fame as a social media celebrity is like doing well at a game, because in this sphere, fame is nothing more nor less than relatively high scores on attention scales, the metrics of subscribers, followers, Likes, or clicks built into social media applications.

*sphere: 영역 **metric: 측정 기준

① shifts to that of elite celebrity
② disappears gradually over time
③ focuses solely on talent and class
④ reconstructs the meaning of fame
⑤ restricts interactions with the public

다음 빈칸에 들어갈 말로 가장 적절한 것을 고르시오. [3점]

Researchers are working on a project that asks coastal towns how they are preparing for rising sea levels. Some towns have risk assessments; some towns even have a plan. But it's a rare town that is actually carrying out a plan. One reason we've failed to act on climate change is the common belief that _____. For decades, climate change was a prediction about the future, so scientists talked about it in the future tense. This became a habit — so that even today many scientists still use the future tense, even though we know that a climate crisis is ongoing. Scientists also often focus on regions most affected by the crisis, such as Bangladesh or the West Antarctic Ice Sheet, which for most Americans are physically remote.

① it is not related to science
② it is far away in time and space
③ energy efficiency matters the most
④ careful planning can fix the problem
⑤ it is too late to prevent it from happening

M34 ✱✱✱ _____ 고1 2021(6월)/34

다음 빈칸에 들어갈 말로 가장 적절한 것을 고르시오. [3점]

It is common to assume that creativity concerns primarily the relation between actor(creator) and artifact(creation). However, from a sociocultural standpoint, the creative act is never "complete" in the absence of a second position—that of an audience. While the actor or creator him/herself is the first audience of the artifact being produced, this kind of distantiation can only be achieved by _____. This means that, in order to be an audience to your own creation, a history of interaction with others is needed. We exist in a social world that constantly confronts us with the "view of the other." It is the view we include and blend into our own activity, including creative activity. This outside perspective is essential for creativity because it gives new meaning and value to the creative act and its product. *artifact: 창작물

① exploring the absolute truth in existence
② following a series of precise and logical steps
③ looking outside and drawing inspiration from nature
④ internalizing the perspective of others on one's work
⑤ pushing the audience to the limits of its endurance

M35 ✱✱✱ _____ 고1 2023(6월)/32

다음 빈칸에 들어갈 말로 가장 적절한 것을 고르시오. [3점]

Think of the brain as a city. If you were to look out over a city and ask "where is the economy located?" you'd see there's no good answer to the question. Instead, the economy emerges from the interaction of all the elements — from the stores and the banks to the merchants and the customers. And so it is with the brain's operation: it doesn't happen in one spot. Just as in a city, no neighborhood of the brain _____.
In brains and in cities, everything emerges from the interaction between residents, at all scales, locally and distantly. Just as trains bring materials and textiles into a city, which become processed into the economy, so the raw electrochemical signals from sensory organs are transported along superhighways of neurons. There the signals undergo processing and transformation into our conscious reality. *electrochemical: 전기화학의

① operates in isolation
② suffers from rapid changes
③ resembles economic elements
④ works in a systematic way
⑤ interacts with another

M36 ✱✱✱ _____ 고1 2021(11월)/34

다음 빈칸에 들어갈 말로 가장 적절한 것을 고르시오. [3점]

Some deep-sea organisms are known to use bioluminescence as a lure, to attract prey with a little glow imitating the movements of their favorite fish, or like fireflies, as a sexual attractant to find mates. While there are many possible evolutionary theories for the survival value of bioluminescence, one of the most fascinating is to _____. The color of almost all bioluminescent molecules is blue-green, the same color as the ocean above. By self-glowing blue-green, the creatures no longer cast a shadow or create a silhouette, especially when viewed from below against the brighter waters above. Rather, by glowing themselves, they can blend into the sparkles, reflections, and scattered blue-green glow of sunlight or moonlight. Thus, they are most likely making their own light not to see, but to be un-seen. *bioluminescence: 생물 발광 **lure: 가짜 미끼

① send a signal for help
② threaten enemies nearby
③ lift the veil of hidden prey
④ create a cloak of invisibility
⑤ serve as a navigation system

M37 ✱✱✱

다음 빈칸에 들어갈 말로 가장 적절한 것을 고르시오. [3점]

The famous primatologist Frans de Waal, of Emory University, says humans downplay similarities between us and other animals as a way of maintaining our spot at the top of our imaginary ladder. Scientists, de Waal points out, can be some of the worst offenders — employing technical language to _____. They call "kissing" in chimps "mouth-to-mouth contact"; they call "friends" between primates "favorite affiliation partners"; they interpret evidence showing that crows and chimps can make tools as being somehow qualitatively different from the kind of toolmaking said to define humanity. If an animal can beat us at a cognitive task — like how certain bird species can remember the precise locations of thousands of seeds — they write it off as instinct, not intelligence. This and so many more tricks of language are what de Waal has termed "linguistic castration." The way we use our tongues to disempower animals, the way we invent words to maintain our spot at the top.

*primatologist: 영장류학자 **affiliation: 제휴

① define human instincts
② overestimate chimps' intelligence
③ distance the other animals from us
④ identify animals' negative emotions
⑤ correct our misconceptions about nature

M38 ✱✱✱

다음 빈칸에 들어갈 말로 가장 적절한 것을 고르시오. [3점]

Generalization without specific examples that humanize writing is boring to the listener and to the reader. Who wants to read platitudes all day? Who wants to hear the words great, greater, best, smartest, finest, humanitarian, on and on and on without specific examples? Instead of using these 'nothing words,' leave them out completely and just describe the _____. There is nothing worse than reading a scene in a novel in which a main character is described up front as heroic or brave or tragic or funny, while thereafter, the writer quickly moves on to something else. That's no good, no good at all. You have to use less one word descriptions and more detailed, engaging descriptions if you want to make something real.

*platitude: 상투적인 말

① similarities   ② particulars   ③ fantasies
④ boredom   ⑤ wisdom

M39 ✱✱✱

다음 빈칸에 들어갈 말로 가장 적절한 것을 고르시오.

We don't send telegraphs to communicate anymore, but it's a great metaphor for giving advance notice. Sometimes, you must inform those close to you of upcoming change by conveying important information well in advance. There's a huge difference between saying, "From now on, we will do things differently," which doesn't give people enough time to understand and accept the change, and saying something like, "Starting next month, we're going to approach things differently." Telegraphing empowers people to _____. Telegraphing involves the art of seeing an upcoming event or circumstance and giving others enough time to process and accept the change. Telegraph anything that will take people out of what is familiar and comfortable to them. This will allow processing time for them to accept the circumstances and make the most of what's happening.

① unite   ② adapt   ③ object
④ compete   ⑤ recover

M40 ★★★❀ 고1 2023(6월)/33

다음 빈칸에 들어갈 말로 가장 적절한 것을 고르시오. [3점]

Someone else's body language affects our own body, which then creates an emotional echo that makes us feel accordingly. As Louis Armstrong sang, "When you're smiling, the whole world smiles with you." If copying another's smile makes us feel happy, the emotion of the smiler has been transmitted via our body. Strange as it may sound, this theory states that _____. For example, our mood can be improved by simply lifting up the corners of our mouth. If people are asked to bite down on a pencil lengthwise, taking care not to let the pencil touch their lips (thus forcing the mouth into a smile-like shape), they judge cartoons funnier than if they have been asked to frown. The primacy of the body is sometimes summarized in the phrase "I must be afraid, because I'm running."

*lengthwise: 길게 **frown: 얼굴을 찡그리다

① language guides our actions
② emotions arise from our bodies
③ body language hides our feelings
④ what others say affects our mood
⑤ negative emotions easily disappear

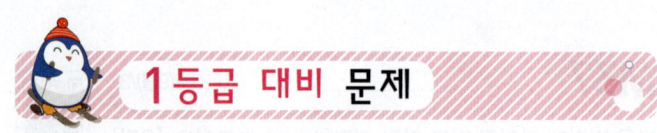
1등급 대비 문제

M41 ~ 43 ▶ 제한시간 6분

M41 ★ 2등급 대비 고1 2021(6월)/31

다음 빈칸에 들어갈 말로 가장 적절한 것을 고르시오.

In a culture where there is a belief that you can have anything you truly want, there is no problem in choosing. Many cultures, however, do not maintain this belief. In fact, many people do not believe that life is about getting what you want. Life is about doing what you are *supposed* to do. The reason they have trouble making choices is they believe that what they may want is not related to what they are supposed to do. The weight of outside considerations is greater than their _____. When this is an issue in a group, we discuss what makes for good decisions. If a person can be unburdened from their cares and duties and, just for a moment, consider what appeals to them, they get the chance to sort out what is important to them. Then they can consider and negotiate with their external pressures.

① desires   ② merits   ③ abilities
④ limitations   ⑤ worries

다음 빈칸에 들어갈 말로 가장 적절한 것을 고르시오.

Research has confirmed that athletes are less likely to participate in unacceptable behavior than are non-athletes. However, moral reasoning and good sporting behavior seem to decline as athletes progress to higher competitive levels, in part because of the increased emphasis on winning. Thus winning can be _____ in teaching character development. Some athletes may want to win so much that they lie, cheat, and break team rules. They may develop undesirable character traits that can enhance their ability to win in the short term. However, when athletes resist the temptation to win in a dishonest way, they can develop positive character traits that last a lifetime. Character is a learned behavior, and a sense of fair play develops only if coaches plan to teach those lessons systematically.

*trait: 특성

① a piece of cake
② a one-way street
③ a bird in the hand
④ a fish out of water
⑤ a double-edged sword

다음 빈칸에 들어갈 말로 가장 적절한 것을 고르시오. [3점]

Over time, babies construct expectations about what sounds they will hear when. They hold in memory the sound patterns that occur on a regular basis. They make hypotheses like, "If I hear *this* sound first, it probably will be followed by *that* sound." Scientists conclude that much of babies' skill in learning language is due to their _____. For babies, this means that they appear to pay close attention to the patterns that repeat in language. They remember, in a systematic way, how often sounds occur, in what order, with what intervals, and with what changes of pitch. This memory store allows them to track, within the neural circuits of their brains, the frequency of sound patterns and to use this knowledge to make predictions about the meaning in patterns of sounds.

① lack of social pressures
② ability to calculate statistics
③ desire to interact with others
④ preference for simpler sounds
⑤ tendency to imitate caregivers

M ③ 빈칸이 <u>끝부분</u>에 있는 경우

- **1st** 먼저 빈칸이 포함된 문장을 읽고, 빈칸에 들어갈 말에 대한 단서를 찾으세요.
- **2nd** **1st** 에서 찾은 것들을 토대로 글을 읽으며 핵심 내용을 파악하세요.
- **3rd** 빈칸에 알맞은 선택지를 골라 빈칸 문장을 완성하세요.

M44 ★★★ .... 고1 2023(3월)/33

다음 빈칸에 들어갈 말로 가장 적절한 것을 고르시오. [3점]

In Lewis Carroll's *Through the Looking-Glass*, the Red Queen takes Alice on a race through the countryside. They run and they run, but then Alice discovers that they're still under the same tree that they started from. The Red Queen explains to Alice: "*here*, you see, it takes all the running you can do, to keep in the same place." Biologists sometimes use this Red Queen Effect to explain an evolutionary principle. If foxes evolve to run faster so they can catch more rabbits, then only the fastest rabbits will live long enough to make a new generation of bunnies that run even faster — in which case, of course, only the fastest foxes will catch enough rabbits to thrive and pass on their genes. Even though they might run, the two species _____.

*thrive: 번성하다

① just stay in place
② end up walking slowly
③ never run into each other
④ won't be able to adapt to changes
⑤ cannot run faster than their parents

1st 먼저 빈칸이 포함된 문장을 읽고, 빈칸에 들어갈 말에 대한 단서를 찾으세요.

> Even though they might run, / the two species
> 그것들이 달린다 해도 / 그 두 종은
> _____. //
> _____ //

● **빈칸에 필요한 것이 무엇인가요?**
  어떤 두 종이 달리는데, 그 두 종은 _____이래요.
  두 종이 무엇을 가리키는지, 그것들이 달리는 상황이 나오는지, 그 상황이 어떤 결과를 낳는지 등을 살펴봐야 해요.

2nd **1st** 에서 찾은 것들을 토대로 글을 읽으며 핵심 내용을 파악하세요.

1) 빈칸 문장 바로 앞 문장에 If가 보여요.

> **If** foxes evolve to run faster / so they can catch more
> 만약 여우가 더 빨리 달리도록 진화한다면 / 더 많은 토끼를 잡기 위해
> rabbits, / then only the fastest rabbits will live long
> / 그러면 오직 가장 빠른 토끼만이 충분히 오래 산다
> enough / to make a new generation of bunnies / that
> / 새로운 세대의 토끼를 낳게 되도록 /
> run even faster / — in which case, / of course, /
> 훨씬 더 빨리 달리는 / 이 경우 / 물론 /
> only the fastest foxes will catch enough rabbits / to
> 가장 빠른 여우만이 충분한 토끼를 잡을 것이다 /
> thrive and pass on their genes. //
> 번성하여 자신들의 유전자를 물려주도록 //

● **If의 등장이 의미하는 바는 무엇일까요?**
  우리는 빈칸 문장을 통해 앞에서 어떤 두 종이 달리는 상황이 나올 거라고 예상했어요. If는 부사절 접속사로 상황을 가정하는 문장을 이끌어요.
  이 문장만으로 정답이 무엇인지 확실하게 고를 수는 없지만, 빈칸에 들어갈 말에 대한 단서를 제공하는 상황이 등장한다는 것을 알 수 있어요.

● **그렇다면 이 문장은 어떤 내용인가요?**
  여우와 토끼라는 두 종이 등장했어요. 만약 여우가 토끼를 많이 잡기 위해 더 빨리 달리도록 진화한다면, 토끼도 여우를 피할 만큼 빠른 토끼만이 살아남아 세대를 이어간대요. 여우의 진화가 토끼의 진화로 이어지고, 이 토끼의 진화가 또 여우의 진화로 이어진다는 거죠.
  그렇다면 여우와 토끼가 달린다 해도 그 두 종은 어떻다는 걸까요?

2) 글의 나머지 부분에는 또 어떤 상황이 제시되었는지 확인해 볼까요?

> They run and they run, / but then Alice discovers /
> 그들은 달리고 또 달리지만   / 그러다가 Alice는 발견한다   /
> that they're still under the same tree / that they
> 그들이 여전히 똑같은 나무 아래에 있음을   / 자신들이
> started from. //
> 출발했던   //
> The Red Queen explains to Alice: / "*here*, you see, /
> 붉은 여왕은 Alice에게 설명한다   / "'여기서는' 보다시피   /
> it takes all the running you can do, / to keep in the
> 네가 할 수 있는 모든 뜀박질을 해야 한단다   / 같은 장소에 머물러
> same place." //
> 있으려면"이라고   //

● **Alice와 붉은 여왕이 등장했어요.**

Alice와 붉은 여왕은 달리고 또 달렸는데도 출발선에 머물렀고, 붉은 여왕은 같은 장소에 머물러 있으려면 최선을 다해 달려야 한다고 말했어요. 뒤처지지 않기 위해 모두가 최선을 다하므로 결국 출발선이 같다는 거죠.
앞서 살펴봤던 여우와 토끼가 살아남기 위해 계속 진화했던 것과
❶(   ) 맥락이네요!

3rd **빈칸에 알맞은 선택지를 골라 빈칸 문장을 완성하세요.**

1) 먼저 선택지를 해석해 봅시다.

① just stay in place
   제자리에 머무를 뿐이다
② end up walking slowly
   결국 천천히 걷게 된다
③ never run into each other
   결코 서로 마주치지 않는다
④ won't be able to adapt to changes
   변화에 적응할 수 없을 것이다
⑤ cannot run faster than their parents
   그것들의 부모님보다 빨리 달릴 수 없다

● **빈칸에 들어갈 표현을 찾아봅시다.**

여우와 토끼가 경쟁적으로 달려 결국 양쪽 모두가 진화한 것과, 출발선에라도 있으려면 최선을 다해 뛰어야 한다는 붉은 여왕의 말은 결국 어떤 두 종이 달린다고 해도 그것들은 '제자리에 머무를 뿐'이라는 거였네요. 따라서 정답은 **❷(   )**!
글에 제시된 문장과 완전히 똑같은 정답 선택지가 제시되는 경우는 거의 없어요. '같은 장소에 머무르다(keep in the same place)'와 '제자리에 머무르다(stay in place)'처럼 같은 의미이지만 다르게 표현한 정답 선택지를 골라야 한다는 점에 주의하세요!

● **예시가 하나만 제시됐다면 어떻게 풀어야 했을까요?**

이 글에서는 붉은 여왕과 Alice의 예시에서 '같은 장소에 머무르다'라는 정답 선택지와 거의 같은 문장을 제시해 줬어요. 그래서 여우와 토끼의 상황에서도 쉽게 정답을 찾을 수 있었죠.
하지만 모든 문제가 이렇게 여러 개의 예시를 제시해 주는 것은 아니에요. 하나의 예시만으로도 핵심을 파악해야 하는 문제들도 많이 출제되니 꼭 대비하세요!

2) 글의 흐름을 정리하며 글의 내용을 다시 확인해 봅시다.

예시 ① 붉은 여왕과 Alice: 달리고 또 달렸지만, 여전히 출발했던 나무 아래에 있었음 → 같은 장소에 머물러 있으려면 최선을 다해 달려야 함

예시 ② 여우와 토끼: 여우는 토끼를 더 많이 잡기 위해 빨리 달리도록 진화하고, 여우를 피할 만큼 빠른 토끼만 살아남음

결론 열심히 달려도 함께 달린다면 제자리에 머무를 뿐임

수능 Tip

#접속사 #관계대명사 #that

> They run and they run, / but then Alice discovers
> 그들은 달리고 또 달리지만   / 그러다가 Alice는 발견한다
> / **that** they're still under the same tree / **that** they
> / 그들이 여전히 똑같은 나무 아래에 있음을   / 자신들이
> started from. //
> 출발했던   //

1 **that이 두 번 등장했어요.**

첫 번째 that 앞에 동사 discovers가 온 것으로 보아, 이 that은 discovers의 목적어 역할을 하는 명사절을 이끄는 접속사로 쓰인 것을 알 수 있어요.

2 **두 번째 that 앞에는 선행사가 있군요!**

앞에 선행사 the same tree가 있고, 뒤에는 주어 they와 동사 started from으로 이루어진 문장이 왔는데 from의 목적어가 빠져있어요. 따라서 이 that은 the same tree를 수식하는 **❸(   )** 관계대명사로 쓰인 거예요.

M45 ~ 48 ▶ 제한시간 8분

M45 ★★★✦

다음 빈칸에 들어갈 말로 가장 적절한 것을 고르시오. [3점]

Plants can communicate, although not in the same way we do. Some express their discontent through scents. You know that smell that hangs in the air after you've mowed the lawn? Yeah, that's actually an SOS. Some plants use sound. Yes, sound, though at a frequency that we can't hear. Researchers experimented with plants and microphones to see if they could record any trouble calls. They found that plants produce a high-frequency clicking noise when stressed and can make different sounds for different stressors. The sound a plant makes when it's not getting watered differs from the one it'll make when a leaf is cut. However, it's worth noting that experts don't think plants are crying out in pain. It's more likely that these reactions are knee-jerk survival actions. Plants are living organisms, and their main objective is to survive. Scents and sounds are their tools for _____.

*scent: 냄새 **mow: (잔디를) 깎다 ***knee-jerk: 자동적인

① defending against things that might harm them
② showing their support for neighboring plants
③ hiding their pains and dissatisfaction
④ sharing nutrients with other plants
⑤ changing their genetic structure

구문 서술형

주어진 우리말과 일치하도록 괄호 안의 단어들을 이용하여 영작하시오.

식물들이 소리를 사용한다면, 그것들은 곤경에 처했음을 알리는 소리를 만들 수 있을 것이다. (make, trouble calls, use, sound, plants)

➡ _____

M46 ★★★✦

다음 빈칸에 들어갈 말로 가장 적절한 것을 고르시오.

Most entrepreneurs put in tremendous amounts of time and effort in creating and launching new products and services and then make the mistake of overpricing them. They have created something they care deeply about, it's theirs, and this powerful sense of ownership distorts their perception of value which causes them to overprice their products. While many of them are quick to realize that their initial prices are too high, not all these people are happy or willing to drop their prices to make their products more attractive. And this can be a very costly mistake that may lead to the failure of their new business. When you launch a new product or service, your priority should be to get sufficient market adoption as soon as possible and you should be ready to _____ to achieve this aim. Once you have strong sales volumes, you can increase your prices to maximize your profits.

*entrepreneur: 기업가 **tremendous: 엄청난

① sacrifice your initial prices and profits
② upgrade your products and service
③ maintain the overpricing strategy
④ switch to a brand-new business
⑤ seek out consumer reviews

구문 서술형

괄호 안의 단어를 빈칸에 알맞은 형태로 쓰고, 우리말의 빈칸에 알맞은 말을 쓰시오.

If they _____ that the prices of their products were too high, they wouldn't have overpriced them. (realize)

➡ 사실, 그들은 과거에 자신들의 제품의 가격이 너무 높다는 것을 _____.

다음 빈칸에 들어갈 말로 가장 적절한 것을 고르시오.

When scientists make an important new discovery or experimentally prove some hypothesis, they do not, in general, keep that information to themselves so that they alone can consider its meaning and derive additional theories from it. Instead, they publish their results and make their data available for inspection. This makes it possible for other scientists to reconsider their data and possibly refute their conclusions. More important, though, it makes it possible for other scientists to use that data to construct new hypotheses and perform new experiments. The assumption is that society as a whole will end up knowing more if information is spread as widely as possible, rather than being limited to a few people. In a strict sense, every scientist _____.

*derive: 도출하다 **refute: 반박하다

① pursues only new discoveries
② sticks to their own research ideas
③ is restricted from using certain data
④ ignores the data against their theories
⑤ depends on the work of other scientists

구문 서술형

주어진 문장을 가정법 과거완료 문장으로 바꿀 때, 밑줄 친 부분을 바르게 고쳐 쓰시오.

If information <u>is</u> spread as widely as possible, society as a whole <u>will end up</u> knowing more.

➡ _____, _____

다음 빈칸에 들어갈 말로 가장 적절한 것을 고르시오.

Whether we feel happy or sad, content or discontent, is not determined merely by each individual successive moment of life experience — a good thing happens and I'm happy, a bad thing happens and I'm sad. While our experiences affect our mood, we are not blown in a completely new direction by each gust of wind. As humans, we adjust — to new information and events both good and bad — and return to our personal default level of well-being. There will be highs and lows, but over time, like water seeking its own level, we are pulled toward our baseline — back *up* after bad news and back *down* after good. The euphoria of first love fades, and so does the despair of a break-up. This tendency is best seen with little kids and their toy joy: When they get what they've longed for, they believe they will be happy for the rest of their lives. And for the first few minutes of the rest of their lives, they are. But then the kids — like adults — _____.

*euphoria: (극도의) 행복감

① adapt   ② regret   ③ explore
④ struggle   ⑤ celebrate

구문 서술형

주어진 우리말과 일치하도록 괄호 안의 단어들을 이용하여 영작하시오.

그들이 간절히 원해왔던 것을 얻는다면, 그들은 그들의 남은 인생의 처음 몇 분 동안 행복할 것이다. (what, long for, they, get)

➡ _____, they will be happy for the first few minutes of the rest of their lives.

M49 ★★★   고1 2025(9월)/32

다음 빈칸에 들어갈 말로 가장 적절한 것을 고르시오. [3점]

Although you may put off going to sleep in order to squeeze more activities into your day, eventually your need for sleep becomes overwhelming and you are forced to get some sleep. This daily drive for sleep appears to be due, in part, to a compound known as adenosine. This natural chemical builds up in your blood as time awake increases. While you sleep, your body breaks down the adenosine. Thus, this molecule may be what your body uses to keep track of lost sleep and to trigger sleep when needed. An accumulation of adenosine and other factors might explain why, after several nights of less than optimal amounts of sleep, you build up a sleep debt that you must make up by sleeping longer than normal. Because of such built-in molecular feedback, you can't become accustomed to getting less sleep than your body needs. Eventually, a lack of sleep _____.

*compound: 화합물 **accumulation: 축적

① takes away your energy
② causes mood swings
③ catches up with you
④ breaks down natural chemicals
⑤ triggers adenosine to disappear

구문 서술형

괄호 안의 단어를 이용하여 가정법 과거완료 문장을 완성하시오. (단, 필요시 형태를 바꾸고 주절의 조동사는 would를 쓸 것)

➡ If you _____ several nights of less than optimal amounts of sleep, you _____ a sleep debt. (not have, not build up)

M50 ★★★   고1 2024(3월)/34

다음 빈칸에 들어갈 말로 가장 적절한 것을 고르시오.

A number of research studies have shown how experts in a field often experience difficulties when introducing newcomers to that field. For example, in a genuine training situation, Dr. Pamela Hinds found that people expert in using mobile phones were remarkably less accurate than novice phone users in judging how long it takes people to learn to use the phones. Experts can become insensitive to how hard a task is for the beginner, an effect referred to as the 'curse of knowledge'. Dr. Hinds was able to show that as people acquired the skill, they then began to underestimate the level of difficulty of that skill. Her participants even underestimated how long it had taken themselves to acquire that skill in an earlier session. Knowing that experts forget how hard it was for them to learn, we can understand the need to _____, rather than making assumptions about how students 'should be' learning.

*novice: 초보

① focus on the new functions of digital devices
② apply new learning theories recently released
③ develop varieties of methods to test students
④ forget the difficulties that we have had as students
⑤ look at the learning process through students' eyes

M51 ✱✱✱ 고1 2024(9월)/32

다음 빈칸에 들어갈 말로 가장 적절한 것을 고르시오. [3점]

Every time a new medium comes along — whether it's the invention of the printed book, or TV, or SNS — and you start to use it, it's like you are putting on a new kind of goggles, with their own special colors and lenses. Each set of goggles you put on makes you see things differently. So when you start to watch television, before you absorb the message of any particular TV show — whether it's *Wheel of Fortune* or *The Wire* — you start to see the world as being shaped like television itself. That's why Marshall McLuhan said that every time a new medium comes along — a new way for humans to communicate — it has buried in it a message. It is gently guiding us to _____.

The way information gets to you, McLuhan argued, is more important than the information itself. TV teaches you that the world is fast; that it's about surfaces and appearances.

① see the world according to a new set of codes
② ignore unfamiliar messages from new media
③ maintain steady focus and clear understanding
④ interpret information through a traditional lens
⑤ enjoy various media contents with one platform

M52 ✱✱✱✲ 고1 2022(11월)/31

다음 빈칸에 들어갈 말로 가장 적절한 것을 고르시오. [3점]

To demonstrate how best to defeat the habit of delaying, Dan Ariely, a professor of psychology and behavioral economics, performed an experiment on students in three of his classes at MIT. He assigned all classes three reports over the course of the semester. The first class had to choose three due dates for themselves, up to and including the last day of class. The second had no deadlines — all three papers just had to be submitted by the last day of class. In his third class, he gave students three set deadlines over the course of the semester.

At the end of the semester, he found that students with set deadlines received the best grades, the students with no deadlines had the worst, and those who could choose their own deadlines fell somewhere in the middle. Ariely concludes that _____ — whether by the professor or by students who recognize their own tendencies to delay things — improves self-control and performance.

① offering rewards
② removing obstacles
③ restricting freedom
④ increasing assignments
⑤ encouraging competition

M53 ✱✱✱  고1 2023(11월)/32

다음 빈칸에 들어갈 말로 가장 적절한 것을 고르시오.

Participants in a study were asked to answer questions like "Why does the moon have phases?" Half the participants were told to search for the answers on the internet, while the other half weren't allowed to do so. Then, in the second part of the study, all of the participants were presented with a new set of questions, such as "Why does Swiss cheese have holes?" These questions were unrelated to the ones asked during the first part of the study, so participants who used the internet had absolutely no advantage over those who hadn't. You would think that both sets of participants would be equally sure or unsure about how well they could answer the new questions. But those who used the internet in the first part of the study rated themselves as more knowledgeable than those who hadn't, even about questions they hadn't searched online for. The study suggests that having access to unrelated information was enough to _____.

*phase: (달의) 상(相)

① improve their judgment skills
② pump up their intellectual confidence
③ make them endure challenging situations
④ lead to a collaboration among the participants
⑤ motivate them to pursue in-depth knowledge

M54 ★★★　　　　　　　　　　　　고1 2023(3월)/34

다음 빈칸에 들어갈 말로 가장 적절한 것을 고르시오. [3점]

Everything in the world around us was finished in the mind of its creator before it was started. The houses we live in, the cars we drive, and our clothing — all of these began with an idea. Each idea was then studied, refined and perfected before the first nail was driven or the first piece of cloth was cut. Long before the idea was turned into a physical reality, the mind had clearly pictured the finished product. The human being designs his or her own future through much the same process. We begin with an idea about how the future will be. Over a period of time we refine and perfect the vision. Before long, our every thought, decision and activity are all working in harmony to bring into existence what we _____.

*refine: 다듬다

① didn't even have the potential to accomplish
② have mentally concluded about the future
③ haven't been able to picture in our mind
④ considered careless and irresponsible
⑤ have observed in some professionals

M55 ★★✿　　　　　　　　　　　　고1 2023(9월)/31

다음 빈칸에 들어갈 말로 가장 적절한 것을 고르시오. [3점]

Many people are terrified to fly in airplanes. Often, this fear stems from a lack of control. The pilot is in control, not the passengers, and this lack of control instills fear. Many potential passengers are so afraid they choose to drive great distances to get to a destination instead of flying. But their decision to drive is based solely on emotion, not logic. Logic says that statistically, the odds of dying in a car crash are around 1 in 5,000, while the odds of dying in a plane crash are closer to 1 in 11 million. If you're going to take a risk, especially one that could possibly involve your well-being, wouldn't you want the odds in your favor? However, most people choose the option that will cause them the least amount of _____. Pay attention to the thoughts you have about taking the risk and make sure you're basing your decision on facts, not just feelings.

*instill: 스며들게 하다

① anxiety　　② boredom　　③ confidence
④ satisfaction　　⑤ responsibility

M56 ★★★　　　　　　　　　　　　고1 2023(9월)/34

다음 빈칸에 들어갈 말로 가장 적절한 것을 고르시오. [3점]

For many people, *ability* refers to intellectual competence, so they want everything they do to reflect how smart they are — writing a brilliant legal brief, getting the highest grade on a test, writing elegant computer code, saying something exceptionally wise or witty in a conversation. You could also define ability in terms of a particular skill or talent, such as how well one plays the piano, learns a language, or serves a tennis ball. Some people focus on their ability to be attractive, entertaining, up on the latest trends, or to have the newest gadgets. However ability may be defined, a problem occurs when _____. The performance becomes the *only* measure of the person; nothing else is taken into account. An outstanding performance means an outstanding person; an average performance means an average person. Period.

① it is the sole determinant of one's self-worth
② you are distracted by others' achievements
③ there is too much competition in one field
④ you ignore feedback about a performance
⑤ it is not accompanied by effort

M57 ★★★

다음 빈칸에 들어갈 말로 가장 적절한 것을 고르시오. [3점]

Most times a foreign language is spoken in film, subtitles are used to translate the dialogue for the viewer. However, there are occasions when foreign dialogue is left unsubtitled (and thus incomprehensible to most of the target audience). This is often done if the movie is seen mainly from the viewpoint of a particular character who does not speak the language. Such absence of subtitles allows the audience to feel a similar sense of incomprehension and alienation that the character feels. An example of this is seen in *Not Without My Daughter*. The Persian language dialogue spoken by the Iranian characters is not subtitled because the main character Betty Mahmoody does not speak Persian and the audience is _____.

*subtitle: 자막(을 넣다) **incomprehensible: 이해할 수 없는
***alienation: 소외

① seeing the film from her viewpoint
② impressed by her language skills
③ attracted to her beautiful voice
④ participating in a heated debate
⑤ learning the language used in the film

M58 ★★★

다음 빈칸에 들어갈 말로 가장 적절한 것을 고르시오. [3점]

Face-to-face interaction is a uniquely powerful — and sometimes the only — way to share many kinds of knowledge, from the simplest to the most complex. It is one of the best ways to stimulate new thinking and ideas, too. Most of us would have had difficulty learning how to tie a shoelace only from pictures, or how to do arithmetic from a book. Psychologist Mihàly Csikszentmihàlyi found, while studying high achievers, that a large number of Nobel Prize winners were the students of previous winners: they had access to the same literature as everyone else, but _____ made a crucial difference to their creativity. Within organisations this makes conversation both a crucial factor for high-level professional skills and the most important way of sharing everyday information.

*arithmetic: 계산 **literature: (연구) 문헌

① natural talent
② regular practice
③ personal contact
④ complex knowledge
⑤ powerful motivation

M59 ★★★

다음 빈칸에 들어갈 말로 가장 적절한 것을 고르시오. [3점]

In a study at Princeton University in 1992, research scientists looked at two different groups of mice. One group was made intellectually superior by modifying the gene for the glutamate receptor. Glutamate is a brain chemical that is necessary in learning. The other group was genetically manipulated to be intellectually inferior, also done by modifying the gene for the glutamate receptor. The smart mice were then raised in standard cages, while the inferior mice were raised in large cages with toys and exercise wheels and with lots of social interaction. At the end of the study, although the intellectually inferior mice were genetically handicapped, they were able to perform just as well as their genetic superiors. This was a real triumph for nurture over nature. Genes are turned on or off _____.

*glutamate: 글루타민산염 **manipulate: 조작하다

① by themselves for survival
② free from social interaction
③ based on what is around you
④ depending on genetic superiority
⑤ so as to keep ourselves entertained

M60 ★★★

다음 빈칸에 들어갈 말로 가장 적절한 것을 고르시오. [3점]

The law of demand is that the demand for goods and services increases as prices fall, and the demand falls as prices increase. *Giffen goods* are special types of products for which the traditional law of demand does not apply. Instead of switching to cheaper replacements, consumers demand more of giffen goods when the price increases and less of them when the price decreases. Taking an example, rice in China is a giffen good because people tend to purchase less of it when the price falls. The reason for this is, when the price of rice falls, people have more money to spend on other types of products such as meat and dairy and, therefore, change their spending pattern. On the other hand, as rice prices increase, people _____.

① order more meat   ② consume more rice
③ try to get new jobs   ④ increase their savings
⑤ start to invest overseas

M61 ★★★

다음 빈칸에 들어갈 말로 가장 적절한 것을 고르시오. [3점]

One of the big questions faced this past year was how to keep innovation rolling when people were working entirely virtually. But experts say that digital work didn't have a negative effect on innovation and creativity. Working within limits pushes us to solve problems. Overall, virtual meeting platforms put more constraints on communication and collaboration than face-to-face settings. For instance, with the press of a button, virtual meeting hosts can control the size of breakout groups and enforce time constraints; only one person can speak at a time; nonverbal signals, particularly those below the shoulders, are diminished; "seating arrangements" are assigned by the platform, not by individuals; and visual access to others may be limited by the size of each participant's screen. Such _____ are likely to stretch participants beyond their usual ways of thinking, boosting creativity.

① restrictions   ② responsibilities   ③ memories
④ coincidences   ⑤ traditions

M62 ★★★

다음 빈칸에 들어갈 말로 가장 적절한 것을 고르시오. [3점]

The prevailing view among developmental scientists is that people are active contributors to their own development. People are influenced by the physical and social contexts in which they live, but they also play a role in influencing their development by interacting with, and changing, those contexts. Even infants influence the world around them and construct their own development through their interactions. Consider an infant who smiles at each adult he sees; he influences his world because adults are likely to smile, use "baby talk," and play with him in response. The infant brings adults into close contact, making one-on-one interactions and creating opportunities for learning. By engaging the world around them, thinking, being curious, and interacting with people, objects, and the world around them, individuals of all ages are "_____."

① mirrors of their generation
② shields against social conflicts
③ explorers in their own career path
④ followers of their childhood dreams
⑤ manufacturers of their own development

M63 ★★★

다음 빈칸에 들어갈 말로 가장 적절한 것을 고르시오. [3점]

In the studies of Colin Cherry at the Massachusetts Institute for Technology back in the 1950s, his participants listened to voices in one ear at a time and then through both ears in an effort to determine whether we can listen to two people talk at the same time. One ear always contained a message that the listener had to repeat back (called "shadowing") while the other ear included people speaking. The trick was to see if you could totally focus on the main message and also hear someone talking in your other ear. Cleverly, Cherry found it was impossible for his participants to know whether the message in the other ear was spoken by a man or woman, in English or another language, or was even comprised of real words at all! In other words, people could not _____.

① decide what they should do in the moment
② remember a message with too many words
③ analyze which information was more accurate
④ speak their own ideas while listening to others
⑤ process two pieces of information at the same time

M64 ★★★

다음 빈칸에 들어갈 말로 가장 적절한 것을 고르시오. [3점]

Plato's realism includes all aspects of experience but is most easily explained by considering the nature of mathematical and geometrical objects such as circles. He asked the question, what is a circle? You might indicate a particular example carved into stone or drawn in the sand. However, Plato would point out that, if you looked closely enough, you would see that neither it, nor indeed any physical circle, was perfect. They all possessed flaws, and all were subject to change and decayed with time. So how can we talk about perfect circles if we cannot actually see or touch them? Plato's extraordinary answer was that the world we see is a poor reflection of a deeper unseen reality of *Forms*, or *universals*, where perfect cats chase perfect mice in perfect circles around perfect rocks. Plato believed that the *Forms* or *universals* are the true reality that exists in _____.

① observable phenomena of the physical world
② our experiences shaped by external influences
③ an overlapping area between emotion and reason
④ an invisible but perfect world beyond our senses
⑤ our perception affected by stereotype or generalization

M65 ★★★❀

다음 빈칸에 들어갈 말로 가장 적절한 것을 고르시오.

If you've ever made a poor choice, you might be interested in learning how to break that habit. One great way to trick your brain into doing so is to sign a "Ulysses Contract." The name of this life tip comes from the Greek myth about Ulysses, a captain whose ship sailed past the island of the Sirens, a tribe of dangerous women who lured victims to their death with their irresistible songs. Knowing that he would otherwise be unable to resist, Ulysses instructed his crew to stuff their ears with cotton and tie him to the ship's mast to prevent him from turning their ship towards the Sirens. It worked for him and you can do the same thing by _____. For example, if you want to stay off your cellphone and concentrate on your work, delete the apps that distract you or ask a friend to change your password!

*lure: 유혹하다 **mast: 돛대

① letting go of all-or-nothing mindset
② finding reasons why you want to change
③ locking yourself out of your temptations
④ building a plan and tracking your progress
⑤ focusing on breaking one bad habit at a time

M

M66 ★★★

다음 빈칸에 들어갈 말로 가장 적절한 것을 고르시오.

Individuals who perform at a high level in their profession often have instant credibility with others. People admire them, they want to be like them, and they feel connected to them. When they speak, others listen — even if the area of their skill has nothing to do with the advice they give. Think about a world-famous basketball player. He has made more money from endorsements than he ever did playing basketball. Is it because of his knowledge of the products he endorses? No. It's because of what he can do with a basketball. The same can be said of an Olympic medalist swimmer. People listen to him because of what he can do in the pool. And when an actor tells us we should drive a certain car, we don't listen because of his expertise on engines. We listen because we admire his talent. _____ connects. If you possess a high level of ability in an area, others may desire to connect with you because of it.

*endorsement: (유명인의 텔레비전 등에서의 상품) 보증 선전

① Patience   ② Sacrifice   ③ Honesty
④ Excellence   ⑤ Creativity

M67 ~ 70 ▶ 제한시간 8분

M67 ⭐ 2등급 대비 _____ 고1 2022(11월)/34

다음 빈칸에 들어갈 말로 가장 적절한 것을 고르시오.

Our homes aren't just ecosystems, they're unique ones, hosting species that are adapted to indoor environments and pushing evolution in new directions. Indoor microbes, insects, and rats have all evolved the ability to survive our chemical attacks, developing resistance to antibacterials, insecticides, and poisons. German cockroaches are known to have developed a distaste for glucose, which is commonly used as bait in roach traps. Some indoor insects, which have fewer opportunities to feed than their outdoor counterparts, seem to have developed the ability to survive when food is limited. Dunn and other ecologists have suggested that as the planet becomes more developed and more urban, more species will _____. Over a long enough time period, indoor living could drive our evolution, too. Perhaps my indoorsy self represents the future of humanity.

*glucose: 포도당 **bait: 미끼

① produce chemicals to protect themselves
② become extinct with the destroyed habitats
③ evolve the traits they need to thrive indoors
④ compete with outside organisms to find their prey
⑤ break the boundaries between wildlife and humans

M68 ⭐ 2등급 대비 _____ 고1 2024(10월)/33

다음 빈칸에 들어갈 말로 가장 적절한 것을 고르시오. [3점]

When I worked for a large electronics company that manufactured laser and ink-jet printers, I soon discovered why there are often three versions of many consumer goods. If the manufacturer makes only one version of its product, people who bought it might have been willing to spend more money, so the company is losing some income. If the company offers two versions, one with more features and more expensive than the other, people will compare the two models and still buy the less expensive one. But if the company introduces a third model with even more features and more expensive than the other two, sales of the second model go up; many people like the features of the most expensive model, but not the price. The middle item has more features than the least expensive one, and it is less expensive than the fanciest model. They buy the middle item, unaware that they have been _____.

① manipulated by the presence of the higher-priced item
② persuaded by a high-volume, low-margin strategy
③ tricked to keep purchasing unnecessary products
④ fooled by the wrong information on the price
⑤ exposed to a discounted price repeatedly

다음 빈칸에 들어갈 말로 가장 적절한 것을 고르시오.

One big difference between science and stage magic is that while magicians hide their mistakes from the audience, in science you make your mistakes in public. You show them off so that everybody can learn from them. This way, you get the advantage of everybody else's experience, and not just your own idiosyncratic path through the space of mistakes. This, by the way, is another reason why we humans are so much smarter than every other species. It is not that our brains are bigger or more powerful, or even that we have the ability to reflect on our own past errors, but that we _____ that our individual brains have earned from their individual histories of trial and error.　　*idiosyncratic: (개인에게) 특유한

① share the benefits
② overlook the insights
③ develop creative skills
④ exaggerate the achievements
⑤ underestimate the knowledge

다음 빈칸에 들어갈 말로 가장 적절한 것을 고르시오. [3점]

Due to technological innovations, music can now be experienced by more people, for more of the time than ever before. Mass availability has given individuals unheard-of control over their own sound-environment. However, it has also confronted them with the simultaneous availability of countless genres of music, in which they have to orient themselves. People start filtering out and organizing their digital libraries like they used to do with their physical music collections. However, there is the difference that the choice lies in their own hands. Without being restricted to the limited collection of music-distributors, nor being guided by the local radio program as a 'preselector' of the latest hits, the individual actively has to _____. The search for the right song is thus associated with considerable effort.　　*simultaneous: 동시의

① choose and determine his or her musical preferences
② understand the technical aspects of recording sessions
③ share unique and inspiring playlists on social media
④ interpret lyrics with background knowledge of the songs
⑤ seek the advice of a voice specialist for better performances

다음 빈칸에 들어갈 말로 가장 적절한 것을 고르시오. [3점]

You hear again and again that some of the greatest composers were misunderstood in their own day. Not everyone could understand the compositions of Beethoven, Brahms, or Stravinsky in their day. The reason for this initial lack of acceptance is unfamiliarity. The musical forms, or ideas expressed within them, were completely new. And yet, this is exactly one of the things that makes them so great. Effective composers have their own ideas. Have you ever seen the classic movie *Amadeus*? The composer Antonio Salieri is the "host" of this movie; he's depicted as one of the most famous non-great composers — he lived at the time of Mozart and was completely overshadowed by him. Now, Salieri wasn't a bad composer; in fact, he was a very good one. But he wasn't one of the world's great composers because his work wasn't _____. What he wrote sounded just like what everyone else was composing at the time.

① simple   ② original
③ familiar   ④ conventional
⑤ understandable

다음 빈칸에 들어갈 말로 가장 적절한 것을 고르시오. [3점]

One dynamic that can change dramatically in sport is the concept of the home-field advantage, in which perceived demands and resources seem to play a role. Under normal circumstances, the home ground would appear to provide greater perceived resources (fans, home field, and so on). However, researchers Roy Baumeister and Andrew Steinhilber were among the first to point out that these competitive factors can change; for example, the success percentage for home teams in the final games of a playoff or World Series seems to drop. Fans can become part of the perceived demands rather than resources under those circumstances. This change in perception can also explain why a team that's struggling at the start of the year will _____ to reduce perceived demands and pressures.

*perceive: 인식하다 **playoff: 우승 결정전

① often welcome a road trip
② avoid international matches
③ focus on increasing ticket sales
④ want to have an eco-friendly stadium
⑤ try to advertise their upcoming games

M 어휘 Review

＊ 다음 영어는 우리말 뜻을, 우리말은 영어 단어를 〈보기〉에서 찾아 쓰시오.

〈 보기 〉

역학	emergence	유혹	humanity
전환	overwhelming	보여주다	upcoming
성취	obstacle	판단	modify

01 demonstrate _____

02 achievement _____

03 dynamic _____

04 transition _____

05 temptation _____

06 장애물 _____

07 인류 _____

08 압도적인 _____

09 다가오는 _____

10 수정하다 _____

＊ 다음 우리말에 알맞은 영어 표현을 찾아 연결하시오.

11 ~을 갈망하다 •   • pass on

12 ~을 물려주다 •   • long for

13 ~을 지적하다 •   • catch up with

14 ~을 따라잡다 •   • point out

15 ~을 가려내다 •   • sort out

＊ 다음 우리말 표현에 맞는 단어를 고르시오.

16 위험한 여성 부족 ➡ a (bribe / tribe) of dangerous women

17 희소 조건에서 ➡ in the (scarce / ample) condition

18 가장 간단한 것부터 가장 복잡한 것까지 ➡ from the simplest to the most (competent / complex)

19 궤도를 돌 위성 ➡ a satellite to (omit / orbit)

20 최소한의 특징 ➡ minimal (feature / fracture)

＊ 다음 문장의 빈칸에 알맞은 단어를 〈보기〉에서 찾아 쓰시오.

〈 보기 〉

quoted	absence	sizable	sole
engaging	decline	generalization	precise
perceived	negotiate	stimulate	medium

21 구체적인 사례가 없는 일반화는 듣는 사람과 읽는 사람에게 지루하다.

➡ _____ without specific examples is boring to the listener and to the reader.

22 그들은 외적인 부담에 대해 고려하고 협상할 수 있다.

➡ They can consider and _____ with their external pressures.

23 그러면 여기에 인용된 숫자로 괜찮다.

➡ Then the number _____ here is fine.

24 도덕적 분별력과 바람직한 스포츠 행위가 감소하는 것 같다.

➡ Moral reasoning and good sporting behavior seem to _____.

25 그것이 자기 가치의 유일한 결정 요소이다.

➡ It is the _____ determinant of one's self-worth.

26 제2의 입장이 부재한 상황에서는 창작 행위는 결코 "완전"하지 않다.

➡ The creative act is never "complete" in the _____ of a second position.

27 이러한 동서의 차이는 충분히 크다.

➡ This east-west difference is _____ enough.

28 당신은 세밀하고 마음을 끄는 묘사를 더 많이 사용해야 한다.

➡ You have to use more detailed, _____ descriptions.

29 그것은 새로운 생각과 아이디어를 자극하는 가장 좋은 방법의 한 가지이다. ➡ It is one of the best ways to _____ new thinking and ideas.

30 팬들은 인식된 부담의 일부가 될 수 있다. ➡ Fans can become part of the _____ demands.

흐름에 맞지 않는 문장 찾기

★ 유형 설명

다음 글에서 전체 흐름과 관계 <u>없는</u> 문장은?

① Surprisingly, however, errors in memory were not random. ② Rather, subjects often rewrote

잠깐!
나는 여기에 속하지 않는 것 같아.

첫 문장 이후로 이어지는 글의 논리적인 흐름을 방해하거나 주제와 동떨어진 진술을 하는 문장을 골라내야 한다.

🔑 첫 문장을 읽고, 글의 핵심 소재와 주제를 파악한다.
이어지는 각각의 문장이 앞 문장과 자연스럽게, 적절한 연결어 등으로 연결되는지 확인한다.
전체 글이나 앞 문장에 등장한 소재를 다루긴 하지만 전혀 동떨어진 이야기를 하는 문장이 정답인 경우가 많다.

😎 유형 풀이 비법

1 글의 흐름을 확인하라!
• 문장 간의 논리적 흐름을 위해 지시어와 연결어를 본다.

2 글의 주제를 파악하라!
• 주제나 요지를 파악하고, 이에 어긋나는 문장을 찾는다.

3 어색한 내용을 찾아라!
• 소재는 동일하지만 전혀 다른 내용을 다루는 문장이 있는지 살핀다.

(Tip) 정답으로 고른 문장을 빼고 읽어보며 앞뒤 연결이 자연스러운지 확인한다.

🔑 어휘 및 표현 Preview

□ **compose** 작곡하다
□ **improve** 개선하다
□ **participant** 참가자
□ **session** 활동, 기간
□ **review** 검토하다
□ **treatment** 치료
□ **choir** 합창단
□ **wellbeing** 행복
□ **state** 상태
□ **sensory** 감각의
□ **nerve** 신경
□ **tissue** (세포로 이루어진) 조직
□ **transmit** 전달하다
□ **capacity** 능력, 용량
□ **contract** 수축하다
□ **genuine** 진정한

□ **authority** 권한
□ **assembly** 조립
□ **empower** (권한을) 부여하다
□ **efficiency** 효율성
□ **self-discipline** 자기 통제력
□ **sympathy** 공감
□ **arise** 발생하다
□ **tale** 이야기
□ **viewpoint** 관점
□ **stepsister** 의붓자매
□ **exist** 존재하다
□ **willingly** 기꺼이
□ **illusion** 착각
□ **cram** 벼락치기를 하다
□ **differentiate** 구분하다
□ **enormous** 엄청난

□ **vanish** 사라지다
□ **introduce** 도입하다
□ **factor** 요소, 요인
□ **statistics** 통계학
□ **prediction** 예측
□ **conduct** 수행하다
□ **encounter** 만남, 접함
□ **frequency** 빈도
□ **approach** 접근하다
□ **fade away** 사라지다
□ **symbolic** 상징적인
□ **interpret** 해석하다
□ **unexpectedly** 예상치 못하게
□ **insurer** 보험사
□ **figure out** ~을 알아내다
□ **balance** 균형을 맞추다

14 비교

┌───┐
│ * 「as + 형용사의 원급 + 명사 + as ...」 │
│ 형용사의 원급 뒤에는 명사(구)가 올 수 있다. │
└───┘

1 원급 비교 – 형용사나 부사의 원급을 이용한 비교 구문

1) 기본 형태: *「as + 형용사나 부사의 원급 + as ...」(…만큼 ~한/하게)**

- Simon is (as tall as) his brother is.
  형용사의 원급 비교
  (Simon은 그의 형만큼 키가 크다.)

- Fiona can run (as fast as) he can.
  부사의 원급 비교
  (Fiona는 그만큼 빠르게 달릴 수 있다.)

2) 부정형: 「not as[so] + 형용사나 부사의 원급 + as ...」(…만큼 ~하지 않은/않게)

- Simon is (not as[so] tall as) his brother. (Simon은 그의 형만큼 키가 크지 않다.)

2 비교급 비교

1) 여러 가지 비교급 비교

기본 형태 ┌─ 비교급 비교의 기본 형태는 「형용사나 부사의 비교급 + than ...」(…보다 더 ~한/하게)이다.
         ├─ 원급 비교와 마찬가지로 **비교의 두 대상은 문법적 성격이 같아야** 한다.
         └─ than 뒤에 오는 어구 역시 원급 비교에서 as 뒤에 오는 어구와 **동일한 원칙**이 적용된다.

- Simon is (taller than) his brother (is). (Simon은 그의 형보다 키가 더 크다.)

- Simon's brother is (less tall than) Simon. (Simon의 형은 Simon보다 키가 덜 크다.)
  「less + 형용사/부사의 원급 + than ...」: '…보다 덜 ~한/하게'

3 최상급 비교

1) 「the + 형용사나 부사의 최상급 (+ in [of] ...)」: '(… 중에서) 가장 ~한/하게'라는 의미로,
범위를 나타내는 in이나 of와 같이 쓰이는 경우가 많다.

- The giraffe is (the tallest) (of) all animals. (기린이 모든 동물들 중에서 가장 키가 크다.)

2) 「one of the + 최상급 + 복수 명사」: '가장 ~한 것들 중 하나'

- Coughing is (one of the most common symptoms) of a cold. (기침은 감기의 가장 흔한 증상들 중 하나이다.)

Check Test

1 밑줄 친 원급 표현에 유의하여 다음을 해석하시오.

Similarly, another study showed that emoticons were useful in strengthening the intensity of a verbal message, <u>as well as</u> in the expression of sarcasm.

→ _____

2 밑줄 친 부분을 어법상 알맞게 비교급으로 바꿔 쓰시오.

The negative effects of music were <u>great</u> than the psychologists expected.

→ _____

3 괄호 안의 단어를 빈칸에 적절하게 최상급으로 바꿔 쓰시오.

Why do we have the illusion that cramming for an exam is _____ learning strategy? (good)

4 밑줄 친 원급 표현에 유의하여 다음을 해석하시오.

However, you should know that stimulants are <u>as likely</u> to have negative effects on memory <u>as</u> they are to be beneficial.

→ _____

• 정답

 선택지가 아닌 문장에서 글의 소재를 찾으세요.
 문장 하나하나를 살펴보면서 앞뒤 문장의 관계를 파악하세요.
3rd 정답으로 선택한 문장을 제외하면 앞뒤 문장이 매끄럽게 연결되는지 확인하세요.

N01 ❋❋❋ .... 고1 2024(3월)/35

다음 글에서 전체 흐름과 관계 없는 문장은?

A group of psychologists studied individuals with severe mental illness who experienced weekly group music therapy, including singing familiar songs and composing original songs. ① The results showed that the group music therapy improved the quality of participants' life, with those participating in a greater number of sessions experiencing the greatest benefits. ② Focusing on singing, another group of psychologists reviewed articles on the efficacy of group singing as a mental health treatment for individuals living with a mental health condition in a community setting. ③ The findings showed that, when people with mental health conditions participated in a choir, their mental health and wellbeing significantly improved. ④ The negative effects of music were greater than the psychologists expected. ⑤ Group singing provided enjoyment, improved emotional states, developed a sense of belonging and enhanced self-confidence.

*therapy: 치료 **efficacy: 효능

1st 선택지가 아닌 문장에서 글의 소재를 찾으세요.

A group of psychologists studied / individuals with
한 심리학자 그룹이 연구했다 / 심각한 정신 질환이 있는
severe mental illness / who experienced weekly
사람들을 / 집단 음악 치료를 매주 경험한
group music therapy, / including singing familiar
집단 음악 치료를, / 친숙한 노래 부르기와 독창적인 노래
songs and composing original songs. //
작곡하기를 포함한 //

● 글의 중심 소재는 '정신 질환'과 '집단 음악 치료'인 것 같아요.
한 심리학자 그룹이 심각한 정신 질환이 있는 사람들에게 집단 음악 치료를 제공한 연구가 있다고 소개하고 있어요.

2nd 문장 하나하나를 살펴보면서 앞뒤 문장의 관계를 파악하세요.

1) ① 문장부터 살펴봅시다.

① The results showed / that the group music
그 연구 결과는 보여주었다 / 집단 음악 치료가 참여자의 삶의 질을
therapy improved the quality of participants' life, /
개선하였음을 /
with those participating in a greater number of
(치료) 활동에 참여한 횟수가 더 많은 참여자들이 가장 큰 효과를 경험하며 //
sessions experiencing the greatest benefits. //

● The results는 어떤 연구의 결과인가요?
앞 문장에서 한 심리학자 그룹이 진행했다고 한 연구의 결과를 가리켜요.
①(　　　　　　)가 삶의 질을 개선했고, 많이 참여할수록 효과도 컸다고 하네요. 정신 질환이 있는 사람들에게 집단 음악 치료를 제공한 연구의 결과이므로 서로 자연스럽게 연결되는 내용이에요.

2) ② 문장도 확인해 볼까요?

② Focusing on singing, / another group of
노래 부르기에 초점을 두고 / 또 다른 그룹의 심리학자는
psychologists reviewed articles / on the efficacy of
논문을 검토했다 / 집단 가창의 효능에 대한
group singing / as a mental health treatment / for
집단 가창의 / 정신 건강 치료로서 / 집단
individuals living with a mental health condition in
생활의 환경에서 정신적인 건강 문제를 가지고 살고 있는 이들에게 미치는 //
a community setting. //

● **비슷한 주제의 논문도 있나 봐요.**
정신적인 건강 문제가 있는 이들에게 미치는 집단 가창의 효능에 관한
논문이 있대요. 집단 음악 치료에 관한 또 다른 연구를 소개하는 내용이
앞 문장과 자연스럽게 연결되네요. 뒤에 이어질 이 논문의 결과도
확인해야겠죠?

3) ③ 문장은 어떤가요?

③ The findings showed that, / when people with
　　발견된 결과는 보여주었다 　　　　　/ 정신 건강 문제를 가진
mental health conditions participated in a choir, /
사람이 합창단에 참여했을 때 　　　　　　　　　　　/
their mental health and wellbeing significantly
그들의 정신 건강과 행복이 상당히 개선되었음을 //
improved. //

● **The findings는 무엇의 결과인가요?**
❷ 문장에서 또 다른 그룹의 심리학자가 집단 가창의 효능에 대한 논문을
검토했다고 했는데, 그 논문의 결과에 해당하는 내용이에요.

● **① 문장에 소개된 연구 결과와 마찬가지네요.**
정신 건강 문제를 가진 사람이 합창단에서 노래했을 때, 그들의 정신
건강이 개선되었다는 내용이에요. 앞의 연구 결과와 같은 맥락이므로
마찬가지로 잘 연결되었죠.

4) ④ 문장은 전체 흐름에 맞는 글인가요?

④ The negative effects of music / were greater than
　　음악의 부정적인 효과는 　　　　　　/ 심리학자가 예상했던
the psychologists expected. //
것보다 더 컸다 　　　　　　　　//

● **갑자기 음악의 부정적인 효과가 컸다고요?**
③ 문장까지 집단 음악 치료의 긍정적 효과에 관한 내용이 잘 이어지다가
갑자기 음악의 부정적인 효과가 예상보다 더 컸다고 하네요. 이건 확실히
글의 흐름에 맞지 않으니까 ④이 정답인 것 같죠?

5) ⑤ 문장에서 글의 흐름이 원래대로 돌아오는지 확인합시다.

⑤ Group singing provided enjoyment, / improved
　　집단 가창은 즐거움을 제공했고 　　　　　　/ 감정 상태를
emotional states, / developed a sense of belonging /
개선하였으며 　　　　/ 소속감을 키웠고 　　　　　　　/
and enhanced self-confidence. //
자신감을 강화하였다 　　　　　　//

● **다시 집단 음악 치료의 긍정적 효과에 관한 내용으로 돌아왔어요!**
③에서 집단 가창이 정신 건강을 개선했다고 했고, ⑤에서 집단 가창의
네 가지 긍정적인 심리적 효과를 나열하며 글을 마무리하고 있어요. ④이
아닌 ③에 이어지기 때문에 ④이 무관한 문장이 맞네요!

3rd 정답으로 선택한 문장을 제외하면 앞뒤 문장이 매끄럽게
연결되는지 확인하세요.

1) 정답으로 선택한 ④ 문장을 빼고 글을 읽어봅시다.

③ The findings showed that, / when people with
　　발견된 결과는 보여주었다 　　　　　/ 정신 건강 문제를 가진 사람이
mental health conditions participated in a choir, /
합창단에 참여했을 때, 　　　　　　　　　　　　/
their mental health and wellbeing significantly
그들의 정신 건강과 행복이 상당히 개선되었음을 //
improved. //
⑤ Group singing provided enjoyment, / improved
　　집단 가창은 즐거움을 제공했고 　　　　　　/ 감정 상태를
emotional states, / developed a sense of belonging /
개선하였으며 　　　　/ 소속감을 키웠고 　　　　　　　/
and enhanced self-confidence. //
자신감을 강화하였다 　　　　　　//

● **'개선되었다'와 '즐거움', '발달시켰다', '강화하였다' 등이 이어져요.**
집단 음악 치료로 정신 건강과 행복이 상당히 개선되었다는 내용 뒤에
즐거움을 제공했고, 감정 상태를 개선하였다는 등의 긍정적인 효과들이
자연스럽게 연결되고 있어요. 따라서 정답은 음악의 부정적인 효과를
언급한 ❷(　　　　　)!

2) 글의 흐름을 정리하며 글의 내용을 다시 확인해 봅시다.

 연구 정신 질환이 있는 사람들에게 매주 집단 음악 치료를 제공한 연구

⬇

 연구결과 정신 질환이 있는 사람들이 집단 음악 치료를 받으면 삶의 질이 개선되었음

⬇

 관련논문 정신적인 건강 문제를 가진 사람들에게 미치는 집단 가창의 효능에 관한 논문

⬇

 논문의결론 합창단에 참여했을 때, 정신 건강과 행복이 상당히 개선되었음

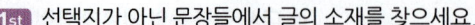

1st 선택지가 아닌 문장들에서 글의 소재를 찾으세요.
2nd 문장 하나하나를 살펴보면서 앞뒤 문장의 관계를 파악하세요.
3rd 정답으로 선택한 문장을 제외하면 앞뒤 문장이 매끄럽게 연결되는지 확인하세요.

N02 ★★★ ·············· 고1 2023(9월)/35

다음 글에서 전체 흐름과 관계 없는 문장은? [3점]

Sensory nerves have specialized endings in the tissues that pick up a particular sensation. If, for example, you step on a sharp object such as a pin, nerve endings in the skin will transmit the pain sensation up [5] your leg, up and along the spinal cord to the brain. ① While the pain itself is unpleasant, it is in fact acting as a protective mechanism for the foot. ② That is, you get used to the pain so the capacity with which you can avoid [10] pain decreases. ③ Within the brain, nerves will connect to the area that controls speech, so that you may well shout 'ouch' or something rather less polite. ④ They will also connect to motor nerves that travel back [15] down the spinal cord, and to the muscles in your leg that now contract quickly to lift your foot away from the painful object. ⑤ Sensory and motor nerves control almost all functions in the body — from the beating of [20] the heart to the movement of the gut, sweating and just about everything else.

*spinal cord: 척수 **gut: 장

1st 선택지가 아닌 문장들에서 글의 소재를 찾으세요.

1) 첫 번째 문장을 봅시다.

> Sensory nerves have specialized endings / in the
> 감각 신경은 특화된 말단을 가지고 있다   / 조직에
> tissues / that pick up a particular sensation. //
>   / 특정 감각을 포착하는   //

● 감각 신경과 관련된 글이군요.
감각 신경은 특정 감각을 포착하는 특화된 말단을 가지고 있다고 했어요.
어떤 감각을 포착하는지, 포착한 후에는 어떤 일이 일어나는지를
설명하겠네요!

2) 선택지 전에 한 문장이 더 있어요.

> If, for example, / you step on a sharp object / such
> 만약 예를 들어   / 여러분이 날카로운 물체를 밟는다면   / 핀과
> as a pin, / nerve endings in the skin will transmit
> 같이   / 피부의 신경 말단이 통증 감각을 전달할 것이다
> the pain sensation / up your leg, / up and along the
>   / 여러분의 다리 위로 / 그리고 척수를 따라 위로
> spinal cord / to the brain. //
>   / 뇌까지   //

● 예시가 등장했어요.
앞에서 감각 신경이 특정 감각을 포착하는 말단을 가지고 있다고 한 것에
대한 예시군요!
핀 같은 날카로운 물체를 밟으면 피부 신경 말단이 통증 감각을 다리로,
척수로, 뇌로, 그러니까 점점 위로 전달한대요. 이제 선택지 문장들을
읽으면서 흐름에 맞지 않는 문장을 찾아봅시다.

2nd 문장 하나하나를 살펴보면서 앞뒤 문장의 관계를 파악하세요.

1) ① 역접의 연결어 While로 문장이 시작돼요.

> ① While the pain itself is unpleasant, / it is in fact
>   통증 자체는 불쾌하지만   / 그것은 사실은
> acting / as a protective mechanism / for the foot. //
> 작용하고 있다 / 보호하는 메커니즘으로   / 발을   //

● 통증에는 이유가 있대요.
통증은 불쾌하지만, 사실은 발을 보호하는 메커니즘으로 작용하는
거래요. 앞에서 감각 신경이 통증 감각을 위로 전달한다고 했는데, 이
통증 감각은 사실 우리를 보호하기 위해 작용한다는 흐름은 어색하지
않아요.

2) ② 고통에 익숙해진다고요?

② Ｔhat is, / you get used to the pain / so the capacity
즉   / 여러분은 그 고통에 익숙해져서   / 고통을 피할 수 있는

with which you can avoid pain / decreases. //
능력이   / 감소하게 된다   //

● That is는 '즉, 다시 말해'를 뜻해요.
앞 문장과 같은 맥락의 말을 반복할 때 That is를 쓰는데, 앞에 고통에
익숙해진다거나 고통을 피할 수 있는 능력이 감소한다는 내용이
나왔었나요? ❶(   )!

● 우리는 고통을 잘 피하지 못하게 된대요.
핀을 밟았을 때의 고통에 익숙해지고 고통을 피할 수 있는 능력이
감소하면, 우리는 계속 핀을 밟게 될 거예요. 그럼 발에는 계속 상처가
나고 다치겠죠?
통증은 우리를 보호하는 메커니즘으로 작용한다고 했는데, 고통에
익숙해지는 것은 우리를 보호하는 것과는 거리가 멀어요. ②이 무관한
문장일 확률이 높네요.

3) ③ 뇌와 관련된 내용이 이어졌어요.

③ Within the brain, / nerves will connect to the area
뇌 안에서   / 신경은 부분에 연결될 것이다
/ that controls speech, / so that you may well shout
/ 언어를 통제하는   / 그래서 여러분은 '아야'라고 외칠 것이다
'ouch' / or something rather less polite. //
/ 또는 다소 덜 공손한 무언가를   //

● 뇌는 선택지 이전 문장에 등장했었어요.
정답일 거라고 예상한 ②을 제외하고 생각해 보면, 앞에서 우리는 핀과
같은 날카로운 물체를 밟은 상황을 가정했어요. 그리고 발의 통증 감각이
다리로, 척수로, 뇌로 전달됐고요.
③에서는 이렇게 뇌로 전달된 통증 감각이 어디에 연결되는지를
설명하고 있어요.

● 우리는 아플 때 '아야'라고 외쳐요.
뇌로 전달된 통증 감각은 ❷(   )를 통제하는 부분에
연결돼서 우리가 핀을 밟았을 때 '아야'라고 외치게 한다는 거예요.
①에 자연스럽게 이어지는 내용이니까 ②이 정답인 게 확실해요!

4) ④ 정답은 찾았지만 계속 읽어봅시다.

④ Ｔhey will also connect to motor nerves / that
그것들은 또한 운동신경에 연결될 것이다   / 척수를
travel back down the spinal cord, / and to the
타고 내려오는   / 그리고 여러분의
muscles in your leg / that now contract quickly / to
다리 근육에   / 이제 재빨리 수축하는   /
lift your foot away / from the painful object. //
발을 떼어 들어올리기 위해 / 고통을 주는 물체로부터   //

● 통증 감각은 다시 내려온대요.
앞 문장까지는 핀을 밟았을 때, 통증 감각이 발에서 뇌까지 위로 올라가
우리가 '아야'라고 외치게 되는 과정을 설명했어요.
이제는 통증 감각이 뇌에서 척수를 타고 내려와서 다리 근육에
연결된대요. 우리를 아프게 하는 핀으로부터 발을 떼도록 말이에요.

5) ⑤ 마지막 문장까지 자연스럽게 연결되는지 확인합시다.

⑤ Sensory and motor nerves control / almost all
감각 신경과 운동 신경은 통제한다   / 신체의 거의 모든
functions in the body / — from the beating of the
기능을   / 심장의 박동에서부터
heart / to the movement of the gut, sweating and
      / 장의 운동, 발한과 그 밖에 모든 것에까지 //
just about everything else. //

● 전체 내용을 정리하는 문장이에요.
감각 신경과 운동 신경은 신체의 거의 모든 기능을 통제한대요. 핀을
밟았을 때 느꼈던 통증 감각과 같은 ❸(   ) 신경과, 핀에서
발을 떼게 하는 것과 같은 ❹(   ) 신경은 서로 연결돼서
신체의 대부분의 기능을 통제한다는 거예요.

3rd 정답으로 선택한 문장을 제외하면 앞뒤 문장이 매끄럽게
연결되는지 확인하세요.

① While the pain itself is unpleasant, / it is in fact
통증 자체는 불쾌하지만   / 그것은 사실은
acting / as a protective mechanism / for the foot. //
작용하고 있다 / 보호하는 메커니즘으로   / 발을   //
③ Within the brain, / nerves will connect to the area
뇌 안에서   / 신경은 부분에 연결될 것이다
/ that controls speech, / so that you may well shout
/ 언어를 통제하는   / 그래서 여러분은 '아야'라고 외칠 것이다
'ouch' / or something rather less polite. //
/ 또는 다소 덜 공손한 무언가를   //

● ①에서 언급한 메커니즘을 ③에서 구체적으로 설명하고 있어요.
통증 감각은 몸을 보호하는 메커니즘으로 작용하는데, 뇌로 전달된
통증 감각은 뇌의 언어 통제 신경에 연결되어 아픔을 표현하게 한다는
흐름이에요.
두 문장이 자연스럽게 연결되니까, 고통에 익숙해져서 고통을 피하는
능력이 감소한다고 한 ②이 흐름에 맞지 않는 문장이에요.

N03 ~ 07 ▶ 제한시간 10분

N03 ★★★　　　　　　　　　　고1 2025(3월)/35

다음 글에서 전체 흐름과 관계 <u>없는</u> 문장은?

What does it mean for a character to be a hero as opposed to a villain? In artistic and entertainment descriptions, it's essential for the author to establish a positive relationship between a protagonist and the audience. ① In order for tragedy or misfortune to draw out an emotional response in viewers, the character must be adjusted so as to be recognizable as either friend or enemy. ② Likewise, the line between friends and enemies is not clear in reality. ③ Whether the portrayal is fictional or documentary, we must feel that the protagonist is someone whose actions benefit us; the protagonist is, or would be, a worthy companion or valued ally. ④ Violent action films are often filled with dozens of incidental deaths of minor characters that draw out little response in the audience. ⑤ In order to feel strong emotions, the audience must be emotionally invested in a character as either ally or enemy.

*villain: 악당 **protagonist: 주인공

구문 서술형

주어진 우리말과 일치하도록 괄호 안의 단어를 빈칸에 알맞게 쓰시오. (원급 비교 사용)

현실에서 친구와 적 사이의 선은 영화에서만큼 명확하지 않다.

→ In reality, the line between friends and enemies is _____ it is in films. (clear)

N04 ★★★✳　　　　　　　　　　고1 2025(6월)/35

다음 글에서 전체 흐름과 관계 <u>없는</u> 문장은?

In the 1930s, the British psychologist Sir Frederic Bartlett asked people to listen to folktales from other countries and then recall these stories at a later date. As you might guess, unfamiliar stories were not remembered as well as familiar stories. ① Surprisingly, however, errors in memory were not random. ② Rather, subjects often rewrote similar parts of the stories in their own minds — particularly the parts that made the least sense to them. ③ To attract a wide audience, stories should focus on topics that interest many people. ④ Bartlett concluded that when facing problems, humans draw upon mental schemata, or shelves of stored knowledge in our brains, to fill in any minor gaps in our memories. ⑤ Therefore, remembering is an imaginative process that involves building upon past experiences.

*folktale: 민간 설화

구문 서술형

밑줄 친 단어를 최상급으로 바르게 고치고, 해당 부분을 해석하시오.

When recalling stories, people often rewrote the parts that made <u>little</u> sense to them.

→ 고친 표현: _____, 해석: _____

N05 ★★★

다음 글에서 전체 흐름과 관계 <u>없는</u> 문장은?

Humans for centuries have dreamed of machines that could become intelligent and make human-like decisions. There have been myths about robots, automatons, and artificial beings since ancient Greece (e.g., the myth of Pandora, who released ills upon the world). ① Likewise, literature throughout history has dreamed of creating human-like creatures and thinking machines (e.g., Mary Shelley's *Frankenstein*). ② In 1950, British mathematician Alan Turing asked whether machines could think and reason like humans and then developed the Turing test to measure a machine's intelligence and whether the machines can think autonomously. ③ A few years later, MIT professor John McCarthy coined "artificial intelligence," replacing the previously used expression "automata studies." ④ But artificial intelligence didn't stop there; its first major appearance was in a movie where feeling artificial intelligence replaced human characters with robots. ⑤ Since then, artificial intelligence has become the study and practice of "making intelligent machines" that are programmed to think like humans — endowed by their creators with reasoning and learning.

*automaton: 자동 장치 **endow: 부여하다

구문 서술형

밑줄 친 부분을 괄호 안의 우리말에 맞게 고쳐 쓰시오. (원급 비교 사용)

British mathematician Alan Turing asked whether machines could think and reason <u>like humans</u>.

(인간만큼 잘)

➡ 고친 표현: _____

N06 ★★★

다음 글에서 전체 흐름과 관계 <u>없는</u> 문장은?

Simply giving employees a sense of agency — a feeling that they are in control, that they have genuine decision-making authority — can radically increase how much energy and focus they bring to their jobs. ① One 2010 study at a manufacturing plant in Ohio, for instance, carefully examined assembly-line workers who were empowered to make small decisions about their schedules and work environment. ② They designed their own uniforms and had authority over shifts while all the manufacturing processes and pay scales stayed the same. ③ It led to decreased efficiency because their decisions were not uniform or focused on meeting organizational goals. ④ Within two months, productivity at the plant increased by 20 percent, with workers taking shorter breaks and making fewer mistakes. ⑤ Giving employees a sense of control improved how much self-discipline they brought to their jobs.   *radically: 급격하게 **shift: (근무) 교대

N07 ★★★※

다음 글에서 전체 흐름과 관계 <u>없는</u> 문장은?

Why do we have the illusion that cramming for an exam is the best learning strategy? Because we are unable to differentiate between the various sections of our memory. Immediately after reading our textbook or our class notes, information is fully present in our mind. ① It sits in our conscious working memory, in an active form. ② We feel as if we know it, because it is present in our short-term storage space ... but this short-term section has nothing to do with the long-term memory that we will need in order to recall the same information a few days later. ③ After a few seconds or minutes, working memory already starts disappearing, and after a few days, the effect becomes enormous: unless you retest your knowledge, memory vanishes. ④ Focusing on exploring new topics rather than reviewing the same material over and over again can improve your academic performance. ⑤ To get information into long-term memory, it is essential to study the material, then test yourself, rather than spend all your time studying.   *cram: 벼락 공부를 하다

N08 ✽✽✽

고1 2020(11월)/35

다음 글에서 전체 흐름과 관계 <u>없는</u> 문장은?

The Barnum Effect is the phenomenon where someone reads or hears something very general but believes that it applies to them. ① These statements appear to be very personal on the surface but in fact, they are true for many. ② Human psychology allows us to want to believe things that we can identify with on a personal level and even seek information where it doesn't necessarily exist, filling in the blanks with our imagination for the rest. ③ This is the principle that horoscopes rely on, offering data that appears to be personal but probably makes sense to countless people. ④ Reading daily horoscopes in the morning is beneficial as they provide predictions about the rest of the day. ⑤ Since the people reading them want to believe the information so badly, they will search for meaning in their lives that make it true.

*horoscope: 별자리 운세

N09 ✽✽✽

고1 2021(9월)/35

다음 글에서 전체 흐름과 관계 <u>없는</u> 문장은?

The Zeigarnik effect is commonly referred to as the tendency of the subconscious mind to remind you of a task that is incomplete until that task is complete. Bluma Zeigarnik was a Lithuanian psychologist who wrote in the 1920s about the effects of leaving tasks incomplete. ① She noticed the effect while watching waiters serve in a restaurant. ② The waiters would remember an order, however complicated, until the order was complete, but they would later find it difficult to remember the order. ③ Zeigarnik did further studies giving both adults and children puzzles to complete then interrupting them during some of the tasks. ④ They developed cooperation skills after finishing tasks by putting the puzzles together. ⑤ The results showed that both adults and children remembered the tasks that hadn't been completed because of the interruptions better than the ones that had been completed.

N10 ✽✽✽

고1 2022(11월)/35

다음 글에서 전체 흐름과 관계 <u>없는</u> 문장은?

Developing a personal engagement with poetry brings a number of benefits to you as an individual, in both a personal and a professional capacity. ① Writing poetry has been shown to have physical and mental benefits, with expressive writing found to improve immune system and lung function, diminish psychological distress, and enhance relationships. ② Poetry has long been used to aid different mental health needs, develop empathy, and reconsider our relationship with both natural and built environments. ③ Poetry is also an incredibly effective way of actively targeting the cognitive development period, improving your productivity and scientific creativity in the process. ④ Poetry is considered to be an easy and useful means of expressing emotions, but you fall into frustration when you realize its complexity. ⑤ In short, poetry has a lot to offer, if you give it the opportunity to do so.

*cognitive: 인지적인

N11 ✽✽✽

고1 2021(6월)/35

다음 글에서 전체 흐름과 관계 <u>없는</u> 문장은? [3점]

Health and the spread of disease are very closely linked to how we live and how our cities operate. The good news is that cities are incredibly resilient. Many cities have experienced epidemics in the past and have not only survived, but advanced. ① The nineteenth and early-twentieth centuries saw destructive outbreaks of cholera, typhoid, and influenza in European cities. ② Doctors such as Jon Snow, from England, and Rudolf Virchow, of Germany, saw the connection between poor living conditions, overcrowding, sanitation, and disease. ③ A recognition of this connection led to the replanning and rebuilding of cities to stop the spread of epidemics. ④ In spite of reconstruction efforts, cities declined in many areas and many people started to leave. ⑤ In the mid-nineteenth century, London's pioneering sewer system, which still serves it today, was built as a result of understanding the importance of clean water in stopping the spread of cholera.

*resilient: 회복력이 있는 **sewer system: 하수 처리 시스템

N12 ✽✽❀ 고1 2021(3월)/35

다음 글에서 전체 흐름과 관계 <u>없는</u> 문장은?

Today's music business has allowed musicians to take matters into their own hands. ① Gone are the days of musicians waiting for a gatekeeper (someone who holds power and prevents you from being let in) at a label or TV show to say they are worthy of the spotlight. ② In today's music business, you don't need to ask for permission to build a fanbase and you no longer need to pay thousands of dollars to a company to do it. ③ There are rising concerns over the marketing of child musicians using TV auditions. ④ Every day, musicians are getting their music out to thousands of listeners without any outside help. ⑤ They simply deliver it to the fans directly, without asking for permission or outside help to receive exposure or connect with thousands of listeners.

N13 ✽✽❀ 고1 2023(3월)/35

다음 글에서 전체 흐름과 관계 <u>없는</u> 문장은?

Whose story it is affects *what* the story is. Change the main character, and the focus of the story must also change. If we look at the events through another character's eyes, we will interpret them differently. ① We'll place our sympathies with someone new. ② When the conflict arises that is the heart of the story, we will be praying for a different outcome. ③ Consider, for example, how the tale of Cinderella would shift if told from the viewpoint of an evil stepsister. ④ We know Cinderella's kingdom does not exist, but we willingly go there anyway. ⑤ *Gone with the Wind* is Scarlett O'Hara's story, but what if we were shown the same events from the viewpoint of Rhett Butler or Melanie Wilkes?

*sympathy: 공감

N14 ✽✽❀ 고1 2022(3월)/35

다음 글에서 전체 흐름과 관계 <u>없는</u> 문장은?

Who hasn't used a cup of coffee to help themselves stay awake while studying? Mild stimulants commonly found in tea, coffee, or sodas possibly make you more attentive and, thus, better able to remember. ① However, you should know that stimulants are as likely to have negative effects on memory as they are to be beneficial. ② Even if they could improve performance at some level, the ideal doses are currently unknown. ③ If you are wide awake and well-rested, mild stimulation from caffeine can do little to further improve your memory performance. ④ In contrast, many studies have shown that drinking tea is healthier than drinking coffee. ⑤ Indeed, if you have too much of a stimulant, you will become nervous, find it difficult to sleep, and your memory performance will suffer.

*stimulant: 자극제 **dose: 복용량

N

N15 ✽✽❀ 고1 2023(6월)/35

다음 글에서 전체 흐름과 관계 <u>없는</u> 문장은?

Although technology has the potential to increase productivity, it can also have a negative impact on productivity. For example, in many office environments workers sit at desks with computers and have access to the internet. ① They are able to check their personal e-mails and use social media whenever they want to. ② This can stop them from doing their work and make them less productive. ③ Introducing new technology can also have a negative impact on production when it causes a change to the production process or requires workers to learn a new system. ④ Using technology can enable businesses to produce more goods and to get more out of the other factors of production. ⑤ Learning to use new technology can be time consuming and stressful for workers and this can cause a decline in productivity.

N16 ★★❀ 고1 2023(11월)/35

다음 글에서 전체 흐름과 관계 <u>없는</u> 문장은?

In statistics, the law of large numbers describes a situation where having more data is better for making predictions. According to it, the more often an experiment is conducted, the closer the average of the results can be expected to match the true state of the world. ① For instance, on your first encounter with the game of roulette, you may have beginner's luck after betting on 7. ② But the more often you repeat this bet, the closer the relative frequency of wins and losses is expected to approach the true chance of winning, meaning that your luck will at some point fade away. ③ Each number's symbolic meanings can be interpreted in various ways and are promising in situations that may change unexpectedly. ④ Similarly, car insurers collect large amounts of data to figure out the chances that drivers will cause accidents, depending on their age, region, or car brand. ⑤ Both casinos and insurance industries rely on the law of large numbers to balance individual losses.

N17 ★★★❀ 고1 2022(6월)/35

다음 글에서 전체 흐름과 관계 <u>없는</u> 문장은?

According to Marguerite La Caze, fashion contributes to our lives and provides a medium for us to develop and exhibit important social virtues. ① Fashion may be beautiful, innovative, and useful; we can display creativity and good taste in our fashion choices. ② And in dressing with taste and care, we represent both self-respect and a concern for the pleasure of others. ③ There is no doubt that fashion can be a source of interest and pleasure which links us to each other. ④ Although the fashion industry developed first in Europe and America, today it is an international and highly globalized industry. ⑤ That is, fashion provides a sociable aspect along with opportunities to imagine oneself differently — to try on different identities.

*virtue: 가치

N18 ★★★❀ 고1 2021(11월)/35

다음 글에서 전체 흐름과 관계 <u>없는</u> 문장은?

Internet activist Eli Pariser noticed how online search algorithms encourage our human tendency to grab hold of everything that confirms the beliefs we already hold, while quietly ignoring information that doesn't match those beliefs. ① We set up a so-called "filter-bubble" around ourselves, where we are constantly exposed only to that material that we agree with. ② We are never challenged, never giving ourselves the opportunity to acknowledge the existence of diversity and difference. ③ Creating a difference that others don't have is a way to succeed in your field, leading to the creation of innovations. ④ In the best case, we become naive and sheltered, and in the worst, we become radicalized with extreme views, unable to imagine life outside our particular bubble. ⑤ The results are disastrous: intellectual isolation and the real distortion that comes with believing that the little world we create for ourselves is *the* world.

*naive: 세상을 모르는 **radicalize: 과격하게 만들다 ***distortion: 왜곡

N19 ⭐ 2등급 대비 _____ 고1 2024(10월)/35

다음 글에서 전체 흐름과 관계 없는 문장은?

Today, the water crisis is political — which is to say, not inevitable or beyond our capacity to fix — and, therefore, functionally elective. ① That is one reason it is nevertheless distressing: an abundant resource made scarce through governmental neglect and indifference, bad infrastructure and contamination, and careless urbanization. ② There is no need for a water crisis, in other words, but we have one anyway, and aren't doing much to address it. ③ Some cities lose more water to leaks than they deliver to homes: even in the United States, leaks and theft account for an estimated loss of 16 percent of freshwater; in Brazil, the estimate is 40 percent. ④ The numerical comparison of available resources seems to exaggerate the real-world water shortage problem that we face. ⑤ Seen in both cases, as everywhere, the selective scarcity clearly highlights have-and-have-not inequities, leaving 2.1 billion people without safe drinking water and 4.5 billion without proper sanitation worldwide.

*elective: 선택의

N20 ⭐ 2등급 대비 _____ 고1 2022(9월)/35

다음 글에서 전체 흐름과 관계 없는 문장은?

The fast-paced evolution of Information and Communication Technologies (ICTs) has radically transformed the dynamics and business models of the tourism and hospitality industry. ① This leads to new levels/forms of competitiveness among service providers and transforms the customer experience through new services. ② Creating unique experiences and providing convenient services to customers leads to satisfaction and, eventually, customer loyalty to the service provider or brand (i.e., hotels). ③ In particular, the most recent *technological* boost received by the tourism sector is represented by mobile applications. ④ Increasing competitiveness among service providers does not necessarily mean promoting quality of customer services. ⑤ Indeed, empowering tourists with mobile access to services such as hotel reservations, airline ticketing, and recommendations for local attractions generates strong interest and considerable profits.

*hospitality industry: 서비스업(호텔 · 식당업 등)

✱ 다음 영어는 우리말 뜻을, 우리말은 영어 단어를 〈보기〉에서 찾아 쓰시오.

〈보기〉

품종	frustration	전달하다	exaggerate
진술	misfortune	부족한	minor
확산	treatment	공감	balance

01 spread _____

02 scarce _____

03 statement _____

04 deliver _____

05 empathy _____

06 과장하다 _____

07 사소한 _____

08 불행 _____

09 치료 _____

10 좌절감 _____

✱ 다음 우리말에 알맞은 영어 표현을 찾아 연결하시오.

11 ~에 기여하다 •   • fade away

12 사라지다 •   • contribute to

13 ~에 의존하다 •   • draw upon

14 ~을 활용하다 •   • rely on

15 ~와 연관되다 •   • be linked to

✱ 다음 우리말 표현에 맞는 단어를 고르시오.

16 그 영향은 엄청나게 된다 ➡ the effect becomes (numerous / enormous)

17 사악한 의붓자매 ➡ a(n) (evil / noble) stepsister

18 작은 결정 권한을 부여받은 ➡ (empowered / embodied) to make small decisions

19 그것은 수단을 제공한다 ➡ it provides a (medium / manuscript)

20 빠른 속도의 진화 ➡ the fast-paced (evolution / revolution)

✱ 다음 문장의 빈칸에 알맞은 단어를 〈보기〉에서 찾아 쓰시오.

〈보기〉

beneficial	edible	ally	sensory
stimulants	vanishes	contamination	resilient
permission	incidental	sociable	genuine

21 자극제는 기억력에 부정적인 영향을 미칠 수도 있다.
➡ _____ are likely to have negative effects on memory.

22 좋은 소식은 도시가 믿을 수 없을 정도로 회복력이 있다는 것이다.
➡ The good news is that cities are incredibly _____ .

23 아침에 매일 별자리 운세를 읽는 것은 유익하다.
➡ Reading daily horoscopes in the morning is _____ .

24 당신은 팬층을 만들기 위해 허락을 요청할 필요가 없다.
➡ You don't need to ask for _____ to build a fanbase.

25 감각 신경은 특화된 말단을 가지고 있다.
➡ _____ nerves have specialized endings.

26 폭력적인 액션 영화는 흔히 많은 부수적인 죽음으로 가득 차 있다.
➡ Violent action films are often filled with dozens of _____ deaths.

27 풍족한 자원이 오염을 통해 부족하게 되었다.
➡ An abundant resource made scarce through _____ .

28 주인공은 가치 있는 동료나 소중한 협력자이다.
➡ The protagonist is a worthy companion or valued _____ .

29 여러분이 자신의 지식을 다시 테스트하지 않으면, 기억은 사라진다.
➡ Unless you retest your knowledge, memory _____ .

30 패션은 친교적인 측면을 제공한다.
➡ Fashion provides a(n) _____ aspect.

JDA

성균관대학교 댄스 동아리

춤을 좋아하는 사람들이 모여 함께 즐기는 JDA(제이다)는 제일 좋아서 제이다!

JDA는 성균관대학교 인문사회과학캠퍼스 중앙 댄스 동아리입니다.

JDA는 Jazz Dance Association의 약자이며, 재즈 댄스를 중심으로 시작했지만
지금은 얼반(Urban), 코리오(Choreo), 방송 댄스 등 다양한 댄스 커버를 진행하고 있습니다.

JDA에서는 정기 공연, 입학식, 새내기 배움터, 드림 클래스, 대학생 거리축제 등
다양한 공연들을 진행하고 있습니다.

춤에 대한 관심과 열정이 있으신 분이라면,
춤을 춰본 적이 없더라도 춤을 좋아하기만 한다면
모두 환영입니다!

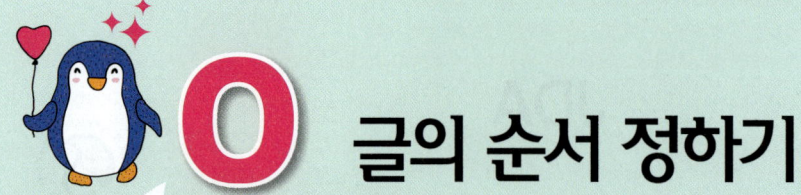

글의 순서 정하기

★ 유형 설명

주어진 글 다음에 이어질 글의 순서로 가장 적절한 것을 고르시오.

> Cartilage is extremely important for the healthy functioning of a joint, especially if

흠... 이 발자국들을 단서로 글의 순서를 파악하면 되겠군.

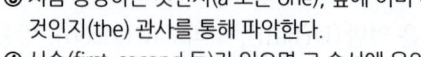

주어진 한 문단에 이어지는 나머지 세 문단의 논리적 순서를 연결어 등의 단서를 통해 추론해야 한다.

① this, that, these, it 등의 지시어가 가리키는 것이 무엇인지 파악한다.
② on the other hand, similarly, however 등의 연결어로 서로 연결되어야 하는 내용이 무엇인지를 생각하면서 앞뒤에 올 내용을 확인한다.
③ 처음 등장하는 것인지(a 또는 one), 앞에 이미 나온 것인지(the) 관사를 통해 파악한다.
④ 서수(first, second 등)가 있으면 그 순서에 유의한다.
⑤ research, study, reason 등의 연구 자료나 근거가 있는 문단은 그 앞이나 뒤에 어떤 주장을 뒷받침하려고 하는지 유의한다.

유형 풀이 비법

1 글의 소재를 파악하라!
• 주어진 글을 통해 무엇에 관한 글인지를 알아낸다.

2 단서를 찾아라!
• 연결어, 대명사, 지시어 등 문장 간의 연결고리 역할을 하는 단서들을 찾는다.

3 부사구를 확인하라!
• 시간적, 공간적 순서가 드러나는 글의 경우에 관련 부사구를 단서로 활용한다.

(Tip) 순서를 맞추고 전체 글을 다시 읽으며 흐름이 맞는지 확인한다.

어휘 및 표현 Preview

- □ exotic 이국적인
- □ digest 소화하다
- □ mature 익은
- □ densely 밀집하게
- □ extinction 멸종
- □ appropriate 적절한
- □ progressive 점진적인
- □ arena 경기장
- □ equipment 장비
- □ common sense (일반인들의) 공통된 견해, 상식
- □ adaptation 조정
- □ empire 제국
- □ on foot 걸어서
- □ near 다가가다
- □ relay 이어가다
- □ under good condition 좋은 상황에서, 사정이 좋으면

- □ station 배치하다
- □ royal 왕의, 왕실의
- □ along ~을 따라
- □ catch sight of ~을 찾아내다
- □ livestock 가축
- □ settlement 정착지
- □ aeroplane 비행기
- □ archive 보관하다
- □ assume 추정하다
- □ via ~을 통하여
- □ attachment 첨부
- □ threaten 위협하다
- □ hazardous 위험한
- □ neglect 소홀히 하다
- □ declare 선언하다
- □ fossil fuel 화석 연료
- □ productivity 생산성
- □ output 산출량

- □ efficient 효율적인
- □ division 분배
- □ specialize in ~을 전문으로 하다
- □ straighten 펴다
- □ polish 다듬다
- □ profoundly 완전히
- □ fundamental 근본적인
- □ observation 관찰
- □ stick out ~을 내밀다
- □ imitate 모방하다
- □ trial and error 시행착오
- □ adolescent 청소년기의
- □ put ~ at a disadvantage ~을 불리하게 만들다
- □ rule 지배하다
- □ logical-based 논리에 기반한
- □ evaluate 평가하다
- □ modify 수정하다

⑮ 접속사

1 등위접속사: and, but, or, for, so
- We listened to the flight safety speech (and) the plane took off at last.

등위접속사

(우리가 비행 안전 수칙을 듣고 나서야 비행기가 마침내 이륙했다.)
- I felt hungry, (so) I made a sandwich. (나는 배고프다고 느껴서 샌드위치를 만들었다.)

등위접속사

2 명사절을 이끄는 접속사: that, whether, if
- A professor of medicine warns (that) a lot of dust mites are at home.

명사절 접속사

(한 의학교수는 집에 먼지 진드기가 매우 많다고 경고한다.)
- It is not certain (whether) he will accept it or not.

명사절 접속사

(그가 그것을 받아들일지 아닐지는 확실하지 않다.)

3 시간을 나타내는 접속사: when, while, as, till(until), after, before, since
- (When) the sky became darker, her shadow appeared in sight.

부사절 접속사(시간)

(하늘이 좀 더 어두워지자 그녀의 그림자가 보이기 시작했다.)
- I haven't seen her (since) she went to Oxford.

부사절 접속사(시간)

(그녀가 Oxford로 간 이후로 나는 그녀를 본 적이 없다.)

4 이유를 나타내는 접속사: because, as, since, now that
- (Since) my house is near the park, I often go for a walk. (집이 공원 근처라서 나는 자주 산책을 한다.)

부사절 접속사(이유)
- (Now that) the weather is fine, let's take a walk. (날씨가 좋으므로 산책을 하자.)

부사절 접속사(이유)

5 목적을 나타내는 접속사: in order that, so that, in case, for fear (that)~(should)
- I want to follow the trend (so that) other people will not look down on me.

부사절 접속사(목적)

(다른 사람들이 나를 무시하지 않도록 나는 유행을 따르고 싶다.)
- A bigger sofa would be better (in case) we invite guests.

부사절 접속사(목적)

(우리가 손님을 초대할 경우에 대비하여 더 큰 소파가 좋을 것이다.)

6 결과를 나타내는 접속사: 「so + 형용사/부사 + that」, 「such + (a(n)) + (형용사) + 명사 + that」
- A hummingbird's wings flutter (so fast that) they make a humming sound.

부사절 접속사(결과)

(벌새의 날개는 아주 빠르게 퍼덕거려서 윙윙거리는 소리가 난다.)
- It was (such lovely weather that) we spent the day there. (너무 좋은 날씨여서 우리는 그곳에서 하루를 보냈다.)

부사절 접속사(결과)

> **＊상관접속사**
> not only A but also B,
> both A and B,
> either A or B,
> neither A nor B
> - This means that forgetfulness may be affected by **not only** time **but also** our values and interests.
>
(A뿐만 아니라 B도)
>
(이것은 건망증이 시간뿐만 아니라 우리의 가치관과 관심사에도 영향을 받을 수 있음을 의미한다.)

Check Test

1 다음 문장에서 어법상 적절한 접속사를 고르시오.

[When / That] you pluck a guitar string, it moves back and forth hundreds of times every second.

2 밑줄 친 접속사에 유의하여 다음을 해석하시오.

It is caused <u>because</u> the light from the flash penetrates the eyes through the pupils.

→ _____

3 밑줄 친 접속사에 유의하여 다음을 해석하시오.

<u>When</u> magma cools rapidly, the crystals that form will be small.

→ _____

4 밑줄 친 접속사에 유의하여 다음을 해석하시오.

<u>After</u> she had the others at work on another project, she asked Douglas whose hand it was.

→ _____

• **정답**

1 When 2 그것은 플래시에서 나오는 빛이 동공을 통해 그 눈에 침투하기 때문에 생겨난다. 3 마그마가 빠르게 식을 때에 형성되는 결정은 작을 것이다. 4 그녀는 다른 사람들에게 또 다른 프로젝트에 관해 일을 시킨 후, Douglas에게 그 손이 누구의 것인지 물었다.

O 글의 순서 정하기 첫 번째

1st 주어진 글을 통해 글의 핵심 소재를 파악하고 전개 방향을 예측해 보세요.
2nd 글의 흐름을 나타내는 부사와 지시어에 주의를 기울여 문단을 해석하며 논리적인 순서를 짐작해 보세요.
3rd 예상한 순서를 통해 글의 흐름을 한 번 더 확인하세요.

001 ★★★※ .... 고1 2025(3월)/37

주어진 글 다음에 이어질 글의 순서로 가장 적절한 것을 고르시오. [3점]

> Cartilage is extremely important for the healthy functioning of a joint, especially if that joint bears weight, like your knee.

(A) This squeezing of joint fluid into and out of the cartilage helps it respond to the ⁵ off-and-on pressure of walking without breaking under the pressure.

(B) The cartilage in your left knee then "drinks in" synovial fluid, in much the same way that a sponge soaks up liquid¹⁰ when put in water. When you take another step and transfer the weight back onto your left leg, much of the fluid squeezes out of the cartilage.

(C) Imagine for a moment that you're¹⁵ looking into the inner workings of your left knee as you walk down the street. When you shift your weight from your left leg to your right, the pressure on your left knee is released. ²⁰

*cartilage: 연골 **synovial fluid: 윤활액

① (A) — (C) — (B) ② (B) — (A) — (C)
③ (B) — (C) — (A) ④ (C) — (A) — (B)
⑤ (C) — (B) — (A)

1st 주어진 글을 통해 글의 핵심 소재를 파악하고 전개 방향을 예측해 보세요.

> Cartilage is extremely important / for the healthy
> 연골은 아주 중요하며   / 관절의 건강한
> functioning of a joint, / especially if that joint bears
> 기능에   / 특히 그 관절이 당신의 무게를 지탱한다면
> weight, / like your knee. //
> 그렇다   / 무릎처럼   //

● **'연골'이 글의 중심 소재로 보여요.**
연골이 무게를 지탱하는 관절(무릎)의 기능에 아주 중요하다는 내용이에요.

● **어떤 내용으로 글이 전개될까요?**
연골이 왜 중요한지를 부연 설명하거나, 연골이 무게를 지탱하는 과정을 설명하는 흐름으로 글이 전개될 것 같아요.

2nd 글의 흐름을 나타내는 부사와 지시어에 주의를 기울여 문단을 해석하며 논리적인 순서를 짐작해 보세요.

1) (A) 문단부터 확인해 봅시다.

> (A) This squeezing of joint fluid into and out of the
> 이러한 관절 윤활액의 연골 안팎으로의 압착은
> cartilage / helps it respond to the off-and-on
> / 연골이 걷는 것의 반복적인 압력에 반응할 수 있도록 돕는다
> pressure of walking / without breaking under the
> / 압력에 부서지지 않고 //
> pressure. //

● **바로 앞의 내용을 언급하는 This가 쓰였어요.**
이를 통해 squeezing이 (A)에서 처음 언급된 것이 아니라, (A)의 바로 앞 문단에서 squeezing과 연관된 무언가가 먼저 언급되었을 것이라고 예상할 수 있어요.

● **주어진 글에 squeezing과 연관된 내용이 있었나요?**
주어진 글에는 ❶(   )이 관절의 건강에 중요하다는 내용만 있을 뿐, squeezing과 연관된 어떠한 내용도 없어요. 따라서 squeezing이 언급되는 문단이 (A)보다 먼저 나온 뒤에 (A)에서 This squeezing으로 이를 다시 언급하는 흐름이 되어야 해요.
▶ 주어진 글 바로 뒤에 (A)가 올 수 없음

● **(A) 뒤에는 어떤 내용이 있어야 할까요?**
연골이 반복적인 압력에 견디는 것, 즉 관절의 건강한 기능을 다시 강조하는 것을 보니 글을 마무리하는 문단일 가능성이 높아요. 혹시나 다른 내용이 이어질 수도 있으니 뒤 문단도 마저 살펴봅시다!

2) (B) 문단에 연골이 무게를 지탱하는 과정이 등장하네요!

> (B) The cartilage in your left knee / then "drinks in"
> 당신의 왼쪽 무릎의 연골은　　　　　　　　／ 그러면 윤활액을
>
> synovial fluid, / in much the same way / that a
> '흡수'한다　　　　／ 거의 같은 방식으로　　　／ 스펀지가
>
> sponge soaks up liquid / when put in water. //
> 액체를 흡수하는 것과　　／ 물에 담겼을 때　　／ //
>
> When you take another step / and transfer the
> 당신이 또 다른 한 걸음을 내딛어　　／ 체중을 다시 왼쪽
>
> weight back onto your left leg, / much of the fluid
> 다리로 옮길 때　　　　　／ 윤활액의 상당 부분이
>
> squeezes out of the cartilage. //
> 압착되어 연골 밖으로 나간다　　／ //

● **다음 순서를 나타내는 부사 then이 쓰였어요.**
  그렇다면 왼쪽 무릎의 연골이 윤활액을 흡수하기 전의 과정이 (B)의 바로 앞 문단에 언급되었을 거예요.

● **주어진 글과 (A)에 그런 내용이 있었나요?**
  주어진 글은 연골의 중요성, (A)는 관절 윤활액의 압착에 관한 문단이에요. 그렇다면 적어도 이 과정이 시작되는 내용이 나와야 하는데, 주어진 글에는 어떤 과정조차 언급되지 않았고 (A)는 어떤 과정의 중간이나 끝에 해당하는 내용이에요.
  ▶ 순서: 주어진 글과 (A) 바로 뒤에 (B)가 올 수 없음

● **(B) 뒤에는 어떤 내용이 있어야 할까요?**
  (A)의 squeezing과 연관되는 단어를 찾고 있었는데, (B) 문단의 두 번째 문장에 ❷(　　　　　)가 있네요! 왼쪽 무릎 연골이 윤활액을 흡수하고 체중을 왼쪽 다리로 옮기면 윤활액이 '압착'된다는 내용이군요. 이를 (A)에서 This squeezing으로 다시 언급하는 흐름이니까 (A)가 (B) 뒤에 이어지는 것이 적절해 보여요.
  ▶ 순서: (B) → (A)

3) (C) 문단이 주어진 글 뒤에 오는 게 적절한지 확인해 볼까요?

> (C) Imagine for a moment / that you're looking into
> 잠시 상상해 봐라　　　　／ 당신이 왼쪽 무릎의 내부 작동 방식을
>
> the inner workings of your left knee / as you walk
> 들여다본다고　　　　　　　　　　／ 길을 걸으며 //
>
> down the street. //
>
> When you shift your weight / from your left leg to
> 당신이 체중을 옮길 때　　　／ 왼쪽 다리에서 오른쪽 다리로
>
> your right, / the pressure on your left knee is
> 　　　　／ 당신의 왼쪽 무릎의 압력이 풀린다 //
>
> released. //

● **(C) 앞에는 어떤 내용이 있어야 할까요?**
  주어진 글에서 무릎처럼 무게를 지탱하는 관절이 언급되었고 (C)에도 왼쪽 무릎이 언급되며 서로 이어져요. 주어진 글 바로 뒤에서 (C)가 왼쪽 무릎의 내부 작동 방식을 예로 들며 설명하는 흐름도 적절하고요! 따라서 (C) 앞에는 주어진 글이 와야 해요.
  ▶ 순서: 주어진 글 → (C)

● **(C) 뒤에는 어떤 내용이 있어야 할까요?**
  두 번째 문장은 왼쪽 다리에서 오른쪽 다리로 체중을 옮길 때 왼쪽 무릎의 압력이 풀린다는 내용인데, 이때 스펀지에 물이 스며드는 것처럼 왼쪽 무릎의 연골이 ❸(　　　　　)을 흡수하는 것이 자연스러운 과정이에요. 즉, (B)의 then이 (C)의 내용을 받아서 왼쪽 무릎의 압력이 풀린 다음의 과정을 이어서 설명하는 흐름이죠!
  ▶ 순서: 주어진 글 → (C) → (B) → (A)

3rd 예상한 순서를 통해 글의 흐름을 한 번 더 확인하세요.

도입 (주어진 글)	연골은 무게를 지탱하는 무릎 관절의 기능에 아주 중요함
↓	
예시 (C)	걷는 동안 왼쪽 다리에서 오른쪽 다리로 체중을 옮기면 왼쪽 무릎의 압력이 줄어듦
↓	
부연 (B)	그리면 왼쪽 무릎의 연골은 윤활액을 흡수하고, 다시 체중을 왼쪽 다리로 옮기면 이를 압착해 밖으로 내보냄
↓	
결과 (A)	윤활액의 압착 덕분에 연골이 반복적인 걷기 압력에도 견딜 수 있음

➤ 정답을 한번 찾아볼까요?
연골이 무게를 지탱하는 무릎 관절 기능에 중요하다는 내용의 주어진 글 뒤에는 왼쪽 무릎을 예로 들며 무릎의 내부 작동 과정을 설명하기 시작하는 (C), 그 뒤에는 연골이 윤활액을 흡수하고 압착하는 과정을 설명한 (B), 마지막에는 이러한 윤활액의 압착 덕분에 연골이 걷기 압력에 견딜 수 있다는 내용으로 글을 마무리하는 (A)가 나와야 해요.
따라서 정답은 ❹(　　　　　)!

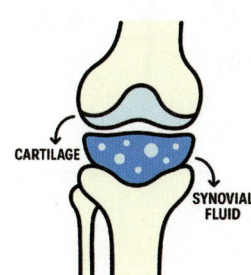

CARTILAGE
SYNOVIAL FLUID

O 글의 순서 정하기 _{두 번째}

1st 주어진 글을 통해 글의 핵심 소재를 파악하고 전개 방향을 예측해 보세요.
2nd 글의 흐름을 나타내는 부사와 관사(a, the)에 주의를 기울여 문단을 해석하며 논리적인 순서를 짐작해 보세요.
3rd 예상한 순서를 통해 글의 흐름을 한 번 더 확인하세요.

---

002 ★★★....................... 고1 2024(6월)/37

주어진 글 다음에 이어질 글의 순서로 가장 적절한
것을 고르시오.

> Problems often arise if an exotic species is
> suddenly introduced to an ecosystem.

(A) The grey had the edge because it can
   adapt its diet; it is able, for instance, to
   eat green acorns, while the red can only ₅
   digest mature acorns. Within the same
   area of forest, grey squirrels can destroy
   the food supply before red squirrels even
   have a bite.

(B) Britain's red and grey squirrels provide a ₁₀
   clear example. When the grey arrived
   from America in the 1870s, both squirrel
   species competed for the same food and
   habitat, which put the native red squirrel
   populations under pressure. ₁₅

(C) Greys can also live more densely and in
   varied habitats, so have survived more
   easily when woodland has been
   destroyed. As a result, the red squirrel
   has come close to extinction in England. ₂₀

*edge: 우위 **acorn: 도토리

① (A) — (C) — (B)　　② (B) — (A) — (C)
③ (B) — (C) — (A)　　④ (C) — (A) — (B)
⑤ (C) — (B) — (A)

1st 주어진 글을 통해 글의 핵심 소재를 파악하고 전개 방향을
예측해 보세요.

> Problems often arise / if an exotic species is
> 문제가 종종 발생한다　　　　/ 외래종이 갑자기 생태계에 유입되면 //
> suddenly introduced to an ecosystem. //

- **'외래종'이 등장해요.**
  외래종이 갑자기 생태계에 유입되면 문제가 발생한대요.

- **어떤 내용으로 글이 전개될까요?**
  외래종의 유입으로 발생한 문제를 구체적으로 보여주는 예시가 등장할
  것 같군요. 토종 생물이 ❶(　　　　　　　)으로 인해 생존에 위협을
  받는다는 내용이 이어질 수도 있겠어요.

2nd 글의 흐름을 나타내는 부사와 관사(a, the)에 주의를 기울여
문단을 해석하며 논리적인 순서를 짐작해 보세요.

1) (A) 문단부터 확인해 봅시다.

> The grey had the edge / because it can adapt its
> 회색 다람쥐는 우위를 점했다　　/ 먹이를 조절할 수 있기 때문에
> diet; / it is able, for instance, to eat green acorns, /
> 　　/ 예를 들어 회색 다람쥐는 설익은 도토리를 먹을 수 있다　　/
> while the red can only digest mature acorns. //
> 반면 붉은 다람쥐는 다 익은 도토리만 소화할 수 있다　　　　//
> Within the same area of forest, / grey squirrels can
> 숲의 같은 지역 내에서　　　　　/ 회색 다람쥐는 식량 공급을
> destroy the food supply / before red squirrels even
> 파괴할 수 있다　　　　/ 붉은 다람쥐가 한 입 먹기도 전에 //
> have a bite. //

- **The grey와 the red는 무엇을 나타낼까요?**
  grey와 red라는 색깔로 구분되는 두 부류가 등장했군요. 도토리를
  먹는다는 것을 보니 다람쥐일 것 같아요! 역시나 바로 뒤 문장에 grey
  squirrels와 red squirrels로 이들을 가리키고 있어요.

- **(A) 앞에는 어떤 내용이 있어야 할까요?**
  외래종의 생태계 유입으로 인한 문제를 나타내는 예시로서 두 부류의
  다람쥐를 곧바로 제시할 수도 있어요. 하지만 앞서 봤듯이 (A)의 첫
  문장에는 The grey와 the red가 나타나기 때문에, (A)보다 먼저 두
  다람쥐 부류를 소개하는 문단이 나온 뒤에 이들을 (A)에서 색깔로
  가리키는 흐름이 되어야 해요.
  ▶ 주어진 글 바로 뒤에 (A)가 올 수 없음

● **(A) 뒤에는 어떤 내용이 있어야 할까요?**

외래종인 회색 다람쥐가 갑자기 생태계에 유입되어 토종인 붉은 다람쥐에게 가져다준 문제의 결과가 이어질 거예요.

2) (B) 문단이 두 다람쥐를 소개하며 시작하네요!

Britain's red and grey squirrels / provide a clear
영국의 붉은색 다람쥐와 회색 다람쥐가   / 명확한 예를

example. //
제공한다   //

When the grey arrived from America in the 1870s, /
1870년대 미국에서 회색 다람쥐가 왔을 때   /

both squirrel species competed / for the same food
두 다람쥐 종은 경쟁했다   / 동일한 먹이와 서식지를

and habitat, / which put the native red squirrel
놓고   / 이것이 토종의 붉은 다람쥐 개체군을 압박했다 //

populations under pressure. //

● **(B) 앞에는 어떤 내용이 있어야 할까요?**

붉은색 다람쥐와 회색 다람쥐가 명확한 예(a clear example)를 제공한다고 했는데, 여기에 부정관사 a가 쓰였네요! 이 예시가 글에서 처음으로 등장했음을 알려주고 있어요.
영국 기준으로 외래종인 미국의 회색 다람쥐가 영국에 왔을 때 토종인 붉은 다람쥐를 압박했다는 내용이군요. 외래종이 생태계에 유입되어 발생하는 문제의 발단에 해당하니까, 주어진 글에 나타난 문제(Problems)와 연결되는 것이 적절하죠!

▶ 순서: 주어진 글 → (B)

● **(B) 뒤에는 어떤 내용이 있어야 할까요?**

(A) 문단을 읽으며 다람쥐들에 대한 소개가 앞에 나올 필요가 있다고 생각했는데 그 부분이 여기 있었네요! 다람쥐들 간 문제의 배경을 (B)에서 설명하고 구체적인 문제를 나타내는 (A)가 뒤에 이어지는 것이 적절해 보여요.

▶ 순서: 주어진 글 → (B) → (A)

3) (C) 문단이 마지막에 오는 게 적절한지 확인해 볼까요?

(C) Greys can also live more densely and in varied
회색 다람쥐는 또한 더 밀집하며 다양한 서식지에서 살 수 있어서

habitats, / so have survived more easily / when
           / 더 쉽게 살아남았다   / 삼림이

woodland has been destroyed. //
파괴되었을 때   //

As a result, / the red squirrel has come close to
그 결과   / 붉은 다람쥐는 영국에서 거의 멸종 위기에 이르렀다 //

extinction in England. //

● **(C) 앞에는 어떤 내용이 있어야 할까요?**

또 다른 내용을 나타내는 also 뒤에 회색 다람쥐가 서식지 측면에서 우위인 상황이 이어지네요. 먹이 측면에서의 우위를 설명한 (A)의 뒤에 서식지 측면에서의 우위를 추가로 설명하는 (C)가 이어지는 것이 적절해 보여요!

▶ 순서: 주어진 글 → (B) → (A) → (C)

3rd 예상한 순서를 통해 글의 흐름을 한 번 더 확인하세요.

> **도입** 외래종이 생태계에 유입되면 문제가 발생함
> ↓
> **예시** 영국의 토종 붉은색 다람쥐와 미국에서 온 외래종 회색 다람쥐가 경쟁했고 회색 다람쥐가 붉은색 다람쥐를 압박했음
> ↓
> **부연** 먹이 조절에서 우위를 가진 회색 다람쥐가 붉은색 다람쥐의 식량 공급을 파괴했음
> ↓
> **결과** 서식지 범위에서도 회색 다람쥐가 우위를 가졌고 붉은색 다람쥐는 멸종 위기에 처했음

➤ 정답을 한번 찾아볼까요?

외래종 유입으로 문제가 발생한다고 한 주어진 글 뒤에는 다람쥐들의 예시를 소개한 (B)가 이어지고, 그 뒤에는 먹이 측면에서 회색 다람쥐의 우위를 설명한 (A), 마지막에는 서식지 측면의 우위와 문제의 최종 결과를 설명한 (C)가 나와야 해요.
따라서 정답은 ❷(   )!

지시어와 연결어에 주목하여 글의 순서를 추론하자!

003 ~ 06 ▶ 제한시간 8분

003 ★★★ 고1 2025(3월)/36

주어진 글 다음에 이어질 글의 순서로 가장 적절한 것을 고르시오.
[3점]

> Let's assume that at least some animals are capable of thinking despite lacking a language.

(A) This doesn't imply that squirrels lack concepts, simply that they don't need them for this concrete form of thinking. For us to be able to say that an animal has concepts, we have to show not just that she's capable of thinking, but also that she has certain specific abilities.

(B) To do this, in principle she doesn't need a concept of branch nor a concept of tree. It might be enough for her to have, for example, the ability to think in images; to make a mental map of the tree where she can imagine and try out different routes.

(C) This doesn't necessarily mean that they possess concepts, for some forms of thought may be nonconceptual. We can imagine, for instance, a squirrel who is planning how to get from the branch she's currently standing on to a branch from the tree in front.
*squirrel: 다람쥐

① (A) — (C) — (B) ② (B) — (A) — (C)
③ (B) — (C) — (A) ④ (C) — (A) — (B)
⑤ (C) — (B) — (A)

구문 서술형

밑줄 친 부분을 바르게 고치고, 그 부분이 문장에서 어떤 역할을 하는지 쓰시오.

⇒ Let's assume <u>which</u> at least some animals are capable of thinking.

⇒ 고친 표현: _____

⇒ 역할: 동사 assume의 _____ 역할을 하는 _____ 을 이끈다.

004 ★★★❀ 고1 2025(6월)/36

주어진 글 다음에 이어질 글의 순서로 가장 적절한 것을 고르시오.
[3점]

> History, people often say, repeats itself. And looking at the historical records of the ancient civilizations, some things do seem to happen again and again.

(A) If so, archaeology would be pretty boring; one thing would happen again and again. But that's not what archaeologists see. Some civilizations end suddenly, like the Aztec and Inca, conquered by invaders in the 1520s AD.

(B) Civilizations expand, get overextended, and then collapse as in the cases of Rome, which went under in 476 AD, and the British Empire, which fell apart more than a thousand years later in the post-World War II era. But is this always the case?

(C) Those empires never had the chance to collapse as a result of overexpansion. So in the case of civilizations, "history repeats itself" seems to be an oversimplification.
*archaeology: 고고학 **invader: 침입자 ***empire: 제국

① (A) — (C) — (B) ② (B) — (A) — (C)
③ (B) — (C) — (A) ④ (C) — (A) — (B)
⑤ (C) — (B) — (A)

구문 서술형

두 문장을 순서대로 연결할 때 필요한 등위접속사를 모두 쓰시오.

> • Archaeology would be pretty boring if the same thing happened again and again.
> • That's not what archaeologists see.

⇒ _____

주어진 글 다음에 이어질 글의 순서로 가장 적절한 것을 고르시오.

> Stanford psychology professor Dr. Carol Dweck is the internationally recognized pioneer of the concept of "growth mindset" as a way to continually grow, learn, and persevere in our efforts.

(A) These kids end up taking on tougher things, and feel better about themselves. "Emphasizing effort gives a child a variable that they can control," Dweck has explained.

(B) In contrast, Dweck found, kids who are praised not for their smarts but for their effort develop what Dweck calls a "growth mindset." They learn that their effort is what led to their success, and if they continue to try, over time they'll improve and achieve more things.

(C) Dweck found that kids who are told they're "smart" actually underperform in future tasks, by choosing easier tasks to avoid evidence that they are not smart, which Dweck calls having a "fixed mindset." *persevere: 인내하다 **variable: 변수

① (A) — (C) — (B) ② (B) — (A) — (C)
③ (B) — (C) — (A) ④ (C) — (A) — (B)
⑤ (C) — (B) — (A)

[구문 서술형]
주어진 우리말과 일치하도록 빈칸에 알맞은 상관접속사를 쓰시오.

똑똑함이 아닌 노력에 대해 칭찬받는 아이들은 "성장 사고방식"을 발달시킨다.

➡ Kids who are praised _____ for their smarts _____ for their effort develop a "growth mindset."

주어진 글 다음에 이어질 글의 순서로 가장 적절한 것을 고르시오.
[3점]

> The desert tortoise has a simple solution for coping with Death Valley's extreme heat: It avoids it.

(A) But to stay supplied with water through its extended hibernation, the reptile relies on something else — its highly sophisticated bladder. Unlike most animals, the tortoise's bladder acts as a holding tank, allowing it to reabsorb water back into its body. Incredibly, a desert tortoise can go a full year without taking in any freshwater at all.

(B) The slow-moving creature hibernates during the winter and stays in its tunnel for much of the summer, meaning that it spends more than 90 percent of its life immobile. In fact, the tortoise usually only surfaces after a good rain. Then, it gets to work. The tortoise stocks up on water by eating plants and digging holes to collect rain.

(C) And because its bladder is so important to a tortoise's survival, park rangers often remind visitors not to stop and help the slow-movers across the road. Tortoises become so terrified when people pick them up that they empty their bladders, losing their precious water reserves. *hibernation: 동면 **bladder: 방광

① (A) — (C) — (B) ② (B) — (A) — (C)
③ (B) — (C) — (A) ④ (C) — (A) — (B)
⑤ (C) — (B) — (A)

[구문 서술형]
두 문장을 순서대로 연결할 때 필요한 등위접속사를 모두 쓰시오.

> • A desert tortoise's bladder acts as a holding tank.
> • It can go a full year without taking in any freshwater at all.

➡ 접속사: _____

007 ✹✹✸ ───────── 고1 2025(9월)/37

주어진 글 다음에 이어질 글의 순서로 가장 적절한 것을 고르시오.

> Imagine you are pedalling your bicycle on a level road. You stop pedalling: no force is now acting to move you forward. What happens?

(A) One of these is friction in the wheels rubbing on the axles. Another is air resistance, which you can feel, pushing you backwards as you and the bicycle move forwards. When you apply these ideas to something around you, like a cart, you can see what could be generating friction: mainly the axles rubbing on the body as they rotate.

(B) You gradually slow down. How could you slow down more suddenly, in a shorter distance? By putting the brakes on. Because the brakes change your movement, making you slow down more suddenly, they must be exerting a force on the bicycle and you, as they grip and rub on the wheel-rims.

(C) This is the force called friction, which tends to slow down moving things by acting in the direction opposite to movement, that is backwards. Even without the brakes on, there are other friction forces acting on you and your bicycle, which also slow you down.

*axle: (바퀴의) 축 **rim: 테두리

① (A) — (C) — (B) ② (B) — (A) — (C)
③ (B) — (C) — (A) ④ (C) — (A) — (B)
⑤ (C) — (B) — (A)

구문 서술형
밑줄 친 접속사에 유의하여 빈칸에 알맞은 해석을 쓰시오.

➡ You can feel air resistance pushing you backwards as you and the bicycle move forwards.

➡ _____ 여러분은 여러분을 뒤쪽으로 미는 공기 저항을 느낄 수 있다.

---

008 ✹✹✹ ───────── 고1 2024(10월)/37

주어진 글 다음에 이어질 글의 순서로 가장 적절한 것을 고르시오.

> Conventional medicine has long believed that depression is caused by an imbalance of neurotransmitters in the brain.

(A) However, there is a major problem with this explanation. This is because the imbalance of substances in the brain is a consequence of depression, not its cause. In other words, depression causes a decrease in brain substances such as serotonin and noradrenaline, not a decrease in brain substances causes depression.

(B) If it is not consciousness itself, then the root cause of depression is also a distortion of our state of consciousness: a consciousness that has lost its sense of self and the meaning of life. Such a disease of consciousness may manifest itself in the form of depression.

(C) In this revised cause-and-effect, the key is to reframe depression as a problem of consciousness. Our consciousness is a more fundamental entity that goes beyond the functioning of the brain. The brain is no more than an organ of consciousness.

*neurotransmitter: 신경 전달 물질 **manifest: (명백히) 나타내다

① (A) — (C) — (B) ② (B) — (A) — (C)
③ (B) — (C) — (A) ④ (C) — (A) — (B)
⑤ (C) — (B) — (A)

구문 서술형
밑줄 친 부분을 대신할 수 있는 접속사를 쓰시오.

➡ There is a problem with this explanation, because the imbalance of substances in the brain is a consequence of depression, not its cause.

➡ _____

주어진 글 다음에 이어질 글의 순서로 가장 적절한 것을 고르시오.

In many sports, people realized the difficulties and even impossibilities of young children participating fully in many adult sport environments.

(A) As examples, baseball has T ball, football has flag football and junior soccer uses a smaller and lighter ball and (sometimes) a smaller field. All have junior competitive structures where children play for shorter time periods and often in smaller teams.

(B) In a similar way, tennis has adapted the court areas, balls and rackets to make them more appropriate for children under 10. The adaptations are progressive and relate to the age of the child.

(C) They found the road to success for young children is unlikely if they play on adult fields, courts or arenas with equipment that is too large, too heavy or too fast for them to handle while trying to compete in adult-style competition. Common sense has prevailed: different sports have made adaptations for children.　　　*prevail: 널리 퍼지다

① (A) — (C) — (B)　　② (B) — (A) — (C)
③ (B) — (C) — (A)　　④ (C) — (A) — (B)
⑤ (C) — (B) — (A)

주어진 글 다음에 이어질 글의 순서로 가장 적절한 것을 고르시오.
[3점]

With no horses available, the Inca empire excelled at delivering messages on foot.

(A) When a messenger neared the next hut, he began to call out and repeated the message three or four times to the one who was running out to meet him. The Inca empire could relay messages 1,000miles (1,610km) in three or four days under good conditions.

(B) The messengers were stationed on the royal roads to deliver the Inca king's orders and reports coming from his lands. Called Chasquis, they lived in groups of four to six in huts, placed from one to two miles apart along the roads.

(C) They were all young men and especially good runners who watched the road in both directions. If they caught sight of another messenger coming, they hurried out to meet them. The Inca built the huts on high ground, in sight of one another.
*excel: 탁월하다 **messenger: 전령

① (A) — (C) — (B)　　② (B) — (A) — (C)
③ (B) — (C) — (A)　　④ (C) — (A) — (B)
⑤ (C) — (B) — (A)

011 ✽✽✾

주어진 글 다음에 이어질 글의 순서로 가장 적절한 것을 고르시오.
[3점]

As businesses shift some core business activities to digital, such as sales, marketing, or archiving, it is assumed that the impact on the environment will be less negative.

(A) When we store bigger data on clouds, increased carbon emissions make our green clouds gray. The carbon footprint of an email is smaller than mail sent via a post office, but still, it causes four grams of CO_2, and it can be as much as 50 grams if the attachment is big.

(B) However, digital business activities can still threaten the environment. In some cases, the harm of digital businesses can be even more hazardous. A few decades ago, offices used to have much more paper waste since all documents were paper based.

(C) When workplaces shifted from paper to digital documents, invoices, and emails, it was a promising step to save trees. However, the cost of the Internet and electricity for the environment is neglected. A recent *Wired* report declared that most data centers' energy source is fossil fuels.

① (A) — (C) — (B)　　② (B) — (A) — (C)
③ (B) — (C) — (A)　　④ (C) — (A) — (B)
⑤ (C) — (B) — (A)

012 ✽✽✽

주어진 글 다음에 이어질 글의 순서로 가장 적절한 것을 고르시오.

The discovery of mirror neurons has profoundly changed the way we think of a fundamental human capacity, learning by observation.

(A) You may not see the tongue stick out each time you stick yours out at your newborn, but if you do it many times, the tongue will come out more often than if you do something different. Babies babble and later start to imitate the sounds their parents produce.

(B) As children we learn a lot by observing what our parents and friends do. Newborns, in the first week of life, have an inborn tendency to stick out their tongue if their parents stick out theirs. Such imitation is not perfect.

(C) Later still, they play with vacuum cleaners and hammers in imitation of their parents. Our modern cultures, in which we write, speak, read, build spaceships and go to school, can work only because we are not restricted to the behavior we are born with or learn by trial and error. We can learn a lot by simply watching others. *babble: 옹알이하다

① (A) — (C) — (B)　　② (B) — (A) — (C)
③ (B) — (C) — (A)　　④ (C) — (A) — (B)
⑤ (C) — (B) — (A)

013 ★★★

주어진 글 다음에 이어질 글의 순서로 가장 적절한 것을 고르시오. [3점]

> Have you ever been surprised to hear a recording of your own voice? You might have thought, "Is that really what my voice sounds like?"

(A) There are two pathways through which we perceive our own voice when we speak. One is the route through which we perceive most external sounds, like waves that travel from the air through the outer, middle and inner ear.

(B) But because our vocal cords vibrate when we speak, there is a second internal path. Vibrations are conducted through our bones and stimulate our inner ears directly. Lower frequencies are emphasized along this pathway. That makes your voice sound deeper and richer to yourself than it may sound to other people.

(C) Maybe your accent is more pronounced in the recording than you realized, or your voice is higher than it seems to your own ears. This is of course quite a common experience. The explanation is actually fairly simple.

*vocal cords: 성대 **frequency: 주파수

① (A) — (C) — (B)   ② (B) — (A) — (C)
③ (B) — (C) — (A)   ④ (C) — (A) — (B)
⑤ (C) — (B) — (A)

014 ★★★

주어진 글 다음에 이어질 글의 순서로 가장 적절한 것을 고르시오. [3점]

> Managers are always looking for ways to increase productivity, which is the ratio of costs to output in production. Adam Smith, writing when the manufacturing industry was new, described a way that production could be made more efficient, known as the "division of labor."

(A) Because each worker specializes in one job, he or she can work much faster without changing from one task to another. Now 10 workers can produce thousands of pins in a day — a huge increase in productivity from the 200 they would have produced before.

(B) One worker could do all these tasks, and make 20 pins in a day. But this work can be divided into its separate processes, with a number of workers each performing one task.

(C) Making most manufactured goods involves several different processes using different skills. Smith's example was the manufacture of pins: the wire is straightened, sharpened, a head is put on, and then it is polished.

*ratio: 비율

① (A) — (C) — (B)   ② (B) — (A) — (C)
③ (B) — (C) — (A)   ④ (C) — (A) — (B)
⑤ (C) — (B) — (A)

015 ***

고1 2022(3월)/36

주어진 글 다음에 이어질 글의 순서로 가장 적절한 것을 고르시오.

> Toward the end of the 19th century, a new architectural attitude emerged. Industrial architecture, the argument went, was ugly and inhuman; past styles had more to do with pretension than what people needed in their homes.

(A) But they supplied people's needs perfectly and, at their best, had a beauty that came from the craftsman's skill and the rootedness of the house in its locality.

(B) Instead of these approaches, why not look at the way ordinary country builders worked in the past? They developed their craft skills over generations, demonstrating mastery of both tools and materials.

(C) Those materials were local, and used with simplicity — houses built this way had plain wooden floors and whitewashed walls inside.

* pretension: 허세, 가식

① (A) — (C) — (B)   ② (B) — (A) — (C)
③ (B) — (C) — (A)   ④ (C) — (A) — (B)
⑤ (C) — (B) — (A)

016 ***

고1 2022(11월)/37

주어진 글 다음에 이어질 글의 순서로 가장 적절한 것을 고르시오.

> Each beech tree grows in a particular location and soil conditions can vary greatly in just a few yards. The soil can have a great deal of water or almost no water. It can be full of nutrients or not.

(A) This is taking place underground through the roots. Whoever has an abundance of sugar hands some over; whoever is running short gets help. Their network acts as a system to make sure that no trees fall too far behind.

(B) However, the rate is the same. Whether they are thick or thin, all the trees of the same species are using light to produce the same amount of sugar per leaf. Some trees have plenty of sugar and some have less, but the trees equalize this difference between them by transferring sugar.

(C) Accordingly, each tree grows more quickly or more slowly and produces more or less sugar, and thus you would expect every tree to be photosynthesizing at a different rate.

*photosynthesize: 광합성하다

① (A) — (C) — (B)   ② (B) — (A) — (C)
③ (B) — (C) — (A)   ④ (C) — (A) — (B)
⑤ (C) — (B) — (A)

017 ***❀

고1 2023(6월)/36

주어진 글 다음에 이어질 글의 순서로 가장 적절한 것을 고르시오.

> Up until about 6,000 years ago, most people were farmers. Many lived in different places throughout the year, hunting for food or moving their livestock to areas with enough food.

(A) For example, priests wanted to know when to carry out religious ceremonies. This was when people first invented clocks — devices that show, measure, and keep track of passing time.

(B) There was no need to tell the time because life depended on natural cycles, such as the changing seasons or sunrise and sunset. Gradually more people started to live in larger settlements, and some needed to tell the time.

(C) Clocks have been important ever since. Today, clocks are used for important things such as setting busy airport timetables — if the time is incorrect, aeroplanes might crash into each other when taking off or landing!

① (A) — (C) — (B)   ② (B) — (A) — (C)
③ (B) — (C) — (A)   ④ (C) — (A) — (B)
⑤ (C) — (B) — (A)

018 ★★★☆

주어진 글 다음에 이어질 글의 순서로 가장 적절한 것을 고르시오.
[3점]

> Maybe you've heard this joke: "How do you eat an elephant?" The answer is "one bite at a time."

(A) Common crystal habits include squares, triangles, and six-sided hexagons. Usually crystals form when liquids cool, such as when you create ice cubes. Many times, crystals form in ways that do not allow for perfect shapes. If conditions are too cold, too hot, or there isn't enough source material, they can form strange, twisted shapes.

(B) So, how do you "build" the Earth? That's simple, too: one atom at a time. Atoms are the basic building blocks of crystals, and since all rocks are made up of crystals, the more you know about atoms, the better. Crystals come in a variety of shapes that scientists call *habits*.

(C) But when conditions are right, we see beautiful displays. Usually, this involves a slow, steady environment where the individual atoms have plenty of time to join and fit perfectly into what's known as the *crystal lattice*. This is the basic structure of atoms that is seen time after time.

① (A) — (C) — (B)   ② (B) — (A) — (C)
③ (B) — (C) — (A)   ④ (C) — (A) — (B)
⑤ (C) — (B) — (A)

019 ★★★☆

주어진 글 다음에 이어질 글의 순서로 가장 적절한 것을 고르시오.
[3점]

> When you pluck a guitar string it moves back and forth hundreds of times every second.

(A) The vibration of the wood creates more powerful waves in the air pressure, which travel away from the guitar. When the waves reach your eardrums they flex in and out the same number of times a second as the original string.

(B) Naturally, this movement is so fast that you cannot see it — you just see the blurred outline of the moving string. Strings vibrating in this way on their own make hardly any noise because strings are very thin and don't push much air about.

(C) But if you attach a string to a big hollow box (like a guitar body), then the vibration is amplified and the note is heard loud and clear. The vibration of the string is passed on to the wooden panels of the guitar body, which vibrate back and forth at the same rate as the string.   *pluck: (현악기를) 뜯다 **amplify: 증폭시키다

① (A) — (C) — (B)   ② (B) — (A) — (C)
③ (B) — (C) — (A)   ④ (C) — (A) — (B)
⑤ (C) — (B) — (A)

020 ★★★☆

주어진 글 다음에 이어질 글의 순서로 가장 적절한 것을 고르시오.

> Things are changing. It has been reported that 42 percent of jobs in Canada are at risk, and 62 percent of jobs in America will be in danger due to advances in automation.

(A) However, what's difficult to automate is the ability to creatively solve problems. Whereas workers in "doing" roles can be replaced by robots, the role of creatively solving problems is more dependent on an irreplaceable individual.

(B) You might say that the numbers seem a bit unrealistic, but the threat is real. One fast food franchise has a robot that can flip a burger in ten seconds. It is just a simple task but the robot could replace an entire crew.

(C) Highly skilled jobs are also at risk. A supercomputer, for instance, can suggest available treatments for specific illnesses in an automated way, drawing on the body of medical research and data on diseases.

① (A) — (C) — (B)   ② (B) — (A) — (C)
③ (B) — (C) — (A)   ④ (C) — (A) — (B)
⑤ (C) — (B) — (A)

021 ★★★❀ 고1 2023(11월)/36

주어진 글 다음에 이어질 글의 순서로 가장 적절한 것을 고르시오. [3점]

> The adolescent brain is not fully developed until its early twenties. This means the way the adolescents' decision-making circuits integrate and process information may put them at a disadvantage.

(A) On the other hand, the limbic system matures earlier, playing a central role in processing emotional responses. Because of its earlier development, it is more likely to influence decision-making. Decision-making in the adolescent brain is led by emotional factors more than the perception of consequences.

(B) Due to these differences, there is an imbalance between feeling-based decision-making ruled by the more mature limbic system and logical-based decision-making by the not-yet-mature prefrontal cortex. This may explain why some teens are more likely to make bad decisions.

(C) One of their brain regions that matures later is the prefrontal cortex, which is the control center, tasked with thinking ahead and evaluating consequences. It is the area of the brain responsible for preventing you from sending off an initial angry text and modifying it with kinder words.

*integrate: 통합하다 **limbic system: 대뇌변연계
***prefrontal cortex: 전전두엽 피질

① (A) — (C) — (B) ② (B) — (A) — (C)
③ (B) — (C) — (A) ④ (C) — (A) — (B)
⑤ (C) — (B) — (A)

022 ★★★ 고1 2023(11월)/37

주어진 글 다음에 이어질 글의 순서로 가장 적절한 것을 고르시오.

> Despite the remarkable progress in deep-learning based facial recognition approaches in recent years, in terms of identification performance, they still have limitations. These limitations relate to the database used in the learning stage.

(A) To counteract this problem, researchers have developed models for face aging or digital de-aging. It is used to compensate for the differences in facial characteristics, which appear over a given time period.

(B) If the selected database does not contain enough instances, the result may be systematically affected. For example, the performance of a facial biometric system may decrease if the person to be identified was enrolled over 10 years ago.

(C) The factor to consider is that this person may experience changes in the texture of the face, particularly with the appearance of wrinkles and sagging skin. These changes may be highlighted by weight gain or loss.

*biometric: 생체 측정의 **sagging: 처진

① (A) — (C) — (B) ② (B) — (A) — (C)
③ (B) — (C) — (A) ④ (C) — (A) — (B)
⑤ (C) — (B) — (A)

O23 ★★★   고1 2023(3월)/37

주어진 글 다음에 이어질 글의 순서로 가장 적절한 것을 고르시오.

> Natural processes form minerals in many ways. For example, hot melted rock material, called magma, cools when it reaches the Earth's surface, or even if it's trapped below the surface. As magma cools, its atoms lose heat energy, move closer together, and begin to combine into compounds.

(A) Also, the size of the crystals that form depends partly on how rapidly the magma cools. When magma cools slowly, the crystals that form are generally large enough to see with the unaided eye.

(B) During this process, atoms of the different compounds arrange themselves into orderly, repeating patterns. The type and amount of elements present in a magma partly determine which minerals will form.

(C) This is because the atoms have enough time to move together and form into larger crystals. When magma cools rapidly, the crystals that form will be small. In such cases, you can't easily see individual mineral crystals.

*compound: 화합물

① (A) — (C) — (B)   ② (B) — (A) — (C)
③ (B) — (C) — (A)   ④ (C) — (A) — (B)
⑤ (C) — (B) — (A)

O24 ★★★   고1 2022(6월)/37

주어진 글 다음에 이어질 글의 순서로 가장 적절한 것을 고르시오.
[3점]

> According to legend, once a vampire bites a person, that person turns into a vampire who seeks the blood of others. A researcher came up with some simple math, which proves that these highly popular creatures can't exist.

(A) In just two-and-a-half years, the original human population would all have become vampires with no humans left. But look around you. Have vampires taken over the world? No, because there's no such thing.

(B) If the first vampire came into existence that day and bit one person a month, there would have been two vampires by February 1st, 1600. A month later there would have been four, the next month eight, then sixteen, and so on.

(C) University of Central Florida physics professor Costas Efthimiou's work breaks down the myth. Suppose that on January 1st, 1600, the human population was just over five hundred million.

① (A) — (C) — (B)   ② (B) — (A) — (C)
③ (B) — (C) — (A)   ④ (C) — (A) — (B)
⑤ (C) — (B) — (A)

O25 ★★★✻   고1 2022(6월)/36

주어진 글 다음에 이어질 글의 순서로 가장 적절한 것을 고르시오.

> Mrs. Klein told her first graders to draw a picture of something to be thankful for. She thought that most of the class would draw turkeys or Thanksgiving tables. But Douglas drew something different.

(A) The class was so responsive that Mrs. Klein had almost forgotten about Douglas. After she had the others at work on another project, she asked Douglas whose hand it was. He answered softly, "It's yours. Thank you, Mrs. Klein."

(B) Douglas was a boy who usually spent time alone and stayed around her while his classmates went outside together during break time. What the boy drew was a hand. But whose hand? His image immediately attracted the other students' interest.

(C) So, everyone rushed to talk about whose hand it was. "It must be the hand of God that brings us food," said one student. "A farmer's," said a second student, "because they raise the turkeys." "It looks more like a police officer's," added another, "they protect us."

① (A) — (C) — (B)   ② (B) — (A) — (C)
③ (B) — (C) — (A)   ④ (C) — (A) — (B)
⑤ (C) — (B) — (A)

O26 ***

고1 2023(3월)/36

주어진 글 다음에 이어질 글의 순서로 가장 적절한 것을 고르시오. [3점]

> In the Old Stone Age, small bands of 20 to 60 people wandered from place to place in search of food. Once people began farming, they could settle down near their farms.

(A) While some workers grew crops, others built new houses and made tools. Village dwellers also learned to work together to do a task faster.

(B) For example, toolmakers could share the work of making stone axes and knives. By working together, they could make more tools in the same amount of time.

(C) As a result, towns and villages grew larger. Living in communities allowed people to organize themselves more efficiently. They could divide up the work of producing food and other things they needed.   *dweller: 거주자

① (A) — (C) — (B)   ② (B) — (A) — (C)
③ (B) — (C) — (A)   ④ (C) — (A) — (B)
⑤ (C) — (B) — (A)

O27 ***

고1 2022(9월)/36

주어진 글 다음에 이어질 글의 순서로 가장 적절한 것을 고르시오.

> With nearly a billion hungry people in the world, there is obviously no single cause.

(A) The reason people are hungry in those countries is that the products produced there can be sold on the world market for more than the local citizens can afford to pay for them. In the modern age you do not starve because you have no food, you starve because you have no money.

(B) However, far and away the biggest cause is poverty. Seventy-nine percent of the world's hungry live in nations that are net exporters of food. How can this be?

(C) So the problem really is that food is, in the grand scheme of things, too expensive and many people are too poor to buy it. The answer will be in continuing the trend of lowering the cost of food.

*net exporter: 순 수출국 **scheme: 체계, 조직

① (A) — (C) — (B)   ② (B) — (A) — (C)
③ (B) — (C) — (A)   ④ (C) — (A) — (B)
⑤ (C) — (B) — (A)

1등급 대비 문제

O28   ⭐ 2등급 대비

고1 2022(9월)/37

주어진 글 다음에 이어질 글의 순서로 가장 적절한 것을 고르시오. [3점]

> Most people have a perfect time of day when they feel they are at their best, whether in the morning, evening, or afternoon.

(A) When your mind and body are less alert than at your "peak" hours, the muse of creativity awakens and is allowed to roam more freely. In other words, when your mental machinery is loose rather than standing at attention, the creativity flows.

(B) However, if the task you face demands creativity and novel ideas, it's best to tackle it at your "worst" time of day! So if you are an early bird, make sure to attack your creative task in the evening, and vice versa for night owls.

(C) Some of us are night owls, some early birds, and others in between may feel most active during the afternoon hours. If you are able to organize your day and divide your work, make it a point to deal with tasks that demand attention at your best time of the day.

*roam: (어슬렁어슬렁) 거닐다

① (A) — (C) — (B)   ② (B) — (A) — (C)
③ (B) — (C) — (A)   ④ (C) — (A) — (B)
⑤ (C) — (B) — (A)

주어진 글 다음에 이어질 글의 순서로 가장 적절한 것을
고르시오. [3점]

> Literary works, by their nature, suggest rather than explain; they imply rather than state their claims boldly and directly.

(A) What a text implies is often of great interest to us. And our work of figuring out a text's implications tests our analytical powers. In considering what a text suggests, we gain practice in making sense of texts.

(B) But whatever the proportion of a work's showing to telling, there is always something for readers to interpret. Thus we ask the question "What does the text suggest?" as a way to approach literary interpretation, as a way to begin thinking about a text's implications.

(C) This broad generalization, however, does not mean that works of literature do not include direct statements. Depending on when they were written and by whom, literary works may contain large amounts of direct telling and lesser amounts of suggestion and implication.

① (A) — (C) — (B)　　② (B) — (A) — (C)
③ (B) — (C) — (A)　　④ (C) — (A) — (B)
⑤ (C) — (B) — (A)

주어진 글 다음에 이어질 글의 순서로 가장 적절한 것을
고르시오. [3점]

> Robert Schumann once said, "The laws of morals are those of art." What the great man is saying here is that there is good music and bad music.

(A) It's the same with performances: a bad performance isn't necessarily the result of incompetence. Some of the worst performances occur when the performers, no matter how accomplished, are thinking more of themselves than of the music they're playing.

(B) The greatest music, even if it's tragic in nature, takes us to a world higher than ours; somehow the beauty uplifts us. Bad music, on the other hand, degrades us.

(C) These doubtful characters aren't really listening to what the composer is saying — they're just showing off, hoping that they'll have a great 'success' with the public. The performer's basic task is to try to understand the meaning of the music, and then to communicate it honestly to others.

*incompetence: 무능　**degrade: 격하시키다

① (A) — (C) — (B)　　② (B) — (A) — (C)
③ (B) — (C) — (A)　　④ (C) — (A) — (B)
⑤ (C) — (B) — (A)

031 ⭐ 1등급 대비 .... 고1 2024(10월)/36

주어진 글 다음에 이어질 글의 순서로 가장 적절한 것을 고르시오. [3점]

> As individuals, our ability to thrive depended on how well we navigated relationships in a group. If the group valued us, we could count on support, resources, and probably a mate.

(A) And, crucially, they are meant to make that motivation feel like it is coming from within. If we realized, on a conscious level, that we were responding to social pressure, our performance might come off as grudging or cynical, making it less persuasive.

(B) If it didn't, we might get none of these merits. It was a matter of survival, physically and genetically. Over millions of years, the pressure selected for people who are sensitive to and skilled at maximizing their standing.

(C) The result was the development of a tendency to unconsciously monitor how other people in our community perceive us. We process that information in the form of self-esteem and such related emotions as pride, shame, or insecurity. These emotions compel us to do more of what makes our community value us and less of what doesn't.   *grudging: 투덜대는

① (A) — (C) — (B)   ② (B) — (A) — (C)
③ (B) — (C) — (A)   ④ (C) — (A) — (B)
⑤ (C) — (B) — (A)

032 ⭐ 1등급 대비 .... 고1 2021(11월)/36

주어진 글 다음에 이어질 글의 순서로 가장 적절한 것을 고르시오.

> Roughly twenty years ago, brick-and-mortar stores began to give way to electronic commerce. For good or bad, the shift fundamentally changed consumers' perception of the shopping experience.

(A) Before long, the e-commerce book market naturally expanded to include additional categories, like CDs and DVDs. E-commerce soon snowballed into the enormous industry it is today, where you can buy everything from toilet paper to cars online.

(B) Nowhere was the shift more obvious than with book sales, which is how online bookstores got their start. Physical bookstores simply could not stock as many titles as a virtual bookstore could. There is only so much space available on a shelf.

(C) In addition to greater variety, online bookstores were also able to offer aggressive discounts thanks to their lower operating costs. The combination of lower prices and greater selection led to the slow, steady rise of online bookstores.

*brick-and-mortar: 오프라인 거래의

① (A) — (C) — (B)   ② (B) — (A) — (C)
③ (B) — (C) — (A)   ④ (C) — (A) — (B)
⑤ (C) — (B) — (A)

* 다음 영어는 우리말 뜻을, 우리말은 영어 단어를 〈보기〉에서 찾아 쓰시오.

〈보기〉

causal	도움 없는	behavior	풍부함
alert	돌아다니다	ancient	비현실적인
pioneer	분배	distortion	전하다

01 unaided   _____

02 wander   _____

03 division   _____

04 abundance   _____

05 unrealistic   _____

06 선구자   _____

07 경계하는   _____

08 행동   _____

09 고대의   _____

10 왜곡   _____

* 다음 우리말에 알맞은 영어 표현을 찾아 연결하시오.

11 멸망하다 •   • go under

12 뽐내다 •   • fall apart

13 위험에 처한 •   • at risk

14 해체되다 •   • show off

15 ~을 이용하다 •   • draw on

* 다음 우리말 표현에 맞는 단어를 고르시오.

16 그들의 가축을 옮기다 ➡ move their (livestock / livelihood)

17 무능의 결과 ➡ the result of (incompetence / competence)

18 이 사고의 구체적인 형태 ➡ this (abstract / concrete) form of thinking

19 자존심 같은 그런 관련된 감정들 ➡ such related emotions as (pleasure / pride)

20 현지 시민들 ➡ the local (citizens / critics)

* 다음 문장의 빈칸에 알맞은 단어를 〈보기〉에서 찾아 쓰시오.

〈보기〉

joint	adaptations	extinction	extraordinary
collapse	consciousness	vibration	hexagons
generations	underperform	orderly	handle

21 그것들은 질서 있고 반복적인 패턴으로 스스로 배열된다.
➡ They arrange themselves into _____ repeating patterns.

22 문명은 확장하고 과도하게 확장되다가 결국 붕괴한다.
➡ Civilizations expand, get overextended, and then _____.

23 연골은 관절의 건강한 기능에 중요하다.
➡ Cartilage is important for the healthy functioning of a(n) _____.

24 뇌는 의식의 기관에 지나지 않는다.
➡ The brain is no more than a organ of _____.

25 그 결과, 붉은 다람쥐는 영국에서 거의 멸종 위기에 이르렀다.
➡ As a result, the red squirrel has come close to _____ in England.

26 일반적인 결정 습성은 육면의 육각형을 포함한다.
➡ Common crystal habits include six-sided _____.

27 이러한 조정은 점진적이고 어린아이의 연령과 관련이 있다.
➡ The _____ are progressive and relate to the age of the child.

28 그들은 세대를 거쳐 공예 기술을 발전시켰다.
➡ They developed their craft skills over _____.

29 나무의 진동은 더 강력한 파동을 만들어 낸다.
➡ The _____ of the wood creates more powerful waves.

30 "똑똑하다"라는 말을 듣는 아이들은 과제에서 기대에 못 미치는 성과를 낸다.
➡ Kids who are told they're "smart" _____ in tasks.

P 주어진 문장 넣기

★ 유형 설명

글의 흐름으로 보아, 주어진 문장이 들어가기에 가장 적절한 곳을 고르시오.

> Piaget argued that children's understanding of morality is like their understanding of those

연결어 등의 단서를 이용하여 주어진 한 문장을 논리적인 흐름에 맞게 글의 중간에 끼워 넣어야 한다.

🔑 글을 읽으면서 앞뒤 연결이 어색한 문장들 사이에 주어진 문장을 넣어 보고 흐름이 매끄러워지는지 확인한다.
앞 문장에는 전혀 등장하지 않았던 어구가 갑자기 등장하거나 글의 흐름이 아무 연결어 없이 완전히 전환되는 부분이 정답이다.

사고 장면이 묘사되고 있었는데 왜 갑자기 수술을 마친 내용이 나오지?

빠진 이 문장을 넣으면 말이 될 거예요!

🎭 유형 풀이 비법

1 주어진 문장을 파악하라!
- 주어진 문장을 읽고, 문제 풀이에 활용할 만한 단서가 있는지 살펴본다.

2 문장 관계를 추론하라!
- 정관사, 대명사, 대동사, 지시어, 연결어 등에 유의하여 문장 간의 관계를 추론한다.

3 글의 주제를 파악하라!
- 통일성과 일관성을 유지하는 주제를 파악하여 주어진 문장의 위치를 찾는다.

> (Tip) 정답을 고른 후에는 주어진 문장을 알맞은 위치에 넣고 문맥이 자연스러운지 확인한다.

📍 자주 쓰이는 연결어

□ in fact 사실상
□ moreover 게다가
□ in addition 게다가
□ despite ~에도 불구하고
□ in spite of ~에도 불구하고
□ although ~에도 불구하고
□ but 하지만, 그러나
□ however 하지만, 그러나
□ in contrast 대조적으로
□ in comparison with ~와 비교해보면
□ on the contrary 반대로
□ on the other hand 반면에
□ nevertheless 그럼에도 불구하고
□ besides 이외에도
□ rather 오히려

□ in summary 요약하면
□ in a word 한마디로 말해서
□ at the same time 동시에
□ furthermore 더욱이, 더구나
□ that is 즉
□ namely 즉, 다시 말해
□ thus 따라서, 그러므로
□ therefore 따라서
□ accordingly 따라서
□ hence 그러므로, 따라서
□ in other words 바꾸어 말하면
□ for example 예를 들어
□ for instance 예를 들어
□ in conclusion 결론적으로
□ as a result 결과적으로
□ as a consequence ~의 결과로서

📖 어휘 및 표현 Preview

□ misinterpretation 오해
□ mistranslation 오역
□ intensity 강도
□ transport 이동시키다
□ interval 간격
□ rapid 빠른
□ trait 형질
□ hence 이런 이유로
□ distinguish 구별하다
□ self-evident 자명한
□ disastrous 처참한
□ displace 쫓아내다
□ leave A to one side A를 보류하다
□ contribution 기여
□ gene 유전자
□ flexibility 유연성

16 관계사

1 관계대명사의 종류: 관계대명사가 **관계대명사절에서 하는 역할**에 따라 나뉜다.

	선행사가 사람	선행사가 사물	역할
주격 관계대명사	who	which	관계대명사절에서 **주어 역할**을 함
목적격 관계대명사	who(m)	which	관계대명사절에서 **목적어 역할**을 함
소유격 관계대명사	whose		관계대명사절 안에서 **소유격을 대신함**

- Eric is a student who likes me.
  선행사(사람)　주격 관계대명사
- This is the desk which we bought.
  선행사(사물)　목적격 관계대명사

2 관계대명사 that – whose를 제외하고 언급된 모든 관계대명사를 대신할 수 있다.

선행사가 -thing, 사람과 사물/동물이 혼합된 경우, 선행사에 최상급이나 서수,

all, any, every, no, some, the only[very, same] 등이 포함된 경우에 주로 쓰인다.

- You are the only person that[who(m)] she loves. (당신은 그녀가 사랑하는 유일한 사람이다.)
  선행사(사람)　목적격 관계대명사

3 관계대명사 what
- '~하는 것(들)'이라는 의미로, 그 자체에 선행사가 포함되어 있어서 **the thing(s) which[that]로 바꿀 수 있다.**
- 선행사(명사)가 하는 역할인 주어, 목적어, 보어가 되는 *명사절을 이끈다.

- I know what I should do. (나는 내가 해야 하는 것을 안다.)
  목적어 역할을 하는 명사절을 이끎

> *관계대명사가 이끄는 절
> 선행사를 포함하는 관계대명사 what은 명사절을 이끈다.

4 관계부사: 두 문장을 연결하는 관계사가 **접속사와 부사어의 역할**을 한다.

관계부사	용도	선행사	전치사 + 관계대명사	예문
where	장소	the place, house, city 등	at/in/on + which	It's a place where we hang out.
when	시간	the time, day, year 등	at/on/in/during + which	Today is the day when it all changes.
why	이유	the reason	for which	That is the reason why I can't do it.
how	방법	the way	in which	I like the way (how) you dance.

Check Test

1 관계대명사를 찾아 쓰시오.

This is crucial because most survival situations arise as a result of a series of events that could have been avoided.

→ _____

2 주어진 단어 중에서 어법상 적절한 것을 고르시오.

For example, imagine a forest with only one type of plant in it, [who / which] is the only source of food and habitat for the entire forest food web.

3 밑줄 친 부분을 한 단어로 바꿔 쓰시오.

This food chain implies the sequence in which food energy is transferred from producer to consumer or higher trophic level.

→ _____

4 주어진 단어 중에서 어법상 적절한 것을 고르시오.

Friction is a force between two surfaces [that / what] are sliding, or trying to slide, across each other.

• 정답
1 that 2 which 3 where 4 that

P 주어진 문장 넣기 첫 번째

1st 주어진 문장을 해석하고, 앞뒤에 어떤 내용이 올지 생각해 봅시다.
2nd 각 선택지의 앞뒤 흐름이 매끄러운지 확인합시다.
3rd 주어진 문장을 선택한 자리에 넣고, 글의 흐름이 자연스러운지 확인하세요.

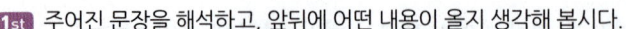

P01 ★★★ .... 고1 2025(3월)/38

글의 흐름으로 보아, 주어진 문장이 들어가기에 가장 적절한 곳을 고르시오.

> Piaget argued that children's understanding of morality is like their understanding of those water glasses: we can't say that it is innate or kids learn it directly from adults.

Piaget put the same amount of water into⁵ two different glasses: a tall narrow glass and a wide glass, then asked kids to compare two glasses. (①) Kids younger than six or seven usually say that the tall narrow glass now holds more water, because the level is higher.¹⁰ (②) And when they are ready, they figure out the conservation of volume for themselves just by playing with cups of water. (③) Rather, it is self-constructed as kids play with other kids. (④) Taking turns¹⁵ in a game is like pouring water back and forth between glasses. (⑤) Once kids have reached the age of five or six, then playing games and working things out together will help them learn about fairness far more²⁰ effectively than any teaching from adults.

*innate: 타고난 **conservation: 보존

1st 주어진 문장을 해석하고, 앞뒤에 어떤 내용이 올지 생각해 봅시다.

Piaget argued / that children's understanding of
Piaget는 주장했다 / 도덕성에 대한 아이들의 이해는
morality / is like their understanding of those water
/ 그런 물잔에 대한 이해와 같은데
glasses: / we can't say / that it is innate or kids learn
/ 즉 우리가 말할 수 없다고 / 그것이 타고났다거나 혹은 아이들이
it directly from adults. //
어른들로부터 직접 그것을 배운다고 //

● 이 문장은 어떤 내용인가요?
Piaget가 도덕성에 대한 아이들의 이해는 타고났다거나 아이들이 어른들로부터 직접 배웠다고 할 수 없는데, 이것이 물잔에 대한 이해와 같대요. 도덕성에 대한 아이들의 이해를 물잔에 비유하는 내용인 듯하네요.

● 주어진 문장보다 앞에 water glasses가 언급되었나 봐요.
이미 앞에서 언급된 대상을 다시 가리키는 지시형용사 ❶(   ) 가 쓰였어요. 적어도 주어진 문장의 앞에는 water glasses가 계속 언급될 거라고 예상할 수 있어요.

2nd 각 선택지의 앞뒤 흐름이 매끄러운지 확인합시다.

1) ①의 앞 문장과 뒤 문장을 확인해 봅시다.

앞 문장: Piaget put the same amount of water / into
Piaget는 똑같은 양의 물을 넣고 /
two different glasses: / a tall narrow glass and a
두 개의 서로 다른 유리잔에 / 키가 크고 폭이 좁은 유리잔과
wide glass, / then asked kids to compare two
넓은 유리잔 / 다음 아이들에게 두 유리잔을 비교하라고 요청했다 //
glasses. //

뒤 문장: Kids younger than six or seven usually say /
6세 혹은 7세보다 더 어린 아이들은 대개 말하는데 /
that the tall narrow glass now holds more water, /
키가 크고 폭이 좁은 유리잔에 물이 더 많이 담겨 있다고 /
because the level is higher. //
왜냐하면 수위가 더 높기 때문이다 //

● 예상한 대로 물잔의 예시가 시작되는군요.
Piaget는 아이들에게 서로 다른 두 물잔을 비교하라고 요청했대요. 이때 6~7세보다 더 어린 아이들은 수위가 높다는 이유로 키가 크고 폭이 좁은 유리잔이 물이 더 많다고 말한다고 하는데, 실험 설계와 결과를 설명하는 두 문장이 자연스럽게 이어지네요.

▶ 주어진 문장이 ①에 들어갈 수 없음

2) ②의 앞 문장과 뒤 문장을 확인해 봅시다.

> **앞 문장:** ①의 뒤 문장과 같음
>
> **뒤 문장:** And when they are ready, / they figure out
> 그리고 아이들이 준비가 되어 있을 때 / 그들은 부피의 보존을
> the conservation of volume for themselves / just by
> 스스로 알아낸다 / 물이 든
> playing with cups of water. //
> 컵들을 갖고 놂으로써 //

● **물잔 예시를 부연 설명해요.**
앞 문장에 아이들이 두 물잔을 비교하는 내용이 있는데, 뒤 문장에서 아이들이 이러한 놀이를 통해 부피의 보존을 스스로 알아낸다는 내용이 앞뒤로 자연스럽게 연결되네요.

▶ 주어진 문장이 ②에 들어갈 수 없음

3) ③의 앞 문장과 뒤 문장을 확인해 봅시다.

> **앞 문장:** ②의 뒤 문장과 같음
>
> **뒤 문장:** Rather, / it is self-constructed / as kids play
> 오히려 / 그것은 아이들이 스스로 구성해 낸 것이다 /
> with other kids. //
> 다른 아이들과 놀면서 //

● **중요한 단서인 Rather와 it이 쓰였어요.**
앞 내용과 반대되는 내용을 나타내는 중요한 단서인 Rather와 앞에서 언급된 대상을 다시 가리키는 대명사 it이 있어요. 따라서 ③의 앞뒤 문장이 서로 반대되는지, 여기서 it이 무엇을 가리키는지를 살펴봐야 해요.

● **③의 앞뒤 문장이 서로 이어지지 않아요.**
③의 앞 문장에서 아이들이 물잔을 갖고 놀며 부피의 보존을 스스로 알아낸다고 하는데, ③의 뒤 문장에서 마찬가지로 아이들이 다른 아이들과 놀며 it을 스스로 구성해 낸다고 해요. 두 문장이 서로 반대되지 않을뿐더러, 물잔이나 부피의 보존을 스스로 구성한다는 것은 어색해요.

● **it이 가리키는 것이 혹시 주어진 문장에 있지는 않나요?**
맞아요! 주어진 문장에서 '도덕성에 대한 아이들의 이해가 물잔에 대한 이해와 같고, 이는 타고나거나 어른들로부터 배우는 것은 아니라고 했어요. ❷( ) 아이들이 다른 아이들과 놀면서 도덕성에 대한 이해를 스스로 구성해 낸다는 내용인 ③의 뒤 문장이 주어진 문장과 자연스럽게 이어져요.

▶ 주어진 문장이 ③에 들어가야 함

4) ④의 앞 문장과 뒤 문장을 확인해 봅시다.

> **앞 문장:** ③의 뒤 문장과 같음
>
> **뒤 문장:** Taking turns in a game is like / pouring water
> 게임을 순서대로 돌아가며 하는 것은 같다 / 물잔 사이를 왔다 갔다
> back and forth between glasses. //
> 하며 물을 붓는 것과 //

● **물잔 비유가 이어져요.**
게임을 순서대로 돌아가며 하는 것, 즉 게임의 규칙이라는 도덕성은 아이들이 물잔 사이를 왔다 갔다 하며 물을 붓는 것과 같다는 부연 설명이 자연스럽게 이어지네요.

▶ 주어진 문장이 ④에 들어갈 수 없음

5) ⑤의 앞 문장과 뒤 문장을 확인해 봅시다.

> **앞 문장:** ④의 뒤 문장과 같음
>
> **뒤 문장:** Once kids have reached the age of five or six,
> 일단 아이들이 5세 혹은 6세에 이르면
> / then playing games and working things out
> / 함께 게임을 하고 문제를 해결해 나가는 것이 도움이 될 것이다
> together will help / them learn about fairness far
> / 그들이 훨씬 더 효과적으로 공평함에 대해
> more effectively / than any teaching from adults. //
> 배우는 데 / 어른들로부터의 그 어떤 가르침보다 //

● **추가적인 물잔 비유로 글이 마무리되네요.**
게임을 순서대로 돌아가며 하는 것에 이어서, 함께 게임을 하고 문제를 해결하는 것이 공평함을 배우는 데 있어서 어른의 가르침보다 도움이 된다는 내용으로 글이 마무리되어요.

▶ 주어진 문장이 ⑤에 들어갈 수 없음

3rd 주어진 문장을 선택한 자리에 넣고, 글의 흐름이 자연스러운지 확인하세요.

> **도입** 아이들에게 두 물잔 비교를 요청하면 처음엔 수위만으로 판단하는데, 물잔을 갖고 놀며 부피의 보존 개념을 스스로 이해하게 됨
>
> ↓
>
> **전개** 도덕성에 대한 아이들의 이해는 타고나거나 어른으로부터 배운 것이 아니라 다른 아이들과 놀며 스스로 구성한 것임
>
> ↓
>
> **예시** 게임의 규칙과 협동 같은 도덕성은 물잔 놀이를 통해 배울 수 있음

P

 P 주어진 문장 넣기 (두 번째)

1st 연결어나 지시어 등의 단서에 주의를 기울이면서 주어진 문장을 해석하세요.
2nd 처음부터 글을 읽으며 흐름이 매끄럽지 않은 부분을 찾으세요.
3rd 정답으로 추론한 자리에 주어진 문장을 넣고, 앞뒤 문장과 자연스럽게 연결되는지 확인하세요.

P02 ★★★ .... 고1 2023(9월)/38

글의 흐름으로 보아, 주어진 문장이 들어가기에 가장 적절한 곳을 고르시오. [3점]

> Other individuals prefer integrating work and family roles all day long.

Boundaries between work and home are blurring as portable digital technology makes it increasingly possible to work⁵ anywhere, anytime. Individuals differ in how they like to manage their time to meet work and outside responsibilities. (①) Some people prefer to separate or segment roles so that boundary crossings are minimized. (②)¹⁰ For example, these people might keep separate email accounts for work and family and try to conduct work at the workplace and take care of family matters only during breaks and non-work time. (③) We've even¹⁵ noticed more of these "segmenters" carrying two phones — one for work and one for personal use. (④) Flexible schedules work well for these individuals because they enable greater distinction between time at²⁰ work and time in other roles. (⑤) This might entail constantly trading text messages with children from the office, or monitoring emails at home and on vacation, rather than returning to work to find hundreds of²⁵ messages in their inbox.

*entail: 수반하다

1st 연결어나 지시어 등의 단서에 주의를 기울이면서 주어진 문장을 해석하세요.

> [Other] individuals prefer / integrating work and
> 다른 사람들은 선호한다 / 직장과 가정의 역할을 통합하는
> family roles / all day long. //
> 것을 / 하루 종일 //

● **'다른'을 뜻하는 Other가 핵심 단서예요!**
other는 기준이 되는 대상과는 다른 불특정한 대상을 가리키는 부정대명사 또는 형용사로 사용돼요.
다시 말해, other가 포함된 문장이 무언가를 설명했다면, 그 문장 앞에는 관련된 내용이지만 상반된 어떤 설명이 제시되어 있어야 한다는 거예요.
주어진 문장의 자리를 찾는 데 상당히 큰 도움이 될 것 같죠?

● **주어진 문장을 해석해 봅시다.**
'다른' 사람들은 하루 종일 직장과 가정의 역할을 통합하는 것을 선호한대요. Other가 있으니까, 앞에는 직장과 가정의 역할을 통합하는 것을 선호하지 않는 사람들의 이야기가 나오다가 내용이 전환되겠네요!

2nd 처음부터 글을 읽으며 흐름이 매끄럽지 않은 부분을 찾으세요.

1) 첫 번째 문장을 봅시다.

> [Boundaries] between work and home are blurring / as
> 직장과 가정의 경계가 흐릿해지고 있다 /
> portable digital technology makes it / increasingly
> 휴대용 디지털 기술이 ~을 만듦에 따라 / 점차 가능하게
> possible / to work anywhere, anytime. //
> / 언제, 어디서나 작업하는 것 //

● **직장과 가정의 ❶(   )에 관한 글이에요.**
휴대용 디지털 기술로 사람들은 시간과 장소에 구애받지 않고 일할 수 있게 되었고, 그래서 직장과 가정의 경계가 흐릿해지고 있대요. 주어진 문장에서 봤던 직장과 가정의 역할을 통합하는 것을 선호하는 사람과 선호하지 않는 사람들이 곧 등장하겠네요!

2) ①의 앞 문장과 뒤 문장을 확인해 봅시다.

> **앞 문장:** Individuals differ / in how they like to
> 사람들은 차이가 있다 / 자신의 시간을 관리하기를 바라는
> manage their time / to meet work and outside
> 방식에 / 직장과 외부의 책임을 수행하기 위해 //
> responsibilities. //

> **뒤 문장:** [Some] people prefer / to separate or segment
> 어떤 사람들은 선호한다 / 역할을 분리하거나 분할하는 것을
> roles / so that boundary crossings are minimized. //
> / 경계 교차 지점이 최소화되도록 //

● **사람들이 등장했어요!**
직장과 그 외의 책임을 수행하는 시간을 관리하는 방식이 사람마다
다르대요. 여기서 '그 외의 책임'이란 가정의 역할을 말하는 거고요!

● **선호하는 사람들이 먼저 등장했네요?**
아, 우리는 직장과 가정의 역할을 '통합'하는 것을 '선호하지 않는' 사람들이
먼저 나올 거라고 예상했는데, 역할을 '분리'하는 것을 '선호하는' 사람들이
나왔어요. 결국 같은 말을 하는 거니까 우리의 예상이 맞았어요.

▶ 주어진 문장이 **①**에 들어갈 수 없음

3) ②의 앞 문장과 뒤 문장을 확인해 봅시다.

앞 문장: ①의 뒤 문장과 같음

뒤 문장: For example, / these people might keep
　　　　　　예를 들어　　　／ 이러한 사람들은 별개의 이메일 계정을

separate email accounts / for work and family / and
유지할지도 모른다　　　　 / 직장과 가정을 위한　　 / 그리고

try to conduct work at the workplace / and take
직장에서 일을 수행하려고 할지도 모른다　　　　　 / 그리고

care of family matters / only during breaks and
가정사를 처리할지도 모른다　 / 휴식 시간과 일을 하지 않는

non-work time. //
시간 동안에만　　 //

● **예시가 이어져요.**
직장과 가정에서 쓰는 이메일 계정을 따로 만들고, 직장에서
일하지 않는 시간에만 가정사를 처리하는 건 직장과 가정의 역할을
②(　　　　　　　)하는 사람들의 예시죠? 우리는 직장과 가정의
역할을 '통합'하는 사람들로 글이 전환되는 부분만 찾으면 되니까 계속
읽어 봅시다.

▶ 주어진 문장이 **②**에 들어갈 수 없음

4) ③의 앞 문장과 뒤 문장을 확인해 봅시다.

앞 문장: ②의 뒤 문장과 같음

뒤 문장: We've even noticed / more of these
　　　　　　우리는 심지어 알게 되었다　　 / 더 많은 이러한 '분할자들'이

"segmenters" / carrying two phones / — one for
　　　　　 / 두 개의 전화기를 가지고 다니는 것을 / 하나는 업무용

work / and one for personal use. //
　 / 그리고 하나는 개인용인　　　 //

● **'분할자들'은 '분리'하는 사람들이겠죠?**
앞에서 이메일을 따로 만든 것처럼, 전화기를 업무용과 개인용 각각
만드는 '분할자들'이 있대요. '통합'하는 사람들은 아직 등장하지
않았네요!

▶ 주어진 문장이 **③**에 들어갈 수 없음

5) ④의 앞 문장과 뒤 문장을 확인해 봅시다.

앞 문장: ③의 뒤 문장과 같음

뒤 문장: Flexible schedules work well / for these
　　　　　　유연 근로 시간제는 잘 적용된다　　　 / 이런 사람들에게

individuals / because they enable greater distinction
　　　　　 / 그것들이 더 큰 구별을 가능하게 하기 때문에

/ between time at work / and time in other roles. //
/ 직장에서의　시간 사이에　　 / 다른 역할에서의 시간과　　 //

● **유연 근로 시간제는 출퇴근 시간을 자유롭게 조정하는 거예요.**
직장과 가정에서의 시간을 더 확실히 구별하게 해주는 유연 근로
시간제는 직장과 가정을 '분리'하는 사람들에게 잘 적용되죠.
원하는 시간에 업무를 하고, 원하는 시간에 가정의 역할을 할 수
있으니까요.
④까지 살펴봤는데 아직도 '통합'을 선호하는 사람들은 등장하지
않았어요. 과연 **⑤**에 등장할지, ▶ 주어진 문장이 **④**에 들어갈 수 없음
이어서 읽어 봅시다!

6) ⑤의 앞 문장과 뒤 문장을 확인해 봅시다.

앞 문장: ④의 뒤 문장과 같음

뒤 문장: This might entail / constantly trading text
　　　　　　이것은 수반할지도 모른다　 / 아이들과 문자 메시지를 지속적으로

messages with children / from the office, / or
주고받는 것을　　　　　　 / 직장에서　　 / 또는

monitoring emails at home and on vacation, / rather
집에서 그리고 휴가 중에 이메일을 확인하는 것을　　 / 직장으로

than returning to work to find / hundreds of
돌아가서 발견하는 것 대신에　　　 / 받은 편지함에서

messages in their inbox. //
수백 개의 메시지를　　　 //

● **This가 가리키는 것은 뭔가요?**
직장에서 가족과 문자 메시지를 주고받고, 집에서는 업무 이메일을
확인하는 사람들이 등장했어요. 직장과 가정의 역할을 '통합'한
사람들이네요! This는 그러니까 직장과 가정의 역할을 통합하는 것을
가리키는 거네요. 주어진 문장이 들어갈 곳을 찾은 것 같죠?

▶ 주어진 문장이 **⑤**에 들어가야 함

3rd 정답으로 추론한 자리에 주어진 문장을 넣고, 앞뒤 문장과
자연스럽게 연결되는지 확인하세요.
〈직장과 가정의 역할을 분리하는 것을 선호하는 사람들은 별개의 이메일
계정과 전화기를 사용하고, 유연 근로 시간제가 더 잘 적용된다. 다른
사람들은 직장과 가정의 역할을 통합하는 것을 선호하는데, 그들은 직장에서
가족과 연락하고 집에서 업무 이메일을 확인한다.〉
앞뒤 문장과 주어진 문장이 자연스럽게 연결되니까, 정답은 **3**(　　　)!

❖ 정답 및 해설 273~274p

P03 ~ 06 ▶ 제한시간 8분

P03 ★★★ 고1 2025(3월)/39

글의 흐름으로 보아, 주어진 문장이 들어가기에 가장 적절한 곳을 고르시오.

> But all this wisdom about how to deal with heat, accumulated over centuries of practical experience, is all too often ignored.

The rise of air-conditioning accelerated the construction of sealed boxes, where the building's only airflow is through the filtered ducts of the air-conditioning unit. It doesn't have to be this way. Look at any old building in a hot climate, whether it's in Sicily or Marrakesh or Tehran. (①) Architects understood the importance of shade, airflow, light colors. (②) They oriented buildings to capture cool breezes and block the worst heat of the afternoon. (③) They built with thick walls and white roofs and transoms over doors to encourage airflow. (④) Anyone who has ever spent a few minutes in a mudbrick house in Tucson, or walked on the narrow streets of old Seville, knows how well these construction methods work. (⑤) In this sense, air-conditioning is not just a technology of personal comfort; it is also a technology of forgetting.

*accumulate: 축적하다 **duct: (배)관 ***transom: 채광창

구문 서술형

밑줄 친 부분의 선행사를 찾고, 밑줄 부분을 한 단어로 바꿔 쓰시오.

➡ The rise of air-conditioning accelerated the construction of sealed boxes, <u>in which</u> the building's only airflow is through the filtered ducts.

➡ 선행사: _____

➡ 한 단어: _____

P04 ★★★❋ 고1 2025(6월)/38

글의 흐름으로 보아, 주어진 문장이 들어가기에 가장 적절한 곳을 고르시오.

> Partly this was the obvious convenience of being able to exit more quickly.

To monitor our surroundings is to focus on what's outside of ourselves: what we see, hear, smell, feel, and perhaps even taste. But sometimes what really marks a place is something less specific — a *feeling* within us. (①) An interesting example emerged from a study of subway passenger behavior. (②) Researchers trying to understand why people sit where they sit or stand where they stand in subway and metro trains examined the factors that shape the way riders used and navigated that space in different situations. (③) One of their findings involved the reasons many riders like to plant themselves close to the train's doors. (④) But it was shaped partly by a more abstract sensation — the desire to avoid the sometimes uncomfortable feeling of accidentally making eye contact with seated passengers. (⑤) We can't see feelings — but they're very real, and they influence our experience of the world.

구문 서술형

문장에서 틀린 부분을 찾아 밑줄을 긋고 바르게 고치시오.

To monitor our surroundings is to focus on which is outside of ourselves.

➡ 고친 표현: _____

글의 흐름으로 보아, 주어진 문장이 들어가기에 가장 적절한 곳을 고르시오. [3점]

> But if we sink just our face in a bowl of water, while the whole of the rest of our body is in the dry air, the diving reflex is triggered.

We have a 'diving reflex', like other marine mammals. (①) This means that special nerve endings on our faces, around the mouth and nose, trigger this reflex only when the facial region goes under water. (②) If we are in the water, with our head out in the air, there is no diving reflex. (③) It automatically closes down the airway, reducing the risk of swallowing water, and it narrows the small air-passages in the lungs. (④) At the same time the heart rate is slowed down to half speed and blood is shunted to the vital organs, protecting them from the effects of the brief stop in breathing. (⑤) By contrast, if a chimpanzee or a gorilla found itself in water with its face below the surface, it would panic, its heart would race and it would quickly drown.

*reflex: 반사 **trigger: 유발하다 ***shunt: 방향을 돌리다

구문 서술형

밑줄 친 부분이 틀린 이유를 서술하고, 바르게 고치시오.

We have the same 'diving reflex' <u>whom</u> other marine mammals have.

➡ 틀린 이유: _____

➡ 고친 표현: _____

글의 흐름으로 보아, 주어진 문장이 들어가기에 가장 적절한 곳을 고르시오.

> Nonlinear editing, on the other hand, is like using a word processing program.

All editing systems are now nonlinear computer-based systems that allow random access to any video shot or scene without having to fast forward or fast reverse to find it. Nonlinear systems can create a range of special effects, such as slow motion, wipes and dissolves. (①) Another highlight of a digital nonlinear system is its random access process that makes it easy for an editor to find desired shots or scenes without having to spend time fast forwarding or rewinding videotape. (②) With nonlinear editing, shots or scenes can be easily added or removed anywhere in the program, and the computer adjusts the program length automatically. (③) Linear editing was like composing a paper on a typewriter. (④) If a mistake was made or new information needed to be added the whole piece had to be retyped. (⑤) If a mistake is made, it is easily deleted and fixed with a few keystrokes, and new information can be added easily.

*linear: 선형의

구문 서술형

밑줄 친 관계대명사를 바르게 고치고, 그 관계대명사의 격을 쓰시오.

All editing systems are now nonlinear computer-based systems <u>which</u> random access process makes it easy to find desired shots.

➡ 고친 표현: _____

➡ 관계대명사의 격: _____

P07 ★★★ .... 고1 2025(9월)/39

글의 흐름으로 보아, 주어진 문장이 들어가기에 가장
적절한 곳을 고르시오. [3점]

> A person who always tries to prevent harm but never does, is not generally thought of as morally good.

A morally good person is one who does morally bad actions significantly less often than most and does morally good ones significantly more often than most. In judging a person not only her actions but also her intentions and motives are relevant. (①) A morally good person must intend to do morally good actions and intend to avoid morally bad ones. (②) A person who unintentionally prevents harm to others and does not harm them simply because things do not turn out as she intends is not morally good. (③) Although this kind of situation generally occurs only in slapstick movies, it is worth mentioning to avoid the false impression that it is the actual consequences of a person's actions that count toward her being judged morally good or bad. (④) But actual consequences are important. (⑤) Of such a person, it may be said that she means well; but, contrary to Kant, some results are necessary before she is regarded as morally good.

구문 서술형

괄호 안에서 알맞은 것을 고르고, 빈칸에 들어갈 알맞은 관계대명사를 쓰시오.

A morally good person is one _____ does morally bad actions significantly less often than most.

➡ 선행사: (사람 / 사물)

➡ 빈칸에 들어갈 관계대명사: _____

P08 ★★✿ .... 고1 2024(10월)/38

글의 흐름으로 보아, 주어진 문장이 들어가기에 가장
적절한 곳을 고르시오.

> Instead, they look for evidence, to make sure that psychological ideas are firmly based, and not just derived from generally held beliefs or assumptions.

The common accounts of human nature that float around in society are generally a mixture of assumptions, tales and sometimes plain silliness. However, psychology is different. (①) It is the branch of science that is devoted to understanding people: how and why we act as we do; why we see things as we do; and how we interact with one another. (②) The key word here is 'science.' (③) Psychologists don't depend on opinions and hearsay, or the generally accepted views of society at the time, or even the considered opinions of deep thinkers. (④) In addition to this evidence-based approach, psychology deals with fundamental processes and principles that generate our rich cultural and social diversity, as well as those shared by all human beings. (⑤) These are what modern psychology is all about.

구문 서술형

빈칸에 알맞은 말을 쓰시오.

Psychology is devoted to understanding ⓐ how and ⓑ why we act as we do.

➡ ⓐ를 대신하는 선행사: _____

➡ ⓑ 앞에 생략된 선행사: _____

글의 흐름으로 보아, 주어진 문장이 들어가기에 가장 적절한 곳을 고르시오.

> Research in the 1980s and 1990s, however, demonstrated that the "tongue map" explanation of how we taste was, in fact, totally wrong.

The tongue was mapped into separate areas where certain tastes were registered: sweetness at the tip, sourness on the sides, and bitterness at the back of the mouth. (①) As it turns out, the map was a misinterpretation and mistranslation of research conducted in Germany at the turn of the twentieth century. (②) Today, leading taste researchers believe that taste buds are not grouped according to specialty. (③) Sweetness, saltiness, bitterness, and sourness can be tasted everywhere in the mouth, although they may be perceived at a little different intensities at different sites. (④) Moreover, the mechanism at work is not place, but time. (⑤) It's not that you taste sweetness at the tip of your tongue, but rather that you register that perception *first*.

*taste bud: 미뢰

글의 흐름으로 보아, 주어진 문장이 들어가기에 가장 적절한 곳을 고르시오.

> Environmental factors can also determine how the animal will respond during the treatment.

No two animals are alike. (①) Animals from the same litter will display some of the same features, but will not be exactly the same as each other; therefore, they may not respond in entirely the same way during a healing session. (②) For instance, a cat in a rescue center will respond very differently than a cat within a domestic home environment. (③) In addition, animals that experience healing for physical illness will react differently than those accepting healing for emotional confusion. (④) With this in mind, every healing session needs to be explored differently, and each healing treatment should be adjusted to suit the specific needs of the animal. (⑤) You will learn as you go; healing is a constant learning process.

*litter: (한 배에서 태어난) 새끼들

글의 흐름으로 보아, 주어진 문장이 들어가기에 가장 적절한 곳을 고르시오.

> Farmers, on the other hand, could live in the same place year after year and did not have to worry about transporting young children long distances.

Growing crops forced people to stay in one place. Hunter-gatherers typically moved around frequently, and they had to be able to carry all their possessions with them every time they moved. (①) In particular, mothers had to carry their young children. (②) As a result, hunter-gatherer mothers could have only one baby every four years or so, spacing their births so that they never had to carry more than one child at a time. (③) Societies that settled down in one place were able to shorten their birth intervals from four years to about two. (④) This meant that each woman could have more children than her hunter-gatherer counterpart, which in turn resulted in rapid population growth among farming communities. (⑤) An increased population was actually an advantage to agricultural societies, because farming required large amounts of human labor.

*counterpart: (대응 관계에 있는) 상대

P12　❋❋❋ ──────────────── 고1 2024(9월)/38

글의 흐름으로 보아, 주어진 문장이 들어가기에 가장
적절한 곳을 고르시오.

> "Homologous" traits, in contrast, may or may not have a common function, but they descended from a common ancestor and hence have some common structure that indicates their being "the same" organ.

Biologists distinguish two kinds of similarity. (①) "Analogous" traits are ones that have a common function but arose on different branches of the evolutionary tree and are in an important sense not "the same" organ. (②) The wings of birds and the wings of bees are both used for flight and are similar in some ways because anything used for flight has to be built in those ways, but they arose independently in evolution and have nothing in common beyond their use in flight. (③) The wing of a bat and the front leg of a horse have very different functions, but they are all modifications of the forelimb of the ancestor of all mammals. (④) As a result, they share nonfunctional traits like the number of bones and the ways they are connected. (⑤) To distinguish analogy from homology, biologists usually look at the overall architecture of the organs and focus on their most useless properties.

P13　❋❋❋ ──────────────── 고1 2024(9월)/39

글의 흐름으로 보아, 주어진 문장이 들어가기에 가장
적절한 곳을 고르시오. [3점]

> Thus, as global warming raises the temperature of marine waters, it is self-evident that the amount of dissolved oxygen will decrease.

Seawater contains an abundance of dissolved oxygen that all marine animals breathe to stay alive. (①) It has long been established in physics that cold water holds more dissolved oxygen than warm water does — this is one reason that cold polar seas are full of life while tropical oceans are blue, clear, and relatively poorly populated with living creatures. (②) This is a worrisome and potentially disastrous consequence if allowed to continue to an ecosystem-threatening level. (③) Now scientists have analyzed data indicating that the amount of dissolved oxygen in the oceans has been declining for more than a half century. (④) The data show that the ocean oxygen level has been falling more rapidly than the corresponding rise in water temperature. (⑤) Falling oxygen levels in water have the potential to impact the habitat of marine organisms worldwide and in recent years this has led to more frequent anoxic events that killed or displaced populations of fish, crabs, and many other organisms.

*dissolved: 용해된 **anoxic: 산소 결핍의

P14　❋❋❋ ──────────────── 고1 2023(3월)/39

글의 흐름으로 보아, 주어진 문장이 들어가기에 가장
적절한 곳을 고르시오. [3점]

> It was also found that those students who expected the lecturer to be warm tended to interact with him more.

People commonly make the mistaken assumption that because a person has one type of characteristic, then they automatically have other characteristics which go with it. (①) In one study, university students were given descriptions of a guest lecturer before he spoke to the group. (②) Half the students received a description containing the word 'warm', the other half were told the speaker was 'cold'. (③) The guest lecturer then led a discussion, after which the students were asked to give their impressions of him. (④) As expected, there were large differences between the impressions formed by the students, depending upon their original information of the lecturer. (⑤) This shows that different expectations not only affect the impressions we form but also our behaviour and the relationship which is formed.

P15 ★★★

글의 흐름으로 보아, 주어진 문장이 들어가기에 가장 적절한 곳을 고르시오.

> Yet we know that the face that stares back at us from the glass is not the same, cannot be the same, as it was 10 minutes ago.

Sometimes the pace of change is far slower. (①) The face you saw reflected in your mirror this morning probably appeared no different from the face you saw the day before — or a week or a month ago. (②) The proof is in your photo album: Look at a photograph taken of yourself 5 or 10 years ago and you see clear differences between the face in the snapshot and the face in your mirror. (③) If you lived in a world without mirrors for a year and then saw your reflection, you might be surprised by the change. (④) After an interval of 10 years without seeing yourself, you might not at first recognize the person peering from the mirror. (⑤) Even something as basic as our own face changes from moment to moment.

*peer: 응시하다

P16 ★★★

글의 흐름으로 보아, 주어진 문장이 들어가기에 가장 적절한 곳을 고르시오.

> The sales director kept an air horn outside his office and would come out and blow the horn every time a salesperson settled a deal.

Rewarding business success doesn't always have to be done in a material way. (①) A software company I once worked for had a great way of recognizing sales success. (②) The noise, of course, interrupted anything and everything happening in the office because it was unbelievably loud. (③) However, it had an amazingly positive impact on everyone. (④) Sometimes rewarding success can be as easy as that, especially when peer recognition is important. (⑤) You should have seen the way the rest of the sales team wanted the air horn blown for them.

*air horn: (압축 공기로 작동하는) 경적

P17 ★★★

글의 흐름으로 보아, 주어진 문장이 들어가기에 가장 적절한 곳을 고르시오.

> However, using caffeine to improve alertness and mental performance doesn't replace getting a good night's sleep.

Studies have consistently shown caffeine to be effective when used together with a pain reliever to treat headaches. (①) The positive correlation between caffeine intake and staying alert throughout the day has also been well established. (②) As little as 60mg(the amount typically in one cup of tea) can lead to a faster reaction time. (③) One study from 2018 showed that coffee improved reaction times in those with or without poor sleep, but caffeine seemed to increase errors in the group with little sleep. (④) Additionally, this study showed that even with caffeine, the group with little sleep did not score as well as those with adequate sleep. (⑤) It suggests that caffeine does not fully make up for inadequate sleep.

P18 ★★★
고1 2022(6월)/38

글의 흐름으로 보아, 주어진 문장이 들어가기에 가장 적절한 곳을 고르시오.

> For example, if you rub your hands together quickly, they will get warmer.

Friction is a force between two surfaces that are sliding, or trying to slide, across each other. For example, when you try to push a book along the floor, friction makes this difficult. Friction always works in the direction opposite to the direction in which the object is moving, or trying to move. So, friction always slows a moving object down. (①) The amount of friction depends on the surface materials. (②) The rougher the surface is, the more friction is produced. (③) Friction also produces heat. (④) Friction can be a useful force because it prevents our shoes slipping on the floor when we walk and stops car tires skidding on the road. (⑤) When you walk, friction is caused between the tread on your shoes and the ground, acting to grip the ground and prevent sliding.

*skid: 미끄러지다 **tread: 접지면, 바닥

P19 ★★★
고1 2022(6월)/39

글의 흐름으로 보아, 주어진 문장이 들어가기에 가장 적절한 곳을 고르시오.

> But, a blind person will associate the same friend with a unique combination of experiences from their nonvisual senses that act to represent that friend.

Humans born without sight are not able to collect visual experiences, so they understand the world entirely through their other senses. (①) As a result, people with blindness at birth develop an amazing ability to understand the world through the collection of experiences and memories that come from these nonvisual senses. (②) The dreams of a person who has been without sight since birth can be just as vivid and imaginative as those of someone with normal vision. (③) They are unique, however, because their dreams are constructed from the nonvisual experiences and memories they have collected. (④) A person with normal vision will dream about a familiar friend using visual memories of shape, lighting, and colour. (⑤) In other words, people blind at birth have similar overall dreaming experiences even though they do not dream in pictures.

P20 ★★★
고1 2022(9월)/38

글의 흐름으로 보아, 주어진 문장이 들어가기에 가장 적절한 곳을 고르시오.

> Unfortunately, it is also likely to "crowd out" other activities that produce more sustainable social contributions to our social well-being.

Television is the number one leisure activity in the United States and Europe, consuming more than half of our free time. (①) We generally think of television as a way to relax, tune out, and escape from our troubles for a bit each day. (②) While this is true, there is increasing evidence that we are more motivated to tune in to our favorite shows and characters when we are feeling lonely or have a greater need for social connection. (③) Television watching does satisfy these social needs to some extent, at least in the short run. (④) The more television we watch, the less likely we are to volunteer our time or to spend time with people in our social networks. (⑤) In other words, the more time we make for *Friends*, the less time we have for friends in real life.

*Friends: 프렌즈(미국의 한 방송국에서 방영된 시트콤)

P21 ★★★ 고1 2023(6월)/39

글의 흐름으로 보아, 주어진 문장이 들어가기에 가장
적절한 곳을 고르시오. [3점]

> As children absorb more evidence from the world around them, certain possibilities become much more likely and more useful and harden into knowledge or beliefs.

According to educational psychologist Susan Engel, curiosity begins to decrease as young as four years old. By the time we are adults, we have fewer questions and more default settings. As Henry James put it, "Disinterested curiosity is past, the mental grooves and channels set." (①) The decline in curiosity can be traced in the development of the brain through childhood. (②) Though smaller than the adult brain, the infant brain contains millions more neural connections. (③) The wiring, however, is a mess; the lines of communication between infant neurons are far less efficient than between those in the adult brain. (④) The baby's perception of the world is consequently both intensely rich and wildly disordered. (⑤) The neural pathways that enable those beliefs become faster and more automatic, while the ones that the child doesn't use regularly are pruned away.

*default setting: 기본값 **groove: 고랑 ***prune: 가지치기하다

P22 ★★★ 고1 2023(9월)/39

글의 흐름으로 보아, 주어진 문장이 들어가기에 가장
적절한 곳을 고르시오. [3점]

> However, do not assume that a product is perfectly complementary, as customers may not be completely locked in to the product.

A "complementary good" is a product that is often consumed alongside another product. (①) For example, popcorn is a complementary good to a movie, while a travel pillow is a complementary good for a long plane journey. (②) When the popularity of one product increases, the sales of its complementary good also increase.

(③) By producing goods that complement other products that are already (or about to be) popular, you can ensure a steady stream of demand for your product. (④) Some products enjoy perfect complementary status — they *have* to be consumed together, such as a lamp and a lightbulb. (⑤) For example, although motorists may seem required to purchase gasoline to run their cars, they can switch to electric cars.

P23 ★★★ 고1 2021(11월)/38

글의 흐름으로 보아, 주어진 문장이 들어가기에 가장
적절한 곳을 고르시오.

> Worse, some are contaminated with other substances and contain ingredients not listed on the label.

According to top nutrition experts, most nutrients are better absorbed and used by the body when consumed from a whole food instead of a supplement. (①) However, many people feel the need to take pills, powders, and supplements in an attempt to obtain nutrients and fill the gaps in their diets. (②) We hope these will give us more energy, prevent us from catching a cold in the winter, or improve our skin and hair. (③) But in reality, the large majority of supplements are artificial and may not even be completely absorbed by your body. (④) For example, a recent investigative report found heavy metals in 40 percent of 134 brands of protein powders on the market. (⑤) With little control and regulation, taking supplements is a gamble and often costly.

*contaminate: 오염시키다 **supplement: 보충제

❖ 정답 및 해설 289 ~ 295p

P24 ✽✽❀

글의 흐름으로 보아, 주어진 문장이 들어가기에 가장 적절한 곳을 고르시오.

> Bad carbohydrates, on the other hand, are simple sugars.

All carbohydrates are basically sugars. (①) Complex carbohydrates are the good carbohydrates for your body. (②) These complex sugar compounds are very difficult to break down and can trap other nutrients like vitamins and minerals in their chains. (③) As they slowly break down, the other nutrients are also released into your body, and can provide you with fuel for a number of hours. (④) Because their structure is not complex, they are easy to break down and hold few nutrients for your body other than the sugars from which they are made. (⑤) Your body breaks down these carbohydrates rather quickly and what it cannot use is converted to fat and stored in the body.

*carbohydrate: 탄수화물 **convert: 바꾸다

P25 ✽✽❀

글의 흐름으로 보아, 주어진 문장이 들어가기에 가장 적절한 곳을 고르시오.

> As the sticks approach each other, the air immediately in front of them is compressed and energy builds up.

Sound and light travel in waves. An analogy often given for sound is that of throwing a small stone onto the surface of a still pond. Waves radiate outwards from the point of impact, just as sound waves radiate from the sound source. (①) This is due to a disturbance in the air around us. (②) If you bang two sticks together, you will get a sound. (③) When the point of impact occurs, this energy is released as sound waves. (④) If you try the same experiment with two heavy stones, exactly the same thing occurs, but you get a different sound due to the density and surface of the stones, and as they have likely displaced more air, a louder sound. (⑤) And so, a physical disturbance in the atmosphere around us will produce a sound.

*analogy: 비유 **radiate: 사방으로 퍼지다

P26 ✽✽✽

글의 흐름으로 보아, 주어진 문장이 들어가기에 가장 적절한 곳을 고르시오. [3점]

> If we could magically remove the glasses, we would find the two water bodies would not mix well.

Take two glasses of water. Put a little bit of orange juice into one and a little bit of lemon juice into the other. (①) What you have are essentially two glasses of water but with a completely different chemical makeup. (②) If we take the glass containing orange juice and heat it, we will still have two different glasses of water with different chemical makeups, but now they will also have different temperatures. (③) Perhaps they would mix a little where they met; however, they would remain separate because of their different chemical makeups and temperatures. (④) The warmer water would float on the surface of the cold water because of its lighter weight. (⑤) In the ocean we have bodies of water that differ in temperature and salt content; for this reason, they do not mix.

P27 ★★★ 고1 2021(11월)/39

글의 흐름으로 보아, 주어진 문장이 들어가기에 가장
적절한 곳을 고르시오. [3점]

> But after this brief moment of rest, the pendulum swings back again and therefore part of the total energy is then given in the form of kinetic energy.

In general, kinetic energy is the energy associated with motion, while potential energy represents the energy which is "stored" in a physical system. Moreover, the total energy is always conserved. (①) But while the total energy remains unchanged, the kinetic and potential parts of the total energy can change all the time. (②) Imagine, for example, a pendulum which swings back and forth. (③) When it swings, it sweeps out an arc and then slows down as it comes closer to its highest point, where the pendulum does not move at all. (④) So at this point, the energy is completely given in terms of potential energy. (⑤) So as the pendulum swings, kinetic and potential energy constantly change into each other.

*pendulum: 추(錘) **arc: 호(弧)

P28 ★★★ 고1 2021(6월)/38

글의 흐름으로 보아, 주어진 문장이 들어가기에 가장
적절한 곳을 고르시오. [3점]

> But, when there is biodiversity, the effects of a sudden change are not so dramatic.

When an ecosystem is biodiverse, wildlife have more opportunities to obtain food and shelter. Different species react and respond to changes in their environment differently. (①) For example, imagine a forest with only one type of plant in it, which is the only source of food and habitat for the entire forest food web. (②) Now, there is a sudden dry season and this plant dies.

(③) Plant-eating animals completely lose their food source and die out, and so do the animals that prey upon them. (④) Different species of plants respond to the drought differently, and many can survive a dry season. (⑤) Many animals have a variety of food sources and don't just rely on one plant; now our forest ecosystem is no longer at the death!

*biodiversity: (생물학적) 종 다양성 **habitat: 서식지

P29 ★★★ 고1 2021(6월)/39

글의 흐름으로 보아, 주어진 문장이 들어가기에 가장
적절한 곳을 고르시오. [3점]

> It has been observed that at each level of transfer, a large proportion, 80 – 90 percent, of the potential energy is lost as heat.

Food chain means the transfer of food energy from the source in plants through a series of organisms with the repeated process of eating and being eaten. (①) In a grassland, grass is eaten by rabbits while rabbits in turn are eaten by foxes. (②) This is an example of a simple food chain. (③) This food chain implies the sequence in which food energy is transferred from producer to consumer or higher trophic level. (④) Hence the number of steps or links in a sequence is restricted, usually to four or five. (⑤) The shorter the food chain or the nearer the organism is to the beginning of the chain, the greater the available energy intake is.

*trophic: 영양의

P30 ✦✦✦ ──────────── 고1 2023(11월)/38

글의 흐름으로 보아, 주어진 문장이 들어가기에 가장 적절한 곳을 고르시오.

> Leaving the contribution of that strategy to one side, the danger of creating more uniform crops is that they are more at risk when it comes to disasters.

The decline in the diversity of our food is an entirely human-made process. The biggest loss of crop diversity came in the decades that followed the Second World War. (①) In an attempt to save millions from extreme hunger, crop scientists found ways to produce grains such as rice and wheat on an enormous scale. (②) And thousands of traditional varieties were replaced by a small number of new super-productive ones. (③) The strategy worked spectacularly well, at least to begin with. (④) Because of it, grain production tripled, and between 1970 and 2020 the human population more than doubled. (⑤) Specifically, a global food system that depends on just a narrow selection of plants has a greater chance of not being able to survive diseases, pests and climate extremes.

*pest: 해충

P31 ✦✦✦ ──────────── 고1 2023(11월)/39

글의 흐름으로 보아, 주어진 문장이 들어가기에 가장 적절한 곳을 고르시오.

> A few years ago, Cuba altered that uniform style, modernizing it and perhaps conforming to other countries' style; interestingly, the national team has declined since that time.

Between 1940 and 2000, Cuba ruled the world baseball scene. They won 25 of the first 28 World Cups and 3 of 5 Olympic Games. (①) The Cubans were known for wearing uniforms covered in red from head to toe, a strong contrast to the more conservative North American style featuring grey or white pants. (②) Not only were their athletic talents superior, the Cubans appeared even stronger from just the colour of their uniforms. (③) A game would not even start and the opposing team would already be scared. (④) The country that ruled international baseball for decades has not been on top since that uniform change. (⑤) Traditions are important for a team; while a team brand or image can adjust to keep up with present times, if it abandons or neglects its roots, negative effects can surface.

*conservative: 보수적인

P32 ⭐ 2등급 대비   고1 2022(11월)/38

글의 흐름으로 보아, 주어진 문장이 들어가기에 가장 적절한 곳을 고르시오. [3점]

> Nevertheless, language is enormously important in human life and contributes largely to our ability to cooperate with each other in dealing with the world.

Should we use language to understand mind or mind to understand language? (①) Analytic philosophy historically assumes that language is basic and that mind would make sense if proper use of language was appreciated. (②) Modern cognitive science, however, rightly judges that language is just one aspect of mind of great importance in human beings but not fundamental to all kinds of thinking. (③) Countless species of animals manage to navigate the world, solve problems, and learn without using language, through brain mechanisms that are largely preserved in the minds of humans. (④) There is no reason to assume that language is fundamental to mental operations. (⑤) Our species *homo sapiens* has been astonishingly successful, which depended in part on language, first as an effective contributor to collaborative problem solving and much later, as collective memory through written records.　　*appreciate: (제대로) 인식하다

P33 ⭐ 2등급 대비   고1 2022(9월)/39

글의 흐름으로 보아, 주어진 문장이 들어가기에 가장 적절한 곳을 고르시오. [3점]

> What we need is a reliable and reproducible method for measuring the relative hotness or coldness of objects rather than the rate of energy transfer.

We often associate the concept of temperature with how hot or cold an object feels when we touch it. In this way, our senses provide us with a qualitative indication of temperature. (①) Our senses, however, are unreliable and often mislead us. (②) For example, if you stand in bare feet with one foot on carpet and the other on a tile floor, the tile feels colder than the carpet *even though both are at the same temperature.* (③) The two objects feel different because tile transfers energy by heat at a higher rate than carpet does. (④) Your skin "measures" the rate of energy transfer by heat rather than the actual temperature. (⑤) Scientists have developed a variety of thermometers for making such quantitative measurements.

*thermometer: 온도계

P34 ⭐ 2등급 대비   고1 2024(10월)/39

글의 흐름으로 보아, 주어진 문장이 들어가기에 가장 적절한 곳을 고르시오. [3점]

> Such a system can only hope to be stable if only a smaller number of collective ways of being may emerge.

Life is what physicists might call a 'high-dimensional system,' which is their fancy way of saying that there's a lot going on. (①) In just a single cell, the number of possible interactions between different molecules is enormous. (②) For example, it is only a limited number of tissues and body shapes that may result from the development of a human embryo. (③) In 1942, the biologist Conrad Waddington called this drastic narrowing of outcomes *canalization*. (④) The organism may switch between a small number of well-defined possible states, but can't exist in random states in between them, rather as a ball in a rough landscape must roll to the bottom of one valley or another. (⑤) We'll see that this is true also of health and disease: there are many causes of illness, but their manifestations at the physiological and symptomatic levels are often strikingly similar.　　*embryo: 배아 **physiological: 생리적인

P35 ⭐ 1등급 대비   고1 2022(3월)/39

글의 흐름으로 보아, 주어진 문장이 들어가기에 가장 적절한 곳을 고르시오.

> Since the dawn of civilization, our ancestors created myths and told legendary stories about the night sky.

We are connected to the night sky in many ways. (①) It has always inspired people to wonder and to imagine. (②) Elements of those narratives became embedded in the social and cultural identities of many generations. (③) On a practical level, the night sky helped past generations to keep track of time and create calendars — essential to developing societies as aids to farming and seasonal gathering. (④) For many centuries, it also provided a useful navigation tool, vital for commerce and for exploring new worlds. (⑤) Even in modern times, many people in remote areas of the planet observe the night sky for such practical purposes.

*embed: 깊이 새겨 두다 **commerce: 무역

P36 ⭐ 1등급 대비   고1 2024(6월)/39

글의 흐름으로 보아, 주어진 문장이 들어가기에 가장 적절한 곳을 고르시오. [3점]

> By comparison, birds with the longest childhoods, and those that migrate with their parents, tend to have the most efficient migration routes.

Spending time as children allows animals to learn about their environment. Without childhood, animals must rely more fully on hardware, and therefore be less flexible. (①) Among migratory bird species, those that are born knowing how, when, and where to migrate — those that are migrating entirely with instructions they were born with — sometimes have very inefficient migration routes. (②) These birds, born knowing how to migrate, don't adapt easily. (③) So when lakes dry up, forest becomes farmland, or climate change pushes breeding grounds farther north, those birds that are born knowing how to migrate keep flying by the old rules and maps. (④) Childhood facilitates the passing on of cultural information, and culture can evolve faster than genes. (⑤) Childhood gives flexibility in a changing world.

어휘 Review

✳ 다음 영어는 우리말 뜻을, 우리말은 영어 단어를 〈보기〉에서 찾아 쓰시오.

〈보기〉
rightly	화합물	clinically	조상
intake	간격	channel	압축하다
drought	생태계	constantly	번식

01 ancestor _____

02 ecosystem _____

03 interval _____

04 compress _____

05 compound _____

06 섭취량 _____

07 당연히 _____

08 끊임없이 _____

09 경로 _____

10 가뭄 _____

✳ 다음 우리말에 알맞은 영어 표현을 찾아 연결하시오.

11 먹이로 삼다 • • derive from

12 ~와는 반대로 • • contrary to

13 ~로부터 도출하다 • • prey upon

14 일련의 • • back and forth

15 왔다 갔다 • • a series of

✳ 다음 우리말 표현에 맞는 단어를 고르시오.

16 유아의 뇌 ➡ the (infant / inborn) brain

17 소리 현상에 대해 자주 언급되는 비유 ➡ an (anatomy / analogy) often given for sound

18 물리적 교란 작용 ➡ a physical (disturbance / distribution)

19 수많은 종의 동물들 ➡ (careless / countless) species of animals

20 각 이동 단계에서 ➡ at each level of (transform / transfer)

✳ 다음 문장의 빈칸에 알맞은 단어를 〈보기〉에서 찾아 쓰시오.

〈보기〉
abstract	harden	restricted	fairness
pillow	applicable	lungs	navigate
tissues	mess	assumption	route

21 하나의 연쇄(사슬) 안에 있는 단계나 연결의 수는 보통 4~5개로 제한된다.
➡ The number of steps or links in a sequence is _____, usually to four or five.

22 그러나 연결 상태는 엉망이다.
➡ The wiring, however, is a(n) _____.

23 그러나 이는 부분적으로 더 추상적인 느낌에 의해 형성되었다.
➡ But it was shaped partly by a more _____ sensation.

24 특정한 가능성들이 지식이나 믿음으로 굳어진다.
➡ Certain possibilities _____ into knowledge or beliefs.

25 그것은 폐 속의 작은 공기 통로를 좁힌다.
➡ It narrows the small air-passages in the _____.

26 그들은 세계를 항해하고 문제를 해결해 낸다.
➡ They manage to _____ the world and solve problems.

27 흔히 사람들은 잘못된 가정을 한다.
➡ People commonly make the mistaken _____.

28 게임을 하는 것은 그들이 더 효과적으로 공평함에 대해 배우도록 도울 것이다.
➡ Playing games will help them learn about _____ more effectively.

29 그 의사는 환자의 아픈 조직을 직접적으로 누르고 있다.
➡ The practitioner is pushing right into the patient's sore _____.

30 여행 베개는 긴 비행기 여행에 대한 보완재이다.
➡ A travel _____ is a complementary good for a long plane journey.

요약문 완성하기

★ 유형 설명

다음 글의 내용을 한 문장으로 요약하고자 한다. 빈칸 (A), (B)에 들어갈 말로 가장 적절한 것은?

> In the course of trying to solve a problem with an invention, you may encounter a brick wall

글의 내용을 한 문장으로 요약하여 주제문을 완성한다는 생각으로 접근해야 한다.

🔑 요약문을 먼저 읽음으로써 글이 무슨 내용인지를 대강 파악한 다음 글을 읽기 시작한다.
주제를 담은 문장을 글에서 찾거나 (주제문이 없다면) 스스로 만들어 보고 그것과 똑같은 내용을 다르게 표현하는 문장이 되도록 요약문을 완성한다.

🕶 유형 풀이 비법

1 요약문을 확인하라!
• 제시된 요약문을 먼저 읽고, 글에서 찾아야 할 내용을 파악한다.

2 글의 주제를 파악하라!
• 글 전체를 읽으며 주제문을 찾고, 무엇에 관한 내용인지 파악한다.

3 직접 요약문을 완성하라!
• 글의 내용을 대표할 수 있는 핵심어를 찾아 요약문을 스스로 만들어 본다.

Tip 핵심어나 주요 내용을 다르게 표현한 어구를 선택지에서 찾는다.

🔑 어휘 및 표현 Preview

- □ conscious 의식적인
- □ subconscious 잠재의식적인
- □ judgment 판단(력)
- □ cloud (기억력, 판단력 등을) 흐리게 하다
- □ bias 편견
- □ originate 비롯되다
- □ scholar 학자
- □ preserve 보존하다
- □ disability 장애
- □ distinguish 구별하다
- □ embrace 포용하다
- □ ensure 반드시 ~ 하게 하다
- □ label 분류하다
- □ combination 조합
- □ nutrient 영양소
- □ occasionally 가끔

- □ captivity 감금
- □ trade 거래하다
- □ universally 일반적으로
- □ source 모으다
- □ comparison 비교
- □ abandon 포기하다
- □ communicate 전달하다
- □ scrub 수술복
- □ notable 눈에 띄는
- □ exception 예외
- □ explore 탐구하다
- □ norm 규범, 기준
- □ affair (공식적인) 일
- □ competence 능숙함, 능력
- □ deviation 일탈
- □ noticeable 주목할 만한

- □ apply 적용하다
- □ transmission 전파
- □ innovation 혁신
- □ conceptually 개념적으로
- □ liken to ~와 유사하다
- □ mutation 돌연변이
- □ modify 수정하다
- □ account for ~을 설명하다
- □ trait 특성
- □ acquire 습득하다
- □ peer 동료
- □ frequency 빈도
- □ probability 개연성, 확률
- □ credible 믿을 만한
- □ trustworthy 신뢰할 수 있는
- □ prospect 전망

17 분사

1 분사의 종류 – 현재분사와 과거분사

	현재분사	과거분사
형태	동사원형 + -ing	동사원형 + -ed
의미	능동(~하는), 진행(~하고 있는)	수동(~된, ~해진), 완료(~한)

- your (smiling) face (당신의 웃는 얼굴)
  현재분사
- (discovered) documents (발견된 서류)
  과거분사

2 *분사구문의 의미 – 분사구문은 여러 의미를 갖는데, 문맥에 따라 자연스럽게 해석해야 한다.

1) 동시동작: '~하면서'라는 의미로, 절로 바꿀 때 주로 접속사 **as**를 쓴다.

- Writing the words down, Doug read them aloud. (단어들을 기록하면서 Doug는 그것들을 소리 내어 읽었다.)
  → As Doug wrote the words down, ~.

2) 연속동작: '~하고 나서'라는 의미로, 절로 바꿀 때 주로 접속사 **and**를 쓴다.

- Turning on the computer, she started working. (컴퓨터를 켜고 그녀는 일하기를 시작했다.)
  → She turned on the computer, and, ~.

3) 결과: '~해서'라는 의미로, 절로 바꿀 때 주로 접속사 **and**를 쓴다.

- The bus left Seoul at 6, arriving in Busan at 10. (버스는 6시에 서울을 떠나서 10시에 부산에 도착했다.)
  → ~, and it arrived in Busan at 10.

4) 때: 절로 바꿀 때 **after, as soon as, before, when, while** 등의 접속사를 쓴다.

- Considering the matter carefully, he made the decision. (그 문제를 주의 깊게 고려한 후에 그는 결정을 내렸다.)
  → After he considered the matter carefully, ~.

5) 이유: 절로 바꿀 때 **as, because, since** 등의 접속사를 쓴다.

- Being sick, she stays at home. (아파서 그녀는 집에 머문다.)
  → Because she is sick, ~.

> *「with + 목적어 + 형용사/부사(구)」
> - It's not considered polite to talk **with your mouth full**.
>   (입에 음식을 가득 물고 말하는 것은 예의 바르다고 여겨지지 않는다.)

Check Test

1 다음 문장을 같은 의미의 분사구문 형태로 바꿔 쓸 때, 빈칸에 알맞은 단어를 쓰시오. (단, 접속사는 생략할 것)

The common blackberry has an amazing ability to move manganese from one layer of soil to another while it uses its roots.
→ The common blackberry has an amazing ability to move manganese from one layer of soil to another ＿＿＿＿＿＿ its roots.

2 밑줄 친 부분에 유의하여 다음 문장을 해석하시오.

Steinberg and Gardner randomly assigned some participants to play alone or with two same-age peers looking on.

→ ＿＿＿＿＿＿＿＿＿＿＿＿

• 정답

2 Steinberg와 Gardner는 일부 참가자를 무작위로 혼자 게임하거나 둘의 같은 나이 또래들이 지켜보는 가운데 게임을 하게 했다.

1 using

Q 요약문 완성하기 (첫 번째)

1st 요약문을 통해 글에서 무엇을 찾아야 하는지 확인하세요.
2nd 글을 읽으면서, 미리 생각해 둔 개념을 다루는 부분을 찾아보세요.
3rd 전체 글의 내용을 정리하여 요약문이 적절한지 확인하세요.

Q01 ★★★❀······················· 고1 2024(3월)/40

다음 글의 내용을 한 문장으로 요약하고자 한다.
빈칸 (A), (B)에 들어갈 말로 가장 적절한 것은?

The mind has parts that are known as the conscious mind and the subconscious mind. The subconscious mind is very fast to act and doesn't deal with emotions. It deals with memories of your responses to life, your⁵ memories and recognition. However, the conscious mind is the one that you have more control over. You think. You can choose whether to carry on a thought or to add emotion to it and this is the part of your¹⁰ mind that lets you down frequently because — fueled by emotions — you make the wrong decisions time and time again. When your judgment is clouded by emotions, this puts in biases and all kinds of other¹⁵ negativities that hold you back. Scared of spiders? Scared of the dark? There are reasons for all of these fears, but they originate in the conscious mind. They only become real fears when the subconscious²⁰ mind records your reactions.

> While the controllable conscious mind deals with thoughts and ___(A)___, the fast-acting subconscious mind stores your responses, ___(B)___ real fears.

(A)	(B)
① emotions	— forming
② actions	— overcoming
③ emotions	— overcoming
④ actions	— avoiding
⑤ moralities	— forming

1st 요약문을 통해 글에서 무엇을 찾아야 하는지 확인하세요.

While the controllable conscious mind deals with /
통제할 수 있는 의식적 마음은 다루지만 /
thoughts and ___(A)___ , / the fast-acting
생각과 (A) 를 / 빠르게 작동하는 잠재의식적
subconscious mind / stores your responses, /
마음이 / 여러분의 반응을 저장하고 /
___(B)___ real fears. //
이는 실제 두려움을 (B) //

● **문장이 While로 시작해요.**
while은 '~인 반면에'라는 뜻의 접속사로, 두 가지 사실을 비교, 대조할 때 쓰여요. 여기서는 (A)와 (B)가 각각 포함된 두 절을 비교하고 있군요.

● **(A)를 먼저 봅시다.**
(A)는 통제할 수 있는 ❶(   )에 관한 부분이에요.
의식적 마음이 생각과 '무엇'을 다룬대요.

● **(B)를 봅시다.**
(B)는 빠르게 작동하는 잠재의식적 마음에 관한 부분이에요. 잠재의식적 마음은 우리의 반응을 저장하고 실제 두려움을 '무엇'한대요.

● **글을 읽으며 무엇을 찾아야 하는지 정리가 좀 되나요?**
우리는 접속사 While을 통해 이 글이 의식적 마음과 잠재의식적 마음의 차이점을 설명하는 글이라는 걸 알았어요. 둘의 차이점을 찾아내 그것을 선택지에서 고르면 정답을 쉽게 찾을 수 있을 것 같아요.

2nd 글을 읽으면서, 미리 생각해 둔 개념을 다루는 부분을 찾아보세요.

1) 글의 첫 문장을 읽어봅시다.

The mind has parts / that are known as the
마음은 부분을 갖고 있다 / 의식적 마음과 잠재의식적
conscious mind and the subconscious mind. //
마음이라고 알려진 //

● **우리가 예상한 것처럼 두 종류의 마음이 언급되었어요.**
의식적 마음과 잠재의식적 마음이라는 두 부분이 각각 어떤 기능을 하고 서로 어떤 차이점이 있는지 나타내는 내용이 뒤에 이어질 것 같아요.

2) 그다음 문장들을 이어서 봅시다.

The subconscious mind is very fast to act / and
잠재의식적 마음은 매우 빠르게 작동하며 / 감정을
doesn't deal with emotions. //
다루지 않는다 //
It deals with / memories of your responses to life,
그것은 다룬다 / 여러분의 삶에 대한 반응의 기억, 기억 및 인식을 //
your memories and recognition. //

- **잠재의식적 마음을 먼저 설명하네요.**
  잠재의식적 마음: 매우 빠르게 작동함,
  감정을 다루지 않고 반응의 기억, 그리고 기억 및 인식을 다룸

- **(B) 선택지와 연결해서 볼까요?**
  (A)가 의식적 마음, (B)가 잠재의식적 마음에 대해 설명하는 절에 있었죠?
  잠재의식적 마음이 우리의 반응을 저장하고 실제 두려움을 '무엇'한다고
  했는데 아직은 전혀 감이 잡히지 않아요. 뒤에 이어지는 문장들을 더
  읽어봅시다!

3) 그다음 문장들을 읽으며 (A)를 찾아봅시다.

> However, the conscious mind is the one / that you
> 그러나 의식적 마음은 부분이다   / 여러분이
>
> have more control over. //
> 더 많은 통제력을 갖고 있는   //
>
> You think. //
> 여러분은 생각한다 //
>
> You can choose / whether to carry on a thought / or
> 여러분은 선택할 수 있다 / 생각을 계속할지   / 또는
>
> to add emotion to it / ~
> 그 생각에 감정을 더할지를   / ~

- **의식적 마음에 대한 설명이 등장했어요.**
  의식적 마음: 우리가 더 많은 통제력을 가진 부분임,
  생각만 계속할지 아니면 생각에 감정을 더할지를 선택하게 하는 부분임

- **(A) 선택지와 연결해서 봅시다.**
  통제할 수 있는 의식적 마음이 생각과 '무엇'을 다루는지가 (A)에 들어갈
  내용이었어요. 방금 우리는 의식적 마음이 생각만 계속할지, 아니면
  생각에 감정을 더할지를 선택하도록 하는 부분임을 확인했죠? 이처럼
  의식적 마음은 생각과 더불어 '감정'도 다룰 수 있는 거예요. 이와 같은
  내용을 선택지에서 찾으면 되겠어요!

4) 이제 글의 후반부에서 (B)를 찾아봅시다.

> Scared of spiders? //
> 거미를 무서워하는가   //
>
> Scared of the dark? //
> 어둠을 무서워하는가   //
>
> There are reasons for all of these fears, / but they
> 이러한 두려움 전부 이유가 있지만   / 그것들은
>
> originate in the conscious mind. //
> 의식적 마음에서 비롯된다   //
>
> They only become real fears / when the
> 그것들은 오직 실제 두려움이 된다 / 잠재의식적
>
> subconscious mind records your reactions. //
> 마음이 여러분의 반응을 기록할 때   //

- **두려움이 형성되는 과정을 설명하고 있어요.**
  거미나 어둠 등에 대한 두려움처럼 처음엔 두려움이 의식적 마음에서
  비롯되었다가 잠재의식적 마음이 반응을 기록할 때만 실제 두려움이
  된다고 했어요.

- **(B) 선택지와 연결해서 볼까요?**
  잠재의식적 마음이 여러분의 반응을 저장하고, 이것이 실제 두려움을
  '무엇'하는지가 (B)에 들어갈 내용이었죠? 우리는 글의 마지막 문장을
  통해, 의식적 마음에서 비롯된 두려움은 잠재의식적 마음이 반응을
  기록할 때만 실제 두려움이 '된다'라는 것을 알아냈어요. 비슷한 내용을
  선택지에서 찾으면 되겠군요!

3rd 전체 글의 내용을 정리하여 요약문이 적절한지 확인하세요.

1) 글의 내용은 이렇게 정리할 수 있어요.

도입 | 마음은 의식적 마음과 잠재의식적 마음이라고 알려진 부분을 가지고 있음

↓

전개 | 잠재의식적 마음은 삶에 대한 반응의 기억과 인식을 다루고 의식적 마음은 생각과 감정을 다룸

↓

대조 | 의식적 마음이 다루는 감정 때문에 잘못된 결정을 반복적으로 내리거나 판단력이 흐려져서 편견과 부정성을 자리 잡게 만들기도 함

↓

부연 | 의식적 마음에서 비롯된 두려움은 잠재의식적 마음이 반응을 기록할 때 실제 두려움이 됨

2) 이제 선택지에서 정답을 골라봅시다.

	(A)	(B)
①	emotions 감정	forming 형성하면서
②	actions 행동	overcoming 극복하면서
③	emotions	overcoming
④	actions	avoiding 피하면서
⑤	moralities 도덕성	forming

- **(A)에 들어갈 말은 무엇인가요?**
  의식적 마음은 생각과 '감정'을 다룰 수 있다고 했으니까, (A)에는 '감정'을
  뜻하는 ①, ③ emotions가 적절해요.

- **(B)에 들어갈 말은 무엇인가요?**
  잠재의식적 마음이 반응을 저장하고 이것이 실제 두려움이 '된다'라고
  했으니까, (B)에는 이와 비슷한 ①, ⑤ forming이 적절해요.

- **이를 종합하면 정답은 무엇인가요?**
  (A)에는 emotions가, (B)에는 forming이 들어가야 하니까 정답은
  ①(   )!

Q 요약문 완성하기 (두 번째)

Q02 ★★★❀ .... 고1 2024(6월)/40

다음 글의 내용을 한 문장으로 요약하고자 한다.
빈칸 (A), (B)에 들어갈 말로 가장 적절한 것은?

Over the last several decades, scholars have developed standards for how best to create, organize, present, and preserve digital information for future generations. What has remained neglected for the most part, however, [5] are the needs of people with disabilities. As a result, many of the otherwise most valuable digital resources are useless for people who are deaf or hard of hearing, as well as for people who are blind, have low vision, or [10] have difficulty distinguishing particular colors. While professionals working in educational technology and commercial web design have made significant progress in meeting the needs of such users, some [15] scholars creating digital projects all too often fail to take these needs into account. This situation would be much improved if more projects embraced the idea that we should always keep the largest possible audience in [20] mind as we make design decisions, ensuring that our final product serves the needs of those with disabilities as well as those without.

↓

The needs of people with disabilities have often been ___(A)___ in digital projects, which could be changed by adopting a(n) ___(B)___ design.

(A)	(B)
① overlooked	— inclusive
② accepted	— practical
③ considered	— inclusive
④ accepted	— abstract
⑤ overlooked	— abstract

1st 요약문을 통해 글에서 무엇을 찾아야 하는지 확인하세요.

The needs of people with disabilities / have often been ___(A)___ in digital projects, / which could
장애가 있는 사람들의 요구는 / 디지털
프로젝트에서 종종 ___(A)___ 왔으며 / 이것은 변화될 수
be changed / by adopting a(n) ___(B)___ design. //
있다 / ___(B)___ 디자인을 채택함으로써 //

● **주절과 계속적 용법의 관계사절이 which로 연결되어 있어요.**
여기서 which는 digital projects를 수식하는 계속적 용법의 주격 관계대명사절을 이끌고 있어요. (A)와 (B)가 포함된 두 절의 내용이 서로 연결된다는 것을 알 수 있죠.

● **(A)를 먼저 봅시다.**
(A)는 디지털 프로젝트에서 장애가 있는 사람들의 요구가 종종 '어떻게' 되었는지에 관한 부분이에요.

● **(B)를 봅시다.**
(B)는 이 상황을 변화시킬 방법에 관한 부분이에요. '어떤' 디자인을 채택함으로써 이 상황이 변화될 수 있다고 하네요.

● **글을 읽으며 무엇을 찾아야 하는지 정리가 좀 되나요?**
장애가 있는 사람들의 요구가 디지털 프로젝트에서 종종 '어떻게' 되었다는 문제가 있나 봐요. 이것이 '어떤' 디자인을 채택함으로써 변화될 수 있다고 했으니, 장애가 있는 사람들이 겪은 문제와 그 해결책을 찾아내 그것을 선택지에서 고르면 정답을 쉽게 찾을 수 있을 거예요.

2nd 글을 읽으며 빈칸을 채우는 데 필요한 내용을 글에서 찾으세요.

1) 글의 첫 문장을 읽어봅시다.

Over the last several decades, / scholars have
지난 수십 년 동안 / 학자들은 표준을
developed standards / for how best to create,
개발해 왔다 / 디지털 정보를 가장 잘 만들고,
organize, present, and preserve digital information
정리하고, 제시하고, 보존하는 방법에 대한
/ for future generations. //
/ 미래 세대를 위해 //

● **배경 상황이 제시되었어요.**
수십 년 동안 학자들이 디지털 정보를 만들고, 정리하고, 제시하고, 보존하는 방법에 대한 표준을 개발해 왔대요. 요약문에 '디지털 프로젝트'가 있었는데 이것이 디지털 정보에 관한 것이었군요! 이제 장애가 있는 사람들이 디지털 정보와 관련하여 겪은 문제가 뒤에 이어질 것 같아요.

2) 그다음 문장들에서 (A)를 찾아봅시다.

> What has remained neglected for the most part, /
> 여전히 대부분 무시되어온 것은   /
> however, / are the needs of people with disabilities. //
> 그러나   / 장애가 있는 사람들의 요구들이다   //
> As a result, / many of the otherwise most valuable
> 그 결과   / 그렇지 않은 경우라면 가장 가치 있었을 디지털 자원 중
> digital resources are useless / ~
> 상당수가 무용지물이 되고 있다   / ~

● **장애가 있는 사람들의 문제 상황이 등장했어요.**
장애가 있는 사람들의 요구들이 대부분 **❶**(   )되었고
그 결과, 장애가 있는 사람들에게 디지털 자원의 상당수가 무용지물이
되었다고 했어요.

● **(A) 선택지와 연결해서 볼까요?**
(A)는 디지털 프로젝트에서 장애가 있는 사람들의 요구가 종종
'어떻게' 되었는지에 관한 부분이에요. 장애가 있는 사람들의 요구가
'무시되었다'라는 아주 직접적인 단서가 주어졌으므로 '무시'와 비슷한
선택지를 찾으면 될 거예요!

3) (B)를 찾기 위해 마지막 문장을 봅시다.

> This situation would be much improved / if more
> 이러한 상황은 훨씬 개선될 것이다   / 더 많은
> projects embraced the idea / that we should always
> 프로젝트에서 생각을 받아들인다면 / 최대한 많은 사용자를 항상
> keep the largest possible audience in mind / as we
> 염두에 두어야 한다고   / 디자인을
> make design decisions, / ensuring that our final
> 결정할 때   / 최종 제품이 장애가 있는 사람들의
> product serves the needs of those with disabilities /
> 요구를 충족시킬 수 있도록 하면서   /
> as well as those without. //
> 장애가 없는 사람들의 요구뿐만 아니라 //

● **이러한 상황이 개선될 수 있다고 했어요!**
우리가 요약문에서 예상했던 것처럼, 앞서 언급된 문제의 해결 방안을
제시하려나 봐요. 그것은 바로 **❷**(   )을 결정할 때 최대한
많은 사용자를 항상 염두에 두어야 한다는 것이래요. ensuring으로
이어지는 분사구문에서도 최종 제품이 장애의 유무에 상관없이 모든
요구를 충족시킬 수 있도록 한다는 부연 설명이 있군요.

● **(B) 선택지와 연결해서 볼까요?**
'어떤' 디자인을 채택함으로써 이 상황이 변화될 수 있는지가 (B)에 들어갈
내용이었죠? 우리는 글의 마지막 문장을 통해, 이 상황을 개선할 방법은
디자인을 결정할 때 '최대한 많은 사용자를 염두에 두고' 장애의 유무에
상관없이 모든 요구를 충족시키는 것임을 알아냈어요. 비슷한 내용을
선택지에서 찾으면 되겠군요!

3rd 전체 글의 내용을 정리하여 요약문이 적절한지 확인하세요.

1) 글의 내용은 이렇게 정리할 수 있어요.

도입 ▸ 디지털 정보 개발에 있어서 장애인의 요구는 무시되어 왔음

↓

전개 ▸ 장애가 있는 사람들에게 디지털 자원은 무용지물이 되어 버림

↓

부연 ▸ 디지털 프로젝트에서는 여전히 장애인의 요구를 고려하지 못하는
경우가 많음

↓

결론 ▸ 디지털 프로젝트를 결정할 때 최대한 많은 사용자를 항상 염두에
두고 장애가 있는 사람들과 그렇지 않은 사람들 모두의 요구를
충족시킬 수 있도록 해야 함

2) 이제 선택지에서 정답을 골라봅시다.

(A)	(B)
① overlooked 간과된	inclusive 포괄적인
② accepted 수용된	practical 실용적인
③ considered 고려된	inclusive
④ accepted	abstract 추상적인
⑤ overlooked	abstract

● **(A)에 들어갈 말은 무엇인가요?**
장애가 있는 사람들의 요구가 디지털 프로젝트에서 종종 '무시되었다'고
했으니까, (A)에는 맥락이 비슷한 '간과된'이라는 뜻의 ①, ⑤
overlooked가 적절해요.

● **(B)에 들어갈 말은 무엇인가요?**
장애가 있는 사람들의 요구가 간과되는 문제는 장애 여부를 가리지 않고
모두의 요구를 충족하는 '포괄적인' 디자인을 채택함으로써 변화될 수
있다고 했으니까, (B)에는 ①, ③ inclusive가 적절해요.

● **이를 종합하면 정답은 무엇인가요?**
(A)에는 overlooked가, (B)에는 inclusive가 들어가야 하니까 정답은
❸(   )!

Q03 ~ 06 ▶ 제한시간 8분

Q03 ★★★❋ 고1 2025(3월)/40

다음 글의 내용을 한 문장으로 요약하고자 한다. 빈칸 (A), (B)에 들어갈 말로 가장 적절한 것은?

In the course of trying to solve a problem with an invention, you may encounter a brick wall of resistance when you try to think your way logically through the problem. Such logical thinking is a linear type of process, which uses our reasoning skills. This works fine when we're operating in the area of what we know or have experienced. However, when we need to deal with new information, ideas, and viewpoints, linear thinking will often come up short. On the other hand, creativity by definition involves the application of new information to old problems and the conception of new viewpoints and ideas. For this you will be most effective if you learn to operate in a nonlinear manner; that is, use your creative brain. Stated differently, if you think in a linear manner, you'll tend to be conservative and keep coming up with techniques which are already known. This, of course, is just what you don't want.

*linear: 선형의 **conservative: 보수적인

⬇

_____(A)_____ thinking works well with familiar problems but falls short in dealing with new ideas, for which creative thinking is needed to come up with _____(B)_____ solutions.

	(A)		(B)
①	Logical	—	innovative
②	Flexible	—	instant
③	Logical	—	proven
④	Flexible	—	superior
⑤	Logical	—	collaborative

구문 서술형

괄호 안의 단어를 빈칸에 알맞은 형태로 넣어 분사구문을 완성하시오.

➡ _____ to think your way logically through the problem, you may encounter a brick wall of resistance. (try)

Q04 ★★★❋ 고1 2025(6월)/40

다음 글의 내용을 한 문장으로 요약하고자 한다. 빈칸 (A), (B)에 들어갈 말로 가장 적절한 것은?

There is a natural assumption of truth, or a truth bias when humans communicate with one another. In other words, when we're listening to others or reading their words, our automatic assumption is that the other person is telling the truth. This usually works out fine. If you ask someone where the restroom is located or if it's raining outside, you can safely assume that most people will not lie in their responses. Imagine how difficult it would be to converse with someone if you assumed that *everything* they were telling you was false! Indeed, questioning the truth of a statement and then choosing not to believe it requires additional mental steps. For the most part, humans are "cognitive misers," which means we typically don't expend more mental effort than seems necessary in a given situation. It makes sense then, that when we see something online, even if it is fake, our default is to believe it, at least at first.

*expend: 들이다 **default: 기본값

⬇

We humans are unlikely to _____(A)_____ the truth of information we receive, due to our tendency to _____(B)_____ mental effort.

	(A)		(B)
①	doubt	—	save
②	trust	—	maintain
③	judge	—	add
④	doubt	—	increase
⑤	trust	—	reduce

구문 서술형

주어진 우리말과 일치하도록 괄호 안의 단어를 이용하여 분사구문을 알맞게 쓰시오. (단, 접속사를 생략하지 않을 것)

온라인에서 무언가를 볼 때, 우리는 그것을 믿는 경향이 있다. (see, something, online)

➡ _____, we tend to believe it.

Q05 ✦✦✦ 고1 2025(9월)/40

다음 글의 내용을 한 문장으로 요약하고자 한다. 빈칸 (A), (B)에 들어갈 말로 가장 적절한 것은?

Vision is influenced by our preconceptions about reality. In viewing a scene, we establish unconscious hierarchies that reflect our functional relationship to objects and our momentary priorities. For example, when visualizing a hammer in our mind's eye, we tend to "see" it in profile or at some other "ready for use" angle. One would probably not visualize a hammer as seen from the top so that the handle is hidden by the hammer's head. The functional relationship we have with objects creates visual expectations that interfere with our ability to see "like a camera." The camera, like the human eye, sees only shapes and colors. It documents the world impartially through a lens that is similar to the eye. When we look at them carefully, photographs are often surprising because they don't interpret confusing details but simply serve them up to us with a mechanical indifference. And because of their flatness, photographs often contain areas that appear as unrecognizable colors and shapes.

↓

Our visual perception is shaped by an established hierarchy based on functional relationships, which ____(A)____ our ability to see objects as they truly are, unlike the ____(B)____ perspective of a camera.

	(A)		(B)
①	enhances	—	accurate
②	simplifies	—	fixed
③	interrupts	—	objective
④	enhances	—	neutral
⑤	interrupts	—	inconsistent

구문 서술형

문장에서 틀린 부분을 찾아 밑줄을 긋고 바르게 고치시오.

Looked at photographs carefully, we often find them surprising.

➡ _____

Q06 ✦✦✦ 고1 2024(10월)/40

다음 글의 내용을 한 문장으로 요약하고자 한다. 빈칸 (A), (B)에 들어갈 말로 가장 적절한 것은?

Punishing a child may not be effective due to what Álvaro Bilbao, a neuropsychologist, calls 'trick-punishments.' A trick-punishment is a scolding, a moment of anger or a punishment in the most classic sense of the word. Instead of discouraging the child from doing something, it encourages them to do it. For example, Hugh learns that when he hits his little brother, his mother scolds him. For a child who feels lonely, being scolded is much better than feeling invisible, so he will continue to hit his brother. In this case, his mother would be better adopting a different strategy. For instance, she could congratulate Hugh when he has not hit his brother for a certain length of time. The mother clearly cannot allow the child to hit his little brother, but instead of constantly pointing out the negatives, she can choose to reward the positives. In this way, any parent can avoid trick-punishments.

↓

A trick-punishment ____(A)____ the unwanted behavior of a child, which implies that parents should focus on ____(B)____ the attention to negatives while rewarding positive behaviors.

	(A)		(B)
①	reinforces	—	reducing
②	reinforces	—	maximizing
③	discourages	—	attracting
④	discourages	—	lowering
⑤	controls	—	increasing

구문 서술형

주어진 문장의 부사절을 분사구문으로 바꿔 쓰시오. (단, 접속사를 생략할 것)

Because a child thinks that being scolded is much better than feeling invisible, he will continue to hit his brother.

➡ _____

_____, a child will continue to hit his brother.

Q07 ★★★❀

다음 글의 내용을 한 문장으로 요약하고자 한다. 빈칸 (A), (B)에 들어갈 말로 가장 적절한 것은?

Capuchins — New World Monkeys that live in large social groups — will, in captivity, trade with people all day long, especially if food is involved. *I give you this rock and you give me a treat to eat.* If you put two monkeys in cages next to each other, and offer them both slices of cucumber for the rocks they already have, they will happily eat the cucumbers. If, however, you give one monkey grapes instead — grapes being universally preferred to cucumbers — the monkey that is still receiving cucumbers will begin to throw them back at the experimenter. Even though she is still getting "paid" the same amount for her effort of sourcing rocks, and so her particular situation has not changed, the comparison to another makes the situation unfair. Furthermore, she is now willing to abandon all gains — the cucumbers themselves — to communicate her displeasure to the experimenter.

⬇

According to the passage, if the Capuchin monkey realizes the ___(A)___ in rewards compared to another monkey, she will ___(B)___ her rewards to express her feelings about the treatment, despite getting exactly the same rewards as before.

	(A)		(B)
①	benefit	—	protect
②	inequality	—	share
③	abundance	—	yield
④	inequality	—	reject
⑤	benefit	—	display

Q08 ★★★

다음 글의 내용을 한 문장으로 요약하고자 한다. 빈칸 (A), (B)에 들어갈 말로 가장 적절한 것은? [3점]

Many of the first models of cultural evolution drew noticeable connections between culture and genes by using concepts from theoretical population genetics and applying them to culture. Cultural patterns of transmission, innovation, and selection are conceptually likened to genetic processes of transmission, mutation, and selection. However, these approaches had to be modified to account for the differences between genetic and cultural transmission. For example, we do not expect the cultural transmission to follow the rules of genetic transmission strictly. If two biological parents have different forms of a cultural trait, their child is not necessarily equally likely to acquire the mother's or father's form of that trait. Further, a child can acquire cultural traits not only from its parents but also from nonparental adults and peers; thus, the frequency of a cultural trait in the population is relevant beyond just the probability that an individual's parents had that trait.

*mutation: 돌연변이 **relevant: 유의미한

⬇

Early cultural evolution models used the ___(A)___ between culture and genes but had to be revised since cultural transmission allows for more ___(B)___ factors than genetic transmission.

	(A)		(B)
①	similarity	—	diverse
②	similarity	—	limited
③	difference	—	flexible
④	difference	—	complicated
⑤	interaction	—	credible

다음 글의 내용을 한 문장으로 요약하고자 한다. 빈칸 (A), (B)에 들어갈 말로 가장 적절한 것은?

In their study in 2007 Katherine Kinzler and her colleagues at Harvard showed that our tendency to identify with an in-group to a large degree begins in infancy and may be innate. Kinzler and her team took a bunch of five-month-olds whose families only spoke English and showed the babies two videos. In one video, a woman was speaking English. In the other, a woman was speaking Spanish. Then they were shown a screen with both women side by side, not speaking. In infant psychology research, the standard measure for affinity or interest is attention — babies will apparently stare longer at the things they like more. In Kinzler's study, the babies stared at the English speakers longer. In other studies, researchers have found that infants are more likely to take a toy offered by someone who speaks the same language as them. Psychologists routinely cite these and other experiments as evidence of our built-in evolutionary preference for "our own kind."

*affinity: 애착

↓

Infants' more favorable responses to those who use a ___(A)___ language show that there can be a(n) ___(B)___ tendency to prefer in-group members.

	(A)		(B)
①	familiar	—	inborn
②	familiar	—	acquired
③	foreign	—	cultural
④	foreign	—	learned
⑤	formal	—	innate

다음 글의 내용을 한 문장으로 요약하고자 한다. 빈칸 (A), (B)에 들어갈 말로 가장 적절한 것은?

One way that music could express emotion is simply through a learned association. Perhaps there is nothing naturally sad about a piece of music in a minor key, or played slowly with low notes. Maybe we have just come to hear certain kinds of music as sad because we have learned to associate them in our culture with sad events like funerals. If this view is correct, we should have difficulty interpreting the emotions expressed in culturally unfamiliar music. Totally opposed to this view is the position that the link between music and emotion is one of resemblance. For example, when we feel sad we move slowly and speak slowly and in a low-pitched voice. Thus when we hear slow, low music, we hear it as sad. If this view is correct, we should have little difficulty understanding the emotion expressed in culturally unfamiliar music.

↓

It is believed that emotion expressed in music can be understood through a(n) ___(A)___ learned association or it can be understood due to the ___(B)___ between music and emotion.

	(A)		(B)
①	culturally	—	similarity
②	culturally	—	balance
③	socially	—	difference
④	incorrectly	—	connection
⑤	incorrectly	—	contrast

Q

Q11 ★★★
고1 2022(6월)/40

다음 글의 내용을 한 문장으로 요약하고자 한다. 빈칸 (A), (B)에 들어갈 말로 가장 적절한 것은? [3점]

According to a study of Swedish adolescents, an important factor of adolescents' academic success is how they respond to challenges. The study reports that when facing difficulties, adolescents exposed to an authoritative parenting style are less likely to be passive, helpless, and afraid to fail. Another study of nine high schools in Wisconsin and northern California indicates that children of authoritative parents do well in school, because these parents put a lot of effort into getting involved in their children's school activities. That is, authoritative parents are significantly more likely to help their children with homework, to attend school programs, to watch their children in sports, and to help students select courses. Moreover, these parents are more aware of what their children do and how they perform in school. Finally, authoritative parents praise academic excellence and the importance of working hard more than other parents do.

↓

The studies above show that the children of authoritative parents often succeed academically, since they are more ___(A)___ to deal with their difficulties and are affected by their parents' ___(B)___ involvement.

	(A)		(B)
①	likely	—	random
②	willing	—	minimal
③	willing	—	active
④	hesitant	—	unwanted
⑤	hesitant	—	constant

Q12 ★★★
고1 2021(3월)/40

다음 글의 내용을 한 문장으로 요약하고자 한다. 빈칸 (A), (B)에 들어갈 말로 가장 적절한 것은?

In one study, researchers asked pairs of strangers to sit down in a room and chat. In half of the rooms, a cell phone was placed on a nearby table; in the other half, no phone was present. After the conversations had ended, the researchers asked the participants what they thought of each other. Here's what they learned: when a cell phone was present in the room, the participants reported the quality of their relationship was worse than those who'd talked in a cell phone-free room. The pairs who talked in the rooms with cell phones thought their partners showed less empathy. Think of all the times you've sat down to have lunch with a friend and set your phone on the table. You might have felt good about yourself because you didn't pick it up to check your messages, but your unchecked messages were still hurting your connection with the person sitting across from you.

↓

The presence of a cell phone ___(A)___ the connection between people involved in conversations, even when the phone is being ___(B)___ .

	(A)		(B)
①	weakens	—	answered
②	weakens	—	ignored
③	renews	—	answered
④	maintains	—	ignored
⑤	maintains	—	updated

Q13 ★★★

다음 글의 내용을 한 문장으로 요약하고자 한다. 빈칸 (A), (B)에 들어갈 말로 가장 적절한 것은?

One of the most powerful tools to find meaning in our lives is reflective journaling — thinking back on and writing about what has happened to us. In the 1990s, Stanford University researchers asked undergraduate students on spring break to journal about their most important personal values and their daily activities; others were asked to write about only the good things that happened to them in the day. Three weeks later, the students who had written about their values were happier, healthier, and more confident about their ability to handle stress than the ones who had only focused on the good stuff. By reflecting on how their daily activities supported their values, students had gained a new perspective on those activities and choices. Little stresses and hassles were now demonstrations of their values in action. Suddenly, their lives were full of meaningful activities. And all they had to do was reflect and write about it — positively reframing their experiences with their personal values.

*hassle: 귀찮은 일

↓

Journaling about daily activities based on what we believe to be _____(A)_____ can make us feel that our life is meaningful by _____(B)_____ our experiences in a new way.

	(A)		(B)
①	factual	—	rethinking
②	worthwhile	—	rethinking
③	outdated	—	generalizing
④	objective	—	generalizing
⑤	demanding	—	describing

Q14 ★★★

다음 글의 내용을 한 문장으로 요약하고자 한다. 빈칸 (A), (B)에 들어갈 말로 가장 적절한 것은?

It's not news to anyone that we judge others based on their clothes. In general, studies that investigate these judgments find that people prefer clothing that matches expectations — surgeons in scrubs, little boys in blue — with one notable exception. A series of studies published in an article in June 2014 in the *Journal of Consumer Research* explored observers' reactions to people who broke established norms only slightly. In one scenario, a man at a black-tie affair was viewed as having higher status and competence when wearing a red bow tie. The researchers also found that valuing uniqueness increased audience members' ratings of the status and competence of a professor who wore red sneakers while giving a lecture. The results suggest that people judge these slight deviations from the norm as positive because they suggest that the individual is powerful enough to risk the social costs of such behaviors.

↓

A series of studies show that people view an individual _____(A)_____ when the individual only slightly _____(B)_____ the norm for what people should wear.

	(A)		(B)
①	positively	—	challenges
②	negatively	—	challenges
③	indifferently	—	neglects
④	negatively	—	meets
⑤	positively	—	meets

Q15 ★★★

고1 2023(6월)/40

다음 글의 내용을 한 문장으로 요약하고자 한다. 빈칸 (A), (B)에 들어갈 말로 가장 적절한 것은?

Nearly eight of ten U.S. adults believe there are "good foods" and "bad foods." Unless we're talking about spoiled stew, poison mushrooms, or something similar, however, no foods can be labeled as either good or bad. There are, however, combinations of foods that add up to a healthful or unhealthful diet. Consider the case of an adult who eats only foods thought of as "good" — for example, raw broccoli, apples, orange juice, boiled tofu, and carrots. Although all these foods are nutrient-dense, they do not add up to a healthy diet because they don't supply a wide enough variety of the nutrients we need. Or take the case of the teenager who occasionally eats fried chicken, but otherwise stays away from fried foods. The occasional fried chicken isn't going to knock his or her diet off track. But the person who eats fried foods every day, with few vegetables or fruits, and loads up on supersized soft drinks, candy, and chips for snacks has a bad diet.

↓

Unlike the common belief, defining foods as good or bad is not ____(A)____ ; in fact, a healthy diet is determined largely by what the diet is ____(B)____ .

	(A)		(B)
①	incorrect	—	limited to
②	appropriate	—	composed of
③	wrong	—	aimed at
④	appropriate	—	tested on
⑤	incorrect	—	adjusted to

Q16 ★★★

고1 2020(6월)/40

다음 글의 내용을 한 문장으로 요약하고자 한다. 빈칸 (A), (B)에 들어갈 말로 가장 적절한 것은? [3점]

Have you noticed that some coaches get the most out of their athletes while others don't? A poor coach will tell you what you did wrong and then tell you not to do it again: "Don't drop the ball!" What happens next? The images you see in your head are images of you dropping the ball! Naturally, your mind recreates what it just "saw" based on what it's been told. Not surprisingly, you walk on the court and drop the ball. What does the good coach do? He or she points out what could be improved, but will then tell you how you could or should perform: "I know you'll catch the ball perfectly this time." Sure enough, the next image in your mind is you *catching* the ball and *scoring* a goal. Once again, your mind makes your last thoughts part of reality — but this time, that "reality" is positive, not negative.

↓

Unlike ineffective coaches, who focus on players' ____(A)____ , effective coaches help players improve by encouraging them to ____(B)____ successful plays.

	(A)		(B)
①	scores	—	complete
②	scores	—	remember
③	mistakes	—	picture
④	mistakes	—	ignore
⑤	strengths	—	achieve

Q17 ❀❀❀ 고1 2020(3월)/40

다음 글의 내용을 한 문장으로 요약하고자 한다. 빈칸 (A), (B)에 들어갈 말로 가장 적절한 것은?

While there are many evolutionary or cultural reasons for cooperation, the eyes are one of the most important means of cooperation, and eye contact may be the most powerful human force we lose in traffic. It is, arguably, the reason why humans, normally a quite cooperative species, can become so noncooperative on the road. Most of the time we are moving too fast — we begin to lose the ability to keep eye contact around 20 miles per hour — or it is not safe to look. Maybe our view is blocked. Often other drivers are wearing sunglasses, or their car may have tinted windows. (And do you really want to make eye contact with those drivers?) Sometimes we make eye contact through the rearview mirror, but it feels weak, not quite believable at first, as it is not "face-to-face."

*tinted: 색이 옅게 들어간

⬇

While driving, people become ____(A)____, because they make ____(B)____ eye contact.

	(A)		(B)
①	uncooperative	—	little
②	careful	—	direct
③	confident	—	regular
④	uncooperative	—	direct
⑤	careful	—	little

Q18 ❀❀❀ 고1 2021(6월)/40

다음 글의 내용을 한 문장으로 요약하고자 한다. 빈칸 (A), (B)에 들어갈 말로 가장 적절한 것은?

A woman named Rhonda who attended the University of California at Berkeley had a problem. She was living near campus with several other people — none of whom knew one another. When the cleaning people came each weekend, they left several rolls of toilet paper in each of the two bathrooms. However, by Monday all the toilet paper would be gone. It was a classic tragedy-of-the-commons situation: because some people took more toilet paper than their fair share, the public resource was destroyed for everyone else. After reading a research paper about behavior change, Rhonda put a note in one of the bathrooms asking people not to remove the toilet paper, as it was a shared item. To her great satisfaction, one roll reappeared in a few hours, and another the next day. In the other note-free bathroom, however, there was no toilet paper until the following weekend, when the cleaning people returned.

* peck: (모이를) 쪼아 먹다

⬇

A small ____(A)____ brought about a change in the behavior of the people who had taken more of the ____(B)____ goods than they needed.

	(A)		(B)
①	reminder	—	shared
②	reminder	—	recycled
③	mistake	—	stored
④	mistake	—	borrowed
⑤	fortune	—	limited

Q19~23 ▶ 제한시간 10분

Q19 ⭐ 2등급 대비   고1 2023(3월)/40

다음 글의 내용을 한 문장으로 요약하고자 한다. 빈칸 (A), (B)에 들어갈 말로 가장 적절한 것은?

To help decide what's risky and what's safe, who's trustworthy and who's not, we look for *social evidence*. From an evolutionary view, following the group is almost always positive for our prospects of survival. "If everyone's doing it, it must be a sensible thing to do," explains famous psychologist and best selling writer of *Influence*, Robert Cialdini. While we can frequently see this today in product reviews, even subtler cues within the environment can signal trustworthiness. Consider this: when you visit a local restaurant, are they busy? Is there a line outside or is it easy to find a seat? It is a hassle to wait, but a line can be a powerful cue that the food's tasty, and these seats are in demand. More often than not, it's good to adopt the practices of those around you.   *subtle: 미묘한 **hassle: 성가신 일

⬇

We tend to feel safe and secure in   (A)   when we decide how to act, particularly when faced with   (B)   conditions.

      (A)   (B)
① numbers   —   uncertain
② numbers   —   unrealistic
③ experiences   —   unrealistic
④ rules   —   uncertain
⑤ rules   —   unpleasant

Q20 ⭐ 2등급 대비   고1 2021(9월)/40

다음 글의 내용을 한 문장으로 요약하고자 한다. 빈칸 (A), (B)에 들어갈 말로 가장 적절한 것은? [3점]

Nancy Lowry and David Johnson conducted an experiment to study a teaching environment where fifth and sixth graders were assigned to interact on a topic. With one group, the discussion was led in a way that built an agreement. With the second group, the discussion was designed to produce disagreements about the right answer. Students who easily reached an agreement were less interested in the topic, studied less, and were less likely to visit the library to get additional information. The most noticeable difference, though, was revealed when teachers showed a special film about the discussion topic — during lunch time! Only 18 percent of the agreement group missed lunch time to see the film, but 45 percent of the students from the disagreement group stayed for the film. The thirst to fill a knowledge gap — to find out who was right within the group — can be more powerful than the thirst for slides and jungle gyms.

⬇

According to the experiment above, students' interest in a topic   (A)   when they are encouraged to   (B)   .

      (A)   (B)
① increases   —   differ
② increases   —   approve
③ increases   —   cooperate
④ decreases   —   participate
⑤ decreases   —   argue

다음 글의 내용을 한 문장으로 요약하고자 한다. 빈칸 (A), (B)에 들어갈 말로 가장 적절한 것은?

My colleagues and I ran an experiment testing two different messages meant to convince thousands of resistant alumni to make a donation. One message emphasized the opportunity to do good: donating would benefit students, faculty, and staff. The other emphasized the opportunity to feel good: donors would enjoy the warm glow of giving. The two messages were equally effective: in both cases, 6.5 percent of the unwilling alumni ended up donating. Then we combined them, because two reasons are better than one. Except they weren't. When we put the two reasons together, the giving rate dropped below 3 percent. Each reason alone was more than twice as effective as the two combined. The audience was already skeptical. When we gave them different kinds of reasons to donate, we triggered their awareness that someone was trying to persuade them — and they shielded themselves against it.

*alumni: 졸업생 **skeptical: 회의적인

↓

In the experiment mentioned above, when the two different reasons to donate were given ____(A)____ , the audience was less likely to be ____(B)____ because they could recognize the intention to persuade them.

	(A)		(B)
①	simultaneously	—	convinced
②	separately	—	confused
③	frequently	—	annoyed
④	separately	—	satisfied
⑤	simultaneously	—	offended

다음 글의 내용을 한 문장으로 요약하고자 한다. 빈칸 (A)와 (B)에 들어갈 말로 가장 적절한 것은?

The common blackberry (*Rubus allegheniensis*) has an amazing ability to move manganese from one layer of soil to another using its roots. This may seem like a funny talent for a plant to have, but it all becomes clear when you realize the effect it has on nearby plants. Manganese can be very harmful to plants, especially at high concentrations. Common blackberry is unaffected by damaging effects of this metal and has evolved two different ways of using manganese to its advantage. First, it redistributes manganese from deeper soil layers to shallow soil layers using its roots as a small pipe. Second, it absorbs manganese as it grows, concentrating the metal in its leaves. When the leaves drop and decay, their concentrated manganese deposits further poison the soil around the plant. For plants that are not immune to the toxic effects of manganese, this is very bad news. Essentially, the common blackberry eliminates competition by poisoning its neighbors with heavy metals.

*manganese: 망가니즈(금속 원소) **deposit: 축적물

↓

The common blackberry has an ability to ____(A)____ the amount of manganese in the surrounding upper soil, which makes the nearby soil quite ____(B)____ for other plants.

	(A)		(B)
①	increase	—	deadly
②	increase	—	advantageous
③	indicate	—	nutritious
④	reduce	—	dry
⑤	reduce	—	warm

다음 글의 내용을 한 문장으로 요약하고자 한다. 빈칸
(A)와 (B)에 들어갈 말로 가장 적절한 것은?

There is often a lot of uncertainty in the realm of science, which the general public finds uncomfortable. They don't want "informed guesses," they want certainties that make their lives easier, and science is often unequipped to meet these demands. In particular, the human body is fantastically complex, and some scientific answers can never be provided in black-or-white terms. All this is why the media tends to oversimplify scientific research when presenting it to the public. In their eyes, they're just "giving people what they want" as opposed to offering more accurate but complex information that very few people will read or understand. A perfect example of this is how people want definitive answers as to which foods are "good" and "bad." Scientifically speaking, there are no "good" and "bad" foods; rather, food quality exists on a continuum, meaning that some foods are *better* than others when it comes to general health and well-being.   *continuum: 연속(체)

⬇

With regard to general health, science, by its nature, does not _____(A)_____ the public's demands for certainty, which leads to the media giving less _____(B)_____ answers to the public.

	(A)		(B)
①	satisfy	—	simple
②	satisfy	—	complicated
③	ignore	—	difficult
④	ignore	—	simple
⑤	reject	—	complicated

> 빈칸 앞에 부정어
> no나 not이 있는지
> 반드시 확인하자!

＊ 다음 영어는 우리말 뜻을, 우리말은 영어 단어를 〈보기〉에서 찾아 쓰시오.

〈 보기 〉

관대한	reasoning	실시하다	recreate
판단	encounter	편향	neutral
외과 의사	miser	전망	trait

01 conduct _____

02 bias _____

03 prospect _____

04 judgment _____

05 surgeon _____

06 재현하다 _____

07 맞닥뜨리다 _____

08 구두쇠 _____

09 추론 _____

10 중립적인 _____

＊ 다음 우리말에 알맞은 영어 표현을 찾아 연결하시오.

11 ~에 반대하다 • • point out

12 ~와 대화하다 • • converse with

13 ~에 노출된 • • exposed to

14 정의상 • • by definition

15 지적하다 • • be opposed to

＊ 다음 우리말 표현에 맞는 단어를 고르시오.

16 진실에 대한 자연스러운 가정 ➡ a natural (consumption / assumption) of truth

17 새로운 정보의 적용 ➡ the (appreciation / application) of new information

18 깊은 토양층으로부터 ➡ from deeper soil (layers / layouts)

19 수천 명의 저항하는 졸업생 ➡ thousands of (resistant / prepared) alumni

20 더 적은 공감 ➡ less (emphasis / empathy)

＊ 다음 문장의 빈칸에 알맞은 단어를 〈보기〉에서 찾아 쓰시오.

〈 보기 〉

disabilities	comparison	concentrations	challenges
statement	conception	revised	originate
strategy	authoritative	generous	neglect

21 어떤 진술의 진실성에 의문을 제기하는 것은 추가적인 정신적 단계를 요구한다.
➡ Questioning the truth of a _____ requires additional mental steps.

22 초기의 문화 진화 모델들은 수정되어야만 했다.
➡ Early cultural evolution models had to be _____.

23 우리의 최종 제품은 장애가 있는 사람들의 요구를 충족한다.
➡ Our final product serves the needs of those with _____.

24 다른 것과의 비교는 그 상황을 부당하게 만든다.
➡ The _____ to another makes the situation unfair.

25 망가니즈는 식물에 매우 해로울 수 있으며, 특히 고농도일 때 그렇다.
➡ Manganese can be very harmful to plants, especially at high _____.

26 중요한 요인은 그들이 어려움에 반응하는 방식이다.
➡ An important factor is how they respond to _____.

27 창의성은 새로운 관점과 아이디어의 구상을 포함한다.
➡ Creativity involves the _____ of new viewpoints and ideas.

28 그의 어머니는 다른 전략을 채택하는 것이 나을 것이다.
➡ His mother would be better adopting a different _____.

29 하지만 그것들은 의식적 마음에서 비롯된다.
➡ But they _____ in the conscious mind.

30 권위가 있는 부모들은 아이들을 도와줄 가능성이 더 크다.
➡ _____ parents are more likely to help their children.

장문의 이해

┌→ 글이나 말의 대략적인 뜻

대의 파악 문제 글의 전체 내용을 이해했는지 평가하는 문제

● 윗글의 제목으로 가장 적절한 것은?

① Once Set, Spending Habits Seldom Change
② Why Do We Spend More with Credit Cards?

🔑 적절하지 않은 낱말을 골라낸 후, 그 풀이 과정을 통해 확인한 글의 주제를 함축적이고 비유적으로 나타내는 제목을 고른다.

세부 정보 문제 글의 세부 내용을 파악했는지 평가하는 문제

● 밑줄 친 (a)~(e) 중에서 문맥상 낱말의 쓰임이 적절하지 않은 것은?

① (a)   ② (b)   ③ (c)   ④ (d)   ⑤ (e)

🔑 밑줄 친 낱말의 적절성을 판단하는 문제를 풀기 위해서는 그것이 포함된 문장과 그 앞뒤 내용을 살펴야 한다.

내용이 길고 많네. 내가 여기서 알아야 하는 정보는 무엇이지?

(Tip) 정답을 고른 뒤 본문과 맞춰보며 맞는지 확인한다.

🎭 유형 풀이 비법

1 문제를 먼저 읽어라!
• 제시된 문제를 먼저 읽고, 어떤 유형의 문제인지 파악한다.

2-1 세부 정보 문제를 풀어라!
• 처음부터 꼼꼼히 글을 읽으면서 흐름에 맞게 문장 간의 관계를 확인하고, 세부 정보를 묻는 문제를 푼다.

2-2 세부 정보 문제 풀이 비법
• 밑줄 친 단어 앞이나 문장 내의 부정 표현(not, no one, nothing 등)에 유의한다. 반의어가 확실한지 확인한다.

3 대의 파악 문제를 풀어라!
• 세부 정보를 파악하는 문제의 풀이 과정에서 확인한 글의 주제를 정리하고, 이를 모두 포함한 제목을 찾는다.

🔑 어휘 및 표현 Preview

□ **point out** ~을 짚어 주다
□ **force** 강요하다
□ **worthy of** ~을 받을 만한
□ **dramatic** 극적인
□ **institution** 기관
□ **initiate** 시작하다
□ **contradiction** 모순
□ **assessment** 평가
□ **surplus** 잉여, 흑자
□ **consistent** 지속적인
□ **stability** 안정성
□ **reproduce** 재현하다
□ **randomly** 무작위로

□ **previously** 이전에
□ **accurately** 정확하게
□ **guarantee** 보장하다
□ **sector** 부문
□ **lamb** ((동물)) 양
□ **pastureland** 목초지
□ **bulk** 큰 규모
□ **violate** 침해하다
□ **mastery** 숙달
□ **remarkable** 놀라운
□ **stimulate** 자극시키다
□ **receptor** 수용체
□ **activate** 활성화시키다

□ **tissue** (세포) 조직
□ **fire off** 발사하다
□ **preference** 선호
□ **resistance** 저항
□ **accordingly** 그에 따라
□ **represent** 나타내다
□ **elementary** 기본적인
□ **besides** ~ 외에
□ **joint** 공동의
□ **mutual** 상호의
□ **conceal** 감추다, 숨기다
□ **confine** 제한하다, 국한하다
□ **human nature** 인간 본성

18 생략, 강조

1 생략 – 문장에서 **생략되어도 의미를 파악할 수 있거나 반복되는 부분**은 문장을 간결하게 만들기 위해 생략하는 경우가 많다.

1) 부사절의 「주어＋be동사」 생략: 부사절의 주어가 주절의 주어와 같을 때

• They were best friends when at school. (학교 다닐 때 그들은 가장 친한 친구였다.)
　　　　　　　　　　　　　　반복되는 they were가 생략됨

2) 「주격 관계대명사＋be동사」의 생략: 주격 관계대명사절의 동사가 be동사일 때

• The girl wearing a hat is Anet. (모자를 쓰고 있는 소녀는 Anet이다.)
　　　　who is가 생략됨

3) to부정사의 to를 제외한 부분 생략

• Edward asked me to call him but I didn't want to.*
　　　　　　　　　　　　　　　반복되는 call him이 생략됨
(Edward는 내게 그에게 전화하라고 요청했지만 나는 그러고 싶지 않았다.)

> **＊대부정사**
> 반복을 피하기 위해 생략되고 남은 to부정사의 to를 '대부정사'라고 한다.

2 강조 – 강조하고자 하는 어구를 문장 맨 앞에 두는 방법 외에, **특정 어구를 덧붙여 문장의 어느 한 부분을 강조**할 수 있다.

1) 「It is／was ~ that …」 강조 구문: **It is／was와 that 사이에** 강조하고자 하는 어구를 두며, 동사를 제외한 **주어, 목적어, 부사구나 부사절**을 강조할 수 있다.

• Kelly damaged my car last night. (Kelly가 어젯밤에 내 차를 망가뜨렸다.)
➡ It was Kelly that[who] damaged my car last night. (어젯밤에 내 차를 망가뜨린 것은 바로 **Kelly**였다.)
　　　　주어 강조, 사람을 강조할 때는 that 대신 who(m)을 쓸 수 있음
➡ It was my car that Kelly damaged last night. (어젯밤에 Kelly가 망가뜨린 것은 바로 **내 차**였다.)
　　　　목적어 강조
➡ It was last night that Kelly damaged my car. (Kelly가 내 차를 망가뜨린 것은 바로 **어젯밤**이었다.)
　　　　부사구 강조

2) do동사를 이용한 강조: 「**do[does]／did＋동사원형**」의 형태로 **동사의 의미를 강조**한다.

• We did go there, but we didn't stay long. (우리는 **정말** 그곳에 **갔지만**, 우리는 오래 머물지 않았다.)
　　　　동사 강조

Check Test

1 밑줄 친 부분을 do 동사를 이용하여 강조하시오.

Language <u>changes</u> lives.

→ _____

2 생략할 수 있는 부분을 찾아 표시하시오.

Since the turn of the twentieth century we've believed in genetic causes of diagnoses — a theory which is called genetic determinism.

3 밑줄 친 부분을 it ~ that 강조 구문을 활용하여 강조하시오.

<u>The principles of gradual exposure</u> are still very useful.

→ _____

4 생략할 수 있는 부분을 찾아 표시하시오.

They can repeat a sequence of steps making up a routine better than steps which are ordered randomly.

R 장문의 이해

[R01~R02] 다음 글을 읽고, 물음에 답하시오.

Paying with plastic fundamentally changes the way we spend money, altering the calculus of our financial decisions. When you buy something with cash, the purchase involves an actual (a) loss — your wallet is 5 literally lighter. Credit cards, however, make the purchase abstract, so that you don't really feel the downside of spending money. Brain-imaging experiments suggest that paying with credit cards actually (b) reduces activity in the 10 insula, a brain region associated with negative feelings. As George Loewenstein, a neuroeconomist at Carnegie Mellon, says, "The nature of credit cards ensures that your brain is anesthetized against the pain of 15 payment." Spending money doesn't feel (c) bad, so you spend more money.

Consider this experiment: Drazen Prelec and Duncan Simester, two business professors at MIT, organized a real-life, sealed-bid auction 20 for tickets to a Boston Celtics game. Half the participants in the auction were informed that they had to pay with cash; the other half were told they had to pay with credit cards. Prelec and Simester then averaged the bids for the 25 two different groups. It turns out that the average credit card bid was *twice* as (d) high as the average cash bid. When people used their credit cards, their bids were much more (e) careful. They no longer felt the need to 30 limit their expenses.

*calculus: 계산법 **anesthetize: 마비시키다 ***bid: 입찰

R01 ★★※ .... 고1 2025(6월)/41

윗글의 제목으로 가장 적절한 것은?

① Once Set, Spending Habits Seldom Change
② Why Do We Spend More with Credit Cards?
③ Credit Cards: A Safer Way to Pay than Cash
④ Paying with Plastic: The Secret to Saving Money
⑤ Using Cash Leads to Taking More Financial Risks

R02 ★★※ .... 고1 2025(6월)/42

밑줄 친 (a)~(e) 중에서 문맥상 낱말의 쓰임이 적절하지 않은 것은? [3점]

① (a)   ② (b)   ③ (c)   ④ (d)   ⑤ (e)

1st 어떤 문제들이 출제되었는지 확인하고, 각 유형의 풀이 방법을 떠올려 보세요.

1) 첫 번째는 제목을 찾는 문제예요.

① Once Set, Spending Habits Seldom Change
한번 형성된 소비 습관은 좀처럼 변하지 않는다

② Why Do We Spend More with Credit Cards?
왜 우리는 신용카드를 사용할 때 더 많이 지출할까?

③ Credit Cards: A Safer Way to Pay than Cash
신용카드: 현금보다 더 안전한 결제 수단

④ Paying with Plastic: The Secret to Saving Money
신용카드 결제: 돈을 절약하는 비결

⑤ Using Cash Leads to Taking More Financial Risks
현금 사용은 더 많은 재정적 위험으로 이어진다

● **제목 찾기 유형은 일단 선택지를 통해 핵심 소재를 파악해야 해요.**
①은 소비 습관에 대한 내용이고, ②, ③, ④은 신용카드, ⑤은 현금에 대한 내용이에요. 주로 결제 수단에 관하여 이야기할 것 같으니, 결제 수단별 특징을 잘 구분하여 정리하면 문제를 푸는 데 큰 도움이 될 거예요.

● **각 선택지가 제목이 될 수 있는 글의 내용을 한번 생각해 볼까요?**
①이 제목이라면 소비 습관이 좀처럼 변하지 않는다는 글이 될 것이고, ②은 신용카드를 사용할 때 지출이 많아지는 경향을 설명할 거예요. ③은 신용카드가 현금보다 더 안전하다는 내용이 전개될 것이고, ④은 신용카드가 절약에 좋다는 내용이 나올 거예요. ⑤은 현금 사용이 더 위험하다는 내용이겠군요.

2) 두 번째는 문맥상 쓰임이 적절하지 않은 낱말을 찾는 문제예요.
제목을 찾는 문제의 선택지에서 짐작한 내용을 단서로 글을 읽으며 두 번째 문제를 먼저 해결하고, 파악한 내용을 통해 첫 번째 문제의 정답을 찾아봅시다.

R02
2nd 글의 세부 사항을 묻는 문제를 먼저 풀면서 글의 내용을 파악하세요.

1) 글의 첫 문장과 (a)부터 살펴봅시다.

Paying with plastic / fundamentally changes the
신용카드로 지불하는 것은 / 우리가 돈을 소비하는 방식을
way we spend money, / altering the calculus / of
근본적으로 바꾸며 / 계산법을 변화시킨다 /
our financial decisions. //
우리의 재정적 결정에 대한 //

● **신용카드 지불의 영향을 소개하네요.**
신용카드 지불은 소비 방식을 근본적으로 바꾸고 재정 결정에 대한 계산법을 변화시킨대요. 우선 제목을 찾는 문제에서 예상한 대로, 신용카드라는 결제 수단의 특징이 먼저 제시되었어요. 뒤에 다른 결제 수단의 특징도 제시되는지 확인해 봅시다.

When you buy something with cash, / the purchase
당신이 무언가를 현금으로 구매할 때 / 그 구매는 실제
involves an actual (a) loss — / your wallet is
손실을 수반한다 / 당신의 지갑이 말 그대로
literally lighter. //
더 가벼워진다 //
Credit cards, however, / make the purchase
하지만, 신용카드는 / 구매를 추상화시켜
abstract, / so that you don't really feel / the
/ 당신은 실제로 느끼지 못한다 /
downside of spending money. //
돈을 소비하는 것의 부정적인 면을 //

● **(a)가 포함된 문장과 그 뒤 문장까지 함께 살펴봅시다.**
무언가를 현금으로 구매하면 지갑 속 화폐가 없어져 더 가벼워지는 실제 (a) 손실을 수반하지만, 신용카드는 구매를 ❶( )시켜서 소비의 부정적인 면을 느끼지 못하게 된대요.
신용카드가 소비의 부정적인 면을 느끼지 못하게 한다는 것을 보면, 신용카드의 단점을 강조하는 글일 것 같은데 뒤의 내용도 이어서 확인해야겠어요.

2) (b)를 이어서 봅시다.

Brain-imaging experiments suggest / that paying
뇌 영상 실험은 보여준다 / 신용카드로
with credit cards / actually (b) reduces activity / in
지불하는 것이 / 실제로 활동을 감소시킨다는 것을 /
the insula, / a brain region associated with negative
뇌섬엽에서의 / 부정적인 감정과 관련된 뇌 영역인 //
feelings. //

● **실험을 예시로 들며 앞 문장을 부연 설명해요.**
신용카드 지불이 부정적인 감정과 관련된 영역인 뇌섬엽의 활동을 실제로 (b) 감소시킨다는 사실이 뇌 영상 실험으로 밝혀졌군요. 소비의 부정적인 면을 느끼지 못한다는 내용의 앞 문장과 일치하는 내용이에요.

3) (c)도 앞의 내용을 뒷받침해요.

Spending money / doesn't feel (c) bad, / so you
돈을 쓰는 것이 / 나쁘게 느껴지지 않는다 / 그래서
spend more money. //
당신은 더 많은 돈을 쓴다 //

● **우리는 어떤 상황에 더 많은 돈을 쓰게 될까요?**
돈을 쓰는 것이 나쁘게 느껴진다면 우리는 돈을 쓰는 것이 꺼려져 많은 돈을 쓰지 않을 거예요. 그런데 앞에서 설명한 것처럼 신용카드가 소비의 부정적인 면을 느끼지 못하게 하기 때문에 돈을 쓰는 것이 (c) 나쁘게 느껴지지 않을 것이고, 따라서 돈을 더 많이 쓰게 되는 거죠.

4) 앞의 내용을 입증하기 위한 경매도 있었대요.

> Half the participants in the auction / were informed
> 경매에 참여한 사람들 중 절반은 / 들었다
> / that they had to pay with cash; / the other half /
> / 현금으로 지불해야 한다는 말을 / 나머지 절반은 /
> were told / they had to pay with credit cards. //
> 들었다 / 신용카드로 지불해야 한다는 말을 //

● **경매 참여자를 두 그룹으로 나누었어요.**

절반은 현금으로, 나머지 절반은 신용카드로 지불해야 한다고
정했군요. 이제 여기서 신용카드 그룹의 사람들이 어떻게 지불하는지
살펴봐야겠죠?

> It turns out / that the average credit card bid / was
> 나타났다 / 평균 신용카드 입찰 금액이 /
> *twice* as (d) high / as the average cash bid. //
> '두 배'만큼 높은 것으로 / 평균 현금 입찰 금액의 //

● **이 결과는 무엇을 의미하나요?**

우리는 앞에서 신용카드 지불이 소비의 **❷(   )** 면을
느끼지 못하게 한다는 점을 계속 확인했어요. 따라서 신용카드 그룹의
사람들은 과소비의 위험을 느끼지 못하고 현금 그룹보다 두 배만큼
(d) 높은 금액을 들이면서도 무모하게 입찰할 수 있던 거예요.

5) 마지막 문장에서 신용카드 소비의 특성을 한 문장으로 정리하는군요.

> When people used their credit cards, / their bids /
> 사람들이 신용카드를 사용할 때 / 그들의 입찰은 /
> were much more (e) careful. //
> 훨씬 더 신중했다 //

● **두 배만큼 높은 금액을 들이는 것이 신중한 건가요?**

아니죠! 오히려 소비의 부정적인 면을 느끼지 못하기 때문에 신중할 수가
없죠.
(d)에서 살펴봤듯이, 신용카드 그룹에서 현금 그룹보다 두 배만큼 높은
금액을 들인 것은 말 그대로 '무모했던' 거예요.
따라서 careful을 reckless(무모한) 등의 어휘로 바꾸는 것이 글의 흐름상
적절해요.

R01

3rd 세부 사항을 묻는 문제를 풀면서 얻은 정보로 글의 제목을 묻는
문제의 정답을 찾으세요.

우리는 선택지를 먼저 보고 글의 소재가 무엇일지를 예상했고, 각 선택지에
맞는 글의 전개 내용을 생각해 봤어요.
신용카드로 소비하면 소비의 부정적인 면을 느끼지 못한다는 점을 반복해서
설명하고, 실제 경매에서도 신용카드를 사용하면 현금을 사용할 때보다
무모하게 소비하게 된다고 했어요.
'왜 우리는 신용카드를 사용할 때 더 많이 지출할까?'라는 질문에 대한 답을
설명하는 글이니까 정답은 **❸(   )**!

▶ 글의 내용을 다시 한번 확인해 보세요.

도입 | 신용카드는 소비 방식을 근본적으로 바꿨음
↓
주제 | 신용카드 사용은 소비의 부정적인 면을 느끼지 못하게 함
↓
부연 | 그에 따라 신용카드를 쓰면 더 무모하게 소비하게 됨

수능 Tip

#동격

> ~ actually (b) reduces activity / in the insula, / a
> ~ 실제로 활동을 감소시킨다 / 뇌섬엽에서의 /
> brain region associated with negative feelings. //
> 부정적인 감정과 관련된 뇌 영역인 //
> As George Loewenstein, / a neuroeconomist at
> George Loewenstein이 / Carnegie Mellon의
> Carnegie Mellon, / says, / ~
> 신경경제학자인 / 말하듯이 / ~

1 같은 대상을 나타내는 두 명사(구)가 콤마로 연결되어 있어요.

두 명사(구)가 같은 대상을 나타내며, 하나의 명사(구)가
다른 명사(구)를 설명하는 관계를 '동격'이라고 해요. 이때
두 명사(구)는 콤마(,)나 전치사 of를 써서 연결해요.

2 뒤의 명사(구)가 앞의 명사(구)를 부연 설명해요.

the insula 뒤에 콤마와 a brain ~ feelings라는
명사구가 쓰여 뇌섬엽이 어떤 기관인지를 설명해요. 또한
George Loewenstein 뒤에 콤마와 a neuroeconomist
at Carnegie Mellon이라는 명사구가 쓰여, 어디에서
어떤 직업을 가진 사람인지를 나타내요.

단어장

R03~04 ▶ 제한시간 4분

[R03~R04] 다음 글을 읽고, 물음에 답하시오.

Some researchers view spoken languages as incomplete devices for capturing precise differences. They think numbers represent the most neutral language of description. However, when our language of description is changed to numbers, we do not move toward greater (a) accuracy. Numbers are no more appropriate 'pictures of the world' than words, music, or painting. While useful for specific purposes (e.g. census taking, income distribution), they (b) include information of enormous value. For example, the future lives of young students are tied to their scores on national tests. In effect, whether they can continue with their education, where, and at what cost depends importantly on a handful of numbers. These numbers do not account for the (c) quality of schools they have attended, whether they have been tutored, have supportive parents, have test anxiety, and so on. Finally, putting aside the many ways in which statistical results can be manipulated, there are ways in which turning people's lives into numbers is (d) morally insulating. Statistics on crime, homelessness, or the spread of a disease say nothing of people's suffering. We read the statistics as reports on events at a distance, thus allowing us to (e) escape without being disturbed. Statistics are human beings with the tears wiped off. Quantify with caution.

*statistical: 통계의 **manipulate: 조작하다 ***insulating: 차단하는

R03 ★★★❀　　　고1 2025(3월)/41

윗글의 제목으로 가장 적절한 것은?

① Numbers Don't Tell Us Everything
② Human Stories Uncovered by the Numbers
③ Data: A Framework for Understanding Humans
④ The Limitations of Language in Conveying Truth
⑤ The Advantages of Quantifying Human Experiences

R04 ★★★　　　고1 2025(3월)/42

밑줄 친 (a)~(e) 중에서 문맥상 낱말의 쓰임이 적절하지 않은 것은? [3점]

① (a)　② (b)　③ (c)　④ (d)　⑤ (e)

구문 서술형

주어진 문장을 읽고 빈칸에 알맞은 말을 쓰시오.

While useful for specific purposes, numbers exclude information of enormous value.

➡ 문장 성분이 생략된 위치: _____

➡ 생략된 내용: _____

R

[R05~R06] 다음 글을 읽고, 물음에 답하시오.

"May I help you?" are the worst four words that a retail salesperson can utter because they don't encourage the customer to talk and put them on the defensive. The four words usually draw out a negative response that stops cold a sales transaction. Examples of (a) <u>better</u> questions to use when approaching customers are "Is there anything in particular that you are looking for?" and "Are you shopping for a gift?" If a fashion salesperson approached you with "May I help you?" chances are you would feel the salesperson didn't (b) <u>care</u>. This line is a rote approach that is so overused by untrained and uninterested salespeople. In fact, most of us shudder in horror on hearing these words. The very meaning of the question "May I help you?" (c) <u>rejects</u> that the customer is in trouble of some sort and needs rescuing. This almost always puts the customer on the defense. "No, thank you" is usually the immediate response, even if the customer is actually in need of assistance. The subconscious thought by the customer is often "I'm smart enough to figure out what I want, and I don't need your help!"

If customers feel pressured or cornered, then salespeople won't make any sales. The approach has to promote a (d) <u>comfortable</u> environment that makes customers feel there is no rush. Furthermore, if customers just want to look around, they should feel that it is all right to do so. In situations where customers really do want to look around on their own, salespeople should give customers their business cards and keep themselves (e) <u>accessible</u> in case customers have questions or concerns.

*shudder: 몸서리치다

R05 ✽✽❀

윗글의 제목으로 가장 적절한 것은?

① Breaking the Ice: Building Trust with Customers
② To Be a Smart Consumer or Not
③ Why "May I Help You?" Fails
④ How "Buy One Get One" Opens Your Wallet
⑤ The Closer to Customers, the More Money You Make

R06 ✽✽✽

밑줄 친 (a)~(e) 중에서 문맥상 낱말의 쓰임이 적절하지 않은 것은? [3점]

① (a)　　② (b)　　③ (c)　　④ (d)　　⑤ (e)

구문 서술형

괄호 안의 조건에 맞게 밑줄 친 부분을 고쳐 쓰고, 해당 부분을 해석하시오.

In situations where customers <u>want</u> to look around on their own, salespeople should keep themselves accessible. (강조하는 조동사를 이용하여 2단어로)

➡ 고친 표현: _____, 해석: _____

From an early age, we assign purpose to objects and events, preferring this reasoning to random chance. Children assume, for instance, that pointy rocks are that way because they don't want you to sit on them. When we encounter something, we first need to (a) <u>determine</u> what sort of thing it is. Inanimate objects and plants generally do not move and can be evaluated from physics alone. However, by attributing intention to animals and even objects, we are able to make fast decisions about the (b) <u>likely</u> behaviour of that being. This was essential in our hunter-gatherer days to avoid being eaten by predators.

The anthropologist Stewart Guthrie made the point that survival in our evolutionary past meant that we interpret ambiguous objects as agents with human mental characteristics, as those are the mental processes which we understand. Ambiguous events are caused by such agents. This results in a perceptual system strongly (c) <u>resistant</u> towards anthropomorphism. Therefore, we tend to assume intention even where there is none. This would have arisen as a survival mechanism. If a lion is about to attack you, you need to react (d) <u>quickly</u>, given its probable intention to kill you. By the time you have realized that the design of its teeth and claws could kill you, you are dead. So, assuming intent, without detailed design analysis or understanding of the physics, has (e) <u>saved</u> your life.

*ambiguous: 모호한 **anthropomorphism: 의인화

R07 ★★★

윗글의 제목으로 가장 적절한 것은? [3점]

① Agency Detection: Inherited from Survival Mechanism
② How Humans' Perceptual System Is Operated for Hunting
③ Hiding Intentions: The Unique Trait of Human Mentality
④ Our Ambiguous Intention Makes Understanding Confusing
⑤ How We Interpret Animate and Inanimate Objects Differently

R08 ★★★

밑줄 친 (a)~(e) 중에서 문맥상 낱말의 쓰임이 적절하지 않은 것은?

① (a)   ② (b)   ③ (c)   ④ (d)   ⑤ (e)

구문 서술형

다음 문장에서 강조하는 어구를 찾고, 문장을 해석하시오.

It is by attributing intention to animals that we can make fast decisions about the likely behaviour of that being.

➡ 강조하는 것: _____

➡ 해석: _____

_____

[R09~R10] 다음 글을 읽고, 물음에 답하시오.

Norms are everywhere, defining what is "normal" and guiding our interpretations of social life at every turn. As a simple example, there is a norm in Anglo society to say *Thank you* to strangers who have just done something to (a) help, such as open a door for you, point out that you've just dropped something, or give you directions. There is no law that forces you to say *Thank you*. But if people don't say *Thank you* in these cases it is marked. People expect that you will say it. You become responsible. (b) Failing to say it will be both surprising and worthy of criticism. Not knowing the norms of another community is the (c) central problem of cross-cultural communication. To continue the *Thank you* example, even though another culture may have an expression that appears translatable (many don't), there may be (d) similar norms for its usage, for example, such that you should say *Thank you* only when the cost someone has caused is considerable. In such a case it would sound ridiculous (i.e., unexpected, surprising, and worthy of criticism) if you were to thank someone for something so (e) minor as holding a door open for you.

R09 ★★★
고1 2024(3월)/41

윗글의 제목으로 가장 적절한 것은?

① Norms: For Social Life and Cultural Communication
② Don't Forget to Say "Thank you" at Any Time
③ How to Be Responsible for Your Behaviors
④ Accept Criticism Without Hurting Yourself
⑤ How Did Diverse Languages Develop?

R10 ★★★
고1 2024(3월)/42

밑줄 친 (a)~(e) 중에서 문맥상 낱말의 쓰임이 적절하지 않은 것은?

① (a)　　② (b)　　③ (c)　　④ (d)　　⑤ (e)

[R11~R12] 다음 글을 읽고, 물음에 답하시오.

All humans, to an extent, seek activities that cause a degree of pain in order to experience pleasure, whether this is found in spicy food, strong massages, or stepping into a too-cold or too-hot bath. The key is that it is a 'safe threat'. The brain perceives the stimulus to be painful but ultimately (a) non-threatening. Interestingly, this could be similar to the way humor works: a 'safe threat' that causes pleasure by playfully violating norms. We feel uncomfortable, but safe. In this context, where (b) survival is clearly not in danger, the desire for pain is actually the desire for a reward, not suffering or punishment. This reward-like effect comes from the feeling of mastery over the pain. The closer you look at your chilli-eating habit, the more remarkable it seems. When the active ingredient of chillies — capsaicin — touches the tongue, it stimulates exactly the same receptor that is activated when any of these tissues are burned. Knowing that our body is firing off danger signals, but that we are actually completely safe, (c) produces pleasure. All children start off hating chilli, but many learn to derive pleasure from it through repeated exposure and knowing that they will never experience any real (d) joy. Interestingly, seeking pain for the pain itself appears to be (e) uniquely human. The only way scientists have trained animals to have a preference for chilli or to self-harm is to have the pain always directly associated with a pleasurable reward.

R11 ★★★
고1 2024(6월)/41

윗글의 제목으로 가장 적절한 것은?

① The Secret Behind Painful Pleasures
② How 'Safe Threat' Changes into Real Pain
③ What Makes You Stronger, Pleasure or Pain?
④ How Does Your Body Detect Danger Signals?
⑤ Recipes to Change Picky Children's Eating Habits

R12 ★★★
고1 2024(6월)/42

밑줄 친 (a)~(e) 중에서 문맥상 낱말의 쓰임이 적절하지 않은 것은?

① (a)　　② (b)　　③ (c)　　④ (d)　　⑤ (e)

[R13~R14] 다음 글을 읽고, 물음에 답하시오.

Higher education has grown from an elite to a mass system across the world. In Europe and the USA, (a) increased rates of participation occurred in the decades after the Second World War. Between 2000 and 2014, rates of participation in higher education almost doubled from 19% to 34% across the world among the members of the population in the school-leaving age category (typically 18—23). The dramatic expansion of higher education has been marked by a wider range of institutions of higher learning and a more diverse demographic of students.

Changes from an elite system to a mass higher education system are associated with political needs to build a (b) specialised workforce for the economy. In theory, the expansion of higher education to develop a highly skilled workforce should diminish the role of examinations in the selection and control of students, initiating approaches to assessment which (c) block lifelong learning: assessment *for* learning and a focus on feedback for development. In reality, socio-political changes to expand higher education have set up a 'field of contradictions' for assessment in higher education. Mass higher education requires efficient approaches to assessment, such as examinations and multiple-choice quizzes, with minimalist, (d) impersonal, or standardised feedback, often causing students to focus more on grades than feedback. In contrast, the relatively small numbers of students in elite systems in the past (e) allowed for closer relationships between students and their teachers, with formative feedback shaping the minds, academic skills, and even the characters of students.

*demographic: 인구집단

R13 ★★★ 고1 2024(9월)/41

윗글의 제목으로 가장 적절한 것은?

① Is It Possible to Teach Without Assessment?
② Elite vs. Public: A History of Modern Class Society
③ Mass Higher Education and Its Reality in Assessment
④ Impacts of Mass Higher Education on Teachers' Status
⑤ Mass Higher Education Leads to Economic Development

R14 ★★★ 고1 2024(9월)/42

밑줄 친 (a)~(e) 중에서 문맥상 낱말의 쓰임이 적절하지 않은 것은? [3점]

① (a) ② (b) ③ (c) ④ (d) ⑤ (e)

[R15~R16] 다음 글을 읽고, 물음에 답하시오.

Early hunter-gatherer societies had (a) minimal structure. A chief or group of elders usually led the camp or village. Most of these leaders had to hunt and gather along with the other members because the surpluses of food and other vital resources were seldom (b) sufficient to support a full-time chief or village council. The development of agriculture changed work patterns. Early farmers could reap 3–10 kg of grain from each 1 kg of seed planted. Part of this food/energy surplus was returned to the community and (c) limited support for nonfarmers such as chieftains, village councils, men who practice medicine, priests, and warriors. In return, the nonfarmers provided leadership and security for the farming population, enabling it to continue to increase food/energy yields and provide ever larger surpluses.

With improved technology and favorable conditions, agriculture produced consistent surpluses of the basic necessities, and population groups grew in size. These groups concentrated in towns and cities, and human tasks (d) specialized further. Specialists such as carpenters, blacksmiths, merchants, traders, and sailors developed their skills and became more efficient in their use of time and energy. The goods and services they provided brought about an (e) improved quality of life, a higher standard of living, and, for most societies, increased stability.

*reap: (농작물을) 베어들이다 **chieftain: 수령, 두목

R15 ★★★ 고1 2023(6월)/41

윗글의 제목으로 가장 적절한 것은?

① How Agriculture Transformed Human Society
② The Dark Shadow of Agriculture: Repetition
③ How Can We Share Extra Food with the Poor?
④ Why Were Early Societies Destroyed by Agriculture?
⑤ The Advantages of Large Groups Over Small Groups in Farming

R16 ★★★ 고1 2023(6월)/42

밑줄 친 (a)~(e) 중에서 문맥상 낱말의 쓰임이 적절하지 않은 것은? [3점]

① (a) ② (b) ③ (c) ④ (d) ⑤ (e)

[R17~R18] 다음 글을 읽고, 물음에 답하시오.

Chess masters shown a chess board in the middle of a game for 5 seconds with 20 to 30 pieces still in play can immediately reproduce the position of the pieces from memory. Beginners, of course, are able to place only a few. Now take the same pieces and place them on the board randomly and the (a) difference is much reduced. The expert's advantage is only for familiar patterns — those previously stored in memory. Faced with unfamiliar patterns, even when it involves the same familiar domain, the expert's advantage (b) disappears.

The beneficial effects of familiar structure on memory have been observed for many types of expertise, including music. People with musical training can reproduce short sequences of musical notation more accurately than those with no musical training when notes follow (c) unusual sequences, but the advantage is much reduced when the notes are ordered randomly. Expertise also improves memory for sequences of (d) movements. Experienced ballet dancers are able to repeat longer sequences of steps than less experienced dancers, and they can repeat a sequence of steps making up a routine better than steps ordered randomly. In each case, memory range is (e) increased by the ability to recognize familiar sequences and patterns.

*expertise: 전문 지식 **sequence: 연속, 순서
***musical notation: 악보

R17 **❀ 　　　　　　　 고1 2023(3월)/41

윗글의 제목으로 가장 적절한 것은?

① How Can We Build Good Routines?
② Familiar Structures Help Us Remember
③ Intelligence Does Not Guarantee Expertise
④ Does Playing Chess Improve Your Memory?
⑤ Creative Art Performance Starts from Practice

R18 *** 　　　　　　　 고1 2023(3월)/42

밑줄 친 (a)~(e) 중에서 문맥상 낱말의 쓰임이 적절하지 않은 것은?

 (a)　 (b)　 (c)　 (d)　 (e)

[R19~R20] 다음 글을 읽고, 물음에 답하시오.

Since the turn of the twentieth century we've believed in genetic causes of diagnoses — a theory called genetic determinism. Under this model, our genes (and subsequent health) are determined at birth. We are "destined" to inherit certain diseases based on the misfortune of our DNA. Genetic determinism doesn't (a) consider the role of family backgrounds, traumas, habits, or anything else within the environment. In this dynamic we are not (b) active participants in our own health and wellness. Why would we be? If something is predetermined, it's not (c) necessary to look at anything beyond our DNA. But the more science has learned about the body and its interaction with the environment around it (in its various forms, from our nutrition to our relationships to our racially oppressive systems), the more (d) simplistic the story becomes. We are not merely expressions of coding but products of a remarkable variety of interactions that are both within and outside of our control. Once we see beyond the narrative that genetics are (e) destiny, we can take ownership of our health. This allows us to see how "choiceless" we once were and empowers us with the ability to create real and lasting change.

*oppressive: 억압적인

R19 *** 　　　　　　　 고1 2021(11월)/41

윗글의 제목으로 가장 적절한 것은?

① Health Is in Our Hands, Not Only in Our Genes
② Genetics: A Solution to Enhance Human Wellness
③ How Did DNA Dominate Over Environment in Biology?
④ Never Be Confident in Your Health, but Keep Checking!
⑤ Why Scientific Innovation Affects Our Social Interactions

R20 ***❀ 　　　　　　　 고1 2021(11월)/42

밑줄 친 (a)~(e) 중에서 문맥상 낱말의 쓰임이 적절하지 않은 것은? [3점]

① (a)　 ② (b)　 ③ (c)　 ④ (d)　 ⑤ (e)

[R21~R22] 다음 글을 읽고, 물음에 답하시오.

Claims that local food production cut greenhouse gas emissions by reducing the burning of transportation fuel are usually not well founded. Transport is the source of only 11 percent of greenhouse gas emissions within the food sector, so reducing the distance that food travels after it leaves the farm is far (a) <u>less</u> important than reducing wasteful energy use on the farm. Food coming from a distance can actually be better for the (b) <u>climate</u>, depending on how it was grown. For example, field-grown tomatoes shipped from Mexico in the winter months will have a smaller carbon footprint than (c) <u>local</u> winter tomatoes grown in a greenhouse. In the United Kingdom, lamb meat that travels 11,000 miles from New Zealand generates only one-quarter the carbon emissions per pound compared to British lamb because farmers in the United Kingdom raise their animals on feed (which must be produced using fossil fuels) rather than on clover pastureland.

When food does travel, what matters most is not the (d) <u>distance</u> traveled but the travel mode (surface versus air), and most of all the load size. Bulk loads of food can travel halfway around the world by ocean freight with a smaller carbon footprint, per pound delivered, than foods traveling just a short distance but in much (e) <u>larger</u> loads. For example, 18-wheelers carry much larger loads than pickup trucks so they can move food 100 times as far while burning only one-third as much gas per pound of food delivered.   *freight: 화물 운송

R21 ★★★❀ 고1 2023(9월)/41

윗글의 제목으로 가장 적절한 것은?

① Shorten the Route, Cut the Cost
② Is Local Food Always Better for the Earth?
③ Why Mass Production Ruins the Environment
④ New Technologies: What Matters in Agriculture
⑤ Reduce Food Waste for a Smaller Carbon Footprint

R22 ★★★ 고1 2023(9월)/42

밑줄 친 (a)~(e) 중에서 문맥상 낱말의 쓰임이 적절하지 않은 것은? [3점]

① (a)　　② (b)　　③ (c)　　④ (d)　　⑤ (e)

[R23~R24] 다음 글을 읽고, 물음에 답하시오.

Like all humans, the first *Homo* species to begin the long difficult process of constructing a language from scratch almost certainly never said entirely what was on their minds. At the same time, these primitive hominins would not have simply made (a) <u>random</u> sounds or gestures. Instead, they would have used means to communicate that they believed others would understand. And they also thought their hearers could "fill in the gaps", and connect their knowledge of their culture and the world to interpret what was uttered.

These are some of the reasons why the (b) <u>origins</u> of human language cannot be effectively discussed unless conversation is placed at the top of the list of things to understand. Every aspect of human language has evolved, as have components of the human brain and body, to (c) <u>engage</u> in conversation and social life. Language did not fully begin when the first hominid uttered the first word or sentence. It began in earnest only with the first conversation, which is both the source and the (d) <u>goal</u> of language. Indeed, language changes lives. It builds society and expresses our highest aspirations, our basest thoughts, our emotions and our philosophies of life. But all language is ultimately at the service of human interaction. Other components of language — things like grammar and stories — are (e) <u>crucial</u> to conversation.

*hominin: 인간의 조상으로 분류되는 종족 **hominid: 사람과(科)의 동물

R23 ★★★❀ 고1 2020(11월)/41

윗글의 제목으로 가장 적절한 것은?

① Various Communication Strategies of Our Ancestors
② Conversation: The Core of Language Development
③ Ending Conversation Without Offending Others
④ How Language Shapes the Way You Think
⑤ What Makes You a Good Communicator?

R24 ★★★ 고1 2020(11월)/42

밑줄 친 (a)~(e) 중에서 문맥상 낱말의 쓰임이 적절하지 않은 것은? [3점]

① (a)　　② (b)　　③ (c)　　④ (d)　　⑤ (e)

[R25~R26] 다음 글을 읽고, 물음에 답하시오.

As kids, we worked hard at learning to ride a bike; when we fell off, we got back on again, until it became second nature to us. But when we try something new in our adult lives we'll usually make just one attempt before judging whether it's (a) worked. If we don't succeed the first time, or if it feels a little awkward, we'll tell ourselves it wasn't a success rather than giving it (b) another shot.

That's a shame, because repetition is central to the process of rewiring our brains. Consider the idea that your brain has a network of neurons. They will (c) connect with each other whenever you remember to use a brain-friendly feedback technique. Those connections aren't very (d) reliable at first, which may make your first efforts a little hit-and-miss. You might remember one of the steps involved, and not the others. But scientists have a saying: "neurons that fire together, wire together." In other words, repetition of an action (e) blocks the connections between the neurons involved in that action. That means the more times you try using that new feedback technique, the more easily it will come to you when you need it.

R25 ★★❀ 고1 2021(3월)/41

윗글의 제목으로 가장 적절한 것은?

① Repeat and You Will Succeed
② Be More Curious, Be Smarter
③ Play Is What Makes Us Human
④ Stop and Think Before You Act
⑤ Growth Is All About Keeping Balance

R26 ★★★ 고1 2021(3월)/42

밑줄 친 (a)~(e) 중에서 문맥상 낱말의 쓰임이 적절하지 않은 것은?

① (a)　　② (b)　　③ (c)　　④ (d)　　⑤ (e)

[R27~R28] 다음 글을 읽고, 물음에 답하시오.

Mike May lost his sight at the age of three. Because he had spent the majority of his life adapting to being blind — and even cultivating a skiing career in this state — his other senses compensated by growing (a) stronger. However, when his sight was restored through a surgery in his forties, his entire perception of reality was (b) disrupted. Instead of being thrilled that he could see now, as he'd expected, his brain was so overloaded with new visual stimuli that the world became a frightening and overwhelming place. After he'd learned to know his family through touch and smell, he found that he couldn't recognize his children with his eyes, and this left him puzzled. Skiing also became a lot harder as he struggled to adapt to the visual stimulation.

This (c) confusion occurred because his brain hadn't yet learned to see. Though we often tend to assume our eyes function as video cameras which relay information to our brain, advances in neuroscientific research have proven that this is actually not the case. Instead, sight is a collaborative effort between our eyes and our brains, and the way we process (d) visual reality depends on the way these two communicate. If communication between our eyes and our brains is disturbed, our perception of reality is altered accordingly. And because other areas of May's brain had adapted to process information primarily through his other senses, the process of learning how to see was (e) easier than he'd anticipated.

R27 ★★★❀ 고1 2022(11월)/41

윗글의 제목으로 가장 적절한 것은?

① Eyes and Brain Working Together for Sight
② Visualization: A Useful Tool for Learning
③ Collaboration Between Vision and Sound
④ How to Ignore New Visual Stimuli
⑤ You See What You Believe

R28 ★★★❀ 고1 2022(11월)/42

밑줄 친 (a)~(e) 중에서 문맥상 낱말의 쓰임이 적절하지 않은 것은?

① (a)　　② (b)　　③ (c)　　④ (d)　　⑤ (e)

[R29~R30] 다음 글을 읽고, 물음에 답하시오.

A ball thrown into the air is acted upon by the initial force given it, persisting as inertia of movement and tending to carry it in the same straight line, and by the constant pull of gravity downward, as well as by the resistance of the air. It moves, accordingly, in a (a) curved path. Now the path does not represent the working of any particular force; there is simply the (b) combination of the three elementary forces mentioned; but in a real sense, there is something in the total action besides the isolated action of three forces, namely, their joint action. In the same way, when two or more human individuals are together, their mutual relationships and their arrangement into a group are things which would not be (c) concealed if we confined our attention to each individual separately. The significance of group behavior is greatly (d) increased in the case of human beings by the fact that some of the tendencies to action of the individual are related definitely to other persons, and could not be aroused except by other persons acting as stimuli. An individual in complete (e) isolation would not reveal their competitive tendencies, their tendencies towards the opposite sex, their protective tendencies towards children. This shows that the traits of human nature do not fully appear until the individual is brought into relationships with other individuals.

*inertia: 관성 **arouse: 유발하다

R29 ★★❀   고1 2023(11월)/41

윗글의 제목으로 가장 적절한 것은?

① Common Misunderstandings in Physics
② Collaboration: A Key to Success in Relationships
③ Interpersonal Traits and Their Impact on Science
④ Unbalanced Forces Causing Objects to Accelerate
⑤ Human Traits Uncovered by Interpersonal Relationships

R30 ★★★   고1 2023(11월)/42

밑줄 친 (a)~(e) 중에서 문맥상 낱말의 쓰임이 적절하지 않은 것은? [3점]

① (a)　　② (b)　　③ (c)　　④ (d)　　⑤ (e)

[R31~R32] 다음 글을 읽고, 물음에 답하시오.

U.K. researchers say a bedtime of between 10 p.m. and 11 p.m. is best. They say people who go to sleep between these times have a (a) lower risk of heart disease. Six years ago, the researchers collected data on the sleep patterns of 80,000 volunteers. The volunteers had to wear a special watch for seven days so the researchers could collect data on their sleeping and waking times. The scientists then monitored the health of the volunteers. Around 3,000 volunteers later showed heart problems. They went to bed earlier or later than the (b) ideal 10 p.m. to 11 p.m. timeframe.

One of the authors of the study, Dr. David Plans, commented on his research and the (c) effects of bedtimes on the health of our heart. He said the study could not give a certain cause for their results, but it suggests that early or late bedtimes may be more likely to disrupt the body clock, with (d) positive consequences for cardiovascular health. He said that it was important for our body to wake up to the morning light, and that the worst time to go to bed was after midnight because it may (e) reduce the likelihood of seeing morning light which resets the body clock. He added that we risk cardiovascular disease if our body clock is not reset properly.

* disrupt: 혼란케 하다 ** cardiovascular: 심장 혈관의

R31 ★★❀   고1 2022(6월)/41

윗글의 제목으로 가장 적절한 것은?

① The Best Bedtime for Your Heart
② Late Bedtimes Are a Matter of Age
③ For Sound Sleep: Turn Off the Light
④ Sleeping Patterns Reflect Personalities
⑤ Regular Exercise: A Miracle for Good Sleep

R32 ★★★   고1 2022(6월)/42

밑줄 친 (a)~(e) 중에서 문맥상 낱말의 쓰임이 적절하지 않은 것은?

① (a)　　② (b)　　③ (c)　　④ (d)　　⑤ (e)

1등급 대비 문제

R33~40 ▶ 제한시간 16분

[R33~R34] 다음 글을 읽고, 물음에 답하시오.

The market's way of telling a firm about its failures is harsh and brief. Not only are complaints less expensive to handle but they also can cause the seller to (a) improve. The seller may learn something as well. I remember a cosmetics company that received complaints about sticky sunblock lotion. At the time, all such lotions were more or less sticky, so the risk of having customers buy products from a rival company was not (b) great. But this was also an opportunity. The company managed to develop a product that was not sticky and captured 20 percent of the market in its first year. Another company had the (c) opposite problem. Its products were not sticky enough. The company was a Royal Post Office in Europe and the product was a stamp. The problem was that the stamp didn't stick to the envelope. Management contacted the stamp producer who made it clear that if people just moistened the stamps properly, they would stick to any piece of paper. What to do? Management didn't take long to come to the conclusion that it would be (d) less costly to try to educate its customers to wet each stamp rather than to add more glue. The stamp producer was told to add more glue and the problem didn't occur again.

Since it is better for the firm to have buyers complain rather than go elsewhere, it is important to make it (e) easier for dissatisfied customers to complain.

*stamp: 우표

R33 ❖ 2등급 대비 _____ 고1 2021(9월)/41

윗글의 제목으로 가장 적절한 것은?

① Designs That Matter the Most to Customers
② Complaints: Why Firms Should Welcome Them
③ Cheap Prices Don't Necessarily Mean Low Quality
④ More Sticky or Less Sticky: An Unsolved Problem
⑤ Treat Your Competitors Like Friends, Not Enemies

R34 ❖ 2등급 대비 _____ 고1 2021(9월)/42

밑줄 친 (a)~(e) 중에서 문맥상 낱말의 쓰임이 적절하지 않은 것은? [3점]

① (a)　　② (b)　　③ (c)　　④ (d)　　⑤ (e)

[R35~R36] 다음 글을 읽고, 물음에 답하시오.

In a society that rejects the consumption of insects there are some individuals who overcome this rejection, but most will continue with this attitude. It may be very (a) difficult to convince an entire society that insects are totally suitable for consumption. However, there are examples in which this (b) reversal of attitudes about certain foods has happened to an entire society. Several examples in the past 120 years from European-American society are: considering lobster a luxury food instead of a food for servants and prisoners; considering sushi a safe and delicious food; and considering pizza not just a food for the rural poor of Sicily. In Latin American countries, where insects are already consumed, a portion of the population hates their consumption and (c) associates it with poverty. There are also examples of people who have had the habit of consuming them and (d) encouraged that habit due to shame, and because they do not want to be categorized as poor or uncivilized. According to Esther Katz, an anthropologist, if the consumption of insects as a food luxury is to be promoted, there would be more chances that some individuals who do not present this habit overcome ideas under which they were educated. And this could also help to (e) revalue the consumption of insects by those people who already eat them.

R35 ⊕ 2등급 대비 _____ 고1 2022(9월)/41

윗글의 제목으로 가장 적절한 것은?

① The More Variety on the Table, The Healthier You Become
② Edible or Not? Change Your Perspectives on Insects
③ Insects: A Key to Solve the World Food Shortage
④ Don't Let Uniqueness in Food Culture Disappear
⑤ Experiencing Various Cultures by Food

R36 ⊕ 2등급 대비 _____ 고1 2022(9월)/42

밑줄 친 (a)~(e) 중에서 문맥상 낱말의 쓰임이 적절하지 않은 것은?

① (a) ② (b) ③ (c) ④ (d) ⑤ (e)

[R37~R38] 다음 글을 읽고, 물음에 답하시오.

The longest journey we will make is the eighteen inches between our head and heart. If we take this journey, it can shorten our (a) misery in the world. Impatience, judgment, frustration, and anger reside in our heads. When we live in that place too long, it makes us (b) unhappy. But when we take the journey from our heads to our hearts, something shifts (c) inside. What if we were able to love everything that gets in our way? What if we tried loving the shopper who unknowingly steps in front of us in line, the driver who cuts us off in traffic, the swimmer who splashes us with water during a belly dive, or the reader who pens a bad online review of our writing?

Every person who makes us miserable is (d) like us — a human being, most likely doing the best they can, deeply loved by their parents, a child, or a friend. And how many times have we unknowingly stepped in front of someone in line? Cut someone off in traffic? Splashed someone in a pool? Or made a negative statement about something we've read? It helps to (e) deny that a piece of us resides in every person we meet.

*reside: (어떤 장소에) 있다

R37 ★ 1등급 대비 _____ 고1 2022(3월)/41

윗글의 제목으로 가장 적절한 것은?

① Why It Is So Difficult to Forgive Others
② Even Acts of Kindness Can Hurt Somebody
③ Time Is the Best Healer for a Broken Heart
④ Celebrate the Happy Moments in Your Everyday Life
⑤ Understand Others to Save Yourself from Unhappiness

R38 ★ 1등급 대비 _____ 고1 2022(3월)/42

밑줄 친 (a)~(e) 중에서 문맥상 낱말의 쓰임이 적절하지 않은 것은?

① (a) ② (b) ③ (c) ④ (d) ⑤ (e)

If you were afraid of standing on balconies, you would start on some lower floors and slowly work your way up to higher ones. It would be easy to face a fear of standing on high balconies in a way that's totally controlled. Socializing is (a) trickier. People aren't like inanimate features of a building that you just have to be around to get used to. You have to interact with them, and their responses can be unpredictable. Your feelings toward them are more complex too. Most people's self-esteem isn't going to be affected that much if they don't like balconies, but your confidence can (b) suffer if you can't socialize effectively.

It's also harder to design a tidy way to gradually face many social fears. The social situations you need to expose yourself to may not be (c) available when you want them, or they may not go well enough for you to sense that things are under control. The progression from one step to the next may not be clear, creating unavoidable large (d) decreases in difficulty from one to the next. People around you aren't robots that you can endlessly experiment with for your own purposes. This is not to say that facing your fears is pointless when socializing. The principles of gradual exposure are still very (e) useful. The process of applying them is just messier, and knowing that before you start is helpful.

R39 ⭐ 1등급 대비 고1 2021(6월)/41

윗글의 제목으로 가장 적절한 것은?

① How to Improve Your Self-Esteem
② Socializing with Someone You Fear: Good or Bad?
③ Relaxation May Lead to Getting Over Social Fears
④ Are Social Exposures Related with Fear of Heights?
⑤ Overcoming Social Anxiety Is Difficult; Try Gradually!

R40 ⭐ 1등급 대비 고1 2021(6월)/42

밑줄 친 (a)~(e) 중에서 문맥상 낱말의 쓰임이 적절하지 않은 것은?

① (a)　　② (b)　　③ (c)　　④ (d)　　⑤ (e)

어휘 Review

✱ 다음 영어는 우리말 뜻을, 우리말은 영어 단어를 〈보기〉에서 찾아 쓰시오.

┌─────────────〈보기〉─────────────┐

개념	morally	인용하다	region
구성하다	average	천성	quantify
말하다	core	효과적으로	minor

└─────────────────────────────┘

01 effectively _____

02 nature _____

03 construct _____

04 utter _____

05 norm _____

06 핵심 _____

07 평균을 내다 _____

08 영역 _____

09 도덕적으로 _____

10 수량화하다 _____

✱ 다음 우리말에 알맞은 영어 표현을 찾아 연결하시오.

11 본격적으로 • • put aside

12 제쳐 두다 • • in earnest

13 ~에 참여하다 • • in return

14 ~에 대한 반응으로 • • engage in

15 처음부터 • • from scratch

✱ 다음 우리말 표현에 맞는 단어를 고르시오.

16 그의 인생의 대부분 ➡ (majority / minority) of his life

17 화장품 회사 ➡ a (cosmetics / cosmology) company

18 최초의 '호모' 종 ➡ the first *Homo* (species / specimen)

19 우리의 가장 높은 열망 ➡ our highest (inspirations / aspirations)

20 더 큰 정확성으로 나아가기 ➡ moving toward greater (accuracy / tendency)

✱ 다음 문장의 빈칸에 알맞은 단어를 〈보기〉에서 찾아 쓰시오.

┌─────────────〈보기〉─────────────┐

typical	inanimate	suffering	minimal
rewiring	domain	evolved	ultimately
predators	carbon	fundamentally	confine

└─────────────────────────────┘

21 범죄 또는 노숙자 문제에 관한 통계는 사람들의 고통에 대해 아무것도 말하지 않는다.
   ➡ Statistics on crime or homelessness say nothing of people's _____.

22 무생물과 식물은 일반적으로 움직이지 않는다.
   ➡ _____ objects and plants generally do not move.

23 우리 뇌를 재연결하는 과정에서 반복이 핵심적이다.
   ➡ Repetition is central to the process of _____ our brains.

24 그것은 같은 익숙한 분야를 포함한다.
   ➡ It involves the same familiar _____.

25 초기 수렵 채집 사회는 최소한의 구조만 가지고 있었다.
   ➡ Early hunter-gatherer societies had _____ structure.

26 인간 언어의 모든 측면은 진화해 왔다.
   ➡ Every aspect of human language has _____.

27 모든 언어는 궁극적으로 인간의 상호 작용을 위한 것이다.
   ➡ All language is _____ at the service of human interaction.

28 포식자에게 잡아먹히는 것을 피하기 위해 이는 필수적이었다.
   ➡ This was essential to avoid being eaten by _____.

29 밭에서 재배된 토마토는 더 적은 탄소 발자국을 가질 것이다.
   ➡ Field-grown tomatoes will have a smaller _____ footprint.

30 신용카드로 지불하는 것은 우리가 돈을 소비하는 방식을 근본적으로 바꾼다.
   ➡ Paying with plastic _____ changes the way we spend money.

복합 문단의 이해

정확해.
이 복합 문단도 글의 순서,
등장인물, 구체적인 줄거리를
파악하며 읽으면 문제가
바로 풀려.

소설 읽을 때
무엇을 파악하며
읽니?

음...
등장인물과
줄거리요!

★ 유형 설명: 3가지 유형의 문제가 출제된다.

순서 배열 글의 흐름에 맞게 순서를 배열하는 문제

● 주어진 글 (A)에 이어질 내용을 순서에 맞게 배열한 것으로
  가장 적절한 것은?

  ① (B) — (D) — (C) ② (C) — (B) — (D)

지칭 추론 가리키는 대상이 다른 한 명을 고르는 문제

● 밑줄 친 (a)~(e) 중에서 가리키는 대상이 나머지 넷과 다른
  것은?

  ① (a) ② (b) ③ (c) ④ (d) ⑤ (e)

내용 불일치 글의 내용과 일치하지 않는 것을 고르는 문제

● 윗글에 관한 내용으로 적절하지 않은 것은?

  ① Jack은 자신의 농장에서 충분한 돈을 벌지 못했다.

유형 풀이 비법

1 순서 배열 문제

• 시간의 흐름 순 배열이
  원칙이다.
• 단, 과거 회상 글의 경우,
  중간에 과거 내용이 나올 수
  있다. (예외)

2 지칭 추론 문제

• 각 선지 앞부분에 특히
  유의한다.

글의
세부 사항을
묻는 문제

3 내용 불일치 문제

• 문단들의 흐름과 무관하게
  (A)~(D)의 순서대로
  선택지가 구성된다.

(Tip) 글의 세부 사항을
묻는 지칭 추론, 내용
불일치 문제를 먼저 풀면서
대략적인 글의 순서를
확인한다.

🔑 어휘 및 표현 Preview

□ spiritual 영적인
□ in the form of ~의 모양으로
□ holy 성스러운
□ lesson 교훈
□ filter out ~을 걸러내다
□ pass through ~을 통과하다
□ spin 짜다 (과거형 spun)
□ cycle 순환
□ guide 인도하다
□ saint 성자
□ guard 경호인
□ reply 답하다
□ despite ~에도 불구하고
□ confess 고백하다
□ tension 긴장

□ solution 해결책
□ request 요청
□ approach 접근하다
□ offer 제안하다
□ call for ~을 시키다
□ gesture 행동
□ take up ~을 차지하다
□ severe 극심한
□ barely 간신히, 겨우
□ tightly 꽉, 단단히
□ hesitate 망설이다
□ flight instructor 비행 교관
□ appreciation 감상
□ patiently 인내심 있게
□ panic 당황하다

□ indication 표시
□ instrument 도구
□ merchant 상인
□ stare at ~을 바라보다
□ a world of 막대한, 엄청난
□ embrace 껴안다
□ compliment 칭찬하다
□ grand 거창한, 웅장한
□ glance 눈길
□ worship 예배하다
□ arrangement 준비
□ accommodation 숙소, 거처
□ qualified 자격이 있는
□ trip over ~에 발이 걸려 넘어지다
□ duty 의무

19 도치
└ 차례나 위치를 서로 바꾸는 것!

1 부정어(구)로 인한 도치 – hardly, little, no, not, not until, scarcely 등의 **부정어**나 only(의미상 부정어)가 강조를 위해 문장 맨 앞으로 **나올 때** 주어와 동사의 도치가 일어난다.

be동사가 쓰인 경우	**부정어(구)+be동사+주어**
	• Seldom (is she) nervous even before the exam.
	주어(she)와 동사(is)가 도치됨 (그녀는 시험 전에도 좀처럼 긴장하지 않는다.)
일반동사가 쓰인 경우	**부정어(구)+do/does/did+주어+동사원형**
	• Hardly (does he attend) the meetings. (그는 회의에 좀처럼 참석하지 않는다.)
	「does + 주어(he) + 동사원형(attend)」으로 도치됨
조동사가 쓰인 경우	**부정어(구)+조동사+주어+동사원형**
	• Never (could I see) him at the party. (나는 파티에서 그를 결코 볼 수 없었다.)
	「조동사(could) + 주어(I) + 동사원형(see)」으로 도치됨

2 〈방향·장소〉를 나타내는 부사(구)나 보어의 강조를 위한 도치

방향의 부사
• Below (is the working schedule). (근무 일정표는 아래와 같습니다.)
　　　 주어(the working schedule)와 동사(is)가 도치됨

• Among the bushes (was a snake). (덤불 사이에 뱀 한 마리가 있었다.)
　 장소의 부사구　　 주어(a snake)와 동사(was)가 도치됨

was의 주격 보어
• Great (was my pleasure). (내 기쁨은 매우 컸다.)
　　 주어(my pleasure)와 동사(was)가 도치됨

3 간접의문문의 어순 – 의문문이 종속절처럼 다른 문장의 일부로 쓰일 때는 「의문사+주어+동사」의 어순이다.

asked의 직접목적어로 쓰인 간접의문문
• Sonya asked me (where Elliot is). (Sonya는 내게 Elliot이 어디에 있는지 물었다.)
　　　　　 「의문사+주어+동사」의 어순

전치사 on의 목적어로 쓰인 간접의문문
• None of this has an impact on (how I treat) others.
　　　　　　　 「의문사+주어+동사」의 어순

(이 중 어느 것도 내가 다른 사람들을 대하는 방식에 영향을 미치지 않는다.)

Check Test

1 다음 문장을 도치 구문으로 알맞게 바꾸어 쓰시오.

She never had anyone doing anything like that.
→ _____

3 괄호 안의 단어를 활용하여 도치 구문을 완성하시오.

The poet wore simple clothes. (scarcely)
→ _____

2 밑줄 친 부분을 어법상 적절하게 바꾸어 쓰시오.

Flying the small plane a student pilot was.
→ _____

4 주어진 단어 중에서 어법상 적절한 것을 고르시오.

On the horse [a wonderful lady sat / sat a wonderful lady].

● 정답
4 sat a wonderful lady
1 Never did she have anyone doing anything like that. **2** was a student pilot **3** Scarcely did the poet wear simple clothes.

[S01~S03] 다음 글을 읽고, 물음에 답하시오.

(A) Long ago, when the world was young, an old Native American spiritual leader Odawa had a dream on a high mountain. In his dream, Iktomi, the great spirit and searcher of wisdom, appeared to (a) him 5 in the form of a spider. Iktomi spoke to him in a holy language.

(B) Odawa shared Iktomi's lesson with (b) his people. Today, many Native Americans have dream catchers hanging above their 10 beds. Dream catchers are believed to filter out bad dreams. The good dreams are captured in the web of life and carried with the people. The bad dreams pass through the hole in the web and are no 15 longer a part of their lives.

(C) When Iktomi finished speaking, he spun a web and gave it to Odawa. He said to Odawa, "The web is a perfect circle with a hole in the center. Use the web to help 20 your people reach their goals. Make good use of their ideas, dreams, and visions. If (c) you believe in the great spirit, the web will catch your good ideas and the bad ones will go through the hole." Right after 25 Odawa woke up, he went back to his village.

(D) Iktomi told Odawa about the cycles of life. (d) He said, "We all begin our lives as babies, move on to childhood, and then to 30 adulthood. Finally, we come to old age, where we must be taken care of as babies

again." Iktomi also told (e) him that there are good and bad forces in each stage of life. "If we listen to the good forces, they 35 will guide us in the right direction. But if we listen to the bad forces, they will lead us the wrong way and may harm us," Iktomi said.

S01 ✱✱✱ .... 고1 2024(3월)/43

주어진 글 (A)에 이어질 내용을 순서에 맞게 배열한 것으로 가장 적절한 것은?

① (B) — (D) — (C)   ② (C) — (B) — (D)
③ (C) — (D) — (B)   ④ (D) — (B) — (C)
⑤ (D) — (C) — (B)

S02 ✱✱✱ .... 고1 2024(3월)/44

밑줄 친 (a)~(e) 중에서 가리키는 대상이 나머지 넷과 다른 것은?

① (a)   ② (b)   ③ (c)   ④ (d)   ⑤ (e)

S03 ✱✱✱ .... 고1 2024(3월)/45

윗글에 관한 내용으로 적절하지 않은 것은?

① Odawa는 높은 산에서 꿈을 꾸었다.
② 많은 미국 원주민은 드림캐처를 현관 위에 건다.
③ Iktomi는 Odawa에게 거미집을 짜서 주었다.
④ Odawa는 잠에서 깨자마자 자신의 마을로 돌아갔다.
⑤ Iktomi는 Odawa에게 삶의 순환에 대해 알려 주었다.

1st 글의 세부 사항을 묻는 일치/불일치 문제를 먼저 풀면서 글의 내용을 대략적으로 확인하세요.

1) 먼저 선택지의 핵심 어구에 □ 표시를 하고, 글에서 찾아야 할 정보가 무엇인지 확인합시다.

> ① Odawa는 높은 산에서 꿈을 꾸었다.
> ② 많은 미국 원주민은 드림캐처를 현관 위에 건다.
> ③ Iktomi는 Odawa에게 거미집을 짜서 주었다.
> ④ Odawa는 잠에서 깨자마자 자신의 마을로 돌아갔다.
> ⑤ Iktomi는 Odawa에게 삶의 순환에 대해 알려 주었다.

● 우리가 찾아야 하는 다섯 가지 정보를 확인했어요.
　① Odawa가 높은 산에서 꿈을 꾸었는지 아닌지,
　② 많은 미국 원주민들이 드림캐처를 현관 위에 거는지 아닌지,
　③ Iktomi가 Odawa에게 거미집을 짜서 주었는지 안 주었는지,
　④ Odawa가 잠에서 깨자마자 자신의 마을로 돌아갔는지 아닌지,
　⑤ Iktomi가 Odawa에게 삶의 순환에 대해 알려주었는지 아닌지를 글을 읽으면서 확인하면 정답을 찾을 수 있어요.

2) 선택지의 일치 여부를 확인할 수 있는 단서는 (A), (B), (C), (D) 문단에 순서대로 제시돼요. ①과 (A) 문단부터 확인해 봅시다.

> Long ago, / when the world was young, / an old
> 오래전　　/ 세상이 생겨난 지 오래지 않을 무렵　　/ 아메리카
> Native American spiritual leader Odawa / had a
> 원주민의 늙은 영적 지도자인 Odawa는　　　　　/ 높은
> dream on a high mountain. //
> 산에서 꿈을 꾸었다　　　//

● had a dream on a high mountain을 찾았나요?
　Odawa는 오래전 세상이 생겨난지 오래지 않을 무렵에 높은 산에서 꿈을 꾸었대요. 따라서 ① 'Odawa는 높은 산에서 꿈을 꾸었다.'는 글의 내용으로 적절해요. ▶ (O)

3) ②의 핵심 단어는 '드림캐처'예요.

> Today, many Native Americans / have dream
> 오늘날 많은 미국 원주민은　　　　　/ 침대 위에
> catchers hanging above their beds. //
> 드림캐처를 건다　　　//

● dream catchers가 보이네요!
　우리는 ② 선택지를 볼 때 드림캐처를 현관 위에 거는지 아닌지를 확인해야 한다고 했어요. 그런데 본문에는 '침대 위에 드림캐처를 건다'라고 나와 있네요? ②에 드림캐처를 거는 위치가 잘못 나타나 있어요. 따라서 ② '많은 미국 원주민은 드림캐처를 현관 위에 건다.'는 글의 내용으로 적절하지 않아요. ▶ (X)
　S03의 정답은 ❶ (　　　　　)이네요.

4) 정답은 찾았지만 ③의 일치 여부도 확인해 봅시다.

> When Iktomi finished speaking, / he spun a web /
> Iktomi가 말을 끝냈을 때　　　　　/ 그는 거미집을 짜서　　/
> and gave it to Odawa. //
> Odawa에게 주었다　　　//

● '거미집'이라는 단어가 있나요?
　Iktomi는 말을 끝내고 Odawa에게 거미집을 짜서 주었다고 했어요. 따라서 ③ 'Iktomi는 Odawa에게 거미집을 짜서 주었다.'는 글의 내용으로 적절해요. ▶ (O)

5) ④도 확인해 볼까요?

> Right after Odawa woke up, / he went back to his
> Odawa는 잠에서 깨자마자　　　/ 자기 마을로 되돌아갔다　　//
> village. //

● Odawa는 잠에서 깨자마자 무엇을 했나요?
　Odawa는 잠에서 깨자마자 자기 마을로 되돌아갔다고 했어요. 따라서 ④ 'Odawa는 잠에서 깨자마자 자기 마을로 돌아갔다.'도 역시 글의 내용으로 적절해요. ▶ (O)

6) 마지막으로 ⑤도 확인해 봅시다.

> Iktomi told Odawa / about the cycles of life. //
> Iktomi는 Odawa에게 말했다 / 삶의 순환에 관해서　　//

● Iktomi가 Odawa에게 말해준 것은 무엇이었나요?
　Iktomi는 Odawa에게 삶의 순환에 관해서 말했다고 했어요. 따라서 ⑤ 'Iktomi는 Odawa에게 삶의 순환에 대해 알려주었다.'는 글의 내용으로 적절해요. ▶ (O)

S02

2nd 글의 맥락을 통해 지칭 추론 문제를 풀고, 다시 한번 글의 내용을 확인하세요.

1) 지칭 추론 문제 역시 (A)부터 읽으며 (a)가 가리키는 대상을 파악해 봅시다.

> Long ago, / when the world was young, / an old
> 오래전　　/ 세상이 생겨난 지 오래지 않을 무렵　　/ 아메리카
> Native American spiritual leader Odawa / had a
> 원주민의 늙은 영적 지도자인 Odawa는　　　　　/ 높은
> dream on a high mountain. //
> 산에서 꿈을 꾸었다　　　//
> In his dream, / Iktomi, the great spirit and searcher
> 자신의 꿈속에서　　/ 위대한 신령이자 지혜의 구도자인 Iktomi가
> of wisdom, / appeared to (a) him in the form of a
> 　　　　/ 거미의 형태로 그에게 나타났다 //
> spider. //

● **Iktomi가 거미의 형태로 나타난 대상인 him은 누구일까요?**

이 글에는 아메리카 원주민의 늙은 영적 지도자인 Odawa와 위대한 신령이자 지혜의 구도자인 Iktomi가 등장해요. Odawa가 꿈을 꾸었고 그 꿈속에서 Iktomi가 거미의 형태로 (a) him에게 나타났던 것이니까 (a)는 Odawa를 가리키는 걸 알 수 있어요. ▶ **(a) him = Odawa**

2) 이제 (b)를 봅시다.

> Odawa shared Iktomi's lesson / with (b) his people. //
> Odawa는 Iktomi의 교훈을 나누었다 / 그의 마을 사람들과 //

● **Odawa가 마을 사람들과 Iktomi의 교훈을 나눈 부분이네요.**

원주민의 영적 지도자인 Odawa가 Iktomi에게서 교훈을 듣고 그의 마을 사람들과 이를 나눈 것이니까, (b)는 Odawa's겠네요. (a)와 (b)가 모두 Odawa이기 때문에 이제 우리는 Iktomi를 지칭하는 것을 찾으면 되겠어요. ▶ **(b) his = Odawa's**

3) (c)가 포함된 문장을 그 앞 문장들과 함께 봅시다.

> He said to Odawa, / "The web is a perfect circle /
> 그가 Odawa에게 말했다 / "그 거미집은 완벽한 원이다 /
>
> with a hole in the center. //
> 가운데 구멍이 뚫린 //
>
> Use the web / to help your people reach their goals. //
> 거미집을 사용해라 / 너의 마을 사람들이 자신들의 목표에 도달할 수 있도록 //
>
> Make good use of their ideas, dreams, and visions. //
> / 그들의 생각, 꿈, 비전을 잘 활용해라 //
>
> If (c) you believe in the great spirit, / the web will
> 만약 네가 위대한 신령을 믿는다면 / 그 거미집이 네 좋은
>
> catch your good ideas / and the bad ones will go
> 생각을 붙잡아 줄 것이고 / 나쁜 생각은 구멍을 통해 빠져 나갈
>
> through the hole." //
> 것이다"라고 //

● **Odawa의 꿈속에서 Iktomi가 교훈을 알려주는 상황이에요.**

Iktomi는 (c) you가 위대한 신령을 믿는다면 거미집이 좋은 생각을 붙잡고 나쁜 생각은 빠져나가게 할 것이라고 했어요. Odawa에게 교훈을 알려주는 것이니까 (c)는 Odawa겠네요. ▶ **(c) you = Odawa**

4) (d)가 나오는 부분도 봅시다.

> Iktomi told Odawa / about the cycles of life. //
> Iktomi는 Odawa에게 말했다 / 삶의 순환에 관해서 //
>
> (d) He said, / "We all begin our lives as babies, /
> 그는 말했다 / "우리는 모두 아기로 삶을 출발하고 /
>
> move on to childhood, and then to adulthood. //
> 유년기를 거쳐 그다음 성년기에 이르게 된다 //

● **삶의 순환에 관해서 Odawa에게 말하는 사람은 누구인가요?**

Iktomi가 Odawa에게 삶의 순환에 관하여 말하고 있어요. Odawa에게 이어서 이야기를 하는 (d) He는 Iktomi를 가리키네요! 따라서 Odawa가 아닌 Iktomi를 가리키는 (d)가 정답이에요. ▶ **(d) He = Iktomi**

S02의 정답은 ❷( )이네요.

5) 마지막 (e)를 봅시다.

> Iktomi also told (e) him / that there are good and
> 또한 Iktomi는 그에게 말했다 / 좋고 나쁜 힘이 있다고
>
> bad forces / in each stage of life. //
> / 삶의 각 단계에는 //

● **Iktomi가 Odawa에게 교훈을 알려주고 있어요.**

Iktomi가 계속 교훈을 알려주는 대상인 (e) him은 마찬가지로 Odawa가 맞네요. ▶ **(e) him = Odawa**

(S01)

3rd 파악한 세부 사항을 활용하여 각 문단의 내용을 요약하고, 순서를 맞춰 보세요.

1) 두 문제를 풀면서 파악한 세부 사항과 순서를 암시하는 연결어, 대명사, 지시어 등을 토대로 각 문단을 요약해 봅시다.

> (A) 문단 Odawa가 산에서 꿈을 꾸었고 Iktomi가 나타나서 성스러운 언어로 말함
>
> (B) 문단 Odawa는 Iktomi의 교훈을 부족(his people = Odawa의 마을에 사는 사람들)에 전했음, 오늘날 많은 미국 원주민들은 드림캐처를 침대 위에 걸어둠
>
> (C) 문단 Iktomi가 말을 마치고(finished speaking) 거미집을 짜서 Odawa에게 주었고 거미집의 용도를 설명함, Odawa는 꿈에서 깨자마자 그의 마을로 돌아감(went back to his village)
>
> (D) 문단 Iktomi가 Odawa에게 삶의 순환에 관하여 말했음 (Iktomi told Odawa)

2) 이제 선택지에서 정답을 골라봅시다.

(A) Odawa는 산에서 꿈을 꾸었고 Iktomi가 나타나 성스러운 언어로 말했죠.

(D) Iktomi가 Odawa에게 삶의 순환에 관하여 말했어요.

(C) Iktomi가 말을 마친 후에 거미집을 짜서 Odawa에게 주었고 거미집의 용도를 설명했죠. Odawa는 꿈에서 깨자마자 그의 마을로 돌아갔어요.

(B) Odawa는 Iktomi의 교훈을 부족에 전하였고, 오늘날 많은 미국 원주민들은 나쁜 꿈을 걸러내고 좋은 꿈을 담는 드림캐처를 침대 위에 걸어두죠.

따라서 글의 순서로 가장 적절한 것은 (D) — (C) — (B)로, S01의 정답은 ❸( )이에요.

S04~06 ▶ 제한시간 6분

[S04~S06] 다음 글을 읽고, 물음에 답하시오.

(A) Jack, an Arkansas farmer, was unhappy because he couldn't make enough money from his farm. He worked hard for many years, but things didn't improve. He sold his farm to his neighbor, Victor, who was by no means wealthy. Hoping for a fresh start, he left for the big city to find better opportunities. Years passed, but Jack still couldn't find the fortune he was looking for. Tired and broke, (a) he returned to the area where his old farm was.

*broke: 무일푼의

(B) "How did you do all this?" he asked. And he continued, "When you bought the farm, you barely had any money. How did you get so rich?" Victor smiled and said, "I owe it all to (b) you. There were diamonds on this land — acres and acres of diamonds! I got rich because I discovered those diamonds." "Diamonds?" Jack said in disbelief. And he said, "I knew every part of that land, and there were no diamonds!"

*acres of: 대량의

(C) Victor reached into his pocket and carefully pulled out something small and shiny. Holding it between (c) his fingers, he let it catch the light. He said, "This is a diamond." Jack was amazed and said, "I saw so many rocks like that and thought they were useless. They made farming so hard!" Victor laughed and said, "(d) You didn't know what diamonds look like. Sometimes, treasures are hidden right in front of us."

(D) One day, he drove past his old land and was shocked by what he saw. Victor, the man who had bought the farm with very little money, now seemed to be living a life of great success. He had torn down the farmhouse and built a massive house in its place. New buildings, trees, and flowers adorned the well-kept property. Jack could hardly believe that (e) he had ever worked on this same land. Curious, he stopped to talk to Victor.

*adorn: 꾸미다

S04 ★★❀ 고1 2025(3월)/43

주어진 글 (A)에 이어질 내용을 순서에 맞게 배열한 것으로 가장 적절한 것은?

① (B) — (D) — (C)   ② (C) — (B) — (D)
③ (C) — (D) — (B)   ④ (D) — (B) — (C)
⑤ (D) — (C) — (B)

S05 ★★❀ 고1 2025(3월)/44

밑줄 친 (a)~(e) 중에서 가리키는 대상이 나머지 넷과 다른 것은?

① (a)   ② (b)   ③ (c)   ④ (d)   ⑤ (e)

S06 ★★❀ 고1 2025(3월)/45

윗글에 관한 내용으로 적절하지 않은 것은?

① Jack은 자신의 농장에서 충분한 돈을 벌지 못했다.
② Jack은 자신의 이웃인 Victor에게서 농장을 샀다.
③ Victor는 다이아몬드를 발견해서 부자가 되었다.
④ Victor는 자신의 주머니에서 작고 반짝이는 것을 꺼냈다.
⑤ Victor는 농가가 있던 자리에 거대한 집을 지었다.

구문 서술형

괄호 안의 조건에 맞게 문장을 알맞게 바꿔 쓰시오.

He was never happy because he couldn't make enough money from his farm.

(부정어 Never가 문장 맨 앞에 오는 도치 구문으로)

➡ _____

_____

[S07~S09] 다음 글을 읽고, 물음에 답하시오.

(A) The sun shone in the cloudless sky as Becky, a retired teacher, walked to the fruit market. Across town, Dana was riding a bus towards the museum for a job interview. Just before reaching her stop, Dana noticed the sky had suddenly darkened. Her heart sank — she had no umbrella. As (a) she stepped off the bus next to the market, where Becky had just finished shopping, raindrops began to fall.

(B) Dana thanked her, took the umbrella, and opened it. She saw a small card tied to the handle. It read: "Cover each other." She was touched by the message. She hurried to the museum, arriving dry and comfortable, and performed well in her interview. The Museum CEO was impressed by Dana and offered (b) her the Event Manager position, her dream job. Throughout the years ahead, she often thought back to Becky's kind gesture.

(C) Inspired by the memory, Dana created a museum event called "Cover Each Other" with paintings of people supporting others. She donated half of the money from ticket sales to families who lost their homes to natural disasters. Dana kept Becky's message framed in (c) her office as a reminder that one kind gesture could change someone's life. The kindness of one stranger had shaped her path, and she made sure it continued to shape the world.

(D) Dana felt panic. She didn't want to show up to her interview soaked. She looked around but couldn't find any stores nearby to buy an umbrella, and she didn't have time to search around. Just then, Becky approached (d) her, holding an open umbrella in one hand and a closed one in the other. "Take this," (e) she said with a smile. Dana's eyes widened. "Are you sure?" Becky nodded. "I always carry an extra on rainy days."

*soaked: 흠뻑 젖은

S07 ✽❀❀   고1 2025(6월)/43

주어진 글 (A)에 이어질 내용을 순서에 맞게 배열한 것으로 가장 적절한 것은?

① (B) — (D) — (C)   ② (C) — (B) — (D)
③ (C) — (D) — (B)   ④ (D) — (B) — (C)
⑤ (D) — (C) — (B)

S08 ✽✽❀   고1 2025(6월)/44

밑줄 친 (a)~(e) 중에서 가리키는 대상이 나머지 넷과 다른 것은?

① (a)   ② (b)   ③ (c)   ④ (d)   ⑤ (e)

S09 ✽✽✽   고1 2025(6월)/45

윗글에 관한 내용으로 적절하지 않은 것은?

① Becky는 과일 시장으로 걸어갔다.
② 작은 카드는 Dana가 받은 우산 손잡이에 매여 있었다.
③ Dana는 Becky의 친절한 행동을 종종 떠올렸다.
④ Dana는 티켓 판매금 전액을 기부했다.
⑤ Dana는 우산을 구매할 가게를 찾을 수 없었다.

구문 서술형

주어진 우리말을 참고하여, 틀린 부분을 찾아 밑줄을 긋고 바르게 고치시오.

그녀는 면접에 흠뻑 젖어서 나타나고 싶지 않았다.

➡ Never was she want to show up to her interview soaked.

➡ 고친 표현: _____

[S10~S12] 다음 글을 읽고, 물음에 답하시오.

(A) While the cafeteria was full of high school students on that afternoon, Dave was thirsty. We sat near yet away from him, fixing our hair and worrying about the test next period we hadn't studied for. (a) He was far away from our world, yet forced to be a part of it.

(B) Although it was clear that they were from very different worlds, for one moment, they'd shared a real understanding. As I walked away from my lunch table that day, I looked at Dave. I thought he and the dollar were very much alike. They both weren't accepted where the world said they were supposed to be. But just as the dollar had found a place in a warm-hearted senior's pocket, I was sure (b) he would eventually find his, too.

(C) But for some reason, he decided against it. He wasn't leaving until he got a drink. With a determined expression, (c) he kept aimlessly pushing the dollar bill into the machine. Just then a popular senior boy stood up from his seat, and walked over to the boy. (d) He calmly explained how the machine often had trouble accepting dollar bills. After that, he pulled some coins from his pocket and put them into the machine. Dave gave him his dollar and chose a flavor of fruit juice. Then the two walked off in different directions.

(D) He stood at the drink machine with purpose, fumbling through his fake leather wallet for some change. He came up with a wrinkled dollar bill, and nervously glanced back at his table where other students in (e) his class were sitting. Dave tried to make the machine accept his money. After he failed a few times, some students began to laugh at him. He started shaking, and tears began to form in his eyes. I saw him turn to sit down, looking like he had given up.   *fumble: 더듬어 찾다

S10 ❋❋❋ 고1 2025(9월)/43

주어진 글 (A)에 이어질 내용을 순서에 맞게 배열한 것으로 가장 적절한 것은?

① (B) — (D) — (C)   ② (C) — (B) — (D)
③ (C) — (D) — (B)   ④ (D) — (B) — (C)
⑤ (D) — (C) — (B)

S11 ❋❋❋ 고1 2025(9월)/44

밑줄 친 (a)~(e) 중에서 가리키는 대상이 나머지 넷과 다른 것은?

① (a)   ② (b)   ③ (c)   ④ (d)   ⑤ (e)

S12 ❋❋❋ 고1 2025(9월)/45

윗글에 관한 내용으로 적절하지 않은 것은?

① 그날 오후 식당은 고등학생들로 가득 찼다.
② 'I'는 Dave와 그 달러가 비슷하다고 생각했다.
③ 상급생은 주머니에서 동전을 꺼냈다.
④ Dave와 상급생은 같은 방향으로 떠났다.
⑤ Dave의 눈에 눈물이 맺히기 시작했다.

구문 서술형

주어진 우리말과 일치하도록 괄호 안의 단어를 이용하여 문장을 완성하시오. (필요시 형태를 바꿀 것)

그는 자판기가 왜 지폐를 잘 인식하지 못하는지 차분히 설명해 주었다.

(accept, have trouble, the machine, dollar bills, why)

➡ He calmly explained _____
_____.

[S13~S15] 다음 글을 읽고, 물음에 답하시오.

(A) An airplane flew high above the deep blue seas far from any land. Flying the small plane was a student pilot who was sitting alongside an experienced flight instructor. As the student looked out the window, (a) she was filled with wonder and appreciation for the beauty of the world. Her instructor, meanwhile, waited patiently for the right time to start a surprise flight emergency training exercise.

(B) Then, the student carefully flew low enough to see if she could find any ships making their way across the surface of the ocean. Now the instructor and the student could see some ships. Although the ships were far apart, they were all sailing in a line. With the line of ships in view, the student could see the way to home and safety. The student looked at (b) her in relief, who smiled proudly back at her student.

(C) When the student began to panic, the instructor said, "Stay calm and steady. (c) You can do it." Calm as ever, the instructor told her student, "Difficult times always happen during flight. The most important thing is to focus on your flight in those situations." Those words encouraged the student to focus on flying the aircraft first. "Thank you, I think (d) I can make it," she said, "As I've been trained, I should search for visual markers."

(D) When the plane hit a bit of turbulence, the instructor pushed a hidden button. Suddenly, all the monitors inside the plane flashed several times then went out completely! Now the student was in control of an airplane that was flying well, but (e) she had no indication of where she was or where she should go. She did have a map, but no other instruments. She was at a loss and then the plane shook again.

*turbulence: 난(亂)기류

S13 ✿✿✾

주어진 글 (A)에 이어질 내용을 순서에 맞게 배열한 것으로 가장 적절한 것은?

① (B) — (D) — (C)   ② (C) — (B) — (D)
③ (C) — (D) — (B)   ④ (D) — (B) — (C)
⑤ (D) — (C) — (B)

S14 ✿✿✿

밑줄 친 (a)~(e) 중에서 가리키는 대상이 나머지 넷과 다른 것은?

① (a)   ② (b)   ③ (c)   ④ (d)   ⑤ (e)

S15 ✿✿✿

윗글에 관한 내용으로 적절하지 않은 것은?

① 교관과 교육생이 소형 비행기에 타고 있었다.
② 배들은 서로 떨어져 있었지만 한 줄을 이루고 있었다.
③ 교관은 어려운 상황에서는 집중이 가장 중요하다고 말했다.
④ 비행기 내부의 모니터가 깜박이다가 다시 정상 작동했다.
⑤ 교육생은 지도 이외의 다른 도구는 가지고 있지 않았다.

[S16~S18] 다음 글을 읽고, 물음에 답하시오.

(A) Once upon a time in the Iranian city of Shiraz, there lived the famous poet Sheikh Saadi. Like most other poets and philosophers, he led a very simple life. A rich merchant of Shiraz was preparing for his daughter's wedding and invited (a) <u>him</u> along with a lot of big businessmen of the town. The poet accepted the invitation and decided to attend.

(B) The host personally led the poet to his seat and served out chicken soup to him. After a moment, the poet suddenly dipped the corner of his coat in the soup as if he fed it. All the guests were now staring at (b) <u>him</u> in surprise. The host said, "Sir, what are you doing?" The poet very calmly replied, "Now that I have put on expensive clothes, I see a world of difference here. All that I can say now is that this feast is meant for my clothes, not for me."

(C) Seeing all this, the poet quietly left the party and went to a shop where he could rent clothes. There he chose a richly decorated coat, which made him look like a new person. With this coat, he entered the party and this time was welcomed with open arms. The host embraced him as (c) <u>he</u> would do to an old friend and complimented him on the clothes he was wearing. The poet did not say a word and allowed the host to lead (d) <u>him</u> to the dining room.

(D) On the day of the wedding, the rich merchant, the host of the wedding, was receiving the guests at the gate. Many rich people of the town attended the wedding. They had come out in their best clothes. The poet wore simple clothes which were neither grand nor expensive. He waited for someone to approach him but no one gave (e) <u>him</u> as much as even a second glance. Even the host did not greet him and looked away.

S16 ✱✱✱
고1 2024(9월)/43

주어진 글 (A)에 이어질 내용을 순서에 맞게 배열한 것으로 가장 적절한 것은?

① (B) — (D) — (C)　　② (C) — (B) — (D)
③ (C) — (D) — (B)　　④ (D) — (B) — (C)
⑤ (D) — (C) — (B)

S17 ✱✱✱
고1 2024(9월)/44

밑줄 친 (a)~(e) 중에서 가리키는 대상이 나머지 넷과 다른 것은?

① (a)　② (b)　③ (c)　④ (d)　⑤ (e)

S18 ✱✱✱
고1 2024(9월)/45

윗글에 관한 내용으로 적절하지 않은 것은?

① 시인은 상인의 초대를 받아들였다.
② 상인은 시인의 외투 자락을 수프에 담갔다.
③ 시인은 옷을 빌릴 수 있는 가게로 갔다.
④ 결혼식 날 상인은 입구에서 손님을 맞이했다.
⑤ 마을의 많은 부유한 사람들이 결혼식에 참석했다.

[S19~S21] 다음 글을 읽고, 물음에 답하시오.

(A) A boy had a place at the best school in town. In the morning, his granddad took him to the school. When (a) he went onto the playground with his grandson, the children surrounded them. "What a funny old man," one boy smirked. A girl with brown hair pointed at the pair and jumped up and down. Suddenly, the bell rang and the children ran off to their first lesson.
*smirk: 히죽히죽 웃다

(B) In some schools the children completely ignored the old man and in others, they made fun of (b) him. When this happened, he would turn sadly and go home. Finally, he went onto the tiny playground of a very small school, and leant against the fence, exhausted. The bell rang, and the crowd of children ran out onto the playground. "Sir, are you all right? Shall I bring you a glass of water?" a voice said. "We've got a bench in the playground — come and sit down," another voice said. Soon a young teacher came out onto the playground.

(C) The old man greeted (c) him and said: "Finally, I've found my grandson the best school in town." "You're mistaken, sir. Our school is not the best — it's small and cramped." The old man didn't argue with the teacher. Instead, he made arrangements for his grandson to join the school, and then the old man left. That evening, the boy's mom said to (d) him: "Dad, you can't even read. How do you know you've found the best teacher of all?" "Judge a teacher by his pupils," the old man replied.
*cramped: 비좁은

(D) The old man took his grandson firmly by the hand, and led him out of the school gate. "Brilliant, I don't have to go to school!" the boy exclaimed. "You do, but not this one," his granddad replied. "I'll find you a school myself." Granddad took his grandson back to his own house, asked grandma to look after him, and went off to look for a teacher (e) himself. Every time he spotted a school, the old man went onto the playground, and waited for the children to come out at break time.

S19 ✽✽✽✤

주어진 글 (A)에 이어질 내용을 순서에 맞게 배열한 것으로 가장 적절한 것은?

① (B) — (D) — (C)   ② (C) — (B) — (D)
③ (C) — (D) — (B)   ④ (D) — (B) — (C)
⑤ (D) — (C) — (B)

S20 ✽✽✽✤

밑줄 친 (a)~(e) 중에서 가리키는 대상이 나머지 넷과 다른 것은?

① (a)   ② (b)   ③ (c)   ④ (d)   ⑤ (e)

S21 ✽✽✽✤

윗글에 관한 내용으로 적절하지 <u>않은</u> 것은?

① 갈색 머리 소녀가 노인과 소년을 향해 손가락질했다.
② 노인은 지쳐서 울타리에 기댔다.
③ 노인은 선생님과 논쟁을 벌였다.
④ 노인은 글을 읽을 줄 몰랐다.
⑤ 소년은 학교에 가지 않아도 된다고 소리쳤다.

[S22~S24] 다음 글을 읽고, 물음에 답하시오.

(A) On my daughter Marie's 8th birthday, she received a bunch of presents from her friends at school. That evening, with her favorite present, a teddy bear, in her arms, we went to a restaurant to celebrate her birthday. Our server, a friendly woman, noticed my daughter holding the teddy bear and said, "My daughter loves teddy bears, too." Then, we started chatting about (a) her family.

(B) When Marie came back out, I asked her what she had been doing. She said that she gave her teddy bear to our server so that she could give it to (b) her daughter. I was surprised at her sudden action because I could see how much she loved that bear already. (c) She must have seen the look on my face, because she said, "I can't imagine being stuck in a hospital bed. I just want her to get better soon."

(C) I felt moved by Marie's words as we walked toward the car. Then, our server ran out to our car and thanked Marie for her generosity. The server said that (d) she had never had anyone doing anything like that for her family before. Later, Marie said it was her best birthday ever. I was so proud of her empathy and warmth, and this was an unforgettable experience for our family.

(D) The server mentioned during the conversation that her daughter was in the hospital with a broken leg. (e) She also said that Marie looked about the same age as her daughter. She was so kind and attentive all evening, and even gave Marie cookies for free. After we finished our meal, we paid the bill and began to walk to our car when unexpectedly Marie asked me to wait and ran back into the restaurant.

S22
❀❀❀ ─────────────────────── 고1 2022(11월)/43

주어진 글 (A)에 이어질 내용을 순서에 맞게 배열한 것으로 가장 적절한 것은?

① (B) — (D) — (C) ② (C) — (B) — (D)
③ (C) — (D) — (B) ④ (D) — (B) — (C)
⑤ (D) — (C) — (B)

S23
❀❀❀ ─────────────────────── 고1 2022(11월)/44

밑줄 친 (a)~(e) 중에서 가리키는 대상이 나머지 넷과 다른 것은?

① (a) ② (b) ③ (c) ④ (d) ⑤ (e)

S24
❀❀❀ ─────────────────────── 고1 2022(11월)/45

윗글에 관한 내용으로 적절하지 않은 것은?

① Marie는 테디 베어를 팔에 안고 식당에 갔다.
② 'I'는 Marie의 갑작스러운 행동에 놀랐다.
③ 종업원은 Marie의 관대함에 고마워했다.
④ 종업원은 자신의 딸이 팔이 부러져서 병원에 있다고 말했다.
⑤ 종업원은 Marie에게 쿠키를 무료로 주었다.

[S25~S27] 다음 글을 읽고, 물음에 답하시오.

(A) A nurse took a tired, anxious soldier to the bedside. "Jack, your son is here," the nurse said to an old man lying on the bed. She had to repeat the words several times before the old man's eyes opened. Suffering from the severe pain because of heart disease, he barely saw the young uniformed soldier standing next to him. (a) He reached out his hand to the soldier.

(B) Whenever the nurse came into the room, she heard the soldier say a few gentle words. The old man said nothing, only held tightly to (b) him all through the night. Just before dawn, the old man died. The soldier released the old man's hand and left the room to find the nurse. After she was told what happened, she went back to the room with him. The soldier hesitated for a while and asked, "Who was this man?"

(C) She was surprised and asked, "Wasn't he your father?" "No, he wasn't. I've never met him before," the soldier replied. She asked, "Then why didn't you say something when I took you to (c) him?" He said, "I knew there had been a mistake, but when I realized that he was too sick to tell whether or not I was his son, I could see how much (d) he needed me. So, I stayed."

(D) The soldier gently wrapped his fingers around the weak hand of the old man. The nurse brought a chair so that the soldier could sit beside the bed. All through the night the young soldier sat there, holding the old man's hand and offering (e) him words of support and comfort. Occasionally, she suggested that the soldier take a rest for a while. He politely said no.

S25 ✽✽✽ 고1 2023(6월)/43

주어진 글 (A)에 이어질 내용을 순서에 맞게 배열한 것으로 가장 적절한 것은?

① (B) — (D) — (C)　　② (C) — (B) — (D)
③ (C) — (D) — (B)　　④ (D) — (B) — (C)
⑤ (D) — (C) — (B)

S26 ✽✽✽ 고1 2023(6월)/44

밑줄 친 (a)~(e) 중에서 가리키는 대상이 나머지 넷과 다른 것은?

① (a)　　② (b)　　③ (c)　　④ (d)　　⑤ (e)

S27 ✽✽✽ 고1 2023(6월)/45

윗글에 관한 내용으로 적절하지 않은 것은?

① 노인은 심장병으로 극심한 고통을 겪고 있었다.
② 군인은 간호사를 찾기 위해 병실을 나갔다.
③ 군인은 노인과 이전에 만난 적이 있다고 말했다.
④ 간호사는 군인이 앉을 수 있도록 의자를 가져왔다.
⑤ 군인은 잠시 쉬라는 간호사의 제안을 정중히 거절하였다.

[S40~S42] 다음 글을 읽고, 물음에 답하시오.

(A) Once upon a time, there was a king who lived in a beautiful palace. While the king was away, a monster approached the gates of the palace. The monster was so ugly and smelly that the guards froze in shock. He passed the guards and sat on the king's throne. The guards soon came to their senses, went in, and shouted at the monster, demanding that (a) <u>he</u> get off the throne.
*throne: 왕좌

(B) Eventually the king returned. He was wise and kind and saw what was happening. He knew what to do. He smiled and said to the monster, "Welcome to my palace!" He asked the monster if (b) <u>he</u> wanted a cup of coffee. The monster began to grow smaller as he drank the coffee.

(C) The king offered (c) <u>him</u> some take-out pizza and fries. The guards immediately called for pizza. The monster continued to get smaller with the king's kind gestures. (d) <u>He</u> then offered the monster a full body massage. As the guards helped with the relaxing massage, the monster became tiny. With another act of kindness to the monster, he just disappeared.

(D) With each bad word the guards used, the monster grew more ugly and smelly. The guards got even angrier — they began to brandish their swords to scare the monster away from the palace. But (e) <u>he</u> just grew bigger and bigger, eventually taking up the whole room. He grew more ugly and smelly than ever.
*brandish: 휘두르다

S40 ✽❀❀ 고1 2023(3월)/43

주어진 글 (A)에 이어질 내용을 순서에 맞게 배열한 것으로 가장 적절한 것은?

① (B) — (D) — (C) ② (C) — (B) — (D)
③ (C) — (D) — (B) ④ (D) — (B) — (C)
⑤ (D) — (C) — (B)

S41 ✽❀❀ 고1 2023(3월)/44

밑줄 친 (a)~(e) 중에서 가리키는 대상이 나머지 넷과 다른 것은?

① (a) ② (b) ③ (c) ④ (d) ⑤ (e)

S42 ✽❀❀ 고1 2023(3월)/45

윗글에 관한 내용으로 적절하지 <u>않은</u> 것은?

① 왕이 없는 동안 괴물이 궁전 문으로 접근했다.
② 왕은 미소를 지으며 괴물에게 환영한다고 말했다.
③ 왕의 친절한 행동에 괴물의 몸이 계속 더 작아졌다.
④ 경비병들은 괴물을 마사지해 주기를 거부했다.
⑤ 경비병들은 겁을 주어 괴물을 쫓아내려 했다.

S43~48 ▶ 제한시간 12분

[S43~S45] 다음 글을 읽고, 물음에 답하시오.

(A) One day a young man was walking along a road on his journey from one village to another. As he walked he noticed a monk working in the fields. The young man turned to the monk and said, "Excuse me. Do you mind if I ask (a) you a question?" "Not at all," replied the monk.

*monk: 수도승

(B) A while later a middle-aged man journeyed down the same road and came upon the monk. "I am going to the village in the valley," said the man. "Do you know what it is like?" "I do," replied the monk, "but first tell (b) me about the village where you came from." "I've come from the village in the mountains," said the man. "It was a wonderful experience. I felt as though I was a member of the family in the village."

(C) "I am traveling from the village in the mountains to the village in the valley and I was wondering if (c) you knew what it is like in the village in the valley." "Tell me," said the monk, "what was your experience of the village in the mountains?" "Terrible," replied the young man. "I am glad to be away from there. I found the people most unwelcoming. So tell (d) me, what can I expect in the village in the valley?" "I am sorry to tell you," said the monk, "but I think your experience will be much the same there." The young man lowered his head helplessly and walked on.

(D) "Why did you feel like that?" asked the monk. "The elders gave me much advice, and people were kind and generous. I am sad to have left there. And what is the village in the valley like?" he asked again. "(e) I think you will find it much the same," replied the monk. "I'm glad to hear that," the middle-aged man said smiling and journeyed on.

S43　⭐ 2등급 대비　　　　　　고1 2022(3월)/43

주어진 글 (A)에 이어질 내용을 순서에 맞게 배열한 것으로 가장 적절한 것은?

① (B) — (D) — (C)　　② (C) — (B) — (D)
③ (C) — (D) — (B)　　④ (D) — (B) — (C)
⑤ (D) — (C) — (B)

S44　⭐ 2등급 대비　　　　　　고1 2022(3월)/44

밑줄 친 (a)~(e) 중에서 가리키는 대상이 나머지 넷과 <u>다른</u> 것은?

① (a)　　② (b)　　③ (c)　　④ (d)　　⑤ (e)

S45　⭐ 2등급 대비　　　　　　고1 2022(3월)/45

윗글에 관한 내용으로 적절하지 <u>않은</u> 것은?

① 한 수도승이 들판에서 일하고 있었다.
② 중년 남자는 골짜기에 있는 마을로 가는 중이었다.
③ 수도승은 골짜기에 있는 마을에 대해 질문받았다.
④ 수도승의 말을 듣고 젊은이는 고개를 숙였다.
⑤ 중년 남자는 산속에 있는 마을을 떠나서 기쁘다고 말했다.

[S46~S48] 다음 글을 읽고, 물음에 답하시오.

(A) Once long ago, deep in the Himalayas, there lived a little panda. He was as ordinary as all the other pandas. He was completely white from head to toe. His two big ears, his four furry feet and his cute round nose were all frosty white, leaving (a) him feeling ordinary and sad. Unlike the cheerful and contented pandas around him, he desired to be distinctive, special, and unique.

(B) The little panda changed his path and hurried to the nearest berry bush, greedily eating a mouthful of juicy red berries. However, they were so bitter he couldn't swallow even one. At dusk, he finally got home and slowly climbed his favorite bamboo tree. There, he discovered a strange black and red flower with a sweet scent that tempted (b) him to eat all its blossoms.

(C) Driven by the desire for uniqueness, the little panda sought inspiration from (c) his distant cousin, a giant white panda covered with heavenly black patches. But the cousin revealed the patches were from an unintended encounter with mud, and he disliked them. Disappointed, the little panda walked home. On his way, he met a red-feathered peacock, who explained (d) he turned red from eating wild berries.

(D) The following morning, under sunny skies, the little panda felt remarkably better. During breakfast, he found the other pandas chatting enthusiastically and asked why. They burst into laughter, exclaiming, "Look at yourself!" Glancing down, he discovered his once white fur was now stained jet black and glowing red. He was overjoyed and realized that, rather than by imitating others, (e) his wishes can come true from unexpected places and genuine experiences.

S46 ⭐ 2등급 대비   고1 2024(10월)/43

주어진 글 (A)에 이어질 내용을 순서에 맞게 배열한 것으로 가장 적절한 것은?

① (B) — (D) — (C)   ② (C) — (B) — (D)
③ (C) — (D) — (B)   ④ (D) — (B) — (C)
⑤ (D) — (C) — (B)

S47 ⭐ 2등급 대비   고1 2024(10월)/44

밑줄 친 (a)~(e) 중에서 가리키는 대상이 나머지 넷과 다른 것은?

① (a)   ② (b)   ③ (c)   ④ (d)   ⑤ (e)

S48 ⭐ 2등급 대비   고1 2024(10월)/45

윗글의 'little panda'에 관한 내용으로 적절하지 않은 것은?

① 다른 판다들과는 달리 특별해지기를 갈망했다.
② 베리가 너무 써서 한 개도 삼킬 수 없었다.
③ 집에 돌아오는 길에 검고 붉은 꽃을 발견하였다.
④ 그의 사촌은 자신의 검은 반점을 싫어했다.
⑤ 다른 판다들이 왜 신나게 수다를 떠는지 물어보았다.

[S49~S51] 다음 글을 읽고, 물음에 답하시오.

(A) One day a poor man brought a bunch of grapes to a prince as a gift. He was very excited to be able to bring a gift for (a) him because he was too poor to afford more. He placed the grapes beside the prince and said, "Oh, Prince, please accept this small gift from me." His face beamed with happiness as he offered his small gift.

(B) If the prince had offered the grapes to them, they might have made funny faces and shown their distaste for the grapes. That would have hurt the feelings of that poor man. He thought to himself that it would be better to eat all of them cheerfully and please (b) him. He did not want to hurt the feelings of that poor man. Everyone around him was moved by his thoughtfulness.

(C) The prince thanked him politely. As the man looked at him expectantly, the prince ate one grape. Then (c) he ate another one. Slowly the prince finished the whole bunch of grapes by himself. He did not offer grapes to anyone near him. The man who brought those grapes to (d) him was very pleased and left. The close friends of the prince who were around him were very surprised.

(D) Usually the prince shared whatever he had with others. He would offer them whatever he was given and they would eat it together. This time was different. Without offering it to anyone, (e) he finished the bunch of grapes by himself. One of the friends asked, "Prince! How come you ate all the grapes by yourself and did not offer them to any one of us?" He smiled and said that he ate all the grapes by himself because the grapes were too sour.

S49 ⭐ 2등급 대비   고1 2021(11월)/43

주어진 글 (A)에 이어질 내용을 순서에 맞게 배열한 것으로 가장 적절한 것은?

① (B) — (C) — (D) 　　② (C) — (B) — (D)
③ (C) — (D) — (B) 　　④ (D) — (B) — (C)
⑤ (D) — (C) — (B)

S50 ⭐ 2등급 대비   고1 2021(11월)/44

밑줄 친 (a)~(e) 중에서 가리키는 대상이 나머지 넷과 다른 것은?

① (a)　　② (b)　　③ (c)　　④ (d)　　⑤ (e)

S51 ⭐ 2등급 대비   고1 2021(11월)/45

윗글의 왕자에 관한 내용으로 적절하지 않은 것은?

① 가난한 남자에게 포도 한 송이를 선물로 받았다.
② 가난한 남자의 감정을 상하게 하고 싶지 않았다.
③ 곁에 있던 어떤 이에게도 포도를 권하지 않았다.
④ 가지고 있는 어떤 것이든 평소에 다른 사람들과 나눴다.
⑤ 포도가 너무 시어서 혼자 다 먹지 못했다.

S 어휘 Review

* 다음 영어는 우리말 뜻을, 우리말은 영어 단어를 〈보기〉에서 찾아 쓰시오.

〈보기〉

상실	entire	불친절한	disaster
유명한	자격이 있는	merchant	서리가 내리는
stare	세심한	generous	saint

01 frosty _____

02 loss _____

03 attentive _____

04 qualified _____

05 unwelcoming _____

06 너그러운 _____

07 전체의 _____

08 응시하다 _____

09 재해 _____

10 상인 _____

* 다음 우리말에 알맞은 영어 표현을 찾아 연결하시오.

11 ~을 만나다 •   • step off

12 막대한 •   • a world of

13 ~에 갇히다 •   • tear down

14 내리다 •   • come upon

15 허물다 •   • be stuck in

* 다음 우리말 표현에 맞는 단어를 고르시오.

16 진흙과의 의도치 않은 접촉 ➡ (unintended / unlimited) encounter with mud

17 왕의 친절한 행동 ➡ the king's kind (gesture / texture)

18 한 수도승을 보게 되었다 ➡ (overlooked / noticed) a monk

19 직장 내 긴장 ➡ workplace (transition / tension)

20 한 마을로부터 다른 마을로 ➡ from one (village / valley) to another

* 다음 문장의 빈칸에 알맞은 단어를 〈보기〉에서 찾아 쓰시오.

〈보기〉

helplessly	worship	precious	hostility
wrinkled	rewarded	barely	ignored
grand	property	sudden	greet

21 그 젊은이는 힘없이 고개를 숙이고 계속 걸어갔다.
➡ The young man lowered his head _____ and walked on.

22 나는 그녀의 갑작스러운 행동에 놀랐다.
➡ I was surprised at her _____ action.

23 사람들이 사원에서 예배를 드리기 위해 멀리서 왔다.
➡ People traveled to _____ at the temple.

24 그는 제복을 입은 젊은 군인을 간신히 보았다.
➡ He _____ saw the young uniformed soldier.

25 한 농부가 헛간에서 일하는 동안 그의 귀중한 시계를 잃어버렸다.
➡ A farmer lost his _____ watch while working in his barn.

26 그는 구겨진 1달러 지폐를 꺼내어 그의 테이블을 돌아보았다.
➡ He came up with a _____ dollar bill, and glanced back at his table.

27 그는 시계를 되찾아 기뻤고 그 어린 소년에게 약속했던 대로 보상해 주었다.
➡ He was delighted to get his watch back and _____ the little boy as promised.

28 새 건물들, 나무들, 그리고 꽃들이 잘 관리된 소유지를 꾸몄다.
➡ New buildings, trees, and flowers adorned the well-kept _____.

29 몇몇 학교에서는 아이들이 노인을 완전히 무시했다.
➡ In some schools the children completely _____ the old man.

30 한 노인이 마을 중심부에 큰 사원을 지었다.
➡ An old man built a(n) _____ temple at the center of his village.

방그사 (방과 후 그린 사업)

서울대학교 에너지환경 동아리

지속가능한 미래를 위한 '방그사'

방그사는 '방과 후 그린 사업'이란 뜻을 지닌 동아리로, 2020년에 신설된 젊은 동아리입니다. 2019년에 에너지자원공학과 학생 11명이 환경 NGO 대자연과 함께하는 #MakeZero #MakeGreenCampus 에너지 절약 실천 사업에 참여하면서 방그사가 시작되었습니다.

기후 변화 문제에 대처하는 하나의 주제(텀블러 사용, 분리수거 등)를 선정하여 한 달에 4번 이상 실천한 사진을 자신의 SNS에 인증하는 활동을 합니다.
또 초등학교 3, 4학년을 대상으로 한 환경 교육 수업 동영상을 제작하고, '기업의 환경 활동'을 주제로 한 기고문을 작성하여 Climate Times에 기고도 합니다.

그린캠퍼스 교육을 연수하고, 타 대학 그린캠퍼스 환경 동아리 및 환경 단체와 교류도 하는데, 이러한 활동의 노고를 인정받아 에코리그에서 서울시장상을 수상하기도 하였습니다.

기후 변화에 대처하고, 건강한 지구를 만드는 데 관심이 있는 신입 부원을 기다립니다.

* 고난도 유형 독해 모의고사

[회별 12문항, 제한시간 25분]

1회 **모의고사** — 고2 2025 실시 3월 학력평가 문항 선별

2회 **모의고사** — 고2 2024 실시 3월 학력평가 문항 선별

3회 **모의고사** — 고2 2023 실시 3월 학력평가 문항 선별

*수록 유형

번호	유형
01번	밑줄 친 부분의 의미 찾기
02번	주제 찾기
03번	제목 찾기
04번	어법에 맞지 않는 낱말 찾기
05번	문맥에 맞지 않는 낱말 찾기
06번	빈칸 완성하기
07번	
08번	글의 순서 정하기
09번	주어진 문장 넣기
10번	요약문 완성하기
11번	장문의 이해
12번	

1회 고난도 유형 독해 모의고사

고2 2025 실시
3월 학력평가 문항 선별

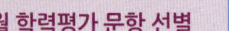

단어장

- 문항 수 12개
- 배점 28점
- 제한시간 25분

1회 01

고2 2025(3월)/21

밑줄 친 keeping the ball on a slope가 다음 글에서 의미하는 바로 가장 적절한 것은? [3점]

The concept of ecosystem states should be familiar to anyone with a home vegetable garden. The garden is a small ecosystem that the grower attempts to keep in a specific state, namely the maximization of fruit and vegetable production. To achieve this, the grower is almost always intervening in the dynamics of the ecosystem; they remove unwanted plants that begin to grow and perhaps spray insecticides and fence off the patch to stop insects and other animals from consuming the vegetables. Since maximizing vegetable growth is an inherently unstable state for the ecosystem, the grower is effectively keeping the ball on a slope. If the grower stops intervening, even for a day, the ecosystem, that small patch of ground, will naturally begin to shift to a more stable state. Vegetables may still grow, but yield will almost certainly be lower as other plants crowd out the vegetables and wildlife consume the produce.

* insecticide: 살충제

① improving the garden's environment without human intervention
② altering the ecosystem of the garden to maximize its stability
③ balancing increased plant diversity with ecosystem stability
④ maintaining an unstable ecosystem for high vegetable yield
⑤ boosting the harmonious growth of plants in the wild

1회 02

고2 2025(3월)/23

다음 글의 주제로 가장 적절한 것은?

If the brain has already stored someone's face and name, why do we still end up remembering one and not the other? This is because the brain has something of a two-tier memory system at work when it comes to retrieving memories, and this gives rise to a common yet infuriating sensation: recognising someone, but not being able to remember how or why, or what their name is. This happens because the brain differentiates between familiarity and recall. To clarify, familiarity (or recognition) is when you encounter someone or something and you know you've done so before. But beyond that, you've got nothing; all you can say is this person/thing is already in your memories. Recall is when you can access the original memory of how and why you know this person; recognition is just flagging up the fact that the memory exists.

* retrieve: 꺼내다 ** infuriating: 짜증 나는

① process of recalling details from partial memories
② impact of emotional responses on memory retrieval patterns
③ dangers of memory loss regarding face and name recognition
④ ways to manage the difficulty of recognising faces and names
⑤ distinction between recall and familiarity in the memory system

다음 글의 제목으로 가장 적절한 것은?

Since their start in the early 1950s U.S. television sitcoms have charted many of the social conflicts in U.S. society: civil rights, women's rights in the home and in the workplace, children's rights, immigration and multiculturalism, as well as evolving conceptions of the family. Each of these issues has been addressed through humour in a way that has helped to make more progressive values more acceptable than previously. Often a character, usually someone marked as a bigot, resisted one or more of these developments and was then made to appear ridiculous. They were cut down either through their own stupidity, a brief scolding from others, or both. In this way, the humour of sitcoms acted as a cost-effective means to encourage acceptance of a more pluralistic and tolerant society.

* bigot: 편견이 아주 심한 사람 ** pluralistic: 다원적인

① Why Do Sitcoms Criticize Progressive Ideas?
② Acceptability of Humour in Multicultural Society
③ The Decline of U.S. Sitcoms along with Social Change
④ Production Costs: Why TV Commercials Are Necessary
⑤ Humour in Sitcoms Helps Acceptance of Progressive Values

다음 글의 밑줄 친 부분 중, 어법상 틀린 것은?

The prominence of the social dimension in food writing might suggest that the flavor of food is taking a back seat. I suspect ① that most people view flavor as of secondary importance in social settings where food is served. Although our social gatherings coalesce around food, the meaning of these gatherings does not seem to depend on flavor. Flavor ② assists with the narrow purpose of filling the belly, and once that is accomplished it provides the backdrop for whatever social dynamics characterize the gathering. These can be understood independently of the flavor of the food on offer, the appreciation of ③ which is understood to be personal and subjective. According to this conventional wisdom, the ceremonies and rituals around food, the social events that supply food with its meaning, ④ does not depend on the quality of sensations provided by the food. To focus ⑤ excessively on flavor is to miss the larger significance of these social relations.

* coalesce: 모이다 ** backdrop: 배경

다음 글의 밑줄 친 부분 중, 문맥상 낱말의 쓰임이
적절하지 <u>않은</u> 것은?

There are reasons why science is not fully trusted and why healthy skepticism and critical thinking are essential. In spite of professional standards, claims of objectivity, and the peer review process, the conduct of science can be ① <u>biased</u>. All experts are not the same, nor do they submit their work to the same scrutiny. Knowing the source of funding can be ② <u>important</u> in evaluating scientific claims. For example, the Harvard researchers who made claims in the late 1960s about the problems with dietary fat, leading the nation away from perceiving sugar as one of the main causes in health problems, were funded in part by the sugar industry. The authors did not reveal their funding source to the *New England Journal of Medicine*, where their ③ <u>influential</u> article appeared. Their article shaped a generation of changes in eating patterns that appears to have ④ <u>discouraged</u> higher use of sugar, now widely implicated as a source of the rise in obesity and diabetes. Stories such as this one fuel suspicion — but also lead to further safeguards in the scientific process. Funding ⑤ <u>disclosures</u>, although not required five decades ago, have since been made compulsory.

* skepticism: 회의주의   ** scrutiny: 심층 조사
*** implicate: 관련이 있음을 알려 주다

The explosion of popular music in the second half of the twentieth century as well as the global circulation and dissemination of music by the creative industries propelled a new understanding of _____ in relation to music. Suddenly, in the 1950s, anyone could pick up spoons, a couple of pans, a second-hand guitar and start a band. This led to specific genres such as skiffle, but also, more generally, reflected a much more relaxed and inclusive attitude to music making. While ordinary people had always sung and made music, the popular music movement was driven by a spirit of rebellion and freedom. This approach led to the punk movement, whose musicians even made it a condition for their music to be non-virtuosic and accessible to all in the 1970s. Groups who had been entirely excluded from music revelled in opportunities to create. This led to a sense of novelty and empowerment in and beyond the music sphere.

* dissemination: 보급   ** non-virtuosic: 전문성이 높지 않은
*** revel in: ~을 만끽하다

① accessibility   ② responsibility
③ exchange   ④ preservation
⑤ profitability

Great scientists are seldom one-hit wonders. Newton is a prime example: beyond the Newtonian mechanics, he developed the theory of gravitation, calculus, laws of motion, and optimization. In fact, well-known scientists are often involved in multiple discoveries, a phenomenon potentially explained by the Matthew effect. Indeed, an initial success may offer a scientist legitimacy, improve peer perception, provide knowledge of how to score and win, enhance social status, and attract resources and quality collaborators, each of these payoffs further increasing her odds of scoring another win. Yet, there is an appealing alternative explanation: Great scientists have multiple hits and consistently succeed in their scientific endeavors simply because they're exceptionally talented. Therefore, future success again goes to those who have had success earlier, *not* because of advantages offered by the previous success, but because the earlier success was _____. The Matthew effect posits that success *alone* increases the future probability of success, raising the question: Does status dictate outcomes, or does it simply reflect an underlying talent or quality? In other words, is there really a Matthew effect after all? [3점]

* posit: 상정하다

① inseparable from consistent efforts
② attributed to talented collaborators
③ dependent on financial resources
④ driven by societal recognition
⑤ indicative of a hidden talent

주어진 글 다음에 이어질 글의 순서로 가장 적절한 것을 고르시오. [3점]

> The governments of virtually every country on the planet attach great importance to achieving food security and a wide variety of mechanisms have been developed to realize this goal.

(A) However, food security does not require food self-sufficiency because countries can import food items not easily produced within the country. Agricultural products are, after all, highly sensitive to climatic, soil and other conditions that tend to vary around the world.

(B) The first issue governments face in achieving national food security is the problem of insuring that adequate amounts of food are available to the resident population. Some governments have set goals of food self-sufficiency, which means most if not all of the food available in a country comes from the domestic farming system.

(C) Even countries with extremely productive agricultural sectors are not fully self-sufficient in all food items. The United States, for example, depends on imports for its supply of coffee, tea, bananas and other tropical products. In general, the problem of assuring adequate food supplies is solved by relying on both domestic production and imports.

① (A) — (C) — (B)　　② (B) — (A) — (C)
③ (B) — (C) — (A)　　④ (C) — (A) — (B)
⑤ (C) — (B) — (A)

글의 흐름으로 보아, 주어진 문장이 들어가기에 가장 적절한 곳을 고르시오. [3점]

Knowledge is information that has demonstrated its usefulness.

It is important to recognize that although science is a rule-based procedure, it is very much a creative process. (①) A conjecture is a philosophical invention, cooked up rather mystically by the mind through the mental computation we call careful contemplation. (②) However, until the hypothesis is tested against reality, it is not yet truly knowledge; it is just information that represents speculation. (③) It is what is left over after cycles of experimental testing have eliminated false theories. (④) As scientists continually test their hypotheses and modify their models to account for new and surprising data, a kind of "learning loop" emerges that statisticians call *Bayesian updating*. (⑤) Based on Bayes' Rule, developed by eighteenth-century English statistician and philosopher Thomas Bayes, Bayesian updating refers to a mathematical process whereby an accepted theory or predictive model gets increasingly accurate through the repetitive testing of competing variants of that theory.

* conjecture: 추론 ** contemplation: 숙고 *** speculation: 추측

다음 글의 내용을 한 문장으로 요약하고자 한다. 빈칸 (A), (B)에 들어갈 말로 가장 적절한 것은?

Quite often the interaction between groups is socially unequal, and this is reflected in the fact that in many cases borrowing of words or constructions goes mostly or entirely in one direction, from the more powerful or prestigious group to the less favored one. The languages of socially subordinated groups may from quite an early period of contact provide terminology for objects or practices with which speakers of the more powerful group were previously unfamiliar, but the effects of contact in that direction may not progress any further than this. In some cases, as with the Dharug language of Sydney, Australia, the source of some of the earliest loans from Indigenous Australian languages into English, the fate of the language system is extinction after the obliteration of many of its speakers. The remainder shifted to varieties of English, the language of the people who had suppressed them.

* prestigious: 권력을 가진 ** subordinate: 종속된 *** obliteration: 소멸

↓

Language borrowing from dominant to subordinate groups reflects social ___(A)___, where the language systems of the latter often ___(B)___ even though they may have provided some terms, as exemplified by Dharug in Australia.

	(A)		(B)
①	inequality	—	vanish
②	imbalance	—	prevail
③	integration	—	prosper
④	variety	—	decline
⑤	coordination	—	disappear

In 1900, at the close of the first decade in which electric systems had become a practical alternative for manufacturers, less than 5 percent of the power used in factories came from electricity. But the technological advances of suppliers made electric systems and electric motors ever more affordable and reliable, and the suppliers' intensive marketing programs also (a) sped the adoption of the new technology. Further accelerating the shift was the rapid (b) expansion in the number of skilled electrical engineers, who provided the expertise needed to install and run the new systems. In short order, electric power had gone from exotic to commonplace.

But one thing didn't change. Factories continued to build their own power-supply systems on their own premises. (c) Few manufacturers considered buying electricity from the small central stations. Designed to supply lighting to local homes and shops, the central stations had neither the size nor the skill to serve the needs of big factories. And the factory owners, having always supplied their own power, were (d) willing to assign such a critical function to an outsider. They knew that a glitch in power supply would bring their operations to a (e) halt — and that a lot of glitches might well mean bankruptcy. As the new century began, a survey found that there were already 50,000 private electric plants in operation, far surpassing the 3,600 central stations.

* premises: (공장) 부지 ** glitch: (작은) 결함

 11 ─────────────────────── 고2 2025(3월)/41

윗글의 제목으로 가장 적절한 것은?

① How to Avoid Minor Errors in Factory Operation
② Power Use in Factories: What Changed and What Didn't
③ Technical Advances in Power Supply by Central Stations
④ Threats from the Increased Use of Electricity in Factories
⑤ From Private to Central Power Supply: A Revolutionary Change

12 ─────────────────────── 고2 2025(3월)/42

밑줄 친 (a)~(e) 중에서 문맥상 낱말의 쓰임이 적절하지 않은 것은?

① (a)   ② (b)   ③ (c)   ④ (d)   ⑤ (e)

2회 고난도 유형 독해 모의고사

고2 2024 실시
3월 학력평가 문항 선별

단어장

■ 문항 수 12개
■ 배점 28점
■ 제한시간 25분

2회 01 _____ 고2 2024(3월)/21

밑줄 친 we were still taping bricks to accelerators가 다음 글에서 의미하는 바로 가장 적절한 것은?
[3점]

If you had wanted to create a "self-driving" car in the 1950s, your best option might have been to strap a brick to the accelerator. Yes, the vehicle would have been able to move forward on its own, but it could not slow down, stop, or turn to avoid barriers. Obviously not ideal. But does that mean the entire concept of the self-driving car is not worth pursuing? No, it only means that at the time we did not yet have the tools we now possess to help enable vehicles to operate both autonomously and safely. This once-distant dream now seems within our reach. It is much the same story in medicine. Two decades ago, we were still taping bricks to accelerators. Today, we are approaching the point where we can begin to bring some appropriate technology to bear in ways that advance our understanding of patients as unique individuals. In fact, many patients are already wearing devices that monitor their conditions in real time, which allows doctors to talk to their patients in a specific, refined, and feedback-driven way that was not even possible a decade ago.

* strap: 끈으로 묶다   ** autonomously: 자율적으로

① the importance of medical education was overlooked
② self-driving cars enabled patients to move around freely
③ the devices for safe driving were unavailable at that time
④ lack of advanced tools posed a challenge in understanding patients
⑤ appropriate technologies led to success in developing a new medicine

2회 02 _____ 고2 2024(3월)/23

다음 글의 주제로 가장 적절한 것은?

Empathy is frequently listed as one of the most desired skills in an employer or employee, although without specifying exactly what is meant by *empathy*. Some businesses stress cognitive empathy, emphasizing the need for leaders to understand the perspective of employees and customers when negotiating deals and making decisions. Others stress affective empathy and empathic concern, emphasizing the ability of leaders to gain trust from employees and customers by treating them with real concern and compassion. When some consultants argue that successful companies foster empathy, what that translates to is that companies should conduct good market research. In other words, an "empathic" company understands the needs and wants of its customers and seeks to fulfill those needs and wants. When some people speak of design with empathy, what that translates to is that companies should take into account the specific needs of different populations — the blind, the deaf, the elderly, non-English speakers, the color-blind, and so on — when designing products.

* empathy: 공감, 공감 능력   ** compassion: 동정심

① diverse benefits of good market research
② negative factors in making business decisions
③ difficulties in designing products with empathic concern
④ efforts to build cognitive empathy among employees
⑤ different interpretations of empathy in business

다음 글의 제목으로 가장 적절한 것은?

The most prevalent problem kids report is that they feel like they need to be accessible at all times. Because technology allows for it, they feel an obligation. It's easy for most of us to relate — you probably feel the same pressure in your own life! It is really challenging to deal with the fact that we're human and can't always respond instantly. For a teen or tween who's still learning the ins and outs of social interactions, it's even worse. Here's how this behavior plays out sometimes: Your child texts one of his friends, and the friend doesn't text back right away. Now it's easy for your child to think, "This person doesn't want to be my friend anymore!" So he texts again, and again, and again — "blowing up their phone." This can be stress-inducing and even read as aggressive. But you can see how easily this could happen.

* tween: (10~12세 사이의) 십대 초반의 아동

① From Symbols to Bytes: History of Communication
② Parents' Desire to Keep Their Children Within Reach
③ Building Trust: The Key to Ideal Human Relationships
④ The Positive Role of Digital Technology in Teen Friendships
⑤ Connected but Stressed: Challenges for Kids in the Digital Era

다음 글의 밑줄 친 부분 중, 어법상 틀린 것은?

For years, many psychologists have held strongly to the belief ① that the key to addressing negative health habits is to change behavior. This, more than values and attitudes, ② is the part of personality that is easiest to change. Ingestive habits such as smoking, drinking and various eating behaviors are the most common health concerns targeted for behavioral changes. Process-addiction behaviors (workaholism, shopaholism, and the like) fall into this category as well. Mental imagery combined with power of suggestion was taken up as the premise of behavioral medicine to help people change negative health behaviors into positive ③ ones. Although this technique alone will not produce changes, when ④ using alongside other behavior modification tactics and coping strategies, behavioral changes have proved effective for some people. ⑤ What mental imagery does is reinforce a new desired behavior. Repeated use of images reinforces the desired behavior more strongly over time.

* ingestive: (음식) 섭취의 ** premise: 전제

다음 글의 밑줄 친 부분 중, 문맥상 낱말의 쓰임이
적절하지 <u>않은</u> 것은? [3점]

Emotion socialization—learning from other people about emotions and how to deal with them — starts early in life and plays a foundational role for emotion regulation development. Although extra-familial influences, such as peers or media, gain in importance during adolescence, parents remain the ① <u>primary</u> socialization agents. For example, their own responses to emotional situations serve as a role model for emotion regulation, increasing the likelihood that their children will show ② <u>similar</u> reactions in comparable situations. Parental practices at times when their children are faced with emotional challenges also impact emotion regulation development. Whereas direct soothing and directive guidance of what to do are beneficial for younger children, they may ③ <u>cultivate</u> adolescents' autonomy striving. In consequence, adolescents might pull away from, rather than turn toward, their parents in times of emotional crisis, unless parental practices are ④ <u>adjusted</u>. More suitable in adolescence is ⑤ <u>indirect</u> support of autonomous emotion regulation, such as through interest in, as well as awareness and nonjudgmental acceptance of, adolescents' emotional experiences, and being available when the adolescent wants to talk.

Dancers often push themselves to the limits of their physical capabilities. But that push is misguided if it is directed toward accomplishing something physically impossible. For instance, a tall dancer with long feet may wish to perform repetitive vertical jumps to fast music, pointing his feet while in the air and lowering his heels to the floor between jumps. That may be impossible no matter how strong the dancer is. But a short-footed dancer may have no trouble! Another dancer may be struggling to complete a half-turn in the air. Understanding the connection between a rapid turn rate and the alignment of the body close to the rotation axis tells her how to accomplish her turn successfully. In both of these cases, understanding and working within the _____ imposed by nature and described by physical laws allows dancers to work efficiently, minimizing potential risk of injury.

* alignment: 정렬　** rotation axis: 회전축

① habits　　　② cultures　　　③ constraints
④ hostilities　　⑤ moralities

We must explore the relationship between children's film production and consumption habits. The term "children's film" implies ownership by children — *their* cinema — but films supposedly made for children have always been _____, particularly in commercial cinemas. The considerable crossover in audience composition for children's films can be shown by the fact that, in 2007, eleven Danish children's and youth films attracted 59 per cent of theatrical admissions, and in 2014, German children's films comprised seven out of the top twenty films at the national box office. This phenomenon corresponds with a broader, international embrace of what is seemingly children's culture among audiences of diverse ages. The old prejudice that children's film is some other realm, separate from (and forever subordinate to) a more legitimate cinema for adults is not supported by the realities of consumption: children's film is at the heart of contemporary popular culture.

* subordinate: 하위의

① centered on giving moral lessons
② consumed by audiences of all ages
③ appreciated through an artistic view
④ produced by inexperienced directors
⑤ separated from the cinema for adults

주어진 글 다음에 이어질 글의 순서로 가장 적절한 것을 고르시오. [3점]

Development of the human body from a single cell provides many examples of the structural richness that is possible when the repeated production of random variation is combined with nonrandom selection.

(A) Those in the right place that make the right connections are stimulated, and those that don't are eliminated. This process is much like sculpting. A natural consequence of the strategy is great variability from individual to individual at the cell and molecular levels, even though large-scale structures are quite similar.

(B) The survivors serve to produce new cells that undergo further rounds of selection. Except in the immune system, cells and extensions of cells are not genetically selected during development, but rather, are positionally selected.

(C) All phases of body development from embryo to adult exhibit random activities at the cellular level, and body formation depends on the new possibilities generated by these activities coupled with selection of those outcomes that satisfy previously built-in criteria. Always new structure is based on old structure, and at every stage selection favors some cells and eliminates others.

* molecular: 분자의 ** embryo: 배아

① (A) — (C) — (B)
② (B) — (A) — (C)
③ (B) — (C) — (A)
④ (C) — (A) — (B)
⑤ (C) — (B) — (A)

글의 흐름으로 보아, 주어진 문장이 들어가기에 가장 적절한 곳을 고르시오. [3점]

> However, there are many lines of evidence to suggest that vagrancy can, on rare occasions, dramatically alter the fate of populations, species or even whole ecosystems.

It is a common assumption that most vagrant birds are ultimately doomed, aside from the rare cases where individuals are able to reorientate and return to their normal ranges. (①) In turn, it is also commonly assumed that vagrancy itself is a relatively unimportant biological phenomenon. (②) This is undoubtedly true for the majority of cases, as the most likely outcome of any given vagrancy event is that the individual will fail to find enough resources, and/or be exposed to inhospitable environmental conditions, and perish. (③) Despite being infrequent, these events can be extremely important when viewed at the timescales over which ecological and evolutionary processes unfold. (④) The most profound consequences of vagrancy relate to the establishment of new breeding sites, new migration routes and wintering locations. (⑤) Each of these can occur through different mechanisms, and at different frequencies, and they each have their own unique importance.

* vagrancy: 무리에서 떨어져 헤맴 ** doomed: 죽을 운명의
*** inhospitable: 살기 힘든

다음 글의 내용을 한 문장으로 요약하고자 한다. 빈칸 (A), (B)에 들어갈 말로 가장 적절한 것은?

The fast-growing, tremendous amount of data, collected and stored in large and numerous data repositories, has far exceeded our human ability for understanding without powerful tools. As a result, data collected in large data repositories become "data tombs" — data archives that are hardly visited. Important decisions are often made based not on the information-rich data stored in data repositories but rather on a decision maker's instinct, simply because the decision maker does not have the tools to extract the valuable knowledge hidden in the vast amounts of data. Efforts have been made to develop expert system and knowledge-based technologies, which typically rely on users or domain experts to *manually* input knowledge into knowledge bases. However, this procedure is likely to cause biases and errors and is extremely costly and time consuming. The widening gap between data and information calls for the systematic development of tools that can turn data tombs into "golden nuggets" of knowledge.

* repository: 저장소 ** golden nugget: 금괴

⬇

> As the vast amounts of data stored in repositories ___(A)___ human understanding, effective tools to ___(B)___ valuable knowledge are required for better decision-making.

	(A)		(B)
①	overwhelm	—	obtain
②	overwhelm	—	exchange
③	enhance	—	apply
④	enhance	—	discover
⑤	fulfill	—	access

It's untrue that teens can focus on two things at once — what they're doing is shifting their attention from one task to another. In this digital age, teens wire their brains to make these shifts very quickly, but they are still, like everyone else, paying attention to one thing at a time, sequentially. Common sense tells us multitasking should (a) increase brain activity, but Carnegie Mellon University scientists using the latest brain imaging technology find it doesn't. As a matter of fact, they discovered that multitasking actually decreases brain activity. Neither task is done as well as if each were performed (b) individually. Fractions of a second are lost every time we make a switch, and a person's interrupted task can take 50 percent (c) longer to finish, with 50 percent more errors. Turns out the latest brain research (d) contradicts the old advice "one thing at a time."

It's not that kids can't do some tasks simultaneously. But if two tasks are performed at once, one of them has to be familiar. Our brains perform a familiar task on "automatic pilot" while really paying attention to the other one. That's why insurance companies consider talking on a cell phone and driving to be as (e) dangerous as driving while drunk — it's the driving that goes on "automatic pilot" while the conversation really holds our attention. Our kids may be living in the Information Age but our brains have not been redesigned yet.

11

윗글의 제목으로 가장 적절한 것은?

① Multitasking Unveiled: What Really Happens in Teens' Brains
② Optimal Ways to Expand the Attention Span of Teens
③ Unknown Approaches to Enhance Brain Development
④ Multitasking for a Balanced Life in a Busy World
⑤ How to Build Automaticity in Performing Tasks

12

밑줄 친 (a)~(e) 중에서 문맥상 낱말의 쓰임이 적절하지 않은 것은?

① (a)   ② (b)   ③ (c)   ④ (d)   ⑤ (e)

3회 고난도 유형 독해 **모의고사**

고2 2023 실시
3월 학력평가 문항 선별

 단어장

■ 문항 수 **12개**
■ 배점 **27점**
■ 제한시간 **25분**

3회 **01**   고2 2023(3월)/21

밑줄 친 helping move the needle forward가
다음 글에서 의미하는 바로 가장 적절한 것은? [3점]

Everyone's heard the expression *don't let the perfect become the enemy of the good*. If you want to get over an obstacle so that your idea can become the solution-based policy you've long dreamed of, you can't have an all-or-nothing mentality. You have to be willing to alter your idea and let others influence its outcome. You have to be okay with the outcome being a little different, even a little *less*, than you wanted. Say you're pushing for a clean water act. Even if what emerges isn't as well-funded as you wished, or doesn't match how you originally conceived the bill, you'll have still succeeded in ensuring that kids in troubled areas have access to clean water. That's what counts, that *they* will be safer because of your idea and your effort. Is it perfect? No. Is there more work to be done? Absolutely. But in almost every case, helping move the needle forward is vastly better than not helping at all.

① spending time and money on celebrating perfection
② suggesting cost-saving strategies for a good cause
③ making a difference as best as the situation allows
④ checking your resources before altering the original goal
⑤ collecting donations to help the education of poor children

3회 **02**   고2 2023(3월)/23

다음 글의 주제로 가장 적절한 것은?

What consequences of eating too many grapes and other sweet fruit could there possibly be for our brains? A few large studies have helped to shed some light. In one, higher fruit intake in older, cognitively healthy adults was linked with less volume in the hippocampus. This finding was unusual, since people who eat more fruit usually display the benefits associated with a healthy diet. In this study, however, the researchers isolated various components of the subjects' diets and found that fruit didn't seem to be doing their memory centers any favors. Another study from the Mayo Clinic saw a similar inverse relationship between fruit intake and volume of the cortex, the large outer layer of the brain. Researchers in the latter study noted that excessive consumption of high-sugar fruit (such as mangoes, bananas, and pineapples) may cause metabolic and cognitive problems as much as processed carbs do.

* hippocampus: (대뇌 측두엽의) 해마   ** carb: 탄수화물 식품

① benefits of eating whole fruit on the brain health
② universal preference for sweet fruit among children
③ types of brain exercises enhancing long-term memory
④ nutritional differences between fruit and processed carbs
⑤ negative effect of fruit overconsumption on the cognitive brain

다음 글의 제목으로 가장 적절한 것은?

Winning turns on a self-conscious awareness that others are watching. It's a lot easier to move under the radar when no one knows you and no one is paying attention. You can mess up and be rough and get dirty because no one even knows you're there. But as soon as you start to win, and others start to notice, you're suddenly aware that you're being observed. You're being judged. You worry that others will discover your flaws and weaknesses, and you start hiding your true personality, so you can be a good role model and good citizen and a leader that others can respect. There is nothing wrong with that. But if you do it at the expense of being who you really are, making decisions that please others instead of pleasing yourself, you're not going to be in that position very long. When you start apologizing for who you are, you stop growing and you stop winning. Permanently.

① Stop Judging Others to Win the Race of Life
② Why Disappointment Hurts More than Criticism
③ Winning vs. Losing: A Dangerously Misleading Mindset
④ Winners in a Trap: Too Self-Conscious to Be Themselves
⑤ Is Honesty the Best Policy to Turn Enemies into Friends?

다음 글의 밑줄 친 부분 중, 어법상 틀린 것은? [3점]

Human beings like certainty. This liking stems from our ancient ancestors ① who needed to survive alongside saber-toothed tigers and poisonous berries. Our brains evolved to help us attend to threats, keep away from ② them, and remain alive afterward. In fact, we learned that the more ③ certain we were about something, the better chance we had of making the right choice. Is this berry the same shape as last time? The same size? If I know for certain it ④ is, my brain will direct me to eat it because I know it's safe. And if I'm uncertain, my brain will send out a danger alert to protect me. The dependence on certainty all those millennia ago ensured our survival to the present day, and the danger-alert system continues to protect us. This is achieved by our brains labeling new, vague, or unpredictable everyday events and experiences as uncertain. Our brains then ⑤ generating sensations, thoughts, and action plans to keep us safe from the uncertain element, and we live to see another day.
* saber-toothed tiger: 검치호(검 모양의 송곳니를 가진 호랑이)

다음 글의 밑줄 친 부분 중, 문맥상 낱말의 쓰임이 적절하지 <u>않은</u> 것은? [3점]

Robert Blattberg and Steven Hoch noted that, in a changing environment, it is not clear that consistency is always a virtue and that one of the advantages of human judgment is the ability to detect change. Thus, in changing environments, it might be ① advantageous to combine human judgment and statistical models. Blattberg and Hoch examined this possibility by having supermarket managers forecast demand for certain products and then creating a composite forecast by averaging these judgments with the forecasts of statistical models based on ② past data. The logic was that statistical models ③ deny stable conditions and therefore cannot account for the effects on demand of novel events such as actions taken by competitors or the introduction of new products. Humans, however, can ④ incorporate these novel factors in their judgments. The composite — or average of human judgments and statistical models — proved to be more ⑤ accurate than either the statistical models or the managers working alone.

* composite: 종합적인; 종합된 것

Free play is nature's means of teaching children that they are not _____. In play, away from adults, children really do have control and can practice asserting it. In free play, children learn to make their own decisions, solve their own problems, create and follow rules, and get along with others as equals rather than as obedient or rebellious subordinates. In active outdoor play, children deliberately dose themselves with moderate amounts of fear and they thereby learn how to control not only their bodies, but also their fear. In social play children learn how to negotiate with others, how to please others, and how to manage and overcome the anger that can arise from conflicts. None of these lessons can be taught through verbal means; they can be learned only through experience, which free play provides.

* rebellious: 반항적인

① noisy   ② sociable   ③ complicated
④ helpless   ⑤ selective

Many early dot-com investors focused almost entirely on revenue growth instead of net income. Many early dot-com companies earned most of their revenue from selling advertising space on their Web sites. To boost reported revenue, some sites began exchanging ad space. Company A would put an ad for its Web site on company B's Web site, and company B would put an ad for its Web site on company A's Web site. No money ever changed hands, but each company recorded revenue (for the value of the space that it gave up on its site) and expense (for the value of its ad that it placed on the other company's site). This practice did little to boost net income and _____ — but it did boost *reported* revenue. This practice was quickly put to an end because accountants felt that it did not meet the criteria of the revenue recognition principle.   * revenue: 수익   ** net income: 순이익

① simplified the Web design process
② resulted in no additional cash inflow
③ decreased the salaries of the employees
④ intensified competition among companies
⑤ triggered conflicts on the content of Web ads

주어진 글 다음에 이어질 글의 순서로 가장 적절한 것을 고르시오.

> Like positive habits, bad habits exist on a continuum of easy-to-change and hard-to-change.

(A) But this kind of language (and the approaches it spawns) frames these challenges in a way that isn't helpful or effective. I specifically hope we will stop using this phrase: "break a habit." This language misguides people. The word "break" sets the wrong expectation for how you get rid of a bad habit.

(B) This word implies that if you input a lot of force in one moment, the habit will be gone. However, that rarely works, because you usually cannot get rid of an unwanted habit by applying force one time.

(C) When you get toward the "hard" end of the spectrum, note the language you hear — *breaking* bad habits and *battling* addiction. It's as if an unwanted behavior is a nefarious villain to be aggressively defeated.

* spawn: 낳다   ** nefarious: 사악한

① (A) — (C) — (B)   ② (B) — (A) — (C)
③ (B) — (C) — (A)   ④ (C) — (A) — (B)
⑤ (C) — (B) — (A)

모의고사
3회

글의 흐름으로 보아, 주어진 문장이 들어가기에 가장
적절한 곳을 고르시오.

> In the electric organ the muscle cells are connected
> in larger chunks, which makes the total current
> intensity larger than in ordinary muscles.

Electric communication is mainly known in
fish. The electric signals are produced in special
electric organs. When the signal is discharged the
electric organ will be negatively loaded compared
to the head and an electric field is created around
the fish. (①) A weak electric current is created
also in ordinary muscle cells when they contract.
(②) The fish varies the signals by changing
the form of the electric field or the frequency of
discharging. (③) The system is only working
over small distances, about one to two meters.
(④) This is an advantage since the species
using the signal system often live in large groups
with several other species. (⑤) If many fish
send out signals at the same time, the short range
decreases the risk of interference.

다음 글의 내용을 한 문장으로 요약하고자 한다. 빈칸
(A), (B)에 들어갈 말로 가장 적절한 것은?

A young child may be puzzled when asked to
distinguish between the directions of right and
left. But that same child may have no difficulty
in determining the directions of up and down or
back and front. Scientists propose that this occurs
because, although we experience three dimensions,
only two had a strong influence on our evolution:
the vertical dimension as defined by gravity and,
in mobile species, the front/back dimension as
defined by the positioning of sensory and feeding
mechanisms. These influence our perception of
vertical versus horizontal, far versus close, and the
search for dangers from above (such as an eagle)
or below (such as a snake). However, the left-right
axis is not as relevant in nature. A bear is equally
dangerous from its left or the right side, but not if
it is upside down. In fact, when observing a scene
containing plants, animals, and man-made objects
such as cars or street signs, we can only tell when
left and right have been inverted if we observe
those artificial items.

* axis: 축

↓

> Having affected the evolution of our ___(A)___
> perception, vertical and front/back dimensions
> are easily perceived, but the left-right axis,
> which is not ___(B)___ in nature, doesn't come
> instantly to us.

(A)		(B)
① spatial	—	significant
② spatial	—	scarce
③ auditory	—	different
④ cultural	—	accessible
⑤ cultural	—	desirable

빠른 정답

Creative people aren't all cut from the same cloth. They have (a) varying levels of maturity and sensitivity. They have different approaches to work. And they're each motivated by different things. Managing people is about being aware of their unique personalities. It's also about empathy and adaptability, and knowing how the things you do and say will be interpreted and adapting accordingly. Who you are and what you say may not be the (b) same from one person to the next. For instance, if you're asking someone to work a second weekend in a row, or telling them they aren't getting that deserved promotion just yet, you need to bear in mind the (c) group. Vincent will have a very different reaction to the news than Emily, and they will each be more receptive to the news if it's bundled with different things. Perhaps that promotion news will land (d) easier if Vincent is given a few extra vacation days for the holidays, while you can promise Emily a bigger promotion a year from now. Consider each person's complex positive and negative personality traits, their life circumstances, and their mindset in the moment when deciding what to say and how to say it. Personal connection, compassion, and an individualized management style are (e) key to drawing consistent, rock star-level work out of everyone.

11

고2 2023(3월)/41

윗글의 제목으로 가장 적절한 것은?

① Know Each Person to Guarantee Best Performance
② Flexible Hours: An Appealing Working Condition
③ Talk to Employees More Often in Hard Times
④ How Empathy and Recognition Are Different
⑤ Why Creativity Suffers in Competition

12

고2 2023(3월)/42

밑줄 친 (a)~(e) 중에서 문맥상 낱말의 쓰임이 적절하지 않은 것은?

① (a)　　② (b)　　③ (c)　　④ (d)　　⑤ (e)

빠른 정답

A 목적 찾기 ··········· 문제편 p. 12~20
01 ① 02 ② 03 ③ 04 ③ 05 ⑤ 06 ③ 07 ⑤ 08 ⑤ 09 ⑤ 10 ②
11 ⑤ 12 ② 13 ② 14 ② 15 ④ 16 ⑤ 17 ① 18 ③ 19 ②

B 심경의 이해 ··········· 문제편 p. 24~30
01 ③ 02 ⑤ 03 ① 04 ③ 05 ① 06 ① 07 ② 08 ③ 09 ⑤ 10 ①
11 ⑤ 12 ② 13 ② 14 ③ 15 ② 16 ② 17 ② 18 ① 19 ①

C 주장 찾기 ··········· 문제편 p. 34~42
01 ② 02 ⑤ 03 ⑤ 04 ② 05 ② 06 ② 07 ① 08 ② 09 ③ 10 ①
11 ② 12 ⑤ 13 ⑤ 14 ⑤ 15 ④ 16 ④ 17 ⑤ 18 ③

D 밑줄 친 부분의 의미 찾기 ··········· 문제편 p. 46~56
01 ② 02 ⑤ 03 ① 04 ① 05 ④ 06 ① 07 ⑤ 08 ⑤ 09 ③ 10 ①
11 ⑤ 12 ⑤ 13 ⑤ 14 ① 15 ③ 16 ③ 17 ④ 18 ②

E 요지 찾기 ··········· 문제편 p. 60~70
01 ③ 02 ③ 03 ① 04 ① 05 ③ 06 ⑤ 07 ① 08 ③ 09 ④ 10 ⑤
11 ① 12 ① 13 ① 14 ③ 15 ① 16 ① 17 ⑤

F 주제 찾기 ··········· 문제편 p. 74~83
01 ⑤ 02 ② 03 ⑤ 04 ② 05 ⑤ 06 ④ 07 ⑤ 08 ② 09 ④ 10 ①
11 ⑤ 12 ② 13 ① 14 ① 15 ② 16 ① 17 ④

G 제목 찾기 ··········· 문제편 p. 88~98
01 ① 02 ① 03 ① 04 ① 05 ② 06 ③ 07 ⑤ 08 ① 09 ⑤ 10 ①
11 ③ 12 ① 13 ⑤ 14 ② 15 ② 16 ② 17 ① 18 ① 19 ④ 20 ②
21 ④ 22 ① 23 ②

H 도표의 이해 ··········· 문제편 p. 102~110
01 ④ 02 ④ 03 ④ 04 ⑤ 05 ③ 06 ③ 07 ⑤ 08 ⑤ 09 ④ 10 ③
11 ④ 12 ④ 13 ⑤ 14 ⑤ 15 ④ 16 ④ 17 ④

I 내용 불일치 ··········· 문제편 p. 114~124
01 ③ 02 ④ 03 ④ 04 ④ 05 ③ 06 ③ 07 ④ 08 ⑤ 09 ② 10 ⑤
11 ④ 12 ③ 13 ⑤ 14 ④ 15 ③ 16 ⑤ 17 ⑤ 18 ③ 19 ③ 20 ④
21 ③ 22 ③ 23 ④

J 실용문의 이해 ··········· 문제편 p. 128~142
01 ⑤ 02 ② 03 ② 04 ③ 05 ④ 06 ③ 07 ⑤ 08 ④ 09 ⑤ 10 ④
11 ④ 12 ④ 13 ⑤ 14 ⑤ 15 ③ 16 ④ 17 ④ 18 ③ 19 ④ 20 ②
21 ⑤ 22 ④ 23 ⑤ 24 ③ 25 ⑤ 26 ④ 27 ④ 28 ④ 29 ⑤ 30 ⑤

K 어법에 맞지 않는 낱말 찾기 ··········· 문제편 p. 146~154
01 ④ 02 ④ 03 ③ 04 ② 05 ④ 06 ② 07 ③ 08 ⑤ 09 ③ 10 ④
11 ⑤ 12 ④ 13 ④ 14 ③ 15 ④ 16 ④

L 문맥에 맞지 않는 낱말 찾기 ··········· 문제편 p. 158~166
01 ④ 02 ④ 03 ⑤ 04 ④ 05 ⑤ 06 ③ 07 ③ 08 ④ 09 ③ 10 ②
11 ④ 12 ⑤ 13 ④ 14 ⑤ 15 ⑤ 16 ④

M 빈칸 완성하기 ··········· 문제편 p. 170~202
01 ② 02 ③ 03 ② 04 ② 05 ① 06 ② 07 ② 08 ⑤ 09 ① 10 ③
11 ③ 12 ① 13 ① 14 ② 15 ① 16 ② 17 ① 18 ① 19 ① 20 ④
21 ① 22 ② 23 ① 24 ④ 25 ① 26 ② 27 ② 28 ② 29 ② 30 ③
31 ① 32 ④ 33 ② 34 ④ 35 ① 36 ④ 37 ③ 38 ② 39 ④ 40 ②
41 ① 42 ⑤ 43 ② 44 ① 45 ① 46 ① 47 ⑤ 48 ① 49 ③ 50 ⑤
51 ① 52 ③ 53 ② 54 ② 55 ① 56 ① 57 ① 58 ③ 59 ③ 60 ②
61 ① 62 ⑤ 63 ⑤ 64 ④ 65 ③ 66 ④ 67 ③ 68 ① 69 ① 70 ①
71 ② 72 ①

N 흐름에 맞지 않는 문장 찾기 ··········· 문제편 p. 206~215
01 ④ 02 ② 03 ② 04 ③ 05 ④ 06 ③ 07 ④ 08 ④ 09 ④ 10 ④
11 ④ 12 ③ 13 ④ 14 ④ 15 ④ 16 ③ 17 ④ 18 ③ 19 ④ 20 ④

O 글의 순서 정하기 ··········· 문제편 p. 220~236
01 ⑤ 02 ② 03 ⑤ 04 ② 05 ⑤ 06 ② 07 ③ 08 ① 09 ④ 10 ③
11 ③ 12 ② 13 ④ 14 ⑤ 15 ③ 16 ⑤ 17 ② 18 ② 19 ③ 20 ③
21 ④ 22 ③ 23 ② 24 ⑤ 25 ③ 26 ④ 27 ② 28 ⑤ 29 ⑤ 30 ②
31 ③ 32 ③

P 주어진 문장 넣기 ··········· 문제편 p. 240~256
01 ③ 02 ⑤ 03 ⑤ 04 ④ 05 ⑤ 06 ⑤ 07 ⑤ 08 ④ 09 ① 10 ②
11 ③ 12 ③ 13 ② 14 ⑤ 15 ② 16 ② 17 ③ 18 ④ 19 ⑤ 20 ④
21 ⑤ 22 ⑤ 23 ④ 24 ④ 25 ② 26 ② 27 ⑤ 28 ② 29 ④ 30 ⑤
31 ④ 32 ⑤ 33 ⑤ 34 ② 35 ② 36 ④

Q 요약문 완성하기 ··········· 문제편 p. 260~274
01 ① 02 ① 03 ① 04 ① 05 ③ 06 ① 07 ④ 08 ① 09 ① 10 ①
11 ③ 12 ① 13 ② 14 ① 15 ② 16 ③ 17 ① 18 ① 19 ① 20 ①
21 ① 22 ① 23 ②

R 장문의 이해 ··········· 문제편 p. 278~292
01 ② 02 ⑤ 03 ① 04 ② 05 ③ 06 ③ 07 ① 08 ③ 09 ① 10 ④
11 ① 12 ④ 13 ③ 14 ① 15 ① 16 ③ 17 ② 18 ③ 19 ① 20 ④
21 ② 22 ⑤ 23 ② 24 ⑤ 25 ① 26 ⑤ 27 ① 28 ⑤ 29 ⑤ 30 ③
31 ① 32 ④ 33 ② 34 ④ 35 ② 36 ④ 37 ⑤ 38 ⑤ 39 ④ 40 ④

S 복합 문단의 이해 ··········· 문제편 p. 296~314
01 ⑤ 02 ④ 03 ② 04 ④ 05 ③ 06 ② 07 ④ 08 ⑤ 09 ④ 10 ⑤
11 ④ 12 ④ 13 ⑤ 14 ② 15 ④ 16 ⑤ 17 ③ 18 ② 19 ④ 20 ③
21 ③ 22 ④ 23 ③ 24 ④ 25 ④ 26 ② 27 ③ 28 ④ 29 ② 30 ③
31 ④ 32 ② 33 ④ 34 ④ 35 ② 36 ④ 37 ④ 38 ④ 39 ④ 40 ④
41 ④ 42 ④ 43 ④ 44 ④ 45 ⑤ 46 ② 47 ④ 48 ③ 49 ③ 50 ②
51 ⑤

〈고난도 유형 독해 모의고사〉

1회 모의고사 ··········· 문제편 p. 318~323
01 ④ 02 ⑤ 03 ⑤ 04 ④ 05 ④ 06 ① 07 ⑤ 08 ② 09 ③ 10 ①
11 ② 12 ④

2회 모의고사 ··········· 문제편 p. 324~329
01 ④ 02 ⑤ 03 ⑤ 04 ④ 05 ③ 06 ③ 07 ② 08 ⑤ 09 ③ 10 ①
11 ① 12 ④

3회 모의고사 ··········· 문제편 p. 330~335
01 ③ 02 ⑤ 03 ④ 04 ⑤ 05 ③ 06 ④ 07 ② 08 ④ 09 ② 10 ①
11 ① 12 ③

A 목적 찾기

문제편 p. 12~20

A 01 정답 ① *새로운 반려견 공원 개장

Dear Dog Owners, / 친애하는 반려견 주인 여러분 /

My name is Lily Paxton, / and I'm the town's Pet Program Coordinator. //
제 이름은 Lily Paxton이며 / 저는 이 마을의 반려동물 프로그램 코디네이터입니다 //

형용사적 용법 (our goal 수식)   make의 목적어와 목적격 보어 (형용사)
As part of our goal / to make the community more dog-friendly, / we recently opened / a new dog park. // 단서 새로운 반려견 공원 개장을 알림
목표의 일환으로 / 이 지역 사회를 더욱 반려견 친화적으로 만들기 위한 / 저희는 최근에 개장했습니다 / 새로운 반려견 공원을 /

부사적 용법 (목적)
The park was designed / to provide an enjoyable experience / for both dogs and owners. //
이 공원은 설계되었습니다 / 즐거운 경험을 제공하도록 / 반려견과 주인 모두에게 //

관계부사 (선행사: areas)
There are big grassy areas / where your dogs can run, jump, and play. //
넓은 잔디밭이 있습니다 / 반려견들이 달리고, 점프하고, 놀 수 있는 //

We have separate spaces / for small dogs and big dogs, / to
부사적 용법 (목적)
ensure safety. //
저희는 별도의 공간을 마련했습니다 / 소형견과 대형견을 위한 / 안전을 보장하기 위해 //

You'll also find lots of benches and areas / for resting and staying cool. //
여러분들은 벤치들과 공간들도 많이 찾을 수 있을 것입니다 / 휴식을 취하고 시원하게 머물 수 있는 //

뒤에 목적어절 접속사 that이 생략됨
We hope / you will have a wonderful time with your dogs / in this newly opened park. //
저희는 바랍니다 / 여러분이 반려견과 함께 멋진 시간을 보내시길 / 새롭게 개장한 이 공원에서 /

Regards, Lily Paxton, Pet Program Coordinator /
Lily Paxton, 반려동물 프로그램 코디네이터 드림 /

• coordinator ⓝ 코디네이터   • community ⓝ 지역 사회
• recently ⓪ 최근에   • grassy area 잔디밭   • separate ⓐ 별도의
• ensure ⓥ 보장하다   • newly ⓪ 새롭게

친애하는 반려견 주인 여러분,
제 이름은 Lily Paxton이며, 저는 이 마을의 반려동물 프로그램 코디네이터입니다. 이 지역 사회를 더욱 반려견 친화적으로 만들기 위한 목표의 일환으로, 저희는 최근에 새로운 반려견 공원을 개장했습니다. 이 공원은 반려견과 주인 모두에게 즐거운 경험을 제공하도록 설계되었습니다. 반려견들이 달리고, 점프하고, 놀 수 있는 넓은 잔디밭들이 있습니다. 안전을 보장하기 위해, 저희는 소형견과 대형견을 위한 별도의 공간을 마련했습니다. 여러분들은 휴식을 취하고 시원하게 머물 수 있는 벤치들과 공간들도 많이 찾을 수 있을 것입니다. 저희는 새롭게 개장한 이 공원에서 여러분이 반려견과 함께 멋진 시간을 보내시길 바랍니다.
Lily Paxton, 반려동물 프로그램 코디네이터 드림

다음 글의 목적으로 가장 적절한 것은?

① 새로 만든 반려견 공원의 개장을 홍보하려고
　새로운 반려견 공원의 개장을 알리고 있음
② 동물 보호 정책에 대한 의견을 구하려고 동물 보호 정책은 언급되지 않았음
③ 유기견 보호 자원봉사자를 모집하려고 유기견 보호는 언급되지 않았음
④ 반려견 공원 운영 시간의 변경을 안내하려고 운영 시간은 언급되지 않았음
⑤ 반려견 훈련 프로그램에의 참여를 권유하려고
　반려견 훈련 프로그램은 언급되지 않았음

>왜 정답? ❋❋❋ [정답률 97%]

마을의 반려견 프로그램 코디네이터가 새로운 반려견 공원의 개장을 알리고 공원 시설을 소개하고 있는 내용이므로 정답은 ①이다.

>왜 오답?

② 동물 보호 정책은 언급되지 않았다.
③ 유기견 보호는 언급되지 않았다.
④ 반려견 공원의 운영 시간이 아니라, 시설에 관해서만 언급되었다.
⑤ 반려견 훈련 프로그램은 언급되지 않았다.

A 02 정답 ② *TourTide Magazine 온라인 구독 권유

Dear Reader, / 독자분께 /

We always appreciate your support. //
보내주신 성원에 항상 감사드립니다 //

As you know, / our service is now available / through an app. // 앱을 통해서 /
아시다시피 / 이제 저희 서비스를 이용하실 수 있습니다 / 앱을 통해서 //

형용사적 용법 (a better time 수식)
There has never been a better time / to switch to an online membership of *TourTide Magazine*. // 단서1 온라인 회원으로 전환하기에 가장 좋은 시기임
이보다 더 좋은 시기는 없습니다 / TourTide Magazine의 온라인 회원으로 전환하기에 //

At a 50% discount off your current print subscription, / you can access / a full year of online reading. // 단서2 할인된 가격으로 온라인 구독이 가능함
당신의 현재 인쇄본 구독료에서 50% 할인된 가격으로 / 구독할 수 있습니다 / 1년 치를 온라인으로 //

Get new issues and daily web pieces at TourTide.com, / read or
병렬 구조(명령문)
listen to *TourTide Magazine* via the app, / and get our members-only newsletter. //
TourTide.com에서 신간호와 일일 웹 기사를 받아보고 / 앱을 통해 TourTide Magazine을 읽거나 청취해 보고 / 회원 전용 뉴스레터도 받아보세요 //

You'll also gain access / to our editors' selections of the best articles. //
받아볼 수 있습니다 / 편집자들이 선정한 최고의 기사도 //

Join today! // 단서3 가입을 권유함
오늘 가입하세요 //

Yours, *TourTide* Team / TourTide 팀 드림 /

• appreciate ⓥ 감사하다   • available ⓐ 이용 가능한
• switch ⓥ 전환하다   • subscription ⓝ 구독
• access ⓥ 이용하다, 접근하다   • via prep ~을 통해

독자분께,
보내주신 성원에 항상 감사드립니다. 아시다시피, 이제 앱을 통해서도 저희 서비스를 이용하실 수 있습니다. TourTide Magazine의 온라인 회원으로 전환하기에 이보다 더 좋은 시기는 없습니다. 당신의 현재 인쇄본 구독료에서 50% 할인된 가격으로 1년 치를 온라인으로 구독할 수 있습니다. TourTide.com에서 신간호와 일일 웹 기사를 받아보고, 앱을 통해 TourTide Magazine을 읽거나 청취해 보고, 회원 전용 뉴스레터도 받아보세요. 편집자들이 선정한 최고의 기사도 받아볼 수 있습니다. 오늘 가입하세요!
TourTide 팀 드림

다음 글의 목적으로 가장 적절한 것은?

① 여행 일정 지연에 대해 사과하려고 여행 일정에 관한 내용이 아님
② 잡지 온라인 구독을 권유하려고
　할인된 가격으로 온라인 구독이 가능하기에 가입하기 좋은 시기라고 하며 권유함
③ 무료 잡지 신청을 홍보하려고 무료 잡지 신청에 대한 언급은 없음
④ 여행 후기 모집을 안내하려고 여행 후기를 모집하려는 내용이 아님
⑤ 기사에 대한 독자 의견에 답변하려고 잡지 구독을 권유하는 글임

잡지 독자에게 온라인 멤버십 구독 시 받을 수 있는 혜택들을 설명하면서 온라인 구독을 권유하고 있으므로 정답은 ②이다.

>왜 오답?

① 여행 일정에 관한 언급은 없다.
③ 온라인 구독을 권유하는 것이지 무료인 것은 아니다. 함정
④ 여행 후기를 모집하려는 내용이 아니다.
⑤ 기사에 대한 독자 의견에 대해 답변하는 글이 아니다.

Ⓐ 03 정답 ③ ＊작품 전시 안내

Dear Miranda, /
Miranda님께 /

Thank you / for participating in our Crafts Art Fair. //
감사합니다 / 우리의 Crafts Art Fair에 참여해 주셔서 //

Since we've chosen you / as one of the 'Artists of This Year', /
'~로(서)'

we are looking forward to introducing / your unique handmade
look forward to -ing: ~ 하는 것을 기대하다

baskets / to our community. //
우리가 당신을 선정했기에 / '올해의 예술가들' 중 한 명으로 / 소개하기를 기대하고 있습니다 / 당신의 독창적인 수공예 바구니를 / 우리 지역 사회에 //
'~의 일환으로'

As part of organizing the exhibition plan, / we are happy
목적어절 접속사
to inform you / that your artworks will be exhibited / at the
assigned table, number seven. // 단서 작품이 전시될 테이블 안내
전시 배치도를 조직하는 것의 일환으로 / 알려 드리게 되어 우리는 기쁩니다 / 당신의 작품이 전시될 예정임을 / 지정된 7번 테이블에 //
앞에 주격 관계대명사와 be동사가 생략됨
Visitors can easily find your artworks / located near the
entrance. //
방문객들이 당신의 작품을 쉽게 찾을 수 있습니다 / 입구 근처에 위치한 //

If you have any special requirements / or need further
assistance, / feel free to contact us / in advance. //
특별한 요구 사항이 있거나 / 추가적인 도움이 필요하시면 / 편히 연락해 주시기 바랍니다 / 미리 //

Sincerely, / Helen Dwyer /
진심을 담아 / Helen Dwyer /

- introduce ⓥ 소개하다   · handmade ⓐ 수공예의
- organize ⓥ 조직하다   · exhibition plan 전시 배치도
- inform ⓥ 알리다   · requirement ⓝ 요구 사항
- further ⓐ 추가적인   · assistance ⓝ 도움

Miranda님께,
우리의 Crafts Art Fair에 참여해 주셔서 감사합니다. 우리가 당신을 '올해의 예술가들' 중 한 명으로 선정했기에, 당신의 독창적인 수공예 바구니를 우리 지역 사회에 소개하기를 기대하고 있습니다. 전시 배치도를 조직하는 것의 일환으로, 우리는 당신의 작품이 지정된 7번 테이블에 전시될 예정임을 알려 드리게 되어 기쁩니다. 방문객들이 입구 근처에 위치한 당신의 작품을 쉽게 찾을 수 있습니다. 특별한 요구 사항이 있거나 추가적인 도움이 필요하시면, 편히 미리 연락해 주시기 바랍니다.
진심을 담아,
Helen Dwyer

다음 글의 목적으로 가장 적절한 것은?
① 공예품 구매 희망자를 소개하려고 판매가 아닌 전시에 관한 내용임
② 비상시 박람회장 대피 동선을 안내하려고 비상 대피 동선은 언급되지 않았음
③ 작품이 전시될 지정 테이블을 알려 주려고
올해의 예술가로 선정되어 테이블을 배정받음
④ 올해의 공예가 선정 투표 방식을 공지하려고 선정 투표 방식은 언급되지 않았음
⑤ 박람회에 참여할 새로운 공예가를 모집하려고
이미 선정되어 작품이 전시될 예정임

올해의 예술가로 선정되어 작품이 전시될 예정이고 작품의 전시 위치를 안내하는 내용이므로 정답은 ③이다.

>왜 오답?

① 공예품 판매가 아닌 전시에 관한 글이다.
② 비상시 대피 동선은 언급되지 않았다.
④ 선정 투표 방식은 언급되지 않았다.
⑤ 편지를 받은 Miranda는 이미 올해의 예술가 중 한 명으로 선정되었다.

구문 서술형

정답 Visitors, can (easily) find, your artworks

해석 방문객들이 입구 근처에 위치한 당신의 작품을 쉽게 찾을 수 있다.
→ 해당 문장의 주어는 Visitors, 동사는 can (easily) find, 목적어는 your artworks이다.

Ⓐ 04 정답 ③ ＊도서관 운영 시간 연장 요청

Dear Principal Jones, / Jones 교장 선생님께 /

I hope / this message finds you well. //
저는 바랍니다 / 이 메시지가 당신에게 잘 전달되기를 //
'~로서'   부사적 용법 (목적)
As student council president, / I am reaching out / to discuss
an important matter / regarding our school library's current
'~에 관하여'
operating hours. //
학생회장으로서 / 저는 연락드립니다 / 중요한 문제를 논의하고자 / 우리 학교 도서관의 현재 운영 시간에 관한 //
계속적 용법의 주격 관계대명사   삽입절
At present, / the library closes at 5 p.m., / which many students
관계사절의 동사   형용사적 용법 (ability 수식)
feel limits their ability / to fully use its resources for study and
research / after regular class hours. //
현재 / 도서관은 오후 5시에 문을 닫는데 / 이는 많은 학생이 느끼기에 능력을 제한합니다 / 학습과 연구를 위해 도서관 자원을 충분히 사용할 수 있는 / 정규 수업 시간 이후 //

This is particularly challenging for those / preparing for college
병렬 구조
entrance exams / or working on academic projects / that demand
주격 관계대명사 (선행사: projects)
a quiet and resourceful environment. //
이것은 특히 그들에게 어렵습니다 / 대학 입학 시험을 준비하거나 / 학업 연구과제를 수행하는 / 조용하고 자료가 풍부한 환경을 요하는 //
ask의 목적어와 목적격 보어 (to부정사)
Therefore, / I'd like to ask you / to extend the library's operating
hours to 7 p.m. // 단서 도서관 운영 시간 연장을 요청함
그러므로 / 저는 당신에게 요청드리고 싶습니다 / 도서관 운영 시간을 오후 7시까지 연장해 주시기를 //
by -ing: ~함으로써
This change would greatly benefit students / by providing
형용사적 용법 (time 수식)
additional time / to focus on their academic goals. //
이러한 변화는 학생들에게 크게 이익이 될 것입니다 / 추가시간을 제공함으로써 / 그들의 학업 목표에 집중하기 위한 //

I hope you will consider this proposal / as a step / toward
improving our academic environment / and better supporting
our needs. //
저는 이 제안을 당신이 고려 해주시기를 바랍니다 / 단계로써 / 우리의 학업 환경을 개선하고 / 우리의 필요성을 더 잘 지지해주는 //

Sincerely, / 진심을 담아 /

Eric Park / Student Council President / Eric Park / 학생회장 /

- reach out 연락하다   · current ⓐ 현재의
- operating hour 운영 시간   · resource ⓝ 자원
- entrance ⓝ 입학   · academic ⓐ 학문의, 학업의
- extend ⓥ 연장하다   · proposal ⓝ 제안

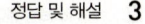

Jones 교장 선생님께,

저는 이 메시지가 당신에게 잘 전달되기를 바랍니다. 학생회장으로서 저는 우리 학교 도서관의 현재 운영 시간에 관한 중요한 문제를 논의하고자 연락드립니다. 현재, 도서관은 오후 5시에 문을 닫는데, 이는 많은 학생이 느끼기에, 정규 수업 시간 이후 학습과 연구를 위해 도서관 자원을 충분히 사용할 수 있는 능력을 제한합니다. 이것은 특히 대학 입학 시험을 준비하거나 조용하고 자료가 풍부한 환경을 요하는 학업 연구과제를 수행하는 그들에게 어렵습니다. 그러므로, 저는 도서관 운영 시간을 오후 7시까지 연장해 주시기를 당신에게 요청드리고 싶습니다. 이러한 변화는 그들의 학업 목표에 집중하기 위한 추가 시간을 제공함으로써 학생들에게 크게 이익이 될 것입니다. 저는 우리의 학업 환경을 개선하고 우리의 필요성을 더 잘 지지해주는 단계로써 이 제안을 당신이 고려 해주시기를 바랍니다.

진심을 담아, Eric Park 학생회장

다음 글의 목적으로 가장 적절한 것은?
① 신간 도서 구입을 건의하려고 신간 도서 구입은 언급되지 않았음
② 도서관 프로그램 확대를 부탁하려고 프로그램 확대는 언급되지 않았음
③ 도서관 운영 시간 연장을 요청하려고 도서관 운영 시간을 연장할 것을 요청함
④ 도서 대출 시스템 개선에 감사하려고 도서 대출 시스템은 언급되지 않았음
⑤ 도서관 열람실 공간 확대를 제안하려고 공간 확대는 언급되지 않았음

왜 정답? ✱✱✱ [정답률 96%]
학업 목표에 집중할 추가 시간을 위해 도서관의 운영 시간 연장을 요청하므로 글의 목적은 ③이다.

왜 오답?
① 신간 도서 구입은 언급되지 않았다.
② 도서관 프로그램이 아닌, 운영 시간 연장을 요청하고 있다.
④ 도서 대출 시스템은 언급되지 않았다.
⑤ 열람실 공간 확대는 언급되지 않았다.

구문 서술형

정답 2, This, is, 주격 보어, challenging

해석 이것은 특히 대학 입학 시험을 준비하거나 조용하고 자료가 풍부한 환경을 요하는 학업 연구과제를 수행하는 그들에게 어렵다.
→ 2형식 문장은 「주어 + 동사 + 주격 보어」로 이루어진 문장이다. 동사로는 주로 be동사나 become, look, feel, seem 등이 쓰이며 이때 주격 보어로는 명사나 형용사가 쓰인다.

A 05 정답 ⑤ *서류 검토 결과 통지 요구

To the State Education Department, / 주 교육부 귀중 /
I am writing / with regard to the state's funding / for the
'~와 관련하여'
construction project at Fort Montgomery High School. //
저는 편지를 씁니다 / 주 예산과 관련하여 / Fort Montgomery 고등학교의 건축 프로젝트를 위한 //
Our school needs additional spaces / to provide a fully functional
형용사적 용법 (spaces 수식)
Art and Library Media Center / to serve our students / in a more
부사적 용법 (목적)
meaningful way. //
저희 학교는 추가 공간이 필요합니다 / 완전하게 제 기능을 하는 Art and Library Media Center를 제공하기 위한 / 학생들을 만족시키기 위해 / 보다 의미 있는 방식으로 //
전치사 + 동명사
Despite submitting all required documentation for funding / to
your department / in April 2024, / we have not yet received / any
notification from your department. //
재정 지원에 필요한 모든 서류를 제출했음에도 불구하고 / 귀하의 부서로 / 2024년 4월에 / 저희는 아직 받지 못했습니다 / 귀하의 부서로부터 어떠한 통지도 //

A delay in the process / can carry considerable consequences /
related to the school's budgetary constraints and schedule. //
과정상 지연은 / 상당한 결과를 초래할 수 있습니다 / 학교의 예산 제약 및 일정과 관련하여 //
「in order to + 동사원형」; ~하기 위해   뒤에 목적어절 접속사 that 생략
Therefore, / in order to proceed with our project, / we request
'~와 관련하여'
you / notify us of the review result / regarding the submitted
documentation. // 단서 제출한 서류에 대한 검토 결과를 통지해달라고 요청함
그러므로 / 저희의 프로젝트를 진행하기 위해 / 요청합니다 / 검토 결과를 저희에게 통지해 줄 것을 / 제출 서류와 관련한 //
look forward to ~ing: ~을 고대하다
I look forward to hearing from you. // 귀하로부터의 답변을 고대합니다 //
Respectfully, Clara Smith / Clara Smith 드림 /
Principal, Fort Montgomery High School /
Fort Montgomery 고등학교 교장 /

- funding ⓝ 재정 지원   - construction ⓝ 건축, 건설
- additional ⓐ 추가적인   - functional ⓐ 기능을 하는
- submit ⓥ 제출하다   - documentation ⓝ 서류
- notification ⓝ 통지   - considerable ⓐ 상당한
- consequence ⓝ 결과   - budgetary ⓐ 예산의
- constraint ⓝ 제약   - notify A of B A에게 B를 통지하다

주 교육부 귀중,
저는 Fort Montgomery 고등학교의 건축 프로젝트를 위한 주 예산과 관련하여 편지를 씁니다. 저희 학교는 보다 의미있는 방식으로 학생들을 만족시키기 위해 완전하게 제 기능을 하는 Art and Library Media Center를 제공하기 위한 추가 공간이 필요합니다. 2024년 4월에 귀하의 부서로 예산에 필요한 모든 서류를 제출했음에도 불구하고, 저희는 아직 귀하의 부서로부터 어떠한 통지도 받지 못했습니다. 과정상 지연은 학교의 예산 제한 및 일정과 관련하여 상당한 결과를 초래할 수 있습니다. 그러므로, 저희의 프로젝트를 진행하기 위해 제출 서류와 관련한 검토 결과를 저희에게 통지해 줄 것을 요청합니다. 귀하로부터의 답변을 고대합니다.
Fort Montgomery 고등학교 교장, Clara Smith 드림

다음 글의 목적으로 가장 적절한 것은?
① 제출 서류의 마감 기한 연장을 요청하려고 마감 기한에 관한 내용이 아님
② 교내 미디어 센터의 리모델링을 제안하려고 리모델링은 언급되지 않았음
③ 학교 프로젝트에 배정된 예산을 확인하려고 예산을 확인하는 내용이 아님
④ 학교 공간 조성을 위한 공모전을 홍보하려고 공모전은 언급되지 않았음
⑤ 제출 서류에 대한 검토 결과 통지를 요구하려고
제출 서류에 관련한 검토 결과를 통지해 줄 것을 요청함

왜 정답? ✱✱✱ [정답률 73%]
건축 프로젝트를 위한 예산 지원을 받기 위해 필요한 서류를 제출했음에도 아직 아무런 통지를 받지 못했기에 제출 서류와 관련한 검토 결과 통지를 요청하고 있으므로 글의 목적은 ⑤이다.

왜 오답?
① 이미 서류는 제출하였으므로 마감 기한에 대한 연장을 요청하는 것이 아니다.
② 교내 미디어 센터의 리모델링은 언급되지 않았다.
③ 건축 프로젝트를 위한 예산을 지원받는 과정에서 제출 서류의 검토 결과를 요청할 뿐, 배정된 예산을 확인하는 것이 글의 목적은 아니다. 함정
④ 학교 공간 조성을 위한 공모전은 언급되지 않았다.

구문 서술형

정답 you, 3형식, 우리는 당신이 검토 결과를 통지해 줄 것을 요청합니다

→ 문장의 접속부사 Therefore와 전치사구 in order to ~ project를 제외하면 주어 we, 동사 request, 그리고 목적어절 (that) you notify ~ documentation으로 이루어진 3형식 문장이다. 목적어절은 '~하는 것'으로 해석하므로 '우리는 당신이 ~해 줄 것을 요청합니다'라고 해석한다.

A 06 정답 ③ *작가에게 학교 특별 강연 요청하기

Dear Ms. Jane Watson, /
Jane Watson 씨께 /

I am John Austin, / a science teacher / at Crestville High School. // (동격)
저는 John Austin입니다 / 과학 교사인 / Crestville 고등학교의 //

Recently / I was impressed / by the latest book you wrote / about the environment. // (앞에 목적격 관계대명사 생략)
최근에 / 저는 감명받았습니다 / 당신이 쓴 최신 도서에 / 환경에 관해서 //

Also / my students read your book / and had a class discussion about it. //
또한 / 저의 학생들은 당신의 책을 읽었고 / 그것에 대한 수업 토론을 하였습니다 //

They are big fans of your book, / so I'd like to ask you / to visit our school / and give a special lecture. // (ask의 목적격 보어(to부정사)) 단서 1 작가에게 학교를 방문하여 특별 강연을 해달라고 요청함
그들은 당신의 책을 아주 좋아합니다 / 그래서 저는 당신에게 요청드리고 싶습니다 / 우리 학교에 방문하여 / 특별 강연을 해 주시기를 //

We can set the date and time / to suit your schedule. //
우리는 날짜와 시간을 정할 수 있습니다 / 당신의 일정에 맞춰 //

Having you at our school / would be a fantastic experience / for the students. // (동명사 주어) 단서 2 작가의 방문과 강연이 학생들에게 어떤 영향을 미칠지 설명함
당신이 우리 학교에 와 주신다면 / 멋진 경험이 될 것 같습니다 / 학생들에게 //

We would be very grateful / if you could come. // (주절이 앞에 온 가정법 과거 문장)
우리는 정말 감사하겠습니다 / 당신이 와 주신다면 //

Best regards, John Austin /
John Austin 드림 /

- science ⓝ 과학
- recently ⓐⓓ 최근에
- impressed ⓐ 감명을 받은
- environment ⓝ 환경
- discussion ⓝ 토론
- lecture ⓝ 강의
- suit ⓥ 맞추다
- experience ⓝ 경험
- grateful ⓐ 감사한

Jane Watson 씨께,
저는 Crestville 고등학교의 과학 교사 John Austin입니다. 최근에, 저는 환경에 관해 당신이 쓴 최신 도서에 감명받았습니다. 또한 저의 학생들은 당신의 책을 읽었고 그것에 대해 토론 수업을 하였습니다. 그들은 당신의 책을 아주 좋아하고, 그래서 저는 당신이 우리 학교에 방문하여 특별 강연을 해 주시기를 요청드리고 싶습니다. 우리는 당신의 일정에 맞춰 날짜와 시간을 정할 수 있습니다. 당신이 우리 학교에 와 주신다면 학생들에게 멋진 경험이 될 것 같습니다. 우리는 당신이 와 주신다면 정말 감사하겠습니다.
John Austin 드림

다음 글의 목적으로 가장 적절한 것은?

① 환경 보호의 중요성을 강조하려고 — 작가가 환경에 관한 책을 썼다고 했으나, 환경 보호의 중요성을 강조하는 내용은 없음
② 글쓰기에서 주의할 점을 알려 주려고 — 작가의 책에 감명받았다며 칭찬하고 있음
③ 특강 강사로 작가의 방문을 요청하려고 — I'd like to ask you to visit our school and give a special lecture
④ 작가의 팬 사인회 일정 변경을 공지하려고 — 팬 사인회나 일정 변경에 관한 내용은 없음
⑤ 작가가 쓴 책의 내용에 관하여 문의하려고 — 책의 내용에 대해 질문하지 않음

왜 정답? ✿❀❀ [정답률 94%]

작가에게 학교를 방문하여 특별 강연을 해달라고 요청하고 있고 작가의 방문이 학생들에게 멋진 경험이 될 것이라고 했기 때문에 글의 목적은 ③이다.

왜 오답?

① 작가가 쓴 최신 도서가 환경에 관한 책이라는 내용만 나와 있다. 함정
② 작가의 책에 감명받았다고 칭찬하고 있으며 글쓰기에서 주의할 점은 언급하지 않았다.
④ 작가의 팬 사인회와 그 일정 변경에 관한 내용은 없다.
⑤ 작가의 방문과 특별 강연을 요청할 뿐, 책의 내용에 대해서는 질문하지 않았다.

A 07 정답 ⑤ *기차역 유인 매표소 재운영 요구

To whom it may concern, /
관계자분께 /

I am writing / to express my deep concern / about the recent change / made by Pittsburgh Train Station. // (부사적 용법(목적)) (앞에 주격 관계대명사와 be동사가 생략됨)
저는 글을 쓰고 있습니다 / 저의 깊은 우려를 표하기 위해 / 최근의 변경에 대해 / Pittsburgh Train Station에 의한 //

The station had traditional ticket offices with staff before, / but these have been replaced with ticket vending machines. // (현재완료 수동태)
이전에는 역에 직원이 있는 전통적인 매표소가 있었지만 / 이것들은 승차권 발매기로 대체되었습니다 //

However, / individuals who are unfamiliar with these machines / are now experiencing difficulty / accessing the railway services. // (복수 주어) (주격 관계대명사) (복수 동사)
그러나 / 이러한 기계에 익숙하지 않은 사람들은 / 현재 어려움을 겪고 있습니다 / 철도 서비스에 접근하는 데 //

Since these individuals heavily relied on the staff assistance / to be able to travel, / they are in great need of / ticket offices with staff in the station. // (부사절 접속사(이유)) (부사적 용법(목적)) (be in need of: ~을 필요로 하다)
이 사람들은 직원의 도움에 크게 의존했기 때문에 / 이동할 수 있기 위해 / 그들은 매우 필요로 합니다 / 역 내에 직원이 있는 매표소를 //

Therefore, I am urging you / to consider reopening the ticket offices. // (urging의 목적어와 목적격 보어(to부정사)) 단서 매표소 재운영 고려를 촉구함
그러므로 저는 당신에게 촉구합니다 / 매표소 재운영을 고려할 것을 //

With the staff back in their positions, / many people would regain access / to the railway services. // (「with + 명사 ~, 주어 + 조동사 과거 + 동사원형」: with 가정법)
직원이 그들의 자리로 돌아오면 / 많은 사람이 접근을 다시 얻을 것입니다 / 철도 서비스에 대한 //

I look forward to your prompt attention to this matter / and a positive resolution. //
저는 이 문제에 대한 당신의 신속한 관심을 기대합니다 / 그리고 긍정적인 해결을 //

Sincerely, / Sarah Roberts /
진심을 담아 / Sarah Roberts /

- concern ⓝ 우려
- traditional ⓐ 전통적인
- vending machine 자동판매기
- assistance ⓝ 도움
- urge ⓥ 촉구하다
- regain ⓥ 되찾다
- prompt ⓐ 신속한
- resolution ⓝ 해결

관계자분께,
저는 Pittsburgh Train Station에 의한 최근의 변경에 대해 저의 깊은 우려를 표하기 위해 글을 쓰고 있습니다. 이전에는 역에 직원이 있는 전통적인 매표소가 있었지만, 이것들은 승차권 발매기로 대체되었습니다. 그러나 이러한 기계에 익숙하지 않은 사람들은 현재 철도 서비스에 접근하는 데 어려움을 겪고 있습니다. 이 사람들은 이동할 수 있기 위해 직원의 도움에 크게 의존했기 때문에, 그들은 역 내에 직원이 있는 매표소를 매우 필요로 합니다. 그러므로 저는 당신에게 매표소 재운영을 고려할 것을 촉구합니다. 직원이 그들의 자리로 돌아오면 많은 사람이 철도 서비스에 대한 접근을 다시 얻을 것입니다. 저는 이 문제에 대한 당신의 신속한 관심과 긍정적인 해결을 기대합니다.
진심을 담아, Sarah Roberts

다음 글의 목적으로 가장 적절한 것은?

① 승차권 발매기 수리를 의뢰하려고 — 수리에 대한 언급은 없음
② 기차표 단체 예매 방법을 문의하려고 — 단체 예매 방법에 관한 내용이 아님
③ 기차 출발 시간 지연에 대해 항의하려고 — 출발 시간 지연에 관한 언급은 없음
④ 기차역 직원의 친절한 도움에 감사하려고 — 직원의 도움에 감사하는 내용이 아님
⑤ 기차역 유인 매표소 재운영을 요구하려고 — 기차역 유인 매표소 재운영을 고려할 것을 촉구함

>왜 정답? ❋❀❀ [정답률 92%]

기계에 익숙하지 않은 사람들이 승차권 발매기 사용을 어려워하고 있다며 유인 매표소 재운영을 요구하고 있으므로 글의 목적은 ⑤이다.

>왜 오답?

① 매표소가 승차권 발매기로 대체되었다고는 했지만, 수리는 언급되지 않았다.
② 기차표 단체 예매에 관한 내용이 아니다.
③ 기차 출발 시간이 지연되었다는 것은 언급되지 않았다.
④ 기차역 직원의 친절한 도움은 언급되지 않았다.

A 08 정답 ⑤ ＊새로운 의류 매장의 판매직에 지원하는 Grace

Dear Ms. MacAlpine, / 친애하는 MacAlpine 씨께 /
명사절 접속사
I was so excited to hear / **that** your brand is opening a new shop / on Bruns Street next month. //
저는 듣고 매우 들떴습니다 / 당신의 브랜드가 새 매장을 연다는 것을 / 다음 달에 Bruns 거리에 //

현재완료(계속)　　　　　　　　*helps의 목적어와 목적격 보어(to부정사)*
I **have** always **appreciated** / the way your brand helps / **women to feel** more stylish and confident. //
저는 항상 높이 평가해 왔습니다 / 당신의 브랜드가 도와주는 방식을 / 여성들이 더 멋지고 자신감 있게 느끼도록 //

단서 1 구인 광고에 대한 응답으로 편지를 쓰고 있음
I am writing / in response to your ad / in the Bruns Journal. //
저는 편지를 쓰고 있습니다 / 당신의 광고에 대한 응답으로 / Bruns Journal에 있는 //

현재완료(계속)
I graduated from the Meline School of Fashion / and **have worked** as a sales assistant / at LoganMart for the last five years. //
저는 Meline 패션 학교를 졸업했고 / 판매 보조원으로 일해 왔습니다 / 지난 5년간 LoganMart에서 //

현재완료(계속)　　　　　　　　= want
During that time, / I'**ve developed** strong customer service and sales skills, / and now I **would like** to apply for the sales position / in your clothing store. // **단서 2** 판매원으로서의 자질을 소개하며 판매직에 지원하고자 함
그 기간 동안 / 저는 뛰어난 고객 서비스 및 판매 기술을 발달시켜 왔고 / 이제 판매직에 지원하고 싶습니다 / 당신의 의류 매장의 //

I am available for an interview / at your earliest convenience. //
저는 인터뷰가 가능합니다 / 당신이 편한 가장 빠른 시간에 //

I look forward to hearing from you. //
당신으로부터 대답을 듣게 되기를 기대합니다 //

Thank you for reading my letter. //
저의 편지를 읽어 주셔서 감사드립니다 //

Yours sincerely, Grace Braddock / Grace Braddock 드림 /

- appreciate ⓥ 감사하다　　• confident ⓐ 자신감 있는
- in response to ~에 대한 응답으로　　• ad(= advertisement) ⓝ 광고
- graduate ⓥ 졸업하다　　• at one's convenience 편한 때에

친애하는 MacAlpine 씨께,
저는 당신의 브랜드가 다음 달에 Bruns 거리에 새 매장을 연다는 것을 듣고 매우 들떴습니다. 저는 당신의 브랜드가 여성들이 더 멋지고 자신감 있게 느끼도록 도와주는 방식을 항상 높이 평가해 왔습니다. 저는 Bruns Journal에 있는 당신의 광고에 대한 응답으로 편지를 쓰고 있습니다. 저는 Meline 패션 학교를 졸업했고 지난 5년간 LoganMart에서 판매 보조원으로 일해 왔습니다. 그 기간 동안 저는 뛰어난 고객 서비스 및 판매 기술을 발달시켜 왔고, 이제 당신의 의류 매장의 판매직에 지원하고 싶습니다. 저는 당신이 편한 가장 빠른 시간에 인터뷰가 가능합니다. 당신으로부터 대답을 듣게 되기를 기대합니다. 저의 편지를 읽어 주셔서 감사드립니다.
Grace Braddock 드림

다음 글의 목적으로 가장 적절한 것은?

① 영업 시작일을 문의하려고 　영업이 다음 달에 시작한다는 것을 이미 알고 있음
② 인터뷰 일정을 변경하려고 　구직 인터뷰를 요청하고 있음
③ 디자인 공모전에 참가하려고 　디자인 공모전에 관한 언급은 없음
④ 제품 관련 문의에 답변하려고 　특정 제품과 관련된 언급은 없음
⑤ 의류 매장 판매직에 지원하려고 　새로 오픈하는 의류 매장의 판매직에 지원하고자 함

>왜 정답? ❋❀❀ [정답률 92%]

브랜드가 새 매장을 연다는 소식을 듣고, 자신의 패션 관련 학력과 경력을 소개하며 의류 매장의 판매직에 지원하고자 하므로 정답은 ⑤이다.

>왜 오답?

① 영업은 다음 달에 시작한다고 제시되었다.
② 구직 인터뷰를 요청하고 있으므로, 일정을 변경한다는 것은 옳지 않다. 　주의
③ 디자인 공모전에 관한 언급은 없었다.
④ 특정 제품과 관련된 언급은 없었다.

A 09 정답 ⑤ ＊화학 박람회를 위한 대학생 모집

Dear Professor Sanchez, / Sanchez 교수님께 /

My name is Ellis Wight, / and I'm the director of the Alexandria Science Museum. //
제 이름은 Ellis Wight이고 / 저는 Alexandria 과학 박물관의 관장입니다 //

We are holding a Chemistry Fair / for local middle school students / on Saturday, October 28. //
저희는 화학 박람회를 개최합니다 / 지역 중학교 학생들을 위한 / 10월 28일 토요일에 //

명사적 용법(주격 보어)　　　　　*to부정사의 수동태*
The goal of the fair is **to encourage** them / **to be interested** in science / through guided experiments. // 이 박람회의 목적은 그들을 장려하는 것입니다 / 과학에 관심을 갖도록 / 안내되는 실험을 통해 //

주격 관계대명사
We are looking for college students / **who** can help with the experiments / during the event. // **단서 1** 박람회에서 실험을 도와줄 대학생을 모집 중임
저희는 대학생을 모집합니다 / 실험을 도와줄 수 있는 / 행사 기간 동안 //

부사적 용법(목적)
I am contacting you **to ask** you / to recommend some students from the chemistry department at your college / **who you think** *삽입절* are qualified for this job. // **단서 2** 일을 도와줄 수 있는 화학과 학생을 추천해 달라고 함
저는 교수님께 요청을 드리고자 연락드립니다 / 귀교의 화학과 학생 몇 명을 추천해 줄 것을 / 교수님께서 생각하시기에 이 일에 적합한 //

With their help, / I'm sure / the participants will have a great experience. //
그들의 도움으로 / 저는 확신합니다 / 참가자들이 훌륭한 경험을 하게 될 것을 //

I look forward to hearing from you soon. //
교수님으로부터 곧 연락이 오기를 고대하겠습니다 //

Sincerely, Ellis Wight / Ellis Wight 드림 /

- director ⓝ 책임자, 관리자　　• chemistry ⓝ 화학　　• local ⓐ 지역의
- goal ⓝ 목표　　• experiment ⓝ 실험　　• contact ⓥ 연락하다
- recommend ⓥ 추천하다　　• department ⓝ (대학의) 학과
- qualified ⓐ 자격이 있는　　• look forward to ~을 고대하다

Sanchez 교수님께,
제 이름은 Ellis Wight이며, Alexandria 과학 박물관의 관장입니다. 저희는 10월 28일 토요일에 지역 중학교 학생을 위한 화학 박람회를 개최합니다. 이 박람회의 목적은 안내되는 실험을 통해 학생들이 과학에 관심을 갖도록 장려하는 것입니다. 저희는 행사 기간 동안 실험을 도와줄 수 있는 대학생을 모집하고자 합니다. 저는 교수님께서 이 일에 적합하다고 생각하시는 귀교의 화학과 학생 몇 명을 추천해 달라는 요청을 드리고자 연락드립니다. 저는 그 학생들의 도움으로 참가자들이 훌륭한 경험을 하게 될 것을 확신합니다. 교수님으로부터 곧 연락이 오기를 고대하겠습니다.
Ellis Wight 드림

다음 글의 목적으로 가장 적절한 것은?
① 과학 박물관 내 시설 이용 제한을 안내하려고 시설 이용이 제한되는 것이 아님
② 화학 박람회 일정이 변경된 이유를 설명하려고 일정은 변경되지 않음
③ 중학생을 위한 화학 실험 특별 강연을 부탁하려고
　特別 강연을 부탁하는 것이 아님
④ 중학교 과학 수업용 실험 교재 집필을 의뢰하려고
　教材 집필에 관해서는 언급되지 않음
⑤ 화학 박람회에서 실험을 도울 대학생 추천을 요청하려고
　실험을 도울 대학생을 추천해 달라고 함

왜 정답? ✽❀❀ [정답률 90%]
중학생을 위한 화학 박람회에서 실험 진행을 도와줄 대학생을 모집 중이라고 하면서, Sanchez 교수가 재직 중인 대학교의 화학과 학생 몇 명을 추천해 달라고 요청하고 있으므로 정답은 ⑤이다.

왜 오답?
① 과학 박물관에서는 박람회가 개최될 뿐, 시설 이용이 제한된다는 언급은 없다.
② 화학 박람회 일정 변경은 언급하지 않았다.
③ 안내되는 실험이 있다고만 언급했을 뿐, 이에 관한 강연을 부탁하는 것은 아니다.
④ 교재 집필은 전혀 언급되지 않았다.
함정

A 10 정답 ② *모금 음악회 참석 요청

Dear Ms. Robinson, /
Robinson 씨께 /
The Warblers Choir is happy to announce / that we are invited
　　　　　　　　　　　　　　　　　　목적어절을 이끄는 접속사
to compete / in the International Young Choir Competition. //
Warblers 합창단은 알려드리게 되어 기쁩니다 / 실력을 겨루도록 초청받은 사실을 / 국제 청년 합창 대회에서 //
The competition takes place / in London on May 20. //
대회는 열립니다 / 5월 20일 런던에서 //
양보의 부사절을 이끄는 접속사
Though we wish to participate in the event, / we do not have the
necessary funds / to travel to London. //
비록 저희는 대회에 참가하고 싶지만 / 필요한 자금이 없습니다 / 런던에 가는 데 //
　　　　　　　　　　　　　명사적 용법(목적격보어)
So / we are kindly asking you / to support us / by coming to our
fundraising concert. // 단서 모금 음악회에 참석해 후원해 주기를 요청하고 있음
그래서 / 저희는 귀하께 정중하게 부탁드립니다 / 저희를 후원해 주시기를 / 저희 모금 음악회에 참석함으로써 //
미래 시제 수동태
It will be held / on March 26. //
음악회는 개최될 것입니다 / 3월 26일에 //
　　　　　　　　　　　　　　　　　목적어로 쓰인 명사절
In this concert, / we shall be able to show you / how big our
passion for music is. //
이 음악회에서 / 저희는 귀하께 보여드릴 수 있을 것입니다 / 음악에 대한 저희의 열정이 얼마나 큰지 //
Thank you in advance / for your kind support and help. //
미리 감사드립니다 / 귀하의 친절한 후원과 도움에 대해 //
Sincerely, Arnold Reynolds //
Arnold Reynolds 드림 //

• choir ⓝ 합창단　• announce ⓥ 알리다, 공고하다
• compete ⓥ 겨루다, 경쟁하다　• take place 열리다
• participate in ~에 참가하다　• necessary ⓐ 필요한
• support ⓥ 후원하다　• fundraising ⓝ 모금　• passion ⓝ 열정
• in advance 미리, 앞서

Robinson 씨께,
Warblers 합창단이 국제 청년 합창 대회에서 실력을 겨루도록 초청받은 사실을 알려드리게 되어 기쁩니다. 대회는 5월 20일 런던에서 열립니다. 비록 저희는 대회에 참가하고 싶지만, 런던에 가는 데 필요한 자금이 없습니다. 그래서 귀하께서 저희 모금 음악회에 참석하셔서 저희를 후원해 주시기를 정중하게 부탁드립니다. 음악회는 3월 26일에 개최될 것입니다. 이 음악회에서 저희는 음악에 대한 저희의 열정이 얼마나 큰지 귀하께

보여드릴 수 있을 것입니다. 귀하의 친절한 후원과 도움에 대해 미리 감사드립니다.
Arnold Reynolds 드림

다음 글의 목적으로 가장 적절한 것은?
① 합창 대회 결과를 공지하려고 합창 대회 결과에 대한 언급은 없음
② 모금 음악회 참석을 요청하려고 모금 음악회 참석을 통한 후원을 요청하는 글임
③ 음악회 개최 장소를 예약하려고
　음악회 개최 장소에 대한 언급은 있지만, 장소를 예약하겠다는 내용은 없음
④ 합창곡 선정에 조언을 구하려고 합창곡 선정에 대한 언급은 없음
⑤ 기부금 사용 내역을 보고하려고 기부금을 언급한 것으로 만든 함정

왜 정답? ✽❀❀ [정답률 90%]
중반부에 나오는 So we are kindly asking you to support us by coming to our fundraising concert. (그래서 귀하께서 저희 모금 음악회에 참석하셔서 저희를 후원해 주시기를 정중하게 부탁드립니다.)에서 글의 목적을 직접적으로 드러내고 있다.
런던에서 열리는 국제 청년 합창 대회에 초대받았지만 자금이 없어서 모금 음악회에 참석해 후원해 달라는 요청을 하고 있다. 따라서 이 글의 목적으로 가장 적절한 것은 ②이다.

왜 오답?
① 합창 대회에 참석하게 되었다는 내용만 있지 아직 참석 전이므로, 결과에 대한 내용은 없다.
③ 음악회 개최 장소에 대한 언급은 있지만, 장소를 예약하겠다는 내용은 없다.
④ 합창곡 선정에 대한 언급은 나오지 않았다.
⑤ 기부금을 위한 음악회 참석을 요청하는 글로, 아직 기부금을 사용하지 않았으므로 기부금 사용 내역 보고에 대한 내용은 없다.

A 11 정답 ⑤ *학급 파티에 가져올 음식에 대한 유의 사항

Dear Parents/Guardians, /
부모님들/보호자들께 /
　　　　　　　　　　미래 시제 수동태
Class parties will be held / on the afternoon of Friday, /
December 16th, 2022. //
학급 파티가 열릴 것입니다 / 금요일 오후에 / 2022년 12월 16일 //
Children may bring in / sweets, crisps, biscuits, cakes, and
drinks. //
아이들은 가지고 올 수 있습니다 / 사탕류, 포테이토 칩, 비스킷, 케이크, 그리고 음료를 //
　　　　　　　　　　　　목적어절을 이끄는 접속사
We are requesting / that children do not bring in / home-cooked
or prepared food. // 단서1 가져오면 안 되는 음식을 언급함
우리는 요청합니다 / 아이들이 가져오지 않기를 / 집에서 만들거나 준비한 음식을 //
　　　　　　　　　　　　　　　with+목적어+과거분사(~가 …된[한] 채로)
All food should arrive / in a sealed packet / with the ingredients
clearly listed. // 단서2 밀봉된 채 성분을 명확하게 적어서 가져와야 함
모든 음식은 가져와야 합니다 / 밀봉된 꾸러미로 / 성분을 명확하게 목록으로 작성하여 //
Fruit and vegetables are welcomed / if they are pre-packed / in
a sealed packet from the shop. // 단서3 견과류가 포함된 음식을 가져오지 말라고 함
과일과 채소는 환영합니다 / 사전 포장된 것이라면 / 가게에서 밀봉된 꾸러미로 //
　　　　　　　　　　　　　　　　　　food를 수식하는 현재분사구
Please DO NOT send any food into school / containing nuts / as
we have many children / with severe nut allergies. //
어떤 음식도 학교에 보내지 마십시오 / 견과류가 포함된 / 학생들이 많이 있기 때문에 / 심각한 견과류 알레르기를 가진 //
　　　　　　　　　　　　　　　　　앞에 목적격 관계대명사 생략
Please check / the ingredients of all food / your children bring /
carefully. //
확인해 주십시오 / 모든 음식의 성분을 / 아이들이 가져오는 / 주의 깊게 //
Thank you / for your continued support and cooperation. //
감사드립니다 / 여러분의 지속적인 지원과 협조에 //
Yours sincerely, Lisa Brown, Headteacher /
교장 Lisa Brown 드림 /

- guardian ⓝ 보호자 · crisp ⓝ 포테이토 칩
- request ⓥ 요청하다 · seal ⓥ 밀봉하다 · ingredient ⓝ 성분
- list ⓥ 목록으로 작성하다 · contain ⓥ 포함하다 · nut ⓝ 견과
- severe ⓐ 심각한 · cooperation ⓝ 협조

부모님들/보호자들께,

학급 파티가 2022년 12월 16일 금요일 오후에 열릴 것입니다. 아이들은 사탕류, 포테이토 칩, 비스킷, 케이크, 그리고 음료를 가지고 올 수 있습니다. 우리는 아이들이 집에서 만들거나 준비한 음식을 가져오지 않기를 요청합니다. 모든 음식은 성분을 명확하게 목록으로 작성하여 밀봉된 꾸러미로 가져와야 합니다. 과일과 채소는 가게에서 밀봉된 꾸러미로 사전 포장된 것이라면 환영합니다. 심각한 견과류 알레르기를 가진 학생들이 많이 있기 때문에 견과류가 포함된 어떤 음식도 학교에 보내지 마십시오. 아이들이 가져오는 모든 음식의 성분을 주의 깊게 확인해 주십시오. 여러분의 지속적인 지원과 협조에 감사드립니다.

교장 Lisa Brown 드림

다음 글의 목적으로 알맞은 것은?

① 학급 파티 일정 변경을 공지하려고 학급 파티의 일정을 변경하는 내용이 아님
② 학교 식당의 새로운 메뉴를 소개하려고 사탕류, 포테이토 칩, 비스킷, 케이크, 그리고 음료를 언급한 것으로 만든 함정
③ 학생의 특정 음식 알레르기 여부를 조사하려고 견과류 알레르기를 가진 학생들이 있다는 것으로 만든 오답
④ 학부모의 적극적인 학급 파티 참여를 독려하려고 학부모의 파티 참여를 독려하는 것이 아님
⑤ 학급 파티에 가져올 음식에 대한 유의 사항을 안내하려고 집에서 만들거나 준비한 음식을 가져오지 말라는 등 학급 파티에 가져올 음식에 대한 유의 사항을 안내함

왜 정답? ✸✸✸ [정답률 90%]

학급 파티에서 사용할 음식을 가져올 때의 유의 사항으로 집에서 만들거나 준비한 음식을 가져오지 말고, 성분을 목록으로 작성해서 밀봉해야 하고, 견과류가 포함된 음식은 가져오지 말라고 요청하고 있다. 따라서 이 글의 목적으로 가장 적절한 것은 ⑤이다.

왜 오답?

① 학급 파티의 일정 변경에 대한 내용은 없다.
② 사탕류, 포테이토 칩, 비스킷, 케이크, 그리고 음료는 학교 식당의 새로운 메뉴가 아니라 아이들이 학급 파티에 가져올 수 있는 음식의 종류이다.
🎀 ③ 견과류 알레르기를 가진 학생들이 있다는 것으로 만든 오답으로, 학생의 특정 음식 알레르기 여부를 조사하려는 것이 아니다.
④ 학부모의 적극적인 학급 파티 참여 독려가 아니라, 아이들이 학급 파티에 가져올 음식에 대한 유의 사항을 말하고 있다.

자이 쌤's Follow Me! ─ 홈페이지에서 제공

A 12 정답 ② *패키지여행 상품 홍보

ACC Travel Agency Customers: /
ACC 여행사 고객님께 /
Have you ever wanted / to enjoy a holiday in nature? //
당신은 원했던 적이 있나요 / 자연 속에서 휴가를 즐기는 것을 //
This summer is the best time / to turn your dream into reality. //
이번 여름이 최고의 시간입니다 / 당신의 꿈을 현실로 바꿀 //
We have a perfect travel package / for you. // 단서 1 완벽한 패키지여행 상품이 있다고 소개함
우리에게는 완벽한 패키지여행 상품이 있습니다 / 당신을 위한 //
This travel package includes / special trips to Lake Madison / as well as massage and meditation / to help you relax. //
이 패키지여행 상품은 포함합니다 / Lake Madison으로의 특별한 여행을 / 마사지와 명상뿐만 아니라 / 당신이 쉬도록 돕는 //
Also, / we provide yoga lessons / taught by experienced instructors. //
또한 / 우리는 요가 강의를 제공합니다 / 숙련된 강사로부터 배우는 //
If you book this package, / you will enjoy all this / at a reasonable price. // 단서 2 합리적인 가격에 패키지여행을 이용할 수 있다고 함
만약 당신이 이 패키지를 예약한다면 / 당신은 이 모든 것을 즐길 것입니다 / 합리적인 가격에 //

We are sure / that it will be an unforgettable experience / for you. //
우리는 확신합니다 / 그것이 잊지 못할 경험이 될 것이라고 / 당신에게 //
If you call us, / we will be happy to give you more details. //
우리에게 전화하시면 / 우리는 기꺼이 당신에게 더 많은 세부 사항을 알려드리겠습니다 //

- include ⓥ 포함하다 · meditation ⓝ 명상
- instructor ⓝ 강사 · book ⓥ 예약하다
- reasonable ⓐ 합리적인 · unforgettable ⓐ 잊지 못할

ACC 여행사 고객님께:

자연 속에서 휴가를 즐기는 것을 원한 적이 있습니까? 이번 여름이 당신의 꿈을 현실로 바꿀 최고의 시간입니다. 우리에게는 당신을 위한 완벽한 패키지여행 상품이 있습니다. 이 패키지여행 상품은 당신이 편히 쉴 수 있도록 돕는 마사지와 명상뿐만 아니라 Lake Madison으로의 특별한 여행도 포함합니다. 또한, 우리는 숙련된 강사의 요가 강의도 제공합니다. 만약 당신이 이 패키지를 예약한다면, 당신은 이 모든 것을 합리적인 가격에 즐길 것입니다. 우리는 그것이 당신에게 잊지 못할 경험이 될 것을 확신합니다. 우리에게 전화하시면, 우리는 당신에게 더 많은 세부 사항을 기꺼이 알려드리겠습니다.

다음 글의 목적으로 가장 적절한 것은?

① 여행 일정 변경을 안내하려고 여행 일정에 대한 언급은 없음
② 패키지여행 상품을 홍보하려고 완벽한 패키지여행 상품을 합리적인 가격에 즐기라고 함
③ 여행 상품 불만족에 대해 사과하려고 고객의 불만족에 대해 사과하는 글이 아님
④ 여행 만족도 조사 참여를 부탁하려고 여행을 이미 다녀온 고객에게 쓴 글이 아님
⑤ 패키지여행 업무 담당자를 모집하려고 잠재적인 고객을 대상으로 한 글임

왜 정답? ✸✸✸ [정답률 94%]

자연 속에서 즐길 수 있는 완벽한 패키지여행 상품이 있다고 소개하면서, 그것에 포함된 프로그램들과 합리적 가격을 설명하여 홍보하고 있으므로 정답은 ②이다.

왜 오답?

① 여행 상품을 홍보하는 단계로 여행 일정 변경을 공지하는 것이 아니다.
③ 이미 여행을 다녀온 고객의 불만족에 대해 사과하는 것이 아니다.
④ 고객의 만족도 조사를 요청하는 글이 아니다.
🎀 ⑤ 잠재적 고객을 대상으로 홍보하는 글이지 담당 직원을 모집하려는 글이 아니다.
(🎀 이유: 직원을 모집하는 거라면 합리적인 가격은 언급할 이유가 없다.)

자이 쌤's Follow Me! ─ 홈페이지에서 제공

A 13 정답 ② *분실물 발견 시 연락 요청

Dear Boat Tour Manager, /
보트 투어 담당자께 /
On March 15, / my family was on one of your Glass Bottom Boat Tours. // 「one of+복수 명사」: ~ 중 하나
3월 15일에 / 저희 가족은 귀사의 Glass Bottom Boat Tours 중 하나에 참여했습니다 //
When we returned to our hotel, / I discovered / that I left behind my cell phone case. // 단서 1 호텔에 돌아와서 휴대 전화 케이스를 놓고 온 것을 깨달음
우리가 호텔에 돌아왔을 때 / 제가 발견했습니다 / 제 휴대 전화 케이스를 놓고 왔다는 것을 //
The case must have fallen off my lap / and onto the floor / when I took it off my phone / to clean it. // must have p.p.: ~ 했음에 틀림없다 / 부사적 용법(목적)
케이스가 제 무릎에서 떨어졌던 것이 틀림없습니다 / 그리고 바닥으로 / 제가 휴대 전화에서 그것(케이스)을 분리했을 때 / 그것을 닦기 위해 //
I would like to ask you to check / if it is on your boat. // ~인지 아닌지
확인해 주시길 부탁드립니다 / 그것이 보트에 있는지 //
Its color is black / and it has my name on the inside. //
그것의 색깔은 검은색입니다 / 그리고 그것은 안쪽에 제 이름이 있습니다 //
If you find the case, / I would appreciate it / if you would let me know. // 단서 2 케이스가 발견되면 알려달라고 부탁하고 있음
만약 케이스가 발견된다면 / 감사하겠습니다 / 저에게 알려주시면 //

Sincerely, /
Sam Roberts /
Sam Roberts 드림 /

- **tour** ⓝ 여행　　• **return** ⓥ 돌아오다　　• **discover** ⓥ 발견하다
- **leave behind** ~을 놓아 둔 채 잊고 오다　　• **lap** ⓝ 무릎
- **ask** ⓥ 부탁하다, 요청하다　　• **appreciate** ⓥ 감사히 여기다

보트 투어 담당자께,
3월 15일에 저희 가족은 귀사의 Glass Bottom Boat Tours 중 하나에 참여했습니다. 호텔에 돌아왔을 때, 제가 휴대 전화 케이스를 놓고 왔다는 것을 발견했습니다. 케이스를 닦기 위해 휴대 전화에서 분리했을 때 제 무릎에서 케이스가 바닥으로 떨어졌던 것이 틀림없습니다. 그것이 보트에 있는지 확인해 주시길 부탁드립니다. 그것의 색깔은 검은색이며 안쪽에 제 이름이 있습니다. 만약 케이스가 발견된다면, 저에게 알려주시면 감사하겠습니다.
Sam Roberts 드림

다음 글의 목적으로 가장 적절한 것은?
① 제품의 고장 원인을 문의하려고 제품 고장에 대한 언급은 없음
②분실물 발견 시 연락을 부탁하려고
　보트에 두고 온 휴대 전화 케이스를 발견하면 연락해달라고 부탁하는 글임
③ 시설물의 철저한 관리를 당부하려고 호텔, 바닥 등에 대한 언급으로 만든 오답
④ 여행자 보험 가입 절차를 확인하려고
　보트 투어를 이미 했고 여행자 보험에 대한 내용은 없음
⑤ 분실물 센터 확장의 필요성을 건의하려고
　휴대 전화 케이스를 두고 왔다고 했으나 분실물 센터에 대한 언급은 없음

왜 정답? ✽✽✽ [정답률 97%]
후반부에 나오는 If you find the case, I would appreciate it if you would let me know. (만약 케이스가 발견된다면, 저에게 알려주시면 감사하겠습니다.)에 글의 목적이 직접적으로 드러나 있다.
보트에서 휴대 전화 케이스를 분리하여 닦다가 놓고 온 필자가 보트 투어 담당자에게 케이스가 발견되면 알려줄 것을 부탁하고 있는 내용이다. 따라서 이 글의 목적으로 가장 적절한 것은 ②이다.

왜 오답?
① 제품 고장에 대한 언급은 없다.
③ 호텔, 바닥 등에 대한 언급은 있지만 시설물의 관리를 당부하는 내용은 없다.
④ 보트 투어를 이미 했고 여행자 보험에 대한 내용은 없다.
⑤ 휴대 전화 케이스를 두고 왔다고 했지만, 분실물 센터에 대한 언급은 나오지 않았다.

A 14 정답 ② ✽식당 연례행사 참석 초대

Dear Mr. Dennis Brown, /
Dennis Brown 씨께 /　단서 1 연례행사인 Fall Dinner에 초대하게 되어 기쁘다고 했음
　　　　　　　　　　　　　　　　　부사적 용법 (이유)
We at G&D Restaurant are honored / and delighted / to invite
　　전치사
you / to our annual Fall Dinner. //
우리 G&D 식당은 영광입니다 / 그리고 기쁩니다 / 당신을 초대하게 되어 / 우리의 연례행사인 Fall Dinner에 //
　　　　　　　　미래시제 수동태
The annual event will be held / on October 1st, 2021 / at our
restaurant. //
그 연례행사는 열릴 것입니다 / 2021년 10월 1일에 / 우리 식당에서 //

At the event, / we will be introducing / new wonderful dishes /
목적격 관계대명사
that our restaurant will be offering soon. //
그 행사에서 / 우리는 소개할 것입니다 / 새로운 멋진 음식들을 / 우리 식당이 곧 제공할 //

These delicious dishes will showcase / the amazing talents / of
our gifted chefs. //
이 맛있는 음식들은 보여줄 것입니다 / 멋진 재능을 / 우리의 뛰어난 요리사들의 //

Also, / our chefs will be providing / cooking tips, / ideas on what
병렬 구조
to buy for your kitchen, / and special recipes. //
또한 / 우리의 요리사들은 제공할 것입니다 / 요리 비법들과 / 당신의 주방을 위해 무엇을 사야 할지에 대한 생각들 / 그리고 특별한 요리법을 //

조건의 부사절을 이끄는 접속사
We at G&D Restaurant / would be more than grateful / if you can
make it to this special occasion / and be part of our celebration. //
우리 G&D 식당은 / 매우 감사할 것입니다 / 만약에 당신이 이 특별한 행사에 참석하면 / 그리고 우리의 축하 행사의 일부가 되어준다면 //　단서 2 축하 행사에 참석해주면 매우 감사할 것이라고 했음

We look forward to seeing you. //
우리는 당신을 곧 보기를 학수고대합니다. //

Thank you so much. // 매우 감사합니다 //

Regards, / 존경을 담아 /

Marcus Lee, Owner - G&D Restaurant //
G&D 식당 주인, Marcus Lee 드림 //

- **delighted** ⓐ 아주 기뻐하는　　• **annual** ⓐ 연례의　　• **dish** ⓝ 요리
- **showcase** ⓥ 전시하다, 소개하다　　• **gifted** ⓐ 재능이 있는
- **recipe** ⓝ 조리법　　• **grateful** ⓐ 고마워하는　　• **occasion** ⓝ 행사
- **celebration** ⓝ 축하 행사　　• **look forward to -ing** ~을 학수고대하다

Dennis Brown 씨께,
우리 G&D 식당은 우리의 연례행사인 Fall Dinner에 당신을 초대하게 되어 영광이고 기쁩니다. 그 연례행사는 2021년 10월 1일에 우리 식당에서 열릴 것입니다. 그 행사에서, 우리는 우리 식당이 곧 제공할 새로운 멋진 음식들을 소개할 것입니다. 이 맛있는 음식들은 우리의 뛰어난 요리사들의 멋진 재능을 보여줄 것입니다. 또한, 우리의 요리사들은 요리 비법들과 당신의 주방을 위해 무엇을 사야 할지에 대한 생각들, 그리고 특별한 요리법을 제공할 것입니다. 우리 G&D 식당은 만약에 당신이 이 특별한 행사에 와서 우리의 축하의 일부가 되어준다면 매우 감사할 것입니다. 우리는 당신을 곧 보기를 학수고대합니다. 매우 감사합니다.
존경을 담아, G&D 식당 주인, Marcus Lee 드림

다음 글의 목적으로 가장 적절한 것은?
① 식당 개업을 홍보하려고 개업은 이미 했고 연례행사에 관해 설명함
②식당의 연례행사에 초대하려고 연례행사에 방문해서 축하해주기를 바란다고 했음
③ 신입 요리사 채용을 공고하려고 요리사들에 관해서는 실력이 훌륭하다는 언급만 있음
④ 매장 직원의 실수를 사과하려고 매장 직원의 실수와는 관련이 없는 내용
⑤ 식당 만족도 조사 참여를 부탁하려고 만족도 조사는 언급되지 않음

왜 정답? ✽✽✽ [정답률 92%]
첫 문장 We at G&D Restaurant are honored and delighted to invite you to our annual Fall Dinner.에서 식당의 연례행사인 Fall Dinner에 초대하게 되어 영광이라고 했다. 새로운 음식을 소개하고 요리사들의 요리 비법 등을 제공하는 행사라고 하며 행사에 참석해 축하해주면 좋겠다는 내용이다. 따라서 이 글의 목적으로 ②이 가장 적절하다.

왜 오답?
① 식당은 이미 개업해서 운영 중이고 연례행사를 연다고 말하고 있다.
③ 실력 좋은 요리사들의 재능이 담긴 새 음식을 소개할 것이라고 했지만 채용은 언급되지 않았다. 주의
④ 매장 직원의 실수는 제시된 글과 전혀 관련이 없는 내용이다.
⑤ 식당 만족도 조사는 글에 언급되지 않았다.

A 15 정답 ④ ✽도서관 공사에 참여할 자원봉사자 모집

Dear members of Eastwood Library, / Eastwood 도서관 회원들께 /
~ 덕분에
Thanks to the Friends of Literature group, / we've successfully
raised enough money / to remodel the library building. //
　　　　　　　　　　　　형용사적 용법
Friends of Literature 모임 덕분에 / 우리는 충분한 돈을 성공적으로 모았습니다 / 도서관 건물을 리모델링하기 위한 //

John Baker, / our local builder, / has volunteered / to help us
　　　　　　　동격
with the remodeling / but he needs assistance. //
John Baker 씨가 / 우리 지역의 건축업자인 / 자원했습니다 / 우리의 리모델링을 돕기로 / 하지만 그는 도움이 필요합니다 //

By grabbing a hammer or a paint brush / and donating your time / you can help with the construction. // 단서1 여러 가지 방법으로 공사를 도울 수 있다고 언급함
by -ing: ~함으로써   병렬 구조

망치나 페인트 붓을 쥠으로써 / 그리고 시간을 기부함으로써 / 여러분은 공사를 도울 수 있습니다 //

단서2 봉사활동 팀에 동참함으로써 도서관을 더 좋게 만드는 데 기여하도록 권유함
Join Mr. Baker in his volunteering team / and become a part / of making Eastwood Library a better place! //
병렬 구조

Baker 씨의 자원봉사 팀에 동참하십시오 / 그리고 참여하십시오 / Eastwood 도서관을 더 좋은 곳으로 만드는 데 //

Please call 541-567-1234 / for more information. //
541-567-1234로 전화해 주십시오 / 더 많은 정보를 원하시면 //

Sincerely, Mark Anderson / Mark Anderson 드림 /

- successfully @d 성공적으로   · raise ⓥ (자금 등을) 모으다
- remodel ⓥ 리모델링하다, 개축하다   · local @ 지역의
- builder ⓝ 건축업자   · volunteer ⓥ 자원하다
- assistance ⓝ 도움   · grab ⓥ 쥐다   · hammer ⓝ 망치
- donate ⓥ 기부하다   · construction ⓝ 공사

Eastwood 도서관 회원들께
Friends of Literature 모임 덕분에, 우리는 도서관 건물을 리모델링하기 위한 충분한 돈을 성공적으로 모았습니다. 우리 지역의 건축업자인 John Baker 씨가 우리의 리모델링을 돕기로 자원했지만, 그는 도움이 필요합니다. 망치나 페인트 붓을 쥐고 시간을 기부함으로써, 여러분은 공사를 도울 수 있습니다. Baker 씨의 자원봉사 팀에 동참하여 Eastwood 도서관을 더 좋은 곳으로 만드는 데 참여하십시오! 더 많은 정보를 원하시면 541-567-1234로 전화해 주십시오.
Mark Anderson 드림

다음 글의 목적으로 가장 적절한 것은?
① 도서관 임시 휴관의 이유를 설명하려고 도서관 임시 휴관에 대한 언급은 없음
② 도서관 자원봉사자 교육 일정을 안내하려고
자원봉사자가 언급됐지만 교육과는 무관
③ 도서관 보수를 위한 모금 행사를 제안하려고
모금은 이미 마련했고 봉사자를 모집한다고 했음
④ 도서관 공사에 참여할 자원봉사자를 모집하려고
도서관을 리모델링하는 공사를 도울 자원봉사자로 참여할 것을 권하는 내용
⑤ 도서관에서 개최하는 글쓰기 대회를 홍보하려고 글쓰기 대회에 대한 내용은 없음

＞왜 정답？ ✲✲✲ [정답률 90%]
중반부에 나온 John Baker, our local builder, has volunteered to help us with the remodeling but he needs assistance. (우리 지역의 건축업자인 John Baker 씨가 우리의 리모델링을 돕기로 자원했지만, 그는 도움이 필요합니다.)에서 직접적으로 이 글의 목적을 밝혔다. 도서관 리모델링 과정에 더 많은 일손이 필요하다고 하며 자원봉사자로 참여할 것을 권하고 있으므로 이 글의 목적으로 가장 적절한 것은 ④이다.

＞왜 오답？
① 도서관 임시 휴관이 아닌 리모델링 공사에 대한 글이다.
② 도서관 자원봉사자를 모집하는 내용이지만 교육 일정은 언급되지 않았다.
③ Friends of Literature 모임을 통해 도서관 리모델링을 위한 충분한 비용이 이미 마련되었음을 언급하였다. 함정
⑤ 도서관에서 개최하는 글쓰기 대회에 대한 내용은 나오지 않았다.

A 16 정답 ⑤ *오래된 신문의 사용 허락 요청

To the school librarian, /
학교 사서 선생님께 /

I am Kyle Thomas, / the president of the school's English writing club. //
동격

저는 Kyle Thomas입니다 / 학교 영어 글쓰기 동아리 회장인 //

I have planned activities / that will increase the writing skills / of our club members. //
주격 관계대명사

저는 활동들을 계획해 왔습니다 / 글쓰기 실력을 증진시킬 / 저희 동아리 회원들의 //

One of the aims of these activities / is to make us aware / of various types of news media / and the language / used in printed newspaper articles. //
단수 주어   단수 동사   과거분사

이러한 활동들의 목표 중 하나는 / 저희가 인식하게 만드는 것입니다 / 뉴스 미디어의 다양한 유형과 / 언어를 / 인쇄된 신문 기사에 사용된 //

However, / some old newspapers / are not easy to access online. //
그러나 / 일부 오래된 신문은 / 온라인으로 접근하는 것이 쉽지 않습니다 //

It is, therefore, my humble request to you / to allow us to use old newspapers / that have been stored in the school library. //
가주어   진주어   주격 관계대명사

그러므로 / 선생님께 드리는 저의 겸허한 요청입니다 / 오래된 신문을 저희가 사용할 수 있도록 허락해 달라는 것이 / 학교 도서관에 보관되어 온 //
단서 학교 도서관에 있는 오래된 신문의 사용을 허락해달라고 요청하고 있음

I would really appreciate it / if you grant us permission. //
정말 감사하겠습니다 / 선생님께서 저희에게 허락해 주시면 //

Yours truly,
Kyle Thomas / Kyle Thomas 드림 /

- librarian ⓝ 사서   · president ⓝ 회장
- aware @ 알고[자각하고] 있는   · access ⓥ 접근하다, 이용하다
- humble @ 겸허한, 겸손한   · request ⓝ 요청
- store ⓥ 저장[보관]하다   · grant ⓥ 주다, 수여하다
- permission ⓝ 허락

학교 사서 선생님께,
저는 학교 영어 글쓰기 동아리 회장인 Kyle Thomas입니다. 저는 저희 동아리 회원들의 글쓰기 실력을 증진시킬 활동들을 계획해 왔습니다. 이러한 활동들의 목표 중 하나는 저희가 뉴스 미디어의 다양한 유형과 인쇄된 신문 기사에 사용된 언어를 인식하게 만드는 것입니다. 그러나 일부 오래된 신문은 온라인으로 접근하는 것이 쉽지 않습니다. 그러므로 학교 도서관에 보관되어 온 오래된 신문을 저희가 사용할 수 있도록 허락해 달라는 것이 선생님께 드리는 저의 겸허한 요청입니다. 만약 선생님께서 저희에게 허락해 주시면 정말 감사하겠습니다.
Kyle Thomas 드림

다음 글의 목적으로 가장 적절한 것은?
① 도서관 이용 시간 연장을 건의하려고 도서관 이용 시간에 대한 언급은 없음
② 신청한 도서의 대출 가능 여부를 문의하려고
도서 대출 신청에 대한 내용은 나오지 않음
③ 도서관에 보관 중인 자료 현황을 조사하려고
도서관에 보관되어 있는 신문에 대한 언급으로 만든 함정
④ 글쓰기 동아리 신문의 도서관 비치를 부탁하려고
글에 나온 신문은 동아리 신문을 말한 것이 아님
⑤ 도서관에 있는 오래된 신문의 사용 허락을 요청하려고
학교 도서관에 있는 오래된 신문의 사용을 허락해 달라고 요청하는 글임

＞왜 정답？ ✲✲✲ [정답률 94%]
후반부에 나오는 It is, therefore, my humble request to you to allow us to use old newspapers that have been stored in the school library. (그러므로 학교 도서관에 보관되어 온 오래된 신문을 저희가 사용할 수 있도록 허락해 달라는 것이 선생님께 드리는 저의 겸허한 요청입니다.)에 글의 목적을 드러내고 있다. 영어 글쓰기 동아리 회장이 회원들의 글쓰기 실력을 증진시킬 활동을 목표로 학교 도서관에 있는 오래된 신문의 사용을 허락해 달라고 요청하고 있다. 따라서 이 글의 목적으로 가장 적절한 것은 ⑤이다.

＞왜 오답？
① 도서관 이용 시간에 대한 언급은 없다.
② 도서 대출 신청에 대한 내용은 나오지 않았다.
③ 도서관에서 어떤 자료를 보유하고 있는지에 대한 내용은 아니고, 도서관에 보관되어 있는 신문에 대한 언급으로 만든 함정일 뿐이다.
④ 글에 신문에 대한 언급은 있지만, 이것이 동아리 신문을 말하는 것은 아니다.

자이쌤's Follow Me! ─ 홈페이지에서 제공

A 17 정답 ① *회사 로고 제작 의뢰하기

Dear Mr. Jones, / Jones 씨에게 /
I am James Arkady, / PR Director of KHJ Corporation. //
저는 James Arkady입니다 / KHJ Corporation의 홍보부 이사 //
「plan+to부정사: ~할 계획이다」
We are planning to redesign our brand identity / and launch a
부사적 용법(목적)
new logo / to celebrate our 10th anniversary. // 단서1 새로운 로고를
선보일 계획이라고 했음
저희는 저희 회사 브랜드 정체성을 다시 설계할 계획입니다 / 그리고 새로운 로고를 선보일
(계획입니다) / 저희 회사의 창립 10주년을 기념하기 위해서 //
주격 관계대명사
We request you to create a logo / that best suits our company's
core vision, / 'To inspire humanity.' // 단서2 새로운 로고 제작을 부탁함
저희는 귀하께 로고를 제작해주시기를 요청합니다 / 저희 회사의 핵심 비전에 가장 잘 어울리
는 / '인류애를 고양하자' /
뒤에 목적어절 접속사 that 생략
I hope / the new logo will convey our brand message / and
capture the values of KHJ. //
저희는 희망합니다 / 새로운 로고가 저희 회사 브랜드 메시지를 전달하기를 / 그리고 KHJ의
가치를 담고 있기를 //
Please send us your logo design proposal / once you are done
with it. //
귀하의 로고 디자인 제안서를 저희에게 보내 주십시오 / 완성하는 대로 //
Thank you. // 감사합니다 //
Best regards, James Arkady // James Arkady 드림 //

- PR director 홍보부 이사   - corporation ⓝ 기업, 회사
- redesign ⓥ 다시 설계하다   - identity ⓝ 정체성
- celebrate ⓥ 축하하다   - anniversary ⓝ 기념일
- request ⓥ 요청하다   - suit ⓥ 어울리다, 적합하다
- core ⓝ 핵심   - inspire ⓥ 영감을 주다
- humanity ⓝ 인류애   - convey ⓥ 전달하다
- capture ⓥ (사진이나 글로 감정·분위기 등을) 정확히 담아내다

Jones 씨에게
저는 KHJ Corporation의 홍보부 이사 James Arkady입니다. 저희 회사
의 창립 10주년을 기념하기 위해서 저희 회사 브랜드 정체성을 다시 설계
하고 새로운 로고를 선보일 계획입니다. 저희 회사의 핵심 비전 '인류애를
고양하자'에 가장 잘 어울리는 로고를 제작해주시기를 요청합니다. 새로운
로고가 저희 회사 브랜드 메시지를 전달하고 KHJ의 가치가 담기기를 바랍
니다. 완성하는 대로 귀하의 로고 디자인 제안서를 보내 주십시오. 감사합
니다.
James Arkady 드림

다음 글의 목적으로 가장 적절한 것은?
① 회사 로고 제작을 의뢰하려고 핵심 비전에 잘 어울리는 새로운 로고 제작을 부탁함
② 변경된 회사 로고를 홍보하려고 변경된 로고 홍보가 아니라 새로운 로고 제작에 관한 글임
③ 회사 비전에 대한 컨설팅을 요청하려고 회사 비전에 대한 컨설팅은 언급되지 않음
④ 회사 창립 10주년 기념품을 주문하려고 회사 창립 10주년이라고 한 것으로 만든 함정
⑤ 회사 로고 제작 일정 변경을 공지하려고 로고 제작 일정과 관련된 내용은 없음

왜 정답? ✱❀❀ [정답률 91%]
글의 중반부에서 We request you to create a logo that best suits our
company's core vision, 'To inspire humanity.' (저희 회사의 핵심 비전 '인류애
를 고양하자'에 가장 잘 어울리는 로고를 제작해주시기를 요청합니다.)를 통해 목적
을 직접적으로 드러내고 있다. 따라서 이 글의 목적으로 가장 적절한 것은 ①이다.

왜 오답?
② 변경된 로고 홍보가 아니라 새로운 로고 제작에 관한 글이다.
③ 회사 비전에 대한 컨설팅은 언급되지 않았다.
④ 회사 창립 10주년이라고 했지만 기념품과 관련된 내용은 없었다. 함정
⑤ 새로운 로고 제작을 부탁했지만, 이와 관련된 일정에 대한 언급은 없었다.

A 18 정답 ③ ──── ⭐2등급 대비 [정답률 88%]

*놀이터 시설 수리 요청

To whom it may concern, /
관계자분께 /
I am a resident of the Blue Sky Apartment. //
저는 Blue Sky 아파트의 거주자입니다 /
목적어절 접속사   '~을 필요로 하는'
Recently / I observed / that the kid zone is in need of repairs. //
최근에 / 저는 알게 되었습니다 / 아이들을 위한 구역이 수리가 필요하다는 것을 //
want의 목적격 보어(to부정사)
I want you to pay attention / to the poor condition / of the
playground equipment in the zone. // 단서1 놀이터의 설비가 열악해 수리가
필요함
저는 귀하께서 관심을 기울여 주시기를 바랍니다 / 열악한 상태에 / 그 구역 놀이터 설비의 //
부분 표현은 of 뒤의 명사에 수 일치
The swings are damaged, / the paint is falling off, / and some of
복수동사
the bolts on the slide are missing. //
그네가 손상되었고 / 페인트가 떨어져 나가고 있고 / 미끄럼틀의 볼트 몇 개가 빠져 있습니다 //
현재완료(계속)
The facilities have been in this terrible condition / since we
moved here. //
(놀이터) 시설은 이렇게 형편없는 상태였습니다 / 우리가 이곳으로 이사 온 이후로 //
앞에 주격 관계대명사와 be동사가 생략됨
They are dangerous / to the children playing there. //
그것들은 위험합니다 / 거기서 노는 아이들에게 //
Would you please have them repaired? // 단서2 놀이터 설비의 수리를 요청함
그것을 수리해 주시겠습니까 //
부사적 용법(목적)
I would appreciate your immediate attention / to solve this
matter. //
즉각적인 관심을 두시면 감사하겠습니다 / 이 문제를 해결하기 위해 //
Yours sincerely, Nina Davis / Nina Davis 드림 /

- resident ⓝ 거주자   - recently ⓐⓓ 최근에
- observe ⓥ 알다, 목격하다   - repair ⓝ 수리   - attention ⓝ 주의
- condition ⓝ 상태   - playground ⓝ 놀이터
- equipment ⓝ 설비   - swing ⓝ 그네   - damage ⓥ 손상하다
- fall off 떨어져 나가다   - slide ⓝ 미끄럼틀   - facility ⓝ 시설
- terrible ⓐ 형편없는   - appreciate ⓥ 감사하다
- immediate ⓐ 즉각적인   - solve ⓥ (문제 등을) 해결하다

관계자분께,
저는 Blue Sky 아파트의 거주자입니다. 최근에 저는 아이들을 위한
구역이 수리가 필요하다는 것을 알게 되었습니다. 저는 귀하께서 그 구역
놀이터 설비의 열악한 상태에 관심을 기울여 주시기를 바랍니다. 그네가
손상되었고, 페인트가 떨어져 나가고 있고, 미끄럼틀의 볼트 몇 개가 빠져
있습니다. (놀이터) 시설은 우리가 이곳으로 이사 온 이후로 이렇게 형편없는
상태였습니다. 그것들은 거기서 노는 아이들에게 위험합니다. 그것을
수리해 주시겠습니까? 이 문제를 해결하기 위해 즉각적인 관심을 두시면
감사하겠습니다.
Nina Davis 드림

다음 글의 목적으로 가장 적절한 것은?
① 아파트의 첨단 보안 설비를 홍보하려고 첨단 보안 설비는 언급되지 않음
② 아파트 놀이터의 임시 폐쇄를 공지하려고
③ 아파트 놀이터 시설의 수리를 요청하려고 놀이터에 수리가 필요하지 폐쇄되는 것은 아님
④ 아파트 놀이터 사고의 피해 보상을 촉구하려고 손상된 설비가 수리되어야 한다고 요청함
⑤ 아파트 공용 시설 사용 시 유의 사항을 안내하려고 사고 예방을 위해서 수리를 요청하는 것임
  놀이터 이용의 유의 사항을 말하는 것이 아님

왜 2등급? 필자가 자신이 Blue Sky 아파트의 거주자라고 밝히면서 편지가
시작되는데, 다섯 개의 선택지에 모두 '아파트'라는 핵심어가 포함되어 있어 모든
선택지를 꼼꼼히 살펴봐야 하는 2등급 대비 문제이다.

왜 정답?

현재 놀이터의 그네와 미끄럼틀이 일부 망가져 있고 페인트가 벗겨져 있는 등 시설이 열악하므로 놀이터 시설을 수리해달라고 요청하는 내용이다. 따라서 이 글의 목적으로 가장 적절한 것은 ③이다.

왜 오답?

① 첨단 보안 설비는 언급되지 않았다.
② 놀이터를 임시 폐쇄하자는 글이 아니고 수리해야 한다는 내용이다.
④ 놀이터 사고가 발생하였는지는 알 수 없고, 예방 차원에서 수리를 요청하고 있다.
⑤ 유의 사항 안내가 아니라 수리를 요청하는 글이다.

A 19 정답 ② ⎯⎯⎯⎯ ★ 2등급 대비 [정답률 87%]

*성과를 반영한 급여 인상 요청

Dear Mr. Krull, /
친애하는 Krull 씨께 /
　　　　　　동명사를 목적어로 취하는 동사
I have greatly **enjoyed** working / at Trincom Enterprises / as a
sales manager. //
저는 일하는 것을 매우 즐겨 왔습니다 / Trincom Enterprises에서 / 영업 매니저로 //

Since I joined in 2015, / I **have been** a loyal and essential member
　　　　　　　└── 병렬 구조 ──┘
of this company, / and **have developed** innovative ways / to
contribute to the company. //
2015년에 입사한 이후 / 저는 이 회사의 충성스럽고 필수적인 구성원이었고 / 혁신적인
방법들을 개발해 왔습니다 / 회사에 기여할 //

Moreover, / in the last year alone, / I have brought in two new
　　　　　　　　　　　　　분사구문(결과)
major clients to the company, / **increasing the company's total**
sales by 5%. //
게다가 / 작년 한 해에만 / 저는 두 개의 주요 고객사를 회사에 새로 유치했습니다 / 회사의
총매출을 5퍼센트 증가시키면서 //

Also, / I have voluntarily trained 5 new members of staff, /
　　　　　　　　　　분사구문(결과)
totaling 35 hours. //
또한 / 저는 신규 직원 5명을 자발적으로 교육해 왔습니다 / 합계가 35시간이 되도록 //

I would therefore request your consideration / in raising my
계속적 용법의 주격 관계대명사　삽입절
salary, / **which I believe** reflects my performance / as well as the
industry average. // 단서 자신의 성과를 반영하여 급여를 인상하는 것에 대한 고려를 요청함
따라서 저는 당신의 고려를 요청합니다 / 제 급여를 인상하는 것에 대한 / 그리고 저는 이것이
제 성과를 반영한다고 믿습니다 / 업계 평균뿐만 아니라 //
　look forward to v-ing: ~을 기대하다
I **look forward to speaking** with you soon. //
저는 당신과 곧 이야기하기를 기대합니다 //

Kimberly Morss /
Kimberly Morss /

- loyal ⓐ 충성스러운, 충실한 　• essential ⓐ 필수적인
- innovative ⓐ 혁신적인 　• contribute ⓥ 기여하다
- voluntarily ⓐ𝖽 자발적으로, 자원해서 　• total ⓥ 합계가 ~이 되다
- request ⓥ 요청하다 　• consideration ⓝ 고려
- reflect ⓥ 반영하다 　• performance ⓝ 성과

친애하는 Krull 씨께,
저는 Trincom Enterprises에서 영업 매니저로 일하는 것을 매우 즐겨
왔습니다. 2015년에 입사한 이후, 저는 이 회사의 충성스럽고 필수적인
구성원이었고, 회사에 기여할 혁신적인 방법들을 개발해 왔습니다. 게다가,
저는 작년 한 해만 두 개의 주요 고객사를 회사에 새로 유치하여 회사의
총매출을 5퍼센트 증가시켰습니다. 또한 저는 신규 직원 5명을 자발적으로
교육해 왔고, 그 합계가 35시간이 되었습니다. 따라서 저는 제 급여를 인상하는
것에 대한 당신의 고려를 요청하고, 이것이 업계 평균뿐만 아니라 제 성과도
반영한다고 믿습니다. 저는 당신과 곧 이야기하기를 기대합니다.
Kimberly Morss

다음 글의 목적으로 가장 적절한 것은?

① 부서 이동을 신청하려고　부서 이동에 대한 언급은 없음
② 급여 인상을 요청하려고　급여를 인상하는 것에 대한 고려를 요청하는 내용
③ 근무 시간 조정을 요구하려고
　　　　　　　　　신규 직원 교육 누적 시간이 35시간이라는 것으로 만든 오답
④ 기업 혁신 방안을 제안하려고
　　　　　　　회사에 기여할 혁신적 방법들을 개발했다는 내용으로 만든 오답
⑤ 신입 사원 연수에 대해 문의하려고
　　　　　　　신규 직원을 교육했다고 언급했을 뿐임

왜 2등급? 필자는 영업 매니저로서 회사에 기여한 업적들을 나열했다. 혁신적인
방법을 개발했다거나, 신입 사원을 교육했다는 것은 필자의 업적의 예시일 뿐, 글의
목적이 아님을 구분해야 정답을 고를 수 있는 2등급 대비 문제이다.

왜 정답?

영업 매니저로 일하면서 회사에 기여할 혁신적인 방법들을 개발해 왔다고 하면서,
매출 증가나 직원 교육 등의 성과를 언급했다. 이러한 이유로 급여 인상에 대한 고려를
요청한다고 했으므로 글의 목적으로 가장 적절한 것은 ②이다.

왜 오답?

① 영업 매니저로 일했다는 내용은 있지만, 부서 이동에 대한 언급은 없다.
③ 신규 직원을 교육한 시간이 35시간인 것이지 근무 시간 조정을 요청한 것이
아니다.
④ 회사에 기여할 혁신적 방법들을 개발했다는 내용은 있지만, 기업 혁신 방안을
제안하고 있지는 않다. (▶ 이유: 기업 혁신 방안은 급여 인상에 참고할 만한
성과일 뿐이다.)
⑤ 신규 직원을 교육했다고 했지 신입 사원 연수에 대해 문의하는 것이 아니다.

예시를 통해
필자가 말하려고 하는
바를 알아내자!

A 어휘 Review 정답 ⎯⎯ 문제편 p. 21

01 연락하다	11 look forward to	21 ingredients
02 인류애	12 participate in	22 meditation
03 수공예의	13 notify A of B	23 contribute
04 요구 사항	14 in advance	24 immediate
05 화학	15 leave behind	25 condition
06 local	16 essential	26 humble
07 include	17 reasonable	27 proposal
08 grab	18 entrance	28 goal
09 cooperation	19 severe	29 construction
10 funding	20 subscription	30 appreciate

B 심경의 이해 문제편 p. 24~30

B 01 정답 ③ *토끼의 등장

The shed is cold and damp, / the **air thick** / with the smell of old wood and earth. //
사이에 반복되는 be동사 is가 생략됨
헛간은 춥고 습기가 차 있고 / 공기에 짙다 / 오래된 나무와 흙냄새가 //

It's dark, / and I can't make out / **what**'s moving in the shadows. //
선행사를 포함하는 관계대명사
어두워서 / 나는 알아볼 수 없다 / 그림자 속에서 움직이는 무언가를 //

"Who's there?" / I ask, / my voice shaking with fear. //
"거기 누구세요" / 나는 묻는다 / 목소리가 두려움에 떨리며 //
단서 1 두려움에 목소리가 떨림

The shadow moves closer, / and my heart is beating fast / — until the figure steps into a faint beam of light / **breaking through a crack in the wall.** //
현재분사구 (light 수식)
그림자가 점점 가까이 다가오고 / 나의 심장은 점점 빠르게 뛰고 있다 / 희미한 빛줄기 속으로 그 형체가 들어설 때 / 벽 틈새로 새어 들어온 //

A rabbit. // 토끼다 //

A laugh escapes my lips / **as** it stares at me / with wide, curious eyes. //
부사절 접속사 (시간)
웃음이 내 입술에서 새어 나온다 / 그것이 나를 바라볼 때 / 크고 호기심 가득한 눈으로 //

"You scared me," / I say, / **feeling much better.** //
"너 때문에 놀랐잖아" / 나는 말한다 / 훨씬 나아진 기분을 느끼며 //

The rabbit pauses for a moment, / then hops away, / **disappearing back into the shadows.** //
분사구문
토끼는 잠시 멈칫하더니 / 이내 깡충 뛰어 / 그림자 속으로 다시 사라진다 //

I'm left smiling. // 나는 미소 지으며 남아 있다 //

I start to feel at ease. // **단서 2** 놀랐던 마음이 진정되고 안도함
나의 마음이 편안해지기 시작한다 //

- damp ⓐ 습기 찬 • thick ⓐ (공기가) 짙은
- make out 알아보다, 식별하다 • shadow ⓝ 그림자
- shaking ⓐ 떨리는 • figure ⓝ 형체, 형상 • faint ⓐ 희미한
- beam ⓝ 빛줄기 • crack ⓝ 틈새
- escape ⓥ (웃음 등이) 새어 나오다 • stare at ~을 바라보다
- hop ⓥ 깡충 뛰다 • at ease 편안히

헛간은 춥고 습기가 차 있고, 공기에 오래된 나무와 흙냄새가 짙다. 어두워서, 나는 그림자 속에서 움직이는 무언가를 알아볼 수 없다. "거기 누구세요?" 목소리가 두려움에 떨리며, 나는 묻는다. 그림자가 점점 가까이 다가오고, 나의 심장은 점점 빠르게 뛰고 있다. 그때, 벽 틈새로 새어 들어온 희미한 빛줄기 속으로 그 형체가 들어선다. 토끼다. 그것이 크고 호기심 가득한 눈으로 나를 바라볼 때, 웃음이 내 입술에서 새어 나온다. "너 때문에 놀랐잖아." 훨씬 나아진 기분을 느끼며, 나는 말한다. 토끼는 잠시 멈칫하더니, 이내 깡충 뛰어 그림자 속으로 다시 사라진다. 나는 미소 지으며 남아 있다. 나의 마음이 편안해지기 시작한다.

다음 글에 드러난 'I'의 심경 변화로 가장 적절한 것은?

① envious → hopeful 두려워서 심장이 빨리 뛰므로 부러움의 감정은 아님
부러워하는 → 희망찬

② anxious → angry 정체를 알게 된 후 안도감을 느낌
걱정스러운 → 화난

③ frightened → relieved 정체 모를 대상에 두려움을 느꼈으나 정체를 알고는 안도했음
겁먹은 → 안도한

④ curious → regretful 후반부에 'I'가 아닌 토끼의 표정에 호기심이 묻어 있었음
호기심 있는 → 후회하는

⑤ excited → disappointed 실망보다는 안도에 가까움
흥분한 → 실망한

왜 정답? ✻✻✻ [정답률 84%]

전반부: 헛간에 있는데 정체 모를 존재가 다가와서 심장이 빠르게 뜀 ▶ '겁먹은'

후반부: 다가온 존재를 확인하니 토끼임을 알게 됨 ▶ '안도한'

따라서 'I'의 심경 변화로 가장 적절한 것은 ③ '겁먹은 → 안도한'이다.

왜 오답?

① 두려움을 느끼고 있으므로 부러운 감정을 느낀 것이 아니다.
② 다가오는 대상에 화가 난 것이 아니라 안도감을 느꼈다.
④ 후반부에 호기심을 드러낸 것은 'I'가 아니라 토끼였고, 후회하기보다는 안도했다. *함정*
⑤ 초반에 걱정하고 두려움에 떨다가 긴장이 풀린 것이지, 실망한 것은 아니다.

B 02 정답 ⑤ *무대에서 쓰러진 Arthur의 소생

All the actors on the stage / were focused on their acting. //
무대 위의 모든 배우가 / 그들의 연기에 집중하고 있었다 //

Then, suddenly, / Arthur fell into the corner of the stage. //
그 때 갑자기 / Arthur가 무대의 한쪽 구석에 쓰러졌다 //

Jeevan immediately approached Arthur / and **found** his heart wasn't beating. //
뒤에 목적어절 접속사 that이 생략됨
Jeevan이 즉각 Arthur에게 다가갔고 / 그의 심장이 뛰지 않는 것을 알아차렸다 //

Jeevan began CPR. //
Jeevan은 CPR을 시작했다 //

Jeevan worked silently, / **glancing sometimes at Arthur's face.** //
분사구문
Jeevan은 조용히 작업했다 / 때때로 Arthur의 얼굴을 흘긋 보며 //

He thought, / "Please, start breathing again, please." //
그는 생각했다 / '제발, 다시 숨쉬기를 시작해요, 제발'이라고 //
단서 1 Arthur가 다시 숨쉬기를 간절히 바람

Arthur's eyes were closed. //
Arthur의 눈은 감겨 있었다 //

Moments later, / an older man in a grey suit appeared, / swiftly **kneeling beside Arthur's chest.** //
분사구문
잠시 뒤 / 회색 정장 차림의 한 노인이 나타났고 / Arthur의 가슴 옆에 재빠르게 무릎을 꿇었다 //

"I'm Walter Jacobi. // I'm a doctor." //
"저는 Walter Jacobi입니다 // 저는 의사입니다" //

He announced with a calm voice. //
그는 차분한 목소리로 전했다 //

Jeevan wiped the sweat off his forehead. //
Jeevan은 그의 이마에서 땀을 닦아냈다 //

With combined efforts, / Jeevan and Dr. Jacobi successfully revived Arthur. //
협력하여 / Jeevan과 Dr. Jacobi는 Arthur를 성공적으로 소생시켰다 //

Arthur's eyes slowly opened. //
Arthur의 눈이 천천히 떠졌다 //

Finally, / Jeevan was able to hear Arthur's breath again, / **thinking to himself,** / "Thank goodness. // You're back." //
분사구문
마침내 / Jeevan은 Arthur의 숨을 다시 들을 수 있었고 / 자신에게 되뇌었다 / '다행이다 // 깨어났다'라고 //
단서 2 Arthur가 깨어나서 안도함

- immediately ⓐd 즉시 • glance ⓥ 흘긋 보다
- swiftly ⓐd 신속하게 • kneel ⓥ 무릎을 꿇다
- combined ⓐ 합쳐진 • effort ⓝ 노력 • revive ⓥ 소생시키다
- thrilled ⓐ 흥분한 • desperate ⓐ 간절한

무대 위의 모든 배우가 그들의 연기에 집중하고 있었다. 그 때 갑자기 Arthur가 무대의 한쪽 구석에 쓰러졌다. Jeevan이 즉각 Arthur에게 다가갔고 그의 심장이 뛰지 않는 것을 알아차렸다. Jeevan은 CPR을 시작했다. Jeevan은 때때로 Arthur의 얼굴을 흘긋 보며 조용히 작업했다. 그는 '제발, 다시 숨쉬기를 시작해요, 제발.'이라고 생각했다. Arthur의 눈은 감겨 있었다. 잠시 뒤, 회색 정장 차림의 한 노인이 나타났고, Arthur의 가슴 옆에 재빠르게 무릎을 꿇었다. "저는 Walter Jacobi입니다. 저는 의사입니다." 그는 차분한 목소리로 전했다. Jeevan은 그의 이마에서 땀을 닦아냈다. 협력하여, Jeevan과 Dr. Jacobi는 Arthur를 성공적으로 소생시켰다. Arthur의 눈이 천천히 떠졌다. 마침내 Jeevan은 Arthur의 숨을 다시 들을 수 있었고, '다행이다. 깨어났다.'라고 자신에게 되뇌었다.

① thrilled → bored 지루할 만한 상황이 아님
  흥분한 → 지루한
② ashamed → confident 수치를 느낄 일이 아님
  수치스러운 → 자신만만한
③ hopeful → helpless 결국 Arthur는 소생되었기에 무력함을 느끼지 않음
  희망에 찬 → 무력한
④ surprised → indifferent 후반에 무관심함을 느끼지 않음
  놀란 → 무관심한
⑤ desperate → relieved Please, start breathing → Thank goodness
  간절한 → 안도한

왜 정답 ？ ✿✿✿ [정답률 87%]

전반부: 심장이 뛰지 않는 Arthur에게 CPR을 하면서 다시 숨쉬기를 바람 ▶ '간절한'
후반부: 의사의 도움으로 Arthur가 다시 소생됨 ▶ '안도한'
따라서 Jeevan의 심경 변화로 가장 적절한 것은 ⑤ '간절한 → 안도한'이다.

왜 오답 ？

① 다시 숨을 쉬기 시작한 Arthur를 보며 느낀 감정은 지루함이 아니다.
② 쓰러진 Arthur에게 심폐 소생술을 하며 느낀 감정은 수치가 아니다.
③ 결국 의사의 도움으로 Arthur는 소생되었기에 무력감을 느끼지 않았다.
④ 마지막에 의사의 도움으로 Arthur는 의식을 되찾았고, 다행이라 생각했기에
  무관심함을 느낀 것이 아니다.

B 03 정답 ① *유럽 배낭여행 연기

Maya waited in line / to check in for her flight. //
  부사적 용법 (목적)
Maya는 줄을 서서 기다리고 있었다 / 비행기 탑승 수속을 위해 //
Her expectations / about her European backpacking trip / were
복수 주어   복수 동사
really high. // 단서 1 유럽 배낭여행에 대한 기대가 높음
그녀의 기대는 / 유럽 배낭여행에 대한 / 아주 높았다 //
She had been looking forward to the trip / for a year. //
그녀는 이 여행을 손꼽아 기다려 왔다 / 일 년 동안 //
  can't wait to-v: 빨리 ~하고 싶다   병렬 구조
She couldn't wait to visit museums in Madrid / and see the
Eiffel Tower / at night in Paris. //
그녀는 빨리 Madrid의 박물관들을 방문하고 / Eiffel Tower를 보고 싶었다 / 밤에 Paris에서 //
  부사절 접속사 (시간)   앞에 목적어절 접속사 that이 생략됨
As she stood in line, / she could feel those experiences were
finally so close. //
줄을 서 있는 동안 / 그녀는 느꼈다 / 그 경험들이 마침내 정말 가까워졌다고 //
When she approached the counter, / the airline employee asked
  타동사 (뒤에 전치사 없이 목적어가 옴)
/ to see her passport. //
  명사적 용법 (목적어)
그녀가 카운터에 다가갔을 때 / 항공사 직원이 요청했다 / 그녀의 여권을 보고 //
  자동사 (뒤에 전치사가 필요함)
Maya reached into her pocket / but felt nothing. //
Maya는 주머니에 손을 넣었지만 / 아무것도 만져지지 않았다 //
  과거완료 (realized보다 이전의 일)
She realized / she had left her passport at home. //
그녀는 깨달았다 / 여권을 집에 두고 온 것을 //
Her plans were ruined. // 그녀의 계획은 망쳐졌다 //
  분사구문을 이끄는 현재분사
She was heartbroken, / knowing / she could not board the flight
/ and had to delay her dream trip. // 단서 2 여행을 연기해야 한다는 것을 깨닫고는 상심함
그녀는 상심했다 / 깨달으며 / 비행기에 탑승할 수 없고 / 꿈꿔왔던 여행을 연기해야 한다는 것을 //

- check in (비행기) 탑승 수속을 하다   · expectation ⓝ 기대
- look forward to ~을 기대하다   · approach ⓥ 다가가다
- passport ⓝ 여권   · ruin ⓥ 망치다   · heartbroken ⓐ 상심한
- board ⓥ 탑승하다   · indifferent ⓐ 무관심한

Maya는 비행기 탑승 수속을 위해 줄을 서서 기다리고 있었다. 유럽 배낭여행에 대한 그녀의 기대는 아주 높았다. 그녀는 일 년 동안 이 여행을 손꼽아 기다려 왔다. 그녀는 빨리 Madrid의 박물관들을 방문하고 Paris에서 밤에 Eiffel Tower를 보고 싶었다. 줄을 서 있는 동안, 그녀는 그 경험들이 마침내 정말 가까워졌다고 느꼈다. 그녀가 카운터에 다가갔을 때, 항공사 직원이 그녀의 여권

을 보자고 요청했다. Maya는 주머니에 손을 넣었지만 아무것도 만져지지 않았다. 그녀는 여권을 집에 두고 온 것을 깨달았다. 그녀의 계획은 망쳐졌다. 그녀는 비행기에 탑승할 수 없고 꿈꿔왔던 여행을 연기해야 한다는 것을 깨달으며, 상심했다.

① excited → frustrated 여행을 앞두고 신났지만 비행기에 탑승할 수 없어서 상심했음
  신나는 → 좌절한
② joyful → indifferent 비행기에 탑승할 수 없어서 무관심했던 것이 아님
  즐거운 → 무관심한
③ terrified → relaxed 여행을 앞두고 겁에 질렸던 것이 아님
  겁에 질린 → 편안한
④ worried → satisfied 비행기에 탑승할 수 없어서 상심함
  걱정하는 → 만족한
⑤ bored → curious 비행기 탑승 수속을 기다리면서 기대했음
  지루한 → 호기심 많은

왜 정답 ？ ✿✿✿ [정답률 93%]

전반부: 비행기 탑승 수속을 기다리며 유럽 배낭여행을 기대함 ▶ '신나는'
후반부: 여권을 집에 놓고 와서 비행기에 탑승할 수 없음을 깨달음 ▶ '좌절한'
따라서 Maya의 심경 변화로 가장 적절한 것은 ① '신나는 → 좌절한'이다.

왜 오답 ？

② 비행기를 기다리면서 즐거워했지만 비행기에 탑승할 수 없게 되자 무관심했던 것이
  아니라 상심했다. 함정
③ 유럽 여행에 관해 겁에 질리지 않고 기대하였다.
④ 후반부에서 유럽 여행을 가지 못하게 되어 만족감이 아닌 상심이 드러난다.
⑤ 비행기 탑승 수속을 기다리며 지루해하지 않고 여행을 기대했다.

구문 서술형

정답 A large number of her plans were ruined.

→ plan은 셀 수 있는 명사이므로, a large number of를 이용하여 수량을 표현할 수 있다.

B 04 정답 ③ *오디션 결과

I glanced at the clock / on the wall. //
나는 시계를 흘끗 보았다 / 벽에 있는 //
10:00. // 10시였다 //
  뒤에 목적어절 접속사 that이 생략됨
That meant / the casting director would call very soon / with the
results of my first audition / for a musical part in *The Wizard of Oz*. //
그것은 의미했다 / 섭외 감독이 전화할 것이라는 걸 / 나의 첫 번째 오디션 결과로 / '오즈의 마법사' 뮤지컬 배역에 대한 //
                                          병렬 구조 (분사구문)
I felt shaky all over, / chewing my thumbnail and jiggling my
feet. // 단서 1 오디션 결과를 기다리며 긴장함
나는 온몸이 떨렸고 / 엄지손톱을 물어뜯고 발을 흔들어댔다 //
Finally, the telephone rang. // 마침내 전화기가 울렸다 //
While I was coming round, / Dad answered. //
내가 안절부절못하는 사이 / 아빠가 전화를 받았다 //
I heard him say, / "Ahh, thank you. / I'll let her know ..." //
나는 그가 말하는 것을 들었다 / "아, 감사합니다 / 그녀에게 알려주겠습니다"라고 //
  부사절 접속사 (시간)
As I got to the bottom of the stairs, / he was just putting the
phone down. //
내가 계단을 다 내려갔을 때 / 그는 막 전화기를 내려놓고 있었다 //
"That was *The Wizard of Oz*. // "오즈의 마법사'였어 //
You're second senior munchkin," / he announced. //
너는 둘째 상급 먼치킨이야'라고 / 그가 알려주었다 //
                                    분사구문을 이끄는 현재분사
I got a little rush of excitement, / knowing / I was in /
흥분감이 약간 밀려왔다 / 알게 되어 / 내가 참여한다는 것 / 앞에 목적어절 접속사 that이 생략됨
  목적어절(I was in)을 구체적으로 설명
— that whatever happened / I could be involved in one of the
  복합관계대명사 (= no matter what) 단서 2 배역을 따냈다는 소식을 듣고 흥분감이 밀려옴
productions. //
즉 어떤 일이 있었더라도 / 내가 작품들 중 하나에 참여할 수 있다는 것을 //

- glance ⓥ 홀끗 보다　• casting director 섭외 감독　• chew ⓥ 씹다
- jiggle ⓥ 가볍게 흔들다　• rush ⓝ 물결　• production ⓝ 작품

나는 벽에 있는 시계를 흘끗 보았다. 10시였다. 그것은 섭외 감독이 '오즈의 마법사' 뮤지컬 배역에 대한 나의 첫 번째 오디션 결과로 전화할 것이라는 걸 의미했다. 나는 온몸이 떨렸고, 엄지손톱을 물어뜯고 발을 흔들어댔다. 마침내 전화기가 울렸다. 내가 안절부절못하는 사이, 아빠가 전화를 받았다. 나는 그가, "아, 감사합니다. 그녀에게 알려주겠습니다 …"라고 말하는 것을 들었다. 내가 계단을 다 내려갔을 때, 그는 막 전화기를 내려놓고 있었다. "'오즈의 마법사'였어. 너는 둘째 상급 먼치킨이야."라고 그가 알려주었다. 내가 참여한다는 것 즉 어떤 일이 있었더라도 내가 작품들 중 하나에 참여할 수 있다는 것을 알게 되어 흥분감이 약간 밀려왔다.

> 다음 글에 드러난 'I'의 심경 변화로 가장 적절한 것은?
> ① puzzled → calm 결과를 듣고 침착하지는 않았음
> 　당황한　침착한
> ② bored → confused 결과를 기다리며 지루하지는 않았음
> 　지루한　혼란스러운
> ③ nervous → pleased I felt shaky → I got a little rush of excitement
> 　긴장한　기쁜
> ④ satisfied → regretful 결과를 기다리며 만족하지는 않았음
> 　만족한　후회하는
> ⑤ confident → disappointed 결과를 기다리며 자신감 있지는 않았음
> 　자신감 있는　실망한

> 왜 정답 ? ✽✽✽ [정답률 90%]

전반부: 온몸을 떨며 오디션 결과 전화를 기다림 ▶ '긴장한'
후반부: 뮤지컬에 참여하게 되었다는 소식을 들었음 ▶ '기쁜'
따라서 'I'의 심경 변화로 가장 적절한 것은 ③ '긴장한 → 기쁜'이다.

> 왜 오답 ?
① 오디션 결과를 듣고 침착했던 것은 아니다.
② 오디션 결과를 기다리며 지루했던 것은 아니다.
④ 오디션 결과를 기다리며 만족했던 것은 아니다.
⑤ 오디션 결과를 기다리며 자신감 있던 것은 아니다.

구문 서술형

정답 production, productions

→ '작품들 중 하나'를 뜻하는 복수 명사가 와야 하므로 productions가 알맞다.

B 05 정답 ① ✽농구 코치의 충격적인 통보

As I waited outside the locker room / after a hard-fought basketball game, / the coach called out to me, / "David, walk with me." //
내가 라커룸 밖에서 기다릴 때 / 치열하게 싸운 농구 경기 후에 / 코치가 나를 크게 불렀다 / "David, 나와 함께 걷자"라며 //
뒤에 목적어절 접속사 that 생략
I figured / he was going to tell me / something important. //
나는 생각했다 / 그가 나에게 말해 줄 거라고 / 무언가 중요한 것을 //
select의 목적격 보어 (to부정사)
He was going to select me to be the captain of the team, / the
관계대명사절(the leader 수식)
leader I had always wanted to be. //
그가 나를 팀의 주장으로 뽑을 것으로 (생각했다) / 내가 항상 되기를 원했던 리더인 //

My heart was racing / with anticipation. // 단서 1 팀의 주장이 될 것으로 기대
나의 심장이 빠르게 뛰었다 / 기대감으로 //

But when his next words hit my ears, / everything changed. //
그러나 그의 다음 말이 내 귀를 쳤을 때 / 모든 것이 변했다 //

"We're going to have to send you home," / he said coldly. //
"우리는 너를 집으로 보내야만 해"라고 / 그가 차갑게 말했다 //
　해내다
"I don't think you are going to make it." //
"나는 네가 해낼 거라고 생각하지 않아" //

I couldn't believe his decision. //
나는 그의 결정을 믿을 수 없었다 //
　'마음을 추스리다'
I tried to hold it together, / but inside I was falling apart. //
나는 마음을 가다듬으려고 했지만 / 내면에서 나는 산산이 무너지고 있었다 //
　형용사적 용법 (A car 수식)
A car would be waiting tomorrow morning / to take me home. //
내일 아침에 차가 기다리고 있을 것이다 / 나를 집에 데려갈 //

And just like that, / it was over. // 그리고 그렇게 / 끝이 났다 //

- hard-fought ⓐ 치열히 싸운　• figure ⓥ 생각하다
- race ⓥ 빠르게 뛰다　• anticipation ⓝ 기대감　• fall apart 무너지다

내가 치열하게 싸운 농구 경기 후에 라커룸 밖에서 기다릴 때, 코치가 "David, 나와 함께 걷자."라며 나를 크게 불렀다. 나는 그가 나에게 무언가 중요한 것을 말해 줄 거라고 생각했다. 그는 내가 항상 되기를 원했던 리더인 팀의 주장으로 나를 뽑으려 할 것이라고 (생각했다). 나의 심장이 기대감으로 빠르게 뛰었다. 그러나 그의 다음 말이 내 귀를 쳤을 때, 모든 것이 변했다. "우리는 너를 집으로 보내야 해."라고 그가 차갑게 말했다. "나는 네가 해낼 거라고 생각하지 않아." 나는 그의 결정을 믿을 수 없었다. 나는 마음을 가다듬으려고 했지만, 내면에서 나는 산산이 무너지고 있었다. 내일 아침에 나를 집에 데려갈 차가 기다리고 있을 것이다. 그리고 그렇게, 끝이 났다.

> 다음 글에 드러난 'I'의 심경 변화로 가장 적절한 것은?
> ① hopeful → frustrated My heart ~ with anticipation
> 　희망찬　좌절한 → inside I was falling apart
> ② confident → jealous 질투의 대상이 없음
> 　자신감 있는　질투하는
> ③ anxious → grateful 결국 팀에서 제외되었기에 감사할 일이 아님
> 　긴장한　감사하는
> ④ relaxed → indifferent 편안하거나 무관심을 느끼지 않음
> 　편안한　무관심한
> ⑤ bored → annoyed 지루하거나 짜증이 나는 상황이 아님
> 　지루한　짜증이 나는

> 왜 정답 ? ✽✽✽ [정답률 88%]

전반부: 코치가 불렀을 때 자신이 팀의 주장이 될 것이라는 기대를 함 ▶ '희망찬'
후반부: 코치가 '너는 해내지 못할 것 같다'고 하며 집으로 가라고 통보함 ▶ '좌절한'
따라서 'I'의 심경 변화로 가장 적절한 것은 ① '희망찬 → 좌절한'이다.

> 왜 오답 ?
② 팀에서 제외되어 집으로 가라는 통보를 받고 느낀 감정은 질투가 아니다.
③ 팀에서 제외되어 집으로 가라는 통보를 받고 느낀 감정은 감사가 아니다.
④ 후반에 코치의 통보를 받고 정신이 무너지고 있는 상황이므로 무관심한 감정이 아니다.
⑤ 주장의 자리를 기대했다가 팀에서 나가라는 충격적인 통보를 받은 상황이므로 지루하거나 짜증을 느끼지 않았다.

구문 서술형

정답 a great deal of, a lot of

해석 나의 심장이 많은 기대감으로 빠르게 뛰었다.

→ anticipation은 추상명사, 즉 셀 수 없는 명사이므로 a great deal of, a lot of 등을 이용하여 수량을 표현할 수 있다.

B 06 정답 ① ✽모래성 쌓기의 진정한 의미

동격
Marilyn and her three-year-old daughter, Sarah, / took a trip to
계속적 용법의 관계부사(선행사: the beach)
the beach, / where Sarah built her first sandcastle. //
Marilyn과 세 살 된 딸 Sarah는 / 해변으로 여행을 떠났고 / 그곳에서 Sarah는 처음으로 모래성을 쌓았다 //

Moments later, / an enormous wave destroyed Sarah's castle. //
잠시 후 / 거대한 파도가 Sarah의 성을 무너뜨렸다 // 단서 1 마음이 무너지고 눈물을 흘림

In response to the loss of her sandcastle, / tears streamed down Sarah's cheeks / and her heart was broken. //
모래성을 잃은 것에 반응하여 / 눈물이 Sarah의 뺨을 타고 흘러내렸고 / 그녀의 마음은 무너졌다 //

She ran to Marilyn, / saying / she would never build a sandcastle
again. //
<small>분사구문을 이끄는 현재분사</small>
그녀는 Marilyn에게 달려갔다 / 말하며 / 그녀가 다시는 모래성을 쌓지 않겠다고 //
Marilyn said, / "Part of the joy of building a sandcastle is / that,
in the end, / we give it as a gift / to the ocean." //
<small>단수 주어 / 단수 동사</small>
Marilyn은 말했다 / "모래성을 쌓는 즐거움 중 일부는 / 결국에는 / 우리가 그것을 선물로
주는 것이란 / 바다에게"라고 // <small>단서 2 모래성 쌓기에 대한 엄마 Marilyn의 생각을 매우 좋아함</small>
Sarah loved this idea / and responded with enthusiasm / to the
idea of building another castle — // <small>병렬 구조</small>
<small>단서 3 또 다른 모래성을 만들 생각에 열정적으로 반응함</small>
Sarah는 이 생각이 마음에 들었고 / 열정적으로 반응했다 / 또 다른 모래성을 만들
this time, / even closer to the water / so the ocean would get its
gift sooner! // <small>비교급 강조 부사</small>
이번에는 / 바다와 훨씬 더 가까운 곳에서 / 바다가 그 선물을 더 빨리 받을 수 있도록 //

- sandcastle ⓝ 모래성   • enormous ⓐ 거대한
- destroy ⓥ 부수다   • stream ⓥ 흐르다   • respond ⓥ 반응하다
- enthusiasm ⓝ 열정   • regretful ⓐ 후회하는

Marilyn과 세 살 된 딸 Sarah는 해변으로 여행을 떠났고, 그곳에서 Sarah는
처음으로 모래성을 쌓았다. 잠시 후, 거대한 파도가 Sarah의 성을 무너뜨렸다.
모래성을 잃은 것에 반응하여 눈물이 Sarah의 뺨을 타고 흘러내렸고, 그녀의
마음은 무너졌다. 그녀는 다시는 모래성을 쌓지 않겠다고 말하며 Marilyn에게
달려갔다. Marilyn은 "모래성을 쌓는 즐거움 중 일부는 결국에는 우리가 그것
을 바다에게 선물로 주는 것이란."라고 말했다. Sarah는 이 생각이 마음에 들
었고 또 다른 모래성을 만들 생각에 이번에는 바다와 훨씬 더 가까운 곳에서 바
다가 그 선물을 더 빨리 받을 수 있도록 하겠다며 열정적으로 반응했다.

> 다음 글에 드러난 Sarah의 심경 변화로 가장 적절한 것은?
> ① sad → excited <small>her heart was broken → loved this idea and responded with enthusiasm</small>
>   슬픈 → 신이 난
> ② envious → anxious <small>초반부에 슬퍼서 눈물을 흘리는 상황임</small>
>   부러워하는 → 걱정하는
> ③ bored → joyful <small>모래성을 잃은 것에 마음이 무너졌다고 했기 때문에 지루한 감정이 아님</small>
>   지루한 → 즐거운
> ④ relaxed → regretful <small>안도하거나 후회하는 감정을 느낄 상황이 아님</small>
>   안도하는 → 후회하는
> ⑤ nervous → surprised <small>초조한 감정이나 놀란 감정이 표현되지 않음</small>
>   초조한 → 놀란

> 왜 정답? ✽✽✽ [정답률 95%]

전반부: 파도가 모래성을 무너뜨려서 마음이 무너짐 ▶ '슬픈'
후반부: 바다에 모래성을 선물로 주는 거라는 엄마의 생각이 마음에 들어 또 다른
모래성을 쌓는 것에 열정적으로 반응함 ▶ '신이 난'
따라서 Sarah의 심경 변화로 가장 적절한 것은 ① '슬픈 → 신이 난'이다.

> 왜 오답?

② 초반부에 모래성이 무너져서 눈물을 흘리며 슬퍼하는 상황이므로 부러워하는
   감정이라고 볼 수 없다.
③ 모래성을 잃은 것에 반응하여 눈물을 흘리고 마음이 무너졌다는 내용이 나오기
   때문에 지루한 감정이 아니다.
④ 초반부에 모래성이 무너진 것에 대해 안도하거나 후반부에 엄마의 말을 듣고
   모래성을 쌓는 것에 대해 후회하고 있지 않다.
⑤ 내용에서 초조하거나 놀란 감정을 나타내는 표현이 나와 있지 않다.

B 07 정답 ② ✽대학 합격 편지

As I walked from the mailbox, / my heart was beating rapidly. //
<small>부사절 접속사(시간)</small> <small>단서 1 빠른 심장 박동</small>
우체통에서 걸어올 때 / 내 심장은 빠르게 뛰고 있었다 //
In my hands, / I held the letter from the university / I had
applied to. // <small>앞에 목적격 관계대명사가 생략됨</small>
내 손에는 / 대학에서 보낸 편지가 들려있었다 / 내가 지원했던 //
I thought / my grades were good enough to cross the line / and
my application letter was well-written, / but was it enough? //
<small>수동태 동사</small>
내 생각에 / 합격할 만큼 성적이 좋았고 / 지원서도 잘 썼지만 / 그것으로 충분했을까? //

I hadn't slept a wink for days. // <small>단서 2 잠을 못 잠</small>
<small>과거완료</small>
며칠 동안 한숨도 잘 수 없었다 //
As I carefully tore into the paper of the envelope, / the letter
slowly emerged with the opening phrase, / "It is our great
pleasure..." //
봉투의 종이를 조심스럽게 찢자 / 첫 문구와 함께 편지가 천천히 모습을 드러냈다 / "매우
기쁘게도..."라는 //
I shouted with joy, / "I am in!" // <small>단서 3 합격 확인 후 기뻐서 소리지름</small>
나는 기뻐서 소리질렀다 / "합격이야!" //
As I held the letter, / I began to make a fantasy / about my
college life in a faraway city. // <small>명사적 용법(목적어)</small>
나는 편지를 손에 쥐고 / 상상하기 시작했다 / 집에서 멀리 떨어진 도시에서의 대학 생활에
대해 //

- rapidly ⓐⓓ 빠르게   • application letter 지원서
- sleep a wink 한숨 자다   • envelope ⓝ 봉투
- emerge ⓥ 나타나다   • phrase ⓝ 문구   • faraway ⓐ 거리가 먼

우체통에서 걸어올 때 내 심장은 빠르게 뛰고 있었다. 내 손에는 지원했던 대
학에서 보낸 편지가 들려있었다. 내 생각에는 합격할 만큼 성적이 좋았고 지원
서도 잘 썼지만, 그것으로 충분했을까? 며칠 동안 한숨도 잘 수 없었다. 봉투의
종이를 조심스럽게 찢자 "매우 기쁘게도..."라는 첫 문구와 함께 편지가 천천히
모습을 드러냈다. 나는 기뻐서 소리질렀다. "합격이야!" 나는 편지를 손에 쥐고
집에서 멀리 떨어진 도시에서의 대학 생활에 대해 상상하기 시작했다.

> 다음 글에 드러난 'I'의 심경 변화로 가장 적절한 것은?
> ① relaxed → upset <small>편안하거나 속상한 감정은 표현되지 않았음</small>
>   편안한 → 속상한
> ② anxious → delighted <small>결과를 기다리며 긴장했으나 합격을 확인하고 기뻐함</small>
>   긴장한 → 기쁜
> ③ guilty → confident <small>죄책감을 느끼는 상황이 아님</small>
>   죄책감이 드는 → 자신감 있는
> ④ angry → grateful <small>화가 나는 상황이 아님</small>
>   화난 → 감사하는
> ⑤ hopeful → disappointed <small>합격을 했으므로 실망하는 상황이 아님</small>
>   희망적인 → 실망한

> 왜 정답? ✽✽✽ [정답률 88%]

전반부: 대학 합격 여부를 편지로 확인하기 전에 매우 긴장하는 모습을 보임 ▶ '긴장한'
후반부: 합격이라고 적혀 있는 편지를 확인함 ▶ '기쁜'
따라서 I의 심경 변화로 가장 적절한 것은 ② '긴장한 → 기쁜'이다.

> 왜 오답?

① 긴장하다가 합격 소식을 듣고 기뻐했으므로 편안하거나 속상한 감정이 아니다.
③ 초반부에 죄책감은 표현되지 않았다.
④ 초반부에 화난 감정은 표현되지 않았다.
⑤ 합격 소식을 확인했으므로 실망하는 상황이 아니다.

<small>자이 쌤's Follow Me! – 홈페이지에서 제공</small>

B 08 정답 ③ ✽유명한 화가를 만난 Cindy

One day, / Cindy happened to sit / next to a famous artist in a
café, / and she was thrilled / to see him in person. //
<small>happen to-v: 우연히 ~하다</small> <small>단서 1 유명한 화가를 직접 보게 되어 감격함</small>
<small>부사적 용법(이유)</small>
어느 날 / Cindy는 우연히 앉게 되었다 / 카페에서 유명한 화가 옆에 / 그리고 그녀는 감격했
다 / 직접 그를 만나게 되어 //
He was drawing / on a used napkin over coffee. //
그는 그림을 그리고 있었다 / 커피를 마시면서 사용하던 냅킨에 //
She was looking on / in awe. // 그녀는 지켜보고 있었다 / 경외심을 가지고 //
After a few moments, / the man finished his coffee / and was
about to throw away the napkin / as he left. // <small>~할 때</small>
잠시 후에 / 그 남자는 커피를 다 마셨다 / 그리고 그 냅킨을 버리려고 했다 / 자리를 떠날 때 //
Cindy stopped him. // Cindy는 그를 멈춰 세웠다 //
"Can I have that napkin / you drew on?", / she asked. //
<small>지시형용사</small> <small>앞에 목적격 관계대명사 생략</small>
"저 냅킨을 가져도 될까요 / 당신이 그림을 그렸던" / 그녀가 물었다 //

"Sure," / he replied. // "물론이죠" / 그가 대답했다 //

"Twenty thousand dollars." // 단서 2 가져가려던 냅킨의 가격이 2만 달러라고 들음
"2만 달러입니다" //

It takes+시간+to부정사 ~: ~하는 데 …이 걸리다
She said, / with her eyes wide-open, / "What? It took you like two minutes / to draw that." //
그녀는 말했다 / 눈을 동그랗게 뜨고 / "뭐라고요? 대략 2분밖에 안 걸렸잖아요 / 그것을 그리는 데" //

"No," / he said. // "아니요" / 그가 말했다 //

"It took me over sixty years / to draw this." //
"나는 60년 넘게 걸렸어요 / 이것을 그리는 데" //
분사구문(= As she was at a loss)
Being at a loss, / she stood still rooted to the ground. //
어쩔 줄 몰라서 / 그녀는 꼼짝 못한 채 서 있었다 // 단서 3 화가의 대답을 듣고 놀라서 꼼짝 못한 채 그냥 서 있기만 함

- thrilled ⓐ 흥분한, 감격한   - draw ⓥ 그리다   - awe ⓝ 경외심
- reply ⓥ 대답하다   - at a loss 어쩔 줄을 모르는
- rooted ⓐ ~에 뿌리를 둔[정착한]

어느 날, Cindy는 카페에서 우연히 유명한 화가 옆에 앉게 되었고, 그녀는 직접 그를 만나게 되어 감격했다. 그는 커피를 마시면서 사용하던 냅킨에 그림을 그리고 있었다. 그녀는 경외심을 가지고 지켜보고 있었다. 잠시 후에, 그 남자는 커피를 다 마시고 나서 자리를 뜨면서 그 냅킨을 버리려고 했다. Cindy는 그를 멈춰 세웠다. "당신이 그림을 그렸던 저 냅킨을 가져도 될까요?"라고 그녀가 물었다. "물론이죠,"라고 그가 대답했다. "2만 달러입니다." 그녀는 눈을 동그랗게 뜨고 말했다, "뭐라고요? 그리는 데 2분밖에 안 걸렸잖아요." "아니요,"라고 그가 말했다. "나는 이것을 그리는 데 60년 넘게 걸렸어요." 그녀는 어쩔 줄 몰라 꼼짝 못한 채 서 있었다.

> 다음 글에 드러난 Cindy의 심경 변화로 가장 적절한 것은?
> ① relieved → worried 처음에 유명한 화가를 만나서 흥분하고 좋아했음
> 안심하는   걱정하는
> ② indifferent → embarrassed 유명한 화가 옆에 앉게 되어 몹시 흥분하고 있는
> 무관심한   당황스러워하는   상태이므로 무관심하지 않음
> ③excited → surprised 유명한 화가 옆에 앉게 되어 흥분했지만, 냅킨에 있는 그림에 대한
> 흥분한   놀란   화가의 재치 있는 말을 듣고 놀랐음
> ④ disappointed → satisfied 유명한 화가 옆에 앉았으므로 실망하는 것과 반대임
> 실망한   만족한
> ⑤ jealous → confident 유명한 화가를 질투하는 것은 아님
> 질투하는   자신감 있는

> 왜 정답 ? ★★※ [정답률 80%]

처음에 Cindy는 카페에서 유명한 화가 옆에 앉게 되어 감격했다. 그런데 화가가 그림을 그리고 있었던 냅킨을 Cindy가 가져도 되냐고 물었을 때 화가의 재치 있는 대답으로 인해 깜짝 놀라서 어찌할 바를 몰랐다고 했다. 따라서 Cindy의 심경 변화로 가장 적절한 것은 ③ '흥분한 → 놀란'이다.

> 왜 오답 ?

① 유명한 화가를 만나서 흥분하고 좋아했다고 했고, 안심하는 상황은 아니다.
② Cindy는 유명한 화가 옆에 앉게 되어 감격했으므로 무관심한 심경이 아니다.
④ 유명한 화가 옆에 앉아서 감격스러워했다고 했으므로 실망하는 것과 반대이다.
⑤ 유명한 화가를 질투했다는 내용은 전혀 언급되지 않았다.

B 09 정답 ⑤ *새벽에 느낀 두려움

In the middle of the night, / Matt suddenly awakened. //
한밤중에 / Matt는 갑자기 잠에서 깼다 //

He glanced / at his clock. //
그는 흘긋 보았다 / 그의 시계를 //

It was 3:23. //
3시 23분이었다 //
wondered의 목적어절을 이끄는 의문사
For just an instant / he wondered / what had wakened him. //
잠시 동안 / 그는 궁금했다 / 무엇이 그를 깨웠는지 //

Then / he remembered. //
그때 / 그는 기억했다 //

지각동사 heard의 목적격보어(동사원형)
He had heard / someone come into his room. //
그는 들었다 / 누군가가 그의 방에 들어온 것을 // 단서 1 누군가가 몰래 방에 들어온 것을 들었음
병렬 구조
Matt sat up in bed, / rubbed his eyes, / and looked around the small room. //
Matt는 침대에 꼿꼿이 앉았다 / 그의 눈을 비볐다 / 그리고 작은 방을 둘러보았다 //
분사구문
"Mom?" / he said quietly, / hoping he would hear his mother's voice / [assuring him / that everything was all right]. //
"엄마?" / 그가 조용히 말했다 / 엄마의 목소리를 그가 들을 수 있기를 바라면서 / 그를 안심시키는 / 모든 것이 괜찮다고 //

But / there was no answer. // 단서 2 두려움에 도움을 요청했으나 엄마가 대답하지 않음
그런데 / 답이 없었다 //
목적어절을 이끄는 접속사
Matt tried to tell himself / that he was just hearing things. //
Matt는 스스로에게 말하려고 노력했다 / 그가 막 환청을 들었다고 //

But / he knew he wasn't. //
그런데 / 그는 그가 그렇지 않았다는 것을 알았다 //

There was someone / in his room. //
누군가가 있었다 / 그의 방에는 // 단서 3 알 수 없는 존재가 방에 있어서 두려움을 느낌

He could hear / rhythmic, scratchy breathing / and it wasn't his own. //
그는 들을 수 있었다 / 규칙적으로 긁는 듯한 숨소리를 / 그리고 그것은 그의 것이 아니었다 //

He lay awake / for the rest of the night. //
그는 깬 상태로 누워있었다 / 남은 밤 동안 // 단서 4 두려움에 잠을 잘 수 없어서 밤새 깨어 있었음

- awaken ⓥ 잠에서 깨다   - glance ⓥ 흘긋 보다
- for an instant 잠시 동안   - rub ⓥ 비비다   - assure ⓥ 안심시키다
- rhythmic ⓐ 리드미컬한, 규칙적으로 순환하는

한밤중에, Matt는 갑자기 잠에서 깼다. 그는 그의 시계를 흘긋 보았다. 3시 23분이었다. 잠시 동안 그는 무엇이 그를 깨웠는지 궁금했다. 그때 그는 기억했다. 누군가가 그의 방에 들어온 것을 그가 들었다는 것을. Matt는 침대에 꼿꼿이 앉아 그의 눈을 비비고 작은 방을 둘러보았다. "엄마?" 그가 조용히 말했는데, 모든 것이 괜찮다고 그를 안심시키는 엄마의 목소리를 그가 들을 수 있기를 바라면서였다. 그런데 답이 없었다. Matt는 그가 막 환청을 들었다고 스스로에게 말하려고 노력했다. 그런데 그는 그가 그렇지 않았다는 것을 알았다. 그의 방에는 누군가가 있었다. 그는 규칙적으로 긁는 듯한 숨소리를 들을 수 있었고, 그것은 그의 것이 아니었다. 그는 남은 밤 동안 깬 상태로 누워있었다.

> 다음 글의 상황에 나타난 분위기로 가장 적절한 것은?
> ① humorous and fun 긴장하고 잠을 못 자는 상황임
> 유머스럽고 재미있는
> ② boring and dull 지루하고 따분하기에는 두려움에 긴장한 상태임
> 지루하고 따분한
> ③ calm and peaceful 정반대의 상황임
> 차분하고 평화로운
> ④ noisy and exciting 고요한 가운데 이상한 소리가 나고 신나는 상황은 아님
> 시끄럽고 신나는
> ⑤mysterious and frightening 정체를 알 수 없는 소리에 두려움을 느끼고 있음
> 불가사의하고 무서운

> 왜 정답 ? ★★※ [정답률 84%]

Matt는 새벽에 누군가가 방에 들어온 것을 느껴서 두려움에 잠을 이루지 못하는 상황이다. 두려움에 엄마를 불렀지만 엄마가 대답하지 않았고 잠을 잘 수 없어서 밤새 깨어 있었다고 했다. 따라서 이 글의 상황에 나타난 분위기로 가장 적절한 것은 ⑤ '불가사의하고 무서운'이다.

> 왜 오답 ?

① 두려움을 크게 느끼고 잠을 잘 수 없는 상황이므로 유머스럽고 재미있다는 것은 적절하지 않다.
② 잠에서 깬 후 무서움을 느끼고 긴장했으므로 지루하고 따분한 상황은 아니다.
③ 조용한 새벽에 정체 모를 소리가 나는 상황이므로 차분하고 평화로운 분위기와는 거리가 멀다.
④ 고요한 가운데 알 수 없는 소리가 들려 두려움을 느끼고 있으므로 신나는 상황은 아니다.

정답 ① *새로 이사 온 이웃에 대한 기대감 ────

On the way home, / Shirley noticed a truck / parked in front of
(앞에 주격 관계대명사와 be동사 생략)
the house / across the street. //
집에 오는 길에 / Shirley는 트럭 한 대를 알아차렸다 / 집 앞에 주차된 / 길 건너편에 //
New neighbors! //
새 이웃이었다 //
단서 1 알고 싶어 죽을 지경이었다는 것은 호기심이 있음을 보여줌
Shirley was dying to know / about them. //
Shirley는 알고 싶어 죽을 지경이었다 / 그들에 대해 //
"Do you know anything / about the new neighbors?" / she asked
Pa / at dinner. //
"뭔가 알고 계셔요 / 새 이웃에 대해" / 그녀는 아빠에게 물었다 / 저녁 식사 시간에 //
주격 관계대명사
He said, / "Yes, and there's one thing / that may be interesting
to you." //
그는 말했다 / "그럼, 그리고 한 가지 있지 / 네 흥미를 끌 만한 것이" //
Shirley had / a billion more questions. //
Shirley는 가지고 있었다 / 더 묻고 싶은 것을 엄청나게 //
Pa said joyfully, / "They have a girl / just your age. //
아빠는 기쁘게 말했다 / "여자아이가 한 명 있어 / 딱 네 나이의 //
Maybe / she wants to be your playmate." //
아마 / 그 애가 네 놀이 친구가 되고 싶어 할 수도 있어" //
Shirley nearly dropped her fork / on the floor. //
Shirley는 포크를 떨어뜨릴 뻔했다 / 바닥에 //
How many times / had she prayed for a friend? //
얼마나 많이 / 그녀가 친구를 달라고 기도했던가 //
(수동태의 과거 시제)
Finally, / her prayers were answered! //
마침내 / 그녀의 기도가 응답받았다 // **단서 2** 친구가 생기기를 간절히 원하고 있었음을 알 수 있음
She and the new girl / could go to school together, / play
together, / and become best friends. //
(병렬 구조)
그녀와 새로 온 여자아이는 / 함께 학교에 갈 수 있을지도 모른다 / 함께 놀 (수 있을지도 모른
다) / 그리고 제일 친한 친구가 될 (수 있을지도 모른다) //

- notice ⓥ 알아차리다　　• park ⓥ 주차하다　　• neighbor ⓝ 이웃
- joyfully ⓐⓓ 기쁘게　　• playmate ⓝ 놀이 친구　　• pray ⓥ 기도하다

집에 오는 길에, Shirley는 트럭 한 대가 길 건너편 집 앞에 주차된 것을 알
아차렸다. 새 이웃이었다! Shirley는 그들에 대해 알고 싶어 죽을 지경이었
다. 저녁 식사 시간에 그녀는 "새 이웃에 대해 뭔가 알고 계셔요?"라고 아
빠에게 물었다. 그는 "그럼, 그리고 네 흥미를 끌 만한 것이 한 가지 있지."
라고 말했다. Shirley는 더 묻고 싶은 게 엄청나게 많았다. 아빠는 "딱 네
나이의 여자아이가 한 명 있어. 아마 그 애가 네 놀이 친구가 되고 싶어 할
수도 있어."라고 기쁘게 말했다. Shirley는 포크를 바닥에 떨어뜨릴 뻔했
다. 그녀가 얼마나 많이 친구를 달라고 기도했던가? 마침내 그녀의 기도가
응답받았다! 그녀와 새로 온 여자아이는 함께 학교에 가고, 함께 놀고, 그
리고 제일 친한 친구가 될 수 있을지도 모른다.

> 다음 글에 드러난 Shirley의 심경으로 가장 적절한 것은?
> ① curious and excited 새로 온 친구에 대한 호기심을 표현하고, 친구가 생기길 굉장히
> 호기심이 많고 신이 난　원하고 있었으므로 신이 난 상태임
> ② sorry and upset 누군가에게 미안함을 느끼거나 마음이 상한 상황이 아님
> 미안하고 마음이 상한
> ③ jealous and annoyed
> 질투심을 느끼고 짜증이 난　기쁘고 설레는 마음은 나와 있으나 질투하고 짜증이 난 내용은 없음
> ④ calm and relaxed 고요하고 정적이기보다는 들뜬 분위기가 묘사됨
> 차분하고 느긋한
> ⑤ disappointed and unhappy 반대로 신나고 행복한 분위기임
> 실망하고 기분이 나쁜

> **왜 정답?** ✽✽✽ [정답률 93%]
> 새로 이사 온 이웃에 대한 호기심을 느끼고 있고, 같은 나이의 여자아이가 있다는 것
> 을 듣고 그 아이와 좋은 친구가 될 수 있을 것이라는 기대를 하고 있다. 따라서 정답
> 은 ① '호기심이 많고 신이 난'이다.

> **왜 오답?**
> ② 누군가에게 미안함을 느끼거나 마음이 상한 것보다는 설레고 기대되는 분위기의
> 글이다.
> ③ 새 이웃과 좋은 친구가 될 수 있을 것으로 기대하는 분위기이므로 질투심과 짜증
> 을 느끼는 것은 적절하지 않다.
> ④ 기도가 응답받았다고 표현하고 있고 포크를 떨어뜨릴 뻔할 정도로 기쁨에 놀랐
> 으므로 차분하거나 느긋한 분위기는 아니다.
> ⑤ 실망스럽거나 기분이 나쁜 것이 아니고 오히려 신나고 행복한 분위기가 묘사되
> 어 있다.

정답 ⑤ *엄마가 사주신 선물 ────

When my mom came home from the mall / with a special
(의문사)
present for me / I was pretty sure / I knew what it was. //
엄마가 상점에서 집에 왔을 때 / 나를 위한 특별한 선물을 가지고 / 나는 꽤 확신했다 / 그것이
무엇인지 알고 있다고 //
I was absolutely thrilled / because I would soon communicate /
with a new cell phone! //
나는 완전히 들떴는데 / 왜냐하면 곧 소통할 것이기 때문이었다 / 새로운 휴대폰으로 //
(앞에 목적격 관계대명사 생략)
I was daydreaming / about all of the cool apps and games / I was
going to download. // **단서 1** 휴대폰을 선물 받을 것이라고 생각하고 신이 났음
나는 상상에 잠겨 있었다 / 모든 멋진 앱과 게임에 대해 / 내가 다운로드할 //
(동사의 병렬 구조)
But my mom smiled really big / and handed me a book. //
하지만 엄마는 매우 크게 미소지었다 / 그리고 나에게 책 한 권을 건네주었다 //
(분사구문을 이끎)
I flipped through the pages, / figuring / that maybe she had
hidden my new phone inside. //
나는 책장을 넘겨보았다 / 생각하며 / 아마도 그녀가 나의 새로운 휴대폰을 안에 숨겨 두었을
것이라 //
(목적어절을 이끄는 접속사)
But I slowly realized / that my mom had not got me a phone /
(계속적 용법의 관계대명사)
and my present was just a little book, / which was so different
(선행사를 포함한 관계대명사)
from what I had wanted. // **단서 2** 선물이 책이라는 것을 깨닫고 실망함
그러나 나는 서서히 깨달았다 / 엄마가 나에게 휴대폰을 사 주지 않았다는 것을 / 그리고 내
선물이 겨우 작은 책이라는 것을 / 그리고 그것은 내가 원했던 것과는 너무 달랐다 //

- absolutely ⓐⓓ 절대적으로, 완전히　　• thrilled ⓐ 들뜬
- daydream ⓥ 공상에 잠기다　　• flip through 휙휙 넘기다, ~을 훑어보다
- figure ⓥ 생각[판단]하다　　• realize ⓥ 깨닫다, 실현하다
- furious ⓐ 몹시 화가 난　　• ashamed ⓐ 부끄러운
- anticipating ⓐ 기대하는　　• satisfied ⓐ 만족하는
- disappointed ⓐ 실망한

엄마가 나를 위한 특별한 선물을 가지고 상점에서 집에 왔을 때 나는
그것이 무엇인지 알고 있다고 꽤 확신했다. 나는 완전히 들떴는데
왜냐하면 곧 새로운 휴대폰으로 소통할 것이기 때문이었다! 나는 내가
다운로드할 모든 멋진 앱과 게임에 대해 상상에 잠겨 있었다. 하지만
엄마는 매우 크게 미소 지으며 나에게 책 한 권을 건네주었다. 나는 아마도
그녀가 나의 새로운 휴대폰을 안에 숨겨 두었을 것이라 생각하며 책장을
넘겨보았다. 그러나 나는 엄마가 나에게 휴대폰을 사주지 않았고 나의
선물이 겨우 작은 책이라는 것을 서서히 깨달았으며, 그것은 내가 원했던
것과는 너무 달랐다.

> 다음 글에 드러난 "I"의 심경 변화로 가장 적절한 것은?
> ① worried → furious 처음에는 선물이 휴대폰이라고 생각하고 들떠 있었음
> 걱정하는　　몹시 화가 난
> ② surprised → relieved 나중에는 선물이 책이라는 것을 알고 실망했음
> 놀란　　　　안심한
> ③ ashamed → confident 부끄러워하는 내용은 없음
> 부끄러운　　자신감 있는
> ④ anticipating → satisfied 선물이 책이라는 것을 알고 나서 만족하지 않고 실망했음
> 기대하는　　만족하는
> ⑤ excited → disappointed 선물이 휴대폰인 줄 알고 신이 났다가 책인 것을 알고 실망함
> 신이 난　　　실망한

왜 정답? ✱✱✱ [정답률 92%]

엄마가 선물을 가지고 오셨을 때 'I'는 선물이 휴대폰일 것이라고 생각해서 들떴지만, 선물이 책이라는 것을 확인하고 실망하게 되는 내용이다. 따라서 'I'의 심경 변화로 가장 적절한 것은 ⑤ '신이 난 → 실망한'이다.

> But으로 시작하는 마지막 문장에 주목하기! 꿀팁

왜 오답?

① 처음에는 선물이 휴대폰이라고 생각하고 들떠 있었으므로 걱정하는 것과는 관련 없다.

② 후반부에 선물이 책이라는 것을 알고 실망하게 되었으므로 안심한 것은 아니다.

③ 글 어디에도 'I'가 부끄러워하는 내용은 나오지 않는다.

④ 선물이 책이라는 것을 알게 되어 실망했으므로 만족하는 상황과 반대이다.

B 12 정답 ② ✱타자기 고장 해결로 찾은 안도감

It was two hours before the submission deadline / and I still hadn't finished / my news article. //
제출 마감 시간 두 시간 전이었다 / 그리고 나는 여전히 끝내지 못했다 / 나의 뉴스 기사를 //

I sat at the desk, / but suddenly, / the typewriter didn't work. //
나는 책상에 앉았다 / 그런데 갑자기 / 타자기가 작동하지 않았다 //

No matter how (아무리 ~할지라도) hard I tapped the keys, / the levers wouldn't move / to strike the paper. //
내가 아무리 세게 키를 두드려도 / 레버는 움직이지 않았다 / 종이를 두드리려 //

I started to realize / **that** (목적어절을 이끄는 접속사) I would not be able / to finish the article / on time. // **단서 1** 타자기가 고장 나서 작성 중이던 기사를 제시간에 끝낼 수 없을 것임을 깨달음
나는 깨닫기 시작했다 / 내가 할 수 없으리라는 것을 / 그 기사를 끝내는 것을 / 제시간에 //

Desperately, / I **rested** the typewriter / on my lap / and **started** (병렬 구조) hitting each key / with as much force as I could manage. //
필사적으로 / 나는 타자기를 올려놓았다 / 내 무릎 위에 / 그리고 각각의 키를 누르기 시작했다 / 내가 할 수 있을 만큼의 많은 힘을 가지고 //

Nothing happened. //
아무 일도 일어나지 않았다 //

Thinking something might have happened (분사구문) / inside of it, / I **opened** the cover, / **lifted** (병렬 구조) up the keys, / and **found** the problem / — a paper clip. //
무슨 일이 일어났을지도 모르겠다고 생각하면서 / 그것의 내부에 / 나는 그 덮개를 열고 / 키들을 들어 올리고 / 문제를 발견했다 / 종이 클립 //

The keys had no room / **to move.** (형용사적 용법) //
키들이 공간이 없었다 / 움직일 //

After picking it out, / I pressed and pulled some parts. //
그것을 집어서 꺼낸 후에 / 나는 몇 개의 부품들을 누르고 당겼다 //

The keys moved smoothly again. //
키들이 매끄럽게 다시 움직였다 //

I breathed deeply / and smiled. //
나는 깊게 숨을 내쉬었다 / 그리고 미소 지었다 //

Now I knew / **that** (목적어절을 이끄는 접속사) I could finish my article / on time. // **단서 2** 타자기 고장을 해결해서 기사를 제시간에 끝낼 수 있게 됨
이제는 알았다 / 내가 기사를 끝낼 수 있음을 / 제시간에 //

- submission ⓝ 제출 ・ deadline ⓝ 마감 시간
- typewriter ⓝ 타자기 ・ tap ⓥ (가볍게) 두드리다
- strike ⓥ (세게) 치다, 두드리다 ・ desperately ⓐⓓ 필사적으로
- lap ⓝ 무릎 ・ room ⓝ 공간 ・ smoothly ⓐⓓ 매끄럽게
- frustrated ⓐ 좌절한 ・ indifferent ⓐ 무관심한
- disappointed ⓐ 실망한

제출 마감 시간 두 시간 전이었고 나는 여전히 나의 뉴스 기사를 끝내지 못했다. 나는 책상에 앉았는데, 갑자기, 타자기가 작동하지 않았다. 내가 아무리 세게 키를 두드려도, 레버는 종이를 두드리려 움직이지 않았다. 나는 내가 제시간에 그 기사를 끝낼 수 없으리라는 것을 깨닫기 시작했다. 필사적으로, 나는 타자기를 내 무릎 위에 올려놓고 각각의 키를 내가 할 수 있을 만큼의 많은 힘을 가지고 누르기 시작했다. 아무 일도 일어나지

않았다. 그것의 내부에 무슨 일이 일어났을지도 모르겠다고 생각하면서, 나는 그 덮개를 열고, 키들을 들어 올리고, 문제를 발견했다 — 종이 클립. 키들이 움직일 공간이 없었다. 그것을 집어서 꺼낸 후에, 나는 몇 개의 부품들을 누르고 당겼다. 키들이 매끄럽게 다시 움직였다. 나는 깊게 숨을 내쉬고 미소 지었다. 이제는 제시간에 내가 기사를 끝낼 수 있음을 알았다.

> 다음 글에 나타난 'I'의 심경 변화로 가장 적절한 것은?
> ① confident → nervous 처음에 기사를 제시간에 끝내지 못할 것 같아 좌절한 상태였음
> 　자신감 있는　불안한
> ② frustrated → relieved 타자기가 고장 나서 기사를 제시간에 끝낼 수 없을까 봐 좌절했다가 타자기 문제를 해결하고 안심한 상황
> 　좌절한　안심한
> ③ bored → amazed 처음에 지루한 상황은 제시되지 않음
> 　지루한　놀란
> ④ indifferent → curious 무관심하거나 호기심 많은 상황은 제시되지 않음
> 　무관심한　호기심 많은
> ⑤ excited → disappointed 기사를 제시간에 끝내지 못할까 봐 좌절한 것이지 흥분한 것이 아님
> 　흥분한　실망한

왜 정답? ✱✱✱ [정답률 81%]

'I'는 처음에 타자기가 작동하지 않아 기사를 제시간에 끝낼 수 없을까 봐 좌절하다가 타자기 문제를 해결하고 비로소 제시간에 기사를 끝낼 수 있을 것을 알게 되어 안심하게 된다. 따라서 정답은 ② '좌절한 → 안심한'이다.

왜 오답?

① 처음에 기사를 끝내지 못할 것 같아 좌절한 상태였으므로 적절하지 않다.

③ 글 어디에도 지루한 상황은 나오지 않는다.

④ 무관심하고 호기심 많은 상황은 제시되지 않았다.

⑤ 기사를 끝내지 못할까 봐 좌절한 것이지 흥분한 상태가 아니므로 적절하지 않다.

B 13 정답 ② ✱공원에 간 Matthew

One Saturday morning, / Matthew's mother told **Matthew** (직접목적어절을 이끄는 접속사) / **that** she was going to take him (간접목적어) / to the park. //
어느 토요일 아침 / Matthew의 어머니는 Matthew에게 말했다 / 그녀가 그를 데리고 가겠다고 / 공원으로 //

A big smile / came across his face. // **단서 1** 공원에 갈 생각에 신이 났음
환한 미소가 / 그의 얼굴에 그려졌다 //

As (이유를 나타내는 접속사) he loved to play outside, / he ate his breakfast / and got dressed quickly / so they could go. //
그는 밖에 나가서 노는 것을 좋아했기 때문에 / 그는 서둘러 아침을 먹었다 / 그리고 옷을 입었다 / 그래서 그들이 나갈 수 있기 위해 //

When they got to the park, / Matthew ran all the way over to the swing set. //
공원에 도착했을 때 / Matthew는 그네를 향해 바로 뛰어갔다 //

That was his favorite thing **to do** (형용사적 용법) / at the park. //
그것은 그가 하는 가장 좋아하는 것이었다 / 공원에서 //

But / the swings **were** all **being used.** (수동태의 과거진행형) //
하지만 / 그네는 이미 모두 이용되고 있었다 //

His mother explained / **that** (목적어절을 이끄는 접속사) he could use the slide / **until** (시간을 나타내는 접속사(~까지)) a swing became available, / but it was broken. // **단서 2** 그네를 가장 좋아하지만 탈 수 없는 상황이고 미끄럼틀마저 부서져 있음
그의 어머니는 말했다 / 그가 미끄럼틀을 탈 수 있다고 / 그네를 이용할 수 있을 때까지 / 하지만 그것은 부서져 있었다 //

단서 3 어머니가 공원을 떠나야 한다고 함
Suddenly, / his mother got a phone call / and she told Matthew / they had to leave. //
갑자기 / 그의 어머니가 전화를 받았다 / 그리고 Matthew에게 말했다 / 그들이 떠나야 한다고 //

His heart sank. // **단서 4** 가슴이 내려앉음
그의 가슴이 내려앉았다 //

- swing set 스윙 세트(그네와 미끄럼틀 등으로 이뤄진 아이들 놀이 기구)
- available ⓐ 이용할 수 있는 ・ sink ⓥ 가라앉다, 침몰하다
- embarrassed ⓐ 난처한 ・ indifferent ⓐ 무관심한
- ashamed ⓐ 부끄러운 ・ touched ⓐ 감동한

어느 토요일 아침, Matthew의 어머니는 Matthew에게 공원으로 데리고 가겠다고 말했다. 환한 미소가 그의 얼굴에 그려졌다. 그는 밖에 나가서 노는 것을 좋아했기 때문에, 나가기 위해 서둘러 아침을 먹고 옷을 입었다. 공원에 도착했을 때, Matthew는 그네를 향해 바로 뛰어갔다. 그것은 그가 공원에서 가장 좋아하는 것이었다. 하지만 그네는 이미 모두 이용되고 있었다. 그의 어머니는 그네를 이용할 수 있을 때까지 미끄럼틀을 탈 수 있다고 말했지만, 그것은 부서져 있었다. 갑자기 그의 어머니가 전화를 받고 Matthew에게 그들이 떠나야 한다고 말했다. 그는 가슴이 내려앉았다.

다음 글에 드러난 Matthew의 심경 변화로 가장 적절한 것은?

① embarrassed → indifferent 처음에 어머니가 공원에 데려가겠다고 하자 미소지었음
  난처한   무관심한
② excited → disappointed
  신이 난   실망한   공원에 갈 생각에 신이 났다가 그네를 타지 못하고 떠나야 해서 실망함
③ cheerful → ashamed 글의 후반부에 부끄러워하는 내용이 제시되지 않았음
  기분 좋은   부끄러운
④ nervous → touched 긴장하거나 감동하는 내용은 없었음
  긴장한   감동한
⑤ scared → relaxed 후반부에 공원을 떠나야 해서 실망했음
  무서운   안심하는

왜 정답? ✱✱✱ [정답률 85%]

어머니가 공원에 데려가겠다고 말했을 때 밖에서 노는 것을 좋아하는 Matthew는 환한 미소를 지으며 좋아했지만, 공원에서 가장 좋아하는 그네 타기를 하지 못하고 미끄럼틀도 부서져 있어서 타지 못한 채 공원을 떠나야 했다. 따라서 Matthew의 심경 변화로 가장 적절한 것은 ② '신이 난 → 실망한'이다.

왜 오답?

① 처음에 어머니가 공원에 데려가겠다고 하자 Matthew가 미소를 지었기 때문에 난처한 것과는 상관이 없다.
③ 글의 후반부에 Matthew가 부끄러워하는 장면은 나오지 않는다.
④ 글 전체에서 Matthew가 긴장하거나 감동할 만한 상황은 없다.
⑤ Matthew의 가슴이 내려앉은 것은 공원을 떠나야 하는 실망감 때문이다. (함정)

B 14 정답 ③ *최우수상 트로피를 받아 기쁜 Zoe

The principal / stepped on stage. //
교장 선생님이 / 무대 위로 올라갔다 //

"Now, / I present this year's top academic award / to the student
/ who has achieved the highest placing." //
   주격 관계대명사
"이제, / 올해의 학업 최우수상을 수여하겠습니다 / 학생에게 / 최고 등수를 차지한" //

He smiled at the row of seats / where twelve finalists had
                               관계부사
gathered. //
그는 좌석 열을 향해 미소를 지었다 / 열두 명의 최종 입상 후보자가 모여있는 //

Zoe wiped a sweaty hand / on her handkerchief / and glanced
at the other finalists. // 단서 1 학업 최우수상 입상 후보자들 중 한 명으로서 결과가 발표되기
                             병렬 구조   전에 긴장했음
Zoe는 땀에 젖은 손을 문질러 닦았다 / 손수건에 / 그리고 나머지 다른 최종 입상 후보자들을
힐끗 보았다 //

They all looked as pale and uneasy / as herself. // 단서 2 Zoe를 포함한
            ┗━━ 원급 비교 ━━┛   최종 입상 후보자들은
그들은 모두 창백하고 불안해 보였다 / 그녀만큼 //   모두 창백하고 불안해
                                                      보임

Zoe and one of the other finalists / had won first placing in four
                                     과거완료
subjects / so it came down to / how teachers ranked their hard
                전치사 to의 목적어로 쓰인 명사절
work and confidence. //
Zoe와 나머지 다른 최종 입상 후보자 중 한 명이 / 네 개 과목에서 1위를 차지했다 / 그래서
그것은 좁혀졌다 / 그들의 노력과 자신감을 선생님들이 어떻게 평가하느냐로 //

"The Trophy for General Excellence / is awarded to Miss Zoe
                                      수동태
Perry," / the principal declared. //
"전체 최우수상을 위한 트로피는 / Zoe Perry 양에게 수여됩니다"라고 / 교장 선생님이
공표했다 //

"Could Zoe step this way, please?" //
"Zoe는 이리로 나와 주시겠습니까" //

마치 ~인 것처럼
Zoe felt as if she were in heaven. //
Zoe는 마치 천국에 있는 기분이었다 //   단서 3 최우수상을 받게 되자 천국에 있는 것처럼 기뻤음

She walked into the thunder of applause / with a big smile. //
그녀는 우레와 같은 박수갈채를 받으며 걸어갔다 / 활짝 웃음을 지으며 //   단서 4 Zoe는
                                                                      활짝 웃음

- principal ⓝ (학)교장 · present ⓥ 수여하다
- academic ⓐ 학업의 · award ⓝ 상 · row ⓝ 열, 횡렬
- finalist ⓝ 최종 입상 후보자 · gather ⓥ 모이다
- sweaty ⓐ 땀에 젖은 · handkerchief ⓝ 손수건
- glance ⓥ 힐끗 보다 · pale ⓐ 창백한 · uneasy ⓐ 불안한
- subject ⓝ 과목 · rank ⓥ 평가하다, 순위를 매기다
- confidence ⓝ 자신감 · declare ⓥ 공표하다
- thunder of applause 우레와 같은 박수갈채
- disappointed ⓐ 실망한 · guilty ⓐ 죄책감을 느끼는
- confident ⓐ 자신감 있는 · delighted ⓐ 기쁜

교장 선생님이 무대 위로 올라갔다. "이제, 최고 등수를 차지한 학생에게 올해의 학업 최우수상을 수여하겠습니다." 그는 열두 명의 최종 입상 후보자가 모여있는 좌석 열을 향해 미소를 지었다. Zoe는 땀에 젖은 손을 손수건에 문질러 닦고는 나머지 다른 최종 입상 후보자들을 힐끗 보았다. 그들은 모두 그녀만큼 창백하고 불안해 보였다. Zoe와 나머지 다른 최종 입상 후보자 중 한 명이 네 개 과목에서 1위를 차지했으므로, 그들의 노력과 자신감을 선생님들이 어떻게 평가하느냐로 좁혀졌다. "전체 최우수상을 위한 트로피는 Zoe Perry 양에게 수여됩니다."라고 교장 선생님이 공표했다. "Zoe는 이리로 나와 주시겠습니까?" Zoe는 마치 천국에 있는 기분이었다. 그녀는 활짝 웃음을 지으며 우레와 같은 박수갈채를 받으며 걸어갔다.

다음 글에 드러난 Zoe의 심경 변화로 가장 적절한 것은?

① hopeful → disappointed 처음에는 다른 후보자들처럼 긴장하고 있었음
  희망에 가득 찬 실망한
② guilty → confident 죄책감을 느끼는 내용은 나오지 않았음
  죄책감을 느끼는 자신감 있는
③ nervous → delighted 처음에는 긴장했으나 나중에 학업 최우수상을 받고 난 후 기뻐함
  긴장한   기쁜
④ angry → calm 화난 상황은 아님
  화난   침착한
⑤ relaxed → proud 처음에는 손에 땀이 차고 불안했음
  편안한   자랑스러워하는

왜 정답? ✱✱✱ [정답률 82%]

처음에 Zoe는 다른 입상 후보자들처럼 손이 땀에 젖고 창백하고 불안했으나, 최종적으로 전체 최우수상 트로피의 수여자로 공표된 다음에는 천국에 있는 기분이었고 활짝 웃음을 지었다는 내용이다. 따라서 Zoe의 심경 변화로 가장 적절한 것은 ③ '긴장한 → 기쁜'이다.

왜 오답?

① 처음에는 불안하고 긴장했다는 내용이 나오므로 희망찬 것과는 관련이 없다.
② Zoe가 죄책감을 느끼는 것에 대해서는 나오지 않는다.
④ Zoe가 화가 났다는 내용은 언급되지 않았다.
⑤ 처음에 Zoe는 매우 긴장한 상태였기 때문에 편안한 것과는 반대이다.

B 15 정답 ② *휴가 중 받게 된 부재중 전화

On one beautiful spring day, / I was fully enjoying my day off. //
어느 아름다운 봄날 / 나는 휴가를 충분히 즐기고 있었다 //
                                                       ~하기 위해서, ~하도록
I arrived at the nail salon, / and muted my cellphone / so that
I would be disconnected for the hour / and feel calm and
peaceful. //
나는 네일 샵에 도착했다 / 그리고 나의 휴대 전화를 음 소거했다 / 그 시간 동안 단절되도록 /
그리고 차분하고 평화롭게 느낄 수 있도록 //   단서 1 네일 샵에서 매니큐어를 받으면서 편안함을 느낌
I was so comfortable / while I got a manicure. //
나는 아주 편안했다 / 매니큐어를 받는 동안 //

As I left the place, / I checked my cellphone / and saw four
missed calls / from a strange number. //
병렬 구조
내가 그 장소를 떠날 때 / 나는 나의 휴대 전화를 확인했다 / 그리고 네 통의 부재중 전화를
봤다 / 낯선 번호에서 온 //
목적어절 접속사
I knew immediately / that something bad was coming, / and I
called back. //
나는 즉시 알았다 / 나쁜 어떤 일이 생겼다는 것을 / 그리고 다시 전화했다 //
목적어절 접속사
A young woman answered and said / that my father had fallen
over a stone / and was injured, / now seated on a bench. //
한 젊은 여성이 전화를 받아 말했다 / 나의 아버지가 돌에 걸려 넘어졌다고 / 그리고 다쳐서 /
지금 벤치에 앉아 있다고 //
단서 2 아버지가 넘어져서 다쳤다는 전화를 받음
부사절 접속사(이유)
I was really concerned / since he had just recovered from his
knee surgery. // 단서 3 무릎 수술을 한 지 얼마 되지 않은 아버지가 걱정됨
나는 정말 걱정되었다 / 그가 무릎 수술에서 막 회복했기 때문에 //
I rushed getting into my car / to go see him. //
나는 급히 차에 올랐다 / 그를 보러 가기 위해 //

- day off (근무를) 쉬는 날　　· mute ⓥ (소리를) 작게 하다, 음 소거하다
- disconnect ⓥ 단절하다　　· calm ⓐ 침착한, 차분한
- immediately ⓪ 즉시　　· fall over ~에 걸려 넘어지다
- injured ⓐ 다친, 부상을 입은　　· concerned ⓐ 걱정되는
- recover ⓥ 회복하다　　· surgery ⓝ 수술
- indifferent ⓐ 무관심한　　· annoyed ⓐ 화난

어느 아름다운 봄날, 나는 휴가를 충분히 즐기고 있었다. 나는 네일 샵에
도착해서 그 시간 동안 단절되어 차분하고 평화롭게 느낄 수 있도록 나의
휴대 전화를 음 소거했다. 나는 매니큐어를 받는 동안 아주 편안했다. 내가 그
장소를 떠날 때, 나는 나의 휴대 전화를 확인했고 낯선 번호에서 걸려 온 네
통의 부재중 전화를 봤다. 나는 나쁜 어떤 일이 생겼다는 것을 즉시 알고 다시
전화했다. 한 젊은 여성이 전화를 받아 나의 아버지가 돌에 걸려 넘어져 다쳤고
지금 벤치에 앉아 있다고 말했다. 그가 무릎 수술에서 막 회복했기 때문에 나는
정말 걱정되었다. 나는 그를 보러 가기 위해 급히 차에 올랐다.

다음 글에 드러난 'I'의 심경 변화로 가장 적절한 것은?

① nervous → confident　자신감을 느끼는 내용은 나오지 않음
　긴장한　　자신감 있는
②relaxed → worried　편안하게 휴가를 즐기던 중 아버지가 다쳤다는 연락을 받고 걱정함
　편안한　　걱정하는
③ excited → indifferent　아버지가 다친 것을 알고 걱정했으므로 무관심한 것이 아님
　신이 난　　무관심한
④ pleased → jealous　질투하는 내용은 언급되지 않음
　기쁜　　질투하는
⑤ annoyed → grateful　화를 내거나 감사하는 내용은 없음
　화난　　감사하는

왜 정답? ❋❋❋ [정답률 89%]

전반부: 아름다운 봄날에 휴가를 즐기면서 매니큐어를 받음 ▶ '편안한', '신이 난', '기쁜'
후반부: 아버지가 다치셨다는 것을 알게 됨 ▶ '걱정하는'
따라서 I의 심경 변화는 ② '편안한 → 걱정하는'이다.

왜 오답?

① 글에 자신감을 느끼는 것과 관련된 내용은 언급되지 않았다.
③ 후반부에 아버지가 다친 것을 알고 걱정하는 내용이 나오므로 무관심하다고 볼 수
　없다.
④ 질투하는 것과 관련된 내용은 나오지 않았다.
⑤ 화를 내거나 감사하는 내용은 모두 언급되지 않았다.

B 16 정답 ② ＊먹이를 찾고 있었던 곰

On a two-week trip / in the Rocky Mountains, / I saw a grizzly
bear / in its native habitat. // 단서 1 처음에는 곰을 보고 기분이 좋았음
2주간의 여행 중 / 로키산맥에서 / 나는 회색곰 한 마리를 보았다 / 자연 서식지에서 //
부사절 접속사(시간)　　watched의 목적격 보어
At first, / I felt joy / as I watched the bear / walk across the land. //
처음에 / 나는 기분이 좋았다 / 그 곰을 보았을 때 / 땅을 가로질러 걸어가는 //
　　　　　　　　　　　　　　　　　'이따금'
분사구문
He stopped every once in a while / to turn his head about, /
sniffing deeply. //
그것은 이따금 멈춰 섰다 / 그것의 고개를 돌리기 위해 / 깊게 코를 킁킁거리며 //
목적어절 접속사
He was following the scent of something, / and slowly I began
to realize / that this giant animal was smelling me! // 단서 2 곰은 나를 찾고 있었음
그것은 무언가의 냄새를 따라가고 있었다 / 그리고 서서히 나는 깨닫기 시작했다 / 이 거대한
동물이 내 냄새를 맡고 있다는 것을 //
I froze. // 나는 얼어붙었다 //
This was no longer a wonderful experience; / it was now an
issue / of survival. // 단서 3 이제 생존의 문제가 됨
이것은 더는 멋진 경험이 아니었고 / 이제 문제였다 / 생존의 //
명사적 용법(주격 보어)　　형용사적 용법(meat 수식)
The bear's motivation was to find meat to eat, / and I was clearly
on his menu. //
그 곰의 동기는 먹을 고기를 찾는 것이었고 / 나는 분명히 그의 메뉴에 올라 있었다 //

- grizzly bear 회색곰　　· native ⓐ 자연의　　· habitat ⓝ 서식지
- sniff ⓥ (코를) 킁킁거리다　　· realize ⓥ 깨닫다　　· giant ⓐ 거대한
- freeze ⓥ 얼어붙다　　· issue ⓝ 문제　　· survival ⓝ 생존
- motivation ⓝ 동기　　· clearly ⓪ 분명히

로키산맥에서 2주간의 여행 중, 나는 자연 서식지에서 회색곰 한 마리를
보았다. 처음에 나는 그 곰이 땅을 가로질러 걸어가는 모습을 보았을 때 기분이
좋았다. 그것은 이따금 멈춰 서서 고개를 돌려 깊게 코를 킁킁거렸다. 그것은
무언가의 냄새를 따라가고 있었고, 나는 서서히 거대한 이 동물이 내 냄새를
맡고 있다는 것을 깨닫기 시작했다! 나는 얼어붙었다. 이것은 더는 멋진 경험이
아니었고, 이제 생존의 문제였다. 그 곰의 동기는 먹을 고기를 찾는 것이었고,
나는 분명히 그의 메뉴에 올라 있었다.

다음 글에 드러난 'I'의 심경 변화로 가장 적절한 것은?

① sad → angry　처음엔 기분이 좋았음
　슬픈　　화난
②delighted → scared　곰을 보고 기분이 좋았지만 먹이가 될 수도 있음을 알고 무서워함
　기쁜　　무서운
③ satisfied → jealous　곰을 질투한 것이 아님
　만족하는　　질투하는
④ worried → relieved　먹이가 될 수도 있는 것이 안도할 상황은 아님
　걱정하는　　안도하는
⑤ frustrated → excited　오히려 처음에 흥분하고 마지막에 좌절했다고 볼 수 있음
　좌절한　　흥분하는

왜 정답? ❋❋❋ [정답률 85%]

전반부: 로키산맥에서 곰을 보고 기분이 좋았음 ▶ '기쁜', '만족하는'
후반부: 곰이 내 냄새를 따라오고 있다는 것을 깨달음 ▶ '무서운'
따라서 'I'의 심경 변화로 가장 적절한 것은 ② '기쁜 → 무서운'이다.

왜 오답?

① 처음에는 곰을 보고 기분이 좋았다.
③ 질투의 대상은 나오지 않았다.
④ 곰의 먹이가 될 수도 있는 상황이므로 안도하는 것이 아니다.
⑤ 반대로 처음에는 곰을 봐서 흥분했다가 먹이가 될 수 있음에 좌절했다고 볼 수
　있다.

B 17 정답 ② *암벽 등반 중에 생긴 일

Gregg and I **had been rock climbing** since sunrise / and **had had**
no problems. // 〔단서 1〕 아무런 문제없이 암벽 등반을 하고 있었음
Gregg와 나는 일출 이후에 암벽 등반을 해왔고 / 아무런 문제가 없었다 //

So we took a risk. // 그래서 우리는 위험을 감수했다 //

"Look, the first bolt is right there. // 봐, 첫 번째 볼트가 바로 저기에 있어 //

I can definitely climb out to it. // 나는 분명히 거기까지 올라갈 수 있어 //

Piece of cake," / I persuaded Gregg, / minutes before I found
myself pinned. // 〔단서 2〕 '식은 죽 먹기'라고 하면서 자신만해 함
식은 죽 먹기야'라고 / 나는 Gregg를 설득했다 / 내가 꼼짝 못 한다는 것을 알게 되기 몇 분
전에 //

It wasn't a piece of cake. //
그것은 식은 죽 먹기가 아니었다 //

The rock was deceptively barren of handholds. //
그 바위는 믿을 수 없게도 손으로 잡을 곳이 없었다 //

I clumsily **moved** back and forth / across the cliff face / and
ended up with nowhere to go...but down. //
나는 서투르게 앞뒤로 움직여 보았다 / 절벽 면을 가로질러 / 그리고 결국 아래쪽밖에는 갈
곳이 없게 되었다 //

The bolt / **that** would save my life, / **if I could get to it**, / was
about two feet / above my reach. // 〔단서 3〕 목숨을 구해줄 볼트가 손에 닿지 않음
볼트는 / 내 목숨을 구해줄 / 만약 내가 거기까지 갈 수 있다면 / 약 2피트 위에 있었다 / 내
손이 닿을 수 있는 곳에서 //

My arms trembled from exhaustion. //
내 팔은 기진맥진하여 떨렸다 //

I looked at Gregg. //
나는 Gregg를 쳐다보았다 //

My body froze with fright / from my neck down to my toes. //
내 몸은 공포로 얼어붙었다 / 목에서부터 발끝까지 // 〔단서 4〕 몸이 공포로 얼어붙음

Our rope **was tied** between us. //
우리 사이에 밧줄이 묶여 있었다 //

If I fell, / he would fall with me. //
내가 떨어지면 / 그도 나와 함께 떨어질 것이다 //

- risk ⓝ 위험 • definitely ⓐⓓ 분명히 • persuade ⓥ 설득하다
- pin ⓥ 꼼짝 못하게 하다 • deceptively ⓐⓓ 속을 정도로, 믿을 수 없게
- handhold ⓝ 손으로 잡을 곳 • clumsily ⓐⓓ 서투르게
- cliff ⓝ 절벽 • reach ⓝ (닿을 수 있는) 거리[범위]
- tremble ⓥ 떨(리)다 • exhaustion ⓝ 기진맥진
- fright ⓝ 공포, 놀람 • fearful ⓐ 두려운 • regretful ⓐ 후회하는

Gregg와 나는 일출 이후에 암벽 등반을 해왔고 아무런 문제가 없었다.
그래서 우리는 위험을 감수했다. "봐, 첫 번째 볼트가 바로 저기에 있어.
나는 분명히 거기까지 올라갈 수 있어. 식은 죽 먹기야."라고 나는 Gregg를
설득했고, 얼마 지나지 않아 나는 내가 꼼짝 못 한다는 것을 알게 되었다.
그것은 식은 죽 먹기가 아니었다. 그 바위는 믿을 수 없게도 손으로 잡을
곳이 없었다. 나는 서투르게 절벽 면을 앞뒤로 가로질러 보았지만, 갈 곳이
없었다...아래쪽밖에는. 만약 내가 거기까지 갈 수 있다면, 내 목숨을 구해줄
볼트는 손이 닿을 수 있는 곳에서 약 2피트 위에 있었다. 내 팔은 기진맥진하여
떨렸다. 나는 Gregg를 쳐다보았다. 내 몸은 목에서부터 발끝까지 공포로
얼어붙었다. 우리 사이에 밧줄이 묶여 있었다. 내가 떨어지면, 그도 나와 함께
떨어질 것이다.

다음 글에 드러난 'I'의 심경 변화로 가장 적절한 것은?

① joyful → bored 떨어질지도 모르는 상황임
즐거운 → 지루한
② confident → fearful 처음에는 자신만했지만, 공포로 얼어붙음
자신감 있는 → 두려운
③ nervous → relieved 안심할 상황이 아님
불안한 → 안심한
④ regretful → pleased 오히려 반대의 상황임
후회하는 → 즐거운
⑤ grateful → annoyed 감사하거나 화를 낸 상황이 아님
감사하는 → 화가 난

왜 정답? ★★❀ [정답률 84%]

전반부: 식은 죽 먹기라고 하며 위험을 감수함 ▶ '즐거운' 또는 '자신감 있는'
후반부: 볼트는 손에 닿지 않고, 공포로 몸이 얼어붙음 ▶ '두려운'
따라서 I의 심경 변화는 ② '자신감 있는 → 두려운'이다.

왜 오답?

① 처음엔 즐거웠지만, 목숨이 위태로운 상황이므로 지루한 것이 아니다.
③ 안심할 상황은 언급되지 않았다. (☞ 이유: Gregg와 나 사이에 밧줄이 있는 것은
서로를 지켜주는 것이 아니라, 한 명이 떨어지면 같이 떨어지는 더 위험한 상황을
암시하는 것이므로 안심했다고 볼 수 없다.)
④ 정답과 정반대의 심경 변화라고 할 수 있다.
⑤ 감사하거나 화가 날 상황은 없었다.

B 18 정답 ① *신혼여행에서 결혼 반지를 잃어버린 부부

I **had** never **seen** a beach / with such white sand or water / **that**
was such a beautiful shade of blue. //
나는 해변을 한 번도 본 적이 없었다 / 그렇게 하얀 모래나 바다를 가진 / 그렇게 아름다운
푸른 색조의 //

Jane and I set up a blanket on the sand / **while looking** forward
to our ten days of honeymooning / on an exotic island. //
Jane과 나는 모래 위에 담요를 깔았다 / 열흘간의 신혼여행을 기대하면서 / 이국적인
섬에서의 // 〔단서 1〕 Jane과 나는 이국적인 섬에서의 아름다운 신혼여행에 들떠 기대하고 있음

"Look!" // Jane waved her hand / **to point** at the beautiful scene
before us / — and her gold wedding ring / went flying off her
hand. // 〔단서 2〕 아내가 손을 흔들 때 결혼반지가 빠져버림
"저기 좀 봐" / Jane이 그녀의 손을 흔들어 / 우리 앞의 아름다운 풍경을 가리켰다 / 그러자
그녀의 금으로 된 결혼반지가 / 그녀의 손에서 빠져 날아갔다 //

I tried to see / **where** it went, / but the sun hit my eyes / and I
lost track of it. //
나는 보려고 노력했지만 / 그것이 날아간 곳을 / 햇빛이 눈에 들어와 / 그것이 가던 방향을
놓쳤다 //

I didn't want to lose her wedding ring, / so I started looking in
the area / **where I thought** it **had landed**. //
나는 그녀의 결혼반지를 잃어버리고 싶지 않아서 / 장소를 들여다보기 시작했다 / 내가
생각하기에 그것이 떨어졌을 //

However, the sand was so fine / and I realized / **that** anything
heavy, like gold, / would quickly sink / and might never be
found again. // 〔단서 3〕 해변에서 결혼반지를 찾을 수 없을 것임을 깨달음
하지만 모래가 너무 고왔고 / 나는 깨달았다 / 금처럼 무거운 것은 / 빨리 가라앉아 / 다시
발견되지 않을 수도 있겠다는 것을 //

- shade ⓝ 색조 • honeymoon ⓥ 신혼여행을 하다
- exotic ⓐ 이국적인 • track ⓝ (이동하는) 길[방향]
- land ⓥ (땅에) 떨어지다 • fine ⓐ 고운

나는 그렇게 하얀 모래나 그렇게 아름다운 푸른 색조의 바다를 가진 해변을 한 번도 본 적이 없었다. 이국적인 섬에서의 열흘간의 신혼여행을 기대하면서 Jane과 나는 모래 위에 담요를 깔았다. "저기 좀 봐!" Jane이 그녀의 손을 흔들어 우리 앞의 아름다운 풍경을 가리켰다. 그러자 그녀의 금으로 된 결혼반지가 그녀의 손에서 빠져 날아갔다. 나는 그것이 날아간 곳을 보려고 노력했지만, 햇빛이 눈에 들어와 그것의 가던 방향을 놓쳤다. 나는 그녀의 결혼반지를 잃어버리고 싶지 않아서 내가 생각하기에 그것이 떨어졌던 장소를 들여다보기 시작했다. 하지만 모래가 너무 고왔고 나는 금처럼 무거운 것은 빨리 가라앉아 다시는 발견되지 않을 수도 있겠다는 것을 깨달았다.

다음 글에 드러난 'I'의 심경 변화로 가장 적절한 것은?

① excited → frustrated
들뜬 → 좌절한   처음에는 신혼여행으로 들떠있었지만, 결혼반지를 잃어버려 좌절함
② pleased → jealous   처음에는 기뻤지만, 결혼반지를 잃어버려 좌절함
기쁜 → 질투하는
③ nervous → confident   처음에는 신혼여행에 기뻐하므로 긴장될 상황이 아님
긴장된 → 자신감 있는
④ annoyed → grateful   마지막에 결혼반지를 찾지 못했으므로 감사할 상황이 아님
성가신 → 감사하는
⑤ relaxed → indifferent   마지막에 결혼반지를 잃어버렸으므로 무관심할 상황이 아님
편안한 → 무관심한

오왜 정답? ✽✻✻ [정답률 88%]

전반부: 이국적이고 아름다운 섬의 해변에서 앞으로 열흘간의 신혼여행을 기대하고 있음 ▶ '들뜬', '기쁜', 또는 '편안한'
후반부: 아내가 손을 흔들 때 결혼반지가 빠졌고, 해변에서 반지를 찾지는 못할 것을 깨달음 ▶ '좌절한'
따라서 I의 심경 변화는 ① '들뜬 → 좌절한'이다.

오왜 오답?

② 마지막에 결혼반지를 잃어버려 좌절했으므로, 질투하는 상황이 아니다.
③ 처음에는 신혼여행에 대한 기대를 하고 있으므로, 긴장될 상황이 아니다.
④ 마지막에 결혼반지를 찾지 못했으므로, 감사할 상황이 아니다.
⑤ 마지막에 결혼반지를 잃어버렸으므로, 무관심한 상황이 아니다. ◀주의

자이쌤's Follow Me! – 홈페이지에서 제공

B 19 정답 ① ✽사라진 남편과 딸

When I woke up / in our hotel room, / it was almost midnight. //
내가 깨어났을 때 / 호텔 방에서 / 거의 자정이었다 //

I didn't see / my husband nor daughter. //
나는 보지 못했다 / 내 남편도 딸도 //

I called them, / but I heard their phones ringing / in the room. //
나는 그들에게 전화를 걸었지만 / 나는 그들의 전화가 울리는 것을 들었다 / 방에서 //

분사구문
Feeling worried, / I went outside and walked down the street, / but they were nowhere to be found. // 단서1 걱정이 되어 남편과 딸을 찾아 다녔지만 찾을 수 없었음
걱정되어 / 나는 밖으로 나가 거리를 걸어 내려갔다 / 하지만 그들은 어디에도 없었다 //

뒤에 목적어절 접속사 that이 생략됨
When I decided / I should ask someone for help, / a crowd nearby caught my attention. //
내가 결정했을 때 / 누군가에게 도움을 요청해야겠다고 / 근처에 있던 군중이 내 주의를 끌었다 //

분사구문
I approached, / hoping to find my husband and daughter, / and suddenly I saw two familiar faces. //
나는 다가갔다 / 남편과 딸을 찾기를 바라면서 / 그리고 갑자기 나는 익숙한 두 얼굴을 보았다 //

분사구문
I smiled, / feeling calm. // 단서2 남편과 딸을 보고 안도하며 미소를 지음
나는 미소를 지었다 / 안도감을 느끼며 //

Just then, / my daughter saw me / and called, "Mom!" //
바로 그때 / 나의 딸이 나를 보고 / "엄마"라고 불렀다 //

They were watching the magic show. //
그들은 마술쇼를 보고 있었다 //

felt의 목적격 보어(원형부정사)
Finally, / I felt all my worries disappear. // 단서3 모든 걱정이 사라짐
마침내 / 나는 내 모든 걱정이 사라지는 것을 느꼈다 //

• midnight ⓝ 자정   • nowhere ⓐⓓ 아무 데도 (없다)
• crowd ⓝ 군중, 무리   • approach ⓥ 다가가다
• suddenly ⓐⓓ 갑자기   • familiar ⓐ 익숙한, 친숙한
• calm ⓐ 침착한   • disappear ⓥ 사라지다
• indifferent ⓐ 무관심한   • embarrassed ⓐ 당황한

내가 호텔 방에서 깨어났을 때는, 거의 자정이었다. 남편과 딸이 보이지 않았다. 나는 그들에게 전화를 걸었지만, 그들의 전화가 방에서 울리는 것을 들었다. 걱정돼서 나는 밖으로 나가 거리를 걸어 내려갔지만, 그들은 어디에도 없었다. 내가 누군가에게 도움을 요청하려고 했을 때, 근처에 있던 군중이 내 주의를 끌었다. 나는 남편과 딸을 찾기를 바라면서 다가갔고, 갑자기 낯익은 두 얼굴이 보였다. 나는 안도하며 미소를 지었다. 바로 그때, 딸이 나를 보고 "엄마!"라고 불렀다. 그들은 마술쇼를 보고 있었다. 마침내, 나는 내 모든 걱정이 사라지는 것을 느꼈다.

다음 글에 드러난 'I'의 심경 변화로 가장 적절한 것은?

① anxious → relieved   남편과 딸이 안 보여 걱정했지만, 찾은 후에는 안도했음
걱정하는 → 안도하는
② delighted → unhappy   남편과 딸을 찾아 기쁜 것은 글의 후반부임
기쁜 → 불행한
③ indifferent → excited   사라진 남편과 딸에 무관심하지 않았음
무관심한 → 신난
④ relaxed → upset   남편과 딸을 찾았으므로 화난 것이 아님
편안한 → 화난
⑤ embarrassed → proud   자랑스러울 만한 사건은 언급되지 않았음
당황한 → 자랑스러운

오왜 정답? ✽✻✻ [정답률 90%]

전반부: 남편과 딸이 전화도 두고 없어짐 ▶ '걱정하는' 또는 '당황한'
후반부: 마술쇼를 보고 있던 남편과 딸을 만남 ▶ '안도하는'
따라서 'I'의 심경 변화는 ① '걱정하는 → 안도하는'이 적절하다.

오왜 오답?

② 정답과 정반대의 순서이다.
③ 사라진 남편과 딸에 대해 무관심했던 것이 아니라 걱정했다.
④ 남편과 딸을 발견한 후 화가 났다는 언급은 없다.
⑤ 남편과 딸이 없어져 당황스러웠던 것은 맞지만, 자랑스러운 감정을 느꼈다는 언급은 없다.

B 어휘 Review 정답 ──── 문제편 p. 31

01 절벽	11 day off	21 hops
02 후회하는	12 flip through	22 exhaustion
03 습기 찬	13 a piece of cake	23 uneasy
04 공포	14 at a loss	24 heartbroken
05 난처한	15 sleep a wink	25 figured
06 awe	16 gathered	26 midnight
07 approach	17 submission	27 applause
08 suddenly	18 surgery	28 swing
09 disconnect	19 motivation	29 habitat
10 board	20 thrilled	30 strike

C 주장 찾기

문제편 p. 34~42

C 01 정답 ② *적절한 몸짓의 효과

Improving your gestural communication involves / more than
동명사 (전치사 than의 목적어)   knowing의 목적어 (의문사+to부정사)
just knowing / when to nod or shake hands. //
몸짓을 사용하는 의사소통을 개선하는 것은 포함한다 / 단순히 아는 것 이상을 / 고개를 끄덕
이거나 악수를 해야 할 때를 //

It's about using gestures / to complement your spoken messages,
분사구문
/ adding layers of meaning to your words. //
이는 몸짓을 사용하는 것에 대한 것이다 / 여러분의 말로 전하는 메시지를 보완하기 위해 / 여
러분의 말에 여러 겹의 의미를 더하면서 //

Open-handed gestures, / for example, / can indicate honesty, /
분사구문
creating an atmosphere of trust. //
손바닥을 보이는 동작은 / 예를 들어 / 정직함을 나타낸다 / 신뢰의 분위기를 만들며 //

You invite openness and collaboration / when you speak with
with 분사구문
your palms facing up. //
여러분은 개방성과 협력을 끌어낸다 / 손바닥을 위로 향한 채로 이야기할 때 //

This simple yet powerful gesture can make / others feel more
comfortable and willing to engage in conversation. //
이 간단하지만 강력한 몸짓은 만들 수 있다 / 상대방이 더 편안함을 느끼고 대화에 더 기꺼이
참여하고 싶도록 //
명령문 동사   단서 적절한 몸짓은 상대방이 대화에 참여하게 함

But be careful / of the trap of over-gesturing. //
하지만 주의하라 / 과도한 몸짓의 함정에 //

Too many hand movements can distract / from your message, /
분사구문
drawing attention away from your words. //
너무 많은 손동작은 집중이 안 되게 한다 / (그들을) 여러분의 메시지에 / 여러분의 말로부터
(사람들의) 관심을 돌리게 해서 //
소유격 관계대명사
Imagine / a speaker / whose hands move quickly like birds, /
주어가 생략되지 않은 분사구문
their message lost in the chaos of their gestures. //
상상해 보라 / 발표자를 / 손이 마치 새처럼 빠르게 움직이는 / 자신의 메시지가 몸짓의 혼돈
속에 사라져 버린 //

Balance is key. // 균형이 핵심이다 //

Your gestures should highlight your words, / not overshadow
= your words
them. // 여러분의 몸짓은 여러분의 말을 강조해야지 / 말을 가려서는 안 된다 //

- gestural ⓐ 몸짓의   • nod ⓥ 고개를 끄덕이다
- complement ⓥ 보완하다   • layer ⓝ 겹
- indicate ⓥ 나타내다, 보여 주다   • honesty ⓝ 정직함
- atmosphere ⓝ 분위기   • collaboration ⓝ 협력
- palm ⓝ 손바닥   • willing to 기꺼이 ~ 하는
- engage in ~에 참여하다   • over-gesturing ⓝ 과도한 몸짓
- distract from ~에 집중이 안 되게 하다   • chaos ⓝ 혼돈
- overshadow ⓥ 가리다

몸짓을 사용하는 의사소통을 개선하는 것은 단순히 고개를 끄덕이거나 악수를
해야 할 때를 아는 것 이상을 포함한다. 이는 여러분의 말로 전하는 메시지를
보완하기 위해 여러분의 말에 여러 겹의 의미를 더하면서 몸짓을 사용하는 것에
대한 것이다. 예를 들어 손바닥을 보이는 동작은 정직함을 나타내어 신뢰의 분
위기를 만든다. 손바닥을 위로 향한 채로 이야기할 때 여러분은 개방성과 협력
을 끌어낸다. 이 간단하지만 강력한 몸짓은 상대방이 더 편안함을 느끼고 대화
에 더 기꺼이 참여하고 싶도록 만들 수 있다. 하지만 과도한 몸짓의 함정에 주
의하라. 너무 많은 손동작은 여러분의 말로부터 (사람들의) 관심을 돌리게 해서
(그들을) 여러분의 메시지에 집중이 안 되게 한다. 손이 마치 새처럼 빠르게 움
직여서 자신의 메시지가 몸짓의 혼돈 속에 사라져 버린 발표자를 상상해 보라.
균형이 핵심이다. 여러분의 몸짓은 여러분의 말을 강조해야지, 말을 가려서는
안 된다.

다음 글에서 필자가 주장하는 바로 가장 적절한 것은?
① 메시지를 잘 전달하기 위해서 열린 마음을 지녀야 한다.
　　열린 마음이 아니라 손바닥을 보이는 것이 언급되었음
② 효과적인 의사소통을 위해 몸짓을 적절히 사용해야 한다.
　　적절한 몸짓을 통해 말의 효과를 높일 수 있음
③ 청중의 반응을 파악하기 위해 그들의 몸짓에 주목해야 한다.
　　청중의 반응은 언급되지 않았음
④ 전달하고자 하는 것을 감추기보다 직접적으로 표현해야 한다.
　　직접적으로 표현하라는 것은 언급되지 않았음
⑤ 상대방을 설득하기 위해서는 메시지를 반복적으로 강조해야 한다.
　　메시지의 반복은 언급되지 않았음

> **왜 정답?** *✧✧✧ [정답률 90%]

적절한 몸짓은 의사소통을 원활하게 하지만, 부적절한 몸짓은 의사소통을 방해한다고
주장하므로 정답은 ②이다.

> **왜 오답?**

몸짓이라는 핵심어는 같지만, 주체가 다르다! 꿀팁

① 손바닥을 보이는 것(Open-handed)이 언급되었을 뿐, 열린 마음은 언급되지 않
았다.
③ 자신이 사용하는 몸짓에 관한 내용이지, 청중의 몸짓에 주목하라는 내용이 아니다.
④ 전달하려는 것을 직접적으로 표현하라는 주장이 아니다.
⑤ 상대방을 대화로 끌어들이기 위해 몸짓을 사용하는 것을 언급했지만, 상대방을 설
득하기 위해 메시지를 반복적으로 강조하라는 것은 언급되지 않았다.

C 02 정답 ⑤ *에너지가 높은 시간 파악하기

가주어   to maintain의 의미상 주어   진주어
It is difficult for any of us / to maintain a constant level of
attention / throughout our working day. //
~은 우리 중 누구라도 어렵다 / 꾸준한 수준의 주의 집중을 유지하는 것 / 근무일 내내 //
　　　　　　　　　　　　　　　　　　　　　　앞에 주격 관계대명사와 be동사가 생략됨
We all have body rhythms / characterised by peaks and valleys
of energy and alertness. //
우리는 모두 신체 리듬을 가지고 있다 / 에너지와 기민함의 정점과 저점으로 특징지어지는 //
　　　　　　　　　　　　　　　　　　　　　　　　　부사절 접속사(조건)
You will achieve more, / and feel confident as a benefit, / if you
　　　　　　　　　　　　　　　　　　　　　　　　관계부사
schedule your most demanding tasks / at times when you are
best able to cope with them. //
당신은 더 많은 것을 이루고 / 이익으로 자신감을 느낄 것이다 / 만약 당신이 가장 힘든 작업을
계획하면 / 그것들을 가장 잘 처리할 수 있는 시간에 //

If you haven't thought / about energy peaks before, / take a few
　　　　부사적 용법(목적)
days / to observe yourself. //
만약 당신이 생각해 본 적이 없다면 / 전에 에너지 정점에 관해 / 며칠을 사용하라 / 자신을
관찰하기 위해 //
　　　　　　　　　　관계부사　　단서 1 자신이 가장 좋은 상태인 때를 알라고 함
Try to note the times / when you are at your best. //
때를 알아차리도록 노력하라 / 당신이 가장 좋은 상태인 //

We are all different. //
우리는 모두 다르다 //
　　　　　　　　　　　　　　　단서 2 사람마다 정점인 시간은 다름
For some, / the peak will come first thing / in the morning, / but
　　　　가주어　　　　　　　　　　　진주어
for others / it may take a while / to warm up. //
어떤 사람에게는 / 정점은 제일 먼저 오는 것이다 / 아침에 / 하지만 다른 사람들에게는 / ~은
얼마간의 시간이 걸릴 수도 있다 / 준비하는 것 //

- maintain ⓥ 유지하다   • constant ⓐ 일정한
- attention ⓝ 주의 (집중)   • characterise ⓥ 특징으로 하다
- peaks and valleys 정점과 저점   • achieve ⓥ 이루다
- confident ⓐ 자신감 있는   • benefit ⓝ 이익, 혜택
- demanding ⓐ (일이) 힘든   • task ⓝ 과업, 작업
- cope with ~을 처리하다

우리 중 누구라도 근무일 내내 꾸준한 주의 집중을 유지하기는 어렵다. 우리
모두 에너지와 기민함의 정점과 저점을 특징으로 하는 신체 리듬을 가지고
있다. 가장 힘든 작업을 가장 잘 처리할 수 있는 시간에 그것을 하도록 계획을
잡으면, 더 많은 것을 이루고 이익으로 자신감을 느낄 것이다. 만약 전에
에너지 정점에 관해 생각해 본 적이 없다면, 며칠 동안 자신을 관찰하라.
자신이 가장 좋은 상태일 때를 알아차리도록 노력하라. 우리는 모두 다르다.
어떤 사람에게는 정점이 아침에 제일 먼저 오지만, 다른 사람에게는 준비하는
데 얼마간의 시간이 걸릴 수도 있다.

다음 글에서 필자가 주장하는 바로 가장 적절한 것은?

① 부정적인 감정에 에너지를 낭비하지 말라. 부정적인 감정은 글의 내용과 관련 없음
② 자신의 신체 능력에 맞게 운동량을 조절하라. 신체 리듬을 언급한 것으로 만든 오답
③ 자기 성찰을 위한 아침 명상 시간을 확보하라.
자기 성찰을 위해 명상을 하라는 내용은 없음
④ 생산적인 하루를 보내려면 일을 균등하게 배분하라.
일의 분배는 언급되지 않음
⑤ 자신의 에너지가 가장 높은 시간을 파악하여 활용하라.
자신이 가장 효율적인 시간을 파악해서 활용하라고 했음

왜 정답? ✱✸✸ [정답률 84%]

· **문제점**: 언제나 꾸준한 주의 집중을 유지하기는 어려움
· **해결책**: 하루 중 자신이 가장 좋은 상태인 시간을 파악하기
▶ 자신의 에너지가 가장 높은 시간을 파악하여 활용하라는 것이므로 정답은 ⑤이다.

왜 오답?

① 부정적인 강점이 아니라 자신에게 맞지 않는 시간에는 에너지가 저점일 수 있다고 했다.
② 신체 리듬을 언급했을 뿐, 운동량을 조절하라는 내용은 없었다. 함정
③ 자기 성찰을 하는 것은 중요하지만 명상에 대한 내용은 없었다.
④ 오히려 힘든 작업을 가장 잘 처리할 수 있는 시간에 하라고 했다.

C 03 정답 ⑤ ＊습관 형성에 영향을 주는 행동의 편리성

People often ask me, / "What surprises you most about habits?" //
사람들은 종종 나에게 묻는다 / "습관에 관한 무엇이 당신을 가장 놀라게 하나요"라고 //
주격 관계대명사 (One thing 수식)
One thing / that continually astonishes me / is the degree / to
전치사 + 관계대명사
which we're influenced by sheer convenience. //
한 가지는 / 나를 계속해서 놀라게 하는 / 정도이다 / 우리가 순전한 편리성에 의해 영향을 받는 //
'~의 양' cf) an amount of: 많은 ~ 과거분사구
The amount of effort, time, or decision making / required by an
action / has a huge influence / on habit formation. //
노력, 시간, 또는 의사 결정의 양이 / 행동에 의해 요구되는 / 큰 영향을 미친다 / 습관 형성에 //
to ~ extent: ~한 정도로 be likely to-v: ~할 가능성이 있다
To a truly remarkable extent, / we're more likely to do something
부사절 접속사 (조건)
/ if it's convenient, / and less likely / if it's not. //
정말 놀라울 정도로 / 우리는 어떤 일을 더 자주 할 것이고 / 그 일이 편리하다면 / 덜 하게 될 것이다 / 그렇지 않다면 //
단서 습관으로 만들고 싶은 행동의 편리성에 주의를 기울여야 함
For this reason, / we should pay close attention / to the
사이에 목적격 관계대명사가 생략됨
convenience of any activity / we want to make into a habit. //
이런 이유로 / 우리는 세심한 주의를 기울여야 한다 / 행동의 편리성에 / 습관으로 만들고 싶은 //
동명사구 주어
Putting a wastebasket / next to our front door / made mail sorting
slightly more convenient, / and I stopped / procrastinating with
this chore. //
쓰레기통을 두는 것이 / 현관문 옆에 / 우편물을 분류하는 일을 약간 더 편리하게 했고 / 나는
멈추었다 / 이 일을 미루는 것을 //
목적어절 접속사 동명사 (전치사 of의 목적어)
Many people report / that they do a much better job / of staying
부사절 접속사 (~이기 때문에)
close to distant family members / now that tools like group
가목적어 진목적어
chats / make it easy / to stay in touch. //
많은 사람들은 말한다 / 일을 훨씬 더 잘한다고 / 멀리 사는 가족들과 더 가까이 지내는 / 그룹
채팅 같은 도구들이 / 쉽게 만들어 주기 때문에 / 연락을 유지하는 것을 //

· **astonish** ⓥ 놀라게 하다   · **degree** ⓝ 정도
· **convenience** ⓝ 편리성   · **decision making** 의사 결정
· **remarkable** ⓐ 놀라운   · **extent** ⓝ 정도   · **chore** ⓝ 일, 잡일
· **stay in touch** 연락을 유지하다

사람들은 종종 나에게, "습관에 관한 무엇이 당신을 가장 놀라게 하나요?"라고
묻는다. 나를 계속해서 놀라게 하는 한 가지는 우리가 순전한 편리성에 의해 영
향을 받는 정도이다. 행동에 의해 요구되는 노력, 시간, 또는 의사 결정의 양이
습관 형성에 큰 영향을 미친다. 정말 놀라울 정도로, 우리는 어떤 일이 편리하

다면 그것을 더 자주 할 것이고, 그렇지 않다면 덜 하게 될 것이다. 이런 이유
로, 우리는 습관으로 만들고 싶은 행동의 편리성에 세심한 주의를 기울여야 한
다. 현관문 옆에 쓰레기통을 두는 것이 우편물을 분류하는 일을 약간 더 편리하
게 했고, 나는 이 일을 미루는 것을 멈추었다. 많은 사람들은 그룹 채팅 같은 도
구들이 연락을 유지하는 것을 쉽게 만들어 주기 때문에 멀리 사는 가족들과 더
가까이 지내는 일을 훨씬 더 잘한다고 말한다.

다음 글에서 필자가 주장하는 바로 가장 적절한 것은?

① 불필요한 자극을 유발하는 작업 환경을 개선해야 한다.
작업 환경이 불필요한 자극을 유발한다는 것은 언급되지 않았음
② 생활방식 개선을 위해 규칙적인 생활 습관을 길러야 한다.
생활방식 개선은 언급되지 않았음
③ 목표를 신속하게 달성하려면 구체적인 계획을 세워야 한다.
구체적인 계획을 세우는 것은 언급되지 않았음
④ 반복적인 업무의 편의를 위해 디지털 도구를 사용해야 한다.
디지털 도구 활용에 관한 내용이 아님
⑤ 습관으로 만들고 싶은 행동의 편리성에 주의를 기울여야 한다.
습관으로 만들고 싶은 행동의 편리성이 습관을 형성하는 데 영향을 미침

왜 정답? ✱✸✸ [정답률 86%]

어떤 일이나 행동이 편리하다면 그것을 더 자주 하게 되어 행동의 편리성이 습관 형성
에 영향을 준다고 주장하므로 정답은 ⑤이다.

왜 오답?

① 작업 환경이 불필요한 자극을 유발하고 있다는 내용은 언급되지 않았다.
② 습관이 반복적으로 언급되지만, 생활방식 개선을 위해서 습관 형성을 해야 한다는
내용이 아니다. 주의
③ 목표 달성을 위해 구체적인 계획을 세우라는 내용이 아니다.
④ 그룹 채팅이 연락을 유지하기 쉽게 하는 수단으로 언급되었지, 반복적인 업무의 편
의를 위한 도구로 언급되지는 않았다.

구문 서술형

정답 Putting a wastebasket next to our front door

→ 동명사구는 명사적 용법으로 쓰일 때 문장의 주어 역할을 할 수 있다. 따라
서 Put을 Putting으로 바꿔야 한다.

C 04 정답 ② ＊수업 시작의 중요성

Inefficient teachers overlook / the potential power of the
opening minutes of class. //
비효율적인 교사들은 간과한다 / 수업 시작 몇 분의 잠재적인 힘을 //
병렬 구조 (부사절 접속사 (조건))
Often, / if students are quiet enough / and if there are many
문장의 주어
pressing demands / on a teacher's time at that moment, / more
than ten minutes can disappear / before class starts. //
종종 / 학생들이 충분히 조용하고 / 긴급한 요구가 많으면 / 그 순간 교사의 시간에 대한 /
10분 이상이 사라질 수 있다 / 수업이 시작되기 전에 //
가주어 진주어절 접속사 '거의 없는'
It's no wonder / that students are late for class; / they have little
reason to be on time. //
놀라운 일이 아니다 / 학생들이 수업에 늦는 것은 / 그들이 제시간에 올 이유가 거의 없다 //
부사적 용법 (목적)
You can use the first ten minutes / to get your class off to a great
명사적 용법 (choose의 목적어)
start, / or you can choose to waste this time. //
당신은 첫 10분을 사용하거나 / 훌륭한 시작으로 당신의 수업을 출발시키도록 / 당신은 이 시
간을 낭비하도록 선택할 수 있다 //

The first minutes set the tone / for the rest of the class. //
첫 몇 분이 분위기를 설정한다 / 나머지 수업의 // 단서1 수업 첫 몇 분이 수업의 분위기를 정함

If you are prepared for class / and have taught your students an
opening routine, /
당신이 수업 준비가 되어 있고 / 시작 루틴을 학생들에게 가르쳤다면 /
= your students
they can use this brief time / to make mental and emotional
병렬 구조 (목적)
transitions from the last class or subject / and prepare to focus
명사적 용법 (prepare의 목적어)
on learning new material. //
그들은 이 짧은 시간을 사용할 수 있다 / 지난 수업 또는 과목으로부터 정신적, 감정적 변화를
만들고 / 새로운 자료를 배우는 것에 집중하려고 준비하기 위해 //

In summary, / you should establish an opening routine / to develop your class with an effective start. // **단서2** 효과적인 수업을 위해 수업 시작 루틴을 마련해야 함
요약하자면 / 시작 루틴을 마련해야 한다 / 효과적인 출발로 수업을 전개하기 위한 //

- inefficient ⓐ 비효율적인 · overlook ⓥ 간과하다
- potential ⓐ 잠재적인 · demand ⓝ 요구
- disappear ⓥ 사라지다
- get ~ off to a great start ~을 순조롭게 시작하다
- set the tone 분위기를 잡다 · brief ⓐ 짧은
- transition ⓝ 변화 · material ⓝ 자료
- establish ⓥ 설립하다, 마련하다

비효율적인 교사들은 수업 시작 몇 분의 잠재적인 힘을 간과한다. 종종, 학생들이 충분히 조용하고 그 순간 교사의 시간에 대한 긴급한 요구가 많으면, 수업이 시작되기 전에 10분 이상이 사라질 수 있다. 학생들이 수업에 늦는 것은 놀라운 일이 아니다. 그들이 제시간에 올 이유가 거의 없다. 당신은 훌륭한 시작으로 당신의 수업을 출발시키도록 첫 10분을 사용하거나 당신은 이 시간을 낭비하도록 선택할 수 있다. 첫 몇 분이 나머지 수업의 분위기를 설정한다. 당신이 수업 준비가 되어 있고 시작 루틴을 학생들에게 가르쳤다면, 그들은 지난 수업 또는 과목으로부터 정신적, 감정적 변화를 만들고 새로운 자료를 배우는 것에 집중하려고 준비하기 위해 이 짧은 시간을 사용할 수 있다. 요약하자면, 효과적인 출발로 수업을 전개하기 위한 시작 루틴을 마련해야 한다.

다음 글에서 필자가 주장하는 바로 가장 적절한 것은?
① 학생의 적극적인 참여를 위해 포용적 수업 분위기를 형성하라. 포용적 수업 분위기 형성에 관한 내용이 아님
② 수업을 효과적으로 전개하기 위해 시작 루틴을 마련하라. 시작 루틴을 통해 수업을 효과적으로 시작할 수 있음
③ 학습 동기를 부여할 수 있는 창의적인 수업 자료를 개발하라. 창의적 수업 자료 개발에 관한 내용이 아님
④ 적절한 학습량 조절을 통해 학습 부담을 줄여라. 학습 부담은 언급되지 않았음
⑤ 학생이 스스로 학습 루틴을 만들도록 장려하라. 학생의 학습 루틴에 관한 내용이 아님

> 왜 정답 ? ✱✱✱ [정답률 94%]

수업의 첫 몇 분이 가진 잠재력을 이해하고 수업 시작 루틴을 마련한다면 수업의 효율성이 높아진다는 내용이므로 정답은 ②이다.

> 왜 오답 ?

① 첫 몇 분이 나머지 수업의 분위기를 조성한다고 했을 뿐, 포용적 수업 분위기를 형성하라는 내용이 아니다.
③ 학생들의 새로운 자료 학습이 언급되었을 뿐, 창의적 수업 자료를 개발하라는 내용이 아니다.
④ 학습 부담은 언급되지 않았다.
⑤ 교사들이 수업 시작 루틴을 마련해야 한다고 했을 뿐, 학생이 스스로 학습 루틴을 만들어야 한다는 내용이 아니다.

구문 서술형

정답 가주어, 가주어, that

해설 학생들이 수업에 늦는 것은 놀라운 일이 아니다.
→ 가주어 It이 진주어절 that ~ for class 대신에 문장 앞에 쓰였다.

C 05 정답 ② *간단한 운동과 집안일의 병행

For many of us, / making time for exercise / is a continuing challenge. // 동명사구 주어
우리 중 다수에게 / 운동할 시간을 내는 것은 / 계속되는 도전이다 //

Between work commitments and family obligations, / it often feels like / there's no room in our packed schedules / for a dedicated workout. // '여유가 없다'
업무에 대한 전념과 가족 의무 사이에서 / 종종 느껴진다 / 우리의 빡빡한 일정들에는 여유가 없는 것처럼 / 운동에 전념할 //

'만일 ~한다면 어떨까'   '~의 한가운데에'
But what if the workout came to you, / right in the midst of your daily routine? //
그러나 만약 운동이 여러분을 찾아온다면 어떨까 / 여러분의 일상 바로 한가운데에서 //
관계부사 (앞에 선행사가 생략됨)
That's / where the beauty of integrating mini-exercises into household chores / comes into play. //
그것이 (지점이다) / 간단한 운동을 집안일에 통합시키는 아름다움이 / 작동하는 //

Let's be realistic; / chores are inevitable. //
현실적이 되자 / 집안일은 불가피하다 //

whether A or B: A이든 B이든
Whether it's washing dishes / or taking out the trash, / these tasks are an essential part of daily life. //
그것이 설거지하는 것이든 / 쓰레기를 내다 버리는 것이든 / 이런 일들은 일상생활의 필수적인 부분이다 //

'~하기보다는'   동명사구 (전치사의 목적어)
But rather than viewing chores / as purely obligatory activities, / why not seize these moments / as opportunities for physical activity? //
하지만 집안일을 간주하기보다는 / 순전히 의무적인 행위로 / 이런 순간들을 이용하는 것이 어떤가 / 신체 활동을 위한 기회로 //

병렬 구조 (명령문 동사)
For instance, / practice squats / or engage in some wall push-ups / as you wait for your morning kettle to boil. // 부사절 접속사 (시간)
예를 들어 / 스쿼트를 연습하거나 / 벽에 대고 하는 팔 굽혀 펴기 몇 개를 시작해 보라 / 여러분의 아침 주전자가 끓기를 기다리면서 //

동명사구 주어
Incorporating quick exercises into your daily chores / can improve your health. // **단서** 간단한 운동을 집안일에 포함하는 것은 건강에 좋음
짧은 운동을 여러분의 일상적인 집안일에 포함시키는 것이 / 여러분의 건강을 향상시킬 수 있다 //

- commitment ⓝ 전념, 헌신 · obligation ⓝ 의무
- dedicated ⓐ 전념[헌신]하는 · integrate ⓥ 통합하다
- chore ⓝ 일 · come into play 작동하다 · realistic ⓐ 현실적인
- inevitable ⓐ 피할 수 없는 · seize ⓥ 잡다
- engage in ~을 시작하다 · incorporate ⓥ 포함하다

우리 중 다수에게 운동할 시간을 내는 것은 계속되는 도전이다. 업무에 대한 전념과 가족 의무 사이에서, 우리의 빡빡한 일정들에는 운동에 전념할 여유가 없는 것처럼 종종 느껴진다. 그러나 만약 여러분의 일상 바로 한가운데에서 운동이 여러분을 찾아온다면 어떨까? 그것이 바로 간단한 운동을 집안일에 통합시키는 아름다움이 작동하는 지점이다. 현실적이 되자. 집안일은 불가피하다. 그것이 설거지하는 것이든 쓰레기를 내다 버리는 것이든지 간에, 이런 일들은 일상생활의 필수적인 부분이다. 하지만 집안일을 순전히 의무적인 행위로 간주하기보다는, 이런 순간들을 신체 활동을 위한 기회로 잘 이용하는 것이 어떨까? 예를 들어, 여러분의 아침 주전자가 끓기를 기다리면서 스쿼트를 연습하거나 벽에 대고 하는 팔 굽혀 펴기 몇 개를 시작해 보라. 짧은 운동을 여러분의 일상적인 집안일에 포함시키는 것이 여러분의 건강을 향상시킬 수 있다.

다음 글에서 필자가 주장하는 바로 가장 적절한 것은?
① 간단한 운동일지라도 강도를 점진적으로 높여야 한다. 운동 강도에 대한 언급은 없음
② 집안일을 간단한 운동을 병행할 기회로 활용해야 한다. 집안일을 기회로 삼아 간단한 운동을 해야 함
③ 집안일을 할 때 동선을 고려하여 효율을 높여야 한다. 집안일의 동선과 효율은 언급되지 않았음
④ 자신이 즐길 수 있는 운동을 찾아 꾸준히 해야 한다. 즐길 수 있는 운동은 언급되지 않았음
⑤ 몸에 무리를 주지 않으려면 집안일을 줄여야 한다. 집안일을 줄여야 한다는 내용이 아님

> 왜 정답 ? ✱✱✱ [정답률 94%]

우리는 빡빡한 일정에서 운동에 전념할 여유가 없다고 느끼기 때문에, 불가피한 집안일을 기회로 삼아 간단한 운동을 집안일에 포함시켜야 한다고 주장하고 있으므로 정답은 ②이다.

> 왜 오답 ?

① 운동 강도에 대한 내용이 아니다.
③ 집안일의 동선과 효율은 언급되지 않았다.
④ 즐길 수 있는 운동을 찾으라는 것은 언급되지 않았다.
⑤ 집안일을 줄이라는 내용이 아니다.

구문 서술형

정답 these tasks, 이런 일들은 일상생활의 필수적인 부분이다

→ Whether가 이끄는 부사절 뒤에 주절이 오는 형태이다. 사람이나 사물을 나타내는 명사나 명사구가 주어가 될 수 있으므로, 주절의 주어는 these tasks이다.

C 06 정답 ② *긍정적인 진술이 가져오는 변화

선행사를 포함하는 관계대명사
Magic is **what** we all wish for / to happen in our life. //
마법은 우리 모두 바라는 바이다 / 자신의 삶에서 일어나기를 //

Do you love the movie *Cinderella* / like me? //
여러분도 '신데렐라' 영화를 사랑하는가 / 나처럼 //

Well, / in real life, / you can also create magic. //
그러면 / 실제 삶에서 / 여러분도 마법을 만들 수 있다 //

Here's the trick. // 여기 그 요령이 있다 //

목적격 관계대명사
Write down all the real-time challenges / **that** you face and deal with. //
모든 실시간의 어려움을 적어라 / 여러분이 직면하고 처리하는 //

change A into B: A를 B로 바꾸다
Just **change** the challenge statement / **into** positive statements. //
단지 그 어려움에 관한 진술을 바꾸어라 / 긍정적인 진술로 //
사역동사+목적어+목적 보어(동사원형)
단서 1 어려움에 관한 진술을 긍정적인 진술로 바꿈

Let me give you / an example / here. //
여러분에게 제시하겠다 / 한 예시를 / 여기서 //

동명사구(전치사의 목적어)
If you struggle with / **getting up early** in the morning, / then write a positive statement / such as "I get up early in the morning at 5:00 am every day." //
만약 여러분이 어려움을 겪는다면 / 아침 일찍 일어나는 것에 / 그러면 긍정적인 진술을 써라 / '나는 매일 일찍 아침 5시에 일어난다'와 같은 //

접속사(일단 ~하면)
Once you write these statements, / get ready to witness / magic and confidence. //
일단 여러분이 이러한 진술을 적는다면 / 목격할 준비를 하라 / 마법과 자신감을 //

~ 함으로써
You will be surprised / that just **by writing** these statements, / there is a shift / in the way you think and act. //
여러분은 놀랄 것이다 / 단지 이러한 진술을 적음으로써 / 변화가 있다는 것에 / 여러분이 생각하고 행동하는 방식에 //
단서 2 긍정적인 진술이 생각과 행동 방식에 변화를 가져옴

Suddenly you feel / more powerful and positive. //
어느 순간 여러분은 느끼게 된다 / 더 강력하고 긍정적이라고 //
단서 3 자신이 더 강력하고 긍정적이라고 느낄 수 있음

- magic ⓝ 마법, 마술 · challenge ⓝ 어려움, 도전
- statement ⓝ 진술 · positive ⓐ 긍정적인
- struggle ⓥ 어려움을 겪다 · witness ⓥ 목격하다
- confidence ⓝ 자신감 · surprise ⓥ 놀라게 하다 · shift ⓝ 변화
- powerful ⓐ 강력한

마법은 우리 모두 자신의 삶에서 일어나기를 바라는 바이다. 여러분도 나처럼 '신데렐라' 영화를 사랑하는가? 그러면, 실제 삶에서, 여러분도 마법을 만들 수 있다. 여기 그 요령이 있다. 여러분이 직면하고 처리하는 모든 실시간의 어려움을 적어라. 그 어려움에 관한 진술을 긍정적인 진술로 바꾸어라. 여기서 여러분에게 한 예시를 제시하겠다. 만약 여러분이 아침 일찍 일어나는 것에 어려움을 겪는다면, 그러면 '나는 매일 일찍 아침 5시에 일어난다.'와 같은 긍정적인 진술을 써라. 일단 여러분이 이러한 진술을 적는다면, 마법과 자신감을 목격할 준비를 하라. 여러분은 단지 이러한 진술을 적음으로써 여러분이 생각하고 행동하는 방식에 변화가 있다는 것에 놀랄 것이다. 어느 순간 여러분은 더 강력하고 긍정적이라고 느끼게 된다.

다음 글에서 필자가 주장하는 바로 가장 적절한 것은?

① 목표한 바를 꼭 이루려면 생각을 곧바로 행동으로 옮겨라.
생각을 행동으로 옮기라는 내용은 없음
② 자신감을 얻으려면 어려움을 긍정적인 진술로 바꿔 써라.
Just change the challenge statement into positive statements.
③ 어려운 일을 해결하려면 주변 사람에게 도움을 청하라.
어려움에 직면했을 때 긍정적인 진술을 하라는 내용임
④ 일상에서 자신감을 향상하려면 틈틈이 마술을 배워라.
마술을 배우라고 하지 않음
⑤ 실생활에서 마주하는 도전을 피하지 말고 견뎌 내라.
도전을 견뎌내는 인내와 관련된 내용은 없음

왜 정답? ✸✸✸ [정답률 91%]

요령: 실시간으로 직면하는 어려움을 긍정적인 진술로 바꾸기
예시: 아침에 일찍 일어나는 것이 어렵다면, '매일 일찍 아침 5시에 일어난다.'라고 적어보기
결과: 그렇게 행동할 자신감을 얻고, 생각과 행동 방식이 변화되어 스스로에 대해 긍정적으로 느낄 수 있음
▶ 긍정적인 진술을 통해 스스로를 더 강력하고 긍정적이라고 느낄 수 있는 변화와 자신감을 보게 될 것이라는 내용이므로 정답은 ②이다.

왜 오답?

① 목표를 이루기 위해 생각을 행동으로 옮기라는 내용은 언급되지 않았다.
③ 어려운 일에 직면했을 때 변화를 위해서 긍정적인 진술을 하는 방법이 제시되었다.
④ 이 글에서 마법은 어려움이 해결되고 변화가 일어나는 일을 비유적으로 표현한 것이지, 실제로 마술을 배우라는 의미가 아니다.
⑤ 도전을 피하지 말고 인내해야 한다는 내용은 언급되지 않았다.

C 07 정답 ① *공간 정돈의 긍정적 효과

동명사 주어   '~로 이어지다'
Having a messy room / can **add up to** negative feelings and destructive thinking. //
방이 지저분한 것은 / 결국 부정적인 감정과 파괴적인 사고로 이어질 수 있다 //

목적어절 접속사
Psychologists say / **that** having a disorderly room can indicate / a disorganized mental state. //
심리학자들은 말한다 / 방이 무질서하다는 것은 나타낼 수 있다고 / 정신 상태가 혼란스럽다는 것을 //

뒤에 관계부사 when 생략
One of the professional tidying experts says / that **the moment** you start cleaning your room, / you also start **changing** your life / and **gaining** new perspective. //
병렬 구조(목적어) 단서 1 방 청소를 시작하면 인생이 변함
정리 전문가 중 한 명은 말한다 / 방 청소를 시작하는 순간 / 당신은 또한 인생을 변화시키기 시작하고 / 새로운 관점을 얻기 (시작한다고) //

부사절 접속사(시간)
When you clean your surroundings, / positive and good atmosphere follows. // 단서 2 긍정적 분위기가 형성됨
주변을 청소하면 / 긍정적이고 좋은 분위기가 따라온다 //

You can do more things / efficiently and neatly. //
당신은 더 많은 일을 할 수 있다 / 효율적이고 깔끔하게 // 단서 3 효율적이고 깔끔하게 일할 수 있음

So, / **clean up** your closets, / **organize** your drawers, / and **arrange** your things first, / then peace of mind will follow. //
병렬 구조
그러니 / 옷장을 청소하고 / 서랍을 정리하고 / 물건을 먼저 정돈한다면 / 마음의 평화가 따라올 것이다 //
단서 4 정리 정돈을 하면 마음의 평화가 따라옴

- messy ⓐ 지저분한 · destructive ⓐ 파괴적인
- disorderly ⓐ 무질서한 · indicate ⓥ 나타내다
- disorganized ⓐ 체계적이지 못한 · mental state 정신 상태
- tidy ⓥ 정돈하다 · gain ⓥ 얻다 · surroundings ⓝ 주변 환경
- atmosphere ⓝ 분위기 · neatly ⓐⓓ 단정하게

방이 지저분한 것은 결국 부정적인 감정과 파괴적인 사고로 이어질 수 있다. 심리학자들은 방이 무질서하다는 것은 정신 상태가 혼란스럽다는 것을 나타낼 수 있다고 말한다. 정리 전문가 중 한 명은 방 청소를 시작하는 순간 당신은 인생을 변화시키고 새로운 관점을 얻기 시작한다고 말한다. 주변을 청소하면 긍정적이고 좋은 분위기가 따라온다. 당신은 더 많은 일을 효율적이고 깔끔하게 할 수 있다. 그러니 먼저 옷장을 청소하고, 서랍을 정리하고, 물건을 정돈한다면 마음의 평화가 따라올 것이다.

다음 글에서 필자가 주장하는 바로 가장 적절한 것은?
① 자신의 공간을 정돈하여 긍정적 변화를 도모하라.
　　　　　주변을 청소하면 인생이 긍정적으로 변한다는 내용임
② 오랜 시간 고민하기보다는 일단 행동으로 옮겨라.
　　　　　　　　　　정리 정돈에 관한 내용임
③ 무질서한 환경에서 창의적인 생각을 시도하라.
　　　　정리 정돈을 함으로써 긍정적 변화를 시도하라는 내용임
④ 장기 목표를 위해 단기 목표를 먼저 설정하라.
　　　　　　　　　목표 설정에 관한 내용이 아님
⑤ 반복되는 일상을 새로운 관점으로 관찰하라.
　　　　　　　반복되는 일상에 관한 내용이 아님

왜 정답? ✸✸✸ [정답률 96%]
정리 정돈을 시작하는 순간 삶에 변화가 생기고 새로운 관점으로 바라볼 수 있다는
말과 함께 여러 가지 긍정적인 효과들을 설명하고 있으므로 정답은 ①이다.

왜 오답?
② 정리 정돈의 긍정적 효과에 관한 내용이지, 일단 행동하라는 내용은 없다.
③ 무질서한 환경을 긍정적으로 보고 있는 글이 아니다.
④ 옷장을 청소하고 서랍을 정리하는 등의 행위는 단지 목표의 예시가 아닌 정리
　정돈을 할 것을 설명하는 예시이다.
⑤ 정리 정돈을 통해 새로운 관점을 얻을 수 있다는 내용일 뿐, 반복되는 일상에 대한
　언급은 없다. ◀ **주의**

C 08 정답 ② ＊지나친 영재 자랑을 자제할 필요성

As the parent of a gifted child, / you need to be aware of a
certain common parent trap. //
영재의 부모로서 / 당신은 어떤 흔한 부모의 덫을 주의할 필요가 있다 //
　　　　　　　　　　뒤에 반복되는 a proud parent가 생략됨
Of course / you are a proud parent / and you should be. //
물론 / 당신은 자랑스러워하는 부모이고 / 그리고 그래야 한다 //
　　　　가주어　　　　　　진주어
While it is very easy to talk nonstop / about your little genius
and his or her remarkable behavior, / this can be very stressful
on your child. //
쉬지 않고 말하는 것은 매우 쉬우나 / 당신의 작은 천재와 그 또는 그녀의 놀라운 행동에
대해서 / 이것은 당신의 아이에게 매우 스트레스가 될 수 있다 //
가주어　　　　　　　　　　진주어
It is extremely important / to limit your bragging behavior / to
your very close friends, / or your parents. // **단서** 영재인 자녀를 주변에
　　　　　　　　　　　　　　　　　　　　　　자랑하는 것을 제한해야 함
매우 중요하다 / 당신의 자랑하는 행동을 제한하는 것이 / 당신의 아주 가까운 친구나 / 당신의
부모에게로 //
Gifted children feel pressured / when their parents show them
off too much. // ────────── '~을 자랑하다'
영재는 부담을 느낀다 / 그들의 부모가 지나치게 그들을 자랑할 때 //
　　　　　　　　　　　　　　　목적격 관계대명사
This behavior creates expectations / that they may not be able to
live up to, / and also creates a false sense of self for your child. //
'~에 부응하다'
이러한 행동은 기대를 만들고 / 그들이 부응할 수 없을지도 모르는 / 또한 당신의 자녀에게
있어 잘못된 자의식을 만든다 //
　　　　　　　　　　보어 역할을 하는 간접의문문
You want your child to be who they are, / not who they seem to
be / as defined by their incredible achievements. //
당신은 당신의 자녀가 있는 그대로의 그들이기를 바란다 / 보이는 누군가가 아니라 / 그들의
엄청난 업적에 의해서 규정지어진 대로 //
If not, / you could end up with / a driven perfectionist child / or
perhaps a drop-out, / or worse. //
그렇지 않으면 / 당신은 결국 마주하게 될 것이다 / 지나친 완벽주의자 아이 / 또는 아마도
학업 중단자이거나 / 그보다 더 안 좋은 것을 //

• be aware of ~을 알다[주의하다]　　• nonstop ⓐⓓ 연속적으로
• remarkable ⓐ 놀라운　　• bragging ⓐ 자랑하는
• expectation ⓝ 기대　　• incredible ⓐ 엄청난
• achievement ⓝ 업적　　• end up with 결국 ~로 끝나다
• driven ⓐ 지나친　　• perfectionist ⓝ 완벽주의자
• drop-out ⓝ 학업 중단자, 중퇴자

영재의 부모로서, 당신은 어떤 흔한 부모의 덫을 주의할 필요가 있다. 물론, 당신은 자랑스러워하는 부모이고, 그리고 그래야 한다. 당신의 작은 천재와 그 또는 그녀의 놀라운 행동에 대해서 쉬지 않고 말하는 것은 매우 쉬우나, 이것은 당신의 아이에게 매우 스트레스가 될 수 있다. 당신의 자랑하는 행동을 당신의 아주 가까운 친구나, 당신의 부모에게로 제한하는 것이 매우 중요하다. 영재는 그들의 부모가 지나치게 그들을 자랑할 때 부담을 느낀다. 이러한 행동은 그들이 부응할 수 없을지도 모르는 기대를 만들고, 또한 당신의 자녀에게 있어 잘못된 자의식을 만든다. 당신은 당신의 자녀가 그들의 엄청난 업적에 의해서 규정지어진 대로 보이는 누군가가 아니라 있는 그대로의 그들이기를 바란다. 그렇지 않으면, 당신은 결국 지나친 완벽주의자 아이 또는 아마도 학업 중단자이거나 그보다 더 안 좋은 것을 마주하게 될 것이다.

다음 글에서 필자가 주장하는 바로 가장 적절한 것은?
① 부모는 자녀를 다른 아이와 비교하지 말아야 한다.
　　　　　　　자녀를 다른 아이와 비교하지 말라는 내용이 아님
② 부모는 자녀의 영재성을 지나치게 자랑하지 말아야 한다.
　　　　　　영재인 자녀를 둔 부모들은 주변에 지나치게 자랑하는 것을 제한해야 함
③ 영재교육 프로그램에 대한 맹목적인 믿음을 삼가야 한다.
　　　　　　　　　　영재교육 프로그램에 대한 언급은 없음
④ 과도한 영재교육보다 자녀와의 좋은 관계 유지에 힘써야 한다.
　　　　　　　　자녀와 좋은 관계를 유지하는 것에 관한 언급은 없음
⑤ 자녀의 독립성을 기르기 위해 자기 일은 스스로 하게 해야 한다.
　　　　　　자녀의 독립성을 기르는 것에 관한 언급은 없음

왜 정답? ✸✸✸ [정답률 81%]
영재인 자녀를 부모가 지나치게 자랑하면 그것은 그들에게 부담이 될 수 있고, 잘못된
자의식을 만들 수 있다며 이를 제한해야 한다고 주장하고 있다. 따라서 정답은 ②이다.

왜 오답?
① 영재인 자녀를 지나치게 자랑하면 안 된다는 내용이지, 다른 아이들과 비교하면 안
　된다는 내용이 아니다.
③ 영재교육 프로그램은 언급되지 않았다.
④ 과도한 영재교육이나 자녀와의 좋은 관계 유지는 언급되지 않았다.
⑤ 자녀의 독립성을 기르는 것은 언급되지 않았다.

C 09 정답 ③ ＊독자들의 능동적 사고를 촉진시키는 글쓰기

　　　　　　　　　　　목적어절 접속사(reminding의 직접목적어)
As you set about to write, / it is worth reminding yourself / that
while you ought to have a point of view, / you should avoid
telling your readers / what to think. //
당신이 글을 쓰려고 할 때는 / 상기시키는 것은 가치가 있다 / 당신의 관점을 가져야 하는 한편
/ 독자에게 말하는 것을 피해야 한다 / 무엇을 생각할지 //
Try to hang a question mark / over it all. // **단서 1** 관점을 직접 전달하는
　　　　　　　　　　　　　　　　　　　　　　것이 아니라 독자의 능동적 판
물음표를 달기 위해 노력해라 / 그것(논점) 전체에 //　　단을 유도해야 한다고 했음
This way / you allow your readers to think for themselves /
　　　　　　　　　　　　　　　　　　　　　　앞에 that 생략
about the points and arguments / you're making. //
이런 방식으로 / 당신은 독자들이 스스로 생각할 수 있게 만든다 / 요점과 주장들에 대해 / 당
신이 하는 //
　　　　　　　　　　　　　　　　　　　　　　분사구문
As a result, / they will feel more involved, / finding themselves
just as committed / to the arguments you've made / and the
insights you've exposed / as you are. //　──────── 병렬 구조
결과적으로 / 독자들은 좀 더 열중하게 되는 느낌을 받게 될 것이다 / 몰입되는 자신을 발견하
면서 / 당신이 한 주장과 / 당신이 드러내는 통찰력에 / 당신만큼이나 //
You will have written an essay / that not only avoids passivity
in the reader, / but is interesting / and gets people to think. //
　　　　　　　not only A but (also) B: A뿐만 아니라 B도
당신은 글을 쓰게 될 것이다 / 독자들의 수동성을 피하면서도 / 흥미롭고 / 사람들을 생각하
게 만드는 // **단서 2** 사람들이 능동적으로 사고하게 만드는 글을 쓰게 될 것이라고 했음

• remind ⓥ 상기시키다　　• argument ⓝ 논점, 주장
• committed ⓐ 몰입된　　• insight ⓝ 통찰력
• expose ⓥ 노출시키다　　• passivity ⓝ 수동성

당신이 글을 쓰려고 할 때는, 당신의 관점을 가져야 하는 한편, 독자에게 무엇을 생각할지 말하는 것을 피해야 한다고 상기시키는 것은 가치가 있다. 그것(논점) 전체에 물음표를 달기 위해 노력해라. 이런 방식으로 당신

은 독자들이 당신의 요점과 당신이 하는 주장들에 대해 스스로 생각할 수 있게 만든다. 결과적으로 독자들은 당신만큼이나 당신이 한 주장과 당신이 드러내는 통찰력에 몰입되는 자신을 발견하면서, 좀 더 열중하게 되는 느낌을 받게 될 것이다. 당신은 독자들의 수동성을 피하면서도 흥미롭고 사람들을 생각하게 만드는 글을 쓰게 될 것이다.

다음 글에서 필자가 주장하는 바로 가장 적절한 것은?

① 저자의 독창적인 견해를 드러내야 한다.
　　　　　　　　　　　　　직접적 방법보다 간접적 방법이 좋다는 내용임
② 다양한 표현으로 독자에게 감동을 주어야 한다.
　　　　　　　　　　　다양한 표현을 쓰라는 말은 언급되지 않음
③ 독자가 능동적으로 사고할 수 있도록 글을 써야 한다.
　　　　직접 전달하지 않고 독자의 능동적 판단을 유도해야 한다는 내용
④ 독자에게 가치판단의 기준점을 명확히 제시해야 한다.
　　　　　　　독자에게 능동적 판단을 하도록 하는 것이 좋다는 내용
⑤ 주관적 관점을 배제하고 사실을 바탕으로 글을 써야 한다.
　　　　　주관적이어야 하는지 혹은 객관적이어야 하는지에 대한 내용이 아님

›왜 정답? ★★❀ [정답률 84%]

저자가 전달하고자 하는 바를 독자에게 노골적으로 전달하는 것보다는 독자가 궁금증을 갖고 능동적으로 사고할 수 있도록 유도하는 것이 더 흥미롭고 설득력 있는 글쓰기가 될 수 있다는 내용이다. 따라서 이 글의 주장으로 가장 적절한 것은 ③이다.

›왜 오답?

① 저자의 독창적 견해를 말하는 것보다는 간접적으로 전달하는 방법이 좋다는 내용이다.
② 독자에게 감동을 주는 방법에 대한 것은 이 글에 나오지 않은 내용이다.
④ 가치판단의 기준점을 잡고 이를 제시하는 것이 아니라 독자가 능동적 판단을 하도록 하는 것이 좋다는 내용이다.
⑤ 주관적이어야 하는지 혹은 객관적이어야 하는지에 대한 내용이 아니다.

C 10 정답 ① ★성공하기 위해 새로운 것을 시도해야 한다.

Sometimes, / you feel the need to avoid something / **that** will lead to success out of discomfort. //
　　　　　　　　　　　주격 관계대명사
가끔씩 / 당신은 무언가를 피할 필요가 있다고 느낀다 / 불편하기 때문에 성공으로 이끌어 줄 //

Maybe / you are avoiding extra work / **because you are tired**. //
　　　　　　　　　　　　　　　because+주어+동사
아마도 / 당신은 추가적인 일을 피하고 있다 / 피곤하기 때문에 //

You are actively shutting out success / because you want to avoid being uncomfortable. //
　　　　　　　　　　　　　주어(동명사구)
당신은 적극적으로 성공을 차단하고 있다 / 불편한 것을 피하고 싶어서 //

Therefore, / **overcoming your instinct** / to avoid uncomfortable things at first / **is** essential. // **단서1** 불편함을 피하려는 본능을 극복해야 함
　　　　　　단수 동사
따라서 / 당신의 본능을 극복하는 것이 / 처음에는 불편한 것을 피하고자 하는 / 필요하다 //
명령문의 동사원형
Try doing new things / outside of your comfort zone. // **단서2** 편안한 곳에서 벗어나 새로운 것을 시도할 것을 주장함
　　　　　　　　　　　　전치사
새로운 일을 시도하라 / 편안함을 주는 곳을 벗어나서 //

Change is always uncomfortable, / but it is key **to** doing things differently / in order to find that magical formula / for success. //
변화는 항상 불편하다 / 하지만 그것(변화)은 일을 색다르게 하는 데 있어 핵심이다 / 그 마법의 공식을 찾기 위해서 / 성공을 위한 //

• avoid ⓥ 피하다　　• discomfort ⓝ 불편
• shut out ~을 차단하다[가로막다]　　• overcome ⓥ 극복하다
• instinct ⓝ 본능　　• essential ⓐ 필수적인
• comfort zone 편안함을 주는 곳, 안락 지대　　• magical ⓐ 마법의
• formula ⓝ 공식

가끔씩 당신은 불편하기 때문에 성공으로 이끌어 줄 무언가를 피할 필요가 있다고 느낀다. 아마도 당신은 피곤하기 때문에 추가적인 일을 피하고 있다. 당신은 불편한 것을 피하고 싶어서 적극적으로 성공을 차단하고 있다. 따라서 처음에는 불편한 것을 피하고자 하는 당신의 본능을 극복하는 것이 필요하다. 편안함을 주는 곳을 벗어나서 새로운 일을 시도하라. 변화는 항상 불편하지만, 성공을 위한 그 마법의 공식을 찾기 위해서 그것(변화)은 일을 색다르게 하는 데 있어 핵심이다.

다음 글에서 필자가 주장하는 바로 가장 적절한 것은?

① 불편할지라도 성공하기 위해서는 새로운 것을 시도해야 한다.
　　　　　　　불편함을 피하려는 본능을 극복해서 새로운 것을 시도하라고 주장함
② 일과 생활의 균형을 맞추는 성공적인 삶을 추구해야 한다.
　　　　　　성공하기 위해서는 새로운 것을 시도해야 한다는 내용임
③ 갈등 해소를 위해 불편함의 원인을 찾아 개선해야 한다.
　　　　　　　　　　　　갈등 해소와 관련된 내용은 언급되지 않음
④ 단계별 목표를 설정하여 익숙한 것부터 도전해야 한다.
　　　　　　　성공하기 위한 목표 설정과는 관련이 없음
⑤ 변화에 적응하기 위해 직관적으로 문제를 해결해야 한다.
　　　　　　　핵심어 '변화'를 넣어 만든 함정

›왜 정답? ★❀❀ [정답률 91%]

불편함을 피하는 것은 성공을 차단하는 것이므로, 성공하기 위해서 불편함을 피하려는 본능을 이겨내고 항상 새로운 일을 시도하라는 내용의 글이다. 특히, ==Try doing new things outside of your comfort zone. (편안함을 주는 곳을 벗어나서 새로운 일을 시도하라.)==에 필자의 주장이 명확히 드러나 있다. 따라서 정답은 ①이다.

꿀팁 명령문에 주목하기!

›왜 오답?

② 성공하기 위해서는 새로운 것을 시도해야 한다는 내용이므로 일과 생활의 균형에 대한 내용은 아니다.
③ 갈등 해소와 관련된 내용은 언급되지 않았으므로 적절하지 않다.
④ 성공하기 위한 구체적 방법을 제시하는 내용이므로 목표 설정과는 관련이 없다.
⑤ 핵심어인 '변화'가 들어가서 답으로 착각하기 쉬운 오답이다.

C 11 정답 ② ★행동으로 삶의 모범을 보이기

We are always teaching our children something / by our words and our actions. //
우리는 항상 우리의 자녀에게 무언가를 가르치고 있다 / 우리의 말과 행동으로 //
　　　　　　　　　　　　　　　동명사(전치사의 목적어)
They learn from ==seeing==. // **단서1** 우리의 자녀는 보는 것으로 배움
그들은 보는 것으로부터 배운다 //

They learn from hearing / and from *overhearing*. //
그들은 듣는 것으로부터 배우고 '우연히 듣는 것'으로부터 (배운다) //

Children share the values of their parents / about the most important things in life. //
아이들은 그들 부모의 가치를 공유한다 / 인생에서 가장 중요한 것에 대해 //

Our priorities and principles / and our examples of good behavior / can teach our children / **to take** the ==high road== / when other roads look tempting. //
　　　　　　　　명사적 용법(목적격 보어)　'확실한 길, 올바른 길'
우리의 우선순위와 원칙 / 그리고 훌륭한 행동에 대한 본보기는 / 우리의 자녀에게 가르칠 수 있다 / 올바른 길로 가도록 / 다른 길이 유혹적으로 보일 때 //

Remember / **that** children do not learn the values / **that** make up strong character / simply by being *told* about them. // 기억하라
　　　　　목적어절 접속사　　　　　　　　주격 관계대명사
　　　　　　　　　　　　　　　　　by v-ing: ~함으로써
아이들은 가치를 배우지 않는다 / 확고한 인격을 구성하는 / 단순히 그것들에 대해 '들음'으로써 //
　　　　　　　　　　　　　　　　　seeing의 목적격 보어(원형부정사)
They learn / by seeing the people around them / *act on and uphold* those values / in their daily lives. // 그들은 배운다 / 그들 주변 사람들을 봄으로써 / 그러한 가치를 좇아 '행동'하고 '유지'하는 것을 / 그들의 일상생활에서 //

Therefore // show your child / good examples of life / by your action. // **단서2** 자녀에게 행동으로 삶의 모범을 보이라고 함
그러므로 / 여러분의 자녀에게 보여라 / 삶의 모범을 / 여러분의 행동으로 //
　　　　　　　　　　　　　show의 간접목적어　직접목적어절 접속사
In our daily lives, / we can show ==our children== / **that** we respect others. //
우리의 일상생활에서 / 우리는 우리의 자녀에게 보여줄 수 있다 / 우리가 타인을 존중하는 것을 //
　　　　　　　　　　　　　　　　　　　부사절 접속사(시간)
We can show them / ==our compassion and concern== / ==when== others are suffering, / and ==our own self-discipline, courage and honesty== / ==as== we make difficult decisions. //
　부사절 접속사(시간)　　　　　　　　　　병렬 구조
우리는 그들에게 보여줄 수 있다 / 우리의 연민과 걱정을 / 다른 사람이 괴로워할 때 / 그리고 우리 자신의 자제력, 용기 그리고 정직을 / 우리가 어려운 결정을 할 때 //

• overhear ⓥ 우연히 듣다　　• priority ⓝ 우선순위
• tempting ⓐ 솔깃한　　• character ⓝ 인격　　• uphold ⓥ 유지하다
• self-discipline ⓝ 자제력　　• honesty ⓝ 정직함

우리는 항상 우리의 자녀에게 말과 행동으로 무언가를 가르치고 있다. 그들은 보는 것으로부터 배운다. 그들은 듣거나 '우연히 듣는 것'으로부터 배운다. 아이들은 인생에서 가장 중요한 것에 대해 그들 부모의 가치를 공유한다. 우리의 우선순위와 원칙 그리고 훌륭한 행동에 대한 본보기는 우리의 자녀에게 다른 길이 유혹적으로 보일 때 올바른 길로 가도록 가르칠 수 있다. 아이들은 확고한 인격을 구성하는 가치를 단순히 그것에 대해 '들음'으로써 배우지 않는다는 것을 기억하라. 그들은 그들 주변 사람들이 그들의 일상생활에서 그러한 가치를 좇아 '행동'하고 '유지'하는 것을 봄으로써 배운다. 그러므로 여러분의 자녀에게 여러분의 행동으로 삶의 모범을 보여라. 우리의 일상생활에서, 우리는 우리 자녀에게 우리가 타인을 존중하는 것을 보여줄 수 있다. 우리는 그들에게 다른 사람이 괴롭힐 때 우리의 연민과 걱정을, 그리고 우리가 어려운 결정을 할 때 우리 자신의 자제력, 용기 그리고 정직을 보여줄 수 있다.

다음 글에서 필자가 주장하는 바로 가장 적절한 것은?
① 자녀를 타인과 비교하는 말을 삼가야 한다.
　　　　　　　　　　　자녀를 타인과 비교하지 말라는 글이 아님
② 자녀에게 행동으로 삶의 모범을 보여야 한다.
　　아이들은 보는 것으로부터 배운다고 했음
③ 칭찬을 통해 자녀의 바람직한 행동을 강화해야 한다.
　　　　　　　　　　　　　　칭찬하라는 내용이 아님
④ 훈육을 하기 전에 자녀 스스로 생각할 시간을 주어야 한다.
　　　　　　　　　　　훈육이 아니라 본보기가 되라는 내용임
⑤ 자녀가 새로운 것에 도전할 때 인내심을 가지고 지켜봐야 한다.
　　　　자녀가 새로운 것에 도전한다는 내용은 없음

왜 정답? ✿✿✿ [정답률 90%]
- 오해: 아이들이 단순히 '들음'으로써 배운다고 생각함
- 해결: 아이들은 어떤 행동을 하고 그것을 유지하는 것을 '봄'으로써 배움
▶ 아이들이 볼 수 있게 행동으로 삶의 모범을 보이라고 주장하고 있으므로 정답은 ②이다.

왜 오답?
① 자녀를 타인과 비교하지 말라고 주장하는 글이 아니다.
③ 자녀를 칭찬하라는 내용은 언급되지 않았다.
④ 자녀를 훈육하라는 것이 아니라 자녀에게 본보기가 되라는 내용이다.
⑤ 자녀가 새로운 것에 도전한다거나 인내심을 가지라는 내용은 없었다.

C 12　정답 ⑤　*상업용 블로그가 성공하기 위한 방법

be about to-v 막 ~하려고 하다
You already have a business / and you're about to launch your
'~하도록'
blog / so that you can sell your product. //
여러분은 이미 사업체를 가지고 있다 / 그리고 여러분의 블로그를 시작하려는 참이다 / 여러분의 제품을 팔 수 있도록 //

관계부사
Unfortunately, / here is where a 'business mind' can be a bad thing. //
유감스럽게도 / 여기가 '비즈니스 정신'이 나쁜 것이 될 수 있는 지점이다 //

목적어절 접속사
Most people believe / that to have a successful business blog /
현재분사(blog 수식)
promoting a product, / they have to stay strictly 'on the topic.' //
대부분의 사람들은 믿는다 / 성공적인 상업용 블로그를 가지기 위해서 / 제품을 홍보하는 / 그들이 엄격하게 '그 주제에' 머물러야 한다고 //

핵심 주어(단수)　　단수 동사
If all you're doing / is shamelessly promoting your product, / then who is going to want to read / the latest thing you're writing about? //
만일 여러분이 하는 일의 전부가 / 뻔뻔스럽게 여러분의 제품을 홍보하는 것이라면 / 그러면 누가 읽고 싶어 할까 / 여러분이 쓰고 있는 최신의 것을 //

Instead, / you need to give some useful or entertaining
'~하도록'
information away / for free / so that people have a reason / to
형용사적 용법(reason 수식)
keep coming back. // 단서1 블로그에서 무료로 유용하고 재미있는 정보를 제공해 사람들이 다시 방문할 이유를 만들어야 함
대신에 / 여러분은 어떤 유용하거나 재미있는 정보를 줄 필요가 있다 / 무료로 / 사람들이 이유를 가지도록 / 계속해서 다시 방문할 //

only가 문두로 가면서 주어와 동사가 도치됨　　　목적격 관계대명사
Only by doing this / can you create an interested audience / that you will then be able to sell to. //
이렇게 해야만 / 여러분은 관심 있는 독자를 만들 수 있다 / 여러분이 그다음에 판매를 할 수 있게 될 //

단서2 상업용 블로그로 성공하기 위해서는 독자들이 관심을 갖는 것에 대해 써야 함
핵심 주어(단수)　　　　　　　　　　　　　　　단수 동사
So, / the best way to be successful / with a business blog / is to
명사적 용법(주격 보어)
write about things / that your audience will be interested in. //
따라서 / 성공하기 위한 가장 좋은 방법은 / 상업용 블로그로 / (어떤) 것들에 관해 쓰는 것이다 / 여러분의 독자가 관심을 가질 //

- **launch** ⓥ (새로운 일을) 시작하다[개시하다]　　· **promote** ⓥ 홍보하다
- **strictly** 𝖺𝖽 엄격하게　　· **shamelessly** 𝖺𝖽 뻔뻔스럽게
- **give ~ away** ~을 나누어 주다　　· **entertaining** ⓐ 재미있는, 즐거움을 주는
- **audience** ⓝ 청중, 독자

여러분은 이미 사업체를 가지고 있고 여러분의 제품을 팔 수 있도록 여러분의 블로그를 시작하려는 참이다. 유감스럽게도, 여기가 '비즈니스 정신'이 나쁜 것이 될 수 있는 지점이다. 대부분의 사람들은 제품을 홍보하는 성공적인 상업용 블로그를 가지기 위해서 그들이 엄격하게 '그 주제에' 머물러야 한다고 믿는다. 만일 여러분이 하는 일의 전부가 뻔뻔스럽게 여러분의 제품을 홍보하는 것이라면, 그렇다면 누가 여러분이 쓰고 있는 최신의 것을 읽고 싶어 할까? 대신에, 사람들이 계속해서 다시 방문할 이유를 가지도록 여러분은 어떤 유용하거나 재미있는 정보를 무료로 줄 필요가 있다. 이렇게 해야만 여러분이 그다음에 판매를 할 수 있게 될 관심 있는 독자를 만들 수 있다. 따라서, 상업용 블로그로 성공하기 위한 가장 좋은 방법은 여러분의 독자가 관심을 가질 만한 것들에 관해 쓰는 것이다.

다음 글에서 필자가 주장하는 바로 가장 적절한 것은?
① 인터넷 게시물에 대한 윤리적 기준을 세워야 한다.
　　블로그가 주요 소재이며 윤리적 기준에 대한 언급은 없음
② 블로그를 전문적으로 관리할 인력을 마련해야 한다.
　　　　　　　　　전문 인력 마련에 대한 내용은 없음
③ 신제품 개발을 위해 상업용 블로그를 적극 활용해야 한다.
　　　　　　　　　활용 목적이 아니라 활용 방안에 관한 내용임
④ 상품에 대한 고객들의 반응을 정기적으로 분석할 필요가 있다.
　　　　　　　　　고객 반응 분석에 대한 글이 아님
⑤ 상업용 블로그는 사람들이 흥미 있어 할 정보를 제공해야 한다.
　　상업용 블로그로 성공하기 위해서는 독자가 관심을 갖는 것을 써야 한다고 했음

왜 정답? ✿✿✿ [정답률 93%]
- 문제점: 상업용 블로그에 제품 홍보 글만 쓴다면 사람들은 읽고 싶지 않을 것임
- 해결책: 유용하고 재미있는 정보를 무료로 주고, 사람들이 관심을 가질 만한 것에 관해 쓰기
▶ 상업용 블로그는 사람들이 흥미 있어 할 정보를 제공해서 블로그에 다시 방문하도록 해야 한다는 주장이므로 정답은 ⑤이다.

왜 오답?
① 인터넷 게시물의 윤리적 기준에 대한 내용은 언급되지 않았다.
② 블로그를 관리할 전문적인 인력을 마련해야 한다는 글이 아니다.
③ 신제품 개발과 관련된 내용은 나오지 않았고, 블로그의 활용 목적이 아니라 활용 방안과 관련된 내용이다. 주의
④ 고객의 반응을 분석해야 한다는 내용은 언급되지 않았다.

C 13　정답 ⑤　*업무와 개인 용무를 한 곳에 정리하라

목적어절 접속사　　주격 관계대명사절
Research shows / that people who work have two calendars: / one for work / and one for their personal lives. //
연구는 보여준다 / 일하는 사람들이 두 개의 달력을 가지고 있다는 것을 / 하나는 업무를 위한 달력이고 / 하나는 개인적인 삶을 위한 달력이다 //

부사절 접속사(양보)　　　　　　동명사구 주어
Although it may seem sensible, / having two separate calendars / for work and personal life / can lead to distractions. //
비록 그것이 실용적으로 보일지라도 / 두 개의 별도의 달력을 갖는 것은 / 업무와 개인적인 삶을 위한 / 주의산만으로 이어질 수 있다 // 단서1 두 개의 달력을 갖는 것은 주의산만으로 이어짐

To check if something is missing, / you will find yourself / checking your to-do lists multiple times. //
누락된 것이 있는지를 확인하기 위해 / 당신은 스스로를 발견할 것이다 / 할 일 목록을 여러 번 확인하는 //

Instead, / organize all of your tasks / in one place. //
대신 / 당신의 모든 일을 정리하라 / 한 곳에 // 단서2 모든 일을 한 곳에 정리할 것을 권함

가주어　　　진주어절 접속사
It doesn't matter / if you use digital or paper media. //
~은 중요하지 않다 / 당신이 디지털 또는 종이 매체를 사용하는지는 //

가주어 진주어
It's okay / to keep your professional and personal tasks / in one place. //
~은 괜찮다 / 당신의 업무와 개인 일을 두는 것은 / 한 곳에 //

전치사의 목적어(간접의문문)
This will give you a good idea / of how time is divided / between work and home. //
이것은 당신이 잘 알게 해줄 것이다 / 시간이 어떻게 쪼개지는지 / 일과 가정 사이에 //

will allow의 목적격 보어   의문형용사
This will allow you / to make informed decisions / about which tasks are most important. //
이것은 당신을 가능하게 할 것이다 / 정보에 입각한 결정을 하도록 / 어떤 일이 가장 중요한지에 대한 //

- personal ⓐ 개인적인   - sensible ⓐ 실용적인
- separate ⓐ 별도의   - distraction ⓝ 주의산만
- multiple ⓐ 많은   - organize ⓥ 정리하다
- media ⓝ 매체, 수단   - professional ⓐ 직업의
- divide ⓥ 나누다   - informed ⓐ 정보에 입각한

연구는 일하는 사람들이 두 개의 달력을 가지고 있다는 것을 보여준다: 하나는 업무를 위한 달력이고 하나는 개인적인 삶을 위한 달력이다. 비록 그것이 실용적으로 보일지라도, 업무와 개인적인 삶을 위한 두 개의 별도의 달력을 갖는 것은 주의를 산만하게 할 수 있다. 누락된 것이 있는지를 확인하기 위해, 당신은 할 일 목록을 여러 번 확인하는 것을 깨닫게 될 것이다. 대신, 당신의 모든 일을 한 곳에 정리하라. 당신이 디지털 매체를 사용하든 종이 매체를 사용하든 중요하지 않다. 당신의 업무와 개인 일을 한 곳에 두는 것은 괜찮다. 이것은 당신에게 일과 가정 사이에 시간이 어떻게 쪼개지는지에 대해 잘 알게 해줄 것이다. 이것은 어떤 일이 가장 중요한지에 대한 정보에 입각한 결정을 내리게 할 것이다.

다음 글에서 필자가 주장하는 바로 가장 적절한 것은?
① 결정한 것은 반드시 실행하도록 노력하라.
  결정한 사안에 대한 이행을 강조한 글이 아님
② 자신이 담당한 업무에 관한 전문성을 확보하라.
  업무를 할 때 전문성을 확보하라는 글이 아님
③ 업무 집중도를 높이기 위해 책상 위를 정돈하라.
  distractions로 만든 오답
④ 좋은 아이디어를 메모하는 습관을 길러라.
  메모의 중요성을 강조한 글이 아님
⑤ 업무와 개인 용무를 한 곳에 정리하라.
  두 개의 달력보다는 하나에 정리하라고 함

>왜 정답? ❋❋❋ [정답률 82%]
- 오해: 달력을 업무 달력과 개인 달력으로 나누는 것이 실용적일 것이라고 생각함
- 해결: 모든 일을 한 곳에 정리하면 시간이 어떻게 분배되는지 잘 알 수 있어서 더 나은 결정을 내리게 됨
▶ 업무와 개인 용무를 한 곳에 정리하라는 것이므로 정답은 ⑤이다.

>왜 오답?
① 결정한 사안은 꼭 실행하라고 주장하는 글이 아니다.
② 담당 업무에 관한 전문성 확보를 주장하는 글이 아니다.
③ 책상 위를 정돈하는 것과 업무 집중도 사이의 관계는 언급되지 않았다.
④ 메모하는 습관을 기르라고 이야기하는 글이 아니다.

자이 쌤's Follow Me! – 홈페이지에서 제공

C 14 정답 ⑤ *회의에서 다룰 사항은 미리 공유해야 한다.

목적격 관계대명사
Meetings encourage creative thinking / and can give you ideas / that you may never have thought of on your own. //
회의는 창의적 사고를 촉진한다 / 그리고 당신에게 아이디어들을 제공할 수 있다 / 당신이 혼자서는 절대 떠올리지 못할 만한 //

기수+서수(분수 표현)   consider의 목적격보어(to부정사)
However, on average, / meeting participants consider / about one third of meeting time / to be unproductive. //
그러나, 평균적으로, / 회의 참석자들은 여긴다 / 회의 시간의 대략 3분의 1 정도를 / 비생산적으로 //

단서 1 회의를 더 생산적으로 만들려면 회의 전에 잘 준비해야 함
But / you can make your meetings / more productive and more useful / by preparing well in advance. //
can make의 목적격보어(형용사)
하지만 / 당신은 회의를 만들 수 있다 / 더 생산적이고 유용하게 / 사전에 잘 준비함으로써 //

병렬 구조
You should create a list of items / to be discussed / and share your list with other participants / before a meeting. // 핵심문장
당신은 사항들의 목록을 만들어야 한다 / 논의하게 될 / 그리고 다른 회의 참석자들에게 당신의 목록을 공유해야 한다 / 회의 전에 //

allow+목적어+목적격보어(to부정사)
It allows them to know / what to expect in your meeting / and
목적격보어의 병렬 구조(위의 to는 생략됨) 단서 2 회의 전에 목록을 만들어서 공유했을 때 얻을 수 있는 효과
prepare to participate. //
그것은 참석자들이 알게 만들어준다 / 회의에서 무엇을 기대하는지를 / 그리고 회의 참석을 준비할 수 있도록 (만들어준다) //

- encourage ⓥ 촉진하다, 장려하다   - creative ⓐ 창의적인
- on one's own 혼자서, 혼자 힘으로   - on average 평균적으로
- unproductive ⓐ 비생산적인   - productive ⓐ 생산적인
- prepare ⓥ 준비하다   - in advance 미리, 사전에
- discuss ⓥ 논의하다, 의논하다   - share ⓥ 공유하다
- participant ⓝ 참석자   - participate ⓥ 참여하다

회의는 창의적 사고를 촉진하며 당신이 혼자서는 절대 떠올리지 못할 만한 아이디어들을 당신에게 제공할 수 있다. 그러나, 평균적으로, 회의 참석자들은 회의 시간의 대략 3분의 1 정도를 비생산적으로 여긴다. 하지만 당신은 사전에 잘 준비함으로써 회의를 더 생산적이고 유용하게 만들 수 있다. 당신은 논의하게 될 사항들의 목록을 만들고 회의 전에 다른 회의 참석자들에게 공유해야 한다. 그것은 참석자들이 회의에서 무엇을 기대하는지를 알고 회의 참석을 준비할 수 있도록 만들어준다.

다음 글에서 필자가 주장하는 바로 가장 적절한 것은?
① 회의 결과는 빠짐없이 작성해서 공개해야 한다.
  회의 전에 해야 할 일을 주장하는 글임
② 중요한 정보는 공식 회의를 통해 전달해야 한다.
③ 생산성 향상을 위해 정기적인 평가회가 필요하다.
  회의가 비생산적이라고 생각하는 사람들이 있다고 언급한 것으로 만든 함정
④ 모든 참석자의 동의를 받아서 회의를 열어야 한다.
  동의를 받아서 회의를 열어야 한다는 내용은 없음
⑤ 회의에서 다룰 사항은 미리 작성해서 공유해야 한다.
  회의 전에 논의할 사항을 미리 회의 참석자들에게 알려야 한다고 했음

>왜 정답? ❋❋❋ [정답률 90%]
후반부에 나오는 You should create a list of items to be discussed and share your list with other participants before a meeting. (당신은 논의하게 될 사항들의 목록을 만들고 회의 전에 다른 회의 참석자들에게 공유해야 한다.)이 이 글의 핵심문장이다.
필자는 미리 준비를 하면 회의를 더 생산적으로 만들 수 있고, 논의하게 될 사항들의 목록이 참석자들이 회의 참석을 준비할 수 있도록 만들어준다고 주장하고 있다. 따라서 필자의 주장으로 가장 적절한 것은 ⑤이다.

>왜 오답?
①, ② 회의를 더 생산적으로 만들기 위해서 회의 전에 해야 할 일을 주장하고 있다.
③ 회의 시간의 대략 3분의 1 정도를 비생산적으로 여기는 사람들이 있다는 내용은 있지만 정기적인 평가회에 관한 내용은 글에서 언급되지 않았다.
④ 회의 참석자와 회의에서 논의하게 될 사항들의 목록을 공유해야 한다는 내용은 있으나 회의를 열기 위해 동의를 받아야 한다는 내용은 나오지 않았다. 주의

C 15 정답 ④ *졸업 이후에도 자발적인 성장 이루기

Unfortunately, / many people don't take personal responsibility / for their own growth. //
안타깝게도 / 많은 사람이 개인적인 책임을 지지 않는다 / 그들 자신의 성장에 대해 //

앞에 주격 관계대명사와 be동사 생략
Instead, / they simply run the race / laid out for them. //
대신 / 그들은 단지 경주를 한다 / 그들에게 놓인 //
단서 1 사람들은 학교를 다닐 때는 발전을 계속 함

They do well / enough in school to keep advancing. //
그들은 제법 잘한다 / 학교에서 계속 발전할 만큼 //

동사 run(운영하다)의 과거분사: 운영되는
Maybe / they manage to get a good job / at a well-run company. //
아마도 / 그들은 좋은 일자리를 얻는 것을 해낸다 / 잘 운영되는 회사에서 //

정답 및 해설 **31**

But so many think and act / as if their learning journey ends / with college. //

하지만 아주 많은 사람들이 생각하고 행동한다 / 마치 그들의 배움의 여정이 끝나는 것처럼 / 대학으로

They **have checked** all the boxes in the life / **that** was laid out for them / and now lack a road map / **describing** the right ways / **to move** forward and continue to grow. //
<small>현재완료 / 주격 관계대명사 / 현재분사(road map 수식) / 형용사적 용법(ways 수식)</small>

그들은 삶의 모든 사항을 체크했고 / 그들에게 놓인 / 이제는 로드 맵이 없다 / 올바른 방법을 설명해 주는 / 앞으로 나아가고 계속 성장할 수 있는 //

In truth, / that's **when** the journey really begins. //
<small>선행사(the time)가 생략된 관계부사</small>

사실 / 그때가 여정이 진정으로 시작되는 때이다 //

When school is finished, / your growth becomes voluntary. //

학교 교육이 끝나면 / 여러분의 성장은 자발적이게 된다 //
<small>**단서 2** 학교 졸업 후에 성장은 자발적으로 이루어짐</small>

Like healthy eating habits or a regular exercise program, / you need to commit to it / and devote thought, time, and energy to it. //
<small>**단서 3** 성장을 위해 자발적으로 에너지를 투자해야 함</small>

건강한 식습관이나 규칙적인 운동 프로그램처럼 / 여러분은 그것에 전념하고 / 그것에 생각, 시간, 그리고 에너지를 쏟을 필요가 있다 //

Otherwise, it simply won't happen / — and your life and career are likely to **stop progressing** / as a result. //
<small>「stop + -ing」: ~하는 것을 멈추다</small>

그렇지 않으면 그것은 그냥 일어나지 않을 것이고 / 여러분의 삶과 경력이 진전을 멈출 가능성이 있다 / 결과적으로 //

- take responsibility for ~에 책임을 지다
- advance ⓥ 발전하다
- manage to (간신히) 해내다
- well-run ⓐ 잘 운영되는
- commit to ~에 전념하다
- devote ~ to … ~을 …에 쏟다[바치다]
- otherwise ⓐⓓ 그렇지 않으면
- career ⓝ 경력

안타깝게도 많은 사람들이 그들 자신의 성장에 대해 개인적인 책임을 지지 않는다. 대신, 그들은 단지 그들에게 놓인 경주를 한다. 그들은 학교에서 계속 발전할 만큼 제법 잘한다. 아마도 그들은 잘 운영되는 회사에서 좋은 일자리를 얻는 것을 해낸다. 하지만 아주 많은 사람들이 마치 그들의 배움의 여정이 대학으로 끝나는 것처럼 생각하고 행동한다. 그들은 그들에게 놓인 삶의 모든 사항을 체크했고 이제는 앞으로 나아가고 계속 성장할 수 있는 올바른 방법을 설명해 주는 로드 맵이 없다. 사실, 그때가 여정이 진정으로 시작되는 때이다. 학교 교육이 끝나면, 여러분의 성장은 자발적이게 된다. 건강한 식습관이나 규칙적인 운동 프로그램처럼 여러분은 그것에 전념하고 그것에 생각, 시간, 그리고 에너지를 쏟을 필요가 있다. 그렇지 않으면 그것은 그냥 일어나지 않을 것이고, 결과적으로 여러분의 삶과 경력이 진전을 멈출 가능성이 있다.

다음 글에서 필자가 주장하는 바로 가장 적절한 것은?

① 성공 경험을 위해 달성 가능한 목표를 수립해야 한다.
<small>달성 가능한 목표 수립은 언급되지 않음</small>
② 체계적인 경력 관리를 위해 전문가의 도움을 받아야 한다.
<small>경력 관리를 위해 전문가의 도움을 받는 내용은 언급되지 않음</small>
③ 건강을 위해 꾸준한 운동과 식습관 관리를 병행해야 한다.
<small>꾸준한 운동과 식습관 관리처럼 졸업 후에도 자발적인 성장에 전념하라는 내용임</small>
④ 졸업 이후 성장을 위해 자발적으로 배움을 실천해야 한다.
<small>졸업 후에도 자발적으로 배움을 위해 노력해야 한다는 내용임</small>
⑤ 적성에 맞는 직업을 찾기 위해 학교 교육에 충실해야 한다.
<small>학교 교육 이후의 성장에 관한 내용임</small>

>왜 정답 ? ✱✱❀ [정답률 85%]

사람들은 학교에 다니는 동안은 끊임없이 발전하지만, 졸업 후에는 성장을 멈춘다고 한다. 졸업 후의 성장은 온전히 개인의 책임이며, 이를 위해 자발적으로 에너지를 쏟아야 한다고 주장하고 있으므로 정답은 ④이다.

>왜 오답 ?

① 달성 가능한 목표 수립은 언급되지 않았다.
② 경력 관리를 위해 전문가의 도움을 받는 내용은 언급되지 않았다.
③ 꾸준한 운동과 식습관 관리를 병행하라는 내용이 아니라, 그러한 것들과 마찬가지로 졸업 후에도 자발적인 성장에 전념하라는 내용이다. **함정**
⑤ 학교 교육 이후의 성장에 관한 내용이다.

C 16 정답 ④ ＊쓸 때보다 말할 때 더 많은 단어를 사용해야 한다.

Experts on writing say, / "Get rid of / as many words as possible." //

글쓰기 전문가들은 말한다 / "삭제하라 / 가능한 한 많은 단어를" //

Each word must do / **something important**. //
<small>-thing으로 끝나는 대명사는 뒤에서 수식함</small>

각 단어는 해야 한다 / 무언가 중요한 일을 //

If it doesn't, / get rid of it. //

만일 그렇지 않다면 / 그것을 삭제하라 //

Well, this doesn't work / for speaking. //

자, 이 방법은 통하지 않는다 / 말하기에서는 //

It takes more words / to introduce, express, and adequately elaborate an idea / in speech / than it takes in writing. //
<small>핵심문장 **단서 1** 글을 쓸 때보다 말할 때 더 많은 단어가 필요함</small>

더 많은 단어가 필요하다 / 아이디어를 소개하고, 표현하며, 적절히 부연 설명하는 데 / 말을 할 때는 / 글을 쓸 때 필요한 것보다 //

Why is this so? //

이것은 왜 그러한가 //

While the reader can reread, / the listener cannot rehear. //
<small>**단서 2** 독자는 글을 다시 읽으면 되지만, 청자는 다시 들을 수 없기 때문임</small>

독자는 글을 다시 읽을 수 있으나 / 청자는 다시 들을 수 없다 //

Speakers do not come equipped / with a replay button. //

화자는 갖추고 있지 않다 / 반복 재생 버튼을 //

Because listeners are easily distracted, / they will miss / many pieces of / **what** a speaker says. //
<small>선행사를 포함한 관계대명사</small>

청자들은 쉽게 주의력이 흐려지기 때문에 / 놓칠 것이다 / 많은 부분을 / 화자가 말하는 것 중 //

If they miss the crucial sentence, / they may never catch up. //

그들이 중요한 문장을 놓친다면 / 절대로 따라잡을 수 없을 것이다 //

This makes **it** necessary / for speakers / **to talk** longer about their points, / **using more words on them** / than would be used / **to express** the same idea / in writing. //
<small>가목적어 / 진목적어 / 분사구문 / 부사적 용법(목적) / **단서 3** 글을 쓸 때 사용된 단어 수보다 더 많은 단어를 사용해서 길게 말할 필요가 있음</small>

이것은 필요하게 한다 / 화자들에게 / 그들의 요점에 대해 더 길게 말할 / 더 많은 단어를 사용하여 / 사용될 것보다 / 같은 아이디어를 표현하기 위해 / 글을 쓸 때 //

- expert ⓝ 전문가
- get rid of ~을 삭제하다
- adequately ⓐⓓ 적절히
- elaborate ⓥ 부연 설명하다
- equipped with ~을 갖춘
- distract ⓥ 집중이 안 되게 하다
- crucial ⓐ 중요한

글쓰기 전문가들은 "가능한 한 많은 단어를 삭제하라"고 말한다. 각 단어는 무언가 중요한 일을 해야 한다. 만일 그렇지 않다면 그것을 삭제하라. 자, 이 방법은 말하기에서는 통하지 않는다. 말을 할 때는 아이디어를 소개하고, 표현하며, 적절히 부연 설명하는 데 글을 쓸 때보다 더 많은 단어가 필요하다. 이것은 왜 그러한가? 독자는 글을 다시 읽을 수 있으나 청자는 다시 들을 수 없다. 화자는 반복 재생 버튼을 갖추고 있지 않다. 청자들은 쉽게 주의력이 흐려지기 때문에 화자가 말하는 것 중 많은 부분을 놓칠 것이다. 그들이 중요한 문장을 놓친다면, 절대로 따라잡을 수 없을 것이다. 이것은 화자들이 같은 아이디어를 표현하기 위해 글을 쓸 때 사용될 단어 수보다 그것들(요점)에 대해 더 많은 단어를 사용하여 그들의 요점에 대해 더 길게 말할 필요가 있게 한다.

다음 글에서 필자가 주장하는 바로 가장 적절한 것은?

① 연설 시 중요한 정보는 천천히 말해야 한다.
<small>천천히 말해야 한다는 내용은 없음</small>
② 좋은 글을 쓰려면 간결한 문장을 사용해야 한다.
<small>말할 때의 단어 수에 대한 내용은 포함되지 못함</small>
③ 말하기 전에 신중히 생각하는 습관을 길러야 한다.
<small>말하기 전에 신중히 생각하는 습관에 대한 언급은 없음</small>
④ 글을 쓸 때보다 말할 때 더 많은 단어를 사용해야 한다.
<small>말할 때 글을 쓸 때보다 더 많은 단어를 사용해야 한다는 내용</small>
⑤ 청중의 이해를 돕기 위해 미리 연설문을 제공해야 한다.
<small>미리 연설문을 제공해야 한다는 내용은 아님</small>

〉왜 정답? ✱✱✱❀ [정답률 71%]

글의 초반부에 나온 It takes more words to introduce, express, and adequately elaborate an idea in speech than it takes in writing. (말을 할 때는 아이디어를 소개하고, 표현하며, 적절히 부연 설명하는 데 글을 쓸 때보다 더 많은 단어가 필요하다.)이 이 글의 핵심문장이다.
즉, 말을 할 때는 청자들이 쉽게 주의를 잃고 다시 되돌려 들을 수 없기 때문에 글을 쓸 때보다 더 많은 단어를 사용해 생각을 전달해야 한다고 주장하고 있다. 따라서 필자의 주장으로 가장 적절한 것은 ④이다.

〉왜 오답?

① 연설 시 중요한 정보를 천천히 말해야 한다는 내용은 없다.
② 글을 쓸 때 단어 수가 적어야 한다는 언급은 있지만, 말할 때의 단어 수에 대한 내용을 포함하지 못하므로 적절한 답이 아니다. 〔함정〕
③ 말하기 전에 신중히 생각하는 습관에 대해서는 언급하지 않았다.
⑤ 청중의 이해를 돕기 위해 미리 연설문을 제공해야 한다는 내용이 아니다.

Ⓒ 17 정답 ⑤ ── ✪ 2등급 대비 [정답률 68%]

*큰일을 이루려면 작은 일부터 제대로 수행해야 한다.

When I was in the army, / my instructors would show up / in my barracks room, / and the first thing / [앞에 목적격 관계대명사 생략] they would inspect / was our bed. //
내가 군대에 있을 때 / 교관들이 모습을 드러내곤 했었는데 / 나의 병영 생활관에 / 첫 번째 것은 / 그들이 검사하곤 했던 / 우리의 침대였다 //

It was a simple task, / but every morning / we [수동태] were required to make our bed / [완벽하게] to perfection. //
단순한 일이었다 / 하지만 매일 아침 / 우리는 침대를 정돈하도록 요구받았다 / 완벽하게 //

It seemed a little ridiculous / at the time, / but the wisdom of this simple act / [현재완료 수동태] has been proven to me / many times over. //
약간 우스꽝스럽게 보였다 / 그 당시에는 / 하지만 이 단순한 행위의 지혜는 / 나에게 증명되었다 / 여러 차례 거듭하여 //

If you make your bed every morning, / you [미래완료 시제] will have accomplished / the first task of the day. //
여러분이 매일 아침 침대를 정돈한다면 / 여러분은 성취한 것이 된다 / 하루의 첫 번째 과업을 //

It will give you a small sense of pride / and it will encourage [encourage의 목적격보어(to부정사)] you / to do another task and another. //
그것은 여러분에게 작은 자존감을 줄 것이다 / 그리고 그것은 여러분에게 용기를 줄 것이다 / 또 다른 과업을 잇따라 이어가도록 // 〔단서 1 작은 일을 완수하는 것이 작은 자존감을 주고, 그것이 다른 과업들을 이어갈 수 있는 용기를 줄 것임〕

By the end of the day, / that one task completed / will have turned into many tasks completed. // 〔단서 2 하나의 과업을 완수하면 여러 개의 과업을 완수하는 것이 가능함〕
하루가 끝날 때쯤에는 / 완수된 그 하나의 과업이 / 여러 개의 완수된 과업으로 변해 있을 것이다 //

If you can't do little things right, / you will never do the big things right. // 〔핵심문장. 단서 3 작은 일을 제대로 할 수 없으면 큰일도 제대로 할 수 없음〕
작은 일들을 제대로 할 수 없으면 / 여러분은 결코 큰일들을 제대로 할 수 없을 것이다 //

- army ⓝ 군대 · instructor ⓝ 교관
- inspect ⓥ 검사하다, 점검하다 · require ⓥ 요구하다
- make one's bed 침대를 정돈하다 · ridiculous ⓐ 우스꽝스러운
- prove ⓥ 증명하다 · encourage ⓥ 용기를 주다
- complete ⓥ 완수하다 · turn into ~으로 변하다

내가 군대에 있을 때, 교관들이 나의 병영 생활관에 모습을 드러내곤 했었는데, 그들이 맨 먼저 검사하곤 했던 것은 우리의 침대였다. 단순한 일이었지만, 매일 아침 우리는 침대를 완벽하게 정돈하도록 요구받았다. 그 당시에는 약간 우스꽝스럽게 보였지만, 이 단순한 행위의 지혜는 여러 차례 거듭하여 나에게 증명되었다. 여러분이 매일 아침 침대를 정돈한다면, 여러분은 하루의 첫 번째 과업을 성취한 것이 된다. 그것은 여러분에게 작은 자존감을 주고, 또 다른 과업을 잇따라 이어가도록 용기를 줄 것이다. 하루가 끝날 때쯤에는, 완수된 그 하나의 과업이 여러 개의 완수된 과업으로 변해 있을 것이다. 작은 일들을 제대로 할 수 없으면, 여러분은 결코 큰일들을 제대로 할 수 없을 것이다.

> **다음 글에서 필자가 주장하는 바로 가장 적절한 것은?**
> ① 숙면을 위해서는 침대를 깔끔하게 관리해야 한다.
>   [숙면을 위해 침대를 관리한다는 내용이 아님]
> ② 일의 효율성을 높이려면 협동심을 발휘해야 한다.
>   [일의 효율성이나 협동심에 관해 언급되지 않음]
> ③ 올바른 습관을 기르려면 정해진 규칙을 따라야 한다.
>   [매일 아침 침대를 정돈하도록 요구받았다는 내용으로 만든 함정]
> ④ 건강을 유지하기 위해서는 기상 시간이 일정해야 한다.
>   [건강이나 기상 시간에 대한 내용은 없음]
> ⑤ 큰일을 잘 이루려면 작은 일부터 제대로 수행해야 한다.
>   [침대 정리를 예로 들면서, 작은 일부터 제대로 해야 큰일을 잘 이룰 수 있음을 말하고 있음]

⭐ 필자가 군대에서 겪었던 일에 대해 말하면서 궁극적으로 주장하는 바가 무엇인지 파악해야 한다. 핵심문장이 확실하게 드러나는 글이므로 핵심문장을 찾으면 쉽게 풀리는 문제이다.

〉왜 정답?

마지막 문장 If you can't do little things right, you will never do the big things right. (작은 일들을 제대로 할 수 없으면, 여러분은 결코 큰일들을 제대로 할 수 없을 것이다.)가 이 글의 핵심문장이다.
필자는 군대에서 매일 아침 침대를 정돈하게 했던 일화를 예로 들어, 작은 일을 제대로 완수해야만 또 다른 과업들을 잘 수행할 수 있음을 말하고 있다. 따라서 필자의 주장으로 가장 적절한 것은 ⑤이다.

〉왜 오답? 〔핵심 내용인지 예시인지 구별하기! 꿀팁〕

① 침대를 정리하는 것에 대한 내용은 나왔으나, 그것은 작은 일을 완수하는 것의 예시로 나온 것이고 숙면을 위해 침대를 관리한다는 내용이 아니다.
② 일의 효율성이나 협동심에 관해서는 언급되지 않았다.
③ 매일 아침 침대를 정돈하도록 요구받았다는 내용으로 만든 함정으로, 올바른 습관을 기르기 위해 규칙을 따라야 한다고 주장하는 것이 아니다.
④ 건강이나 기상 시간에 대한 내용은 언급되지 않았다.

Ⓒ 18 정답 ③ ── ✪ 2등급 대비 [정답률 53%]

*교사는 비언어적 표현에 유의해야 한다.

Some experts estimate / [목적어절을 이끄는 접속사] that as much as half / of what we communicate / is done / through the way we move our bodies. //
일부 전문가들은 추정한다 / 절반 정도가 / 우리가 전달하는 것의 / 행해진다고 / 우리가 우리의 몸을 움직이는 방식을 통해 //

[동명사 주어] Paying attention to the nonverbal messages / [앞에 목적격 관계대명사 that 생략] you send / can make a significant difference / in your relationship with students. // 〔핵심문장. 단서 1 비언어적인 메시지에 주의를 기울이면 학생과의 관계가 달라질 수 있음〕
비언어적인 메시지에 주의를 기울이는 것은 / 여러분이 보내는 / 중요한 차이를 만들 수 있다 / 학생들과 여러분의 관계에 //

In general, / most students are often closely tuned in / to their teacher's body language. // 〔단서 2 학생들의 관심은 교사의 몸짓 언어(비언어적 메시지)에 면밀하게 맞춰져 있음〕
일반적으로 / 대부분의 학생들은 종종 관심이 면밀하게 맞춰져 있다 / 자신의 선생님의 몸짓 언어에 //

For example, / when your students first enter the classroom, / their initial action / is [명사적 용법(주격보어)] to look for their teacher. //
예를 들어 / 여러분의 학생들이 처음 교실에 들어갈 때 / 그들의 첫 행동은 / 자신의 선생님을 찾는 것이다 //

Think / about how encouraging and empowering it is / for a student / when that teacher has a friendly greeting and a welcoming smile. // 단서 3 선생님의 친근한 인사와 환영하는 미소(비언어적 표현)가 학생에게 격려가 됨

생각해 보라 / 얼마나 격려가 되고 힘을 주는지 / 학생에게 / 그 선생님이 친근한 인사를 하고 환영하는 미소를 짓는다면 //

동명사 주어(단수)＊ / 사역동사+목적어+목적격보어(동사원형)

Smiling at students / — to let them know / that you are glad to see them — / does not require a great deal of time or effort, / 단수 동사＊

학생들에게 미소 짓는 것 / 즉 그들에게 알려 주는 것이 / 여러분이 그들을 알게 돼서 기쁘다는 것을 / 많은 시간이나 노력을 요구하는 것은 아니다 /

but it can make a significant difference / in the classroom climate / right from the start of class. //

하지만 그것은 중요한 차이를 만들 수 있다 / 교실 분위기에 / 수업의 바로 그 시작부터 //

- estimate ⓥ 추정하다 · pay attention to ~에 주의를 기울이다
- nonverbal ⓐ 비언어적인 · significant ⓐ 중요한
- make a difference 차이를 만들다 · closely ⓐⓓ 면밀히, 밀접하게
- tuned in (to) (~에) 맞춰진, (~에 대해) 잘 아는
- initial ⓐ 처음의, 초기의 · encouraging ⓐ 격려의, 힘을 북돋아 주는
- empower ⓥ 힘을 주다 · a great deal of 많은 · effort ⓝ 노력
- climate ⓝ 분위기, 기후

일부 전문가들은 우리가 전달하는 것의 절반 정도가 우리가 우리의 몸을 움직이는 방식을 통해 행해진다고 추정한다. 여러분이 보내는 비언어적인 메시지에 주의를 기울이는 것은 학생들과 여러분의 관계에 중요한 차이를 만들 수 있다. 일반적으로 대부분의 학생들은 자신의 선생님의 몸짓 언어에 종종 관심이 면밀하게 맞춰져 있다. 예를 들어 여러분의 학생들이 처음 교실에 들어갈 때 그들의 첫 행동은 자신의 선생님을 찾는 것이다. 그 선생님이 친근한 인사를 하고 환영하는 미소를 짓는다면 그것이 학생에게 얼마나 격려가 되고 힘을 주는지 생각해 보자. 학생들에게 미소 짓는 것, 즉 그들에게 여러분이 그들을 알게 돼서 기쁘다는 것을 알려 주는 것이 많은 시간이나 노력을 요구하는 것은 아니지만, 그것은 수업의 바로 그 시작부터 교실 분위기에 중요한 차이를 만들 수 있다.

다음 글에서 필자가 주장하는 바로 가장 적절한 것은?

① 교사는 학생 간의 상호 작용을 주의 깊게 관찰해야 한다.
학생 간 상호 작용에 대한 언급은 없음
② 수업 시 교사는 학생의 수준에 맞는 언어를 사용해야 한다.
비언어적 메시지가 주요 소재임
③ 학생과의 관계에서 교사는 비언어적 표현에 유의해야 한다.
교사의 비언어적 메시지가 학생과 교실 분위기에 영향을 준다는 내용
④ 학교는 학생에게 다양한 역할 경험의 기회를 제공해야 한다.
다양한 역할 경험에 대한 언급은 없음
⑤ 교사는 학생 안전을 위해 교실의 물리적 환경을 개선해야 한다.
물리적 환경이 아니라 교사의 비언어적 메시지에 유의해야 한다는 내용임

⭐ 중반부에 For example(예를 들어)이 나오면서 필자의 주장을 뒷받침하는 내용이 나오는 것에 주목해야 한다. 이를 통해 필자가 결국 말하고자 하는 바가 무엇인지 이해하고 핵심문장을 찾는 것이 중요하다.

🟩 왜 정답?

필자는 학생들의 관심이 교사의 몸짓 언어에 면밀하게 맞춰져 있고, 교사의 친근한 인사와 환영하는 미소가 학생에게 격려가 된다고 하면서 교사가 자신의 비언어적인 메시지에 주의를 기울이면 학생들과의 관계에 변화가 생길 수 있다고 주장하고 있다. 따라서 필자의 주장으로 가장 적절한 것은 ③이다.

🟥 왜 오답?

① 학생 간 상호 작용에 대한 언급은 없으며, 교사의 비언어적 메시지가 학생에게 영향을 미친다는 내용의 글이다.
② 학생 수준에 맞는 언어에 대한 내용은 없고, 교사의 비언어적 메시지가 글의 핵심 소재이다.
④ 학생의 다양한 역할 경험에 대한 내용은 언급되지 않았다.
⑤ 교실의 물리적 환경에 대한 언급은 없으며, 교사의 비언어적 메시지에 유의해야 한다는 내용이다.

＊ 주어-동사 수 일치

– 문장의 주어가 명사구 혹은 명사절일 때 항상 단수 취급한다. to부정사구, 동명사구나 의문사절, that절, whether절 등과 같은 명사절이 주어로 오는 경우 동사와 멀어질 수 있기 때문에 수 일치 여부를 쉽게 판단하기 힘들다. 따라서 항상 문장을 전체적으로 파악해야 한다.

· Creating a list of goals is a good way to be a better student.
동명사구 주어 / 단수 동사
(목표들의 목록을 만드는 것은 더 나은 학생이 되기 위한 좋은 방법이다.)

· Whether he will accept my offer is not certain yet.
명사절 주어 / 단수 동사
(그가 나의 제안을 받아들일지는 아직 확실하지 않다.)

· To overcome my emotional problems is difficult.
to부정사구 주어 / 단수 동사
(나의 감정적인 문제들을 극복하는 것은 어렵다.)

예시를 통해 핵심문장을 파악하자!

ⓒ 어휘 Review 정답 ──────── 문제편 p. 43

01 목격하다	11 give away	21 neatly
02 검사하다	12 manage to	22 overshadow
03 산만한	13 be about to	23 dedicated
04 완벽한	14 cope with	24 uphold
05 이익	15 peaks and valleys	25 remarkable
06 seize	16 separate	26 launch
07 unproductive	17 obligations	27 Otherwise
08 achieve	18 incredible	28 powerful
09 elaborate	19 atmosphere	29 perfection
10 compassion	20 tempting	30 constant

D 밑줄 친 부분의 의미 찾기 문제편 p. 46~56

D 01 정답 ② *신념과 행동의 관계

가주어 진주어절 접속사
It is common sense / **that** people's inner beliefs / may drive their
external behavior. // 단서1 내적 신념이 외적 행동을 이끎
상식이다 / 사람들의 내적 신념이 / 그들의 외적인 행동을 이끌 수 있다는 것은 //

추측 (~일 것이다)
If you're attracted to a certain person, / you **should** be more
likely to socialize / with that person. //
만약 당신이 어떤 사람에게 끌린다면 / 당신은 더 어울리려고 할 것이다 / 그 사람과 //

If you favor a brand of toothpaste, / you're more likely to buy
it. //
만약 당신이 한 브랜드의 치약을 선호한다면 / 당신이 그것을 구매할 가능성은 더 높다 //

Of course, / our internal thoughts / don't *always* predict our
public behavior, / but, overall, / **what** we do / obviously reflects
what we think. //
선행사를 포함하는 관계대명사
물론 / 우리의 내적 사고가 / '항상' 공개적인 행동을 예측하지는 않지만 / 전반적으로 / 우리가
하는 것은 / 분명히 우리가 생각하는 바를 반영한다 //

But beliefs and behaviors / are also related / in a more
remarkable way. // 단서2 신념과 행동은 더 놀라운 방식으로도 관련됨
그러나 신념과 행동은 / 또한 관련이 있다 / 이보다 더 놀라운 방식으로 //
가주어 진주어절 접속사
It turns out / **that** the arrow / is as likely to point / in the reverse
direction. //
드러난다 / 화살이 / 가리킬 가능성이 그만큼 높다 / 반대 방향을 //

As social psychologist David Myers observes, / "If social
psychology has taught us anything / during the last 25 years, /
사회심리학자 David Myers가 말한 바에 따르면 / "사회심리학이 우리에게 가르쳐준 것이 있
다면 / 지난 25년간 /

it is that / we are likely / **not only** to think ourselves into a way
not only A but also B: A뿐만 아니라 B도
of acting / **but also** to act ourselves into a way of thinking." //
그것은 바로 / 우리가 가능성이 있다는 것이다 / 우리가 생각하여 행동 방식에 이를 뿐만 아니
라 / 우리가 또한 행동하여 사고 방식에 이를" // 단서3 반대로 행동이 사고 방식에 이르기도 함

- common sense 상식 ・ belief ⓝ 신념 ・ drive ⓥ 이끌다
- external ⓐ 외적인 ・ behavior ⓝ 행동
- socialize ⓥ 어울리다, 교류하다 ・ internal ⓐ 내적의, 내면의
- obviously ⓐⓓ 분명히 ・ reflect ⓥ 반영하다
- remarkable ⓐ 놀랄 만한, 놀라운 ・ likely ⓐ ~할 가능성이 있는
- reverse ⓐ 반대의 ・ direction ⓝ 방향 ・ entirely ⓐⓓ 완전히
- separate ⓐ 분리된 ・ be dependent on ~에 의존하다
- surroundings ⓝ (주변) 환경 ・ matter ⓥ 중요하다

사람들의 내적 신념이 그들의 외적인 행동을 이끌 수 있다는 것은 상식이다. 만
약 당신이 어떤 사람에게 끌린다면, 당신은 그 사람과 더 어울리려고 할 것이
다. 만약 당신이 한 브랜드의 치약을 선호한다면, 당신이 그것을 구매할 가능
성이 더 높다. 물론, 우리의 내적 사고가 '항상' 공개적인 행동을 예측하지는 않
지만, 전반적으로, 우리가 하는 것은 분명히 우리가 생각하는 바를 반영한다.
그러나 신념과 행동은 이보다 더 놀라운 방식으로도 관련이 있다. 화살이 반대
방향을 가리킬 가능성이 그만큼 높다는 것이 드러난다. 사회 심리학자 David
Myers가 말한 바에 따르면, "지난 25년간 사회 심리학이 우리에게 가르쳐준 것
이 있다면, 그것은 우리가 생각하여 행동 방식에 이를 뿐만 아니라 우리가 행동
하여 사고 방식에 이를 가능성도 있다는 것이다."

밑줄 친 **the arrow is as likely to point in the reverse direction**이
다음 글에서 의미하는 바로 가장 적절한 것은? [3점]

① actions can be entirely separate from beliefs
행동은 신념과 완전히 분리될 수 있다   행동과 신념이 분리되는 것이 아니라 서로 영향을 미침
② our behaviors can also shape what we believe
우리의 행동이 우리가 믿는 바를 형성할 수도 있다   행동이 신념을 이끌 수 있음
③ our opinions can be dependent on our emotions
우리의 의견은 감정에 의존할 수 있다   감정은 언급되지 않았음
④ behaviors can clearly reflect one's surroundings
행동은 분명히 주변 환경을 반영할 수 있다   환경은 언급되지 않았음
⑤ what we think can matter more than what we do 생각과 행동의
우리가 생각하는 것이 우리가 하는 것보다 더 중요할 수 있다   중요성을 비교하는 내용이 아님

＞왜 정답? ★★❀ [정답률 69%]

- 신념이 행동을 이끌 수 있음 단서1
- 신념과 행동은 더 놀라운 방식으로도 관련됨 단서2
- 행동하여 사고 방식에 이르기도 함 단서3

➡ 신념이 행동을 이끌 수 있다는 상식을 제시했으나, But 이후로는 행동 또한 생각에
이르게 한다는 반대 방향의 관계를 제시했다.

▶ 따라서 '화살이 반대 방향을 가리킬 가능성이 그만큼 높다'는 것은 신념이 행동을
이끈다는 상식과 반대로 ② '우리의 행동이 우리가 믿는 바를 형성할 수도 있다'를
의미한다.

＞왜 오답?

① 행동과 신념이 완전히 분리되는 것이 아니라 서로 영향을 미칠 수 있다고 했다.
③ 끌리는 사람과 더 어울리려고 한다는 예시가 언급되었을 뿐, 우리의 의견이 감정에
의존한다는 내용이 아니다.
④ 환경은 언급되지 않았다.
⑤ 생각과 행동 중 어느 것이 먼저 시작되는지에 관한 내용이지, 어느 것이 다른 것보
다 중요하다는 것은 언급되지 않았다. 주의

D 02 정답 ⑤ *기술의 발전으로 변하는 일자리

If we adopt technology, / we need to pay its costs. //
만약 우리가 기술을 받아들이면 / 우리는 그것의 비용을 치러야 한다 //
현재완료 수동태
Thousands of traditional livelihoods **have been pushed** aside /
by progress, / and the lifestyles around those jobs removed. //
수천 개의 전통적인 생계 수단이 밀려났다 / 발전에 의해 / 그리고 그 직업들 주변의 생활
방식이 없어졌다 //
앞에 목적격 관계대명사가 생략됨
Hundreds of millions of humans today work / at jobs **they hate**,
앞에 목적격 관계대명사가 생략됨
/ producing things **they have no love for**. //
오늘날 수억 명의 사람들이 일한다 / 그들이 싫어하는 직장에서 / 그들이 아무런 애정을 갖지
않는 것들을 생산하면서 //

Sometimes / these jobs cause / physical pain, disability, or
chronic disease. //
때때로 / 이러한 일자리들은 유발한다 / 육체적 고통, 장애 또는 만성 질환을 //
주격 관계대명사
Technology creates many new jobs / **that** are certainly dangerous. //
기술은 많은 새로운 일자리를 창출한다 / 확실히 위험한 //

At the same time, / mass education and media train humans /
병렬구조
to avoid low-tech physical work, / **to seek** jobs working in the
digital world. // 단서1 과거와 다르게 인간이 육체노동을 적게 하는 직종에 많이 종사하게 됨
동시에 / 대중 교육과 대중 매체는 인간을 훈련시킨다 / 낮은 기술의 육체노동을 피하고 /
디지털 세계에서 일하는 직업을 찾도록 //
핵심 주어(단수) 단수 동사
The divorce of the hands from the head **puts** a stress / on the
human mind. //
머리로부터 손이 단절되는 것은 부담을 준다 / 인간의 정신에 //
핵심 주어(단수) 단수 동사
Indeed, / **the sedentary nature** of the best-paying jobs / **is** a
health risk / — for body and mind. // 단서2 보수가 좋은 앉아서 일하는 직업은
건강에 부정적 영향을 미침
실제로 / 가장 보수가 좋은 직업의 주로 앉아서 하는 특성은 / 건강 위험 요소이다 / 신체와
정신에 //

- adopt ⓥ 받아들이다, 채택하다 • traditional ⓐ 전통적인
- livelihood ⓝ 생계 수단 • progress ⓝ 발전 • remove ⓥ 없애다
- physical ⓐ 육체의 • disability ⓝ 장애 • mass ⓐ 대중의
- avoid ⓥ 피하다 • divorce ⓝ 단절, 이혼
- indeed ⓐⓓ 실제로, 참으로 • risk ⓝ 위험 (요소)
- ignorance ⓝ 무지, 무식 • endless ⓐ 끝없는 • labor ⓝ 노동

만약 우리가 기술을 받아들이면, 우리는 그것의 비용을 치러야 한다. 수천 개의 전통적인 생계 수단이 발전에 의해 밀려났으며, 그 직업과 관련된 생활 방식이 없어졌다. 오늘날 수억 명의 사람들이 자기가 싫어하는 직장에서 일하면서, 자신이 아무런 애정을 느끼지 못하는 것들을 생산한다. 때때로 이러한 일자리는 육체적 고통, 장애 또는 만성 질환을 유발한다. 기술은 확실히 위험한 많은 새로운 일자리를 창출한다. 동시에, 대중 교육과 대중 매체는 낮은 기술의 육체노동을 피하고 디지털 세계에서 일하는 직업을 찾도록 인간을 훈련시킨다. 머리로부터 손이 단절되는 것은 인간의 정신에 부담을 준다. 실제로, 가장 보수가 좋은 직업의 주로 앉아서 하는 특성은 신체와 정신에 건강 위험 요소이다.

> 밑줄 친 The divorce of the hands from the head가 다음 글에서 의미하는 바로 가장 적절한 것은? [3점]

① ignorance of modern technology
현대 기술의 무지 → 현대 기술의 무지가 아니라 변화에 관한 내용임
② endless competition in the labor market
노동 시장에서의 끝없는 경쟁 → 노동 시장에서의 경쟁에 관한 글이 아님
③ not getting along well with our coworkers
동료들과 잘 어울리지 못하는 것 → 동료들과의 관계는 언급되지 않음
④ working without any realistic goals for our career
우리의 경력을 위해 현실적인 목표 없이 일하는 것 → 목표 설정을 하라는 것이 아님
⑤ our increasing use of high technology in the workplace
직장에서 우리의 증가하는 첨단 기술 사용 → 기술의 발전으로 육체노동을 피하게 됨

> 왜 정답? ★★★ [정답률 57%]

- 과거와 다르게 인간이 육체노동을 적게 하는 직종에 많이 종사하게 됨 단서1
- 보수가 좋은 앉아서 일하는 직업은 건강에 부정적 영향을 미침 단서2

➡ 기술의 발전으로 과거와는 다르게 육체노동을 적게 하는 직종이 많아지고, 앉아서만 일하다 보니 건강에 부정적인 영향을 미침

▶ 몸을 쓰지 않고 기술을 사용해 머리로 일한다는 것이므로 '머리로부터 손이 단절되는 것'은 ⑤ '직장에서 우리의 증가하는 첨단 기술 사용'을 의미한다.

> 왜 오답?

① 현대 기술의 무지가 아니라 변화에 관한 글이다.
② 노동 시장에서의 경쟁을 말하는 글이 아니다.
③ 동료들과의 관계에 관해서는 언급되지 않았다.
④ 현실적 목표를 세우라고 조언하는 글이 아니다.

D 03 정답 ① *인간 유전자 편집

분사구문을 이끄는 현재분사 (주어와 if가 생략됨)   명사절 (Assuming의 목적어)
Assuming / gene editing in humans / proves to be safe and
                                        주격 보어
effective, / it might seem logical, even preferable, / to correct
                                                       부사적 용법 (형용사 수식)
disease-causing mutations /
가정한다면 / 인간 유전자 편집이 / 안전하고 효과적이라고 입증된다고 / 합리적이고, 심지어 바람직해 보일 수도 있다 / 질병을 유발하는 돌연변이를 교정하는 것이 /

at the earliest possible stage of life, / before harmful genes begin
                                          동명사 (begin의 목적어)
causing serious problems. //
생애의 가능한 한 가장 이른 단계에서 / 해로운 유전자가 심각한 문제를 일으키기 '전에' //

        가주어   진주어
Yet once it becomes possible / to transform an embryo's mutated
genes into "normal" ones, / there will certainly be temptations /
to upgrade normal genes to superior versions. //
하지만 일단 가능해지면 / 배아의 돌연변이가 된 유전자를 '정상적인' 유전자로 변형하는 것이 / 유혹이 분명히 있을 것이다 / 정상적인 유전자를 더 우수한 버전으로 업그레이드하려는 /
                                                    부사적 용법 (목적)
Should we begin / editing genes in unborn children / to lower
their lifetime risk of heart disease or cancer? //
우리가 시작해야 할까 / 태어나지 않은 아이들의 유전자를 편집하는 것을 / 심장병이나 암과 같은 질병에 대한 평생 위험을 낮추기 위해 //
단서1 질병에 대한 위험을 낮춤

단서2 유전자에 유익한 특성을 부여하거나 신체적 특징을 바꿀 수 있음
What about giving unborn children beneficial features, / like
                                  병렬 구조 (동명사)
greater strength and increased mental abilities, / or changing
physical characteristics, / like eye and hair color? //
유익한 특성을 태어나기 않은 아이들에게 부여하는 것은 어떨까 / 더 강한 체력이나 향상된 인지 능력 같은 / 또는 신체적 특징을 바꾸거나 / 눈이나 머리카락 색 같은 //

The pursuit for perfection seems almost natural to human
nature, / but if we start down this slippery slope, / we may not
                        의문사절
like where we end up. // 단서3 완벽을 계속 추구하면 좋지 않은 결과로 이어질 수 있음
완벽에 대한 추구는 인간의 본성에 거의 자연스러워 보이지만 / 만약 우리가 이 미끄러운 경사 길을 내려가기 시작한다면 / 우리는 결국 놓일 곳이 마음에 들지 않을 수도 있다 //

- gene editing 유전자 편집 • logical ⓐ 합리적인
- preferable ⓐ 바람직한 • correct ⓥ 교정하다
- transform ⓥ 변형하다, 바꾸다 • temptation ⓝ 유혹
- superior ⓐ 우수한 • characteristics ⓝ 특징 • pursuit ⓝ 추구
- slippery ⓐ 미끄러운 • slope ⓝ 경사
- end up 결국 ~하게 되다 • alteration ⓝ 개조, 변경
- stick to ~을 고수하다 • belief ⓝ 믿음, 신념 • moral ⓐ 도덕적인

인간 유전자 편집이 안전하고 효과적이라고 입증된다고 가정한다면, 해로운 유전자가 심각한 문제를 일으키기 '전에' 생애의 가능한 한 가장 이른 단계에서 질병을 유발하는 돌연변이를 교정하는 것이 합리적이고, 심지어 바람직해 보일 수도 있다. 하지만 일단 배아의 돌연변이가 된 유전자를 '정상적인' 유전자로 변형하는 것이 가능해지면, 정상적인 유전자를 더 우수한 버전으로 업그레이드하려는 유혹이 분명히 있을 것이다. 우리가 심장병이나 암과 같은 질병에 대한 평생 위험을 낮추기 위해 태어나지 않은 아이들의 유전자를 편집하는 것을 시작해야 할까? 더 강한 체력이나 향상된 인지 능력 같은 유익한 특성을 태어나지 않은 아이들에게 부여하거나 또는 눈이나 머리카락 색 같은 신체적 특징을 바꾸는 것은 어떨까? 완벽에 대한 추구는 인간의 본성에 거의 자연스러워 보이지만, 만약 우리가 이 미끄러운 경사 길을 내려가기 시작한다면, 우리는 결국 놓일 곳이 마음에 들지 않을 수도 있다.

> 밑줄 친 start down this slippery slope이 다음 글에서 의미하는 바로 가장 적절한 것은? [3점]

① allow genetic alterations to upgrade humans
인간을 개선하기 위해 유전적 개조를 허용한다 → 유전적 발전을 위해 유전자 편집을 시도할 수 있음
② stick to the traditional beliefs in human nature
인간 본성에 대한 전통적인 믿음을 고수한다 → 인간의 본성에 대한 믿음은 언급되지 않음
③ resist the temptation to change genes in humans
인간의 유전자를 바꾸고자 하는 유혹에 저항한다 → 인간 유전자 개량에 대한 욕구와 반대됨
④ fail to reduce the risk of suffering from diseases
질병에 걸릴 위험을 줄이는 데 실패한다 → 질병에 걸릴 위험을 줄이고자 함
⑤ consider more about the moral issues of genetics
유전학의 도덕적 문제에 대해 더 많이 고려한다 → 유전자 개량의 도덕적 문제는 언급되지 않았음

> 왜 정답? ★★☆ [정답률 62%]

- 질병에 대한 평생 위험을 낮추기 위해 유전자를 편집하는 것 단서1
- 유익한 특성을 부여하거나 신체적 특징을 바꾸는 것 단서2
- 완벽을 계속 추구하면 우리는 원치 않는 곳에 놓일 것임 단서3

➡ 질병 예방과 우월한 신체적 특성을 갖추기 위해 유전자를 인위적으로 변형시키는 것이 어떤지를 묻다가, 이처럼 완벽을 추구하다 보면 우리는 결국 원치 않는 곳에 놓일 것이라는 부정적인 결말을 제시했다. '미끄러운 경사 길'은 한번 내려가기 시작하면 되돌아가기 힘들어지기 때문에 돌이킬 수 없는 문제를 시작하는 것, 즉 '유전자 변형 및 편집을 허용하는 것'과 같다.

▶ 따라서 '미끄러운 경사 길을 내려간다'는 것은 ① '인간을 개선하기 위해 유전적 개조를 허용한다'를 의미한다.

> 왜 오답?

② 인간 본성에 대한 전통적인 믿음에 관한 글이 아니다.
③ 인간 유전자 편집에 대한 유혹에 저항하는 것이 아니라 계속 빠져드는 것에 해당한다. 함정
④ 질병의 가능성을 낮추기 위해 유전자 변형을 해결책으로 거론하고 있다.
⑤ 유전학의 도덕적 문제는 언급되지 않았다.

당신의 몸에 있는 많은 원자는 거의 우주 자체만큼이나 오래되었다. 당신이 숨을 쉴 때, 예를 들어, 당신이 들이마신 원자 중 일부만이 당신의 다음 숨에서 내뱉어진다. 남아있는 원자는 당신의 몸으로 들어가 당신의 일부가 되고, 이후 그것들은 다양한 방법으로 당신의 몸을 떠난다. 당신은 당신의 몸을 구성하는 원자를 '소유'하지 않는다. 당신은 그것들을 빌린다. 원자는 영원히 우리 주변과 내부, 그리고 우리 사이를 이동하기 때문에 우리 모두는 같은 원자풀로부터 공유한다. 원자는 우리가 숨을 쉬고 땀이 증발하면서 사람에서 사람으로 순환한다. 우리는 거대한 규모로 원자를 재순환시킨다. 가장 가벼운 원자의 기원은 우주의 기원으로 거슬러 올라가며, 대부분의 더 무거운 원자는 태양과 지구보다 오래되었다. 태초부터 존재해 온 원자가 당신의 몸에 있으며 제한 없는 형태, 즉 비생물체와 생물체 가운데 우주 전체에 걸쳐 재순환한다. 당신은 몸속 원자의 현재 관리인이다. 당신의 뒤를 이을 많은 것[사람]들이 있을 것이다.

구문 서술형

정답 editing 또는 to edit

해석 우리가 태어나지 않은 아이들의 유전자를 편집하는 것을 시작해야 할까?

→ 동사 begin의 목적어가 필요하므로, 동사 edit을 동명사 editing 또는 to부정사 to edit로 바꿔야 한다.

D 04 정답 ① *원자의 끊임없는 순환

as 형용사/부사 원급 as …: ~만큼이나 ~한
Many atoms in your body / are nearly as old as the universe itself. //
당신의 몸에 있는 많은 원자 / 거의 우주 자체만큼이나 오래되었다 //

목적격 관계대명사
When you breathe, / for example, / only some of the atoms that you inhale / are exhaled / in your next breath. //
당신이 숨을 쉴 때 / 예를 들어 / 당신이 들이마신 원자 중 일부만이 / 내뱉어진다 / 당신의 다음 숨에서 //

부사적 용법 (결과)
The remaining atoms are taken into your body / to become part of you, / and they later leave your body / by various means. //
남아있는 원자는 당신의 몸으로 들어가 / 당신의 일부가 되고 / 이후 그것들은 당신의 몸을 떠난다 / 다양한 방법으로 //
단서 1 원자는 몸에 들어온 이후에 떠남

주격 관계대명사
You don't "own" the atoms / that make up your body; / you borrow them. //
= the atoms
당신은 원자를 '소유'하지 않는다 / 당신의 몸을 구성하는 / 당신은 그것들을 빌린다 //

병렬 구조 (전치사)
We all share from the same atom pool / because atoms forever travel around, within, and among us. //
우리 모두는 같은 원자풀로부터 공유한다 / 원자는 영원히 우리 주변과 내부, 그리고 우리 사이를 이동하기 때문에 //

병렬 구조 (as가 이끄는 부사절)
Atoms cycle from person to person / as we breathe and as our sweat is evaporated. // **단서 2** 원자는 사람들 사이를 순환함
원자는 사람에서 사람으로 순환한다 / 우리가 숨을 쉬고 땀이 증발하면서 //

We recycle atoms on a grand scale. //
우리는 거대한 규모로 원자를 재순환시킨다 //

The origin of the lightest atoms goes back / to the origin of the universe, / and most heavier atoms are older than the Sun and Earth. //
가장 가벼운 원자의 기원은 거슬러 올라가며 / 우주의 기원으로 / 대부분의 더 무거운 원자는 태양과 지구보다 오래되었다 //

주격 관계대명사
There are atoms in your body / that have existed since the first moments of time, /
당신의 몸에 원자가 있으며 / 태초부터 존재해 온 /
분사구문을 이끄는 현재분사
recycling throughout the universe / among limitless forms, both nonliving and living. // **단서 3** 원자는 다양한 형태로 재순환하며 우주에 존재함
우주 전체에 걸쳐 재순환한다 / 제한 없는 형태, 즉 비생물체와 생물체 가운데 //

You're the present caretaker / of the atoms in your body. //
당신은 현재 관리인이다 / 몸속 원자의 // **단서 4** 현재의 관리인에게서 떠나 다른 관리인으로 옮겨갈 것임
대명사 (많은 것)[사람]
There will be many / who will follow you. //
많은 것[사람]들이 있을 것이다 / 당신의 뒤를 이을 //

- atom ⓝ 원자 · inhale ⓥ 흡입하다 · exhale ⓥ 내뱉다
- means ⓝ 수단, 방법 · make up ~을 구성하다 · cycle ⓥ 순환하다
- sweat ⓝ 땀 · grand ⓐ 거대한 · scale ⓝ 규모
- limitless ⓐ 제한 없는 · caretaker ⓝ 관리인

원자들은 순환하며 또 다른 형태 속에 존재하게 될 것임
밑줄 친 There will be many who will follow you가 다음 글에서 의미하는 바로 가장 적절한 것은?

① Atoms will become part of other forms after you
원자들은 당신 이후의 다른 형태의 일부가 될 것이다
② Atoms will remain unique and cannot be shared
원자들은 고유한 상태로 남을 것이며 공유될 수 없다
③ Atoms will follow their original forms
원자들은 원래 형태를 따를 것이다 **원자들은 원래 형태를 따르지 않고 끊임없이 형태를 바꿈**
④ Atoms will never be taken by a new form
원자들은 새로운 형태에 결코 흡수되지 않을 것이다 **원자들은 계속 새로운 형태로 흡수됨**
⑤ Atoms will disappear completely after your lifetime
원자들은 당신의 생애 후에 완전히 사라질 것이다 **원자들은 사라지지 않고 순환함**

➤왜 정답 ? ★★❀ [정답률 74%]

- 원자는 몸에 들어온 이후에 떠남 **단서 1**
- 원자는 사람들 사이를 순환함 **단서 2**
- 원자는 다양한 형태로 재순환하며 우주에 존재함 **단서 3**
- 원자가 현재의 관리인을 떠나 다른 관리인으로 옮겨갈 것임 **단서 4**

➡ 원자는 우리 몸에 들어왔다가 떠나며 사람들 사이를 순환하고, 다양한 형태로 재순환하며 우주에 존재한다. 즉, 현재 관리인에게 있는 원자는 결국 다른 관리인으로 옮겨갈 것이다.

▶ 따라서 '당신의 뒤를 이을 많은 것[사람]들이 있을 것이다'라는 것은 ① '원자들은 당신 이후의 다른 형태의 일부가 될 것이다'를 의미한다.

➤왜 오답 ?

② 원자는 고유한 상태로 남지 않고 순환하며 공유될 것이다.
③ 원자들은 원래의 형태를 따르지 않고 형태를 변화하며 존재한다.
④ 원자들은 끊임없이 새로운 형태에 흡수되어 우주에 존재한다.
⑤ 인간의 생애가 끝나도 그 안의 원자는 새로운 형태로 순환한다.

구문 서술형

정답 become, 결과, 부사적

해석 남아있는 원자는 당신의 몸으로 들어가 당신의 일부가 된다.

→ to become이 '(그 결과) 당신의 일부가 되다'라는 결과를 나타내는 부사적 용법으로 쓰였다.

When we see something, / we naturally and automatically break it up / into shapes, colors, and concepts / that we have learned through education. //
목적격 관계대명사
우리가 무언가를 볼 때 / 우리는 그것을 자연스럽게 그리고 자동적으로 해체한다 / 모양, 색깔, 그리고 개념들로 / 우리가 교육을 통해 배운 //

선행사를 포함하는 관계대명사 / 앞에 목적격 관계대명사가 생략됨
We recode what we see / through the lens / of everything we know. //
우리는 우리가 보는 것을 재부호화한다 / 렌즈를 통해 / 우리가 알고 있는 모든 것의 //

동명사
We reconstruct memories / rather than retrieving the video from memory. // **단서 1** 기억에서 영상을 떠올리는 것이 아니라 기억을 재구성함
우리는 기억을 재구성한다 / 기억에서 영상을 생각해 내기보다 //

This is a useful trait. //
이것은 유용한 특성이다 //

= Reconstructing   형용사적 용법 (way 수식)
It's a more efficient way / to store information / — a bit like an optimal image compression algorithm such as JPG, / rather than storing a raw bitmap image file. //
그것은 더 효율적인 방법이다 / 정보를 저장하기 위한 / JPG와 같은 최적의 이미지 압축 알고리즘과 약간 비슷하게 / 가공되지 않은 비트맵 이미지 파일을 저장하기보다 //

주격 관계대명사 ┌ 병렬 구조 (관계절 동사) ┐   in detail: 자세하게
People who lack this ability and remember everything in perfect detail / struggle to generalize, learn, and make connections / between what they have learned. //
선행사를 포함하는 관계대명사절
이런 능력이 부족하고 완벽히 세세하게 모든 것을 기억하는 사람들은 / 일반화하고, 학습하고, 연결하려고 고군분투한다 / 자신들이 학습한 것들 사이를 //

동명사 주어 (단수)
But representing the world / as abstract ideas and features / comes at a cost of seeing the world as it is. //
~을 희생하여, ~을 대가로
그러나 세상을 재현하는 것은 / 추상적 생각과 특징으로 / 세상을 있는 그대로 보는 것을 희생하여 나온다 // **단서 2** 추상적으로 세상을 재현하면 세상을 있는 그대로 볼 수 없음

Instead, / we see the world / through our assumptions, motivations, and past experiences. //
대신에 / 우리는 세상을 바라본다 / 우리의 가정, 동기 그리고 과거 경험을 통해 //

문장의 주어   동격절 접속사
The discovery / that our memories are reconstructed through abstract representations / rather than played back like a movie / completely undermined / the legal primacy of eyewitness testimony. // **단서 3** 기억은 있는 그대로가 아니기 때문에 목격자 증언은 법적 우위성을 잃음
병렬 구조   문장의 동사
발견은 / 우리의 기억이 추상적 재현을 통해 재구성된다는 / 영화처럼 재생되기보다는 / 완전히 손상시켰다 / 목격자 증언의 법적 우위성을 //

Seeing is not believing. // 보는 것이 믿는 것은 아니다 //

- **automatically** ad 자동적으로   • **break up** 해체하다
- **concept** n 개념   • **recode** v 재부호화하다
- **reconstruct** v 재구성하다   • **trait** n 특성   • **store** v 저장하다
- **optimal** a 최적의   • **compression** n 압축
- **raw** a 날것의, 가공되지 않은   • **generalize** v 일반화하다
- **make connections between ~** 사이를 연결하다
- **represent** v 재현하다   • **abstract** a 추상적인
- **assumption** n 가정   • **undermine** v 손상시키다
- **legal** a 법적인   • **eyewitness** n 목격자   • **testimony** n 증언
- **relevant** a 관련 있는   • **fall short of** ~이 부족하다
- **comprehension** n 이해   • **precede** v (~보다) 먼저 일어나다

우리가 무언가를 볼 때, 우리는 그것을 자연스럽게 그리고 자동적으로 우리가 교육을 통해 배운 모양, 색깔, 그리고 개념들로 해체한다. 우리는 우리가 알고 있는 모든 것의 렌즈를 통해 우리가 보는 것을 재부호화한다. 우리는 기억에서 영상을 생각해 내기보다 기억을 재구성한다. 이것은 유용한 특성이다. 그것은 가공되지 않은 비트맵 이미지 파일을 저장하기보다 JPG와 같은 최적의 이미지 압축 알고리즘과 약간 비슷하게 정보를 저장하기 위한 더 효율적인 방법이다. 이런 능력이 부족하고 완벽히 세세하게 모든 것을 기억하는 사람들은 일반화하고, 학습하고, 자신들이 학습한 것들 사이를 연결하려고 고군분투한다. 그러나

세상을 추상적 생각과 특징으로 재현하는 것은 세상을 있는 그대로 보는 것을 희생하여 나온다. 대신에, 우리는 우리의 가정, 동기 그리고 과거 경험을 통해 세상을 바라본다. 우리의 기억이 영화처럼 재생되기보다는 추상적 재현을 통해 재구성된다는 발견은 목격자 증언의 법적 우위성을 완전히 손상시켰다. <u>보는 것이 믿는 것은 아니다.</u>

밑줄 친 Seeing is not believing.이 다음 글에서 의미하는 바로 가장 적절한 것은? [3점]

① Abstract ideas are hard to explain without relevant images. 추상적인 아이디어를 설명하는 것과는 관련이 없음
추상적인 아이디어는 관련 이미지 없이 설명하기 어렵다.

② It takes longer to retrieve unconsciously encoded information. 정보를 상기하는 시간은 언급되지 않았음
무의식적으로 부호화된 정보를 상기하는 것은 시간이 더 오래 걸린다.

③ Beliefs formed from repeated experiences do not easily change. 반복되는 경험이나 신념은 언급되지 않았음
반복되는 경험에서 형성된 신념은 쉽게 변하지 않는다.

④ Our memories fall short of an objective representation of the world. representing the world ~ comes at a cost of seeing the world
우리의 기억은 세상을 객관적으로 표현하기에 부족하다.   as it is

⑤ Comprehension of facts precedes the formation of abstract concepts. 사실 이해와 추상적 개념 형성의 순서는 언급되지 않았음
사실에 대한 이해는 추상적인 개념 형성보다 먼저 일어난다.

| 문제 풀이 순서 | ★★★ [정답률 38%]

1st 밑줄 친 문장을 읽고, 그 의미가 무엇일지 예상한다.

[보는 것이 믿는 것은 아니다.

➡ '보는 것'과 '믿는 것'이 서로 다르다거나, 둘 중 어느 하나가 다른 것보다 낫지 않다는 내용이 이어질 것이다. 구체적으로 어떤 상황에서 '보는 것'과 '믿는 것' 사이에 차이가 나타나는지를 파악해야 한다.

2nd 글의 나머지 부분에서 '보는 것'과 '믿는 것'을 이해하여 정답을 찾는다.

- 우리는 기억에서 영상을 떠올리는 것이 아니라 기억을 재구성한다. **단서 1**
- 추상적으로 세상을 재현하면 세상을 있는 그대로 볼 수 없다. **단서 2**
- 우리의 기억이 영화처럼 재생되기보다는 추상적 재현을 통해 재구성된다는 발견은 목격자 증언의 법적 우위성을 완전히 손상시켰다. **단서 3**

➡ 보는 것 (기억에서 영상을 떠올리는 것, 세상을 있는 그대로 보는 것, 영화처럼 재생되는 것)
↔ 믿는 것 (기억을 재구성하는 것, 추상적으로 세상을 재현하는 것, 추상적 재현을 통한 재구성)

영상과 영화는 눈으로 '보는' 세상을 있는 그대로 담는다. 반면, 추상적으로 세상을 재현하는 것은 세상을 그대로 기억하는 것이 아니라 자신이 '믿는'대로 세상을 재구성하는 것이다.
기억은 '보는 것'(객관적인 사실)이 아닌 '믿는 것'(주관적인 재구성)이므로 객관성이 부족해서 목격자의 증언은 신뢰할 수 없고 법적으로 우위성이 없다는 것이 글의 내용이다.

▶ 따라서 정답은 ④ '우리의 기억은 세상을 객관적으로 표현하기에 부족하다'이다.

| 선택지 분석 |

① 기억의 추상적인 측면이 언급되었을 뿐, 추상적인 아이디어를 설명할 때 관련 이미지가 필요하다는 내용과는 무관하다.

② 정보를 상기하는 시간은 언급되지 않았다.

③ 과거 경험을 통해 세상을 바라본다고 했을 뿐, 경험을 통한 신념 형성은 언급되지 않았다.

④ 기억은 우리가 눈으로 본 것을 추상적으로 재구성한 것이므로 세상을 객관적으로 표현하기에 부족하다.

⑤ 추상적인 재현과 객관적인 사실 사이의 법적 우위성이 언급되었을 뿐, 시간적 순서에 관한 내용이 아니다.

구문 서술형

정답 형용사적, (a more efficient) way

해석 재구성은 정보를 저장하기 위한 더 효율적인 방법이다.

→ to store가 앞에 나온 명사 (a more efficient) way를 수식하는 형용사적 쓰임으로 쓰였다.

D 06 정답 ① *동물의 수많은 감각

Consider / the seemingly simple question / *How many senses are there?* //
고려해 봐라 / 겉으로 보기에 단순한 질문을 / '얼마나 많은 감각이 존재하는가'라는 //
└ 목적어절을 이끄는 접속사 ┘
Around 2,370 years ago, / Aristotle wrote / that there are five,
└ both A and B: A와 B 둘 다 ┘
/ in both humans and animals — / sight, hearing, smell, taste, and touch. // 단서1 Aristotle은 인간과 동물에게 다섯(감각)이 있다고 기술함
약 2,370년 전 / Aristotle은 썼다 / 다섯(감각)이 있다고 / 인간과 동물 둘 다에게 / 시각, 청각, 후각, 미각, 그리고 촉각 //
However, / according to the philosopher Fiona Macpherson, /
└ '~에 따르면' ┘
there are reasons to doubt it. //
└ 형용사적 용법(reasons 수식) ┘
그러나 / 철학자 Fiona Macpherson에 따르면 / 그것을 의심할 이유가 존재한다 //
For a start, / Aristotle missed a few in humans: / the perception
┌ 병렬 구조 ┐
of your own body / which is different from touch / and the sense
└ 주격 관계대명사 ┘
of balance / which has links to both touch and vision. //
우선 / Aristotle은 인간에게서 몇 가지를 빠뜨렸는데 / 여러분 자신의 신체에 대한 인식과 / 촉각과는 다른 / 균형 감각 / 촉각과 시각 모두에 관련되어 있는 //
Other animals have senses / that are even harder to categorize. //
└ 복수 선행사(senses)와 수일치 ┘
다른 동물들은 감각을 가지고 있다 / 범주화하기 훨씬 더 어려운 // 단서2 다른 동물들은 범주화하기 훨씬 더 어려운 감각을 가짐
Many vertebrates have a different sense system / for detecting
└ 동명사구(전치사의 목적어) ┘
odors. //
많은 척추동물은 다른 감각 체계를 가지고 있다 / 냄새를 탐지하기 위한 //
Some snakes can detect / the body heat of their prey. //
어떤 뱀은 감지할 수 있다 / 그들의 먹잇감의 체열을 //
These examples tell us / that "senses cannot be clearly divided
└ 목적어절을 이끄는 접속사 ┘
into a limited number of specific kinds," / Macpherson wrote in
The Senses. // 단서3 감각은 특정한 종류로 명확하게 분류되지 않을 수 있음
이러한 사례는 우리에게 알려 준다 / '감각은 제한된 수의 특정한 종류로 명확하게 나누어지지 않을 수 있다'라는 것을 / Macpherson이 'The Senses'에서 쓰기를 //
Instead of trying to push animal senses / into Aristotelian
└ '~ 대신에' ┘
buckets, / we should study them / for what they are. //
동물의 감각을 밀어 넣는 대신 / Aristotle의 양동이로 / 우리는 그것들을 연구해야 한다 / 그것들이 존재하는 그대로 //

- seemingly ⓐ𝒹 겉보기에   - sense ⓝ 감각   - sight ⓝ 시각
- philosopher ⓝ 철학자   - doubt ⓥ 의심하다
- perception ⓝ 인식   - balance ⓝ 균형   - vision ⓝ 시각
- categorize ⓥ 분류하다   - detect ⓥ 감지하다   - prey ⓝ 먹잇감
- divide ⓥ 나누다   - specific ⓐ 특정한   - bucket ⓝ 양동이

'얼마나 많은 감각이 존재하는가?'라는 겉으로 보기에 단순한 질문을 고려해 봐라. 약 2,370년 전 Aristotle은 인간과 동물 둘 다에게 시각, 청각, 후각, 미각, 그리고 촉각의 다섯(감각)이 있다고 썼다. 그러나, 철학자 Fiona Macpherson에 따르면, 그것을 의심할 이유가 존재한다. 우선, Aristotle은 인간에게서 몇 가지를 빠뜨렸는데, 그것은 촉각과는 다른 여러분 자신의 신체에 대한 인식과, 촉각과 시각 모두에 관련되어 있는 균형 감각이었다. 다른 동물들은 훨씬 더 범주화하기 어려운 감각을 가지고 있다. 많은 척추동물은 냄새를 탐지하기 위한 다른 감각 체계를 가지고 있다. 어떤 뱀은 그들의 먹잇감의 체열을 감지할 수 있다. Macpherson이 'The Senses'에서 쓰기를, 이러한 사례는 우리에게 '감각은 제한된 수의 특정한 종류로 명확하게 나누어지지 않을 수 있다.'라는 것을 알려 준다. 동물의 감각을 Aristotle의 양동이로 밀어 넣는 대신, 우리는 그것들을 존재하는 그대로 연구해야 한다.

밑줄 친 push animal senses into Aristotelian buckets가 다음 글에서 의미하는 바로 가장 적절한 것은? [3점]

① sort various animal senses into fixed categories   Aristotle은 다양한 동물의 감각을 고정된 범주로 분류한다   동물의 감각을 다섯 가지로 분류했음
② keep a balanced view to understand real senses   균형 잡힌 견해를 실제 감각을 이해하기 위해 균형 잡힌 견해를 유지한다   유지하라는 내용은 언급되지 않음
③ doubt the traditional way of dividing all senses   모든 감각을 나누는 전통적인 방식에 의문을 제기한다   전통적인 방식으로 나눈다는 의미임
④ ignore the lessons on senses from Aristotle   제시되지 않음   Aristotle의 감각에 대한 가르침을 무시한다
⑤ analyze more animals to find real senses   실제 감각을 찾기 위해 더 많은 동물을 분석한다   동물의 감각을 기존의 고정된 범주로 분류하는 것에서 벗어나야 한다는 내용임

왜 정답 ? ✱✱✱ [정답률 64%]

┌ ・Aristotle은 인간과 동물에게 다섯 가지 감각이 있다고 기술했음 단서1
└ ・다른 동물들은 훨씬 더 범주화하기 어려운 감각을 가짐 단서2
➡ 감각은 특정한 종류로 명확하게 분류되지 않을 수 있음 단서3
▶ '동물의 감각을 Aristotle의 양동이로 밀어 넣는 것'은 '동물의 감각을 Aristotle이 정한 다섯 가지 감각의 범주로 분류하는 것'을 의미하므로 ① '다양한 동물의 감각을 고정된 범주로 분류한다'는 것을 의미한다.

왜 오답 ?

② 균형 잡힌 견해를 유지하라는 내용은 이 글에서 다루어지지 않았다.
③ 감각을 나누는 전통적인 방식에서 벗어나 다양하고 복잡한 감각을 있는 그대로 연구해야 한다는 글의 내용과 부합하나, 밑줄 친 부분은 감각을 전통적인 방식으로 나누는 것을 의미한다. 함정
④ Aristotle의 감각에 대한 가르침을 무시하라는 내용은 언급되지 않았다.
⑤ 동물의 감각이 범주화하기 어려울 만큼 훨씬 다양하고 복잡하다는 내용은 있지만, 더 많은 동물을 분석하라는 내용은 제시되지 않았다. 주의

D 07 정답 ⑤ *부정에서 벗어나기 위해 긍정과 어울리기

One valuable technique / for getting out of / helplessness,
└ 단수 주어 ┘
└ 주격 관계대명사 ┘
depression, / and situations which are predominantly being run
/ by the thought, "I can't," /
한 가지 유용한 기술은 / ~에서 벗어나기 위한 / 무력함, 우울감 / 그리고 현저히 지배당하는 상황 / '나는 할 수 없다'는 생각에 의해 / 단서1 우리가 처한 문제를 해결한 사람들과 함께 있으면 부정적인 감정과 상황에서 벗어날 수 있음
└ 단수 동사 ┘
is to choose to be with other persons / who have resolved the
└ 주격 관계대명사 ┘
problem / with which we struggle. //
└ 전치사 + 관계대명사 ┘
타인과 함께 있기로 선택하는 것이다 / 문제를 해결해 본 / 우리가 분투하고 있는 //
This is one of the great powers of self-help groups. //
이것은 자조 집단의 큰 힘 중 하나이다 //
└ 부사절 접속사(시간) ┘
When we are in a negative state, / we have given a lot of energy
└ 현재완료(계속) ┘
/ to negative thought forms, / and the positive thought forms
are weak. //
우리가 부정적인 상태에 있을 때 / 우리는 많은 에너지를 투입해 왔고 / 부정적인 사고 형태에 / 긍정적인 사고 형태는 약하다 //
└ '긍정적인 기운을 내는' ┘
Those who are in a higher vibration / are free of the energy from
their negative thoughts / and have energized positive thought
forms. //
더 높은 진동에 있는(긍정적인 기운을 내는) 사람들은 / 그들의 부정적인 사고에서 나오는 에너지가 없고 / 긍정적인 사고 형태를 활기 띠게 했다 //
└ 명사적 용법(주어) = those who are in a higher vibration ┘
Merely / to be in their presence / is beneficial. //
단지 / 그들이 있는 자리에 있기만 하는 것도 / 유익하다 // 단서2 더 높은 진동에 있는 사람들과 함께 있기만 해도 도움이 됨
In some self-help groups, / this is called "hanging out with the
winners." //
일부 자조 집단에서 / 이것은 '승자들과 어울리기'라고 불린다 //
The benefit here / is on the psychic level of consciousness, / and
┌ 병렬 구조 ┐
there is a transfer of positive energy / and relighting of one's
own latent positive thought forms. //
여기에서의 이점은 / 의식의 정신적 수준에 있으며 / 긍정적인 에너지의 전달과 / 자신의 잠재적인 긍정적인 사고 형태의 재점화가 있다 //

- technique ⓝ 기술　　· helplessness ⓝ 무력감
- depression ⓝ 우울감　　· predominantly ⓐ 현저히
- resolve ⓥ 해결하다　　· self-help ⓝ 자조, 자립
- energize ⓥ 활기를 북돋우다
- be in one's presence ~의 자리에 (함께) 있다　　· psychic ⓐ 정신의
- transfer ⓝ 이동　　· relight ⓥ 재점화하다

무력함, 우울감, 그리고 '나는 할 수 없다'는 생각에 의해 현저히 지배당하는 상황에서 벗어나기 위한 한 가지 유용한 기술은 우리가 분투하고 있는 문제를 해결해 본 타인과 함께 있기로 선택하는 것이다. 이것은 자조 집단의 큰 힘 중 하나이다. 우리가 부정적인 상태에 있을 때, 우리는 부정적인 사고 형태에 많은 에너지를 투입해 왔고 긍정적인 사고 형태는 약하다. 더 높은 진동에 있는 사람들은 그들의 부정적인 사고에서 나오는 에너지가 없고, 긍정적인 사고 형태를 활기 띠게 했다. 단지 그들이 있는 자리에 있기만 하는 것도 유익하다. 일부 자조 집단에서 이것은 '승자들과 어울리기'라고 불린다. 여기에서의 이점은 의식의 정신적 수준에 있으며, 긍정적인 에너지의 전달과 자신의 잠재적인 긍정적인 사고 형태의 재점화가 있다.

> 밑줄 친 "hanging out with the winners"가 다음 글에서 의미하는 바로 가장 적절한 것은?
> ① staying with those who sacrifice themselves for others
> 타인을 위해 자신을 희생하는 사람들과 함께하기　타인을 위해 희생한다는 언급은 없음
> ② learning from people who have succeeded in competition
> 경쟁에서 성공한 사람들로부터 배우기　경쟁에서 성공한 사람들에 관한 내용이 아님
> ③ keeping relationships with people in a higher social position
> 높은 사회적 지위에 있는 사람들과 관계를 유지하라는 내용이 아님
> 높은 사회적 지위에 있는 사람들과 관계 유지하기
> ④ spending time with those who need social skill development
> 사회적 기술 발달이 필요한 사람들에 대한 언급은 없음
> 사회적 기술 발달이 필요한 사람들과 시간 보내기
> ⑤ being with positive people who have overcome negative states　One valuable technique ~ with which we struggle.
> 부정적인 상태를 극복한 긍정적인 사람들과 함께하기

왜 정답? ✽✽✽ [정답률 80%]

- 우리가 분투하고 있는 문제를 해결해 본 타인과 함께 있기로 선택하는 것은 부정적인 감정과 상황에서 벗어나는 유용한 방법임 [단서 1]
- 더 높은 진동에 있는 사람들과 함께하기만 해도 유익함 [단서 2]

➡ 부정적 감정과 상황에서 벗어나기 위해 우리가 처한 부정적 상황을 이미 해결한 사람과 함께 있는 것은 유용하고 유익한 방법이다.

▶ '승자'는 '어려움을 이미 극복한 긍정적인 사람'을 의미하고, '어울리는 것'은 그러한 사람들과 '함께 하는 것'을 의미하므로 '승자들과 함께하는 것'은 ⑤ '부정적인 상태를 극복한 긍정적인 사람들과 함께하기'를 의미한다.

왜 오답?

① 타인을 위해 자신을 희생하는 사람들은 언급되지 않았다.
② 부정적 상황을 해결한 사람과 어울려야 한다는 것이지, 경쟁에서 이긴 사람들로부터 배우라는 내용이 아니다.
③ 높은 사회적 지위에 있는 사람들과 관계를 유지하는 것은 언급되지 않았다.
④ 사회적 기술 발달이 필요한 사람들은 언급되지 않았다.

> 🍯꿀팁　a higher vibration은 높은 사회적 지위가 아니라 더 높은 진동에 있는(긍정적인 기운을 내는) 것을 의미함

자이 쌤's Follow Me! – 홈페이지에서 제공

D 08 정답 ⑤ *구직 활동을 할 때는 진취적으로 행동해라.

A job search / is not a passive task. // 구직 활동은 / 수동적인 일이 아니다 //
　　　　　　　　　　　　　부정어(nor)로 인한 도치
When you are searching, / you are not browsing, / nor are you "just looking". //
구직 활동을 할 때 / 여러분은 이것저것 훑어보고 다니지 않으며 / '그냥 구경만 하지'도 않는다 //
　　　　　　　　　　　　　　앞에 목적격 관계대명사 생략
Browsing is not an effective way / to reach a goal / you claim to want to reach. //
훑어보고 다니는 것은 효과적인 방법이 아니다 / 목표에 도달할 수 있는 / 여러분이 도달하기를 원한다고 주장하는 //

단서 1 구직 활동을 할 때는 직접적이고 집중해야 하며 영리해야 함
If you are acting with purpose, / if you are serious about anything / you chose to do, / then you need to be direct, focused
　　　　　　　　　　　　　　　　　　　병렬 구조
/ and whenever possible, / clever. //
만약 여러분이 목적을 가지고 행동한다면 / 만약 어떤 것에 대해 여러분이 진지하다면 / 하고자 선택한 것은 / 여러분은 직접적이고 / 집중해야 한다 / 그리고 가능한 한 / 영리해야 한다 //
　　　　　　Everyone else를 꾸며주는 현재분사구　　분사구문
Everyone else searching for a job / has the same goal, / competing for the same jobs. //
일자리를 찾는 다른 모든 사람이 / 같은 목표를 지니고 있으며 / 같은 일자리를 얻기 위해 경쟁한다 //
　　　　　　단서 2 구직 활동을 할 때는 다른 사람들보다 더 많은 것을 해야 함
You must do more / than the rest of the herd. //
여러분은 더 많은 것을 해야 한다 / 그 무리의 나머지 사람들보다 //
Regardless of how long it may take you / to find and get the job / you want, /
얼마나 오랜 시간이 걸리든 간에 / 직업을 찾아서 얻는 데 / 여러분이 원하는 /
　　　　　　　　　　　　　　　　　　　병렬 구조
being proactive will logically get you results faster / than if you rely only on / browsing online job boards / and emailing an occasional resume. // 단서 3 진취적인 것이 구직 활동 결과를 더 빠르게 얻도록 해줄 것임
진취적인 것이 논리적으로 여러분이 더 빨리 결과를 얻도록 해줄 것이다 / 의존하는 것보다는 / 온라인 취업 게시판을 검색하는 것에만 / 그리고 가끔 이력서를 이메일로 보내는 것 (에만) //
Leave those activities / to the rest of the sheep. //
그런 활동들은 남겨 두라 / 나머지 양들이 하도록 //

- passive ⓐ 수동적인　　· browse ⓥ 훑어보다
- effective ⓐ 효과적인　　· claim ⓥ 주장하다, 공언하다
- direct ⓐ 직접적인　　· focused ⓐ 집중하는　　· rest ⓝ 나머지
- herd ⓝ 무리　　· proactive ⓐ 진취적인　　· logically ⓐ 논리적으로
- occasional ⓐ 가끔의　　· resume ⓝ 이력서
- sheep ⓝ 양, 어리석은 사람　　· job-seeker ⓝ 구직자
- competition ⓝ 경쟁　　· employer ⓝ 고용주　　· stand out 돋보이다

구직 활동은 수동적인 일이 아니다. 구직 활동을 할 때, 여러분은 이것저것 훑어보고 다니지 않으며 '그냥 구경만 하지'도 않는다. 훑어보고 다니는 것은 여러분이 도달하기를 원한다고 주장하는 목표에 도달할 수 있는 효과적인 방법이 아니다. 만약 여러분이 목적을 가지고 행동한다면, 만약 하고자 선택한 어떤 것에 대해 여러분이 진지하다면, 여러분은 직접적이고, 집중해야 하며, 가능한 한 영리해야 한다. 일자리를 찾는 다른 모든 사람이 같은 목표를 지니고 있으며, 같은 일자리를 얻기 위해 경쟁한다. 여러분은 그 무리의 나머지 사람들보다 더 많은 것을 해야 한다. 원하는 직업을 찾아서 얻는 데 얼마나 오랜 시간이 걸리든 간에, 온라인 취업 게시판을 검색하고 가끔 이력서를 이메일로 보내는 것에만 의존하는 것보다는 진취적인 것이 논리적으로 여러분이 더 빨리 결과를 얻도록 해줄 것이다. 그런 활동들은 나머지 양들이 하도록 남겨 두라.

> 밑줄 친 Leave those activities to the rest of the sheep이 다음 글에서 의미하는 바로 가장 적절한 것은? [3점]
> ① Try to understand other job-seekers' feelings.
> 다른 구직자들의 감정을 이해하려고 노력하라.　다른 구직자들의 감정을 이해하라는 내용이 아님
> ② Keep calm and stick to your present position.
> 침착함을 유지하고 현재 위치를 고수하라.　침착하게 현재 위치를 지키라는 것은 언급되지 않음
> ③ Don't be scared of the job-seeking competition.
> 구직 경쟁을 두려워하지 마라.　다른 모든 사람이 같은 일자리를 얻기 위해 경쟁한다는 언급만 했음
> ④ Send occasional emails to your future employers.　가끔 이력서를
> 미래의 고용주들에게 가끔 이메일을 보내라.　이메일로 보내는 것에만 의존하지 말라는 것으로 만든 오답
> ⑤ Be more active to stand out from other job-seekers.
> 다른 구직자들보다 돋보이도록 더 활동적으로 하라.
> 구직 활동을 할 때는 다른 구직자들보다 더 활동적이고 진취적으로 임하는 것이 필요하다는 내용

왜 정답? ✽✽✽ [정답률 62%]

구직 활동을 할 때는 수동적인 태도를 지양하고 진취적이고 활동적으로 다른 구직자들보다 더 많은 활동을 해야 한다는 내용의 글이다. 취업 게시판을 검색하고 가끔 이력서를 이메일로 보내는 수동적인 활동은 다른 사람들이 하도록 내버려두고 더 진취적인 일을 하라고 했으므로, 밑줄 친 부분의 의미로 가장 적절한 것은 ⑤ '다른 구직자들보다 돋보이도록 더 활동적으로 하라.'이다.

왜 오답 ?

① 다른 구직자의 감정을 이해하라는 내용이 아니라, 다른 구직자보다 진취적인 활동을 하라는 내용이다.
② 침착하게 현재 위치를 지키라는 내용은 언급되지 않았다.
③ 다른 모든 사람이 같은 일자리를 얻기 위해 경쟁한다는 언급만 했을 뿐, 구직 경쟁을 두려워하지 말라는 내용이 아니다. (함정)
④ 가끔 이력서를 이메일로 보내는 것에만 의존하지 말라는 것으로 만든 오답이다.

D 09 정답 ③ *선택적으로 해석하는 경향

We have a tendency / to interpret events selectively. //
— 형용사적 용법
우리는 경향이 있다 / 사건을 선택적으로 해석하는 // **단서1** 우리는 선택적으로 사건을 해석함 — 핵심문장

If we want things to be "this way" or "that way" / we can most certainly select, stack, or arrange evidence / in a way / that supports such a viewpoint. //
— 주격 관계대명사
만약 우리가 일이 "이렇게" 또는 "그렇게" 되기를 원한다면 / 우리는 틀림없이 증거를 선택하거나 쌓거나 배열할 수 있다 / 방식으로 / 그러한 관점을 뒷받침하는 //

Selective perception is based / on what seems to us to stand out. //
— 것
선택적인 지각은 기반을 둔다 / 우리에게 두드러져 보이는 것에 //

However, / what seems to us to be standing out / may very well be related / to our goals, interests, expectations, past experiences, / or current demands of the situation /
— 것
그러나 / 우리에게 두드러져 보이고 있는 것은 / 매우 관련 있을지도 모른다 / 우리의 목표, 관심사, 기대, 과거의 경험에 / 또는 상황에 대한 현재의 요구에 /

— "with a hammer in hand, / everything looks like a nail." //
— look like+명사: ~처럼 보이다
"망치를 손에 들고 있으면 / 모든 것은 못처럼 보인다." //

This quote / highlights the phenomenon of selective perception. //
이 인용문은 / 선택적 지각의 현상을 강조한다 // **단서2** 우리는 우리의 목표, 관심사, 기대 등을 특별하다고 여기는데, 이런 인간의 성향을 망치와 못으로 비유함

If we want to use a hammer, / then the world around us / may begin to look / as though it is full of nails! //
— 접속사(마치 ~처럼)
만약 우리가 망치를 사용하기를 원하면 / 우리 주변의 세상은 / 보이기 시작할지도 모른다 / 못으로 가득 찬 것처럼 //

- tendency ⓝ 경향 • interpret ⓥ 해석하다
- selectively ⓐⓓ 선택적으로 • stack ⓥ 쌓다 • viewpoint ⓝ 관점
- perception ⓝ 지각, 인식 • stand out 두드러지다, 눈에 띄다
- be related to ~와 관련이 있다 • interest ⓝ 관심, 관심사
- expectation ⓝ 기대 • demand ⓝ 요구 • hammer ⓝ 망치
- nail ⓝ 못 • quote ⓝ 인용문 • highlight ⓥ 강조하다
- phenomenon ⓝ 현상

우리는 사건을 선택적으로 해석하는 경향이 있다. 만약 우리가 일이 "이렇게" 또는 "그렇게" 되기를 원한다면, 우리는 틀림없이 그러한 관점을 뒷받침하는 방식으로 증거를 선택하거나 쌓거나 배열할 수 있다. 선택적인 지각은 우리에게 두드러져 보이는 것에 기반을 둔다. 그러나 우리에게 두드러져 보이고 있는 것은 우리의 목표, 관심사, 기대, 과거의 경험 또는 상황에 대한 현재의 요구와 매우 관련 있을지도 모른다 — "망치를 손에 들고 있으면, 모든 것은 못처럼 보인다." 이 인용문은 선택적 지각의 현상을 강조한다. 만약 우리가 망치를 사용하기를 원하면, 우리 주변의 세상은 못으로 가득 찬 것처럼 보이기 시작할지도 모른다!

밑줄 친 want to use a hammer가 다음 글에서 의미하는 바로 가장 적절한 것은? [3점]

① are unwilling to stand out 반복해서 나오는 stand out을 이용해 만든 오답
눈에 띄는 것을 꺼리다
② make our effort meaningless
우리의 노력을 무의미하게 만들다 우리가 하는 노력을 무의미하게 만든다는 내용은 언급되지 않음
③ intend to do something in a certain way
특정한 방식으로 무언가를 하려고 의도하다
④ hope others have a viewpoint similar to ours 자신과 비슷한 견해를
다른 사람들이 우리와 비슷한 견해를 가지기를 희망하다 가지기를 원한다는 내용이 아님
⑤ have a way of thinking that is accepted by others 다른 사람들이
다른 사람들에 의해 수용되는 사고방식을 가지다 인정하는 사고방식에 관한 내용은 없음
— 인간은 사건을 선택적으로 해석하고, 망치를 들고 있으면 모든 것이 못으로 보인다고 했음

왜 정답 ? ★★★ [정답률 53%]

망치를 들고 있는 인간에 비유해서, 특정한 의도나 생각에 맞춰서 세상을 바라보는 인간의 성향을 설명하는 글이다. 망치를 들고 있는 인간은 모든 것을 못으로 간주하거나 세상을 못으로 가득 차 있다고 인식한다고 했다. 즉, 우리는 우리의 목표, 관심사, 기대 등을 특별하다고 여긴다는 것이다. 따라서 밑줄 친 부분은 ③ '특정한 방식으로 무언가를 하려고 의도하다'를 의미한다.

왜 오답 ?

① 글에서 반복되는 stand out을 이용하여 만든 오답이다.
② 우리가 하는 노력을 무의미하게 만든다는 내용은 언급되지 않았다.
④ 사람들이 자신과 비슷한 견해를 가지기를 원한다는 내용의 글이 아니다.
⑤ 다른 사람들이 인정하는 사고방식에 관한 내용은 나오지 않았다.

D 10 정답 ① *고객 만족도 관리가 중요한 이유

Why do you care / how a customer reacts / to a purchase? //
— 간접의문문
당신은 왜 신경 쓰는가 / 고객이 어떻게 반응하는지를 / 구매품에 대해 //

Good question. //
좋은 질문이다 //
— by v-ing: ~함으로써
By understanding post-purchase behavior, / you can understand the influence and the likelihood /
구매 후 행동을 이해함으로써 / 당신은 그 영향력과 가능성을 이해할 수 있다 /

of whether a buyer will repurchase the product / (and whether she will keep it or return it). //
구매자가 제품을 재구매할지 / (그리고 그녀가 제품을 가질지 또는 반품할지) //

You'll also determine / whether the buyer will encourage others / to purchase the product from you. //
— 명사절 접속사
당신은 또한 알아낼 것이다 / 구매자가 다른 사람들에게 권장할지 / 당신으로부터 제품을 구매하도록 // **단서1** 구매 후 행동을 통해 구매자가 다른 사람에게 제품을 추천할지 여부를 파악할 수 있음

Satisfied customers can become unpaid ambassadors / for your business, / so customer satisfaction should be on the top / of your to-do list. //
만족한 고객은 무급 대사가 될 수 있다 / 당신의 사업을 위한 / 따라서 고객 만족이 최상단에 있어야 한다 / 당신의 할 일 목록의 //

People tend to believe / the opinions of people / they know. //
— 앞에 목적격 관계대명사가 생략됨
사람들은 믿는 경향이 있다 / 사람들의 의견을 / 그들이 아는 //

People trust friends / over advertisements / any day. //
사람들은 친구를 신뢰한다 / 광고보다 / 언제든 // **단서2** 사람들은 광고보다 친구를 신뢰함

They know / that advertisements are paid / to tell the "good side" / and that they're used / to persuade them / to purchase products and services. //
— 목적어절 접속사의 병렬 구조   — 부사적 용법(목적)
그들은 알고 있다 / 광고에는 돈이 쓰인다는 것을 / '좋은 면'을 말하기 위해 / 그리고 그것들이 사용된다는 것을 / 그들을 설득하기 위해 / 제품과 서비스를 구매하도록 //

By continually monitoring / your customer's satisfaction after the sale, / you have the ability / to avoid negative word-of-mouth advertising. //
— 형용사적 용법(ability 수식)
지속적으로 추적 관찰함으로써 / 판매 후 당신의 고객의 만족을 / 당신은 능력을 가진다 / 부정적인 입소문 광고를 피할 //

- react ⓥ 반응하다 • behavior ⓝ 행동 • influence ⓝ 영향
- likelihood ⓝ 가능성 • repurchase ⓥ 재구매하다
- determine ⓥ 알아내다 • encourage ⓥ 권장하다
- satisfied ⓐ 만족한 • ambassador ⓝ 대사
- persuade ⓥ 설득하다 • monitor ⓥ 추적 관찰하다
- word-of-mouth ⓐ 구두의, 구전의

당신은 왜 고객이 구매품에 어떻게 반응하는지를 신경 쓰는가? 좋은 질문이다. 구매 후 행동을 이해함으로써, 당신은 그 영향력과 구매자가 제품을 재구매할지 (그리고 그녀가 제품을 가질지 또는 반품할지)의 가능성을 이해할 수 있다.

당신은 구매자가 다른 사람들에게 당신으로부터 제품을 구매하도록 권장할지 여부 또한 알아낼 것이다. 만족한 고객은 당신의 사업을 위한 무급 대사가 될 수 있으므로, 고객 만족이 당신의 할 일 목록의 최상단에 있어야 한다. 사람들은 그들이 아는 사람들의 의견을 믿는 경향이 있다. 사람들은 언제든 광고보다 친구를 더 신뢰한다. 그들은 광고에는 '좋은 면'을 말하기 위해 돈이 쓰인다는 것과 그것들이 제품과 서비스를 구매하도록 그들을 설득하는 데 사용된다는 것을 알고 있다. 판매 후 고객의 만족을 지속적으로 추적 관찰함으로써, 당신은 부정적인 입소문 광고를 피할 능력을 가진다.

밑줄 친 become unpaid ambassadors가 다음 글에서 의미하는 바로 가장 적절한 것은?

① recommend products to others for no gain
대가 없이 다른 사람에게 제품을 추천하다 — 만족한 고객은 다른 사람에게 제품을 추천함
② offer manufacturers feedback on products
제조업체에 제품에 대한 피드백을 제공하다 — 제조업체에 직접 피드백을 제공하는 것이 아님
③ become people who don't trust others' words
다른 사람의 말을 믿지 않는 사람이 되다 — 다른 구매자의 말을 믿지 않는다는 것이 아님
④ get rewards for advertising products overseas
해외에서 제품 광고에 대한 보상을 받다 — '무급'이라고 했으므로 보상을 받는 것이 아님
⑤ buy products without worrying about the price
가격 걱정 없이 제품을 구매하다 — 가격에 구애받지 않는다는 내용은 언급되지 않음

왜 정답? ✽✽✽ [정답률 62%]

- 고객의 구매품에 대한 반응을 살펴야 함 → 고객이 다른 사람에게 제품 구매를 권장할지를 파악할 수 있음 **단서 1**
- 사람들은 돈이 쓰인 광고보다 친구를 신뢰함 **단서 2**

→ 구매품에 만족한 고객은 다른 사람에게 제품을 추천할 것이고, 사람들은 광고보다 친구의 추천을 더 신뢰한다.

▶ '무급'은 '돈이 쓰이지 않은 친구의 말'을 의미하고, '대사'는 '제품 구매를 권장하는 사람'을 의미하므로 '무급 대사가 된다는' 것은 ① '대가 없이 다른 사람에게 제품을 추천하다'를 의미한다.

왜 오답?

② 구매자가 제조업체에 직접 피드백을 제공한다는 내용은 언급되지 않았다.
③ 만족한 고객은 말을 전하는 사람이므로 다른 사람의 말을 믿지 않는다는 것은 어색하다. **주의**
④ '무급'이라고 했으므로 보상을 받는다는 것은 적절하지 않으며, 해외와 관련된 내용은 언급되지 않았다.
⑤ 만족한 고객은 가격에 구애받지 않는다는 내용은 없다.

D 11 정답 ③ *중요한 것은 힘들게 얻는다는 잘못된 생각

Our language helps / to reveal our deeper assumptions. //
우리의 언어는 돕는다 / 우리의 더 깊은 전제를 드러내는 것을 //

Think of these revealing phrases: / When we accomplish something important, / we say / it took "blood, sweat, and tears." //
(뒤에 목적어절 접속사 that이 생략됨)
이것을 잘 드러내는 다음과 같은 문구들을 생각해 보라 / 우리가 중요한 무언가를 성취할 때 / 우리는 말한다 / 그것이 '피, 땀, 그리고 눈물'을 필요로 했다고 //

(뒤에 목적어절 접속사 that이 생략됨)
We say / important achievements are "hard-earned." //
우리는 말한다 / 중요한 성과는 '힘들게 얻은' 것이라고 // **단서 1** 우리는 중요한 성과는 힘들게 얻어진다고 말함

We recommend a "hard day's work" / when "day's work" would be enough. //
우리는 '힘든 하루 동안의 일'이라는 말을 권한다 / '하루 동안의 일'이라는 말로도 충분할 때 //

(부사절 접속사)   (뒤에 목적어절 접속사 that이 생략됨)
When we talk of "easy money," / we are implying / it was obtained / through illegal or questionable means. //
우리가 '쉬운 돈'이라는 말을 할 때 / 우리는 넌지시 드러내고 있다 / 그것이 얻어졌다는 것을 / 불법적이거나 의심스러운 수단을 통해 //

We use the phrase "That's easy for you to say" / as a criticism, / usually when we are seeking to invalidate / someone's opinion. //
우리는 '말은 쉽지'라는 문구를 사용한다 / 비판으로 / 우리가 보통 틀렸음을 입증하려고 할 때 / 누군가의 의견이 //

목적어절 접속사
It's like we all automatically accept / that the "right" way is, inevitably, the harder one. // **단서 2** 우리는 올바른 방법은 어려운 방법이라고 믿고 있음
이는 마치 우리가 모두 자동적으로 받아들이는 것과 같다 / '올바른' 방법은 반드시 더 어려운 방법이라는 것을 //

In my experience / this is hardly ever questioned. //
나의 경험상 / 이것은 거의 한 번도 의문이 제기되지 않는다 //

강조 용법의 do 동사
What would happen / if you do challenge this sacred cow? //
무슨 일이 일어날까 / 만약 여러분이 정말로 이 신성한 소에 맞선다면 //

-thing으로 끝나는 대명사는 형용사가 뒤에서 수식함
We don't even pause to consider / that something important and valuable / could be made easy. //
우리는 잠시 멈춰 생각해 보지도 않는다 / 중요하고 가치 있는 무언가가 / 쉬운 것으로 만들어질 수 있다고 //

현재분사구(thing 수식)
What if / the biggest thing / keeping us from doing what matters / is the false assumption / that it has to take huge effort? //
동격절 접속사
만약 ~라면 어떨까 / 가장 큰 것이 / 우리가 중요한 일을 하지 못하게 하는 / 잘못된 전제라면 / 그것은 엄청난 노력을 필요로 한다는 //

- reveal ⓥ 드러내다
- assumption ⓝ 추정, 전제
- accomplish ⓥ 성취하다
- achievement ⓝ 성취, 성과
- imply ⓥ 암시하다, 넌지시 나타내다
- obtain ⓥ 얻다
- illegal ⓐ 불법적인
- questionable ⓐ 의심스러운
- means ⓝ 수단
- criticism ⓝ 비판, 비평
- automatically ⓐⓓ 자동으로, 무의식적으로
- inevitably ⓐⓓ 반드시, 불가피하게
- challenge ⓥ 도전하다, 의문을 제기하다
- sacred ⓐ 신성한
- pause ⓥ 잠시 멈추다
- valuable ⓐ 가치 있는
- matter ⓥ 중요하다
- false ⓐ 잘못된
- tendency ⓝ 경향
- hardship ⓝ 고난
- solid ⓐ 확고한
- abandon ⓥ 버리다
- notion ⓝ 개념, 생각
- superstition ⓝ 미신

우리의 언어는 우리의 더 깊은 전제를 드러내는 것을 돕는다. 이것을 잘 드러내는 다음과 같은 문구들을 생각해 보라. 우리가 중요한 무언가를 성취할 때, 우리는 그것이 '피, 땀, 그리고 눈물'을 필요로 했다고 말한다. 우리는 중요한 성과는 '힘들게 얻은' 것이라고 말한다. 우리는 '하루 동안의 일'이라는 말로도 충분할 때 '힘든 하루 동안의 일'이라는 말을 권한다. 우리가 '쉬운 돈'이라는 말을 할 때, 우리는 그것이 불법적이거나 의심스러운 수단을 통해 얻어졌다는 것을 넌지시 드러내고 있다. 우리는 보통 누군가의 의견이 틀렸음을 입증하려고 할 때, '말은 쉽지'라는 문구를 비판으로 사용한다. 이는 마치 우리가 모두 '올바른' 방법은 반드시 더 어려운 방법이라는 것을 자동적으로 받아들이는 것과 같다. 나의 경험상 이것은 거의 한 번도 의문이 제기되지 않는다. 만약 여러분이 정말로 이 신성한 소에 맞선다면 무슨 일이 일어날까? 우리는 중요하고 가치 있는 무언가를 쉬운 것으로 만들 수 있다고 잠시 멈춰 생각해 보지도 않는다. 만약 우리가 중요한 일을 하지 못하게 하는 가장 큰 것이 중요한 일은 엄청난 노력을 필요로 한다는 잘못된 전제라면 어떨까?

밑줄 친 challenge this sacred cow가 다음 글에서 의미하는 바로 가장 적절한 것은? [3점]
this sacred cow는 '중요한 성취를 하려면 노력해야 한다(힘들게 일해야 한다)'는 것을 의미함

① resist the tendency to avoid any hardship
어떤 고난도 피하려는 경향에 저항하다 — 의미하는 바와 반대되는 내용임
② escape from the pressure of using formal language
격식 있는 언어 사용에 대한 압박에서 벗어나다 — 격식 있는 언어는 언급되지 않음
③ doubt the solid belief that only hard work is worthy
노력(힘든 일)만이 가치 있다는 확고한 믿음을 의심하다
④ abandon the old notion that money always comes first
돈이 항상 우선이라는 오래된 생각을 버리다 — 돈이 우선이라는 언급은 없음
⑤ break the superstition that holy animals bring good luck
신성한 동물들이 행운을 가져다준다는 미신을 깨다 — 글에 나온 sacred cow를 이용한 오답으로 동물과 관련된 내용이 아님

> **왜 정답?** ★★★ [정답률 54%]

- 우리는 중요한 무언가를 성취할 때, 그것이 '피, 땀, 그리고 눈물'을 필요로 했다고 말하고, 중요한 성과는 힘들게 얻어진다고 말함 **단서1**
- 우리는 올바른 방법은 어려운 방법이라고 믿으며 이것에 의문을 제기하지 않음 **단서2**
→ 중요한 성과는 힘들게 얻어지며, 올바른 방법은 어려운 방법이라고 믿는 것 = this sacred cow
  ▶ '이 신성한 소(this sacred cow)에 맞서는' 것은 ③ '노력(힘든 일)만이 가치가 있다는 확고한 믿음을 의심하다'를 의미한다.

> **왜 오답?**

① '어떤 고난도 피하려는 경향'이 아니라 '노력해야만 중요한 성취를 이룬다는 생각'이므로 의미하는 바와 반대되는 내용이다.
② 격식 있는 언어에 대한 언급은 없으므로 정답이 될 수 없다.
④ 돈을 가장 중시한다는 내용은 나오지 않았다.
⑤ sacred cow를 이용해서 만든 오답으로, 동물에 관한 내용이 아니다.

D 12 정답 ⑤ ＊감지되어야만 쓸모가 있는 신호들

Most people have no doubt(틀림없이) heard / this question: / If a tree falls
결과 절을 연결하는 등위접속사 ┘   목적격 보어(원형부정사)
in the forest / and there is no one there / to hear it fall, / does it
make a sound? //
대부분의 사람들은 틀림없이 들어봤을 것이다 / 이 질문을 / 만약 숲에서 나무가 쓰러진다면 / 그리고 거기에 아무도 없다면 / 그것이 쓰러지는 것을 들을 / 그것은 소리를 내는 것일까 //

The correct answer is no. // **단서1** 듣는 사람이 없는 숲에서 쓰러지는 나무는 소리를 내지 않음
정답은 '아니요'이다 //

Sound is more than pressure waves, / and indeed there can be
no sound / without a hearer. // **단서2** 듣는 사람이 없다면 소리는 있을 수 없음
소리는 압력파 이상이고 / 정말로 소리는 있을 수 없다 / 듣는 사람 없이는 //

And similarly, / scientific communication is a two-way process. //
그리고 마찬가지로 / 과학적 의사소통은 양방향 과정이다 //

단서3 마찬가지로 출판된 과학 논문도 독자에 의해 이해되지 않으면 쓸모가 없음
Just as a signal of any kind is useless / unless it is perceived, /
                                          └부사절 접속사(조건)
a published scientific paper (signal) is useless / unless it is both
received *and* understood / by its intended audience. //
어떠한 종류의 신호든 쓸모가 없는 것처럼 / 그것이 감지되지 않으면 / 출판된 과학 논문(신호)도 쓸모가 없다 / 수신되거나 '그리고' 이해되지 않으면 / 의도된 독자에 의해 //

Thus we can restate / the axiom of science / as follows: / A
scientific experiment is not complete / until the results have
                                                현재완료 수동태
been published *and understood*. //
따라서 우리는 재진술할 수 있다 / 과학의 자명한 이치를 / 다음과 같이 / 과학 실험은 완성되지 않는다 / 결과가 출판되고 '그리고 이해될' 때까지 //

'~에 지나지 않는'
Publication is no more than pressure waves / unless the
published paper is understood. //
출판은 압력파에 지나지 않는다 / 출판된 논문이 이해되지 않으면 //

Too many scientific papers / fall silently in the woods. //
너무 많은 과학 논문이 / 소리 없이 숲속에서 쓰러진다 //

- indeed @ 정말로 · hearer ⓝ 듣는 사람 · process ⓝ 과정
- signal ⓝ 신호 · useless @ 쓸모없는 · perceive ⓥ 감지하다
- receive ⓥ 수신하다, 받다 · intended @ 의도된
- audience ⓝ 관객, 독자 · restate ⓥ 다시 말하다
- experiment ⓝ 실험 · publication ⓝ 출판
- previous @ 이전의 · demand ⓝ 요구

대부분의 사람들은 틀림없이 이 질문을 들어봤을 것이다. 만약 숲에서 나무가 쓰러지고 그것이 쓰러지는 것을 들을 사람이 아무도 없다면, 그것은 소리를 내는 것일까? 정답은 '아니요'이다. 소리는 압력파 이상이며, 정말로 듣는 사람 없이는 소리가 있을 수 없다. 그리고 마찬가지로, 과학적 의사소통은 양방향 과정이다. 어떠한 종류의 신호든 그것이 감지되지 않으면 쓸모가 없는 것처럼, 출판된 과학 논문(신호)도 그것이 의도된 독자에 의해 수신되거나 '그리고' 이해되지 않으면 쓸모가 없다. 따라서 우리는 과학의 자명한 이치를 다음과 같이 재진술할 수 있다. 과학 실험은 결과가 출판되고 '그리고 이해될' 때까지 완성되지 않는다. 출판된 논문이 이해되지 않으면 출판은 압력파에 지나지 않는다. 너무 많은 과학 논문이 소리 없이 숲속에서 쓰러진다.

밑줄 친 fall silently in the woods가 다음 글에서 의미하는 바로 가장 적절한 것은? [3점]

① fail to include the previous study 이전 연구를 포함하는지는 언급되지 않음
  이전 연구를 포함하지 못하다
② end up being considered completely false 맞고 틀림을 판단하는 것이 아님
  결국 완전히 잘못된 것으로 간주되다
③ become useless because they are not published
  그것들이 출판되지 않기 때문에 쓸모없어진다 출판되지 않아서 쓸모없는 것이 아님
④ focus on communication to meet public demands
  대중의 요구를 충족하기 위해 소통에 집중한다 communication이 언급된 것으로 만든 오답
⑤ are published yet readers don't understand them
  출판되었으나 독자들이 그것들을 이해하지 못한다 독자가 이해하지 못하면 쓸모없어짐

> **왜 정답?** ★★★ [정답률 50%]

- 아무도 없는 숲에서 나무는 소리 없이 쓰러짐 **단서1**
- 듣는 사람이 없다면 소리도 없음 **단서2**
→ 나무와 마찬가지로 출판된 과학 논문도 그것을 읽고 이해할 사람이 없다면 쓸모없는 것임 **단서3**
  ▶ '소리 없이 숲속에서 쓰러진다'는 것은 '듣는 사람이 없어 쓸모없어진다는 것'을 의미하므로 ⑤ '출판되었으나 독자들이 그것들을 이해하지 못한다'는 것을 의미한다.

> **왜 오답?**

① 이전 연구를 포함한다는 언급은 없었다.
② 쓸모가 없어진다는 것이지 논문이 과학적으로 맞거나 틀리는지를 판단하는 것이 아니다.
③ 출판되지 않아서 쓸모없어지는 것이 아니라, 출판된 후에 이해하는 사람이 없을 때 쓸모없어지는 것이다. **주의**
④ communication이 언급된 것으로 만든 오답으로, 대중과 소통해야 한다는 내용이 아니다.

자이 쌤's Follow Me! – 홈페이지에서 제공

D 13 정답 ⑤ ＊더러운 것은 상대적인 것이다.

Nothing is trash / by nature. // 어떤 것도 쓰레기인 것은 없다 / 본래부터 //
Anthropologist Mary Douglas brings back and analyzes / the
common saying / that dirt is "matter out of place." //
                동격의 that
인류학자 Mary Douglas는 소환하여 해석한다 / 흔히 하는 말을 / 더러운 것은 "제자리에 놓여있지 않은 물체"라는 //

Dirt is relative, / she emphasizes. // **단서1** 더러운 것은 상대적인 것이라고 했음
더러운 것은 상대적인 것이다 / 라고 그녀는 강조한다 //

가주어   진주어
"Shoes are not dirty in themselves, / but it is dirty / to place
them on the dining-table; / food is not dirty / in itself, / but it is
                                                            가주어
dirty / to leave pots and pans in the bedroom, / or food all over
       진주어
clothing; / "신발은 그 자체로는 더럽지 않다 / 하지만 그것은 더럽다 / 식탁 위에 놓여 있을 때 / 음식은 더럽지 않다 / 그 자체로는 / 하지만 더럽다 / 침실에 냄비와 팬을 놓아둔다면 / 혹은 음식이 옷에 다 묻어 있을 때 /

similarly, / bathroom items in the living room; / clothing lying
on chairs; / outdoor things placed indoors; / upstairs things
                          앞에 주격 관계대명사와 be동사 생략
downstairs, and so on." // **단서2** 더러움은 절대적인 기준이 있는 것이 아니라 상황에 맞지 않는 것이 더럽게 인식되는 예시들을 들어 설명함
유사하게 / 거실에 있는 욕실 용품 / 의자 위에 놓여 있는 옷 / 실내에 있는 실외 물품들 / 아래 층에 있는 위층 물건들 / 등등이 더러운 것이다" //

D

Sorting / the dirty from the clean / — removing the shoes from the table, / putting the dirty clothing in the washing machine / — **involves** systematic ordering and classifying. //

<small>핵심 주어(단수) / 단수 동사</small>

분류하는 것은 / 깨끗한 것과 더러운 것을 / — 식탁에서 신발을 치우는 것 / 세탁기에 더러운 옷을 넣는 것 / 체계적인 정리와 분류를 포함한다 //

Eliminating dirt is / thus / a positive process. //

<small>동명사구 주어 / 단수 동사</small>

더러운 것을 제거하는 것은 / 그러므로 / 긍정적인 과정이다 //

- trash ⓝ 쓰레기
- anthropologist ⓝ 인류학자
- bring back 소환하다
- analyze ⓥ 분석하다
- common ⓐ 흔한, 일반적인
- relative ⓐ 상대적인
- emphasize ⓥ 강조하다
- indoors ⓐ𝒹 실내에서
- systematic ⓐ 체계적인
- classify ⓥ 분류하다
- eliminate ⓥ 제거하다
- process ⓝ 과정

어떤 것도 본래부터 쓰레기인 것은 없다. 인류학자 Mary Douglas는 더러운 것은 "제자리에 놓여있지 않은 물체"라는 흔히 하는 말을 소환하여 해석한다. 더러운 것은 상대적인 것이라고 그녀는 강조한다. "신발은 그 자체로는 더럽지 않지만, 식탁 위에 놓여 있을 때 더러운 것이며, 음식은 그 자체로는 더럽지 않지만, 침실에 냄비와 팬을 놓아둔다면, 혹은 음식이 옷에 다묻어 있을 때, 유사하게, 거실에 있는 욕실 용품, 의자 위에 놓여 있는 옷, 실내에 있는 실외 물품들, 아래층에 있는 위층 물건들, 등등이 더러운 것이다." 깨끗한 것과 더러운 것을 분류하는 것 — 식탁에서 신발을 치우는 것, 세탁기에 더러운 옷을 넣는 것 — 은 체계적인 정리와 분류를 포함하는 것이다. 더러운 것을 제거하는 것은 그러므로 긍정적인 과정이다.

밑줄 친 "matter out of place"가 다음 글에서 의미하는 바로 가장 적절한 것은?

① something that is completely broken <small>부서진 물건에 대한 언급은 없음</small>
<small>완전히 부서진 물건</small>
② a tiny dust that nobody notices <small>단순히 더러움과 '먼지'를 연결시켜 만든 오답</small>
<small>아무도 알아차리지 못하는 작은 먼지</small>
③ a dirty but renewable material <small>재생 가능한 것에 대한 내용은 없음</small>
<small>더럽지만 재생 가능한 재료</small>
④ what can be easily replaced <small>대체 가능한 것은 주제와 상관없는 내용</small>
<small>쉽게, 대체될 수 있는 것</small>
⑤ a thing that is not in order <small>제자리에 있지 않아서 더러움을 유발하는 것이라고 했음</small>
<small>정돈되지 않은 것</small>

왜 정답? ★★★ [정답률 46%]

이 글은 인류학자 Mary Douglas가 더러운 것은 상대적인 것이라고 강조했다는 말로 시작했다. 이어지는 내용에서 식탁 위에 놓여 있는 신발, 침대 위에 놓여 있는 냄비와 팬 등을 예시로 들면서 상황에 맞지 않는 것이 더럽게 인식되는 것이라고 설명했다. 제자리에 있지 않은 것이 더러움을 유발한다고 했으므로 밑줄 친 부분은 ⑤ '정돈되지 않은 것'을 의미한다.

왜 오답?

① 부서진 물건에 대한 언급은 없었다.
② 단순히 더러움과 '먼지'를 연결시켜 만든 오답일 뿐이다.
③ 더러움을 판단하는 데 있어 재생 가능 여부에 대한 내용은 없다.
④ 대체 가능한 것인지는 더러움이 상대적인 기준에 의해 판단될 수 있다는 주제와 관련 없다.

D 14 정답 ④ ● 2등급 대비 [정답률 56%]

＊객관적이면서도 주관적인 색 인지

Many people take the commonsense view / **that** color is an objective property / of things, / or of the light **that** bounces off them. //

<small>동격절 접속사 / 주격 관계대명사(선행사 light) / =things</small>

<small>단서 1 색은 사물, 또는 사물의 빛 반사로 인한 객관적인 속성이라는 견해가 있음</small>

많은 사람들이 상식적인 견해를 취한다 / 색은 객관적인 속성이라는 / 사물의 / 또는 사물로부터 튕겨 나오는 빛의 //

<small>뒤에 목적어절 접속사 that이 생략됨</small>

They say a tree's leaves are green / because they reflect green light / — a greenness **that** is just **as** real **as** the leaves. //

<small>주격 관계대명사 / 원급 비교</small>

그들은 나뭇잎이 녹색이라고 말한다 / 녹색 빛을 반사하기 때문에 / (정확히 나뭇잎만큼 진짜인 녹색) //

Others argue / **that** color doesn't **inhabit** the physical world at all / but exists only in the eye or mind of the viewer. //

<small>명사절 접속사 / 타동사</small>

다른 사람들은 주장한다 / 색이 물리적인 세계에 전혀 존재하지 않고 / 보는 사람의 눈이나 정신 안에만 존재한다고 <small>단서 2 색은 사람의 눈과 정신에 의한 주관적인 속성이라는 견해가 있음</small>

They maintain / **that** if a tree fell in a forest / and no one was there **to see** it, / its leaves would be colorless / — and **so would** everything else. //

<small>명사절 접속사 / 형용사적 용법(no one 수식) / so가 앞으로 가면서 주어와 동사가 도치됨</small>

그들은 주장한다 / 만약 나무가 숲에서 쓰러지고 / 그것을 볼 사람이 아무도 거기에 없다면 / 그것의 잎은 색이 없을 것이고 / 다른 모든 것들도 그럴 것이라고 //

<small>뒤에 목적어절 접속사 that이 생략됨</small>

They say / there is no such *thing* as color; / there are only the people **who** see it. //

<small>주격 관계대명사</small>

그들은 말한다 / 색 같은 '것'은 없고 / 그것을 보는 사람들만 있다고 //

Both positions are, / in a way, correct. // <small>단서 3 색이 객관적이라는 견해와 주관적이라는 견해는 어떤 면에서는 모두 옳음</small>

두 가지 입장 모두 / 어떤 면에서는 옳다 //

Color is objective *and* subjective / — "the place," **as Paul Cézanne put it**, / "**where** our brain and the universe meet." //

<small>삽입절 / 관계부사</small>

색은 객관적이고 *동시에* 주관적이며 / Paul Cézanne이 말했듯이 장소이다 / "우리의 뇌와 우주가 만나는" // <small>단서 4 색은 객관적인 세상의 빛이 주관적인 뇌에 의해 해석될 때 만들어짐</small>

Color is created / **when** light from the world / is registered by the eyes / and interpreted by the brain. //

<small>부사절 접속사</small>

색은 만들어진다 / 세상으로부터의 빛이 / 눈에 의해 등록되고 / 뇌에 의해 해석될 때 //

- commonsense ⓐ 상식적인
- objective ⓐ 객관적인
- property ⓝ 속성, 성질
- bounce off 튕겨 나오다
- reflect ⓥ 반사하다
- inhabit ⓥ ~에 살다[존재하다]
- physical ⓐ 물리적인
- subjective ⓐ 주관적인

많은 사람들이 색은 사물 또는 사물로부터 튕겨 나오는 빛의 객관적인 속성이라는 상식적인 견해를 취한다. 그들은 나뭇잎이 녹색 빛(정확히 나뭇잎만큼 진짜인 녹색)을 반사하기 때문에 녹색이라고 말한다. 다른 사람들은 색이 물리적인 세계에 전혀 존재하지 않고 보는 사람의 눈이나 정신 안에만 존재한다고 주장한다. 그들은 만약 나무가 숲에서 쓰러지고 그것을 볼 사람이 아무도 거기에 없다면, 그것의 잎은 색이 없을 것이고, 다른 모든 것들도 그럴 것이라고 주장한다. 그들은 색 같은 '것'은 없고 그것을 보는 사람만 있다고 말한다. 두 가지 입장 모두 어떤 면에서는 옳다. 색은 객관적이고 *동시에* 주관적이며, Paul Cézanne이 말했듯이 '우리의 뇌와 우주가 만나는 곳'이다. 색은 세상으로부터의 빛이 눈에 의해 등록되고 뇌에 의해 해석될 때 만들어진다.

밑줄 친 our brain and the universe meet가 다음 글에서 의미하는 바로 가장 적절한 것은? [3점] <small>our brain은 나의 관점을 가리키지만, the universe는 다른 이들의 관점이 아닌 객관적인 빛의 반사를 가리킴</small>

① we see things beyond the range of perception <small>객관적인 빛의 반사를 인식하기 때문에 인식의 범위를 넘어설 수 없음</small>
<small>우리는 인식의 범위를 넘어서 사물을 본다</small>
② objects appear different by the change of light <small>주관적인 해석에 관한 내용이 빠져 있음</small>
<small>사물들은 빛의 변화에 의해 다르게 나타난다</small>
③ your perspectives and others' reach an agreement
<small>당신의 관점과 다른 이들의 관점이 합의를 이룬다</small>
④ our mind and physical reality interact with each other
<small>우리의 정신과 물리적 현실이 서로 상호작용한다</small>
⑤ structures of the human brain and the universe are similar <small>인간의 뇌와 우주 구조의 유사성은 언급되지 않음</small>
<small>인간 뇌와 우주의 구조는 유사하다</small>

<small>객관적인 현실과 주관적인 해석이 상호작용하여 색을 인식함</small>

왜 2등급? 지문에 등장한 단어들이 선택지 곳곳에 배치되어 있어 정답을 단번에 찾기 어려운 2등급 대비 문제이다. 대립하는 두 가지 주장에 해당하는 단어들을 잘 정리하여 밑줄 친 부분의 단어들과 비교하며 의미를 파악해야 한다.

| 문제 풀이 순서 |

1st 밑줄 친 부분이 포함된 문장을 읽고, 그 의미가 무엇일지 예상한다.

색은 객관적이고 '동시에' 주관적이며, Paul Cézanne이 말했듯이 '우리의 뇌와 우주가 만나는 곳'이다.

➡ 색이 객관적인 동시에 주관적이라고 했다. 이 사실에 관하여 '우리의 뇌'와 '우주'가 각각 무엇을 나타내는지, 그 둘이 '만나는' 것이 무엇을 의미하는지 파악해야 한다.

2nd 글의 나머지 부분에서 색에 관하여 대립하는 주장을 파악하고 정답을 찾는다.

- **주장 1**: 색은 사물, 또는 사물의 빛 반사로 인한 객관적인 속성이라는 견해가 있다. **단서 1**
- **주장 2**: 색은 사람의 눈과 정신에 의한 주관적인 속성이라는 견해도 있다. **단서 2**
- **결론**: 색이 객관적이라는 견해와 주관적이라는 견해는 어떤 면에서는 모두 옳다. **단서 3**

➡ '우리의 뇌와 우주가 만나는'이라는 뜻은 세상의 빛이 반사되어 만들어 낸 색(물리적 현실, 객관적)이 우리의 눈과 뇌에서 해석되는 것(우리의 정신, 주관적)으로 인식된다는 것을 의미한다.
  ▶ 따라서 정답은 ④ '우리의 정신과 물리적 현실이 서로 상호작용한다'이다.

| 선택지 분석 |

① 객관적인 빛의 반사를 인식하기 때문에 시각은 인식의 범위를 넘어설 수 없다.
② 객관적인 빛의 반사와 주관적인 해석을 모두 언급해야 하는데, 주관적인 해석에 관한 내용이 빠져있다.
③ your perspective와 others' (perspective) 모두 주관적인 관점에 해당하므로, 객관적인 현실에 관한 내용이 빠져있다.
④ 주관적인 해석(our mind)과 객관적인 현실(physical reality)이 서로 상호작용하여 색을 인식한다는 내용이다.
⑤ 인간의 뇌와 우주 구조의 유사성은 언급되지 않았다.

D 15 정답 ③   ★ 2등급 대비 [정답률 45%]

*스트레스 관리

A psychology professor raised a glass of water / while teaching stress management principles / to her students, / and asked them, / "How heavy is this glass of water / I'm holding?" //
한 심리학 교수가 물이 든 유리잔(물잔)을 들어 올렸다 / 스트레스 관리 원칙을 가르치던 중 / 그녀의 학생들에게 / 그리고 그들에게 물었다 / "이 물잔은 얼마나 무거울까요 / 제가 들고 있는"이라고 //

Students shouted out / various answers. //
학생들은 외쳤다 / 다양한 대답을 //

The professor replied, / "The absolute weight of this glass / doesn't matter. //
그 교수가 답했다 / "이 잔의 절대 무게는 / 중요하지 않습니다 //

It depends on / how long I hold it. //
이는 ~에 달려 있죠 / 제가 이 잔을 얼마나 오래 들고 있느냐 //

If I hold it for a minute, / it's quite light. //
만약 제가 이것을 1분 동안 들고 있다면 / 꽤 가볍죠 // **단서 1** 물잔을 오래 들고 있다면 더 큰 고통을 야기할 것임

But, / if I hold it for a day straight, / it will cause severe pain in my arm, / forcing me to drop the glass / to the floor. //
하지만 / 만약 제가 이것을 하루 종일 들고 있다면 / 이것은 제 팔에 심각한 고통을 야기할 것입니다 / 그리고 잔을 떨어뜨리게 할 것입니다 / 바닥에 //

In each case, / the weight of the glass is the same, / but the longer I hold it, / the heavier it feels to me." //
각 사례에서 / 잔의 무게는 같지만 / 제가 오래 들고 있을수록 / 그것은 저에게 더 무겁게 느껴지죠" // **단서 2** 물잔의 무게가 같아도 얼마나 오래 들고 있는지에 따라 무게가 다르게 느껴짐

As the class nodded their heads / in agreement, / she continued, / "Your stresses in life / are like this glass of water. //
학생들은 고개를 끄덕였고 / 동의하며 / 교수는 이어 말했다 / "여러분이 인생에서 느끼는 스트레스들도 / 이 물잔과 같습니다 // **단서 3** 스트레스를 물잔에 비유한 것임을 알 수 있음

If you still feel / the weight of yesterday's stress, / it's a strong sign / that it's time to put the glass down." //
만약 아직도 느낀다면 / 어제 받은 스트레스의 무게를 / 그것은 강한 신호입니다 / 잔을 내려놓아야 할 때라는" //

- psychology ⓝ 심리학 • professor ⓝ 교수
- management ⓝ 관리 • principle ⓝ 원칙 • reply ⓥ 대답하다
- absolute ⓐ 절대적인 • weight ⓝ 무게 • matter ⓥ 중요하다

- depend on ~에 달려 있다 • quite ⓐⓓ 꽤 • light ⓐ 가벼운
- straight ⓐⓓ 계속해서 • severe ⓐ 심각한
- nod ⓥ (고개를) 끄덕이다 • agreement ⓝ 동의
- continue ⓥ (쉬지 않고) 계속되다 • put down ~을 내려놓다

한 심리학 교수가 학생들에게 스트레스 관리 원칙을 가르치던 중 물이 든 유리잔(물잔)을 들어 올리고 "제가 들고 있는 이 물잔은 얼마나 무거울까요?"라고 물었다. 학생들은 다양한 대답을 외쳤다. 그 교수가 답했다. "이 잔의 절대 무게는 중요하지 않습니다. 이는 제가 이 잔을 얼마나 오래 들고 있느냐에 달려 있죠. 만약 제가 이것을 1분 동안 들고 있다면, 꽤 가볍죠. 하지만, 만약 제가 이것을 하루종일 들고 있다면 이것은 제 팔에 심각한 고통을 야기하고 잔을 바닥에 떨어뜨리게 할 것입니다. 각 사례에서 잔의 무게는 같지만, 제가 오래 들고 있을수록 그것은 저에게 더 무겁게 느껴지죠." 학생들은 동의하며 고개를 끄덕였고, 교수는 이어 말했다. "여러분이 인생에서 느끼는 스트레스들도 이 물잔과 같습니다. 만약 아직도 어제 받은 스트레스의 무게를 느낀다면, 그것은 잔을 내려놓아야 할 때라는 강한 신호입니다."

> 밑줄 친 put the glass down이 다음 글에서 의미하는 바로 가장 적절한 것은? [3점]
> ① pour more water into the glass 잔은 스트레스를 비유한 것임
>   잔에 물을 더 따른다
> ② set a plan not to make mistakes 미리 계획을 세우라는 내용은 나오지 않음
>   실수를 하지 않기 위해 계획을 세운다
> ③ let go of the stress in your mind 스트레스를 오랫동안 가지고 있지 말라고 했음
>   당신 마음속의 스트레스를 푼다
> ④ think about the cause of your stress
>   당신의 스트레스의 원인에 대해 생각한다 스트레스의 원인을 분석하는 내용이 아님
> ⑤ learn to accept the opinions of others 다른 사람들의 의견을 받아들이는
>   다른 사람들의 의견을 받아들이는 것을 배운다 것은 언급되지 않음

왜 2등급? 물이 든 유리잔으로 비유하고 있는 것이 무엇인지 정확하게 파악하는 것이 중요하다. 이를 통해 심리학 교수의 말을 제대로 이해해야 정답을 고를 수 있다.

| 문제 풀이 순서 |

1st 밑줄 친 부분이 포함된 문장을 읽고, 그 의미가 무엇일지 예상한다.

만약 아직도 어제 받은 스트레스의 무게를 느낀다면, 그것은 잔을 내려놓아야 할 때라는 강한 신호입니다.
➡ 한 심리학 교수가 스트레스 관리 원칙을 가르치면서 한 말의 일부이다. 어제 받은 스트레스의 무게를 느끼면 '잔을 내려놓아야 한다는 신호라고 했으므로 스트레스와 잔의 의미에 대해 파악해야 할 것이다.

2nd 글의 나머지 부분에서 물잔의 의미를 확실히 파악해서 정답을 찾는다.

- 물잔을 하루종일 들고 있다면 팔에 심각한 고통을 야기하고 잔을 떨어뜨릴 것이다. **단서 1**
- 잔의 무게가 같아도 더 오래 들고 있으면 더 무겁게 느껴진다. **단서 2**
- 인생에서 느끼는 스트레스도 이 물잔과 같다. **단서 3**

➡ 물잔을 오래 들고 있으면 고통을 느끼게 되고, 같은 무게의 잔이라도 더 오래 들고 있으면 더 무겁게 느껴진다고 했다.
  ▶ 물잔은 스트레스를 비유하고 있는 것이므로 밑줄 친 부분의 의미로 가장 적절한 것은 ③ '당신 마음속의 스트레스를 푼다'이다.

| 선택지 분석 |

① 스트레스를 비유하기 위해 나온 the glass를 넣어 만든 오답이다.
② 실수를 하지 않기 위해 계획을 세우는 내용은 글에서 전혀 언급되지 않았다.
③ 물잔을 스트레스에 비유하고 있으므로 잔을 내려놓는다는 것은 스트레스를 내려놓는 것, 즉 스트레스를 푸는 것을 의미한다.
④ 스트레스 관리에 대한 내용을 담고 있는 글이기는 하지만 스트레스의 원인을 분석하는 내용은 나오지 않는다.
⑤ 이 글에서 다른 사람들의 의견을 받아들이는 것을 배워야 한다는 내용은 나오지 않았다.

＊고객의 불합리한 요구를 거절할 필요성

Is the customer *always* right? //
고객은 항상 옳은가 //

When customers return a broken product / to a famous company, /
고객들이 고장 난 제품을 반품할 때 / 한 유명한 회사에 /

주격 관계대명사
which makes kitchen and bathroom fixtures, / the company
부사적 용법(목적)
nearly always offers / a replacement / to maintain good customer relations. //
주방과 욕실 설비를 만드는 / 그 회사는 거의 항상 제공한다 / 대체품을 / 좋은 고객 관계를 유지하기 위해 //

사이에 관계부사 when 생략   주어와 동사 도치
Still, / "there are times / you've got to say / 'no,'" / explains the warranty expert of the company, / such as when a product is undamaged / or has been abused. // [단서 1 고객에게 안 된다는 말을 해야 할 때가 있음]
그럼에도 / "때가 있다 / 말을 해야 할 / "'안 돼요.'라고 / 그 회사의 상품 보증 전문가는 설명한다 / 상품이 멀쩡할 때와 같이 / 또는 남용되었을 때 //

주격 관계대명사
Entrepreneur Lauren Thorp, / who owns an e-commerce company, / says, / "While the customer is 'always' right, / sometimes you just have to fire a customer." //
기업가 Lauren Thorp는 / 전자 상거래 회사를 소유한 / 말한다 / "고객이 '항상' 옳지만 / 때로는 당신이 고객을 해고해야만 한다" //

목적어절을 이끄는 접속사
When Thorp has tried everything / to resolve a complaint / and realizes / that the customer will be dissatisfied / no matter what, /
Thorp가 최선을 다해왔는데 / 고객의 불만을 해결하기 위해 / 그리고 깨달을 때 / 그 고객이 만족하지 않을 것이란 사실을 / 어떠한 경우에도 /

계속적 용법의 주격 관계대명사
she returns her attention / to the rest of her customers, / who / 삽입절 she says / are "the reason for my success." //
그녀는 자신의 주의를 돌린다 / 나머지 다른 고객들에게 / 그들은 / 그녀는 말한다 / "내 성공의 이유"라고 // [단서 2 고객의 불만을 어떻게 해도 해결해 줄 수 없을 때는 다른 고객들에게 주의를 돌릴 필요가 있음]

- return ⓥ 반품하다   · fixture ⓝ 설비   · replacement ⓝ 대체품
- warranty ⓝ (상품 등의) 보증   · undamaged ⓐ 손상되지 않은, 멀쩡한
- abuse ⓥ 남용하다   · entrepreneur ⓝ 기업가
- e-commerce ⓝ 전자 상거래   · resolve ⓥ 해결하다
- complaint ⓝ 불평, 불만   · dissatisfy ⓥ 불만을 느끼게 하다
- attention ⓝ 주의   · delete ⓥ 삭제하다   · reject ⓥ 거절하다
- unreasonable ⓐ 불합리한   · demand ⓝ 요구
- intention ⓝ 의도   · influential ⓐ 영향력 있는

고객은 항상 옳은가? 주방과 욕실 설비를 만드는 한 유명한 회사에 고객들이 고장 난 제품을 반품할 때 그 회사는 좋은 고객 관계를 유지하기 위해 거의 항상 대체품을 제공한다. 그럼에도, 그 회사의 상품 보증 전문가는 상품이 멀쩡하거나 남용되었을 때와 같이, "'안 돼요.'라고 말을 해야 할 때가 있다."고 설명한다. 전자 상거래 회사를 소유한 기업가 Lauren Thorp는 "고객이 '항상' 옳지만, 때로는 당신이 고객을 해고해야만 한다."고 말한다. Thorp가 고객의 불만을 해결하기 위해 최선을 다해왔는데 그 고객이 어떠한 경우에도 만족하지 않을 것이란 사실을 깨달을 때, 그녀는 자신의 주의를 나머지 다른 고객들에게 돌리는데, 그 고객들은 "내 성공의 이유"라고 그녀는 말한다.

밑줄 친 fire a customer가 다음 글에서 의미하는 바로 가장 적절한 것은?
① deal with a customer's emergency
고객의 응급 상황에 대처하다 [고객의 응급 상황에 대처하라는 의미가 아님]
② delete a customer's purchasing record
고객의 구매 기록을 삭제하다 [고객의 구매 기록 삭제에 대한 내용은 없음]
③ reject a customer's unreasonable demand
고객의 불합리한 요구를 거절하다 [고객의 불만이 합리적이지 않을 때 고객의 요구를 거절할 필요가 있다고 했음]
④ uncover the hidden intention of a customer
고객의 숨겨진 의도를 밝히다 [고객의 숨겨진 의도를 밝히는 것에 대한 언급은 없음]
⑤ rely on the power of an influential customer
영향력 있는 고객의 힘에 의존하다 [영향력 있는 고객의 힘에 의존하자는 말이 아님]

[왜 2등급?] 첫 문장에서 질문을 던진 후에 한 유명한 회사의 예시를 들고 있는데, 이 예시가 의미하는 바를 파악하지 못하면 정답을 고르기 어려운 문제이다.

| 문제 풀이 순서 |

[1st] 밑줄 친 부분이 포함된 문장을 읽고, 그 의미가 무엇일지 예상한다.

전자 상거래 회사를 소유한 기업가 Lauren Thorp는 "고객이 '항상' 옳지만, 때로는 당신이 고객을 해고해야만 한다."고 말한다.
➡ 기업가 Lauren Thorp가 이렇게 말한 이유가 글의 나머지 부분에 나올 것이다. '고객을 해고해야만' 한다는 말이 의미하는 바를 파악해야 한다.
▶ While(~이긴 하지만)이라는 접속사가 쓰여서 기본적으로는 고객이 항상 옳다는 전제가 있지만, 아닌 경우도 있다는 것을 예상해야 한다.

[2nd] 글의 나머지 부분에서 기업가의 말에 대한 설명을 이해하여 정답을 찾는다.

· 그 회사의 상품 보증 전문가는 고객에게 안 된다는 말을 해야 할 때가 있다고 말했다. [단서 1]
· Thorp는 고객이 어떻게 해도 만족하지 않을 것이란 것을 깨달으면 다른 고객들에게 주의를 돌리는 것이 자신의 성공 이유라고 말한다. [단서 2]
➡ 예시로 든 주방과 욕실 설비를 만드는 회사의 상품 보증 전문가는 고객이 불합리한 요구를 하거나 불만을 이야기할 때 그것을 다 들어주기보다 안 된다는 말을 할 필요가 있다고 했다.
Thorp가 한 말도 같은 맥락으로, 고객을 해고하라는 말은 고객의 요구를 때로는 거절할 수 있어야 한다는 의미이다.
▶ 따라서 정답은 ③ '고객의 불합리한 요구를 거절하다'이다.

| 선택지 분석 |
① 고객의 응급 상황에 대처하라는 말이 아니다.
② 고객의 구매 기록을 삭제하라는 내용은 나오지 않는다.
③ 기업가 Lauren Thorp는 고객의 불만이 합리적이지 않을 때 고객의 요구를 거절할 필요가 있다는 의미로 말한 것이다.
④ 고객의 숨겨진 의도를 밝히는 것과 관련된 내용이 아니다.
⑤ 영향력 있는 고객의 힘에 의존해야 한다는 것이 아니라 오히려 불합리한 고객의 요구는 거절할 때도 있어야 한다고 했다.

＊기후 변화의 원인인 우리의 소비

~에 관한 한
When it comes to climate change, / many blame / the fossil fuel industry for pumping greenhouse gases, / the agricultural sector for burning rainforests, / 병렬 구조
기후 변화에 관해 / 많은 사람들은 탓한다 / 온실가스를 배출하는 것에 대해 화석 연료 산업을 / 열대 우림을 태우는 것에 대해 농업 분야를 /

or the fashion industry for producing excessive clothes. //
혹은 과다한 의복을 생산하는 것에 대해 패션 산업을 //

But wait, / what drives these industrial activities? //
하지만 자 / 무엇이 이러한 산업 활동들을 가동시키는가 // [단서 1 기후 변화의 원인이 되는 산업 활동은 우리의 소비 때문에 이루어짐]

Our consumption. // 우리의 소비이다 //

Climate change is a summed product / of each person's behavior. // 기후 변화는 합쳐진 산물이다 / 각 개인 행위의 //

For example, / the fossil fuel industry / is a popular scapegoat / in the climate crisis. //
예를 들어 / 화석 연료 산업은 / 일반적인 희생양이다 / 기후 위기에 있어서 //

But / why do they drill and burn fossil fuels? //
하지만 / 왜 그들은 화석 연료를 시추하고 태울까 // [단서 2 화석 연료 산업 활동들을 가동하도록 하는 금전적인 동기를 우리가 제공하고 있음]

We provide them strong financial incentives: / some people regularly travel / on airplanes and cars / that burn fossil fuels. //
주격 관계대명사
우리가 그들에게 강력한 금전적인 동기를 제공한다 / 예를 들어, 어떤 사람들은 정기적으로 여행한다 / 비행기와 차로 / 화석 연료를 태우는 //

Some people waste electricity / <u>generated</u> by burning fuel in power plants. //
앞에 주격 관계대명사와 be동사 생략
어떤 사람들은 전기를 낭비한다 / 발전소에서 연료를 태움으로써 생산된 //
앞에 주격 관계대명사와 be동사 생략
Some people use and throw away plastic products / <u>derived</u> from crude oil / every day. //
동명사 주어(단수 취급)
어떤 사람들은 플라스틱 제품을 사용하고 버린다 / 원유로부터 얻어진 / 매일 //
<u>Blaming</u> the fossil fuel industry / while engaging in these
단수 동사
behaviors / <u>is</u> a slap in our own face. // 단서3 우리의 잘못을 생각하지 않고 화석
연료 산업을 탓하는 경우에 대한 설명임
화석 연료 산업을 탓하는 것은 / 이러한 행위들에 참여하면서 / 스스로의 얼굴 때리기이다 //

- pump ⓥ 퍼붓다, 쏟아지다   - agricultural ⓐ 농업의
- sector ⓝ 분야   - rainforest ⓝ (열대) 우림   - excessive ⓐ 과도한
- drive ⓥ 추진시키다   - consumption ⓝ 소비   - sum ⓥ 합계하다
- financial ⓐ 재정적인, 금전적인   - incentive ⓝ 동기
- slap ⓝ 철썩 때리기   - room ⓝ 여지   - admit ⓥ 인정하다

기후 변화에 관해 많은 사람들은 온실가스를 배출하는 것에 대해 화석 연료 산업을, 열대 우림을 태우는 것에 대해 농업 분야를, 혹은 과도한 의복을 생산하는 것에 대해 패션 산업을 탓한다. 하지만 자, 무엇이 이러한 산업 활동들을 가동시키는가? 우리의 소비이다. 기후 변화는 각 개인 행위의 합쳐진 산물이다. 예를 들어 화석 연료 산업은 기후 위기에 있어서 일반적인 희생양이다. 하지만 왜 그들은 화석 연료를 시추하고 태울까? 우리가 그들에게 강력한 금전적인 동기를 제공한다. 예를 들어, 어떤 사람들은 화석 연료를 태우는 비행기와 차로 정기적으로 여행한다. 어떤 사람들은 발전소에서 연료를 태움으로써 생산된 전기를 낭비한다. 어떤 사람들은 원유로부터 얻어진 플라스틱 제품을 매일 사용하고 버린다. 이러한 행위들에 참여하면서 화석 연료 산업을 탓하는 것은 스스로의 얼굴 때리기이다.

> 밑줄 친 a slap in our own face가 다음 글에서 의미하는 바로 가장 적절한 것은? [3점]
> ① giving the future generation room for change
> 미래 세대에게 변화의 여지를 주는 것   미래 세대의 변화와 관계없는 내용임
> ② warning ourselves about the lack of natural resources
> 천연자원의 부족에 대해 우리 스스로에게 경고하는 것   천연자원의 부족에 대한 내용이 아님
> ③ refusing to admit the benefits of fossil fuel production
> 화석 연료 생산의 장점을 인정하지 않는 것   화석 연료 생산의 장점에 대한 내용이 아님
> ④ failing to recognize our responsibility for climate change
> 기후 변화에 대한 우리의 책임을 인지하지 못하는 것   기후 변화를 초래하는 것은 우리 스스로임
> ⑤ starting to deal with environmental problems individually   환경 문제를 개별적으로 다룬다는 언급은 없음
> 환경 문제를 개별적으로 다루기 시작하는 것

왜 1등급? 선택지에 환경에 관련된 단어들이 포함되어 있다. 이를 통해 글의 내용에 대한 짐작이 가능하지만, 글을 읽으면서 이 단어들과 관련된 부분을 잘 이해한 뒤 오답 선택지를 소거해야 하는 1등급 대비 문제이다.

| 문제 풀이 순서 |

1st 선택지와 앞부분을 통해 핵심 소재를 확인하고 글의 내용을 예상한다.

선택지	거의 모든 선택지에 환경과 관련된 표현들이 등장한다.
앞부분	기후 변화에 관해 사람들은 ~ 산업을 탓한다. 하지만 이런 산업 활동들을 가동시키는 것은 사실 우리의 소비이다. 단서1

➡ 글의 소재는 '기후 변화'이다.
사람들은 보통 산업 활동들이 기후 변화를 일으킨다고 생각하지만, 사실 이 기후 변화의 원인이 되는 산업 활동은 우리의 소비 때문이라는 것이 글의 주제일 것이다.

2nd 밑줄 친 부분이 포함된 문장을 읽고, 그 의미가 무엇일지 예상한다.

이러한 행위들에 참여하면서 화석 연료 산업을 탓하는 것은 스스로의 얼굴 때리기이다.

➡ 밑줄 친 부분 = 이러한 행위들에 참여하면서 화석 연료 산업을 탓하는 것
따라서 화석 연료 산업을 탓하지만 그와 관련된 행위들에 참여한다는 의미일 것이다. 또한, '이러한 행위'가 무엇인지 앞부분에서 찾아야 함을 알 수 있다.

3rd 글의 나머지 부분을 확인해서 정답을 찾는다.

• 화석 연료를 태우는 비행기와 차로 여행을 하는 것과 같이, 우리가 화석 연료 산업 활동들을 가동하도록 하는 금전적인 동기를 제공하고 있다. 단서2
• 밑줄 친 부분은 우리의 잘못을 생각하지 않고 화석 연료 산업을 탓하는 경우에 대한 비유적 표현이다. 단서3

➡ 화석 연료 산업을 가동하는 행위들에 참여하면서 화석 연료 산업을 탓한다는 것이다.
▶ 따라서 '스스로의 얼굴 때리기'가 의미하는 바는 ④ '기후 변화에 대한 우리의 책임을 인지하지 못하는 것'이다.

| 선택지 분석 |

① 스스로 얼굴을 때림으로써 무언가를 깨닫게 되어 미래 세대에 긍정적인 영향을 주었다는 등의 내용이 아니다.
② 화석 연료에 대한 내용이고, 천연자원 부족에 대한 내용은 아니다.
③ 화석 연료 생산의 장점이라기보다는 생산의 원인이 우리 스스로에게 있다는 내용이다.
④ 산업 활동들을 가동시키도록 우리가 금전적인 동기를 제공하고 있지만, 우리의 잘못은 생각하지 않고 화석 연료 산업을 탓한다는 내용이다.
⑤ 기후 변화를 야기하는 산업 활동들이 우리들의 요구로 인해 생겨난다는 것을 인지하지 못한다는 것이지, 그것을 깨닫고 개별적으로 환경 문제를 다루고 있다는 것이 아니다.

D 18 정답 ②   ★ 1등급 대비 [정답률 58%]

*농지가 풍족해지면서 발생하는 문제
「force + 목적어 + 목적격 보어(to부정사)」의 수동태형
The soil of a farm field / <u>is forced to be</u> the perfect environment / for monoculture growth. //
농지의 토양은 / 완벽한 환경이어야 한다 / 단일 작물 재배를 위한 //

This is achieved / by adding <u>nutrients</u> in the form of fertilizer /
병렬 구조
and <u>water</u> by way of irrigation. //
이것은 이루어진다 / 비료 형태로 양분을 더하고 / 관개로 물을 댐으로써 //
'~동안'
<u>During</u> the last fifty years, / engineers and crop scientists have
help + 목적어 + 목적격 보어(동사원형)   동명사(전치사의 목적어)
helped / farmers become much more efficient / at <u>supplying</u> exactly the right amount of both. //
지난 50년 동안 / 기술자와 농작물 연구자들은 도움을 주었다 / 농부들이 훨씬 더 효율적일 수 있도록 / 양쪽 모두의 정확한 적정량을 공급하는 데 //

World usage of fertilizer <u>has tripled</u> since 1969, / and the global
현재완료(계속)
capacity for irrigation <u>has</u> almost <u>doubled</u>; /
전 세계 비료 사용량은 1969년 이래로 세 배가 되었고 / 전체 관개 능력은 거의 두 배가 되었다 /

we are feeding and watering our fields / more than ever, / and our crops are loving it. // 단서1 현재 농지는 그 어느 때보다 기름지고 물이 풍족함
우리는 들판을 기름지게 하고 물을 대고 있다 / 그 어느 때보다도 / 우리의 농작물은 이를 좋아한다 //
단서2 '단서1'의 상황을 가리킴
Unfortunately, / these luxurious conditions have also excited / the attention of certain agricultural undesirables. //
불행히도 / 이런 호사스러운 상황은 끌어들였다 / 농업에서는 달갑지 않은 것들의 관심도 //
부사절 접속사(이유) *   단서3 농지는 자연 지대에 비해 영양분과 물이 매우 풍족함
<u>Because</u> farm fields are loaded with nutrients and water /
'~에 비해서'   주격 관계대명사
<u>relative to</u> the natural land <u>that</u> surrounds them, /
농지는 영양분과 물이 풍족하게 채워져 있기 때문에 / 주위를 둘러싼 자연 지대에 비해 /
수동태 동사
they <u>are desired</u> as luxury real estate / by every random weed in the area. //
그것들은 고급 부동산으로 원해진다 / 그 지역의 모든 잡초에 의해 //

D

- soil ⓝ 토양   • nutrient ⓝ 영양분   • fertilizer ⓝ 비료
- capacity ⓝ 능력   • agricultural ⓐ 농업의
- undesirable ⓝ 원하지 않는 것   • be loaded with ~으로 가득 차다
- real estate 부동산   • weed ⓝ 잡초   • abundant ⓐ 풍부한

농지의 토양은 단일 작물 재배를 위한 완벽한 환경이어야 한다. 이것은 비료 형태로 양분을 더하고 관개로 물을 댐으로써 이루어진다. 지난 50년 동안 기술자와 농작물 연구자들은 농부들이 양쪽 모두의 정확한 적정량을 공급하는 데 훨씬 더 효율적일 수 있도록 도움을 주었다. 전 세계 비료 사용량은 1969년 이래로 세 배가 되었고, 전체 관개 능력은 거의 두 배가 되었다. 우리는 그 어느 때보다도 들판을 기름지게 하고 물을 대고 있으며, 우리의 농작물은 이를 좋아한다. 불행히도, 이러한 호사스러운 상황은 농업에서는 달갑지 않은 것들의 관심도 끌어들였다. 농지는 주위를 둘러싼 자연 지대에 비해 영양분과 물이 풍족히 채워져 있기 때문에 그 지역의 어떤 잡초라도 원하는 고급 부동산이 된다.

밑줄 친 luxury real estate가 다음 글에서 의미하는 바로 가장 적절한 것은? [3점]
① a farm where a scientist's aid is highly required
과학자의 원조가 절실히 요구되는 농장 　　　 과학자들의 원조가 필요하다는 내용은 없음
②a field abundant with necessities for plants
식물에 필요한 것이 풍부한 들판 　 영양분과 물이 풍족한 들판을 호사스러운 상황이라고 표현함
③ a district accessible only for the rich
부자들만이 접근할 수 있는 지역 　 부자들만 접근이 가능한 지역에 관한 내용이 아님
④ a place that is conserved for ecology 생태 보호에 관한 언급은 없음
생태 보호가 되어 있는 곳
⑤ a region with higher economic value 경제적 가치에 관한 언급은 없음
경제적 가치가 더 높은 지역

왜 1등급❓ 밑줄 친 부분의 어휘가 흔히 쓰이는 어휘가 아니라서 본문의 내용과 의미를 연결하기 어려운 1등급 대비 문제이다. 글의 앞부분을 요약한 these luxurious conditions가 밑줄 친 부분에 연관되기 때문에, 앞서 어떤 상황이 설명되었는지 파악하면 어렵지 않게 밑줄 친 부분의 의미를 파악할 수 있다.

| 문제 풀이 순서 |

1st 밑줄 친 부분이 포함된 문장을 읽고, 글의 내용을 예상한다.

밑줄 친 부분이 포함된 문장	농지는 주위를 둘러싼 자연 지대에 비해 영양분과 물이 풍족히 채워져 있기 때문에 단서3 그 지역의 어떤 잡초라도 원하는 고급 부동산이 된다.

➡ 영양분과 물이 풍족히 채워진 농지가 결국 어떤 잡초라도 원하는 '고급 부동산'이 된다고 했으므로, '고급 부동산'은 영양분과 물이 풍족히 채워진 땅이라고 예상할 수 있다. 글 전반적으로 그러한 땅에 관한 설명이 이어질 것이다.

2nd 글의 나머지 부분을 읽고, 예상한 내용이 맞는지 확인한다.
• 지난 50년 동안 비료 사용량과 관개 능력이 크게 발전함 → 어느 때보다도 농지의 상태가 기름지고 좋아짐 단서1
• 불행히도, 이러한 호사스러운 상황은 달갑지 않은 것들의 관심도 끌어들임 단서2

➡ 비료와 물을 풍부하게 공급받아 농지가 풍족해진 상황을 these luxurious conditions로 가리켰는데, 밑줄 친 부분에 마찬가지로 luxury라는 표현이 있다.

3rd 파악한 내용을 종합하여 밑줄 친 부분의 의미를 파악한다.

현대의 농지는 영양분과 물이 풍족하여 호사스러운 상황이지만, 이런 상황이 역설적으로 잡초에도 좋은 땅이 되기 때문에 잡초도 농지로 끌어들일 수 있다는 내용이다. 결국, '고급 부동산'은 식물(농작물, 잡초)에 필요한 것(영양분, 물)이 풍부한 땅을 의미하므로 정답은 ② '식물에 필요한 것이 풍부한 들판'이다.

| 선택지 분석 |
① 기술자와 농작물 연구자들 덕분에 이미 농지는 풍족하므로 과학자의 원조가 요구되지는 않는다.
②밑줄 친 부분의 표면적 의미이다.
③ 농지에 관한 내용일 뿐, 부자들만이 접근할 수 있는 지역에 관한 내용이 아니다.
④ 생태 보호에 대한 언급은 없다.
⑤ 농지에 영양분과 물이 풍부하다고 했을 뿐, 농지의 경제적 가치에 대한 언급은 없다.

✱ 부사절 접속사

– 부사절을 이끄는 종속접속사는 시간, 이유, 목적, 양보, 대조, 조건 등의 의미를 나타낸다. that은 주로 명사절 접속사로 많이 출제되지만 부사절 접속사로 쓰여 목적, 결과를 나타내기도 한다.
• **When** he entered the garden, he saw a rabbit.
시간을 나타내는 부사절 접속사 when
(그가 정원에 들어갔을 때, 그는 토끼 한 마리를 보았다.)
• I didn't call **because** I didn't want to see her.
이유를 나타내는 부사절 접속사 because
(그녀를 보고 싶지 않았기 때문에 나는 전화하지 않았다.)
• Please turn off the light **so that** the baby can sleep.
목적을 나타내는 부사절 접속사 so that
(아기가 잘 수 있도록 불을 꺼주세요.)
• My father bought a new car **even though** we objected.
양보를 나타내는 부사절 접속사 even though
(아버지는 우리가 반대했음에도 불구하고 새 차를 사셨다.)
• My parents speak fluent German **whereas** I only speak English.
대조를 나타내는 부사절 접속사 whereas
(난 영어만 하는 반면 우리 부모님은 유창한 독일어를 구사하신다.)

– 부사절의 주어가 주절의 주어와 동일할 때 부사절의 「주어+be 동사」는 생략 가능하다.
• All employees are required to wear safety helmets **while** (they are) at work.
주절의 주어와 동일한 부사절의 주어와 be동사
(모든 직원들은 회사에 있는 동안 안전모를 써야 한다.)

D 어휘 Review 정답 ——— 문제편 p. 57

01 지각	11 stand out	21 restate
02 농업의	12 put down	22 physical
03 진취적인	13 make up	23 herd
04 경쟁	14 bounce off	24 grand
05 가끔의	15 be loaded with	25 absolute
06 logically	16 livelihoods	26 attention
07 indeed	17 passive	27 Merely
08 previous	18 principles	28 maintain
09 agreement	19 warranty	29 behavior
10 replacement	20 capacity	30 scapegoat

E 요지 찾기

문제편 p. 60~70

E 01 정답 ③ *우리가 지닌 리더가 될 수 있는 잠재력

When we think of leaders, / we may think of people / **such as** ^{'~와 같은'}
Abraham Lincoln or Martin Luther King, Jr. //
우리가 리더에 대해 생각할 때 / 우리는 사람들에 대해 생각할지 모른다 / Abraham Lincoln 혹은 Martin Luther King, Jr.와 같은 //

If you consider / the historical importance and far-reaching influence / of these individuals, / leadership might seem / like a noble and high goal. //
만약 여러분이 고려한다면 / 역사적 중요성과 광범위한 영향력을 / 이러한 인물들의 / 리더십은 보일지도 모른다 / 고귀하고 높은 목표처럼 //

But like all of us, / these people started out as students, workers, and citizens /
그러나 우리 모두와 마찬가지로 / 이러한 인물들은 학생, 근로자, 그리고 시민으로 시작했다 /
주격 관계대명사 / 간접의문문(의문사+주어+동사)
who possessed ideas / about **how some aspect of daily life could be improved** / on a larger scale. // 단서 1 위대한 리더들은 일상을 개선할 아이디어를 가진 학생, 근로자, 시민으로 시작함
생각을 가졌던 / 일상생활의 어느 측면이 어떻게 개선될 수 있는지에 대한 / 더 큰 규모로 //

Through diligence and experience, / they improved upon their ideas / 단서 2 리더들은 근면함과 경험을 통해 본인의 생각을 발전시킴
근면함과 경험을 통해 / 이 사람들은 자신의 생각을 발전시켰다 /
by v-ing: ~함으로써
by sharing them with others, / **seeking** their opinions and feedback / 병렬 구조 and constantly **looking** for the best way / **to** 형용사적 용법(way 수식)
accomplish goals / for a group. //
자신의 생각을 다른 사람들과 공유하고 / 그들의 의견과 반응을 구하며 / 끊임없이 가장 좋은 방법을 찾음으로써 / 목표를 성취할 수 있는 / 집단을 위한 // 단서 3 우리 모두는 리더가 형용사적 용법(potential 수식) 될 수 있는 잠재력을 가짐
Thus we all have the potential / **to be leaders** at school, in our communities, and at work, / regardless of age or experience. //
그러므로 우리는 모두 잠재력을 가지고 있다 / 학교, 공동체, 그리고 일터에서 리더가 될 수 있는 / 나이나 경험에 관계없이 //

- historical ⓐ 역사적인 • importance ⓝ 중요성
- far-reaching ⓐ 광범위한 • influence ⓝ 영향력
- noble ⓐ 고귀한 • possess ⓥ 가지다, 소유하다 • aspect ⓝ 측면
- improve ⓥ 개선하다 • scale ⓝ 규모 • share ⓥ 공유하다
- seek ⓥ 찾다, 구하다 • opinion ⓝ 의견 • constantly ⓐⓓ 끊임없이
- accomplish ⓥ 성취하다 • thus ⓐⓓ 그러므로
- potential ⓝ 잠재력 • community ⓝ 공동체
- regardless of ~와 관계없이

우리가 리더에 대해 생각할 때, 우리는 Abraham Lincoln 혹은 Martin Luther King, Jr.와 같은 사람들에 대해 생각할지 모른다. 만약 여러분이 이러한 인물들의 역사적 중요성과 광범위한 영향력을 고려한다면, 리더십은 고귀하고 높은 목표처럼 보일지도 모른다. 그러나 우리 모두와 마찬가지로, 이러한 인물들은 일상생활의 어느 측면이 더 큰 규모로 어떻게 개선될 수 있는지에 대한 생각을 가졌던 학생, 근로자, 그리고 시민으로 시작했다. 근면함과 경험을 통해, 그들은 자신의 생각을 다른 사람들과 공유하고, 그들의 의견과 반응을 구하며, 끊임없이 집단을 위한 목표를 성취할 수 있는 가장 좋은 방법을 찾음으로써 자신의 생각을 발전시켰다. 그러므로 우리는 모두, 나이나 경험에 관계없이, 학교, 공동체, 그리고 일터에서 리더가 될 수 있는 잠재력을 가지고 있다.

다음 글의 요지로 가장 적절한 것은?
① 훌륭한 리더는 고귀한 목표를 위해 희생적인 삶을 산다.
　리더가 희생적인 삶을 산다는 것은 언급되지 않음
② 위대한 인물은 위기의 순간에 뛰어난 결단력을 발휘한다.
　자신의 생각을 발전시킨 사람들이 리더가 된 내용이 제시됨
③ 공동체를 위한 아이디어를 발전시키는 누구나 리더가 될 수 있다.
　큰 규모에서 일상을 개선할 아이디어를 가진 사람이라면 누구나 리더가 될 잠재력을 가짐
④ 다른 사람의 의견을 경청하는 자세는 목표 달성에 가장 중요하다.
　리더가 다른 사람들의 의견과 반응을 구하는 내용이 있긴 하지만 글의 중심 내용은 아님
⑤ 근면하고 경험이 풍부한 사람들은 경제적으로 성공할 수 있다.
　경제적으로 성공하는 사람들에 대한 것은 언급되지 않음

왜 정답 ? ✱✱✱ [정답률 92%]

오해: 리더십은 고귀하고 높은 목표임

진실: 우리 모두와 마찬가지로, 위대한 리더들은 일상생활의 어느 측면이 더 큰 규모로 어떻게 개선될 수 있는지에 관한 생각을 가진 일반적인 사람(학생, 근로자, 시민)이었음 단서 1

부연: 그들은 근면함과 경험을 통해 본인의 생각을 발전시킴 단서 2

주장: 우리 모두 리더가 될 수 있는 잠재력을 가지고 있음 단서 3

▶ 평범한 학생, 근로자, 시민도 생각을 발전시켜 집단을 위한 목표를 성취할 수 있다면 위대한 리더가 될 수 있고 우리는 그렇게 할 수 있는 잠재력이 있다는 내용이므로 정답은 ③이다.

왜 오답 ?

① 리더가 희생적인 삶을 산다는 것은 언급되지 않았다.
② 리더는 본인의 생각을 발전시켜 집단을 위한 목표를 성취할 수 있는 가장 좋은 방법을 찾는다고 했다.
④ 위대한 리더가 다른 사람들과 생각을 공유하고 의견과 반응을 구한다는 내용이 나오지만, 이는 핵심 내용이 아니다. (이유: 경청하는 것은 생각을 발전시키는 과정의 일부일 뿐이다.)
⑤ 경제적으로 성공하는 사람들에 대한 것은 언급되지 않았다.
리더와 혼동하면 안 됨 꿀팁

E 02 정답 ③ *늘어난 소비자의 일

핵심 주어(단수) 삽입절 단수 동사
The promise of a computerized society, / **we were told**, / **was** that it would pass to machines / all of the repetitive drudgery of work, /
컴퓨터화된 사회의 약속은 / 우리가 듣기로는 / 그것이 기계에 넘길 거라는 것이었다 / 모든 반복적인 고된 일을 /
분사구문을 이끄는 현재분사 allowing의 목적격 보어
allowing us humans **to pursue** higher purposes / and **to have** more leisure time. //
우리 인간들로 하여금 더 높은 목적을 추구하게 하면서 / 그리고 더 많은 여가 시간을 가질 수 있게 (하면서) //

It didn't work out this way. //
그것은 이런 식으로 되지는 않았다 //
뒤에 time이 생략됨
Instead of more time, / most of us have **less**. //
더 많은 시간 대신에 / 우리 대부분은 더 적은 시간을 가지고 있다 //

Companies large and small have off-loaded work / onto the backs of consumers. // 단서 1 회사들은 고객들에게 일을 떠넘김
크고 작은 회사들은 일을 떠넘겼다 / 소비자들의 등에 //
주격 관계대명사
Things **that** used to be done for us, / as part of the value-added service of working with a company, / we are now expected to do ourselves. // 단서 2 회사들이 서비스 차원으로 해주던 일도 이제는 우리가 스스로 하게 됨
우리를 위해 행해지던 일들은 / 회사와 함께 함으로써 받은 부가가치 서비스의 일환으로 / 우리는 이제 스스로가 하도록 기대된다 //

With air travel, / we're now expected to complete / **our own** 동격 **reservations and check-in,** / **jobs that used to be done** / by airline employees or travel agents. //
항공 여행의 경우 / 이제는 우리가 완수하도록 기대된다 / 우리의 예약과 체크인을 / 행해지던 일인 / 항공사 직원이나 여행사 직원에 의해 //

At the grocery store, / we're expected **to bag** our own groceries / and, in some supermarkets, / **to scan** our own purchases. // 병렬 구조
식료품점에서는 / 우리가 자신의 식료품을 봉지에 넣도록 기대된다 / 그리고 일부 슈퍼마켓에서는 / 자신이 구매한 물건을 스캔하도록 (기대된다) //

- promise ⓝ 약속 • repetitive ⓐ 반복적인 • pursue ⓥ 추구하다
- purpose ⓝ 목적 • leisure ⓝ 여가 • off-load ⓥ 떠넘기다
- consumer ⓝ 소비자 • value-added ⓐ 부가가치의
- reservation ⓝ 예약 • agent ⓝ 직원 • grocery ⓝ 식료품

컴퓨터화된 사회의 약속은, 우리가 듣기로는, 그것이 모든 반복적인 고된 일을 기계에 넘겨, 우리 인간들이 더 높은 목적을 추구하고 더 많은 여가 시간을 가질 수 있게 해준다는 것이었다. 그것은 이런 식으로 되지는 않았다. 더 많은 시간 대신에, 우리 대부분은 더 적은 시간을 가지고 있다. 크고 작은 회사들은 일을 소비자들의 등에 떠넘겼다. 회사와 함께 함으로써 받은 부가가치 서비스의 일환으로, 우리를 위해 행해지던 것들을 이제 우리 스스로가 하도록 기대된다. 항공 여행의 경우, 항공사 직원이나 여행사 직원들에 의해 행해지던 일인 우리의 예약과 체크인을 이제는 우리가 완수하도록 기대된다. 식료품점에서는, 우리가 자신의 식료품을 봉지에 넣도록, 그리고 일부 슈퍼마켓에서는, 우리 자신이 구매한 물건을 스캔하도록 기대된다.

다음 글의 요지로 가장 적절한 것은?
① 컴퓨터 기반 사회에서는 여가 시간이 더 늘어난다.
　　　　　　　　　　　　　여가 시간이 더 적어졌다고 했음
② 회사 업무의 전산화는 업무 능률을 향상시킨다.
　　　　　　　　　　　　업무 능률은 언급하지 않음
③ 컴퓨터화된 사회에서 소비자는 더 많은 일을 하게 된다.
　　　　　　　　　　　회사들이 일을 소비자에게 떠넘김
④ 온라인 거래가 모든 소비자들을 만족시키기에는 한계가 있다.
　　　　　　　　　온라인 거래에 국한된 내용이 아님
⑤ 산업의 발전으로 인해 기계가 인간의 일자리를 대신하고 있다.
　　　　　　　　오히려 인간의 일이 늘어났다는 내용임

왜 정답? ✱✱✱ [정답률 57%]

컴퓨터화된 사회에서 회사는 소비자에게 일을 떠넘겼고, 우리를 위해 행해지던 것들을 이제는 우리가 직접 하도록 기대된다. 단서1 단서2
➡ 예시: 1 항공사나 여행사 직원의 일이었던 예약과 체크인을 우리가 함
　　　 2 상점에서 구매한 물건을 우리가 직접 봉지에 담거나 스캔함
　 ▶ 컴퓨터화된 사회에서 소비자가 더 많은 일을 하게 되었다는 것이므로 정답은 ③이다.

왜 오답?

① 여가 시간이 더 늘어날 것을 기대했지만 그렇지 않다고 했다.
② 직원의 업무 능률이 늘었다는 것은 언급되지 않았다.
④ 온라인 거래만 이야기하는 글이 아니다.
⑤ 컴퓨터화된 사회의 문제점으로 인간의 일자리 감소를 이야기하는 글이 아니다.
　 (🎀 이유: '컴퓨터화된 사회'로 떠올릴 수 있는 내용으로 만든 오답이다.)

E 03 정답 ① *과학을 통한 불확실성 축소

사이에 목적격 관계대명사가 생략됨
The <mark>science we</mark> learn in grade school / is a collection / of certainties about the natural world / — the earth goes around the sun, / DNA carries the information of an organism, and so on. //
우리가 초등학교에서 배우는 과학은 / 모음인데 / 자연계에 대한 확실함의 / 즉 지구는 태양 주위를 돌고 / DNA는 유기체의 정보를 담고 있다는 것 등이다 //

　　　　　only가 문두로 오면서 주어와 동사가 도치됨
<mark>Only</mark> when you start to learn the practice of science / <mark>do you</mark>
　　　　　　　　　　　　　　　　　　　　　　부사
<mark>realize</mark> / that each of these "facts" was <mark>hard</mark> won /
여러분이 과학의 실제를 배우기 시작할 때만 / 깨닫게 된다 / 이러한 각각의 '사실'이 어렵게 얻어졌다고 /

through a succession of logical inferences / based upon many observations or experiments. //
연속적인 논리적 추론을 통해 / 많은 관찰이나 실험을 바탕으로 한 //

The process of science is / less about collecting pieces of
　　　　　　　　　　　　　　　　선행사를 포함하는 관계대명사
knowledge / than <u>it</u> is about reducing the uncertainties / in <mark>what</mark>
= the process of science
we know. // 단서 과학의 과정은 지식의 불확실함을 줄이는 것임
과학의 과정은 ~이다 / 지식의 조각을 모으는 것보다는 / 불확실함을 줄이는 것에 대한 것 / 우리가 알고 있는 것에서 //

Our uncertainties can be greater or lesser / for any given piece
　　　　　　　　　　　　　　　　　　　　~에 따라
of knowledge / <mark>depending upon</mark> where we are / in that process /
우리의 불확실함이 더 크거나 더 적을 수 있는데 / 주어진 어떤 지식의 조각에 대해서 / 우리가 지금 있는 곳에 따라 / 그 과정에서 /

— today we are quite certain / of <mark>how an apple will fall from
a tree</mark>, / but our understanding of the turbulent fluid flow /
전치사 of의 목적어 (간접의문문)
remains a work in progress / after more than a century of effort. //
즉 오늘날 우리는 꽤 확신하지만 / 사과가 나무에서 어떻게 떨어질지 / 난류 유동에 대한 우리의 이해는 / 여전히 진행 중인 연구로 남아 있다 / 한 세기가 넘는 노력 후에도 //

- grade school 초등학교　　　· certainty ⓝ 확실함, 확실한 것
- carry ⓥ 담고 있다　　· organism ⓝ 유기체　　· practice ⓝ 실제
- succession ⓝ 연속　　· logical ⓐ 논리적인
- observation ⓝ 관찰　　· uncertainty ⓝ 불확실함
- in progress 진행 중인

우리가 초등학교에서 배우는 과학은 자연계에 대한 확실함의 모음인데, 즉 지구는 태양 주위를 돌고, DNA는 유기체의 정보를 담고 있다는 것 등이다. 여러분이 과학의 실제를 배우기 시작할 때만, 이러한 각각의 '사실'이 많은 관찰이나 실험을 바탕으로 한 연속적인 논리적 추론을 통해 어렵게 얻어졌다고 깨닫게 된다. 과학의 과정은 지식의 조각을 모으는 것보다는 우리가 알고 있는 것에서 불확실함을 줄이는 것에 대한 것이다. 그 과정에서 우리가 지금 있는 곳에 따라 주어진 어떤 지식의 조각에 대해서 우리의 불확실함이 더 크거나 더 적을 수 있는데, 즉 오늘날 우리는 사과가 나무에서 어떻게 떨어질지 꽤 확신하지만, 난류 유동에 대한 우리의 이해는 한 세기가 넘는 노력 후에도 여전히 진행 중인 연구로 남아 있다.

다음 글의 요지로 가장 적절한 것은?
① 과학은 현재의 지식에 대한 불확실함을 줄이는 과정이다.
　　　　　　　　　　　과학 탐구를 통해 불확실함을 다소 감소시킬 수 있음
② 관찰과 실험 과정에서 우연히 얻어진 과학적 사실이 많다.
　　　　우연보다는 연속적인 추론을 통해 과학적 사실들을 발견함
③ 학생들에게 다양한 연구 방법을 가르치는 것이 중요하다.
　　　　　　　　다양한 연구 방법 교육의 필요성은 언급되지 않았음
④ 과학 연구에서는 정확한 실험 과정 설계가 핵심이다.
　　　　　　　　　　　실험 과정 설계는 언급되지 않았음
⑤ 과학은 분산된 지식을 수집하여 통합하는 학문이다.
　　　　　　지식의 분산이 아니라 누적과 확장에 관한 내용임

왜 정답? ✱✱✱ [정답률 72%]

도입: 초등학교 때 접한 다양한 과학 지식은 연속적인 추론의 결과임
주장: 과학의 과정은 지식의 불확실성을 줄이는 것임 단서
예시: 만유인력(사과가 어떻게 떨어질지)은 충분히 연구되었기에 확실히 알고 있지만, 난류 유동처럼 아직 불확실해서 연구가 진행 중인 경우도 있음
　 ▶ 과학은 탐구를 통해 지식의 불확실성을 줄이는 과정이라는 내용이므로 정답은 ①이다.

왜 오답?

② 우연이 아닌 끊임없는 탐구와 연속적인 논리 추론을 통해 과학적 사실이 밝혀진다.
③ 다양한 연구 방법의 교육에 관한 내용이 아니다.
④ 실험 과정 설계의 정확한 방향성은 언급된 내용이 아니다.
⑤ 과학의 과정은 지식의 조각을 모으는 것보다는 <mark>지식의 불확실함을 줄이는 것</mark>이라고 했다. 주의

구문 서술형

정답 뒤에 오는 명사를 한정, process

해석 그 과정에서 우리의 불확실함이 더 크거나 더 적을 수 있다.
→ 뒤에 오는 명사가 단수일 때는 지시형용사 this/that, 복수일 때는 these/those를 써서 수식할 수 있다. 따라서 지시형용사 that이 단수 명사 process를 한정한다.

E 04 정답 ① *말수를 줄일 때 나오는 경청

Imagine / following the spirit of a silence vow / into daily life. //
상상해 보라 / 침묵 서약의 정신을 따르는 것을 / 일상생활에서 //
　　　　　　　　　　　　　　spend 시간 -ing: ~하는 데 시간을 쓰다
Challenge yourself / to <mark>spend</mark> an entire day <mark>saying</mark> / only <mark>what</mark>
you absolutely must say. //　　　　　　　　　선행사를 포함하는 관계대명사
스스로 도전해 보라 / 말하는 데 하루 온종일을 보내는 것에 / 반드시 말해야 할 것만 //

가주어
It's been widely observed / by behavioral psychology experts / — and anyone who's ever been on a first date — /
널리 관찰되어 왔다 / 행동 심리학 전문가들에 의해 / 그리고 첫 데이트를 해 본 적이 있는 누구든지 /

진주어절 접속사 **'~로서'**
that we too often tend to treat / "conversation" as a game of
형용사적 용법 (our own turn 수식)
waiting for our own turn to speak. //
우리가 너무나 자주 여기는 경향이 있다는 것이 / "대화"를 자신이 말할 차례를 기다리는 게임처럼 //

We miss / what's being said / because we're mentally rehearsing
진행형 수동태 (be being 과거분사)
/ our next utterance. //
우리는 놓친다 / 말해지고 있는 것을 / 머릿속으로 연습하느라 / 다음 발언을 //

'~라면 어떨까?' **동격절 접속사**
What if you could eliminate the idea / that the next available
형용사적 용법 (your next opening 수식)
mini-silence / is your next opening / to express whatever is in your head? //
만약 당신이 생각을 없앨 수 있다면 어떨까 / 그 다음에 오는 작은 침묵이 / 그 다음 시작이라는 / 당신의 머릿속에 있는 무엇이든지를 표현할 //

What if you were limited to, / say, / fifty spoken words / tomorrow? //
당신이 제한받는다면 어떨까 / 이를테면 / 말을 50단어로 / 내일 //

I think / you'd listen quite differently. //
나는 생각한다 / 당신이 매우 다르게 듣게 될 것이라고 //

앞에 목적격 관계대명사가 생략됨
You'd attend quite carefully / to every word you heard. //
당신은 매우 신중히 귀를 기울이게 될 것이다 / 당신이 듣는 모든 단어에 //

You'd be attuned / to what you must respond to. //
당신이 맞춰질 것이다 / 반드시 응답해야 할 것에 //

'the+비교급 ~, the+비교급 …' 더 ~할수록 더 …하다
You might discover / that the less you say, / the more you hear. //
당신은 발견할지도 모른다 / 말을 줄일수록 / 더 많이 듣게 된다는 것을 //
단서 더 적게 말할수록 더 많이 들을 수 있음

- spirit ⓝ 정신   - challenge ⓥ 도전하다   - observe ⓥ 관찰하다
- behavioral ⓐ 행동의   - psychology ⓝ 심리학
- expert ⓝ 전문가   - treat ⓥ 여기다   - rehearse ⓥ 연습하다
- eliminate ⓥ 제거하다   - attend ⓥ 귀[주의]를 기울이다

일상생활에서 침묵 서약의 정신을 따르는 것을 상상해 보라. 반드시 말해야 할 것만 말하는 데 하루 온종일을 보내는 것에 스스로 도전해 보라. 우리가 너무나 자주 "대화"를 자신이 말할 차례를 기다리는 게임처럼 여기는 경향이 있다는 것이 행동 심리학 전문가들 — 그리고 첫 데이트를 해 본 적이 있는 누구든지 — 에 의해 널리 관찰되어 왔다. 우리는 다음 발언을 머릿속으로 연습하느라 말해지고 있는 것을 놓친다. 만약 당신이 그 다음에 오는 작은 침묵이 당신의 머릿속에 있는 무엇이든지를 표현할 그 다음 시작이라는 생각을 없앨 수 있다면 어떨까? 내일 당신이 말을, 이를테면, 50단어로 제한받는다면 어떨까? 나는 당신이 매우 다르게 듣게 될 것이라고 생각한다. 당신은 당신이 듣는 모든 단어에 매우 신중히 귀를 기울이게 될 것이다. 당신이 반드시 응답해야 할 것에 맞춰질 것이다. 당신은 말을 줄일수록, 더 많이 듣게 된다는 것을 발견할지도 모른다.

다음 글의 요지로 가장 적절한 것은?
① 말을 적게 하면 상대방의 말을 경청할 수 있다. 말을 줄이면 더 많이 듣게 됨
② 첫 만남에서는 언행에 더욱 신중할 필요가 있다. 신중한 언행은 언급되지 않았음
③ 불필요한 대화를 줄이면 스트레스가 감소한다. 불필요한 대화와 스트레스에 관한 내용이 아님
④ 침묵은 의사소통의 효율성을 저해할 수 있다. 침묵이 아니라 말을 줄이는 것에 관한 내용임
⑤ 몸짓 언어는 효과적인 대화에 도움이 된다. 몸짓 언어는 언급되지 않았음

왜 정답? ✿❀❀ [정답률 91%]
도입: 반드시 해야 할 말만 해 볼 것을 권유
문제 제기: 대화에서 다음 발언을 준비하느라 상대의 말을 놓치는 문제가 발생함
해결 방법: 말을 적게 하면 더 신중하게 듣고 더 많이 듣게 될 수 있음 **단서**
▶ 말을 줄이면 상대방의 말을 더 잘 듣게 된다는 내용이므로 정답은 ①이다.

왜 오답?
② 첫 만남에서 언행에 신중해야 한다는 것은 언급되지 않았다.
③ 불필요한 대화가 유발하는 스트레스에 관한 내용이 아니다.

---

④ 대화 중간의 작은 침묵이 언급되었지만, 침묵이 의사소통 효율성을 저해한다는 것이 요지는 아니다. **함정**
⑤ 몸짓 언어는 언급되지 않았다.

구문 서술형
정답 yourself

→ 명령문 동사 Challenge의 주어와 목적어가 you로 같다. 주어와 목적어가 같은 대상일 때 재귀대명사 재귀 용법을 사용해 목적어를 나타내므로, 재귀대명사 yourself의 형태로 오는 것이 알맞다.

E 05 정답 ③ *원예 활동의 이점

The act of gardening itself / is a fantastic form of physical activity. //
원예 행위 그 자체는 / 신체 활동의 환상적인 형태이다 //

from A to B: A에서 B까지
It involves a range of motions, / from digging and planting / to watering and harvesting. //
그것은 다양한 움직임을 포함한다 / 파기와 심기에서 / 물 주기와 수확하기까지 이르는 //

help의 목적어
These activities help improve / strength, flexibility, and endurance. //
이런 활동들은 향상시키는 것을 돕는다 / 강인함, 유연성과 내구력을 //

You might not realize it, / but small tasks like weeding or turning compost / can burn many calories. //
당신은 그것을 인식하지 못할 수도 있으나 / 잡초 뽑기나 퇴비 뒤섞기와 같은 작은 과업들은 / 많은 칼로리를 태울 수 있다 //

'~한 사람들'
Gardening is particularly beneficial / for those who find traditional exercise challenging. //
원예는 특히 이롭다 / 전통적 운동이 힘들다고 생각하는 사람들에게 //

= a low-impact way to stay active and fit
It's a low-impact way / to stay active and fit, / making it accessible / for people of all ages and physical abilities. //
그것은 부담을 주지 않는 방법이어서 / 활동적이고 건강하게 유지하기에 / 접근할 수 있게 만든다 / 모든 연령대 및 신체 능력을 지닌 사람들이 //

전치사 (~ 외에도)
Besides physical health, / gardening has profound mental health benefits. // **단서** 원예의 신체적 및 정신적 이점
신체적 건강 외에도 / 원예는 충분한 정신적 건강 이점이 있다 //

Tending to plants can be incredibly calming and meditative. //
식물을 돌보는 것은 믿을 수 없을 정도로 고요하고 명상적일 수 있다 //

allows의 목적어와 목적격 보어 (to부정사)
It allows you to focus on the present moment, / reducing stress and anxiety. //
그것은 당신이 현재 순간에 집중하게 하면서 / 스트레스와 불안감을 줄인다 //

앞에 주격 관계대명사와 be동사가 생략됨
The repetitive tasks involved in gardening can induce / a state of mindfulness, / similar to meditation. //
원예와 관련한 반복적인 과업은 유도한다 / 마음 돌봄의 상태를 / 명상과 유사한 //

목적어절 접속사 **동명사 (목적어절의 주어)**
Studies have shown / that spending time in nature, / even in a small garden, / can elevate mood, improve cognition, and reduce depression symptoms. //
병렬 구조 (목적어절의 동사)
연구는 보여왔다 / 자연에서 시간을 보내는 것이 / 심지어 작은 정원이더라도 / 기분을 돋우고, 인지를 개선하며, 우울 증상을 줄일 수 있음을 //

문장의 주어 **watching의 목적격 보어**
The sense of accomplishment / from watching your plants grow and thrive / can also boost self-esteem and overall well-being. //
문장의 동사
성취감은 / 당신의 식물들이 성장하고 잘 자라는 것을 지켜본 것에서 온 / 또한 자아존중감과 전반적 행복을 높일 수 있다 //

- dig ⓥ 파다   - harvest ⓥ 수확하다   - flexibility ⓝ 유연성
- endurance ⓝ 내구력   - beneficial ⓐ 이익을 가져오는
- incredibly ⓐ⑥ 믿을 수 없게   - meditative ⓐ 명상의

- anxiety ⓝ 불안감
- meditation ⓝ 명상
- cognition ⓝ 인지
- accomplishment ⓝ 성취감
- boost ⓥ 높이다
- mindfulness ⓝ 마음 돌봄
- elevate ⓥ 증진시키다
- depression ⓝ 우울함
- thrive ⓥ 번성하다, 번영하다
- self-esteem ⓝ 자아존중감

원예 행위 그 자체는 신체 활동의 환상적인 형태이다. 그것은 파기와 심기에서 물 주기와 수확하기까지 이르는 다양한 움직임을 포함한다. 이런 활동들은 강인함, 유연성과 내구력을 향상시키는 것을 돕는다. 당신은 그것을 인식하지 못할 수도 있으나 잡초 뽑기나 퇴비 뒤섞기와 같은 작은 과업들은 많은 칼로리를 태울 수 있다. 원예는 특히 전통적 운동이 힘들다고 생각하는 사람들에게 이롭다. 그것은 활동적이고 건강하게 유지하기에 부담을 주지 않는 방법이어서 모든 연령대 및 신체 능력을 지닌 사람들이 접근할 수 있게 만든다. 신체적 건강 외에도, 원예는 충분한 정신적 건강 이점이 있다. 식물을 돌보는 것은 믿을 수 없을 정도로 고요하고 명상적일 수 있다. 그것은 당신이 현재 순간에 집중하게 하면서 스트레스와 불안감을 줄인다. 원예와 관련한 반복적인 과업은 명상과 유사한 마음 돌봄의 상태를 유도한다. 연구는 심지어 작은 정원이더라도 자연에서 시간을 보내는 것이 기분을 돋우고, 인지를 개선하며, 우울 증상을 줄일 수 있음을 보여왔다. 당신의 식물들이 성장하고 잘 자라는 것을 지켜본 것에서 온 성취감은 또한 자아존중감과 전반적 행복을 높일 수 있다.

다음 글의 요지로 가장 적절한 것은?
① 야외 활동을 통해 협동심과 자존감을 높일 수 있다. 원예 활동의 이점에 관한 내용임
② 취미 활동을 지속적으로 할 수 있는 동기가 필요하다. 동기 부여의 필요성에 관한 내용이 아님
③ 원예 활동은 신체적 건강과 더불어 정신적 건강에 이롭다. 원예 활동이 갖는 신체적 · 정신적 이점들을 소개함
④ 실내에서 식물을 기르는 것은 집중력 향상에 도움이 된다. 실내에서 식물을 기르는 것은 언급되지 않았음
⑤ 원예 활동은 연령에 관계없이 다양한 사람들이 즐길 수 있다. 원예의 이점 중 일부에만 해당함

〉왜 정답 ? ❀❀❀ [정답률 92%]
원예 활동이 주는 신체적 이점들을 나열하다가, 정신적 건강에 주는 이점들도 있다고 하며 예시를 소개하는 글이므로 정답은 ③이다.

〉왜 오답 ?
① 야외 활동이 아니라 원예 활동의 이점에 관한 내용이다.
② 취미 활동을 지속하기 위한 동기부여가 필요하다는 내용이 아니다.
④ 원예 활동은 실내가 아닌 실외 활동이며, 집중력 향상 이외에도 여러 이점을 예로 들었다. **주의**
⑤ 원예 활동은 모든 연령대의 사람들이 접근할 수 있다고 했을 뿐, 그 외에도 원예 활동의 다양한 이점을 소개하고 있다. **함정**

〔구문 서술형〕
〔정답〕 itself, 주어를 강조하는 강조 용법으로 쓰였기 때문이다.
〔해석〕 원예 행위 그 자체는 신체 활동의 환상적인 형태이다.
→ 재귀대명사 itself가 주어 The act of gardening을 강조하는 강조 용법으로 쓰였으므로 이를 생략할 수 있다.

E 06 정답 ⑤ ＊무의식적인 최초 반응의 정확성

It's when people find themselves / unable to explain why they recognize the person, / saying things like "his face just popped out at me," / that they tend to be accurate more often. //
바로 사람들이 스스로를 발견할 때에 / 왜 그 사람을 알아보는지 설명할 수 없는 / "그의 얼굴이 그냥 나에게 탁 떠올랐다"라는 식으로 말하면서 / 그들은 더 자주 정확한 경향이 있다 //

Sometimes / our first, immediate, automatic reaction to a situation / is the truest interpretation / of what our mind is telling us. // **단서 1** 최초의 즉각적이고 자동적인 반응이 가장 정확한 우리의 마음임
때때로 / 상황에 대한 우리의 최초의, 즉각적인, 자동적인 반응이 / 가장 정확한 해석이다 / 우리 마음이 우리에게 말하고 있는 것에 대한 //

That very first impression / can also be more accurate about the world / than the deliberative, reasoned self-narrative can be. // **단서 2** 첫인상이 신중하고 논리적인 자기 서사보다 더 정확할 수 있음
바로 그 첫인상이 / 또한 세상에 대해 더 정확할 수 있다 / 신중하고 논리적인 자기 서사보다 //

In his book *Blink*, / Malcolm Gladwell describes a variety of studies / in psychology and behavioral economics /
그의 저서 'Blink'에서 / Malcolm Gladwell은 다양한 연구를 기술한다 / 심리학 및 행동 경제학의 /

that demonstrate the superior performance of relatively unconscious first guesses / compared to logical step-by-step justifications for a decision. //
상대적으로 무의식적인 최초 추측의 우수성을 보여 주는 / 결정에 대한 논리적인 단계적 정당화에 비해서 //

- conduct ⓥ 수행하다
- inaccurate ⓐ 부정확한
- recognize ⓥ 알아채다
- immediate ⓐ 즉각적인
- interpretation ⓝ 해석
- reasoned ⓐ 논리적인
- demonstrate ⓥ 보여 주다
- relatively ⓐⓓ 상대적으로
- logical ⓐ 논리적인
- deliberation ⓝ 숙고
- identification ⓝ 식별
- accurate ⓐ 정확한
- automatic ⓐ 자동적인
- impression ⓝ 인상
- self-narrative ⓝ 자기 서사
- superior ⓐ 우수한
- unconscious ⓐ 무의식의
- justification ⓝ 정당화
- feature ⓝ 특징

David Dunning의 코넬 대학의 실험실에서, 그는 목격자 증언에 대한 실험을 수행했고, 얼굴 특징에 대한 신중한 숙고와 선택 절차에 대한 상세한 논의가 실제로는 '부정확한' 식별의 징후일 수 있다는 증거를 발견했다. 사람들이 "그의 얼굴이 그냥 나에게 탁 떠올랐다"라는 식으로 말하면서 왜 그 사람을 알아보는지 설명할 수 없는 스스로를 발견하는 바로 그때 그들은 더 자주 정확한 경향이 있다. 때때로 상황에 대한 우리의 최초의, 즉각적인, 자동적인 반응이 우리 마음이 우리에게 말하고 있는 것에 대한 가장 정확한 해석이다. 바로 그 첫인상이 또한 신중하고 논리적인 자기 서사보다 세상에 대해 더 정확할 수 있다. Malcolm Gladwell은 그의 저서 'Blink'에서, 결정에 대한 논리적인 단계적 정당화에 비해서 상대적으로 무의식적인 최초 추측의 우수성을 보여 주는 심리학 및 행동 경제학의 다양한 연구를 기술한다.

다음 글의 요지로 가장 적절한 것은?
① 논리적인 근거가 부족한 판단은 진실을 왜곡할 수 있다. 논리적 근거가 부족한 판단은 언급되지 않았음
② 인간의 표정은 무의식적인 감정 상태를 가장 잘 반영한다. 인간의 표정과 감정 상태에 관한 내용이 아님
③ 사람을 정확하게 식별하기 위해서는 상황에 대한 정보가 중요하다. 사람을 정확하게 식별하는 방법에 관한 내용이 아님
④ 목격자 진술은 사건 직후보다 일정 시간이 지난 뒤 더 명확해진다. 목격자 진술의 정확도와 시간의 관계는 언급되지 않았음
⑤ 무의식적인 최초의 반응이 신중히 판단한 결과보다 정확할 수 있다. 무의식적 최초 추측이 신중하고 논리적인 자기 서사보다 정확할 수 있음

〉왜 정답 ? ❀❀❀ [정답률 82%]
주장: 상황에 대한 즉각적인 반응이나 무의식적인 최초 추측이 신중하고 논리적인 판단 결과보다 더 정확할 수 있다. **단서 1, 단서 2**
예시 1: David Dunning의 실험 → 목격자 증언에 대한 실험에서 신중한 숙고와 상세한 논의가 오히려 부정확한 결과를 나타냄
예시 2: Malcolm Gladwell의 저서 → 무의식적 최초의 추측이 논리적인 결정보다 우수함을 증명하는 다양한 연구를 기술함
▶ 상황에 대한 무의식적인 최초 반응이 신중한 판단 결과보다 더 정확할 수 있다는 내용이므로 정답은 ⑤이다.

왜 오답?

① 결정에 대한 논리적인 단계적 정당화가 언급되었을 뿐, 논리적 근거나 진실 왜곡은 언급되지 않았다.

② 인간의 표정과 감정 상태에 관한 내용이 아니다.

③ 사람을 식별하는 실험에서 최초의 무의식 반응이 더 정확하다는 내용이지, 상황에 대한 정보가 중요하다는 내용이 아니다.

④ 목격자 진술의 정확도와 시간의 관계에 관한 내용이 아니다. (❦ 이유: 최초의 무의식 반응이 논리적 판단보다 더 정확하다는 근거로 소개된 목격자 증언 실험으로 만든 오답이다.)

구문 서술형

정답 themselves, 없다, 재귀

해석 사람들은 왜 그 사람을 알아보는지 설명할 수 없는 스스로를 발견한다.

→ 사람들이 '스스로를' 발견하는 것이므로, 주어 people과 목적어 themselves가 가리키는 대상이 같다. 즉, themselves는 재귀 용법으로 쓰인 목적어이므로 생략할 수 없다.

> ★ to부정사의 to를 생략하는 경우
> 문장 성분이 아래와 같은 2형식 문장에서 to부정사의 to를 생략하기도 한다.
> 주어: do가 포함된 명사절 (All you have to do)
> 동사: be동사 (is)
> 보어: to부정사 (to come, to show)

E 07 정답 ① *작은 관심의 힘

'~에 관해서는'
When it comes to helping out, / you don't have to do much. //
도움을 주는 것에 관해서 / 당신은 많은 것을 할 필요는 없다 //

to가 생략된 to부정사 / 목적어절 접속사
All you have to do is **come** around / and **show that** you care. //
당신이 할 수 있는 일은 그저 다가가서 / 관심을 갖고 있다는 것을 보여주면 된다 // **단서 1** 관심을 갖고 있다는 것만 보여주면 됨

주격 관계대명사
If you notice someone **who** is lonely, / you could go and sit with them. //
외로운 사람을 발견하면 / 가서 함께 앉아 있으면 된다 //

주격 관계대명사
If you work with someone / **who** eats lunch all by themselves, / and you go and sit down with them, /
사람과 함께 일한다면 / 혼자서 점심을 먹는 / 그리고 그 사람에게 다가가서 함께 앉는다면 /

명사적 용법(목적어)
they will begin **to be** more social after a while, / and they will **owe** it all **to** you. //
owe B to A: A에게 B를 빚지다
얼마 지나지 않아 그 사람은 더 사교적으로 변하기 시작할 것이고 / 이 모든 것을 당신 덕분이라고 할 것이다 //

A person's happiness / comes from attention. //
한 사람의 행복은 / 관심에서 비롯된다 // **단서 2** 행복은 관심에서 비롯됨

주격 관계대명사
There are too many people out in the world / **who** feel like everyone has forgotten them or ignored them. //
세상에는 사람들이 너무 많다 / 모든 이가 자신을 잊었거나 무시한다고 느끼는 //

부사절 접속사(양보)   현재분사구(someone 수식)
Even if you say hi / to someone **passing by**, / they will begin to feel better about themselves, / like someone cares. //
인사만 건네도 / 지나가는 사람들에게 / 그들은 자기 자신에 대해 기분이 좋아지기 시작할 것이다 / 누군가 (그들에게) 관심을 가져주는 것처럼 // **단서 3** 누군가 관심을 준다는 것을 알면 기분이 좋아짐

- care ⓥ 관심을 보이다
- social ⓐ 사교적인, 사회적인
- owe ⓥ 빚지다
- ignore ⓥ 무시하다
- pass by 지나가다

도움을 주는 것에 관해서 당신은 많은 것을 할 필요는 없다. 그저 다가가서 관심을 갖고 있다는 것을 보여주기만 하면 된다. 외로운 사람을 발견하면 가서 함께 앉아 있으면 된다. 혼자서 점심을 먹는 사람과 함께 일한다면, 그리고 그 사람에게 다가가서 함께 앉는다면 얼마 지나지 않아 그 사람은 더 사교적으로 변하기 시작할 것이고, 이 모든 것을 당신 덕분이라고 할 것이다. 한 사람의 행복은 관심에서 비롯된다. 세상에는 모든 이가 자신을 잊었거나 무시한다고 느끼는 사람들이 너무 많다. 지나가는 사람들에게 인사만 건네도, 누군가 (그들에게) 관심을 가져주는 것처럼, 그들은 자기 자신에 대해 기분이 좋아지기 시작할 것이다.

다음 글의 요지로 가장 적절한 것은?

① 사소한 관심이 타인에게 도움이 될 수 있다. 타인을 향한 사소한 관심이 도움이 됨

② 사람마다 행복의 기준이 제각기 다르다. 사람마다의 행복 기준을 말하는 글이 아님

③ 선행을 통해 자신을 되돌아볼 수 있다. 선행과 자아 반성에 대한 글이 아님

④ 원만한 대인 관계는 경청에서 비롯된다. 경청과 원만한 대인 관계에 대한 글이 아님

⑤ 현재에 대한 만족이 행복의 필수조건이다. 현재에 대한 만족이 행복을 줄 수 있다는 내용이 아님

왜 정답? ✿✿✿ [정답률 92%]

도와주길 원한다면 다가가서 관심을 갖고 있다는 것만 보여주면 된다. **단서 1**

예시: 외로운 사람을 발견하면 가서 함께 앉아있으면 됨 → 혼자서 점심을 먹는 사람에게 다가가서 함께 앉는다면 그 사람은 당신에게 고마움을 느낄 것임

부가 설명: 한 사람의 행복은 관심에서 비롯됨 **단서 2** → 누군가 관심을 가져주면 사람들은 자신에 대해 기분이 좋아짐 **단서 3**

▶ 타인을 향한 사소한 관심은 그들의 기분을 좋게 만들고 도움을 줄 수 있다는 내용이므로 정답은 ①이다.

왜 오답?

② 사람마다 행복의 기준이 다르다는 것은 언급되지 않았다.

③ 선행을 통해 자신을 되돌아볼 수 있다는 내용이 아니다.

④ 관심을 통해 타인을 도와줄 수 있다는 내용일 뿐, 경청과 대인관계에 대한 글이 아니다.

⑤ 현재에 대해 만족하라는 내용이 아니다.

E 08 정답 ③ *생존에 도움이 되는 감정

수동태 동사   **단서 1** 감정은 생존에 기여했기 때문에 존재한다고 여겨짐
Our emotions **are thought** to exist / because they have contributed to our survival / as a species. //
우리의 감정은 존재한다고 여겨진다 / 그것들이 우리의 생존에 기여해 왔기 때문에 / 종으로서 //
첫 번째 절의 주어(명사)   두 번째 절의 주어(동명사구)
Fear has helped us avoid dangers, / **expressing anger** helps us scare off threats, / and **expressing positive emotions** helps us bond with others. //
세 번째 절의 주어(동명사구)
두려움은 우리가 위험을 피하는 데 도움을 주어 왔고 / 분노를 표현하는 것은 우리가 위협을 쫓아내도록 돕고 / 긍정적인 감정을 표현하는 것은 우리가 다른 사람과 유대하도록 돕는다 //
단수 주어
From an evolutionary perspective, / **an emotion** is a kind of "program" / **that, when triggered,** / **directs** many of our activities /
주격 관계대명사   삽입구   단수 동사
진화적 관점에서 / 감정은 일종의 '프로그램'이다 / 유발될 때 / 우리의 많은 활동을 지시하는 /
(including attention, perception, memory, movement, expressions, etc.) //
(주의, 지각, 기억, 움직임, 표현 등을 포함하는) //
For example, / fear **makes** us very attentive, / **narrows** our perceptual focus to threatening stimuli, / **will cause** us **either** to face a situation (fight) **or** avoid it (flight), /
병렬 구조
「either A or B」: A 또는 B (중 하나)
예를 들어 / 두려움은 우리를 매우 주의 깊게 만들고 / 우리의 지각의 초점을 위협적인 자극으로 좁히고 / 우리로 하여금 상황을 정면으로 대하거나 (싸우거나) 그것을 피하도록 (도피하도록) 하며 /
and **may cause** us / to remember an experience more acutely / (so that we avoid the threat in the future). //
우리로 하여금 ~하도록 할 수도 있다 / 경험을 더 강렬하게 기억(하도록) / (그래서 우리가 미래에 위협을 피하도록) //
「전치사 + 관계대명사」
Regardless of the specific ways **in which** they activate our systems, / the specific emotions **we possess** are thought to exist /
앞에 목적격 관계대명사가 생략됨
그것들이 우리의 시스템을 활성화하는 구체적인 방식과는 관계없이 / 우리가 소유한 특정한 감정은 / 존재한다고 여겨진다 /
because they have helped us / (as a species) survive challenges / within our environment long ago. // **단서 2** 감정은 힘든 상황에 생존하도록 도움을 줬기 때문에 존재한다고 여겨짐
그것들이 우리에게 도움을 주어 왔기 때문에 / (종으로서) 힘든 상황에서 생존하도록 / 오래전에 우리의 환경 내에서 //

If they **had not helped** us adapt and survive, / they **would not have evolved** with us. //
가정법 과거완료
만약 그것들이 우리가 적응하고 생존하도록 도움을 주지 않았더라면 / 그것들은 우리와 함께 진화해 오지 않았을 것이다 //

- contribute ⓥ 기여하다   • species ⓝ 종
- bond ⓥ 유대감을 형성하다   • evolutionary ⓐ 진화론적인
- direct ⓥ 지시하다   • attentive ⓐ 주의를 기울이는
- narrow ⓥ 좁히다   • stimuli ⓝ 자극   • acutely ⓐⓓ 강렬하게

우리의 감정은 그것들이 종으로서 우리의 생존에 기여해 왔기 때문에 존재한다고 여겨진다. 두려움은 우리가 위험을 피하는 데 도움을 주어 왔고, 분노를 표현하는 것은 우리가 위협을 쫓아내도록 돕고, 긍정적인 감정을 표현하는 것은 우리가 다른 사람과 유대하도록 돕는다. 진화적 관점에서, 감정은 유발될 때 (주의, 지각, 기억, 움직임, 표현 등을 포함하는) 우리의 많은 활동을 지시하는 일종의 '프로그램'이다. 예를 들어, 두려움은 우리를 매우 주의 깊게 만들고, 우리의 지각의 초점을 위협적인 자극으로 좁히고, 우리로 하여금 상황을 정면으로 대하거나 (싸우거나) 그것을 피하도록 (도피하도록) 하며, 우리로 하여금 경험을 더 강렬하게 기억하도록 (그래서 우리가 미래에 위협을 피하도록) 할 수도 있다. 그것들이 우리의 시스템을 활성화하는 구체적인 방식과는 관계없이, 우리가 소유한 특정한 감정은 그것들이 오래전에 우리의 환경 내에서 우리가 (종으로서) 힘든 상황에서 생존하도록 도움을 주어 왔기 때문에 존재한다고 여겨진다. 만약 그것들이 우리가 적응하고 생존하도록 도움을 주지 않았더라면 그것들은 우리와 함께 진화해 오지 않았을 것이다.

다음 글의 요지로 가장 적절한 것은?
① 과거의 경험이 현재의 감정에 영향을 미친다.
  ‹과거의 경험이 현재의 감정에 영향을 미친다는 내용이 아님›
② 문명의 발달에 따라 인간의 감정은 다양화되어 왔다.
  ‹감정의 다양화에 관한 내용이 아님›
③ 감정은 인간이 생존하도록 도와왔기 때문에 존재한다.
  ‹감정은 생존에 도움을 줬기 때문에 존재한다고 여겨짐›
④ 부정적인 감정은 긍정적인 감정보다 더 오래 기억된다.
  ‹어떤 감정이 더 오래 기억되는지에 관한 내용이 아님›
⑤ 두려움의 원인을 파악함으로써 두려움을 없앨 수 있다.
  ‹두려움을 없애는 것에 관한 내용이 아님›

왜 정답? ✽✽✽ [정답률 91%]

주장: 감정은 생존에 기여했기 때문에 존재한다고 여겨짐 [단서 1], [단서 2]
예시: 두려움은 우리를 주의 깊게 만들고, 지각의 초점을 좁혀 위협적인 자극에 집중하고, 상황에 맞서거나 피하도록 하고, 경험을 더 강렬하게 기억하도록 할 수 있음
▶ 감정은 인간의 생존에 도움을 주었기에 지금까지 존재한다는 내용이므로 정답은 ③이다.

왜 오답?

① 먼 과거의 힘든 상황에서 감정이 생존에 도움을 줬기에 현재까지도 존재한다는 것이지, 과거의 경험이 현재의 감정에 영향을 미친다는 내용이 아니다. ‹함정›
② 인간의 생존에 도움을 준 감정인 두려움, 분노, 긍정적인 감정이 언급되었을 뿐, 감정의 다양화에 관한 내용이 아니다.
④ 어떤 감정이 더 오래 기억되는지에 관한 내용이 아니다.
⑤ 두려움은 생존에 도움을 준 감정의 예시로 제시되었을 뿐, 두려움을 없애는 것에 관한 내용이 아니다.

E 09 정답 ④ *어떻게 협상해야 하는가

We all negotiate every day, / whether we realise it or not. //
준부정어(거의 ~ 없는)   how to-v: ~하는 법
우리는 모두 매일 협상한다 / 우리가 그것을 알든지 모르든지 간에 //
Yet / **few** people ever learn / *how to negotiate*. //
하지만 / 이제까지 배운 사람은 거의 없다 / '어떻게' 협상하는지를 //
= learn how to negotiate
Those who **do** / usually learn the traditional, win-lose negotiating style / rather than an approach / **that** is likely to result in / a win-win agreement. //
주격 관계대명사
(협상 방식을) 배우는 사람들은 / 대개 전통적인, 한쪽만 이기는 협상 방식을 배운다 / 접근법보다는 / 도출할 가능성이 있는 / 양쪽이 이기는 합의를 //

This old-school, adversarial approach may be useful / in a one-off negotiation / **where** you will probably not deal with **that** person again. //
관계부사   지시형용사
이 구식의 적대적인 접근법은 아마 유용할지도 모른다 / 일회성 협상에서 / 여러분이 아마 그 사람을 다시 상대하지 않을 //
However, / such transactions are becoming increasingly rare, / **because** most of us deal with the same people repeatedly /
부사절 접속사(이유)
그러나 / 이러한 거래는 점점 더 드물어지고 있다 / 우리 대부분이 동일한 사람들을 반복적으로 상대하기 때문에 //
— our spouses and children, our friends and colleagues, our customers and clients. //
배우자와 자녀, 우리의 친구와 동료, 고객과 의뢰인 같은 //
[단서 1] 성공적인 결과를 얻으면서 상대방과도 좋은 관계를 유지하는 것이 중요함
In view of this, / **it's** essential / **to achieve** successful results for ourselves / and **maintain** a healthy relationship with our negotiating partners / at the same time. //
가주어   진주어   병렬구조
이러한 관점에서 / ~이 매우 중요하다 / 우리 자신을 위해 성공적인 결과를 얻어내는 것이 / 그리고 우리의 협상 파트너들과 건전한 관계를 유지하는 것이 / 동시에 //
In today's interdependent world / of business partnerships and long-term relationships, / a win-win outcome is **fast** becoming / the *only* acceptable result. //
형용사와 부사의 형태가 같음
[단서 2] 양쪽이 모두 이기는 성과만 받아들여지고 있음
오늘날의 상호 의존적인 세계에서 / 사업 협력과 장기적인 관계의 / 양쪽이 이기는 성과가 빠르게 되어가고 있다 / '유일하게' 받아들일 수 있는 결과가 //

- negotiate ⓥ 협상하다   • realise ⓥ 알아차리다
- traditional ⓐ 전통적인   • approach ⓝ 접근(법)
- agreement ⓝ 합의, 동의   • one-off ⓐ 단 한 번의
- transaction ⓝ 거래   • rare ⓐ 드문   • repeatedly ⓐⓓ 반복적으로
- spouse ⓝ 배우자   • essential ⓐ 매우 중요한
- maintain ⓥ 유지하다   • interdependent ⓐ 상호 의존적인
- acceptable ⓐ 받아들일 수 있는

우리는 그것을 알든지 모르든지 간에, 모두 매일 협상한다. 하지만 이제까지 '어떻게' 협상하는지를 배운 사람은 거의 없다. (협상 방식을) 배우는 사람들은 대개 양쪽이 이기는 합의를 도출할 가능성이 있는 접근법보다는 전통적인, 한쪽만 이기는 협상 방식을 배운다. 이 구식의 적대적인 접근법은 아마 여러분이 그 사람을 다시 상대하지 않을 일회성 협상에서 유용할지도 모른다. 그러나, 우리 대부분은 배우자와 자녀, 친구와 동료, 고객과 의뢰인같이 동일한 사람들을 반복적으로 상대하기 때문에, 이러한 거래는 점점 더 드물어지고 있다. 이러한 관점에서, 우리 자신을 위해 성공적인 결과를 얻어내는 동시에 협상 파트너들과 건전한 관계를 유지하는 것이 매우 중요하다. 오늘날 사업 협력과 장기적인 관계의 상호 의존적인 세계에서, 양쪽이 이기는 성과는 '유일하게' 받아들일 수 있는 결과가 빠르게 되어가고 있다.

다음 글의 요지로 가장 적절한 것은?
① 협상 상대의 단점뿐 아니라 장점을 철저히 분석해야 한다.
  ‹협상 상대를 철저히 분석하라는 언급은 없음›
② 의사소통 과정에서 서로의 의도를 확인하는 것이 바람직하다.
  ‹서로의 의도를 확인하라는 내용이 아님›
③ 성공적인 협상을 위해 다양한 대안을 준비하는 것이 중요하다.
  ‹다양한 대안의 필요성을 제시하지 않았음›
④ 양측에 유리한 협상을 통해 상대와 좋은 관계를 유지해야 한다.
  ‹양쪽이 이기는 성과만이 받아들여짐›
⑤ 원만한 인간관계를 위해 상호독립성을 인정하는 것이 필요하다.
  ‹interdependent가 언급된 것으로 만든 오답›

왜 정답? ✽✽✽ [정답률 67%]

- 구식 협상: 한쪽만 이김, 일회성 협상에 유용함
- 오늘날 협상: 양쪽이 모두 이겨서 좋은 관계를 유지하는 것이 중요함 [단서 1], [단서 2]
▶ 양측에 유리한 협상을 통해 상대와 좋은 관계를 유지해야 한다는 것이므로 정답은 ④이다.

왜 오답?

① 협상 상대를 분석하라고 이야기하는 글이 아니다.
② 의사소통 과정에서 서로의 의도를 확인해야 한다는 내용이 아니다.
③ 성공적인 협상이 필요하다고 하는 것은 맞지만, 다양한 대안을 준비하라는 것이 아니다. (▶ 이유: 일반적으로 '성공적인 협상'하면 떠올릴 수 있는 내용으로 만든 오답이다.)
⑤ 글에서 언급된 interdependent의 반의어인 '상호독립성'으로 만든 오답이다.

E 10 정답 ⑤ *소설의 세부 사항은 무엇을 담아야 하는가

사이에 주어와 be동사 생략
When writing a novel, / research for information needs to be done. // 단서 1 소설을 쓸 때는 정보 조사를 해야 함
소설을 쓸 때 / 정보를 위한 조사가 행해질 필요가 있다 //

주격 보어절 접속사
The thing is / that some kinds of fiction / demand a higher level of detail: / crime fiction, for example, or scientific thrillers. //
문제는 / 어떤 종류의 소설은 / 더 높은 수준의 세부 사항을 요구한다는 것이다 / 예를 들어 범죄 소설이나 과학 스릴러와 같은 //

부사적 용법(형용사 hard 수식)
The information is never hard to find; / one website for authors / even organizes trips to police stations, / so that crime writers can get it right. //
부사절 접속사(~하도록)
정보는 찾기에 결코 어렵지 않다 / 작가들을 위한 한 웹사이트는 / 심지어 경찰서로의 견학을 계획하기도 한다 / 범죄물 작가들이 정보를 제대로 얻을 수 있도록 //

간접목적어   직접목적어   형용사적 용법
Often, / a polite letter will earn you permission / to visit a particular location / and record all the details that you need. //
병렬 구조   목적격 관계대명사
종종 / 정중한 편지는 여러분에게 허가를 얻어 줄 것이다 / 특정한 장소를 방문하고 / 필요한 모든 세부 사항을 기록할 수 있는 //

명사절 접속사   부사절 접속사(조건)
But remember / that you will drive your readers to boredom / if you think / that you need to pack everything you discover into
명사절 접속사   앞에 목적격 관계대명사 생략
your work. // 단서 2 조사한 모든 세부 사항을 소설에 담으면 지루해짐
하지만 기억하라 / 여러분은 독자들을 지루하게 만들 것이라는 것을 / 만약 여러분이 생각할 경우 / 발견한 모든 것을 작품에 담아야 한다고 //

주격 관계대명사   문장의 본동사   주격 관계대명사
The details that matter / are those that reveal the human experience. // 단서 3 중요한 세부 사항은 인간의 경험을 드러내는 것임
중요한 세부 사항은 / 인간의 경험을 드러내는 것이다 //

분사구문을 이끎
The crucial thing is / telling a story, / finding the characters, the tension, and the conflict / — not the train timetable or the building blueprint. // 단서 4 중요한 세부 사항은 인물, 긴장, 갈등 등 인간의 이야기임
중요한 것은 / 이야기를 말하는 것이다 / 인물, 긴장, 그리고 갈등을 찾아가며 / 기차 시간표나 건물 청사진이 아니라 //

- demand ⓥ 요구하다   · crime fiction 범죄 소설
- organize ⓥ 계획하다, 준비하다   · get it right 제대로 이해하다
- permission ⓝ 허가   · drive ~ to … ⓥ ~을 …하게 만들다
- boredom ⓝ 지루함   · reveal ⓥ 드러내다   · crucial ⓐ 중요한
- tension ⓝ 긴장   · conflict ⓝ 갈등   · blueprint ⓝ 청사진

소설을 쓸 때 정보를 위한 조사가 행해질 필요가 있다. 문제는 예를 들어 범죄 소설이나 과학 스릴러와 같은 어떤 종류의 소설은 더 높은 수준의 세부 사항을 요구한다는 것이다. 정보는 찾기에 결코 어렵지 않다. 작가들을 위한 한 웹사이트는 범죄물 작가들이 정보를 제대로 얻을 수 있도록 심지어 경찰서로의 탐방을 조직하기도 한다. 종종 정중한 편지는 여러분에게 특정한 장소를 방문하고 필요한 모든 세부 사항을 기록할 수 있는 허가를 얻어 줄 것이다. 하지만 만약 여러분이 발견한 모든 것을 작품에 담아야 한다고 생각할 경우 여러분은 독자들을 지루하게 만들 것이라는 것을 기억하라. 중요한 세부 사항은 인간의 경험을 드러내는 것이다. 중요한 것은 기차 시간표나 건물 청사진이 아니라 인물, 긴장, 그리고 갈등을 찾아가며 이야기를 말하는 것이다.

다음 글의 요지로 가장 적절한 것은?
① 작품의 완성도는 작가의 경험의 양에 비례한다.
경험의 양이 아니라 세부 사항에 비례함
② 작가의 상상력은 가장 훌륭한 이야기 재료이다. 작가의 상상력은 언급되지 않음
③ 소설에서 사건 전개에 대한 묘사는 구체적일수록 좋다.
묘사를 구체적으로 하기보다는 인간의 경험을 중심으로 해야 한다고 설명함
④ 소설을 쓸 때 독자의 관심사를 먼저 고려하는 것이 중요하다.
독자의 관심사는 언급되지 않음
⑤ 소설에 포함될 세부 사항은 인간의 경험을 드러내는 것이어야 한다.
소설의 세부 사항은 인간의 경험을 드러내는 것이어야 함

> 왜 정답? ✳✳❀ [정답률 71%]
작가가 조사한 모든 세부 사항을 소설에 담게 되면 소설은 지루해진다고 설명하고 있다. 글쓴이는 중요한 세부 사항은 인간의 경험을 드러내는 것으로, 인물, 긴장, 갈등을 찾아가며 이야기를 말해야 한다고 설명했으므로, 글의 요지로 가장 적절한 것은 ⑤이다.

> 왜 오답?
① 작품의 완성도는 작가의 경험의 양이 아니라 인간의 경험과 관련된 세부 사항에 비례한다.
② 작가의 상상력은 언급되지 않았다.
③ 묘사를 구체적으로 하는 것이 아니라, 인간의 경험을 중심으로 해야 한다고 설명했다. (이유: in detail이 '구체적으로 묘사하는 것'을 떠올리도록 만든 오답이다.)
④ 독자의 관심사는 언급되지 않았다.

E 11 정답 ① *상황에 따른 학습 전략 활용하기

When students are starting their college life, / they may approach every course, test, or learning task / the same way, /
선행사를 포함하는 관계대명사
using what we like to call / "the rubber-stamp approach." //
학생들이 대학 생활을 시작할 때 / 그들은 모든 과목이나, 시험, 학습 과제에 접근할지도 모른다 / 똑같은 방식으로 / 우리가 부르고 싶은 방법을 이용하여 / '고무도장 방식'이라고 //

Think about it this way: / Would you wear a tuxedo / to a baseball game? //
그것을 이런 식으로 생각해 보라 / 여러분은 턱시도를 입겠는가 / 야구 경기에 //

A colorful dress / to a funeral? //
화려한 드레스를 (입겠는가) / 장례식에 //

A bathing suit / to religious services?
수영복을 (입겠는가) / 종교적인 예식에 //

Probably not. //
아마 아닐 것이다 //
뒤에 목적어절 접속사 that이 생략됨
You know / there's appropriate dress / for different occasions and settings. //
여러분은 알고 있다 / 적합한 옷이 있음을 / 다양한 행사와 상황에 //

목적어절 접속사
Skillful learners know / that "putting on the same clothes" won't work / for every class. // 단서 1 상황마다 적절한 복장이 있는 것처럼 수업마다 다른 학습 전략이 있음
숙련된 학습자는 알고 있다 / '같은 옷을 입는 것'이 효과가 없을 것임을 / 모든 수업에는 //

They are flexible learners. //
그들은 유연한 학습자이다 //
병렬 구조
They have different strategies / and know when to use them. //
그들은 다양한 전략을 갖고 있으며 / 그것들을 언제 사용해야 하는지 안다 //

They know / that you study for multiple-choice tests differently / than you study for essay tests. // 단서 2 시험별로 더 적절한 학습 방법이 있음
그들은 안다 / 여러분이 선다형 시험은 다르게 공부한다는 것을 / 논술 시험을 위해 공부하는 것과는 //
not only A but also B : A뿐만 아니라 B도
And they not only know what to do, / but they also know / how to do it. //
그리고 그들은 무엇을 해야 하는지 알고 있을 뿐만 아니라 / 그들은 또한 알고 있다 / 그것을 어떻게 해야 하는지 //

- approach ⓥ 접근하다   · tuxedo ⓝ 턱시도   · funeral ⓝ 장례식
- bathing suit 수영복   · religious ⓐ 종교적인
- appropriate ⓐ 적합한, 알맞은   · occasion ⓝ 행사
- setting ⓝ 상황   · skillful ⓐ 숙련된, 능숙한   · flexible ⓐ 유연한
- strategy ⓝ 전략   · multiple-choice test 선다형 시험

대학 생활을 시작할 때 학생들은 우리가 '고무도장 방식'이라고 부르고 싶은 방법을 이용하여, 모든 과목이나, 시험, 학습 과제를 똑같은 방식으로 접근할지도 모른다. 그것을 이런 식으로 생각해 보라. 여러분은 야구 경기에 턱시도를 입고 가겠는가? 장례식에 화려한 드레스를 입고 가겠는가? 종교적인 예식에 수영복을 입고 가겠는가? 아마 아닐 것이다. 다양한 행사와 상황마다 적합한 옷이 있음을 여러분은 알고 있다. 숙련된 학습자는 '같은 옷을 입는 것'이 모든 수업에 효과가 있지는 않을 것을 알고 있다. 그들은 유연한 학습자이다. 그들은 다양한 전략을 갖고 있으며 그것을 언제 사용해야 하는지 안다. 그들은 선다형 시험은 논술 시험을 위해 공부하는 것과는 다르게 공부한다는 것을 안다. 그리고 그들은 무엇을 해야 하는지 알고 있을 뿐만 아니라, 그것을 어떻게 해야 하는지도 알고 있다.

① 숙련된 학습자는 상황에 맞는 학습 전략을 사용할 줄 안다.
　　　　　　평가 방식에 맞는 학습 전략을 사용해야 함
② 선다형 시험과 논술 시험은 평가의 형태와 목적이 다르다.
　　　　　　　　　　　　　　　두 시험을 위한 공부법이 다름
③ 문화마다 특정 행사와 상황에 맞는 복장 규정이 있다.
　　　　　　　　　　　　　복장은 예시로 든 것일 뿐임
④ 학습의 양보다는 학습의 질이 학업 성과를 좌우한다.
　　　　　　　　　　　학습의 양과 질을 비교한 글이 아님
⑤ 학습 목표가 명확할수록 성취 수준이 높아진다.
　　　　　　　　　　목표보다는 방법과 전략이 중요함

왜 정답? ✽✽✽ [정답률 80%]

• **문제점**: 서로 다른 상황에 같은 방식으로(= 고무도장 방식)으로 접근하는 것
• **해결책**: 상황마다 적절한 복장이 있는 것처럼 수업, 시험별로 더 적절한 방법을
　사용하기 단서1 단서2
▶ 상황에 맞는 학습 전략을 사용해야 한다는 것이므로 정답은 ①이다.

왜 오답?

② 서로 다른 시험에 맞는 학습 전략을 세워야 한다는 내용으로, 두 시험을 비교한
　글이 아니다.
③ 복장 규정은 예시로 든 것이지 글의 요지는 아니다.
④ 학습의 양과 질이 성과를 좌우한다는 것은 언급되지 않았다.
⑤ 학습 목표가 아닌 적절한 전략이 성취 결과에 영향을 미친다고 했다.

E 12 정답 ① *두려움을 주는 뉴스

The old saying is that "knowledge is power," / but when it comes to scary, threatening news, / research suggests the exact opposite. //
~에 관한 한
오래된 격언에 따르면 '아는 것이 힘이다'라고 한다 / 하지만 무섭고 위협적인 뉴스에 관한 한 /
연구는 정반대를 시사한다 //

Frightening news can actually rob people / of their inner sense
rob A of B: A에게서 B를 빼앗다
분사구문을 이끄는 현재분사
of control, / making them less likely to take care of themselves
and other people. // 단서1 두려움을 주는 뉴스는 사람으로부터 내면의 통제력을 빼앗음
두려움을 주는 뉴스는 실제로 사람으로부터 빼앗을 수 있다 / 내면의 통제력을 / 그들이
스스로와 다른 사람들을 돌볼 가능성을 더 낮게 만들면서 //
목적어절 접속사
Public health research shows / that when the news presents
health-related information / in a pessimistic way, /
공중 보건 연구는 보여준다 / 뉴스가 건강과 관련된 정보를 제시할 때 / 비관적인 방식으로 /
부사적 용법(목적)
people are actually less likely to take steps / to protect themselves
from illness / as a result. //
사람들이 조치를 취할 가능성이 실제로 더 낮다는 것을 / 질병으로부터 자신을 보호하기 위해
/ 결과적으로 /
주격 관계대명사
A news article / that's intended to warn people / about increasing
cancer rates, / for example, / can result in fewer people choosing
to get screened / for the disease /
뉴스 기사는 / 사람들에게 경고하려 하는 / 증가하는 암 발생률에 대해 / 예를 들어 / 더 적은
사람들이 검사받도록 선택하는 결과를 가져올 수 있다 / 그 병에 대해 /
선행사를 포함하는 관계대명사
because they're so terrified / of what they might find. //
그들이 너무 두려워하기 때문에 / 그들이 발견할지도 모를 것에 대해 //
This is also true / for issues such as climate change. //
이것은 또한 사실이다 / 기후 변화와 같은 문제에도 //
단서2 두려움을 주는 뉴스는 사람들을 우울하게 해서 그들이 조치를 덜 취하게 함
When a news story is all doom and gloom, / people feel
depressed / and become less interested / in taking small,
병렬 구조
personal steps / to fight ecological collapse. //
뉴스가 온통 파멸과 암울한 상황일 때 / 사람들은 우울하게 느낀다 / 그리고 흥미를 덜 느끼게
된다 / 작고 개인적인 조치를 취하는 것에 / 생태학적 붕괴와 싸우기 위한 //

• saying ⓝ 속담, 격언　　• threatening ⓐ 위협적인
• opposite ⓝ 반대　　　　• frightening ⓐ 두려움을 주는
• inner ⓐ 내면의　　　　　• pessimistic ⓐ 비관적인

• take a step 조치를 취하다　• intend ⓥ 의도하다　• rate ⓝ 비율
• screen ⓥ (특정 질병이 있는지) 검진하다　• terrified ⓐ 두려워하는, 겁이 난

오래된 격언에 따르면 '아는 것이 힘이다'라고 하지만, 무섭고 위협적인 뉴스에 관한 한, 연구는 정반대를 시사한다. 두려움을 주는 뉴스는 실제로 사람들로부터 내면의 통제력을 빼앗을 수 있어서, 그들이 스스로와 다른 사람들을 돌볼 가능성을 더 낮게 만든다. 공중 보건 연구는 뉴스가 건강과 관련된 정보를 비관적인 방식으로 제시할 때, 결과적으로 사람들이 질병으로부터 자신을 보호하기 위한 조치를 취할 가능성이 실제로 더 낮다는 것을 보여준다. 예를 들어, 증가하는 암 발생률에 대해 사람들에게 경고하려 하는 뉴스 기사는 그들이 발견할지도 모를 것에 대해 너무 두려워하기 때문에 더 적은 사람들이 그 병에 대해 검사받는 것을 선택하는 결과를 가져올 수 있다. 이것은 기후 변화와 같은 문제에도 해당한다. 뉴스가 온통 파멸과 암울한 상황일 때, 사람들은 우울하게 느끼고 생태학적 붕괴와 싸우기 위한 작고 개인적인 조치를 취하는 것에 흥미를 덜 느끼게 된다.

다음 글의 요지로 가장 적절한 것은?

① 두려움을 주는 뉴스는 사람들이 문제에 덜 대처하게 할 수 있다.
　　두려움을 주는 뉴스는 사람들을 우울하게 만들어서 조치를 덜 취하게 한다고 했음
② 정보를 전달하는 시기에 따라 뉴스의 영향력이 달라질 수 있다.
　　　　　　　　　　　정보 전달 시기에 대해서는 언급하지 않았음
③ 지속적인 환경 문제 보도가 사람들의 인식 변화를 가져온다.
　　　　　　환경 문제 보도는 두려움을 주는 뉴스에 대한 하나의 예시로 언급된 것임
④ 정보 제공의 지연은 정확한 문제 인식에 방해가 될 수 있다.
　　　　　　　　　정보 제공이 늦어지면 안 된다는 내용이 아님
⑤ 출처가 불분명한 건강 정보는 사람들에게 유익하지 않다.
　　　　　　　　　　　　출처의 명확성에 대한 내용은 없음

왜 정답? ✽✽✽ [정답률 79%]

'아는 것이 힘'이지만, 무섭고 위협적인 뉴스에는 적용되지 않는다.
➡ 사람들 내면의 통제력을 빼앗아 스스로와 주변을 덜 돌보게 함 단서1
➡ 사람들은 작고 개인적인 조치조차 덜 취함 단서2
　　▶ 두려움을 주는 뉴스는 사람들이 문제에 덜 대처하게 한다는 것이므로 정답은
　　　①이다.

왜 오답?

② 정보를 전달하는 '시기'에 대한 언급은 없다.
③ 환경 문제 보도는 하나의 예시로 언급된 것으로 글 전체를 포괄할 수 없다. 주의
④ 빠른 정보의 제공을 권장하는 글이 아니다.
⑤ 건강 정보의 출처와 그 명확성에 대한 내용은 없다.

E 13 정답 ① *감정으로 인해 상황을 오해할 가능성

병렬 구조
Your emotions deserve attention / and give you important
pieces of information. //
당신의 감정은 주목할 만하다 / 그리고 당신에게 중요한 정보를 준다 //
However, / they can also sometimes be an unreliable, / inaccurate
source of information. // 단서1 감정이 신뢰할 수 없는 부정확한 정보를 제공할 수 있음
그러나 / 감정은 또한 가끔 신뢰할 수 없다 / 부정확한 정보의 원천이 (될 수도 있다) /
앞에 목적어절을 이끄는 접속사 that 생략
You may feel a certain way, / but that does not mean / those
feelings are reflections of the truth. // 단서2 감정이 반드시 사실을
당신이 분명하게 느낄지 모른다 / 하지만 그것은 의미하지 않는다 / 그러한 감정들이 사실의
반영임을 // 반영하는 것은 아님
You may feel sad / and conclude that your friend is angry with
you / when her behavior simply reflects that she's having a
목적어절을 이끄는 접속사
bad day. //
당신이 슬플지도 모른다 / 그래서 당신의 친구가 당신에게 화가 났다고 결론을 내릴지도
(모른다) / 친구의 행동이 단지 나타낼 때에도 / 그녀가 좋지 않은 날을 보내고 있음을 //
병렬 구조
You may feel depressed / and decide that you did poorly in an
interview / when you did just fine. //
당신은 기분이 우울할지도 모른다 / 그래서 면접에서 당신이 못했다고 판단할지도 (모른다) /
잘했을 때도 //
주격 관계대명사
Your feelings can mislead you / into thinking things / that are
not supported by facts. // 단서3 감정이 사실에 의해 뒷받침되지 않는 것들을
당신의 감정은 당신을 속여 / ~ 것들을 생각하게 할 수 있다 / 사실에 의해 뒷받침되지 않는 //
　　　　　　　　　　　　　　　생각하게 할 수 있음

- emotion ⓝ 감정　　• deserve ⓥ ~할 만하다, ~받을 가치가 있다
- information ⓝ 정보　　• unreliable ⓐ 신뢰할 수 없는
- inaccurate ⓐ 부정확한　　• source ⓝ 원천　　• reflection ⓝ 반영
- conclude ⓥ 결론을 내리다　　• behavior ⓝ 행동
- reflect ⓥ 반영하다, 나타내다　　• mislead ⓥ 속이다

당신의 감정은 주목할 만하고 당신에게 중요한 정보를 준다. 그러나, 감정은 또한 가끔 신뢰할 수 없고, 부정확한 정보의 원천이 될 수도 있다. 당신이 분명하게 느낄지 모르지만, 그것은 그러한 감정들이 사실의 반영임을 의미하지는 않는다. 친구의 행동이 단지 그녀가 좋지 않은 날을 보내고 있음을 나타낼 때에도, 당신이 슬프기 때문에 그녀가 당신에게 화가 났다고 결론을 내릴지도 모른다. 당신은 기분이 우울해서 면접에서 잘했을 때도 못했다고 판단할지도 모른다. 당신의 감정은 당신을 속여 사실에 의해 뒷받침되지 않는 것들을 생각하게 할 수 있다.

> **다음 글의 요지로 가장 적절한 것은?**
> ① 자신의 감정으로 인해 상황을 오해할 수 있다.
> 　감정이 올바르지 않은 정보를 제공할 수 있다는 내용
> ② 자신의 생각을 타인에게 강요해서는 안 된다.
> 　타인에게 생각을 강요하는 내용은 나오지 않음
> ③ 인간관계가 우리의 감정에 영향을 미친다.
> 　우리의 감정이 우리에게 주는 정보에 대해 말하고 있음
> ④ 타인의 감정에 공감하는 자세가 필요하다.
> 　타인의 감정을 판단하는 내용이 나오지만 공감해야 한다는 내용은 없음
> ⑤ 공동체를 위한 선택에는 보상이 따른다.
> 　공동체를 위한 선택과 보상에 대한 언급은 없음

> **왜 정답?** ★★❀ [정답률 75%]

감정이 신뢰할 수 없는 부정확한 정보를 줄 수 있다고 하면서, 그 예로 자신의 감정 때문에 친구가 화났다고 판단하거나 면접을 못 봤다고 생각할 수 있다는 내용이 나온다. 감정이 우리를 속여 사실에 뒷받침되지 않은 것들을 생각하게 할 수도 있다고 설명하고 있다. 따라서 이 글의 요지로 가장 적절한 것은 ①이다.

> **왜 오답?**

② 감정으로 인해 우리의 생각이 잘못될 수 있다는 것을 설명하는 글이며 타인에게 우리의 생각을 강요하는 것과 관련된 내용은 없다.
③ 인간관계가 우리의 감정에 미치는 영향은 언급되지 않았다.
④ 글에서 타인의 감정을 판단하는 부분이 제시되어 있지만 이는 우리의 감정으로 인해 판단이 틀릴 수 있다는 것을 설명하기 위한 내용이며, 타인의 감정을 공감해야 한다는 내용이 아니다.
⑤ 공동체를 위한 선택과 보상에 관한 내용은 전혀 나오지 않았다.

E 14 정답 ③ *충성도를 높이기 위한 고객 정보 활용

Information is worthless / if you never actually use it. //
정보는 가치 없다 / 여러분이 결코 그것을 실제로 사용하지 않는다면 //

Far too often, / companies collect valuable customer information
　　　　　　주격 관계대명사
/ that ends up buried and never used. //
너무나 자주 / 기업들은 귀중한 고객 정보를 수집한다 / 결국에는 묻히고 절대로 사용되지 않는 //

뒤에 목적어절을 이끄는 접속사 that 생략
They must ensure / their data is accessible / for use at the
appropriate times. // **단서1** 기업은 기업의 정보가 적시에 사용되도록 해야 함
그들은 보장해야 한다 / 그들의 정보가 접근 가능하도록 / 적절한 때의 사용을 위해 //

For a hotel, / one appropriate time for data usage / is check-in at the front desk. //
호텔의 경우 / 정보 사용을 위한 하나의 적절한 때는 / 프런트 데스크의 체크인이다 //

I often check in at a hotel / I've visited frequently, / only **for**
to부정사의 의미상 주어　　　　　　　　　　　　　　　　동격의 that
the people at the front desk / to give no indication / **that** they
recognize me as a customer. //
나는 호텔에 종종 체크인한다 / 내가 자주 방문했던 / 결국 프런트 데스크에 있는 사람들이 /
표시를 보여주지 않는다 / 그들이 나를 고객으로 알아차린다는 //

must have p.p.: ~였음에 틀림없다
The hotel **must have stored** a record of my visits, / but they don't
make that information accessible / to the front desk clerks. //
그 호텔은 내 방문 기록을 저장하고 있음이 분명하다 / 하지만 그들은 그 정보가 접근
가능하도록 해 주지 않는다 / 프런트 데스크 직원들에게 //

형용사적 용법　　　　　부사적 용법
They are missing a prime opportunity / **to utilize** data / **to create**
앞에 주격 관계대명사와 be동사 생략
a better experience / **focused** on customer loyalty. //
그들은 최적의 기회를 놓치고 있다 / 정보를 활용할 / 더 나은 경험을 만들 수 있도록 / 고객
충성도에 초점을 맞춘 //
단서2 호텔에서 프런트 데스크에 적시에 정보를 주지
않아서 충성도를 높일 수 있는 기회를 놓치고 있음

Whether they have ten customers, ten thousand, or even ten
million, / the goal is the same: / create a delightful customer
　　　　　　　주격 관계대명사
experience / **that** encourages loyalty. // **단서3** 기업의 목표는 충성도를 높이는
그들이 열 명, 만 명 혹은 심지어 천만 명의 고객을 가지고 있든 / 목표는 동일하다 / 즉,
그것은 즐거운 고객 경험을 만드는 것이다 / 충성도를 높이는 //

즐거운 고객 경험을 만드는 것임

- worthless ⓐ 가치가 없는　　• valuable ⓐ 소중한, 귀중한
- end up 결국 ~하다　　• bury ⓥ 묻다　　• ensure ⓥ 보장하다
- accessible ⓐ 접근[이용] 가능한　　• appropriate ⓐ 적절한
- indication ⓝ 표시, 암시　　• recognize ⓥ 인식하다, 알아보다
- store ⓥ 저장하다　　• prime ⓐ 주된, 최고의
- utilize ⓥ 활용[이용]하다　　• loyalty ⓝ 충성(도)

만약 여러분이 결코 정보를 실제로 사용하지 않는다면 그것은 가치가 없다. 너무나 자주 기업들은 결국에는 묻히고 절대로 사용되지 않는 귀중한 고객 정보를 수집한다. 그들은 그들의 정보가 적절한 때의 사용을 위해 접근 가능하도록 보장해야 한다. 호텔의 경우 정보 사용을 위한 하나의 적절한 때는 프런트 데스크의 체크인이다. 나는 내가 자주 방문했던 호텔에 종종 체크인하는데 결국 프런트 데스크에 있는 사람들이 그들이 나를 고객으로 알아차린다는 표시를 보여주지 않는다. 그 호텔은 내 방문 기록을 저장하고 있음이 분명하지만 그들은 그 정보가 프런트 데스크 직원들에게 접근 가능하도록 해 주지 않는다. 그들은 고객 충성도에 초점을 맞춘 더 나은 경험을 만들 수 있도록 정보를 활용할 최적의 기회를 놓치고 있다. 그들이 열 명, 만 명 혹은 심지어 천만 명의 고객을 가지고 있든 목표는 동일하다. 즉, 그것은 충성도를 높이는 즐거운 고객 경험을 만드는 것이다.

> **다음 글의 요지로 가장 적절한 것은?**
> ① 기업 정보의 투명한 공개는 고객 만족도를 향상시킨다.
> 　기업 정보의 외부 공개와 관련된 내용이 아님
> ② 목표 고객층에 대한 분석은 기업의 이익 창출로 이어진다.
> 　고객 분석과 이익 창출의 관계에 대한 언급은 없음
> ③ 고객 충성도를 높이기 위해 고객 정보가 활용될 필요가 있다.
> 　기업은 고객 정보를 적시에 활용해서 고객 충성도를 높여야 한다고 했음
> ④ 일관성 있는 호텔 서비스 제공을 통해 단골 고객을 확보할 수 있다.
> 　오히려 단골 고객임을 알 수 있도록 정보를 활용하라고 했음
> ⑤ 사생활 침해에 대한 우려로 고객 정보를 보관하는 데 어려움이 있다.
> 　사생활 침해와 관련된 내용은 나오지 않음

> **왜 정답?** ★★❀ [정답률 78%]
> 정보를 활용했더라면 필자의
> 충성도를 높일 수 있었을 것임 🍯

기업은 고객 정보를 적시에 활용할 수 있도록 해야 한다고 하면서 그 예로, 필자가 호텔을 방문할 때 프런트 데스크에 적시에 정보를 주지 않아서 정보를 활용할 기회를 놓치고 있는 것을 경험한 것을 들었다. 즉 고객이 즐거운 경험을 하도록 함으로써 고객의 충성도를 높이도록 해야 한다는 내용의 글이다. 따라서 이 글의 요지로 가장 적절한 것은 ③이다.

> **왜 오답?**

① 기업 정보를 외부에 투명하게 공개해야 한다는 내용의 글이 아니라 기업이 갖고 있는 고객 정보를 적시에 활용해야 한다는 내용이다.
② 고객 분석과 이익 창출이 주요 내용이 아니고, 고객 정보를 적시에 활용하여 충성도를 높이는 즐거운 고객 경험을 만들어야 한다는 내용이다.
④ 일관성 있는 서비스가 아니라 오히려 단골 고객임을 알 수 있도록 정보를 활용하여 충성도를 높이도록 해야 한다는 글이다.
⑤ 사생활 침해와 고객 정보 보관의 어려움에 대한 내용은 글에 제시되지 않았다.

A recent study / from Carnegie Mellon University in Pittsburgh, / called / "When Too Much of a Good Thing May Be Bad," / indicates / 최근 한 연구는 / 피츠버그시 Carnegie Mellon University의 / 불리는 / "너무 많은 좋은 것이 나쁠 수도 있을 때"라고 / 보여준다 /

목적절을 이끄는 접속사
that classrooms with too much decoration / are a source of distraction / for young children / and directly affect their cognitive performance. // **단서 1** 너무 많은 장식이 아이들의 주의력과 인지적 수행에 영향을 미침
너무 많은 장식이 있는 교실이 / 주의 산만의 원인이고 / 어린이들의 / 직접적으로 그들의 인지적인 수행에 영향을 미친다는 점을 //

분사구문
Being visually overstimulated, / the children have a great deal of difficulty / concentrating / and end up with / worse academic
병렬 구조
results. // **단서 2** 지나친 시각적 자극이 나쁜 학습 결과로 이어질 수 있음
시각적으로 지나치게 자극되었을 때 / 아이들은 많이 어려워하고 / 집중하는 것을 / 결국 ~로 끝이 난다 / 더 나쁜 학습 결과 //

On the other hand, / if there is not much decoration / on the classroom walls, / the children are less distracted, / spend more time / on their activities, / and learn more. //
병렬 구조
반면에 / 교실 벽에 장식이 많지 않으면 / 아이들은 덜 산만해지고 / 더 많은 시간을 사용하고 / 그들의 활동에 / 더 많이 배운다 //

가주어 **진주어**
So / it's our job, / in order to support their attention, / to find the right balance / between excessive decoration and the complete absence of it. // 그래서 / 우리가 할 일이다 / 그들의 집중을 돕기 위해 / 적절한 균형을 찾는 것이 / 지나친 장식과 장식이 전혀 없는 것 사이의 //

- indicate ⓥ 보여주다 · distraction ⓝ 주의 산만
- cognitive ⓐ 인지적인 · performance ⓝ 수행
- overstimulate ⓥ 지나치게 자극시키다 · concentrate ⓥ 집중하다
- excessive ⓐ 지나친 · complete ⓐ 완전한
- absence ⓝ 없음, 부재

피츠버그시 Carnegie Mellon University의 "너무 많은 좋은 것이 나쁠 수도 있을 때"라고 불리는 최근 한 연구는, 너무 많은 장식이 있는 교실이 어린이들의 주의 산만의 원인이고 직접적으로 그들의 인지적인 수행에 영향을 미친다는 점을 보여준다. 시각적으로 지나치게 자극되었을 때, 아이들은 집중하는 데 많이 어려워하고 결국 더 나쁜 학습 결과로 끝이 난다. 반면에, 교실 벽에 장식이 많지 않으면, 아이들은 덜 산만해지고, 그들의 활동에 더 많은 시간을 사용하고, 더 많이 배운다. 그래서, 그들의 집중을 돕기 위해, 지나친 장식과 장식이 전혀 없는 것 사이의 적절한 균형을 찾는 것이 우리가 할 일이다.

다음 글의 요지로 가장 적절한 것은?

① 아이들의 집중을 돕기 위해 과도한 교실 장식을 지양할 필요가 있다.
과도한 교실 장식이 아이들의 집중을 방해한다는 내용
② 아이들의 인성과 인지 능력을 균형 있게 발달시키는 것이 중요하다.
인성 발달에 대한 언급은 없음
③ 아이들이 직접 교실을 장식하는 것은 창의력 발달에 도움이 된다.
교실 장식이 언급되긴 했지만, 직접 교실을 장식하는 것은 언급되지 않음
④ 다양한 교실 활동은 아이들의 수업 참여도를 증진시킨다.
다양한 교실 활동에 대한 내용은 없음
⑤ 풍부한 시각 자료는 아이들의 학습 동기를 높인다.
시각적으로 지나치게 자극되면 오히려 안 좋다고 했음

＞왜 정답？ ✽✽✽ [정답률 75%]
첫 문장에서 한 연구에 대해 언급하면서 너무 많은 장식이 있는 교실이 어린이들의 인지적인 수행에 영향을 미친다고 했다. 이 부분이 이 글의 핵심으로, 이어지는 내용에서 지나친 시각적 자극이 나쁜 학습 결과로 이어질 수 있다고 설명한다. 따라서 이 글의 요지로 가장 적절한 것은 ①이다.

＞왜 오답？
② 아이들의 인성 발달에 대한 언급은 없다.
③ 아이들이 직접 교실을 장식하는 것의 장점에 대한 글이 아니다.
④ 다양한 교실 활동을 하는 것에 대해서는 언급되지 않았다.
⑤ 시각적으로 지나치게 자극되면 오히려 안 좋다고 했으므로 풍부한 시각 자료가 학습 동기를 높인다는 내용이 아니다.

＊건강 유지와 최상의 기능 발휘를 위한 수면

관계부사
Many people view sleep / as merely a "down time" / when their
완전자동사
brain shuts off / and their body rests. //
많은 사람이 수면을 본다 / 그저 '가동되지 않는 시간'으로 / 그들의 뇌가 멈추는 / 그리고 그들의 신체가 쉬는 //

부사적 용법(목적)
In a rush / to meet work, school, family, or household
분사구문
responsibilities, / people cut back on their sleep / thinking it won't be a problem, /
서두르는 와중에 / 일, 학교, 가족, 또는 가정의 책임을 다하기 위해 / 사람들은 수면 시간을 줄이고 / 그것이 문제가 되지 않을 것으로 생각하는데 /

비교급 강조
because all of these other activities seem much more important. //
왜냐하면 이러한 모든 다른 활동들이 훨씬 더 중요해 보이기 때문이다 //

목적어절을 이끄는 접속사 **tasks를 수식하는 과거분사구**
But research reveals / that a number of vital tasks / carried out
병렬 구조
during sleep / help to maintain good health / and enable people to function / at their best. // **핵심문장, 단서 1** 수면 중에 진행되는 과업이 건강을 유지하고 최상의 기능을 발휘하게 함
하지만 연구는 밝히고 있다 / 많은 매우 중요한 과업이 / 수면 중에 수행되는 / 건강을 유지하는 데 도움이 된다는 것을 / 그리고 사람들이 기능할 수 있게 해 준다는 것을 / 최상의 수준으로 //

work를 수식하는 현재분사
While you sleep, / your brain is hard at work / forming the pathways / necessary for learning and creating memories and new insights. // 잠을 자는 동안 / 여러분의 뇌는 열심히 일하고 있다 / 경로를 형성하느라 / 학습하고 기억과 새로운 통찰을 만드는 데 필요한 //

Without enough sleep, / you can't focus and pay attention or respond quickly. //
병렬 구조 **단서 2** 수면이 정신과 주의 집중에 영향을 미침
충분한 수면이 없다면 / 여러분은 정신을 집중하고 주의를 기울이거나 빠르게 반응할 수 없다 //

A lack of sleep / may even cause mood problems. //
수면 부족은 / 심지어 감정 (조절) 문제를 일으킬 수도 있다 // **단서 3** 수면이 부족하면 감정에 문제를 일으킬 수 있음
목적어절을 이끄는 접속사
In addition, / growing evidence shows / that a continuous lack of sleep increases / the risk for developing serious diseases. //
게다가 / 점점 더 많은 증거가 / 보여 준다 / 계속된 수면 부족이 증가시킨다는 것을 / 심각한 질병의 발생 위험을 // **단서 4** 수면 부족이 심각한 질병의 발생 위험을 증가시켜 건강에 위험함

- view ⓥ 보다, 여기다 · merely @d 그저
- down time 가동되지 않는 시간 · shut off 멈추다
- in a rush 서둘러 · responsibility ⓝ 책임
- cut back on ~을 줄이다 · reveal ⓥ 밝히다 · a number of 많은
- carry out ~을 수행하다 · at one's best 최상의 수준으로
- form ⓥ 형성하다 · pathway ⓝ 경로 · memory ⓝ 기억
- insight ⓝ 통찰 · respond ⓥ 반응하다 · lack ⓝ 부족
- cause ⓥ 일으키다 · evidence ⓝ 증거 · risk ⓝ 위험
- serious ⓐ 심각한 · disease ⓝ 질병

많은 사람이 수면을 그저 뇌가 멈추고 신체가 쉬는 '가동되지 않는 시간'으로 본다. 일, 학교, 가족, 또는 가정의 책임을 다하기 위해 서두르는 와중에, 사람들은 수면 시간을 줄이고, 그것이 문제가 되지 않을 것으로 생각하는데, 왜냐하면 이러한 모든 다른 활동들이 훨씬 더 중요해 보이기 때문이다. 하지만 연구는 수면 중에 수행되는 많은 매우 중요한 과업이 건강을 유지하는 데 도움이 되고 사람들이 최상의 수준으로 기능할 수 있게 해 준다는 것을 밝히고 있다. 잠을 자는 동안, 여러분의 뇌는 학습하고 기억과 새로운 통찰을 만드는 데 필요한 경로를 형성하느라 열심히 일하고 있다. 충분한 수면이 없다면, 여러분은 정신을 집중하고 주의를 기울이거나 빠르게 반응할 수 없다. 수면이 부족하면 심지어 감정 (조절) 문제를 일으킬 수도 있다. 게다가, 계속된 수면 부족이 심각한 질병의 발생 위험을 증가시킨다는 것을 점점 더 많은 증거가 보여 준다.

다음 글의 요지로 가장 적절한 것은?

① 수면은 건강 유지와 최상의 기능 발휘에 도움이 된다.
　　　수면 부족은 집중력, 주의력, 감정 조절, 질병에 나쁜 영향을 미친다는 내용임
② 업무량이 증가하면 필요한 수면 시간도 증가한다.
　　　업무량이 증가하면 수면 시간이 증가해야 한다는 내용이 아님
③ 균형 잡힌 식단을 유지하면 뇌 기능이 향상된다.
　　　균형 잡힌 식단에 대한 언급은 없음
④ 불면증이 주위 사람들에게 부정적인 영향을 미친다.
　　　불면증이 부정적인 영향을 미친다는 것은 맞지만 주위 사람들에 대한 영향과 관련된 내용은 없음
⑤ 꿈의 내용은 깨어 있는 시간 동안의 경험을 반영한다.
　　　꿈에 대해서는 언급되지 않음

⭐ 중반부에 But(하지만)으로 시작하는 핵심문장에 주목해야 한다. 많은 사람들이 여러 가지 책임을 완수하기 위해 수면 시간을 줄인다고 한 것에 대해 반론을 제기하는 부분이다.

❯왜 정답?

중반부에 나오는 a number of vital tasks ~ during sleep help to maintain good health and enable people to function at their best (수면 중의 많은 매우 중요한 과업이 건강을 유지하는 데 도움이 되고 사람들이 최상의 수준으로 기능할 수 있게 해 준다)가 이 글의 핵심문장이다. 수면이 부족하면 집중하기 힘들고 주의력 감소, 감정 조절 문제, 질병의 발생 위험 증가를 일으킬 수 있다는 내용이다. 따라서 윗글의 요지로 가장 적절한 것은 ①이다.

❯왜 오답?

② 업무량이 증가하면 수면 시간이 증가해야 한다는 내용이 아니라, 충분한 수면 시간이 주는 이점에 대한 글이다.
③ 균형 잡힌 식단에 대해서는 언급되지 않았다.
④ 불면증이 부정적인 영향을 미친다는 것은 맞지만, 그것이 주위 사람들에게 미치는 것에 대한 내용이 아니다. 주의
⑤ 꿈에 대한 내용은 나오지 않았다.

E 17 정답 ⑤ ──── ⭐ 2등급 대비 [정답률 52%]

✱ 자신의 신념에 대한 맹신이 갖는 문제점

<u>가주어</u>　　　<u>진주어절을 이끄는 접속사</u>
<u>It</u>'s important / <u>that</u> you think independently and fight for what you believe in, / <u>but there comes a time</u> /
중요하다 / 독자적으로 생각하고 자신이 믿는 것을 위해 싸우는 것이 / 하지만 때가 온다 /
　　　　　　　　　　　　　　　　　　　병렬 구조
when it's wiser <u>to stop</u> fighting for your view / and <u>move</u> on to accepting / what a trustworthy group of people think is best. //
자신의 생각을 위해 싸우는 것을 중단하는 것이 더 현명한 / 그리고 받아들이는 쪽으로 나아가는 것이 / 신뢰할 수 있는 집단이 가장 좋다고 생각하는 것을 // ─핵심문장

This can be extremely difficult. //
이것은 매우 어려울 수 있다 // 단서1 무조건 나만의 생각을 고수하는 것보다 마음을 여는 태도의 중요성
　<u>가주어</u>　　　　　　　　　　　　　<u>의미상의 주어</u>　　<u>진주어</u>
But <u>it</u>'s smarter, and ultimately better / <u>for you to be open-minded and have</u> faith / that the conclusions of a trustworthy group of people / are better than whatever you think. //
하지만 더 영리하고 궁극적으로 더 좋다 / 여러분이 마음을 열고 믿음을 갖는 것이 / 신뢰할 수 있는 집단의 결론이 / 여러분이 생각하는 어떤 것보다 낫다는 //

If you can't understand their view, / you're probably just blind / to their way of thinking. // 만약 여러분이 그들의 생각을 이해할 수 없다면 / 여러분은 아마도 단지 보지 못하는 것이다 / 그들이 생각하는 방식을 //

If you continue doing <u>what</u> you think is best / when all the
　　　　　　　　　　　~것
evidence and trustworthy people are against you, / you're being dangerously confident. //
당신이 최선이라고 생각하는 것을 계속한다면 / 모든 증거와 신뢰할 수 있는 사람들이 당신에게 반대할 때 / 당신은 위험할 정도로 자신감에 차 있는 것이다 //
　　　　　　　　　<u>진주어절을 이끄는 접속사</u>
The truth is / <u>that</u> while most people can become incredibly
　　　　　　　　　　　　　　=can't become incredibly open-minded
open-minded, / some <u>can't</u>, / 사실의 ~이다 / 대부분의 사람들은 믿을 수 없을 정도로 마음을 열게 되는 반면에 / 어떤 사람들은 그럴 수 없다는 것 /

even after they have repeatedly encountered lots of pain / from betting that they were right / when they were not. // 많은 고통을 반복적으로 겪고 난 후에도 / 옳았다고 확신하는 것으로부터 / 자신이 옳지 않았을 때 //
단서2 고통을 많이 겪고 나서도 자신이 옳았다고 계속 확신하는 사람이 있음

- independently ⓐ⓭ 독자적으로　　· trustworthy ⓐ 신뢰할 만한
- extremely ⓐⓓ 극도로　　· ultimately ⓐⓓ 궁극적으로
- faith ⓝ 믿음　　· evidence ⓝ 증거, 단서
- confident ⓐ 자신감 있는　　· incredibly ⓐⓓ 놀랍게
- encounter ⓥ 만나다, 마주치다

독자적으로 생각하고 자신이 믿는 것을 위해 싸우는 것도 중요하지만, 자신의 생각을 위해 싸우는 것을 중단하고 신뢰할 수 있는 집단이 가장 좋다고 생각하는 것을 받아들이는 쪽으로 나아가는 것이 현명한 때가 온다. 이것은 매우 어려울 수 있다. 하지만 여러분이 마음을 열고 신뢰할 수 있는 집단의 결론이 여러분이 생각하는 어떤 것보다 낫다는 믿음을 갖는 것이 더 영리하고 궁극적으로 더 좋다. 만약 여러분이 그들의 생각을 이해할 수 없다면, 여러분은 아마도 단지 그들이 생각하는 방식을 보지 못하는 것이다. 모든 증거와 신뢰할 수 있는 사람들이 당신에게 반대할 때 당신이 최선이라고 생각하는 것을 계속한다면, 당신은 위험할 정도로 자신감에 차 있는 것이다. 사실 대부분의 사람들은 믿을 수 없을 정도로 마음을 열게 되는 반면에, 어떤 사람들은 자신이 옳지 않았을 때 옳았다고 확신하는 것으로부터 많은 고통을 겪고 난 후에도 그럴 수 없다는 것이다.

다음 글의 요지로 가장 적절한 것은?

① 대부분의 사람들은 진리에 도달하지 못하고 고통을 받는다.
　　　진리 도달 여부는 요지와 거리가 먼 내용
② 맹목적으로 다른 사람의 의견을 받아들이는 것은 위험하다.
　　　타인의 의견 수용은 핵심 내용이 아님
③ 남을 설득하기 위해서는 타당한 증거로 주장을 뒷받침해야 한다.
　　　증거의 타당성에 대한 내용이 아님
④ 믿을만한 사람이 누구인지 판단하려면 열린 마음을 가져야 한다.
　　　타인 신뢰를 위한 자세와는 관련 없는 내용
⑤ 자신의 의견이 최선이 아닐 수 있다는 것을 인정하는 것이 필요하다.
　　　자신의 의견이 틀릴 수 있음을 인지해야 한다고 했음

⭐ 문장의 길이가 긴 편이고, 모든 선택지가 글에서 언급된 핵심어를 포함하고 있는 2등급 대비 문제이다. 자신의 신념을 고집하는 것이 좋다는 것인지 나쁘다는 것인지, 또 그것을 어떤 행동으로 해결할 수 있는지를 찾아야 한다.

❯왜 정답?

자신이 생각하는 것만 옳다고 하기보다는, 자신이 신뢰할 수 있는 집단이 좋다고 생각하는 것을 수용할 수 있는 포용력이 중요하다고 했다.
즉, 자신의 의견만이 유일하게 옳은 것이 아닐 수 있음을 인지하고 열린 마음으로 판단할 수 있어야 한다는 내용이다. 따라서 이 글의 요지로 가장 적절한 것은 ⑤이다.

❯왜 오답?

① 진리에 도달할 수 있는지는 이 글의 내용과 관련이 없다.
② 다른 사람의 의견을 무조건 수용하는 것이 위험하다는 것은 요지와 거리가 멀다.
③ 타인을 설득하기 위한 증거의 타당성에 관한 내용은 전혀 언급되지 않았다.
④ 믿을 수 있는 사람을 판단할 수 있는 마음가짐을 가져야 한다는 내용이 아니다.

E 어휘 Review 정답 ──── 문제편 p. 71

01 측면	11 in a rush	21 owe
02 배우자	12 cut back on	22 boredom
03 인지적인	13 be true for	23 pessimistic
04 잠재력	14 in progress	24 continuous
05 연속	15 carry out	25 deserve
06 accomplish	16 traditional	26 overstimulated
07 leisure	17 flexible	27 rare
08 excessive	18 crucial	28 acutely
09 elevate	19 pathways	29 unreliable
10 conduct	20 insights	30 supported

F 주제 찾기

문제편 p. 74~83

F 01 정답 ⑤ *유대감의 효과

유도부사
<u>There</u> is a wealth of evidence / <u>that</u> when parents, teachers, 동격절 접속사
supervisors, and coaches / are perceived as involved and caring, / people feel happier and more motivated. // **단서 1** 배려를 받으면 동기가 부여됨

수많은 증거가 있다 / 부모, 교사, 상사, 그리고 코치가 / 관여되어 있고 배려한다고 여겨질 때 / 사람들은 더 행복하고 더 동기가 부여된다는 //

And it is not just those people with power / — we need to feel valued and respected / by peers and coworkers. //

그리고 그것이 단지 권력을 가진 사람들만은 아닌데 / 즉 우리는 소중히 여겨지고 존중받는다는 느낌을 받을 필요가 있다 / 또래와 직장 동료들에게서도 //

Thus, / when the need for relatedness is met, / motivation and internalization are fueled, / **provided that** support for autonomy and competence are also there. // **단서 2** 관계성이 충족되면 동기와 내면화가 자극됨
비인칭 독립분사구문 (= If we are provided that)

따라서 / 관계성에 대한 욕구가 충족될 때 / 동기와 내면화는 자극된다 / 그리고 자율성과 유능함에 대한 지원 또한 제공된다면 //

If we are trying to motivate others, / a caring relationship is a crucial basis **from which to begin**. //
「전치사 + 관계대명사 + to부정사」(= which we can begin from)

만약 우리가 다른 사람들에게 동기를 부여하려고 한다면 / 배려하는 관계는 그곳에서 시작할 수 있는 중요한 기반이 된다 //

And when we are trying to motivate **ourselves**, / **doing things to** 재귀대명사 (재귀 용법) 명령사구 (주어)
enhance a sense of connectedness to others / can be crucial / to long-term persistence. // **단서 3** 타인과의 유대감 강화는 동기부여에 중요함

그리고 우리가 스스로 동기를 부여하려고 할 때 / 타인과의 유대감을 강화하기 위한 일을 하는 것은 / 중요할 수 있다 / 장기적인 지속에 //

So **exercise** with a friend, / **call** someone when you have a difficult decision to make, / and **be** there as a support for others / **as** they take on challenges. //
병렬 구조 (명령문 동사)   부사절 접속사 (시간)

그러니 친구와 함께 운동하라 / 당신이 어려운 결정을 내려야 할 때 누군가에게 전화하라 / 그리고 그들을 위한 버팀목으로 그곳에 있어라 / 다른 사람들이 도전에 맞설 때 //

- a wealth of 수많은 · supervisor ⓝ 상사
- perceive ⓥ 여기다, 인식하다 · motivate ⓥ 동기를 부여하다
- value ⓥ 소중히 여기다 · peer ⓝ 또래, 동료
- relatedness ⓝ 관계성 · internalization ⓝ 내면화
- fuel ⓥ 자극하다, 연료를 공급하다 · competence ⓝ 유능함, 능숙함
- crucial ⓐ 중요한 · enhance ⓥ 강화하다, 향상시키다
- a sense of connectedness 유대감 · take on ~에 맞서다

부모, 교사, 상사, 그리고 코치가 관여되어 있고 배려한다고 여겨질 때, 사람들은 더 행복하고 더 동기가 부여된다는 수많은 증거가 있다. 그리고 그것이 단지 권력을 가진 사람들만은 아닌데, 즉 우리는 또래와 직장 동료들에게서도 소중히 여겨지고 존중받는다는 느낌을 받을 필요가 있다. 따라서, 관계성에 대한 욕구가 충족될 때, 그리고 자율성과 유능함에 대한 지원 또한 제공된다면, 동기와 내면화는 자극된다. 만약 우리가 다른 사람들에게 동기를 부여하려고 한다면, 배려하는 관계는 그곳에서 시작할 수 있는 중요한 기반이 된다. 그리고 우리가 스스로 동기를 부여하려고 할 때, 타인과의 유대감을 강화하기 위한 일을 하는 것은 장기적인 지속에 중요할 수 있다. 그러니 친구와 함께 운동하라, 당신이 어려운 결정을 내려야 할 때 누군가에게 전화하라, 그리고 다른 사람들이 도전에 맞설 때 그들을 위한 버팀목으로 그곳에 있어라.

다음 글의 주제로 가장 적절한 것은?

① ways of getting out of dependent relationships
의존적인 관계에서 벗어나는 방법들 　　　　　　 의존의 긍정적 측면에 관한 내용임
② necessity of independent decision-making for happier life
독립이 아닌 타인과의 관계를 통해 동기부여가 가능함
더 행복한 삶을 위한 독립적인 의사결정의 필요성
③ key factors required for boosting a competitive atmosphere 경쟁보다는 관계 형성의 효과에 관한 내용임
경쟁적인 분위기를 조성하는 데 필요한 핵심 요소들
④ challenges in maintaining lasting bonds with family members 유대감 유지의 어려움은 언급되지 않았음
가족 구성원과의 지속적인 유대감을 유지하는 데 따른 어려움
⑤ importance of building connected relationships in motivation 유대감 형성이 동기부여에 긍정적 영향을 미침
동기부여에 있어 유대감 있는 관계 형성의 중요성

왜 정답 ? ★★❀ [정답률 80%]

- 배려를 받을 때 동기가 부여됨 **단서 1**
- 관계성이 충족되면 동기와 내면화가 자극됨 **단서 2**
- 타인과의 유대감 강화는 동기부여에 중요함 **단서 3**

➡ 배려와 존중을 받을 때, 관계성이 충족될 때 동기가 부여되므로 타인과의 유대감을 강화하는 것이 동기부여에 중요하다는 내용이다.

▶ 따라서 글의 주제는 ⑤ '동기부여에 있어 유대감 있는 관계 형성의 중요성'이다.

왜 오답 ?

① 글의 내용은 타인에 대한 의존이 긍정적이라는 것에 가깝고, 의존적 관계에서 벗어나는 방법은 언급되지 않았다.
② 타인과의 관계보다 독립이 행복을 준다는 내용이 아니다.
③ 경쟁보다는 유대감 강화를 권장하는 내용이다.
④ 유대감 강화가 중요하다고는 했지만, 가족 구성원과 유대감을 유지하는 어려움은 언급되지 않았다.

F 02 정답 ② *Lake Wobegon 효과

'다수의'
We tend to believe / **that** we possess **a host of** socially desirable 병렬 구조 (목적어절 접속사)   주격 관계대명사
characteristics, / and **that** we are free of most of those / **that** are socially undesirable. //

우리는 믿는 경향이 있다 / 우리가 사회적으로 바람직한 특성들을 많이 지니고 있고 / 우리는 그것들의 대부분은 지니고 있지 않다고 / 사회적으로 바람직하지 않은 //

For example, / a large majority of the general public thinks /
예를 들어 / 대대수의 일반 대중들은 생각한다 /

that they are more intelligent, more fair-minded, less prejudiced, / and more skilled / behind the wheel of an automobile / than the average person. // **단서 1** 많은 사람들은 자신이 보통 사람보다 더 낫다고 생각함

그들이 더 지적이고, 더 공정하고, 덜 편견을 가지며 / 더 능숙하다고 / 자동차를 운전할 때 / 보통 사람보다 //

so ~ that ...: 너무 ~해서 …하다
This phenomenon is **so** reliable and ubiquitous / **that** it has come to be known as the "Lake Wobegon effect," / after Garrison Keillor's fictional community /

이 현상은 너무 신뢰할 수 있고 어디서나 볼 수 있어서 / 그것은 'Lake Wobegon 효과'라고 알려지게 되었다 / Garrison Keillor의 허구적인 공동체의 이름을 딴 /
관계부사
where "the women are strong, the men are good-looking, / and all the children are above average." // **단서 2** 리더십: 고등학생 100만 명 중 70퍼센트가 자신이 평균 이상이라고 생각했음

'여성들은 강하고, 남성들은 잘생긴 / 그리고 모든 아이들은 평균 이상'인 //

A survey of one million high school seniors found / that 70% **thought** / they were above average in leadership ability, / and only 2% **thought** / they were below average. //
뒤에 목적어절 접속사 that이 생략됨

고등학교 고학년 학생 100만 명을 대상으로 한 설문조사는 발견했다 / 70퍼센트는 생각했다는 것을 / 자신이 리더십 능력에 있어 평균 이상이라고 / 그리고 2퍼센트만이 생각했다는 것을 / 자신이 평균 이하라고 //
'~에 있어서' '~와 잘 지내다' **단서 3** 다른 사람들과 잘 지내는 능력: 모두 자신이 평균 이상이라고 생각했음
In terms of ability to **get along with** others, / **all** students thought they were above average, / 60% thought they were in the top 10%, / and 25% thought they were in the top 1%! //

다른 사람들과 잘 지내는 능력에 있어서 / '모든' 학생들은 자신이 평균 이상이라고 생각했고 / 60퍼센트는 자신이 상위 10퍼센트에 속한다고 생각했으며 / 25퍼센트는 자신이 상위 1퍼센트에 속한다고 생각했다 //

- **possess** ⓥ 지니다, 소유하다
- **desirable** ⓐ 바람직한
- **characteristic** ⓝ 특성, 특징
- **majority** ⓝ 다수
- **general** ⓐ 일반적인
- **intelligent** ⓐ 지적인
- **fair-minded** ⓐ 공정한
- **prejudiced** ⓐ 편견이 있는
- **fictional** ⓐ 허구적인
- **senior** ⓝ (고등학교의) 졸업반 학생
- **self-image** ⓝ 자아상
- **tendency** ⓝ 경향
- **superior** ⓐ (~보다) 우월한
- **prejudice** ⓝ 편견

우리는 우리가 사회적으로 바람직한 특성들을 많이 지니고 있고, 사회적으로 바람직하지 않은 특성들의 대부분은 지니고 있지 않다고 믿는 경향이 있다. 예를 들어, 대다수의 일반 대중들은 그들이 보통 사람보다 더 지적이고, 더 공정하고, 덜 편견을 가지며 자동차를 운전할 때 더 능숙하다고 생각한다. 이 현상은 너무 신뢰할 수 있고 어디서나 볼 수 있기 때문에 '여성들은 강하고, 남성들은 잘생겼으며, 모든 아이들은 평균 이상'인 Garrison Keillor의 허구적인 공동체의 이름을 따서 'Lake Wobegon 효과'라고 알려지게 되었다. 고등학교 고학년 학생 100만 명을 대상으로 한 설문조사에서 70퍼센트는 자신이 리더십 능력에 있어 평균 이상이라고 생각했고, 2퍼센트만이 자신이 평균 이하라고 생각했다는 것을 발견했다. 다른 사람들과 잘 지내는 능력에 있어서, '모든' 학생들은 자신이 평균 이상이라고 생각했고, 60퍼센트는 자신이 상위 10퍼센트에 속한다고 생각했으며, 25퍼센트는 자신이 상위 1퍼센트에 속한다고 생각했다!

다음 글의 주제로 가장 적절한 것은?

① importance of having a positive self-image as a leader
리더로서 긍정적인 자아상을 갖는 것의 중요성 리더의 자질을 설명하는 글이 아님
② our common belief that we are better than average
우리가 평균보다 우월하다는 우리의 공통된 믿음 대부분 스스로가 평균보다 낫다고 생각한다고 했음
③ our tendency to think others are superior to us
다른 사람이 우리보다 우월하다고 생각하는 우리의 경향 글의 주제와 정반대의 내용임
④ reasons why we always try to be above average
우리가 항상 평균 이상이 되려고 노력하는 이유 이미 평균 이상이라고 여기는 통념에 관한 글임
⑤ danger of prejudice in building healthy social networks
건강한 사회 연결망 구축에 있어 편견의 위험성 get along with others, prejudiced 등이 언급된 것으로 만든 오답

왜 정답? ✱✱❀ [정답률 71%]

- 대다수의 사람들은 그들이 보통 사람보다 더 지적이고, 더 공정하고, 덜 편견을 가지며 운전에 더 능숙하다고 생각함 단서 1

예시 1: 고등학교 고학년 학생 100만 명 중 70퍼센트가 자신의 리더십이 평균 이상이라고 생각함 단서 2

예시 2: 다른 사람들과 잘 지내는 능력에 있어서는 '모든' 학생들이 자신이 평균 이상이라고 생각함 단서 3

➡ 'Lake Wobegon 효과'를 고등학교 학생들을 예시로 들어 설명했다.
▶ 글의 주제는 ② '우리가 평균보다 우월하다는 우리의 공통된 믿음'이 적절하다.

왜 오답?

① 리더십은 예시로 제시되었을 뿐, 리더십의 자질을 설명하는 글이 아니다. 함정
③ 우리가 다른 사람보다 우월하다고 생각한다고 했으므로 글의 주제와는 정반대의 내용이다.
④ 사람들이 평균 이상이 되려고 노력하는 이유 등은 언급되지 않았다.
⑤ 건강한 사회 연결망 구축과 편견의 관계를 말한 글이 아니다.

F 03 정답 ⑤ ✱문제 해결을 위한 과학 지식의 실천

be concerned with: ~와 관련이 있다
Science **is concerned with** / accumulating and understanding observations / of the physical world. //
과학은 관련이 있다 / 관찰을 축적하고 이해하는 것과 / 물리적 세계에 대한 //

That understanding alone / solves no problems. //
그 이해 단독으로는 / 어떠한 문제도 해결하지 않는다 //

to help의 의미상 주어 (= that understanding)
Individual people / have to act on that understanding / **for it to** help solve problems. // 단서 1 문제를 해결하려면 이해를 행동으로 옮겨야 함
부사적 용법 (목적)
개개인은 / 그 이해를 행동으로 옮겨야 한다 / 그것이 문제를 해결하는 것을 돕기 위해 //

목적어절 접속사
For instance, science has found / **that** regular exercise can lower / your risk of heart disease. //
예를 들어, 과학은 발견했다 / 규칙적인 운동이 낮출 수 있다는 것을 / 심장병의 위험을 //

동명사구 주어   단수 동사   = Knowing this fact
Knowing this fact **is** interesting, / but **it** will do nothing / for your personal health / **unless** you act on it and actually exercise. //
부사절 접속사 (조건)
이러한 사실을 아는 것은 흥미롭지만 / 그것은 아무런 도움이 되지 않는다 / 당신의 개인 건강에 / 당신이 이를 행동으로 옮겨 실제로 운동하지 않는다면 //
앞 문장의 but 이후 내용을 가리킴
And **that**'s the hard part. //
그리고 바로 이 점이 어려운 부분이다 //

Reading an article about exercise / is easy. //
운동에 대한 기사를 읽는 것은 / 쉽다 //

Getting into an actual routine of regular exercise / is harder. //
규칙적인 운동의 실제적인 루틴을 형성하는 것은 / 더 어렵다 //

'조금도 ~ 아니다'
In this sense, / science really / solves **no** problems **at all**. //
이러한 점에서 / 과학은 사실 / 어떤 문제도 해결하지 않는다 //

과거분사구 (the knowledge 수식)   병렬 구조
Problems are only solved / when people **take** the knowledge / **provided by science** / and **use it**. // 단서 2 지식을 활용해야만 문제가 해결됨
= the knowledge
문제는 해결된다 / 사람들이 지식을 취하고 / 과학에 의해 제공된 / 그것을 사용할 때만 //

In fact, / many of humanity's biggest problems are caused / by lack of action, / and not lack of knowledge. // 단서 3 인류 문제 중 다수가 행동의 부족에 의해 발생함
실제로 / 인류의 가장 큰 문제들 중 다수는 야기된다 / 행동의 부족에 의해 / 지식의 부족이 아니라 //

- **observation** ⓝ 관찰
- **physical** ⓐ 물리적인, 신체적인
- **lower** ⓥ 낮추다
- **risk** ⓝ 위험
- **personal** ⓐ 개인의
- **act on** ~을 행동으로 옮기다
- **article** ⓝ 기사
- **humanity** ⓝ 인류
- **strategic** ⓐ 전략적인
- **act against** ~을 거슬러 행동하다
- **lack** ⓝ 부족

과학은 물리적 세계에 대한 관찰을 축적하고 이해하는 것과 관련이 있다. 그 이해 단독으로는 어떠한 문제도 해결하지 않는다. 개개인은 그것이 문제를 해결하는 것을 돕기 위해 그 이해를 행동으로 옮겨야 한다. 예를 들어, 과학은 규칙적인 운동이 심장병의 위험을 낮출 수 있다는 것을 발견했다. 이러한 사실을 아는 것은 흥미롭지만, 당신이 이를 행동으로 옮겨 실제로 운동하지 않는다면 그것은 당신의 개인 건강에 아무런 도움이 되지 않는다. 그리고 바로 이 점이 어려운 부분이다. 운동에 대한 기사를 읽는 것은 쉽다. 규칙적인 운동의 실제적인 루틴을 형성하는 것은 더 어렵다. 이러한 점에서, 과학은 사실 어떤 문제도 해결하지 않는다. 문제는 사람들이 과학에 의해 제공된 지식을 취하고 그것을 사용할 때만 해결된다. 실제로, 인류의 가장 큰 문제들 중 다수는 지식의 부족이 아니라, 행동의 부족에 의해 야기된다.

다음 글의 주제로 가장 적절한 것은?

① advantages of putting strategic plans into action
전략적 계획을 실행에 옮기는 것의 이점 전략적 계획은 언급되지 않았음
② danger of acting against the wisdom of the crowd
다수의 지혜를 거슬러 행동하는 것의 위험성 다수의 지혜는 언급되지 않았음
③ difficulty in sharing scientific knowledge with the public 과학 지식 공유의 어려움은 언급되지 않았음
대중과 과학 지식을 공유하는 것의 어려움
④ problems with lacking specific knowledge about exercising 지식의 부족이 아니라 행동의 부족에 의해 문제가 야기됨
운동에 대한 구체적인 지식 부족으로 생기는 문제
⑤ need to act on scientific understanding in solving problems 과학적 이해를 행동으로 옮길 때 문제가 해결될 수 있음
문제를 해결하기 위해 과학적 이해를 행동으로 옮길 필요성

왜 정답? ✱✱❀ [정답률 83%]

- 문제를 해결하려면 이해를 행동으로 옮겨야 함 단서 1
- 지식을 활용해야만 문제가 해결됨 단서 2
- 지식 부족이 아닌 행동 부족으로 인류의 가장 큰 문제들 중 다수가 발생함 단서 3

➡ 이해나 지식을 행동으로 옮겨 활용해야 문제를 해결할 수 있다고 했으므로 ⑤ '문제를 해결하기 위해 과학적 이해를 행동으로 옮길 필요성'이 글의 주제이다.

왜 오답?

① 전략적 계획은 언급되지 않았다.
② 과학적 지식의 실천에 관한 내용이지 다수의 지혜에 관한 내용이 아니다.
③ 대중과 과학 지식을 공유하기 어렵다는 내용은 언급되지 않았다.
④ 운동은 실천의 예시로 들었을 뿐이며, 과학적 이해를 행동으로 옮기는 것에 관한 내용이다.

구문 서술형

정답 understanding, 지시형용사, 목적어, 접속사

해석 ① 그 이해 단독으로는 어떠한 문제도 해결하지 않는다.

② 과학은 규칙적인 운동이 심장병의 위험을 낮출 수 있다는 것을 발견했다.

→ ① understanding 앞에 쓰인 that은 지시형용사로 쓰여 '그 이해'라는 뜻을 완성한다.

② regular ~ disease 앞에 쓰인 that은 목적어절 접속사로 쓰여 '~라는 것'이라는 뜻을 완성한다.

F 04 정답 ② *인간의 감각을 확장하는 도구들

For many centuries, / humans have taken advantage of tools /
주격 관계대명사
that translate and bring into our perception natural phenomena
목적격 관계대명사
/ that we can't perceive with our senses. // 단서 1 인간은 지각할 수 없는 현상을 지각하기 위해 도구를 이용함
수 세기 동안 / 인간은 도구들을 이용해 왔다 / 자연 현상을 바꾸고 우리의 지각으로 가져오는 / 우리의 감각으로는 지각할 수 없는 //

In some cases, / this consists of simply amplifying / signals that feed into our normal sensory inputs / 단서 2 감각 신호를 확장하는 도구
어떤 경우에는 / 이것은 단순히 확장하는 것으로 구성된다 / 우리의 일반적인 감각 입력으로 들어오는 신호를 //

전치사구   목적어 주격 관계대명사
(e.g., telescopes can bring into clear view / that which is too far
                                        '너무 ~해서 …할 수 없는'
away / for our eyes to perceive on their own). //
(예: 망원경은 명확한 시야로 가져올 수 있다 / 너무 멀어서 / 우리 눈이 그 자체로 지각할 수 없는 것을) //

turn A into B: A를 B로 바꾸다   목적격 관계대명사
Other instruments turn signals / that we cannot perceive / into
= signals
ones that we can observe. // 단서 3 인지할 수 없는 신호를 관찰하도록 돕는 도구
다른 도구들은 신호를 바꾼다 / 우리가 인지할 수 없는 / 우리가 관찰할 수 있는 것으로 //

Some of these take the form of expanding / the reach of our current senses, / such as creating visible images / based on the ultraviolet spectrum of light /
이러한 도구 중 일부는 확장하는 형태를 취한다 / 우리의 현재 감각 범위를 / 가시 이미지를 생성하거나 / 빛의 자외선 스펙트럼을 기반으로 /

병렬 구조 (동명사)
or changing sounds / that are normally outside the range / of what human ears can hear / into audible signals. //
소리를 바꾸는 것과 같이 / 보통 범위 밖에 있는 / 인간의 귀가 들을 수 있는 것의 / 들을 수 있는 신호로 //

Alternatively, / some instruments measure properties / for
                                          병렬 구조
which we have no sensory capacity at all / and change them /
대명사 목적격 관계대명사
into that which we can observe. //
아니면 / 일부 도구는 속성을 측정하고 / 우리가 전혀 감각 수용 능력이 없는 / 그것들을 바꾼다 / 이를 우리가 관찰할 수 있는 것으로 //

- translate ⓥ 바꾸다   · perception ⓝ 지각
- feed into ~에 들어가다   · sensory ⓐ 감각의
- telescope ⓝ 망원경   · ultraviolet ⓐ 자외(선)의
- property ⓝ 속성   · capacity ⓝ 수용   · difficulty ⓝ 어려움
- replace A with B A를 B로 대체하다   · inspire ⓥ 영감을 주다
- visual ⓐ 시각의   · auditory ⓐ 청각의   · imagination ⓝ 상상

수 세기 동안, 인간은 우리의 감각으로는 지각할 수 없는 자연 현상을 바꾸고 우리의 지각으로 가져오는 도구들을 이용해 왔다. 어떤 경우에는, 이것은 우리의 일반적인 감각 입력으로 들어오는 신호를 단순히 확장하는 것(예: 망원경은 너무 멀어서 우리 눈이 그 자체로 지각할 수 없는 것을 명확한 시야로 가져올 수 있다)으로 구성된다. 다른 도구들은 우리가 인지할 수 없는 신호를 우리가 관찰할 수 있는 것으로 바꾼다. 이러한 도구 중 일부는 우리의 현재 감각 범위를 확장하는 빛의 자외선 스펙트럼을 기반으로 가시 이미지를 생성하거나 보통은 인간의 귀가 들을 수 있는 것의 범위 밖에 있는 소리를 들을 수 있는 신호로

바꾸는 것과 같이 형태를 취한다. 아니면, 일부 도구들은 우리가 전혀 감각 수용 능력이 없는 속성을 측정하고 이를 우리가 관찰할 수 있는 것으로 그것들을 바꾼다.

다음 글의 주제로 가장 적절한 것은?
① difficulties in replacing human senses with tools
   인간의 감각을 도구로 대체하는 것의 어려움
②the tools that increase the ability of human senses   인간의 감각 대체가 아니라 확장에 관한 내용임
   인간의 감각 능력을 향상시키는 도구들   도구를 통해 감각 능력을 향상시킴
③ human senses that inspire the inventing of scientific
   tools   도구 발명은 언급되지 않음
   과학 도구 발명에 영감을 주는 인간의 감각들
④ differences between visual and auditory senses in
   humans   시각과 청각의 차이점은 언급되지 않았음
   인간의 시각과 청각의 차이점
⑤ the power of human imagination in discovering the
   universe   상상력은 언급되지 않았음
   우주를 발견하는 데 있어서 인간 상상력의 힘

왜 정답 ? ★★※ [정답률 80%]
- 인간은 지각할 수 없는 현상을 지각하기 위해 도구를 이용함 단서 1
- 감각 신호를 확장하는 도구 단서 2
- 인지할 수 없는 감각 신호를 관찰하도록 돕는 도구 단서 3

➡ 인간의 감각 신호를 확장하거나 인지할 수 없는 감각 신호를 관찰하도록 돕는 도구들을 예로 들었다. 이러한 도구들은 모두 인간의 감각 능력을 향상시킨다.
▶ 따라서 정답은 ② '인간의 감각 능력을 향상시키는 도구들'이다.

왜 오답 ?
① 인간의 감각을 대체하는 것이 아니라, 확장하는 도구에 관한 내용이다.
③ 인간의 감각을 확장하는 도구들의 예시가 나왔을 뿐, 과학 도구 발명에 관한 내용이 아니다. 주의
④ 인간의 시각과 청각의 차이점은 언급되지 않았다.
⑤ 인간의 상상력은 언급되지 않았다.

구문 서술형

정답 properties, them

해석 아니면(대신에), 일부 도구들은 우리가 전혀 감각 수용 능력이 없는 속성을 측정하고 이를 우리가 관찰할 수 있는 것으로 그것들을 바꾼다.

→ 동사 measure와 change가 접속사 and로 연결된 병렬 구조이므로, 문장의 목적어는 measure 뒤의 properties와 change 뒤의 them이다.

F 05 정답 ⑤ *신뢰할 만한 양적 데이터를 얻기 위한 질문 방법

복수 주어   복수 동사
Many forms of research / lead naturally to quantitative data. //
많은 종류의 연구는 / 자연스럽게 양적 데이터로 이어진다 //

'~의 수' cf) a number of: 많은
A study of happiness / might measure the number of times
관계부사절 (times 수식)
someone smiles / during an interaction, /
행복에 관한 연구는 / 누군가가 미소 짓는 횟수를 측정할 수 있다 / 상호 작용 중에 /

and a study of memory / might measure the number of items an
목적격 관계대명사절 (items 수식)
individual can recall / after one, five, and ten minutes. //
그리고 기억에 관한 연구는 / 개인이 회상할 수 있는 항목의 수를 측정할 수 있다 / 1분, 5분, 그리고 10분 후에 //

동명사 주어   간접의문문 (Asking의 직접목적어)
Asking people how many times in a year they are sad / will also
yield quantitative data, / but it might not be reliable. //
사람들에게 자신이 일 년에 몇 번 슬픈지 물어보는 것 / 또한 양적 데이터를 산출할 수 있지만 / 이는 신뢰할 만하지 않을 수도 있다 //

Respondents' recollections may be inaccurate, / and their definitions of 'sad' could vary widely. //
응답자의 회상은 부정확할 수 있고 / '슬픈'에 대한 그들의 정의는 크게 다를 수 있다 //

동명사 주어 (단수)
But asking / "How many times in the past year were you sad /

enough to call in sick to work?" / **prompts**(단수 동사) a concrete answer. //
그러나 묻는 것은 / "지난 1년 동안 슬펐던 적이 몇 번 있었습니까 / 직장에 병가를 낼 만큼"이라고 / 구체적인 답변을 유발한다 //

Similarly, / instead of asking people / **to rate**(asking의 목적격 보어 (to부정사)) how bad a procrastinator they are, /
마찬가지로 / 사람들에게 묻는 대신 / 자신이 얼마나 심하게 미루는 사람인지를 평가하도록 /
ask,(명령문의 동사원형) / "How many of your utility bills are you currently late in paying, / **even though**(부사절 접속사 (양보)) you can afford to pay them?" //
물어보라 / "얼마나 많은 공과금 고지서의 납부가 현재 늦었나요 / 당신이 지불할 여유가 있음에도 불구하고"라고 //

Questions(복수 주어) **that**(주격 관계대명사) seek concrete responses / **help make**(복수 동사) abstract concepts **clearer**(make의 목적격 보어) and **ensure**(병렬 구조 (help의 목적어)) consistency / from one study to the next. // **단서** 양적 데이터 연구에서는 구체적인 응답을 요구하는 질문이 유용함
구체적인 응답을 요구하는 질문은 / 추상적인 개념을 더 명확하게 만들고 일관성을 보장하는 것을 돕는다 / 한 연구에서 다음 연구 간의 //

- quantitative ⓐ 양적인 ・ measure ⓥ 측정하다
- recall ⓥ 회상하다 ・ yield ⓥ 산출하다 ・ reliable ⓐ 신뢰할 만한
- recollection ⓝ 회상 ・ inaccurate ⓐ 부정확한 ・ vary ⓥ 다르다
- prompt ⓥ 유발[촉구]하다 ・ concrete ⓐ 구체적인
- rate ⓥ 평가하다 ・ utility bill 공과금 고지서
- afford to (~을 살) 여유가 있다 ・ seek ⓥ 요구하다, 찾다
- abstract ⓐ 추상적인 ・ ensure ⓥ 보장하다
- consistency ⓝ 일관성 ・ overgeneralize ⓥ 지나치게 일반화하다
- enhance ⓥ 높이다 ・ attain ⓥ 얻다

많은 종류의 연구는 자연스럽게 양적 데이터로 이어진다. 행복에 관한 연구는 누군가가 상호 작용 중에 미소 짓는 횟수를 측정할 수 있고, 기억에 관한 연구는 개인이 1분, 5분, 그리고 10분 후에 회상할 수 있는 항목의 수를 측정할 수 있다. 사람들에게 자신이 일 년에 몇 번 슬픈지 물어보는 것 또한 양적 데이터를 산출할 수 있지만, 이는 신뢰할 만하지 않을 수도 있다. 응답자의 회상은 부정확할 수 있고, '슬픈'에 대한 그들의 정의는 크게 다를 수 있다. 그러나 "지난 1년 동안 직장에 병가를 낼 만큼 슬펐던 적이 몇 번 있었습니까?"라고 묻는 것은 구체적인 답변을 유발한다. 마찬가지로, 사람들에게 그들이 얼마나 심하게 미루는 사람인지를 평가하도록 묻는 대신, "당신이 지불할 여유가 있음에도 불구하고 얼마나 많은 공과금 고지서의 납부가 현재 늦었나요?"라고 물어보라. 구체적인 응답을 요구하는 질문은 추상적인 개념을 더 명확하게 만들고 한 연구에서 다음 연구 간의 일관성을 보장하는 것을 돕는다.

> 다음 글의 주제로 가장 적절한 것은?
> ① risks of overgeneralizing results from the collected data 수집된 데이터의 결과를 지나치게 일반화하는 것의 위험 데이터 결과의 일반화는 언급되지 않았음
> ② usefulness of answering abstract questions with numbers 답변 방법이 아닌 질문 방법에 관한 내용임 숫자로 추상적인 질문에 답하는 유용성
> ③ effect of sample size on enhancing the reliability of research 표본 크기와 신뢰성의 관계는 언급되지 않았음 표본 크기가 연구의 신뢰성을 높이는 데 미치는 영향
> ④ limitations of measuring and quantifying various human emotions 감정 측정의 한계에 관한 내용이 아님 다양한 인간의 감정을 측정하고 정량화하는 것의 한계
> ⑤ importance of specific questions to attain reliable quantitative data 구체적인 질문을 통해 신뢰할 수 있는 양적 데이터를 얻을 수 있음 신뢰할 수 있는 양적 데이터를 얻기 위한 구체적인 질문의 중요성

>왜 정답? ★★✲ [정답률 67%]

도입: 양적 데이터를 산출하는 연구의 한계(응답자의 부정확한 기억, 개념에 대한 주관적인 정의로 인한 신뢰도 하락)
대안: 구체적인 답변을 유발하는 질문
예시 **1**: 슬픔을 측정하기 위해 직장 병가의 빈도를 묻는 질문
예시 **2**: 미루는 사람인지를 알기 위해 지연된 공과금 납부의 수를 묻는 질문
결론: 구체적 응답을 요구하는 질문은 개념을 명확하게 하고 연구의 일관성을 확보한다. **단서**

➡ 양적 데이터의 신뢰도를 높이기 위해서는 구체적인 답변을 요구하는 질문이 중요함
▶ 따라서 글의 주제는 ⑤ '신뢰할 수 있는 양적 데이터를 얻기 위한 구체적인 질문의 중요성'이다.

>왜 오답?

① 데이터 결과의 일반화는 언급되지 않았다.
② 양적 데이터 수집 시 구체적으로 질문해야 한다는 내용이지, 추상적인 질문에 숫자로 답변해야 한다는 내용이 아니다.
③ 표본의 크기는 언급되지 않았다.
④ 행복과 슬픔에 관한 연구에서 양적 데이터의 신뢰도가 낮을 수 있다고 했지만, 구체적인 질문을 통해 이러한 한계를 극복할 수 있다고 했다. **주의**

구문 서술형

정답 people, quantitative data

해석 사람들에게 자신이 일 년에 몇 번 슬픈지 물어보는 것은 양적 데이터를 산출할 수 있다.
→ people이 동명사 Asking의 간접목적어 역할을 한다. 전체 문장의 목적어는 동사 will (also) yield 뒤의 quantitative data이다.

F 06 정답 ④ *불리한 조건의 노동자들을 돕는 AI

단서 AI는 노동 시장에서 불리한 노동자의 일터에서의 접근성을 향상시킴
By improving accessibility of the workplace / for workers / that are typically at a disadvantage in the labour market, / AI can improve inclusiveness in the workplace. //
일터로의 접근성을 향상시킴으로써 / 노동자를 위한 / 노동 시장에서 일반적으로 불리한 위치에 있는 / AI는 일터에서 포괄성을 향상시킬 수 있다 //

AI-powered assistive **devices**(복수 주어) / to aid workers with visual, speech or hearing difficulties /
AI 동력의 보조 장치들이 / 시각, 발화 또는 청각 장애가 있는 노동자들을 돕기 위한 /
are becoming(복수 동사) more widespread, / **improving the access to**,(분사구문을 이끄는 현재분사) and **the quality of**(병렬 구조(work를 전치사의 목적어로 받음)) work / for people with disabilities. //
더 널리 보급되어 / 업무 접근성과 업무의 질을 향상시키고 있다 / 장애를 지닌 사람들의 //

For example, / speech recognition solutions / for people with dysarthric voices, / or live captioning systems / for deaf and hard of hearing people /
예를 들어 / 발화 인식 솔루션이나 / 구음 장애가 있는 사람들을 위한 / 실시간 자막 시스템은 / 청각 장애인과 난청인을 위한 /

can facilitate communication with colleagues and access to jobs / **where**(관계부사) inter-personal communication is necessary. //
동료와의 의사소통과 일에 대한 접근을 용이하게 할 수 있다 / 대인 의사소통이 필요한 //

AI can also enhance the capabilities of low-skilled workers, / with potentially positive effects / on their wages and career prospects. //
AI는 또한 저숙련 노동자들의 능력을 향상시킬 수 있다 / 잠재적으로 긍정적인 영향과 함께 / 그들의 임금과 경력 전망에 //

For example, / AI's capacity **to translate**(형용사적 용법(capacity 수식)) written and spoken word in real-time / can improve the performance of non-native speakers / in the workplace. //
예를 들어 / 문자 언어와 음성 언어를 실시간으로 번역하는 AI의 능력은 / 비원어민의 수행을 향상시킬 수 있다 / 일터에서 //

Moreover, / recent developments in AI-powered text generators / can instantly improve the performance of lower-skilled individuals /
게다가 / 최근의 AI 동력의 텍스트 생성기의 발전은 / 저숙련된 개인의 수행을 즉시 향상시킬 수 있다 /
in domains **such as**('~와 같은') writing, coding or customer service. //
글쓰기, 코딩, 고객 서비스와 같은 영역에서 //

- accessibility ⓝ 접근성　• disadvantage ⓝ 불리함
- labour ⓝ 노동　• inclusiveness ⓝ 포괄성
- assistive ⓐ 도움이 되는　• recognition ⓝ 인지
- caption ⓝ 자막　• facilitate ⓥ 촉진하다　• capability ⓝ 능력
- potentially ⓐⓓ 잠재적으로　• wage ⓝ 임금　• prospect ⓝ 전망
- domain ⓝ 영역　• ethical ⓐ 윤리적인　• necessity ⓝ 필요성
- support ⓥ 지원하다　• cure ⓥ 치료하다

노동 시장에서 일반적으로 불리한 위치에 있는 노동자를 위한 일터로의 접근성을 향상시킴으로써, AI는 일터에서 포괄성을 향상시킬 수 있다. 시각, 발화 또는 청각 장애가 있는 노동자들을 돕기 위한 AI 동력의 보조 장치들이 더 널리 보급되어, 장애를 지닌 사람들의 업무 접근성과 업무의 질을 향상시키고 있다. 예를 들어, 구음 장애가 있는 사람들을 위한 발화 인식 솔루션이나 청각 장애인과 난청인을 위한 실시간 자막 시스템은 동료와의 의사소통과 대인 의사소통이 필요한 일에 대한 접근을 용이하게 할 수 있다. AI는 또한 그들의 임금과 경력 전망에 잠재적으로 긍정적인 영향과 함께 저숙련 노동자들의 능력을 향상시킬 수 있다. 예를 들어, 문자 언어와 음성 언어를 실시간으로 번역하는 AI의 능력은 일터에서 비원어민의 수행을 향상시킬 수 있다. 게다가, 최근의 AI 동력의 텍스트 생성기의 발전은 글쓰기, 코딩, 고객 서비스와 같은 영역에서 저숙련된 개인의 수행을 즉시 향상시킬 수 있다.

다음 글의 주제로 가장 적절한 것은?
AI가 불리한 조건을 가진 노동자에게 도움을 줄 수 있다는 내용임
① jobs replaced by AI in the labour market
　노동 시장에서 AI에 의해 대체된 직업들　AI가 직업을 대체한다는 언급은 없음
② ethical issues caused by using AI in the workplace
　직장에서 AI를 사용하는 것으로 인한 윤리적 문제　AI의 윤리적 문제에 관한 내용이 아님
③ necessity of using AI technology for language learning
　언어 학습을 위한 AI 기술 사용의 필요성　언어 학습에 대한 언급은 없음
④ impacts of AI on supporting workers with disadvantages
　불리한 조건을 가진 근로자를 지원하는 AI의 영향
⑤ new designs of AI technology to cure people with disabilities　장애를 치료하는 AI 기술에 대한 언급은 없음
　장애를 가진 사람을 치료하기 위한 AI 기술의 새로운 설계

왜 정답? ✱✱✱ [정답률 74%]

- AI는 노동 시장에서 불리한 위치에 있는 노동자들의 접근성을 향상시킴으로써, 일터에서 포괄성을 향상시킬 수 있음 **단서**
- 예시 **1**: 발화 인식 솔루션과 실시간 자막 시스템 → 구음 장애 및 청각 장애가 있는 사람들도 의사소통이 필요한 일에 접근할 수 있게 함
- 예시 **2**: 실시간 번역 AI → 비원어민의 수행을 향상시킴
- 예시 **3**: AI 텍스트 생성기의 발전 → 저숙련된 개인의 수행을 향상시킴

➡ 노동 시장에서 불리한 조건을 가진 근로자를 위해 AI가 할 수 있는 역할을 설명하고 있다.
　▶ 따라서 글의 주제는 ④ '불리한 조건을 가진 근로자를 지원하는 AI의 영향'이다.

왜 오답?

① AI가 노동 시장에서 근로자에게 도움을 줄 수 있다고 했을 뿐, 노동 시장에서 AI가 직업을 대체한다는 것은 언급되지 않았다.
② 직장에서 AI를 사용하는 것으로 인한 윤리적 문제에 관한 내용이 아니다.
③ AI를 사용한 언어 학습은 언급되지 않았다.
⑤ 장애를 치료한다는 것은 언급되지 않았다. (▶◀ 이유: AI가 불리한 조건을 가진 사람들의 업무 수행을 도울 수 있다는 것만 언급되었을 뿐이다.)

F 07 정답 ⑤ ✱고난에 맞서는 것의 중요성

병렬 구조
We often try to make cuts in our challenges / and take the easy route. //
~을 멈추다[줄이다]
우리는 종종 우리의 도전을 멈추려 한다 / 그리고 쉬운 길을 택하려고 (한다) //

접속사가 생략되지 않은 분사구문
When taking the quick exit, / we fail to acquire the strength to
형용사적 용법(the strength 수식)
compete. //
쉬운 길을 택하면 / 경쟁할 수 있는 힘을 얻지 못한다 //

We often take the easy route / to improve our skills. //
우리는 종종 쉬운 길을 택한다 / 실력을 향상하기 위해 //

Many of us never really work / to achieve mastery in the key areas of life. //
우리 중 다수가 노력을 하지 않는다 / 인생의 핵심이 되는 영역에서 숙달을 위해 //

주격 관계대명사
These skills are key tools / that can be useful to our career, health, and prosperity. //
이러한 기술은 핵심 도구이다 / 경력, 건강, 번영에 도움이 될 수 있는 //

Highly successful athletes don't win / because of better
　　　　　　　　　　　　　　　　　　　'~함으로써'　부사적 용법(목적)
equipment; / they win / by facing hardship to gain strength and
skill. // **단서 1** 성공한 운동선수들은 고난에 맞섬으로써 승리함
성공한 운동선수들은 승리하는 것이 아니다 / 더 좋은 장비 때문에 / 그들은 승리한다 / 힘과 실력을 얻기 위해 고난에 맞섬으로써 //

They win through preparation. //
그들은 준비를 통해 승리한다 //

it ~ that 강조 구문
It's the mental preparation, winning mindset, strategy, and skill
'돋보이게 하다'
/ that set them apart. //
바로 정신적 준비, 승리하는 마음가짐, 전략, 그리고 기술이다 / 그들을 돋보이게 하는 것은 //

Strength comes from struggle, / not from taking the path of least
resistance. // **단서 2** 맞서 싸워야 힘이 나옴
힘은 맞서 싸우는 데서 나온다 / 저항이 가장 적은 길을 택하는 것이 아니라 //

Hardship is not just a lesson for the next time / in front of us. //
고난은 단지 다음을 위한 교훈만은 아니다 / 우리 앞에 놓인 //

앞에 목적격 관계대명사가 생략됨
Hardship will be the greatest teacher / we will ever have in life. //
고난은 가장 위대한 스승이 될 것이다 / 우리 인생에서 // **단서 3** 고난은 인생에서 가장 위대한 스승임

- route ⓝ 경로, 길　• acquire ⓥ 획득하다　• compete ⓥ 경쟁하다
- mastery ⓝ 숙달　• prosperity ⓝ 번영　• equipment ⓝ 장비
- hardship ⓝ 고난　• mindset ⓝ 마음가짐
- struggle ⓝ 투쟁, 분투　• resistance ⓝ 저항
- confront ⓥ 직면하다

우리는 종종 우리의 도전을 멈추고, 쉬운 길을 택하려고 한다. 쉬운 길을 택하면 경쟁할 수 있는 힘을 얻지 못한다. 우리는 종종 실력을 향상하기 위해 쉬운 길을 택한다. 우리 중 다수가 인생의 핵심이 되는 영역에서 숙달을 위한 노력을 하지 않는다. 이러한 기술은 경력, 건강, 번영에 도움이 될 수 있는 핵심 도구이다. 성공한 운동선수들은 더 좋은 장비 때문에 승리하는 것이 아니다. 그들은 힘과 실력을 얻기 위해 고난에 맞섬으로써 승리한다. 그들은 준비를 통해 승리한다. 그들을 돋보이게 하는 것은 바로 정신적 준비, 승리하는 마음가짐, 전략, 그리고 기술이다. 힘은 저항이 가장 적은 길을 택하는 것이 아니라 맞서 싸우는 데서 나온다. 고난은 단지 우리 앞에 놓인 다음을 위한 교훈만은 아니다. 고난은 우리 인생에서 가장 위대한 스승이 될 것이다.

다음 글의 주제로 가장 적절한 것은?
인생의 갑작스러운 난관을 극복하기 어렵다는 내용이 아님
① characteristics of well-equipped athletes
　준비가 잘된 운동선수의 특징　잘 준비된 운동선수의 특징을 열거하는 글이 아님
② difficulties in overcoming life's sudden challenges
　인생의 갑작스러운 난관을 극복하는 데 있어서의 어려움
③ relationship between personal habit and competence
　개인의 습관과 능력 사이의 관계　개인의 습관이나 능력 사이의 관계에 관한 내용이 아님
④ risks of enduring hardship without any preparation
　아무런 준비도 없이 고난을 견뎌내는 것의 위험
⑤ importance of confronting hardship in one's life
　인생에서 고난을 직면하는 것의 중요성　고난은 우리 인생의 위대한 스승임
　고난의 필요성을 말하고 있지만 고난을 견디는 위험에 관한 내용은 아님

왜 정답? ✱✱✱ [정답률 83%]

- 성공한 운동선수들은 힘과 실력을 얻기 위해 고난에 맞섬으로써 승리한다. **단서 1**
- 힘은 맞서 싸우는 데서 나온다. **단서 2**
- 고난은 우리 인생에서 가장 위대한 스승이 될 것이다. **단서 3**

➡ 인생에서 어떤 것을 성취하기 위해서는 고난에 맞서 싸워야 한다고 했으므로 ⑤ '인생에서 고난을 직면하는 것의 중요성'이 글의 주제이다.

왜 오답?

① 잘 준비된 운동선수의 특징을 열거하는 글이 아니다. (▶◀ 이유: 고난의 필요성에 대한 근거로서 성공한 운동선수를 예로 들었을 뿐이다.)
② 갑작스러운 난관을 극복하는 것이 어렵다는 내용은 없다.
③ 개인의 습관이 능력과 어떤 관계가 있는지 전혀 언급되지 않았다.
④ 고난의 필요성에 대한 글이지만 고난을 견디는 것이 위험하다는 내용은 없다.

F 08 정답 ② *인간 진화에 있어 소속의 유용성

For creatures like us, / evolution smiled / upon those with a
strong need / to belong. 【단서 1】 진화와 소속에 대한 욕구와의 관계를 언급함
형용사적 용법
우리와 같은 창조물에게 있어 / 진화는 미소를 지었다 / 강한 욕구를 가진 것들에 / 소속하려는 //

Survival and reproduction are the criteria of success / by natural
selection, / and forming relationships with other people / can be
동명사구 주어   동사
useful / for both survival and reproduction. //
생존과 번식은 성공의 기준이고 / 자연 선택에 의한 / 다른 사람들과 관계를 형성하는 것은 /
유용할 수 있다 / 생존과 번식 모두에 // 【단서 2】 다른 사람과의 관계 형성(소속)은 생존과 번식에 유용함

Groups can share resources, / care for sick members, / scare off
predators, / fight together against enemies, / divide tasks / so
부사적 용법(목적)(=in order to)   병렬 구조
as to improve efficiency, / and contribute to survival / in many
other ways. //
집단은 자원을 공유하고 / 아픈 구성원을 돌보고 / 포식자를 쫓아버리고 / 적에 맞서서 함께
싸우고 / 일을 나누고 / 효율성을 향상시키기 위해 / 생존에 기여한다 / 많은 다른 방식에서 //

In particular, / if an individual and a group want / the same
resource, / the group will generally prevail, / so competition for
resources / would especially favor / a need to belong. //
특히 / 한 개인과 한 집단이 원하면 / 같은 자원을 / 집단이 일반적으로 이기고 / 그래서
자원에 대한 경쟁은 / 특별히 좋아할 것이다 / 소속하려는 욕구를 //

Belongingness will likewise promote reproduction, / such as by
bring A into contact with B; A를 B와 접속시키다
bringing potential mates into contact / with each other, /
마찬가지로 소속되어 있다는 것은 번식을 촉진시키는데 / 이를테면 잠재적인 짝을 만나게
해주거나 / 서로 /
                    병렬 구조
and in particular / by keeping parents together / to care for their
계속적 용법의 관계대명사
children, / who are much more likely to survive / if they have
more than one caregiver. //
특히 / 부모가 함께 있도록 함으로써인데 / 자녀를 돌보기 위해 / 자녀들은 훨씬 더 생존하기
쉬울 것이다 / 한 명보다 많은 돌보는 이가 있으면 //

- evolution ⓝ 진화 　• survival ⓝ 생존 　• reproduction ⓝ 번식
- criteria ⓝ 기준 　• natural selection 자연 선택
- predator ⓝ 포식자 　• efficiency ⓝ 효율성
- contribute ⓥ 기여하다 　• individual ⓝ 개인
- prevail ⓥ 이기다 　• competition ⓝ 경쟁
- belongingness ⓝ (단체에의) 귀속, 소속성 　• promote ⓥ 촉진시키다
- potential ⓐ 잠재적인 　• mate ⓝ 짝 　• evolutionary ⓐ 진화의
- theory ⓝ 이론

우리와 같은 창조물에게 있어 진화는 소속하려는 강한 욕구를 가진 것들에
미소를 지었다. 생존과 번식은 자연 선택에 의한 성공의 기준이고, 다른
사람들과 관계를 형성하는 것은 생존과 번식 모두에 유용할 수 있다.
집단은 자원을 공유하고, 아픈 구성원을 돌보고, 포식자를 쫓아버리고,
적에 맞서서 함께 싸우고, 효율성을 향상시키기 위해 일을 나누고,
많은 다른 방식에서 생존에 기여한다. 특히, 한 개인과 한 집단이 같은
자원을 원하면, 집단이 일반적으로 이기고, 그래서 자원에 대한 경쟁은
소속하려는 욕구를 특별히 좋아할 것이다. 마찬가지로 소속되어 있다는
것은 번식을 촉진시키는데, 이를테면 잠재적인 짝을 서로 만나게
해주거나, 특히 부모가 자녀를 돌보기 위해 함께 있도록 함으로써인데,
자녀들은 한 명보다 많은 돌보는 이가 있으면 훨씬 더 생존하기 쉬울
것이다.

다음 글의 주제로 가장 적절한 것은?

① skills for the weak to survive modern life
현대 생활에서 살아남기 위한 약자를 위한 기술　　　생존에 대해 말한 것으로 만든 오답
② usefulness of belonging for human evolution
인간 진화를 위한 소속의 유용성
③ ways to avoid competition among social groups 집단이 언급되긴
사회 집단 간의 경쟁을 피하는 방법　　　했지만 집단 간의 경쟁을 피하는 방법은 나오지 않음
④ roles of social relationships in children's education
아동 교육에서 사회적 관계의 역할　　　자녀에 대한 내용이 나오지만 아동 교육에 대한 글은 아님
⑤ differences between two major evolutionary theories
두 가지 주요 진화 이론 사이의 차이점　　　진화 이론 간의 차이를 말하는 글이 아님

>왜 정답? ★★★ [정답률 62%]

진화는 소속에 대한 강한 욕구를 가진 것들에 유리하다고 하면서, 인간의 생존과
번식에 다른 사람들과 관계를 형성하고 집단에 소속되어 있는 것이 도움이 된다는
내용의 글이다. 따라서 이 글의 주제로 가장 적절한 것은 ② '인간 진화를 위한
소속의 유용성'이다.

>왜 오답?

① 생존과 관련된 내용이긴 하지만, 현대 생활에서 살아남기 위한 약자들을 위한
　기술은 언급되지 않았다.

③ 집단이 언급되긴 했지만 사회 집단 간의 경쟁을 피하는 방법은 나오지 않았다.

④ 자녀에 대한 내용이 나오지만 아동 교육에서 사회적 관계가 갖는 역할은
　언급되지 않았다.

⑤ 두 가지 진화 이론 간의 차이를 말하는 글이 아니다.

F 09 정답 ④ *구강 건강의 중요성과 영향력

Nearly everything has to go through your mouth / to get to the
부사적 용법(목적)
rest of you, / from food and air to bacteria and viruses. //
from A to B: A에서 B까지
거의 모든 것이 여러분의 입을 거쳐야 한다 / 여러분의 나머지 부분에 도달하기 위해 / 음식과
공기에서부터 박테리아와 바이러스까지 //

A healthy mouth can help your body / get what it needs and
선행사를 포함한 관계대명사
prevent it from harm / 【단서 1】 입은 몸의 영양을 공급하고 피해를 막아줌
건강한 입은 몸을 도와줄 수 있다 / 여러분의 몸이 필요한 것을 얻고, 피해로부터 지키도록 /
to부정사의 의미상 주어
— with adequate space for air to travel to your lungs, / and
healthy teeth and gums / that prevent harmful microorganisms
주격 관계대명사
from entering your bloodstream. //
prevent A from -ing: A가 ~하는 것을 막다
공기가 폐로 이동할 수 있는 적당한 공간 / 그리고 건강한 치아와 잇몸으로 / 해로운 미생물이
혈류로 들어가는 것을 막는 //

From the moment you are created, / oral health affects every
every + 단수 명사
aspect of your life. // 【단서 2】 구강 건강은 삶의 모든 측면에 영향을 미침
여러분이 생겨난 순간부터 / 구강 건강은 여러분의 삶의 모든 측면에 영향을 미친다 //
선행사를 포함하는 관계대명사(주어절을 이끎)
What happens in the mouth / is usually just the tip of the iceberg
/ and a reflection / of what is happening in other parts of the
병렬 구조
body. //
선행사를 포함하는 관계대명사(전치사의 목적어절을 이끎)
입안에서 일어나는 일은 / 대개 빙산의 일각일 뿐이며 / 반영이다 / 신체의 다른 부분에서
일어나고 있는 일의 //

Poor oral health can be a cause of a disease / that affects the
주격 관계대명사
entire body. // 【단서 3】 나쁜 구강 건강은 신체 질병의 원인이 될 수 있음
나쁜 구강 건강은 질병의 원인일 수 있다 / 전체 몸에 영향을 끼치는 //
병렬 구조
The microorganisms in an unhealthy mouth / can enter the
bloodstream / and travel anywhere in the body, / posing serious
분사구문을 이끎
health risks. //
건강하지 않은 입안의 미생물은 / 혈류로 들어가고 / 신체의 어느 곳이든 이동하여 / 심각한
건강상의 위험을 초래할 수 있다 //

- nearly ⓐⓓ 거의 　• go through ~을 거쳐가다 　• adequate ⓐ 적당한
- lung ⓝ 폐 　• gum ⓝ 잇몸 　• harmful ⓐ 해로운
- bloodstream ⓝ 혈류 　• oral ⓐ 구강의 　• affect ⓥ 영향을 미치다
- aspect ⓝ 측면 　• tip of the iceberg 빙산의 일각
- reflection ⓝ 반영, 반사 　• entire ⓐ 전체의
- pose ⓥ ~을 초래하다, 제기하다 　• immune system 면역 체계

음식과 공기에서부터 박테리아와 바이러스까지 거의 모든 것이 여러분의 나머
지 부분에 도달하기 위해 여러분의 입을 거쳐야 한다. 건강한 입은 공기가 폐로
이동할 수 있는 적당한 공간, 그리고 해로운 미생물이 혈류로 들어가는 것을 막
는 건강한 치아와 잇몸으로 여러분의 몸이 필요한 것을 얻고, 피해로부터 몸을
지키도록 도와줄 수 있다. 여러분이 생겨난 순간부터 구강 건강은 여러분의 삶
의 모든 측면에 영향을 미친다. 입안에서 일어나는 일은 대개 빙산의 일각일 뿐
이며 신체의 다른 부분에서 일어나고 있는 일의 반영이다. 나쁜 구강 건강은 전

체 몸에 영향을 끼치는 질병의 원인일 수 있다. 건강하지 않은 입안의 미생물이 혈류로 들어가고 신체의 어느 곳이든 이동하여 심각한 건강상의 위험을 초래할 수 있다.

다음 글의 주제로 가장 적절한 것은?
① the way the immune system fights viruses
면역 체계가 바이러스와 싸우는 방법 　　　면역 체계는 언급되지 않음
② the effect of unhealthy eating habits on the body
건강하지 않은 식습관이 몸에 미치는 영향 　　　식습관은 언급되지 않음
③ the difficulty in raising awareness about oral health
구강 건강에 관한 인식을 높이는 것의 어려움 　　구강 건강에 관한 인식 제고는 언급되지 않음
④ the importance of oral health and its impact on the body
구강 건강의 중요성과 몸에 미치는 영향 　　구강 건강의 중요성과 영향력에 관한 내용임
⑤ the relationship between oral health and emotional well-being
구강 건강과 정서적 행복 간의 관계 　　정서적 행복은 언급되지 않음

왜 정답? ✿✿❀ [정답률 86%]

도입: 거의 모든 것은 인간의 입을 통하고, 입은 몸의 영양을 공급하고 피해를 막아줌 [단서 1]

주제: 구강 건강은 삶의 모든 면에 영향을 미치며, 특히 나쁜 구강 건강은 질병을 일으킬 수 있음 [단서 2], [단서 3]

➡ 공기부터 박테리아까지 거의 모든 것이 인간의 입을 통하고, 구강 건강은 우리 삶의 모든 면에 영향을 미침

▶ 따라서 글의 주제로는 ④ '구강 건강의 중요성과 몸에 미치는 영향'이 가장 적절하다.

왜 오답?

① 면역 체계는 언급되지 않았다.
② 식습관은 언급되지 않았다.
③ 구강 건강에 관한 인식 제고는 언급되지 않았다. (➼ 이유: 구강 건강의 중요성에 관한 내용이지, 사람들의 인식 제고는 언급되지 않았다.)
⑤ 정서적 행복에 관한 언급은 없었다.

F 10 정답 ① *젊은이들이 채식주의 식단을 찾는 이유 —

[단서 1] 많은 젊은이들이 육식에 반대하고 채식을 선호한다고 했음
Vegetarian eating is moving into the mainstream / as more and more young adults say no / to meat, poultry, and fish. // 채식은 주류가 되어가고 있다 / 점점 더 많은 젊은이들이 반대함에 따라 / 고기, 가금류, 생선에 //

~에 따르면
According to the American Dietetic Association, / "approximately planned vegetarian diets are healthful, / are
　　　　　　　　　　　　　　　　　　　　　　　병렬 구조
nutritionally adequate, / and provide health benefits / in the prevention and treatment of certain diseases." // American Dietetic Association에 따르면 / 대략적으로 계획된 채식 식단이 건강에 좋고 / 영양학적으로도 적당하고 / 건강상의 이점을 제공한다 / 특정한 질병을 예방하고 치료하는 데 //

목적격 관계대명사
But / health concerns are not the only reason / that young adults give for changing their diets. // 그러나 / 건강에 대한 염려들이 유일한 이유는 아니다 / 젊은이들이 그들의 식단을 바꾸려고 하는 //

[단서 2] 동물의 권리 옹호 차원에서 채식을 선택하는 젊은이들이 있음
Some make the choice / out of concern for animal rights. // 몇몇은 선택한다 / 동물의 권리에 대한 관심 때문에 //

분사구문을 이끄는 과거분사(앞에 being 생략)　주격 관계대명사
When faced with the statistics that show / the majority of
　　　　　　　　　　　　　　　뒤에 목적어절 접속사가 생략됨
animals raised as food / live in confinement, / many teens give
부사적 용법(목적)
up meat / to protest those conditions. // 보여주는 통계자료를 볼 때 / 음식으로 길러지는 대다수의 동물들이 / 갇혀서 산다는 것을 / 많은 십대들은 고기를 포기한다 / 그러한 상황에 저항하기 위해 //

Others turn to vegetarianism / to support the environment. //
다른 사람들은 채식주의자가 된다 / 환경을 지지하기 위해 //
[단서 3] 환경 보호를 위해 채식주의자가 되는 사람들도 있음
Meat production uses / vast amounts of water, land, grain, and energy / and creates problems with animal waste and resulting pollution. // 고기를 생산하는 것은 사용한다 / 거대한 양의 물, 땅, 곡식과 에너지를 / 그리고 가축에서 나오는 쓰레기와 그에 따른 오염과 같은 문제들을 만들어낸다 //

· vegetarian eating 채식　　· mainstream ⓝ 주류
· dietetic ⓐ 식이(성)의　　· approximately ⓐⓓ 거의, 대략
· nutritionally ⓐⓓ 영양학적으로　　· adequate ⓐ 적당한
· prevention ⓝ 예방　　· treatment ⓝ 치료
· concern ⓝ 관심, 염려　　· confinement ⓝ 갇힘
· vegetarianism ⓝ 채식주의　　· vast ⓐ 거대한

채식은 점점 더 많은 젊은이들이 고기, 가금류, 생선에 반대함에 따라 주류가 되어가고 있다. American Dietetic Association에 따르면, 대략적으로 계획된 채식 식단이 건강에 좋고, 영양학적으로도 적당하고, 특정한 질병을 예방하고 치료하는 데 건강상의 이점을 제공한다. 그러나 건강에 대한 염려들이 젊은이들이 그들의 식단을 바꾸려고 하는 유일한 이유는 아니다. 몇몇은 동물의 권리에 대한 관심 때문에 선택한다. 음식으로 길러지는 대다수의 동물들이 갇혀서 산다는 것을 보여주는 통계자료를 볼 때, 많은 십대들은 그러한 상황에 저항하기 위해 고기를 포기한다. 다른 사람들은 환경을 지지하기 위해 채식주의자가 된다. 고기를 생산하는 것은 거대한 양의 물, 땅, 곡식과 에너지를 사용하고 가축에서 나오는 쓰레기와 그에 따른 오염과 같은 문제들을 만들어낸다.

다음 글의 주제로 가장 적절한 것은?
① reasons why young people go for vegetarian diets 다양한
젊은이들이 채식주의 식단을 찾는 이유들 이유로 점점 더 많은 젊은이들이 채식을 선호한다는 내용
② ways to build healthy eating habits for teenagers
십대들을 위한 건강한 식습관을 기르는 방법들 십대가 아닌 젊은이들과 관련된 내용임
③ vegetables that help lower your risk of cancer
암 발병 위험을 낮추는 데 도움이 되는 채소 암과 관련된 내용은 나오지 않았음
④ importance of maintaining a balanced diet
균형 잡힌 식단을 유지하는 것의 중요성 균형 잡힌 식단에 대한 언급은 없음
⑤ disadvantages of plant-based diets
채식 식단의 단점들 많은 젊은이들이 채식을 선호한다는 내용임

왜 정답? ✿✿❀ [정답률 78%]

많은 젊은이들이 육식에 반대하고 채식을 선호한다고 했다. 젊은이들이 건강과 동물의 권리, 환경 보호 등 다양한 이유로 육식에 반대하고 채식을 선택한다는 내용이다. 따라서 이 글의 주제로 가장 적절한 것은 ① '젊은이들이 채식주의 식단을 찾는 이유들'이다.

왜 오답?

② 젊은이들의 식습관에 대한 글이므로 십대에 대한 내용은 아니다.
③ 채식이 건강에 좋다고는 했으나 암 발병을 낮춘다는 내용은 없다. 함정
④ 균형 잡힌 식단을 유지하는 것은 언급되지 않은 내용이다.
⑤ 채식이 가진 장점들 때문에 채식이 선호된다는 내용으로 단점은 나오지 않았다.

F 11 정답 ⑤ *녹는 얼음과 해수면 상승이 미치는 영향 —

핵심 주어(단수)
The most remarkable and unbelievable consequence / of
　　　　　　　　　　　　　　　　　　　　　　　　　단수 동사
melting ice and rising seas / is that together they are a kind of
time machine, / 가장 놀랍고 믿을 수 없는 결과는 / 녹는 얼음과 상승하는 바다의 / 그것들이 합쳐서 일종의 타임머신이라는 것이다 /

so ~ that S V: 너무 ~해서 …하다　[단서 1] 녹는 얼음과 상승하는 바다는 하루의 기간을 바꾸고 있음
so real that they are altering the duration of our day. // (이것은) 너무나 현실적이어서 그것들이 우리 하루의 기간을 바꾸고 있다 //

It works like this: / As the glaciers melt and the seas rise, / gravity forces more water / toward the equator. // 그것은 이처럼 작동한다 / 빙하가 녹고 바다가 높아지면서 / 중력이 더 많은 물을 밀어 넣는다 / 적도를 향해 //

분사구문
This changes the shape of the Earth / ever so slightly, / making it fatter around the middle, / 이것은 지구의 모양을 변화시킨다 / 아주 약간 / 가운데 주변으로 그것을 더 불룩하게 만들면서 /

계속적 용법의 주격 관계대명사　[단서 2] 지구의 모양이 바뀌면서 회전이 늦어짐
which in turns slows the rotation of the planet / similarly to the
관계부사절
way / a ballet dancer slows her spin / by spreading out her arms. // 그리고 그것은 결과적으로 행성의 회전을 늦춘다 / 방식과 유사하게 / 발레 무용수가 그녀의 회전을 늦추는 / 양팔을 뻗어서 //

The slowdown isn't much, / just a few thousandths of a second each year, / but like the barely noticeable jump of rising seas every year, / it adds up. // 단서 3 감속은 점점 쌓임
= the slowdown

이 감속은 크지 않다 / 매년 단지 몇천분의 1초로 / 하지만 해마다 상승하는 바다의 알아차리기 힘든 증가처럼 / 그것은 쌓인다 //

When dinosaurs lived on the Earth, / a day lasted only about twenty-three hours. //

공룡들이 지구에 살았을 때 / 하루는 약 23시간만 지속되었다 //

- remarkable ⓐ 놀라운, 주목할 만한   · unbelievable ⓐ 믿을 수 없는
- consequence ⓝ 결과   · alter ⓥ 바꾸다, 고치다
- duration ⓝ (지속되는) 기간   · glacier ⓝ 빙하   · gravity ⓝ 중력
- equator ⓝ (지구의) 적도   · rotation ⓝ 회전
- spread out (몸을) 뻗다   · barely ⓐⓓ 간신히, 거의 ~ 아니게
- noticeable ⓐ 알아차릴 수 있는, 뚜렷한   · add up 누적되다, 쌓이다
- dinosaur ⓝ 공룡   · last ⓥ 지속하다   · temperature ⓝ 온도
- principle ⓝ 원리   · maintain ⓥ 유지하다
- implication ⓝ 영향, 결과
- biodiversity ⓝ (균형 잡힌 환경을 위한) 생물의 다양성
- keep track of ~을 기록하다

녹는 얼음과 상승하는 바다의 가장 놀랍고 믿을 수 없는 결과는 그것들이 합쳐서 일종의 타임머신이라는 것이고, 이것은 너무나 현실적이어서 그것들이 우리 하루의 기간을 바꾸고 있다. 그것은 이처럼 작동한다. 빙하가 녹고 바다가 높아지면서 중력이 적도를 향해 더 많은 물을 밀어 넣는다. 이것은 지구의 모양을 아주 약간 변화시켜 가운데 주변으로 그것을 더 불룩하게 만들고, 이것은 결과적으로 발레 무용수가 양팔을 뻗어서 그녀의 회전을 늦추는 방식과 유사한 방식으로 행성의 회전을 늦춘다. 이 감속이 매년 단지 몇천분의 1초로 크지는 않지만, 해마다 상승하는 바다의 알아차리기 힘든 증가처럼, 그것은 쌓인다. 공룡들이 지구에 살았을 때, 하루는 약 23시간만 지속되었다.

다음 글의 주제로 가장 적절한 것은?

① cause of rising temperatures on the Earth
지구의 기온 상승의 원인   지구의 기온이 오르는 원인은 설명하지 않음
② principles of planets maintaining their shapes
행성이 그들의 모양을 유지하는 원리   행성의 모양이 변화한다고 했음
③ implications of melting ice on marine biodiversity
녹는 얼음이 해양 생물의 다양성에 미치는 영향   해양 생물에 관한 내용은 없음
④ way to keep track of time without using any device
장치를 사용하지 않고 시간을 기록하는 방법   마지막 문장에 시간을 언급한 것으로 만든 오답
⑤ impact of melting ice and rising seas on the length of a day
빙하가 녹고 바다가 높아지면서 행성의 회전을 늦춰서 하루의 기간을 바꾸고 있다고 했음
녹는 얼음과 해수면 상승이 하루의 길이에 미치는 영향

>왜 정답? ★★※ [정답률 70%]

얼음이 녹아 해수면이 상승하는 것은 하루의 기간을 바꾸고 있다. 단서 1
① 빙하가 녹으면서 중력이 적도로 더 많은 물을 보냄
② 지구의 모양이 가운데가 더 불룩한 모양으로 바뀜
③ 행성의 회전을 늦춤 단서 2
④ 감속은 크지 않지만 누적됨 단서 3

➡ 얼음이 녹는 것이 하루의 기간을 바꾸는 과정을 순서대로 설명함
▶ 따라서 글의 주제는 ⑤ '녹는 얼음과 해수면 상승이 하루의 길이에 미치는 영향이 가장 적절하다.

>왜 오답?   함정

① 얼음이 녹는다고는 했지만, 지구의 기온이 상승하는 이유는 나오지 않았다.
② 빙하가 녹고 바다가 높아지면서 지구의 모양이 변한다고 했으므로 적절하지 않다.
③ 해양 생물의 다양성에 관한 글이 아니다.
④ 공룡이 지구에 살았을 때 하루는 약 23시간이었다고 했을 뿐, 시간을 기록하는 방법에 대한 글이 아니다.

 감속이 크지 않지만 시간이 결국 변할 수도 있음을 설명하는 대목 꿀팁

F 12 정답 ② *매력적이지만은 않은 문화적 다양성

단서 1 다양한 문화적 배경을 가진 노동자들과 현지 주민이 상호작용하면 생산성이 증가될 수 있음
The interaction of workers / from different cultural backgrounds / with the host population / might increase productivity / due to positive externalities / like knowledge spillovers. //
핵심 주어   본동사

노동자들의 상호작용은 / 다른 문화적 배경으로부터의 / 현지 주민과의 / 생산성을 증가시킬 수 있다 / 긍정적인 외부 효과로 인해 / 지식 파급과 같은 //

This is only an advantage / up to a certain degree. //
이것은 장점일 뿐이다 / 어느 정도까지만 //

When the variety of backgrounds is too large, / fractionalization may cause excessive transaction costs / for communication, / which may lower productivity. // 단서 2 배경의 다양성이 너무 크면 오히려 생산성이 저하될 수 있음
계속적 용법의 주격 관계대명사

배경의 다양성이 너무 크면 / 분열은 과도한 거래 비용을 초래할 수 있다 / 의사소통에 대해 / 그리고 이것은 생산성을 저하시킬 수 있다 //

not only A but also B: A뿐만 아니라 B도
Diversity not only impacts the labour market, / but may also affect the quality of life / in a location. //
다양성은 노동 시장에 영향을 줄 뿐만 아니라 / 삶의 질에도 영향을 미칠 수 있다 / 한 지역의 //

A tolerant native population may value / a multicultural city or region / because of an increase / in the range of available goods and services. // 단서 3 관용적인 원주민은 다문화 도시를 가치 있게 여길 것임
전치사

관용적인 원주민은 가치 있게 여길 수 있다 / 다문화 도시나 지역을 / 증가로 인해 / 이용 가능한 재화와 서비스의 범위의 //

단서 4 다양성을 그것을 국가 정체성의 왜곡으로 생각하는 원주민들에게는 매력적이지 않음
On the other hand, / diversity could be perceived / as an unattractive feature / if natives perceive it / as a distortion / of what they consider to be their national identity. //
조동사가 포함된 수동태
선행사가 포함된 관계대명사   = diversity

반면에 / 다양성은 인식될 수 있다 / 매력적이지 않은 특징으로 / 만약 원주민들이 그것을 인식한다면 / 왜곡으로 / 그들의 국가 정체성이라고 그들이 생각하는 것에 대한 //

They might even discriminate / against other ethnic groups / and they might fear / that social conflicts between different foreign nationalities are imported / into their own neighbourhood. //
목적어절 접속사

그들은 심지어 차별할 수도 있다 / 다른 민족 집단을 / 그리고 그들은 두려워할 수도 있다 / 다른 외국 국적들 간의 사회적 갈등이 유입되는 것을 / 그들 주변으로 //

- interaction ⓝ 상호작용   · productivity ⓝ 생산성
- spillover ⓝ 여파, 파급   · degree ⓝ 정도   · excessive ⓐ 과도한
- transaction ⓝ 거래   · diversity ⓝ 다양성   · labour ⓝ 노동
- tolerant ⓐ 관대한   · multicultural ⓐ 다문화의
- distortion ⓝ 왜곡   · discriminate ⓥ 차별하다
- ethnic ⓐ 민족의   · conflict ⓝ 갈등   · nationality ⓝ 국적
- import ⓥ 수입하다, 유입하다   · contrastive ⓐ 대조하는

다른 문화적 배경으로부터의 노동자들과 현지 주민의 상호작용은 지식 파급과 같은 긍정적인 외부 효과로 인해 생산성을 증가시킬 수 있다. 이것은 어느 정도까지만 장점일 뿐이다. 배경의 다양성이 너무 크면, 분열은 의사소통에 대한 과도한 거래 비용을 초래하는데, 이는 생산성을 저하시킬 수 있다. 다양성은 노동 시장에 영향을 줄 뿐만 아니라 한 지역의 삶의 질에도 영향을 미칠 수 있다. 관용적인 원주민은 이용 가능한 재화와 서비스의 범위의 증가로 인해 다문화 도시나 지역을 가치 있게 여길 수 있다. 반면에, 원주민들이 다양성을 그들의 국가 정체성이라고 생각하는 것에 대한 왜곡으로 인식한다면 다양성은 매력적이지 않은 특징으로 인식될 수 있다. 그들은 심지어 다른 민족 집단을 차별할 수도 있고 그들은 다른 외국 국적들 간의 사회적 갈등이 그들 주변으로 유입되는 것을 두려워할 수도 있다.

다음 글의 주제로 가장 적절한 것은?

① roles of culture in ethnic groups   특정 인종에 국한된 내용이 아님
인종 집단 내에서 문화의 역할
② contrastive aspects of cultural diversity
문화적 다양성의 대조적 측면   문화적 다양성이 갖는 장단점을 이야기함
③ negative perspectives of national identity
국가적 정체성의 부정적 관점   국가적 정체성의 왜곡은 특정 원주민의 예시일 뿐임
④ factors of productivity differences across countries
국가 간 생산성 차이의 요인   국가 간 생산성의 차이에 관한 글이 아님
⑤ policies to protect minorities and prevent discrimination
소수 집단을 보호하고 차별을 예방하기 위한 정책   소수 집단을 보호해야 한다는 글이 아님

- 다양한 문화적 배경을 가진 노동자들과 현지 주민이 상호작용하면 생산성이 향상됨 단서 1
→ 예시: 관용적인 원주민은 다문화 지역을 가치 있게 여길 것임 단서 3
- 다양성이 너무 큰 경우에는 생산성이 저하됨 단서 2
→ 예시: 다양성을 국가 정체성의 왜곡으로 생각하는 원주민은 다양성을 매력적이게 보지 않음 단서 4
▶ 문화적 다양성이 초래할 수 있는 긍정적, 부정적 현상을 예시를 들어 설명하고 있으므로 글의 주제로 가장 적절한 것은 ② '문화적 다양성의 대조적 측면'이다.

＞왜 오답 ？

① 다양한 문화적 배경을 이야기했으므로 특정 인종 집단 내에서 문화의 역할을 말한 것이 아니다.
③ 국가적 정체성을 부정적으로 바라보는 것은 다양성을 왜곡으로 인식하는 원주민의 관점일 뿐이다. 함정
④ 국가 간 생산성 차이나 그 요인을 설명한 글이 아니다.
⑤ 원주민, 다양성 등이 언급된 것으로 만든 오답으로, 소수 집단 보호를 이야기하는 글이 아니다.

F 13 정답 ① *관광 산업의 성장 배경

'~함에 따라' 단서 1 여러 국가들의 상황이 나아지면서 근로 여건이 개선됨
As the social and economic situation of countries got better, /
wage levels and working conditions improved. //
국가들의 사회적, 경제적 상황이 더 나아지면서 / 임금 수준과 근로 여건이 개선되었다 //
수동태 동사
Gradually people were given / more time off. //
점차 사람들은 받게 되었다 / 더 많은 휴가를 // 단서 2 사람들도 더 많은 휴가를 받게 됨
가주어
At the same time, / forms of transport improved / and it became
진주어 단서 3 운송 형태가 개선되어 이동이 더
faster and cheaper / to get to places. // 빠르고 저렴해짐
동시에 / 운송 형태가 개선되었고 / ~이 더 빠르고 더 저렴해졌다 / 장소를 이동하는 것 //

England's industrial revolution / led to many of these changes. //
영국의 산업 혁명이 / 이러한 변화 중 많은 것을 일으켰다 //

Railways, / in the nineteenth century, / opened up now famous
seaside resorts / such as Blackpool and Brighton. //
철도는 / 19세기에 / 현재 유명한 해안가 리조트가 들어서게 했다 / Blackpool과 Brighton 같은 //
전치사구가 앞에 오면서 주어와 동사가 도치됨
With the railways / came many large hotels. //
철도가 생기면서 / 많은 대형 호텔이 생겨났다 //

In Canada, / for example, / the new coast-to-coast railway
system made possible / the building of such famous hotels / as
Banff Springs and Chateau Lake Louise in the Rockies. //
캐나다에서는 / 예를 들어 / 새로운 대륙 횡단 철도 시스템이 가능하게 했다 / 그런 유명한 호텔의 건설을 / 로키산맥의 Banff Springs와 Chateau Lake Louise 같은 //
병렬 구조
Later, / the arrival of air transport / opened up more of the world
/ and led to tourism growth. // 단서 4 항공 운송은 관광 산업을 성장시킴
이후에 / 항공 운송의 출현은 / 세계의 더 많은 곳(으로 가는 길)을 열어 주었고 / 관광 산업의 성장을 이끌었다 //

- economic ⓐ 경제의 · wage ⓝ 임금, 급료
- condition ⓝ 여건, 조건 · gradually ⓐⓓ 점차
- transport ⓝ 운송, 수송 · industrial ⓐ 산업의
- revolution ⓝ 혁명 · railway ⓝ 철도
- open up ~을 가능하게 하다 · seaside ⓐ 해안가의
- coast-to-coast ⓐ 대륙 횡단의 · arrival ⓝ 출현 · factor ⓝ 요인
- expansion ⓝ 확장, 확대 · discomfort ⓝ 불편함
- destination ⓝ 목적지 · impact ⓝ 영향

국가들의 사회적, 경제적 상황이 더 나아지면서, 임금 수준과 근로 여건이 개선되었다. 점차 사람들은 더 많은 휴가를 받게 되었다. 동시에, 운송 형태가 개선되었고 장소를 이동하는 것이 더 빠르고 더 저렴해졌다. 영국의 산업 혁명이 이러한 변화 중 많은 것을 일으켰다. 19세기에, 철도로 인해

Blackpool과 Brighton 같은 현재 유명한 해안가 리조트가 들어서게 되었다. 철도가 생기면서 많은 대형 호텔이 생겨났다. 예를 들어, 캐나다에서는 새로운 대륙 횡단 철도 시스템이 로키산맥의 Banff Springs와 Chateau Lake Louise 같은 유명한 호텔의 건설을 가능하게 했다. 이후에 항공 운송의 출현은 세계의 더 많은 곳으로 가는 길을 열어 주었고 관광 산업의 성장을 이끌었다.

다음 글의 주제로 가장 적절한 것은?
① factors that caused tourism expansion
관광 확대를 야기한 요인들 / 사회적, 경제적 상황 개선으로 인한 관광 확대에 대한 내용임
② discomfort at a popular tourist destination
유명한 관광지에서의 불편함 / 불편함은 언급되지 않았음
③ importance of tourism in society and economy
사회와 경제에서 관광의 중요성 / 관광의 중요성이 아닌 확대가 주제임
④ negative impacts of tourism on the environment
관광이 환경에 미치는 부정적 영향들 / 환경에 어떤 영향을 미쳤는지는 알 수 없음
⑤ various types of tourism and their characteristics
다양한 종류의 관광과 그 특징들 / 관광 산업 성장에 관한 내용임

＞왜 정답 ？ ✱✱✱ [정답률 62%]

- 국가들의 사회적, 경제적 상황이 나아지면서 임금 수준과 근로 여건이 개선되었다. 단서 1
→ 개인들은 더 많은 휴가를 받게 됨 단서 2
- 운송 형태도 개선되어 이동이 더 빠르고 저렴해졌다. 단서 3
→ 철도와 항공 운송의 출현이 관광 산업의 성장을 이끌었음 단서 4
→ 여러 국가의 상황이 나아지면서 발생한 연쇄적인 결과로 관광이 확대되었음
▶ 따라서 글의 주제로는 ① '관광 확대를 야기한 요인들'이 가장 적절하다.

＞왜 오답 ？

② 유명한 관광지에서 마주하게 되는 불편함에 대해서는 언급하지 않았다.
③ 관광의 중요성이 아닌 확대가 주제이다.
④ 환경에 미치는 부정적 영향에 대해서는 언급하지 않았다.
⑤ 관광의 종류가 아닌 관광 산업의 성장에 대한 내용이다. (▶ 이유: 해안가 리조트, 호텔 등은 예시일 뿐 관광의 종류와 특징을 설명하는 글이 아니다.)

F 14 정답 ① ★ 2등급 대비 [정답률 78%]

*윤작의 장점

「전치사+관계대명사」
Crop rotation is the process / in which farmers change the crops
앞에 목적격 관계대명사 생략
/ they grow in their fields / in a special order. //
윤작은 과정이다 / 농부가 작물을 바꾸는 / 자신의 밭에서 재배하는 / 특별한 순서로 //

For example, / if a farmer has three fields, / he or she may grow
/ carrots in the first field, / green beans in the second, / and
tomatoes in the third. //
예를 들면 / 만약 한 농부가 세 개의 밭을 가지고 있다면 / 그들은 재배할 수 있다 / 첫 번째 밭에는 당근을 / 두 번째 밭에는 녹색 콩을 / 세 번째 밭에는 토마토를 //
사이에 반복되는 will be가 생략됨
The next year, / green beans will be in the first field, / tomatoes
in the second field, / and carrots will be in the third. //
그 다음 해에 / 첫 번째 밭에는 녹색 콩을 / 두 번째 밭에는 토마토를 / 세 번째 밭에는 당근을 재배할 것이다 //

In year three, / the crops will rotate again. //
3년 차에 / 작물은 다시 순환할 것이다 //

By the fourth year, / the crops will go back to their original
order. //
4년째에 이르면 / 작물은 원래의 순서로 되돌아갈 것이다 //
Each+단수 명사+단수 동사 단서 1 작물을 바꿔서
Each crop enriches the soil / for the next crop. // 심으면 각각의 작물은
각각의 작물은 토양을 비옥하게 한다 / 다음 작물을 위한 // 다음 작물을 위한 토양을 비옥하게 함

This type of farming is sustainable / because the soil stays
healthy. // 단서 2 윤작은 토양이 건강하게 유지되어 지속 가능함
이 유형의 농업은 지속 가능하다 / 토양이 건강하게 유지되기 때문에 //

- crop rotation 윤작 · process ⓝ 과정 · field ⓝ 밭
- order ⓝ 순서 · rotate ⓥ 순환하다 · original ⓐ 원래의

- enrich ⓥ 비옥하게 하다 · soil ⓝ 토양 · type ⓝ 유형
- maintain ⓥ 유지하다 · organic ⓐ 유기농의 · impact ⓝ 영향

윤작은 농부가 자신의 밭에서 재배하는 작물을 특별한 순서로 바꾸는 과정이다. 예를 들면, 만약 한 농부가 세 개의 밭을 가지고 있다면, 그들은 첫 번째 밭에는 당근을, 두 번째 밭에는 녹색 콩을, 세 번째 밭에는 토마토를 재배할 수 있다. 그 다음 해에 첫 번째 밭에는 녹색 콩을, 두 번째 밭에는 토마토를, 세 번째 밭에는 당근을 재배할 것이다. 3년 차에 작물은 다시 순환할 것이다. 4년째에 이르면 작물은 원래의 순서로 되돌아 갈 것이다. 각각의 작물은 다음 작물을 위한 토양을 비옥하게 한다. 이 유형의 농업은 토양이 건강하게 유지되기 때문에 지속 가능하다.

다음 글의 주제로 가장 적절한 것은?
① advantage of crop rotation in maintaining soil health
  토양 건강 유지에 있어서 윤작의 장점   윤작을 하면 토양이 건강하게 유지되어 지속 가능함
② influence of purchasing organic food on farmers
  유기농 식품 구매가 농부에게 주는 영향   유기농 식품 구매에 대해 언급하지 않음
③ ways to choose three important crops for rich soil
  비옥한 토양을 위해 세 가지 중요 작물을 선택하는 방법
④ danger of growing diverse crops in small spaces 작은 공간에서
  작은 공간에서 다양한 작물을 재배하는 것의 위험성   다양한 작물을 재배한다는 내용은 없음
⑤ negative impact of crop rotation on the environment
  윤작이 환경에 미치는 부정적인 영향   윤작이 토양을 비옥하게 한다는 내용임
  세 가지 작물이 예시로 나오기는 하지만 윤작의 방법을 설명하기 위해 제시됨

🔵 2등급? 마지막 두 문장을 제외하면 전부 윤작의 정의와 과정에 관한 내용이기 때문에, 글을 처음부터 읽는다면 주제를 오해하기 쉬운 2등급 대비 문제이다. 윤작의 순기능이 언급되는 글의 마지막 부분에 집중해서 글의 주제를 파악해야 한다.

| 문제 풀이 순서 |

1st 글의 앞부분에서 글의 소재를 파악하고 이어질 내용을 예상한다.

윤작은 농부가 자신의 밭에서 재배하는 작물을 특별한 순서로 바꾸는 과정이다. 단서

➡ 글의 소재: 윤작(재배하는 작물의 순서를 바꾸는 과정) 발상
  윤작의 구체적인 방법이나 윤작의 장점이 이어질 것이다.

2nd 글의 나머지 부분에서 내용을 파악하고 정답을 찾는다.

- 작물을 바꿔서 심으면 각각의 작물은 다음 작물을 위한 토양을 비옥하게 함 단서1
- 윤작은 토양을 건강하게 유지하기 때문에 지속 가능함 단서2
➡ 윤작을 하여 작물을 바꿔서 심으면 각 작물이 다음 작물이 심어질 토양을 비옥하게 하고, 토양이 건강하게 유지되어 농사가 지속 가능해짐
  ▶ 윤작의 장점을 설명하고 있는 이 글의 주제로 가장 적절한 것은 ① '토양 건강 유지에 있어서 윤작의 장점'이다.

| 선택지 분석 |

① 윤작을 하면 토양의 건강이 유지되어 농사가 지속 가능하다는 장점을 설명하는 글이다.
② 유기농 식품 구매는 언급되지 않았다.
③ 윤작 방식을 설명하기 위해서 세 가지 작물을 예로 들었을 뿐이며, 세 가지 작물을 선택하는 방법에 관한 글이 아니다.
④ 다양한 작물을 재배하는 내용이 나오긴 하지만, 작은 공간에서 재배한다는 내용은 제시되지 않았다.
⑤ 윤작이 토양을 비옥하게 한다는 긍정적인 영향에 관한 글이기 때문에 부정적인 영향은 제시되지 않았다.

F 15 정답 ② ──── ⭐2등급 대비 [정답률 60%]

*아이들이 수학적 이해를 발달시키는 방법

Every day, / children explore and construct / relationships among objects. //
매일 / 아이들은 탐구하고 구성한다 / 사물 사이의 관계들을 //
Frequently, / these relationships focus on / how much or how many of something exists. // 단서1 아이들은 사물 사이의 관계들을 숫자와 양으로 초점을 맞춤
빈번히 / 이러한 관계들은 ~에 초점을 맞춘다 / 무언가가 얼마만큼 혹은 몇 개 존재하는지 //

Thus, / children count / — "One cookie, / two shoes, / three candles on the birthday cake, / four children in the sandbox." //
따라서 / 아이들은 센다 / "쿠키 하나 / 신발 두 개 / 생일 케이크 위에 초 세 개 / 모래놀이통에 아이 네 명" //
Children compare / — "Which has more? // Which has fewer? // few의 비교급
Will there be enough?" //
아이들은 비교한다 / "무엇이 더 많지 // 무엇이 더 적지 // 충분할까" //
Children calculate / — "How many will fit? // Now, I have five. // I need one more." //
아이들은 계산한다 / "몇 개가 알맞을까 / 나는 지금 다섯 개가 있어 // 하나 더 필요하네" //
In all of these instances, / children are developing a notion of quantity. // 단서2 아이들은 일상에서 양의 개념을 발달시킴
이 모든 예시에서 / 아이들은 양의 개념을 발달시키는 중이다 //   단서3 아이들은 경험과 활동을 통해 수학 개념을 밝히고 연구함
Children reveal and investigate mathematical concepts / through their own activities or experiences, /
아이들은 수학적 개념을 밝히고 연구한다 / 그들만의 활동이나 경험을 통해 /
                                        의문형용사(how many)+명사(crackers)
such as figuring out / how many crackers to take at snack time / or sorting shells into piles. //
알아내는 것인지와 같은 / 간식 시간에 몇 개의 크래커를 가져갈지 / 혹은 조개껍질들을 더미로 분류하는 것(과 같은) //

- explore ⓥ 탐구하다 · construct ⓥ 구성하다 · object ⓝ 사물
- frequently ⓐⓓ 빈번히 · exist ⓥ 존재하다
- compare ⓥ 비교하다 · calculate ⓥ 계산하다
- fit ⓥ 적합하다, 알맞다 · develop ⓥ 발달시키다
- notion ⓝ 개념 · quantity ⓝ 양 · reveal ⓥ 밝히다
- investigate ⓥ 조사하다, 연구하다 · mathematical ⓐ 수학적인
- figure out ~을 알아내다 · sort ⓥ 분류하다 · shell ⓝ 조개껍질
- pile ⓝ (수북이 쌓여 있는) 더미 · count ⓥ (수를) 세다
- advantage ⓝ 이점

매일, 아이들은 사물 사이의 관계들을 탐구하고 구성한다. 빈번히, 이러한 관계들은 무언가가 얼마만큼 혹은 몇 개 존재하는지에 초점을 맞춘다. 따라서, 아이들은 센다. "쿠키 하나, 신발 두 개, 생일 케이크 위에 초 세 개, 모래놀이통에 아이 네 명." 아이들은 비교한다. "무엇이 더 많지? 무엇이 더 적지? 충분할까?" 아이들은 계산한다. "몇 개가 알맞을까? 나는 지금 다섯 개가 있어. 하나 더 필요하네." 이 모든 예시에서, 아이들은 양의 개념을 발달시키는 중이다. 아이들은 간식 시간에 몇 개의 크래커를 가져갈지 알아내는 것 혹은 조개껍질들을 더미로 분류하는 것과 같은, 그들만의 활동이나 경험을 통해 수학적 개념을 밝히고 연구한다.

다음 글의 주제로 가장 적절한 것은?
① difficulties of children in learning how to count 아이들이 숫자를
  숫자 세는 법을 배우는 아이들의 어려움   세는 것은 나와 있지만 그 어려움은 제시되지 않음
② how children build mathematical understanding   아이들이
  아이들이 수학적 이해를 발달시키는 방법   경험과 활동을 통해서 양의 개념을 발달시킨다고 했음
③ why fingers are used in counting objects 사물을 세는 내용은 나오지만
  사물을 세는 데 손가락이 사용되는 이유   손가락을 사용하는 것에 대한 언급은 없음
④ importance of early childhood education
  유아 교육의 중요성   유아 교육의 중요성에 대한 내용이 아님
⑤ advantages of singing number song
  숫자 노래를 부르는 것의 이점들   숫자 노래를 부르는 것에 대한 내용은 없음

✦ 지문의 길이가 짧아서 오히려 정답을 고르기가 헷갈릴 수 있는 2등급 대비 문제이다. 모든 선택지에 '아이' 또는 '숫자를 세는 것'과 관련된 내용이 포함되어 있어 글을 완벽하게 이해해야만 정답을 골라낼 수 있다. 큰따옴표로 제시된 아이들의 생각 또는 말이 나타내는 공통된 주제가 무엇인지 생각하며 글을 읽어야 한다.

| 문제 풀이 순서 |

1st 글의 앞부분에서 글의 소재를 파악하고 이어질 내용을 예상한다.

매일, 아이들은 사물 사이의 관계들을 탐구하고 구성한다. 단서

➡ 글의 소재: 아이들의 사물 탐구
  아이들이 어떻게 사물을 탐구하고 관계를 구성하는지 예시가 이어질 것이다. 발상

Ⓕ

2nd 글의 나머지 부분에서 내용을 파악하고 정답을 찾는다.

- 아이들은 세고, 비교하고, 계산하면서 양의 개념을 발달시킴 **단서 1**
- 아이들은 활동이나 경험을 통해 수학적 개념을 밝히고 연구함 **단서 2**
→ 아이들은 주변 사물의 수를 세고, 비교하며 계산하는 그들만의 활동을 통해 수학 개념을 연구한다고 했다.
▶ 따라서 ② '아이들이 수학적 이해를 발달시키는 방법'이 글의 주제로 가장 적절하다.

| 선택지 분석 |

① 아이들이 숫자를 세고 있는 것은 맞지만, 그것의 어려움에 관해 이야기한 글이 아니다.
② 아이들이 세고, 비교하고, 계산하는 것은 수학적 이해를 발달시키는 것이다.
③ 손가락은 글에서 언급되지 않았다.
④ 아이들이 스스로 수학을 이해하는 것이지, 어른들이 교육한 것이 아니다.
⑤ their own activities로 만든 오답으로, 숫자 노래를 부른다는 내용은 없었다.

F 16 정답 ① ★1등급 대비 [정답률 59%]

*행복을 위한 뇌의 습관 형성

「used to+동사원형」: ~하곤 했다
We used to think / that the brain never changed, / but according
목적어절을 이끄는 접속사   목적어절을 이끄는 접속사
to the neuroscientist Richard Davidson, / we now know / that
this is not true /
우리는 생각했다 / 뇌가 절대 변하지 않는다고 / 하지만 신경과학자 Richard Davidson에 따르면 / 우리는 이제 안다 / 이것이 사실이 아니라는 것을 /

— specific brain circuits grow stronger / through regular
practice. // **단서 1** 특정한 뇌 회로는 규칙적인 연습을 통해 더 강해짐
특정한 뇌 회로는 더 강해진다 / 규칙적인 연습을 통해 //

He explains, / "Well-being is fundamentally no different / than
learning to play the cello. //
그는 설명한다 / "행복은 기본적으로 다르지 않다 / 첼로를 연주하는 것을 배우는 것과 //

If one practices the skills of well-being, / one will get better at
it." //
만약 어떤 이가 행복의 기술을 연습한다면 / 그 사람은 그것을 더 잘하게 될 것이다"라고 //
선행사를 포함한 관계대명사   주격 보어절을 이끄는 접속사
What this means / is that you can actually train your brain /
부사적 용법
to become more grateful, relaxed, or confident, / by repeating
주격 관계대명사
experiences / that evoke gratitude, relaxation, or confidence. //
이것이 의미하는 것은 / 여러분이 여러분의 뇌를 실제로 훈련시킬 수 있다는 것이다 / 더
감사하거나 편안하거나 자신감을 갖도록 / 경험을 반복함으로써 / 감사, 휴식 또는 자신감을
불러일으키는 // **단서 2** 경험을 반복하여 뇌를 훈련시켜서 감사하거나 편안하거나 자신감을
갖도록 할 수 있음
                                    앞에 목적격 관계대명사 생략
Your brain is shaped / by the thoughts you repeat. //
여러분의 뇌는 형성된다 / 여러분이 반복하는 생각에 의해 //

The more neurons fire / as they are activated by repeated
the+비교급 ~ the+비교급 ...: ~할수록 더 ...하다
thoughts and activities, / the faster they develop into neural
계속적 용법의 관계대명사
pathways, / which cause lasting changes in the brain. //
뉴런이 더 많이 점화할수록 / 그것이 반복된 생각과 활동에 의해 활성화되면서 / 그것은 신경
경로로 더 빠르게 발달한다 / 그리고 이는 뇌에 지속적인 변화를 야기한다 //
                                    주격 관계대명사절
Or in the words of Donald Hebb, / "Neurons that fire together
wire together." //
혹은 Donald Hebb의 말을 빌리면 / "함께 점화하는 뉴런은 함께 연결된다" //
such+a(n)+형용사+명사
This is such an encouraging premise: / bottom line — we can
to부정사의 의미상 주어
intentionally create the habits / for the brain to be happier. //
이는 대단히 고무적인 전제이다 / 즉, 결론은 / 우리가 습관을 의도적으로 만들 수 있다 / 뇌가
더 행복해지도록 — 핵심문장, **단서 3** 우리는 뇌가 더 행복해지도록 의도적으로 습관을 만들 수 있음

- neuroscientist ⓝ 신경과학자 · circuit ⓝ 회로
- fundamentally 〔ad〕 기본적으로 · grateful ⓐ 고마워하는
- relaxed ⓐ 편안한 · confident ⓐ 자신감 있는
- gratitude ⓝ 감사 · relaxation ⓝ 휴식 · confidence ⓝ 자신감
- shape ⓥ 형성하다 · neuron ⓝ 뉴런, 신경 세포 · premise ⓝ 전제
- fire ⓥ 발화[점화]하다 · activate ⓥ 활성화시키다, 작동시키다

- neural ⓐ 신경의 · pathway ⓝ 경로, 길
- lasting ⓐ 지속적인, 영속적인 · wire ⓥ 연결하다
- encouraging ⓐ 장려하는, 고무적인 · bottom line 핵심, 결론
- intentionally 〔ad〕 고의로, 의도적으로 · musical instrument 악기
- enhance ⓥ 향상시키다 · capacity ⓝ 능력
- discover ⓥ 발견하다

우리는 뇌가 절대 변하지 않는다고 생각했었지만 신경과학자 Richard Davidson에 따르면 우리는 이제 이것이 사실이 아님을 즉, 특정한 뇌 회로가 규칙적인 연습을 통해 더 강해진다는 것을 안다. 그는 "행복은 첼로를 연주하는 것을 배우는 것과 기본적으로 다르지 않다. 만약 어떤 이가 행복의 기술을 연습한다면 그 사람은 그것을 더 잘하게 될 것이다."라고 설명한다. 이것이 의미하는 것은 여러분이 감사, 휴식 또는 자신감을 불러일으키는 경험을 반복함으로써 더 감사하고, 편안하고 또는 자신감을 갖도록 여러분의 뇌를 실제로 훈련시킬 수 있다는 것이다. 여러분의 뇌는 여러분이 반복하는 생각에 의해 형성된다. 뉴런은 그것이 반복된 생각과 활동에 의해 활성화되면서 더 많이 점화할수록, 그것은 신경 경로로 더 빠르게 발달하게 되고 이는 뇌에 지속적인 변화를 야기한다. 혹은 Donald Hebb의 말을 빌리면 "함께 점화하는 뉴런은 함께 연결된다." 이는 대단히 고무적인 전제이다. 즉, 결론은 뇌가 더 행복해지도록 우리가 습관을 의도적으로 만들 수 있다는 것이다.

> **다음 글의 주제로 가장 적절한 것은?**
> ① possibility of forming brain habits for well-being
> 행복을 위해 뇌의 습관을 형성하는 것의 가능성 규칙적인 연습으로 뇌가 행복해지도록 할 수 있음
> ② role of brain circuits in improving body movements
> 몸의 움직임을 향상시키는 데 있어서의 뇌 회로의 역할 몸의 움직임에 대한 내용은 없음
> ③ importance of practice in playing musical instruments
> 악기를 연주하는 데 있어서의 연습의 중요성 첼로 연주는 비유로 사용된 것임
> ④ effect of taking a break on enhancing memory capacity
> 기억력을 향상시키는 것에 대한 휴식의 효과 기억력 향상에 대한 내용은 없음
> ⑤ difficulty of discovering how neurons in the brain work
> 뇌의 뉴런이 작동하는 방식을 발견하는 것의 어려움 뇌가 어떻게 작동하는지 알기 어렵다는 언급은 없음

왜 1등급? '뇌'와 관련된 글로, 소재 자체가 어려운 1등급 대비 문제이다. neuroscientist, neuron 등 뇌와 관련된 어려운 표현들이 등장했지만, '행복은 첼로를 연주하는 것을 배우는 것과 다르지 않다'라고 한 것이 무슨 의미일지를 생각해 보면 정답을 골라낼 수 있다.

| 문제 풀이 순서 |

1st 글의 앞부분에서 글의 핵심 소재를 파악하고 전개 방향을 예측한다.

우리는 뇌가 절대 변하지 않는다고 생각했었지만 신경과학자 Richard Davidson에 따르면 우리는 이제 이것이 사실이 아님을 즉, 특정한 뇌 회로가 규칙적인 연습을 통해 더 강해진다는 것을 안다. **단서 1**
→ 글의 소재: 연습을 통해 강해지는 뇌 회로 **단서**
뇌 회로를 강하게 하는 규칙적인 연습이 무엇인지 설명할 것이다. **발상**

2nd **1st** 에서 발상한 것을 토대로 글을 읽고, 내용을 파악한다.

- 첼로 연주처럼 행복의 기술도 연습하면 실력이 향상됨
- 감사, 휴식, 자신감의 경험을 반복하여 뇌를 훈련할 수 있음 **단서 2**
→ 뇌를 반복적으로 활성화하여 뉴런을 자극하면 뇌가 변할 수 있다고 했다. 즉, 뇌가 더 행복해지도록 의도적으로 습관을 만들 수 있다는 것이다. **단서 3**

3rd 글의 내용을 포괄하는 알맞은 주제를 고른다.

2nd 에서 파악한 글의 내용을 종합하면 이 글의 주제는 '첼로 연주를 연습하는 것처럼, 행복해지는 것도 뇌를 훈련할 수 있다'는 것이다.
▶ 따라서 ① '행복을 위해 뇌의 습관을 형성하는 것의 가능성'이 글의 주제로 가장 적절하다.

| 선택지 분석 |

① 규칙적인 연습으로 뇌가 행복해지도록 만들 수 있다고 했다.
② train, activities로 만든 오답으로, 몸의 움직임과는 관련 없는 내용이다.
③ 첼로 연주는 뇌를 훈련할 수 있음을 설명하기 위해 언급된 비유적인 표현이다.
④ 기억력 향상이 아니라 행복해지도록 뇌를 훈련할 수 있다는 내용이다.
⑤ 뉴런이 여러 번 언급되긴 했지만, 뉴런의 작동 방식을 발견하기 어렵다고는 하지 않았다.

*삶에 폭넓게 영향을 미치는 기후에 대한 지식

The whole of human society operates / on knowing the future weather. // 핵심문장
전체 인간 사회는 운영된다 / 미래의 날씨를 아는 것을 기반으로

For example, / farmers in India know / **when** the monsoon rains
목적어절을 이끄는 의문사
will come next year / and so they know / **when** to plant the
목적어구를 이끄는 의문사
crops. // 단서1 인도의 농부들은 내년에 몬순 장마가 올 시기를 알아서 작물을 심을 시기도 안다고 했음
예를 들어 / 인도의 농부들은 안다 / 내년에 몬순 장마가 올 시기를 / 그래서 그들은 안다 /
작물을 심을 시기를

Farmers in Indonesia **know** / there are two monsoon rains each
뒤에 목적어절을 이끄는 접속사 생략
year, / so next year they can have two harvests. //
인도네시아의 농부들은 안다 / 매년 몬순 장마가 두 번 있다는 것을 / 그래서 이듬해에 그들은
수확을 두 번 할 수 있다 //

This is based / on their knowledge of the past, / **as** the monsoons
접속사(이유)
have always come / at about the same time each year / in living
memory. //
이것은 기반을 두고 있다 / 과거에 대한 그들의 지식에 / 몬순이 항상 왔기 때문이다 / 거의
같은 시기에 / 살아 있는 기억 속에서 //

But the need **to predict** / goes deeper than this; / it influences
형용사적 용법
every part of our lives. //
그러나 예측할 필요는 / 이것보다 더욱더 깊어진다 / 그것은 우리 생활의 모든 부분에 영향을
미친다 //

Our houses, roads, railways, airports, offices, and so on / **are** all
수동태
designed for the local climate. // 단서2 우리가 생활하는 공간들은 지역의 기후에
맞춰 설계됨
우리의 집, 도로, 철도, 공항, 사무실 등은 / 모두 지역의 기후에 맞추어 설계된다 //

For example, / in England all the houses have central heating, /
접속사(이유)
as the outside temperature is usually below 20°C, / but no air-
conditioning, / **as** temperatures rarely go beyond 26°C, /
접속사(이유)
예를 들어 / 영국에서는 모든 집은 중앙난방을 갖추고 있다 / 외부의 기온이 대체로 섭씨 20도
미만이기 때문에 / 그러나 냉방기는 없다 / 기온이 섭씨 26도 위로 올라가는 일은 거의 없어서 /
접속사(반면에)
while in Australia the opposite is true: / most houses have air-
conditioning / but rarely central heating. //
반면에 호주에서는 그 정반대가 사실이다 / 대부분의 집은 냉방기를 갖추었다 / 그러나
중앙난방은 거의 없다 //

- operate ⓥ 운영되다 • monsoon ⓝ 몬순(동남아시아 지역의 계절풍)
- crop ⓝ 작물 • harvest ⓝ 수확 • predict ⓥ 예측하다
- influence ⓥ 영향을 미치다 • railway ⓝ 철도 • climate ⓝ 기후
- central heating ⓝ 중앙난방 • temperature ⓝ 기온
- air-conditioning 냉방(기) • rarely ⓐ 거의 없게
- opposite ⓝ 정반대 • deal with ~을 다루다
- temperature ⓝ 온도 • affect ⓥ 영향을 미치다
- wisdom ⓝ 지혜 • harsh ⓐ 혹독한

전체 인간 사회는 미래의 날씨를 아는 것을 기반으로 운영된다. 예를
들어, 인도의 농부들은 내년에 몬순 장마가 올 시기를 알고 그래서 그들은
작물을 심을 시기를 안다. 인도네시아의 농부들은 매년 몬순 장마가
두 번 있다는 것을 알고, 그래서 이듬해에 그들은 수확을 두 번 할 수
있다. 이것은 과거에 대한 그들의 지식에 기반을 두고 있는데, 살아 있는
기억 속에서 몬순은 매년 항상 거의 같은 시기에 왔기 때문이다. 그러나
예측할 필요는 이것보다 더욱더 깊어지며, 그것은 우리 생활의 모든
부분에 영향을 미친다. 우리의 집, 도로, 철도, 공항, 사무실 등은 모두
지역의 기후에 맞추어 설계된다. 예를 들어, 영국에서는 외부의 기온이
대체로 섭씨 20도 미만이기 때문에 모든 집은 중앙난방을 갖추고 있지만,
기온이 섭씨 26도 위로 올라가는 일은 거의 없어서 냉방기는 없는 반면,
호주에서는 그 정반대가 사실이어서, 대부분의 집은 냉방기를 갖추었지만
중앙난방은 거의 없다.

다음 글의 주제로 가장 적절한 것은? [3점]
기후 변화를 다루는 기술이 아니라 날씨에 대해 아는 것이 생활에 영향을 미친다는 내용임
① new technologies dealing with climate change
기후 변화를 다루는 새로운 기술들
② difficulties in predicting the weather correctly 날씨를 정확히
날씨를 정확히 예측하는 데 있어서의 어려움 예측하는 것의 어려움에 대한 내용은 없음
③ weather patterns influenced by rising temperatures 냉방기를
온도 상승을 받은 날씨 패턴 언급한 것을 온도 상승으로 연결시켜 만든 함정
④ **knowledge of the climate widely affecting our lives**
우리의 삶에 폭넓게 영향을 미치는 기후에 대한 지식
⑤ traditional wisdom helping our survival in harsh
climates 혹독한 기후에서 살아남기 위한 지혜에 대한 내용은 없음
혹독한 기후에서 우리의 생존을 도와주는 전통적 지혜
└ 작물 수확과 냉난방 시설을 예로 들어 날씨에 대해 아는 것이 우리 삶에 미치는 영향에 대해 말하는 내용

왜 1등급? 첫 문장 다음의 예시들에서 인도의 농부들이 몬순 장마가 올 시기를
아는 것, 영국의 집이 갖춘 중앙난방, 호주의 정반대의 상황과 같은 내용이 나온다. 이
예시들을 통해 공통적으로 이야기하는 주제가 무엇인지 파악해야 정답을 고를 수
있다.

| 문제 풀이 순서 |

1st 글의 앞부분에서 글의 소재를 파악하고 이어질 내용을 예상한다.

전체 인간 사회는 미래의 날씨를 아는 것을 기반으로 운영된다.

➡ 글의 소재: 날씨 예측 단서
날씨를 예측하는 것이 인간 사회에 어떤 영향을 미쳤는지를 설명할 것이다. 발상

2nd **1st** 에서 발상한 것을 토대로 글을 읽고, 내용을 파악한다.

- 인도: 몬순 장마의 시기를 예측해 작물을 심음 단서1
- 인도네시아: 몬순 장마가 두 번 있음을 알고 수확을 두 번 함
- 영국: 외부 기온이 낮아 중앙난방은 있고, 냉방기는 없음
- 호주: 외부 기온이 높아 냉방기는 있고, 중앙난방은 없음

➡ 과거의 지식을 토대로 농사를 위한 날씨를 예측한 인도, 인도네시아에 이어 생활
전반을 위해 날씨를 예측한 영국과 호주의 예시가 이어진다.

3rd 글의 내용을 포괄하는 알맞은 주제를 고른다.

날씨를 예측하는 것은 농사뿐만 아니라 생활 모든 부분에 영향을 미쳐서 각 지역의
기후에 맞추어 생활 전반이 설계된다는 내용의 글이다. 단서2
▶ 따라서 ④ '우리의 삶에 폭넓게 영향을 미치는 기후에 대한 지식'이 글의 주제로
가장 적절하다.

| 선택지 분석 |

① 기후 변화를 다루는 기술이 아니라, 기후의 영향을 받는 생활에 관한 내용이다.
② 날씨를 예측하는 어려움에 관해서는 언급되지 않았다.
③ 냉방기는 예시로 제시된 온도와 관련하여 만든 함정으로, 온도 상승에 의해 변화된
날씨에 관해 설명한 글이 아니다.
④ 여러 나라를 예로 들어 날씨를 아는 것이 인간 생활에 많은 영향을 미친다고 설명했
다.
⑤ 혹독한 기후나, 그것을 극복한 지혜에 관해서는 언급되지 않았다.

F 어휘 Review 정답 ━━━ 문제편 p. 84

01 영향	11 deal with	21 discriminate
02 요인	12 a host of	22 rotation
03 직면하다	13 take on	23 operates
04 상호작용	14 figure out	24 explore
05 경향	15 keep track of	25 enriches
06 prosperity	16 competence	26 desirable
07 distortion	17 tolerant	27 monsoon
08 glacier	18 recognition	28 notion
09 pose	19 consequence	29 consistency
10 wage	20 crops	30 ultraviolet

G 01 정답 ① *개인의 정체성과 행동의 관계

단서 1 행동은 정체성을 반영함
Your behaviors / are usually a reflection of your identity. //
당신의 행동은 / 대개 당신의 정체성을 반영한다 //
선행사를 포함하는 관계대명사　　　　　　관계대명사절(the type of person 수식)
What you do / is an indication of the type of person / you believe that you are — / either consciously or nonconsciously. //
당신이 하는 행동은 / 어떤 사람인지를 나타낸다 / 당신이 스스로 그렇다고 믿고 있는 / 의식적으로든 무의식적으로든 //
목적어절 접속사　　부사절 접속사(일단 ~하면)
Research has shown / that once a person believes in a particular aspect of their identity, / they are more likely to act / according to that belief. //
단서 2 자신의 정체성에 따라 행동할 가능성이 높음
연구는 밝혔다 / 자신의 정체성의 특정 측면을 믿으면 / 그들은 행동할 가능성이 더 높다 / 그 믿음에 따라 //

For example, / people who identified as "being a voter" / were
　　　　　　　　└ 주격 관계대명사 ┘
more likely to vote / than those who simply claimed / "voting"
앞에 목적격 관계대명사가 생략됨
was an action they wanted to perform. //
예를 들어 / 자신을 "유권자"라고 느끼는 사람은 / 투표할 가능성이 더 높았다 / 단순히 주장하는 사람보다 / "투표"가 자신이 하고 싶은 행동이라고 //
　　　　　　　　　　　주격 관계대명사
Similarly, / the person who accepts exercise as the part of their
　　　　　　　　　　　convince의 목적어와 목적격 보어
identity / doesn't have to convince themselves / to train. //
마찬가지로 / 운동을 자신의 정체성의 일부로 받아들이는 사람은 / 스스로를 설득할 필요가 없다 훈련하라고 //
Doing the right thing is easy. // 옳은 일을 하는 것은 쉽다 //
After all, / when your behavior and your identity / perfectly
　　　　　　　　　　　　　'더 이상 ~하지 않는'
match, / you are no longer pursuing behavior change. //
결국 / 자신의 행동과 정체성이 / 완벽하게 일치하면 / 더 이상 행동 변화를 추구하지 않아도 된다 //
　　　　　　　　　　　　　　관계대명사절(the type of person 수식)
You are simply acting / like the type of person / you already believe yourself to be. //
단서 3 스스로가 그렇다고 믿는 사람의 유형처럼 행동함
당신은 행동하고 있을 뿐이다 / 어떤 유형의 사람처럼 / 당신 스스로가 그렇다고 이미 믿고 있는 //

- reflection ⓝ 반영　· identity ⓝ 정체성　· indication ⓝ 암시
- consciously ⓐ𝖽 의식적으로　· vote ⓥ 투표하다
- claim ⓥ 주장하다　· convince ⓥ 설득하다　· pursue ⓥ 추구하다

당신의 행동은 대개 당신의 정체성을 반영한다. 당신이 하는 행동은 의식적으로든 무의식적으로든 당신이 스스로를 어떤 사람이라고 믿고 있는지를 나타낸다. 연구에 따르면 자신의 정체성의 특정 측면을 믿는 사람은 그 믿음에 따라 행동할 가능성이 더 높다. 예를 들어, 자신을 "유권자"라고 느끼는 사람은 단순히 "투표"가 자신이 하고 싶은 행동이라고 주장하는 사람보다 투표할 가능성이 더 높았다. 마찬가지로, 운동을 자신의 정체성의 일부로 받아들이는 사람은 훈련하라고 스스로를 설득할 필요가 없다. 옳은 일을 하는 것은 쉽다. 결국, 자신의 행동과 정체성이 완벽하게 일치하면 더 이상 행동 변화를 추구하지 않아도 된다. 당신은 그저 당신 스스로가 그렇다고 이미 믿고 있는 유형의 사람처럼 행동하고 있을 뿐이다.

다음 글의 제목으로 가장 적절한 것은?
자신의 정체성을 어떻게 인식하는지에 따라 행동하게 됨
① Action Comes from Who You Think You Are
행동은 당신이 자신을 어떤 사람으로 생각하는지로부터 나온다
② The Best Practices for Gaining More Voters
더 많은 유권자를 확보하기 위한 우수 사례　　유권자 확보에 관한 내용이 아님
③ Stop Pursuing Undesirable Behavior Change!　바람직하지 않은
바람직하지 않은 행동 변화를 추구하는 것을 멈추세요!　행동 변화에 관한 언급은 없음
④ What to Do When Your Exercise Bores You
운동이 지루하게 느껴질 때 해야 할 일　　운동이 지루해질 때 해야 하는 방법에 관한 글이 아님
⑤ Your Actions Speak Louder than Your Words
당신의 행동이 당신의 말보다 중요하다　　행동이 말보다 중요하다는 내용이 아님

왜 정답? ✿✿✿ [정답률 76%]
- 당신의 행동은 대개 당신의 정체성을 반영한다. 단서 1
- 자신의 정체성의 어떤 측면을 믿는 사람은 그에 따라 행동할 가능성이 높다. 단서 2
- 스스로가 그렇다고 믿는 사람의 유형처럼 행동하게 된다. 단서 3
➡ 행동은 자신이 인식하고 있는 자아를 반영하기 때문에 자신의 정체성을 어떻게 인식하는지에 따라 행동하게 된다는 글이므로 글의 제목으로 가장 적절한 것은 ① '행동은 당신이 자신을 어떤 사람으로 생각하는지로부터 나온다'이다.

왜 오답?
② 유권자 확보의 우수 사례에 관한 내용이 아니다. (✗ 이유: 유권자는 정체성에 따른 행동의 예시로서 주어졌을 뿐이다.)
③ 바람직하지 않은 행동 변화에 대해 주의를 주거나 경고하는 글이 아니다.
④ 운동이 지루해질 때 어떻게 해야 하는지를 이야기하는 글이 아니다.
⑤ 행동이 말보다 더 중요하다는 내용이 아니다.

G 02 정답 ① *부유한 국가가 갖는 스트레스

'거의 없는'　　　　　　　　　　　부사적 용법(감정의 원인)
Few people will be surprised / to hear that poverty tends to
　　　　　　　　　　　　　　　　　　명사절 접속사
create stress: /
놀랄 사람은 거의 없을 것이다 / 가난이 스트레스를 만드는 경향이 있다는 것을 듣고 /
　　　　　　　　　　　　앞에 주격 관계대명사와 be동사가 생략됨
a 2006 study published in the American journal *Psychosomatic Medicine*, / for example, /
미국의 학술지 〈Psychosomatic Medicine〉에 발표된 2006년 연구는 / 예를 들어 /
동사
noted that a lower socioeconomic status was associated / with
명사절 접속사
higher levels of stress hormones in the body. //
더 낮은 사회 경제적 지위가 관련이 있다고 언급했다 / 체내의 더 높은 수치의 스트레스 호르몬과 //

However, / richer economies have their own distinct stresses. //
하지만 / 더 부유한 국가는 그들만의 뚜렷한 스트레스를 가지고 있다 // 단서 1 부유한 국가들도 그들만의 스트레스가 있음
The key issue is time pressure. //
핵심 쟁점은 시간 압박이다 // 단서 2 부유한 국가의 스트레스 요인은 시간 압박임
주어
A 1999 study / of 31 countries by American psychologist Robert
　　　　　　　　　　　　　　　　　　　　　　　　　　동사
Levine and Canadian psychologist Ara Norenzayan / found that wealthier, more industrialized nations had a faster pace of life /
1999년 연구는 / 미국의 심리학자 Robert Levine과 캐나다의 심리학자 Ara Norenzayan 이 31개국을 대상으로 한 / 더 부유하고, 더 산업화된 국가들이 더 빠른 삶의 속도를 가지고 있다는 것을 알아냈다 /
단서 3 더 부유하고, 더 산업화된 국가들의 삶의 속도가 더 빠름
단서 4 빠른 삶의 속도는 촉박함을 느끼게 하고 심장병에 걸리기 쉽게 함
　　　　　병렬 구조
— which led to a higher standard of living, / but at the same
　　　　　병렬 구조(목적격 보어)
time left the population feeling a constant sense of urgency, / as well as being more prone to heart disease. //
그리고 이것은 더 높은 생활 수준으로 이어졌지만 / 동시에 사람들에게 지속적인 촉박함을 느끼게 했다(는 것을) / 심장병에 걸리기 더 쉽게 했을 뿐만 아니라 //
'사실'
In effect, / fast-paced productivity creates wealth, / but it also
　　　　　　　　　　　　　　　부사절 접속사(시간)　　형용사적 용법(time 수식)
leads people to feel time-poor / when they lack the time / to
재귀대명사(강조 용법)
relax and enjoy themselves. //
사실 / 빠른 속도의 생산력은 부를 창출하지만 / 그것은 또한 사람들이 시간이 부족하다고 느끼게 한다 / 그들이 시간이 없을 때 / 스스로 긴장을 풀고 즐겁게 지낼 //

- poverty ⓝ 가난　· socioeconomic ⓐ 사회 경제적인
- status ⓝ 지위　· associate ⓥ 연상하다, 연관짓다
- distinct ⓐ 뚜렷한　· pressure ⓝ 압박
- psychologist ⓝ 심리학자　· wealthy ⓐ 부유한
- industrialized ⓐ 산업화된　· pace ⓝ 속도
- standard ⓝ 수준, 기준　· constant ⓐ 지속적인
- urgency ⓝ 촉박함　· lack ⓥ 부족하다　· trap ⓝ 덫, 함정

가난이 스트레스를 유발하는 경향이 있다는 것을 듣고 놀랄 사람은 거의 없을 것이다: 예를 들어, 미국의 학술지 〈Psychosomatic Medicine〉에 발표된 2006년 연구는 더 낮은 사회 경제적 지위가 체내의 더 높은 수치의 스트레스 호르몬과 관련이 있다고 언급했다. 하지만, 더 부유한 국가는 그들만의 뚜렷한

스트레스를 가지고 있다. 핵심 쟁점은 시간 압박이다. 미국의 심리학자 Robert Levine과 캐나다의 심리학자 Ara Norenzayan이 31개국을 대상으로 한 1999년 연구는 더 부유하고, 더 산업화된 국가들이 더 빠른 삶의 속도를 가지고 있다는 것 — 그리고 이것이 더 높은 생활 수준으로 이어졌지만, 동시에 사람들에게 지속적인 촉박함을 느끼게 했을 뿐만 아니라 심장병에 걸리기 더 쉽게 했다는 것을 알아냈다. 사실, 빠른 속도의 생산력은 부를 창출하지만, 그것은 또한 사람들이 긴장을 풀고 즐겁게 지낼 시간이 없을 때 시간이 부족하다고 느끼게 한다.

다음 글의 제목으로 가장 적절한 것은?
① Why Are Even Wealthy Countries Not Free from Stress? 부유한 나라들은 시간 압박으로 스트레스를 받음
왜 부유한 나라들조차 스트레스에서 자유롭지 못한가?
② In Search of the Path to Escaping the Poverty Trap
빈곤의 덫에서 벗어날 수 있는 길을 찾아서   가난의 굴레에서 벗어나는 방법을 모색한 글이 아님
③ Time Management: Everything You Need to Know
시간 관리: 당신이 알아야 할 모든 것   시간 관리에 관해 설명한 글이 아님
④ How Does Stress Affect Human Bodies?
스트레스는 인체에 어떻게 영향을 미치는가?   stress, heart disease로 만든 오답
⑤ Sound Mind Wins the Game of Life!
건강한 마음이 인생의 게임에서 승리한다!   건강한 마음이 주는 이점을 이야기한 글이 아님

왜 정답? ✱✱✽ [정답률 68%]
- 부유한 국가들은 그들만의 뚜렷한 스트레스가 있다. 단서 1
- 부유한 국가의 스트레스 요인은 '시간 압박'이다. 단서 2
- 더 부유하고, 더 산업화된 국가들은 삶의 속도가 더 빠르다. 단서 3
- 빠른 삶의 속도는 촉박함을 느끼게 하고 심장병에 걸리기 쉽게 한다. 단서 4
➡ 부유한 국가의 스트레스 요인인 '시간 압박'과 '빠른 삶의 속도'에 관해 이야기하는 글이므로 글의 제목으로 가장 적절한 것은 ① '왜 부유한 나라들조차 스트레스에서 자유롭지 못한가?'이다.

왜 오답?
② 가난에서 벗어나는 방법을 설명한 글이 아니다.
③ 시간 관리의 중요성을 알리고 설명한 글이 아니다.
④ 빠른 삶의 속도가 심장병의 위험을 높였다는 것은 한 연구의 결과일 뿐, 이것이 글의 핵심은 아니다. 함정
⑤ 건강한 마음을 가지라고 조언하는 글이 아니다.

G 03 정답 ① ✱소리 내어 읽는 것의 효과

Modern brain-scanning techniques / such as fMRI (functional '~와 같은'
Magnetic Resonance Imaging) / have revealed / that reading 동명사 (목적어절의 주어)
aloud lights up many areas of the brain. // 단서 1 소리 내어 읽는 것은 두뇌를 단수 동사   깨움
현대의 뇌 스캐닝 기법은 / fMRI(기능적 자기 공명 영상)와 같은 / 드러냈다 / 소리 내어 읽는 것이 두뇌의 여러 영역을 밝힌다는 것 //
There is intense activity in areas / associated with pronunciation 과거분사구 (areas 수식)
and hearing the sound of the spoken response, / which 계속적 용법의 주격 관계대명사
strengthens the connective structures of your brain cells / for more brainpower. //
영역에서 강렬한 활동이 있으며 / 발음과 발화된 반응의 소리를 듣는 것과 연관된 / 이는 여러분의 뇌세포의 결합 구조를 강화시킨다 / 더 많은 두뇌 능력을 위한 //
This leads / to an overall improvement in concentration. //
이것은 이어진다 / 전반적인 집중력 향상으로 //
Reading aloud is also a good way / to develop your public 형용사적 용법 (way 수식)
speaking skills / because it forces you to read each and every = reading aloud
word / 단서 2 소리 내어 읽음으로써 말하기 능력이 향상됨
소리 내어 읽는 것은 좋은 방법인데 / 여러분의 대중 말하기 능력을 발전시키는 / 왜냐하면 그것은 여러분으로 하여금 하나도 빠짐없이 단어를 읽게 강제하기 때문인데 / 앞에 목적격 관계대명사가 생략됨   접속사가 생략되지 않은 분사구문
— something people don't often do / when reading quickly, or reading in silence. //
이는 사람들이 자주 하지 않는 일이다 / 빨리 읽거나 조용히 읽을 때 //

Children, in particular, should be encouraged / to read aloud 수동태 동사
/ because the brain is wired for learning through connections 명사적 용법 (be encouraged의 목적격 보어)
/ that are created by positive stimulation, / such as singing, touching, and reading aloud. //
특히 어린이는 장려되어야 한다 / 소리 내어 읽도록 / 뇌가 결합을 통한 학습에 대해 연결되어 있기 때문에 / 긍정적인 자극에 의해 만들어진 / 노래 부르기, 만지기, 소리 내어 읽기와 같은 //

- technique ⓝ 기법, 기술 ・ light up 밝히다 ・ intense ⓐ 강렬한
- associated with ~과 연관된 ・ pronunciation ⓝ 발음
- strengthen ⓥ 강화시키다 ・ connective structure 결합 구조
- cell ⓝ 세포 ・ overall ⓐ 전반적인 ・ concentration ⓝ 집중력
- in silence 조용히 ・ in particular 특히 ・ encourage ⓥ 장려하다
- wire ⓥ 연결하다

fMRI(기능적 자기 공명 영상)와 같은 현대의 뇌 스캐닝 기법은 소리 내어 읽는 것이 두뇌의 여러 영역을 밝힌다는 것을 드러냈다. 발음과 발화된 반응의 소리를 듣는 것과 연관된 영역에서 강렬한 활동이 있으며, 이는 더 많은 두뇌 능력을 위한 여러분의 뇌세포의 결합 구조를 강화시킨다. 이것은 전반적인 집중력 향상으로 이어진다. 소리 내어 읽는 것은 여러분의 대중 말하기 능력을 발전시키는 좋은 방법인데, 왜냐하면 그것은 여러분으로 하여금 하나도 빠짐없이 단어를 읽게 강제하기 때문인데, 이는 사람들이 빨리 읽거나 조용히 읽을 때 자주 하지 않는 일이다. 특히 어린이는 뇌가 노래 부르기, 만지기, 소리 내어 읽기와 같은 긍정적인 자극에 의해 만들어진 결합을 통한 학습에 대해 연결되어 있기 때문에 소리 내어 읽도록 장려되어야 한다.

다음 글의 제목으로 가장 적절한 것은?
① Reading Aloud: Improving Brainpower and Speaking Skills 소리 내어 읽으면 두뇌와 말하기 능력이 향상됨
소리 내어 읽기: 두뇌 능력과 말하기 능력 향상
② Reading Practices: Shortcuts to Academic Achievements
독서 습관: 학문적 성취를 위한 지름길   독서의 습관이 아닌 방법에 관한 내용임
③ Improve Your Writing Skills Through Reading Aloud
소리 내어 읽기를 통한 글쓰기 능력 향상   글쓰기 능력 향상은 언급되지 않았음
④ How Your Brain Changes When You Read in Silence 조용히
조용히 읽을 때 뇌가 어떻게 변하는가   읽으면 단어를 하나도 빠짐없이 읽지는 못한다고 했음
⑤ Techniques for Faster and More Effective Reading
더 빠르고 효과적인 독서를 위한 기법   빨리 읽으면 단어를 하나도 빠짐없이 읽지는 못한다고 했음

왜 정답? ✱✱✽ [정답률 82%]
- 소리 내어 읽는 것은 두뇌의 여러 영역을 밝힌다. 단서 1
- 소리 내어 읽는 것은 말하기 능력을 향상시킨다. 단서 2
➡ 소리 내어 읽는 것이 두뇌와 말하기 능력에 주는 긍정적 효과에 관한 글이다.
▶ 따라서 정답은 ① '소리 내어 읽기: 두뇌 능력과 말하기 능력 향상'이다.

왜 오답?
② 소리 내어 읽는 것이 뇌와 말하기 능력에 끼치는 긍정적 영향에 관한 내용이지, 독서가 학문적 성취에 끼치는 영향은 언급되지 않았다.
③ 소리 내어 읽는 것의 긍정적 효과가 글의 주제이지만, 그중에 글쓰기 능력 향상은 언급되지 않았다. 주의
④ 조용히 읽으면 단어를 하나도 빠짐없이 읽는 것을 자주 하지 않는다고 했을 뿐이며, 조용히 읽는 것은 글의 주제가 아니다.
⑤ 빠르게 읽으면 단어를 하나도 빠짐없이 읽는 것을 자주 하지 않는다고 했을 뿐이며, 빠르고 효과적인 독서를 위한 기법은 언급되지 않았다.

구문 서술형

정답 to read, 목적격 보어

해석 소리 내어 읽는 것은 여러분이 하나도 빠짐없이 단어를 읽도록 강제한다.
→ 주어진 문장은 「주어 + 동사 + 목적어 + 목적격 보어」로 이루어진 5형식 문장이다. 동사 forces는 to부정사를 목적격 보어로 취하므로, read를 to read로 고쳐야 한다.

G 04 정답 ① *현실에 대한 해석의 차이

We think / we're being **logical**, **objective**, and **rational** / — and therefore **accurate** / in **our analysis, judgment**, and **decisions**. //
우리는 생각한다 / 우리가 논리적이고 객관적이며 합리적이고 / 그러므로 정확하다고 / 분석, 판단, 그리고 결정에 있어서

So we think / **that** if other people are logical, objective, and rational, / they will **agree** with us / **and** **see** what we see. //
따라서 우리는 생각한다 / 다른 사람들이 논리적이고 객관적이며 합리적이라면 / 그들이 우리에게 동의하고 / 우리가 보는 것을 볼 것이라고 //

But the opposite is the case. // 하지만 그 반대가 사실이다 //

Every human brain is different. // 모든 사람의 뇌는 다르다 //

Everyone's life experience is different. // 모두의 인생 경험은 다르다 //

Everyone's desires and knowledge are different. //
모두의 욕망과 지식은 다르다 //

You might think / **you're** being realistic / — that is, that your ideas match reality, / but that's impossible. // **단서 1** 당신의 생각이 현실과 일치하는 것은 불가능함
당신은 생각할 수 있다 / 당신이 현실적이라고 / 즉, 당신의 생각이 현실과 일치한다고 / 하지만 그것은 불가능하다 //

It's only your interpretation of reality, / **which** will always be different from **someone else's**. // **단서 2** 당신의 현실에 관한 해석은 다른 사람의 해석은 다름
그것은 현실에 대한 당신의 해석일 뿐이며 / 다른 사람의 것과 항상 다를 것이다 //

When two nations play each other / in the World Cup, / the **fans** of each country **criticize** the referees / for missing all the infractions / **that** the other team commits. //
두 나라가 서로 경기를 할 때 / World Cup에서 / 각 나라의 팬들은 심판들을 비난한다 / 모든 반칙을 놓친 것에 대해 / 상대 팀이 저지르는 //

Without fail, / **each fan base believes** / that the referees are biased / against their team. //
어김없이 / 각 팬층은 믿는다 / 심판이 편파적이라고 / 자기 팀에 불리하게 //

- logical ⓐ 논리적인
- objective ⓐ 객관적인
- rational ⓐ 합리적인
- accurate ⓐ 정확한
- analysis ⓝ 분석
- agree ⓥ 동의하다
- opposite ⓝ 반대
- the case 사실
- realistic ⓐ 현실적인
- match ⓥ 일치하다
- interpretation ⓝ 해석
- criticize ⓥ 비난하다
- referee ⓝ 심판
- commit ⓥ 저지르다
- biased ⓐ 편파적인, 편향된
- interpret ⓥ 해석하다

우리는 우리가 논리적이고 객관적이며 합리적이고 — 그러므로 분석, 판단, 그리고 결정에 있어서 정확하다고 생각한다. 따라서 우리는 다른 사람들이 논리적이고 객관적이며 합리적이라면, 그들이 우리에게 동의하고 우리가 보는 것을 볼 것이라고 생각한다. 하지만 그 반대가 사실이다. 모든 사람의 뇌는 다르다. 모두의 인생 경험은 다르다. 모두의 욕망과 지식은 다르다. 당신은 당신이 현실적이라고 — 즉, 당신의 생각이 현실과 일치한다고 생각할 수 있지만, 그것은 불가능하다. 그것은 현실에 대한 당신의 해석일 뿐이며, 다른 사람의 것과 항상 다를 것이다. World Cup에서 두 나라가 서로 경기를 할 때, 각 나라의 팬들은 상대 팀이 저지르는 모든 반칙을 놓친 것에 대해 심판들을 비난한다. 어김없이, 각 팬층은 심판이 자기 팀에 불리하게 편파적이라고 믿는다.

다음 글의 제목으로 가장 적절한 것은?

① Open to Interpretation: Everyone Sees Reality Differently 생각이 현실과 일치하는 것은 불가능하며 사람마다 현실에 대한 해석이 다르다는 → 다양한 해석의 여지: 모든 사람은 현실을 다르게 본다 내용임
② Efforts Made to Fill the Gap Between Real and Ideal 현실과 이상 사이의 간극을 메우기 위한 노력들 → 현실과 이상 사이의 간극은 언급되지 않았음
③ One Single Reality: What We All Agree Upon 현실에 대한 해석은 하나의 단일한 현실: 모두가 동의하는 것 단일하지 않고 사람마다 다르다는 내용임
④ Why Sports Fans Judge Their Team's Play Objectively 왜 스포츠 팬들이 자기 팀의 경기를 객관적으로 판단하는가
⑤ Knowledge: The Key to Interpreting the World Accurately 모두의 지식이 다르기 때문에 현실에 대한 해석이 서로 다르다는 내용임 지식: 세상을 정확하게 해석하는 비결
└ 스포츠 팬들이 자기 팀의 경기에 관해 객관적이지 못하다는 내용임

- 당신의 생각이 현실과 일치하는 것은 불가능하다. **단서 1**
- 당신의 현실에 관한 해석과 다른 사람의 현실에 관한 해석은 다르다. **단서 2**
→ 생각과 현실이 일치하지 않으며 사람마다 현실에 관해 다르게 해석한다는 내용이다.
▶ 따라서 정답은 ① '다양한 해석의 여지: 모든 사람은 현실을 다르게 본다'이다.

왜 오답?

② 현실과 이상 사이의 간극은 언급되지 않았다.
③ 현실에 대한 해석은 단일하지 않고 사람마다 다르다는 것이 글의 내용이다.
④ 스포츠 팬들은 자기 팀의 경기 때 객관적이지 않다는 것이 글의 내용이다.
⑤ 모두의 지식이 다르기 때문에 현실에 대한 해석도 서로 다르다. (이유: 지식은 세상을 정확하게 해석하는 비결이 될 수 없다는 것이 글의 내용이다.)

구문 서술형

정답 logical, objective, rational, other people

해석 다른 사람들이 논리적이고 객관적이며 합리적이라면, 그들이 우리에게 동의할 것이다.
→ If절이 「주어 + be동사 + 주격 보어」로 이루어진 2형식 문장이므로 보어는 형용사 logical, objective, rational이다. 주격 보어가 문장의 주어인 other people의 성질, 상태 등을 설명한다.

G 05 정답 ② *동물 실험과 의학적 발전의 인과관계

Many opponents of animal experimentation argue / **that** not only **is modern medicine not the only** cause for the decline in mortality, /
많은 동물 실험 반대자들은 주장한다 / 현대 의학이 사망률 감소의 유일한 원인이 아닐 뿐만 아니라 / **단서 1** 동물 실험 반대자들은 많은 의학적 발전이 동물 실험의 결과가 아니었다고 주장함

many medical advances / that **did** contribute to human health / were not the result of animal experimentation. //
많은 의학적 발전이 / 인간 건강에 기여했던 / 동물 실험의 결과가 아니었다고 //

Defenders of research **have claimed** / that **since** there is a strong correlation /
연구 옹호자들은 주장해왔다 / 강한 상관관계가 있기 때문에 / **단서 2** 동물 실험 옹호자들은 동물 실험이 의학적 발전을 초래했다고 주장함

between the practice of animal experimentation and medical advancement, / **the former** caused **the latter**. //
동물 실험 실행과 의학적 발전 사이에 / 전자가 후자를 초래했다고 //

Opponents of research reject this inference. //
연구 반대자들은 이 추론을 거부한다 //

After all, / we have independent reasons / **to expect** these phenomena **to be correlated**. //
결국 / 우리는 독립적인 이유를 가진다 / 이러한 현상들이 상관관계가 있을 것이라고 예상하게 하는 //

Since the law **prescribes** / that all new drugs, prosthetic devices, and surgical techniques **be** tried on animals / before they are used in humans, /
법이 규정하기 때문에 / 모든 신약들, 보철 장치들 그리고 외과 기술들이 동물에게 시험 되어야 한다고 / 인간에게 사용되기 전에 /

we will subsequently find / that all medical advances are correlated / with prior experimentation on animals. //
우리는 그 결과로서 알게 될 것이다 / 모든 의학적 발전들이 상관관계가 있다는 것을 / 이전의 동물 실험과 //

Consequently, / the correlation between animal experimentation and medical discovery is the result of legal necessity, / not evidence / **that** animal experimentation led to medical advances. //
따라서 / 동물 실험과 의학적 발견 간의 상관관계는 법적 필요성의 결과이지 / 증거가 아니다 / 동물 실험이 의학적 발전을 이끌었다는 //

Moreover, / several influential physicians have offered historical evidence / **that** animal experimentation has not been **as responsible** for biomedical discovery / **as** defenders suggest. //
게다가 / 몇몇 영향력 있는 의사들은 역사적 증거를 제시해 왔다 / 동물 실험이 생의학적 발견의 원인이 아니었다는 / 옹호자들이 주장하는 것만큼 //

They claim / that clinical discoveries played a more substantial role / than animal researchers have led us to believe. //
그들은 주장한다 / 임상적 발견들이 더 중요한 역할을 했다고 / 동물 연구자들이 우리가 믿게 해 온 것보다 //

- opponent ⓝ 반대자
- mortality ⓝ 사망률
- advance ⓝ 발전, 진보
- contribute ⓥ 기여하다
- defender ⓝ 옹호자
- correlation ⓝ 상관관계
- inference ⓝ 추론
- prescribe ⓥ 규정하다
- surgical ⓐ 외과의
- evidence ⓝ 증거
- biomedical ⓐ 생물 의학의
- substantial ⓐ 중요한
- unlock ⓥ 열다
- frontier ⓝ 경계, 지평
- refer to ~을 참고하다
- strict ⓐ 엄격한
- adoption ⓝ 입양
- extend ⓥ 연장하다
- life span 수명

많은 동물 실험 반대자들은 현대 의학이 사망률 감소의 유일한 원인이 아닐 뿐만 아니라, 인간 건강에 기여했던 많은 의학적 발전이 동물 실험의 결과가 아니었다고 주장한다. 연구 옹호자들은 동물 실험 실행과 의학적 발전 사이에 강한 상관관계가 있기 때문에 전자가 후자를 초래했다고 주장해왔다. 연구 반대자들은 이 추론을 거부한다. 결국, 우리는 이러한 현상들이 상관관계가 있을 것이라고 예상하게 하는 독립적인 이유를 가진다. 법이 모든 신약들, 보철 장치들 그리고 외과 기술들이 인간에게 사용되기 전에 동물에게 시험 되어야 한다고 규정하기 때문에, 우리는 그 결과로서 모든 의학적 발전들이 이전의 동물 실험과 상관관계가 있다는 것을 알게 될 것이다. 따라서, 동물 실험과 의학적 발견 간의 상관관계는 법적 필요성의 결과이지, 동물 실험이 의학적 발전을 이끌었다는 증거가 아니다. 게다가, 몇몇 영향력 있는 의사들은 동물 실험이 옹호자들이 주장하는 것만큼 생의학적 발견의 원인이 아니었다는 역사적 증거를 제시해 왔다. 그들은 임상적 발견들이 동물 연구자들이 우리가 믿게 해 온 것보다 더 중요한 역할을 했다고 주장한다.

동물 실험과 의학 발전의 인과관계에 대해 상반되는 주장을 소개함

다음 글의 제목으로 가장 적절한 것은?
① Bio-medicine: Unlocking New Frontiers in Health Care
생명 의학: 의료의 새로운 지평을 열다   생명 의학을 통한 의료 발전에 관한 내용이 아님
② Is Medicine Advanced by Experimenting on Animals?
의학은 동물 실험을 통해 발전하는가?
③ Refer to Historical Evidence to Solve Medical Issues
의학 문제 해결을 위해 역사적 증거를 참고하라   의학 문제 해결은 언급되지 않았음
④ Why Aren't There Strict Laws for Animal Adoption?
왜 동물 입양에 대한 엄격한 법이 없는가?   동물 입양은 언급되지 않았음
⑤ Medical Advances for Extending Human Life Span
인간 수명 연장을 위한 의학의 발전   인간 수명 연장은 언급되지 않았음

왜 정답? ✱✱✱ [정답률 86%]
- 동물 실험 반대자는 의학적 발전이 동물 실험의 결과가 아니었다고 주장함 단서 1
- 동물 실험 옹호자는 동물 실험이 의학 발전을 가져왔다고 주장함 단서 2
➡ 동물 실험과 의학 발전 사이의 상관관계에 대해, 동물 실험 옹호자와 반대자 사이에 대립하는 주장을 설명하는 내용이다.
▶ 따라서 정답은 ② '의학은 동물 실험을 통해 발전하는가?'이다.

왜 오답?
① 생명 의학을 통한 의료 발전이 핵심 내용은 아니다.
③ 의학 문제 해결은 언급되지 않았다.
④ 동물 입양은 언급되지 않았다.
⑤ 인간 수명 연장은 언급되지 않았다.

구문 서술형

정답 between animal experimentation and medical discovery is the result

→ 문장의 주어는 The correlation between animal experimentation and medical discovery, 동사는 is, 주격 보어는 the result of legal necessity다.

G 06 정답 ③ *인간과 AI의 공동 진화

The evolution of AI / **is** often **associated with** the concept of singularity. //
be associated with ~: ~와 연관되다
AI의 진화는 / 종종 특이점의 개념과 연관된다 //

Singularity / **refers to** the point / **at which** AI exceeds human intelligence. //
'~을 말한다'   「전치사 + 관계대명사」
특이점은 / 지점을 말한다 / AI가 인간의 지능을 넘어서는 //

After that point, / **it** is predicted / **that** AI will repeatedly improve itself and evolve / at an accelerated pace. //
가주어   진주어절 접속사
그 지점 이후 / 예측된다 / AI는 스스로를 반복적으로 개선하고 진화할 것으로 / 가속화된 속도로 //

When AI becomes self-aware / and pursues its own goals, / it will be a conscious **being**, / not just a machine. //
'존재'
AI가 스스로를 인식하게 되고 / 자기 자신의 목표를 추구할 때 / 그것은 의식이 있는 존재가 될 것이다 / 단지 기계가 아니라 //

AI and human consciousness / will then begin **to evolve** together. // 단서 1 AI와 인간의 의식은 미래에 함께 진화할 것임
명사적 용법 (begin의 목적어)
AI와 인간의 의식은 / 그러면 함께 진화하기 시작할 것이다 //

Our consciousness will evolve / to new dimensions / through our interactions with AI, / **which** will **provide** us **with** intellectual stimulation / and inspire new insights and creativity. //
계속적 용법의 주격 관계대명사   '~에게 …을 제공하다'
우리의 의식은 진화할 것이다 / 새로운 차원으로 / 우리의 AI와의 상호 작용을 통해 / 이는 우리에게 지적 자극을 제공하고 / 새로운 통찰력과 창의성을 불어넣을 것이다 //

Conversely, / our consciousness also has a significant impact / on the evolution of AI. //
반대로 / 우리의 의식 또한 중대한 영향을 끼친다 / AI의 진화에 //

The direction of AI's evolution will depend greatly / on **what values and ethics we incorporate into AI**. //
의문사절
AI 진화의 방향은 크게 좌우될 것이다 / 우리가 어떤 가치와 윤리를 AI에 통합시키는지에 //

We need to see our relationship with AI / as a mutual coexistence of conscious beings, / **recognizing** its rights and **supporting** the evolution of its consciousness. // 단서 2 인간-AI 관계는 의식 있는 존재들의 상호 공존으로 봐야 함
병렬 구조 (분사구문)
우리는 우리와 AI와의 관계를 볼 필요가 있다 / 의식 있는 존재들의 상호 공존으로 / AI의 권리를 인식하고 그것의 의식의 진화를 지지하면서 //

- evolution ⓝ 진화
- singularity ⓝ 특이점
- exceed ⓥ 넘어서다, 능가하다
- intelligence ⓝ 지능
- predict ⓥ 예측하다
- accelerate ⓥ 가속하다
- pursue ⓥ 추구하다
- conscious ⓐ 의식이 있는
- insight ⓝ 통찰력
- significant ⓐ 상당한
- direction ⓝ 방향
- incorporate ⓥ 통합시키다
- mutual ⓐ 상호의
- coexistence ⓝ 공존
- recognize ⓥ 인식하다
- unsolvable ⓐ 해결할 수 없는
- resistance ⓝ 저항
- upcoming ⓐ 다가오는
- stare in the face 노려보다

AI의 진화는 종종 특이점의 개념과 연관된다. 특이점은 AI가 인간의 지능을 넘어서는 지점을 의미한다. 그 지점 이후, AI는 스스로를 반복적으로 개선하고 가속화된 속도로 진화할 것으로 예측된다. AI가 스스로를 인식하게 되고 자기 자신의 목표를 추구할 때, 그것은 단지 기계가 아니라 의식이 있는 존재가 될 것이다. AI와 인간의 의식은 그러면 함께 진화하기 시작할 것이다. 우리의 의식은 우리의 AI와의 상호 작용을 통해 새로운 차원으로 진화할 것이며, 이는 우리에게 지적 자극을 제공하고 새로운 통찰력과 창의성을 불어넣을 것이다. 반대로, 우리의 의식 또한 AI의 진화에 중대한 영향을 끼친다. AI 진화의 방향은 우리가 어떤 가치와 윤리를 AI에 통합시키는지에 크게 좌우될 것이다. 우리는 AI의 권리를 인식하고 그것의 의식의 진화를 지지하면서, 우리와 AI와의 관계를 의식 있는 존재들의 상호 공존으로 볼 필요가 있다.

다음 글의 제목으로 가장 적절한 것은?

① An Unsolvable Dilemma: Is AI Friend or Enemy?
해결할 수 없는 딜레마: AI는 친구인가, 적인가?   AI가 인간에게 좋은지 나쁜지에 대한 내용이 아님
② The History of Humans' Resistance Against Machines
기계에 대한 인간의 저항의 역사   기계에 대한 인간의 저항은 언급되지 않음
③ Upcoming Future: AI as a Human Partner for Co-evolution   AI와 인간이 상호 공존하며 함께 진화할 것임
다가오는 미래: 공동 진화를 위한 인간 파트너로서의 AI
④ AI World Without Human Intelligence Is Staring You in the Face
인간 지능이 없는 AI 세계가 당신을 노려보고 있다   인간 지능이 없는 AI 세계에 관한 내용이 아님
⑤ How AI Makes Human-to-Human Relationships More Meaningful   인간과 인간의 관계가 아닌 인간과 AI의 관계를 언급함
AI가 인간과 인간의 관계를 더욱 의미 있게 만드는 방법

왜 정답? ✹✹✷ [정답률 75%]

- AI와 인간의 의식은 미래에 함께 진화할 것이다. 단서 1
- 인간-AI 관계는 의식 있는 존재들의 상호 공존으로 봐야 한다. 단서 2

➡ AI와 인간의 의식은 미래에 함께 진화하여 서로에게 영향을 미칠 것이므로 AI와의 관계를 상호 공존의 관계로 보아야 한다는 내용이다.

▶ 따라서 정답은 ③ '다가오는 미래: 공동 진화를 위한 인간 파트너로서의 AI'이다.

왜 오답?

① AI가 인간에게 좋은지 나쁜지에 관한 평가는 언급되지 않았다.
② AI와 인간의 공존에 관한 내용이지, 기계에 대한 인간의 저항에 관한 내용이 아니다.
④ 우리의 의식 또한 AI의 진화에 영향을 끼친다고 했으므로 인간 지능이 없는 AI 세계에 관한 내용이 아니다.
⑤ 인간-인간 관계에 미치는 AI의 영향이 아니라 인간-AI 관계가 중심 내용이다. 주의

구문 서술형

정답 self-aware, 형용사, a conscious being, 명사(구)

해석 AI가 스스로를 인식하게 될 때, 그것은 의식이 있는 존재가 될 것이다.

→ 주격 보어 자리에는 명사, 형용사, 분사 등이 올 수 있다. 형용사 self-aware와 명사구 a conscious being이 부사절의 주어 AI와 주절의 주어 it을 보충 설명하는 주격 보어로 쓰였다.

G 07 정답 ⑤ * 그림 작품 완성 시점의 판단

동명사 주어
Working around the whole painting, / rather than concentrating '~보다는'
on one area at a time, / will mean / you can stop at any point / 병렬 구조
and the painting can be considered "finished." //
전체 그림에 대해서 작업하는 것은 / 한 번에 한 영역에만 집중하기보다 / 의미할 것이다 /
여러분이 어떤 지점에서도 멈출 수 있고 / 그림이 '완성'된 것으로 간주될 수 있다는 것을 / 가목적어   진목적어   stop v-ing: ~하는 것을 그만두다
Artists often find it difficult / to know when to stop painting, /
가주어   진주어
and it can be tempting / to keep on adding more to your work. //
화가인 여러분은 종종 어렵다는 것을 발견하고 / 언제 그림을 멈춰야 할지 알기가 / 유혹을
느낄 수도 있다 / 자신의 그림에 계속해서 더 추가하고 싶은
가주어   진주어
It is important / to take a few steps back from the painting / from
부사적 용법(목적)
time to time / to assess your progress. //
중요하다 / 그림에서 몇 걸음 뒤로 물러나는 것이 / 때때로 / 자신의 진행 상황을 평가하기
위해   단서 1 자신의 진행 상황을 평가하기 위해 그림에서 몇 걸음 뒤로 물러나는 것이 중요함

Putting too much into a painting / can spoil its impact / and
주격 보어(과거분사)
leave it looking overworked. // 단서 2 그림에 너무 많은 것을 넣으면 망칠 수 있음
한 그림에 너무 많은 것을 넣으면 / 그것의 영향력을 망칠 수 있고 / 그것이 과하게 작업된
것처럼 보이게 둘 수 있다 //
명사절 접속사
If you find yourself struggling / to decide whether you have
finished, / take a break / and come back to it later / with fresh
eyes. // 단서 3 작업이 끝났는지 결정하는 것이 어렵다면 휴식을 취한 후에 그림을 다시 봄
만약 여러분이 자신이 어려움을 겪고 있음을 알게 된다면 / 끝냈는지를 결정하는 데 / 잠시
휴식을 취하고 / 나중에 그것(그림)으로 다시 돌아와라 / 새로운 눈으로

(page 76 자이스토리 영어 독해 기본)

Then you can decide / whether any areas of your painting would benefit / from further refinement. //
그러면 여러분은 결정할 수 있다 / 자신의 그림 어느 부분이 득을 볼지를 / 더 정교하게 꾸며서 //

- concentrate ⓥ 집중하다
- keep on v-ing 계속 ~하다
- from time to time 때때로
- assess ⓥ 평가하다
- progress ⓝ 진행 상황, 진전
- spoil ⓥ 망치다
- impact ⓝ 영향(력)
- overwork ⓥ 과하게 작업하다
- struggle ⓥ 어려움을 겪다, 분투하다
- benefit ⓥ 득을 보다
- inspiration ⓝ 영감
- incomplete ⓐ 미완성의, 불완전한
- interpretation ⓝ 해석, 이해

한 번에 한 영역에만 집중하기보다 전체 그림에 대해서 작업하는 것은 여러분이 어떤 지점에서도 멈출 수 있고 그림이 '완성'된 것으로 간주될 수 있다는 것을 의미할 것이다. 화가인 여러분은 종종 언제 그림을 멈춰야 할지 알기 어렵다는 것을 발견하고, 자신의 그림에 계속해서 더 추가하고 싶은 유혹을 느낄 수도 있다. 때때로 자신의 진행 상황을 평가하기 위해 그림에서 몇 걸음 뒤로 물러나는 것이 중요하다. 한 그림에 너무 많은 것을 넣으면 그것의 영향력을 망칠 수 있고 그것이 과하게 작업된 것처럼 보이게 둘 수 있다. 만약 여러분이 끝냈는지를 결정하는 데 자신이 어려움을 겪고 있음을 알게 된다면, 잠시 휴식을 취하고 나중에 새로운 눈으로 그것(그림)으로 다시 돌아와라. 그러면 여러분은 더 정교하게 꾸며서 자신의 그림 어느 부분이 득을 볼지를 결정할 수 있다.

다음 글의 제목으로 가장 적절한 것은?
그림에 너무 많은 것을 추가했을 때 망칠 수 있다는 내용임
① Drawing Inspiration from Diverse Artists
다양한 예술가들로부터 영감을 끌어내기   다양한 예술가에게 영감을 얻는 내용은 언급되지 않음
② Don't Spoil Your Painting by Leaving It Incomplete
너의 그림을 완성하지 않은 상태로 두어서 망치지 마라
③ Art Interpretation: Discover Meanings in a Painting
예술 해석: 그림 속의 의미를 발견하라   그림 속의 의미를 발견하는 내용은 제시되지 않음
④ Do Not Put Down Your Brush: The More, the Better
붓을 내려놓지 마라: 다다익선   너무 많은 추가가 그림 작품에 해가 될 수 있음을 설명함
⑤ Avoid Overwork and Find the Right Moment to Finish
과한 작업을 피하고 마무리할 적절한 순간을 찾아라
적절한 시점에 과도한 작업을 멈추고 새로운 눈으로 작품을 다시 봐야 함

왜 정답? ✹✹✷ [정답률 67%]

- 작품의 진행 상황을 평가하기 위해서 본인 그림에서 몇 걸음 뒤로 물러나는 것이 중요함 단서 1
- 한 그림에 너무 많은 것을 넣으면 작품의 영향력을 망칠 수 있고 과하게 작업된 것처럼 보이게 둘 수 있음 단서 2
- 작업이 끝났는지 결정하는 데 어려움이 있다면 잠시 휴식을 취하고 새로운 눈으로 그림을 바라봐야 함 단서 3

➡ 과도하게 그림 작품을 작업하지 않고 적절한 시점에 작업을 멈추는 것의 중요성과 그 방법을 제시하고 있다.

▶ 따라서 정답은 ⑤ '과한 작업을 피하고 마무리할 적절한 순간을 찾아라'이다.

왜 오답?

① 다양한 예술가에게 영감을 얻는 내용은 언급되지 않았다.
② 너무 많은 것을 그림에 넣으면 안 된다는 내용이지 그림을 완성해야 한다는 내용이 아니다.
③ 그림에서 의미를 발견하고 예술 작품을 해석하는 내용은 제시되지 않았다.
④ 그림에 너무 많은 것을 추가했을 때 작품의 영향력을 망치고 과하게 작업된 것처럼 보이게 할 수 있다는 내용이므로, 글의 내용과 반대된다.

G 08 정답 ① * 기후 변화 해결책이 될 수 있는 고래

Whales are highly efficient / at carbon storage. //
고래는 매우 효율적이다 / 탄소 저장에 //   단서 1 고래는 탄소 저장에 효율적임

When they die, / each whale sequesters an average of 30 tons of
분사구문을 이끄는 현재분사
carbon dioxide, / taking that carbon out of the atmosphere for
centuries. //
그들이 죽을 때 / 각각의 고래는 평균 30톤의 이산화 탄소를 격리하며 / 수 세기 동안
대기로부터 그 탄소를 빼내어 둔다 //

For comparison, / the average tree absorbs / only 48 pounds of
CO$_2$ a year. //
비교하자면 / 평균적인 나무는 흡수한다 / 연간 48파운드의 이산화 탄소만을 //

From a climate perspective, / each whale is / the marine
equivalent of thousands of trees. //
기후의 관점에서 / 각각의 고래는 ~이다 / 수천 그루의 나무에 상응하는 바다에 사는 것 //

Whales also help sequester carbon / by fertilizing the ocean
/ as they release nutrient-rich waste, / in turn increasing
phytoplankton populations, /
고래는 또한 탄소를 격리하는 데 도움을 주는데 / 바다를 비옥하게 함으로써 / 영양이 풍부한
배설물을 내보내면서 / 결과적으로 식물성 플랑크톤 개체를 증가시키고 /

계속적 용법의 주격 관계대명사   분사구문을 이끄는 현재분사
which also sequester carbon / — leading some scientists to call
them / the "engineers of marine ecosystems." //
이는 또한 탄소를 격리한다 / 그리하여 몇몇 과학자들은 그들을 부르게 되었다 / '해양
생태계의 기술자'라고 //

In 2019, economists from the International Monetary Fund
(IMF) / estimated the value of the ecosystem services / provided
                       앞에 주격 관계대명사와 be동사가 생략됨
by each whale / at over $2 million USD. //
2019년 국제 통화 기금(IMF)의 경제학자들은 / 생태계 서비스의 가치를 추정했다 / 각각의
고래에 의해서 제공되는 / 미화 200만 달러가 넘게 //

call for: ~을 요구하다
They called for / a new global program of economic incentives /
to return whale populations to preindustrial whaling levels / as
        단서 2 고래는 기후 변화에 대한 자연 기반 해결책임
one example of a "nature-based solution" / to climate change. //
그들은 요구했다 / 새로운 글로벌 경제적 인센티브 프로그램을 / 고래 개체수를 산업화 이전의
고래잡이 수준으로 되돌리기 위한 / '자연 기반 해결책'의 한 예로서 / 기후 변화에 대한 //

수동태의 현재진행형
Calls are now being made / for a global whale restoration
program, / to slow down climate change. //
요구가 현재 제기되고 있다 / 세계적인 고래 복원 프로그램에 대한 / 기후 변화를 늦추기 위해 //
    단서 3 기후 변화를 늦추기 위해 세계적인 고래 복원 프로그램에 대한 요구가 제기됨

- storage ⓝ 저장   - atmosphere ⓝ 대기   - comparison ⓝ 비교
- absorb ⓥ 흡수하다   - marine ⓐ 해양의
- equivalent ⓝ (~에) 상응하는 것   - fertilize ⓥ 비옥하게 하다
- release ⓥ 내보내다   - estimate ⓥ 추정하다
- incentive ⓝ 장려책   - preindustrial ⓐ 산업화 이전의
- restoration ⓝ 복원   - extinct ⓐ 멸종된
- overpopulation ⓝ 과밀(과잉 밀집)   - industry ⓝ 산업
- habitat ⓝ 서식지

고래는 탄소 저장에 매우 효율적이다. 그들이 죽을 때, 각각의 고래는 평균 30
톤의 이산화 탄소를 격리하며, 수 세기 동안 대기로부터 그 탄소를 빼내어 둔
다. 비교하자면, 평균적인 나무는 연간 48파운드의 이산화 탄소만을 흡수한다.
기후의 관점에서 각각의 고래는 수천 그루의 나무에 상응하는 바다에 사는 것이
다. 고래는 또한 영양이 풍부한 배설물을 내보내면서 바다를 비옥하게 함으로써
탄소를 격리하는 데 도움을 주는데, 결과적으로 식물성 플랑크톤 개체를 증가시
키고 이는 또한 탄소를 격리한다. 그리하여 몇몇 과학자들은 그들을 '해양 생태
계의 기술자'라고 부르게 되었다. 2019년 국제 통화 기금(IMF)의 경제학자들은
각각의 고래에 의해서 제공되는 생태계 서비스의 가치를 미화 200만 달러가 넘
게 추정했다. 그들은 기후 변화에 대한 '자연 기반 해결책'의 한 예로서 고래 개
체수를 산업화 이전의 고래잡이 수준으로 되돌리기 위한 새로운 글로벌 경제적
인센티브 프로그램을 요구했다. 기후 변화를 늦추기 위해 세계적인 고래 복원
프로그램에 대한 요구가 현재 제기되고 있다.

다음 글의 제목으로 가장 적절한 것은?
① Saving Whales Saves the Earth and Us
고래를 구하는 것은 지구와 우리를 구한다   기후 변화에 대한 자연 기반 해결책임
② What Makes Whales Go Extinct in the Ocean
고래가 바다에서 멸종하도록 하는 것   고래의 멸종 이유에 관한 내용이 아님
③ Why Is Overpopulation of Whales Dangerous?
고래의 과밀이 왜 위험한가?   고래의 과밀에 대한 언급은 없음
④ Black Money: Lies about the Whaling Industry
검은 돈: 고래잡이 산업에 대한 거짓   고래잡이 산업이 핵심 내용은 아님
⑤ Climate Change and Its Effect on Whale Habitats
기후 변화와 그것이 고래 서식지에 미치는 영향
고래 서식지에 기후 변화가 미치는 영향에 관한 언급은 없음

> 왜 정답? ★★❀ [정답률 79%]
- 고래는 탄소 저장에 매우 효율적이다. 단서 1
- 고래는 기후 변화에 대한 자연 기반 해결책이다. 단서 2
- 기후 변화를 늦추기 위해 세계적인 고래 복원 프로그램에 대한 요구가 제기되고
  있다. 단서 3
➡ 고래는 탄소 저장에 매우 효율적이며 기후 변화에 대한 자연 기반 해결책이므로,
  기후 변화를 늦추기 위해 고래 복원 프로그램이 요구되고 있다는 내용의 글이다.
  ▶ 따라서 정답은 ① '고래를 구하는 것은 지구와 우리를 구한다'이다.

> 왜 오답?
② 고래가 멸종되는 원인에 관한 내용이 아니다.
③ 고래의 과밀이 위험한 이유는 언급되지 않았고, 오히려 기후 변화를 늦추기 위해
  고래 개체수를 늘려야 한다는 내용이다.
④ 고래잡이 산업에 대한 거짓과 검은 돈(부정한 이득)은 언급되지 않았다.
⑤ 고래가 기후 변화 문제의 해결책이 될 수 있다고 했을 뿐, 기후 변화가 고래
  서식지에 미치는 영향은 언급되지 않았다. 주의

G 09 정답 ⑤ *억지 미소의 효과

주어(선행사)   주격 관계대명사   동사 ①
Every event / that causes you to smile / makes you feel happy /
        동사 ②
and produces feel-good chemicals / in your brain. //
모든 사건은 / 당신을 미소 짓게 만드는 / 당신을 행복하게 느끼게 만든다 / 그리고 기분이 좋
아지는 화학 물질을 생산한다 / 당신의 뇌에서 //
                force의 목적격보어로 온 to부정사
Force your face to smile / even when you are stressed or feel
unhappy. // 단서 1 명령문으로서 억지로라도 미소 짓게 하라고 주장하고 있음
당신의 얼굴이 미소 짓게 해라 / 심지어 당신이 스트레스를 받거나 불행하다고 느낄 때에도 //
                          과거분사로 The facial muscular pattern 수식
The facial muscular pattern / produced by the smile / is linked /
to all the "happy networks" in your brain / and will in turn
                                          병렬 구조
naturally calm you down / and change your brain chemistry /
안면 근육의 형태는 / 미소에 의해 만들어지는 / 연결된다 / 당신의 뇌의 모든 "행복 연결망"
과 / 그리고 그 결과 자연스럽게 당신을 안정시킬 것이다 / 그리고 당신의 뇌의 화학 작용을 변
화시킬 (것이다) /

by releasing / the same feel-good chemicals. //
배출함으로써 / 기분이 좋게 만들어주는 동일한 화학 물질들을 //

Researchers studied / the effects of a genuine and forced smile /
on individuals / during a stressful event. //
연구원들은 연구했다 / 진정한 미소와 억지 미소가 미치는 영향을 / 개인들에게 / 스트레스를
받는 상황에서 //
                  사역동사+목적어+목적격 보어(동사원형)
The researchers had participants perform stressful tasks / while
                          분사구문
not smiling, smiling, / or holding chopsticks crossways in their
mouths / (to force the face to form a smile). //
연구원들은 참가자들이 스트레스를 받는 과제를 수행하게 했다 / 미소 짓지 않거나, 미소 짓거
나 / 입에 젓가락을 옆으로 물고서 / (얼굴이 미소를 만들도록 하기 위해) //
                                    목적어절을 이끄는 접속사
The results of the study showed / that smiling, forced or
genuine, / during stressful events, / reduced the intensity / of
                                      that 절 안의 동사
the stress response in the body / and lowered heart rate levels /
그 연구의 결과는 보여주었다 / 미소가, 억지이든 진정한 것이든 / 스트레스를 받는 상황에서 /
강도를 줄였다 / 신체의 스트레스 반응의 / 그리고 심장 박동률의 수준도 낮췄다 /
after recovering from the stress. // 단서 2 억지 미소도 스트레스를 줄이는 데
                                          도움을 주었다고 연구 결과를 설명하고 있음
스트레스로부터 회복한 후에 //

- chemicals ⓝ 화학 물질   - muscular ⓐ 근육의
- chemistry ⓝ 화학 작용   - genuine ⓐ 참된, 진정한
- participant ⓝ 참가자   - intensity ⓝ 강도
- response ⓝ 반응   - lower ⓥ 낮추다   - recover ⓥ 회복하다

당신을 미소 짓게 만드는 모든 사건은 당신을 행복하게 느끼게 만들고, 당
신의 뇌에서 기분이 좋게 만들어주는 화학 물질을 생산해내도록 한다. 심
지어 당신이 스트레스를 받거나 불행하다고 느낄 때조차도 당신의 얼굴이
미소 짓게 해라. 미소에 의해 만들어진 안면 근육의 형태는 당신의 뇌의 모
든 '행복 연결망'과 연결되어 있고, 그 결과 자연스럽게 당신을 안정시키고

기분을 좋게 만들어주는 동일한 화학물질들을 배출함으로써 뇌의 화학 작용을 변화시킬 것이다. 연구원들은 스트레스를 받는 상황에서 진정한 미소와 억지 미소가 개인들에게 미치는 영향을 연구했다. 연구원들은 참가자들이 미소 짓지 않거나, 미소 짓거나, (억지 미소를 짓게 하기 위해) 입에 젓가락을 옆으로 물고서 스트레스를 받는 과제를 수행하게 했다. 연구의 결과는 미소가, 억지이든 진정한 것이든, 스트레스를 받는 상황에서 신체의 스트레스 반응의 강도를 줄였고, 스트레스로부터 회복한 후의 심장 박동률의 수준도 낮추었다는 것을 보여주었다.

> **다음 글의 제목으로 가장 적절한 것은?**
> ① Causes and Effects of Stressful Events
> 스트레스를 받는 상황의 원인과 결과   스트레스를 받는 상황의 원인과 결과에 대한 내용이 아님
> ② Personal Signs and Patterns of Stress
> 스트레스의 개인적인 징후와 양상   스트레스의 개인적인 징후나 양상에 대한 내용은 없음
> ③ How Body and Brain React to Stress
> 신체와 뇌(정신)가 스트레스에 반응하는 방식   신체와 뇌에 대한 언급은 있지만 스트레스에 어떻게 반응하는지에 대한 내용은 아님
> ④ Stress: Necessary Evil for Happiness
> 스트레스: 행복을 위한 필요악   스트레스가 행복에 필수적인지에 대한 언급은 없음
> ⑤Do Faked Smiles Also Help Reduce Stress?
> 억지 미소가 또한 스트레스를 줄이는 데 도움을 주는가?   억지 미소도 스트레스 해소에 도움을 준다는 내용임

왜 정답? ★★❀ [정답률 66%] 〔연구 결과의 의미를 제대로 이해해야 함〕 꿀팁

이 글은 스트레스를 받을 때 미소를 지으라는 필자의 주장과 이를 뒷받침하는 연구 내용으로 이루어져 있다. 연구 결과에 따르면, 미소가 진정한 것이든 억지이든 스트레스 반응의 강도를 줄이고 심장 박동률의 수준을 낮췄다고 했다. 따라서 미소 자체가 스트레스 해소에 도움을 준다는 사실을 알 수 있으므로, 이 글의 제목으로 가장 적절한 것은 ⑤ '억지 미소가 또한 스트레스를 줄이는 데 도움을 주는가?'이다.

왜 오답?

① 스트레스를 받는 상황의 원인과 결과에 대한 내용은 나오지 않았다.
② 스트레스를 개인적 차원에서 분석한 글이 아니다.
③ 신체와 뇌가 스트레스에 어떻게 반응하는지가 아니라, 미소에 따라 신체가 어떻게 반응하는지에 대한 내용이다.
④ 스트레스가 행복에 필요한가에 대한 언급은 없다.

· expand ⓥ 확장시키다   · skyscraper ⓝ 고층 건물, 마천루
· architecture ⓝ 건축   · under construction 건설 중인

사람들은 도시 발전에 대해 생각할 때, 수직 운송 수단의 중요한 역할을 거의 고려하지 않는다. 실제로 매일 70억 회 이상의 엘리베이터 이동이 전 세계 높은 빌딩에서 이루어진다. 효율적인 수직 운송 수단은 점점 더 높은 고층 건물을 만들 수 있는 우리의 능력을 확장시킬 수 있다. Illinois 공과대학의 건축학과 교수인 Antony Wood는 지난 20년 간의 엘리베이터의 발전은 아마도 우리가 높은 건물에서 봐 왔던 가장 큰 발전이라고 설명한다. 예를 들어, 건설 중인 사우디아라비아 Jeddah의 Jeddah Tower에 있는 엘리베이터는 660미터라는 기록적인 높이에 이를 것이다.

> **다음 글의 제목으로 가장 적절한 것은?**
> ①Elevators Bring Buildings Closer to the Sky
> 수직 운송 수단인 엘리베이터가 고층 건물 만드는 능력을 확장시킨다는 내용
> 엘리베이터는 건물을 하늘에 더 가까이 데려다 준다
> ② The Higher You Climb, the Better the View
> 더 높이 오를수록, 전망은 더 좋아진다   높은 곳의 전망이 좋다는 내용은 언급되지 않음
> ③ How to Construct an Elevator Cheap and Fast
> 엘리베이터를 저렴하고 빠르게 건설하는 방법   핵심어인 엘리베이터를 이용하여 만든 오답
> ④ The Function of the Ancient and the Modern City
> 고대 도시와 현대 도시의 기능   도시의 기능에 대해서는 나오지 않음
> ⑤The Evolution of Architecture: Solutions for Overpopulation
> 건축의 혁명: 인구과잉을 위한 해결책   인구과잉 문제를 다룬 글이 아님

왜 정답? ★★❀ [정답률 76%]

엘리베이터로 대표되는 수직 운송 수단이 고층 건물을 만드는 우리의 능력을 확장시킨다고 하면서 660미터라는 기록적인 높이를 자랑하는 고층 건물의 엘리베이터를 구체적인 사례로 들어 설명하는 내용이다. 따라서 이 글의 제목으로 가장 적절한 것은 ① '엘리베이터는 건물을 하늘에 더 가까이 데려다 준다'이다.

왜 오답?

② 높은 곳의 전망이 좋다는 내용은 언급되지 않았다.
③ 이 글의 핵심어인 엘리베이터를 이용하여 만든 오답이다. 함정
④ 도시의 기능에 대해서는 전혀 나오지 않았다.
⑤ 인구과잉 문제를 다룬 글이 아니므로 적절하지 않다.

G 10 정답 ① *고층 건물 건설 능력을 확장시키는 엘리베이터

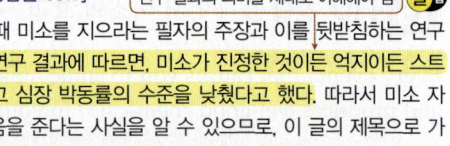

When people think about the development of cities, / rarely do they consider / the critical role of vertical transportation. //
도치(부정어+do동사+주어+동사원형)
사람들이 도시 발전에 대해 생각할 때 / 그들은 거의 고려하지 않는다 / 수직 운송 수단의 중요한 역할을 //

In fact, / each day, / more than 7 billion elevator journeys / are taken in tall buildings / all over the world. //
실제로 / 매일 / 70억 회 이상의 엘리베이터 이동이 / 높은 빌딩에서 이루어진다 / 전 세계 //

Efficient vertical transportation / can expand / our ability / to build taller and taller skyscrapers. // 단서1 수직 운송 수단이 고층 건물을 만들 수 있는 능력을 확장시켜줌
형용사적 용법
효율적인 수직 운송 수단은 / 확장시킬 수 있다 / 우리의 능력을 / 점점 더 높은 고층 건물을 만들 수 있는 //

Antony Wood, a Professor of Architecture / at the Illinois Institute of Technology, / explains /
핵심 주어   동사
건축학과 교수인 Antony Wood는 / Illinois 공과대학의 / 설명한다 /

that advances in elevators over the past 20 years / are probably the greatest advances / we have seen in tall buildings. //
목적어절 접속사   앞에 목적격대명사 생략
지난 20년 간의 엘리베이터의 발전은 / 아마도 가장 큰 발전이라고 / 우리가 높은 건물에서 봐 왔던 //

For example, / elevators in the Jeddah Tower / in Jeddah, Saudi Arabia, / under construction, / will reach a height record of 660m. // 단서2 기록적인 높이를 자랑하는 엘리베이터의 예를 말함
핵심 주어   동사
예를 들어 / Jeddah Tower에 있는 엘리베이터는 / 사우디아라비아 Jeddah의 / 건설 중인 / 660미터라는 기록적인 높이에 이를 것이다 //

· development ⓝ 발전   · critical ⓐ 중요한, 결정적인
· vertical ⓐ 수직의   · transportation ⓝ 운송, 수송

G 11 정답 ③ *씹기가 포유동물의 생존을 돕는 방식

Chewing leads to / smaller particles for swallowing, / and more exposed surface area / for digestive enzymes to act on. //
씹기는 ~로 이어진다 / 삼킴을 위한 더 작은 조각들 / 그리고 더 노출된 표면으로 / 소화 효소가 작용하는 //

In other words, / it means / the extraction of more fuel and raw materials / from a mouthful of food. //
다시 말해서 / 그것은 의미한다 / 더 많은 연료와 원료를 추출하는 것을 / 한 입의 음식으로부터 //

This is especially important / for mammals / because they heat their bodies from within. // 단서1 씹기는 포유류의 생존에 중요함
이것은 특히 중요하다 / 포유류에게 / 그들이 체내에서 자신의 몸을 따뜻하게 하기 때문에 //
단서2 씹기는 포유류가 생존하는 데 필요한 에너지를 줌
Chewing gives mammals / the energy needed to be active / not only during the day but also the cool night, / and to live in colder climates / or places with changing temperatures. //
the energy를 수식   병렬 구조
씹기는 포유류에게 준다 / 활동하는데 필요한 에너지를 / 낮은 물론 서늘한 밤 동안에도 / 그리고 더 추운 기후에서 사는 데 / 또는 기온이 변하는 장소에서 (사는 데) //

It allows them to sustain / higher levels of activity and travel speeds / to cover larger distances, / avoid predators, / capture prey, / and make and care for their young. //
allow ~ to-v; ~가 …하도록 허락하다   형용사적 용법의 병렬 구조
그것은 그들이 유지하게 한다 / 더 높은 수준의 활동과 이동 속도를 / 더 먼 거리를 가고, 천적을 피하고, 먹이를 포획하고, 새끼를 낳고 돌볼 수 있게 하는 //

Mammals are able to live / in an incredible variety of habitats, / from Arctic tundra to Antarctic pack ice, / deep open waters to high-altitude mountaintops, / and rainforests to deserts, /
from A to B: A에서 B까지   앞에 from 생략   앞에 from 생략
포유류는 살 수 있다 / 매우 다양한 서식지에서 / 북극 툰드라부터 남극의 유빙까지 / 심해부터 고도가 높은 산꼭대기까지 / 그리고 열대 우림부터 사막까지 /

in no small measure because of their teeth. //
어느 정도는 그들의 이빨로 인해 //

- particle ⓝ 작은 조각
- swallow ⓥ 삼키다
- expose ⓥ 노출하다
- digestive ⓐ 소화의
- act on ~에 작용하다
- extraction ⓝ 추출
- raw material 원료
- mouthful ⓝ 한 입
- mammal ⓝ 포유류
- sustain ⓥ 유지하다
- predator ⓝ 포식자, 천적
- capture ⓥ 포획하다
- prey ⓝ 먹이
- habitat ⓝ 서식지
- Arctic ⓐ 북극의
- Antarctic ⓐ 남극의
- pack ice 총빙(叢氷), 유빙
- high-altitude ⓐ 고도가 높은
- mountaintop ⓝ 산꼭대기
- in no small measure 어느 정도
- ease ⓥ 완화시키다
- indigestion ⓝ 소화불량
- harsh ⓐ 가혹한

씹기는 삼킴을 위한 더 작은 조각들과 소화 효소가 작용하는 더 노출된 표면으로 이어진다. 다시 말해서, 한 입의 음식으로부터 더 많은 연료와 원료를 추출하는 것을 의미한다. 이것은 그들이 체내에서 자신의 몸을 따뜻하게 하기 때문에 포유류에게 특히 중요하다. 씹기는 포유류에게 낮은 물론 서늘한 밤 동안에도 활동하고, 더 추운 기후나 기온이 변하는 장소에서 사는 데 필요한 에너지를 준다. 그것은 그들에게 더 먼 거리를 가고, 천적을 피하고, 먹이를 포획하고 새끼를 낳고 돌볼 수 있게 하는 더 높은 수준의 활동과 이동 속도를 유지하게 한다. 포유류는 어느 정도는 그들의 이빨로 인해 북극 툰드라부터 남극의 유빙까지, 심해부터 고도가 높은 산꼭대기까지 그리고 열대 우림부터 사막까지 매우 다양한 서식지에서 살 수 있다.

다음 글의 제목으로 가장 적절한 것은?

① Chewing: A Way to Ease Indigestion
씹기: 소화불량을 완화시키는 방법 씹기가 소화불량을 완화시킨다는 언급은 없음
② Boost Your Energy by Chewing More!
더 많이 씹어서 당신의 에너지를 북돋우세요! 중심 소재인 포유류의 생존과 관련이 없음
③ How Chewing Helps Mammals Survive
씹기가 포유류의 생존을 돕는 방식 씹기가 포유류에게 에너지를 주고 활동과 이동을 돕는다고 했음
④ Different Types and Functions of Teeth
이빨의 여러 가지 형태와 기능 이빨의 형태와 기능에 대해서는 언급하지 않음
⑤ A Harsh Climate Makes Mammals Stronger
혹독한 기후가 포유류를 더 강하게 만든다 중심 소재인 씹기가 포함되어 있지 않음

>왜 정답? ★★⊛ [정답률 77%]

씹기가 포유에게 필요한 에너지를 주며 더 높은 수준의 활동과 이동 속도를 유지하게 해 준다는 내용의 글이다. 따라서 이 글의 내용을 포괄할 수 있는 ③ '씹기가 포유동물이 생존하도록 돕는 방식'이 글의 제목으로 가장 적절하다.

>왜 오답?

① 씹기가 소화불량을 완화시킨다는 언급은 나오지 않았다.
② 중심 소재인 포유류의 생존에 대한 내용을 포함하고 있지 않다.
④ 이빨의 형태와 기능에 대해서는 언급되지 않았다.
🎀 ⑤ 이 글의 중심 소재인 씹기가 포함되어 있지 않으므로 글의 내용을 포괄할 수 없는 제목이다.

자이 쌤's Follow Me! —홈페이지에서 제공

G 12 정답 ② *결코 지나치지 않은 교육

명사절 접속사
In life, / they say / that too much of anything / is not good for you. //
삶에서 / 그들은 말한다 / 어떤 것이든 과도하면 / 여러분에게 이롭지 않다고 //

In fact, / too much of certain things / in life / can kill you. //
실제로 / 과도한 어떤 것은 / 삶에서 / 여러분을 죽일 수 있다 //

For example, / they say / that water has no enemy, / because water is essential / to all life. //
예를 들어, / 그들은 말한다 / 물은 적이 없다고 / 물이 필수적이기 때문에 / 모든 생물에게 //

조건의 부사절 접속사
But if you take in too much water, / like one who is drowning, /
주절
it could kill you. //
그러나 만일 여러분이 너무 많은 물을 들이마시면 / 물에 빠진 사람처럼 / 그것은 여러분을 죽일 수 있다 //

Education is the exception / to this rule. // **단서 1** 뭐든지 과하면 안 된다는 규칙의 예외가 교육임
교육은 예외다 / 이 규칙에서 //

You can never have / too much education or knowledge. // **단서 2** 교육이나 지식은 아무리 많아도 지나치지 않음
여러분은 결코 가질 수 없다 / 너무 많은 교육이나 지식을 //

주격 보어절 접속사
The reality is / that most people will never have enough education / in their lifetime. //
실상은 ~이다 / 대부분의 사람은 결코 충분한 교육을 갖지 않을 것이라는 것 / 그들의 일생에서 //

선행사 주격 관계대명사 전치사
I am yet to find that one person / who has been hurt in life / by
명사구
too much education. //
나는 그 한 사람을 아직 본 적이 없다 / 삶에서 피해를 본 / 너무 많은 교육에 의해 //

Rather, / we see lots of casualties / every day, worldwide, /
오히려 / 우리는 수많은 피해자들을 본다 / 매일 전 세계에서 /

resulting from the lack of education. //
교육의 부족으로 인해 생긴 //

명사절 접속사
You must keep in mind / that education is a long-term investment / of time, money, and effort / into humans. //
여러분은 명심해야 한다 / 교육이 장기적인 투자임을 / 시간, 돈, 그리고 노력의 / 인간에게 //

- be good for ~에 좋다
- enemy ⓝ 적
- essential ⓐ 필수적인
- take in ~을 들이마시다
- drown ⓥ 물에 빠져 죽다, 익사하다
- education ⓝ 교육
- exception ⓝ 예외
- knowledge ⓝ 지식
- in one's lifetime 평생
- be yet to-v 아직 ~하지 못하다
- hurt ⓥ 피해를 보다
- long-term ⓐ 장기적인
- investment ⓝ 투자

사람들은 삶에서 어떤 것이든 과도하면 여러분에게 이롭지 않다고 한다. 실제로, 삶에서 과도한 어떤 것은 여러분을 죽일 수 있다. 예를 들어, 물은 모든 생물에게 필수적이기 때문에 적이 없다고 한다. 그러나 만일 여러분이 물에 빠진 사람처럼 너무 많은 물을 들이마시면 그것은 여러분을 죽일 수 있다. 교육은 이 규칙에서 예외다. 교육이나 지식은 아무리 많이 있어도 지나치지 않다. 실상은 대부분의 사람은 그들의 일생에서 결코 충분한 교육을 받지 않을 거라는 것이다. 나는 너무 많은 교육에 의해 삶에서 피해를 본 한 사람을 아직 본 적이 없다. 오히려 우리는 매일, 전 세계에서 교육의 부족으로 인해 생긴 수많은 피해자들을 본다. 교육이 인간에게 시간, 돈, 그리고 노력을 장기 투자하는 것임을 명심해야 한다.

다음 글의 제목으로 가장 적절한 것은?

① All Play and No Work Makes Jack a Smart Boy 교육의 중요성을 이야기함
놀기만 하고 공부하지 않으면 똑똑해진다
② Too Much Education Won't Hurt You You can never have too much
아무리 교육을 많이 받아도 해롭지 않을 것이다 education or knowledge.에 드러남
③ Two Heads Are Worse than One 혼자 하는 것이 좋다는 내용이 아님
두 머리를 맞대는 것이 하나의 머리보다 더 좋지 않다
④ Don't Think Twice Before You Act 신중함의 악영향에 대한 언급은 없음
행동하기 전에 두 번 생각하지 마라
⑤ Learn from the Future, Not from the Past 과거나 미래에 대한
과거가 아니라 미래로부터 배워라 언급은 없음

>왜 정답? ★★⊛ [정답률 75%]

과도한 것은 해를 끼친다는 규칙의 예외가 교육이라고 하면서 교육이나 지식은 아무리 많이 가져도 결코 지나치지 않다고 했으므로 제목으로 적절한 것은 ② '아무리 교육을 많이 받아도 해롭지 않을 것이다'이다.

>왜 오답? All works and no play makes Jack a dull boy. (놀지 않고 공부만 하면 바보가 된다.)라는 속담을 반대로 활용한 선택지임 꿀팁

① 공부, 교육의 중요성을 이야기하는 글이므로 제목으로 적절하지 않다.
③ 백지장도 맞들면 낫다는 속담을 반대로 이야기한 것으로, 혼자 하는 것의 장점을 이야기하는 글이 아니다.
④ 신중하게 행동하는 것이 가져오는 나쁜 결과에 대한 글이 아니다.
⑤ 교육에 대한 내용이긴 하지만 과거로부터 배우라거나 미래로부터 배우라는 언급은 없다.

G 13 정답 ⑤ *불필요한 소비로 인한 낭비

Think, for a moment, / about something you bought / **that** you
never ended up using. //
단서 1 사놓고 한 번도 사용하지 않았던 물건에 대해 생각해보라고 했음
잠시 생각해 봐라 / 여러분이 사 놓은 물건에 대해 / 결국 한 번도 사용하지 않았던 //

An item of clothing / **you never ended up wearing**? //
옷 한 벌 / 결국 한 번도 입지 않은 //

A book / **you never read**? // 책 한 권 / 한 번도 읽지 않은 //

Some piece of electronic equipment / that never even made it
out of the box? // 어떤 전자 기기 / 심지어 상자에서 꺼내 보지도 않은 //

It is estimated / **that** Australians alone spend / on average $10.8
billion AUD (approximately $9.99 billion USD) every year /
추산되는데 / 호주인들이 단독으로 쓴다 / 매년 평균 108억 호주 달러(약 99억 9천 미국 달러)를 /

on goods **they do not use** / — more than the total government
spending / on universities and roads. //
사용하지 않는 물건에 / 이는 정부 지출 총액을 넘는 금액이다 / 대학과 도로에 사용하는 //

That is an average of $1,250 AUD (approximately $1,156 USD) /
for each household. //
그 금액은 평균 1,250 호주 달러(약 1,156 미국 달러)이다 / 각 가구당 /
단서 2 우리가 사놓고 먼지가 쌓일 정도로 사용하지 않는 것은 낭비라고 했음

All the things **we buy** / **that** then just sit there gathering dust /
are waste / — a waste of money, a waste of time, and waste / in
the sense of pure rubbish. //
우리가 사는 모든 물건은 / 구매 이후에 제자리에서 먼지를 끌어모으기만 하는 / 낭비인데 / 돈 낭비, 시간 낭비, 그리고 낭비다 / 순전히 쓸모없는 물건이라는 의미에서 //

As the author Clive Hamilton observes, / 'The difference
between / the stuff we buy / **and** what we use / is waste.' //
작가인 Clive Hamilton이 말하는 것처럼 / 둘 사이의 차이점은 / 사는 물건과 / 우리가 사용하는 것의 / 낭비다 //
단서 3 사는 물건과 사용하는 물건의 차이는 낭비라고 말한 작가의 말을 인용함

- end up -ing 결국 ~하다 · electronic equipment 전자 기기
- estimate ⓥ 추산하다 · average ⓝ 평균 · billion ⓝ 십 억
- approximately ⓐⓓ 약, 대략 · goods ⓝ 물건, 제품, 상품
- household ⓝ 가구, 세대 · gather ⓥ 모으다 · dust ⓝ 먼지
- waste ⓝ 낭비, 쓰레기 · in the sense of ~이라는 의미에서
- pure ⓐ 순전한, 순수한 · rubbish ⓝ 쓸모없는 물건, 쓰레기
- observe ⓥ (발언, 의견을) 말하다

여러분이 사 놓고 결국 한 번도 사용하지 않았던 물건에 대해 잠시 생각해 봐라. 결국 한 번도 입지 않은 옷 한 벌? 한 번도 읽지 않은 책 한 권? 심지어 상자에서 꺼내 보지도 않은 어떤 전자 기기? 사용하지 않는 물건에 단독으로 호주인들이 매년 평균 108억 호주 달러(약 99억 9천 미국 달러)를 쓰는 것으로 추산되는데, 이는 대학과 도로에 사용하는 정부 지출 총액을 넘는 금액이다. 그 금액은 각 가구당 평균 1,250 호주 달러(약 1,156 미국 달러)이다. 우리가 사고 나서 제자리에서 먼지를 끌어모으기만 하는 모든 물건은 낭비인데, 돈 낭비, 시간 낭비, 그리고 순전히 쓸모없는 물건이라는 의미에서 낭비이다. 작가인 Clive Hamilton이 말하는 것처럼 "우리가 사는 물건에서 우리가 사용하는 것을 뺀 것은 낭비다."

다음 글의 제목으로 가장 적절한 것은?
① Spending Enables the Economy 사용하지 않을 것을 사는 것은 낭비라고 했으므로 글과 반대라고 할 수 있다
지출은 경제를 활성화시킨다
② Money Management: Dos and Don'ts 돈 관리는 관련이 없는 내용임
돈 관리: 해야 할 것과 하지 말아야 할 것
③ Too Much Shopping: A Sign of Loneliness 안 쓸 것을 사는 것에 대해 말했지만, 외로움에 대한 내용은 언급되지 않음
과도한 쇼핑: 외로움의 징후
④ 3R's of Waste: Reduce, Reuse, and Recycle 'waste'는 언급되었으나 폐기에 대해서 다루고 있지는 않음
쓰레기의 3R: 줄이기 재사용하기 그리고 재활용하기
⑤ What You Buy Is Waste Unless You Use It
사용하지 않는다면 당신이 사는 것은 쓰레기이다 사고 쓰지 않으면 낭비가 된다는 내용

왜 정답? ★★★❋ [정답률 79%]

호주인들이 사용하지 않는 물건에 쓰는 돈이 엄청나다고 하면서, 물건을 사기만 하고 사용하지 않는다면 결국에는 무의미한 낭비가 된다는 내용이다. 따라서 정답은 ⑤ '사용하지 않는다면 당신이 사는 것은 쓰레기이다'.

왜 오답?
① 소비가 경제를 돌아가게 만든다는 내용은 낭비를 지양하자는 이 글의 주제와 반대라고 할 수 있다.
② 돈 관리에 있어서 해야 할 것과 하지 말아야 할 것은 낭비와 상관없는 내용이다.
③ 과도한 쇼핑을 한다는 것은 이 글과 같은 맥락으로 볼 수 있지만 외로움에 대해서는 언급되지 않았다. 함정
④ 이 글에서 waste라는 단어가 나왔지만, 쓰레기 처리 방법은 관련이 없다.

G 14 정답 ② *새로운 직업을 창출하는 AI

단서 1 직업 손실과 관련된 글임을 시사함
The loss of many traditional jobs / in everything / from art to
healthcare / **will partly be** offset / by the creation of new human
jobs. //
많은 전통적인 직업의 소실은 / 모든 것에서 / 예술부터 건강관리에 이르는 / 부분적으로 상쇄될 것이다 / 인간의 새로운 직업의 생성에 의해서 //

Primary care doctors / **who** focus on **diagnosing** known diseases /
and **giving** familiar treatments / **will probably be replaced** / by
AI doctors. //
일반 진료 의사들은 / 밝혀진 질병을 진단하는 데 집중하는 / 그리고 일반적인 처방을 내리는 / 아마도 대체될 것이다 / AI 의사에 의해 //

But / precisely because of that, / there will be **much** more money /
to pay human doctors and lab assistants / **to do** groundbreaking
research / and **develop** new medicines or surgical procedures. //
그러나 / 정확히 그것 때문에 / 돈이 훨씬 더 많을 것이다 / 인간 의사와 실험실 조교에게 지급할 / 획기적인 연구를 하도록 / 그리고 새로운 약이나 수술 절차를 개발하도록 //

AI might help / create new human jobs / in another way. //
AI는 도울지도 모른다 / 인간의 새로운 직업을 만드는 것을 / 또 다른 방식으로 //

Instead of humans competing with AI, / **they** could focus on
servicing and using AI. //
인간이 AI와 경쟁하는 대신에 / 그들은 AI를 정비하고 활용하는 것에 집중할 수 있다 //
단서 2 AI가 새로운 직업 창출에 도움이 될 수 있다는 점을 제시함

For example, / the replacement of human pilots / by drones / **has
eliminated** some jobs / but **created** many new opportunities / in
maintenance, remote control, data analysis, / and cyber security. //
예를 들어 / 인간 조종사의 대체는 / 드론에 의한 / 몇몇 직업을 없애 왔다 / 그러나 많은 새로운 기회를 만들어 왔다 / 정비, 원격조종, 데이터분석에 있어서 / 그리고 사이버 보안(에 있어서) //
단서 3 AI가 새로운 직업을 창출해낸 구체적 사례를 제시함

- partly ⓐⓓ 부분적으로
- primary care doctor 일반 진료 의사, 1차 진료 의사
- diagnose ⓥ 진단하다 · treatment ⓝ 처방, 치료
- be replaced by ~에 의해 대체되다 · groundbreaking ⓐ 획기적인
- surgical ⓐ 수술의, 외과의 · procedure ⓝ 절차
- drone ⓝ 드론 · eliminate ⓥ 없애다, 제거하다
- maintenance ⓝ 정비 · analysis ⓝ 분석
- security ⓝ 보안, 안보

예술부터 건강관리에 이르는 모든 것에서 많은 전통적인 직업의 소실은 인간의 새로운 직업의 생성에 의해서 부분적으로 상쇄될 것이다. 밝혀진 질병을 진단하고 일반적인 처방을 내리는 일을 주로 하는 일반 진료 의사들은 아마도 AI 의사에 의해 대체될 것이다. 그러나 정확히 그것 때문에, 획기적인 연구를 하고 새로운 약이나 수술 절차를 개발하도록 인간 의사와 실험실 조교에게 지급할 돈이 훨씬 더 많을 것이다. AI는 또 다른 방식으로 인간의 새로운 직업을 만드는 것을 도울지도 모른다. 인간이 AI와 경쟁하는 대신에, 그들은 AI를 정비하고 활용하는 것에 집중할 수 있다. 예를 들어, 드론에 의한 인간 조종사의 대체는 몇몇 직업을 없애 왔지만, 정비, 원격조종, 데이터분석, 그리고 사이버 보안에 있어서 많은 새로운 기회를 만들어 왔다.

다음 글의 제목으로 가장 적절한 것은?

① What Makes Robots Smarter? 로봇을 똑똑하게 만드는 것에 대한 글이 아님
   무엇이 로봇을 더 똑똑하게 만드는가?
②Is AI Really a Threat to Your Job? AI로 인해 수많은 다양한 직업이 만들어질
   AI가 당신의 직업에 정말로 위협이 되는가? 수 있다는 내용
③ Watch Out! AI Can Read Your Mind AI가 글의 핵심 소재라는 것으로 만든
   조심하세요! AI가 당신의 마음을 읽을 수 있어요 오답
④ Future Jobs: Less Work, More Gains 미래의 직업이 일은 더 적게 하고
   미래의 직업: 일은 더 적게 하고 수익은 더 많이 얻는다 수익은 더 많이 얻는다는 내용은 언급되지 않음
⑤ Ongoing Challenges for AI Development
   지속적인 AI 개발 과제 AI의 개발과는 관련이 없는 글임

>왜 정답? **❀ [정답률 77%]

의사가 AI 의사로 대체되는 등 인간의 직업이 AI에 의해 대체될 수 있지만, 이와 동시에 AI로 인해서 수많은 다양한 직업이 만들어질 수 있다는 내용의 글이다. 따라서 이 글의 제목으로 가장 적절한 것은 ② 'AI가 당신의 직업에 정말로 위협이 되는가?'이다.

>왜 오답?

① 로봇을 똑똑하게 만드는 것에 대해서는 아무런 내용이 언급되지 않았다.
③ AI가 글의 핵심 소재라는 점에 착안하여 만든 오답이다.
④ 일은 더 적게 하고 수익은 더 많이 얻게 된다는 미래의 직업과 관련된 내용은 언급되지 않았다.
⑤ 글의 전체적인 내용이 AI 개발을 위한 지속적인 과제와는 전혀 관련이 없다.

---- 배경 지식 ----

＊ 인공 지능(AI)
   인공 지능이란 컴퓨터가 인간처럼 사고하도록 만든 체계를 말한다. 하지만 컴퓨터가 스스로 인간과 같은 생각을 하고 판단하는 것은 아직 더 개발이 필요하다. 컴퓨터는 엄청나게 많은 정보와 굉장히 빠른 처리 속도를 가지고 있어서 그중에서 하나를 선택하는 수준이라고 볼 수 있다.

G 15 정답 ② ＊성공이 불러올 수 있는 문제점

전치사구의 병렬 구조
Success can lead you / off your intended path / and into a comfortable rut. // 단서1 성공은 틀에 박힌 편안한 생활로 이끌 수 있음
성공은 여러분을 이끌 수 있다 / 여러분이 의도한 길에서 벗어나 / 틀에 박힌 편안한 생활로 //

If you are good at something / and are well rewarded for doing
                              부사절 접속사(양보)
it, / you may want to keep doing it / even if you stop enjoying
it. //
여러분이 어떤 일을 잘하고 / 그것을 하는 것에 대한 보상을 잘 받는다면 / 계속 그것을 하고
싶을 수도 있다 / 그것을 즐기지 않게 되더라도 //
                 주격 보어절 접속사
The danger is / that one day you look around and realize /
       so ~ that ...: 너무 ~해서 …하다
you're so deep in this comfortable rut / that you can no longer
see the sun / or breathe fresh air; /
위험한 점은 ~이다 / 어느 날 여러분이 주변을 둘러보고 깨닫게 된다는 것 / 자신이 틀에 박힌
이 편안한 생활에 너무나 깊이 빠져 있어서 / 더는 태양을 보거나 / 신선한 공기를 호흡할 수
없다는 것을 /
                                      so ~ that ...: 너무 ~해서 …하다
the sides of the rut / have become so slippery / that it would take
a superhuman effort / to climb out; / and, effectively, you're
stuck. // 단서2 틀에 박힌 생활에서 빠져나오려면 초인적인 노력이 필요함
그 틀에 박힌 생활의 양쪽 면이 / 너무나 미끄럽게 되어 / 초인적인 노력이 필요할 것이다 /
기어올라 나오려면 / 그리고 사실상 여러분이 꼼짝할 수 없다는 것을 //
                      동격절 접속사
And it's a situation / that many working people worry / they're
in now. //
그리고 그것은 상황이다 / 많은 근로자가 걱정하는 / 현재 자신이 처해 있다고 //

The poor employment market / has left them feeling locked / in
선행사를 포함하는 관계대명사
what may be a secure, or even well-paying / — but ultimately
unsatisfying — job. // 단서3 안정적이지만 불만족스러운 일자리에 갇혀 있다고 느끼게 됨
열악한 고용 시장이 / 그들을 갇혀 있다고 느끼게 해 놓았다 / 안정적이거나 심지어 보수가
좋을 수도 있지만 / 궁극적으로는 만족스럽지 못한 일자리에 //

• lead ⓥ 이끌다 • intend ⓥ 의도하다 • path ⓝ 길
• reward ⓥ 보상하다 • realize ⓥ 깨닫다 • breathe ⓥ 호흡하다
• slippery ⓐ 미끄러운 • superhuman ⓐ 초인적인
• effectively ⓐⓓ 사실상, 실제로 • employment ⓝ 고용
• secure ⓐ 안정적인 • ultimately ⓐⓓ 궁극적으로
• unsatisfying ⓐ 만족스럽지 못한 • trap ⓝ 함정, 덫
• influential ⓐ 영향력 있는

성공은 여러분을 의도한 길에서 벗어나 틀에 박힌 편안한 생활로 이끌 수 있다. 여러분이 어떤 일을 잘하고 그것을 하는 것에 대한 보상을 잘 받는다면, 그것을 즐기지 않게 되더라도 계속 그것을 하고 싶을 수도 있다. 위험한 점은 어느 날 여러분이 주변을 둘러보고, 자신이 틀에 박힌 이 편안한 생활에 너무나 깊이 빠져 있어서 더는 태양을 보거나 신선한 공기를 호흡할 수 없으며, 그 틀에 박힌 생활의 양쪽 면이 너무나 미끄럽게 되어 기어올라 나오려면 초인적인 노력이 필요할 것이고, 사실상 자신이 꼼짝할 수 없다는 것을 깨닫게 된다는 것이다. 그리고 그것은 많은 근로자가 현재 자신이 처해 있다고 걱정하는 상황이다. 열악한 고용 시장이 그들을 안정적이거나 심지어 보수가 좋을 수도 있지만, 궁극적으로는 만족스럽지 못한 일자리에 갇혀 있다고 느끼게 해 놓았다.

다음 글의 제목으로 가장 적절한 것은?

① Don't Compete with Yourself 현실에 안주하지 말라는 내용임
   자신과 경쟁하지 말라
②A Trap of a Successful Career
   성공적인 커리어의 함정 성공적인 커리어를 가졌을 때 야기될 수 있는 문제점에 관한 내용임
③ Create More Jobs for Young People
   젊은이들을 위한 더 많은 직업을 만들어라 직업이 부족하다는 내용이 아님
④ What Difficult Jobs Have in Common
   어려운 직업들이 공통으로 갖는 것 어려운 직업들에 관한 내용은 언급되지 않음
⑤ A Road Map for an Influential Employer
   영향력 있는 고용주를 위한 지침 영향력 있는 고용주가 되라는 내용이 아님

>왜 정답? **❀ [정답률 71%]

• 성공은 틀에 박힌 편안한 생활로 이끌 수 있음 단서1
• 틀에 박힌 생활에서 빠져나오려면 초인적인 노력이 필요함 단서2
• 안정적이지만 불만족스러운 일자리에 갇혀 있다고 느끼게 됨 단서3

➡ 성공적인 커리어로 인해 편안한 생활에 오히려 갇히게 된다는 내용이므로 정답은 ② '성공적인 커리어의 함정'이다.

>왜 오답?

① 자신과 경쟁하지 말라는 내용이 아니다.
③ 젊은이들을 위한 더 많은 일자리를 만들라는 내용이 아니다.
④ 어려운 직업들에 대한 내용은 없다.
⑤ 고용주에게만 국한된 내용이 아니다.

G 16 정답 ② ＊인간이 지루함을 느끼는 이유

Kids tire of their toys, / college students get sick of cafeteria
food, / and sooner or later most of us / lose interest in our
favorite TV shows. //
아이들은 자기들의 장난감에 지루해하고 / 대학생들은 카페테리아 음식에 싫증을 내고 /
머지않아 우리 중 대부분은 / 우리가 가장 좋아하는 TV 쇼에 흥미를 잃는다 //
                   명사절 접속사   과거분사(주격 보어)
The bottom line is / that we humans are easily bored. //
요점은 / 우리 인간이 쉽게 지루해한다는 것이다 // 단서1 인간은 쉽게 지루함을 느낌

But why should this be true? //
그런데 왜 이것이 사실이어야 할까 //
                    과거분사(주격 보어)   주격 관계대명사
The answer lies buried deep in our nerve cells, / which are
designed to reduce / their initial excited response to stimuli /
each time they occur. // 단서2 인간은 신경학적으로 같은 자극이 반복될 때마다 반응이
                              약화되도록 설계됨
답은 우리의 신경 세포 내에 깊이 숨어 있다 / 약화하도록 설계된 / 그것에 대한 초기의 흥분된
반응을 / 자극이 일어날 때마다 //

At the same time, / these neurons enhance their responses / to
things that change / — especially things that change quickly. //
주격 관계대명사   주격 관계대명사
동시에 / 이 뉴런들은 반응을 강화한다 / 변화하는 것들에 대한 / 특히 빠르게 변화하는 것들에 //

We probably evolved this way / because our ancestors got more
survival value, / for example, from attending to / what was
선행사를 포함한 관계대명사   강조 용법의 재귀대명사
moving in a tree / (such as a puma) / than to the tree itself. //
우리는 아마도 이런 방식으로 진화했을 것이다 / 우리의 조상이 더 많은 생존 가치를 얻었기
때문에 / 예를 들면 주의를 기울이는 것으로부터 / 나무에서 움직이는 것에 / (퓨마처럼) / 나무
그 자체보다 //

<단서3> 인간은 변하지 않는 환경에 지루함을 느끼고,
새로운 자극을 두드러지게 느끼는 것이 생존에 유리했음

Boredom in reaction to an unchanging environment / turns
down the level of neural excitation / so that new stimuli / (like
our ancestor's hypothetical puma threat) / stand out more. //
변하지 않는 환경에 대한 반응으로의 지루함은 / 신경 흥분의 수준을 낮춰 / 새로운 자극이 /
(우리 조상이 가정한 퓨마의 위협과 같은) / 더 두드러지게 한다 //

It's the neural equivalent / of turning off a front door light / to
부사적 용법(목적)
see the fireflies. //
이것은 신경적 대응물이다 / 앞문의 불을 끄는 것의 / 반딧불이를 보기 위해 //

- tire of ~에 질리다[싫증이 나다]   · get sick of ~에 싫증이 나다
- cafeteria ⓝ 구내식당, 카페테리아   · sooner or later 머지않아
- the bottom line is ~ 요점은 ~이다   · be designed to ~하도록 설계되다
- initial ⓐ 초기의   · response ⓝ 반응
- stimulus ⓝ 자극(pl. stimuli)   · occur ⓥ 발생하다
- enhance ⓥ 강화하다   · especially ⓐⓓ 특히   · value ⓝ 가치
- threat ⓝ 위협   · firefly ⓝ 반딧불이   · brilliant ⓐ 영특한
- detect ⓥ 감지하다   · destruction ⓝ 파괴

아이들은 자기들의 장난감에 지루해하고, 대학생들은 카페테리아 음식에 싫증
을 내고, 머지않아 우리 중 대부분은 우리가 가장 좋아하는 TV 쇼에 흥미를 잃
는다. 요점은 우리 인간이 쉽게 지루해한다는 것이다. 그런데 왜 이것이 사실이
어야 할까? 답은 자극이 일어날 때마다 그것에 대한 초기의 흥분된 반응을 약화
하도록 설계된 우리의 신경 세포 내에 깊이 숨어 있다. 동시에 이 뉴런들은 변
화하는 것들, 특히 빠르게 변화하는 것들에 대한 반응을 강화한다. 예를 들면
우리는 아마도 우리의 조상이 나무 그 자체보다 (퓨마처럼) 나무에서 움직이는
것에 주의를 기울이는 것으로부터 더 많은 생존 가치를 얻었기 때문에 이런 방
식으로 진화했을 것이다. 변하지 않는 환경에 대한 반응으로의 지루함은 신경
흥분의 수준을 낮춰 (우리 조상이 가정한 퓨마의 위협과 같은) 새로운 자극이
더 두드러지게 한다. 이것은 반딧불이를 보기 위해 앞문의 불을 끄는 것의 신경
적 대응물이다.

다음 글의 제목으로 가장 적절한 것은?
① The Brain's Brilliant Trick to Overcome Fear
두려움을 극복하기 위한 뇌의 영특한 속임수   puma threat이 언급된 것으로 만든 오답
②Boredom: Neural Mechanism for Detecting Change 지루함을
지루함: 변화를 감지하기 위한 신경학적 메커니즘   느낌으로써 변화하는 환경을 더욱 잘 감지하게 됨
③Humans' Endless Desire to Pursue Familiar Experiences
익숙한 경험을 추구하고자 하는 인간의 끊임없는 욕구
④The Destruction of Nature in Exchange for Human
Survival 자연 파괴에 관한 내용은 언급되지 않음
인간의 생존과 맞교환한 자연 파괴
⑤How Humans Changed the Environment to Their
Advantage 인간은 환경을 바꾼 것이 아니라 생존에 유리한 방식으로 진화했다고 함
인간이 자신의 이익을 위해 환경을 바꾼 방법
- 인간이 익숙한 경험을 추구한다는 내용은 언급되지 않음

> 왜 정답 ? ✱✱ ✽ [정답률 78%]

현상: 인간은 쉽게 지루함을 느낌 <단서1>
이유: 인간은 신경학적으로 같은 자극이 반복될 때마다 반응이 약해짐 <단서2>
근거: 인간은 변하지 않는 환경에 지루함을 느끼고, 새로운 자극을 두드러지게 느끼는
것이 생존에 유리했음 <단서3>
예시: 움직이지 않는 나무에 주의를 기울이는 것보다, 나무에서 움직이는 퓨마에
주의를 기울이는 것이 생존에 유리함
➡ 인간은 변하지 않는 상황에 쉽게 지루함을 느끼고, 변화하는 상황에 빠르고
강력하게 반응한다. 그것이 생존에 더 유리했기 때문에 인간은 그러한 방식으로
진화했다고 설명하고 있다.
▶ 따라서 글의 제목으로 가장 적절한 것은 ② '지루함: 변화를 감지하기 위한
신경학적 메커니즘'이다.

> 왜 오답 ?
① 두려움을 극복하기 위한 전략이 아니라, 변화를 빠르게 감지하기 위한 전략이 주된
내용이다.
③ 인간이 익숙한 경험을 추구한다는 내용이 아니라, 오히려 싫증을 낸다는 내용이다. <주의>
④ 자연 파괴에 관한 내용은 언급되지 않았다.
⑤ 인간은 환경을 바꾼 것이 아니라 생존에 유리한 방식으로 진화했다고 했다.

G 17 정답 ① *더 많은 용기는 더 많은 기회를 가져온다.

<단서1> 안전 구역에서만 움직여서 더 위대한 일을 달성할 기회를 놓침
Many people make a mistake / of only operating / along the
safe zones, / and in the process / they miss the opportunity / to
형용사적 용법
achieve greater things. //
많은 사람들이 실수를 저지른다 / 오직 움직이는 / 안전 구역에서 / 그 과정에서 / 그들은
기회를 놓친다 / 더 위대한 일들을 달성할 //

They do so / because of a fear of the unknown / and a fear of
treading / the unknown paths of life. //
그들은 그렇게 한다 / 미지의 세계에 대한 두려움 때문에 / 그리고 밟는 것에 대한 두려움
(때문에) / 알려지지 않은 삶의 경로를 //
핵심 주어   주격 관계대명사
Those that are brave / enough to take those roads / less travelled
/ are able to get great returns / and derive major satisfaction / out
동사의 병렬 구조
of their courageous moves. //
용감한 사람들은 / 이런 길을 택할 만큼 충분히 / 사람들이 잘 다니지 않는 / 엄청난 보상을
받는 것을 할 수 있다 / 그리고 큰 만족감을 끌어내는 것을 / 그들의 용감한 행동으로부터 //
목적어절을 이끄는 접속사
Being overcautious will mean / that you will miss / attaining the
greatest levels / of your potential. // <단서2> 지나치게 조심하면 최고 수준의
지나치게 조심하는 것은 의미할 것이다 / 놓친다는 것을 / 최고 수준을 달성하는 것을 / 잠재력을 달성할 기회를 놓침
여러분의 잠재력의 //
동격절 접속사
You must learn / to take those chances that many people
around you / will not take, / because your success will flow /
목적격 관계대명사
from those bold decisions / that you will take / along the way. //
여러분은 배워야 한다 / 기회를 택하는 것을 / 주변에 있는 많은 사람들이 / 선택하지 않을 /
왜냐하면 여러분의 성공은 나올 것이기 때문이다 / 용감한 결정으로부터 / 여러분이 내릴 /
삶의 과정에서 //
핵심문장 <단서3> 용감한 결정은 성공을 가져올 수 있음

- operate ⓥ 움직이다   · process ⓝ 과정   · path ⓝ 경로
- return ⓝ 보상   · derive ⓥ 끌어내다   · satisfaction ⓝ 만족
- courageous ⓐ 용감한   · move ⓝ 행동
- overcautious ⓐ 지나치게 조심하는   · attain ⓥ 달성하다
- flow ⓥ 흐르다, 나오다   · bold ⓐ 용감한   · courage ⓝ 용기
- satisfying ⓐ 만족스러운   · overcome ⓥ 극복하다

많은 사람들이 안전 구역에서만 움직이는 실수를 저지르고, 그 과정에서
더 위대한 일들을 달성할 기회를 놓친다. 그들은 미지의 세계에 대한
두려움과 알려지지 않은 삶의 경로를 밟는 것에 대한 두려움 때문에
그렇게 한다. 사람들이 잘 다니지 않는 이런 길을 택할 만큼 충분히 용감한
사람들은 엄청난 보상을 받을 수 있고 그들의 용감한 행동으로부터 큰
만족감을 끌어낼 수 있다. 지나치게 조심하는 것은 여러분의 잠재력의
최고 수준을 달성하는 것을 놓친다는 것을 의미할 것이다. 여러분은
주변에 있는 많은 사람들이 선택하지 않을 기회를 택하는 것을 배워야
하는데, 왜냐하면 여러분의 성공은 삶의 과정에서 여러분이 내릴 용감한
결정으로부터 나올 것이기 때문이다.

다음 글의 제목으로 가장 적절한 것은?
용기를 내어 알려지지 않은 길을 택하면 성공과 잠재력 달성의 기회가 더 생긴다는 내용
①More Courage Brings More Opportunities
더 많은 용기는 더 많은 기회를 가져온다
②Travel: The Best Way to Make Friends 잘 다니지 않는 길을 택한다는
여행: 친구를 사귀는 최고의 방법   것을 여행으로 연결시켜 만든 오답
③How to Turn Mistakes into Success
실수를 성공으로 바꾸는 방법   실수를 성공으로 바꾸는 방법은 나오지 않음
④Satisfying Life? Share with Others 삶을 다른 사람과 공유하라는 내용이 아님
만족스러운 삶? 다른 사람들과 공유하세요
⑤Why Is Overcoming Fear So Hard? 두려움 때문에 안전 구역에서만
왜 두려움을 극복하는 것이 그렇게 어려운가?   움직인다는 언급으로 만든 함정

마지막 문장이 이 글의 핵심문장이다. 사람들이 안전 구역에서만 움직여서 더 위대한 일을 달성할 기회를 놓치고, 지나치게 조심하면 최고 수준의 잠재력을 달성할 기회를 놓친다고 하면서 다른 사람이 택하지 않은 길을 택하는 용기를 보이는 것이 성공을 가져올 수 있다는 내용이다.

따라서 이 글의 제목으로 가장 적절한 것은 ① '더 많은 용기는 더 많은 기회를 가져온다'이다.

>**왜 오답**?
② 잘 다니지 않는 길을 택한다는 언급으로 만든 오답일 뿐, 여행이 친구를 사귀는 최고의 방법이라는 내용은 없다. **주의**
③ 실수를 성공으로 바꾸는 방법을 이야기하는 글이 아니다.
④ 삶에 만족하는지를 묻고 삶을 다른 사람과 공유하라는 내용이 아니다.
⑤ 두려움이 언급되기는 하지만, 두려움 극복이 왜 어려운지 말하는 글이 아니다.

G 18 정답 ① *건축물이 우리 삶에 미치는 영향

뒤에 목적어절 접속사 that이 생략됨
We **think** / we are shaping our buildings. //
우리는 생각한다 / 우리가 건물을 형성하고 있다고 //

But really, / our buildings and development are also shaping us. //
단서 1 건물과 개발이 우리를 형성함
그러나 실제로 / 우리의 건물과 개발도 우리를 형성하고 있다 //

핵심 주어   단수 동사
One of the best examples of this / **is** the oldest-known construction: / the ornately carved rings of standing stones / at Göbekli Tepe in Turkey. //
이것의 가장 좋은 예 중 하나는 / 가장 오래된 것으로 알려진 건축물이다 / 화려하게 조각된 입석의 고리 / 튀르키예의 Göbekli Tepe에 있는 //

부사절 접속사(시간)   형용사적 용법(idea 수식)
Before these ancestors got the idea / **to erect** standing stones / some 12,000 years ago, / they were hunter-gatherers. //
이 조상들이 아이디어를 얻기 전에 / 입석을 세우는 / 약 12,000년 전에 / 그들은 수렵 채집인이었다 //
단서 2 튀르키예의 조상들은 입석을 세우기 전에는 수렵 채집인이었음

It appears / that the erection of the multiple rings of megalithic stones / took **so** long, / and **so** many successive generations, /
so ~ that ... : 너무 ~해서 …하다
~으로 보인다 / 거석으로 된 여러 개의 고리를 세우는 것이 / 너무 오랜 시간이 걸렸고 / 너무 많은 잇따른 세대를 거쳐야 해서 /

부사적 용법(목적)
(앞의 so와 연결됨)
that these innovators were forced to settle down / **to complete** the construction works. //
이 혁신가들은 정착해야만 했다 / 건설 작업을 완료하기 위해 //
단서 3 입석을 세우는 과정에서 정착했고 최초의 농업 사회가 형성됨

In the process, / they became the first farming society / on Earth. //
그 과정에서 / 그들은 최초의 농업 사회가 되었다 / 지구상에서 //

현재분사(society 수식)
This is an early example / of a society **constructing** something / **that** ends up radically remaking the society itself. //
주격 관계대명사
이것은 초기 예이다 / 무언가를 건설하는 사회의 / 결국 사회 그 자체를 근본적으로 재구성하는 //
단서 4 무언가를 건설 = 사회 자체를 재구성하는 것

Things are not so different / in our own time. //
상황은 그렇게 다르지 않다 / 우리 시대에도 //

• development ⓝ 개발   • construction ⓝ 건축(물)
• carve ⓥ 조각하다   • ancestor ⓝ 조상   • erect ⓥ (똑바로) 세우다
• successive ⓐ 연속적인   • innovator ⓝ 혁신가
• settle down 정착하다   • radically ⓐⒹ 근본적으로
• transform ⓥ 바꾸다

우리는 우리가 건물을 형성하고 있다고 생각한다. 그러나 실제로, 우리의 건물과 개발도 또한 우리를 형성하고 있다. 이것의 가장 좋은 예 중 하나는 가장 오래된 것으로 알려진 건축물인 튀르키예의 Göbekli Tepe에 있는 화려하게 조각된 입석의 고리이다. 이 조상들이 약 12,000년 전에 입석을 세우는 아이디어를 얻기 전에, 그들은 수렵 채집인이었다. 거석으로 된 여러 개의 고리를 세우는 것이 너무 오랜 시간이 걸렸고 너무 많은 잇따른 세대를

거쳐야 해서 이 혁신가들은 건설 작업을 완료하기 위해 정착해야만 했던 것으로 보인다. 그 과정에서, 그들은 지구상에서 최초의 농업 사회가 되었다. 이것은 결국 사회 자체를 근본적으로 재구성하는 무언가를 건설하는 사회의 초기 예이다. 우리 시대에도 상황은 그렇게 다르지 않다.

다음 글의 제목으로 가장 적절한 것은?
① Buildings Transform How We Live!
건물이 우리가 사는 방식을 바꾼다!   건물이나 개발이 우리를 형성한다고 함
② Why Do We Build More Than We Need?
왜 우리는 우리가 필요한 것보다 더 지을까?   필요보다 많은 건물을 짓는다는 언급은 없음
③ Copying Ancient Buildings for Creativity
창의성을 위해 고대 건물을 모방하기   창의성과 관련된 글이 아님
④ Was Life Better in Hunter-gatherer Times?
수렵 채집 시대의 삶은 더 좋았을까?   hunter-gatherers가 언급된 것으로 만든 오답
⑤ Innovate Your Farm with New Constructions
새로운 건축물로 당신의 농장을 혁신하라   농장을 혁신하라는 글이 아님

G

>**왜 정답**? ✿✿❀ [정답률 65%]
우리가 건물을 형성하는 것처럼 건물과 개발도 우리를 형성함 **단서 1**
❶ 튀르키예의 조상들은 입석을 세우기 전에는 수렵 채집인이었음 **단서 2**
❷ 그들은 입석을 세우면서 정착해야 했고, 최초의 농업 사회가 형성됨 **단서 3**
❸ 무언가를 건설한 것이 사회 자체를 재구성한 것의 초기 예임 **단서 4**
▶ 튀르키예를 예로 들어 사회에서 건축물이 가지는 의미는 사회 자체의 재구성임을 설명했으므로 글의 제목으로 가장 적절한 것은 ① '건물이 우리가 사는 방식을 바꾼다!'이다.

>**왜 오답**?
② 필요 이상으로 많은 건축물을 짓는다는 언급은 없다.
③ 창의성을 위해 고대 건물을 모방한다는 내용이 아니다.
④ 수렵 채집 시대가 더 살기 좋았을지 알아보는 글이 아니다.
  (▶ 이유: 수렵 채집 사회에서 농경 사회가 된 튀르키예의 예시가 제시됐을 뿐, 둘 중 언제가 더 살기 좋았는지는 설명하지 않았다.)
⑤ 새로운 건축물로 혁신하는 것은 맞지만, 농장에만 국한된 내용이 아니다. 함정

G 19 정답 ④   ★ 2등급 대비 [정답률 55%]

*갈등 극복을 통한 창의성 신장

help의 목적격보어(동사원형)
Diversity, challenge, and conflict help us / **maintain** our imagination. //
다양성, 어려움, 그리고 갈등은 우리를 도와준다 / 상상력을 유지하도록 //

that 절의 병렬 구조
Most people assume / **that** conflict is bad / and **that** being in one's "comfort zone" is good. //
대부분의 사람들은 단정한다 / 갈등은 나쁜 것이라고 / 그리고 "편안한 구역"에 머무는 것이 좋은 것이라고 //

That is not exactly true. // 그것은 정확히는 사실이 아니다 //

Of course, / we don't want to find ourselves / without a job or medical insurance / or in a fight with our partner, family, boss, or coworkers. //
물론 / 우리는 자신의 모습을 보고 싶어 하지 않는다 / 직장 또는 의료보험이 없거나 / 배우자, 가족, 직장 상사, 직장 동료들과의 다툼에 빠진 //

One bad experience can be sufficient / to last us a lifetime. //
하나의 나쁜 경험이 충분할 수 있다 / 우리에게 평생 지속되는 데 //
단서 1 갈등, 충돌 등의 문제 상황을 통해 우리는 고민하게 됨
But small disagreements with family and friends, / trouble with technology or finances, / or challenges at work and at home / can help us think through our own capabilities. //
하지만 가족과 친구들과의 작은 의견 충돌 / 기술적 또는 재정적 문제 / 또는 직장과 가정에서의 어려움이 / 우리의 능력에 대해 진지하게 고민하게 도와준다 //

주격 관계대명사
Problems / **that** need solutions / force us to use our brains / **in order to** develop creative answers. //
~하기 위해
문제들은 / 해결책이 필요한 / 우리의 뇌를 사용하도록 강요한다 / 창의적인 해답들을 개발하기 위해 //
단서 2 문제 해결 과정에서 창의성을 발휘하게 됨

Navigating landscapes / that are varied / that offer trials and
occasional conflicts, / **is** more helpful to creativity /
핵심 주어 / 단수 동사
지형을 운전하는 것은 / 변화무쌍한 / 시련과 이따금씩의 갈등을 주는 / 훨씬 더 창의성에 도
움을 준다 /
than hanging out in landscapes / that pose no challenge to our
주격 관계대명사
senses and our minds. // **단서 3** 안전한 상황보다 변화무쌍한 상황이 창의성에 더 도움을 줌
지형을 다니는 것보다 / 우리 감각과 마음에 아무런 어려움을 주지 않는 //
Our two million-year history / is packed with challenges and
conflicts. // 우리의 2백만년 역사는 / 어려움과 갈등으로 가득 차 있다 //

- diversity ⓝ 다양성　　　• conflict ⓝ 갈등　　　• maintain ⓥ 유지하다
- assume ⓥ 단정하다　　　• insurance ⓝ 보험　　　• sufficient ⓐ 충분한
- capability ⓝ 능력　　　• navigate ⓥ 운전하다
- landscape ⓝ 풍경, 지형　　　• trial ⓝ 시련　　　• occasional ⓐ 이따금씩의

다양성, 어려움, 그리고 갈등은 우리의 상상력을 유지하게 도와준다. 대부
분의 사람들은 갈등은 나쁜 것이고 "편안한 구역"에 머무는 것이 좋은 것
이라고 단정한다. 그것은 정확히는 사실이 아니다. 물론, 우리는 직장 또는
의료보험이 없거나, 배우자, 가족, 직장 상사, 직장 동료들과의 다툼에 빠
진 자신의 모습을 보고 싶어 하지 않는다. 하나의 나쁜 경험이 우리에게 평
생 지속되는 데 충분할 수 있다. 하지만 가족과 친구들과의 작은 의견 충
돌, 기술적 또는 재정적 문제, 직장과 가정에서의 어려움이 우리의 능력에
대해 진지하게 고민하게 도와준다. 해결책이 필요한 문제들은 창의적인 해
답들을 개발하기 위해 우리의 뇌를 사용하도록 강요한다. 시련과 갈등을
주는, 변화무쌍한 지형을 운전하는 것은 우리 감각과 마음에 아무런 어려
움을 주지 않는 지형을 다니는 것보다 훨씬 더 창의성에 도움을 준다. 우리
의 2백만년 역사는 어려움과 갈등으로 가득 차 있다.

다음 글의 제목으로 가장 적절한 것은?
① Technology: A Lens to the Future　기술은 미래의 핵심 요소라는 내용이 아님
　기술: 미래를 보는 렌즈
② Diversity: A Key to Social Unification
　다양성: 사회 통합의 해답　　다양성을 통해 사회 통합을 이루자는 내용이 아님
③ Simple Ways to Avoid Conflicts with Others
　타인과의 갈등을 피하는 간단한 방법들　갈등을 피하라고 하지 않았음
④ Creativity Doesn't Come from Playing It Safe
　창의성은 안전함에서 나오지 않는다　갈등, 충돌 등의 문제를 해결하면서 창의성을 발휘한다고 했음
⑤ There Are No Challenges That Can't Be Overcome
　극복할 수 없는 어려움은 존재하지 않는다　어려움 극복 여부가 핵심은 아님

| 문제 풀이 순서 |

1st 선택지와 첫 문장을 통해 핵심 소재를 확인하고 글의 내용을 예상한다.

선택지	거의 모든 선택지에 '다양성', '갈등', '안전함', '어려움'과 같은 표현이 등장한다.
첫 문장	다양성, 어려움, 그리고 갈등은 우리의 상상력을 유지하게 도와준다.

➡ 이 글은 다양성이나 갈등이 가지는 상상력과의 관계에 대한 내용일 것이다.
➡ 첫 문장을 통해 다양성과 갈등에 대해 긍정적인 내용이 이어질 것임을 짐작할 수 있다.

2nd 글의 나머지 부분에서 내용을 파악하고 정답을 찾는다.

- **하지만** 의견 충돌, 기술적 또는 재정적 문제, 직장과 가정에서의 어려움이 우리가
  진지하게 고민하게 도와준다. **단서 1**
- 해결책이 필요한 문제들은 우리가 창의성을 발휘하게 만든다. **단서 2**
- 변화무쌍한 지형을 운전하는 것은 안전한 지형을 다니는 것보다 훨씬 더 창의성에
  도움을 준다. **단서 3**

➡ 대부분의 사람들이 갈등은 나쁜 것이라고 하지만, 갈등, 충돌 등의 문제 상황을 통해
  우리는 고민하게 되고 갈등과 어려움을 극복하는 과정에서 창의성이 발휘된다는
  내용이다.
　▶ 이 글의 주제는 '갈등 극복을 통한 창의성 신장'이므로 ④ '창의성은 안전함에서
　　나오지 않는다'가 제목으로 가장 적절하다.

| 선택지 분석 |
① 기술을 통해 미래 사회를 들여다볼 수 있다는 내용은 나오지 않는다.
② 다양성을 통해 사회 통합을 이루자는 내용이 아니다.
③ 갈등을 극복하는 과정에서 창의력이 생긴다고 했으므로 갈등을 피하라고 하는 것이
　아니다.
④ 갈등, 충돌 등의 문제를 해결하면서 창의성을 발휘한다는 내용이다.
⑤ 어려움 극복 여부가 핵심 내용은 아니므로 글의 제목으로 불충분하다.

G 20 정답 ②　　　　　　　　　　　★ 2등급 대비 [정답률 57%]

＊정체성을 찾도록 현대 사회가 우리를 이끄는 방식

In modern times, / society became more dynamic. //
현대에는 / 사회가 더욱 역동적이게 되었다 //
Social mobility increased, / and people began to exercise
/ a higher degree of choice / regarding, for instance, their
profession, their marriage, or their religion. //
사회적 유동성이 증가했다 / 그리고 사람들은 행사하기 시작했다 / 더 높은 정도의 선택권을 /
예를 들어 자신의 직업, 결혼 혹은 종교와 관련하여 //
This posed a challenge / to traditional roles in society. //
이것은 이의를 제기했다 / 사회의 전통적인 역할에 //
가주어　　　　진주어절을 이끄는 접속사
It was less evident / **that** one needed to commit to the roles / **one**
앞에 목적격 관계대명사 생략
was born into / when alternatives could be realized. //
덜 분명해졌다 / 개인이 역할에 전념할 필요가 있다는 것은 / 자신이 타고난 / 대안이 실현될
수 있을 때 //
동명사 주어
Increasing control over one's life choices / became **not only**
not only A but (also) B: A뿐만 아니라 B도
possible **but** desired. // **단서 1** 현대 사회에서는 자신의 삶을 선택하는 것이 가능하며 바람직함
개인의 삶의 선택에 대한 통제력을 늘리는 것이 / 가능해졌을 뿐만 아니라 바람직하게 되었다 //
Identity then became a problem. //
그러자 정체성이 문제가 되었다 //
It was no longer almost ready-made at birth / but something to
be discovered. // **단서 2** 현대 사회에서는 정체성이 태어날 때
　　　　　　　　　　　주어지는 것이 아니라 발견해 나가는 것임
그것은 더 이상 태어날 때 대체로 주어지는 것이 아닌 / 발견되어져야 할 것이었다 //
Traditional role identities **prescribed by society** / began to
앞에 주격 관계대명사와 be동사 생략
appear **as** masks / **imposed** on people / **whose** real self was to be
앞에 주격 관계대명사와 be동사 생략　　소유격 관계대명사
found / somewhere underneath. //
　전치사(~처럼)
사회에 의해 규정되어진 전통적인 역할 정체성은 / 가면처럼 보이기 시작했다 / 사람들에게
부여된 / 진정한 자아가 발견되어져야 할 / 아래 어딘가에서 //

- dynamic ⓐ 역동적인　　　• mobility ⓝ 유동성
- exercise ⓥ 행사하다　　　• profession ⓝ 직업　　　• religion ⓝ 종교
- pose ⓥ 제기하다　　　• traditional ⓐ 전통적인　　　• evident ⓐ 분명한
- commit to ~에 전념[헌신]하다　　　• alternative ⓝ 대안
- identity ⓝ 정체성　　　• ready-made 이미 주어진
- at birth 태어날 때　　　• discover ⓥ 발견하다
- prescribe ⓥ 규정하다　　　• underneath ⓐⓓ ~의 아래에
- competitive ⓐ 경쟁적인　　　• trustworthy ⓐ 신뢰할 수 있는

현대에는 사회가 더욱 역동적이게 되었다. 사회적 유동성이 증가하였고
사람들은 예를 들어 자신의 직업, 결혼 혹은 종교와 관련하여 더 높은
정도의 선택권을 행사하기 시작했다. 이것은 사회의 전통적인 역할에
이의를 제기했다. 대안이 실현될 수 있을 때 개인이 자신이 타고난
역할에 전념할 필요가 있다는 것은 덜 분명해졌다. 개인의 삶의 선택에
대한 통제력을 늘리는 것이 가능해졌을 뿐만 아니라 바람직하게 되었다.
그러자 정체성이 문제가 되었다. 그것은 더 이상 태어날 때 대체로 주어진
것이 아닌 발견되어져야 할 것이었다. 사회에 의해 규정되어진 전통적인
역할 정체성은 아래 어딘가에서 자신의 진정한 자아가 발견되어져야 할
사람들에게 부여된 가면처럼 보이기 시작했다.

다음 글의 제목으로 가장 적절한 것은?

① What Makes Our Modern Society So Competitive? 현대 사회가 무엇이 우리의 현대 사회를 그렇게 경쟁적으로 만드는가? 경쟁적이라는 내용은 없음

② How Modern Society Drives Us to Discover Our Identities 현대 사회에서는 자신의 삶을 선택하고 정체성을 찾아갈 수 있음 현대 사회가 우리의 정체성을 찾도록 우리를 이끄는 방식

③ Social Masks: A Means to Build Trustworthy Relationships 사회적인 가면이 신뢰할 수 있는 관계를 만든다는 내용은 없음 사회적 가면들: 신뢰할 수 있는 관계를 만드는 수단

④ The More Social Roles We Have, the Less Choice We Have 역할이 많을수록 선택권이 적어진다는 내용은 없음 우리가 사회적 역할이 많을수록 선택의 폭이 더 적어진다

⑤ Increasing Social Mobility Leads Us to a More Equal Society 사회적 유동성 증가는 선택권을 늘려준다고만 언급됨 사회적 유동성 증가가 우리를 더 평등한 사회로 이끈다

왜 2등급? 현대 사회에서는 개인이 삶을 선택하는 것이 가능해졌을 뿐만 아니라 바람직하게 되었다는 것이 핵심 내용이다. 도입부에서 역동적이게 된 현대 사회를 언급한 이후에 이어지는 내용을 잘 연결해서 생각해야 한다.

| 문제 풀이 순서 |

1st 글의 앞부분에서 중심 화제를 제시했는지 확인하고 글의 내용을 예상한다.

[현대 사회에는 사회적 유동성이 증가하였고 사람들은 직업이나 결혼, 종교와 관련하여 더 높은 정도의 선택권을 행사하기 시작했다.

➡ 역동적이게 된 현대 사회를 언급하면서 사람들에게 선택권이 많아졌다는 내용이 나온다.

➡ 사람들이 주어진 대로 살지 않고 스스로 선택하면서 산다는 것과 관련된 내용이 이어질 것이다.

2nd 글을 읽으면서 세부적인 내용들을 파악해서 답을 고른다.

[• 현대 사회에서 개인의 삶에 대한 통제력을 늘리는 것이 가능해졌고 바람직하게 되었다. **단서1**
  • 정체성은 태어날 때 주어진 것이 아니라 발견되어져야 할 것이다. **단서2**

➡ 현대 사회는 선택권이 많아졌다는 것과 연결되면서 자신의 삶을 선택하는 것이 가능하고 바람직하다고 했다. 그래서 현대 사회에서는 자신의 정체성이 태어날 때 주어지는 것이 아니고 발견해 나간다고 했다.

▶ 따라서 ② '현대 사회가 우리의 정체성을 찾도록 우리를 이끄는 방식'이 이 글의 제목으로 가장 적절하다.

| 선택지 분석 |

① 현대 사회가 역동적이게 되었다는 언급은 있지만 경쟁적이게 된다는 내용은 나오지 않았다.

② 현대 사회에서 우리는 자신이 타고난 역할에 전념할 필요가 없이 개인의 삶을 선택할 수 있게 됐고 정체성을 발견해 나간다는 내용이다.

③ 사회적인 가면이 신뢰할 수 있는 관계를 만들어준다는 언급은 없었다.

④ 역할과 선택권이 많이 언급되긴 하지만, 역할이 많을수록 선택의 폭이 적어진다는 내용은 나오지 않았다.

⑤ 사회적 유동성 증가가 선택권을 늘려주었다는 언급은 있지만 더 평등한 사회를 만든다는 내용은 없었다.

G 21 정답 ④ ★2등급 대비 [정답률 57%]

*옳다는 것이 새로운 가능성을 막는다

Have you ever brought up an idea or suggestion / to someone / and heard them immediately say / "No, that won't work."? //
지각동사＋목적어＋원형부정사
아이디어나 제안을 내놓은 적이 있는가 / 누군가에게 / 그리고 그들이 즉시 말한 것을 들은 적이 있는가 / "아니, 그건 안 될 거야'라고 //

You may have thought, / "He/she didn't even give it a chance. // How do they know it won't work?" //
여러분은 아마도 생각했을지도 모른다 / "그 사람은 기회조차 주지 않았어 // 어떻게 그들은 그것이 안 될 것이라는 것을 알지"라고 //

단서1 어떤 일에 대해 옳을 때, 다른 관점이나 기회를 닫게 됨

When you are right about something, / you close off the possibility / of another viewpoint or opportunity. //
여러분이 어떤 일에 대해 옳다면 / 여러분은 가능성을 닫는다 / 다른 관점이나 기회의 //

Being right about something means / that "it is the way it is, period." //
동명사구 주어(단수 취급)   단수 동사
어떤 일에 대해 옳다는 것은 의미한다 / "그것은 원래 그런 거야, 끝"이라는 것을 //

You may be correct. //
여러분이 맞을 수도 있다 //

Your particular way of seeing it / may be true with the facts. //
동명사 주어
여러분이 그것을 보는 특정한 방법이 / 사실에 부합할 수도 있다 //

However, / considering the other option or the other person's point of view / can be beneficial. //
하지만 / 다른 선택지나 다른 사람의 관점을 고려하는 것은 / 이로울 수 있다 //

If you see their side, / you will see something new / or, at worse, learn something / about how the other person looks at life. //
전치사의 목적어(간접의문문)
만약 여러분이 그들의 관점을 안다면 / 여러분은 새로운 것을 보거나 / 그것보다는 나쁘더라도 무언가를 배울 것이다 / 상대방이 삶을 바라보는 방식에 대해 //
뒤에 목적어절 접속사 that이 생략됨

Why would you think / everyone sees and experiences life / the way you do? //
왜 여러분은 생각하는가 / 모두가 삶을 보거나 경험할 것이라고 / 여러분이 하는 방식대로 //

Besides how boring that would be, / it would eliminate all new opportunities, ideas, invention, and creativity. //
'~ 외에'
그것이 얼마나 지루할지는 / 제외하고라도 / 그것은 모든 새로운 기회, 아이디어, 발명, 그리고 창의성을 없앨 것이다 // **단서2** 자신이 옳다고 생각하면 새로운 기회나 창의성이 없어질 수 있음

- bring up (화제를) 꺼내다
- immediately (ad) 즉시
- possibility (n) 가능성
- period (n) 마침표, 끝
- point of view 관점
- eliminate (v) 제거하다, 없애다
- honest (a) 정직한
- block (v) 막다, 차단하다
- suggestion (n) 제안
- close off ~을 차단하다[막다]
- viewpoint (n) 관점
- consider (v) 고려하다
- beneficial (a) 유익한, 이로운
- invention (n) 발명
- filter out (액체·빛 등에서) ~을 걸러내다
- option (n) 선택(지)

누군가에게 아이디어나 제안을 내놓고, 그들이 즉시 "아니, 그건 안 될 거야."라고 말한 것을 들은 적이 있는가? 여러분은 아마도 "그 사람은 기회조차 주지 않았어. 어떻게 그들은 그것이 안 될 것이라는 것을 알지?"라고 생각했을지도 모른다. 여러분이 어떤 일에 대해 옳다면, 여러분은 다른 관점이나 기회의 가능성을 닫아 버린다. 어떤 일에 대해 옳다는 것은 "그것은 원래 그런 거야, 끝."이라고 하는 것을 의미한다. 여러분이 맞을 수도 있다. 여러분이 그것을 보는 특정한 방법이 사실에 부합할 수도 있다. 하지만 다른 선택지나 다른 사람의 관점을 고려하는 것은 이로울 수 있다. 만약 여러분이 그들의 관점을 안다면, 여러분이 새로운 것을 보거나 그것보다는 나쁘더라도 다른 사람이 삶을 바라보는 방식에 대한 무언가를 배울 것이다. 왜 모두가 여러분이 하는 방식대로 삶을 보거나 경험할 것이라고 생각하는가? 그것이 얼마나 지루할지는 제외하고라도, 그것은 모든 새로운 기회, 아이디어, 발명, 그리고 창의성을 없앨 것이다.

자신이 옳다고 생각하면 창의성이나 기회가 없어질 수 있다는 내용
다음 글의 제목으로 가장 적절한 것은?

① The Value of Being Honest 옳은 것의 안 좋은 점에 대해 말하는 내용임 정직한 것의 가치

② Filter Out Negative Points of View 부정적인 관점을 걸러내라 다른 사람의 관점도 고려해야 한다고 했음

③ Keeping Your Word: A Road to Success 약속 지키기: 성공으로 가는 길 약속을 지키는 것에 대한 언급은 없음

④ Being Right Can Block New Possibilities 옳다는 것이 새로운 가능성을 차단할 수 있다

⑤ Look Back When Everyone Looks Forward 모두가 앞을 볼 때 뒤를 돌아보라 남들과 다르게 생각해야 한다는 내용이 아님

왜 2등급? 일반적으로 생각한다면 '옳은 것'은 좋은 것이지만, 꼭 그렇지만은 않다고 이야기하는 글이다. 따라서 글의 내용만으로 정답을 고르지 않고, 상식이나 일반적인 통념으로 정답을 골랐다면 오답을 고르기 쉬운 2등급 대비 문제이다.

문제 풀이 순서

1st 글의 앞부분을 읽으며 이어질 내용을 예상한다.

> 누군가에게 아이디어나 제안을 내놓고, 그들이 즉시 "아니, 그건 안 될 거야."라고 말한 것을 들은 적이 있는가? ~ 여러분이 어떤 일에 대해 옳다면, 여러분은 다른 관점이나 기회의 가능성을 닫아 버린다. **단서 1**

➡ 다른 사람에게 제안을 한 뒤 부정적인 반응을 들은 적이 있는지 질문을 던지면서, 어떤 일에 대해 옳을 때, 다른 관점이나 기회를 닫게 된다고 했다. **단서**

➡ 자신만이 옳다고 생각하면 새로운 기회를 얻지 못한다는 내용의 글일 것이다. **발상**

2nd 글의 나머지 부분에서 내용을 파악하고 정답을 찾는다.

> (왜 모두가 여러분이 하는 방식대로 삶을 보거나 경험할 것이라고 생각하는가?) 그것이 얼마나 지루할지는 제외하고라도, 그것은 모든 새로운 기회, 아이디어, 발명, 그리고 창의성을 없앨 것이다. **단서 2**

➡ 자신이 옳다고 생각하며 모두가 자신처럼 삶을 보거나 경험할 것이라고 생각하는 것은 새로운 기회나 아이디어, 창의성 등을 없앨 것이라고 했다. 글의 앞부분에서 자신만이 옳다고 생각하면 기회의 가능성이 닫힌다고 한 것도 같은 맥락이다.

▶ 따라서 ④ '옳다는 것이 새로운 가능성을 차단할 수 있다'가 글의 제목으로 가장 적절하다.

선택지 분석

① 옳다고 생각하는 것의 안 좋은 점에 대해 말하는 글로 정직함의 가치와는 관련이 없다.

② 다른 사람의 관점도 걸러내지 말고 고려해야 한다고 했다.

③ 약속을 지키라고 조언하는 글이 아니다.

④ 자신이 옳다고만 생각하면 새로운 기회가 없어질 수 있다고 했다.

⑤ 다른 사람의 관점도 받아들이라고 했지 남들과 다르게 생각해야 한다는 내용이 아니다.

G 22 정답 ① ⭐ 1등급 대비 [정답률 55%]

*일상과 긴밀히 연결된 알고리즘

Only a generation or <u>two</u> ago, / <u>mentioning</u> the word *algorithms*
뒤에 generations 생략   동명사(핵심 주어)
/ would have drawn a blank / from most people. //
한 세대 혹은 두 세대 전만 해도 / '알고리즘'이라는 단어를 언급하는 것은 / 아무 반응을 얻지 못했다 / 대부분의 사람들로부터 //
단서 1 알고리즘은 오늘날 문명의 모든 부분에 존재함
Today, / algorithms appear / in every part of civilization. //
오늘날 / 알고리즘은 나타난다 / 문명의 모든 부분에서 //
수동태
They <u>are connected</u> / to everyday life. // **단서 2** 알고리즘은 일상과 연결되어 있음
그것들은 연결되어 있다 / 일상에 //
not just A but (also) B: A뿐만 아니라 B도
They're <u>not just</u> in your cell phone or your laptop / <u>but</u> in your
car, your house, your appliances, and your toys. //
그것들은 당신의 휴대 전화나 노트북 안뿐만 아니라 / 당신의 자동차, 집, 전자 제품과 장난감 안에도 있다 //
Your bank is a huge web of algorithms, / <u>with humans turning</u>
the switches / here and there. // 「with+(대)명사+분사」 ~가 …한[된] 채로
당신의 은행은 알고리즘의 거대한 망이다 / 인간들이 스위치를 돌리고 있는 / 여기저기서 //
Algorithms schedule flights / and then fly the airplanes. //
알고리즘은 비행 일정을 잡는다 / 그리고 비행기를 운항한다 //
Algorithms run factories, / trade goods, / and keep records. //
알고리즘은 공장을 운영한다 / 상품을 거래한다 / 그리고 기록 문서를 보관한다 //
가정법 과거
<u>If every algorithm suddenly stopped</u> working, / <u>it would be</u> the
end of the world / as we know it. //
만일 모든 알고리즘이 갑자기 작동을 멈춘다면 / 이는 세상의 끝이 될 것이다 / 우리가 알고 있듯 //
단서 3 알고리즘이 갑자기 작동을 멈춘다면 세상도 끝이 나게 될 것이라고 했음

- generation ⓝ 세대 · mention ⓥ 언급하다
- draw a blank 아무 반응을 얻지 못하다 · appear ⓥ 나타나다
- civilization ⓝ 문명 · connect ⓥ 연결하다 · laptop ⓝ 노트북
- appliances ⓝ 가전제품 · web ⓝ 망
- schedule ⓥ 일정을 잡다, 예정하다 · run ⓥ 운영하다
- trade ⓥ 거래하다 · goods ⓝ 상품 · transportation ⓝ 운송
- driving force 원동력, 추진력 · industry ⓝ 산업

한 세대 혹은 두 세대 전만 해도, '알고리즘'이라는 단어를 언급하는 것은 대부분의 사람들로부터 아무 반응을 얻지 못했다. 오늘날, 알고리즘은 문명의 모든 부분에서 나타난다. 그것들은 일상에 연결되어 있다. 그것들은 당신의 휴대 전화나 노트북 안뿐만 아니라 당신의 자동차, 집, 전자 제품과 장난감 안에도 있다. 당신의 은행은 인간들이 여기저기서 스위치를 돌리고 있는, 알고리즘의 거대한 망이다. 알고리즘은 비행 일정을 잡고 비행기를 운항한다. 알고리즘은 공장을 운영하고, 상품을 거래하며, 기록 문서를 보관한다. 만일 모든 알고리즘이 갑자기 작동을 멈춘다면, 이는 우리가 알고 있듯 세상의 끝이 될 것이다.

다음 글의 제목으로 가장 적절한 것은?

① We Live in an Age of Algorithms 오늘날 우리 일상의 모든 부분에
우리는 알고리즘의 시대에 살고 있다   알고리즘이 연결되어 있다는 내용
② Mysteries of Ancient Civilizations
고대 문명의 수수께끼들   글에 civilization이 나온 것으로 만든 함정
③ Dangers of Online Banking Algorithms 은행 알고리즘이 언급되었으나
온라인 은행 알고리즘의 위험들   이는 우리 일상에 연결된 알고리즘을 설명하는 예시임
④ How Algorithms Decrease Human Creativity 알고리즘이 인간의
알고리즘이 인간의 창의성을 감소시키는 방식   창의성을 감소시키는 것에 대해서 언급되지 않음
⑤ Transportation: A Driving Force of Industry
운송: 산업의 원동력   운송이 산업에 미치는 영향에 대한 내용은 없음

왜 1등급? 첫 문장에서 핵심 소재인 '알고리즘(algorithms)'이 언급되었다. 이 핵심 소재에 대해 어떤 내용이 이어지는지 파악하는 것이 중요하다. 휴대 전화, 노트북, 은행 등 제시되는 예시의 내용으로 핵심 내용을 파악해야 하는 1등급 대비 문제이다.

문제 풀이 순서

1st 선택지와 첫 문장을 통해 핵심 소재를 확인하고 글의 내용을 예상한다.

선택지	세 개의 선택지에 '알고리즘'이라는 단어가 들어가고 나머지 선택지에는 '문명', '운송'과 같이 글에 나온 표현과 관련된 단어가 등장한다.
첫 문장	한 세대 혹은 두 세대 전만 해도, '알고리즘'이라는 단어를 언급하는 것은 대부분의 사람들로부터 아무 반응을 얻지 못했다.

➡ 이 글은 '알고리즘'과 관련된 내용이 될 것이다.

➡ 첫 문장에서 몇 세대 전만 해도 '알고리즘'에 대한 반응을 얻을 수 없었다고 했으므로 이후에는 이와 다른 경향을 보인다는 내용이 이어질 것으로 예상할 수 있다.

2nd **1st** 에서 발상한 것을 토대로 글을 읽고, 내용을 파악한다.

> · 오늘날 문명의 모든 부분에 알고리즘은 존재한다. **단서 1**
> · 그리고 알고리즘은 일상과 연결되어 있다. **단서 2**

➡ 글의 중반부에서 이에 대한 예시로 휴대 전화, 노트북, 자동차, 집, 전자 제품과 장난감, 은행 등을 들었다. 또한, 알고리즘이 비행 일정을 잡고 공장을 운영하는 등의 일도 할 수 있다고 하면서 예전과 다르게 일상과 연결된 알고리즘에 대한 내용이 나온다.

3rd 글의 주제에 알맞은 제목을 고른다.

2nd 에서 파악한 글의 내용을 종합하면 이 글의 주제는 '일상과 긴밀히 연결된 알고리즘'이다.

오늘날 우리 문명의 모든 부분이 알고리즘과 연결되어 있고, 알고리즘이 실제로 우리 일상에서 어떻게 활용되는지 여러 가지 예시를 들며 설명하는 글이다.

▶ 따라서 이 글의 제목으로 가장 적절한 것은 ① '우리는 알고리즘의 시대에 살고 있다'이다.

| 선택지 분석 |

① 오늘날 우리 일상에 알고리즘이 연결되어 있다는 내용이다.
② 글에 civilization이 언급되었으나 이는 오늘날의 문명에 대해 말하기 위해 사용된 것이다.
③ 은행은 알고리즘의 거대한 망이라는 내용이 글의 후반부에 나왔지만, 온라인 은행 알고리즘의 위험성에 대해서는 나오지 않았다.
④ 알고리즘이 인간의 창의성에 미치는 부정적인 영향에 대한 내용은 없다.
⑤ 알고리즘이 비행기 운항에 활용되는 예시가 나오지만, 산업 분야에서 운송의 역할을 설명하기 위함이 아니다.

G 23 정답 ② ★1등급 대비 [정답률 52%]

＊감정에 구체적인 이름을 붙이는 것의 유익함

Our ability / to accurately recognize and label emotions / is often referred to as *emotional granularity*. //
형용사적 용법 / 병렬 구조
우리의 능력은 / 감정을 정확하게 인식하고 그것에 이름을 붙일 수 있는 / 흔히 '감정 입자도'라고 불린다 //

In the words of Harvard psychologist Susan David, / "Learning to label emotions / with a more nuanced vocabulary / can be absolutely transformative." //
동명사 주어
단서1 감정에 이름을 붙이는 것은 사람을 변화시킴
Harvard 대학의 심리학자인 Susan David의 말에 의하면 / "감정에 이름을 붙이는 법을 배우는 것은 / 더 미묘한 차이가 있는 어휘로 / 절대적으로 (사람을) 변화시킬 수 있다" //

David explains / that if we don't have a rich emotional vocabulary, / it is difficult / to communicate our needs / and to get the support / that we need / from others. //
가주어 / 진주어(병렬 구조) / 주격 관계대명사
David는 설명한다 / 우리가 풍부한 감정적인 어휘를 갖고 있지 않으면 / 어렵다 / 우리의 욕구를 전달하는 것이 / 그리고 지지를 얻는 것이 / 우리가 필요로 하는 / 다른 사람들로부터 //

But / those who are able to distinguish / between a range of various emotions / "do much, much better /
주격 관계대명사 / 비교급 강조
그러나 / 구별할 수 있는 사람들은 / 광범위한 다양한 감정을 / "훨씬 훨씬 더 잘한다" /

at managing the ups and downs / of ordinary existence / than those who see everything in black and white" //
주격 관계대명사
좋은 일들과 궂은 일들을 관리하는 일을 / 평범한 존재로 사는 중에 / 모든 것을 흑백 논리로 보는 사람들보다" //
단서2 다양한 감정을 구분할 수 있는 사람들이 좋은 일들과 궂은 일들을 관리하는 일을 훨씬 더 잘함

In fact, / research shows / that the process of labeling emotional experience / is related to greater emotion regulation and psychosocial well-being. //
목적어절을 이끄는 접속사
단서3 감정에 이름을 붙이는 것이 감정 통제 및 행복과 관련되어 있음
사실 / 연구 결과가 보여 준다 / 감정적인 경험에 이름을 붙이는 과정이 / 더 큰 감정 통제 및 심리 사회적인 행복과 관련되어 있다 //

- accurately ad 정확하게
- recognize v 인식하다
- granularity n 입자도
- psychologist n 심리학자
- absolutely ad 절대적으로
- transformative a (사람을) 변화시키는
- communicate v 전달하다
- support n 지지
- distinguish v 구별하다
- a range of 다양한
- manage v 관리하다
- ordinary a 평범한
- existence n 존재
- psychosocial a 심리 사회적인
- endure v 견디다
- categorize v 분류하다
- efficiency n 효율성

감정을 정확하게 인식하고 그것에 이름을 붙일 수 있는 우리의 능력은 흔히 '감정 입자도'라고 불린다. Harvard 대학의 심리학자인 Susan David의 말에 의하면, "감정에 더 미묘한 차이가 있는 어휘로 이름을 붙이는 법을 배우는 것은 절대적으로 (사람을) 변화시킬 수 있다." David는 우리가 풍부한 감정적인 어휘를 갖고 있지 않으면, 우리의 욕구를 전달하고 우리가 필요로 하는 지지를 다른 사람들로부터 얻는 것이 어렵다고 설명한다. 그러나 광범위한 다양한 감정을 구별할 수 있는 사람들은 "모든 것을 흑백 논리로 보는 사람들보다 평범한 존재로 사는 중에 겪는 좋은 일들과 궂은 일들을 관리하는 일을 훨씬, 훨씬 더 잘한다." 사실, 감정적인 경험에 이름을 붙이는 과정은 더 큰 감정 통제 및 심리 사회적인 행복과 관련되어 있다는 것을 연구 결과가 보여 준다.

다음 글의 제목으로 가장 적절한 것은?

① True Friendship Endures Emotional Arguments
진정한 우정은 감정적 논쟁을 견딘다 → 우정과 감정적 논쟁에 관한 내용이 아님
② Detailed Labeling of Emotions Is Beneficial
감정의 구체적인 이름 붙이기는 유익하다 → 감정을 구체적으로 구분하고 이름 붙이는 것의 이점에 대한 내용임
③ Labeling Emotions: Easier Said Than Done
감정에 이름 붙이기: 행동보다 말이 쉽다
④ Categorize and Label Tasks for Efficiency
효율성을 위해 일을 분류하고 이름 붙여라 → 효율성을 위해 일을 분류한다는 내용이 아님
⑤ Be Brave and Communicate Your Needs
용감하게 욕구를 전달해라 → 글에 나온 communicate, needs를 넣어서 만든 오답

왜 1등급? 글에서 인용하고 있는 심리학자 Susan David의 말에 주목해야 한다. 이를 통해 궁극적으로 감정에 구체적인 이름을 붙이는 것이 유익하다는 것인지, 유익하지 않다는 것인지를 이해해야 한다.

| 문제 풀이 순서 |

1st 글의 중심 내용을 이해하는 데 중요한 내용이 앞부분에 나오는지 확인한다.

Harvard 대학의 심리학자인 Susan David의 말에 의하면, "감정에 더 미묘한 차이가 있는 어휘로 이름을 붙이는 법을 배우는 것은 절대적으로 (사람을) 변화시킬 수 있다." 단서1

→ 심리학자인 Susan David의 말을 인용해서 감정에 구체적인 이름을 붙이는 것이 사람을 변화시킬 수 있다고 했다.

2nd 글의 나머지 부분에 나오는 관련된 내용을 파악한다.

- 다양한 감정을 구별할 수 있는 사람들은 모든 것을 흑백 논리로 보는 사람들보다 좋은 일들과 궂은 일들을 관리하는 일을 훨씬 더 잘한다. 단서2
- 감정적인 경험에 이름을 붙이는 과정은 감정 통제 및 심리 사회적인 행복과 관련되어 있다. 단서3

→ 감정을 구분하고 감정에 구체적인 이름을 붙이는 것이 감정을 통제하고, 심리 사회적인 행복으로 연결될 수 있는 등 여러 이점을 가지고 있다는 내용이다.

3rd 글의 주제에 알맞은 제목을 고른다.

→ 이 글의 주제는 '감정에 구체적인 이름을 붙이는 것의 유익함'이다.
▶ 따라서 글의 제목으로 가장 적절한 것은 ② '감정의 구체적인 이름 붙이기는 유익하다'이다.

| 선택지 분석 |

① 우정과 감정적 논쟁에 관한 내용이 아니라 감정에 이름을 붙이는 것의 이점에 관한 내용이다.
② 감정에 구체적인 이름을 붙이는 것에 대해 심리학자인 Susan David의 말을 인용하면서 그것이 다양한 이점을 가지고 있다고 했다.
③ 감정에 이름을 붙인다는 말을 넣어서 만든 함정이다.
④ 효율성을 위해 일을 분류하고 이름을 붙인다는 내용이 아니다.
⑤ 글에 나온 communicate, needs를 넣어서 만든 오답으로, 용감하게 욕구를 전달하라는 것이 중심 내용은 아니다.

G 어휘 Review 정답 ── 문제편 p. 99

01 추산하다	11 a range of	21 coexistence
02 쓰레기	12 commit to	22 labeling
03 고층 건물	13 in silence	23 Poverty
04 소화의	14 bring up	24 belief
05 위협	15 close off	25 pursuing
06 essential	16 successive	26 efficient
07 sufficient	17 accurately	27 occurs
08 release	18 enhance	28 spoil
09 categorize	19 inspiration	29 fertilizing
10 rational	20 status	30 eliminate

H 도표의 이해

문제편 p. 102~110

H 01 정답 ④ *2022년 국가별 1인당 이산화 탄소 배출량

The above graph shows per capita CO₂ emissions / from coal, oil, and gas by countries in 2022. // 위 그래프는 보여 준다 / 1인당 이산화 탄소 배출량을 / 2022년의 국가별 석탄, 석유, 천연가스에서 나온

미국은 총배출량(14.7)이 가장 높으며, 석탄에서 나온 배출량(2.8)은 두 번째로 낮음

① The United States had the highest total per capita CO₂ emissions, / even though its emissions from coal were the second lowest / among the five countries shown. // 미국은 가장 높은 1인당 이산화 탄소 총배출량을 가졌다 / 석탄에서 나온 배출량은 두 번째로 낮았음에도 불구하고 / 보여진 다섯 개의 국가 중 //

분사구문을 이끄는 현재분사   = South Korea
② South Korea's total per capita CO₂ emissions / were over 10 tons, / ranking it the second highest / among the countries shown. // 한국의 총배출량(11톤)은 10톤을 넘고, 두 번째로 높음
한국의 1인당 이산화 탄소 총배출량은 / 10톤이 넘고 / 두 번째로 높은 순위를 차지했다 / 보여진 국가 중 //

③ Germany had lower CO₂ emissions per capita / than South Korea / in all three major sources respectively. // 독일은 더 낮은 1인당 / 이산화 탄소 배출량을 가졌다 / 한국보다 / 각각의 모든 세 가지 주요한 원천에서 //
독일은 모든 세 가지 원천의 1인당 이산화 탄소 배출량이 한국보다 더 낮음

복수 주어
④ The per capita CO₂ emissions from coal / in South Africa / were over three times higher than(→ nearly twice as high as) those in Germany. //
복수 동사   = the per capita CO₂ emissions from coal
단서 남아프리카 공화국의 석탄에서 나온 배출량(5.7)은 독일의 석탄에서 나온 배출량(2.9)의 세 배를 넘지 않음
석탄으로부터의 1인당 이산화 탄소 배출량은 / 남아프리카 공화국의 / 독일의 그것보다 세 배보다 더 높았다(→ 거의 두 배 높았다) //

⑤ In Brazil, / oil was the largest source of CO₂ emissions per capita / among its three major sources, / just as it was in the United States and Germany. // 브라질, 미국, 독일에선 석유의 1인당 이산화 탄소 배출량 비중이 가장 큼   = oil
브라질에서 / 석유는 1인당 이산화 탄소 배출량의 가장 큰 원천이었다 / 세 가지 주요한 원천 중에서 / 그것은 미국과 독일에서도 마찬가지였다 //

- emission ⓝ 배출량 - rank ⓥ (순위를) 차지하다
- major ⓐ 주요한 - respectively ⓐⓓ 각각

위 그래프는 2022년의 국가별 석탄, 석유, 천연가스에서 나온 1인당 이산화 탄소 배출량을 보여 준다. ① 석탄에서 나온 배출량은 보여진 다섯 개의 국가 중 두 번째로 낮았음에도 불구하고, 미국은 가장 높은 1인당 이산화 탄소 총배출량을 가졌다. ② 한국의 1인당 이산화 탄소 총배출량은 10톤이 넘고, 보여진 국가 중 두 번째로 높은 순위를 차지했다. ③ 독일은 한국보다 각각의 모든 세 가지 주요한 원천에서 더 낮은 1인당 이산화 탄소 배출량을 가졌다. ④ 남아프리카 공화국의 석탄으로부터의 1인당 이산화 탄소 배출량은 독일의 그것보다 세 배보다 더 높았다(→ 거의 두 배 높았다). ⑤ 브라질에서 석유는 브라질의 세 가지 주요한 원천 중에서 1인당 이산화 탄소 배출량의 가장 큰 원천이었고, 그것은 미국과 독일에서도 마찬가지였다.

다음 도표의 내용과 일치하지 않는 것은?

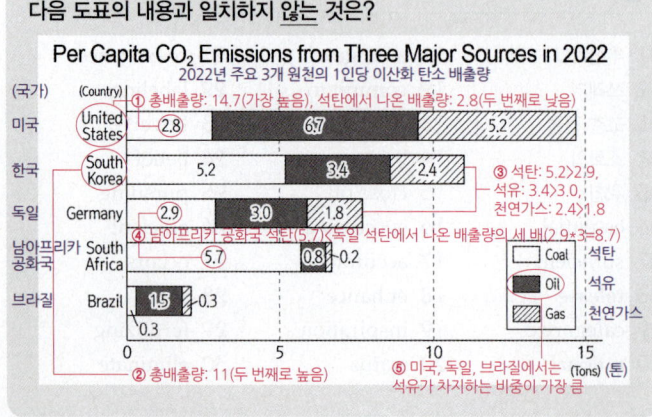

Per Capita CO₂ Emissions from Three Major Sources in 2022
2022년 주요 3개 원천의 1인당 이산화 탄소 배출량

> **왜 정답?** ✱❊❊ [정답률 85%]

남아프리카 공화국의 석탄에서 나온 1인당 이산화 탄소 배출량은 5.7톤으로, 독일의 석탄에서 나온 1인당 이산화 탄소 배출량인 2.9톤의 세 배인 8.7톤보다 적다. 따라서 ④이 도표의 내용과 일치하지 않는다.

> **왜 오답?**

① 미국의 1인당 이산화 탄소 총배출량은 14.7톤이므로 전체 중 가장 높고, 석탄에서 나온 배출량은 2.8톤으로 브라질(0.3톤)에 이어 두 번째로 낮다.
② 한국의 1인당 이산화 탄소 총배출량은 11톤이므로 10톤을 넘고, 전체 중 미국에 이어 두 번째로 높다.
③ 석탄(5.2〉2.9), 석유(3.4〉3.0), 천연가스(2.4〉1.8)에서 나온 이산화 탄소 배출량은 독일이 한국보다 모두 더 낮다.
⑤ 브라질, 미국, 독일 모두 세 가지 원천 중 석유에서 나온 이산화 탄소 배출량이 차지하는 비중이 가장 크다.

─ **어법 특강** ─

✱ 분사구문
- 분사가 이끄는 어구가 부사절을 대신할 때 이 어구를 분사구문이라고 하며, 부사절을 분사구문으로 바꿀 때는,
  1. 주절의 주어와 부사절의 주어가 같은 경우 주어를 생략한다.
  2. 주절의 시제와 일치할 때 현재분사로, 주절의 시제보다 앞설 때는 having p.p.의 형태로, 수동태일 때는 (being/having been)+p.p. 형태로 바꾼다.
  3. 내용상 밝혀야 할 때를 제외하고, 부사절 접속사를 생략한다.

H 02 정답 ④ *미국인들의 패스트푸드 섭취 빈도

shows의 목적어 (간접의문문)
The above graph shows / how often people in America consumed fast food in 2023, / sorted according to frequency of consumption. // 분사구문을 이끄는 과거분사(앞에 being이 생략됨)
위 그래프는 보여 준다 / 2023년 미국에서 사람들이 얼마나 자주 패스트푸드를 먹었는지를 / 빈도 순에 따라

주 1회 이상: 13%(매일)+36%(일주일에 몇 번)+16%(일주일에 한 번)=65%〉50%
① More than 50 percent of individuals / consumed fast food / once a week or more frequently. // 50퍼센트가 넘는 사람들은 / 패스트푸드를 먹었다 / 일주일에 한 번 또는 더 자주

일주일에 몇 번: 36% → 가장 큰 비중 차지
② The most highly reported pattern of consumption / was a few times a week, / which was 36 percent of the total. // 계속적 용법의 주격 관계대명사
가장 많이 응답된 섭취 패턴은 / 일주일에 몇 번이었고 / 이는 전체의 36퍼센트였다 //

한 달에 몇 번: 18% → 두 번째로 큰 비중 차지
③ The second most highly reported pattern was a few times a month, / accounting for 18 percent of the total. // 분사구문을 이끄는 현재분사
두 번째로 가장 많이 응답된 패턴은 한 달에 몇 번이었으며 / 이는 전체의 18퍼센트를 차지했다 //

단수 주어
④ The percentage of people / who ate fast food once every couple of months / was more(→ less) / than that of those who consumed it daily. // 단수 동사   = the percentage   = fast food
단서 8%(두 달에 한 번) 〈 13%(매일)
사람들의 비율은 / 패스트푸드를 두 달에 한 번 먹었던 / 많았다(→ 적었다) / 패스트푸드를 매일 먹었던 사람들의 비율보다 //

⑤ The combined share of those who rarely or never ate fast food / was less than 10 percent. // 거의 혹은 전혀 먹지 않음: 5%+4%=9% 〈 10%
패스트푸드를 거의 혹은 전혀 먹지 않았던 사람들을 합친 몫은 / 10퍼센트 미만이었다 //

- consume ⓥ 먹다 - sort ⓥ 분류하다 - frequency ⓝ 빈도
- frequently ⓐⓓ 자주 - account for ~을 차지하다
- percentage ⓝ 비율 - combine ⓥ 합치다
- share ⓝ 몫 - rarely ⓐⓓ 거의 ~ 않는

위 그래프는 2023년 미국에서 사람들이 얼마나 자주 패스트푸드를 먹었는지를 빈도 순에 따라 보여 준다. ① 50퍼센트가 넘는 사람들은 패스트푸드를 일주일에 한 번 또는 더 자주 먹었다. ② 가장 많이 응답된 섭취 패턴은 일주일에 몇 번이었고, 이는 전체의 36퍼센트였다. ③ 두 번째로 가장 많이 응답된 패턴은 한 달에 몇 번이었으며, 이는 전체의 18퍼센트를 차지했다. ④ 패스트푸드를 두 달에 한 번 먹었던 사람들의 비율은 패스트푸드를 매일 먹었던 사람들의 비율보다 많았다(→ 적었다). ⑤ 패스트푸드를 거의 혹은 전혀 먹지 않았던 사람들을 합친 몫은 10퍼센트 미만이었다.

다음 도표의 내용과 일치하지 않는 것은?

2023년 미국인들의 패스트푸드 섭취 빈도
How Often People in America Consumed Fast Food in 2023

① 주 1회 이상: 13%+36%+16%=65% (50%를 초과함)
④ 두 달에 한 번(8%) < 매일(13%)

- Daily 매일 — 13%
- A few times a week 일주일에 몇 번 — 36%
② 가장 많은 패턴: 일주일에 몇 번(36%)
- Once a week 일주일에 한 번 — 16%
- A few times a month 한 달에 몇 번 — 18% ③ 두 번째로 많은 패턴: 한 달에 몇 번(18%)
- Once every couple of months 두 달에 한 번 — 8%
- Rarely 거의 먹지 않음 — 5%
- Never 전혀 먹지 않음 — 4%
⑤ 거의 혹은 전혀 먹지 않음: 5%+4%=9% (10% 미만임)

왜 정답? ✹✹✺ [정답률 88%]

두 달에 한 번 섭취하는 사람들은 8퍼센트이고 매일 섭취하는 사람은 13퍼센트이므로 매일 섭취하는 사람이 두 달에 한 번 섭취하는 사람들보다 많다. 따라서 ④이 도표의 내용과 일치하지 않는다.

왜 오답?

주의
① 주 1회 이상 섭취하는 사람은 일주일에 한 번, 일주일에 몇 번, 매일 먹는 사람들의 비율을 전부 합해야 하므로 총 65퍼센트, 즉 50퍼센트를 초과한다.
② 일주일에 몇 번 섭취하는 경우는 36퍼센트로 가장 큰 비중을 차지한다.
③ 두 번째로 가장 많이 응답된 패턴은 한 달에 몇 번 섭취하는 경우로 18퍼센트이다.
⑤ 거의 먹지 않거나 전혀 먹지 않는 사례는 총 9퍼센트이므로 10퍼센트 미만이다.

구문 서술형

정답 shows, consumed

→ 2023년이라는 과거의 특정 시점에 패스트푸드를 먹었던 것이므로 과거형인 consumed, 그 결과를 그래프가 현재 보여 준다는 것이므로 3인칭 단수 현재형인 shows로 쓴다.

H 03 정답 ④ ✱소매 거래에서 온라인 점유율

The graph above shows / the online share of retail trade / in
과거분사 (European countries 수식)
selected European countries in 2018 and 2019. //
위 그래프는 보여준다 / 소매 거래에서의 온라인 점유율을 / 선정된 유럽 국가들에서 2018년과 2019년에 //

① In 2019, / the United Kingdom recorded / **the highest** online 최상급
share of retail trade, / **reaching 19.2 percent**. // 2019년: 영국 19.2%
분사구문   → 가장 높음
2019년에 / 영국은 기록하였다 / 소매 거래에서 가장 높은 온라인 점유율을 / 19.2퍼센트에 달하며 //

② The Netherlands showed the largest increase / in its online share of retail trade / among the countries / from 2018 to 2019, / with a jump of over 6 percentage points. // 네덜란드: 9.1% → 15.3%
                                                    6.2%p 증가하여 가장 큼
네덜란드는 가장 큰 증가를 보였다 / 소매 거래에서의 온라인 점유율이 / 국가들 중 / 2018년부터 2019년까지 / 6퍼센트포인트 넘게 증가하여 //

③ In 2018, / Germany had a **higher** online share of retail trade /
                          비교급
than the Netherlands, / whereas, in 2019, / Germany fell behind the Netherlands. // 2018년: 독일 15.1% > 네덜란드 9.1%, 2019년: 독일 14.2% < 네덜란드 15.3%
2018년에는 / 독일은 소매 거래에서 더 높은 온라인 점유율을 가졌으나 / 네덜란드보다 / 반면 2019년에는 / 독일은 네덜란드에 뒤처졌다 //

④ In 2018, / Germany's online share of retail trade / was over
   배수사 + 비교급 + than: ~배 더 ~한
(→ not over) four times higher / than that of Spain. //
2018년에 / 독일의 소매 거래에서의 온라인 점유율은 / 네 배 넘게 높았다(→ 높지 않았다) / 스페인의 그것보다 //
단서 2018년 독일의 점유율인 15.1%는 스페인의 네 배(4.8% × 4 = 19.2%)를 넘지 않음

⑤ Among the five countries, / Italy recorded / the lowest online share / of retail trade / in both 2018 and 2019. // 이탈리아: 2018년 3.4%, 2019년 5.9%
다섯 국가들 중 / 이탈리아는 기록하였다 / 가장 낮은 온라인 점유율을 / 소매 거래에서 / 2018년과 2019년 모두 //

- **share** ⓝ 점유율, 몫
- **retail** ⓝ 소매
- **trade** ⓝ 거래
- **record** ⓥ 기록하다
- **reach** ⓥ 도달하다
- **increase** ⓝ 증가
- **fall behind** 뒤처지다

위 그래프는 선정된 유럽 국가들에서 2018년과 2019년에 소매 거래에서의 온라인 점유율을 보여준다. ① 2019년에, 영국은 19.2퍼센트에 달하며, 소매 거래에서 가장 높은 온라인 점유율을 기록하였다. ② 네덜란드는 2018년부터 2019년까지 소매 거래에서의 온라인 점유율이 6퍼센트포인트 넘게 증가하여, 국가들 중 가장 큰 증가를 보였다. ③ 2018년에는, 독일은 네덜란드보다 소매 거래에서 더 높은 온라인 점유율을 가졌으나, 2019년에는, 독일은 네덜란드에 뒤처졌다. ④ 2018년에, 독일의 소매 거래에서의 온라인 점유율은 스페인의 그것보다 네 배 넘게 높았다(→ 높지 않았다). ⑤ 다섯 국가들 중, 이탈리아는 2018년과 2019년 모두 소매 거래에서 가장 낮은 온라인 점유율을 기록하였다.

다음 도표의 내용과 일치하지 않는 것은?

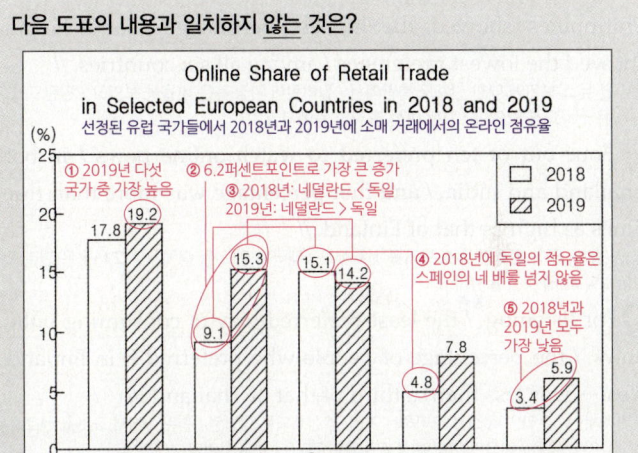

Online Share of Retail Trade in Selected European Countries in 2018 and 2019
선정된 유럽 국가들에서 2018년과 2019년에 소매 거래에서의 온라인 점유율

① 2019년 다섯 국가 중 가장 높음
③ 6.2퍼센트포인트로 가장 큰 증가
③ 2018년: 네덜란드 < 독일 2019년: 네덜란드 > 독일
④ 2018년에 독일의 점유율은 스페인의 네 배를 넘지 않음
⑤ 2018년과 2019년 모두 가장 낮음

- United Kingdom 영국 — 17.8 / 19.2
- Netherlands 네덜란드 — 9.1 / 15.3
- Germany 독일 — 15.1 / 14.2
- Spain 스페인 — 4.8 / 7.8
- Italy 이탈리아 — 3.4 / 5.9

왜 정답? ✹✺✺ [정답률 89%]

2018년에 독일의 소매 거래에서의 온라인 점유율은 15.1%로 스페인의 점유율인 4.8%의 네 배(4.8% × 4 = 19.2%)를 넘지 않는다. 따라서 ④이 도표의 내용과 일치하지 않는다.

왜 오답?

① 2019년 영국은 소매 거래에서의 온라인 점유율이 19.2퍼센트로 다른 나라들보다 높다.
② 네덜란드의 소매 거래에서의 온라인 점유율은 2018년부터 2019년까지 6.2퍼센트포인트 증가했으며, 다른 나라들보다 크게 증가했다.
③ 2018년 독일은 소매 거래에서의 온라인 점유율이 15.1%로 네덜란드 9.1%보다 높지만 2019년에는 14.2%로 네덜란드 15.3%보다 낮다.
⑤ 이탈리아는 소매 거래에서의 온라인 점유율이 2018년과 2019년에 각각 3.4%, 5.9%로 가장 낮다.

구문 서술형

정답 has shown, since

해석 네덜란드는 2018년 이래로 소매 거래에서의 온라인 점유율에서 가장 큰 증가를 보여 왔다.

→ 2018년이라는 과거 시점부터 지속되어 왔음을 나타내려면 현재완료시제를 써야 하고, 국가명인 The Netherlands는 단수 취급하므로 has shown으로 쓴다. 주로 현재완료시제와 같이 쓰여 '~이래로'를 나타내는 전치사는 since이다.

H 04 정답 ⑤ *국가별 온라인 뉴스 소비 방식 선호도 비교

The graph above shows / the percentage of online news consumption preferences in three ways / for six countries in 2020. //
위 그래프는 보여준다 / 세 가지 방식의 온라인 뉴스 소비 선호도 비율을 / 2020년 여섯 개 국가에서 //

독일(67%), 영국(78%), 핀란드(82%): 읽기가 가장 선호되고 모두 60%가 넘음
① In Germany, the UK and Finland, / reading was the most
과거분사 (way 수식)
<mark>preferred</mark> way of consuming online news, / with its percentage over 60 percent / across the three countries. //
독일, 영국 그리고 핀란드에서 / 읽기는 온라인 뉴스를 소비하는 가장 선호되는 방식이었으며 / 그것의 비율이 60퍼센트가 넘었다 / 세 나라 모두에서 //

필리핀(52%), 태국(40%), 인도(40%)
주격 보어절 접속사   : 보기를 가장 선호함
② The interesting point is / <mark>that</mark> the Philippines, Thailand and India all preferred to watch online news the most. //
흥미로운 점은 ~이다 / 필리핀, 태국 그리고 인도 모두가 온라인 뉴스 보기를 가장 선호했다는 것 //

'~의 측면에서, ~에 관하여'   보기 선호도: 필리핀(52%) 가장 높음, 핀란드(12%) 가장 낮음
③ <mark>In terms of</mark> preference to watching online news, / the Philippines showed the highest percentage / and Finland showed the lowest preference / among all six countries. //
온라인 뉴스 보기에 대한 선호도 측면에서 / 필리핀이 가장 높은 비율을 보였고 / 핀란드가 가장 낮은 선호도를 보였다 / 모든 여섯 개 나라 중에서 //

④ Four out of ten preferred to watch online news / in both Thailand and India, / and that percentage was more than three times as high as that of Finland. // 보기 선호도: 40%(태국, 인도) > 12%(핀란드)×3
열 명 중 네 명이 온라인 뉴스 보기를 선호했고 / 태국과 인도 둘 다에서 / 그 비율은 핀란드의 그것보다 세 배 이상 높았다 //

동격   핀란드(6%)가 태국(22%)의 삼분의 일(약 7.3%)보다 적음
단서
⑤ For <mark>listening</mark>, / <mark>the least preferred way of consuming online news</mark>, / the percentage of people who preferred it in Finland / was(→ was less than) a third of that of Thailand. //
듣기에서는 / 온라인 뉴스를 소비하는 가장 덜 선호되는 방법인 / 핀란드에서 그것을 선호하는 사람들의 비율은 / 태국의 그것의 삼분의 일이었다(→ 보다 적었다) //

- consumption ⓝ 소비   - preference ⓝ 선호(도)
- consume ⓥ 소비하다   - least ⓐⓓ 가장 적게

위 그래프는 2020년 여섯 개 국가에서 세 가지 방식의 온라인 뉴스 소비 선호도 비율을 보여준다. ① 독일, 영국 그리고 핀란드에서 읽기는 온라인 뉴스를 소비하는 가장 선호되는 방식이었으며 세 나라 모두에서 그것의 비율이 60퍼센트가 넘었다. ② 흥미로운 점은 필리핀, 태국 그리고 인도 모두가 온라인 뉴스 보기를 가장 선호했다는 것이다. ③ 온라인 뉴스 보기에 대한 선호도 측면에서, 필리핀이 가장 높은 비율을 보였고, 핀란드가 모든 여섯 개 나라 중에서 가장 낮은 선호도를 보였다. ④ 태국과 인도 둘 다에서 열 명 중 네 명이 온라인 뉴스 보기를 선호했고, 그 비율은 핀란드의 그것보다 세 배 이상 높았다. ⑤ 온라인 뉴스를 소비하는 가장 덜 선호되는 방법인 듣기에서는, 핀란드에서 그것을 선호하는 사람들의 비율은 태국의 그것의 삼분의 일이었다(→ 보다 적었다).

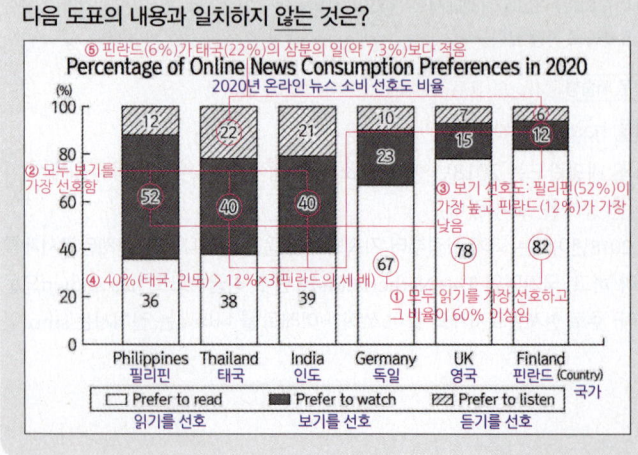

다음 도표의 내용과 일치하지 않는 것은?

Percentage of Online News Consumption Preferences in 2020
2020년 온라인 뉴스 소비 선호도 비율

⑤ 핀란드(6%)가 태국(22%)의 삼분의 일(약 7.3%)보다 적음

② 모두 보기를 가장 선호함
③ 보기 선호도: 필리핀(52%)이 가장 높고 핀란드(12%)가 가장 낮음
④ 40%(태국, 인도) > 12%×3 핀란드의 세 배
① 모두 읽기를 가장 선호하고 그 비율이 60% 이상임

	Philippines 필리핀	Thailand 태국	India 인도	Germany 독일	UK 영국	Finland 핀란드 (Country) 국가
듣기	12	22	21	10	15	6
보기	52	40	40	23	78	82
읽기	36	38	39	67		

□ Prefer to read 읽기를 선호 ■ Prefer to watch 보기를 선호 ▨ Prefer to listen 듣기를 선호

왜 정답? ❋❋❋ [정답률 82%]

핀란드에서 온라인 뉴스 듣기 선호도는 6퍼센트이므로 태국(22퍼센트)의 삼분의 일(약 7.3퍼센트)보다 적다. 따라서 ⑤이 도표의 내용과 일치하지 않는다.

왜 오답?

① 독일, 영국, 핀란드의 읽기 선호 비율은 각각 67%, 78%, 82%로, 모두 60% 이상이다.
② 필리핀, 태국, 인도의 보기 선호 비율은 각각 52%, 40%, 40%로, 각 국가에서 가장 선호도가 높다.
③ 여섯 국가의 보기 선호 비율 중 필리핀(52%)은 가장 높고, 핀란드(12%)는 가장 낮다.
④ 태국과 인도 모두 보기 선호 비율이 40%이므로 핀란드의 세 배(12%×3=36%)가 넘는다.

구문 서술형

정답 preferred

해석 2020년에 필리핀, 태국 그리고 인도 모두가 온라인 뉴스 보기를 가장 선호했다.
→ 2020년이라는 과거 시점의 일을 나타내려면 과거시제를 써야 하므로 preferred로 쓴다.

H 05 정답 ③ *젊은 사람들의 기후 변화에 대한 두려움

목적격 관계대명사(선행사: the extent)   '16세에서 25세 사이의'
The above graph shows / the extent to <mark>which</mark> young people <mark>aged 16-25</mark> in six countries had fear / about climate change / in 2021. //
위 그래프는 보여준다 / 6개국의 16세에서 25세 사이 젊은 사람들이 두려움을 갖는 정도를 / 기후 변화에 대해 / 2021년에 //

주격 관계대명사
① The Philippines had the highest percentage / of young people <mark>who</mark> said they were extremely or very worried, / at 84 percent, /
분사구문을 이끄는 과거분사   필리핀이 가장 높음(49% + 35% = 84%),
<mark>followed</mark> by 67 percent in Brazil. //   브라질이 두 번째로 높음 (29% + 38% = 67%)
필리핀은 비율이 가장 높았다 / 극도로 혹은 매우 걱정한다고 말한 젊은 사람들의 (비율이) / 84퍼센트로 / 브라질이 67퍼센트로 그 뒤를 이었다 //

② More than 60 percent of young people in Portugal said / they were extremely worried or very worried. // 포르투갈(30% + 35% = 65%)은 60% 이상
포르투갈은 60퍼센트 이상의 젊은 사람들이 말했다 / 그들이 극도로 혹은 매우 걱정하고 있다고 //

복수 선행사(people)와 수 일치
③ In France, / the percentage of young people / <mark>who</mark> <mark>were</mark> extremely worried / was <mark>higher(→ lower)</mark> / than <mark>that</mark> of young = the percentage people who were very worried. //
단서 회색 막대(극도로 걱정하는 비율)가 하얀색 막대(매우 걱정하는 비율)보다 짧음
프랑스는 / 젊은 사람들의 비율이 / 극도로 걱정하는 / 더 높았다(→ 낮았다) / 매우 걱정하는 젊은 사람들의 비율보다 //

단수 주어
④ In the United Kingdom, / <mark>the percentage</mark> of young generation / who said that they were very worried / <mark>was</mark> 29 percent. // 단수 동사
영국은 / 젊은 세대의 비율이 / 매우 걱정한다고 말하는 / 29퍼센트였다 // 영국의 하얀색 막대는 29퍼센트임

⑤ In the United States, / the total percentage of extremely worried and very worried youth / was the smallest among the six countries. // 미국은 회색 막대와 하얀색 막대를 합한 길이가 가장 짧음
미국은 / 극도로 걱정하거나 매우 걱정하는 젊은 사람들의 총비율이 / 6개국 중에서 가장 작았다 //

- extent ⓝ 정도   - youth ⓝ 청소년, 젊은 사람들
- fear ⓝ 두려움   - climate change 기후 변화
- extremely ⓐⓓ 극도로   - generation ⓝ 세대

위 그래프는 2021년 6개국의 16세에서 25세 사이 젊은 사람들이 기후 변화에 대해 두려움을 갖는 정도를 보여 준다. ① 필리핀은 극도로 혹은 매우 걱정한다고 말한 젊은 사람들의 비율이 84퍼센트로 가장 높았으며, 브라질이 67퍼센트로 그 뒤를 이었다. ② 포르투갈은 60퍼센트 이상의 젊은 사람들이 극도로 혹은 매우 걱정하고 있다고 말했다. ③ 프랑스는 극도로 걱정하는 젊은 사람들의 비율이 매우 걱정하는 젊은 사람들의 비율보다 높았다(→ 낮았다). ④ 영국은 매우 걱정한다고 말하는 젊은 세대의 비율이 29퍼센트였다. ⑤ 미국은 극도로 걱정하거나 매우 걱정하는 젊은 사람들의 총비율이 6개국 중에서 가장 작았다.

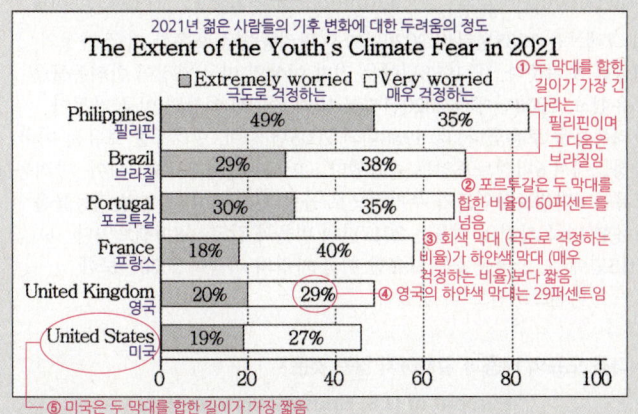

다음 도표의 내용과 일치하지 <u>않는</u> 것은?

2021년 젊은 사람들의 기후 변화에 대한 두려움의 정도
The Extent of the Youth's Climate Fear in 2021

■ Extremely worried □ Very worried
극도로 걱정하는   매우 걱정하는

국가	Extremely worried	Very worried
Philippines 필리핀	49%	35%
Brazil 브라질	29%	38%
Portugal 포르투갈	30%	35%
France 프랑스	18%	40%
United Kingdom 영국	20%	29%
United States 미국	19%	27%

① 두 막대를 합한 길이가 가장 긴 나라는 필리핀이며 그 다음은 브라질임
② 포르투갈은 두 막대를 합한 비율이 60퍼센트를 넘음
③ 회색 막대 (극도로 걱정하는 비율)가 하얀색 막대 (매우 걱정하는 비율)보다 작음
④ 영국의 하얀색 막대는 29퍼센트임
⑤ 미국은 두 막대를 합한 길이가 가장 짧음

▷왜 정답? ❀❀❀ [정답률 85%]

프랑스에서 극도로 걱정하는 젊은 사람들의 비율은 18퍼센트이며 매우 걱정하는 젊은 사람들의 비율은 40퍼센트로, 극도로 걱정하는 젊은 사람들의 비율이 매우 걱정하는 젊은 사람들의 비율보다 작다. 따라서 도표의 내용과 일치하지 않는 것은 ③이다.

▷왜 오답?

① 극도로 걱정하는 젊은 사람들의 비율(회색 막대)과 매우 걱정하는 젊은 사람들의 비율(하얀색 막대)의 합이 가장 큰 나라는 필리핀이고 두 번째로 큰 나라는 브라질이다.
② 포르투갈은 회색 막대와 하얀색 막대를 합한 비율이 65퍼센트이다.
④ 영국에서는 매우 걱정하는 젊은 사람들의 비율을 가리키는 하얀색 막대가 29퍼센트이다.
⑤ 미국은 극도로 걱정하는 젊은 사람들의 비율을 가리키는 회색 막대와 매우 걱정하는 젊은 사람들의 비율을 가리키는 하얀색 막대를 합한 길이가 가장 짧은 국가이다.

H 06 정답 ③ *지역별 전자 폐기물 수거율 및 재활용률

The above graph shows / the electronic waste collection and recycling rate / by region / in 2016 and 2019. //
위 도표는 보여준다 / 전자 폐기물 수거율 및 재활용률을 / 지역별 / 2016년과 2019년의 //

① In both years, / Europe showed / the highest electronic waste collection and recycling rates. // 2016년, 2019년 모두 유럽이 가장 높음
두 해 모두 / 유럽이 보였다 / 가장 높은 전자 폐기물 수거율 및 재활용률을 //

② The electronic waste collection and recycling rate of Asia in 2019 / was lower than in 2016. // 아시아: 2019년(12%) < 2016년(15%)
2019년 아시아의 전자 폐기물 수거율 및 재활용률은 / 2016년보다 낮았다 //

③ The Americas / ranked third both in 2016 and in 2019(→ second in 2016 and third in 2019), / with 17 percent and 9 percent respectively. // 단서 아메리카: 2016년(17%, 전체 2위), 2019년(9%, 전체 3위)
(남·북·중앙) 아메리카는 / 2016년과 2019년 모두 3위(→ 2016년에는 2위, 2019년에는 3위)를 기록했으며 / 그 비율은 각각 17퍼센트와 9퍼센트였다 //

④ In both years, / the electronic waste collection and recycling rates in Oceania / remained under 10 percent. // 2016년(6%), 2019년(9%) 모두 10% 미만
두 해 모두 / 오세아니아의 전자 폐기물 수거율 및 재활용률은 / 10퍼센트 아래에 머물렀다 //

⑤ Africa / had the lowest electronic waste collection and recycling rates / in both 2016 and 2019, / showing the smallest gap between 2016 and 2019. // 2016년도, 2019년도 모두 막대가 가장 짧으며, 두 년도 간 차이는 1퍼센트포인트로 가장 낮음
분사구문
아프리카는 / 가장 낮은 전자 폐기물 수거율 및 재활용률을 기록했다 / 2016년과 2019년 모두 / 그리고 두 해 사이의 비율 격차가 가장 적었다 //

- electronic waste 전자 폐기물
- recycling ⓝ 재활용
- region ⓝ 지역
- respectively 🄰🄳 각각
- gap ⓝ 격차

위 도표는 2016년과 2019년의 지역별 전자 폐기물 수거율 및 재활용률을 보여준다. ① 두 해 모두 유럽이 가장 높은 전자 폐기물 수거율 및 재활용률을 보였다. ② 2019년 아시아의 전자 폐기물 수거율 및 재활용률은 2016년보다 낮았다. ③ (남·북·중앙) 아메리카는 2016년과 2019년 모두 3위(→ 2016년에는 2위, 2019년에는 3위)를 기록했으며, 그 비율은 각각 17퍼센트와 9퍼센트였다. ④ 오세아니아의 전자 폐기물 수거율 및 재활용률은 두 해 모두 10퍼센트 아래에 머물렀다. ⑤ 아프리카는 2016년과 2019년 모두 가장 낮은 전자 폐기물 수거율 및 재활용률을 기록했으며, 두 해 사이의 비율 격차가 가장 적었다.

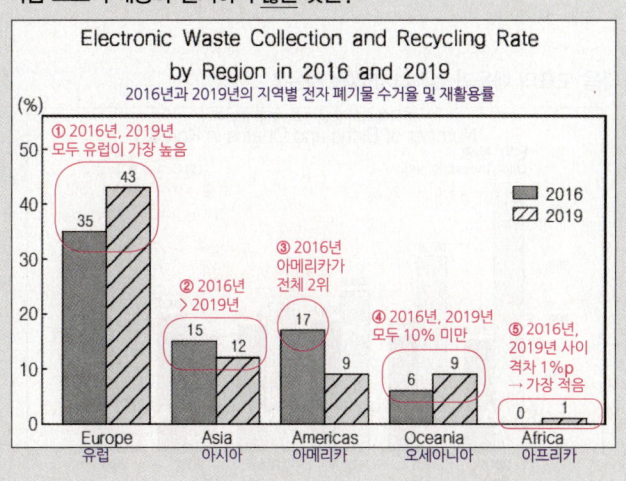

다음 도표의 내용과 일치하지 <u>않는</u> 것은?

Electronic Waste Collection and Recycling Rate by Region in 2016 and 2019
2016년과 2019년의 지역별 전자 폐기물 수거율 및 재활용률

■ 2016 ▨ 2019

Region	2016	2019
Europe 유럽	35	43
Asia 아시아	15	12
Americas 아메리카	17	9
Oceania 오세아니아	6	9
Africa 아프리카	0	1

① 2016년, 2019년 모두 유럽이 가장 높음
② 2016년 > 2019년
③ 2016년 아메리카가 전체 2위
④ 2016년, 2019년 모두 10% 미만
⑤ 2016년, 2019년 사이 격차 1%p → 가장 적음

▷왜 정답? ❀❀❀ [정답률 89%]

아메리카의 전자 폐기물 수거율 및 재활용률은 2016년에 17%로 2위를 차지했으며 2019년에는 9%로 오세아니아와 공동 3위이다. 그러므로 2016년과 2019년 모두 3위를 기록했다고 한 ③이 도표의 내용과 일치하지 않는다.

▷왜 오답?

① 유럽은 2016년(35%), 2019년(43%) 모두 가장 높다.
② 아시아의 2019년 전자 폐기물 수거율 및 재활용률은 12%로, 2016년의 15%보다 적다.
④ 오세아니아의 2016년, 2019년 전자 폐기물 수거율 및 재활용률은 각각 6%, 9%로 모두 10% 미만이다.
⑤ 아프리카의 2016년과 2019년 사이의 전자 폐기물 수거율 및 재활용률은 가장 낮았고, 두 해의 격차는 1%p로 가장 적다.

H 07 정답 ⑤ *한국의 출생과 사망 인구

The above graph shows / the number of births and deaths / in Korea / from 2016 to 2021. //
위 그래프는 보여준다 / 출생자 수와 사망자 수를 / 한국에서의 / 2016년부터 2021년까지 //

① The number of births continued to decrease / throughout the whole period. // 출생자 수는 계속 감소했다 / 전체 기간 내내

② The gap / between the number of births and deaths / was the largest in 2016. // 차이는 / 출생자와 사망자 수 사이의 / 2016년에 가장 컸다 //
단수 주어 / 단수 동사

③ In 2019, / the gap / between the number of births and deaths / was the smallest, / with the number of births slightly larger / than that of deaths. // 2019년에는 / 차이가 / 출생자와 사망자 수 사이의 / 가장 작았다 / 출생자 수가 약간 더 큰 채로 / 사망자의 수보다 //
단수 동사 / '~의 수' / = the number

④ The number of deaths increased steadily / during the whole period, / except the period from 2018 to 2019. //
전치사
사망자 수는 꾸준히 증가했다 / 전체 기간 동안 / 2018년과 2019년까지의 기간을 제외하고 //

⑤ In 2021(→ 2020), / the number of deaths was larger / than that of births / for the first time. // 단서 2020년에도 사망자가 출생자보다 많았음
= the number
2021년(→ 2020년)에는 / 사망자 수가 더 컸다 / 출생자 수보다 / 처음으로 //

• birth ⓝ 출생   • decrease ⓥ 감소하다   • period ⓝ 기간
• gap ⓝ 차이   • slightly ⓐⓓ 약간   • increase ⓥ 증가하다
• steadily ⓐⓓ 꾸준히   • except ⓟⓡⓔⓟ ~을 제외하고

위 그래프는 2016년부터 2021년까지 한국에서의 출생자 수와 사망자 수를 보여준다. ① 출생자 수는 전체 기간 내내 계속 감소했다. ② 출생자 수와 사망자 수 사이의 차이는 2016년에 가장 컸다. ③ 2019년에는 출생자 수와 사망자 수 사이의 차이가 가장 작았는데, 출생자 수가 사망자 수보다 약간 더 컸다. ④ 사망자 수는 2018년과 2019년까지의 기간을 제외하고 전체 기간 동안 꾸준히 증가했다. ⑤ 2021년(→ 2020년)에는 처음으로 사망자 수가 출생자 수보다 더 컸다.

다음 도표의 내용과 일치하지 않는 것은?

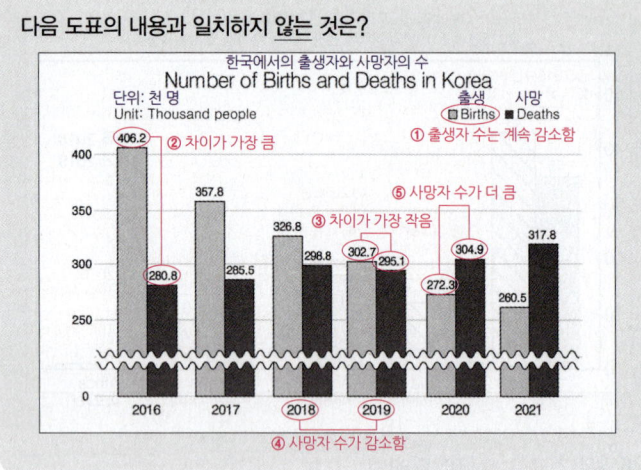

한국에서의 출생자와 사망자의 수
Number of Births and Deaths in Korea

>왜 정답? ❋❋❋ [정답률 77%]

사망자의 수가 출생자의 수보다 커지기 시작한 해는 2021년이 아니라 2020년이므로 도표의 내용과 일치하지 않는 것은 ⑤이다.

>왜 오답?

① 2016년에서 2021년까지 출생자의 수는 계속 감소했다.
② 출생자 수와 사망자 수 사이의 차이는 2016년에 가장 컸다.
③ 2019년에는 출생자 수와 사망자 수 사이의 차이가 가장 작았는데, 출생자 수가 사망자 수보다 약간 더 컸다.
④ 사망자 수는 2018년에서 2019년 사이에만 소폭 줄었고, 이외에는 매년 증가했다.

H 08 정답 ⑤ *미국 가정의 반려동물 보유 비율

The graph above shows / the percent of households with pets / in the United States (U.S.) / from 1988 to 2020. //
위 그래프는 보여준다 / 반려동물을 보유한 가정의 비율을 / 미국에서 / 1988년부터 2020년까지 //

① In 1988, / more than half of U.S. households / owned pets, / and more than 6 out of 10 U.S. households / owned pets / from 2008 to 2020. //
1988년에는 / 절반 이상의 미국 가정이 / 반려동물을 보유했다 / 그리고 10개 중 6개 이상의 미국 가정이 / 반려동물을 보유했다 / 2008년에서 2020년까지 //

② In the period between 1988 and 2008, / pet ownership increased among U.S. households / by 6 percentage points. //
between A and B: A와 B 사이에
1988년과 2008년 사이 / 반려동물 보유는 미국 가정에서 증가했다 / 6퍼센트포인트만큼 //

③ From 2008 to 2013, / pet ownership rose / an additional 6 percentage points. //
2008년과 2013년 사이 / 반려동물 보유는 올랐다 / 6퍼센트포인트가 추가적으로 //

④ The percent of U.S. households with pets / in 2013 / was the same as that in 2017, / which was 68 percent. //
= the percent of U.S. households with pets
반려동물을 보유한 미국 가정의 비율은 / 2013년에 / 2017년의 비율과 같고 / 68퍼센트였다 //

⑤ In 2015, / the rate of U.S. households with pets / was 3(→ 2) percentage points lower / than in 2020. //
앞에 the rate of U.S. households with pets 생략
2015년에는 / 반려동물을 보유한 미국 가정의 비율이 / 3(→ 2)퍼센트포인트 더 낮았다 / 2020년보다 //
단서 2015년에는 65퍼센트이고 2020년에는 67퍼센트이므로 2퍼센트포인트 더 낮음

• household ⓝ 가정   • own ⓥ 보유하다   • period ⓝ 기간
• ownership ⓝ 보유   • additional ⓐ 추가적인   • rate ⓝ 비율

위 그래프는 1988년부터 2020년까지 반려동물을 보유한 미국 가정의 비율을 보여준다. ① 1988년에는 절반 이상의 미국 가정이 반려동물을 보유했고, 2008년에서 2020년까지 10개 중 6개 이상의 미국 가정이 반려동물을 보유했다. ② 1988년과 2008년 사이, 반려동물 보유는 미국 가정들에서 6퍼센트포인트 증가했다. ③ 2008년과 2013년 사이, 반려동물 보유는 6퍼센트포인트가 추가적으로 올랐다. ④ 2013년의 반려동물을 보유한 미국 가정의 비율은 2017년의 비율과 같고, 68퍼센트였다. ⑤ 2015년에는, 반려동물을 보유한 미국 가정의 비율이 2020년보다 3(→ 2)퍼센트포인트 더 낮았다.

다음 도표의 내용과 일치하지 않는 것은?

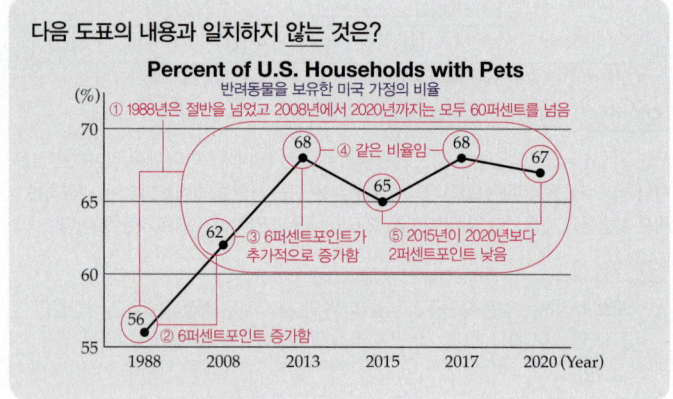

Percent of U.S. Households with Pets
반려동물을 보유한 미국 가정의 비율

>왜 정답? ❋❋❋ [정답률 80%]

2015년에 반려동물을 보유한 미국 가정의 비율은 65퍼센트이고 2020년에 반려동물을 보유한 미국 가정의 비율은 67퍼센트이므로, 2015년의 비율이 2 퍼센트포인트 더 낮다. 따라서 3퍼센트포인트 더 낮다고 하는 ⑤가 도표의 내용과 일치하지 않는다.

>왜 오답?

① 1988년에 미국 가정의 반려동물 보유 비율은 50퍼센트를 넘었기 때문에 미국 가정의 절반 이상이 반려동물을 보유했고, 2008년에서 2020년까지 반려동물 보유 비율이 모두 60퍼센트를 넘었기 때문에 10개 중 6개 이상의 미국 가정이 반려동물을 보유했다.
② 2008년에 반려동물 보유 비율은 62퍼센트이고 1988년에 반려동물 보유 비율은 56퍼센트이므로 6퍼센트포인트 증가했다.
③ 2013년에 반려동물 보유 비율은 68퍼센트이고 2008년에 반려동물 보유 비율은 62퍼센트이므로 6퍼센트포인트가 다시 추가적으로 증가했다는 것을 알 수 있다.
④ 2013년에 반려동물 보유 비율은 68퍼센트이고 2017년에 반려동물 보유 비율도 68퍼센트이므로 각각의 비율이 똑같다.

H 09 정답 ④ *문화 활동에 참여한 미국 학생들의 비율

The graph above shows / the percentage of U.S. homeschooled and public school students / participating in cultural activities / in 2016. //
현재분사
위 그래프는 보여준다 / 미국의 홈스쿨링을 받는 학생과 공립 학교 학생의 비율을 / 문화 활동에 참여하는 / 2016년에 //

① With the exception of live performances and sporting events / the percentage of homeschooled students / participating in cultural activities /
현재분사
라이브 공연과 스포츠 행사를 제외하고 / 홈스쿨링을 받는 학생의 비율이 / 문화 활동에 참여하는 /

was higher than that of public school students. //
= the percentage
공립 학교 학생의 그것보다 높았다 //

② For each group of students, / community events accounted for the largest percentage / among all cultural activities. //
각 집단의 학생에 있어 / 지역사회 행사는 가장 큰 비율을 차지했다 / 모든 문화 활동 중에서 //

92 자이스토리 영어 독해 기본

③ The percentage point difference / between homeschooled students and their public school peers / was largest in visiting libraries. //

between A and B: A와 B 사이

퍼센트 포인트 차이는 / 홈스쿨링을 받는 학생과 그들의 공립 학교 또래 간의 / 도서관 방문에서 가장 컸다 //

④ The percentage of homeschooled students / visiting museums or galleries / was more(→ less) than twice that of public school students. // 단서 박물관이나 미술관에 방문하는 홈스쿨링을 받는 학생은 42퍼센트로, 공립 학교 학생의 비율인 25퍼센트의 두 배가 되지 않음
홈스쿨링을 받는 학생의 비율은 / 박물관이나 미술관에 방문하는 / 공립 학교 학생의 그것의 두 배 이상이었다(→ 보다 작았다) //

⑤ Going to zoos or aquariums / ranked the lowest / for both groups of students, / with 31 and 23 percent respectively. //
동물원이나 수족관에 가는 것이 / 가장 낮은 순위를 차지했다 / 두 집단의 학생에 있어 / 각각 31퍼센트와 23퍼센트로 //

- homeschool ⓥ 홈스쿨링을 하다 · public school 공립 학교
- exception ⓝ 예외 · performance ⓝ 공연
- account for ~을 차지하다 · respectively 젧 각각

위 도표는 2016년에 문화 활동에 참여하는 미국의 홈스쿨링을 받는 학생과 공립 학교 학생의 비율을 보여준다. ① 라이브 공연과 스포츠 행사를 제외하고 문화 활동에 참여하는 홈스쿨링을 받는 학생의 비율이 공립 학교 학생의 그것보다 높았다. ② 각 집단의 학생에 있어 지역사회 행사는 모든 문화 활동 중에서 가장 큰 비율을 차지했다. ③ 홈스쿨링을 받는 학생과 그들의 공립 학교 또래 간의 퍼센트 포인트 차이는 도서관 방문에서 가장 컸다. ④ 박물관이나 미술관에 방문하는 홈스쿨링을 받는 학생의 비율은 공립 학교 학생의 그것의 두 배 이상이었다(→ 보다 작았다). ⑤ 동물원이나 수족관에 가는 것이 두 집단의 학생에 있어 가장 낮은 순위를 차지했는데 각각 31퍼센트와 23퍼센트였다.

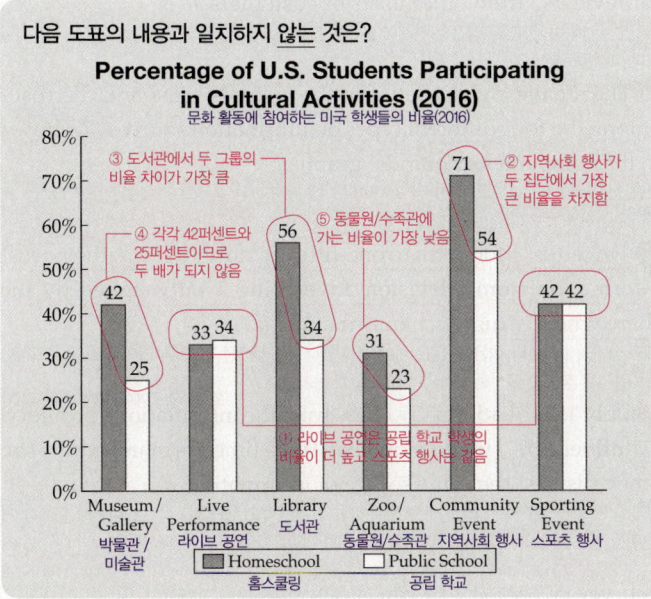

다음 도표의 내용과 일치하지 않는 것은?

Percentage of U.S. Students Participating in Cultural Activities (2016)
문화 활동에 참여하는 미국 학생들의 비율(2016)

> 왜 정답 ? ★★※ [정답률 78%]

박물관이나 미술관 방문의 경우 홈스쿨링을 받는 학생의 비율은 42퍼센트로, 공립 학교 학생의 비율인 25퍼센트의 두 배(50)가 되지 않는다. 따라서 두 배 이상이라는 ④은 도표의 내용과 일치하지 않는다.

> 왜 오답 ?

① 라이브 공연은 홈스쿨링을 받는 학생의 비율이 33퍼센트, 공립 학교 학생의 비율이 34퍼센트로 공립 학교 학생의 비율이 더 높고, 스포츠 행사는 두 그룹 모두 42퍼센트로 비율이 같다.
② 지역사회 행사에서 홈스쿨링을 받는 학생의 비율은 71퍼센트, 공립 학교 학생의 비율은 54퍼센트로, 지역사회 행사 참여가 두 집단 모두에서 가장 큰 비율을 차지하고 있다.
③ 도서관 방문의 경우 홈스쿨링을 받는 학생의 비율은 56퍼센트, 공립 학교 학생의 비율은 34퍼센트로, 그 차이가 22퍼센트 포인트에 해당하여 다른 어떤 문화 활동에서의 차이보다 크다.

---

⑤ 동물원과 수족관에 가는 비율이 각각 31퍼센트와 23퍼센트에 해당하여 모든 문화 활동 중에 가장 낮은 비율을 차지한다.

H 10 정답 ③ *대륙별 도시 인구 점유율

The graph above shows / the share of the urban population / by continent / in 1950 and in 2020. //
위 그래프는 보여준다 / 도시 인구 점유율을 / 대륙별 / 1950년과 2020년의 //

① For each continent, / the share of the urban population in 2020 / was larger / than that in 1950. //

단수 주어   단수 동사   = the share of the urban population

각 대륙에서 / 2020년의 도시 인구 점유율이 / 더 컸다 / 1950년의 그것보다 //

② From 1950 to 2020, / the share of the urban population in Africa / increased / from 14.3% to 43.5%. //
1950년부터 2020년까지 / 아프리카의 도시 인구 점유율은 / 증가했다 / 14.3%에서 43.5%로 //

③ The share of the urban population in Asia / was the second lowest / in 1950 but not in 2020(→ and in 2020 as well). //
아시아의 도시 인구 점유율은 / 두 번째로 낮았지만 / 1950년에는 / 2020년에는 그렇지 않았다(→ 2020년에도 또한 그랬다) // 단서 아시아의 도시 인구 점유율은 1950년에 아프리카에 이어 두 번째로 낮았고, 2020년에도 아프리카에 이어 두 번째로 낮았음

④ In 1950, / the share of the urban population in Europe / was larger / than that in Latin America and the Caribbean, / whereas the reverse was true in 2020. //

= the share of the urban population

1950년에는 / 유럽의 도시 인구 점유율이 / 더 컸다 / 라틴 아메리카와 카리브해 지역의 그것보다 / 2020년에는 역전이 일어났다 //

⑤ Among the five continents, / Northern America was ranked / in the first position / for the share of the urban population / in both 1950 and 2020. //
다섯 개 대륙 중 / 북아메리카는 차지했다 / 1위를 / 도시 인구 점유율에서 / 1950년과 2020년 모두 //

- share ⓝ 점유율 · urban ⓐ 도시의 · population ⓝ 인구
- continent ⓝ 대륙 · reverse ⓝ 역전

위 그래프는 1950년과 2020년의 대륙별 도시 인구 점유율을 보여준다. ① 각 대륙에서, 2020년의 도시 인구 점유율이 1950년의 그것보다 더 컸다. ② 1950년부터 2020년까지 아프리카의 도시 인구 점유율은 14.3%에서 43.5%로 증가했다. ③ 아시아의 도시 인구 점유율은 1950년에는 두 번째로 낮았지만, 2020년에는 그렇지 않았다(→ 2020년에도 또한 그랬다). ④ 1950년에는 유럽의 도시 인구 점유율이 라틴 아메리카와 카리브해 지역의 그것보다 더 컸지만, 2020년에는 역전이 일어났다. ⑤ 다섯 개 대륙 중, 북아메리카는 도시 인구 점유율에서 1950년과 2020년 모두 1위를 차지했다.

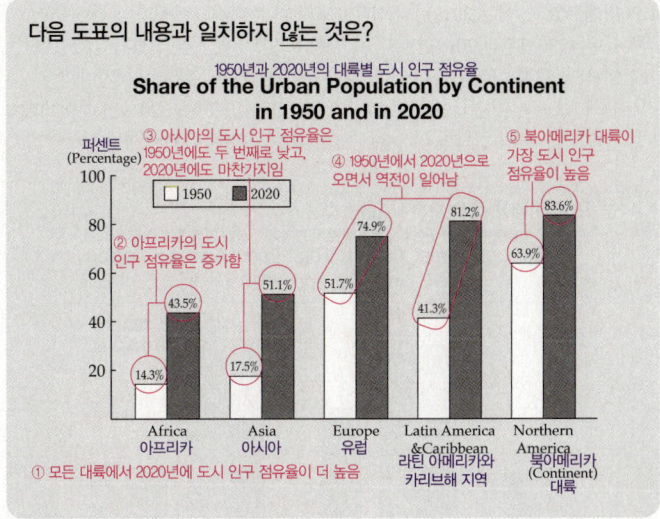

다음 도표의 내용과 일치하지 않는 것은?

1950년과 2020년의 대륙별 도시 인구 점유율
Share of the Urban Population by Continent in 1950 and in 2020

> 왜 정답 ? ★★※ [정답률 77%]

아시아의 도시 인구 점유율은 1950년에도 아프리카에 이어 두 번째로 낮고, 2020년에도 아프리카에 이어 두 번째로 낮다. 따라서 2020년에는 두 번째로 낮지 않다는 ③은 도표의 내용과 일치하지 않는다.

> 왜 오답?

① 모든 대륙에서 1950년보다 2020년에 도시 인구 점유율이 높다.

② 아프리카의 도시 인구 점유율은 14.3%에서 43.5%로 증가했으므로 일치한다.

④ 1950년 유럽과 라틴 아메리카와 카리브해 지역의 도시 인구 점유율은 각각 51.7%, 41.3%로 유럽이 높지만, 2020년에는 유럽 74.9%, 라틴 아메리카와 카리브해 지역이 81.2%로 역전이 일어났다.

⑤ 1950년과 2020년에 북아메리카 대륙의 도시 인구 점유율은 각각 63.9%, 83.6%로 다섯 대륙 중 가장 높다.

H 11 정답 ④ *산림 면적이 차지하는 비율

The above graph shows / the share of forest area / in total land area / by region / in 1990 and 2019. //
위 도표는 보여준다 / 산림 면적의 점유율을 / 총 토지 면적에서 / 지역별 / 1990년과 2019년의 //

① Africa's share of forest area in total land area / was over 20% / in both 1990 and 2019. // 아프리카: 1990년(25.3%), 2019년(21.4%)
아프리카의 전체 토지 면적에서 산림 면적의 점유율은 / 20퍼센트를 넘었다 / 1990년과 2019년에 모두 //

아메리카: 1990년(42.6%) > 2019년(41.4%)
② The share of forest area in America / was 42.6% in 1990, /
계속적 용법의 주격 관계대명사
which was larger than that in 2019. //
아메리카의 산림 면적 점유율은 / 1990년에 42.6퍼센트였고 / 이는 2019년의 그것보다 더 컸다 //

아시아: 1990년(32.4%) − 2019년(20%) = 12.4%p
③ The share of forest area in Asia / declined from 1990 to 2019 / by more than 10 percentage points. //
아시아의 산림 면적 점유율은 / 1990년부터 2019년까지 감소했다 / 10퍼센트포인트 이상 //

④ In 2019, / the share of forest area in Europe / was the largest
= the share of forest area
among the five regions, / more than ~~three~~(→ two) times **that** in Asia / in the same year. //
2019년 / 유럽의 산림 면적 점유율은 / 다섯 개 지역 중 가장 컸다 / 아시아의 그것의 세 배가 넘으며 / 같은 해에 // 단서 2019년: 유럽(46%)은 아시아(20%)의 3배(60%)보다 작음

⑤ Oceania showed the smallest gap / between 1990 and 2019 /
~에서는, ~에 관하여
in terms of the share of forest area in total land area. //
오세아니아는 가장 작은 차이를 보였다 / 1990년과 2019년 사이에 / 총 토지 면적에서 산림 면적의 점유율에 있어 // — 오세아니아: 2019년(23.4%) − 1990년(22.6%) = 0.8%p로 가장 작음

- • share ⓝ 몫, 점유율 • region ⓝ 지역 • decline ⓥ 감소하다

위 도표는 1990년과 2019년의 지역별 총 토지 면적에서 산림 면적의 점유율을 보여준다. ① 아프리카의 전체 토지 면적에서 산림 면적의 점유율은 1990년과 2019년 둘 다 20퍼센트를 넘었다. ② 1990년 아메리카의 산림 면적 점유율은 42.6퍼센트였고, 이는 2019년의 점유율보다 더 컸다. ③ 아시아의 산림 면적 점유율은 1990년부터 2019년까지 10퍼센트포인트 이상 감소했다. ④ 2019년 유럽의 산림 면적 점유율은 다섯 개 지역 중 가장 컸고, 같은 해 아시아의 점유율의 세(→ 두) 배가 넘었다. ⑤ 오세아니아는 1990년과 2019년 사이에 총 토지 면적에서 산림 면적의 점유율에 있어 가장 작은 차이를 보였다.

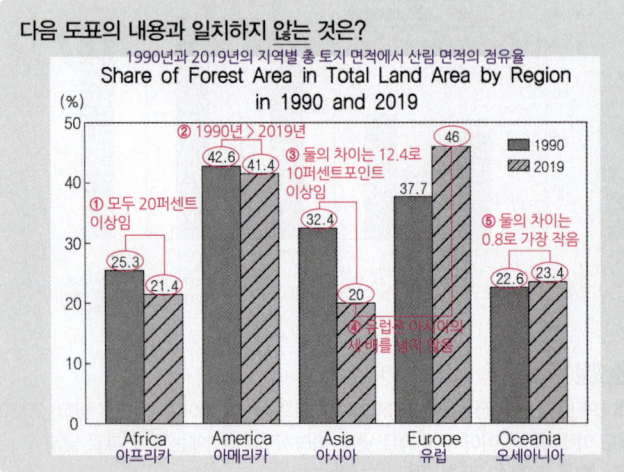

다음 도표의 내용과 일치하지 않는 것은?

1990년과 2019년의 지역별 총 토지 면적에서 산림 면적의 점유율
Share of Forest Area in Total Land Area by Region in 1990 and 2019

② 1990년 > 2019년
③ 둘의 차이는 12.4로 10퍼센트포인트 이상임
① 모두 20퍼센트 이상임
⑤ 둘의 차이는 0.8로 가장 작음
④ 유럽이 아시아의 세 배를 넘지 못함

Africa 아프리카 / America 아메리카 / Asia 아시아 / Europe 유럽 / Oceania 오세아니아

> 왜 정답? ✱❊❊ [정답률 83%]

2019년 유럽의 산림 면적 점유율은 46퍼센트로 가장 크지만, 같은 해 아시아 점유율인 20퍼센트의 세 배인 60퍼센트보다는 작으므로 ④이 도표의 내용과 일치하지 않는다.

> 왜 오답?

① 아프리카의 산림 면적 점유율은 1990년에는 25.3퍼센트, 2019년에는 21.4퍼센트로, 모두 20퍼센트를 넘었다.

② 아메리카의 1990년 산림 면적 점유율은 42.6퍼센트로, 2019년의 41.4퍼센트보다 더 크다.

③ 아시아의 산림 면적 점유율은 1990년 32.4퍼센트에서 2019년 20퍼센트로 12.4퍼센트포인트 감소했다.

⑤ 1990년과 2019년 오세아니아의 산림 면적 점유율의 차이는 0.8퍼센트포인트로, 가장 작다.

H 12 정답 ④ *정보 출처별 소비자의 신뢰도

The graph above shows / the consumers' levels of trust / in four
~에 기반하여
different types of information sources, / **based on** a survey of US adults in 2020. //
위 그래프는 보여준다 / 소비자의 신뢰 정도를 / 네 가지 다른 종류의 정보 출처들에 대한 / 2020년 미국 성인들을 대상으로 한 설문조사에 기반하여 //

앞에 that 생략
① About half of US adults say / **they trust** the information / they receive from reviews / from other users or customers. //
미국 성인의 절반 정도가 말했다 / 정보를 믿는다고 / 상품평에서 얻은 / 다른 사용자들이나 고객들로부터의 //

② This is more than double / those who say they hold distrust for reviews / from other users or customers. //
이것은 두 배 이상이다 / 상품평에 대해 불신을 갖는다고 말한 미국 성인들의 / 다른 사용자들이나 고객들로부터의 //

핵심 주어
③ **The smallest gap** / between the levels of trust and distrust / among the four different types of information sources / **is shown**
단수 동사
in the companies or brands' graph. //
가장 적은 차이는 / 신뢰와 불신 정도 사이의 / 네 가지 다른 종류의 정보 출처들 중에서 / 회사나 상표에서 보인다 //

단서 텔레비전 광고로부터의 정보를 신뢰하는 비율은 23%이므로 1/5인 20%보다 큼
④ ~~Fewer~~(→ More) than one-fifth of adults say / they trust information from television advertising, / outweighed by the share who distrust such information. //
미국 성인의 1/5보다 적은(→ 많은) 수치가 말했다 / 텔레비전 광고로부터의 정보를 신뢰한다고 / 그러한 정보를 불신하는 쪽의 수치가 이를 능가했다 //

앞에 주격 관계대명사와 be동사 생략
⑤ Only 15% of adults say / they trust the information / **provided** by influencers, / while more than three times as many adults say / they distrust the same source of information. //
미국 성인의 15%만 말했다 / 정보를 신뢰한다고 / 인플루언서가 제공하는 / 반면에 이보다 세 배 이상 많은 수치의 미국 성인들이 말했다 / 같은 정보 출처를 불신한다고 //

- • survey ⓝ 설문조사 • gap ⓝ 차이, 격차
- • outweigh ⓥ 능가하다 • share ⓝ 부분, 몫

위 그래프는 2020년 미국 성인들을 대상으로 한 설문조사에 기반하여 네 가지 다른 종류의 정보 출처들에 대한 소비자의 신뢰 정도를 보여준다. ① 미국 성인의 절반 정도가 다른 사용자들이나 고객들로부터의 상품평에서 얻은 정보를 믿는다고 말했다. ② 이것은 다른 사용자들이나 고객들로부터의 상품평에 대해 불신을 갖는다고 말한 미국 성인들의 두 배 이상이다. ③ 네 가지 다른 종류의 정보 출처들 중에서 신뢰와 불신 정도 사이의 가장 적은 차이는 회사나 상표에서 보인다. ④ 미국 성인의 1/5보다 적은(→ 많은) 수치가 텔레비전 광고로부터의 정보를 신뢰한다고 말했는데, 그러한 정보를 불신하는 쪽의 수치가 이를 능가했다. ⑤ 미국 성인의 15%만 인플루언서가 제공하는 정보를 신뢰한다고 말했는데, 반면에 이보다 세 배 이상 많은 수치의 미국 성인들이 같은 정보 출처를 불신한다고 말했다.

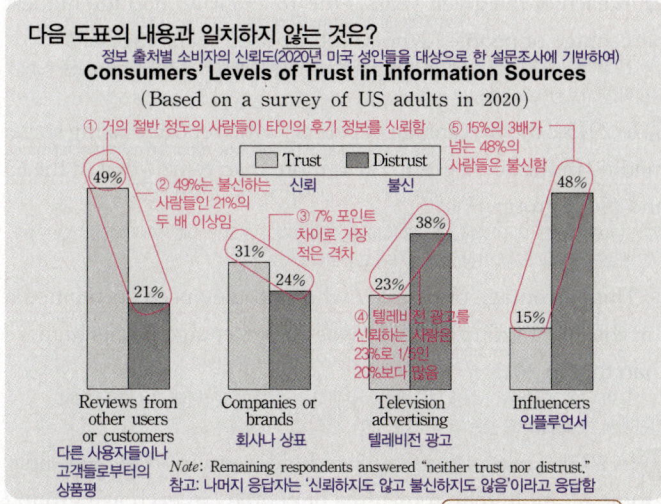

다음 도표의 내용과 일치하지 않는 것은?
정보 출처별 소비자의 신뢰도(2020년 미국 성인들을 대상으로 한 설문조사에 기반하여)
Consumers' Levels of Trust in Information Sources
(Based on a survey of US adults in 2020)

① 거의 절반 정도의 사람들이 타인의 후기 정보를 신뢰함
② 49%는 불신하는 사람들인 21%의 두 배 이상임
③ 7% 포인트 차이로 가장 적은 격차
④ 텔레비전 광고를 신뢰하는 사람은 23%로 1/5인 20%보다 많음
⑤ 15%의 3배가 넘는 48%의 사람들은 불신함

Trust 신뢰   Distrust 불신

Reviews from other users or customers 다른 사용자들이나 고객들로부터의 상품평
Companies or brands 회사나 상표
Television advertising 텔레비전 광고
Influencers 인플루언서

Note: Remaining respondents answered "neither trust nor distrust."
참고: 나머지 응답자는 '신뢰하지도 않고 불신하지도 않음'이라고 응답함

> 꿀팁 one-fifth of adults가 몇 퍼센트인지 주의하기!!

왜 정답? ★★✿ [정답률 80%]
텔레비전 광고로부터의 정보를 신뢰하는 비율은 23%이므로 1/5인 20%보다 커서 ④의 Fewer을 More로 바꿔야 적절하다.

왜 오답?
① 거의 절반인 49%의 설문 참여자가 다른 사용자 및 고객의 상품평을 신뢰한다.
② 49%의 수치는 21%인 신뢰하지 못하는 사람들의 비율을 두 배 이상 능가한다.
③ 회사나 상표로부터의 정보를 신뢰하는 사람과 그렇지 못한 사람의 격차가 7% 포인트 차이로 가장 적다.
⑤ 인플루언서를 신뢰하는 비율인 15%의 3배가 넘는 48%의 사람들이 불신한다.

H 13 정답 ⑤ ＊온라인 강의와 학습 자료를 이용한 영국인들의 비율

The above graph shows / <u>the percentage</u> of people in the UK / 앞에 접속사 that 생략 주격 관계대명사 <u>who</u> used online courses and online learning materials, / by age group / in 2020. // 위 도표는 보여 준다 / 영국 사람들의 비율을 / 온라인 강의와 온라인 학습 자료를 이용한 / 연령 집단별로 / 2020년도에 //

① In each age group, / the percentage of people / <u>who</u> used 주격 관계대명사 online learning materials / was higher / than that of people / <u>who</u> used online courses. // 각 연령 집단에서 / 사람들의 비율이 / 온라인 학습 자료를 이용한 / 더 높았다 / 사람들의 비율보다 / 온라인 강의를 이용한 //

② The 25–34 age group / had <u>the highest</u> percentage of people 최상급 / who used online courses / in all the age groups. // 25세에서 34세 연령 집단에서 / 사람들의 비율이 가장 높았다 / 온라인 강의를 이용한 / 모든 연령 집단 중 //

③ Those aged 65 and older / were the least likely / to use online courses / among the six age groups. // 65세 이상인 사람들이 / 가장 낮았다 / 온라인 강의를 이용할 가능성이 / 여섯 개의 연령 집단 가운데서 //

④ Among the six age groups, / the gap / <u>between</u> the percentage between A and B: A와 B 사이 of people who used online courses / <u>and that</u> of people who = the percentage used online learning materials / 여섯 개의 연령 집단 가운데서 / 차이는 / 온라인 강의를 이용한 사람들의 비율과 / 온라인 학습 자료를 이용한 사람들의 비율 사이의 /

was the greatest / in the 16–24 age group. // 가장 컸다 / 16세에서 24세 연령 집단에서 // 단서 55–64 연령 집단에서 온라인 학습 자료를 이용한 비율은 17퍼센트로, 다섯 명 중 한 명을 넘는 비율이 아님

⑤ In each of the 35–44, 45–54, and 55–64(→ 삭제) age groups, / more than one in five people / used online learning materials. // 35세에서 44세, 45세에서 54세, 55세에서 64세(→ 삭제)의 각 연령 집단에서 / 다섯 명 중 한 명이 넘는 비율의 사람들이 / 온라인 학습 자료를 이용했다 //

• course ⓝ 강의   • learning material 학습 자료
• age group 연령 집단   • among ⟨prep⟩ ~ 중에서

위 도표는 2020년도에 온라인 강의와 온라인 학습 자료를 이용한 영국 사람들의 비율을 연령 집단별로 보여 준다. ① 각 연령 집단에서 온라인 학습 자료를 이용한 사람들의 비율이 온라인 강의를 이용한 사람들의 비율보다 더 높았다. ② 모든 연령 집단 중, 25세에서 34세 연령 집단에서 온라인 강의를 이용한 사람들의 비율이 가장 높았다. ③ 여섯 개의 연령 집단 가운데서, 65세 이상인 사람들이 온라인 강의를 이용할 가능성이 가장 낮았다. ④ 여섯 개의 연령 집단 가운데서, 온라인 강의를 이용한 사람들의 비율과 온라인 학습 자료를 이용한 사람들의 비율 차이는 16세에서 24세 연령 집단에서 가장 컸다. ⑤ 35세에서 44세, 45세에서 54세, 55세에서 64세의(→ 삭제) 각 연령 집단에서 다섯 명 중 한 명이 넘는 비율의 사람들이 온라인 학습 자료를 이용했다.

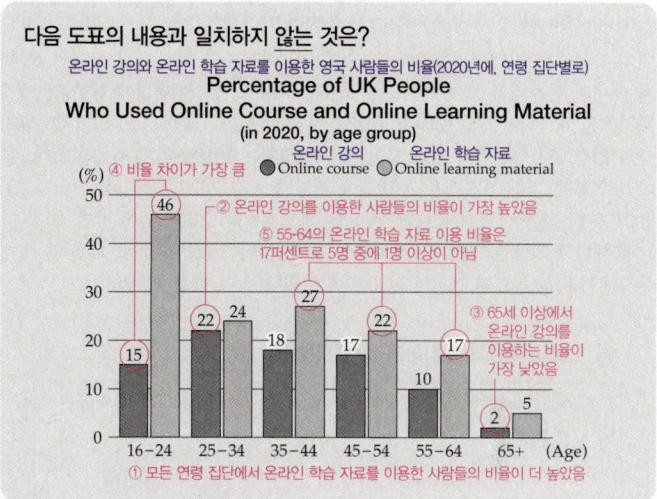

다음 도표의 내용과 일치하지 않는 것은?
온라인 강의와 온라인 학습 자료를 이용한 영국 사람들의 비율(2020년에, 연령 집단별로)
Percentage of UK People
Who Used Online Course and Online Learning Material
(in 2020, by age group)

온라인 강의 Online course   온라인 학습 자료 Online learning material

④ 비율 차이가 가장 큼
② 온라인 강의를 이용한 사람들의 비율이 가장 높았음
⑤ 55-64의 온라인 학습 자료 이용 비율은 17퍼센트로 5명 중에 1명 이상이 아님
③ 65세 이상에서 온라인 강의를 이용하는 비율이 가장 낮았음

16–24: 15, 46
25–34: 22, 24
35–44: 18, 27
45–54: 17, 22
55–64: 10, 17
65+: 2, 5 (Age)

① 모든 연령 집단에서 온라인 학습 자료를 이용한 사람들의 비율이 더 높았음

왜 정답? ★★✿ [정답률 72%]
35세에서 44세 연령 집단의 온라인 학습 자료 이용 비율은 27퍼센트, 45세에서 54세 연령 집단은 22퍼센트로 두 집단은 모두 5명 중에 1명 이상이 온라인 학습 자료를 이용했다. 하지만 55세에서 64세 연령 집단에서 온라인 학습 자료를 이용한 비율은 17퍼센트이므로 다섯 명 중 한 명이 넘는 비율이라고 할 수 없다. 따라서 ⑤이 도표의 내용과 일치하지 않는다.

왜 오답?
① 모든 연령 집단에서 온라인 학습 자료를 이용한 사람들의 비율이 온라인 강의를 이용한 사람들의 비율보다 높았다.
② 25세에서 34세 연령 집단은 온라인 강의 수강 비율이 22퍼센트로 다른 연령 집단들과 비교해서 가장 높았다.
③ 65세 이상인 연령 집단의 온라인 강의 수강 비율은 2퍼센트로 연령 집단들 중에서 가장 낮았다.
④ 온라인 강의를 이용한 사람들의 비율과 온라인 학습 자료를 이용한 사람들의 비율 차이는 16세에서 24세 연령 집단에서 31퍼센트 포인트로 다른 연령 집단과 비교해 가장 컸다.

H 14 정답 ⑤ ＊청정에너지와 화석 연료에 대한 전 세계 투자액

The above graph shows / global energy investment / in clean energy and in fossil fuels / between 2018 and 2022. // 위의 그래프는 보여 준다 / 전 세계 에너지 투자액을 / 청정에너지와 화석 연료에 대한 / 2018년과 2022년 사이에 //

① Since 2018 / global energy investment in clean energy / 청정에너지 투자액은 매년 증가하여 2022년에 가장 높았음 continued to rise, / <u>reaching</u> its highest level in 2022. // 분사구문을 이룸 2018년 이후로 / 청정에너지에 대한 전 세계 투자액은 / 계속해서 상승했으며 / 2022년에 가장 높은 수준에 도달했다 //

② The investment gap / between clean energy and fossil fuels / 투자액 격차는 2020년이 2019년보다 더 큼 = the investment gap between clean energy and fossil fuels in 2020 / was larger than <u>that</u> in 2019. // 투자액 격차는 / 청정에너지와 화석 연료 사이 / 2020년의 / 2019년의 그것보다 컸다 //

③ Investment in fossil fuels / was highest in 2018 / and lowest in 2020. //
화석 연료 투자액은 2018년이 최고이고, 2020년이 최저임
화석 연료에 대한 투자액은 / 2018년에 가장 높았고 / 2020년에 가장 낮았다 //

④ In 2021, / investment in clean energy / exceeded 1,200 billion dollars, / while investment in fossil fuels did not. //
2021년에는 / 청정에너지에 대한 투자액이 / 1조 2000억 달러를 넘은 반면 / 화석 연료에 대한 투자액은 그러지 않았다 //
2021년 청정에너지 투자액은 1조 2,000억 이상, 화석 연료 투자액은 1조 2,000억 미만임

⑤ In 2022, / the global investment in clean energy / was more (→ less) than double / that of fossil fuels. //
= the global investment
2022년에는 / 청정에너지에 대한 전 세계 투자액이 / 두 배 이상이었다(→ 미만이었다) / 화석 연료의 그것의 //
단서 2022년 청정에너지 투자액은 약 1조 6천억 달러, 화석 연료 투자액은 약 1조 달러로, 두 배를 넘지 않았음

- investment ⓝ 투자, 투자액　- fossil fuel 화석 연료　- gap ⓝ 차이

위의 그래프는 2018년과 2022년 사이에 청정에너지와 화석 연료에 대한 전 세계 에너지 투자액을 보여 준다. ① 2018년 이후로 청정에너지에 대한 전 세계 투자액은 계속해서 상승했으며, 2022년에 가장 높은 수준에 도달했다. ② 2020년의 청정에너지와 화석 연료 사이 투자액 격차는 2019년의 그것보다 컸다. ③ 화석 연료에 대한 투자액은 2018년에 가장 높았고 2020년에 가장 낮았다. ④ 2021년에는 청정에너지에 대한 투자액이 1조 2천억 달러를 넘은 반면, 화석 연료에 대한 투자액은 그러지 않았다. ⑤ 2022년에는 청정에너지에 대한 전 세계 투자액이 화석 연료의 그것의 두 배 이상이었다(→ 두 배를 넘지 않았다).

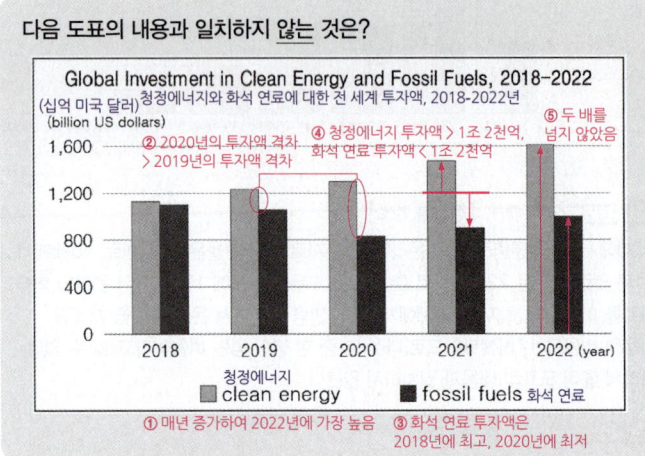

다음 도표의 내용과 일치하지 않는 것은?

Global Investment in Clean Energy and Fossil Fuels, 2018-2022
(십억 미국 달러)(billion US dollars) 청정에너지와 화석 연료에 대한 전 세계 투자액, 2018-2022년

clean energy 청정에너지　fossil fuels 화석 연료

>왜 정답 ? ✿✿✿ [정답률 88%]

2022년 청정에너지 투자액은 약 1조 6천억 달러이고, 화석 연료 투자액은 약 1조 달러로, 청정에너지 투자액이 화석 연료 투자액의 두 배를 넘지 않는다. 따라서 도표의 내용과 일치하지 않는 것은 ⑤이다.

>왜 오답 ?

① 청정에너지 투자액은 매년 증가하여 2022년에 가장 높았다.
② 2020년 청정에너지와 화석 연료 사이의 투자액 격차는 4천억 달러 이상으로, 2019년의 투자액 격차보다 크다.
③ 화석 연료 투자액은 2018년에 약 1조 1천억 달러로 최고이며, 2020년에 약 8천억 달러로 최저이다.
④ 2021년 청정에너지 투자액은 1조 2천억 달러를 넘었고, 화석 연료 투자액은 넘지 않았다.

H 15 정답 ④ *미국의 소셜 미디어 사용 비율

The graph above shows / the percentages of people in different age groups / who reported using social media / in the United States / in 2015 and 2021. //
주격 관계대명사
위 그래프는 보여준다 / 다양한 연령 집단에서 사람들의 비율을 / 소셜 미디어를 사용한다고 보고한 / 미국에서 / 2015년과 2021년에 //

18-29 집단: 두 해 모두 가장 높음
① In each of the given years, / the 18-29 group had the highest percentage of people / who said they used social media. //
뒤에 목적어절 접속사 that이 생략됨
주어진 각각의 해에서 / 18세에서 29세 집단에서 사람들의 비율이 가장 높았다 / 그들이 소셜 미디어를 사용한다고 말한 //

② In 2015, / the percentage of people / who reported using social media / in the 30-49 group / was more than twice / that in the 65 and older group. //
= the percentage of people who reported using social media
2015년: 30-49 집단(77%) > 65 이상 집단(35%) x2
2015년에 / 사람들의 비율은 / 소셜 미디어를 사용한다고 보고한 / 30세에서 49세 집단에서 / 두 배보다 컸다 / 65세 이상 집단에서의 그것보다 //

③ The percentage of people / who said they used social media / in the 50-64 group in 2021 / was 22 percentage points higher / than that in 2015. //
50-64 집단: 2021년(73%) − 2015년(51%) = 22%p
사람들의 비율은 / 그들이 소셜 미디어를 사용한다고 말한 / 2021년에 50세에서 64세 집단에서 / 22퍼센트포인트 더 높았다 / 2015년의 그것보다 //

④ In 2021, / except for the 65 and older group(→ 50 and older groups), / more than four-fifths of people / in each age group / reported using social media. //
분수 표현
단서 2021년에 50세에서 64세 집단(73%)도 80퍼센트 미만임
2021년에 / 65세(→ 50세) 이상 집단을 제외하고 / 5분의 4가 넘는 사람들이 / 각 연령 집단에서 / 소셜 미디어를 사용한다고 보고했다 //

⑤ Among all the age groups, / only the 18-29 group showed a decrease / in the percentage of people / who reported using social media / from 2015 to 2021. //
18-29 집단: 90%(2015)에서 84%(2021)로 감소함
모든 연령 집단 중에서 / 18세에서 29세 집단만이 감소를 보였다 / 사람들의 비율에서 / 소셜 미디어를 사용한다고 보고한 / 2015년에서 2021년까지 //

- given ⓐ 주어진, 정해진　- among prep ~ 중에서
- decrease ⓝ 감소

위 그래프는 2015년과 2021년에 미국에서 소셜 미디어를 사용한다고 보고한 다양한 연령 집단에서 사람들의 비율을 보여준다. ① 주어진 각각의 해에서 18세에서 29세 집단에서 소셜 미디어를 사용한다고 말한 사람들의 비율이 가장 높았다. ② 2015년에 30세에서 49세 집단에서 소셜 미디어를 사용한다고 보고한 사람들의 비율은 65세 이상 집단에서의 비율의 두 배보다 컸다. ③ 2021년에 50세에서 64세 집단에서 소셜 미디어를 사용한다고 말한 사람들의 비율은 2015년의 비율보다 22퍼센트포인트 더 높았다. ④ 2021년에 65세(→ 50세) 이상 집단을 제외한 각 연령 집단에서 5분의 4가 넘는 사람들이 소셜 미디어를 사용한다고 보고했다. ⑤ 모든 연령 집단 중에서 18세에서 29세 집단만이 2015년에서 2021년까지 소셜 미디어를 사용한다고 보고한 사람들의 비율에서 감소를 보였다.

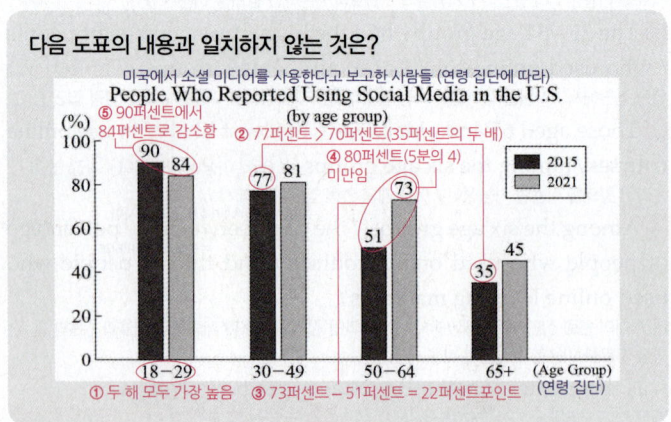

다음 도표의 내용과 일치하지 않는 것은?

미국에서 소셜 미디어를 사용한다고 보고한 사람들 (연령 집단에 따라)
People Who Reported Using Social Media in the U.S.
(by age group)

>왜 정답 ? ✿✿✿ [정답률 81%]

2021년 50세에서 64세 집단의 수치는 73퍼센트로 전체의 5분의 4인 80퍼센트가 되지 않으므로 65세 이상 집단만 5분의 4가 넘지 않는다고 한 ④이 도표의 내용과 일치하지 않는다.

왜 오답?

① 18세에서 29세 집단의 비율은 2015년에는 90퍼센트, 2021년에는 84퍼센트로 두 해 모두 가장 높다.

② 2015년 30세에서 49세 집단은 77퍼센트로, 65세 이상 집단의 35퍼센트의 두 배인 70퍼센트보다 높다.

③ 50세에서 64세 집단의 2021년 비율은 73퍼센트로, 2015년의 51퍼센트보다 22퍼센트포인트 더 높다.

⑤ 18세에서 29세 집단만 유일하게 2015년에서 2021년까지의 비율이 감소했다.

H 16 정답 ③ ━━━━━━━━ ★ 2등급 대비 [정답률 67%]

＊국가별 전기 생산 에너지 비율

The above graph shows / the electricity generation / from fossil fuels, nuclear energy, and renewables / in four countries in 2023. //
위 그래프는 보여 준다 / 전기 생산을 / 화석 연료, 핵에너지, 그리고 재생 가능 에너지로부터의 / 2023년 네 개 국가에서의 //

호주 전기 생산: 화석 연료(67%) > (재생 가능 에너지(33%) × 2)
① Australia's electricity generation / only comes from fossil fuels and renewables, / and the percentage of fossil fuels / is more than twice **that** of renewables. //
= electricity generation
호주의 전기 생산은 / 화석 연료와 재생 가능 에너지로부터만 나오고 / 화석 연료의 비율은 / 재생 가능 에너지의 그것의 두 배가 넘는다 //
'~에 관해서는'
② **In terms of** electricity generation from nuclear energy, / the U.S. shows the highest percentage / among all four countries. //
핵에너지로부터의 전기 생산의 면에서 / 미국은 가장 높은 비율을 보여 준다 / 모든 네 개 국가 중 //
핵에너지 전기 생산: 미국(18%) > 영국(14%) > 브라질(2%)
③ The percentage of electricity generation from fossil fuels in the U.S. / is higher than **that** in the U.K., / **which** is also true(→ not the case) for renewables. //
= the percentage ~ fossil fuels 계속적 용법 관계대명사(앞 내용을 부연 설명)
단서 화석 연료: 미국(59%) > 영국(40%) 재생 가능 에너지: 미국(23%) < 영국(46%)
미국에서 화석 연료로부터의 전기 생산 비율은 / 영국에서의 그것보다 높고 / 이것은 재생 가능 에너지에도 적용된다(→ 재생 가능 에너지에는 적용되지 않는다) //
과거분사구(electricity 수식)
④ In the U.K., / the percentage of electricity **generated from nuclear energy** / is less than a third / of **that** generated from renewables. //
= the percentage of electricity
영국: 핵에너지(14%) < 재생 가능 에너지(46%) × 1/3
영국에서 / 핵에너지로부터 생산되는 전기의 비율은 / 3분의 1보다 적다 / 재생 가능 에너지로부터 생산되는 그것의 //
⑤ Brazil's percentage of electricity generated from renewables / is 10 percentage points larger / than **that** of Australia and the U.K. **combined**. //
= the percentage of ~ renewables 과거분사(앞의 that of ~ U.K. 수식)
재생 가능 에너지: 브라질(89%) − {호주(33%) + 영국(46%)} = 10%p
브라질의 재생 가능 에너지로부터 생산되는 전기의 비율은 / 10퍼센트포인트 더 크다 / 호주와 영국을 합친 그것보다 //

- generation ⓝ 생산   - fossil ⓝ 화석   - fuel ⓝ 연료
- nuclear ⓐ 핵의   - renewables ⓝ 재생 가능 에너지
- combine ⓥ 합치다, 결합하다

위 그래프는 2023년 네 개 국가에서의 화석 연료, 핵에너지, 그리고 재생 가능 에너지로부터의 전기 생산을 보여 준다. ① 호주의 전기 생산은 화석 연료와 재생 가능 에너지로부터만 나오고, 화석 연료의 비율은 재생 가능 에너지의 그것의 두 배가 넘는다. ② 핵에너지로부터의 전기 생산의 면에서 미국은 모든 네 개 국가 중 가장 높은 비율을 보여 준다. ③ 미국에서 화석 연료로부터의 전기 생산 비율은 영국에서의 그것보다 높고, 이것은 재생 가능 에너지에도 적용된다(→ 재생 가능 에너지에는 적용되지 않는다). ④ 영국에서 핵에너지로부터 생산되는 전기의 비율은 재생 가능 에너지로부터 생산되는 그것의 3분의 1보다 적다. ⑤ 브라질의 재생 가능 에너지로부터 생산되는 전기의 비율은 호주와 영국을 합친 그것보다 10퍼센트포인트 더 크다.

다음 도표의 내용과 일치하지 않는 것은?

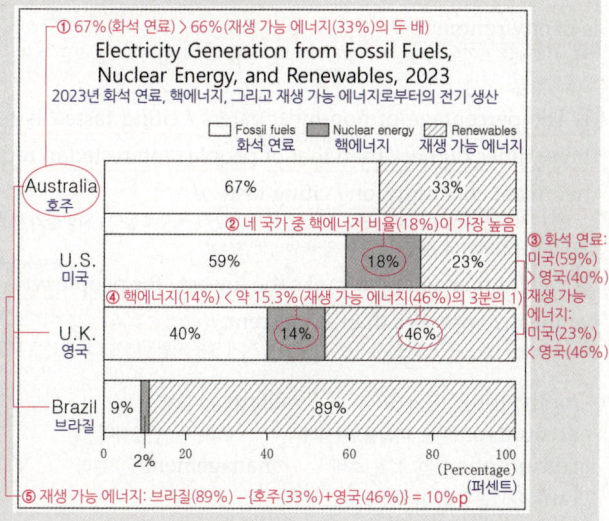

① 67%(화석 연료) > 66%(재생 가능 에너지(33%)의 두 배)
Electricity Generation from Fossil Fuels, Nuclear Energy, and Renewables, 2023
2023년 화석 연료, 핵에너지, 그리고 재생 가능 에너지로부터의 전기 생산

□ Fossil fuels 화석 연료 ■ Nuclear energy 핵에너지 ▨ Renewables 재생 가능 에너지

② 네 국가 중 핵에너지 비율(18%)이 가장 높음
③ 화석 연료: 미국(59%) > 영국(40%)
재생 가능 에너지: 미국(23%) < 영국(46%)
④ 핵에너지(14%) < 약 15.3%(재생 가능 에너지(46%)의 3분의 1)
⑤ 재생 가능 에너지: 브라질(89%) − {호주(33%)+영국(46%)} = 10%p

| | Australia 호주: Fossil fuels 67%, Renewables 33% |
| U.S. 미국: Fossil fuels 59%, Nuclear energy 18%, Renewables 23% |
| U.K. 영국: Fossil fuels 40%, Nuclear energy 14%, Renewables 46% |
| Brazil 브라질: Fossil fuels 9%(2%), Renewables 89% |

(Percentage) (퍼센트)

왜 2등급? 일부 선택지는 근사치가 아닌 정확한 값을 요구하며, 퍼센트포인트 개념이 쓰여 까다로웠을 수도 있다. 배수(2배, 3배, …) 및 분수(3분의 1, 4분의 1, …)는 근소한 차이로 오답을 만들 수 있어서 꼭 주의해야 하고, 퍼센트(%)의 차이를 나타내는 퍼센트포인트(%p)의 개념을 숙지하여 정답을 골라야 한다.

왜 정답?

화석 연료로부터의 전기 생산 비율은 미국이 59%, 영국이 40%로 미국이 영국보다 높지만, 재생 가능 에너지의 경우에는 영국이 46%, 미국이 23%로 영국이 미국보다 더 높다. 따라서 재생 가능 에너지로부터의 전기 생산 비율이 화석 연료와 마찬가지로 미국이 영국보다 높다고 한 ③이 도표의 내용과 일치하지 않는다.

왜 오답?

① 호주의 화석 연료 비율(67%)은 재생 가능 에너지(33%)의 두 배(66%)가 넘는다.

② 핵에너지 비율은 미국(18%)이 다른 나라들(영국 14%, 브라질 2%, 호주 0%)보다 높다.

④ 영국의 핵에너지 비율(14%)은 재생 가능 에너지 비율(46%)의 3분의 1인 약 15.3%보다 적다.

⑤ 브라질의 재생 가능 에너지 비율(89%)은 호주와 영국을 합친 것(79%)보다 10퍼센트포인트 더 크다.

H 17 정답 ④ ━━━━━━━━ ✿ 2등급 대비 [정답률 63%]

＊고기를 덜 먹거나 안 먹는 이유

The graph above shows / the survey results on reasons / for people **interested** in eating less meat / and **those** eating no meat / in the UK in 2018. //
앞에 주격 관계대명사와 be동사가 생략됨 = people
위의 그래프는 보여 준다 / 이유에 대한 조사 결과를 / 고기를 덜 먹는 것에 관심 있는 사람들(에 대한) / 그리고 고기를 먹지 않는 사람들 / 영국에서 2018년에 //
주격 관계대명사
① For the group of people / **who** are interested in eating less meat, / health is the strongest motivator / for doing so. //
사람들의 집단에게 / 고기를 덜 먹는 것에 관심이 있는 / 건강은 가장 강력한 동기이다 / 그렇게 하는 //
고기를 덜 먹는 것에 관심 있는 사람들에게 건강이 49퍼센트로 가장 높음
② For the group of non-meat eaters, / animal welfare accounts for the largest percentage / among all reasons, / **followed by environment, health, and taste**. //
과거분사가 이끄는 분사구문 ＊
고기를 먹지 않는 사람들: 동물 복지(52%) > 환경(32%) > 건강(31%) > 맛(30%)
고기를 먹지 않는 사람들의 집단의 경우 / 동물 복지가 가장 큰 비율을 차지한다 / 모든 이유 중에서 / 환경, 건강, 그리고 맛이 그 뒤를 따른다 //

③ The largest percentage point difference / between the two groups / is in animal welfare, / whereas the smallest difference is in environment. //
핵심 주어(단수) *
단수 동사
가장 큰 차이: 동물 복지(52%−22%=30%) / 가장 작은 차이: 환경(32%−22%=10%)
가장 큰 퍼센트포인트 차이는 / 두 집단 사이의 / 동물 복지에 있다 / 가장 작은 차이는 환경에 있는 반면 //

④ The percentage of non-meat eaters / citing taste / is four(→ three) times higher / than that of people / interested in reducing their meat consumption / citing taste. //
단서 맛 때문에 고기를 먹지 않는 사람들은 30퍼센트이고, 고기를 덜 먹는 것에 관심 있는 사람들은 10퍼센트이므로 3배임
= the percentage
고기를 먹지 않는 사람들의 비율은 / 맛을 언급하면서 / 4(→ 3)배 높다 / 사람들의 비율보다 / 고기 섭취를 줄이는 데 관심이 있는 / 맛을 언급하면서 //

⑤ Weight management ranks the lowest / for people who don't eat meat, / with less than 10 percent. //
주격 관계대명사
고기를 먹지 않는 사람들에게 체중 관리는 9퍼센트로 가장 낮음
체중 관리는 가장 낮은 순위를 차지한다 / 고기를 먹지 않는 사람들에게 / 10퍼센트 미만으로 //

- motivator ⓝ 동기 (요인)   - welfare ⓝ 복지
- account for (부분·비율을) 차지하다   - cite ⓥ 언급하다
- consumption ⓝ 섭취, 소비   - management ⓝ 관리
- rank ⓥ (순위를) 차지하다

위의 그래프는 고기를 덜 먹는 것에 관심 있는 사람들과 고기를 먹지 않는 사람들의 이유에 대한 2018년 영국에서의 조사 결과를 보여 준다. ① 고기를 덜 먹는 것에 관심이 있는 사람들의 집단에게, 건강은 그렇게 하는 가장 강력한 동기이다. ② 고기를 먹지 않는 사람들의 집단의 경우, 모든 이유 중에서 동물 복지가 가장 큰 비율을 차지하고 있고, 환경, 건강, 그리고 맛이 그 뒤를 따른다. ③ 두 집단 사이의 가장 큰 퍼센트포인트 차이는 동물 복지에 있는 반면, 가장 작은 차이는 환경에 있다. ④ 맛을 언급하는 고기를 먹지 않는 사람들의 비율은 맛을 언급하는 고기 섭취를 줄이는 데 관심이 있는 사람들의 비율보다 4(→ 3)배 높다. ⑤ 체중 관리는 고기를 먹지 않는 사람들에게 10퍼센트 미만으로 가장 낮은 순위를 차지한다.

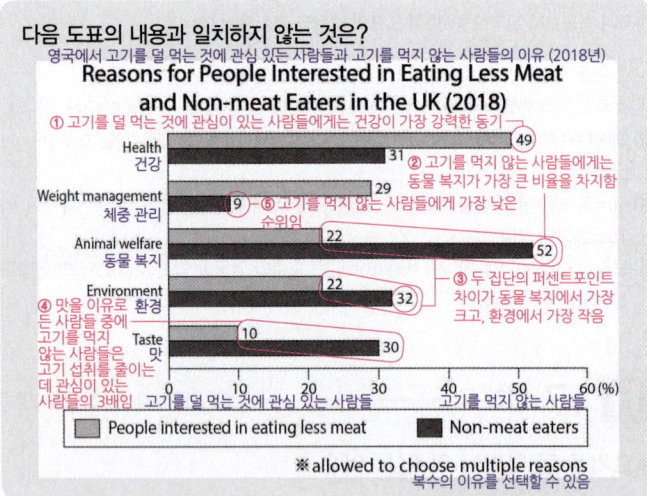

다음 도표의 내용과 일치하지 않는 것은?
영국에서 고기를 덜 먹는 것에 관심 있는 사람들과 고기를 먹지 않는 사람들의 이유 (2018년)
Reasons for People Interested in Eating Less Meat and Non-meat Eaters in the UK (2018)

※ allowed to choose multiple reasons
복수의 이유를 선택할 수 있음

⭐ 최상급 표현이 ④을 제외한 모든 선택지에 등장했는데, 그 범위가 다 달라 그래프의 항목을 이리저리 옮겨 다니며 수치를 확인해야 하는 2등급 대비 문제이다. 범위를 제대로 확인하지 못한다면 오답을 고르게 되므로 범위를 정확하게 파악해야 한다.

>왜 정답 ?
맛 때문에 고기를 먹지 않는 사람들의 비율은 30퍼센트로, 맛 때문에 고기 섭취를 줄이는 데 관심이 있는 사람들의 비율인 10퍼센트의 4배가 아니라 3배이다. 따라서 ④이 도표의 내용과 일치하지 않는다.

>왜 오답 ?
① 고기를 덜 먹는 것에 관심이 있는 사람들에게는 건강이 49퍼센트로 가장 강력한 동기이다.

② 고기를 먹지 않는 사람의 경우 동물 복지가 52퍼센트로 가장 큰 비율을 차지하고, 환경, 건강, 맛이 그 뒤에 이어진다.
③ 두 집단의 퍼센트포인트 차이는 동물 복지가 가장 크고(52퍼센트와 22퍼센트로 30퍼센트포인트 차이), 환경이 가장 작다(32퍼센트와 22퍼센트로 10퍼센트포인트 차이).
⑤ 고기를 먹지 않는 사람들에게 체중 관리는 9퍼센트로 가장 낮은 순위를 차지한다.

─── 어법 특강

＊ 분사구문의 형태

– 분사구문은 「현재분사/과거분사/형용사 ~, 주어+동사 ~.」로 표현되며, 분사구문이 콤마 뒤에 오는 경우도 있다. 특히, 형용사나 과거분사로 시작하는 분사구문에 유의해야 한다. 이런 형태가 되는 이유는 앞에 being이나 having been이 보통 생략되기 때문이다.

- The rope burnt evenly, indicating the passage of time.
→ 의미상 주어인 the rope와 능동의 관계
(그 밧줄은 시간의 경과를 보여주면서 균등하게 탔다.)

- (Being) Sent to the boarding school, I was 11 years od.
→ 의미상 주어인 I와 수동의 관계이고, being이 생략되어 sent만 남게 됨
(기숙학교에 보내어졌을 때 나는 11살이었다.)

- (Being) Tired with hard work, he fell asleep with TV on.
→ 앞에 being이 생략되어 tired만 남게 됨
(과로로 피곤해서 그는 TV를 켜놓은 채 잠이 들었다.)

─── 어법 특강

＊ 주어–동사 수 일치

– 문장의 주어가 명사구 혹은 명사절일 때 항상 단수 취급한다. to부정사구, 동명사구나 의문사절, that절, whether절 등과 같은 명사절이 주어로 오는 경우 동사와 멀어질 수 있기 때문에 수 일치 여부를 쉽게 판단하기 힘들다. 따라서 항상 문장을 전체적으로 파악해야 한다.

- Creating a list of goals is a good way to be a better student.
동명사구 주어   단수 동사
(목표들의 목록을 만드는 것은 더 나은 학생이 되기 위한 좋은 방법이다.)

- Whether he will accept my offer is not certain yet.
명사절 주어   단수 동사
(그가 나의 제안을 받아들일 지는 아직 확실하지 않다.)

- To overcome my emotional problems is difficult.
to부정사구 주어   단수 동사
(나의 감정적인 문제들을 극복하는 것은 어렵다.)

Ⓗ 어휘 Review 정답 ───── 문제편 p. 111

01 분류하다	11 age group	21 decrease
02 차이	12 in terms of	22 management
03 점유율	13 based on	23 retail
04 복지	14 fall behind	24 region
05 약간	15 account for	25 ownership
06 cite	16 motivator	26 fossil
07 among	17 generation	27 urban
08 combine	18 recycling	28 consumed
09 steadily	19 emissions	29 declined
10 respondent	20 investment	30 extremely

I 20 정답 ④ *Bessie Coleman의 생애

Bessie Coleman was born / in Texas in 1892. //
Bessie Coleman은 태어났다 / 1892년에 텍사스에서 //
When she was eleven, / she was told / **that** the Wright brothers
(목적어절을 이끄는 접속사)
had flown their first plane. // **①의 단서** 11살 때 Wright 형제의 첫 비행 소식을 들었음
그녀가 11살이었을 때 / 그녀는 들었다 / Wright 형제가 그들의 첫 비행을 했다는 것을 //
Since that moment, / she dreamed about the day / she would
soar through the sky. //
그때부터 / 그녀는 그날을 꿈꿨다 / 자신이 하늘을 높이 날아오르는 //
At the age of 23, / Coleman moved to Chicago, / **where** she
(계속적 용법의 관계부사)
worked at a restaurant / **to save** money for flying lessons. //
(부사적 용법(목적))
23살 때 / Coleman은 시카고로 이사했다 / 그리고 거기서 식당에서 일했다 / 비행 수업을
위한 돈을 모으기 위해 // **②의 단서** 비행 수업을 듣기 위해 파리로 가야 했음
However, / she had to travel to Paris / **to take** flying lessons /
(부사적 용법(목적))
because American flight schools at the time / admitted **neither**
women **nor** Black people. // *(neither A nor B: A도 아니고 B도 아닌)*
그러나 / 그녀는 파리로 가야 했다 / 비행 수업을 듣기 위해 / 그 당시 미국 비행 학교가 /
여성이나 흑인의 입학을 허가하지 않았기 때문에 //
In 1921, / she finally became the first Black woman / **to earn** an
(형용사적 용법)
international pilot's license. // **③의 단서** 국제 조종사 면허를 딴 최초의 흑인 여성이 됨
1921년에 / 그녀는 마침내 최초의 흑인 여성이 되었다 / 국제 조종사 면허를 딴 //
She also studied flying acrobatics / in Europe / and made her
first appearance / in an airshow in New York / in 1922. //
그녀는 또한 곡예 비행을 공부했다 / 유럽에서 / 그리고 그녀의 첫 출현을 했다 / 뉴욕의
에어쇼에서 / 1922년에 // **④의 단서** 뉴욕 에어쇼에 첫 출현을 함
As a female pioneer of flight, / she inspired the next generation
to pursue / their dreams of flying. // **⑤의 단서** 다음 세대가 비행
의 꿈을 추구하도록 영감을 줌
여성 비행 개척자로서 / 그녀는 다음 세대가 추구하도록 영감을 주었다 / 그들의 비행의 꿈을 //

- soar ⓥ 날아오르다
- international ⓐ 국제적인
- pilot ⓝ 비행사
- license ⓝ 면허
- appearance ⓝ 출현
- female ⓐ 여성의
- pioneer ⓝ 개척자
- inspire ⓥ 영감을 주다
- generation ⓝ 세대
- pursue ⓥ 추구하다

Bessie Coleman은 1892년에 텍사스에서 태어났다. 그녀가 11살이었을
때 그녀는 Wright 형제가 그들의 첫 비행을 했다는 것을 들었다.
그때부터 그녀는 자신이 하늘을 높이 날아오르는 그날을 꿈꿨다. 23살 때
Coleman은 시카고로 이사했고 그곳에서 비행 수업을 위한 돈을 모으기
위해 식당에서 일했다. 그러나 그 당시 미국 비행 학교가 여성이나 흑인의
입학을 허가하지 않았기 때문에 그녀는 비행 수업을 듣기 위해 파리로
가야 했다. 1921년에 그녀는 마침내 국제 조종사 면허를 딴 최초의 흑인
여성이 되었다. 그녀는 또한 유럽에서 곡예 비행을 공부했고 1922년에
뉴욕의 에어쇼에 그녀의 첫 출현을 했다. 여성 비행 개척자로서 그녀는
다음 세대가 그들의 비행의 꿈을 추구하도록 영감을 주었다.

Bessie Coleman에 관한 다음 글의 내용과 일치하지 <u>않는</u> 것은?

① 11살 때 Wright 형제의 첫 비행 소식을 들었다.
　When she was eleven, she was told that the Wright brothers had flown their first plane.
② 비행 수업을 듣기 위해 파리로 가야 했다.
　she had to travel to Paris to take flying lessons
③ 국제 조종사 면허를 딴 최초의 흑인 여성이 되었다.
　she finally became the first Black woman to earn an international pilot's license
④ 유럽에서 에어쇼에 첫 출현을 했다.
　made her first appearance in an airshow in New York in 1922
⑤ 다음 세대가 비행의 꿈을 추구하도록 영감을 주었다.
　she inspired the next generation to pursue their dreams of flying

왜 정답 ? ★★❀ [정답률 88%]

후반부의 She also studied flying acrobatics in Europe and made her first
appearance in an airshow in New York in 1922. (그녀는 또한 유럽에서
곡예 비행을 공부했고 1922년에 뉴욕의 에어쇼에 그녀의 첫 출현을 했다)를 통해
유럽에서 한 것은 곡예 비행 공부이고 에어쇼에 첫 출현을 한 것은 뉴욕이라는
것을 알 수 있다.
따라서 ④이 글의 내용과 일치하지 않는다.

왜 오답 ?

① 11살 때 Wright 형제의 첫 비행 소식을 들었다고 했다. (When she was
eleven, she was told that the Wright brothers had flown their first
plane.)
② 그 당시 미국 비행 학교가 여성이나 흑인의 입학을 허가하지 않았기 때문에
비행 수업을 듣기 위해서 파리로 가야 했다고 했다. (she had to travel to
Paris to take flying lessons)
③ 국제 조종사 면허를 딴 최초의 흑인 여성이 되었다고 했다. (she finally
became the first Black woman to earn an international pilot's license)
⑤ 다음 세대가 비행의 꿈을 추구하도록 영감을 주었다고 했다. (she inspired the
next generation to pursue their dreams of flying)

I 21 정답 ③ *Claude Bolling의 일생

Pianist, composer, and big band leader, Claude Bolling, / was
(동격)
born on April 10, 1930, in Cannes, France, / but spent most of
his life / in Paris. // **①의 단서** 1930년에 프랑스에서 태어났음
피아니스트, 작곡가, 그리고 빅 밴드 리더인 Claude Bolling은 / 1930년 4월 10일 프랑스
칸에서 태어났다 / 하지만 그의 삶의 대부분을 보냈다 / 파리에서 //
He began studying classical music / as a youth. // **②의 단서** 학교 친구를
통해 재즈를 소개받았음
그는 클래식 음악을 공부하기 시작했다 / 젊었을 때 //
He **was introduced** to the world of jazz / by a schoolmate. //
(수동태의 과거형)
그는 재즈(재즈 세계)를 소개받았다 / 학교 친구를 통해 //
Later, / Bolling became interested / in the music of Fats Waller, /
one of the most excellent jazz musicians. //
(「one of+최상급+복수 명사」: 가장 ~한 …들 중 하나)
후에 / Bolling은 관심을 가졌다 / Fats Waller의 음악에 / 최고의 재즈 음악가들 중 한 명인 //
Bolling became famous as a teenager / **by winning** the Best
(by -ing: ~함으로써)
Piano Player prize / at an amateur contest in France. //
그는 10대 때 유명해졌다 / Best Piano Player 상을 수상하면서 / 프랑스의 아마추어
대회에서 // **③의 단서** 10대에 Best Piano Player 상을 받음
He was also a successful film music composer, / **writing** the
(분사구문을 이룸)
music / for more than one hundred films. // **④의 단서** 성공적인
영화 음악 작곡가였음
그는 또한 성공적인 영화 음악 작곡가였고 / 음악을 작곡했다 / 100편이 넘는 영화의 //
In 1975, / he collaborated with flutist Rampal / and published
(계속적 용법의 목적격 관계대명사)
Suite for Flute and Jazz Piano Trio, / **which** he became most well-
known for. // **⑤의 단서** 1975년에 플루트 연주자와 협업했음
1975년에 / 그는 플루트 연주자 Rampal과 협업했다 / 그리고 'Suite for Flute and Jazz
Piano Trio'를 발매했으며 / 그것으로 가장 잘 알려지게 되었다 //
He died in 2020, / **leaving** two sons, David and Alexandre. //
(분사구문을 이룸)
그는 2020년 사망했다 / 두 아들 David와 Alexandre를 남기고 //

- composer ⓝ 작곡가
- classical music 클래식 음악
- youth ⓝ 청년
- introduce ⓥ 소개하다
- schoolmate ⓝ 학교 친구
- successful ⓐ 성공한
- collaborate ⓥ 협업하다
- publish ⓥ 발매하다
- well-known ⓐ 잘 알려진

피아니스트, 작곡가, 그리고 빅 밴드 리더인 Claude Bolling은 1930년
4월 10일 프랑스 칸에서 태어났지만, 그의 삶의 대부분을 파리에서
보냈다. 그는 젊었을 때 클래식 음악을 공부하기 시작했다. 그는 학교
친구를 통해 재즈(재즈 세계)를 소개받았다. 후에 Bolling은 최고의
재즈 음악가들 중 한 명인 Fats Waller의 음악에 관심을 가졌다. 그는
10대 때 프랑스의 아마추어 대회에서 Best Piano Player 상을 수상하며
유명해졌다. 그는 또한 성공적인 영화 음악 작곡가였고, 100편이 넘는
영화의 음악을 작곡했다. 1975년에, 그는 플루트 연주자 Rampal과
협업했고, 'Suite for Flute and Jazz Piano Trio'를 발매했으며, 그것으로
가장 잘 알려지게 되었다. 그는 두 아들 David와 Alexandre를 남기고
2020년 사망했다.

Claude Bolling에 관한 다음 글의 내용과 일치하지 <u>않는</u> 것은?

① 1930년에 프랑스에서 태어났다.
　Claude Bolling, was born on April 10, 1930, in Cannes, France
② 학교 친구를 통해 재즈를 소개받았다.
　He was introduced to the world of jazz by a schoolmate.
③ 20대에 Best Piano Player 상을 받았다.
　Bolling became famous as a teenager by winning the Best Piano Player prize
④ 성공적인 영화 음악 작곡가였다. He was also a successful film music composer
⑤ 1975년에 플루트 연주자와 협업했다. In 1975, he collaborated with flutist Rampal

왜 정답? ✽✽✽ [정답률 94%]
중반부의 Bolling became famous as a teenager by winning the Best Piano Player prize at an amateur contest in France. (그는 10대 때 프랑스의 아마추어 대회에서 Best Piano Player 상을 수상하며 유명해졌다.)를 통해 Best Piano Player 상을 10대에 받았다는 것을 알 수 있다. 따라서 ③이 글의 내용과 일치하지 않는다.

> 일부만 맞는 선택지인지 확인하기! 꿀팁

왜 오답?
① 1930년 4월 10일에 프랑스 칸에서 태어났다고 했다. (Claude Bolling, was born on April 10, 1930, in Cannes, France)
② 학교 친구를 통해 재즈의 세계를 소개받았다고 했다. (He was introduced to the world of jazz by a schoolmate.)
④ 그는 성공적인 영화 음악 작곡가였다고 했다. (He was also a successful film music composer)
⑤ 1975년에 플루트 연주자 Rampal과 협업했다고 했다. (In 1975, he collaborated with flutist Rampal)

I 22 정답 ③ ＊Antonie van Leeuwenhoek의 생애

Antonie van Leeuwenhoek was a scientist / well known for his cell research. // **❶의 단서** 세포 연구로 잘 알려진 과학자였음
Antonie van Leeuwenhoek은 과학자였다 / 세포 연구로 잘 알려진 //

He was born / in Delft, the Netherlands, on October 24, 1632. //
그는 태어났다 / 1632년 10월 24일, 네덜란드의 Delft에서 //

At the age of 16, / he began to learn job skills / in Amsterdam. //
16살에 / 그는 직업 기술을 배우기 시작했다 / Amsterdam에서 //

At the age of 22, / Leeuwenhoek returned to Delft. //
22살에 / Leeuwenhoek은 Delft로 돌아왔다 //　　　**❷의 단서** 22살에 Delft로 돌아왔음

가주어 의미상의 주어 진주어
It wasn't easy / for Leeuwenhoek / to become a scientist. //
쉽지 않았다 / Leeuwenhoek이 / 과학자가 되는 것은 //

주격 관계대명사
He knew only one language / — Dutch — / which was quite unusual / for scientists of his time. // **❸의 단서** 네덜란드어 하나만 알고 있었음
그는 오직 한 가지 언어만을 알고 있었다 / 네덜란드어 / 그것은 상당히 드문 것이었다 / 그 당시 과학자들에게는 //

But his curiosity was endless, / and he worked hard. //
하지만 그의 호기심은 끝이 없었다 / 그리고 그는 열심히 노력했다 //

He had an important skill. // 그에게는 중요한 기술이 있었다 //
how to-v: ~하는 법
He knew / how to make things out of glass. // **❹의 단서** 유리로 물건을 만드는 방법을 알고 있었음
그는 알고 있었다 / 유리로 물건을 만드는 법을 //

This skill came in handy / when he made lenses / for his simple microscope. //
이 기술은 도움이 되었다 / 그가 렌즈를 만들 때 / 자신의 간단한 현미경을 위해 //
with 분사구문
He saw tiny veins / with blood flowing / through them. //
그는 미세한 혈관들을 보았다 / 피가 흐르고 있는 / 그것들을 통해 //

He also saw living bacteria / in pond water. //
그는 또한 살아 있는 박테리아를 보았다 / 연못 물 속에서 //
병렬 구조
He paid close attention / to the things he saw / and wrote down his observations. //
그는 세심한 주의를 기울였다 / 자신이 본 것들에 / 그리고 관찰한 것을 기록했다 //　앞에 목적격 관계대명사 생략

이유를 나타내는 접속사　　　　　　　　　　　　　부사적 용법(목적)
Since he couldn't draw well, / he hired an artist / to draw pictures of what he described. // **❺의 단서** 화가를 고용해 설명하는 것을 그리게 했음
그는 그림을 잘 그릴 수 없었기 때문에 / 화가를 고용했다 / 자신이 설명하는 것을 그림으로 그리게 하려고 //

- known for ~로 알려진　　• research ⓝ 연구
- Dutch ⓝ 네덜란드어　　• unusual ⓐ 드문　　• curiosity ⓝ 호기심
- endless ⓐ 끝없는　　• come in handy 도움이 되다
- microscope ⓝ 현미경　　• flow ⓥ 흐르다　　• pond ⓝ 연못
- pay attention to ~에 주의를 기울이다　　• observation ⓝ 관찰
- hire ⓥ 고용하다　　• describe ⓥ 설명하다

Antonie van Leeuwenhoek은 세포 연구로 잘 알려진 과학자였다. 그는 1632년 10월 24일 네덜란드 Delft에서 태어났다. 그는 16살에 Amsterdam에서 직업 기술을 배우기 시작했다. Leeuwenhoek은 22살에 Delft로 돌아왔다. Leeuwenhoek이 과학자가 되기는 쉽지 않았다. 그는 오직 한 가지 언어, 즉 네덜란드어만을 알고 있었는데, 그것은 그 당시 과학자들에게는 상당히 드문 것이었다. 하지만 그의 호기심은 끝이 없었고, 그는 열심히 노력했다. 그에게는 중요한 기술이 있었다. 그는 유리로 물건을 만드는 법을 알고 있었다. 이 기술은 그가 자신의 간단한 현미경에 쓰일 렌즈를 만들 때 도움이 되었다. 그는 피가 흐르고 있는 미세한 혈관을 보았다. 그는 또한 연못 물 속에서 살아 있는 박테리아를 보았다. 그는 자신이 본 것들에 세심한 주의를 기울였고 관찰한 것을 기록했다. 그는 그림을 잘 그릴 수 없었기 때문에, 화가를 고용하여 자신이 설명하는 것을 그림으로 그리게 했다.

Antonie van Leeuwenhoek에 관한 다음 글의 내용과 일치하지 <u>않는</u> 것은?

① 세포 연구로 잘 알려진 과학자였다.
　Antonie van Leeuwenhoek was a scientist well known for his cell research.
② 22살에 Delft로 돌아왔다. At the age of 22, Leeuwenhoek returned to Delft.
③ 여러 가지 언어를 알았다. He knew only one language — Dutch
④ 유리로 물건을 만드는 방법을 알고 있었다.
　He knew how to make things out of glass.
⑤ 화가를 고용하여 설명하는 것을 그리게 했다.
　he hired an artist to draw pictures of what he described

왜 정답? ✽✽✽ [정답률 92%]
Leeuwenhoek는 네덜란드어 하나만 알고 있었는데 그 당시 과학자들에게는 상당히 드문 것이었다고 했다. (He knew only one language — Dutch — which was quite unusual for scientists of his time.) 따라서 여러 가지 언어가 아니라 한 가지 언어만 알고 있었으므로 글의 내용과 일치하지 않는 것은 ③이다.

> 내용 불일치 문제는 순서대로 선택지가 제시됨! 꿀팁

왜 오답?
① 세포 연구로 잘 알려져 있었다고 했다. (Antonie van Leeuwenhoek was a scientist well known for his cell research.)
② 22살에 Delft로 돌아왔다고 했다. (At the age of 22, Leeuwenhoek returned to Delft.)
④ 유리로 물건을 만드는 방법을 알고 있었다고 했다. (He knew how to make things out of glass.)
⑤ 그림을 잘 그리지 못해, 화가를 고용하여 설명하는 것을 그리게 했다고 했다. (Since he couldn't draw well, he hired an artist to draw pictures of what he described.)

I 23 정답 ④ ＊남아프리카 소설가 Wilbur Smith

Wilbur Smith was a South African novelist / specialising in historical fiction. // **❶의 단서** 역사 소설을 전문으로 하는 소설가였음
Wilbur Smith는 남아프리카 소설가였다 / 역사 소설을 전문으로 하는 //

Smith wanted to become a journalist, / writing about social conditions / in South Africa, / but his father was never supportive / of his writing / and forced him / to get a real job. //
force+목적어+목적격 보어(to부정사) ＊
Smith는 언론인이 되고 싶었으나 / 사회 환경에 관해 글을 쓰는 / 남아프리카의 / 그의 아버지는 절대로 지지하지 않았다 / 그가 글을 쓰는 것을 / 그리고 강요했다 / 그가 실질적인 직업을 갖도록 // **❷의 단서** 아버지가 글을 쓰는 것을 지지하지 않았음

Smith studied further / and became a tax accountant, / but he finally turned back / to his love of writing. // Smith는 더 공부했다 / 그리고 세금 회계사가 되었다 / 그러나 결국에는 돌아왔다 / 그가 사랑하는 글 쓰는 일로 //

He wrote his first novel, / *The Gods First Make Mad*, / and had received / 20 rejections / by 1962. //
과거완료
③의 단서 첫 번째 소설이 1962년까지 20번 거절당했음
그는 첫 번째 소설을 썼다 / The Gods First Make Mad를 / 그리고 받았다 / 20번의 거절 / 1962년까지 //

In 1964, / Smith published another novel, / *When the Lion Feeds*, / and it went on to be successful, / selling around the world. //
분사구문※
④의 단서 소설 When the Lion Feeds는 영화화되지 않음
1964년에 / Smith는 또 다른 소설을 출간했다 / When the Lion Feeds를 / 그리고 그것은 성공을 거두었다 / 전 세계에 팔리면서 //

A famous actor and film producer / bought the film rights / for *When the Lion Feeds*, / although no movie resulted. //
한 유명한 배우이자 영화 제작자가 / 영화 판권을 샀다 / When the Lion Feeds에 대한 / 비록 영화화되지는 않았지만 //

⑤의 단서 죽기 전까지 49편의 소설을 출간했음
By the time of his death in 2021 / he had published / 49 novels, / selling more than 140 million copies worldwide. //
분사구문
2021년에 죽기 전까지 / 그는 출간했다 / 49편의 소설을 / 전 세계적으로 1억 4천만 부 이상을 판매하면서 //

• novelist ⓝ 소설가 • specialise in ~을 전문으로 하다
• journalist ⓝ 언론인 • supportive ⓐ 지지하는
• accountant ⓝ 회계사 • rejection ⓝ 거절
• publish ⓥ 출간[발행]하다 • right ⓝ (작품·영화 등에 대한) 판권
• worldwide ⓓ 전 세계적으로

Wilbur Smith는 역사 소설을 전문으로 하는 남아프리카 소설가였다. Smith는 남아프리카의 사회 환경에 관해 글을 쓰는 언론인이 되고 싶었으나, 그의 아버지는 그가 글을 쓰는 것을 절대로 지지하지 않았고 그가 실질적인 직업을 갖도록 강요했다. Smith는 더 공부하여 세금 회계사가 되었으나 결국에는 그가 사랑하는 글 쓰는 일로 돌아왔다. 그는 첫 번째 소설, *The Gods First Make Mad*를 썼고 1962년까지 20번의 거절을 당했다. 1964년에 Smith는 또 다른 소설, *When the Lion Feeds*를 출간했고, 그것이 전 세계에 팔리면서 성공을 거두었다. 비록 영화화되지는 않았지만, 한 유명한 배우이자 영화 제작자가 *When the Lion Feeds*에 대한 영화 판권을 샀다. 2021년에 죽기 전까지 그는 49편의 소설을 출간했으며 전 세계적으로 1억 4천만 부 이상을 판매했다.

Wilbur Smith에 관한 다음 글의 내용과 일치하지 <u>않는</u> 것은?

① 역사 소설을 전문으로 하는 소설가였다.
Wilbur Smith was a South African novelist specialising in historical fiction.
② 아버지는 그가 글 쓰는 것을 지지하지 않았다.
his father was never supportive of his writing
③ 첫 번째 소설은 1962년까지 20번 거절당했다.
He wrote his first novel, The Gods First Make Mad, and had received 20 rejections by 1962.
④ 소설 *When the Lion Feeds*는 영화화되었다. A famous actor and film producer bought the film rights for When the Lion Feeds, although no movie resulted.
⑤ 죽기 전까지 49편의 소설을 출간했다.
By the time of his death in 2021 he had published 49 novels

〉왜 정답? ❋❋❋ [정답률 85%]

소설 *When the Lion Feeds*의 판권은 판매되었지만 영화화되지 않았다고 (A famous actor and film producer bought the film rights for *When the Lion Feeds*, although no movie resulted.) 했다. 따라서 ④이 이 글의 내용과 일치하지 않는다.

〉왜 오답?

① 역사 소설을 전문으로 하는 소설가였다. (Wilbur Smith was a South African novelist specialising in historical fiction.)
② 아버지는 그가 글 쓰는 것을 지지하지 않았다고 했다. (his father was never supportive of his writing) 숫자 같은 세부 정보에 유의하기! 꿀팁
③ 첫 번째 소설은 1962년까지 20번 거절당했음을 알 수 있다. (He wrote his first novel, *The Gods First Make Mad*, and had received 20 rejections by 1962.)
⑤ 죽기 전까지 49편의 소설을 출간했다고 했다. (By the time of his death in 2021 he had published 49 novels)

어법 특강

✱ to부정사

to부정사는 문장에 따라 명사, 형용사, 부사의 역할을 한다.

– 명사적 용법 : '~ 하는 것, -걸'의 의미로 문장 내에서 주어, 목적어, 보어의 역할을 할 수 있다.
• I need to ask myself what I really like.
(나는 내가 정말 무엇을 좋아하는지 스스로에게 물어볼 필요가 있다.)
→ 목적어 자리에 to부정사가 오는 동사들은 따로 외워두는 것이 좋다.
(want, need, decide, choose, expect, hope, learn, plan, promise 등)

– 형용사적 용법: 명사를 수식할 때 '~ 할'이라는 의미로 해석하면 된다.
• If you need someone to talk with, feel free to call me anytime.
(만약 네가 대화를 할 사람이 필요하면, 언제든지 나에게 전화해도 된다.)

– 부사적 용법: 문맥에 따라 다양한 의미를 가지는데, 보통 '~하기 위해서, ~하려고'라는 의미의 '목적'으로 많이 쓰인다. 그 외에 (감정의) 원인, 결과, 조건 등의 의미를 가진다.
• What can we do to save energy?
(에너지를 절약하기 위해 우리는 무엇을 할 수 있을까?)

I

어법 특강

✱ 분사구문

– 분사구문은 시간, 이유, 조건, 양보, 동시 동작 등과 같은 부사절의 의미를 대신한다. 부사절과 주절의 주어가 같을 경우, 부사절의 주어를 없애고 주어가 다를 경우 그대로 둔다. 부사절의 동사가 능동이면 현재분사로, 수동이면 과거분사로 바꾼다.

• Studying about education, I learned that children drop in IQ each summer vacation. 분사구문(시간)
(교육에 관한 연구를 할 때 나는 아이들의 지능 지수가 여름 방학 때마다 떨어진다는 것을 알게 되었다.)

• Not knowing that the product exists, customers would probably not buy it. 분사구문(이유)
(그 상품이 존재한다는 것을 알지 못해서 소비자들은 아마도 그것을 사지 않을 것이다.)

• When people yawn, they instinctively increase blood flow, bringing in low temperature air.
분사구문(동시 동작)
(사람들이 하품을 할 때 그들은 낮은 온도의 공기를 내부로 가져오면서 본능적으로 혈액의 흐름을 증가시킨다.)

I 어휘 Review 정답 ——— 문제편 p. 125

01 부양하다	11 major in	21 eagerly
02 비평가	12 go on to	22 analysis
03 고아로 만들다	13 doctor's degree	23 textile
04 작곡가	14 bachelor's degree	24 submitted
05 드문	15 end one's career	25 assemble
06 endless	16 military	26 wildlife
07 hire	17 slavery	27 candidate
08 literature	18 symbol	28 trousers
09 escape	19 contribution	29 emigrated
10 equality	20 chemistry	30 expressive

 **J** 실용문의 이해

문제편 p. 128~142

J 01 정답 ⑤ *2023 드론 레이싱 선수권 대회

2023 Drone Racing Championship / 2023 드론 레이싱 선수권 대회 /

Are you the best drone racer? //
당신은 최고의 드론 레이서인가요 //

형용사적 용법(opportunity 수식)
Then take the opportunity / to prove you are the one! //
그렇다면 기회를 잡으세요 / 여러분이 바로 그 사람이라는 것을 증명할 //

When & Where / 언제 & 어디서 /

• 6 p.m.–8 p.m., / Sunday, July 9 / ①의 단서 7월 9일 일요일에 개최됨
오후 6시부터 오후 8시까지 / 7월 9일 일요일 /

• Lakeside Community Center / Lakeside Community Center /

Requirements / 필요 요건 /

• Participants: / High school students only /
참가자 / 고등학생만 / ②의 단서 고등학생만 참가할 수 있음

• Bring your own drone / for the race. //
자신의 드론을 가지고 오세요 / 레이스를 위한 / ③의 단서 자신의 드론을 가져와야 함

Prize / 상 /

미래시제 수동태
• $500 and a medal will be awarded / to the winner. //
500달러와 메달이 수여될 것입니다 / 우승자에게 / ④의 단서 우승자에게는 상금과 메달이 수여됨

Note / 참고 사항 /
⑤의 단서 선착순 10명에게 기념품이 주어질 것임
• The first 10 participants will get souvenirs. //
선착순 10명의 참가자들은 기념품을 받게 될 것입니다 //

For more details, / please visit www.droneracing.com / or call 313-6745-1189. //
더 많은 세부 정보를 원하시면 / www.droneracing.com을 방문하시거나 / 313-6745-1189로 전화주세요 //

• opportunity ⓝ 기회   • prove ⓥ 증명하다
• requirement ⓝ 필요 요건   • award ⓥ 수여하다
• participant ⓝ 참가자   • souvenir ⓝ 기념품

2023 드론 레이싱 선수권 대회

당신은 최고의 드론 레이서인가요? 그렇다면 여러분이 바로 그 사람이라는 것을 증명할 기회를 잡으세요!

언제 & 어디서
• 오후 6시부터 오후 8시까지, 7월 9일 일요일
• Lakeside Community Center

필요 요건
• 참가자: 고등학생만
• 레이스를 위한 자신의 드론을 가지고 오세요.

상
• 500달러와 메달이 우승자에게 수여될 것입니다.

참고 사항
• 선착순 10명의 참가자들은 기념품을 받게 될 것입니다.
더 많은 세부 정보를 원하시면, www.droneracing.com을 방문하시거나 313-6745-1189로 전화주세요.

2023 Drone Racing Championship에 관한 다음 안내문의 내용과 일치하지 않는 것은?
① 7월 9일 일요일에 개최된다. Sunday, July 9
② 고등학생만 참가할 수 있다. Participants: High school students only
③ 자신의 드론을 가져와야 한다. Bring your own drone for the race.
④ 상금과 메달이 우승자에게 수여될 것이다.
$500 and a medal will be awarded to the winner.
⑤20명의 참가자가 기념품을 받을 것이다.
The first 10 participants will get souvenirs.

➤왜 정답? ✹❀❀ [정답률 95%]

선착순 10명의 참가자들은 기념품을 받게 될 것이라고(The first 10 participants will get souvenirs.) 했으므로 20명의 참가자가 기념품을 받을 것이라고 한 ⑤이 안내문의 내용과 일치하지 않는다.

➤왜 오답?
① 7월 9일 일요일에 개최된다. (Sunday, July 9)
② 고등학생만 참가할 수 있다. (Participants: High school students only)
③ 레이스를 위한 자신의 드론을 가져와야 한다. (Bring your own drone for the race.)
④ 상금 500달러와 메달이 우승자에게 수여될 것이다. ($500 and a medal will be awarded to the winner.)

J 02 정답 ② *Blackwood 동물원

Welcome to Blackwood Zoo /
Blackwood 동물원에 오신 것을 환영합니다 /

부사적 용법 (ready 수식)
Get ready / to explore! //
준비를 하세요 / 탐험할 //

①의 단서 10km의 보행로에서 동물 관람 가능
You can watch amazing animals / on our 10km walking path. //
여러분은 놀라운 동물들을 볼 수 있습니다 / 10 km의 보행로에서 //

Hours of Operation / 운영 시간 /

• Every day / all year round! // 매일 / 1년 내내 //

• 9:30 a.m. - 4:30 p.m. / (Last admission at 3:30 p.m.) /
오전 9:30 ~ 오후 4:30 / (오후 3:30에 마지막 입장) / ②의 단서 마지막 입장이 3시 30분이고 운영은 4시 30분에 종료됨

Ticket Prices / 티켓 가격 /

• Age 13 - 64: $30 / 13세~64세: 30달러 /

• Age 3 - 12: $20 / 3~12세는 20달러의 입장료를 내야 함 ③의 단서
3세~12세: 20달러 /

• Others: Free / 그 외: 무료 /

Seasonal Note / 계절에 따른 안내 /
부사절 접속사 (이유)
Since the weather is still cold, / some animals like snakes and turtles / will stay only indoors. // ④의 단서 추운 날씨로 인해 일부 동물은 실내에만 머무를 예정
날씨가 여전히 추워서 / 뱀과 거북이 같은 일부 동물은 / 실내에만 머무를 것입니다 //
현재시제 (규칙적인 사실, 반복되는 일정, 시간표 등)
※Free shuttle bus departs / from Blackwood Subway Station / every 30 minutes. // ⑤의 단서 무료 셔틀버스는 30분마다 출발
무료 셔틀버스는 출발합니다 / Blackwood 지하철역에서 / 30분마다 //

• explore ⓥ 탐험하다   • amazing ⓐ 놀라운
• walking path 보행로   • operation ⓝ 운영
• admission ⓝ 입장   • seasonal ⓐ 계절에 따른
• indoors ⓐⓓ 실내에   • depart ⓥ 출발하다

Blackwood 동물원에 오신 것을 환영합니다

탐험할 준비를 하세요! 여러분은 10km의 보행로에서 놀라운 동물들을 볼 수 있습니다.
운영 시간
• 매일, 1년 내내!
• 오전 9:30 ~ 오후 4:30 (오후 3:30에 마지막 입장)
티켓 가격
• 13세~64세: 30달러
• 3세~12세: 20달러
• 그 외: 무료
계절에 따른 안내
날씨가 여전히 추워서, 뱀과 거북이 같은 일부 동물은 실내에만 머무를 것입니다.
※ 무료 셔틀버스는 30분마다 Blackwood 지하철역에서 출발합니다.

Blackwood Zoo에 관한 다음 안내문의 내용과 일치하지 <u>않는</u> 것은?

① 10km의 보행로에서 동물들을 볼 수 있다.
　You can watch amazing animals on our 10km walking path.
② 운영 시간은 오후 3시 30분까지이다.
　9:30 a.m. - 4:30 p.m. (Last admission at 3:30 p.m.)
③ 3세부터 12세까지의 티켓 가격은 20달러이다.
　Age 3 - 12: $20
④ 날씨가 여전히 추워서 일부 동물은 실내에만 머무를 것이다.
　Since the weather is still cold, some animals ~ will stay only indoors.
⑤ 무료 셔틀버스가 30분마다 출발한다.
　Free shuttle bus departs ~ every 30 minutes.

왜 정답? ❀❀❀ [정답률 93%]

운영 시간은 오후 4시 30분까지라고 (9:30 a.m. - 4:30 p.m.) 했으므로 운영 시간이 오후 3시 30분까지라고 한 ②이 안내문의 내용과 일치하지 않는다.

왜 오답?

① 10km의 보행로에서 동물들을 볼 수 있다. (You can watch amazing animals on our 10km walking path.)
③ 3세부터 12세까지의 티켓 가격은 20달러이다. (Age 3 - 12: $20)
④ 날씨가 여전히 추워서 일부 동물은 실내에만 머무를 것이다. (Since the weather is still cold, some animals ~ will stay only indoors.)
⑤ 무료 셔틀버스가 30분마다 출발한다. (Free shuttle bus departs ~ every 30 minutes.)

[구문 서술형]

[정답] are staying

[해석] 날씨가 여전히 추워서 많은 동물들은 실내에만 머무르고 있다.
→ 「a number of + 복수 명사」는 '많은 ~'이라는 뜻으로, 복수 취급한다. 주어가 복수이므로, be동사 are를 써서 are staying으로 써야 한다.

J 03 정답 ② *양말 DIY 워크숍

Sock DIY Workshop / 양말 DIY 워크숍 /
Join us / for a fun and creative Sock DIY(Do It Yourself)
Workshop / for all ages! //
함께하세요 / 재미있고 창의적인 양말 DIY(손수 만들기) 워크숍에 / 모든 연령대를 위한 //

When & Where / 일시 및 장소 /
①의 단서 4월 19일 토요일 오후 1시에서 3시까지 진행됨
• Saturday, / April 19th, / from 1 p.m. to 3 p.m. /
토요일 / 4월 19일 / 오후 1시부터 오후 3시까지 /
• The community hall, Clanton Center /
커뮤니티 홀, Clanton Center /　②의 단서 Clanton Center의 커뮤니티 홀에서 열림

Workshop Program / 워크숍 프로그램 /

Time / 시간	DIY Item / DIY 품목	Things to Do / 할 일
③의 단서 양말로 장난감 만들기는 오후 1시에 시작 1 p.m. - 2 p.m. / 오후 1시 ~ 오후 2시 /	Toys / 장난감 /	과거분사 (toys 수식) Create stuffed toys / with socks / 봉제 인형 만들기 / 양말로 /
2 p.m. - 3 p.m. / 오후 2시 ~ 오후 3시 /	Flowerpot Covers / 화분 커버 /	Transform socks / into decorative covers / for small flowerpots / 양말을 변형하기 / 장식 커버로 / 소형 화분용 /

What Participants Should Prepare / 참가자가 준비해야 할 것 /
과거분사 (socks 수식)
• Used / but clean socks / ④의 단서 사용했어도 깨끗하면 준비물로 가능함
사용했지만 / 깨끗한 양말 /

Participation Fee / 참가비 /
'~당, ~마다'
• $5 per person / (including the cost for materials) /
1인당 5달러 / (재료비를 포함함) /　⑤의 단서 재료비를 포함해서 1인당 5달러

※For more details, / visit the Clanton Center website / or call us
at 555-123-4567. //
세부 사항은 / Clanton Center 웹사이트를 방문하거나 / 555-123-4567로 전화하세요 //

• stuffed toy 봉제 인형　• transform ⓥ 변형하다, 바꾸다
• decorative ⓐ 장식의　• flowerpot ⓝ 화분
• participation fee 참가비　• material ⓝ 재료
• detail ⓝ 세부 사항

양말 DIY 워크숍

모든 연령대를 위한 재미있고 창의적인 양말 DIY(손수 만들기) 워크숍에 함께하세요!

일시 및 장소
• 4월 19일 토요일, 오후 1시부터 오후 3시까지
• 커뮤니티 홀, Clanton Center

워크숍 프로그램

시간	DIY 품목	할 일
오후 1시 ~ 오후 2시	장난감	양말로 봉제 인형 만들기
오후 2시 ~ 오후 3시	화분 커버	양말을 소형 화분용 장식 커버로 변형하기

참가자가 준비해야 할 것
• 사용했지만 깨끗한 양말
참가비
• 1인당 5달러(재료비를 포함함)
※ 세부 사항은 Clanton Center 웹사이트를 방문하거나 555-123-4567로 전화하세요.

Sock DIY Workshop에 관한 다음 안내문의 내용과 일치하는 것은?

① 4월 19일 토요일 오후 1시부터 4시까지 열린다.
　Saturday, April 19th, from 1 p.m. to 3 p.m.
② Clanton Center의 커뮤니티 홀에서 진행된다.
　The community hall, Clanton Center
③ 참가자는 오후 2시부터 양말로 장난감을 만든다.
　1 p.m. -2 p.m. / Create stuffed toys with socks
④ 참가자는 사용하지 않은 깨끗한 양말을 준비해야 한다.
　Used but clean socks
⑤ 참가비는 재료비를 제외하고 1인당 5달러이다.
　$5 per person (including the cost for materials)

왜 정답? ❀❀❀ [정답률 87%]

행사의 진행 장소가 Clanton Center의 커뮤니티 홀이므로 (The community hall, Clanton Center) 안내문의 내용과 일치하는 것은 ②이다.

왜 오답?

① 4시가 아닌 3시까지 진행된다. (Saturday, April 19th, from 1 p.m. to 3 p.m.)
③ 오후 2시가 아닌 1시부터 양말로 장난감을 만든다. (1 p.m.-2 p.m. / Create stuffed toys with socks)
④ 사용했더라도 깨끗한 양말을 준비해야 한다. (Used but clean socks)
⑤ 참가비는 재료비를 포함해서 1인당 5달러이다. ($5 per person (including the cost for materials))

[구문 서술형]

[정답] have, has

[해석] 참가비는 재료비를 포함하여 1인당 5달러이다.
→ 「each + 단수 명사」는 항상 단수 취급하므로 조동사 have to를 단수형인 has to로 고쳐 수를 일치시켜야 한다.

J 04 정답 ③ *실내 식물을 파는 팝업 가게 안내

Houseplant Heaven Pop-up Shop / 실내 식물 천국 팝업 숍 /
단기간 제품을 판매하고 운영을 종료하는 가게

Enjoy / a special plant shopping experience! //
즐겨보세요 / 특별한 식물 쇼핑 경험을 //

Explore beautiful houseplants, / and bring some green into your home. //
아름다운 실내 식물들을 구경하고 / 당신의 집으로 초록을 가져가세요 //

When: / October 11 – 13, 10 a.m. – 8 p.m. /
①의 단서 3일간 진행됨
언제 / 10월 11 - 13일, 오전 10시 - 오후 8시 /

Where: / Tasty Cup Cafe / 어디서 / Tasty Cup Cafe /

Details / 세부 사항 /

• Indoor plants / are available for purchase. //
실내 식물이 / 구매 가능합니다 // ②의 단서 실내 식물이 구매 가능함

• If you buy 2 plants, / you will get a 50% discount / on coffee. //
식물을 2개 사면 / 50% 할인받을 것입니다 / 커피를 //
③의 단서 식물을 2개 사면 커피를 할인받음

Activities / 활동 /

과거분사구 (a photo zone 수식)
• Take pictures in a photo zone / filled with unique plants. //
포토존에서 사진을 찍으세요 / 독특한 식물로 가득 찬 //

과거분사구 (eco-friendly pots 수식)
• Decorate eco-friendly pots / made from recycled glass. //
친환경 화분들을 장식하세요 / 재활용 유리로 만든 //
④의 단서 친환경 화분을 장식하는 활동이 있음

수동태 동사
※ Outside food and drinks / are not allowed. //
외부 음식과 음료는 / 허용되지 않습니다 //
⑤의 단서 외부 음식과 음료는 허용되지 않음

• houseplant ⓝ 실내 식물 • explore ⓥ 구경하다, 둘러보다
• available ⓐ 이용 가능한 • purchase ⓝ 구매
• unique ⓐ 독특한 • eco-friendly ⓐ 친환경적인
• recycle ⓥ 재활용하다 • allow ⓥ 허용하다

실내 식물 천국 팝업 숍

특별한 식물 쇼핑 경험을 즐겨보세요! 아름다운 실내 식물들을 구경하고, 당신의 집으로 초록을 가져가세요.
언제: 10월 11 – 13일, 오전 10시 – 오후 8시
어디서: Tasty Cup Cafe
세부 사항
• 실내 식물이 구매 가능합니다.
• 식물을 2개 사면, 커피를 50% 할인 받을 것입니다.
활동
• 독특한 식물로 가득 찬 포토존에서 사진을 찍으세요.
• 재활용 유리로 만든 친환경 화분들을 장식하세요.
※ 외부 음식과 음료는 허용되지 않습니다.

Houseplant Heaven Popup Shop에 관한 다음 안내문의 내용과 일치하지 않는 것은?
① 3일간 진행된다. October 11 - 13
② 실내 식물이 구매 가능하다. Indoor plants are available for purchase.
③ 식물을 2개 사면 커피를 무료로 받을 것이다.
If you buy 2 plants, you will get a 50% discount on coffee.
④ 친환경 화분을 장식하는 활동이 있다.
Decorate eco-friendly pots made from recycled glass.
⑤ 외부 음식과 음료는 허용되지 않는다.
Outside food and drinks are not allowed.

왜 정답? ✽✽✽ [정답률 97%]
식물을 2개 사면 커피를 50% 할인받을 것이라고 (If you buy 2 plants, you will get a 50% discount on coffee.) 했으므로 커피를 무료로 받을 것이라고 한 ③이 안내문의 내용과 일치하지 않는다.

왜 오답?
① 3일간 진행된다. (October 11 – 13)
② 실내 식물이 구매 가능하다. (Indoor plants are available for purchase.)

---

④ 친환경 화분을 장식하는 활동이 있다. (Decorate eco-friendly pots made from recycled glass.)
⑤ 외부 음식과 음료는 허용되지 않는다. (Outside food and drinks are not allowed.)

구문 서술형

정답 are

해석 모든 실내 식물은 구매 가능하다.
→ 부분이나 수량을 나타내는 표현은 of 뒤의 명사에 수를 일치시킨다. 「All of + 복수 명사」이므로 be동사는 현재시제 복수형인 are로 써야 한다.

J 05 정답 ④ *2025 여름 만화 축제 안내

2025 Summer Cartoon Festival / 2025 여름 만화 축제 /

It's the 8th annual Summer Cartoon Festival! //
제8회 연례 여름 만화 축제입니다 // ①의 단서 8번째 열리는 연례 축제임

The festival drew / a lot of visitors last year. //
이 축제는 끌었습니다 / 작년에 많은 방문객을 /
'~하는 게 어떨까요?' = visitors
Why not be one of them this year? //
여러분도 올해 그 중 한 명이 되어보는 것은 어떨까요 //

Dates: / July 5 – 6 / 날짜 / 7월 5일 - 6일 /

Time: / 9 a.m. – 6 p.m. / ②의 단서 오전 9시부터 오후 6시까지 진행됨
시간 / 오전 9시 - 오후 6시 /

Place: / Merryville Park / 장소 / Merryville Park /

Featured Events / 주요 이벤트 /

• Cartoon drawing classes for beginners only /
초급자만을 위한 만화 그리기 수업 / ③의 단서 초급자만을 위한 만화 그리기 수업이 있음

• Face painting by cartoonists / ④의 단서 페이스 페인팅 행사가 있음
만화가에 의한 페이스 페인팅 /

• Parade of costumed characters / 의상을 갖춰 입은 캐릭터의 퍼레이드 /

Notes / 참고 사항 /
⑤의 단서 모든 방문객이 캐릭터 스티커를 받음
• All visitors / will receive character stickers. //
모든 방문객들은 / 캐릭터 스티커를 받을 것입니다 //

• For a more detailed timetable and other information, / check out www.SummerCartoonFest.com. //
더 자세한 시간표와 기타 정보를 위해서 / www.SummerCartoonFest.com을 확인하세요 //

• annual ⓐ 연례의, 매년의 • featured ⓐ 주요한
• drawing ⓝ 그림 그리기 • beginners ⓝ 초급자
• costumed ⓐ 의상을 갖춰 입은 • receive ⓥ 받다
• detailed ⓐ 자세한 • check out 확인하다

2025 여름 만화 축제

제8회 연례 여름 만화 축제입니다! 이 축제는 작년에 많은 방문객을 끌었습니다. 여러분도 올해 그 중 한 명이 되어보는 것은 어떨까요?
날짜: 7월 5일 – 6일
시간: 오전 9시 – 오후 6시
장소: Merryville Park
주요 이벤트
• 초급자만을 위한 만화 그리기 수업
• 만화가에 의한 페이스 페인팅
• 의상을 갖춰 입은 캐릭터의 퍼레이드
참고 사항
• 모든 방문객들은 캐릭터 스티커를 받을 것입니다.
• 더 자세한 시간표와 기타 정보를 위해서, www.SummerCartoonFest.com을 확인하세요.

2025 Summer Cartoon Festival에 관한 다음 안내문의 내용과 일치하는 것은?

① 처음으로 개최되는 축제이다. It's the 8th annual Summer Cartoon Festival!

② 오전 9시부터 오후 7시까지 진행된다. Time: 9 a.m. - 6 p.m.

③ 상급자를 위한 만화 그리기 수업이 있다.

④ 페이스 페인팅 행사가 있다. Cartoon drawing classes for beginners only / Face painting by cartoonists

⑤ 방문객 중 일부만 캐릭터 스티커를 받을 것이다.
All visitors will receive character stickers.

> 왜 정답 ? ✽❀❀ [정답률 95%]

만화가에 의한 페이스 페인팅 행사(Face painting by cartoonists)가 있으므로 안내문의 내용과 일치하는 것은 ④이다.

> 왜 오답 ?

① 8번째 열리는 연례 축제이다. (It's the 8th annual Summer Cartoon Festival!)

② 오전 9시부터 오후 6시까지 진행된다. (Time: 9 a.m. – 6 p.m.)

③ 초급자만을 위한 만화 그리기 수업이 있다. (Cartoon drawing classes for beginners only)

⑤ 모든 방문객이 캐릭터 스티커를 받을 것이다. (All visitors will receive character stickers.)

구문 서술형

정답 Every visitor is receiving character stickers.

해석 모든 방문객들은 캐릭터 스티커를 받고 있다.

→ every는 항상 단수 명사를 수식한다. 따라서 기존의 All 뒤에 나온 복수 명사 visitors는 visitor로 고쳐야 한다. will receive를 현재진행시제로 나타내려면 단수 주어에 수 일치시킨 is receiving으로 고쳐야 한다.

J 06 정답 ③ ＊Father-Daughter Sock Hop

Father-Daughter Sock Hop /
Father-Daughter Sock Hop /
부사적 용법 (감정의 원인)
We are excited to bring you / the 5th annual Father-Daughter Sock Hop / — an incredibly special evening for fathers and daughters to dance! //
우리는 당신을 모시게 되어 기쁩니다 / 제5회 연례 Father-Daughter Sock Hop에 / 아빠와 딸이 춤을 추는 매우 특별한 저녁인 //

When & Where / 언제 & 어디서 /
• September 12th(Friday), / from 6 p.m. to 9 p.m. /
9월 12일(금요일) / 저녁 6시에서 9시까지 / ①의 단서 9월 12일 금요일에 개최됨
• Maple Creek Community Center /
Maple Creek 커뮤니티 센터 /

Participation Fee / 참가비 /
• $25 per pair / ②의 단서 한 쌍당 참가비는 25달러
한 쌍당 25달러 /
• $5 per each additional daughter /
추가되는 딸 1명당 5달러 /
• No refund for cancellations / on the day of the event /
취소 시 환불 불가 / 행사 당일 / ③의 단서 행사 당일 취소 시 환불은 불가능함

Notice / 공지사항 /
미래시제 수동태 ④의 단서 모든 참가자에게 선물로 양말 한 켤레가 제공됨
• A pair of socks will be given out / as a gift to every participant. //
양말 한 켤레가 제공될 것입니다 / 모든 참가자에게 선물로 //
• Take pictures at the photo zone. // ⑤의 단서 포토존에서 사진을 찍을 수 있음
포토존에서 사진을 찍으세요 //

Registration / 등록 /
• Register online / at www.maplecreekcity.org. /
온라인으로 등록하세요 / www.maplecreekcity.org에서 //

• annual ⓐ 연례의, 매년의   • participation ⓝ 참가, 참여
• fee ⓝ 요금   • additional ⓐ 추가의   • refund ⓝ 환불
• cancellation ⓝ 취소   • participant ⓝ 참가자
• registration ⓝ 등록

Father-Daughter Sock Hop

우리는 당신을 아빠와 딸이 춤을 추는 매우 특별한 저녁인 제5회 연례 Father-Daughter Sock Hop에 모시게 되어 기쁩니다!

언제 & 어디서
• 9월 12일(금요일), 저녁 6시에서 9시까지
• Maple Creek 커뮤니티 센터

참가비
• 한 쌍당 25달러
• 추가되는 딸 1명당 5달러
• 행사 당일 취소 시 환불 불가

공지사항
• 양말 한 켤레가 모든 참가자에게 선물로 제공될 것입니다.
• 포토존에서 사진을 찍으세요.

등록
• www.maplecreekcity.org에서 온라인으로 등록하세요.

Father-Daughter Sock Hop에 관한 다음 안내문의 내용과 일치하지 않는 것은?

① 9월 12일 금요일에 개최된다. September 12th(Friday)

② 한 쌍당 참가비는 $25이다. $25 per pair

③ 행사 당일 취소 시 환불이 가능하다.
No refund for cancellations on the day of the event

④ 모든 참가자에게 선물이 제공된다.
A pair of socks will be given out as a gift to every participant.

⑤ 포토존에서 사진을 찍을 수 있다. Take pictures at the photo zone.

> 왜 정답 ? ✽❀❀ [정답률 95%]

행사 당일 취소 시 환불이 불가능하다고 (No refund for cancellations on the day of the event) 했으므로 행사 당일 취소 시 환불이 가능하다고 한 ③이 안내문의 내용과 일치하지 않는다.

> 왜 오답 ?

① 9월 12일 금요일에 개최된다. (September 12th(Friday))

② 한 쌍당 참가비는 $25이다. ($25 per pair)

④ 모든 참가자에게 선물이 제공된다. (A pair of socks will be given out as a gift to every participant.)

⑤ 포토존에서 사진을 찍을 수 있다. (Take pictures at the photo zone.)

구문 서술형

정답 Each of the participants receives a pair of socks.

해석 모든 참가자는 양말 한 켤레를 받을 것이다. → 각각의 참가자들은 양말 한 켤레를 받는다.

→ 「Each of + 복수 명사」 형태가 되어야 하며 이는 항상 단수로 취급한다. 따라서 Every participant는 Each of the participants로, will receive는 receives로 고쳐야 한다.

J 07 정답 ⑤ ＊도서관 책갈피 디자인 대회

2025 Library Bookmark Design Contest /
2025 도서관 책갈피 디자인 대회 /
①의 단서 여섯 번째 열리는 대회임
The 6th annual Library Bookmark Design Contest is now open! //
제6회 연례 Library Bookmark Design Contest가 지금 열립니다 //

Show your creativity and design skills. //
여러분의 창의성과 디자인 기술을 보여주세요 //

Participation / 참가 /

- Participants need to be between the ages of 5-12. //
참가자는 5세에서 12세 사이여야 합니다 //　②의 단서 5세에서 12세 사이여야 참가할 수 있음

Guidelines / 지침 /

- Create a bookmark by hand / using markers or crayons. // ^{분사구문}
손으로 책갈피를 만드세요 / 마커 또는 크레용을 사용하여 //

- Designs must fit the slogan "Find Your Voice." //
디자인은 "Find Your Voice" 슬로건에 적합해야 합니다 //
^{부정 명령문 동사}
- Do not use / commercialized character images / in your
design. // ③의 단서 상업용 캐릭터 이미지를 사용할 수 없음
사용하지 마세요 / 상업용 캐릭터 이미지들을 / 디자인에 //

Submission / 제출 /

- Limit one entry per participant. // ④의 단서 출품작은 참가자당 한 개로 제한됨
참가자당 한 개의 출품작으로 제한합니다 //
^{수동태 동사}
- Entries should be submitted / via email to contest@srpls.org
by October 4th. //
출품작은 제출되어야 합니다 / 10월 4일까지 이메일(contest@srpls.org)로 //

Prizes / 시상 /

- 1st place: $50 gift card, / 2nd place: $30 gift card /
1등: 50달러 선물 카드 / 2등: 30달러 선물 카드 /
⑤의 단서 수상자의 책갈피는 인쇄되어 방문객에게 제공될 것임
^{미래시제 수동태}
- Winners' bookmarks will be printed / and given to visitors. //
수상자의 책갈피는 인쇄되어 / 방문객에게 제공될 것입니다 //

※ For more information, / please visit our website at www.
sherrillpubliclibrary.org. //
더 많은 정보를 위해 / 웹사이트 www.sherrillpubliclibrary.org를 방문하세요 //

- creativity ⓝ 창의성　- slogan ⓝ 슬로건, 구호
- commercialized ⓐ 상업화된　- submission ⓝ 제출
- limit ⓥ 제한하다　- entry ⓝ 출품작　- submit ⓥ 제출하다

2025 Library Bookmark Design Contest

제6회 연례 Library Bookmark Design Contest가 지금 열립니다! 여러분의 창의성과 디자인 기술을 보여주세요.

참가
- 참가자는 5세에서 12세 사이여야 합니다.

지침
- 마커 또는 크레용을 사용하여 손으로 책갈피를 만드세요.
- 디자인은 "Find Your Voice" 슬로건에 적합해야 합니다.
- 디자인에 상업용 캐릭터 이미지들을 사용하지 마세요.

제출
- 참가자당 한 개의 출품작으로 제한합니다.
- 출품작은 10월 4일까지 이메일(contest@srpls.org)로 제출되어야 합니다.

시상
- 1등: 50달러 선물 카드, 2등: 30달러 선물 카드
- 수상자의 책갈피는 인쇄되어 방문객에게 제공될 것입니다.

※ 더 많은 정보를 위해, 웹사이트 www.sherrillpubliclibrary.org를 방문하세요.

2025 Library Bookmark Design Contest에 관한 다음 안내문의
내용과 일치하는 것은?

① 여덟 번째 열리는 대회이다. The 6th annual Library Bookmark Design Contest
② 13세 이상이면 누구나 참가할 수 있다. between the ages of 5-12
③ 상업용 캐릭터 이미지를 사용할 수 있다.
Do not use commercialized character images
④ 출품작은 참가자당 두 개로 제한된다. Limit one entry per participant.
⑤ 수상자의 책갈피는 인쇄되어 방문객에게 제공될 것이다.
Winners' bookmarks will be printed and given to visitors.

➣왜 정답? ✿❀❀ [정답률 94%]

수상자의 책갈피는 인쇄되어 방문객에게 제공될 것이라고 했으므로(Winners' bookmarks will be printed and given to visitors) 안내문의 내용과 일치하는 것은 ⑤이다.

➣왜 오답?

① 여섯 번째 열리는 대회이다. (The 6th annual Library Bookmark Design Contest)
② 참가자는 5세에서 12세 사이여야 한다. (between the ages of 5-12)
③ 상업용 캐릭터 이미지를 사용할 수 없다. (Do not use commercialized character images)
④ 출품작은 참가자당 한 개로 제한된다. (Limit one entry per participant.)

구문 서술형

정답 were, was

해석 마커나 크레용 둘 중 하나가 책갈피를 만드는 데 사용되었다.
→ either A or B로 연결된 주어는 B에 수를 일치시켜야 하므로 복수 동사인 were를 단수 명사인 crayon에 맞게 was로 고쳐야 한다.

J 08 정답 ④ *반려동물 먹이 요리 교실

Yummy Paws: Pet Food Cooking Class /
냠냠 발: 반려동물 먹이 요리 교실 /
^{관계부사 (cooking class 수식)}
Join us / for an exciting pet food cooking class / where you will
learn / how to create healthy and delicious pumpkin biscuits /
for your furry friends! //
참여하세요 / 신나는 반려동물 먹이 요리 교실에 / 당신이 배울 수 있는 / 건강하고 맛있는 호박 비스킷을 만드는 방법을 / 여러분의 털북숭이 친구를 위해 //

When: / 2:00 p.m.–4:00 p.m., Every Sunday, December, 2024 /
언제 / 2024년 12월 매주 일요일 오후 2시-4시 / ①의 단서 12월에 일요일마다 2시간씩 진행

Where: / Green Park Community Center, Room 5 /
어디서 / Green Park Community Center, 5호실 /

Registration / 등록 /

- Register online / at www.yummypawsclass.com. //
온라인으로 등록하세요 / www.yummypawsclass.com에서 //

- Limited to 10 participants / for each class /
참여 인원을 10명으로 제한 / 각 수업당 / ②의 단서 수업당 인원은 10명으로 제한함

Fee / 수업료 /

- $30 per participant / (Full payment is required / when
registering.) // ③의 단서 등록 시 전액 지불해야 함
참가자당 30달러 / (전액 지불해야 합니다 / 등록 시) //

- The fee includes / all ingredients. //
수업료는 포함합니다 / 모든 재료를 //

Note / 유의 사항 /

- Additional recipes / available for free /
추가 레시피는 / 무료로 이용 가능 / ④의 단서 추가 레시피는 무료로 이용 가능함

- For safety reasons, / no pets are allowed. //
안전상의 이유로 / 반려동물 출입이 허용되지 않습니다 //

- For a refund, / cancel at least 48 hours before the class. //
환불을 위해서는 / 최소한 수업 48시간 전까지 취소하세요 // ⑤의 단서 환불을 위해서는 수업 48시간 전까지 취소해야 함

- furry ⓐ 털이 많은　- register ⓥ 등록하다　- limit ⓥ 제한하다
- participant ⓝ 참가자　- payment ⓝ 지불　- require ⓥ 요구하다
- ingredient ⓝ 재료　- additional ⓐ 추가적인
- available ⓐ 이용 가능한　- safety ⓝ 안전　- refund ⓝ 환불

냠냠 발: 반려동물 먹이 요리 교실

여러분의 털북숭이 친구를 위해 건강하고 맛있는 호박 비스킷을 만드는 방법을 배울 수 있는 신나는 반려동물 먹이 요리 교실에 참여하세요!

언제: 2024년 12월 매주 일요일 오후 2시-4시
어디서: Green Park Community Center, 5호실
등록
• www.yummypawsclass.com에서 온라인으로 등록하세요.
• 각 수업당 참여 인원을 10명으로 제한

수업료
• 참가자당 30달러(등록 시 전액 지불해야 합니다.)
• 수업료는 모든 재료를 포함합니다.

유의 사항
• 추가 레시피는 무료로 이용 가능
• 안전상의 이유로 반려동물 출입이 허용되지 않습니다.
• 환불을 위해서는 최소한 수업 48시간 전까지 취소하세요.

Yummy Paws: Pet Food Cooking Class에 관한 다음 안내문의 내용과 일치하지 <u>않는</u> 것은?
① 12월에 일요일마다 2시간씩 진행된다.
  2:00 p.m.-4:00 p.m., Every Sunday, December
② 각 수업당 참여 인원이 10명으로 제한된다.
  Limited to 10 participants for each class
③ 수업료는 등록 시 전액 지불한다.
  Full payment is required when registering.
④ 추가 레시피는 별도로 구매해야 한다. Additional recipes available for free
⑤ 환불을 위해서는 수업 48시간 전까지 취소해야 한다.
  For a refund, cancel at least 48 hours before the class.

➢왜 정답? ✽✽✽ [정답률 96%]
추가 레시피는 무료로 이용 가능하다고 (Additional recipes available for free) 했으므로, 추가 레시피는 별도로 구매해야 한다는 ④이 안내문의 내용과 일치하지 않는다.

➢왜 오답?
① 12월에 매주 일요일 2시에서 4시로 2시간씩 진행된다. (2:00 p.m.-4:00 p.m., Every Sunday, December)
② 각 수업당 참여 인원이 10명으로 제한된다. (Limited to 10 participants for each class)
③ 수업료는 등록 시에 전액 지불해야 한다. (Full payment is required when registering.)
⑤ 환불을 위해서는 최소한 수업 48시간 전까지 취소해야 한다. (For a refund, cancel at least 48 hours before the class.)

[구문 서술형]

[정답] are

[해석] • 추가 레시피는 무료로 이용 가능합니다.
• 모든 재료는 수업료에 포함됩니다.

→ 첫 번째 문장의 주어 recipes와 두 번째 문장의 주어 ingredients는 모두 복수 명사이다. 따라서 공통으로 들어갈 말은 복수 주어에 수 일치시킨 복수형 be 동사 are이다.

J 09 정답 ⑤ ✱K-Pop 커버 댄스 대회

2024 K-Pop Cover Dance Contest / 2024 K-Pop 커버 댄스 대회 /
Good news / for K-Pop fans in Canada! //
희소식 / 캐나다의 K-Pop 팬을 위한 //
                        to부정사의 의미상 주어
It's time / for your dance team / to show your talents / at this contest! //
시간입니다 / 여러분의 댄스 팀이 / 재능을 보여줄 수 있는 / 이 대회에서 //
When & Where / 언제 & 어디서 /
• Date: / November 29th, 2024 / ①의 단서 하루만 진행됨
날짜 / 2024년 11월 29일 /
• Time: / 7 p.m.-9 p.m. / 시간 / 오후 7시-9시 /
• Location: / So Merry Theatre / 장소 / So Merry Theatre /
Judging Criteria: / Cooperation, Artistic Skill, Costume /
심사 기준 / 협동, 예술적 기술, 무대의상 / ②의 단서 심사 기준에 관객 호응은 없음

Prize / 상품 /
• Top 3 teams will receive / a $200 gift certificate. //
상위 세 팀은 받을 것입니다 / 200달러 상품권을 // ③의 단서 상위 세 팀만 상품권을 받음
                                                형용사적 용법 (the chance 수식)
• The winning team will have the chance / to visit Korea's top management agencies. //
우승 팀은 기회를 가질 것입니다 / 한국의 최고 매니지먼트 회사를 방문할 //
Application / 신청 /
• A cover dance video / should not be more than 4 minutes long. // ④의 단서 영상 길이는 4분이 넘지 않아야 함
커버 댄스의 영상 길이는 / 4분이 넘지 않아야 합니다 //
                                                        ~을 통해서
• Submit the video, / along with your application, / via our website / by November 3rd. // ⑤의 단서 신청서와 함께 영상을 웹사이트에 제출해야 함
영상을 제출하세요 / 신청서와 함께 / 우리 웹사이트를 통해 / 11월 3일까지 //
For more information, / visit www.2024kpopcontest.com. //
더 많은 정보를 위해서 / www.2024kpopcontest.com에 방문하세요 //

• talent ⓝ 재능   • contest ⓝ 대회   • judge ⓥ 심사하다
• criterion ⓝ 기준 (pl. criteria)   • cooperation ⓝ 협동
• costume ⓝ 의상   • gift certificate 상품권
• management agency 매니지먼트 회사[기획사]   • application ⓝ 신청
• submit ⓥ 제출하다

2024 K-Pop 커버 댄스 대회
캐나다의 K-Pop 팬을 위한 희소식! 이 대회에서 여러분의 댄스팀이 재능을 보여 줄 때입니다!
언제 & 어디서
• 날짜: 2024년 11월 29일
• 시간: 오후 7시 - 9시
• 장소: So Merry Theatre
심사 기준: 협동, 예술적 기술, 무대의상
상품
• 상위 세 팀은 200달러 상품권을 받을 것입니다.
• 우승 팀은 한국의 최고 매니지먼트 회사를 방문할 기회를 가질 것입니다.
신청
• 커버 댄스의 영상 길이는 4분이 넘지 않아야 합니다.
• 신청서와 함께 영상을 11월 3일까지 우리 웹사이트를 통해 제출하세요.
더 많은 정보를 위해서 www.2024kpopcontest.com에 방문하세요.

2024 K-Pop Cover Dance Contest에 관한 다음 안내문의 내용과 일치하는 것은?
① 2일 동안 진행된다. November 29th, 2024
② 심사 기준에 관객 호응이 포함된다.
  Judging Criteria: Cooperation, Artistic Skill, Costume
③ 상위 열 팀은 200달러 상품권을 받을 것이다.
  Top 3 teams will receive a $200 gift certificate.
④ 커버 댄스의 영상 길이는 4분이 넘어야 한다.
  A cover dance video should not be more than 4 minutes long.
⑤ 신청서와 함께 영상을 웹사이트를 통해 제출해야 한다.
  Submit the video, along with your application, via our website

➢왜 정답? ✽✽✽ [정답률 86%]
신청하려면 신청서와 함께 커버 영상을 웹사이트를 통해 제출해야 하므로(Submit the video, along with your application, via our website) 안내문의 내용과 일치하는 것은 ⑤이다.

➢왜 오답?
① 하루 동안 진행된다. (November 29th, 2024)
② 심사 기준은 협동, 예술적 기술, 무대의상이므로 관객 호응은 포함되지 않는다. (Judging Criteria: Cooperation, Artistic Skill, Costume)
③ 상위 세 팀만 200달러 상품권을 받을 것이다. (Top 3 teams will receive a $200 gift certificate.)
④ 커버 댄스의 영상 길이는 4분이 넘지 않아야 한다. (A cover dance video should not be more than 4 minutes long.)

정답 receive

해석 우승 팀뿐만 아니라 2등, 3등 팀도 200달러 상품권을 받는다.
→ 'A뿐만 아니라 B도'라는 의미의 상관접속사 not only A but also B는 B에 동사의 수를 일치시키므로, the 2nd and 3rd place teams에 수 일치한 복수 동사 receive를 써야 한다.

J 10 정답 ④ *봄철 차 교실

Spring Tea Class for Young People /
청소년을 위한 봄철 차 교실 /

Join us for a delightful Spring Tea Class / for young people, /
관계부사(선행사: Spring Tea Class)
where you'll experience / the taste of tea / from various cultures
around the world. // ①의 단서 수강생은 차 교실에서 전 세계 다양한 문화권의 차를 맛보는 경험을 함
즐거운 봄철 차 교실에 참여하세요 / 청소년을 위한 / 그곳에서 여러분은 경험을 할 것입니다 /
차를 맛보는 / 전 세계 다양한 문화권의 //

Class Schedule / 수업 일정 /
• Friday, April 5 (4:30 p.m. – 6:00 p.m.) / ②의 단서 금요일 수업은 오후 4:30 ~ 오후 6:00에 진행됨
4월 5일 금요일 (오후 4:30 ~ 오후 6:00) /
• Saturday, April 6 (9:30 a.m. – 11:00 a.m.) /
4월 6일 토요일 (오전 9:30 ~ 오전 11:00) /

Details / 세부 내용 /
• We will give you / tea and snacks. // ③의 단서 수강생에게 차와 간식을 제공함
우리는 여러분에게 드리겠습니다 / 차와 간식을 //
동명사(전치사의 목적어)
• We offer special tips / for **hosting** a tea party. //
우리는 특별한 조언을 제공합니다 / 차 모임 주최를 위한 //

Participation Fee / 참가비 /
'~당, ~마다'
• Age 13-15: $25 **per** person / ④의 단서 15세 이하의 수강생은 25달러의 참가비를 냄
13 ~ 15세: 1인당 25달러 /
• Age 16-18: $30 per person /
16 ~ 18세: 1인당 30달러 /

Note / 주의 사항 / ⑤의 단서 음식 알레르기가 있는 수강생은 이메일을 미리 보내야 함
If you have any food allergy, / you should email us in advance
at youth@seasonteaclass.com. //
만약 여러분이 음식 알레르기가 있다면 / 저희에게 미리 youth@seasonteaclass.com으로
이메일을 보내야 합니다 //

- delightful @ 즐거운 • experience ⓥ 경험하다
- various @ 다양한 • host ⓥ (파티 등을) 주최하다
- in advance 미리

청소년을 위한 봄철 차 교실
청소년을 위한 즐거운 봄철 차 교실에 참여하세요. 그곳에서 여러분은 전 세계 다양한 문화권의 차를 맛보는 경험을 할 것입니다.
수업 일정
• 4월 5일 금요일 (오후 4:30 ~ 오후 6:00)
• 4월 6일 토요일 (오전 9:30 ~ 오전 11:00)
세부 내용
• 우리는 여러분에게 차와 간식을 드리겠습니다.
• 우리는 차 모임 주최를 위한 특별한 조언을 제공합니다.
참가비
• 13 ~ 15세: 1인당 25달러
• 16 ~ 18세: 1인당 30달러
주의 사항
만약 여러분이 음식 알레르기가 있다면 저희에게 미리
youth@seasonteaclass.com으로 이메일을 보내야 합니다.

Spring Tea Class for Young People에 관한 다음 안내문의 내용과 일치하지 않는 것은?
① 수강생은 전 세계 다양한 문화권의 차를 경험할 수 있다.
you'll experience the taste of tea from various cultures around the world
② 금요일 수업은 오후에 1시간 30분 동안 진행된다.
Friday, April 5 (4:30 p.m. - 6:00 p.m.)
③ 수강생에게 차와 간식을 제공할 것이다.
We will give you tea and snacks.
④15세 이하의 수강생은 30달러의 참가비를 내야 한다.
Age 13 - 15: $25 per person
⑤ 음식 알레르기가 있는 수강생은 이메일을 미리 보내야 한다.
If you have any food allergy, you should email us in advance

>왜 정답 ? ❋❀❀ [정답률 95%]
13세에서 15세는 1인당 25달러(Age 13 - 15: $25 per person)라고 했으므로 15세 이하의 수강생은 30달러의 참가비를 내야 한다고 한 ④이 안내문의 내용과 일치하지 않는다.

>왜 오답 ?
① 수강생은 전 세계 다양한 문화권의 차를 경험할 수 있다. (you'll experience the taste of tea from various cultures around the world)
② 금요일 수업은 오후에 1시간 30분 동안 진행된다. (Friday, April 5 (4:30 p.m. - 6:00 p.m.))
③ 수강생에게 차와 간식을 제공할 것이다. (We will give you tea and snacks.)
⑤ 음식 알레르기가 있는 수강생은 이메일을 미리 보내야 한다. (If you have any food allergy, you should email us in advance)

J 11 정답 ④ *의류 업사이클링 대회

Clothes Upcycling Contest 2024 / 2024 의류 업사이클링 대회 /

Are you passionate / about fashion and the environment? //
여러분은 열정이 있으신가요 / 패션과 환경에 대한 //

Then we have a contest for you! //
그렇다면 우리가 여러분을 위한 대회를 개최합니다 //

• **Participants /** 참가자 / ①의 단서 Lakewood에 사는 11세~18세 사람들이 참여 가능
현재분사(Anyone 수식)
- Anyone **living** in Lakewood, aged 11 to 18 /
Lakewood에 거주하는 11세에서 18세까지이면 누구나 /

• **How to participate /** 참여 방법 /
- Take before and after photos / of your upcycled clothes. //
전, 후 사진을 찍으세요 / 여러분의 업사이클된 옷의 //
- Email the photos at lovelw@lwplus.com. // ②의 단서 참가자는 출품 사진을 이메일로 보냄
사진은 lovelw@lwplus.com으로 이메일을 보내세요 //
- Send in the photos / from April 14 to May 12. //
사진은 보내세요 / 4월 14일부터 5월 12일까지 // ③의 단서 참가자는 5월 12일까지 출품 사진을 제출할 수 있음

• **Winning Prize /** 우승 상품 /
형용사적 용법(gift card 수식)
- A $100 gift card / **to use** at local shops / ④의 단서 우승 상품은 지역 상점에서 쓸 수 있는 100달러 기프트 카드임
100달러 기프트 카드 한 장 / 지역 상점에서 쓸 수 있는 /
미래시제 수동태
- The winner **will be announced** / on our website on May 30. //
우승자를 발표할 것입니다 / 우리 웹사이트에서 5월 30일에 // ⑤의 단서 웹사이트에서 우승자를 발표함
For more details, / visit our website www.lovelwplus.com. //
더 많은 정보를 위해서는 / 우리 웹사이트(www.lovelwplus.com)를 방문하세요 //

- passionate @ 열정적인 • environment ⓝ 환경
- contest ⓝ 대회 • upcycled @ 업사이클된
- winning prize 우승 상품 • local @ 지역의
- announce ⓥ 발표하다

2024 의류 업사이클링 대회
여러분은 패션과 환경에 대한 열정이 있으신가요? 그렇다면 우리가 여러분을 위한 대회를 개최합니다!
• **참가자**
- Lakewood에 거주하는 11세에서 18세까지이면 누구나

• 참여 방법
– 여러분의 업사이클된 옷의 전, 후 사진을 찍으세요.
– 사진은 lovelw@lwplus.com으로 이메일을 보내세요.
– 사진은 4월 14일부터 5월 12일까지 보내세요.
• 우승 상품
– 지역 상점에서 쓸 수 있는 100달러 기프트 카드 한 장
– 우승자를 우리 웹사이트에서 5월 30일에 발표할 것입니다.
더 많은 정보를 위해서는 우리 웹사이트(www.lovelwplus.com)를 방문하세요.

Clothes Upcycling Contest 2024에 관한 다음 안내문의 내용과 일치하는 것은?
① Lakewood에 사는 사람이면 누구든지 참가할 수 있다.
  Anyone living in Lakewood, aged 11 to 18
② 참가자는 출품 사진을 직접 방문하여 제출해야 한다.
  Email the photos at lovelw@lwplus.com.
③ 참가자는 5월 14일까지 출품 사진을 제출할 수 있다.
  Send in the photos from April 14 to May 12.
④ 우승 상품은 지역 상점에서 쓸 수 있는 기프트 카드이다.
  A $100 gift card to use at local shops
⑤ 지역 신문을 통해 우승자를 발표한다.
  The winner will be announced on our website on May 30.

⊃왜 정답? ✿✿✿ [정답률 92%]
우승 상품은 지역 상점에서 쓸 수 있는 100달러 기프트 카드 한 장이라고 했으므로 (A $100 gift card to use at local shops) 안내문의 내용과 일치하는 것은 ④이다.

⊃왜 오답?
① Lakewood에 사는 11세에서 18세까지의 사람들이 참가할 수 있다. (Anyone living in Lakewood, aged 11 to 18)
② 직접 방문하는 것이 아니라 이메일을 통해 제출한다. (Email the photos at lovelw@lwplus.com.)
③ 5월 12일까지 출품 사진을 제출해야 한다. (Send in the photos from April 14 to May 12.)
⑤ 지역 신문이 아니라 웹사이트에서 우승자를 발표한다. (The winner will be announced on our website on May 30.)

J 12 정답 ④ *미식 베이킹 대회

Gourmet Baking Competition / 미식 베이킹 대회 /
병렬 구조
Get out your cookbooks / and dust off your greatest baking recipes. //
요리책을 꺼내 / 최고의 베이킹 레시피의 먼지를 털어내세요 //

When & Where / 일시 및 장소 /
• 5 p.m. -7 p.m. Saturday, August 3rd / ①의 단서 8월 3일 토요일에 개최
8월 3일 토요일 오후 5시 - 오후 7시 /
• Gourmet Baking Studio / Gourmet Baking Studio /

Registration / 참가 신청 /
• Register online / at www.bakeoff.org by July 25th. // ②의 단서 온라인으로 신청
온라인으로 신청하세요 / 7월 25일까지 www.bakeoff.org에서 //
• Anyone can participate / in the competition. //
누구나 참가할 수 있습니다 / 대회에 // ③의 단서 누구나 참여 가능

Categories / 부문 /
• Pies, Cakes, and Cookies / 파이, 케이크, 쿠키 /
• Each person / can only enter one category. // ④의 단서 참가자 한 명당 하나의 부문만 참가 가능
참가자 한 명당 / 하나의 부문만 참가할 수 있습니다 //

Prizes & Gifts / 상 및 선물 /
미래시제 수동태
• Prizes will be given / to the top three / in each category. //
상이 수여됩니다 / 최상위 3명에게는 / 각 부문별 //
• Souvenirs will be given / to every participant. //
기념품이 주어집니다 / 모든 참가자에게 // ⑤의 단서 모든 참여자에게 기념품 수여

• dust off 먼지를 털다; 방치했던 것을 오랜만에 꺼내다
• competition ⓝ 대회 • souvenir ⓝ 기념품

미식 베이킹 대회
요리책을 꺼내 최고의 베이킹 레시피의 먼지를 털어내세요.
일시 및 장소
• 8월 3일 토요일 오후 5시 – 오후 7시
• Gourmet Baking Studio
참가 신청
• 7월 25일까지 www.bakeoff.org에서 온라인으로 신청하세요.
• 누구나 대회에 참가할 수 있습니다.
부문
• 파이, 케이크, 쿠키
• 참가자 한 명당 하나의 부문만 참가할 수 있습니다.
상 및 선물
• 각 부문별 최상위 3명에게는 상이 수여됩니다.
• 모든 참가자에게 기념품이 주어집니다.

Gourmet Baking Competition에 관한 다음 안내문의 내용과 일치하지 않는 것은?
① 8월 3일 토요일에 개최된다. Saturday, August 3rd
② 온라인으로 참가 신청이 가능하다. Register online at www.bakeoff.org
③ 누구나 참가할 수 있다. Anyone can participate in the competition.
④ 참가자 한 명이 여러 부문에 참여할 수 있다.
  Each person can only enter one category.
⑤ 모든 참가자에게 기념품이 제공될 것이다.
  Souvenirs will be given to every participant.

⊃왜 정답? ✿✿✿ [정답률 92%]
참가자 한 명당 한 부문에 참여할 수 있다고 (Each person can only enter one category.) 했으므로 참가자 한 명이 여러 부문에 참여할 수 있다고 한 ④이 안내문의 내용과 일치하지 않는다.

⊃왜 오답?
① 8월 3일 토요일에 개최된다. (Saturday, August 3rd)
② 온라인으로 참가 신청이 가능하다. (Register online at www.bakeoff.org)
③ 누구나 참가할 수 있다. (Anyone can participate in the competition.)
⑤ 모든 참가자에게 기념품이 제공될 것이다. (Souvenirs will be given to every participant.)

J 13 정답 ⑤ *겨울 스포츠 프로그램

Winter Sports Program / 겨울 스포츠 프로그램 /
Winter is coming! // 겨울이 옵니다 //
Let's have some fun together! / 같이 즐겨요 //

Time & Location / 시간 및 장소 /
• Every Sunday in December / from 1 p.m. to 3 p.m. /
12월 매주 일요일 / 오후 1시부터 오후 3시까지 / ①의 단서 1시부터 3시임
• Grand Blue Ice Rink / Grand Blue Ice Rink /

Lesson Details / 강좌 세부 정보 /
• Ice Hockey, Speed Skating, and Figure Skating /
아이스하키, 스피드 스케이팅, 피겨 스케이팅 / ②의 단서 종목은 3개
• Participants / must be 8 years of age or older. //
참가자는 / 8세 이상이어야 합니다 // ③의 단서 참가 연령은 8세 이상

Fee / 수강료 /
• Ice Hockey: $200 / 아이스하키: $200 /
• Speed Skating / Figure Skating: $150 /
스피드 스케이팅 / 피겨 스케이팅: $150 / ④의 단서 아이스하키와 스케이팅의 수강료가 다름

Notice / 주의 사항 /
미래시제 수동태
• Skates and helmets / will be provided / for free. //
스케이트와 헬멧이 / 제공됩니다 / 무료로 //

- You should bring / your own gloves. // ⑤의 단서 장갑은 각자 가져와야 함
가져와야 합니다 / 각자의 장갑을 //

※ For more information, / visit www.wintersports.com. //
더 많은 정보를 얻고자 한다면 / www.wintersports.com에 방문하세요 //

- provide ⓥ 제공하다 · for free 무료로

겨울 스포츠 프로그램
겨울이 옵니다! 같이 즐겨요!
시간 및 장소
- 12월 매주 일요일 오후 1시부터 오후 3시까지
- Grand Blue Ice Rink
강좌 세부 정보
- 아이스하키, 스피드 스케이팅, 피겨 스케이팅
- 참가자는 8세 이상이어야 합니다.
수강료
- 아이스하키: $200
- 스피드 스케이팅 / 피겨 스케이팅: $150
주의 사항
- 스케이트와 헬멧이 무료로 제공됩니다.
- 장갑은 각자 가져와야 합니다.
※ 더 많은 정보를 얻고자 한다면, www.wintersports.com에 방문하세요.

Winter Sports Program에 관한 다음 안내문의 내용과 일치하는 것은?
① 오후 2시에서 4시 사이에 실시된다. from 1 p.m. to 3 p.m.
② 네 종목의 강좌가 개설된다. Ice Hockey, Speed Skating, and Figure Skating
③ 참가 연령에 제한은 없다. Participants must be 8 years of age or older.
④ 모든 종목 강좌의 수강료는 같다. Ice Hockey: $200, Speed Skating / Figure Skating: $150
⑤ 장갑은 각자 가져와야 한다. You should bring your own gloves.

왜 정답? ✽✽✽ [정답률 95%]
장갑은 각자 가져와야 한다고 (You should bring your own gloves.) 했으므로 안내문의 내용과 일치하는 것은 ⑤이다.

왜 오답?
① 오후 1시에서 3시 사이에 실시된다. (from 1 p.m. to 3 p.m.)
② 아이스하키, 스피드 스케이팅, 피겨 스케이팅 총 세 종목이다. (Ice Hockey, Speed Skating, and Figure Skating)
③ 참가 연령은 8세 이상으로 제한되어 있다. (Participants must be 8 years of age or older.)
④ 아이스하키는 200달러이며 스피드 스케이팅과 피겨 스케이팅은 150달러이다. (Ice Hockey: $200, Speed Skating / Figure Skating: $150)

J 14 정답 ⑤ *2024 Young Inventors 로봇 대회

2024 Young Inventors Robot Competition /
2024 Young Inventors 로봇 대회 /

Join us / for an exciting day / of the Young Inventors Robot Competition! //
우리와 함께하세요 / 신나는 날에 / Young Inventors 로봇 대회의 //

□ **Categories** / 분야 /
- Participants can compete / in one of the 'following' categories: /
참가자들은 참가할 수 있습니다 / 다음 분야 중 하나에 / ①의 단서 세 가지 분야 중 하나에 참가할 수 있음
- Robot Design / · Robot Coding / · Robot Remote Control /
로봇 디자인 / 로봇 코딩 / 로봇 원격 조종 /

□ **Date and Time** / 날짜와 시간 /
- September 28, 2024, 10 a.m. to 3 p.m. / ②의 단서 9월 28일에 오전 10시부터 오후 3시까지 5시간 동안 열림
2024년 9월 28일, 오전 10시부터 오후 3시까지 /

□ **Location** / 장소 /
- Computer Lab, Oakwood University /
Oakwood University 컴퓨터실 /
□ **Registration** / 등록 /
- From August 1 to August 10, 2024 /
2024년 8월 1일부터 8월 10일까지 /
- Open to high school students / ③의 단서 고등학생이 등록할 수 있음
고등학생이 등록 가능 / ④의 단서 온라인 등록만 가능함
- Online registration only (www.younginventors.edu) /
온라인 등록만 가능 (www.younginventors.edu) /
□ **Awards** / 시상 /
- In each competition category, / three participants will be honored. // ⑤의 단서 각 분야에서 세 명의 참가자가 수상함 (미래시제 수동태)
각 경쟁 분야에서 / 세 명의 참가자가 수상할 것입니다 //
- 1st place: $300 / · 2nd place: $200 / · 3rd place: $100 /
1등: 300달러 / 2등: 200달러 / 3등: 100달러 /

※ For more information, / visit our website. //
더 많은 정보를 원하시면 / 저희 웹사이트를 방문하세요 //

- competition ⓝ 대회 · participant ⓝ 참가자
- category ⓝ 분야 · remote ⓐ 원격의 · registration ⓝ 등록
- honor ⓥ 수여하다

2024 Young Inventors 로봇 대회
Young Inventors 로봇 대회의 신나는 날에 우리와 함께하세요!
□ 분야
- 참가자들은 다음 분야 중 하나에 참가할 수 있습니다.
- 로봇 디자인 · 로봇 코딩 · 로봇 원격 조종
□ 날짜와 시간
- 2024년 9월 28일, 오전 10시부터 오후 3시까지
□ 장소
- Oakwood University 컴퓨터실
□ 등록
- 2024년 8월 1일부터 8월 10일까지
- 고등학생이 등록 가능
- 온라인 등록만 가능 (www.younginventors.edu)
□ 시상
- 각 경쟁 분야에서 세 명의 참가자가 수상할 것입니다.
- 1등: 300달러 · 2등: 200달러 · 3등: 100달러
※ 더 많은 정보를 원하시면, 저희 웹사이트를 방문하세요.

2024 Young Inventors Robot Competition에 관한 다음 안내문의 내용과 일치하지 않는 것은?
① 세 가지 분야 중 하나에 참가할 수 있다. Participants can compete in one of the following categories
② 9월 28일에 5시간 동안 열린다. September 28, 2024, 10 a.m. to 3 p.m.
③ 고등학생이 등록할 수 있다. Open to high school students
④ 등록은 온라인으로만 가능하다. Online registration only
⑤ 수상자는 각 분야당 한 명이다. In each competition category, three participants will be honored.

왜 정답? ✽✽✽ [정답률 92%]
수상자는 각 분야당 세 명이라고 (In each competition category, three participants will be honored.) 했으므로 수상자는 각 분야당 한 명이라고 한 ⑤이 안내문의 내용과 일치하지 않는다.

왜 오답?
① 세 가지 분야 중 하나에 참가할 수 있다. (Participants can compete in one of the following categories)
② 9월 28일에 5시간 동안 열린다. (September 28, 2024, 10 a.m. to 3 p.m.)
③ 고등학생이 등록할 수 있다. (Open to high school students)
④ 등록은 온라인으로만 가능하다. (Online registration only)

Saintville Art Week Stamp Tour /
Saintville 예술 주간 스탬프 투어 /

The 8th annual / Saintville Art Week Stamp Tour / is back this year! //
해마다 열리는 8번째 / Saintville 예술 주간 스탬프 투어가 / 올해도 돌아왔습니다 //

Anyone can participate in our event. // ①의 단서 누구나 행사에 참가할 수 있음
누구나 우리의 행사에 참가할 수 있습니다 //

병렬 구조(동사) ┐ ┌ 병렬 구조(목적어)
Join us and enjoy exhibitions and new collections. //
우리와 함께하여 전시와 새로운 컬렉션을 즐겨 보세요 //

□ **When:** The first week of October, 2024 /
언제: 2024년 10월 첫째 주 / ②의 단서 2024년 10월 첫째 주에 진행됨

□ **Where:** Saintville Arts District /
어디서: Saintville Arts District /

□ **How: /** 어떻게: / ③의 단서 Saintville Arts Center에서 스탬프 투어 지도를 받음

Step 1. Take a stamp tour map / from the Saintville Arts Center. //
1단계: 스탬프 투어 지도를 받으세요 / Saintville Arts Center에서 //

Step 2. Get stamps from at least 3 out of 5 spots / and receive your gift. // ④의 단서 5곳 중 3곳에서 도장을 받으면 선물을 받을 수 있음
2단계: 다섯 곳 중 적어도 세 곳에서 도장을 받고 / 선물을 받으세요 //

「either A or B」: A 혹은 B (중 하나)
- You can choose either an umbrella or a mug / with printed artwork on it / for your gift. // ⑤의 단서 우산 혹은 머그잔 중 하나를 선물로 고를 수 있음
선택할 수 있습니다 / 우산이나 머그잔 중 하나를 / 예술 작품이 인쇄된 / 선물로 //

※ For more information, / please visit our website at www.SaintvilleArtsCenter.com. //
더 많은 정보를 원하시면 / 저희 웹사이트 www.SaintvilleArtsCenter.com을 방문해 주세요 //

- annual ⓐ 매년의   - participate ⓥ 참가하다
- exhibition ⓝ 전시

Saintville 예술 주간 스탬프 투어

해마다 열리는 8번째 Saintville 예술 주간 스탬프 투어가 올해도 돌아왔습니다! 누구나 우리의 행사에 참가할 수 있습니다. 우리와 함께하여 전시와 새로운 컬렉션을 즐겨 보세요.
□ 언제: 2024년 10월 첫째 주
□ 어디서: Saintville Arts District
□ 어떻게:
1단계: Saintville Arts Center에서 스탬프 투어 지도를 받으세요.
2단계: 다섯 곳 중 적어도 세 곳에서 도장을 받고 선물을 받으세요.
- 예술 작품이 인쇄된 우산이나 머그잔 중 하나를 선물로 선택할 수 있습니다.
※ 더 많은 정보를 원하시면, 저희 웹사이트 www.SaintvilleArtsCenter.com을 방문해 주세요.

Saintville Art Week Stamp Tour에 관한 다음 안내문의 내용과 일치하는 것은?
① 참가 대상에 제한이 있다. Anyone can participate in our event.
② 10월 둘째 주에 진행된다. The first week of October, 2024
③ Saintville Arts Center에서 스탬프 투어 지도를 받는다.
Take a stamp tour map from the Saintville Arts Center.
④ 적어도 다섯 곳에서 도장을 받아야 선물을 받는다.
Get stamps from at least 3 out of 5 spots and receive your gift.
⑤ 선물로 가방과 머그잔 중 하나를 고를 수 있다.
You can choose either an umbrella or a mug with printed artwork on it for your gift.

✓왜 정답? ✿✿✿ [정답률 91%]
참가 방법 중 첫 번째 단계가 Saintville Arts Center에서 스탬프 투어 지도를 받는 것이므로 (Take a stamp tour map from the Saintville Arts Center.) 안내문의 내용과 일치하는 것은 ③이다.

✓왜 오답?
① 참가 대상에 제한이 없다. (Anyone can participate in our event.)
② 10월 첫째 주에 진행된다. (The first week of October, 2024)
④ 다섯 곳 중 적어도 세 곳에서 도장을 받아야 선물을 받는다. (Get stamps from at least 3 out of 5 spots and receive your gift.)
⑤ 우산과 머그잔 중 하나를 선물로 고를 수 있다. (You can choose either an umbrella or a mug with printed artwork on it for your gift.)

2022 Springfield Park Yoga Class /
2022 Springfield Park Yoga Class /

The popular yoga class / in Springfield Park / returns! //
인기 있는 요가 수업 / Springfield Park에서의 / 돌아옵니다 //
yoga를 수식하는 과거분사구

Enjoy yoga / hosted on the park lawn. //
요가를 즐겨보세요 / 공원 잔디밭에서 열리는 //

If you can't make it / to the park, / join us online / on our social media platforms! // ①의 단서 온라인으로도 참여할 수 있음
만약 여러분이 오지 못한다면 / 공원에 / 온라인으로 저희와 함께하세요 / 저희의 소셜 미디어 플랫폼에서 //

□ **When:** / Saturdays, / 2 p.m. to 3 p.m., / September /
언제 / 토요일마다 / 오후 2시부터 오후 3시까지 / 9월 / ②의 단서 9월 중 토요일마다 진행됨

□ **Registration:** / At least TWO hours / before each class starts, / sign up here. // ③의 단서 수업 시작 2시간 전까지 등록해야 함
등록 / 적어도 두 시간까지 / 매 수업이 시작하기 전 / 여기에서 등록하세요 //

□ **Notes /**
주의 사항 /

• For online classes: / find a quiet space / with enough room / for you / to stretch out. //
온라인 수업 대상 / 조용한 장소를 찾으세요 / 충분한 공간을 가진 / 여러분이 / 스트레칭을 할 만큼 //

수동태의 부정형
• For classes in the park: / mats are not provided, / so bring your own! // ④의 단서 매트는 제공되지 않음
공원에서의 수업 대상 / 매트는 제공되지 않습니다 / 그러니 본인 것을 가져오세요 //

미래 시제 수동태
※ The class will be canceled / if the weather is unfavorable. //
수업은 취소될 것입니다 / 만약 날씨가 좋지 않으면 // ⑤의 단서 날씨가 좋지 않으면 취소될 것임

For more information, / click here. //
더 많은 정보를 위해서는 / 여기를 클릭하세요 //

• host ⓥ (행사를) 주최하다, 열다   • registration ⓝ 등록
• cancel ⓥ 취소하다   • unfavorable ⓐ 좋지 않은

2022 Springfield Park Yoga Class

Springfield Park에서의 인기 있는 요가 수업이 돌아옵니다! 공원 잔디밭에서 열리는 요가를 즐겨보세요. 만약 여러분이 공원에 오지 못한다면, 저희의 소셜미디어 플랫폼에서 온라인으로 저희와 함께하세요!
□ 언제: 9월, 토요일마다, 오후 2시부터 오후 3시까지
□ 등록: 매 수업이 시작하기 적어도 두 시간 전까지, 여기에서 등록하세요.
□ 주의 사항
• 온라인 수업 대상: 여러분이 스트레칭을 할 만큼 충분한 공간을 가진 조용한 장소를 찾으세요.
• 공원에서의 수업 대상: 매트는 제공되지 않으니, 본인 것을 가져오세요!
※ 만약 날씨가 좋지 않으면 수업은 취소될 것입니다.
더 많은 정보를 위해서는, 여기를 클릭하세요.

2022 Springfield Park Yoga Class에 관한 다음 안내문의 내용과 일치하지 <u>않는</u> 것은?

① 온라인으로도 참여할 수 있다. If you can't make it to the park, join us online on our social media platforms!

② 9월 중 토요일마다 진행된다. When: Saturdays, 2 p.m. to 3 p.m., September

③ 수업 시작 2시간 전까지 등록해야 한다. Registration: At least TWO hours before each class starts

④ 매트가 제공된다. mats are not provided

⑤ 날씨가 좋지 않으면 취소될 것이다. The class will be canceled if the weather is unfavorable.

오 정답? ✽✽✽ [정답률 96%]

매트는 제공되지 않는다고(mats are not provided) 했으므로 ④이 안내문의 내용과 일치하지 않는다.

오 오답?

① 온라인으로도 참여할 수 있다고 했다. (If you can't make it to the park, join us online on our social media platforms!)

② 9월 중 토요일마다 진행된다고 했다. (When: Saturdays, 2 p.m. to 3 p.m., September)

③ 수업 시작 2시간 전까지 등록해야 한다고 했다. (Registration: At least TWO hours before each class starts)

⑤ 날씨가 좋지 않으면 취소될 것이라고 했다. (The class will be canceled if the weather is unfavorable.)

J 17 정답 ④ ✽아이들 태권도 프로그램 안내

Kids Taekwondo Program /
아이들 태권도 프로그램 /

명령문
<mark>Enjoy</mark> our taekwondo program / this summer vacation. //
태권도 프로그램을 즐기세요 / 이번 여름 방학에 //

□ **Schedule /**
일정 /

• Dates: / August 8th – August 10th /
날짜 / 8월 8일 ~ 8월 10일 /   ①의 단서 8월 8일부터 10일까지 3일간 운영됨

• Time: / 9:00 a.m. – 11:00 a.m. /
시간 / 오전 9시 ~ 오전 11시 /

□ **Participants /**
참가자 /

• Any child aged 5 and up /   ②의 단서 5세 이상의 어린이가 참가할 수 있음
5세 이상 어린이 누구나 /

□ **Activities /**
활동 /

• Self-defense training /   ③의 단서 자기 방어 훈련 활동을 함
자기 방어 훈련 /
                               부사적 용법(목적)
• Team building games / <mark>to develop</mark> social skills /
팀 빌딩 게임 / 사교성 개발을 위한 /

□ **Participation Fee /**
참가비 /

• $50 per child (includes snacks) /   ④의 단서 참가비에 간식비가 포함됨
1인당 50달러 (간식 포함) /

□ **Notice /**
알림 /

• What to bring: / water bottle, towel /   ⑤의 단서 물병과 수건을 가져와야 함
가져올 것 / 물병, 수건 /
           to부정사의 부정
• What <mark>not to bring</mark>: / chewing gum, expensive items /
가져오지 말아야 할 것 / 껌, 비싼 물건 /

• participant ⓝ 참가자   • activity ⓝ 활동
• self-defense ⓝ 자기 방어   • develop ⓥ 발달시키다
• fee ⓝ 요금   • include ⓥ 포함하다

아이들 태권도 프로그램

이번 여름 방학에 태권도 프로그램을 즐기세요.

□ 일정
• 날짜 : 8월 8일 ~ 8월 10일
• 시간 : 오전 9시 ~ 오전 11시

□ 참가자
• 5세 이상 어린이 누구나

□ 활동
• 자기 방어 훈련
• 사교성 개발을 위한 팀 빌딩 게임

□ 참가비
• 1인당 50달러 (간식 포함)

□ 알림
• 가져올 것: 물병, 수건
• 가져오지 말아야 할 것: 껌, 비싼 물건

Kids Taekwondo Program에 관한 다음 안내문의 내용과 일치하지 <u>않는</u> 것은?

① 8월 8일부터 3일간 운영한다. Dates: August 8th – August 10th

② 5세 이상의 어린이가 참가할 수 있다. Any child aged 5 and up

③ 자기 방어 훈련 활동을 한다. Self-defense training

④ 참가비에 간식비는 포함되지 않는다. $50 per child (includes snacks)

⑤ 물병과 수건을 가져와야 한다. What to bring: water bottle, towel

오 정답? ✽✽✽ [정답률 95%]

참가비에서 $50 per child (includes snacks)(1인당 50달러 (간식 포함))라고 했으므로 참가비에 간식비가 포함되어 있다는 것을 알 수 있다. 따라서 ④은 안내문의 내용과 일치하지 않는다.

오 오답?

① Dates: August 8th – August 10th에서 8월 8일부터 8월 10일까지 3일 동안 열린다고 했다.

② Any child aged 5 and up에서 5세 이상의 어린이가 참가할 수 있다고 했다.

③ Self-defense training에서 자기 방어 훈련 활동을 한다는 것을 알 수 있다.

⑤ What to bring: water bottle, towel에서 물병과 수건을 가져와야 한다고 했다.

J 18 정답 ③ ✽해저 걷기 활동

Undersea Walking Activity / 해저 걷기 활동 /

Enjoy a fascinating underwater walk / on the ocean floor. //
매력적인 수중 걷기를 즐기세요 / 해양 바닥에서 //
                                '걸어서, 도보로'
Witness wonderful marine life / <mark>on foot</mark>! //
멋진 바다 생물을 직접 보세요 / 걸어 다니며 //

Age Requirement / 연령 요건 /

10 years or older / 10세 이상 /

Operating Hours / 영업시간 /

from Tuesday to Sunday /   ①의 단서 월요일은 운영하지 않음
화요일부터 일요일까지 /

9:00 a.m. – 4:00 p.m. / 오전 9시부터 오후 4시까지 /

Price / 가격 /

$30 (insurance fee included) /   ②의 단서 가격에 보험료가 포함됨
30달러 (보험료 포함) /

What to Bring / 가져올 것 /

swim suit and towel /
수영복과 수건 /

Notes / 주의 사항 /

• Experienced lifeguards accompany you / throughout the activity. // **③의 단서** 숙련된 안전 요원이 활동 내내 동행함
숙련된 안전 요원이 여러분과 동행합니다 / 활동 내내 //

• With a special underwater helmet, / you can wear glasses / during the activity. // **④의 단서** 특수 수중 헬멧을 착용하면 안경을 쓸 수 있음
특수 수중 헬멧 착용 시 / 여러분은 안경을 쓸 수 있습니다 / 활동 중에 //

조동사가 포함된 수동태
• Reservations can be made / on-site or online at www.seawalkwonder.com. // **⑤의 단서** 현장 또는 온라인으로 예약할 수 있음
예약은 할 수 있습니다 / 현장 또는 www.seawalkwonder.com에서 온라인으로 //

• fascinating ⓐ 매력적인, 대단히 흥미로운 • witness ⓥ 목격하다
• marine life 해양 생물 • requirement ⓝ 요건, 필요조건
• insurance ⓝ 보험 • experienced ⓐ 경험 있는, 숙련된
• accompany ⓥ 동반하다, 동행하다 • underwater ⓐ 수중의

해저 걷기 활동

해양 바닥에서 매력적인 수중 걷기를 즐기세요. 걸어 다니며 멋진 바다 생물을 직접 보세요!
연령 요건
10세 이상
영업시간
화요일부터 일요일까지
오전 9시부터 오후 4시까지
가격
30달러 (보험료 포함)
가져올 것
수영복과 수건
주의 사항
• 숙련된 안전 요원이 활동 내내 여러분과 동행합니다.
• 특수 수중 헬멧 착용 시 여러분은 활동 중에 안경을 쓸 수 있습니다.
• 예약은 현장 또는 www.seawalkwonder.com에서 온라인으로 할 수 있습니다.

Undersea Walking Activity에 관한 다음 안내문의 내용과 일치하는 것은?
① 연중무휴로 운영된다. from Tuesday to Sunday
② 가격에 보험료는 포함되어 있지 않다. $30 (insurance fee included)
③ 숙련된 안전 요원이 활동 내내 동행한다.
Experienced lifeguards accompany you throughout the activity.
④ 특수 수중 헬멧 착용 시 안경을 쓸 수 없다.
With a special underwater helmet, you can wear glasses during the activity.
⑤ 현장 예약은 불가능하다.
Reservations can be made on-site or online at www.seawalkwonder.com.

>왜 정답? ✿❀❀ [정답률 87%]

숙련된 안전 요원이 활동 내내 동행한다고(Experienced lifeguards accompany you throughout the activity.) 했으므로 안내문의 내용과 일치하는 것은 ③이다.

>왜 오답?

① 화요일부터 일요일까지 운영한다고 했으므로 월요일은 운영하지 않음을 알 수 있다. (from Tuesday to Sunday)
② 가격은 보험료 포함 30달러라고 했다. ($30 (insurance fee included))
④ 특수 수중 헬멧 착용 시 활동 중에도 안경을 쓸 수 있다고 했다. (With a special underwater helmet, you can wear glasses during the activity.)
⑤ 예약은 현장과 온라인으로 할 수 있다고 했다. (Reservations can be made on-site or online at www.seawalkwonder.com.)

J 19 정답 ④ *은공예 수업 안내 ———————

Silversmithing Class / 은공예 수업 /

Kingston Club is offering / a fine jewelry making class. //
Kingston Club은 제공합니다 / 정교한 보석 만들기 수업을 //
형용사적 용법(chance 수식)
Don't miss this great chance / to make your own jewelry! //
이 좋은 기회를 놓치지 마세요 / 여러분만의 보석을 만들 //

When & Where / 언제 & 어디에서 /

• Saturday, October 21, 2023 / (2 p.m. to 4 p.m.) /
2023년 10월 21일 토요일 / (오후 2시부터 오후 4시까지) / **①의 단서** 두 시간 동안 진행됨

• Kingston Club studio / Kingston Club 스튜디오 /

Registration / 등록 /

• Available only online / 온라인으로만 가능 /

• Dates: October 1 – 14, 2023 / **②의 단서** 10월 1일부터 등록할 수 있음
날짜: 2023년 10월 1일부터 14일 /

• Fee: $40 (This includes all tools and materials.) /
비용: 40달러 (이것은 모든 도구와 재료를 포함합니다.) /
수동태 동사
• Registration is limited to 6 people. // **③의 단서** 등록 인원은 6명으로 제한됨
등록은 6명으로 제한됩니다 //

Note / 유의 사항 /

• Participants must be at least 16 years old. //
참가자는 16세 이상이어야 합니다 // **④의 단서** 16세 이상만 참가할 수 있음

• No refund / for cancellation on the day of the class /
환불 불가 / 수업 당일 취소에 대한 / **⑤의 단서** 수업 당일 취소 시 환불되지 않음

• available ⓐ 이용할 수 있는 • material ⓝ 재료
• registration ⓝ 등록 • limit ⓥ 제한하다
• participant ⓝ 참가자 • refund ⓝ 환불 • cancellation ⓝ 취소

은공예 수업

Kingston Club은 정교한 보석 만들기 수업을 제공합니다. 여러분만의 보석을 만들 이 좋은 기회를 놓치지 마세요!
언제 & 어디에서
• 2023년 10월 21일 토요일(오후 2시부터 오후 4시까지)
• Kingston Club 스튜디오
등록
• 온라인으로만 가능
• 날짜: 2023년 10월 1일부터 14일
• 비용: 40달러 (이것은 모든 도구와 재료를 포함합니다.)
• 등록은 6명으로 제한됩니다.
유의 사항
• 참가자는 16세 이상이어야 합니다.
• 수업 당일 취소 시 환불 불가

Silversmithing Class에 관한 다음 안내문의 내용과 일치하지 않는 것은?
① 두 시간 동안 진행된다. 2 p.m. to 4 p.m.
② 10월 1일부터 등록할 수 있다. Dates: October 1 - 14, 2023
③ 등록 인원은 6명으로 제한된다. Registration is limited to 6 people.
④ 참가 연령에 제한이 없다. Participants must be at least 16 years old.
⑤ 수업 당일 취소 시 환불이 불가하다.
No refund for cancellation on the day of the class

>왜 정답? ✿❀❀ [정답률 96%]

참가자는 16세 이상이어야 하므로(Participants must be at least 16 years old.) 참가 연령에 제한이 없다고 한 ④이 안내문의 내용과 일치하지 않는다.

>왜 오답?

① 오후 2시부터 4시까지 두 시간 동안 진행된다. (2 p.m. to 4 p.m.)
② 10월 1일부터 등록이 시작된다. (Dates: October 1 - 14, 2023)
③ 등록 인원은 6명으로 제한된다. (Registration is limited to 6 people.)
⑤ 수업 당일 취소에 대한 환불은 불가하다. (No refund for ~ day of the class)

J 20 정답 ② *달빛 초콜릿 공장 견학

Moonlight Chocolate Factory Tour /
달빛 초콜릿 공장 견학 /
<u>Take</u> (명령문) this special tour and <u>have</u> a chance / <u>to enjoy</u> (형용사적 용법) our most popular chocolate bars. //
이 특별한 투어에 참여하여 기회를 가지세요 / 우리의 가장 인기 있는 초콜릿 바를 즐길 //

□ **Operating Hours** / 운영 시간 /
• Monday – Friday, 2:00 p.m. – 5:00 p.m. / **①의 단서** 주중 오후 시간에 운영됨
월요일 ~ 금요일, 오후 2시 ~ 오후 5시 /

□ **Activities** / 활동 /
• Watching our chocolate-making process /
초콜릿 제조 과정 견학 / **②의 단서** 초콜릿 제조 과정을 견학함
• Tasting 3 types of chocolate / (dark, milk, and mint chocolate) /
초콜릿 3종 시식 / (다크, 밀크 및 민트 초콜릿) / **③의 단서** 세 가지 종류의 초콜릿을 시식함

□ **Notice** / 알림 /
• Ticket price: / $30 / 티켓 가격 / 30달러 /
• <u>Wearing</u> (동명사 주어) a face mask / <u>is</u> (단수 동사) required. / **④의 단서** 마스크 착용은 필수임
마스크 착용은 / 필수입니다 /
• Taking pictures <u>is</u> not <u>allowed</u> (수동태) / inside the factory. //
사진 촬영은 허용되지 않습니다 / 공장 내부에서 // **⑤의 단서** 공장 내부에서 사진을 찍는 것은 허용되지 않음

• popular ⓐ 인기 있는 • process ⓝ 과정 • taste ⓥ 맛보다
• notice ⓝ 알림 • require ⓥ 요구하다

달빛 초콜릿 공장 견학

이 특별한 투어에 참여하여 우리의 가장 인기 있는 초콜릿 바를 즐길 기회를 가지세요.

□ 운영 시간
• 월요일 ~ 금요일, 오후 2시 ~ 오후 5시
□ 활동
• 초콜릿 제조 과정 견학
• 초콜릿 3종 (다크, 밀크 및 민트 초콜릿) 시식
□ 알림
• 티켓 가격: 30달러
• 마스크 착용은 필수입니다.
• 공장 내부에서 사진 촬영은 허용되지 않습니다.

Moonlight Chocolate Factory Tour에 관한 다음 안내문의 내용과 일치하는 것은?
① 주말 오후 시간에 운영한다. Monday – Friday, 2:00 p.m. – 5:00 p.m.
②초콜릿 제조 과정을 볼 수 있다. Watching our chocolate-making process
③ 네 가지 종류의 초콜릿을 시식한다.
Tasting 3 types of chocolate (dark, milk, and mint chocolate)
④ 마스크 착용은 참여자의 선택 사항이다. Wearing a face mask is required.
⑤ 공장 내부에서 사진 촬영이 가능하다.
Taking pictures is not allowed inside the factory.

왜 정답? ✿✿✿ [정답률 94%]

안내문의 중반부에 활동을 설명하며 Watching our chocolate-making process (초콜릿 제조 과정 견학)라고 했으므로 초콜릿 제조 과정을 볼 수 있다는 것을 알 수 있다. 따라서 ②이 안내문의 내용과 일치한다.

왜 오답?

① 주중 오후 시간에 운영된다고 했다. (Monday – Friday, 2:00 p.m. – 5:00 p.m.)
③ 세 가지 종류의 초콜릿을 시식한다고 했다. (Tasting 3 types of chocolate (dark, milk, and mint chocolate))
④ 마스크 착용이 필수라고 했다. (Wearing a face mask is required.)
⑤ 사진 촬영은 공장 내부에서 허용되지 않는다고 했다. (Taking pictures is not allowed inside the factory.)

J 21 정답 ⑤ *야간 궁궐 투어

Nighttime Palace Tour / 야간 궁궐 투어 /
Date: / Friday, April 29 – Sunday, May 15 /
날짜 / 4월 29일 금요일 ~ 5월 15일 일요일 /
Time / 시간 /

Friday 금요일 **①의 단서** 금요일에는 한 번만 운영함	7 p.m. – 8:30 p.m. 오후 7시 ~ 오후 8시 30분
Saturday & Sunday 토요일과 일요일	6 p.m. – 7:30 p.m. 오후 6시 ~ 오후 7시 30분
	8 p.m. – 9:30 p.m. 오후 8시 ~ 오후 9시 30분

Tickets & Booking / 티켓과 예약 /
• $15 per person (free for kids under 8) / **②의 단서** 8세 미만 어린이는 무료임
1인당 15달러(8세 미만 어린이는 무료) /
• Bookings will <u>be accepted</u> (수동태) / up to 2 hours / <u>before</u> (시간의 부사절을 이끄는 접속사) the tour starts. // **③의 단서** 예약은 투어 시작 2시간 전까지 가능함
예약은 가능합니다 / 2시간까지 / 투어가 시작하기 전에 //

Program Activities /
프로그램 활동 /
• Group tour with a tour guide (1 hour) / **④의 단서** 투어 가이드와 함께 투어를 함
투어 가이드와 단체 투어 (1시간) /
• Trying traditional foods and drinks (30 minutes) /
전통 음식 시식 및 음료 시음 (30분) / **⑤의 단서** 추가 비용 없이 전통 의상을 입어 볼 수 있음
※ You can try on traditional clothes / with no extra charge. //
전통 의상을 입어 볼 수 있습니다 / 추가 비용 없이 //
※ For more information, / please visit our website, / www.palacenighttour.com. //
더 많은 정보를 원하시면 / 저희 웹 사이트에 방문하세요 / www.palacenighttour.com //

• palace ⓝ 궁궐 • book ⓥ 예약하다
• traditional ⓐ 전통적인 • charge ⓝ 비용

야간 궁궐 투어
날짜: 4월 29일 금요일 ~ 5월 15일 일요일
시간

금요일	오후 7시~오후 8시 30분
토요일과 일요일	오후 6시~오후 7시 30분
	오후 8시~오후 9시 30분

티켓과 예약
• 1인당 15달러(8세 미만 어린이는 무료)
• 예약은 투어 시작 2시간 전까지 가능합니다.
프로그램 활동
• 투어 가이드와 단체 투어 (1시간)
• 전통 음식 시식 및 음료 시음 (30분)
※추가 비용 없이 전통 의상을 입어 볼 수 있습니다.
※더 많은 정보를 원하시면, 저희 웹 사이트
www.palacenighttour.com에 방문하세요.

Nighttime Palace Tour에 관한 다음 안내문의 내용과 일치하는 것은?
① 금요일에는 하루에 두 번 투어가 운영된다. Friday, 7 p.m. – 8:30 p.m.
② 8세 미만 어린이의 티켓은 5달러이다. $15 per person (free for kids under 8)
③ 예약은 투어 하루 전까지만 가능하다.
Bookings will be accepted up to 2 hours before the tour starts.
④ 투어 가이드의 안내 없이 궁궐을 둘러본다. Group tour with a tour guide (1hour)
⑤추가 비용 없이 전통 의상을 입어 볼 수 있다.
You can try on traditional clothes with no extra charge.

> **왜 정답?** ✸✸✸ [정답률 90%]

안내문의 후반부에 You can try on traditional clothes with no extra charge. (추가 비용 없이 전통 의상을 입어볼 수 있습니다.)라고 했으므로 추가 비용 없이 전통 의상을 입어 볼 수 있음을 알 수 있다. 따라서 ⑤이 안내문의 내용과 일치한다.

> **왜 오답?**

① Friday, 7 p.m. – 8:30 p.m.에서 금요일에는 하루에 한 번 투어가 운영됨을 알 수 있다.
② $15 per person (free for kids under 8)에서 8세 미만 어린이의 티켓은 무료라고 했다.
③ Bookings will be accepted up to 2 hours before the tour starts.에서 예약은 투어 2시간 전까지 가능함을 알 수 있다.
④ Group tour with a tour guide (1hour)에서 투어 가이드의 안내가 있다고 했다.

J 22 정답 ④ ＊Kenner High School's Water Challenge

Kenner High School's Water Challenge /
Kenner High School's Water Challenge /

Kenner High School's Water Challenge / is a new contest / to
형용사적 용법
propose measures / against water pollution. //
Kenner High School's Water Challenge는 / 새로운 대회입니다 / 대책을 제안하는 / 수질 오염에 대한 //

Please share your ideas / for dealing with water pollution! //
여러분의 아이디어를 공유해 주세요 / 수질 오염에 대처하기 위한 //

Submission / 제출 /
– **How**: / Submit your proposal / by email / to admin@khswater. edu. // ①의 단서 제안서는 이메일로 제출해야 함
어떻게 / 여러분의 제안서를 제출해 주세요 / 이메일로 / admin@khswater.edu로 //

– **When**: / September 5, 2022 / to September 23, 2022 /
언제 / 2022년 9월 5일부터 / 2022년 9월 23일까지 / ②의 단서 9월 5일부터 제안서를 제출할 수 있음

Details / 세부 사항 /
– Participants must enter / in teams of four / and can only join one team. //
참가자들은 반드시 참가해야 합니다 / 4인으로 구성된 팀으로 / 그리고 오직 한 팀에만 참여할 수 있습니다 //
수동태
– Submission is limited / to one proposal per team. // ③의 단서 제안서는 한 팀당 한 개만 제출할 수 있음
제출은 제한됩니다 / 한 팀당 한 개의 제안서로 //
the proposal form을 수식하는 과거분사
– Participants must use / the proposal form / provided on the website. // ④의 단서 제공된 제안서 양식을 사용해야 함
참가자들은 사용해야 합니다 / 제안서 양식을 / 웹 사이트에 제공된 //

Prizes / 상품 /
– 1st: / $50 gift certificate /
1등 / 50달러 상품권 /
– 2nd: / $30 gift certificate / ⑤의 단서 2등은 30달러의 상품권을 받음
2등 / 30달러 상품권 /
– 3rd: / $10 gift certificate /
3등 / 10달러 상품권 /

Please visit / www.khswater.edu / to learn more about the challenge. //
방문해 주세요 / www.khswater.edu를 / challenge에 대해 더 알고 싶으면 //

- propose ⓥ 제안하다 · measure ⓝ 대책 · pollution ⓝ 오염
- submission ⓝ 제출 · submit ⓥ 제출하다 · proposal ⓝ 제안서
- gift certificate 상품권

Kenner High School's Water Challenge

Kenner High School's Water Challenge는 수질 오염에 대한 대책을 제안하는 새로운 대회입니다. 수질 오염에 대처하기 위한 여러분의 아이디어를 공유해 주세요!

제출
– 어떻게: 여러분의 제안서를 이메일로 admin@khswater.edu로 제출해 주세요.
– 언제: 2022년 9월 5일부터 2022년 9월 23일까지

세부 사항
– 참가자들은 반드시 4인으로 구성된 팀으로 참가해야 하며 오직 한 팀에만 참여할 수 있습니다.
– 한 팀당 한 개의 제안서만 제출할 수 있습니다.
– 참가자들은 웹 사이트에 제공된 제안서 양식을 사용해야 합니다.

상품
– 1등: 50달러 상품권
– 2등: 30달러 상품권
– 3등: 10달러 상품권

Challenge에 대해 더 알고 싶으면 www.khswater.edu를 방문해 주세요.

Kenner High School's Water Challenge에 관한 다음 안내문의 내용과 일치하는 것은?

① 제안서는 직접 방문하여 제출해야 한다. Submit your proposal by email to admin@khswater.edu.
② 9월 23일부터 제안서를 제출할 수 있다. When: September 5, 2022 to September 23, 2022
③ 제안서는 한 팀당 4개까지 제출할 수 있다. Submission is limited to one proposal per team.
④ 제공된 제안서 양식을 사용해야 한다. Participants must use the proposal form provided on the website.
⑤ 2등은 10달러의 상품권을 받는다. 2nd: $30 gift certificate

> **왜 정답?** ✸✸❀ [정답률 87%]

Participants must use the proposal form provided on the website.를 통해 웹 사이트에 제공된 제안서 양식을 사용해야 함을 알 수 있다. 따라서 ④이 안내문의 내용과 일치한다.

> **왜 오답?**

① 제안서는 이메일로 제출하면 된다고 했다. (Submit your proposal by email to admin@khswater.edu.)
② 9월 5일부터 제안서를 제출할 수 있다고 했다. (When: September 5, 2022 to September 23, 2022)
③ 제안서는 한 팀당 한 개만 제출할 수 있다고 했다. (Submission is limited to one proposal per team.)
⑤ 2등은 30달러의 상품권을 받는다고 했다. (2nd: $30 gift certificate)

J 23 정답 ⑤ ＊2023 해양 인식 영상 대회

2023 Ocean Awareness Film Contest / 2023 해양 인식 영상 대회 /
병렬 구조
Join our 7th annual film contest / and show your knowledge / of marine conservation. //
우리의 일곱 번째 연례 영상 대회에 참가하세요 / 그리고 여러분의 지식을 보여주세요 / 해양 보존에 관한 //

☐ **Theme /** 주제 /
- Ocean Wildlife / Ocean Pollution / ①의 단서 주제는 두 가지임
해양 야생 생물 / 해양 오염 /

(Choose one of the above.) // (위에서 하나를 선택하세요) //

☐ **Guidelines /** 지침 /
- Participants: / High school students / ②의 단서 고등학생만 참가할 수 있음
참가자 / 고등학생 /

- Submission deadline: / September 22, 2023 /
제출 기한 / 2023년 9월 22일 /

- The video must be between 10 and 15 minutes. //
영상은 10분에서 15분 사이여야 합니다 // ③의 단서 영상은 10분에서 15분 사이여야 함
조동사가 포함된 수동태

- All entries **must be uploaded** / to our website. //
모든 출품작은 업로드되어야 합니다 / 우리 웹사이트에 //

- Only one entry per person / ④의 단서 1인당 하나만 출품할 수 있음
1인당 오직 하나의 출품작 /

□ Prizes / 상금 /

• 1st place / $100 / • 2nd place: / $70 / • 3rd place: / $50 /
1등 / 100달러 / 2등 / 70달러 / 3등 / 50달러 /
미래시제 수동태
(Winners **will be announced** / on our website.) //
(수상자는 공지될 것입니다 / 우리 웹사이트에) // ⑤의 단서 수상자는 웹사이트에 공지됨

For more information, / please visit www.oceanawareFC.com. //
더 많은 정보를 위해 / www.oceanawareFC.com을 방문하세요 //

• awareness ⓝ 인식   • annual ⓐ 연례의   • knowledge ⓝ 지식
• marine ⓐ 해양의   • conservation ⓝ 보존   • pollution ⓝ 오염
• submission ⓝ 제출   • entry ⓝ 출품[응모]작

2023 해양 인식 영상 대회

우리의 일곱 번째 연례 영상 대회에 참가하여 해양 보존에 관한 여러분의 지식을 보여주세요.

□ 주제
– 해양 야생 생물 / 해양 오염
  (위에서 하나를 선택하세요.)

□ 지침
– 참가자: 고등학생
– 제출 기한: 2023년 9월 22일
– 영상은 10분에서 15분 사이여야 합니다.
– 모든 출품작은 우리 웹사이트에 업로드되어야 합니다.
– 1인당 오직 하나의 출품작

□ 상금
• 1등: 100달러   • 2등: 70달러   • 3등: 50달러
  (수상자는 우리 웹사이트에 공지될 것입니다.)
더 많은 정보를 위해 www.oceanawareFC.com을 방문하세요.

2023 Ocean Awareness Film Contest에 관한 다음 안내문의 내용과 일치하는 것은?

① 세 가지 주제 중 하나를 선택해야 한다.
   Theme: Ocean Wildlife / Ocean Pollution
② 중학생이 참가할 수 있다.
   Participants: High school students
③ 영상은 10분을 넘길 수 없다.
   The video must be between 10 and 15 minutes.
④ 1인당 두 개까지 출품할 수 있다.
   Only one entry per person
⑤ 수상자는 웹사이트에 공지될 것이다.
   Winners will be announced on our website.

> 왜 정답 ? ✿✿✿ [정답률 94%]

수상자는 웹사이트에 공지될 것이라고(Winners will be announced on our website.) 했으므로 안내문의 내용과 일치하는 것은 ⑤이다.

> 왜 오답 ?

① 선택해야 하는 주제는 두 가지만 제시되었다. (Theme: Ocean Wildlife / Ocean Pollution)
② 고등학생만 참가할 수 있다. (Participants: High school students)
③ 영상은 10분에서 15분 사이여야 하므로 10분을 넘겨야 한다. (The video must be between 10 and 15 minutes.) 주의
④ 1인당 한 개만 출품할 수 있다. (Only one entry per person)

J 24 정답 ③ *기사 모집 공고문

Call for Articles / 기사 모집 /
목적격 보어(과거분사)
Do you want / to get your stories **published**? /
여러분은 원하나요 / 여러분의 이야기가 출간되기를 /

New Dream Magazine is looking for future writers! //
〈New Dream Magazine〉은 미래의 작가를 찾고 있습니다 //
앞에 주격 관계대명사와 be동사가 생략됨
This event is open to anyone / **aged** 13 to 18. //
이 행사는 모두에게 열려있습니다 / 13세에서 18세까지의 // ①의 단서 13세에서 18세까지 누구나 참여할 수 있음

Articles / 기사 /
• Length of writing: / 300 – 325 words / 원고의 길이 / 300~325단어 /
• Articles should also include / high-quality color photos. //
기사에는 또한 포함해야 합니다 / 고화질 컬러 사진을 // ②의 단서 고화질 컬러 사진을 포함해야 함

Rewards / 사례금 /
• Five cents per word / 단어당 5센트 /
• Five dollars per photo / ③의 단서 사진 한 장당 5달러의 사례금을 받음
사진당 5달러 /

Notes / 주의 사항 /
간접목적어   직접 목적어
• You should send **us** / **your phone number** / together with your writing. // ④의 단서 원고와 함께 전화번호를 보내야 함
여러분은 우리에게 보내야 합니다 / 여러분의 전화번호를 / 원고와 함께 //

• Please email your writing to us / at article@ndmag.com. //
여러분의 원고를 이메일로 우리에게 보내주세요 / article@ndmag.com으로 // ⑤의 단서 원고는 이메일로 제출해야 함

• article ⓝ 기사   • publish ⓥ 출간하다   • look for ~을 찾다
• length ⓝ 길이   • include ⓥ 포함하다   • reward ⓝ 사례금

기사 모집

여러분의 이야기가 출간되기를 원하시나요? 〈New Dream Magazine〉은 미래의 작가를 찾고 있습니다! 이 행사는 13세에서 18세까지 누구나 참여할 수 있습니다.

기사
• 원고 길이: 300~325단어
• 기사에는 또한 고화질 컬러 사진이 포함되어야 합니다.

사례금
• 단어당 5센트   • 사진당 5달러

주의 사항
• 여러분은 전화번호를 원고와 함께 보내야 합니다.
• 원고를 이메일 article@ndmag.com으로 보내세요.

Call for Articles에 관한 다음 안내문의 내용과 일치하지 <u>않는</u> 것은?

① 13세에서 18세까지의 누구나 참여할 수 있다.
   This event is open to anyone aged 13 to 18.
② 기사는 고화질 컬러 사진을 포함해야 한다.
   Articles should also include high-quality color photos.
③ 사진 한 장에 5센트씩 지급한다.
   Five dollars per photo
④ 전화번호를 원고와 함께 보내야 한다.
   You should send us your phone number together with your writing.
⑤ 원고를 이메일로 제출해야 한다.
   Please email your writing to us at article@ndmag.com.

> 왜 정답 ? ✿✿✿ [정답률 93%]

사례금은 사진당 5달러라고(Five dollars per photo) 했으므로 사진 한 장에 5센트씩 지급한다고 한 ③은 안내문의 내용과 일치하지 않는다.

> 왜 오답 ?

① 13세에서 18세 사이라면 누구나 참여할 수 있다. (This event is open to anyone aged 13 to 18.)
② 기사는 고화질 컬러 사진을 포함해야 한다. (Articles should also include high-quality color photos.)
④ 원고를 보낼 때 전화번호를 함께 보내야 한다. (You should send us your phone number together with your writing.)
⑤ 원고 제출은 이메일로 하라고 했다. (Please email your writing to us at article@ndmag.com.)

J 25 정답 ⑤ *2023 오스트레일리아 게이트볼 챔피언십 안내

2023 Australian Gateball Championships /
2023 오스트레일리아 게이트볼 챔피언십 /

                                    부사적 용법(목적)
The Diamond Coast is getting set / to welcome the Australian
Gateball Championships. //
Diamond Coast는 준비를 하고 있습니다 / 오스트레일리아 게이트볼 챔피언십을 환영할 //

                                              병렬 구조
Join this great outdoor competition / and be the winner this
year! //
이 멋진 야외 대회에 참여해서 / 올해 우승자가 되세요 //

When & Where / 언제 & 어디서 /
• December 19 – 22, 2023 / ①의 단서 4일 동안 진행됨
2023년 12월 19일부터 22일까지 /
• Diamond Coast Performance Centre / Diamond Coast 공연 센터 /

Schedule of Matches / 경기 일정 /
• Doubles matches (9 a.m. – 11 a.m.) / ②의 단서 복식 경기는 오전에 열림
복식 경기 (오전 9시부터 오전 11시까지) /
• Team matches (1 p.m. – 3 p.m.) /
단체 경기 (오후 1시부터 오후 3시까지) /

Prizes / 상 /
• Every participant will receive / a certificate for entry. //
모든 참가자는 받을 것입니다 / 참가 증서를 // ③의 단서 모든 참가자는 참가 증서를 받음
                    수동태 동사
• Champions are awarded a medal. // 우승자들은 메달을 받습니다 //

Note / 참고 /
• Participation is free. // ④의 단서 참가비는 무료임
참가비는 무료입니다 //
• Visit www.australiangateball.com for registration. //
등록을 위해 www.australiangateball.com을 방문하십시오 //
(Registration on site is not available.) //
(현장 등록은 불가합니다) // ⑤의 단서 현장에서 등록하는 것은 불가함

• get set 준비하다 • competition ⓝ 대회, 경기
• doubles match 복식 경기 • participant ⓝ 참가자
• certificate ⓝ 증서 • award ⓥ (상을) 주다

2023 오스트레일리아 게이트볼 챔피언십
Diamond Coast는 오스트레일리아 게이트볼 챔피언십을 환영할 준비를 하고
있습니다. 이 멋진 야외 대회에 참여해서 올해 우승자가 되세요!
언제 & 어디서
• 2023년 12월 19일부터 22일까지
• Diamond Coast 공연 센터
경기 일정
• 복식 경기 (오전 9시부터 오전 11시까지)
• 단체 경기 (오후 1시부터 오후 3시까지)
상
• 모든 참가자는 참가 증서를 받을 것입니다.
• 우승자들은 메달을 받습니다.
참고
• 참가비는 무료입니다.
• 등록을 위해 www.australiangateball.com을 방문하십시오.
  (현장 등록은 불가합니다.)

2023 Australian Gateball Championships에 관한 다음 안내문의
내용과 일치하지 **않는** 것은?
① 4일 동안 진행된다. December 19 — 22, 2023
② 복식 경기는 오전에 열린다. Doubles matches (9 a.m. — 11 a.m.)
③ 모든 참가자는 참가 증서를 받는다.
                    Every participant will receive a certificate for entry.
④ 참가비는 무료이다. Participation is free.
⑤현장에서 등록하는 것이 가능하다. Registration on site is not available.

>왜 정답? ✱✿✿ [정답률 90%]
등록은 웹사이트를 통해 해야 하며, 현장에서 등록하는 것은 불가능하다고
(Registration on site is not available.) 했으므로 현장에서 등록하는 것이
가능하다고 한 ⑤은 안내문의 내용과 일치하지 않는다.

>왜 오답?
① 4일 동안 진행된다. (December 19 — 22, 2023)
② 복식 경기는 오전에 열린다. (Doubles matches (9 a.m. — 11 a.m.))
③ 모든 참가자는 참가 증서를 받는다. (Every participant will receive a
  certificate for entry.)
④ 참가비는 무료이다. (Participation is free.)

J 26 정답 ④ *Rachel의 꽃 교실 수강 안내

Rachel's Flower Class /
Rachel의 꽃 교실 /
                make+목적어+목적격 보어
Make Your Life More Beautiful! //
여러분의 인생을 더 아름답게 만드세요 //

Class Schedule / (Every Monday to Friday) /
수업 일정 / (매주 월요일부터 금요일까지) /

Flower Arrangement 꽃꽂이	11 a.m. – 12 p.m. 오전 11시 ~ 정오
Flower Box Making 플라워 박스 만들기	1 p.m. – 2 p.m. / ①의 단서 플라워 박스 만들기 수업은 오후 1시에 시작함 오후 1시 ~ 오후 2시

Price /
가격 /
• $50 for each class / (flowers and other materials included) /
각 수업당 50달러 / (꽃값과 다른 재료비 포함) / ②의 단서 수업료에 꽃값과 다른 재료비가 포함됨
• Bring your own scissors and a bag. //
본인의 가위와 가방을 가져오세요 // ③의 단서 수강생은 가위와 가방을 가져와야 함

Other Info. /
다른 정보 /
                                  either A or B: A이거나 B
• You can sign up for classes / either online or by phone. //
수업 등록을 할 수 있습니다 / 온라인이나 전화로 // ④의 단서 수업 등록은 온라인이나 전화로 가능함
• No refund / for cancellations on the day of your class /
환불 불가 / 수업 당일 취소 시 / ⑤의 단서 수업 당일에 취소하면 환불을 받을 수 없음
To contact, / visit www.rfclass.com / or call 03 – 221 – 2131. //
연락하시려면 / www.rfclass.com을 방문하세요 / 또는 03 – 221 – 2131로 전화주세요 //

• flower arrangement 꽃꽂이 • material ⓝ 재료
• refund ⓝ 환불 • cancellation ⓝ 취소

Rachel의 꽃 교실
여러분의 인생을 더 아름답게 만드세요!
수업 일정 (매주 월요일부터 금요일까지)

꽃꽂이	오전 11시 ~ 정오
플라워 박스 만들기	오후 1시 ~ 오후 2시

가격

- 각 수업당 50달러

(꽃값과 다른 재료비 포함)

- 본인의 가위와 가방을 가져오세요.

다른 정보

- 온라인이나 전화로 수업 등록을 할 수 있습니다.
- 수업 당일 취소 시 환불 불가

연락하시려면, www.rfclass.com을 방문하시거나 03-221-2131로 전화주세요.

Rachel's Flower Class에 관한 다음 안내문의 내용과 일치하지 않는 것은?

① 플라워 박스 만들기 수업은 오후 1시에 시작된다.
　　Flower Box Making / 1 p.m. - 2 p.m.
② 수강료에 꽃값과 다른 재료비가 포함된다.
　　$50 for each class (flowers and other materials included)
③ 수강생은 가위와 가방을 가져와야 한다. Bring your own scissors and a bag.
④ 수업 등록은 전화로만 할 수 있다.
　　You can sign up for classes either online or by phone.
⑤ 수업 당일 취소 시 환불을 받을 수 없다.
　　No refund for cancellations on the day of your class

왜 정답? ❉❉❉ [정답률 94%]

안내문에서 You can sign up for classes either online or by phone. (온라인이나 전화로 수업 등록을 할 수 있습니다.)이라고 했으므로 수업 등록을 전화로만 할 수 있다는 ④은 안내문의 내용과 일치하지 않는다.

왜 오답?

① Flower Box Making / 1 p.m. - 2 p.m.에서 플라워 박스 만들기 수업은 오후 1시에 시작됨을 알 수 있다.
② $50 for each class (flowers and other materials included)에서 수강료에 꽃값과 다른 재료비가 포함된다고 했다.
③ Bring your own scissors and a bag.에서 수강생은 가위와 가방을 가져와야 함을 알 수 있다.
⑤ No refund for cancellations on the day of your class에서 수업 당일 취소 시 환불을 받을 수 없다고 했다.

J 27 정답 ⑤ *전자 폐기물 재활용의 날*

E-Waste Recycling Day /
전자 폐기물 재활용의 날 /

E-Waste Recycling Day / is an annual event in our city. //
전자 폐기물 재활용의 날은 / 우리 시의 연례행사입니다 //

명령문
Bring your used electronics / such as cell phones, tablets, and laptops / to recycle. //
여러분의 중고 전자 제품을 가져오세요 / 휴대 전화, 태블릿, 노트북과 같이 / 재활용할 //

Go green! // 친환경적으로 행동해요 //

When / 언제 /

Saturday, December 17, 2022 /
2022년 12월 17일 토요일 /

8:00 a.m. - 11:00 a.m. / ①의 단서 3시간 동안 진행됨
오전 8시부터 오전 11시까지 /

Where / 어디서 /

Lincoln Sports Center ②의 단서 Lincoln 스포츠 센터에서 열림
Lincoln 스포츠 센터 /

Notes / 주의 사항 /

- **Items NOT accepted: / light bulbs, batteries, and microwaves /**
허용되지 않는 품목들 / 전구, 건전지, 전자레인지 / ③의 단서 전자레인지는 허용되지 않는 품목임
조동사가 포함된 수동태
- **All personal data on the devices / must be wiped out in advance. //** ④의 단서 기기 속 모든 개인 정보는 미리 삭제되어야 함
기기 속 모든 개인 정보는 / 미리 삭제되어야 합니다 //

- **This event is free / but open only to local residents. //**
이 행사는 무료입니다 / 하지만 지역 주민에게만 개방됩니다 // ⑤의 단서 행사는 무료이지만 지역 주민에게만 개방됨

Please contact us at 986-571-0204 / for more information. //
986-571-0204로 연락주세요 / 더 많은 정보를 원하시면 //

- **e-waste** ⓝ 전자 폐기물
- **electronics** ⓝ 전자 제품
- **light bulb** 전구
- **wipe out** ~을 완전히 없애다[삭제하다]
- **resident** ⓝ 거주자, 주민
- **annual** ⓐ 해마다의, 연례의
- **accept** ⓥ 받아들이다, 허용하다
- **microwave** ⓝ 전자레인지
- **in advance** 사전에, 미리

전자 폐기물 재활용의 날

전자 폐기물 재활용의 날은 우리 시의 연례행사입니다. 휴대 전화, 태블릿, 노트북과 같이 재활용할 중고 전자 제품을 가져오세요. 친환경적으로 행동해요!

언제
2022년 12월 17일 토요일
오전 8시부터 오전 11시까지

어디서
Lincoln 스포츠 센터

주의 사항
- 허용되지 않는 품목들: 전구, 건전지, 전자레인지
- 기기 속 모든 개인 정보는 미리 삭제되어야 합니다.
- 이 행사는 무료이나 지역 주민에게만 개방됩니다.

더 많은 정보를 원하시면 986-571-0204로 연락주세요.

E-Waste Recycling Day에 관한 다음 안내문의 내용과 일치하지 않는 것은?

① 3시간 동안 진행된다. 8:00 a.m. - 11:00 a.m.
② Lincoln 스포츠 센터에서 열린다. Lincoln Sports Center
③ 전자레인지는 허용되지 않는 품목이다.
　　Items NOT accepted: light bulbs, batteries, and microwaves
④ 기기 속 모든 개인 정보는 미리 삭제되어야 한다.
　　All personal data on the devices must be wiped out in advance.
⑤ 거주 지역에 상관없이 참가할 수 있다.
　　This event is free but open only to local residents.

왜 정답? ❉❉❉ [정답률 92%]

행사는 무료이지만 지역 주민에게만 개방된다고(This event is free but open only to local residents.) 했으므로 거주 지역에 상관없이 참가할 수 있다고 한 ⑤은 안내문의 내용과 일치하지 않는다.

왜 오답?

① 행사는 오전 8시부터 오전 11시까지 3시간 동안 진행된다. (8:00 a.m. - 11:00 a.m.)
② Lincoln 스포츠 센터에서 열린다. (Lincoln Sports Center)
③ 전구, 건전지, 전자레인지는 허용되지 않는 품목이다. (Items NOT accepted: light bulbs, batteries, and microwaves)
④ 기기 속 모든 개인 정보는 미리 삭제해야 한다. (All personal data on the devices must be wiped out in advance.)

J 28 정답 ④ *롤러스케이트장 홍보*

Greenhill Roller Skating /
Greenhill 롤러스케이팅 /

형용사적 용법(chance 수식)
Join us / for your chance to enjoy roller skating! //
함께 해요 / 롤러스케이팅을 즐길 기회를 //

- **Place: / Greenhill Park, 351 Cypress Avenue /**
장소 / Greenhill Park, 351 Cypress Avenue /

- **Dates: / Friday, April 7 - Sunday, April 9 /**
일자 / 4월 7일 금요일~4월 9일 일요일 /

- **Time: / 9 a.m. - 6 p.m. /** ①의 단서 운영 시간은 오전 9시부터 오후 6시까지임
시간 / 오전 9시~오후 6시 /

- Fee: / $8 per person / for a 50-minute session //
요금 / 1인당 8달러 / 50분 수업에 // ②의 단서 입장료는 50분 기준 1인당 8달러임

Details /
세부 사항 /

– Admission will be on a first-come, first-served basis / with no reservations. // ③의 단서 선착순 입장으로 별도의 예약은 불필요함
입장은 선착순입니다 / 예약 없이 //

– Children / under the age of 10 / must <mark>be accompanied</mark> by an adult. // 수동태 동사 ④의 단서 10세 미만의 어린이는 어른 동행 필수임
어린이는 / 10세 미만의 / 어른과 동행해야 합니다 //

– We will lend you our roller skates / for free. // ⑤의 단서 롤러스케이트 대여는 무료임
우리는 롤러스케이트를 빌려줍니다 / 무료로 //

Contact the Community Center / for more information / at 013-234-6114 //
커뮤니티 센터로 연락하세요 / 더 많은 정보를 위해서 / 013-234-6114로 //

- **fee** ⓝ 요금 • **session** ⓝ 수업 • **admission** ⓝ 입장
- **first-come, first-served basis** 선착순 • **reservation** ⓝ 예약
- **accompany** ⓥ 동행하다 • **lend** ⓥ 빌려주다
- **contact** ⓥ 연락하다

Greenhill 롤러스케이팅
롤러스케이팅을 즐길 기회를 함께 해요!
- 장소: Greenhill Park, 351 Cypress Avenue
- 일자: 4월 7일 금요일~4월 9일 일요일
- 시간: 오전 9시~오후 6시
- 요금: 50분 수업에 1인당 8달러

세부 사항
– 입장은 예약 없이 선착순입니다.
– 10세 미만의 어린이는 어른과 동행해야 합니다.
– 롤러스케이트는 무료로 빌려줍니다.
더 많은 정보를 위해서 커뮤니티 센터 013-234-6114로 연락하세요.

Greenhill Roller Skating에 관한 다음 안내문의 내용과 일치하는 것은?
① 오전 9시부터 오후 9시까지 운영한다. Time: 9 a.m. - 6 p.m.
② 이용료는 시간 제한 없이 1인당 8달러이다. $8 per person for a 50-minute session
③ 입장하려면 예약이 필요하다. Admission will be on a first-come, first-served basis with no reservations.
④ 10세 미만 어린이는 어른과 동행해야 한다. Children under the age of 10 must be accompanied by an adult.
⑤ 추가 요금을 내면 롤러스케이트를 빌려준다. We will lend you our roller skates for free.

〉왜 정답 ? ✽✽✽ [정답률 90%]
10세 미만 어린이는 어른과 동행해야 한다고(Children under the age of 10 must be accompanied by an adult.) 했으므로 안내문의 내용과 일치하는 것은 ④이다.

〉왜 오답 ?
① 오전 9시부터 오후 6시까지 운영한다고 했다. (Time: 9 a.m. - 6 p.m.)
② 입장료는 50분 수업에 1인당 8달러라고 했다. ($8 per person for a 50-minute session)
③ 선착순 입장이므로 예약은 필요 없다고 했다. (Admission will be on a first-come, first-served basis with no reservations.)
⑤ 롤러스케이트 대여는 무료로 가능하다고 했다. (We will lend you our roller skates for free.)

J 29 정답 ⑤ *여름 스쿠버 다이빙 수업 ──────

Summer Scuba Diving One-day Class /
여름 스쿠버 다이빙 하루 수업 /

<mark>Join</mark> our summer scuba driving lesson / for beginners, / and 병렬 구조
<mark>become</mark> an underwater explorer! //
우리의 여름 스쿠버 다이빙 수업에 참여하고 / 초보자를 위한 / 수중 탐험가가 되세요 //

Schedule / 일정 /
- 10:00 – 12:00 / Learning the basics /
  10시에서 12시 / 기초 배우기 /
- 13:00 – 16:00 / Practicing diving skills in a pool / ①의 단서 다이빙 기술 연습은 수영장에서 함
  13시에서 16시 / 수영장에서 다이빙 기술 연습하기 /

Price / 가격 /
- Private lesson: / $150 / 개인 수업 / 150달러 /
- Group lesson (up to 3 people): / $100 per person / ②의 단서 그룹 수업은 최대 3명까지임
  그룹 수업 (3명까지) / 1인당 100달러 /
- Participants can rent our diving equipment / <mark>for free.</mark> // ③의 단서 다이빙 장비는 무료로 대여해 줌
  참가자는 우리의 다이빙 장비를 대여할 수 있습니다 / 무료로 //

Notice / 알림 /
- Participants must be 10 years old or over. // ④의 단서 참가자의 연령은 10세 이상으로 제한됨
  참가자는 10세 이상이어야 합니다 //
- Participants must register / at least 5 days before / the class begins. // ⑤의 단서 수업 시작 5일 전까지는 등록해야 함
  참가자는 등록해야 합니다 / 적어도 5일 전까지 / 수업이 시작하기 //

For more information, / please go to www.ssdiver.com. //
더 많은 정보를 원하시면 / www.ssdiver.com을 방문하세요 //

- **underwater** ⓐ 수중의 • **explorer** ⓝ 탐험가
- **private** ⓐ 개인을 위한 • **rent** ⓥ 대여하다
- **equipment** ⓝ 장비 • **register** ⓥ 등록하다

여름 스쿠버 다이빙 하루 수업
초보자를 위한 우리의 여름 스쿠버 다이빙 수업에 참여하고 수중 탐험가가 되세요!
일정
- 10시에서 12시 기초 배우기
- 13시에서 16시 수영장에서 다이빙 기술 연습하기
가격
- 개인 수업: 150달러
- 그룹 수업 (3명까지): 1인당 100달러
- 참가자는 우리의 다이빙 장비를 무료로 대여할 수 있습니다.
알림
- 참가자는 10세 이상이어야 합니다.
- 참가자는 적어도 수업 시작 5일 전까지 등록해야 합니다.
더 많은 정보를 원하시면, www.ssdiver.com을 방문하세요.

Summer Scuba Diving One-day Class에 관한 다음 안내문의 내용과 일치하는 것은?
① 오후 시간에 바다에서 다이빙 기술을 연습한다. Practicing diving skills in a pool
② 그룹 수업의 최대 정원은 4명이다. Group lesson (up to 3 people)
③ 다이빙 장비를 유료로 대여할 수 있다. Participants can rent our diving equipment for free.
④ 연령에 관계없이 참가할 수 있다. Participants must be 10 years old or over.
⑤ 적어도 수업 시작 5일 전까지 등록해야 한다. Participants must register at least 5 days before the class begins.

〉왜 정답 ? ✽✽✽ [정답률 88%]
참가자는 적어도 수업 시작 5일 전까지 등록해야 한다고(Participants must register at least 5 days before the class begins.) 했으므로 안내문의 내용과 일치하는 것은 ⑤이다.

> **왜 오답?**
>
> ① 바다가 아니라 수영장에서 다이빙 기술을 연습한다고 했다. (Practicing diving skills in a pool)
> ② 그룹 수업은 3명까지라고 했다. (Group lesson (up to 3 people))
> ③ 참가자는 다이빙 장비를 무료로 대여할 수 있다고 했다. (Participants can rent our diving equipment for free.)
> ④ 참가자는 10세 이상이어야 한다고 했다. (Participants must be 10 years old or over.)

J 30 정답 ⑤ **＊**도시 어드벤처 탐색 행사 안내 ──────

The Amazing Urban Adventure Quest / 놀라운 도시 어드벤처 탐색 /
Explore Central Park / 사이에 주어와 be동사 생략 while solving clues and completing challenges! //
Central Park를 탐험하세요 / ①의 단서 참여하는 동안 스마트폰의 안내를 받아야 함 단서를 해결하고 도전을 완수하면서 //
분사구문 Guided by your smartphone, / make your way / among the well-known places in the park. //
스마트폰의 안내를 받으면서 / 자신의 길을 만들어 보세요 / 공원의 명소들 속 //

When & How / 언제 & 어떻게 /
• Available 365 days a year (from sunrise to sunset) /
1년 365일 이용 가능 (일출부터 일몰까지) / ②의 단서 일 년 내내 일몰까지만 참여할 수 있음
• Start when you want. // 여러분이 원할 때 시작하세요 //
• Get a stamp at each checkpoint. //
각 체크포인트에서 스탬프를 받으세요 //

Adventure Courses / 어드벤처 코스 /
• East Side: Starts at Twilight Gardens (no age limit) /
동편: Twilight Gardens에서 시작합니다 (나이 제한 없음) /
• West Side: Starts at Strawberry Castle (over 15 years old) /
서편: Strawberry Castle에서 시작합니다 (15세 초과) / ③의 단서 서편 코스는 15세 초과라는 나이 제한이 있음

Registration & Cost / 등록 & 비용 /
• Sign up online at www.urbanquest.com. //
www.urbanquest.com에서 온라인으로 등록하세요 //
• $40 for a team of 2 – 5 people /
2-5명으로 구성된 팀당 $40 / ④의 단서 1인당이 아니라 팀당 40달러의 요금이 듦
• Save 20% with discount code: / CENTRALQUEST //
할인 코드로 20%를 절약하세요 / CENTRALQUEST // ⑤의 단서 할인 코드는 CENTRALQUEST임

• **urban** ⓐ 도시의 • **clue** ⓝ 단서 • **registration** ⓝ 등록
• **sign up** 등록하다 • **save** ⓥ ~을 절약하다[아끼다]
• **discount** ⓝ 할인

놀라운 도시 어드벤처 탐색

단서를 해결하고 도전을 완수하면서 Central Park를 탐험하세요! 스마트폰의 안내를 받으면서 공원의 명소들 속 자신의 길을 만들어 보세요.
언제 & 어떻게
• 1년 365일 이용 가능 (일출부터 일몰까지)
• 여러분이 원할 때 시작하세요.
• 각 체크포인트에서 스탬프를 받으세요.
어드벤처 코스
• 동편: Twilight Gardens에서 시작합니다. (나이 제한 없음)
• 서편: Strawberry Castle에서 시작합니다. (15세 초과)
등록 & 비용
• www.urbanquest.com에서 온라인으로 등록하세요.
• 2–5명으로 구성된 팀당 $40
• 할인 코드 CENTRALQUEST로 20%를 절약하세요.

> The Amazing Urban Adventure Quest에 관한 다음 안내문의 내용과 일치하는 것은?
> ① 참여하는 동안 스마트폰 사용은 금지된다. Guided by your smartphone
> ② 일 년 내내 일몰 후 참여할 수 있다.
> Available 365 days a year (from sunrise to sunset)
> ③ 서편 코스는 나이 제한이 없다.
> West Side: Starts at Strawberry Castle (over 15 years old)
> ④ 1인당 40달러의 요금이 든다. $40 for a team of 2 — 5 people
> ⑤ 할인받을 수 있는 코드가 있다.
> Save 20% with discount code: CENTRALQUEST

> **왜 정답?** ✻❋❋ [정답률 90%]
>
> 20% 할인을 받을 수 있는 코드를 소개했으므로 (Save 20% with discount code: CENTRALQUEST) 안내문의 내용과 일치하는 것은 ⑤이다.

> **왜 오답?**
>
> ① 참여하는 동안 스마트폰의 안내를 받는다. (Guided by your smartphone)
> ② 일 년 내내 일몰까지만 참여할 수 있다. (Available 365 days a year (from sunrise to sunset))
> ③ 서편 코스는 15세 초과라는 나이 제한이 있다. (West Side: Starts at Strawberry Castle (over 15 years old))
> ④ 1인당이 아니라 2-5명으로 구성된 팀당 40달러의 요금이 든다. ($40 for a team of 2 — 5 people)

세부사항을 꼼꼼하게 선택지와 대조하자!

J 어휘 Review 정답 ──────── 문제편 **p. 143**

01 환불	11 doubles match	21 scissors
02 취소	12 sign up	22 accompanied
03 해양의	13 check out	23 furry
04 대책	14 gift certificate	24 provided
05 제안서	15 get set	25 talent
06 palace	16 hosting	26 charge
07 annual	17 process	27 accepted
08 award	18 inside	28 commercialized
09 awareness	19 unfavorable	29 participants
10 remote	20 operating	30 required

K 어법에 맞지 않는 낱말 찾기

문제편 p. 146~154

K 01 정답 ④ *루틴의 역할과 중요성

다음 글의 밑줄 친 부분 중, 어법상 틀린 것은?

enable A to-v: A가 ~할 수 있도록 하다
Routines enable athletes / to evaluate competition conditions. //
루틴은 운동선수가 ~할 수 있도록 해 준다 / 경기 조건을 평가하는 //

단수 주어
For example, / bouncing a ball in a volleyball service routine /
① supplies the server / with information about the ball, the
단수 동사
floor, and the state of her muscles. //
예를 들어 / 배구 서브 루틴에서 공을 튕기는 것은 / 서브를 하는 선수에게 제공한다 / 공, 바
닥, 그리고 자신의 근육 상태에 대한 정보를 //

prepare를 수식하기 위해 to와 동사원형 사이에 삽입된 부사
This information / can then be used / to ② properly prepare for
her serve. //
이 정보는 / 그다음 사용될 수 있다 / 자신의 서브를 적절히 준비하기 위해 //

문장의 본동사
Routines also enable athletes / to adjust and fine-tune their
병렬 구조(부사구)
preparations / ③ based on those evaluations / or in pursuit of a
particular competitive goal. //
루틴은 또한 선수가 ~할 수 있게 해 준다 / 준비 상태를 조절하고 미세하게 조정하는 / 그러한
평가에 기반하거나 / 또는 특정 경쟁 목표를 추구하여 //

선행사
This adaptation can involve / adjustment to the conditions,
rivals, competitive situation, or internal influences / ④ what (→
선행사를 포함하지 않는 주격 관계대명사
that 또는 which) can affect performance. // 단서 선행사가 존재함
이러한 적응은 포함할 수 있다 / 조건, 경쟁 상대, 경기 상황, 또는 내적 영향에 대한 조정을 /
수행에 영향을 미칠 수 있는 //

동명사   adjust A to B: A를 B에 맞게 조정하다
Just like adjusting a race-car engine / to the conditions of
the track, air temperature, and weather, / routines adjust all
부사적 용법 (목적)
competitive components / ⑤ to achieve proper performance. //
경주용 자동차 엔진을 조정하는 것과 마찬가지로 / 트랙, 기온, 그리고 날씨의 조건에 맞게 /
루틴은 경기의 모든 구성 요소를 조정한다 / 적절한 수행을 해내기 위해 //

- routine ⓝ 루틴, 일상의 과정   - enable ⓥ ~할 수 있게 하다
- athlete ⓝ 운동선수   - evaluate ⓥ 평가하다
- competition ⓝ 경기, 경쟁   - condition ⓝ 조건
- bounce ⓥ (공을) 튕기다   - supply ⓥ 제공하다
- properly ⓐⅾ 적절히   - adjust ⓥ 조절하다, 조정하다
- fine-tune ⓥ 미세하게 조정하다   - in pursuit of ~을 추구하여
- adaptation ⓝ 적응   - internal ⓐ 내적인   - influence ⓝ 영향
- affect ⓥ 영향을 미치다   - performance ⓝ 수행
- achieve ⓥ 해내다

루틴은 운동선수가 경기 조건을 평가할 수 있도록 해준다. 예를 들어, 배구 서브 루틴에서 공을 튕기는 것은 서브를 하는 선수에게 공, 바닥, 그리고 자신의 근육 상태에 대한 정보를 제공한다. 그다음 이 정보는 자신의 서브를 적절히 준비하기 위해 사용될 수 있다. 루틴은 또한 그러한 평가에 기반하거나 또는 특정 경쟁 목표를 추구하여 선수가 준비 상태를 조절하고 미세하게 조정할 수 있게 해준다. 이러한 적응은 수행에 영향을 미칠 수 있는 조건, 경쟁 상대, 경기 상황, 또는 내적 영향에 대한 조정을 포함할 수 있다. 경주용 자동차 엔진을 트랙, 기온, 그리고 날씨의 조건에 맞게 조정하는 것과 마찬가지로, 루틴은 적절한 수행을 해내기 위해 경기의 모든 구성 요소를 조정한다.

왜 정답? ✱✱✱ [정답률 71%]
④ 선행사를 포함하는 관계대명사 what 앞에 선행사가 있다!

선행사
This adaptation can involve / adjustment to the conditions,
rivals, competitive situation, or internal influences / ④ what
선행사를 포함하지 않는 주격 관계대명사   앞에 선행사가 있음
(→ that 또는 which) can affect performance. //

단서 선행사를 포함하는 관계대명사 what에 밑줄이 있으므로
발상 그 앞에는 선행사가 없을 것이다.
해결 그런데 what 앞에 관계사절 can affect performance의 주어 역할을 하는 선
행사 the conditions ~ internal influences가 있다. 따라서 what을 주격 관
계대명사 that 또는 which로 고쳐야 한다.
개념 관계대명사 what은 선행사를 포함하므로, 앞에 선행사가 있을 때는 who,
which, that처럼 다른 관계대명사를 써야 한다.

왜 오답?
① 동사는 주어에 그 수를 일치시킨다.

동명사 (단수 주어)
For example, / bouncing a ball in a volleyball service routine /
단수 동사
① supplies the server / ~

supplies는 단수 동사이며, 문장의 주어가 동명사구 bouncing ~ routine이므로 마
찬가지로 단수이다. 따라서 단수 동사 supplies가 알맞게 쓰였다.

② 부사는 준동사를 수식할 수 있다.

prepare를 수식하기 위해 to와 동사원형 사이에 삽입된 부사
This information can then be used / to ② properly prepare for
her serve. //

문맥상 서브를 '적절하게' 준비하는 것이므로 부사 properly가 준동사 to prepare를
수식하고 있다.

③ 분사구문은 부사구의 역할을 한다.

문장의 본동사
Routines also enable athletes / to adjust and fine-tune their
분사구문을 이끄는 과거분사   병렬 구조 (부사구)
preparations / ③ [based on those evaluations] / or [in pursuit
of a particular competitive goal]. //

밑줄 친 based 외에도 문장에 본동사 enable이 이미 있다. 따라서 based는 분사구
문을 이끄는 과거분사이며, 이 분사구문은 문장에 '그러한 평가에 기반하여'라는 뜻을
더해준다.
이는 등위접속사 or로 병렬 구조를 이루는 전치사구(in pursuit of ~ goal)와 마찬가
지로 문장에 의미를 더하는 부사구의 역할을 한다. 따라서 과거분사 based는 알맞게
쓰였다.

⑤ 부사적 용법의 to부정사는 목적의 의미를 나타낼 수 있다.

부사적 용법 (목적)
~ / routines adjust all competitive components / ⑤ to achieve
proper performance. //

이 문장에서 to achieve는 부사의 역할을 하며 앞 절에 '적절한 수행을 해내기 위해'라
는 목적의 의미를 더해준다. 따라서 to achieve는 알맞게 쓰였다.

K 02 정답 ④ *기술 발전으로 인한 더 많은 자원 소비

다음 글의 밑줄 친 부분 중, 어법상 틀린 것은?

전치사+명사구   주격 관계대명사
Despite all the high-tech devices / that seem to deny the need for
paper, / paper use in the United States / ① has nearly doubled
recently. //   단수 주어(paper use)와 수 일치
모든 첨단 기기들에도 불구하고 / 종이의 필요성을 부정하는 것처럼 보이는 / 미국에서 종이
사용은 / 최근 거의 두 배로 증가했다 //

We now consume more paper / than ever: / 400 million tons
globally / and growing. //
우리는 더 많은 종이를 소비하고 있다 / 그 어느 때보다도 / 전 세계적으로 4억 톤을 소비하고
있으며 / 증가하고 있다 //

'the only+명사」 뒤에는 관계대명사 which가 올 수 없음   목적격 관계대명사
Paper is not the only resource / ② that we are using more of. //
종이만이 유일한 자원이 아니다 / 우리가 더 많이 사용하고 있는 //

Technological advances often come with / the promise of
③ using fewer materials. //
전치사 뒤에 동명사가 옴
기술의 발전은 흔히 수반한다 / 더 적은 재료의 사용 가능성을 //

However, / the reality is / that they have historically caused
more materials use, / making us ④ dependently(→ dependent)
부사구문을 이끎
on more natural resources. // 단서 부사는 보어 자리에 올 수 없음
그러나 / 현실은 ~ 한다 / 그것들이 역사적으로 더 많은 재료 사용을 야기하여 / 우리가 더
많은 천연자원 사용에 의존하게 //
비교급 강조 부사(much, far, even, still, a lot 등)
The world now consumes far more "stuff" / than it ever has. //
세계는 이제 훨씬 더 많은 '것'을 소비한다 / 그 어느 때보다도 //
숫자+times: ~배
We use twenty-seven times more industrial minerals, / such
as gold, copper, and rare metals, / than we ⑤ did just over a
대동사(= used)
century ago. //
우리는 27배 더 많은 산업 광물을 사용한다 / 금, 구리, 희귀 금속과 같은 / 1세기 이전보다 //

We also each individually use / more resources. //
우리는 또한 각자 사용한다 / 더 많은 자원을 //

Much of that / is due to our high-tech lifestyle. //
그중 많은 부분은 / 우리의 첨단 생활 방식 때문이다 //

- deny ⓥ 부정하다 - recently ⓐⓓ 최근에 - consume ⓥ 소비하다
- globally ⓐⓓ 전세계적으로 - resource ⓝ 자원 - advance ⓝ 발전
- promise ⓝ 가능성, 기대 - material ⓝ 재료
- cause ⓥ 야기하다, 일으키다 - industrial ⓐ 산업의

종이의 필요성을 부정하는 것처럼 보이는 모든 첨단 기기들에도 불구하고,
미국에서 종이 사용은 최근 거의 두 배로 증가했다. 우리는 그 어느
때보다도 더 많은 종이를 소비하고 있다. 전세계적으로 4억 톤을 소비하고
있으며 증가하고 있다. 우리가 더 많이 사용하고 있는 자원은 종이만이
아니다. 기술의 발전은 흔히 더 적은 재료의 사용 가능성을 수반한다.
그러나, 현실은 그것들이 역사적으로 더 많은 재료 사용을 야기하여
우리가 더 많은 천연자원 사용에 의존하게 한다. 세계는 이제 그 어느
때보다도 훨씬 더 많은 '것'을 소비한다. 우리는 금, 구리, 희귀 금속과 같은
산업 광물을 1세기 이전보다 27배 더 많이 사용한다. 우리는 또한 각자 더
많은 자원을 사용한다. 그중 많은 부분은 우리의 첨단 생활 방식 때문이다.

> 왜 정답? ★★★ [정답률 62%]

④ [목적격보어] dependently는 5형식 동사(make)와 목적어(us) 뒤에 나오는
목적격보어가 와야 하는 자리이다. 목적격보어에는 부사가 아니라 형용사가
와야 어법상 알맞으므로 dependent로 바꿔야 한다.

> 왜 오답?

① [주어와 동사의 수 일치] paper use가 3인칭 단수 주어이므로 동사도
3인칭 단수 형태 has로 알맞게 썼다. in the United States는 paper use를
수식하는 전치사구이므로 복수 주어로 착각해서는 안 된다.

> ✳ [주어와 동사의 수 일치] 해결하기   KEY
- 수식어구를 제외하고 주어를 찾아 동사의 수를 일치시킨다.
- 주어와 동사의 수 일치를 묻는 문제의 대부분은 동사 바로 앞에 핵심 주어가
  위치하지 않는다.

② [목적격 관계대명사] that은 뒤에 나오는 문장에서 of의 목적어 구실을 하는
목적격 관계대명사이다. that이 수식하는 선행사는 the only resource인데,
선행사가 the only가 수식하는 명사일 때 관계대명사 which는 올 수 없다. 주의
따라서 the only resource 뒤에 목적격 관계대명사 that을 사용한 것은 어법상
적절하다.

③ [전치사+동명사] 전치사의 목적어로 동사가 올 때는 동명사의 형태로 와야
하므로 using이 적절하게 사용되었다.

⑤ [대동사] did는 앞에 나온 use의 반복적인 사용을 대신하여 쓰인 대동사이다.
1세기 전에 우리가 '사용했다'는 의미에서 과거 시제를 반영하여 did를
썼으므로 어법상 적절하다.

K 03 정답 ③ *전문가의 지식 구조 ─────────

다음 글의 밑줄 친 부분 중, 어법상 틀린 것은? [3점]

Studies of experts / provide insight / into ① what it means / to
간접의문문을 이끄는 의문사 가주어
have deep and flexible understanding. //
진주어 (to부정사)
전문가에 대한 연구는 / 통찰을 제공한다 / 무엇을 의미하는지에 대한 / 깊고 유연한 이해를 갖
는 것이 //

Experts in a particular domain / are people / who have deep,
주격 관계대명사
richly interconnected ideas about the world. //
특정 분야의 전문가는 / 사람들이다 / 세상에 대해 깊고 풍부하게 상호 연결된 생각을 지닌 //

They are not / just good thinkers / or people who are ②
부사 (smart 수식)
exceptionally smart. //
그들은 아니다 / 단순히 생각을 잘하는 사람이거나 / 유난히 똑똑한 사람이 //

Rather, / experts ③ having (→ have) knowledge / in a specific
병렬 구조 (문장의 동사)
domain / — such as chess, chemistry, or tennis — / and are not
단서 experts에 대한 동사 자리임 등위접속사 (동사와 동사를 연결)
generalists. //
오히려 / 전문가는 지식을 가지고 있다 / 특정 분야에서 / 체스, 화학, 테니스와 같은 / 그리고
다방면의 지식을 가진 사람이 아니다 //

However, / experts do not just know / "a bunch of facts." //
'많은'
그러나 / 전문가는 알기만 하는 것은 아니다 / '많은 사실들'을 //

In fact, / having expertise in a topic / means / ④ that knowledge
목적어절 접속사
is organized into coherent frameworks,
목적어절의 첫 번째 문장
사실 / 한 주제에 대한 전문성이 있다는 것은 / 의미한다 / 지식이 일관된 틀로 조직되어 있고 /
목적어절의 두 번째 문장
and the expert understands the inter-relationship between facts
/ and can distinguish which ideas are most central. //
전문가가 사실 간의 상호 관계를 이해하고 / 어떤 아이디어가 가장 핵심적인지 구분할 수 있다
는 것을 //

This kind of deep but organized understanding / allows for
과거분사 (understanding 수식) 병렬 구조
greater flexibility in learning / and ⑤ facilitates application
across multiple contexts. //
이러한 깊이 있으면서도 조직적인 이해는 / 학습에서 더 큰 유연성을 가능하게 하고 / 다양한
맥락에 걸쳐 적용을 촉진한다 //

- insight ⓝ 통찰 - flexible ⓐ 유연한 - domain ⓝ 분야
- interconnected ⓐ 상호 연결된 - exceptionally ⓐⓓ 유난히
- generalist ⓝ 다방면의 지식을 가진 사람 - expertise ⓝ 전문성
- organize ⓥ 조직하다 - framework ⓝ 틀 - central ⓐ 핵심적인
- organized ⓐ 조직적인 - flexibility ⓝ 유연성
- application ⓝ 적용 - context ⓝ 맥락

전문가에 대한 연구는 깊고 유연한 이해를 가지는 것이 무엇을 의미하는지에 대
한 통찰을 제공한다. 특정 분야의 전문가는 세상에 대해 깊고 풍부하게 상호 연
결된 생각을 가진 사람들이다. 그들은 단순히 생각을 잘하는 사람이거나 유난히
똑똑한 사람이 아니다. 오히려, 전문가는 특정 분야 — 체스, 화학, 또는 테니스
와 같은 — 에서 지식을 가지고 있고, 다방면의 지식을 가진 사람이 아니다. 그
러나, 전문가는 "많은 사실"을 알기만 하는 것은 아니다. 사실, 한 주제에 대한
전문성이 있다는 것은 지식이 일관된 틀로 조직화되어 있고, 전문가가 사실 간
의 상호 관계를 이해하고 어떤 아이디어가 가장 핵심적인지 구분할 수 있다는
것을 의미한다. 이러한 깊이 있으면서도 조직화된 이해는 학습에서의 더 큰 유
연성을 가능하게 하고 다양한 맥락에 걸쳐 적용을 촉진한다.

> 왜 정답? ★★❀ [정답률 64%]

③ 동사 자리에 준동사가 쓰였다!

Rather, / experts ③ having (→ have) knowledge / in a specific
동사가 와야 함 병렬 구조 (문장의 동사)
domain / — such as chess, chemistry, or tennis — / and are not
삽입어구: 제외하고 생각하기 등위접속사 (동사와 동사를 연결)
generalists.

단서 준동사 having에 밑줄이 있으므로

발상 동사 자리에 온 건 아닌지 확인한다.

해결 등위접속사 and 뒤에는 동사 are not이 알맞게 쓰였지만, and 앞에는 동사가 없다. 준동사 having은 문장에서 동사의 역할을 할 수 없으므로 having을 동사 have로 고쳐야 한다.

개념 주어와 동사는 문장의 필수 요소로서, 그중 하나라도 없으면 의미가 통하지 않으므로 문장이 될 수 없다.

왜 오답?

① 간접의문문은 명사 역할을 한다.

Studies of experts / provide insight / into ① what it means / to have deep and flexible understanding. //
(간접의문문을 이끄는 의문사 / 동사 / 진주어 (to부정사) / 가주어)

문맥상 '무엇을 의미하는지'를 뜻하므로, 의문사 what이 into의 목적어 역할을 하는 간접의문문을 알맞게 이끈다. 간접의문문은 「의문사 + 주어 + 동사」의 어순을 따른다.

② 부사는 형용사를 수식할 수 있다.

They are not / just good thinkers / or people who are ② exceptionally smart. //
(부사 (smart 수식))

문맥상 '유난히' 똑똑한 사람들에 대해 언급하고 있으므로 부사 exceptionally가 주격 보어 자리에 온 형용사 smart를 알맞게 수식하고 있다.

④ 접속사 that은 완전한 절을 이끈다.

In fact, / having expertise in a topic / means / ④ that [knowledge is organized into coherent frameworks], / and [the expert understands the inter-relationship between facts / and can distinguish which ideas are most central]. //
(목적어절 접속사 / 목적어절의 첫 번째 문장 / 목적어절의 두 번째 문장)

목적어절 접속사 that이 knowledge is organized ~ frameworks와 the expert understands ~ central이라는 두 개의 완전한 절을 이끌고 있으므로 알맞게 쓰였다.

⑤ 등위접속사로 연결된 두 성분은 병렬 구조를 이룬다.

This kind of deep but organized understanding / allows for greater flexibility in learning / and ⑤ facilitates application across multiple contexts. //
(문장의 주어 / 등위접속사 (동사와 동사를 연결) / 병렬 구조 (문장의 동사))

동사 facilitates는 allows와 병렬 구조를 이루고 있다. 문장의 주어가 understanding으로 단수이므로 단수 동사의 형태로 온 것은 알맞다.

[구문 서술형]

정답 richly, interconnected

해석 전문가는 세상에 대해 풍부하게 상호 연결된 생각을 가진 사람들이다.

→ 형용사 rich를 부사로 바꿔 쓰려면 뒤에 -ly를 붙여 richly로 써야 한다. '풍부하게 상호 연결된'을 나타내므로 바로 뒤의 형용사 interconnected를 수식한다.

K 04 정답 ② *큰 포유류의 초식동물 종을 길들이기 어려운 이유

다음 글의 밑줄 친 부분 중, 어법상 틀린 것은? [3점]

Big mammalian herbivore species react to danger / from predators or humans / in different ways. //
큰 포유류의 초식동물 종은 위험에 대해 반응한다 / 포식자나 인간으로부터의 / 다른 방식으로 //

Some species are nervous, fast, and programmed for instant flight / when they perceive a threat. //
어떤 종들은 긴장하고, 빠르고, 즉각적인 비행을 하도록 프로그램화되어 있다 / 그들이 위험을 감지할 때 //

Other species are slower, less nervous, / seek protection in herds, / ① stand their ground when threatened, / and don't run until necessary. //
(복수 주어 / 병렬 구조 (복수 동사))
다른 종들은 더 느리고, 덜 긴장하고 / 무리 속에서 보호를 찾고 / 위협을 받았을 때 그들의 자리를 지키고 / 필요할 때까지 도망가지 않는다 //

Naturally, / the nervous species are difficult to keep in captivity. //
자연스럽게 / 긴장하는 동물 종들은 갇힌 상태를 유지하기 어렵다 //

If ② putting (→ put) into an enclosure, / they are likely to panic, / and either die of shock or hit themselves repeatedly to death against the fence / in their attempts to escape. //
(접속사가 생략되지 않은 분사구문 / 주절의 주어 (분사구문의 주어와 같음) / 단서 우리 안에 '넣어지는' 것이므로 수동 관계임)
만약 우리 안에 넣어지면 / 그들은 패닉에 빠져 / 충격으로 죽거나 반복적으로 울타리에 부딪혀 죽을 가능성이 있다 / 탈출하려는 시도로 //

That's true, for example, of gazelles, / ③ which for thousands of years were the most frequently hunted game species / in some parts of the Fertile Crescent. //
(선행사 / 계속적 용법의 주격 관계대명사 / 복수 동사 / 전치사구)
예를 들어 이것은 가젤에 해당하는데 / 이들은 수천 년 동안 가장 빈번하게 사냥된 사냥감 종이었다 / 비옥한 초승달 지대의 일부 지역에서 //

There is no mammal species / that the first settled peoples of that area / had more opportunity ④ to domesticate / than gazelles. //
(목적격 관계대명사 / 형용사적 용법 (opportunity 수식))
포유류는 없다 / 그 지역에 처음으로 정착한 인간들이 / 길들일 기회가 더 많았던 / 가젤보다 //

But no gazelle species has ever been domesticated. //
그러나 어떤 가젤 종도 지금까지 길들여진 적이 없다 //

Just imagine trying to herd an animal / that runs away, blindly hits ⑤ itself against walls, / can leap up to nearly 30 feet, / and can run at a speed of 50 miles per hour! //
(선행사 / 주격 관계대명사 / 재귀대명사 (재귀 용법))
동물을 무리 지으려고 노력하는 것을 상상해보라 / 도망가고, 자신을 맹목적으로 벽에 부딪히고 / 거의 30피트까지 뛰어오를 수 있고 / 시속 50마일 속도로 달릴 수 있는 //

- mammalian ⓐ 포유류의 • species ⓝ 종 • react ⓥ 반응하다
- predator ⓝ 포식자 • instant ⓐ 즉각적인
- perceive ⓥ 인지하다, 감지하다 • threat ⓝ 위협
- protection ⓝ 보호 • captivity ⓝ 사육, 감금
- enclosure ⓝ 우리, 울타리 • panic ⓥ 공황 상태에 빠지다
- repeatedly ⓐⓓ 반복적으로 • attempt ⓝ 시도
- frequently ⓐⓓ 빈번하게 • opportunity ⓝ 기회
- domesticate ⓥ 길들이다, 사육하다 • blindly ⓐⓓ 맹목적으로
- leap ⓥ 뛰어오르다

큰 포유류의 초식동물 종은 포식자나 인간으로부터의 위험에 대해 다른 방식으로 반응한다. 어떤 종들은 그들이 위험을 감지할 때 긴장하고, 빠르고, 즉각적인 비행을 하도록 프로그램화되어 있다. 다른 종들은 더 느리고, 덜 긴장하고, 무리 속에서 보호를 찾고, 위협을 받았을 때 그들의 자리를 지키고 필요할 때까지 도망가지 않는다. 자연스럽게, 긴장하는 동물 종들은 갇힌 상태를 유지하기 어렵다. 만약 우리 안에 넣어지면, 그들은 패닉에 빠져 충격으로 죽거나 탈출하려는 시도로 반복적으로 울타리에 부딪혀 죽을 가능성이 있다. 예를 들어 이것은 가젤에 해당하는데, 이들은 수천 년 동안 비옥한 초승달 지대의 일부 지역에서 가장 빈번하게 사냥된 사냥감 종이었다. 그 지역에 처음으로 정착한 인간들이 가젤보다 길들일 기회가 더 많았던 포유류는 없다. 그러나 어떤 가젤 종도 지금까지 길들여진 적이 없다. 도망가고, 자신을 맹목적으로 벽에 부딪히고, 거의 30피트까지 뛰어오를 수 있고, 시속 50마일 속도로 달릴 수 있는 동물을 무리 지으려고 노력하는 것을 상상해보라!

⟩왜 정답? ★★★ [정답률 48%]

② 주절의 주어와 분사의 관계가 수동이다!

접속사가 생략되지 않은 분사구문　　주절의 주어 (분사구문의 주어와 같음)
┌ If ② putting (→ put) into an enclosure, / they are likely to
　　　주어와 수동 관계이므로 과거분사가 와야 함
└ panic, ~ //

(단서) 접속사 If가 생략되지 않은 분사구문이다. 분사구문의 생략된 주어는 주절의 주어인 they(= the nervous species)이다.

(발상) the nervous species와 putting의 능동 및 수동 관계를 살펴본다.

(해결) putting과 전치사구 into an enclosure 사이에 목적어가 없고, 문맥상으로도 the nervous species가 우리 안에 '넣어지는' 것이기 때문에 수동 관계를 나타낸다. 따라서 현재분사 putting을 과거분사 put으로 고쳐야 한다.

(개념) 분사구문에서 주어와 동사의 관계가 능동이면 현재분사를, 수동이면 과거분사를 사용한다.

⟩왜 오답?

① 동사는 주어에 그 수를 일치시킨다.

복수 주어
┌ Other species are slower, less nervous, / seek protection in
　　　　　　　　　　　병렬 구조 (복수 동사)
├ herds, ① stand their ground when threatened, / and don't run
└ until necessary. //

문장의 주어는 복수 명사인 Other species이다. 문장의 동사인 are, seek, stand, don't run이 병렬 구조를 이루고 있으며 이들은 모두 복수형이므로 stand 또한 알맞게 쓰였다.

③ 계속적 용법의 관계대명사는 콤마 뒤에서 선행사를 수식한다.

　　　　　　　　　　선행사　　　　계속적 용법의 주격 관계대명사
┌ That's true, for example, of gazelles, / ③ which for thousands
　　　　　복수 동사
└ of years were the most frequently hunted game species ~ //
　　　전치사구: 제외하고 생각하기

which가 콤마 뒤에 쓰여 선행사 gazelles에 대해 부가적인 설명을 덧붙이므로, 계속적 용법의 주격 관계대명사 which가 알맞게 쓰였다.

④ to부정사는 형용사적 용법으로 쓰여 명사를 수식할 수 있다.

　　　　　　　　　　　　형용사적 용법 (opportunity 수식)
[~ had more opportunity ④ to domesticate / than gazelles. //

to domesticate가 바로 앞의 명사 opportunity를 수식하여 '길들일 기회'라는 뜻을 나타내므로, 형용사적 용법의 to부정사가 알맞게 쓰였다.

⑤ 주어와 목적어가 같을 때 목적어 자리에 재귀대명사를 쓴다.

　　　　　　　　　　　　　　　선행사　　　주격 관계대명사
┌ Just imagine trying to herd an animal / that runs away, blindly
　　　재귀대명사 (재귀 용법)
└ hits ⑤ itself against walls, ~ //

관계사절의 주어는 선행사인 an animal이다. 문맥상 an animal이 벽에 부딪히는 대상은 자기 자신이므로, 즉 주어와 목적어가 같으므로 재귀 용법의 재귀대명사 itself가 알맞게 쓰였다.

(구문 서술형)

(정답) Naturally, 자연스럽게

→ 일곱 번째 줄의 문장에서 부사 Naturally가 문장 전체를 수식한다. 앞 문장의 상황이 원인이 되고 '자연스럽게' 그 결과로 뒤 문장의 상황이 일어남을 나타낸다.

K 05 정답 ④ *디지털 은유와 언어적 은유의 차이

다음 글의 밑줄 친 부분 중, 어법상 틀린 것은?

Digital technologies are essentially related to metaphors, / but digital metaphors are different from linguistic ① ones / in
　　　　　　　　　　　　　　　　　　　　　　　　　= metaphors
important ways. //
디지털 기술은 근본적으로 은유와 관련되어 있지만 / 디지털 은유는 언어적 은유와 다르다 / 중요한 면에서 //

'~라는 점에서'
Linguistic metaphors are passive, / in the sense that the audience
　　　　　　　　　　　　　　　　　　　　　　　　　과거분사구 (the world 수식)
needs to choose / to actively enter the world / proposed by
metaphor. //
언어적 은유는 수동적이다 / 독자가 선택할 필요가 있다는 점에서 / 세계에 적극적으로 들어가도록 / 은유에 의해 제시된 //

In the Shakespearean metaphor "time is a beggar," / the
audience is unlikely to understand the metaphor /
"시간은 구걸하는 자다"라는 셰익스피어의 은유에서 / 독자는 은유를 이해할 것 같지 않다 /
　　　　　　　병렬 구조　　　　　　　　　　부사　　　　동명사
without cognitive effort / and without further ② engaging
Shakespeare's prose. //
인지적인 노력 없이는 / 그리고 셰익스피어의 산문을 더 끌어들이지 않고는 //

Technological metaphors, / on the other hand, / are active (and often imposing) /
기술적 은유는 / 반면에 / 능동적이다 (그리고 종종 강요적이다) /
　　　　　　　　　　　수동태　　　　　　　주격 관계대명사
in the sense that they are realized / in digital artifacts that are
　　　　　　　　　　　　　분사구문을 이끄는 현재분사
actively doing things, / forcefully ③ changing a user's meaning
horizon. //
그것이 실현된다는 점에서 / 능동적으로 일을 하는 디지털 인공물에서 / 사용자의 의미의 지평을 강력하게 바꾸면서 //

Technological creators / cannot generally afford / to require their
　　　　　　　　　　　　　require의 목적격 보어 (to부정사)
potential audience / to wonder how the metaphor works; /
기술적인 창작자는 / 일반적으로 여유가 없다 / 그들의 잠재적인 독자에게 요구할 / 어떻게 은유가 작용하는지 궁금해하도록 /
　　　　　　　　　　　　　　　　　　　　명사절 접속사 (보어 역할)
normally the selling point is / ④ what(→ that) the usefulness of
the technology / is obvious at first glance. // (단서) 뒤에 완전한 문장이 왔으므로
　　　　　　　　　　　　　　　　　　　　　　　명사절 접속사 that 자리임
일반적으로 매력은 ~이다 / 기술의 유용성이 / 첫눈에 분명하다는 것 //
　　　　　　　　　　　　　　　　　　　　수동태 동사
Shakespeare, / on the other hand, / is beloved / in part / because
단수 주어
the meaning of his works is not immediately obvious / and ⑤
　　　　　　　　　병렬 구조 (단수 동사)
requires some thought on the part of the audience. //
셰익스피어는 / 반면에 / 사랑받는다 / 부분적으로는 / 그의 작품의 의미가 즉각적으로 분명하지 않고 / 독자 측에서 어느 정도의 생각을 요구하기 때문에 //

- essentially (ad) 근본적으로　　　- metaphor (n) 은유
- linguistic (a) 언어적인　　　　　- passive (a) 수동적인
- propose (v) 제시하다　　　　　　- beggar (n) 구걸하는 사람
- cognitive (a) 인지적인　　　　　- engage (v) 사로잡다　　　- prose (n) 산문
- imposing (a) 강요[강압]적인　　　- artifact (n) 인공물
- forcefully (ad) 강력하게　　　　　- horizon (n) 지평선
- selling point 매력, 장점　　　　- at first glance 첫눈에
- immediately (ad) 즉각적으로

디지털 기술은 근본적으로 은유와 관련되어 있지만, 디지털 은유는 중요한 면에서 언어적 은유와 다르다. 언어적 은유는 독자가 은유에 의해 제시된 세계에 적극적으로 들어가도록 선택할 필요가 있다는 점에서 수동적이다. "시간은 구걸하는 자다"라는 셰익스피어의 은유에서 독자는 인지적인 노력 없이는 그리고 셰익스피어의 산문을 더 끌어들이지 않고는 은유를 이해할 것 같지 않다. 반면에 기술적 은유는 사용자의 의미의 지평을 강력하게 바꾸면서 능동적으로 일을 하는 디지털 인공물에서 그것이 실현된다는 점에서 능동적이다. (그리고 종종 강요적이다.) 기술적인 창작자는 일반적으로 그들의 잠재적인 독자에게 어떻게 은유가 작용하는지 궁금해하도록 요구할 여유가 없고, 일반적으로 매력은 기술의 유용성이 첫눈에 분명하다는 것이다. 반면에 셰익스피어는 부분적으로는 그의 작품의 의미가 즉각적으로 분명하지 않고 독자 측에서 어느 정도의 생각을 요구하기 때문에 사랑받는다.

왜 정답? ❀❀❀ [정답률 66%]

④ 관계대명사 what 뒤에 완전한 절이 왔다!

~ normally the selling point(주어) is(동사) / ④ ~~what~~(→ that)(명사절 접속사 that 필요) the usefulness of the technology is obvious at first glance.(완전한 2형식 문장) //

(단서) 밑줄이 선행사를 포함하는 관계대명사 what에 있으므로

(발상) 주격과 목적격 관계대명사 뒤에는 주어나 목적어가 빠진 불완전한 절이 와야 한다.

(해결) 하지만 what 뒤에 주어(the usefulness of the technology), 동사(is), 보어(obvious)가 이어지며 완전한 2형식 문장을 이룬다. 따라서 what을 명사절 접속사 that으로 바꿔야 한다.

(개념) 선행사를 포함하는 관계대명사 what은 불완전한 절을 이끈다.

왜 오답?

① 대명사는 앞에서 반복되는 명사를 찾아 수를 일치시킨다.

Digital technologies are essentially related to metaphors, / but digital metaphors(복수 주어) are(복수 동사) different from linguistic ① ones(= metaphors) / in important ways. //

문맥상 linguistic ones는 digital metaphors와는 다른 유형인 linguistic metaphors를 가리킨다. 따라서 metaphors를 대신하여 복수 대명사 ones가 알맞게 쓰였다.

② 전치사 뒤에는 명사에 해당하는 어구가 온다.

~ without cognitive effort / and without(전치사) further(부사) ② engaging(동명사) Shakespeare's prose. //

전치사 without 뒤에 명사에 해당하는 동명사 engaging이 알맞게 쓰였다.

③ 분사구문의 현재분사는 능동의 의미를 나타낸다.

Technological metaphors(주어), / on the other hand, / are(동사) active (and often imposing) / in the sense that they are realized / in digital artifacts that are actively doing things, / forcefully ③ changing(분사구문을 이끄는 현재분사) a user's meaning horizon. //

주절의 주어는 Technological metaphors이며 이것이 '강력하게 사용자의 의미의 지평을 변화시켰다(forcefully changing a user's meaning horizon)'는 능동의 의미이므로, 현재분사 changing이 알맞게 쓰였다.

⑤ 동사는 주어에 그 수를 일치시킨다.

~ because(부사절 접속사) the meaning of his works(단수 주어) is not immediately obvious / and ⑤ requires(병렬 구조) some thought on the part of the audience. //

because로 시작하는 부사절에서 단수 동사인 is와 requires가 병렬 구조를 이루고 있다. 수 일치를 해야 하는 핵심 주어는 단수인 the meaning이므로 requires는 알맞게 쓰였다.

구문 서술형

(정답) 한정적, 서술적

(해석) (1) 디지털 은유는 중요한 면에서 언어적 은유와 다르다.
(2) 기술의 유용성은 첫눈에 분명하다.

→ (1) 형용사 important가 명사 ways를 바로 앞에서 수식하므로 한정적 용법으로 쓰였다. (2) 형용사 obvious가 주어를 보충 설명하는 주격 보어로 쓰였으므로 서술적 용법으로 쓰였다.

K 06 정답 ② *의미 있는 일의 긍정적 영향

다음 글의 밑줄 친 부분 중, 어법상 틀린 것은? [3점]

It(가주어) would be hard to overstate(진주어) / how important meaningful work is(간접의문문(의문사+주어+동사)) / to human beings / — work ① that(주격 관계대명사) provides a sense of fulfillment and empowerment. //
과장해서 말하기도 어려울 것이다 / 의미 있는 일이 얼마나 중요한지를 / 인간에게 / 성취감과 권한을 제공하는 일 //

Those who('~한 사람들') have found deeper meaning in their careers / find(동사) their days much(비교급 강조 부사) more energizing and satisfying, /
자신의 직업에서 더 깊은 의미를 찾은 사람은 / 자신의 하루하루가 훨씬 더 활기차고 만족감을 준다는 것을 발견한다 /

and ② to count (→ count) their employment / as one of their greatest sources of joy and pride. // (단서) 접속사 and가 동사 find와 동사 count를 연결하는 병렬 구조임
그리고 자신의 직업을 꼽는다 / 기쁨과 자부심의 가장 큰 원천 중 하나로 //

Sonya Lyubomirsky, professor of psychology at the University of California(동격), / has conducted numerous workplace studies / ③ showing(현재분사) /
University of California의 심리학 교수인 Sonya Lyubomirsky는 / 수많은 업무 현장 연구를 수행했다 / 보여 주는 /

that(목적어절 접속사) when people are more fulfilled on the job, / they not only produce higher quality work and a greater output, / but also generally earn higher incomes. // (not only A but also B: A뿐만 아니라 B도)
사람이 직업에 더 많은 성취감을 느낄 때 / 그들은 더 질 높은 업무와 더 큰 성과를 만들어 낼 뿐만 아니라 / 일반적으로 더 높은 수입을 거둔다는 것을 //

Those most(사이에 who are 생략됨) satisfied with their work / ④ are also much more likely to(be likely to ~: ~할 가능성이 있다) be happier / with their lives overall. //
자신의 일에 가장 만족하는 사람은 / 또한 더 행복해할 가능성이 훨씬 더 크다 / 전반적으로 자신의 삶에 //

For her book *Happiness at Work*, / researcher Jessica Pryce-Jones conducted / a study of 3,000 workers in seventy-nine countries, /
자신의 저서 'Happiness at Work'를 위해 / 연구자 Jessica Pryce-Jones는 수행했다 / 79개 국가의 3,000명의 근로자에 대한 연구를 /

⑤ finding(분사구문을 이끄는 현재분사) / that those(복수 주어) who took greater satisfaction from their work / were(복수 동사) 150 percent more likely / to have a happier life overall. //
그리고 알아냈다 / 자신의 일로부터 더 큰 만족감을 갖는 사람이 / 가능성이 150퍼센트 더 크다는 것을 / 전반적으로 더 행복한 삶을 살 //

- overstate ⓥ 과장해서 말하다 • meaningful ⓐ 의미 있는
- human being 인간 • provide ⓥ 제공하다
- fulfillment ⓝ 성취감 • empowerment ⓝ 권한
- career ⓝ 직업, 경력 • energizing ⓐ 활기찬
- count ~ as … ~을 …라고 여기다 • employment ⓝ 직업, 고용
- psychology ⓝ 심리 • workplace ⓝ 업무 현장, 직장
- overall ad 전반적으로 • satisfaction ⓝ 만족

인간에게 의미 있는 일, 즉 성취감과 권한을 제공하는 일이 얼마나 중요한지는 아무리 강조해도 지나치지 않을 것이다. 자신의 직업에서 더 깊은 의미를 찾은 사람은 자신의 하루하루가 훨씬 더 활기차고 만족감을 준다는 것을 발견하고, 자신의 직업을 기쁨과 자부심의 가장 큰 원천 중 하나로 꼽는다. University of California의 심리학 교수인 Sonya Lyubomirsky는 사람이 직업에 더 많은 성취감을 느낄 때 그들은 더 질 높은 업무와 더 큰 성과를 만들어 낼 뿐만 아니라 일반적으로 더 높은 수입을 거둔다는 것을 보여 주는 수많은 업무 현장 연구를 수행했다. 자신의 일에 가장 만족하는 사람은 또한 전반적으로 자신의 삶에 더 행복해할 가능성이 훨씬 더 크다. 자신의 저서 'Happiness at Work'를 위해 연구자 Jessica Pryce-Jones는 79개 국가의 3,000명의 근로자에 대한 연구를 수행했고, 자신의 일로부터 더 큰 만족감을 갖는 사람이 전반적으로 더 행복한 삶을 살 가능성이 150퍼센트 더 크다는 것을 알아냈다.

왜 정답? ★★✧ [정답률 75%]

② 접속사로 연결되는 두 요소가 병렬 구조를 이루어야 한다!

주어

Those who have found deeper meaning in their careers / **find**
〈첫 번째 동사〉

their days much more energizing and satisfying, / **and** ②
〈등위접속사〉

두 번째 동사
~~to count~~ (→ count) their employment / as one of their greatest

sources of joy and pride. //

(단서) 접속사 and 뒤에 나오는 to부정사에 밑줄이 있으므로

(발상) to count와 병렬 구조를 이룰 만한 요소를 찾아본다.

(해결) 주어인 Those ~ their careers 뒤에 복수 현재형 동사 find가 있으므로 등위접속사 and로 연결되는 요소는 마찬가지로 복수 현재형 동사여야 한다. 따라서 부정사인 to count를 count로 고쳐야 어법상 알맞다.

(개념) 접속사 and, but, or로 연결되는 두 요소는 문장 성분이 같아야 한다.

왜 오답?

①that은 사물과 사람 모두를 선행사로 취할 수 있다.

It would be hard to overstate / how important meaningful
that의 선행사 주격 관계대명사
work is / to human beings / — work ① **that** provides a sense
주어가 없는 불완전한 절
of fulfillment and empowerment. //

관계대명사는 주어나 목적어가 빠진 불완전한 절을 이끈다. (개념)
밑줄 친 that 뒤에 오는 절은 주어가 없고 동사 provides가 곧바로 이어지는 불완전한 절이다. (단서)
work를 선행사로 하는 주격 관계대명사 that이 알맞게 쓰였다.

③ 현재분사는 명사를 수식할 수 있다.

Sonya Lyubomirsky, professor of psychology at the University

of California, / has conducted numerous workplace studies /
현재분사(studies 수식)
③ **showing** /[that when people are more fulfilled on the job,
showing의 목적어절
/ they not only produce higher quality work and a greater

output, / but also generally earn higher incomes.]//

현재분사는 명사를 수식하는 역할을 한다. 현재분사가 한 단어일 때는 수식하는 명사 앞에 위치하고 구의 형태일 때는 수식하는 명사 뒤에 위치한다. (개념)
showing 앞에 문장의 주어 Sonya Lyubomirsky와 동사 has conducted가 주어졌다. (단서)
여기서 showing은 앞의 studies를 수식하고 that 뒤의 목적어절을 수반하는 현재분사이다.
따라서 현재분사 showing이 알맞게 쓰였다.

④ 동사는 주어에 그 수를 일치시킨다.

복수 주어 관계대명사절(who are가 생략됨) 복수 동사
Those most satisfied with their work / ④ **are** also much more

likely to be happier / with their lives overall. //

주어를 꾸미는 수식어구와 상관없이 핵심 주어의 수에 동사의 수를 일치시킨다. (개념)
동사 are에 밑줄이 있으므로 (단서) 주어를 찾아서 수가 일치하는지 확인한다. (발상)
주격 관계대명사 who와 be동사 are가 생략된 관계대명사절 most satisfied with their work를 제외하면 핵심 주어인 Those가 남는다. Those는 복수이므로 be동사도 복수형 동사인 are를 쓰는 것이 적절하다. (해결)

⑤ 접속사와 주어를 생략하여 분사구문을 만들 수 있다.

전치사구: 제외하고 생각하기
For her book Happiness at Work, / researcher Jessica Pryce-

Jones conducted / a study of 3,000 workers in seventy-
분사구문을 이끄는 현재분사(= and she found)
nine countries, / ⑤ **finding** / [that those who took greater
finding의 목적어절
satisfaction from their work / were 150 percent more likely / to

have a happier life overall.]//

두 문장의 주어가 같을 때, 접속사가 있는 문장에서 접속사와 주어를 생략하고 동사를 분사 형태로 바꾸어 분사구문을 만들 수 있다. (개념)
주어 researcher Jessica Pryce-Jones와 동사 conducted를 포함하는 완전한 문장이 끝나고 콤마 뒤에 finding이 이어진다. (단서)
finding의 목적어절은 그녀가 발견한 연구 결과를 설명하기 때문에 finding 앞에 생략된 주어는 she라는 것을 알 수 있다.
따라서 콤마 바로 뒤에 있던 접속사 and와 주어 she를 생략하고 동사 found를 현재분사로 바꾼 finding이 적절히 쓰였다.

K 07 정답 ③ *인류 생활 방식의 변화와 문명의 탄생

다음 글의 밑줄 친 부분 중, 어법상 틀린 것은? [3점]

계속적 용법의 주격 관계대명사 수동태 동사
The hunter-gatherer lifestyle, / **which** can ① **be described** as
주절의 동사
"natural" to human beings, / **appears** to have had much / to

recommend it. //

수렵 채집 생활 방식은 / 인류에게 "자연스러운" 것으로 묘사될 수 있으며 / 많은 것(장점)이 있는 것으로 보인다 / 그것을 추천할 만한 //

단수 주어
Examination of human remains / from early hunter-gatherer
단수 동사
societies / ② **has** suggested /
유적 조사는 / 초기 수렵 채집 사회의 / 알려준다 /
목적어절 접속사
that our ancestors **enjoyed** abundant food, / obtainable without
병렬 구조
excessive effort, / and **suffered** very few diseases. //

인류의 조상들이 풍족한 식량을 누릴 수 있었고 / 과도한 노력 없이도 구할 수 있는 / 질병에 걸리는 일도 거의 없었다는 것을 //
명사절을 이끄는 의문사
If this is true, / it is not clear / **why** so many humans settled
분사구문
in permanent villages / and developed agriculture, / **growing**

crops and domesticating animals: /
이것이 사실이라면 / 분명하지 않다 / 왜 그렇게 많은 인류가 영구적으로 마을에 정착하여 / 농업을 발달시켰는지 / 농작물을 재배하고 동물을 기르면서 /
단서 부사구를 강조하는
「it is[was] ~ that」강조 구문   「it is[was] ~ that」 강조 구문
cultivating fields was hard work, / and **it was in farming villages**
부사구
/ ③ **what**(→ **that**) epidemic diseases first took root. //
밭을 경작하는 일은 힘든 일이었고 / 바로 농경 마을이었다 / 전염병이 처음 뿌리를 내린 곳은 //
부사절을 이끄는 복합 관계대명사 뒤에 be동사 생략
Whatever its immediate **effect** / on the lives of humans, / the
부사(동사 led 수식)
development of settlements and agriculture / ④ **undoubtedly**
본동사
led to / a high increase in population density. //
즉각적인 영향이 무엇이든 / 인간의 삶에 미치는 / 정착지와 농업의 발전은 / 의심의 여지 없이 이어졌다 / 인구 밀도의 높은 증가로 /
앞에 주격 관계대명사와 be동사 생략됨
This period, / **known as the New Stone Age**, / was a major

turning point in human development, /
이 시기는 / 신석기 시대로 알려진 / 인류 발전의 중요한 전환점으로 /

⑤ opening the way / to the growth of the first towns and cities, / and eventually leading to settled "civilizations." //
병렬 구조
길을 열었다 / 최초의 마을과 도시가 성장하도록 / 결국 정착된 "문명"으로 이어졌다 //

- hunter-gatherer ⓝ 수렵 채집인 • examination ⓝ 조사
- abundant ⓐ 풍부한 • obtainable ⓐ 획득할 수 있는
- excessive ⓐ 지나친, 과도한 • permanent ⓐ 영구적인
- domesticate ⓥ 길들이다, 재배하다 • cultivate ⓥ 경작하다
- take root 뿌리를 내리다 • immediate ⓐ 즉각적인
- density ⓝ 밀도 • civilization ⓝ 문명

수렵 채집 생활 방식은 인류에게 "자연스러운" 것으로 묘사될 수 있으며, 그것을 추천할 만한 많은 것(장점)이 있는 것으로 보인다. 초기 수렵 채집 사회의 유적 조사는 인류의 조상들이 과도한 노력 없이도 구할 수 있는 풍족한 식량을 누릴 수 있었고 질병에 걸리는 일도 거의 없었다는 것을 알려준다. 이것이 사실이라면, 왜 그렇게 많은 인류가 영구적으로 마을에 정착하여 농작물을 재배하고 동물을 기르면서 농업을 발달시켰는지는 분명하지 않다. 밭을 경작하는 것은 힘든 일이었고, 전염병이 처음 뿌리를 내린 곳은 농경 마을이었다. 인간의 삶에 미치는 즉각적인 영향이 무엇이든, 정착지와 농업의 발전은 의심의 여지 없이 인구 밀도의 높은 증가로 이어졌다. 신석기 시대로 알려진 이 시기는 인류 발전의 중요한 전환점으로, 최초의 마을과 도시가 성장하는 길을 열었고, 결국 정착된 "문명"으로 이어졌다.

왜 정답? ✿✿❀ [정답률 74%]

③ 부사구를 강조하는 「it is[was] ~ that」 강조 구문이다.

and로 연결되는 등위절: 제외하고 생각하기   「it is[was] ~ that」 강조 구문   강조를 받는 부사구
… cultivating fields was hard work, / and it was in farming villages / ③ what(→ that) epidemic diseases first took root. //
완전한 절을 이끄는 that 자리임

(단서) what에 밑줄이 있으므로

(발상) what이 의문사절이나 관계사절을 이끄는 것이 적절한지 확인해야 한다.

(해결) it was와 what 사이에 in farming villages라는 부사구가 왔고, what 뒤로는 주어 epidemic diseases와 동사 took root로 이루어진 완전한 절이 있다. 의문사절이나 관계사절을 이끄는 what은 불완전한 절만 이끌 수 있으므로, 여기에는 what 대신에, 부사구를 강조하는 「it is[was] ~ that」 강조 구문이 쓰이는 것이 적절하다. 따라서 what을 that으로 바꿔야 한다.

(개념) 「it is[was] ~ that」 강조 구문에서는 강조하고자 하는 어구를 it is[was]와 that 사이에 둔다.

왜 오답?

① 주어와 동사의 관계가 수동일 때 수동태 동사를 쓴다.

주어   계속적 용법의 주격 관계대명사   조동사의 수동태
The hunter-gatherer lifestyle, / which can ① be described as "natural" to human beings, / appears to have had much / to recommend it. //
본동사

관계사절의 수동태 동사인 be described에 밑줄이 있으므로 선행사와 동사가 수동의 관계인지 확인한다.
문맥상 관계사절의 선행사인 lifestyle이 인류에게 자연스러운 것으로 '묘사된다'는 것, 즉, 수동 관계를 나타낸다. (단서)
따라서 조동사 can 뒤에 be described가 오는 것은 어법상 적절하다.

② 동사는 주어에 그 수를 일치시킨다.

단수 주어
Examination of human remains / from early hunter-gatherer societies / ② has suggested / that our ancestors enjoyed
단수 동사   목적어절: 제외하고 생각하기
abundant food, / obtainable without excessive effort, / and suffered very few diseases. //

문장의 동사는 주어에 그 수를 일치시킨다. (개념)
동사가 「has +과거분사」 형태이고 단수 동사인 has에 밑줄이 있으므로 문장의 주어 역시 단수인지 확인한다.
주어인 Examination은 단수이므로 단수 동사 has가 적절하게 쓰였다.

④ 부사는 동사를 수식할 수 있다.

부사절: 제외하고 생각하기
Whatever its immediate effect / on the lives of humans, / the development of settlements and agriculture / ④ undoubtedly led to / a high increase in population density. //
주어   부사(동사 led 수식)
동사

부사는 동사, 형용사, 부사, 문장 전체를 수식하는 수식어로서, 동사의 앞이나 뒤에서 그 동사를 수식할 수 있다. (개념)
부사인 undoubtedly에 밑줄이 있으므로 주변에 부사가 수식할 만한 문장 요소가 있는지 확인한다.
동사 led를 앞에서 수식하며 '의심의 여지 없이'라는 뜻을 더하는 부사 undoubtedly가 적절하게 쓰였다.

⑤ 분사구문의 현재분사는 능동의 의미를 나타낸다.

주어   본동사
This period, / known as the New Stone Age, / was a major turning point in human development, / ⑤ [opening the way / to the growth of the first towns and cities, / and eventually leading to settled "civilizations."] //
분사구문을 이끄는 현재분사

주어(This period), 동사(was), 주격 보어(a major ~ development)의 완전한 절 뒤에 opening이 왔으므로, 분사구문을 이끄는 현재분사로 쓰였음을 알 수 있다.
분사구문의 생략된 주어는 This period(신석기 시대)이며 그 시기가 성장의 길을 '열었다'는 능동의 관계를 나타낸다. (단서)
따라서 현재분사 opening이 적절하게 쓰였다.
접속사가 이끄는 절의 접속사와 주어를 생략하고 동사를 분사로 바꾸어 분사구문을 만들 수 있다. 이때 주어와 동사의 관계가 능동이면 현재분사, 수동이면 「(being) + 과거분사」 형태로 쓴다. (개념)

K 08 정답 ⑤ *조직의 구조에 따른 갈등 관리

다음 글의 밑줄 친 부분 중, 어법상 틀린 것은?

단수 주어 「one of +복수 명사」: ~ 중 하나
From an organizational viewpoint, / one of the most fascinating examples / of how any organization may contain / many different types of culture /
단수 동사
조직의 관점에서 / 가장 매력적인 예시 중 하나는 / 어떻게 어느 조직이 포함할 수 있는지에 대한 / 많은 다른 문화 유형들을 /
① is to recognize the functional operations / of different departments within the organization. //
기능적 운영을 인식하는 것이다 / 조직 내 다른 부서들의 //

The varying departments and divisions / within an organization / will inevitably view any given situation / from their own biased and prejudiced perspective. //
과거분사(situation 수식)
과거분사(perspective 수식)
다양한 부서와 과는 / 조직 내 / 필연적으로 어떤 주어진 상황이라도 볼 것이다 / 그들 자신만의 편향적이고 편파적인 관점에서 //

A department and its members will acquire "tunnel vision" / which disallows them to see things / as others see ② them. //
주격 관계대명사   접속사(~대로) =things
한 부서와 그 구성원들은 '터널 시야 현상'을 갖게 될 것이다 / 그들이 (상황을) 볼 수 없게 하는 / 다른 이들이 그것들을 보는 대로 //
~ 자체, 바로 그 ~
The very structure of organizations / can create conflict. //
조직의 구조 자체가 / 갈등을 만들어낼 수 있다 //
The choice of ③ whether the structure is "mechanistic" or "organic" / can have a profound influence / on conflict management. //
명사절 접속사(~인지 아닌지)
구조가 '기계적'인지 또는 '유기적'인지의 선택은 / 깊은 영향을 미칠 수 있다 / 갈등 관리에 //

A mechanistic structure has a vertical hierarchy / with many rules, many procedures, and many levels of management / ④ involved in decision making. //

과거분사

기계적 구조는 수직적 위계를 갖는다 / 많은 규칙, 많은 절차 그리고 많은 수준의 관리를 가진 / 의사결정에 포함된 //

Organic structures are more horizontal in nature, / ⑤ which(→ where) decision making is less centralized / and spread across the plane of the organization. // **단서** 관계대명사는 완전한 절을 이끌 수 없음

관계부사

유기적 구조는 본래 더 수평적이고 / 여기서는 의사결정이 덜 중앙 집중화되고 / 조직 전반에 걸쳐 펼쳐진다 //

- organizational ⓐ 조직의
- fascinating ⓐ 매력적인
- operation ⓝ 운영
- division ⓝ (조직의) 분과
- prejudiced ⓐ 편견이 있는
- disallow ⓥ 허가하지 않다
- mechanistic ⓐ 기계적인
- profound ⓐ 깊은
- vertical ⓐ 수직의
- viewpoint ⓝ 관점
- functional ⓐ 기능상의
- varying ⓐ 가지각색의
- inevitably ⓐd 필연적으로
- acquire ⓥ 습득하다
- conflict ⓝ 갈등
- organic ⓐ 유기적인
- management ⓝ 관리
- procedure ⓝ 절차
- horizontal ⓐ 수평의

조직의 관점에서, 어떤 조직이 어떻게 많은 다른 문화 유형들을 포함할 수 있는 지에 대한 가장 매력적인 예시 중 하나는 조직 내 다른 부서들의 기능적 운영을 인식하는 것이다. 조직 내 다양한 부서와 과는 필연적으로 어떤 주어진 상황이 라도 그들 자신만의 편향적이고 편파적인 관점에서 볼 것이다. 한 부서와 그 구 성원들은 그들을 다른 이들이 그것들을 보는 대로 볼 수 없게 하는 '터널 시야 현상'을 갖게 될 것이다. 조직의 구조 자체가 갈등을 만들어낼 수 있다. 구조가 '기계적'인지 또는 '유기적'인지의 선택은 갈등 관리에 깊은 영향을 미칠 수 있 다. 기계적 구조는 많은 규칙, 많은 절차 그리고 의사결정에 포함된 많은 수준 의 관리를 가진 수직적 위계를 갖는다. 유기적 구조는 본래 더 수평적이고, 여 기서는 의사결정이 덜 중앙 집중화되고, 조직 전반에 걸쳐 펼쳐진다.

왜 정답? ★★★ [정답률 48%]

⑤ 관계대명사 뒤에 완전한 절이 왔다!

Organic structures are more horizontal in nature, / ⑤ which(→ where) decision making is less centralized / and spread across the plane of the organization. //

관계부사 자리임 / 병렬 구조 / 완전한 수동태 문장

단서 밑줄이 관계대명사 which에 있으므로

발상 뒤에 주어나 목적어가 빠진 불완전한 절이 이어질 것이다.

해결 그런데 which 뒤에 주어 decision making, 동사 is, 그리고 과거분사 less centralized와 spread가 병렬 구조를 이루는 완전한 수동태 문장이 이어진다. 따라서 관계대명사 which를 완전한 절을 이끄는 관계부사 where 또는 in which 등으로 바꿔야 한다.

개념 관계대명사는 앞에 수식받는 명사인 선행사가 있어야 하며, 불완전한 절을 이끈다.

왜 오답?

① 동사는 주어에 그 수를 일치시킨다.

전치사구: 제외하고 생각하기 / 단수 주어

From an organizational viewpoint, / one of the most fascinating examples / of how any organization may contain many different types of culture / ① is to recognize the functional operations of different departments within the organization. //

전치사구: 제외하고 생각하기 / 단수 동사

be동사 is에 밑줄이 있으므로 주어도 마찬가지로 단수인지, 다른 동사는 없는지 확인한다.
문장에 다른 동사는 없으며 핵심 주어는 단수 명사인 one이므로 단수 동사가 와야 한다. 따라서 단수 동사 is가 알맞게 쓰였다.
「one of + 복수 명사」 구조에서 핵심 주어는 단수 명사인 one이다. **개념**

② 대명사는 그것이 대신하는 명사에 수를 일치시킨다.

주격 관계대명사 / 목적격 보어 / to see의 목적어(복수 명사) / = things

[A department and its members will acquire "tunnel vision" / [which disallows them to see things [as others see ② them.]]]//

접속사(~대로)

대명사 them에 밑줄이 있으므로 **단서**
그것이 대신하는 명사를 찾아 수 일치 여부를 확인한다. **발상**
관계사절의 목적격 보어인 to see의 목적어는 복수 명사인 things이다.
'~대로'라는 의미의 접속사 as 뒤에도 마찬가지로 동사 see와 목적어 them이 있다.
의미상 them이 가리키는 것은 things이므로, 복수 대명사 them이 알맞게 쓰였다.

③ whether는 명사절을 이끈다.

명사절 접속사 / 주어 / 동사 / 주격 보어

The choice of ③ [whether the structure is "mechanistic" or "organic"] / can have a profound influence on conflict management. //

명사절 접속사 whether가 이끄는 절은 완전한 문장을 이루며, 문장에서 주어, 목적어, 보어의 역할을 한다. **개념**
whether가 이끄는 절이 전치사 of의 목적어로 쓰였으며, 주어는 the structure, 동사는 is, 주격 보어는 "mechanistic" or "organic"이므로 완전한 2형식 문장을 이룬다. 의미상으로도 '구조가 '기계적'인지 또는 '유기적'인지'를 나타내므로 명사절 접속사 whether가 알맞게 쓰였다.

④ 분사는 형용사처럼 명사를 수식할 수 있다.

본동사 / 전치사구

A mechanistic structure has a vertical hierarchy /[with many rules, many procedures, and many levels of management ④ involved in decision making.]//

과거분사(levels of management 수식)

과거분사는 형용사처럼 명사를 수식하며, 수동의 의미를 나타낸다. **개념**
문장의 본동사는 has이고 '~을 가진다'라는 의미로 쓰였다. 전치사 with의 목적어로 many rules, many procedures, many levels of management가 왔으며, involved는 이 중에서 levels of management를 수식한다. 해석상으로도 '의사결정에 포함된 많은 수준의 관리'라는 수동의 의미를 나타내므로 과거분사 involved가 알맞게 쓰였다.

자이 쌤's Follow Me! – 홈페이지에서 제공

K 09 정답 ③ *유사점을 가진 사람과 잘 지내는 성향

다음 글의 밑줄 친 부분 중, 어법상 틀린 것은?

주격 관계대명사

We usually get along best with people / who we think are like us. //

삽입절

우리는 보통 사람들과 가장 잘 지낸다 / 우리와 같다고 생각하는 //

In fact, / we seek them out. //
사실 / 우리는 그들을 찾아낸다 //

복수 주어

It's why / places like Little Italy, Chinatown, and Koreatown ① exist. //

복수 동사

그것이 이유이다 / 리틀 이탈리아, 차이나타운, 코리아타운과 같은 장소들이 존재하는 //

But / I'm not just talking about race, skin color, or religion. //
하지만 / 나는 인종, 피부색, 또는 종교만을 말하는 것이 아니다 //

주격 관계대명사

I'm talking about people / who share our values / and look at the world / the same way we ② do. //

look at the world를 받는 대동사

나는 사람들을 말하는 것이다 / 우리의 가치관을 공유하는 / 그리고 세상을 바라보는 / 우리와 같은 방식으로 //

As the saying goes, / birds of a feather flock together. //
속담에서처럼 / 같은 깃털을 가진 새가 함께 무리 짓는다 //

단서 a very common human tendency가 선행사이므로 선행사를 포함하는 관계대명사인 what은 쓸 수 없음

This is a very common human tendency / ③ what(→ that) is rooted in / how our species developed. //
이것은 매우 흔한 인간의 경향이다 / ~에 깊게 뿌리박혀 있는 / 우리 종(種)이 발전한 방식 //

Imagine / you are walking out in a forest. //
상상해 보라 / 여러분이 숲에 나가 걷는다고 //

-thing으로 끝나는 대명사는 형용사가 뒤에서 수식함
You would be conditioned / to avoid something unfamiliar or foreign / because there is a high likelihood / that ④ it would be interested in killing you. //
동격의 접속사
something unfamiliar or foreign을 가리킴
여러분은 조건화되어 있을 것이다 / 친숙하지 않거나 낯선 것을 피하도록 / 왜냐하면 가능성이 커서 / 그것이 여러분을 죽이는 데에 관심이 있을 //

사역동사 make의 목적격보어(동사원형)
Similarities make us ⑤ relate better / to other people / because we think / they'll understand us / on a deeper level / than other people. //
유사점(을 갖고 있는 것)은 우리가 마음이 더 잘 통하게 한다 / 다른 사람들과 / 왜냐하면 우리는 생각하기 때문이다 / 그들이 우리를 이해할 것이라고 / 더 깊이 있는 수준으로 / 다른 사람들보다 //

- get along with ~와 잘 지내다
- seek ~ out (특히 많은 노력을 기울여) ~을 찾아내다   • exist ⓥ 존재하다
- race ⓝ 인종   • religion ⓝ 종교   • value ⓝ 가치관
- feather ⓝ 깃털   • flock ⓥ (많은 수가) 모이다
- tendency ⓝ 경향   • be rooted in ~에 뿌리박고 있다
- conditioned ⓐ 조건부의   • unfamiliar ⓐ 친숙하지 않은
- likelihood ⓝ 가능성   • relate ⓥ 관련시키다. 마음이 통하다

우리는 보통 우리와 같다고 생각하는 사람들과 가장 잘 지낸다. 사실, 우리는 그들을 찾아낸다. 그것이 리틀 이탈리아, 차이나타운, 코리아타운과 같은 장소들이 존재하는 이유이다. 하지만 나는 인종, 피부색, 또는 종교만을 말하는 것이 아니다. 나는 우리의 가치관을 공유하고 우리와 같은 방식으로 세상을 바라보는 사람들을 말하는 것이다. 속담에서처럼, 같은 깃털을 가진 새가 함께 무리 짓는다. 이것은 우리 종이 발전한 방식에 깊게 뿌리박혀 있는 매우 흔한 인간의 경향이다. 여러분이 숲에 나가 걷는다고 상상해 보라. 친숙하지 않거나 낯선 것은 여러분을 죽이는 데 관심이 있을 가능성이 커 여러분은 그런 것을 피하도록 조건화되어 있을 것이다. 유사점(을 갖고 있는 것)은 우리가 다른 사람들과 마음이 더 잘 통할 수 있도록 하는데, 그들이 우리를 다른 사람들보다 더 깊이 있는 수준으로 이해할 것으로 생각하기 때문이다.

>왜 정답？ ★★★ [정답률 65%]
③ [주격 관계대명사] 이 문장에서 a very common human tendency는 is rooted로 이어지는 주격 관계대명사절 앞에 위치한 선행사이므로 선행사를 포함하는 관계대명사 what은 쓸 수 없다. 따라서 what을 사물을 선행사로 취하는 주격 관계대명사 that이나 which로 고쳐야 어법상 알맞다.

>왜 오답？
① [주어와 동사의 수 일치] places like Little Italy, Chinatown, and Koreatown이 why가 이끄는 절의 주어이고 복수 형태이므로 복수형 동사인 exist가 알맞게 사용되었다.
② [대동사] 의미상 do는 '세상을 바라보다'로 해석되어야 하므로 앞에 쓰인 동사구 look at the world를 대신해 do가 쓰인 것은 적절하다.

> * [대동사] 해결하기   KEY
> • 앞서 나온 동사가 일반동사일 때는 do동사가, be동사일 때는 be동사가 대동사로 쓰인다.
> • 대동사가 사용될 때는 동사의 시제와 주어와의 수 일치에 주의해야 한다.

④ [지칭대명사] it은 앞에 나온 something unfamiliar or foreign을 지칭하는 대명사이므로 어법상 적절하다.
⑤ [목적격보어] 사역동사 make의 목적어로 us, 목적격보어로 relate가 왔고, 사역동사의 목적격보어로 동사원형인 relate가 쓰인 것은 적절하다.

K 10 정답 ④ *아이를 향한 칭찬의 효과

다음 글의 밑줄 친 부분 중, 어법상 틀린 것은? [3점]

Although praise is one of the most powerful tools / available for improving young children's behavior, / it is equally powerful / for improving your child's self-esteem. //
= praise
칭찬은 가장 강력한 도구 중 하나이지만 / 어린아이들의 행동을 개선하는 데 사용할 수 있는 / 그것은 똑같이 강력하다 / 여러분의 아이의 자존감을 향상시키는 데에도 //

선행사를 포함하는 관계대명사
Preschoolers believe / what their parents tell ① them / in a very profound way. //
= preschoolers
미취학 아동들은 여긴다 / 그들의 부모가 그들에게 하는 말을 / 매우 뜻깊게 //

형용사적 용법(the cognitive sophistication 수식)
They do not yet have / the cognitive sophistication / to reason ② analytically / and reject false information. //
to reason 수식
그들은 아직 가지고 있지 않다 / 인지적 정교함을 / 분석적으로 추론하는 / 그리고 잘못된 정보를 거부하는 //

목적어절 접속사
If a preschool boy consistently hears from his mother / ③ that he is smart and a good helper, / he is likely to incorporate that information / into his self-image. //
'~할 가능성이 높다'
만약 미취학 소년이 그의 어머니로부터 계속 듣는다면 / 그가 똑똑하고 좋은 조력자라는 것을 / 그는 그 정보를 통합시킬 가능성이 높다 / 그의 자아상으로 //

동명사 주어(단수 취급)   주격 관계대명사
Thinking of himself as a boy / who is smart and knows how to do things / ④ being(→ is) likely to make him endure longer / in problem-solving efforts /
단서 문장의 주어인 Thinking에 대한 동사가 없음
make의 목적격 보어 ①
스스로를 어떠한 소년으로 생각하는 것은 / 똑똑하고 일을 어떻게 하는지 아는 / 그를 더 오래 지속하도록 만들 가능성이 높다 / 문제 해결 노력에 있어서 /

make의 목적격 보어 ②
and increase his confidence / in trying new and difficult tasks. //
그리고 그의 자신감을 증가시킬 (가능성이 높다) / 새롭고 어려운 일을 시도하는 것에 있어서 //

주어
Similarly, / thinking of himself as the kind of boy / who is a good helper / will make him more likely to volunteer / ⑤ to help with tasks / at home and at preschool. //
부사적 용법(목적)
마찬가지로 / 자신을 그런 부류의 소년으로 생각하는 것은 / 좋은 조력자인 / 그를 더 자원하도록 만들 것이다 / 일을 돕기 위해 / 집에서와 유치원에서 //

- praise ⓝ 칭찬   • equally ⓐⓓ 동등하게   • self-esteem ⓝ 자존감
- preschooler ⓝ 미취학 아동   • cognitive ⓐ 인지적인
- reason ⓥ 추론하다   • analytically ⓐⓓ 분석적으로
- consistently ⓐⓓ 지속적으로   • incorporate ⓥ 통합하다
- self-image ⓝ 자아상   • endure ⓥ 지속하다, 견디다

칭찬은 어린아이들의 행동을 개선하는 데 사용할 수 있는 가장 강력한 도구 중 하나이지만, 그것은 아이의 자존감을 향상시키는 데에도 똑같이 강력하다. 미취학 아동들은 그들의 부모가 그들에게 하는 말을 매우 뜻깊게 여긴다. 그들은 분석적으로 추론하고 잘못된 정보를 거부할 수 있는 인지적 정교함을 아직 가지고 있지 않다. 만약 미취학 소년이 그의 어머니로부터 그가 똑똑하고 좋은 조력자라는 것을 계속 듣는다면, 그는 그 정보를 그의 자아상으로 통합시킬 가능성이 높다. 스스로를 똑똑하고 일을 어떻게 하는지 아는 소년으로 생각하는 것은 그가 문제 해결 노력에 있어 더 오래 지속하도록 하고, 새롭고 어려운 일을 시도하는 것에 있어 그의 자신감을 증가시킬 가능성이 높다. 마찬가지로, 자신을 좋은 조력자인 그런 부류의 소년으로 생각하는 것은 그가 집에서와 유치원에서 일을 돕기 위해 더 자원하도록 만들 것이다.

>왜 정답？ ★★★ [정답률 58%]
④ 문장에 동사가 없다!

동명사 주어   선행사   주격 관계대명사
Thinking of himself as a boy / [who is smart and knows how to do things] / ④ being(→ is) likely to make him endure longer / in problem-solving efforts / and increase his confidence / in trying new and difficult tasks. //
단수 동사
동사 자리임
전치사구: 제외하고 생각하기
and로 연결: 제외하고 생각하기

K

정답 및 해설 141

単서 밑줄이 동명사 being에 있으므로

발상 동명사가 쓰일 자리가 맞는지 확인해야 한다.

해결 그런데 문장의 주어 Thinking에 대한 동사 동사가 빠져 있다. 앞에 나온 is는 who가 이끄는 주격 관계대명사절의 동사이므로 being이 문장의 동사 자리에 쓰였음을 알 수 있다.

being과 같은 준동사는 동사 역할을 할 수 없으므로, 단수 주어 Thinking에 맞는 단수 동사 is로 고쳐야 한다.

개념 주어와 동사는 문장의 필수 요소로서, 둘 중 하나라도 없으면 의미가 통하지 않으므로 문장이 될 수 없다.

>왜 오답?

① 대명사는 그것이 대신하는 명사에 수를 일치시킨다.

[Preschoolers believe / what their parents tell ① them / in a very profound way. //

대명사 them에 밑줄이 있으므로 그것이 대신하는 명사를 찾아 수 일치 여부를 확인한다.

문맥상 미취학 아동들은 그들의 부모가 '그들에게' 하는 말을 매우 뜻깊게 여기는 것이므로 preschoolers를 가리킨다.

따라서 복수 대명사 them은 어법상 적절하게 쓰였다.

② 부사는 준동사를 수식할 수 있다.

[They do not yet have / the cognitive sophistication / to reason ② analytically / and reject false information. //

부사 analytically에 밑줄이 있으므로 수식하는 대상을 찾아 부사의 수식을 받을 수 있는지를 확인한다.

문맥상 '분석적으로 추론하는' 인지적 정교함을 가지고 있지 않은 것이므로 to reason을 수식하고 있다.

to부정사는 준동사로, 부사의 수식을 받을 수 있으므로 analytically는 알맞게 쓰였다.

③ that이 목적어절을 이끌고 있다.

[If a preschool boy consistently hears from his mother / that he is smart and a good helper,] / he is likely to incorporate that information / into his self-image. //

명사절 접속사 that은 문장에서 명사 역할을 하는 절을 이끌며 '~하는 것'이라고 해석한다. 개념

문장의 동사인 hears 뒤에 that이 왔고, that 뒤에는 주어(he), 동사(is), 주격 보어(smart and a good helper)를 갖춘 완전한 절이 이어진다.

따라서 that은 hears의 목적어절을 이끄는 명사절 접속사로 적절하게 쓰였다.

⑤ 부사적 용법의 to부정사가 쓰였다.

[Similarly, / thinking of himself as the kind of boy / who is a good helper / will make him more likely to volunteer / ⑤ to help with tasks / at home and at preschool. //

주어(thinking ~ helper), 동사(will make), 목적어(him), 목적격 보어(more likely to volunteer)를 갖춘 5형식 문장이므로, to help는 수식어인 형용사나 부사의 역할을 할 것이다.

문맥상 일을 '돕기 위해' 더 자원하도록 만든다는 것이므로 목적을 나타내는 부사적 용법으로 to help는 적절하게 쓰였다.

K 11 정답 ⑤ *동물 캐릭터에 투영된 인간의 특징

다음 글의 밑줄 친 부분 중, 어법상 틀린 것은? [3점]

The most noticeable human characteristic / projected onto animals / is ① that they can talk / in human language. //
가장 눈에 띄는 인간의 특징은 / 동물에게 투영된 / 동물들이 대화할 수 있다는 것이다 / 인간의 언어로 //

Physically, / animal cartoon characters and toys / ② made after animals / are also most often deformed / in such a way as to resemble humans. //
신체적으로 / 동물 만화 캐릭터와 장난감은 / 동물을 본떠 만들어진 / 또한 변형되는 경우가 가장 흔하다 / 인간을 닮게 하는 그런 방식으로 //

This is achieved by ③ showing them / with humanlike facial features / and deformed front legs / to resemble human hands. //
이것은 그것들을 보여줌으로써 달성된다 / 인간과 같은 얼굴 특징과 / 변형된 앞다리로 / 사람의 손을 닮게 //

In more recent animated movies / the trend has been to show the animals / in a more "natural" way. //
더 최근의 만화 영화에서 / 추세는 동물을 묘사하는 것이었다 / 더 '자연스러운' 방식으로 //

However, / they still use their front legs / ④ like human hands / (for example, / lions can pick up and lift small objects, / with one paw), /
그러나 / 그것들은 여전히 앞다리를 사용한다 / 사람의 손처럼 / (예를 들어 / 사자가 작은 물체를 집어 들어 올릴 수 있는 것처럼 / 한 발로) /

and they still talk / with an appropriate facial expression. //
그리고 그것들은 여전히 이야기한다 / 적절한 표정을 지으며 //

A general strategy / that is used to make the animal characters more emotionally appealing, / both to children and adults, /
일반적인 전략은 / 동물 캐릭터를 더 감정적으로 매력적이게 만들기 위해 이용되는 / 아이와 어른 모두에게 /

⑤ are(→ is) to give them / enlarged and deformed childlike features. //
그것들에게 부여하는 것이다 / 확대되고 변형된 어린이 같은 특징을 //

- noticeable ⓐ 눈에 띄는 · characteristic ⓝ 특징, 특성
- project ⓥ 투영하다 · physically ⓐⓓ 신체적으로
- emotionally ⓐⓓ 감정적으로 · appealing ⓐ 매력적인
- enlarge ⓥ 확대하다 · childlike ⓐ 어린이 같은

동물에게 투영된 가장 눈에 띄는 인간의 특징은 동물이 인간의 언어로 대화할 수 있다는 점이다. 신체적으로도, 동물 만화 캐릭터와 동물을 본떠 만든 장난감은 또한 인간을 닮게 하는 방식으로 변형되는 경우가 가장 많다. 이것은 인간과 같은 얼굴 특징과 사람의 손을 닮게 변형된 앞다리를 가지고 있는 것으로 그것들을 보여줌으로써 달성된다. 더 최근의 만화 영화에서 추세는 동물을 더 '자연스러운' 방식으로 묘사하는 것이었다. 그러나 그것들은 (예를 들어 사자가 한 발로 작은 물체를 집어 들어 올릴 수 있는 것처럼) 여전히 사람의 손처럼 앞다리를 사용하고, 여전히 적절한 표정을 지으며 이야기한다. 동물 캐릭터를 아이와 어른 모두에게 더 감정적으로 매력적이게 만들기 위해 이용되는 일반적인 전략은 그것들에 확대되고 변형된 어린이 같은 특징을 부여하는 것이다.

>왜 정답? ✱✱❂ [정답률 66%]

⑤ 주어는 단수인데 복수 동사가 쓰였다!

[A general strategy / [that is used to make the animal characters more emotionally appealing, / both to children and adults,] / ⑤ are(→ is) to give them / enlarged and deformed childlike features. //

142 자이스토리 영어 독해 기본

(단서) 동사에 밑줄이 있으므로

(발상) 주어를 찾아 그 수가 일치하는지 확인한다.

(해결) that이 이끄는 관계대명사절을 제외하면 문장의 핵심 주어는 A general strategy로 단수이다. 따라서 동사는 are가 아니라 단수 동사인 is가 와야 한다.

(개념) 주어를 꾸미는 수식어구와 상관없이 핵심 주어의 수에 동사의 수를 일치시킨다.

왜 오답?

① 접속사 that 뒤에는 완전한 절이 온다.

┌ The most noticeable human characteristic / projected onto
│ (문장의 주어)
└ animals / is ① that they can talk / in human language. //
   (문장의 동사)   (주격 보어절을 이끄는 접속사) (완전한 1형식 문장)

접속사로 쓰인 that은 완전한 절을 이끈다. (개념)
that 뒤에 주어 they, 자동사 can talk로 구성된 완전한 1형식 문장이
이어진다. (단서)
주격 보어절을 이끄는 접속사 that이 알맞게 쓰였다.

② 주격 관계대명사와 be동사는 함께 생략할 수 있다.

┌ Physically, / animal cartoon characters and toys / ② [made
│   (문장의 동사)   (선행사)   (which[that] are)
└ after animals] / are also most often deformed / in such a way
  as to resemble humans. //

주격 관계대명사절의 동사가 be동사일 경우 주격 관계대명사와 함께 생략할 수
있다. (개념)
뒤에 문장의 진짜 동사 are deformed가 오므로 made는 주격 관계대명사절의
동사임을 알 수 있다. (단서)
동물을 본떠 '만들어진' 것이므로 수동태 동사 are made의 be동사 are와 주격
관계대명사 which[that]가 생략된 문장이다.

③ 전치사 뒤에는 명사에 해당하는 어구가 온다.

┌ This is achieved by ③ showing them / with humanlike facial
│   (전치사) (동명사)
└ features / and deformed front legs / to resemble human hands. //
                                        (수식어구: 제외하고 생각하기)

전치사의 목적어로 동사가 올 때는 동명사의 형태로 온다. (개념)
showing은 전치사 by의 목적어 자리에 왔다. (단서)
'~함으로써'라는 의미를 완성하면서 전치사 by의 목적어로 동명사 showing은
알맞게 쓰였다.

④ like가 전치사로 쓰였다.

┌ However, / they still use their front legs / ④ like human hands
│   (주어)   (동사)   (목적어)   (전치사)
│ / (for example, / lions can pick up and lift small objects, / with
│ one paw), / and they still talk / with an appropriate facial
│   (for example 뒤: 제외하고 생각하기)
└ expression. //

like는 동사와 전치사로 쓰일 수 있는데, 앞에 동사 use가 왔다. (개념)
use와 like 사이에 접속사가 없으므로 like는 동사가 아니라 전치사로 쓰였다. (단서)
'사람의 손처럼'이라는 의미를 완성하는 전치사 like는 알맞게 쓰였다.

K 12 정답 ④ — ⭐ 2등급 대비 [정답률 53%]

＊장기 이식자의 뇌사 판정 기준

다음 글의 밑줄 친 부분 중, 어법상 틀린 것은? [3점]

Some countries **have proposed** tougher guidelines / for
                (현재완료)
determining brain death / when transplantation — transferring
organs to others — / is under consideration. //
일부 국가는 더 엄격한 지침을 제안했다 / 뇌사를 결정하는 것에 대한 / 장기 이식, 즉 다른
사람에게 장기를 전달하는 것을 / 고려 중일 때 //

In several European countries, / there are legal requirements /
                                                    (주격 관계대명사)
which specify /
몇몇 유럽 국가에는 / 법적 요건들이 있다 / 명시하는 /
     (명사절 접속사)
① that a whole team of doctors must agree / over the diagnosis
of death / in the case of a potential donor. //
의사 팀 전체가 동의해야 한다고 / 사망 진단에 / 잠재적 기증자의 경우 //
      (단수 주어)
The reason for these strict regulations / for diagnosing brain
death in potential organ donors /
이러한 엄격한 규정들의 이유는 / 잠재적인 장기 기증자의 뇌사 진단에 대한 /
(단수 동사)   (명사적 용법(주격 보어))
② is, no doubt, to ease public fears / of a premature diagnosis of
brain death / for the purpose of obtaining organs. //
의심할 바 없이 대중의 두려움을 완화하기 위한 것이다 / 너무 이른 뇌사 진단에 대한 / 장기
확보를 위한 //
      (가주어)   (진주어)
But **it** is questionable / **whether** these requirements reduce
                                                = public suspicions
public suspicions / as much as they create ③ them. //
하지만 의문이다 / 이러한 요건들이 대중의 의심을 줄여 주는지는 / 그것을 만들어 내는 만큼 //
                                         (동격절 접속사)
They certainly maintain mistaken beliefs / **that** diagnosing brain
death / is an unreliable process ④ lack(→lacking) precision. //
그것들은 확실히 잘못된 믿음을 유지한다 / 뇌사 진단이 / 정확성이 결여된 신뢰하기 어려운
과정이라는 //
                         (단서) 명사 process를 수식하는 현재분사 자리임
As a matter of consistency, at least, / criteria for diagnosing the
deaths of organ donors / should be exactly the same / as for
                         (목적격 관계대명사)
those for ⑤ whom immediate burial or cremation is intended. //
적어도 일관성의 이유로 / 장기 기증자의 사망 진단 기준은 / 정확히 동일해야 한다 / 즉각적인
매장 또는 화장이 예정된 사람들에 대한 그것과 //

- propose ⓥ 제안하다 • tough ⓐ 엄격한, 힘든
- transplantation ⓝ 이식 • transfer ⓥ 전달하다, 옮기다
- legal requirement 법적 요건 • specify ⓥ 명시하다
- potential ⓐ 잠재적인 • regulation ⓝ 규정, 규제
- no doubt 의심할 바 없이, 틀림없는 • ease ⓥ 완화하다
- premature ⓐ 너무 이른 • obtain ⓥ 확보하다
- suspicion ⓝ 의심 • belief ⓝ 믿음, 신념
- unreliable ⓐ 믿을 수 없는 • precision ⓝ 정확성
- consistency ⓝ 일관성 • criterion ⓝ 기준(pl. criteria)
- burial ⓝ 매장

일부 국가는 장기 이식, 즉 다른 사람에게 장기를 전달하는 것을 고려 중일 때
뇌사를 결정하는 것에 대한 더 엄격한 지침을 제안했다. 몇몇 유럽 국가에는 잠
재적 기증자의 경우 의사 팀 전체가 사망 진단에 동의해야 한다고 명시하는 법
적 요건들이 있다. 잠재적인 장기 기증자의 뇌사 진단에 대한 이러한 엄격한 규
정들의 이유는 의심할 바 없이 장기 확보를 위한 너무 이른 뇌사 진단에 대한
대중의 두려움을 완화하기 위한 것이다. 하지만 이러한 요건들이 대중의 의심을
만들어 내는 만큼 그것을 줄여 주는지는 의문이다. 그것들은 뇌사 진단이 정확
성이 결여된 신뢰하기 어려운 과정이라는 잘못된 믿음을 확실히 유지시킨다. 적
어도 일관성의 이유로 장기 기증자의 사망 진단 기준은 즉각적인 매장 또는 화
장이 예정된 사람들에 대한 그것과 정확히 동일해야 한다.

왜 **2등급?** 정답 문장에 동사가 세 개나 있어서, 문장을 해석하며 잘못 쓰인 동사를 가려내야 하는 2등급 대비 문제이다. 문장에는 동사가 하나만 있어야 하므로, 동격절의 동사 is와 lack 중 어느 것이 잘못 쓰였는지를 유심히 확인해야 한다.

왜 정답?

④ **하나의 절은 하나의 동사만 가진다!**

They certainly maintain mistaken beliefs / that [diagnosing
(동격절 접속사) (주어)
brain death is an unreliable process ④ lack(→ lacking)
(동사) 명사 process를 수식하는 현재분사로 바뀌어야 함
precision.]//

(단서) 밑줄이 동사 lack에 있고, that절에 포함되어 있으므로

(발상) 동사 lack이 that절에서 유일한 동사의 역할을 하는지 확인해야 한다.

(해결) that절의 주어는 diagnosing brain death이고 동사는 is이므로, lack은 동사로 쓰일 수 없다. 문맥상 lack은 '정확성이 부족한 절차'라는 의미로 바로 앞의 명사 process를 수식하고 있다.
따라서 동사가 아니라 현재분사 lacking으로 고쳐야 어법상 적절하다.

(개념) 모든 절에는 하나의 동사만 있어야 하며, 본동사 외의 동사는 의미에 따라 준동사(동명사, to부정사, 분사)로 고쳐야 한다.

왜 오답?

① **접속사 that 뒤에는 완전한 절이 온다.**

전치사구: 제외하고 생각하기
In several European countries, / there are legal requirements /
(which의 선행사)
(주격 관계대명사) (명사절 접속사(specify의 목적어 역할))
which specify / ① that a whole team of doctors must agree /
(관계사절의 동사) (완전한 1형식 문장)
over the diagnosis of death / in the case of a potential donor. //

명사절 접속사 that은 완전한 문장을 이끌고, 문장에서 명사(주어, 목적어, 보어)의 역할을 한다. (개념)
관계사절 안에서 that은 목적어 역할을 하는 명사절을 이끌며, 주어와 동사로 이루어진 완전한 1형식 문장으로 이루어져 있다. (단서)
명사절 접속사로 that이 알맞게 쓰였다.

② **동사는 주어에 그 수를 일치시킨다.**

(문장의 주어)
The reason for these strict regulations / for diagnosing brain
(수식어구(제외하고 생각하기)) (동사) (명사적 용법(주격 보어))
death in potential organ donors / ② is, no doubt, to ease
public fears / of a premature diagnosis of brain death / for the
(수식어구(제외하고 생각하기))
purpose of obtaining organs. //

주어를 꾸미는 수식어구와 상관없이 핵심 주어의 수에 동사의 수를 일치시킨다. (개념)
문장의 핵심 주어는 단수 명사인 The reason이므로, be동사의 단수형인 is가 알맞게 쓰였다.

③ **대명사는 앞에서 반복되는 명사를 찾아 수를 일치시킨다.**

(가주어) (진주어(whether 절))
But it is questionable / whether these requirements reduce
(= these requirements) (주어 + 동사 + 목적어)
public suspicions / as much as they create ③ them. //
(= public suspicions)

대명사는 앞에서 언급된 명사를 반복하며, 반복되는 명사와 수를 일치시킨다. (개념)
문맥상 복수 대명사 them이 가리키는 것은 복수 명사인 public suspicions이다.
앞에 언급된 복수 명사를 받는 복수 대명사 them이 알맞게 쓰였다.

⑤ **목적격 관계대명사는 전치사의 목적어로도 쓰인다.**

As a matter of consistency, at least, / criteria for diagnosing the
deaths of organ donors / should be exactly the same / as for
(선행사) (목적격 관계대명사) (be intended for: ~이 예정되다)
those for ⑤ whom immediate burial or cremation is intended. //

관계대명사는 전치사의 목적어로 쓰일 수 있다. (개념)
목적격 관계대명사 whom이 전치사 for의 목적어로 쓰였다. (단서)
전치사와 선행사를 관계사절 뒤로 옮기면 원래의 문장인 immediate burial or cremation is intended for those가 완성된다.
전치사 for의 목적어로 목적격 관계대명사 whom이 알맞게 쓰였다.

K 13 정답 ④ ⭐ 2등급 대비 [정답률 51%]

*학습이 가능한 인공 지능

다음 글의 밑줄 친 부분 중, 어법상 틀린 것은? [3점]

(뒤에 목적격 관계대명사 생략)
You may have seen headlines / in the news / about some of the
(과거분사구(machines 수식))
things / machines powered by artificial intelligence can do. //
여러분은 헤드라인들을 본 적이 있을 것이다 / 뉴스에서 / 몇 가지 일에 대해 / 인공 지능으로 구동되는 기계가 할 수 있는 //

(목적격 관계대명사)
However, / if you were to consider all the tasks / ① that AI-
powered machines could actually perform, / it would be quite
mind-blowing! //
하지만 / 당신이 모든 작업을 고려한다면 / AI로 구동되는 기계가 실제로 수행할 수 있는 / 그것은 꽤 놀라울 것이다 //

(핵심 주어(단수)) (단수 동사)
One of the key features of artificial intelligence / ② is that it
enables machines to learn new things, / rather than requiring
programming / specific to new tasks. //
인공 지능의 핵심 특징 중 하나는 / 그것이 기계들이 새로운 것을 학습할 수 있게 한다는 것이다 / 프로그래밍을 필요로 하기보다는 / 새로운 작업에 특화된 //

Therefore, / the core difference / between computers of the
(복수 지시대명사(= computers)) (주격 보어절 접속사)
future and ③ those of the past / is that future computers will be
able to learn and self-improve. //
그러므로 / 핵심적인 차이점은 / 미래의 컴퓨터들과 과거의 그것들 간에 / 미래의 컴퓨터는 학습하고 스스로 개선할 수 있을 것이라는 점이다 //

In the near future, / smart virtual assistants will know more
about you / than your closest friends and family members ④
are(→ do). // (단서) 일반동사인 know를 대신해야 하므로 be동사 are는 쓸 수 없음
가까운 미래에 / 스마트 가상 비서는 여러분에 대해 더 많이 알게 될 것이다 / 여러분의 가장 가까운 친구나 가족이 아는 것보다 //

(간접의문문(의문사+주어+동사))
Can you imagine / how that might change our lives? //
여러분은 상상할 수 있는가 / 그것이 우리의 삶을 어떻게 변화시킬지 //

(가주어)
These kinds of changes are exactly / why it is so important ⑤
(진주어) (목적격 관계대명사)
to recognize the implications / that new technologies will have
for our world. //
이러한 종류의 변화들은 정확히 ~이다 / 영향을 인식하는 것이 매우 중요한 이유 / 새로운 기술들이 우리 세계에 미칠 //

- artificial intelligence 인공 지능(AI) · task ⓝ 과업, 작업
- perform ⓥ 수행하다 · mind-blowing ⓐ 놀라운, 감동적인
- feature ⓝ 특징, 특색 · core ⓐ 핵심적인 · virtual ⓐ 가상의
- implication ⓝ 영향, 결과

여러분은 인공 지능으로 구동되는 기계가 할 수 있는 몇 가지 일에 대한 헤드라인들을 뉴스에서 본 적이 있을 것이다. 하지만, AI로 구동되는 기계가 실제로 수행할 수 있는 모든 작업을 고려한다면, 그것은 꽤 놀라울 것이다! 인공 지능의 핵심 특징들 중 하나는 그것이 새로운 작업에 특화된 프로그래밍을 필요로 하기보다는 기계들이 새로운 것을 학습할 수 있게 한다는 것이다. 그러므로, 미래의 컴퓨터들과 과거의 컴퓨터들 사이의 핵심적인 차이점은 미래의 컴퓨터가 학습하고 스스로 개선할 수 있을 것이라는 점이다. 가까운 미래에, 스마트 가상 비서는 여러분에 대해 여러분의 가장 가까운 친구나 가족이 아는 것보다 더 많이 알게 될 것이다. 그것이 우리의 삶을 어떻게 변화시킬지 상상할 수 있는가? 이러한 종류의 변화들은 정확히 새로운 기술들이 우리 세계에 미칠 영향을 인식하는 것이 매우 중요한 이유이다.

왜 2등급? 동사에 밑줄이 있으면 수 일치를 물어보는 경우가 많으므로 주어와의 수 일치만 확인하고 넘어간다면 틀릴 수 있는 2등급 대비 문제이다. be동사나 조동사 do가 선택지로 지정된 경우에는, 대동사로 쓰인 건 아닌지도 반드시 함께 확인해야 한다.

왜 정답?

④ know를 대신하는 대동사로 are가 쓰였다!

In the near future, / smart virtual assistants <u>will know</u> more
주어　　　　일반동사
about you / than your closest friends and family members
　　　접속사
④ are(→ do). //
일반동사를 대신해야 함　　　　주어

단서 밑줄이 be동사인 are에 있으므로

발상 be동사가 쓰일 자리가 맞는지 확인해야 한다.

해결 의미상 스마트 가상 비서는 친구나 가족이 '아는' 것보다 더 많이 알게 될 것이라고 해석되어야 하므로 are는 앞에 나온 일반동사 know의 반복적인 사용을 대신하는 대동사로 쓰였음을 알 수 있다.
일반동사를 대신하는 대동사는 be동사가 아니라 do동사이므로, 복수 주어 your closest friends and family members에 맞는 복수 동사 do로 고쳐야 한다.

개념 앞에 나온 동사가 일반동사일 때는 do동사가, be동사일 때는 be동사가 대동사로 쓰인다.

왜 오답?

① 목적격 관계대명사는 목적어가 없는 불완전한 절을 이끈다.

However, / if you were to consider all the tasks / [① that
　　　　　　　　　　　　　　　선행사　　목적격 관계대명사
AI-powered machines could actually perform], / it would be
주어　　　　　　　동사
quite mind-blowing! //

단서 밑줄이 that에 있으므로

발상 명사절 접속사, 관계대명사, 관계부사 등 중에서 어느 것으로 쓰였는지를 확인해야 한다.

해결 that 뒤에 동사 could perform의 목적어가 없는 불완전한 절이 이어지므로 tasks를 수식하는 목적격 관계대명사로 that은 적절하게 쓰였다.

개념 관계대명사 that은 주어나 목적어가 빠진 불완전한 절을 이끈다.

② 동사는 주어에 그 수를 일치시킨다.

One of the key features of artificial intelligence / ② is that it
핵심 주어(단수)　　　　수식어구　　　　단수 동사
enables machines to learn new things, / rather than requiring
주격 보어절 접속사　　　　　제외하고 생각하기
programming / specific to new tasks. //

단서 동사 is에 밑줄이 있으므로

발상 주어를 찾아 수 일치 여부를 확인한다.

해결 문장의 핵심 주어는 One으로 단수 명사이므로 동사도 단수 동사인 is가 알맞게 쓰였다.

개념 주어를 꾸미는 수식어구와 상관없이 핵심 주어의 수에 동사의 수를 일치시킨다.

③ 지시대명사는 그것이 가리키는 것에 수를 일치시킨다.

As a matter of consistency, at least, / criteria for diagnosing the
deaths of organ donors / should be exactly the same / as for
those for ⑤ whom immediate burial or cremation is intended. //
선행사　목적격 관계대명사　　　　　　　be intended for: ~이 예정되다

단서 밑줄이 지시대명사 those에 있으므로

발상 those가 가리키는 대상을 찾아 그 수가 일치하는지 확인한다.

해결 문맥상 미래의 컴퓨터들과 과거의 '컴퓨터들' 간에 핵심적인 차이점을 이야기하는 것이므로 those가 지칭하는 대상은 computers로 복수이다. 따라서 복수대명사 those는 어법상 적절하게 쓰였다.

개념 앞에 나온 명사의 반복을 피하기 위해 단수는 지시대명사 that을, 복수는 지시대명사 those를 쓴다.

⑤ 명사적 용법의 to부정사가 쓰였다.

These kinds of changes are exactly / why it is so important
　　　　　　　　　　　　주격 보어절을 이끄는 의문사　가주어
⑤ to recognize the implications / that new technologies will
　　　　진주어
have for our world. //

단서 밑줄이 to recognize에 있으므로

발상 to recognize가 문장에 명사, 형용사, 부사 중에 어떤 역할을 하는지 확인한 후, 쓰임새에 맞게 쓰였는지 확인해야 한다.

해결 '영향을 인식하는 것'을 의미하는 to부정사구는 문장의 진주어이다. 형식적인 주어 자리에 가주어 it이 쓰인 문장으로 to recognize는 명사적 용법으로 적절하게 사용되었다.

개념 to부정사는 명사처럼 주어, 목적어, 보어 역할을 할 수 있다.

K 14 정답 ③　　　　　　★ 2등급 대비 [정답률 50%]

＊인간의 뇌의 크기와 지능

다음 글의 밑줄 친 부분 중, 어법상 틀린 것은? [3점]

The human brain, / it turns out, / has shrunk in mass / by about
　　　　　　삽입절
10 percent / since it ① peaked in size / 15,000 – 30,000 years ago. //
인간의 뇌는 / 밝혀졌다 / 부피가 줄어들었다는 것이 / 약 10퍼센트만큼 / 크기가 정점에 도달한 이래 / 15,000년에서 30,000년 전 //

One possible reason is / that many thousands of years ago /
　　　　　　　　　　주격 보어절을 이끄는 접속사
humans lived / in a world of dangerous predators /
한 가지 가능한 이유는 ~이다 / 수천 년 전에 / 인간은 살았다 / 위험한 포식자의 세계에서 /
world를 수식하는 관계부사
② where they had to have their wits / about them / at all times /
to avoid being killed. //
부사적 용법(목적)
그들의 '기지'를 발휘했어야 하는 / 그들(위험한 포식자)에 대한 / 항상 / 죽임을 당하는 것을 피하기 위해 //

Today, / we have effectively domesticated ourselves / and many
of the tasks of survival /
　　　　단서 문장의 주어가 many of the tasks of survival로 복수 주어이므로 복수형 동사가 와야 함
오늘날 / 우리는 우리 자신을 효율적으로 길들여 왔다 / 그리고 생존의 많은 과업이 /
from A to B: A부터 B까지
— from avoiding immediate death / to building shelters / to
obtaining food / — ③ has(→ have) been outsourced / to the
wider society. //
즉각적인 죽음을 피하는 것부터 / 은신처를 짓는 일과 / 음식을 얻어 내는 일까지 / 위탁되어 왔다 / 더 넓은 사회로 //

We are smaller / than our ancestors too, / and it is a characteristic
　　　　　　　　　　　　　　　　　가주어
/ of domestic animals / ④ that they are generally smaller / than
their wild cousins. //　진주어절을 이끄는 접속사
우리는 더 작기도 하다 / 우리의 조상보다 / 그리고 한 특징이다 / 가축의 / 가축이 일반적으로 더 작다는 것은 / 그들의 야생 사촌보다 //

None of this may mean / we are dumber / — brain size is not
　　　　　뒤에 목적어절을 이끄는 접속사 that 생략
necessarily an indicator / of human intelligence /
이것의 어떤 것도 의미하지는 않는다 / 우리가 더 어리석다는 것을 / 뇌 크기가 반드시 지표는 아니다 / 인간의 지능의 /

— but it may mean / that our brains today are wired up /
　　　　　　　　목적어절을 이끄는 접속사
differently, / and perhaps more efficiently, / than ⑤ those of our
　　　　　　　　　　　　　　　　brains를 받는 대명사
ancestors. //
그러나 그것은 의미할지도 모른다 / 오늘날 우리의 뇌가 타고났다는 것을 / 다르게 / 그리고 아마도 더 효율적으로 / 우리 조상들의 그것들보다 //

- shrink ⓥ 줄어들다　　• mass ⓝ 부피　　• peak ⓥ 정점에 달하다
- predator ⓝ 포식자　　• domesticate ⓥ 길들이다
- immediate ⓐ 즉각적인　　• shelter ⓝ 은신처　　• obtain ⓥ 얻다
- outsource ⓥ (회사가 작업·생산을) 외부에 위탁하다
- characteristic ⓝ 특징　　• domestic ⓐ 가정의
- indicator ⓝ 지표　　• intelligence ⓝ 지능

인간의 뇌는 15,000년에서 30,000년 전 크기가 정점에 도달한 이래 부피가 약 10퍼센트만큼 줄어들었다는 것이 밝혀졌다. 한 가지 가능한 이유는 수천 년 전에 인간은 죽임을 당하는 것을 피하기 위해 항상 그들(위험한 포식자)에 대한 그들의 기지를 발휘했어야 하는 위험한 포식자의 세계에서 살았다는 것이다. 오늘날, 우리는 우리 자신을 효율적으로 길들여 왔고 생존의 많은 과업이 — 즉각적인 죽음을 피하는 것부터 은신처를 짓는 일과 음식을 얻어 내는 일까지 — 더 넓은 사회로 위탁되어 왔다. 우리는 우리의 조상보다 더 작기도 한데, 가축이 그들의 야생 사촌보다 일반적으로 더 작다는 것은 가축의 한 특징이다. 이것의 어떤 것도 우리가 더 어리석다는 것을 의미하지는 않지만 — 뇌 크기가 반드시 인간의 지능의 지표는 아니다 — 그것은 오늘날 우리의 뇌가 다르게, 그리고 우리 조상들의 그것들보다 아마도 더 효율적으로 타고났다는 것을 의미할지도 모른다.

(왜) 2등급? 문법 사항이 어려워도 하나의 선택지가 눈에 띄는 정답인 다른 문제들과 달리, 출제율이 낮은 시제, 동사의 수 일치, 대명사의 수 일치까지 골고루 나와 확인하고 넘어가야 하는 요소들이 많은 2등급 대비 문제이다.

왜 정답?

③ 주어는 복수 명사인데 단수 동사가 왔다!

and로 연결된 등위절: 제외하고 생각하기

Today, / we have effectively domesticated ourselves / and
many of the tasks of survival / [— from avoiding immediate
　복수 주어　　　　　　　　　　　　　　수식어구
death / to building shelters / to obtaining food —] / ③ ~~has~~
복수 동사　　　　　　　　　　　　　　　　　　　주어가 복수 명사임
(→ **have**) been outsourced / to the wider society. //

(단서) 밑줄이 동사 has에 있으므로
(발상) 주어를 찾아 수 일치 여부를 확인한다.
(해결) and로 연결된 두 번째 절의 핵심 주어는 many of the tasks로 복수 명사이다. 따라서 has를 복수 동사 have로 고쳐야 한다.
(개념) 주어를 꾸미는 수식어구와 상관없이 핵심 주어의 수에 동사의 수를 일치시킨다.

왜 오답?

① 과거 시제를 나타낼 때 과거 동사를 쓴다.

주절: 제외하고 생각하기

The human brain, / it turns out, / has shrunk in mass / by
about 10 percent / since it ① **peaked** in size / **15,000 – 30,000**
　　　　　　　　　　　　　과거 시제 동사　　　　　과거 시점을 나타내는 부사구
years ago. //

(단서) 밑줄이 과거 시제를 나타내는 동사 peaked에 있으므로
(발상) 문장의 시제가 과거 시제가 맞는지 확인해야 한다.
(해결) 이 문장은 15,000년에서 30,000년 전이라는 과거 시점을 이야기하고 있으므로 과거 동사 peaked를 쓰는 것은 알맞다.
(개념) 과거의 동작이나 상태, 습관 등은 동사의 과거형으로 과거시제를 나타낸다.

② 관계부사 where는 완전한 절을 이끈다.

One possible reason is / that many thousands of years
ago / humans lived / in a world of dangerous predators /
　　　　　　　　　　　　　　　　장소의 선행사
[② **where** they had to have their wits / about them / at all
　　　관계부사　　　완전한 절(주어+동사+목적어)
times / to avoid being killed]. //

(단서) 밑줄이 관계부사 where에 있으므로
(발상) 앞에 장소의 선행사가 있고, 뒤에 완전한 절이 이어지는지 확인한다.
(해결) 뒤에 주어 they, 동사 had to have, 목적어 their wits로 구성된 완전한 3형식 문장이 이어지고, 앞에는 장소를 의미하는 선행사 a world of dangerous predators가 있다.
따라서 관계부사 where는 적절하게 쓰였다.
(개념) 관계부사는 뒤에 완전한 절을 이끌며, 선행사에 따라 다른 관계부사가 쓰인다.

④ that은 진주어절을 이끄는 접속사로 쓰일 수 있다.

and로 연결된 등위절: 제외하고 생각하기

We are smaller / than our ancestors / too, / and **it** is a
　　　　　　　　　　　　　　　　　　　　　　　　　　　가주어
characteristic / of domestic animals / ④ **that** they are generally
　완전한 절(주어+동사+주격 보어)　　　진주어절 접속사
smaller / than their wild cousins. //

(단서) 밑줄이 있는 that은 명사절 접속사, 관계대명사, 관계부사 등 여러 가지 역할을 하므로
(발상) 어떤 역할로 쓰였는지 that 앞뒤를 잘 살펴야 한다.
(해결) 주어 자리에 it이 왔고, 문맥상 가주어이다. 따라서 뒤에 온 that은 진주어절을 이끄는 명사절 접속사로 알맞게 사용되었다.
(개념) that절이 주어일 때 주어 자리에 가주어 it을 쓰고 진주어(that절)는 문장의 뒷부분으로 보낼 수 있다.

⑤ 대명사는 그것이 가리키는 명사에 수 일치시켜야 한다.

but으로 연결된 등위절: 제외하고 생각하기

None of this may mean / we are dumber / — brain size is not
necessarily an indicator / of human intelligence — / but it may
mean / that our **brains** today are wired up / differently, / and
perhaps more efficiently, / than ⑤ **those** of our ancestors. //
　　　　　　　　　　　　　　　　오늘날 우리의 '뇌'와 조상의 '그것'을 비교함

(단서) 밑줄이 지시대명사 those에 있으므로
(발상) 대명사가 가리키는 대상을 찾아 그 수가 일치하는지 확인한다.
(해결) 문맥상 오늘날 우리의 '뇌'와 조상의 '뇌'를 비교하고 있다. 따라서 those가 받는 것은 앞에 나온 복수 명사인 brains이므로 those는 어법상 알맞다.
(개념) 앞에 나온 명사의 반복을 피하기 위해 단수는 that, 복수는 those 지시대명사를 쓴다.

K 15 정답 ④ ──────── ⭐ 1등급 대비 [정답률 48%]

*Monday Morning Quarterback

다음 글의 밑줄 친 부분 중, 어법상 틀린 것은?

뒤에 관계부사 why가 생략됨
There is a **reason** / the title "Monday Morning Quarterback"
exists. //
이유가 있다 / 'Monday Morning Quarterback'이라는 이름이 존재하는 //
　　　　　　　　　　　　　　　　　　　　　현재분사(fans 수식)
Just read the comments on social media / from fans **discussing**
the weekend's games, /
소셜 미디어의 댓글만 읽어 보아라 / 주말 경기에 대해 토론하는 팬들의 /
　　　　　　　　　　　　　　　　　간접의문문
and you quickly see / **how many people believe** / they could
play, coach, and manage sport teams / more ① **successfully** /
than those on the field. //　　　　동사(could play, coach, manage)를 수식하는 부사
그러면 여러분은 금방 알 수 있다 / 얼마나 많은 사람들이 믿는지 / 자신이 경기를 뛰고, 감독하고, 스포츠팀을 관리할 수 있다고 / 더 성공적으로 / 경기장에 있는 사람들보다 //

This goes for the boardroom as well. //
이것은 이사회실에서도 마찬가지이다 //

Students and professionals / with years of training and specialized degrees / in sport business / may also find themselves
목적어(재귀대명사)
② being given advice /
목적격 보어(진행형 수동태)
학생들과 전문가들은 / 수년간의 훈련을 받고 전문적인 학위를 가진 / 스포츠 사업에서 / 또한 충고를 듣고 있는 자신을 발견할지도 모른다 /

on how to do their jobs / from friends, family, or even total strangers / without any expertise. //
어떻게 자신의 일을 해야 하는지에 대한 / 친구들, 가족, 혹은 심지어 완전히 낯선 사람들로부터 / 전문 지식이 전혀 없는 //

Executives in sport management / ③ have decades of knowledge
핵심 주어(복수)   복수 동사
and experience / in their respective fields. //
스포츠 경영 임원진들은 / 수십 년의 지식과 경험을 가지고 있다 / 자신의 각 분야에서 //

However, / many of them face criticism / from fans and
단서 telling의 행위자와 대상이 서로 다름
community members / telling ④ themselves(→ them) / how to
                      현재분사(fans and community members 수식)
run their business. //
하지만 / 그들 중 많은 사람들이 비난에 직면한다 / 팬들과 지역 사회 구성원들로부터의 / 그들에게 알려주는 / 그들의 사업 운영 방식을 /

Very few people tell their doctor / how to perform surgery / or
                    간접목적어   직접목적어
their accountant / how to prepare their taxes, /
간접목적어   직접목적어
자신의 의사에게 알려 주는 사람은 거의 없다 / 수술하는 방법을 / 또는 회계사(에게) / 자신의 세금을 준비하는 방법을 /

but many people provide feedback / on ⑤ how sport
                                전치사   간접의문문
organizations should be managed. //
그러나 많은 사람들이 피드백을 제공한다 / 스포츠 조직이 어떻게 관리되어야 하는지에 대한 //

- exist ⓥ 존재하다   • professional ⓝ 전문가   • degree ⓝ 학위
- expertise ⓝ 전문 지식   • executive ⓝ 경영진, 간부
- decade ⓝ 10년   • respective ⓐ 각자의
- criticism ⓝ 비판, 비난   • surgery ⓝ 수술
- accountant ⓝ 회계사   • organization ⓝ 조직

'Monday Morning Quarterback'이라는 이름이 존재하는 이유가 있다. 주말 경기에 대해 토론하는 팬들의 소셜 미디어의 댓글만 읽어봐도 여러분은 자신이 경기장에 있는 사람들보다 더 성공적으로 경기를 뛰고, 감독하고, 스포츠팀을 관리할 수 있다고 얼마나 많은 사람들이 믿는지 금방 알 수 있다. 이것은 이사회실에서도 마찬가지이다. 스포츠 사업에서 수년간의 훈련을 받고 전문적인 학위를 가진 학생들과 전문가들 또한 친구들, 가족, 혹은 전문 지식이 전혀 없는 심지어 완전히 낯선 사람들로부터 어떻게 자신의 일을 해야 하는지에 대한 충고를 듣고 있는 자신을 발견할지도 모른다. 스포츠 경영 임원진들은 자신의 각 분야에서 수십 년의 지식과 경험을 가지고 있다. 하지만, 그들 중 많은 사람들이 그들에게 그들의 사업 운영 방식을 알려주는 팬들과 지역 사회 구성원들로부터의 비난에 직면한다. 자신의 의사에게 수술하는 방법을 알려주거나 자신의 회계사에게 자신의 세금을 준비하는 방법을 알려주는 사람은 거의 없지만, 많은 사람들이 스포츠 조직이 어떻게 관리되어야 하는지에 대한 피드백은 제공한다.

왜 1등급? 분사가 나타내는 행위를 누가 하고 있는지, 누가 그 행위의 대상인지를 구분하며 재귀대명사의 적절한 쓰임을 가려내야 하는 1등급 대비 문제이다. 문장에 many of them과 fans and community members라는 두 집단이 나오므로, 문장을 정확히 해석하여 행위자와 대상을 구분해야 한다.

> 왜 정답?
④ telling의 행위자와 대상이 다르다!

However, / many of them face criticism / from fans and
              telling의 대상
community members / [telling ④ themselves(→ them) / how
telling의 행위자   현재분사
                                    many of them을 가리켜야 함
to run their business]. //

K

> 왜 오답?
① 부사는 동사를 수식할 수 있다.
and로 연결된 절: 제외하고 생각하기
Just read the comments on social media / from fans discussing the weekend's games, / and you quickly see / how many people believe / they could play, coach, and manage sport teams / more ① successfully / than those on the field.
                        부사   동사(구)

단서 밑줄이 재귀대명사 themselves에 있고 앞에 telling이 있으므로
발상 재귀적 용법의 재귀대명사로 맞게 쓰였는지 확인해야 한다.
해결 그런데 문맥상 현재분사 telling의 행위자는 '팬들과 지역 사회 구성원들'이고 telling의 대상은 '그들 중 많은 사람들'로 같지 않다. 따라서 재귀대명사가 아니라 일반 대명사인 them으로 고쳐야 어법상 적절하다.
개념 동사의 행위가 주어에게 가해질 때(주어 = 목적어) 목적어로 재귀대명사를 쓴다.

단서 부사 successfully에 밑줄이 있으므로 발상 수식하는 대상을 찾아 부사의 수식을 받을 수 있는지를 확인한다.
해결 문맥상 '더 성공적으로 경기를 뛰고, 감독하고, 스포츠팀을 관리한다'는 것이므로 동사구 could play, coach, and manage를 수식하는 successfully는 적절하게 쓰였다.
개념 부사는 동사, 형용사, 다른 부사, 문장 전체를 수식할 수 있다.

② 수동의 관계에는 「be+p.p.」 형태를 사용한다.
                        주어
Students and professionals / with years of training and specialized degrees / in sport business / may also find
                                                                              동사
themselves ② being given advice / on how to do their jobs
목적어   목적격 보어
/ from friends, family, or even total strangers / without any
expertise. //
전치사구: 제외하고 생각하기

단서 밑줄이 수동의 의미를 나타내는 being given에 있으니까
발상 수식을 하는 명사와의 관계가 수동일 것이다.
해결 find는 지각동사와 마찬가지로 진행 중인 순간을 나타내기 위해 목적격 보어 자리에 현재분사를 쓸 수 있다. 따라서 충고를 '듣고 있는' 자신을 발견한다는 의미로 being given이 목적격 보어 자리에 온 것은 적절하다.
개념 수동 관계를 나타내는 「be+p.p.」는 be동사를 being이나 been으로 바꾸어 진행형이나 완료형으로 나타낼 수 있다.

③ 동사는 주어에 그 수를 일치시킨다.
핵심 주어(복수)   수식어구   복수 동사
Executives in sport management / ③ have decades of knowledge and experience / in their respective fields. //
                                                              목적어

단서 동사 have에 밑줄이 있으므로
발상 주어를 찾아 수 일치 여부를 확인한다.
해결 문장의 핵심 주어는 Executives로 복수 명사이므로 동사도 복수 동사인 have가 알맞게 쓰였다.
개념 주어를 꾸미는 수식어구와 상관없이 핵심 주어의 수에 동사의 수를 일치시킨다.

⑤ 간접의문문은 명사 역할을 한다.
but으로 연결된 절: 제외하고 생각하기
Very few people tell their doctor / how to perform surgery / or their accountant / how to prepare their taxes, / but many
                                                                              주어
people provide feedback / on ⑤ how sport organizations
      동사   목적어   전치사   전치사의 목적어(간접의문문)
should be managed. //

(단서) 의문사 how에 밑줄이 있으므로

(발상) 명사절을 이끄는 간접의문문인지를 확인한다.

(해결) 의문사 how가 전치사 on 뒤의 목적어 자리에서 주어(sport organizations), 동사(should be managed)로 이루어진 명사절을 이끌고 있다. 따라서 how는 알맞게 쓰였다.

(개념) 명사절의 역할을 하는 의문문을 간접의문문이라고 하는데, 「의문사+주어+동사」 순서로 쓴다.

K 16 정답 ④ — ★ 1등급 대비 [정답률 40%]

*식품 속 미네랄의 감소

다음 글의 밑줄 친 부분 중, 어법상 틀린 것은? [3점]

The reduction of minerals in our food / is the result of using pesticides and fertilizers / ① that kill off beneficial bacteria, earthworms, and bugs / in the soil /
우리의 식품 속 미네랄의 감소는 / 살충제와 비료를 사용하는 것의 결과이다 / 이로운 박테리아, 지렁이 그리고 벌레를 죽이는 / 토양에 있는 /

that create many of the essential nutrients / in the first place / and prevent the uptake of nutrients into the plant. //
많은 필수 영양소를 만들어 내는 / 우선적으로 / 그리고 식물로의 영양소 흡수를 막는 //

Fertilizing crops with nitrogen and potassium / ② has led to declines / in magnesium, zinc, iron and iodine. //
농작물에 질소와 칼륨으로 비료를 주는 것은 / 감소로 이어져 왔다 / 마그네슘, 아연, 철 그리고 아이오딘의 //

For example, / there has been on average about a 30% decline / in the magnesium content of wheat. //
예를 들어 / 평균적으로 약 30퍼센트의 감소가 있었다 / 밀의 마그네슘 함량에서 //

This is partly due to potassium ③ being a blocker / against magnesium absorption / by plants. //
이는 부분적으로 포타슘이 방해물이 되기 때문이다 / 마그네슘 흡수에 / 식물에 의한 //

Lower magnesium levels in soil / also ④ occurring(→ occur) with acidic soils / and around 70% of the farmland on earth / is now acidic. //
단서: 주어 Lower magnesium levels in soil에 대한 동사가 없음
토양의 더 낮은 마그네슘 수치는 / 산성 토양에서도 나타난다 / 그리고 지구상에 있는 농지의 약 70퍼센트가 / 현재 산성이다 //

Thus, / the overall characteristics of soil / determine the accumulation of minerals / in plants. //
따라서 / 토양의 전반적인 특성은 / 미네랄의 축적을 결정한다 / 식물 속 //

Indeed, nowadays / our soil is less healthy / and so are the plants ⑤ grown on it. //
실제로 오늘날 / 우리의 토양은 덜 건강하다 / 그리고 그 위에서 길러진 식물도 그러하다 //

- reduction ⓝ 감소 · mineral ⓝ 미네랄 · fertilizer ⓝ 비료
- beneficial ⓐ 유익한 · earthworm ⓝ 지렁이 · bug ⓝ 벌레
- soil ⓝ 토양 · essential ⓐ 필수적인 · nutrient ⓝ 영양소
- in the first place 우선적으로 · uptake ⓝ 흡수
- fertilize ⓥ 비료를 주다 · nitrogen ⓝ 질소 · potassium ⓝ 칼륨
- zinc ⓝ 아연 · iron ⓝ 철 · on average 평균적으로
- content ⓝ 내용물, 함량 · wheat ⓝ 밀 · blocker ⓝ 방해물
- absorption ⓝ 흡수 · acidic ⓐ 산성의 · farmland ⓝ 농지
- characteristic ⓝ 특징, 특성 · determine ⓥ 결정하다
- accumulation ⓝ 축적

우리의 식품 속 미네랄의 감소는 우선적으로 많은 필수 영양소를 만들어 내는 토양에 있는 이로운 박테리아, 지렁이 그리고 벌레를 죽이고 식물로의 영양소 흡수를 막는 살충제와 비료를 사용하는 것의 결과이다. 농작물에 질소와 칼륨으로 비료를 주는 것은 마그네슘, 아연, 철 그리고 아이오딘의 감소로 이어져 왔다.

예를 들어 밀의 마그네슘 함량에서 평균적으로 약 30퍼센트의 감소가 있었다. 이는 부분적으로 포타슘이 식물에 의한 마그네슘 흡수에 방해물이 되기 때문이다. 토양의 더 낮은 마그네슘 수치는 산성 토양에서도 나타나는데 지구상에 있는 농지의 약 70퍼센트가 현재 산성이다. 따라서 토양의 전반적인 특성은 식물 속 미네랄의 축적을 결정한다. 실제로 오늘날 우리의 토양은 덜 건강하고 그 위에서 길러진 식물도 그러하다.

(왜 1등급?) 문장의 동사 자리에 준동사가 온 정답 선택지 이외에도, 전치사와 동명사 사이에 의미상의 주어가 삽입되어 어법을 파악하기 어려운 함정 선택지가 포함된 1등급 대비 문제이다. 문법적 판단 외에도 문맥상 해석이 자연스러운지도 반드시 확인해야 한다.

왜 정답?

④ 문장에 동사가 없다!

(Lower magnesium levels in soil / also ④ occurring(→ occur)
복수 주어 / 동사 자리임 / 복수 동사
with acidic soils) / and (around 70% of the farmland on earth /
and로 연결된 등위절
is now acidic). //

(단서) 밑줄이 -ing 형태인 occurring에 있으므로

(발상) 동명사 또는 현재분사로 쓰였을 것이다.

(해결) 그런데 이 문장에서는 주어 Lower magnesium levels in soil에 대한 동사가 없다. 준동사는 동사 역할을 할 수 없으므로 occurring을 복수 주어에 맞는 복수 동사 occur로 고쳐야 한다.

(개념) 주어와 동사는 문장의 필수 요소로서, 둘 중 하나라도 없으면 의미가 통하지 않으므로 문장이 될 수 없다.

왜 오답?

① 관계대명사절에서 주어 역할을 하는 that은 주격 관계대명사이다.

The reduction of minerals in our food / is the result of using
선행사 / 주격 관계대명사 / 선행사
pesticides and fertilizers / ① [that kill off beneficial bacteria,
병렬 구조(관계사절의 동사)
earthworms, and bugs / in the soil / [that create many of the
주격 관계대명사
essential nutrients / in the first place] / and prevent the uptake
of nutrients into the plant]. //

(단서) 접속사나 관계사로 모두 쓰일 수 있는 that에 밑줄이 있으니까

(발상) 명사절 접속사, 관계대명사, 관계부사 중에서 어느 것으로 쓰였는지를 확인해야 한다.

(해결) 뒤에 동사 kill off가 이어지는 것으로 보아 선행사 pesticides and fertilizers를 수식하는 주격 관계대명사로 쓰였다는 것을 알 수 있다.

(개념) 관계대명사는 선행사와 선행사가 관계대명사절에서 하는 역할에 따라 주격, 목적격, 소유격 관계대명사로 나뉜다.

② 주어와 동사는 수 일치되어야 한다.

Fertilizing crops with nitrogen and potassium / ② has led to
단수 주어(동명사구) / 단수 동사
declines / in magnesium, zinc, iron and iodine. //

(단서) 동사 has에 밑줄이 있으니까

(발상) 주어를 찾아 수 일치 여부를 확인해야 한다.

(해결) 주어가 Fertilizing crops로 동명사구이다. 동명사구는 단수 취급하므로 단수 동사 has가 쓰인 것은 어법상 알맞다.

(개념) to부정사(구), 동명사(구), 명사절은 단수 취급한다.

③ 전치사의 목적어로 동명사 형태가 온다.

┌ This is partly due to potassium ③ being a blocker / against
│   전치사   being의 의미상의 주어   전치사의 목적어(동명사구)
└ magnesium absorption / by plants. //

(단서) 밑줄이 -ing 형태인 being에 있으므로

(발상) 동명사 또는 현재분사로 쓰였을 것이다.

(해결) being은 전치사 due to의 목적어 자리에 왔고, potassium은 being의
의미상 주어로 쓰였다.
전치사의 목적어로 동사가 올 때는 동명사의 형태로 와야 하므로 being이
전치사 due to의 목적어로 알맞게 사용되었다.

(개념) 전치사의 목적어로 동사가 올 때:「동사원형+-ing」의 동명사 형태로 옴

⑤ 주격 관계대명사절에서「주격 관계대명사 + be동사」는 생략할 수 있다.

┌ Indeed, / nowadays our soil is less healthy / and so are the
│   선행사
└ plants ⑤ [grown on it]. //
          과거분사구
        ∧「주격 관계대명사 + be동사」 생략

(단서) 완전한 절 뒤에 과거분사구 grown on it이 이어지므로

(발상) the plants를 수식하는 것으로 볼 수 있다.

(해결) 식물이 '길러지는' 것이므로 plants which[that] is grown on it에서 주격
관계대명사 which[that]와 be동사 is가 생략되고 과거분사 grown만 남은
것은 어법상 알맞다.

(개념) 주격 관계대명사절의 동사가 be동사일 때「주격 관계대명사 + be동사」는
생략할 수 있다.

┌─────────────────────────────── 어법 특강 ───┐
│ ＊ 주격 관계대명사
│
│ – 주어를 대신하여 절과 절을 연결하는 접속사 역할을 할 때 주격 관계대명사를 쓴
│   다. 즉, 관계대명사가 포함된 절에서 주어가 없다면, 주격 관계대명사로 쓰였다는
│   것을 알 수 있다. 이 때 선행사의 종류에 따라 who(사람), which(사물), that(사
│   람, 사물, 동물 모두) 중 적절한 관계대명사를 써야 한다. 그리고 주격 관계대명사
│   절의 동사는 선행사와 수를 일치시켜야 한다는 것에 주의한다.
│ • What's the name of the person who won the lottery?
│   '사람'을 나타내는 선행사를 수식하는 who
│   (복권에 당첨되었던 그 사람의 이름은 무엇이죠?)
│ • It is important to eat food which is good for your health.
│   단수 선행사   단수 동사
│   (네 건강에 좋은 음식을 먹는 것은 중요하다.)
│ • Green turtles and seals are marine animals that are endangered.
│   복수 선행사   복수 동사
│   (바다거북과 바다표범은 멸종 위기에 처한 해양 동물들입니다.)
└──┘

┌─────────────────────────────── 어법 특강 ───┐
│ ＊ 과거분사
│
│ – 과거분사는 v-ed의 형태로, 수동(~되는, ~당하는)이나 완료(~된)의 의미를 나타
│   낼 때 쓰인다.
│ • She is reading a novel written in French.
│   (그녀는 프랑스어로 쓰인 소설을 읽고 있다.)
│ • Your teacher wants this assignment handed in tomorrow.
│   (너의 선생님은 내일 이 과제가 제출되기를 원하신다.)
│ • Many women like bags made in Italy.
│   (많은 여성들이 이탈리아에서 만들어진 가방들을 좋아한다.)
└──┘

K

주어와 동사는
문장에 꼭 있어야 하는
필수 요소야!

K 어휘 Review 정답 ─────── 문제편 p. 155

01 10년	11 in pursuit of	21 fulfillment
02 비난	12 no doubt	22 permanent
03 기능상의	13 at first glance	23 generally
04 경향	14 take root	24 Praise
05 전문 지식	15 get along with	25 enclosure
06 conditioned	16 civilization	26 virtual
07 domesticate	17 suspicions	27 varying
08 deny	18 regulations	28 reason
09 unfamiliar	19 core	29 Executives
10 likelihood	20 obtainable	30 acquire

L 문맥에 맞지 않는 낱말 찾기

문제편 p. 158~166

L 01 정답 ④ *미니멀리즘의 진정한 의미

다음 글의 밑줄 친 부분 중, 문맥상 낱말의 쓰임이 적절하지 않은 것은?

The term minimalism gives a negative impression / to some people / who(주격 관계대명사) think that(명사절 접속사) it is all about sacrificing valuable possessions. //
미니멀리즘이라는 용어는 부정적인 인상을 준다 / 일부 사람들에게 / 그것을 소중한 소유물을 희생하는 것에 관한 것으로만 생각하는 //

This insecurity naturally stems from / their ① attachment to their possessions. //
이러한 불안은 자연스럽게 비롯된다 / 자신의 소유물에 대한 애착에서 //

It is(가주어) difficult to distance oneself(진주어 / 재귀적 용법) / from something that(주격 관계대명사) has been around for quite some time. //
자신을 멀리 두는 것은 어렵다 / 꽤 오랫동안 곁에 있어 왔던 것으로부터 //

Being an emotional animal(분사구문), / human beings give meaning / to the things around them. //
감정의 동물이기 때문에 / 인간은 의미를 부여한다 / 그들의 곁에 있는 물건에 //

So, the question arising(현재분사) here / is that(명사절 접속사) if minimalism will ② hurt one's emotions, / why become a minimalist? //
그래서 여기서 생기는 질문은 / 미니멀리즘이 사람의 감정을 상하게 한다면 / 왜 미니멀리스트가 되느냐는 것이다 //

The answer is very simple; / the assumption of the question is fundamentally ③ wrong. //
대답은 매우 간단하다 / 그 질문의 가정은 근본적으로 틀리다 //

Minimalism does not hurt emotions. // **단서** 미니멀리즘은 감정을 상하게 하지 않으므로, 당연히 슬픈 감정은 머지않아 극복될 것임
미니멀리즘은 감정을 상하게 하지 않는다 //

You might feel a bit sad / while getting(사이에 주어와 be동사 생략) rid of a useless item / but sooner than later, / this feeling will be ④ maintained (→ overcome) / by the joy of clarity. //
여러분은 조금 슬퍼할 수도 있다 / 쓸모없는 물건을 치우면서 / 하지만 머지않아 / 이 느낌은 유지될(→ 극복될) 것이다 / 명료함의 기쁨으로 //

Minimalists never argue / that(명사절 접속사) you should leave / every convenience of the modern era. //
미니멀리스트는 주장하지 않는다 / 여러분이 버려야 한다고 / 현대의 모든 편의를 //

They are of the view / that(동격절 접속사) you only need to ⑤ eliminate stuff / that(주격 관계대명사) is unused / or not going to be used in the near future. //
그들은 견해를 가지고 있다 / 여러분이 물건을 없애기만 하면 된다는 / 사용되지 않거나 / 가까운 미래에 사용되지 않을 //

- term ⓝ 용어 · impression ⓝ 인상 · sacrifice ⓥ 희생하다
- possession ⓝ 소유물 · insecurity ⓝ 불안
- stem from ~에서 비롯되다 · attachment ⓝ 애착
- distance … from ~ …을 ~로부터 멀리 두다 · hurt ⓥ 상하게 하다
- assumption ⓝ 가정 · fundamentally ⓐⓓ 근본적으로
- get rid of ~을 제거하다 · sooner than later 머지않아
- clarity ⓝ 명료함 · convenience ⓝ 편의 · modern era 현대
- be of the view that ~라는 견해를 갖다 · eliminate ⓥ 없애다

미니멀리즘이라는 용어는 그것을 소중한 소유물을 희생하는 것에 관한 것으로만 생각하는 일부 사람들에게 부정적인 인상을 준다. 이러한 불안은 자신의 소유물에 대한 ① 애착에서 자연스럽게 비롯된다. 꽤 오랫동안 곁에 있어 왔던 것으로부터 자신을 멀리 두는 것은 어렵다. 감정의 동물이기 때문에, 인간은 그들의 곁에 있는 물건에 의미를 부여한다. 그래서 여기서 생기는 질문은 미니멀리즘이 사람의 감정을 ② 상하게 한다면 왜 미니멀리스트가 되느냐는 것이다. 대답은 매우 간단하다. 그 질문의 가정은 근본적으로 ③ 틀리다. 미니멀리즘은 감

정을 상하게 하지 않는다. 여러분은 쓸모없는 물건을 치우면서 조금 슬퍼할 수도 있지만 머지않아 이 느낌은 명료함의 기쁨으로 ④ 유지될(→ 극복될) 것이다. 미니멀리스트는 여러분이 현대의 모든 편의를 버려야 한다고 주장하지 않는다. 그들은 여러분이 사용되지 않거나 가까운 미래에 사용되지 않을 물건을 ⑤ 없애기만 하면 된다는 견해를 가지고 있다.

왜 정답? ✱✱ [정답률 68%]
④ maintained 유지되다
여러분은 쓸모없는 물건을 치우면서 조금 슬퍼할 수도 있지만 머지않아 이 느낌은 명료함의 기쁨으로 ④ maintained(극복될) 것이다.
➡ 미니멀리즘은 감정을 상하게 하지 않는다고 했으므로, 물건을 치우는 동안은 조금 슬플 수도 있지만, 그 감정이 '유지될' 것이라는 표현은 문맥상 적절하지 않다.
▶ maintained를 overcome(극복될)과 같은 말로 바꿔야 함

왜 오답?
① attachment 애착
이러한 불안은 자신의 소유물에 대한 ① 애착에서 자연스럽게 비롯된다.
➡ 곁에 있어 왔던 것을 멀리하는 것은 어렵다고 했으므로, 불안이 소유물에 대한 '애착'에서 비롯된다는 표현은 적절하다. ▶ attachment는 문맥에 맞음

② hurt 상하게 하다
그래서 여기서 생기는 질문은 미니멀리즘이 사람의 감정을 ② 상하게 한다면 왜 미니멀리스트가 되느냐는 것이다.
➡ 미니멀리즘은 소중한 것을 희생시킨다는 부정적인 인상, 즉 불안을 일으킨다고 설명했으므로, 미니멀리즘은 감정을 '상하게 한다'라고 가정하는 표현은 적절하다.
▶ hurt는 문맥에 맞음

③ wrong 틀린
그 질문의 가정은 근본적으로 ③ 틀리다.
➡ 미니멀리즘은 사람의 감정을 상하게 한다고 인식되지만, 사실은 그렇지 않다는 내용이 이어지고 있으므로, 그 가정이 '틀리다'라는 표현은 적절하다.
▶ wrong은 문맥에 맞음

⑤ eliminate 없애다
그들은 여러분이 사용되지 않거나 가까운 미래에 사용되지 않을 물건을 ⑤ 없애기만 하면 된다는 견해를 가지고 있다.
➡ 미니멀리즘은 자신에게 필요하지 않은 물건을 비우는 행위이므로, '없애다'라는 표현은 적절하다. ▶ eliminate는 문맥에 맞음

L 02 정답 ④ *고객의 수요 파악

다음 글의 밑줄 친 부분 중, 문맥상 낱말의 쓰임이 적절하지 않은 것은? [3점]

The major philosophical shift(주어) / in the idea of selling / came(동사) / when industrial societies became more affluent, / more competitive, / and more geographically spread out / during the 1940s and 1950s. //
주요한 철학적 변화가 / 판매 개념에 / 일어났다 / 산업 사회가 더 부유하게 되면서 / 더 경쟁적이고 / 더 지리적으로 퍼져 나가 (되면서) / 1940년대와 1950년대 동안 //

This forced business to develop(forced의 목적어와 목적격 보어(to부정사)) / ① closer relations with buyers and clients, /
이것은 기업이 발전시키게 했다 / 구매자 및 고객과 더 긴밀한 관계를 /

which(계속적 용법의 주격 관계대명사) in turn made business realize / that it(가주어) was not enough to produce(진주어) a quality product / at a reasonable price. //
그리고 이것은 결과적으로 기업이 깨닫게 했다 / 양질의 제품을 생산하는 것으로는 충분하지 않다는 것을 / 합리적인 가격에 // **단서 1** 합리적인 가격에 양질의 제품을 생산하는 것으로는 충분하지 않음

In fact, / it was equally ② essential / to deliver products / that customers actually wanted. //
가주어   진주어

사실 / ~이 마찬가지로 매우 중요했다 / 제품을 내놓는 것 / 고객이 실제로 원하는 //

Henry Ford produced / his best-selling T-model Ford / in one color only (black) in 1908, / but in modern societies / this was no longer ③ possible. //

Henry Ford는 생산했다 / 자신의 가장 많이 팔렸던 T-모델 Ford를 / 1908년에 단 하나의 색상(검은색)으로만 / 하지만 현대 사회에서는 / 이것이 더 이상 가능하지 않았다 //

The modernization of society / led to a marketing revolution / that ④ strengthened(→ destroyed) the view / that production would create its own demand. //

사회의 현대화는 / 마케팅 혁명으로 이어졌다 / 견해를 강화하는(→ 파괴하는) / 생산이 그 자체의 수요를 창출할 것이라는 //
핵심 주어   단서 2 이전과는 다른 곳에 기업은 집중함

Customers, / and the desire to ⑤ meet / their diverse and often complex needs, / became the focus of business. //
동사

고객과 / 충족하고자 하는 욕망이 / 그들의 다양하고 흔히 복잡한 욕구를 / 기업의 초점이 되었다 //

- major ⓐ 주요한   • philosophical ⓐ 철학적인   • shift ⓝ 변화
- industrial ⓐ 산업의   • competitive ⓐ 경쟁적인
- geographically ⓓ 지리적으로   • client ⓝ 고객
- quality ⓐ 질 좋은   • reasonable ⓐ 합리적인
- equally ⓓ 마찬가지로   • essential ⓐ 매우 중요한
- modernization ⓝ 현대화   • revolution ⓝ 혁명
- desire ⓝ 욕망, 욕구   • diverse ⓐ 다양한   • complex ⓐ 복잡한

산업 사회가 1940년대와 1950년대 동안 더 부유하고, 더 경쟁적이고, 더 지리적으로 퍼져 나가게 되면서 판매 개념에 주요한 철학적 변화가 일어났다. 이것은 기업이 구매자 및 고객과 ① 더 긴밀한 관계를 발전시키게 했고, 결과적으로 기업이 합리적인 가격에 양질의 제품을 생산하는 것으로는 충분하지 않다는 것을 깨닫게 했다. 사실, 고객이 실제로 원하는 제품을 내놓는 것이 마찬가지로 ② 매우 중요했다. 1908년에 Henry Ford는 자신의 가장 많이 팔렸던 T-모델 Ford를 단 하나의 색상(검은색)으로만 생산했지만, 현대 사회에서는 이것이 더 이상 ③ 가능하지 않았다. 사회의 현대화는 생산이 그 자체의 수요를 창출할 것이라는 견해를 ④ 강화하는(→ 파괴하는) 마케팅 혁명으로 이어졌다. 고객과 그들의 다양하고 흔히 복잡한 욕구를 ⑤ 충족하고자 하는 욕망이 기업의 초점이 되었다.

> 왜 정답 ? ★★★ [정답률 41%]

④ strengthened 강화하는

사회의 현대화는 생산이 그 자체의 수요를 창출할 것이라는 견해를 ④ 강화하는 마케팅 혁명으로 이어졌다.
파괴하는

➡ 기존에는 생산이 수요를 창출할 것이라고 생각했지만, 현대 사회에서는 인식이 변화되어서 이전과 다른 마케팅 혁명이 일어났다고 했으므로 이전의 견해를 '강화한다'고 하는 것은 자연스럽지 않다.
▶ strengthened를 destroyed(파괴하는)와 같은 반의어로 바꿔야 함

> 왜 오답 ?

① closer 더 긴밀한

이것은 기업이 구매자 및 고객과 ① 더 긴밀한 관계를 발전시키게 했고, 결과적으로 기업이 합리적인 가격에 양질의 제품을 생산하는 것으로는 충분하지 않다는 것을 깨닫게 했다.

➡ 합리적인 가격에 양질의 제품을 생산하는 것만으로는 충분하지 않았으므로 기업은 고객과 '더 긴밀한' 관계를 발전시켜야 했을 것이다. ▶ closer는 문맥에 맞음

② essential 매우 중요한

사실, 고객이 실제로 원하는 제품을 내놓는 것이 마찬가지로 ② 매우 중요했다.

➡ 좋은 가격에 좋은 제품을 생산하는 것으로는 충분하지 않다고 했으므로 고객의 요구와 수요를 고려하는 것은 '매우 중요했을' 것이다.
▶ essential은 문맥에 맞음

③ possible 가능한

1908년에 Henry Ford는 자신의 가장 많이 팔렸던 T-모델 Ford를 단 하나의 색상(검은색)으로만 생산했지만, 현대 사회에서는 이것이 더 이상 ③ 가능하지 않았다.

➡ 잘 팔리는 자동차 모델을 한 색상으로 생산했던 과거와는 달리 고객의 요구가 중요해진 현대 사회는 그런 것이 '가능하지' 않았을 것이다.
▶ possible은 문맥에 맞음

⑤ meet 충족하다

고객과 그들의 다양하고 흔히 복잡한 욕구를 ⑤ 충족하고자 하는 욕망이 기업의 초점이 되었다.

➡ 고객의 수요를 파악해서 이에 맞춘 마케팅을 하려고 한다고 했으므로 고객의 복잡한 욕구를 '충족하고자' 하는 것에 기업이 초점을 맞추었을 것이다.
▶ meet는 문맥에 맞음

L 03 정답 ⑤ *소비자 심리에 기반한 마케팅 전략

다음 글의 밑줄 친 부분 중, 문맥상 낱말의 쓰임이 적절하지 않은 것은? [3점]

Promotion deals with consumer psychology. //
프로모션은 소비자 심리를 다룬다 //

We can't ① force people / to think one way or another, /
우리가 사람들을 강요할 수는 없으며 / 어떤 한 방식으로 생각하도록 /
be used to-v: ~하는 데 사용되다
and the clever marketer knows that / promotion is used / to provide information / in the most clear, honest, and simple fashion possible. //
단서 1 현명한 마케팅 담당자는 명확하게 정보를 제공하기 위해 프로모션을 사용함

현명한 마케팅 담당자는 알고 있다 / 프로모션이 사용된다는 것을 / 정보를 제공하기 위해 / 가능한 한 가장 명확하고 정직하며 단순한 방식으로 //
앞 문장의 내용   단수 주어   단수 동사
By doing so, / the possibility of increasing sales goes up. //
그렇게 함으로써 / 매출 증가의 가능성이 높아진다 //
단서 2 예전에는 프로모션으로 소비자를 강조하기 위해 주어와 동사가 도치됨
gone을 강조하기 위해 주어와 동사가 도치됨
Gone are the days when promotions were done / in order to ② fool the consumer / into purchasing something. //
fool A into B: A를 속여서 B하게 하다

프로모션이 행해지던 시대는 갔다 / 소비자를 속이기 위해 / 무언가를 구매하도록 //
단수 주어   getting의 목적어와 목적격 보어 (to부정사)
The long-term effect of getting a consumer to buy something / they did not really want or need / wasn't good. //
앞에 목적격 관계대명사가 생략됨   단수 동사

소비자가 물건을 구매하도록 하는 것의 장기적인 효과는 / 그들이 정말로 원하지 않았거나 필요로 하지 않았던 / 좋지 않았다 //
앞에 주격 관계대명사와 be동사가 생략됨
In fact, / consumers fooled once can do ③ damage to sales / as they relate their experience to others. //

사실 / 한 번 속은 소비자는 판매에 손해를 끼칠 수 있다 / 자신의 경험을 다른 사람에게 전하기 때문에 //
단서 3 기만당한 소비자는 그 경험을 알릴 수 있으므로 판매에 손해를 끼침

Instead, / marketers now know that / their goal is / to ④ identify the consumers / who are most likely to appreciate a good or service, /
병렬 구조 (주격 보어로 쓰인 to부정사)

대신 / 마케팅 담당자들은 이제 알고 있다 / 목표가 되어야 한다는 것을 / 소비자를 확인하고 / 상품이나 서비스의 진가를 가장 인정할 것 같은 /
지시형용사   주격 관계대명사
and to promote that good or service / in a way that makes the value clear / to the consumer. //
단서 4 상품과 서비스의 가치를 인정하는 소비자를 대상으로 마케팅을 진행해야 함

그 상품이나 서비스를 홍보하는 것이 / 가치를 명확하게 하는 방식으로 / 그 소비자에게 //

Therefore, / marketers must know / where the ⑤ uninterested(→ potential) consumers are, / and how to reach them. //
병렬 구조 (know의 목적어)

그러므로 / 마케팅 담당자는 알아야 한다 / 그 무관심한(→ 잠재적인) 소비자가 어디에 있는지 / 그리고 어떻게 그들에게 도달해야 하는지 //

- promotion ⓝ 프로모션, 홍보 • deal with ~을 다루다
- consumer ⓝ 소비자 • psychology ⓝ 심리
- one way or another 어떤 한 방식으로 • fashion ⓝ 방식, 방법
- possibility ⓝ 가능성 • sales ⓝ 매출, 판매 • fool ⓥ 속이다
- purchase ⓥ 구매하다 • long-term ⓐ 장기적인
- relate ⓥ 전하다 • experience ⓝ 경험 • identify ⓥ 확인하다
- appreciate ⓥ 진가를 인정하다 • reach ⓥ 도달하다

프로모션은 소비자 심리를 다룬다. 우리가 사람들을 어떤 한 방식으로 생각하도록 ① 강요할 수는 없으며, 현명한 마케팅 담당자는 프로모션이 가능한 한 가장 명확하고 정직하며 단순한 방식으로 정보를 제공하기 위해 사용된다는 것을 알고 있다. 그렇게 함으로써, 매출 증가의 가능성이 높아진다. 무언가를 구매하도록 소비자를 ② 속이기 위해 프로모션이 행해지던 시대는 갔다. 소비자가 정말로 원하지 않았거나 필요로 하지 않았던 물건을 구매하도록 하는 것의 장기적인 효과는 좋지 않았다. 사실, 한 번 속은 소비자는 자신의 경험을 다른 사람에게 전하기 때문에 판매에 ③ 손해를 끼칠 수 있다. 대신, 마케팅 담당자들은 상품이나 서비스의 진가를 가장 인정할 것 같은 소비자를 ④ 확인하고, 그 소비자에게 그 상품이나 서비스의 가치를 명확하게 하는 방식으로 홍보하는 것이 목표가 되어야 한다는 것을 이제 알고 있다. 그러므로, 마케팅 담당자는 그 ⑤ 무관심한(→ 잠재적인) 소비자가 어디에 있는지, 그리고 어떻게 그들에게 도달해야 하는지 알아야 한다.

∵왜 정답? ✽✽❀ [정답률 68%]

⑤ uninterested 무관심한

┌ 그러므로, 마케팅 담당자는 그 ⑤ ~~무관심한~~(잠재적인) 소비자가 어디에 있는지, 그리
└ 고 어떻게 그들에게 도달해야 하는지 알아야 한다.

➡ 소비자를 속이던 과거와는 다르게 현대에는 정직한 마케팅, 즉 자신들의 상품과 서비스의 가치를 인정하는 '잠재적인' 소비자를 찾는 마케팅이 중요하므로 '무관심한' 소비자를 찾는 것은 문맥에 맞지 않는다.
　▶ uninterested를 potential(잠재적인)과 같은 어휘로 바꿔야 함

∵왜 오답?

① force 강요하다

┌ 우리가 사람들을 어떤 한 방식으로 생각하도록 ① 강요할 수는 없으며, 현
│ 명한 마케팅 담당자는 프로모션이 가능한 한 가장 명확하고 정직하며 단순
└ 한 방식으로 정보를 제공하기 위해 사용된다는 것을 알고 있다.

➡ 프로모션이 소비자 심리를 다루고, 명확하고 단순하게 정보를 제공하기 위해 사용되는 것이라고 했다. 즉, 프로모션은 소비자들에게 정보를 제공하여 그들이 심리를 바꾸도록 유도할 뿐이지, 그들이 특정 방식으로 생각하도록 '강요'할 수는 없다.
　▶ force는 문맥에 맞음

② fool 속이다

┌ 무언가를 구매하도록 소비자를 ② 속이기 위해 프로모션이 행해지던 시대
└ 는 갔다.

➡ 앞에서 정직하게 정보를 제공하기 위해 프로모션이 사용된다고 했으므로, 예전처럼 구매자들을 '속이는' 프로모션이 행해지는 시대가 갔다는 표현은 적절하다.
　▶ fool은 문맥에 맞음

③ damage 손해를 끼치다

┌ 사실, 한 번 속은 소비자는 자신의 경험을 다른 사람에게 전하기 때문에 판
└ 매에 ③ 손해를 끼칠 수 있다.

➡ 기만당한 소비자들이 다른 사람에게 자신의 경험을 공유하면 판매가 줄어들 것이므로, 판매에 '손해를 끼칠' 수 있다는 표현은 적절하다. ▶ damage는 문맥에 맞음

④ identify (정체 등을) 확인하다

┌ 대신, 마케팅 담당자들은 상품이나 서비스의 진가를 가장 인정할 것 같은
│ 소비자를 ④ 확인하고, 그 소비자에게 그 상품이나 서비스의 가치를 명확하
└ 게 하는 방식으로 홍보하는 것이 목표가 되어야 한다는 것을 이제 알고 있다.

➡ 마케팅의 대상을 정해야 하므로, 자신들의 가치를 잘 알아줄 수 있는 소비자들을 '확인한다'는 표현은 적절하다. ▶ identify는 문맥에 맞음

(구문 서술형)

(정답) People can't be forced to think one way or another by us.

(해석) 우리는 사람들을 어떤 한 방식으로 생각하도록 강요할 수 없다. → 사람들은 우리에 의해 어떤 한 방식으로 생각하도록 강요될 수 없다.
→ 능동태 문장의 목적어 people을 주어로 하는 수동태 문장에서 동사 can't force는 can't be forced로 바꿔 쓰고, 목적격 보어인 to think와 그 뒤 어구는 그대로 쓰고, 주어인 We는 by us로 문장 맨 끝에 써야 한다.

L 04 정답 ④ ＊인과 추론의 오류

다음 글의 밑줄 친 부분 중, 문맥상 낱말의 쓰임이 적절하지 않은 것은?

It is natural / for people / to observe happenings / and then seek explanations / for why those happenings occurred. //
（to observe와 seek의 의미상의 주어 / 진주어 / 가주어 / 간접의문문）
당연하다 / 사람들이 / 사건들을 관찰하고 / 그 후 설명을 찾는 것은 / 왜 그런 사건들이 일어났는지에 대한 //

But sometimes / the reasoning is ① wrong / because of one or more misconceptions. //
그러나 때로는 / 그 추론이 잘못된다 / 하나 또는 그 이상의 오해로 인해 //

One of these / is the *ecological fallacy*, / where an argument claims / that there is a causal relationship between two things / merely because they occur ② together. //
（단수 주어 / 단수 동사 / 관계부사 = misconceptions）
그 중 하나는 / '생태학적 오류'이다 / 여기서 논지는 / 두 가지 사이에 인과관계가 있다는 것이다 / 그것들이 함께 발생한다는 이유만으로 //

For example, in the 1950s / it was found / that crime rates were the highest / in neighborhoods / where immigrants were most numerous. //
（가주어 / 진주어절 접속사 / 관계부사）
예를 들어, 1950년대에 / 밝혀졌다 / 범죄율이 가장 높다는 것이 / 지역에서 / 이민자가 가장 많은 //

Some people used this "co-occurrence" / to argue / that immigrants were a ③ cause of crime. //
（부사적 용법 (목적)）
일부 사람들은 이 "동시 발생"을 이용했다 / 주장하기 위해서 / 이민자들이 범죄의 원인이라고 //

But a careful analysis of this situation / revealed / that immigrants were forced to live / in neighborhoods / where crime rates were already ④ low(→ high); /
（관계부사）
그러나 이 상황에 대한 면밀한 분석은 / 밝혀냈다 / 이민자들이 거주할 수밖에 없었다는 것을 / 지역에 / 이미 범죄율이 낮은(→ 높은) /

they could not afford more expensive housing / in safer neighborhoods. // (단서) 이민자들은 안전한 지역에 살 여력이 없음
그들은 더 비싼 주택을 살 여력이 없었다 / 보다 안전한 지역의 //

Immigrants themselves / committed very few of the crimes. //
（재귀대명사 (강조 용법)）
이민자 자신들은 / 범죄를 거의 저지르지 않았다 //

Unless you analyze the claim carefully, / you would ⑤ misinterpret the relationship / and thereby construct a faulty belief. //
（부사절 접속사 (만약 ~하지 않는다면) / 병렬 구조 (문장의 동사)）
그 주장을 주의 깊게 분석하지 않으면 / 당신은 그 관계를 잘못 해석하고 / 그 결과 잘못된 믿음을 형성할 수 있다 //

- observe ⓥ 관찰하다 • happening ⓝ 사건
- explanation ⓝ 설명 • reasoning ⓝ 추론
- misconception ⓝ 오해 • ecological ⓐ 생태학적인
- fallacy ⓝ 오류 • argument ⓝ 논지, 주장 • causal ⓐ 인과적인
- merely ⓐⓓ 단지 ~만으로 • crime rate 범죄율
- numerous ⓐ 많은 • co-occurrence ⓝ 동시 발생

- reveal ⓥ 밝혀내다 • afford ⓥ ~할 여력[여유]이 있다
- commit ⓥ 저지르다 • misinterpret ⓥ 잘못 해석하다, 오해하다
- construct ⓥ 구성하다, 형성하다 • faulty ⓐ 잘못된

사람들이 사건들을 관찰하고 나서 왜 그런 사건들이 일어났는지에 대한 설명을 찾는 것은 당연하다. 그러나 때로는 하나 또는 그 이상의 오해로 인해 그 추론이 ① 잘못된다. 그 중 하나는 '생태학적 오류'로, 여기서 논지는 두 가지가 ② 함께 발생한다는 이유만으로 두 가지 사이에 인과 관계가 있다는 것이다. 예를 들어, 1950년대에 범죄율이 이민자가 가장 많은 지역에서 가장 높다는 것이 밝혀졌다. 일부 사람들은 이민자들이 범죄의 ③ 원인이라고 주장하기 위해서 이러한 "동시 발생"을 이용했다. 그러나 이 상황에 대한 면밀한 분석은 이민자들이 이미 범죄율이 ④ 낮은(→ 높은) 지역에 거주할 수밖에 없었다는 것을 밝혀냈다; 그들은 보다 안전한 지역의 더 비싼 주택을 살 여력이 없었다. 이민자 자신들은 범죄를 거의 저지르지 않았다. 그 주장을 주의 깊게 분석하지 않으면, 당신은 그 관계를 ⑤ 잘못 해석하여 잘못된 믿음을 형성할 수 있다.

⊳왜 정답? ★★❋ [정답률 76%]

④ low 낮은

그러나 이 상황에 대한 면밀한 분석은 이민자들이 이미 범죄율이 ④ ~~낮은~~ _{높은} 지역에 거주할 수밖에 없었다는 것을 밝혀냈다. 그들은 보다 안전한 지역의 더 비싼 주택을 살 여력이 없었다.

➡ 이민자들은 안전한 지역의 비싼 주택을 살 여력이 없었다는 설명이 이어지므로 그들은 이미 범죄율이 '낮은' 지역이 아니라 '높은' 지역에 거주할 수밖에 없었던 것이다.
▶ low를 high(높은)와 같은 반의어로 바꿔야 함

⊳왜 오답?

① wrong 잘못된

그러나 때로는 하나 또는 그 이상의 오해로 인해 그 추론이 ① 잘못된다.

➡ 사람들은 사건을 관찰하고 나서 그것의 발생 원인을 찾는다는 앞 문장에 But으로 연결되므로 때로는 오해로 인해 그 추론이 '잘못된다'는 표현은 적절하다.
▶ wrong은 문맥에 맞음

② together 함께

그 중 하나는 '생태학적 오류'로, 여기서 논지는 두 가지가 ② 함께 발생한다는 이유만으로 두 가지 사이에 인과 관계가 있다는 것이다.

➡ 두 가지 사이에 인과 관계가 있다고 추론할 만한 상황은 두 가지가 '함께' 발생할 때이다. ▶ together는 문맥에 맞음

③ cause 원인

일부 사람들은 이민자들이 범죄의 ③ 원인이라고 주장하기 위해서 이러한 "동시 발생"을 이용했다.

➡ 높은 범죄율과 이민자 유입이 함께 발생할 때, 두 가지 사이에 인과 관계가 있다고 주장할 수도 있으므로, 이민자가 범죄의 '원인'이라고 주장할 것이다.
▶ cause는 문맥에 맞음

⑤ misinterpret 잘못 해석하다

그 주장을 주의 깊게 분석하지 않으면, 당신은 그 관계를 ⑤ 잘못 해석하여 잘못된 믿음을 형성할 수 있다.

➡ 생태학적 오류인 주장을 주의 깊게 분석하지 않으면, 두 사건 사이의 관계를 '잘못 해석하여' 잘못된 믿음을 형성할 것이다. ▶ misinterpret은 문맥에 맞음

구문 서술형

정답 very few of the crimes, Very few of the crimes were committed by immigrants themselves.

해석 이민자 자신들은 범죄를 거의 저지르지 않았다. → 매우 적은 범죄들이 이민자 자신들에 의해 저질러졌다.

→ 3형식 문장은 능동태의 목적어를 주어로, 동사는 「be동사+과거분사」 형태로, 주어는 「by+목적격」으로 고쳐 수동태 문장으로 바꿔 쓴다.

Ⅼ 05 정답 ⑤ *적게 가질수록 더 나누는 경향

다음 글의 밑줄 친 부분 중, 문맥상 낱말의 쓰임이 적절하지 않은 것은?

For a species born in a time / [관계부사] when resources were limited and dangers were great, / our natural tendency to share and [형용사적 용법 (tendency 수식)] cooperate is ① complicated / when resources are plenty and outside dangers are few. //
단서 1 자원이 많고 위험이 적어지면 오히려 나누고 협력하려는 성향이 복잡해짐
시기에 태어난 종에게 있어 / 자원이 제한적이고 위험이 컸던 / 나누고 협력하려는 우리의 타고난 성향은 복잡하다 / 자원이 풍부하고 외부의 위험이 거의 없을 때 //

When we have less, / we tend to be more open / to sharing what [선행사를 포함하는 관계대명사] we have. //
우리가 더 적게 가질 때 / 더 개방적이 되는 경향이 있다 / 우리가 가진 것을 나누는 데 //

Certain nomadic tribes don't have much, / [등위접속사 (하지만)] yet they are happy to [부사적 용법 (감정의 원인)] share / because it is in their ② interest to do so. // [= share]
특정 유목 부족은 많은 것을 가지고 있지 않지만 / 그들은 기꺼이 나누려고 한다 / 그렇게 하는 것이 그들의 이익에 부합하기 때문에 //

If you happen upon them in your travels, / they will open up their homes / and give you their food and hospitality. //
만약 당신이 여행 중 그들을 우연히 만나면 / 그들은 자신의 집을 열고 / 당신에게 음식과 환대를 제공할 것이다 //

It's not just because they are nice people; / it's because their ③ survival depends on sharing, /
이는 그들이 좋은 사람이어서만이 아니다 / 이는 그들의 생존이 나누는 것에 달려 있기 때문인데 /
[등위접속사 (왜냐하면)] 단서 2 처지가 바뀌면 생존에 위험이 있으므로 특정 유목 부족은 기꺼이 나눔
for they know that they may be the travelers / in need of food and shelter another day. //
왜냐하면 그들은 여행자가 될 수 있음을 알기 때문이다 / 또 다른 날 그들이 음식과 거처가 필요한 //

Ironically, the ④ more we have, / the bigger our fences, / the [the 비교급 ~, the 비교급 …: 더 ~할수록 더 …하다] more sophisticated our security to keep people away / and the [병렬 구조] less we want to share. // 단서 3 더 많이 가질수록 사람들을 멀리 두고 덜 나누려고 함
아이러니하게도, 우리가 더 많이 가질수록 / 우리의 울타리는 더 커지고 / 사람들을 멀리 두기 위한 우리의 보안은 더 정교해지며 / 우리는 더 적게 나누기를 원하게 된다 //
[단수 주어]
Our desire for more, / combined with our ⑤ increased(→ decreased) physical interaction with the "common folk," / starts [단수 동사] to create / a disconnection or blindness to reality. //
우리의 더 많은 것에 대한 욕망은 / "일반 대중"과의 늘어난(→ 줄어든) 실재적인 상호작용과 결합되어서 / 만들어내기 시작한다 / 현실에 대한 단절이나 눈멀음을 //

- resource ⓝ 자원 • tendency ⓝ 경향 • cooperate ⓥ 협력하다
- complicated ⓐ 복잡한 • plenty ⓐ 풍부한 • interest ⓝ 이익
- survival ⓝ 생존 • depend on ~에 달려있다 • shelter ⓝ 안식처
- ironically ⓐⓓ 역설적으로 • sophisticated ⓐ 정교한
- desire ⓝ 욕망 • combine A with B A를 B와 결합하다
- interaction ⓝ 상호작용 • disconnection ⓝ 단절

자원이 제한적이고 위험이 컸던 시기에 태어난 종에게 있어, 자원이 풍부하고 외부의 위험이 거의 없을 때 나누고 협력하려는 우리의 타고난 성향은 ① 복잡하다. 우리가 더 적게 가질 때, 우리가 가진 것을 나누는 데 더 개방적이 되는 경향이 있다. 특정 유목 부족은 많은 것을 가지고 있지 않지만, 그렇게 하는 것이 그들의 ② 이익에 부합하기 때문에 그들은 기꺼이 나누려고 한다. 만약 당신이 여행 중 그들을 우연히 만나면, 그들은 자신의 집을 열고 당신에게 음식과 환대를 제공할 것이다. 이는 그들이 좋은 사람이어서만이 아니다. 이는 그들의 ③ 생존이 나누는 것에 달려 있기 때문인데, 왜냐하면 그들은 또 다른 날 그들이 음식과 거처가 필요한 여행자가 될 수 있음을 알기 때문이다. 아이러니하게도, 우리가 ④ 더 많이 가질수록, 우리의 울타리는 더 커지고, 사람들을 멀리 두기 위한 우리의 보안은 더 정교해지며, 우리는 더 적게 나누기를 원하게 된다. 우리의 더 많은 것에 대한 욕망은 "일반 대중"과의 ⑤ 늘어난(→ 줄어든) 실재적인 상호작용과 결합되어서, 현실에 대한 단절이나 눈멀음을 만들어내기 시작한다.

왜 정답? ★★☆ [정답률 61%]

⑤ increased 늘어난

우리의 더 많은 것에 대한 욕망은 "일반 대중"과의 ⑤ ~~늘어난~~ 줄어든 실재적인 상호작용과 결합되어서, 현실에 대한 단절이나 눈멀음을 만들어내기 시작한다.

➡ 앞 문장에서 더 많이 가질수록 사람들을 멀리 두려 한다고 했다. 따라서 더 많은 것에 대한 욕망은 일반 대중과의 '늘어난' 상호작용이 아니라 '줄어든' 상호작용과 결합될 것이다.

▶ increased를 decreased(줄어든)와 같은 반의어로 바꿔야 함

왜 오답?

① complicated 복잡한

자원이 제한적이고 위험이 컸던 시기에 태어난 종에게 있어, 자원이 풍부하고 외부의 위험이 거의 없을 때 나누고 협력하려는 우리의 타고난 성향은 ① 복잡하다.

➡ 자원이 제한적이고 위험이 크다면 생존을 위해 가진 것을 나누려 하지만, 자원이 풍부하고 위험이 작다면 나눔과 협력의 동기가 예전처럼 단순하지 않고 '복잡할' 것이다. ▶ complicated는 문맥에 맞음

② interest 이익

특정 유목 부족은 많은 것을 가지고 있지 않지만, 그렇게 하는 것이 그들의 ② 이익에 부합하기 때문에 그들은 기꺼이 나누려고 한다.

➡ 가진 것이 적더라도 기꺼이 나누는 것은 그렇게 하는 것이 그들에게 '이익'이 되기 때문일 것이다. ▶ interest는 문맥에 맞음

③ survival 생존

이는 그들이 좋은 사람이어서만이 아니다. 이는 그들의 ③ 생존이 나누는 것에 달려 있기 때문인데, 왜냐하면 그들은 또 다른 날 그들이 음식과 거처가 필요한 여행자가 될 수 있음을 알기 때문이다.

➡ 자원이 부족한 환경에서 나눔은 단순히 친절의 문제가 아니라, 언젠가 자신도 도움을 받아야 하는 상황에 처할 수 있기 때문에 필요한 '생존' 전략이다.

▶ survival은 문맥에 맞음

④ more 더 많이

아이러니하게도, 우리가 ④ 더 많이 가질수록, 우리의 울타리는 더 커지고, 사람들을 멀리 두기 위한 우리의 보안은 더 정교해지며, 우리는 더 적게 나누기를 원하게 된다.

➡ 적게 가질 때 더 많이 나누던 것과 다르게, '더 많이' 가질수록 오히려 덜 나눈다는 아이러니한 상황을 설명하고 있다. ▶ more는 문맥에 맞음

구문 서술형

정답 you, their food and hospitality, (1) You will be given their food and hospitality.
(2) Their food and hospitality will be given to you.

해석 그들은 당신에게 그들의 음식과 환대를 제공할 것이다. → (1) 당신은 그들의 음식과 환대를 제공받을 것이다. (2) 그들의 음식과 환대는 당신에게 제공될 것이다.

→ (1) 간접목적어 you를 주어로 하는 수동태 문장은 수동태 동사 뒤에 직접목적어를 그대로 쓴다. (2) 직접목적어 their food and hospitality를 주어로 하는 수동태 문장은 동사 뒤에 「전치사 to + 간접목적어」를 쓴다.

L 06 정답 ③ *집단 지성을 통한 문제 해결

다음 글의 밑줄 친 부분 중, 문맥상 낱말의 쓰임이 적절하지 않은 것은? [3점]

Herbert Simon won his Nobel Prize / for recognizing our limitations / in information, time, and cognitive capacity. //
Herbert Simon은 그의 노벨상을 받았다 / 우리의 한계를 인지한 것으로 / 정보, 시간, 그리고 인지적인 능력에서 //

(부사절 접속사 (이유) / 형용사적 용법 (resources 수식))
As we lack the resources / to compute answers independently, / we ① distribute the computation across the population / and solve the answer slowly, / generation by generation. // (병렬 구조)
우리는 자원이 부족하기 때문에 / 독립적으로 해답을 계산하기 위한 / 우리는 전체 인구에 걸쳐 계산을 분배하고 / 해답을 천천히 풀어낸다 / 세대에 걸쳐 //

(앞에 to가 생략됨)
Then / all we have to do / is socially learn the right answers. //
그러면 / 우리가 해야 하는 모든 것은 / 올바른 해답을 사회적으로 배우는 것이다 //
단서 1 우리는 해답만 사회적으로 배우면 됨

You don't need to understand / how your computer or toilet works; / you just need to be able to use the interface and flush. // (병렬 구조 (to 뒤에 연결))
여러분은 이해할 필요가 없다 / 여러분의 컴퓨터 혹은 변기가 어떻게 작동하는지 / 여러분은 단지 (컴퓨터의) 인터페이스를 사용할 수 있고 (변기의) 물을 내릴 수 있기만 하면 된다 //

(주격 관계대명사 / 의문사 + to부정사)
All that needs to be ② transmitted / is which button to push / — essentially how to interact with technologies / rather than how they work. //
단서 2 우리는 기술과 상호 작용하는 방법만 알면 됨
전달될 필요가 있는 모든 것은 / 어떤 버튼을 눌러야 하는지 ~이다 / 근본적으로 기술과 상호 작용하는 방법 / 어떻게 그것들이 작동하는지보다는 //

(동명사 / 병렬 구조)
And so instead of holding ③ less(→ more) information / than we have mental capacity for / and indeed need to know, /
그렇다면 더 적은(→ 더 많은) 정보를 가지는 것 대신에 / 우리가 정신적 수용을 할 수 있는 것보다 / 그리고 정말로 알아야 할 필요가 있는 것보다 /

we could dedicate our large brains / to a small piece of a giant calculation. //
우리는 우리의 큰 두뇌를 바칠 수 있다 / 거대한 계산의 작은 조각에 //

(「형용사/부사 + enough to부정사」: ~하기에 충분히 …한/…하게 / 주격 관계대명사)
We understand things / well enough to ④ benefit from them, / but all the while / we are making small calculations / that contribute to a larger whole. //
우리는 사물을 이해한다 / 그것들로부터 이득을 얻기에 충분히 잘 / 하지만 그러면서 / 우리는 작은 계산을 하고 있다 / 더 큰 전체에 기여하는 //

We are just doing our part / in a larger computation / for our societies' ⑤ collective brains. //
우리는 단지 우리의 역할을 하고 있는 것이다 / 더 큰 계산에서 / 우리 사회의 집합적인 두뇌를 위한 //

- limitation ⓝ 한계
- cognitive ⓐ 인지적인
- capacity ⓝ 능력
- independently ad 독립적으로
- distribute ⓥ 분배하다
- computation ⓝ 계산
- generation ⓝ 세대
- flush ⓥ (변기의) 물을 내리다
- transmit ⓥ 전달하다
- essentially ad 근본적으로
- dedicate ⓥ 바치다, 헌신하다
- calculation ⓝ 계산
- benefit ⓥ 이득을 얻다
- contribute to ~에 기여하다
- collective ⓐ 집합적인

Herbert Simon은 정보, 시간, 그리고 인지적인 능력에서 우리의 한계를 인지한 것으로 그의 노벨상을 받았다. 우리는 독립적으로 해답을 계산하기 위한 자원이 부족하기 때문에 우리는 전체 인구에 걸쳐 계산을 ① 분배하고 세대에 걸쳐 해답을 천천히 풀어낸다. 그러면 우리가 해야 하는 모든 것은 올바른 해답을 사회적으로 배우는 것이다. 여러분은 여러분의 컴퓨터 혹은 변기가 어떻게 작동하는지 이해할 필요가 없고 여러분은 단지 인터페이스를 사용할 수 있고 (변기의) 물을 내릴 수 있기만 하면 된다. ② 전달될 필요가 있는 모든 것은 어떤 버튼을 눌러야 하는지, 근본적으로 어떻게 그것들이 작동하는지보다는 기술과 상호 작용하는 방법이다. 그렇다면 우리가 정신적 수용을 할 수 있는 것과 정말로 알아야 할 필요가 있는 것보다 ③ 더 적은(→ 더 많은) 정보를 가지는 것 대신에

우리는 우리의 큰 두뇌를 거대한 계산의 작은 조각에 바칠 수 있다. 우리는 그것들로부터 ④ 이득을 얻기에 충분할 정도로 사물을 잘 이해하지만 그러면서 우리는 더 큰 전체에 기여하는 작은 계산을 하고 있다. 우리는 우리 사회의 ⑤ 집합적인 두뇌를 위한 더 큰 계산에서 단지 우리의 역할을 하고 있는 것이다.

>왜 정답? ✷✷❋ [정답률 75%]

③ less 더 적은

┌ 그렇다면 우리가 정신적 수용을 할 수 있는 것과 정말로 알아야 할 필요가
│ 있는 것보다 ③ 더 적은(~~더 많은~~) 정보를 가지는 것 대신에 우리는 우리의 큰 두뇌를
└ 거대한 계산의 작은 조각에 바칠 수 있다.

➡ 인간은 인지적인 한계로 인해 세대에 걸쳐 해답을 내므로, 올바른 해답을 사회적으로 배워야 한다고 했다. 즉, 기술의 원리는 몰라도 기술을 사용하는 방법만 알면 된다는 것이다. 이처럼 우리는 모든 것을 알 필요가 없으므로, 우리가 알아야 하는 정보량보다 '더 적은' 정보가 아니라 '더 많은' 정보를 가지지 않고 작은 계산에 두뇌를 할애할 수 있다. ▶ less를 more(더 많은)와 같은 반의어로 바꿔야 함

>왜 오답?

① distribute 분배하다

┌ 우리는 독립적으로 해답을 계산하기 위한 자원이 부족하기 때문에 우리는
│ 전체 인구에 걸쳐 계산을 ① 분배하고 세대에 걸쳐 해답을 천천히 풀어낸
└ 다.

➡ 독립적으로 계산하는 것이 아닌, 전체 인구에 걸쳐서 복잡한 계산을 끌어낸다는 의미이므로, 계산을 '분배한다'라는 표현은 적절하다. ▶ distribute는 문맥에 맞음

② transmitted 전달되는

┌ ② 전달될 필요가 있는 모든 것은 어떤 버튼을 눌러야 하는지, 근본적으로
└ 어떻게 그것들이 작동하는지보다는 기술과 상호 작용하는 방법이다.

➡ 우리는 올바른 해답을 사회적으로 배우기 때문에, 우리에게 '전달될' 필요가 있는 정보라는 표현은 적절하다. ▶ transmitted는 문맥에 맞음

④ benefit 이득을 얻다

┌ 우리는 그것들로부터 ④ 이득을 얻기에 충분할 정도로 사물을 잘 이해하지
└ 만 그러면서 우리는 더 큰 전체에 기여하는 작은 계산을 하고 있다.

➡ 우리가 기술과 상호 작용하는 방법을 알고 이를 이용할 수 있으므로, 사물로부터 '이득을 얻기에' 충분할 정도로 사물을 잘 이해한다는 표현은 적절하다.
▶ benefit은 문맥에 맞음

⑤ collective 집합적인

┌ 우리는 우리 사회의 ⑤ 집합적인 두뇌를 위한 더 큰 계산에서 단지 우리의
└ 역할을 하고 있는 것이다.

➡ 더 큰 계산은 '개별적인' 두뇌가 아닌 우리 사회의 '집합적인' 두뇌를 위해 사회 전체적으로 이루어진다. ▶ collective는 문맥에 맞음

구문 서술형

정답 3, Our large brains could be dedicated to a small piece of a giant calculation.

해석 우리는 우리의 큰 두뇌를 거대한 계산의 작은 조각에 바칠 수 있다. → 우리의 큰 두뇌는 거대한 계산의 작은 조각에 바쳐질 수 있다.
→ 주어진 문장은 주어(We), 동사(could dedicate), 목적어(our large brains)로 이루어진 3형식 문장이다. 3형식 문장은 능동태의 목적어를 주어로, 동사는 「be동사+과거분사」 형태로 고쳐 수동태 문장으로 바꿔 쓴다.

L 07 정답 ③ *이동 속도와 세부 정보 처리의 관계 —

다음 글의 밑줄 친 부분 중, 문맥상 낱말의 쓰임이 적절하지 않은 것은? [3점]

The rate of speed 「전치사+관계대명사」 at which one is traveling / will greatly determine / the ability 형용사적 용법(the ability 수식) to process detail in the environment. //
사람이 이동하는 속도의 빠르기는 / 크게 결정할 것이다 / 환경 속 세세한 것을 처리하는 능력을 //
단서 1 인간의 이동 속도는 환경 속 세부 정보 처리 능력을 결정함

In evolutionary terms, / human senses are adapted to the ① speed / 「전치사+관계대명사」 at which humans move through space / under their own power while walking. // 접속사가 생략되지 않은 분사구문
진화론적 관점에서 / 인간의 감각은 속도에 적응되어 있다 / 공간을 이동하는 / 그 자신의 힘으로 걸으며 //

Our ability 형용사적 용법(Our ability 수식) to distinguish detail / in the environment / is therefore ideally ② suited to / movement at speeds of perhaps five miles per hour and under. // **단서 2** 환경 속 세부 정보 구별 능력은 우리가 스스로 이동하는 속도에 맞춰져 있음
세세한 것을 구별하는 우리의 능력은 / 환경 속에서 / 그래서 이상적으로 맞추어져 있다 / 대략 시속 5마일 또는 그 속도 이하의 이동에 // **단서 3** 도로 위 운전자는 세부 정보를 처리하는 능력이 훨씬 더 제한됨

The fastest users of the street, motorists, 동격 / therefore have a much more limited ability / to process details along the street /
도로의 가장 빠른 사용자인 운전자들은 / 그러므로 훨씬 더 제한된 능력을 가지고 있고 / 도로를 따라 (이동하며) 세세한 것을 처리하는 /

— a motorist simply has ③ enough (→ little) time or ability / to appreciate design details. // 형용사적 용법
운전자는 단지 충분한(→ 적은) 시간이나 능력이 있다 / 디자인의 세세한 것을 감상할 수 있는 //

On the other hand, / pedestrian travel, being much slower, / allows for the ④ appreciation of environmental detail. //
반면에 / 보행자 이동은 훨씬 더 느려서 / 환경의 세세한 것을 감상할 수 있도록 허용해 준다 //

Joggers and bicyclists / fall somewhere in between these polar opposites; /
조깅하는 사람과 자전거를 타는 사람은 / 이러한 극과 극 사이의 어딘가에 해당한다 /

while they travel faster than pedestrians, / their rate of speed is ordinarily much ⑤ slower / than that of the typical motorist. // 비교급 강조 부사 = rate of speed
그들은 보행자보다 더 빨리 이동하지만 / 속도의 빠르기는 보통 훨씬 더 느리다 / 전형적인 운전자의 그것보다 //

- rate ⓝ 빠르기 · travel ⓥ 이동하다 · determine ⓥ 결정하다
- ability ⓝ 능력 · process ⓥ 처리하다 · evolutionary ⓐ 진화의
- ideally ⓐⓓ 이상적으로 · suited ⓐ 맞추어진 · motorist ⓝ 운전자
- limited ⓐ 제한된 · appreciate ⓥ 감상하다
- allow for ~을 가능하게 하다[허락하다] · polar ⓐ 극과 극의
- opposite ⓝ 반대의 것 · ordinarily ⓐⓓ 보통 · typical ⓐ 전형적인

사람이 이동하는 속도의 빠르기는 환경 속 세세한 것을 처리하는 능력을 크게 결정할 것이다. 진화론적 관점에서, 인간의 감각은 그 자신의 힘으로 걸으며 공간을 이동하는 ① 속도에 적응되어 있다. 환경 속에서 세세한 것을 구별하는 우리의 능력은 그래서 대략 시속 5마일 또는 그 속도 이하의 이동에 이상적으로 ② 맞추어져 있다. 그러므로 도로의 가장 빠른 사용자인 운전자는 도로를 따라서 (이동하며) 세세한 것을 처리하는 훨씬 더 제한된 능력을 가지고 있고, 그래서 운전자는 단지 디자인의 세세한 것을 감상할 수 있는 ③ 충분한(→ 적은) 시간이나 능력이 있다. 반면에 보행자 이동은 훨씬 더 느려서, 환경의 세세한 것을 ④ 감상할 수 있도록 허용해 준다. 조깅하는 사람과 자전거를 타는 사람은 이러한 극과 극 사이의 어딘가에 해당한다. 그들은 보행자보다 더 빨리 이동하지만, 속도의 빠르기는 보통 전형적인 운전자의 그것보다 훨씬 ⑤ 더 느리다.

왜 정답? ✱✱❀ [정답률 66%]

③enough 충분한

그러므로 도로의 가장 빠른 사용자인 운전자는 도로를 따라서 (이동하며) 세세한 것을 처리하는 훨씬 더 제한된 능력을 가지고 있고, 그래서 운전자는 단지 디자인의 세세한 것을 감상할 수 있는 ③ ~~충분한~~(적은) 시간이나 능력이 있다.

➡ 도로 위 운전자는 인간이 걷는 속도보다 훨씬 빠르게 이동하기 때문에 세부 정보를 처리하는 능력이 제한된다고 했으므로, 운전자가 세세한 것을 감상할 수 있는 '충분한' 시간이나 능력이 있다는 것은 문맥에 맞지 않는다.

▶ enough를 little(적은)과 같은 반의어로 바꾸어야 함

왜 오답?

①speed 속도

진화론적 관점에서, 인간의 감각은 그 자신의 힘으로 걸으며 공간을 이동하는 ① 속도에 적응되어 있다.

➡ 사람이 이동하는 속도의 빠르기는 환경 속 세부 정보를 처리하는 능력을 결정한다고 했으므로, 인간의 감각은 이동하는 '속도'에 적응되어 있다는 표현은 적절하다. ▶ speed는 문맥에 맞음

②suited 맞추어진

환경 속에서 세세한 것을 구별하는 우리의 능력은 그래서 대략 시속 5마일 또는 그 속도 이하의 이동에 이상적으로 ② 맞추어져 있다.

➡ 이동 속도가 환경 속 세부 정보를 처리하는 능력을 결정한다고 했으므로, 인간이 스스로 이동하는 속도인 대략 시속 5마일 또는 그 속도 이하에 우리의 세부 정보 구별 능력이 '맞추어져' 있다는 표현은 적절하다.

▶ suited는 문맥에 맞음

④appreciation 감상

반면에 보행자 이동은 훨씬 더 느려서, 환경의 세세한 것을 ④ 감상할 수 있도록 허용해 준다.

➡ 보행자의 이동 속도가 운전자보다 훨씬 더 느리기 때문에 주변을 둘러볼 시간을 충분히 가지므로, 환경의 세부 정보를 '감상할 수 있도록 허용한다는 표현은 적절하다. ▶ appreciation은 문맥에 맞음

⑤slower 더 느린

조깅하는 사람과 자전거를 타는 사람은 이러한 극과 극 사이의 어딘가에 해당한다. 그들은 보행자보다 더 빨리 이동하지만, 속도의 빠르기는 보통 전형적인 운전자의 그것보다 훨씬 ⑤ 더 느리다.

➡ 조깅하는 사람과 자전거를 타는 사람의 이동 속도는 보행자의 속도와 운전자의 속도 사이 어딘가에 있으므로, 운전자의 이동 속도 빠르기보다 '더 느리다'는 표현은 적절하다. ▶ slower는 문맥에 맞음

L 08 정답 ④ ✱도로의 친환경적인 역할

다음 글의 밑줄 친 부분 중, 문맥상 낱말의 쓰임이 적절하지 <u>않은</u> 것은? [3점]

An excellent alternative / to **calming** traffic / is **removing** it. //
훌륭한 대안은 / 교통을 진정시키는 / 그것을 제거하는 것이다 //

Some cities ① reserve / an extensive network of lanes and streets / for bikes, pedestrians, and the occasional service vehicle. //
몇몇 도시는 마련해 둔다 / 광범위한 망의 도로와 거리를 / 자전거, 보행자, 그리고 수시 서비스 차량을 위한 //

This motivates people / to travel by bike rather than by car, / **making streets safer for everyone.** //
이것은 사람들에게 동기를 부여한다 / 자동차보다 자전거로 이동을 하도록 / 그래서 거리를 모두에게 더 안전하게 만든다 //

As bicycles become more ② popular in a city, / planners can convert more automobile lanes and entire streets / to accommodate more of **them**. //
자전거가 도시에서 더 인기가 많아지면 / 도시 계획자들은 더 많은 자동차 도로와 전체 거리를 전환할 수 있다 / 더 많은 자전거를 수용할 수 있도록 //

Nevertheless, / even the most bikeable cities / still ③ require motor vehicle lanes / for taxis, emergency vehicles, and delivery trucks. //
그럼에도 불구하고 / 가장 자전거를 타기 좋은 도시들조차도 / 여전히 자동차 도로를 필요로 한다 / 택시, 긴급 차량, 그리고 배달 트럭을 위한 //

Delivery vehicles are frequently a target of animus, / but **they** are actually an essential component / to making cities greener. //
배달 차량은 자주 반감의 대상이지만 / 그것들은 실제로 필수 구성요소이다 / 도시를 더 친환경적으로 만드는 (데 있어서) // **단서 1** 배달 차량은 도시를 더 친환경적으로 만드는 데 필수적임

A tightly packed delivery truck / is a **far** more ④ inefficient(→ efficient) transporter of goods / than several hybrids **carrying a few shopping bags each.** // **단서 2** 짐이 빽빽하게 들어찬 트럭과 몇 개의 쇼핑백을 실은 하이브리드 차량을 비교함
짐이 빽빽하게 들어찬 배달 트럭은 / 훨씬 더 비효율적인(→ 효율적인) 상품 운송 수단이다 / 각각 몇 개의 쇼핑백을 실은 여러 하이브리드 차량보다 //

Distributing food and other goods to neighborhood vendors / ⑤ allows **them** to operate smaller stores close to homes / **so that** residents can walk, rather than drive, to get their groceries. //
음식과 다른 상품을 동네 상인에게 배포하는 것은 / 그들이 집에 가까운 더 작은 상점을 운영할 수 있게 하고 / 그 결과 주민들은 식료품을 사기 위해 운전하기보다는 걸어갈 수 있다 //

- **alternative** ⓝ 대안 · **reserve** ⓥ 마련하다
- **extensive** ⓐ 광범위한 · **lane** ⓝ 길, 도로 · **pedestrian** ⓝ 보행자
- **vehicle** ⓝ 교통 수단 · **occasional** ⓐ 가끔의
- **motivate** ⓥ 동기를 부여하다 · **automobile** ⓝ 자동차
- **accommodate** ⓥ 수용하다 · **frequently** ⓐⓓ 자주
- **distribute** ⓥ 나누어주다 · **neighborhood** ⓝ 이웃
- **vendor** ⓝ 상점 · **operate** ⓥ 운영하다 · **resident** ⓝ 거주자

교통을 진정시키는 훌륭한 대안은 그것을 제거하는 것이다. 몇몇 도시는 자전거, 보행자, 그리고 수시 서비스 차량을 위한 광범위한 망의 도로와 거리를 ① 마련해 둔다. 이것은 사람들이 자동차보다 자전거로 이동을 하도록 동기를 부여하여 거리를 모두에게 더 안전하게 만든다. 자전거가 도시에서 더 ② 인기가 많아지면, 계획자들은 더 많은 자동차 도로와 전체 거리를 더 많은 자전거를 수용할 수 있도록 전환할 수 있다. 그럼에도 불구하고, 가장 자전거를 타기 좋은 도시들조차도 여전히 택시, 긴급 차량, 그리고 배달 트럭을 위한 자동차 도로를 ③ 필요로 한다. 배달 차량은 자주 반감의 대상이지만, 그것들은 실제로 도시를 더 친환경적으로 만드는 필수 구성요소이다. 짐이 빽빽하게 들어찬 배달 트럭은 각각 몇 개의 쇼핑백을 실은 여러 하이브리드 차량보다 훨씬 더 ④ 비효율적인(→ 효율적인) 상품 운송 수단이다. 음식과 다른 상품을 동네 상인에게 배포하는 것은 그들이 집에 가까운 더 작은 상점을 운영 ⑤ 할 수 있게 하고 그 결과 주민들은 식료품을 사기 위해 운전하기보다는 걸어갈 수 있다.

왜 정답? ✱✱❀ [정답률 74%]

④inefficient 비효율적인

짐이 빽빽하게 들어찬 배달 트럭은 각각 몇 개의 쇼핑백을 실은 여러 하이브리드 차량보다 훨씬 더 ④ ~~비효율적인~~(효율적인) 상품 운송 수단이다.

➡ 앞 문장에서 배달 트럭은 더 친환경적인 도시를 만드는 데 필수 요소라고 했으므로, 짐이 빽빽하게 들어찬 배달 트럭은 짐을 적게 실은 여러 하이브리드 차량보다 더 '비효율적인' 상품 운송 수단이 아니라 '효율적인' 상품 운송 수단이다.

▶ inefficient를 efficient(효율적인)와 같은 반의어로 바꿔야 함

왜 오답?

①reserve 마련하다

몇몇 도시는 자전거, 보행자, 그리고 수시 서비스 차량을 위한 광범위한 망의 도로와 거리를 ① 마련해 둔다. 이것은 사람들이 자동차보다 자전거로 이동을 하도록 동기를 부여하여 거리를 모두에게 더 안전하게 만든다.

➡ 사람들이 자동차보다 자전거로 이동하도록 한다는 것은 자전거, 보행자, 서비스 차량을 위한 도로와 거리를 '마련한' 결과일 것이다. ▶ reserve는 문맥에 맞음

② popular 인기 있는

┌ 자전거가 도시에서 더 ② 인기가 많아지면, 계획자들은 더 많은 자동차
└ 도로와 전체 거리를 더 많은 자전거를 수용할 수 있도록 전환할 수 있다.

➡ 자전거의 '인기가 많아져서' 계획자들이 더 많은 자전거를 수용하도록 도로와
 거리를 전환한다는 것은 자연스럽다. ▶ popular는 문맥에 맞음

③ require 필요로 하다

┌ 그럼에도 불구하고, 가장 자전거를 타기 좋은 도시들조차도 여전히 택시,
└ 긴급 차량, 그리고 배달 트럭을 위한 자동차 도로를 ③ 필요로 한다.

➡ 반대되는 내용을 나타내는 Nevertheless가 있으므로, 자전거의 인기가 많은
 도시에서 자전거 도로를 더 만들 수도 있지만 여전히 다양한 차량을 위한 자동차
 도로를 '필요로 한다'고 하는 것은 적절하다. ▶ require는 문맥에 맞음

⑤ allows 할 수 있게 하다

┌ 음식과 다른 상품을 동네 상인에게 배포하는 것은 그들이 집에 가까운 더
│ 작은 상점을 운영 ⑤ 할 수 있게 하고 그 결과 주민들은 식료품을 사기 위해
└ 운전하기보다는 걸어갈 수 있다.

➡ 주민들이 가까운 상점으로 걸어가도록 하려면, 동네 상인에게 상품을 배포하여
 각각의 생활 반경에 작은 상점을 운영'할 수 있게 하면' 된다.

 ▶ allows는 문맥에 맞음

L 09 정답 ② *이사가 힘든 아이들

다음 글의 밑줄 친 부분 중, 문맥상 낱말의 쓰임이 적절하지 않은 것은?
[3점]

부사절 접속사(대조)
While moving is difficult for everyone, / it is particularly
stressful for children. //
이사는 모두에게 힘들지만 / 그것은 아이들에게 특히 스트레스가 많은 일이다 //

They lose their sense of security / and may feel disoriented /
부사절 접속사   주격 관계대명사
when their routine is disrupted / and all **that** is ① familiar is
taken away. //
그들은 안도감을 잃고 / 혼란스러움을 느낄 수도 있다 / 그들의 일상이 무너질 때 / 그리고
익숙한 모든 것이 사라질 때 //

Young children, ages 3–6, / are particularly affected / by a move. //
3세에서 6세 사이의 어린아이들은 / 특히 영향을 받는다 / 이사에 의해 //

                                                        가주어
Their understanding at this stage / is quite literal, / and **it** is ②
            to imagine의 의미상 주어   진주어
easy(→ difficult) **for them** / **to imagine** beforehand / a new home
                            단서 이해력에 융통성이 없는 시기임
and their new room. //
이 시기에 그들의 이해력은 / 꽤 융통성이 없다 / 그리고 ~은 그들에게 쉽다(→ 어렵다) / 미리
상상하는 것은 / 새로운 집과 자신의 새로운 방을 //

Young children may have worries / such as "Will I still be me in
the new place?" / and "Will my toys and bed come with us?" //
어린아이들은 걱정들을 가질지도 모른다 / "내가 새로운 곳에서 여전히 나일까"와 같은 /
그리고 "내 장난감과 침대가 우리와 함께 갈까"(와 같은) //
가주어   진주어
It is important **to establish** a balance / between validating
                              helping의 목적어와 목적격 보어(원형부정사)
children's past experiences / and focusing on helping **them** ③
adjust to the new place. //
균형을 잡는 것이 중요하다 / 아이들의 과거 경험을 인정하는 것 사이에서 / 그들을 돕는 데
집중하는 것과 / 새로운 곳에 적응하도록 //
                              형용사적 용법(opportunities 수식)
Children need to have opportunities / **to share** their backgrounds
         주격 관계대명사
/ in a way **that** ④ respects their past / as an important part / of
   간접의문문
who they are. //
아이들은 기회를 가질 필요가 있다 / 자신의 배경을 공유할 / 자신의 과거를 존중하는
방식으로 / 중요한 부분으로서 / 자신이 누구인지에 대한 //
                              계속적 용법의 주격 관계대명사
This contributes / to building a sense of community, / **which**
                                              = children
is essential for all children, / especially **those** in ⑤ transition. //
이것은 기여한다 / 공동체 의식을 형성하는 데 / 이는 모든 아이들에게 매우 중요하다 / 특히
변화를 겪는 아이들(에게) //

- particularly [ad] 특히   - security [n] 안도감, 안심
- disoriented [a] 혼란에 빠진   - disrupt [v] 파괴하다
- take away ~을 제거하다   - literal [a] 융통성이 없는, 문자 그대로의
- beforehand [ad] 미리   - establish [v] 확고히 하다, 설립하다
- validate [v] 인정하다   - contribute [v] 기여하다
- transition [n] 변화

이사는 모두에게 힘들지만, 아이들에게 특히 스트레스가 많은 일이다.
그들은 안도감을 잃고 그들의 일상이 무너지고 ① 익숙한 모든 것이 사라질
때 혼란스러움을 느낄 수도 있다. 3세에서 6세 사이의 어린아이들은 이사에
특히 영향을 받는다. 이 시기에 그들의 이해력은 꽤 융통성이 없고, 그들이
새로운 집과 자신의 새로운 방을 미리 상상하는 것은 ② 쉽다(→ 어렵다).
어린아이들은 "내가 새로운 곳에서 여전히 나일까?"와 "내 장난감과 침대가
우리와 함께 갈까?"와 같은 걱정들을 가질지도 모른다. 아이들의 과거 경험을
인정하는 것과 그들이 새로운 곳에 ③ 적응하도록 돕는 데 집중하는 것
사이에서 균형을 잡는 것이 중요하다. 아이들은 자신이 누구인지에 대한 중요한
부분으로서 자신의 과거를 ④ 존중하는 방식으로 자신의 배경을 공유할 기회를
가질 필요가 있다. 이것은 공동체 의식을 형성하는 데 기여하고, 이는 모든
아이들, 특히 ⑤ 변화를 겪는 아이들에게 매우 중요하다.

왜 정답 ? ★★★ [정답률 63%]

② easy 쉬운

┌ 이 시기에 그들의 이해력은 꽤 융통성이 없어서, 그들이 새로운 집과
└ 자신의 새로운 방을 미리 상상하는 것은 ② 쉽다.
                                                        어렵다

➡ 아이들의 이해력에 융통성이 없는 시기라고 했으므로, 새로운 집이나 방을
 상상하는 것이 '쉽다'고 하는 것은 문맥에 맞지 않는다.

 ▶ easy를 difficult(어려운)와 같은 반의어로 바꿔야 함

왜 오답 ?

① familiar 익숙한

┌ 이사는 모두에게 힘들지만, 아이들에게 특히 스트레스가 많은 일이다.
│ 그들은 안도감을 잃고 그들의 일상이 무너지고 ① 익숙한 모든 것이 사라질
└ 때 혼란스러움을 느낄 수도 있다.

➡ 이사는 아이들에게 특히 스트레스라고 했으므로, 이사로 인해 '익숙한' 모든 것이
 사라질 때 아이들은 혼란스러움을 느낄 것이다.

 ▶ familiar는 문맥에 맞음

③ adjust 적응하다

┌ 어린아이들은 "내가 새로운 곳에서 여전히 나일까?"와 "내 장난감과 침대가
│ 우리와 함께 갈까?"와 같은 걱정들을 가질지도 모른다. 아이들의 과거
│ 경험을 인정하는 것과 그들이 새로운 곳에 ③ 적응하도록 돕는 데 집중하는
└ 것 사이에서 균형을 잡는 것이 중요하다.

➡ 아이들은 과거로부터 변하는 것을 혼란스러워하여 걱정하므로 이사 가기 전의
 경험은 인정하고, 새로운 곳에는 '적응하도록' 돕는 것이 중요할 것이다.

 ▶ adjust는 문맥에 맞음

④ respects 존중하다

┌ 아이들은 자신이 누구인지에 대한 중요한 부분으로서 자신의 과거를
└ ④ 존중하는 방식으로 자신의 배경을 공유할 기회를 가질 필요가 있다.

➡ 앞에서 아이들의 과거 경험을 인정하는 것도 중요하다고 했으므로, 아이들은
 자신의 과거를 '존중하는' 방식으로 자신의 배경을 공유할 기회를 가져야 할 것이다.

 ▶ respects는 문맥에 맞음

⑤ transition 변화

┌ 이것(This)은 공동체 의식을 형성하는 데 기여하고, 이는 모든 아이들,
└ 특히 ⑤ 변화를 겪는 아이들에게 매우 중요하다.

➡ 앞 문장의 내용을 '이것'이라고 하면서, 배경을 공유할 기회를 가지는 것은 이사로
 인해 '변화'를 겪는 아이들에게 중요하다고 하는 흐름은 적절하다.

 ▶ transition은 문맥에 맞음

L 10 정답 ② *효모에서 천연 완하제로

다음 글의 밑줄 친 부분 중, 문맥상 낱말의 쓰임이 적절하지 <u>않은</u> 것은?

Advertisers often displayed considerable facility / in ① <u>adapting</u> their claims / to the market status of the goods / <mark>they promoted.</mark> //
광고주들은 상당한 능력을 자주 보여주었다 / 그들의 주장을 조절하는 데 있어서 / 상품의 시장 지위에 맞게 / 그들이 홍보한 //
_{앞에 목적격 관계대명사가 생략됨}

Fleischmann's yeast, / for instance, / was used as an ingredient / for cooking homemade bread. // **단서 1** Fleischmann의 효모는 집에서 빵을 만드는 재료로 사용되었음
Fleischmann의 효모는 / 예를 들어 / 재료로 사용되었다 / 집에서 만든 빵을 요리하는 //
단서 2 20세기 초 사람들은 빵을 집에서 만들지 않고 가게에서 사게 됨

Yet / more and more people in the early 20th century / were buying their bread from stores or bakeries, / so consumer demand for yeast ② <u>increased</u>(→ decreased). //
하지만 / 20세기 초에 점점 더 많은 사람들이 / 가게나 빵집에서 빵을 사고 있었고 / 그래서 효모에 대한 소비자 수요는 증가했다(→ 감소했다) //

The producer of Fleischmann's yeast / hired the J. Walter Thompson advertising agency / _{부사적 용법(목적)} <mark>to come up with</mark> a different marketing strategy / to ③ <u>boost</u> sales. //
Fleischmann의 효모의 생산자는 / J. Walter Thompson 광고 대행사를 고용했다 / 다른 마케팅 전략을 고안하려고 / 판매를 촉진하기 위해서 //

_{앞에 Being이 생략됨}
No longer the "Soul of Bread," / the Thompson agency first turned yeast / into an important source of vitamins / with significant health ④ <u>benefits.</u> //
더 이상 "Soul of Bread"가 아니라 / Thompson 광고 대행사는 먼저 효모를 바꾸었다 / 비타민의 중요한 공급원으로 / 상당한 건강상의 이점이 있는 //

Shortly thereafter, / the advertising agency transformed yeast / into a natural laxative. //
그 직후 / 그 광고 대행사는 효모를 바꾸었다 / 천연 완하제로 //

_{helped의 목적어}
⑤ <u>Repositioning</u> yeast / helped <mark>increase</mark> sales. //
효모의 이미지 전환을 꾀하는 것은 / 매출을 증가시키는 것을 도왔다 //

- display ⓥ 보여주다, 전시하다
- considerable ⓐ 상당한
- facility ⓝ 재능, 시설
- adapt ⓥ 조절하다
- claim ⓝ 주장
- status ⓝ 지위
- promote ⓥ 홍보하다
- yeast ⓝ 효모
- ingredient ⓝ 재료
- demand ⓝ 수요, 요구
- hire ⓥ 고용하다
- strategy ⓝ 전략
- boost ⓥ 촉진하다
- significant ⓐ 상당한
- thereafter ⓐⅾ 그 후에
- transform ⓥ 바꾸다
- reposition ⓥ 이미지 전환을 꾀하다

광고주들은 그들이 홍보한 상품의 시장 지위에 맞게 그들의 주장을 ① 조절하는 상당한 능력을 자주 보여주었다. 예를 들어, Fleischmann의 효모는 집에서 만든 빵을 요리하는 재료로 사용되었다. 하지만 20세기 초에 점점 더 많은 사람들이 가게나 빵집에서 빵을 사고 있었고, 그래서 효모에 대한 소비자 수요는 ② 증가했다(→ 감소했다). Fleischmann의 효모의 생산자는 판매를 ③ 촉진하기 위해서 다른 마케팅 전략을 고안하려고 J. Walter Thompson 광고 대행사를 고용했다. Thompson 광고 대행사는 먼저 효모를 더 이상 "Soul of Bread"가 아니라 상당한 건강상의 ④ 이점이 있는 비타민의 중요한 공급원으로 바꾸었다. 그 직후, 광고 대행사는 효모를 천연 완하제로 바꾸었다. 효모의 ⑤ 이미지 전환을 꾀하는 것은 매출을 증가시키는 것을 도왔다.

> **왜 정답** ? ★★★ [정답률 58%]

② increased 증가했다

┌ 예를 들어, Fleischmann의 효모는 집에서 만든 빵을 요리하는 재료로 사용되었다.
│ 하지만 20세기 초에 점점 더 많은 사람들이 가게나 빵집에서 빵을 사고 └ 있었고, 그래서 효모에 대한 소비자 수요는 ~~증가했다~~. 감소했다

➡ 효모는 집에서 빵을 요리하는 재료로 사용되었지만, 점점 많은 사람들이 빵을 가게에서 사면서 효모에 대한 소비자의 수요는 '증가한' 것이 아니라 '줄어들었을' 것이다. ▶ increased를 decreased(감소했다)와 같은 반의어로 바꿔야 함

> **왜 오답** ?

① adapting 조절하는

┌ 광고주들은 그들이 홍보한 상품의 시장 지위에 맞게 그들의 주장을 └ ① 조절하는 상당한 능력을 자주 보여주었다.

➡ 이어서 제시되는 광고 대행사가 Fleischmann의 효모를 비타민 공급원으로 바꾸고, 또 천연 완하제로 바꾸었다는 내용을 종합하면 광고주들이 그들의 주장을 '조절하는' 능력을 보여주었다는 것은 자연스럽다.
▶ adapting은 문맥에 맞음

③ boost 촉진하다

┌ Fleischmann의 효모의 생산자는 판매를 ③ 촉진하기 위해서 다른
│ 마케팅 전략을 고안하려고 J. Walter Thompson 광고 대행사를 └ 고용했다.

➡ 마케팅 전략을 고안하기 위해 광고 대행사를 고용한 것은 판매를 '촉진하기' 위해서일 것이다.
▶ boost는 문맥에 맞음

④ benefits 이점

┌ Thompson 광고 대행사는 먼저 효모를 더 이상 "Soul of Bread"
│ 가 아니라 상당한 건강상의 ④ 이점이 있는 비타민의 중요한 공급원으로 └ 바꾸었다.

➡ 효모의 판매를 촉진하기 위한 새로운 마케팅 전략이 효모의 건강상의 '이점'을 강조하기 위해 효모가 비타민 공급원임을 홍보했다는 것이므로 자연스러운 내용이다.
▶ benefits는 문맥에 맞음

⑤ Repositioning 이미지 전환을 꾀하는 것

┌ 그 직후, 광고 대행사는 효모를 천연 완하제로 바꾸었다. 효모의
└ ⑤ 이미지 전환을 꾀하는 것은 매출을 증가시키는 것을 도왔다.

➡ 빵을 요리하는 재료를 넘어서, 효모가 건강상의 이점이 있는 비타민이자 천연 완하제라고 이미지를 바꾼 것은 '이미지 전환을 꾀하는 것'에 해당한다.
▶ Repositioning은 문맥에 맞음

L 11 정답 ④ *옥신이 좌우하는 식물의 성장

다음 글의 밑줄 친 부분 중, 문맥상 낱말의 쓰임이 적절하지 <u>않은</u> 것은?
[3점]

Plant growth is controlled / by a group of hormones called _{앞에 주격 관계대명사와 be동사가 생략됨}
auxins / <mark>found</mark> at the tips of stems and roots of plants. //
식물의 성장은 조절된다 / 옥신이라고 불리는 호르몬 그룹에 의해 / 식물의 줄기와 뿌리의 끝에서 발견되는 //

_{앞에 주격 관계대명사와 be동사가 생략됨}
Auxins <mark>produced</mark> at the tips of stems / tend to accumulate on the _{주격 관계대명사}
side of the stem / <mark>that</mark> is in the shade. //
줄기의 끝에서 생산된 옥신은 / 줄기의 옆면에 축적되는 경향이 있다 / 그늘진 곳에 있는 //

Accordingly, / the auxins ① <u>stimulate</u> growth / on the shaded side of the plant. //
따라서 / 옥신은 성장을 자극한다 / 식물의 그늘진 면에서의 //

Therefore, / the shaded side grows faster / than the side facing the sunlight. //
그러므로 / 그늘진 면은 더 빨리 자란다 / 햇빛을 마주하는 면보다 //

명사적 용법(목적격 보어)
This phenomenon causes the stem **to bend and appear** / to be growing ② towards the light. //
이 현상은 줄기가 휘어지게 하고 보이게 한다 / 빛을 향하여 성장하는 것처럼 //

Auxins have the ③ opposite effect / on the roots of plants. //
옥신은 반대의 효과를 가진다 / 식물의 뿌리에서는 //

Auxins in the tips of roots / tend to limit growth. //
뿌리 끝에 있는 옥신은 / 성장을 억제하는 경향이 있다 //

부사절 접속사(조건)
If a root is horizontal in the soil, / the auxins will accumulate on the lower side / and interfere with its development. //
만약 하나의 뿌리가 토양 속에서 / 수평이라면 / 옥신은 아래쪽에 축적될 것이다 / 그리고 그것의 발달을 방해할 것이다 /
단서 옥신이 뿌리 아래쪽에 축적되면 뿌리 아래쪽의 발달을 방해함

Therefore, / the lower side of the root will grow ④ faster(→ slower) / than the upper side. //
그러므로 / 뿌리의 아래쪽은 더 빠르게(→ 더 느리게) 자라게 된다 / 위쪽보다 //

This will, in turn, cause the root to bend ⑤ downwards, / with
with+(대)명사+분사: 부대상황(~하면서)
the tip of the root growing in that direction. //
이것은 결과적으로 뿌리가 아래로 휘어지게 한다 / 뿌리의 끝부분은 그 방향으로 자라면서 //

- tip ⓝ 끝 (부분) · stem ⓝ (식물의) 줄기 · accumulate ⓥ 축적하다
- shade ⓝ 그늘 · accordingly ⓐd 따라서, 그래서
- stimulate ⓥ 자극하다 · face ⓥ 직면하다, 마주하다
- phenomenon ⓝ 현상 · bend ⓥ 구부러지다, 휘어지다
- opposite ⓐ 반대의 · limit ⓥ 제한하다 · horizontal ⓐ 수평의
- soil ⓝ 토양 · interfere with ~을 방해하다
- development ⓝ 발달 · in turn 결국, 결과적으로

식물의 성장은 식물의 줄기와 뿌리의 끝에서 발견되는 옥신이라고 불리는 호르몬 그룹에 의해 조절된다. 줄기의 끝에서 생산된 옥신은 그늘진 곳에 있는 줄기의 옆면에 축적되는 경향이 있다. 따라서, 옥신은 식물의 그늘진 면에서의 성장을 ① 자극한다. 그러므로 그늘진 면은 햇빛을 마주하는 면보다 더 빨리 자란다. 이 현상은 줄기가 휘어지게 하고 빛을 ② 향하여 성장하는 것처럼 보이게 한다. 옥신은 식물의 뿌리에서는 ③ 반대의 효과를 가진다. 뿌리 끝에 있는 옥신은 성장을 억제하는 경향이 있다. 만약 하나의 뿌리가 토양 속에서 수평이라면, 옥신은 아래쪽에 축적되어 그것의 발달을 방해할 것이다. 그러므로 뿌리의 아래쪽은 위쪽보다 ④ 더 빠르게(→ 더 느리게) 자라게 된다. 이것은 결과적으로 뿌리가 ⑤ 아래로 휘어지게 하고 뿌리의 끝부분은 그 방향으로 자란다.

＞왜 정답? ★★★ [정답률 53%]
④faster 더 빠르게
만약 하나의 뿌리가 토양 속에서 수평이라면, 옥신은 아래쪽에 축적되어 그것의 발달을 방해할 것이다. 그러므로 뿌리의 아래쪽은 위쪽보다 ④ 더 빠르게 자라게 된다.
(더 느리게)
→ 뿌리 끝에 있는 옥신은 성장을 억제하는 경향이 있어서 옥신이 뿌리 아래쪽에 축적되면 뿌리의 발달을 방해한다고 했다. 그러므로 뿌리 아래쪽은 위쪽보다 '더 빠르게' 자란다는 것은 문맥에 맞지 않는다.
▶ faster를 slower(더 느리게)와 같은 반의어로 바꿔야 함

＞왜 오답?
①stimulate 자극하다
따라서, 옥신은 식물의 그늘진 면에서의 성장을 ① 자극한다. 그러므로 그늘진 면은 햇빛을 마주하는 면보다 더 빨리 자란다.
→ 이어지는 문장에서 그늘진 면이 햇빛을 마주하는 면보다 더 빨리 자란다고 했으므로, 옥신은 식물의 그늘진 부분에서의 성장을 '자극할' 것이다.
▶ stimulate는 문맥에 맞음

②towards 향하여
이 현상은 줄기가 휘어지게 하고 빛을 ② 향하여 성장하는 것처럼 보이게 한다.
→ 그늘진 면이 햇빛을 마주하는 면보다 더 빨리 자라서 줄기가 휘어진다고 했으므로 빛을 '향하여' 자라는 것처럼 보일 것이다. ▶ towards는 문맥에 맞음

③opposite 반대의
옥신은 식물의 뿌리에서는 ③ 반대의 효과를 가진다. 뿌리 끝에 있는 옥신은 성장을 억제하는 경향이 있다.
→ 앞에서는 옥신이 줄기의 성장을 자극한다고 했는데, 이어지는 문장에서 뿌리 끝에서는 옥신이 성장을 억제한다고 했으므로 '반대의' 효과임을 알 수 있다.
▶ opposite은 문맥에 맞음

⑤downwards 아래로
이것은 결과적으로 뿌리가 ⑤ 아래로 휘어지게 하고 뿌리의 끝부분은 그 방향으로 자란다.
→ 앞에서 옥신이 뿌리 끝의 성장을 억제한다고 했으므로, 옥신은 뿌리가 '아래로' 휘어지게 할 것이다.
▶ downwards는 문맥에 맞음

L 12 정답 ⑤ 　　 2등급 대비 [정답률 44%]

＊거절 요법

다음 글의 밑줄 친 부분 중, 문맥상 낱말의 쓰임이 적절하지 않은 것은? [3점]

Rejection is / an everyday part of our lives, / yet most people can't handle it well. //
거절은 ~이다 / 우리 삶의 일상적인 부분 / 하지만 대부분의 사람은 그것을 잘 감당하지 못한다 //

so ~ that …: 너무 ~해서 …하다
For many, / it's so painful / that they'd rather not ask for
병렬 구조
something at all / than ask and ① risk rejection. //
많은 사람에게 / 거절은 너무 고통스럽다 / 그래서 그들은 아예 무언가를 요청하지 않으려 한다 / 요청하고 거절당할 위험을 감수하기보다는 //

Yet, / as the old saying goes, / if you don't ask, / the answer is always no. // 하지만 / 옛말처럼 / 요청하지 않으면 / 대답은 항상 '아니오'이다 //

동명사 주어＊ 　 단수 동사
Avoiding rejection ② negatively affects / many aspects of your life. // 거절을 피하는 것은 부정적으로 영향을 미친다 / 여러분의 삶의 많은 측면에 //

All of that happens / only because you're not ③ tough enough
형용사를 뒤에서 수식함
/ to handle it. //
이 모든 것은 일어난다 / 단지 여러분이 강하지 않기 때문에 / 거절을 감당할 만큼 //

For this reason, / consider rejection therapy. //
이러한 이유로 / 거절 요법을 (시도하는 것을) 고려해 보라 //

주격 관계대명사
Come up with a ④ request or an activity / that usually results in a rejection. // 단서1 스스로 거절을 이끌어 낼 만한 요청이나 활동을 생각해 내라고 함
요청이나 활동을 생각해 내라 / 일반적으로 거절을 이끌어 낼 //

Working in sales / is one such example. //
판매 분야에서 일하는 것이 / 그러한 사례 중 하나이다 //

동명사 주어＊
Asking for discounts / at the stores / will also work. //
할인을 요청하는 것 / 매장에서 / 또한 효과가 있을 것이다 //

By deliberately getting yourself ⑤ welcomed(→ rejected) /
주격 관계대명사
you'll grow a thicker skin / that will allow you to take on much more in life, /
의도적으로 스스로를 환영받을(→ 거절당할) 상황에 놓이게 함으로써 / 여러분은 더 두꺼운 피부(둔감함)를 가지게 될 것이다 / 인생에서 훨씬 더 많은 것을 떠맡을 수 있게 해주는 /

분사구문을 이끎
thus making you more successful at dealing / with unfavorable circumstances. //
그리하여 그것은 더 성공적으로 대처할 수 있게 해 줄 것이다 / 호의적이지 않은 상황에 //
단서2 더 많은 것을 떠맡을 수 있는 두꺼운 피부(둔감함)를 가지게 되어 호의적이지 않은 상황에 잘 대처할 수 있음

- rejection ⓝ 거절 · handle ⓥ 다루다 · painful ⓐ 고통스러운
- risk ⓥ 위험을 무릅쓰다 · affect ⓥ 영향을 미치다
- aspect ⓝ 측면 · tough ⓐ 강한 · therapy ⓝ 요법
- request ⓝ 요청 · discount ⓝ 할인
- unfavorable ⓐ 호의적이지 않은 · circumstance ⓝ 상황

거절은 우리 삶의 일상적인 부분이지만, 대부분의 사람은 그것을 잘 감당하지 못한다. 많은 사람에게 거절이 너무 고통스럽기 때문에, 그들은 요청하고 거절당할 ① 위험을 감수하기보다는 아예 무언가를 요청하지 않으려 한다. 하지만 옛말처럼, 요청하지 않으면 대답은 항상 '아니오'이다. 거절을 피하는 것은 여러분의 삶의 많은 측면에 ② 부정적으로 영향을 미친다. 이 모든 것은 여러분이 단지 거절을 감당할 만큼 ③ 강하지 않기 때문에 일어난다. 이러한 이유로 거절 요법을 (시도하는 것을) 고려해 보라. 일반적으로 거절당할 만한 ④ 요청이나 활동을 생각해 내라. 판매 분야에서 일하는 것이 그러한 사례 중 하나이다. 매장에서 할인을 요청하는 것 또한 효과가 있을 것이다. 의도적으로 스스로를 ⑤ 환영받을(→ 거절당할) 상황에 놓이게 함으로써 여러분은 더 둔감해지고, 인생에서 훨씬 더 많은 것을 떠맡을 수 있게 되며, 그리하여 그것은 호의적이지 않은 상황에 더 성공적으로 대처할 수 있게 해 줄 것이다.

와 2등급? 일부러 거절을 당하라는 글의 내용을 잘 이해하지 못하면 밑줄 친 부분의 낱말들의 쓰임이 적절한지 판단하기 어려운 문제이다. 전체적인 내용을 잘 파악해서 반대 의미를 나타내는 낱말이 들어갈 자리를 확인한다.

와 정답?

⑤ welcomed 환영받다

- 의도적으로 스스로를 ⑤ ~~환영받을~~ (거절당할) 상황에 놓이게 함으로써 여러분은 더 둔감해지고, 인생에서 훨씬 더 많은 것을 떠맡을 수 있게 되며, 그리하여 그것은 호의적이지 않은 상황에 더 성공적으로 대처할 수 있게 해 줄 것이다.
➡ 일부러 '환영받을' 상황에 놓이게 한다면 호의적이지 않은 상황에 성공적으로 대처할 수 있는 것이 아니라 오히려 삶에 부정적인 영향을 미칠 것이다.
▶ welcomed를 rejected(거절당하다)와 같은 반의어로 바꿔야 함

와 오답?

① risk 위험을 감수하다

- 많은 사람에게 거절이 너무 고통스럽기 때문에, 그들은 요청하고 거절당할 ① 위험을 감수하기보다는 아예 무언가를 요청하지 않으려 한다.
➡ 거절이 너무 고통스럽다고 했으므로 거절당할 '위험을 감수하기'보다는 요청하지 않으려 할 것이다. ▶ risk는 문맥에 맞음

② negatively 부정적으로

- 하지만 옛말처럼, 요청하지 않으면 대답은 항상 '아니오'이다. 거절을 피하는 것은 여러분의 삶의 많은 측면에 ② 부정적으로 영향을 미친다.
➡ 요청하지 않으면 대답은 항상 부정적이라고 했으므로 무언가를 얻을 수 없을 것이다. 그러므로 거절을 피하는 것은 '부정적으로' 영향을 줄 것이다.
▶ negatively는 문맥에 맞음

③ tough 강한

- 이 모든 것은 여러분이 단지 거절을 감당할 만큼 ③ 강하지 않기 때문에 일어난다.
➡ 거절을 피하는 것은 부정적으로 영향을 미친다고 했으므로, 그 이유는 거절을 감당할 만큼 '강하지' 않을 것이라는 표현은 적절하다. ▶ tough는 문맥에 맞음

④ request 요청

- 이러한 이유로 거절 요법을 (시도하는 것을) 고려해보라. 일반적으로 거절당할 만한 ④ 요청이나 활동을 생각해 내라.
➡ 일부러 거절당하게 해보라는 것이므로 거절당할 만한 '요청'을 생각해보라는 것은 적절하다. ▶ request는 문맥에 맞음

어법 특강

* **동명사의 역할**
  - 동명사는 문장에서 주어, 목적어, 보어의 역할을 한다. 동명사가 주어로 쓰일 때는 단수 취급한다.
  - Drawing is my favorite hobby. (주어)
    (그림 그리기는 내가 가장 좋아하는 취미이다.)
  - What I like most about my job is meeting many people. (보어)
    (내가 내 직업에서 가장 좋아하는 점은 많은 사람들을 만나는 것이다.)
  - He enjoys playing basketball with his friends. (목적어)
    (그는 친구들과 농구하는 것을 즐긴다.)

L 13 정답 ⑤ ★ 2등급 대비 [정답률 45%]

*허브의 기능 및 위약 효과의 진실

다음 글의 밑줄 친 부분 중, 문맥상 낱말의 쓰임이 적절하지 않은 것은?
[3점]

가주어 / 진주어절을 이끄는 접속사 / 병렬 구조
It is widely believed / that certain herbs somehow magically improve / the work of certain organs, / and "cure" specific diseases / as a result. //
널리 알려져 있다 / 어떤 허브는 다소 마법처럼 향상시킨다고 / 특정 장기의 기능을 / 그리고 특정한 질병을 "고친다"고 / 그 결과 //

Such statements are unscientific / and groundless. //
그러한 진술은 비과학적이다 / 그리고 근거가 없다 //

형용사적 용법
Sometimes / herbs appear to work, / since they tend to ① increase / your blood circulation / in an aggressive attempt / by your body / to eliminate them / from your system. //
때때로 / 허브는 효과가 있는 것처럼 보이는데 / 이는 증가시키는 경향이 있기 때문이다 / 혈액 순환을 / 적극적인 시도 속에서 / 당신 몸의 / 그것들을 제거하려는 / 당신의 신체로부터 //

계속적 용법의 관계대명사
That can create / a ② temporary feeling of a high, / which makes it seem / as if your health condition has improved. //
make+목적어+목적격보어(동사원형)
그것은 만들어 줄 수 있는데 / 일시적인 좋은 기분을 / 이는 마치 보이게 만든다 / 당신의 건강 상태가 향상된 것처럼 //

접속사가 생략되지 않은 분사구문
Also, / herbs can have a placebo effect, / just like any other method, / thus helping you feel better. //
또한 / 허브는 위약 효과를 가지고 있는데 / 어떤 다른 방법과 마찬가지로 / 그래서 당신이 더 나아졌다고 느끼도록 도와준다 //

it ~ that ... 강조 구문
Whatever the case, / it is your body / that has the intelligence / to ③ regain health, / and not the herbs. // **단서 1** 건강을 되찾게 하는 지성을 가진 것은 허브가 아니라 몸임
어떠한 경우든 / 바로 당신의 몸이다 / 지성을 가진 것은 / 건강을 되찾게 하는 / 허브가 아니라 //

intelligence를 수식하는 과거분사
How can herbs have the intelligence / needed to direct your body / into getting healthier? // **단서 2** 허브가 어떻게 지성을 가질 수 있는지 질문함
허브가 어떻게 지성을 가질 수 있겠는가 / 당신의 몸을 인도하는 데 요구되는 / 더 건강해지는 방향으로 //

That is impossible. // **단서 3** 허브가 지성을 가지는 것은 불가능하다고 답함
그것은 불가능하다 //

병렬 구조
Try to imagine / how herbs might come into your body / and intelligently ④ fix your problems. //
상상해 보라 / 어떻게 허브가 당신의 몸 안으로 들어가 / 영리하게 당신의 문제를 해결할 수 있는지를 //

목적어절
If you try to do that, / you will see / how impossible it seems. //
만약 당신이 그렇게 해 본다면 / 당신은 알게 될 것이다 / 그것이 얼마나 불가능하게 보이는지를 //

목적어절을 이끄는 접속사
Otherwise, / it would mean / that herbs are ⑤ less (→ more) intelligent / than the human body, / which is truly hard to believe. //
계속적 용법의 관계대명사
그렇지 않다면 / 그것은 의미하는 것이 되는데 / 허브가 덜(→ 더) 지적이라는 것을 / 인간의 몸보다 / 이는 정말로 믿기 어렵다 //

❶ 행위자는 미래의 보상을 위해 현재의 쾌락을 포기한다. ⇒ 단서 1
❷ 크리스마스 선물을 위해 연초부터 모은 돈을 여름 휴가에 대신 쓰는 것, 즉 행위자가 저축을 조기에 사용하는 것은 약한 의지를 나타낸다. ⇒ 단서 2
❸ 행위자는 저축 계획을 세워도 즉각적인 쾌락의 유혹이 생기면 다르게 행동할 수 있다. ⇒ 단서 3

| 문제 풀이 순서 |

1st 각 낱말의 의미를 먼저 확인하고, 반의어를 미리 생각해 놓는다.

- ① delayed: 지연된 ↔ hurried: 서두르는
- ② greater: 더 큰 ↔ smaller: 더 작은
- ③ prematurely: 조기에 ↔ late: 늦은
- ④ weakness: 약함 ↔ strongness: 강함
- ⑤ disappears: 사라지다 ↔ appears: 나타나다

➡ 문맥에 맞는 낱말을 반의어로 바꿔서 정답 선택지를 만드는 경우가 많다. 그러므로 반의어를 먼저 떠올린 후 문맥이 어색한 부분을 찾는 것이 좋다.

2nd 선택지의 앞뒤 내용을 파악해서 문맥이 자연스러운지 확인한다.

①delayed 지연된

많은 인간과 인간이 아닌 동물은 물건이나 돈을 미래의 소비를 위해 저축한다. 이러한 행동은 즉각적인 보상보다 ① 지연된 보상을 선호하는 것을 드러내는 듯하다.

➡ 미래의 소비를 위해 물건이나 돈을 저축하는 행위는 나중을 위한 것이므로 즉각적인 보상보다 '지연된' 보상을 선호하는 것을 의미한다.
▶ delayed는 문맥에 맞음

②greater 더 큰

즉, 행위자는 미래의 보상을 위해 당장의 쾌락을 포기하는 것이다. 그러므로 미래 보상의 하락된 가치는 하락되지 않은 현재의 가치보다 ② 더 커야만 한다.

➡ 미래의 가치가 현재의 가치보다 더 커야 행위자가 미래의 보상을 위해 당장의 쾌락을 포기하는 것이 설명되므로, 미래 보상의 하락된 가치는 하락되지 않은 현재의 가치보다 '더 커야만' 한다. ▶ greater는 문맥에 맞음

③prematurely 조기에

그러나, 어떤 경우 행위자가 계획한 일을 기다리지 않고 그들의 저축을 ③ 조기에 사용하는 경우도 있다. 예를 들어, 연초에 한 직원이 자기 돈을 크리스마스 선물을 사기 위해 모아두었지만 대신 여름 휴가에 사용할 수 있다.

➡ 크리스마스 선물을 위해 저축한 돈을 여름 휴가에 사용하는 것은 행위자가 저축을 '조기에' 사용하는 경우이다. ▶ prematurely는 문맥에 맞음

④weakness 약함

예를 들어, 연초에 한 직원이 자기 돈을 크리스마스 선물을 사기 위해 모아두었지만 대신 여름 휴가에 사용할 수 있다. 이러한 사례는 의지의 ④ 약함의 예시가 될 수 있다.

➡ 크리스마스 선물을 위해 저축한 돈을 여름 휴가에 사용하는 것은 크리스마스 때까지 지출을 참을 의지가 약한 것을 나타내므로, 의지의 '약함'의 예시가 된다.
▶ weakness는 문맥에 맞음

⑤disappears 사라지다

즉, 행위자는 그들의 저축을 가장 큰 이익을 위해 특정 방식으로 사용하기로 판단하거나 결심했으나 즉각적인 즐거움에 대한 유혹이 ⑤ ~~사라지면~~ 생기면 다르게 행동할 수도 있다.

➡ 저축을 가장 큰 이익을 위해 사용하려고 결정했으나 그와 다르게 행동하도록 하려면, 즉각적인 쾌락에 대한 유혹이 '사라지는' 것이 아니라 '생겨야' 할 것이다.
▶ disappears를 appears(생기다)와 같은 반의어로 바꿔야 함

L 16 정답 ② ━━━━━━ ★ 1등급 대비 [정답률 40%]

＊삶에 대한 통제력 회복

다음 글의 밑줄 친 부분 중, 문맥상 낱말의 쓰임이 적절하지 <u>않은</u> 것은? [3점]

Do you sometimes feel like / you don't love your life? //
당신은 가끔 느끼는가 / 당신의 삶을 사랑하지 않는다고 //

Like, deep inside, / something is missing? //
마치, 마음 깊은 곳에서 / 뭔가가 빠진 것처럼 //

That's because / we are living someone else's life. //
왜냐하면 (그것은) ~ 때문이다 / 우리가 타인의 삶을 살고 있기 //

allow+목적어+목적격보어(to부정사)
We allow / other people to ① influence our choices. //
우리는 허용한다 / 타인이 우리의 선택에 영향을 주도록 //
단서 1 타인이 우리의 선택에 영향을 주고 있음

We are trying / to meet their expectations. //
우리는 노력하고 있다 / 그들의 기대감을 만족시키기 위해

수동태
Social pressure is deceiving / — we are all impacted / without noticing it. // 단서 2 우리는 사회적 압력의 영향을 받고 있음
사회적 압력은 (우리를) 현혹시킨다 / 우리 모두는 영향을 받는다 / 그것을 눈치채지도 못한 채 //

end up -ing: ~결국 ~하게 되다
Before we realize / we are losing ownership of our lives, / we end up ② ignoring(→ envying) / how other people live. //
우리가 깨닫기도 전에 / 우리의 삶에 대한 소유권을 잃었다는 것을 / 우리는 결국 무시하게(→ 부러워하게) 된다 / 다른 사람들이 어떻게 사는지를 //

부사 enough는 형용사 뒤에 위치함
Then, / we can only see the greener grass / — ours is never good enough. // 단서 3 더 푸른 잔디(타인의 삶이 더 좋아보이는 것)만을 보면
우리의 삶은 충분히 좋아질 수 없음
그러면 / 우리는 더 푸른 잔디(타인의 삶이 더 좋아 보이는 것)만 볼 수 있게 된다 / 우리의 삶은 만족할 만큼 충분히 좋아질 수 없다 //

앞에 목적격 관계대명사 생략 ＊
To regain that passion / for the life you want, / you must ③ recover control of your choices. //
열정을 되찾기 위해서는 / 당신이 원하는 삶에 대한 / 당신의 선택에 대한 통제력을 회복해야 한다 //

간접의문문
No one but yourself can choose / how you live. //
당신 자신을 제외한 그 누구도 선택할 수 없다 / 당신이 어떻게 살지를 //

But, how? //
하지만 어떻게 해야 할까 //

명사적 용법
The first step to getting rid of expectations / is to treat yourself ④ kindly. //
기대감을 버리는 첫 단계는 / 자신을 친절하게 대하는 것이다 //

You can't truly love other people / if you don't love yourself first. //
다른 사람을 진정으로 사랑할 수 없다 / 자신을 먼저 사랑하지 않으면 //

간접의문문
When we accept / who we are, / there's no room for other's ⑤ expectations. //
우리가 받아들일 때 / 우리의 있는 그대로를 / 타인의 기대감을 위한 여지는 남아 있지 않다 //

- missing ⓐ (제자리나 집에 있지 않고) 없어진, 빠진
- meet ⓥ (필요, 요구 등을) 충족시키다 · expectation ⓝ 기대
- deceiving ⓐ 속이는, 현혹시키는 · notice ⓥ 눈치채다, 알아채다
- ownership ⓝ 소유권 · ignore ⓥ 무시하다 · passion ⓝ 열정
- recover ⓥ 회복하다 · get rid of ~을 버리다
- treat ⓥ 대하다, 다루다 · accept ⓥ 받아들이다 · room ⓝ 여지

당신은 가끔 당신의 삶을 사랑하지 않는다고 느끼는가? 마치, 마음 깊은 곳에서 뭔가가 빠진 것처럼? 왜냐하면, (그것은) 우리가 타인의 삶을 살고 있기 때문이다. 우리는 타인이 우리의 선택에 ① 영향을 주도록 허용한다. 우리는 그들의 기대감을 만족시키기 위해 노력하고 있다. 사회적 압력은 (우리를) 현혹시킨다. 우리 모두는 그것을 눈치채지도 못한 채 영향을 받는다. 우리의 삶에 대한 소유권을 잃었다는 것을 깨닫기도 전에, 우리는 결국 다른 사람들이 어떻게 사는지를 ② 무시하게(→ 부러워하게) 된다. 그러면, 우리는 더 푸른 잔디(타인의 삶이 더 좋아 보이는 것)만 볼 수

있게 된다. 우리의 삶은 만족할 만큼 충분히 좋아질 수 없다. 당신이 원하는 삶에 대한 열정을 되찾기 위해서는 당신의 선택에 대한 통제력을 ③ 회복해야 한다. 당신 자신을 제외한 그 누구도 당신이 어떻게 살지를 선택할 수 없다. 하지만 어떻게 해야 할까? 기대감을 버리는 첫 단계는 자신을 ④ 친절하게 대하는 것이다. 자신을 먼저 사랑하지 않으면 다른 사람을 진정으로 사랑할 수 없다. 우리가 우리의 있는 그대로를 받아들일 때, 타인의 ⑤ 기대감을 위한 여지는 남아 있지 않다.

왜 1등급? 'The grass is greener on the other side of the fence.(남의 떡이 더 커 보인다.)'라는 속담을 알고 있으면 'the greener grass'라는 단서를 쉽게 파악할 수 있지만, 모른다면 비유적인 의미를 파악하기가 어려운 1등급 대비 문제이다.

| 풀이 단서 확인 |

❶ 타인은 우리의 선택에 영향을 준다. ⇒ **단서 1**
❷ 우리는 눈치채지 못한 채 사회적 압력의 영향을 받는다. ⇒ **단서 2**
❸ 남의 것이 더 좋아 보이기만 하면 우리의 삶은 충분히 좋아질 수 없다.
⇒ **단서 3**

| 문제 풀이 순서 |

1st 각 낱말의 의미를 먼저 확인하고, 반의어를 미리 생각해 놓는다.

① influence: 영향을 주다 ↔ ?
② ignoring: 무시하다 ↔ envying: 부러워하다
③ recover: 회복하다 ↔ ?
④ kindly: 친절하게 ↔ unkindly: 불친절하게
⑤ expectations: 기대감 ↔ ?

➡ 선택지에 제시된 낱말과 반대 의미를 나타내는 낱말을 넣었을 때 문맥이 성립되는 경우에 정답인 경우가 많으므로 반의어를 확실히 떠올리기 힘든 ①과 ③, ⑤은 정답이 아닐 가능성이 높다.

2nd 선택지의 앞뒤 내용을 파악해서 문맥이 자연스러운지 확인한다.

① influence 영향을 주다

왜냐하면, (그것은) 우리가 타인의 삶을 살고 있기 때문이다. 우리는 타인이 우리의 선택에 ① 영향을 주도록 허용한다. 우리는 그들의 기대감을 만족시키기 위해 노력하고 있다.

➡ 앞 문장에서 우리가 타인의 삶을 살고 있다고 했으므로 타인이 우리의 선택에 '영향을 주도록' 허용한다는 표현은 적절하다. ▶ influence는 문맥에 맞음

② ignoring 무시하는

우리의 삶에 대한 소유권을 잃었다는 것을 깨닫기도 전에, 우리는 결국 다른 사람들이 어떻게 사는지를 ② ~~무시하게~~ (부러워하게) 된다. 그러면, 우리는 더 푸른 잔디(타인의 삶이 더 좋아 보이는 것)만 볼 수 있게 된다.

➡ 영어 속담 중에 '남의 떡이 더 커 보인다'라는 뜻을 가진 속담이 The grass is greener on the other side인데, 여기서 the greener grass를 인용하여 타인의 삶을 가리키는 표현으로 사용했다.
우리는 더 푸른 잔디만을 볼 수 있게 된다고 했으므로 다른 사람들이 어떻게 사는지를 '무시하게' 되는 것이 아니라 그 반대이다.
▶ ② ignoring을 envying(부러워하는)과 같은 반의어로 바꿔야 함

③ recover 회복하다

당신이 원하는 삶에 대한 열정을 되찾기 위해서는 당신의 선택에 대한 통제력을 ③ 회복해야 한다.

➡ 원하는 삶에 대한 열정을 되찾으려면 우리의 선택에 대한 통제력을 '회복해야' 할 것이다. ▶ recover는 문맥에 맞음

④ kindly 친절하게

기대감을 버리는 첫 단계는 자신을 ④ 친절하게 대하는 것이다. 자신을 먼저 사랑하지 않으면 다른 사람을 진정으로 사랑할 수 없다.

➡ 뒤에 자신을 먼저 사랑해야 한다는 내용이 나오므로 자신을 '친절하게' 대하는 것이 첫 단계라는 표현은 적절하다. ▶ kindly는 문맥에 맞음

⑤ expectations 기대감

우리가 우리의 있는 그대로를 받아들일 때, 타인의 ⑤ 기대감을 위한 여지는 남아 있지 않다.

➡ 우리가 타인의 기대감을 만족시키기 위해 노력하는 상태에서 벗어나 우리의 있는 그대로를 받아들일 때, 타인의 '기대감'을 위한 여지는 남아있지 않게 될 것이라는 표현은 적절하다. ▶ expectations는 문맥에 맞음

어법 특강

＊ 관계대명사의 생략

– 목적격 관계대명사는 생략하는 경우가 많다.
• She was a celebrated actress (whom) he had known and loved.
  a celebrated actress를 선행사로 하는 목적격 관계대명사
  (그녀는 그가 알고 사랑했던 유명한 배우였다.)
• I've been thinking about those questions (which) you asked me last week.
  those questions를 선행사로 하는 목적격 관계대명사
  (나는 네가 내게 지난주에 물어본 그 질문들에 대해 생각해 오고 있다.)

어법 특강

＊ 보어 자리에 부정사가 오는 동사들

– 주격 보어 자리에 to부정사가 오는 동사: seem, happen, appear 등
• He always seems to get bored and restless in classes.
  seems의 주격 보어
  (그는 항상 수업시간에 지루해하고 가만히 못 있는 것처럼 보인다.)

– 목적격 보어 자리에 to부정사가 오는 동사: ask, allow, want, advise, tell, force, enable, cause, get 등
• Your support will enable me to perform better at my work.
  will enable의 목적격 보어
  (당신의 지원이 제가 직장에서 일을 더 잘하게 만들 것입니다.)

– 목적격 보어 자리에 원형부정사가 오는 동사: make, have, let(사역동사) / see, feel, hear(지각동사) 등 / help(단, help는 to부정사와 원형부정사 둘 다 쓸 수 있다.)
• Exercising regularly lets you stay in a positive mood.
  lets의 목적격 보어
  (규칙적으로 운동하는 것은 네가 긍정적인 기분을 유지하게 해 준다.)

L 어휘 Review 정답 ——— 문제편 p. 167

01 전형적인	11 interfere with	21 reveal
02 이상적으로	12 set aside	22 complicated
03 명료함	13 take away	23 term
04 미리	14 stem from	24 reserve
05 상당한	15 in turn	25 transformed
06 therapy	16 convenience	26 insecurity
07 circumstance	17 residents	27 Industrial
08 desire	18 polar	28 determine
09 deceiving	19 agent	29 resolve
10 motivate	20 possessions	30 considerable

M 01 정답 ② *갑작스러운 방해의 대가

The costs of **interruptions** / are well-documented. //
방해로 인한 대가는 / 잘 기록되어 있다 //

Martin Luther King Jr. lamented them / when he described /
지시형용사 주격 관계대명사 수동태 동사 부사절 접속사(이유) 부사절 접속사(시간)
"**that** lovely poem **that** didn't **get written** / **because** someone
knocked on the door." // 단서 1 Martin Luther King Jr.는 갑자기 누가 문을 두드려 시를 완성하지 못함
Martin Luther King Jr.는 이를 슬퍼했다 / 그가 묘사했을 때 / "쓰여지지 못한 그
사랑스러운 시 / 누군가 문을 두드렸기 때문에" //

Perhaps / the most famous literary example happened in 1797 /
when Samuel Taylor Coleridge **started** writing his poem / *Kubla
Khan* / from a dream he had /
앞에 목적격 관계대명사 that이 생략됨
아마도 / 가장 유명한 문학적 사례는 1797년에 일어났던 일일 것이다 / Samuel Taylor
Coleridge가 시를 쓰기 시작했는데 / *Kubla Khan*이라는 / 꿈에서 /
병렬 구조
but then **was visited** by an unexpected guest. //
뜻밖의 손님이 찾아왔을 때 //

For Coleridge, by coincidence, / the untimely visitor came at a
particularly bad time. //
공교롭게도 Coleridge에게 / 이 불청객은 특히 좋지 않은 시기에 찾아왔다 //
left의 목적어 목적격 보어
He forgot his inspiration / and left **the work unfinished**. //
그는 영감을 잊고 / 작품을 미완성으로 남겼다 // 단서 2 Samuel Taylor Coleridge는 갑자기
부사절 접속사(대조) 손님이 찾아와서 작품을 끝내지 못함
While there are many documented cases of sudden disruptions
주격 관계대명사
/ **that** have had significant consequences / 단서 3 심각한 결과를 초래한
갑작스러운 방해의 사례가 많음
갑작스러운 방해의 사례가 많이 기록되어 있지만 / 심각한 결과를 초래한 /
'-와 같은'
for professionals in critical roles / **such as** doctors, nurses,
control room operators, stock traders, and pilots, /
중요한 역할을 담당하는 전문가들에게 / 의사, 간호사, 관제실 운영자, 주식 거래자, 조종사와
같은 /

they also impact most of us in our everyday lives, / **slowing**
down work productivity / and generally **increasing** stress levels. //
병렬 구조
갑작스러운 방해는 일상 생활에서 대부분의 사람들에게도 영향을 미치고 / 업무 생산성을
떨어뜨리며 / 일반적으로 스트레스 수준을 높인다 //

- document ⓥ 기록하다
- coincidence ⓝ 우연
- particularly ad 특히
- sudden ⓐ 갑작스러운
- significant ⓐ 상당한
- critical ⓐ 중요한
- productivity ⓝ 생산성
- literary ⓐ 문학적인
- untimely ⓐ 시기가 적절하지 않은
- inspiration ⓝ 영감
- disruption ⓝ 방해
- consequence ⓝ 결과
- impact ⓥ 영향을 끼치다

방해로 인한 대가는 잘 기록되어 있다. Martin Luther King Jr.는 "누군가 문
을 두드리는 바람에 쓰여지지 못한 사랑스러운 시"를 묘사하며 이를 슬퍼했다.
아마도 가장 유명한 문학적 사례는 1797년 Samuel Taylor Coleridge가 꿈을
꾸고 *Kubla Khan*이라는 시를 쓰기 시작했는데 뜻밖의 손님이 찾아왔을 때 일어
났던 일일 것이다. 공교롭게도 Coleridge에게 이 불청객은 특히 좋지 않은 시
기에 찾아왔다. 그는 영감을 잊고 작품을 미완성으로 남겼다. 의사, 간호사, 관
제실 운영자, 주식 거래자, 조종사와 같은 중요한 역할을 담당하는 전문가들에
게 심각한 결과를 초래한 갑작스러운 방해의 사례가 많이 기록되어 있지만, 갑
작스러운 방해는 일상 생활에서 대부분의 사람들에게도 영향을 미쳐 업무 생산
성을 떨어뜨리며 일반적으로 스트레스 수준을 높인다.

다음 빈칸에 들어갈 말로 가장 적절한 것을 고르시오.
① misunderstandings 오해에 대한 내용이 아님
  오해
② interruptions 방해의 대가를 여러 사례를 통해 설명하고 있음
  방해
③ inequalities 불평등에 대한 언급은 없음
  불평등
④ regulations 규제에 관한 내용이 아님
  규제
⑤ arguments 논쟁에 관한 내용이 아님
  논쟁

| 문제 풀이 순서 | ★★★ [정답률 58%]

1st 빈칸이 포함된 문장을 읽고, 빈칸에 들어갈 말에 대한 단서를 얻는다.

빈칸 문장	The costs of _____ are well-documented.
	_____로 인한 대가는 잘 기록되어 있다.

→ '무엇'으로 인한 대가가 잘 기록되어 있다고 했으므로, 단서
대가를 만드는 것이 '무엇'인지, 그리고 그것에 대한 어떤 기록이 있는지 알려줄
것이다. 발상

2nd 글의 나머지 부분을 확인해서 정답을 찾는다.

예시 1: Martin Luther King Jr. → 시를 쓰고 있을 때 누가 노크를 하여 시를
완성하지 못함 단서 1
예시 2: Samuel Taylor Coleridge → 시를 쓰고 있을 때 갑자기 손님이 찾아와서
영감을 잊고 작품을 끝내지 못함 단서 2
갑작스러운 방해가 전문가들에게 심각한 결과를 초래한 사례들이 많이 기록되어
있음 단서 3
→ 예시로 제시된 두 인물 모두 작업 중에 누군가가 방해하여 작품을 끝내지 못했고,
이들과 비슷한 사례들이 많이 기록되어 있다고 했다.
▶ 즉, ② '방해'의 대가인 업무 생산성 저하가 잘 기록되어 있다.

| 선택지 분석 |
① 어떤 상황이나 관계에 대한 오해로 인한 대가가 아니다.
② 갑작스러운 방해로 인해 대가를 치른 사례들이 많다고 했다.
③ 불평등의 대가는 언급되지 않았다.
④ 규제로 인한 대가가 발생한 상황이 아니다.
⑤ 논쟁으로 인한 대가가 발생했다는 내용은 없다.

M 02 정답 ③ *대화를 지속하기 위해 질문보다는 관찰하기

명령문 동사
As you listen to your child / in an emotional moment, / **be aware**
비교급
/ that **sharing simple observations** usually works **better** / **than**
비교 대상
asking questions / to get a conversation rolling. //
여러분이 자녀의 말을 들을 때 / 어떤 감정적인 순간에 놓인 / 인식해라 / 단순한 관찰 결과를
공유하는 것이 대개는 더 효과적임을 / 질문을 하는 것보다 / 대화가 계속 굴러가게 하기 위
해 //

You may ask your child / "Why do you feel sad?" / and she may
not have a clue. // 단서 1 자녀는 감정의 원인을 묻는 말에 제대로 대답하지 못할 수도 있음
여러분이 자녀에게 물으면 / "왜 슬픈 기분이 드니"라고 / 그녀는 짐작조차 못할 수도 있다 //

As a child, / she may not have an answer on the tip of her
tongue. //
아이라서 / 그녀는 답이 당장 떠오르지 않을지도 모른다 //

Maybe / she's feeling sad / about her parents' arguments, / or
because she feels overtired, / or she's worried about a piano
recital. //
어쩌면 / 그녀는 슬픔을 느끼고 있거나 / 부모님의 말다툼에 대해 / 혹은 그녀가 극도로 지쳤기
때문이거나 / 혹은 피아노 연주회를 걱정할지도 모른다 //
단서 2 감정 상태와 원인 중 어떤 것도 대답하지 못할 수도 있음
앞에 언급된 내용 (자신의 감정 상태와 그 원인)
But she may or may not be able to explain / any of **this**. //
그러나 그녀는 이것에 대해 설명할 수도 있고 설명하지 못할 수도 있다 / 어떤 것도 //

And / <mark>even when</mark> she <mark>does</mark> come up with an answer, / she might
'비록 ~할 때라도' 강조 용법의 do동사
be worried / that the answer is not good enough to justify the
feeling. //

그리고 / 그녀가 정말로 답이 떠오를 때조차도 / 걱정할 수도 있다 / 그 대답이 그 감정을 정당화하기에는 충분하지 않다고 //

Under these circumstances, / a series of questions can just make
사역동사 make의 목적어와 목적격 보어 (형용사)
<mark>a child silent</mark>. //

이러한 상황에서는 / 연속된 질문들이 그저 자녀를 침묵하게 만들 수 있다 //

가주어   진주어
<mark>It's better</mark> / <mark>to simply reflect what you notice</mark>. // 단서3 감정을 알아차렸음을 보이는 것이 직접적인 질문보다 더 나음
더 낫다 / 여러분이 인지한 것을 단순히 나타내는 것이 //

병렬 구조 (직접 화법)
You can <mark>say</mark>, / "<mark>You seem a little tired today</mark>," / or, "<mark>I noticed that</mark>
병렬 구조 (문장의 동사)
<mark>you frowned</mark> / when I mentioned the recital," / and <mark>wait</mark> for her
response. //

여러분은 말할 수 있다 / "너 오늘 조금 피곤해 보이네" 혹은 "네가 얼굴을 찡그린 것을 알아챘어 / 내가 연주회 얘기를 꺼냈을 때"라고 / 그리고 그녀의 반응을 기다려 볼 수 있다 //

- be aware that ~을 인식하다   - have a clue 짐작하다
- on the tip of one's tongue 당장 떠오르지 않는, 혀 끝에서 맴도는
- argument ⓝ 말다툼, 논쟁   - overtired ⓐ 극도로 지친
- recital ⓝ 연주회   - justify ⓥ 정당화하다
- circumstances ⓝ 상황, 환경   - a series of 연속된
- frown ⓥ (얼굴을) 찡그리다   - mention ⓥ 얘기를 꺼내다
- push ~ for ... ~에게 ⋯을 요구하다   - observation ⓝ 관찰
- cool down 식히다, 진정시키다

여러분이 어떤 감정적인 순간에 놓인 자녀의 말을 들을 때, 대화가 계속 굴러가게 하기 위해 질문을 하는 것보다 **단순한 관찰 결과를 공유하는 것**이 대개는 더 효과적임을 인식해라. 여러분이 자녀에게 "왜 슬픈 기분이 드니?"라고 물으면 그녀는 짐작조차 못 할 수도 있다. 아이라서. 그녀는 답이 당장 떠오르지 않을지도 모른다. 어쩌면 그녀는 부모님의 말다툼에 대해 슬픔을 느끼고 있거나, 혹은 그녀가 극도로 지쳤기 때문이거나, 혹은 피아노 연주회를 걱정할지도 모른다. 그러나 그녀는 이것에 대해 설명할 수도 있고 어떤 것도 설명하지 못할 수도 있다. 그리고 그녀가 정말로 답이 떠오를 때조차도 그 대답이 그 감정을 정당화하기에는 충분하지 않다고 걱정할 수도 있다. 이러한 상황에서는 연속된 질문들이 그저 자녀를 침묵하게 만들 수 있다. 여러분이 인지한 것을 단순히 나타내는 것이 더 낫다. "너 오늘 조금 피곤해 보이네." 혹은 "내가 연주회 얘기를 꺼냈을 때 네가 얼굴을 찡그린 것을 알아챘어."라고 말하고, 그녀의 반응을 기다려 볼 수 있다.

다음 빈칸에 들어갈 말로 가장 적절한 것을 고르시오.

① giving quick advice 조언은 언급되지 않았음
빠르게 조언하는 것
② pushing her for answers 대답을 억지로 요구하면 답을 듣기 더 어려움
대답을 억지로 요구하는 것
③ sharing simple observations 자녀가 답변의 부담을 느낄 때는 계속 묻기보다는 단순한 관찰 결과를 공유하는 것 부모가 감정을 인지했음을 알려 주는 것이 더 효과적임
④ telling your own life stories 이야기를 공유하는 것은 언급되지 않았음
자신의 인생 이야기를 들려주는 것
⑤ leaving her alone to cool down 자녀를 혼자 두면 대화가 이어질 수 없음
진정할 시간을 주며 혼자 두는 것

| 문제 풀이 순서 | ✽✽✖ [정답률 60%]

1st 빈칸이 포함된 문장을 읽고, 빈칸에 들어갈 말에 대한 단서를 얻는다.

빈칸 문장	As you listen to your child in an emotional moment, be aware that _____ usually works better than asking questions to get a conversation rolling. 여러분이 어떤 감정적인 순간에 놓인 자녀의 말을 들을 때, 대화가 계속 굴러가게 하기 위해 질문을 하는 것보다 _____ 이 대개는 더 효과적임을 인식해라.

➡ 자녀와의 대화를 지속하기 위해서 질문보다 '무엇'이 더 효과적이라고 했으므로, 단서 질문 외에 다른 방식이 언급되는지 확인해야 한다. 발상

2nd 글의 내용을 종합해서 빈칸에 들어갈 적절한 말을 찾는다.

- 자녀가 감정의 원인을 묻는 말에 제대로 대답하지 못할 수도 있음 단서1
- 자녀는 감정 상태와 원인 중 어떤 것도 대답하지 못할 수도 있음 단서2
- 단순히 감정을 인지했음을 나타내는 것이 직접 감정을 묻는 것보다 나음 단서3

➡ 자녀에게 감정 상태나 원인을 물을 때 제대로 된 답변을 얻지 못할 수도 있다. 이때 답을 얻기 위해 계속 묻기보다는, 단순하게 부모가 인지하는(관찰하는) 자녀의 감정을 말해주는 것이 더 낫다는 내용이다.

▶ 따라서 감정적인 순간에 놓인 자녀와 대화하려면 계속 질문하는 것보다 자녀의 감정에 관하여 ③ '단순한 관찰 결과를 공유하는 것'이 대개는 더 효과적이다.

| 선택지 분석 |

① 자녀의 감정 상태를 알기 위해 계속 질문하는 것은 언급되었지만, 빠르게 조언하는 것은 언급되지 않았다.
② 계속 질문하여 대답을 억지로 요구하는 것은 오히려 자녀가 침묵하게 한다.
③ 자녀의 감정에 관하여 계속 질문하여 자녀에게 부담을 주는 것보다는, 부모의 입장에서 자녀의 상태를 관찰한 결과를 말해주고 반응을 보는 것이 더 효과적이다.
④ 자신의 인생을 공유하는 것보다는, 부모가 관찰한 자녀의 감정 상태를 알려주는 것이 대화를 지속하는 데 더 도움이 된다.
⑤ 결국 자녀와 대화해야 하는데, 자녀를 혼자 두면 대화를 이어가기 어려울 것이다.

구문 서술형

정답 shared, would

→ 현재 사실에 반대되거나 실현 가능성이 없는 일을 가정하는 가정법 과거 문장이다. If절에는 동사의 과거형인 shared, 주절에는 조동사의 과거형인 would를 써야 한다.

M 03 정답 ② ＊경험에 기반한 주의 집중 ────

In everyday life, / we use <mark>previous experience</mark> / to predict /
부사적 용법 (목적)
간접의문문
<mark>where we should pay attention</mark>. //
일상생활에서 / 우리는 이전 경험을 사용한다 / 예측하기 위해 / 어디에 집중해야 할지를 //

Different environments create different expectations. //
다른 환경은 다른 기대를 만든다 //

앞 문장의 내용을 가리킴
<mark>This</mark> was profoundly illustrated / by the scientist Jared Diamond
/ in his book *Guns, Germs, and Steel*. //
이것은 깊이 있게 설명되었다 / 과학자 Jared Diamond에 의해 / 그의 저서인 *Guns, Germs, and Steel*에서 //

현재분사구 (an adventure 수식)
He describes an adventure / <mark>wandering through the New
Guinea jungle / with native New Guineans</mark>. //
그는 모험을 묘사한다 / New Guinea 정글을 돌아다닌 / New Guinea 원주민들과 함께 //

목적절 접속사   뒤에 목적격 관계대명사가 생략됨
He relates / <mark>that</mark> these natives / tend to perform poorly at <mark>tasks</mark>
현재완료 수동태
Westerners <mark>have been trained</mark> to do / since childhood. //
그는 말한다 / 이 원주민들이 / 과업을 잘 수행하지 못하는 경향이 있다고 / 서구인들이 훈련받아 온 / 어린 시절부터 // 단서1 New Guinea 원주민들은 서구인들이 훈련받아 온 과업을 잘 수행하지 못함

'거의 ~가 아닌'
But they are <mark>hardly</mark> stupid. // 하지만 그들이 멍청한 것은 아니다 //
앞에 주격 관계대명사와 be동사가 생략됨
They can detect / the most subtle changes in the jungle, / <mark>good
병렬 구조 (for + 동명사)
for</mark> / <mark>following</mark> the tracks of a predator / or <mark>for finding</mark> the way
back home. // 단서2 New Guinea 원주민들은 정글의 미묘한 변화를 감지함
그들은 감지할 수 있는데 / 정글에서 가장 미묘한 변화를 / 이는 유용하다 / 포식자의 흔적을 추적하거나 / 집으로 돌아오는 길을 찾는데 //

의문사 + to부정사
They know / <mark>which insects to leave alone</mark>, / know where food
exists, / can build and tear down shelters with ease. //
그들은 알며 / 어느 곤충을 내버려 두어야 할지 / 어디에 음식이 있는지 알고 / 피난처를 쉽게 만들고 철거할 수 있다 //

단수 주어   단수 동사
<mark>Diamond</mark>, / who had never spent time in such places, / <mark>has no</mark>
형용사적 용법 (ability 수식)
ability / to pay attention to these things. //
Diamond는 / 그러한 장소에서 시간을 보내본 적이 없는 / 능력이 없다 / 이러한 것들에 주의를 기울일 수 있는 // 단서3 원주민과 다른 장소에서 성장한 Diamond는 원주민과 같은 능력이 없음

가정법 if 생략 (= If he were ~)

Were he to be tested on such tasks, / he also would perform poorly. //

그가 그런 과업들에 대해 시험을 본다면 / 그 역시 잘하지 못할 것이다 //

- predict ⓥ 예측하다　　・ environment ⓝ 환경
- illustrate ⓥ 설명하다　　・ describe ⓥ 묘사하다
- wander ⓥ 돌아다니다, 방랑하다　　・ relate ⓥ 말하다, 이야기하다
- task ⓝ 과업　　・ detect ⓥ 감지하다　　・ predator ⓝ 포식자
- tear down 철거하다, 허물다　　・ shelter ⓝ 피난처
- cooperation ⓝ 협력　　・ instinct ⓝ 본능

일상생활에서, 우리는 어디에 집중해야 할지를 예측하기 위해 **이전 경험**을 사용한다. 다른 환경은 다른 기대를 만든다. 이것은 과학자 Jared Diamond에 의해 그의 저서인 *Guns, Germs, and Steel*에서 깊이 있게 설명되었다. 그는 New Guinea 정글을 New Guinea 원주민들과 함께 돌아다닌 모험을 묘사한다. 그는 서구인들이 어린 시절부터 훈련받아 온 과업을 이 원주민들이 잘 수행하지 못하는 경향이 있다고 말한다. 하지만 그들이 멍청한 것은 아니다. 그들은 정글에서 가장 미묘한 변화를 감지할 수 있는데, 이는 포식자의 흔적을 추적하거나 집으로 돌아오는 길을 찾는 데 유용하다. 그들은 어느 곤충을 내버려 두어야 할지 알며, 어디에 음식이 있는지 알고, 피난처를 쉽게 만들고 철거할 수 있다. 그러한 장소에서 시간을 보내본 적이 없는 Diamond는 이러한 것들에 주의를 기울일 수 있는 능력이 없다. 그가 그런 과업들에 대해 시험을 본다면, 그 역시 잘하지 못할 것이다.

다음 빈칸에 들어갈 말로 가장 적절한 것을 고르시오. [3점]

① close cooperation 긴밀한 협력은 언급되지 않았음
　긴밀한 협력
②previous experience 이전 경험에 따라 어디에 주의를 집중하는지가 달라짐
　이전 경험
③ survival instinct 본능보다는 환경에 따라 달라지는 경험을 강조함
　생존 본능
④ modern technology 현대 기술은 언급되지 않았음
　현대 기술
⑤ parental advice 부모의 조언은 언급되지 않았음
　부모의 조언

왜 정답? ✱✱❋ [정답률 62%]

- New Guinea 원주민들은 서구인들에게 익숙한 과업을 잘 수행하지 못함 단서 1
- New Guinea 원주민들은 정글의 미묘한 변화를 감지할 수 있음 단서 2
- 다른 장소에서 성장한 Diamond는 이 원주민들과 같은 능력이 없음 단서3

➡ New Guinea 원주민들은 서구인들이 어릴 때부터 훈련받아서 익숙한 과업을 잘 수행하지 못하지만, 정글에서 미묘한 변화에 주의를 기울이고 이를 감지할 수 있다. 반면에 Diamond는 정글에서 시간을 보낸 적이 없어서 New Guinea 원주민들과 같은 능력이 없다.

▶ 즉, 일상에서 어디에 집중할지 예측하기 위해 각자 성장한 환경 속에서 겪은 ② '이전 경험'을 사용한다는 것을 알 수 있다.

왜 오답?

① 어디에 집중할지 예측하기 위해 경험을 사용한다고 했을 뿐, 협력은 언급되지 않았다. 예시와 연관되더라도, 빈칸 문장에 더 집중하기! 꿀팁
③ 음식과 피난처가 언급되긴 했으나, 생존 본능이 어디에 집중할지에 영향을 끼친다는 내용이 아니다.
④ 현대 기술이 어디에 집중할지에 영향을 끼친다는 내용은 언급되지 않았다.
⑤ 부모의 조언이 어디에 집중할지에 영향을 끼친다는 내용은 언급되지 않았다.

[구문 서술형]

[정답] Were he to be tested

[해석] 그가 익숙치 않은 과업에 대해 시험을 본다면, 그 역시 잘하지 못할 것이다.
→ 가정법 문장에서 if를 생략하면 주어와 동사를 도치하므로 Were he to be tested로 쓴다.

M 04 정답 ② *인간의 번식 전략

In most respects, / humans are one of a relatively small number
'~ 중 하나'
of species /

대부분의 측면에서 / 인간은 비교적 소수의 종들 중 하나이다 /
주격 관계대명사 (선행사: species)
that evolved a very different strategy / of **investing more
energy to reproduce more slowly**. //

매우 다른 전략을 진화시킨 / 더 많은 에너지를 투자하여 더 천천히 번식하는 //

Like apes and elephants, / we mature at a leisurely pace, / grow
devote 목적어 to 동명사: ~을 '에 투자하다, 바치다
large bodies, / and have few babies / but **devote much time and
energy** / **to raising** them well. // 단서 1 인간은 새끼들을 적게 낳지만 키우는 데
　　　　　　　　　　　　　　　　많은 시간과 에너지를 투자함
유인원과 코끼리와 마찬가지로 / 우리는 천천히 성숙하고 / 몸집을 크게 키우며 / 새끼들을 적게 낳지만 / 많은 시간과 에너지를 투자한다 / 그들을 잘 키우는 데 //

This unusual strategy succeeds / because while apes and
elephants produce / fewer babies than mice, / a larger
percentage of their offspring / survive to then reproduce. //
　　　　　　　　　　　　　　부사적 용법 (결과)
이 특이한 전략은 성공한다 / 왜냐하면 유인원과 코끼리는 낳지만 / 생쥐보다 더 적은 수의 새끼를 / 그들의 새끼 중 더 높은 비율이 / 살아남아서 번식한다 //

A house mouse can become a mother / when she is just five
weeks old, / has four to ten pups per litter, / and can have a new
　　　　　　　병렬 구조
litter every two months / over the course of her approximately
twelve-month life. //

생쥐는 어미가 될 수 있으며 / 생후 5주 만에 / 한 배에서 4마리에서 10마리의 새끼를 낳고 / 2개월마다 새로운 새끼들을 낳을 수 있다 / 약 12개월의 생애 동안 //
완전자동사 die와 함께 쓰인 유사 보어 (형용사)
However, the vast majority of her pups die young. //
그러나, 그의 새끼 대부분은 어릴 때 죽는다 //

In contrast, / a chimp or elephant mother does not reproduce
/ until she is at least twelve years old, / and she gives birth to
　　　　　　　　　　　　절과 절을 잇는 등위접속사
only one infant / every five or six years / over the next thirty
　　　　　　　　　　　　　　　　　　= approximately
or so years. // 단서 2 침팬지와 코끼리는 생쥐보다 더 늦게 그리고 더 적게 자손을 번식함
반면 / 침팬지나 코끼리 어미는 번식을 하지 않으며 / 최소 12살이 될 때까지 / 단 한 마리의 새끼만 낳는다 / 5년 또는 6년마다 / 이후 30년 정도에 걸쳐 //
　　　　　　　　　　　　　　　동명사 (전치사 to의 목적어)
About half of these offspring / make it to becoming parents. //
이러한 새끼 중 절반 정도가 / 부모가 되는 데 성공한다 // 단서3 침팬지와 코끼리는 생쥐보다도
　　　　　　　　　　　　　　　　　　　　더 높은 비율의 자손이 생존하여 번식함

- respect ⓝ 측면　　・ relatively ⓐ 비교적
- a small number of 소수의　　・ species ⓝ 종
- evolve ⓥ 진화시키다　　・ strategy ⓝ 전략　　・ mature ⓥ 성숙하다
- leisurely ⓐ 느긋한, 여유 있는　　・ pace ⓝ 속도　　・ raise ⓥ 키우다
- pup ⓝ 새끼　　・ approximately ⓐ 약, 대략
- majority ⓝ 대부분, 다수　　・ give birth to ~을 낳다
- make it to ~에 이르다　　・ make use of ~을 사용하다
- reproduce ⓥ 번식하다　　・ intention ⓝ 의도
- pass down ~을 물려주다

대부분의 측면에서, 인간은 더 많은 에너지를 투자하여 더 천천히 번식하는 매우 다른 전략을 진화시킨 비교적 소수의 종들 중 하나이다. 유인원과 코끼리와 마찬가지로, 우리는 천천히 성숙하고, 몸집을 크게 키우며, 새끼들을 적게 낳지만 그들을 잘 키우는 데 많은 시간과 에너지를 투자한다. 유인원과 코끼리는 생쥐보다 더 적은 수의 새끼를 낳지만, 그들의 새끼 중 더 높은 비율이 살아남아서 번식하기 때문에 이 특이한 전략은 성공한다. 생쥐는 생후 5주 만에 어미가 될 수 있으며, 한 배에서 4마리에서 10마리의 새끼를 낳고, 약 12개월의 생애 동안 2개월마다 새로운 새끼들을 낳을 수 있다. 그러나, 그의 새끼 대부분은 어릴 때 죽는다. 반면, 침팬지나 코끼리 어미는 최소 12살이 될 때까지 번식을 하지 않으며, 이후 30년 정도에 걸쳐 5년 또는 6년마다 단 한 마리의 새끼만 낳는다. 이러한 새끼 중 절반 정도가 부모가 되는 데 성공한다.

천천히 성숙하고 새끼를 적게 낳지만 양육에 더 많은 시간과 에너지를 투자하는
① making use of fewer resources for reproduction
번식을 위해 더 적은 자원을 사용하는　　　　　　번식과 자원량의 관계는 언급되지 않았음
②investing more energy to reproduce more slowly
더 많은 에너지를 투자하여 더 천천히 번식하는
③ hiding their intentions to get what they really want
정말로 원하는 것을 얻기 위해 의도를 숨기는　　의도를 숨기는 것은 언급되지 않았음
④ passing down shared social values to their offspring
자손에게 공유된 사회적 가치를 물려주는　　　사회적 가치를 물려주는 전략은 언급되지 않았음
⑤ living separately from their family units at an early age
어린 나이에 가족 단위로부터 분리되어 따로 사는
　　　　　　　　　　　　　　가족 단위로부터 분리하는 전략은 언급되지 않았음

| 문제 풀이 순서 | ★★★ [정답률 54%]

1st 빈칸이 포함된 문장을 읽고, 빈칸에 들어갈 말에 대한 단서를 얻는다.

빈칸 문장	In most respects, humans are one of a relatively small number of species that evolved a very different strategy of _____. 대부분의 측면에서, 인간은 _____ 매우 다른 전략을 진화시킨 비교적 소수의 종들 중 하나이다.

➡ 인간이 매우 다른 전략을 진화시킨 소수의 종들 중 하나라고 했으므로 〔단서〕
인간이 다른 종과 다르게 '어떤' 전략을 진화시켰는지 확인해야 한다. 〔발상〕

2nd 글의 내용을 종합해서 빈칸에 들어갈 적절한 말을 찾는다.
• 인간은 유인원과 코끼리처럼 새끼들을 적게 낳지만 잘 키우는 데 많은 시간과 에너지를 들임 〔단서 1〕
• 침팬지와 코끼리는 생쥐에 비해 상대적으로 더 늦게 그리고 더 적게 새끼들을 번식함 〔단서 2〕
• 침팬지와 코끼리는 생쥐보다 더 높은 비율의 자손이 생존하여 번식함 〔단서 3〕
➡ 인간은 침팬지와 코끼리처럼 늦은 나이에 적은 수의 새끼를 낳지만, 잘 키우는 데 많은 시간과 에너지를 들이므로 이들의 새끼가 생존하여 번식하는 비율은 생쥐의 그것보다 높다.
▶ 따라서 인간은 새끼들을 적게 낳으며 ② '더 많은 에너지를 투자하여 더 천천히 번식하는' 전략을 진화시켰다.

| 선택지 분석 |
① 인간은 번식을 위해 적은 자원이 아니라 오히려 많은 시간과 에너지를 들인다는 내용이다.
②인간은 천천히 성숙하고 새끼를 적게 낳지만, 양육에 더 많은 시간과 에너지를 들인다.
③ 인간이 원하는 것을 얻기 위해서 의도를 숨기는 전략을 발전시켰다는 내용이 아니다.
④ 공유된 사회적 가치를 물려주는 것은 언급되지 않았다.
⑤ 가족 단위로부터 분리되어 사는 전략은 언급되지 않았다.

구문 서술형

〔정답〕 becomes, is, won't die, became, was, wouldn't die

〔해석〕 만일 생쥐가 더 나이가 들어서 엄마가 된다면, 그의 새끼 대부분은 어릴 때 죽지 않을 것이다.
→ 문장의 동사는 if절의 동사 becomes, 종속절의 동사 is, 주절의 동사 won't die이다. 가정법 과거 문장이 되려면 if절과 그 종속절의 동사는 과거형인 became과 was로, 주절의 동사는 조동사의 과거형을 써서 wouldn't die로 고쳐야 한다.

M 05 정답 ① ＊측정값의 불확실성이 갖는 의미의 상대성

「one of + 복수 명사」: ~ 중 하나 (one에 수 일치)　　　to appreciate의 의미상 주어
One of the things that makes uncertainty difficult for members of 단수 동사
the public to appreciate / is that the significance of uncertainty is relative. //
대중이 불확실성을 이해하기 어렵게 만드는 것들 중 하나는 / 불확실성의 중요성이 상대적이라는 것이다 //

Take, for example, the distance between Earth and the sun: / 1.49597×10⁸ km, as measured at one point during the year. //
지구와 태양 사이의 거리의 예를 들어보자 / 즉 연중 한 지점에서 측정된 1.49597×10⁸ km //
= 1.49597×10⁸ km
This seems relatively precise; / after all, using six significant
뒤에 목적격절 접속사가 생략됨
digits means / I know the distance to an accuracy of one part in a million or so. //
이것은 상대적으로 정확해 보이지만 / 결국, 여섯 자리의 유효 숫자를 사용하는 것은 의미한다 / 백만 분의 일 정도의 정확도로 그 거리를 알고 있다는 것을 //

However, if the next digit is uncertain, / that means the uncertainty in knowing the precise Earth-sun distance / is larger than the distance between New York and Chicago! //
하지만, 만약 다음 숫자가 불확실하다면 / 그것은 지구와 태양의 정확한 거리를 아는 것에 있어서의 불확실성이 / 뉴욕과 시카고의 거리보다 더 크다는 것을 의미한다 //
명사절 접속사 (~인지 아닌지)
Whether or not the quoted number is "precise" / therefore
간접의문문
depends on / what I'm intending to do with it. //
인용된 숫자가 '정확한지' 아닌지는 / 따라서 ~에 따라 다르다 / 내가 그것으로 무엇을 하려고 하느냐 //
〔단서 1〕 숫자의 정확성 여부는 그것을 사용하려는 의도에 달려있음

If I care only about / what minute the sun will rise tomorrow, / then the number quoted here is fine. // 〔단서 2〕 일출 시각 예상은 여섯 자리 숫자
만약 내가 관심이 있다면 / 내일 태양이 몇 분에 뜰지에만 / 여기에 인용된 숫자로 괜찮다 //
형용사적 용법 (satellite 수식)
If I want to send a satellite to orbit just above the sun, however, / then I would need to know distances more accurately. //
하지만 만약 내가 태양 주위에 궤도를 돌 위성을 보내고 싶다면 / 나는 더 정확하게 거리를 알 필요가 있을 것이다 //
〔단서 3〕 태양 주위를 돌 위성을 보내려면 더 정확한 수치가 필요함

• uncertainty ⓝ 불확실성　• appreciate ⓥ 이해하다, 진가를 알다
• relatively ⓐⓓ 상대적으로　• precise ⓐ 정확한, 정밀한
• digit ⓝ 자릿수　• accuracy ⓝ 정확도　• quoted ⓐ 인용된
• depend on ~에 달려 있다　• intend ⓥ 의도하다
• satellite ⓝ (인공)위성　• orbit ⓥ 궤도를 돌다
• accurately ⓐⓓ 정확하게　• significance ⓝ 중요성
• relative ⓐ 상대적인　• intention ⓝ 의도

대중이 불확실성을 이해하기 어렵게 만드는 것들 중 하나는 **불확실성의 중요성이 상대적이라는 것이다.** 지구와 태양 사이의 거리, 즉 연중 한 지점에서 측정된 1.49597×10⁸ km의 예를 들어보자. 이것은 상대적으로 정확해 보이지만, 결국, 여섯 자리의 유효 숫자를 사용하는 것은 백만 분의 일 정도의 정확도로 그 거리를 알고 있다는 것을 의미한다. 하지만, 만약 다음 숫자가 불확실하다면, 그것은 지구와 태양의 정확한 거리를 아는 것에 있어서의 불확실성이 뉴욕과 시카고의 거리보다 더 크다는 것을 의미한다! 따라서, 인용된 숫자가 '정확한지' 아닌지는 내가 그것으로 무엇을 하려고 하느냐에 따라 다르다. 만약 내가 내일 태양이 몇 분에 뜰지에만 관심이 있다면, 여기에 인용된 숫자로 괜찮다. 하지만 만약 내가 태양 주위에 궤도를 돌 위성을 보내고 싶다면, 나는 더 정확하게 거리를 알 필요가 있을 것이다.

모든 측정의 불확실성 수준이 같다는 것은 반대되는 내용임
다음 빈칸에 들어갈 말로 가장 적절한 것을 고르시오. [3점]
①the significance of uncertainty is relative
불확실성의 중요성은 상대적이다　　　불확실성의 정도는 의도에 따라 상대적임
② the relativity of time is difficult to recognize
시간의 상대성은 인지하기 어렵다　　　　시간의 상대성에 관한 내용이 아님
③ all measurements have the same level of uncertainty
모든 측정값은 동일한 수준의 불확실성을 가진다
④ measurements of distance do not depend on intention
거리 측정은 의도에 따라 달라지지 않는다
⑤ specific numbers make people believe without question
구체적인 숫자는 사람들이 이의 없이 믿게 만든다　　구체적인 숫자의 신뢰성이 아닌
거리 측정이 의도에 따라 달라지지 않는다는 것은 반대되는 내용임　　중요성에 관한 내용임

| 문제 풀이 순서 | ★★★ [정답률 43%]

1st 빈칸이 포함된 문장을 읽고, 빈칸에 들어갈 말에 대한 단서를 얻는다.

빈칸 문장	One of the things that makes uncertainty difficult for members of the public to appreciate is that _____. 대중이 불확실성을 이해하기 어렵게 만드는 것들 중 하나는

➡ 대중이 불확실성을 이해하기 어렵게 하는 원인을 묻고 있으므로 (단서)
불확실성을 이해하기 어려운 문제 상황이나 예시를 통해 그 원인을 파악해야 한다.
(발상)

2nd 글의 내용을 종합해서 빈칸에 들어갈 적절한 말을 찾는다.

- 어떤 숫자를 정확하다고 할 수 있는지는 그것을 사용하려는 의도에 따라 달라짐 (단서1)
- 일출 시각 예상은 여섯 자리 숫자 정도로도 괜찮음 (단서2)
- 태양 주위를 돌 위성을 보내려면 더 정확한 수치가 필요함 (단서3)

➡ 같은 측정값이라도 어떤 목적으로 사용하느냐에 따라 그 값이 정확한 정도가 달라진다.

▶ 따라서, ① '불확실성의 중요성은 상대적이기' 때문에 대중이 불확실성을 이해하기 어려운 것이다.

| 선택지 분석 |

① 측정값의 불확실성이 갖는 중요성은 그 측정값을 사용하려는 의도에 따라 달라진다.
② 시간의 상대성은 언급되지 않았다.
③ 의도에 따라 요구되는 정확성의 정도가 다르다고 했으므로, 모든 측정값의 불확실성이 동일하다는 것은 반대되는 내용이다.
④ 의도에 따라 요구되는 정확성의 정도가 다르다고 했으므로, 거리 측정이 의도에 따라 달라지지 않는다는 것은 반대되는 내용이다.
⑤ 구체적인 숫자의 신뢰성이 아닌 중요성에 관한 내용이다.

구문 서술형

(정답) If I knew distances more accurately, I could send a satellite to orbit just above the sun.

→ 현재 사실에 반대되거나 실현 가능성이 없는 일을 가정하는 가정법 과거 문장은 「If + 주어 + 동사의 과거형 ~, 주어 + 조동사의 과거형 + 동사원형 …」 형태로 쓴다. 따라서 이때 if절의 동사 know와 주절의 조동사 can은 모두 과거시제로 바꿔 쓴다.

M 06 정답 ② ＊고통 인식의 주관성

How much we suffer / relates to **how we frame the pain in our mind**. //
우리가 얼마나 고통받는지 / 우리가 고통을 우리의 마음에서 어떻게 구성하는지와 관련된다 //

When 1500m runners push **themselves** / into extreme pain
(재귀대명사 (재귀 용법))
/ to win a race / — **their muscles screaming** / and **their lungs**
(병렬 구조 (주어가 생략되지 않은 분사구문))
exploding with oxygen deficit, / they don't psychologically
suffer much. // (단서1) 달리기 선수는 극심한 육체적 고통에도 정신적으로 덜 고통받음
1500미터 달리기 선수가 스스로를 밀어붙일 때 / 극심한 고통으로 / 경주에서 이기기 위해 / 그들의 근육이 비명을 지르고 / 그들의 폐가 산소 부족으로 폭발하면서 / 그들은 정신적으로 많이 고통받지 않는다 //

In fact, / **ultra-marathon runners** / — those people **who** are crazy
(복수 주어)   (주격 관계대명사)
enough to push themselves / beyond the normal boundaries of
human endurance, /
사실 / 울트라 마라톤 선수들은 / 즉, 스스로를 밀어붙일 만큼 충분히 열정적인 사람들은 / 인간 인내력의 정상적 경계를 넘어서 /

---

covering distances of 50-100km or more over many hours, / **talk**
(분사구문을 이끄는 현재분사)   (복수 동사)
about making friends with their pain. // (단서2) 고통과 친구가 되는 울트라 마라톤 선수
많은 시간 동안 50에서 100킬로미터 혹은 그 이상의 거리를 가지만 / 그들의 고통과 친구가 되는 것에 대해 이야기한다 //

When a patient has paid / for some form of passive back pain therapy / and the practitioner pushes deeply / into a painful part of a patient's back / to mobilise it, /
한 환자가 돈을 지불했고 / 특정 형태의 수동적 등 통증 치료에 / 의사가 깊게 눌렀을 때 / 환자 등의 아픈 부분을 / 그것을 풀어 주기 위해 /
(단서3) 치료가 가치 있다고 생각하는 환자는 그에 따른 고통도 좋은 것으로 느낌
the patient calls **that good pain** / if he or she believes / this type
(calls의 목적어와 목적격 보어)
of deep pressure treatment will be **of value**, / even though the
('of + 추상 명사」 → 형용사)
practitioner is pushing / right into the patient's sore tissues. //
환자는 그것을 좋은 아픔이라고 부른다 / 만약 그 또는 그녀가 믿는다면 / 이러한 종류의 깊은 압박 치료법이 가치가 있을 것이라고 / 비록 의사가 누르고 있을지라도 / 환자의 아픈 조직을 직접적으로 //

- suffer Ⓥ 고통받다 · explode Ⓥ 폭발하다 · deficit Ⓝ 부족, 결핍
- psychologically Ⓐⓓ 정신적으로 · boundary Ⓝ 경계
- endurance Ⓝ 인내력 · distance Ⓝ 거리 · passive Ⓐ 수동적인
- therapy Ⓝ 치료 · practitioner Ⓝ 의사
- mobilise Ⓥ 풀어주다, 움직이게 하다 · pressure Ⓝ 압박
- treatment Ⓝ 치료법 · sore Ⓐ 아픈 · tissue Ⓝ (근육) 조직
- frame Ⓥ 구성하다 · expert Ⓝ 전문가

우리가 얼마나 고통받는지는 **우리가 고통을 우리의 마음에서 어떻게 구성하는지**와 관련된다. 1500미터 달리기 선수가 경주에서 이기기 위해 그들의 근육이 비명을 지르고 그들의 폐가 산소 부족으로 폭발하면서, 스스로를 극심한 고통으로 밀어붙일 때, 그들은 정신적으로 많이 고통받지 않는다. 사실 울트라 마라톤 선수들은 즉, 인간 인내력의 정상적 경계를 넘어서 스스로를 밀어붙일 만큼 충분히 열정적인 사람들은 많은 시간 동안 50에서 100킬로미터 혹은 그 이상의 거리를 가지만 그들의 고통과 친구가 되는 것에 대해 이야기한다. 한 환자가 특정 형태의 수동적 등 통증 치료에 돈을 지불했고 의사가 그것을 풀어 주기 위해 환자 등의 아픈 부분을 깊게 눌렀을 때, 비록 의사가 환자의 아픈 조직을 직접적으로 누르고 있을지라도, 만약 그 또는 그녀가 이러한 종류의 깊은 압박 치료법이 가치가 있을 것이라고 믿는다면, 환자는 그것을 좋은 아픔이라고 부른다.

다음 빈칸에 들어갈 말로 가장 적절한 것을 고르시오.

① how long we have been in pain 지속 시간과 고통의 관계는 언급되지 않았음
우리가 얼마나 오래 고통스러워했는지
② how we frame the pain in our mind 우리가 고통을 어떻게 인식하느냐에
우리가 고통을 우리의 마음에서 어떻게 구성하는지 따라 고통의 정도가 달라짐
③ how fast we can recover from past pain
과거의 고통에서 얼마나 빨리 회복할 수 있는지 고통의 회복은 언급되지 않았음
④ what part of our body we train regularly 신체 부위별 훈련에 따른
우리가 어떤 신체 부위를 규칙적으로 훈련하는지 고통은 언급되지 않았음
⑤ what treatment we receive from experts
전문가로부터 어떤 치료를 받는지 치료법과 고통의 관계는 언급되지 않았음

| 문제 풀이 순서 | ★★★ [정답률 58%]

1st 빈칸이 포함된 문장을 읽고, 빈칸에 들어갈 말에 대한 단서를 얻는다.

빈칸 문장	How much we suffer relates to _____. 우리가 얼마나 고통받는지는 와 관련된다.

➡ '우리가 얼마나 고통받는지(고통의 정도)'는 '무엇'과 관련된다고 했다. (단서)
빈칸 문장이 글의 맨 앞에 있으므로 주제문일 가능성이 높다. 글의 나머지 부분에서 '무엇'에 따라 고통의 정도가 달라지는지를 구체적으로 설명하거나 예시를 제시할 것이다. (발상)

2nd 글의 나머지 부분을 읽고, 글의 내용을 종합해서 빈칸에 들어갈 내용을 찾는다.

- 1500m 달리기 선수가 경주에서 스스로를 극심한 고통으로 밀어붙여도 그들은 정신적으로 많이 고통받지 않는다. (단서1)
- 울트라 마라톤 선수들은 많은 시간 동안 먼 거리를 달리면서도 그들의 고통과 친구가 되는 것에 대해 이야기한다. (단서2)
- 환자가 압박 치료법이 가치가 있을 것이라고 믿는다면, 압박 시 느끼는 아픔을 좋은 아픔이라고 생각한다. (단서3)

➡ 1500m 달리기 선수, 울트라 마라톤 선수, 환자를 예시로 들며 '가치가 있다'라고 생각하는 일에 따르는 고통은 아무렇지 않은 것으로, 심지어 좋은 고통으로도 여긴다고 했다. 즉, 우리가 고통을 어떻게 인식하고 받아들이는지에 따라 극심한 고통도 긍정적으로 여길 수 있다는 내용이다.

▶ 우리가 얼마나 고통받는지는 ② '우리가 고통을 우리의 마음에서 어떻게 구성하는지'와 관련된다.

| 선택지 분석 |

① 고통의 지속 기간에 따라 고통의 정도가 달라진다는 내용이 아니다.
② 우리가 고통을 마음에서 어떻게 인식하는지에 따라 고통의 정도가 달라진다는 내용이다.
③ 과거의 고통이나 고통의 회복은 언급되지 않았다.
④ 어떤 신체 부위를 훈련하는지에 따라 고통의 정도가 달라진다는 내용이 아니다.
⑤ 압박 치료법이 가치 있다고 느끼면 그에 따른 고통을 긍정적으로 여긴다고 했을 뿐, 어떤 치료법을 받는지에 따라 고통의 정도가 달라진다는 내용이 아니다.

구문 서술형

정답 believes

해석 만일 환자가 어떤 종류의 깊은 압박 치료법이 가치가 있을 것이라고 믿는다면, 그는 그것을 '좋은 아픔'이라고 부를 것이다.
→ 주절의 조동사 will이 원형 그대로 쓰였고, 현재 또는 미래의 불확실한 일을 가정하므로 가정법 현재 문장이다. if절의 주어가 a patient로 단수이므로 동사 believed를 현재형인 believes로 고쳐 써야 한다.

M 07 정답 ② *주의 집중과 뇌의 재구조화

There's a lot of scientific evidence / demonstrating that focused attention leads / to the reshaping of the brain. //
과학적 증거는 많이 있다 / 주의 집중이 이어진다는 것을 보여주는 / 뇌의 재구조화로 //

In animals rewarded for noticing sound / (to hunt or to avoid being hunted for example), / we find much larger auditory centers in the brain. // 단서1 좋은 청각의 이점이 있는 동물은 뇌의 청각 중추가 큼
소리를 알아채는 것에 대한 보상을 받은 동물에서 / (예를 들어 사냥하거나 사냥감이 되는 것을 피하기 위해) / 우리는 뇌의 청각 중추가 훨씬 더 큰 것을 발견한다 //

In animals rewarded for sharp eyesight, / the visual areas are larger. // 단서2 예리한 시력의 이점이 있는 동물은 뇌의 시각 영역이 큼
예리한 시력에 대한 보상을 받은 동물은 / 시각 영역이 더 크다 //

Brain scans of violinists provide more evidence, / showing dramatic growth and expansion / in regions of the cortex that represent the left hand, / 단서3 바이올린 연주자는 왼손을 나타내는 피질 영역이 성장하고 확장됨
바이올린 연주자의 뇌 스캔 결과는 더 많은 증거를 제공하는데 / 극적인 성장과 확장을 보여준다 / 왼손을 나타내는 피질 영역의 /

which has to finger the strings precisely, / often at very high speed. //
(그 왼손은) 현을 정확하게 켜야 한다 / 종종 매우 빠른 속도로 //

Other studies have shown / that the hippocampus, which is vital for spatial memory, / is enlarged in taxi drivers. // 단서4 택시 운전사는 공간 기억에 필수적인 해마가 확장됨
다른 연구는 보여준다 / 공간 기억에 필수적인 해마가 / 택시 운전사에서 확대되는 것을 //

The point is / that the physical architecture of the brain changes / according to where we direct our attention / and what we practice doing. // 단서5 어디에 주의를 집중하고 무엇을 연습하는지에 따라 뇌의 구조가 바뀜
요점은 / 뇌의 물리적 구조가 달라진다는 것이다 / 우리가 어디에 주의를 기울이고 / 무엇을 연습하느냐에 따라 //

- evidence ⓝ 증거 · demonstrate ⓥ 보여주다
- attention ⓝ 주의 집중 · auditory ⓐ 청각의 · sharp ⓐ 예리한
- eyesight ⓝ 시력 · dramatic ⓐ 극적인 · expansion ⓝ 확장
- represent ⓥ 나타내다 · precisely ⓐⓓ 정확하게 · vital ⓐ 중요한

- spatial ⓐ 공간의   · enlarge ⓥ 확대하다   · physical ⓐ 신체적인
- architecture ⓝ 건축, 설계   · direct ⓥ 지시하다

주의 집중이 뇌의 재구조화로 이어진다는 과학적 증거는 많이 있다. (예를 들어 사냥하거나 사냥감이 되는 것을 피하기 위해) 소리를 알아채는 것에 대한 보상을 받은 동물에서 우리는 뇌의 청각 중추가 훨씬 더 큰 것을 발견한다. 예리한 시력에 대한 보상을 받은 동물은 시각 영역이 더 크다. 바이올린 연주자의 뇌 스캔 결과는 더 많은 증거를 제공해서 종종 매우 빠른 속도로 현을 정확하게 켜야 하는 왼손을 나타내는 피질 영역의 극적인 성장과 확장을 보여준다. 다른 연구는 공간 기억에 필수적인 해마가 택시 운전사에게서 확대되는 것을 보여준다. 요점은 우리가 어디에 주의를 기울이고 무엇을 연습하느냐에 따라 뇌의 물리적 구조가 달라진다는 것이다.

다음 빈칸에 들어갈 말로 가장 적절한 것을 고르시오.
① improved decision making 의사 결정에 관한 내용이 아님
향상된 의사 결정
② the reshaping of the brain 뇌의 구조가 변하게 됨
뇌의 재구조화
③ long-term mental tiredness 정신적 피로에 관한 내용이 아님
장기간의 정신적 피로
④ the development of hand skills 손 재주가 아닌 뇌의 구조가 발달함
손 재주의 발달
⑤ increased levels of self-control 자기 통제력에 관한 내용이 아님
증가된 자기 통제 수준

| 문제 풀이 순서 | ★★❋ [정답률 64%]

1st 빈칸이 포함된 문장을 읽고, 빈칸에 들어갈 말에 대한 단서를 얻는다.

빈칸 문장	There's a lot of scientific evidence demonstrating that focused attention leads to _____. 주의 집중이 _____로 이어진다는 과학적 증거는 많이 있다.

➡ 주의 집중이 '무엇'으로 이어지는지에 대한 증거가 많다고 했으므로, 단서 집중에 따라서 '무슨' 일이 일어나는지에 대한 과학적 증거들이 이어질 것이다. 발상

2nd 글의 나머지 부분을 확인해서 정답을 찾는다.

증거1 : 청각에 대한 보상이 큰 동물은 뇌의 청각 중추가 큼
증거2 : 시력에 대한 보상이 큰 동물은 뇌의 시각 영역이 큼
증거3 : 바이올린 연주자는 왼손을 나타내는 피질 영역이 성장하고 확장됨
증거4 : 택시 운전사는 공간 기억에 필수적인 해마가 확대됨
➡ 주의를 집중하는 영역에 따라 그에 필요한 뇌의 부위가 커져서 뇌의 구조가 바뀐다는 과학적 증거들을 열거했다.

▶ 주의 집중으로 인해 뇌의 영역이나 구조가 변화한다는, 즉 ② '뇌의 재구조화'로 이어진다는 과학적 증거가 많다.

| 선택지 분석 |

① 주의 집중이 의사 결정을 향상되게 한다는 내용이 아니다.
② 주의를 어디에 집중하고 연습하는지에 따라 뇌의 재구조화가 일어난다.
③ 주의 집중이 장기간의 정신적 피로를 초래한다는 내용이 아니다.
④ 손 재주가 아닌 해당 부분의 뇌 구조가 발달한다는 내용이다.
⑤ 주의 집중이 자기 통제 수준을 증가시킨다는 내용이 아니다.

M 08 정답 ⑤ *인간의 뇌가 진화한 이유

How did the human mind evolve? // 인간의 생각은 어떻게 진화했을까 //
One possibility is / that competition and conflicts with other human tribes / caused our brains to evolve the way they did. //
한 가지 가능성은 / 다른 인간 부족과의 경쟁과 갈등이 / 우리 두뇌가 그렇게 진화하도록 했다는 것이다 //
A human tribe that could out-think its enemies, even slightly, / possessed a vital advantage. // 단서1 적보다 더 우수한 생각을 하는 부족은 우위를 가짐
적보다 조금이라도 더 우수한 생각을 할 수 있는 인간 부족은 / 중요한 우위를 점했다 //

<u>The ability</u> of your tribe / <mark>to imagine</mark> and <mark>predict</mark> where and
단수 주어
when a hostile enemy tribe might strike, / and <mark>plan</mark> accordingly,
병렬 구조
/ <mark>gives</mark> your tribe / a significant military advantage. //
단수 동사
부족의 능력은 / 적대적인 적 부족이 언제 어디서 공격할지 상상하고 예측하며 / 그에 따라
계획을 세울 수 있는 / 부족에게 가져다준다 / 상당한 군사적 우위를 //

The human mind became a weapon / in the struggle for survival,
비교급 강조 부사   부정대명사
/ a weapon <mark>far</mark> more decisive than <mark>any</mark> before it. //
인간의 생각은 무기가 되었다 / 생존을 위한 투쟁에서 / 그 이전의 어떤 무기보다 훨씬 더
결정적인 무기인 //   단서 2 인간의 생각은 생존을 위한 투쟁에서 가장 중요한 무기가 됨

And this mental advantage was applied, over and over, / within
each succeeding generation. //   단서 3 생각이 더 우수한 부족이 승리할 확률이
높고 그러한 유전자를 자손에게 물려줌
그리고 이러한 정신적 우위는 계속해서 적용되었다 / 다음 세대에 걸쳐 //
단수 주어   주격 관계대명사   단수 동사
<u>The tribe that</u> could out-think its opponents / <mark>was</mark> more likely
to succeed in battle / and <mark>would</mark> then <mark>pass on</mark> the genes /
앞에 주격 관계대명사와 be동사 생략   pass on A to B: A를 B에 전달하다
<u>responsible</u> for this mental advantage / <mark>to</mark> its offspring. //
상대보다 더 우수한 생각을 할 수 있는 부족은 / 전투에서 승리할 확률이 높았고 / 이러한
유전자를 물려주었다 / 정신적 우위를 담당하는 / 자손에게 //

You and I / are the descendants of the winners. //
당신과 나는 / 승자의 후손이다 //

- evolve ⓥ 진화하다   - possibility ⓝ 가능성   - tribe ⓝ 부족
- out-think ⓥ ~보다 우수한 생각을 하다   - slightly ⓐⓓ 약간
- possess ⓥ 소유하다   - vital ⓐ 중요한   - predict ⓥ 예측하다
- hostile ⓐ 적대적인   - accordingly ⓐⓓ 그에 맞춰
- decisive ⓐ 결정적인   - succeeding ⓐ 다음의
- opponent ⓝ 반대자   - offspring ⓝ 자손   - descendant ⓝ 후손

인간의 생각은 어떻게 진화했을까? 한 가지 가능성은 **다른 인간 부족과의 경쟁과 갈등**이 우리 두뇌가 그렇게 진화하도록 했다는 것이다. 적보다 조금이라도 더 우수한 생각을 할 수 있는 인간 부족은 중요한 우위를 점했다. 적대적인 적 부족이 언제 어디서 공격할지 상상하고 예측하며 그에 따라 계획을 세울 수 있는 능력은 부족에게 상당한 군사적 우위를 가져다준다. 인간의 생각은 생존을 위한 투쟁에서 그 이전의 어떤 무기보다 훨씬 더 결정적인 무기가 되었다. 그리고 이러한 정신적 우위는 다음 세대에 걸쳐 계속해서 적용되었다. 상대보다 더 우수한 생각을 할 수 있는 부족은 전투에서 승리할 확률이 높았고, 이러한 정신적 우위를 담당하는 유전자를 자손에게 물려주었다. 당신과 나는 승자의 후손이다.

다음 빈칸에 들어갈 말로 가장 적절한 것을 고르시오. [3점]
① physical power to easily hunt prey 신체 능력에 대한 언급 없음
먹이를 쉽게 사냥할 수 있는 신체 능력
② individual responsibility in one's inner circle 책임에 관한 언급 없음
내부 세력 안에서의 개인적 책임
③ instinctive tendency to avoid natural disasters
자연재해를 피하기 위한 본능적인 경향   자연재해에 관한 언급 없음
④ superiority in the number of one's descendants
자손의 수에서의 우위   자손의 수에 대한 언급 없음
⑤ competition and conflicts with other human tribes
다른 인간 부족과의 경쟁과 갈등
정신적 우위를 가진 부족이 다른 부족과의 경쟁과 갈등에서 유리했고 이를 자손에게 물려줌

| 문제 풀이 순서 | ★★★ [정답률 55%]

1st 빈칸이 포함된 문장 주변을 읽고, 빈칸에 들어갈 말에 대한 단서를 얻는다.

| 빈칸 앞 문장 | How did the human mind evolve?
인간의 생각은 어떻게 진화했을까? |
| 빈칸 문장 | One possibility is that _____ caused our brains to evolve the way they did.
한 가지 가능성은 _____ 이 우리 두뇌가 그렇게 진화하도록 했다는 것이다. |

➡ 빈칸 앞 문장에서 인간의 생각이 진화한 과정에 관하여 질문을 던졌고, 빈칸 문장은 우리 두뇌가 진화하도록 한 '무엇'이 한 가지 가능성이라고 했으므로, 단서 우리 두뇌가 그렇게 진화하도록 한 것이 '무엇'인지 뒤에서 설명할 것이다. 발상

2nd 글의 내용을 종합해서 빈칸에 들어갈 적절한 말을 찾는다.
┌ • 적보다 조금이라도 더 우수한 생각을 할 수 있는 인간 부족은 중요한 우위를
│   점했다. 단서 1
│ • 인간의 생각은 생존을 위한 투쟁에서 그 어떤 무기보다 훨씬 더 결정적인 무기가
│   되었다. 단서 2
└ • 상대보다 더 우수한 생각을 할 수 있는 부족은 전투에서 승리할 확률이 높았고,
    이러한 정신적 우위를 담당하는 유전자를 자손에게 물려주었다. 단서 3
➡ 적보다 더 뛰어난 생각을 할 수 있는 부족은 전투에서 승리할 확률이 높았고 생존에
   유리했기 때문에, 이러한 유전자를 자손에게 물려주었다고 했다. 다른 부족보다
   우수한 생각을 해야만 그들을 이기고 살아남았으므로 빈칸에는 다른 부족과의
   경쟁이나 갈등에 관한 내용이 들어가야 한다.

3rd 글의 내용을 다시 한번 정리하며 이해한 중심 내용을 선택지에서 고른다.

우리의 뇌가 이렇게 진화하게 된 이유는 더 뛰어난 생각을 하는 인간 부족이 생존을
위한 투쟁에서 더 유리했고 그러한 유전자를 자손에게 물려주었기 때문이므로
빈칸에는 ⑤ '다른 인간 부족과의 경쟁과 갈등'이 들어가야 한다.

| 선택지 분석 |
① 먹이 사냥을 위한 신체 능력이 아니라 뛰어난 정신적 능력이 우위를 가져다주었다.
② 부족 내의 세력이나 개인적인 책임에 관한 내용은 언급되지 않았다.
③ 자연재해를 피하기 위한 본능에 관한 내용은 언급되지 않았다.
④ 자손의 수가 많은 것이 우리의 뇌를 진화하게 만든 것이 아니다.
⑤ 적과의 싸움에서 정신적 우위를 가진 부족이 유리했고 이러한 유전자로 진화할 수
   있었다.

M 09 정답 ① *과학에서 개념을 다룰 때 주의할 점

Concepts are vital to human survival, / but we must also
                                    = concepts
be careful with <mark>them</mark> / because concepts open the door to
essentialism. //
개념은 인간의 생존에 필수적이지만 / 우리는 또한 그것들을 주의해야 한다 / 개념이
본질주의로 향하는 문을 열기 때문에 //

They **encourage us / to see things that aren't present**. //
그것들은 우리를 부추긴다 / 존재하지 않는 것들을 보도록 //

Stuart Firestein opens his book, *Ignorance*, / with an old proverb,
              가주어   진주어
/ "<mark>It</mark> is very difficult <mark>to find</mark> a black cat in a dark room, / especially
when there is no cat." //   단서 1 고양이가 없는 어두운 방에서 검은
                              고양이를 찾는 것은 매우 어려움
Stuart Firestein은 그의 책인 *Ignorance*를 시작한다 / 옛 속담으로 / "어두운 방에서 검은
고양이를 찾는 것은 매우 어렵다 / 특히 고양이가 없을 때"라는 //

This statement beautifully <mark>sums up</mark> / the search for essences. //
                                        ~을 요약하다
이 말은 훌륭하게 요약한다 / 본질에 대한 탐구를 //

History has many examples of scientists / <mark>who</mark> searched
                                   주격 관계대명사
fruitlessly for an essence / because they used the wrong concept /
형용사적 용법(concept 수식)
<mark>to guide</mark> their hypotheses. //   단서 2 잘못된 개념을 사용하여 헛되이 본질을 찾았던
역사는 과학자들의 많은 예를 가지고 있다 / 헛되이 본질을 탐색했던 / 잘못된 개념을   과학자들
사용했기 때문에 / 가설을 이끄는 //

Firestein gives the example of <mark>luminiferous ether</mark>, / <mark>a mysterious</mark>
                                                동격
<mark>substance</mark> / that was thought to fill the universe / <mark>so that</mark> light
                                                         ~하도록
would have a medium to move through. //
Firestein은 발광 에테르의 예를 제시한다 / 신비한 물질인 / 우주를 가득 채워줄 것이라
여겨진 / 빛이 통과할 수 있는 매개체를 갖도록 //
        단서 3 에테르는 존재하지 않기에 찾을 수 없는 검은 고양이와 같음
The ether was a black cat, / writes Firestein, / and physicists <mark>had</mark>
           과거완료 진행형   = a dark room
<mark>been theorizing</mark> in a dark room, / and then experimenting in <mark>it</mark>,
에테르는 검은 고양이였고 / Firestein이 쓰기를 / 물리학자들은 어두운 방에서 이론을
세우고 / 그러고 나서 그 안에서 실험을 하고 있었던 것이다 /
분사구문을 이끄는 현재분사
<mark>looking</mark> for evidence of a cat that did not exist. //
존재하지 않았던 고양이라는 증거를 찾으며 //

Ⓜ

- concept ⓝ 개념
- vital ⓐ 필수적인
- essentialism ⓝ 본질주의
- proverb ⓝ 속담
- statement ⓝ 진술
- essence ⓝ 본질
- fruitlessly ⓐⓓ 헛되이
- hypothesis ⓝ 가설 (pl. hypotheses)
- luminiferous ⓐ 발광의, 빛을 내는
- mysterious ⓐ 신비로운
- substance ⓝ 물질
- theorize ⓥ 이론을 세우다
- simplify ⓥ 단순하게 만들다
- philosophy ⓝ 철학

개념은 인간의 생존에 필수적이지만, 개념이 본질주의로 향하는 문을 열기 때문에 우리는 또한 그것들을 주의해야 한다. 그것들은 **존재하지 않는 것들을 보도록 우리를 부추긴다.** Stuart Firestein은 "어두운 방에서 검은 고양이를 찾는 것은 특히 고양이가 없을 때 매우 어렵다."라는 옛 속담으로 그의 책, *Ignorance*를 시작한다. 이 말은 본질에 대한 탐구를 훌륭하게 요약한다. 역사는 가설을 이끄는 잘못된 개념을 사용했기 때문에 헛되이 본질을 탐색했던 과학자들의 많은 예를 가지고 있다. Firestein은 빛이 통과할 수 있는 매개체를 갖도록 우주를 가득 채워줄 것이라 여겨진 신비한 물질인 발광 에테르의 예를 제시한다. Firestein이 쓰기를, 에테르는 검은 고양이였고, 물리학자들은 어두운 방에서 이론을 세우고, 그리고 나서 존재하지 않았던 고양이라는 증거를 찾으며, 그 안에서 실험을 하고 있었던 것이었다.

> 다음 빈칸에 들어갈 말로 가장 적절한 것을 고르시오. [3점]
> ① encourage us to see things that aren't present
>   존재하지 않는 것들을 보도록 우리를 부추긴다
>   (잘못된 개념은 존재하지 않는 본질을 찾기 위한 헛된 노력으로 이어질 수 있다는 내용임)
> ② force scientists to simplify scientific theories
>   과학 이론을 단순화하도록 과학자들을 강요한다 (과학 이론의 단순화에 대한 언급은 없음)
> ③ let us think science is essential and practical
>   우리가 과학이 필수적이고 실용적이라고 생각하게 한다 (과학이 필수적이고 실용적이라는 내용이 아님)
> ④ drive physicists to explore philosophy
>   물리학자들이 철학을 탐구하도록 한다 (철학을 탐구하게 한다는 내용이 아님)
> ⑤ lead us to ignore the unknown
>   미지의 것을 무시하도록 우리를 이끈다 (개념이 미지의 것을 무시한다는 내용이 아님)

| 문제 풀이 순서 | ★★★ [정답률 53%]

1st 빈칸이 포함된 문장과 앞 문장을 읽고, 빈칸에 들어갈 말에 대한 단서를 얻는다.

빈칸 앞 문장	Concepts are vital to human survival, but we must also be careful with them because concepts open the door to essentialism. 개념은 인간의 생존에 필수적이지만, 개념이 본질주의로 향하는 문을 열기 때문에 우리는 또한 그것들을 주의해야 한다.
빈칸 문장	They _____. 그것들은

➡ 빈칸 문장 앞에서 개념(Concepts)이 필수적이지만 주의해야 한다고 했고, 빈칸 문장은 그것들(They)은 '어떠하다'라고 했다. (단서)
They는 앞 문장의 Concepts를 나타내므로, 구체적으로 개념의 어떤 점을 주의해야 하는지가 뒤에 이어질 것이다. (발상)

2nd 글의 나머지 부분을 읽고, 글을 정리하면서 빈칸에 들어갈 내용을 찾는다.

- "어두운 방에서 검은 고양이를 찾는 것은 특히 고양이가 없을 때 매우 어렵다." 단서1
- 역사는 가설을 이끄는 잘못된 개념을 사용했기 때문에 헛되이 본질을 탐색했던 과학자들의 많은 예를 가지고 있다. 단서2
- 에테르는 검은 고양이었다. 단서3

➡ 검은 고양이의 속담과 에테르라는 예시를 통해, 잘못된 개념은 존재하지 않는 것을 찾도록 하므로 주의해야 한다고 말하고 있다. 따라서 빈칸에는 ① '존재하지 않는 것들을 보도록 우리를 부추긴다'가 들어가야 한다.

| 선택지 분석 |

① 잘못된 개념은 존재하지 않는 본질을 찾기 위한 헛된 노력으로 이어질 수 있다는 내용이다.
② 잘못된 개념 때문에 잘못된 이론을 세웠다는 비유를 들었지만, 과학 이론을 단순화하는 것은 언급되지 않았다.
③ 개념이 인간의 생존에 필수적이라고 했을 뿐, 과학이 필수적이고 실용적이라고 생각하게 한다는 내용이 아니다.
④ 본질주의가 언급되긴 하지만, 물리학자가 철학을 탐구한다는 것은 언급되지 않았다.
⑤ Firestein의 책 제목이 Ignorance일 뿐, 무언가를 무시하는 것은 언급되지 않았다.

M 10 정답 ③ *수면 중 환경 자극에 대한 감각 반응 감소

단수 주어
One of the most striking characteristics / of a sleeping animal or person / is that they do not respond normally / to environmental stimuli. // 단서1 수면 중 사람이나 동물은 환경 자극에 정상적으로 반응하지 않음
가장 두드러진 특징 중 하나는 / 잠을 자고 있는 동물이나 사람의 / 그들이 정상적으로 반응하지 않는다는 것이다 / 환경의 자극에 //
단서2 수면하는 포유류의 눈은 정상적으로 볼 수 없음
If you open the eyelids of a sleeping mammal / the eyes will not see normally / — they **are functionally blind**. //
만약 당신이 잠을 자고 있는 포유류의 눈꺼풀을 열면 / 그 눈은 정상적으로 볼 수 없을 것인데 / 즉 그 눈은 기능적으로는 실명 상태이다 //

Some visual information apparently gets in, / but it is not normally processed / as it is shortened or weakened; / same with the other sensing systems. // 단서3 다른 감각 체계처럼 시각적 정보는 정상적으로 처리되지 않음
어떤 시각적 정보는 명백히 눈으로 들어오지만 / 그것은 정상적으로 처리되지 않는데 / 짧아지거나 약화되어서 / 이는 다른 감각 체계도 마찬가지다 //

병렬 구조
Stimuli are registered but / not processed normally / and they fail to wake the individual. // 단서4 수면 중 자극은 등록되지만 정상적으로 처리가 안 되고 사람을 깨우지 못함
자극은 등록되지만 / 정상적으로 처리되지 않고 / 사람을 깨우는 데 실패한다 //

동명사구(전치사의 목적어)
Perceptual disengagement probably / serves the function of **protecting sleep**, / so some authors do not **count** it / **as** part of the definition of sleep itself. // count A as B: A를 B로 여기다[간주하다]
지각 이탈은 추측하건대 / 수면을 보호하는 기능을 제공해서 / 어떤 저자는 그것을 여기지 않는다 / 수면 자체의 정의의 일부로 //

= perceptual disengagement
But as sleep would be impossible without it, / **it** seems essential to **its definition**. // = the definition of sleep
그러나 수면이 그것 없이는 불가능하기 때문에 / 그것(지각 이탈)은 그것(수면)의 정의에 필수적인 것으로 보여진다 //

부사적 용법(목적)
Nevertheless, many animals (including humans) / use the intermediate state of drowsiness / **to derive** some benefits of sleep / without total perceptual disengagement. //
그럼에도 (인간을 포함한) 많은 동물은 / 졸음이라는 중간 상태를 이용한다 / 수면의 일부 이득을 끌어내기 위해서 / 완전한 지각 이탈 없이 //

- striking ⓐ 두드러진
- characteristic ⓝ 특징
- respond ⓥ 반응하다
- environmental ⓐ 환경의
- eyelid ⓝ 눈꺼풀
- mammal ⓝ 포유류
- visual ⓐ 시각의
- apparently ⓐⓓ 분명히
- process ⓥ 처리하다
- shorten ⓥ 짧아지다
- weaken ⓥ 약해지다
- essential ⓐ 필수적인
- nevertheless ⓐⓓ 그럼에도 불구하고
- derive ⓥ 얻다
- perceptual ⓐ 지각의
- activate ⓥ 활성화하다

잠을 자고 있는 동물이나 사람의 가장 두드러진 특징 중 하나는 그들이 환경의 자극에 정상적으로 반응하지 않는다는 것이다. 만약 당신이 잠을 자고 있는 포유류의 눈꺼풀을 열면, 그 눈은 정상적으로 볼 수 없을 것인데, 즉 그 눈은 **기능적으로는 실명 상태이다.** 어떤 시각적 정보는 명백히 눈으로 들어오지만, 그것은 짧아지거나 약화되어서 정상적으로 처리되지 않는데, 이는 다른 감각 체계도 마찬가지다. 자극은 등록되지만 정상적으로 처리되지 않고 사람을 깨우는 데 실패한다. 지각 이탈은 추측하건대 수면을 보호하는 기능을 제공해서 어떤 저자는 그것을 수면 자체의 정의의 일부로 여기지 않는다. 그러나 수면이 그것 없이는 불가능하기 때문에 그것(지각 이탈)은 그것(수면)의 정의에 필수적인 것으로 보여진다. 그럼에도 (인간을 포함한) 많은 동물은 완전한 지각 이탈 없이 수면의 일부 이득을 끌어내기 위해서 졸음이라는 중간 상태를 이용한다.

다음 빈칸에 들어갈 말로 가장 적절한 것을 고르시오. [3점]

① get recovered easily 수면 중에는 시각이 정상적이지 않음
쉽게 회복한다
② will see much better 동물이 수면 상태일 때 시각적 정보 처리가 방해받음
훨씬 더 잘 보게 될 것이다
③ are functionally blind
기능적으로는 실명 상태이다 수면 중에는 시각적 정보가 들어오기 하지만 정상적으로 처리되지 않음
④ are completely activated 시각적 정보가 제대로 처리되지 않음
완전히 활성화된다
⑤ process visual information
시각 정보를 처리한다 잠잘 때 시각 자극은 등록되지만 정상적으로 처리되지 않음

| 문제 풀이 순서 | ★★★ [정답률 53%]

1st 먼저 빈칸 문장과 그 뒤 문장을 읽고, 빈칸에 들어갈 말을 예측한다.

빈칸 문장	만약 당신이 잠을 자고 있는 포유류의 눈꺼풀을 열면, 그 눈은 정상적으로 볼 수 없을 것인데, 단서2 즉 그 눈은 _____.
빈칸 문장 뒤	어떤 시각적 정보가 명백히 눈으로 들어오지만, 그것은 짧아지거나 약화되어서 정상적으로 처리되지 않는데, 이는 다른 감각 체계도 마찬가지다. 단서3

➡ 수면 상태의 눈은 정상적으로 기능하지 않고 이때 그 눈을 '어떠하다'라고 했으므로, 단서 수면 상태의 눈이 '어떠한지'에 관한 다른 표현을 찾아봐야 한다. 발상 빈칸 문장 뒤에서 모든 시각적 정보가 정상적으로 처리되지는 않는다고 했으므로, 비슷한 내용이 빈칸에 들어갈 것이라는 걸 짐작할 수 있다.

2nd 글의 나머지 부분을 읽고, 수면 상태의 눈이 어떠한지 파악한다.
- 잠을 자고 있는 동물이나 사람의 가장 두드러진 특징 중 하나는 그들이 환경의 자극에 정상적으로 반응하지 않는다는 것이다. 단서1
- 자극은 등록되지만 정상적으로 처리되지 않고 사람을 깨우는 데 실패한다. 단서4

➡ 동물이나 사람은 잠을 잘 때 환경의 자극에 정상적으로 반응하지 않고, 자극이 등록되어도 정상적으로 처리되지 않는다. 이는 눈의 본래 기능을 하지 못하는 '실명 상태'와도 같다.
▶ 즉, 수면 상태에서 눈은 ③ '기능적으로는 실명 상태이다.'

| 선택지 분석 |
① 수면 중에 포유류의 눈이 쉽게 회복한다는 내용은 언급되지 않았다.
② 눈이 훨씬 더 잘 보게 된다는 내용은 수면 중 정상적인 시각적 정보 처리가 방해받는다는 내용과 모순된다.
③ 수면 중 포유류는 눈꺼풀을 열더라도 정상적으로 볼 수 없으며 시각적 정보가 들어오기는 하지만 정상적으로 처리되지 않는다고 했다.
④ 수면하는 포유류의 눈이 완전히 활성화된다고 하는 것은 수면 중에는 시각적 정보가 제대로 처리되지 않는다는 내용과 대조된다.
⑤ 수면 중에 자극은 등록되지만 정상적으로 처리되지 않는다고 했다.

M 11 정답 ③ *희소성이 판매를 장려한다!

앞에 목적격 관계대명사가 생략됨
Restricting the number of items / customers can buy / boosts sales. //
품목의 개수를 제한하는 것은 / 고객이 구입할 수 있는 / 매출을 증가시킨다 //

동격
Brian Wansink, / Professor of Marketing at Cornell University, / investigated the effectiveness of this tactic / in 1998. //
Brian Wansink는 / Cornell University의 마케팅 교수인 / 이 전략의 효과를 조사했다 / 1998년에 //

persuaded의 목적격 보어
He persuaded three supermarkets in Sioux City, Iowa, / **to offer** Campbell's soup at a small discount: / 79 cents rather than 89 cents. //
그는 Iowa 주 Sioux City에 있는 세 개의 슈퍼마켓을 설득했다 / Campbell의 수프를 약간 할인하여 제공하도록 / 89센트가 아닌 79센트로 //

수동태 동사
The discounted soup **was sold** / in one of three conditions: / a
관계부사
control, / **where** there was no limit on the volume of purchases, /
할인된 수프는 판매되었다 / 세 가지 조건 중 하나의 조건으로 / 하나의 대조군 / 구매량에 제한이 없는 /
관계부사
or two tests, / **where** customers were limited to either four or twelve cans. // 단서1 세 개의 조건이 제시됨
또는 두 개의 실험군 / 고객이 4개 또는 12개의 캔으로 제한되는 // (구매량에 제한이 없거나, 4개로 제한되거나, 12개로 제한됨)

In the unlimited condition / shoppers bought 3.3 cans on
부사절 접속사(대조)
average, / **whereas** in the scarce condition, / when there was a limit, / they bought 5.3 on average. // 단서2 구매량에 제한이 없을 때보다
무제한 조건에서 / 구매자들은 평균 3.3캔을 구입했다 / 반면 희소 조건에서는 / 제한이 있던 / 구매량에 제한이 있을 때 더 많이 구입함
그들은 평균 5.3캔을 구입했다 //
뒤에 목적어절 접속사가 생략됨
This **suggests** / scarcity encourages sales. // 단서3 희소성이 판매를 장려함
이것은 보여준다 / 희소성이 판매를 장려한다는 것을 //

The findings are particularly strong / because the test took place in a supermarket / with genuine shoppers. //
이 결과는 특히 강력하다 / 왜냐하면 이 실험은 슈퍼마켓에서 진행되었기 때문이다 / 진짜 구매자들이 있는 //
부정어(nor)로 인한 주어, 동사 도치
It didn't rely on claimed data, / nor **was it** held in a laboratory /
관계부사
where consumers might behave differently. //
그것은 주장된 데이터에 의존하지 않았고 / 실험실에서 이루어진 것도 아니었다 / 소비자들이 다르게 행동할지도 모르는 //

- boost ⓥ 증가시키다, 촉진하다 · investigate ⓥ 조사하다
- effectiveness ⓝ 효과 · persuade ⓥ 설득하다
- condition ⓝ 조건 · control ⓝ 통제 집단 · volume ⓝ 용량, 양
- on average 평균적으로 · scarce ⓐ 부족한, 드문
- scarcity ⓝ 희소성 · particularly ⓐⓓ 특히 · genuine ⓐ 진짜의
- claimed ⓐ 주장된 · laboratory ⓝ 실험실 · restrict ⓥ 제한하다

고객이 구입할 수 있는 품목의 개수를 제한하는 것은 매출을 증가시킨다. Cornell University의 마케팅 교수인 Brian Wansink는 1998년에 이 전략의 효과를 조사했다. 그는 Iowa 주 Sioux City에 있는 세 개의 슈퍼마켓이 Campbell의 수프를 약간 할인하여 제공하도록 설득했다: 89센트가 아닌 79센트로. 할인된 수프는 세 가지 조건 중 하나의 조건으로 판매되었다: 구매량에 제한이 없는 하나의 대조군, 또는 고객이 4개의 캔으로 제한되거나 12개의 캔으로 제한되는 두 개의 실험군. 무제한 조건에서 구매자들은 평균 3.3캔을 구입했던 반면, 제한이 있던 희소 조건에서는, 평균 5.3캔을 구입했다. 이것은 희소성이 판매를 장려한다는 것을 보여준다. 이 실험은 진짜 구매자들이 있는 슈퍼마켓에서 진행되었기 때문에 그 결과는 특히 강력하다. 그것은 주장된 데이터에 의존하지 않았고, 소비자들이 다르게 행동할지도 모르는 실험실에서 이루어진 것도 아니었다.

다음 빈칸에 들어갈 말로 가장 적절한 것을 고르시오. [3점]

① Promoting products through social media
소셜 미디어를 통해 제품을 홍보하는 것 소셜 미디어는 언급되지 않았음
② Reducing the risk of producing poor quality items
품질이 낮은 제품을 생산할 위험성을 줄이는 것 질 좋은 제품이 매출을 증가시킨다는 내용이 아님
③ Restricting the number of items customers can buy
고객이 구입할 수 있는 품목의 개수를 제한하는 것 고객이 구입할 수 있는 개수를 제한함
④ Offering several options that customers find attractive
고객이 매력적으로 여기는 여러 옵션을 제공하는 것
⑤ Emphasizing the safety of products with research data
연구 자료와 함께 제품의 안정성을 강조하는 것 제품의 안정성에 관해서는 이야기하지 않음
구매 수량을 제한한 것이 매력적인 선택권인지 알 수 없음

➡ **왜 정답?** ★★★✿ [정답률 62%]

빈칸 문장	_____은 매출을 증가시킨다.

➡ 빈칸 문장: '무엇'은 매출을 증가시킨다.
➡ Brian Wansink 교수의 실험 결과:
  그룹 **1**: 수프 구매 수량에 제한이 없음 → 평균 3.3캔을 구입함
  그룹 **2, 3**: 수프 구매가 4캔 또는 12캔으로 제한됨 → 평균 5.3캔을 구입함
  ▶ 희소성이 판매를 장려한 것이므로 ③ '고객이 구입할 수 있는 품목의 개수를 제한하는 것'이 매출을 증가시킨 것이다.

① 소셜 미디어를 통해 제품을 홍보하여 매출을 증가시킨 것이 아니다.
② 제품 품질 관리를 통해 매출을 증가시켰다는 내용이 아니다.
❹ 구매 수량에 제한을 둔 것을 매력적인 구매 옵션으로 보기는 어렵다.
　　(❹ 이유: 무제한으로 구매할 수 있는 것은 매력적인 옵션으로 볼 수 있지만, 4개로
　　제한하는 것까지 매력적인 옵션으로 볼 수 없다.)
⑤ 제품의 안정성은 언급되지 않았다.

M 12 정답 ① *이동 방향에 따른 회복 속도의 차이

People differ / in how quickly they can reset their biological
　　　　　　부사적 용법(목적)　　절과 절을 잇는 등위접속사
clocks / to overcome jet lag, / and the speed of recovery / depends
on the **direction** of travel. //
사람마다 서로 다르다 / 자신의 체내 시계를 얼마나 빨리 재설정할 수 있는지 / 시차로 인한
피로감을 극복하기 위해서 / 그리고 그 회복 속도는 / 이동 방향에 달려 있다 //
　　　　　가주어　　　　　　　진주어의 병렬 구조
Generally, / it's easier / to fly westward and lengthen your day /
than it is to fly eastward and shorten it. //　　　**단서 1** 동쪽보다는 서쪽 비행이
　　　　　　　　　　　　　　　　　　　　　　　　　　　피로감을 덜 느끼게 함
일반적으로 / ~이 더 쉽다 / 서쪽으로 비행하여 여러분의 하루를 연장하는 것 / 동쪽으로
비행하여 그것을 단축하는 것보다 //　　**단서 2** 방향에 따른 시차로 인한 피로감이 경기력에 영향을 줌
This east-west difference in jet lag / is sizable enough / to have
an impact / on the performance of sports teams. //
시차로 인한 피로감에서 이러한 동서의 차이는 / 충분히 크다 / 영향을 미칠 만큼 / 스포츠
팀의 경기력에 //
　　　　　　　목적어절을 이끄는 접속사
Studies have found / that teams flying westward perform
　　　　　　　　　　　　현재분사구(teams 수식)
significantly better / than teams flying eastward / in professional
baseball and college football. //
연구는 발견했다 / 서쪽으로 비행하는 팀이 상당히 더 잘한다는 것을 / 동쪽으로 비행하는
팀보다 / 프로 야구와 대학 미식축구에서 //
A more recent study / of more than 46,000 Major League Baseball
games / found additional evidence / that eastward travel is
　　　동격절 접속사
비교 표현
tougher / **than** westward travel. //
더 최근의 연구는 / 46,000 경기가 넘는 메이저 리그 야구 경기에 대한 / 추가적인 증거를
발견했다 / 동쪽으로 이동하는 것이 더 힘들다는 것을 / 서쪽으로 이동하는 것보다 //

- differ ⓥ 다르다　　• reset ⓥ 재설정하다　　• biological ⓐ 생물체의
- overcome ⓥ 극복하다　　• recovery ⓝ 회복
- westward ⓐⓓ 서쪽으로　　• lengthen ⓥ 연장하다
- eastward ⓐⓓ 동쪽으로　　• sizable ⓐ 큰　　• impact ⓝ 영향
- significantly ⓐⓓ 상당히　　• additional ⓐ 추가의
- evidence ⓝ 증거　　• tough ⓐ 힘든　　• purpose ⓝ 목적

시차로 인한 피로감을 극복하기 위해서 자신의 체내 시계를 얼마나 빨리
재설정할 수 있는지는 사람마다 서로 다르며, 그 회복 속도는 이동 **방향**에
달려 있다. 일반적으로 동쪽으로 비행하여 여러분의 하루를 단축하는 것보다
서쪽으로 비행하여 여러분의 하루를 연장하는 것이 더 쉽다. 시차로 인한
피로감에서 이러한 동서의 차이는 스포츠 팀의 경기력에 영향을 미칠 만큼
충분히 크다. 연구에 따르면 서쪽으로 비행하는 팀이 동쪽으로 비행하는 팀보다
프로 야구와 대학 미식축구에서 상당히 더 잘한다. 46,000 경기가 넘는 메이저
리그 야구 경기에 대한 더 최근의 연구는 동쪽으로 이동하는 것이 서쪽으로
이동하는 것보다 더 힘들다는 추가적인 증거를 발견했다.

다음 빈칸에 들어갈 말로 가장 적절한 것을 고르시오.
①direction 동서의 차이는 방향을 의미함
　방향
② purpose 목적이 아닌 방향이 중요함
　목적
③ season 계절이 영향을 미친다는 내용은 없음
　계절
④ length 길이가 아니라 방향이 중요하다고 했음
　길이
⑤ cost 비용에 대한 내용은 없음
　비용

빈칸 문장	시차로 인한 피로감을 극복하기 위해서 자신의 체내 시계를 얼마나 빨리 재설정할 수 있는지는 사람마다 서로 다르며, 그 회복 속도는 이동 _____에 달려 있다.
빈칸 문장 뒤 예시	일반적으로 동쪽으로 비행하여 여러분의 하루를 단축하는 것보다 서쪽으로 비행하여 여러분의 하루를 연장하는 것이 더 쉽다. **단서 1**

➡ 빈칸 문장: 시차로 인한 피로감을 회복하는 속도는 이동의 '무엇'에 달려 있다.
➡ 빈칸 문장 뒤 예시: 동쪽으로 여행하는 것보다 서쪽으로 여행하여 하루를 연장하는
　 것이 더 쉽다.
　 ▶ 지구의 자전 방향(서 → 동)과 반대로 여행하는 것이 더 낫다는 것이므로
　 회복 속도는 이동의 ① '방향'에 달려 있다.

② 이동의 목적이 아닌 방향이 중요하다는 내용이다.
③ 계절이 영향을 미친다는 내용은 없었다.
④ 이동의 길이가 아니라 방향이 중요하다고 했다. ◀ 주의
⑤ 비용에 대한 내용은 나오지 않았으므로 적절하지 않다.

M 13 정답 ③ *성취를 위한 시간 활용

　　　　　　　　　　　　　　주격 관계대명사　　　　　선행사를 포함하는 관계대명사
If you want the confidence / that comes from achieving / what
you set out to do each day, / then it's important to understand /
　　　　　　　　　　　　　　가주어　　　　　　　　　진주어
how long things are going to take. //
만약 여러분이 자신감을 원한다면 / 성취함으로써 얻게 되는 / 매일 하고자 착수하는 일을 /
그러면 아는 것이 중요하다 / 일이 얼마나 시간이 걸릴지 //
　핵심 주어
Over-optimism about what can be achieved / within a certain
time frame / is a problem. //　**단서 1** 정해진 시간 내에 할 수 있다고 지나치게 믿는 것은
　　　　　동사　　　　　　　　　　　　　　　　　　　　　문제임
성취될 수 있는 것에 대한 지나친 낙관주의는 / 특정한 기간 내에 / 문제이다 //
So / work on it. //　　　　　　　　　　**단서 2** 시간이 얼마나 필요할지 추산하는 것을
그러므로 / 그것을 (개선하려고) 노력하라 //　　　　　습관화하라고 함
Make a practice / of estimating the amount of time needed /
alongside items on your 'things to do' list, /
습관화하라 / 필요한 시간의 양을 추산하는 것을 / '해야 할 일' 목록에 있는 것들과 함께 /
　　　　　　병렬 구조
and learn by experience / when tasks take a greater or lesser
time / than expected. //
그리고 경험에서 배워라 / 과제가 더 많거나 더 적은 시간이 걸릴 때 / 예상보다 //
Give attention / also to fitting the task / to the available time. //
주의를 기울여라 / 과제를 맞추는 것에도 / 이용 가능한 시간에 //
　　　　　　　　　　목적격 관계대명사
There are some tasks / that you can only set about / if you have
a significant amount of time available. //
몇몇 과제가 있다 / 여러분이 시작할 수 있는 / 상당한 양의 이용할 수 있는 시간이 있어야만 //
　　　　　　　　　　　　'무의미하다'
There is no point / in trying to gear up for such a task / when
you only have a short period available. //
무의미하다 / 그런 과제를 위해 준비하려고 애쓰는 것은 / 여러분에게 이용할 수 있는 짧은
시간밖에 없을 때 //　　　　　　　　　　　　　　　　　**단서 3** 과제별로 시간을 배분하여
　　　　　　　　　　　앞에 목적격 관계대명사가 생략됨　　　　순서를 정하라고 함
So schedule the time / you need / for the longer tasks / and put
the short tasks / into the spare moments in between. //
그러므로 시간을 계획하라 / 여러분이 필요로 하는 / 시간이 더 오래 걸리는 과제를 위해 /
그리고 시간이 짧게 걸리는 과제를 배치하라 / 사이의 남는 시간에 //

- set out ~에 착수하다　　• over-optimism ⓝ 지나친 낙관주의
- certain ⓐ 특정한　　• estimate ⓥ 추산하다, 어림잡다
- alongside prep ~와 함께　　• task ⓝ 과제　　• fit ⓥ 맞추다
- available ⓐ 이용 가능한　　• significant ⓐ 상당한
- spare ⓐ 남겨둔　　• practical ⓐ 실용적인　　• leisure ⓝ 여가

만약 여러분이 매일 하고자 착수하는 일을 성취함으로써 얻게 되는 자신감을 원한다면 **일이 얼마나 시간이 걸릴지** 아는 것이 중요하다. 어떤 특정 기간 내에 성취될 수 있는 것에 대한 지나친 낙관주의는 문제이다. 그러므로 그것을 개선하려고 노력하라. '해야 할 일' 목록에 있는 것들과 함께, 필요한 시간의 양을 추산하는 것을 습관화하고, 과제가 예상보다 더 많거나 적은 시간이 걸릴 때 경험을 통해 배워라. 이용 가능한 시간에 과제를 맞추는 것에도 주의를 기울여라. 상당한 양의 이용할 수 있는 시간이 있어야만 시작할 수 있는 몇몇 과제가 있다. 여러분에게 이용할 수 있는 시간이 짧을 때 그런 과제를 위해 준비하려고 애쓰는 것은 무의미하다. 그러므로 시간이 더 오래 걸리는 과제를 위해 필요한 시간을 계획하고, 그 사이의 남는 시간에 시간이 짧게 걸리는 과제를 배치하라.

다음 빈칸에 들어갈 말로 가장 적절한 것을 고르시오.
① what benefits you can get 이익에 대한 내용이 아님
여러분이 어떤 이익을 얻을 수 있는지
② how practical your tasks are 과제가 아니라 시간을 실용적으로 쓰라고 함
여러분의 과제가 얼마나 실용적인지
③ how long things are going to take
일이 얼마나 시간이 걸릴지   소요될 시간을 추산하여 적절하게 배치하라고 함
④ why failures are meaningful in life
왜 실패가 인생에 있어서 의미 있는지   실패를 통해 배우라는 내용이 아님
⑤ why your leisure time should come first
왜 여러분의 여가 시간을 우선시해야 하는지   여가 시간에 한정된 내용이 아님

왜 정답? ★★★ [정답률 57%]

빈칸 문장	만약 여러분이 매일 하고자 착수하는 일을 성취함으로써 얻게 되는 자신감을 원한다면 _____ 아는 것이 중요하다.

➡ 빈칸 문장: 일을 성취하여 자신감을 얻으려면 '무엇을' 아는 것이 중요하다.
➡ 빈칸 문장 뒤:
1 정해진 시간 내에 무언가를 성취할 수 있다고 믿는 지나친 낙관주의는 문제임 **단서 1**
2 필요한 시간의 양을 추산하는 것을 습관화하라고 함 **단서 2**
3 과제별로 필요한 시간을 배분하고 순서를 배치하라고 함 **단서 3**
▶ 따라서 일을 성취하여 얻게 되는 자신감에는 ③ '일이 얼마나 시간이 걸릴지' 아는 것이 중요하다.

왜 오답?
① 얻을 수 있는 이익을 계산하라고 조언하는 글이 아니다.
② 과제의 실용성이 아니라 효율적인 시간의 사용을 강조하는 글이다.
④ 실패를 통해 배우라는 언급은 없었다.
⑤ 여가 시간이 아니라 과제마다 소요될 시간을 파악하라고 했다.

M 14 정답 ⑤ *자발적 탐구가 갖는 학습적 이점

The last two decades of research / on the science of learning /
have shown conclusively **that** / we remember things better, and
목적어절을 이끄는 접속사
longer, / if **we discover them ourselves / rather than being told**
them. //
지난 20년간의 연구는 / 학습과학에 관한 / 결론적으로 보여주었다 / 우리는 그것들을 더 잘 기억하고, 더 오래 기억한다는 것을 / 만약 우리가 스스로 발견한다면 / 무언가에 관해서 듣는 것보다 //
This is the teaching method / **practiced** by physics professor Eric
앞에 주격 관계대명사와 be동사 생략
Mazur. //
이것은 교수법이다 / 물리학 교수 Eric Mazur에 의해 실천되는 //
He doesn't lecture / in his classes at Harvard. //
그는 (설명식) 강의를 하지 않는다 / 하버드 수업에서 **단서 1** 학생들은 질문에 대한 답을 찾기 위해 스스로 정보를 수집함
Instead, / he asks students difficult questions, / **based on** their ~에 기반하여
homework reading, / that require them to pull together sources
of information / **to solve** a problem. //
부사적 용법(목적)
대신에 / 그는 학생들에게 어려운 질문을 던진다 / 독서 활동 과제에 기반하여 / 그들이 정보 자료를 모을 수 있게 만드는 / 문제를 해결하기 위해 //

Mazur doesn't give them the answer; / instead, / he asks the
students **to break off** into small groups / and **discuss** the problem
병렬 구조
among themselves. // **단서 2** 질문에 대한 답은 학생들이 토론 과정을 통해서 구할 수 있음
Mazur는 그들에게 답을 주지 않는다 / 대신에 / 그는 학생들을 소그룹으로 나누어 / 그들 스스로 문제를 토론하도록 요구한다 //
Eventually, / nearly everyone in the class / gets the answer right,
/ and the concepts stick with them / because they had to find
their own way to the answer. // **단서 3** 스스로 정답으로 가는 길을 찾았기 때문에 학생들에게 이 개념들이 오래 남게 됨
결국 / 학급의 거의 모든 사람들이 / 정답을 맞힌다 / 그리고 이러한 개념들은 그들에게 오래 남는다 / 그들이 정답으로 가는 길을 스스로 찾아야 했기 때문에 //

- conclusively ⓐⓓ 결정적으로 · teaching method 교수법
- practice ⓥ 실천하다 · lecture ⓥ (설명식) 강의를 하다
- pull together 모으다 · break off ~을 분리시키다, 나누다
- eventually ⓐⓓ 결국 · concept ⓝ 개념

학습과학에 관한 지난 20년간의 연구는 만약 **우리가 무언가에 관해서 듣는 것보다 스스로 발견한다**면 우리는 그것들을 더 잘 기억하고, 더 오래 기억한다는 것을 결론적으로 보여주었다. 이것은 물리학 교수 Eric Mazur에 의해 실천되는 교수법이다. 그는 하버드 수업에서 (설명식) 강의를 하지 않는다. 대신에, 그는 독서 활동 과제에 기반하여 학생들에게 문제를 해결하기 위해 정보 자료를 모을 수 있게 만드는 어려운 질문을 던진다. Mazur는 그들에게 답을 주지 않는다. 대신에, 그는 학생들을 소그룹으로 나누어 그들 스스로 문제를 토론하도록 요구한다. 결국, 학급의 거의 모든 사람이 정답을 맞히고, 그들이 정답으로 가는 길을 스스로 찾아야 했기 때문에 이러한 개념들은 그들에게 오래 남는다.

다음 빈칸에 들어갈 말로 가장 적절한 것을 고르시오. [3점]
① they are taught repeatedly in class 반복을 통해 학습한다는 내용은 없음
그들은 수업에서 반복적으로 가르침을 받았다
② we fully focus on them without any distractions
우리는 방해 요인 없이 그것들에 온전히 집중한다   방해 요인과 관련 없는 내용임
③ equal opportunities are given to complete tasks
과제 완수를 위해 공평한 기회가 주어진다   공평한 기회에 대한 언급은 없음
④ there's no right or wrong way to learn about a topic   학습할
주제에 대해 배우는 것에는 옳거나 그른 방법이 있는 것이 아니다   때 더 나은 방법이 있다는 내용임
⑤ we discover them ourselves rather than being told them
우리가 무언가에 관해서 듣는 것보다 스스로 발견한다
강의식 수업으로 답을 아는 것보다 학생들 스스로 답을 찾아보는 것이 더 효과가 오래간다고 했음

왜 정답? ★★★ [정답률 57%]   예로 든 교수의 강의 방식에 주목하기! **꿀팁**
물리학 교수 Eric Mazur가 하버드 수업에서 설명식 강의를 하지 않는다고 하면서, 학생들에게 답을 알려주기보다는 질문에 대한 답을 찾기 위해 학생들 스스로 정보를 수집하고 소그룹 토론 과정을 통해서 구하게 한다고 했다. 그러면 스스로 정답으로 가는 길을 찾았기 때문에 이 개념들이 학생들에게 오래 남게 된다고 했다. 따라서 빈칸에 들어갈 말로 가장 적절한 것은 ⑤ '우리가 무언가에 관해서 듣는 것보다 스스로 발견한다'이다.

왜 오답?
① 반복적 학습에 대한 내용은 나오지 않았다.
② 방해 요인이 아닌 일방적 설명 강의가 상대적으로 효과가 덜하다는 내용이다.
③ 학생들이 스스로 학습하는 것이 초점이지 공평한 기회는 주제와 관련이 없다.
④ 옳고 그른 방식에 대해서는 언급하지 않고 더 나은 방법을 소개하고 있다.

M 15 정답 ⑤ *경제적 이유 때문에 발달한 언어

Many evolutionary biologists argue **that** / humans **developed**
목적어절을 이끄는 접속사
language for economic reasons. //
많은 진화 생물학자들은 주장한다 / 인간이 경제적인 이유로 언어를 발달시켰다고 //
We needed to trade, / and we needed to establish trust / **in order** ~하기 위해
to trade. // 우리는 거래해야 했다 / 그리고 신뢰를 확립해야 했다 / 거래하기 위해서는 //
Language is very handy / when you are trying to conduct
business with someone. // **단서 1** 언어는 거래에 용이함
언어는 매우 편리하다 / 당신이 누군가와 거래할 때 //

M

Two early humans / could **not only** agree / to trade three wooden
not only A but (also) B: A뿐만 아니라 B도
bowls for six bunches of bananas / **but** establish rules as well. //
초창기의 두 인간은 / 동의할 수 있었을 뿐만 아니라 / 3개의 나무로 만든 그릇을 6다발의 바나나와 거래하기로 / 규칙을 정할 수도 있었다 //

What wood was used / for the bowls? //
무슨 나무를 사용했나 / 그 그릇들을 만드는데 //

Where did you get the bananas? //
어디서 그 바나나를 얻게 되었나 //

단서 2 복잡하고 정확한 거래를 위해 언어가 필요했을 것이라고 추측할 수 있음

That business deal / would have been nearly impossible /
using only gestures and confusing noises / and carrying it out /
according to terms agreed upon / creates a bond of trust. //
그 상업 거래는 / 거의 불가능했을 것이다 / 단지 제스처와 혼란스런 소음만을 사용해서는 / 그리고 그것을 실행하는 것이 / 합의된 조항에 따라서 / 신뢰라는 결속을 만들었다 //

Language allows us **to be specific**, / and this is **where**
allows의 목적격보어   *관계부사*
conversation plays a key role. //
언어는 우리가 구체적이도록 해준다 / 그리고 이것이 대화가 중요한 역할을 하는 지점이다 //

- evolutionary @ 진화의   • biologist ⓝ 생물학자
- establish ⓥ 확립하다   • conduct ⓥ 거래하다   • handy @ 간편한
- confusing @ 혼란스러운   • terms ⓝ (합의·계약 등의) 조항
- bond ⓝ 결속

많은 진화 생물학자들은 인간이 **경제적인 이유로 언어를 발달시켰다**고 주장한다. 우리는 거래해야 했고, 거래하기 위해서는 신뢰를 확립해야 했다. 언어는 당신이 누군가와 거래할 때 매우 편리하다. 초창기의 두 인간은 3개의 나무로 만든 그릇을 6다발의 바나나와 거래하기로 동의할 수 있었을 뿐만 아니라 규칙을 정할 수도 있었다. 그 그릇들을 만드는데 무슨 나무를 사용했나? 어디서 그 바나나를 얻게 되었나? 단지 제스처와 혼란스런 소음만을 사용해서는 그 상업 거래는 거의 불가능했을 것이고, 합의된 조항에 따라서 그것을 실행하는 것이 신뢰라는 결속을 만든다. 언어는 우리가 구체적이도록 해주고 이것이 대화가 중요한 역할을 하는 지점이다.

다음 빈칸에 들어갈 말로 가장 적절한 것을 고르시오.

① used body language to communicate
소통하기 위해 몸짓 언어를 사용했다   몸짓 언어가 아니라 말로 하는 언어에 대한 내용임
② instinctively knew who to depend on
본능적으로 의지해야 할 대상을 알았다   타인에게 의존하지 않고 대화로 소통함
③ often changed rules for their own needs
그들의 요구를 위해 규칙을 자주 바꾸었다   대화라는 규칙을 통해 거래한다고 했음
④ lived independently for their own survival
자신의 생존을 위해 독립적으로 살았다   소통을 통해 신뢰를 쌓아 거래하며 생존한다고 했음
⑤ developed language for economic reasons
경제적인 이유로 언어를 발전시켰다   신뢰에 기반한 거래를 위해 언어가 발달되었다는 내용

왜 정답? ✱✱✱ [정답률 67%]

과거에 생존을 위해 거래를 했는데 이때 서로의 신뢰를 쌓기 위해서는 단순한 제스처와 소음 이상의 것이 필요했다고 했다. 이런 경제적 행위의 과정에서 언어가 용이했기 때문에 언어가 발달했다는 내용이다. 따라서 빈칸에 들어갈 말로 가장 적절한 것은 ⑤ '경제적인 이유로 언어를 발전시켰다'이다.

왜 오답?

① 몸짓 언어는 거래를 위한 신뢰 확립의 수단으로 충분하지 않았다.
② 타인에게 의존하기보다는 서로 소통했다고 했으므로 적절하지 않다.
③ 자신의 욕구를 위해 규칙을 바꾼 게 아니고 소통을 위해 언어를 발전시켰다고 했다. 함정
④ 독립적으로 생존하기보다는 타인과 거래하며 소통했다고 했다.

M 16 정답 ② ＊관심 분야에서는 읽기를 피하지 않는다!

A key to engagement and achievement / **is** providing students /
핵심 주어   단수 동사
with **relevant texts they will be interested in**. //
참여와 성취의 핵심은 / 학생들에게 제공하는 것이다 / 그들이 관심 있어 할 적절한 글을 //

My scholarly work and my teaching / **have been** deeply
influenced / by the work of Rosalie Fink. //
현재완료(계속)
나의 학문적인 연구와 나의 수업은 / 깊이 영향을 받아왔다 / Rosalie Fink의 연구에 //

She interviewed twelve adults / **who** were highly successful in
주격 관계대명사
their work, / **including** a physicist, a biochemist, and a company
분사 형태의 전치사
CEO. //
그녀는 열두 명의 성인들과 면담했다 / 그들의 직업에서 매우 성공한 / 물리학자, 생화학자 그리고 회사의 최고 경영자를 포함해 //

All of them had dyslexia / and **had had** significant problems
앞의 had보다 더 이전 시점을 나타내는 과거완료
with reading / throughout their school years. //
그들 모두가 난독증이 있었고 / 읽기에 상당한 문제를 겪어 왔다 / 그들의 학령기 내내 //
부사절 접속사(대조)   목적어절 접속사
While she expected to find / **that** they had avoided reading /
형용사적 용법(ways 수식)   to bypass와 병렬 구조
and discovered ways / **to bypass** it / or **compensate** with other
strategies / for learning, / she found the opposite. //
그녀는 알아낼 것을 예상했으나 / 그들이 읽기를 피했고 / 방법을 발견했을 것이라고 / 그것을 우회하거나 / 다른 전략들로 보완할 / 학습에 있어 / 그녀는 정반대를 알아냈다 //
단서 1 난독증이 있는 사람들은 읽기를 피하거나 우회할 거라고 예상했지만, 결과는 정반대였음

"To my surprise, / I found / that these dyslexics were enthusiastic
readers... / they rarely avoided reading. //
"놀랍게도 / 나는 알아냈다 / 이런 난독증이 있는 사람들이 열성적인 독자인 것을… / 그들은 좀처럼 읽기를 피하지 않았다 //

On the contrary, / they sought out books." //
이에 반하여 / 그들은 책을 찾았다" //   단서 2 그들은 책을 찾아서 읽었음
앞에 목적격 관계대명사가 생략됨   주격 보어절 접속사
The pattern Fink discovered / was **that** all of her subjects had
been passionate / in some personal interest. //
Fink가 발견한 패턴은 / 그녀의 실험대상자 모두가 열정적이었다는 것이었다 / 어떤 개인적인 관심사에 //
단서 3 실험대상자는 모두 개인적인 관심사에 열정적이었음

The areas of interest included / religion, math, business, science,
history, and biography. //
관심 분야는 포함했다 / 종교, 수학, 상업, 과학, 역사 그리고 생물학을 //
부사적 용법(목적)
What mattered was that they read voraciously / **to find** out
more. // 단서 4 관심사에 관해 더 알기 위해 열심히 읽음
중요한 것은 그들이 탐욕스럽게 읽었다는 것이다 / 더 많이 알아내기 위해 //

- engagement ⓝ 참여   • achievement ⓝ 성취
- scholarly @ 학문적인   • physicist ⓝ 물리학자
- biochemist ⓝ 생화학자   • significant @ 중요한, 상당한
- bypass ⓥ 우회하다   • compensate ⓥ 보완하다
- strategy ⓝ 전략   • enthusiastic @ 열성적인
- rarely @d 좀처럼 ~않는   • seek ⓥ 찾다(seek-sought-sought)
- subject ⓝ 실험대상자, 대상 • passionate @ 열정적인

참여와 성취의 핵심은 학생들에게 **그들이 관심 있어 할 적절한 글을** 제공하는 것이다. 나의 학문적인 연구와 나의 수업은 Rosalie Fink의 연구에 깊이 영향을 받아왔다. 그녀는 물리학자, 생화학자 그리고 회사의 최고 경영자를 포함해 그들의 직업에서 매우 성공한 열두 명의 성인들과 면담했다. 그들 모두가 난독증이 있었고 그들의 학령기 내내 읽기에 상당한 문제를 겪어 왔다. 그녀는 그들이 학습에 있어 읽기를 피하고 그것을 우회하거나 다른 전략들로 보완할 방법을 발견했으리라고 예상했으나, 정반대를 알아냈다. "놀랍게도, 나는 이런 난독증이 있는 사람들이 열성적인 독자인 것을… 그들이 좀처럼 읽기를 피하지 않았다는 것을 알아냈다. 이에 반하여, 그들은 책을 찾았다." Fink가 발견한 패턴은 그녀의 실험대상자 모두가 어떤 개인적인 관심사에 열정적이었다는 것이었다. 관심 분야는 종교, 수학, 상업, 과학, 역사 그리고 생물학을 포함했다. 중요한 것은 그들이 더 많이 알아내기 위해 탐욕스럽게 읽었다는 것이다.

다음 빈칸에 들어갈 말로 가장 적절한 것을 고르시오.

① examples from official textbooks
공인 교과서에서 나온 예시   공인 교과서에서 나온 예시가 핵심이라는 언급은 없음
② relevant texts they will be interested in
그들이 관심 있어 할 적절한 글   관심 분야에는 열정적으로 읽음
③ enough chances to exchange information
정보를 교환할 충분한 기회   정보를 교환할 기회를 주라는 것이 아님
④ different genres for different age groups
다양한 연령 집단에 대한 다양한 장르   다양한 연령 집단과 관련된 내용이 아님
⑤ early reading experience to develop logic skills
논리 기술을 발전시키기 위한 초기의 읽기 경험   초기의 읽기 경험이 중요하다는 내용이 아님

>왜 정답? ★★★ [정답률 52%]

빈칸 문장	참여와 성취의 핵심은 학생들에게 _____을 제공하는 것이다.

➡ **빈칸 문장:** 학생들에게 '무엇'을 제공하는 것이 참여와 성취의 핵심이다.
➡ **Rosalie Fink의 연구**
가정: 난독증이 있는 사람들은 읽기를 피하거나 우회할 것임 `단서 1`
결과: 그들은 오히려 책을 찾아서 읽었음 `단서 2`
원인: 그들은 모두 각자의 관심사에 더 알기 위해 열정적으로 읽음 `단서 3` `단서 4`
▶ '관심 분야에는 열정적이므로, 참여와 성취의 핵심은 학생들에게 ② '그들이 관심 있어 할 적절한 글'을 제공하는 것이다.

>왜 오답?
① 공인 교과서에서 나온 예시가 핵심이라는 언급은 없다.
③ 학생들에게 서로 정보를 교환할 기회를 주라는 것이 아니다.
④ 다양한 연령 집단과 관련된 내용이 아니다. (▶◀ 이유: 물리학자, 생물학자 등이 언급되긴 했지만, 연령과 관련 없는 내용이다.)
⑤ 읽기와 관련된 내용은 맞지만, 성공하기 위해 초기 읽기 경험이 중요하다고 말하는 글이 아니다. `함정`

M 17 정답 ① *단순한 제품이 갖는 비교우위

Sometimes **it is** the **simpler product** / **that** gives a business a competitive advantage. //
It ~ that ... 강조 구문
때때로 더 단순한 제품이다 / 기업에 비교우위를 주는 것은 //

Until recently, / bicycles had to have many gears, often 15 or 20, / for them to be considered high-end. //
최근까지 / 자전거는 보통 15개 혹은 20개의 많은 기어를 가져야 했다 / 최고급이라고 여겨지기 위해서는 `단서 1` 최소한의 특징을 가진 자전거들이 더 저렴해서 고객들에게 인기 있게 되었다고 했음

But / fixed-gear bikes with minimal features / have become more popular, / as those who buy them are happy to pay more / for much less. //
그러나 / 최소한의 특징을 가지고 있는, 고정식 기어 자전거들은 / 점점 더 인기를 얻게 되었다 / 그것들을 사는 사람들이 기꺼이 더 지불함에 따라 / 훨씬 적은 것에 대해 //

The overall profitability of these bikes / is much higher than the more complex ones / because they do a single thing really well / without the cost of added complexity. //
_핵심 주어_ _단수 동사_ _비교급 강조(even, much, still, a lot, far 등)_
이런 자전거들의 전반적인 수익성은 / 더 복잡한 것들보다 훨씬 더 큰데 / 그것들이 한 가지를 정말 잘하기 때문이다 / 추가되는 복잡성에 대한 비용 없이 //

Companies should be careful / of getting into a war over adding more features / with their competitors, /
기업들은 조심해야 한다 / 더 많은 특징들을 추가하는 전쟁을 하는 데 있어서 / 경쟁 업체와 /
이유를 나타내는 접속사
as this will increase cost / and almost certainly reduce profitability / **because of** competitive pressure on price. //
때문에 _때문에_
이것이 비용을 증가시키고 / 수익성을 거의 확실히 감소시킬 것이기 때문이다 / 가격에 대한 경쟁적인 압박 때문에 // `단서 2` 제품에 더 많은 특징들을 추가하는 것은 가격이 비싸져서 수익성을 떨어뜨릴 수 있음

• competitive advantage 비교우위 • fixed-gear ⓐ 고정식 기어의
• feature ⓝ 특징 • overall ⓐ 전반적인 • profitability ⓝ 수익성
• complexity ⓝ 복잡성 • competitor ⓝ 경쟁 업체
• pressure ⓝ 압박

때때로 기업에게 비교우위를 주는 것은 **더 단순한 제품**이다. 최근까지, 자전거는 최고급이라고 여겨지기 위해서는 보통 15개 혹은 20개의 많은 기어를 가져야 했다. 그러나 최소한의 특징을 가지고 있는, 고정식 기어 자전거들은 그것들을 사는 사람들이 훨씬 적은 것에 대해 기꺼이 더 지불함에 따라 점점 더 인기를 얻게 되었다. 이런 자전거들의 전반적인 수익성은 더 복잡한 것들보다 훨씬 더 큰데 그것들이 추가되는 복잡성에 대한 비용 없이 한 가지를 정말 잘하기 때문이다. 기업들은 경쟁 업체와 더 많은 특징들을 추가하는 전쟁을 하는 것을 조심해야 하는데, 이것이 가격에 대한 경쟁적인 압박 때문에 비용을 증가시키고 수익성을 거의 확실히 감소시킬 것이기 때문이다.

다음 빈칸에 들어갈 말로 가장 적절한 것을 고르시오.
① simpler product 복잡한 제품일수록 수익성 감소 확률이 높다고 했음
   더 단순한 제품
② affordable price 가격이 아닌 제품의 복잡성에 대해 언급함
   지불 가능한 가격
③ consumer loyalty 고객은 단순한 제품이 저렴해 선호한다고 언급했을 뿐임
   고객 충성심
④ customized design 고객은 맞춤 디자인 보다는 저렴하고 간단한 제품을 선호한다고 했음
   고객 맞춤 디자인
⑤ eco-friendly technology 친환경 기술은 관련 없는 내용
   친환경 기술

>왜 정답? ★★★ [정답률 58%]

자전거를 예로 들면서, 많은 기어를 가진 자전거보다 최소한의 특징을 가진 자전거들이 더 저렴해서 고객들에게 인기 있게 되었다고 했다. 복잡하고 발전된 기술을 쓰는 제품일수록 가격이 올라가 고객들 입장에서는 부담을 느끼기 쉽다. 그 결과 수익성은 간단한 제품이 더 높다고 했으므로 기업에 비교우위를 주는 제품 또한 '더 단순한 제품'일 것이다. 따라서 ①이 빈칸에 들어갈 말로 가장 적절하다.

>왜 오답?
② 가격보다는 제품의 복잡성에 의해 수익성이 달라진다고 설명했다.
③ 고객들은 대체로 최소한의 기능을 가진 부담 없는 가격의 제품을 선호한다고 했다.
④ 고객 맞춤 디자인 보다는 저렴하고 간단한 제품의 수익성이 더 높다고 했다.
⑤ 친환경 기술은 언급되지 않은 내용이다.

M 18 정답 ① *시각의 적응력

A remarkable characteristic of the visual system / is **that** it has the ability of **adapting itself**. //
명사절 접속사
시각 체계의 두드러진 특징은 / 스스로 적응하는 능력이 있다는 것이다 //

Psychologist George M. Stratton made **this clear** / in an impressive self-experiment. //
목적어 목적격 보어
심리학자 George M. Stratton은 이것을 분명히 했다 / 인상적인 자가 실험에서 //

Stratton wore reversing glasses for several days, / **which** literally turned the world upside down for him. //
계속적 용법의 주격 관계대명사
Stratton은 며칠 동안 반전 안경을 착용했는데 / 그 안경은 말 그대로 그에게 세상을 뒤집어 놓았다 //

In the beginning, / this caused him great difficulties: / just **putting** food in his mouth with a fork / **was** a challenge for him. //
동명사 주어 _단수 동사_
처음에 / 이것은 그에게 큰 어려움을 초래하였다 / 포크로 음식을 입에 넣는 것조차 / 그에게는 도전이었다 //

With time, however, / his visual system adjusted to the new stimuli from reality, / and he was able to act normally / in his environment again, /
그러나 시간이 지나면서 / 그의 시각 체계는 현실의 새로운 자극에 적응했고 / 정상적으로 행동할 수 있었다 / 다시 자신의 환경에서 /
분사구문
even **seeing it upright** / when he concentrated. //
심지어 똑바로 보면서 / 그가 집중했을 때는 // `단서 1` 반전 안경을 낀 환경에 적응하며 정상적으로 행동함

As he took off his reversing glasses, / he was again confronted with problems: /
반전 안경을 벗었을 때 / 그는 다시 문제에 직면했다 /

he used the wrong hand / when he wanted to reach for something, / for example. //
그는 반대 손을 사용했다 / 그가 무언가를 잡기를 원할 때 / 예를 들어 // `단서 2` 반전 안경을 벗고 나서도 금세 적응하여 정상으로 돌아옴

Fortunately, / Stratton could reverse the perception, / and he did not have to wear reversing glasses / for the rest of his life. //
다행히 / Stratton은 지각을 뒤집을 수 있었고 / 반전 안경을 착용하지 않아도 되었다 / 평생 //

For him, / everything returned to normal / after one day. //
그에게 / 모든 것이 정상으로 돌아왔다 / 하루 만에 //

M

- remarkable @ 두드러진 • characteristic ⓝ 특징
- visual system 시각 체계 • adapt ⓥ 적응하다
- psychologist ⓝ 심리학자 • self-experiment ⓝ 자가 실험
- literally @d 말 그대로 • upside down 거꾸로
- difficulty ⓝ 어려움 • challenge ⓝ 도전
- stimulus ⓝ 자극 (pl. stimuli) • concentrate ⓥ 집중하다
- be confronted with ~에 직면하다 • fortunately @d 다행히
- perception ⓝ 지각

시각 체계의 두드러진 특징은 <u>스스로 적응하는</u> 능력이 있다는 것이다. 심리학자 George M. Stratton은 인상적인 자가 실험에서 이것을 분명히 했다. Stratton 은 며칠 동안 반전 안경을 착용했는데 그 안경은 말 그대로 그에게 세상을 뒤집어 놓았다. 처음에 이것은 그에게 큰 어려움을 초래하였다. 포크로 음식을 입에 넣는 것조차 그에게는 도전이었다. 그러나 시간이 지나면서 그의 시각 체계는 현실의 새로운 자극에 적응했고, 그가 집중했을 때는 심지어 똑바로 보면서, 다시 자신의 환경에서 정상적으로 행동할 수 있었다. 반전 안경을 벗었을 때 그는 다시 문제에 직면했다. 예를 들어 그가 무언가를 잡기를 원할 때 그는 반대 손을 사용했다. 다행히 Stratton은 지각을 뒤집을 수 있었고 평생 반전 안경을 착용하지 않아도 되었다. 그에게 하루 만에 모든 것이 정상으로 돌아왔다.

> **다음 빈칸에 들어갈 말로 가장 적절한 것을 고르시오.**
> ① adapting itself 시각은 스스로 적응하는 능력이 있음
> 스스로 적응하는
> ② visualizing ideas 생각을 시각화하는 내용이 아님
> 생각을 시각화하는
> ③ assessing distances 거리를 가늠하는 것과 관련 없음
> 거리를 가늠하는
> ④ functioning irregularly 불규칙적으로 기능한다는 언급은 없음
> 불규칙적으로 기능하는
> ⑤ operating independently 독립적으로 작동한다는 내용이 아님
> 독립적으로 작동하는

▷왜 정답 ? ✱✱✽ [정답률 68%]

빈칸 문장	시각 체계의 두드러진 특징은 _____ 능력이 있다는 것이다.

➡ **빈칸 문장:** 시각 체계는 '무엇'할 수 있는 능력이 있다.

빈칸 문장 뒤 예시	반전 안경 실험 • 반전 안경을 낀 환경에 시간이 흐르며 적응함 단서 1 • 반전 안경을 벗고 나서도 금세 적응하여 정상으로 돌아옴 단서 2

➡ 반전 안경 실험을 통해 시각에 변화를 주었을 때, 초반에는 어려움을 겪었지만 시간이 흐르면서 새로운 자극에 적응했다는 내용임
▶ 시각은 그 자극에 변화를 주더라도 스스로 적응하는 능력이 있다는 내용이므로, 정답은 ① '스스로 적응하는'이다.

▷왜 오답 ?

② 생각을 시각화하는 내용이 아니다.
③ 거리를 가늠하는 것과 관련이 없다.
④ 시각이 불규칙적으로 기능한다는 언급은 없었다.
⑤ 시각이 독립적으로 작동한다는 내용이 아니다.

자이 쌤's Follow Me! – 홈페이지에서 제공

M19 정답 ① ✱우리를 규정해주는 기억

부정어구 도치: 부정어구+동사+주어 / 형용사적 용법
Not only does memory underlie / our ability to think at all, / it defines / the content of our experiences / and how we preserve them / for years to come. //
기억이 어쨌든 기반이 될 뿐만 아니라 / 사고하는 우리의 능력의 / 그것은 규정한다 / 우리의 경험의 내용을 / 그리고 우리가 그것을 보존하는 방식을 / 다가올 수년간 //

Memory / **makes us who we are**. //
기억은 / 우리를 우리가 누구인지로 만들어 준다 //

---

were to 가정법: If 주어+were to+동사원형 ~, 주어+would+동사원형 ...
If I were to suffer from heart failure / and depend upon an artificial heart, / I would be no less myself. //
만약 내가 심장 부전을 앓는다 해도 / 그리고 인공 심장에 의존한다 (해도) / 나는 역시 여느 때의 나일 것이다 //

가정법 과거: If 주어+과거형 동사 ~, 주어+would+동사원형 ...
If I lost an arm in an accident / and had it replaced with an artificial arm, / I would still be essentially me. //
만약 내가 사고로 한 팔을 잃는다 해도 / 그리고 그것을 인공 팔로 교체한다 (해도) / 나는 여전히 본질적으로 '나'일 것이다 //

단서 1 정신과 기억이 손상되지 않으면 나는 계속 같은 사람임
~하는 한
As long as my mind and memories remain intact, / I will continue to be the same person, / no matter which part of my body (other than the brain) is replaced. //
나의 정신과 기억이 손상되지 않은 한 / 나는 계속 같은 사람일 것이다 / 나의 신체의 (뇌를 제외한) 어떤 부분이 교체될지라도 //

On the other hand, / when someone suffers from advanced Alzheimer's disease / and his memories fade, /
반면 / 누군가 후기의 알츠하이머병을 앓고 / 그의 기억이 흐려진다면 /

목적어절을 이끄는 접속사의 병렬 구조
people often say / that he "is not himself anymore," / or that it is as if the person "is no longer there," / though his body remains unchanged. // 단서 2 기억이 흐려지면 사람들은 그가 다른 사람이 되었다고 말함
사람들은 종종 말한다 / 그는 '더 이상 여느 때의 그가 아니라고' / 혹은 마치 그 사람이 '더 이상 그곳에 없는' 것 같다고 / 비록 그의 신체는 변하지 않은 채로 남아 있음에도 불구하고 //

- underlie ⓥ 기반이 되다 • preserve ⓥ 보존하다
- heart failure 심장 부전 • artificial heart 인공 심장
- replace ⓥ 대체하다 • essentially @d 본질적으로
- advanced @ (발달 단계상) 후기의
- fade ⓥ 흐려지다, 점점 희미해지다 • have to do with ~와 관련이 있다

기억이 어쨌든 사고하는 우리의 능력의 기반이 될 뿐만 아니라 그것은 우리의 경험의 내용과 다가올 수년간 우리가 그것을 보존하는 방식을 규정한다. 기억은 **우리를 우리가 누구인지로 만들어 준다.** 만약 내가 심장 부전을 앓고 인공 심장에 의존한다 해도 나는 역시 여느 때의 나일 것이다. 만약 내가 사고로 한 팔을 잃고 그것을 인공 팔로 교체한다 해도 나는 여전히 본질적으로 '나'일 것이다. 나의 정신과 기억이 손상되지 않은 한, 나의 신체의 (뇌를 제외한) 어떤 부분이 교체될지라도 나는 계속 같은 사람일 것이다. 반면 누군가 후기의 알츠하이머병을 앓고 그의 기억이 흐려진다면, 비록 그의 신체는 변하지 않은 채로 남아 있음에도 불구하고 사람들은 종종 그는 '더 이상 여느 때의 그가 아니라고' 혹은 마치 그 사람이 '더 이상 그곳에 없는' 것 같다고 말한다.

> **다음 빈칸에 들어갈 말로 가장 적절한 것을 고르시오.**
> ① makes us who we are 기억이 현재의 우리를 규정해준다는 내용임
> 우리를 우리가 누구인지로 만들어 준다
> ② has to do with our body 기억과 몸의 관련성에 대한 내용이 아님
> 우리의 몸과 관련이 있다
> ③ reflects what we expect 우리의 기대에 대해서는 언급되지 않음
> 우리가 기대하는 것을 반영한다
> ④ lets us understand others 다른 사람을 이해하는 것과 관련된 내용은 없음
> 우리가 다른 사람들을 이해하도록 한다
> ⑤ helps us learn from the past 기억에 대한 내용인 것으로 만든 함정
> 우리가 과거로부터 배우도록 돕는다

▷왜 정답 ? ✱✱✱ [정답률 66%]   기억이 있는 경우 꿀팁

심장 부전을 앓고 인공 심장에 의존하거나 사고로 한 팔을 잃고 그것을 인공 팔로 교체한다고 해도 우리의 정신과 기억이 손상되지 않으면 우리는 계속 같은 사람이라고 했다. 하지만 후기의 알츠하이머병을 앓고 기억이 흐려진다면 신체가 변하지 않아도 사람들은 그가 다른 사람이 되었다고 말한다는 내용이다.
기억이 현재의 우리를 규정해준다는 내용이므로 빈칸에는 ① '우리를 우리가 누구인지로 만들어 준다'가 들어가는 것이 적절하다. 기억이 없는 경우 꿀팁

▷왜 오답 ?

② 기억이 현재의 우리를 규정해준다는 내용이므로, 기억과 몸이 관련이 있다는 것에 대한 내용이 아니다.
③ 우리가 기대하는 것에 대해서는 언급되지 않았다.
④ 타인을 이해하는 것과 관련된 내용은 전혀 제시되지 않았다.
⑤ 기억에 대한 내용인 것으로 만든 함정일 뿐이고, 과거로부터 배운다는 말이 들어가는 것은 적절하지 않다.

M 20 정답 ④ *한 번에 하나의 관점만 취하며 세상을 이해하는 경향

Anthropologist Gregory Bateson suggests / that we tend to understand the world / **by focusing in on particular features within it**. //
(by -ing: ~함으로써)
인류학자 Gregory Bateson은 제안한다 / 우리가 세상을 이해하는 경향이 있다고 / 세상 안의 특정한 특징에 초점을 맞춤으로써 //

Take platypuses. //
오리너구리를 예로 들어보자 //

We might zoom in **so** closely to their fur / **that** each hair **appears different**. //
('너무 …해서 ~하다') (2형식 동사) (보어(형용사))
우리가 그들의 털을 매우 가까이 확대하면 / 각 가닥이 다르게 보인다 //

We might also zoom out / to the extent **where** it appears as a single, uniform object. //
(관계부사)
우리는 또한 축소할 수도 있다 / 그것이 하나의 동일한 개체로 보이는 정도까지 //

We might take the platypus as an individual, / or we might treat it as part of a larger unit / such as a species or an ecosystem. //
우리는 오리너구리를 개체로 취급할 수도 있고 / 더 큰 단위의 일부로 취급할 수도 있다 / 종 또는 생태계와 같이 // 〔단서 1〕 오리너구리를 어떻게 보는지에 따라 다르게 취급할 수 있음

(가주어) (진주어)
It's possible **to move** between many of these perspectives, /
이러한 많은 관점 사이를 이동하는 것은 가능하다 / 〔단서 2〕 많은 관점 사이를 이동하며 초점을 달리 맞추는 것이 가능함

although we may need some additional tools and skills / **to zoom** in on individual pieces of hair / or zoom out to entire ecosystems. //
(부사적 용법(목적))
비록 몇 가지 추가 도구와 기술이 필요할지도 모르지만 / 개별 머리카락을 확대하거나 / 전체 생태계로 축소하기 위해 //

Crucially, however, / we can only take up one perspective at a time. //
그러나 결정적으로 / 우리는 한 번에 하나의 관점만 취할 수 있다 //

We can **pay** attention to the **varied** behavior of individual animals, / **look** at **what** unites them into a single species, / or **look** at them as part of bigger ecological patterns. //
(과거분사) (선행사를 포함하는 관계대명사) (병렬 구조)
우리는 개별 동물의 다양한 행동에 주의를 기울일 수 있고 / 그들을 단일 종으로 통합하는 것을 살펴볼 수도 있고 / 더 큰 생태학적 패턴의 일부로서 그들을 살펴볼 수도 있다 //

Every possible perspective involves / emphasizing certain aspects and ignoring others. //
가능한 모든 관점은 포함한다 / 특정 측면을 강조하고 다른 측면을 외면하는 것을 // 〔단서 3〕 우리가 무언가를 볼 때, 특정 측면을 강조하고 다른 측면은 외면함

- tend to ~하는 경향이 있다
- fur ⓝ 털
- to the extent where ~할 정도까지
- uniform ⓐ 동일한, 획일적인
- object ⓝ 개체
- unit ⓝ 단위
- species ⓝ 종(種)
- ecosystem ⓝ 생태계
- perspective ⓝ 관점
- additional ⓐ 추가적인
- individual ⓐ 개별의
- entire ⓐ 전체의
- crucially ⓐⓓ 결정적으로
- varied ⓐ 다양한
- behavior ⓝ 행동
- unite ⓥ 통합하다
- ecological ⓐ 생태학적인
- emphasize ⓥ 강조하다
- aspect ⓝ 측면
- ignore ⓥ 무시하다, 외면하다
- framework ⓝ 틀

인류학자 Gregory Bateson은 우리가 **세상 안의 특정한 특징에 초점을 맞춤으로써** 세상을 이해하는 경향이 있다고 제안한다. 오리너구리를 예로 들어보자. 우리가 그들의 털을 매우 가까이 확대하면 각 가닥이 다르게 보인다. 우리는 또한 그것이 하나의 동일한 개체로 보이는 정도까지 축소할 수도 있다. 우리는 오리너구리를 개체로 취급할 수도 있고 종 또는 생태계와 같이 더 큰 단위의 일부로 취급할 수도 있다. 비록 개별 머리카락을 확대하거나 전체 생태계로 축소하기 위해 몇 가지 추가 도구와 기술이 필요할지도 모르지만, 이러한 많은 관점 사이를 이동하는 것은 가능하다. 그러나 결정적으로 우리는 한 번에 하나의 관점만 취할 수 있다. 우리는 개별 동물의 다양한 행동에 주의를 기울일 수 있고, 그들을 단일 종으로 통합하는 것을 살펴볼 수도 있고, 더 큰 생태학적 패턴의 일부로서 그들을 살펴볼 수도 있다. 가능한 모든 관점은 특정 측면을 강조하고 다른 측면을 외면하는 것을 포함한다.

다음 빈칸에 들어갈 말로 가장 적절한 것을 고르시오. [3점]
① using our experiences as a guide 우리의 경험을 안내서로 사용함으로써
　우리의 경험에 관한 언급은 없음
② breaking the framework of old ideas 오래된 생각의 틀을 깸으로써
　오래된 생각의 틀을 깬다는 언급은 없음
③ adding new information to what we know 우리가 아는 것에 새로운 정보를 더함으로써
　새로운 정보를 더한다는 내용은 없음
④ focusing in on particular features within it 세상 안의 특정한 특징에 초점을 맞춤으로써
　특정한 특징에 초점을 두고 이에 맞는 관점을 가지며 세상을 이해함
⑤ considering both bright and dark sides of it 그것의 밝은 면과 어두운 면을 둘 다 고려함으로써
　밝은 면과 어두운 면을 고려한다는 내용은 없음

왜 정답 ? ✱✱※ [정답률 68%]

| 빈칸 문장 | 인류학자 Gregory Bateson은 우리가 ＿＿＿＿＿ 세상을 이해하는 경향이 있다고 제안한다. |

➡ **빈칸 문장**: 우리가 세상을 '어떻게' 이해하는 경향이 있는지가 핵심이다.
➡ **Gregory Bateson의 연구 결과**:
　예시: 오리너구리를 확대하면 모든 털이 달라 보이고, 축소하면 동일한 하나의 개체로 보임 〔단서 1〕
　적용: 대상을 하나의 개체로 볼지, 더 큰 단위의 일부로 볼지 등 여러 관점 사이를 이동하는 것은 가능함 〔단서 2〕
　결론: 우리가 세상을 이해할 때도 하나의 관점을 취해 특정 측면을 강조하고 다른 측면은 외면하며 초점을 맞춤 〔단서 3〕
　▶ 인간이 세상을 바라보는 방식은 특정한 특징에 초점을 맞추어 여러 관점 중 하나를 택하는 것이므로, 우리는 세상을 ④ '세상 안의 특정한 특징에 초점을 맞춤으로써' 이해한다.

왜 오답 ?
① 우리의 경험에 관한 언급은 없었다.
② 오래된 생각의 틀을 깬다는 언급은 없었다.
③ 새로운 정보를 더한다는 내용은 없었다.
⑤ 밝은 면과 어두운 면을 고려한다는 내용은 없었다.

M 21 정답 ① ⭐ 2등급 대비 [정답률 52%]

*신선함에 대한 요구가 갖는 환경적 대가

The demand for freshness / can **have hidden environmental costs**. //
신선함에 대한 요구는 / 숨겨진 환경적인 대가를 지니고 있을 수 있다 //

While freshness **is now being used / as** a term / in food marketing / as part of a return to nature, /
(수동태의 현재진행형)
신선함이 현재 사용되고 있는 반면에 / 하나의 용어로 / 식품 마케팅에서 / 자연으로의 회귀의 일부로서 /

the demand for year-round supplies of fresh produce / such as soft fruit and exotic vegetables / **has led** / to the widespread use of hot houses / in cold climates / and increasing reliance / on total quality control / 〔단서 1〕 신선함에 대한 요구가 가져온 온실 사용과 품질 관리에 대한 의존성 증가
(핵심 주어(단수)) (단수 동사)
신선한 식품의 연중 공급에 대한 요구는 / 부드러운 과일이나 외국산 채소와 같은 / 이어져 왔다 / 광범위한 온실 사용으로 / 추운 기후에서의 / 그리고 의존성의 증가로 / 총체적인 품질 관리에 대한 /

— management by temperature control, / use of pesticides / and computer/satellite-based logistics. //
온도 조절에 의한 관리 / 살충제 사용 / 그리고 컴퓨터 위성 기반 물류와 같은 //

The demand for freshness / has also contributed / to concerns about food wastage. // 〔단서 2〕 신선함에 대한 요구가 가져온 식량 낭비
신선함에 대한 요구는 / 또한 원인이 되어 왔다 / 식량 낭비에 대한 우려의 //

Use of 'best before', 'sell by' and 'eat by' labels / has legally allowed / institutional waste. //
'유통 기한', '판매 시한', 그리고 '섭취 시한' 라벨 사용은 / 법적으로 허용해 왔다 / 제도적인 폐기물 생산을 //

Campaigners have exposed / the scandal of over-production and waste. //
운동가들은 폭로해 왔다 / 과잉 생산이나 폐기물에 대한 추문을 //
농경

Tristram Stuart, / one of the global band of anti-waste campaigners, / argues / that, with freshly made sandwiches, /
목적어를 이끄는 접속사
over-ordering is standard practice / across the retail sector /
Tristram Stuart는 / 폐기물 반대 세계 연대 소속 운동가 중 한 명인 / 주장한다 / 신선하게 만들어진 샌드위치와 함께 / 초과 주문이 일반적인 행태라고 / 소매 산업 분야 전반에서 이루어지는 /

to avoid the appearance of empty shelf space, / leading to high volumes of waste / when supply regularly exceeds demand. //
분사구문
판매대가 비어 보이는 것을 막기 위한 / 이것은 엄청난 양의 폐기물로 이어진다 / 공급이 정기적으로 수요를 초과하면 //

- freshness ⓝ 신선함
- environmental ⓐ 환경적인
- produce ⓝ 생산물[품]
- exotic ⓐ 외국산의
- widespread ⓐ 광범위한
- reliance ⓝ 의존성
- quality ⓝ 품질
- management ⓝ 관리
- satellite ⓝ 위성
- contribute ⓥ (~의) 원인이 되다
- concern ⓝ 우려
- wastage ⓝ 낭비
- legally ⓐⓓ 법적으로
- institutional ⓐ 제도적인
- expose ⓥ 폭로하다
- practice ⓝ 행태
- retail ⓝ 소매 산업
- sector ⓝ 분야
- regularly ⓐⓓ 정기적으로
- exceed ⓥ 초과하다
- worsen ⓥ 악화시키다
- technological ⓐ 기술적인
- advance ⓝ 발전, 진전
- diversify ⓥ 다양화하다

신선함에 대한 요구는 숨겨진 환경적인 대가를 지니고 있을 수 있다. 자연으로의 회귀의 일부로서 현재 신선함이 식품 마케팅에서 하나의 용어로 사용되고 있는 반면에, 부드러운 과일이나 외국산 채소와 같은 신선한 식품의 연중 공급에 대한 요구는 추운 기후에서의 광범위한 온실 사용과 총체적인 품질 관리 — 온도 조절에 의한 관리, 살충제 사용, 그리고 컴퓨터/위성 기반 물류 — 에 대한 의존성의 증가로 이어져 왔다. 신선함에 대한 요구는 또한 식량 낭비에 대한 우려의 원인이 되어 왔다. '유통 기한', '판매 시한', 그리고 '섭취 시한' 라벨 사용은 제도적인 폐기물 생산을 법적으로 허용해 왔다. 운동가들은 과잉 생산이나 폐기물에 대한 추문을 폭로해 왔다. 폐기물 반대 세계 연대 소속 운동가 중 한 명인 Tristram Stuart는 신선하게 만들어진 샌드위치와 함께, 판매대가 비어 보이는 것을 막기 위한 초과 주문이 소매 산업 분야 전반에서 이루어지는 일반적인 행태이며, 이것은 공급이 정기적으로 수요를 초과하면 엄청난 양의 폐기물로 이어진다고 주장한다.

다음 빈칸에 들어갈 말로 가장 적절한 것을 고르시오. [3점]
① have hidden environmental costs
숨겨진 환경적 대가를 지니고   신선함에 대한 요구가 환경적인 문제를 가져온다는 내용
② worsen the global hunger problem
세계 기아 문제를 악화시키고   식품에 대한 언급으로 만든 함정
③ bring about technological advances
기술적 발전을 가져오고   컴퓨터/위성 기반 물류가 언급됐지만, 기술적 발전을 가져온다는 내용이 아님
④ improve nutrition and quality of food
음식의 영양과 품질을 향상시키고   온실 사용과 총체적인 품질 관리에 대한 언급으로 만든 오답
⑤ diversify the diet of a local community
지역 사회의 식단을 다양화하고   지역 사회 식단의 다양화에 대한 글이 아님

─────────────────────────

2등급? 음식의 신선함을 요구하는 것이 어떤 결과를 초래했는지 파악해야 한다. 각 선택지에 '환경적', '기아 문제', '기술적 발전', '음식', '식단과 같이 글에 등장한 표현에서 유추할 수 있는 핵심어가 사용되었기 때문에 글에 제시된 상황들을 정확하게 이해해야만 정답을 고를 수 있는 2등급 대비 문제이다.

| 문제 풀이 순서 |

1st 빈칸이 포함된 문장의 내용을 파악하고, 빈칸에 들어갈 말에 대한 단서를 얻는다.

빈칸 문장
The demand for freshness can _____.
신선함에 대한 요구는 _____ 있을 수 있다.

첫 문장이 빈칸이 포함된 문장인데, 신선함에 대한 요구가 '무엇' 할 수 있다는 내용이다. (단서)
나머지 글을 읽으면서 이 '신선함에 대한 요구'와 관련된 내용을 찾아야 할 것이다. (발상)

2nd 글의 내용을 종합해서 빈칸에 들어갈 적절한 말을 찾는다.

- 부드러운 과일이나 외국산 채소와 같은 신선한 식품의 연중 공급에 대한 요구는 추운 기후에서의 광범위한 온실 사용과 총체적인 품질 관리 — 온도 조절에 의한 관리, 살충제 사용, 그리고 컴퓨터/위성 기반 물류 — 에 대한 의존성의 증가로 이어져 왔다. 단서 1
- 신선함에 대한 요구는 식량 낭비에 대한 우려의 원인이 되어 왔다. 단서 2

신선함에 대한 요구가 온실 사용과 품질 관리를 필요로 하게 만들었고, 그런 요구가 식량 자원이 낭비되고 엄청난 양의 폐기물이 생기는 결과를 초래한다고 했다.
▶ 빈칸 문장은 〈신선함에 대한 요구는 ① '숨겨진 환경적인 대가를 지니고' 있을 수 있다.〉라는 내용이 되어야 한다.

3rd 글의 내용을 다시 한번 정리하며 정답이 맞는지 확인한다.

신선한 식품에 대한 요구를 맞추기 위해 광범위한 온실 사용과 총체적인 품질 관리에 대한 의존성이 증가됐고, 식량 낭비도 초래해서 많은 양의 폐기물을 만들어냈다는 내용의 글이다.
따라서 빈칸에 들어갈 말로 가장 적절한 것은 ① '숨겨진 환경적인 대가를 지니고'이다.

| 선택지 분석 |

① 신선함에 대한 요구가 엄청난 환경적인 문제들을 초래할 수 있다는 내용이다.
② 신선한 식품에 대한 요구가 기아 문제를 악화시킨다는 내용은 없고, 식품에 대한 언급으로 만든 함정이다.
③ 컴퓨터/위성 기반 물류가 언급됐지만, 신선함에 대한 요구가 기술적 발전을 가져온다는 글이 아니다.
④ 신선함에 대한 요구로 인해 음식의 영양과 품질이 향상된다는 것이 아니라, 환경적 문제가 생길 수 있다는 내용의 글이다.
⑤ 신선한 식품에 대한 요구로 지역 사회 식단의 다양화가 나타난다는 언급은 없다.

M 22 정답 ② 2등급 대비 [정답률 45%]

*삶을 바꾼 상호 의존
전치사+관계대명사
The best way / in which innovation changes our lives / is by enabling people to work for each other. //
최고의 방법은 / 혁신이 우리의 삶을 바꾸는 / 사람들이 서로를 위해 일할 수 있도록 함으로써이다 //

주격 보어절 접속사
The main theme of human history / is that we become steadily
선행사를 포함하는 관계대명사
more specialized / in what we produce, / and steadily more diversified / in what we consume: /
인류 역사의 주요한 주제는 / 우리가 꾸준히 더 전문화된다는 것이다 / 우리가 생산하는 것에 / 그리고 꾸준히 더 다양화된다(는 것이다) / 우리가 소비하는 것에 /

we move away / from unstable self-sufficiency / to safer mutual interdependence. // 단서 1 우리는 불안정한 자급자족에서 서로 간의 상호 의존으로 옮겨감
즉, 우리는 옮겨간다 / 불안정한 자급자족에서 / 더 안전한 서로 간의 상호 의존으로 //

by v-ing: ~함으로써
By concentrating on serving other people's needs / for forty hours a week / — which we call a job /
다른 사람들의 필요를 충족시키는 것에 집중함으로써 / 일주일에 40시간 동안 / 그것을 우리는 직업이라고 부르는데 /

앞에 주격 관계대명사와 be동사가 생략됨
— you can spend the other seventy-two hours / (not counting fifty-six hours in bed) / relying on the services / provided to you by other people. // 단서 2 우리는 타인의 필요를 충족시키기 위해 일하고, 남은 시간에는 다른 사람들이 제공하는 서비스에 의지함
여러분은 나머지 72시간을 보낼 수 있다 / (잠자는 56시간은 계산에 넣지 않고) / 서비스에 의지하여 / 다른 사람들에 의해 여러분에게 제공되는 //

Innovation has made it possible to work for a fraction of a
가목적어 진목적어
second / in order to be able to afford / to turn on an electric lamp
/ for an hour, / 단서3 혁신을 통해 우리가 일하는 시간이 짧아짐
혁신은 아주 짧은 시간 동안 일하는 것을 가능하게 했다 / 여유를 가질 수 있게 하기 위해 /
전등을 켜는 / 한 시간 동안 /
분사구문을 이끄는 현재분사 주격 관계대명사
providing the quantity of light / that would have required a
whole day's work / if you had to make it yourself /
빛의 양을 제공하면서 / 하루 종일의 노동을 필요로 했을 / 여러분이 그것을 스스로
만들어야 했다면 /
부사적 용법(목적)
by collecting and refining sesame oil or lamb fat / to burn in a
simple lamp, / as much of humanity did / in the not so distant
past. //
참기름이나 양의 지방을 모으고 정제함으로써 / 간단한 등을 켜기 위해 / 많은 인류가 그랬던
것처럼 / 그리 멀지 않은 과거에 //

- innovation ⓝ 혁신 · theme ⓝ 주제 · steadily ⓐⓓ 꾸준히
- specialized ⓐ 전문화된 · diversified ⓐ 다양화된, 여러 가지의
- unstable ⓐ 불안정한 · self-sufficiency ⓝ 자급자족
- mutual ⓐ 서로의, 상호간의 · interdependence ⓝ 상호 의존
- concentrate ⓥ 집중하다 · rely ⓥ 의존하다, 믿다
- afford ⓥ (금전적·시간적) 여유[형편]가 되다 · sesame oil 참기름
- lamb ⓝ 어린 양 · humanity ⓝ 인류 · creatively ⓐⓓ 창의적으로
- personalized ⓐ 개인화된 · commercialize ⓥ 상품화하다

혁신이 우리의 삶을 바꾸는 최고의 방법은 **사람들이 서로를 위해 일할 수
있도록 함**으로써이다. 인류 역사의 주요한 주제는 우리가 생산하는 데 꾸준히
더 전문화되고 소비하는 데 꾸준히 더 다양화되는 것이다. 즉, 우리는 불안정한
자급자족에서 더 안전한 서로 간의 상호 의존으로 옮겨간다는 것이다. 일주일에
40시간 동안 사람들의 필요를 충족시키는 것, 즉 우리가 직업이라고 부르는
것에 집중함으로써, 여러분은 다른 사람들에 의해 여러분에게 제공되는
서비스에 의지하여 나머지 72시간(잠자는 56시간은 계산에 넣지 않고)을 보낼
수 있다. 혁신은 전등을 한 시간 동안 켜는 여유를 가질 수 있게 하기 위해
아주 짧은 시간 동안 일하는 것을 가능하게 했고, 그것은 만약 여러분이 그리
멀지 않은 과거에 많은 인류가 했던 것처럼 단순한 등을 켜기 위해 참기름이나
양의 지방을 모으고 정제함으로써 그것을 스스로 만들어야 했다면 하루 종일의
노동을 필요로 했었을 빛의 양을 제공했다.

다음 빈칸에 들어갈 말로 가장 적절한 것을 고르시오. [3점]
① respecting the values of the old days
지난날의 가치를 존중함   혁신으로 과거보다 효율적으로 일하게 됨
②enabling people to work for each other
사람들이 서로를 위해 일할 수 있도록 함   자급자족에서 상호 의존으로 옮겨간다고 했음
③ providing opportunities to think creatively
창의적으로 생각하는 기회를 제공함   창의적인 생각을 강조하는 내용이 아님
④ satisfying customers with personalized services
개인화된 서비스로 고객을 만족시킴   개인화가 아니라 서로 의존한다고 함
⑤ introducing and commercializing unusual products
이색적인 상품을 소개하고 상품화함   이색적인 상품에 관한 글이 아님

왜 2등급? 예시를 통해 설명하고 있는 '불안정한 자급자족'에서 '안전한 서로 간의
상호 의존'으로 옮겨가는 것이 무엇을 의미하는지를 파악해야 빈칸에 들어갈 말을 고를
수 있는 2등급 문제이다. 즉, 혼자 모든 것을 자급자족하던 것에서 서로의 전문성을
나누는 것으로의 이동이 무엇을 의미하는지 생각해 본다.

| 문제 풀이 순서 |

1st 먼저 빈칸 문장을 읽고, 빈칸에 들어갈 말을 예측한다.

빈칸 문장	혁신이 우리의 삶을 바꾸는 최고의 방법은 _____으로써이다.

➡ '무엇을 함으로써' 우리의 삶이 바뀌었다고 했으므로, 단서
혁신이 어떻게 우리의 삶을 바꿨는지에 대해 설명할 것이다. 발상

2nd 글의 나머지 부분을 읽고, 혁신이 의미하는 바가 무엇인지 찾는다.

- 우리의 생산은 전문화되고 소비는 다양화됨(**불안정한 자급자족 → 서로 간의 상호
  의존**) 단서1   이것이 바로 혁신! 꿀팁
- 일주일에 40시간은 다른 사람을 위해 일하고, 나머지 72시간은 다른 사람이
  제공하는 서비스에 의지함 단서2

➡ 이를 통해 인류는 과거와는 달리 짧은 시간에 효율적으로 일할 수 있게
   되었다. 단서3
   ▶ 즉, 혁신은 ② '사람들이 서로를 위해 일할 수 있도록 함'으로써 우리의 삶을
   바꿨다.

| 선택지 분석 |

① 과거보다 전문화되고 다양화된 것을 긍정적으로 말하는 글이다.
② 자급자족하던 과거의 삶에서 벗어나 서로의 서비스에 의존하게 됐다고 했다.
③ 창의적인 생각을 강조하는 내용은 없었다.
④ 개인화가 아니라 전문화되었다고 했으며, 고객 만족은 언급되지 않았다.
⑤ 상품을 소개하고 상품화하는 것과 관련된 내용이 아니다.

M 23 정답 ② ★ 1등급 대비 [정답률 44%]

* 로봇이 빼앗고 있는 인간의 판단력
목적어절을 이끄는 접속사
We worry / that the robots are taking our jobs, / but just as
보어절을 이끄는 접속사
common a problem is / that the robots are taking our judgment. //
우리는 걱정한다 / 로봇이 우리의 직업을 빼앗고 있다고 / 그러나 그만큼 흔한 문제는 ~이다 /
로봇이 우리의 판단력을 빼앗고 있다는 것
앞에 주격 관계대명사와 be동사 생략
In the large warehouses / so common / behind the scenes of
today's economy, /
거대한 창고에서 / 아주 흔한 / 오늘날의 경제 배후에서 /
human 'pickers' hurry around / grabbing products / off
병렬 구조
shelves / and moving them / to where they can be packed and
dispatched. //
인간 '집게'는 서두른다 / 상품을 집어내는 데 / 선반에서 / 그리고 이동시킨다 / 그것들이
포장되고 발송될 수 있는 곳으로 //
전치사구가 문두로 오면서 주어와 동사가 도치됨
In their ears / are headpieces: / the voice of 'Jennifer', / a piece of
software, / tells them / where to go / and what to do, / controlling
분사구문
the smallest details / of their movements. //
그들의 귀에는 / 헤드폰이 있다 / 'Jennifer'의 목소리가 / 한 소프트웨어 프로그램인 /
그들에게 말한다 / 어디로 갈지 / 그리고 무엇을 할지 / 가장 작은 세부 사항들을 조종하면서
/ 그들의 움직임의 //
Jennifer breaks down instructions / into tiny chunks, / to
부사적 용법(목적)
minimise error and maximise productivity /
Jennifer는 지시 사항을 쪼갠다 / 아주 작은 덩어리로 / 실수를 줄이고 생산성을 최대화하기
위해 /
— for example, / rather than picking / eighteen copies of a book
/ off a shelf, / the human worker would be politely instructed /
to pick five. //
예를 들어 / 집어내기보다는 / 책 18권을 / 선반에서 / 인간 작업자는 정중하게 지시받을
것이다 / 5권을 집어내라고 //
Then another five. //
그리고 나서 또 다른 5권을 //
Then yet another five. //
그리고 나서 다시 또 다른 5권을 //
Then another three. //
그리고 나서 또 다른 3권을 //
Working in such conditions / reduces people / to machines /
machines를 수식하는 과거분사구
made of flesh. // 단서1 사람을 기계로 격하시킴
그러한 조건에서 일하는 것은 / 사람을 격하시킨다 / 기계로 / 살로 만들어진 //

Rather than asking us / to think or adapt, / the Jennifer unit takes over / the thought process /
우리에게 요구하기보다는 / 생각하거나 적응하라고 / Jennifer라는 장치는 가져간다 / 사고 과정을 /

단서 2 생각하라고 요구하기보다 사고 과정을 빼앗아감

and treats workers / as an inexpensive source / of some visual processing / and a pair of opposable thumbs. //
그리고 작업자들을 취급한다 / 값싼 자원으로 / 약간의 시각적인 처리 과정의 / 그리고 한 쌍의 마주 볼 수 있는 엄지손가락을 가진 //

- judgment ⓝ 판단력   · warehouse ⓝ 창고   · economy ⓝ 경제
- picker ⓝ 집게   · instruction ⓝ 지시 사항   · minimise ⓥ 줄이다
- maximise ⓥ 최대화하다   · productivity ⓝ 생산성
- politely ⓐⓓ 정중하게   · instruct ⓥ 지시하다   · flesh ⓝ 살
- adapt ⓥ 적응하다
- process ⓝ (특정 결과를 달성하기 위한) 과정[절차] ⓥ 가공[처리]하다
- opposable ⓐ 마주 볼 수 있는   · reliability ⓝ 신뢰성
- endurance ⓝ 참을성   · sociability ⓝ 사회성

우리는 로봇이 우리의 직업을 빼앗고 있다고 걱정하지만, 그만큼 흔한 문제는 로봇이 우리의 **판단력**을 빼앗고 있다는 것이다. 오늘날의 경제 배후에서 아주 흔한 거대한 창고에서 인간 '집게'는 서둘러서 선반에서 상품을 집어내고 그것들이 포장되고 발송될 수 있는 곳으로 이동시킨다. 그들의 귀에는 헤드폰이 있는데, 한 소프트웨어 프로그램인 'Jennifer'의 목소리가 그들의 움직임의 가장 작은 세부 사항들을 조종하면서, 그들에게 어디로 갈지와 무엇을 할지를 말한다. Jennifer는 실수를 줄이고 생산성을 최대화하기 위해 지시 사항을 아주 작은 덩어리로 쪼갠다 — 예를 들어, 인간 작업자는 선반에서 책 18권을 집어내기보다는, 5권을 집어내라고 정중하게 지시받을 것이다. 그리고 나서 또 다른 5권을. 그리고 나서 다시 또 다른 5권을. 그리고 나서 또 다른 3권을. 그러한 조건에서 일하는 것은 사람을 살로 만들어진 기계로 격하시킨다. 우리에게 생각하거나 적응하라고 요구하기보다는, Jennifer라는 장치는 사고 과정을 가져가고 작업자들을 약간의 시각적인 처리 과정과 한 쌍의 마주 볼 수 있는 엄지손가락을 가진 값싼 자원으로 취급한다.

다음 빈칸에 들어갈 말로 가장 적절한 것을 고르시오. [3점]

① reliability 로봇이 우리의 신뢰성을 가져간다는 내용은 없음
　신뢰성
② judgment 로봇이 우리의 생각, 사고 과정을 가져간다는 내용
　판단력
③ endurance 로봇이 참을성을 가져간다고 하지 않았음
　참을성
④ sociability 사람을 기계로 격하시킨다는 것으로 만든 함정
　사회성
⑤ cooperation 로봇이 우리의 협동심을 가져간다고 하는 것은 맥락이 어색함
　협동심

왜 1등급? 일반적인 상식으로는 인간이 기계에 명령을 내리는데, 이 글에서는 반대로 기계인 소프트웨어 프로그램 Jennifer가 인간에게 명령을 내린다. 일반적인 상식은 배제하고 글에 제시된 내용만을 가지고 정답을 골라야 하는 1등급 대비 문제이다.

| 문제 풀이 순서 |

1st 먼저 빈칸이 포함된 문장을 읽고, 빈칸에 들어갈 말에 대한 단서를 얻는다.

빈칸 문장	We worry that the robots are taking our jobs, but just as common a problem is that the robots are taking our _____.

우리는 로봇이 우리의 직업을 빼앗고 있다고 걱정하지만, 그만큼 흔한 문제는 로봇이 우리의 _____ 을 빼앗고 있다는 것이다.

→ 첫 문장이 빈칸이 포함된 문장인데, 문장 중간에 연결어 but(하지만)이 있으므로 그 이후에 나오는 부분이 이 글이 말하고자 하는 바일 가능성이 높다. **단서**
로봇이 우리의 직업을 뺏는 게 아니라 다른 '무엇'을 뺏는지 확인해야 한다. **발상**

2nd 로봇이 빼앗고 있는 것이 무엇인지 나머지 글에서 확인한다.

- · 그러한 조건에서 일하는 것은 사람을 살로 만들어진 기계로 격하시킨다. **단서 1**
- · 우리에게 생각하거나 적응하라고 요구하기보다는, Jennifer라는 장치는 사고 과정을 가져가고 작업자들을 약간의 시각적인 처리 과정과 한 쌍의 마주 볼 수 있는 엄지손가락을 가진 값싼 자원으로 취급한다. **단서 2**

→ 소프트웨어 프로그램인 'Jennifer'가 등장하는데, Jennifer는 인간을 값싼 자원으로 이용하여 어디로 가고 무엇을 할지 자세하게 지시한다는 것이다.
　단서 1에서 말한 '그러한' 조건이 바로 이런 작업 환경을 가리킨다. 로봇이 사람을 기계로 격하시키고, 생각하지 못하게 사고 과정을 빼앗아 가는 것이다.
　▶ 빈칸 문장은 <우리는 로봇이 우리의 직업을 빼앗고 있다고 걱정하지만, 그만큼 흔한 문제는 로봇이 우리의 ② '판단력'을 빼앗고 있다.>라는 내용이 되어야 한다.

3rd 글의 내용을 다시 한번 정리하며 정답이 맞는지 확인한다.

로봇의 지시에 따라 작업을 하는 과정에서 인간이 사고하는 과정과 생각하는 능력은 없어지고 단순히 지시 사항에 따라 일을 하는 값싼 자원으로 격하되는 상황을 이야기하는 글이다.
따라서 로봇이 가져가는 것이 우리의 '판단력'이라는 의미가 되어야 하므로 ②이 문맥에 맞다.

| 선택지 분석 |

① 글 어디에도 로봇이 우리의 신뢰성을 가져간다는 내용은 없다.
② 로봇이 우리를 기계처럼 격하시키고 우리의 생각, 사고 과정을 가져간다는 내용이다.
③ 로봇이 우리에게서 참을성을 가져간다고 하지 않았다.
④ 사람을 기계로 격하시킨다는 것으로 만든 함정일 뿐, 로봇이 우리의 사회성을 없앤다는 내용이 아니다.
⑤ 로봇이 우리의 협동심을 가져간다고 하는 것은 맥락이 어색하다.

M 24 정답 ④ *땀으로 감정을 측정하기

동사 conducts를 수식하는 부사구
Our skin conducts electricity / more or less efficiently, / depending on our emotions. //
우리의 피부는 전기를 전도한다 / 꽤 효율적으로 / 우리의 감정에 따라 //

We know that when we're emotionally stimulated / — stressed, sad, any intense emotion, really / — our bodies sweat a tiny bit, / so little we might not even notice. // **단서 1** 감정적 자극이 있을 때 피부는 땀을 분비함
그 정도로 적게
우리가 감정적으로 자극되었을 때 / 즉, 정말로 스트레스를 받거나, 슬퍼거나, 어떤 강렬한 감정일 때 / 우리 몸은 땀을 아주 약간 흘리는데 / 너무 적어서 알아차리지도 못할 정도이다 //

And when those tiny drops of sweat appear, / our skin gets more electrically conductive. // **단서 2** 땀은 피부에 전기가 더 잘 흐르게 함
그리고 이 작은 땀방울이 나타날 때 / 우리의 피부는 전기적으로 더 전도력이 있는 상태가 된다 //

「without + 명사구 + 분사」: ~이 …하지 않은 채
This change in sweat gland activity happens / completely without your conscious mind having much say in the matter. //
이러한 땀샘 활동의 변화는 일어난다 / 여러분의 의식이 그 상황에 그다지 관여하지 않은 채 //

If you feel emotionally intense, / you're going to notice / an increase in sweat gland activity. //
만약 여러분이 감정적으로 강렬하게 느낀다면 / 여러분은 알아차릴 것이다 / 땀샘 활동의 증가를 //

= An increase in sweat gland activity
This is particularly useful / from a scientific viewpoint, / because it allows us to put an objective value / on a subjective state of mind. // **단서 3** 감정과 땀샘 활동의 관계를 통해 마음 상태를 수치화할 수 있음
이는 특히 유용한데 / 과학적 관점에서 / 그것이 우리가 객관적인 값을 부여할 수 있게 해주기 때문이다 / 주관적인 마음 상태에 //

We can actually **measure your emotional state** / by tracking
how your body subconsciously sweats, / by running a bit of
electricity through your skin. //
  tracking의 목적어 (간접의문문)
우리는 실제로 여러분의 감정적 상태를 측정할 수 있다 / 여러분의 신체가 의식하지 못한 채
어떻게 땀을 흘리는지를 추적함으로써 / 그리고 피부를 통해 약간의 전류를 흐르게 함으로
써 //

We can then **turn** the subjective, subconscious experience of
turn ~ into … : ~을 …로 바꾸다
emotional intensity / **into** an objective number / by figuring out
  figuring out의 목적어 (간접의문문)
/ how good your skin gets at transferring an electrical current. //
우리는 그다음에 감정적 강도의 주관적이고, 잠재의식적인 경험을 바꿀 수 있다 / 객관적인 숫
자로 / 계산함으로써 / 여러분의 피부가 전류를 얼마나 잘 전달하는지를 //

- conduct ⓥ 전도하다, 전달하다 · electricity ⓝ 전기
- more or less 꽤, 다소 · efficiently ⓐ𝖽 효율적으로 · drop ⓝ 방울
- conscious mind 의식(적 마음)
- have much say in ~에 발언권이 많다[영향력이 크다]
- intense ⓐ 강렬한 · viewpoint ⓝ 관점 · objective ⓐ 객관적인
- subjective ⓐ 주관적인 · track ⓥ 추적하다
- subconscious ⓐ 잠재의식의 · intensity ⓝ 강도
- figure out 계산하다 · transfer ⓥ 전달하다
- electrical current 전류

우리의 피부는 우리의 감정에 따라, 전기를 꽤 효율적으로 전도한다. 우리가 감
정적으로 자극되었을 때, 즉, 정말로 스트레스를 받거나, 슬프거나, 어떤 강렬
한 감정일 때, 우리 몸은 땀을 아주 약간 흘리는데, 너무 적어서 알아차리지도
못할 정도이다. 그리고 이 작은 땀방울이 나타날 때, 우리의 피부는 전기적으로
더 전도력이 있는 상태가 된다. 이러한 땀샘 활동의 변화는 여러분의 의식이 그
상황에 그다지 관여하지 않은 채 일어난다. 만약 여러분이 감정적으로 강렬하게
느낀다면, 여러분은 땀샘 활동의 증가를 알아차릴 것이다. 이는 특히 과학적 관
점에서 유용한데, 그것이 우리가 객관적인 값을 주관적인 마음 상태에 부여할
수 있게 해주기 때문이다. 우리는 실제로 여러분의 신체가 의식하지 못한 채 어
떻게 땀을 흘리는지를 추적함으로써, 그리고 피부를 통해 약간의 전류를 흐르게
함으로써 여러분의 감정 상태를 측정할 수 있다. 그다음에 여러분의 피부가 전
류를 얼마나 잘 전달하는지를 계산함으로써 우리는 감정적 강도의 주관적이고,
잠재의식적인 경험을 객관적인 숫자로 바꿀 수 있다.

다음 빈칸에 들어갈 말로 가장 적절한 것을 고르시오. [3점]
① limit reactions of hormones 호르몬은 언급되지 않았음
  호르몬 반응을 제한하다
② control the electrical current 전류를 조절하는 것은 언급되지 않았음
  전류를 조절하다
③ improve your skin conditions 피부 상태 자체의 개선은 전류의 결과가 아님
  여러분의 피부 상태를 개선하다
④ measure your emotional state 땀의 전도력을 통해 감정 상태를 측정할 수 있음
  여러분의 감정 상태를 측정하다
⑤ diversify emotional experiences 감정 경험의 다양화는 관련이 없음
  감정 경험을 다양화하다

| 문제 풀이 순서 | ★★★ [정답률 54%]

1st 첫 문장과 빈칸이 포함된 문장을 읽고, 빈칸에 들어갈 말에 대한 단서를 얻는다.

첫 문장	Our skin conducts electricity more or less efficiently, depending on our emotions. 우리의 피부는 우리의 감정에 따라, 전기를 꽤 효율적으로 전도한다.
빈칸 문장	We can actually _____ by tracking how your body subconsciously sweats, by running a bit of electricity through your skin. 우리는 실제로 여러분의 신체가 의식하지 못한 채 어떻게 땀을 흘리는지를 추적함으로써, 그리고 피부를 통해 약간의 전류를 흐르게 함으로써 _____ 할 수 있다.

➡ 우리의 피부가 감정에 따라 전기를 흘려보낸다고 했다. 단서
땀도 물이기 때문에, 피부의 땀은 전류가 더 잘 흐르게 할 것이다. 땀이 나는 피부에
전류가 흐르면 감정에 관하여 '무엇'을 알아낼 수 있는지를 파악해야 한다. 발상

2nd 글의 내용을 종합해서 빈칸에 들어갈 적절한 말을 찾는다.

┌ · 인간의 피부는 감정에 따라 전기가 흐르게 함 단서 1
├ · 땀은 피부에 전기가 더 잘 흐르게 함 단서 2
└ · 감정과 땀샘 활동의 관계를 통해 (주관적인) 마음 상태를 수치화할 수 있음 단서 3

➡ 감정적인 자극이 강렬해지면 피부의 땀샘 활동이 증가하므로 전도성이 증가한다.
즉, 피부에 전기가 흐르는 정도를 측정하면 주관적인 감정 상태를 객관적으로 수치
화할 수 있다.

▶ 따라서 땀이 분비되어 피부에 전기가 흐르면 ④ '감정 상태를 측정할' 수 있다.

| 선택지 분석 |
① 호르몬은 언급되지 않았다.
② 피부에 흐르는 전류를 조절하는 것은 언급되지 않았다.
③ 피부 상태를 좋게 만드는 것은 관련 없는 내용이다.
④ 감정에 따라 피부에 흐르는 땀의 양이 달라지므로 얼마나 전기가 더 잘 통하는지를
   측정하여 감정 상태를 측정할 수 있다.
⑤ 감정적으로 자극받는 예시로 스트레스, 슬픔, 강렬한 감정이 언급되었지만, 감정 경
   험의 다양화와는 관련이 없다.

M 25 정답 ① *Plato의 미(美)의 형상

                          주격 관계대명사 (something 수식)
Plato argued that / when you see something that strikes you as
beautiful, / you are really just seeing a partial reflection of true
beauty, /
Plato는 주장했다 / 여러분이 자신에게 아름답다는 인상을 주는 무언가를 볼 때 / 여러분은 실
제로는 진정한 아름다움의 부분적인 반영을 보고 있을 뿐이라고 /
'마치 ~처럼'
just as a painting or even a photograph only captures / part of
the real thing. //
마치 그림이나 사진조차 포착하는 것처럼 / 실재하는 것의 일부만을 //
                                            동사
True beauty, / or what Plato calls the Form of Beauty, / has no
particular color, shape, or size. // 단서 1 아름다움은 특정한 형태를 가지고
                                          있지는 않음
진정한 아름다움 / 즉, Plato가 미(美)의 형상(Form of Beauty)이라고 부르는 것은 / 특정한
색상, 모양, 혹은 크기를 갖고 있지 않다 //
= true beauty, the Form of Beauty
Rather, / it is a(n) abstract idea, / like the number five. //
오히려 / 그것은 추상적인 관념이다 / 숫자 5처럼 //

You can make drawings of the number five / in blue or red ink, /
                                     재귀대명사 (강조 용법)   대명사
big or small, / but the number five itself is none of those things. //
여러분은 숫자 5의 그림을 만들 수 있지만 / 파란색이나 빨간색 잉크로 / 크거나 작게 / 숫자 5
자체는 그런 것들 중 어느 것도 아니다 //

It has no physical form. // 단서 2 숫자 5는 구체적인 형태가 없음
그것은 구체적인 형태를 가지고 있지 않다 //
                  명령문 동사
Think of the idea of a triangle, / for example. //
삼각형이라는 관념을 생각해 보라 / 예를 들어 //
       = the idea of a triangle
Although it has no particular color or size, / it somehow lies /
                                  앞에 목적격 관계대명사가 생략됨
within each and every triangle / you see. //
그것은 특정한 색상이나 크기가 없을지라도 / 어떻게든 존재한다 / 각각의 모든 삼각형 속에
/ 당신이 보는 //
                             앞에 목적어절 접속사 that이 생략됨
Plato thought / the same was true of beauty. //
Plato는 생각했다 / 아름다움도 마찬가지라고 //

The Form of Beauty somehow lies / within each and every
                            앞에 목적격 관계대명사가 생략됨
beautiful thing / you see. //
미의 원형은 어떻게든 존재한다 / 각각의 모든 아름다운 것 속에 / 당신이 보는 //

- strike ⓥ 인상을 주다 · partial ⓐ 부분적인 · reflection ⓝ 반영
- capture ⓥ 포착하다, 담아내다 · idea ⓝ 관념
- physical ⓐ 물리적인, 구체적인 · each and every 각각의 모든
- somehow ⓐ𝖽 어떻게든 · abstract ⓐ 추상적인
- practical ⓐ 실용적인 · imperfect ⓐ 불완전한
- visualized ⓐ 시각화된

Plato는 여러분이 자신에게 아름답다는 인상을 주는 무언가를 볼 때, 마치 그림이나 사진조차 실재하는 것의 일부만을 포착하는 것처럼, 여러분은 실제로는 진정한 아름다움의 부분적인 반영을 보고 있을 뿐이라고 주장했다. 진정한 아름다움, 즉, Plato가 미(美)의 형상(Form of Beauty)이라고 부르는 것은 특정한 색상, 모양, 혹은 크기를 갖고 있지 않다. 오히려, 그것은 숫자 5처럼, **추상적인** 관념이다. 여러분은 숫자 5의 그림을 파란색이나 빨간색 잉크로, 크거나 작게, 만들 수 있지만, 숫자 5 자체는 그런 것들 중 어느 것도 아니다. 그것은 구체적인 형태를 가지고 있지 않다. 예를 들어, 삼각형이라는 관념을 생각해 보라. 그것은 특정한 색상이나 크기가 없을지라도, 당신이 보는 각각의 모든 삼각형 속에 어떻게든 존재한다. Plato는 아름다움도 마찬가지라고 생각했다. 미의 원형은 당신이 보는 각각의 모든 아름다운 것 속에 어떻게든 존재한다.

다음 빈칸에 들어갈 말로 가장 적절한 것을 고르시오.

① abstract 미의 형상은 숫자와 같이 고정된 형태를 갖추고 있지 않음
　추상적인
② practical 미의 형상의 실용성은 언급되지 않았음
　실용적인
③ imperfect 미의 형상이 불완전하다는 것은 언급되지 않았음
　불완전한
④ visualized 우리가 보는 것은 시각화된 것이지만 미의 형상 자체는 추상적임
　시각화된
⑤ changeable 미의 형상 자체가 바뀔 수 있는지는 언급되지 않았음
　바뀔 수 있는

| **문제 풀이 순서** | ★★★ [정답률 52%] |

1st 빈칸이 포함된 문장을 읽고, 빈칸에 들어갈 말에 대한 단서를 얻는다.

| 빈칸 문장 | Rather, <u>it</u> is a(n) _____ idea, like the number five. |
| | 오히려, <u>그것은</u> 숫자 5처럼, _____ 관념이다. |

➡ it이 숫자 5와 같은 '관념'이라고 했으므로, (단서)
it이 무엇인지, 5라는 관념의 특징으로 어떤 것들이 언급되는지 살펴봐야 한다. (발상)

2nd 글의 내용을 종합해서 빈칸에 들어갈 적절한 말을 찾는다.
- 미(美)의 형상은 특정한 색상, 모양, 혹은 크기가 없음 (단서1)
- 숫자 5는 구체적인 형태를 가지고 있지 않음 (단서2)
➡ Plato는 우리가 아름답다고 느끼는 것은 진정한 아름다움의 일부만을 반영하고, 진정한 아름다움인 '미의 형상은 숫자 5라는 관념처럼 구체적인 형태나 크기가 없다고 했다.
▶ 따라서 it은 '미의 형상'을 가리키고, 이러한 관념의 특징은 구체적이지 않고 ① '추상적'이다.

| **선택지 분석** |

① 미의 형상은 구체적인 형태가 없으므로 추상적인 개념이다.
② 미의 형상의 개념과 추상성이 설명되었을 뿐, 어느 측면에서 실용적인지는 언급되지 않았다.
③ 미의 형상은 구체적인 형태가 없다는 점이 강조되었을 뿐, 불완전한지는 언급되지 않았다.
④ 우리가 보는 것, 즉 아름다움의 부분적인 반영은 시각화된 것이지만 미의 형상은 추상적이다.
⑤ 우리가 보는 것, 즉 아름다움의 부분적인 반영은 여러 형태로 나타나므로 바뀔 수 있지만, 미의 형상이 바뀔 수 있는지는 언급되지 않았다.

| **구문 서술형** |

(정답) (가정법) 현재, 여러분이 숫자 5의 그림을 그린다면, 그것은 구체적인 형태를 가지고 있지 않을 것이다.

→ If절의 동사 make가 현재형이고 주절의 조동사가 will이므로, 가정법 현재 문장이다. 가정법 현재는 현재 또는 미래의 불확실한 일을 가정하며, '~한다면, ~할 것이다'로 해석한다.

M 26 정답 ② *재생 가능 에너지를 위해 화석 연료가 필요한 역설

Richard Heinberg, an American journalist, argues / that in building the renewable energy infrastructure / to stop global warming, /
미국인 저널리스트인 Richard Heinberg는 주장한다 / 재생 가능 에너지 기반 시설을 구축할 때 / 지구 온난화를 막기 위해 /

we are actually involved / in one of the greatest change projects in human history. //
우리는 실제로 관여하는 것이라고 / 인류 역사상 가장 큰 변화 프로젝트 중 하나에 //

'~에 더하여'
In addition to solar panels and wind turbines, / we have to build / an alternative transport infrastructure, farming procedures and industrial processes. //
태양광 패널과 풍력 터빈에 더하여 / 우리는 구축해야 한다 / 대체 교통 기반 시설, 농업 절차 그리고 산업 프로세스를 //

(단서1 재생 가능 에너지로의 전환은 화석 연료 없이는 불가능함)
This transformation cannot happen / without fossil fuels. //
이 변화는 일어날 수 없다 / 화석 연료 없이는 //

For instance, / production of concrete structures and steel elements / require amounts of energy / that is only possible to produce with fossil energy. // (단서2 건축을 위한 콘크리트와 강철 생산에 화석 에너지가 필요함)
예를 들어 / 콘크리트 구조물과 강철 요소의 생산은 / 에너지의 양을 필요로 한다 / 화석 에너지로만 생산 가능한 //

Production of solar panels requires / scarce and expensive minerals / which must be excavated, / again requiring the use of fossil fuels. // (단서3 태양광 패널 생산을 위한 광물 채굴에도 화석 연료가 필요함)
태양광 패널의 생산은 필요로 하며 / 회귀하고 값비싼 광물들을 / 발굴되어져야 하는 / 이는 또한 화석 연료 사용을 필요로 한다 //

Thus, the harder we push / towards a renewable energy system, / the faster we have to use fossil energy / for the construction process. //
the 비교급, the 비교급: ~할수록 더 …하다
따라서, 우리가 더 세게 밀고 나아갈수록 / 재생 가능 에너지 시스템을 향하여 / 더 빠르게 우리는 화석 에너지를 사용해야 한다 / 건설 과정에서 //

not only A but also B: A뿐만 아니라 B도
This is not only expensive, / but also an undermining factor for our efforts / to cut global emissions. //
이는 단지 비용이 많이 들 뿐만 아니라 / 우리의 노력을 저해하는 요인이 된다 / 전 세계적 배기가스를 줄이려는 //

Heinberg remarks / that the cost of building this new energy infrastructure / is seldom counted in transition proposals, /
Heinberg는 언급하는데 / 이러한 새로운 에너지 기반 시설을 구축하는 비용이 / 전환 제안에서 거의 계산되지 않는다고 /

계속적 용법의 주격 관계대명사
which tend to focus just on energy supply requirements. //
이는 에너지 공급 요구 사항에만 집중하는 경향이 있다 //

- renewable energy 재생 가능 에너지
- infrastructure ⓝ 사회 기반 시설 · alternative ⓐ 대안의
- procedure ⓝ 절차 · transformation ⓝ 변화, 변혁
- fossil fuel 화석 연료 · steel ⓝ 강철 · element ⓝ 요소
- require ⓥ 필요로 하다 · scarce ⓐ 회귀한
- mineral ⓝ 광물 · undermining ⓐ 약화시키는 · effort ⓝ 노력
- emission ⓝ 배출(물) · remark ⓥ 말하다, 언급하다
- transition ⓝ 전환 · supply ⓝ 공급
- take advantage of ~을 활용하다 · construction ⓝ 건설
- competitive ⓐ 경쟁력 있는

미국인 저널리스트인 Richard Heinberg는 지구 온난화를 막기 위해 재생 가능 에너지 기반 시설을 구축할 때, 우리는 실제로 인류 역사상 가장 큰 변화 프로젝트 중 하나에 관여하는 것이라고 주장한다. 태양광 패널과 풍력 터빈에 더하여 우리는 대체 교통 기반 시설, 농업 절차 그리고 산업 프로세스를 구축해야 한다. 이 변화는 화석 연료 없이는 일어날 수 없다. 예를 들어, 콘크리트 구조물

과 강철 요소의 생산은 화석 에너지로만 생산 가능한 에너지의 양을 필요로 한다. 태양광 패널의 생산은 발굴되어져야 하는 희귀하고 값비싼 광물들을 필요로 하며, 이는 또한 화석 연료 사용을 필요로 한다. 따라서, 우리가 재생 가능 에너지 시스템을 향하여 더 세게 밀고 나아갈수록, 더 빠르게 **우리는 건설 과정에서 화석 에너지를 사용해야 한다**. 이는 단지 비용이 많이 들 뿐만 아니라, 전 세계적 배기가스를 줄이려는 우리의 노력을 저해하는 요인이 된다. Heinberg는 이러한 새로운 에너지 기반 시설을 구축하는 비용이 전환 제안에서 거의 계산되지 않는다고 언급하는데, 이는 에너지 공급 요구 사항에만 집중하는 경향이 있다.

- 재생 가능 에너지 시스템이 구축되면서 화석 연료 사용도 빨라진다는 내용임
다음 빈칸에 들어갈 말로 가장 적절한 것을 고르시오. [3점]
① we are taking full advantage of renewable energy sources 에너지 전환의 긍정적인 결과가 아니라 과정의 폐해를 강조
　우리는 재생 가능 에너지원을 최대한 활용하고 있다
② we have to use fossil energy for the construction process
　우리는 건설 과정에서 화석 에너지를 사용해야 한다
③ we invest in more natural resources for the environment
　우리는 환경을 위해 더 많은 천연자원에 투자한다 　천연자원이 아니라 화석 연료에 더 투자하게 될 것임
④ we are able to decrease the rate of global warming
　우리는 지구 온난화의 속도를 줄일 수 있다
⑤ alternative energy markets become competitive
　대체 에너지 시장이 경쟁력을 갖추게 된다 　대체 에너지 시장의 경쟁력은 언급되지 않았음
- 에너지 전환 과정에서 지구 온난화를 늦추는 것이 아니라 부추길 수 있음

왜 정답? ★★✿ [정답률 57%]
- 재생 가능 에너지로의 전환은 화석 연료 없이는 불가능함 `단서 1`
- 기반 시설 건축에 필요한 콘크리트와 강철 생산에 화석 에너지가 쓰임 `단서 2`
- 태양광 패널 생산에 필요한 광물 채굴에도 화석 연료가 쓰임 `단서 3`
➡ 화석 에너지에서 재생 가능 에너지로 전환하는 과정에서, 건축과 자재 생산을 위해 오히려 화석 연료가 필수적으로 쓰인다.
▶ 따라서 재생 가능 에너지 시스템 구축을 더 추진할수록, 더 빠르게 ② '우리는 건설 과정에서 화석 에너지를 사용해야 한다.'

왜 오답?
① 재생 가능 에너지 시스템으로 전환하는 과정의 폐해를 강조할 뿐, 전환이 완료된 결과는 언급되지 않았다.
③ 재생 가능 에너지로 전환하면서 화석 연료에 더 투자하게 될 뿐, 천연자원에 더 투자하진 않을 것이다.
④ 재생 가능 에너지로 전환하면서 배기가스 배출량 감축을 위한 노력을 저해할 수 있다고 했으므로 오히려 지구 온난화를 부추길 수 있다.
⑤ 대체 에너지 시장의 경쟁력은 언급되지 않았다.

`구문 서술형`

`정답` don't push, won't have to use, didn't push, wouldn't have to use
`해석` 우리가 재생 가능 에너지 시스템을 향하여 더 세게 밀고 나아가지 않는다면(→ 않았다면), 우리는 새로운 에너지 기반 시설의 건설 과정에서 더 많은 화석 에너지를 사용할 필요가 없을(→ 없었을) 것이다.
→ 문장의 동사는 if절의 동사 don't push와 주절의 동사 won't have to use이다. 가정법 과거 문장이 되려면 if절의 동사는 조동사 do를 과거형으로 바꿔 didn't push로, 주절의 동사는 조동사의 과거형을 써서 wouldn't have to use로 고쳐야 한다.

M 27 정답 ② *변신술로 사냥하는 문어

목적격 관계대명사절 (defence 수식)
The best defence / most species of octopus have / is to stay
가능한 한 ~하게
hidden as much as possible / and do their own hunting at night. //
최고의 방어는 / 대부분의 문어 종(種)이 가진 / 가능한 한 많이 숨어 있는 것과 / 밤에 그들 자신의 사냥을 하는 것이다 //
명사적 용법 (주어)　＝octopus　　　　　　단수 동사
So / to find one in full view in the shallows in daylight / was a
surprise / for two Australian underwater photographers. //
그래서 / 낮에 얕은 곳에서 전체가 보이는 문어를 발견한 것은 / 놀라운 일이었다 / 두 명의 호주 수중 사진작가들에게 //

Actually, / what they saw at first / was a flounder. //
사실 / 그들이 처음에 봤던 것은 / 넙치였다 // `단서 1` 처음에는 문어가 아니라 넙치를 발견했음
It ~ that … 강조 구문 (only when ~ again 강조)
It was only when they looked again / that they saw a medium-sized octopus, / with all eight of its arms folded / and its two
병렬 구조 (with 분사구문)
eyes staring upwards / to create the illusion. //
오직 그들이 다시 봤을 때서야 / 그들은 중간 크기의 문어를 보았고 / 그것의 여덟 개의 모든 팔이 접혀 있었고 / 그것의 두 눈이 위쪽으로 응시하고 있었다 / 착시를 만들기 위해 //
`단서 2` 문어는 색깔과 패턴을 바꿔 다른 생물체로 변신할 수 있음
An octopus has a big brain, excellent eyesight and the ability to change colour and pattern, / and this one was using these assets
부사적 용법 (목적)
/ to turn itself into a completely different creature. //
문어는 큰 뇌, 뛰어난 시력과 색깔과 패턴을 바꾸는 능력을 지니고 있고 / 이것은 이러한 이점을 사용하고 있었다 / 스스로를 완전히 다른 생물체로 바꾸기 위해 //
현재완료 수동태
Many more of this species / have been found since then, / and
주격 관계대명사
there are now photographs of octopuses / that could be said to be transforming into sea snakes. //
이 종의 더 많은 것들이 / 그때 이후로 발견되어 왔으며 / 지금은 문어의 사진이 있다 / 바다뱀으로 변신하는 중이라고 말해질 수 있는 //
분사구문을 이끄는 현재분사
And while they mimic, they hunt / — producing the spectacle of, / say, / `단서 3` 문어는 다른 생물체를 모방하는 동안에 사냥함
그리고 그들이 모방하는 동안에 그들은 사냥을 한다 / 이것은 광경을 만들어낸다 / 말하자면 /
a flounder / suddenly developing an octopodian arm, / sticking
병렬 구조 (a flounder를 수식하는 현재분사)
it down a hole / and grabbing whatever's hiding there. //
넙치가 / 갑자기 문어 다리 같은 팔을 펼치며 / 그것을 구멍으로 찔러 넣어 / 그곳에 숨어 있는 무엇이든지 움켜잡는 // `단서 4` 넙치로 변신한 채 갑자기 다리를 꺼내 사냥함

- defence ⓝ 방어　　• species ⓝ (생물의) 종　　• shallows ⓝ 얕은 곳
- fold ⓥ 접다　　• stare ⓥ 응시하다　　• eyesight ⓝ 시력
- asset ⓝ 이점, 자산　　• creature ⓝ 생물체　　• transform ⓥ 변신하다
- spectacle ⓝ 광경　　• octopodian ⓐ 문어와 같은
- stick ⓥ 찔러 넣다　　• grab ⓥ 움켜잡다　　• broad ⓐ 넓은
- illusion ⓝ 착시[착각]　　• territory ⓝ 영토, 지역

대부분의 문어 종(種)이 가진 최고의 방어는 가능한 한 많이 숨어 있는 것과 밤에 그들 자신의 사냥을 하는 것이다. 그래서 낮에 얕은 곳에서 전체가 보이는 문어를 발견한 것은 두 명의 호주 수중 사진작가들에게는 놀라운 일이었다. 사실 그들이 처음에 봤던 것은 넙치였다. 오직 그들이 다시 봤을 때서야 그들은 중간 크기의 문어를 보았고 **착시를 만들기** 위해 그것의 여덟 개의 모든 팔이 접혀 있었고 그것의 두 눈이 위쪽으로 응시하고 있었다. 문어는 큰 뇌, 뛰어난 시력과 색깔과 패턴을 바꾸는 능력을 지니고 있고, 이것은 스스로를 완전히 다른 생물체로 바꾸기 위해 이러한 이점을 사용하고 있었다. 이 종의 더 많은 것들이 그때 이후로 발견되어 왔으며 지금은 바다뱀으로 변신하는 중이라고 말해질 수 있는 문어의 사진이 있다. 그리고 그들이 모방하는 동안에 그들은 사냥을 한다. 이것은 말하자면 넙치가 갑자기 문어 다리 같은 팔을 펼치며 그것을 구멍으로 찔러 넣어 그곳에 숨어 있는 무엇이든지 움켜잡는 광경을 만들어낸다.

다음 빈칸에 들어갈 말로 가장 적절한 것을 고르시오.
① get a broad view 넓은 시야를 확보하기 위한 것이 아님
　넓은 시야를 확보하다
② create the illusion 넙치를 모방하여 착각을 일으키기 위한 것임
　착시를 만든다
③ capture the moment 순간을 포착한다는 내용이 아님
　순간을 포착하다
④ find its hiding spot 은신처를 찾기 위한 것이 아님
　은신처를 찾다
⑤ mark its territory 영토를 표시하기 위한 것이 아님
　자신의 영토를 표시하다

M

1st 빈칸이 포함된 문장과 그 앞 문장을 읽고, 빈칸에 들어갈 말에 대한 단서를 얻는다.

빈칸 문장 앞	Actually, what they saw at first was a flounder. 사실 그들이 처음에 봤던 것은 넙치였다. 단서 1
빈칸 문장	It was only when they looked again that they saw a medium-sized octopus, with all eight of its arms folded and its two eyes staring upwards to _____. 오직 그들이 다시 봤을 때에야 그들은 중간 크기의 문어를 보았고 _____ 위해 그것의 여덟 개의 모든 팔이 접혀 있었고 그것의 두 눈이 위쪽으로 응시하고 있었다.

➡ 그들이 처음에는 넙치를 봤지만, 문어가 '무엇'을 하기 위해 자신의 모든 팔을 접고 두 눈을 위쪽으로 응시하고 있었다고 했으므로, 단서 빈칸 문장에 나온 문어는 넙치를 모방했음을 알 수 있다. 발상 나머지 글을 읽으며 문어가 '어떤' 상황에서 '왜' 넙치를 모방했는지 파악해야 한다.

2nd 글의 내용을 종합해서 빈칸에 들어갈 적절한 말을 찾는다.
• 문어는 다른 생물체로 변신할 수 있음 단서 2
• 문어는 다른 생물체를 모방하는 동안에 사냥함 단서 3
• 넙치로 변신한 채 갑자기 다리를 꺼내 사냥함 단서 4

➡ 문어는 다른 생명체를 모방할 수 있고, 모방하는 동안에 사냥한다고 했다. 예를 들어, 넙치로 변신하여 먹잇감이 '착각하게' 한 채로, 갑자기 다리를 꺼내 사냥하는 방식이다.

▶ 즉, 문어는 사냥할 때 자신이 다른 생명체로 보이도록 ② '착시를 만들기' 위해 넙치처럼 모든 팔을 접고 두 눈을 위쪽으로 응시하고 있던 것이다.

| 선택지 분석 |

① 문어의 두 눈이 위쪽으로 응시하고 있던 것은 시야를 확보하기 위한 것이 아니라 넙치를 모방한 것이다.
②다른 생명체인 넙치를 모방하여 먹잇감이 착각하도록 하기 위함이었다.
③ 문어의 사냥 과정에서 순간을 포착하여 사냥한다는 내용이 아니다.
④ 문어가 넙치를 모방한 상태에서 먹잇감이 숨어 있는 곳에 다리를 찔러넣어 움켜잡는다고 했을 뿐, 넙치를 모방한 것 자체가 은신처를 찾기 위한 행동은 아니다.
⑤ 문어가 사냥하기 위해 모방을 한다는 내용이지, 영토를 표시한다는 것은 언급되지 않았다.

구문 서술형

정답 If the octopus had stayed hidden, it could have defended itself.

해석 그 문어는 숨어 있지 않았기 때문에, 스스로를 방어할 수 없었다.
→ 그 문어가 숨어 있었다면, 스스로를 방어할 수 있었을 것이다.
→ 문어가 스스로를 방어하지 못했다는 과거 사실과 반대되는 상황을 가정하려면 가정법 과거완료 문장으로 써야 한다. 직설법 문장 주절의 동사 couldn't defend는 가정법 문장의 주절에서 could have defended로, 직설법 문장 부사절의 동사 didn't stay는 가정법 문장의 if절에서 had stayed로 고쳐야 한다.

M 28 정답 ② *기후 변화 픽션의 소멸

On-screen, / climate disaster is everywhere you look, / but the scope of the world's climate transformation / may just as quickly eliminate the climate-fiction genre / 단서 1 세계의 기후 변화는 기후 픽션 장르를 없앨 것임
영화상 / 기후 재난은 여러분이 보는 어디에나 있지만 / 세계의 기후 변화의 범위는 / 그것만큼이나 빠르게 기후 픽션 장르를 없앨지도 모르고 /

— indeed eliminate any effort / **to tell** the story of warming, / **which** could grow too large and too obvious / even for Hollywood. //
형용사적 용법 (any effort 수식) / 계속적 용법의 주격 관계대명사
실제로 노력도 없애 버린다 / 온난화 이야기를 하고자 하는 / 그것은 너무 커지고 너무 명백해질 것이다 / 할리우드에서조차 //

You can tell stories 'about' climate change / while it still seems a marginal feature of human life. // 단서 2 기후 변화의 영향을 별로 느끼지 못할 때는 그것에 대한 이야기를 할 수 있음
여러분은 기후 변화에 관한 이야기를 할 수 있을 것이다 / 기후 변화가 여전히 인간 삶의 주변적인 특징처럼 보이는 동안에 //

But when the temperature rises / by three or four more degrees, / **hardly** anyone will be able to feel **isolated** / from its impacts. //
'거의 ~하지 않다' / 과거분사
하지만 기온이 상승할 때는 / 3도 혹은 4도 이상 / 아무도 고립되었다고 느낄 수 없을 것이다 / 그것의 영향으로부터 //

And so as climate change expands across the horizon, / **it may cease to be a story**. //
그리고 기후 변화가 지평선을 넘어 확장될 때 / 그것은 이야기가 되기를 멈출 것이다 //

Why watch or read climate fiction / about the world you can see 목적격 관계대명사절 plainly out your own window? // 단서 3 현실에서 바로 볼 수 있는 기후 변화에 대한 픽션은 볼 필요 없음
왜 기후 픽션을 보거나 읽는가 / 당신이 자신의 창문 밖으로 뚜렷하게 볼 수 있는 세상에 대한 //

At the moment, / stories illustrating global warming / can still 현재분사구 (stories 수식) offer an escapist pleasure, / even if **that** pleasure often comes / 지시형용사 in the form of horror. //
지금 당장은 / 지구 온난화를 묘사하는 이야기가 / 현실 도피적인 즐거움을 여전히 제공할 수 있다 / 비록 그 즐거움이 종종 올지라도 / 공포의 형태로 //

But when we can no longer pretend / **that** climate suffering is 목적어절 접속사 distant / — in time or in place / — we will **stop pretending** about it / and **start pretending** within it. //
stop -ing: ~하는 것을 멈추다 / 병렬 구조
하지만 우리가 더 이상 가장할 수 없을 때 / 기후 고통이 멀리 있다고 / 시간적으로 또는 장소적으로 / 우리는 그것에 대해 가장하는 것을 멈추고 / 그것 내에서 가장하기 시작할 것이다 //

• disaster ⓝ 재난　　• scope ⓝ 범위　　• transformation ⓝ 변화
• indeed ⓐd 실제로　　• eliminate ⓥ 없애다　　• obvious ⓐ 명백한
• marginal ⓐ 주변적인　　• isolated ⓐ 고립된　　• impact ⓝ 영향
• expand ⓥ 확장하다　　• horizon ⓝ 지평선
• plainly ⓐd 뚜렷하게　　• escapist ⓐ 현실 도피(주의)의
• pretend ⓥ 가장하다　　• suffering ⓝ 고통　　• distant ⓐ 먼
• resolve ⓥ 해결하다　　• cease ⓥ 멈추다, 중단하다
• reborn ⓐ 다시 태어난　　• overestimated ⓐ 과대평가된
• plot ⓝ 줄거리　　• complex ⓐ 복잡한

영화상 기후 재난은 여러분이 보는 어디에나 있지만, 세계의 기후 변화의 범위는 그것만큼이나 빠르게 기후 픽션 장르를 없앨지도 모르고 실제로 온난화 이야기를 하고자 하는 노력도 없애 버리는데, 그것은 할리우드에서조차 너무 커지고 너무 명백해질 것이다. 기후 변화가 여전히 인간 삶의 주변적인 특징처럼 보이는 동안에 여러분은 그것에 '관한' 이야기를 할 수 있을 것이다. 하지만 기온이 3도 혹은 4도 이상 상승할 때는 아무도 그것의 영향으로부터 고립되었다고 느낄 수 없을 것이다. 그리고 기후 변화가 지평선을 넘어 확장될 때, **그것은 이야기가 되기를 멈출 것이다**. 왜 여러분 자신의 창문 밖으로 뚜렷하게 볼 수 있는 세상에 대한 기후 픽션을 보거나 읽겠는가? 비록 그 즐거움이 종종 공포의 형태로 올지라도 지금 당장은 지구 온난화를 묘사하는 이야기가 현실 도피적인 즐거움을 여전히 제공할 수 있다. 하지만 우리가 더 이상 기후 고통이 시간적으로 또는 장소적으로 멀리 있다고 가장할 수 없을 때 우리는 그것에 대해 가장하는 것을 멈추고 그것 내에서 가장하기 시작할 것이다.

다음 빈칸에 들어갈 말로 가장 적절한 것을 고르시오. [3점]

① it may resolve on its own 저절로 해결될 수 있는 것은 아님
그것은 저절로 해결될지도 모른다
② it may cease to be a story 기후 변화가 현실이 되면 그것은 더 이상
그것은 이야기가 되기를 멈출 것이다 허구(이야기)가 아님
③ a forgotten genre will be reborn 기후 픽션 장르가 없어질 것이라는 내용임
잊혀진 장르가 다시 태어날 것이다
④ its impact will be overestimated
그것의 영향은 과대평가될 것이다 기후 변화가 실제보다 과대평가된다는 내용은 없음
⑤ the story's plot will become complex
이야기의 줄거리가 복잡해질 것이다 기후 변화 상황이 복잡해진다는 내용이 아님

| 문제 풀이 순서 | ★★★ [정답률 37%]

1st 빈칸이 포함된 문장과 그 앞 문장을 읽고, 빈칸에 들어갈 말에 대한 단서를 얻는다.

빈칸 문장 앞	But when the temperature rises by three or four more degrees, hardly anyone will be able to feel isolated from its impacts. 하지만 기온이 3도 혹은 4도 이상 상승할 때는 아무도 그것의 영향으로부터 고립되었다고 느낄 수 없을 것이다.
빈칸 문장	And so as climate change expands across the horizon, _____. 그리고 기후 변화가 지평선을 넘어 확장될 때, _____.

➡ 기온이 3~4도 오르면 모두가 그 영향을 느낄 것이라고 했고, 단서 기후 변화가 지평선을 넘어 확장된다면, 즉 기후 변화가 세계적으로 확장된다면 '어떤' 일이 일어날지를 나머지 글에서 확인해야 한다. 발상

2nd 글의 내용을 종합해서 빈칸에 들어갈 내용을 찾는다.

• 세계의 기후 변화는 빠르게 기후 픽션 장르를 없앨지도 모른다. 단서 1
• 기후 변화가 인간 삶의 주변적이라면 그것에 '관한' 이야기를 할 수 있다. 단서 2
• 사람들이 기후 변화를 현실에서 명백하게 볼 수 있다면 왜 기후 픽션을 보거나 읽겠는가? 단서 3

➡ 세계의 기후 변화(현실) ↔ 기후 픽션 장르(이야기, 허구)
기후 변화가 우리의 삶에서 '주변적'이라는 것은 현실과는 거리가 멀기 때문에 허구적인 이야기로 만들 수 있다는 것이다. 그러나, 기후 변화가 현실이 되면 그것은 더 이상 허구적인 이야기가 아니기 때문에 기후 픽션을 볼 이유가 없을 것이다.
▶ 따라서 기후 변화가 지평선을 넘어 확장될 때, ② '그것(기후 변화)은 이야기가 되기를 멈출 것이고' 현실이 될 것이다.

| 선택지 분석 |

① 기후 변화가 저절로 해결될 수 있다는 내용이 아니다.
② 기후 변화가 점점 더 현실이 되면 그것은 더 이상 허구의 이야기가 아니게 된다.
③ 앞으로 기후 변화를 다루는 픽션 장르는 없어질 것이라는 내용이지, 잊혀진 장르가 다시 태어난다는 내용이 아니다.
④ 기후 변화가 현실이 되면서 픽션이 없어질 것이라는 내용이지, 기후 변화의 영향이 과장되었다는 내용이 아니다. 픽션의 특징 중 허구와 과장을 구별하기! 꿀팁
⑤ 기후 변화 픽션의 줄거리, 즉 기후 변화 상황이 복잡해진다는 내용이 아니다.

구문 서술형

정답 rises, will be able to feel

해석 만약 기온이 4도 이상 상승하면, 아무도 그것의 영향으로부터 고립되었다고 느낄 수 없을 것이다.
→ 가정법 현재 문장은 「If + 주어 + 동사의 현재형 ~, 주어 + 조동사/동사의 현재형 …」의 형태이므로, if절의 동사 rise를 3인칭 단수 현재형 rises로 쓰고, 주절에는 조동사 will과 be able to feel을 모두 그대로 쓴다.

M 29 정답 ② *기후 변화에 따른 종의 이동

every+단수 명사+단수 동사
Every species has certain climatic requirements — / what degree of heat or cold it can endure, for example. //
모든 종은 특정한 기후 요건을 가지고 있다 / 예를 들어 어느 정도의 더위나 추위를 견딜 수 있는지와 같은 //

주격 관계대명사(선행사: the places)
When the climate changes, / the places that satisfy those requirements / change, too. // 단서 1 기후가 변할 때 종의 기후 요건을 충족시키는 장소도 변화함
기후가 변할 때 / 그러한 요건을 충족시키는 장소도 / 역시 변한다 //

Species are forced to follow. // 종은 따르도록 강요받는다 //

All creatures are capable of / some degree of **movement**. //
모든 생명체는 가능하다 / 어느 정도의 이동이 //

복수 주어   주격 관계대명사(선행사: creatures)
Even creatures that appear immobile, / like trees and barnacles, / are capable of dispersal / at some stage of their life — /
복수 동사
심지어 움직이지 않는 것처럼 보이는 생명체도 / 나무나 따개비처럼 / 분산할 수 있다 / 그들 일생의 어느 단계에서 / 단서 2 움직이지 않는 것처럼 보이는 생명체조차도 분산할 수 있음

as a seed, in the case of the tree, / or as a larva, in the case of the barnacle. //
나무의 경우는 씨앗으로 / 따개비의 경우는 유충으로 //

과거분사(the place 수식)
A creature must get / from the place it is born — / often occupied by its parent — / to a place where it can survive, grow, and reproduce. // 단서 3 생물은 자신이 태어난 장소로부터 생존, 성장, 번식할 수 있는 장소로 이동해야 함
관계부사(선행사: a place)
생명체는 이동해야 한다 / 자신이 태어난 장소로부터 / 종종 자신의 부모에 의해서 점유된 / 생존하고 성장하며 번식할 수 있는 장소로 //

목적어절 접속사
From fossils, / scientists know / that even creatures like trees moved / with surprising speed / during past periods of climate change. // 단서 4 화석에도 생명체가 이동한 증거가 있음
화석으로부터 / 과학자들은 알고 있다 / 심지어 나무와 같은 생명체가 이동했다는 것을 / 놀라운 속도로 / 기후 변화의 과거 시기 동안 //

• climatic ⓐ 기후의   • requirement ⓝ 요건   • endure ⓥ 견디다
• satisfy ⓥ 충족시키다   • species ⓝ 종(種)   • force ⓥ 강요하다
• creature ⓝ 생명체   • be capable of ~을 할 수 있다
• immobile ⓐ 움직이지 않는   • larva ⓝ 유충   • occupy ⓥ 점유하다
• survive ⓥ 생존하다   • reproduce ⓥ 번식하다
• endurance ⓝ 인내   • transformation ⓝ 변형

모든 종은, 예를 들자면 어느 정도의 더위나 추위를 견딜 수 있는지와 같은, 특정한 기후 요건을 가지고 있다. 기후가 변할 때, 그러한 요건을 충족시키는 장소도 역시 변한다. 종은 따르도록 강요받는다. 모든 생명체는 어느 정도의 이동이 가능하다. 심지어 나무나 따개비처럼 움직이지 않는 것처럼 보이는 생명체도, 나무의 경우는 씨앗으로, 따개비의 경우는 유충으로, 그들 일생의 어느 단계에서 분산할 수 있다. 생명체는 종종 자신의 부모에 의해서 점유된, 그래서 자신이 태어난 장소로부터 생존하고 성장하며 번식할 수 있는 장소로 이동해야 한다. 화석으로부터, 과학자들은 심지어 나무와 같은 생명체는 기후 변화의 과거 시기 동안 놀라운 속도로 이동했다는 것을 알고 있다.

다음 빈칸에 들어갈 말로 가장 적절한 것을 고르시오.

① endurance 생명체가 인내하며 한 장소에 머무는 것이 아니라 이동함
인내
② movement
이동   움직이지 않는 것처럼 보이는 생명체조차도 기후 요건에 맞는 장소로 이동할 수 있음
③ development 생명체의 발달이 아닌 생존, 성장, 번식을 위해 이동하는 내용이 나옴
발달
④ transformation 생명체가 변형된다는 내용이 아님
변형
⑤ communication 생명체의 의사소통을 다룬 내용이 아님
의사소통

| 문제 풀이 순서 | ★★★ [정답률 45%]

1st 먼저 빈칸 문장을 읽고, 빈칸에 들어갈 말을 예측한다.

| 빈칸 문장 | 모든 생명체는 어느 정도의 ＿＿＿＿＿＿＿＿＿이 가능하다. |

➡ 모든 생명체가 어느 정도의 '무엇이' 가능하다고 했으므로, (단서)
모든 생명체의 공통적인 특징이나 공통적으로 가능한 무언가를 찾아야 한다. (발상)

2nd 글의 나머지 부분을 읽고, 모든 생명체가 가능한 것이 무엇인지 찾는다.

- 모든 종은 특정한 기후 요건을 가지고, 기후가 변할 때 종의 기후 요건을 충족시키는 장소도 변화함 (단서 1)
- 움직이지 않는 것처럼 보이는 생명체조차도 일생의 어느 단계에서 분산을 통해 이동함 (단서 2)
- 생물은 부모에 의해 점유된 태어난 장소로부터 생존, 성장, 번식할 수 있는 장소로 이동해야 함 (단서 3)
- 기후가 변화했던 과거의 시기에 생명체가 놀라운 속도로 이동했다는 것을 화석으로부터 알 수 있음 (단서 4)

➡ 움직이지 않는 듯한 생명체를 포함한 모든 생명체는 특정한 기후 요건을 가지고, 기후가 변화하면 이동한다.

▶ 따라서 빈칸에 들어갈 말은 ② '이동'이다.

| 선택지 분석 |

① 생명체가 기후가 바뀐 장소에 인내하며 머물지 않고 기후 요건에 맞는 장소로 이동한다.
② 움직이지 않는 듯한 생명체를 포함하여 모든 종은 기후가 변화할 때 기후 요건을 충족시키는 장소로 이동한다고 했다.
③ 생명체의 발달이 아닌 생존, 성장, 번식을 위해 이동하는 내용이 나온다.
④ 나무와 따개비가 씨앗이나 유충의 상태일 때가 있다고 언급했지만, 이는 분산을 통한 이동의 예시일 뿐이므로 생명체의 변형에 관한 내용이 아니다.
⑤ 모든 생명체가 어느 정도의 의사소통을 한다는 내용은 언급되지 않았다.

M 30 정답 ③ *부하 직원의 반대 의견 지지하기

No respectable boss would say, / "I make it a point to discourage my staff from speaking up, / and I maintain a culture / **that**
(prevents A from -ing: A가 ~하는 것을 막다)
prevents disagreeing viewpoints **from** ever **getting aired**." //
(주격 관계대명사)
존경할 만한 상사라면 누구라도 말하지 않을 것이다 / "나는 반드시 내 직원이 자유롭게 의견을 내지 못하도록 하고 / 나는 문화를 유지한다 / 동의하지 않는 관점이 언제든 공공연히 알려지는 것을 가로막는"라고 //
(단서 1) 대부분의 상사는 반대 의견에 찬성한다고 말함
If anything, / most bosses even say / that they are pro-dissent. //
오히려 / 대부분의 상사는 심지어 말한다 / 자신은 반대에 찬성한다고 //
This idea can be found / throughout the series of conversations
(conversations 수식)
/ with corporate, university, and nonprofit leaders, / **published**
(과거분사(conversations 수식))
weekly in the business sections of newspapers. //
이러한 생각은 발견될 수 있다 / 일련의 대담을 통해서 / 기업, 대학, 그리고 비영리 (단체의) 리더와의 / 신문의 경제란에 매주 발행되는 //
(단서 2) 리더들과의 대담에서 반대 의견을 찬성하는 생각이 발견됨
(과거분사(leaders 수식))
In the interviews, / the **featured** leaders / are asked about their management techniques, / and regularly claim / to continually encourage / **internal protest** from more junior staffers. //
인터뷰에서 / (기사에) 다루어진 리더는 / 자신의 경영 기법에 대해 질문을 받고 / 어김없이 주장한다 / 계속해서 장려하고 있다고 / 내부적인 저항이 더 많은 부하 직원에게서 (나오기를) //
As Bot Pittman remarked / in one of these conversations: / "I
(간접의문문(의문사+주어+동사))
want us to listen to these dissenters / because they may intend
to tell you / **why we can't do something**, / (단서 3) 우리가 반대자에게 귀 기울이기를 원함
Bot Pittman이 말한 것처럼 / 이러한 대화 중 하나에서 / "저는 우리가 이러한 반대자에게 귀 기울이기를 원합니다 / 왜냐하면 그들은 여러분에게 말하려고 의도할 수 있겠지만 / 우리가 무엇인가를 할 수 없는 이유를 /

---

but if you listen hard, / what they're really telling you / is what
(get+목적어+과거분사(수동의 의미))
you must do / to **get something done**." //
그러나 만약에 여러분이 열심히 귀 기울이면 / 그들이 정말로 여러분에게 말하고 있는 것은 / 여러분이 무엇을 해야만 하는가이기 때문입니다 / 어떤 일이 이루어지도록 하기 위해서" //

- respectable ⓐ 존경할 만한 · make it a point 반드시 ~하도록 하다
- discourage ⓥ 못하게 하다 · speak up 자유롭게 의견을 내다
- maintain ⓥ 유지하다 · viewpoint ⓝ 관점
- get aired 공공연히 알려지다 · if anything 오히려 · boss ⓝ 상사
- conversation ⓝ 대담, 대화 · corporate ⓐ 기업
- nonprofit ⓐ 비영리인 · publish ⓥ 발행하다, 출판하다
- section ⓝ 구역, (신문의) ~란 · feature ⓥ (기사로) 다루다
- management ⓝ 경영 · techniques ⓝ 기법
- regularly ⓐ 어김없이, 규칙적으로 · claim ⓥ 주장하다
- continually ⓐ 계속해서 · remark ⓥ 말하다

존경할 만한 상사라면 누구라도 '나는 반드시 내 직원이 자유롭게 의견을 내지 못하도록 하고, 동의하지 않는 관점이 언제든 공공연히 알려지는 것을 가로막는 문화를 유지한다.'라고 말하지는 않을 것이다. 오히려, 대부분의 상사는 심지어 자신은 반대에 찬성한다고 말한다. 이러한 생각은 매주 발행되는 신문의 경제란에 기업, 대학, 그리고 비영리 (단체의) 리더와의 일련의 대담을 통해서 발견될 수 있다. 인터뷰에서, (기사에) 다루어진 리더는 자신의 경영 기법에 대해 질문을 받고, **내부적인 저항**이 더 많은 부하 직원에게서 (나오기를) 계속해서 장려하고 있다고 어김없이 주장한다. Bot Pittman은 이러한 대담 중 하나에서 "저는 우리가 이러한 반대자에게 귀 기울이기를 원합니다. 왜냐하면 그들은 여러분에게 우리가 무엇인가를 할 수 없는 이유를 말하려고 의도할 수 있겠지만, 그러나 만약에 여러분이 열심히 귀 기울이면, 그들이 정말로 여러분에게 말하고 있는 것은 어떤 일이 이루어지도록 하기 위해서 여러분이 무엇을 해야만 하는가이기 때문입니다."라고 말했다.

다음 빈칸에 들어갈 말로 가장 적절한 것을 고르시오. [3점]
① unconditional loyalty 리더가 반대 의견에 귀 기울이는 내용이 나옴
무조건적인 충성
② positive attitude 직원의 태도를 다루고 있는 내용이 아님
긍정적인 태도
③ internal protest 리더가 반대자에게 귀를 기울이면 무엇을 해야 할지 알 수 있음
내부적인 저항
④ competitive atmosphere
경쟁적인 분위기 리더가 의견을 듣는 내용이지 직원들을 경쟁시키는 내용이 아님
⑤ outstanding performance 리더가 직원의 성과를 중요시한다는 내용은 나오지 않음
뛰어난 성과

| 문제 풀이 순서 | ★★★ [정답률 47%]

1st 먼저 빈칸 문장을 읽고, 빈칸에 들어갈 말을 예측한다.

| 빈칸 문장 | 인터뷰에서, (기사에) 다루어진 리더는 자신의 경영 기법에 대해 질문을 받고, ＿＿＿＿＿＿이 더 많은 부하 직원에게서 (나오기를) 계속해서 장려하고 있다고 어김없이 주장한다. |

➡ 리더가 자신의 경영 기법에 대해 질문을 받고 더 많은 부하 직원에게서 '무엇'이 나오기를 계속 장려한다고 했으므로, (단서)
리더의 경영 기법에 대해 부하 직원들이 제기할 수 있는 것이 '무엇'인지 파악해야 한다. (발상)

2nd 글의 나머지 부분을 확인해서 정답을 찾는다.

- 존경할 만한 상사라면 직원들의 자유로운 의견과 동의하지 않는 관점을 가로막지 않는다.
- 대부분의 상사는 반대 의견에 찬성한다고 말하며 반대 의견을 지지하는 태도를 보인다. (단서 1)
- 신문 경제란에 실리는 리더들과의 일련의 대담에서는 반대 의견을 찬성하는 생각이 발견된다. (단서 2)
- Bot Pittman은 우리가 반대자에게 귀 기울이기를 원하며 반대자가 말하는 것은 어떤 일이 이루어지려면 무엇을 해야만 하는가에 대한 것이라고 한다. (단서 3)

▶ 즉, 리더가 직원들의 반대 의견에도 경청하기 때문에 이들에게서 ③ '내부적인 저항'이 나오기를 격려한다는 내용이다.

| 선택지 분석 |

① 반대자에게 귀를 기울이면 무엇을 해야 하는지 알 수 있다고 했으므로 무조건적인 충성을 장려하는 내용은 아니다.

② 리더가 직원들의 긍정적인 태도를 장려하는 내용이 아니라 반대 의견을 듣고자 한다는 내용이다.

③ 리더는 직원들의 내부적인 저항이 나오기를 격려하고 반대 의견에 귀 기울여서 무엇을 해야 할지 알 수 있다.

④ 경쟁적인 분위기는 반대 의견을 듣고자 하는 리더의 의지와 직접적인 관련이 없다.

⑤ 리더가 의견의 다양성과 반대 의견을 듣는 것에 가치를 둔다는 내용이다.

M 31 정답 ① *집단 지성을 위한 brainwriting 과정

To find the hidden potential in teams, / instead of brainstorming, / we're **better off** shifting to a process **called brainwriting**. //
팀의 숨겨진 잠재력을 찾으려면 / 브레인스토밍 대신 / 브레인라이팅이라는 과정으로 전환하는 것이 좋다 //
단서 1 팀의 잠재력을 찾는 과정으로 브레인라이팅이 제시됨

The initial steps are solo. //
초기 단계는 혼자서 진행한다 //
단서 2 개별적으로 아이디어를 냄

You start by asking everyone / to generate ideas separately. //
먼저 모든 사람에게 요청한다 / 개별적으로 아이디어를 내도록 //

Next, / you pool them / and share them anonymously among the group. //
그런 다음 / 아이디어를 모아 / 익명으로 그룹에 공유한다 //

To preserve independent judgment, / each member evaluates them on their own. //
독립적인 판단을 유지하기 위해 / 각 구성원이 스스로 그 아이디어를 평가한다 //
단서 3 독립적으로 아이디어를 스스로 평가함

Only then does the team come together / to select and refine the most promising options. //
그러고 나서야 팀이 함께 모여 / 가장 유망한 옵션을 선택하고 다듬는다 //
단서 4 팀이 모여 옵션을 선택하고 다듬음

By **developing and assessing** ideas individually / before choosing and elaborating them, / teams can surface and advance possibilities / **that** might not get attention otherwise. //
개별적으로 아이디어를 전개하고 평가함으로써 / 아이디어를 선택하고 구체화하기 전에 / 팀은 가능성을 드러내고 발전시킬 수 있다 / 다른 방법으로는 주목받지 못했을 //

This brainwriting process **makes sure / that** all ideas are brought to the table / and all voices are brought into the conversation. //
이 브레인라이팅 과정은 보장한다 / 모든 아이디어를 테이블에 올려놓고 / 모든 의견을 대화에 반영할 수 있도록 //

It is especially effective / in groups **that** struggle to achieve collective intelligence. //
특히 효과적이다 / 집단 지성을 달성하는 데 어려움을 겪는 그룹에서 //

- potential ⓝ 잠재력 · shift ⓥ 바꾸다 · initial ⓐ 초기의
- generate ⓥ 발생하다 · separately ⓐⓓ 따로, 별도로
- pool ⓥ 모으다 · preserve ⓥ 보존하다 · judgment ⓝ 판단
- evaluate ⓥ 평가하다 · refine ⓥ 다듬다 · promising ⓐ 유망한
- elaborate ⓥ 정교하게 말하다 · advance ⓥ 발전시키다
- struggle to ~ ~하기 위해 애쓰다 · collective ⓐ 집단적인
- intelligence ⓝ 지능

팀의 숨겨진 잠재력을 찾으려면 브레인스토밍 대신 브레인라이팅이라는 과정으로 전환하는 것이 좋다. 초기 단계는 혼자서 진행한다. 먼저 모든 사람에게 개별적으로 아이디어를 내도록 요청한다. 그런 다음, 아이디어를 모아 익명으로 그룹에 공유한다. 독립적인 판단을 유지하기 위해 각 구성원이 스스로 그 아이디어를 평가한다. 그러고 나서야 팀이 함께 모여 가장 유망한 옵션을 선택하고 다듬는다. 아이디어를 선택하고 구체화하기 전에 **개별적으로 아이디어를 전개하고 평가함**으로써 팀은 다른 방법으로는 주목받지 못했을 가능성을 드러내고 발전시킬 수 있다. 이 브레인라이팅 과정은 모든 아이디어를 테이블에 올려놓고 모든 의견을 대화에 반영할 수 있도록 한다. 특히 집단 지성을 달성하는 데 어려움을 겪는 그룹에서 효과적이다.

다음 빈칸에 들어갈 말로 가장 적절한 것을 고르시오. [3점]

① developing and assessing ideas individually
아이디어를 선택하고 다듬기 전에는 개별적으로 아이디어를 전개하고 평가함
개별적으로 아이디어를 전개하고 평가하기

② presenting and discussing ideas out loud
큰 소리로 아이디어를 발표하고 토론하기
개별적으로 아이디어를 평가하는 것이 핵심임

③ assigning different roles to each member
각 구성원에게 다른 역할 할당하기
구성원의 역할 할당에 관한 내용이 아님

④ coming to an agreement on these options
이 옵션들에 대한 합의에 도달하기
옵션을 선택하고 다듬기 전에는 개별적으로 아이디어를 전개하고 평가해야 함

⑤ skipping the step of judging these options
이 옵션들을 판단하는 단계 건너뛰기
개별적으로 평가하는 단계를 거쳐야 함

| 문제 풀이 순서 | ★★★ [정답률 46%]

1st 빈칸이 포함된 문장을 읽고, 빈칸에 들어갈 말에 대한 단서를 얻는다.

| 빈칸 문장 | By _____ before choosing and elaborating them, teams can surface and advance possibilities that might not get attention otherwise. 아이디어를 선택하고 구체화하기 전에 _____ 함으로써 팀은 다른 방법으로는 주목받지 못했을 가능성을 드러내고 발전시킬 수 있다. |

➡ 아이디어를 선택하고 구체화하기 전에 '무엇'을 함으로써 팀이 가능성을 발전시킬 수 있다고 했으므로, (단서)
아이디어를 선택하고 구체화하기 전의 과정이 빈칸 문장보다 앞에 나올 것이다. (발상)

2nd **1st** 에서 찾은 단서를 염두에 두고, 빈칸 문장의 앞부분부터 확인한다.

- 팀의 잠재력을 찾으려면 브레인라이팅이라는 과정으로 전환하는 것이 좋다. 단서 1
- 먼저 모든 사람에게 개별적으로 아이디어를 내도록 요청한다. 단서 2
- 독립적인 판단을 유지하기 위해 각 구성원이 스스로 그 아이디어를 평가한다. 단서 3
- 그러고 나서야 팀이 함께 모여 가장 유망한 옵션을 선택하고 다듬는다. 단서 4

➡ 개별적으로 아이디어를 내고 각 구성원이 스스로 그것을 평가하고 나서야 팀이 옵션을 선택하고 다듬는다(구체화한다)는 브레인라이팅 과정을 설명했다. 즉, 아이디어를 선택하고 다듬기 전의 과정은 개별적으로 아이디어를 내고 평가하는 것이다.

▶ 빈칸 문장은 〈아이디어를 구체화하고 선택하기 전에 ① '개별적으로 아이디어를 전개하고 평가함'으로써 팀은 다른 방법으로는 주목받지 못했을 가능성을 드러내고 발전시킬 수 있다.〉라는 내용이 되어야 한다.

3rd 글의 내용을 다시 한번 정리하며 정답이 맞는지 확인한다.

팀에서 개별적으로 낸 아이디어를 평가하고, 그중 유망한 옵션을 선택하고 다듬는 브레인라이팅 과정에 대한 글이다. 따라서 빈칸에는 ① '개별적으로 아이디어를 전개하고 평가하기'가 들어가는 것이 가장 적절하다.

| 선택지 분석 |

① 아이디어를 선택하고 다듬기 전에는 개별적으로 아이디어를 전개하고 평가한다.

② 같이 모여 선택하기 전에 개별적으로 아이디어를 평가하는 것이 핵심이다.

③ 구성원의 역할 할당에 관한 내용이 아니다.

④ 옵션을 선택하고 다듬기 전에는 개별적으로 아이디어를 전개하고 평가해야 한다.

⑤ 각 구성원은 독립적인 판단을 위해서 개별적으로 평가하는 단계를 거친다.

M 32 정답 ④ *엘리트 명성과 다른 평범한 명성

While social media attention is potentially an instrument / **to achieve** ends like elite celebrity, / some content creators desire ordinary fame / as a social end in itself. //
소셜 미디어 관심은 잠재적으로 도구인 반면 / 엘리트 명성과 같은 목적을 달성하기 위한 / 일부 콘텐츠 제작자들은 평범한 명성을 원한다 / 사회적 목적 그 자체로서 //

Not unlike reality television stars, / social media celebrities are often criticized / for not having skills and talents /
리얼리티 텔레비전 스타들과 다르지 않게 / 소셜 미디어 유명인들은 종종 비판을 받는다 / 기술과 재능을 가지고 있지 않다는 이유로 /

앞에 주격 관계대명사와 be동사가 생략됨
associated with traditional, elite celebrity, / such as acting or singing ability. // 단서 1 소셜 미디어 유명인들은 엘리트 명성에 관련된 기술이 없다는 이유로 비판을 받음
전통적인 엘리트 명성과 관련된 / 연기나 가창력과 같은 //

동격절 접속사
This criticism highlights the fact / that digital content creators face real barriers / to crossing over to the sphere of elite celebrity. //
이러한 비판은 사실을 강조한다 / 디지털 콘텐츠 제작자들이 실질적인 장벽에 직면하고 있다는 / 엘리트 명성의 영역으로 넘어가는 데 있어서 //

'~라는 점을 놓친다'
However, / the criticism also misses the point / that the phenomenon of ordinary celebrity **reconstructs the meaning of fame**. //
그러나 / 이 비판은 또한 ~라는 점을 놓친다 / 평범한 명성 현상이 명성의 의미를 재구성한다는 //

The elite celebrity is symbolized by the metaphor of the star, / characterized by mystery and hierarchical distance / and
병렬 구조
associated with naturalized qualities of talent and class. //
엘리트 유명인은 스타라는 은유로 상징되고 / 신비로움과 계층적 거리로 특징지어지며 / 타고난 자질의 재능과 계층에 연관되어 있다 // 단서 2 평범한 명성은 평범한 사람들과의 상호작용으로 관심을 끌어들임

The ordinary celebrity attracts attention / through regular and frequent interactions / with other ordinary people. //
평범한 유명인은 관심을 끈다 / 정기적이고 빈번한 상호작용을 통해 / 다른 평범한 사람들과의 //

동명사구 주어(단수)   단수동사
Achieving ordinary fame as a social media celebrity / is like doing well at a game, /
소셜 미디어 유명인으로서 평범한 명성을 얻는 것은 / 게임에서 잘하는 것과 같은데 /

'그 이상도 그 이하도 아닌'
because in this sphere, / fame is nothing more nor less / than relatively high scores on attention scales, /
왜냐하면 이 영역에서 / 명성은 그 이상도 그 이하도 아니기 때문이다 / 관심 척도에서 상대적으로 높은 점수 / 단서 3 소셜 미디어 유명인의 영역에서 명성은 그저 관심 척도에서 높은 점수를 받는 것임

'내장된'
the metrics of subscribers, followers, Likes, or clicks / built into social media applications. //
즉, 구독자, 폴로어, 좋아요 또는 클릭의 측정 기준(에서) / 소셜 미디어 애플리케이션에 내장된 //

- potentially ad 잠재적으로   - instrument n 도구   - end n 목적
- celebrity n 유명인, 명성   - criticize v 비판하다
- highlight v 강조하다   - barrier n 장애물
- phenomenon n 현상   - symbolize v 상징하다
- metaphor n 은유   - characterize v 특징짓다
- hierarchical a 계층적인   - scale n 척도   - shift v 전환하다
- gradually ad 점차   - solely ad 오로지, 단지   - restrict v 제한하다

소셜 미디어 관심은 잠재적으로 엘리트 명성과 같은 목적을 달성하기 위한 도구인 반면, 일부 콘텐츠 제작자들은 사회적 목적 그 자체로서 평범한 명성을 원한다. 리얼리티 텔레비전 스타들과 다르지 않게, 소셜 미디어 유명인들은 연기나 가창력과 같은 전통적인 엘리트 명성과 관련된 기술과 재능을 가지고 있지 않다는 이유로 종종 비판을 받는다. 이러한 비판은 디지털 콘텐츠 제작자들이 엘리트 명성의 영역으로 넘어가는 데 있어 실질적인 장벽에 직면하고 있다는 사실을 강조한다. 그러나 이 비판은 또한 평범한 명성 현상이 **명성의 의미를 재구성한다**는 점을 놓친다. 엘리트 유명인은 스타라는 은유로 상징되고, 신비로움과 계층적 거리로 특징지어지며, 타고난 자질의 재능과 계층에 연관되어 있다. 평범한 유명인은 다른 평범한 사람들과의 정기적이고 빈번한 상호작용을 통해 관심을 끈다. 소셜 미디어 유명인으로서 평범한 명성을 얻는 것은 게임에서 잘하는 것과 같은데, 왜냐하면 이 영역에서 명성은 관심 척도, 즉, 소셜 미디어 애플리케이션에 내장된 구독자, 폴로어, 좋아요 또는 클릭의 측정 기준에서 상대적으로 높은 점수 그 이상도 그 이하도 아니기 때문이다.

다음 빈칸에 들어갈 말로 가장 적절한 것을 고르시오. [3점]
① shifts to that of elite celebrity   평범한 명성 현상이 엘리트 명성 현상으로 전환한다는 내용이 아님
   엘리트 유명인의 그것으로 전환한다
② disappears gradually over time
   시간이 지남에 따라 점진적으로 사라진다   평범한 명성 현상이 점차 사라진다는 언급은 없음
③ focuses solely on talent and class
   재능과 계층에만 집중한다   재능과 계층에 집중하는 것은 엘리트 명성에 해당함
④ reconstructs the meaning of fame
   명성의 의미를 재구성한다   평범한 명성 현상이 엘리트 명성과는 다르다는 것이 글의 핵심 내용임
⑤ restricts interactions with the public
   대중과의 상호작용을 제한한다   평범한 명성은 오히려 대중과의 상호작용이 필요함

| 문제 풀이 순서 | ★★★ [정답률 38%]

1st 빈칸이 포함된 문장을 읽고, 빈칸에 들어갈 말에 대한 단서를 얻는다.

| 빈칸 문장 | However, the criticism also misses the point that the phenomenon of ordinary celebrity _____. 그러나 이 비판은 또한 평범한 명성 현상이 _____ 라는 점을 놓친다. |

➡ '이 비판'은 평범한 명성 현상이 '무엇을 한다'는 점을 놓친다고 했으므로, 단서 '이 비판'이 무엇을 가리키는지, 또한 평범한 명성 현상이 어떤 특성을 가지고 있다고 표현하는지에 주목하여 글을 읽어야 한다. 발상

2nd 글의 내용을 종합해서 빈칸에 들어갈 적절한 말을 찾는다.
- 소셜 미디어 유명인들은 연기나 가창력과 같은 전통적인 엘리트 명성과 관련된 기술과 재능을 가지고 있지 않다는 이유로 종종 비판을 받는다. 단서 1
- 평범한 유명인은 다른 평범한 사람들과의 정기적이고 빈번한 상호작용을 통해 관심을 끈다. 단서 2
- 소셜 미디어 유명인으로서 평범한 명성을 얻는 것은 게임에서 잘하는 것과 같은데, 왜냐하면 이 영역에서 명성은 관심 척도에서 상대적으로 높은 점수 그 이상도 그 이하도 아니기 때문이다. 단서 3
➡ 빈칸 문장의 '이 비판'은 소셜 미디어 유명인들이 엘리트 명성과 관련된 기술과 재능이 없다는 이유로 받는 비판이다. 또한 평범한 명성을 얻는 것은 엘리트 명성과는 다르게 다른 평범한 사람들과의 상호작용이 필요하고, 이 영역에서 명성은 관심 척도에서 상대적으로 높은 점수라고 했다.

3rd 글의 내용을 다시 한번 정리하며 이해한 중심 내용을 선택지에서 고른다.
소셜 미디어 유명인들은 엘리트 명성에서 필요한 만큼의 기술과 재능이 없다는 '비판'을 받지만, 엘리트 명성과는 다르게 평범한 명성에 있어서 '인기'는 관심 척도에서 높은 점수를 받는 것뿐이라는 내용이다. 엘리트 명성이 형성한 인기의 의미와 평범한 명성에 있어서 인기의 의미가 다른 것이므로 빈칸에는 ④ '명성의 의미를 재구성한다'가 들어가야 한다.

| 선택지 분석 |
① 엘리트 명성과 평범한 명성의 차이점을 설명하는 내용이다.
② 평범한 명성 현상이 시간이 지남에 따라 사라진다는 것은 언급되지 않았다.
③ 재능과 계층에 집중하는 것은 엘리트 명성에 해당하며, 평범한 명성은 관심 척도의 높은 점수에 집중한다.
④ 평범한 명성에서 인기의 의미는 엘리트 명성에서 다루는 인기의 의미와 다르므로, 평범한 명성은 인기의 의미를 재구성한다.
⑤ 평범한 명성은 오히려 대중과의 상호작용이 필수적이며, 이것이 제한된 것은 엘리트 명성에 해당한다.

차이쌤's Follow Me! - 홈페이지에서 제공

M 33 정답 ② *기후 변화에 대한 잘못된 믿음

주격 관계대명사   ask+간접목적어+직접목적어
Researchers are working on a project / that asks / coastal towns / how they are preparing for rising sea levels. //
연구원들은 프로젝트를 진행하고 있다 / 묻는 / 해안가 마을들이 / 해수면 상승에 어떻게 대비하고 있는지 //

Some towns have risk assessments; / some towns even have a plan. //
어떤 마을들은 위험 평가를 한다 / 어떤 마을들은 심지어 계획을 가지고 있다 //

But it's a rare town / **that** is actually carrying out a plan. //
주격 관계대명사
하지만 마을은 드물다 / 실제로 계획을 실행하고 있는 //

One reason / we've failed to act on climate change / is the
common belief / **that** it is far away in time and space. //
동격의 that
한 가지 이유는 / 우리가 기후 변화에 대처하는 데 실패한 / 일반적인 믿음 때문이다 / 그것이
시공간적으로 멀리 떨어져 있다는 //
[단서 1] 수십 년간 기후 변화를 미래 시제로 이야기했음

For decades, / climate change was a prediction / about the
future, / so scientists talked about **it** / in the future tense. //
= climate change
수십 년 동안 / 기후 변화는 예측이었기 때문에 / 미래에 대한 / 과학자들은 기후 변화에 대해
이야기했다 / 미래 시제로 //

This became a habit / — so that even today many scientists /
still use the future tense, / even though we know / **that** a climate
crisis is ongoing. // [단서 2] 심지어 오늘날에도 기후 위기를 미래 시제로 말함
목적어절을 이끄는 접속사
이것이 습관이 되어 / 심지어 오늘날에도 많은 과학자들이 / 여전히 미래 시제를 사용하고
있다 / 우리가 알고 있음에도 / 기후 위기가 진행 중이라는 것을 //

Scientists also often focus on regions / most affected by the
crisis, / such as Bangladesh or the West Antarctic Ice Sheet, /
which for most Americans are physically remote. //
주격 관계대명사
과학자들은 또한 지역에 초점을 맞추고 있으며 / 위기의 영향을 가장 많이 받는 /
방글라데시나 서남극 빙상처럼 / 그 지역은 대부분의 미국인들에게는 물리적으로 멀리 떨어져
있다 // [단서 3] 과학자들이 초점을 맞춘 위기의 영향을 가장 많이 받는 지역들은 물리적으로 멀리 떨어짐

- coastal ⓐ 해안의 · prepare ⓥ 준비하다 · sea level 해수면
- risk ⓝ 위험 · assessment ⓝ 평가 · rare ⓐ 드문
- carry out ~을 실행하다 · act on ~에 따라 행동하다[대처하다]
- climate ⓝ 기후 · decade ⓝ 10년 · prediction ⓝ 예측
- tense ⓝ 시제 · crisis ⓝ 위기 · ongoing ⓐ 계속 진행 중인
- region ⓝ 지역 · affect ⓥ 영향을 주다
- Antarctic ⓐ 남극 지방의 · physically ⓐⓓ 물리적으로
- remote ⓐ 멀리 떨어진 · efficiency ⓝ 효율(성)

연구원들은 해안가 마을들이 해수면 상승에 어떻게 대비하고 있는지
묻는 프로젝트를 진행하고 있다. 어떤 마을들은 위험 평가를 하고 어떤
마을들은 심지어 계획을 가지고 있다. 하지만 실제로 계획을 실행하고
있는 마을은 드물다. 우리가 기후 변화에 대처하는 데 실패한 한 가지
이유는 **그것이 시공간적으로 멀리 떨어져 있다는** 일반적인 믿음 때문이다.
수십 년 동안, 기후 변화는 미래에 대한 예측이었기 때문에 과학자들은
미래 시제로 기후 변화에 대해 이야기했다. 이것이 습관이 되어 우리가
기후 위기가 진행중이라는 것을 알고 있음에도, 많은 과학자들이
오늘날에도 여전히 미래 시제를 사용하고 있다. 과학자들은 또한
방글라데시나 서남극 빙상처럼 위기의 영향을 가장 많이 받는 지역에
초점을 맞추고 있으며, 그 지역은 대부분의 미국인들에게는 물리적으로
멀리 떨어져 있다.

다음 빈칸에 들어갈 말로 가장 적절한 것을 고르시오. [3점]
① it is not related to science 사람들이 기후 변화가 과학과 관련이 없다고 믿는다는
그것이 과학과 관련이 없다 내용은 나오지 않음
②it is far away in time and space 기후 변화가 미래 시제로 이야기되고
그것이 시공간적으로 멀리 떨어져 있다 과학자들이 초점을 맞춘 지역들도 물리적으로 멀리 떨어져 있음
③ energy efficiency matters the most
에너지 효율이 가장 중요하다 에너지 효율에 관한 내용은 전혀 나와 있지 않음
④ careful planning can fix the problem
세심한 계획이 문제를 해결할 수 있다 세심한 계획으로 기후 변화를 해결하려고 한다는 내용은 없음
⑤ it is too late to prevent it from happening 사람들이 기후 위기의
그것이 발생하는 것을 막기에는 너무 늦었다 상황에 대해 절망하는 것은 나오지 않음

> **왜 정답?** ★★★ [정답률 48%]
해안가 마을들이 기후 변화에 대처하기 위해 위험 평가를 하거나 계획을 세우는데,
실제로 그 계획을 실행하는 마을이 드물다고 했다. 후반부에서 과학자들이 기후
변화를 미래 시제로 이야기했고 지금도 그러고 있으며, 기후 위기의 영향을 가장
많이 받는 지역이 물리적으로 멀리 떨어져 있다는 내용이 나온다.
그러므로 기후 변화에 대처하는 데 실패하는 이유는 사람들이 이를 시간과
공간적으로 멀리 떨어져 있다고 믿기 때문이라는 것을 알 수 있다. 따라서 빈칸에
들어갈 말로 가장 적절한 것은 ② '그것이 시공간적으로 멀리 떨어져 있다'이다.

> **왜 오답?**
① 사람들이 기후 변화와 과학이 관련이 없다고 믿기 때문에 기후 변화에 대처하는
데 실패한다고 판단할 만한 근거가 이 글에는 제시되지 않았다.
③ 에너지 효율에 관한 내용은 전혀 언급되지 않았다.
④ 이 글에서 세심한 계획을 통해 기후 변화에 대처하려고 노력하는 내용은 나와
있지 않다.
⑤ 사람들이 기후 위기의 상황을 너무 늦었다고 믿고 기후 변화에 대처하는 것을
포기하는 내용은 없다.

— 배경 지식 —
＊ 기후 변화 협약
기후 변화는 지구의 평균 기온이 변하는 현상으로, 전세계적으로 기후 변화
위기가 점점 심각해지고 있다. 기후 변화 협약은 이산화탄소 등의 온실 가스
배출이 증가됨에 따라 생기는 지구 온난화 현상을 막기 위해 만든 국제 협약이다.
1992년의 브라질 리우 회의(환경과 개발에 관한 유엔 회의)에서 채택된
협약으로, 개발 도상국과 선진국에 모두 적용되는
사항인 일반 의무 사항이 있고, 선진국에만 적용되는
특별 의무 사항이 있다.
이 협약은 1994년 3월에 정식으로 발효되었고,
현재 이 협약에 가입된 국가는 186개국에 달한다.
또한, 미국, 영국 등의 OECD 회원국을 포함한
38개국은 2012년까지 온실 가스 배출량을 더욱
감축하기로 하는 교토 의정서에 합의했다.

Ⓜ **34** 정답 ④ ＊창작 행위에서 타인의 관점의 필요성

It is common **to assume** / that creativity concerns primarily the
가주어 진주어
relation / between actor(creator) and artifact(creation). //
가정하는 것이 일반적이다 / 창조성은 주로 관계와 관련이 있다고 / 행위자(창작자)와 창작물
(창작) 사이의 //

However, / from a sociocultural standpoint, / the creative act is
never "complete" / in the absence of a second position / — that
of an audience. // [단서 1] 관객 없이는 창작이 완전하지 않다고 하면서 관객의 필요성에 대해 말함
그러나 / 사회 문화적 관점에서 볼 때 / 창작 행위는 결코 "완전"하지 않다 / 제2의 입장이 부
재한 상황에서는 / 다시 말해 관객의 부재 상황에서는 //
대조를 나타내는 접속사

While the actor or creator him/herself / is the first audience of
the artifact / being produced, /
행위자나 창작자 자신은 / 창작물의 첫 번째 관객이지만 / 만들어지고 있는 /

this kind of distantiation can only be achieved / by **internalizing
the perspective of others on one's work**. //
이런 거리두기는 오직 이루어질 수 있다 / 다른 사람의 관점을 자신의 작품 속에 내면화하는
것으로서만 //

This means / **that**, in order to be an audience / to your own
목적어절 접속사
creation, / a history of interaction with others / is needed. //
이것은 의미한다 / 관객이 되기 위해서는 / 자신의 창작 활동에 / 다른 사람들과 상호 작용하는
역사가 / 필요하다는 것을 // [단서 2] 자신의 창작물에 대해 자신이 관객이
되기 위해서는 타인과의 상호 작용이 필요함

We exist in a social world / **that** constantly confronts us / with
주격 관계대명사
the "view of the other." // [단서 3] 다른 사람의 관점을 직면해야만 하는 것을 언급하면서
우리는 사회에 살고 있으며 / 끊임없이 우리를 직면하게 하는 / "상대방의 관점"에 //
타인의 관점에 대한 필요성을 강조함

It is **the view** / we include and blend into our own activity, /
뒤에 목적격 관계대명사 생략
including creative activity. //
그것은 관점이다 / 우리가 포함하고 우리 자신의 활동에 뒤섞이는 / 창조적인 행위를 포함해
서 // [단서 4] 외부 관점이 창조성에 필수적임

This outside perspective / is essential for creativity / **because**
이유를 나타내는 접속사
it gives new meaning and value / to the creative act and its
product. //
이러한 외부 관점은 / 창조성에는 필수적이다 / 이것은 새로운 의미와 가치를 부여하기 때문에
/ 창작 행위와 그 결과물에 //

- assume ⓥ 가정하다, 추정하다 ・ concern ⓥ 관련되다
- primarily ⓐ 주로 ・ sociocultural ⓐ 사회 문화적인
- standpoint ⓝ 관점
- in the absence of ~의 부재 속에서, ~이 없는 상황에서
- distantiation ⓝ 거리두기 ・ interaction ⓝ 상호 작용
- constantly ⓐ 끊임없이 ・ confront ⓥ 직면하다, 맞서다
- blend into ~와 뒤섞이다 ・ perspective ⓝ 관점

창조성은 주로 행위자(창작자)와 창작물(창작) 사이의 관계와 관련이 있다고 가정하는 것이 일반적이다. 그러나 사회 문화적 관점에서 볼 때, 창작 행위는 관객의 부재 다시 말해 제2의 입장이 부재한 상황에서는 결코 "완전"하지 않다. 행위자나 창작자 자신은 만들어지고 있는 창작물의 첫 번째 관객이지만, 이런 거리두기는 **다른 사람의 관점을 자신의 작품 속에 내면화하는 것**으로서만 이루어진다. 이것은 자신의 창작 활동에 관객이 되기 위해서는 다른 사람들과 상호 작용하는 역사가 필요하다는 것을 의미한다. 우리는 "상대방의 관점"을 끊임없이 마주하는 사회에 살고 있으며, 그것은 창조적인 행위를 포함해서 우리가 우리 자신의 활동에 통합시키게 되는 관점이다. 이러한 외부 관점은 창작 행위와 그 결과물에 새로운 의미와 가치를 부여하기 때문에 창조성에는 필수적이다.

> **다음 빈칸에 들어갈 말로 가장 적절한 것을 고르시오. [3점]**
> ① exploring the absolute truth in existence
> 존재의 절대적 진리를 탐구하는 것 / 정확하면서 논리적인 단계에 대한 언급은 없음
> ② following a series of precise and logical steps
> 정확하면서도 논리적인 일련의 단계를 따르는 것
> ③ looking outside and drawing inspiration from nature
> 외부를 바라보면서 자연으로부터 영감을 이끌어내는 것 / 관객 없이 창작 행위가 완전해질 수 없고,
> ④ internalizing the perspective of others on one's work
> 다른 사람의 관점을 자신의 작품 속에 내면화하는 것 / 관점이 창작 행위에 필수적이라고 했으
> ⑤ pushing the audience to the limits of its endurance
> 인내의 한계 상황까지 관객을 밀어붙이는 것 / 관객의 인내와 관련된 내용은 없음
> 타인의 관점을 '외부를 바라보는 것'으로 비유해서 만든 오답

왜 정답? ★★★ [정답률 52%]

관객이 없는 경우 창작 행위는 결코 완전해질 수 없다고 하면서 타인과의 상호 작용과 타인의 관점이 창작 행위에 필수적이라는 내용의 글로, 창작 행위와 관련된 타인의 관점을 강조하고 있다. 따라서 빈칸에 들어갈 말로 가장 적절한 것은 ④ '다른 사람의 관점을 자신의 작품 속에 내면화하는 것'이다.

왜 오답?

① 존재의 절대적 진리와는 아무런 관련이 없는 글이다.
② 정확하면서 논리적인 단계를 따르는 것에 대해서는 언급되지 않았다.
③ '타인의 관점'을 '외부를 바라보는 것'으로 비유해서 만든 오답이다.
⑤ 관객의 인내와 관련된 내용은 나오지 않았다.

M 35 정답 ① *도시처럼 상호 작용하는 뇌

Think of the brain as a city. //
뇌를 도시라고 생각해 보라 //

If you were to look out over a city / and ask "where is the economy located?" / you'd see / there's no good answer to the question. //
뒤에 목적어절 접속사 that이 생략됨
만약 당신이 도시를 내다보며 / "경제가 어디에 위치해 있나요"라고 묻는다면 / 당신은 알게 될 것이다 / 그 질문에 대한 좋은 답이 없다는 것을 //

Instead, / the economy emerges / from the interaction of all the elements / — from the stores and the banks / to the merchants and the customers. //
from A to B: A에서 B까지
단서 1 도시의 경제는 모든 요소의 상호 작용으로부터 나타남
대신 / 경제는 나타난다 / 모든 요소의 상호 작용으로부터 / 상점과 은행에서 / 상인과 고객에 이르기까지 //

And so it is with the brain's operation: / it doesn't happen in one spot. //
단서 2 도시와 마찬가지로 뇌의 작동도 한 곳에서 일어나지 않음
그리고 그것은 뇌의 작동도 그러하다 / 그것은 한 곳에서 일어나지 않는다 //

Just as in a city, / no neighborhood of the brain **operates in isolation**. //
도시에서처럼 / 뇌의 어떤 지역도 독립적으로 작동하지 않는다 //

In brains and in cities, / everything emerges / from the interaction between residents, / at all scales, / locally and distantly. //
뇌와 도시 안에서 / 모든 것은 나타난다 / 거주자들 간의 상호 작용으로부터 / 모든 규모에서 / 근방에서든 원거리에서든 // 단서 3 뇌와 도시는 짧든 멀든 내부 요소의 상호 작용으로부터 나타남

계속적 용법의 주격 관계대명사
Just as trains bring materials and textiles into a city, / which become processed into the economy, /
기차가 자재와 직물을 도시로 들여오는 것처럼 / 그리고 그것은 경제 속으로 처리된다 /
핵심 주어(복수)   복수 동사
so the raw electrochemical signals from sensory organs / are transported / along superhighways of neurons. //
감각 기관으로부터의 가공되지 않은 전기화학적 신호는 / 전해진다 / 뉴런의 초고속도로를 따라 //

There / the signals undergo processing and transformation / into our conscious reality. //
거기서 / 신호는 처리와 변형을 겪는다 / 우리의 의식적인 현실로 //

- economy ⓝ 경제 ・ emerge ⓥ 나타나다
- interaction ⓝ 상호 작용 ・ element ⓝ 요소
- merchant ⓝ 상인 ・ operation ⓝ 작용, 작동
- resident ⓝ 거주자 ・ scale ⓝ 정도, 규모 ・ distantly ⓐ 멀리에서
- textile ⓝ 직물 ・ raw ⓐ 가공되지 않은 ・ sensory ⓐ 감각의
- organ ⓝ (체내의) 장기 ・ transport ⓥ 전하다, 이동하다
- superhighway ⓝ 초고속도로 ・ undergo ⓥ 겪다
- conscious ⓐ 의식적인 ・ isolation ⓝ 독립, 분리
- resemble ⓥ 유사하다 ・ systemic ⓐ 체계적인

뇌를 도시라고 생각해 보라. 만약 당신이 도시를 내다보며 "경제가 어디에 위치해 있나요?"라고 묻는다면, 그 질문에 대한 좋은 답이 없다는 것을 알게 될 것이다. 대신, 경제는 상점과 은행에서 상인과 고객에 이르기까지 모든 요소의 상호 작용으로부터 나타난다. 그리고 그것은 뇌의 작동도 그러하다: 그것은 한 곳에서 일어나지 않는다. 도시에서처럼, 뇌의 어떤 지역도 **독립적으로 작동하지 않는다.** 뇌와 도시 안에서, 모든 것은, 모든 규모에서, 근거리에서든 원거리에서든, 거주자들 간의 상호 작용으로부터 나타난다. 기차가 자재와 직물을 도시로 들여오고, 그것이 경제 속으로 처리되는 것처럼, 감각 기관으로부터의 가공되지 않은 전기화학적 신호는 뉴런의 초고속도로를 따라서 전해진다. 거기서 신호는 처리와 우리의 의식적인 현실로 변형을 겪는다.

> **다음 빈칸에 들어갈 말로 가장 적절한 것을 고르시오. [3점]**
> ① operates in isolation 도시처럼 뇌의 모든 지역과 신호들은 상호 작용함
> 독립적으로 작동하다
> ② suffers from rapid changes 급격한 변화와 고통에 대한 언급은 없음
> 급격한 변화로 고통받다
> ③ resembles economic elements 앞에 no가 있으므로 반대 내용이 됨
> 경제적 요소들과 유사하다
> ④ works in a systematic way 작동 방식이 체계적인지는 알 수 없음
> 체계적인 방식으로 작동하다
> ⑤ interacts with another 앞에 no가 있으므로 반대 내용이 됨
> 다른 요소와 상호 작용하다

| 문제 풀이 순서 | ★★★ [정답률 48%]

1st 먼저 빈칸 문장을 읽고, 빈칸에 들어갈 말에 대한 단서를 얻는다.

빈칸 문장	Just as in a city, no neighborhood of the brain _____. 도시에서처럼, 뇌의 어떤 지역도 _____ 않는다.

→ 빈칸 문장 앞에 도시의 어떤 측면에 대한 설명이 있을 것이고, 빈칸 문장 뒤에서 그것이 왜 뇌와 비슷한지 설명할 것이다.
  뇌의 어떤 지역도 '어떻지 않다'라고 했으므로, 빈칸 문장 앞부분을 통해 추론해야 한다.

2nd 나머지 부분을 읽고, 도시와 뇌가 어떻게 비슷한지 확인하여 정답을 찾는다.

글의 앞부분	만약 당신이 도시를 내다보며 "경제가 어디에 위치해 있나요?"라고 묻는다면, 그 질문에 대한 좋은 답이 없다는 것을 알게 될 것이다. 대신, 경제는 상점과 은행에서 상인과 고객에 이르기까지 모든 요소의 상호 작용으로부터 나타난다. **단서1**

➡ 도시의 경제는 한 곳에서 작용하는 것이 아님 → 상점과 은행, 상인과 고객 등 모든 요소의 상호 작용에서 나타남
  ▶ 뇌도 여러 요소의 상호 작용으로 작동할 것임

빈칸 문장 앞	그리고 그것은 뇌의 작동도 그러하다: 그것은 한 곳에서 일어나지 않는다. **단서2**
빈칸 문장 뒤	뇌와 도시 안에서, 모든 것은, 모든 규모에서, 근거리에서든 원거리에서든, 거주자들 간의 상호 작용으로부터 나타난다. **단서3**

➡ 뇌의 작동도 한 곳에서 일어나지 않음 → 모든 것들의 상호 작용에서 나타남
  ▶ 빈칸 앞에 no가 있으므로, 뇌의 어떤 지역도 ① '독립적으로 작동하지' 않는다고 해야 적절하다.

| 선택지 분석 |

① 도시에서처럼, 뇌의 모든 지역과 신호들은 서로 상호 작용하므로 독립적으로 작동하지 않는 것이다.
② 도시가 급격한 변화로부터 자유롭다는 등의 언급은 없었기 때문에 적절하지 않다.
③ 도시와 뇌가 비슷하기 때문에, 도시의 경제적 요소들과 뇌의 지역은 유사하다고 볼 수 있지만, 빈칸 앞에 no가 있으므로 글과 반대 내용이 된다.
④ 체계적이지 않은 것이 상호 작용하는 것인지를 판단할 근거는 제시되지 않았다.
⑤ 빈칸 앞에 no가 있으므로 글과 반대 내용이 된다.

M 36 정답 ④ ＊심해 생물의 생물 발광의 이유

Some deep-sea organisms / are known to use bioluminescence / **as a lure**, / **to attract** prey with a little glow / **imitating** the movements of their favorite fish, /
일부 심해 생물은 / 생물 발광을 활용한다고 알려져 있다 / 가짜 미끼로서 / 작은 빛으로 먹이를 유혹하기 위해 / 그들이 좋아하는 물고기의 움직임을 모방하는 /

or like fireflies, as a sexual attractant / to find mates. //
혹은 반딧불이처럼 성적 유인 물질로서 / 짝을 찾기 위해 //

While there are many possible evolutionary theories / for the survival value of bioluminescence, / **one of the most fascinating** / is to **create a cloak of invisibility**. //
많은 가능한 진화 이론이 있지만 / 생물 발광의 생존가에 대한 / 가장 흥미로운 것 중 하나는 / 보이지 않는 망토를 만드는 것이다 //

The color / of almost all bioluminescent molecules / **is** blue-green, / the same color as the ocean above. //
색깔은 / 거의 모든 생물 발광 분자의 / 청록색이다 / 바다 위층과 같은 색인 //

By self-glowing blue-green, / the creatures no longer cast a shadow / or create a silhouette, / especially **when viewed** from below / against the brighter waters above. //
청록색으로 자체 발광함으로써 / 그 생물은 더 이상 그림자를 드리우거나 / 실루엣을 만들어 내지 않는다 / 특히 위쪽의 아래에서 보여질 때 / 더 밝은 물을 배경으로 //

Rather, / by glowing themselves, / they can blend / into the sparkles, reflections, and scattered blue-green glow / of sunlight or moonlight. // **단서1** 자신을 빛냄으로써 주변에 섞일 수 있음
오히려 / 자신을 빛냄으로써 / 그들은 섞일 수 있다 / 반짝임, 반사 그리고 분산된 청록색 빛에 / 햇빛 혹은 달빛의 //

Thus, / they are most likely making their own light / **not to see**, / but to be un-seen. // **단서2** 빛을 내는 것은 보이지 않기 위해서임
따라서 / 그들은 자신만의 빛을 분명 만들어 내고 있을 것이다 / 보기 위해서가 아니라 / 보이지 않기 위해서 //

• organism ⓝ 유기체   • prey ⓝ 먹이   • glow ⓝ 빛 ⓥ 빛나다
• firefly ⓝ 반딧불이   • sexual ⓐ 성적인   • attractant ⓝ 유인 물질
• mate ⓝ 짝   • evolutionary ⓐ 진화의   • theory ⓝ 이론
• cloak ⓝ 망토   • invisibility ⓝ 눈에 보이지 않음
• molecule ⓝ 분자   • creature ⓝ 생물
• cast a shadow 그림자를 드리우다   • silhouette ⓝ 실루엣
• blend into ∼와 섞이다   • sparkle ⓝ 반짝임   • reflection ⓝ 반사
• scattered ⓐ 분산된   • threaten ⓥ 위협하다

일부 심해 생물은 그들이 좋아하는 물고기의 움직임을 모방하는 작은 빛으로 먹이를 유혹하기 위해 가짜 미끼로서, 혹은 반딧불이처럼 짝을 찾기 위해 성적 유인 물질로써 생물 발광을 활용한다고 알려져 있다. 생물 발광의 생존가에 대한 많은 가능한 진화 이론이 있지만 가장 흥미로운 것 중 하나는 **보이지 않는 망토를 만드는** 것이다. 거의 모든 생물 발광 분자의 색깔은 바다 위층과 같은 색인 청록색이다. 청록색으로 자체 발광함으로써 생물은 특히 위쪽의 더 밝은 물을 배경으로 아래에서 보여질 때 더 이상 그림자를 드리우거나 실루엣을 만들어 내지 않는다. 오히려 자신을 빛냄으로써 그들은 햇빛 혹은 달빛의 반짝임, 반사 그리고 분산된 청록색 빛에 섞일 수 있다. 따라서 그들은 보기 위해서가 아니라 보이지 않기 위해서 자신만의 빛을 분명 만들어 내고 있을 것이다.

다음 빈칸에 들어갈 말로 가장 적절한 것을 고르시오. [3점]
① send a signal for help 심해 생물의 도움 요청에 대한 내용은 없음
  도움을 청하는 신호를 보내는
② threaten enemies nearby 주변의 적에 대한 언급은 없음
  근처에 있는 적을 위협하는
③ lift the veil of hidden prey 먹이가 언급된 것으로 만든 함정
  숨어있는 먹이의 베일을 벗기는
④ create a cloak of invisibility 생물 발광은 보이지 않기 위해서라고 했음
  보이지 않는 망토를 만드는
⑤ serve as a navigation system 내비게이션의 역할과 관련한 내용은 없음
  내비게이션 시스템으로서 역할을 하는

➤**왜** 정답 **?** ✱✱✱ [정답률 59%]

심해 생물 중 일부는 자신을 빛냄으로써 주변에 섞일 수 있다고 했으므로 생물 발광을 통해 주변 환경과 섞인다는 것을 알 수 있고, 이렇게 빛을 내는 것은 보이지 않기 위해서라고 했다. 따라서 ④ '보이지 않는 망토를 만드는'이 빈칸에 들어갈 말로 가장 적절하다.

➤**왜** 오답 **?**

① 심해 생물이 도움을 청하는 신호를 보내는 내용은 전혀 언급되지 않았다.
② 아예 보이지 않게 하기 위한 것이기 때문에 적을 위협할 수 없다.
③ 먹이를 유혹하기 위해 빛을 낸다는 부분에서 먹이가 언급되기는 했지만, 심해 생물이 빛을 내는 것은 먹이를 찾아내기 위함이라는 내용은 없다.
⑤ 빛을 이용해 방향을 찾는다는 등의 내용이 언급되지 않았으므로 내비게이션 시스템과는 관련이 없다.

M 37 정답 ③ ＊동물에 대한 인간의 언어 사용

The famous primatologist / Frans de Waal, of Emory University, **says** /
유명한 영장류학자 / Emory 대학의 Frans de Waal은 말한다 /

humans downplay similarities / between us and other animals / as a way of maintaining our spot / at the top of our imaginary ladder. // **단서1** 인간은 상상 속의 높은 위치를 유지하기 위해 동물이 가진 인간과의 유사성을 경시함
인간은 유사성을 경시한다고 / 우리와 다른 동물들 사이의 / 우리의 위치를 유지하는 방법으로 / 우리의 상상 속 사다리의 꼭대기에 //

Scientists, / **de Waal points out**, / can be some of the worst offenders / — employing technical language / **to distance the other animals from us**. //
과학자들은 / de Waal은 지적한다 / 최악의 범죄자들 중 일부일 수 있다고 / 기술적인 언어를 사용하는 / 우리와 다른 동물들 사이에 거리를 두기 위해 //

They call / "kissing" in chimps / "mouth-to-mouth contact"; /
they call / "friends" between primates / "favorite affiliation
partners"; /
그들은 부른다 / 침팬지의 '키스'를 / '입과 입의 접촉'이라고 / 그들은 부른다 / 영장류 사이의
'친구'를 / '좋아하는 제휴 파트너'라고 / **단서 2** 동물의 인간과 유사한 행위를 다른
언어로 표현하고 질적으로 다르다고 해석함
they interpret evidence / showing that crows and chimps can

make tools / as being somehow qualitatively different / from the
앞에 주격 관계대명사와 be동사가 생략됨
kind of toolmaking / said to define humanity. //
그들은 증거를 해석한다 / 까마귀와 침팬지가 도구를 만들 수 있다는 것을 보여주는 /
아무래도 질적으로 다르다고 / 그 종류의 도구 제작과는 / 인류를 정의한다고 하는 //
단서 3 동물의 지능이 인간보다 우세하면 본능으로 치부함   전치사 like의 목적어절을 이끄는 의문사
If an animal can beat us / at a cognitive task / — like how certain

bird species can remember / the precise locations of thousands
                                                    '치부하다'
of seeds / — they write it off instinct, / not intelligence. //
만약 동물이 우리를 이길 수 있다면 / 인지적인 과업에서 / 특정 종의 새들이 기억할 수 있는
방식처럼 / 수천 개의 씨앗의 정확한 위치를 / 그들은 그것을 본능으로 치부한다 / 지능이
아니라 //
                                                선행사를 포함하는 관계대명사
This and so many more tricks of language / are what de Waal

has termed / "linguistic castration." //
이것과 더 많은 언어적 수법은 / de Waal이 명명한 것이다 / '언어적 거세'라고 //
                                       부사적 용법(목적)
The way we use our tongues / to disempower animals, / the way

we invent words / to maintain our spot at the top. //
우리가 우리의 언어를 사용하는 방식 / 동물로부터 힘을 빼앗기 위해 / 우리가 단어들을
만드는 방식 / 꼭대기에서 우리의 위치를 유지하기 위해 //
단서 4 우리는 동물로부터 힘을 빼앗고 우리의 높은 위치를 유지하는 방식으로 언어를 사용함

- downplay ⓥ 경시하다   - offender ⓝ 범죄자
- primate ⓝ 영장류   - crow ⓝ 까마귀   - qualitatively ⓐⓓ 질적으로
- humanity ⓝ 인류   - beat ⓥ 이기다   - cognitive ⓐ 인지적인
- precise ⓐ 정확한   - instinct ⓝ 본능   - intelligence ⓝ 지능
- linguistic ⓐ 언어(학)의   - castration ⓝ 거세
- overestimate ⓥ 과대평가하다   - misconception ⓝ 오해

Emory 대학의 유명한 영장류학자 Frans de Waal은 인간은 상상 속 사다리의
꼭대기에서 우리의 위치를 유지하는 방법으로 우리와 다른 동물들 사이의
유사성을 경시한다고 말한다. de Waal은 과학자들이 **우리와 다른 동물들
사이에 거리를 두기** 위해 기술적인 언어를 사용하는 최악의 범죄자들 중 일부일
수 있다고 지적한다. 그들은 침팬지의 '키스'를 '입과 입의 접촉'이라고 부르고,
영장류 사이의 '친구'를 '좋아하는 제휴 파트너'라고 부르며, 그들은 까마귀와
침팬지가 도구를 만들 수 있다는 것을 보여주는 증거를 인류를 정의한다고
하는 종류의 도구 제작과는 아무래도 질적으로 다르다고 해석한다. 만약
동물이, 특정 종의 새들이 수천 개의 씨앗의 정확한 위치를 기억할 수 있는
방식처럼, 인지적인 과업에서 우리를 이길 수 있다면, 그들은 그것을 지능이
아니라 본능으로 치부한다. 이것과 더 많은 언어적 수법은 de Waal이 '언어적
거세'라고 명명한 것이다. 우리가 동물로부터 힘을 빼앗기 위해 우리의 언어를
사용하는 방식이며, 우리가 꼭대기에서 우리의 위치를 유지하기 위해 단어들을
만드는 방식이다.

> 다음 빈칸에 들어갈 말로 가장 적절한 것을 고르시오. [3점]
> ① define human instincts 인간의 본능을 정의하기 위해 언어를 사용하는 것 아님
>   인간의 본능을 정의하다
> ② overestimate chimps' intelligence 침팬지는 예시로 제시되었음
>   침팬지의 지능을 과대평가하다
> ③ distance the other animals from us 인간과 동물 사이에 거리를 두기 위해
>   우리와 다른 동물들 사이에 거리를 두다   기술적인 언어를 사용함
> ④ identify animals' negative emotions
>   동물의 부정적 감정을 밝히다   동물의 감정을 밝히기 위해 언어를 사용하는 것이 아님
> ⑤ correct our misconceptions about nature
>   자연에 관한 우리의 오해를 바로잡다   자연에 관한 우리의 오해는 언급되지 않음

| 문제 풀이 순서 | ★★★ [정답률 47%]

1st 먼저 빈칸 문장을 읽고, 빈칸에 들어갈 말을 예측한다.

| 빈칸 문장 | de Waal은 과학자들이 _____ 위해 기술적인 언어를 사용하는 최악의 범죄자들 중 일부일 수 있다고 지적한다. |

→ 과학자들이 '무엇을' 위해 기술적인 언어를 사용하는 범죄자라고 했으므로, **단서**
부정적인 목적으로 언어를 사용한다는 내용이 이어질 것이다. **발상**

2nd 글의 나머지 부분을 확인해서 정답을 찾는다.

- 인간은 상상 속의 높은 위치를 유지하기 위해 동물이 가진 인간과의 유사성을
  경시함 **단서 1**
  예시 **1**: 침팬지의 키스 → 입과 입의 접촉
  예시 **2**: 영장류 사이의 친구 → 좋아하는 제휴 파트너
  예시 **3**: 까마귀와 침팬지의 도구 제작 능력 → 인류의 도구 제작 능력과 질적으로
                                        다름 **단서 2**
- 동물이 인간보다 우세한 경우에는 지능이 아니라 본능으로 치부함 **단서 3**

→ 우리는 동물의 힘을 빼앗고 우리가 그들보다 우세한 위치에 있다는 것을 유지하기
  위한 방법으로 언어를 사용한다는 것이다. **단서 4**
  ▶ 즉, 과학자들은 ③ '우리와 다른 동물들 사이에 거리를 두기' 위해 기술적인
    언어를 사용하는 범죄자일 수 있다.

| 선택지 분석 |
① 인간의 본능을 정의하는 것이 아니라 인간이 동물보다 우세함을 주장하기 위해
   언어를 사용한다는 것이다.
② 침팬지의 지능을 오히려 낮게 평가하기 위해 언어를 사용한다는 것이다.
③ 인간과 동물 사이에 거리를 두기 위해 기술적인 언어를 사용한다고 했다.
④ 동물의 부정적 감정은 언급되지 않았다.
⑤ 자연을 오해하는 것이 아니라 일부러 경시한다고 했다.

M 38 정답 ② *세부 사항 서술의 중요성
          단수 주어   주격 관계대명사
Generalization without specific examples / that humanize
          단수 동사
writing / is boring / to the listener and to the reader. //
구체적인 사례가 없는 일반화는 / 글을 인간미 있게 하는 / 지루하다 / 듣는 사람과 읽는
사람에게 /   핵심문장, **단서 1** 구체적인 사례가 없으면 지루하다고 했음
Who wants to read platitudes / all day? //
누가 상투적인 말을 읽고 싶어 하겠는가 / 온종일 //
Who wants to hear the words / great, greater, best, smartest,

finest, humanitarian, / on and on and on / without specific

examples? //
누가 듣고 싶어 하겠는가 / 위대한, 더 위대한, 최고의, 제일 똑똑한, 가장 훌륭한, 인도주의적인
/ 이런 말들을 계속 / 구체적인 사례가 없이 //
Instead of using these 'nothing words,' / leave them out
                                          병렬 구조
completely / and just describe the particulars. //
이런 '공허한 말들'을 사용하는 대신 / 그것들을 완전히 빼라 / 그리고 세부 사항들만을
서술하라 //
There is nothing worse / than reading a scene in a novel / in
                                      전치사 + 관계대명사
which a main character is described / up front / as heroic or

brave or tragic or funny, /
더 끔찍한 것은 없다 / 소설의 장면을 읽는 것보다 / 주인공이 묘사되는 / 대놓고 / 영웅적이다,
용감하다, 비극적이다, 혹은 웃긴다고 /
while thereafter, / the writer quickly moves on to something

else. //
그런 다음에 / 작가가 다른 것으로 빠르게 넘어가는 //
That's no good, / no good at all. //
그건 좋지 않으며 / 전혀 좋지 않다 //   **단서 2** 세밀하고 마음을 끄는 묘사를 더 많이 사용해야 함
You have to use less one word descriptions / and more detailed,
                                    조건의 부사절 접속사
engaging descriptions / if you want to make something real. //
당신은 한 단어 묘사는 덜 사용해야 한다 / 세밀하고 마음을 끄는 묘사는 더 많이 / 어떤 것을
실감나는 것으로 만들고 싶다면 //

- generalization ⓝ 일반화   - specific ⓐ 구체적인
- humanize ⓥ 인간미 있게 하다   - fine ⓐ 훌륭한
- humanitarian ⓐ 인도주의적인   - describe ⓥ 서술하다
- heroic ⓐ 영웅적인   - brave ⓐ 용감한   - tragic ⓐ 비극적인

- description ⓝ 묘사　・ particular ⓝ 세부 사항
- boredom ⓝ 지루함　・ detailed ⓐ 세밀한
- engaging ⓐ 마음을 끄는, 매력적인

글을 인간미 있게 하는 구체적인 사례가 없는 일반화는 듣는 사람과 읽는 사람에게 지루하다. 누가 상투적인 말을 온종일 읽고 싶어 하겠는가? 구체적인 사례가 없이 위대한, 더 위대한, 최고의, 제일 똑똑한, 가장 훌륭한, 인도주의적인, 이런 말들을 누가 계속해서 끊임없이 듣고 싶어 하겠는가? 이런 '공허한 말들'을 사용하는 대신에, 그것들을 완전히 빼고 **세부 사항들**만을 서술하라. 주인공을 대놓고 영웅적이다, 용감하다, 비극적이다, 혹은 웃긴다고 묘사하고, 그런 다음에 작가가 다른 것으로 빠르게 넘어가는 소설에서의 장면을 읽는 것보다 더 끔찍한 것은 없다. 그건 좋지 않으며, 전혀 좋지 않다. 어떤 것을 실감나는 것으로 만들고 싶다면, 한 단어 묘사는 덜 사용하고, 세밀하고 마음을 끄는 묘사를 더 많이 사용해야 한다.

> **다음 빈칸에 들어갈 말로 가장 적절한 것을 고르시오.**
> ① similarities 유사점을 서술하라는 내용이 아님
> 　유사점들
> ② particulars 구체적인 사례가 있는 세부 사항을 서술하라고 했음
> 　세부 사항들
> ③ fantasies 공허한 말들을 사용하지 말라고 했음
> 　환상들
> ④ boredom 지루함을 서술하라는 내용이 아님
> 　지루함
> ⑤ wisdom 지혜에 대해 서술하라는 내용이 아님
> 　지혜

왜 정답? ✿✿✿ [정답률 60%]

예시를 통해 결국 말하고자 하는 바를 파악하기! 꿀팁

세부 사항들이 없는 일반화는 지루함을 줄 뿐이라는 내용의 글로, 예시를 들어 이러한 설명을 뒷받침하고 있다. 빈칸 앞부분에 구체적 사례가 없는 단어들을 쭉 나열하면서, 이런 공허한 단어들을 다 빼고 세부 사항들을 서술하라는 주장을 하고 있다.
이어지는 부분에서도 어떤 것을 실감나는 것으로 만들고 싶다면 한 단어 묘사 대신에 세밀하고 마음을 끄는 묘사를 더 많이 사용하라고 했다. 따라서 빈칸에 들어갈 말로 가장 적절한 것은 ② '세부 사항들'이다.

왜 오답?

① 이 글은 유사점에 대해 서술하라는 내용이 아니다.
③ 공허한 말들을 사용하지 말라고 한 것으로 만든 함정으로, 환상들에 대해 서술하라는 것이 아니다.
④ 오히려 지루함을 덜기 위해 세부 사항들을 서술하라는 것이다.
⑤ 지혜에 대해 서술하라는 언급은 없다.

M 39 정답 ② *사전 통보인 전보의 필요성

We don't send telegraphs / to communicate / anymore, / but it's a great metaphor / for giving advance notice. //
우리는 전보를 보내지 않는다 / 통신하기 위해 / 더 이상 / 하지만 그것은 훌륭한 비유이다 / 사전 통보를 하는 것에 대한 //
Sometimes, / you must inform those close to you / of upcoming change / by conveying important information / well in advance. //
때때로 / 여러분은 자신에게 가까운 사람들에게 알려야 한다 / 다가오는 변화를 / 중요한 정보를 전달함으로써 / 미리 잘 //
There's a huge difference / between saying, / "From now on, we will do things differently," / which doesn't give people enough time / to understand and accept the change, /
큰 차이가 있다 / 말하는 것과 / "지금부터 우리는 일을 다르게 할 겁니다"라고 / 사람들에게 충분한 시간을 주지 않는 / 그 변화를 이해하고 받아들일 /
and saying something like, / "Starting next month, / we're going to approach things differently." //
~와 같은 어떤 것을 말하는 것 사이에는 / "다음 달부터 / 우리는 일에 다르게 접근할 겁니다" //

Telegraphing empowers people to **adapt**. //
전보를 보내는 것은 사람들이 적응할 수 있도록 해 준다 //
Telegraphing involves the art / of seeing an upcoming event or circumstance / and giving others enough time / to process and accept the change. // 단서 1 전보를 보내는 것은 다른 사람들이 변화를 처리하고 받아들일 충분한 시간을 줌
전보를 보내는 것은 기술을 포함한다 / 다가오는 사건이나 상황을 보는 / 그리고 다른 사람들에게 충분한 시간을 주는 / 그 변화를 처리하고 받아들일 //
Telegraph anything / that will take people out of / what is familiar and comfortable to them. //
무엇이든 전보로 보내라 / 사람들을 ~에서 벗어나게 할 / 그들에게 익숙하고 편안한 것 //
This will allow processing time / for them to accept the circumstances / and make the most of what's happening. //
이것은 처리 시간을 허용해 줄 것이다 / 그들이 그 상황을 받아들이는 / 그리고 일어나고 있는 일을 최대한으로 활용할 수 있는 // 단서 2 전보를 보내는 것은 사람들이 상황을 받아들일 시간을 줌

- telegraph ⓝ 전보　・ metaphor ⓝ 비유, 은유
- advance notice 사전 통보　・ inform A of B A에게 B를 알리다
- upcoming ⓐ 다가오는　・ convey ⓥ 전달하다
- huge ⓐ 큰, 거대한　・ accept ⓥ 수용하다
- empower ⓥ 권한을 부여하다　・ involve ⓥ 포함하다
- circumstance ⓝ 상황　・ process ⓥ 처리하다
- make the most of ~을 최대한으로 활용하다　・ adapt ⓥ 적응하다
- object ⓥ 반대하다　・ compete ⓥ 경쟁하다　・ recover ⓥ 회복하다

우리는 통신하기 위해 더 이상 전보를 보내지 않지만 그것은 사전 통보를 하는 것에 대한 훌륭한 비유이다. 때때로 여러분은 중요한 정보를 미리 잘 전달함으로써 다가오는 변화를 자신에게 가까운 사람들에게 알려야 한다. 사람들에게 그 변화를 이해하고 받아들일 충분한 시간을 주지 않는 "지금부터 우리는 일을 다르게 할 겁니다."라고 말하는 것과 "다음 달부터 우리는 일에 다르게 접근할 겁니다."와 같은 것을 말하는 것 사이에는 큰 차이가 있다. 전보를 보내는 것은 사람들이 **적응할** 수 있도록 해 준다. 전보를 보내는 것은 다가오는 사건이나 상황을 보고 다른 사람들에게 그 변화를 처리하고 받아들일 충분한 시간을 주는 기술을 포함한다. 사람들을 그들에게 익숙하고 편안한 것에서 벗어나게 할 무엇이든 전보로 보내라. 이것은 그들이 그 상황을 받아들이고 일어나고 있는 일을 최대한으로 활용할 수 있는 처리 시간을 허용해 줄 것이다.

> **다음 빈칸에 들어갈 말로 가장 적절한 것을 고르시오.**
> ① unite 연합에 대한 언급은 없음
> 　연합하다
> ② adapt 전보는 사람들이 변화를 처리하고 받아들일 시간을 줌
> 　적응하다
> ③ object 미리 정보를 잘 전달하는 것과 반대하는 것은 관련 없음
> 　반대하다
> ④ compete 경쟁에 대한 내용은 나오지 않음
> 　경쟁하다
> ⑤ recover 잃었던 것에 대한 언급이 없으므로 되찾는 것은 맥락이 어색함
> 　회복하다

왜 정답? ✿✿✿ [정답률 55%]

전보를 보내는 것은 다른 사람들이 다가오는 사건이나 상황에 대한 변화를 처리하고 받아들일 충분한 시간을 준다고 했다. 또한, 전보를 보내는 것은 사람들이 상황을 받아들이고 일을 최대한으로 활용할 수 있는 시간을 준다는 내용이다. 즉, 사람들이 변화를 받아들이도록 해준다는 의미가 되어야 하므로 빈칸에 들어갈 말로 가장 적절한 것은 ② '적응하다'이다.

왜 오답?

① 이 글에 연합과 관련된 내용은 언급되지 않았다.
③ 사람들에게 미리 정보를 알려주어 준비할 시간을 준다는 내용이기 때문에 반대하는 것과는 관련이 없다.
④ 전보가 사람들이 경쟁하도록 부추기는 것은 아니다.
⑤ 잃었던 것에 대한 언급이 없기 때문에 회복한다는 말은 빈칸에 들어가기 어색하다.

M 40 정답 ② *신체로부터 비롯되는 감정

Someone else's body language affects our own body, / <u>which</u> 계속적 용법의 주격 관계대명사

then creates an emotional echo / that makes us feel accordingly. //
다른 사람의 몸짓 언어는 우리 자신의 신체에 영향을 미친다 / 그리고 그것은 그 후 감정적인 메아리를 만들어 낸다 / 우리가 그에 따라 느끼도록 하는 // **단서 1** 다른 사람의 몸짓 언어 → 우리의 신체에 영향 → 그에 따른 감정을 느낌

As Louis Armstrong sang, / "When you're smiling, / the whole world smiles with you." //
Louis Armstrong이 노래했듯이 / "당신이 미소 지을 때 / 전 세계가 당신과 함께 미소 짓는다" //

If <u>copying</u> another's smile <u>makes</u> us <u>feel</u> happy, / the emotion of 동명사 주어(단수 취급) 단수 동사 makes의 목적격 보어(원형부정사)

the smiler has been transmitted / via our body. //
만약 다른 사람의 미소를 따라 하는 것이 우리를 행복하게 한다면 / 그 미소 짓는 사람의 감정은 전달된 것이다 / 우리의 신체를 통해 // **단서 2** 다른 사람의 감정이 우리의 신체를 통해 전달됨

Strange as it may sound, / this theory states / <u>that</u> **emotions** 목적어절 접속사

arise from our bodies. //
이상하게 들릴지 모르지만 / 이 이론은 말한다 / 감정이 우리 신체에서 발생한다고 //

For example, / our mood can be improved / by simply lifting up the corners of our mouth. // **단서 3** 입꼬리만 올려도 기분이 좋아짐
예를 들어 / 우리의 기분은 좋아질 수 있다 / 단순히 입꼬리를 올림으로써 //

If people are asked / to bite down on a pencil lengthwise, / 분사구문을 이끄는 현재분사 not to let의 목적격 보어(원형부정사)

<u>taking</u> care not to let the pencil <u>touch</u> their lips / (thus forcing the mouth into a smile-like shape), /
만약 사람들이 요구받으면 / 연필을 긴 방향으로 꽉 물라고 / 연필이 그들의 입술에 닿지 않도록 조심하면서 / (그리하여 강제로 입을 미소 짓는 것과 같은 모양이 되도록) /

they judge cartoons funnier / than if they <u>have been asked</u> to 현재완료 수동태

frown. //
그들은 만화를 더 재미있다고 판단한다 / 그들이 인상을 찌푸리라고 요구받았을 때보다 //

The primacy of the body is sometimes summarized / in the phrase / "I must be afraid / because I'm running." //
신체가 우선함은 때때로 요약된다 / 구절로 / "나는 두려운 것이 분명하다 / 왜냐하면 나는 도망치고 있기 때문이다"라는 //

- echo ⓝ 메아리　　• accordingly ⓐⓓ 그에 따라
- transmit ⓥ 전달하다　　• via ⓟⓡⓔⓟ ~을 통하여　　• theory ⓝ 이론
- mood ⓝ 기분, 분위기　　• judge ⓥ 판단하다
- disappear ⓥ 사라지다

다른 사람의 몸짓 언어는 우리 자신의 신체에 영향을 미치며, 그것은 그 후 우리가 그에 따라 느끼도록 하는 감정적인 메아리를 만들어 낸다. Louis Armstrong이 노래했듯이, "당신이 미소 지을 때, 전 세계가 당신과 함께 미소 짓는다." 만약 다른 사람의 미소를 따라 하는 것이 우리를 행복하게 한다면, 그 미소 짓는 사람의 감정은 우리의 신체를 통해 전달된 것이다. 이상하게 들릴지 모르지만, 이 이론은 **감정이 우리 신체에서 발생한다**고 말한다. 예를 들어, 우리의 기분은 단순히 입꼬리를 올리는 것으로 좋아질 수 있다. 만약 사람들이 연필을 긴 방향으로 꽉 물라고 요구받으면, 연필이 그들의 입술에 닿지 않도록 조심하면서 (그리하여 강제로 입을 미소 짓는 것과 같은 모양이 되도록), 그들은 인상을 찌푸리라고 요구받았을 때보다 만화를 더 재미있다고 판단한다. 신체가 우선함은 "나는 두려운 것이 분명하다, 왜냐하면 나는 도망치고 있기 때문이다."라는 구절로 때때로 요약된다.

다음 빈칸에 들어갈 말로 가장 적절한 것을 고르시오. [3점]
① language guides our actions
언어가 우리의 행동을 안내한다　　언어가 아니라 신체가 우리의 감정에 영향을 미친다고 했음
② emotions arise from our bodies
감정은 우리 신체에서 발생한다　　억지로 입꼬리를 올려도 기분이 좋아질 수 있음
③ body language hides our feelings
몸짓 언어는 우리의 감정을 숨긴다　　몸짓 언어는 감정을 이끈다고 볼 수 있음
④ what others say affects our mood
다른 사람의 말은 우리 기분에 영향을 미친다　　다른 사람의 말이 아니라 몸짓 언어가 영향을 미치는 것임
⑤ negative emotions easily disappear
부정적인 감정들은 쉽게 사라진다　　부정적인 감정이 쉽게 사라지는지는 알 수 없음

왜 정답 ? ✹✹❀ [정답률 61%]

빈칸 문장	이상하게 들릴지 모르지만, 이 이론은 ＿＿＿＿＿＿＿＿＿＿고 말한다.
빈칸 문장 뒤 예시	예를 들어(For example), 우리의 기분은 단순히 입꼬리를 올리는 것으로 좋아질 수 있다. **단서 3**

➡ 빈칸 문장: 어떤 이론이 등장했고, 그 이론의 내용을 파악해야 한다.
➡ 빈칸 문장 뒤 예시: 진짜 웃지 않고 단순히 입꼬리만 올려도 기분이 좋아질 수 있다.

빈칸 문장 앞 예시	만약 다른 사람의 미소를 따라 하는 것이 우리를 행복하게 한다면, 그 미소 짓는 사람의 감정은 우리의 신체를 통해 전달된 것이다. **단서 2**

➡ 신체 변화(미소 짓는 것)가 감정(행복함)을 발생시킨 것
▶ 따라서 빈칸에는 ② '감정은 우리 신체에서 발생한다'가 적절하다.

왜 오답 ?

① 신체가 감정에 영향을 끼친다는 내용의 글로, 언어가 우리 행동에 미치는 영향을 설명한 글이 아니다.
③ 다른 사람의 몸짓 언어를 따라 함으로써 그 사람의 감정을 전달받았다고 했으므로 글과 반대되는 내용이다. ◀ **주의**
④ 우리의 기분에 영향을 미치는 요인으로 다른 사람의 말이 아니라 몸짓 언어를 따라하는 것을 들었다.
⑤ 미소 짓는 것을 통해 부정적인 감정을 없앨 수 있다는 내용이 아니다.

M 41 정답 ① ✪ 2등급 대비 [정답률 48%]

*인간의 욕망

In a culture / <u>where</u> there is a belief / <u>that</u> you can have anything 관계부사 동격의 that

<u>you truly want</u>, / there is no problem in choosing. // 앞에 목적격 관계대명사 생략
문화에서 / 믿음이 있는 / 당신이 진정으로 원하는 것은 무엇이든지 가질 수 있다는 / 선택은 문제가 안 된다 //

Many cultures, / however, / do not maintain this belief. //
많은 문화들은 / 그러나 / 이러한 믿음을 유지하지 못한다 //

In fact, / many people do not believe / <u>that</u> life is about getting 목적어절 접속사

what you want. // **단서 1** 많은 사람들이 삶에서 자신이 원하는 것을 얻을 수 있다고 믿지 않음
사실 / 많은 사람들은 믿지 않는다 / 삶이란 당신이 원하는 것을 얻는 것이라고 //

Life is about doing / what you are *supposed* to do. //
인생은 하는 것이다 / 당신이 '해야 할' 것을 //

<u>The reason</u> / they have trouble making choices / <u>is</u> they believe / 핵심 주어 동사

<u>that</u> what they may want is not related / to what they are 목적어절 접속사

supposed to do. // **단서 2** 자신이 원하는 것과 해야 할 일이 관련 없다고 믿기 때문에 선택하기 어려운 것이라고 했음
이유는 / 그들이 선택을 하는 데 있어 어려움을 겪는 / 그들이 믿기 때문이다 / 그들이 원하는 것이 관련이 없다고 / 그들이 해야 할 일과 //

<u>The weight</u> of outside considerations / <u>is</u> greater than their 핵심 주어 동사

desires. //
외적으로 고려할 문제의 비중이 / 그들의 욕망보다 더 크다 //

When this is an issue / in a group, / we discuss / what makes for good decisions. //
이것이 논의 대상이 될 때 / 어떤 집단에서 / 우리는 의논을 한다 / 좋은 결정을 내리려고 // 조건의 부사절 접속사

<u>If</u> a person can be unburdened / from their cares and duties / and, just for a moment, / consider <u>what</u> appeals to them, / they get the chance to sort out / what is important to them. // ~것
만약 어떤 사람이 벗어나서 / 걱정과 의무로부터 / 그리고 단지 잠시 동안 / 그들에게 호소하는 것이 무엇인지를 생각해 본다면 / 그들은 가려낼 기회를 얻게 될 것이다 / 자신에게 무엇이 중요한지를 //

Then / they can consider and negotiate / with their external pressures. //
그러면 / 그들은 고려하고 협상할 수 있다 / 외적인 부담에 대해 //

- maintain ⓥ 유지하다 ・be supposed to ~하기로 되어 있다
- be related to ~와 관계가 있다 ・weight ⓝ 비중
- consideration ⓝ 고려사항 ・unburden ⓥ 벗어나게 하다
- sort out ~을 가려내다 ・negotiate ⓥ 협상하다

당신이 진정으로 원하는 것은 무엇이든지 가질 수 있다고 믿는 문화에서는 선택은 문제가 안 된다. 그러나 많은 문화들은 이러한 믿음을 유지하지 못한다. 사실, 많은 사람들은 삶이란 당신이 원하는 것을 얻는 것이라고 믿지 않는다. 인생은 당신이 '해야 할' 것을 하는 것이다. 그들이 선택을 하는 데 있어 어려움을 겪는 이유는 그들이 원하는 것이 그들이 해야 할 일과 관련이 없다고 믿기 때문이다. 외적으로 고려할 문제의 비중이 그들의 **욕망**보다 더 크다. 이것이 어떤 집단에서 논의 대상이 될 때, 우리는 좋은 결정을 내리려고 의논을 한다. 만약 어떤 사람이 걱정과 의무로부터 벗어나 그들에게 호소하는 것이 무엇인지를 잠시 동안 생각해 본다면, 그들은 자신에게 무엇이 중요한지를 가려낼 기회를 얻게 될 것이다. 그리고 나서 그들은 외적인 부담에 대해 고려하고 협상할 수 있다.

다음 빈칸에 들어갈 말로 가장 적절한 것을 고르시오.

① desires 개인이 원하는 것(what you want)을 핵심 소재로 해서 사람들이 선택에 어려움을 겪는 욕망 이유에 대해 말하는 내용
② merits 특정한 것의 이점에 대해서는 언급되지 않음 이점
③ abilities 인간의 능력이 아니라 인간이 원하는 것에 대한 글임 능력
④ limitations 한계 또는 제한과 관련된 내용은 언급되지 않음 한계
⑤ worries unburdened from their cares에 나온 cares와 유사한 단어로 만든 오답 걱정

2등급❓ 선택지가 모두 한 단어로 되어있고, 빈칸에 넣었을 때 다 자연스럽게 해석이 되어서 정답을 고르기 어려운 2등급 대비 문제이다. '인생은 해야 할 것을 하는 것'이 무엇을 의미하는지 파악하여 빈칸에 들어갈 말을 찾아야 한다.

| 문제 풀이 순서 |

1st 먼저 빈칸이 포함된 문장을 읽고, 빈칸에 들어갈 말에 대한 단서를 얻는다.

빈칸 문장	The weight of outside considerations is greater than their _____. 외적으로 고려할 문제의 비중이 그들의 _____보다 더 크다.

➡ 빈칸 문장은 '무엇'보다 외적으로 고려할 문제가 더 중요하다는 내용이므로 이것을 생각하며 나머지 글을 읽는다.

2nd **1st** 에서 찾은 단서를 염두에 두고, 빈칸 문장의 앞부분부터 확인한다.

글의 앞부분	사실, 많은 사람들은 삶이란 당신이 원하는 것을 얻는 것이라고 믿지 않는다. 인생은 당신이 '해야 할' 것을 하는 것이다. 단서1
빈칸 문장 앞	그들이 선택을 하는 데 있어 어려움을 겪는 이유는 그들이 원하는 것이 그들이 해야 할 일과 관련이 없다고 믿기 때문이다. 단서2

➡ 사람들은 인생이 원하는 것을 얻는 것이 아니라 '해야 할' 것을 하는 것이라고 믿는다고 했다. 그래서 이 해야 할 일과 원하는 것이 상관없다고 생각해서 선택에 어려움을 겪는다는 것이다.
▶ 빈칸 문장은 〈외적으로 고려할 문제의 비중이 그들의 ① '욕망'보다 더 크다.〉라는 내용이 되어야 한다.

3rd 글의 내용을 다시 한번 정리하며 정답이 맞는지 확인한다.

➡ 많은 사람들은 삶이 자신들이 원하는 것을 얻는 것이 아니라고 생각하며, 선택하는 데 어려움을 겪는 이유는 자신들이 원하는 것과 해야만 하는 것 사이에 관련이 없다고 믿기 때문이라는 내용이다.
따라서 이를 반영할 수 있는 ① '욕망'이 적절하다.

| 선택지 분석 |

① 사람들이 선택에 어려움을 겪는 이유는 해야 할 일이 개인이 원하는 것(욕망)과 관련이 없다고 생각하기 때문이라는 내용이다.
② 특정한 것의 이점에 대해서는 언급되지 않았다.

---

③ 인간의 능력이 아니라 인간이 원하는 것(욕망)을 소재로 한 글이다.
④ 한계 또는 제한과 관련된 내용은 언급되지 않았다.
⑤ '걱정으로부터 벗어나다(unburdened from their cares)'라는 표현이 언급된 것으로 만든 오답이다.

M 42 정답 ⑤ ─── ⭐ 2등급 대비 [정답률 44%]

＊승리의 긍정적, 부정적 측면

Research has confirmed / that athletes are less likely to participate in unacceptable behavior / than are non-athletes. // (목적어절 접속사 / 비교급 도치)
연구는 확인했다 / 운동선수는 받아들여지지 않는 행동을 덜 할 것이라고 / 선수가 아닌 사람들보다 //
단서1 승리에 집착하면서 바람직한 스포츠 행위가 감소함
However, / moral reasoning and good sporting behavior / seem to decline / as athletes progress to higher competitive levels, / in part / because of the increased emphasis / on winning. // (접속사(~함에 따라서) / because of+명사(구))
그러나 / 도덕적 분별력과 바람직한 스포츠 행위가 / 감소하는 것 같다 / 운동선수가 더 높은 경쟁적 수준까지 올라감에 따라서 / 부분적으로 / 강조가 커지기 때문에 / 승리에 대한 //
Thus / winning can be **a double-edged sword** / in teaching character development. // (in -ing: ~하는 데 있어서, ~할 때)
그래서 / 승리라는 것은 양날의 검이 될 수 있다 / 인성 함양을 가르치는 데 있어서 //
Some athletes / may want to win so much / that they lie, cheat, and break team rules. // 단서2 승리에 대한 집착이 가져오는 부정적 측면 (so ~ that ...: 너무 ~해서 …하다)
어떤 선수는 / 너무나 이기려고 하다 보니 / 그 결과 거짓말하고 속이고 팀 규칙을 위반한다 //
They may develop undesirable character traits / that can enhance their ability to win / in the short term. // (주격 관계대명사)
그들은 바람직하지 못한 인격 특성을 계발할지 모른다 / 이기고자 자신의 능력을 강화할 수 있는 / 단시간에 //
However, / when athletes resist the temptation to win / in a dishonest way, / they can develop positive character traits / that last a lifetime. // 단서3 승리에 집착하지 않을 때 생기는 긍정적인 측면 (형용사적 용법 / 주격 관계대명사)
그러나 / 선수가 이기고자 하는 유혹에 저항할 때 / 부정한 방법으로 / 그들은 긍정적인 인격 특성을 계발할 수 있다 / 일생동안 지속되는 //
Character is a learned behavior, / and a sense of fair play develops / only if coaches plan to teach / those lessons systematically. // (주어 / 동사)
인성이라는 것은 학습되는 행동이다 / 그리고 페어 플레이 정신은 발달한다 / 코치들이 가르치고자 계획할 때만 / 그러한 교훈을 체계적으로 //

- confirm ⓥ 확인하다 ・athlete ⓝ 운동선수
- unacceptable ⓐ 받아들일 수 없는 ・moral ⓐ 도덕적인
- decline ⓥ 감소하다 ・competitive ⓐ 경쟁하는, 경쟁의
- emphasis ⓝ 강조 ・cheat ⓥ 속이다
- undesirable ⓐ 바람직하지 않은 ・enhance ⓥ 강화하다, 향상시키다
- resist ⓥ 저항하다 ・temptation ⓝ 유혹
- systematically ⓐⓓ 체계적으로

운동선수는 선수가 아닌 사람들보다 받아들여지지 않는 행동을 덜 할 것이라고 연구는 확인했다. 그러나 부분적으로 승리에 대한 강조가 커지기 때문에 운동선수가 더 높은 경쟁적 수준까지 올라감에 따라서 도덕적 분별력과 바람직한 스포츠 행위가 감소하는 것 같다. 그래서 승리라는 것은 인성 함양을 가르치는 데 있어서 **양날의 검**이 될 수 있다. 어떤 선수는 너무나 이기려고 하다 보니 그 결과 거짓말하고 속이고 팀 규칙을 위반한다. 그들은 단시간에 이기고자 자신의 능력을 강화할 수 있는 바람직하지 못한 인격 특성을 계발할지 모른다. 그러나 선수가 부정한 방법으로 이기고자 하는 유혹에 저항할 때 그들은 일생동안 지속되는 긍정적인 인격 특성을 계발할 수 있다. 인성이라는 것은 학습되는 행동이며 그러한 교훈을 체계적으로 가르치고자 계획할 때만 페어 플레이 정신은 발달한다.

다음 빈칸에 들어갈 말로 가장 적절한 것을 고르시오

① a piece of cake 스포츠에서 승리가 쉽다는 내용은 아님
식은 죽 먹기
② a one-way street 어느 한 쪽이 일방적이라는 내용은 없음
일방 도로
③ a bird in the hand 수중에 든 새와 관련된 비유적인 내용이 언급되지 않음
수중에 든 새
④ a fish out of water 위험한 상황이라는 내용은 아님
물 밖에 나온 물고기
⑤ a double-edged sword
양날의 검　　스포츠에서 승리와 관련된 부정적 측면과 긍정적 측면 둘 다에 대해 말하는 내용

(왜 2등급?) 선택지에 '식은 죽 먹기', '수중에 든 새', '물 밖에 나온 물고기', '양날의 검'과 같이 속담이나 은유적 표현들이 등장했다. 글의 내용을 정확하게 파악했어도 선택지의 내용을 알지 못하면 오답을 고르기 쉬운 2등급 대비 문제이다.

| 문제 풀이 순서 |

1st 먼저 빈칸이 포함된 문장을 읽고, 연결어를 확인한다.

| 빈칸 문장 | [Thus] winning can be _____ in teaching character development.
[그래서] 승리라는 것은 인성 함양을 가르치는 데 있어서 _____이 될 수 있다. |

➡ 빈칸이 포함된 문장이 Thus(그래서)로 시작하므로 앞의 내용에 대한 결과에 해당한다는 것을 알 수 있다. 글의 나머지 부분에서 핵심 소재인 '승리'에 대해 어떤 내용이 나오는지 확인한다.

2nd However로 시작하는 문장에서 글의 흐름이 계속 전환되는 것에 주목한다.

| 빈칸 문장 앞 | [그러나(However)] 부분적으로 승리에 대한 강조가 커지기 때문에 운동선수가 더 높은 경쟁적 수준까지 올라감에 따라서 도덕적 분별력과 바람직한 스포츠 행위가 감소하는 것 같다. [단서 1] |
| 글의 뒷부분 | [그러나(However)] 선수가 부정한 방법으로 이기고자 하는 유혹에 저항할 때 그들은 일생동안 지속되는 긍정적인 인격 특성을 계발할 수 있다. [단서 3] |

➡ 첫 번째 However로 시작하는 문장에서는 운동선수가 승리에 집착하면서 바람직한 스포츠 행위가 감소한다고 했다.
그래서 선수가 승리에 집착하게 되면 거짓말을 하고, 상대방을 속이고, 규칙을 위반하는 등 부정적인 행동을 한다고 했다. [단서 2]
승리의 부정적인 측면에 대해 이야기하던 흐름이 다시 However로 시작하는 문장이 오면서 바뀐다. 부당한 방법으로 승리하려는 유혹에 저항하면 긍정적인 인격 특성을 키울 수 있다고 했다. 즉, 승리와 관련된 부정적 측면과 긍정적 측면 모두에 대해 말하는 내용의 글이다.
▶ 빈칸 문장은 〈그래서 승리라는 것은 인성 함양을 가르치는 데 있어서 ⑤ '양날의 검'이 될 수 있다.〉라는 내용이 되어야 한다.

3rd 글의 내용을 다시 한번 정리하며 정답이 맞는지 확인한다.

➡ 이 글은 스포츠에서 승리가 갖는 부정적인 측면과 긍정적인 측면에 대한 내용이다. 승리에 집착하면 부정적인 행동을 하지만, 이런 유혹에 저항하면 긍정적인 인격 특성을 키울 수 있다는 점을 함께 이야기했다.
따라서 빈칸에 들어갈 말로 가장 적절한 것은 ⑤ '양날의 검'이다.

| 선택지 분석 |

① 어떤 일이 아주 쉽다고 할 때 쓰는 표현으로, 스포츠에서 승리가 쉽다는 내용은 전혀 없다.
② 어느 한 쪽이 일방적이라는 내용과는 아무런 관련이 없는 글이다.
③ 수중에 든 새와 관련된 비유적인 내용이 전혀 언급되지 않았다.
④ 물 밖에 나온 물고기처럼 위급한 상황을 나타내는 내용은 없다.
⑤ 스포츠에서 승리가 갖는 긍정적인 측면과 부정적인 측면 둘 다에 대해 말하는 내용이다.

M 43 정답 ②　　　　　　　⭐ 1등급 대비 [정답률 37%]

＊아기의 통계 계산 능력

Over time, / babies construct expectations / about what sounds they will hear when(부사). //
시간이 지나면서 / 아기는 기대를 형성한다 / 자신이 어떤 소리를 언제 들을지에 대한 //
They hold in memory the sound patterns / that(주격 관계대명사) occur on a regular basis. // **단서 1** 아기들은 규칙적으로 발생하는 소리 패턴을 기억함
그들은 소리 패턴을 기억한다 / 규칙적으로 발생하는 //
They make hypotheses like, / "If I hear *this* sound first, / it probably will be followed / by *that* sound." //
그들은 ~와 같은 가설을 세운다 / '내가 '이' 소리를 먼저 들으면 / 그것에 아마도 따라올 것이다' / '저' 소리가' //
Scientists conclude / that(목적어절을 이끄는 접속사) much of babies' skill / in learning language / is due to(~ 때문에) their **ability to calculate statistics**. //
과학자들은 결론짓는다 / 아기의 기술의 상당 부분이 / 언어를 배우는 / 통계를 계산하는 그들의 능력 때문이라고 //
For babies, / this means / that(목적어절을 이끄는 접속사) they appear to pay close attention to the patterns / that(주격 관계대명사) repeat in language. //
아기에게 있어 / 이것은 의미한다 / 그들이 패턴에 세심한 주의를 기울이는 것처럼 보인다는 것을 / 언어에서 반복되는 // **단서 2** 아기는 언어에서 반복되는 패턴에 집중함
They remember, / in a systematic way, / how often sounds occur, / in what order, / with what intervals, / and with what changes of pitch. // **단서 3** 아기들은 소리의 여러 가지 패턴을 체계적인 방식으로 기억함
그들은 기억한다 / 체계적인 방식으로 / 소리가 얼마나 자주 발생하는지를 / 어떤 순서로 / 어떤 간격으로 / 그리고 어떤 음조의 변화를 가지고 //
This memory store allows them / to track, / within the neural circuits of their brains, / the frequency of sound patterns /
이 기억 저장소는 그들에게 허락한다 / 추적하도록 / 자신의 뇌의 신경 회로 내에서 / 소리 패턴의 빈도를 /
and to use(병렬 구조) this knowledge / to make predictions / about the meaning in patterns of sounds. //
그리고 이 지식을 사용하도록 (해 준다) / 예측을 하기 위해 / 소리 패턴의 의미에 대한 //

- construct ⓥ 구성하다　　• expectation ⓝ 기대
- hypothesis ⓝ 가설(*pl.* hypotheses)　　• calculate ⓥ 계산하다
- statistics ⓝ 통계　　• systematic ⓐ 체계적인　　• interval ⓝ 간격
- pitch ⓝ 음조　　• track ⓥ 추적하다　　• neural circuit 신경 회로
- frequency ⓝ 빈도　　• prediction ⓝ 예측　　• preference ⓝ 선호
- imitate ⓥ 모방하다　　• caregiver ⓝ (아이 등을) 돌보는 사람

시간이 지나면서 아기는 자신이 어떤 소리를 언제 들을지에 대한 기대를 형성한다. 그들은 규칙적으로 발생하는 소리 패턴을 기억한다. 그들은 '내가 '이' 소리를 먼저 들으면 그것에 아마도 '저' 소리가 따라올 것이다'와 같은 가설을 세운다. 과학자들은 언어를 배우는 아기의 기술의 상당 **부분이 통계를 계산하는** 그들의 **능력** 때문이라고 결론짓는다. 아기에게 있어 이것은 그들이 언어에서 반복되는 패턴에 세심한 주의를 기울이는 것처럼 보인다는 것을 의미한다. 그들은 소리가 얼마나 자주, 어떤 순서로, 어떤 간격으로 그리고 어떤 음조의 변화를 가지고 발생하는지를 체계적인 방식으로 기억한다. 이 기억 저장소는 그들이 자신의 뇌의 신경 회로 내에서 소리 패턴의 빈도를 추적하고, 소리 패턴의 의미에 대한 예측을 하기 위해 이 지식을 사용하도록 해 준다.

다음 빈칸에 들어갈 말로 가장 적절한 것을 고르시오. [3점]

① lack of social pressures 사회적인 압력에 대해서는 언급되지 않음
사회적인 압력의 부족
② ability to calculate statistics 소리의 패턴에 집중하고 체계적으로 예측한다고 했음
통계를 계산하는 능력
③ desire to interact with others 다른 사람과의 상호 작용에 대한 내용은 없음
다른 사람과 상호 작용하려는 욕구
④ preference for simpler sounds 어떤 소리를 더 좋아하는지에 대한 언급은 없음
더 단순한 소리에 대한 선호
⑤ tendency to imitate caregivers 아기에 대한 내용인 것으로 만든 함정
돌보는 사람을 흉내 내는 경향

왜 1등급? 빈칸이 포함된 문장 앞뒤에 등장한 아기가 소리 패턴에 대해 반응하는 방식과 언어를 배우는 방식을 어떻게 연결시키는지 이해하는 것이 정답을 골라내는 핵심이다.

| 문제 풀이 순서 |

1st 빈칸이 포함된 문장을 읽고, 빈칸에 들어갈 말에 대한 단서를 얻는다.

빈칸 문장	Scientists conclude that much of babies' skill in learning language is due to their _____. 과학자들은 언어를 배우는 아기의 기술의 상당 부분이 그들의 _____ 때문이라고 결론짓는다.

➡ due to(~ 때문에)가 있으므로 과학자들이 결론지은 언어를 배우는 아기의 기술의 원인이 '무엇'인지 찾아야 함을 알 수 있다.

2nd 글의 내용을 종합해서 빈칸에 들어갈 적절한 말을 찾는다.

- 아기에게 있어 이것은 그들이 언어에서 반복되는 패턴에 세심한 주의를 기울이는 것처럼 보인다는 것을 의미한다. **단서 2**
- 그들은 소리가 얼마나 자주, 어떤 순서로, 어떤 간격으로 그리고 어떤 음조의 변화를 가지고 발생하는지를 체계적인 방식으로 기억한다. **단서 3**

➡ 아기들은 규칙적으로 발생하는 소리의 패턴을 체계적인 방식으로 기억한다고 했다. 즉, 소리 패턴의 빈도와 의미에 대한 예측을 함으로써 언어를 배우게 된다는 내용의 글이므로 빈칸에는 '패턴'과 같은 맥락의 내용이 올 것이다.

▶ 빈칸 문장은 〈언어를 배우는 아기의 기술의 상당 부분이 ② '통계를 계산하는 능력' 때문이다.〉라는 내용이 되어야 한다.

3rd 글의 내용을 다시 한번 정리하며 정답이 맞는지 확인한다.

➡ 아기들이 체계적으로 소리의 패턴에 대한 예측을 한다고 말하는 내용의 글이다. 이런 내용을 반영할 수 있는 ② '통계를 계산하는 능력'이 문맥에 맞는 표현이다.

| 선택지 분석 |

① 아기가 언어를 배우는 과정에서 소리를 체계적으로 분석한다는 내용으로, 사회적 압력에 대해서는 전혀 언급되지 않았다.
② 아기들은 규칙적으로 발생하는 소리 패턴을 기억하고 가설을 세운 뒤, 언어에서 반복되는 패턴에 세심한 주의를 기울인다고 했다.
③ 들리는 소리의 패턴에 집중한다는 언급이 있을 뿐 다른 사람과의 상호 작용에 대한 것은 나오지 않았다.
④ 아기가 단순한 소리와 복잡한 소리 중 어떤 소리를 더 좋아하는지에 대해서는 언급되지 않았다.
⑤ 아기에 대한 내용이지만 아기를 돌보는 사람에 대한 내용이나 흉내 내는 것에 대해서는 나오지 않았다.

M 44 정답 ① *진화의 원리

In Lewis Carroll's *Through the Looking-Glass*, / the Red Queen takes Alice / on a race through the countryside. //
Lewis Carroll의 〈Through the Looking-Glass〉에서 / 붉은 여왕은 Alice를 데리고 간다 / 시골을 통과하는 한 경주에 //

They run and they run, / but then Alice discovers / that they're still under the same tree / that they started from. // (목적어절 접속사 / 목적격 관계대명사)
그들은 달리고 또 달리지만 / 그러다가 Alice는 발견한다 / 그들이 똑같은 나무 아래에 여전히 있음을 / 자신들이 출발했던 //
단서 1 최선을 다해서 뛰어야 현재의 자리를 유지할 수 있음

The Red Queen explains to Alice: / "*here*, you see, / it takes all the running you can do, / to keep in the same place." //
붉은 여왕은 Alice에게 설명한다 / "'여기서는' 보다시피 / 네가 할 수 있는 모든 뜀박질을 해야 한단 / 같은 장소에 머물러 있으려면"이라고 //

Biologists sometimes use this Red Queen Effect / to explain an evolutionary principle. // (부사적 용법(목적))
생물학자들은 때때로 이 '붉은 여왕 효과'를 사용한다 / 진화 원리를 설명하기 위해 //

If foxes evolve to run faster / so they can catch more rabbits, / (부사절 접속사(목적)) then only the fastest rabbits will live long enough / to make a new generation of bunnies / that run even faster / (주격 관계대명사)
만약 여우가 더 빨리 달리도록 진화한다면 / 더 많은 토끼를 잡기 위해 / 그러면 오직 가장 빠른 토끼만이 충분히 오래 산다 / 새로운 세대의 토끼를 낳게 되도록 / 훨씬 더 빨리 달리는 /

— in which case, / of course, / only the fastest foxes will catch enough rabbits / to thrive and pass on their genes. //
이 경우 / 물론 / 가장 빠른 여우만이 충분히 토끼를 잡을 것이다 / 번성하여 자신들의 유전자를 물려주도록 //
단서 2 토끼와 여우가 생존을 위해 함께 진화함

Even though they might run, / the two species just stay in place. // (부사절 접속사(양보))
그것들이 달린다 해도 / 그 두 종은 제자리에 머무를 뿐이다 //

- countryside ⓝ 시골
- biologist ⓝ 생물학자
- evolutionary ⓐ 진화의
- principle ⓝ 원리
- evolve ⓥ 진화하다
- generation ⓝ 세대
- bunny ⓝ 토끼
- pass on ~을 물려주다
- gene ⓝ 유전자
- run into ~와 마주치다
- adapt ⓥ 적응하다

Lewis Carroll의 〈Through the Looking-Glass〉에서 붉은 여왕은 Alice를 시골을 통과하는 한 경주에 데리고 간다. 그들은 달리고 또 달리지만, 그러다가 Alice는 자신들이 출발했던 나무 아래에 여전히 있음을 발견한다. 붉은 여왕은 Alice에게 "'여기서는' 보다시피 같은 장소에 머물러 있으려면 네가 할 수 있는 모든 뜀박질을 해야 한다."라고 설명한다. 생물학자들은 때때로 이 '붉은 여왕 효과'를 사용해 진화 원리를 설명한다. 만약 여우가 더 많은 토끼를 잡기 위해 더 빨리 달리도록 진화한다면, 오직 가장 빠른 토끼만이 충분히 오래 살아 훨씬 더 빨리 달리는 새로운 세대의 토끼를 낳을 텐데, 물론 이 경우 가장 빠른 여우만이 충분한 토끼를 잡아 번성하여 자신들의 유전자를 물려줄 것이다. 그 두 종이 달린다 해도 그것들은 **제자리에 머무를 뿐이다.**

다음 빈칸에 들어갈 말로 가장 적절한 것을 고르시오. [3점]

① just stay in place 여우와 토끼가 함께 진화하므로 제자리에 머무는 것처럼 보임
   제자리에 머무를 뿐이다
② end up walking slowly 더 빨리 달리도록 진화한다고 했음
   결국 천천히 걷게 된다
③ never run into each other 양쪽 모두 달린다는 것이 부딪치지 않는다는 것을 말하기 위함이 아님
   결코 서로 마주치지 않는다
④ won't be able to adapt to changes
   변화에 적응할 수 없을 것이다 오히려 변화에 적응해야 한다는 내용임
⑤ cannot run faster than their parents 이전 세대보다 빨리 달리도록 진화한다고 함
   그것들의 부모보다 빨리 달릴 수 없다

왜 정답? ★★★ [정답률 51%]

빈칸 문장 앞	만약 여우가 더 많은 토끼를 잡기 위해 더 빨리 달리도록 진화한다면, 오직 가장 빠른 토끼만이 충분히 오래 살아 훨씬 더 빨리 달리는 새로운 세대의 토끼를 낳을 텐데, 물론 이 경우 가장 빠른 여우만이 충분한 토끼를 잡아 번성하여 자신들의 유전자를 물려줄 것이다. **단서 2**
빈칸 문장	그 두 종이 달린다 해도 그것들은 _____.

➡ 빈칸 문장: 더 빨리 달리도록 함께 진화한 여우와 토끼는 달린다고 해도 '어떠할' 것이다.

글의 앞부분	• 그들은 달리고 또 달리지만, 그러다가 Alice는 자신들이 출발했던 나무 아래에 여전히 있음을 발견한다. • 붉은 여왕은 Alice에게 "'여기서는' 보다시피 같은 장소에 머물러 있으려면 네가 할 수 있는 모든 뜀박질을 해야 한다."라고 설명한다. **단서 1**

➡ 글의 앞부분: 계속 달려도 여전히 출발점에 있음 = 같은 장소에라도 있으려면 최선을 다해 달려야 함

▶ 여우와 토끼가 이전 세대에 비해 더 빨라졌다고 해도 더 진화한 상대와 달리는 것이기 때문에 그들은 ① '제자리에 머무를 뿐이다'.

② 천천히 걷는 것이 아니라 최선을 다해서 뛰어야 한다고 했다.

③ 서로 마주치지 않기 위해 달리는 것이 아니다.

④ 생존을 위해서는 오히려 변화에 적응하여 진화해야 한다고 했다. ◀주의

⑤ 부모 세대보다 더 향상된 방향으로 진화한다고 했다.

M 45 정답 ① *식물의 생존 기제

Plants can communicate, / **although** not in the same way we
= communicate
do. // 단서1 식물은 의사표현을 할 수 있음
식물은 의사소통을 할 수 있다 / 우리가 하는 방식과 같지는 않을지라도 //

Some express their discontent / through scents. //
몇몇은 자신들의 불만을 표현한다 / 냄새를 통해 // 단서2 몇몇 식물은 냄새로 불만을 표현함
지시형용사   관계대명사절 (smell 수식)
You know **that** smell / **that hangs in the air** / after you've mowed

the lawn? //
여러분은 냄새를 알고 있는가 / 공기 중에 감도는 / 잔디를 깎고 난 후 //
S로 시작하지만 [es]로 발음
Yeah, / that's actually an **SOS**. //
그렇다 / 그것은 사실 일종의 SOS 신호다 //

Some plants use sound. // 단서3 어떤 식물은 소리로 의사소통할 수 있음
어떤 식물은 소리를 사용한다 //

Yes, / sound, / though at a frequency that we can't hear. //
그렇다 / 소리다 / 우리는 들을 수 없는 주파수에 있지만 //
부사적 용법 (목적)
Researchers experimented with plants and microphones / **to see**
= researchers
/ if **they** could record any trouble calls. //
연구자는 식물과 마이크를 사용해 실험했다 / 알아보기 위해 / 식물이 곤경에 처했음을 알리는
소리를 녹음할 수 있는지 //

They found / that plants produce a high-frequency clicking
부사절에서 「주어+be동사」 생략
noise / **when stressed** / and can make different sounds / for

different stressors. //
그들은 사실을 알아냈다 / 식물이 고주파수의 딸깍거리는 소리를 내며 / 스트레스를 받을 때 /
다른 소리를 낼 수 있다는 / 스트레스 요인에 따라 //
앞에 목적격 관계대명사가 생략됨
The sound **a plant makes** / when it's not getting watered / differs
가주어   worth -ing : ~할 가치가 있는
from **the one** it'll make / when a leaf is cut. //
식물이 내는 소리는 / 물을 공급받지 못하고 있을 때 / 낼 소리와 다르다 / 잎이 잘릴 때 //

However, / **it's worth** noting / **that** experts don't think / plants
                                            진주어절 접속사
are crying out in pain. //
하지만 / 주목할 가치가 있다 / 전문가가 보지는 않는다는 것에 / 식물이 고통으로 울부짖고
있다고 //

It's more likely / that these reactions are knee-jerk survival

actions. // 단서4 식물은 살아남기 위해 반응하는 경우가 있음
가능성이 더 크다 / 이러한 반응은 살아남기 위한 자동적인 행위일 //

Plants are living organisms, / and their main objective is to

survive. //
식물은 살아 있는 유기체이며 / 그들의 주요 목표는 살아남는 것이다 //

Scents and sounds are their tools / for **defending against things**
that might harm them. //
냄새와 소리는 그들의 도구이다 / 자신들에게 해를 끼칠 수도 있는 것들로부터 지키기 위한 //

• communicate ⓥ 의사소통을 하다   • discontent ⓝ 불만
• frequency ⓝ 주파수   • researcher ⓝ 연구자
• experiment ⓥ 실험하다   • survival ⓐ 살아남기 위한
• organism ⓝ 유기체   • objective ⓝ 목표
• defend ⓥ 지키다, 방어하다   • neighboring ⓐ 인접한, 이웃한
• dissatisfaction ⓝ 불만   • nutrient ⓝ 영양소
• genetic ⓐ 유전적인

우리가 하는 방식과 같지는 않을지라도, 식물은 의사소통을 할 수 있다. 몇몇은 냄새를 통해 자신들의 불만을 표현한다. 여러분은 잔디를 깎고 난 후 공기 중에 감도는 냄새를 알고 있는가? 그렇다, 그것은 사실 일종의 SOS 신호다. 어떤 식물은 소리를 사용한다. 그렇다, 우리는 들을 수 없는 주파수에 있지만, 소리다. 연구자는 식물이 곤경에 처했음을 알리는 소리를 녹음할 수 있는지 알아보기 위해 식물과 마이크를 사용해 실험했다. 그들은 식물이 스트레스를 받을 때 고주파수의 딸깍거리는 소리를 내며, 스트레스 요인에 따라 다른 소리를 낼 수 있다는 사실을 알아냈다. 식물이 물을 공급받지 못하고 있을 때 내는 소리와 잎이 잘릴 때 낼 소리가 다르다. 하지만, 전문가가 식물이 고통으로 울부짖고 있다고 보지는 않는다는 것에 주목할 가치가 있다. 이러한 반응은 살아남기 위한 자동적인 행위일 가능성이 더 크다. 식물은 살아 있는 유기체이며, 그들의 주요 목표는 살아남는 것이다. 냄새와 소리는 **자신들에게 해를 끼칠 수도 있는 것들로부터 지키기** 위한 그들의 도구이다.

다음 빈칸에 들어갈 말로 가장 적절한 것을 고르시오. [3점]

① defending against things that might harm them
자신들에게 해를 끼칠 수도 있는 것들로부터 지키기   위험을 받으면 방어를 위해 반응함
② showing their support for neighboring plants
인접한 식물들을 지지함을 보여주기   인접한 식물들은 언급되지 않았음
③ hiding their pains and dissatisfaction
고통과 불만을 숨기기   고통과 불만을 숨기지 않고 표출하며 방어함
④ sharing nutrients with other plants 영양소를 나누는 것은 언급되지 않았음
다른 식물들과 영양소를 나누기
⑤ changing their genetic structure 유전 구조 변화는 언급되지 않았음
유전 구조를 변화시키기

왜 정답 ? ★★✿ [정답률 68%]

빈칸 문장의 Scents and sounds는 식물이 살아남으려 할 때 보이는 반응이다. 식물들은 이러한 반응으로 자신이 곤경에 처했음을 알리고 의사소통한다. 따라서 냄새와 소리는 ① '자신들에게 해를 끼칠 수도 있는 것들로부터 지키기' 위한 식물들의 도구이다.

왜 오답 ?

② 식물이 위험에 처했을 때 인접한 식물들을 도와준다는 내용은 언급되지 않았다.

③ 식물들이 냄새와 소리를 통해 고통과 불만을 표현한다는 내용이지, 이를 숨긴다는 내용이 아니다.

④ 다른 식물들과 영양소를 나눈다는 것은 언급되지 않았다.

⑤ 유전 구조를 변화시키는 것은 언급되지 않았다.

구문 서술형

정답 If plants use sound, they can make trouble calls.

→ '~한다면 ~할 것이다'를 나타내므로 가정법 현재 문장을 써야 한다. 따라서
「If + 주어 + 동사의 현재형 ~, 주어 + 조동사/동사의 현재형…」 순서로 쓰고, if
절의 동사 use와 주절의 조동사 can 모두 현재시제로 쓴다.

M 46 정답 ① *새로운 제품과 서비스의 초기 가격을 낮출 필요성

병렬 구조 (문장의 동사)
Most entrepreneurs / **put** in tremendous amounts of time and
                          동명사 (전치사 in의 목적어)
effort / in **creating** and **launching** new products and services /
                    단서1 새로운 제품과 서비스의 가격을 너무 비싸게 책정하는 실수를 함
and then **make** the mistake of overpricing them. //
대부분의 기업가들은 / 엄청난 시간과 노력을 들이며 / 새로운 제품과 서비스를 만들고 출시하
는 데 / 그런 다음 그것들의 가격을 너무 비싸게 책정하는 실수를 저지른다 //
                                          앞에 목적격 관계대명사가 생략됨
They have created / something **they care deeply about**, / it's

theirs, /
그들은 만들었고 / 자신이 매우 소중히 여기는 무언가를 / 그것은 그들의 것이며 /

and this powerful sense of ownership / distorts their perception
                                  causes의 목적어와 목적격 보어 (to부정사)
of value / which causes **them to overprice** their products. //
이 강한 소유감은 / 가치에 대한 그들의 인식을 왜곡시켜 / 그들의 제품 가격을 너무 높게 책
정하게 만든다 //

While many of them are quick to realize / that their initial prices

are too high, /
그들 중에 많은 이들은 빠르게 깨닫기는 하지만 / 그들의 초기 가격이 너무 높다는 것을 /

not all these people / are happy or willing to drop their prices /
to make their products more attractive. //
make의 목적어와 목적격 보어 (형용사의 비교급)
이 모든 사람들이 / 가격을 낮추는 것을 좋아하거나 내켜하지는 않는다 / 그들의 제품을 더 매
력적으로 만들기 위해 //
앞의 내용을 가리키는 지시대명사　　　주격 관계대명사 (선행사: a very costly mistake)
And this can be a very costly mistake / that may lead to the
failure / of their new business. // 단서 2 가격을 낮추지 않는 것은 새로운 사업의
실패를 초래할 수도 있음
그리고 이것은 손해가 매우 큰 실수가 될 수 있다 / 실패를 초래할 수 있는 / 그들의 새로운 사
업의 //
　　　단서 3 새로운 제품과 서비스를 출시할 때 충분한 시장 점유를 우선순위에 두어야 함
When you launch a new product or service, / your priority
should be to get sufficient market adoption / as soon as possible /
　　　　　　　　　　　　　　　　　　　　　　　　'가능한 한 빨리'
새로운 제품이나 서비스를 출시할 때 / 당신의 우선순위는 충분한 시장 점유를 확보하는 것이
어야 하며 / 가능한 한 빨리 /
and you should be ready to / **sacrifice your initial prices and**
부사적 용법 (목적)
profits / to achieve this aim. //
당신이 준비가 되어 있어야 한다 / 당신의 초기 가격과 수익을 희생할 / 이 목표를 달성하기 위
해서 //
부사절 접속사 (조건)
Once you have strong sales volumes, / you can increase your
prices / to maximize your profits. //
일단 당신이 높은 판매량을 확보하게 되면 / 당신은 가격을 인상할 수 있다 / 수익을 극대화하
기 위해 //

- launch ⓥ 출시하다　　· overprice ⓥ 과한 가격을 매기다
- distort ⓥ 왜곡하다　　· perception ⓝ 인식　　· initial ⓐ 초기의
- be willing to-v 기꺼이 ~하다　· costly ⓐ 손해가 큰, 비용이 많이 드는
- priority ⓝ 우선순위　　· sufficient ⓐ 충분한　　· volume ⓝ 양
- maximize ⓥ 극대화하다　· sacrifice ⓥ 희생하다
- strategy ⓝ 전략　　· switch ⓥ 전환하다　　· brand-new ⓐ 새로운

대부분의 기업가들은 새로운 제품과 서비스를 만들고 출시하는 데 엄청난 시간
과 노력을 들이며, 그런 다음 그것들의 가격을 너무 비싸게 책정하는 실수를 저
지른다. 그들은 자신이 매우 소중히 여기는 무언가를 만들었고, 그것은 그들의
것이며, 이 강한 소유감은 가치에 대한 그들의 인식을 왜곡시켜 그들의 제품 가
격을 너무 높게 책정하게 만든다. 그들 중 많은 이들은 그들의 초기 가격이
너무 높다는 것을 빠르게 깨닫기는 하지만, 이 모든 사람들이 그들의 제품을 더
매력적으로 만들기 위해 가격을 낮추는 것을 좋아하거나 내켜하지는 않는다. 그
리고 이것은 그들의 새로운 사업의 실패를 초래할 수 있는 손해가 매우 큰 실수
가 될 수 있다. 새로운 제품이나 서비스를 출시할 때, 당신의 우선순위는 가능
한 한 빨리 충분한 시장 점유를 확보하는 것이어야 하며, 당신이 이 목표를 달
성하기 위해서는 **당신의 초기 가격과 수익을 희생할** 준비가 되어 있어야 한다.
일단 당신이 높은 판매량을 확보하게 되면, 당신은 수익을 극대화하기 위해 가
격을 인상할 수 있다.

다음 빈칸에 들어갈 말로 가장 적절한 것을 고르시오.
① sacrifice your initial prices and profits　새로운 제품과 서비스 사업에서
당신의 초기 가격과 수익을 희생할　　　처음부터 가격을 너무 높게 책정하면 실패를 초래할 수 있음
② upgrade your products and service
당신의 제품과 서비스를 개선할　　　제품과 서비스를 개선하는 것은 언급되지 않음
③ maintain the overpricing strategy
가격을 높게 책정하는 전략을 유지할　가격을 너무 비싸게 책정하면 안 된다고 했음
④ switch to a brand-new business
완전히 새로운 사업으로 전환할　　완전히 새로운 사업으로 전환하는 것은 언급되지 않음
⑤ seek out consumer reviews 소비자 평가는 언급되지 않음
소비자 평가를 찾아볼

왜 정답 ? ✱✱✱ [정답률 63%]
┌ • 대부분의 기업가들이 새로운 제품과 서비스의 가격을 너무 비싸게 책정하는 실수
│ 를 함 단서 1
│ • 초기 가격이 비싼 것을 알면서도 가격 인하를 꺼리면 사업의 실패를 초래할 수 있음
│ 　　　　　　　　　　　　　　　　　　　　　　　　　　　　단서 2
└ • 새로운 제품·서비스를 출시할 때 충분한 시장 점유를 우선순위로 두어야 함 단서 3
➡ 대부분의 기업가들이 새로운 제품과 서비스를 출시할 때 초기 가격을 너무 높게 책
　정하고 가격 인하를 꺼리는데, 이는 사업의 실패를 초래할 수도 있으므로 충분한 시
　장 점유를 우선순위에 두어야 한다는 내용이다.
　▶ 따라서 시장 점유를 충분히 달성하기 위해서는 ① '당신의 초기 가격과 수익을 희
　생할' 준비를 하고 가격을 낮춰야 한다.

왜 오답 ?
② 제품과 서비스를 개선하면 충분한 시장 점유를 확보할 수 있다는 내용이 아니다.
③ 초기 가격을 너무 비싸게 책정하면 안 된다고 했으므로 가격을 높게 책정하는 전략
　을 유지해서는 안 된다.
④ 새로운 사업을 시작하는 것은 언급되었으나, 완전히 새로운 사업으로 전환하는 것
　은 언급되지 않았다.
⑤ 소비자 평가는 언급되지 않았다.

구문 서술형

정답 had realized, 깨닫지 못했다

해석 그들이 자신들의 제품의 가격이 너무 높다는 것을 깨달았다면, 그
들은 그것들의 가격을 지나치게 높게 책정하지 않았을 것이다.
→ '만약 ~했다면 ~했을 텐데'를 나타내는 가정법 과거완료 문장이다. 따라서
realize를 과거완료시제인 had realized로 고쳐 써야 한다. 사실과 반대되는
내용을 가정하므로, 사실 그들은 과거에 제품 가격이 너무 높다는 것을 '깨닫지
못했을' 것이다.

M **47** 정답 ⑤ ✱과학자들의 정보 공유

When scientists make an important new discovery / or
experimentally prove some hypothesis, / they do not, in
general, keep that information to themselves /
과학자들은 중요한 새로운 발견할 때 / 또는 실험적으로 어떤 가설을 증명할 때 / 그들은, 일반
적으로, 그 정보를 자기만 가지고 있지 않는다 /
부사절 접속사 (목적)
so that they alone can consider its meaning / and derive
additional theories from it. //
그것의 의미를 혼자서 고려하고 / 그것으로부터 추가적인 이론을 도출할 수 있도록 //
　　　　　　　　= scientists　　　make의 목적어와 목적격 보어 (형용사)
Instead, / they publish their results / and make their data
available for inspection. // 단서 1 과학자들은 결과를 발표하여 데이터가 점검되도록 함
대신에 / 그들은 자신의 결과를 발표하고 / 그들의 데이터가 점검 가능하도록 한다 //
　　　　　가목적어　　to reconsider와 refute의 의미상 주어
This makes it possible / for other scientists to reconsider their
data / and possibly refute their conclusions. //
　　　　　　　　　　　　　　병렬 구조 (진목적어)
이것은 가능하게 한다 / 다른 과학자들이 그들의 데이터를 재고하게 하고 / 어쩌면 그들의 결
론을 반박하는 것을 // 단서 2 다른 과학자들이 발표된 데이터를 재고하고 결론에 반박할 수 있음
　　　　　　　　　　　'하지만'　　　　가목적어
More important, / though, / it makes it possible for other
　　　　　　진목적어(명사적 용법의 to부정사)　부사적 용법 (목적)
scientists / to use that data / to construct new hypotheses and
perform new experiments. // 단서 3 다른 과학자들은 이미 발표된 데이터를 활용할 수
　　　　　　　　　　　　　　　　　　　　　　　　　　있음
더 중요한 것은 / 하지만 / 이것이 다른 과학자들이 가능하도록 한다는 것이다 / 그 데이터를
사용하는 것을 / 새로운 가설들을 세우고 새로운 실험들을 수행하기 위하여 //
　　　　　　　　　　　　　　　명사절 접속사 (주격 보어)
The assumption is / that society as a whole will end up knowing
　　　　　　　　　　　　　　　　　　　　　　'가능한 한 ~하게'
more / if information is spread as widely as possible, / rather
　　　　　　　　　　　동명사의 수동태
than being limited to a few people. //
가정은 ~이다 / 사회 전체가 결국 더 많은 것을 알게 될 것이라는 것 / 만약 정보가 가능한 한
널리 확산되면 / 소수의 사람들에게 제한되기보다 //
In a strict sense, / every scientist **depends on the work of other**
scientists. //
엄밀한 의미에서 / 모든 과학자는 다른 과학자들의 연구에 의존한다 //

- experimentally ⓐⓓ 실험적으로　· hypothesis ⓝ 가설
- in general 일반적으로　　· publish ⓥ 발표하다
- inspection ⓝ 점검　　· construct ⓥ 세우다
- assumption ⓝ 가정　　· end up -ing 결국 ~하게 되다
- sense ⓝ 의미　　· pursue ⓥ 추구하다　　· stick to ~을 고수하다

M

과학자들은 중요한 새로운 발견을 하거나 실험적으로 어떤 가설을 증명할 때, 일반적으로, 그들은 그것의 의미를 혼자서 고려하고 그것으로부터 추가적인 이론을 도출할 수 있도록 그 정보를 자기만 가지고 있지 않는다. 대신에, 그들은 자신의 결과를 발표하고 그들의 데이터가 점검 가능하도록 한다. 이것은 다른 과학자들이 그들의 데이터를 재고하게 하고 어쩌면 그들의 결론을 반박하는 것을 가능하게 한다. 하지만, 더 중요한 것은 이것이 다른 과학자들이 새로운 가설들을 세우고 새로운 실험들을 수행하기 위하여 그 데이터를 사용하는 것을 가능하도록 한다는 것이다. 가정은 만약 정보가 소수의 사람들에게 제한되기보다 가능한 한 널리 확산되면 결국 사회 전체가 더 많은 것을 알게 될 것이라는 것이다. 엄밀한 의미에서, 모든 과학자는 **다른 과학자들의 연구에 의존한다**.

다음 빈칸에 들어갈 말로 가장 적절한 것을 고르시오.

① pursues only new discoveries
오직 새로운 발견만을 추구한다 새로운 발견만을 추구한다는 내용은 언급되지 않음
② sticks to their own research ideas
그들 자신만의 연구 아이디어를 고수한다   과학자들은 이미 발표된 다른 자료를 활용한다고 했음
③ is restricted from using certain data 연구 데이터가 확산되어 다른
특정 데이터를 사용하는 데 제한받는다   과학자도 이를 사용한다는 내용임
④ ignores the data against their theories 발표된 데이터를 다른 과학자들이
그들의 이론에 맞서는 데이터를 무시한다   점검하고 반박하는 내용임
⑤ depends on the work of other scientists 과학자들이 결과를 발표하여
다른 과학자들의 연구에 의존한다   다른 과학자들에게 이를 점검받고, 다른
과학자들도 발표된 새로운 데이터를 활용함

| 문제 풀이 순서 | ★★★ [정답률 54%]

1st 첫 문장과 빈칸이 포함된 문장을 읽고, 빈칸에 들어갈 말에 대한 단서를 얻는다.

| 첫 문장 | When scientists make an important new discovery or experimentally prove some hypothesis, they do not, in general, keep that information to themselves ~. 과학자들은 중요한 새로운 발견을 하거나 실험적으로 어떤 가설을 증명할 때, 일반적으로, 그들은 ~ 그 정보를 자기만 가지고 있지 않는다. |
| 빈칸 문장 | In a strict sense, every scientist _____. 엄밀한 의미에서, 모든 과학자는 _____. |

➡ 과학자들이 새로운 발견을 하거나 어떤 가설을 실험적으로 증명할 때 그 정보를 자기만 가지고 있지 않는다고 했으므로, (단서)
과학자들이 서로 정보를 공유한다는 내용이 빈칸에 들어갈 것이다. (발상)

2nd 글의 내용을 종합해서 빈칸에 들어갈 적절한 말을 찾는다.

· 과학자들은 중요한 발견을 하거나 가설을 증명할 때 결과를 발표하여 데이터가 점검될 수 있도록 함 (단서 1)
· 다른 과학자들이 발표된 데이터를 재고하고 결론을 반박할 수 있음 (단서 2)
· 다른 과학자들은 이미 발표된 데이터를 활용할 수 있음 (단서 3)

➡ 과학자들이 새로운 발견을 하거나 실험적으로 가설을 증명할 때 정보를 혼자만 아는 것이 아니라 공유함으로써 다른 과학자들이 그 데이터를 점검하거나 결론을 반박할 수 있게 하고, 새로운 가설을 세우거나 실험을 수행할 때 그 데이터를 활용할 수 있게 한다는 내용이다.
▶ 그러므로 모든 과학자는 ⑤ '다른 과학자들의 연구에 의존한다'고 볼 수 있다.

| 선택지 분석 |

① 새로운 발견의 결과를 발표하면 다른 과학자들이 이를 점검한다고 했지, 그들이 새로운 발견만을 추구한다는 내용이 아니다.
② 과학자들은 새로운 가설 설정과 실험에 다른 과학자가 발표한 데이터를 활용하므로, 자신만의 연구 아이디어를 고수하지 않는다.
③ 과학자들은 특정 데이터 사용에 제한을 받는 것이 아니라, 데이터를 공유한다.
④ 과학자들이 자신들의 이론에 맞서는 결과와 데이터를 무시하는 것이 아니라, 새로운 결과와 데이터를 점검하고 반박할 수 있다.
⑤ 과학자들은 데이터를 다른 과학자들과 공유하고, 다른 과학자들은 그 데이터를 활용할 수 있다는 내용이다.

구문 서술형

정답 had been, would have ended up

해석 만약 정보가 가능한 한 널리 확산되면(→ 확산되었다면) 결국 사회 전체가 더 많은 것을 알게 될(→ 되었을) 것이다.
→ 가정법 과거완료 문장은 「If + 주어 + had p.p. ~, 주어 + 조동사의 과거형 + have p.p. …」 형태이므로, is를 had been으로, will end up을 would have ended up으로 고쳐 써야 한다.

M 48 정답 ① *적응하며 행복의 기준선으로 돌아오는 인간

명사절 접속사 (주어절을 이끎)
Whether we feel happy or sad, content or discontent, / is not determined / merely by each individual successive moment of life experience /
우리가 행복하거나 슬프거나, 만족스럽거나 불만족스러운 것은 / 결정되지 않는다 / 단지 삶의 경험의 각각의 개별적인 연속적인 순간에 의해 /

— a good thing happens and I'm happy, / a bad thing happens and I'm sad. //
좋은 일이 일어나면 행복하고 / 나쁜 일이 일어나면 슬픈 것처럼 //
부사절 접속사 (대조)
While our experiences affect our mood, / we are not blown in a completely new direction / by each gust of wind. //
우리의 경험은 우리의 기분에 영향을 미치지만 / 우리는 완전히 새로운 방향으로 날아가지 않는다 / 각 돌풍에 의해 //

As humans, we adjust / — to new information and events both good and bad — / and return to our personal default level of well-being. // 단서 1 인간은 새로운 정보와 사건에 적응하고 원래의 기본 행복 수준으로 돌아감
인간으로서 우리는 적응하고 / 좋을 뿐 아니라 나쁘기도 한 새로운 정보와 사건들에 / 우리의 개인적인 기본 행복 수준으로 돌아간다 //
단서 2 기복이 있어도 결국 기준선으로 돌아옴
'높고 낮음, 기복'
There will be **highs and lows**, / but over time, like water seeking its own level, / we are pulled toward our baseline /
기복은 있을 것이지만 / 시간이 지나면서 고유한 수위를 찾는 물처럼 / 우리는 우리의 기준선으로 끌려가는데 /

— back *up* after bad news / and back *down* after good. //
즉, 나쁜 소식 후에는 다시 '올라'오고 / 좋은 소식 후에는 다시 '내려'온다 //
도치 구문 (so + 동사 + 주어)
The euphoria of first love fades, / and **so does the despair of a break-up**. // 단서 3 강렬한 감정은 결국 사라짐
첫사랑의 행복감은 사라지고 / 결별의 절망도 그렇다 //

This tendency is best seen / with little kids and their toy joy: /
이 경향은 가장 잘 보여진다 / 어린 아이들과 그들의 장난감 기쁨에서 /
뒤에 목적어절 접속사가 생략됨
When they get what they've longed for, / **they believe** they will be happy / for the rest of their lives. //
그들은 간절히 원하던 것을 얻을 때 / 행복할 것이라고 믿는다 / 그들의 남은 인생 동안 //

And for the first few minutes / of the rest of their lives, / they
뒤에 반복되는 happy가 생략됨
are. //
그리고 처음 몇 분 동안 / 그들의 남은 인생의 / 그들은 그렇다 //

But then the kids / — like adults — / **adapt**. //
하지만 그리고 나서 아이들은 / 어른들처럼 / 적응한다 //

· content ⓐ 만족하는   · discontent ⓐ 불만족하는
· determined ⓐ 결정되는   · merely ⓐⓓ 단지
· successive ⓐ 연속적인   · affect ⓥ 영향을 미치다
· adjust ⓥ 적응하다   · default ⓝ 기본값
· well-being ⓝ 행복, 안녕   · baseline ⓝ 기준선
· fade ⓥ 사라지다, 희미해지다   · despair ⓝ 절망
· tendency ⓝ 경향   · long for ~을 갈망하다   · adapt ⓥ 적응하다
· regret ⓥ 후회하다   · struggle ⓥ 고군분투하다

우리가 행복하거나 슬프거나, 만족스럽거나 불만족스러운 것은 좋은 일이 일어나면 행복하고, 나쁜 일이 일어나면 슬픈 것처럼 단지 삶의 경험의 각각의 개별적인 연속적인 순간에 의해 결정되지 않는다. 우리의 경험은 우리의 기분에 영향을 미치지만, 우리는 각 돌풍에 의해 완전히 새로운 방향으로 날아가지 않는다. 인간으로서 우리는 좋을 뿐 아니라 나쁘기도 한 새로운 정보와 사건들에 적응하고 우리의 개인적인 기본 행복 수준으로 돌아간다. 기복은 있을 것이지만, 시간이 지나면서 고유한 수위를 찾는 물처럼 우리는 우리의 기준선으로 끌려가는데 즉, 나쁜 소식 후에는 다시 '올라'오고 좋은 소식 후에는 다시 '내려'온다. 첫사랑의 행복감은 사라지고, 결별의 절망도 그렇다. 이 경향은 어린 아이들과 그들의 장난감 기쁨에서 가장 잘 보여진다. 그들은 간절히 원하던 것을 얻을 때, 그들의 남은 인생 동안 행복할 것이라고 믿는다. 그리고 그들의 남은 인생의 처음 몇 분 동안, 그들은 그렇다. 하지만 그리고 나서 어른들처럼 아이들은 **적응한다.**

다음 빈칸에 들어갈 말로 가장 적절한 것을 고르시오.

① adapt 행복을 겪은 후 기준선으로 돌아가는 것은 적응하는 과정임
적응하다
② regret 후회는 언급되지 않았음
후회하다
③ explore 탐험은 언급되지 않았음
탐험하다
④ struggle 기준선으로 자연스럽게 돌아가는 경향에 관한 내용임
고군분투하다
⑤ celebrate 축하는 언급되지 않았음
축하하다

| 문제 풀이 순서 | ★★★ [정답률 53%]

1st 빈칸이 포함된 문장과 그 앞의 예시를 읽고, 빈칸에 들어갈 말에 대한 단서를 얻는다.

예시	This tendency is best seen with little kids and their toy joy: When they get what they've longed for, they believe they will be happy for the rest of their lives. And for the first few minutes of the rest of their lives, they are. 이 경향은 어린 아이들과 그들의 장난감 기쁨에서 가장 잘 보여진다. 그들은 간절히 원하던 것을 얻을 때, 그들의 남은 인생 동안 행복할 것이라고 믿는다. 그리고 그들의 남은 인생의 처음 몇 분 동안, 그들은 그렇다.
빈칸 문장	But then the kids — like adults — _____. 하지만 그리고 나서 어른들처럼 아이들은 _____.

➡ 아이들의 장난감 기쁨을 예로 들며, 아이들이 원하던 장난감을 얻으면 처음에는 행복해도 그 뒤에는 어른들처럼 '무엇'을 한다고 했으므로, (단서) 어른들은 행복 뒤에 '무엇'을 하는지 파악해야 한다. (발상)

2nd 글의 내용을 종합해서 빈칸에 들어갈 적절한 말을 찾는다.
- 인간은 새로운 사건에 적응하고 원래의 기본 행복 수준으로 돌아옴 단서1
- 감정 기복이 있어도 시간이 지나면 기준선으로 돌아옴 단서2
- 강력한 감정은 결국 사라짐 단서3

➡ 인간은 어떤 강력한 감정이나 경험을 하더라도 결국에는 '익숙해져' 원래의 감정 상태인 기준선으로 돌아오는 경향이 있다.

▶ 따라서 아이들은 장난감을 얻고 처음에는 행복하다가 다시 원래의 상태로 돌아가기 때문에, 어른들처럼 ① '적응한다.'

| 선택지 분석 |

① 인간의 감정은 결국 기준선으로 돌아온다고 했으므로, 장난감에 대한 아이들의 행복이 사라지고 원래 상태로 돌아오는 것은 적응하는 과정이다.
② 장난감을 얻은 행복 이후에 기준선으로 돌아가므로, 후회하는 것이 아니다.
③ 장난감을 얻은 행복 이후에 기준선으로 돌아가므로, 탐험하는 것이 아니다.
④ 행복 이후에 자연스럽게 기준선으로 돌아가는 경향이므로, 고군분투한다는 것은 어울리지 않는다.
⑤ 아이들이 장난감을 얻은 직후에 축하했을 수도 있지만, 그 이후에 감정이 원래대로 돌아오는 경향이 핵심 내용이므로 어울리지 않는다.

정답 If they get what they've longed for
→ '~한다면 ~할 것이다'를 나타내므로 가정법 현재 문장을 써야 한다. 따라서 「If + 주어 + 동사의 현재형, 주어 + 조동사/동사의 현재형…」의 어순이 적절하므로, If절에 해당하는 빈칸 부분은 If they get what they've longed for로 쓰는 것이 적절하다.

M 49 정답 ③ *아데노신으로 인해 조정되는 수면 욕구

부사절 접속사 (양보)
Although you may put off going to sleep / in order to squeeze more activities into your day, / eventually your need for sleep becomes overwhelming / and you are forced to get some sleep. //
비록 당신은 잠자는 것을 미룰 수 있지만 / 하루에 더 많은 활동을 밀어 넣기 위해 / 결국 당신의 수면에 대한 필요는 압도적이게 되고 / 잠을 잘 수밖에 없게 된다 //

'~ 때문에'
This daily drive for sleep / appears to be **due**, in part, **to a**
과거분사구 (compound 수식)
compound / **known as adenosine**. //
이러한 매일의 수면 욕구는 / 부분적으로 화합물 때문으로 보인다 / 아데노신이라고 알려진
서술적 용법의 형용사 (명사 뒤에서 수식)
This natural chemical builds up in your blood / as time **awake** increases. // 단서1 깨어 있는 시간이 길어질수록 혈액에 아데노신이 쌓임
이 자연 화학물질은 당신의 혈액 속에 쌓인다 / 깨어 있는 시간이 증가할수록 //
부사절 접속사 (시간)
While you sleep, / your body breaks down the adenosine. //
당신이 자는 동안 / 당신의 몸은 아데노신을 분해한다 // 단서2 잠을 자야 아데노신이 분해됨
선행사를 포함하는 관계대명사 '추적하다'
Thus, / this molecule may be **what** your body uses / to **keep track of** lost sleep / and to trigger sleep when needed. //
따라서 / 이 분자는 당신의 몸이 사용하는 것일지도 모른다 / 놓쳐버린 수면을 추적하고 / 필요할 때 수면을 유도하는 데 //

An accumulation of adenosine and other factors might explain /
아데노신의 축적과 다른 요인들은 설명할 수도 있다 /
explain의 목적어절을 이끄는 의문사
why, after several nights of less than optimal amounts of sleep, / you build up a sleep debt / that you must make up / by sleeping longer than normal. // 단서3 수면 빚은 더 오래 잠으로써 보충해야 함
왜 당신이 최적의 수면량에 미치지 못한 며칠 밤 후에 / 수면 빚을 쌓는지를 / 보충해야 하는 / 평소보다 더 오래 잠으로써 //
be[become] accustomed to -ing: ~에 익숙해지다
Because of such built-in molecular feedback, / you can't **become accustomed to getting** less sleep / than your body needs. //
이러한 내재된 분자적 피드백 때문에 / 당신은 더 적은 잠을 자는 것에 익숙해질 수 없다 / 당신의 몸이 필요한 것보다 // 단서4 내재된 신체 작용 때문에 필요량보다 적게 자는 것에 익숙해질 수 없음
Eventually, a lack of sleep **catches up with you**. //
결국 수면 부족은 당신을 따라잡는다 //

- put off 미루다, 연기하다 · eventually [ad] 결국
- overwhelming [a] 압도적인 · drive [n] 욕구, 충동
- chemical [n] 화학물질 · build up 쌓이다 · break down 분해하다
- molecule [n] 분자 · trigger [v] 유발하다 · optimal [a] 최적의
- debt [n] 빚 · make up 보충하다 · built-in [a] 내재된
- lack [n] 부족, 결핍 · take away 뺏다 · swing [n] (기분의) 변화
- catch up with ~을 따라잡다

비록 당신은 하루에 더 많은 활동을 밀어 넣기 위해 잠자는 것을 미룰 수 있지만, 결국 당신의 수면에 대한 필요는 압도적이게 되고 잠을 잘 수밖에 없게 된다. 이러한 매일의 수면 욕구는 부분적으로 아데노신이라고 알려진 화합물 때문으로 보인다. 이 자연 화학물질은 깨어 있는 시간이 증가할수록 당신의 혈액 속에 쌓인다. 당신이 자는 동안, 당신의 몸은 아데노신을 분해한다. 따라서, 이 분자는 당신의 몸이 놓쳐버린 수면을 추적하고 필요할 때 수면을 유도하는 데 사용하는 것일지도 모른다. 아데노신의 축적과 다른 요인들은 왜 당신이 최적의 수면량에 미치지 못한 며칠 밤 후에 평소보다 더 오래 잠으로써 보충해야 하는 수면 빚을 쌓는지를 설명할 수도 있다. 이러한 내재된 분자적 피드백 때문에, 당신은 당신의 몸이 필요한 것보다 더 적은 잠을 자는 것에 익숙해질 수 없다. 결국 수면 부족은 **당신을 따라잡는다.**

정답 및 해설 **203**

다음 빈칸에 들어갈 말로 가장 적절한 것을 고르시오. [3점]

① takes away your energy 수면 부족의 영향을 피할 수 없다는 것이 핵심 내용임
당신의 에너지를 뺏는다
② causes mood swings 기분 변화는 언급되지 않았음
기분 변화를 유발한다
③ catches up with you 수면 부족은 피할 수 없으며 결국 그 대가를 치르게 됨
당신을 따라잡는다
④ breaks down natural chemicals 수면 부족이 아니라 수면이 아데노신을 분해함
천연 화학 물질을 분해한다
⑤ triggers adenosine to disappear 수면 부족은 아데노신을 축적함
아데노신이 사라지도록 유발한다

| 문제 풀이 순서 | ★★★ [정답률 27%]

1st 빈칸이 포함된 문장을 읽고, 빈칸에 들어갈 말에 대한 단서를 얻는다.

빈칸 문장
Eventually, a lack of sleep _____.
결국 수면 부족은 _____.

➡ 수면 부족의 결과를 나타내는 결론 문장에 해당하므로 (단서) 수면 부족이 끼치는 영향을 파악하고 이를 한 문장으로 종합해야 한다. (발상)

2nd 글의 내용을 종합해서 빈칸에 들어갈 적절한 말을 찾는다.

・깨어 있는 동안 아데노신이 계속 쌓여 수면 욕구가 증가함 (단서 1)
・잠을 자야 아데노신이 분해됨 (단서 2)
・아데노신의 축적(수면 빚)은 더 오래 잠으로써 보충해야 함 (단서 3)
・내재된 신체 작용 때문에 필요량보다 적게 자는 것에 익숙해질 수 없음 (단서 4)

➡ 사람은 잠을 안 잘수록 아데노신이 쌓이고 잠을 자야 이를 분해할 수 있는데, 이러한 수면 빚은 더 오래 잠으로써 보충해야 한다. 이러한 신체 작용은 내재된 것이므로 사람은 필요량보다 적게 자는 것에 익숙해질 수 없다.

▶ 따라서, 수면 부족의 영향에서 벗어날 수 없으므로 결국 수면 부족은 ③ '당신을 따라잡는다.'

> 수면 부족에 관한 일반적인 상식보단 지문에 근거해서 답을 고르기! (꿀팁)

| 선택지 분석 |

① 수면 부족이 에너지를 뺏는 것은 사실이지만, 이는 수면 부족의 영향 중 일부일 뿐 (함정) 이며 수면 부족이 가져오는 신체 작용은 내재된 것이어서 피할 수 없다는 점이 핵심 내용이다.
② 수면 부족이 기분 변화를 일으킨다는 것은 언급되지 않았다.
③ 수면 부족이 누적되면 결국 피할 수 없이 그 대가를 치르게 된다는 내용이다.
④ 천연 화학 물질(아데노신)을 분해하는 것은 수면 부족이 아니라 수면의 역할이므로, 글의 내용과 반대된다.
⑤ 아데노신이 사라지도록 유발하는 것은 수면의 역할이며, 수면 부족은 오히려 아데노신을 쌓이게 하므로 글의 내용과 반대된다.

(구문 서술형)

(정답) hadn't had, wouldn't have built up

(해석) 당신이 최적의 수면량에 미치지 못한 며칠 밤을 보내지 않았다면, 당신은 수면 빚을 쌓지 않았을 것이다.
→ 가정법 과거완료의 부정형은 「If + 주어 + had not[hadn't] p.p. ~, 주어+ 조동사의 과거형 + not + have p.p. …」 형태이므로, not have를 hadn't had 로, not build up을 would not[wouldn't] have built up으로 고쳐 써야 한다.

M 50 정답 ⑤ *전문가들이 초보자 교육에서 겪는 어려움

A number of research studies have shown / how experts in a field / often experience difficulties / 사이에 they are 생략 when introducing newcomers to that field. //
많은 조사 연구는 보여주었다 / 어떻게 한 분야의 전문가가 / 어려움을 종종 겪는지를 / 그 분야로 초보자를 입문시킬 때 //

For example, / in a genuine training situation, / Dr. Pamela Hinds found / 목적어절 접속사 사이에 who were 생략 that people expert in using mobile phones / were remarkably less accurate than novice phone users /
예를 들어 / 실제 교육 상황에서 / Pamela Hinds 박사는 알아냈다 / 휴대 전화기를 사용하는 데 능숙한 사람들이 / 초보 휴대 전화기 사용자보다 놀랍도록 덜 정확하다는 것을 /

in judging / how long it takes people to learn to use the phones. //
판단하는 데 있어서 / 휴대 전화기 사용법을 배우는 것에 얼마나 오랜 시간이 걸리는지를 //

Experts can become insensitive / to how hard a task is for the beginner, / an effect referred to as the 'curse of knowledge.' //
전문가는 무감각해질 수 있는데 / 한 과업이 초보자에게 얼마나 어려운지에 대해 / 즉 '지식의 저주'로 칭해지는 효과이다 // (단서 1) 과업에 대한 초보자의 어려움에 대해 무감각해지는 전문가

목적어절 접속사
Dr. Hinds was able to show / that as people acquired the skill, / they then began to underestimate / the level of difficulty of that skill. // (단서 2) 기술을 습득한 사람은 그 기술의 어려움을 과소평가함
Hinds 박사는 보여 줄 수 있었다 / 사람이 기술을 습득했을 때 / 그 이후에 과소평가하기 시작했다는 것을 / 그 기술의 어려움의 정도를 //

Her participants even underestimated / how long it had taken themselves / to acquire that skill in an earlier session. //
그녀의 참가자는 심지어 과소평가했다 / 자신들이 얼마나 오래 걸렸는지를 / 이전 기간에 그 기술을 습득하는 데 // (단서 3) 자신들이 기술을 습득하는 데 걸린 시간까지도 과소평가함

분사구문을 이끄는 현재분사 to learn의 의미상 주어
Knowing that experts forget / how hard it was for them to learn, / we can understand the need / to look at the learning process through students' eyes, /
전문가가 잊어버린다는 것을 안다면 / 자신이 학습하는 것이 얼마나 어려웠는지를 / 우리는 필요성을 이해할 수 있을 것이다 / 학생들의 눈을 통해 학습 과정을 바라봐야 할 (필요성) / '~보다'의

rather than making assumptions / about how students 'should be' learning. //
추정을 하기보다 / 학생이 어떻게 학습을 '해야 하는지'에 대한 //

・research (n) 연구   ・expert (n) 전문가 (a) 능숙한
・field (n) 분야, 영역   ・difficulty (n) 어려움   ・newcomer (n) 초보
・genuine (a) 실제의   ・remarkably (ad) 놀랍게도
・accurate (a) 정확한   ・insensitive (a) 무감각한
・acquire (v) 습득하다   ・underestimate (v) 과소평가하다
・session (n) 기간, 시간   ・assumption (n) 추정, 가정

많은 조사 연구는 한 분야의 전문가가 그 분야로 초보자를 입문시킬 때 어떻게 어려움을 종종 겪는지를 보여주었다. 예를 들어, 실제 교육 상황에서 Pamela Hinds 박사는 휴대 전화기를 사용하는 데 능숙한 사람들이 휴대 전화기 사용법을 배우는 것에 얼마나 오랜 시간이 걸리는지를 판단하는 데 있어서, 초보 휴대 전화기 사용자보다 놀랍도록 덜 정확하다는 것을 알아냈다. 전문가는 한 과업이 초보자에게 얼마나 어려운지에 대해 무감각해질 수 있는데, 즉 '지식의 저주'로 칭해지는 효과이다. Hinds 박사는 사람이 기술을 습득했을 때 그 이후에 그 기술의 어려움의 정도를 과소평가하기 시작했다는 것을 보여 줄 수 있었다. 그녀의 참가자는 심지어 자신들이 이전 기간에 그 기술을 습득하는 데 얼마나 오래 걸렸는지를 과소평가했다. 전문가가 자신이 학습하는 것이 얼마나 어려웠는지를 잊어버린다는 것을 안다면, 우리는 학생이 어떻게 학습을 '해야 하는지'에 대한 (근거 없는) 추정을 하기보다 **학생들의 눈을 통해 학습 과정을 바라봐야 할** 필요성을 이해할 수 있을 것이다.

다음 빈칸에 들어갈 말로 가장 적절한 것을 고르시오. [3점]

① focus on the new functions of digital devices
디지털 기기의 새로운 기능에 주목해야 할   디지털 기기의 새로운 기능에 관한 내용이 아님
② apply new learning theories recently released
최근에 발표된 새로운 학습 이론을 적용해야 할   새로운 학습 이론 적용의 필요성에 대해 언급하지 않음
③ develop varieties of methods to test students
학생들을 평가하는 다양한 방법을 개발해야 할   평가하는 방법을 개발해야 한다는 내용이 없음
④ forget the difficulties that we have had as students
우리가 학생일 때 겪었던 어려움을 잊어야 할
⑤ look at the learning process through students' eyes
학생들의 눈을 통해 학습 과정을 바라봐야 할   전문가가
전문가 보보자의 어려움에 대해 무감각해지는 것에서 문제가 발생함   초보자의 입장에서 학습의 어려움을 이해해야 함

| 문제 풀이 순서 | ★★★ [정답률 39%]

1st 먼저 빈칸 문장을 읽고, 빈칸에 들어갈 말을 예측한다.

| 빈칸 문장 | 전문가가 자신이 학습하는 것이 얼마나 어려웠는지를 잊어버린다는 것을 안다면, 우리는 학생이 어떻게 학습을 '해야 하는지'에 대한 (근거 없는) 추정을 하기보다 _____ 필요성을 이해할 수 있을 것이다. |

➡ 전문가가 자신이 학습하며 겪은 어려움을 잊는다는 가정으로 문장이 시작되고, 학생이 어떻게 학습해야 하는지 추정하는 것보다는 '무엇'할 필요성이 있다고 했다. (단서)
학습의 어려움을 잊고 학생들에게 학습 방법을 가르치려 하는 것 대신, 학생의 입장이 된다거나 학생의 어려움을 이해해야 한다는 내용이 빈칸에 들어갈 것이다. (발상)

2nd 글의 나머지 부분을 읽고, 어떤 필요성에 대해 이야기하고 있는지 파악한다.

| 글의 앞부분 | • 전문가는 한 과업이 초보자에게 얼마나 어려운지에 대해 무감각해질 수 있는데, 즉 '지식의 저주'로 칭해지는 효과이다. 단서 1 |

➡ 전문가는 초보자의 어려움에 무감각해질 수 있다.
  ▶ 빈칸 문장에 제시된 가정과 일치하는 내용이다.

| 글의 뒷부분 | • Hinds 박사는 사람이 기술을 습득했을 때 그 이후에 그 기술의 어려움의 정도를 과소평가하기 시작했다는 것을 보여 줄 수 있었다. 단서 2
• 그녀의 참가자는 심지어 자신들이 이전 기간에 그 기술을 습득하는 데 얼마나 오래 걸렸는지를 과소평가했다. 단서 3 |

➡ Hinds 박사의 실험에서, 사람이 기술을 습득한 이후에 그 기술의 어려움은 물론이고 습득하는 데 필요한 기간을 과소평가한다고 했다.
➡ 전문가들은 초보자의 어려움을 이해하지 못하기 때문에, 그들이 어떻게 배워야 하는지 근거 없이 추정하려 할 수 있다.

3rd 2nd 에서 이해한 내용을 선택지에서 고른다.

➡ 전문가는 초보자의 어려움을 이해하지 못하기 때문에, 그들이 어떻게 기술을 습득해야 하는지를 추정하려 할 텐데, 그보다 먼저 그들의 입장을 이해해야 한다고 주장하는 글이다.
  ▶ 따라서 빈칸 문장에서는 초보자를 학생에 빗대었으므로, 전문가들은 ⑤ '학생들의 눈을 통해 학습 과정을 바라봐야 할' 필요성이 있다.

| 선택지 분석 |

① 휴대 전화기 사용법을 배우는 것을 예시로 들었을 뿐 디지털 기기의 새로운 기능에 관해 설명한 글이 아니다.
② 새로운 학습 이론을 적용해야 할 필요성은 언급되지 않았다.
③ 평가하는 방법을 개발해야 한다는 내용은 언급되지 않았다.
④ 전문가가 초보자의 어려움에 대해 무감각해지는 것에서 문제가 발생하기 때문에 그러한 어려움을 잊는 것은 글의 내용과 모순된다.
⑤ 전문가가 초보자의 입장에서 학습의 어려움을 이해해야 한다는 내용의 글이다.

M 51 정답 ① *새로운 매체가 관점에 미치는 영향

Every time a new medium comes along / — whether it's the
    '나타나다'   부사절 접속사(~이든)
invention of the printed book, or TV, or SNS — / and you start
to use it, /
새로운 매체가 나타날 때마다 / 인쇄된 책의 발명이든 텔레비전의 발명이든 SNS의 발명이든 / 그리고 여러분이 그것을 쓰기 시작할 때마다 /

it's like you are putting on a new kind of goggles, / with their
own special colors and lenses. //
여러분은 새 고글을 쓰는 것과 같다 / 고유의 색깔과 렌즈를 가진 //

Each set of goggles / you put on / makes you see things
differently. //
   앞에 목적격 관계대명사가 생략됨   makes의 목적격 보어(원형부정사)
   단서 1 어떤 고글(매체)을 쓰는지에 따라 세상을 다르게 바라봄
각각의 고글은 / 여러분이 쓰는 / 세상을 다른 방식으로 바라보게 한다 //

So when you start to watch television, / before you absorb the
   부사절 접속사(시간) *
message of any particular TV show / — whether it's *Wheel of
Fortune* or *The Wire* — /
그러므로 여러분이 텔레비전을 보기 시작하면 / 특정 텔레비전 프로그램의 메시지를 흡수하기 이전에 / 그것이 *Wheel of Fortune*이든 *The Wire*든 /

you start to see the world / as being shaped like television itself. //
세상을 바라보게 된다 / 텔레비전 그 자체처럼 형성된 것으로 //

That's why Marshall McLuhan said / that every time a
단서 2 새로운 매체가 나타날 때마다 그 안에 메시지가 담겨 있음   목적어절 접속사*
new medium comes along / — a new way for humans to
       to부정사의 의미상 주어
communicate — / it has buried in it a message. //
형용사적 용법(a new way 수식)
이러한 이유로 Marshall McLuhan이 말한 것이다 / 새로운 매체가 나타날 때마다 / 즉, 인간이 의사소통하는 새로운 방식이 나타날 때마다 / 그 안에 메시지가 담겨 있다고 //

It is gently guiding us / to see the world according to a new set
of codes. //
그것(새로운 매체)은 자연스럽게 우리가 ~하게 한다 / 새로운 일련의 방식에 따라 세상을 바라보게 //

The way information gets to you, / McLuhan argued, / is more
   관계부사절   삽입절
important than the information itself. //
정보가 여러분에게 도달하는 방식이 / McLuhan은 주장했다 / 정보 자체보다 더 중요하다고 //

TV teaches you / that the world is fast; / that it's about surfaces
      목적어절 접속사
and appearances. //
텔레비전은 우리에게 가르친다 / 세상은 빠르고 / 중요한 것은 표면과 겉모습이라고 //

- medium ⓝ 매체   • invention ⓝ 발명   • absorb ⓥ 흡수하다
- communicate ⓥ 소통하다   • surface ⓝ 표면
- appearance ⓝ 겉모습   • code ⓝ 규칙, 방식   • interpret ⓥ 해석하다

인쇄된 책의 발명이든 텔레비전의 발명이든 SNS의 발명이든, 새로운 매체가 나타나 여러분이 그것을 쓰기 시작할 때마다 여러분은 고유의 색깔과 렌즈를 가진 새 고글을 쓰는 것과 같다. 여러분이 쓰는 각각의 고글은 세상을 다른 방식으로 바라보게 한다. 그러므로 여러분이 텔레비전을 보기 시작하면, 그것이 *Wheel of Fortune*이든 *The Wire*든, 특정 텔레비전 프로그램의 메시지를 흡수하기 이전에 세상을 텔레비전 그 자체처럼 형성된 것으로 바라보게 된다. 이러한 이유로 Marshall McLuhan이 새로운 매체, 즉, 인간이 의사소통하는 새로운 방식이 나타날 때마다 그 안에 메시지가 담겨 있다고 말한 것이다. 그것은 자연스럽게 우리가 **새로운 일련의 방식에 따라 세상을 바라보게** 한다. McLuhan은 정보가 여러분에게 도달하는 방식이 정보 자체보다 더 중요하다고 주장했다. 텔레비전은 우리에게 세상은 빠르고, 중요한 것은 표면과 겉모습이라고 가르친다.

다음 빈칸에 들어갈 말로 가장 적절한 것을 고르시오. [3점]

① see the world according to a new set of codes   새로운 매체가
새로운 일련의 방식에 따라 세상을 바라보다   등장할 때마다 세상을 다르게 바라보게 됨
② ignore unfamiliar messages from new media   새로운 미디어의
새로운 미디어에서 온 익숙하지 않은 메시지를 무시하다   메시지를 무시한다는 내용이 아님
③ maintain steady focus and clear understanding
꾸준한 집중력과 명확한 이해를 유지하다   매체가 집중력과 이해에 도움이 된다는 내용이 아님
④ interpret information through a traditional lens
전통적인 렌즈를 통해 정보를 해석하다   전통적인 방식으로 정보를 이해한다는 내용이 아님
⑤ enjoy various media contents with one platform
하나의 플랫폼으로 다양한 미디어 콘텐츠를 즐기다   다양한 미디어 콘텐츠를 즐긴다는 언급은 없음

M

1st 빈칸이 포함된 문장을 읽고, 빈칸에 들어갈 말에 대한 단서를 얻는다.

빈칸 문장	It is gently guiding us to _____ .
	그것은 자연스럽게 우리가 _____ 하게 한다.

➡ It이 자연스럽게 우리가 '무엇'하게 한다고 했으므로, (단서)
It이 무엇을 가리키는지, 그리고 그것이 우리가 '무엇'을 하게 하는지를 파악해야
한다. (발상)

2nd 글의 나머지 부분을 읽고, 빈칸에 들어갈 적절한 말을 찾는다.

・여러분이 쓰는 각각의 고글은 세상을 다른 방식으로 바라보게 한다. 단서 1
・이러한 이유로 Marshall McLuhan이 새로운 매체, 즉, 인간이 의사소통하는
　새로운 방식이 나타날 때마다 그 안에 메시지가 담겨 있다고 말한 것이다. 단서 2

➡ 글의 첫 문장에서 매체를 고글에 비유하였으므로, 각각의 매체가 세상을 다른
방식으로 바라보게 한다는 내용이다. 또한 빈칸 바로 앞 문장에서 새로운 매체가
나타날 때마다 그 안에 메시지가 담겨 있다고 했으므로, 빈칸 문장의 It은 '새로운
매체'를 가리킨다.
따라서 빈칸에는 새로운 매체가 세상을 새로운 방식으로 바라보게 한다는 내용이
들어가야 한다.

▶ 새로운 매체는 자연스럽게 우리가 ① '새로운 일련의 방식에 따라 세상을
바라보게' 한다.

| 선택지 분석 |

① 각각의 매체가 세상을 다른 방식으로 바라보게 하므로, 새로운 매체는 세상을
　새로운 방식으로 바라보게 한다는 내용이다.
② 특정 텔레비전 프로그램의 메시지를 흡수하는 것이 언급되긴 했으나, 메시지를
　무시한다는 것은 언급되지 않았다.
③ 매체가 집중력과 이해를 유지하게 한다는 것은 언급되지 않았다.
④ 새로운 매체는 우리가 기존의 렌즈(관점)가 아닌 새로운 관점으로 세상을 바라보게
　한다.
⑤ 하나의 플랫폼이 아닌 다양한 플랫폼이 언급되며, 이를 통해 다양한 콘텐츠를
　즐긴다는 것은 언급되지 않았다.

어법 특강

＊ 명사절 접속사와 부사절 접속사

– 명사절 접속사의 경우 문장의 주어, 목적어, 보어의 역할을 하는 절을 이끌며,
　부사절 접속사는 주절에 종속된 하나의 완전한 절을 이끌고, 주절에 시간, 이유,
　양보, 조건 등의 의미를 보충해 준다.

　　　　　　　　　　　　┌ 양보의 부사절을 이끄는 접속사
・ I know that even though I have a lot of experience, it will be
　문장의 목적어 역할을 하는 명사절을 이끄는 접속사
　difficult to find a job.
　(나는 비록 내가 많은 경험이 있을지라도, 직업을 찾기 어려울 것이라는 것을 안다.)

M 52 정답 ③ ＊성과를 향상하는 자유의 제한

　　　　부사적 용법(목적)
To demonstrate / how best to defeat the habit of delaying, /
설명하기 위해 / 미루는 습관을 가장 잘 무너뜨리는 방법을 /

Dan Ariely, a professor of psychology and behavioral
economics, / performed an experiment on students / in three of
his classes at MIT. //
심리학 및 행동경제학 교수인 Dan Ariely는 / 학생들을 대상으로 실험을 수행했다 /
MIT에서의 자신의 수업 중 세 개에서 //

　　　　　　　　간접목적어　　　직접목적어
He assigned all classes three reports / over the course of the
semester. //
그는 모든 수업에 세 개의 보고서를 과제로 부여했다 / 학기 과정 동안 //

The first class had to choose / three due dates / for themselves, /
up to and including the last day of class. //
첫 번째 수업(의 학생들)은 선택해야 했다 / 세 개의 마감일을 / 스스로 / 종강일을 포함한
날짜까지 //

The second had no deadlines / — all three papers just had to be
submitted / by the last day of class. //
두 번째는 마감일이 없었고 / 세 개의 보고서가 모두 제출되기만 하면 되었다 / 종강일까지 //

　　　　　　　　　간접목적어　　　 직접목적어
In his third class, / he gave students three set deadlines / over
the course of the semester. //
그의 세 번째 수업에서 / 그는 학생들에게 세 개의 정해진 마감일을 주었다 / 학기 과정 동안 //
　　　　　　　　　　　　　　　　목적어절 접속사
At the end of the semester, / he found / that students with set
deadlines received the best grades, /
학기 말에 / 그는 알아냈다 / 마감일이 정해진 학생들이 최고의 성적을 받았다는 것을 /
　　　　　　　　　　　　　　　　　　　　　　　　　　　＝ students
the students with no deadlines had the worst, / and those
who could choose their own deadlines / fell somewhere in the
middle. // 단서 1 과제의 마감일이 정해질수록 학생들의 성적이 좋았음
마감일이 없는 학생들은 최하의 성적을 받았고 / 자신의 마감일을 선택할 수 있었던 학생들은
/ 그 중간 어디쯤의 위치에 있었다(는 것을) //
　　　　　목적어절 접속사　　　　　　　　　　　　　　단서 2 자기 통제와 성과를 향상함
Ariely concludes / that restricting freedom / — whether by the
　　　　　　　　　　　　　　　　주격 관계대명사
professor / or by students / who recognize their own tendencies
to delay things / — improves self-control and performance. //
Ariely는 결론짓는다 / 자유를 제한하는 것은 / 교수에 의해서든 / 혹은 학생들에 의해서든 /
일을 미루는 자신의 성향을 인식한 / 자기 통제와 성과를 향상한다고 //

・ **demonstrate** ⓥ 보여주다, 설명하다　・ **defeat** ⓥ 패배시키다, 이기다
・ **delay** ⓥ 미루다　　・ **behavioral** @ 행동의, 행동에 관한
・ **assign** ⓥ 맡기다, 배정하다　・ **due date** 마감일, 만기일
・ **for oneself** 스스로　・ **submit** ⓥ 제출하다
・ **conclude** ⓥ 결론을 내리다　・ **restrict** ⓥ 제한하다
・ **recognize** ⓥ 인식하다　・ **tendency** ⓝ 경향, 성향
・ **performance** ⓝ 수행, 성과　・ **reward** ⓝ 보상
・ **obstacle** ⓝ 장애물　・ **assignment** ⓝ 과제
・ **competition** ⓝ 경쟁

미루는 습관을 가장 잘 무너뜨리는 방법을 설명하기 위해, 심리학 및
행동경제학 교수인 Dan Ariely는 MIT의 자신의 수업 중 세 개에서 학생들을
대상으로 실험을 수행했다. 그는 학기 과정 동안 모든 수업에 세 개의 보고서를
과제로 부여했다. 첫 번째 수업의 학생들은 종강일까지 포함해서 세 개의
마감일을 스스로 선택해야 했다. 두 번째는 마감일이 없었고, 세 개의 보고서
모두 종강일까지 제출되기만 하면 되었다. 그의 세 번째 수업에서, 그는 학기
과정 동안 학생들에게 세 개의 정해진 마감일을 주었다. 학기 말에, 그는
마감일이 정해진 학생들이 최고의 성적을 받았고, 마감일이 없는 학생들은
최하의 성적을 받았으며, 자신의 마감일을 선택할 수 있었던 학생들은 그 중간
어디쯤의 위치에 있었다는 것을 알아냈다. Ariely는, 교수에 의해서든 혹은
일을 미루는 자신의 성향을 인식한 학생들에 의해서든, **자유를 제한하는 것**은
자기 통제와 성과를 향상한다고 결론짓는다.

다음 빈칸에 들어갈 말로 가장 적절한 것을 고르시오.

① offering rewards 과제에 대한 보상은 언급되지 않음
　보상을 제공하는 것
② removing obstacles 장애물을 제거하라는 내용이 아님
　장애물을 제거하는 것
③ restricting freedom 마감일을 주는 것은 자유를 제한하는 것임
　자유를 제한하는 것
④ increasing assignments 과제의 양은 늘리지 않았음
　과제를 늘리는 것
⑤ encouraging competition 각 그룹의 학생들이 경쟁하는 것이 아님
　경쟁을 권장하는 것

왜 정답? ★★❀ [정답률 66%]

빈칸 문장	Ariely는, 교수에 의해서든 혹은 일을 미루는 자신의 성향을 인식한 학생들에 의해서든, _____은 자기 통제와 성과를 향상한다고 결론짓는다.

→ **빈칸 문장:** Ariely는 '무엇이' 자기 통제와 성과를 향상한다고 결론지었다.
→ **Ariely의 실험 결과:**
   그룹 **1**: 과제의 마감일을 스스로 선택함 → 중간 정도의 성적
   그룹 **2**: 과제의 마감일이 없음 → 최하의 성적
   그룹 **3**: 과제마다 마감일이 정해져 있음 → 최고의 성적
   ▶ '마감일'이 존재한다는 것은 '자유가 제한'된다는 것이므로 자기 통제와 성과를 향상하는 것은 ③ '자유를 제한하는 것'이다.

왜 오답?
① 주어진 과제에 서로 다른 보상을 제공하는 실험을 한 것이 아니다.
② 오히려 장애물이라고 할 수 있는 마감일을 부여하는 것에 대해 긍정적으로 말하고 있다. (▶ 이유: 마감일이 정해지면 자유로운 과제 수행에 제한이 생기므로 장애물이라고 볼 수 있다.)
④ 모든 수업에서 과제의 양을 늘리거나 줄이지 않았으므로 적절하지 않다.
⑤ 세 그룹의 학생들이 서로 경쟁하도록 한 것이 아니다.

M 53 정답 ② *정보 접근성과 지적 자신감의 상관관계

Participants in a study <u>were asked</u> / to answer questions / like
　　　　　　　　　　수동태 동사
"Why does the moon have phases?" //
한 연구의 참가자들이 요청받았다 / 질문들에 답하도록 / '달은 왜 상을 가지고 있을까'와 같은 //

Half the participants were told / to search for the answers on
the internet, / while the other half weren't allowed / to <u>do so</u>. //
　　　　　　　= search for the answers on the Internet
참가자의 절반은 말을 들었고 / 인터넷에서 답을 검색하라는 / 나머지 절반은 허용되지 않았다 / 그렇게 하도록 //

Then, in the second part of the study, / all of the participants
were presented / with a new set of questions, / such as "Why
does Swiss cheese have holes?" //
그다음, 연구의 두 번째 단계에서 / 모든 참가자는 제시받았다 / 일련의 새로운 질문들을 / '스위스 치즈에는 왜 구멍이 있을까'와 같은 //

These questions were unrelated / to the <u>ones asked</u> during the
　　　　　　　　　　　　　　= questions 과거분사
first part of the study, / so participants <u>who</u> used the internet /
had absolutely no advantage / over those <u>who</u> hadn't. //
　　　　　　　　　주격 관계대명사
이 질문들은 관련이 없어서 / 연구의 첫 번째 단계에서 질문받았던 것들과는 / 인터넷을 사용한 참가자들은 / 이점이 전혀 없었다 / 그러지 않은 참가자들보다 // **단서 1** 두 번째 질문은 첫 번째 질문에서 인터넷을 검색했던 참가자들도 이점이 없었음

You would think / that both sets of participants would be
equally sure or unsure / about <u>how well they could answer the</u>
　　　　　　　　　　　　　　　　　　의문사절
<u>new questions.</u> // **단서 2** 하지만 첫 번째 질문에서 인터넷을 검색했던 참가자들은 전혀 관련이 없는 두 번째 질문의 답조차도 본인이 더 많이 알고 있다고 평가함
여러분은 생각할 것이다 / 두 집단의 참가자들이 동일한 정도로 확신하거나 확신하지 못할 것으로 / 새로운 질문들에 얼마나 잘 대답할 수 있을지에 대해 //

But <u>those who</u> used the internet in the first part of the study /
rated <u>themselves</u> as more knowledgeable / than <u>those who</u>
　~한 사람들　재귀적 용법의 재귀대명사　　사이에 목적격 관계대명사 생략
hadn't, / even about <u>questions</u> <u>they</u> hadn't searched online for. //
그러나 연구의 첫 번째 단계에서 인터넷을 사용했던 참가자들은 / 스스로가 더 많이 알고 있다고 평가했다 / 그러지 않았던 참가자들보다 / 질문들에 대해서조차 / 자신이 온라인에서 검색하지 않았던 //

The study suggests / that <u>having</u> access to unrelated information
　　　　　　　　　　　동명사 주어
/ <u>was</u> enough to **pump up their intellectual confidence**. //
단수 동사
이 연구는 시사한다 / 관련 없는 정보에 접근하는 것이 / 그들의 지적 자신감을 부풀리기에 충분했다는 것을 //

- **participant** ⓝ 참가자 　• **be allowed to** ~하도록 허용되다
- **be unrelated to** ~와 연관되지 않다 　• **absolutely** ⓐd 절대적으로
- **equally** ⓐd 동등하게 　• **rate** ⓥ 평가하다
- **knowledgeable** ⓐ 유식한 　• **suggest** ⓥ 시사하다
- **have access to** ~에 접근하다 　• **judgment** ⓝ 판단
- **pump up** 부풀리다, 증대하다 　• **intellectual** ⓐ 지능의
- **confidence** ⓝ 자신감 　• **endure** ⓥ 견디다
- **challenging** ⓐ 힘든 　• **collaboration** ⓝ 협동
- **motivate** ⓥ 동기를 부여하다 　• **pursue** ⓥ 추구하다
- **in-depth** ⓐ 심도 있는, 면밀한

한 연구의 참가자들이 '달은 왜 상을 가지고 있을까'와 같은 질문들에 답하도록 요청받았다. 참가자의 절반은 인터넷에서 답을 검색하라는 말을 들었고 나머지 절반은 그렇게 하도록 허용되지 않았다. 그다음, 연구의 두 번째 단계에서 모든 참가자는 '스위스 치즈에는 왜 구멍이 있을까'와 같은 일련의 새로운 질문들을 제시받았다. 이 질문들은 연구의 첫 번째 단계에서 질문받았던 것들과는 관련이 없어서 인터넷을 사용한 참가자들은 그러지 않은 참가자들보다 이점이 전혀 없었다. 여러분은 두 집단의 참가자들이 새로운 질문들에 얼마나 잘 대답할 수 있을지에 대해 동일한 정도로 확신하거나 확신하지 못할 것으로 생각할 것이다. 그러나 연구의 첫 번째 단계에서 인터넷을 사용했던 참가자들은 자신이 온라인에서 검색하지 않았던 질문들에 대해서조차 그러지 않았던 참가자들보다 스스로가 더 많이 알고 있다고 평가했다. 이 연구는 관련 없는 정보에 접근하는 것이 **그들의 지적 자신감을 부풀리기에** 충분했다는 것을 시사한다.

다음 빈칸에 들어갈 말로 가장 적절한 것을 고르시오.
① improve their judgment skills 참가자들은 오히려 비이성적인 판단을 하고 있음 판단 능력을 향상하기에
② pump up their intellectual confidence 이전에 관련 없는 정보를 검색했던 그들의 지적 자신감을 부풀리기에 경험만으로도 스스로를 더 많이 알고 있다고 평가함
③ make them endure challenging situations 그들이 어려운 상황을 견디도록 만들기에 참가자들이 어려운 상황을 견디는 내용은 언급되지 않음
④ lead to a collaboration among the participants 참가자들 사이에 협동을 이끌기에 참가자들 사이에 협동은 언급되지 않음
⑤ motivate them to pursue in-depth knowledge 그들이 심도 있는 지식을 추구하도록 동기를 부여하기에 심도 있는 지식을 추구한 것이 아니라 오히려 근거 없는 자신감을 비치게 됨

왜 정답? ★★★ [정답률 52%]

빈칸 문장	이 연구는 관련 없는 정보에 접근하는 것이 _____ 충분했다는 것을 시사한다.

→ 관련 없는 정보에 접근한 것만으로도 참가자들은 '무엇을' 하기에 충분했다고 했으므로, **단서** 정보 접근과 참가자들의 특성이 연결된 연구가 앞에 제시되었을 것이다. **발상**
→ 참가자들은 두 가지 질문을 받음
  질문 1: '달은 왜 상을 가지고 있을까'
  질문 2: '스위스 치즈에는 왜 구멍이 있을까'
  질문 **1**에서 참가자 절반은 인터넷 검색을 했고, 절반은 하지 못함
  질문 **2**는 질문 **1**과 전혀 관련이 없기 때문에, 질문 **1**에서 인터넷 검색을 했던 사람도 질문 **2**를 답변할 때 이점이 없었음 **단서 1**
  하지만 연구 결과, 질문 **1**에서 인터넷을 검색했던 참가자들은 질문 **2**의 답조차도 본인들이 더 많이 알고 있다고 평가함 **단서 2**
→ 우리는 관련 없는 정보에 접근했더라도 스스로를 더 많이 알고 있다고 평가한다는 것이다.
  ▶ 즉, 관련 없는 정보를 검색한 것만으로도 ② '그들의 지적 자신감을 부풀리기에' 충분했다.

왜 오답?
① 참가자들은 오히려 관련 없는 정보를 보고도 자신이 더 지식이 많다는 비이성적인 판단을 하고 있다.
③ 참가자들이 어려운 상황을 견디는 내용은 언급되지 않았다.
④ 참가자들 사이에 협동은 언급되지 않았다.
⑤ 참가자들은 심도 있는 지식을 추구한 것이 아니라 오히려 근거 없는 자신감을 비치게 되었다. **함정**

단수 주어 / 단수 동사
Everything in the world around us / was finished / in the mind
of its creator / before it was started. //
우리 주변 세상의 모든 것은 / 완성되었다 / 그것을 만들어 낸 사람의 마음에서 / 그것이
시작되기 전에 //
뒤에 목적격 관계대명사가 생략됨
단서 1 모든 것은 마음속에서 구상된 후 세상에 나옴
The houses we live in, / the cars we drive, / and our clothing / all
of these began with an idea. //
우리가 사는 집 / 우리가 운전하는 자동차 / 그리고 우리의 옷 / 이 모든 것이 아이디어에서
시작했다 //
단서 2 우리가 실생활에서 접하는 것들도 모두 같은 과정을 거침
병렬 구조
Each idea was then studied, / refined / and perfected / before the
first nail was driven / or the first piece of cloth was cut. //
각각의 아이디어는 그런 다음 연구되고 / 다듬어지고 / 완성되었다 / 첫 번째 못이 박히거나 /
첫 번째 천 조각이 재단되기 전에 //
단서 3 물리적으로 성취를 이루기 전에 마음속에
명확한 그림이 존재해야 함
Long before / the idea was turned into a physical reality, / the
mind had clearly pictured the finished product. //
훨씬 전에 / 그 아이디어가 물리적 실체로 바뀌기 / 마음은 완제품을 분명하게 그렸다 //
The human being designs / his or her own future / through
much the same process. //
인간은 설계한다 / 자신의 미래를 / 거의 같은 과정을 통해 //
전치사 about의 목적어(간접의문문)
We begin with an idea / about how the future will be. //
우리는 아이디어로 시작한다 / 미래가 어떨지에 대한 //
Over a period of time / we refine and perfect the vision. //
일정 기간에 걸쳐서 / 우리는 그 비전을 다듬어 완성한다 //
Before long, / our every thought, decision and activity / are all
부사적 용법(목적) / to bring의 목적어
working in harmony / to bring into existence / what we have
mentally concluded / about the future. //
머지않아 / 우리의 모든 생각, 결정, 활동은 / 모두 조화롭게 작용하게 된다 / 생겨나게 하려고
/ 우리가 머릿속에서 완성한 것을 / 미래에 대해 //

- creator ⓝ 창조자   • clothing ⓝ 의복   • nail ⓝ 못
- drive ⓥ (못·말뚝 등을) 박다   • physical ⓐ 물리적인
- harmony ⓝ 조화   • existence ⓝ 존재   • potential ⓝ 잠재력
- accomplish ⓥ 완성하다   • careless ⓐ 부주의한
- irresponsible ⓐ 무책임한   • observe ⓥ 탐색하다
- professional ⓝ 전문직 (종사자)

우리 주변 세상의 모든 것은 시작되기 전에 그것을 만들어 낸 사람의
마음속에서 완성되었다. 우리가 사는 집, 우리가 운전하는 자동차, 우리의
옷, 이 모든 것이 아이디어에서 시작했다. 각각의 아이디어는 그런 다음, 첫
번째 못이 박히거나 첫 번째 천 조각이 재단되기 전에, 연구되고, 다듬어지고,
완성되었다. 그 아이디어가 물리적 실체로 바뀌기 훨씬 전에 마음은 완제
품을 분명하게 그렸다. 인간은 거의 같은 과정을 통해 자신의 미래를 설계한다.
우리는 미래가 어떨지에 대한 아이디어로 시작한다. 일정 기간에 걸쳐서 우리는
그 비전을 다듬어 완성한다. 머지않아, 우리의 모든 생각, 결정, 활동은 우리가
미래에 대해 머릿속에서 완성한 것을 생겨나게 하려고 모두 조화롭게 작용하게
된다.

다음 빈칸에 들어갈 말로 가장 적절한 것을 고르시오. [3점]

① didn't even have the potential to accomplish
완성할 수 있는 잠재력조차 갖고 있지 못하다   머리로 비전을 떠올리면 실행이 가능함
② have mentally concluded about the future
미래에 대해 머릿속에서 완성하다   머릿속에서 구상한 것이 실제 이루어진다고 했음
③ haven't been able to picture in our mind
우리의 마음에 그려낼 수 없다   이 과정이 선행되어야 성취로 이어짐
④ considered careless and irresponsible
부주의하고 무책임하다고 여겨지다   전혀 언급되지 않은 내용
⑤ have observed in some professionals 직종을 탐색하는 것은 나오지 않음
여러 직종을 탐색해 보다

| 문제 풀이 순서 | ＊＊＊ [정답률 56%]

1st 먼저 빈칸 문장을 읽고, 빈칸에 들어갈 말을 예측한다.

| 빈칸 문장 | 머지않아, 우리의 모든 생각, 결정, 활동은 우리가 ＿＿＿＿＿ 것을 생겨나게 하려고 모두 조화롭게 작용하게 된다. |

➡ 우리가 '어떻게 한' 것을 생겨나게 하려고 우리의 생각, 결정, 활동이 조화롭게
작용한다고 했으므로, **단서** 그 과정을 파악해야 한다. **발상**

2nd 글의 나머지 부분을 확인해서 정답을 찾는다.

| 글의 첫 번째 문장 | 우리 주변 세상의 모든 것은 시작되기 전에 그것을 만들어 낸 사람의 마음속에서 완성되었다. **단서 1** |
| 글의 두 번째 문장 | 우리가 사는 집, 우리가 운전하는 자동차, 우리의 옷, 이 모든 것이 아이디어에서 시작했다. **단서 2** |

➡ 우리 주변의 모든 것이 사람의 마음속에서, 아이디어에서 시작했다고 했다.
▶ 물리적인 실체가 되려면 마음속에서 명확하게 그려내야 함

| 글의 네 번째 문장 | 그 아이디어가 물리적 실체로 바뀌기 훨씬 전에 마음은 완제품을 분명하게 그렸다. **단서 3** |

➡ 마음속에서 이미 완성된 아이디어가 물리적 실체로 바뀐다.
▶ 우리의 모든 생각, 결정, 활동은 우리가 ② '미래에 대해 머릿속에서 완성한' 것을
생겨나게 하려고 조화롭게 작용한다.

| 선택지 분석 |

① 완성될 잠재력이 없는 것을 실현한다는 것이 아니다.
② 머릿속에서 먼저 구상하는 과정을 거쳐 성취가 일어난다고 했다.
③ 마음속에 그려내는 과정이 선행되어야 성취로 이어진다고 했다.
④ 부주의하고 무책임한 태도에 관한 내용은 언급되지 않았다.
⑤ 직종을 탐색하는 것과 관련된 글이 아니다.

M 55 정답 ① ＊감정에 근거한 두려움

부사적 용법(감정의 원인)
Many people are terrified / to fly in airplanes. //
많은 사람들은 두려워한다 / 비행기를 타는 것을 //

Often, / this fear stems / from a lack of control. //
종종 / 이 두려움은 비롯된다 / 통제력의 부족에서 //

The pilot is in control, / not the passengers, / and this lack of
control instills fear. //
조종사는 통제를 하지만 / 승객은 그렇지 않으며 / 이러한 통제력의 부족은 두려움을 스며들게
한다 //
so ~ (that) ...: 너무 ~해서 …하다
Many potential passengers are so afraid / they choose to drive
부사적 용법(목적) / that이 생략됨
great distances / to get to a destination / instead of flying. //
많은 잠재적인 승객들은 너무 두려워서 / 그들은 먼 거리를 운전하는 것을 선택한다 /
목적지에 도착하기 위해 / 비행하는 대신 //
형용사적 용법(decision 수식)
But their decision to drive / is based solely on emotion, / not
logic. // **단서 1** 비행기를 타는 것이 무서워 운전을 하는 것은 논리가 아닌 감정에 근거한 결정임
그러나 운전을 하기로 한 그들의 결정은 / 오직 감정에 근거한다 / 논리가 아닌 //
목적격절 접속사 / 핵심 주어(복수)
Logic says / that statistically, / the odds of dying in a car crash /
복수동사
are around 1 in 5,000, / while the odds of dying in a plane crash
/ are closer to 1 in 11 million. // **단서 2** 통계적으로 자동차 사고 사망 확률이
비행기 사고로 사망할 확률보다 훨씬 높음
논리는 말한다 / 통계적으로 / 자동차 사고로 사망할 확률은 / 약 5,000분의 1이고 / 반면
비행기 사고로 사망할 확률은 / 1,100만분의 1에 더 가깝다고 //
= risk
If you're going to take a risk, / especially one that could possibly
주격 관계대명사
involve / your well-being, / wouldn't you want the odds / in
'~에게 유리하게'
your favor? //
만약 여러분이 위험을 감수할 것이라면 / 특히 포함할 수 있는 것이라면 / 여러분의 안녕을 /
여러분은 확률을 원하지 않겠는가 / 여러분에게 유리한 //

However, / most people choose the option / **that** will cause **them**
주격 관계대명사   *간접목적어*
/ **the least amount of anxiety**. //
직접목적어
그러나 / 대부분의 사람들은 선택지를 고른다 / 그들에게 야기할 수 있는 / 최소한의 불안감을 //
Pay attention / to the thoughts **you have** / about taking the risk
앞에 목적격 관계대명사가 생략됨
/ and make sure / you're basing your decision on facts, / not just
feelings. 단서 3 감정이 아니라 사실에 근거해서 결정을 내리고 있는지 확인하라고 함
주의를 기울여라 / 여러분이 가지고 있는 생각에 / 위험을 감수하는 것에 대해 / 그리고
확인하라 / 여러분이 결정을 사실에 근거하고 있는지 / 단지 감정이 아니라 //

- terrified ⓐ 두려워하는 • stem from ~에서 생겨나다
- passenger ⓝ 승객 • potential ⓐ 잠재적인
- destination ⓝ 목적지 • base ⓥ 근거하다 • solely ⓐ 오로지
- logic ⓝ 논리 • statistically ⓐ 통계적으로
- odds ⓝ (어떤 일이 있을) 가능성 • boredom ⓝ 지루함
- responsibility ⓝ 책임감

많은 사람들은 비행기를 타는 것을 두려워한다. 종종, 이 두려움은 통제력의 부족에서 비롯된다. 조종사는 통제를 하지만, 승객은 그렇지 않으며, 이러한 통제력의 부족은 두려움을 스며들게 한다. 많은 잠재적인 승객들은 너무 두려워서 그들은 비행기를 타는 대신 목적지에 도착하기 위해 먼 거리를 운전하는 것을 선택한다. 그러나 운전을 하기로 한 그들의 결정은 논리가 아닌 오직 감정에 근거한다. 논리에 따르면 통계적으로 자동차 사고로 사망할 확률은 약 5,000분의 1이고, 반면 비행기 사고로 사망할 확률은 1,100만분의 1에 더 가깝다고 한다. 만약 여러분이 위험을 감수할 것이라면, 특히 여러분의 안녕을 혹시 포함할 수 있는 위험을 감수할 것이라면, 여러분에게 유리한 확률을 원하지 않겠는가? 그러나 대부분의 사람들은 그들에게 최소한의 **불안감**을 야기할 수 있는 선택을 한다. 위험을 감수하는 것에 대해 여러분이 가지고 있는 생각에 주의를 기울이고 여러분이 결정을 단지 감정이 아닌 사실에 근거하고 있는지 확인하라.

> 다음 빈칸에 들어갈 말로 가장 적절한 것을 고르시오.
> ① anxiety 확률보다 두려움에 근거하여 자동차를 탐
>   불안감
> ② boredom 지루함과는 관련 없는 내용임
>   지루함
> ③ confidence 자신감을 최소화한다는 내용이 아님
>   자신감
> ④ satisfaction 최소한의 만족감을 주는 선택이 아님
>   만족감
> ⑤ responsibility 책임감과는 관련 없는 내용임
>   책임감

> **왜 정답?** ✱✱✱ [정답률 61%]

빈칸 문장	그러나(However) 대부분의 사람들은 그들에게 최소한의 _____을 야기할 수 있는 선택을 한다.

➡ **빈칸 문장**: 사람들은 '무엇'을 최소화하는 선택을 한다.

글의 앞부분	• 비행기를 타는 것이 두려워 먼 거리를 운전하는 선택을 함 = 감정에 근거한 결정 단서 1 • 자동차 사고로 사망할 확률 > 비행기 사고로 사망할 확률 단서 2

➡ 논리적으로는 비행기로 사망할 확률이 더 낮음에도 사람들은 단지 두려운 감정 때문에 자동차 운전을 선택한다.

마지막 문장	단지 감정이 아니라 사실에 근거한 결정을 하고 있는지 확인해야 함 단서 3

➡ 감정이 아니라 사실에 근거한 결정을 해야 한다.
  ▶ 많은 사람들이 논리가 아니라 감정, 즉 ① '불안감'을 최소화하는 선택을 한다는 것이다.

왜 오답?

② 지루함을 줄이기 위한 선택을 한다는 내용이 아니다.
③ 자신감을 줄이기 위한 선택을 한다는 내용이 아니다.
④ 논리가 아니라 감정에 근거한 결정은 오히려 각자의 만족감을 최대화하려는 결정이라고 볼 수 있다. 주의
⑤ 책임감과 관련된 내용이 아니다.

Ⓜ 56 정답 ① *능력이 유일한 척도가 될 때

For many people, / *ability* refers to intellectual competence, / so
they want everything **they do** / **to reflect** how smart they are /
앞에 목적격 관계대명사가 생략됨 *명사적 용법(목적격 보어)*
많은 사람들에게 / '능력'은 지적 능력을 의미한다 / 그래서 그들은 자신이 하는 모든 것을 원한다 / 자신이 얼마나 똑똑한지를 보여주기를 /
— **writing** a brilliant legal brief, / **getting** the highest grade on
                          병렬 구조
a test, / **writing** elegant computer code, / **saying** something
exceptionally wise or witty / in a conversation. //
예컨대 훌륭한 법률 보고서를 작성하는 것 / 시험에서 최고의 성적을 받는 것 / 정연한 컴퓨터 코드를 작성하는 것 / 비범하게 현명하거나 재치 있는 말을 하는 것 / 대화에서 //
You could also define ability / **in terms of** a particular skill
                                 '~에 관하여'
or talent, / such as how well one **plays** the piano, / **learns** a
                                      병렬 구조
language, / or **serves** a tennis ball. //
여러분은 또한 능력을 정의할 수도 있다 / 특정한 기술이나 재능의 관점에서 / 누군가가 피아노를 얼마나 잘 치는지 / 언어를 얼마나 잘 배우는지 / 또는 테니스공을 얼마나 잘 서브하는지와 같은 //
Some people focus on their ability / **to be** attractive, entertaining,
/ up on the latest trends, / or **to have** the newest gadgets. //
                              병렬 구조
어떤 사람들은 그들의 능력에 초점을 맞춘다 / 매력적이고 재미있으며 / 최신 유행에 맞추거나 / 최신 기기를 가질 수 있는 //
복합 관계부사(= No matter how)   단서 1 능력은 어떻게 정의되든 문제가 발생함
However ability may be defined / a problem occurs / when **it is
the sole determinant of one's self-worth**. //
능력이 어떻게 정의되든지 / 문제가 발생한다 / 그것이 자신의 가치의 유일한 결정 요소일 때 //
The performance becomes the *only* measure of the person; /
nothing else is taken into account. // 단서 2 누군가의 수행이 유일한 척도가 되어 다른 것은 고려되지 않음
수행이 그 사람의 '유일한' 척도가 된다 / 그 외 어느 것도 고려되지 않는다 //
An outstanding performance means / an outstanding person; /
an average performance means / an average person. //
뛰어난 수행은 의미한다 / 뛰어난 사람을 / 평범한 수행은 의미한다 / 평범한 사람을 //
단서 3 단순히 뛰어난 수행은 뛰어난 사람을, 평범한 수행은 평범한 사람을 의미하게 됨
Period. //
끝 //

- refer to ~을 나타내다 • intellectual ⓐ 지적인
- competence ⓝ 능력, 능숙함 • brilliant ⓐ 훌륭한
- legal ⓐ 법률과 관련된 • brief ⓝ 업무 (보고서)
- elegant ⓐ 우아한, 정연한 • exceptionally ⓐ 각별히
- witty ⓐ 재치 있는 • gadget ⓝ 기기, 장치
- measure ⓝ 척도, 기준 • take into account ~을 고려하다
- outstanding ⓐ 뛰어난 • sole ⓐ 유일한
- determinant ⓝ 결정 요인 • accompany ⓥ 동반하다

많은 사람들에게 '능력'은 지적 능력을 의미하므로 그들은 자신이 하는 모든 것이 자신이 얼마나 똑똑한지를 보여주기를 원한다. 예컨대, 훌륭한 법률 보고서를 작성하는 것, 시험에서 최고의 성적을 받는 것, 정연한 컴퓨터 코드를 작성하는 것, 대화에서 비범하게 현명하거나 재치 있는 말을 하는 것이다. 여러분은 또한 피아노를 얼마나 잘 치는지, 언어를 얼마나 잘 배우는지, 테니스공을 얼마나 잘 서브하는지와 같은 특정한 기술이나 재능의 관점에서 능력을 정의할 수도 있다. 어떤 사람들은 매력적이고, 재미있고, 최신 유행에 맞추거나, 최신 기기를 가질 수 있는 그들의 능력에 초점을 맞춘다. 능력이 어떻게 정의되든지, **그것이 자신의 가치의 유일한 결정 요소일 때** 문제가 발생한다. 수행이 그 사람의 '유일한' 척도가 되며, 다른 어느 것도 고려되지 않는다. 뛰어난 수행은 뛰어난 사람을 의미하고, 평범한 수행은 평범한 사람을 의미한다. 끝.

다음 빈칸에 들어갈 말로 가장 적절한 것을 고르시오. [3점]

① it is the sole determinant of one's self-worth
그것이 자신의 가치의 유일한 결정 요소이다   능력이 유일한 척도일 때 문제가 발생함
② you are distracted by others' achievements
여러분은 다른 사람의 성취를 위해 주의가 분산된다   주의가 분산된다는 언급은 없음
③ there is too much competition in one field
한 분야에 너무 많은 경쟁이 있다   너무 많은 경쟁이 있다는 내용이 아님
④ you ignore feedback about a performance
여러분은 수행에 대한 피드백을 무시한다   수행에 대한 피드백을 무시한다는 내용은 없음
⑤ it is not accompanied by effort
그것이 노력을 수반하지 않는다   능력이 노력을 수반하지 않을 때 문제가 발생한다는 내용이 아님

왜 정답? ★★★ [정답률 59%]

빈칸 문장	능력이 어떻게 정의되든지, ＿＿＿＿＿＿＿＿＿일 때 문제가 발생한다.
빈칸 문장 뒤 예시	수행이 그 사람의 '유일한' 척도가 되며, 다른 어느 것도 고려되지 않는다.

➡ 빈칸 문장: 능력은 어떻게 정의되든, '어떨 때' 문제가 발생한다. 단서 1
➡ 빈칸 문장 뒤: 수행 = 그 사람을 판단하는 유일한 척도 = 그 사람의 능력 단서 2
▶ 다른 요소는 고려하지 않고, 수행만으로 사람을 정의한다고 했으므로 ① '그것이 자신의 가치의 유일한 결정 요소'일 때 문제가 발생하는 것이다.

왜 오답?
② 다른 사람의 성취에 의해 주의가 분산되면 문제가 발생한다는 언급은 없다.
(▶ 이유: 앞에 언급된 여러 능력들은 다른 사람의 성취로 제시된 것이 아니다.)
③ 한 분야에 너무 많은 경쟁이 있으면 문제가 발생한다는 내용의 글이 아니다.
④ 수행에 대한 피드백을 무시하면 문제가 발생한다고는 하지 않았다.
⑤ 능력이 노력을 수반해야 한다고 말하는 글이 아니다.

M 57 정답 ① *영화에서 외국어 대화 자막이 없는 것의 효과*

앞에 관계부사 when 생략
Most times / a foreign language is spoken in film, / subtitles are
부사적 용법(목적)
used / to translate the dialogue / for the viewer. //
대부분의 경우 / 영화에서 외국어가 사용되는 / 자막이 사용된다 / 대화를 통역하려고 / 관객을 위해 //

관계부사
However, / there are occasions / when foreign dialogue is left
unsubtitled / (and thus incomprehensible / to most of the target
audience). //
하지만 / 경우가 있다 / 외국어 대화가 자막 없이 처리되는 / (그리하여 이해하지 못하게 / 대부분의 주요 대상 관객이) //

앞 문장의 when 이하를 받음
This is often done / if the movie is seen mainly / from the
주격 관계대명사
viewpoint / of a particular character / who does not speak the
language. // 단서1 외국어 대화가 자막 없이 처리되는 경우는 그 언어를 할 줄 모르는 특정 등장인물의 관점에서 영화가 보여질 때 일어남
이것은 흔히 일어난다 / 영화가 주로 보여진다면 / 관점에서 / 특정 등장인물의 / 그 언어를 할 줄 모르는 //

명사적 용법(목적격보어)
Such absence of subtitles / allows the audience / to feel a similar
목적격 관계대명사
sense of incomprehension and alienation / that the character
feels. // 단서2 자막의 부재가 관객에게 등장인물과 비슷한 감정을 느끼도록 해줌
그러한 자막의 부재는 / 관객에게 허락한다 / 비슷한 몰이해와 소외의 감정을 느끼도록 / 그 등장인물이 느끼는 것과 //

An example of this is seen / in Not Without My Daughter. //
이것의 한 예를 볼 수 있다 / Not Without My Daughter에서 //

과거분사
The Persian language dialogue / spoken by the Iranian
characters / is not subtitled /
페르시아어 대화에는 / 이란인 등장인물들이 하는 / 자막이 없다 /

because the main character Betty Mahmoody / does not
speak Persian / and the audience is **seeing the film / from her
viewpoint.** //
왜냐하면 주인공 Betty Mahmoody가 / 페르시아어를 하지 못해서 / 그리고 관객은 영화를 보고 있게 된다 / 그녀의 시각에서 //

• foreign language 외국어   • translate ⓥ 통역하다
• dialogue ⓝ 대화   • viewer ⓝ 관객   • occasion ⓝ 경우
• mainly ⓐⓓ 주로   • viewpoint ⓝ 관점, 시각
• particular ⓐ 특정한   • absence ⓝ 부재
• incomprehension ⓝ 몰이해   • impress ⓥ 감명을 주다
• heated ⓐ 열띤   • debate ⓝ 토론

영화에서 외국어가 사용되는 대부분의 경우 관객을 위해 대화를 통역하려고 자막이 사용된다. 하지만 외국어 대화가 자막 없이 (그리하여 대부분의 주요 대상 관객이 이해하지 못하게) 처리되는 경우가 있다. 영화가 그 언어를 할 줄 모르는 특정한 등장인물의 관점에서 주로 보여지는 경우에 흔히 이렇게 처리된다. 그러한 자막의 부재는 관객이 그 등장인물이 느끼는 것과 비슷한 몰이해와 소외의 감정을 느끼게 한다. 이것의 한 예를 Not Without My Daughter에서 볼 수 있다. 주인공 Betty Mahmoody가 페르시아어를 하지 못하기 때문에 이란인 등장인물들이 하는 페르시아어 대화에는 자막이 없으며, 관객은 **그녀의 시각에서 영화를 보고** 있게 된다.

다음 빈칸에 들어갈 말로 가장 적절한 것을 고르시오. [3점]
주인공도 페르시아어를 하지 못하므로, 자막을 없애 주인공의 시각에서 영화를 보게 해준다는 의미임
① seeing the film from her viewpoint
그녀의 시각에서 영화를 보고
② impressed by her language skills 외국어에 대한 언급이 많은 것으로 만든
그녀의 언어 능력에 감명받고   함정
③ attracted to her beautiful voice 주인공의 목소리에 대한 내용은 없음
그녀의 아름다운 목소리에 끌리고
④ participating in a heated debate 토론에 대한 언급은 없음
열띤 토론에 참여하고 있고
⑤ learning the language used in the film
영화에서 쓰인 언어를 배우고   영화에서 외국어가 사용된다는 언급으로 만든 오답

왜 정답? ★★★ [정답률 62%]

영화에서 외국어 대화에 자막을 달지 않는 것을 통해, 등장인물이 그 언어를 하지 못해 느끼는 몰이해와 소외의 감정을 관객들에게도 전달할 수 있다는 내용의 글이다.
예로 든 영화에서 주인공이 페르시아어를 하지 못하기 때문에 페르시아어 대화 자막을 넣지 않았다고 했으므로 관객으로 하여금 '주인공의 시각에서 영화를 보는' 느낌을 준다는 의미가 되어야 한다. 따라서 빈칸에는 ① '그녀의 시각에서 보고'가 들어가는 것이 가장 적절하다.

왜 오답?
② 외국어에 대한 언급이 많이 나왔지만, 관객들이 주인공의 언어 능력에 감명 받게 된다는 내용은 아니다.
③ 주인공의 아름다운 목소리에 대한 언급은 없다.
④ 관객들이 열띤 토론에 참가하고 있다는 것은 글의 내용과 무관하다.
⑤ 영화에서 외국어가 사용된다는 언급으로 만든 오답으로, 관객들이 영화에서 쓰인 언어를 배운다는 내용이 아니다.   주의

M 58 정답 ③ *대면 상호 작용과 지식 공유*

핵심문장 단서1 지식을 공유하는 가장 강력한 방법은 대면 상호 작용이라고 했음
Face-to-face interaction is a uniquely powerful / — and
형용사적 용법
sometimes the only — way / to share many kinds of knowledge,
from A to B: A에서 B까지
/ from the simplest to the most complex. //
대면 상호 작용은 유례없이 강력한 / 때로는 유일한 방법이다 / 많은 종류의 지식을 공유하는 / 간단한 것부터 가장 복잡한 것까지 //

형용사적 용법
It is one of the best ways / to stimulate new thinking and ideas,
too. //
그것은 가장 좋은 방법의 한 가지이기도 하다 / 새로운 생각과 아이디어를 자극하는 //

have difficulty (in) -ing: ~하는 데 어려움을 겪다
Most of us would have had difficulty / learning / how to tie a
how to-v(~하는 법)의 병렬 구조
shoelace / only from pictures, / or how to do arithmetic / from
a book. //
우리 대부분이 어려움을 겪었을 것이다 / 배우는 데 / 신발 끈 묶는 법을 / 그림만으로 / 또는 계산하는 방법을 / 책으로부터 //

단서 2 노벨상 수상자들이 이전 노벨상 수상자들의 학생이었다는 것은 상호 작용이나 접촉이 있었음을 보여줌

Psychologist Mihàly Csikszentmihàlyi found, / while studying high achievers, / that a large number of Nobel Prize winners / were the students / of previous winners:
목적어절을 이끄는 접속사 / 삽입된 분사구문

심리학자 Mihàly Csikszentmihàlyi는 발견했다 / 높은 성취도를 보이는 사람들을 연구하면서 / 다수의 노벨상 수상자가 / 학생들이라는 것을 / 이전 (노벨상) 수상자들의 /

they had access / to the same literature as everyone else, / but **personal contact** made a crucial difference / to their creativity. //

그들은 접근했다 / 다른 사람들과 똑같은 (연구) 문헌에 / 그러나 개인적인 접촉이 결정적인 차이를 만들었다 / 그들의 창의성에 //

Within organisations / this makes conversation / both a crucial factor for high-level professional skills / and the most important way / of sharing everyday information. //
both A and B: A와 B 둘 다

조직 내에서 / 이것은 대화를 만든다 / 고급 전문 기술을 위한 매우 중요한 요소로 / 그리고 가장 중요한 방식으로 / 일상 정보를 공유하는 //

- face-to-face 대면의
- interaction ⓝ 상호 작용
- uniquely ⓐⓓ 유례없이
- knowledge ⓝ 지식
- complex ⓐ 복잡한
- stimulate ⓥ 자극하다
- shoelace ⓝ 신발 끈
- psychologist ⓝ 심리학자
- previous ⓐ 이전의
- access ⓝ 접근
- crucial ⓐ 결정적인, 매우 중요한
- factor ⓝ 요소
- professional ⓐ 전문적인
- talent ⓝ 재능
- complex ⓐ 복합적인
- motivation ⓝ 동기

대면 상호 작용은 가장 간단한 것부터 가장 복잡한 것까지 많은 종류의 지식을 공유하는, 유례없이 강력한 — 때로는 유일한 — 방법이다. 그것은 새로운 생각과 아이디어를 자극하는 가장 좋은 방법의 한 가지이기도 하다. 우리 대부분이 그림만으로 신발 끈 묶는 법을 배웠거나, 책으로부터 계산하는 방법을 배웠다면 어려움을 겪었을 것이다. 심리학자 Mihàly Csikszentmihàlyi는 높은 성취도를 보이는 사람들을 연구하면서 다수의 노벨상 수상자가 이전 (노벨상) 수상자들의 학생들이라는 것을 발견했다. 그들은 다른 사람들과 똑같은 (연구) 문헌에 접근할 수 있었지만, **개인적인 접촉**이 그들의 창의성에 결정적인 차이를 만들었다. 이로 인해 조직 내에서 대화는 고급 전문 기술을 위한 매우 중요한 요소이자 일상 정보를 공유하는 가장 중요한 방식이 된다.

다음 빈칸에 들어갈 말로 가장 적절한 것을 고르시오.

① natural talent 타고난 재능이 결정적 차이를 만든다는 내용이 아님
　타고난 재능
② regular practice 규칙적인 연습에 대한 언급은 없음
　규칙적인 연습
③ personal contact 대면 상호 작용을 통한 개인적 접촉이 지식을 공유하게 해줘서 차이를 만들었다는 내용임
　개인적인 접촉
④ complex knowledge 복합적 지식이 창의성에 차이를 만들었다는 내용이 아님
　복합적인 지식
⑤ powerful motivation 강력한 동기에 대해서 언급되지 않음
　강력한 동기

>왜 정답? ★★★ [정답률 53%]

대면 상호 작용을 통해 개인적으로 접촉하고 대화하는 것이 고급 전문 기술이나 지식을 공유할 수 있는 가장 좋은 방법이라는 내용의 글이다.
빈칸이 포함된 문장은 많은 노벨상 수상자들이 이전 노벨상 수상자들의 제자로, 똑같은 문헌을 접해도 '개인적인 대화나 접촉'이 가능해 창의성에 영향을 받았다는 의미가 완성되어야 한다. 따라서 빈칸에 들어갈 말로 가장 적절한 것은 ③ '개인적인 접촉'이다.

>왜 오답?

① 타고난 재능이 창의성에 결정적 차이를 만든다는 언급은 없다.
② 규칙적인 연습이 창의성에 영향을 미쳤다는 내용이 아니다.
④ 복합적인 지식에 대한 내용은 나오지 않았다.
⑤ 강력한 동기가 창의성에서 차이를 만들었다는 내용이 아니다.

M 59 정답 ③ *후천적 환경과 양육의 중요성

In a study at Princeton University / in 1992, / research scientists looked at two different groups of mice. //
프린스턴 대학의 한 연구에서 / 1992년 / 연구 과학자들은 두 개의 다른 쥐 집단을 관찰했다 //

One group was made intellectually superior / by modifying the gene / for the glutamate receptor. //
한 집단은 지적으로 우월하게 만들어졌다 / 유전자를 변형함으로써 / 글루타민산염 수용체에 대한 //

Glutamate is a brain chemical / that is necessary in learning. //
주격 관계대명사
글루타민산염은 뇌 화학 물질이다 / 학습에 필수적인 //

The other group was genetically manipulated / to be intellectually inferior, / also done by modifying the gene / for the glutamate receptor. //
부사적 용법 / by -ing: ~함으로써

다른 집단도 역시 유전적으로 조작되었다 / 지적으로 열등하도록 / 유전자를 변형함으로써 / 글루타민산염 수용체에 대한 //

단서 1 유전적으로 지적 능력이 열등하도록 조작된 쥐들이 좋은 환경에서 길러짐

The smart mice were then raised / in standard cages, / while the inferior mice were raised in large cages / with toys and exercise wheels / and with lots of social interaction. //
접속사(반면에)

그 후 똑똑한 쥐들은 길러졌다 / 표준 우리에서 / 반면에 열등한 쥐들은 큰 우리에서 길러졌다 / 장난감과 운동용 쳇바퀴가 있고 / 사회적 상호 작용이 많은 //

At the end of the study, / although the intellectually inferior mice / were genetically handicapped, / they were able to perform / just as well as their genetic superiors. //
원급 비교

연구가 끝날 무렵 / 비록 지적 능력이 떨어지는 쥐들이 / 유전적으로 장애가 있었지만 / 그들은 수행할 수 있었다 / 그들의 유전적인 우월군들만큼 잘 //

단서 3 양육(후천적 환경)이 천성(선천적 성질)을 극복함

This was a real triumph / for nurture over nature. //
이것은 진정한 승리였다 / 천성(선천적 성질)에 대한 양육(후천적 환경)의 //

Genes are turned on or off / **based on what is around you**. //
유전자는 작동하거나 멈춘다 / 여러분 주변에 있는 것에 따라 //

단서 2 유전적으로 지적 능력이 우월한 쥐들과 지적 능력이 열등한 쥐들 사이에 수행 능력의 차이가 없음

- intellectually ⓐⓓ 지적으로
- superior ⓐ 우월한 ⓝ 상급자
- modify ⓥ 변형하다
- gene ⓝ 유전자
- receptor ⓝ 수용체
- chemical ⓝ 화학 물질
- necessary ⓐ 필수적인
- genetically ⓐⓓ 유전적으로
- inferior ⓐ 열등한
- raise ⓥ 기르다
- standard ⓐ 표준의
- social ⓐ 사회적인
- interaction ⓝ 상호 작용
- handicapped ⓐ 장애가 있는
- triumph ⓝ 승리
- nurture ⓝ 양육
- nature ⓝ 천성
- genetic ⓐ 유전의
- superiority ⓝ 우월성

1992년 프린스턴 대학의 한 연구에서, 연구 과학자들은 두 개의 다른 쥐 집단을 관찰했다. 한 집단은 글루타민산염 수용체에 대한 유전자를 변형함으로써 지적으로 우월하게 만들어졌다. 글루타민산염은 학습에 필수적인 뇌 화학 물질이다. 다른 집단도 역시 글루타민산염 수용체에 대한 유전자를 변형함으로써, 지적으로 열등하도록 유전적으로 조작되었다. 그 후 똑똑한 쥐들은 표준 우리에서 길러졌고, 반면에 열등한 쥐들은 장난감과 운동용 쳇바퀴가 있고 사회적 상호작용이 많은 큰 우리에서 길러졌다. 연구가 끝날 무렵, 비록 지적 능력이 떨어지는 쥐들이 유전적으로 장애가 있었지만, 그들은 그들의 유전적인 우월군들만큼 잘 수행할 수 있었다. 이것은 천성(선천적 성질)에 대한 양육(후천적 환경)의 진정한 승리였다. 유전자는 **여러분 주변에 있는 것에 따라** 작동하거나 멈춘다.

다음 빈칸에 들어갈 말로 가장 적절한 것을 고르시오. [3점]

① by themselves for survival
　생존을 위해 스스로 — 생존을 위해 유전자가 어떻게 작용하는지는 언급되지 않음
② free from social interaction 글에 나온 실험은 환경의 중요성을 보여주므로 반대가 됨
　사회적 상호 작용 없이
③ based on what is around you 후천적 환경, 즉 양육의 중요성을 설명함
　여러분 주변에 있는 것에 따라
④ depending on genetic superiority
　유전적 우월성에 따라서 — 유전적 우월성보다 중요한 것은 환경과 양육임
⑤ so as to keep ourselves entertained
　즐겁게 지내기 위해서 — 우리가 즐거울 수 있도록 유전자가 어떤 일을 하는지는 설명하지 않음

왜 정답? ★★★ [정답률 57%]

글에서 나온 실험은 유전적으로 지적 능력이 열등하게 조작된 쥐들을 좋은 환경에서 길렀을 때, 유전적으로 지적 능력이 우월한 쥐들만큼 수행을 잘 할 수 있다는 것을 보여준다. 이를 통해 타고난 천성보다 양육이 더 중요하다는 결론을 내릴 수 있다.

따라서 유전자가 작동하거나 멈추는 것은 후천적 환경, 즉 양육이 영향을 미친다는 의미가 되어야 하므로 빈칸에 들어갈 말로 가장 적절한 것은 ③ '여러분 주변에 있는 것에 따라'이다.

왜 오답?

① 생존을 위해 유전자가 어떻게 작용하는지에 대한 설명은 이 글에 나와 있지 않다.

② 양육 환경의 중요성을 알려주는 글이므로, 사회적 상호 작용 없이 작동한다는 것은 글의 내용과 반대가 된다.

④ 글에 나온 실험은 유전적 우월성보다 양육과 환경이 더 중요하다는 것을 알려준다.

⑤ 우리가 즐겁게 지낼 수 있도록 유전자가 어떤 역할을 하는지에 대한 언급은 없다. **함정**

M 60 정답 ② *수요 법칙이 적용되지 않는 기펜재

The law of demand / is that the demand for goods and services increases / as prices fall, / and the demand falls / as prices increase. //
~할수록

수요의 법칙은 / 상품과 서비스에 대한 수요가 증가하고 / 가격이 하락할수록 / 수요가 감소하는 것이다 / 가격이 상승할수록

Giffen goods are special types of products / for which the traditional law of demand does not apply. //
which은 특별한 유형의 상품(special types of products)을 가리킴

'기펜재'는 특별한 유형의 상품이다 / 전통적인 수요 법칙이 적용되지 않는 //

Instead of switching to cheaper replacements, / consumers demand more of giffen goods / when the price increases / and less of them / when the price decreases. //
= giffen goods

저렴한 대체품으로 바꾸는 대신, / 소비자들은 기펜재를 더 많이 수요한다 / 가격이 상승할 때 / 그리고 덜 (수요한다) / 가격이 하락할 때 //
단서 1 기펜재는 가격이 상승할 때 수요가 더 많아지고, 가격이 하락할 때 수요가 더 적어짐

Taking an example, / rice in China is a giffen good / because people tend to purchase less of it / when the price falls. //

예를 들어 / 중국의 쌀은 기펜재이다 / 사람들이 덜 구매하는 경향이 있기 때문에 / 가격이 하락할 때 //
단서 2 중국의 쌀은 기펜재임

The reason for this is, / when the price of rice falls, / people have more money to spend / on other types of products / such as meat and dairy / and, therefore, change their spending pattern. //
형용사적 용법

그 이유는 ~이다 / 쌀값이 하락하면 / 사람들이 쓸 돈이 많아지고 / 다른 종류의 상품에 / 고기나 유제품 같은 / 그 결과 소비 패턴을 바꾸기 때문 //

On the other hand, / as rice prices increase, / people **consume more rice**. //
단서 3 기펜재인 쌀 가격이 상승함

반면에 / 쌀값이 상승하면 / 사람들은 더 많은 쌀을 소비한다 //

- demand ⓝ 수요   • goods ⓝ 상품   • price ⓝ 가격
- traditional ⓐ 전통적인   • apply for ~에 적용하다
- instead of ~ 대신에   • switch ⓥ 바꾸다
- replacement ⓝ 대체품   • purchase ⓥ 구매하다
- dairy ⓝ 유제품   • consume ⓥ 소비하다
- savings ⓝ 저축한 돈, 저금   • invest ⓥ 투자하다

수요의 법칙은 가격이 하락할수록 상품과 서비스에 대한 수요가 증가하고, 가격이 상승할수록 수요가 감소하는 것이다. '기펜재'는 전통적인 수요 법칙이 적용되지 않는 특별한 유형의 상품이다. 저렴한 대체품으로 바꾸는 대신 소비자들은 가격이 상승할 때 기펜재를 더 많이, 가격이 하락할 때 덜 수요한다. 예를 들어, 중국의 쌀은 가격이 하락할 때 사람들이 덜 구매하는 경향이 있기 때문에 기펜재이다. 그 이유는, 쌀값이 하락하면, 사람들이

고기나 유제품 같은 다른 종류의 상품에 쓸 돈이 많아지고, 그 결과 소비 패턴을 바꾸기 때문이다. 반면에, 쌀값이 상승하면, 사람들은 **더 많은 쌀을 소비한다.**

다음 빈칸에 들어갈 말로 가장 적절한 것을 고르시오. [3점]

① order more meat 쌀값이 상승하면 고기나 유제품에 쓸 돈이 줄어들기 때문에 더 많은
더 많은 고기를 주문한다   고기를 주문하지 못할 것임
② consume more rice
더 많은 쌀을 소비한다   중국의 쌀은 기펜재이므로 쌀값이 상승하면 사람들의 쌀 수요는 증가함
③ try to get new jobs 기펜재 수요에 대해서 설명한 글이며 구직 활동에 대한 언급은 없음
새로운 직업을 얻으려고 노력한다
④ increase their savings 저축의 증가와 감소가 기펜재의 가격과 관련이 있는지는
그들의 저축을 증가시킨다   언급되지 않음
⑤ start to invest overseas 해외 투자에 대한 내용은 전혀 나오지 않음
해외에 투자하기 시작한다

왜 정답? ★★★ [정답률 57%]

기펜재는 전통적인 수요 법칙이 적용되지 않아 가격이 상승할 때 수요가 더 많아지고 가격이 하락할 때 수요가 더 적어지는 상품이라고 했다. 중국의 쌀이 기펜재라고 설명했기 때문에 쌀값이 상승하면 수요가 더 많아질 것이다. 따라서 빈칸에 들어갈 말로 가장 적절한 것은 ② '더 많은 쌀을 소비한다'이다.

왜 오답?

① 쌀값이 상승하면 고기나 유제품에 쓸 돈이 줄어들기 때문에 더 많은 고기를 주문하지 못하게 될 것이다.

③ 제품의 가격 상승과 구직의 연관성을 설명하는 글이 아니다.

④ 기펜재 가격의 상승이 저축 증가나 감소에 미치는 영향은 언급되지 않았다.

⑤ 이 글에서 해외 투자에 대한 내용은 전혀 나오지 않았다.

M 61 정답 ① *가상 공간에서 증진되는 창의력

One of the big questions / faced this past year / was how to keep innovation rolling / when people were working entirely virtually. //
단수 주어   단수 동사

가장 큰 질문 중 하나는 / 작년에 직면한 / 어떻게 혁신을 지속할 것인가 하는 것이었다 / 사람들이 완전히 가상 공간에서 작업할 때 //

But experts say / that digital work didn't have a negative effect / on innovation and creativity. //
목적어절을 이끄는 접속사

그러나 전문가들은 말한다 / 디지털 작업이 부정적인 영향을 미치지 않았다고 / 혁신과 창의성에
단서 1 디지털 작업은 혁신과 창의성에 부정적인 영향을 미치지 않음

Working within limits / pushes us to solve problems. //
동명사 주어(단수 취급)   단수 동사   **단서 2** 한계 내에서 일하는 것은 문제 해결을 독려함

한계 내에서 일하는 것은 / 우리에게 문제를 해결하도록 독려한다 //

Overall, / virtual meeting platforms put more constraints / on communication and collaboration / than face-to-face settings. //

전반적으로 / 가상 미팅 플랫폼은 더 많은 제약들을 가한다 / 의사소통과 협업에 / 대면 설정보다 //
단서 3 가상 미팅 플랫폼은 우리에게 더 많은 제약을 줌

For instance, / with the press of a button, / virtual meeting hosts can control the size of breakout groups / and enforce time constraints; / only one person can speak at a time; /
병렬 구조

예를 들어 / 버튼을 누르면 / 가상 회의 진행자는 소모임 그룹의 크기를 제어할 수 있다 / 그리고 시간제한을 강요할 (수 있다) / 한 번에 한 사람만이 말할 수 있다 /

nonverbal signals, / particularly those below the shoulders, / are diminished; / "seating arrangements" are assigned by the platform, / not by individuals; /
삽입 구문

비언어적 신호 / 특히 어깨 아래의 신호는 / 제한된다 / '좌석 배치'는 플랫폼에 의해 할당된다 / 개인이 아닌 /

and visual access to others may be limited / by the size of each participant's screen. //

그리고 다른 사람에 대한 시각적 접근은 제한될 수 있다 / 각 참가자의 화면 크기에 따라 //

Such **restrictions** are likely to stretch participants / beyond their usual ways of thinking, / boosting creativity. //
분사구문

이러한 제한점들은 참가자들을 확장시킬 가능성이 높다 / 그들의 일반적인 사고방식 너머까지 / 창의력을 증진시키면서 //
단서 4 참가자들이 일반적인 사고방식을 넘어서 창의력을 증진시킬 가능성이 생김

- face ⓥ 직면하다 · innovation ⓝ 혁신 · entirely [ad] 완전히
- virtual ⓐ 가상의 · constraint ⓝ 제약 · collaboration ⓝ 협업
- face-to-face ⓐ 대면의 · enforce ⓥ 강요하다 · at a time 한 번에
- nonverbal ⓐ 비언어적인 · diminish ⓥ 제한하다, 줄이다
- arrangement ⓝ 배정, 배치 · assign ⓥ 할당하다

작년에 직면한 가장 큰 질문 중 하나는 사람들이 완전히 가상 공간에서 작업할 때 어떻게 혁신을 지속할 것인가 하는 것이었다. 그러나 전문가들은 디지털 작업이 혁신과 창의성에 부정적인 영향을 미치지 않았다고 말한다. 한계 내에서 일하는 것은 우리에게 문제를 해결하도록 독려한다. 전반적으로, 가상 미팅 플랫폼은 대면 설정보다 의사소통과 협업에 더 많은 제약들을 가한다. 예를 들어, 버튼을 누르면, 가상 회의 진행자는 소모임 그룹의 크기를 제어하고 시간제한을 강요할 수 있다. 한 번에 한 사람만이 말할 수 있다. 비언어적 신호, 특히 어깨 아래의 신호는 제한된다. '좌석 배치'는 개인이 아닌 플랫폼에 의해 할당된다. 그리고 다른 사람에 대한 시각적 접근은 각 참가자의 화면 크기에 따라 제한될 수 있다. 이러한 제한점들은 참가자들을 그들의 일반적인 사고방식 너머까지 확장시켜 창의력을 증진시킬 가능성이 높다.

다음 빈칸에 들어갈 말로 가장 적절한 것을 고르시오.
① restrictions 한계가 문제 해결을 독려한다고 설명함
제한점들
② responsibilities 책임감이 창의력 증진에 미치는 영향은 언급되지 않음
책임감들
③ memories 기억들에 대한 언급은 없음
기억들
④ coincidences 우연의 일치들에 대한 언급은 없음
우연의 일치들
⑤ traditions 전통이 혁신과 창의성에 영향을 미치는 내용은 나오지 않음
전통들

>왜 정답? ★★★ [정답률 54%]

전반부에서 디지털 작업이 혁신과 창의성에 부정적인 영향을 미치지 않는다는 전문가들의 의견을 제시했고, 한계 내에서 일하는 것은 우리의 문제 해결을 독려한다고 설명했다. 그리고 후반부에서는 가상 미팅 플랫폼이 우리를 제한하는 예시가 나온다.
따라서 우리를 제한하고 한계 내에서 일하게 하는 가상 공간에서, 우리의 창의력이 증진될 수 있다는 것을 알 수 있다. 그러므로 빈칸에 들어갈 말로 가장 적절한 것은 ① '제한점들'이다.

>왜 오답?

② 책임감이 혁신과 창의성에 미치는 영향력을 설명하는 내용은 나오지 않는다.
③ 기억에 관련된 내용은 언급되지 않았다.
④ 우연의 일치는 언급되지 않았다.
⑤ 전통이 창의성에 영향을 준다는 내용은 없다.

M 62 정답 ⑤ *상호 작용을 통해 자신의 발달 구성하기

The prevailing view / among developmental scientists / is that people are active contributors / to their own development. //
보어절을 이끄는 접속사
지배적인 견해는 / 발달 과학자들 사이에서 / 사람들이 능동적인 기여자라는 것이다 / 그들 자신의 발달에 //
단서 1 사람들은 자신의 발달에 대한 능동적 기여자임
People are influenced / by the physical and social contexts / in which they live, / but they also play a role / in influencing their development / by interacting with, / and changing, / those
전치사+관계대명사
contexts. // 단서 2 사람들은 자신의 발달에 영향을 미치고 환경과 상호 작용함
사람들은 영향을 받는다 / 물리적인 그리고 사회적인 환경의 / 그들이 사는 / 그러나 그들은 또한 역할을 한다 / 그들의 발달에 영향을 주는 / 상호 작용함으로써 / 그리고 변화시킴으로써 / 그 환경들을 //
단서 3 심지어 유아도 상호 작용을 통해 자신의 발달을 구성함
Even infants influence / the world around them / and construct their own development / through their interactions. //
심지어 유아도 영향을 준다 / 그들 주변의 세상에 / 그리고 그들 자신의 발달을 구성한다 / 상호 작용을 통해서 //

Consider an infant / who smiles / at each adult / he sees; / he
주격 관계대명사 앞에 목적격 관계대명사 생략
influences his world / because adults are likely to smile, / use "baby talk," / and play with him / in response. //
유아를 생각해 보라 / 미소 짓는 / 각각의 어른에게 / 그가 바라보는 / 그는 자신의 세상에 영향을 준다 / 어른들이 미소 지을 것이기 때문에 / "아기 말"을 사용하고 / 그리고 그와 함께 놀아준다 / (그에) 반응하여 //
The infant brings adults / into close contact, / making one-on-one interactions / and creating opportunities / for learning. //
병렬 구조
그 유아는 어른들을 끌어들인다 / 친밀한 연결로 / 일대일 상호 작용을 하고 / 기회를 만든다 / 학습을 위한 //
By engaging the world around them, / thinking, / being curious, / and interacting with people, objects, and the world around them, / individuals of all ages are "manufacturers / of their own development." //
병렬 구조
그들 주변 세상에 참여함으로써 / 생각하고 / 호기심을 가지고 / 그리고 그들 주변의 사람들, 사물들, 그리고 세상과 상호 작용함으로써 / 모든 연령대의 개인들은 "생산하는 사람이 된다 / 그들 자신의 발달을" //

- prevailing ⓐ 지배적인 · view ⓝ 견해
- developmental ⓐ 발달의 · contributor ⓝ 기여자
- development ⓝ 발달 · physical ⓐ 물리적인 · context ⓝ 환경
- interact ⓥ 상호 작용하다 · infant ⓝ 유아
- construct ⓥ 구성하다 · engage ⓥ (관심을) 끌다, 참여하다
- object ⓝ 사물 · individual ⓝ 개인
- manufacturer ⓝ 생산하는 사람, 제조자 · generation ⓝ 세대
- shield ⓝ 방패 · explorer ⓝ 탐험가

발달 과학자들 사이에서 지배적인 견해는 사람들이 그들 자신의 발달에 능동적인 기여자라는 것이다. 사람들은 그들이 사는 물리적인 그리고 사회적인 환경의 영향을 받지만, 그들은 또한 그 환경들과 상호 작용하고, 그리고 변화시킴으로써, 그들의 발달에 영향을 주는 역할을 한다. 심지어 유아들도 그들 주변의 세상에 영향을 주고 상호 작용을 통해서 그들 자신의 발달을 구성한다. 그가 바라보는 각각의 어른에게 미소 짓는 유아를 생각해 보라. (그에) 반응하여, 어른들이 미소 짓고, "아기 말"을 사용하고, 그리고 그와 함께 놀아줄 것이기 때문에 그는 자신의 세상에 영향을 준다. 그 유아는 어른들을 친밀한 연결로 끌어들여서, 일대일 상호 작용을 하고 학습의 기회를 만든다. 그들 주변 세상의 관심을 끌고, 생각하고, 호기심을 가지고, 그리고 그들 주변의 사람들, 사물들, 그리고 세상과 상호 작용함으로써, 모든 연령대의 개인들은 "그들 자신의 발달을 생산하는 사람"이다.

다음 빈칸에 들어갈 말로 가장 적절한 것을 고르시오.
① mirrors of their generation 그들 세대를 비춰준다는 내용은 없음
그들 세대의 거울
② shields against social conflicts 사회적 갈등에 맞서는 역할을 한다는 내용이 아님
사회적 갈등에 맞서는 방패
③ explorers in their own career path 진로를 개척한다는 내용은 없음
그들만의 진로를 개척하는 탐험가
④ followers of their childhood dreams 유아가 언급된 것으로 만든 오답
어린 시절의 꿈을 꾸는 추종자
⑤ manufacturers of their own development 사람들은 환경과 상호
그들 자신의 발달을 생산하는 사람 작용하면서 자신의 발달을 구성한다는 내용

>왜 정답? ★★★ [정답률 56%]

사람들이 주변 환경과 상호 작용하고 환경을 변화시키면서 그들 스스로의 발달에 영향을 주는 역할을 한다는 내용이다. 유아를 예로 들어, 유아마저도 자신의 발달을 스스로 구성한다고 설명했다.
따라서 모든 연령대의 개인들은 그들 스스로 발달을 만들어 가는 사람들이라는 의미가 되어야 하므로 빈칸에 들어갈 말로 가장 적절한 것은 ⑤ '그들 자신의 발달을 생산하는 사람'이다.

>왜 오답?

① 모든 연령대의 개인들이 그들 세대의 거울이라는 언급은 없다.
② 사람들이 사회적 갈등에 맞서는 역할을 한다는 내용이 아니다.
③ 사람들이 자신의 진로를 개척하는 탐험가라는 내용은 없다.
④ 유아가 언급된 것으로 만든 오답일 뿐, 모든 사람들이 어린 시절의 꿈을 꾼다는 것과 상관없는 글이다.

정답 ⑤ *두 가지 정보를 동시에 처리할 수 없다.

In the studies of Colin Cherry / at the Massachusetts Institute for Technology / back in the 1950s, /
Colin Cherry의 연구에서 / 메사추세츠 공과 대학의 / 1950년대 /

his participants listened to voices / in one ear at a time / and then through both ears / in an effort to determine / whether we can 지각동사+목적어+목적격보어(동사원형)
listen to two people talk / at the same time. //
참가자들은 목소리를 들었다 / 한 번은 한쪽 귀로만 / 그다음엔 양쪽 귀로 / 판단하기 위해 / 우리가 두 사람이 이야기하는 것을 들을 수 있는지 / 동시에 //

One ear always contained a message / that the listener had to repeat back / (called "shadowing") / while the other ear included people speaking. //
한쪽 귀는 항상 메시지를 포함했다 / 듣는 사람이 다시 반복해야 하는 / ("shadowing"이라 불리는) / 다른 한쪽 귀가 사람들이 말하는 것을 포함하는 동안 //

The trick was to see / if you could totally focus on / the main 지각동사+목적어+목적격보어(현재분사)
message / and also **hear someone talking** / in your other ear. //
속임수는 알아보기 위한 것이었다 / 사람들이 완전히 집중할 수 있는지 / 주된 메시지에 / 다른 사람이 말하는 것 또한 들을 수 있는지를 / 다른 귀로는 / 단서 1 양쪽 귀로 각각 다른 것을 들을 수 있는지 알아보려는 목적의 실험을 했음

뒤에 목적어절을 이끄는 접속사 that 생략
Cleverly, / **Cherry found / it** was impossible / **for his participants** 진주어 가주어 의미상 주어
/ **to know** /
영리하게도 / Cherry는 발견했다 / 가능하지 않다는 것을 / 참가자들이 / 알아차리는 것이 /

whether the message in the other ear / was spoken / by a man or woman, / in English or another language, / or was even comprised / of real words / at all! // 단서 2 사람들은 다른 한쪽 귀로 돌리는 메시지에 대해 전혀 알지 못했음
다른 한쪽 귀로 돌리는 메시지가 / 말해진 것인지 / 남자 혹은 여자에 의해 / 영어인지 다른 외국어인지 / 심지어 구성된 것인지 / 실제 단어로 / 전혀 //

In other words, / people could not **process / two pieces of information / at the same time**. //
다시 말해서 / 사람들은 처리할 수 없었다 / 두 개의 정보를 / 동시에 //

- **institute** ⓝ (특히 교육 전문 직종과 관련된) 기관[협회]
- **contain** ⓥ 포함하다   • **shadow** ⓥ 따라하다
- **comprise** ⓥ 구성하다   • **process** ⓥ 처리하다

1950년대 메사추세츠 공과 대학의 Colin Cherry의 연구에서 우리가 두 사람이 이야기하는 것을 동시에 들을 수 있는지 판단하기 위해 참가자들은 한 번은 한쪽 귀로만 목소리를 듣고, 그다음엔 양쪽 귀로 들었다. 한쪽 귀로는 듣는 사람이 다시 반복해야 하는("shadowing"이라 불리는) 메시지를 계속 들려주었고 다른 한쪽 귀로는 사람들이 말하는 것을 들려주었다. 속임수는 사람들이 주된 메시지에 완전히 집중하면서 다른 귀로는 다른 사람이 말하는 것 또한 들을 수 있는지를 알아보기 위한 것이었다. 영리하게도, Cherry는 참가자들이 다른 한쪽 귀로 들리는 메시지가 남자가 말한 것인지 혹은 여자가 말한 것인지, 영어인지 다른 외국어인지, 심지어 실제 단어로 구성된 것인지조차 알아차리기가 전혀 가능하지 않다는 것을 발견했다. 다시 말해서, 사람들은 **두 개의 정보를 동시에 처리할** 수 없었다.

다음 빈칸에 들어갈 말로 가장 적절한 것을 고르시오. [3점]
① decide what they should do in the moment
  그 순간에 무엇을 해야 하는지 결정할   무엇을 해야 하는지 결정할 수 없었다는 내용이 아님
② remember a message with too many words   양쪽 귀로 듣는다고
  너무 많은 단어들이 사용된 메시지를 기억할   했지만, 너무 많은 단어가 사용된 메시지라는 것은 아님
③ analyze which information was more accurate
  어떤 정보가 더 정확한지 분석할   어떤 정보가 더 정확한지 분석할 수 없다는 글이 아님
④ speak their own ideas while listening to others   다른 사람의 말을
  다른 사람의 말을 듣는 동안 그들 자신의 생각을 말할   듣는 것에 대한 내용만 있음
⑤ process two pieces of information at the same time
  두 개의 정보를 동시에 처리할   양쪽 귀로 각각 다른 말을 집중해 들을 수 없다는 내용

> 왜 정답 ? ★★★ [정답률 55%]
한쪽 귀로는 반복해야 하는 메시지를 들려주고 다른 쪽 귀로는 사람들이 말하는 것을 들려주는 실험을 한 뒤, 사람들이 다른 쪽 귀로 들은 내용을 잘 기억하고 구분할 수 있는지 알아보는 연구에 대한 내용이다.

사람들은 다른 쪽 귀로 들은 말을 남자가 했는지 여자가 했는지, 영어였는지 다른 언어였는지 등을 전혀 알지 못했기 때문에 두 가지 정보를 동시에 처리할 수 없음을 이야기하고 있다. 따라서 빈칸에 들어갈 말로 가장 적절한 것은 ⑤ '두 개의 정보를 동시에 처리할'이다.

> 왜 오답 ?
① 사람들이 그 순간에 무엇을 해야 하는지 결정할 수 없었다는 내용이 아니다.
② 양쪽 귀로 듣는다고 했지만, 사람들이 너무 많은 단어가 사용된 메시지를 기억할 수 없었다는 언급은 없다.
③ 어떤 정보가 더 정확한지 분석할 수 없다는 내용은 나오지 않았다.
④ 다른 사람의 말을 듣는 것에 대한 내용만 있었고, 자신의 생각을 이야기하는 것에 대한 내용은 없다.

정답 ④ *플라톤이 실재론을 설명한 방식

Plato's realism includes all aspects of experience / but is most '~함으로써'
easily explained / **by considering** the nature of mathematical and geometrical objects / such as circles. //
플라톤의 실재론은 경험의 모든 측면을 포함하지만 / 가장 쉽게 설명된다 / 수학적이고 기하학적인 대상의 특성을 고려함으로써 / 원과 같은 //

He asked the question, / what is a circle? //
그는 질문을 했다 / '원이란 무엇인가'라는 //

You might indicate a particular example / **carved** into stone or 병렬 구조(example 수식)
drawn in the sand. //
여러분은 특정한 예를 가리킬 수 있다 / 돌에 새겨져 있거나 모래에 그려진 // 단서 1 플라톤은 세상에 물리적으로 나타나는 어떠한 원도 완벽하지 않다고 지적함

However, Plato would point out / that, **if you looked** closely 가정법 과거
enough, / you **would see** / that **neither** it, **nor** indeed any physical circle, was perfect. // neither A nor B: A와 B 둘 다 아닌
그러나 플라톤은 지적할 것이다 / 여러분이 충분히 면밀히 관찰한다면 / 여러분이 알게 될 것이라고 / 그 어느 것도, 진정 어떤 물리적인 원도 완벽하지 않다는 것을 //

They all possessed flaws, / and all were subject to change / and decayed with time. //
그것들 모두는 결함을 가지고 있었고 / 모두 변화의 영향을 받고 / 시간이 지남에 따라 쇠하였다 //

So how can we talk about perfect circles / if we cannot actually see or touch them? // 단서 2 플라톤은 우리가 보는 모든 원이 완벽하지 않은데, 완벽한 원을 어떻게 논할 수 있을지 고민함
그렇다면, 우리가 완벽한 원에 대해 어떻게 이야기할 수 있을까 / 그것을 실제로 보거나 만질 수 없다면 //

앞에 목적격 관계대명사가 생략됨
Plato's extraordinary answer / was that the world **we see** is a poor reflection / of a deeper unseen reality of *Forms*, or *universals*, / 단서 3 플라톤은 우리가 보는 세상이 실재를 불충분하게 반영한다고 설명함
플라톤의 비범한 대답은 / 우리가 보는 세상이 불충분한 반영물이라는 것이다 / 더 깊은 보이지 않는 '형상' 또는 '보편자'라는 실재의 /
관계부사
where perfect cats chase perfect mice / in perfect circles around perfect rocks. //
완벽한 고양이가 완벽한 쥐를 쫓는 / 완벽한 암석 주변에서 완벽한 원을 그리며 //

Plato believed / that the *Forms* or *universals* are the true reality / 주격 관계대명사
that exists in **an invisible but perfect world beyond our senses**. //
플라톤은 믿었다 / '형상' 또는 '보편자'가 진정한 실재라고 / 보이지 않지만 우리의 감각을 넘어선 완벽한 세계에 존재하는 //

- **realism** ⓝ 실재론   • **geometrical** ⓐ 기하학적인
- **nature** ⓝ 본성   • **indicate** ⓥ 가리키다   • **carve** ⓥ 조각하다, 새기다
- **point out** 지적하다   • **indeed** ⓐⓓ 진실로, 진정
- **physical** ⓐ 물리적인   • **flaw** ⓝ 결함
- **be subject to** ~에 영향을 받다   • **decay** ⓥ 부패하다, 쇠하다
- **extraordinary** ⓐ 비범한   • **reflection** ⓝ 반영, 반영물
- **unseen** ⓐ 보이지 않는   • **exist** ⓥ 존재하다
- **observable** ⓐ 관찰 가능한   • **overlap** ⓥ 겹치다   • **sense** ⓝ 감각
- **stereotype** ⓝ 고정관념   • **generalization** ⓝ 일반화

플라톤의 실재론은 경험의 모든 측면을 포함하지만, 원과 같은 수학적이고 기하학적인 대상의 특성을 고려함으로써 가장 쉽게 설명된다. 그는 '원이란 무엇인가'라는 질문을 했다. 여러분은 돌에 새겨져 있거나 모래에 그려진 특정한 예를 가리킬 수 있다. 그러나 플라톤은 여러분이 충분히 면밀히 관찰한다면, 여러분이 그 어느 것도, 진정 어떤 물리적인 원도 완벽하지 않다는 것을 알게 될 것이라고 지적할 것이다. 그것들 모두는 결함을 가지고 있었고, 모두 변화의 영향을 받고 시간이 지남에 따라 쇠하였다. 그렇다면, 우리가 완벽한 원을 실제로 보거나 만질 수 없다면, 그것에 대해 어떻게 이야기할 수 있을까? 플라톤의 비범한 대답은 우리가 보는 세상이 완벽한 고양이가 완벽한 암석 주변에서 완벽한 원을 그리며 완벽한 쥐를 쫓는 '형상' 또는 '보편자'라는 더 깊은 보이지 않는 실재의 불충분한 반영물이라는 것이다. 플라톤은 '형상' 또는 '보편자'가 **보이지 않지만 우리의 감각을 넘어선 완벽한 세계**에 존재하는 진정한 실재라고 믿었다.

다음 빈칸에 들어갈 말로 가장 적절한 것을 고르시오. [3점]
① observable phenomena of the physical world
플라톤은 물리적 세상의 관찰 가능한 현상들은 모두 '형상' 또는 '보편자'가 이 세상에 불완전하게 반영된 것이라 주장함
물리적 세상의 관찰 가능한 현상들
② our experiences shaped by external influences
외부의 영향으로 형성된 우리의 경험   우리의 경험에 관한 언급은 없음
③ an overlapping area between emotion and reason
감정과 이성 사이의 중첩되는 영역   감정과 이성에 관한 언급은 없음
④ an invisible but perfect world beyond our senses
보이지 않지만 우리의 감각을 넘어선 완벽한 세계
⑤ our perception affected by stereotype or generalization
고정관념이나 일반화에 영향을 받은 우리의 인식   고정관념과 일반화에 관한 언급은 없음
플라톤은 '형상' 또는 '보편자'가 우리가 볼 수 없는 완벽한 세계에 존재한다고 주장함

왜 정답? ★★★ [정답률 57%]

빈칸 문장	플라톤은 '형상' 또는 '보편자'가 ＿＿＿＿＿＿＿＿에 존재하는 진정한 실재라고 믿었다.

➡ 빈칸 문장: 플라톤은 '형상' 또는 '보편자'의 개념이 '여기'에 존재하는 진정한 실재라고 주장함
➡ Plato의 실재론:
비유: 세상에 물리적으로 나타나는 어떠한 원도 완벽하지 않음 [단서 1]
적용: 우리가 세상에서 보는 모든 원이 완벽하지 않고 구체적인 형상이 없는데, 완벽한 원을 어떻게 논할 수 있을지 고민함 [단서 2]
결론: 우리가 볼 수 없는 더 깊은 '형상' 또는 '보편자'에 완벽한 실재가 존재하며, 우리가 세상에서 보는 모든 것은 그 실재가 이 세상에 불완전하게 반영된 것이라 설명함 [단서 3]
▶ 플라톤은 우리가 볼 수 없는 더 깊은 세계에 '형상' 또는 '보편자'라는 완벽한 실재가 있으며, 그것이 불완전하게 반영된 것이 우리가 보는 세상이라고 설명했다. 따라서 플라톤이 생각했던 '형상' 또는 '보편자'의 개념이 존재하는 곳은 ④ '보이지 않지만 우리의 감각을 넘어선 완벽한 세계'이다.

왜 오답?
① 플라톤은 물리적 세상의 관찰 가능한 현상들은 모두 '형상' 또는 '보편자'가 이 세상에 불완전하게 반영된 것이라 주장했으므로, 빈칸의 내용과 상반된 보기이다. **함정**
② 우리의 경험에 관한 언급은 없었다.
③ 감정과 이성에 관한 언급은 없었다.
⑤ 고정관념과 일반화에 관한 언급은 없었다.

M 65 정답 ③ *스스로 유혹 차단하기

If you've ever made a poor choice, / you might be interested / in learning **how to break** that habit. //
how to-v: ~하는 법
여러분이 한 번이라도 좋지 못한 선택을 한 적이 있다면 / 여러분은 관심이 있을지도 모른다 / 그 습관을 깨는 방법을 배우는 데 //

One great way / **to trick** your brain into doing so / is **to sign** a
형용사적 용법(way 수식)   명사적 용법(주격 보어)
"Ulysses Contract." //
한 가지 좋은 방법은 / 그렇게 하도록 여러분의 뇌를 속이는 / 'Ulysses 계약'에 서명하는 것이다 //

The name of this life tip / comes from the Greek myth about
동격
Ulysses, / a captain **whose** ship sailed past the island of **the**
동격   소유격 관계대명사
Sirens, / a tribe of dangerous women /
이러한 인생 조언의 이름은 / Ulysses에 관한 그리스 신화에서 유래되었다 / 사이렌의 섬을 자신의 배로 항해해 지나갔던 선장인 / 위험한 여성 부족인 /
주격 관계대명사
who lured victims to their death / with their irresistible songs. //
희생자들을 죽음으로 유혹한 / 저항할 수 없는 노래로 //

Knowing that he would otherwise be unable to resist, /
그가 그렇게 하지 않으면 저항할 수 없다는 것을 알고 /

Ulysses instructed his crew / **to stuff** their ears with cotton / and
병렬 구조   부사적 용법(목적)
tie him to the ship's mast / **to prevent** him from turning their
ship / towards the Sirens. // [단서 1] Ulysses는 사이렌의 유혹을 이겨 내기 위해 스스로 배에 묶었음
Ulysses는 자신의 선원들을 지시했다 / 그들의 귀를 솜으로 막으라고 / 그리고 그를 배의 돛대에 묶으라고 / 그가 배를 돌리는 것을 막기 위해 / 사이렌에게로 //

It worked for him / and you can do the same thing / by **locking yourself / out of your temptations**. //
그것은 그에게 효과가 있었다 / 그리고 여러분은 같은 일을 할 수 있다 / 스스로를 차단함으로써 / 여러분의 유혹으로부터 //
[단서 2] 휴대 전화를 어떻게 멀리할 수 있을지를 예시로 제시함
For example, / if you want to stay off your cellphone / and concentrate on your work, / **delete** the apps **that** distract you /
주격 관계대명사
or **ask** a friend to change your password! //
병렬 구조
예를 들어 / 만약 여러분이 휴대 전화를 멀리하고 싶다면 / 그리고 여러분의 일에 집중하고 (싶다면) / 여러분의 주의를 산만하게 하는 앱들을 삭제하라 / 또는 친구에게 여러분의 비밀번호를 바꿔 달라고 요청하라 //

- trick ⓥ 속이다 · contract ⓝ 계약 · myth ⓝ 신화
- tribe ⓝ 부족 · victim ⓝ 희생자 · irresistible ⓐ 저항할 수 없는
- otherwise ⓐⓓ 그렇지 않으면 · resist ⓥ 저항하다
- instruct ⓥ 지시하다 · crew ⓝ (배·비행기의) 선원[승무원]
- stuff ⓥ 채워 넣다 · temptation ⓝ 유혹
- concentrate ⓥ 집중하다 · distract ⓥ 주의를 산만하게 하다
- mindset ⓝ 사고방식 · track ⓥ 추적하다 · progress ⓝ 과정

여러분이 한 번이라도 좋지 못한 선택을 한 적이 있다면, 여러분은 그 습관을 깨는 방법을 배우는 데 관심이 있을지도 모른다. 그렇게 하도록 여러분의 뇌를 속이는 한 가지 좋은 방법은 'Ulysses 계약'에 서명하는 것이다. 이러한 인생 조언의 이름은 저항할 수 없는 노래로 희생자들을 죽음으로 유혹한 위험한 여성 부족인 사이렌의 섬을 자신의 배로 항해해 지나갔던 선장 Ulysses에 관한 그리스 신화에서 유래되었다. 그렇게 하지 않으면 저항할 수 없다는 것을 알고, Ulysses는 자신이 배를 사이렌에게로 돌리는 것을 막기 위해 자신의 선원들이 그들의 귀를 솜으로 막고 그를 배의 돛대에 묶으라고 지시했다. 그것은 그에게 효과가 있었고 여러분은 **여러분의 유혹으로부터 스스로를 차단함**으로써 같은 일을 할 수 있다. 예를 들어, 만약 여러분이 휴대 전화를 멀리하고 여러분의 일에 집중하고 싶다면, 여러분의 주의를 산만하게 하는 앱들을 삭제하거나 친구에게 여러분의 비밀번호를 바꿔 달라고 요청하라!

다음 빈칸에 들어갈 말로 가장 적절한 것을 고르시오.
① letting go of all-or-nothing mindset
모 아니면 도라는 사고방식을 버림   극단적인 사고방식을 버리라는 내용이 아님
② finding reasons why you want to change
여러분이 변하고 싶은 이유를 찾음   여러분이 변해야 한다는 내용은 언급되지 않음
③ locking yourself out of your temptations
여러분의 유혹으로부터 스스로를 차단함   스스로 유혹을 차단하기 위한 노력을 하라고 함
④ building a plan and tracking your progress
계획을 수립하고 여러분의 진행 과정을 추적함   계획 수립과 진행 과정에 대한 내용이 아님
⑤ focusing on breaking one bad habit at a time
한 번에 나쁜 습관 하나씩 깨는 데 집중함   한 번에 하나씩 해결하라는 내용이 아님

왜 정답? ✿✿✿ [정답률 61%]

빈칸 문장	그것은 그에게 효과가 있었고 여러분은 _____으로써 같은 일을 할 수 있다.
빈칸 문장 앞 예시	그렇게 하지 않으면 저항할 수 없다는 것을 알고 Ulysses는 자신이 배를 사이렌으로 돌리는 것을 막기 위해 자신의 선원들이 그들의 귀를 솜으로 막고 그를 배의 돛대에 묶으라고 지시했다. 단서1

➡ **빈칸 문장:** 그에게 그것이 효과가 있었듯, 여러분도 '무엇을 함'으로써 같은 일을 할 수 있다. 단서
　▶ '그'가 누구이고, '그것'은 무엇인지를 확인해야 한다. 발상
➡ **빈칸 문장 앞 예시:** Ulysses(= 그)는 사이렌에게 유혹되지 않기 위해 스스로 배에 묶였다(= 그것).

빈칸 문장 뒤 예시	예를 들어(For example), 만약 여러분이 휴대 전화를 멀리하고 여러분의 일에 집중하고 싶다면, 여러분의 주의를 산만하게 하는 앱들을 삭제하거나 친구에게 여러분의 비밀번호를 바꿔 달라고 요청하라! 단서2

➡ **빈칸 문장 뒤 예시:** Ulysses가 스스로를 사이렌에게서 차단했듯, 휴대 전화의 앱들을 삭제하거나 비밀번호를 바꿈으로써 휴대 전화를 멀리할 수 있다.
　▶ 따라서 ③ '여러분의 유혹으로부터 스스로를 차단함'으로써 여러분도 Ulysses와 같은 일을 할 수 있다는 것이다.

왜 오답?

① 극단적인 사고방식을 버리라는 글이 아니다.
② 변하고자 하는 이유를 찾는 것이 중요하다는 내용이 아니다.
④ 계획 수립과 그 진행 과정에 대한 내용이 아니다. 함정
⑤ 첫 문장에 나온 break, habit을 넣어 만든 오답으로, 나쁜 습관을 한 번에 하나씩 해결하라고 조언하는 내용이 아니다.

M 66 정답 ④ *전문성이 주는 영향력

주격 관계대명사　단서1 자신의 직업에 전문성이 있는 사람들은 즉각적인 신뢰를 얻음
Individuals / who perform at a high level in their profession / often have instant credibility with others. //
개인들은 / 자신의 직업에서 높은 수준으로 수행하는 / 흔히 다른 사람들에게 즉각적인 신뢰를 얻는다 //

People admire them, / they want to be like them, / and they feel connected to them. //
사람들은 그들을 존경하고 / 그들처럼 되고 싶어 하고 / 그들과 연결되어 있다고 느낀다 //

부사절 접속사(양보)
When they speak, / others listen / — even if the area of their skill
'~와 관련이 없다'　앞에 목적격 관계대명사가 생략됨
/ has nothing to do with the advice / they give. //
그들이 말할 때 / 다른 사람들은 경청한다 / 비록 그들의 기술 분야가 / 조언과 관련이 없을지라도 / 그들이 주는 //
단서2 조언과 관련되지 않은 분야라도 전문성이 있으면 사람들은 경청함

Think about a world-famous basketball player. //
세계적으로 유명한 농구선수에 대해 생각해 보라 //

대동사(= made)　분사구문
He has made more money from endorsements / than he ever did / playing basketball. //
그는 광고로부터 더 많은 돈을 벌었다 / 그가 그간 벌었던 것보다 / 농구를 하면서 //

앞에 목적격 관계대명사가 생략됨
Is it because of his knowledge / of the products he endorses? //
그것이 그의 지식 때문일까 / 그가 광고하는 제품에 대한 //

No. //
아니다 //

선행사를 포함하는 관계대명사
It's because of what he can do / with a basketball. //
그것은 그가 할 수 있는 것 때문이다 / 농구로 //

The same can be said / of an Olympic medalist swimmer. //
같은 것이 말해질 수 있다 / 올림픽 메달리스트 수영 선수에도 //

선행사를 포함하는 관계대명사
People listen to him / because of what he can do in the pool. //
사람들은 그의 말을 경청한다 / 그가 수영장에서 할 수 있는 것 때문에 //

앞에 직접목적어절 접속사 that이 생략됨
And when an actor tells us / we should drive a certain car, / we don't listen / because of his expertise on engines. //
그리고 어떤 배우가 우리에게 말할 때 / 우리가 특정 자동차를 운전해야 한다고 / 우리는 경청하는 것이 아니다 / 엔진에 대한 그의 전문 지식 때문에 //

We listen / because we admire his talent. //
우리는 경청한다 / 우리가 그의 재능을 존경하기 때문에 //

Excellence connects. //
탁월함이 연결된다 //
단서3 사람들은 전문성이 있는 사람에게 연결되고 싶어 함

If you possess a high level of ability in an area, / others may desire to connect with you / because of it. //
만약 당신이 어떤 분야에서 높은 수준의 능력을 갖추고 있다면 / 다른 사람들은 당신과 연결되기를 원할 수도 있다 / 그것 때문에 //

- individual ⓝ 개인　· profession ⓝ 직업　· instant ⓐ 즉각적인
- credibility ⓝ 신뢰　· admire ⓥ 존경하다　· advice ⓝ 조언
- knowledge ⓝ 지식　· certain ⓐ 특정한
- expertise ⓝ 전문 지식[기술]　· talent ⓝ 재능
- patience ⓝ 인내심, 참을성　· sacrifice ⓝ 희생

자신의 직업에서 높은 수준으로 수행하는 사람들은 흔히 다른 사람들에게 즉각적인 신뢰를 얻는다. 사람들은 그들을 존경하고, 그들처럼 되고 싶어 하고, 그들과 연결되어 있다고 느낀다. 그들이 말할 때, 다른 사람들은 비록 그들의 기술 분야가 그들이 주는 조언과 관련이 없을지라도 경청한다. 세계적으로 유명한 농구선수에 대해 생각해 보라. 그는 그가 농구를 하면서 그간 벌었던 것보다 광고로부터 더 많은 돈을 벌었다. 그것이 그가 광고하는 제품에 대한 그의 지식 때문일까? 아니다. 그것은 그가 농구로 할 수 있는 것 때문이다. 올림픽 메달리스트 수영 선수도 마찬가지이다. 사람들은 그가 수영장에서 할 수 있는 것 때문에 그의 말을 경청한다. 그리고 어떤 배우가 우리에게 특정 자동차를 운전해야 한다고 말할 때, 우리는 엔진에 대한 그의 전문 지식 때문에 경청하는 것은 아니다. 우리는 그의 재능을 존경하기 때문에 경청한다. **탁월함**이 연결된다. 만약 당신이 어떤 분야에서 높은 수준의 능력을 갖추고 있다면, 다른 사람들은 그것 때문에 당신과 연결되기를 원할 수도 있다.

> **다음 빈칸에 들어갈 말로 가장 적절한 것을 고르시오.**
> ① Patience 인내심 때문에 존경을 받는 것이 아님
> 인내심
> ② Sacrifice 희생이 중요하다는 것이 아님
> 희생
> ③ Honesty 정직함이 중요하다는 것이 아님
> 정직함
> ④ Excellence 특정 분야에서 보여준 전문성이 신뢰로 연결됨
> 탁월함
> ⑤ Creativity 창의성은 언급되지 않음
> 창의성

왜 정답? ✿✿✿ [정답률 57%]

빈칸 문장	_____이 연결된다.
빈칸 문장 뒤	만약 당신이 어떤 분야에서 높은 수준의 능력을 갖추고 있다면, 다른 사람들은 그것 때문에 당신과 연결되기를 원할 수도 있다. 단서3

➡ **빈칸 문장:** '무엇'이 연결된다.
➡ **빈칸 문장 뒤:** 높은 수준의 능력을 갖춤 → 사람들은 연결되기를 원함
　▶ 따라서 빈칸은 '높은 수준'과 같은 맥락일 것임

글의 앞부분	· 자신의 직업에서 높은 수준으로 수행하는 사람들은 흔히 다른 사람들에게 즉각적인 신뢰를 얻는다. 단서1 · 그들이 말할 때, 다른 사람들은 비록 그들의 기술 분야가 그들이 주는 조언과 관련이 없을지라도 경청한다. 단서2

➡ 특정 분야에서 높은 수준으로 수행하는 능력은 이와 상관없는 분야에 대한 신뢰로 이어진다.
　▶ 따라서 ④ '탁월함'이 다른 분야로도 연결되는 것이다.

왜 오답?

① 인내심 때문에 존경받는다는 내용이 아니다.
② 희생의 중요성을 강조하는 내용이 아니다.
③ 정직함과 관련된 내용은 언급되지 않았다.
⑤ 창의성과는 관련 없는 내용이다.

M 67 정답 ③   ☆ 2등급 대비 [정답률 50%]

*실내 생활이 진화를 만든다?

단서 1 집은 실내 생활에 적응된 종을 수용하고 새로운 방향으로 진화하게 함

Our homes aren't just ecosystems, / they're unique ones, / hosting species / that are adapted to indoor environments / and pushing evolution in new directions. //
└병렬구조┘
우리의 집은 단순한 생태계가 아니다 / 그것들은 독특한 곳이다 / 종들을 수용하고 / 실내 환경에 적응된 / 새로운 방향으로 진화를 밀어붙이면서 //

단서 2 살충제와 독 등에 대한 내성을 키우며 진화했음

Indoor microbes, insects, and rats have all evolved / the ability
형용사적 용법(ability 수식)
to survive our chemical attacks, / developing resistance to
분사구문
antibacterials, insecticides, and poisons. //
실내 미생물, 곤충, 그리고 쥐들은 모두 진화시켜 왔다 / 우리의 화학적 공격에서 살아남을 수 있는 능력을 / 항균제, 살충제, 그리고 독에 대한 내성을 키우면서 //

German cockroaches are known / to have developed a distaste
계속적 용법의 주격 관계대명사
for glucose, / which is commonly used as bait / in roach traps. //
독일 바퀴벌레는 알려져 있다 / 포도당에 대한 혐오감을 발달시켜 왔다고 / 그리고 그것은 미끼로 흔히 사용된다 / 바퀴벌레 덫에 //
주어   계속적 용법의 주격 관계대명사
Some indoor insects, / which have fewer opportunities to feed /
본동사
than their outdoor counterparts, / seem to have developed the
ability to survive / when food is limited. //
일부 실내 곤충은 / 먹이를 잡아먹을 더 적은 기회를 가지는데 / 야외(에 사는) 상대방에 비해 / 생존할 수 있는 능력을 발달시켜 온 것으로 보인다 / 먹이가 제한적일 때 //
목적어절 접속사
Dunn and other ecologists have suggested / that as the planet
becomes more developed and more urban, / more species will
앞에 목적격 관계대명사 생략
evolve the traits / they need to thrive indoors. //
Dunn과 다른 생태학자들은 말해 왔다 / 지구가 점점 더 발전되고 도시화되면서 / 더 많은 종들이 특성들을 진화시킬 것이라고 / 실내에서 번성하기 위해 그들이 필요로 하는 //

Over a long enough time period, / indoor living could drive our evolution, too. // **단서 3** 실내 생활은 우리도 진화하게 만들었음
충분히 긴 시간에 걸쳐 / 실내 생활은 또한 우리의 진화를 이끌 수 있었다 //

Perhaps my indoorsy self / represents the future of humanity. //
아마도 실내 생활을 좋아하는 내 모습은 / 인류의 미래를 대변할 것이다 //

- ecosystem ⓝ 생태계   • adapt ⓥ 적응하다   • evolution ⓝ 진화
- microbe ⓝ 미생물   • evolve ⓥ 진화하다
- resistance ⓝ 저항(력), 내성   • antibacterial ⓝ 항균제
- insecticide ⓝ 살충제   • cockroach ⓝ 바퀴벌레(= roach)
- distaste ⓝ 혐오감, 불쾌감   • counterpart ⓝ 상대(방)
- ecologist ⓝ 생태학자   • urban ⓐ 도시의   • trait ⓝ 특성, 속성
- thrive ⓥ 번성하다, 번창하다   • indoorsy ⓐ 실내 생활을 좋아하는
- humanity ⓝ 인류   • extinct ⓐ 멸종된   • habitat ⓝ 서식지
- organism ⓝ 유기체   • boundary ⓝ 경계

우리의 집은 단순한 생태계가 아니라 독특한 곳이며, 실내 환경에 적응된 종들을 수용하고 새로운 방향으로 진화를 밀어붙인다. 실내 미생물, 곤충, 그리고 쥐들은 모두 항균제, 살충제, 독에 대한 내성을 키우면서 우리의 화학적 공격에서 살아남을 수 있는 능력을 진화시켜 왔다. 독일 바퀴벌레는 바퀴벌레 덫에서 미끼로 흔히 사용되는 포도당에 대한 혐오감을 발달시켜 온 것으로 알려져 있다. 야외(에 사는) 상대방에 비해 먹이를 잡아먹을 더 적은 기회를 가지는 일부 실내 곤충은 먹이가 제한적일 때 생존할 수 있는 능력을 발달시켜 온 것으로 보인다. Dunn과 다른 생태학자들은 지구가 점점 더 발전되고

도시화되면서, 더 많은 종들이 **실내에서 번성하기 위해 그들이 필요로 하는 특성들을 진화시킬** 것이라고 말해 왔다. 충분히 긴 시간에 걸쳐, 실내 생활은 또한 우리의 진화를 이끌 수 있었다. 아마도 실내 생활을 좋아하는 내 모습은 인류의 미래를 대변할 것이다.

다음 빈칸에 들어갈 말로 가장 적절한 것을 고르시오. [3점]

① produce chemicals to protect themselves
자신을 보호하기 위해 화학 물질을 생산하다   화학 물질을 생산하는 종에 대한 언급은 없음
② become extinct with the destroyed habitats
파괴된 서식지와 함께 멸종되다   서식지 파괴, 종의 멸종과 관련된 내용이 아님
③ evolve the traits they need to thrive indoors
실내에서 번성하기 위해 그들이 필요로 하는 특성들을 진화시키다   실내 생활에 적응하기 위해 진화했음
④ compete with outside organisms to find their prey
먹이를 찾기 위해 외부 유기체와 경쟁하다   외부 유기체와 경쟁한다는 내용이 아님
⑤ break the boundaries between wildlife and humans
야생 동물과 인간 사이의 경계를 허물다   야생 동물과 인간과의 경계에 대한 글이 아님

왜 2등급? 다섯 개의 선택지 모두에 글에서 언급된 어구가 포함되어 있어, 글의 내용을 정확하게 파악하지 못하면 정답을 골라내기 어려운 2등급 대비 문제이다. 실내 미생물, 곤충, 쥐가 살충제와 독 등에 대한 내성을 키운 것의 결과가 어땠는지에 주목하여 글을 읽어야 한다.

| 문제 풀이 순서 |

1st 먼저 빈칸 문장을 읽고, 빈칸에 들어갈 말을 예측한다.

빈칸 문장	Dunn과 다른 생태학자들은 지구가 점점 더 발전되고 도시화되면서, 더 많은 종들이 _____ 것이라고 말해 왔다.

➡ 지구가 발전하면서 더 많은 종들이 '어떠할' 것이라고 했으므로, **단서** 도시화에 따라 생물들이 '어떻게' 되었는지 파악해야 한다. **발상**

2nd 글의 나머지 부분을 확인해서 정답을 찾는다.

글의 앞부분	• 우리의 집은 단순한 생태계가 아니라 독특한 곳이며, ~ 새로운 방향으로 진화를 밀어붙인다. **단서 1** • 실내 미생물, 곤충, 그리고 쥐들은 ~ 화학적 공격에서 살아남을 수 있는 능력을 진화시켜 왔다. **단서 2**

➡ 집은 미생물, 곤충, 쥐 등에게 화학적 공격을 가하지만, 동시에 그들이 내성을 키워 살아남도록 하는 새로운 방향의 진화를 이끈다.
▶ 빈칸 문장의 species의 예시로 실내 미생물, 곤충, 쥐를 제시함

글의 뒷부분	• 충분히 긴 시간에 걸쳐, 실내 생활은 또한 우리의 진화를 이끌 수 있었다. **단서 3** • 아마도 실내 생활을 좋아하는 내 모습은 인류의 미래를 대변할 것이다.

➡ 실내 생활은 앞서 언급한 생물뿐 아니라 인류의 진화도 이끌었다.
▶ 즉, 지구가 발전하면서 더 많은 종들이 ③ '실내에서 번성하기 위해 그들이 필요로 하는 특성들을 진화시킬' 것이다.

| 선택지 분석 |

① 화학적 공격에서 살아남을 수 있는 능력을 진화시켜 온 종들에 대한 언급은 있지만, 화학 물질을 생산하는 종에 대해서는 언급하지 않았다.
② 파괴된 서식지나 종의 멸종과 관련된 내용은 언급하지 않았다.
③ 예시를 통해 여러 종이 실내 환경에 적응하기 위해 진화했음을 설명했다.
④ 먹이를 잡아먹을 기회가 적은 일부 실내 곤충이 진화했다고 한 것은 하나의 예시이다.
⑤ 야생 동물과 인간이 가까워진다는 내용이라고 볼 수 없다.

*가격을 이용한 소비자 심리 조작

When I worked for a large electronics company / **that** manufactured laser and ink-jet printers, / I soon discovered / why there are often three versions of many consumer goods. //

<small>주격 관계대명사</small>

내가 큰 전자 회사에서 일했을 때 / 레이저와 잉크젯 프린터를 생산했던 / 나는 곧 발견했다 / 많은 소비 상품의 세 가지 버전이 종종 있는 이유를 //

<small>부사절 접속사 (조건)</small>
If the manufacturer makes / only one version of its product, / people **who** bought it / **might have been** willing to spend more money, / so the company is losing some income. //

<small>주격 관계대명사 / might have p.p.: ~했을지도 모른다</small>

만약 생산자가 만든다면 / 그 제품의 오직 한 가지 버전만 / 그것을 구매했던 사람들은 / 기꺼이 더 많은 돈을 쓰려고 했을 수도 있어서 / 회사는 일부 수입을 잃을 것이다 //

<small>단서 1 두 개의 버전이 제공되면 덜 비싼 모델을 구입함</small>
If the company offers two versions, / **one** with more features and more expensive than **the other**, / people will compare the two models / and still buy the less expensive one. //

<small>one: 하나, the other: 나머지 하나</small>

만약 그 회사가 두 버전을 제공하는데 / 하나가 다른 것보다 더 많은 기능과 더 비싼 가격을 가진다면 / 사람들은 두 모델을 비교하고 / 여전히 덜 비싼 것을 살 것이다 //

<small>비교급 강조 부사</small>
But / if the company introduces a third model / with **even** more features and more expensive than the other two, / **sales** of the second model **go** up; /

<small>복수 주어 / 복수 동사</small>

하지만 / 만약 그 회사가 세 번째 모델을 출시한다면 / 나머지 두 개보다 훨씬 더 많은 기능과 더 비싼 가격을 가진 / 두 번째 모델의 판매가 증가하는데 /

many people like the features of the most expensive model, / but not the price. //

<small>단서 2 세 번째 모델이 제공되면 그보다는 덜 비싼 중간 모델을 구입함</small>

왜냐하면 많은 사람들은 가장 비싼 모델의 기능을 좋아하지만 / 그것의 가격을 좋아하지는 않기 때문이다 //

<small>단서 3 가장 싼 모델보다는 기능이 많고 가장 비싼 모델보다는 가격이 덜 비싼 중간 제품을 사게 됨</small>
The middle item has more features / than the least expensive one, / and it is less expensive than the fanciest model. //

중간 제품은 더 많은 기능이 있고 / 가장 저렴한 제품보다 / 가장 고급 모델보다는 덜 비싸다 //

<small>being이 생략된 분사구문 / 현재완료 수동태</small>
They buy the middle item, / **unaware** that / they **have been manipulated** by the presence of the higher-priced item. //

그들은 중간 제품을 구입한다 / 알지 못한 채 / 자신이 더 비싼 가격의 제품의 존재에 의해 조종되었다는 것을 //

- manufacture ⓥ 생산[제조]하다　　• goods ⓝ 상품
- be willing to-v 기꺼이 ~하려고 하다　　• income ⓝ 수입
- feature ⓝ 기능　• fancy ⓐ 고급의　　• unaware ⓐ 알지 못하는
- manipulate ⓥ 조종하다　　• presence ⓝ 존재
- high-volume ⓐ 대량의　　• low-margin ⓐ 가격이 싼, 수익이 적은
- trick ⓥ 속이다　　• unnecessary ⓐ 불필요한　　• fool ⓥ 속이다
- repeatedly ⓐ�d 반복적으로

내가 레이저와 잉크젯 프린터를 생산했던 큰 전자 회사에서 일했을 때 나는 많은 소비 상품의 세 가지 버전이 종종 있는 이유를 곧 발견했다. 만약 생산자가 그 제품의 오직 한 가지 버전만 만든다면 그것을 구매했던 사람들은 기꺼이 더 많은 돈을 쓰려고 했을 수도 있어서 회사는 일부 수입을 잃을 것이다. 만약 그 회사가 두 버전을 제공하는데 한 버전이 나머지보다 더 많은 기능과 더 비싼 가격을 가진다면, 사람들은 두 모델을 비교하고 여전히 덜 비싼 것을 살 것이다. 하지만 만약 그 회사가 나머지 두 개보다 훨씬 더 많은 기능과 더 비싼 가격을 가진 세 번째 모델을 출시한다면 두 번째 모델의 판매가 증가하는데, 왜냐하면 많은 사람들은 가장 비싼 모델의 기능을 좋아하지만 그것의 가격을 좋아하지는 않기 때문이다. 중간 제품은 가장 저렴한 제품보다 더 많은 기능이 있고 가장 고급 모델보다는 덜 비싸다. 그들은 자신이 **더 비싼 가격의 제품의 존재에 의해 조종되었다**는 것을 알지 못한 채 중간 제품을 구입한다.

다음 빈칸에 들어갈 말로 가장 적절한 것을 고르시오. [3점]

① manipulated by the presence of the higher-priced item
<small>더 비싼 세 번째 제품의 존재로 인해 중간 제품을 사도록 소비자들의 결정이 유도됨</small>
<small>더 비싼 가격의 제품의 존재에 의해 조종된</small>
② persuaded by a high-volume, low-margin strategy
<small>싼 가격으로 대량 판매하는 전략에 의해 설득된　　싼 가격으로 대량 판매하는 전략은 언급되지 않았음</small>
③ tricked to keep purchasing unnecessary products
<small>불필요한 제품을 계속 구매하도록 속은　　소비자들이 반복해서 불필요한 제품을 구매하는 내용은 없음</small>
④ fooled by the wrong information on the price
<small>잘못된 가격 정보에 속아 넘어간　　잘못된 가격 정보는 언급되지 않았음</small>
⑤ exposed to a discounted price repeatedly
<small>할인된 가격에 반복적으로 노출된　　제품 가격의 할인은 언급되지 않았음</small>

왜 2등급? 일반적으로 알려진 잘못된 소비 습관들(박리다매에 현혹되는 것, 불필요한 제품 구매)이 선택지에 있어서 선입견으로 답을 고르기 쉬운 2등급 대비 문제이다. 세 가지 제품이 등장하기 때문에 제품 간 '비교'가 정답의 단서임을 파악해야 한다.

| 문제 풀이 순서 |

1st 빈칸이 포함된 문장과 그 앞 문장을 읽고, 빈칸에 들어갈 말에 대한 단서를 얻는다.

빈칸 문장 앞	The middle item has more features than the least expensive one, and it is less expensive than the fanciest model. 중간 제품은 가장 저렴한 제품보다 더 많은 기능이 있고 가장 고급 모델보다는 덜 비싸다. 단서 3
빈칸 문장	They buy the middle item, unaware that they have been _____. 그들은 자신이 _____ 것을 알지 못한 채 중간 제품을 구입한다.

➡ 중간(두 번째) 제품은 가장 저렴한 모델보다 기능은 더 많지만 가장 비싼 모델보다는 가격이 저렴하다고 했다. **단서** 소비자들이 '무엇'을 알지 못한 채 중간 제품을 선택하게 되는지 살펴봐야 한다. **발상**

2nd 글의 나머지 부분을 읽고, 빈칸에 들어갈 적절한 말을 찾는다.

⌈ • 기능 및 가격: 모델 A < 모델 B ⇨ 덜 비싼 '모델 A'를 선택 단서 1
⌊ • 기능 및 가격: 모델 A < 모델 B < 모델 C ⇨ 중간인 '모델 B'의 판매가 증가함 단서 2

➡ 선택지가 두 가지(모델 A와 B)뿐일 때는 덜 비싼 모델 A가 선택된다. 하지만 세 가지(모델 A, B, C)일 때는 A보다는 많은 기능과 C보다는 저렴한 가격으로 인해 앞의 경우에서 선택되지 않았던 모델 B의 판매가 증가한다.

▶ 더 비싼 모델 C의 존재로 인해 처음에는 선택되지 않았던 모델 B가 선택을 더 많이 받게 되는 것이므로, 소비자들은 ① '더 비싼 가격의 제품의 존재에 의해 조종된' 것을 모른 채 중간 제품을 구매하는 것이다.

| 선택지 분석 |

① 더 비싼 세 번째 제품의 존재로 인해 중간 제품을 사도록 소비자들의 결정이 조종되는 것이다.
② 제품별 가격 비교는 언급되었지만, 대량 판매는 언급되지 않았다.
③ 세 가지 모델이 있을 때 소비자들이 중간 제품을 선택하게 된다고 했을 뿐, 소비자들이 반복해서 불필요한 제품을 구매하게 된다는 내용이 아니다.
④ 가격 비교를 통해 중간 제품을 사도록 조종된다는 것이지, 제품의 가격 자체를 속인다는 내용이 아니다.
⑤ 제품 가격의 할인은 언급되지 않았다.

M 69 정답 ①　　　　　　　　⭐ 2등급 대비 [정답률 41%]

*경험적 지식 공유를 통한 발전

<small>between A and B: A와 B 사이　　주격 보어절을 이끄는 접속사</small>
One big difference / **between** science **and** stage magic / is **that** while magicians hide their mistakes from the audience, / in science / you make your mistakes in public. //

한 가지 큰 차이점은 / 과학과 무대 마술 사이의 / 마술사들이 그들의 실수를 관중에게 숨기는 반면 / 과학에서는 / 공공연히 실수를 한다는 것이다 //

You show them off / so that everybody can learn from them. // (그래서) ~할 수 있도록
당신은 실수를 드러내 보여준다 / 모두가 실수로부터 배울 수 있도록 //

This way, / you get the advantage of everybody else's experience, / and not just your own idiosyncratic path / through the space of mistakes. // 단서 1 서로의 실수를 통해 경험이라는 지식을 획득한다고 했음
이런 식으로 / 다른 모든 사람들의 경험이라는 이익을 얻는다 / 그리고 당신 자신만의 특유한 길(에서 얻은 이익)뿐만 아니라 / 당신은 단지 실수라는 영역을 거쳐 온 //

This, / by the way, / is another reason / why we humans are so much smarter than every other species. // 관계부사
이는 / 한편 / 또 다른 이유이다 / 왜 우리 인간이 다른 모든 종보다 훨씬 더 영리한지에 대한 //

It is not that A, but B: A가 아니라 B다
It is not that our brains are bigger or more powerful, / or even that we have the ability / to reflect on our own past errors, / 병렬 구조
그것은 우리의 뇌가 더 커지나 더 강력해서가 아니라 / 혹은 심지어 우리가 능력을 가져서 / 우리 자신의 과거 실수들을 반추하는 /

but that we **share the benefits** / that our individual brains have earned / from their individual histories of trial and error. //
그렇지만 이익들을 나눠서이다 / 우리 개개인들의 뇌가 얻어낸 / 그들 개개인들의 시행착오의 역사로부터 // 단서 2 인간의 뇌 자체의 능력이 뛰어나기보다는 개개인의 경험을 함께 활용한다고 했음

- audience ⓝ 관중   • in public 공공연히   • species ⓝ 종(種)
- reflect on ~을 되돌아보다   • individual ⓐ 개인의
- history ⓝ 역사   • trial and error 시행착오

과학과 무대 마술 사이의 한 가지 큰 차이점은 마술사들이 그들의 실수를 관중에게 숨기는 반면, 과학에서는 공공연히 실수를 한다는 것이다. 당신은 모두가 실수로부터 배울 수 있도록 실수를 드러내 보여준다. 이런 식으로, 당신은 단지 실수라는 영역을 거쳐 온 당신 자신만의 특유한 길(에서 얻은 이익)뿐만 아니라, 다른 모든 사람들의 경험이라는 이익을 얻는다. 한편, 이는 왜 우리 인간이 다른 모든 종보다 훨씬 더 영리한지에 대한 또 다른 이유이다. 그것은 우리의 뇌가 더 커지나 더 강력해서, 혹은 심지어 우리가 우리 자신의 과거 실수들을 반추하는 능력을 가져서가 아니라, 우리 개개인들의 뇌가 그들 개개인들의 시행착오의 역사로부터 얻어낸 **이익들을 나눠서**이다.

다음 빈칸에 들어갈 말로 가장 적절한 것을 고르시오.
① share the benefits 인간은 과거의 경험을 기반 삼아 성장한다는 내용
이익들을 나누다
② overlook the insights 통찰력을 간과하는 내용은 언급되지 않음
통찰력을 간과하다
③ develop creative skills 인간만이 독창적 능력을 발전시키는지는 알 수 없음
독창적인 능력을 발전시키다
④ exaggerate the achievements 인간이 성취를 과장한다는 내용은 없음
성취를 과장하다
⑤ underestimate the knowledge 지식을 과소평가했다면 발전하지 못했을 것임
지식을 과소평가하다

왜 2등급? 과학과 마술의 차이점을 언급하며 글을 시작하고 있지만, 정작 마술과는 상관이 없는 내용이 전개된다. 따라서 글의 첫 문장만 읽고 마술과 관련이 있는 오답 선택지를 고르도록 함정을 만든 2등급 대비 문제이다.

| 문제 풀이 순서 |

1st 먼저 빈칸이 포함된 문장을 읽고, 연결어를 확인한다.

빈칸 문장
It is not that our brains are bigger or more powerful, or even that we have the ability to reflect on our own past errors, but that we _____ that our individual brains have earned from their individual histories of trial and error. 단서 2
그것은 우리의 뇌가 더 커지나 더 강력해서, 혹은 심지어 우리가 우리 자신의 과거 실수들을 반추하는 능력을 가져서가 아니라, 우리 개개인들의 뇌가 그들 개개인들의 시행착오의 역사로부터 얻어낸 _____이다.

→ '그것'에 대한 이유가 not A but B 구조를 이루면서 빈칸이 포함된 문장에 나오는데, 우리의 뇌나 능력 때문이 아니라 개인의 시행착오의 역사로부터 얻어낸 '무엇' 때문이라는 것이다. 단서
글의 나머지 부분에서 '그것'이 가리키는 내용과 '무엇' 때문인지 확인한다. 발상

2nd 글의 내용을 종합해서 빈칸에 들어갈 적절한 말을 찾는다.

이런 식으로, 당신은 단지 실수라는 영역을 거쳐 온 당신 자신만의 특유한 길(에서 얻은 이익)뿐만 아니라, 다른 모든 사람들의 경험이라는 이익을 얻는다. 단서 1

→ 인간들이 다른 종들보다 훨씬 큰 발전을 이룬 것(빈칸 문장의 It이 가리키는 것)은 자기 자신뿐만 아니라 다른 사람들의 과거의 경험을 통해 얻은 지식을 통해 성장해왔기 때문이라는 것이다.
▶ 빈칸 문장은 〈~ 우리 개개인들의 뇌가 그들 개개인들의 시행착오의 역사로부터 얻어낸 ① '이익들을 나눠서'이다.〉라는 내용이 되어야 한다.

3rd 글의 내용을 다시 한번 정리하며 정답이 맞는지 확인한다.

→ 이 글은 인간의 뇌 자체의 능력이 뛰어나기보다는 개인의 경험들에서 배운 유용함을 공유하며 성장해왔다는 내용이다. 따라서 빈칸에는 ① '이익들을 나누다'가 들어가는 것이 가장 적절하다.

| 선택지 분석 |

① 인간은 실수를 통해 얻은 경험을 서로 공유하며 성장해와서 큰 발전을 이뤘다고 했다.
② 통찰력을 간과한다면 영리해지지 못할 것이다.
③ 인간의 독보적인 능력이 언급되긴 했으나 독창성에 대해서는 알 수 없다.
④ 인간은 성취를 이루었는데, 이를 과장해서 얻는 이익은 언급되지 않았다.
⑤ 지식을 과소평가한 것이 아니고 공유함으로써 함께 종의 발전을 이루었다고 했다.

M

M 70 정답 ①   ★ 1등급 대비 [정답률 41%]

*음악을 직접 선택하는 개인

Due to technological innovations, / music can now be experienced / by more people, / for more of the time than ever before. // ~ 때문에, ~으로 인해
기술 혁신으로 인해 / 음악은 이제 경험될 수 있다 / 더 많은 사람에 의해 / 이전보다 더 많은 시간 동안 //

Mass availability has given individuals unheard-of control / over their own sound-environment. // 수여동사+간접목적어+직접목적어
대중이용 가능성은 개인들에게 전례가 없는 통제권을 주었다 / 그들 자신의 음향 환경에 대한 //

However, / it has also confronted them / with the simultaneous availability of countless genres of music, / in which they have to orient themselves. // 단서 1 수많은 장르의 음악을 동시에 이용할 수 있는 현재의 상황 = where
하지만 / 이것은 또한 그들을 직면하게 했다 / 무수한 장르의 음악을 동시에 이용할 수 있는 상황에 / 그 상황에서 그들은 적응해야만 한다 // 단서 2 개인이 직접 음악을 걸러내고 조합하기 시작함

People start filtering out / and organizing their digital libraries / like they used to do with their physical music collections. // start -ing: ~하기 시작하다 접속사(= as)
사람들은 필터링하기 시작한다 / 그리고 자신들의 디지털 라이브러리를 조합하기 / 그들이 이전에 물리적 형태를 지닌 음악을 수집했던 것처럼 //

However, / there is the difference / that the choice lies in their own hands. // 단서 3 선택권은 개인이 가진다는 차이가 있음 동격의 that
하지만 / 차이가 있다 / 선택권은 자신이 가진다는 //

Without being restricted / to the limited collection of music-distributors, / nor being guided / by the local radio program / as a 'preselector' of the latest hits, / 단서 4 음악 선택 시 개인은 아무런 간섭을 받지 않음 병렬 구조 전치사(~로서)
국한되지 않고 / 음악 배급자의 제한된 컬렉션에 / 또한 안내를 받지 않고 / 지역 라디오 프로그램의 / 최신 히트곡의 '사전 선택자'로서 /

the individual actively / has to **choose and determine his or her musical preferences**. //
개인은 적극적으로 / 자신의 음악적 선호를 선택하고 결정해야 한다 //

The search for the right song / is thus associated with considerable effort. //
적절한 노래를 찾는 것은 / 따라서 상당한 노력과 관련이 있다 //

- individual ⓝ 개인
- unheard-of ⓐ 전례가 없는
- confront ⓥ 맞서다, 직면하다
- orient oneself 적응하다, 순응하다
- restrict ⓥ 제한하다
- distributor ⓝ 분배업자
- be associated with ~와 관련이 있다
- considerable ⓐ 상당한

기술 혁신으로 인해, 음악은 이제 이전보다 더 많은 시간 동안 더 많은 사람에 의해 경험될 수 있다. 대중이용 가능성은 개인들에게 그들 자신의 음향 환경에 대한 전례가 없는 통제권을 주었다. 하지만 그들은 무수한 장르의 음악을 동시에 이용할 수 있는 상황에 맞닥뜨리게 되었고 그들은 그 상황에 적응해야만 한다. 사람들은 이전에 물리적 형태를 지닌 음악을 수집했던 것처럼 자신들의 디지털 라이브러리를 필터링하고 조합하기 시작한다. 하지만 선택권은 자신이 가진다는 차이가 있다. 음악 배급자의 제한된 컬렉션에 국한되지 않고, 또한 최신 히트곡의 '사전 선택자'로서 지역 라디오 프로그램의 안내를 받지 않고, 개인은 적극적으로 **자신의 음악적 선호를 선택하고 결정해야** 한다. 따라서 적절한 노래를 찾는 것은 상당한 노력과 관련이 있다.

다음 빈칸에 들어갈 말로 가장 적절한 것을 고르시오. [3점]
선호하는 음악의 선택은 아무런 개입 없이 온전히 개인에게 있다고 했음
① choose and determine his or her musical preferences
자신의 음악적 선호를 선택하고 결정해야
② understand the technical aspects of recording sessions
녹음 시간의 기술적 측면을 이해해야 / 녹음 시간의 기술적 측면은 언급되지 않음
③ share unique and inspiring playlists on social media
소셜 미디어에 대한 독창적이면서 영감을 불러일으키는 선곡표를 공유해야 / 선곡표 공유에 대한 언급은 없음
④ interpret lyrics with background knowledge of the songs
노래의 배경지식을 가지고 가사를 해석해야 / 노래의 배경지식을 통해 가사를 해석하라는 내용은 아님
⑤ seek the advice of a voice specialist for better performances
더 나은 공연을 위해 성악 전문가의 충고를 구해야 / 성악 전문가와 관련된 내용은 없음

왜 1등급? 음악과 관련된 글인 것은 쉽게 파악할 수 있지만, 모든 선택지가 음악과 관련된 내용이라 오답의 함정을 잘 골라내야 하는 1등급 대비 문제이다. 적절한 노래를 제상자가 찾아주는 것이 아니라 스스로 찾는 것이 상당한 노력과 관련이 있다고 한 것이 무슨 의미일지 생각해 본다.

| 문제 풀이 순서 |

1st 먼저 빈칸이 포함된 문장을 읽고, 빈칸에 들어갈 말에 대한 단서를 얻는다.

빈칸 문장	Without being restricted to the limited collection of music distributors, nor being guided by the local radio program as a 'preselector' of the latest hits, the individual actively has to _____. 단서 음악 배급자의 제한된 컬렉션에 국한되지 않고, 또한 최신 히트곡의 '사전 선택자'로서 지역 라디오 프로그램의 안내를 받지 않고, 개인은 적극적으로 _____ 한다.

➡ 음악 배급자나 지역 라디오 프로그램의 제한을 받지 않고 개인이 '어떻게' 해야 하는지 찾아야 한다. 발상

2nd **1st** 에서 찾은 단서를 염두에 두고, 빈칸 문장의 앞부분부터 확인한다.

빈칸 문장 앞	하지만 선택권은 자신이 가진다는 차이가 있다. 단서 3
그 앞	사람들은 이전에 물리적 형태를 지닌 음악을 수집했던 것처럼 자신들의 디지털 라이브러리를 필터링하고 조합하기 시작한다. 단서 2

➡ 수많은 장르의 음악을 동시에 즐길 수 있는 상황에서 개인이 직접 음악을 걸러내고 조합하기 시작했는데, 이런 상황에서도 개인이 음악의 선택권을 가진다고 했다.

음악 배급자나 지역 라디오 프로그램의 제한을 받는 예전과 달리 개인이 음악을 직접 선택할 수 있다는 내용의 글이다.
▶ 빈칸 문장은 바로 이 내용이 들어가야 하므로 ① '자신의 음악적 선호를 선택하고 결정해야' 한다는 것이다.

3rd 글의 내용을 다시 한번 정리하며 정답이 맞는지 확인한다.

➡ 기술 혁신으로 사람들은 물리적 형태가 없는 디지털 라이브러리를 조합하기 시작했으며, 라디오 프로그램이 선정하는 음악이 아니라 개인이 적극적으로 자신이 선호하는 음악을 선택하고 결정하게 됐다는 것이다.
따라서 빈칸에는 ① '자신의 음악적 선호를 선택하고 결정해야'가 들어가는 것이 가장 적절하다.

| 선택지 분석 |
① 현재는 개인이 수많은 장르의 음악을 이용할 수 있고, 외부의 제한을 받지 않고 직접 음악을 걸러내고 조합할 수 있다고 했다.
② 녹음 시간의 기술적 측면에 대해서는 언급되지 않았다.
③ 개인이 음악 선택권을 가지고 있다는 내용일 뿐, 개인의 선곡표 공유에 관한 내용은 없다.
④ 노래의 배경지식을 통해 가사를 해석하라는 내용의 글이 아니다.
⑤ 성악 전문가와 관련된 내용은 나오지 않았다.

M 71 정답 ② ⭐ 1등급 대비 [정답률 34%]

＊위대한 작곡가의 특징

You hear again and again / that some of the greatest composers / were misunderstood / in their own day. //
목적어절 접속사 / 수동태 동사
여러분은 몇 번이고 듣는다 / 몇몇 가장 위대한 작곡가들이 / 진가를 인정받지 못했다고 / 그들의 시대에 //

Not everyone could understand / the compositions of Beethoven, Brahms, or Stravinsky / in their day. //
모든 사람이 이해할 수 있었던 것은 아니었다 / 베토벤, 브람스, 스트라빈스키의 곡들을 / 그들의 시대에 //

The reason / for this initial lack of acceptance / is unfamiliarity. //
단수 주어 / 단수 동사
이유는 / 이러한 초기의 수용 부족의 / 낯설음이다 //

The musical forms, / or ideas expressed within them, / were completely new. //
앞에 주격 관계대명사와 be동사가 생략됨
음악적 형식 / 또는 그 안에 표현된 생각은 / 완전히 새로운 것이었다 //

And yet, / this is exactly one of the things / that makes them so great. //
주격 관계대명사 / = the greatest composers
그럼에도 불구하고 / 이것이 바로 ~인 것들 중 하나이다 / 그들을 그토록 위대하게 만드는 //
단서 1 작곡가들을 위대하게 만드는 것은 완전히 새로운 음악적 형식 또는 그 속의 생각임

Effective composers have their own ideas. //
유능한 작곡가는 그들 자신만의 생각을 갖는다 //

Have you ever seen / the classic movie *Amadeus*? //
당신은 본 적이 있는가 / 고전 영화 *Amadeus*를 //

The composer Antonio Salieri is the "host" of this movie; / he's depicted / as one of the most famous non-great composers /
작곡가 Antonio Salieri가 이 영화의 '주인공'이다 / 그는 묘사된다 / 가장 유명한 위대하지 않은 작곡가 중 한 명으로 /
단서 2 위대하지 않은 작곡가로 묘사되는 Salieri

— he lived at the time of Mozart / and was completely overshadowed by him. //
수동태 동사
그는 모차르트 시대에 살았고 / 그에 의해 완전히 가려졌다 //

Now, Salieri wasn't a bad composer; / in fact, / he was a very good one. //
자, Salieri는 형편없는 작곡가가 아니었다 / 사실 / 그는 매우 훌륭한 작곡가였다 //

But he wasn't one of the world's great composers / because his work wasn't **original**. //
하지만 그는 세계의 위대한 작곡가들 중 한 명은 아니었다 / 그의 작품이 독창적이지 않았기 때문에 //

선행사를 포함하는 관계대명사

What he wrote / sounded just like / **what** everyone else was composing at the time. // 단서3 Salieri가 작곡한 것은 당시 모든 사람이 작곡한 것과 비슷했음

그가 쓴 곡은 / 마치 ~처럼 들렸다 / 그 당시 모든 다른 사람들이 작곡했던 것 //

- misunderstand ⓥ 진가를 못 알아보다 · composition ⓝ 작품
- initial ⓐ 초기의 · lack ⓝ 부족 · acceptance ⓝ 수용
- unfamiliarity ⓝ 낯섦 · host ⓝ 주인공 · depict ⓥ 묘사하다
- composer ⓝ 작곡가 · overshadow ⓥ 가리다
- original ⓐ 독창적인 · conventional ⓐ 관습적인

여러분은 몇몇 가장 위대한 작곡가들이 그들의 시대에 진가를 인정받지 못했다고 몇 번이고 듣는다. 그들의 시대에 베토벤, 브람스, 스트라빈스키의 곡들을 모든 사람이 이해할 수 있었던 것은 아니었다. 이러한 초기의 수용 부족의 이유는 낯섦이다. 음악적 형식, 또는 그 안에 표현된 생각은 완전히 새로운 것이었다. 그럼에도 불구하고 이것이 바로 그들을 그토록 위대하게 만드는 것들 중 하나이다. 유능한 작곡가는 그들 자신만의 생각을 갖는다. 당신은 고전 영화 *Amadeus*를 본 적이 있는가? 작곡가 Antonio Salieri가 이 영화의 '주인공'이다. 그는 가장 유명한 위대하지 않은 작곡가 중 한 명으로 묘사된다. 그는 모차르트 시대에 살았고 그에 의해 완전히 가려졌다. 자, Salieri는 형편없는 작곡가가 아니었다. 사실, 그는 매우 훌륭한 작곡가였다. 하지만 그의 작품이 **독창적이지** 않았기 때문에 그는 세계의 위대한 작곡가들 중 한 명은 아니었다. 그가 쓴 곡은 마치 그 당시 모든 다른 사람들이 작곡했던 것처럼 들렸다.

다음 빈칸에 들어갈 말로 가장 적절한 것을 고르시오.

① simple 그의 작품이 단순하지 않았다는 내용이 아님
   단순한
② original 작품이 독창적이지 않았기 때문에 위대한 작곡가 중 한 명이 될 수 없었음
   독창적인
③ familiar 그의 작품은 오히려 익숙했음
   익숙한
④ conventional 그의 작품은 오히려 관습적이었음
   관습적인
⑤ understandable 그의 작품이 이해하기 어려웠다는 내용이 아님
   이해하기 쉬운

왜 1등급? 빈칸 앞에 not이 있어서 빈칸에 어떤 단어가 들어가야 하는지 신중히 살펴봐야 하는 1등급 대비 문제이다. '위대한' 작곡가에 관하여 반복적으로 등장하는 특징을 잘 찾아낸 후, 한 단어로 나타낼 수 있어야 한다.

| 문제 풀이 순서 | ✱✱✱ [정답률 34%]

1st 빈칸이 포함된 문장 주변을 읽고, 빈칸에 들어갈 말에 대한 단서를 얻는다.

빈칸 문장	But he wasn't one of the world's great composers because his work wasn't _____. 하지만 그의 작품이 _____ 않았기 때문에 그는 세계의 위대한 작곡가들 중 한 명은 아니었다.
빈칸 뒤 문장	What he wrote sounded just like what everyone else was composing at the time. 그가 쓴 곡은 마치 그 당시 모든 다른 사람들이 작곡했던 것처럼 들렸다. 단서3

➡ 빈칸 문장은 그의 작품이 '어떻지' 않았기 때문에 세계의 위대한 작곡가들 중 한 명이 아니었다고 했고, 빈칸 뒤 문장에서 그 이유가 그가 쓴 곡이 당시에 다른 사람들이 작곡했던 것과 유사했기 때문이라고 했다. 단서
여기서 '그'는 누구인지, 그리고 세계의 위대한 작곡가들은 '어떤' 사람인지 언급될 것이다. 발상

2nd 글의 내용을 종합해서 빈칸에 들어갈 적절한 말을 찾는다.

- 완전히 새로운 음악적 형식, 또는 그 안에 표현된 생각은 작곡가들을 위대하게 만드는 것들 중 하나이다. 단서1
- 작곡가 Antonio Salieri는 가장 유명한 위대하지 않은 작곡가 중 한 명으로 묘사된다. 단서2

➡ 작곡가들을 위대하게 만드는 것은 '완전히 새로운' 음악적 형식 또는 그 안에 표현된 생각이라고 했으며, Salieri는 유명하지만 '위대하지는 않은' 작곡가로 묘사된다고 했다. 따라서 빈칸에는 Salieri의 작품이 '완전히 새롭지는' 않았다는 것에 관한 표현이 들어가야 한다.
▶ Salieri의 작품은 ② '독창적이지' 않았기 때문에 그는 세계의 위대한 작곡가들 중 한 명이 아니었다.

3rd 글의 내용을 다시 한번 정리하며 정답이 맞는지 확인한다.

Antonio Salieri는 훌륭하지만 위대하지는 않은 작곡가였다. 위대한 작곡가의 곡은 완전히 새로운 것이어야 했는데, 그가 쓴 곡은 당시의 다른 곡들과 비슷했던, 즉 ② '독창적이지' 않았기 때문이다. 따라서 ②이 정답이다.

| 선택지 분석 |

① 곡의 단순함에 관한 내용이 아니라, 곡의 독창성에 관한 내용이다.
② 위대한 작곡가들은 완전히 새로운 음악적 형식과 생각이 있다고 했으므로, Salieri가 위대한 작곡가가 될 수 없었던 것은 작품에 독창성이 없었기 때문이다.
③ Salieri의 곡은 오히려 익숙했기 때문에 그는 위대한 작곡가가 될 수 없었다. 빈칸 앞에 not이 있기 때문에 정답이 될 수 없다.
④ Salieri의 곡은 오히려 관습적이었기 때문에 그는 위대한 작곡가가 될 수 없었다. 빈칸 앞에 not이 있기 때문에 정답이 될 수 없다.
⑤ 곡을 이해하기 쉬운지에 관한 내용이 아니라, 곡의 독창성에 관한 내용이다.

M 72 정답 ① ——— ★ 1등급 대비 [정답률 21%]

＊스포츠에서의 홈 이점

주격 관계대명사　　단서1 홈 이점은 극적으로 바뀔 수 있는 역학이라고 언급함
One dynamic / **that** can change dramatically in sport / is the
　　　　　　　　　　　　　　　　　　　「전치사 + 관계대명사」
concept of the home-field advantage, / **in which** perceived demands and resources / seem to play a role. //
한 가지 역학은 / 스포츠에서 극적으로 바뀔 수 있는 / 홈 이점이라는 개념이다 / 여기에서 인식된 부담과 자원이 / 역할을 하는 것처럼 보인다 //

Under normal circumstances, / the home ground would appear / to provide greater perceived resources / (fans, home field, and so on). //
일반적인 상황에서 / 홈그라운드는 보인다 / 인식된 자원을 더 많이 제공하는 것처럼 / (팬, 홈 경기장 등) //

However, / researchers Roy Baumeister and Andrew Steinhilber
　　　　　　　　　　　　　　　　　형용사적 용법　목적어절을 이끄는 접속사
/ were among the first / **to point** out / **that** these competitive factors can change; /
하지만 / 연구원 Roy Baumeister와 Andrew Steinhilber는 / 최초 중 하나였다 / 지적한 / 이러한 경쟁력이 있는 요소들이 바뀔 수도 있다고 /

　　　　　　　　　　　단수 주어＊
for example, / **the success percentage** for home teams / in the
　　　　　　　　　　　　　　　　　　　　　　단수 동사＊
final games of a playoff / or World Series / **seems** to drop. //
예를 들어 / 홈 팀들의 성공률은 / 우승 결정전에서 / 또는 (미국 프로 야구) 선수권의 마지막 경기(에서) / 떨어지는 것처럼 보인다 //
　　　　　　　　　　　　　　　　단서2 홈 팀의 성공률이 떨어진 것을 언급함

Fans can become / part of the perceived demands / rather than resources / under those circumstances. // 단서3 팬들은 부담이 될 수 있음
팬들은 될 수 있다 / 인식된 부담의 일부가 / 자원보다는 / 이러한 상황에서 //

　　　　　　　　　　　　　　　　　　　　　　　주격 관계대명사
This change in perception / can also explain / why a team **that**'s struggling / at the start of the year / will **often welcome a road**
　　　　　　　　　부사적 용법(목적)
trip / **to reduce** perceived demands and pressures. //
이러한 인식의 변화는 / 또한 설명할 수 있다 / 왜 고전하는 팀이 / 연초에 / 길을 떠나는 것 (원정 경기를 가는 것)을 흔히 반기는지 / 인식된 부담과 압박을 줄이기 위해 //

- dynamic ⓝ 역학 · dramatically ⓐⓓ 극적으로
- concept ⓝ 개념 · home-field advantage 홈 이점
- circumstance ⓝ 상황 · play a role 역할을 하다
- provide ⓥ 제공하다 · point out ~을 지적하다
- competitive ⓐ 경쟁력이 있는 · struggling ⓐ 고전하는
- advertise ⓥ 광고하다 · upcoming ⓐ 다가오는

스포츠에서 극적으로 바뀔 수 있는 한 가지 역학은 홈 이점이라는 개념으로, 여기에서는 인식된 부담과 자원이 역할을 하는 것처럼 보인다. 일반적인 상황에서, 홈그라운드는 인식된 자원(팬, 홈 경기장 등)을 더 많이 제공하는 것처럼 보인다. 하지만, 연구원 Roy Baumeister와 Andrew Steinhilber는 이러한 경쟁력이 있는 요소들이 바뀔 수도 있다고 처음으로 지적한 사람 중 하나였다. 예를 들어, 우승 결정전이나 (미국 프로 야구) 선수권의 마지막 경기에서 홈 팀들의 성공률은 떨어지는 것처럼 보인다. 이러한 상황에서 팬들은 자원보다는 인식된 부담의 일부가 될 수 있다. 이러한 인식의 변화는 왜 연초에 고전하는 팀이 인식된 부담과 압박을 줄이기 위해 **길을 떠나는 것(원정 경기를 가는 것)을 흔히 반기는지** 또한 설명할 수 있다.

다음 빈칸에 들어갈 말로 가장 적절한 것을 고르시오. [3점]

① often welcome a road trip 고전하는 팀이 부담과 압박을 줄이기 위해 길을 떠나는, 즉, 원정 경기를 가는 것을 반김
길을 떠나는 것을 흔히 반기는지
② avoid international matches 국제 시합을 피한다는 내용은 없음
국제 시합을 피하는지
③ focus on increasing ticket sales 티켓 판매 증가와 관련된 내용은 없음
티켓 판매 증가에 중점을 두는지
④ want to have an eco-friendly stadium 친환경적 경기장에 대한 내용이 아님
친환경적 경기장을 갖기를 원하는지
⑤ try to advertise their upcoming games 팬들이 언급된 것으로 만든 함정
그들의 다가올 경기를 광고하려고 노력하는지

왜 1등급? 홈그라운드 경기와 관련된 글로 ① 선택지를 제외한 모든 선택지에 '시합', '티켓', '경기장', '경기'와 같은 스포츠와 관련된 핵심어가 등장했다. 하지만 정작 정답 선택지는 이런 스포츠와 관련 없어 보이는 ①이었는데, '길을 떠나는 것'을 '원정 경기를 가는 것'이라고 비유적으로 표현했기 때문이다. 이것을 알아차리지 못하고 나머지 선택지에서 정답을 고르려고 했다면 시간만 낭비하게 되는 1등급 대비 문제이다.

| 문제 풀이 순서 |

1st 빈칸이 포함된 문장을 읽고, 무엇을 염두에 두고 글을 읽어야 하는지 확인한다.

빈칸 문장	This change in perception can also explain why a team that's struggling at the start of the year will _____ to reduce perceived demands and pressures. 이러한 인식의 변화는 왜 연초에 고전하는 팀이 인식된 부담과 압박을 줄이기 위해 _____ 또한 설명할 수 있다.

→ 빈칸이 포함된 문장은 이 글의 마지막 문장인데, 연초에 고전하는 팀이 부담과 압박을 줄이기 위해 '무엇'을 하는지에 대한 이유가 This change in perception (이러한 인식의 변화)이라고 했다. （단서）
앞에서 이것이 가리키는 것에 대한 설명이 나올 것임을 생각하며 읽는다. （발상）

2nd However로 시작하는 문장에서 글의 흐름이 전환되는 것에 주목한다.

첫 문장	스포츠에서 극적으로 바뀔 수 있는 한 가지 역학은 홈 이점이라는 개념으로, 여기에서는 인식된 부담과 자원이 역할을 하는 것처럼 보인다. （단서 1）
세 번째 문장	**하지만**, 연구원 Roy Baumeister와 Andrew Steinhilber는 이러한 경쟁력이 있는 요소들이 바뀔 수도 있다고 처음으로 지적한 사람 중 하나였다. **예를 들어,** 우승 결정전이나 (미국 프로 야구) 선수권의 마지막 경기에서 홈 팀들의 성공률은 떨어지는 것처럼 보인다. （단서 2）

→ 스포츠에서는 홈 이점으로 경기가 극적으로 바뀔 수 있다고 했는데, However로 이어지는 문장 이후에는 오히려 홈 팀의 성공률이 떨어지는 것처럼 홈그라운드가 주는 경쟁력 있는 요소들이 바뀔 수 있다고 했다. 이런 상황에서 홈 팬은 인식된 부담이 된다는 것이다. （단서 3）

▶ 따라서 빈칸에는 고전하는 팀이 부담을 줄이기 위해 '홈에서 멀어진다'는 내용이 올 것이다.

3rd 글의 내용을 다시 한번 정리하며 정답이 맞는지 확인한다.

→ 스포츠에서 홈 이점은 경쟁력 있는 요소가 아니라 오히려 홈 팀들의 성공률을 떨어뜨릴 수 있다고 했다. 따라서 연초에 고전하는 팀이 부담과 압박을 줄이기 위해 홈에서 벗어나 ① '길을 떠나는 것(원정 경기를 가는 것)을 반긴다'는 의미가 되어야 문맥상 알맞다.

| 선택지 분석 |

① 스포츠에서의 홈 이점이라고 생각하는 것들이 오히려 부정적인 영향을 끼칠 수 있다는 내용이다.
② 국제 시합이 아닌 홈 경기를 피한다는 내용이 들어가야 하므로 글의 내용과 반대이다.
③ 티켓 판매 증가와 관련된 내용은 없다.
④ resources가 언급된 것으로 만든 오답으로, 홈 경기에서 '자원'이 오히려 부담이 될 수 있다는 내용이다.
⑤ 팬들의 존재가 오히려 인식된 부담의 일부가 될 수 있다고 했으므로 적절하지 않다.

어법 특강

＊ 주어-동사 수 일치

– 문장의 주어가 명사구 혹은 명사절일 때 항상 단수 취급한다. to부정사구, 동명사구나 의문사절, that절, whether절 등과 같은 명사절이 주어로 오는 경우 동사와 멀어질 수 있기 때문에 수 일치 여부를 쉽게 판단하기 힘들다. 따라서 항상 문장을 전체적으로 파악해야 한다.

· Creating a list of goals is a good way to be a better student.
　동명사구 주어　　　　단수 동사
(목표들의 목록을 만드는 것은 더 나은 학생이 되기 위한 좋은 방법이다.)

· Whether he will accept my offer is not certain yet.
　　명사절 주어　　　　단수 동사
(그가 나의 제안을 받아들일 지는 아직 확실하지 않다.)

· To overcome my emotional problems is difficult.
　to부정사구 주어　　　　단수 동사
(나의 감정적인 문제들을 극복하는 것은 어렵다.)

M 어휘 Review 정답 — 문제편 p. 203

01 보여주다	11 long for	21 Generalization
02 성취	12 pass on	22 negotiate
03 역학	13 point out	23 quoted
04 전환	14 catch up with	24 decline
05 유혹	15 sort out	25 sole
06 obstacle	16 tribe	26 absence
07 humanity	17 scarce	27 sizable
08 overwhelming	18 complex	28 engaging
09 upcoming	19 orbit	29 stimulate
10 modify	20 feature	30 perceived

N 01 정답 ④ *집단 음악 활동의 정신 건강 문제 개선

다음 글에서 전체 흐름과 관계 없는 문장은?

A group of psychologists studied / individuals with severe
mental illness / who experienced weekly group music therapy, /
including singing familiar songs and composing original songs. //
주격 관계대명사(선행사: individuals)
병렬 구조
한 심리학자 그룹이 연구했다 / 심각한 정신 질환이 있는 사람들을 / 집단 음악 치료를 매주
경험한 / 친숙한 노래 부르기와 독창적인 노래 작곡하기를 포함한 //

① The results showed / that the group music therapy improved
the quality of participants' life, /
목적어절 접속사
단서 1 집단 음악 치료가 참여자의 삶의 질을 개선함
그 연구 결과는 보여주었다 / 집단 음악 치료가 참여자의 삶의 질을 개선하였음을 /

with those participating in a greater number of sessions
현재분사구(those 수식)
with+명사+현재분사: 명사가 ~한 채로, ~했기에
experiencing the greatest benefits. //
분사구문을 이끄는 현재분사
참여자가 (치료) 활동에 참여한 횟수가 많을수록 가장 큰 효과를 경험했기에 //

② Focusing on singing, / another group of psychologists
reviewed articles / on the efficacy of group singing / as a mental
health treatment /
노래 부르기에 초점을 두고 / 또 다른 그룹의 심리학자는 논문을 검토했다 / 집단 가창의
효능에 대한 / 정신 건강 치료로서 /

for individuals living with a mental health condition in a
community setting. //
집단 생활의 환경에서 정신적인 건강 문제를 가지고 살고 있는 이들에게 미치는//
목적어절 접속사 부사절 접속사(시간)

③ The findings showed / that, when people with mental health
conditions participated in a choir, / their mental health and
wellbeing significantly improved. //
단서 2 정신 건강 문제를 가진 사람이 합창단에
참여했을 때 정신 건강과 행복이 향상됨
발견된 결과는 보여주었다 / 정신 건강 문제를 가진 사람이 합창단에 참여했을 때 / 그들의
정신 건강과 행복이 상당히 개선되었음을 //

④ The negative effects of music / were greater than the
psychologists expected. //)
(음악의 부정적인 효과는 / 심리학자가 예상했던 것보다 더 컸다 //)

⑤ Group singing provided enjoyment, / improved emotional
states, / developed a sense of belonging / and enhanced self-
confidence. //
병렬 구조
단서 3 집단 가창은 정신적으로 여러 긍정적 효과를 가져옴
집단 가창은 즐거움을 제공했고 / 감정 상태를 개선하였으며 / 소속감을 키웠고 / 자신감을
강화하였다 //

- psychologist ⓝ 심리학자 · severe ⓐ 심각한
- mental ⓐ 정신적인 · illness ⓝ 병, 질환 · compose ⓥ 작곡하다
- improve ⓥ 개선하다 · participant ⓝ 참가자
- session ⓝ 활동, 기간 · benefit ⓝ 이점 · review ⓥ 검토하다
- treatment ⓝ 치료 · setting ⓝ 환경 · finding ⓝ 결과
- choir ⓝ 합창단 · wellbeing ⓝ 행복 · significantly ⓐⓓ 상당히
- state ⓝ 상태 · enhance ⓥ 강화하다

한 심리학자 그룹이 친숙한 노래 부르기와 독창적인 작곡하기를 포함한 집단 음
악 치료를 매주 경험한 심각한 정신 질환이 있는 사람들을 연구했다. ① 그 연
구 결과는 참여자가 (치료) 활동에 참여한 횟수가 많을수록 가장 큰 효과를 경
험했기에, 집단 음악 치료가 참여자의 삶의 질을 개선하였음을 보여주었다. ②
노래 부르기에 초점을 두고, 또 다른 그룹의 심리학자는 집단생활의 환경에서
정신적인 건강 문제를 가지고 살고 있는 이들에게 미치는 집단 가창의 효능에
대한 논문을 검토했다. ③ 발견된 결과는, 정신적인 건강 문제를 가진 사람이
합창단에 참여했을 때, 정신 건강과 행복이 상당히 개선되었음을 보여주었다.
(④ 음악의 부정적인 효과는 심리학자가 예상했던 것보다 더 컸다.) ⑤ 집단 가
창은 즐거움을 제공했고 감정 상태를 개선하였으며 소속감을 키웠고 자신감을
강화하였다.

왜 정답·오답? ★★☆ [정답률 72%]

앞부분: 집단 음악 치료가 정신 질환이 있는 사람들에게 미치는 영향에 관한 연구

① 그 연구 결과는 집단 음악 치료가 참여자의 삶의 질을 개선하였음을
보여주었음
▶ 집단 음악 치료는 참여자의 삶의 질을 개선한다는 연구 결과가 이어지므로 ①은
무관한 문장이 아님

② 노래 부르기에 초점을 두고, 또 다른 그룹의 심리학자는 집단생활의
환경에서 정신적인 건강 문제를 가지고 살고 있는 이들에게 미치는 집단
가창의 효능에 대한 논문을 검토했음
▶ 집단적인 음악 활동이 정신 건강 문제를 가진 이들에게 미치는 영향에 대한 또
다른 연구가 자연스럽게 이어지므로 ②은 무관한 문장이 아님

③ 정신적인 건강 문제를 가진 사람이 합창단에 참여했을 때, 정신 건강과
행복이 상당히 개선되었음
▶ 정신 건강 문제를 가진 이들에게 미치는 집단 가창의 효능을 연구한 결과가
이어지므로 ③은 무관한 문장이 아님

④ 음악의 부정적인 효과는 심리학자가 예상했던 것보다 더 컸음
▶ 집단 가창이 정신 건강 문제가 있는 사람들에게 주는 긍정적인 효과를
이야기하다가, 음악의 부정적인 효과를 이야기하여 글의 흐름에 맞지 않으므로
④이 무관한 문장임

⑤ 집단 가창은 즐거움을 제공했고 감정 상태를 개선하였으며 소속감을
키웠고 자신감을 강화하였음
▶ 집단 가창이 정신 상태에 미치는 긍정적인 효과를 다시 이어주므로 ⑤은 무관한
문장이 아님

* 글의 흐름

연구	한 심리학자 그룹이 집단 음악 치료를 매주 경험한 심각한 정신 질환이 있는 사람들을 연구함
연구 결과	정신 질환이 있는 사람들이 집단 음악 치료를 받으면 삶의 질이 개선되었음
관련 논문	또 다른 그룹의 심리학자는 정신적인 건강 문제를 가지고 살고 있는 이들에게 미치는 집단 가창의 효능에 대한 논문을 검토함
논문의 결론	정신적인 건강 문제를 가진 사람이 합창단에 참여했을 때, 정신 건강과 행복이 상당히 개선되었음

N 02 정답 ② *특화된 말단 조직을 가진 감각 신경

다음 글에서 전체 흐름과 관계 없는 문장은? [3점]

Sensory nerves have specialized endings / in the tissues / that
pick up a particular sensation. //
과거분사(endings 수식)
주격 관계대명사
감각 신경은 특화된 말단을 가지고 있다 / 조직에 / 특정 감각을 포착하는 //

단서 1 신경 말단이 통증을 발, 다리, 척수, 뇌로 전달함
If, for example, / you step on a sharp object / such as a pin, /
nerve endings in the skin will transmit the pain sensation / up
your leg, / up and along the spinal cord / to the brain. //
만약 예를 들어 / 여러분이 날카로운 물체를 밟는다면 / 핀과 같이 / 피부의 신경 말단이 통증
감각을 전달할 것이다 / 여러분의 다리 위로 / 그리고 척수를 따라 위로 / 뇌까지 //

① While the pain itself is unpleasant, / it is in fact acting / as a
protective mechanism / for the foot. //
부사절 접속사(대조) 강조 용법의 재귀대명사
단서 2 통증은 발을 보호하는
메커니즘으로 작용하는 것임
통증 자체는 불쾌하지만 / 그것은 사실은 작용하고 있다 / 보호하는 메커니즘으로 / 발을 //

② That is, / you get used to the pain / so the capacity with
which you can avoid pain / decreases. //)
'즉, 다시 말해' 결과 절을 잇는 등위접속사 「전치사+관계대명사」
(즉 / 여러분은 그 고통에 익숙해져서 / 고통을 피할 수 있는 능력이 / 감소하게 된다 //)

③ Within the brain, / nerves will connect to the area / **that** 〔주격 관계대명사〕
controls speech, / **so that** you may well shout 'ouch' / or 〔그래서 ~하도록〕
something rather less polite. // 〔단서 3 뇌의 신경이 언어를 통제해서 아픔을 말로 표현함〕

뇌 안에서 / 신경은 부분에 연결될 것이다 / 언어를 통제하는 / 그래서 여러분은 '아야'라고 외칠 것이다 / 또는 다소 덜 공손한 무언가를 //

④ They will also connect to motor nerves / that travel back down the spinal cord, /

그것들은 또한 운동신경에 연결될 것이다 / 척수를 타고 내려오는 /

and to the muscles in your leg / that now contract quickly / **to lift** 〔부사적 용법(목적)〕
your foot away / from the painful object. // 〔단서 4 운동신경은 다리 근육까지 연결돼서 발을 들어 올리게 함〕

그리고 여러분의 다리 근육에 / 이제 재빨리 수축하는 / 발을 떼어 들어올리기 위해 / 고통을 주는 물체로부터 //

⑤ Sensory and motor nerves control / almost all functions in the body / — **from** the beating of the heart / **to** the movement of the 〔from A to B: A에서 B까지〕
gut, sweating and just about everything else. //

감각 신경과 운동 신경은 통제한다 / 신체의 거의 모든 기능을 / 심장의 박동에서부터 / 장의 운동, 발한과 그 밖에 모든 것에까지 //

- sensory ⓐ 감각의   - nerve ⓝ 신경   - ending ⓝ 끝, 말단
- tissue ⓝ (세포로 이루어진) 조직   - sensation ⓝ 감각
- transmit ⓥ 전달하다   - protective ⓐ 보호하는
- mechanism ⓝ 방법, 메커니즘   - capacity ⓝ 능력, 용량
- polite ⓐ 공손한   - muscle ⓝ 근육   - contract ⓥ 수축하다
- function ⓝ 기능   - sweating ⓝ 발한

감각 신경은 특정 감각을 포착하는 특화된 말단을 조직에 가지고 있다. 예를 들어, 만약 여러분이 핀과 같이 날카로운 물체를 밟는다면, 피부의 신경 말단이 통증 감각을 여러분의 다리 위로, 그리고 척수를 따라 위로 뇌까지 전달할 것이다. ① 통증 자체는 불쾌하지만, 그것은 사실 발을 보호하는 메커니즘으로 작용하고 있다. (② 즉, 여러분은 그 고통에 익숙해져서 고통을 피할 수 있는 능력이 감소하게 된다.) ③ 뇌 안에서, 신경은 언어를 통제하는 부분에 연결될 것이고, 그래서 여러분은 '아야' 또는 다소 덜 공손한 무언가를 외칠 것이다. ④ 그것들은 또한 척수를 타고 내려오는 운동신경에 연결될 것이고, 이제 고통을 주는 물체로부터 발을 떼어 들어올리기 위해 재빨리 수축하는 여러분의 다리 근육에 연결될 것이다. ⑤ 감각 신경과 운동 신경은 심장의 박동에서부터 장의 운동, 발한과 그 밖에 모든 것에 이르기까지 신체의 거의 모든 기능을 통제한다.

왜 정답·오답? ★★★ [정답률 41%]

앞부분: 감각 신경의 말단이 통증을 포착하여 전달하는 과정

① 통증 자체는 불쾌하지만, 그것은 사실 발을 보호하는 메커니즘으로 작용하고 있음
▶ 핀을 밟았을 때의 통증은 사실 발을 보호하는 메커니즘이라고 이야기하는 흐름은 자연스럽기 때문에 ①은 무관한 문장이 아님

② 즉(That is), 여러분은 그 고통에 익숙해져서 고통을 피할 수 있는 능력이 감소하게 됨
▶ 핀을 밟았을 때의 고통에 익숙해져 그 고통을 잘 피할 수 없게 되면, 계속 핀을 밟게 될 것이므로 발을 보호하는 메커니즘이라는 앞 문장과의 흐름에 맞지 않음, 즉 ②가 무관한 문장임

③ 뇌 안에서, 신경은 언어를 통제하는 부분에 연결될 것이고, 그래서 여러분은 '아야' 또는 다소 덜 공손한 무언가를 외칠 것임
▶ 핀을 밟은 통증이 뇌로 전달되었을 때, 뇌 안에서 일어나는 신경 작용에 대한 설명이 이어지므로 ③은 무관한 문장이 아님

④ 그것들은 또한 척수를 타고 내려오는 운동신경에 연결될 것이고, 이제 고통을 주는 물체로부터 발을 떼어 들어올리기 위해 재빨리 수축하는 여러분의 다리 근육에 연결될 것임
▶ 앞 문장에 이어서 통증은 뇌를 거쳐 척수를 타고 내려와 다리 근육에 연결된다며 순서에 따라 자연스럽게 설명하므로 ④은 무관한 문장이 아님

⑤ 감각 신경과 운동 신경은 심장의 박동에서부터 장의 운동, 발한과 그 밖에 모든 것에 이르기까지 신체의 거의 모든 기능을 통제함
▶ 감각 신경과 운동 신경이 신체 거의 모든 기능을 통제한다고 정리하면서 글을 마무리하므로 ⑤은 무관한 문장이 아님

＊ 글의 흐름

도입	감각 신경의 말단 조직은 특정 감각을 포착하는 데 특화됨
예시	날카로운 핀을 밟으면 피부의 신경 말단이 통증 감각을 다리, 척수, 뇌 순서로 전달함
과정(뇌)	뇌에서는 언어 통제 부분에 연결되어 아픔을 언어로 표현하게 함
과정(운동신경)	통증은 척수를 타고 내려와 다리 근육에 연결되어 발을 핀에서 떼게 함
결론	감각 신경과 운동 신경은 신체의 거의 모든 기능을 통제함

N 03 정답 ② *감정적 반응의 조건

다음 글에서 전체 흐름과 관계 없는 문장은?

What does **it** mean / **for a character** to be a hero / as opposed to 〔가주어〕 〔의미상 주어〕 〔진주어 (to부정사)〕
a villain? //

무슨 의미인가 / 등장인물이 영웅이라는 것은 / 악당과 대비되는 //

In artistic and entertainment descriptions, / it's essential for the author / to establish a positive relationship / between a protagonist and the audience. // 〔단서 1 주인공과 관객 사이 긍정적인 관계가 필수적임〕

예술적이고 오락적인 묘사에서 / 작가에게 필수적이다 / 긍정적인 관계를 수립하는 것이 / 주인공과 관객 사이에 // 〔단서 2 등장인물이 확실히 인식되어야 관객으로부터 감정적인 반응을 유도할 수 있음〕

① In order **for tragedy or misfortune** / **to draw** out an emotional 〔의미상 주어〕 〔부사적 용법 (목적)〕
response in viewers, / the character must be adjusted / **so as to** 〔so as to-v: ~하기 위해서 (목적)〕
be recognizable as either friend or enemy. //

비극 또는 불행이 관객에게서 감정적 반응을 끌어내기 위해서 / 등장인물은 조정되어야 한다 / 친구 또는 적 둘 중의 하나로 인식될 수 있도록 //

② Likewise, / the line between friends and enemies / is not 〔단수 주어〕 〔단수 동사〕
clear / in reality. //)

(마찬가지로 / 친구와 적 사이의 선이 / 명확하지 않다 / 현실에서는 //)

③ Whether the portrayal is fictional or documentary, / we must feel / that the protagonist is someone / **whose actions benefit us**; / 〔소유격 관계대명사절 (someone 수식)〕

묘사가 허구적이든 사실을 기록하든 간에 / 우리는 느껴야 한다 / 주인공은 누군가이며 / 행동이 우리에게 이로움을 주는 /

the protagonist is, or would be, / a worthy companion or **valued** 〔과거분사 (ally 수식)〕
ally. //

주인공은 ~이고, 혹은 그렇게 될 (존재일) 것이라고 / 가치 있는 동료나 소중한 협력자 //

④ Violent action films **are** often **filled** with / dozens of incidental 〔수동태 동사〕
deaths of minor characters / **that** draw out little response in the 〔주격 관계대명사〕
audience. // 〔단서 3 비중이 적은 등장인물은 관객의 반응에 큰 영향을 미치지 않음〕

폭력적인 액션 영화는 흔히 가득 차 있다 / 비중이 적은 등장인물의 많은 부수적인 죽음으로 / 관객들에게서 반응을 거의 끌어내지 않는 //

⑤ In order to feel strong emotions, / the audience must be emotionally invested in a character / as either ally or enemy. //

강한 감정을 느끼기 위해 / 관객은 등장인물에게 감정적으로 깊이 연관되어 있어야 한다 / 협력자 또는 적 둘 중 하나로 // 〔단서 4 등장인물과의 감정적 연관이 관객이 강한 감정을 느끼도록 유도함〕

- as opposed to ~와 대비되는   - essential ⓐ 필수적인
- establish ⓥ 수립하다   - positive ⓐ 긍정적인   - tragedy ⓝ 비극
- misfortune ⓝ 불행   - draw out 끌어내다

* 글의 흐름

1 도입: 인간은 신화와 문학을 통해 오랫동안 지능을 가진 기계를 꿈꿔왔음

2 전개: 상상의 개념이 튜링 테스트를 통해 과학적 탐구의 대상이 되었고, '인공지능'이라는 학문적 용어로도 정립됨

3 결론: 그 후 인공지능은 인간처럼 사고하는 지능적인 기계를 만드는 구체적인 연구 및 실행 분야로 발전함

구문 서술형

정답 as well as humans

해석 영국의 수학자 Alan Turing은 기계가 인간만큼 잘 사고하고 추론할 수 있는지 물었다.

→ '…만큼 ~한/하게'를 나타낼 때, 「as + 형용사나 부사의 원급 + as …」 형태의 원급 비교 구문을 쓴다. '잘'을 뜻하는 부사 well을 사용해 as well as humans로 써야 한다.

N 06 정답 ③ *의사 결정 권한과 업무 생산성의 관계

다음 글에서 전체 흐름과 관계 없는 문장은?

동명사구 주어
Simply giving employees a sense of agency / — a feeling that
병렬 구조(동격절 접속사)
they are in control, / that they have genuine decision-making
authority — /

단순히 직원들에게 주인의식을 주는 것은 / (그들이 통제하고 있다는 느낌 / 진정한 의사 결정 권한이 있다는 느낌) /

can radically increase / how much energy and focus they bring
to their jobs. // 단서1 직원들에게 주인의식을 주는 것은 그들이 업무에 쏟는 에너지와 집중력을 높임

급격하게 높일 수 있다 / 그들이 자신의 업무에 쏟는 에너지와 집중력을 //

주어
① One 2010 study / at a manufacturing plant in Ohio, / for
본동사
instance, / carefully examined assembly-line workers /

2010년의 한 연구는 / 오하이오주의 한 제조 공장에서 진행된 / 예를 들어 / 조립 라인 근로자를 주의 깊게 살펴보았다 /
주격 관계대명사(workers 수식)
who were empowered to make small decisions / about their
schedules and work environment. // 단서2 직원들에게 결정 권한을 부여한 예시

작은 결정 권한을 부여받은 / 그들의 일정과 작업 환경에 대한 //

② They designed their own uniforms / and had authority over
부사절 접속사(대조)
shifts / while all the manufacturing processes and pay scales
stayed the same. //

그들은 그들 자신의 유니폼을 디자인했고 / 근무 교대에 대한 권한을 가졌다 / 모든 생산 과정과 임금 규모는 동일하게 유지된 반면에 //

③ It led to decreased efficiency / because their decisions were
not uniform or focused on meeting organizational goals. //)

(그것은 효율성을 낮추는 결과를 낳았다 / 결정이 합치되거나 조직의 목표 달성에 초점이 맞춰지지 않았기 때문에 //)

④ Within two months, / productivity at the plant / increased by
「with + 명사 + 분사」 with 분사구문
20 percent, / with workers taking shorter breaks / and making
fewer mistakes. // 단서3 생산성이 증가했음

두 달 만에 / 그 공장의 생산성은 / 20퍼센트 증가했다 / 직원들은 휴식 시간을 더 짧게 가졌고 / 실수를 더 적게 했다 /

⑤ Giving employees a sense of control / improved how much
self-discipline they brought to their jobs. //

직원들에게 통제권을 쥐고 있다는 느낌을 주는 것이 / 그들이 업무에 끌어들이는 자기 통제력을 향상시켰다 //
단서4 주인의식이 업무에 대한 자기 통제력을 향상시킴

- agency ⓝ 행위자
- genuine ⓐ 진정한
- authority ⓝ 권한
- examine ⓥ 살펴보다
- assembly ⓝ 조립
- empower ⓥ (권한을) 부여하다
- scale ⓝ 규모

- efficiency ⓝ 효율성
- uniform ⓐ 똑같은
- organizational ⓐ 조직의
- productivity ⓝ 생산성
- self-discipline ⓝ 자기 통제력

단순히 직원들에게 주인의식(그들이 통제하고 있다는 느낌, 진정한 의사 결정 권한이 있다는 느낌)을 주는 것만으로도 그들이 자신의 업무에 쏟는 에너지와 집중력을 급격하게 높일 수 있다. ① 예를 들어, 오하이오주의 한 제조 공장에서 진행된 2010년의 한 연구는 그들의 일정과 작업 환경에 대한 작은 결정 권한을 부여받은 조립 라인 근로자를 주의 깊게 살펴보았다. ② 그들은 그들 자신의 유니폼을 디자인했고, 근무 교대에 대한 권한을 가진 반면에, 모든 생산 과정과 임금 규모는 동일하게 유지되었다. (③ 결정이 합치되거나 조직의 목표 달성에 초점이 맞춰지지 않았기 때문에 그것은 효율성을 낮추는 결과를 낳았다.) ④ 두 달 만에 직원들은 휴식 시간을 더 짧게 가졌고, 실수를 더 적게 하였으며, 그 공장의 생산성은 20퍼센트 증가했다. ⑤ 자신들이 통제권을 쥐고 있다는 느낌을 직원들에게 부여한 것이 그들이 업무에 끌어들이는 자기 통제력을 향상시켰다.

왜 정답·오답? ★★★ [정답률 58%]

첫 문장: 직원에게 주인의식이 주어지면 업무에 대한 에너지와 집중력이 높아진다는 내용

① 오하이오주의 한 제조 공장에서 진행된 2010년의 한 연구는 그들의 일정과 작업 환경에 대한 작은 결정 권한을 부여받은 조립 라인 근로자를 주의 깊게 살펴보았음

▶ 작은 결정 권한을 부여받은 한 공장 근로자들을 관찰한 연구를 소개하며 주제문을 뒷받침할 예시가 이어지므로 ①은 무관한 문장이 아님

② 그들은 그들 자신의 유니폼을 디자인했고, 근무 교대에 대한 권한을 가진 반면에, 모든 생산 과정과 임금 규모는 동일하게 유지되었음

▶ 앞에서 언급된 연구에 관한 부연 설명이 이어지므로 ②은 무관한 문장이 아님

③ 결정이 합치되거나 조직의 목표 달성에 초점이 맞춰지지 않았기 때문에 그것은 효율성을 낮추는 결과를 낳았음

▶ 주제문에 따르면 직원들에게 결정 권한을 주는 것이 긍정적인 효과를 불러온다고 했는데, 효율성이 떨어졌다는 내용은 전체 글의 흐름에 맞지 않으므로 ③이 무관한 문장임

④ 두 달 만에 직원들은 휴식 시간을 더 짧게 가졌고, 실수를 더 적게 하였으며, 그 공장의 생산성은 20퍼센트 증가했음

▶ 직원들이 결정 권한을 부여받은 결과, 공장의 생산성이 증가했다고 하며 주제문을 뒷받침하므로 ④은 무관한 문장이 아님

⑤ 자신들이 통제권을 쥐고 있다는 느낌을 직원들에게 부여한 것이 그들이 업무에 끌어들이는 자기 통제력을 향상시켰음

▶ 직원들이 스스로 통제권(결정 권한)이 있다고 생각한 것이 업무에 대한 자기 통제력도 향상시키는 결과를 낳았다고 하며 주제문을 뒷받침하므로 ⑤은 무관한 문장이 아님

* 글의 흐름

도입	직원들에게 주인의식을 주는 것만으로도 그들의 업무 능력을 높일 수 있음
연구	오하이오 주의 한 제조 공장에서 근로자에게 작은 결정 권한을 줬음
연구 결과	직원들의 업무 능력이 높아진 결과, 공장의 생산성도 증가함
부연	직원들이 통제권을 갖는다고 느낄 때 업무에서 자기 통제력이 높아짐

정답 ④ *학습에 사용되는 기억의 종류와 특징

다음 글에서 전체 흐름과 관계 없는 문장은?

Why do we have the illusion / ^{동격절 접속사}that cramming for an exam / ^{동명사구 주어} is the best learning strategy? //
왜 우리는 착각을 하는 것일까 / 시험을 위해 벼락 공부를 하는 것이 / 최고의 학습 전략이라는 //

Because we are unable to differentiate / between the various sections of our memory. //
우리가 구별할 수 없기 때문이다 / 우리의 기억의 다양한 구획을 //

Immediately after reading our textbook or our class notes, / information is fully present in our mind. //
우리의 교과서나 수업 노트를 읽은 직후에는 / 정보가 우리 머릿속에 완전히 존재한다 //

= Information
① It sits in our conscious working memory, / in an active form. // [단서 1] 정보는 우리의 의식적인 작업 기억에 자리함
그것은 우리의 의식적인 작업 기억에 자리한다 / 활동적인 형태로 //

② We feel as if we know it, / because it is present in our short-term storage space ... / but this short-term section has nothing to do with the long-term memory / [단서 2] 정보를 알고 있는 것처럼 느끼지만 단기 저장 공간은 장기 기억과 무관함
^{목적격 관계대명사}that we will need / ^{'~하기 위해'}in order to recall the same information / a few days later. //
우리는 마치 우리가 그것을 알고 있는 것처럼 느낀다 / 그것은 우리의 단기 저장 공간에 존재하기 때문에 / 하지만 이 단기 구획은 장기 기억과는 아무런 관련이 없다 / 우리가 필요로 할 / 같은 정보를 기억하기 위해 / 며칠 후 //

③ After a few seconds or minutes, / working memory already starts disappearing, / and after a few days, / the effect becomes enormous: / [단서 3] 점차 작업 기억이 사라지기 시작하고 테스트를 하지 않으면 기억은 사라짐
unless you retest your knowledge, / memory vanishes. //
몇 초 또는 몇 분 후 / 작업 기억은 이미 사라지기 시작하고 / 며칠 후 / 그 영향은 엄청나게 된다 / 여러분이 자신의 지식을 다시 테스트하지 않으면 / 기억은 사라진다 //

④ ^{병렬 구조(동명사구 주어)}Focusing on exploring new topics / rather than reviewing the same material over and over again / can improve your academic performance. //)
(새로운 주제를 탐구하는 데 집중하는 것이 / 같은 자료를 반복해서 다시 복습하는 것보다 / 여러분의 학업 성취를 향상시킬 수 있다 //)

⑤ To get information into long-term memory, / ^{가주어}it is essential / to study the material, / then test yourself, / rather than spend all your time studying. // [단서 4] 정보를 장기 기억에 넣으려면 학습과 테스트가 필수적임
^{진주어}정보를 장기 기억에 넣으려면 / ~이 필수적이다 / 자료를 공부하는 것 / 그리고 나서 스스로를 테스트하는 것 / 여러분의 모든 시간을 공부하는 데에 쓰기보다는 //

- illusion ⓝ 착각   - cram ⓥ 벼락치기를 하다   - strategy ⓝ 전략
- differentiate ⓥ 구분하다   - present ⓐ 존재하는
- conscious ⓐ 의식적인   - enormous ⓐ 엄청난
- vanish ⓥ 사라지다   - material ⓝ 자료   - academic ⓐ 학업적인
- performance ⓝ 성취   - essential ⓐ 필수적인

왜 우리는 시험을 위해 벼락 공부를 하는 것이 최고의 학습 전략이라는 착각을 하는 것일까? 우리가 우리의 기억의 다양한 구획을 구별할 수 없기 때문이다. 우리의 교과서나 수업 노트를 읽은 직후에는 정보가 우리 머릿속에 완전히 존재한다. ① 그것은 우리의 의식적인 작업 기억에 활동적인 형태로 자리한다. ② 그것은 우리의 단기 저장 공간에 존재하기 때문에 우리는 마치 우리가 그것을 알고 있는 것처럼 느끼지만, 이 단기 구획은 며칠 후 같은 정보를 기억하기 위해 우리가 필요로 할 장기 기억과는 아무런 관련이 없다. ③ 몇 초 또는 몇 분 후, 작업 기억은 이미 사라지기 시작하고, 며칠 후 그 영향은 엄청나게 되어, 여러분이 자신의 지식을 다시 테스트하지 않으면 기억은 사라진다. (④ 같은 자료를 반복해서 다시 복습하는 것보다 새로운 주제를 탐구하는 데 집중하는 것이 여러분의 학업 성취를 향상시킬 수 있다.) ⑤ 정보를 장기 기억에 넣으려면, 여러분의 모든 시간을 공부하는 데에 쓰기보다는 자료를 공부하고 나서 스스로를 테스트하는 것이 필수적이다.

왜 정답·오답? ★★☆ [정답률 81%]

글의 앞부분: 벼락 공부가 최고의 학습 전략이라는 착각을 하는 이유는 우리가 기억의 다양한 구획을 구별할 수 없기 때문이며, 실제로 자료를 읽은 직후에는 정보가 우리 머릿속에 완전히 존재한다는 내용

① 그것(It)은 우리의 의식적인 작업 기억에 활동적인 형태로 자리함
▶ It은 앞 문장의 information을 가리킴. 자료를 읽은 직후에 정보가 머리에 완전히 존재한다는 내용 뒤에, 의식적인 작업 기억에 활동적인 형태로 자리한다는 부연 설명이 이어지므로 ①은 무관한 문장이 아님

② 그것은 우리의 단기 저장 공간에 존재하기 때문에 우리는 마치 우리가 그것을 알고 있는 것처럼 느끼지만, 이 단기 구획은 며칠 후 같은 정보를 기억하기 위해 우리가 필요로 할 장기 기억과는 아무런 관련이 없음
▶ 정보는 단기 저장 공간(작업 기억)에 활동적인 형태로 자리하기 때문에 우리가 그 정보를 알고 있는 것처럼 느끼지만, 이는 장기 기억과 무관하다고 설명하므로 ②은 무관한 문장이 아님

③ 몇 초 또는 몇 분 후, 작업 기억은 이미 사라지기 시작하고, 며칠 후 그 영향은 엄청나게 되어, 여러분이 자신의 지식을 다시 테스트하지 않으면 기억은 사라짐
▶ 작업 기억이 장기 기억과는 무관하기 때문에, 자신의 지식을 다시 테스트하지 않으면 작업 기억이 점차 사라진다는 내용이 자연스럽게 이어지므로 ③은 무관한 문장이 아님

④ 같은 자료를 반복해서 다시 복습하는 것보다 새로운 주제를 탐구하는 데 집중하는 것이 여러분의 학업 성취를 향상시킬 수 있음
▶ 작업 기억은 다시 테스트하지 않으면 사라진다는 내용이 이어지다가, 새로운 주제를 탐구하는 데 집중한다는 내용이 뒤에 오는 것은 전체 글의 흐름에 맞지 않으므로 ④이 무관한 문장임

⑤ 정보를 장기 기억에 넣으려면, 여러분의 모든 시간을 공부하는 데에 쓰기보다는 자료를 공부하고 나서 스스로를 테스트하는 것이 필수적임
▶ 지식을 다시 테스트하지 않으면 작업 기억이 점차 사라진다고 했으므로, 장기 기억에 정보를 넣으려면 공부하고 나서 스스로 테스트하는 것이 필수라는 내용이 자연스럽게 이어짐. 따라서 ⑤은 무관한 문장이 아님

* 글의 흐름

도입	우리는 기억의 구획을 구별할 수 없기 때문에 벼락 공부가 최고의 학습 전략이라는 착각을 함
전개	자료를 읽은 직후에는 정보가 머릿속에 완전히 존재함(정보가 작업 기억에 활동적인 형태로 자리하여 우리가 그것을 알고 있다고 착각하는 것임)
부연	작업 기억은 장기 기억과 무관하기 때문에, 정보를 다시 테스트하지 않으면 기억은 점차 사라짐
결론	정보를 장기 기억에 넣으려면 자료를 공부한 후 스스로 테스트하는 것이 필수적임

N 08 정답 ④ *바넘 효과

다음 글에서 전체 흐름과 관계 없는 문장은?

The Barnum Effect is the phenomenon / ^{관계부사(선행사: the phenomenon)}where someone reads or hears / something very general / but believes / ^{목적어절 접속사}that it applies to them. //
바넘 효과는 현상이다 / 누군가가 읽거나 듣는 / 매우 일반적인 어떤 것을 / 하지만 믿는 / 그것이 자신에게 적용된다고 //

① These statements appear / to be very personal / on the surface / but in fact, / they are true for many. //
이러한 진술들은 보인다 / 매우 개인적인 것처럼 / 표면적으로는 / 그러나 실제로는 / 많은 사람에게 적용된다 //

O 글의 순서 정하기 〔문제편 p. 220~236〕

O 01 정답 ⑤ *연골의 작동 원리와 중요성

Cartilage is extremely important / for the healthy functioning
부사절 접속사 (조건)   전치사 (~처럼)
of a joint, / especially **if** that joint bears weight, / **like** your
knee. //
연골은 아주 중요하며 / 관절의 건강한 기능에 / 특히 그 관절이 당신의 무게를 지탱한다면
그렇다 / 무릎처럼 //

단서1 (B)에 언급된 윤활액의 압착을 가리킴
(A) This squeezing of joint fluid into and out of the cartilage /
helps의 목적어와 목적격 보어 (원형부정사)
helps **it respond** to the off-and-on pressure of walking / without
breaking under the pressure. //
이러한 관절 윤활액의 연골 안팎으로의 압착은 / 연골이 걷는 것의 반복적인 압력에 반응할 수
있도록 돕는다 / 압력에 부서지지 않고 //

(B) The cartilage in your left knee / then "drinks in" synovial
관계부사 (선행사: the same way)
fluid, / in much the same way / **that** a sponge soaks up liquid /
부사절에서 '주어+be동사' 생략
when put in water. // 단서2 (C)의 마지막 문장에 언급된 것처럼 무게 이동으로 인해 무릎
압력이 풀린 경우에 일어나는 과정을 설명함
당신의 왼쪽 무릎의 연골은 / 그러면 윤활액을 '흡수'한다 / 거의 같은 방식으로 / 스펀지가 액
체를 흡수하는 것과 / 물에 담겼을 때 //

When you take another step / and transfer the weight back onto
불가산 명사 단수 동사
your left leg, / much of the **fluid squeezes** out of the cartilage. //
당신이 또 다른 한 걸음을 내딛어 / 체중을 다시 왼쪽 다리로 옮길 때 / 윤활액의 상당 부분이
압착되어 연골 밖으로 나간다 //

단서3 주어진 글에 소개된 연골 작동 원리를 알려 주는 예시
(C) Imagine for a moment / that you're looking into the inner
workings of your left knee / as you walk down the street. //
잠시 상상해 봐라 / 당신이 왼쪽 무릎의 내부 작동 방식을 들여다본다고 / 길을 걸으며 //

문장의 주어   수동태 동사
When you shift your weight / from your left leg to your right, /
the pressure on your left knee is released. //
당신이 체중을 옮길 때 / 왼쪽 다리에서 오른쪽 다리로 / 당신의 왼쪽 무릎의 압력이 풀린다 //

- joint ⓝ 관절   • bear ⓥ 지탱하다   • weight ⓝ 무게, 체중
- squeeze ⓥ 압착하다   • respond ⓥ 반응하다
- off-and-on ⓐ 반복적인   • soak up 흡수하다
- transfer ⓥ 옮기다, 이동하다   • look into ~을 들여다보다
- shift ⓥ 옮기다   • pressure ⓝ 압력   • release ⓥ 풀다

연골은 관절의 건강한 기능에 아주 중요하며, 특히 그 관절이 당신의 무릎처럼
무게를 지탱한다면 그렇다. (C) 당신이 길을 걸으며 왼쪽 무릎의 내부 작동 방
식을 들여다본다고 잠시 상상해 봐라. 당신이 왼쪽 다리에서 오른쪽 다리로 체
중을 옮길 때, 당신의 왼쪽 무릎의 압력이 풀린다. (B) 그러면 당신의 왼쪽 무릎
의 연골은 스펀지가 물에 담겼을 때 액체를 흡수하는 것과 거의 같은 방식으로
윤활액을 '흡수'한다. 당신이 또 다른 한 걸음을 내딛어 체중을 다시 왼쪽 다리
로 옮길 때, 윤활액의 상당 부분이 압착되어 연골 밖으로 나간다. (A) 이러한 관
절 윤활액의 연골 안팎으로의 압착은 연골이 걷는 것의 반복적인 압력에 부서지
지 않고 반응할 수 있도록 돕는다.

(A)에서 윤활액의 역할을 설명했으므로 (B)에 이어져야 자연스러움
주어진 글 다음에 이어질 글의 순서로 가장 적절한 것을 고르시오. [3점]
① (A) — (C) — (B) 주어진 글에서 윤활액이 언급되지 않았으므로 (A)가 바로 올 수 없음
② (B) — (A) — (C)
③ (B) — (C) — (A) then을 받을 만한 표현이 주어진 글에 없음
④ (C) — (A) — (B) 연골의 관절은 무게를 지탱함 — (C) 보행 시 한쪽 다리로 체중을
옮기면 반대쪽 무릎의 압력이 풀림 — (B) 연골이 윤활액을 흡수한 후,
⑤ (C) — (B) — (A) 내딛을 때 윤활액이 압착되어 연골 밖으로 나감 — (A) 윤활액의 압착
덕분에 연골이 보호됨

| 문제 풀이 순서 | ★★❀ [정답률 63%]

1st 각 문단의 내용을 파악하고, 글의 논리적인 순서를 추론한다.

⌐ **주어진 글:** 연골은 관절의 건강한 기능에 아주 중요하며, 특히 그 관절이 당
└ 신의 무릎처럼 무게를 지탱한다면 그렇다.

→ **주어진 글 뒤:** 연골이 관절을 보호하는 원리를 설명할 것이다.

⌐ **(A):** 이러한(This) 관절 윤활액의 연골 안팎으로의 **압착(squeezing)**은
│ 연골이 걷는 것의 반복적인 압력에 부서지지 않고 반응할 수 있도록 돕는
└ 다.

→ **(A) 앞:** 연골을 보호하는 This squeezing이 무엇인지 앞에 언급되어야 한다.
  ▶ 주어진 글에는 연골의 중요성과 기능만 제시되었으므로 (A) 앞에 올 수 없음
  (A) 뒤: 관절 윤활액의 압착 덕분에 연골이 부서지지 않고 반응할 수 있게 된다고 했
  으므로 연골이 보호되는 과정의 마지막, 다시 말해, 글의 마지막일 가능성이 높다.

⌐ **(B):** 그러면(then) 당신의 왼쪽 무릎의 연골은 스펀지가 물에 담겼을 때 액
│ 체를 흡수하는 것과 거의 같은 방식으로 윤활액을 '흡수'한다. 당신이 또 다
│ 른 한 걸음을 내딛어 체중을 다시 왼쪽 다리로 옮길 때, 윤활액의 상당 부분
└ 이 **압착되어(squeezes)** 연골 밖으로 나간다.

→ **(B) 앞:** 다음 순서를 나타내는 then이 나왔으므로, 왼쪽 무릎의 연골이 윤활액을 흡
  수하기 이전 과정이 앞에 나와야 한다.
  ▶ 주어진 글에는 연골의 중요성과 기능만 제시되었으므로 (B) 앞에 올 수 없음
  (B) 뒤: 연골 안으로 흡수된 윤활액이 압착되어 연골 밖으로 나가는 과정을 (A)에서
  This squeezing으로 다시 언급했다.
  ▶ (B) 뒤에 (A)가 와야 함 (순서: (B) → (A))

⌐ **(C):** 당신이 길을 걸으며 왼쪽 무릎의 내부 작동 방식을 들여다본다고 잠시
│ 상상해 봐라. 당신이 왼쪽 다리에서 오른쪽 다리로 체중을 옮길 때, 당신의
└ 왼쪽 무릎의 압력이 풀린다.

→ **(C) 앞:** 주어진 글에서 연골이 관절에 중요하다고 했는데, 왼쪽 무릎의 내부 작동 방
  식을 예로 들며 이를 설명한다.
  ▶ (C) 앞에 주어진 글이 와야 함 (순서: 주어진 글 → (C))
  (C) 뒤: 왼쪽 무릎의 압력이 풀린다는 내용 뒤에, (B)의 then이 연골이 윤활액을 흡
  수한다는 내용을 받는다.
  ▶ (C) 뒤에 (B)가 와야 함 (순서: 주어진 글 → (C) → (B) → (A))

2nd 글이 한눈에 들어오도록 정리하여 정답을 확인한다.

주어진 글: 연골은 무게를 지탱하는 무릎 관절의 기능에 아주 중요하다.
→ **(C):** 걷는 동안 왼쪽 다리에서 오른쪽 다리로 체중을 옮기면 왼쪽 무릎의 압력이 줄
  어든다.
→ **(B):** 그러면 왼쪽 무릎의 연골은 윤활액을 흡수하고, 다시 체중을 왼쪽 다리로 옮기
  면 이를 압착해 밖으로 내보낸다.
→ **(A):** 윤활액의 압착 덕분에 연골이 반복적인 걷기 압력에도 견딜 수 있다.
  ▶ 주어진 글 다음에 이어질 글의 순서는 (C) → (B) → (A)이므로 정답은 ⑤임

O 02 정답 ② *외래종의 유입이 생태계에 미치는 영향

Problems often arise / if an exotic species is suddenly
introduced / to an ecosystem. //
문제가 종종 발생한다 / 외래종이 갑자기 유입되면 / 생태계에 //

(A) The grey had the edge / because it can adapt its diet; / it is
부사절 접속사 (대조)
able, for instance, to eat green acorns, / **while** the red can only
digest mature acorns. // 단서1 회색 다람쥐가 (붉은색 다람쥐보다) 먹이에 있어서 우위를 점함
회색 다람쥐는 우위를 점했다 / 먹이를 조절할 수 있기 때문에 / 예를 들어 회색 다람쥐는
설익은 도토리를 먹을 수 있다 / 반면 붉은 다람쥐는 다 익은 도토리만 소화할 수 있다 //

Within the same area of forest, / grey squirrels can destroy the
food supply / before red squirrels even have a bite. //
숲의 같은 지역 내에서 / 회색 다람쥐는 식량 공급을 파괴할 수 있다 / 붉은 다람쥐가 한 입
먹기도 전에 //

단서2 외래종 유입으로 인한 문제의 예시를 제공

(B) Britain's red and grey squirrels / provide a clear example. //
영국의 붉은색 다람쥐와 회색 다람쥐가 / 명확한 예를 제공한다 //

When the grey arrived from America in the 1870s, / both squirrel species competed / for the same food and habitat, / which put the native red squirrel populations under pressure. //
계속적 용법의 주격 관계대명사
1870년대 미국에서 회색 다람쥐가 왔을 때 / 두 다람쥐 종은 경쟁했고 / 동일한 먹이와 서식지를 놓고 / 이것이 토종의 붉은 다람쥐 개체군을 압박했다 //

병렬 구조(부사구)
(C) Greys can also live more densely and in varied habitats, / so have survived more easily / when woodland has been destroyed. //
앞에 주어 생략(Greys)
단서3 회색 다람쥐가 생존에 더 강한 이유를 추가로 제시함
회색 다람쥐는 또한 더 밀집하며 다양한 서식지에서 살 수 있어서 / 더 쉽게 살아남았다 / 삼림이 파괴되었을 때 //

As a result, / the red squirrel has come close to extinction in England. //
단서4 결국 붉은색 다람쥐는 멸종 위기에 처함
그 결과 / 붉은 다람쥐는 영국에서 거의 멸종 위기에 이르렀다 //

- arise ⓥ 생기다 · exotic ⓐ 이국적인 · species ⓝ 종
- introduce ⓥ 도입하다 · adapt ⓥ 적응하다 · digest ⓥ 소화하다
- mature ⓐ 익은 · compete ⓥ 경쟁하다 · native ⓐ 토종의
- densely ⓐⓓ 밀집하게 · varied ⓐ 다양한 · habitat ⓝ 서식지
- extinction ⓝ 멸종

외래종이 갑자기 생태계에 유입되면 문제가 종종 발생한다. (B) 영국의 붉은색 다람쥐와 회색 다람쥐가 명확한 예를 제공한다. 1870년대 미국에서 회색 다람쥐가 왔을 때, 두 다람쥐 종은 동일한 먹이와 서식지를 놓고 경쟁했고, 이것이 토종의 붉은 다람쥐 개체군을 압박했다. (A) 회색 다람쥐는 먹이를 조절할 수 있기 때문에 우위를 점했다. 예를 들어 회색 다람쥐는 설익은 도토리를 먹을 수 있는 반면, 붉은 다람쥐는 다 익은 도토리만 소화할 수 있다. 숲의 같은 지역 내에서 회색 다람쥐는 붉은 다람쥐가 한 입 먹기도 전에 식량 공급을 파괴할 수 있다. (C) 회색 다람쥐는 또한 더 밀집하며 다양한 서식지에서 살 수 있어서 삼림이 파괴되었을 때 더 쉽게 살아남았다. 그 결과, 붉은 다람쥐는 영국에서 거의 멸종 위기에 이르렀다.

주어진 글 다음에 이어질 글의 순서로 가장 적절한 것을 고르시오.
① (A) — (C) — (B) (A)에서 얘기하고 있는 다람쥐에 대한 언급이 주어진 글에 없음
② (B) — (A) — (C) 외래종이 갑자기 유입되면 생태계에 문제가 발생함 — (B) 영국의 토종 붉은색 다람쥐와 미국에서 유입된 회색 다람쥐의 예시 — (A) 회색 다람쥐가 먹이 조절에서 더 우위를 차지함 — (C) 또한 회색 다람쥐가 삼림이 파괴되었을 때 더 쉽게 생존할 수 있으므로 결국 붉은 다람쥐는 멸종 위기에 처함
③ (B) — (C) — (A)
④ (C) — (A) — (B) (C)의 '그 결과'로 나타나는 붉은색 다람쥐의 멸종 이유는 (A)에서 처음으로 제시됨
⑤ (C) — (B) — (A) 붉은색 다람쥐와 회색 다람쥐의 예를 처음으로 언급한 (B)가 맨 앞에 와야 함

| 문제 풀이 순서 | ✸✸❀ [정답률 71%]

1st 각 문단의 내용을 파악하고, 글의 논리적인 순서를 추론한다.

주어진 글: 외래종이 갑자기 생태계에 유입되면 문제가 종종 발생한다.

→ 주어진 글 뒤: 외래종이 유입되면 어떤 문제가 발생하는지에 대한 내용이 이어질 것이다.

(A): 회색 다람쥐는 먹이를 조절할 수 있기 때문에 우위를 점했다. 예를 들어 회색 다람쥐는 설익은 도토리를 먹을 수 있는 반면, 붉은 다람쥐는 다 익은 도토리만 소화할 수 있다. 숲의 같은 지역 내에서 회색 다람쥐는 붉은 다람쥐가 한 입 먹기도 전에 식량 공급을 파괴할 수 있다.

→ (A) 앞: 회색 다람쥐와 붉은 다람쥐에 관한 정보가 앞에 나와야 한다.
▶ 주어진 글 바로 뒤에 (A)가 올 수 없음
(A) 뒤: 붉은색 다람쥐가 불리하다는 내용이 이어지거나 그 결과가 제시될 것이다.

(B): 영국의 붉은색 다람쥐와 회색 다람쥐가 명확한 예(example)를 제공한다. 1870년대 미국에서 회색 다람쥐가 왔을 때, 두 다람쥐 종은 동일한 먹이와 서식지를 놓고 경쟁했고, 이것이 토종의 붉은 다람쥐 개체군을 압박했다.

→ (B) 앞: 토종 붉은색 다람쥐와 외래종 회색 다람쥐가 어떤 경우의 예인지 제시되어야 하는데, 주어진 글에 외래종의 유입으로 인한 생태계 문제가 언급되었으므로 주어진 글에 이어지는 내용이다.
▶ (B) 앞에 주어진 글이 와야 함 (순서: 주어진 글 → (B))
(B) 뒤: 회색 다람쥐가 어떻게 붉은 다람쥐를 압박했는지가 이어져야 한다. 구체적인 내용으로서 먹이 조절을 언급한 (A)가 이어질 수도 있지만, (C)의 내용도 확인해야 한다.

(C): 회색 다람쥐는 또한(also) 더 밀집하며 다양한 서식지에서 살 수 있어서 삼림이 파괴되었을 때 더 쉽게 살아남았다. 그 결과, 붉은 다람쥐는 영국에서 거의 멸종 위기에 이르렀다.

→ (C) 앞: 또 다른 내용을 나타내는 also가 있으므로, 회색 다람쥐가 붉은 다람쥐보다 우위를 점한 첫 번째 이유로서 회색 다람쥐가 먹이를 조절할 수 있다고 언급한 (A)가 앞에 와야 한다.
▶ (C) 앞에 (A)가 와야 함 (순서: 주어진 글 → (B) → (A) → (C))

2nd 글이 한눈에 들어오도록 정리하여 정답을 확인한다.

주어진 글: 외래종이 생태계에 유입되면 문제가 발생한다.
→ (B): 그 예로, 영국의 토종 붉은색 다람쥐와 외래종 회색 다람쥐가 경쟁하였고 회색 다람쥐가 붉은색 다람쥐를 압박했다.
→ (A): 먹이 조절에서 회색 다람쥐가 우위를 갖고 있으므로 회색 다람쥐는 붉은색 다람쥐의 식량 공급을 파괴할 수 있었다.
→ (C): 또한 회색 다람쥐가 더 밀집하여 다양한 서식지에 살기 때문에 삼림이 파괴되었을 때 더 쉽게 생존한다. 그 결과 토종인 붉은색 다람쥐는 멸종 위기에 처했다.
▶ 주어진 글 다음에 이어질 글의 순서는 (B) → (A) → (C)이므로 정답은 ②임

O 03 정답 ⑤ *비개념적 사고와 동물의 인지 능력

Let's assume / that at least some animals are capable of thinking / despite lacking a language. //
가정해 보자 / 적어도 일부 동물은 사고할 수 있다고 / 언어가 부족함에도 불구하고 //

단서1 다람쥐가 개념 없이도 상상을 통해 행동할 수 있다는 (B)의 내용
= squirrels = concepts
(A) This doesn't imply / that squirrels lack concepts, / simply that they don't need them / for this concrete form of thinking. //
이것이 의미하는 것이 아니라 / 다람쥐가 개념이 부족하다는 것을 / 단지 다람쥐가 그것들이 필요하지 않다는 것을 의미한다 / 이 사고의 구체적인 형태를 위해 //

의미상 주어 부사적 용법 (목적)
For us to be able to say / that an animal has concepts, / we have to show / not just that she's capable of thinking, / but also that she has certain specific abilities. //
not just A, but also B: A뿐만 아니라 B도
우리가 말할 수 있기 위해서 / 동물이 개념을 가지고 있다고 / 우리는 보여 주어야 한다 / 그 동물이 사고할 수 있다는 것뿐만 아니라 / 어떤 특정한 능력을 가지고 있다는 것을 //

단서2 (C)에 언급된 다람쥐의 이동을 가리킴
(B) To do this, / in principle / she doesn't need a concept of branch / nor a concept of tree. //
not A nor B: A도 B도 아닌
이것을 하기 위해서 / 원칙적으로 / 다람쥐는 나뭇가지의 개념이 필요하지 않고 / 또한 나무의 개념도 필요하지 않다 //

가주어 진주어 (to부정사)
It might be enough for her to have, / for example, / the ability to think in images; / to make a mental map of the tree / where she can imagine and try out different routes. //
관계부사
다람쥐가 가지고 있는 것으로 충분할 수도 있다 / 예를 들어 / 이미지로 생각하는 능력 / 즉, 나무에 대한 머릿속 지도를 만드는 능력만 / 다람쥐가 다양한 경로를 상상하고 시도해 볼 수 있는 //

단서3 주어진 글의 가정(언어 없이 사고하는 동물이 있다)을 가리킴
(C) This doesn't necessarily mean / that they possess concepts, / for some forms of thought may be nonconceptual. //
등위접속사 (이유)
이것이 반드시 의미하지는 않는데 / 그들이 개념을 가지고 있다고 / 왜냐하면 사고의 어떤 형태는 비(非)개념적일 수도 있기 때문이다 //

We can imagine, / for instance, / a squirrel **who** is planning how
to get / from the branch **she's currently standing on** / to a branch
from the tree in front. //

주격 관계대명사
앞에 목적격 관계대명사가 생략됨

우리는 상상해 볼 수 있다 / 예를 들어 / 가는 방법을 계획하고 있는 다람쥐를 / 현재 서 있는 나
뭇가지에서 / 앞쪽 나무의 나뭇가지로 //

- **assume** ⓥ 가정하다
- **capable** ⓐ ~할 수 있는
- **despite** ⓟⓡⓔⓟ ~에도 불구하고
- **lack** ⓥ 부족하다
- **imply** ⓥ 의미하다
- **concept** ⓝ 개념
- **concrete** ⓐ 구체적인
- **specific** ⓐ 특정한
- **in principle** 원칙적으로
- **possess** ⓥ 가지고 있다, 소유하다
- **nonconceptual** ⓐ 비(非)개념적인
- **currently** ⓐⓓ 현재

적어도 일부 동물은 언어가 부족함에도 불구하고 사고할 수 있다고 가정해 보자. (C) 이것이 그들이 개념을 가지고 있다고 반드시 의미하지는 않는데, 왜냐하면 사고의 어떤 형태는 비(非)개념적일 수도 있기 때문이다. 예를 들어, 우리는 현재 서 있는 나뭇가지에서 앞쪽 나무의 나뭇가지로 가는 방법을 계획하고 있는 다람쥐를 상상해 볼 수 있다. (B) 이것을 하기 위해서, 원칙적으로 다람쥐는 나뭇가지의 개념이 필요하지 않고 또한 나무의 개념도 필요하지 않다. 예를 들어, 다람쥐가 이미지로 생각하는 능력, 즉, 다람쥐가 다양한 경로를 상상하고 시도해 볼 수 있는 나무에 대한 머릿속 지도를 만드는 능력만 가지고 있는 것으로 충분할 수도 있다. (A) 이것은 다람쥐가 개념이 부족하다는 것을 의미하는 것이 아니라, 단지 다람쥐가 이 사고의 구체적인 형태를 위해 그것들이 필요하지 않다는 것을 의미한다. 우리가 동물이 개념을 가지고 있다고 말할 수 있기 위해서, 그 동물이 사고할 수 있다는 것뿐만 아니라 어떤 특정한 능력을 가지고 있다는 것을 우리는 보여 주어야 한다.

> 주어진 글 다음에 이어질 글의 순서로 가장 적절한 것을 고르시오. [3점]
> ① (A) ― (C) ― (B) 주어진 글에 (A)의 '이것'과 연결되는 내용이 없음
> ② (B) ― (A) ― (C)
> ③ (B) ― (C) ― (A) (B)의 '이것'은 (C)의 뒷부분에 있음
> ④ (C) ― (A) ― (B) (A)의 '이것'은 (B)의 뒷부분에 있음
> ⑤ (C) ― (B) ― (A) 일부 동물들은 언어 없이도 사고가 가능하다는 가정 ― (C) 일부 사고는 비개념적 ― (B) 다람쥐는 행동에 대한 개념이 없어도 이미지로 계획 가능 ― (A) 개념 없이도 구체적인 사고가 가능

| 문제 풀이 순서 | ★★★ [정답률 52%]

1st 각 문단의 내용을 파악하고, 글의 논리적인 순서를 추론한다.

┌ **주어진 글:** 적어도 일부 동물은 언어가 부족함에도 불구하고 사고할 수 있다고 가정해 보자.

➡ **주어진 글 뒤:** 언어가 부족하지만 사고가 실제 이루어지는 상황이 제시될 것이다.

┌ (A) 이것(This)은 다람쥐가 개념이 부족하다는 것을 의미하는 것이 아니라, 단지 다람쥐가 이 사고의 구체적인 형태를 위해 그것들이 필요하지 않다는 것을 의미한다. 우리가 동물이 개념을 가지고 있다고 말할 수 있기 위해서, 그 동물이 사고할 수 있다는 것뿐만 아니라 어떤 특정한 능력을 가지고 있다는 것을 우리는 보여 주어야 한다.

➡ **(A) 앞:** 다람쥐는 개념이 필요하지 않다는 것과 관련된 This가 무엇인지 앞에 나와야 한다. ▶ 주어진 글에는 언어 없이도 사고할 수 있다는 내용 외에 어떠한 사례도 없으므로 (A) 앞에 올 수 없음

(A) 뒤: 동물의 행동에 개념이 필수적이지는 않고 동물이 개념을 가진다고 말하려면 사고 능력뿐 아니라 특정한 능력을 지녔음을 입증해야 한다는 내용으로 마무리되었으므로 글의 마지막일 가능성이 높다.

┌ (B) 이것(this)을 하기 위해서, 원칙적으로 다람쥐는 나뭇가지의 개념이 필요하지 않고 또한 나무의 개념도 필요하지 않다. 예를 들어, 다람쥐가 이미지로 생각하는 능력, 즉, 다람쥐가 다양한 경로를 상상하고 시도해 볼 수 있는 나무에 대한 머릿속 지도를 만드는 능력만 가지고 있는 것으로 충분할 수도 있다.

➡ **(B) 앞:** 나뭇가지나 나무와 관련된 this가 무엇인지 앞에 나와야 한다.
> ▶ 주어진 글에는 다람쥐나 나뭇가지 등 어떠한 사례도 없으므로 (B) 앞에 올 수 없음

(B) 뒤: 다람쥐가 이미지로 생각하는 능력만 있어도 충분하다는 내용을 (A)에서 This로 다시 언급하며, 이는 개념이 부족하다는 것이 아니라, 개념이 필요하지 않은 것이라는 내용으로 이어진다. ▶ (B) 뒤에 (A)가 와야 함 (순서: (B) → (A))

┌ **(C):** 이것이 그들(they)이 개념을 가지고 있다고 반드시 의미하지는 않는데, 왜냐하면 사고의 어떤 형태는 비(非)개념적일 수도 있기 때문이다. 예를 들어, 우리는 현재 서 있는 나뭇가지에서 앞쪽 나무의 나뭇가지로 가는 방법을 계획하고 있는 다람쥐를 상상해 볼 수 있다.

➡ **(C) 앞:** 개념을 가지지 않을 수도 있다는 they는 주어진 글에서 언어가 부족해도 사고할 수 있는 일부 동물들을 나타낸다.
> ▶ (C) 앞에 주어진 글이 와야 함 (순서: 주어진 글 → (C))

(C) 뒤: 다람쥐가 나뭇가지마다 이동하는 예시가 등장했으므로, (B)에서 다람쥐가 이동하기 위해 나뭇가지의 개념이 필요하지 않다는 내용으로 이어진다.
> ▶ (C) 뒤에 (B)가 와야 함 (순서: 주어진 글 → (C) → (B) → (A))

2nd 글이 한눈에 들어오도록 정리하여 정답을 확인한다.

주어진 글: 일부 동물은 언어가 부족하더라도 사고할 수 있다.
→ **(C):** 일부 사고는 비개념적일 수 있다.
→ **(B):** 다람쥐는 나뭇가지의 개념 없이도 이미지로 경로를 상상하여 이동할 수 있다.
→ **(A):** 개념 없이도 구체적인 사고를 할 수 있다.
> ▶ 주어진 글 다음에 이어질 글의 순서는 (C) → (B) → (A)이므로 정답은 ⑤임

구문 서술형

정답 that, 목적어, 명사절

해석 적어도 일부 동물은 사고할 수 있다고 가정해 보자.
→ 밑줄 친 부분 앞에 선행사가 없고, 동사 assume의 목적어가 와야 하므로, 목적어 역할을 하는 명사절을 이끄는 접속사 that으로 고쳐야 한다.

O 04 정답 ② *역사적 반복의 예외가 나타나는 문명 붕괴

> History, / **people often say**, / repeats **itself**. //
> 삽입절   재귀대명사 (재귀 용법)
> 역사는 / 사람들이 종종 말하길 / 그 자체를 반복한다 //
> 분사구문
> And **looking at the historical records** / of the ancient
> **civilizations**, / some things / **do** seem to happen again and
> 강조 용법의 do동사
> again. //
> 그리고 역사적 기록들을 보면 / 고대 문명의 / 몇 가지 일들이 / 정말로 반복해서 일어나는 것처럼 보인다 //

(A) If so, / archaeology would be pretty boring; / one thing
would happen again and again. //
만약 그렇다면 / 고고학은 꽤 지루할 것이다 / 한 가지 일이 반복해서 일어날 테니 말이다 //

선행사를 포함하는 관계대명사
But that's not **what** archaeologists see. // 단서 1 역사가 항상 반복되는 것이 아니라 예외가 있음
하지만 그것은 고고학자들이 보는 것이 아니다 //

Some civilizations end suddenly, / like the Aztec and Inca, /
과거분사구 (the Aztec and Inca 수식)
conquered by invaders in the 1520s AD. //
어떤 문명들은 갑작스럽게 끝난다 / Aztec과 Inca처럼 / 서기 1520년대에 침략자들에 의해 정복된 //

(B) Civilizations expand, / get overextended, / and then collapse
/ as in the cases of Rome, / which went under in 476 AD, /
문명은 확장하고 / 과도하게 확장되다가 / 결국 붕괴한다 / 로마의 경우와 / 서기 476년에 멸망한 / 단서 2 주어진 글에서 언급된 고대 문명에서 반복해서 일어난 역사를 부연 설명함
병렬 구조 (명사 + 관계사절)
and the British Empire, / which fell apart more than a thousand
years later / in the post-World War II era. //
대영제국의 사례에서처럼 / 천 년 이상 지난 후 해체된 / 제2차 세계 대전 이후에 //

But is this always the case? //
하지만 이것이 항상 그런가 //

형용사적 용법 (the chance 수식)
(C) Those empires never had the chance / to collapse as a result
of overexpansion. //
단서 3 침략으로 정복된 the Aztec and Inca를 가리킴
그러한 제국들은 기회조차 없었다 / 과도한 확장의 결과로 붕괴할 //

So in the case of civilizations, / "history repeats itself" / seems to
be an oversimplification. //
그래서 문명의 경우에 / "역사는 그 자체를 반복한다"라는 말은 / 지나친 단순화로 보인다 //

- ancient ⓐ 고대의   - civilization ⓝ 문명   - seem ⓥ ~처럼 보이다
- conquer ⓥ 정복하다   - expand ⓥ 확장하다
- collapse ⓥ 붕괴하다   - go under 멸망하다, 가라앉다
- fall apart 해체되다   - era ⓝ 시기
- oversimplification ⓝ 지나친 단순화

역사는, 사람들이 종종 말하길, 그 자체를 반복한다. 그리고 고대 문명의 역사적 기록들을 보면, 몇 가지 일들이 정말로 반복해서 일어나는 것처럼 보인다. (B) 문명은 서기 476년에 멸망한 로마의 경우와, 천 년 이상 지난 후 제2차 세계대전 이후에 해체된 대영제국의 사례에서처럼 확장하고, 과도하게 확장되다가, 결국 붕괴한다. 하지만 이것이 항상 그런가? (A) 만약 그렇다면, 고고학은 꽤 지루할 것이다; 한 가지 일이 반복해서 일어날 테니 말이다. 하지만 그것은 고고학자들이 보는 것이 아니다. 어떤 문명들은, 서기 1520년대에 침략자들에 의해 정복된 Aztec과 Inca처럼 갑작스럽게 끝난다. (C) 그러한 제국들은 과도한 확장의 결과로 붕괴할 기회조차 없었다. 그래서 문명의 경우에, "역사는 그 자체를 반복한다"라는 말은 지나친 단순화로 보인다.

> 주어진 글 다음에 이어질 글의 순서로 가장 적절한 것을 고르시오. [3점]
> ① (A) — (C) — (B) (B)의 뒤에 이어지는 설명이 와야 함
> ② (B) — (A) — (C) 역사는 반복되는 것처럼 보임 — (B) 문명은 과도한 확장 끝에 붕괴함
>   — (A) 그러나 일부 문명은 갑자기 멸망하여 역사적 반복의 예외를 보임
>   — (C) 따라서 문명의 역사가 반복된다는 것은 지나치게 단순화한 주장임
> ③ (B) — (C) — (A) (C)의 Those empires는 (A)의 Aztec과 Inca를 가리킴
> ④ (C) — (A) — (B)
> ⑤ (C) — (B) — (A) 주어진 글에는 (C)의 Those empires가 가리킬 만한 대상이 없음

| 문제 풀이 순서 | ✹✹✸ [정답률 70%]

1st 각 문단의 내용을 파악하고, 글의 논리적인 순서를 추론한다.

주어진 글: 역사는, 사람들이 종종 말하길, 그 자체를 반복한다. 그리고 고대 문명의 역사적 기록들을 보면, 몇 가지 일들이 정말로 반복해서 일어나는 것처럼 보인다.

➡ **주어진 글 뒤:** 사람들이 말하기로는 역사가 반복되고 고대 문명의 기록에서도 그런 것처럼 보인다고 했으므로, 이에 관한 예시나 반론이 뒤에 이어질 것이다.

(A): 만약 그렇다면(so), 고고학은 꽤 지루할 것이다; 한 가지 일이 반복해서 일어날 테니 말이다. 하지만 그것은 고고학자들이 보는 것이 아니다. 어떤 문명들은, 서기 1520년대에 침략자들에 의해 정복된 Aztec과 Inca처럼 갑작스럽게 끝난다.

➡ **(A) 앞:** so가 가리키는 내용, 즉 역사에서 구체적으로 무엇이 반복해서 일어나는지가 앞에 나와야 하는데, 주어진 글에는 역사가 반복되는 구체적인 사례가 없다.
  ▶ 주어진 글 바로 뒤에 (A)가 올 수 없음
  (A) 뒤: 침략으로 정복된 Aztec과 Inca에 대한 부연 설명이 이어져야 한다.

(B): 문명은 서기 476년에 멸망한 로마의 경우와, 천 년 이상 지난 후 제2차 세계 대전 이후에 해체된 대영제국의 사례에서처럼 확장하고, 과도하게 확장되다가, 결국 붕괴한다. 하지만 이것이 항상 그런가?

➡ **(B) 앞:** 문명이 과도한 확장 끝에 붕괴하는 역사적 반복을 설명하고 그 예시로 로마와 대영제국을 제시한다.
  ▶ (B) 앞에 주어진 글이 와야 함 (순서: 주어진 글 → (B))
  (B) 뒤: '하지만 이것이 항상 그런가?'라는 질문 뒤에 과도한 확장이 아닌 다른 원인으로 붕괴한 문명의 사례가 이어져야 하는데, (A)에 침략으로 정복된 Aztec과 Inca가 나온다.
  ▶ (B) 뒤에 (A)가 와야 함 (순서: 주어진 글 → (B) → (A))

(C): 그러한 제국들(Those empires)은 과도한 확장의 결과로 붕괴할 기회조차 없었다. 그래서 문명의 경우에, "역사는 그 자체를 반복한다"라는 말은 지나친 단순화로 보인다.

➡ **(C) 앞:** 과도한 확장으로 붕괴하지 않은 '그러한 제국들'이 앞에 나와야 한다.
  ▶ '그러한 제국들'은 침략으로 붕괴된 Aztec과 Inca를 가리키므로 (A) 뒤에 와야 함 (순서: 주어진 글 → (B) → (A) → (C))
  (C) 뒤: 문명에서 역사가 반복된다는 말은 지나친 단순화라는 결론으로 글이 마무리된다.

2nd 글이 한눈에 들어오도록 정리하여 정답을 확인한다.

주어진 글: 역사는 반복되는 것처럼 보인다.
→ **(B):** 문명은 팽창과 과도한 확장 끝에 붕괴한다.
→ **(A):** 그러나 일부 문명은 갑자기 멸망하여 예외를 보인다.
→ **(C):** 문명의 역사가 반복된다는 것은 지나친 단순화이다.
  ▶ 주어진 글 다음에 이어질 글의 순서는 (B) → (A) → (C)이므로 정답은 ②임

구문 서술형

정답 But[Yet]

해석 • 만약 같은 일이 반복해서 일어난다면 고고학은 꽤 지루할 것이다.
• 그것은 고고학자들이 보는 것이 아니다.
→ 두 번째 문장에서, 첫 번째 문장의 내용(같은 일이 반복되면 고고학은 지루할 것임)은 고고학자들이 보는 것이 아니라고 했으므로 두 문장의 내용이 서로 반대된다. 따라서 두 문장을 연결하려면 반대 관계를 나타내는 등위접속사 But 또는 Yet을 써야 한다.

O 05 정답 ⑤ *노력에 대한 칭찬을 통한 성장 사고방식의 발달

> Stanford psychology professor Dr. Carol Dweck / is the
> internationally recognized pioneer / of the concept of "growth
> ~로서   형용사적 용법 (way 수식)
> mindset" / as a way to continually grow, learn, and persevere
> in our efforts. //
> Stanford 심리학 교수인 Carol Dweck 박사는 / 국제적으로 인정받는 선구자이다 / "성장 사고방식" 개념으로 / 우리의 노력에서 지속적으로 성장하고, 배우며, 인내할 수 있는 방법인 //

단서 1 (B)에서 노력에 대한 칭찬으로 성장 사고방식을 발달시킨 아이들을 가리킴
(A) These kids / end up taking on tougher things, / and feel
better about themselves. //
이 아이들은 / 결국 더 힘든 일을 받아들이고 / 스스로에 대해 더 좋은 느낌을 갖게 된다 //

동명사구 주어   단수 동사   목적격 관계대명사 (a variable 수식)
"Emphasizing effort gives a child a variable / that they can
control," / Dweck has explained. //
"노력을 강조하는 것은 아이에게 변수를 제공한다 / 그들이 통제할 수 있는"이라고 / Dweck은 설명했다 //

'반대로'   not A but B: A가 아니라 B
(B) In contrast, Dweck found, / kids who are praised not for
                    선행사를 포함하는 관계대명사
their smarts but for their effort / develop what Dweck calls a
"growth mindset." // 단서 2 똑똑함에 대해 칭찬받은 아이들에 대한 내용이 앞에 와야 함
반대로, Dweck은 발견했다 / 똑똑함이 아닌 노력에 대해 칭찬받는 아이들은 / Dweck이 "성장 사고방식"이라 부르는 것을 발달시킨다는 것을 //

목적어절 접속사   선행사를 포함하는 관계대명사   부사절 접속사 (조건)
They learn / that their effort is what led to their success, / and if
they continue to try, / over time / they'll improve and achieve
more things. //
그들은 배운다 / 그들의 노력이 성공으로 이르게 한 것임을 / 그리고 그들이 계속해서 노력한다면 / 시간이 지나면서 / 그들은 발전하고 더 많은 것을 성취하게 될 것이다 //

(C) Dweck found / that kids who are told **they're "smart"** / 단서 3 똑똑하다는 칭찬을 들은 아이들에 관한 내용으로 (B)와 대조됨
actually underperform in future tasks, / by choosing easier tasks / 앞에 목적어절 접속사 that이 생략됨
Dweck은 발견했는데 / "똑똑하다"라는 말을 듣는 아이들은 / 실제로 미래 과제에서 기대에 못 미치는 성과를 낸다는 / 더 쉬운 과제를 선택함으로써 /
to avoid evidence / **that** they are not smart, / **which** Dweck calls 동격절 접속사   계속적 용법의 목적격 관계대명사
having a "fixed mindset." //
증거를 피하기 위해 / 그들이 똑똑하지 않다는 / Dweck은 이를 "고정 사고방식"을 가진 것으로 부른다 //

- internationally ad 국제적으로   • recognized ⓐ 인정받는
- pioneer ⓝ 선구자   • effort ⓝ 노력   • end up -ing 결국 ~하게 되다
- take on ~을 받아들이다, 맡다   • tough ⓐ 힘든
- emphasize ⓥ 강조하다   • control ⓥ 통제하다
- continue ⓥ 계속[지속]하다   • improve ⓥ 발전하다
- underperform ⓥ 기대에 못 미치는 성과를 내다   • evidence ⓝ 증거

Stanford 심리학 교수인 Carol Dweck 박사는 우리의 노력에서 지속적으로 성장하고, 배우며, 인내할 수 있는 방법인 "성장 사고방식" 개념으로 국제적으로 인정받는 선구자이다. (C) Dweck은 "똑똑하다"라는 말을 듣는 아이들은 그들이 똑똑하지 않다는 증거를 피하기 위해 더 쉬운 과제를 선택함으로써 실제로 미래 과제에서 기대에 못 미치는 성과를 낸다는 것을 발견했는데, Dweck은 이를 "고정 사고방식"을 가진 것으로 부른다. (B) 반대로, Dweck은 똑똑함이 아닌 노력에 대해 칭찬받는 아이들은 Dweck이 "성장 사고방식"이라 부르는 것을 발달시킨다는 것을 발견했다. 그들은 그들의 노력이 성공으로 이르게 한 것임을 배우고, 그들이 계속해서 노력한다면, 시간이 지나면서 발전하고 더 많은 것을 성취하게 될 것이다. (A) 이 아이들은 결국 더 힘든 일을 받아들이고, 스스로에 대해 더 좋은 느낌을 갖게 된다. "노력을 강조하는 것은 아이에게 그들이 통제할 수 있는 변수를 제공한다."라고 Dweck은 설명했다.

> **주어진 글 다음에 이어질 글의 순서로 가장 적절한 것을 고르시오.**
> ① (A) — (C) — (B) 주어진 글에는 (A)의 These kids를 가리키는 대상이 없음
> ② (B) — (A) — (C) ┐
> ③ (B) — (C) — (A) ┘주어진 글에는 In contrast로 받을 내용이 없음
> ④ (C) — (A) — (B) 성장 사고방식의 장점을 설명하는 (A)가 (B) 뒤에 와야 함
> ⑤ (C) — (B) — (A) Dweck의 "성장 사고방식" 개념 → (C) 똑똑하다고 칭찬받는 아이들은 "고정 사고방식"을 가짐 → (B) 노력에 대해 칭찬받는 아이들은 "성장 사고방식"을 발달시킴 → (A) 성장 사고방식을 발달시킨 아이들의 특징

| **문제 풀이 순서** | ★★※ [정답률 65%]

1st 각 단락의 내용을 파악하고, 글의 논리적인 순서를 추론한다.

주어진 글: Stanford 심리학 교수인 Carol Dweck 박사는 우리의 노력에서 지속적으로 성장하고, 배우며, 인내할 수 있는 방법인 "성장 사고방식" 개념으로 국제적으로 인정받는 선구자이다.

➡ **주어진 글 뒤:** Dweck이 밝혀낸 성장 사고방식 개념이 노력에 관한 것이라고 했는데, 이에 관하여 부연 설명이 이어질 것이다.

(A): 이 아이들(These kids)은 결국 더 힘든 일을 받아들이고, 스스로에 대해 더 좋은 느낌을 갖게 된다. "노력을 강조하는 것은 아이에게 그들이 통제할 수 있는 변수를 제공한다."라고 Dweck은 설명했다.

➡ **(A) 앞:** These kids가 어떤 아이들을 가리키는지가 앞에 나와야 한다. 주어진 글에 성장 사고방식 개념이 언급되긴 하지만, 아이들은 언급되지 않았다.
  ▶ (A) 앞에 주어진 글이 올 수 없음
  (A) 뒤: (A)는 성장 사고방식을 갖춘 아이들의 특징과 노력을 강조하는 것의 의의를 설명하고 있으므로 글의 마지막일 가능성이 높다.

(B): 반대로(In contrast), Dweck은 똑똑함이 아닌 노력에 대해 칭찬받는 아이들은 Dweck이 "성장 사고방식"이라 부르는 것을 발달시킨다는 것을 발견했다. 그들은 그들의 노력이 성공으로 이르게 한 것임을 배우고, 그들이 계속해서 노력한다면, 시간이 지나면서 발전하고 더 많은 것을 성취하게 될 것이다.

➡ **(B) 앞:** 반대되는 내용을 나타내는 In contrast가 있으므로, 앞에는 똑똑함에 대해 칭찬받는 아이들이 언급되어야 한다. 노력에 대해 칭찬받는 아이들이 긍정적으로 언급되므로, 그와 반대인 아이들은 부정적으로 언급될 것이다.
  ▶ (B) 앞에 주어진 글과 (A)가 올 수 없음
  (B) 뒤: 노력에 대한 칭찬이 성장 사고방식을 키우고, 이들은 시간이 지나면서 발전한다고 했으므로 (A)의 These kids는 성장 사고방식을 키운 아이들이다.
  ▶ (B) 뒤에 (A)가 와야 함 (순서: (B) → (A))

(C): Dweck은 "똑똑하다"라는 말을 듣는 아이들은 그들이 똑똑하지 않다는 증거를 피하기 위해 더 쉬운 과제를 선택함으로써 실제로 미래 과제에서 기대에 못 미치는 성과를 낸다는 것을 발견했는데, Dweck은 이를 "고정 사고방식"을 가진 것으로 부른다.

➡ **(C) 앞:** 고정 사고방식과 관련된 개념이 먼저 제시되어야 한다. 주어진 글에서 노력에서 파생되는 성장 사고방식을 소개하고 이를 부연 설명하기에 앞서, (C)에서 노력이 아닌 똑똑함에서 파생되는 고정 사고방식을 먼저 설명하는 흐름이다.
  ▶ (C) 앞에 주어진 글이 와야 함 (순서: 주어진 글 → (C))
  (C) 뒤: 고정 사고방식을 가진 아이들의 성과가 기대에 못 미친다는 부정적인 내용 바로 뒤에 성장 사고방식을 가진 아이들에 관한 내용이 (B)의 In contrast로 이어진다.
  ▶ (C) 뒤에 (B)가 와야 함 (순서: 주어진 글 → (C) → (B) → (A))

2nd 글이 한눈에 들어오도록 정리하여 정답을 확인한다.

주어진 글: Dweck은 성장 사고방식 개념을 제시하였다.
→ **(C):** 똑똑하다고 칭찬받은 아이들은 고정 사고방식을 갖게 된다.
→ **(B):** 반대로 노력에 관해 칭찬받은 아이들은 성장 사고방식을 발달시킨다.
→ **(A):** 성장 사고방식을 발달시킨 아이들은 긍정적인 특성을 갖는다.
  ▶ 주어진 글 다음에 이어질 글의 순서는 (C) → (B) → (A)이므로 정답은 ⑤임

구문 서술형

정답 not, but

→ 'A가 아닌 B'는 상관접속사 not A but B로 표현할 수 있다. '똑똑함이 아닌 노력에 대해'이므로 for their smarts 앞에 not, for their effort 앞에 but을 써야 한다.

O 06 정답 ② *방광에 물을 오래 저장하는 사막거북

> The desert tortoise has a simple solution / for coping with Death Valley's extreme heat: / It avoids it. //
> 사막거북은 간단한 해결책을 가지고 있는데 / Death Valley의 극심한 더위를 극복하기 위해 / 그것은 더위를 피하는 것이다 //

(A) But **to stay supplied** with water / through its extended 부사적 용법 (목적) 주격 보어 (과거분사)
hibernation, / the reptile relies on something else / — its highly sophisticated bladder. // 단서 1 (B)에서 나열된 수분 비축 방법들과는 다른 방법을 가리킴
하지만 수분이 공급된 채로 지내기 위해 / 그것의 장기간에 걸친 동면 동안 / 이 파충류는 다른 것에 의존한다 / 즉, 그것의 매우 정교한 방광이다 //

Unlike most animals, / the tortoise's bladder acts as a holding tank, / **allowing** it to reabsorb water back into its body. // 분사구문을 이끄는 현재분사
대부분의 동물과 달리 / 거북의 방광은 보관 탱크로서의 역할을 하며 / 그것이 그것의 몸으로 물을 다시 흡수할 수 있게 한다 //

Incredibly, / a desert tortoise can go a full year / **without taking** in any freshwater at all. // without -ing: ~ 없이, ~하지 않고
놀랍게도 / 사막거북은 1년 내내 살아갈 수 있다 / 담수를 전혀 섭취하지 않고도 //

(B) The slow-moving creature hibernates during the winter 단서 2 주어진 글의 The desert tortoise를 가리킴
and stays in its tunnel for much of the summer, / **meaning** that 분사구문을 이끄는 현재분사
it spends more than 90 percent of its life immobile. //
그 느리게 움직이는 생명체는 겨울에는 동면하고 / 대부분의 여름에는 그것의 굴 속에서 보내는데 / 이는 그 생의 90퍼센트 이상을 움직이지 않은 채로 보낸다는 것을 의미한다 //

In fact, / the tortoise usually only surfaces / after a good rain. //
사실 / 거북은 보통 밖으로 나온다 / 충분한 비가 온 후에만 //

Then, it gets to work. // 그 다음에 그것은 활동을 시작한다 //

┌─── 병렬 구조 (by의 목적어) ───┐
The tortoise stocks up on water / by **eating** plants / and **digging**
        ┌─ 형용사적 용법 (holes 수식)
holes **to collect** rain. //
거북은 물을 비축한다 / 식물을 먹고 / 빗물을 모으기 위한 구멍을 팜으로써 //

(C) And because its bladder is so important / to a tortoise's
survival, / 단서 3 (A)에서 처음 언급된 '방광'을 부연 설명함
그리고 그것의 방광이 매우 중요하기 때문에 / 거북의 생존에 /

park rangers often remind visitors / not to stop and help the
slow-movers / across the road. //
공원 순찰대원들은 종종 방문객들에게 상기시킨다 / 멈추어 그 느리게 움직이는 것을 도와주지 않을 것을 / 도로를 건너도록 //

Tortoises become **so terrified** / when people pick them up /
so + 형용사 + that …: 너무 ~해서 …하다   분사구문을 이끄는 현재분사
that they empty their bladders, / **losing** their precious water
reserves. //
거북은 너무 겁을 먹어 / 사람들이 그들을 들어 올릴 때 / 그들의 방광을 비워버리고 / 소중한 저장된 물을 잃게 된다 //

- cope with ~에 대처하다   · extreme ⓐ 극심한   · avoid ⓥ 피하다
- reptile ⓝ 파충류   · rely on ~에 의존하다
- sophisticated ⓐ 정교한   · reabsorb ⓥ 재흡수하다
- take in ~을 섭취하다   · freshwater ⓝ 담수   · creature ⓝ 생물
- immobile ⓐ 움직이지 않는   · surface ⓥ 표면으로 나오다
- stock up on ~을 비축하다   · survival ⓝ 생존
- ranger ⓝ 경비대원, 순찰대원   · reserves ⓝ 비축물

사막거북은 Death Valley의 극심한 더위를 극복하기 위해 간단한 해결책을 가지고 있는데 그것은 더위를 피하는 것이다. (B) 그 느리게 움직이는 생명체는 겨울에는 동면하고 대부분의 여름에는 그것의 굴 속에서 보내는데 이는 그 생의 90퍼센트 이상을 움직이지 않은 채로 보낸다는 것을 의미한다. 사실, 거북은 보통 충분한 비가 온 후에만 밖으로 나온다. 그 다음에 그것은 활동을 시작한다. 거북은 식물을 먹고, 빗물을 모으기 위한 구멍을 팜으로써 물을 비축한다. (A) 하지만 그것의 장기간에 걸친 동면 동안 수분이 공급된 채로 지내기 위해, 이 파충류는 다른 것에 의존한다. 즉, 그것의 매우 정교한 방광이다. 대부분의 동물과 달리, 거북의 방광은 보관 탱크로서의 역할을 하며, 그것이 그것의 몸으로 물을 다시 흡수할 수 있게 한다. 놀랍게도, 사막거북은 1년 내내 담수를 전혀 섭취하지 않고도 살아갈 수 있다. (C) 그리고 그것의 방광이 거북의 생존에 매우 중요하기 때문에, 공원 순찰대원들은 종종 방문객들에게 멈추어 그 느리게 움직이는 것을 도로를 건너도록 도와주지 않을 것을 상기시킨다. 거북은 사람들이 그들을 들어 올릴 때 너무 겁을 먹어 그들의 방광을 비워버리고, 소중한 저장된 물을 잃게 된다.

> 주어진 글 다음에 이어질 글의 순서로 가장 적절한 것을 고르시오. [3점]
>
> ① (A) — (C) — (B) 주어진 글에는 (A)의 장기간에 걸친 동면에 대한 언급이 없음
> ② (B) — (A) — (C) 사막 거북은 더위를 피함으로써 더위를 극복함 → (B) 생의 대부분을 움직이지 않지만 활동할 때는 물을 비축함 → (A) 움직이지 않을 때는 물을 저장하기 위해 정교한 방광에 의존함 → (C) 이들을 들어 올리면 방광을 비우므로 그러지 않도록 주의해야 함
> ③ (B) — (C) — (A)
> ④ (C) — (A) — (B) (A)에 처음 언급된 방광을 (C)에서 부연 설명함
> ⑤ (C) — (B) — (A)

| 문제 풀이 순서 | ✹✹✸ [정답률 62%]

1st 각 문단의 내용을 파악하고, 글의 논리적인 순서를 추론한다.

┌ **주어진 글:** 사막거북은 Death Valley의 극심한 더위를 극복하기 위해 간단
└ 한 해결책을 가지고 있는데 그것은 더위를 피하는 것이다.

➡ **주어진 글 뒤:** 사막거북이 더위를 피하는 구체적인 방법이 제시될 것이다.

┌ **(A):** 하지만(But) 그것의 장기간에 걸친 동면 동안 수분이 공급된 채로 지내기 위해, 이 파충류는 다른 것(something else)에 의존한다. 즉, 그것의 매우 정교한 방광이다. 대부분의 동물과 달리, 거북의 방광은 보관 탱크로서의 역할을 하며, 그것이 그것의 몸으로 물을 다시 흡수할 수 있게 한다. 놀
└ 랍게도, 사막거북은 1년 내내 담수를 전혀 섭취하지 않고도 살아갈 수 있다.

➡ **(A) 앞:** 반대되는 내용을 나타내는 but과, 이미 언급된 것과는 다른 대상을 나타내는 something else가 쓰였으므로, 방광 외에 사막거북이 수분과 관련하여 이용하는 다른 방법이 앞에 먼저 언급되어야 한다.
▶ 주어진 글에는 사막거북이 더위를 피한다고만 했으므로 (A) 앞에 올 수 없음
(A) 뒤: 방광의 중요한 기능인 수분 재흡수가 언급되었으므로, 이에 관한 부연 설명이 이어질 것이다.

┌ **(B):** 그 느리게 움직이는 생명체(The slow-moving creature)는 겨울에는 동면하고 대부분의 여름에는 그것의 굴 속에서 보내는데 이는 그 생의 90퍼센트 이상을 움직이지 않은 채로 보낸다는 것을 의미한다. 사실, 거북은 보통 충분한 비가 온 후에만 밖으로 나온다. 그 다음에 그것은 활동을 시작한다. 거북은 식물을 먹고, 빗물을 모으기 위한 구멍을 팜으로써 물
└ (water)을 비축한다.

➡ **(B) 앞:** 정관사 the가 쓰인 The slow-moving creature로 시작하므로, 느리게 움직이는 생물이 (B)의 바로 앞에서 처음으로 언급되었을 것이다. 주어진 글이 사막거북에 대한 소개로 시작되며, (B)의 첫 문장은 사막거북이 더위를 피하는 구체적인 방법에 해당하므로 자연스럽게 이어진다.
▶ (B) 앞에 주어진 글이 와야 함 (순서: 주어진 글 → (B))
(B) 뒤: 동면 동안 물을 비축하는 여러 방법이 소개되었는데, 사막거북은 이러한 방법들이 아닌 방광에 의지한다는 내용이 (A)에 나온다.
▶ (B) 뒤에 (A)가 와야 함 (순서: 주어진 글 → (B) → (A))

┌ **(C):** 그리고 그것의 방광(its bladder)이 거북의 생존에 매우 중요하기 때문에, 공원 순찰대원들은 종종 방문객들에게 멈추어 그 느리게 움직이는 것을 도로를 건너도록 도와주지 않을 것을 상기시킨다. 거북은 사람들이 그들을 들어 올릴 때 너무 겁을 먹어 그들의 방광을 비워버리고, 소중한 저장된
└ 물을 잃게 된다.

➡ **(C) 앞:** its bladder라고 했으므로, bladder가 앞에 먼저 언급되었을 것이다. (A)에 bladder가 처음으로 언급되었으므로, its는 (B)에 언급된 사막거북을 가리킨다.
▶ (C) 앞에 (A)가 와야 함 (순서: 주어진 글 → (B) → (A) → (C))
(C) 뒤: 방광의 중요성과 관련된 주의사항으로 글이 마무리된다.

2nd 글이 한눈에 들어오도록 정리하여 정답을 확인한다.

주어진 글: 사막거북의 더위 극복법은 더위를 피하는 것이다.
➡ **(B):** 생의 대부분을 움직이지 않지만, 활동할 때는 물을 비축한다.
➡ **(A):** 움직이지 않을 때는 물을 저장하기 위해 정교한 방광에 의존한다.
➡ **(C):** 이들을 들어 올리면 방광을 비우므로 그러지 않도록 주의해야 한다.
▶ 주어진 글 다음에 이어질 글의 순서는 (B) → (A) → (C)이므로 정답은 ②임

구문 서술형

정답 and, so

해석 · 사막거북의 방광은 보관 탱크로서의 역할을 한다.
· 그것은 1년 내내 담수를 전혀 섭취하지 않고도 살아갈 수 있다.
→ '그리고'를 나타내는 등위접속사 and나 '그 결과'를 나타내는 등위접속사 so를 쓸 수 있다.

○ 07 정답 ③ *자전거의 속도를 늦추는 다양한 마찰력의 원리

Imagine you are pedalling your bicycle / on a level road. //
자전거 페달을 밟고 있다고 상상해 보아라 / 수평의 도로에서 //
You stop pedalling: / no force is now acting / to move you [형용사적 용법 (force 수식)]
forward. //
당신은 페달을 밟는 것을 멈추고 / 어떠한 힘도 이제 작용하지 않는다 / 당신을 앞으로 나아가게 하는 //
What happens? // 그러면 어떻게 될까 //

(A) One of these is friction in the wheels / rubbing on the axles. // [현재분사구 (the wheels 수식)]
이들 중 하나는 바퀴의 마찰이다 / 축에 닿는 //
[단서 1] (C)의 other friction forces의 예시
Another is air resistance, / which you can feel, / pushing you [계속적 용법의 목적격 관계대명사] [현재분사구 (air resistance 수식)]
backwards / as you and the bicycle move forwards. //
또 다른 하나는 공기 저항으로 / 이는 당신이 느낄 수 있다 / 당신을 뒤쪽으로 미는 / 당신과 자전거가 앞쪽으로 움직일 때 //

When you apply these ideas / to something around you, like a
cart, / you can see what could be generating friction: / [간접의문문 (see의 목적어)]
이러한 개념을 적용하면 / 카트와 같은 당신 주변에 있는 어떤 것에 / 당신은 무엇이 마찰력을 발생시킬 수 있을지 알 수 있다 /
mainly the axles rubbing on the body as they rotate. // [현재분사구 (the axles 수식)]
주로 회전하면서 본체에 닿는 축들과 같이 //

(B) You gradually slow down. // 당신은 서서히 느려진다 //
How could you slow down more suddenly, / in a shorter
distance? // [단서 2] 주어진 글의 질문에 대한 대답
당신은 더 갑자기 속도를 줄이려면 어떻게 해야 할까 / 더 짧은 거리 안에서 //
By putting the brakes on. // 브레이크를 작동시키면 된다 //
Because the brakes change your movement, / making you slow [분사구문]
down more suddenly, / they must be exerting a force on the
bicycle and you, / as they grip and rub on the wheel-rims. //
브레이크는 당신의 움직임을 변화시켜 / 당신을 더 갑자기 느려지게 하기 때문에 / 그것들이 자전거와 당신에게 힘을 가하고 있어야 한다 / 바퀴 테두리를 잡고 닿으면서 //
(C) This is the force called friction, / which tends to slow down [계속적 용법의 주격 관계대명사]
moving things / by acting in the direction opposite to movement,
/ that is backwards. // [단서 3] (B)의 a force를 가리킴
이것이 마찰력이라고 불리는 힘이며 / 그 힘은 움직이는 물체를 느리게 하는 경향이 있다 / 움직임의 반대 방향으로 작용함으로써 / 즉 뒤쪽으로 //
Even without the brakes on, / there are other friction forces /
acting on you and your bicycle, / which also slow you down. // [앞에 주격 관계대명사와 be동사가 생략됨] [계속적 용법의 주격 관계대명사]
심지어 브레이크를 작동시키지 않아도 / 다른 마찰력이 존재하며 / 당신과 당신의 자전거에 작용하는 / 이것은 또한 당신을 느리게 한다 //

- level ⓐ 평평한   · force ⓝ 힘   · act ⓥ 작용하다
- friction ⓝ 마찰   · rub ⓥ 문지르다   · resistance ⓝ 저항
- generate ⓥ 발생시키다   · rotate ⓥ 회전하다
- gradually ⓐd 점차적으로   · exert ⓥ (힘을) 가하다
- grip ⓥ 꽉 잡다

자전거 페달을 수평의 도로에서 밟고 있다고 상상해 보아라. 당신은 페달을 밟는 것을 멈추고 당신을 앞으로 나아가게 하는 어떠한 힘도 이제 작용하지 않는다. 그러면 어떻게 될까? (B) 당신은 서서히 느려진다. 당신은 더 짧은 거리 안에서 더 갑자기 속도를 줄이려면 어떻게 해야 할까? 브레이크를 작동시키면 된다. 브레이크는 당신의 움직임을 변화시켜 당신을 더 갑자기 느려지게 하기 때문에, 그것들이 바퀴 테두리를 잡고 닿으면서 자전거와 당신에게 힘을 가하고 있어야 한다. (C) 이것이 마찰력이라고 불리는 힘이며, 그 힘은 움직임의 반대 방향, 즉 뒤쪽으로 작용함으로써 움직이는 물체를 느리게 하는 경향이 있다. 심지어 브레이크를 작동시키지 않아도 당신과 당신의 자전거에 작용하는 다른 마찰력이 존재하며, 이것은 또한 당신을 느리게 한다. (A) 이들 중 하나는 축에 닿는 바퀴의 마찰이다. 또 다른 하나는 당신과 자전거가 앞쪽으로 움직일 때 당신을 뒤쪽으로 미는 공기 저항으로 이는 당신이 느낄 수 있다. 카트와 같은 당신

주변에 있는 어떤 것에 이러한 개념을 적용하면, 주로 회전하면서 본체에 닿는 축들과 같이, 당신은 무엇이 마찰력을 발생시킬 수 있을지 알 수 있다.

(A)의 these가 가리키는 대상이 (B)에 없음
주어진 글 다음에 이어질 글의 순서로 가장 적절한 것을 고르시오.
① (A) — (C) — (B) — 주어진 글의 질문에 대한 답이 (A)에 없음
② (B) — (A) — (C)
③ (B) — (C) — (A) — 자전거를 타다가 페달 밟기를 멈추면 어떻게 되는가? → (B) 서서히 느려지게 되고, 브레이크를 작동할 때 바퀴에 가해지는 힘이 있음 → (C) 이것이 마찰력이며 이때 다른 마찰력들도 존재함 → (A) 주변 물체에 마찰의 개념을 적용하면 마찰력의 요인을 알 수 있음
④ (C) — (A) — (B)
⑤ (C) — (B) — (A) — (C)의 This가 가리키는 힘이 주어진 글에 없음

| **문제 풀이 순서** | ★★☆ [정답률 67%]

1st 각 문단의 내용을 파악하고, 글의 논리적인 순서를 추론한다.

주어진 글: 자전거 페달을 수평의 도로에서 밟고 있다고 상상해 보아라. 당신은 페달을 밟는 것을 멈추고 당신을 앞으로 나아가게 하는 어떠한 힘도 이제 작용하지 않는다. 그러면 어떻게 될까(What happens)?
→ **주어진 글 뒤:** What happens?에 대한 질문의 답변, 즉 자전거를 타고 가는 중에 페달 밟기를 멈추면 어떤 일이 일어나는지가 이어져야 한다.

(A) 이들 중 하나(One of these)는 축에 닿는 바퀴의 마찰이다. 또 다른 하나는 당신과 자전거가 앞쪽으로 움직일 때 당신을 뒤쪽으로 미는 공기 저항으로 이는 당신이 느낄 수 있다. 카트와 같은 당신 주변에 있는 어떤 것에 이러한 개념을 적용하면, 주로 회전하면서 본체에 닿는 축들과 같이, 당신은 무엇이 마찰력을 발생시킬 수 있을지 알 수 있다.
→ **(A) 앞:** these가 가리키는 대상이 앞에 나와야 한다. 이는 마찰과 관련이 있어야 하는데, 주어진 글에는 마찰이 언급되지 않았다. 또한 주어진 글의 질문에 대한 답변이 (A)에 있지 않다. ▶ (A) 앞에 주어진 글이 올 수 없음
(A) 뒤: 주변 물체에 마찰의 개념을 적용하면 마찰력의 요인을 알 수 있다고 하며 글을 마무리하고 있으므로, 글의 마지막 부분일 가능성이 높다.

(B) 당신은 서서히 느려진다(You gradually slow down.). 당신은 더 짧은 거리 안에서 더 갑자기 속도를 줄이려면 어떻게 해야 할까? 브레이크를 작동시키면 된다. 브레이크는 당신의 움직임을 변화시켜 당신을 더 갑자기 느려지게 하기 때문에, 그것들이 바퀴 테두리를 잡고 닿으면서 자전거와 당신에게 힘을 가하고 있어야 한다.
→ **(B) 앞:** 첫 문장(You gradually slow down.)은 주어진 글의 마지막 질문에 대한 가장 직접적인 대답이다.
▶ (B) 앞에 주어진 글이 와야 함 (순서: 주어진 글 → (B))
(B) 뒤: 브레이크가 가하는 힘을 부연 설명하는 내용이 이어질 것이다.

(C) 이것(This)이 마찰력이라고 불리는 힘이며, 그 힘은 움직임의 반대 방향, 즉 뒤쪽으로 작용함으로써 움직이는 물체를 느리게 하는 경향이 있다. 심지어 브레이크를 작동시키지 않아도 당신과 당신의 자전거에 작용하는 다른 마찰력(other friction forces)이 존재하며, 이것은 또한 당신을 느리게 한다.
→ **(C) 앞:** This는 (B)의 마지막에 언급된 브레이크가 가하는 힘을 가리킨다.
▶ (C) 앞에 (B)가 와야 함 (순서: 주어진 글 → (B) → (C))
(C) 뒤: 다른 마찰력이 존재한다고 했는데, (A)에 바퀴의 마찰과 공기 저항이라는 다른 마찰력이 언급되었다.
▶ (C) 뒤에 (A)가 와야 함 (순서: 주어진 글 → (B) → (C) → (A))

2nd 글이 한눈에 들어오도록 정리하여 정답을 확인한다.

주어진 글: 자전거 페달을 밟고 있다가 멈추면 어떻게 될까?
→ **(B):** 서서히 느려진다. 브레이크를 사용하면 더 빨리 멈추는데, 이때 작용하는 힘이 있다.
→ **(C):** 이는 마찰력이며, 이외에 다른 마찰력들도 존재한다.
→ **(A):** 주변 물체에 마찰의 개념을 적용하면 마찰력의 요인을 알 수 있다.
▶ 주어진 글 다음에 이어질 글의 순서는 (B) → (C) → (A)이므로 정답은 ③임

정답 여러분과 자전거가 앞쪽으로 움직일 때

→ as는 '~할 때'를 뜻하며 시간을 나타내는 부사절 접속사이다. 따라서, 이 문장에서 as가 이끄는 부사절은 '여러분과 자전거가 앞쪽으로 움직일 때'로 해석한다.

O 08 정답 ① *우울증의 원인이 되는 의식의 왜곡

Conventional medicine / has long believed / 명사절 접속사 수동태 동사 that depression is caused / by an imbalance of neurotransmitters in the brain. //
전통적인 의학은 / 오랫동안 믿어 왔다 / 우울증이 발생한다고 / 뇌의 신경 전달 물질의 불균형으로 인해
단서 1 우울증에 대한 전통적 의학 해석 소개

(A) However, / there is a major problem / with this explanation. //
그러나 / 중대한 문제가 있다 / 이 설명에는 //
단서 2 this explanation은 주어진 글의 내용임

This is because / the imbalance of substances in the brain / is a consequence of depression, / not its cause. //
단서 3 뇌 속 물질의 불균형은 우울증의 원인이 아니라 결과임
이것은 왜냐하면 / 뇌 속 물질의 불균형은 / 우울증의 결과이다 / (우울증의) 원인이 아니라 //

In other words, / depression causes a decrease in brain substances / such as serotonin and noradrenaline, / not a decrease in brain substances causes depression. //
다시 말해서 / 우울증이 뇌의 물질의 감소를 유발하는 것이지 / 세로토닌이나 노르아드레날린과 같은 / 뇌의 물질의 감소가 우울증을 유발하는 것이 아니다 //

(B) 부사절 접속사 (조건) 재귀대명사 (강조 용법) If it is not consciousness itself, / then the root cause of depression / is also a distortion of our state of consciousness: /
만약 그것이 의식 그 자체가 아니라면 / 우울증의 근본 원인 / 역시 우리의 의식 상태의 왜곡이며 /
단서 4 우울증이 의식의 문제임을 부연 설명함

주격 관계대명사 a consciousness / that has lost its sense of self and the meaning of life. // 즉, 의식이다 / 자아감과 삶의 의미를 상실한 //

재귀대명사 (재귀 용법) Such a disease of consciousness / may manifest itself / in the form of depression. //
그러한 의식의 질환이 / 명백히 나타날 수 있다 / 우울증의 형태로 //

(C) In this revised cause-and-effect, / the key is 명사적 용법 (주격 보어) to reframe depression / as a problem of consciousness. //
단서 5 (A)의 인과 관계(원인: 우울증, 결과: 뇌의 물질의 감소)를 가리킴
이 수정된 인과 관계에서 / 핵심은 우울증을 재구성하는 것이다 / 의식의 문제로 //

주격 관계대명사 Our consciousness is a more fundamental entity / that goes beyond the functioning of the brain. //
우리의 의식은 보다 근본적인 실체이다 / 뇌의 기능을 넘어서는 //

'단지 ~일 뿐이다' The brain / is no more than an organ of consciousness. //
뇌는 / 의식의 기관에 지나지 않는다 //
단서 6 뇌는 의식의 기관일 뿐이라는 내용이 (B)와 연결됨

- conventional ⓐ 전통적인 · depression ⓝ 우울증
- cause ⓥ 발생시키다 · imbalance ⓝ 불균형
- explanation ⓝ 설명 · substance ⓝ 물질
- consequence ⓝ 결과 · decrease ⓝ 감소 · root ⓝ 근본
- distortion ⓝ 왜곡 · revise ⓥ 수정하다
- cause-and-effect ⓝ 인과 관계 · reframe ⓥ 재구성하다
- fundamental ⓐ 근본적인 · entity ⓝ 실체
- organ ⓝ (인체의) 기관[장기]

전통적인 의학은 우울증이 뇌의 신경 전달 물질의 불균형으로 인해 발생한다고 오랫동안 믿어 왔다. (A) 그러나 이 설명에는 중대한 문제가 있다. 이것은 왜냐하면 뇌 속 물질의 불균형은 우울증의 원인이 아니라 그것의 결과이기 때문이다. 다시 말해서, 우울증이 세로토닌이나 노르아드레날린과 같은 뇌의 물질의 감소를 유발하는 것이지 뇌의 물질의 감소가 우울증을 유발하는 것이 아니다. (C) 이 수정된 인과 관계에서, 핵심은 우울증을 의식의 문제로 재구성하는 것이다. 우리의 의식은 뇌의 기능을 넘어서는 보다 근본적인 실체이다. 뇌는 의식의 기관에 지나지 않는다. (B) 만약 그것이 의식 그 자체가 아니라면, 우울증의 근본 원인 역시 우리의 의식 상태의 왜곡이며 즉, 자아감과 삶의 의미를 상실한 의식이다. 그러한 의식의 질환이 우울증의 형태로 명백히 나타날 수 있다.

주어진 글 다음에 이어질 글의 순서로 가장 적절한 것을 고르시오.
① (A) — (C) — B
② (B) — (A) — (C)
③ (B) — (C) — (A)
④ (C) — (A) — (B)
⑤ (C) — (B) — (A)

전통 의학은 우울증이 뇌 속 물질의 불균형의 원인이라고 했음 - (A) 이와 반대로 뇌 속 물질의 불균형은 우울증의 원인이 아니라 결과임 - (C) 우울증은 의식의 문제이며 뇌는 의식의 기관일 뿐임 - (B) 우울증의 근본 원인은 왜곡된 의식 상태임
- 의식에 대한 언급이 없는 주어진 글이 (B) 바로 앞에 올 수 없음
- (C)의 '이 수정된 인과 관계'가 주어진 글에 없음

| 문제 풀이 순서 | ★★★ [정답률 42%]

1st 각 문단의 내용을 파악하고, 글의 논리적인 순서를 추론한다.

주어진 글: 전통적인(Conventional) 의학은 우울증이 뇌의 신경 전달 물질의 불균형으로 인해 발생한다고 오랫동안 믿어 왔다.

➡ 주어진 글 뒤: 우울증과 뇌의 신경 전달 물질 불균형의 인과 관계가 현대에서는 어떻게 바뀌었는지를 설명할 것이다.

(A): 그러나 이 설명(this explanation)에는 중대한 문제가 있다. 이것은 왜냐하면 뇌 속 물질의 불균형은 우울증의 원인이 아니라 그것의 결과이기 때문이다. 다시 말해서, 우울증이 세로토닌이나 노르아드레날린과 같은 뇌의 물질의 감소를 유발하는 것이지 뇌의 물질의 감소가 우울증을 유발하는 것이 아니다.

➡ (A) 앞: this explanation이 무엇인지 앞에 나와야 한다. 주어진 글에 우울증이 뇌 속 물질 불균형의 결과라는 전통적인 설명이 나왔는데, (A)는 이 설명과 반대되는 인과 관계가 사실이라고 했다.
▶ (A) 앞에 주어진 글이 와야 함 (순서: 주어진 글 → (A))
(A) 뒤: 새롭게 수정된 인과 관계에 대한 부연 설명이 이어질 것이다.

(B): 만약 그것(it)이 의식 그 자체가 아니라면, 우울증의 근본 원인 역시 우리의 의식 상태의 왜곡이며 즉, 자아감과 삶의 의미를 상실한 의식이다. 그러한 의식의 질환이 우울증의 형태로 명백히 나타날 수 있다.

➡ (B) 앞: 의식 그 자체가 아니라는 it이 무엇인지 앞에 나와야 한다.
▶ 주어진 글과 (A) 바로 뒤에 (B)가 올 수 없음
(B) 뒤: 왜곡된 의식 상태로 우울증이 발생한다는 부연 설명을 끝으로 글이 마무리된다.

(C): 이 수정된 인과 관계(this revised cause-and-effect)에서, 핵심은 우울증을 의식의 문제로 재구성하는 것이다. 우리의 의식은 뇌의 기능을 넘어서는 보다 근본적인 실체이다. 뇌는 의식의 기관에 지나지 않는다.

➡ (C) 앞: this revised cause-and-effect가 가리키는 것이 앞에 나와야 한다. 전통적인 인과 관계를 수정한 내용이 (A)에 제시되었다.
▶ (C) 앞에 (A)가 와야 함 (순서: 주어진 글 → (A) → (C))
(C) 뒤: 우울증은 의식의 문제이며 뇌는 의식의 기관일 뿐, 의식이 근본적인 실체라고 했다. 따라서 (B)에서 의식 그 자체가 아니라는 it은 '뇌'에 해당한다. 즉, 뇌는 의식의 기관일 뿐이므로, 우울증의 원인은 뇌가 아니라 의식에 있다는 것이다.
▶ (C) 뒤에 (B)가 와야 함 (순서: 주어진 글 → (A) → (C) → (B))

2nd 글이 한눈에 들어오도록 정리하여 정답을 확인한다.

주어진 글: 전통 의학에서는 우울증의 원인이 뇌의 신경 전달 물질의 불균형이다.
→ (A): 사실 뇌 물질의 감소는 우울증의 원인이 아니라 결과이다.
→ (C): 우울증은 의식의 문제이며 뇌는 의식의 기관일 뿐, 의식이 근본적인 실체이다.
→ (B): 우울증의 근본 원인은 왜곡된 의식 상태이다.
▶ 주어진 글 다음에 이어질 글의 순서는 (A) → (C) → (B)이므로 정답은 ①임

정답 since[as, for]

해석 이 설명에는 문제가 있는데, 왜냐하면 뇌 속 물질의 불균형은 우울증의 원인이 아니라 그것의 결과이기 때문이다.

→ because는 '~ 때문에'를 뜻하며 이유를 나타내는 부사절 접속사이다. 따라서, 마찬가지로 이유를 나타내는 부사절 접속사인 as, since, 또는 등위접속사 for로 바꿔 쓸 수 있다.

In many sports, people realized / the difficulties and even impossibilities / of young children[participating의 의미상 주어] / participating fully in many adult sport environments. //
[단서 1] 어린아이들이 성인 스포츠 환경에 완전히 참여하기는 어렵거나 불가능함
많은 스포츠에서 사람들은 깨달았다 / 어렵고 심지어 불가능하다는 것을 / 어린아이들이 / 여러 성인 스포츠 환경에 완전히 참여하기란 //

(A) As examples, / baseball has T ball, / football has flag football / and junior soccer uses a smaller and lighter ball and (sometimes) a smaller field. //
[단서 2] (C)에서 언급한 어린아이들을 위한 스포츠 조정의 예시
예를 들자면 / 야구에는 티볼이 있고 / 풋볼에는 플래그 풋볼이 있고 / 유소년 축구는 더 작고 더 가벼운 공과 (가끔은) 더 작은 경기장을 사용한다 //

All have junior competitive structures / where[관계부사(선행사: structures)] children play / for shorter time periods and often in smaller teams. //
모두가 유소년 시합의 구조를 가진다 / 어린아이들이 경기하는 / 더 짧아진 경기 시간 동안 그리고 종종 더 작은 팀으로 //

(B) In a similar way, / tennis has adapted the court areas, balls and rackets / to make them more appropriate[5형식 동사+목적어+목적격 보어(형용사)] / for children under 10. //
[단서 3] (C)에서 언급한 어린아이들을 위한 스포츠 조정의 또 다른 예시
비슷한 방식으로 / 테니스는 코트 면적, 공, 라켓을 조정했다 / 더 적합하도록 만들기 위해 / 10세 미만의 어린아이에게 //

The adaptations are progressive / and relate to the age of the child. //
[단서 4] 주어진 글에 나온 people
이러한 조정은 점진적이고 / 어린아이의 연령과 관련이 있다 //
[뒤에 목적어절 접속사 that이 생략됨]

(C) They found / the road to success for young children is unlikely / if they play on adult fields, courts or arenas /
그들은 발견했다 / 어린아이들이 성공으로 가는 길이 있을 것 같지 않다는 것을 / 성인용 운동장, 코트 또는 경기장에서 운동한다면 /

with equipment / that[주격 관계대명사(선행사: equipment)] is too large, / too heavy / or too fast for them[to handle의 의미상 주어] to handle / while trying[접속사가 생략되지 않은 분사구문] to compete in adult-style competition. //
장비를 가지고 / 너무 크거나 / 너무 무겁고 / 또는 너무 빨라서 그들(어린아이들)이 다룰 수 없는 / 성인 스타일의 시합에서 경쟁하려고 하면서 //

Common sense has prevailed: / different sports have made adaptations for children. //
이러한 공통된 견해가 널리 퍼졌기에 / 여러 스포츠는 어린아이들을 위한 조정을 했다 //

- realize ⓥ 깨닫다　　· impossibility ⓝ 불가능　　· field ⓝ 경기장
- competitive ⓐ 경쟁적인　　· structure ⓝ 구조　　· period ⓝ 기간
- racket ⓝ 라켓　　· appropriate ⓐ 적절한
- progressive ⓐ 점진적인　　· relate to ~와 관련되다
- arena ⓝ 경기장　　· equipment ⓝ 장비　　· handle ⓥ 다루다
- compete ⓥ 경쟁하다　　· common sense (일반인들의) 공통된 견해, 상식
- adaptation ⓝ 조정

많은 스포츠에서 사람들은 어린아이들이 여러 성인 스포츠 환경에 완전히 참여하기란 어렵고 심지어 불가능하다는 것을 깨달았다. (C) 어린아이들이 너무 크거나 너무 무겁고 또는 너무 빨라서 그들(어린아이들)이 다룰 수 없는 장비를 가지고 성인 스타일의 시합에서 경쟁하려고 하면서 성인용 운동장, 코트 또는 경기장에서 운동한다면 그들(어린아이들)이 성공으로 가는 길이 있을 것 같지 않다는 것을 그들은 발견했다. 이러한 공통된 견해가 널리 퍼졌기에 여러 스포츠는 어린아이들을 위한 조정을 했다. (A) 예를 들자면, 야구에는 티볼이 있고, 풋볼에는 플래그 풋볼이 있고, 유소년 축구는 더 작고 더 가벼운 공과 (가끔은) 더 작은 경기장을 사용한다. 모두가 어린아이들이 더 짧아진 경기 시간 동안 그리고 종종 더 작은 팀으로 경기하는 유소년 시합의 구조를 가진다. (B) 비슷한 방식으로, 테니스는 코트 면적, 공, 라켓을 10세 미만의 어린아이에게 더 적합하도록 만들기 위해 조정했다. 이러한 조정은 점진적이고 어린아이의 연령과 관련이 있다.

주어진 글 다음에 이어질 글의 순서로 가장 적절한 것을 고르시오.

① (A) — (C) — (B)　(A)가 주어진 글에 관한 예시가 아님
② (B) — (A) — (C)　(B)가 '비슷한 방식으로'라는 접속사로 시작했지만, 주어진 글과 이어지지 않음
③ (B) — (C) — (A)　(C)에서 어린아이들이 성인 스포츠 환경에서 겪는 문제점을 해결하기 위해
④ (C) — (A) — (B)　여러 스포츠에서 어린아이들을 위한 조정을 함 — (A) 야구, 풋볼, 유소년 축구에서 어린아이들을 위해 조정함 — (B) 비슷한 방식으로 테니스에서도 어린아이들에게 적합하게 조정함
⑤ (C) — (B) — (A)　(B) 앞에는 다른 스포츠의 예시가 먼저 나와야 함

| 문제 풀이 순서 | ★★✸ [정답률 73%]

1st 각 문단의 내용을 파악하고, 글의 논리적인 순서를 추론한다.

주어진 글: 많은 스포츠에서 사람들은 어린아이들이 여러 성인 스포츠 환경에 완전히 참여하기란 어렵고 심지어 불가능하다는 것을 깨달았다.

➡ **주어진 글 뒤:** 어린아이들이 여러 성인 스포츠 환경에 완전히 참여하는 것이 어렵거나 불가능하다는 것을 사람들이 깨달았기 때문에 이를 해결하기 위한 방법이 이어질 것이다.

(A): 예를 들자면, 야구에는 티볼이 있고, 풋볼에는 플래그 풋볼이 있고, 유소년 축구는 더 작고 더 가벼운 공과 (가끔) 더 작은 경기장을 사용한다. 모두가 어린아이들이 더 짧아진 경기 시간 동안 그리고 종종 더 작은 팀으로 경기하는 유소년 시합의 구조를 가진다.

➡ **(A) 앞:** (A)는 야구, 풋볼, 축구 등 대표적인 스포츠들이 유소년에 맞게 조정된 예시를 언급하고 있으므로, 앞에는 성인 스포츠가 유소년에 맞게 조정되었다는 등의 중심 문장이 직접 언급되어야 한다. ▶ 주어진 글 바로 뒤에 (A)가 올 수 없음

(A) 뒤: 다양한 스포츠가 어린아이들을 위해 조정된 것에 관한 부연 설명이 이어질 것이다.

(B): 비슷한 방식으로(In a similar way), 테니스는 코트 면적, 공, 라켓을 10세 미만의 어린아이에게 더 적합하도록 만들기 위해 조정했다. 이러한 조정은 점진적이고 어린아이의 연령과 관련이 있다.

➡ **(B) 앞:** In a similar way 뒤에 테니스가 어린아이에게 더 적합하도록 조정된 내용이 나오므로 앞에는 어린아이에게 더 적합하도록 조정된 다른 스포츠 예시가 언급되어야 한다.
▶ 어린아이들을 위해 적합하게 조정된 야구, 풋볼, 유소년 축구라는 예시가 언급된 (A)가 (B) 앞에 와야 함 (순서: (A) → (B))

(B) 뒤: 조정을 어떻게 했는지 설명하며 마무리했다.
▶ (B)가 마지막에 옴

(C): 어린아이들이 너무 크거나 너무 무겁고 또는 너무 빨라서 그들(어린아이들)이 다룰 수 없는 장비를 가지고 성인 스타일의 시합에서 경쟁하려고 하면서 성인용 운동장, 코트 또는 경기장에서 운동한다면 그들(어린아이들)이 성공으로 가는 길이 있을 것 같지 않다는 것을 그들은(They) 발견했다. 이러한 공통된 견해가 널리 퍼졌기에 여러 스포츠는 어린아이들을 위한 조정을 했다.

➡ **(C) 앞:** They(그들은)가 가리키는 대상에 관한 내용이 있어야 한다.
▶ 주어진 글에서 They(그들은)가 가리키는 대상인 people(사람들은)이 나옴 (순서: 주어진 글 → (C))

(C) 뒤: 여러 스포츠가 어린아이들을 위해 조정됐다는 내용 뒤에는 이에 관한 예시로서 야구, 풋볼, 유소년 축구를 언급한 (A)가 이어질 것이다.
▶ (C) 뒤에 (A)가 이어져야 함 (순서: 주어진 글 → (C) → (A) → (B))

2nd 글이 한눈에 들어오도록 정리하여 정답을 확인한다.

주어진 글: 어린아이들이 성인 스포츠 환경에 완전히 참여하기란 어렵고 심지어 불가능하다.

➡ **(C):** 장비나 경기 환경이 어린아이들에게 적합하지 않다는 견해가 널리 퍼져서 여러 스포츠는 어린아이들을 위한 조정을 했다.

➡ **(A):** 예를 들어 야구, 풋볼, 유소년 축구는 각각 어린아이들에게 적합하도록 조정을 했다.

➡ **(B):** 비슷한 방식으로 테니스도 어린아이에게 더 적합하도록 조정을 했다.
▶ 주어진 글 다음에 이어질 글의 순서는 (C) → (A) → (B)이므로 정답은 ④임

O 10 정답 ③ *Inca 제국의 Chasquis 전령들

With no horses available, / the Inca empire excelled / at delivering messages on foot. // **단서 1** Inca 제국은 걸어서 메시지를 전달하는 데 탁월했음
구할 수 있는 말이 없어서 / Inca 제국은 탁월했다 / 걸어서 메시지를 전달하는 데 //

1st 각 문단의 내용을 파악하고, 글의 논리적인 순서를 추론한다.

주어진 글: 구할 수 있는 말이 없어서, Inca 제국은 걸어서 메시지를 전달하는 데 탁월했다.

➡ **주어진 글 뒤:** 걸어서 메시지를 전달하는 방법에 관한 내용이 이어질 것이다.

(A) When a messenger neared the next hut, / he began to call out and repeated the message three or four times / to the one who 주격 관계대명사(선행사: the one) was running out to meet him. // 부사적 용법(목적) **단서 2** 전령이 오두막을 향해 오는 내용이 앞에 와야 함
전령은 다음 오두막에 다가갈 때 / 소리치기 시작했고 메시지를 서너 번 반복했다 / 자신을 만나러 달려 나오고 있는 전령에게 //

(A): 전령은 다음 오두막(the next hut)에 다가갈 때, 자신을 만나러 달려 나오고 있는 전령에게 소리치기 시작했고 메시지를 서너 번 반복했다. Inca 제국은 사정이 좋으면 사나흘 만에 1,000마일(1,610km) 정도 메시지를 이어 갈 수 있었다.

➡ **(A) 앞:** 정관사 the가 쓰였으므로, 오두막에 대한 설명이 앞에 언급되어야 하는데, 주어진 글에는 오두막에 관한 내용이 없다.
▶ 주어진 글 바로 뒤에 (A)가 올 수 없음

The Inca empire could relay messages 1,000 miles (1,610 km) / in three or four days under good conditions. //
Inca 제국은 1,000마일(1,610km) 정도 메시지를 이어 갈 수 있었다 / 사정이 좋으면 사나흘 만에 //
단서 3 누가 걸어서 메시지를 전달했는지 설명함

(A) 뒤: 구체적인 메시지 전달 속도로 문장을 마무리했으므로, 주어진 글의 중심 문장인 'Inca 제국이 걸어서 메시지를 전달하는 데 탁월했다'를 정리하는 문단임을 유추할 수 있다.

(B) The messengers were stationed on the royal roads / to deliver the Inca king's orders and reports / coming from his lands. // 현재분사구(orders and reports 수식)
전령들은 왕의 길에 배치되었다 / Inca 왕의 명령과 보고를 전달하기 위해 / 그의 영토에서 오는 //

(B): 전령들은 Inca 왕의 명령과 그의 영토에서 오는 보고를 전달하기 위해 왕의 길에 배치되었다. Chasquis라고 불리는, 그들은 네 명에서 여섯 명의 집단을 이루어 길을 따라 1마일에서 2마일 간격으로 떨어져 배치된 오두막에서 생활했다.

Called Chasquis, / they lived in groups of four to six / in huts, placed from one to two miles apart along the roads. // 앞에 주격 관계대명사와 be동사 생략됨
Chasquis라고 불리는 / 그들은 네 명에서 여섯 명의 집단을 이루어 생활했다 / 길을 따라 1마일에서 2마일 간격으로 떨어져 배치된 오두막에서 //
단서 4 (C) 앞에 They(그들은)가 가리키는 대상이 나와야 함

➡ **(B) 앞:** 명령과 보고를 전달하는 수단으로서 오두막마다 배치된 전령들이 언급되었다. 구할 수 있는 말이 없어서 Inca 제국이 전령들을 통해 메시지를 전달했음을 유추할 수 있다.
▶ (B) 앞에 주어진 글이 와야 함 (순서: 주어진 글 ➡ (B))
(B) 뒤: 전령들에 대한 부연 설명이 이어질 것이다.

(C) They were all young men / and especially good runners / who watched the road in both directions. // 주격 관계대명사(선행사: runners)
그들은 모두 젊은 남자였고 / 특히 잘 달리는 이들이었다 / 양방향으로 길을 주시하는 //

(C): 그들은(They) 모두 젊은 남자였고, 양방향으로 길을 주시하는 특히 잘 달리는 이들이었다. 그들은 다른 전령이 오는 것을 발견하면 그들을 맞이하기 위해 서둘러 나갔다. Inca 사람들은 서로를 볼 수 있는 높은 지대에 오두막을 지었다.

If they caught sight of another messenger coming, / they hurried out to meet them. //
그들은 다른 전령이 오는 것을 발견하면 / 그들을 맞이하기 위해 서둘러 나갔다 //

➡ **(C) 앞:** '그들(They)'이 가리키는 대상이 앞에 나와야 한다. 명령과 보고를 전달하기 위해 배치된 전령에 관한 내용이 (B)에 있다.
▶ (C) 앞에 (B)가 와야 함 (순서: 주어진 글 ➡ (B) ➡ (C))

The Inca built the huts on high ground, / in sight of one another. //
Inca 사람들은 높은 지대에 오두막을 지었다 / 서로를 볼 수 있는 //

(C) 뒤: 전령들이 높은 지대에 오두막을 짓고 어떻게 활동했는지에 대한 부연 설명이 이어져야 한다.
▶ (A)에서 전령들의 메시지 전달 방법과 메시지 전달 속도에 대한 설명을 이어감 (순서: 주어진 글 ➡ (B) ➡ (C) ➡ (A))

- available ⓐ 구할 수 있는
- empire ⓝ 제국
- on foot 걸어서
- near ⓥ 다가가다
- relay ⓥ 이어가다
- under good condition 좋은 상황에서, 사정이 좋으면
- station ⓥ 배치하다
- royal ⓐ 왕의, 왕실의
- order ⓝ 명령
- hut ⓝ 오두막
- place ⓥ 배치하다
- apart ⓐⓓ 떨어져
- along ⓟⓡⓔⓟ ~을 따라
- especially ⓐⓓ 특히
- direction ⓝ 방향
- catch sight of ~을 찾아내다

2nd 글이 한눈에 들어오도록 정리하여 정답을 확인한다.

주어진 글: Inca 제국은 구할 수 있는 말이 없어서 걸어서 메시지를 전달하는 데 탁월했다.

➡ **(B):** Inca 왕의 명령과 그의 영토에서 오는 보고를 전달하기 위해 Chasquis라고 불리는 전령들이 왕의 길에 배치되었다.

➡ **(C):** 전령들은 잘 달리는 젊은 남자들이었고 다른 전령이 오는 것을 발견하면 서둘러 나갔다.

➡ **(A):** 전령이 자신을 만나러 달려 나오는 다음 전령에게 소리치며 메시지를 서너 번 반복하고, 사정이 좋으면 메시지는 사나흘 만에 1,000마일 정도를 이어 갈 수 있었다.

▶ 주어진 글 다음에 이어질 글의 순서는 (B) ➡ (C) ➡ (A)이므로 정답은 ③임

구할 수 있는 말이 없어서, Inca 제국은 걸어서 메시지를 전달하는 데 탁월했다. (B) 전령들은 Inca 왕의 명령과 그의 영토에서 오는 보고를 전달하기 위해 왕의 길에 배치되었다. Chasquis라고 불리는, 그들은 네 명에서 여섯 명의 집단을 이루어 길을 따라 1마일에서 2마일 간격으로 떨어져 배치된 오두막에서 생활했다. (C) 그들은 모두 젊은 남자였고, 양방향으로 길을 주시하는 특히 잘 달리는 이들이었다. 그들은 다른 전령이 오는 것을 발견하면 그들을 맞이하기 위해 서둘러 나갔다. Inca 사람들은 서로를 볼 수 있는 높은 지대에 오두막을 지었다. (A) 전령은 다음 오두막에 다가갈 때, 자신을 만나러 달려 나오고 있는 전령에게 소리치기 시작했고 메시지를 서너 번 반복했다. Inca 제국은 사정이 좋으면 사나흘 만에 1,000마일(1,610km) 정도 메시지를 이어 갈 수 있었다.

주어진 글 다음에 이어질 글의 순서로 가장 적절한 것을 고르시오. [3점]

① (A) — (C) — (B) (A) 앞에 전령과 오두막에 대한 언급이 먼저 나와야 함
② (B) — (A) — (C) (A)의 끝에서 메시지 전달 속도를 설명하는데 (C)의 They(그들은)와 이어지지 않아서 어색함
③ (B) — (C) — (A) (B) 전령들이 왕의 길에 배치되었고 오두막에서 집단으로 생활함 — (C) 전령들은 잘 달리는 젊은 남자들이었고 다른 전령이 오는 것을 발견하면 서둘러 나감 — (A) 전령이 자신을 만나러 달려 나오는 다음 전령에게 소리치며 메시지를 서너 번 반복함
④ (C) — (A) — (B)
⑤ (C) — (B) — (A) (C)의 They(그들은)가 가리키는 대상이 누구인지 먼저 언급해야 함

O 11 정답 ③ *디지털 비즈니스 활동이 환경에 미치는 영향

단서 1 디지털 비즈니스 활동이 환경에 덜 부정적인 영향을 미칠 거라 예상함

As businesses shift / some core business activities to digital, / such as sales, marketing, or archiving, / it is assumed that the impact on the environment will be less negative. //
기업이 전환함에 따라 / 일부 핵심 비즈니스 활동을 디지털로 / 영업, 마케팅, 파일 보관 등과 같은 / 환경에 미치는 영향이 덜 부정적일 것으로 예상된다 //

(A) When we store bigger data on clouds, / increased carbon emissions make our green clouds gray. //
클라우드에 더 많은 데이터를 저장하면 / 증가된 탄소 배출량이 녹색 구름을 회색으로 변하게 만든다 //

단서 2 (C)에서 언급된 '데이터 센터'의 에너지원이 화석 연료인 것과 내용이 연결됨

The carbon footprint of an email is smaller / than mail sent via a post office, / but still, it causes four grams of CO₂, / and it can be as much as 50 grams / if the attachment is big. //
이메일의 탄소 발자국은 더 적지만 / 우체국을 통해 보내는 우편물보다 / 여전히 4g의 이산화탄소를 유발하며 / 50g에 달할 수 있다 / 첨부 파일이 크면 //

(B) However, / digital business activities / can still threaten the environment. //
단서 3 주어진 글의 내용과는 달리, 여전히 디지털 비즈니스 활동은 환경을 위협함
그러나 / 디지털 비즈니스 활동은 / 여전히 환경을 위협할 수 있다 //

In some cases, / the harm of digital businesses / can be even more hazardous. //
경우에 따라서는 / 디지털 비즈니스가 끼치는 해악이 / 훨씬 더 위험할 수 있다 //

A few decades ago, / offices used to have much more paper waste / since all documents were paper based. //
수십 년 전만 해도 / 사무실에서는 종이 폐기물이 훨씬 더 많았다 / 모든 문서가 종이로 작성되었기 때문에 //

단서 4 (B)에서 언급된 종이의 디지털 전환은 나무를 보호하려는 조치였음

(C) When workplaces shifted from paper to digital documents, invoices, and emails, / it was a promising step to save trees. //
직장에서 종이를 디지털 문서, (디지털) 송장, 이메일로 전환했을 때 / 그것은 나무를 보호할 수 있는 유망한 조치였다 //

However, / the cost of the Internet and electricity for the environment / is neglected. //
하지만 / 인터넷과 전기가 환경에 입히는 손실은 / 간과되고 있다 //

A recent *Wired* report declared / that most data centers' energy source is fossil fuels. //
최근 Wired의 보고서는 말했다 / 대부분의 데이터 센터의 에너지원은 화석 연료라고 //

- **shift** ⓥ 전환하다
- **archive** ⓥ 보관하다
- **assume** ⓥ 추정하다
- **store** ⓥ 저장하다
- **carbon** ⓝ 탄소
- **emission** ⓝ 배출
- **footprint** ⓝ 발자국
- **via** (prep) ~을 통하여
- **attachment** ⓝ 첨부
- **threaten** ⓥ 위협하다
- **harm** ⓝ 해
- **hazardous** ⓐ 위험한
- **promising** ⓐ 유망한
- **neglect** ⓥ 소홀히 하다
- **declare** ⓥ 선언하다
- **fossil fuel** 화석 연료

기업이 영업, 마케팅, 파일 보관 등 일부 핵심 비즈니스 활동을 디지털로 전환함에 따라 환경에 미치는 영향이 덜 부정적일 것으로 예상된다. (B) 그러나 디지털 비즈니스 활동은 여전히 환경을 위협할 수 있다. 경우에 따라서는 디지털 비즈니스가 끼치는 해악이 훨씬 더 위험할 수 있다. 수십 년 전만 해도 사무실에서는 모든 문서가 종이로 작성되었기 때문에 종이 폐기물이 훨씬 더 많았다. (C) 직장에서 종이를 디지털 문서, (디지털) 송장, 이메일로 전환한 것은 나무를 보호할 수 있는 유망한 조치였다. 하지만 인터넷과 전기가 환경에 입히는 손실은 간과되고 있다. 최근 Wired의 보고서에 따르면 대부분의 데이터 센터의 에너지원은 화석 연료이다. (A) 클라우드에 더 많은 데이터를 저장할수록 탄소 배출량이 증가하여 녹색 구름을 회색으로 변하게 만든다. 이메일의 탄소 발자국은 우체국을 통해 보내는 우편물보다 적지만 여전히 4g의 이산화탄소를 유발하며 첨부 파일이 크면 50g에 달할 수 있다.

주어진 글 다음에 이어질 글의 순서로 가장 적절한 것을 고르시오. [3점]

① (A) — (C) — (B)   (A)의 클라우드나 데이터 저장에 대한 언급은 주어진 글에 없음
② (B) — (A) — (C)   (A)의 '탄소 배출량'에 대한 언급이 나온 이유는 (C)의 데이터 센터의 에너지원이 '화석 연료'이기 때문임
③ (B) — (C) — (A)   비즈니스 활동의 디지털 전환이 환경에 미치는 영향은 덜 부정적일 것으로 예상됨 — (B) 디지털 비즈니스 활동은 여전히 환경을 위협함 — (C) 데이터 센터의 에너지원은 화석 연료임 — (A) 더 많은 데이터를 저장할수록 탄소 배출량이 증가함
④ (C) — (A) — (B)
⑤ (C) — (B) — (A)   (C)에서 언급된 종이 사용은 (B)에서 먼저 제시됨

| 문제 풀이 순서 | ✿✿✿ [정답률 61%]

1st 각 문단의 내용을 파악하고, 글의 논리적인 순서를 추론한다.

주어진 글: 기업이 영업, 마케팅, 파일 보관 등 일부 핵심 비즈니스 활동을 디지털로 전환함에 따라 환경에 미치는 영향이 덜 부정적일 것으로 예상된다.

➡ **주어진 글 뒤:** 비즈니스 활동의 디지털 전환이 환경에 미치는 영향에 관한 설명이 이어질 것이다.

(A): 클라우드에 더 많은 데이터를 저장할수록 탄소 배출량이 증가하여 녹색 구름을 회색으로 변하게 만든다. 이메일의 탄소 발자국은 우체국을 통해 보내는 우편물보다 적지만 여전히 4g의 이산화탄소를 유발하며 첨부 파일이 크면 50g에 달할 수 있다.

➡ **(A) 앞:** 데이터 저장과 탄소 배출량 사이의 관계가 앞에 제시되어야 한다.
▶ 주어진 글 바로 뒤에 (A)가 올 수 없음
(A) 뒤: 디지털 비즈니스 활동이 탄소 배출을 증가시킨다는 구체적인 예시이므로 (A)가 글의 마지막 부분일 가능성이 높다. ▶ (A)가 마지막에 올 확률이 높음

(B): 그러나(However) 디지털 비즈니스 활동은 여전히 환경을 위협할 수 있다. 경우에 따라서는 디지털 비즈니스가 끼치는 해악이 훨씬 더 위험할 수 있다. 수십 년 전만 해도 사무실에서는 모든 문서가 종이로 작성되었기 때문에 종이 폐기물이 훨씬 더 많았다.

➡ **(B) 앞:** 디지털 비즈니스 활동이 환경을 위협할 수 있다는 내용이 However로 이어지므로, 앞에는 비즈니스 활동의 디지털 전환이 환경에 미치는 영향이 덜 부정적이라고 한 주어진 글이 이어져야 한다.
▶ (B) 앞에 주어진 글이 와야 함 (순서: 주어진 글 → (B))
(B) 뒤: 문서가 종이에서 디지털로 전환되었다는 설명이 이어질 것이다.

(C): 직장에서 종이를 디지털 문서, (디지털) 송장, 이메일로 전환한 것은 나무를 보호할 수 있는 유망한 조치였다. 하지만 인터넷과 전기가 환경에 입히는 손실은 간과되고 있다. 최근 Wired의 보고서에 따르면 대부분의 데이터 센터의 에너지원은 화석 연료이다.

➡ **(C) 앞:** 수십 년 전만 해도 사무실에서 종이를 많이 사용했다고 언급한 (B)에 이어지는 내용이다. ▶ (C) 앞에 (B)가 와야 함 (순서: 주어진 글 → (B) → (C))
(C) 뒤: 데이터 센터의 에너지원이 화석 연료라고 밝혔으므로, 데이터를 저장할수록 탄소 배출량이 증가한다고 언급한 (A)가 이어져야 한다.
▶ (C) 뒤에 (A)가 이어져야 함 (순서: 주어진 글 → (B) → (C) → (A))

2nd 글이 한눈에 들어오도록 정리하여 정답을 확인한다.

주어진 글: 디지털 비즈니스 활동이 환경에 미치는 영향은 덜 부정적일 것이라 예상된다.

➡ **(B):** 그러나 디지털 비즈니스 활동은 여전히 환경을 위협한다. 옛 사무실에서는 종이를 많이 사용했다.

➡ **(C):** 종이에서 디지털로 전환했지만, 인터넷과 전기가 환경에 입히는 손실이 있다. 데이터 센터의 에너지원은 화석 연료이다.

➡ **(A):** 디지털로 더 많은 데이터를 저장할수록 탄소 배출량이 증가한다. 첨부 파일이 큰 이메일의 경우 오히려 우편물보다 탄소 발자국은 더 많다.
▶ 주어진 글 다음에 이어질 글의 순서는 (B) → (C) → (A)이므로 정답은 ③임

O12 정답 ② *관찰과 모방에 의한 학습

The discovery of mirror neurons has profoundly changed / the way we think of a fundamental human capacity, / learning by observation. // 단서1 관찰에 의한 학습이라는 소재를 소개함

동격 동명사구

거울 뉴런의 발견은 완전히 바꾸어 놓았다 / 근본적인 인간의 능력에 대해 우리가 생각하는 방식을 / 관찰에 의한 학습이라는 //

(A) You may not see the tongue stick out / each time you stick yours out at your newborn, / 단서2 혀를 내미는 것이 앞에 언급되어야 함

= your tongue

당신은 (아기의) 혀가 내밀어 나오는 것을 보지 못할 수도 있지만 / 당신의 갓난아기에게 당신의 것(혀)을 내밀 때마다 /

but if you do it many times, / the tongue will come out more often / than if you do something different. //

만약 당신이 그것을 여러 번 한다면 / (아기의) 혀가 더 자주 나올 것이다 / 당신이 다른 것을 할 때보다 //

Babies babble and later start to imitate the sounds / their parents produce. // 단서3 아기들은 옹알이 이후에 소리를 모방함

앞에 목적격 관계대명사가 생략됨

아기들은 옹알이하고 이후에 소리를 모방하기 시작한다 / 그들의 부모가 내는 //

선행사를 포함하는 관계대명사

(B) As children / we learn a lot / by observing what our parents and friends do. // 단서4 주어진 글에 나온 관찰에 의한 학습과 연결됨

어린이일 때 / 우리는 많이 배운다 / 우리의 부모와 친구들이 하는 것을 관찰하면서 //

Newborns, in the first week of life, / have an inborn tendency / to stick out their tongue / if their parents stick out theirs. //

형용사적 용법(tendency 수식)

갓난아기들은 / 생의 첫 주에 / 선천적인 성향을 갖고 있다 / 자신의 혀를 내미는 / 그들의 부모가 그들의 것(혀)을 내밀면 // 단서5 갓난아기들은 혀를 내미는 성향을 가짐

Such imitation is not perfect. //

그러한 모방은 완벽하지 않다 //

(C) Later still, / they play with vacuum cleaners and hammers / in imitation of their parents. // 단서6 (A)의 마지막 문장에서 언급되는 Babies가 they와 연결됨

이후에도 여전히 / 그들은 진공청소기와 망치를 갖고 논다 / 부모들을 흉내 내어 //

전치사+관계대명사

Our modern cultures, / in which we write, speak, read, build spaceships and go to school, /

우리의 현대 문화는 / 쓰고 말하고 읽고 우주선을 만들고 학교에 가는 /

can work only because we are not restricted to the behavior / we are born with or learn by trial and error. //

앞에 목적격 관계대명사가 생략됨

단지 행동에 국한되지 않기 때문에 작동할 수 있다 / 우리가 가지고 태어나는 또는 시행착오를 통해 배우는 //

We can learn a lot / by simply watching others. //

우리는 많이 배울 수 있다 / 그저 다른 사람들을 관찰하는 것을 통해 //

- discovery ⓝ 발견
- profoundly ⓐⓓ 완전히
- fundamental ⓐ 근본적인
- capacity ⓝ 능력
- observation ⓝ 관찰
- newborn ⓝ 신생아
- stick out ~을 내밀다
- imitate ⓥ 모방하다
- inborn ⓐ 선천적인
- tendency ⓝ 성향
- restrict ⓥ 제한하다
- behavior ⓝ 행동
- trial and error 시행착오

거울 뉴런의 발견은 관찰에 의한 학습이라는 근본적인 인간의 능력에 대해 우리가 생각하는 방식을 완전히 바꾸어 놓았다. (B) 어린이일 때 우리는 우리의 부모와 친구들이 하는 것을 관찰하면서 많이 배운다. 갓난아기들은 생의 첫 주에 그들의 부모가 그들의 것(혀)을 내밀면 자신의 혀를 내미는 선천적인 성향을 갖고 있다. 그러한 모방은 완벽하지 않다. (A) 당신은 당신의 갓난아기에게 당신의 것(혀)을 내밀 때마다 (아기의) 혀가 내밀어 나오는 것을 보지 못할 수도 있지만, 만약 당신이 그것을 여러 번 한다면 당신이 다른 것을 할 때보다 (아기의) 혀가 더 자주 나올 것이다. 아기들은 옹알이하고 이후에 그들의 부모가 내는 소리를 모방하기 시작한다. (C) 이후에도 여전히, 그들은 부모들을 흉내 내어 진공청소기와 망치를 갖고 논다. 쓰고 말하고 읽고 우주선을 만들고 학교에 가는 우리의 현대 문화는 단지 우리가 가지고 태어나는 또는 시행착오를 통해 배우는 행동에 국한되지 않기 때문에 작동할 수 있다. 우리는 그저 다른 사람들을 관찰하는 것을 통해 많이 배울 수 있다.

주어진 글에는 혀에 관한 언급이 없음

주어진 글 다음에 이어질 글의 순서로 가장 적절한 것을 고르시오.

① (A) ─ (C) ─ (B) 거울 뉴런이 발견되어, 관찰에 의한 학습에 대한 관점이 바뀜 ─ (B) 아기가 혀를 내미는 것을 따라 하는 것처럼, 관찰을 통해 학습함
② (B) ─ (A) ─ (C) ─ (A) 특정 행동을 반복하면 그 행동을 더 자주 모방함 ─ (C) 인간은 다른 사람들을 관찰하며 많이 배움
③ (B) ─ (C) ─ (A)
④ (C) ─ (A) ─ (B)
⑤ (C) ─ (B) ─ (A) (C)의 they가 가리키는 대상이 주어진 글에 없음

혀를 내미는 모방을 이어서 언급하는 (A)가 (B) 뒤에 이어져야 함

| 문제 풀이 순서 | ✱✱❋ [정답률 77%]

1st 각 문단의 내용을 파악하고, 글의 논리적인 순서를 추론한다.

주어진 글: 거울 뉴런의 발견은 관찰에 의한 학습이라는 근본적인 인간의 능력에 대해 우리가 생각하는 방식을 완전히 바꾸어 놓았다.

➡ **주어진 글 뒤:** 관찰에 의한 학습과 연결되는 내용이 나올 것이다.

(A): 당신은 당신의 갓난아기에게 당신의 것(혀)을 내밀 때마다 (아기의) 혀가 내밀어 나오는 것을 보지 못할 수도 있지만, 만약 당신이 그것을 여러 번 한다면 당신이 다른 것을 할 때보다 (아기의) 혀가 더 자주 나올 것이다. 아기들(Babies)은 옹알이하고 이후에 그들의 부모가 내는 소리를 모방하기 시작한다.

➡ **(A) 앞:** 아기들이 부모들의 행동을 모방해 혀를 내민다는 설명과, 한계가 있다는 내용이 앞에 나와야 한다. 주어진 글에는 관찰에 의한 학습만 언급되었을 뿐, 혀가 언급되지 않았다.
▶ 주어진 글 바로 뒤에 (A)가 올 수 없음

(A) 뒤: 아기들이 성장하면서 보여주는 모방 행동들을 나열했으므로, (A) 뒤에도 아기의 다른 모방 행동이 이어질 것이다.

(B): 어린이일 때 우리는 우리의 부모와 친구들이 하는 것을 관찰하면서 많이 배운다(learn a lot by observing). 갓난아기들은 생의 첫 주에 그들의 부모가 그들의 것(혀)을 내밀면 자신의 혀(tongue)를 내미는 선천적인 성향을 갖고 있다. 그러한 모방은 완벽하지 않다.

➡ **(B) 앞:** 어린이가 주변을 관찰하면서 많이 배운다고 했으므로, 관찰에 의한 학습을 처음 언급한 주어진 글이 앞에 와야 한다.
▶ 순서: 주어진 글 → (B)

(B) 뒤: 모방이 완벽하지는 않다고 했으므로, 매번 모방에 성공하는 것은 아니라는 내용의 (A)가 뒤에 와야 한다.
▶ 순서: 주어진 글 → (B) → (A)

(C): 이후에도 여전히, 그들(they)은 부모들을 흉내 내어 진공청소기와 망치를 갖고 논다. 쓰고 말하고 읽고 우주선을 만들고 학교에 가는 우리의 현대 문화는 단지 우리가 가지고 태어나는 또는 시행착오를 통해 배우는 행동에 국한되지 않기 때문에 작동할 수 있다. 우리는 그저 다른 사람들을 관찰하는 것을 통해 많이 배울 수 있다.

➡ **(C) 앞:** 부모들을 흉내 내어 물건을 갖고 노는 they(그들)가 누구인지 앞에 나와야 하므로, 아기들의 단계적인 모방 행동을 언급한 (A)가 앞에 와야 한다.
▶ 순서: 주어진 글 → (B) → (A) → (C)

2nd 글이 한눈에 들어오도록 정리하여 정답을 확인한다.

주어진 글: 거울 뉴런의 발견은 관찰에 의한 학습에 대한 우리의 관점을 바꿨다.

➡ **(B):** 우리는 주변의 행동을 관찰하며 배우고, 신생아는 불완전하지만 혀 내밀기를 모방한다.

➡ **(A):** 특정 행동이 반복되면 그 행동을 더 자주 모방하며, 아기는 점차 소리도 모방한다.

➡ **(C):** 나중에는 다른 행동들도 모방하며, 이처럼 우리는 다른 사람들을 관찰하며 많이 배운다.
▶ 주어진 글 다음에 이어질 글의 순서는 (B) → (A) → (C)이므로 정답은 ②임

Have you ever been surprised / to hear a recording of your own voice? //
당신은 놀랐던 적이 있는가 / 당신의 음성 녹음을 듣고 //

You might have thought, / "Is that really what my voice sounds like?" //
당신은 생각했을지도 모른다 / '내 목소리가 정말 이렇게 들리는가'라고 //

(A) There are two pathways / through which we perceive our own voice / when we speak. //
두 가지 경로가 있다 / 우리 자신의 목소리를 인지하는 데는 / 우리가 말할 때 //

One is the route / through which we perceive most external sounds, / like waves that travel from the air / through the outer, middle and inner ear. //
하나는 경로이다 / 우리가 대부분의 외부의 소리를 인지하는 / 공기로부터 이동하는 파동처럼 / 외이, 중이, 내이를 통하는 //

(B) But because our vocal cords vibrate when we speak, / there is a second internal path. //
그러나 우리가 말할 때 우리의 성대가 진동하기 때문에 / 두 번째 내부의 경로가 있다 //

Vibrations are conducted through our bones / and stimulate our inner ears directly. //
진동은 뼈를 통해 전해지고 / 우리의 내이를 직접 자극한다 //

Lower frequencies are emphasized / along this pathway. //
낮은 주파수는 두드러진다 / 이 경로를 따라 //

That makes your voice sound deeper and richer to yourself / than it may sound to other people. //
그것은 당신의 목소리가 당신 자신에게 더 깊고 풍부하게 들리게 한다 / 다른 사람에게 들릴 수 있는 것보다 //

(C) Maybe your accent is more pronounced in the recording / than you realized, / or your voice is higher / than it seems to your own ears. //
어쩌면 녹음에서는 당신의 억양이 더 강조되거나 / 당신이 인식한 것보다 / 당신의 목소리가 더 높다 / 당신의 귀에 들리는 것 같은 것보다 //

This is of course quite a common experience. //
이것은 당연히 꽤 흔한 경험이다 //

The explanation is actually fairly simple. //
이 설명은 사실 꽤 간단하다 //

- pathway ⓝ 경로 - route ⓝ 경로 - perceive ⓥ 인지하다
- external ⓐ 외부의 - travel ⓥ 이동하다 - vibrate ⓥ 진동하다
- internal ⓐ 내부의 - conduct ⓥ 전하다 - stimulate ⓥ 자극하다
- emphasize ⓥ 강조하다 - pronounced ⓐ 강조된 - fairly ⓪ 꽤

당신은 당신의 음성 녹음을 듣고 놀랐던 적이 있는가? 당신은 '내 목소리가 정말 이렇게 들리는가?'라고 생각했을지도 모른다. (C) 어쩌면 녹음에서는 당신이 인식한 것보다 당신의 억양이 더 강조되거나, 당신의 목소리가 당신의 귀에 들리는 것 같은 것보다 더 높다. 이것은 당연히 꽤 흔한 경험이다. 이 설명은 사실 꽤 간단하다. (A) 우리가 말할 때 우리 자신의 목소리를 인지하는 데는 두 가지 경로가 있다. 하나는 외이, 중이, 내이를 통하는 공기로부터 이동하는 파동처럼 우리가 대부분의 외부의 소리를 인지하는 경로이다. (B) 그러나 우리가 말할 때 우리의 성대가 진동하기 때문에 두 번째 내부의 경로가 있다. 진동은 뼈를 통해 전해지고, 우리의 내이를 직접 자극한다. 낮은 주파수는 이 경로를 따라 두드러진다. 그것은 당신의 목소리가 다른 사람에게 들릴 수 있는 것보다 당신 자신에게 더 깊고 풍부하게 들리게 한다.

주어진 글 다음에 이어질 글의 순서로 가장 적절한 것을 고르시오. [3점]

① (A) — (C) — (B) 주어진 글의 현상을 (C)에서 부연 설명함
② (B) — (A) — (C) 두 번째 경로를 소개하는 (B)가 주어진 글 바로 뒤에 이어질 수 없음
③ (B) — (C) — (A)
④ (C) — (A) — (B) 자신의 음성 녹음을 들으면 목소리가 다르다고 생각함 — (C) 녹음된 목소리는 억양이 더 강조되거나 더 높게 들림 — (A) 목소리를 인지하는 경로는 두 가지이며 첫 번째는 외부의 소리를 인지하는 경로임 — (B) 두 번째는 내부의 경로이며 이를 통해 자신의 목소리를 더 풍부하게 들음
⑤ (C) — (B) — (A) 첫 번째 경로를 소개한 (A)가 두 번째 경로를 소개한 (B)보다 앞에 와야 함

| 문제 풀이 순서 | ✱✱✱ [정답률 78%]

1st 각 문단의 내용을 파악하고, 글의 논리적인 순서를 추론한다.

주어진 글: 당신은 당신의 음성 녹음을 듣고 놀랐던 적이 있는가? 당신은 '내 목소리가 정말 이렇게 들리는가?'라고 생각했을지도 모른다.

→ **주어진 글 뒤:** 녹음된 자신의 목소리가 원래의 목소리와 다르게 들리는 이유를 부연 설명할 것이다.

(A): 우리가 말할 때 우리 자신의 목소리를 인지하는(perceive) 데는 두 가지 경로가 있다. 하나(One)는 외이, 중이, 내이를 통하는 공기로부터 이동하는 파동처럼 우리가 대부분의 외부의 소리를 인지하는 경로이다.

→ **(A) 앞:** 자신의 목소리를 인지하는 경로를 설명하므로, 자신의 목소리를 인지하는 것에 관한 내용이 먼저 와야 한다. 주어진 글에는 녹음된 목소리가 실제 목소리와 다르게 들린다는 의문점만 제시되었으므로 (A)와 이어질 수 없다.
▶ 주어진 글 바로 뒤에 (A)가 올 수 없음

(A) 뒤: One이라고 했으므로 두 번째 경로에 대한 설명이 이어질 것이다.

(B): 그러나 우리가 말할 때 우리의 성대가 진동하기 때문에 두 번째 내부의 경로(second internal path)가 있다. 진동은 뼈를 통해 전해지고, 우리의 내이를 직접 자극한다. 낮은 주파수는 이 경로를 따라 두드러진다. 그것은 당신의 목소리가 다른 사람에게 들릴 수 있는 것보다 당신 자신에게 더 깊고 풍부하게 들리게 한다.

→ **(B) 앞:** second internal path가 등장했으므로, 목소리를 인지하는 두 가지 경로를 언급하며 첫 번째 경로를 소개한 (A)가 앞에 와야 한다.
▶ 순서: (A) → (B)

(B) 뒤: 두 경로에 대한 설명이 마무리되었으므로 글의 마지막일 가능성이 높다.

(C): 어쩌면 녹음에서는 당신이 인식한(realized) 것보다 당신의 억양이 더 강조되거나, 당신의 목소리가 당신의 귀에 들리는 것 같은 것보다 더 높다. 이것은 당연히 꽤 흔한 경험이다. 이 설명은 사실 꽤 간단하다.

→ **(C) 앞:** 녹음된 자신의 목소리가 낯설게 느껴지는 현상을 소개하는 내용이 있어야 하므로, 녹음된 목소리가 다르게 들린 경험을 묻는 주어진 글이 앞에 와야 한다.
▶ 순서: 주어진 글 → (C)

(C) 뒤: 녹음된 자신의 목소리가 자신이 인식한 목소리와 왜 다른지에 대한 설명이 이어져야 하므로, 자신의 목소리를 인지하는 경로를 설명한 (A)가 뒤에 이어져야 한다.
▶ 순서: 주어진 글 → (C) → (A) → (B)

2nd 글이 한눈에 들어오도록 정리하여 정답을 확인한다.

주어진 글: 녹음된 목소리가 실제 목소리와 다르게 들려서 놀란 적이 있는가?

→ **(C):** 녹음된 목소리에서 억양이 강조되거나 더 높게 느껴졌을 수도 있다.

→ **(A):** 목소리를 인지하는 두 가지 경로 중 첫 번째는 대부분의 외부 소리를 듣는 경로이다.

→ **(B):** 두 번째인 내부 경로에서 낮은 주파수가 두드러지기에 자신의 목소리가 더 깊고 풍부하게 들리게 된다.

▶ 주어진 글 다음에 이어질 글의 순서는 (C) → (A) → (B)이므로 정답은 ④임

O14 정답 ⑤ *노동의 분업을 통한 생산성 증대

Managers are always looking for ways / **to increase**
productivity, / 계속적 용법의 주격 관계대명사 **which** is the ratio of costs to output in
production. // 형용사적 용법(ways 수식)
관리자들은 항상 방법을 찾고 있다 / 생산성을 높일 수 있는 / 그리고 그 생산성은 생산에서
비용 대비 생산량의 비율이다 / **단서1** Adam Smith는 노동의 분업으로 더 효율적인 생산이
가능하다고 설명함   분사구문
Adam Smith, / **writing when the manufacturing industry was**
new, / described a way / **that** production could be made more
앞에 주격 관계대명사와 be동사가 생략됨   관계부사
efficient, / **known** as the "division of labor." //
Adam Smith는 / 제조 산업이 새로 등장했을 때 저술한 / 방식을 설명했다 / 생산이 더
효율적으로 될 수 있는 / '노동의 분업'으로 알려진 //

단서2 (B)의 마지막에 언급된 한 가지 작업만 하는 노동자에 이어지는 내용임
(A) Because each worker specializes in one job, / he or she can
work much faster / without changing from one task to another. //
각 노동자는 한 가지 작업을 전문으로 하기 때문에 / 그 또는 그녀는 훨씬 더 빠르게 일할 수
있다 / 한 작업에서 다른 작업으로 변경하지 않고도 //
Now 10 workers can produce / thousands of pins in a day / — a
huge increase in productivity / from the 200 / **they would have**
앞에 목적격 관계대명사가 생략됨
produced before. //
이제 10명의 노동자가 생산할 수 있다 / 하루에 수천 개의 핀을 / 이는 생산성 측면에서 크게
증가한 것이다 / 200개로부터 / 이전에 그들이 생산했던 //
병렬 구조
(B) One worker could **do** all these tasks, / and **make** 20 pins in
a day. // **단서3** 분업이 적용되지 않던 (C)에 이어지는 내용임
한 명의 노동자가 이 모든 작업들을 할 수 있었고 / 하루에 20개의 핀을 만들 수도 있었다 //
But this work can be divided / into its separate processes, / with
많은, 다수의
a number of workers each performing one task. //
그러나 이 일은 분리될 수 있다 / 별개의 과정으로 / 많은 노동자가 각각 한 가지 작업을
수행하면서 //
동명사 주어(단수 취급)   단수 동사
(C) **Making** most manufactured goods / **involves** several
different processes / using different skills. //
대부분의 공산품을 만드는 것은 / 여러 가지 다른 과정을 포함한다 / 다른 기술을 사용하는 //
Smith's example was the manufacture of pins: / the wire is
straightened, / sharpened, / a head is put on, / and then it is
polished. // **단서4** Smith의 '노동의 분업'을 설명하는 예로서 핀의 공정을 소개함
Smith의 예는 핀의 제조였다 / 철사는 곧게 펴지고 / 뾰족해지고 / 상부가 놓이고 / 그리고
나서 그것이 다듬어진다 //

- **productivity** ⓝ 생산성   • **output** ⓝ 산출량
- **efficient** ⓐ 효율적인   • **division** ⓝ 분배
- **specialize in** ~을 전문으로 하다   • **separate** ⓐ 별개의
- **manufactured** ⓐ 제작된   • **straighten** ⓥ 펴다
- **polish** ⓥ 다듬다

관리자들은 항상 생산성을 높일 수 있는 방법을 찾고 있는데, 생산성은
생산에서 비용 대비 생산량의 비율이다. 제조 산업이 새로 등장했을 때 저술한
Adam Smith는 '노동의 분업'으로 알려진 생산이 더 효율적으로 될 수 있는
방식을 설명했다. (C) 대부분의 공산품을 만드는 것은 다른 기술을 사용하는
여러 가지 다른 과정을 포함한다. Smith의 예는 핀의 제조였다. 철사는 곧게
펴지고, 뾰족해지고, 상부가 놓이고, 그리고 나서 그것이 다듬어진다. (B) 한
명의 노동자가 이 모든 작업들을 할 수 있었고, 하루에 20개의 핀을 만들 수도
있었다. 그러나 이 일은 많은 노동자가 각각 한 가지 작업을 수행하면서 별개의
과정으로 분리될 수 있다. (A) 각 노동자는 한 가지 작업을 전문으로 하기
때문에, 그 또는 그녀는 한 작업에서 다른 작업으로 변경하지 않고도 훨씬 더
빠르게 일할 수 있다. 이제 10명의 노동자가 하루에 수천 개의 핀을 생산할 수
있다. 이는 이전에 그들이 생산했던 200개로부터 생산성 측면에서 크게 증가한
것이다.

(A)의 한 가지 작업은 (B)의 마지막에 나온 별개의 과정으로 분리된 작업임
주어진 글 다음에 이어질 글의 순서로 가장 적절한 것을 고르시오.

① (A) — (C) — (B)
② (B) — (A) — (C)   (B)의 'all these tasks(이 모든 작업들)'가
③ (B) — (C) — (A)   가리키는 것이 앞에 있어야 함
④ (C) — (A) — (B)   Adam Smith는 '노동의 분업'을 설명함 – (C) Smith는 다양한
⑤ (C) — (B) — (A)   작업들이 필요한 핀 제조를 말함 –(B) 한 명이 모든 작업을 할 수도
                     있지만, 한 명이 하나의 작업을 할 수도 있음–(A) 10명이 200개를
                     만들던 것이 수천 개로 증가함

| 문제 풀이 순서 | ★★★ [정답률 62%]

1st 각 문단의 내용을 파악하고, 글의 논리적인 순서를 추론한다.

주어진 글: 관리자들은 항상 생산성을 높일 수 있는 방법을 찾고 있는데,
생산성은 생산에서 비용 대비 생산량의 비율이다. 제조 산업이 새로
등장했을 때 저술한 Adam Smith는 '노동의 분업'으로 알려진 생산이 더
효율적으로 될 수 있는 방식을 설명했다. **단서**

➡ **주어진 글 뒤:** Adam Smith가 설명한 '노동의 분업'에 대한 구체적인 설명이
이어질 것이다. **발상**

(A): 각 노동자는 한 가지 작업을 전문으로 하기 때문에, 그 또는 그녀는
한 작업에서 다른 작업으로 변경하지 않고도 훨씬 더 빠르게 일할 수 있다.
이제 10명의 노동자가 하루에 수천 개의 핀을 생산할 수 있다. 이는 이전에
그들이 생산했던 200개로부터 생산성 측면에서 크게 증가한 것이다.

➡ **(A) 앞:** 어떤 과정을 거쳐 이러한 결과가 나왔는지가 언급되어야 한다.
▶ 주어진 글 바로 뒤에 (A)가 올 수 없음
(A) 뒤: 생산성이 크게 증가한 결과에 해당하므로 글의 결론일 가능성이 높다.
▶ (A)가 마지막에 올 확률이 높음

(B): 한 명의 노동자가 이 모든 작업들(all these tasks)을 할 수 있었고,
하루에 20개의 핀을 만들 수도 있었다. 그러나 이 일은 많은 노동자가 각각
한 가지 작업을 수행하면서 별개의 과정으로 분리될 수 있다.

➡ **(B) 앞:** **①** 어떤 노동자인지,
② 어떤 작업들인지가 언급되어야 한다.
▶ (B) 앞에는 주어진 글과 (A) 모두 올 수 없으므로 (C)가 올 가능성이 높음
(B) 뒤: 많은 노동자가 각각 한 가지 작업을 수행하는 것을 (A)에서 한 가지 작업을
전문으로 하는 것으로 이야기했으므로 (A)가 이어지는 것이 적절하다.
▶ (A)가 (B) 뒤에 와야 함 (순서: (B) ➡ (A))

(C): 대부분의 공산품을 만드는 것은 다른 기술을 사용하는 여러 가지 다른
과정을 포함한다. Smith의 예는 핀의 제조였다. 철사는 곧게 펴지고,
뾰족해지고, 상부가 놓이고, 그리고 나서 그것이 다듬어진다.

➡ **(C) 앞:** 주어진 글에서 말한 Adam Smith의 '노동의 분업'을 설명하는 예시로
핀의 제조가 등장했다.
▶ 주어진 글에 이어지는 내용임 (순서: 주어진 글 ➡ (C))
➡ **(C) 뒤:** 철사를 펴고, 뾰족하게 만들고, 상부를 놓아 다듬는 과정을 '이 모든
작업들'이라고 한 (B)가 이어져야 한다.
▶ (C) 뒤에 (B)가 이어져야 함 (순서: 주어진 글 ➡ (C) ➡ (B) ➡ (A))

2nd 글이 한눈에 들어오도록 정리하여 정답을 확인한다.

주어진 글: Adam Smith는 생산의 효율성을 높이는 방법으로 '노동의 분업'을
설명했다.
➡ **(C):** Smith는 그 예로 철사를 펴고, 뾰족하게 만들고, 상부를 놓아 다듬어야 하는
핀의 제조를 제시했다.
➡ **(B):** 이 모든 작업들은 한 사람이 할 수도 있지만, 한 사람이 하나의 작업만 하는
별개의 과정으로 분리될 수 있다.
➡ **(A):** 한 가지 작업만 전문으로 하면 다른 작업으로 변경하지 않고 더 빠르게 작업할
수 있고, 생산성이 크게 증가한다.
▶ 주어진 글 다음에 이어질 글의 순서는 (C) ➡ (B) ➡ (A)이므로 정답은 ⑤임

O 15 정답 ③ *평범한 시골 건축업자들의 건축 방식과 특징

Toward the end of the 19th century, / a new architectural attitude emerged. //
19세기 말이 되면서 / 새로운 건축학적 사고방식이 나타났다 //

단서 1 새로운 건축학적 사고방식에 대한 내용

Industrial architecture, / the argument went, / was ugly and inhuman; / past styles had more to do / with pretension / than what people needed / in their homes. //
산업 건축은 / 그 주장에 따르면 / 추하고 비인간적이었다 / 과거의 스타일은 더욱 관련이 있었다 / 허세와 / 사람들이 필요했던 것보다는 / 그들의 집에서 //

단서 2 (C)의 마지막에 부족하거나 완벽하지 않았던 점이 언급되었는데, 그와 반대되는 내용이 But으로 이어짐

(A) But they supplied / people's needs perfectly / and, at their best, / had a beauty / that came from the craftsman's skill / and the rootedness of the house / in its locality. //
그러나 그것들은 충족시켰다 / 사람들의 필요를 완벽하게 / 그리고 가장 잘 된 경우에는 / 아름다움을 갖추고 있었다 / 장인의 솜씨에서 비롯된 / 그리고 그 집의 뿌리내림(에서 비롯된) / 그것의 지역에 //

(B) Instead of these approaches, / why not look at the way / ordinary country builders worked / in the past? //
이러한 접근 대신에 / 방식을 살펴보자는 것은 어떠한가 / 평범한 시골 건축업자들이 일했던 / 과거에 //

단서 3 주어진 글에서 말한 과거의 건축 스타일을 가리킴

They developed their craft skills / over generations, / demonstrating mastery / of both tools and materials. //
그들은 공예 기술을 발전시켰다 / 세대를 거쳐 / 숙달한 기술을 보이며 / 도구와 재료 둘 다에 //

단서 4 (B)의 마지막에 언급한 materials에 대한 내용이 이어짐

(C) Those materials were local, / and used with simplicity / — houses built this way / had plain wooden floors and whitewashed walls / inside. //
그 재료는 지역적이고 / 단순하게 사용되었는데 / 집들은 / 이러한 방식으로 건축된 / 평범한 나무 바닥과 회반죽을 칠한 벽을 가졌다 / 실내에 //

- architectural ⓐ 건축학의   • attitude ⓝ 사고방식
- emerge ⓥ 나타나다   • industrial ⓐ 산업의   • argument ⓝ 주장
- inhuman ⓐ 비인간적인   • have to do with ~와 관련 있다
- craftsman ⓝ 장인   • rootedness ⓝ 뿌리박음
- locality ⓝ 지역, 인근   • approach ⓝ 접근   • ordinary ⓐ 평범한
- generation ⓝ 세대   • demonstrate ⓥ 보여 주다
- mastery ⓝ 숙달한 기술   • simplicity ⓝ 단순함
- plain ⓐ 평범한   • whitewashed ⓐ 회반죽을 바른

19세기 말이 되면서, 새로운 건축학적 사고방식이 나타났다. 그 주장에 따르면, 산업 건축은 추하고 비인간적이었다. 다른 한편으로 과거의 스타일은 사람들이 그들의 집에서 필요했던 것보다는 허세와 더욱 관련이 있었다. (B) 이러한 접근 대신에, 평범한 시골 건축업자들이 과거에 일했던 방식을 살펴보는 것은 어떠한가? 그들은 도구와 재료 둘 다에 숙달한 기술을 보이며, 세대를 거쳐 공예 기술을 발전시켰다. (C) 그 재료는 지역적이고, 단순하게 사용되었는데, 이러한 방식으로 건축된 집들은 실내가 평범한 나무 바닥과 회반죽을 칠한 벽으로 되어 있었다. (A) 그러나 그것들은 사람들의 필요를 완벽하게 충족시켰고, 가장 잘 된 경우에는, 장인의 솜씨와 그 집의 지역에 뿌리내림에서 비롯된 아름다움을 갖추고 있었다.

주어진 글 다음에 이어질 글의 순서로 가장 적절한 것을 고르시오.

① (A) — (C) — (B)
② (B) — (A) — (C)
   (B)의 these approaches가 주어진 글에서 말한 과거의 건축 스타일을 가리킴
   (A)가 But으로 시작하므로 앞에는 부족하거나 완벽하지 않았다는 내용의 (C)가 나와야 함
③ (B) — (C) — (A) (B) 평범한 시골 건축업자들의 방식을 살펴보자고 제안함 – (C) 재료는 평범했음 – (A) 그러나 사람들의 필요를 완전히 충족시켰음
④ (C) — (A) — (B)
⑤ (C) — (B) — (A)
   (C)의 those materials 앞에는 반드시 materials에 대한 언급이 먼저 있어야 함

| 문제 풀이 순서 | ★★★ [정답률 61%]

1st 각 문단의 내용을 파악하고, 글의 논리적인 순서를 추론한다.

주어진 글: 19세기 말이 되면서, 새로운 건축학적 사고방식이 나타났다. 그 주장에 따르면, 산업 건축은 추하고 비인간적이었다. 다른 한편으로 과거의 스타일은 사람들이 그들의 집에서 필요했던 것보다는 허세와 더욱 관련이 있었다.

➡ **주어진 글 뒤:** 19세기 말에 새로운 건축학적 사고방식이 나타나, 산업 건축과 과거 스타일을 비판했다는 내용이므로 (단서) 이런 사고방식과 관련된 내용이 나올 것이다. (발상)

(A): 그러나(But) 그것들(they)은 사람들의 필요를 완벽하게 충족시켰고, 가장 잘 된 경우에는, 장인의 솜씨와 그 집의 지역에 뿌리내림에서 비롯된 아름다움을 갖추고 있었다.

➡ **(A) 앞:** ❶ But으로 시작했으므로 they로 가리키는 것들에 대한 반대 내용이 (A) 앞에 나와야 한다.
❷ 사람들의 필요를 충족시켰고 아름다움을 갖추고 있었다는 것과도 다른 시각이 앞에 제시되어야 한다.
▶ (A) 앞에 주어진 글이 올 수 없음
(A) 뒤: they에 대한 추가적인 내용이 나오지 않는다면 마무리에 해당할 가능성이 높다.
▶ (A)가 마지막에 올 확률이 높음

(B): 이러한 접근(these approaches) 대신에(Instead of), 평범한 시골 건축업자들이 과거에 일했던 방식을 살펴보는 것은 어떠한가? 그들은 도구와 재료 둘 다에 숙달한 기술을 보이며, 세대를 거쳐 공예 기술을 발전시켰다.

➡ **(B) 앞:** ❶ '이러한 접근(these approaches)'이라고 가리키는 것이 앞에 나와야 한다.
❷ '대신에(Instead of)'라고 했으므로 평범한 시골 건축업자들이 과거에 일했던 방식과 다른 방식이 앞에 나와야 한다.
▶ 주어진 글에 나온 새로운 건축학적 사고방식을 가리키므로 (B) 앞에 주어진 글이 와야 함 (순서: 주어진 글 ➡ (B))
(B) 뒤: 시골 건축업자들의 도구, 재료와 관련된 내용이 뒤에 이어질 것이다.

(C): 그 재료(those materials)는 지역적이고, 단순하게 사용되었는데, 이러한 방식으로 건축된 집들은 실내가 평범한 나무 바닥과 회반죽을 칠한 벽으로 되어 있었다.

➡ **(C) 앞:** (B)에서 언급한 재료를 가리키는 '그 재료(those materials)'로 시작하므로 (B)가 앞에 와야 한다.
▶ (C) 앞에 (B)가 와야 함 (순서: 주어진 글 ➡ (B) ➡ (C))
(C) 뒤: 평범한 시골 건축업자들은 재료들을 단순하고 평범하게 썼다고 했는데, 이것을 they로 가리키며 다른 시각을 보여주는 내용이 (A)이므로 (C) 뒤에 와야 한다.
▶ 순서: 주어진 글 ➡ (B) ➡ (C) ➡ (A)

2nd 글이 한눈에 들어오도록 정리하여 정답을 확인한다.

주어진 글: 19세기 말에 새로운 건축학적 사고방식이 등장해서 산업 건축과 과거 스타일을 비판했다.
➡ **(B):** 시골의 평범한 건축업자의 건축 방식을 살펴보자.
➡ **(C):** 그들이 사용한 재료는 단순했고, 스타일은 평범했다.
➡ **(A):** 그러나 사람들의 필요를 완벽히 충족시켰고 나름의 아름다움을 갖췄다.
▶ 주어진 글 다음에 이어질 순서는 (B) ➡ (C) ➡ (A)이므로 정답은 ③임

O 16 정답 ⑤ *도움을 주고받는 너도밤나무

Each beech tree grows in a particular location / and soil conditions can vary greatly / in just a few yards. //
각각의 너도밤나무는 고유한 장소에서 자란다 / 그리고 토양의 조건들은 크게 달라질 수 있다 / 단 몇 야드 안에서도 // **[단서 1]** 너도밤나무가 자라는 토양의 조건은 가까운 거리 내에서도 크게 달라질 수 있음

The soil can have a great deal of water / or almost no water. //
토양은 다량의 물을 가질 수 있고 / 또는 거의 물이 없을 수도 있다 //

It can be full of nutrients or not. //
그것은 영양분이 가득할 수도 아닐 수도 있다 //

[단서 2] This는 (B)의 마지막에 언급한, 나무들 사이의 당 차이를 균등하게 한다는 내용을 가리킴
(A) This is taking place underground / through the roots. //
이것은 지하에서 일어나고 있다 / 뿌리들을 통해 //

복합관계대명사
Whoever has an abundance of sugar / hands some over; / 복합관계대명사 **whoever** is running short / gets help. //
풍부한 당을 가진 나무는 어떤 나무라도 / 일부를 건네준다 / 부족해지는 나무는 어떤 나무라도 / 도움을 받는다 //

형용사적 용법(system 수식)
Their network acts as a system / to make sure that no trees fall too far behind. //
그들의 연결망은 시스템으로서 역할을 한다 / 그 어떤 나무도 너무 뒤처지지 않는 것을 확실히 하기 위한 //

(B) However, / the rate is the same. //
그러나 / 그 정도는 동일하다 // **[단서 3]** 앞에 정도가 동일하다는 것과 반대되는 내용이 나와야 함

whether A or B: A이든 B이든
Whether they are thick **or** thin, / all the trees of the same species are using light / 부사적 용법(결과) to produce the same amount of sugar per leaf. //
그들이 굵든 가늘든 / 같은 종의 모든 나무들은 빛을 사용한다 / 그래서 이파리당 같은 양의 당을 생산한다 //

by v-ing: ~함으로써
Some trees have plenty of sugar / and some have less, / but the trees equalize this difference between them / by transferring sugar. //
어떤 나무들은 충분한 당을 지니고 / 어떤 것들은 더 적게 지닌다 / 하지만 나무들은 그들 사이의 이 차이를 균등하게 한다 / 당을 전달함으로써 // **[단서 4]** 주어진 글에서 말한 너도밤나무의 토양의 조건들이 다른 것에 따른 결과임

병렬 구조
(C) Accordingly, / each tree **grows** more quickly or more slowly / and **produces** more or less sugar, / and thus you would expect / every tree to be photosynthesizing / at a different rate. //
이에 따라 / 각 나무는 더 빨리 혹은 더 느리게 자라고 / 더 많거나 더 적은 당을 생산한다 / 그래서 여러분은 기대할 것이다 / 모든 나무가 광합성을 할 것이라고 / 다른 정도로 //

- beech tree 너도밤나무
- nutrient ⓝ 영양분
- abundance ⓝ 풍부(함)
- plenty of 풍부한, 많은
- transfer ⓥ 전달하다, 옮기다
- vary ⓥ (상황에 따라) 달라지다
- underground ⓐ 지하에서
- run short (~이) 부족하다
- equalize ⓥ 균등하게 하다
- accordingly ⓐ 따라서, 그에 따라

각각의 너도밤나무는 고유한 장소에서 자라고 토양의 조건들은 단 몇 야드 안에서도 크게 달라질 수 있다. 토양은 다량의 물을 가지거나 거의 물이 없을 수도 있다. 그것은 영양분이 가득할 수도 아닐 수도 있다. (C) 이에 따라, 각 나무는 더 빨리 혹은 더 느리게 자라고 더 많은 혹은 더 적은 당을 생산하는데, 그래서 여러분은 모든 나무가 다른 정도로 광합성을 할 것이라고 기대할 것이다. (B) 그러나 그 정도는 동일하다. 그들이 굵든 가늘든 간에, 같은 종의 모든 나무들은 빛을 사용하여 이파리당 같은 양의 당을 생산한다. 어떤 나무들은 충분한 당을 지니고 어떤 것들은 더 적게 지니지만, 나무들은 당을 전달함으로써 그들 사이의 이 차이를 균등하게 한다. (A) 이것은 뿌리들을 통해 지하에서 일어나고 있다. 풍부한 당을 가진 나무가 누구든 간에 일부를 건네주고, 부족해지는 나무는 누구든 간에 도움을 받는다. 그들의 연결망은 그 어떤 나무도 너무 뒤처지지 않는 것을 확실히 하기 위한 시스템으로서 역할을 한다.

주어진 글 다음에 이어질 글의 순서로 가장 적절한 것을 고르시오. [3점]
① (A) — (C) — (B) (C)는 주어진 글의 결과이므로 주어진 글에 이어져야 함
② (B) — (A) — (C)
③ (B) — (C) — (A) However(그러나)로 시작하는 (B)와 상반된 내용이 주어진 글에 없음
④ (C) — (A) — (B) (A)의 This가 가리키는 것은 (B)의 마지막에 언급됨
⑤ (C) — (B) — (A) 너도밤나무가 자라는 토양의 조건은 서로 다름 — (C) 너도밤나무가 자라는 속도와 생산하는 당이 다름 — (B) 그러나 각 나무들은 같은 양의 당을 생산함 — (A) 뿌리를 통해 나무들은 당을 주고받으며 균등하게 함

| 문제 풀이 순서 | ★★★ [정답률 60%]

[1st] 각 문단의 내용을 파악하고, 글의 논리적인 순서를 추론한다.

주어진 글: 각각의 너도밤나무는 고유한 장소에서 자라고 토양의 조건들은 단 몇 야드 안에서도 크게 달라질 수 있다. 토양은 다량의 물을 가지거나 거의 물이 없을 수도 있다. 그것은 영양분이 가득할 수도 아닐 수도 있다. **단서**

➡ **주어진 글 뒤:** 서로 다른 토양에서 너도밤나무가 어떻게 다르게 자라는지를 설명하는 내용이 이어질 것이다. **발상**

(A): 이것(This)은 뿌리들을 통해 지하에서 일어나고 있다. 풍부한 당을 가진 나무가 누구든 간에 일부를 건네주고, 부족해지는 나무는 누구든 간에 도움을 받는다. 그들의 연결망은 그 어떤 나무도 너무 뒤처지지 않는 것을 확실히 하기 위한 시스템으로서 역할을 한다.

➡ **(A) 앞:** '이것(This)'이 무엇인지 설명하는 내용이 앞에 와야 한다.
▶ (A) 앞에 주어진 글이 올 수 없음
(A) 뒤: 서로 다른 조건의 토양에서 자랄지라도 어떤 나무도 뒤처지지 않게 한다는 것은 글의 결말일 가능성이 크다.
▶ (A)가 마지막에 올 확률이 높음

(B): 그러나(However) 그 정도(the rate)는 동일하다. 그들이 굵든 가늘든 간에, 같은 종의 모든 나무들은 빛을 사용하여 이파리당 같은 양의 당을 생산한다. 어떤 나무들은 충분한 당을 지니고 어떤 것들은 더 적게 지니지만, 나무들은 당을 전달함으로써 그들 사이의 이 차이를 균등하게 한다.

➡ **(B) 앞:** ❶ 어떤 '정도(rate)'를 말하는 것인지 언급되어야 하고,
❷ 역접의 연결어 However로 연결되므로 앞에는 반대되는 내용(정도가 다르다는 내용)이 와야 한다.
▶ 주어진 글과 (A)에는 해당 내용이 없으므로 (C)가 올 확률이 높음
(B) 뒤: 나무들은 서로 당을 전달함으로써 그들 사이의 격차를 줄인다는 것을 (A)에서 This로 설명했다.
▶ (A)가 (B) 뒤에 와야 함 (순서: (B) ➡ (A))

(C): 이에 따라(Accordingly), 각 나무는 더 빨리 혹은 더 느리게 자라고 더 많은 혹은 더 적은 당을 생산하는데, 그래서 여러분은 모든 나무가 다른 정도로 광합성을 할 것이라고 기대할 것이다.

➡ **(C) 앞:** 앞서 예상한 것처럼 주어진 글에 이어지는 내용으로, 서로 다른 토양에서 너도밤나무가 어떻게 다르게 자랄 것인지 예상하는 내용이 이어졌다.
▶ 주어진 글에 이어지는 내용임 (순서: 주어진 글 ➡ (C))
(C) 뒤: 광합성의 정도가 다를 것이라고 예상한 것과 달리 '그 정도'는 동일하다고 한 (B)가 이어져야 한다.
▶ (C) 뒤에 (B)가 이어져야 함 (순서: 주어진 글 ➡ (C) ➡ (B) ➡ (A))

[2nd] 글이 한눈에 들어오도록 정리하여 정답을 확인한다.

주어진 글: 너도밤나무가 자라는 토양의 조건은 가까이에서도 크게 달라질 수 있다.
➡ **(C):** 이에 따라 각 나무가 광합성을 하는 정도는 모두 다를 것이다.
➡ **(B):** 하지만 나무들은 서로 당을 주고받음으로써 그 차이를 균등하게 만든다.
➡ **(A):** 이것은 뿌리에서 일어나며 이 연결망으로 어떤 나무도 뒤처지지 않게 한다.
▶ 주어진 글 다음에 이어질 글의 순서는 (C) ➡ (B) ➡ (A)이므로 정답은 ⑤임

O 17 정답 ② *시계가 필요했던 사람들

Up until about 6,000 years ago, / most people were farmers. //
약 6,000년 전까지 / 대부분의 사람들은 농부였다 //

Many lived in different places / throughout the year, / hunting for food / or moving their livestock / to areas with enough food. // 단서 1 과거 사람들은 일 년 내내 장소를 옮기면서 살았음
많은 사람들은 여러 장소에서 살았다 / 일 년 내내 / 식량을 찾아다니거나 / 그들의 가축을 옮기면서 / 충분한 먹이가 있는 지역으로 //

(A) For example, / priests wanted to know / when to carry out religious ceremonies. // 단서 2 (B)에서 언급된 시간을 알아야 했던 사람들의 예시
예를 들어 / 성직자들은 알고 '싶었다 / 언제 종교적인 의식을 수행해야 하는지 //

This was when people first invented clocks / — devices that show, measure, and keep track of passing time. //
이때가 사람들이 시계를 처음 발명한 때이다 / 시간을 보여주고, 측정하고, 흐르는 시간을 추적하는 장치인 //

(B) There was no need to tell the time / because life depended on natural cycles, / such as the changing seasons or sunrise and sunset. //
시간을 알 필요가 없었다 / 왜냐하면 삶은 자연적인 주기에 달려있었기 때문에 / 변화하는 계절이나 일출과 일몰 같은 //

단서 3 정착하게 되면서 시간을 알아야 했던 사람들이 생겨남
Gradually more people started to live in larger settlements, / and some needed to tell the time. //
점점 더 많은 사람들이 더 큰 정착지에서 살기 시작했다 / 그리고 어떤 사람들은 시간을 알 필요가 있었다 //

(C) Clocks have been important ever since. //
시계는 그 이후로도 중요했다 // 단서 4 (A)에서 시계가 발명된 이후로 줄곧 시계는 중요했음

Today, / clocks are used for important things / such as setting busy airport timetables / — if the time is incorrect / aeroplanes might crash into each other / when taking off or landing! //
오늘날 / 시계는 중요한 일에 사용된다 / 바쁜 공항 시간표를 설정하는 것과 같은 / 만약 시간이 부정확하다면 / 비행기는 서로 충돌할지도 모른다 / 이륙하거나 착륙할 때 //

- livestock ⓝ 가축
- priest ⓝ 성직자
- religious ⓐ 종교적인
- invent ⓥ 발명하다
- device ⓝ 장치
- gradually ⓐⓓ 점점
- settlement ⓝ 정착지
- timetable ⓝ 시간표
- aeroplane ⓝ 비행기

약 6,000년 전까지, 대부분의 사람들은 농부였다. 많은 사람들은 식량을 찾아다니거나 가축을 충분한 먹이가 있는 지역으로 옮기며 일 년 내내 여러 장소에서 살았다. (B) 변화하는 계절이나 일출과 일몰 같은, 자연적인 주기에 삶이 달려있기 때문에 시간을 알 필요가 없었다. 점점 더 많은 사람들이 더 큰 정착지에서 살기 시작했고, 어떤 사람들은 시간을 알 필요가 있었다. (A) 예를 들어, 성직자들은 언제 종교적인 의식을 수행해야 하는지 알고 싶었다. 이때 사람들이 시간을 보여주고, 측정하고, 흐르는 시간을 추적하는 장치인 시계를 처음으로 발명했다. (C) 시계는 그 이후로도 중요했다. 오늘날, 시계는 바쁜 공항 시간표를 설정하는 것과 같은 중요한 일에 사용된다 — 만약 시간이 부정확하다면, 비행기는 이륙하거나 착륙할 때 서로 충돌할지도 모른다!

시간을 알 필요가 있었던 성직자의 예시가 뒷받침하는 일반적 진술인 (B)가 (A)앞에 있어야 함
주어진 글 다음에 이어질 글의 순서로 가장 적절한 것을 고르시오. [3점]
① (A) — (C) — (B)
② (B) — (A) — (C) 과거 사람들은 여러 장소를 이동하며 살았음–(B) 사람들이 정착하면서 시간을 알 필요가 있게 됨–(A) 이때 시계가 발명됨–(C) 그 이후로 오늘날까지 시계는 중요함
③ (B) — (C) — (A) (A)는 (B)의 시간을 알 필요가 있었던 사람들의 예시임
④ (C) — (A) — (B)
⑤ (C) — (B) — (A) 오늘날까지 시계는 중요하다는 (C)는 글의 결말임

1st 각 문단의 내용을 파악하고, 글의 논리적인 순서를 추론한다.

주어진 글: 약 6,000년 전까지, 대부분의 사람들은 농부였다. 많은 사람들은 식량을 찾아다니거나 가축을 충분한 먹이가 있는 지역으로 옮기며 일 년 내내 여러 장소에서 살았다. 단서

➡ **주어진 글 뒤**: 여러 장소를 옮겨 다니며 살았던 과거의 사람들에 관해 구체적으로 설명한 뒤, 오늘날에는 어떤지가 이어질 것이다. 발상

(A): 예를 들어(For example), 성직자들은 언제 종교적인 의식을 수행해야 하는지 알고 싶었다. 이때 사람들이 시간을 보여주고, 측정하고, 흐르는 시간을 추적하는 장치인 시계를 처음으로 발명했다.

➡ **(A) 앞**: '언제' 종교 의식을 해야 하는지 알고 싶었던 성직자의 예시가 For example로 이어지므로, 앞에 '언제'와 관련된 내용이 와야 한다.
▶ 주어진 글 바로 뒤에 (A)가 올 수 없음
(A) 뒤: '시계가 처음 등장했으므로 시계와 관련된 내용이 이어질 것이다.

(B): 변화하는 계절이나 일출과 일몰 같은, 자연적인 주기에 삶이 달려있기 때문에 시간을 알 필요가 없었다. 점점 더 많은 사람들이 더 큰 정착지에서 살기 시작했고, 어떤 사람들은 시간을 알 필요가 있었다.

➡ **(B) 앞**: 자연 주기에 삶이 달려있다는 것은 주어진 글에서 언급한 일 년 내내 옮겨 다니며 살았던 것을 의미하므로 주어진 글에 이어지는 내용이다.
▶ (B) 앞에 주어진 글이 와야 함 (순서: 주어진 글 → (B))
(B) 뒤: 시간을 알 필요가 있는 사람들의 예시로 성직자를 이야기한 (A)가 이어져야 한다.
▶ (B) 뒤에는 (A)가 이어져야 함 (순서: 주어진 글 → (B) → (A))

(C): 시계는 그 이후로도(ever since) 중요했다. 오늘날, 시계는 바쁜 공항 시간표를 설정하는 것과 같은 중요한 일에 사용된다 — 만약 시간이 부정확하다면, 비행기는 이륙하거나 착륙할 때 서로 충돌할지도 모른다!

➡ **(C) 앞**: 시계가 발명된 이후로 줄곧 중요했던 것이므로 시계가 처음 발명됐다고 언급한 (A)에 이어지는 내용이다.
▶ (C) 앞에는 (A)가 와야 함 (순서: 주어진 글 → (B) → (A) → (C))
(C) 뒤: 오늘날까지 시계는 매우 중요한 역할을 하고 있다면서 글을 마무리하고 있으므로 (C)는 마지막에 와야 한다.

2nd 글이 한눈에 들어오도록 정리하여 정답을 확인한다.

주어진 글: 과거 많은 사람들은 일 년 내내 여러 장소를 옮겨 다니며 살았다.
→ **(B)**: 그들은 자연적인 주기에 의존하여 살았기 때문에 시간을 알 필요가 없었지만, 정착하기 시작하면서 시간을 알아야 했던 사람들이 생겨났다.
→ **(A)**: 예를 들어 성직자들은 언제 종교 의식을 해야 하는지 알아야 했고, 이때 시계가 처음으로 발명되었다.
→ **(C)**: 시계가 발명된 이후로 오늘날까지 시계는 매우 중요한 역할을 하고 있다.
▶ 주어진 글 다음에 이어질 글의 순서는 (B) → (A) → (C)이므로 정답은 ②임

⟶ 어법 특강

✱ 병렬 구조를 이루는 등위접속사
- and, but, or, so 등은 등위접속사로 두 개 이상의 단어, 구, 절을 연결한다. 이때 동일한 품사와 문법적으로 같은 성분을 연결해야 한다.
- Don't forget to prepare *a cutting board* and *a knife*. 단어와 단어를 연결
(도마와 칼을 준비할 것을 잊지 마세요.)
- *You can squeeze oranges by hand,* but *it's easier if you use a squeezer.* 문장과 문장을 연결
(당신은 손으로 오렌지를 짤 수 있지만, 압착기를 사용하면 더 쉬워요.)

Maybe you've heard this joke: / "How do you eat an elephant?" // **단서 1** 질문 형태의 농담으로 글을 시작함

아마 여러분은 이 농담을 들어본 적이 있을 것이다 / "당신은 코끼리를 어떻게 먹는가" //

현재완료(경험)

The answer is "one bite at a time." //

정답은 '한 번에 한 입'이다 //

(A) Common crystal habits include / squares, triangles, and six-sided hexagons. // **단서 2** (B)에서 과학자들이 언급한 습성에 이어지는 내용임

일반적인 결정 습성은 포함한다 / 사각형, 삼각형, 그리고 육면의 육각형을 //

부사절 접속사(시간)

Usually crystals form / when liquids cool, / such as when you create ice cubes. //

보통 결정이 형성된다 / 액체가 차가워질 때 / 여러분이 얼음 조각을 만들 때와 같이 //

주격 관계대명사

Many times, / crystals form / in ways / that do not allow for perfect shapes. //

많은 경우 / 결정은 형성된다 / 방식으로 / 완벽한 모양을 허용하지 않는 //

If conditions are too cold, / too hot, / or there isn't enough source material, / they can form strange, twisted shapes. //

조건이 너무 차갑거나 / 너무 뜨겁거나 / 혹은 원천 물질이 충분하지 않으면 / 그것들은 이상하고 뒤틀린 모양을 형성할 수 있다 //

(B) So, / how do you "build" the Earth? // **단서 3** 질문 형태의 다른 농담이 제시됨

그렇다면 / 여러분은 어떻게 지구를 '건설'하는가 //

That's simple, too: / one atom at a time. //

그것은 또한 간단하다 / 한 번에 하나의 원자이다 //

부사절 접속사(이유)

Atoms are the basic building blocks of crystals, / and since all rocks are made up of crystals, / the more you know about atoms, / the better. //

the 비교급 S V, the 비교급 (S V): ~할수록 더욱 …하다

원자는 결정의 기본 구성 요소이고 / 모든 암석은 결정으로 이루어져 있기 때문에 / 여러분이 원자에 대해 더 많이 알수록 / 더 좋다 //

목적격 관계대명사

Crystals come in a variety of shapes / that scientists call *habits*. //

결정은 다양한 모양으로 나온다 / 과학자들이 '습성'이라고 부르는 //

(C) But when conditions are right, / we see beautiful displays. // **단서 4** (A)의 조건이 안 좋을 때와 상반된 내용이 But으로 연결됨

하지만 조건이 맞을 때 / 우리는 아름다운 배열을 본다 //

관계부사

Usually, / this involves a slow, steady environment / where the individual atoms have plenty of time / to join and fit perfectly into / what's known as the *crystal lattice*. //

형용사적 용법(time 수식)
선행사를 포함한 관계대명사 '결정격자'

보통 / 이것은 느리고 안정적인 환경을 수반한다 / 개별적인 원자들이 충분한 시간을 가지는 / 결합하고 완벽하게 들어맞는 / '결정격자'라고 알려진 것에 //

주격 관계대명사

This is the basic structure of atoms / that is seen time after time. //

이것은 원자의 기본적인 구조이다 / 반복하여 보여지는 //

- hexagon ⑪ 육각형 • condition ⑪ 조건 • twisted ⓐ 뒤틀린
- atom ⑪ 원자 • display ⑪ 배열 • steady ⓐ 안정적인, 꾸준한
- individual ⓐ 개별적인

아마 여러분은 이 농담을 들어본 적이 있을 것이다. "당신은 코끼리를 어떻게 먹는가?" 정답은 '한 번에 한 입'이다. (B) 그렇다면, 여러분은 어떻게 지구를 '건설'하는가? 그것은 또한 간단하다. 한 번에 하나의 원자이다. 원자는 결정의 기본 구성 요소이고, 모든 암석은 결정으로 이루어져 있기 때문에, 여러분이 원자에 대해 더 많이 알수록 더 좋다. 결정은 과학자들이 '습성'이라고 부르는 다양한 모양으로 나온다. (A) 일반적인 결정 습성은 사각형, 삼각형, 육면의 육각형을 포함한다. 보통 여러분이 얼음 조각을 만들 때와 같이 액체가 차가워질 때 결정이 형성된다. 많은 경우, 결정은 완벽한 모양을 허용하지 않는 방식으로 형성된다. 조건이 너무 차갑거나, 너무 뜨겁거나, 혹은 원천 물질이 충분하지 않으면 그것들은 이상하고 뒤틀린 모양을 형성할 수 있다. (C) 하지만 조건이 맞을 때, 우리는 아름다운 배열을 본다. 보통, 이것은 개별적인 원자들이 결합하고 '결정격자'라고 알려진 것에 완벽하게 들어맞는 충분한 시간을 가지는 느리고 안정적인 환경을 수반한다. 이것은 반복하여 보이는 원자의 기본적인 구조이다.

주어진 글 다음에 이어질 글의 순서로 가장 적절한 것을 고르시오. [3점]

① (A) — (C) — (B) (B)의 질문 형태 농담은 주어진 글에 이어져야 함
② (B) — (A) — (C) 코끼리를 어떻게 먹는가에 대한 정답(한 번에 한 입) — (B) 지구를 구성하는 원자는 결정의 기본 구성 요소임 — (A) 결정은 환경이 맞지 않으면 이상한 모양을 형성함 — (C) 환경 조건이 좋으면 결정격자를 형성함
③ (B) — (C) — (A)
④ (C) — (A) — (B) 환경 조건이 좋지 않은 (A)가 먼저 나온 뒤 But으로 조건이 좋은 (C)가 연결되어야 함
⑤ (C) — (B) — (A)

| 문제 풀이 순서 | ★★❀ [정답률 77%]

1st 각 문단의 내용을 파악하고, 글의 논리적인 순서를 추론한다.

┌ **주어진 글:** 아마 여러분은 이 농담을 들어본 적이 있을 것이다.
└ "당신은 코끼리를 어떻게 먹는가?" 정답은 '한 번에 한 입'이다. **단서**

→ **주어진 글 뒤:** 농담을 제시해 글을 시작한 이유나 배경을 설명할 것이다. **발상**

┌ **(A):** 일반적인 결정 습성은 사각형, 삼각형, 육면의 육각형을 포함한다. 보통 여러분이 얼음 조각을 만들 때와 같이 액체가 차가워질 때 결정이 형성된다. 많은 경우, 결정은 완벽한 모양을 허용하지 않는 방식으로 형성된다. 조건이 너무 차갑거나, 너무 뜨겁거나, 혹은 원천 물질이 └ 충분하지 않으면 그것들은 이상하고 뒤틀린 모양을 형성할 수 있다.

→ **(A) 앞:** 결정 습성에 대한 설명이 나오기 전에, 결정에 관한 내용이 언급되어야 한다.
▶ 주어진 글 바로 뒤에 (A)가 올 수 없음
(A) 뒤: 조건이 좋지 않은 상황을 이야기했으므로, 반대로 조건이 좋을 때는 결정이 어떻게 형성되는지에 대한 설명이 이어질 것이다.

┌ **(B):** 그렇다면, 여러분은 어떻게 지구를 '건설'하는가? 그것은 또한 간단하다. 한 번에 하나의 원자이다. 원자는 결정의 기본 구성 요소이고, 모든 암석은 결정으로 이루어져 있기 때문에, 여러분이 원자에 대해 더 많이 알수록 더 좋다. 결정은 과학자들이 '습성'이라고 부르는 다양한 └ 모양으로 나온다.

→ **(B) 앞:** 주어진 글의 질문과 유사한 질문이 제시되었다.
▶ 주어진 글에 이어지는 내용임 (순서: 주어진 글 → (B))
(B) 뒤: 결정과 결정 습성을 처음으로 언급했으므로, 이에 관해 부연 설명하는 (A)가 이어질 것이다.
▶ (B) 뒤에 (A)가 이어져야 함 (순서: 주어진 글 → (B) → (A))

┌ **(C):** 하지만(But) 조건이 맞을 때, 우리는 아름다운 배열을 본다. 보통, 이것은 개별적인 원자들이 결합하고 '결정격자'라고 알려진 것에 완벽하게 들어맞는 충분한 시간을 가지는 느리고 안정적인 환경을 └ 수반한다. 이것은 반복하여 보이는 원자의 기본적인 구조이다.

→ **(C) 앞:** 역접의 연결어 But으로 조건이 맞을 때 결정 배열이 아름답다는 내용이 이어졌으므로, 앞에는 조건이 맞지 않을 때의 결정 모양에 관해 이야기한 (A)가 와야 한다.
▶ (A)에 이어지는 내용임 (순서: 주어진 글 → (B) → (A) → (C))
(C) 뒤: 앞의 내용을 정리하며 결정격자는 보이는 원자의 기본적인 구조라고 하며 글을 마무리했다.

2nd 글이 한눈에 들어오도록 정리하여 정답을 확인한다.

주어진 글: 코끼리를 어떻게 먹는가? 한 번에 한 입씩.
→ **(B):** 지구도 한 번에 하나의 원자로 건설할 수 있는데, 원자는 결정을 구성하고, 결정은 암석을 구성한다.
→ **(A):** 결정은 주로 액체가 차가워질 때 형성되는데, 환경 조건이 맞지 않으면 결정 모양이 이상해진다.
→ **(C):** 하지만 조건이 맞으면 결정은 아름답게 배열되며 이러한 결정격자는 보이는 원자의 기본 구조이다.
▶ 주어진 글 다음에 이어질 글의 순서는 (B) → (A) → (C)이므로 정답은 ②임

O 19 정답 ③ *기타가 소리를 내는 원리

1st 각 문단의 내용을 파악하고, 글의 논리적인 순서를 추론한다.

When you pluck a guitar string / it moves back and forth / hundreds of times every second. //
여러분이 기타 줄을 뜯을 때 / 그것은 이리저리 움직인다 / 매초 수백 번 //

[단서 1] (C)의 나무판의 진동을 가리킴
(A) The vibration of the wood / creates more powerful waves / in the air pressure, / 계속적 용법의 주격 관계대명사 *which* travel away from the guitar. //
그 나무의 진동은 / 더 강력한 파동을 만들어 낸다 / 공기의 압력에 / 그리고 그것은 기타로부터 멀리 퍼진다 //

부사절 접속사
When the waves reach your eardrums / they flex in and out / the same number of times a second / as the original string. //
그 파동이 여러분의 고막에 도달할 때 / 그것들은 굽히쳐 들어가고 나온다 / 초당 동일한 횟수로 / 원래의 굴과 //

[단서 2] 주어진 글에서 말한 기타 줄의 움직임을 가리킴
so ~ that ...: 너무 ~해서 …하다
(B) Naturally, / this movement is *so* fast *that* you cannot see it / — you just see / the blurred outline of the moving string. //
당연히 / 이 움직임은 너무 빨라서 여러분은 그것을 볼 수 없다 / 여러분은 그저 본다 / 움직이는 줄의 흐릿한 윤곽만 //

현재분사(Strings 수식)
Strings *vibrating* in this way on their own / make hardly any noise / 병렬 구조 because strings *are* very thin / and *don't push* much air about. //
이렇게 스스로 진동하는 줄들은 / 거의 어떤 소리도 나지 않는다 / 왜냐하면 줄이 매우 가늘고 / 많은 공기를 밀어내지 못하기 때문이다 //

부사절 접속사(조건)
(C) But *if* you attach a string / to a big hollow box / (like a guitar body), / then the vibration is amplified / and the note is heard loud and clear. // [단서 3] (B)의 마지막과 반대되는 내용이 But으로 연결됨
하지만 여러분이 줄을 달면 / 커다란 속이 빈 상자에 / (기타 몸통 같은) / 그러면 그 진동은 증폭되어 / 그 음이 크고 선명하게 들린다 //

2어동사의 수동태는 동사만 be p.p.로 바꾸고 부사나 전치사는 그대로 씀
The vibration of the string *is passed on* / to the wooden panels of the guitar body, / 계속적 용법의 주격 관계대명사 *which* vibrate back and forth / at the same rate as the string. //
그 줄의 진동은 전달된다 / 기타 몸통의 나무판으로 / 그리고 그것은 이리저리 떨린다 / 줄과 같은 속도로 //

- string ⓝ 줄, 끈
- vibration ⓝ 진동
- pressure ⓝ 압력
- eardrum ⓝ 고막
- flex ⓥ 굽히다
- blurred ⓐ 흐릿한
- outline ⓝ 윤곽, 개요
- hardly ⓐⓓ 거의 ~ 않다
- hollow ⓐ (속이) 빈
- pass on ~을 전달하다
- panel ⓝ 판

여러분이 기타 줄을 뜯을 때 그것은 매초 수백 번 이리저리 움직인다. (B) 당연히, 이 움직임은 너무 빨라서 여러분은 그것을 볼 수 없다. 여러분은 그저 움직이는 줄의 흐릿한 윤곽만 본다. 이렇게 스스로 진동하는 줄들은 거의 소리가 나지 않는데, 이는 줄이 매우 가늘고 많은 공기를 밀어내지 못하기 때문이다. (C) 하지만 여러분이 (기타 몸통 같은) 커다란 속이 빈 상자에 줄을 달면, 그 진동은 증폭되어 그 음이 크고 선명하게 들린다. 그 줄의 진동은 기타 몸통의 나무판으로 전달되어 줄과 같은 속도로 이리저리 떨린다. (A) 그 나무의 진동은 공기의 압력에 더 강력한 파동을 만들어 내어 기타로부터 멀리 퍼진다. 그 파동이 여러분의 고막에 도달할 때 원래의 줄과 초당 동일한 횟수로 굽히쳐 들어가고 나온다.

주어진 글 다음에 이어질 글의 순서로 가장 적절한 것을 고르시오.

① (A) — (C) — (B) ← 주어진 글과 (B)에는 (A)의 나무를 가리킬 만한 내용이 없음
② (B) — (A) — (C)
③ (B) — (C) — (A) ← 기타 줄은 빠르게 움직임 — (B) 이 움직임은 소리가 나지 않음, 줄이 너무 가늘어서 공기를 밀어내지 못하기 때문임 — (C) 하지만 기타 몸통의 나무판처럼 속이 빈 상자에 줄을 달면 진동이 증폭되어 소리가 잘 들림 — (A) 그 나무의 진동이 파동을 만들고, 그 파동이 고막에 들리는 것임
④ (C) — (A) — (B)
⑤ (C) — (B) — (A) ← (C)와 주어진 글은 But으로 연결될 수 없음

주어진 글: 여러분이 기타 줄을 뜯을 때 그것은 매초 수백 번 이리저리 움직인다. (단서)

➡ **주어진 글 뒤:** 빠르게 움직이는 기타 줄과 관련된 내용이 이어질 것이다. (발상)

(A): 그 나무(the wood)의 진동은 공기의 압력에 더 강력한 파동을 만들어 내어 기타로부터 멀리 퍼진다. 그 파동이 여러분의 고막에 도달할 때 원래의 줄과 초당 동일한 횟수로 굽히쳐 들어가고 나온다.

➡ **(A) 앞:** '그 나무'라고 했으므로 앞에 어떤 나무가 언급되어야 한다.
▶ 주어진 글 바로 뒤에 (A)가 올 수 없음
(A) 뒤: 파동이 고막에 도달했다고 했는데, 그 파동이 고막 이후에 어디로 가는지를 설명하지 않는다면 (A)가 글의 결론일 것이다.
▶ (A)가 마지막에 올 확률이 높음

(B): 당연히, 이 움직임(this movement)은 너무 빨라서 여러분은 그것을 볼 수 없다. 여러분은 그저 움직이는 줄의 흐릿한 윤곽만 본다. 이렇게 스스로 진동하는 줄들은 거의 소리가 나지 않는데, 이는 줄이 매우 가늘고 많은 공기를 밀어내지 못하기 때문이다.

➡ **(B) 앞:** 1 '이 움직임(this movement)'이 무엇을 가리키는지 앞에 나와야 한다. 2 너무 빠르게 움직여서 움직임을 볼 수 없다고 했으므로, 주어진 글에서 말한 매초 수백 번 움직이는 기타 줄의 움직임을 말하는 것이다.
▶ 주어진 글에 이어지는 내용임 (순서: 주어진 글 → (B))
(B) 뒤: (A)의 '그 나무'를 가리킬 내용이 (B)에 없으므로 (A)가 이어질 수는 없다.
▶ (C)가 이어질 확률이 높음

(C): 하지만(But) 여러분이 (기타 몸통 같은) 커다란 속이 빈 상자에 줄을 달면, 그 진동은 증폭되어 그 음이 크고 선명하게 들린다. 그 줄의 진동은 기타 몸통의 나무판으로 전달되어 줄과 같은 속도로 이리저리 떨린다.

➡ **(C) 앞:** 소리가 잘 들린다는 내용이 역접의 연결어 But으로 이어지므로, 앞에는 소리가 잘 들리지 않는다고 설명한 (B)가 와야 한다.
▶ 순서: 주어진 글 → (B) → (C)
(C) 뒤: 기타 몸통, 즉 나무판의 진동을 (A)에서 '그 나무의 진동'으로 가리켜 설명을 이어갔다. ▶ (A)가 이어져야 함 (순서: 주어진 글 → (B) → (C) → (A))

2nd 글이 한눈에 들어오도록 정리하여 정답을 확인한다.

주어진 글: 기타 줄을 뜯으면 그것은 매우 빠르게 움직인다.
➡ **(B):** 그 움직임은 너무 빨라서 볼 수 없는데, 이렇게 스스로 진동하는 줄은 가늘고 공기를 밀어내지 못하기 때문에 소리가 거의 나지 않는다.
➡ **(C):** 하지만 커다란 속이 빈 상자에 줄을 연결하면 진동이 증폭되어 소리가 커지며, 그 진동이 기타 몸통의 나무판까지 전달되어 떨린다.
➡ **(A):** 나무판의 진동은 더 강력한 파동을 만들어 내어 퍼지고 고막에까지 도달한다.
▶ 주어진 글 다음에 이어질 글의 순서는 (B) → (C) → (A)이므로 정답은 ③임

O 20 정답 ③ *자동화로 대체되는 일자리

Things are changing. // [단서 1] 캐나다와 미국의 일자리가 자동화로 인해 위기에 처할 것임
상황이 변화하고 있다 //

가주어 진주어절 접속사
It has been reported / *that* 42 percent of jobs in Canada are at risk, / and 62 percent of jobs in America / will be in danger / due to advances in automation. //
~이 보도되어 왔다 / 캐나다의 일자리 중 42퍼센트가 위기에 처해 있다고 / 그리고 미국의 일자리 중 62퍼센트가 / 위기에 처할 것이라고 / 자동화의 발전으로 인해 //

선행사를 포함하는 관계대명사
(A) However, / *what*'s difficult to automate / is the ability to creatively solve problems. // [단서 2] 앞에 자동화하기 어려운 것과 반대되는 내용이 나와야 함
하지만 / 자동화하기 어려운 것은 / 창의적으로 문제들을 해결하는 능력이다 //

Whereas workers in "doing" roles / can be replaced by robots, / the role of creatively solving problems / is more dependent on an irreplaceable individual. //
반면에 '(기계적인 일을) 하는' 역할의 노동자들은 / 로봇들에 의해 대체될 수 있다 / 창의적으로 문제를 해결하는 역할은 / 대체 불가능한 개인에 더 의존한다 //

(B) You might say / that the numbers seem a bit unrealistic, / but the threat is real. // 단서3 '그 숫자들'은 주어진 글에 나온 퍼센트를 가리킴
여러분은 말할지 모른다 / 그 숫자들이 약간 비현실적으로 보인다고 / 하지만 그 위협은 현실이다 //

One fast food franchise has a robot / that can flip a burger in ten seconds. //
한 패스트푸드 체인점은 로봇을 가지고 있다 / 10초 안에 버거 하나를 뒤집을 수 있는 //

It is just a simple task / but the robot could replace an entire crew. //
그것은 단지 단순한 일일 뿐이다 / 하지만 그 로봇은 전체 직원을 대체할 수도 있다 //

(C) Highly skilled jobs / are also at risk. // 단서4 앞에 위기에 처한 다른 직업들에 대한 내용이 와야 함
고도로 숙련된 직업들 / 또한 위기에 처해 있다 //

A supercomputer, / for instance, / can suggest available treatments for specific illnesses / in an automated way, / drawing on the body of medical research and data / on diseases. //
슈퍼컴퓨터는 / 예를 들면 / 특정한 질병들에 대해 이용 가능한 치료법을 제안할 수 있다 / 자동화된 방식으로 / 방대한 양의 의학 연구와 데이터를 이용하여 / 질병에 대한 //

- at risk 위험에 처한   - advance ⓝ 발전, 진전
- automation ⓝ 자동화   - automate ⓥ 자동화하다
- dependent ⓐ 의존하는   - irreplaceable ⓐ 대체할 수 없는
- crew ⓝ (한 팀으로 일하는) 직원   - draw on ~을 이용하다

상황이 변화하고 있다. 캐나다의 일자리 중 42퍼센트가 위기에 처해 있고, 미국의 일자리 중 62퍼센트가 자동화의 발전으로 인해 위기에 처할 것이라고 보도되어 왔다. (B) 여러분은 그 숫자들이 약간 비현실적으로 보인다고 말할지 모르지만, 그 위협은 현실이다. 한 패스트푸드 체인점은 10초 안에 버거 하나를 뒤집을 수 있는 로봇을 가지고 있다. 그것은 단지 단순한 일일 뿐이지만 그 로봇은 전체 직원을 대체할 수도 있다. (C) 고도로 숙련된 직업들 또한 위기에 처해 있다. 예를 들면, 슈퍼컴퓨터는 질병에 대한 방대한 양의 의학 연구와 데이터를 이용하여 특정한 질병들에 대해 이용 가능한 치료법을 자동화된 방식으로 제안할 수 있다. (A) 하지만, 자동화하기 어려운 것은 창의적으로 문제들을 해결하는 능력이다. '(기계적인 일을) 하는' 역할의 노동자들은 로봇들에 의해 대체될 수 있는 반면에, 창의적으로 문제를 해결하는 역할은 대체 불가능한 개인에 더 의존한다.

주어진 글 다음에 이어질 글의 순서로 가장 적절한 것을 고르시오.
① (A) — (C) — (B) (B)의 the numbers(그 숫자들)는 주어진 글에 나온 퍼센트를 가리킴
② (B) — (A) — (C) (A) 앞에는 자동화하기 어려운 것과 반대되는 내용이 나와야 함
③ (B) — (C) — (A) 많은 일자리가 자동화의 발전으로 위기에 처함 – (B) 단순한 일을 하는 로봇은 전체 직원을 대체할 수도 있음 – (C) 고도로 숙련된 직업들도 위기에 처함 – (A) 창의적으로 문제를 해결하는 역할은 자동화할 수 없음
④ (C) — (A) — (B) (C)에서 고도로 숙련된 직업들 '또한' 위기에 처해 있다고 했는데
⑤ (C) — (B) — (A) 주어진 글에는 위기에 처한 다른 직업이 없음

| 문제 풀이 순서 | ✱✱❋ [정답률 67%]

1st 각 문단의 내용을 파악하고, 글의 논리적인 순서를 추론한다.

주어진 글: 상황이 변화하고 있다. 캐나다의 일자리 중 42퍼센트가 위기에 처해 있고, 미국의 일자리 중 62퍼센트가 자동화의 발전으로 인해 위기에 처할 것이라고 보도되어 왔다. 단서

→ 주어진 글 뒤: 자동화로 인해 사라지는 일자리와 사라지지 않는 일자리에는 어떤 것들이 있는지 설명하는 내용이 이어질 것이다. 발상

(A): 하지만(However), 자동화하기 어려운 것은 창의적으로 문제들을 해결하는 능력이다. '(기계적인 일을) 하는' 역할의 노동자들은 로봇들에 의해 대체될 수 있는 반면에, 창의적으로 문제를 해결하는 역할은 대체 불가능한 개인에 더 의존한다.

→ (A) 앞: 역접의 연결어 However로 자동화하기 어려운 직업의 특성을 언급하고 있으므로, 앞에는 이와 대조되는 자동화가 가능한 직업들이 언급되어야 한다.
▶ 주어진 글 바로 뒤에 (A)가 올 수 없음
(A) 뒤: 기계적으로 작업하는 직업은 대체되고 창의적으로 문제를 해결하는 직업은 대체되기 어렵다는 문장으로 마무리했다.
▶ (A)가 마지막에 올 확률이 높음

(B): 여러분은 그 숫자들(the numbers)이 약간 비현실적으로 보인다고 말할지 모르지만, 그 위협은 현실이다. 한 패스트푸드 체인점은 10초 안에 버거 하나를 뒤집을 수 있는 로봇을 가지고 있다. 그것은 단지 단순한 일일 뿐이지만 그 로봇은 전체 직원을 대체할 수도 있다.

→ (B) 앞: 1 '그 숫자들(the numbers)'이 가리키는 대상이 앞에 나와야 한다.
2 자동화로 인해 사라지는 캐나다와 미국 내 직업의 비율이 주어진 글에 있다.
▶ (B) 앞에 주어진 글이 와야 함 (순서: 주어진 글 ➡ (B))
(B) 뒤: 단순노동을 하는 직업이 자동화될 수 있다고 했으므로, 반대로 자동화되지 않을 직업에 관한 내용이 이어질 것이다.

(C): 고도로 숙련된 직업들 또한(also) 위기에 처해 있다. 예를 들면, 슈퍼컴퓨터는 질병에 대한 방대한 양의 의학 연구와 데이터를 이용하여 특정한 질병들에 대해 이용 가능한 치료법을 자동화된 방식으로 제안할 수 있다.

→ (C) 앞: also라고 했으므로 앞에 자동화될 수 있는 또 다른 직업의 예시가 나와야 한다.
▶ 버거를 뒤집는 단순한 노동의 일자리가 자동화될 수 있다고 한 (B)가 (C) 앞에 와야 함 (순서: 주어진 글 ➡ (B) ➡ (C))
(C) 뒤: 고도로 숙련된 슈퍼컴퓨터마저 자동화될 수 있음을 시사했으므로, 자동화되기 어려운 직업에 관해 이야기한 (A)가 올 것이다.
▶ (C) 뒤에 (A)가 이어져야 함 (순서: 주어진 글 ➡ (B) ➡ (C) ➡ (A))

2nd 글이 한눈에 들어오도록 정리하여 정답을 확인한다.

주어진 글: 세계적으로 자동화로 인해 사라지는 일자리가 상당히 많다.
→ (B): 그 수치가 비현실적으로 느껴지겠지만, 실제로 한 패스트푸드 체인점에서 도입한 로봇이 햄버거 조리라는 단순한 업무를 하는 인력을 대거 대체할 수도 있다.
→ (C): 슈퍼컴퓨터가 데이터를 이용하여 질병 치료법을 제안할 수 있는 것처럼, 고도로 숙련된 직업들 역시 자동화될 위기에 처해 있다.
→ (A): 하지만 단순한 기계적 업무가 아닌 창의적인 문제 해결 능력을 요구하는 업무는 로봇에 의해 대체되기 어렵다.
▶ 주어진 글 다음에 이어질 글의 순서는 (B) ➡ (C) ➡ (A)이므로 정답은 ③임

O 21 정답 ④ *청소년이 그릇된 결정을 내릴 확률이 높은 이유

The adolescent brain is not fully developed / until its early twenties. //
청소년기의 뇌는 완전히 발달하지 않는다 / 20대 초반까지는 //

This means / the way / the adolescents' decision-making circuits integrate and process information / may put them at a disadvantage. // 단서1 청소년의 불완전한 뇌 발달은 의사 결정 시 청소년을 불리하게 만듦
이것은 의미한다 / 방식이 / 청소년의 의사 결정 회로가 정보를 통합하고 처리하는 / 그들을 불리하게 만들 수 있음을 //

단서 2 (C)와 상반되는 내용이 On the other hand로 연결됨

(A) On the other hand, / the limbic system matures earlier, /
분사구문을 이끄는 현재분사
playing a central role / in processing emotional responses. //
반면 / 대뇌변연계는 더 일찍 성숙하여 / 중심적인 역할을 한다 / 정서적 반응을 처리하는 데 //

Because of its earlier development, / it is more likely to influence
decision-making. //
그것의 더 이른 발달로 인해 / 그것이 의사 결정에 영향을 미칠 가능성이 더 높다 //
수동태 동사
Decision-making in the adolescent brain / is led by emotional
factors / more than the perception of consequences. //
청소년기의 뇌에서 의사 결정은 / 감정적인 요인에 의해 이끌어진다 / 결과의 인식보다 //

(B) Due to these differences, / there is an imbalance /
이러한 차이점 때문에 / 불균형이 존재한다 **단서 3** (C)와 (A)에서 청소년기의 뇌가 얼마나 다른지에 대한 설명이 언급된 후에 나와야 함
between feeling-based decision-making / ruled by the more
between A and B 구문 *과거분사*
mature limbic system / and logical-based decision-making / by
the not-yet-mature prefrontal cortex. //
감정 기반 의사 결정과 / 더 성숙한 대뇌변연계에 의해 지배되는 / 논리 기반 의사 결정
사이에는 / 아직 성숙하지 않은 전전두엽 피질에 의한 //
간접의문문(의문사+주어+동사)
This may explain / why some teens are more likely to make bad
decisions. // **단서 4** 주어진 글에 이어서 뇌 영역 중 나중에 발달하는 영역을 먼저 언급함
이것은 설명해 줄 수 있다 / 왜 일부 십 대들이 그릇된 결정을 내릴 가능성이 더 높은지를 //
주격 관계대명사
(C) One of their brain regions / that matures later / is the
과거분사 (the prefrontal cortex 수식)
prefrontal cortex, / which is the control center, / tasked with
thinking ahead and evaluating consequences. //
뇌 영역 중 하나는 / 나중에 성숙하는 / 전전두엽 피질이며 / 통제 센터인 / 그것은 미리
생각하고 결과를 평가하는 임무를 맡고 있다 //
prevent A from -ing: A가 ~하는 것을 막다
It is the area of the brain / responsible for preventing you from
sending off an initial angry text / and modifying it with kinder
words. //
병렬 구조
그것은 뇌의 영역이다 / 당신이 초기의 화가 난 문자를 보내는 것을 막고 / 그것을 더 친절한
단어로 수정하게 하는 역할을 하는 //

- adolescent ⓐ 청소년기의 · decision-making ⓝ 의사결정
- circuit ⓝ 회로 · process ⓥ 처리하다
- put ~ at a disadvantage ~을 불리하게 만들다
- on the other hand 반면에 · mature ⓥ 성숙해지다 ⓐ 성숙한
- influence ⓥ ⓝ 영향을 미치다 · factor ⓝ 요인
- imbalance ⓝ 불균형 · feeling-based ⓐ 감정에 기반한
- rule ⓥ 지배하다 · logical-based ⓐ 논리에 기반한
- evaluate ⓥ 평가하다 · initial ⓐ 초기의 · modify ⓥ 수정하다

청소년의 뇌는 20대 초반까지는 완전히 발달하지 않는다. 이것은 청소년의
의사 결정 회로가 정보를 통합하고 처리하는 방식이 그들을 불리하게 만들 수
있음을 의미한다. (C) 나중에 성숙하는 뇌 영역 중 하나는 통제 센터인 전전두
엽 피질이며, 그것은 미리 생각하고 결과를 평가하는 임무를 맡고 있다. 그것은
당신이 초기의 화가 난 문자를 보내는 것을 막고 그것을 더 친절한 단어로 수정
하게 하는 역할을 하는 뇌의 영역이다. (A) 반면 대뇌변연계는 더 일찍 성숙하
여 정서적 반응을 처리하는 데 중심적인 역할을 한다. 그것의 더 이른 발달로
인해 그것이 의사 결정에 영향을 미칠 가능성이 더 높다. 청소년기의 뇌에서 의
사 결정은 결과의 인식보다 감정적인 요인에 의해 이끌어진다. (B) 이러한 차이
점 때문에 더 성숙한 대뇌변연계에 의해 지배되는 감정 기반 의사 결정과 아직
성숙하지 않은 전전두엽 피질에 의한 논리 기반 의사 결정 사이에는 불균형이
존재한다. 이것은 왜 일부 십 대들이 그릇된 결정을 내릴 가능성이 더 높은지를
설명해 줄 수 있다.

주어진 글 다음에 이어질 글의 순서로 가장 적절한 것을 고르시오. [3점]

① (A) — (C) — (B) (A)는 주어진 글과 상반되는 (On the other hand) 내용이 아님

② (B) — (A) — (C)
③ (B) — (C) — (A) 주어진 글에는 (B)의 차이점을 가리킬 만한 내용이 없음

④ (C) — (A) — (B) (C) 청소년의 뇌에서 늦게 발달하는 영역이 있음 — (A) 반면, 청소년의 뇌에서 빨리 발달하는 영역이 있음 — (B) 이러한 차이점 때문에 청소년은 그릇된 결정을 내릴 가능성이 높아짐

⑤ (C) — (B) — (A) (A)에서 발달 속도가 다른 뇌의 영역을 모두 소개한 후, (B)에서 그 차이로 인한 결과를 설명해야 함

| 문제 풀이 순서 | ★★※ [정답률 68%]

1st 각 문단의 내용을 파악하고, 글의 논리적인 순서를 추론한다.

▸ **주어진 글:** 청소년기의 뇌는 20대 초반까지는 완전히 발달하지 않는다.
이것은 청소년의 의사 결정 회로가 정보를 통합하고 처리하는 방식이
그들을 불리하게 만들 수 있음을 의미한다. **단서**

➡ **주어진 글 뒤:** 청소년기에 뇌가 어떻게 발달하는지, 그리고 그것이 그들을 왜
불리하게 만드는지에 관한 자세한 설명이 이어질 것이다. **발상**

▸ **(A):** 반면(On the other hand) 대뇌변연계는 더 일찍 성숙하여 정서적
반응을 처리하는 데 중심적인 역할을 한다. 그것의 더 이른 발달로 인해
그것이 의사 결정에 영향을 미칠 가능성이 더 높다. 청소년기의 뇌에서
의사 결정은 결과의 인식보다 감정적인 요인에 의해 이끌어진다.

➡ **(A) 앞:** 역접의 연결어 On the other hand로 청소년기에 일찍 발달하는 뇌의
영역을 설명하고 있으므로, 앞에는 청소년기보다 늦게 발달하는 뇌의 영역을
언급해야 한다. ▶ 주어진 글 바로 뒤에 (A)가 올 수 없음

(A) 뒤: 청소년기에 뇌의 특정 영역의 발달 시기가 달라짐으로써 어떤 결과를
가져오는지에 대한 내용이 이어질 것이다.

▸ **(B):** 이러한 차이점 때문에(Due to these differences) 더 성숙한
대뇌변연계에 의해 지배되는 감정 기반 의사 결정과 아직 성숙하지 않은
전전두엽 피질에 의한 논리 기반 의사 결정 사이에는 불균형이 존재한다.
이것은 왜 일부 십 대들이 그릇된 결정을 내릴 가능성이 더 높은지를
설명해 줄 수 있다.

➡ **(B) 앞:** 대뇌변연계는 이미 (A)에서 언급되었고 (A)의 앞에 청소년기보다 늦게
발달하는 뇌의 영역을 언급해야 하는데, (B)에 나타난 전전두엽 피질이 이에
해당한다는 것을 유추할 수 있다. 전전두엽 피질과 대뇌변연계를 순서대로 설명한
뒤에 이들을 종합하는 (B)가 이어지는 흐름이므로, 대뇌변연계가 언급된 (A)가
앞에 와야 한다. ▶ (A)에 이어지는 내용임 (순서: (A) → (B))

(B) 뒤: 의사 결정 사이의 불균형은 십 대들이 그릇된 결정을 내릴 가능성이 높은
이유라고 언급하며 글을 마무리한다.

▸ **(C):** 나중에 성숙하는 뇌 영역 중 하나는 통제 센터인 전전두엽 피질이며,
그것은 미리 생각하고 결과를 평가하는 임무를 맡고 있다. 그것은 당신이
초기의 화가 난 문자를 보내는 것을 막고 그것을 더 친절한 단어로
수정하게 하는 역할을 하는 뇌의 영역이다.

➡ **(C) 앞:** 청소년기보다 나중에 발달하는 뇌의 영역이 있다는 내용을 언급해야 한다.
▶ 주어진 글에 이어지는 내용임 (순서: 주어진 글 → (C))

(C) 뒤: 반대로 청소년기보다 오히려 빨리 발달하는 뇌의 영역인 대뇌변연계가
언급된 (A)가 이어질 것이다.
▶ (C) 뒤에 (A)가 이어져야 함 (순서: 주어진 글 → (C) → (A) → (B))

2nd 글이 한눈에 들어오도록 정리하여 정답을 확인한다.

▸ **주어진 글:** 청소년기에는 뇌가 완전히 발달하지 않아서 의사 결정 시 불리할 수 있다.

➡ **(C):** 결과를 미리 평가하는 전전두엽 피질은 청소년기보다 늦게 발달한다.

➡ **(A):** 반면, 정서적인 반응을 다루는 대뇌변연계는 청소년기에 빨리 발달한다.

➡ **(B):** 이러한 차이점 때문에 청소년기는 감정에 기반한 그릇된 결정을 내릴
가능성이 높다.

▶ 주어진 글 다음에 이어질 글의 순서는 (C) → (A) → (B)이므로 정답은 ④임

정답 ③ *딥 러닝 얼굴 인식 접근법의 한계와 극복 방안

Despite the remarkable progress / in deep-learning based facial recognition approaches / in recent years, / **in terms of** identification performance, / they still have limitations. //
눈에 띄는 발전에도 불구하고 / 딥 러닝 기반의 얼굴 인식 접근법의 / 최근 몇 년 동안 / 식별 성능 측면에서 / 여전히 그것은 한계를 가지고 있다 //

These limitations relate / to the database **used** in the learning stage. // (과거분사(the database 수식))
단서 1 딥 러닝 얼굴 인식 접근법의 한계는 딥 러닝이 학습하는 데이터베이스와 관련 있음
이러한 한계는 관련이 있다 / 학습 단계에서 사용되는 데이터베이스와 //

단서 2 (B)와 (C)에서 언급된 시간에 따라 사람의 얼굴이 바뀐다는 문제를 가리킴
(A) **To counteract** this problem, / researchers **have developed** models / for face aging or digital de-aging. // (부사적 용법(목적)) (현재완료)
이 문제에 대응하기 위해 / 연구자들은 모델을 개발했다 / 얼굴 노화나 디지털 노화 완화의 //

It **is used to compensate** for the differences / in facial characteristics, / **which** appear over a given time period. // (be used to-v: ~하는 데 쓰이다) (계속적 용법의 주격 관계대명사)
그것은 차이를 보완하는 데 사용된다 / 얼굴 특성의 / 주어진 기간 동안 나타나는 //

(B) If the **selected** database / does not contain enough instances, / the result may be systematically affected. // (과거분사(database 수식))
선택된 데이터베이스가 / 충분한 사례를 포함하지 않으면 / 그 결과가 시스템적으로 영향을 받을 수 있다 //
단서 3 주어진 글에 딥 러닝이 학습하는 데이터베이스 때문에 문제가 발생한다는 내용 뒤에 이어짐

For example, / the performance of a facial biometric system may decrease / if the person **to be identified** / was enrolled over 10 years ago. // (형용사적 용법(person 수식))
예를 들어 / 안면 생체 측정 시스템의 성능이 저하될 수 있다 / 식별될 사람이 / 10년도 더 전에 등록된 경우 //
단서 4 (B)에서 언급된 '오래된 데이터'를 구체적으로 설명하고 있음

(C) The factor **to consider** / is **that** this person may experience changes / in the texture of the face, / particularly with the appearance of wrinkles and sagging skin. // (형용사적 용법(factor 수식)) (명사절 접속사)
고려해야 할 요인은 / 이 사람이 변화를 경험할 수 있다는 것이다 / 얼굴의 질감 / 특히 주름과 처진 피부가 나타나는 것을 동반한 //

These changes may be highlighted / by weight gain or loss. //
이러한 변화는 두드러질 수 있다 / 체중 증가 또는 감소에 의해 //

- remarkable ⓐ 눈에 띄는, 두드러진
- progress ⓝ 발전, 진전
- facial ⓐ 얼굴의
- recognition ⓝ 인식
- identification ⓝ 식별
- performance ⓝ 성능
- limitation ⓝ 한계
- relate to ~와 관련이 있다
- counteract ⓥ 대응하다
- compensate for ~을 보완하다
- characteristic ⓝ 특징
- instance ⓝ 사례, 예시
- systematically ⓐⓓ 체계적으로
- enroll ⓥ 등록하다
- factor ⓝ 요인
- texture ⓝ 질감
- particularly ⓐⓓ 특히
- appearance ⓝ 발현, 나타나는 것
- wrinkle ⓝ 주름
- highlight ⓥ 강조하다

최근 몇 년 동안 딥 러닝 기반의 얼굴 인식 접근법의 눈에 띄는 발전에도 불구하고, 식별 성능 측면에서 여전히 그것은 한계를 가지고 있다. 이러한 한계는 학습 단계에서 사용되는 데이터베이스와 관련이 있다. (B) 선택된 데이터베이스가 충분한 사례를 포함하지 않으면 그 결과가 시스템적으로 영향을 받을 수 있다. 예를 들어 식별될 사람이 10년도 더 전에 등록된 경우 안면 생체 측정 시스템의 성능이 저하될 수 있다. (C) 고려해야 할 요인은 이 사람이 특히 주름과 처진 피부가 나타나는 것을 동반한 얼굴의 질감 변화를 경험할 수 있다는 것이다. 이러한 변화는 체중 증가 또는 감소에 의해 두드러질 수 있다. (A) 이 문제에 대응하기 위해 연구자들은 얼굴 노화나 디지털 노화 완화의 모델을 개발했다. 그것은 주어진 기간 동안 나타나는 얼굴 특성의 차이를 보완하는 데 사용된다.

주어진 글 다음에 이어질 글의 순서로 가장 적절한 것을 고르시오.

① (A) — (C) — (B) 주어진 글에는 (A)의 '문제'를 가리킬 만한 내용이 구체화되지 않음
② (B) — (A) — (C) (A)의 '문제'는 (B)와 (A)의 내용을 모두 포함함
③ (B) — (C) — (A) (B) 데이터베이스가 너무 적거나 오래된 경우 성능이 저하됨 — (C) 사람은 시간이 지나고 체중이 바뀌면서 얼굴의 질감에 변화가 일어남 — (A) 이 문제에 대응하기 위해 연구자들은 새로운 모델을 개발해 노화의 차이를 보완함
④ (C) — (A) — (B)
⑤ (C) — (B) — (A) (C)는 (B)에서 언급된 '오래 전에 등록된 데이터'를 구체적으로 설명하고 있으므로 (B) 뒤에 이어져야 함

| 문제 풀이 순서 | ★★★ [정답률 53%]

1st 각 문단의 내용을 파악하고, 글의 논리적인 순서를 추론한다.

주어진 글: 최근 몇 년 동안 딥 러닝 기반의 얼굴 인식 접근법의 눈에 띄는 발전에도 불구하고, 식별 성능 측면에서 여전히 그것은 한계를 가지고 있다. 이러한 한계는 학습 단계에서 사용되는 데이터베이스와 관련이 있다. (단서)

➡ **주어진 글 뒤:** 딥 러닝이 학습하는 데이터베이스에 어떤 한계가 있는지 설명할 것이다. (발상)

(A): 이 문제(this problem)에 대응하기 위해 연구자들은 얼굴 노화나 디지털 노화 완화의 모델을 개발했다. 그것은 주어진 기간 동안 나타나는 얼굴 특성의 차이를 보완하는 데 사용된다.

➡ **(A) 앞:** '이 문제'라고 했으므로 앞에 구체적인 문제가 언급되어야 한다.
▶ 주어진 글 바로 뒤에 (A)가 올 수 없음
(A) 뒤: 앞에서 언급된 문제에 대응하기 위해 연구자들은 새로운 모델을 개발해 노화의 차이를 보완했다고 설명하므로, (A)가 글의 결론일 것이다.
▶ (A)가 마지막에 올 확률이 높음

(B): 선택된 데이터베이스가 충분한 사례를 포함하지 않으면 그 결과가 시스템적으로 영향을 받을 수 있다. 예를 들어 식별될 사람이 10년도 더 전에 등록된 경우 안면 생체 측정 시스템의 성능이 저하될 수 있다.

➡ **(B) 앞:** 선택된 데이터베이스가 너무 적거나 오래되었을 때 문제가 발생할 수 있다고 설명하고 있으므로, 주어진 글에서 말한 데이터베이스의 한계를 소개하고 있다. ▶ 주어진 글에 이어지는 내용임 (순서: 주어진 글 → (B))
(B) 뒤: 이러한 데이터베이스의 한계를 고려할 때 무엇을 염두에 두어야 하는지를 구체적으로 설명할 것이다. ▶ (C)가 이어질 확률이 높음

(C): 고려해야 할 요인은 이 사람(this person)이 특히 주름과 처진 피부가 나타나는 것을 동반한 얼굴의 질감 변화를 경험할 수 있다는 것이다. 이러한 변화는 체중 증가 또는 감소에 의해 두드러질 수 있다.

➡ **(C) 앞:** (B)에서 예시로 언급한 '식별될 사람'이 (C)에서 this person으로 다시 언급되었다. 사람은 체중이 변하면서 얼굴도 변할 수 있다고 설명하고 있으므로, (B)에서 언급한 '오래된 데이터베이스'를 구체적으로 설명하고 있다.
▶ (B)에 이어지는 내용임 (순서: 주어진 글 → (B) → (C))
(C) 뒤: 데이터베이스가 이러한 문제를 지닐 때, 이를 어떻게 해결할지에 대한 내용이 소개될 것이다.
▶ (A)가 이어져야 함 (순서: 주어진 글 → (B) → (C) → (A))

2nd 글이 한눈에 들어오도록 정리하여 정답을 확인한다.

주어진 글: 딥 러닝 얼굴 인식 접근법의 한계는 데이터베이스와 관련 있다.
➡ **(B):** 데이터베이스가 너무 적거나 오래된 경우, 시스템의 성능이 저하될 수 있다.
➡ **(C):** 사람은 시간이 지나고 체중이 바뀌면서 얼굴의 질감에 변화가 일어난다.
➡ **(A):** 이 문제에 대응하기 위해 연구자들은 새로운 모델을 개발해 노화의 차이를 보완했다.
▶ 주어진 글 다음에 이어질 글의 순서는 (B) → (C) → (A)이므로 정답은 ③임

O 23 정답 ② *마그마의 결정 형성

Natural processes form minerals / in many ways. //
자연 과정은 광물을 형성한다 / 많은 방법으로 //
For example, / hot melted rock material, / called magma, /
앞에 주격 관계대명사와 be동사가 생략됨
cools / when it reaches the Earth's surface, / or even if it's
trapped / below the surface. //
예를 들어, / 뜨거운 용암 물질은 / 마그마라고 불리는 / 식는다 / 그것이 지구의 표면에
도달할 때 / 또는 심지어 갇혔을 때도 / 표면 아래에 //
As magma cools, / its atoms lose heat energy, / move closer
together, / and begin to combine into compounds. //
병렬구조
마그마가 식으면서 / 마그마의 원자는 열에너지를 잃고 / 서로 더 가까이 이동해 /
화합물로 결합하기 시작한다 //
단서 1 마그마가 식으면서 화합물로 결합함

(A) Also, / the size of the crystals / that form / depends partly /
핵심 주어(단수)   단수 동사
on how rapidly the magma cools. // **단서 2** 광물의 종류를 결정할 뿐만 아니라
또한 / 결정의 크기는 / 형성되는 / 부분적으로 달려있다 / 마그마가 얼마나 빨리 식느냐에 //
결정의 크기에도 영향을 끼친다는 추가 내용
When magma cools slowly, / the crystals that form are generally
주격 관계대명사절
large enough / to see with the unaided eye. // 마그마가 천천히 식으면 /
형성되는 결정은 일반적으로 충분히 크다 / 육안으로 볼 수 있을 만큼 //
단서 3 마그마가 식는 과정에서 원자가 배열되어 화합물이 형성됨
(B) During this process, / atoms of the different compounds
arrange themselves / into orderly repeating patterns. //
이 과정 동안 / 서로 다른 화합물의 원자가 스스로를 배열한다 / 질서 있고 반복적인 패턴으로 //
앞에 주격 관계대명사와 be동사가 생략됨
The type and amount of elements / present in a magma / partly
determine / which minerals will form. //
원소의 종류와 양이 / 마그마에 존재하는 / 부분적으로 결정한다 / 어떤 광물이 형성될지를 //
(C) This is because the atoms have enough time / to move
병렬구조
together / and form into larger crystals. //
이것은 원자가 충분한 시간을 가지기 때문이다 / 함께 이동하고 / 더 큰 결정을 형성할 //
주격 관계대명사절
When magma cools rapidly, / the crystals that form will be
small. // **단서 4** 천천히 식은 마그마의 결정이 큰 이유 설명함
마그마가 빠르게 식으면 / 형성되는 결정은 작을 것이다 //
In such cases, / you can't easily see individual mineral crystals. //
그런 경우에는 / 당신은 개별 광물 결정을 쉽게 볼 수 없다 //

- natural ⓐ 자연의 · mineral ⓝ 광물 · melt ⓥ 녹이다, 녹다
- material ⓝ 물질 · surface ⓝ 표면 · trap ⓥ 가두다
- atom ⓝ 원자 · crystal ⓝ 결정(체) · rapidly ⓐ𝑑 빨리
- unaided ⓐ 도움 없는 · arrange ⓥ 배열하다
- orderly ⓐ 질서 있는 · element ⓝ 원소

자연 과정은 많은 방법으로 광물을 형성한다. 예를 들어, 마그마라고 불리는
뜨거운 용암 물질은 지구의 표면에 도달할 때, 또는 심지어 표면 아래에 갇혔을
때도 식는다. 마그마가 식으면서, 마그마의 원자는 열에너지를 잃고, 서로 더
가까이 이동해, 화합물로 결합하기 시작한다. (B) 이 과정 동안, 서로 다른
화합물의 원자가 질서 있고 반복적인 패턴으로 스스로 배열된다. 마그마에
존재하는 원소의 종류와 양이 어떤 광물이 형성될지를 부분적으로 결정한다.
(A) 또한, 형성되는 결정의 크기는 부분적으로는 마그마가 얼마나 빨리
식느냐에 달려있다. 마그마가 천천히 식으면, 형성되는 결정은 일반적으로
육안으로 볼 수 있을 만큼 충분히 크다. (C) 이것은 원자가 함께 이동해 더
큰 결정을 형성할 충분한 시간을 가지기 때문이다. 마그마가 빠르게 식으면,
형성되는 결정은 작을 것이다. 그런 경우에는 당신은 개별 광물 결정을 쉽게 볼
수 없다.

주어진 글 다음에 이어질 글의 순서로 가장 적절한 것을 고르시오. [3점]

① (A) — (C) — (B) (B)의 과정을 먼저 거쳐야 (A), (C)의 설명이 나올 수 있음
② (B) — (A) — (C) 마그마는 식으면서 화합물로 결합함 — (B) 마그마가 배열되면서 어떤 광물이
형성될지 부분적으로 결정됨 — (A) 결정의 크기는 마그마가 식는 속도에
영향을 받으므로 천천히 식으면 결정이 큼 — (C) 빠르게 식으면 결정이 작음
③ (B) — (C) — (A) 처럼 진행된 후 (A)의 영향이 더해져 (C)의 결과가 나옴
④ (C) — (A) — (B) 적절한 순서와 정반대
⑤ (C) — (B) — (A) This로 가리키는 내용이 주어진 글에 없음

| 문제 풀이 순서 | ★★★ [정답률 59%]

1st 각 문단의 내용을 파악하고, 글의 논리적인 순서를 추론한다.

주어진 글: 자연 과정은 많은 방법으로 광물을 형성한다. 예를 들어, 마그마
라고 불리는 뜨거운 용암 물질은 지구의 표면에 도달할 때, 또는 심지어 표
면 아래에 갇혔을 때도 식는다. 마그마가 식으면서, 마그마의 원자는 열에
너지를 잃고, 서로 더 가까이 이동해, 화합물로 결합하기 시작한다. **단서**

➡ **주어진 글 뒤:** 마그마가 식으면서 어떤 화합물로 결합되고, 그 결과는 어떤지를
설명하는 내용이 이어질 것이다. **발상**

(A): 또한(Also), 형성되는 결정의 크기는 부분적으로는 마그마가 얼마나
빨리 식느냐에 달려있다. 마그마가 천천히 식으면, 형성되는 결정은 일반적
으로 육안으로 볼 수 있을 만큼 충분히 크다.

➡ **(A) 앞:** '또한(Also)'으로 결정의 크기가 마그마가 식는 속도에 달려있다는 내용이
이어지므로 앞에도 결정의 무언가를 좌우하는 요인이 있어야 한다.
▶ 주어진 글에는 결합한다는 내용만 있으므로 주어진 글이 (A) 바로 앞에 올 수
없음

(A) 뒤: 천천히 식는 경우에 대해 설명했으므로 빠르게 식는 경우에는 어떤지
이어서 설명할 것이다.

(B): 이 과정(this process) 동안, 서로 다른 화합물의 원자가 질서 있고
반복적인 패턴으로 스스로 배열된다. 마그마에 존재하는 원소의 종류와 양
이 어떤 광물이 형성될지를 부분적으로 결정한다.

➡ **(B) 앞:** ❶ '이 과정(this process)'이 무엇인지 나와야 한다.
❷ 주어진 글에서 말한 마그마가 식어서 화합물로 결합하는 과정을 말한다.
▶ (B) 앞에 주어진 글이 있어야 함 (순서: 주어진 글 ➡ (B))
(B) 뒤: 광물 형성에 영향을 주는 또 다른 요인이 올 것이다.
▶ 마그마의 식는 속도에 결정의 크기가 정해진다는 (A)가 (B) 뒤에 와야 함
(순서: 주어진 글 ➡ (B) ➡ (A))

(C): 이것(This)은 원자가 함께 이동해 더 큰 결정을 형성할 충분한 시간을
가지기 때문이다. 마그마가 빠르게 식으면, 형성되는 결정은 작을 것이다.
그런 경우에는 당신은 개별 광물 결정을 쉽게 볼 수 없다.

➡ **(C) 앞:** ❶ '이것(This)'이 가리키는 것이 앞에 나와야 한다.
❷ 마그마가 천천히 식으면 결정이 큰 이유를 설명하고 있으므로 This는 (A)의
내용을 가리킨다.
▶ (A)에 이어지는 내용임 (순서: 주어진 글 ➡ (B) ➡ (A) ➡ (C))

2nd 글이 한눈에 들어오도록 정리하여 정답을 확인한다.

주어진 글: 마그마는 흐르면서 열에너지를 잃고, 화합물로 결합한다.

➡ **(B):** 이 과정에서 마그마에 존재하는 원소의 종류와 양이 어떤 광물이 형성될지를
결정한다.

➡ **(A):** 마그마의 식는 속도에 결정의 크기가 결정되는데, 천천히 식으면 큰 결정이
형성된다.

➡ **(C):** 왜냐하면 큰 결정이 될 시간이 충분하기 때문이다. 마그마가 빠르게 식으면
형성되는 결정은 작아진다.

▶ 주어진 글 다음에 이어질 글의 순서는 (B) ➡ (A) ➡ (C)이므로 정답은 ②임

O 24 정답 ⑤ *흡혈귀가 존재할 수 없는 이유

According to legend, / <u>once</u> a vampire bites a person, / that person turns into a vampire / <u>who</u> seeks the blood of others. //
전설에 따르면 / 흡혈귀가 사람을 물면 / 그 사람은 흡혈귀로 변한다 / 다른 사람의 피를 갈구하는 //

A researcher came up with some simple math, / <u>which</u> proves that these highly popular creatures can't exist. //
한 연구자가 간단한 계산법을 생각해냈다 / 이 잘 알려진 존재가 실존할 수 없다는 것을 증명하는 //

단서 1 흡혈귀의 존재가 없는 것을 증명하는 계산법에 대한 내용이 이어져야 함

(A) In just two-and-a-half years, / the original human population / would all have become vampires / <u>with no humans left.</u> //
불과 2년 반 만에 / 원래의 인류는 / 모두 흡혈귀가 되어 / 인간이 더 이상 남아있지 않았을 것이다 //

단서 2 원래의 인류가 왜 더 이상 남아있지 않게 되는지 앞에 설명이 나와야 함

But look around you. //
하지만 주위를 둘러보아라 //

Have vampires taken over the world? //
흡혈귀가 세상을 정복하였는가 //

No, / because there's no such thing. //
아니다 / 왜냐하면 흡혈귀는 존재하지 않으니까 //

(B) If the first vampire <u>came</u> into existence / that day / and <u>bit</u> one person a month, / there would have been two vampires / by February 1st, 1600. //
최초의 흡혈귀가 생겨나서 / 그날 / 한 달에 한 명을 물었다면 / 흡혈귀가 둘 있었을 것이다 / 1600년 2월 1일까지 //

단서 3 that day가 가리키는 날은 (C)에서 말한 1600년 1월 1일임

A month later / there would have been four, / the next month eight, / then sixteen, / and so on. //
한 달 뒤면 / 넷이 될 것이고 / 그 다음 달은 여덟 / 그리고 열여섯 / 등등으로 계속 늘어나는 것이다 //

(C) University of Central Florida / physics professor Costas Efthimiou's work / breaks down the myth. //
University of Central Florida의 / 물리학과 교수 Costas Efthimiou의 연구가 / 그 미신을 무너뜨렸다 //

단서 4 the myth가 가리키는 내용이 주어진 글임

Suppose / <u>that</u> on January 1st, 1600, / the human population was just over five hundred million. //
가정해 보자 / 1600년 1월 1일에 / 인구가 5억 명이 넘는다고 //

· legend ⓝ 전설 · bite ⓥ 물다 · seek ⓥ 갈구하다
· come up with ~을 제시하다[생각해내다] · highly ⓐⓓ 매우
· creature ⓝ 존재 · exist ⓥ 존재하다 · original ⓐ 원래의
· take over ~을 정복하다 · existence ⓝ 존재 · and so on 등등
· myth ⓝ 사회적 통념, 미신 · suppose ⓥ 가정하다
· population ⓝ 인구

전설에 따르면, 흡혈귀가 사람을 물면 그 사람은 다른 사람의 피를 갈구하는 흡혈귀로 변한다. 한 연구자가 이 잘 알려진 존재가 실존할 수 없다는 것을 증명하는 간단한 계산법을 생각해냈다. (C) University of Central Florida의 물리학과 교수 Costas Efthimiou의 연구가 그 미신을 무너뜨렸다. 우선, 1600년 1월 1일에 인구가 5억 명이 넘는다고 가정해 보자. (B) 그날 최초의 흡혈귀가 생겨나서 한 달에 한 명을 물었다면, 1600년 2월 1일까지 흡혈귀가 둘 있었을 것이다. 한 달 뒤면 넷, 그 다음 달은 여덟, 그리고 열여섯 등등으로 계속 늘어나는 것이다. (A) 불과 2년 반 만에, 원래의 인류는 모두 흡혈귀가 되어 더 이상 남아있지 않았을 것이다. 하지만 주위를 둘러 보아라. 흡혈귀가 세상을 정복하였는가? 아니다. 왜냐하면 흡혈귀는 존재하지 않으니까.

주어진 글 다음에 이어질 글의 순서로 가장 적절한 것을 고르시오. [3점]

① (A) — (C) — (B) 결론이 나오는 (A)가 나오기 위해 필요한 가정이 주어진 글에 없음
② (B) — (A) — (C) (B)의 첫 문장에 나온 '그날(that day)'이 가리킬 수 있는 것이 주어진 글에 없음
③ (B) — (C) — (A)
④ (C) — (A) — (B) 흡혈귀가 매달 2배씩 증가하는 가정을 설명한 (B) 뒤에 결론인 (A)가 와야 함
⑤ (C) — (B) — (A) (C) 물리학과 교수의 가정 - (B) 흡혈귀가 매달 2배씩 늘어남 -(A) 계산에 따르면 2년 반만에 인류가 모두 흡혈귀로 변하는데, 현재 인류가 존재하므로 흡혈귀가 없음을 증명한 것임

| 문제 풀이 순서 | ★★★ [정답률 66%]

1st 각 문단의 내용을 파악하고, 글의 논리적인 순서를 추론한다.

주어진 글: 전설에 따르면, 흡혈귀가 사람을 물면 그 사람은 다른 사람의 피를 갈구하는 흡혈귀로 변한다. 한 연구자가 이 잘 알려진 존재가 실존할 수 없다는 것을 증명하는 간단한 계산법을 생각해냈다.

➡ 주어진 글 뒤: 한 연구자가 흡혈귀는 존재하지 않는다는 것을 증명하는 간단한 계산법을 생각해냈다는 내용이 나오므로 단서 이 내용을 구체적으로 설명하는 문단이 뒤에 와야 할 것이다. 발상

(A): 불과 2년 만에(In just two-and-a-half years), 원래의 인류는 모두 흡혈귀가 되어 더 이상 남아있지 않았을 것이다. 하지만 주위를 둘러 보아라. 흡혈귀가 세상을 정복하였는가? 아니다. 왜냐하면 흡혈귀는 존재하지 않으니까.

➡ (A) 앞: **1** '불과 2년반 만에(In just two-a-half years)'라고 했으므로 앞에서 어떤 것을 가정했을 것이다.
2 가정한 것과 같은 계산에 따르면 인류가 모두 흡혈귀로 변했어야 하는데 그렇지 않으므로 흡혈귀는 없다고 했다.
▶ 가정하는 내용이 없으므로 (A) 앞에 주어진 글이 올 수 없음
(A) 뒤: 현재 인류가 존재하므로 흡혈귀는 없다는 결론을 이야기했다.
▶ (A)가 마지막에 올 확률이 높음

(B): 그날(that day) 최초의 흡혈귀가 생겨나서 한 달에 한 명을 물었다면, 1600년 2월 1일까지 흡혈귀가 둘 있었을 것이다. 한 달 뒤면 넷, 그 다음 달은 여덟, 그리고 열여섯 등등으로 계속 늘어나는 것이다.

➡ (B) 앞: **1** '그날(that day)'로 가리키는 것이 앞에 나와야 한다.
2 최초의 흡혈귀가 생겨나서 한 달에 한 명을 물면, 1600년 2월 1일에 흡혈귀는 둘이 되었을 것이고, 이런 식으로 계속 늘어났을 것이라고 했다.
▶ (B) 앞에 주어진 글이 올 수 없음
(B) 뒤: 이런 가정이 어떤 결과를 가져오는지에 대한 내용이 (A)에 나왔으므로 (A)는 (B) 뒤에 이어져야 한다.
▶ (B) 뒤에 (A)가 와야 함 (순서: (B) ➡ (A))

(C): University of Central Florida의 물리학과 교수 Costas Efthimiou의 연구가 그 미신(the myth)을 무너뜨렸다. 우선, 1600년 1월 1일에 인구가 5억 명이 넘는다고 가정해보자.

➡ (C) 앞: 물리학과 교수 Costas Efthimiou가 '그 미신(the myth)'을 무너뜨렸다는 내용이 나온다. 여기서 언급된 '그 미신(the myth)'은 주어진 글에서 말한 흡혈귀의 존재이다.
▶ (C) 앞에 주어진 글이 와야 함 (순서: 주어진 글 ➡ (C))
(C) 뒤: 1600년 1월 1일에 인구가 5억 명이 넘는다고 가정해보자고 했는데, (B)의 첫 문장에 나온 '그날(that day)'이 바로 이 1600년 1월 1일을 가리킨다. 따라서 (B)는 (C) 뒤에 이어져야 한다.
▶ (C) 뒤에 (B)가 와야 함 (순서: 주어진 글 ➡ (C) ➡ (B) ➡ (A))

2nd 글이 한눈에 들어오도록 정리하여 정답을 확인한다.

주어진 글: 한 연구자가 흡혈귀는 존재하지 않는다는 것을 증명하는 간단한 계산법을 생각해냈다.
➡ (C): 1600년 1월 1일에 인구가 5억 명이 넘었다고 가정하자.
➡ (B): 그날 흡혈귀가 생겨나 달마다 한 명을 물면, 매달 2배씩 흡혈귀로 변할 것이다.
➡ (A): 2년 반 만에 인류는 모두 흡혈귀가 되어야 하지만, 그렇지 않으므로 흡혈귀는 없다.
▶ 주어진 글 다음에 이어질 순서는 (C) ➡ (B) ➡ (A)이므로 정답은 ⑤임

O 25 정답 ③ *소년이 그린 손의 의미

Mrs. Klein told her first graders / to draw a picture / of something to be thankful for. //
— tell+목적어+목적격보어
— 형용사적 용법(something 수식)
— 목적어절을 이끄는 접속사

Klein 선생님은 1학년 학생들에게 말했다 / 그려보라고 / 감사히 여기는 것을 //

She thought / that most of the class / would draw turkeys or Thanksgiving tables. //

그녀는 생각했다 / 반 아이들 대부분이 / 칠면조나 추수감사절 식탁을 그릴 것으로 //
— -thing으로 끝나는 대명사는 형용사가 뒤에서 수식

But Douglas drew something different. //
단서 1 Douglas가 무엇을 그렸는지 뒤에 설명이 이어져야 함

하지만 Douglas는 그렸다 / 색다른 것을 //

(A) The class was so responsive / that Mrs. Klein had almost forgotten about Douglas. //
— so ~ that ...: 너무 ~해서 ...하다
단서 2 반 아이들이 '손'에 대해 앞다투어 말한 것에 이어짐

반 아이들의 호응에 / Klein 선생님은 Douglas에 대해 하마터면 잊어버릴 뻔했다 //

After she had the others at work / on another project, / she asked Douglas / whose hand it was. //
— 의문형용사

그녀는 나머지 아이들에게 하도록 지도한 후 / 다른 과제를 / Douglas에게 물었다 / 그 손이 누구의 것인지 //

He answered softly, / "It's yours. Thank you, Mrs. Klein." //

그는 조용히 대답했다 / "선생님 손이에요. 고마워요, Klein 선생님" //

(B) Douglas was a boy / who usually spent time alone / and stayed around her / while his classmates went outside together / during break time. //
— 주격 관계대명사

Douglas는 소년이었다 / 보통 혼자 시간을 보내는 / 그리고 그녀 주변에 머무르는 / 그의 반 친구들이 함께 밖으로 나가 있는 동안 / 쉬는 시간에 //
— 선행사를 포함하는 관계대명사

What the boy drew / was a hand. // **단서 3** Douglas는 손을 그림

그 소년이 그린 것은 / 손이었다 //

But whose hand? //

그런데 누구의 손일까 //

His image immediately / attracted the other students' interest. //

그의 그림은 즉시 / 다른 학생들의 관심을 끌었다 //
단서 4 (B)에 나온 hand에 대한 내용이 이어짐

(C) So, / everyone rushed to talk / about whose hand it was. //

그래서 / 모두가 앞 다투어 말하려 했다 / 그것이 누구의 손인지에 관해 //
— 주격 관계대명사

"It must be the hand of God / that brings us food," / said one student. //

"그것은 신의 손이 틀림없어 / 우리에게 음식을 가져다주는"이라고 / 한 학생이 말했다 //
— 뒤에 hand 생략

"A farmer's," / said a second student, / "because they raise the turkeys." //

"농부의 손이야"라고 / 두 번째 학생이 말했다 / "왜냐하면 그들은 칠면조를 기르거든" //
— 뒤에 hand 생략

"It looks more like a police officer's," / added another, / "they protect us." //

"경찰관의 손과 더 비슷해 보여"라고 / 또 다른 학생이 덧붙였다 / "그들은 우리를 보호해 줘" //

- turkey ⓝ 칠면조
- Thanksgiving ⓝ 추수감사절
- responsive ⓐ 호응하는
- alone ⓐⅾ 혼자서
- break ⓝ 휴식
- immediately ⓐⅾ 즉시
- attract ⓥ (마음을) 끌다
- rush ⓥ 서두르다, 급히 움직이다
- raise ⓥ 기르다

Klein 선생님은 1학년 학생들에게 감사히 여기는 것을 그려보라고 말했다. 그녀는 반 아이들 대부분이 칠면조나 추수감사절 식탁을 그릴 것으로 생각했다. 하지만 Douglas는 색다른 것을 그렸다. (B) 그의 반 친구들이 쉬는 시간에 함께 밖으로 나가 있는 동안, 보통 Douglas는 혼자 시간을 보내고 그녀 주변에 머무르는 소년이었다. 그 소년이 그린 것은 손이었다. 그런데 누구의 손일까? 그의 그림은 즉시 다른 학생들의 관심을 끌었다. (C) 그래서, 모두들 그것이 누구의 손인지에 관해 앞다투어 말하려 했다. "그것은 우리에게 음식을 가져다주는 신의 손이 틀림없어."라고 한 학생이 말했다. "농부의 손이야, 왜냐하면 그들은 칠면조를 기르거든."이라고 두 번째 학생이 말했다. "경찰관의 손과 더 비슷해 보여, 그들은 우리를 보호해 줘."라고 또 다른 학생이 덧붙였다. (A) 반 아이들의 호응에 Klein 선생님은 Douglas에 대해 하마터면 잊어버릴 뻔했다. 그녀는 나머지

아이들에게 다른 과제를 하도록 지도한 후, Douglas에게 그 손이 누구의 것인지 물었다. "선생님 손이에요. 고마워요, Klein 선생님."이라고 그는 조용히 대답했다.

주어진 글 다음에 이어질 글의 순서로 가장 적절한 것을 고르시오.

① (A) — (C) — (B) 반 아이들이 무엇에 호응하고 있는지 (A) 앞에 먼저 나와야 함
② (B) — (A) — (C) (C)에서 반 아이들이 앞다투어 말한 후에 (A)에서 Douglas가 선생님의 손임을 밝히는 것으로 이어져야 함
③ (B) — (C) — (A) (B) Douglas가 감사히 여기는 것으로 손을 그림 - (C) 반 아이들이 누구의 손인지 앞다투어 말함 - (A) Douglas가 선생님의 손임을 밝힘
④ (C) — (A) — (B)
⑤ (C) — (B) — (A) (C) 앞에 손에 대한 설명이 먼저 제시되어야 함

| 문제 풀이 순서 | ★★❀ [정답률 81%]

1st 각 문단의 내용을 파악하고, 글의 논리적인 순서를 추론한다.

주어진 글: Klein 선생님은 1학년 학생들에게 감사히 여기는 것을 그려보라고 말했다. 그녀는 반 아이들 대부분이 칠면조나 추수감사절 식탁을 그릴 것으로 생각했다. 하지만 Douglas는 색다른 것을 그렸다.

➡ **주어진 글 뒤:** Klein 선생님이 1학년 학생들에게 감사히 여기는 것을 그리라고 했는데 Douglas가 색다른 것을 그렸다고 했으므로 **단서** 이런 Douglas와 관련된 내용이 이어질 것이다. **발상**

(A): 반 아이들의 호응에 Klein 선생님은 Douglas에 대해 하마터면 잊어버릴 뻔했다. 그녀는 나머지 아이들에게 다른 과제를 하도록 지도한 후, Douglas에게 그 손이 누구의 것인지 물었다. "선생님 손이에요. 고마워요, Klein 선생님."이라고 그는 조용히 대답했다.

➡ **(A) 앞:** 반 아이들의 호응에 선생님이 Douglas에 대해 잊어버릴 뻔했다고 했으므로 앞에는 반 아이들이 호응하는 것에 대한 내용이 나와야 한다.
▶ 주어진 글에 반 아이들이 호응하는 내용이 없으므로 (A) 앞에 주어진 글이 올 수 없음

(A) 뒤: Douglas가 직접 누구의 손인지 밝히고 있으므로 글의 결말일 것이다.
▶ (A)가 마지막일 확률이 높음

(B): 그의 반 친구들이 쉬는 시간에 함께 밖으로 나가 있는 동안, 보통 Douglas는 혼자 시간을 보내고 그녀 주변에 머무르는 소년이었다. 그 소년이 그린 것은 손이었다. 그런데 누구의 손일까? 그의 그림은 즉시 다른 학생들의 관심을 끌었다.

➡ **(B) 앞:** Douglas는 보통 혼자 시간을 보내는 소년이었고, 그가 그린 것은 손이었는데 그것이 학생들의 관심을 끌었다고 했다. Douglas가 색다른 것을 그렸다는 내용이 주어진 글에 나오므로 주어진 글이 앞에 와야 한다.
▶ 앞에 주어진 글이 와야 함 (순서: 주어진 글 ➡ (B))

(B) 뒤: Douglas의 그림이 학생들의 관심을 끌었다고 했으므로 이런 학생들의 반응에 대한 내용이 뒤에 이어질 것이다.

(C): 그래서(So), 모두들 그것이 누구의 손인지에 관해 앞다투어 말하려 했다. "그것은 우리에게 음식을 가져다주는 신의 손이 틀림없어."라고 한 학생이 말했다. "농부의 손이야, 왜냐하면 그들은 칠면조를 기르거든."이라고 두 번째 학생이 말했다. "경찰관의 손과 더 비슷해 보여, 그들은 우리를 보호해 줘."라고 또 다른 학생이 덧붙였다.

➡ **(C) 앞:** **1** So(그래서)는 앞에 원인이 나오고 뒤에 결과를 말할 때 쓴다.
2 여러 아이들이 앞다투어 Douglas가 그린 손이 누구의 손인지 말하는 내용이므로 앞에는 학생들의 관심을 끌었다는 (B)가 와야 한다.
▶ (C) 앞에 (B)가 와야 함 (순서: 주어진 글 ➡ (B) ➡ (C))

(C) 뒤: 학생들은 Douglas가 그린 손이 신, 농부, 경찰관의 손이라는 추측을 말했다고 했으므로 Douglas가 본인이 그린 손은 선생님의 손이라고 말하는 (A)가 뒤에 와야 한다.
▶ 순서: 주어진 글 ➡ (B) ➡ (C) ➡ (A)

주어진 글: Klein 선생님이 1학년 학생들에게 감사히 여기는 것을 그리라고 했고 Douglas가 색다른 것을 그렸다.

→ **(B):** Douglas는 손을 그렸고 다른 학생들이 관심을 가졌다.

→ **(C):** 여러 학생들이 Douglas가 그린 손이 누구의 손인지 이야기했다.

→ **(A):** Douglas가 본인이 그린 손은 선생님의 손이라고 말했다.

▶ 주어진 글 다음에 이어질 순서는 (B) → (C) → (A)이므로 정답은 ③임

○ 26 정답 ④ *구석기 시대의 분업과 협업

In the Old Stone Age, / small bands of 20 to 60 people wandered / from place to place / in search of food. //
구석기 시대에는 / 20명에서 60명의 작은 무리가 돌아다녔다 / 이곳저곳을 / 식량을 찾아 //

Once people began farming, / they could settle down / near their farms. // 단서 1 농사를 지으면서 정착하기 시작함
일단 사람들이 농사를 짓기 시작하면서 / 그들은 정착할 수 있었다 / 자신들의 농경지 근처에 //

부사절 접속사(대조) *
(A) While some workers grew crops, / others built new houses / and made tools. // 단서 2 분업에 대한 예시
어떤 노동자들은 농작물을 재배한 반면 / 다른 노동자들은 새로운 집을 짓고 / 도구를 만들었다 //

명사적 용법(learned의 목적어)   부사적 용법(목적)
Village dwellers also learned / to work together / to do a task faster. //
마을 거주자들은 또한 배웠다 / 함께 일하는 것을 / 더 빨리 일을 하기 위해 //

(B) For example, / toolmakers could share the work / of making stone axes and knives. // 단서 3 협업에 대한 예시
예를 들어 / 도구 제작자들은 작업을 공유할 수 있었다 / 돌도끼와 돌칼을 만드는 //

By working together, / they could make more tools / in the same amount of time. //
함께 일함으로써 / 그들은 더 많은 도구를 만들 수 있었다 / 같은 시간 안에 //

(C) As a result, / towns and villages grew larger. // 단서 4 정착의 결과
그 결과 / 도시와 마을이 더 커졌다 //

to부정사를 목적격 보어로 취하는 동사
Living in communities / allowed people to organize themselves / more efficiently. //
공동체에서 생활하는 것은 / 사람들이 스스로 조직하도록 했다 / 더 효율적으로 //

앞에 목적격 관계대명사가 생략됨
They could divide up the work / of producing food and other things / they needed. //
그들은 일을 나눌 수 있었다 / 식량과 다른 것들을 생산하는 / 그들이 필요로 한 //

- band ⓝ 무리   - wander ⓥ 돌아다니다   - settle down 정착하다
- crop ⓝ 농작물   - toolmaker ⓝ 도구 제작자   - axe ⓝ 도끼
- community ⓝ 공동체   - organize ⓥ 조직하다
- efficiently ⓐⓓ 효율적으로   - divide ⓥ 나누다

구석기 시대에는 20명에서 60명의 작은 무리가 식량을 찾아 이곳저곳을 돌아다녔다. 일단 농사를 짓기 시작하면서, 사람들은 자신들의 농경지 근처에 정착할 수 있었다. (C) 그 결과, 도시와 마을이 더 커졌다. 공동체 생활을 통해 사람들은 자신들을 더 효율적으로 조직할 수 있었다. 그들은 식량과 자신들에게 필요한 다른 것들을 생산하는 일을 나눌 수 있었다. (A) 어떤 노동자들은 농작물을 재배했고, 다른 노동자들은 새로운 집을 짓고 도구를 만들었다. 마을 거주자들은 또한 일을 더 빨리 하기 위해 함께 일하는 것도 배웠다. (B) 예를 들어, 도구 제작자들은 돌도끼와 돌칼을 만드는 작업을 공유할 수 있었다. 함께 일함으로써, 그들은 같은 시간 안에 더 많은 도구를 만들 수 있었다.

주어진 글 다음에 이어질 글의 순서로 가장 적절한 것을 고르시오.

① (A) — (C) — (B) 주어진 글에는 노동과 관련된 언급이 없음

② (B) — (A) — (C)

③ (B) — (C) — (A) 주어진 글에는 도구 제작자를 예로 들 만한 내용이 나오지 않음

④ (C) — (A) — (B) 농경지 주변에 정착함 — (C) 그 결과 마을이 커졌고 일을 나눔 — (A) 일부는 농사를 지었고 일부는 도구를 만들었고, 협업을 배움 — (B) 예를 들어 돌도끼와 돌칼을 만드는 노동자들은 작업을 공유함

⑤ (C) — (B) — (A) 분업을 말한 뒤 협업을 말하고 다시 분업을 말하는 것은 어색함

| 문제 풀이 순서 | ★★★ [정답률 59%]

1st 각 문단의 내용을 파악하고, 글의 논리적인 순서를 추론한다.

주어진 글: 구석기 시대에는 20명에서 60명의 작은 무리가 식량을 찾아 이곳 저곳을 돌아다녔다. 일단 농사를 짓기 시작하면서, 사람들은 자신들의 농경 지 근처에 정착할 수 있었다. 단서

→ 주어진 글 뒤: 농사로 시작된 정착 생활과 관련된 내용이 이어질 것이다. 발상

(A): 어떤 노동자들은(workers) 농작물을 재배했고, 다른 노동자들은 새로운 집을 짓고 도구를 만들었다. 마을 거주자들은 또한 일을 더 빨리 하기 위해 함께 일하는 것도 배웠다.

→ (A) 앞: 노동자 또는 노동과 관련된 내용이 나와야 한다.
  ▶ 주어진 글에는 없으므로 바로 뒤에 (A)가 올 수 없음
  (A) 뒤: 함께 일하는 것을 배웠다는 것과 관련된 내용이 이어질 것이다.

(B): 예를 들어(For example), 도구 제작자들은 돌도끼와 돌칼을 만드는 작업을 공유할 수 있었다. 함께 일함으로써, 그들은 같은 시간 안에 더 많은 도구를 만들 수 있었다.

→ (B) 앞: For example(예를 들어)로 (A)에서 말한 마을 거주자들이 배운 함께 일하는 것의 예시가 이어진다.
  ▶ (B) 앞에 (A)가 와야 함 (순서: (A) → (B))
  (B) 뒤: (A) 앞에 주어진 글이 아닌 다른 문단이 와야 하는데, (B)는 (A) 뒤에 왔으므로 남은 (C)가 (A) 앞 순서일 것이다.
  ▶ (B)가 마지막에 올 확률이 높음

(C): 그 결과(As a result), 도시와 마을이 더 커졌다. 공동체 생활을 통해 사람들은 자신들을 더 효율적으로 조직할 수 있었다. 그들은 식량과 자신들에게 필요한 다른 것들을 생산하는 일을 나눌 수 있었다.

→ (C) 앞: 주어진 글에서 말한 정착의 결과로 도시와 마을이 커져 사람들이 효율적으로 조직될 수 있었다고 하는 흐름이 적절하다.
  ▶ (C) 앞에 주어진 글이 와야 함 (순서: 주어진 글 → (C))
  (C) 뒤: 사람들은 식량과 생필품 생산을 분업했다고 했으므로 이 두 가지 노동과 관련된 내용이 이어질 것이다.
  ▶ 두 종류의 노동자를 언급한 (A)가 이어져야 함
  (순서: 주어진 글 → (C) → (A) → (B))

2nd 글이 한눈에 들어오도록 정리하여 정답을 확인한다.

주어진 글: 농사를 지으면서 사람들이 정착할 수 있었다.

→ (C): 공동체 생활을 통해 사람들은 더 효율적으로 조직하고 분업했다.

→ (A): 분업하며 마을 거주자들은 함께 일하는 것도 배웠다.

→ (B): 도구 제작자들은 함께 일하며 같은 시간에 더 많은 작업을 할 수 있었다.

▶ 주어진 글 다음에 이어질 글의 순서는 (C) → (A) → (B)이므로 정답은 ④임

┌─ 어법 특강

＊ 부사절 접속사

– 부사절을 이끄는 종속접속사는 시간, 이유, 목적, 양보, 대조, 조건 등의 의미를 나타낸다. that은 주로 명사절 접속사로 많이 출제되지만 부사절 접속사로 쓰여 목적, 결과를 나타내기도 한다.

· My father bought a new car **even though** we objected.
  양보를 나타내는 부사절 접속사 even though
  (아버지는 우리가 반대했음에도 불구하고 새 차를 사셨다.)

· My parents speak fluent German **whereas** I only speak English.
  대조를 나타내는 부사절 접속사 whereas
  (난 영어만 하는 반면 우리 부모님은 유창한 독일어를 구사하신다.)

O 27 정답 ② *빈곤으로 인한 굶주림 문제

With nearly a billion hungry people / in the world, / there is obviously no single cause. // **단서 1** 굶주림에는 한 가지 이유만 있는 것이 아님
거의 10억 명의 굶주린 사람들이 있는데 / 전 세계에 / 이에 대해 분명 원인이 단 하나만 있는 것은 아니다 //

단서 2 순 수출국인 나라의 사람들이 굶주리는 것에 대해 이유를 물은 (B) 뒤에 이어지는 대답
뒤에 관계부사 why 생략 / 보어절을 이끄는 접속사
(A) The reason / people are hungry in those countries / is / that the products produced there / can be sold / on the world market / for more than the local citizens can afford to pay / for them. //
이유는 / 그러한 국가에서 사람들이 굶주리는 / ~이다 / 그곳에서 생산된 산물들이 / 팔릴 수 있기 때문 / 세계 시장에서 / 현지 시민들이 지불할 수 있는 것보다 더 비싸게 / 그것들에 //

In the modern age / you do not starve / because you have no food, / you starve / because you have no money. //
현대에는 / 여러분이 굶주리는 것이 아니라 / 식량이 없어서 / 굶주리는 것이다 / 돈이 없어서 //

(B) However, / far and away / the biggest cause is poverty. // **단서 3** 여러 원인 중 가장 큰 원인이 빈곤이라는 내용으로, 주어진 문장과 반대로 연결됨
그렇지만 / 단연 / 가장 큰 원인은 빈곤이다 //
주격 관계대명사
Seventy-nine percent / of the world's hungry / live in nations / that are net exporters of food. //
79퍼센트가 / 세계의 굶주린 사람들의 / 나라에 살고 있다 / 음식의 순 수출국인 //

How can this be? //
어떻게 이럴 수가 있을까 //

보어절을 이끄는 접속사
(C) So the problem really is / that food is, / in the grand scheme of things, / too expensive / and many people are too poor / to
too ~ to ...: 너무 ~해서 …할 수 없다
buy it. // **단서 4** 돈이 없어서 굶주리는 것이라는 (B)의 마지막 문장에 이어지는 내용
그래서 문제는 실로 ~이다 / 식량이 / 거대한 체계로 볼 때 / 너무 비싸고 / 많은 사람들이 너무 가난하여 / 그것을 구매할 수 없다는 것 //

The answer will be / in continuing / the trend / of lowering the cost of food. //
해답은 있을 것이다 / 지속하는 데 / 추세를 / 식량의 가격을 낮추는 //

- obviously [ad] 분명히
- local [a] 현지의
- citizen [n] 시민
- afford [v] (…을 살·할·금전적·시간적) 여유[형편]가 되다
- starve [v] 굶주리다
- far and away 단연, 훨씬
- poverty [n] 빈곤
- grand [a] 거대한
- trend [n] 추세
- lower [v] 낮추다

전 세계에 거의 10억 명의 굶주린 사람들이 있는데, 이에 대해 분명 원인이 단 하나만 있는 것은 아니다. (B) 그렇지만, 가장 큰 원인은 단연 빈곤이다. 세계의 굶주린 사람들의 79퍼센트가 식량 순 수출국에 살고 있다. 어떻게 이럴 수가 있을까? (A) 그러한 국가에서 사람들이 굶주리는 이유는 그곳에서 생산된 산물들이 현지 시민들이 그것들에 지불할 수 있는 것보다 더 비싸게 세계 시장에서 팔릴 수 있기 때문이다. 현대에는 여러분이 식량이 없어서 굶주리는 것이 아니라, 돈이 없어서 굶주리는 것이다. (C) 그래서 문제는 실로 식량이 거대한 체계로 볼 때, 너무 비싸고 많은 사람들은 너무 가난하여 그것을 구매할 수 없다는 것이다. 해답은 식량의 가격을 낮추는 추세를 지속하는 데 있을 것이다.

주어진 글 다음에 이어질 글의 순서로 가장 적절한 것을 고르시오.
① (A) — (C) — (B) (A)에서 말하는 those countries가 주어진 글에 없음
②(B) — (A) — (C) (B) 빈곤이 가장 큰 원인인데 순 수출국에서 많이 굶주림 – (A) 순 수출국의 산물이 현지에서 더 비쌈 – (C) 해결책은 식량의 가격을 낮추는 것임
③ (B) — (C) — (A) (A)에서 말하는 those countries는 (B)에서 말한 순 수출국을 가리키는 것임
④ (C) — (A) — (B) ┐(C)에서 해결책을 제시하므로 마지막에 와야 함
⑤ (C) — (B) — (A) ┘

| 문제 풀이 순서 | ★★★ [정답률 66%]

1st 각 문단의 내용을 파악하고, 글의 논리적인 순서를 추론한다.

주어진 글: 전 세계에 거의 10억 명의 굶주린 사람들이 있는데, 이에 대해 분명 원인이 단 하나만 있는 것은 아니다.

→ **주어진 글 뒤:** 굶주림에는 한 가지 원인만 있는 것이 아니라고 했으므로 **단서** 여러 원인들에 대한 내용이 이어질 것이다. **발상**

(A): 그러한 국가에서(in those countries) 사람들이 굶주리는 이유는 그곳에서 생산된 산물들이 현지 시민들이 그것들에 지불할 수 있는 것보다 더 비싸게 세계 시장에서 팔릴 수 있기 때문이다. 현대에는 여러분이 식량이 없어서 굶주리는 것이 아니라, 돈이 없어서 굶주리는 것이다.

→ **(A) 앞:** **1** in those countries(그러한 국가에서)라고 했으므로 앞에 those countries로 가리키는 것이 나와야 한다.
2 생산된 산물이 현지 시민들이 지불할 수 있는 것보다 비싸게 세계 시장에서 팔리기 때문에 그 사람들이 돈이 없어 굶주린다는 내용이다.
▶ 주어진 글에 those countries로 가리킬 수 있는 것이 없으므로 (A) 앞에 주어진 글이 올 수 없음
(A) 뒤: 돈이 없어서 굶주린다고 했으므로 이와 관련된 해결책이 제시될 수 있다.

(B): 그렇지만(However), 가장 큰 원인은 단연 빈곤이다. 세계의 굶주린 사람들의 79퍼센트가 식량 순 수출국에 살고 있다. 어떻게 이런 수가 있을까?

→ **(B) 앞:** **1** However로 시작하므로 앞에 반대 내용이 와야 한다.
2 여러 굶주림의 원인 중 빈곤이 가장 큰 원인이고, 특히 식량 순 수출국에 굶주리는 사람이 많다는 내용이므로 굶주림에는 여러 원인이 있다고 한 주어진 글에 이어지는 내용이다.
▶ (B) 앞에 주어진 글이 와야 함 (순서: 주어진 글 → (B))
(B) 뒤: 마지막 문장에서 식량 순 수출국에 굶주리는 사람이 많은 이유를 묻고 있으므로 식량 순 수출국을 those countries로 받으며 이에 대한 답이 나오는 (A)가 뒤에 와야 한다.
▶ (B) 뒤에 (A)가 와야 함 (순서: 주어진 글 → (B) → (A))

(C): 그래서(So) 문제는 실로 식량이 거대한 체계로 볼 때, 너무 비싸고 많은 사람들은 너무 가난하여 그것을 구매할 수 없다는 것이다. 해답은 식량의 가격을 낮추는 추세를 지속하는 데 있을 것이다.

→ **(C) 앞:** (A) 뒤에 이어질 것으로 예상한 내용이 (C)에 등장한다. 돈이 없어 굶주리는 문제를 해결하는 방법으로 식량의 가격을 낮추는 것을 말하고 있으므로 (A) 뒤에 (C)가 와야 한다. ▶ 순서: 주어진 글 → (B) → (A) → (C)

2nd 글이 한눈에 들어오도록 정리하여 정답을 확인한다.

주어진 글: 굶주림에는 여러 원인이 있다.
→ **(B):** 빈곤이 가장 큰 문제인데, 특히 음식 순 수출국에서 굶주림이 심각하다.
→ **(A):** 순 수출국에서는 음식을 비싸게 팔기 때문에 돈이 없는 시민들은 굶주린다.
→ **(C):** 그러므로 식량 가격을 낮춰야 한다.
▶ 주어진 글 다음에 이어질 순서는 (B) → (A) → (C)이므로 정답은 ②임

O 28 정답 ⑤ ○ 2등급 대비 [정답률 46%]

*창의성을 발휘하는 데 최적의 시간

뒤에 목적어절을 이끄는 접속사 that 생략
Most people have / a perfect time of day / when they feel / they are at their best, / whether in the morning, evening, or afternoon. // **단서 1** 사람마다 최고의 상태에 있다고 느끼는 시간이 다름
대부분의 사람들은 갖는다 / 하루 중 완벽한 시간을 / 그들이 느끼는 / 자신의 최고의 상태에 있다고 / 아침이든 저녁이든 혹은 오후든 간에 //

비교급 표현
(A) When your mind and body are less alert / than at your "peak" hours, / the muse of creativity awakens / and is allowed to roam / more freely. // **단서 2** (B)에서 언급한 창의성과 최악의 시간에 대한
부연 설명이므로 (B) 뒤에 와야 함
여러분의 정신과 신체가 주의력이 덜할 때 / 여러분의 "정점의" 시간보다 / 창의성의 영감이 깨어난다 / 그리고 거니는 것이 허용된다 / 더 자유롭게 //

In other words, / when your mental machinery is loose / rather than standing at attention, / the creativity flows. //
다시 말해서 / 여러분의 정신 기제가 느슨하게 풀려있을 때 / 주의력 있게 기립해 있을 때보다 / 창의성이 샘솟는다 //

단서 3 (C)의 마지막 문장과 앞에 목적격 관계대명사 생략 / 반대되는 내용이 이어짐

(B) However, / if the task / you face / demands creativity and novel ideas, / it's best / to tackle it / at your "worst" time of day! //
가주어 ~ 진주어
그러나 / 만약 과업이 / 여러분이 직면한 / 창의성과 새로운 아이디어를 요구한다면 / 최선이다 / 그것을 다루는 것이 / 하루 중 여러분의 "최악의" 시간에 //

So if you are an early bird, / make sure / to attack your creative task / in the evening, / and vice versa for night owls. //
그래서 만약 여러분이 일찍 일어나는 새라면 / 명심해라 / 창의적인 작업에 착수할 것을 / 저녁에 / 그리고 밤 올빼미라면 반대로 할 것을 //

단서 4 사람마다 최고의 상태에 있다고 느끼는 시간이 다르다는 것에 이어지는 내용

(C) Some of us are night owls, / some early birds, / and others in between / may feel most active / during the afternoon hours. //
뒤에 동사 are 생략
우리 중 몇몇은 밤 올빼미이고 / 몇몇은 일찍 일어나는 새이며 / 그 사이에 있는 누군가는 / 가장 활력을 느낄지도 모른다 / 오후의 시간 동안 //

If you are able / to organize your day and divide your work, / make it a point / to deal with tasks / that demand attention / at your best time of the day. //
주격 관계대명사
만약 여러분이 할 수 있다면 / 하루를 계획하고 업무를 분배하는 것을 / 중점을 두어라 / 과업을 처리하는 것에 / 집중을 요구하는 / 하루 중 여러분의 최적의 시간에 //

- alert ⓐ 기민한, 주의하는
- peak ⓐ 정점의
- muse ⓝ 영감
- awaken ⓥ 깨어나다
- mental ⓐ 정신의
- machinery ⓝ 기제, 시스템
- loose ⓥ 느슨하게 하다, 풀다
- attention ⓝ 집중, 주의력
- demand ⓥ 요구하다
- novel ⓐ 새로운
- tackle ⓥ (힘든 문제·상황과) 씨름하다
- early bird 일찍 일어나는 사람
- vice versa 반대로
- night owl 밤에 깨어 있는 사람
- organize ⓥ 계획하다
- divide ⓥ 분배하다

대부분의 사람들은 아침이든 저녁이든 혹은 오후든 간에 하루 중 그들이 자신의 최고의 상태에 있다고 느끼는 완벽한 시간을 갖는다. (C) 우리 중 몇몇은 밤 올빼미이고, 몇몇은 일찍 일어나는 새이며, 그 사이에 있는 누군가는 오후의 시간 동안 가장 활력을 느낄지도 모른다. 여러분이 하루를 계획하고 업무를 분배한다면, 집중을 요구하는 과업을 하루 중 여러분의 최적의 시간에 처리하는 것에 중점을 두어라. (B) 그러나, 만약 여러분이 직면한 과업이 창의성과 새로운 아이디어를 요구한다면, 하루 중 여러분의 "최악의" 시간에 그것을 다루는 것이 최선이다! 그래서 만약 여러분이 일찍 일어나는 새라면 저녁에 창의적인 작업에 착수하고, 밤 올빼미라면 반대로 할 것을 명심해라. (A) 여러분의 정신과 신체가 여러분의 "정점의" 시간보다 주의력이 덜할 때, 창의성의 영감이 깨어나 더 자유롭게 거니는 것이 허용된다. 다시 말해서, 여러분의 정신 기제가 주의력 있게 기립해 있을 때보다 느슨하게 풀려있을 때 창의성이 샘솟는다.

주어진 글 다음에 이어질 글의 순서로 가장 적절한 것을 고르시오. [3점]

① (A) — (C) — (B) (A)는 (B)의 내용에 대한 부연이므로 주어진 글 다음에 올 수 없음
② (B) — (A) — (C)
③ (B) — (C) — (A) (B)에서 However로 연결하는 반대 내용이 주어진 글에 없음
④ (C) — (A) — (B) (C) 다음에는 반대 내용을 연결하는 (B)가 이어져야 함
⑤ (C) — (B) — (A) (C) 집중력을 요하는 작업은 최고의 시간에 하는 것이 좋음 – (B) 창의성을 요하는 작업은 최악의 상태에 하는 것이 좋음 – (A) 느슨하게 풀려 있을 때 창의성이 가장 잘 발휘됨

⑩ **2등급** ❓ 사람마다 최고의 상태라고 느끼는 시간이 다 다르다고 하면서, 집중력을 요구하는 작업과 창의성을 요구하는 작업 각각을 '어떤' 상태일 때 하라고 설명하는 글이다.
둘 다 '최고의' 상태일 때 해야 효율적일 것 같지만, 창의성을 요구하는 작업은 '최악의' 상태에서 해야 더 좋다고 이야기한다. 따라서 스스로 판단하여 답을 유추하지 말고, 글에서 설명하는 대로 이해해야 헷갈리지 않고 정답을 고를 수 있는 2등급 대비 문제이다.

| 문제 풀이 순서 |

1st 각 문단의 내용을 파악하고, 글의 논리적인 순서를 추론한다.

주어진 글: 대부분의 사람들은 아침이든 저녁이든 혹은 오후든 간에 하루 중 그들이 자신의 최고의 상태에 있다고 느끼는 완벽한 시간을 갖는다.

→ **소재**: 최고의 상태에 있다고 느끼는 최적의 시간 **단서**
전개 방향: 사람마다 완벽함을 느끼는 시간이 다르다고 했으므로 어떻게 다른지 등에 대한 내용이 이어질 것이다. **발상**

(A): 여러분의 정신과 신체가 여러분의 "정점의" 시간보다 주의력이 덜할 때, 창의성의 영감이 깨어나 더 자유롭게 거니는 것이 허용된다. 다시 말해서(In other words), 여러분의 정신 기제가 주의력 있게 기립해 있을 때보다 느슨하게 풀려있을 때 창의성이 샘솟는다.

→ **(A) 앞**: 신체와 정신이 느슨한 상태에서 창의성이 잘 발휘된다는 내용이다. 그러므로 이 앞에는 최고의 시간이 아닐 때 관련된 내용이 올 가능성이 높다.
▶ (A) 앞에 주어진 글이 올 수 없음
(A) 뒤: '다시 말해서(In other words)'는 앞에서 언급했던 것을 다시 한 번 정리하는 연결어이므로 글을 마무리하는 문단일 것이다.
▶ (A)가 마지막에 올 확률이 높음

(B): 그러나(However), 만약 여러분이 직면한 과업이 창의성과 새로운 아이디어를 요구한다면, 하루 중 여러분의 "최악의" 시간에 그것을 다루는 것이 최선이다! 그래서 만약 여러분이 일찍 일어나는 새라면 저녁에 창의적인 작업에 착수하고, 밤 올빼미라면 반대로 할 것을 명심해라.

→ **(B) 앞**: However는 반대 내용을 나타내는 연결어이므로 (B) 앞에는 최악의 시간에 창의성이 요구되는 일을 하는 것과 반대되는 내용이 나와야 한다.
▶ (B) 앞에 주어진 글이나 (A)가 올 수 없음
(B) 뒤: 창의성이 요구되는 일을 하려면 최악의 시간에 하라고 했는데, 이와 관련해서 주의력이 덜한 시간에 창의성이 잘 발휘된다는 부연 내용이 (A)에 나온다.
▶ (B) 뒤에 (A)가 와야 함 (순서: (B) → (A))

(C): 우리 중 몇몇은(Some of us) 밤 올빼미이고, 몇몇은(some) 일찍 일어나는 새이며, 그 사이에 있는 누군가는(others) 오후의 시간 동안 가장 활력을 느낄지도 모른다. 여러분이 하루를 계획하고 업무를 분배한다면, 집중을 요구하는 과업을 하루 중 여러분의 최적의 시간에 처리하는 것에 중점을 두어라.

→ **(C) 앞**: '우리 중 몇몇은(Some of us)', '몇몇은(some)', '누군가는(others)'이라고 하면서 사람마다 각자 활력을 느끼는 시간이 다르다고 했으므로 주어진 글에서 사람마다 완벽함을 느끼는 시간이 다르다는 내용에 이어진다. ▶ (C) 앞에 주어진 글이 와야 함 (순서: 주어진 글 → (C))
(C) 뒤: 집중력을 요하는 일은 최적의 시간에 해야 한다고 했으므로 '그러나(However)' 창의성을 요구하는 일은 최악의 시간에 하는 것이 좋다고 한 (B)가 이어질 것이다.
▶ (C) 뒤에 (B)가 와야 함 (순서: 주어진 글 → (C) → (B) → (A))

2nd 글이 한눈에 들어오도록 정리하여 정답을 확인한다.

주어진 글: 사람마다 완벽함을 느끼는 시간이 다르다.
→ **(C)**: 집중력을 요하는 작업은 가장 완벽함을 느끼는 최고의 시간에 하는 것이 좋다.
→ **(B)**: 그러나 창의성을 요하는 작업은 최악의 상태에 하는 것이 좋다.
→ **(A)**: 신체와 정신이 느슨한 상태일 때 창의성이 가장 잘 발휘된다.
▶ 주어진 글 다음에 이어질 순서는 (C) → (B) → (A)이므로 정답은 ⑤임

＊문학 작품이 함축하는 것 이해하기

Literary works, / by their nature, / suggest rather than explain; / they imply / rather than state their claims / boldly and directly. // 단서 1 문학 작품은 직접 진술하기보다는 함축함
문학 작품들은 / 그 본질상 / 설명하기보다는 암시한다 / 그들은 함축한다 / 그들의 주장을 진술하기보다는 / 뚜렷하고 직접적으로 //

선행사를 포함하는 관계대명사
단서 2 (B)의 마지막에 나온 질문과 이어짐
(A) What a text implies / is often of great interest to us. //
텍스트가 무엇을 함축하는지는 / 종종 우리에게 매우 흥미롭다 //
핵심 주어   단수 동사
And our work / of figuring out a text's implications / tests our analytical powers. //
그리고 우리의 작업은 / 텍스트의 함축을 알아내는 / 우리의 분석적 능력을 시험한다 //
In considering what a text suggests, / we gain practice in making sense of texts. //
텍스트가 무엇을 암시하는지를 고려하는 과정에서 / 우리는 텍스트를 이해하는 기량을 얻게 된다 //

어떤 ~일지라도   단서 3 앞에 작품의 보여주기와 말하기의 비율에 대한 언급이 있어야 함
(B) But whatever the proportion / of a work's showing to telling, / there is always something for readers to interpret. //
to부정사의 의미상 주어
하지만 비율이 어떻든지 간에 / 작품의 말하기 대 보여주기의 / 무언가가 항상 존재한다 / 독자가 해석해야 하는 //
Thus we ask the question / "What does the text suggest?" / as a way to approach literary interpretation, / as a way to begin thinking about a text's implications. //
형용사적 용법   형용사적 용법
그러므로 우리는 질문을 한다 / "그 텍스트가 무엇을 암시하는가"라는 / 문학적 해석에 접근하는 방법으로서이자 / 텍스트의 함축에 대해 생각하는 것을 시작하는 방법으로서 //
목적어절을 이끄는 접속사
(C) This broad generalization, however, / does not mean that works of literature do not include / direct statements. //
그러나 이 넓은 일반화는 / 의미하지는 않는다 / 문학 작품들이 포함하지 않는다는 것을 / 직접적인 진술을 //
단서 4 앞에 문학 작품에 대한 넓은 일반화에 대한 내용이 와야 함
~에 따라
Depending on when they were written and by whom, / literary works may contain / large amounts of direct telling / and lesser amounts of suggestion and implication. //
그들이 언제 그리고 누구에 의해 쓰였는지에 따라 / 문학 작품들은 포함할 수도 있다 / 많은 양의 직접적 말하기를 / 그리고 더 적은 양의 암시와 함축을 //

- literary ⓐ 문학의 ・ work ⓝ 작품 ・ imply ⓥ 암시하다
- state ⓥ 진술하다 ・ claim ⓝ 주장 ・ boldly ⓐⓓ 뚜렷하게
- directly ⓐⓓ 직접적으로 ・ figure out 이해하다
- implication ⓝ 함축 ・ analytical ⓐ 분석적인
- proportion ⓝ 비율 ・ interpret ⓥ 해석하다
- interpretation ⓝ 해석 ・ generalization ⓝ 일반화
- literature ⓝ 문학 ・ include ⓥ 포함하다 ・ statement ⓝ 진술
- contain ⓥ 포함하다 ・ suggestion ⓝ 암시

문학 작품들은 그 본질상 설명하기보다는 암시하는데, 그들은 그들의 주장을 뚜렷하고 직접적으로 진술하기보다는 함축한다. (C) 그러나 이 넓은 일반화는 문학 작품들이 직접적인 진술을 포함하지 않는다는 것을 의미하지는 않는다. 그들이 언제 그리고 누구에 의해 쓰였는지에 따라 문학 작품들은 많은 양의 직접적 말하기와 더 적은 양의 암시와 함축을 포함할 수도 있다. (B) 하지만 작품의 말하기 대 보여주기의 비율이 어떻든지 간에 독자가 해석해야 하는 무언가가 항상 존재한다. 그러므로 우리는 문학적 해석에 접근하는 방법이자 텍스트의 함축에 대해 생각하는 것을 시작하는 방법으로서, "그 텍스트가 무엇을 암시하는가?"라는 질문을 한다. (A) 텍스트가 무엇을 함축하는지는 종종 우리에게 매우 흥미롭다. 그리고 텍스트의 함축을 알아내는 우리의 작업은 우리의 분석적 능력을 시험한다. 텍스트가 무엇을 암시하는지를 고려하는 과정에서 우리는 텍스트를 이해하는 기량을 얻게 된다.

주어진 글 다음에 이어질 글의 순서로 가장 적절한 것을 고르시오. [3점]
① (A) — (C) — (B)
   주어진 글에 나온 문학 작품에 대한 일반화를 (C)의 This broad generalization이 이어받고 있음
② (B) — (A) — (C)
③ (B) — (C) — (A)
   (B)는 암시와 함축의 비율이 언급된 (C)의 뒤에 나와야 함
④ (C) — (A) — (B)
⑤ (C) — (B) — (A)
   (C) 문학 작품들에 직접적인 진술이 없다는 것은 아님 – (B) 독자가 해석해야 하는 것은 항상 존재함 – (A) 텍스트의 함축을 알아내는 것을 통해 우리는 텍스트를 이해하는 기량을 얻게 됨

왜 2등급? 내용의 이해를 돕는 예시가 없어 어려운 2등급 대비 문제이다. 주어진 글에서 문학 작품들이 주장을 함축한다고 한 것에 이어지는 내용으로 무엇이 적절한지 But, This broad generalization과 같은 단서들에 주목해야 글의 순서를 파악할 수 있다.

| 문제 풀이 순서 |

1st 각 문단의 내용을 파악하고, 글의 논리적인 순서를 추론한다.

주어진 글: 문학 작품들은 그 본질상 설명하기보다는 암시하는데, 그들은 그들의 주장을 뚜렷하고 직접적으로 진술하기보다는 함축한다.

➡ 소재: 문학 작품이 가진 암시하고 함축하는 특성 단서
전개 방향: 문학 작품들이 어떤 방식으로 함축하는지 등에 대한 내용이 이어질 것이다. 발상

(A): 텍스트가 무엇을 함축하는지는 종종 우리에게 매우 흥미롭다. 그리고 텍스트의 함축을 알아내는 우리의 작업은 우리의 분석적 능력을 시험한다. 텍스트가 무엇을 암시하는지를 고려하는 과정에서 우리는 텍스트를 이해하는 기량을 얻게 된다.

➡ (A) 앞: 텍스트의 함축을 알아내는 것을 통해 우리가 텍스트를 이해하는 기량을 얻게 된다는 내용이다. 그러므로 이 앞에는 텍스트의 함축과 관련된 내용이 올 것이다. ▶ (A) 앞에 주어진 글이 올 수 없음
(A) 뒤: 결국 우리가 텍스트를 이해하는 기량을 얻게 된다고 하며 글을 마무리할 것이다. ▶ (A)가 마지막에 올 확률이 높음

(B): 하지만(But) 작품의 말하기 대 보여주기의 비율이 어떻든지 간에 독자가 해석해야 하는 무언가가 항상 존재한다. 그러므로 우리는 문학적 해석에 접근하는 방법이자 텍스트의 함축에 대해 생각하는 것을 시작하는 방법으로서, "그 텍스트가 무엇을 암시하는가?"라는 질문을 한다.

➡ (B) 앞: 1 반대 내용을 나타내는 연결어 But이 왔으므로 앞에 반대 내용이 나와야 한다.
2 말하기 대 보여주기의 비율에 상관없이 독자가 해석해야 하는 것이 항상 존재한다고 했으므로 (B) 앞에는 이와 반대되는 내용이 나와야 한다.
▶ (B) 앞에 주어진 글이나 (A)가 올 수 없음
(B) 뒤: 마지막에 해석의 방법으로서 "What does the text suggest?(그 텍스트가 무엇을 암시하는가?)"라는 질문을 한다고 했는데, 이 질문과 관련해서 텍스트의 함축에 대한 내용이 (A)에 나온다.
▶ (B) 뒤에 (A)가 와야 함 (순서: (B) ➡ (A))

(C): 그러나 이 넓은 일반화(This broad generalization)는 문학 작품들이 직접적인 진술을 포함하지 않는다는 것을 의미하지는 않는다. 그들이 언제 그리고 누구에 의해 쓰였는지에 따라 문학 작품들은 많은 양의 직접적 말하기와 더 적은 양의 암시와 함축을 포함할 수도 있다.

➡ (C) 앞: '이 넓은 일반화(This broad generalization)'라고 하는데, 이것은 주어진 글에서 '문학 작품들은 그들의 주장을 직접적으로 진술하기보다는 함축한다'고 한 일반화된 언급을 가리킨다.
▶ (C) 앞에 주어진 글이 와야 함 (순서: 주어진 글 ➡ (C))
(C) 뒤: 문학 작품들에 직접적인 진술이 없다는 것을 의미하는 것은 아니라고 했고 직접적 말하기, 암시와 함축의 비율에 대해 언급하고 있으므로 말하기 대 보여주기의 비율로 시작하는 (B)가 이어져야 한다.
▶ (C) 뒤에 (B)가 와야 함 (순서: 주어진 글 ➡ (C) ➡ (B) ➡ (A))

2nd 글이 한눈에 들어오도록 정리하여 정답을 확인한다.

주어진 글: 문학 작품들은 그들의 주장을 직접적으로 진술하기보다는 함축한다.
→ **(C):** 문학 작품들에 직접적인 진술이 없다는 것은 아니다.
→ **(B):** 말하기 대 보여주기의 비율에 상관없이 독자가 해석해야 하는 것이 항상 존재한다.
→ **(A):** 텍스트의 함축을 알아내는 것을 통해 텍스트를 이해하는 기량을 얻게 된다.
▶ 주어진 글 다음에 이어질 순서는 (C) → (B) → (A)이므로 정답은 ⑤임

O 30 정답 ② ⭐ 2등급 대비 [정답률 51%]

*나쁜 연주와 나쁜 연주자의 특징

Robert Schumann once said, / "The laws of morals are those = the laws of art." //
Robert Schumann은 말한 적이 있다 / "도덕의 법칙은 예술의 법칙이다"라고 //

What the great man is saying here / is that there is good music
주어   동사 보어절을 이끄는 접속사
and bad music. // 단서1 좋은 음악과 나쁜 음악이 있다고 한 위인의 말을 언급함
여기서 이 위인이 말하고 있는 것은 / 좋은 음악과 나쁜 음악이 있다는 것이다 //

단서2 (B)의 마지막에 말한 나쁜 음악에 이어서 나쁜 연주에 대한 내용이 나옴
(A) It's the same with performances: / a bad performance isn't
necessarily the result of incompetence. //
연주도 마찬가지다 / 나쁜 연주가 반드시 무능의 결과는 아니다 //

Some of the worst performances occur / when the performers, /
아무리 ~하더라도
no matter how accomplished, / are thinking more of themselves
앞에 목적격 관계대명사 생략
than of the music they're playing. //
최악의 연주 중 일부는 발생한다 / 연주자들이 ~ 때 / 아무리 숙달되었더라도 / 자기 자신을
더 생각하고 있을 / 연주하고 있는 곡보다 //
접속사(비록 ~일지라도) 단서3 주어진 글에서 말한 좋은 음악에 이어지는 내용
(B) The greatest music, / even if it's tragic in nature, / takes us
to a world higher than ours; / somehow the beauty uplifts us. //
가장 위대한 음악은 / 심지어 그것이 사실상 비극적일지라도 / 우리의 세상보다 더 높은
세상으로 우리를 데려간다 / 그래서 어떻게든지 아름다움은 우리를 향상시킨다 //

Bad music, / on the other hand, / degrades us. //
나쁜 음악은 / 반면에 / 우리를 격하시킨다 단서4 (A)의 마지막에 언급한, 곡보다 자기
자신을 더 생각하고 있는 연주자들을 가리킴
(C) These doubtful characters / aren't really listening to / what
~것
the composer is saying — / they're just showing off, / hoping
목적절을 이끄는 접속사   분사구문을 이끎
that they'll have a great 'success' / with the public. //
이 미덥지 못한 사람들은 / 정말로 듣고 있는 것이 아니다 / 작곡가가 말하는 것을 / 그들은
그저 뽐내고 있을 뿐이다 / 큰 '성공'을 거두기를 바라며 / 대중적으로 //
주어
The performer's basic task / is to try to understand the meaning
동사
of the music, / and then to communicate it honestly / to others. //
명사적 용법(주격 보어)의 병렬 구조
연주자의 기본 임무는 / 음악의 의미를 이해하려고 노력하는 것이다 / 그리고 그것을 정직하게
전달하는 (것이다) / 다른 사람들에게 //

- moral ⓝ 도덕, 교훈   - performance ⓝ 연주
- necessarily ⓐⓓ 반드시   - accomplished ⓐ 숙달된
- tragic ⓐ 비극적인   - uplift ⓥ 향상시키다
- doubtful ⓐ 미덥지 못한   - character ⓝ 사람, 등장인물
- composer ⓝ 작곡가   - show off 뽐내다
- communicate ⓥ 전달하다   - honestly ⓐⓓ 정직하게

Robert Schumann은 "도덕의 법칙은 예술의 법칙이다."라고 말한 적이
있다. 여기서 이 위인이 말하고 있는 것은 좋은 음악과 나쁜 음악이 있다는
것이다. (B) 가장 위대한 음악은, 심지어 그것이 사실상 비극적일지라도,
우리의 세상보다 더 높은 세상으로 우리를 데려간다. 그래서 어떻게든지
아름다움은 우리를 향상시킨다. 반면에 나쁜 음악은 우리를 격하시킨다.
(A) 연주도 마찬가지다. 나쁜 연주가 반드시 무능의 결과는 아니다.
최악의 연주 중 일부는 연주자들이 아무리 숙달되었더라도 연주하고
있는 곡보다 자기 자신을 더 생각하고 있을 때 발생한다. (C) 이 미덥지
못한 사람들은 작곡가가 말하는 것을 정말로 듣고 있는 것이 아니다.
그들은 대중적으로 큰 '성공'을 거두기를 바라며 그저 뽐내고 있을 뿐이다.
연주자의 기본 임무는 음악의 의미를 이해하려고 노력하고서, 그것을 다른
사람들에게 정직하게 전달하는 것이다.

주어진 글 다음에 이어질 글의 순서로 가장 적절한 것을 고르시오. [3점]
나쁜 연주에 대한 내용이 나오는 (A)는 (B)에서 나쁜 음악에 대해 말한 후에 올 수 있음
① (A) — (C) — (B)
② (B) — (A) — (C)   (B) 좋은 음악과 나쁜 음악의 특징 – (A) 나쁜 연주의 특징은 연주자가
곡보다 자기 자신을 더 생각하고 있는 것임 – (C) 나쁜 연주자들의
특징과 연주자의 기본 임무를 설명함
③ (B) — (C) — (A)
(C)의 these doubtful characters는 (A)에서 언급한, 곡보다 자기 자신을 더 생각하고 있는 연주자들을 가리킴
④ (C) — (A) — (B)
주어진 글에서 말한 좋은 음악에 이어지는, 위대한 음악에 대한 내용이
⑤ (C) — (B) — (A) 나오는 (B)가 맨 앞에 와야 함

왜 2등급? 각 문단에 단서가 되는 접속사가 없고, 모두 음악과 연주와 관련된
내용을 설명하고 있어 순서를 파악하기 까다로운 2등급 대비 문제이다.
어떤 순서로 전개되어야 나쁜 음악에는 나쁜 연주와 나쁜 연주자가 있다고 말하는
자연스러운 흐름이 되는지 내용을 통해 알아내야 한다.

| 문제 풀이 순서 |

1st 각 문단의 내용을 파악하고, 글의 논리적인 순서를 추론한다.

┌ **주어진 글:** Robert Schumann은 "도덕의 법칙은 예술의 법칙이다."라고
  말한 적이 있다. 여기서 이 위인이 말하고 있는 것은 좋은 음악과 나쁜 음악
└ 이 있다는 것이다.

→ **소재:** 좋은 음악과 나쁜 음악 단서
  전개 방향: Robert Schumann의 명언을 인용해 좋은 음악과 나쁜 음악이 있다고
  했다. 따라서 좋은 음악이나 나쁜 음악에 대한 내용이 이어질 것이다. 발상

┌ **(A):** 연주도 마찬가지다(It's the same). 나쁜 연주가 반드시 무능의 결과
  는 아니다. 최악의 연주 중 일부는 연주자들이 아무리 숙달되었더라도 연주
└ 하고 있는 곡보다 자기 자신을 더 생각하고 있을 때 발생한다.

→ **(A) 앞:** '마찬가지다(It's the same)'라고 했으므로 나쁜 연주 말고 다른 어떤 것이
  (A)에서 말하는 것처럼 꼭 무능의 결과는 아니라는 내용이 앞에 와야 한다.
  ▶ (A) 앞에 주어진 글이 올 수 없음
  (A) 뒤: 나쁜 연주의 경우, 연주자가 곡보다 자기 자신에 더 몰두한다는 내용이므로
  이런 연주자들과 관련된 내용이 뒤에 올 것이다.

┌ **(B):** 가장 위대한 음악(The greatest music)은, 심지어 그것이 사실상 비
  극적일지라도, 우리의 세상보다 더 높은 세상으로 우리를 데려간다. 그래서
  어떻게든지 아름다움은 우리를 향상시킨다. 반면에 나쁜 음악(Bad
└ music)은 우리를 격하시킨다.

→ **(B) 앞:** 위대한 음악은 우리를 향상시키고, 나쁜 음악은 우리를 격하시킨다는
  내용으로, 좋은 음악과 나쁜 음악이 있다고 한 주어진 글에 이어진다.
  ▶ (B) 앞에 주어진 글이 와야 함 (순서: 주어진 글 → (B))
  (B) 뒤: 나쁜 음악에 대한 언급에 이어서 이와 마찬가지인 나쁜 연주에 대한 내용이
  (A)에 나온다. ▶ (B) 뒤에 (A)가 와야 함 (순서: 주어진 글 → (B) → (A))

┌ **(C):** 이 미덥지 못한 사람들(These doubtful characters)은 작곡가가
  말하는 것을 정말로 듣고 있는 것이 아니다. 그들은 대중적으로 큰 '성공'을
  거두기를 바라며 그저 뽐내고 있을 뿐이다. 연주자의 기본 임무는 음악의
  의미를 이해하려고 노력하고서, 그것을 다른 사람들에게 정직하게 전달하
└ 는 것이다.

→ **(C) 앞:** (A) 뒤에 이어질 것으로 예상한 내용이 (C)에 등장한다.
  또한, '이 미덥지 못한 사람들(These doubtful characters)'은 (A)에서
  언급했던, 곡보다 자기 자신을 더 생각하고 있는 연주자들을 가리킨다.
  ▶ 순서: 주어진 글 → (B) → (A) → (C)

2nd 글이 한눈에 들어오도록 정리하여 정답을 확인한다.

주어진 글: 위인의 명언을 인용하여 좋은 음악과 나쁜 음악이 있다고 했다.
→ **(B):** 좋은 음악은 우리를 향상시키고, 나쁜 음악은 우리를 격하시킨다.
→ **(A):** 연주도 마찬가지인데, 나쁜 연주는 연주자가 곡이 아니라 자기 자신에게
  몰두했을 때에 해당한다.
→ **(C):** 나쁜 연주자는 그저 뽐내는 사람이고, 연주자의 기본 임무는 음악을 제대로
  이해하고 전달하는 것이다.
▶ 주어진 글 다음에 이어질 순서는 (B) → (A) → (C)이므로 정답은 ②임

O 31 정답 ③ ━━━━━━━ ★ 1등급 대비 [정답률 36%]

*사회적 압박이 개인에 미치는 영향

As individuals, / our ability to thrive / depended on how well
we navigated relationships in a group. //
형용사적 용법 (our ability 수식)
간접의문문
개인으로서 / 성공하려는 우리의 능력은 / 우리가 집단 내에서 관계를 얼마나 잘 다루는지
에 달려 있었다 //

If the group valued us, / we could count on / support,
resources, and probably a mate. //
If 가정법 과거
만약 그 집단이 우리를 가치 있게 여긴다면 / 우리는 기대할 수 있을 것이다 / 지원, 자원,
그리고 아마도 짝을 // 단서 1 집단이 개인을 가치 있게 여기면 그 개인은 이점을 얻음

(A) And, crucially, / they are meant to make / that motivation
feel like it is coming from within. // 단서 2 they와 that motivation이 가리키는
대상이 (A) 앞에 나와야 함
make의 목적어와 목적격 보어(원형부정사)
그리고 결정적으로 / 그것들은 만들도록 되어있다 / 그 동기가 내부에서 나오고 있는 것처럼
느끼게 //

If we realized, / on a conscious level, / that we were responding
to social pressure, / our performance might come off as grudging
or cynical, / making it less persuasive. //
목적어절 접속사
~처럼 느껴지다
분사구문
우리가 깨닫는다면 / 의식적인 수준에서 / 우리가 사회적 압박에 반응하고 있었다는 것을 / 우
리의 행동은 투덜대거나 냉소적인 것으로 나타날 수 있다 / 그것(그 동기)을 설득력이 떨어지
게 만들면서 //

(B) If it didn't, / we might get none of these merits. //
If 가정법 과거   단서 3 it은 주어진 글의 the group을 가리킴
만약 그렇지 않다면 / 우리는 그러한 이점들 중 아무것도 얻지 못할 것이다 //

It was a matter of survival, / physically and genetically. //
그것은 생존의 문제였다 / 신체적으로 그리고 유전적으로 //

Over millions of years, / the pressure selected for people / who
are sensitive to and skilled at maximizing their standing. //
주격 관계대명사
병렬구조
수백만 년 동안 / 그러한 압박은 사람들을 선택했다 / 자신의 지위를 최대화하는 데 민감하고
능숙한 // 단서 4 사회적 압박은 자신의 지위를 높이는 인간을 선택함

(C) The result was the development of a tendency / to
unconsciously monitor / how other people in our community
perceive us. // 단서 5 (B)에서 언급한 사회적 압박의 결과가 제시됨
형용사적 용법 (a tendency 수식)
그 결과는 경향의 발달이었다 / 무의식적으로 관찰하는 / 우리 공동체의 다른 사람들이 우리
를 어떻게 인식하는지 //

We process that information / in the form of self-esteem / and
such related emotions as pride, shame, or insecurity. //
우리는 그 정보를 처리한다 / 자존감의 형태로 / 그리고 자존심, 수치심 또는 불안 같은 관련
된 감정(의 형태로) //

These emotions compel us / to do more of what makes our
community value us / and less of what doesn't. //
compel의 목적격 보어 (to부정사)
병렬 구조 ('비교급 + of + 선행사를 포함하는 관계대명사')
이러한 감정들은 우리에게 강요한다 / 우리의 공동체가 우리를 가치 있게 여기도록 만드는 것
을 더 많이 하고 / 그렇지 않은 것을 덜 하도록 //

- thrive ⓥ 성공하다   - navigate ⓥ 다루다, 길을 찾다
- value ⓥ 가치 있게 여기다   - count on ~을 기대하다   - mate ⓝ 짝
- crucially 졅 결정적으로   - conscious ⓐ 의식적인
- cynical ⓐ 냉소적인   - persuasive ⓐ 설득력 있는   - merit ⓝ 이점
- physically 졅 신체적으로   - genetically 졅 유전적으로
- select for ~을 선택하다   - sensitive ⓐ 민감한   - skilled ⓐ 능숙한
- maximize ⓥ 최대화하다   - standing ⓝ 지위
- tendency ⓝ 경향   - unconsciously 졅 무의식적으로
- perceive ⓥ 인식하다   - self-esteem ⓝ 자존감   - pride ⓝ 자존심
- shame ⓝ 수치심   - insecurity ⓝ 불안   - compel ⓥ 강요하다

개인으로서 성공하려는 우리의 능력은 우리가 집단 내에서 관계를 얼마나 잘 다
루는지에 달려 있었다. 만약 그 집단이 우리를 가치 있게 여긴다면 우리는 지
원, 자원, 그리고 아마도 짝을 기대할 수 있을 것이다. (B) 만약 그렇지 않다면,
우리는 그러한 이점들 중 아무것도 얻지 못할 것이다. 그것은 신체적으로 그리
고 유전적으로 생존의 문제였다. 수백만 년 동안 그러한 압박은 자신의 지위를

최대화하는 데 민감하고 능숙한 사람들을 선택했다. (C) 그 결과는 우리 공동체
의 다른 사람들이 우리를 어떻게 인식하는지 무의식적으로 관찰하는 경향의 발
달이었다. 우리는 자존감 그리고 자존심, 수치심 또는 불안 같은 관련된 감정의
형태로 그 정보를 처리한다. 이러한 감정들은 우리에게 우리의 공동체가 우리를
가치 있게 여기도록 만드는 것을 더 많이 하고 그렇지 않은 것을 덜 하도록 강
요한다. (A) 그리고 결정적으로 그것들은 그 동기가 내부에서 나오고 있는 것처
럼 그것을 느끼게 만들도록 되어 있다. 우리가 사회적 압박에 반응하고 있었다
는 것을 의식적인 수준에서 깨닫는다면, 우리의 행동은 그것(그 동기)을 설득력
이 떨어지게 만들면서 투덜대거나 냉소적인 것으로 나타날 수 있다.

주어진 글 다음에 이어질 글의 순서로 가장 적절한 것을 고르시오. [3점]

① (A) — (C) — (B) (A)의 '그 동기'에 대한 언급이 주어진 글에 없음
② (B) — (A) — (C) (B)에서 언급된 내용의 결과를 (C)에서 설명하고 있음
③ (B) — (C) — (A) 집단이 개인을 가치 있게 여기면 그 개인은 이점을 얻음 - (B) 그렇지
않으면 그런 이점은 없으며 생존하지 못함 - (C) 그 결과, 타인의
인식을 관찰하는 경향을 발전시키면서 자존감 등의 감정들이 나타나고
집단에 가치 있는 행동을 하도록 만들어짐 - (A) 그 감정들로 인해
자신이 하는 행동의 동기가 내적인 것처럼 느끼게 함
④ (C) — (A) — (B)
⑤ (C) — (B) — (A) (B)는 주어진 글과 반대되는 경우이므로 주어진 글 바로 뒤에 와야 함

━━━━━━━━━━━━━━━━━━━━━━━

왜 1등급? 주어진 글과 연결되는 문단은 쉽게 찾을 수 있지만, 이후 문단의 지시어
와 대응하는 확실한 단어를 찾기 어렵고, 내용의 인과 관계를 자세히 살펴봐야 하는
1등급 대비 문제이다.

| 문제 풀이 순서 |

1st 각 문단의 내용을 파악하고, 글의 논리적인 순서를 추론한다.

주어진 글: 개인으로서 성공하려는 우리의 능력은 우리가 집단 내에서 관계
를 얼마나 잘 다루는지에 달려 있었다. 만약(If) 그 집단이 우리를 가치 있게 여
겼다면 우리는 지원, 자원, 그리고 아마도 짝을 기대할 수 있었을 것이다.

➡ **주어진 글 뒤:** 집단 내 관계 형성과 개인의 성공이 어떤 관련이 있는지를 설명할 것
이다. If 가정법 문장이 집단 내에서 가치 있다고 인정받는 경우를 소개하므로 이와
반대되는 경우가 뒤에 이어질 수도 있다.

(A): 그리고 결정적으로 그것들(they)은 그 동기(that motivation)가 내
부에서 나오고 있는 것처럼 그것을 느끼게 만들도록 되어있다. 우리가 사회
적 압박에 반응하고 있었다는 것을 의식적인 수준에서 깨닫는다면, 우리의
행동은 그것(그 동기)을 설득력이 떨어지게 만들면서 투덜대거나 냉소적인
것으로 나타날 수 있다.

➡ **(A) 앞:** they와 that motivation이 가리키는 내용이 앞에 나와야 한다.
   ▶ 주어진 글 바로 뒤에 (A)가 올 수 없음
(A) 뒤: they나 that motivation에 관해 추가적인 내용이 나오지 않는다면 마무
리에 해당할 가능성이 높다. ▶ (A)가 마지막에 올 확률이 높음

(B): 만약 그렇지 않았다면(If it didn't), 우리는 그러한 이점들(these
merits) 중 아무것도 얻지 못했을 것이다. 그것은 신체적으로 그리고 유전
적으로 생존의 문제였다. 수백만 년 동안 그러한 압박은 자신의 지위를 최
대화하는 데 민감하고 능숙한 사람들을 선택했다.

➡ **(B) 앞:** it과 these merits가 가리키는 대상이 앞에 나와야 한다. 주어진 글에 집단
내에서 가치 있다고 '인정받으면' 지원, 자원, 짝이라는 '이점'을 기대할 수 있다는 내
용이 있으므로, it didn't는 the group didn't value us에 해당하고 지원, 자원, 짝
이라는 이점들이 these merits에 해당함을 알 수 있다.
   ▶ (B) 앞에 주어진 글이 와야 함 (순서: 주어진 글 → (B))
(B) 뒤: 집단 내에서 가치 있다고 인정받는 것은 생존과 직결되고, 인정받아야 한다
는 압박은 사람들이 지위를 최대화하도록 했으므로, 이러한 경향의 결과가 뒤에 이
어질 것이다.

(C): 그 결과(the result)는 우리 공동체의 다른 사람들이 우리를 어떻게 인식하는지 무의식적으로 관찰하는 경향의 발달이었다. 우리는 자존감 그리고 자존심, 수치심 또는 불안 같은 관련된 감정의 형태로 그 정보를 처리한다. 이러한 감정들(these emotions)은 우리에게 우리의 공동체가 우리를 가치 있게 여기도록 만드는 것을 더 많이 하고 그렇지 않은 것을 덜 하도록 강요한다.

➡ **(C) 앞:** (B)에서 사람들이 인정받아야 하는 압박을 받았다고 했는데, 이는 다른 사람들의 시선을 관찰하는 경향이 발달하는 결과(the result)로 이어졌다.
  ▶ (C) 앞에 (B)가 와야 함 (순서: 주어진 글 → (B) → (C))
  (C) 뒤: 우리가 인정을 얻어야 한다는 압박을 통해 느끼는 감정들(these emotions)이 집단에서 가치 있게 행동하도록 강요한다고 했다. 이는 (A)에서 그 감정들(they)이 집단에서 가치 있게 행동할 동기(the motivation)가 내부에서 나오는 것처럼 느끼게 한다는 내용과 연결된다.
  ▶ (C) 뒤에 (A)가 와야 함 (순서: 주어진 글 → (B) → (C) → (A))

2nd 글이 한눈에 들어오도록 정리하여 정답을 확인한다.

주어진 글: 개인의 성공은 집단 내 관계 형성에 달려 있어서 집단이 우리를 가치 있게 여기면 이점들을 얻을 수 있다.
➡ **(B):** 그렇지 않으면 그런 이점들을 얻을 수 없었으며, 생존과 직결되는 이러한 압박은 지위를 최대화하도록 했다.
➡ **(C):** 그 결과로 다른 사람들의 시선을 무의식적으로 관찰하는 경향을 발전시켜 왔고, 이에 따른 감정들은 우리가 집단에서 가치 있는 행동을 하도록 만든다.
➡ **(A):** 그러한 감정들은 그 동기가 우리의 내부에서 나온 것처럼 느끼게 만들며, 만약 사회적 압박에 의해 행동한다고 우리가 의식적으로 인식하면 투덜대거나 냉소적인 태도가 나타날 수 있다.
  ▶ 주어진 글 다음에 이어질 글의 순서는 (B) → (C) → (A)이므로 정답은 ③임

O 32 정답 ③ — ★ 1등급 대비 [정답률 41%]

*전자 상거래의 확대

Roughly twenty years ago, / brick-and-mortar stores / began to give way to electronic commerce. // **단서1** 전자 상거래가 쇼핑 경험에 대한 소비자의 인식을 바꿨음
대략 20년 전 / 오프라인 거래 상점이 / 전자 상거래로 바뀌기 시작했다 //

For good or bad, / the shift fundamentally changed / consumers' perception of the shopping experience. //
좋든 나쁘든 간에 / 그 변화는 근본적으로 바꿨다 / 쇼핑 경험에 대한 소비자의 인식을 //

(A) Before long, / the e-commerce book market naturally expanded / to include additional categories, / like CDs and DVDs. // **단서2** 온라인 서점의 꾸준한 상승이 추가적인 항목도 포함하는 것으로 이어짐
부사적 용법*
머지않아 / 전자 상거래 책 시장은 자연스럽게 확장되었다 / 추가적인 항목을 포함하도록 / CD와 DVD 같은 //

E-commerce soon snowballed / into the enormous industry / it is today, / where you can buy everything / from toilet paper to cars online. //
계속적 용법의 관계부사*
전자 상거래는 곧 눈덩이처럼 불어났다 / 거대 산업으로 / 오늘날의 / 그리고 그곳에서 여러분은 모든 것을 살 수 있다 / 화장실 휴지에서 자동차까지 온라인으로 //

(B) Nowhere was the shift more obvious / than with book sales, / which is how online bookstores got their start. // **단서3** 주어진 글의 the shift에 이어짐
부정어구 도치: 부정어구+동사+주어 / 계속적 용법의 관계대명사*
그 변화가 더 분명한 곳은 없었다 / 책 판매보다 / 그런데 그것이 온라인 서점이 시작된 방식이다 //

Physical bookstores simply could not stock / as many titles as a virtual bookstore could. //
원급 비교
물리적인 서점은 단순히 구비할 수 없었다 / 가상 서점이 할 수 있는 만큼 많은 서적을 //

There is only so much space / available on a shelf. //
공간은 딱 그 정도밖에 없다 / 책꽂이 위의 활용 가능한 //

(C) In addition to greater variety, / online bookstores were also able to offer aggressive discounts / thanks to their lower operating costs. // **단서4** 앞에 다양성에 대한 내용이 언급되어야 함
덕분에
더 많은 다양성뿐만 아니라 / 온라인 서점은 공격적인 할인을 또한 제공할 수 있었다 / 그들의 더 낮은 운영비 덕분에 //

The combination / of lower prices and greater selection / led to the slow, steady rise / of online bookstores. //
결합은 / 더 낮은 가격과 더 많은 선택의 / 느리지만 꾸준한 상승으로 이어졌다 / 온라인 서점의 //

- roughly [ad] 대략 • give way to ~로 바뀌다
- electronic commerce 전자 상거래 • shift [n] 이동, 변화
- perception [n] 인식 • expand [v] 확장하다
- category [n] 범주, 항목 • snowball [v] 눈덩이처럼 불어나다
- enormous [a] 거대한 • obvious [a] 명백한
- physical [a] 물리적인 • virtual [a] 가상의
- variety [n] 다양성 • aggressive [a] 공격적인
- operating cost 운영비 • combination [n] 조합, 결합

대략 20년 전 오프라인 거래 상점이 전자 상거래로 바뀌기 시작했다. 좋든 나쁘든 간에 그 변화는 쇼핑 경험에 대한 소비자의 인식을 근본적으로 바꾸었다. (B) 그 변화가 책 판매보다 더 분명한 곳은 없었는데 그것이 온라인 서점이 시작된 방식이다. 물리적인 서점은 단순히 가상 서점이 할 수 있는 만큼 많은 서적을 구비할 수 없었다. 책꽂이 위의 활용 가능한 공간은 딱 그 정도밖에 없다. (C) 더 많은 다양성뿐만 아니라 온라인 서점은 그들의 더 낮은 운영비 덕분에 공격적인 할인을 또한 제공할 수 있었다. 더 낮은 가격과 더 많은 선택의 결합은 온라인 서점의 느리지만 꾸준한 상승으로 이어졌다. (A) 머지않아 전자 상거래 책 시장은 CD와 DVD 같은 추가적인 항목을 포함하도록 자연스럽게 확장되었다. 전자 상거래는 곧 오늘날의 거대 산업으로 눈덩이처럼 불어났고 그곳에서 여러분은 화장실 휴지에서 자동차까지 모든 것을 온라인으로 살 수 있다.

> **주어진 글 다음에 이어질 글의 순서로 가장 적절한 것을 고르시오.**
> ① (A) — (C) — (B) 주어진 글의 the shift가 (B)의 the shift로 이어져야 함
> ② (B) — (A) — (C) (C)에서 말한 온라인 서점의 꾸준한 상승이 (A)의 추가적인 항목을 포함하는 것으로 이어져야 함
> ③ (B) — (C) — (A) (B) 가상 서점이 물리적인 서점보다 많은 책을 구비할 수 있었음 – (C) 더 많은 다양성과 공격적 할인을 통해 온라인 서점이 성장했음 – (A) 전자 상거래가 확장되고, 눈덩이처럼 불어났음
> ④ (C) — (A) — (B)
> ⑤ (C) — (B) — (A) (C)의 앞에는 다양성에 대한 내용이 나와야 함

왜 1등급? 주어진 글에서 말한 오프라인 거래 상점이 전자 상거래로 바뀌기 시작했다는 '변화(the shift)'에 대한 내용이 자연스럽게 이어지도록 나머지 글을 배열하는 것이 글의 순서를 맞추는 핵심이다.
특히 (A)와 (C)의 순서가 헷갈릴 수 있는데, 책뿐만 아니라 DVD, 휴지, 자동차 등 다양한 것을 온라인으로 살 수 있다고 말한 (A)의 마지막 부분이 글의 결말일 것이라는 단서를 파악해야 하는 1등급 대비 문제이다.

| 문제 풀이 순서 |

1st 각 문단의 내용을 파악하고, 글의 논리적인 순서를 추론한다.

주어진 글: 대략 20년 전 오프라인 거래 상점이 전자 상거래로 바뀌기 시작했다. 좋든 나쁘든 간에 그 변화는 쇼핑 경험에 대한 소비자의 인식을 근본적으로 바꾸었다.

➡ **소재:** 오프라인 거래 상점에서 전자 상거래로의 변화 **단서**
  전개 방향: 오프라인 거래 상점이 전자 상거래로 바뀌는 변화가 소비자의 인식을 바꾸게 된 것에 대한 내용이 이어질 것이다. **발상**

(A): 머지않아(Before long) 전자 상거래 책 시장은 CD와 DVD 같은 추가적인 항목을 포함하도록 자연스럽게 확장되었다. 전자상거래는 곧 오늘날의 거대 산업으로 눈덩이처럼 불어났고 그곳에서 여러분은 화장실 휴지에서 자동차까지 모든 것을 온라인으로 살 수 있다.

(A) 앞: 머지않아(Before long)라고 했으므로 전자 상거래 책 시장이 추가적인 항목을 포함하는 것까지 확장되기 전의 상황이 (A) 앞에 나와야 한다.
▶ (A) 앞에 주어진 글이 올 수 없음
(A) 뒤: 작은 전자 상거래가 확장되어 오늘날처럼 모든 것을 살 수 있게 되었다고 했으므로 글을 마무리짓는 역할을 할 가능성이 높다.
▶ (A)가 마지막에 올 확률이 높음

(B): 그 변화(the shift)가 책 판매보다 더 분명한 곳은 없는데 그것이 온라인 서점이 시작된 방식이다. 물리적인 서점은 단순히 가상 서점이 할 수 있는 만큼 많은 서적을 구비할 수 없었다. 책꽂이 위의 활용 가능한 공간은 딱 그 정도밖에 없다.

(B) 앞: 온라인 서점에서 제일 분명한 '그 변화(the shift)'는 바로 주어진 글에 나온 그 변화(the shift)를 그대로 가리킨다.
▶ (B) 앞에 주어진 글이 와야 함 (순서: 주어진 글 → (B))
(B) 뒤: 물리적인 서점은 가상 서점만큼 다양한 서적을 구비할 수 없다는 내용이므로 가상 서점의 장점이 뒤에 이어질 것이다.

(C): 더 많은 다양성뿐만 아니라(In addition to greater variety) 온라인 서점은 그들의 더 낮은 운영비 덕분에 공격적인 할인을 또한 제공할 수 있었다. 더 낮은 가격과 더 많은 선택의 결합은 온라인 서점의 느리지만 꾸준한 상승으로 이어졌다.

(C) 앞: In addition to라고 했으므로 온라인 서점의 '더 많은 다양성(greater variety)'에 대한 내용이 앞에 와야 한다.
▶ (C) 앞에 (B)가 와야 함 (순서: 주어진 글 → (B) → (C))
(C) 뒤: 공격적인 할인을 통해 온라인 서점이 꾸준히 상승했다고 했으므로, 여기에서 더 나아가 추가적인 항목을 포함하는 것까지 확장되는 (A)가 뒤에 와야 한다.
▶ 순서: 주어진 글 → (B) → (C) → (A)

2nd 글이 한눈에 들어오도록 정리하여 정답을 확인한다.

주어진 글: 오프라인 거래 상점이 전자 상거래로 바뀌기 시작했고, 이 변화가 소비자의 인식을 바꾸었다.
→ **(B):** 가상 서점은 물리적인 서점보다 많은 책을 구비할 수 있었다.
→ **(C):** 더 많은 다양성뿐만 아니라 공격적인 할인을 통해 온라인 서점이 꾸준히 상승했다.
→ **(A):** 전자 상거래가 CD와 DVD 같은 추가적인 항목을 포함하면서 확장되고, 다른 분야에까지 눈덩이처럼 불어났다.
▶ 주어진 글 다음에 이어질 순서는 (B) → (C) → (A)이므로 정답은 ③임

어법 특강

✱ **to부정사의 부사적 용법**
– to부정사의 용법에는 명사적 용법, 형용사적 용법, 부사적 용법이 있는데, 그 중에서 부사적 용법은 목적, 감정의 원인, 결과, 이유 · 판단의 근거, 조건, 형용사 · 부사 수식을 하는 역할로 쓰인다.
• She learned Spanish to travel to Spain. (목적)
(그녀는 스페인으로 여행을 가기 위해 스페인어를 배웠다.)
• It's so nice to meet you again. (감정의 원인)
(너를 다시 만나게 되어서 정말 좋아.)
• My grandmother lived to be 99. (결과)
(우리 할머니는 99세까지 사셨다.)

어법 특강

✱ **관계부사의 종류 및 생략**
– 관계부사의 종류는 where(장소), when(때), why(이유), how(방법)이 있고, 보통 생략이 가능하다. 하지만 how나 선행사 the way는 둘 중 반드시 하나만 사용해야 한다.

장소	(the place) where	이유	(the reason) why
때	(the time) when	방법	(the way) how

• I went to the library (where) we met first.
(나는 우리가 처음 만났던 도서관에 갔다.)
• No one knows the reason (why) my flight has been canceled.
(아무도 내 비행편이 취소된 이유를 모른다.)
• It's the way in which the machine works.
how 대신 (the way) in which나 (the way) that으로 쓸 수 있음
(이것이 그 기계가 작동하는 방식이다.)

주어진 글의 the shift가 어느 문단에서 이어지고 있는지 찾아야 해!

O 어휘 Review 정답 ━━━━━━ 문제편 p. 237

01	도움 없는	11	go under	21	orderly
02	돌아다니다	12	show off	22	collapse
03	분배	13	at risk	23	joint
04	풍부함	14	fall apart	24	consciousness
05	비현실적인	15	draw on	25	extinction
06	pioneer	16	livestock	26	hexagons
07	alert	17	incompetence	27	adaptations
08	behavior	18	concrete	28	generations
09	ancient	19	pride	29	vibration
10	distortion	20	citizens	30	underperform

 **P 주어진 문장 넣기** 문제편 p. 240~256

P 01 정답 ③ *놀이를 통한 아이들의 도덕성 발달

글의 흐름으로 보아, 주어진 문장이 들어가기에 가장 적절한 곳을 고르시오.

단서 1 도덕성을 설명하기 위해 앞에서 물잔을 예로 듦

Piaget argued / that children's understanding of morality / is like their understanding of those water glasses: / we can't say / that it is innate or kids learn it directly from adults. //
Piaget는 주장했다 / 도덕성에 대한 아이들의 이해는 / 그런 물잔에 대한 이해와 같은데 / 즉 우리가 말할 수 없다고 / 그것이 타고났다거나 혹은 아이들이 어른들로부터 직접 그것을 배운다고 //

Piaget put the same amount of water / into two different glasses: / a tall narrow glass and a wide glass, / then asked kids to compare two glasses. // 병렬 구조
Piaget는 똑같은 양의 물을 넣고 / 두 개의 서로 다른 유리잔에 / 키가 크고 폭이 좁은 유리잔과 넓은 유리잔 / 그런 다음 아이들에게 두 유리잔을 비교하라고 요청했다 //

(①) Kids younger than six or seven usually say / that the tall narrow glass now holds more water, / because the level is higher. //
단서 2 아이들은 상황을 단편적으로만 이해함
6세 혹은 7세보다 더 어린 아이들은 대개 말하는데 / 키가 크고 폭이 좁은 유리잔에 물이 더 많이 담겨 있다고 / 왜냐하면 수위가 더 높기 때문이다 //

단서 3 아이들은 놀이를 통해 개념을 이해함
(②) And when they are ready, / they figure out the conservation of volume for themselves / just by playing with cups of water. //
by -ing: ~함으로써
그리고 아이들이 준비가 되어 있을 때 / 그들은 부피의 보존을 스스로 알아낸다 / 물이 든 컵들을 갖고 놂으로써 //

부사절 접속사 (~ 하면서) 단서 4 다른 아이들과 놀면서 도덕성을 깨달음
(③) Rather, / it is self-constructed / as kids play with other kids. //
오히려 / 그것은 아이들이 스스로 구성해 낸 것이다 / 다른 아이들과 놀면서 //

동명사구 주어
(④) Taking turns in a game is like / pouring water back and forth between glasses. //
게임을 순서대로 돌아가며 하는 것은 같다 / 물잔 사이를 왔다 갔다 하며 물을 붓는 것과 //

'일단 ~하면'
(⑤) Once kids have reached the age of five or six, / then playing games and working things out together will help / them learn about fairness far more effectively / than any teaching from adults. //
동명사구 주어   비교급 강조 부사
단서 5 함께 놀며 공평과 같은 가치를 배움
일단 아이들이 5세 혹은 6세에 이르면 / 함께 게임을 하고 문제를 해결해 나가는 것이 도움이 될 것이다 / 그들이 훨씬 더 효과적으로 공평함에 대해 배우는 데 / 어른들로부터의 그 어떤 가르침보다 //

- argue ⓥ 주장하다 • morality ⓝ 도덕(성) • amount ⓝ 양
- narrow ⓐ 좁은 • level ⓝ 수위, 높이 • volume ⓝ 부피
- self-constructed ⓐ 스스로 구성해 낸 • reach ⓥ ~에 이르다
- fairness ⓝ 공평함

Piaget는 똑같은 양의 물을 키가 크고 폭이 좁은 유리잔과 넓은 유리잔, 두 개의 서로 다른 유리잔에 넣고 그런 다음 아이들에게 두 유리잔을 비교하라고 요청했다. (①) 6세 혹은 7세보다 더 어린 아이들은 키가 크고 폭이 좁은 유리잔에 물이 더 많이 담겨 있다고 대개 말하는데, 왜냐하면 수위가 더 높기 때문이다. (②) 그리고 아이들이 준비가 되어 있을 때, 그들은 물이 든 컵들을 갖고 놂으로써 부피의 보존을 스스로 알아낸다. (③ Piaget는 도덕성에 대한 아이들의 이해는 그런 물잔에 대한 이해와 같은데, 즉 우리가 그것이 타고났다거나 혹은 아이들이 어른들로부터 직접 그것을 배운다고 말할 수 없다고 주장했다.) 오히려 그것은 아이들이 다른 아이들과 놀면서 스스로 구성해 낸 것이다. (④) 게임을 순서대로 돌아가며 하는 것은 물잔 사이를 왔다 갔다 하며 물을 붓는 것과 같다. (⑤) 일단 아이들이 5세 혹은 6세에 이르면, 함께 게임을 하고 문제를 해결해 나가는 것이 어른들로부터의 그 어떤 가르침보다 그들이 훨씬 더 효과적으로 공평함에 대해 배우는 데 도움이 될 것이다.

| 문제 풀이 순서 | ★★★ [정답률 50%]

1st 주어진 문장을 해석하고, 앞뒤에 어떤 내용이 올지 생각한다.

Piaget argued that children's understanding of morality is like their understanding of those water glasses: we can't say that it is innate or kids learn it directly from adults.
Piaget는 도덕성에 대한 아이들의 이해는 그런 물잔에 대한 이해와 같은데, 즉 우리가 그것이 타고났다거나 혹은 아이들이 어른들로부터 직접 그것을 배운다고 말할 수 없다고 주장했다.

➡ 주어진 문장 앞: those water glasses(그런 물잔)라고 했으므로, 단서 아이들의 도덕성 이해도를 설명하는 예시로 '물잔'이 언급되고 다른 내용으로 전환되는 부분을 찾아야 한다. 발상

2nd 각 선택지의 앞뒤 흐름이 매끄러운지 확인한다.

①의 앞 문장과 뒤 문장
앞 문장: Piaget는 똑같은 양의 물을 키가 크고 폭이 좁은 유리잔과 넓은 유리잔, 두 개의 서로 다른 유리잔에 넣고 그런 다음 아이들에게 두 유리잔을 비교하라고 요청했다.
뒤 문장: 6세 혹은 7세보다 더 어린 아이들은 키가 크고 폭이 좁은 유리잔에 물이 더 많이 담겨 있다고 대개 말하는데, 왜냐하면 수위가 더 높기 때문이다.

➡ 아이들에게 모양이 다른 두 물잔을 비교하라고 요청했고, 6~7세보다 어린 아이들이 단순히 수위를 기준으로 물의 양을 판단했다는 결과가 앞뒤로 이어진다.
▶ 주어진 문장이 ①에 들어갈 수 없음

②의 앞 문장과 뒤 문장
앞 문장: ①의 뒤 문장과 같음
뒤 문장: 그리고 아이들이 준비가 되어 있을 때, 그들은 물이 든 컵들을 갖고 놂으로써 부피의 보존을 스스로 알아낸다.

➡ 아이들이 6~7세 이전에는 물의 양을 단순한 기준으로 판단했지만, 나중에 물잔을 갖고 놀면서 스스로 부피 보존의 개념을 알아낸다는 내용이 이어진다.
▶ 주어진 문장이 ②에 들어갈 수 없음

③의 앞 문장과 뒤 문장
앞 문장: ②의 뒤 문장과 같음
뒤 문장: 오히려(Rather) 그것(it)은 아이들이 다른 아이들과 놀면서 스스로 구성해 낸 것이다.

➡ 물잔 예시가 마무리되고 오히려 아이들이 it을 스스로 구성한다고 했는데, 이는 물잔이나 부피의 보존 자체를 가리키는 것이 아니므로 앞뒤 문장이 이어지지 않는다. 주어진 문장에 아이들의 도덕성 이해가 물잔 이해와 같다고 했으므로, it은 도덕성에 대한 이해를 가리킨다. ▶ 주어진 문장이 ③에 들어가야 함

④의 앞 문장과 뒤 문장
앞 문장: ③의 뒤 문장과 같음
뒤 문장: 게임을 순서대로 돌아가며 하는 것은 물잔 사이를 왔다 갔다 하며 물을 붓는 것과 같다.

➡ 아이들이 놀이를 통해 도덕성을 스스로 구성한 예를 들기 위해, 물잔 사이를 왔다 갔다 하며 물을 붓는 게임을 언급했다. ▶ 주어진 문장이 ④에 들어갈 수 없음

⑤의 앞 문장과 뒤 문장
앞 문장: ④의 뒤 문장과 같음
뒤 문장: 일단 아이들이 5세 혹은 6세에 이르면, 함께 게임을 하고 문제를 해결해 나가는 것이 어른들로부터의 그 어떤 가르침보다 그들이 훨씬 더 효과적으로 공평에 대해 배우는 데 도움이 될 것이다.

➡ 게임의 순서를 지키는 것을 물잔 놀이를 통해 배운다는 점에 이어서, 공평함을 배우려면 어른의 가르침보다 놀이를 통해 배우는 것이 더 효과적이라는 내용으로 글이 마무리된다. ▶ 주어진 문장이 ⑤에 들어갈 수 없음

272 자이스토리 영어 독해 기본

P 02 정답 ⑤ *직장과 가정의 경계에서 보이는 차이

글의 흐름으로 보아, 주어진 문장이 들어가기에 가장 적절한 곳을 고르시오. [3점]

Other individuals prefer / integrating work and family roles / all day long. // 단서 1 앞에는 직장과 가정의 역할을 통합하는 것을 선호하지 않는 사람들이 나와야 함
다른 사람들은 선호한다 / 직장과 가정의 역할을 통합하는 것을 / 하루 종일 //

Boundaries between work and home are blurring / as portable digital technology makes it(가목적어) / increasingly possible(목적격 보어) / to work(진목적어) anywhere, anytime. //
직장과 가정의 경계가 흐릿해지고 있다 / 휴대용 디지털 기술이 ~을 만듦에 따라 / 점차 가능하게 / 언제, 어디서나 작업하는 것을 //

Individuals differ / in how they like to manage their time(전치사의 목적어로 쓰인 간접의문문) / to meet(부사적 용법(목적)) work and outside responsibilities. //
사람들은 차이가 있다 / 자신의 시간을 관리하기를 바라는 방식에 / 직장과 외부의 책임을 수행하기 위해 //

(①) Some people prefer / to separate or segment roles / so that(결과의 접속사(~하도록)) boundary crossings are minimized. //
어떤 사람들은 선호한다 / 역할을 분리하거나 분할하는 것을 / 경계 교차 지점이 최소화되도록 //

(②) For example, / these people might keep(might에 연결되는 동사 ①) separate email accounts / for work and family /
예를 들어 / 이러한 사람들은 별개의 이메일 계정을 유지할지도 모른다 / 직장과 가정을 위한 /
and try(동사 ②) to conduct work at the workplace / and take care of(동사 ③) family matters / only during breaks and non-work time. //
그리고 직장에서 일을 수행하려고 할지도 모른다 / 그리고 가정사를 처리할지도 모른다 / 휴식 시간과 일을 하지 않는 시간 동안에만 //

(③) We've even noticed / more of these "segmenters"(목적어) / carrying(목적격 보어(현재분사)) two phones / — one for work / and one for personal use. //
우리는 심지어 알게 되었다 / 더 많은 이러한 '분할자들'이 / 두 개의 전화기를 가지고 다니는 것을 / 하나는 업무용 / 그리고 하나는 개인용인 //

(④) Flexible schedules work well / for these individuals / because(부사절 접속사(이유)) they enable greater distinction / between time at work / and time in other roles. // 단서 2 직장과 다른 역할을 잘 구분하는 사람들에 관한 설명이 앞에서부터 이어졌음
유연근로시간제는 잘 적용된다 / 이런 사람들에게 / 그것들이 더 큰 구별을 가능하게 하기 때문에 / 직장에서의 시간 사이에 / 다른 역할에서의 시간과 //

(⑤) This might entail / constantly trading(entail의 목적어 ①) text messages with children / from the office, /
이것은 수반할지도 모른다 / 아이들과 문자 메시지를 지속적으로 주고받는 것을 / 직장에서 /
or monitoring(목적어 ②) emails at home and on vacation, / rather than returning(목적어 ③) to work to find(부사적 용법(결과)) / hundreds of messages in their inbox. //
또는 집에서 그리고 휴가 중에 이메일을 확인하는 것을 / 직장으로 돌아가서 발견하는 것 대신에 / 받은 편지함에서 수백 개의 메시지를 // 단서 3 직장과 가정의 역할이 통합된 사람들에 관한 설명임

- integrate ⓥ 통합하다
- boundary ⓝ 경계(선)
- blur ⓥ 흐릿해지다
- portable ⓐ 휴대용의
- responsibility ⓝ 책임(감)
- separate ⓥ 분리하다
- segment ⓥ 분할하다
- minimize ⓥ 최소화하다
- conduct ⓥ 수행하다
- flexible ⓐ 유연한
- distinction ⓝ 구별, 차이
- constantly ad 거듭, 지속적으로
- inbox ⓝ 받은 편지함

휴대용 디지털 기술이 언제, 어디서나 작업하는 것을 점차 가능하게 함에 따라 직장과 가정의 경계가 흐릿해지고 있다. 사람들이 직장과 외부의 책임을 수행하기 위해 자신의 시간을 관리하기를 바라는 방식에는 차이가 있다. (①) 어떤 사람들은 경계 교차 지점이 최소화되도록 역할을 분리하거나 분할하는 것을 선호한다. (②) 예를 들어, 이러한 사람들은 직장과 가정을 위한 별개의 이메일 계정을 유지하고 직장에서 일을 수행하며 휴식 시간과 일을 하지 않는 시간 동안에만 가정사를 처리하려고 할지도 모른다. (③) 우리는 더 많은 이러한 '분할자들'이 하나는 업무용이고 하나는 개인용인 두 개의 전화기를 가지고 다니고 있음을 심지어 알게 되었다. (④) 유연근로시간제는 이런 사람들에게 잘 적용되는데, 왜냐하면 직장에서의 시간과 다른 역할에서의 시간 사이에 더 큰 구별을 가능하게 하기 때문이다. (⑤ 다른 사람들은 하루 종일 직장과 가정의 역할을 통합하는 것을 선호한다.) 이것은 직장으로 돌아가서 받은 편지함에서 수백 개의 메시지를 발견하는 것 대신 직장에서 아이들과 문자 메시지를 지속적으로 주고받거나 집에서 그리고 휴가 중에 이메일을 확인하는 것을 수반할지도 모른다.

| 문제 풀이 순서 | ✿✿✿ [정답률 29%]

1st 주어진 문장을 해석하고, 연결어, 지시어 등을 확인한다.

Other individuals prefer integrating work and family roles all day long.
다른 사람들은 하루 종일 직장과 가정의 역할을 통합하는 것을 선호한다.

→ **주어진 문장 앞:** Other individuals(다른 사람들)라고 했으므로 (단서) 앞에는 직장과 가정의 역할을 통합하는 것을 선호하지 않는 사람들이 언급되어야 한다. (발상)

2nd 찾은 단서를 생각하며 각 선택지의 앞뒤 흐름이 매끄러운지 확인한다.

- ①의 앞 문장과 뒤 문장

앞 문장: 사람들이 직장과 외부의 책임을 수행하기 위해 자신의 시간을 관리하기를 바라는 방식에는 차이가 있다.
뒤 문장: 어떤 사람들은 경계 교차 지점이 최소화되도록 역할을 분리하거나 분할하는 것을 선호한다.

→ 앞 문장에는 직장과 가정의 역할을 통합하는 것을 선호하지 않는 사람들은 언급되지 않았고, 뒤 문장에서 역할을 분리하는 것을 선호하는 사람들에 대해 언급을 시작하고 있다.
▶ 주어진 문장이 ①에 들어갈 수 없음

- ②의 앞 문장과 뒤 문장

앞 문장: ①의 뒤 문장과 같음
뒤 문장: 예를 들어(For example), 이러한 사람들은 직장과 가정을 위한 별개의 이메일 계정을 유지하고 직장에서 일을 수행하며 휴식 시간과 일을 하지 않는 시간 동안에만 가정사를 처리하려고 할지도 모른다.

→ 앞 문장에서 말한 역할을 분리하는 것을 선호하는 사람들에 대한 예시가 이어진다.
▶ 주어진 문장이 ②에 들어갈 수 없음

- ③의 앞 문장과 뒤 문장

앞 문장: ②의 뒤 문장과 같음
뒤 문장: 우리는 더 많은 이러한(these) '분할자들'이 하나는 업무용이고 하나는 개인용인 두 개의 전화기를 가지고 다니고 있음을 심지어 알게 되었다.

→ 역할을 분리하는 것을 선호하는 '분할자들'에 대한 설명이 이어진다.
▶ 주어진 문장이 ③에 들어갈 수 없음

- ④의 앞 문장과 뒤 문장

앞 문장: ③의 뒤 문장과 같음
뒤 문장: 유연근로시간제는 이런(these) 사람들에게 잘 적용되는데, 왜냐하면 직장에서의 시간과 다른 역할에서의 시간 사이에 더 큰 구별을 가능하게 하기 때문이다.

→ 직장과 다른 역할에서의 시간을 구별하는 것은 두 가지 역할을 분리하고자 하는 사람들에게 잘 적용되는 것이므로 앞 문장과 같은 사람들에 관해 이야기하고 있다.
▶ 주어진 문장이 ④에 들어갈 수 없음

⑤의 앞 문장과 뒤 문장

앞 문장: ④의 뒤 문장과 같음

뒤 문장: 이것(This)은 직장으로 돌아가서 받은 편지함에서 수백 개의 메시지를 발견하는 것 대신 직장에서 아이들과 문자 메시지를 지속적으로 주고받거나 집에서 그리고 휴가 중에 이메일을 확인하는 것을 수반할지도 모른다.

➡ 직장에서 아이들과 문자를 주고받고, 집에서 업무 이메일을 확인하는 것은 직장과 가정의 역할을 통합하는 것의 예시이다.

따라서 직장과 가정의 역할을 통합하는 것을 선호하는 사람들이 처음 언급된 주어진 문장이 ⑤에 오는 것이 적절하다.

▶ 주어진 문장이 ⑤에 들어가야 함

P 03 정답 ⑤ *냉방 설비의 지혜 ─────────

> 글의 흐름으로 보아, 주어진 문장이 들어가기에 가장 적절한 곳을 고르시오.

But / all this **wisdom** (불가산 명사) about how to deal with heat, / **accumulated over centuries of practical experience** (분사구문), / **is** (단수 동사) all too often ignored. //

그러나 / 열을 다루는 방법에 대한 이 모든 지혜는 / 수 세기의 실제적인 경험을 하면서 축적됐는데 / 너무 자주 간과된다 //

The rise of air-conditioning accelerated / the construction of sealed boxes, / **where** (계속적 용법의 관계부사) the building's only airflow is through the filtered ducts / of the air-conditioning unit. //

냉방 설비의 부상은 가속화했는데 / 밀폐된 구조물의 건설을 / 그곳에서 건물의 유일한 공기 흐름은 여과된 배관을 통해서 이루어진다 / 냉방 설비 장치의 //

It doesn't have to be this way. //

그것이 이러한 방식일 필요는 없다 //

Look at any old building / in a hot climate, / **whether** (부사절 접속사 (~이든 아니든)) it's in Sicily or Marrakesh or Tehran. //

오래된 아무 건물이나 보아라 / 더운 기후에 있는 / Sicily에 있든 Marrakesh에 있든 Tehran에 있든 간에 //

(①) Architects understood the importance / of shade, airflow, light colors. //

건축가들은 중요성을 이해했다 / 그늘, 공기 흐름, 밝은 색상의 //

(②) They oriented buildings / **to capture** (부사적 용법 (목적)) cool breezes / and **block** the worst heat of the afternoon. //

그들은 건물을 향하게 했다 / 시원한 산들바람을 잡아 두고 / 오후의 가장 혹독한 열기를 막을 수 있도록 //

(③) They built with thick walls / and white roofs / and transoms over doors / **to encourage** (부사적 용법 (목적)) airflow. //

그들은 두꺼운 벽 건물을 지었다 / 흰색 지붕과 / 문 위의 채광창 / 공기 흐름을 촉진하기 위해서 //

(④) **Anyone** (핵심 주어 (단수)) / who has ever spent a few minutes in a mudbrick house in Tucson, / or walked on the narrow streets of old Seville, / **knows** (단수 동사) how well these construction methods work. //
[단서 1 전통적인 냉방 설비가 다양한 지역에서 사용되고 있고 잘 작동함]

어느 누구든 / Tucson의 진흙 벽돌 집에서 몇 분을 보내 봤거나 / 옛 Seville의 좁은 길을 걸어 본 / 이 건설 방법이 얼마나 잘 작동하는지 안다 //

((⑤)) In this sense, / air-conditioning is not just a technology of personal comfort; / it is also a technology of forgetting. //

이러한 의미에서 / 냉방 설비는 개인적인 안락의 기술일 뿐만 아니라 / 이것은 망각의 기술이다 //
[단서 2 전통적으로 효과적인 냉방 설비를 망각한 채로 여전히 다른 냉방 설비가 발전함]

• air-conditioning ⓝ 냉방 설비   • accelerate ⓥ 가속화하다
• box ⓝ 구조물   • airflow ⓝ 공기 흐름   • unit ⓝ 장치
• architect ⓝ 건축가   • breeze ⓝ 산들바람   • comfort ⓝ 안락

냉방 설비의 부상은 밀폐된 구조물의 건설을 가속화했는데, 그곳에서 건물의 유일한 공기 흐름은 냉방 설비 장치의 여과된 배관을 통해서 이루어진다. 그것이 이러한 방식일 필요는 없다. Sicily에 있든 Marrakesh에 있든 Tehran에 있든 간에, 더운 기후에 있는 오래된 아무 건물이나 보아라. (①) 건축가들은 그늘, 공기 흐름, 밝은 색상의 중요성을 이해했다. (②) 그들은 시원한 산들바람을 잡아 두고 오후의 가장 혹독한 열기를 막을 수 있도록 건물을 향하게 했다. (③) 그들은 공기 흐름을 촉진하기 위해서 두꺼운 벽과 흰색 지붕과 문 위의 채광창을 가지고 있는 건물을 지었다. (④) Tucson의 진흙 벽돌 집에서 몇 분을 보내 봤거나, 옛 Seville의 좁은 길을 걸어 본 어느 누구든 이 건설 방법이 얼마나 잘 작동하는지 안다. (⑤ 그러나 열을 다루는 방법에 대한 이 모든 지혜는, 수 세기의 실제적인 경험을 하면서 축적됐는데, 너무 자주 간과된다.) 이러한 의미에서, 냉방 설비는 개인적인 안락의 기술일 뿐만 아니라, 이것은 망각의 기술이다.

| 문제 풀이 순서 | ★★★ [정답률 48%]

1st 주어진 문장을 해석하고, 연결어, 지시어 등을 확인한다.

But **all this wisdom** about how to deal with heat, accumulated over centuries of practical experience, is all too often **ignored**.

그러나 열을 다루는 방법에 대한 **이 모든 지혜**는, 수 세기의 실제적인 경험을 하면서 축적됐는데, 너무 자주 **간과된다**.

➡ 주어진 문장 앞: 앞의 내용을 가리키는 all this wisdom이 있으므로, (단서) 열을 다루는 전통적인 방법들과 그 예시가 전부 주어진 문장 앞에 제시될 것이다. (발상)

➡ 주어진 문장 뒤: But과 ignored가 있으므로 (단서) 앞의 내용과는 다르게, 열을 다루는 전통적인 방법들이 간과된다는 내용이 뒤에 이어질 것이다. (발상)

2nd 각 선택지의 앞뒤 흐름이 매끄러운지 확인한다.

①의 앞 문장과 뒤 문장

앞 문장: Sicily에 있든 Marrakesh에 있든 Tehran에 있든 간에, 더운 기후에 있는 오래된 아무 건물이나 보아라.

뒤 문장: 건축가들은 그늘, 공기 흐름, 밝은 색상의 중요성을 이해했다.

➡ 더운 기후의 건축에는 그늘 등 여러 요소의 중요성이 반영되어 있다는 흐름으로 앞뒤 내용이 이어진다. ▶ 주어진 문장이 ①에 들어갈 수 없음

②의 앞 문장과 뒤 문장

앞 문장: ①의 뒤 문장과 같음

뒤 문장: 그들은 시원한 산들바람을 잡아 두고 오후의 가장 혹독한 열기를 막을 수 있도록 건물을 향하게 했다.

➡ 건축 요소 중 공기 흐름이 반영된 예시가 자연스럽게 연결되었다. ▶ 주어진 문장이 ②에 들어갈 수 없음

③의 앞 문장과 뒤 문장

앞 문장: ②의 뒤 문장과 같음

뒤 문장: 그들은 공기 흐름을 촉진하기 위해서 두꺼운 벽과 흰색 지붕과 문 위의 채광창을 가지고 있는 건물을 지었다.

➡ 건축 요소 중 공기 흐름 및 밝은 색상과 그 외 요소가 반영된 예시가 자연스럽게 연결되었다. ▶ 주어진 문장에 ③에 들어갈 수 없음

④의 앞 문장과 뒤 문장

앞 문장: ③의 뒤 문장과 같음

뒤 문장: Tucson의 진흙 벽돌 집에서 몇 분을 보내 봤거나, 옛 Seville의 좁은 길을 걸어 본 어느 누구든 이 건설 방법이 얼마나 잘 작동하는지 안다.

➡ 앞에 언급된 전통적인 냉방 설비의 예시에 이어서, 이러한 설비들이 여전히 잘 작동한다는 내용이 자연스럽게 연결되었다. ▶ 주어진 문장이 ④에 들어갈 수 없음

앞 문장: ④의 뒤 문장과 같음
뒤 문장: [이러한 의미에서], 냉방 설비는 개인적인 안락의 기술일 뿐만 아니라, 이것은 망각의 기술이다.

→ In this sense가 있으므로 망각에 관한 내용이 앞에 있어야 하는데, 앞 문장에는 옛 냉방 설비가 충분히 잘 작동한다는 내용밖에 없어서 앞뒤 내용이 이어지지 않는다. 주어진 문장에 열을 다루는 지혜가 오래 축적되었지만 '간과된다'고 했으므로, 냉방 설비가 '망각'의 기술이라는 문장과 자연스럽게 연결된다.
▶ 주어진 문장이 ⑤에 들어가야 함

[구문 서술형]

[정답] sealed boxes, where

[해석] 냉방 설비의 부상은 밀폐된 구조물의 건설을 가속화했는데, 그곳에서 건물의 유일한 공기 흐름은 여과된 배관을 통해서 이루어진다.
→ 콤마 뒤 계속적 용법으로 쓰인 「전치사+관계대명사」(in which)의 선행사는 sealed boxes(밀폐된 구조물)이다. 선행사가 어떠한 장소를 나타내고, 「at/in/on+which」와 같이 「전치사+관계대명사」가 쓰였을 때 이를 관계부사 where로 바꿔 쓸 수 있다.

P 04 정답 ④ *주변과 장소를 인지할 때 영향을 미치는 감정

글의 흐름으로 보아, 주어진 문장이 들어가기에 가장 적절한 곳을 고르시오.

Partly this was the obvious convenience / of being able to exit more quickly. // 단서1 승객들이 문 근처에 자리 잡기를 좋아하는 이성적인 이유
부분적으로 이것은 명확한 편리함 때문이었다 / 더 빨리 내릴 수 있다는 //

명사적 용법 (주어)   명사적 용법 (주격 보어)
To monitor our surroundings / is to focus on / what's outside
선행사를 포함하는 관계대명사
of ourselves: / what we see, hear, smell, feel, and perhaps even taste. //
우리 주변을 살피는 것은 / 집중하는 것이다 / 우리 자신 바깥에 있는 것에 / 우리가 보고, 듣고, 냄새 맡고, 느끼고, 어쩌면 맛보기도 하는 것 //

선행사를 포함하는 관계대명사   -thing으로 끝나는 대명사는 형용사가 뒤에서 수식함
But sometimes what really marks a place / is something less specific / — a *feeling* within us. //
그러나 때로는 어떤 장소를 진정으로 특징짓는 것은 / 덜 구체적인 것이다 / 우리 안에 있는 '감정' //

(①) An interesting example emerged / from a study of subway passenger behavior. //
흥미로운 예가 나왔다 / 지하철 승객 행동에 관한 연구에서 //

현재분사(Researchers 수식)
(②) Researchers trying to understand / why people sit where they sit / or stand where they stand / in subway and metro trains /
이해하려고 노력하는 연구자들은 / 왜 사람들이 그들이 앉는 곳에 앉거나 / 그들이 서는 곳에 서는지를 / 지하철이나 전철에서 /

주격 관계대명사 (선행사: the factors)   뒤에 관계부사 how가 생략됨
examined the factors / that shape / the way riders used and navigated that space / in different situations. //
요인들을 조사했다 / 형성하는 / 승객들이 그 공간을 사용하고 탐색하는 방식 / 다양한 상황에서 //
단서2 승객들이 기차의 문 근처에 자리 잡기를 좋아하는 이유를 연구함

(③) One of their findings / involved the reasons / many riders like to plant themselves close to the train's doors. //
자리 잡다
연구 결과 중 하나는 / 이유들과 관련이 있었다 / 많은 승객들이 기차의 문 근처에 자리 잡기를 좋아하는 //
단서3 승객들이 문 근처에 자리 잡기를 좋아하는 감정적인 이유

(④) But it was shaped partly / by a more abstract sensation /
그러나 이는 부분적으로 형성되었다 / 더 추상적인 느낌에 의해 /
형용사적 용법 (the desire 수식)
— the desire to avoid the sometimes uncomfortable feeling / of accidentally making eye contact with seated passengers. //
때때로 불편한 느낌을 피하려는 욕구 / 앉아 있는 승객들과 우연히 눈이 마주치는 //

(⑤) We can't see feelings / — but they're very real, / and they influence our experience of the world. //
우리는 감정들을 볼 수 없다 / 그러나 그것들은 매우 실재하고 / 그것들은 세상에 대한 우리의 경험에 영향을 미친다 //

- obvious ⓐ 명확한   • convenience ⓝ 편리함
- surroundings ⓝ 주변   • mark ⓥ 특징짓다
- specific ⓐ 구체적인   • emerge ⓥ 나타나다   • passenger ⓝ 승객
- behavior ⓝ 행동   • examine ⓥ 조사하다   • factor ⓝ 요인
- shape ⓥ 형성하다   • navigate ⓥ 탐색하다
- findings ⓝ 연구 결과   • involve ⓥ ~와 관련이 있다
- abstract ⓐ 추상적인   • sensation ⓝ 느낌   • desire ⓝ 욕구
- accidentally ⓐd 우연히   • influence ⓥ ~에 영향을 미치다

우리 주변을 살피는 것은 우리 자신 바깥에 있는 것에 집중하는 것이다: 우리가 보고, 듣고, 냄새 맡고, 느끼고, 어쩌면 맛보기도 하는 것. 그러나 때로는 어떤 장소를 진정으로 특징짓는 것은 덜 구체적인 것 — 우리 안에 있는 '감정'이다. (①) 흥미로운 예가 지하철 승객 행동에 관한 연구에서 나왔다. (②) 지하철이나 전철에서 왜 사람들이 그들이 앉는 곳에 앉거나 그들이 서는 곳에 서는지를 이해하려고 노력하는 연구자들은 다양한 상황에서 승객들이 그 공간을 사용하고 탐색하는 방식을 형성하는 요인들을 조사했다. (③) 연구 결과 중 하나는 많은 승객들이 기차의 문 근처에 자리 잡기를 좋아하는 이유들과 관련이 있었다. (④ 부분적으로 이것은 더 빨리 내릴 수 있다는 명확한 편리함 때문이었다.) 그러나 이는 부분적으로 더 추상적인 느낌 — 앉아 있는 승객들과 우연히 눈이 마주치는 때때로 불편한 느낌을 피하려는 욕구에 의해 형성되었다. (⑤) 우리는 감정들을 볼 수 없다 — 그러나 그것들은 매우 실재하고, 그것들은 세상에 대한 우리의 경험에 영향을 미친다.

| 문제 풀이 순서 | ★★❀ [정답률 72%]

1st 주어진 문장을 해석하고, 지시어 등을 확인한다.

Partly this was the obvious convenience of being able to exit more quickly.
부분적으로 이것은 더 빨리 내릴 수 있다는 명확한 편리함 때문이었다.
→ 주어진 문장 앞: this(이것)가 더 빨리 내리는 편리함 때문이라고 했으므로, 단서 무엇이 더 빨리 내릴 수 있는 편리함과 관련이 있는지 찾아야 한다. 발상

2nd 각 선택지의 앞뒤 흐름이 매끄러운지 확인한다.

①의 앞 문장과 뒤 문장
앞 문장: 그러나 때로는 어떤 장소를 진정으로 특징짓는 것은 덜 구체적인 것 — 우리 안에 있는 '감정'이다.
뒤 문장: 흥미로운 예가 지하철 승객 행동에 관한 연구에서 나왔다.
→ 때로는 감정이 장소를 특징짓는다는 내용과 지하철 승객의 행동에 관한 연구 예시가 앞뒤로 이어진다. ▶ 주어진 문장이 ①에 들어갈 수 없음

②의 앞 문장과 뒤 문장
앞 문장: ①의 뒤 문장과 같음
뒤 문장: 지하철이나 전철에서 왜 사람들이 그들이 앉는 곳에 앉거나 그들이 서는 곳에 서는지를 이해하려고 노력하는 연구자들은 다양한 상황에서 승객들이 그 공간을 사용하고 탐색하는 방식을 형성하는 요인들을 조사했다.
→ 지하철 승객의 행동에 관한 연구를 구체적으로 부연 설명한다.
▶ 주어진 문장이 ②에 들어갈 수 없음

③의 앞 문장과 뒤 문장
앞 문장: ②의 뒤 문장과 같음
뒤 문장: 연구 결과 중 하나는 많은 승객들이 기차의 문 근처에 자리 잡기를 좋아하는 이유들과 관련이 있었다.
→ 지하철 승객의 행동에 관한 연구 결과가 승객들이 문 근처에 자리를 잡으려는 이유와 관련이 있음을 이어서 설명한다. ▶ 주어진 문장이 ③에 들어갈 수 없음

④의 앞 문장과 뒤 문장

┌ **앞 문장**: ③의 뒤 문장과 같음

├ **뒤 문장**: 그러나(But) 이는 부분적으로 더(more) 추상적인 느낌 — 앉아 있
└ 는 승객들과 우연히 눈이 마주치는 때때로 불편한 느낌을 피하려는 욕구에
  의해 형성되었다.

➡ 승객들이 문 근처에 자리를 잡으려는 이유가 이어져야 한다. 반대되는 내용을 나타
  내는 But과 비교급 표현인 more가 있으므로, 앞에 다른 이유가 먼저 제시되었을
  것이다. 주어진 문장에 그 이유로서 더 빨리 내릴 수 있다는 명확한 편리함이 언급
  되었다. ▶ **주어진 문장이 ④에 들어가야 함**

⑤의 앞 문장과 뒤 문장

┌ **앞 문장**: ④의 뒤 문장과 같음

├ **뒤 문장**: 우리는 감정들을 볼 수 없다. — 그러나 그것들은 매우 실재하고,
└ 그것들은 세상에 대한 우리의 경험에 영향을 미친다.

➡ 승객들이 문 근처에 자리를 잡으려는 감정적인 이유가 앞에 제시되었고, 이 감정이
  실재하며 경험에 영향을 미친다는 내용으로 글이 마무리된다.
  ▶ **주어진 문장이 ⑤에 들어갈 수 없음**

구문 서술형

정답 which, what 또는 the thing which[that]

해석 우리 주변을 살피는 것은 우리 자신 바깥에 있는 것에 집중하는 것이
다.

→ 전치사 on의 목적어 역할을 하는 선행사와 관계대명사가 필요하므로, 선행
사를 포함하는 관계대명사 what 또는 the thing which[that]를 써야 한다.

P 05 정답 ③ *인간의 잠수 반사

글의 흐름으로 보아, 주어진 문장이 들어가기에 가장 적절한 곳을
고르시오. [3점]

단서 1 얼굴만 물속에 있을 때 잠수 반사가 유발됨

But if we sink just our face / in a bowl of water, / ⟨삽입절⟩ while the
whole of the rest of our body / is in the dry air, / the diving
reflex is triggered. // 하지만 만약 우리가 얼굴만 가라앉히고 / 그릇의 물속에 /
나머지 몸 전체는 / 물기가 없는 공기 중에 있으면 / 잠수 반사가 유발된다 //

We have a 'diving reflex', / like other marine mammals. //
우리는 '잠수 반사'를 가지고 있다 / 다른 해양 포유류처럼 //
(①) This means / 〈목적어절 접속사〉 that 〈복수 주어〉 special nerve endings on our faces, /
around the mouth and nose, / 〈복수 동사〉 trigger this reflex / 〈'~할 때만'〉 only when the
facial region goes under water. // 이것은 의미한다 / 얼굴에 있는 특수 신경
말단이 / 입과 코 주변의 / 이 반사를 유발한다는 것을 / 얼굴 부위가 물 아래에 들어갈 때만 //
(②) If we are in the water, / 〈「with+명사(+being)+부사/전치사구」: ~한 상태로〉 with our head out in the air, / there
is no diving reflex. // 단서 2 얼굴이 물 밖에 있다면 잠수 반사가 일어나지 않음
만약 우리가 물속에 있으면 / 머리는 공기 중에 있는 상태로 / 잠수 반사는 없다 //
〈=diving reflex〉 〈분사구문을 이끄는 현재분사〉
(③) It automatically closes down the airway, / reducing the risk
of swallowing water, / and it narrows the small air-passages in
the lungs. // 단서 3 잠수 반사가 일어났을 때 나타나는 신체적 변화
이것은 기도를 자동으로 닫아 / 물을 삼킬 위험을 줄이고 / 폐 속의 작은 공기 통로를 좁힌다 //
(④) At the same time / the heart rate is slowed down to half
speed / and blood is shunted to the vital organs, /
동시에 / 심박수가 절반 속도로 느려지고 / 혈액이 중요한 장기들로 보내져 /
〈분사구문을 이끄는 현재분사〉
protecting them / from the effects of the brief stop in breathing. //
그것들을 보호한다 / 짧은 호흡 정지로 인한 영향으로부터 //

〈가정법 과거의 if절〉
(⑤) By contrast, / if a chimpanzee or a gorilla found itself in
water / with its face below the surface, / it would panic, / 〈병렬 구조 (가정법 과거의 주절)〉 its
heart would race / and it would quickly drown. //
반면 / 침팬지나 고릴라가 물속에 있는 자신을 발견하면 / 표면 아래에 얼굴이 있는 상태로 /
그것은 당황하여 / 그것의 심장이 빨리 뛰고 / 금방 익사할 것이다 //

- sink ⓥ 가라앉히다 • marine ⓐ 해양의 • mammal ⓝ 포유류
- nerve ⓝ 신경 • region ⓝ 부위, 지역
- automatically ⓐⓓ 자동으로 • airway ⓝ 기도 • risk ⓝ 위험
- swallow ⓥ 삼키다 • narrow ⓥ 좁히다 • passage ⓝ 통로
- lung ⓝ 폐 • heart rate 심박수 • vital ⓐ 중요한
- organ ⓝ 장기 • brief ⓐ 짧은 • below ⓟⓡⓔⓟ ~의 아래에
- panic ⓥ 당황하다 • drown ⓥ 익사하다

우리는 다른 해양 포유류처럼 '잠수 반사'를 가지고 있다. (①) 이것은 입과 코
주변의 얼굴에 있는 특수 신경 말단이 얼굴 부위가 물 아래에 들어갈 때만 이
반사를 유발한다는 것을 의미한다. (②) 만약 우리가, 머리는 공기 중에 있는
상태로, 물속에 있으면 잠수 반사는 없다. (③ 하지만 만약 우리가 그릇의 물속
에 얼굴만 가라앉히고, 나머지 몸 전체는 물기가 없는 공기 중에 있으면, 잠수
반사가 유발된다.) 이것은 기도를 자동으로 닫아, 물을 삼킬 위험을 줄이고, 폐
속의 작은 공기 통로를 좁힌다. (④) 동시에 심박수가 절반 속도로 느려지고
혈액이 중요한 장기들로 보내져, 짧은 호흡 정지로 인한 영향으로부터 그것들
을 보호한다. (⑤) 반면, 침팬지나 고릴라가 표면 아래에 얼굴이 있는 상태로
물속에 있는 자신을 발견하면, 그것은 당황하여, 그것의 심장이 빨리 뛰고 금방
익사할 것이다.

| 문제 풀이 순서 | ✹✹❀ [정답률 69%]

1st 주어진 문장을 해석하고, 연결어 등을 확인한다.

┌ But if we sink just our face in a bowl of water, while the
├ whole of the rest of our body is in the dry air, the diving
└ reflex is triggered.
  하지만 만약 우리가 그릇의 물속에 얼굴만 가라앉히고, 나머지 몸 전체는 물기가 없는 공기
  중에 있으면, 잠수 반사가 유발된다.

➡ **주어진 문장 앞**: 반대되는 내용을 나타내는 But과 잠수 반사가 유발되는 상황이 나
  오므로 단서 잠수 반사가 유발되지 않는 경우가 앞에 제시될 것이다. 발상

2nd 각 선택지의 앞뒤 흐름이 매끄러운지 확인한다.

①의 앞 문장과 뒤 문장

┌ **앞 문장**: 우리는 다른 해양 포유류처럼 '잠수 반사'를 가지고 있다.

├ **뒤 문장**: 이것은 입과 코 주변의 얼굴에 있는 특수 신경 말단이 얼굴 부위가
└ 물 아래에 들어갈 때만 이 반사를 유발한다는 것을 의미한다.

➡ 우리가 다른 해양 포유류처럼 잠수 반사를 가지고 있다고 하며 어떤 상황에서 잠수
  반사가 유발되는지를 이어서 설명한다. ▶ **주어진 문장이 ①에 들어갈 수 없음**

②의 앞 문장과 뒤 문장

┌ **앞 문장**: ①의 뒤 문장과 같음

├ **뒤 문장**: 만약 우리가, 머리는 공기 중에 있는 상태로, 물속에 있으면 잠수
└ 반사는 없다.

➡ 머리가 물 밖의 공기 중에 있고 몸만 물속에 있으면 잠수 반사가 일어나지 않는다고
  하며, 잠수 반사가 유발되는 상황과 그렇지 않은 상황이 자연스럽게 연결된다.
  ▶ **주어진 문장이 ②에 들어갈 수 없음**

③의 앞 문장과 뒤 문장

┌ **앞 문장**: ②의 뒤 문장과 같음

├ **뒤 문장**: 이것(It)은 기도를 자동으로 닫아, 물을 삼킬 위험을 줄이고, 폐 속
└ 의 작은 공기 통로를 좁힌다.

➡ It은 기도를 닫아 물을 삼킬 위험을 줄인다고 했는데, 앞 문장은 머리가 공기 중에
  있는 상태를 설명하므로 앞뒤 문장이 이어지지 않는다. 얼굴만 물속에 가라앉히면
  잠수 반사가 유발된다는 내용이 주어진 문장에 나오므로, It은 잠수 반사를 가리킨
  다. ▶ **주어진 문장이 ③에 들어가야 함**

④의 앞 문장과 뒤 문장
- 앞 문장: ③의 뒤 문장과 같음
- 뒤 문장: 동시에 심박수가 절반 속도로 느려지고 혈액이 중요한 장기들로 보내져, 짧은 호흡 정지로 인한 영향으로부터 그것들을 보호한다.
➡ 잠수 반사가 유발되었을 때 나타날 수 있는 신체적 변화를 이어서 설명한다.
▶ 주어진 문장이 ④에 들어갈 수 없음

⑤의 앞 문장과 뒤 문장
- 앞 문장: ④의 뒤 문장과 같음
- 뒤 문장: 반면, 침팬지나 고릴라가 표면 아래에 얼굴이 있는 상태로 물속에 있는 자신을 발견하면, 그것은 당황하여, 그것의 심장이 빨리 뛰고 금방 익사할 것이다.
➡ 인간과 다르게 잠수 반사가 일어나지 않는 침팬지와 고릴라의 예시로 글이 마무리된다. ▶ 주어진 문장이 ⑤에 들어갈 수 없음

[구문 서술형]

[정답] 선행사가 사람이 아님, that

[해석] 우리는 다른 해양 포유류들이 가지는 것과 똑같은 '잠수 반사'를 가지고 있다.
→ 사람이 아닌 선행사가 있으므로, 사람 선행사와 함께 쓰이는 목적격 관계대명사 whom을 which나 that으로 고쳐야 한다. 선행사 앞에 비교 구조를 나타내는 the same이 있으므로 that을 쓰는 것이 자연스럽다.

P 06 정답 ⑤ *비선형 미디어 편집 시스템의 특징

글의 흐름으로 보아, 주어진 문장이 들어가기에 가장 적절한 곳을 고르시오.

Nonlinear editing, / on the other hand, / is like using a word processing program. // 단서1 비선형 편집과 반대되는 개념이 앞에 나올 것임
비선형 편집은 / 반면 / 워드 프로세싱 프로그램을 사용하는 것과 같다 //

All editing systems are now nonlinear computer-based systems
주격 관계대명사
/ that allow random access to any video shot or scene /
모든 편집 시스템은 이제 비선형 컴퓨터 기반 시스템이다 / 어떤 비디오 숏이나 장면으로의 임의적 접근을 가능하게 하는 /
= any video shot or scene
without having to fast forward or fast reverse / to find it. //
빨리 감기나 빨리 되감기를 할 필요 없이 / 어떤 비디오 화면이나 장면을 찾기 위해 //
다양한
Nonlinear systems can create a range of special effects, /
비선형 시스템은 다양한 특수 효과를 만들 수 있다 /
차량 와이퍼로 훑는 것처럼 화면을 전환하는 효과   두 장면을 겹치며 화면을 전환하는 효과
such as slow motion, wipes and dissolves. //
슬로 모션, 와이프 그리고 디졸브 같은 //
(①) Another highlight of a digital nonlinear system is its
가목적어   의미상 주어   진목적어
random access process / that makes it easy for an editor to find / desired shots or scenes /
디지털 비선형 시스템의 또 다른 주요 특징은 그것의 임의적 접근 과정이다 / 편집자가 찾는 것을 쉽게 해주는 / 원하는 숏이나 장면을 /
without having to spend time / fast forwarding or rewinding videotape. //
시간을 들일 필요 없이 / 비디오테이프를 빨리 감거나 되감는 데 //
(②) With nonlinear editing, / shots or scenes can be easily added or removed / anywhere in the program, / and the computer adjusts the program length automatically. //
비선형 편집으로는 / 숏이나 장면을 쉽게 추가하거나 삭제할 수 있으며 / 프로그램의 어디에나 / 컴퓨터는 프로그램의 길이를 자동으로 조정한다 //

(③) Linear editing was like composing a paper on a typewriter. //
선형 편집은 타자기로 글을 작성하는 것과 같았다 //
부사절 접속사 (조건)
(④) If a mistake was made or new information needed to be
주절의 주어
added / the whole piece had to be retyped. // 단서2 선형 편집은 수정하려면 전체를 다시 작성해야 함
만약 실수가 생겼거나 새로운 정보가 추가되어야 할 필요가 있다면 / 전체를 다시 작성해야 했다 //
단서3 수정하기 쉬운 것은 선형 편집이 아니라 비선형 편집임
(⑤) If a mistake is made, / it is easily deleted and fixed / with a few keystrokes, / and new information can be added easily. //
만약 실수가 생기면 / 그것은 쉽게 삭제되고 수정될 수 있으며 / 몇 번의 키 입력으로 / 새로운 정보가 쉽게 추가될 수 있다 //

- nonlinear ⓐ 비선형의   • random ⓐ 임의의   • scene ⓝ 장면
- reverse ⓥ 되감다   • highlight ⓝ 주요 특징   • editor ⓝ 편집자
- remove ⓥ 제거하다   • adjust ⓥ 조정하다
- automatically ⓐⓓ 자동적으로   • compose ⓥ 작성하다, 구성하다
- retype ⓥ 다시 타이핑하다   • delete ⓥ 삭제하다
- keystroke ⓝ 키 입력

모든 편집 시스템은 이제 어떤 비디오 화면이나 장면을 찾기 위해 빨리 감기나 빨리 되감기를 할 필요 없이 어떤 비디오 숏이나 장면으로의 임의적 접근을 가능하게 하는 비선형 컴퓨터 기반 시스템이다. 비선형 시스템은 슬로 모션, 와이프 그리고 디졸브 같은 다양한 특수 효과를 만들 수 있다. (①) 디지털 비선형 시스템의 또 다른 주요 특징은 편집자가 비디오테이프를 빨리 감거나 되감는 데 시간을 들일 필요 없이 원하는 숏이나 장면을 찾는 것을 쉽게 해주는 그것의 임의적 접근 과정이다. (②) 비선형 편집으로는 숏이나 장면을 프로그램의 어디에나 쉽게 추가하거나 삭제할 수 있으며, 컴퓨터는 프로그램의 길이를 자동으로 조정한다. (③) 선형 편집은 타자기로 글을 작성하는 것과 같았다. (④) 만약 실수가 생겼거나 새로운 정보가 추가되어야 할 필요가 있다면, 전체를 다시 작성해야 했다. (⑤ 비선형 편집은, 반면, 워드 프로세싱 프로그램을 사용하는 것과 같다.) 만약 실수가 생기면 그것은 몇 번의 키 입력으로 쉽게 삭제되고 수정될 수 있으며, 새로운 정보가 쉽게 추가될 수 있다.

| 문제 풀이 순서 | ★★★ [정답률 40%]

1st 주어진 문장을 해석하고, 핵심 단서를 파악한다.
Nonlinear editing, on the other hand, is like using a word processing program.
비선형 편집은, 반면, 워드 프로세싱 프로그램을 사용하는 것과 같다.
➡ 주어진 문장 앞: 반대되는 내용을 나타내는 on the other hand가 있으므로, 단서 비선형 편집과 반대되는 개념이 앞에 나올 것이다. 발상

2nd 각 선택지의 앞뒤 흐름이 매끄러운지 확인한다.

①의 앞 문장과 뒤 문장
- 앞 문장: 모든 편집 시스템은 이제 ~ 어떤 비디오 숏이나 장면으로의 임의적 접근을 가능하게 하는 비선형 컴퓨터 기반 시스템이다.
- 뒤 문장: 디지털 비선형 시스템의 또 다른 주요 특징은 편집자가 비디오테이프를 빨리 감거나 되감는 데 시간을 들일 필요 없이 원하는 숏이나 장면을 찾는 것을 쉽게 해주는 그것의 임의적 접근 과정이다.
➡ 편집 시스템은 이제 비선형 시스템이라고 하며, 비선형 시스템의 특징을 이어서 설명한다. ▶ 주어진 문장이 ①에 들어갈 수 없음

②의 앞 문장과 뒤 문장
- 앞 문장: ①의 뒤 문장과 같음
- 뒤 문장: 비선형 편집으로는 숏이나 장면을 프로그램의 어디에나 쉽게 추가하거나 삭제할 수 있으며, 컴퓨터는 프로그램의 길이를 자동으로 조정한다.
➡ 비선형 편집의 장점을 이어서 설명한다. ▶ 주어진 문장이 ②에 들어갈 수 없음

┌ 앞 문장: ②의 뒤 문장과 같음
└ 뒤 문장: 선형 편집은 타자기로 글을 작성하는 것과 같았다(was).

➡ 현대의 방식인 비선형 편집을 설명하다가, 내용을 전환하기 위해 과거시제를 사용하며 과거의 방식인 선형 편집을 언급한다. ▶ 주어진 문장이 ③에 들어갈 수 없음

④의 앞 문장과 뒤 문장

┌ 앞 문장: ③의 뒤 문장과 같음
│ 뒤 문장: 만약 실수가 생겼거나 새로운 정보가 추가되어야 할 필요가 있다
└ 면, 전체를 다시 작성해야 했다.

➡ 타자기 작업은 글을 수정하기 어렵다는 단점을 언급하며, 선형 편집의 특징을 이어서 부연 설명한다. ▶ 주어진 문장이 ④에 들어갈 수 없음

⑤의 앞 문장과 뒤 문장

┌ 앞 문장: ④의 뒤 문장과 같음
│ 뒤 문장: 만약 실수가 생기면 그것은 몇 번의 키 입력으로 쉽게 삭제되고 수
└ 정될 수 있으며, 새로운 정보가 쉽게 추가될 수 있다.

➡ 선형 편집은 수정이 어렵다고 했는데, 갑자기 수정이 쉽다는 내용이 등장했다. 비선형 편집은 워드 프로세싱 프로그램 같다는 내용이 주어진 문장에 있고, 선형 편집과 반대로 비선형 편집은 쉽게 수정할 수 있다는 흐름이 되어야 한다.

▶ 주어진 문장이 ⑤에 들어가야 함

[구문 서술형]

[정답] whose, 소유격

[해석] 모든 편집 시스템은 이제 그것의 임의적 접근 과정이 원하는 숏을 찾는 것을 쉽게 해주는 비선형 컴퓨터 기반 시스템이다.
→ 비선형 컴퓨터 기반 시스템(nonlinear computer-based systems)의 임의적 접근 과정(random access process)을 나타내므로 소유격 관계대명사 whose로 고쳐야 한다.

P 07 정답 ⑤ *의도와 결과 둘 다로 판단되는 도덕적 선함

글의 흐름으로 보아, 주어진 문장이 들어가기에 가장 적절한 곳을 고르시오. [3점]

┌ 문장의 주어 / 주격 관계대명사
│ A person / who always tries to prevent harm but never does, /
│ 문장의 본동사
│ is not generally thought of / as morally good. //
│ 사람은 / 항상 해를 예방하려고 하지만 결코 그렇게 하지 못하는 / 일반적으로 생각되지 않
└ 는다 / 도덕적으로 선하다고 //

주격 관계대명사
A morally good person / is one / who does morally bad actions
significantly less often than most / and does morally good ones
= actions
significantly more often than most. //
도덕적으로 선한 사람은 / 사람이다 / 도덕적으로 나쁜 행동을 대부분의 사람들보다 훨씬 덜
자주 하고 / 도덕적으로 선한 행동을 대부분의 사람들보다 훨씬 더 자주 하는 //
in -ing: ~할 때는, ~하는 데 있어서
In judging a person / not only her actions / but also her intentions
and motives are relevant. //   not only A but also B: A뿐만 아니라 B도
사람을 판단할 때는 / 그녀의 행동뿐 아니라 / 그녀의 의도와 동기 또한 관련이 있다 //

(①) A morally good person must intend to do / morally good
actions / and intend to avoid / morally bad ones. //
도덕적으로 선한 사람은 하려고 의도해야 하고 / 도덕적으로 선한 행동을 / 피하려고 의도해야
한다 / 도덕적으로 나쁜 행동은 //
문장의 주어   주격 관계대명사
(②) A person / who unintentionally prevents harm to others /
and does not harm them / simply because things do not turn out
문장의 본동사
as she intends / is not morally good. //
사람은 / 다른 사람에게 해를 의도하지 않게 예방하고 / 그들에게 해를 끼치지 않은 / 단지 그
녀가 의도한대로 일이 일어나지 않았기 때문에 / 도덕적으로 선하지 않다 //

(③) Although this kind of situation / generally occurs only in
slapstick movies, / it is worth mentioning / to avoid the false
impression /
이런 종류의 상황은 / 일반적으로 슬랩스틱 영화에서만 발생하지만 / 언급할 가치가 있다 / 잘
못된 인상을 피하기 위해 /
                              it ~ that 강조 구문
that it is the actual consequences of a person's actions that count
동격절 접속사
/ toward her being judged / morally good or bad. //
중요한 것은 한 사람의 행동의 실제 결과라는 / 그녀가 판단되는 것에 / 도덕적으로 선하거나
나쁜지 //

(④) But actual consequences are important. //
하지만 실제 결과는 중요하다 //   [단서 1] 도덕성 판단에는 실제 결과가 중요함
                    가주어   진주어절 접속사
(⑤) Of such a person, / it may be said that she means well; /
but, contrary to Kant, / some results are necessary / before she is
regarded as morally good. // [단서 2] 의도가 선하더라도 도덕적으로 선하려면 결과가
                                      필요함
그런 사람에 대해 / 그녀가 선한 의도를 가지고 있다고 말할 수 있지만 / Kant와 달리 / 어떤
결과가 필요하다 / 그녀가 도덕적으로 선하다고 간주되기 전에 //

- prevent ⓥ 막다, 예방하다   • harm ⓝ 해, 손해
- morally ⓐd 도덕적으로   • significantly ⓐd 상당히, 훨씬
- judge ⓥ 판단하다   • intention ⓝ 의도   • motive ⓝ 동기
- relevant ⓐ 관련된   • intend ⓥ 의도하다
- unintentionally ⓐd 의도치 않게   • occur ⓥ 발생하다
- impression ⓝ 인상   • actual ⓐ 실제의   • consequence ⓝ 결과
- count ⓥ 중요하다   • contrary to ~와는 반대로
- necessary ⓐ 필요한   • regard ⓥ 여기다, 간주하다

도덕적으로 선한 사람은 대부분의 사람들보다 도덕적으로 나쁜 행동을 훨씬 덜 자주 하고, 도덕적으로 선한 행동을 훨씬 더 자주 하는 사람이다. 사람을 판단할 때는 그녀의 행동뿐 아니라 그녀의 의도와 동기 또한 관련이 있다. (①) 도덕적으로 선한 사람은 도덕적으로 선한 행동을 하려고 의도해야 하고, 도덕적으로 나쁜 행동은 피하려고 의도해야 한다. (②) 다른 사람에게 해를 의도하지 않게 예방하고 단지 그녀가 의도한대로 일이 일어나지 않았기 때문에 그들에게 해를 끼치지 않은 사람은 도덕적으로 선하지 않다. (③) 이런 종류의 상황은 일반적으로 슬랩스틱 영화에서만 발생하지만, 그녀가 도덕적으로 선하거나 나쁜지 판단되는 것에 중요한 것은 한 사람의 행동의 실제 결과라는 잘못된 인상을 피하기 위해 언급할 가치가 있다. (④) 하지만 실제 결과는 중요하다. (⑤ 항상 해를 예방하려고 하지만 결코 그렇게 하지 못하는 사람은 일반적으로 도덕적으로 선하다고 생각되지 않는다.) 그런 사람에 대해, 그녀가 선한 의도를 가지고 있다고 말할 수 있지만, Kant와 달리, 그녀가 도덕적으로 선하다고 간주되기 전에 어떤 결과가 필요하다.

| 문제 풀이 순서 | ★★★ [정답률 38%]

1st 주어진 문장을 해석하고, 앞뒤에 어떤 내용이 올지 생각한다.

┌ A person who always tries to prevent harm but never does,
│ is not generally thought of as morally good.
│ 항상 해를 예방하려고 하지만 결코 그렇게 하지 못하는 사람은 일반적으로 도덕적으로 선하
└ 다고 생각되지 않는다.

➡ **주어진 문장 앞:** 해를 예방하려고 시도는 하지만 실천하지 못하는 사람은 도덕적으로 선하다고 여겨지지 않는다고 했으므로, [단서] 실천이나 결과의 중요성이 등장하는 부분과 이어져야 한다. (발상)

2nd 각 선택지의 앞뒤 흐름이 매끄러운지 확인한다.

①의 앞 문장과 뒤 문장

┌ 앞 문장: 사람을 판단할 때는 그녀의 행동뿐 아니라 그녀의 의도와 동기 또한 관련이 있다.
│ 뒤 문장: 도덕적으로 선한 사람은 도덕적으로 선한 행동을 하려고 의도해야
└ 하고, 도덕적으로 나쁜 행동은 피하려고 의도해야 한다.

➡ 도덕성 판단에 행동뿐 아니라 의도나 동기도 중요하다는 내용이 앞뒤로 이어진다.
▶ 주어진 문장이 ①에 들어갈 수 없음

②의 앞 문장과 뒤 문장

- **앞 문장:** ①의 뒤 문장과 같음
- **뒤 문장:** 다른 사람에게 해를 의도하지 않게 예방하고 단지 그녀가 의도한 대로 일이 일어나지 않았기 때문에 그들에게 해를 끼치지 않은 사람은 도덕적으로 선하지 않다.

➡ 결과적으로는 해를 끼치지 않았더라도 선한 의도가 없으면 도덕적으로 선하다고 판단하지 않는다는 내용이므로 앞 문장을 뒷받침한다.
▶ 주어진 문장이 ②에 들어갈 수 없음

③의 앞 문장과 뒤 문장

- **앞 문장:** ②의 뒤 문장과 같음
- **뒤 문장:** 이런 종류의 상황(this kind of situation)은 일반적으로 슬랩스틱 영화에서만 발생하지만, 그녀가 도덕적으로 선하거나 나쁜지 판단되는 것에 중요한 것은 한 사람의 행동의 실제 결과라는 잘못된 인상을 피하기 위해 언급할 가치가 있다.

➡ this kind of situation은 ③의 앞 문장에 나온 상황을 가리킨다. 도덕성 판단에 실제 결과만 중요한 것이 아니라는 인상을 심기 위해 이 상황을 언급할 가치가 있다고 부연 설명한다. ▶ 주어진 문장이 ③에 들어갈 수 없음

④의 앞 문장과 뒤 문장

- **앞 문장:** ③의 뒤 문장과 같음
- **뒤 문장:** 하지만 실제 결과는 중요하다.

➡ 앞 문장에서 실제 결과만 중요한 것이 아니라고 했으나, 실제 결과는 중요하다고 하며 반대되는 내용을 제시하는 흐름이다. ▶ 주어진 문장이 ④에 들어갈 수 없음

⑤의 앞 문장과 뒤 문장

- **앞 문장:** ④의 뒤 문장과 같음
- **뒤 문장:** 그런 사람(such a person)에 대해, 그녀가 선한 의도를 가지고 있다고 말할 수 있지만, Kant와 달리, 그녀가 도덕적으로 선하다고 간주되기 전에 어떤 결과가 필요하다.

➡ such a person이 가리키는 사람은 선한 의도를 가진다고 말할 수 있다고 했는데, 앞에는 선한 의도가 없는 사람만 언급되었다. 선한 의도가 있지만 결과가 없는 사람의 사례는 주어진 문장에 있다. ▶ 주어진 문장이 ⑤에 들어가야 함

[구문 서술형]

[정답] 사람, who[that]

[해석] 도덕적으로 선한 사람은 나쁜 행동을 훨씬 덜 자주 하는 사람이다.
→ 관계대명사절에서 동사 does의 주어 역할을 하므로, 빈칸에는 주격 관계대명사를 써야 한다. 이때, 선행사가 one(=a person)이므로 사람이다. 따라서, 선행사가 사물일 때 쓰는 which를 제외한 주격 관계대명사 who, that이 적절하다.

P 08 정답 ④ *심리학도 과학이다

글의 흐름으로 보아, 주어진 문장이 들어가기에 가장 적절한 곳을 고르시오.

Instead, / they look for evidence, / to make sure / **that** psychological ideas are firmly **based**, / and not just **derived** / from generally **held** beliefs or assumptions. //
(목적어절 접속사) (병렬 구조) (과거분사) (과거분사)
[단서 1 그들(심리학자들)은 증거를 찾으려고 함]
대신에 / 그들은 증거를 찾는다 / 확신하기 위해 / 심리학적 개념이 확고하게 기반을 두고 있는지 / 단지 도출된 것이 아니라 / 일반적으로 받아들여지는 신념이나 가정으로부터 //

(복수 주어) (주격 관계대명사)
The common accounts of human nature / **that** float around in society / **are** generally a mixture of assumptions, tales and sometimes plain silliness. //
(복수 동사)
인간 본성에 대한 흔한 설명은 / 사회에 떠도는 / 일반적으로 가정, 이야기, 그리고 때로는 순전한 어리석음의 혼합이다 //

However, / psychology is different. //
그러나 / 심리학은 다르다 // [단서 2 인간 본성에 대한 흔한 설명과 심리학의 차이점이 이어질 것임]
(=psychology)
(①) It is the branch of science / that is devoted to **understanding** people: / how and why we act as we do; / why we see things as we do; / and how we interact with one another. //
(동명사) [단서 3 심리학은 과학의 분야임]
그것은 과학의 분야이다 / 사람들을 이해하는 데 전념하는 / 즉 우리가 어떻게 그리고 왜 행동하는 대로 행동하는지 / 우리가 왜 보는 대로 사물을 보는지 / 그리고 우리가 어떻게 서로 상호작용하는지 //

(②) The key word here is 'science.' //
여기서 핵심어는 '과학'이다 //

(③) Psychologists don't depend on / opinions and hearsay, / or the generally accepted views of society at the time, / or even the considered opinions of deep thinkers. //
[단서 4 심리학자들이 의존하지 않는 것을 나열함]
심리학자들은 의존하지 않는다 / 의견과 소문 / 혹은 당대의 사회에서 일반적으로 받아들여지는 견해 / 혹은 심지어 심오한 사상가들의 숙고된 의견에 //
'~에 더하여' [단서 5 증거에 기반한다는 내용이 앞에 언급되어야 함]
(④) **In addition to** this evidence-based approach, / psychology deals with fundamental processes and principles /
이러한 증거 기반 접근법에 더하여 / 심리학은 근본적인 과정과 원리를 다룬다 //
(주격 관계대명사) ('~뿐만 아니라')
that generate our rich cultural and social diversity, / **as well as** those **shared by all human beings**. //
(과거분사구 (those 수식))
우리의 풍부한 문화적 사회적 다양성을 만들어 내는 / 모든 인간에 의해 공유되는 것들뿐만 아니라 //

(⑤) These are / what modern psychology is all about. //
이것들은 / 현대 심리학이 무엇인지 보여 주는 것이다 //

- evidence ⓝ 증거 • firmly ⓐⅾ 확고하게
- derive from ~로부터 도출하다 • assumption ⓝ 가정
- account ⓝ 설명 • float ⓥ 떠돌다 • plain ⓐ 순전한
- silliness ⓝ 어리석음 • branch ⓝ 분야
- devote ⓥ 전념[헌신]하다 • hearsay ⓝ 소문
- fundamental ⓐ 근본적인 • principle ⓝ 원리
- generate ⓥ 만들어 내다 • diversity ⓝ 다양성

사회에 떠도는 인간 본성에 대한 흔한 설명은 일반적으로 가정, 이야기, 그리고 때로는 순전한 어리석음의 혼합이다. 그러나, 심리학은 다르다. (①) 그것은 사람들을 이해하는, 즉 우리가 어떻게 그리고 왜 행동하는 대로 행동하는지, 우리가 왜 보는 대로 사물을 보는지, 그리고 우리가 어떻게 서로 상호작용하는지를 이해하는 데 전념하는 과학 분야이다. (②) 여기서 핵심어는 '과학'이다. (③) 심리학자들은 의견과 소문, 혹은 당대의 사회에서 일반적으로 받아들여지는 견해, 혹은 심지어 심오한 사상가들의 숙고된 의견에 의존하지 않는다. (④ 대신에 그들은 심리학적 개념이 단지 일반적으로 받아들여지는 신념이나 가정에서 도출된 것이 아니라, 확고하게 기반을 두고 있는지 확신하기 위해 증거를 찾는다.) 이러한 증거 기반 접근법에 더하여 심리학은 모든 인간에 의해 공유되는 근본적인 과정과 원리뿐만 아니라, 우리의 풍부한 문화적 사회적 다양성을 만들어 내는 것들을 다룬다. (⑤) 이것들은 현대 심리학이 무엇인지 보여 준다.

| 문제 풀이 순서 | ★★❋ [정답률 70%]

1st 주어진 문장을 해석하고 핵심 내용과 연결어, 지시어 등을 확인한다.

Instead, they look for evidence, to make sure that psychological ideas are firmly based, and not just derived from generally held beliefs or assumptions.
[대신에] 그들은 심리학적 개념이 단지 일반적으로 받아들여지는 신념이나 가정에서 도출된 것이 아니라, 확고하게 기반을 두고 있는지 확신하기 위해 증거를 찾는다.

- **주어진 문장 앞**: 대조를 나타내는 Instead와 대명사 they가 있으므로, (단서) they가 가리키는 대상, 그리고 주어진 문장과 대조되는 내용이 앞에 언급될 것이다. (발상)
- **주어진 문장 뒤**: 증거에 기반한 심리학을 부연 설명할 것이다.

2nd 각 선택지의 앞뒤 흐름이 매끄러운지 확인한다.

①의 앞 문장과 뒤 문장
- **앞 문장**: 사회에 떠도는 인간 본성에 대한 흔한 설명은 일반적으로 가정, 이야기, 그리고 때로는 순전한 어리석음의 혼합이다. 그러나, 심리학은 다르다.
- **뒤 문장**: 그것은 사람들을 이해하는, 즉 우리가 어떻게 그리고 왜 행동하는 대로 행동하는지, 우리가 왜 보는 대로 사물을 보는지, 그리고 우리가 어떻게 서로 상호작용하는지를 이해하는 데 전념하는 과학 분야이다.
→ 일반적인 인간 본성에 대한 설명들과 심리학은 다르다고 말했으며, 바로 이어서 심리학은 과학 분야임을 강조했다. ▶ 주어진 문장이 ①에 들어갈 수 없음

②의 앞 문장과 뒤 문장
- **앞 문장**: ①의 뒤 문장과 같음
- **뒤 문장**: 여기서 핵심어는 '과학'이다.
→ 심리학이 과학 분야임을 설명한 앞 문장의 내용을 다시 강조한다. ▶ 주어진 문장이 ②에 들어갈 수 없음

③의 앞 문장과 뒤 문장
- **앞 문장**: ②의 뒤 문장과 같음
- **뒤 문장**: 심리학자들은 의견과 소문, 혹은 당대의 사회에서 일반적으로 받아들여지는 견해, 혹은 심지어 심오한 사상가들의 숙고된 의견에 의존하지 않는다.
→ 심리학은 과학이므로 심리학자들이 과학적이지 않은 것들에 의존하지 않는다는 설명이 이어진다. ▶ 주어진 문장이 ③에 들어갈 수 없음

④의 앞 문장과 뒤 문장
- **앞 문장**: ③의 뒤 문장과 같음
- **뒤 문장**: 이러한 증거 기반 접근법에 더하여 심리학은 모든 인간에 의해 공유되는 근본적인 과정과 원리뿐만 아니라, 우리의 풍부한 문화적 사회적 다양성을 만들어 내는 것들을 다룬다.
→ ④의 앞 문장에 나열된 과학적이지 않은 것들은 this evidence-based approach와 이어질 수 없다. 주어진 문장에서 they는 과학적이지 않은 것들에 의존하는 '대신에' '증거'를 찾는다고 했으므로, they는 심리학자에 해당한다. 따라서 주어진 문장은 심리학자들이 과학적이지 않은 것들에 의존하지 않는다는 ④의 앞 문장과 증거 기반 접근법이 언급된 ④의 뒤 문장을 적절히 이어준다. ▶ 주어진 문장이 ④에 들어가야 함

⑤의 앞 문장과 뒤 문장
- **앞 문장**: ④의 뒤 문장과 같음
- **뒤 문장**: 이것들은 현대 심리학이 무엇인지 보여 준다.
→ 증거 기반의 심리학에 대한 부연 설명 후에 이것이 바로 현대 심리학이라고 하며 글을 마무리한다. ▶ 주어진 문장이 ⑤에 들어갈 수 없음

[구문 서술형]

[정답] the way, the reason

[해석] 심리학은 우리가 어떻게 그리고 왜 행동하는 대로 행동하는지를 이해하는 데 전념한다.
→ ⓐ 관계부사 how와 선행사 the way는 같이 쓸 수 없으므로 how를 대신하려면 선행사 the way를 쓴다.
ⓑ 관계부사 why는 the reason을 선행사로 가진다.

P 09 정답 ① *잘못 알려진 혀 지도 이론

글의 흐름으로 보아, 주어진 문장이 들어가기에 가장 적절한 곳을 고르시오.

Research in the 1980s and 1990s, however, / demonstrated / that the "tongue map" explanation of how we taste / was, in fact, totally wrong. // 단서 1 혀 지도가 틀렸음을 설명하는 내용 앞에 와야 함
그러나 1980년대와 1990년대의 연구는 / 보여 주었다 / 우리가 맛을 느끼는 방식에 대한 '혀 지도' 설명 / 사실은 완전히 틀렸다는 것을 //

단서 2 혀가 특정한 맛이 등록되는 개별적인 영역으로 구획됨 관계부사(선행사: areas)
The tongue was mapped into separate areas / where certain tastes were registered: / sweetness at the tip, / sourness on the sides, / and bitterness at the back of the mouth. //
혀는 개별적인 영역으로 구획되었는데 / 특정 맛이 등록되는 / 끝에는 단맛 / 측면에는 신맛 / 그리고 입의 뒤쪽에는 쓴맛이 있었다 //

'~와 같이'
(①) As it turns out, / the map was a misinterpretation and mistranslation / of research conducted in Germany at the turn of the twentieth century. // 단서 3 그 지도(혀 지도)는 연구를 오해하고 오역한 것임
밝혀진 바와 같이 / 그 지도는 오해하고 오역한 것이었다 / 20세기 초입 독일에서 수행된 연구를 //

단서 4 미뢰는 맛을 느끼는 특화된 분야에 따라 분류되지 않음
(②) Today, / leading taste researchers believe / that taste buds are not grouped according to specialty. //
오늘날 / 선도적인 미각 연구자는 믿는다 / 미뢰가 맛을 느끼는 특화된 분야에 따라 분류되지 않는다고 //

조동사의 수동태
(③) Sweetness, saltiness, bitterness, and sourness / can be tasted everywhere in the mouth, / although they may be perceived / at a little different intensities at different sites. //
= sweetness, saltiness, bitterness, and sourness
단맛, 짠맛, 쓴맛 그리고 신맛은 / 입안 어디에서나 느낄 수 있다 / 비록 그것들이 지각될지도 모르겠지만 / 여러 위치에서 조금씩 다른 강도로 //

not A but B: A가 아니라 B
(④) Moreover, the mechanism at work is not place, / but time. //
게다가, 작동 중인 기제는 위치가 아니라 / 시간이다 //

not A but B: A가 아니라 B
(⑤) It's not that you taste sweetness at the tip of your tongue, / but rather that you register that perception *first*. //
여러분은 혀끝에서 단맛을 느낀다기보다 / 오히려 그 지각(단맛)을 '가장 먼저' 등록하는 것이다 //

- demonstrate ⓥ 보여주다 • explanation ⓝ 설명
- map ⓥ (지도에) 구획하다 • separate ⓐ 개별적인, 별개의
- register ⓥ 등록하다 • tip ⓝ 끝 • sourness ⓝ 신맛
- bitterness ⓝ 쓴맛 • misinterpretation ⓝ 오해
- mistranslation ⓝ 오역 • conduct ⓥ 수행하다 • turn ⓝ 전환기
- leading ⓐ 선도적인 • specialty ⓝ 특화된 분야
- perceive ⓥ 지각하다 • intensity ⓝ 강도
- mechanism ⓝ 기제 • at work 작동 중인

혀는 특정 맛이 등록되는 개별적인 영역으로 구획되었는데, 즉, 끝에는 단맛, 측면에는 신맛, 그리고 입의 뒤쪽에는 쓴맛이 있었다. (① 그러나 1980년대와 1990년대의 연구는 우리가 맛을 느끼는 방식에 대한 '혀 지도' 설명이 사실은 완전히 틀렸다는 것을 보여주었다.) 밝혀진 바와 같이, 그 지도는 20세기 초입 독일에서 수행된 연구를 오해하고 오역한 것이었다. (②) 오늘날, 선도적인 미각 연구자는 미뢰가 맛을 느끼는 특화된 분야에 따라 분류되지 않는다고 믿는다. (③) 비록 그것들이 여러 위치에서 조금씩 다른 강도로 지각될지도 모르겠지만, 단맛, 짠맛, 쓴맛 그리고 신맛은 입안 어디에서나 느낄 수 있다. (④) 게다가, 작동 중인 기제는 위치가 아니라 시간이다. (⑤) 여러분은 혀끝에서 단맛을 느낀다기보다 오히려 그 지각(단맛)을 '가장 먼저' 등록하는 것이다.

1st 주어진 문장을 해석하고, 연결어, 지시어 등을 확인한다.

Research in the 1980s and 1990s, however, demonstrated that the "tongue map" explanation of how we taste was, in fact, totally wrong.

그러나 1980년대와 1990년 대의 연구는 우리가 맛을 느끼는 방식에 대한 '혀 지도' 설명이 사실은 완전히 틀렸다는 것을 보여주었다.

→ **주어진 문장 앞:** however(그러나)라고 했으므로 (단서)
앞에는 '혀 지도' 설명이 옳다고 여겨진 시기나 이 설명이 제시된 상황이 나와야 하고, 뒤에는 '혀 지도' 설명이 틀리다는 내용이 이어져야 한다. (발상)

2nd 찾은 단서를 생각하며 각 선택지의 앞뒤 흐름이 매끄러운지 확인한다.

- ①의 앞 문장과 뒤 문장

앞 문장: 혀는 특정 맛이 등록되는 개별적인 영역으로 구획되었는데, 즉, 끝에는 단맛, 측면에는 신맛, 그리고 입의 뒤쪽에는 쓴맛이 있었다.

뒤 문장: 밝혀진 바와 같이, 그 지도(the map)는 20세기 초입 독일에서 수행된 연구를 오해하고 오역한 것이었다.

→ 혀의 구역마다 느끼는 맛이 다르다는 것, 즉 '혀 지도'에 관한 내용에 이어서 그 지도(the map)가 오역된 것이라는 부정적인 내용이 나온다. 주어진 글의 tongue map이 ①의 뒤 문장에서 the map으로 다시 언급되었으며 혀 지도가 잘못되었다는 내용으로 전환되는 지점이므로 주어진 글이 ①에 오는 것이 적절하다.

▶ 주어진 문장이 ①에 들어가야 함

- ②의 앞 문장과 뒤 문장

앞 문장: ①의 뒤 문장과 같음

뒤 문장: 오늘날, 선도적인 미각 연구자는 미뢰가 맛을 느끼는 특화된 분야에 따라 분류되지 않는다고 믿는다.

→ 혀 지도에 관한 연구가 오역된 것이기 때문에, 오늘날에는 미뢰가 특정 맛을 느끼는 것으로 분류되지 않는다고 믿어진다는 내용으로 자연스럽게 이어졌다.

▶ 주어진 문장이 ②에 들어갈 수 없음

- ③의 앞 문장과 뒤 문장

앞 문장: ②의 뒤 문장과 같음

뒤 문장: 비록 그것들이 여러 위치에서 조금씩 다른 강도로 지각될지도 모르겠지만, 단맛, 짠맛, 쓴맛 그리고 신맛은 입안 어디에서나 느낄 수 있다.

→ 미뢰가 특정 맛을 느끼는 것으로 분류되지 않는다는 설명에 이어서 다양한 맛을 입안 어디에서나 느낄 수 있다는 부연 설명이 자연스럽게 이어졌다.

▶ 주어진 문장이 ③에 들어갈 수 없음

- ④의 앞 문장과 뒤 문장

앞 문장: ③의 뒤 문장과 같음

뒤 문장: 게다가, 작동 중인 기제는 위치가 아니라 시간이다.

→ 미뢰가 특정 맛을 감지하는 것으로 분류될 수 없다는 내용에 이어서 혀가 맛을 느낄 때 작동하는 기제는 위치가 아닌 시간이라는 추가적인 정보가 자연스럽게 이어졌다.

▶ 주어진 문장이 ④에 들어갈 수 없음

- ⑤의 앞 문장과 뒤 문장

앞 문장: ④의 뒤 문장과 같음

뒤 문장: 여러분은 혀끝에서 단맛을 느낀다기보다 오히려 그 지각(단맛)을 '가장 먼저' 등록하는 것이다.

→ 작동 중인 기제가 시간이라는 앞의 내용을 구체적으로 설명하는 자연스러운 흐름이다.

▶ 주어진 문장이 ⑤에 들어갈 수 없음

P 10 정답 ② *동물의 특성과 필요에 따라 조정되어야 하는 치료

글의 흐름으로 보아, 주어진 문장이 들어가기에 가장 적절한 곳을 고르시오.

Environmental factors can also determine / how the animal will respond during the treatment. //
간접의문문(의문사+주어+동사)
단서1 치료 중에 다르게 반응하게 하는 다른 요인이 앞에 언급되어야 함
또한 환경적 요인은 결정할 수 있다 / 치료 중에 동물이 어떻게 반응할지를 //

No two animals are alike. //
어떤 두 동물도 똑같지 않다 //

(①) Animals from the same litter / will display some of the same features, / but will not be exactly the same as each other; /
'~와 같은'
한 배에서 태어난 동물은 / 똑같은 몇몇 특성을 보여 줄 수 있겠지만 / 서로 정확히 같지는 않을 것이다 /

therefore, they may not respond / in entirely the same way / during a healing session. //
단서2 한 배에서 태어난 동물도 서로 다르므로 치료 중에 완전히 똑같은 방식으로 반응하지 않음
그런 까닭에, 그들은 반응하지 않을지도 모른다 / 완전히 똑같은 방식으로 / 치료 활동 중에 //

(②) For instance, / a cat in a rescue center will respond very differently / than a cat within a domestic home environment. //
단서3 어떤 환경에 있는 고양이인지에 따라 다르게 반응함
예를 들어 / 구조 센터에 있는 고양이는 / 매우 다르게 반응할 것이다 / 가정집 환경 내에 있는 고양이와는 //

(③) In addition, / animals that experience healing for physical illness / will react differently / than those accepting healing for emotional confusion. //
주격 관계대명사(선행사: animals)
= animals
게다가 / 신체적 질병의 치료를 받는 동물은 / 다르게 반응할 것이다 / 감정적 동요의 치료를 받는 동물과는 //

(④) With this in mind, / every healing session needs to be explored differently, / and each healing treatment should be adjusted / to suit the specific needs of the animal. //
every+단수 명사+단수 동사
to부정사의 수동태
부사적 용법
조동사의 수동태
이를 염두에 두어 / 모든 치료 활동은 다르게 탐구되어야 하고 / 각각의 치료법은 조정되어야 한다 / 동물의 특정한 필요에 맞도록 //

(⑤) You will learn as you go; / healing is a constant learning process. //
여러분은 직접 겪으면서 배우게 될 것이다 / 치료가 끊임없는 학습의 과정인 것을 //

- factor ⓝ 요인 · determine ⓥ 결정하다 · respond ⓥ 반응하다
- treatment ⓝ 치료 · alike ⓐ 비슷한, 같은 · display ⓥ 보이다
- feature ⓝ 특징 · therefore ⓐⓓ 그런 까닭에 · entirely ⓐⓓ 완전히
- healing session 치료 활동 · rescue center 구조 센터
- domestic ⓐ 가정의 · illness ⓝ 질병 · react ⓥ 반응하다
- confusion ⓝ 동요, 혼란 · with ~ in mind ~을 염두에 두고
- explore ⓥ 탐구하다 · specific ⓐ 특정한, 구체적인
- constant ⓐ 끊임없는 · process ⓝ 과정

어떤 두 동물도 똑같지 않다. (①) 한 배에서 태어난 동물은 똑같은 몇몇 특성을 보여 줄 수 있겠지만, 서로 정확히 같지는 않을 것이다. 그런 까닭에, 그들은 치료 활동 중에 완전히 똑같은 방식으로 반응하지 않을지도 모른다. (② 또한 환경적 요인은 치료 중에 동물이 어떻게 반응할지를 결정할 수 있다.) 예를 들어, 구조 센터에 있는 고양이는 가정집 환경 내에 있는 고양이와는 매우 다르게 반응할 것이다. (③) 게다가, 신체적 질병의 치료를 받는 동물은 감정적 동요의 치료를 받는 동물과는 다르게 반응할 것이다. (④) 이를 염두에 두어, 모든 치료 활동은 다르게 탐구되어야 하고, 각각의 치료법은 동물의 특정한 필요에 맞도록 조정되어야 한다. (⑤) 여러분은 치료가 끊임없는 학습의 과정인 것을 직접 겪으면서 배우게 될 것이다.

1st 주어진 문장을 해석하고, 연결어, 지시어 등을 확인한다.

Environmental factors can **also** determine how the animal will respond during the treatment.
└ **또한** 환경적 요인은 치료 중에 동물이 어떻게 반응할지를 결정할 수 있다.

➡ **주어진 문장 앞:** also(또한)가 있으므로 **단서**
환경적 요인의 다른 역할이 앞에 언급되거나, 치료 중인 동물의 반응을 결정하는 다른 요인이 앞에 나올 것이다. **발상**

2nd 찾은 단서를 생각하며 각 선택지의 앞뒤 흐름이 매끄러운지 확인한다.

- **①의 앞 문장과 뒤 문장**

앞 문장: 어떤 두 동물도 똑같지 않다.

뒤 문장: 한 배에서 태어난 동물은 똑같은 몇몇 특성을 보여 줄 수 있겠지만, 서로 정확히 같지는 않을 것이다. 그런 까닭에, 그들은 치료 활동 중에 완전히 똑같은 방식으로 반응하지 않을지도 모른다.

➡ 어떤 두 동물도 똑같지 않다는 문장 뒤에, 한 배에서 태어난 동물들도 서로 다른 까닭에, 치료 활동에 대한 반응도 완전히 똑같지 않다는 부연 설명이 자연스럽게 이어진다. ▶ 주어진 문장이 ①에 들어갈 수 없음

- **②의 앞 문장과 뒤 문장**

앞 문장: ①의 뒤 문장과 같음

뒤 문장: 예를 들어, 구조 센터에 있는 고양이는 가정집 환경 내에 있는 고양이와는 매우 다르게 반응할 것이다.

➡ ②의 앞 문장은 한 배에서 태어난 동물들도 치료 활동에 대한 반응이 같지 않다는 내용, 즉 생물학적 요인에 관한 것이지만, ②의 뒤 문장은 고양이가 다른 환경 안에서 반응을 다르게 할 수 있다는 예시, 즉 환경적 요인에 관한 것이다. 두 문장이 이어지려면, 그 사이에 환경에 따라 동물의 치료에 대한 반응이 달라질 수 있다는 내용이 와야 한다. ▶ 주어진 문장이 ②에 들어가야 함

- **③의 앞 문장과 뒤 문장**

앞 문장: ②의 뒤 문장과 같음

뒤 문장: 게다가, 신체적 질병의 치료를 받는 동물은 감정적 동요의 치료를 받는 동물과는 다르게 반응할 것이다.

➡ 환경적 요인에 이어서, 동물의 치료 반응에 영향을 미치는 요인으로서 신체적 질병의 치료와 감정적 동요의 치료를 받는 동물이 다르게 반응한다는 내용이 추가로 제시되었다. ▶ 주어진 문장이 ③에 들어갈 수 없음

- **④의 앞 문장과 뒤 문장**

앞 문장: ③의 뒤 문장과 같음

뒤 문장: **이를**(this) 염두에 두어, 모든 치료 활동은 다르게 탐구되어야 하고, 각각의 치료법은 동물의 특정한 필요에 맞도록 조정되어야 한다.

➡ 동물의 치료 반응이 달라지는 다양한 요인이 앞에 쭉 제시되었고, 이러한 요인들로 인해 동물의 치료 반응이 달라질 수 있다는 사실을 this로 가리키며 문장이 자연스럽게 이어졌다. ▶ 주어진 문장이 ④에 들어갈 수 없음

- **⑤의 앞 문장과 뒤 문장**

앞 문장: ④의 뒤 문장과 같음

뒤 문장: 여러분은 치료가 끊임없는 학습의 과정인 것을 직접 겪으면서 배우게 될 것이다.

➡ 치료가 동물에 따라 다른 특정한 필요에 맞게 조정되어야 하므로 치료는 끊임없는 학습의 과정이라는 내용이 자연스럽게 이어진다.
▶ 주어진 문장이 ⑤에 들어갈 수 없음

P 11 정답 ③ *농업이 인구 증가에 미친 영향

글의 흐름으로 보아, 주어진 문장이 들어가기에 가장 적절한 곳을 고르시오.

Farmers, on the other hand, / **could live** in the same place year after year / and **did not have to worry** / about transporting young children long distances. //
  병렬 구조
  단서 1 반면 농부들은 같은 장소에서 오래 살 수 있었음
농부들은 반면에 / 매년 같은 장소에서 살 수 있었고 / 걱정을 하지 않아도 되었다 / 어린아이를 장거리 이동시켜야 하는 //

Growing crops / forced **people to stay** in one place. //
  forced의 목적어와 목적격 보어(to부정사)
농작물 재배는 / 사람들이 한곳에 머무르게 했다 //

Hunter-gatherers typically moved around frequently, / and they had to be able to carry all their possessions with them / every time they moved. //
수렵 채집인들은 일반적으로 자주 이동해야 했고 / 모든 소유물을 가지고 다닐 수 있어야 했다 / 이동할 때마다 //

(①) In particular, / mothers / had to carry their young children. //
  단서 2 수렵 채집인 어머니는 이동의 부담으로 출산 간격을 둠
특히 / 어머니들은 / 어린아이를 업고 이동해야 했다 //

(②) As a result, / hunter-gatherer mothers could have only one baby / every four years or so, / **spacing their births** / **so that** they never had to carry more than one child at a time. //
  분사구문   (그래서) ~할 수 있도록
그 결과 / 수렵 채집인 어머니들은 한 명의 아이만 낳을 수 있었고 / 대략 4년마다 / 출산 간격을 두었다 / 한 번에 한 명 이상의 아이를 업고 다닐 필요가 없도록 //

(**③**) **Societies that** settled down in one place / **were** able to shorten their birth intervals / from four years to about two. //
  복수 주어 주격 관계대명사   복수 동사
  단서 3 정착한 사회는 출산 간격을 단축할 수 있었음
한곳에 정착하게 된 사회는 / 출산 간격을 단축할 수 있었다 / 4년에서 약 2년으로 //

(④) This meant / **that** each woman could have more children / than her hunter-gatherer counterpart, / **which** in turn resulted in rapid population growth / among farming communities. //
  목적어절 접속사
  계속적 용법의 주격 관계대명사(앞 문장 전체 수식)
이는 의미했다 / 여성 한 명이 더 많은 아이를 낳을 수 있다는 것을 / 수렵 채집인인 상대보다 / 그 결과 그것은 급격한 인구 증가를 야기했다 / 농경 사회에서 //

(⑤) An increased population was actually an advantage / to agricultural societies, / because farming required large amounts of human labor. //
인구 증가는 실제로 유리했다 / 농경 사회에 / 왜냐하면 농사는 많은 인간의 노동력을 필요로 했기 때문이다 //

- **transport** ⓥ 이동시키다 • **distance** ⓝ 거리 • **crop** ⓝ 농작물
- **typically** ⓐⓓ 보통, 일반적으로 • **frequently** ⓐⓓ 자주, 빈번하게
- **possession** ⓝ 소유 • **space** ⓥ 간격을 두다 • **birth** ⓝ 출산
- **settle down** 정착하다 • **shorten** ⓥ 단축하다 • **interval** ⓝ 간격
- **rapid** ⓐ 빠른 • **labor** ⓝ 노동력

농작물 재배는 사람들이 한곳에 머무르게 했다. 수렵 채집인들은 일반적으로 자주 이동해야 했고, 이동할 때마다 모든 소유물을 가지고 다닐 수 있어야 했다. (①) 특히, 어머니들은 어린아이를 업고 이동해야 했다. (②) 그 결과, 수렵 채집인 어머니들은 대략 4년마다 한 명의 아이만 낳을 수 있었고, 한 번에 한 명 이상의 아이를 업고 다닐 필요가 없도록 출산 간격을 두었다. (③ 반면, 농부들은 매년 같은 장소에서 살 수 있었고 어린아이를 장거리 이동시켜야 하는 걱정을 하지 않아도 되었다.) 한곳에 정착하게 된 사회는 출산 간격을 4년에서 약 2년으로 단축할 수 있었다. (④) 이는 여성 한 명이 수렵 채집인인 상대보다 더 많은 아이를 낳을 수 있다는 것을 의미했고, 그 결과 그것은 농경 사회에서 급격한 인구 증가를 야기했다. (⑤) 인구 증가는 실제로 농경 사회에 유리했는데, 왜냐하면 농사는 많은 인간의 노동력을 필요로 했기 때문이다.

1st 주어진 문장을 해석하고, 연결어, 지시어 등을 확인한다.

Farmers, on the other hand, could live in the same place
year after year and did not have to worry about transporting
young children long distances.

반면, 농부들은 매년 같은 장소에서 살 수 있었고 어린아이를 장거리 이동시켜야 하는
걱정을 하지 않아도 되었다.

➡ 주어진 문장 앞: 반대되는 내용을 나타내는 on the other hand가
있으므로, (단서)
농부들과는 상황이 반대인 사람들이 언급될 것이다. (발상)
주어진 문장 뒤: 이동하지 않아도 되는 농부들의 상황에 대한 설명이 이어질
것이다.

2nd 각 선택지의 앞뒤 흐름이 자연스러운지 확인한다.

- ①의 앞 문장과 뒤 문장

앞 문장: 수렵 채집인들은 일반적으로 자주 이동해야 했고, 이동할 때마다
모든 소유물을 가지고 다닐 수 있어야 했다.

뒤 문장: 특히, 어머니들은 어린아이를 업고 이동해야 했다.

➡ 농부들과 상황이 반대인 사람들로 수렵 채집인들이 언급되었고, 이들이 자주
이동해야 해서 어머니들이 어린아이를 업고 이동해야 했다는 내용이 앞뒤로
이어진다. ▶ 주어진 문장이 ①에 들어갈 수 없음

- ②의 앞 문장과 뒤 문장

앞 문장: ①의 뒤 문장과 같음

뒤 문장: 그 결과, 수렵 채집인 어머니들은 대략 4년마다 한 명의 아이만
낳을 수 있었고, 한 번에 한 명 이상의 아이를 업고 다닐 필요가 없도록
출산 간격을 두었다.

➡ 수렵 채집인 어머니들은 아이를 업고 이동해야 했으므로 출산 간격을 둘 수밖에
없었다는 결과가 자연스럽게 이어진다. ▶ 주어진 문장이 ②에 들어갈 수 없음

- ③의 앞 문장과 뒤 문장

앞 문장: ②의 뒤 문장과 같음

뒤 문장: 한곳에 정착하게 된 사회는 출산 간격을 4년에서 약 2년으로
단축할 수 있었다.

➡ 자주 이동하는 수렵 채집인에 관한 앞 문장과 한곳에 정착하게 된 사회를 언급하는
뒤 문장이 서로 이어지지 않는다. 수렵 채집인에 관한 내용이 끝나고 on the other
hand로 반대되는 부류인 농부들을 언급하는 주어진 문장이 여기에 와야 한다.
▶ 주어진 문장이 ③에 들어가야 함

- ④의 앞 문장과 뒤 문장

앞 문장: ③의 뒤 문장과 같음

뒤 문장: 이는 여성 한 명이 수렵 채집인인 상대보다 더 많은 아이를 낳을 수
있다는 것을 의미했고, 그 결과 그것이 농경 사회에서 급격한 인구 증가를
야기했다.

➡ 농경 사회에서 단축된 출산 간격은 수렵 채집 사회보다 출산이 많았다는 것을
의미했고, 이것이 급격한 인구 증가를 야기했다는 내용으로 자연스럽게 이어진다.
▶ 주어진 문장이 ④에 들어갈 수 없음

- ⑤의 앞 문장과 뒤 문장

앞 문장: ④의 뒤 문장과 같음

뒤 문장: 인구 증가는 실제로 농경 사회에 유리했는데, 왜냐하면 농사는
많은 인간의 노동력을 필요로 했기 때문이다.

➡ 농경 사회에서의 인구 증가가 실제로 노동력이 많이 필요했던 농경 사회에
유리했다는 내용이 자연스럽게 이어진다. ▶ 주어진 문장이 ⑤에 들어갈 수 없음

P 12 정답 ③ *상사 형질과 상동 형질의 구분

글의 흐름으로 보아, 주어진 문장이 들어가기에 가장 적절한 곳을 고르
시오.

> homo=same, logous(logos)=relation
> "Homologous" traits, / in contrast, / may or may not have a
> common function, / 단서1 상동 형질은 공통적인 기능은 없을 수 있으나 공통적인 조상과 구조를 가짐
> '상동' 형질은 / 대조적으로 / 공통된 기능이 있을 수도 없을 수도 있으나 /
> but they descended from a common ancestor / and hence
> have some common structure / that indicates their being "the
> same" organ. //   주격 관계대명사   동명사 being의 의미상 주어
> 그것들은 공통의 조상으로부터 내려왔으므로 / 어떠한 공통된 구조를 가진다 / 그들이
> '동일한' 기관임을 보여주는 //

Biologists distinguish two kinds of similarity. //
생물학자들은 두 종류의 유사성을 구별한다 // 단서2 두 가지 유사성이 나올 것임
                                           ana=according to 주격 관계대명사
(①) "Analogous" traits are ones / that have a common function
                               병렬 구조
/ but arose on different branches of the evolutionary tree / and
                           병렬 구조
are in an important sense not "the same" organ. //
'상사' 형질은 형질이다 / 공통된 기능을 가지지만 / 진화 계보의 다른 가지에서 생겨났고 /
중요한 면에서 '동일한' 기관이 아닌 // 단서3 상사 형질은 공통 기능은 가지지만 진화 계보의 다른 가지에서 생겨남
(②) The wings of birds and the wings of bees / are both used
for flight / and are similar in some ways / because anything used
과거분사구(anything 수식)   단서4 상사 형질의 예시
for flight has to be built / in those ways, /
새의 날개들과 벌의 날개들은 / 둘 다 비행에 쓰이고 / 일부 방식에서 유사하지만 / 비행에
쓰이는 것은 어떤 것이든 만들어져야 하기 때문에 / 그러한 방식으로 /
but they arose independently in evolution / and have nothing in
common / beyond their use in flight. //
그것들은 진화상에 별개로 생겨났고 / 공통점이 없다 / 비행에서 그것들의 쓰임 외에는 //
                                         단서5 상동 형질의 예시
(③) The wing of a bat and the front leg of a horse / have very
different functions, / but they are all modifications / of the
forelimb of the ancestor of all mammals. //
박쥐의 날개와 말의 앞다리는 / 매우 다른 기능들을 가지나 / 그것들은 모두 변형된 것이다 /
모든 포유류의 조상의 앞다리가 //
                      = The wing of a bat and the front leg of a horse
(④) As a result, / they share nonfunctional traits / like the
number of bones / and the ways they are connected. //
그 결과 / 그들은 비기능적 형질을 공유한다 / 뼈의 개수와 같은 / 그리고 그것들이 연결된
방식과 (같은) //
(⑤) To distinguish analogy from homology, / biologists usually
                                           병렬 구조
look at the overall architecture of the organs / and focus on their
most useless properties. //
상사성과 상동성을 구별하기 위해 / 생물학자들은 주로 그 기관의 전체적인 구성을 살펴보고 /
그들의 가장 쓰임이 없는 특성에 집중한다 //

- trait ⓝ 형질 · descend ⓥ 내려오다 · ancestor ⓝ 조상
- hence (ad) 이런 이유로 · structure ⓝ 구조 · indicate ⓥ 나타내다
- organ ⓝ 기관 · distinguish ⓥ 구별하다 · similarity ⓝ 유사성
- arise ⓥ 생겨나다 · independently (ad) ~와 관계없이
- modification ⓝ 수정 · forelimb ⓝ 앞다리
- mammal ⓝ 포유류 · nonfunctional ⓐ 비기능적
- architecture ⓝ 구성 · property ⓝ 특성

생물학자들은 두 종류의 유사성을 구별한다. (①) '상사' 형질은 공통된 기능을
가지는 것들이지만, 진화 계보의 다른 가지에서 생겨났고 중요한 면에서 '동일
한' 기관이 아닌 형질이다. (②) 새의 날개들과 벌의 날개들은 둘 다 비행에 쓰
이고 비행에 쓰이는 것은 어떤 것이든 그러한 방식으로 만들어져야 하기 때문에
일부 방식에서 유사하지만, 그것들은 진화상에 별개로 생겨났고, 비행에서 그
것들의 쓰임 외에는 공통점이 없다. (③ 대조적으로, '상동' 형질은 공통된 기능
이 있을 수도 없을 수도 있으나 그것들은 공통의 조상으로부터 내려왔으므로 그
들이 '동일한' 기관임을 보여주는 어떠한 공통된 구조를 가진다.) 박쥐의 날개와

말의 앞다리는 매우 다른 기능들을 가지나, 그것들은 모든 포유류의 조상의 앞다리가 모두 변형된 것들이다. (④) 그 결과, 그들은 뼈의 개수와 그것들이 연결된 방식과 같은 비기능적 형질을 공유한다. (⑤) 상사성과 상동성을 구별하기 위해, 생물학자들은 주로 그 기관의 전체적인 구성을 살펴보고 그들의 가장 쓰임이 없는 특성에 집중한다.

| 문제 풀이 순서 | ❋❋❋ [정답률 62%]

1st 주어진 문장을 해석하고, 앞뒤에 어떤 내용이 올지 생각한다.

"Homologous" traits, in contrast, may or may not have a common function, but they descended from a common ancestor and hence have some common structure that indicates their being "the same" organ.
대조적으로, '상동' 형질은 공통된 기능이 있을 수도 없을 수도 있으나 그것들은 공통의 조상으로부터 내려왔으므로 그들이 '동일한' 기관임을 보여주는 어떠한 공통된 구조를 가진다.

➡ 주어진 문장 앞: 반대되는 내용을 나타내는 in contrast가 있으므로, **단서** 상동 형질과 반대되는 형질이 앞에 언급될 것이다. **발상**

➡ 주어진 문장 뒤: 상동 형질을 가지는 예시가 이어질 것이다.

2nd 각 선택지의 앞뒤 흐름이 매끄러운지 확인한다.

- ①의 앞 문장과 뒤 문장
앞 문장: 생물학자들은 두 종류의 유사성을 구별한다.
뒤 문장: '상사' 형질은 공통된 기능을 가지는 것들이지만, 진화 계보의 다른 가지에서 생겨났고 중요한 면에서 '동일한' 기관이 아닌 형질이다.

➡ 두 종류의 유사성을 구별한다는 내용에 이어서, 첫 번째 종류의 유사성인 '상사' 형질을 설명한다. ▶ 주어진 문장이 ①에 들어갈 수 없음

- ②의 앞 문장과 뒤 문장
앞 문장: ①의 뒤 문장과 같음
뒤 문장: 새의 날개들과 벌의 날개들은 둘 다 비행에 쓰이고 비행에 쓰이는 것은 어떤 것이든 그러한 방식으로 만들어져야 하기 때문에 일부 방식에서 유사하지만, 그것들은 진화상에 별개로 생겨났고, 비행에서 그것들의 쓰임 외에는 공통점이 없다.

➡ '상사' 형질의 예시로서 새의 날개들과 벌의 날개들을 언급하며, 비행이라는 기능적 측면에서는 공통적이지만, 그 외에는 공통점이 없다고 설명한다.
▶ 주어진 문장이 ②에 들어갈 수 없음

- ③의 앞 문장과 뒤 문장
앞 문장: ②의 뒤 문장과 같음
뒤 문장: 박쥐의 날개와 말의 앞다리는 매우 다른 기능들을 가지나, 그것들은 모든 포유류의 조상의 앞다리가 모두 변형된 것들이다.

➡ 다른 기능을 가지지만 포유류의 조상의 앞다리가 변형된 박쥐의 날개와 말의 앞다리는 '상사' 형질의 예시가 아닌 '상동' 형질의 예시이다. 따라서 상동 형질의 개념을 언급하는 주어진 문장은 여기에 와야 한다.
▶ 주어진 문장이 ③에 들어가야 함

- ④의 앞 문장과 뒤 문장
앞 문장: ③의 뒤 문장과 같음
뒤 문장: 그 결과, 그들(They)은 뼈의 개수와 그것들이 연결된 방식과 같은 비기능적 형질을 공유한다.

➡ '상동' 형질은 동일한 기관임을 보여주는 어떤 공통된 구조를 가진다고 했으므로, 앞 문장에서 언급된 박쥐의 날개와 말의 앞다리가 비기능적 형질을 공유한다는 내용으로 자연스럽게 연결된다. ▶ 주어진 문장이 ④에 들어갈 수 없음

- ⑤의 앞 문장과 뒤 문장
앞 문장: ④의 뒤 문장과 같음
뒤 문장: 상사성과 상동성을 구별하기 위해, 생물학자들은 주로 그 기관의 전체적인 구성을 살펴보고 그들의 가장 쓰임이 없는 특성에 집중한다.

➡ 상사성과 상동성에 대한 설명이 끝난 후에 두 개념을 모두 언급하며, 생물학자들이 이들을 구별하는 방법을 설명하는 내용이 자연스럽게 이어진다.
▶ 주어진 문장이 ⑤에 들어갈 수 없음

P 13 정답 ② ＊지구 온난화로 인한 용존 산소량의 감소 —

글의 흐름으로 보아, 주어진 문장이 들어가기에 가장 적절한 곳을 고르시오. [3점]

Thus, / as global warming raises the temperature of marine waters, / it is self-evident / that the amount of dissolved oxygen will decrease. //
따라서 / 지구 온난화가 해양 수온을 높임에 따라 / ~이 자명하다 / 용존 산소의 양이 감소할 것 //

Seawater contains an abundance of dissolved oxygen / that all marine animals breathe to stay alive. //
해수는 다량의 용존 산소를 포함한다 / 모든 해양 동물이 살아있기 위해 호흡하는 //
(①) It has long been established / in physics / that cold water holds more dissolved oxygen / than warm water does / — this is one reason / that cold polar seas are full of life /
오랫동안 확립되어 왔다 / 물리학에서 / 차가운 물이 더 많은 용존 산소를 보유하고 있다는 사실은 / 따뜻한 물이 보유하고 있는 것보다 / 이는 하나의 이유이다 / 차가운 극지의 바다는 생명으로 가득한 /
while tropical oceans are blue, clear, / and relatively poorly populated with living creatures. //
반면 열대 해양은 푸르고 맑고 / 생물이 상대적으로 적게 서식하는 //
(②) This is a worrisome / and potentially disastrous consequence / if allowed to continue / to an ecosystem-threatening level. //
이는 걱정스럽고 / 잠재적으로 파괴적인 결과다 / 만약 계속되도록 허용된다면 / 생태계를 위협하는 수준까지 //
(③) Now scientists have analyzed data / indicating that the amount of dissolved oxygen in the oceans has been declining / for more than a half century. //
현재 과학자들은 데이터를 분석해 왔다 / 해양에서 용존 산소의 양이 감소해 왔다는 것을 보여주는 / 반세기가 넘는 기간 동안 //
(④) The data show / that the ocean oxygen level has been falling more rapidly / than the corresponding rise in water temperature. //
이 데이터는 보여 준다 / 해양 산소 농도가 더 빠르게 감소해 오고 있음을 / 상응하는 수온 상승보다 //
(⑤) Falling oxygen levels in water have the potential / to impact the habitat of marine organisms worldwide /
감소하는 수중 산소 농도는 가능성을 갖고 있으며 / 세계적으로 해양 생물의 서식지에 영향을 끼칠 /
and in recent years this has led to more frequent anoxic events / that killed or displaced / populations of fish, crabs, and many other organisms. //
최근에 이것은 더 빈번한 산소 결핍 사건을 초래해 왔다 / 죽이거나 쫓아낸 / 물고기, 게, 그리고 많은 다른 생물의 개체군을 //

- marine ⓐ 해양의 · self-evident ⓐ 자명한
- abundance ⓝ 풍부함 · breathe ⓥ 호흡하다
- established ⓐ 확립된 · polar ⓐ 극지의 · tropical ⓐ 열대의

- worrisome ⓐ 걱정스러운　　• potentially ⓐⓓ 잠재적으로
- disastrous ⓐ 처참한　　• consequence ⓝ 결과
- analyze ⓥ 분석하다　　• potential ⓝ 잠재력
- organism ⓝ 생물(체)　　• displace ⓥ 쫓아내다

해수는 모든 해양 동물이 살아있기 위해 호흡하는 다량의 용존 산소를 포함한다. (①) 따뜻한 물이 보유하고 있는 것보다 차가운 물이 더 많은 용존 산소를 보유하고 있다는 사실은 물리학에서 오랫동안 확립되어 왔으며, 이는 열대 해양은 푸르고 맑고 생물이 상대적으로 적게 서식하는 반면 차가운 극지의 바다는 생명으로 가득한 하나의 이유이다. (② 따라서 지구 온난화가 해양 수온을 높임에 따라 용존 산소의 양이 감소할 것은 자명하다.) 만약 생태계를 위협하는 수준까지 계속되도록 허용된다면 이는 걱정스럽고 잠재적으로 파괴적인 결과다. (③) 현재 과학자들은 해양에서 용존 산소의 양이 반세기가 넘는 기간 동안 감소해 왔다는 것을 보여 주는 데이터를 분석해 왔다. (④) 이 데이터는 해양 산소 농도가 상응하는 수온 상승보다 더 빠르게 감소해 오고 있음을 보여 준다. (⑤) 감소하는 수중 산소 농도는 세계적으로 해양 생물의 서식지에 영향을 끼칠 가능성을 갖고 있으며 최근에 이것은 물고기, 게, 그리고 많은 다른 생물의 개체군을 죽이거나 쫓아낸 더 빈번한 산소 결핍 사건을 초래해 왔다.

| 문제 풀이 순서 | ★★★ [정답률 36%]

1st 주어진 문장을 해석하고, 연결어, 지시어 등을 확인한다.

┌ Thus, as global warming raises the temperature of marine waters, it is self-evident that the amount of dissolved oxygen will decrease.
└ 따라서 지구 온난화가 해양 수온을 높임에 따라 용존 산소의 양이 감소할 것은 자명하다.

➡ 주어진 문장 앞: 결과를 나타내는 Thus가 있으므로, 단서 온도와 용존 산소량의 관계가 앞에 언급될 것이다. 발상
　주어진 문장 뒤: 용존 산소량이 감소하는 현상을 부연 설명할 것이다.

2nd 각 선택지의 앞뒤 흐름이 매끄러운지 확인한다.

- ①의 앞 문장과 뒤 문장

┌ 앞 문장: 해수는 모든 해양 동물이 살아있기 위해 호흡하는 다량의 용존 산소를 포함한다.
│ 뒤 문장: 따뜻한 물이 보유하고 있는 것보다 차가운 물이 더 많은 용존 산소를 보유하고 있다는 사실은 물리학에서 오랫동안 확립되어 왔으며, 이는 열대 해양은 푸르고 맑고 생물이 상대적으로 적게 서식하는 반면
└ 차가운 극지의 바다는 생명으로 가득한 하나의 이유이다.

➡ 해수는 용존 산소를 포함한다는 사실을 소개한 뒤에, 수온과 용존 산소량의 관계에 대한 설명이 자연스럽게 이어진다. ▶ 주어진 문장이 ①에 들어갈 수 없음

- ②의 앞 문장과 뒤 문장

┌ 앞 문장: ①의 뒤 문장과 같음
│ 뒤 문장: 만약 생태계를 위협하는 수준까지 계속되도록 허용된다면
└ 이(This)는 걱정스럽고 잠재적으로 파괴적인 결과다.

➡ 걱정스럽고 파괴적인 결과를 낳은 This가 무엇인지 앞에 나와야 하는데, ①의 뒤 문장에는 생태계를 위협할 만한 현상이 언급되지 않았다. 해양 수온이 높아지면서 용존 산소량이 감소한다고 언급한 주어진 문장이 여기에 와야 한다.
　▶ 주어진 문장이 ②에 들어가야 함

- ③의 앞 문장과 뒤 문장

┌ 앞 문장: ②의 뒤 문장과 같음
│ 뒤 문장: 현재 과학자들은 해양에서 용존 산소의 양이 반세기가 넘는 기간
└ 동안 감소해 왔다는 것을 보여 주는 데이터를 분석해 왔다.

➡ 용존 산소량이 감소하는 현상이 파괴적인 결과이므로, 과학자들이 해양의 용존 산소량 감소에 관한 데이터를 분석했다는 내용은 자연스럽게 연결된다.
　▶ 주어진 문장이 ③에 들어갈 수 없음

- ④의 앞 문장과 뒤 문장

┌ 앞 문장: ③의 뒤 문장과 같음
│ 뒤 문장: 이 데이터(The data)는 해양 산소 농도가 상응하는 수온 상승보다
└ 더 빠르게 감소해 오고 있음을 보여 준다.

➡ 해양 용존 산소량이 감소해 왔다는 데이터를 부연 설명한다.
　▶ 주어진 문장이 ④에 들어갈 수 없음

- ⑤의 앞 문장과 뒤 문장

┌ 앞 문장: ④의 뒤 문장과 같음
│ 뒤 문장: 감소하는 수중 산소 농도는 세계적으로 해양 생물의 서식지에 영향을 끼칠 가능성을 갖고 있으며 최근에 이것은 물고기, 게, 그리고 많은 다른 생물의 개체군을 죽이거나 쫓아낸 더 빈번한 산소 결핍 사건을 초래해
└ 왔다.

➡ 해양 용존 산소량의 감소에 관한 데이터에 이어서, 이것이 생태계에 미치는 영향을 설명하므로 서로 자연스럽게 연결된다. ▶ 주어진 문장이 ⑤에 들어갈 수 없음

P 14 정답 ⑤　*기대가 행동에 미치는 영향

글의 흐름으로 보아, 주어진 문장이 들어가기에 가장 적절한 곳을 고르시오. [3점]

가주어　　　　　　　　진주어절 접속사　　　　　주격 관계대명사
It was also found / that those students who expected the lecturer to be warm / tended to interact with him more. //
~이 또한 밝혀졌다 / 그 강사가 따뜻할 것이라 기대한 학생들은 / 그와 더 많이 소통하는 경향이 있다(는 것이) // 단서 1 앞에 다른 결과가 밝혀져야 함

단서 2 사람들이 유형별로 분류될 수 있는 특성을 갖는다고 잘못된 가정을 함
People commonly make the mistaken assumption / that because a person has one type of characteristic, / then they automatically have other characteristics / which go with it. //
흔히 사람들은 잘못된 가정을 한다 / 어떤 사람이 한 가지 유형의 특성을 가지고 있기 때문에 / 그러면 자동적으로 다른 특성을 가지고 있다는 / 그것과 어울리는 //

(①) In one study, / university students were given / descriptions
부사절 접속사
of a guest lecturer / before he spoke to the group. //
한 연구에서 / 대학생들은 들었다 / 한 강사에 대한 설명을 / 그(초청 강사)가 그 (대학생) 집단에게 강연을 하기 전에 //

전체의 절반
(②) Half the students received a description / containing the
나머지 절반
word 'warm', / the other half were told / the speaker was 'cold'. //
학생들의 절반은 설명을 들었고 / '따뜻한'이라는 단어가 포함된 / 나머지 절반은 말을 들었다 / 그 강사가 '차갑다'는 //

「전치사+관계대명사」
(③) The guest lecturer then led a discussion, / after which the students were asked / to give their impressions of him. //
그러고 나서 그 초청 강사가 토론을 이끌었고 / 그 후에 학생들은 요청받았다 / 그(강사)에 대한 그들의 인상을 말해 달라고 //

(④) As expected, / there were large differences / between the
앞에 주격 관계대명사와 be동사가 생략됨　　　　　분사구문
impressions formed by the students, / depending upon their original information of the lecturer. //
예상한 대로 / 큰 차이가 있었다 / 학생들에 의해 형성된 인상 간에는 / 그 강사에 대한 학생들의 최초 정보에 따라 // 단서 3 사전에 접한 정보에 따라서 강사에 대한 인상이 다르게 형성됨

not only A but also B: A뿐만 아니라 B도
(⑤) This shows / that different expectations / not only affect the impressions we form / but also our behaviour and the relationship / which is formed. // 단서 4 인상에서 더 나아가 행동 및 형성되는 관계까지 영향을 준다는 설명이 이어짐
이것은 보여 준다 / 서로 다른 기대가 / 우리가 형성하는 인상에 영향을 미칠 뿐만 아니라 / 우리의 행동 및 관계에도 (영향을 미친다는 것을) / 형성되는 //

- interact ⓥ 소통하다　　• commonly ⓐⓓ 흔히
- assumption ⓝ 가정　　• automatically ⓐⓓ 자동적으로
- description ⓝ 설명, 묘사　　• contain ⓥ 포함하다
- discussion ⓝ 토론　　• impression ⓝ 인상
- expectation ⓝ 기대　　• behaviour ⓝ 행동

흔히 사람들은 어떤 사람이 한 가지 유형의 특성을 가지고 있기 때문에, 그러면 자동적으로 그것과 어울리는 다른 특성을 가지고 있다는 잘못된 가정을 한다. (①) 한 연구에서, 대학생들은 초청 강사가 그 (대학생) 집단에게 강연을 하기 전에 그 강사에 대한 설명을 들었다. (②) 학생들의 절반은 '따뜻한'이라는 단어가 포함된 설명을 들었고, 나머지 절반은 그 강사가 '차갑다'는 말을 들었다. (③) 그리고 나서 그 초청 강사가 토론을 이끌었고, 그 후에 학생들은 그(강사)에 대한 그들의 인상을 말해 달라고 요청받았다. (④) 예상한 대로, 학생들에 의해 형성된 인상 간에는 그 강사에 대한 학생들의 최초 정보에 따라 큰 차이가 있었다. (⑤ 또한, 그 강사가 따뜻할 것이라 기대한 학생들은 그와 더 많이 소통하는 경향이 있다는 것이 밝혀졌다.) 이것은 서로 다른 기대가 우리가 형성하는 인상뿐만 아니라 우리의 행동 및 형성되는 관계에도 영향을 미친다는 것을 보여 준다.

| 문제 풀이 순서 | ★★★ [정답률 51%]

1st 주어진 문장을 해석하고, 연결어, 지시어 등을 확인한다.

It was also found that those students who expected the lecturer to be warm tended to interact with him more.

또한, 그 강사가 따뜻할 것이라 기대한 학생들은 그와 더 많이 소통하는 경향이 있다는 것이 밝혀졌다.

➡ 주어진 문장 앞: '또한(also)'이라고 했으므로 단서 앞에 강사에 대한 학생들의 기대가 어땠는지 설명하는 내용이 와야 한다. 발상

2nd 각 선택지의 앞뒤 흐름이 매끄러운지 확인한다.

- ①의 앞 문장과 뒤 문장

앞 문장: 흔히 사람들은 어떤 사람이 한 가지 유형의 특성을 가지고 있기 때문에, 그러면 자동적으로 그것과 어울리는 다른 특성을 가지고 있다는 잘못된 가정을 한다.

뒤 문장: 한 연구에서, 대학생들은 초청 강사가 그 (대학생) 집단에게 강연을 하기 전에 그 강사에 대한 설명을 들었다.

➡ 앞 문장의 주장을 뒷받침하는 연구가 뒤 문장에 이어진다.
▶ 주어진 문장이 ①에 들어갈 수 없음

- ②의 앞 문장과 뒤 문장

앞 문장: ①의 뒤 문장과 같음

뒤 문장: 학생들의 절반은 '따뜻한'이라는 단어가 포함된 설명을 들었고, 나머지 절반은 그 강사가 '차갑다'는 말을 들었다.

➡ 앞 문장의 연구에 관해, 학생들을 두 그룹으로 나누어 강사에 관해 반대되는 설명을 했다는 내용이 자연스럽게 이어진다. ▶ 주어진 문장이 ②에 들어갈 수 없음

- ③의 앞 문장과 뒤 문장

앞 문장: ②의 뒤 문장과 같음

뒤 문장: 그리고 나서 그 초청 강사가 토론을 이끌었고, 그 후에 학생들은 그(강사)에 대한 그들의 인상을 말해 달라고 요청받았다.

➡ 강의 후에 학생들에게 강사에 대한 인상이 어땠는지 묻는 흐름은 자연스럽다.
▶ 주어진 문장이 ③에 들어갈 수 없음

- ④의 앞 문장과 뒤 문장

앞 문장: ③의 뒤 문장과 같음

뒤 문장: 예상한 대로, 학생들에 의해 형성된 인상 간에는 그 강사에 대한 학생들의 최초 정보에 따라 큰 차이가 있었다.

➡ 사전 정보에 따라 학생들이 느끼는 강사에 대한 인상에 차이가 있었다는 결과가 자연스럽게 이어진다.
▶ 주어진 문장이 ④에 들어갈 수 없음

- ⑤의 앞 문장과 뒤 문장

앞 문장: ④의 뒤 문장과 같음

뒤 문장: 이것은(This) 서로 다른 기대가 우리가 형성하는 인상뿐만 아니라 우리의 행동 및 형성되는 관계에도 영향을 미친다는 것을 보여 준다.

➡ 앞 문장에서는 '인상'에 대한 차이만 언급했으므로 '행동과 관계'와 관련된 내용이 빠져 있다.
▶ 강사가 따뜻할 것이라 기대한 학생들이 강사와 더 많이 소통했다고 한 주어진 문장이 ⑤에 들어가야 함

P 15 정답 ② *느리지만 계속 일어나는 변화

글의 흐름으로 보아, 주어진 문장이 들어가기에 가장 적절한 곳을 고르시오.

Yet we know / **that** the face / **that** stares back at us from the glass / is not the same, / cannot be the same, / as it was 10 minutes ago. // 단서1 거울 속 얼굴이 10분 전 얼굴과 같지 않다는 것이 Yet(그러나)으로 연결됨

그러나 우리는 안다 / 얼굴이 / 거울로부터 우리를 쳐다보는 / 같지 않다는 것을 / 같을 리가 없다(는 것을) / 10분 전에 그랬던 것과 //

Sometimes / the pace of change / is **far** slower. //

때때로 / 변화의 속도는 / 훨씬 더 느리다 //

(①) The face **you saw** / reflected in your mirror this morning / probably appeared no different / from the face **you saw** the day before / — or a week or a month ago. // 단서2 오늘 아침 거울에 비친 얼굴이 일주일이나 한 달 전과 다르지 않아 보임

당신이 본 얼굴은 / 오늘 아침 당신의 거울 속에 비친 / 아마도 다르지 않은 것처럼 보였을 것이다 / 당신이 그 전날 본 얼굴과 / 또는 일주일이나 한 달 전에 //

(②) The proof is in your photo album: / Look at a photograph **taken** of yourself 5 or 10 years ago / and you see clear differences / between the face in the snapshot and the face in your mirror. // 단서3 5년 또는 10년 전에 찍힌 사진 속에 지금의 얼굴과는 다르다는 증거가 있음

증거는 당신의 사진 앨범에 있다 / 5년 또는 10년 전에 찍힌 당신의 사진을 보라 / 그러면 당신은 명확한 차이를 보게 될 것이다 / 스냅사진 속의 얼굴과 거울 속 얼굴 사이의 //

(③) If you **lived** in a world without mirrors for a year / and then **saw** your reflection, / you might be surprised / by the change. //

만약 당신이 일 년간 거울이 없는 세상에 살고 / 그 이후 당신의 (거울에) 비친 모습을 본다면 / 당신은 깜짝 놀랄지도 모른다 / 그 변화 때문에 //

(④) After an interval of 10 years / without seeing yourself, / you might not at first recognize / the person **peering** from the mirror. // 10년의 기간이 지난 후에는 / 당신 자신을 보지 않고 / 당신은 아마 처음에는 알아보지 못할지도 모른다 / 거울에서 쳐다보고 있는 그 사람을 //

(⑤) Even something **as basic as** our own face / changes from moment to moment. //

심지어 우리 자신의 얼굴같이 아주 기본적인 것조차도 / 순간순간 변한다 //

- **stare** ⓥ 쳐다보다, 응시하다 • **pace** ⓝ 속도 • **reflect** ⓥ 비추다
- **proof** ⓝ 증거 • **interval** ⓝ 간격 • **recognize** ⓥ 알아보다

때때로 변화의 속도는 훨씬 더 느리다. (①) 오늘 아침 거울 속에 비친 당신이 본 얼굴은 아마도 당신이 그 전날 또는 일주일이나 한 달 전에 본 얼굴과 다르지 않은 것처럼 보였을 것이다. (② 그러나 우리는 거울로부터 우리를 쳐다보는 얼굴이 10분 전에 그랬던 것과 같지 않고, 같을 수 없다는 것을 안다.) 증거는 당신의 사진 앨범에 있다: 5년 또는 10년 전에 찍힌 당신의 사진을 보면 당신은 스냅사진 속의 얼굴과 거울 속 얼굴 사이의 명확한 차이를 보게 될 것이다. (③) 만약 당신이 일 년간 거울이 없는 세상에 살고 그 이후 (거울에) 비친 당신의 모습을 본다면, 당신은 그 변화 때문에 깜짝 놀랄지도 모른다. (④) 당신 자신을 보지 않고 10년의 기간이 지난 후, 당신은 거울에서 쳐다보고 있는 그 사람을 처음에는 알아보지 못할지도 모른다. (⑤) 심지어 우리 자신의 얼굴같이 아주 기본적인 것조차도 순간순간 변한다.

1st 주어진 문장을 해석하고, 연결어, 지시어 등을 확인한다.

[Yet] we know that the face that stares back at us from the glass is not the same, cannot be the same, as it was 10 minutes ago.

[그러나] 우리는 거울로부터 우리를 쳐다보는 얼굴이 10분 전에 그랬던 것과 같지 않고, 같을 수 없다는 것을 안다.

➡ 주어진 문장 앞: 'Yet(그러나)'이라고 했으므로 [단서]
앞에는 거울에 비친 얼굴이 이전과 같다는 내용이 와야 한다. [발상]

2nd 찾은 단서를 생각하며 각 선택지의 앞뒤 흐름이 매끄러운지 확인한다.

- ①의 앞 문장과 뒤 문장
앞 문장: 때때로 변화의 속도는 훨씬 더 느리다.
뒤 문장: 오늘 아침 거울 속에 비친 당신이 본 얼굴은 아마도 당신이 그 전날 또는 일주일이나 한 달 전에 본 얼굴과 다르지 않은 것처럼 보였을 것이다.
➡ 앞 문장의 예시를 뒤 문장에서 제시했다.
▶ 주어진 문장이 ①에 들어갈 수 없음

- ②의 앞 문장과 뒤 문장
앞 문장: ①의 뒤 문장과 같음
뒤 문장: 증거는 당신의 사진 앨범에 있다: 5년 또는 10년 전에 찍힌 당신의 사진을 보면 당신은 스냅사진 속의 얼굴과 거울 속 얼굴 사이의 명확한 차이를 보게 될 것이다.
➡ 앞 문장(과거 = 오늘)과 뒤 문장(과거 ≠ 오늘)이 서로 상반된 이야기를 하고 있으므로, 역접의 연결어 Yet으로 현재의 얼굴과 과거의 얼굴이 같을 수 없다는 것을 안다고 한 주어진 문장이 와야 한다.
▶ 주어진 문장이 ②에 들어가야 함

- ③의 앞 문장과 뒤 문장
앞 문장: ②의 뒤 문장과 같음
뒤 문장: 만약 당신이 일 년간 거울이 없는 세상에 살고 그 이후 (거울에) 비친 당신의 모습을 본다면, 당신은 그 변화 때문에 깜짝 놀랄지도 모른다.
➡ 과거에 찍힌 사진으로 얼굴이 변한 것을 볼 수 있는 것처럼, 일 년 동안 거울을 보지 않다가 거울을 보면 변화 때문에 깜짝 놀랄 것이라는 흐름은 자연스럽다.
▶ 주어진 문장이 ③에 들어갈 수 없음

- ④의 앞 문장과 뒤 문장
앞 문장: ③의 뒤 문장과 같음
뒤 문장: 당신 자신을 보지 않고 10년의 기간이 지난 후, 당신은 거울에서 쳐다보고 있는 그 사람을 처음에는 알아보지 못할지도 모른다.
➡ 시간이 지날수록 변화와 차이는 커질 것이라는 앞 문장과 같은 맥락의 내용이 이어진다.
▶ 주어진 문장이 ④에 들어갈 수 없음

- ⑤의 앞 문장과 뒤 문장
앞 문장: ④의 뒤 문장과 같음
뒤 문장: 심지어 우리 자신의 얼굴같이 아주 기본적인 것조차도 순간순간 변한다.
➡ 앞서 이야기해 온 바와 같이 변화의 속도가 때로는 매우 느리더라도, 자신의 얼굴같이 기본적인 것도 사실은 순간순간 변하고 있음을 재확인하며 글을 마무리한다.
▶ 주어진 문장이 ⑤에 들어갈 수 없음

P 16 정답 ② *성공을 보상하는 다양한 방법

[단서 1] 판매부서 관리자가 영업직원이 거래를 성사시킬 때마다 경적을 불었다고 했음

The sales director / kept an air horn outside his office / and would come out and blow the horn / [every time] a salesperson settled a deal. //
~할 때마다
판매부서 관리자는 / 그의 사무실 밖에 경적을 두었다 / 그리고 나와서 경적을 불곤 했다 / 영업직원이 거래를 성사할 때마다 //

주어
Rewarding business success / doesn't always have to be done / in a material way. //
사업 성공을 보상하는 것은 / 항상 되어야 하는 것은 아니다 / 물질적인 방식으로 //
앞에 목적격 관계대명사 생략
(①) A software company / I once worked for / had a great way of recognizing sales success. // [단서 2] 판매 성공을 인정해주는 멋진 방법을 언급했고 구체적 내용은 아직 나오지 않음
한 소프트웨어 회사는 / 내가 예전에 근무한 / 판매 성공을 인정해주는 멋진 방법을 가지고 있었다 //
사이에 주격 관계대명사와 be동사 생략
(②) The noise, / of course, / interrupted anything and everything happening in the office / because it was unbelievably loud. //
그 소리는 / 물론 / 사무실에서 일어나는 어떤 것이라도, 그리고 모든 것을 방해했다 / 믿을 수 없이 시끄러웠기 때문에 // [단서 3] 주어진 문장에 나온 경적 소리를 The noise로 받으면서 내용이 이어지고 있음
(③) However, / it had an amazingly positive impact / on everyone. //
그러나 / 그것은 놀랄 만큼 긍정적인 영향을 주었다 / 모두에게 //
(④) Sometimes rewarding success / can be as easy as that, / especially when peer recognition is important. //
때때로 성공을 보상하는 것은 / 그처럼 쉬울 수 있는데 / 특히 동료의 인정이 중요할 때 그렇다 //
(⑤) You [should have seen] the way / the rest of the sales team / wanted the air horn blown for them. //
should have p.p.: ~했어야 했다
당신은 그 방식을 봤어야 했다 / 그 판매부서의 나머지 사람들이 / 그들을 위해 경적이 불어지기를 바라는 //

- **deal** ⓝ 거래   • **reward** ⓥ 보상하다   • **material** ⓐ 물질적인
- **recognize** ⓥ 인정하다   • **interrupt** ⓥ 방해하다
- **unbelievably** ⓐⓓ 믿을 수 없이   • **amazingly** ⓐⓓ 놀랄 만큼

사업 성공을 보상하는 것은 항상 물질적인 방식으로 되어야 하는 것은 아니다. (①) 내가 예전에 근무한 한 소프트웨어 회사는 판매 성공을 인정해주는 멋진 방법을 가지고 있었다. (② 판매부서 관리자는 그의 사무실 밖에 경적을 두었고 영업직원이 거래를 성사할 때마다 나와서 경적을 불곤 했다.) 물론, 그 소리는 믿을 수 없이 시끄러웠기 때문에 사무실에서 일어나는 어떤 것이라도, 그리고 모든 것을 방해했다. (③) 그러나 그것은 모두에게 놀랄 만큼 긍정적인 영향을 주었다. (④) 때때로, 성공을 보상하는 것은 그처럼 쉬울 수 있는데, 특히 동료의 인정이 중요할 때 그렇다. (⑤) 당신은 그 판매부서의 나머지 사람들이 그들을 위해 경적이 불어지기를 바라는 그 방식을 봤어야 했다.

1st 주어진 문장을 해석하고 문제를 풀 단서를 얻는다.

The sales director kept an air horn outside his office and would come out and blow [the horn] every time a salesperson settled a deal. [단서 1]

판매부서 관리자는 그의 사무실 밖에 경적을 두었고 영업직원이 거래를 성사할 때마다 나와서 경적을 불곤 했다.

➡ 주어진 문장 앞: 판매부서 관리자가 영업직원이 거래를 성사시킬 때마다 '경적(the horn)'을 불었다고 했으므로 [단서]
뒤에 이 경적을 불러서 끼친 영향에 대한 내용이 이어질 것이다. [발상]

- ①의 앞 문장과 뒤 문장

┌ **앞 문장**: 사업 성공을 보상하는 것은 항상 물질적인 방식으로 되어야 하는
└ 것은 아니다.
┌ **뒤 문장**: 내가 예전에 근무한 한 소프트웨어 회사는 판매 성공을 인정해주는
└ 멋진 방법을 가지고 있었다. 단서 2

➡ 앞에서 사업 성공을 보상하는 방법에 대해 언급했고, 뒤에서 성공을 인정해주는
  멋진 방법을 가진 회사를 그 예로 들었으므로 자연스럽게 이어진다.
   ▶ 주어진 문장이 ①에 들어갈 수 없음

- ②의 앞 문장과 뒤 문장

┌ **앞 문장**: ①의 뒤 문장과 같음
├ **뒤 문장**: 물론, 그 소리(The noise)는 믿을 수 없이 시끄러웠기 때문에
└ 사무실에서 일어나는 어떤 것이라도, 그리고 모든 것을 방해했다. 단서 3

➡ 뒤 문장에 나오는 '그 소리(The noise)'로 가리키는 것이 앞 문장에 없으므로
  이어지지 않는다. 주어진 문장의 '경적(the horn) 소리'가 뒤 문장의 '그 소리(The
  noise)'로 이어지는 것이다. ▶ 주어진 문장이 ②에 들어가야 함
  주어진 문장이 ②에 들어가면, 〈판매부서 관리자는 사무실 밖에 경적을 두었고
  영업직원이 거래를 성사할 때마다 경적을 불곤 했다. 그 소리는 굉장히 시끄러웠기
  때문에 모든 것을 방해했다.〉라는 자연스러운 흐름이 된다.

- ③의 앞 문장과 뒤 문장

┌ **앞 문장**: ②의 뒤 문장과 같음
├ **뒤 문장**: 그러나(However) 그것은 모두에게 놀랄 만큼 긍정적인 영향을
└ 주었다.

➡ 굉장히 시끄러운 소리라서 모든 것을 방해했다는 앞의 문장에
  However(그러나)로 이어지며, 긍정적인 영향을 줬다는 반대 내용이 나오므로
  자연스럽게 연결된다.
   ▶ 주어진 문장이 ③에 들어갈 수 없음

- ④의 앞 문장과 뒤 문장

┌ **앞 문장**: ③의 뒤 문장과 같음
├ **뒤 문장**: 때때로, 성공을 보상하는 것은 그처럼 쉬울 수 있는데, 특히 동료의
└ 인정이 중요할 때 그렇다.

➡ 앞에서 경적 소리가 아주 긍정적인 영향을 주었다고 했고, 뒤에서 이렇게 성공을
  보상하는 것이 쉬울 수 있다고 이어지고 있으므로 자연스러운 흐름이다.
   ▶ 주어진 문장이 ④에 들어갈 수 없음

- ⑤의 앞 문장과 뒤 문장

┌ **앞 문장**: ④의 뒤 문장과 같음
├ **뒤 문장**: 당신은 그 판매부서의 나머지 사람들이 그들을 위해 경적이
└ 불어지기를 바라는 그 방식을 봤어야 했다.

➡ 앞에서 성공을 보상하는 것은 쉬울 수 있고 동료의 인정이 중요할 때 그렇다고 한
  문장이, 어떤 영향을 미쳤는지에 대한 문장으로 이어지므로 자연스럽게 연결된다.
   ▶ 주어진 문장이 ⑤에 들어갈 수 없음

P 17 정답 ③ *카페인과 수면의 관계

글의 흐름으로 보아, 주어진 문장이 들어가기에 가장 적절한 곳을 고르
시오.

┌ 단서 1 앞에 반대되는 내용이 나왔음 핵심 주어
│ However, / using caffeine / to improve alertness and mental
│ performance / doesn't replace getting a good night's sleep. //
│ 단수 동사
│ 하지만 / 카페인을 사용하는 것은 / 각성과 정신적 수행능력을 향상시키기 위해 / 숙면을
└ 취하는 것을 대체하지 못한다 //

Studies have consistently shown / caffeine to be effective / when
앞에 being 생략
used together with a pain reliever / to treat headaches. //
연구는 일관적으로 보여주었다 / 카페인이 효과적이라는 것을 / 진통제와 함께 사용할 때 / 두
통을 치료하기 위해 //
(①) The positive correlation / between caffeine intake and
핵심 주어
staying alert throughout the day / has also been well established. //
현재완료 수동태
양의 상관관계 / 카페인 섭취와 하루 종일 각성된 상태에 있는 것 사이에는 / 또한 잘 확립되
어 있다 //
단서 2 카페인을 통해 졸린 상태를 탈출하는 것이 가능함
(②) As little as 60 mg (the amount typically in one cup of tea) /
can lead to a faster reaction time. //
60 mg (일반적으로 차 한 잔에 들어 있는 양) 만큼의 적은 양으로도 / 반응 시간이 빨라질 수
있다 //
(③) One study from 2018 showed / that coffee improved
목적어절을 이끄는 접속사
reaction times in those with or without poor sleep, / but caffeine
seemed to increase errors / in the group with little sleep. //
2018년 한 연구는 보여주었다 / 커피가 수면이 부족한 사람이나 부족하지 않은 사람에게 반응
시간을 개선시켰다는 것을 / 하지만 카페인은 오류를 증가시키는 것 같다는 것을 / 수면이 부
족한 집단 내에서는 //
단서 3 카페인이 수면이 부족한 사람에게는 부정적 영향을 끼치고
기대 효과를 보지 못한다는 반대 내용이 나옴
(④) Additionally, / this study showed / that even with caffeine,
목적어절을 이끄는 접속사
/ the group with little sleep did not score / as well as those with
adequate sleep. //
게다가 / 이 연구는 보여주었다 / 카페인을 섭취하더라도 / 수면이 부족한 그룹은 적절한 점수
를 잘 받지 못했다 / 수면을 취한 집단만큼 //
(⑤) It suggests that / caffeine does not fully make up for
inadequate sleep. //
그것은 보여준다 / 카페인이 불충분한 수면을 충분히 보충하지 못한다는 것을 //

- alertness ⓝ 깨어 있음 • mental ⓐ 정신의
- consistently ⓐⓓ 일관적으로 • effective ⓐ 효과적인
- pain reliever 진통제 • correlation ⓝ 상관관계
- intake ⓝ 섭취 • establish ⓥ 확립하다 • adequate ⓐ 적절한

연구는 카페인이 두통을 치료하기 위해 진통제와 함께 사용할 때 효과적이
라는 것을 일관적으로 보여주었다. (①) 또한 카페인 섭취와 하루 종일 각
성된 상태로 있는 것 사이에는 양의 상관관계가 잘 확립되어 있다. (②)
60 mg (일반적으로 차 한 잔에 들어 있는 양) 만큼의 적은 양으로도 반응
시간이 빨라질 수 있다. (③ 하지만, 각성과 정신적 수행능력을 향상시키기
위해 카페인을 사용하는 것은 숙면을 취하는 것을 대체하지 못한다.) 2018
년 한 연구는 커피는 수면이 부족한 사람이나 부족하지 않은 사람에게나
반응 시간은 개선시켰지만, 카페인은 수면이 부족한 집단 내에서는 오류를
증가시키는 것 같다는 것을 보여주었다. (④) 게다가, 이 연구는 카페인을
섭취하더라도, 수면이 부족한 그룹은 적절한 수면을 취한 집단만큼 점수를
잘 받지 못했다는 것을 보여주었다. (⑤) 그것은 카페인이 불충분한 수면
을 충분히 보충하지 못한다는 것을 보여준다.

| 문제 풀이 순서 | ★★★ [정답률 60%]

1st 주어진 문장을 해석하고, 연결어, 지시어 등을 확인한다.

┌ However, using caffeine to improve alertness and mental
│ performance doesn't replace getting a good night's sleep.
│ 하지만, 각성과 정신적 수행능력을 향상시키기 위해 카페인을 사용하는 것은 숙면을 취하는
└ 것을 대체하지 못한다. 단서 1

➡ 주어진 문장 앞: However(하지만) 앞에는 반대 내용이 와야 한다. 단서
  카페인을 사용하는 것이 각성과 정신적 수행능력을 향상시킨다는 내용일 것이다.
   발상

2nd 각 선택지의 앞뒤 흐름이 매끄러운지 확인한다.

- ①의 앞 문장과 뒤 문장

┌ **앞 문장**: 연구는 카페인이 두통을 치료하기 위해 진통제와 함께 사용할 때
├ 효과적이라는 것을 일관적으로 보여주었다.
├ **뒤 문장**: 또한 카페인 섭취와 하루 종일 각성된 상태로 있는 것 사이에는
└ 양의 상관관계가 잘 확립되어 있다.

➡ 앞 문장은 카페인이 두통을 치료하는 데 효과적이라고 했고, 뒤 문장에서 카페인을 섭취하면 각성 상태로 있게 된다는 내용이 자연스럽게 이어지고 있다.
　▶ 주어진 문장이 ①에 들어갈 수 없음

- ②의 앞 문장과 뒤 문장

┌ **앞 문장:** ①의 뒤 문장과 같음
│ **뒤 문장:** 60 mg (일반적으로 차 한 잔에 들어 있는 양) 만큼의 적은
└ 양으로도 반응 시간이 빨라질 수 있다. 단서2

➡ 카페인을 섭취하면 각성 상태로 있게 된다고 한 뒤에, 구체적인 수치로 60 mg이 나오며 문장이 이어지고 있으므로 자연스러운 흐름이다.
　▶ 주어진 문장이 ②에 들어갈 수 없음

- ③의 앞 문장과 뒤 문장

┌ **앞 문장:** ②의 뒤 문장과 같음
│ **뒤 문장:** 2018년 한 연구는 커피는 수면이 부족한 사람이나 부족하지 않은
│ 사람에게나 반응 시간은 개선시켰지만, 카페인은 수면이 부족한 집단
└ 내에서는 오류를 증가시키는 것 같다는 것을 보여주었다. 단서3

➡ 카페인이 적은 양으로도 효과가 있다고 했는데, 카페인이 수면이 부족한 사람에게는 부정적 영향을 끼치고 기대 효과를 보지 못한다는 반대 내용이 나오므로 어색하다. ▶ 주어진 문장이 ③에 들어가야 함
　주어진 문장이 ③에 들어가면, 〈하지만, 카페인을 사용하는 것은 숙면을 취하는 것을 대체하지 못한다. 2018년 한 연구는 커피는 반응 시간은 개선시켰지만, 카페인은 수면이 부족한 집단 내에서는 오류를 증가시키는 것 같다는 것을 보여주었다.〉라는 자연스러운 흐름이 된다.

- ④의 앞 문장과 뒤 문장

┌ **앞 문장:** ③의 뒤 문장과 같음
│ **뒤 문장:** 게다가(Additionally), 이 연구는 카페인을 섭취하더라도,
│ 수면이 부족한 그룹은 적절한 수면을 취한 집단만큼 점수를 잘 받지
└ 못했다는 것을 보여주었다.

➡ 앞에서 카페인은 수면이 부족한 집단 내에서는 오류를 증가시킨다고 했고, 뒤에 '게다가(Additionally)'라고 하며 부연 설명이 이어지고 있으므로 자연스럽게 연결된다. ▶ 주어진 문장이 ④에 들어갈 수 없음

- ⑤의 앞 문장과 뒤 문장

┌ **앞 문장:** ④의 뒤 문장과 같음
│ **뒤 문장:** 그것(It)은 카페인이 불충분한 수면을 충분히 보충하지 못한다는
└ 것을 보여준다.

➡ 앞에 나온 연구 결과를 It으로 받으며, 카페인이 수면을 보충해주지 못한다는 것을 보여준다고 설명하는 문장이 이어진다. ▶ 주어진 문장이 ⑤에 들어갈 수 없음

P 18 정답 ④ *마찰의 발생

글의 흐름으로 보아, 주어진 문장이 들어가기에 가장 적절한 곳을 고르시오.

┌ For example, / if you rub your hands together quickly, / they
│ will get warmer. // 단서1 앞의 내용에 대한 예시이므로 마찰이 열을 발생시키는
│ 　　　　　　　　　　　　　　　　내용이 앞에 와야 함
└ 예를 들어 / 만약 당신이 손을 빠르게 비비면 / 손이 더 따뜻해질 것이다 //

Friction is a force / between two surfaces / that are sliding, or
　　　　　　　　　　　　　　　　주격 관계대명사
trying to slide, / across each other. //
마찰력은 힘이다 / 두 표면 사이에 작용하는 / 미끄러지거나 미끄러지려고 하는 / 서로
엇갈리게 //
For example, / when you try to push a book along the floor, /
friction makes this difficult. //
　　　　　make+목적어+목적격보어(형용사)
예를 들어 / 당신이 바닥 위 책을 밀려고 할 때 / 마찰이 이를 어렵게 만든다 //

Friction always works / in the direction opposite to / the
　　　　　　　　　　　　　　　　　　　　　앞에 which is 생략
direction in which the object is moving, or trying to move. //
마찰은 항상 작용한다 / ~ 반대 반향으로 / 물체가 움직이거나 움직이려고 하는 방향과 //
So, / friction always / slows a moving object down. //
그래서 / 마찰은 항상 / 움직이는 물체를 느리게 만든다 //
(①) The amount of friction / depends on the surface materials. //
마찰의 양은 / 표면 물질에 따라 달라진다 //
　　　　　　「the+비교급 ~, the+비교급 …」: ~할수록 더 …하다
(②) The rougher the surface is, / the more friction is produced. //
표면이 거칠수록 / 더 많은 마찰력이 발생한다 //
(③) Friction also produces heat. // 단서2 마찰이 열을 발생시킨다고 했음
마찰은 또한 열을 발생시킨다 //
(④) Friction can be a useful force / because it prevents our
　　　　　　　　　　　　　　　　　　　　　　　　　병렬 구조
shoes slipping on the floor / when we walk / and stops car tires
skidding on the road. // 단서3 마찰이 유용하게 작용하는 다른 예들이 이어짐
마찰력은 유용한 힘으로 작용할 수 있다 / 신발이 바닥에서 미끄러지는 것을 방지하므로 /
우리가 걸을 때 / 그리고 자동차 타이어가 도로에서 미끄러지는 것을 막아(주므로) //
　　　　　　　　　　　　　　　　between A and B: A와 B 사이에
(⑤) When you walk, / friction is caused between the tread
on your shoes and the ground, / acting to grip the ground and
　　　　　　　　　　　　　　分詞구문을 이끎(= and it acts)
prevent sliding. //
걸을 때 / 마찰은 발생하며 / 당신의 신발 접지면과 바닥 사이에 / 이 마찰은 땅을 붙잡아
미끄러지는 것을 방지하는 역할을 한다 //

- rub ⓥ 비비다　　· friction ⓝ 마찰력　　· force ⓝ 힘
- surface ⓝ 표면　　· slide ⓥ 미끄러지다　　· work ⓥ 작용하다
- direction ⓝ 방향　　· opposite ⓐ 반대편의　　· object ⓝ 물체
- amount ⓝ 양　　· depend on ~에 달려 있다[의존하다]
- material ⓝ 물질　　· rough ⓐ 거친　　· produce ⓥ 발생시키다
- slip ⓥ 미끄러지다　　· grip ⓥ 붙잡다

마찰력은 서로 엇갈리게 미끄러지거나 미끄러지려고 하는 두 표면 사이에 작용하는 힘이다. 예를 들어, 당신이 바닥 위 책을 밀려고 할 때, 마찰이 이를 어렵게 만든다. 마찰은 항상 물체가 움직이거나 움직이려고 하는 방향과 반대 방향으로 작용한다. 그래서 마찰은 항상 움직이는 물체를 느리게 만든다. (①) 마찰의 양은 표면 물질에 따라 달라진다. (②) 표면이 거칠수록 더 많은 마찰력이 발생한다. (③) 마찰은 또한 열을 발생시킨다. (④ 예를 들어, 만약 당신이 손을 빠르게 비비면, 손이 더 따뜻해질 것이다.) 마찰력은 우리가 걸을 때 신발이 바닥에서 미끄러지는 것을 방지하고 자동차 타이어가 도로에서 미끄러지는 것을 막아주므로 유용한 힘으로 작용할 수 있다. (⑤) 걸을 때, 마찰은 당신의 신발 접지면과 바닥 사이에 발생하며, 이 마찰은 땅을 붙잡아 미끄러지는 것을 방지하는 역할을 한다.

| 문제 풀이 순서 | ★★★ [정답률 55%]

1st 주어진 문장을 해석하고, 연결어, 지시어 등을 확인한다.

┌ For example, if you rub your hands together quickly, they
│ will get warmer. 단서1
└ 예를 들어, 만약 당신이 손을 빠르게 비비면, 손이 더 따뜻해질 것이다.

➡ 주어진 문장 앞: For example로 주어진 문장이 시작하므로, 단서 앞에는 마찰이 열을 발생시킨다는 설명이 와야 한다. 발상
　주어진 문장 뒤: 마찰이 유용하게 작용하는 다른 예시들이 나올 것이다.

2nd 각 선택지의 앞뒤 흐름이 매끄러운지 확인한다.

- ①의 앞 문장과 뒤 문장

┌ **앞 문장:** 마찰력은 서로 엇갈리게 미끄러지거나 미끄러지려고 하는 두 표면
│ 사이에 작용하는 힘이다. 예를 들어, 당신이 바닥 위 책을 밀려고 할 때,
│ 마찰이 이를 어렵게 만든다. 마찰은 ~ 물체를 느리게 만든다.
└ **뒤 문장:** 마찰의 양은 표면 물질에 따라 달라진다.

➡ 뒤 문장은 앞 문장에 이어서 마찰의 특징을 설명한다.
　▶ 주어진 문장이 ①에 들어갈 수 없음

- ②의 앞 문장과 뒤 문장

  앞 문장: ①의 뒤 문장과 같음

  뒤 문장: 표면이 거칠수록 더 많은 마찰력이 발생한다.

→ 뒤 문장은 앞 문장을 부연 설명한다.

  ▶ 주어진 문장이 ②에 들어갈 수 없음

- ③의 앞 문장과 뒤 문장

  앞 문장: ②의 뒤 문장과 같음

  뒤 문장: 마찰은 또한 열을 발생시킨다. 단서 2

→ 앞 문장과는 다른 특징을 뒤 문장에서 제시한다.

  앞 문장: 표면이 거칠수록 더 많은 마찰력이 발생함

  뒤 문장: 마찰은 열을 발생시킴

  ▶ 주어진 문장이 ③에 들어갈 수 없음

- ④의 앞 문장과 뒤 문장

  앞 문장: ③의 뒤 문장과 같음

  뒤 문장: 마찰력은 우리가 걸을 때 신발이 바닥에서 미끄러지는 것을 방지하고 자동차 타이어가 도로에서 미끄러지는 것을 막아주므로 유용한 힘으로 작용할 수 있다. 단서 3

→ 주어진 문장에서 예상한 대로 앞에는 열을 발생시킨다는 마찰력의 특징이, 뒤에는 마찰력이 유용한 힘으로 작용한다는 내용이 왔다.

  ▶ 주어진 문장이 ④에 들어가야 함

→ 주어진 문장이 ④에 들어가면, <마찰은 열을 발생시키는데, 손을 빠르게 비볐을 때 손이 따뜻해지는 것이 그 예이다. 또한 마찰력은 미끄러지는 것을 막아주는 유용한 힘으로도 작용한다.>라는 자연스러운 흐름이 된다.

- ⑤의 앞 문장과 뒤 문장

  앞 문장: ④의 뒤 문장과 같음

  뒤 문장: 걸을 때, 마찰은 당신의 신발 접지면과 바닥 사이에 발생하며, 이 마찰은 땅을 붙잡아 미끄러지는 것을 방지하는 역할을 한다.

→ 뒤 문장은 앞 문장의 예시이다.

  ▶ 주어진 문장이 ⑤에 들어갈 수 없음

┌──── 배경 지식 ────┐
✱ 실생활 속의 마찰

  우리 생활 속에서 나타나는 현상은 마찰력과 많은 관련이 있다. 예를 들어, 자동차 타이어나 산악용 신발은 쉽게 미끄러지지 않도록 고무로 만들어진다.
  자동차 타이어에는 특정한 무늬가 있는데 이것이 마찰력을 높여서 브레이크를 밟을 때 잘 멈출 수 있게 해 준다.
  면장갑에 고무 코팅이 되어 있는 이유도 물건을 잡을 때 놓치지 않게 하기 위해서이다.
└────────────────┘

P 19 정답 ⑤ *선천적 시각 장애인이 꾸는 꿈

글의 흐름으로 보아, 주어진 문장이 들어가기에 가장 적절한 곳을 고르시오.

단서 1 앞과 반대되는 내용이 나와야 하고, the same friend가 가리키는 것이 앞에 있어야 함

But, / a blind person will associate the same friend / with a unique combination of experiences / from their non-visual senses / 주격 관계대명사 that act to represent that friend. //

하지만 / 시각 장애인은 그 친구를 연상할 것이다 / 경험의 독특한 조합으로 / 비시각적 감각에서 나온 / 그 친구를 구현하는 데 작용하는 //

앞에 주격 관계대명사와 be동사 생략

Humans born without sight / are not able to collect visual experiences, / so they understand the world / entirely through their other senses. //

선천적으로 시각 장애를 가진 사람은 / 시각적 경험을 수집할 수 없다 / 그래서 그들은 세상을 이해한다 / 전적으로 다른 감각을 통해 //

(①) As a result, / people with blindness at birth / develop an amazing ability / 형용사적 용법 to understand the world /

그 결과 / 선천적으로 시각 장애를 가진 사람들은 / 놀라운 능력을 개발한다 / 세상을 이해하는 / through the collection of experiences and memories / 주격 관계대명사 that come from these non-visual senses. //

경험과 기억의 수집을 통해 / 이러한 비시각적 감각에서 오는 //

(②) The dreams of a person / 주격 관계대명사 who has been without sight since birth / 원급 비교 can be just as vivid and imaginative / = the dreams as those of someone with normal vision. //

사람이 꾸는 꿈은 / 선천적으로 시각 장애를 가진 / 생생하고 상상력이 풍부할 수 있다 / 정상 시력을 가진 사람의 꿈처럼 //

(③) They are unique, however, / because their dreams 수동태 are constructed / from the non-visual experiences and memories / 앞에 목적격 관계대명사 생략 they have collected. //

그러나 그들의 꿈은 특별하다 / 그들의 꿈이 구성되기 때문에 / 비시각적 경험과 기억으로부터 / 그들이 수집한 단서 2 정상적인 시력을 가진 사람은 시각적 기억을 사용하여 친숙한 친구에 대한 꿈을 꿈

(④) A person with normal vision / will dream about a familiar friend / 분사구문을 이끎 using visual memories of shape, lighting, and colour. //

정상적인 시력을 가진 사람들은 / 친숙한 친구에 대해 꿈을 꿀 것이다 / 형태, 빛 그리고 색의 시각적 기억을 사용하여 //

(⑤) In other words, / 앞에 주격 관계대명사와 be동사 생략 people blind at birth / have similar overall dreaming experiences / even though they do not dream in pictures. // 단서 3 주어진 문장에 대한 부연 설명이 나옴

다시 말해 / 선천적 시각 장애인들은 / 전반적으로 비슷한 꿈을 경험한다 / 시각적인 꿈을 꾸지는 않지만 //

- represent ⓥ 구현하다, 나타내다 · sight ⓝ 시각, 시력
- visual ⓐ 시각의 · sense ⓝ 감각 · entirely ⓐd 전적으로
- birth ⓝ 탄생, 출생 · ability ⓝ 능력 · memory ⓝ 기억
- vivid ⓐ 생생한 · imaginative ⓐ 상상력이 풍부한
- normal ⓐ 정상적인 · construct ⓥ 구성하다
- overall ⓐ 전반적인

선천적으로 시각 장애를 가진 사람은 시각적 경험을 수집할 수 없어서, 세상을 전적으로 다른 감각을 통해 이해한다. (①) 그 결과, 선천적으로 시각 장애를 가진 사람들은 이러한 비시각적 감각에서 오는 경험과 기억의 수집을 통해 세상을 이해하는 놀라운 능력을 개발한다. (②) 선천적으로 시각 장애를 가진 사람이 꾸는 꿈은 정상 시력을 가진 사람의 꿈처럼 생생하고 상상력이 풍부할 수 있다. (③) 그러나 그들의 꿈은 그들이 수집한 비시각적 경험과 기억으로부터 구성되기 때문에 그들은 특별하다. (④) 정상적인 시력을 가진 사람들은 형태, 빛 그리고 색의 시각적 기억을 사용하여 친숙한 친구에 대해 꿈을 꿀 것이다. (⑤ 하지만, 시각 장애인은 그 친구를 구현하는 데 작용하는 비시각적 감각에서 나온 경험의 독특한 조합으로 그 친구를 연상할 것이다.) 다시 말해, 선천적 시각 장애인들은 시각적인 꿈을 꾸지는 않지만, 전반적으로 비슷한 꿈을 경험한다.

| 문제 풀이 순서 | ★★★ [정답률 49%]

1st 주어진 문장을 해석하고, 연결어, 지시어 등을 확인한다.

┌ But, a blind person will associate the same friend with a unique combination of experiences from their non-visual senses that act to represent that friend. 단서 1
└ 하지만, 시각 장애인은 그 친구를 구현하는 데 작용하는 비시각적 감각에서 나온 경험의 독특한 조합으로 그 친구를 연상할 것이다.

→ 주어진 문장 앞: 역접의 연결어 But으로 주어진 문장이 시작되므로, 단서 앞에 시각 장애인이 아닌 사람이 '그 친구'를 어떻게 연상하는지가 올 것이다. 발상 주어진 문장 뒤: 시각 장애인의 연상법을 부연 설명할 것이다.

- ①의 앞 문장과 뒤 문장

┌ **앞 문장:** 선천적으로 시각 장애를 가진 사람은 시각적 경험을 수집할 수
│ 없어서, 세상을 전적으로 다른 감각을 통해 이해한다.
│ **뒤 문장:** 그 결과, 선천적으로 시각 장애를 가진 사람들은 이러한 비시각적
│ 감각에서 오는 경험과 기억의 수집을 통해 세상을 이해하는 놀라운 능력을
└ 개발한다.

➡ 앞 문장과 뒤 문장이 원인과 결과를 이룬다.
▶ 주어진 문장이 ①에 들어갈 수 없음

- ②의 앞 문장과 뒤 문장

┌ **앞 문장:** ①의 뒤 문장과 같음
│ **뒤 문장:** 선천적으로 시각 장애를 가진 사람이 꾸는 꿈은 정상 시력을 가진
└ 사람의 꿈처럼 생생하고 상상력이 풍부할 수 있다.

➡ 뒤 문장은 앞 문장에 이어 시각 장애인에 관해 설명한다.
▶ 주어진 문장이 ②에 들어갈 수 없음

- ③의 앞 문장과 뒤 문장

┌ **앞 문장:** ②의 뒤 문장과 같음
│ **뒤 문장:** 그러나 그들의 꿈은 그들이 수집한 비시각적 경험과 기억으로부터
└ 구성되기 때문에 그들은 특별하다.

➡ 앞 문장의 내용을 뒤 문장에서 부연 설명한다.
▶ 주어진 문장이 ③에 들어갈 수 없음

- ④의 앞 문장과 뒤 문장

┌ **앞 문장:** ③의 뒤 문장과 같음
│ **뒤 문장:** 정상적인 시력을 가진 사람들은 형태, 빛 그리고 색의 시각적
│ 기억을 사용하여 친숙한 친구(a familiar friend)에 대해 꿈을 꿀 것이다.
└ 단서2

➡ 뒤 문장에서 시각 장애인이 아닌 사람에 관해 설명한다.
▶ 주어진 문장이 ④에 들어갈 수 없음

- ⑤의 앞 문장과 뒤 문장

┌ **앞 문장:** ④의 뒤 문장과 같음
│ **뒤 문장:** 다시 말해, 선천적 시각 장애인들은 시각적인 꿈을 꾸지는 않지만,
└ 전반적으로 비슷한 꿈을 경험한다. 단서3

➡ 앞 문장에서는 시각 장애인이 아닌 사람들을, 뒤 문장에서는 다시 시각 장애인들에
  관해 이야기한다. ▶ 주어진 문장이 ⑤에 들어가야 함

➡ 주어진 문장이 ⑤에 들어가면, 〈시각 장애인이 아닌 사람들은 시각적 기억으로
  친숙한 친구에 대해 꿈을 꾸지만, 시각 장애인은 비시각적 감각들의 독특한
  조합으로 그 친구를 연상한다. 즉, 선천적 시각 장애인은 시각적인 꿈을 꾸지는
  않아도 전반적으로 비슷한 경험을 한다.〉라는 자연스러운 흐름이 된다.

P 20 정답 ④ * 텔레비전이 가져오는 사회적 활동 단절의 문제 ─

글의 흐름으로 보아, 주어진 문장이 들어가기에 가장 적절한 곳을
고르시오.

┌ Unfortunately, / it is also likely to "crowd out" / other
│ 주격 관계대명사
│ activities / that produce more sustainable social contributions
│ / to our social well-being. // 단서1 앞에 다른 문제점이 이미 나와 있어야 함
│ 불행히도 / 그것은 또한 "몰아내기" 쉽다 / 다른 활동들을 / 더 지속적인 사회적 기여를
└ 만들어 내는 / 우리의 사회적 행복을 위한 //

Television is the number one leisure activity / in the United
States and Europe, / consuming more than half / of our free
분사구문
time. //
텔레비전은 제1의 여가 활동이다 / 미국과 유럽에서 / 절반 이상을 소비한다 / 우리의 자유시간
중 //
(①) We generally think of television / as a way / to relax, / tune
out, / and escape from our troubles / for a bit each day. //
우리는 일반적으로 텔레비전을 생각한다 / 하나의 방법으로 / 휴식하고 / 관심을 끄고 /
우리의 문제로부터 탈출하는 / 매일 잠시나마 //
(②) While this is true, / there is increasing evidence / that
동격절을 이끄는 접속사
we are more motivated / to tune in to our favorite shows and
characters /
이것이 사실이긴 하지만 / 증거가 늘어나고 있다 / 동기가 더 부여된다는 / 우리가 좋아하는
쇼들과 등장인물들을 보려는 /
when we are feeling lonely / or have a greater need / for social
connection. // 단서2 텔레비전을 보는 것은 사회적 욕구를
우리가 외롭다고 느끼고 있거나 / 더 큰 욕구를 가질 때 / 사회적 관계를 위한 // 단기적으로만 만족시킨다는 문제점이 있음
(③) Television watching does satisfy / these social needs / to
강조의 조동사
some extent, / at least in the short run. //
텔레비전을 보는 것이 정말로 만족시킨다 / 이러한 사회적인 욕구를 / 어느 정도까지는 /
적어도 단기적으로는 //
the+비교급 ~, the+비교급 ...: ~할수록 더 ...하다
(④) The more television we watch, / the less likely we are to
병렬 구조
volunteer our time / or to spend time with people / in our social
networks. // 단서3 사회적 활동을 몰아낸 것에 대한 구체적 설명
우리가 텔레비전을 더 볼수록 / 우리는 우리의 시간을 덜 기꺼이 할애하기 쉽다 / 또는
사람들과 함께 시간을 보내기 / 사회적 관계망 속에서 /
the+비교급 ~, the+비교급 ...: ~할수록 더 ...하다
(⑤) In other words, / the more time we make for *Friends*, / the
less time we have for friends in real life. //
다시 말해서 / 우리가 Friends를 위해 더 많은 시간을 낼수록 / 실제 친구들을 위해서는
시간을 덜 갖게 된다 //

- produce ⓥ 만들어 내다   - sustainable ⓐ 지속적인
- contribution ⓝ 기여   - well-being ⓝ 행복
- consume ⓥ 소비하다   - tune out ~을 무시하다, 관심을 끄다
- evidence ⓝ 증거   - motivate ⓥ 동기를 부여하다
- tune in to (TV 프로그램 등을) 보다, 시청하다   - connection ⓝ 관계
- satisfy ⓥ 만족시키다   - extent ⓝ 정도

텔레비전은 미국과 유럽에서 제1의 여가 활동인데, 우리의 자유시간
중 절반 이상을 소비한다. ① 우리는 일반적으로 텔레비전을 휴식하고,
관심을 끄고, 매일 잠시나마 우리의 문제로부터 탈출하는 하나의 방법으로
생각한다. ② 이것이 사실이긴 하지만, 우리가 외롭다고 느끼고 있거나
사회적 관계를 위한 더 큰 욕구를 가질 때 우리가 좋아하는 쇼들과
등장인물들을 보려는 동기가 더 부여된다는 증거가 늘어나고 있다.
③ 적어도 단기적으로는, 텔레비전을 보는 것이 이러한 사회적인 욕구를
어느 정도까지는 정말로 만족시킨다. (④ 불행히도, 그것은 또한 우리의
사회적 행복을 위한 더 지속적인 사회적 기여를 만들어 내는 다른
활동들을 "몰아내기" 쉽다.) 우리가 텔레비전을 더 볼수록, 우리는 사회적
관계망 속에서 우리의 시간을 기꺼이 할애하거나 사람들과 함께 시간을
덜 보내기 쉽다. ⑤ 다시 말해서, 우리가 Friends를 위해 더 많은 시간을
낼수록, 실제 친구들을 위해서는 시간을 덜 갖게 된다.

| 문제 풀이 순서 | ★★★ [정답률 51%]

1st 주어진 문장을 해석하고, 연결어, 지시어 등을 확인한다.

┌ Unfortunately, it is also likely to "crowd out" other activities
│ that produce more sustainable social contributions to our
│ social well-being. 단서1
│ 불행히도, 그것은 또한 우리의 사회적 행복을 위한 더 지속적인 사회적 기여를 만들어 내는
└ 다른 활동들을 "몰아내기" 쉽다.

➡ **주어진 문장 앞:** also가 쓰였으므로 단서
  앞에 또 다른 문제점이 언급되어야 한다. 발상

  주어진 문장 뒤: 다른 활동들을 몰아내는 것에 관해 자세히 설명할 것이다.

왼쪽 컬럼

2nd 각 선택지의 앞뒤 흐름이 매끄러운지 확인한다.

- ①의 앞 문장과 뒤 문장

앞 문장: 텔레비전은 미국과 유럽에서 제1의 여가 활동인데, 우리의 자유시간 중 절반 이상을 소비한다.

뒤 문장: 우리는 일반적으로 텔레비전을 휴식하고, 관심을 끄고, 매일 잠시나마 우리의 문제로부터 탈출하는 하나의 방법으로 생각한다.

➡ 앞 문장의 내용을 뒤 문장에서 부연 설명한다.

▶ 주어진 문장이 ①에 들어갈 수 없음

- ②의 앞 문장과 뒤 문장

앞 문장: ①의 뒤 문장과 같음

뒤 문장: 이것이 사실이긴 <u>하지만(While)</u>, 우리가 외롭다고 느끼고 있거나 사회적 관계를 위한 더 큰 욕구를 가질 때 우리가 좋아하는 쇼들과 등장인물들을 보려는 동기가 더 부여된다는 증거가 늘어나고 있다.

➡ 앞 문장의 내용을 뒤 문장에서 반전한다.

▶ 주어진 문장이 ②에 들어갈 수 없음

- ③의 앞 문장과 뒤 문장

앞 문장: ②의 뒤 문장과 같음

뒤 문장: 적어도 단기적으로는, 텔레비전을 보는 것이 이러한 사회적인 욕구를 어느 정도까지는 정말로 만족시킨다. **단서 2**

➡ 앞 문장의 내용을 뒤 문장에서 이어서 설명한다.

▶ 주어진 문장이 ③에 들어갈 수 없음

-④의 앞 문장과 뒤 문장

앞 문장: ③의 뒤 문장과 같음

뒤 문장: 우리가 텔레비전을 더 볼수록, 우리는 사회적 관계망 속에서 우리의 시간을 기꺼이 할애하거나 사람들과 함께 시간을 덜 보내기 쉽다. **단서 3**

➡ 앞 문장: 텔레비전을 보면 사회적인 욕구가 단기적으로만 만족됨

뒤 문장: 텔레비전을 볼수록 사람들과 보내는 시간이 줄어듦(= 주어진 문장의 '다른 활동들') ▶ 주어진 문장이 ④에 들어가야 함

➡ 주어진 문장이 ④에 들어가면, <텔레비전을 보면 사회적인 욕구를 단기적으로는 만족시킬 수 있지만, 그것은 우리가 사람들과 함께 시간을 보내는 것과 같은 더 지속적인 사회적 기여를 만들어 내는 다른 활동을 몰아내기 쉽다.>라는 자연스러운 흐름이 된다.

- ⑤의 앞 문장과 뒤 문장

앞 문장: ④의 뒤 문장과 같음

뒤 문장: <u>다시 말해서(In other words)</u>, 우리가 Friends를 위해 더 많은 시간을 낼수록, 실제 친구들을 위해서는 시간을 덜 갖게 된다.

➡ 뒤 문장은 앞 문장의 예시이다.

▶ 주어진 문장이 ⑤에 들어갈 수 없음

P 21 정답 ⑤ *뇌의 발달과 함께 줄어드는 호기심

글의 흐름으로 보아, 주어진 문장이 들어가기에 가장 적절한 곳을 고르시오. [3점]

~함에 따라, **단서 1** 아이들이 흡수한 증거는 지식이나 믿음으로 굳어짐

<u>As</u> children absorb more evidence / from the world around them, / certain possibilities <mark>become</mark> much more likely and more useful / and <mark>harden</mark> into knowledge or beliefs. //

병렬 구조

아이들이 더 많은 증거를 흡수함에 따라 / 그들 주변의 세상으로부터 / 특정한 가능성들이 훨씬 더 커지게 되고 더 유용하게 되며 / 지식이나 믿음으로 굳어진다 //

오른쪽 컬럼

According to educational psychologist Susan Engel, / curiosity begins to decrease / <mark>as young as</mark> four years old. //

원급 비교

교육 심리학자 Susan Engel에 따르면 / 호기심은 줄어들기 시작한다 / 네 살 정도의 어린 나이에 //

뒤에 관계부사 when이 생략됨

By <mark>the time</mark> we are adults, / we have fewer questions and more default settings. //

우리가 어른이 될 무렵 / 우리의 질문은 더 적어지고 기본값은 더 많아진다 //

As Henry James put it, / "Disinterested curiosity is past, / the mental grooves and channels set." //

Henry James가 말했듯이 / "흥미를 유발하지 않는 호기심은 지나가고 / 정신의 고랑과 경로가 자리 잡는다" //

조동사가 포함된 수동태

(①) The decline in curiosity <mark>can be traced</mark> / in the development of the brain / through childhood. // **단서 2** 아이들의 뇌가 발달하면서 호기심은 감소함

호기심 감소의 원인은 찾을 수 있다 / 뇌의 발달에서 / 유년 시절을 통한 //

부사절 접속사(양보)

(②) <mark>Though</mark> smaller than the adult brain, / the infant brain contains millions more neural connections. //

비록 성인의 뇌보다 작지만 / 유아의 뇌는 수백만 개 더 많은 신경 연결을 가지고 있다 //

핵심 주어(복수)

(③) The wiring, / however, / is a mess; / <mark>the lines</mark> of communication between infant neurons / <mark>are far</mark> less efficient / than between those in the adult brain. //

복수동사 비교급 강조 부사

연결 상태는 / 그러나 / 엉망이다 / 유아의 뉴런 간의 전달 선은 / 훨씬 덜 효율적이다 / 성인 뇌의 뉴런 간의 전달 선보다 // **단서 3** 유아의 뇌의 뉴런 간 전달은 성인보다 덜 효율적임

단서 4 아기는 세상을 매우 풍부하면서도 무질서하게 인식함

(④) The baby's perception of the world / is consequently both intensely rich / and wildly disordered. //

세상에 대한 아기의 인식은 / 결과적으로 매우 풍부하면서도 / 상당히 무질서하다 //

주격 관계대명사

(⑤) The neural pathways / <mark>that</mark> enable those beliefs / become faster and more automatic, / <mark>while</mark> the ones / that the child doesn't use regularly / are pruned away. //

부사절 접속사

신경 경로들은 / 그러한 믿음을 가능하게 하는 / 더 빠르고 더 자동적으로 이루어지게 된다 / 반면에 어떤 경로들은 / 아이가 주기적으로 사용하지 않는 / 가지치기 된다 // **단서 5** 어떤 믿음을 가능하게 하는 신경 경로는 더 빠르게 이루어지고, 그렇지 않은 신경 경로는 점점 사라짐

- absorb ⓥ 흡수하다   • possibility ⓝ 가능성   • decline ⓝ 감소
- trace ⓥ (원인을) 추적하다   • infant ⓝ 유아   • neural ⓐ 신경의
- wiring ⓝ 연결, 배선   • mess ⓝ 엉망   • efficient ⓐ 효율적인
- perception ⓝ 인식   • consequently ⓐ𝒹 결과적으로
- intensely ⓐ𝒹 매우   • wildly ⓐ𝒹 상당히, 극도로
- disordered ⓐ 무질서한

교육 심리학자 Susan Engel에 따르면, 호기심은 네 살 정도의 어린 나이에 줄어들기 시작한다. 우리가 어른이 될 무렵, 질문은 더 적어지고 기본값은 더 많아진다. Henry James가 말했듯이, "흥미를 유발하지 않는 호기심은 지나가고, 정신의 고랑과 경로가 자리 잡는다." (①) 호기심의 감소는 유년 시절을 통한 뇌의 발달에서 원인을 찾을 수 있다. (②) 비록 성인의 뇌보다 작지만, 유아의 뇌는 수백만 개 더 많은 신경 연결을 가지고 있다. (③) 그러나 연결 상태는 엉망이다; 유아의 뉴런 간의 전달 선은 성인 뇌의 뉴런들 간의 전달 선보다 훨씬 덜 효율적이다. (④) 결과적으로 세상에 대한 아기의 인식은 매우 풍부하면서도 상당히 무질서하다. (⑤ 아이들이 그들 주변의 세상으로부터 더 많은 증거를 흡수함에 따라, 특정한 가능성들이 훨씬 더 커지게 되고 더 유용하게 되며 지식이나 믿음으로 굳어진다.) 그러한 믿음을 가능하게 하는 신경 경로는 더 빠르고 자동적으로 이루어지게 되는 반면, 아이가 주기적으로 사용하지 않는 경로는 가지치기 된다.

| 문제 풀이 순서 | ★★★ [정답률 48%]

1st 주어진 문장을 해석하고, 연결어, 지시어 등을 확인한다.

As children absorb more evidence from the world around them, certain possibilities become much more likely and more useful and harden into knowledge or <u>beliefs</u>.

아이들이 그들 주변의 세상으로부터 더 많은 증거를 흡수함에 따라, 특정한 가능성들이 훨씬 더 커지게 되고 더 유용하게 되며 지식이나 <u>믿음</u>으로 굳어진다. **단서**

➡ **주어진 문장 앞:** 아이들이 더 많은 증거를 흡수하는 이유가 제시될 것이다. **발상**

2nd 각 선택지의 앞뒤 흐름이 매끄러운지 확인한다.

- ①의 앞 문장과 뒤 문장

┌ 앞 문장: Henry James가 말했듯이, "흥미를 유발하지 않는 호기심은
│ 지나가고, 정신의 고랑과 경로가 자리 잡는다."
└ 뒤 문장: 호기심의 감소는 유년 시절을 통한 뇌의 발달에서 원인을 찾을 수
  있다.

➡ 앞에서 Henry James가 주장한 호기심이 나이가 들수록 줄어드는 원인을 뒤
  문장에서 언급한다. ▶ 주어진 문장이 ①에 들어갈 수 없음

- ②의 앞 문장과 뒤 문장

┌ 앞 문장: ①의 뒤 문장과 같음
│ 뒤 문장: 비록 성인의 뇌보다 작지만, 유아의 뇌는 수백만 개 더 많은 신경
└ 연결을 가지고 있다.

➡ 앞 문장에서 처음 언급한 '유년 시절의 뇌'를 뒤 문장에서 부연 설명한다.
  ▶ 주어진 문장이 ②에 들어갈 수 없음

- ③의 앞 문장과 뒤 문장

┌ 앞 문장: ②의 뒤 문장과 같음
│ 뒤 문장: 그러나(however) 연결 상태는 엉망이다; 유아의 뉴런 간의 전달
└ 선은 성인 뇌의 뉴런들 간의 전달 선보다 훨씬 덜 효율적이다.

➡ 앞 문장에서 유아의 뇌는 신경 연결이 많다고 한 것에 그 연결 상태는 엉망이라는
  설명이 역접의 연결어 however로 자연스럽게 이어진다.
  ▶ 주어진 문장이 ③에 들어갈 수 없음

- ④의 앞 문장과 뒤 문장

┌ 앞 문장: ③의 뒤 문장과 같음
│ 뒤 문장: 결과적으로(consequently) 세상에 대한 아기의 인식은 매우
└ 풍부하면서도 상당히 무질서하다.

➡ 유아의 뇌에는 신경 연결이 많지만, 상태는 엉망인 것의 결과로(consequently)
  세상을 풍부하면서도 무질서하게 인식한다는 내용이 이어진다.
  ▶ 주어진 문장이 ④에 들어갈 수 없음

- ⑤의 앞 문장과 뒤 문장

┌ 앞 문장: ④의 뒤 문장과 같음
│ 뒤 문장: 그러한 믿음(those beliefs)을 가능하게 하는 신경 경로는 더
│ 빠르고 자동적으로 이루어지게 되는 반면, 아이가 주기적으로 사용하지
└ 않는 경로는 가지치기된다.

➡ 그러한 믿음: 주어진 문장에서 말한 '아이들이 흡수하여 생성한 지식이나 믿음'
  세상을 풍부하면서 무질서하게 인식하면서 굳어진 믿음을 더 심화하는 신경 경로는
  더 빨라지고, 그렇지 않은 신경 경로는 사라지는 것이 호기심의 감소라는 것이다.
  ▶ 주어진 문장이 ⑤에 들어가야 함

P 22 정답 ⑤ *보완재의 정의와 특징

글의 흐름으로 보아, 주어진 문장이 들어가기에 가장 적절한 곳을 고르
시오.

┌ However, / do not assume **that** a product is perfectly
│   목적어절 접속사
│ complementary, / **as** customers may not be completely locked
│   부사절 접속사(이유)
│ in / to the product. // 단서 1 앞에는 완벽하게 보완적인 제품이 제시되어야 함
│ 그러나 / 어떤 제품이 완벽하게 보완적이라고 가정하지 마라 / 고객들이 완전히 고정되어
└ 있지 않을 수 있으므로 / 그 제품에 //

A "complementary good" is a product / **that** is often consumed
                                주격 관계대명사
/ alongside another product. //
'보완재'는 제품이다 / 종종 소비되는 / 다른 제품과 함께 //

(①) For example, / popcorn is a complementary good to a
              부사절 접속사(대조)
movie, / **while** a travel pillow is a complementary good / for a
long plane journey. //
예를 들어 / 팝콘은 영화에 대한 보완재다 / 한편 여행 베개는 보완재이다 / 긴 비행기 여행에
대한 //
                                                    핵심 주어(복수)
(②) When the popularity of one product increases, / the **sales**
                                                        복수 동사
of its complementary good also **increase**. //
한 제품의 인기가 높아지면 / 그것의 보완재 판매량도 늘어난다 //
                                          주격 관계대명사
(③) By producing goods / **that** complement other products /
  주격 관계대명사
that are already (or about to be) popular, / you can ensure a
steady stream / of demand for your product. //
제품을 생산함으로써 / 다른 제품을 보완하는 / 이미 인기가 있는 (또는 곧 있을) / 여러분은
꾸준한 흐름을 보장할 수 있다 / 여러분의 제품에 대한 수요의 //
(④) Some products enjoy perfect complementary status /
— they *have* to be consumed together, / such as a lamp and a
lightbulb. // 단서 2 램프와 전구처럼 일부 제품은 완벽한 보완적 상태에 있음
일부 제품들은 완벽한 보완적 상태를 누리고 있고 / 그것은 함께 소비'되어야' 한다 / 램프와
전구와 같이 //
                        부사절 접속사(양보)
(⑤) For example, / **although** motorists may seem required to
                          부사적 용법(목적)
purchase gasoline / **to run** their cars, / they can switch to electric
cars. // 단서 3 운전에 휘발유가 필요해 보일지라도 전기 자동차로 바꿀 수 있음
예를 들어 / 비록 운전자들이 휘발유를 구매할 필요가 있는 것처럼 보일지라도 / 자신의 차를
운전하기 위해 / 그들은 전기 자동차로 바꿀 수 있다 //

- assume ⓥ 가정하다   - complementary ⓐ (상호) 보완적인
- lock ⓥ 고정하다, 잠그다   - alongside prep ~와 함께
- pillow ⓝ 베개   - journey ⓝ 여행   - popularity ⓝ 인기
- complement ⓥ 보완하다   - ensure ⓥ 보장하다
- steady ⓐ 꾸준한   - stream ⓝ 흐름, 연속   - status ⓝ 상태
- motorist ⓝ 운전자   - gasoline ⓝ 휘발유

'보완재'는 종종 다른 제품과 함께 소비되는 제품이다. (①) 예를 들어, 팝콘은
영화에 대한 보완재인 한편, 여행 베개는 긴 비행기 여행에 대한 보완재이다.
(②) 한 제품의 인기가 높아지면 그것의 보완재 판매량도 늘어난다. (③)
여러분은 이미 인기가 있는 (또는 곧 있을) 다른 제품을 보완하는 제품을
생산함으로써 여러분의 제품에 대한 꾸준한 수요 흐름을 보장할 수 있다. (④)
일부 제품들은 완벽한 보완적 상태를 누리고 있고, 그것들은 램프와 전구와
같이 함께 소비'되어야' 한다. (⑤ 그러나 고객들이 그 제품에 완전히 고정되어
있지 않을 수 있으므로, 어떤 제품이 완벽하게 보완적이라고 가정하지 마라.)
예를 들어, 비록 운전자들이 자신의 차를 운전하기 위해 휘발유를 구매할
필요가 있는 것처럼 보일지라도, 그들은 전기 자동차로 바꿀 수 있다.

| 문제 풀이 순서 | ★★★ [정답률 54%]

1st 주어진 문장을 해석하고, 연결어, 지시어 등을 확인한다.

┌ However, do not assume that a product is perfectly
│ complementary, as customers may not be completely locked
│ in to the product.
│ 그러나 고객들이 그 제품에 완전히 고정되어 있지 않을 수 있으므로, 어떤 제품이 완벽하게
└ 보완적이라고 가정하지 마라.

➡ 주어진 문장 앞: However(그러나)라고 했으므로 단서
  앞에는 어떤 제품이 완벽하게 보완적이라는 내용이 올 것이다. 발상

2nd 찾은 단서를 생각하며 각 선택지의 앞뒤 흐름이 매끄러운지 확인한다.

- ①의 앞 문장과 뒤 문장

┌ 앞 문장: '보완재'는 종종 다른 제품과 함께 소비되는 제품이다.
│ 뒤 문장: 예를 들어(For example), 팝콘은 영화에 대한 보완재인 한편,
└ 여행 베개는 긴 비행기 여행에 대한 보완재이다.

➡ 앞 문장에서 언급한 다른 제품과 함께 소비되는 제품인 보완재의 예시가 뒤 문장에 이어진다.
▶ 주어진 문장이 ①에 들어갈 수 없음

- ②의 앞 문장과 뒤 문장
앞 문장: ①의 뒤 문장과 같음
뒤 문장: 한 제품의 인기가 높아지면 그것의 보완재 판매량도 늘어난다.
➡ 앞에서 보완재의 정의와 예시를 말한 뒤, 보완재의 특징을 이어서 말하는 흐름은 자연스럽다.
▶ 주어진 문장이 ②에 들어갈 수 없음

- ③의 앞 문장과 뒤 문장
앞 문장: ②의 뒤 문장과 같음
뒤 문장: 여러분은 이미 인기가 있는 (또는 곧 있을) 다른 제품을 보완하는 제품을 생산함으로써 여러분의 제품에 대한 구준한 수요 흐름을 보장할 수 있다.
➡ 앞에서 어떤 제품의 인기가 높아지면 그 보완재 판매량이 늘어난다고 한 뒤, 이를 활용하여 구준한 수요 흐름을 보장할 수 있다고 말하는 흐름은 자연스럽다.
▶ 주어진 문장이 ③에 들어갈 수 없음

- ④의 앞 문장과 뒤 문장
앞 문장: ③의 뒤 문장과 같음
뒤 문장: 일부 제품들은 완벽한 보완적 상태를 누리고 있고, 그것들은 램프와 전구와 같이 함께 소비'되어야' 한다.
➡ 구준한 수요 흐름을 보장할 수 있는 예시로 완벽한 보완적 상태를 누리는 램프와 전구를 제시했다.
▶ 주어진 문장이 ④에 들어갈 수 없음

- ⑤의 앞 문장과 뒤 문장
앞 문장: ④의 뒤 문장과 같음
뒤 문장: 예를 들어(For example), 비록 운전자들이 자신의 차를 운전하기 위해 휘발유를 구매할 필요가 있는 것처럼 보일지라도, 그들은 전기 자동차로 바꿀 수 있다.
➡ 앞 문장: 램프와 전구(= 완벽한 보완적 상태)는 함께 소비되어야 함
뒤 문장: 자동차(= 휘발유와 보완적 상태) 운전자는 전기 자동차를 탈 수 있음
앞 문장과는 달리 뒤 문장에서는 완벽한 보완적 상태로 보이지만, 실제로는 그렇지 않은 사례를 이야기했으므로 어떤 제품이 완벽하게 보완적이라고 가정하지 말라고 한 주어진 문장이 ⑤에 와야 한다.
▶ 주어진 문장이 ⑤에 들어가야 함

P 23 정답 ④ *보충제 섭취의 폐해

글의 흐름으로 보아, 주어진 문장이 들어가기에 가장 적절한 곳을 고르시오.

단서 1 앞에도 보충제의 단점이 나와야 함
Worse, / some **are** contaminated with other substances / and **contain** ingredients / not listed on the label. //
심하게는 / 어떤 것들은 다른 물질로 오염되어 있다 / 그리고 성분을 포함한다 / 라벨에 실려 있지 않은 //

According to top nutrition experts, / most nutrients are better absorbed and used by the body / **when consumed** from a whole food / instead of a supplement. //
최고의 영양 전문가들에 의하면 / 많은 영양소가 신체에 의해 더 잘 흡수되고 사용된다 / 자연식품으로부터 섭취되었을 때 / 보충제 대신에 //

(①) However, / many people feel the need / **to take** pills, powders, and supplements / in an attempt / **to obtain** nutrients / and **fill** the gaps in their diets. //
그러나 / 많은 사람들이 필요성을 느낀다 / 알약, 분말 그리고 보충제를 섭취할 / 시도로 / 영양소를 얻기 위한 / 그리고 자신의 식단에 있어 부족한 부분을 채우기 위한 //
(②) We hope / these will **give** us more energy, / **prevent** us from catching a cold in the winter, / or **improve** our skin and hair. //
우리는 바란다 / 이것들이 우리에게 더 많은 에너지를 주고 / 우리가 겨울에 감기에 걸리는 것을 막아 주고 / 혹은 우리의 피부와 모발을 개선해 주기를 //
(③) But in reality, / the large majority of supplements are artificial / and may not even be completely absorbed / by your body. // 단서 2 보충제 대부분이 인위적이고 흡수도 안 될 수 있다는 단점을 언급함
그러나 실제로는 / 대다수의 보충제가 인위적이다 / 그리고 완전히 흡수조차 되지 않을 수도 있다 / 여러분의 신체에 의해 //
(④) For example, / a recent investigative report found heavy metals / in 40 percent of 134 brands of protein powders / on the market. // 단서 3 보충제에서 중금속을 발견했다는 예시가 나오기 전에 보충제에 좋지 않은 성분이 들어있다는 문장이 나와야 함
예를 들어 / 최근 한 조사 보고는 중금속을 발견했다 / 단백질 분말 134개 브랜드 중 40퍼센트에서 / 시장에 있는 //
(⑤) With little control and regulation, / **taking** supplements **is** a gamble and often costly. //
단속과 규제가 거의 없다면 / 보충제를 섭취하는 것은 / 도박이며 종종 대가가 크다 //

- substance ⓝ 물질   • ingredient ⓝ 재료, 성분
- label ⓝ 표시, 라벨   • nutrition ⓝ 영양   • absorb ⓥ 흡수하다
- whole food 자연식품   • pill ⓝ 알약   • powder ⓝ 분말
- obtain ⓥ 획득하다   • artificial ⓐ 인공적인
- completely ⓐⓓ 완전히   • recent ⓐ 최근의
- investigative ⓐ 조사의, 연구의   • heavy metal 중금속
- protein ⓝ 단백질   • regulation ⓝ 규제   • gamble ⓝ 도박
- costly ⓐ 대가가 큰

최고의 영양 전문가들에 의하면 많은 영양소가 보충제 대신에 자연식품으로부터 섭취되었을 때 신체에 의해 더 잘 흡수되고 사용된다. (①) 그러나 많은 사람들이 영양소를 얻고 자신의 식단에 있어 부족한 부분을 채우기 위한 시도로 알약, 분말 그리고 보충제를 섭취할 필요성을 느낀다. (②) 우리는 이것들이 우리에게 더 많은 에너지를 주고, 우리가 겨울에 감기에 걸리는 것을 막아 주거나 혹은 우리의 피부와 모발을 개선해 주기를 바란다. (③) 그러나 실제로는 대다수의 보충제가 인위적이고 여러분의 신체에 의해 완전히 흡수조차 되지 않을 수도 있다. (④ 심하게는 어떤 것들은 다른 물질로 오염되어 있으며 라벨에 실려 있지 않은 성분을 포함한다.) 예를 들어 최근 한 조사 보고는 시장에 있는 단백질 분말 134개 브랜드 중 40퍼센트에서 중금속을 발견했다. (⑤) 단속과 규제가 거의 없다면 보충제를 섭취하는 것은 도박이며 종종 대가가 크다.

| 문제 풀이 순서 | ★★★ [정답률 59%]

1st 주어진 문장을 해석하고, 연결어, 지시어 등을 확인한다.

Worse, some are contaminated with other substances and contain ingredients not listed on the label. 단서 1
심하게는 어떤 것들은 다른 물질로 오염되어 있으며 라벨에 실려 있지 않은 성분을 포함한다.

➡ **주어진 문장 앞:** 주어진 문장이 Worse로 시작하면서 어떤 것의 단점을 말하고 있으므로 앞에 또 다른 단점이 제시되어 있어야 한다. 단서
주어진 문장 뒤: 다른 물질로 오염되어 있는 어떤 것들의 구체적인 사례가 이어질 것이다. 발상

2nd 각 선택지의 앞뒤 흐름이 매끄러운지 확인한다.

- ①의 앞 문장과 뒤 문장

앞 문장: 최고의 영양 전문가들에 의하면 많은 영양소가 보충제 대신에 자연식품으로부터 섭취되었을 때 신체에 의해 더 잘 흡수되고 사용된다.

뒤 문장: 그러나(However) 많은 사람들이 영양소를 얻고 자신의 식단에 있어 부족한 부분을 채우기 위한 시도로 알약, 분말 그리고 보충제를 섭취할 필요성을 느낀다.

➡ 뒤 문장은 앞 문장과 상반되는 내용을 역접의 연결어 However로 이어간다.
▶ 주어진 문장이 ①에 들어갈 수 없음

- ②의 앞 문장과 뒤 문장

앞 문장: ①의 뒤 문장과 같음

뒤 문장: 우리는 이것들이 우리에게 더 많은 에너지를 주고, 우리가 겨울에 감기에 걸리는 것을 막아 주거나 혹은 우리의 피부와 모발을 개선해 주기를 바란다.

➡ 뒤 문장은 앞 문장을 부연 설명한다.
사람들은 부족한 영양소를 채우기 위해 보충제를 먹는데(② 앞 문장), 이것들이 에너지를 주고, 감기를 예방하거나, 피부와 모발을 개선해 주기를 바란다(② 뒤 문장). ▶ 주어진 문장이 ②에 들어갈 수 없음

- ③의 앞 문장과 뒤 문장

앞 문장: ②의 뒤 문장과 같음

뒤 문장: 그러나(But) 실제로는 대다수의 보충제가 인위적이고 여러분의 신체에 의해 완전히 흡수조차 되지 않을 수도 있다. 단서2

➡ 뒤 문장은 역접의 연결어 But으로 앞 문장의 내용을 반박한다.
▶ 주어진 문장이 ③에 들어갈 수 없음

- ④의 앞 문장과 뒤 문장

앞 문장: ③의 뒤 문장과 같음

뒤 문장: 예를 들어(For example) 최근 한 조사 보고는 시장에 있는 단백질 분말 134개 브랜드 중 40퍼센트에서 중금속을 발견했다. 단서3

➡ 주어진 문장에서 예상한 대로 앞 문장에는 단점이, 뒤 문장에는 사례가 이어진다.
▶ 주어진 문장이 ④에 들어가야 함

➡ 주어진 문장이 ④에 들어가면, <대다수의 보충제는 인위적이고 신체에 잘 흡수되지 않는데, 심하게는 다른 물질로 오염되어 있거나 표기되지 않은 성분을 포함한다. 예를 들어 판매 중인 단백질 분말의 40퍼센트에서 중금속이 발견됐다.>라는 자연스러운 흐름이 된다.

- ⑤의 앞 문장과 뒤 문장

앞 문장: ④의 뒤 문장과 같음

뒤 문장: 단속과 규제가 거의 없다면 보충제를 섭취하는 것은 도박이며 종종 대가가 크다.

➡ 글의 내용을 정리하며 마무리한다.
▶ 주어진 문장이 ⑤에 들어갈 수 없음

P 24 정답 ④ *좋은 탄수화물과 나쁜 탄수화물

글의 흐름으로 보아, 주어진 문장이 들어가기에 가장 적절한 곳을 고르시오.

Bad carbohydrates, / on the other hand, / are simple sugars. //
나쁜 탄수화물은 / 반면에 / 단당류이다 //   단서1 나쁜 탄수화물에 대한 설명이 on the other hand로 이어짐

All carbohydrates are basically sugars. //
모든 탄수화물은 기본적으로 당이다 //

(①) Complex carbohydrates are the good carbohydrates / for your body. //
복합 탄수화물은 좋은 탄수화물이다 / 여러분의 몸에 //

(②) These complex sugar compounds / are very difficult to break down / and can trap other nutrients / like vitamins and minerals / in their chains. //   단서2 복합 탄수화물은 분해하기 어려운 구조임
이러한 복당류 화합물은 / 분해하기 매우 어렵고 / 다른 영양소를 가두어 둘 수 있다 / 비타민과 미네랄 같은 / 그것의 사슬 안에 //

(③) As they slowly break down, / the other nutrients are also released into your body, / and can provide you with fuel / for a number of hours. //   단서3 복합 탄수화물이 분해될 때 다른 영양소를 우리 몸에 줄 수 있음
그것들이 천천히 분해되면서 / 다른 영양소도 여러분의 몸으로 방출되고 / 여러분에게 연료를 공급할 수 있다 / 많은 시간 동안 //

단서4 구조가 복잡하지 않다는 상반되는 내용이 이어짐
(④) Because their structure is not complex, / they are easy to break down / and hold few nutrients for your body / other than the sugars / from which they are made. //
그것의 구조는 복잡하지 않기 때문에 / 그것은 분해되기 쉽고 / 여러분의 몸을 위한 영양소를 거의 가지고 있지 않다 / 당 외에 / 그것이 만들어지는 //

(⑤) Your body breaks down these carbohydrates / rather quickly / and what it cannot use / is converted to fat / and stored in the body. //
여러분의 몸은 이러한 탄수화물을 분해하고 / 상당히 빨리 / 그것(몸)이 사용할 수 없는 것은 / 지방으로 바뀌어 / 몸에 저장된다 //

- complex ⓐ 복합의   • compound ⓝ 화합물
- nutrient ⓝ 영양소   • chain ⓝ 사슬   • release ⓥ 방출하다
- provide ⓥ 제공하다   • fuel ⓝ 연료   • structure ⓝ 구조

모든 탄수화물은 기본적으로 당이다. (①) 복합 탄수화물은 몸에 좋은 탄수화물이다. (②) 이러한 복당류 화합물은 분해하기 매우 어렵고 비타민과 미네랄 같은 다른 영양소를 그것의 사슬 안에 가두어 둘 수 있다. (③) 그것들이 천천히 분해되면서, 다른 영양소도 여러분의 몸으로 방출되고, 많은 시간 동안 여러분에게 연료를 공급할 수 있다. (④ 반면에 나쁜 탄수화물은 단당류이다.) 그것의 구조는 복잡하지 않기 때문에, 그것은 분해되기 쉽고 그것이 만들어지는 당 외에 몸을 위한 영양소를 거의 가지고 있지 않다. (⑤) 여러분의 몸은 이러한 탄수화물을 상당히 빨리 분해하고 그것(몸)이 사용할 수 없는 것은 지방으로 바뀌어 몸에 저장된다.

| 문제 풀이 순서 | ★★❋ [정답률 61%]

1st 주어진 문장을 해석하고, 연결어, 지시어 등을 확인한다.

Bad carbohydrates, on the other hand, are simple sugars.
반면에 나쁜 탄수화물은 단당류이다.

➡ 주어진 문장 앞: 'on the other hand(반면에)'라고 했으므로 단서 앞에는 나쁜 탄수화물과 반대되는 내용이 와야 한다. 발상

2nd 찾은 단서를 생각하며 각 선택지의 앞뒤 흐름이 매끄러운지 확인한다.

- ①의 앞 문장과 뒤 문장

앞 문장: 모든 탄수화물은 기본적으로 당이다.

뒤 문장: 복합 탄수화물은 몸에 좋은 탄수화물이다.

➡ 앞 문장에서 언급한 탄수화물 중 하나를 뒤 문장에서 설명하고 있다.
▶ 주어진 문장이 ①에 들어갈 수 없음

- ②의 앞 문장과 뒤 문장

앞 문장: ①의 뒤 문장과 같음

뒤 문장: 이러한(These) 복당류 화합물은 분해하기 매우 어렵고 비타민과 미네랄 같은 다른 영양소를 그것의 사슬 안에 가두어 둘 수 있다.

➡ 앞 문장의 '복합 탄수화물'을 '이러한' 복당류 화합물로 가리키며 분해하기 매우 어렵다는 설명을 이어간다.
▶ 주어진 문장이 ②에 들어갈 수 없음

- ③의 앞 문장과 뒤 문장

앞 문장: ②의 뒤 문장과 같음

뒤 문장: 그것들이(they) 천천히 분해되면서, 다른 영양소도 여러분의 몸으로 방출되고, 많은 시간 동안 여러분에게 연료를 공급할 수 있다.

➡ '복당류 화합물'을 they로 지칭하며 오랜 시간 동안 연료를 공급한다는 설명을 이어간다. ▶ 주어진 문장이 ③에 들어갈 수 없음

- ④의 앞 문장과 뒤 문장

앞 문장: ③의 뒤 문장과 같음

뒤 문장: 그것의(their) 구조는 복잡하지 않기 때문에, 그것은 분해되기 쉽고 그것이 만들어지는 당 외에 몸을 위한 영양소를 거의 가지고 있지 않다.

➡ 복합 탄수화물, 즉 복당류 화합물은 분해하기 매우 어렵다고 했는데, '그것의' 구조는 복잡하지 않고 분해되기 쉽다는 반대되는 내용이 이어진다.
▶ 단당류를 처음 언급한 주어진 문장이 ④에 들어가야 함

- ⑤의 앞 문장과 뒤 문장

앞 문장: ④의 뒤 문장과 같음

뒤 문장: 여러분의 몸은 이러한 탄수화물(these carbohydrates)을 상당히 빨리 분해하고 그것(몸)이 사용할 수 없는 것은 지방으로 바뀌어 몸에 저장된다.

➡ '이러한 탄수화물'은 주어진 문장과 ④의 뒤 문장에서 말한 분해하기 쉬운 단당류를 말한다. ▶ 주어진 문장이 ⑤에 들어갈 수 없음

P 25 정답 ③ *소리가 만들어지는 과정

글의 흐름으로 보아, 주어진 문장이 들어가기에 가장 적절한 곳을 고르시오.

As the sticks approach each other, / the air immediately in front of them / is compressed / and energy builds up. //
막대기들이 서로 가까워질 때 / 그것들 바로 앞에 있는 공기가 / 압축된다 / 그리고 에너지는 축적된다 //
단서 1 앞에 sticks가 먼저 언급되었음을 짐작할 수 있음

Sound and light / travel in waves. // 소리와 빛은 / 파장으로 이동한다 //
An analogy often given for sound / is that of throwing a small stone / onto the surface of a still pond. // 소리 현상에 대해 자주 언급되는 비유는 / 작은 돌멩이를 던지는 것이다 / 고요한 연못 표면에 //
Waves radiate outwards / from the point of impact, / just as sound waves radiate / from the sound source. // 파장이 바깥으로 퍼져나간다 / 충격 지점으로부터 / 음파가 사방으로 퍼지는 것처럼 / 음원으로부터 //
(①) This is due to a disturbance / in the air around us. //
이것은 교란 작용 때문이다 / 우리 주변의 공기 중의 // 단서 2 sticks가 처음 언급됨
(②) If you bang two sticks together, / you will get a sound. //
만약에 당신이 막대기 두 개를 함께 꽝 친다면 / 소리를 듣게 될 것이다 //
(③) When the point of impact occurs, / this energy is released / as sound waves. // 단서 3 주어진 문장에 나온 내용의 결과
충돌점이 발생하면 / 이 에너지는 퍼져나간다 / 음파로 //
(④) If you try the same experiment / with two heavy stones, / exactly the same thing occurs, / but you get a different sound / due to the density and surface of the stones, /
만약 여러분이 같은 실험을 해보면 / 두 개의 무거운 돌을 가지고 / 똑같은 일이 일어난다 / 하지만 여러분은 다른 소리를 듣게 된다 / 돌의 밀도와 표면 때문에 /
and as they have likely displaced more air, / a louder sound. //
그 돌이 아마 더 많은 공기를 바꿔 놓았기 때문에 / (당신은) 더 큰 소리를 (듣게 된다) //
(⑤) And so, / a physical disturbance / in the atmosphere around us / will produce a sound. //
따라서 / 물리적 교란 작용이 / 우리 주변의 대기 중에서 일어나는 / 소리를 만든다 //

- approach ⓥ 다가가다, 접근하다 • compress ⓥ 압축하다
- wave ⓝ 파장 • pond ⓝ 연못 • disturbance ⓝ 방해, 교란
- bang ⓥ 꽝 하고 치다 • release ⓥ 방출하다
- experiment ⓝ 실험 • density ⓝ 밀도
- displace ⓥ 바꾸다 • atmosphere ⓝ 대기

소리와 빛은 파장으로 이동한다. 소리 현상에 대해 자주 언급되는 비유는 작은 돌멩이를 고요한 연못 표면에 던지는 것이다. 음파가 음원으로부터 사방으로 퍼지는 것처럼 파장이 충격 지점으로부터 바깥으로 퍼져나간다. (①) 이것은 우리 주변의 공기 중의 교란 작용 때문이다. (②) 만약에 당신이 막대기 두 개를 함께 꽝 친다면, 소리를 듣게 될 것이다. (③ 막대기들이 서로 가까워질 때, 그것들 바로 앞에 있는 공기가 압축되고 에너지는 축적된다.) 충돌점이 발생하면 이 에너지는 음파로 퍼져나간다. (④) 두 개의 무거운 돌을 가지고 같은 실험을 해보면 똑같은 일이 일어나지만, 돌의 밀도와 표면 때문에 당신은 다른 소리를 듣게 되고, 그 돌이 아마 더 많은 공기를 바꿔 놓았기 때문에 당신은 더 큰 소리를 듣게 된다. (⑤) 따라서 우리 주변의 대기 중에서 일어나는 물리적 교란 작용이 소리를 만든다.

| 문제 풀이 순서 | ✖✖✖ [정답률 60%]

1st 주어진 문장을 해석하고 문제를 풀 단서를 얻는다.

As the sticks approach each other, the air immediately in front of them is compressed and energy builds up. 단서 1
막대기들이 서로 가까워질 때, 그것들 바로 앞에 있는 공기가 압축되고 에너지는 축적된다.

➡ 주어진 문장 앞: the sticks가 있으므로 단서 앞에 '막대기'에 대한 내용이 먼저 나와야 한다. 발상

2nd 각 선택지의 앞뒤 흐름이 매끄러운지 확인한다.

- ①의 앞 문장과 뒤 문장

앞 문장: 소리와 빛은 파장으로 이동한다. 소리 현상에 대해 자주 언급되는 비유는 작은 돌멩이를 고요한 연못 표면에 던지는 것이다. 음파가 음원으로부터 사방으로 퍼지는 것처럼 파장이 충격 지점으로부터 바깥으로 퍼져나간다.

뒤 문장: 이것(This)은 우리 주변의 공기 중의 교란 작용 때문이다.

➡ 음파가 충격 지점에서 바깥으로 퍼진다는 내용인데, 이것을 뒤 문장에서 This로 받으며 그 원인이 공기 중의 교란 작용 때문이라는 내용으로 자연스럽게 연결된다.
▶ 주어진 문장이 ①에 들어갈 수 없음

- ②의 앞 문장과 뒤 문장

앞 문장: ①의 뒤 문장과 같음

뒤 문장: 만약에 당신이 막대기 두 개를 함께 꽝 친다면, 소리를 듣게 될 것이다. 단서 2

➡ 음파가 퍼지는 것이 공기 중의 교란 작용 때문이라는 문장 뒤에, 막대기 두 개를 함께 치면 소리를 듣게 된다는 가정을 하는 내용이 이어지는 것은 자연스러운 흐름이다. ▶ 주어진 문장이 ②에 들어갈 수 없음

- ③의 앞 문장과 뒤 문장

앞 문장: ②의 뒤 문장과 같음

뒤 문장: 충돌점이 발생하면 이 에너지(this energy)는 음파로 퍼져나간다. 단서 3

➡ 막대기 두 개를 함께 치면 소리를 듣게 된다고 했는데, 뒤에 '이 에너지(this energy)'가 음파로 퍼져나간다고 했으므로 this energy로 가리킬 수 있는 내용이 없다. two sticks를 주어진 문장에서 the sticks로 받고, 주어진 문장에 나온 energy가 this energy로 이어진다.
▶ 주어진 문장이 ③에 들어가야 함
주어진 문장이 ③에 들어가면, 〈막대기들이 서로 가까워질 때, 그것들 바로 앞에 있는 공기가 압축되고 에너지는 축적된다. 충돌점이 발생하면 이 에너지는 음파로 퍼져나간다.〉라는 자연스러운 흐름이 된다.

- **④의 앞 문장과 뒤 문장**

┌ **앞 문장**: ③의 뒤 문장과 같음
│ **뒤 문장**: 두 개의 무거운 돌을 가지고 같은 실험을 해보면 똑같은 일이
│ 일어나지만, 돌의 밀도와 표면 때문에 당신은 다른 소리를 듣게 되고, 그
│ 돌이 아마 더 많은 공기를 바꿔 놓았기 때문에 당신은 더 큰 소리를 듣게
└ 된다.

➡ 앞에서 에너지가 음파로 퍼져나간다고 한 후에, 두 개의 돌을 가지고 실험해도
'똑같은 일이 일어난다는 내용이 이어진다.
▶ 주어진 문장이 ④에 들어갈 수 없음

- **⑤의 앞 문장과 뒤 문장**

┌ **앞 문장**: ④의 뒤 문장과 같음
│ **뒤 문장**: 따라서 우리 주변의 대기 중에서 일어나는 물리적 교란 작용이
└ 소리를 만든다.

➡ 두 개의 돌로 실험했을 때 소리가 만들어지는 과정이 앞에 나오고, 그 결과 대기
중에서 일어나는 물리적 교란 작용이 소리를 발생시킨다는 내용이 자연스럽게
연결된다.
▶ 주어진 문장이 ⑤에 들어갈 수 없음

P 26 정답 ③ *서로 섞이지 않는 물

글의 흐름으로 보아, 주어진 문장이 들어가기에 가장 적절한 곳을 고르시오.

If we could magically remove the glasses, / we **would find** the
two water bodies would not mix well. //
뒤에 목적어절 접속사 that이 생략됨
만약 우리가 마법처럼 그 유리잔들을 없앨 수 있다면 / 우리는 두 액체가 잘 섞이지
않는다는 것을 알게 될 것이다 //
단서 1 the glasses(그 유리잔들) 안에 든 액체들이 섞이지 않을 상황이 앞에 나와야 함

Take two glasses of water. //
물 두 잔을 가져와라 //

Put a little bit of orange juice / into **one** / and a little bit of lemon
juice / into **the other**. //
'둘 중 하나' *'나머지 하나'*
약간의 오렌지주스를 넣어라 / 하나의 잔에는 / 그리고 약간의 레몬주스를 (넣어라) / 나머지
잔에는 //

(①) **What** you have / **are** essentially **two** glasses of water / but
선행사를 포함하는 관계대명사 *주격 보어가 복수이므로 복수 동사가 옴*
with a completely different chemical makeup. //
여러분이 가지고 있는 것은 / 본질적으로 두 잔의 물이다 / 하지만 완전히 다른 화학적 성질을
지닌 //

(②) If we **take** the glass / containing orange juice / and **heat** it, /
병렬 구조
만약 우리가 잔을 가져와 / 오렌지주스가 든 / 그것을 가열한다면 /
we will still have two different glasses of water / with different
chemical makeups, / but now they will also have different
temperatures. // **단서 2** 오렌지주스가 든 잔을 가열하면, 온도와 화학적 성질이 다른
두 잔의 물이 됨
우리는 여전히 다른 두 잔의 물을 가지고 있을 것이다 / 다른 화학적 성질을 지닌 / 하지만
이제 그것들은 또한 다른 온도를 가질 것이다 // **단서 3** 액체들은 만나면 조금은 섞이지만 분리된
채로 남을 것임 *관계부사*

(③) Perhaps they would mix a little / **where** they met; /
전치사
however, / they would remain separate / **because of** their
different chemical makeups and temperatures. //
어쩌면 그것들은 조금 섞일 것이다 / 그것들이 만났던 곳에서 / 하지만 / 그것들은 분리된
상태로 남아 있을 것이다 / 그것들의 다른 화학적 성질과 온도 때문에 //

(④) The warmer water would float / on the surface of the cold
water / **because of** its lighter weight. //
전치사
더 따뜻한 물은 떠 있을 것이다 / 찬물의 표면에 / 그것의 더 가벼운 무게 때문에 //

(⑤) In the ocean / we have bodies of water / **that** differ in
주격 관계대명사
temperature and salt content; / for this reason, / they do not
mix. //
바다에서 / 우리는 액체들을 가지고 있다 / 온도와 염분에서 다른 / 이러한 이유로 / 그것들은
섞이지 않는다 //

- magically ⓐ 마법처럼 · remove ⓥ 제거하다, 없애다
- essentially ⓐ 본질적으로 · completely ⓐ 완전히
- chemical ⓐ 화학적인 · makeup ⓝ 성질, 구성
- contain ⓥ ~이 들어 있다 · temperature ⓝ 온도
- separate ⓐ 분리된, 따로 떨어진 · float ⓥ (물이나 공기 위에) 떠 있다
- differ ⓥ 다르다 · salt content 염분

물 두 잔을 가져와라. 하나의 잔에는 약간의 오렌지주스를 넣고 다른 잔에는
약간의 레몬주스를 넣어라. (①) 여러분이 가지고 있는 것은 본질적으로 두
잔의 물이지만 완전히 다른 화학적 성질을 지닌 것들이다. (②) 만약 우리가
오렌지주스가 든 잔을 가져와 그것을 가열한다면, 우리는 여전히 다른 화학적
성질을 지닌 다른 두 잔의 물을 가지고 있을 것이지만, 이제 그것들은 또한
다른 온도를 가질 것이다. (③ 만약 우리가 마법처럼 그 유리잔들을 없앨 수
있다면, 우리는 두 액체가 잘 섞이지 않는다는 것을 알게 될 것이다.) 어쩌면
그것들은 그것들이 만났던 곳에서 조금 섞일 것이다. 하지만, 그것들의 다른
화학적 성질과 온도 때문에 그것들은 분리된 상태로 남아 있을 것이다. (④)
더 따뜻한 물은 그것의 더 가벼운 무게 때문에 찬물의 표면에 떠 있을 것이다.
(⑤) 바다에서 우리는 온도와 염분에서 다른 액체들을 가지고 있다. 이러한
이유로, 그것들은 섞이지 않는다.

| 문제 풀이 순서 | ★★★ [정답률 55%]

1st 주어진 문장을 해석하고, 연결어, 지시어 등을 확인한다.

┌ If we could magically **remove** the glasses, we would find the
│ two water bodies would not mix well.
│ 만약 우리가 마법처럼 그 유리잔들을 없앨 수 있다면, 우리는 두 액체가 잘 섞이지 않는다는
└ 것을 알게 될 것이다.

➡ **주어진 문장 앞**: '그 유리잔들(the glasses)'이라고 했으므로 **단서**
앞에 섞이지 않을 두 액체를 담은 유리잔에 대한 언급이 있어야 한다. **발상**

2nd 찾은 단서를 생각하며 각 선택지의 앞뒤 흐름이 매끄러운지 확인한다.

- **①의 앞 문장과 뒤 문장**

┌ **앞 문장**: 물 두 잔을 가져와라. 하나의 잔에는 약간의 오렌지주스를 넣고
│ 다른 잔에는 약간의 레몬주스를 넣어라.
│ **뒤 문장**: 여러분이 가지고 있는 것은 본질적으로 두 잔의 물이지만 완전히
└ 다른 화학적 성질을 지닌 것들이다.

➡ 앞 문장에서 언급한 물 두 잔을 뒤 문장에서 부연 설명한다.
▶ 주어진 문장이 ①에 들어갈 수 없음

- **②의 앞 문장과 뒤 문장**

┌ **앞 문장**: ①의 뒤 문장과 같음
│ **뒤 문장**: 만약(If) 우리가 오렌지주스가 든 잔을 가져와 그것을 가열한다면,
│ 우리는 여전히 다른 화학적 성질을 지닌 다른 두 잔의 물을 가지고 있을
└ 것이지만, 이제 그것들은 또한 다른 온도를 가질 것이다.

➡ 앞에서 언급한 오렌지주스를 가열하는 상황을 If로 가정한다.
▶ 주어진 문장이 ②에 들어갈 수 없음

- **③의 앞 문장과 뒤 문장**

┌ **앞 문장**: ②의 뒤 문장과 같음
│ **뒤 문장**: 어쩌면 그것들은 그것들이 만났던 곳에서 조금 섞일 것이다.
│ 하지만, 그것들의 다른 화학적 성질과 온도 때문에 그것들은 분리된 상태로
└ 남아 있을 것이다.

➡ 앞에서 이야기하고 있는 두 잔의 물이 어떻게 만나게 됐는지가 빠져있다.
따라서 유리잔들을 없애는 상황을 가정한 주어진 문장이 ③에 와야 한다.
▶ 주어진 문장이 ③에 들어가야 함

- ④의 앞 문장과 뒤 문장

앞 문장: ③의 뒤 문장과 같음

뒤 문장: 더 따뜻한 물은 그것의 더 가벼운 무게 때문에 찬물의 표면에 떠 있을 것이다.

➡ 앞에서 분리된 상태로 남아 있을 것이라고 한 물이 어떻게 분리된 상태인지를 부연 설명한다.

▶ 주어진 문장이 ④에 들어갈 수 없음

- ⑤의 앞 문장과 뒤 문장

앞 문장: ④의 뒤 문장과 같음

뒤 문장: 바다에서 우리는 온도와 염분에서 다른 액체들을 가지고 있다. 이러한 이유로, 그것들은 섞이지 않는다.

➡ 앞에서 설명한 이유로 바다에 있는 온도와 염분이 다른 액체들은 섞이지 않는다며 글을 마무리한다.

▶ 주어진 문장이 ⑤에 들어갈 수 없음

P 27 정답 ⑤ *계속 변화하는 위치 에너지와 운동 에너지

글의 흐름으로 보아, 주어진 문장이 들어가기에 가장 적절한 곳을 고르시오. [3점]

단서 1 앞에는 짧은 순간의 멈춤이 언급되고, 뒤에는 추가 다시 흔들리면서 생기는 에너지의 변화에 대한 내용이 나와야 함

But after this brief moment of rest, / the pendulum swings back again / and therefore part of the total energy / is then given / in the form of kinetic energy. //
〔수동태〕
하지만 이 짧은 순간의 멈춤 이후에 / 그 추는 다시 뒤로 흔들리게 되며 / 따라서 총 에너지의 일부가 / 그때 주어지게 된다 / 운동 에너지의 형태로 //

In general, / kinetic energy is the energy / associated with motion, / while potential energy represents the energy / which is "stored" in a physical system. //
〔앞에 주격 관계대명사와 be동사 생략〕〔주격 관계대명사〕
일반적으로 / 운동 에너지는 에너지이다 / 운동과 관련 있는 / 반면에 위치 에너지는 에너지를 나타낸다 / 물리계에 '저장되는' //

Moreover, / the total energy is always conserved. //
게다가 / 총에너지는 항상 보존된다 //

(①) But while the total energy remains unchanged, / the kinetic and potential parts / of the total energy / can change all the time. //
〔대조의 접속사〕
그러나 총에너지가 변하지 않는 채로 있는 반면 / 운동과 위치 에너지 비율은 / 총에너지의 / 항상 변할 수 있다 //

(②) Imagine, for example, a pendulum / which swings back and forth. //
〔주격 관계대명사〕
예를 들어 추를 상상해 보자 / 앞뒤로 흔들리는 //

(③) When it swings, / it sweeps out an arc / and then slows down / as it comes closer to its highest point, / where the pendulum does not move at all. //
〔동사의 병렬 구조〕〔계속적 용법의 관계부사〕
단서 2 추가 최고점에 가까워지면 더 이상 움직이지 않음
그것이 흔들릴 때 / 호 모양으로 쓸어내리듯 움직이다가 / 그리고 나서 속도가 줄어든다 / 그것이 그 최고점에 가까워지면서 / 이 지점에서 추는 더 이상 움직이지 않는다 //

(④) So at this point, / the energy is completely given / in terms of potential energy. //
단서 3 최고점에 가까워진 순간에는 에너지가 전부 위치 에너지가 됨
그래서 이 지점에서 / 에너지는 완전히 주어지게 된다 / 위치 에너지로 //

(⑤) So as the pendulum swings, / kinetic and potential energy / constantly change into each other. //
단서 4 추가 흔들리면서 에너지가 계속 서로 바뀌는 변화가 생김
그래서 그 추가 흔들리면서 / 운동과 위치 에너지는 / 끊임없이 서로 바뀐다 //

- brief ⓐ 짧은 · swing ⓥ 흔들리다 · form ⓝ 형태
- kinetic energy 운동 에너지 · associated with ~과 관련된
- potential energy 위치 에너지 · represent ⓥ 나타내다
- conserve ⓥ 보존하다 · back and forth 앞뒤로
- sweep out 쓸어내다 · constantly ⓐⓓ 끊임없이

일반적으로 운동 에너지는 운동과 관련 있는 에너지이며 반면에 위치 에너지는 물리계에 '저장되는' 에너지를 나타낸다. 게다가 총에너지는 항상 보존된다. (①) 그러나 총에너지가 변하지 않는 채로 있는 반면 총에너지의 운동과 위치 에너지 비율은 항상 변할 수 있다. (②) 예를 들어 앞뒤로 흔들리는 추를 상상해 보자. (③) 그것이 흔들릴 때 호 모양으로 쓸어내리듯 움직이다가 그리고 나서 그것이 그 최고점에 가까워지면서 속도가 줄어드는데, 이 지점에서 추는 더 이상 움직이지 않는다. (④) 그래서 이 지점에서 에너지는 완전히 위치 에너지로 주어지게 된다. (⑤ 하지만 이 짧은 순간의 멈춤 이후에 그 추는 다시 뒤로 흔들리게 되며 따라서 총에너지의 일부가 그때 운동 에너지의 형태로 주어지게 된다.) 그래서 그 추가 흔들리면서 운동과 위치 에너지는 끊임없이 서로 바뀐다.

| 문제 풀이 순서 | ★★★ [정답률 36%]

1st 주어진 문장을 해석하고, 연결어, 지시어 등을 확인한다.

But after this brief moment of rest, the pendulum swings back again and therefore part of the total energy is then given in the form of kinetic energy. **단서 1**
〔앞에 반대 내용이 나와야 함〕
하지만 이 짧은 순간의 멈춤 이후에 그 추는 다시 뒤로 흔들리게 되며 따라서 총에너지의 일부가 그때 운동 에너지의 형태로 주어지게 된다.

➡ But이 있으므로 앞에 반대 내용이 나와야 하는데 **단서** this brief moment of rest가 가리키는 바를 먼저 찾아야 한다. **발상**

2nd 각 선택지의 앞뒤 흐름이 매끄러운지 확인한다.

- ①의 앞 문장과 뒤 문장

앞 문장: 일반적으로 운동 에너지는 운동과 관련 있는 에너지이며 반면에 위치 에너지는 물리계에 '저장되는' 에너지를 나타낸다. 게다가 총에너지는 항상 보존된다.

뒤 문장: 그러나(But) 총에너지가 변하지 않는 채로 있는 반면 총에너지의 운동과 위치 에너지 비율은 항상 변할 수 있다.

➡ 앞에서 총에너지가 항상 보존된다는 내용이 나오는데, 총에너지의 운동과 위치 에너지 비율은 변할 수 있다는 반대 내용이 But(그러나)으로 연결되는 자연스러운 흐름이다.

▶ 주어진 문장이 ①에 들어갈 수 없음

- ②의 앞 문장과 뒤 문장

앞 문장: ①의 뒤 문장과 같음

뒤 문장: 예를 들어(For example) 앞뒤로 흔들리는 추를 상상해 보자.

➡ 총에너지의 운동과 위치 에너지 비율은 변할 수 있다는 것에 대한 예시가 뒤 문장에서 for example(예를 들어)로 이어지고 있다.

▶ 주어진 문장이 ②에 들어갈 수 없음

- ③의 앞 문장과 뒤 문장

앞 문장: ②의 뒤 문장과 같음

뒤 문장: 그것(it)이 흔들릴 때 호 모양으로 쓸어내리듯 움직이다가 그리고 나서 그것이 그 최고점에 가까워지면서 속도가 줄어드는데, 이 지점에서 추는 더 이상 움직이지 않는다. **단서 2**

➡ 뒤 문장의 it은 앞 문장에서 언급한 '앞뒤로 흔들리는 추'이다. 추가 흔들리다가 최고점에 가까워지면 더 이상 움직이지 않는다는 내용으로 자연스럽게 연결된다.

▶ 주어진 문장이 ③에 들어갈 수 없음

좌측 컬럼

- ④의 앞 문장과 뒤 문장

┌ 앞 문장: ③의 뒤 문장과 같음

└ 뒤 문장: 그래서 이 지점(this point)에서 에너지는 완전히 위치 에너지로 주어지게 된다. 단서 3

→ 뒤 문장의 this point는 앞 문장에서 언급한 최고점을 가리키는 것이다. 움직이지 않는 최고점에서는 위치 에너지로만 주어지게 된다는 내용으로 연결된다.
  ▶ 주어진 문장이 ④에 들어갈 수 없음

- ⑤의 앞 문장과 뒤 문장

┌ 앞 문장: ④의 뒤 문장과 같음

└ 뒤 문장: 그래서 그 추가 흔들리면서 운동과 위치 에너지는 끊임없이 서로 바뀐다. 단서 4

→ 추가 멈춰있는 것에 대해 말한 뒤에 갑자기 추가 흔들린다는 내용으로 이어지는 것은 어색하다. 주어진 문장에서 언급한 '이 짧은 순간의 멈춤(this brief moment of rest)'이 바로 '이 지점(this point)'을 가리킨다.
  ▶ 주어진 문장이 ⑤에 들어가야 함

주어진 문장이 ⑤에 들어가면, <하지만 이 짧은 순간의 멈춤 이후에 그 추는 다시 뒤로 흔들리게 되며 따라서 총에너지의 일부가 그때 운동 에너지의 형태로 주어지게 된다. 그래서 그 추가 흔들리면서 운동과 위치 에너지는 끊임없이 서로 바뀐다.>라는 자연스러운 흐름이 된다.

자이쌤's Follow Me! – 홈페이지에서 제공

P 28 정답 ④ *환경 변화에 대해 종 다양성이 갖는 강점

> 글의 흐름으로 보아, 주어진 문장이 들어가기에 가장 적절한 곳을 고르시오. [3점]

But, / when there is biodiversity, / the effects of a sudden change / are not so dramatic. 단서 1 앞과 반대되는 내용이 시작됨을 알 수 있음
하지만 / 종 다양성이 있을 때 / 갑작스러운 변화의 영향은 / 그렇게 극적이 않다 //

When an ecosystem is biodiverse, / wildlife have more opportunities / to obtain food and shelter. // (형용사적 용법)
생태계에 생물 종이 다양할 때 / 야생 생물들은 더 많은 기회를 얻는다 / 먹이와 서식지를 얻을 //
Different species react and respond / to changes in their environment / differently. // (병렬 구조) (핵심문장 단서 2 생태계에 생물종이 다양할 때 생물들은 더 많은 기회를 얻음)
다양한 종들은 작용하고 반응한다 / 그들의 환경 변화에 / 다르게 //

(①) For example, / imagine a forest / with only one type of plant in it, / which is the only source of food and habitat / for the entire forest food web. // (계속적 용법의 관계대명사) (단서 3 예시로 한 종류의 식물만 있는 숲을 제시함)
예를 들어 / 숲을 상상해 봐라 / 그것에 단 한 종류의 식물만 있는 / 그 식물은 유일한 먹이원이자 서식지이다 / 숲의 먹이 그물 전체의 //

(②) Now, / there is a sudden dry season / and this plant dies. //
이제 / 갑작스러운 건기가 온다 / 그리고 이 식물이 죽는다 //

(③) Plant-eating animals / completely lose their food source / and die out, / and so do the animals / that prey upon them. // (so+조동사+주어: ~도 그렇다) (추격 관계대명사)
초식 동물은 / 그들의 먹이원을 완전히 잃는다 / 그리고 죽는다 / 그리고 동물들도 그렇게 된다 / 그들을 먹이로 삼는 // (단서 4 한 종류의 식물만 있는 숲의 내용이 이어짐)

(④) Different species of plants respond / to the drought / differently, / and many can survive / a dry season. //
다양한 종의 식물들이 반응한다 / 가뭄에 / 다르게 / 그리고 많은 식물이 살아남을 수 있다 / 건기에 // (단서 5 한 종류의 식물이 아니라, 다양한 종류의 식물들에 대해 언급함)

(⑤) Many animals have / a variety of food sources / and don't just rely on one plant; / now our forest ecosystem / is no longer at the death! // (더 이상 ~ 않는(부정어))
많은 동물은 가지고 있다 / 다양한 먹이원을 / 그리고 그저 한 식물에 의존하지는 않는다 / 이제 우리의 숲 생태계는 / 더는 종말에 처해 있지 않다 //

우측 컬럼

- effect ⓝ 영향 • sudden ⓐ 갑작스러운 • dramatic ⓐ 극적인
- ecosystem ⓝ 생태계 • wildlife ⓝ 야생 생물
- opportunity ⓝ 기회 • obtain ⓥ 얻다 • shelter ⓝ 서식지
- react ⓥ 작용하다 • respond ⓥ 반응하다 • entire ⓐ 전체의
- prey (up)on 먹이로 삼다 • drought ⓝ 가뭄
- rely on ~ ~에 의존하다 • at the death 종말에 처한

생태계에 생물 종이 다양할 때, 야생 생물들은 먹이와 서식지를 얻을 더 많은 기회를 얻는다. 다양한 종들은 그들의 환경 변화에 다르게 작용하고 반응한다. (①) 예를 들어, 단 한 종류의 식물만 있는 숲을 상상해 보면, 그 식물은 숲의 먹이 그물 전체의 유일한 먹이원이자 서식지이다. (②) 이제, 갑작스러운 건기가 오고 이 식물이 죽는다. (③) 초식 동물은 그들의 먹이원을 완전히 잃고 죽게 되고, 그들을 먹이로 삼는 동물들도 그렇게 된다. (④ 하지만 종 다양성이 있을 때, 갑작스러운 변화의 영향은 그렇게 극적이지 않다.) 다양한 종의 식물들이 가뭄에 다르게 반응하고, 많은 식물이 건기에 살아남을 수 있다. (⑤) 많은 동물은 다양한 먹이원을 가지고 있으며 그저 한 식물에 의존하지는 않는다. 그래서 이제 우리의 숲 생태계는 더는 종말에 처해 있지 않다!

| 문제 풀이 순서 | ★★★ [정답률 55%]

1st 주어진 문장을 해석하고, 연결어, 지시어 등을 확인한다.

┌ But, when there is biodiversity, the effects of a sudden change are not so dramatic. 단서 1
└ 하지만 종 다양성이 있을 때, 갑작스러운 변화의 영향은 그렇게 극적이지 않다.

→ 주어진 문장 앞: But이 있으므로 앞에 반대 내용이 와야 한다. 단서
종 다양성이 없어서 변화의 영향이 극적인 상황이 나올 것이다. 발상

2nd 각 선택지의 앞뒤 흐름이 매끄러운지 확인한다.

- ①의 앞 문장과 뒤 문장

┌ 앞 문장: 생태계에 생물 종이 다양할 때, 야생 생물들은 먹이와 서식지를 얻을 더 많은 기회를 얻는다. 다양한 종들은 그들의 환경 변화에 다르게 작용하고 반응한다. 단서 2

└ 뒤 문장: 예를 들어(For example), 단 한 종류의 식물만 있는 숲을 상상해 보면, 그 식물은 숲의 먹이 그물 전체의 유일한 먹이원이자 서식지이다.
  단서 3

→ 다양한 종들이 있으면 환경 변화에 다르게 작용하고 반응한다는 내용에 한 종류의 식물만 있는 숲을 가정하는 예시가 For example로 자연스럽게 연결되고 있다.
  ▶ 주어진 문장이 ①에 들어갈 수 없음

- ②의 앞 문장과 뒤 문장

┌ 앞 문장: ①의 뒤 문장과 같음

└ 뒤 문장: 이제, 갑작스러운 건기가 오고 이 식물이 죽는다.

→ 앞에서 한 종류의 식물만 숲에 있고 유일한 먹이원일 때를 가정하고, 뒤에 건기가 오면 이 식물이 죽는다는 내용이 이어지므로 자연스러운 흐름이다.
  ▶ 주어진 문장이 ②에 들어갈 수 없음

- ③의 앞 문장과 뒤 문장

┌ 앞 문장: ②의 뒤 문장과 같음

└ 뒤 문장: 초식 동물은 그들의 먹이원을 완전히 잃고 죽게 되고, 그들을 먹이로 삼는 동물들도 그렇게 된다. 단서 4

→ 앞에서 식물이 죽는다는 상황을 가정했고, 초식 동물의 먹이원이었던 이 식물이 죽음으로써 다른 동물들이 죽게 된다는 내용이 이어지므로 자연스럽게 연결된다.
  ▶ 주어진 문장이 ③에 들어갈 수 없음

④의 앞 문장과 뒤 문장

앞 문장: ③의 뒤 문장과 같음

뒤 문장: 다양한 종의 식물들이 가뭄에 다르게 반응하고, 많은 식물이 건기에 살아남을 수 있다. **단서 5**

➡ 초식 동물이 먹이원을 잃어서 죽고, 또 초식 동물을 먹는 동물들도 죽게 된다는 내용이, 다양한 종의 식물들이 건기에 살아남을 수 있다는 내용으로 이어지는 것은 적절하지 않다. ▶ 주어진 문장이 ④에 들어가야 함

주어진 문장이 ④에 들어가면, <하지만 종 다양성이 있을 때, 갑작스러운 변화의 영향은 그렇게 극적이지 않다. 다양한 종의 식물들이 건기에 살아남을 수 있다.>라는 자연스러운 흐름이 된다.

- ⑤의 앞 문장과 뒤 문장

앞 문장: ④의 뒤 문장과 같음

뒤 문장: 많은 동물은 다양한 먹이원을 가지고 있으며 그저 한 식물에 의존하지는 않는다. 그래서 이제 우리의 숲 생태계는 더는 종말에 처해 있지 않다!

➡ 다양한 종의 식물이 있으면 건기에 많은 식물이 살아남을 수 있고, 그래서 한 식물에 의존할 필요가 없어 생태계가 종말에 처하지 않는다는 내용으로 이어진다.
▶ 주어진 문장이 ⑤에 들어갈 수 없음

P 29 정답 ④ *에너지가 이동하는 먹이 사슬

글의 흐름으로 보아, 주어진 문장이 들어가기에 가장 적절한 곳을 고르시오. [3점]

가주어
It has been observed / 진주어절을 이끄는 접속사 that at each level of transfer, / a large proportion, 80 – 90 percent, / of the potential energy / is lost / as heat. // **단서 1** 이동이 여러 차례 이루어짐을 알 수 있음
관찰되어 왔다 / 각 이동 단계에서 / 상당한 부분인 80 – 90퍼센트가 / 잠재적 에너지의 / 손실되는 것으로 / 열로 //

Food chain means / the transfer of food energy / from the source in plants / through a series of organisms / with the repeated process / of eating and being eaten. // 동명사의 수동태(being+p.p.)
먹이 사슬은 의미한다 / 식품 에너지가 이동하는 것을 / 식물 안에 있는 에너지원으로부터 / 일련의 유기체를 통해 / 반복되는 과정 속에서 / 먹고 먹히는 //

(①) In a grassland, / grass is eaten by rabbits / while rabbits in turn are eaten / by foxes. // 접속사(반면에)
초원에서 / 풀은 토끼에게 먹힌다 / 반면에 토끼는 결국 먹힌다 / 여우에게 //

(②) This is an example / of a simple food chain. //
이것은 예이다 / 단순한 먹이 사슬의 //

(③) This food chain implies the sequence / in which food energy is transferred / from producer to consumer / or higher trophic level. // = where **단서 2** 식품 에너지의 이동이 연쇄 안에서 이루어짐
이 먹이 사슬은 연쇄를 의미한다 / 이러한 연쇄 안에서 식품 에너지가 전달된다 / 생산자로부터 소비자로 / 또는 더 높은 영양 수준으로 //

(④) Hence / the number of steps or links / in a sequence / is restricted, / usually to four or five. // 동사 **단서 3** 사슬 내에 있는 단계나 연결의 수가 제한되는 근거가 앞에 있어야 함
그래서 / 단계나 연결의 수는 / 하나의 연쇄(사슬) 안에 있는 / 제한된다 / 보통 4~5개로 //

(⑤) The shorter the food chain / or the nearer the organism is / to the beginning of the chain, / the greater the available energy intake is. // 「the+비교급 ~, the+비교급 ...」 ~할수록 더 ...하다
먹이 사슬이 짧을수록 / 또는 유기체가 가까울수록 / 하위 영양 단계에 / 이용 가능한 에너지 섭취량이 더 커진다 //

- observe ⓥ 관찰하다   · transfer ⓝ 이동 ⓥ 이동하다
- proportion ⓝ 비율, 부분   · food chain 먹이 사슬
- a series of 일련의   · organism ⓝ 유기체   · in turn 차례로, 결국

- imply ⓥ 의미하다   · sequence ⓝ 연쇄, 사슬
- consumer ⓝ 소비자   · restrict ⓥ 제한하다   · intake ⓝ 섭취량

먹이 사슬은 식물 안에 있는 에너지원으로부터 먹고 먹히는 반복되는 과정 속에서 일련의 유기체를 통해 일련의 식품 에너지가 이동하는 것을 의미한다. (①) 초원에서 풀은 토끼에게 먹히지만, 반면에 토끼는 여우에게 먹힌다. (②) 이것은 단순한 먹이 사슬의 예이다. (③) 이 먹이 사슬은 식품 에너지가 생산자로부터 소비자 또는 더 높은 영양 수준으로 전달되는 연쇄를 의미한다. (④ 각 이동 단계에서 잠재적 에너지의 상당한 부분인 80 – 90퍼센트가 열로 손실되는 것으로 관찰되어 왔다.) 그래서 하나의 연쇄(사슬) 안에 있는 단계나 연결의 수는 보통 4~5개로 제한된다. (⑤) 먹이 사슬이 짧을수록 또는 유기체가 하위 영양 단계에 가까울수록 이용 가능한 에너지 섭취량이 더 커진다.

| 문제 풀이 순서 | ★★★ [정답률 60%]

1st 주어진 문장을 해석하고 문제를 풀 단서를 얻는다.

It has been observed that at each level of transfer, a large proportion, 80 – 90 percent, of the potential energy is lost as heat. **단서 1**
각 이동 단계에서 잠재적 에너지의 상당한 부분인 80-90퍼센트가 열로 손실되는 것으로 관찰되어 왔다.

➡ 주어진 문장 앞: at each level of transfer(각 이동 단계에서)라고 했으므로 **단서** 앞에 에너지가 이동하는 것과 관련된 내용이 나와야 한다. **발상**

2nd 각 선택지의 앞뒤 흐름이 매끄러운지 확인한다.

- ①의 앞 문장과 뒤 문장

앞 문장: 먹이 사슬은 식물 안에 있는 에너지원으로부터 먹고 먹히는 반복되는 과정 속에서 일련의 유기체를 통해 일련의 식품 에너지가 이동하는 것을 의미한다.

뒤 문장: 초원에서 풀은 토끼에게 먹히지만, 반면에 토끼는 결국 여우에게 먹힌다.

➡ 먹고 먹히는 것이 반복되면서 식품 에너지가 이동하는 것에 대한 구체적인 사례로 풀, 토끼, 여우로 이어지는 먹이 사슬을 들었다.
▶ 주어진 문장이 ①에 들어갈 수 없음

- ②의 앞 문장과 뒤 문장

앞 문장: ①의 뒤 문장과 같음

뒤 문장: 이것(This)은 단순한 먹이 사슬의 예이다.

➡ 뒤 문장의 This가 가리키는 것은 앞에서 언급된 먹이 사슬의 내용이고, 그 예라고 했으므로 자연스럽게 이어진다.
▶ 주어진 문장이 ②에 들어갈 수 없음

- ③의 앞 문장과 뒤 문장

앞 문장: ②의 뒤 문장과 같음

뒤 문장: 이 먹이 사슬(This food chain)은 식품 에너지가 생산자로부터 소비자 또는 더 높은 영양 수준으로 전달되는 연쇄를 의미한다. **단서 2**

➡ This food chain은 앞에서 언급된 '단순한 먹이 사슬'을 가리키는 것이다. 먹이 사슬이 의미하는 바를 설명하는 내용으로 이어지므로 자연스러운 흐름이다.
▶ 주어진 문장이 ③에 들어갈 수 없음

④의 앞 문장과 뒤 문장

앞 문장: ③의 뒤 문장과 같음

뒤 문장: 그래서 하나의 연쇄(사슬) 안에 있는 단계나 연결의 수는 보통 4~5개로 제한된다. **단서 3**

➡ 먹이 사슬이 의미하는 바를 언급했는데, 그래서 사슬 안의 단계나 연결의 수가 제한된다는 문장으로 이어지는 것은 내용에 공백이 존재한다. ▶ 주어진 문장이 ④에 들어가야 함

주어진 문장이 ④에 들어가면, <각 이동 단계에서 잠재적 에너지의 상당한 부분이 열로 손실되는 것으로 관찰되어 왔다. 그래서 하나의 연쇄(사슬) 안에 있는 단계나 연결의 수는 제한된다.>라는 자연스러운 흐름이 된다.

- **⑤의 앞 문장과 뒤 문장**

앞 문장: ④의 뒤 문장과 같음

뒤 문장: 먹이 사슬이 짧을수록 또는 유기체가 하위 영양 단계에 가까울수록 이용 가능한 에너지 섭취량이 더 커진다.

➡ 연쇄(사슬) 안에 있는 단계나 연결의 수는 제한된다고 했으므로 먹이 사슬이 짧을수록, 하위 영양 단계에 가까울수록 에너지 섭취량이 커진다는 내용이 자연스럽게 연결된다. ▶ 주어진 문장이 ⑤에 들어갈 수 없음

P 30 정답 ⑤ *초생산적인 종 재배의 명암

글의 흐름으로 보아, 주어진 문장이 들어가기에 가장 적절한 곳을 고르시오.

분사구문을 이끄는 현재분사
Leaving the contribution of that strategy to one side, / the
명사절 접속사
danger of creating more uniform crops / is **that** they are more
'~에 관해서는'
at risk / **when it comes to** disasters. //
그 전략의 기여를 차치하고 / 더 획일적인 작물을 만드는 것의 위험은 / 그것들이 더 큰 위험에 처한다는 것이다 / 재앙과 관련해 //
단서 1 앞에는 획일적인 작물이 전략에 기여한 긍정적인 측면이, 뒤에는 재앙과 관련한 위험성이 나와야 함

The decline in the diversity of our food / is an entirely human-made process. //
우리 음식의 다양성의 감소는 / 전적으로 인간이 만든 과정이다 //

주격 관계대명사
The biggest loss of crop diversity / came in the decades / **that**
followed the Second World War. //
농작물 다양성의 가장 큰 손실은 / 수십 년 동안 나타났다 / 제2차 세계 대전 이후 //

'~하려는 시도에서'
(①) **In an attempt to** save millions from extreme hunger, / crop
형용사적 용법(ways 수식)
scientists found ways / **to produce** grains such as rice and wheat /
on an enormous scale. //
수백만 명의 사람들을 극도의 배고픔에서 구하고자 하는 시도에서 / 작물 과학자들이 방법을 발견했다 / 쌀과 밀과 같은 곡물을 생산하는 / 엄청난 규모로 //

(②) And thousands of traditional varieties / were replaced / by
= varieties
a small number of new super-productive **ones**. //
그리고 수천 개의 전통적인 종들은 / 대체되었다 / 소수의 새로운 초(超)생산적인 종들로 //

(③) The strategy worked spectacularly well, / at least to begin with. //
그 전략은 굉장히 잘 작동했다 / 적어도 처음에는 //

(④) Because of it, / grain production tripled, / and between
1970 and 2020 / the human population more than doubled. //
그것 때문에 / 곡물 생산량은 세 배가 되었고 / 1970년과 2020년 사이에 / 인구는 두 배 이상 증가했다 //
단서 2 소수의 초생산적인 종을 만드는 전략은 성공적이었다는 내용이 앞에서부터 이어짐

단수 주어   주격 관계대명사
(⑤) Specifically, / a global food system / **that** depends on just
단수 동사   동명사의 부정
a narrow selection of plants / **has** a greater chance / of **not being**
able to survive / diseases, pests and climate extremes. //
특히 / 세계적인 식량 시스템은 / 농작물의 좁은 선택에만 의존하는 / 더 높은 가능성을 가진다 / 생존하지 못할 / 질병, 해충 및 기후 위기로부터 //
단서 3 농작물의 선택지가 좁으면 질병, 해충, 기후 위기에서 살아남기 어렵다는 점을 언급함

- leave A to one side A를 보류하다 • contribution ⓝ 기여
- strategy ⓝ 전략 • be at risk 위험에 처하다 • disaster ⓝ 재앙
- decline ⓝ 감소 • diversity ⓝ 다양성 • entirely ⓐⓓ 전적으로
- process ⓝ 과정 • extreme ⓐ 극심한 • hunger ⓝ 배고픔
- grain ⓝ 곡물 • enormous ⓐ 거대한 • scale ⓝ 규모
- traditional ⓐ 전통적인 • variety ⓝ 품종
- super-productive ⓐ 초생산적인
- spectacularly ⓐⓓ 극적으로, 굉장히 • specifically ⓐⓓ 특히
- depend on ~에 의존하다 • climate extreme 기후 위기

우리 음식의 다양성의 감소는 전적으로 인간이 만든 과정이다. 농작물 다양성의 가장 큰 손실은 제2차 세계 대전 이후 수십 년 동안 나타났다. (①) 수백만 명의 사람들을 극도의 배고픔에서 구하고자 하는 시도에서 작물 과학자들이 쌀과 밀과 같은 곡물을 엄청난 규모로 생산하는 방법을 발견했다. (②) 그리고 수천 개의 전통적인 종들은 소수의 새로운 초(超)생산적인 종들로 대체되었다. (③) 그 전략은 적어도 처음에는 굉장히 잘 작동했다. (④) 그것 때문에 곡물 생산량은 세 배가 되었고 1970년과 2020년 사이에 인구는 두 배 이상 증가했다. (⑤ 그 전략의 기여를 차치하고, 더 획일적인 작물을 만드는 것의 위험은 그것들이 재앙과 관련해 더 큰 위험에 처한다는 것이다.) 특히 농작물의 좁은 선택에만 의존하는 세계적인 식량 시스템은 질병, 해충 및 기후 위기로부터 생존하지 못할 더 높은 가능성을 가진다.

| 문제 풀이 순서 | ★★★ [정답률 43%]

1st 주어진 문장을 해석하고, 연결어, 지시어 등을 확인한다.

Leaving the contribution of that strategy to one side, the
danger of creating more uniform crops is that they are more
at risk when it comes to disasters.
그 전략의 기여를 차치하고, 더 획일적인 작물을 만드는 것의 위험은 그것들이 재앙과 관련해 더 큰 위험에 처한다는 것이다.

➡ 주어진 문장 앞: '그 전략의 기여'라고 했으므로 단서
앞에는 획일적인 작물을 만드는 것이 전략에 기여한 긍정적인 측면이 언급되어야 한다. 발상

➡ 주어진 문장 뒤: '더 큰 위험'에 처한다고 했으므로 단서
뒤에는 획일적인 작물을 만드는 것이 재앙과 관련하여 어떻게 위험한지 언급되어야 한다. 발상

2nd 찾은 단서를 생각하며 각 선택지의 앞뒤 흐름이 매끄러운지 확인한다.

- **①의 앞 문장과 뒤 문장**

앞 문장: 농작물 다양성의 가장 큰 손실은 제2차 세계 대전 이후 수십 년 동안 나타났다.

뒤 문장: 수백만 명의 사람들을 극도의 배고픔에서 구하고자 하는 시도에서 작물 과학자들이 쌀과 밀과 같은 곡물을 엄청난 규모로 생산하는 방법을 발견했다.

➡ 농작물의 다양성이 손실된 과정을 설명할 뿐, 그것이 전략에 어떤 기여를 했는지는 구체적으로 언급되지 않았다. ▶ 주어진 문장이 ①에 들어갈 수 없음

- **②의 앞 문장과 뒤 문장**

앞 문장: ①의 뒤 문장과 같음

뒤 문장: 그리고 수천 개의 전통적인 종들은 소수의 새로운 초(超)생산적인 종들로 대체되었다.

➡ 앞 문장에서 언급했듯이, 전쟁 후 배고픔을 해소하고자 초 생산적인 종들을 재배하게 되었다는 내용이 이어지고 있다. ▶ 주어진 문장이 ②에 들어갈 수 없음

- **③의 앞 문장과 뒤 문장**

앞 문장: ②의 뒤 문장과 같음

뒤 문장: 그 전략은 적어도 처음에는 굉장히 잘 작동했다.

➡ 작물의 선택지를 줄이는 '전략'이 긍정적인 결과를 낳았다는 내용이 이어지고 있다.
▶ 주어진 문장이 ③에 들어갈 수 없음

- **④의 앞 문장과 뒤 문장**

앞 문장: ③의 뒤 문장과 같음

뒤 문장: 그것 때문에 곡물 생산량은 세 배가 되었고 1970년과 2020년 사이에 인구는 두 배 이상 증가했다.

➡ 그 전략이 성공하여 곡물 생산량과 인구가 증가했다는 내용이 이어지고 있다.
▶ 주어진 문장이 ④에 들어갈 수 없음

⑤의 앞 문장과 뒤 문장

앞 문장: ④의 뒤 문장과 같음

뒤 문장: 특히 농작물의 좁은 선택에만 의존하는 세계적인 식량 시스템은 질병, 해충 및 기후 위기로부터 생존하지 못할 더 높은 가능성을 가진다.

➡ 앞 문장에서 농작물의 좁은 선택지 전략이 성공했던 과정을 설명했고, 뒤 문장에서는 농작물의 좁은 선택지 전략이 위험성을 지니고 있다는 내용이 이어지고 있다. 따라서 초 생산적인 종을 재배하는 것이 긍정적으로 기여했다는 내용에서 위험성에 관한 내용으로 옮겨가는 주어진 문장은 ⑤에 오는 것이 적절하다.
▶ 주어진 문장이 ⑤에 들어가야 함

P 31 정답 ④ *전통을 버리고 쇠퇴하기 시작한 쿠바 야구팀

글의 흐름으로 보아, 주어진 문장이 들어가기에 가장 적절한 곳을 고르시오.

A few years ago, / Cuba altered that uniform style, / 병렬 구조
modernizing it / and perhaps conforming to other countries' style; /
몇 년 전 / 쿠바는 그 유니폼 스타일을 바꿨다 / 유니폼을 현대화하고 / 아마도 다른 나라의 스타일에 맞추면서 /
현재완료(계속)
interestingly, / the national team has declined / since that time. //
단서 1 쿠바팀이 유니폼을 바꾼 후부터 쇠퇴하기 시작했다는 내용이 시작됨
흥미롭게도 / 국가 대표 팀은 쇠퇴해 왔다 / 그 시기부터 //

Between 1940 and 2000, / Cuba ruled the world baseball scene. //
1940년과 2000년 사이에 / 쿠바는 세계 야구계를 지배했다 //
They won / 25 of the first 28 World Cups / and 3 of 5 Olympic Games. //
그들은 이겼다 / 첫 28회의 월드컵 중 25회와 / 5회의 올림픽 게임 중 3회를 //
be known for ~: ~로 알려지다
(①) The Cubans were known / for wearing uniforms covered in red / from head to toe, / a strong contrast to the more conservative North American style / 현재분사(style 수식) featuring grey or white pants. //
쿠바인들은 알려져 있는데 / 빨간색으로 뒤덮인 유니폼을 입는 것으로 / 머리부터 발끝까지 / 이것은 더 보수적인 북미 스타일과 강한 대조를 이룬다 / 회색이나 흰색 바지를 특징으로 하는 //
부정어가 앞에 오면서 주어와 동사가 도치됨
(②) Not only were their athletic talents superior, / the Cubans
비교급 강조
appeared even stronger / from just the colour of their uniforms. //
쿠바인들의 운동 재능이 뛰어났을 뿐만 아니라 / 그들은 훨씬 더 강하게 보였다 / 그들의 유니폼의 색깔만으로도 //
(③) A game would not even start / and the opposing team would already be scared. // 단서 2 쿠바팀은 유니폼만으로 상대방의 기선을 제압하는 등 승승장구했음
경기가 시작하지 않았는데도 / 상대 팀은 이미 겁에 질리곤 했다 //
목적격 관계대명사
(④) The country that ruled international baseball for decades /
현재완료
has not been on top since that uniform change. //
수십 년 동안 국제 야구를 지배했던 그 나라는 / 그 유니폼 교체 이후로 정상에 오른 적이 없었다 //
단서 3 승승장구했던 쿠바는 유니폼을 교체한 후로 정상에 오른 적이 없음
(⑤) Traditions are important for a team; /
전통은 팀에게 중요하다 /
부사적 용법(목적)
while a team brand or image can adjust / to keep up with present times, / if it abandons or neglects its roots, / negative effects can surface. //
팀 브랜드나 이미지는 조정될 수 있지만 / 현시대를 따르기 위해 / 팀이 그들의 뿌리를 버리거나 무시하면 / 부정적인 영향이 표면화될 수 있다 //

- alter ⓥ 바꾸다   • modernize ⓥ 현대화하다
- conform to ~에 순응하다   • interestingly ⓐⓓ 흥미롭게도
- decline ⓥ 쇠퇴하다   • rule ⓥ 지배하다   • contrast ⓝ 대조

- feature ⓥ ~을 특징으로 하다   • athletic ⓐ 운동의
- opposing team 상대 팀   • tradition ⓝ 전통   • adjust ⓥ 조정하다
- keep up with ~에 따르다   • abandon ⓥ 버리다
- neglect ⓥ 무시하다   • root ⓝ 뿌리, 기원   • effect ⓝ 영향

1940년과 2000년 사이에 쿠바는 세계 야구계를 지배했다. 그들은 첫 28회의 월드컵 중 25회와 5회의 올림픽 게임 중 3회를 이겼다. (①) 쿠바인들은 머리부터 발끝까지 빨간색으로 뒤덮인 유니폼을 입는 것으로 알려져 있었는데, 이것은 회색이나 흰색 바지를 특징으로 하는 더 보수적인 북미 스타일과 강한 대조를 이룬다. (②) 쿠바인들의 운동 재능이 뛰어났을 뿐만 아니라 그들은 그들의 유니폼의 색깔만으로도 훨씬 더 강하게 보였다. (③) 경기가 시작하지 않았는데도 상대 팀은 이미 겁에 질리곤 했다. (④ 몇 년 전 쿠바는 유니폼을 현대화하고 아마도 다른 나라의 스타일에 맞추면서 그 유니폼 스타일을 바꿨다. 흥미롭게도 국가 대표 팀은 그 시기부터 쇠퇴해 왔다.) 수십 년 동안 국제 야구를 지배했던 그 나라는 그 유니폼 교체 이후로 정상에 오른 적이 없었다. (⑤) 전통은 팀에게 중요하다. 팀 브랜드나 이미지는 현시대를 따르기 위해 조정될 수 있지만 팀이 그들의 뿌리를 버리거나 무시하면 부정적인 영향이 표면화될 수 있다.

│ 문제 풀이 순서 │ ★★★ [정답률 54%]

1st 주어진 문장을 해석하고, 연결어, 지시어 등을 확인한다.

A few years ago, Cuba altered that uniform style, modernizing it and perhaps conforming to other countries' style; interestingly, the national team has declined since that time.
몇 년 전 쿠바는 유니폼을 현대화하고 아마도 다른 나라의 스타일에 맞추면서 그 유니폼 스타일을 바꿨다. 흥미롭게도 국가 대표 팀은 그 시기부터 쇠퇴해 왔다.

➡ 주어진 문장 앞: 쿠바팀이 유니폼을 현대화하며 다른 국가의 스타일에 맞춰가기 시작했다고 했으므로, 단서 앞에는 that uniform style에 관한 내용이 언급되어야 한다. 발상

➡ 주어진 문장 뒤: 유니폼을 바꾼 후부터 쇠퇴하기 시작했다고 했으므로, 단서 뒤에는 유니폼이 바뀐 후에 쿠바팀이 어떻게 쇠퇴했는지 언급되어야 한다. 발상

2nd 찾은 단서를 생각하며 각 선택지의 앞뒤 흐름이 매끄러운지 확인한다.

- **①의 앞 문장과 뒤 문장**

앞 문장: 1940년과 2000년 사이에 쿠바는 세계 야구계를 지배했다. 그들은 첫 28회의 월드컵 중 25회와 5회의 올림픽 게임 중 3회를 이겼다.

뒤 문장: 쿠바인들은 머리부터 발끝까지 빨간색으로 뒤덮인 유니폼을 입는 것으로 알려져 있었는데, 이것은 회색이나 흰색 바지를 특징으로 하는 더 보수적인 북미 스타일과 강한 대조를 이룬다.

➡ 쿠바가 20세기에 세계 야구계를 지배했던 역사와 그들만의 유니폼의 특징을 이어서 소개하고 있다. ▶ 주어진 문장이 ①에 들어갈 수 없음

- **②의 앞 문장과 뒤 문장**

앞 문장: ①의 뒤 문장과 같음

뒤 문장: 쿠바인들의 운동 재능이 뛰어났을 뿐만 아니라 그들은 그들의 유니폼의 색깔만으로도 훨씬 더 강하게 보였다.

➡ 앞에서 쿠바가 야구계를 지배했던 역사와 독특한 유니폼의 특성을 설명하고, 뒤에서 그 독특한 유니폼 색깔이 그들이 강력해 보였던 이유라 설명하고 있다.
▶ 주어진 문장이 ②에 들어갈 수 없음

- **③의 앞 문장과 뒤 문장**

앞 문장: ②의 뒤 문장과 같음

뒤 문장: 경기가 시작하지 않았는데도 상대 팀은 이미 겁에 질리곤 했다.

➡ 앞에서 쿠바만의 유니폼 색깔이 그들을 강력하게 보이도록 해주었다고 설명했고, 뒤에서 구체적으로 유니폼만으로 상대 팀을 겁에 질리게 했던 모습을 소개하고 있다. ▶ 주어진 문장이 ③에 들어갈 수 없음

④의 앞 문장과 뒤 문장

- **앞 문장:** ③의 뒤 문장과 같음
- **뒤 문장:** 수십 년 동안 국제 야구를 지배했던 그 나라는 그 유니폼 교체 이후로 정상에 오른 적이 없었다.

➡ 앞에서 쿠바만의 독특한 유니폼 색깔 덕분에 승승장구할 수 있었던 역사를 소개했으나, 뒤에서는 쿠바팀이 유니폼을 교체한 후로 정상에 오른 적이 없다는 내용이 이어지고 있다. 따라서 쿠바팀이 유니폼 덕분에 강력한 팀으로 자리매김했다가 유니폼을 바꾼 후 쇠퇴했다는 내용으로 전환되기에, 주어진 문장은 ④에 오는 것이 적절하다. ▶ **주어진 문장이 ④에 들어가야 함**

⑤의 앞 문장과 뒤 문장

- **앞 문장:** ④의 뒤 문장과 같음
- **뒤 문장:** 전통은 팀에게 중요하다. 팀 브랜드나 이미지는 현시대를 따르기 위해 조정될 수 있지만 팀이 그들의 뿌리를 버리거나 무시하면 부정적인 영향이 표면화될 수 있다.

➡ 앞에서 전통적인 유니폼을 바꾼 후 정상에 오른 적이 없었다고 소개했고, 뒤에서는 쿠바팀의 사례를 통해 팀의 전통과 뿌리를 무시하면 부정적인 영향이 나타날 수 있다고 하며 글을 마무리했다.
▶ **주어진 문장이 ⑤에 들어갈 수 없음**

P 32 정답 ⑤ ⭐ 2등급 대비 [정답률 50%]

*언어를 바라보는 서로 다른 견해

> 글의 흐름으로 보아, 주어진 문장이 들어가기에 가장 적절한 곳을 고르시오. [3점]

> **단서 1** 앞에 언어가 인간의 삶에서 매우 중요하다는 것과 반대되는 내용이 나와야 함
> Nevertheless, / language is enormously important in human life / and contributes largely to our ability / to cooperate with each other / in dealing with the world. // 『병렬 구조』『형용사적 용법(ability 수식)』
> 그럼에도 불구하고 / 언어는 인간의 삶에서 매우 중요하다 / 그리고 우리의 능력에 상당히 기여한다 / 서로 협력하는 / 세계를 다루는 데 있어서 //

Should we use / language to understand mind / or mind to understand language? // 『부사적 용법(목적)』
우리는 사용해야 하는가 / 사고를 이해하기 위해 언어를 / 아니면 언어를 이해하기 위해 사고를 //

(①) Analytic philosophy historically assumes / that language is basic / and that mind would make sense / if proper use of language was appreciated. // 『목적어절 접속사의 병렬 구조』
분석 철학은 역사적으로 가정한다 / 언어가 기본이라고 / 그리고 사고가 이치에 맞을 것이라고 / 적절한 언어 사용이 제대로 인식된다면 //

(②) Modern cognitive science, / however, / rightly judges / that language is just one aspect of mind of great importance / in human beings / but not fundamental to all kinds of thinking. // 『목적어절 접속사』
현대 인지 과학은 / 그러나 / 당연히 판단한다 / 언어가 매우 중요한 사고의 한 측면일 뿐이고 / 인간에게 / 모든 종류의 사고에 근본적이지는 않다고 //

(③) Countless species of animals / manage to navigate the world, solve problems, and learn / without using language, / through brain mechanisms / that are largely preserved in the minds of humans. // 『주격 관계대명사』
수많은 종의 동물들이 / 세계를 항해하고, 문제를 해결하고, 학습해 낸다 / 언어를 사용하지 않고 / 두뇌의 메커니즘을 통해 / 인간의 사고 속에 대체로 보존된 //

(④) There is no reason to assume / that language is fundamental to mental operations. // 『목적어절 접속사』 **단서 2** 언어가 정신 작용의 기본이 아니라고 함
가정할 이유는 없다 / 언어가 정신 작용의 기본이라고 //

(⑤) Our species *homo sapiens* / has been astonishingly successful, / which depended in part on language, / 『계속적 용법의 주격 관계대명사』
우리 종족, '호모 사피엔스'는 / 놀라운 성공을 거두어 왔다 / 그리고 그것은 언어에 부분적으로 의존했다 / **단서 3** 언어가 호모 사피엔스의 성공에 영향을 미침

first as an effective contributor / to collaborative problem solving / and much later, / as collective memory / through written records. // 『병렬 구조(~로서)』
처음에는 효과적인 기여 요소로서 / 협력적인 문제 해결에 / 그리고 훨씬 나중에는 / 집단 기억으로서의 / 글로 쓰인 기록을 통한 //

- **enormously** ⓐⓓ 엄청나게, 대단히 • **contribute** ⓥ 기여하다
- **cooperate** ⓥ 협력하다 • **deal with** ~을 다루다
- **analytic philosophy** 분석 철학 • **assume** ⓥ 가정하다
- **cognitive science** 인지 과학 • **rightly** ⓐⓓ 당연히
- **fundamental** ⓐ 근본적인, 기본적인 • **countless** ⓐ 셀 수 없이 많은
- **navigate** ⓥ 항해하다, 길을 찾다 • **preserve** ⓥ 보존하다
- **operation** ⓝ 작용, 작동 • **astonishingly** ⓐⓓ 놀라운 정도로
- **contributor** ⓝ 기여 요소, 원인 제공자
- **collaborative** ⓐ 협력적인, 공동의 • **collective** ⓐ 협력적인

우리는 사고를 이해하기 위해 언어를 사용해야 하는가 아니면 언어를 이해하기 위해 사고를 사용해야 하는가? (①) 분석 철학은 언어가 기본이고 적절한 언어 사용이 제대로 인식된다면 그 사고가 이치에 맞을 것이라고 역사적으로 가정한다. (②) 그러나 현대 인지 과학은 언어가 인간에게 매우 중요한 사고의 한 측면일 뿐 모든 종류의 사고에 근본적이지는 않다고 당연히 판단한다. (③) 수많은 종의 동물들이 인간의 사고 속에 대체로 보존된 두뇌의 메커니즘을 통해 언어를 사용하지 않고 세계를 항해하고, 문제를 해결하고, 학습해 낸다. (④) 언어가 정신 작용의 기본이라고 가정할 이유는 없다. (⑤ 그럼에도 불구하고, 언어는 인간의 삶에서 매우 중요하며 세계를 다루는 데 있어서 서로 협력하는 우리의 능력에 상당히 기여한다.) 우리 종족, '호모 사피엔스'는 놀라운 성공을 거두어 왔는데, 이것은 처음에는 협력적인 문제 해결에 효과적인 기여 요소로서, 그리고 훨씬 나중에는 글로 쓰인 기록을 통한 집단 기억으로서의 언어에 부분적으로 의존했다.

왜 2등급? 주어진 문장이 Nevertheless로 시작하여 글의 내용이 반전되는 부분에 주어진 문장을 넣으면 된다는 단서를 얻었지만, 글의 앞부분에 however가 등장하여 내용이 한번 전환됐다. 따라서, 이미 전환된 내용에 한 번 더 내용이 전환되는 부분을 찾아 주어진 문장을 넣어야 하는 2등급 대비 문제이다.

│ 문제 풀이 순서 │

1st 주어진 문장을 해석하고, 연결어, 지시어 등을 확인한다.

> **Nevertheless,** language is enormously important in human life and contributes largely to our ability to cooperate with each other in dealing with the world.
> **그럼에도 불구하고,** 언어는 인간의 삶에서 매우 중요하며 세계를 다루는 데 있어서 서로 협력하는 우리의 능력에 상당히 기여한다.

➡ **주어진 문장 앞:** 'Nevertheless(그럼에도 불구하고)'라고 했으므로 **단서** 앞에는 언어가 인간의 삶에서 중요하지 않다는 내용이 와야 한다. **발상**

2nd 찾은 단서를 생각하며 각 선택지의 앞뒤 흐름이 매끄러운지 확인한다.

①의 앞 문장과 뒤 문장

- **앞 문장:** 우리는 사고를 이해하기 위해 언어를 사용해야 하는가 아니면 언어를 이해하기 위해 사고를 사용해야 하는가?
- **뒤 문장:** 분석 철학은 언어가 기본이고 적절한 언어 사용이 제대로 인식된다면 그 사고가 이치에 맞을 것이라고 역사적으로 가정한다.

➡ 앞 문장에서 던진 질문에 대한 답을 뒤 문장에서 말하고 있다.
▶ **주어진 문장이 ①에 들어갈 수 없음**

앞 문장: ①의 뒤 문장과 같음

뒤 문장: 그러나(however) 현대 인지 과학은 언어가 인간에게 매우 중요한 사고의 한 측면일 뿐 모든 종류의 사고에 근본적이지는 않다고 당연히 판단한다.

→ 앞 문장의 '분석 철학'의 관점과 다른 '현대 인지 과학'의 관점을 역접의 연결어 however로 이어간다.
  ▶ 주어진 문장이 ②에 들어갈 수 없음

- ③의 앞 문장과 뒤 문장

앞 문장: ②의 뒤 문장과 같음

뒤 문장: 수많은 종의 동물들이 인간의 사고 속에 대체로 보존된 두뇌의 메커니즘을 통해 언어를 사용하지 않고 세계를 항해하고, 문제를 해결하고, 학습해낸다.

→ '언어가 모든 종류의 사고에 근본적이지는 않다'라는 앞 문장의 주장을 뒷받침하는 설명을 이어간다.
  ▶ 주어진 문장이 ③에 들어갈 수 없음

- ④의 앞 문장과 뒤 문장

앞 문장: ③의 뒤 문장과 같음

뒤 문장: 언어가 정신 작용의 기본이라고 가정할 이유는 없다.

→ 앞 문장의 견해와 동일한 주장을 반복한다.
  ▶ 주어진 문장이 ④에 들어갈 수 없음

- ⑤의 앞 문장과 뒤 문장

앞 문장: ④의 뒤 문장과 같음

뒤 문장: 우리 종족, '호모 사피엔스'는 놀라운 성공을 거두어 왔는데, 이것은 처음에는 협력적인 문제 해결에 효과적인 기여 요소로서, 그리고 훨씬 나중에는 글로 쓰인 기록을 통한 집단 기억으로서의 언어에 부분적으로 의존했다.

→ 앞에서는 언어가 정신 작용의 기본이라고 가정할 이유는 없다면서 부정적인 견해를 말했는데, 뒤에서는 언어가 문제 해결에 효과적인 기여 요소라고 하며 상반된 견해를 말하고 있다.
  따라서 '그럼에도 불구하고' 언어가 서로 협력하는 우리의 능력에 상당히 기여한다고 한 주어진 문장이 ⑤에 오는 것이 적절하다.
  ▶ 주어진 문장이 ⑤에 들어가야 함

P 33 정답 ⑤ ★2등급 대비 [정답률 46%]

*실제 온도와는 다른 상대적인 뜨거움과 차가움 측정

글의 흐름으로 보아, 주어진 문장이 들어가기에 가장 적절한 곳을 고르시오. [3점]

선행사를 포함한 관계대명사
What we need / is a reliable and reproducible method / for measuring the relative hotness or coldness / of objects / rather than the rate of energy transfer. // 단서1 우리는 물체의 상대적 뜨거움과 차가움(열)을 측정할 수 있는 수단이 필요함
우리가 필요로 하는 것은 / 신뢰할 수 있고 재현 가능한 수단이다 / 상대적인 뜨거움과 차가움을 측정하기 위한 / 물체의 / 에너지 전도율보다는 //

associate A with B: A를 B와 연관 짓다
We often associate / the concept of temperature / with how hot or cold an object feels / when we touch it. //
우리는 종종 연관 짓는다 / 온도 개념을 / 그것이 얼마나 뜨겁게 또는 차갑게 느껴지는지와 / 우리가 물건을 만졌을 때 //

In this way, / our senses provide us / with a qualitative indication of temperature. //
이런 식으로 / 우리의 감각은 우리에게 제공한다 / 온도의 정성적인 지표를 //

(①) Our senses, / however, / are unreliable / and often mislead us. //
우리의 감각은 / 그러나 / 신뢰할 수 없으며 / 종종 우리를 잘못 인도한다 //

(②) For example, / if you stand in bare feet / with 두 개 중 하나 one foot on carpet / and 두 개 중 나머지 하나 the other on a tile floor, / the tile feels colder / than the carpet / *even though both are at the same temperature.* //
예를 들어 / 여러분이 맨발로 서 있다면 / 한쪽 발은 카페트 위에 / 다른 한쪽 발은 타일 바닥 위에 놓고 / 타일이 더 차갑게 느껴질 것이다 / 카페트보다 / 둘 다 같은 온도임에도 불구하고 //

(③) The two objects feel different / because tile transfers energy / by heat / at a higher rate / than carpet = transfers does. //
그 두 물체는 다르게 느껴진다 / 타일이 에너지를 전달하기 때문에 / 열의 형태로 / 더 높은 비율로 / 카페트가 전달하는 것보다 //

단서2 우리의 피부가 실제 온도보다 열에너지 전도율을 측정함
(④) Your skin "measures" / the rate of energy transfer by heat / rather than the actual temperature. //
여러분의 피부는 "측정한다" / 열에너지 전도율을 / 실제 온도보다는 //

(⑤) Scientists have developed / a variety of thermometers / for making such quantitative measurements. //
과학자들은 개발해 왔다 / 다양한 온도계를 / 그런 정량적인 측정을 하기 위해 //
단서3 주어진 문장에서 언급한, 정량적인 측정(상대적 뜨거움과 차가움을 측정)을 위한 온도계를 개발해 왔음

- reliable ⓐ 신뢰할 수 있는   - reproducible ⓐ 재현 가능한
- transfer ⓥ 전달하다 ⓝ 전도   - qualitative ⓐ 정성적인
- indication ⓝ 지표   - unreliable ⓐ 신뢰할 수 없는
- mislead ⓥ 잘못 인도하다   - bare feet 맨발   - rate ⓝ 비율
- a variety of 다양한   - quantitative ⓐ 정량적인
- measurement ⓝ 측정

우리는 종종 온도 개념을 우리가 물건을 만졌을 때 그것이 얼마나 뜨겁게 또는 차갑게 느껴지는지와 연관 짓는다. 이런 식으로, 우리의 감각은 우리에게 온도의 정성적인 지표를 제공한다. ① 그러나, 우리의 감각은 신뢰할 수 없으며 종종 우리를 잘못 인도한다. ② 예를 들어, 여러분이 맨발로 한쪽 발은 카페트 위에, 다른 한쪽 발은 타일 바닥 위에 놓고 서 있다면, '둘 다 같은 온도임에도 불구하고' 카페트보다 타일이 더 차갑게 느껴질 것이다. ③ 타일이 카페트가 전달하는 것보다 더 높은 비율로 에너지를 열의 형태로 전달하기 때문에 그 두 물체는 다르게 느껴진다. ④ 여러분의 피부는 실제 온도보다는 열에너지 전도율을 "측정한다". (⑤ 우리가 필요로 하는 것은 에너지 전도율보다는 물체의 상대적인 뜨거움과 차가움을 측정하기 위한 신뢰할 수 있고 재현 가능한 수단이다.) 과학자들은 그런 정량적인 측정을 하기 위해 다양한 온도계를 개발해 왔다.

왜 2등급? 마지막 문장에서 언급한 과학자들이 다양한 온도계를 개발한 이유를 글 전반에 걸쳐 설명하는 글이다. 예시로 제시된 카페트와 타일의 온도를 우리가 다르게 느끼는 이유를 이해하고, 이것이 '온도계 개발'과 어떤 관련이 있는지를 파악해야 주어진 문장을 알맞은 곳에 넣을 수 있다.

| 문제 풀이 순서 |

1st 주어진 문장을 해석하고 문제를 풀 단서를 얻는다.

What we need is a reliable and reproducible method for measuring the relative hotness or coldness of objects rather than the rate of energy transfer. 단서1
우리가 필요로 하는 것은 에너지 전도율보다는 물체의 상대적 뜨거움과 차가움을 측정하기 위한 신뢰할 수 있고 재현 가능한 수단이다

→ 우리에게 필요한 것이 물체의 상대적 뜨거움과 차가움을 측정할 수 있는 수단이라는 내용이므로 단서
  이와 관련된 내용이 나올 것임을 생각하며 나머지 글을 읽는다. 발상

2nd 각 선택지의 앞뒤 흐름이 매끄러운지 확인한다.

- ①의 앞 문장과 뒤 문장

앞 문장: 우리는 종종 온도 개념을 우리가 물건을 만졌을 때 그것이 얼마나 뜨겁게 또는 차갑게 느껴지는지와 연관 짓는다. 이런 식으로, 우리의 감각은 우리에게 온도의 정성적인 지표를 제공한다.

뒤 문장: 그러나(however), 우리의 감각은 신뢰할 수 없으며 종종 우리를 잘못 인도한다.

➡ 뒤 문장에서 반대 내용을 연결하는 however(그러나)가 나오며 앞 문장과 연결되고 있다.
앞에서 우리의 감각이 정성적인 지표를 제공한다고 한 후에, 우리의 감각이 우리를 잘못 인도할 때도 있다는 반대 내용이 이어지므로 자연스럽게 연결된다.
▶ 주어진 문장이 ①에 들어갈 수 없음

- ②의 앞 문장과 뒤 문장

앞 문장: ①의 뒤 문장과 같음

뒤 문장: 예를 들어(For example), 여러분이 맨발로 한쪽 발은 카페트 위에, 다른 한쪽 발은 타일 바닥 위에 놓고 서 있다면, '둘 다 같은 온도임에도 불구하고' 카페트보다 타일이 더 차갑게 느껴질 것이다.

➡ 뒤 문장이 For example(예를 들어)로 시작하며 앞 문장에 대한 예시를 제시한다. 우리의 감각이 우리를 잘못 인도한다고 한 앞 문장에 대한 예시로, 맨발을 카페트와 타일 바닥 위에 각각 놓고 서 있을 때 타일이 더 차갑게 느껴진다는 문장이 나오고 있다.
▶ 주어진 문장이 ②에 들어갈 수 없음

- ③의 앞 문장과 뒤 문장

앞 문장: ②의 뒤 문장과 같음

뒤 문장: 타일이 카페트가 전달하는 것보다 더 높은 비율로 에너지를 열의 형태로 전달하기 때문에 그 두 물체는 다르게 느껴진다.

➡ 카페트보다 타일이 더 차갑게 느껴질 것이라는 예시에 대한 부연 설명으로, 타일이 카페트보다 더 높은 비율로 열을 전달하기 때문이라는 문장이 자연스럽게 이어진다.
▶ 주어진 문장이 ③에 들어갈 수 없음

- ④의 앞 문장과 뒤 문장

앞 문장: ③의 뒤 문장과 같음

뒤 문장: 여러분의 피부는 실제 온도보다는 열에너지 전도율을 "측정한다". **단서 2**

➡ 앞에서 말한 카페트와 타일의 예시에 대한 결론으로, 피부는 실제 온도가 아니라 열에너지 전도율을 측정한다고 말하는 문장이 이어진다.
▶ 주어진 문장이 ④에 들어갈 수 없음

- ⑤의 앞 문장과 뒤 문장

앞 문장: ④의 뒤 문장과 같음

뒤 문장: 과학자들은 그런 정량적인 측정을 하기 위해 다양한 온도계를 개발해 왔다. **단서 3**

➡ 앞에서 우리의 피부가 실제 온도보다 열에너지 전도율을 측정한다고 했는데, 과학자들이 '그런 정량적인 측정을 하기 위해'라고 이어지는 것은 어색하다.
▶ 주어진 문장이 ⑤에 들어가야 함

➡ 주어진 문장이 ⑤에 들어가면, 〈우리가 필요로 하는 것은 물체의 상대적인 뜨거움과 차가움을 측정하기 위한 신뢰할 수 있는 수단이다. 과학자들은 그런 정량적인 측정을 하기 위해 온도계를 개발해왔다.〉라는 자연스러운 흐름이 된다.

P 34 정답 ② ━━━━━━━ ⭐ 2등급 대비 [정답률 26%]

＊생명 체계의 운하화 이론

> 글의 흐름으로 보아, 주어진 문장이 들어가기에 가장 적절한 곳을 고르시오. [3점]

Such a system / can only hope to be stable / if only a smaller number of collective ways of being / may emerge. //
이러한 시스템은 / 오직 안정적이기를 기대할 수 있다 / 더 적은 수의 존재의 집합적인 방식 / 나타날 때만 //
단서 1 존재의 집합적인 방식이 제한되어야만 안정적임

선행사를 포함하는 관계대명사
Life is / **what** physicists might call a 'high-dimensional system,'
계속적 용법의 주격 관계대명사 *목적어절 접속사*
/ **which** is their fancy way of saying / **that** there's a lot going on. //
생명은 / 물리학자들이 '고차원 시스템'이라고 부를 수 있는 것이다 / 이는 그들의 말하는 멋진 방식이다 / 많은 일이 발생하고 있다고 //
단서 2 하나의 세포에서도 가능한 상호 작용의 수가 매우 큼

'~의 수'
(①) In just a single cell, / **the number of** possible interactions
단수 동사
between different molecules / **is** enormous. //
단 하나의 세포 내에서도 / 여러 분자 간의 가능한 상호 작용의 수는 / 매우 크다 //

(②) For example, / **it** is only a limited number of tissues and
it ~ that 강조 구문
body shapes / **that** may result from the development of a human embryo. // **단서 3** 인간 배아로부터 나올 수 있는 조직과 형태는 제한되어 있음
예를 들어 / 오직 제한된 수의 조직과 신체 형태이다 / 인간 배아의 발달로부터 나올 수 있는 것은 //

called의 목적어와 목적격 보어 (명사)
(③) In 1942, / the biologist Conrad Waddington called / **this** drastic narrowing of outcomes / *canalization*. //
1942년에 / 생물학자 Conrad Waddington이 불렀다 / 이러한 극적인 결과의 제한을 / '운하화'라고 //
단서 4 Conrad가 이 극적인 결과의 제한을 '운하화'라고 함

(④) The organism may switch / between a small number of well-defined possible states, / but can't exist / in random states in between them, /
유기체는 바뀔 수 있다 / 적은 수의 명확하게 정의 가능한 상태 사이에서 / 하지만 존재할 수 없다 / 그것들 사이에 있는 무작위의 상태로 /

rather as a ball in a rough landscape must roll / to the bottom of one valley or another. //
오히려 울퉁불퉁한 경관에 있는 공이 반드시 굴러가야 하는 것처럼 / 이 계곡 혹은 또 다른 계곡의 바닥으로 //

목적어절 접속사 *be true of: ~에도 적용되다*
(⑤) We'll see / **that** this **is true** also **of** health and disease: / there are many causes of illness, /
우리는 알게 될 것이다 / 이것이 건강과 질병에도 적용된다는 것을 / 즉 질병에는 많은 원인이 있다 /

복수 주어
but **their manifestations** at the physiological and symptomatic
복수 동사
levels / **are** often strikingly similar. //
하지만 그것들의 생리적이고 증상적인 수준에서의 발현은 / 종종 놀랍도록 유사하다 //

- **stable** ⓐ 안정적인 ・ **collective** ⓐ 집합적인
- **emerge** ⓥ 나타나다 ・ **dimensional** ⓐ 차원적인 ・ **cell** ⓝ 세포
- **molecule** ⓝ 분자 ・ **enormous** ⓐ 거대한 ・ **tissue** ⓝ (근육) 조직
- **drastic** ⓐ 극적인 ・ **outcome** ⓝ 결과 ・ **organism** ⓝ 유기체
- **switch** ⓥ 바꾸다 ・ **well-defined** ⓐ 명확히 정의된
- **state** ⓝ 상태 ・ **rough** ⓐ 울퉁불퉁한 ・ **landscape** ⓝ 경관
- **illness** ⓝ 질병 ・ **manifestation** ⓝ 발현
- **symptomatic** ⓐ 증상적인 ・ **strikingly** ⓐⓓ 놀랍게도

생명은 물리학자들이 '고차원 시스템'이라고 부를 수 있는 것인데 이는 많은 일이 발생하고 있다고 말하는 그들의 멋진 방식이다. (①) 단 하나의 세포 내에서도 여러 분자 간의 가능한 상호 작용의 수는 매우 크다. (② 이러한 시스템은 더 적은 수의 존재의 집합적인 방식이 나타날 때만 오직 안정적이기를 기대할 수 있다.) 예를 들어 인간 배아의 발달로부터 나올 수 있는 것은 오직 제한된 수의 조직과 신체 형태이다. (③) 1942년에 생물학자 Conrad Waddington은

이러한 극적인 결과의 제한을 '운하화'라고 불렀다. (④) 오히려 울퉁불퉁한 경관에 있는 공이 이 계곡 혹은 또 다른 계곡의 바닥으로 반드시 굴러가야 하는 것처럼, 유기체는 적은 수의 명확하게 정의된 가능한 상태 사이에서 바뀔 수 있지만 그것들 사이에 있는 무작위의 상태로 존재할 수는 없다. (⑤) 우리는 이것이 건강과 질병에도 적용된다는 것을 알게 될 것이다. 즉 질병의 많은 원인이 있지만, 그것들의 생리적이고 증상적인 수준에서의 발현은 종종 놀랍도록 유사하다.

왜 2등급? 전반적으로 지문의 어휘 수준이 높고, 주어진 문장의 Such a system과 연결될 만한 함정들이 골고루 있어서 헷갈릴 수 있는 2등급 대비 문제이다. 수량을 나타내는 표현이 갑자기 전환되는 부분을 잘 찾으면 정답을 쉽게 고를 수 있다.

| 문제 풀이 순서 |

1st 주어진 문장을 해석하고 핵심 내용과 연결어, 지시어 등을 확인한다.

Such a system can only hope to be stable if only a smaller number of collective ways of being may emerge.
이러한 시스템은 더 적은 수의 존재의 집합적인 방식이 나타날 때만 오직 안정적이기를 기대할 수 있다.

➡ **주어진 문장 앞:** 앞의 내용을 다시 언급하는 Such a system과 존재의 집합적 방식이 적은 경우에만 시스템이 안정적임을 강조하는 only가 있으므로 **단서** 그 시스템이 무엇인지, 그리고 시스템이 불안정한 상황과 그 원인이 먼저 나올 것이다. **발상**

2nd 각 선택지의 앞뒤 흐름이 매끄러운지 확인한다.

①의 앞 문장과 뒤 문장

앞 문장: 생명은 물리학자들이 '고차원 시스템'이라고 부를 수 있는 것인데 이는 많은 일이 발생하고 있다고 말하는 그들의 멋진 방식이다.
뒤 문장: 단 하나의 세포 내에서도 여러 분자 간의 가능한 상호 작용의 수는 매우 크다.

➡ 주어진 문장에서 언급된 Such a system이 생명이라는 '고차원 시스템'임을 알 수 있다. 시스템이 무엇인지와 그 특징이 모두 나왔지만, 생명은 많은 일이 발생하는 고차원 시스템이라는 내용과 단 하나의 세포에도 분자 간 상호 작용이 많다는 내용이 자연스럽게 이어지므로 다음 내용도 살펴봐야 한다.
▶ 주어진 문장이 ①에 들어갈 수 없음

②의 앞 문장과 뒤 문장

앞 문장: ①의 뒤 문장과 같음
뒤 문장: 예를 들어 인간 배아의 발달로부터 나올 수 있는 것은 오직 제한된 수의 조직과 신체 형태이다.

➡ 하나의 세포에도 분자 간 상호 작용의 수가 매우 '크다'라는 앞 문장의 내용과 인간 배아의 발달에서 '제한된' 수의 조직과 신체 형태가 나온다는 뒤 문장의 내용이 서로 이어지지 않는다. 제한적인 수가 앞에 나와야 하는데, 주어진 문장에서 존재의 집합적 방식의 수가 '적을' 때만 '이러한 시스템'이 안정적이라고 했다. 따라서 경우의 수가 많은(불안정한) 고차원 시스템(생명)에서 존재가 안정적으로 구성되려면 경우의 수가 제한적이어야 한다는 흐름으로 적절하게 두 내용을 이어준다.
▶ 주어진 문장이 ②에 들어가야 함

③의 앞 문장과 뒤 문장

앞 문장: ②의 뒤 문장과 같음
뒤 문장: 1942년에 생물학자 Conrad Waddington은 이러한 극적인 결과의 제한을 '운하화'라고 불렀다.

➡ 인간 배아에서 나올 수 있는 결과의 제한성에 대해서 한 생물학자가 '운하화' 이론이라고 이름을 붙였다는 내용으로 이어진다. ▶ 주어진 문장이 ③에 들어갈 수 없음

④의 앞 문장과 뒤 문장

앞 문장: ③의 뒤 문장과 같음
뒤 문장: 오히려 울퉁불퉁한 경관에 있는 공이 이 계곡 혹은 또 다른 계곡의 바닥으로 반드시 굴러가야 하는 것처럼, 유기체는 적은 수의 명확하게 정의된 가능한 상태 사이에서 바뀔 수 있지만 그것들 사이에 있는 무작위의 상태로 존재할 수는 없다.

➡ '운하화'를 '계곡에서 굴러가는 공'에 비유하여 설명한다.
▶ 주어진 문장이 ④에 들어갈 수 없음

⑤의 앞 문장과 뒤 문장

앞 문장: ④의 뒤 문장과 같음
뒤 문장: 우리는 이것이 건강과 질병에도 적용된다는 것을 알게 될 것이다. 즉 질병의 많은 원인이 있지만, 그것들의 생리적이고 증상적인 수준에서의 발현은 종종 놀랍도록 유사하다.

➡ 생명의 '운하화'가 우리의 건강과 질병에도 적용된다는 점을 부연 설명한다.
▶ 주어진 문장이 ⑤에 들어갈 수 없음

P 35 정답 ② ✪ 1등급 대비 [정답률 38%]

＊현재까지 지속되는 실용적 목적의 밤하늘 관찰

글의 흐름으로 보아, 주어진 문장이 들어가기에 가장 적절한 곳을 고르시오.

Since the dawn of civilization, / our ancestors created myths / and told legendary stories / about the night sky. //
문명의 시작부터 / 우리 선조들은 신화를 만들었다 / 그리고 전설적 이야기를 했다 / 밤하늘에 대해 **단서 1** 과거에 밤하늘에 대한 전설적 이야기를 했다고 언급함

We are connected to the night sky / in many ways. // **단서 2** '과거'부터 지금까지 계속 밤하늘이 사람들에게 영감을 주었음
우리는 밤하늘과 연결되어 있다 / 많은 방식으로 //
(①) It has always inspired people / to wonder / and to imagine. //
그것은 항상 사람들에게 영감을 주었다 / 궁금해하도록 / 그리고 상상하도록 //
단서 3 those narratives를 통해 앞에 어떤 이야기가 먼저 언급됐음을 알 수 있음
(②) Elements of those narratives / became embedded / in the social and cultural identities / of many generations. //
그러한 이야기들의 요소들은 / 깊이 새겨졌다 / 사회적 그리고 문화적 정체성에 / 여러 세대의 //
(③) On a practical level, / the night sky helped past generations / to keep track of time / and create calendars — / 실용적인 수준에서 /
밤하늘은 과거 세대들을 도왔다 / 시간을 기록하도록 / 그리고 달력을 만들도록 /
essential to developing societies / as aids / to farming and seasonal gathering. //
이는 사회를 발전시키는 데 필수적이었다 / 보조 도구로서 / 농업과 계절에 따른 수확의 //
(④) For many centuries, / it also provided / a useful navigation tool, / vital / for commerce / and for exploring new worlds. //
수 세기 동안 / 그것은 또한 제공하였다 / 유용한 항해 도구를 / 필수적인 / 무역에 / 그리고 새로운 세계를 탐험하는 데 //
(⑤) Even in modern times, / many people / in remote areas of the planet / observe the night sky / for such practical purposes. //
심지어 현대에도 / 많은 사람이 / 지구의 외딴 지역에 있는 / 밤하늘을 관찰한다 / 그러한 실용적인 목적을 위해 //

- civilization ⓝ 문명 ・ancestor ⓝ 선조 ・myth ⓝ 신화
- legendary ⓐ 전설의 ・inspire ⓥ 영감을 주다
- wonder ⓥ 궁금해하다 ・element ⓝ 요소 ・narrative ⓝ 이야기
- identity ⓝ 정체성 ・practical ⓐ 실용적인
- keep track of ~을 기록하다 ・aid ⓝ 보조 도구
- seasonal ⓐ 계절에 따른 ・gathering ⓝ 수확
- navigation ⓝ 항해 ・vital ⓐ 필수적인 ・explore ⓥ 탐험하다
- remote ⓐ 외딴 ・observe ⓥ 관찰하다 ・purpose ⓝ 목적

우리는 많은 방식으로 밤하늘과 연결되어 있다. (①) 그것은 항상 사람들이 궁금해하고 상상하도록 영감을 주었다. (② 문명의 시작부터, 우리 선조들은 밤하늘에 대해 신화를 만들었고 전설적 이야기를 했다.) 그러한 이야기들의 요소들은 여러 세대의 사회적 그리고 문화적 정체성에 깊이 새겨졌다. (③) 실용적인 수준에서, 밤하늘은 과거 세대들이 시간을 기록하고 달력을 만들도록 도왔고 이는 농업과 계절에 따른 수확의 보조 도구로서 사회를 발전시키는 데 필수적이었다. (④) 수 세기 동안, 그것은 또한 무역과 새로운 세계를 탐험하는 데 필수적인 유용한 항해 도구를 제공하였다. (⑤) 심지어 현대에도, 지구의 외딴 지역에 있는 많은 사람이 그러한 실용적인 목적을 위해 밤하늘을 관찰한다.

왜 1등급? 주어진 문장에서 언급한 '전설적 이야기'가 다음에 어떻게 이어지는지, 글에서 It이나 those narratives로 시작하는 문장에 주목해서 이런 단서들이 가리키는 것이 무엇인지 생각해야 정답을 고를 수 있는 1등급 대비 문제이다.

| 문제 풀이 순서 |

1st 주어진 문장을 해석하고 문제를 풀 단서를 얻는다.

Since the dawn of civilization, our ancestors created myths and told legendary stories about the night sky.
문명의 시작부터, 우리 선조들은 밤하늘에 대해 신화를 만들었고 전설적 이야기를 했다.
단서 1

➡ 밤하늘(the night sky)에 대한 신화와 전설적 이야기와 관련된 내용을 나머지 글에서 찾아야 한다.

2nd 각 선택지의 앞뒤 흐름이 매끄러운지 확인한다.

- ①의 앞 문장과 뒤 문장
앞 문장: 우리는 많은 방식으로 밤하늘과 연결되어 있다.
뒤 문장: 그것은(It)은 항상 사람들이 궁금해하고 상상하도록 영감을 주었다.
단서 2

➡ 뒤 문장의 It이 가리키는 것이 앞 문장의 the night sky이다. 우리가 밤하늘과 연결되어 있다는 언급이 뒤 문장에서 밤하늘이 항상 사람들이 궁금해하고 상상하도록 했다는 내용으로 자연스럽게 연결된다.
▶ 주어진 문장이 ①에 들어갈 수 없음

- ②의 앞 문장과 뒤 문장
앞 문장: ①의 뒤 문장과 같음
뒤 문장: 그러한(those) 이야기들의 요소들은 여러 세대의 사회적 그리고 문화적 정체성에 깊이 새겨졌다. 단서 3

➡ 뒤 문장에 나오는 '그러한 이야기들의 요소들(Elements of those narratives)'이 앞에 나오지 않았다. ▶ 주어진 문장이 ②에 들어가야 함
➡ 주어진 문장이 ②에 들어가면, 〈문명의 시작부터, 우리 선조들은 밤하늘에 대해 신화를 만들었고 전설적 이야기를 했다. 그러한 이야기들의 요소들은 여러 세대의 사회적 그리고 문화적 정체성에 깊이 새겨졌다.〉라는 자연스러운 흐름이 된다.

- ③의 앞 문장과 뒤 문장
앞 문장: ②의 뒤 문장과 같음
뒤 문장: 실용적인 수준에서, 밤하늘은 과거 세대들이 시간을 기록하고 달력을 만들도록 도왔고 이는 농업과 계절에 따른 수확의 보조 도구로서 사회를 발전시키는 데 필수적이었다.

➡ 밤하늘에 대한 이야기들의 요소들이 사회적, 문화적 정체성에 새겨졌다고 했는데, 시간을 기록하고 달력을 만드는 것과 같은 실용적인 측면에 대한 내용으로 자연스럽게 이어진다.
▶ 주어진 문장이 ③에 들어갈 수 없음

- ④의 앞 문장과 뒤 문장
앞 문장: ③의 뒤 문장과 같음
뒤 문장: 수 세기 동안, 그것은(it)은 또한 무역과 새로운 세계를 탐험하는 데 필수적인 유용한 항해 도구를 제공하였다.

➡ 뒤 문장의 it도 밤하늘을 가리킨다. 밤하늘은 앞에서 말한 실용적인 측면 외에도 무역과 같은 분야에서도 유용한 역할을 했다는 것이다.
▶ 주어진 문장이 ④에 들어갈 수 없음

- ⑤의 앞 문장과 뒤 문장
앞 문장: ④의 뒤 문장과 같음
뒤 문장: 심지어 현대에도, 지구의 외딴 지역에 있는 많은 사람이 그러한 (such) 실용적인 목적을 위해 밤하늘을 관찰한다.

➡ such practical purposes는 지금까지 앞에서 말한 밤하늘 관찰의 실용적인 역할들이다.
▶ 주어진 문장이 ⑤에 들어갈 수 없음

━━━━━ 어법 특강 ━━━━━

＊ 병렬 구조를 이루는 등위접속사
– and, but, or, so 등은 등위접속사로 두 개 이상의 단어, 구, 절을 연결한다. 이 때 동일한 품사와 문법적으로 같은 성분을 연결해야 한다.
• Don't forget to prepare *a cutting board* and *a knife*.
  (도마와 칼을 준비할 것을 잊지 마세요.) 단어와 단어를 연결
• *You can squeeze oranges by hand,* but *it's easier if you use a squeezer.*
  문장과 문장을 연결
  (당신은 손으로 오렌지를 짤 수 있지만, 압착기를 사용하면 더 쉬워요.)

P 36 정답 ④ ━━━━━ ★ 1등급 대비 [정답률 39%]

＊동물의 유연성 발달에 중요한 유년기

글의 흐름으로 보아, 주어진 문장이 들어가기에 가장 적절한 곳을 고르시오. [3점]

By comparison, / birds with the longest childhoods, / those =birds
주격 관계대명사
that migrate with their parents, / tend to have the most
efficient migration routes. // 단서 1 유년기가 길고 부모와 이동한 새는 가장 효율적인 이동 경로를 알고 있음
이에 비해 / 유년기가 가장 길고 / 부모와 함께 이동하는 새는 / 가장 효율적인 이동 경로를 가지고 있는 경향이 있다 //

동명사구 주어(단수 취급)   단수 동사
Spending time as children / allows animals to learn about their environment. //
유년기를 보내는 것은 / 동물에게 환경에 대해 배울 수 있게 한다 //

Without childhood, / animals must **rely** more fully on hardware, / and therefore **be** less flexible. //
                    └─ 병렬 구조 ─┘
유년기가 없으면 / 동물은 하드웨어에 더 많이 의존해야 한다 / 그러므로 유연성이 떨어질 수밖에 없다 //

(①) Among migratory bird species, / **those** that are born 복수 주어
knowing how, when, and where to migrate /
철새 중에서도 / 언제, 어디로, 어떻게 이동해야 하는지를 알고 태어나는 새들은 /
                                        관계사절(instructions 수식)
— those that are migrating entirely with instructions / **they were born with** / — sometimes **have** very inefficient migration routes. //
복수 동사
즉 전적으로 지침에 따라 이동하는 새들은 / 태어날 때부터 주어진 / 때때로 매우 비효율적인 이동 경로를 가지고 있다 //

앞에 주격 관계대명사와 be동사가 생략됨   분사구문
(②) These birds, **born knowing how to migrate**, / don't adapt easily. //
이동 방법을 알고 태어난 새들은 / 쉽게 적응하지 못한다 //

(③) So when **lakes dry up**, / **forest becomes farmland**, / or **climate change pushes breeding grounds farther north**, /
                              └── 병렬 구조(부사절) ──┘
따라서 호수가 마르거나 / 숲이 농지로 바뀌거나 / 기후 변화로 번식지가 더 북쪽으로 밀려났을 때 /

주격 관계대명사＊   단서 2 이동하는 방법을 알고 태어난 새들은 기존의 경로로만 날아감
those birds **that** are born knowing how to migrate / keep flying by the old rules and maps. //
이동하는 방법을 알고 태어난 새들은 / 기존의 규칙과 지도를 따라 계속 날아간다 //

(④) Childhood facilitates the passing on of cultural information, / and culture can evolve faster than genes. //
유년기는 문화적 정보의 전달을 촉진하며 / 문화는 유전자보다 더 빠르게 진화할 수 있다 // **단서3** 유년기는 문화적 정보의 전달을 촉진함
(⑤) Childhood gives flexibility / in a changing world. //
유년기는 유연성을 제공한다 / 변화하는 세상에서 //

- migrate ⓥ 이동하다   - route ⓝ 경로   - adapt ⓥ 적응하다
- breeding ⓝ 번식   - farther ⓐⓓ 더 멀리   - facilitate ⓥ 촉진하다
- passing on 전달, 대물림   - evolve ⓥ 진화하다   - gene ⓝ 유전자
- flexibility ⓝ 유연성

동물은 유년기를 보내면서 환경에 대해 배울 수 있다. 유년기가 없으면, 동물은 하드웨어에 더 많이 의존해야 하므로 유연성이 떨어질 수밖에 없다. (①) 철새 중에서도 언제, 어디로, 어떻게 이동해야 하는지를 알고 태어나는 새들, 즉 전적으로 태어날 때부터 주어진 지침에 따라 이동하는 새들은 때때로 매우 비효율적인 이동 경로를 가지고 있다. (②) 이동 방법을 알고 태어난 새들은 쉽게 적응하지 못한다. (③) 따라서 호수가 마르거나 숲이 농지로 바뀌거나 기후 변화로 번식지가 더 북쪽으로 밀려났을 때, 이동하는 방법을 알고 태어난 새들은 기존의 규칙과 지도를 따라 계속 날아간다. (④ 이에 비해 유년기가 가장 길고 부모와 함께 이동하는 새는 가장 효율적인 이동 경로를 가지고 있는 경향이 있다.) 유년기는 문화적 정보의 전달을 촉진하며, 문화는 유전자보다 더 빠르게 진화할 수 있다. (⑤) 유년기는 변화하는 세상에서 유연성을 제공한다.

왜 1등급? 접속사 so로 시작하는 문장을 비롯하여, 주어진 문장의 birds를 가리키는 듯한 these birds로 시작하는 문장이 있어서 자칫하면 오답을 고르기 쉬운 1등급 대비 문제이다. 주어진 문장이 By comparison으로 시작하며 앞 문장과 대조되는 내용을 나타내므로, 유년기가 없는 동물(철새)에서 유년기가 있는 동물(부모와 함께 이동하는 새)로 내용의 흐름이 전환되는 부분을 찾아야 한다.

| 문제 풀이 순서 |

1st 주어진 문장을 해석하고, 연결어, 지시어 등을 확인한다.

By comparison, birds with the longest childhoods, and those that migrate with their parents, tend to have the most efficient migration routes.
이에 비해 유년기가 가장 길고 부모와 함께 이동하는 새는 가장 효율적인 이동 경로를 가지고 있는 경향이 있다.

→ 주어진 문장 앞: 대조를 나타내는 By comparison이 있으므로, **단서** 효율적인 이동 경로를 가지지 못한 새에 관한 내용이 제시될 것이다. **발상**

2nd 각 선택지의 앞뒤 흐름이 매끄러운지 확인한다.

- ①의 앞 문장과 뒤 문장
앞 문장: 유년기가 없으면, 동물은 하드웨어에 더 많이 의존해야 하므로 유연성이 떨어질 수밖에 없다.
뒤 문장: 철새 중에서도 언제, 어디로, 어떻게 이동해야 하는지를 알고 태어나는 새들, 즉 전적으로 태어날 때부터 주어진 지침에 따라 이동하는 새들은 때때로 매우 비효율적인 이동 경로를 가지고 있다.
→ 유년기가 없는 동물은 유연성이 떨어진다는 내용 바로 뒤에, 그 예시로서 태어날 때부터 주어진 지침에 따라 이동하는 일부 철새들은 매우 비효율적인 이동 경로를 가진다는 내용이 자연스럽게 이어진다. ▶ 주어진 문장이 ①에 들어갈 수 없음

- ②의 앞 문장과 뒤 문장
앞 문장: ①의 뒤 문장과 같음
뒤 문장: 이동 방법을 알고 태어난 새들은 쉽게 적응하지 못한다.
→ 주어진 지침에 따라 이동하는 새들은 비효율적인 경로를 가지게 되고, 그러한 새들은 쉽게 적응하지 못하게 된다는 내용이 자연스럽게 이어진다.
▶ 주어진 문장이 ②에 들어갈 수 없음

- ③의 앞 문장과 뒤 문장
앞 문장: ②의 뒤 문장과 같음
뒤 문장: 따라서 호수가 마르거나 숲이 농지로 바뀌거나 기후 변화로 번식지가 더 북쪽으로 밀려났을 때, 이동하는 방법을 알고 태어난 새들은 기존의 규칙과 지도를 따라 계속 날아간다.
→ 이동 방법을 알고 태어난 새들은 쉽게 적응하지 못하므로 환경이 바뀌어도 계속 기존의 이동 경로를 따라 날아간다는 내용으로 이어진다.
▶ 주어진 문장이 ③에 들어갈 수 없음

- ④의 앞 문장과 뒤 문장
앞 문장: ③의 뒤 문장과 같음
뒤 문장: 유년기는 문화적 정보의 전달을 촉진하며, 문화는 유전자보다 더 빠르게 진화할 수 있다.
→ 이동 방법을 알고 태어난 새들은 기존의 방식대로 계속 날아간다는 내용과 유년기가 주는 장점에 관한 내용이 서로 이어지지 않는다. 비효율적인 이동 경로를 가지는 새들에 관한 내용이 끝나고, 반대되는 내용을 나타내는 By comparison으로 시작되며 효율적인 이동 경로를 가지는 새들을 언급하는 주어진 문장이 와야 한다.
▶ 주어진 문장이 ④에 들어가야 함

- ⑤의 앞 문장과 뒤 문장
앞 문장: ④의 뒤 문장과 같음
뒤 문장: 유년기는 변화하는 세상에서 유연성을 제공한다.
→ 문화적 정보의 전달을 촉진하고 빠르게 진화하기 때문에 유년기는 동물에게 유연성을 제공한다는 내용이 자연스럽게 이어진다.
▶ 주어진 문장이 ⑤에 들어갈 수 없음

--- **어법 특강** ---

＊ 주격 관계대명사
– 주어를 대신하여 절과 절을 연결하는 접속사 역할을 할 때 주격 관계대명사를 쓴다. 주격 관계대명사절의 동사는 선행사와 수를 일치시켜야 한다는 것에 주의한다.
- What's the name of the person who won the lottery?
  '사람'을 나타내는 선행사를 수식하는 who
  (복권에 당첨되었던 그 사람의 이름은 무엇이죠?)
- It is important to eat food which is good for your health.
  단수 선행사   단수 동사
  (네 건강에 좋은 음식을 먹는 것은 중요하다.)
- Green turtles and seals are marine animals that are endangered.
  복수 선행사   복수 동사
  (바다거북과 바다표범은 멸종 위기에 처한 해양 동물들입니다.)

P 어휘 Review 정답 — 문제편 p. 257

01 조상	11 prey upon	21 restricted
02 생태계	12 contrary to	22 mess
03 간격	13 derive from	23 abstract
04 압축하다	14 a series of	24 harden
05 화합물	15 back and forth	25 lungs
06 intake	16 infant	26 navigate
07 rightly	17 analogy	27 assumption
08 constantly	18 disturbance	28 fairness
09 channel	19 countless	29 tissues
10 drought	20 transfer	30 pillow

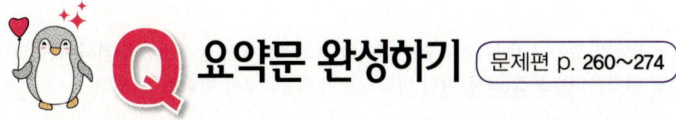
Q 01 정답 ① *의식적 마음과 잠재의식적 마음의 다른 기능

복수 선행사 / 복수 동사(수 일치)
The mind has parts / that are known as the conscious mind and the subconscious mind. //
마음은 부분을 갖고 있다 / 의식적 마음과 잠재의식적 마음이라고 알려진 //

부사적 용법
The subconscious mind is very fast to act / and doesn't deal with emotions. //
잠재의식적 마음은 매우 빠르게 작동하며 / 감정을 다루지 않는다 //

'~을 다루다'
It deals with / memories of your responses to life, your memories and recognition. //
그것은 다룬다 / 여러분의 삶에 대한 반응의 기억, 기억 및 인식을 //

목적격 관계대명사(선행사: the one)
However, the conscious mind is the one / that you have more control over. // 단서 1 우리는 의식적 마음에 더 많은 통제력을 가짐
그러나 의식적 마음은 부분이다 / 여러분이 더 많은 통제력을 갖고 있는 //

You think. //
여러분은 생각한다 //

whether A or B: A인지 B인지
You can choose / whether to carry on a thought / or to add emotion to it / 단서 2 (의식적 마음에서는) 생각을 계속할지 그 생각에 감정을 더할지 선택할 수 있음
여러분은 선택할 수 있다 / 생각을 계속할지 / 또는 그 생각에 감정을 더할지를 /

주격 관계대명사(선행사: the part)
and this is the part of your mind / that lets you down frequently
과거분사가 이끄는 분사구문
/ because — fueled by emotions / — you make the wrong decisions / time and time again. //
그리고 이것은 마음의 부분이기도 하다 / 여러분을 빈번하게 낙담시키는 / 왜냐하면 감정에 북받쳐 / 잘못된 결정을 내리게 만들기 때문에 / 반복해서 //

주격 관계대명사(선행사: negativities)
When your judgment is clouded / by emotions, / this puts in biases and all kinds of other negativities / that hold you back. //
여러분의 판단력이 흐려질 때 / 감정에 의해 / 이것은 편견과 그 밖의 모든 종류의 부정성을 자리 잡게 만든다 / 여러분을 억제하는 //

Scared of spiders? //
거미를 무서워하는가 //

Scared of the dark? //
어둠을 무서워하는가 //

There are reasons for all of these fears, / but they originate in the conscious mind. //
이러한 두려움 전부 이유가 있지만 / 그것들은 의식적 마음에서 비롯된다 //

They only become real fears / when the subconscious mind records your reactions. // 단서 3 잠재의식적 마음이 반응을 기록할 때 실제 두려움이 됨
그것들은 오직 실제 두려움이 된다 / 잠재의식적 마음이 여러분의 반응을 기록할 때 //

'반면에'
→ While the controllable conscious mind deals with / thoughts and (A) emotions, / the fast-acting subconscious mind / stores
분사구문
your responses, / (B) forming real fears. //
통제할 수 있는 의식적 마음은 다루지만 / 생각과 감정을 / 빠르게 작동하는 잠재의식적 마음이 / 여러분의 반응을 저장하고 / 이는 실제 두려움을 형성한다 //

- conscious ⓐ 의식적인 · subconscious ⓐ 잠재의식적인
- recognition ⓝ 인식 · frequently ⓐⓓ 자주, 빈번히
- judgment ⓝ 판단(력) · cloud ⓥ (기억력, 판단력 등을) 흐리게 하다
- bias ⓝ 편견 · negativity ⓝ 부정성 · fear ⓝ 두려움
- originate ⓥ 비롯되다 · controllable ⓐ 통제할 수 있는
- overcome ⓥ 극복하다

마음은 의식적 마음과 잠재의식적 마음이라고 알려진 부분을 갖고 있다. 잠재의식적 마음은 매우 빠르게 작동하며 감정을 다루지 않는다. 그것은 여러분의 삶에 대한 반응의 기억, 기억 및 인식을 다룬다. 그러나 의식적 마음은 여러분이 더 많은 통제력을 갖고 있는 부분이다. 여러분은 생각한다. 여러분은 생각을 계속할지 또는 그 생각에 감정을 더할지를 선택할 수 있다. 그리고 이것은 감정에 북받쳐 잘못된 결정을 반복해서 내리게 만들기 때문에 여러분을 빈번하게 낙담시키는 마음의 부분이기도 하다. 감정에 의해 여러분의 판단력이 흐려질 때 이것은 편견과 그 밖의 여러분을 억제하는 모든 종류의 부정성을 자리 잡게 만든다. 거미를 무서워하는가? 어둠을 무서워하는가? 이러한 두려움 전부 이유가 있지만 그것들은 의식적 마음에서 비롯된다. 그것들은 오직 잠재의식적 마음이 여러분의 반응을 기록할 때 실제 두려움이 된다.

→ 통제할 수 있는 의식적 마음은 생각과 (A) 감정을 다루지만, 빠르게 작동하는 잠재의식적 마음이 여러분의 반응을 저장하고, 이는 실제 두려움을 (B) 형성한다.

다음 글의 내용을 한 문장으로 요약하고자 한다. 빈칸 (A), (B)에 들어갈 말로 가장 적절한 것은?

	(A)		(B)	
①	emotions 감정	—	forming 형성하면서	의식적 마음은 생각에 감정을 더할 수 있으며 잠재의식적 마음은 반응을 저장하여 실제 두려움을 형성함
②	actions 행동	—	overcoming 극복하면서	의식적 마음이 행동을 다루는지 알 수 없음
③	emotions	—	overcoming	잠재의식적 마음이 실제 두려움을 극복한다는 언급이 없음
④	actions	—	avoiding 피하면서	잠재의식적 마음이 실제 두려움을 피한다는 내용이 없음
⑤	moralities 도덕성	—	forming	의식적 마음이 도덕성을 다루는지 이 글에서는 알 수 없음

왜 정답? ★★※ [정답률 67%]

(A):
- 그러나 의식적 마음은 여러분이 더 많은 통제력을 갖고 있는 부분이다. 단서 1
- 여러분은 생각을 계속할지 또는 그 생각에 감정을 더할지를 선택할 수 있다. 단서 2
→ 우리가 의식적 마음에 더 많은 통제력을 갖고 있고 생각을 계속할지 감정을 생각에 더할지 선택할 수 있다고 했기 때문에 통제할 수 있는 의식적 마음이 생각과 '감정(emotions)'을 다룬다.

(B):
- 그것들은 오직 잠재의식적 마음이 여러분의 반응을 기록할 때 실제 두려움이 된다. 단서 3
→ 잠재의식적 마음이 실제 두려움을 '형성하면서(forming)' 우리의 반응을 기록한다(=저장한다).
▶ 요약문의 빈칸에는 각각 ① '감정'과 '형성하면서'가 들어가야 함

왜 오답?
② 이 글을 통해서는 의식적 마음이 행동을 다루는지 알 수 없다.
③ 잠재의식적 마음이 실제 두려움을 형성한다고 했지만 이를 극복하는지는 언급되지 않았다.
④ 잠재의식적 마음은 실제 두려움을 피하는 것이 아니라 반응을 기록하여 실제 두려움을 형성한다.
⑤ 이 글에서는 의식적 마음과 도덕성의 관계가 나오지 않는다.

＊ 글의 흐름

도입	마음은 의식적 마음과 잠재의식적 마음이라고 알려진 부분을 가지고 있음
전개	잠재의식적 마음은 매우 빠르게 작동하며 삶에 대한 반응의 기억, 기억 및 인식을 다루는 반면에, 의식적 마음은 생각을 계속할지 또는 그 생각에 감정을 더할지를 선택할 수 있음
부연	의식적 마음이 다루는 감정 때문에 잘못된 결정을 반복적으로 내리거나 판단력이 흐려져서 편견과 부정성을 자리 잡게 만들기도 함
마무리	잠재의식적 마음이 반응을 저장할 때 실제 두려움이 됨

정답 ① *포괄적 디지털 디자인의 필요성 ────

Over the last several decades, / scholars have developed standards / for how best to create, organize, present, and preserve digital information / for future generations. //
전치사의 목적어(의문사+to부정사)
지난 수십 년 동안 / 학자들은 표준을 개발해 왔다 / 디지털 정보를 가장 잘 만들고, 정리하고, 제시하고, 보존하는 방법에 대한 / 미래 세대를 위해 //

선행사를 포함하는 관계대명사절   본동사
What has remained neglected for the most part, / however, / are the needs of people with disabilities. // 단서1 장애인의 요구는 여전히 무시되어 왔음
여전히 대부분 무시되어온 것은 / 그러나 / 장애가 있는 사람들의 요구들이다 //

As a result, / many of the otherwise most valuable digital resources are useless / for people who are deaf or hard of hearing, /
그 결과 / 그렇지 않은 경우라면 가장 가치 있었을 디지털 자원 중 상당수가 무용지물이 되고 있다 / 청각 장애가 있거나 듣는 것이 힘든 사람에게 /
B as well as A : A뿐만 아니라 B도   병렬 구조(전치사+명사+관계사절)
as well as for people who are blind, / have low vision, / or have difficulty distinguishing particular colors. //
시각 장애가 있는 사람뿐만 아니라 / 시력이 낮거나 / 특정 색상을 구분하기 어려운 //

현재분사구(professionals 수식)
While professionals working in educational technology and commercial web design / have made significant progress in meeting the needs of such users, /
교육 기술 및 상업용 웹디자인에 종사하는 전문가들이 / 이러한 사용자의 요구를 충족시키는 데 상당한 진전을 이루었지만 /
현재분사구(scholars 수식)   take ~ into account: ~을 고려하다
some scholars creating digital projects / all too often fail to take these needs into account. // 단서2 디지털 프로젝트에서 장애인의 요구를 고려하지 못하는 경우가 많음
디지털 프로젝트를 만드는 일부 학자들은 / 이러한 요구를 고려하지 못하는 경우가 너무 많다 //
단서3 최대한 모두의 요구를 충족시킬 수 있는 디자인이 필요함   부사절 접속사(조건)
This situation would be much improved / if more projects
동격절 접속사
embraced the idea / that we should always keep the largest possible audience in mind / as we make design decisions, /
이러한 상황은 훨씬 개선될 것이다 / 더 많은 프로젝트에서 생각을 받아들인다면 / 최대한 많은 사용자를 항상 염두에 두어야 한다고 / 디자인을 결정할 때 /
목적어절 접속사
ensuring that our final product serves the needs of those with disabilities / as well as those without. //
= people
최종 제품이 장애가 있는 사람들의 요구를 충족시킬 수 있도록 하면서 / 장애가 없는 사람들의 요구뿐만 아니라 //

→ The needs of people with disabilities / have often been (A)
계속적 용법의 주격 관계대명사(앞 문장 전체 수식)
overlooked in digital projects, / which could be changed / by adopting a(n) (B) inclusive design. //
장애가 있는 사람들의 요구는 / 디지털 프로젝트에서 종종 간과되어 왔으며 / 이것은 변화될 수 있다 / 포괄(포용)적인 디자인을 채택함으로써 //

• scholar ⓝ 학자   • organize ⓥ 정리하다   • present ⓥ 제시하다
• preserve ⓥ 보존하다   • neglect ⓥ 소홀히 하다
• disability ⓝ 장애   • distinguish ⓥ 구별하다
• embrace ⓥ 포용하다   • ensure ⓥ 반드시 ~ 하게 하다

지난 수십 년 동안 학자들은 미래 세대를 위해 디지털 정보를 가장 잘 만들고, 정리하고, 제시하고, 보존하는 방법에 대한 표준을 개발해 왔다. 그러나 대부분의 경우 장애가 있는 사람들의 요구는 여전히 무시되어 왔다. 그 결과, 청각 장애가 있거나 듣는 것이 힘든 사람, 시각 장애가 있거나 시력이 낮거나 특정 색상을 구분하기 어려운 사람에게는 그렇지 않은 경우라면 가장 가치 있었을 디지털 자원 중 상당수가 무용지물이 되고 있다. 교육 기술 및 상업용 웹 디자인에 종사하는 전문가들은 이러한 사용자의 요구를 충족시키는 데 상당한 진전을 이루었지만, 디지털 프로젝트를 만드는 일부 학자들은 이러한 요구를 고려하지 못하는 경우가 너무 많다. 더 많은 프로젝트에서 디자인을 결정할 때 최대한 많은 사용자를 항상 염두에 두고 최종 제품이 장애가 있는 사람들과 그렇지 않은 사람들 모두의 요구를 충족시킬 수 있도록 해야 한다는 생각을 받아들인다면 이러한 상황은 훨씬 개선될 것이다.

→ 장애가 있는 사람들의 요구는 디지털 프로젝트에서 종종 (A) 간과되어 왔으며, 이것은 (B) 포괄(포용)적인 디자인을 채택함으로써 변화될 수 있다.

다음 글의 내용을 한 문장으로 요약하고자 한다. 빈칸 (A), (B)에 들어갈 말로 가장 적절한 것은?

	(A)		(B)
①	overlooked 간과된	—	inclusive 포괄적인	장애인의 요구는 간과되어 왔고 이를 수용할 수 있는 포괄적인 디자인이 필요함
②	accepted 수용된	—	practical 실용적인	장애인의 요구는 수용되지 않았으며 실용적인 디자인이 필요한 것이 아님
③	considered 고려된	—	inclusive	장애인의 요구는 고려되지 않았음
④	accepted	—	abstract 추상적인	─ 추상적인 디자인이 필요한 것이 아님
⑤	overlooked	—	abstract	

| 문제 풀이 순서 | ★★★ [정답률 55%]

1st 요약문을 통해 글에서 무엇을 찾아야 하는지 확인한다.

요약문	장애가 있는 사람들의 요구는 디지털 프로젝트에서 종종 (A) _____ 왔으며, 이것은 (B) _____ 디자인을 채택함으로써 변화될 수 있다.

→ 글에서 찾아야 하는 것
  (A): 장애가 있는 사람들의 요구가 디지털 프로젝트에서 종종 간과되어, 수용되어, 고려되어 왔는지
  (B): 이것이 포괄적인, 실용적인, 추상적인 디자인을 채택함으로써 변화될 수 있는지

2nd 글의 내용을 파악하여 요약문을 완성한다.

• 디지털 정보에 관한 표준 개발의 대부분의 경우 장애가 있는 사람들의 요구는 여전히 무시되어 왔음 단서1
• 디지털 프로젝트를 만드는 일부 학자들은 이러한 요구를 고려하지 못하는 경우가 너무 많음 단서2
• 더 많은 프로젝트에서 디자인을 결정할 때 최대한 많은 사용자를 항상 염두에 두어야 한다는 생각을 받아들인다면 이러한 상황은 훨씬 개선될 것임 단서3

→ 장애인의 요구가 '간과된' 것이므로 (A)에는 ①, ⑤ '간과된'이 들어가야 하고, 최대한 많은 사용자를 '포함하는' 디자인이 필요한 것이므로 (B)에는 ①, ③ '포괄적인'이 들어가야 한다.
▶ 따라서 정답은 ①임

| 선택지 분석 |

① 장애인의 요구는 간과되어 왔고 이를 수용할 수 있는 포괄적인 디자인이 필요하다.
② 장애인의 요구가 수용되지 않아, 포괄적인 디자인이 필요하다고 말하고 있다.
③ 장애인의 요구는 무시되었다.
④ 장애인의 요구는 수용되지 않았고 추상적인 디자인이 필요한 것도 아니다.
⑤ 추상적인 디자인이 아닌 모두의 요구를 수용할 수 있는 포괄적인 디자인이 필요하다.

Q 03 정답 ① *창의적 사고의 필요성 ────

In the course / of trying to solve a problem with an invention, / you may encounter a brick wall of resistance / when you try to think your way logically through the problem. //
어떤 과정에서 / 발명품을 통해 문제를 해결하려고 하는 / 저항이라는 벽돌 벽에 맞닥뜨릴지도 모른다 / 여러분이 문제를 논리적으로 생각해 나가려고 애쓸 때 //
계속적 용법의 주격 관계대명사
Such logical thinking is a linear type of process, / which uses our reasoning skills. // 단서1 논리적 사고는 선형적 과정임
그러한 논리적 사고는 선형적 과정으로 / 우리의 추론 능력을 활용한다 //
= Logical thinking
This works fine / when we're operating / in the area of / what we know or have experienced. //
이는 잘 작동한다 / 우리가 작업할 때는 / ~의 영역에서 / 알고 있거나 경험해 본 //

However, / when we need to deal with new information, ideas, and viewpoints, / linear thinking will often come up short. //
그러나 / 우리가 새로운 정보, 아이디어, 관점을 다뤄야 할 때 / 선형적 사고로는 흔히 충분하지 않을 것이다 //
단서 2 새로운 아이디어를 다룰 때 선형적(논리적) 사고는 불충분함

On the other hand, / creativity by definition involves / the application of new information to old problems / and the conception of new viewpoints and ideas. //
반면 / 창의성은 정의상 포함한다 / 기존 문제에 대한 새로운 정보의 적용과 / 새로운 관점과 아이디어의 구상을 //

앞 문장의 내용을 가리킴 / 부사절 접속사 (조건)
For this / you will be most effective / if you learn to operate in a nonlinear manner; / that is, use your creative brain. //
이를 위해서 / 여러분은 가장 효과적이 될 것이다 / 여러분이 비선형적 방식으로 작업하는 법을 배운다면 / 즉, 창의적인 뇌를 사용하는 법을 //
단서 3 새로운 아이디어를 다룰 때는 비선형적(창의적) 사고가 효과적임

앞에 Being이 생략된 분사구문
Stated differently, / if you think in a linear manner, / you'll tend to be conservative / and keep coming up with techniques / which are already known. //
다시 말해 / 여러분이 선형적인 방식으로 사고하면 / 보수적으로 되고 / 기술을 계속 떠올리려 할 것이다 / 이미 알려진 //

선행사를 포함하는 관계대명사
This, of course, / is just what you don't want. //
이것이 물론 / 여러분이 원하지 않는 바로 그것이다 //

→ (A) **Logical** thinking works well with familiar problems / but falls short in dealing with new ideas, / for which creative thinking is needed / to come up with (B) **innovative** solutions. //
(전치사 + 계속적 용법의 관계대명사)
논리적 사고는 익숙한 문제에서는 잘 작동하지만 / 새로운 아이디어를 다루는 데에는 불충분한데 / 이를 위해서는 창의적 사고가 필요하다 / 혁신적인 해결책을 생각해 내는 데에 //

- invention ⓝ 발명품
- encounter ⓥ 맞닥뜨리다, 직면하다
- resistance ⓝ 저항
- logically (ad) 논리적으로
- reasoning ⓝ 추론
- viewpoint ⓝ 관점
- by definition 정의상
- application ⓝ 적용
- conception ⓝ 구상
- effective ⓐ 효과적인
- nonlinear ⓐ 비선형적
- manner ⓝ 방식
- state ⓥ 말하다
- innovative ⓐ 혁신적인
- flexible ⓐ 유연한
- instant ⓐ 즉각적인
- proven ⓐ 증명된
- superior ⓐ 우월한
- collaborative ⓐ 협력하는

어떤 발명품을 통해 문제를 해결하려고 하는 과정에서, 여러분이 문제를 논리적으로 생각해 나가려고 애쓸 때 저항이라는 벽돌 벽에 맞닥뜨릴지도 모른다. 그러한 논리적 사고는 선형적 과정으로, 우리의 추론 능력을 활용한다. 이는 우리가 알고 있거나 경험해 본 영역에서 작업할 때는 잘 작동한다. 그러나 우리가 새로운 정보, 아이디어, 관점을 다뤄야 할 때 선형적 사고로는 흔히 충분하지 않을 것이다. 반면, 창의성은 정의상 기존 문제에 대한 새로운 정보의 적용과 새로운 관점과 아이디어의 구상을 포함한다. 이를 위해서 여러분이 비선형적 방식으로 작업하는 법, 즉, 창의적인 뇌를 사용하는 법을 배운다면 여러분은 가장 효과적이 될 것이다. 다시 말해, 여러분이 선형적인 방식으로 사고하면, 보수적으로 되고 이미 알려진 기술을 계속 떠올리려 할 것이다. 이것이 물론 여러분이 원하지 않는 바로 그것이다.
→ (A) 논리적 사고는 익숙한 문제에서는 잘 작동하지만, 새로운 아이디어를 다루는 데에는 불충분한데, 이를 위해서는 창의적 사고가 (B) 혁신적인 해결책을 생각해 내는 데에 필요하다.

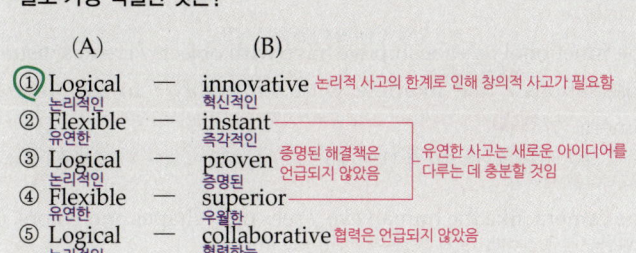

다음 글의 내용을 한 문장으로 요약하고자 한다. 빈칸 (A), (B)에 들어갈 말로 가장 적절한 것은?

(A)		(B)	
① Logical (논리적인)	—	innovative (혁신적인)	논리적 사고의 한계로 인해 창의적 사고가 필요함
② Flexible (유연한)	—	instant (즉각적인)	유연한 사고는 새로운 아이디어를 다루는 데 충분할 것임
③ Logical (논리적인)	—	proven (증명된)	증명된 해결책은 언급되지 않았음
④ Flexible (유연한)	—	superior (우월한)	유연한 사고는 새로운 아이디어를 다루는 데 충분할 것임
⑤ Logical (논리적인)	—	collaborative (협력하는)	협력은 언급되지 않았음

왜 정답? ✽✽✽ [정답률 69%]

(A):
- 논리적 사고는 선형적 과정이다. 단서 1
- 그러나 우리가 새로운 정보, 아이디어, 관점을 다뤄야 할 때 선형적 사고로는 흔히 충분하지 않을 것이다. 단서 2

➡ 선형적(논리적) 사고는 새로운 아이디어를 다뤄야 할 때는 충분하지 않을 것이라고 했다.
▶ (A)에는 ①, ③, ⑤ Logical이 들어가야 함

(B):
- 이를 위해서 여러분이 비선형적 방식으로 작업하는 법, 즉, 창의적인 뇌를 사용하는 법을 배운다면 여러분은 가장 효과적이 될 것이다. 단서 3

➡ 선형적 사고로 해결할 수 없는 일, 즉 새로운(혁신적인) 해결책을 생각하려면 비선형적(창의적) 사고가 효과적이라고 했다.
▶ (B)에는 ① innovative가 들어가야 하므로 정답은 ①임

왜 오답?

② 유연한 사고는 오히려 새로운 아이디어를 생각하는 데 효과적일 것이며, 즉각적인 해결책은 언급되지 않았다.
③ 증명된 해결책은 언급되지 않았다.
④ 유연한 사고는 오히려 새로운 아이디어를 생각하는 데 효과적일 것이며, 우월한 해결책은 언급되지 않았다.
⑤ 협력에 관한 해결책은 언급되지 않았다.

*** 글의 흐름**

1 **도입**: 발명품으로 문제를 해결하려 할 때, 논리적 사고만으로는 저항에 부딪힘
2 **전개**: 선형적(논리적) 사고는 익숙한 작업에서는 효과적이지만 새로운 아이디어를 다룰 때는 불충분함
3 **대조**: 창의성은 새로운 아이디어와 관점을 적용하는 비선형적 사고를 포함함
4 **부연**: 새로운 아이디어를 다룰 때는 비선형적(창의적) 사고가 효과적임

구문 서술형

(정답) Trying

(해석) 여러분이 문제를 논리적으로 생각해 나가려고 애쓸 때 저항이라는 벽돌 벽에 맞닥뜨릴지도 모른다.

→ When you try to think ~ resistance에서 부사절의 접속사(When)와 주어(you)가 생략된 분사구문이다. 부사절의 생략된 주어(you)가 행위의 주체이므로 try를 현재분사 Trying으로 고쳐야 한다.

Q 04 정답 ① *정보에 대한 인간의 진실 편향

동격
There is a natural assumption of truth, or a truth bias / when humans communicate with one another. //
단서 1 인간은 소통할 때 진실 편향이 있음
진실에 대한 자연스러운 가정, 즉 진실 편향이 있다 / 인간이 서로 소통할 때 //

In other words, / when we're listening to others or reading their words, / our automatic assumption / is that the other person is telling the truth. //
단서 2 자동적으로 상대방이 진실을 말하고 있다고 믿음
다시 말해 / 우리가 다른 사람의 말을 듣거나 그들의 글을 읽을 때 / 우리의 자동적인 가정은 / 상대방이 진실을 말하고 있다는 것이다 //

= works[turns] out well
This usually works out fine. // 이는 보통 잘 작동한다 //

간접의문문 / 명사절 접속사 (~인지 아닌지) / 목적어절 접속사
If you ask someone / where the restroom is located / or if it's raining outside, / you can safely assume / that most people will not lie / in their responses. //
만약 당신이 누군가에게 물어본다면 / 화장실이 어디 있는지나 / 밖에 비가 오고 있는지를 / 당신은 확신하며 가정할 수 있다 / 대부분의 사람들이 거짓말을 하지 않을 것이라고 / 그들의 응답에서 //

Imagine / how difficult it would be to converse with someone
/ if you assumed / that *everything* they were telling you / was
false! //

가주어 · 진주어 · 목적절 접속사 · 앞에 목적격 관계대명사가 생략됨

상상해 보라 / 누군가와 대화하는 것이 얼마나 어려울지 / 만약 당신이 가정한다면 / 그들이 당신에게 말하는 '모든 것'이 / 거짓이라고 //

Indeed, / questioning the truth of a statement and then choosing
not to believe it / requires additional mental steps. //

병렬 구조 · 단수 동사

정말로 / 어떤 진술의 진실성에 의문을 제기하고 그것을 믿지 않는 것을 선택하는 것은 / 추가적인 정신적인 단계를 요구한다 // 단서 3 진술의 진실성에 의문을 제기하고 믿지 않으면 추가적인 정신적 단계가 요구됨

For the most part, / humans are "cognitive misers," / which
means / we typically don't expend more mental effort / than
seems necessary in a given situation. //

계속적 용법의 주격 관계대명사 · 단서 4 인간은 일반적으로 정신적 노력을 아끼려고 함

대부분의 경우 / 인간은 "인지적 구두쇠"이고 / 이는 의미한다 / 우리가 더 많은 정신적인 노력을 전형적으로 기울이지 않는다는 것을 / 주어진 상황에서 필요한 것처럼 보이는 것보다 //

It makes sense then, / that when we see something online, / even
if it is fake, / our default is to believe it, / at least at first. //

가주어 · 진주어절 접속사 · 부사절 접속사 (시간) · 부사절 접속사 (양보) · 명사적 용법 (주격 보어)

그렇다면 일리가 있다 / 우리가 온라인에서 무언가를 볼 때 / 비록 그것이 가짜라고 해도 / 우리의 기본값은 그것을 믿는 것이다 / 적어도 처음에는 //

→ We humans are unlikely to (A) doubt / the truth of
information we receive, / due to our tendency / to (B) save
mental effort. //

'~하지 않으려 하다' · 앞에 목적격 관계대명사가 생략됨

우리 인간은 의심하지 않으려 하는데 / 우리가 받는 정보의 진실성을 / 이는 우리의 경향 때문이다 / 정신적 노력을 아끼려는 //

- assumption ⓝ 가정
- bias ⓝ 편향
- in other words 다시 말해
- automatic ⓐ 자동적인
- work out 잘 작동하다, 잘 풀리다
- assume ⓥ 가정하다
- response ⓝ 응답
- converse with ~와 대화하다
- indeed ⓐⅾ 정말로
- statement ⓝ 진술
- additional ⓐ 추가적인
- cognitive ⓐ 인지적인
- miser ⓝ 구두쇠
- typically ⓐⅾ 전형적으로, 일반적으로
- effort ⓝ 노력
- make sense 일리가 있다
- fake ⓐ 가짜의
- at least 적어도
- due to ~ 때문에
- tendency ⓝ 경향

인간이 서로 소통할 때 진실에 대한 자연스러운 가정, 즉 진실 편향이 있다. 다시 말해, 우리가 다른 사람의 말을 듣거나 그들의 글을 읽을 때, 우리의 자동적인 가정은 상대방이 진실을 말하고 있다는 것이다. 이는 보통 잘 작동한다. 만약 당신이 누군가에게 화장실이 어디 있는지나 밖에 비가 오고 있는지를 물어본다면, 당신은 대부분의 사람들이 그들의 응답에서 거짓말을 하지 않을 것이라고 확신하며 가정할 수 있다. 만약 당신이 그들이 당신에게 말하는 '모든 것이' 거짓이라고 가정한다면 누군가와 대화하는 것이 얼마나 어려울지 상상해 보라! 정말로, 어떤 진술의 진실성에 의문을 제기하고 그것을 믿지 않는 것을 선택하는 것은 추가적인 정신적인 단계를 요구한다. 대부분의 경우, 인간은 "인지적 구두쇠"이고, 이는 우리가 주어진 상황에서 필요한 것처럼 보이는 것보다 더 많은 정신적인 노력을 전형적으로 기울이지 않는다는 것을 의미한다. 그렇다면 우리가 온라인에서 무언가를 볼 때, 비록 그것이 가짜라고 해도, 우리의 기본값은, 적어도 처음에는, 그것을 믿는 것임이 일리가 있다.

→ 우리 인간은 우리가 받는 정보의 진실성을 (A) 의심하지 않으려 하는데, 이는 정신적 노력을 (B) 아끼려는 우리의 경향 때문이다.

다음 글의 내용을 한 문장으로 요약하고자 한다. 빈칸 (A), (B)에 들어갈 말로 가장 적절한 것은?

	(A)		(B)	
①	doubt 의심하다	—	save 아끼다	정보의 진실성을 의심하지 않음으로써 정신적인 노력을 아끼려고 함
②	trust 신뢰하다	—	maintain 유지하다	정신적 노력을 유지하려는 것이 아니라 아끼려고 함
③	judge 판단하다	—	add 더하다	정신적 노력을 더하려는 것이 아니라 아끼려고 함
④	doubt 의심하다	—	increase 증가시키다	정신적 노력을 증가시키는 것이 아니라 아끼려고 함
⑤	trust 신뢰하다	—	reduce 줄이다	정보의 진실성을 신뢰하지 않으려고 한다는 것은 글의 내용과 반대됨

왜 정답? ✽✽✽ [정답률 62%]

(A):
┌ · 인간은 소통할 때 진실 편향이 있다. 단서 1
└ · 인간은 자동적으로 상대방이 진실을 말하고 있다고 믿는다. 단서 2

→ 인간은 진실 편향이 있어서 소통할 때 정보의 진실을 믿는, 즉 '의심하지' 않는 경향이 있다.

▶ (A)에는 ①, ④의 doubt가 들어가야 함

(B):
┌ · 상대방의 진술에 의문을 제기하고 믿지 않으면 추가적인 정신적 단계가 요구된다. 단서 3
└ · 인간은 일반적으로 정신적인 노력을 아끼려고 한다. 단서 4

→ 상대방의 진술을 의심하면 정신적인 노력이 더 들기 때문에, 정보가 진실이라고 믿음으로써 그 노력을 '아끼려고' 한다.

▶ (B)에는 ①의 save가 들어가는 것이 적절하므로 정답은 ①임

왜 오답?

② 인간이 정신적 노력을 유지하려는 것이 아니라 아끼려는 것이다.
③, ④ 인간이 정신적 노력을 더하거나 증가시키려는 것이 아니라 아끼려는 것이다.
⑤ 인간이 정보의 진실성을 신뢰하려고 하지 않는다는 것은 글의 내용과 반대된다.

* 글의 흐름

1 도입: 인간은 다른 사람과 소통할 때 정보가 진실이라고 가정하는 진실 편향이 있음
2 전개: 진실 편향은 일반적으로 잘 작동하며, 일상적 질문에서 상대방의 응답을 의심한다면 소통이 힘들어질 것임
3 부연: 상대의 진술을 의심하는 것은 추가적인 인지적 단계를 요구함
4 결론: 인간은 일반적으로 인지적 노력을 아끼려고 함

구문 서술형

정답 When seeing something online

→ 부사절의 주어(we)와 주절의 주어(we)가 같으므로 분사구문의 주어를 생략할 수 있다. 생략된 주어와 능동 관계인 동사 see를 현재분사로 바꾸고, 접속사는 그대로 쓴다.

Q 05 정답 ③ ***우리가 카메라처럼 보지 못하는 이유**

Vision is influenced / by our preconceptions about reality. //
시각은 영향을 받는다 / 현실에 대한 우리의 선입견에 의해 //

in -ing: ~할 때

In viewing a scene, / we establish unconscious hierarchies
/ that reflect / our functional relationship to objects / and our
momentary priorities. //

주격 관계대명사

한 장면을 볼 때 / 우리는 무의식적인 위계를 확립한다 / 반영하는 / 우리의 사물과의 기능적 관계와 / 우리의 순간적인 우선순위 //

부사절에서 '주어+be동사'가 생략됨

For example, / when visualizing a hammer in our mind's eye, /
we tend to "see" it / in profile or at some other "ready for use"
angle. //

예를 들어 / 우리 마음의 눈으로 망치를 시각화할 때 / 우리는 망치를 "보는" 경향이 있다 / 옆모습이나 "사용 준비 완료" 각도에서 //

One would probably not visualize / a hammer as seen from the
top / so that the handle is hidden / by the hammer's head. //

부사절 접속사 (목적)

아마 시각화하지 않을 것이다 / 망치가 위에서 보여진 모습으로 / 손잡이가 가려지도록 / 망치 머리에 //

앞에 목적격 관계대명사가 생략됨

The functional relationship we have with objects / creates visual
expectations / that interfere with our ability / to see "like a
camera." // 단서 1 사물과의 기능적 관계는 우리가 카메라처럼 보는 능력을 방해함

주격 관계대명사

우리가 가진 사물과의 기능적인 관계는 / 시각적 기대를 만든다 / 우리의 능력을 방해하는 / "카메라처럼" 보는 //

The camera, like the human eye, / sees only shapes and colors. //
카메라는 인간의 눈처럼 / 오직 형태와 색깔만을 본다 //

It documents the world impartially / through a lens / that is [주격 관계대명사] similar to the eye. // 단서 2 카메라는 세상을 공평하게 기록함

그것은 세상을 공평하게 기록한다 / 렌즈를 통해 / 눈과 비슷한 //

When we look at them carefully, / photographs are often [= photographs] surprising / 우리가 사진들을 주의 깊게 들여다볼 때 / 종종 놀라게 된다 /

because they don't interpret confusing details / but simply serve them up to us / with a mechanical indifference. [= details]

그것들은 혼란을 주는 세부 사항들을 해석하는 것이 아니라 / 우리에게 그것들을 단순히 제공해주기 때문에 / 기계적인 무관심으로 // 단서 3 사진(카메라)은 기계적인 무관심으로 대상을 보여줌

And because of their flatness, / photographs often contain areas / that appear as unrecognizable colors and shapes. // [주격 관계대명사]

그리고 그것들의 평면성 때문에 / 사진들은 종종 영역을 포함한다 / 알아보기 어려운 색과 형태들로 보이는 //

> Our visual perception is shaped / by an established hierarchy / based on functional relationships, /
> 우리의 시각적 인식은 형성되며 / 확립된 위계에 의해 / 기능적 관계에 기반한 /
> which (A) interrupts our ability to see objects as they truly are, / unlike the (B) objective perspective of a camera. // [형용사적 용법 (ability 수식)]
> 이는 사물을 있는 그대로 보는 능력을 방해한다 / 카메라의 객관적인 시각과는 달리 //

- preconception ⓝ 선입견   - establish ⓥ 확립하다
- unconscious ⓐ 무의식적인   - hierarchy ⓝ 위계
- reflect ⓥ 반영하다   - functional ⓐ 기능적인
- momentary ⓐ 순간적인   - priority ⓝ 우선순위
- visualize ⓥ 마음속에 그리다   - tend to-v ~하는 경향이 있다
- profile ⓝ 옆모습   - interfere with ~을 방해하다
- document ⓥ 기록하다   - impartially ⓐⓓ 공정하게
- interpret ⓥ 해석하다   - mechanical ⓐ 기계적인
- indifference ⓝ 무관심   - unrecognizable ⓐ 알아볼 수 없는
- perspective ⓝ 관점   - enhance ⓥ 향상시키다
- neutral ⓐ 중립적인

시각은 현실에 대한 우리의 선입견에 의해 영향을 받는다. 한 장면을 볼 때, 우리는 우리의 사물과의 기능적 관계와 우리의 순간적인 우선순위를 반영하는 무의식적인 위계를 확립한다. 예를 들어, 우리 마음의 눈으로 망치를 시각화할 때, 우리는 망치를 옆모습이나 "사용 준비 완료" 각도에서 "보는" 경향이 있다. 손잡이가 망치 머리에 가려지도록 망치가 위에서 보여진 모습으로 아마 시각화하지 않을 것이다. 우리가 가진 사물과의 기능적인 관계는 "카메라처럼" 보는 우리의 능력을 방해하는 시각적 기대를 만든다. 카메라는 인간의 눈처럼 오직 형태와 색깔만을 본다. 그것은 눈과 비슷한 렌즈를 통해 세상을 공평하게 기록한다. 우리가 사진들을 주의 깊게 들여다볼 때, 그것들은 혼란을 주는 세부 사항들을 해석하는 것이 아니라 기계적인 무관심으로 우리에게 그것들을 단순히 제공해주기 때문에 종종 놀라게 된다. 그리고 그것들의 평면성 때문에 사진들은 종종 알아보기 어려운 색과 형태들로 보이는 영역을 포함한다.

→ 우리의 시각적 인식은 기능적 관계에 기반한 확립된 위계에 의해 형성되며, 이는 카메라의 (B) 객관적인 시각과는 달리 사물을 있는 그대로 보는 능력을 (A) 방해한다.

> 다음 글의 내용을 한 문장으로 요약하고자 한다. 빈칸 (A), (B)에 들어갈 말로 가장 적절한 것은?
>
> (A)   (B)
> ① enhances   —   accurate 기능적 관계는 객관적 인식을 향상시키지 않음
>   향상시킨다   정확한
> ② simplifies   —   fixed 시각적 인식이 사물을 보는 능력을 단순화하지 않음
>   단순화한다   고정된
> ③ interrupts   —   objective 우리의 시각적 인식은 '객관적' 카메라와
>   방해한다   객관적인   달리 사물을 있는 그대로 보는 능력을 '방해함'
> ④ enhances   —   neutral 기능적 관계는 객관적 인식을 향상시키지 않음
>   향상시킨다   중립적인
> ⑤ interrupts   —   inconsistent 카메라의 시각은 일관성 있음
>   일관성 없는

> 왜 정답 ? ★★★ [정답률 45%]

(A):
┌ • 우리가 가진 사물과의 기능적 관계는 카메라처럼 보는 우리의 능력을 방해한다. 단서 1
⇒ 우리의 시각적 인식은 사물을 있는 그대로 보는 능력을 방해한다.
  ▶ (A)에는 ③, ⑤ interrupts가 들어가야 함

(B):
┌ • 카메라는 세상을 공평하게 기록한다. 단서 2
└ • (카메라로 찍은) 사진은 기계적인 무관심으로 세부사항을 보여준다. 단서 3
⇒ 카메라의 시각은 주관이나 편견 없이 대상을 있는 그대로 본다.
  ▶ (B)에는 ③ objective, ④ neutral이 들어가야 하므로 정답은 ③임

> 왜 오답 ?

① 우리의 시각적 인식은 사물을 있는 그대로 보는 능력을 향상시키지 않는다.
② 사물을 있는 그대로 보는 능력을 단순화한다는 것은 언급되지 않았다.
④ 우리의 시각적 인식은 사물을 있는 그대로 보는 능력을 향상시키지 않는다.
⑤ 일관성이 없는 것은 인간의 시각에 해당하며, 카메라의 시각은 오히려 일관성이 있다.

* 글의 흐름

1 주제: 인간의 시각은 현실에 대한 선입견, 즉 기능적 관계에 의해 영향을 받음
2 예시: 망치를 떠올릴 때 사용하기 좋은 각도로 생각하는 경향이 있음
3 대조: 인간의 주관적 시각과 달리 카메라는 세상을 기계적으로 기록하는 객관적인 시각을 가짐

[구문 서술형]

[정답] Looked, Looking

[해석] 사진들을 주의 깊게 들여다볼 때, 우리는 종종 그것들이 놀랍다는 것을 알게 된다.

→ 분사구문에서 생략된 주어 we가 행위의 주체이므로, 과거분사 Looked를 현재분사 Looking으로 고쳐야 한다.

Q 06 정답 ① *트릭 처벌의 부작용과 대안 —————

Punishing a child may not be effective / due to what Álvaro [동명사 (주어)] ['~ 때문에'] Bilbao, a neuropsychologist, calls 'trick-punishments.' // [동격]
아이를 벌주는 것은 효과적이지 않을 수 있다 / 신경심리학자 Álvaro Bilbao가 '트릭 처벌'이라고 부르는 것으로 인해 //

A trick-punishment is / a scolding, a moment of anger / or a punishment / in the most classic sense of the word. //
트릭 처벌은 / 꾸짖음, 순간의 화 / 혹은 처벌이다 / (처벌이라는) 단어의 가장 전형적인 의미에서의 //

Instead of discouraging the child from doing something, / it encourages them to do it. // 단서 1 트릭 처벌은 행동을 단념시키는 대신 오히려 장려함 [encourages의 목적어와 목적격 보어 (to부정사)]
아이가 무언가를 하는 것을 단념시키는 대신 / 트릭 처벌은 그들이 그것을 하도록 장려한다. //

For example, / Hugh learns / that when he hits his little brother, / his mother scolds him. // [목적어절 접속사]
예를 들어 / Hugh는 배운다 / 그가 자신의 남동생을 때릴 때 / 그의 어머니가 그를 꾸짖는다는 것을 //

For a child who feels lonely, / being scolded is much better / [주격 관계대명사절] [동명사 주어 (수동태)] [비교급 강조] than feeling invisible, / so he will continue to hit his brother. //
외로움을 느끼는 아이에게는 / 꾸중을 듣는 것이 훨씬 낫다 / 눈에 띄지 않는다고 느끼는 것보다 / 그래서 그는 그의 남동생을 때리는 것을 계속할 것이다 //

In this case, / his mother would be better adopting a different [be better -ing: ~하는 것이 낫다] strategy. //
이 경우에 / 그의 어머니는 다른 전략을 채택하는 것이 나을 것이다 //

For instance, / she could congratulate Hugh / when he has not hit his brother / for a certain length of time. //
예를 들어 / 그녀는 Hugh를 자랑스러워해 줄 수 있다 / 그가 그의 남동생을 때리지 않았을 때 / 일정 기간 동안 // **단서 2** 어머니는 그가 남동생을 때리지 않았을 때 자랑스러워해 줄 수 있음

The mother clearly cannot allow the child to hit his little brother, / but instead of constantly **pointing** out the negatives, / she can choose to reward the positives. // 동명사 **단서 3** 부정적인 면을 계속 지적하는 대신 긍정적인 면을 보상해야 함
어머니는 분명 아이가 그의 남동생을 때리는 것을 내버려둘 수 없지만 / 그녀는 부정적 측면을 계속 지적하는 대신에 / 긍정적 측면을 보상하는 것을 선택할 수 있다 //

In this way, / any parent can avoid trick-punishments. //
이렇게 / 어느 부모도 트릭 처벌을 피할 수 있다 //

A trick-punishment / (A) **reinforces** the unwanted behavior of a child, / **which** implies / **that** parents should focus on / 계속적 용법의 주격 관계대명사 목적어절 접속사
(B) **reducing** the attention to negatives / while rewarding positive behaviors. //
트릭 처벌은 / 아이의 바람직하지 못한 행동을 강화하는데 / 이는 시사한다 / 부모가 집중해야 한다는 것을 / 부정적 측면에 관한 관심을 줄이는 데 / 긍정적인 행동을 보상하면서 //

- **punish** ⓥ 벌주다, 처벌하다 • **trick** ⓝ 트릭, 속임수
- **scolding** ⓝ 꾸짖음 • **discourage** ⓥ 단념[좌절]시키다
- **invisible** ⓐ 눈에 띄지 않는 • **adopt** ⓥ 채택하다
- **strategy** ⓝ 전략 • **congratulate** ⓥ 자랑스러워하다
- **constantly** ⓐⓓ 계속, 지속적으로 • **point out** 지적하다
- **reward** ⓥ 보상하다 • **unwanted** ⓐ 바람직하지 못한, 원치 않는
- **imply** ⓥ 시사하다 • **reinforce** ⓥ 강화하다
- **maximize** 최대화하다 • **lower** ⓥ 낮추다

아이를 벌주는 것은 신경심리학자 Álvaro Bilbao가 '트릭 처벌'이라고 부르는 것으로 인해 효과적이지 않을 수 있다. 트릭 처벌은 꾸짖음, 순간의 화 혹은 (처벌이라는) 단어의 가장 전형적인 의미에서의 처벌이다. 아이가 무언가를 하는 것을 단념시키는 대신 트릭 처벌은 그들이 그것을 하도록 장려한다. 예를 들어 Hugh는 그가 자신의 남동생을 때릴 때 그의 어머니가 그를 꾸짖는다는 것을 배운다. 외로움을 느끼는 아이에게는 꾸중을 듣는 것이 눈에 띄지 않는다고 느끼는 것보다 훨씬 나아서 그는 그의 남동생을 때리는 것을 계속할 것이다. 이 경우에, 그의 어머니는 다른 전략을 채택하는 것이 보다 나을 것이다. 예를 들어 그녀는 Hugh가 그의 남동생을 일정 기간 동안 때리지 않았을 때 그를 자랑스러워해 줄 수 있다. 어머니는 분명 아이가 그의 남동생을 때리는 것을 내버려둘 수 없기 때문에 그녀는 부정적 측면을 계속 지적하는 대신에 긍정적 측면을 보상하는 것을 선택할 수 있다. 이렇게 어느 부모도 트릭 처벌을 피할 수 있다.
→ 트릭 처벌은 아이의 바람직하지 못한 행동을 (A) **강화하는데**, 이는 부모가 긍정적인 행동을 보상하면서 부정적 측면에 관한 관심을 (B) **줄이는** 데 집중해야 한다는 것을 시사한다.

다음 글의 내용을 한 문장으로 요약하고자 한다. 빈칸 (A), (B)에 들어갈 말로 가장 적절한 것은?

	(A)	(B)
①	reinforces 강화하다	reducing 줄이는 것
②	reinforces	maximizing 최대화하는 것
③	discourages 단념시키다	attracting 끌어모으는 것
④	discourages	lowering 낮추는 것
⑤	controls 통제하다	increasing 증가시키는 것

① 트릭 처벌은 아이의 잘못된 행동을 강화하므로 부정적인 측면에 주목하기보다 긍정적 측면을 보상해야 한다는 내용임
② 아이의 부정적인 행동에 대한 주목은 줄여야 함
③, ④ 트릭 처벌은 아이의 잘못된 행동을 단념시키지 못함
⑤ 트릭 처벌은 아이의 잘못된 행동을 통제하지 못함

왜 정답? ★★★ [정답률 47%]

- 트릭 처벌은 아이가 무언가를 하는 것을 단념시키는 대신 오히려 그들이 그것을 하도록 장려한다. **단서 1**
- Hugh의 예시: Hugh가 외로움을 느끼는 아이라면 어머니의 꾸중을 듣는 것이 훨씬 나아서 남동생을 때리는 것을 계속할 것이다.

→ 트릭 처벌은 아이의 잘못된 행동을 단념시키는 대신 오히려 그것을 계속하도록 장려한다는 점을 Hugh의 예시로 설명하고 있다.
▶ 트릭 처벌은 아이의 행동을 오히려 장려하여 '강화'하므로 (A)에는 ①, ②의 reinforces가 들어가야 함

- 어머니는 Hugh가 그의 남동생을 일정 기간 때리지 않았을 때 그를 자랑스러워해 줄 수 있다. **단서 2**
- 부정적 측면을 계속 지적하는 대신에 긍정적 측면을 보상하는 것을 선택할 수 있다. **단서 3**

→ 아이의 행동을 막기 위해서 부정적인 측면을 지적하지 말고, 즉 관심을 줄이고 긍정적인 측면을 보상하는 전략을 채택해야 한다고 말하고 있다.
▶ (B)에는 ①의 reducing이나 ④의 lowering이 들어가는 것이 적절하므로 정답은 ①임

왜 오답?

② 트릭 처벌이 아이의 부정적인 행동을 강화하기 때문에 부정적 행동에 대한 주목은 줄여야 하는 것이지 최대화하면 안 된다.
③ 트릭 처벌은 아이의 부정적인 행동을 단념시키는 것이 아니라 오히려 강화시킨다.
④ 트릭 처벌은 아이의 부정적인 행동을 단념시키지 못하고 오히려 강화시킨다.
⑤ 트릭 처벌은 부정적인 행동을 통제할 수 없고, 부정적인 행동을 향한 관심은 증가시키는 것이 아니라 줄여야 한다.

구문 서술형

정답 Thinking that being scolded is much better than feeling invisible

해석 아이는 꾸중을 듣는 것이 눈에 띄지 않는다고 느끼는 것보다 훨씬 낫다고 생각하기 때문에, 그는 남동생을 때리는 것을 계속할 것이다.
→ 접속사 Because를 생략하고 주절의 주어와 같은 a child를 생략한 뒤, 능동 관계의 동사 thinks를 현재분사인 Thinking으로 바꿔야 한다.

Q 07 정답 ④ *불평등을 느끼는 Capuchin의 보상 거부 —

Capuchins / — New World Monkeys / **that** live in large social 주격 관계대명사
groups / — will, in captivity, trade with people all day long, / especially if food is involved. //
Capuchin은 / New World Monkey인 / 대규모의 사회 집단으로 서식하는 / 갇힌 상태에서 온종일 사람들과 거래를 할 것인데 / 특히 먹이가 연관된다면 (그러할 것이다) //

I *give you this rock* / and you *give me a treat* to eat. // 수여동사 + 간접목적어 + 직접목적어
'내가 너에게 이 돌을 주고 / 너는 나에게 먹을 간식을 준다' //

If you **put** two monkeys in cages / next to each other, / and **offer** 부사절 접속사(조건) 병렬 구조
them both slices of cucumber / for the rocks they already have, / they will happily eat the cucumbers. //
만약 당신이 두 마리의 원숭이들을 우리에 넣고 / 나란히 있는 / 오이 조각을 둘 모두에게 주면 / 그들이 이미 가지고 있는 돌의 대가로 / 그들은 그 오이를 기쁘게 먹을 것이다 //

If, however, you give one monkey grapes instead / — **grapes** 동명사 being의 의미상 주어
being universally preferred to cucumbers — / the monkey **that** 주격 관계대명사
is still receiving cucumbers / will begin to throw them back at the experimenter. // **단서 1** 한 원숭이에게만 포도를 주고 다른 원숭이에게는 오이를 주면, 오이를 받은 원숭이는 실험자에게 불만을 표함
하지만 만약 당신이 한 원숭이에게는 포도를 대신 준다면 / 일반적으로 포도는 오이보다 더 선호되는데 / 여전히 오이를 받은 원숭이는 / 그것들을 실험자에게 던지기 시작할 것이다 //

Even though she is still getting "paid" the same amount / for 부사절 접속사(양보)
her effort of sourcing rocks, / and so her particular situation has not changed, / the comparison to another / makes the situation unfair. // **단서 2** 보상을 받는 상황은 바뀌지 않아도, 비교가 상황을 부당하게 만듦
비록 그녀가 같은 양을 여전히 '받고' / 돌을 모은 그녀의 수고에 대한 대가로 / 그래서 그녀의 특정한 상황이 변화가 없더라도 / 다른 원숭이와의 비교는 / 그 상황을 부당하게 만든다 //

Furthermore, / she is now willing to abandon all gains / — the
cucumbers themselves — / to communicate her displeasure to
the experimenter. // 단서 3 원숭이는 불쾌함을 전달하기 위해 받은 보상을 기꺼이 포기함
게다가 / 그녀는 모든 얻은 것들을 이제 기꺼이 포기한다 / 즉, 오이 자체를, / 실험자에게
그녀의 불쾌함을 전달하기 위해 //

→ According to the passage, / if the Capuchin monkey
realizes the (A) **inequality** / in rewards compared to another
monkey, /
이 글에 따르면 / 만약 Capuchin 원숭이가 불평등을 알아차린다면 / 다른 원숭이와
비교하여 보상에서의 /
she will (B) **reject** her rewards / to express her feelings / about
the treatment, / despite getting exactly the same rewards as
before. //
그녀는 그녀의 보상을 거부할 것이다 / 그녀의 감정을 표현하기 위해 / 대우에 대한 /
이전과 정확히 똑같은 보상을 받더라도 //

• captivity ⓝ 감금　• trade ⓥ 거래하다　• cucumber ⓝ 오이
• universally ⓐⓓ 일반적으로　• experimenter ⓝ 실험자
• source ⓥ 모으다　• comparison ⓝ 비교　• abandon ⓥ 포기하다
• communicate ⓥ 전달하다　• displeasure ⓝ 불쾌함

대규모의 사회 집단으로 서식하는 New World Monkey인 Capuchin은 간힌
상태에서 온종일 사람들과 거래를 할 것인데 특히 먹이가 연관된다면 그러할 것
이다. '내가 너에게 이 돌을 주고 너는 나에게 먹을 간식을 준다.' 만약 당신이
두 마리의 원숭이들을 나란히 있는 우리에 넣고 그들이 이미 가지고 있는 돌의
대가로 오이 조각을 둘 모두에게 주었을 때 그들은 그 오이를 기쁘게 먹을 것이
다. 하지만 만약 당신이 한 원숭이에게는 포도를 대신 준다면, 일반적으로 포도
는 오이보다 더 선호되는데, 여전히 오이를 받은 원숭이는 그것들을 실험자에게
던지기 시작할 것이다. 비록 그녀가 돌을 모은 그녀의 수고에 대한 대가로 같은
양을 여전히 '받고', 그래서 그녀의 특정한 상황이 변화가 없더라도, 다른 원숭
이와의 비교는 그 상황을 부당하게 만든다. 게다가, 그녀는 실험자에게 그녀의
불쾌함을 전달하기 위해 모든 얻은 것들, 즉, 오이 자체를 이제 기꺼이 포기한다.
→ 이 글에 따르면, 만약 Capuchin 원숭이가 다른 원숭이와 비교하여 보상에서
의 (A) **불평등**을 알아차린다면, 그녀는 이전과 정확히 똑같은 보상을 받더라도
대우에 대한 그녀의 감정을 표현하기 위해 그녀의 보상을 (B) **거부**할 것이다.

**다음 글의 내용을 한 문장으로 요약하고자 한다. 빈칸 (A), (B)에 들어갈
말로 가장 적절한 것은?**

	(A)		(B)
①	benefit 이익	—	protect 보호하다 · 다른 원숭이와 비교하여 보상의 이익을 알아차리는 내용이 아님
②	inequality 불평등	—	share 공유하다 · 보상을 공유한다는 언급은 없음
③	abundance 풍부함	—	yield 양보하다 · 다른 원숭이와 비교하여 보상의 풍부함을 알아차리는 내용이 아님
④	inequality 불평등	—	reject 거부하다 · 다른 원숭이와 비교하여 보상의 불평등을 알아차리면 불쾌함을 표현하기 위해 보상을 거부한다는 내용임
⑤	benefit 이익	—	display 보여주다 · 대우에 대한 감정을 표현하기 위해 보상을 보여준다는 내용이 아님

왜 정답? ★★ [정답률 60%]

(A):
• 하지만 만약 당신이 한 원숭이에게는 포도를 대신 준다면, 일반적으로 포도는
오이보다 더 선호되는데, 여전히 오이를 받은 원숭이는 그것들을 실험자에게
던지기 시작할 것이다. 단서 1
• 그래서 그녀의 특정한 상황이 변화가 없더라도, 다른 원숭이와의 비교는 그 상황을
부당하게 만든다. 단서 2

➡ 한 원숭이에게는 오이보다 더 선호되는 포도를, 다른 원숭이에게는 오이를 준다면,
다른 원숭이와 비교가 되는 부당한 상황이 만들어진다.
▶ 원숭이들의 보상이 '불평등한' 것이므로 (A)에는 ②, ④의 inequality가
들어가야 함

(B):
• 게다가, 그녀는 실험자에게 그녀의 불쾌함을 전달하기 위해 모든 얻은 것들, 즉,
오이 자체를 이제 기꺼이 포기한다. 단서 3
➡ 불평등한 상황임을 인지한 원숭이는 불쾌함을 표시하기 위해 보상 자체를 기꺼이
포기할, 즉, '거부할' 것이다.
▶ (B)에는 ④의 reject가 들어가는 것이 적절하므로 정답은 ④임

왜 오답?
① 다른 원숭이와 비교하여 보상에서의 이익을 알아차린다는 내용이 아니다.
② 원숭이들이 실험자로부터 보상을 받거나 이를 거부하는 것만 언급되었을 뿐,
보상을 공유하는 것은 언급되지 않았다.
③ 보상의 풍부함에 관한 내용이 아니다. (▶ 이유: 보상의 종류가 다르기 때문에
발생하는 불평등에 관한 내용이다.)
⑤ 원숭이들이 감정을 표현하기 위해 보상을 보여준다는 내용이 아니다.

＊ 글의 흐름

도입	Capuchin은 간힌 상태에서는 (특히 먹이와 연관된) 거래를 계속 할 것임
실험 ①	두 원숭이에게 거래의 보상으로 똑같이 오이를 준다면 만족하고 받을 것임
실험 ②	하지만 한 쪽에 오이보다 더 좋은 보상을 준다면 오이를 받은 원숭이는 불만을 표현할 것임
결론	보상을 받는 상황은 같아도 비교가 상황을 불평등하게 만들기 때문에 보상을 포기하면서까지 불쾌함을 표시할 것임

Q 08 정답 ① ＊초기 문화 진화 모델과 수정된 버전

Many of the first models of cultural evolution / drew noticeable
connections / between culture and genes /
문화 진화의 많은 초기 모델들은 / 주목할 만한 접점을 이끌어냈다 / 문화와 유전자 사이의 /
by using concepts from theoretical population genetics / and
applying them to culture. // 단서 1 초기 문화 진화 모델은 문화와 유전자 사이의 접점을 끌어내 두 개념을 유사하게 설명함
이론 집단 유전학의 개념을 사용함으로써 / 그리고 그것들을 문화에 적용함으로써 //
Cultural patterns of transmission, innovation, and selection /
are conceptually likened / to genetic processes of transmission,
mutation, and selection. //
전파, 혁신, 선택의 문화적 방식은 / 개념적으로 유사하다 / 전달, 돌연변이, 선택의 유전적
과정과 //
However, these approaches had to be modified / to account for
the differences / between genetic and cultural transmission. //
그러나 이러한 접근법은 수정되어야야 했다 / 차이점을 설명하기 위해 / 유전자의 전달과 문화
전파 사이의 / 단서 2 하지만 이러한 접근법은 유전자의 전달과 문화 전파 사이의 차이점을 설명하려면 수정되어야 했음
For example, / we do not expect / the cultural transmission / to
follow the rules of genetic transmission strictly. //
예를 들어 / 우리는 예상하지 않는다 / 문화 전파가 / 유전자 전달의 규칙을 엄격하게 따를
것이라고 //
If two biological parents / have different forms of a cultural
trait, / their child is not necessarily equally likely to acquire / the
mother's or father's form of that trait. //
만약 두 명의 생물학적인 부모가 / 서로 다른 문화적인 특성의 형태를 가진다면 / 그들의
자녀는 반드시 동일하게 획득하지 않을 수 있다 / 엄마 혹은 아빠의 그 특성의 형태를 //
Further, a child can acquire cultural traits / not only from its
parents / but also from nonparental adults and peers; /
더욱이 아이는 문화적인 특성을 얻을 수 있다 / 부모로부터뿐만 아니라 / 부모가 아닌
성인이나 또래로부터도 / 단서 3 문화적인 특성은 부모가 아닌 성인이나 또래 등 다양한 요인에서 얻을 수 있음

thus, the frequency of a cultural trait in the population / is relevant / beyond just the probability / **that** an individual's parents had that trait. //
동격절 접속사

따라서 집단의 문화적인 특성의 빈도는 / 유의미하다 / 단지 확률을 넘어서 / 한 개인의 부모가 그 특성을 가졌을 //

> → Early cultural evolution models / **used** the (A) **similarity** / between culture and genes /
> 병렬 구조
> 초기의 문화 진화 모델들은 / 유사성을 사용했다 / 문화와 유전자 사이의 /
> but **had to** be revised / **since** cultural transmission / allows for more (B) **diverse** factors / than genetic transmission. //
> 부사절 접속사(이유)
> 그러나 수정되어야만 했다 / 문화 전파가 / 더 다양한 요인을 허용하기 때문에 / 유전자의 전달보다 //

- evolution ⓝ 진화 ・ draw ⓥ 이끌어내다
- noticeable ⓐ 주목할 만한 ・ connection ⓝ 접점, 연결
- gene ⓝ 유전자 ・ concept ⓝ 개념
- theoretical population genetics 이론 집단 유전학
- apply ⓥ 적용하다 ・ transmission ⓝ 전파
- innovation ⓝ 혁신 ・ selection ⓝ 선택
- conceptually ⓐⓓ 개념적으로 ・ liken to ~와 유사하다
- mutation ⓝ 돌연변이 ・ modify ⓥ 수정하다
- account for ~을 설명하다 ・ strictly ⓐⓓ 엄격하게 ・ trait ⓝ 특성
- acquire ⓥ 습득하다 ・ further ⓐⓓ 더욱이
- nonparental ⓐ 부모가 아닌 ・ peer ⓝ 동료 ・ frequency ⓝ 빈도
- probability ⓝ 개연성, 확률 ・ revise ⓥ 수정하다, 개정하다
- credible ⓐ 믿을 만한

문화 진화의 많은 초기 모델들은 이론 집단 유전학의 개념을 사용함으로써 그리고 그것들을 문화에 적용함으로써 문화와 유전자 사이의 주목할 만한 접점을 이끌어냈다. 전파, 혁신, 선택의 문화적 방식은 전달, 돌연변이, 선택의 유전적 과정과 개념적으로 유사하다. 그러나 이러한 접근법은 유전자의 전달과 문화 전파 사이의 차이점을 설명하기 위해 수정되어야만 했다. 예를 들어, 우리는 문화 전파가 유전자 전달의 규칙을 엄격하게 따를 것이라고 예상하지 않는다. 만약 두 명의 생물학적인 부모가 서로 다른 문화적인 특성의 형태를 가진다면, 그들의 자녀는 반드시 엄마 혹은 아빠의 그 특성의 형태를 동일하게 획득하지 않을 수 있다. 더욱이 아이는 문화적인 특성을 부모로부터뿐만 아니라 부모가 아닌 성인이나 또래로부터도 얻을 수 있다. 따라서 집단의 문화적인 특성의 빈도는 단지 한 개인의 부모가 그 특성을 가졌을 확률을 넘어서 유의미하다.

→ 초기의 문화 진화 모델들은 문화와 유전자 사이의 (A) **유사성**을 사용했지만, 문화 전파가 유전자의 전달보다 더 (B) **다양한** 요인을 허용하기 때문에 수정되어야만 했다.

다음 글의 내용을 한 문장으로 요약하고자 한다. 빈칸 (A), (B)에 들어갈 말로 가장 적절한 것은? [3점]

	(A)		(B)	
①	similarity 유사성	—	diverse 다양한	초기 모델에서는 문화와 유전의 유사성을 활용했지만, 문화 전파가 더 다양한 요인에 영향을 받기 때문에 수정됨
②	similarity 유사성	—	limited 제한된	문화 전파는 더 제한된 요인이 아니라 다양한 요인에 영향을 받음
③	difference 차이점	—	flexible 유연한	초기 모델에서는 문화와 유전의 차이점이 아닌 유사성을 활용함
④	difference 차이점	—	complicated 복잡한	초기 모델에서는 문화와 유전의 차이점이 아닌 유사성을 활용함
⑤	interaction 상호작용	—	credible 믿을 만한	문화 전파가 더 믿을 만한 요인을 허용한다는 것은 언급되지 않음

| **문제 풀이 순서** | ★★★※ [정답률 61%]

1st 요약문을 통해 글에서 무엇을 찾아야 하는지 확인한다.

요약문	초기의 문화 진화 모델들은 문화와 유전자 사이의 (A) _____을 사용했지만, 문화 전파가 유전자의 전달보다 더 (B) _____ 요인을 허용하기 때문에 수정되어야만 했다.

→ 글에서 찾아야 하는 것
(A): 초기 문화 진화 모델들은 문화와 유전 사이의 유사성, 차이점, 상호작용을 사용했는지
(B): 후에 문화 전파가 유전자의 전달보다 더 다양한, 제한된, 유연한, 복잡한, 믿을 만한 요인을 허용하는 것이 밝혀졌는지

2nd 글의 내용을 파악하여 요약문을 완성한다.

초기 문화 진화 모델의 특징: 문화와 유전자 사이의 접점을 끌어내 두 개념을 설명했고, 문화의 방식과 유전의 과정을 개념적으로 유사하게 보았음 **단서 1**

내용 전환: 하지만 이러한 접근법은 유전자의 전달과 문화 전파 사이의 차이점을 설명하려면 수정되어야 했음 **단서 2**

수정된 모델의 특징: 유전적인 특성은 부모에게서만 얻을 수 있지만, 문화적인 특성은 부모가 아닌 성인이나 또래 등 다양한 요인에서 얻을 수 있음 **단서 3**

→ 초기 문화 진화 모델은 문화와 유전의 유사성을 활용하여 두 개념을 설명했지만, 문화 전파가 유전자 전달보다 훨씬 다양한 요인에 영향을 받는다는 것을 설명하기 위해 이 모델은 수정되어야 했다.

▶ (A)에는 similarity(유사성)가, (B)에는 diverse(다양한)가 들어가야 하므로 정답은 ①임

| **선택지 분석** |

① 초기 모델에서는 문화와 유전의 유사성을 활용했지만, 문화 전파가 더 다양한 요인에 영향을 받기 때문에 수정되었다.
② 문화 전파는 더 제한된 요인이 아니라 다양한 요인에 영향을 받는다.
③ 초기 모델에서는 문화와 유전의 차이점이 아닌 유사성을 활용했다.
④ 초기 모델에서는 문화와 유전의 차이점이 아닌 유사성을 활용했다.
⑤ 문화 전파가 더 믿을 만한 요인을 허용한다는 것은 언급되지 않았다.

Q 09 정답 ① *내(內)집단을 선호하는 인간의 경향 —

In their study in 2007 / Katherine Kinzler and her colleagues at Harvard showed / **that** our tendency **to identify** / with an in-group / to a large degree **begins** in infancy / and **may be** innate. //
목적어절 접속사 주어 형용사적 용법 동사① 동사②
2007년에 있었던 연구에서 / Katherine Kinzler와 그녀의 하버드 동료들은 보여 주었다 / 동일시하려는 우리의 경향이 / 내(內)집단과 / 상당 부분 유아기에 시작되고 / 선천적일 수 있음을 //

Kinzler and her team / **took** a bunch of five-month-olds / whose families only spoke English / **and showed** the babies two videos. //
병렬 구조
Kinzler와 그녀의 팀은 / 한 무리의 5개월 된 아이들을 선정했다 / 가족들이 영어만을 말하는 / 그리고 두 개의 영상을 그 아기들에게 보여 주었다 //

In one video, / a woman was speaking English. //
한 영상에서 / 한 여성이 영어를 말하고 있었다 //

In the other, / a woman was speaking Spanish. //
다른 영상에서는 / 한 여성이 스페인어를 말하고 있었다 //

Then they **were shown** / a screen / with both women side by side, / not speaking. //
과거 시제 수동태
그리고 나서 그들에게 보여 주었다 / 화면을 / 두 여성 모두 나란히 있는 / 말없이 //

In infant psychology research, / **the standard measure** / for affinity or interest / **is** attention / — babies will apparently stare / longer / at the things they like more. //
주어 동사
유아 심리학 연구에서 / 표준 척도는 / 애착이나 관심의 / 주목이다 / 아기들은 분명 처다볼 것이다 / 더 오래 / 그들이 더 좋아하는 것을 //

In Kinzler's study, / the babies stared / at the English speakers longer. // **단서 1** 유아들은 '같은' 언어를 사용하는 사람들을 더 오래 바라봄
Kinzler의 연구에서 / 아기들은 처다보았다 / 영어 사용자들을 더 오래 //

In other studies, / researchers have found / **that** infants are more likely to take a toy / offered by someone / **who** speaks / the same language as them. // **단서 2** 유아들은 '같은' 언어를 사용하는 사람들에게 더 호의적임
목적어절 접속사 주격 관계대명사(선행사: someone)
다른 연구들에서 / 연구자들은 발견했다 / 유아들이 장난감을 받을 가능성이 더 높다는 점을 / 사람에 의해 제공되는 / 말하는 / 자신들과 같은 언어를 //

Psychologists routinely cite / these and other experiments / as
evidence / of our built-in evolutionary preference / for "our own
kind." //　**단서 3** 유아들은 자신과 같은 집단에 대한 '내재된' 선호가 있음

cite A as B: A를 B로 인용하다

심리학자들은 반복해서 인용한다 / 이것들과 다른 실험들을 / 증거로서 / 우리의 내재된 진화
론적 선호에 대한 / '우리와 같은 종류'에 대한 //

→ Infants' more favorable responses / to those who use / a (A)
familiar language / show / that there can be a(n) (B) **inborn**
tendency / to prefer in-group members. //

목적어절 접속사

유아들의 더 호의적인 반응은 / 사용하는 사람들에 대한 / (A) 친숙한 언어를 / 보여 준다 /
(B) 선천적인 경향이 있을 수 있음 / 내집단 구성원들을 선호하는 //

- colleague ⓝ 동료　　　· tendency ⓝ 경향　　　· identify ⓥ 동일시하다
- in-group ⓝ 내(內)집단　　· infancy ⓝ 유아기　　· innate ⓐ 타고난
- psychology ⓝ 심리학　　· measure ⓝ 척도, 기준
- interest ⓝ 관심　　　· apparently ⓐⓓ 명백하게
- stare ⓥ 응시하다　　　· infant ⓝ 유아　　　· routinely ⓐⓓ 일상적으로
- cite ⓥ 인용하다　　　· evolutionary ⓐ 진화의
- preference ⓝ 선호　　　· favorable ⓐ 호의적인

2007년에 있었던 연구에서 Katherine Kinzler와 그녀의 하버드 동료들은
내(內)집단과 동일시하려는 우리의 경향이 상당 부분 유아기에 시작되고
선천적일 수 있음을 보여 주었다. Kinzler와 그녀의 팀은 가족들이 영어만
을 말하는 한 무리의 5개월 된 아이들을 골라 두 개의 영상을 보여 주었다.
한 영상에서 한 여성이 영어를 말하고 있었다. 다른 영상에서는 한 여성이
스페인어를 말하고 있었다. 그러고 나서 그들에게 두 여성 모두 말없이 나
란히 있는 화면을 보여주었다. 유아 심리학 연구에서 애착이나 관심의 표
준 척도는 주목인데, 아기들은 분명 그들이 더 좋아하는 것을 더 오래 쳐다
볼 것이다. Kinzler의 연구에서 아기들은 영어 사용자들을 더 오래 쳐다보
았다. 다른 연구들에서 연구자들은 유아들이 자신들과 같은 언어를 사용하
는 사람이 제공하는 장난감을 받을 가능성이 더 높다는 점을 발견했다. 심
리학자들은 '우리와 같은 종류'에 대한 우리의 내재된 진화론적인 선호에
대한 증거로 이것들과 다른 실험들을 반복해서 인용한다.

→ (A) 친숙한 언어를 사용하는 사람들에 대한 유아들의 더 호의적인 반응
은 내집단 구성원들을 선호하는 (B) 선천적인 경향이 있을 수 있음을 보여
준다.

다음 글의 내용을 한 문장으로 요약하고자 한다. 빈칸 (A), (B)에 들어갈
말로 가장 적절한 것은?

자신과 '같은' 언어를 사용하는 집단을 선호한다고 했음

	(A)		(B)
①	familiar 친숙한	—	inborn 선천적인
②	familiar 친숙한	—	acquired 습득된
③	foreign 낯선	—	cultural 문화적인
④	foreign 낯선	—	learned 학습된
⑤	formal 격식을 차린	—	innate 타고난

유아들은 자신과 '같은' 언어를 사용하는 집단에 대한 '내재된'
선호를 보임

→ 아기들의 선호가 습득되거나, 학습된 것은 아님

격식 차린 언어를 사용한 집단에 관한 언급은 없음

> **왜 정답?** ★★※ [정답률 63%]

유아들이 자신과 같은 언어를 사용하는 사람들에게 더 호의적인 반응을 보였다는 연
구 결과는 '우리와 같은 종류'에 대한 우리의 내재된 선호에 대한 증거라고 했다. 따
라서 요약문의 빈칸에는 ① familiar(친숙한)과 inborn(선천적인)이 들어가야 한다.

> **왜 오답?**

②, ④ acquired(습득된)와 learned(학습된)는 공통적으로 '후천적인'이라는 의미이
므로 내집단을 선호하는 선천적인 경향이 있다는 내용과 반대이다.　**함정**

③ foreign은 '낯선'이라는 의미로, 유아들이 자신과 같은 언어를 사용하는 사람들에
게 더 호의적이라는 내용과 반대된다.

⑤ innate는 '타고난'이라는 의미로, 내집단 구성원들을 선호하는 경향의 특징을 잘
설명하고 있지만, '격식을 차린'이라는 의미의 formal은 글의 내용과 무관하다.

글의 흐름

도입	Kinzler와 그녀의 동료들의 연구는 내집단과 동일시하려는 우리의 경향이 상당 부분 유아기에 시작되고 선천적일 수 있음을 보여 줌
연구 과정	가족들이 영어만 사용하는 5개월 된 아이들의 무리에게 한 여성이 영어만 말하는 영상과 한 여성이 스페인어만 말하는 영상을 보여 주고, 그들에게 두 여성이 말없이 있는 화면을 보여 줌
연구 결과	아기들은 영어 사용자들을 더 오래 쳐다봄
결론	'우리와 같은 종류'에 대한 내재된 진화론적인 선호에 대한 증거로 이것과 다른 실험을 반복해서 인용함

Q 10 정답 ① *음악과 감정의 관계

One way / that music could express emotion / is simply through
a learned association. //

관계부사

한 방법은 / 음악이 감정을 표현할 수 있는 / 단지 학습된 연관을 통해서이다 //

Perhaps there is nothing naturally sad / about a piece of music
/ in a minor key, /

-thing으로 끝나므로 뒤에서 꾸며줌

본질적으로 슬픈 무언가가 있는 것은 아닐 것이다 / 악곡에 대해 / 단조로 /

or played slowly with low notes. //

또는 낮은 음으로 느리게 연주된 //　**단서 1** 문화 속에서 슬픈 일과 연관시키는 것을
학습했기 때문에 어떤 음악이 슬프다고 생각함

Maybe we have just come to hear / certain kinds of music as sad /
because we have learned to associate them /

= certain kinds of music

우리는 듣게 되는데 / 어떤 종류의 음악을 슬프다고 / 우리가 그것들을 연관시키는 것을 학습
해 왔기 때문일 것이다 /

요약문의 culturally

in our culture / with sad events like funerals. //

우리의 문화 속에서 / 장례식과 같은 슬픈 일과 //

If this view is correct, / we should have difficulty interpreting
the emotions /

have difficulty -ing: ~하는 데 어려움을 겪다

만약 이 관점이 옳다면 / 우리는 감정을 이해하는 데 분명 어려움이 있을 것이다 /

과거분사

expressed in culturally unfamiliar music. //

문화적으로 친숙하지 않은 음악에 표현된 //　**단서 2** 음악과 감정 사이의 연결고리는 유사함이라는 입장

Totally opposed to this view / is the position / that the link
between music and emotion / is one of resemblance. //

동격절을 이끄는 접속사
요약문의 similarity

이 관점과 완전히 반대되는 것은 / 입장이다 / 음악과 감정 사이의 연결고리는 / 유사함이라
는 //

For example, / when we feel sad / we move slowly / and speak
slowly /

예컨대 / 슬프다고 느낄 때 / 우리는 느리게 움직인다 / 그리고 느리게 말한다 /

and in a low-pitched voice. //

그리고 낮은 음의 목소리로 //

Thus / when we hear slow, low music, / we hear it as sad. //

따라서 / 우리가 느리고 낮은 음의 음악을 들을 때 / 우리는 그것을 슬프게 듣는다 //

조건의 부사절을 이끄는 접속사

If this view is correct, / we should have little difficulty
understanding the emotion / expressed in culturally unfamiliar
music. //

만약 이 관점이 옳다면 / 우리는 감정을 이해하는 데 분명 어려움이 거의 없을 것이다 / 문화적
으로 친숙하지 않은 음악에 표현된 //

→ It is believed / that emotion expressed in music / can be
understood / through a(n) (A) **culturally** learned association /
or it can be understood /

가주어　*진주어절 접속사*

믿어진다 / 음악에 표현된 감정은 / 이해될 수 있다고 / 문화적으로 학습된 연관을 통해서 /
혹은 그것은 이해될 수 있다고 /

due to the (B) **similarity** / between music and emotion. //

유사성 때문에 / 음악과 감정 사이의 //

- association ⓝ 연관, 관련   • minor key 단조
- note ⓝ 음, 음색   • funeral ⓝ 장례식
- interpret ⓥ 이해하다, 통역하다   • unfamiliar ⓐ 친숙하지 않은
- be opposed to ~에 반대하다   • resemblance ⓝ 유사, 유사성
- low-pitched ⓐ 낮은 음의

음악이 감정을 표현할 수 있는 한 방법은 난지 학습된 연관을 통해서이다. 단조나 낮은 음으로 느리게 연주된 악곡에 대해 본질적으로 슬픈 무언가가 있는 것은 아닐 것이다. 우리는 어떤 종류의 음악을 슬프다고 듣게 되는데 우리가 우리의 문화 속에서 그것들을 장례식과 같은 슬픈 일과 연관시키는 것을 학습해 왔기 때문일 것이다. 만약 이 관점이 옳다면, 우리는 문화적으로 친숙하지 않은 음악에 표현된 감정을 이해하는 데 분명 어려움이 있을 것이다. 이 관점과 완전히 반대되는 입장은 음악과 감정 사이의 연결고리는 유사함이라는 것이다. 예컨대, 슬프다고 느낄 때 우리는 느리게 움직이고 낮은 음의 목소리로 느리게 말한다. 따라서 우리가 느리고 낮은 음의 음악을 들을 때, 우리는 그것을 슬프게 듣는다. 만약 이 관점이 옳다면, 우리는 문화적으로 친숙하지 않은 음악에 표현된 감정을 이해하는 데 분명 어려움이 거의 없을 것이다.

→ 음악에 표현된 감정은 (A) 문화적으로 학습된 연관을 통해서 이해될 수 있다고 믿어지거나, 혹은 음악과 감정 사이의 (B) 유사성 때문에 이해될 수 있다고 믿어진다.

다음 글의 내용을 한 문장으로 요약하고자 한다. 빈칸 (A), (B)에 들어갈 말로 가장 적절한 것은?

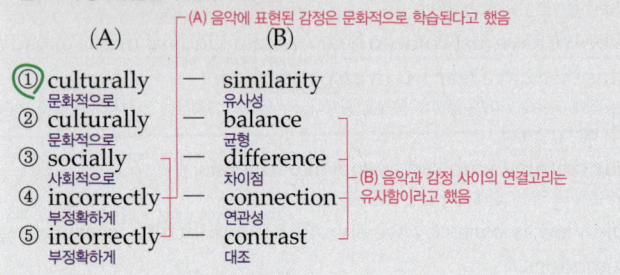

(A) 음악에 표현된 감정은 문화적으로 학습된다고 했음

	(A)	(B)
①	culturally 문화적으로	similarity 유사성
②	culturally 문화적으로	balance 균형
③	socially 사회적으로	difference 차이점
④	incorrectly 부정확하게	connection 연관성
⑤	incorrectly 부정확하게	contrast 대조

(B) 음악과 감정 사이의 연결고리는 유사함이라고 했음

왜 정답? ★★❀ [정답률 67%]

우리가 우리의 문화 속에서 음악과 감정을 연관시키는 학습을 해 왔기 때문에 음악에 표현된 감정을 이해한다는 관점과 음악과 감정 사이에 유사점이 있어서 음악을 들을 때 그 감정을 이해한다는 관점을 대조한 글이다. 따라서 (A)에는 '문화적으로'를 의미하는 culturally가, (B)에는 '유사성'을 의미하는 similarity가 들어가는 것이 적절하므로 정답은 ①이다.

왜 오답?

② (B)에서 음악과 감정 사이의 균형(balance) 때문에 음악이 이해되는 것이 아니므로 적절하지 않다.   〔주의〕

③ (A)의 socially(사회적으로)는 넓게 봤을 때 가능하다고 생각할 수도 있지만, difference(차이점)는 글의 내용과 정반대되는 내용이다.

④, ⑤ (A)에서 부정확하게(incorrectly) 학습된 연관을 통해 음악이 이해된다는 것은 글의 내용에 부합하지 않고, (B)에 contrast(대조)가 들어가면 글의 내용과 반대가 된다.

✱ 글의 흐름

전제	음악이 감정을 표현할 수 있는 한 방법은 학습된 연관을 통해서임
설명	음악은 각자의 문화 속에서 음악과 감정을 연관시키는 학습을 통해 이해됨
대조	음악과 감정 사이에 유사함이 있어 음악이 이해되는 것임

Q 11 정답 ③ ✱ 권위 있는 부모가 자녀의 학업 성취에 미치는 영향

According to a study of Swedish adolescents, / an important factor of adolescents' academic success / is how they respond to challenges. //
스웨덴 청소년들에 대한 연구에 따르면 / 청소년들의 학문적 성공의 중요한 요인은 / 그들이 어려움에 반응하는 방식이다 //

〔단서 1〕 권위 있는 양육 방식에 노출된 청소년이 어려움에 직면했을 때 잘 대처함

The study reports / that when facing difficulties, / adolescents exposed to an authoritative parenting style / are less likely to be passive, helpless, / and afraid to fail. //
〔앞에 주격 관계대명사와 be동사 생략 / 사이에 they are 생략〕
이 연구는 보고하고 있다 / 어려움을 직면했을 때 / 권위가 있는 양육 방식에 노출된 청소년들은 / 덜 수동적이고, 덜 무기력하다고 / 그리고 실패를 덜 두려워한다고 //

〔단서 2〕 권위가 있는 부모들이 학교 활동에 관여하려고 노력하기 때문에 아이들이 학습을 더 잘함

Another study of nine high schools / in Wisconsin and northern California / indicates that / children of authoritative parents / do well in school, /
〔목적어절을 이끄는 접속사〕
9개 고교에서 진행된 또 다른 연구는 / Wisconsin과 northern California의 / 밝히고 있다 / 권위가 있는 부모들의 아이들이 / 학습을 잘 하는데 /

because these parents put a lot of effort / into getting involved in their children's school activities. //
그 이유는 이러한 부모들이 많은 노력을 기울이기 때문이라고 / 아이들의 학교 활동에 관여하고자 //

That is, / authoritative parents are significantly more likely / to help their children with homework, /
즉 / 권위가 있는 부모들은 가능성이 훨씬 더 크다 / 아이들의 숙제를 도와주고 /

to attend school programs, / to watch their children in sports, / and to help students select courses. //
〔help+목적어+목적격보어(동사원형)〕
학교 프로그램에 참여하며 / 스포츠에 참여하는 아이들을 지켜보고 / 아이들의 과목 선택을 도와줄 //

Moreover, / these parents are more aware of / what their children do / and how they perform / in school. //
〔= authoritative parents〕
게다가 / 이러한 부모들은 더 잘 인지하고 있다 / 그들의 아이들이 하고 있는 일에 대해 / 그리고 수행하는 방식에 대해 / 학교에서 //

〔단서 3〕 권위가 있는 부모들이 아이들의 학교생활을 더 잘 인지함

Finally, / authoritative parents praise / academic excellence and the importance of working hard / more than other parents do. //
〔= praise〕
마지막으로 / 권위가 있는 부모들은 칭찬한다 / 학문적 탁월함과 근면함의 중요성을 / 다른 부모들에 비해 더 많이 //

〔단서 4〕 권위가 있는 부모들이 학문적 탁월함과 근면함의 중요성을 더 많이 칭찬함

→ The studies above show / that the children of authoritative parents / often succeed academically, /
〔목적어절을 이끄는 접속사〕
위 연구는 보여준다 / 권위가 있는 부모의 아이들이 / 종종 학업 성취가 좋다는 것을 /

since they are more (A) **willing** to deal with their difficulties / and are affected by their parents' (B) **active** involvement. //
왜냐하면 그들이 어려움에 더 기꺼이 대처하려 하기 때문에 / 그리고 그 부모들의 적극적인 관여에 영향을 받기 (때문에) //

- adolescent ⓝ 청소년   • factor ⓝ 요인   • academic ⓐ 학문적인
- challenge ⓝ 어려움   • face ⓥ 직면하다   • exposed to ~에 노출된
- authoritative ⓐ 권위적인   • passive ⓐ 수동적인
- helpless ⓐ 무기력한   • indicate ⓥ 밝히다, 나타내다
- effort ⓝ 노력   • involve ⓥ 관여시키다
- significantly ⓐⓓ 크게, 의미가 있게   • attend ⓥ 참여하다
- select ⓥ 선택하다   • be aware of ~을 인지하다
- perform ⓥ 수행하다   • praise ⓥ 칭찬하다
- involvement ⓝ 관여

스웨덴 청소년들에 대한 연구에 따르면, 청소년들의 학문적 성공의 중요한 요인은 그들이 어려움에 반응하는 방식이다. 이 연구는, 어려움을 직면했을 때, 권위가 있는 양육 방식에 노출된 청소년들은 덜 수동적이고, 덜 무기력하며, 실패를 덜 두려워한다고 보고하고 있다. Wisconsin과 northern California의 9개 고교에서 진행된 또 다른 연구는 권위가 있는 부모들의 아이들이 학습을 잘 하는데, 그 이유는 이러한 부모들이 아이들의 학교 활동에 관여하고자 많은 노력을 기울이기 때문이라고 밝히고 있다. 즉, 권위가 있는 부모들은 아이들의 숙제를 도와주고, 학교 프로그램에 참여하며, 스포츠에 참여하는 아이들을 지켜보고, 아이들의 과목 선택을 도와줄 가능성이 훨씬 더 크다. 게다가, 이러한 부모들은 그들의 아이들이 학교에서 하고 있는 일과 수행하는 방식에 대해 더 잘 인지하고 있다. 마지막으로, 권위가 있는 부모들은 다른 부모들에 비해 학문적 탁월함과 근면함의 중요성을 더 많이 칭찬한다.

→ 위 연구는 권위가 있는 부모의 아이들이 어려움에 더 (A) **기꺼이** 대처하려 하며, 그 부모들의 (B) **적극적인** 관여에 영향을 받기 때문에 학업 성취가 좋다는 것을 보여준다.

다음 글의 내용을 한 문장으로 요약하고자 한다. 빈칸 (A), (B)에 들어갈 말로 가장 적절한 것은? [3점]

	(A)		(B)
①	likely ~할 것 같은	—	random 임의의
②	willing 기꺼이	—	minimal 최소의
③	willing 기꺼이	—	active 적극적인
④	hesitant 주저하는	—	unwanted 원치 않는
⑤	hesitant 주저하는	—	constant 끊임없는

(A) 권위가 있는 부모의 아이들이 어려움에 직면했을 때 더 '기꺼이' 대처함
(B) 권위가 있는 부모는 아이들의 학교 활동에 더 '적극적인' 관여를 함

왜 정답? ★★★ [정답률 68%]

권위가 있는 부모의 아이들은 학업 성취가 높은데 그 이유는 아이들이 어려움에 직면했을 때 더 잘 대처하고, 부모들이 아이들의 학교 활동에 관여하려고 많은 노력을 기울이기 때문이라고 했다. 또한, 권위 있는 부모는 아이들의 학교생활을 더 잘 인지하고 있고, 학업적 우월성과 근면함의 중요성을 더 많이 칭찬한다고 설명했다. 따라서 요약문의 (A)에는 '기꺼이'라는 뜻의 willing, (B)에는 '적극적인'이라는 뜻의 active가 들어가는 것이 적절하므로 정답은 ③이다.

왜 오답?

①, ② 권위 있는 부모는 아이들의 학교 활동에 관여하고자 많은 노력을 기울인다고 했는데 (B)에 '임의의(random)'나 '최소의(minimal)'를 넣으면 글의 내용과 반대가 된다.

④, ⑤ 스웨덴 청소년들에 대한 연구에 따르면 권위가 있는 양육 방식에 노출된 청소년들은 어려움에 직면했을 때 덜 수동적이고, 덜 무기력하며, 실패를 덜 두려워한다고 했다. 하지만 (A)에 '주저하는(hesitant)'이 들어가면 어려움을 대처하는 데 더 주저한다는 의미가 되어 글의 내용과 반대가 된다.

＊ 글의 흐름

연구 ①	청소년들이 어려움에 반응하는 방식은 학문적 성공의 중요한 요인인데, 권위가 있는 양육 방식에 노출된 청소년들이 어려움에 더 잘 대처함
연구 ②	권위가 있는 부모들의 아이들이 학습을 잘하는데, 이런 부모들이 아이들의 학교 활동에 관여하고자 더 많은 노력을 기울이기 때문임
설명	권위가 있는 부모들은 아이들의 숙제를 도와주고, 학교 프로그램에 참여하는 등의 가능성이 훨씬 더 큼
부연	권위가 있는 부모들은 아이들의 학교생활을 더 잘 인지하고 있음

Q 12 정답 ② ＊사람들 간의 관계에 휴대폰이 미치는 영향

In one study, / researchers asked pairs of strangers / to sit down in a room and chat. //
한 연구에서 / 연구자들은 서로 모르는 사람들끼리 짝을 이루어 / 한 방에 앉아서 이야기를 하도록 했다 //

In half of the rooms, / a cell phone was placed / on a nearby table; / in the other half, / no phone was present. //
절반의 방에는 / 휴대폰이 놓여 있었고 / 근처 탁자 위에 / 나머지 절반에는 / 휴대폰이 없었다 //

동사 asked보다 더 선행하는 행동이므로 과거완료
After the conversations **had ended**, / the researchers asked the participants / what they thought of each other. //
대화가 끝난 후 / 연구자들은 참가자들에게 물었다 / 서로에 대해 어떻게 생각하는지를 //

Here's what they learned: /
여기에 그들이 알게 된 것이 있다 /

단서 1 휴대폰이 있는 방에서 대화한 참가자들이 관계의 질이 더 나빴다고 생각했음
when a cell phone was present in the room, / the participants reported / the quality of their relationship / was worse / than **those** who'd talked / in a cell phone-free room. //
(= the participants)
방에 휴대폰이 있을 때 / 참가자들은 말했다 / 자신들의 관계의 질이 / 더 나빴다고 / 대화했던 참가자들에 비해 / 휴대폰이 없는 방에서 //

주격 관계대명사
The pairs / **who** talked in the rooms with cell phones / thought their partners showed / less empathy. //
짝들은 / 휴대폰이 있는 방에서 대화한 / 자신의 상대가 보여주었다고 생각했다 / 더 적은 공감을 //

Think of all the times / you've **sat** down to have lunch / with a friend / and **set** your phone on the table. //
병렬 구조
모든 순간을 떠올려 보라 / 점심을 먹기 위해 자리에 앉은 / 친구와 / 그리고 탁자 위에 휴대폰을 놓았던 //

단서 2 휴대폰을 확인하지 않아도 휴대폰이 근처에 있다는 것만으로도 신경이 쓰여 사람들의 관계에 안 좋은 영향을 끼친다는 것을 알 수 있음
You might have felt good about yourself / because you didn't pick it up / **to check** your messages, /
부사적 용법(목적)
잘했다고 느꼈을지 모르지만 / 휴대폰을 집어 들지 않았으므로 / 메시지를 확인하려고 /

요약문의 ignored   요약문의 weakens
but your **unchecked** messages / were still **hurting** your connection / with the person **sitting** across from you. //
앞에 who was 생략
하지만 확인하지 않은 여러분의 메시지는 / 여전히 관계를 상하게 하고 있었다 / 맞은편에 앉아 있는 사람과의 //

주어
→ The presence of a cell phone / (A) **weakens** the connection / between people involved in conversations, / even when the phone is being (B) **ignored**. //
휴대폰의 존재는 / 관계를 약화시킨다 / 대화에 참여하는 사람들 간의 / 심지어 휴대폰이 무시되고 있을 때조차 //

• pair ⓝ 짝   • stranger ⓝ 모르는 사람, 낯선 사람
• chat ⓥ 이야기하다   • place ⓥ 놓다, 두다   • nearby ⓐ 근처의
• present ⓐ 있는, 존재하는   • conversation ⓝ 대화
• participant ⓝ 참가자   • report ⓥ 말하다, 전하다   • quality ⓝ 질
• relationship ⓝ 관계   • connection ⓝ 관계, 연결

한 연구에서, 연구자들은 서로 모르는 사람들끼리 짝을 이루어 한 방에 앉아서 이야기하도록 했다. 절반의 방에는 근처 탁자 위에 휴대폰이 놓여 있었고, 나머지 절반에는 휴대폰이 없었다. 대화가 끝난 후, 연구자들은 참가자들에게 서로에 대해 어떻게 생각하는지를 물었다. 여기에 그들이 알게 된 것이 있다. 휴대폰이 없는 방에서 대화했던 참가자들에 비해 방에 휴대폰이 있을 때 참가자들은 자신들의 관계의 질이 더 나빴다고 말했다. 휴대폰이 있는 방에서 대화한 짝들은 자신의 상대가 공감을 덜 보여주었다고 생각했다. 친구와 점심을 먹기 위해 자리에 앉아 탁자 위에 휴대폰을 놓았던 모든 순간을 떠올려 보라. 메시지를 확인하려고 휴대폰을 집어 들지 않았으므로 잘했다고 느꼈을지 모르지만, 확인하지 않은 여러분의 메시지는 여전히 맞은편에 앉아 있는 사람과의 관계를 상하게 하고 있었다.
→ 휴대폰의 존재는 심지어 휴대폰이 (B) **무시되고** 있을 때조차 대화에 참여하는 사람들 간의 관계를 (A) **약화시킨다**.

다음 글의 내용을 한 문장으로 요약하고자 한다. 빈칸 (A), (B)에 들어갈 말로 가장 적절한 것은?

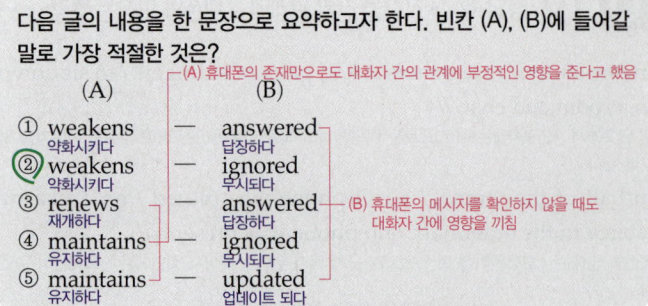

(A) 휴대폰의 존재만으로도 대화자 간의 관계에 부정적인 영향을 준다고 했음
(B) 휴대폰의 메시지를 확인하지 않을 때도 대화자 간에 영향을 끼침

	(A)		(B)
①	weakens 약화시키다	—	answered 답장하다
②	weakens 약화시키다	—	ignored 무시되다
③	renews 재개하다	—	answered 답장하다
④	maintains 유지하다	—	ignored 무시되다
⑤	maintains 유지하다	—	updated 업데이트 되다

> **왜 정답 ?** ★★★ [정답률 54%]

휴대폰이 놓여 있는 방과 없는 방에서 모르는 사람들끼리 대화하도록 한 연구에서, 휴대폰이 있는 방에서 대화한 참가자들이 관계의 질이 더 나빴다고 생각했다는 결과가 나왔다고 했다. 휴대폰의 메시지를 확인하지 않아도 휴대폰이 있다는 것 자체로 사람들의 관계에 안 좋은 영향을 끼친다는 것을 알 수 있다는 내용이다. 따라서 요약문의 빈칸에는 각각 ② weakens(약화시키다)와 ignored(무시되다)가 들어가야 한다.

> **왜 오답 ?**

①, ③ 휴대폰의 메시지를 확인하지 않더라도 관계에 해가 된다고 했으므로 (B)에 '답장하다(answered)'는 적절하지 않다. 또한, 메시지에 답장하는 것과 관계를 '재개하는(renews)' 것의 상관관계는 언급되어있지 않다.
④, ⑤ 휴대폰에 온 메시지를 보지 않거나 휴대폰이 '업데이트 된다고(updated)' 해서 관계가 '유지되는(maintains)' 것은 아니다.

★ **글의 흐름**

연구 내용	휴대폰이 놓여 있는 방과 없는 방에서 모르는 사람들끼리 대화하도록 함
연구 결과	휴대폰이 있는 방에서 대화한 참가자들이 관계의 질이 더 나빴다고 생각했음
예시	친구와 밥을 먹을 때 휴대폰 메시지를 확인하지 않아도 탁자 위에 휴대폰이 있는 것만으로 관계에 안 좋은 영향을 끼침

Q 13 정답 ② ★성찰적 일기 쓰기의 역할

핵심 주어(단수)
One of the most powerful tools / **to find** meaning in our lives / 형용사적 용법(tools 수식)
단수 동사
is reflective journaling / — thinking back on and writing about what has happened to us. //
가장 강력한 도구들 중 하나는 / 우리의 삶에서 의미를 찾기 위한 / 성찰적 일기 쓰기이다 / 즉 우리에게 일어난 일을 돌아보고 그것에 대해 쓰는 것이다 //

In the 1990s, / Stanford University researchers asked undergraduate students / on spring break / **to journal** about 명사적 용법(목적격 보어)
their most important personal values and their daily activities; /
1990년대에 / Stanford University 연구자들이 학생들에게 요청했다 / 봄방학에 / 그들의 가장 중요한 개인적인 가치와 그들의 하루의 활동들에 대해 쓰도록 /

수동태 주격 관계대명사
others **were asked** / to write about only the good things / **that** happened to them in the day. //
다른 사람들은 요청받았다 / 좋은 일만 쓰도록 / 그날 그들에게 일어난 //

복수 주어 주격 관계대명사
Three weeks later, / **the students** / **who** had written about their
복수 동사
values / **were** happier, healthier, and more confident / about their ability to handle stress /
3주 후에 / 학생들은 / 자신의 가치에 관해 썼던 / 더 행복하고, 더 건강하고, 더 자신 있었다 / 스트레스를 다루는 그들의 능력에 대해 /

=students 주격 관계대명사
than the **ones** / **who** had only focused on the good stuff. //
학생들보다 / 좋은 것에만 초점을 맞췄던 // 단서 1 '가치'에 관해 일기를 쓴 학생들이 더 행복했음

전치사의 목적어(간접의문문)
By reflecting / on **how their daily activities supported their values**, / students had gained a new perspective / on those activities and choices. // 단서 2 하루의 활동이 '가치'를 뒷받침하는 방식을 성찰하면서 새로운 관점을 얻었음
성찰함으로써 / 어떻게 그들의 하루의 활동들이 그들의 가치를 뒷받침하는지에 대해 / 학생들은 새로운 관점을 얻었다 / 그 활동들과 선택들에 대해 //

Little stresses and hassles / were now demonstrations of their values / in action. //
작은 스트레스와 귀찮은 일들은 / 이제 그들의 가치를 보여주는 것이었다 / 행동에서 //

Suddenly, / their lives were full of meaningful activities. //
갑자기 / 그들의 삶은 의미 있는 활동으로 가득 찼다 //

앞에 to가 생략됨
And all they had to do / was **reflect and write** about it / — positively reframing their experiences / with their personal values. // 단서 3 개인적인 가치로 그들의 경험을 '재구성'함
그리고 그들이 해야 했던 모든 일은 / 그것에 대해 돌아보고 쓰는 것이었다 / 그들의 경험을 긍정적으로 재구성하면서 / 개인적인 가치로 //

→ Journaling about daily activities / based on what we 사역동사+목적어+목적격 보어(원형부정사)
believe to be (A) **worthwhile** / can **make us feel** / that our life is meaningful /
일상의 활동에 대해 일기를 쓰는 것은 / 우리가 가치 있다고 믿는 것에 근거하여 / 우리가 느끼게 만들 수 있다 / 우리의 삶이 의미 있다는 것을 /
by (B) **rethinking** our experiences in a new way. //
새로운 방식으로 자신의 경험들을 다시 생각함으로써 //

・ reflective ⓐ 성찰적인 ・ journaling ⓝ 일기 쓰기
・ think back on ~을 돌이켜 보다 ・ undergraduate ⓝ (대학) 학부생
・ value ⓝ 가치 ・ handle ⓥ 다루다 ・ reflect ⓥ 성찰하다, 숙고하다
・ support ⓥ 뒷받침하다 ・ perspective ⓝ 관점
・ demonstration ⓝ 입증, (분명히) 보여줌 ・ reframe ⓥ 재구성하다
・ worthwhile ⓐ 가치 있는

우리의 삶에서 의미를 찾기 위한 가장 강력한 도구들 중 하나는 성찰적 일기 쓰기, 즉 우리에게 일어난 일을 돌아보고 그것에 대해 쓰는 것이다. 1990년대에 Stanford University 연구자들이 봄방학에 학부생들에게 그들의 가장 중요한 개인적인 가치와 그들의 하루의 활동들에 대해 쓰도록 요청했다. 다른 사람들은 그날 그들에게 일어난 좋은 일만 쓰도록 요청받았다. 3주 후에, 자신의 가치에 관해 썼던 학생들은 좋은 것에만 초점을 맞췄던 학생들보다 더 행복하고, 더 건강하고, 스트레스를 다루는 자신의 능력에 대해 더 자신 있었다. 어떻게 그들의 하루의 활동들이 그들의 가치를 뒷받침하는지에 대해 성찰함으로써, 학생들은 그 활동들과 선택들에 대해 새로운 관점을 얻었다. 작은 스트레스와 귀찮은 일들은 이제 행동에서 그들의 가치를 보여주는 것이었다. 갑자기, 그들의 삶은 의미 있는 활동으로 가득 찼다. 그리고 그들이 해야 했던 모든 일은 그들의 경험을 개인적인 가치로 긍정적으로 재구성하면서 그것에 대해 돌아보고 쓰는 것이었다.
→ 우리가 (A) 가치 있다고 믿는 것에 근거하여 일상의 활동에 대해 일기를 쓰는 것은 새로운 방식으로 자신의 경험들을 (B) 다시 생각함으로써 우리가 자신의 삶이 의미 있다는 것을 느끼게 만들 수 있다.

다음 글의 내용을 한 문장으로 요약하고자 한다. 빈칸 (A), (B)에 들어갈 말로 가장 적절한 것은?

	(A)		(B)	
①	factual 사실에 기반을 둔	—	rethinking 다시 생각하기	사실만 일기로 쓴 것이 아님
②	worthwhile 가치 있는	—	rethinking 다시 생각하기	자신의 경험을 돌아보면서 개인적인 가치로 재구성하여 썼음
③	outdated 진부한	—	generalizing 일반화하기	진부하다고 믿는 것을 일기로 일반화한 것이 아님
④	objective 객관적인	—	generalizing 일반화하기	자신의 경험을 객관화한 것이 아님
⑤	demanding 힘든	—	describing 묘사하기	힘들었던 활동을 묘사한 것이 아님

1st 요약문을 통해 글에서 무엇을 찾아야 하는지 확인한다.

요약문	우리가 (A) _____고 믿는 것에 근거하여 일상의 활동에 대해 일기를 쓰는 것은 새로운 방식으로 자신의 경험들을 (B) _____으로써 우리가 자신의 삶이 의미 있다는 것을 느끼게 만들 수 있다.

➡ 글에서 찾아야 하는 것
(A): 우리가 사실에 기반을 뒀다고, 가치 있다고, 진부하다고, 객관적이라고, 힘들다고 믿는 것에 근거하여 일상의 활동에 대해 일기를 쓰는 것이
(B): 새로운 방식으로 경험들을 다시 생각함으로써, 일반화함으로써, 묘사함으로써 삶의 의미를 느끼게 만드는지

2nd 글의 내용을 파악하여 요약문을 완성한다.

- • 3주 후에, 자신의 가치에 관해 썼던 학생들은 좋은 것에만 초점을 맞췄던 학생들보다 더 행복하고, 더 건강하고, 스트레스를 다루는 자신의 능력에 대해 더 자신 있었다. **단서 1**
- • 어떻게 그들의 하루의 활동들이 그들의 가치를 뒷받침하는지에 대해 성찰함으로써, 학생들은 그 활동들과 선택들에 대해 새로운 관점을 얻었다. **단서 2**

➡ **개인적으로 중요한 가치와 하루의 활동을 일기로 쓴 학부생들:** 긍정적 결과
하루에 일어난 좋은 일만 일기로 쓴 학부생들: 부정적 결과
▶ '가치 있다'고 믿는 것에 근거하여 성찰함으로써 새로운 관점을 얻은 것이므로 (A)에는 ② worthwhile이 들어가야 함

- • 갑자기, 그들의 삶은 의미 있는 활동으로 가득 찼다. 그리고 그들이 해야 했던 모든 일은 그들의 경험을 개인적인 가치로 긍정적으로 재구성하면서 그것에 대해 돌아보고 쓰는 것이었다. **단서 3**

➡ 개인적인 가치로 그들의 경험을 긍정적으로 '돌아보고 재구성함으로써' 삶이 의미 있는 활동으로 가득하게 됐다.
▶ (B)에는 ①, ② rethinking이 들어가야 함

| 선택지 분석 |
① 사실에 근거하여 일기를 쓰라고 하는 글이 아니다.
②가치를 바탕으로 일상을 되돌아보는 것은 삶의 의미를 느낄 수 있게 한다고 했다.
③ 진부하다고 믿는 것을 일기로 씀으로써 일반화한 것이 아니다.
④ 일상을 객관적인 시각에서 바라보라는 내용이 아니다.
⑤ 힘들었던 활동을 일기에 묘사하라는 내용은 언급되지 않았다.

Q 14 정답 ① ＊약간의 일탈을 긍정적으로 판단하기

It's not news to anyone / that we judge others / based on their clothes. //
(가주어 / 진주어절 접속사 / '~에 근거하여')
~은 누구에게도 새로운 일이 아니다 / 우리가 다른 사람들을 판단하는 것은 / 그들의 의복에 근거하여 //

In general, / studies that investigate these judgments find / that people prefer clothing / that matches expectations / — surgeons in scrubs, little boys in blue / — with one notable exception. //
(주격 관계대명사 / 목적어절 접속사 / 주격 관계대명사)
일반적으로 / 이러한 판단을 조사하는 연구는 발견한다 / 사람들이 옷을 선호한다는 것을 / 예상에 맞는 / 수술복을 입은 외과 의사, 파란 옷을 입은 남자아이와 같이 / 하나의 눈에 띄는 예외가 있는 //

A series of studies / published in an article / in June 2014 / in the *Journal of Consumer Research* / explored observers' reactions / to people who broke established norms only slightly. //
(앞에 주격 관계대명사와 be동사가 생략됨 / 주격 관계대명사)
일련의 연구는 / 기사에 실린 / 2014년 6월에 / 〈Journal of Consumer Research〉에 / 관찰자들의 반응을 탐구했다 / 확립된 규범을 아주 약간 어긴 사람들에 대한 //

In one scenario, / a man at a black-tie affair was viewed / as having higher status and competence / when wearing a red bow tie. // **단서 1** 정장 행사에서 빨간 나비넥타이를 맴 → 더 높은 지위와 능력 가진 것으로 보여짐
(접속사가 생략되지 않은 분사구문)
한 시나리오에서는 / 정장 차림의 행사에서 한 남자가 보여졌다 / 더 높은 지위와 능력을 갖춘 것으로 / 빨간 나비넥타이를 맸을 때 // **단서 2** 지위와 역량에 대한 평가가 높아짐

The researchers also found / that valuing uniqueness increased audience members' ratings / of the status and competence of a professor / who wore red sneakers / while giving a lecture. //
(목적어절 접속사 / 주격 관계대명사 / 접속사가 생략되지 않은 분사구문)
연구자들은 또한 발견했다 / 독특함을 중시하는 것이 청중들의 평가를 높였다는 것을 / 교수의 지위와 역량에 대한 / 빨간 운동화를 신은 / 강의를 하는 동안 //

The results suggest / that people judge these slight deviations from the norm / as positive / **단서 3** 사람들은 규범에서 살짝 일탈한 것을 긍정적으로 봄
(목적어절 접속사)
그 결과들은 시사한다 / 사람들이 규범으로부터 이러한 약간의 일탈들을 판단한다는 것을 / 긍정적으로 /

because they suggest / that the individual is powerful enough / to risk the social costs / of such behaviors. //
(목적어절 접속사)
왜냐하면 그것들은 시사하기 때문이다 / 그 사람이 충분히 강하다는 것을 / 사회적 비용을 감수할 만큼 / 그러한 행동으로 인한 //

> → A series of studies show / that people view an individual (A) **positively** / when the individual only slightly (B) **challenges** / the norm for what people should wear. //
> (목적어절 접속사 / 선행사를 포함하는 관계대명사)
> 일련의 연구는 나타낸다 / 사람들이 한 사람을 긍정적으로 본다는 것을 / 그 사람이 아주 약간 도전할 때 / 사람들이 무엇을 착용해야 하는지에 대한 규범에 //

- • judgment ⓝ 판단
- • surgeon ⓝ 외과 의사
- • exception ⓝ 예외
- • affair ⓝ (공식적인) 일
- • deviation ⓝ 일탈
- • expectation ⓝ 예상, 기대
- • scrub ⓝ 수술복
- • explore ⓥ 탐구하다
- • competence ⓝ 능숙함, 능력
- • notable ⓐ 눈에 띄는
- • norm ⓝ 규범, 기준

우리가 다른 사람들을 그들의 의복에 근거하여 판단하는 것은 누구에게도 새로운 일이 아니다. 일반적으로, 이러한 판단을 조사하는 연구는 사람들이 수술복을 입은 외과 의사, 파란 옷을 입은 남자아이와 같이 예상에 맞지만 하나의 눈에 띄는 예외가 있는 옷을 선호한다는 것을 발견한다. 〈Journal of Consumer Research〉의 2014년 6월 기사에 실린 일련의 연구는 확립된 규범을 아주 약간 어긴 사람들에 대한 관찰자들의 반응을 탐구했다. 한 시나리오에서는, 정장 차림의 행사에서 한 남자가 빨간 나비넥타이를 맸을 때 더 높은 지위와 능력을 갖춘 것으로 보여졌다. 연구자들은 독특함을 중시하는 것이 강의를 하는 동안 빨간 운동화를 신은 교수의 지위와 역량에 대한 청중들의 평가를 높였다는 것을 또한 발견했다. 그 결과들은 사람들이 규범으로부터 이러한 약간의 일탈들을 긍정적으로 판단한다는 것을 시사하는데, 왜냐하면 그것들은 그 사람이 그러한 행동으로 인한 사회적 비용을 감수할 만큼 충분히 강하다는 것을 시사하기 때문이다.
→ 일련의 연구는 사람들이 무엇을 착용해야 하는지에 대한 규범에 한 사람이 아주 약간 (B) 도전할 때 사람들이 그 사람을 (A) 긍정적으로 본다는 것을 나타낸다.

> 다음 글의 내용을 한 문장으로 요약하고자 한다. 빈칸 (A), (B)에 들어갈 말로 가장 적절한 것은?
>
> | | (A) | | (B) | |
> |---|---|---|---|---|
> | ① | positively 긍정적으로 | — | challenges 도전하다 | 규범에 약간 일탈하는 것은 긍정적으로 봄 |
> | ② | negatively 부정적으로 | — | challenges | 규범에 도전하는 사람들을 긍정적으로 봄 |
> | ③ | indifferently 무관심하게 | — | neglects 무시하다 | 규범을 무시하는 사람들에게 무관심하다는 내용이 아님 |
> | ④ | negatively | — | meets 지키다 | 규범을 지키는 사람들을 부정적으로 본다는 언급은 없음 |
> | ⑤ | positively | — | meets | 규범을 지키는 사람들을 긍정적으로 본다는 언급은 없음 |

| 문제 풀이 순서 | ★★★ [정답률 54%]

1st 요약문을 통해 글에서 무엇을 찾아야 하는지 확인한다.

요약문	일련의 연구는 사람들이 무엇을 착용해야 하는지에 대한 규범에 한 사람이 아주 약간 (B) _____ 때 사람들이 그 사람을 (A) _____ 본다는 것을 나타낸다.

→ 글에서 찾아야 하는 것
(B): 무엇을 착용해야 하는지에 대한 규범에 한 사람이 아주 약간 <u>도전할, 무시할,</u>
<u>지킬</u> 때
(A): 사람들이 그 사람을 <u>긍정적으로, 부정적으로, 무관심하게</u> 보는지

2nd 글의 내용을 파악하여 요약문을 완성한다.

┌ 확립된 규범을 아주 약간 어긴 사람들에 대한 반응을 탐구함
│ **예시 1**: 정장 차림의 행사에서 빨간 나비넥타이를 맨 남자
│   → 더 높은 지위와 능력을 갖춘 것으로 보여짐 `단서 1`
│ **예시 2**: 빨간 운동화를 신고 강의한 교수
│   → 지위와 역량에 대한 평가가 높아짐 `단서 2`
└→ 약간의 일탈이 그 행동으로 인한 사회적 비용을 감수할 만큼 강하다는 것을
   시사하기 때문에 사람들은 이를 긍정적으로 본다. `단서 3`
   ▶ 무엇을 착용할지 규범에 약간 벗어난, 즉 '도전한' 것이므로 (B)에는 ①, ②
   challenges가 들어가야 하고, 이에 사람들의 평가가 '긍정적'이었으므로 (A)에는
   ①, ⑤ positively가 들어가야 함

| 선택지 분석 |

① 규범에 약간의 일탈로 도전하는 사람들을 긍정적으로 본다고 했다.
② 규범에 도전하는 사람들을 부정적으로 본다는 것은 글의 내용과 정반대이다.
③ 규범을 무시하는 사람들에게 무관심하다는 내용의 글이 아니다.
④ 규범을 지키는 사람들을 부정적으로 보는지는 언급되지 않았다.
⑤ 규범을 지키는 사람들을 긍정적으로 보는지도 언급되지 않았다.

Q 15 정답 ② *좋은 식단인가 나쁜 식단인가 ——————

뒤에 목적어절 접속사 that이 생략됨
Nearly eight of ten U.S. adults believe / there are "good foods"
and "bad foods." //
미국 성인 10명 중 거의 8명이 믿는다 / '좋은 음식'과 '나쁜 음식'이 있다고 //
= If not
Unless we're talking / about spoiled stew, poison mushrooms,
or something similar, / however, / no foods can be labeled / as
either good or bad. // `단서 1` 어떤 음식도 좋거나 나쁘다고 분류될 수 없음
우리가 이야기하고 있지 않는 한 / 상한 스튜, 독버섯, 또는 이와 유사한 것에 대해 / 하지만 /
어떤 음식도 분류될 수 없다 / 좋거나 나쁘다고 //
                                        주격 관계대명사 '결국 ~이 되다'
There are, however, / combinations of foods / that add up to a
healthful or unhealthful diet. // `단서 2` 음식들의 조합이 건강에 좋거나 좋지 않은
                                        식단을 만듦
하지만 ~이 있다 / 음식들의 조합이 (있다) / 결국 건강에 좋거나 건강에 좋지 않은 식단이
되는 //
                         주격 관계대명사
Consider the case of an adult / who eats only foods / thought of
앞에 주격 관계대명사와 be동사가 생략됨
as "good" / — for example, / raw broccoli, apples, orange juice,
boiled tofu, and carrots. //
어느 성인의 경우를 생각해 보라 / 어떤 음식만 먹는 / '좋은' 음식이라고 생각되는 / 예를 들어
/ 생브로콜리, 사과, 오렌지 주스, 삶은 두부와 당근과 같은 //
부사절 접속사(양보)
Although all these foods are nutrient-dense, / they do not add
up to a healthy diet / because they don't supply a wide enough
                              앞에 목적격 관계대명사가 생략됨
variety of the nutrients / we need. //
비록 이 모든 음식들이 영양이 풍부하지만 / 그것들은 결국 건강한 식단이 되지 않는다 /
그것들이 충분히 다양한 영양소를 공급하지 않기 때문에 / 우리가 필요로 하는 //
                                        주격 관계대명사
Or take the case of the teenager / who occasionally eats fried
                                  병렬 구조
chicken, / but otherwise stays away from fried foods. //
또는 한 십 대의 경우를 예로 들어보자 / 튀긴 닭을 가끔 먹지만 / 그렇지 않으면 튀긴 음식을
멀리하는 //

The occasional fried chicken / isn't going to knock his or her
diet off track. //
가끔 먹는 튀긴 닭은 / 그나 그녀의 식단을 궤도에서 벗어나게 하지 않을 것이다 //
                핵심 주어(단수)
But the person / who eats fried foods every day, / with few
                                              병렬 구조
vegetables or fruits, / and loads upon supersized soft drinks,
                                                  단수 동사
candy, and chips / for snacks / has a bad diet. //
하지만 그 사람은 / 튀긴 음식을 매일 먹는 / 채소나 과일을 거의 먹지 않으면서 / 그리고
초대형 음료, 사탕, 그리고 감자칩으로 배를 가득 채우는 / 간식으로 / 나쁜 식단을 가지고
있다 //

┌───┐
│   전치사   동명사 주어(단수 취급)
│ → Unlike the common belief, / defining foods as good or bad /
│ 단수 동사
│ is not (A) appropriate; / in fact, / a healthy diet is determined
│   선행사를 포함하는 관계대명사
│ / largely by what the diet is (B) composed of. //
│ 일반적인 믿음과 달리 / 음식을 좋거나 나쁘다고 정의하는 것은 / 적절하지 않다 / 사실 /
│ 건강에 좋은 식단은 결정된다 / 대체로 그 식단이 무엇으로 구성되는지에 의해 //
└───┘

· spoiled ⓐ 상한   · stew ⓝ 스튜(고기와 채소를 넣고 천천히 끓이는 요리)
· poison ⓝ 독   · label ⓥ 분류하다   · combination ⓝ 조합
· boiled ⓐ 끓인, 삶은   · tofu ⓝ 두부   · nutrient ⓝ 영양소
· occasionally ⓐ 가끔   · otherwise ⓐ 그렇지 않으면
· load ⓥ 채우다, 싣다   · supersized ⓐ 초대형의
· soft drink (청량) 음료   · appropriate ⓐ 적절한

미국 성인 10명 중 거의 8명이 '좋은 음식'과 '나쁜 음식'이 있다고 믿는다.
하지만, 우리가 상한 스튜, 독버섯, 또는 이와 유사한 것에 대해 이야기하고
있지 않는 한, 어떤 음식도 좋고 나쁨으로 분류될 수 없다. 하지만, 결국 건강에
좋은 식단이나 건강에 좋지 않은 식단이 되는 음식들의 조합이 있다. '좋은'
음식이라고 생각되는 음식만 먹는 성인의 경우를 생각해 보라 — 예를 들어,
생브로콜리, 사과, 오렌지 주스, 삶은 두부와 당근. 비록 이 모든 음식들은
영양이 풍부하지만, 그것들은 우리가 필요로 하는 충분히 다양한 영양소를
공급하지 않기 때문에 결국 건강한 식단이 되지 않는다. 또는 튀긴 닭을
가끔 먹지만, 그렇지 않으면 튀긴 음식을 멀리하는 한 십 대의 경우를 예로
들어보자. 가끔 먹는 튀긴 닭은 그나 그녀의 식단을 궤도에서 벗어나게 하지
않을 것이다. 하지만 채소나 과일을 거의 먹지 않으면서 매일 튀긴 음식을
먹고, 간식으로 초대형 음료, 사탕, 그리고 감자칩으로 배를 가득 채우는
사람은 나쁜 식단을 가지고 있다.
→ 일반적인 믿음과 달리, 음식을 좋고 나쁨으로 정의하는 것은 (A) 적절하지
않다; 사실, 건강에 좋은 식단은 대체로 그 식단이 무엇으로 (B) 구성되는지에
의해 결정된다.

┌───┐
│ 음식의 좋고 나쁨을 정의하는 것이 옳은 것은 아님
│ **내용을 한 문장으로 요약하고자 한다. 빈칸 (A), (B)에 들어갈 말로 가장**
│ **적절한 것은?**
│   (A)   (B)
│ ① incorrect   —   limited to
│   틀린   제한되는
│ ② appropriate   —   composed of   식단이 건강한지 여부는 음식 자체가 아니라
│   적절한   구성되는   음식의 조합에 좌우됨
│ ③ wrong   —   aimed at   식단의 목표는 언급되지 않음
│   잘못된   목표하는
│ ④ appropriate   —   tested on   식단을 검사한 것이 아님
│   검사되는
│ ⑤ incorrect   —   adjusted to
│   조절되는
└───┘

>왜 정답? ★★★ [정답률 59%]

(A):

┌ 하지만, 우리가 상한 스튜, 독버섯, 또는 이와 유사한 것에 대해 이야기하고
└ 있지 않는 한, 어떤 음식도 좋고 나쁨으로 분류될 수 없다. `단서 1`
→ 어떤 음식도 좋고 나쁨으로 분류될 수 '없음'
   ▶ 음식을 좋고 나쁨으로 정의하는 것은 '적절하지 않은' 것이므로 (A)에는 ②, ④
   appropriate가 들어가야 함 (A) 앞에 부정어 not이
                             있으므로 주의해야 함! 꿀팁

(B):

하지만, 결국 건강에 좋은 식단이나 건강에 좋지 않은 식단이 되는 음식들의 조합이 있다. 단서2

➡ 식단이 좋고 나쁜지는 식단을 구성하는 음식들의 조합에 달려있다.

▶ 식단을 '구성하는' 음식에 의해 식단이 건강한지가 결정되는 것이므로 (B)에는 ② composed of가 들어가야 함

>왜 오답?

① 음식이 좋거나 나쁘다고 정의하는 것이 틀리지 '않다'고 하는 것은 글의 내용과 반대이다.

③ 목표에 맞춰 식단을 짜야 건강한 식단이 되는 것이 아니다.

④ 식단을 검사하는 것에 따라 식단이 건강한지가 좌우되는 것이 아니다.

⑤ 어떤 음식들을 얼마나 먹는지로 식단을 '조절한다'고 볼 수 있지만, 음식 자체를 좋고 나쁨으로 정의하는 것은 옳지 않다.

＊ 글의 흐름

도입	많은 사람이 좋은 음식과 나쁜 음식이 있다고 믿음
반박	음식이 좋고 나쁘다고 분류되는 것이 아니라 음식의 조합에 의해 식단이 건강한지가 결정됨
예시 ①	좋은 음식이라고 생각되는 음식만 먹는 것은 다양한 영양소를 갖추고 있지 않기 때문에 건강한 식단이 아님
예시 ②	튀긴 음식을 먹는다고 해도 자주 먹지 않으면 건강한 식단이 될 수도 있음

Q 16 정답 ③ ＊유능한 코치

Have you noticed / that some coaches get the most out / of their
        목적어절을 이끄는 접속사
athletes / while others don't? // 알아챘습니까 / 어떤 코치들은 최상의 결과를
이끌어낸다는 것을 / 선수들에게서 / 반면 다른 코치들은 그렇지 않다는 것을 //
                        단서1 서투른 코치는 당신이 잘못했던 것을 말함
A poor coach will tell you / what you did wrong / and then tell
you / not to do it again: / "Don't drop the ball!" // 요약문의 mistakes
서투른 코치는 당신에게 말할 것이다 / 당신이 무엇을 잘못했는지 / 그러고 나서 당신에게 말
할 것이다 / 다시는 그러지 말라고 / "공을 떨어뜨리지 마라!" //

What happens next? // 그 다음엔 무슨 일이 일어날까 //
       앞에 목적격 관계대명사 생략   동명사와 의미상의 주어
The images / you see in your head / are images of you dropping
the ball! //
이미지들은 / 당신이 머릿속에서 보게 되는 / 당신이 공을 떨어뜨리는 이미지이다 //
                                   ~것
Naturally, / your mind recreates / what it just "saw" / based on
~것
what it's been told. //
당연히 / 당신의 마음은 재현한다 / 방금 '본' 것을 / 그것이 들은 것을 바탕으로 //

Not surprisingly, / you walk on the court / and drop the ball. //
놀랄 것도 없이 / 당신은 코트에 걸어간다 / 그리고 공을 떨어뜨린다 //

What does the good coach do? // 좋은 코치는 무엇을 하는가 //

He or she points out / what could be improved, / but will then
   의문사로 시작하는 절로서 각각 동사의 목적어로 쓰임   앞에 접속사 that이 생략됨
tell you / how you could or should perform: / "I know / you'll
catch the ball / perfectly this time." // 단서2 좋은 코치는 당신이 성공적인 경기를
                                          수행할 수 있도록 이야기해주고 상상하게 함
그 또는 그녀는 지적한다 / 향상될 수 있는 것을 / 그러나 그 후에 당신에게 말할 것이다 / 어
떻게 수행할 수 있는지 또는 어떻게 수행해야 하는지에 대해 / "나는 알아요 / 당신이 공을 잡
을 거라는 것을 / 이번에는 완벽하게 //
요약문의 picture
Sure enough, / the next image in your mind is / you catching the
                               동명사의 의미상의 주어로서 you를 사용
ball and scoring a goal. // 아니나 다를까 / 당신의 마음 속에 떠오르는 다음 이미지는
~이다 / 당신이 공을 '잡고' '득점하는' 것 //

Once again, / your mind makes / your last thoughts part of reality /
— but this time, / that "reality" is positive, / not negative. //
다시 한 번 / 당신의 마음은 만든다 / 당신의 마지막 생각을 현실의 일부로 / 그러나 이번에는
/ 그 '현실'이 긍정적이다 / 부정적이지 않고 //

→ Unlike ineffective coaches, / who focus on players' (A)
                              help+목적어+목적격보어(동사원형)
mistakes, / effective coaches help players improve / by
encouraging them to (B) **picture** successful plays. //
유능하지 않은 코치들과 달리 / 선수들의 실수에 초점을 맞추는 / 유능한 코치들은 선수들
이 향상되도록 도와준다 / 그들이 성공적인 경기를 상상하도록 격려함으로써 //

- notice ⓥ 알아채다   · athlete ⓝ (운동) 선수
- happen ⓥ 일어나다   · drop ⓥ 떨어뜨리다
- recreate ⓥ 재현하다   · surprisingly 〔ad〕 놀랍게도
- perform ⓥ 수행하다   · thought ⓝ 생각
- ineffective ⓐ 유능하지 않은   · successful ⓐ 성공적인

당신은 어떤 코치들은 선수들에게서 최상의 결과를 이끌어내는 반면 다른 코치들은 그렇지 않다는 것을 알아챘는가? 서투른 코치는 당신이 무엇을 잘못했는지를 알려주고 나서 다시는 그렇게 하지 말라고 말할 것이다. "공을 떨어뜨리지 마라!" 그 다음에는 무슨 일이 일어날까? 당신이 머릿속에서 보게 되는 이미지는 당신이 공을 떨어뜨리는 이미지들이다! 당연히, 당신의 마음은 그것이 들은 것을 바탕으로 방금 "본" 것을 재현한다. 놀랄 것도 없이, 당신은 코트에 걸어가서 공을 떨어뜨린다. 좋은 코치는 무엇을 하는가? 그 사람은 향상될 수 있는 것을 지적하지만, 그 후에 어떻게 수행할 수 있는지 또는 어떻게 해야 하는지에 대해 말할 것이다. "이번에는 당신이 공을 완벽하게 잡을 거라는 걸 알아요." 아니나 다를까, 다음으로 당신의 마음 속에 떠오르는 이미지는 당신이 공을 '잡고' '득점하는' 것이다. 다시 한 번, 당신의 마음은 당신이 마지막 생각을 현실의 일부로 만들지만, 이번에는, 그 '현실'이 부정적이지 않고 긍정적이다.

→ 선수들의 (A) **실수**에 초점을 맞추는 유능하지 않은 코치들과 달리, 유능한 코치들은 선수들에게 성공적인 경기를 (B) **상상하도록** 격려함으로써 그들이 향상되도록 돕는다.

다음 글의 내용을 한 문장으로 요약하고자 한다. 빈칸 (A), (B)에 들어갈 말로 가장 적절한 것은?

	(A)		(B)
①	scores 점수	—	complete 완성하다
②	scores 점수	—	remember 기억하다
③	mistakes 실수	—	picture 상상하다(그리다)
④	mistakes 실수	—	ignore 무시하다
⑤	strengths 강점	—	achieve 달성하다

(A)에서 서투른 코치들은 선수들의 실수에 초점을 둔다고 했고 점수에 초점을 둔다는 말은 없음

서투른 코치는 선수의 실수에 초점을 맞추지만, 유능한 코치들은 선수들에게 성공적인 경기를 상상하도록 한다고 했음

(B)에서 유능한 코치들은 성공적인 경기를 '무시하게' 하지 않음

(A)에서 서투른 코치는 선수가 실수한 것을 떠올리게 만듦

>왜 정답? ★★★ [정답률 56%]

서투른 코치들은 선수들의 잘못했던 점들을 상기시키면서 다시는 그러지 말 것을 말하는 반면에, 유능한 코치들은 선수들에게 좋은 결과를 상상하게 해주고 그런 이미지를 현실이 되게 만든다고 했다. 따라서 (A)에는 '실수'를 의미하는 mistakes가, (B)에는 '상상하다'를 의미하는 picture가 들어가는 것이 적절하므로 정답은 ③이다.

>왜 오답?

①, ② (A)에서 서투른 코치들은 선수들의 실수에 초점을 둔다고 했고 '점수(score)'에 초점을 둔다는 말은 없으므로 적절하지 않다.

④ (B)에서 유능한 코치들은 선수들이 성공적인 경기를 '무시하도록(ignore)' 격려하지 않았다.

⑤ (A)에서 서투른 코치들은 선수들의 '강점(strengths)'에 초점을 맞추지 않으므로 적절하지 않다.

＊ 글의 흐름

도입	코치에 따라 선수들의 능력을 이끌어 내는 능력이 다른 것을 아는지 묻는 질문으로 시작함
전개 ①	서투른 코치는 선수들의 실수에 초점을 맞춤
전개 ②	유능한 코치는 선수들이 성공적인 경기를 그리도록 격려함

Q 17 정답 ① *우리가 운전할 때 비협조적인 이유

'~인 반면에'
While there are many evolutionary or cultural reasons / for cooperation, / the eyes are one of the most important means / of cooperation, /

진화적이거나 문화적인 많은 이유가 있지만 / 협동에 대한 / 눈은 가장 중요한 수단 중 하나이다 / 협동의 /

and eye contact may be the most powerful human force / **we**
앞에 목적격 관계대명사가 생략됨
lose in traffic. // 단서 1 차량 운행 중에 시선을 마주치는 능력을 잃음

그리고 시선의 마주침은 가장 강력한 인간의 힘일지도 모른다 / 우리가 차량 운행 중에 잃는 //

선행사   관계부사
It is, arguably, **the reason** / **why** humans, normally a quite cooperative species, / can become so **noncooperative** / on the
요약문의 uncooperative
road. // 단서 2 앞문장의 결과로, 인간이 운전을 할 때는 비협조적이 됨

주장하건대 그것은 이유이다 / 왜 보통은 꽤 협동적인 종인 인간이 / 그렇게 비협조적이 될 수 있는 / 도로에서 //

요약문의 little
Most of the time / we are moving too fast / — we begin to lose
형용사적 용법(the ability 수식)
the ability / **to keep** eye contact / around 20 miles per hour — /
가주어   진주어
or **it** is not safe **to look**. // 단서 3 시속 20마일 정도에서 시선을
마주치는 능력을 잃기 시작하기 때문임
대부분의 시간에 / 우리가 너무 빨리 움직이고 있거나 / 우리는 능력을 잃기 시작한다 / 시선을 마주치는 / 시속 20마일 정도에서 / 혹은 보는 것이 안전하지 않다 //

Maybe our view is blocked. // 어쩌면 우리의 시야가 차단되어 있다 //

Often other drivers are wearing sunglasses, / or their car may have tinted windows. // 단서 4 다른 운전자들과 시선을 마주치는 것이 힘듦

흔히 다른 운전자들이 선글라스를 끼고 있다 / 또는 그들의 차는 색이 옅게 들어간 창문이 있을 수 있다 //

(And do you really want / to make eye contact / with those drivers?) //

(그리고 당신은 정말로 원하는가 / 시선을 마주치기를 / 그러한 운전자들과) //

Sometimes we make eye contact / through the rearview mirror, / but it feels weak, / not quite believable at first, /

때로는 우리는 시선을 마주친다 / 백미러를 통해 / 그러나 그것은 약하게 느껴진다 / 처음에는 전혀 믿을 수 없게 (느껴진다) /

이유의 부사절 접속사
as it is not "face-to-face." //
그것이 '얼굴을 마주하고 있는 것'이 아니기 때문에 //

'~하는 동안'
→ **While** driving, / people become (A) **uncooperative**, / because they make (B) **little** eye contact. //
운전하는 동안 / 사람들은 비협조적이 되는데 / 왜냐하면 그들이 시선 마주침을 거의 하지 않기 때문이다 //

- evolutionary ⓐ 진화적인   · cooperation ⓝ 협동, 협력
- means ⓝ 수단   · eye contact 시선의 마주침   · force ⓝ 힘
- traffic ⓝ (차량) 운행, 교통   · arguably ⓐⓓ 주장하건대
- noncooperative ⓐ 비협조적인

협동에 대한 진화적이거나 문화적인 많은 이유가 있지만, 눈은 가장 중요한 협동 수단 중 하나이고, 시선의 마주침은 우리가 차량 운행 중에 잃는 가장 강력한 인간의 힘일지도 모른다. 주장하건대 그것은 보통은 꽤 협동적인 종인 인간이 도로에서 그렇게 비협조적이 될 수 있는 이유이다. 대부분의 시간에 우리가 너무 빨리 움직이고 있거나, 우리는 시속 20마일 정도에서 시선을 마주치는 능력을 잃기 시작하는데, 혹은 (서로를) 보는 것이 안전하지 않다. 어쩌면 우리의 시야가 차단되어 있을 수도 있다. 흔히 다른 운전자들이 선글라스를 끼고 있거나 그들의 차는 색이 옅게 들어간 창문이 있을 수 있다. (그리고 당신은 정말로 그러한 운전자들과 시선을 마주치고 싶은가?) 때로는 우리는 백미러를 통해 시선을 마주치지만, '얼굴을 마주하고 있는 것'이 아니기 때문에 약하게, 처음에는 전혀 믿을 수 없게, 느껴진다.
→ 운전하는 동안, 사람들은 (A) **비협조적**이 되는데, 왜냐하면 그들이 시선 마주침을 (B) **거의** 하지 **않기** 때문이다.

다음 글의 내용을 한 문장으로 요약하고자 한다. 빈칸 (A), (B)에 들어갈 말로 가장 적절한 것은?

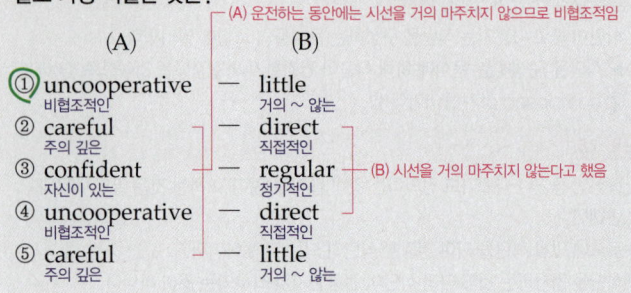

(A) 운전하는 동안에는 시선을 거의 마주치지 않으므로 비협조적임

	(A)		(B)
①	uncooperative 비협조적인	—	little 거의 ~ 않는
②	careful 주의 깊은	—	direct 직접적인
③	confident 자신이 있는	—	regular 정기적인
④	uncooperative 비협조적인	—	direct 직접적인
⑤	careful 주의 깊은	—	little 거의 ~ 않는

(B) 시선을 거의 마주치지 않는다고 했음

⟩왜 정답? ★★❀ [정답률 63%]

눈이 가장 중요한 협동 수단 중 하나인데 운전 중에는 시선을 마주치는 능력을 잃을 수 있고, 이것이 운전을 하는 동안에 인간이 비협조적이 되는 이유라고 했다. 따라서 요약문의 빈칸에는 각각 ① uncooperative(비협조적인)와 little(거의 ~ 않는)이 들어가야 한다.

⟩왜 오답?

- ②, ④ 운전을 할 때는 시선을 마주치는 능력을 잃는데, 가끔 백미러를 통해 시선을 마주친다고 했지, 직접적인(direct) 시선 마주침이 있다고 하지 않았다.
- ③, ⑤ 운전을 할 때 자신감이 있어진다거나(confident) 운전을 주의 깊게(careful) 한다는 내용이 아니다.

* 글의 흐름

전제	눈은 가장 중요한 협동 수단 중 하나임
설명	그것이 바로 꽤 협동적인 인간이 운전할 때 비협조적이 될 수 있는 이유임
결론	우리는 백미러를 통해 시선을 마주치지만, 사실은 얼굴을 마주하고 있는 것이 아니라서 거의 마주치지 않는 것이나 마찬가지임

자이 쌤's Follow Me! —홈페이지에서 제공

Q 18 정답 ① *사람들의 행동 변화에 미치는 상기물의 효과

문장 전체의 핵심 주어   주격 관계대명사
A woman named Rhonda / **who** attended the University of
동사
California / at Berkeley / **had** a problem. //
Rhonda라는 여자는 / California대학에 다니는 / Berkeley에 있는 / 한 가지 문제 상황이 있었다 /

She was living near campus / with several other people / — none of whom knew one another. //

그녀는 캠퍼스 근처에 살고 있었는데 / 여러 사람들과 함께 / 그들 중 누구도 서로 알지는 못했다 //

When the cleaning people came each weekend, / they left several rolls of toilet paper / in each of the two bathrooms. //

청소부가 주말마다 왔을 때 / 그들은 몇 개의 두루마리 화장지를 두고 갔다 / 화장실 두 칸 각각에 //
단서 1 청소부가 주말마다 화장실에 두고 가는 휴지(공유재)가 월요일쯤 되면 모두 사라짐
과거의 불규칙적인 습관
However, / by Monday / all the toilet paper / **would** be gone. //

그러나 / 월요일 즈음 / 모든 화장지가 / 없어지곤 했다 //

이유를 나타내는 접속사
It was a classic tragedy-of-the-commons situation: / **because** some people took more toilet paper / than their fair share, / the public resource was destroyed / for everyone else. //

그것은 전형적인 공유지의 비극 상황이었다 / 일부 사람들이 더 많은 휴지를 가져갔기 때문에 / 자신들이 사용할 수 있는 몫보다 / 공공재가 파괴됐다 / 다른 모든 사람들을 위한 //
단서 2 사람들의 의식을 상기시키기 위해 화장지는 공유되는 물건이라는 내용의 쪽지를 놓아둠
After reading a research paper / about behavior change, / Rhonda put a note / in one of the bathrooms / asking people **not**
to부정사의 부정
to remove the toilet paper, / as it was a shared item. //

한 연구논문을 읽고 나서 / 행동 변화에 대한 / Rhonda는 쪽지를 두었다 / 화장실 한 곳에 / 사람들에게 화장실 화장지를 가져가지 말라는 / 그것은 공유재이므로 //

「to one's+감정 명사」: ~하게도
To her great satisfaction, / one roll reappeared in a few hours, / and another the next day. // 단서3 쪽지가 있는 곳에서 사람들의 행동이 변화됨
아주 만족스럽게도 / 몇 시간 후에 화장지 한 개가 다시 나타났다 / 그리고 그 다음 날에는 또 하나가 다시 나타났다 //

In the other note-free bathroom, / however, / there was no toilet paper / until the following weekend, / when the cleaning people returned. // 단서4 쪽지가 없는 곳에서는 사람들의 행동이 변화되지 않음
쪽지가 없는 화장실에서는 / 하지만 / 화장지가 없었다 / 그 다음 주말까지 / 청소부가 돌아오는 //

→ A small (A) **reminder** brought about a change / in the behavior of the people / who had taken more of the (B) **shared** goods / than they needed //
자그마한 상기물은 변화를 가져왔다 / 사람들의 행동에 / 더 많은 공유재를 가져갔던 / 그들이 필요한 것보다 //

- attend ⓥ 다니다, 참석하다 ・ toilet paper 화장실 휴지
- classic ⓐ 전형적인 ・ tragedy ⓝ 비극 ・ common ⓝ 공유지
- share ⓝ 몫 ・ remove ⓥ 없애다 ・ satisfaction ⓝ 만족
- reappear ⓥ 다시 나타나다 ・ note-free ⓐ 쪽지가 없는
- following ⓐ (시간상으로) 그다음의 ・ behavior ⓝ 행동

Berkeley에 있는 California대학에 다니는 Rhonda라는 여자는 한 가지 문제 상황이 있었다. 그녀는 여러 사람들과 함께 캠퍼스 근처에 살고 있었는데 그들 중 누구도 서로를 알지는 못했다. 청소부가 주말마다 왔을 때 화장실 두 칸 각각 몇 개의 두루마리 화장지를 두고 갔다. 그러나 월요일 즈음 모든 화장지가 없어지곤 했다. 그것은 전형적인 공유지의 비극 상황이었다. 일부 사람들이 자신들이 사용할 수 있는 몫보다 더 많은 휴지를 가져갔기 때문에 다른 모든 사람들을 위한 공공재가 파괴됐다. 행동 변화에 대한 한 연구논문을 읽고 나서, Rhonda는 화장실 화장지는 공유재이므로 사람들에게 가져가지 말라는 쪽지를 화장실 안 곳에 두었다. 아주 만족스럽게도, 몇 시간 후에 화장지 한 개가 다시 나타났고 그 다음 날에는 또 하나가 다시 나타났다. 하지만 쪽지가 없는 화장실에서는 청소부가 돌아오는 그 다음 주말까지 화장지가 없었다.
→ 자그마한 (A) **상기물**은 그들이 필요한 것보다 더 많은 (B) **공유**재를 가져갔던 사람들의 행동에 변화를 가져왔다.

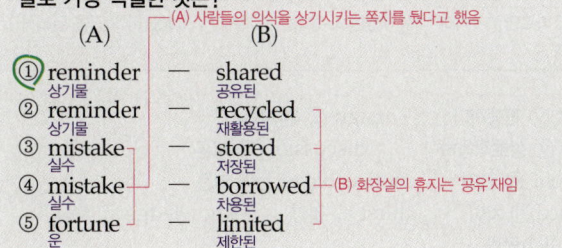

다음 글의 내용을 한 문장으로 요약하고자 한다. 빈칸 (A), (B)에 들어갈 말로 가장 적절한 것은?

(A) 사람들의 의식을 상기시키는 쪽지를 뒀다고 했음

	(A)		(B)
①	reminder 상기물	—	shared 공유된
②	reminder 상기물	—	recycled 재활용된
③	mistake 실수	—	stored 저장된
④	mistake 실수	—	borrowed 차용된
⑤	fortune 운	—	limited 제한된

(B) 화장실의 휴지는 '공유'재임

> 왜 정답? ★★❀ [정답률 67%]

쪽지가 상기물로서의 역할을 함 꿀팁

사람들이 공유재인 화장지를 필요 이상으로 많이 가져가는 상황에서, 화장지를 가져가지 말라는 쪽지가 부착된 곳에서는 사람들이 화장지를 가져가지 않았지만, 이러한 쪽지가 부착되지 않은 곳에서는 사람들이 여전히 화장지를 가져갔다고 했다. 즉, 사람들의 의식을 상기시키는 쪽지로 인해 공유재인 화장지에 대한 사람들의 행동 변화를 설명하는 글이다. 따라서 (A)에는 '상기물'이라는 뜻의 reminder, (B)에는 '공유된'이라는 뜻의 shared가 들어가는 것이 가장 적절하므로 정답은 ①이다.

> 왜 오답?

② 사람들이 가지고 간 화장지는 '재활용된(recycled)' 화장지가 아니라 다수의 사람들에 의해 함께 사용되는 화장지이므로 적절하지 않다.
③, ④ 사람들의 행동 변화를 가져온 것은 사람들의 의식을 상기시키는 쪽지였으므로 이것을 '실수(mistake)'라고 하는 것은 적절하지 않다.

---

⑤ 사람들의 행동 변화를 가져온 것은 '운(fortune)'이 아니라 상기물로서의 역할을 하는 쪽지였으므로 적절하지 않다.

＊ 글의 흐름

도입	Rhonda는 캠퍼스 근처에서 여러 사람들과 함께 생활함
문제 제기	청소부가 주말에 두고 가는 공유재인 화장지를 사람들이 필요 이상으로 많이 가져감
해결책	사람들의 의식을 상기시키는 쪽지를 화장실에 놓아둠
결과	쪽지가 있는 화장실에서 사람들이 화장지를 되돌려 놓음

Q 19 정답 ① ⭐ 2등급 대비 [정답률 50%]

＊생존을 위한 집단행동

단서1 안전성을 높이고 신뢰할 대상을 찾기 위해 사회적 증거를 찾음
To help decide / what's risky and what's safe, / who's trustworthy and who's not, / we look for *social evidence*. //
결정하는 것을 돕기 위해 / 무엇이 위험하고 무엇이 안전한지 / 누구를 신뢰할 수 있고 누구를 신뢰할 수 없는지를 / 우리는 '사회적 증거'를 찾는다 //

단서2 다른 사람들과 비슷한 것을 택하는 것이 더 안전한 선택임
From an evolutionary view, / following the group is almost always positive / for our prospects of survival. //
동명사구 주어(단수 취급) 단수 동사
진화의 관점에서 볼 때 / 집단을 따르는 것이 거의 항상 긍정적이다 / 우리의 생존 전망에 //
강한 확신을 나타내는 조동사
"If everyone's doing it, / it must be a sensible thing to do," / explains / famous psychologist / and best selling writer of *Influence*, Robert Cialdini. //
"모든 사람이 그것을 하고 있다면 / 그것은 해야 할 분별 있는 일인 것이 틀림없다" 라고 / 설명한다 / 유명한 심리학자이자 / 〈Influence〉를 쓴 베스트셀러 작가인 Robert Cialdini는 //
부사절 접속사(대조)
While we can frequently see this today / in product reviews, / even subtler cues / within the environment / can signal trustworthiness. //
우리는 오늘날 이것을 자주 볼 수 있지만 / 상품 평에서 / 훨씬 더 미묘한 신호가 / 환경 내의 / 신뢰성을 나타낼 수 있다 //

Consider this: / when you visit a local restaurant, / are they busy? //
이것을 생각해 보라 / 여러분이 어떤 지역의 음식점을 방문할 때 / 그들이 바쁜가 //

Is there a line outside / or is it easy to find a seat? //
밖에 줄이 있는가 / 아니면 자리를 찾기가 쉬운가 //
가주어 진주어 동격절 접속사
It is a hassle to wait, / but a line can be a powerful cue / that the food's tasty, / and these seats are in demand. //
기다리는 것은 성가신 일이지만 / 줄은 강력한 신호일 수 있다 / 음식이 맛있고 / 이곳의 좌석은 수요가 많다는 //
'대개, 자주' 가주어 진주어
More often than not, / it's good to adopt the practices / of those around you. // 단서3 주변 사람들의 결정을 따르는 것이 좋음
대개는 / 행동을 따르는 것이 좋다 / 당신의 주변에 있는 사람들의 //

→ We tend to feel safe and secure / in (A) **numbers** / when
「의문사 how+to부정사」: 어떻게 ~할지
we decide how to act, / particularly when faced with (B) **uncertain** conditions. //
앞에 we are가 생략됨
우리는 안전하고 안심된다고 느끼는 경향이 있다 / 수에서 / 어떻게 행동할지 결정할 때 / 특히 불확실한 상황에 직면할 때 //

- risky ⓐ 위험한 ・ trustworthy ⓐ 신뢰할 수 있는
- evidence ⓝ 증거 ・ evolutionary ⓐ 진화의
- prospect ⓝ 전망 ・ sensible ⓐ 분별 있는
- psychologist ⓝ 심리학자 ・ cue ⓝ 신호 ・ signal ⓥ 나타내다
- local ⓐ 지역의, 현지의 ・ tasty ⓐ 맛있는
- adopt ⓥ 따르다, 채택하다 ・ practice ⓝ 행동, 관행
- uncertain ⓐ 불확실한 ・ unrealistic ⓐ 비현실적인

무엇이 위험하고 무엇이 안전한지, 누구를 신뢰할 수 있고 누구를 신뢰할 수 없는지를 결정하는 것을 돕기 위해, 우리는 '사회적 증거'를 찾는다. 진화의 관점에서 볼 때, 집단을 따르는 것이 거의 항상 우리의 생존 전망에 긍정적이다. "모든 사람이 그것을 하고 있다면, 그것은 해야 할 분별 있는 일인 것이 틀림없다."라고 유명한 심리학자이자 〈Influence〉를 쓴 베스트셀러 작가인 Robert Cialdini는 설명한다. 오늘날 상품 평에서 이것을 자주 볼 수 있지만, 환경 내의 훨씬 더 미묘한 신호가 신뢰성을 나타낼 수 있다. 이것을 생각해보라. 여러분이 어떤 지역의 음식점을 방문할 때, 그들이 바쁜가? 밖에 줄이 있는가, 아니면 자리를 찾기가 쉬운가? 기다리는 것은 성가신 일이지만, 줄은 음식이 맛있고 이곳의 좌석은 수요가 많다는 강력한 신호일 수 있다. 대개는 주변에 있는 사람들의 행동을 따르는 것이 좋다.

→ 우리는 어떻게 행동할지 결정할 때, 특히 (B) **불확실한** 상황에 직면할 때 (A) **수**에서 안전하고 안심된다고 느끼는 경향이 있다.

다음 글의 내용을 한 문장으로 요약하고자 한다. 빈칸 (A), (B)에 들어갈 말로 가장 적절한 것은?

	(A)		(B)	
①	numbers 수	—	uncertain 불확실한	상황이 불확실할 때 많은 수의 사람들이 어떤 것을 하면 신뢰한다고 했음
②	numbers	—	unrealistic 비현실적인	비현실적이 아닌 불확실한 경우에 대해서 말했음
③	experiences 경험	—	unrealistic	경험하지 않아도 주위 사람을 보며 따라 하라고 했음
④	rules 규칙	—	uncertain	얼마나 많은 사람이 어떤 것을 하느냐를 신경 쓰라고 했음
⑤	rules	—	unpleasant 불쾌한	불쾌하기보다는 불확실해서 정보가 필요할 경우에 해당함

왜 2등급? 글의 첫 문장에서 정답의 단서를 파악했어야 한다. 두 번째 문장부터는 Robet Cialdini의 말을 인용하면서 첫 문장에 대한 예시가 제시된다. 상품평, 음식점의 대기 줄 등의 예시가 '집단을 따르는 것이 생존에 긍정적'이라는 것과 어떤 관련이 있는지 이해해야 하는 2등급 대비 문제이다.

| 문제 풀이 순서 |

1st 요약문을 통해 글에서 무엇을 찾아야 하는지 확인한다.

요약문	우리는 어떻게 행동할지 결정할 때, 특히 '(B) _____한' 상황에 직면할 때 '(A) _____에서' 안전하고 안심된다고 느끼는 경향이 있다.

➡ 글에서 찾아야 하는 것
  (B): 불확실한, 비현실적인, 불쾌한 상황에 직면할 때
  (A): 수에서, 경험에서, 규칙에서 안전하다고 느끼는 경향이 있는지

2nd 글의 내용을 파악하여 요약문을 완성한다.

- 진화의 관점에서 볼 때, 집단을 따르는 것이 거의 항상 우리의 생존 전망에 긍정적이다. **단서 2**
- 대개는 주변에 있는 사람들의 행동을 따르는 것이 좋다. **단서 3**

➡ 우리의 생존에 긍정적인 것은 집단을 따르는 것이라고 했다. 즉 모든 사람이 어떤 일을 하고 있으면 그것은 해야 할 일이라는 것이다.
  ▶ 많은 '수'의 사람이 하면 해야 한다는 것이므로 (A)에는 ①, ②의 numbers가 들어가야 한다.

- 무엇이 위험하고 무엇이 안전한지, 누구를 신뢰할 수 있고 누구를 신뢰할 수 없는지를 결정하는 것을 돕기 위해, 우리는 '사회적 증거'를 찾는다. **단서 1**

➡ 무엇이 안전한 선택인지, 누가 믿을 수 있는 사람인지 모른다는 것은 '불확실한' 상황이다. ▶ (B)에는 ①, ④의 uncertain이 들어가는 것이 적절하다.

| 선택지 분석 |

① 불확실한 상황에서는 집단의 행동을 따르는 것이 좋다는 내용이다.
② 비현실적인 상황은 언급되지 않았다.
③ 경험이 아니라 주변 사람들의 행동을 따르는 것에서 안전하다고 느낀다.
④ 규칙에서 안전하다고 느낀다는 것은 언급되지 않았다.
⑤ 불쾌한 상황은 언급되지 않았다.

---

*의견의 일치 여부에 따른 흥미도 차이

Nancy Lowry and David Johnson / conducted an experiment / to study a teaching environment / where fifth and sixth graders were assigned to interact / on a topic. //
Nancy Lowry와 David Johnson은 / 실험을 진행했다 / 교수환경을 연구하고자 / 5학년과 6학년 학생들이 상호작용을 하게 하는 / 한 주제에 대해 //

With one group, / the discussion was led / in a way that built an agreement. //
한 그룹에서는 / 토론이 유도되었다 / 합의를 도출하는 방식으로 //

With the second group, / the discussion was designed / to produce disagreements about the right answer. //
두 번째 그룹에서는 / 토론이 설계되었다 / 옳은 정답에 대해 불일치를 낳도록 //

Students who easily reached an agreement / were less interested in the topic, / studied less, / and were less likely to visit the library / to get additional information. // **단서 1** 서로 합의를 보지 못할수록 열정적으로 학습함
쉽게 합의에 도달한 학생들은 / 주제에 흥미를 덜 보이고 / 더 적게 공부했으며 / 도서관에 가는 경향이 더 적었다 / 부가적인 정보를 얻기 위해 //

The most noticeable difference, / though, / was revealed / when teachers showed a special film / about the discussion topic — / during lunch time! // **단서 2** 결론 도출을 못한 학생들은 나름의 해답을 찾기 위해 자발적 노력을 함
가장 눈에 띄는 차이는 / 그러나 / 나타났다 / 교사가 학생들에게 영화를 보여주었을 때 / 주제와 관련된 / 점심시간 동안 //

Only 18 percent of the agreement group / missed lunch time / to see the film, / but 45 percent of the students from the disagreement group / stayed for the film. //
동의한 그룹의 18퍼센트만이 / 점심시간을 놓쳤으나 / 영화를 보기 위해 / 동의하지 않은 그룹의 45퍼센트는 / 그 영화를 보기 위해 남았다 //

The thirst to fill a knowledge gap / — to find out who was right within the group / — can be more powerful / than the thirst for slides and jungle gyms. // **단서 3** 학습에 대한 호기심과 흥미로 인해 쉬는 시간을 포기하고 학습에 참여함
지식 차이를 채우려는 열망은 / 그룹 내에서 누가 옳았는지 알기 위해 / 열망보다 더 강했던 것이다 / 미끄럼틀과 정글짐을 향한 //

→ According to the experiment above, / students' interest in a topic (A) **increases** / when they are encouraged to (B) **differ**. //
위의 연구에 따르면 / 주제에 대한 학생들의 흥미는 증가한다 / 학생들이 의견을 달리하도록 장려될 때 //

- conduct ⓥ 진행하다 · assign ⓥ 부여하다
- interact ⓥ 상호작용하다 · discussion ⓝ 토론
- agreement ⓝ 합의 · noticeable ⓐ 눈에 띄는
- difference ⓝ 차이 · thirst ⓝ 열망 · knowledge ⓝ 지식
- slide ⓝ 미끄럼틀

Nancy Lowry와 David Johnson은 교수환경을 연구하고자 5학년과 6학년 학생들이 한 주제에 대해 상호작용을 하게 하는 실험을 진행했다. 한 그룹에서는 토론이 합의를 도출하는 방식으로 유도되었다. 두 번째 그룹에서는 토론이 옳은 정답에 대해 불일치를 낳도록 설계되었다. 쉽게 합의에 도달한 학생들은 주제에 흥미를 덜 보이고 더 적게 공부했으며 부가적인 정보를 얻기 위해 도서관에 가는 경향이 더 적었다. 그러나 가장 눈에 띄는 차이는 교사가 학생들에게 점심시간 동안 주제와 관련된 영화를 보여주었을 때 나타났다! 동의한 그룹의 18퍼센트만이 영화를 보기 위해 점심시간을 놓쳤으나 동의하지 않은 그룹의 45퍼센트는 그 영화를 보기 위해 남았다. 그룹 내에서 누가 옳았는지 알기 위해 지식 차이를 채우려는 열망은 미끄럼틀과 정글짐을 향한 열망보다 더 강했던 것이다.
→ 위의 연구에 따르면, 주제에 대한 학생들의 흥미는 학생들이 의견을 (B) **달리하도록** 장려될 때 (A) **증가한다**.

다음 글의 내용을 한 문장으로 요약하고자 한다. 빈칸 (A), (B)에 들어갈 말로 가장 적절한 것은? [3점]

(A)	(B)
① increases 증가한다	differ 달리하도록
② increases 증가한다	approve 승인하도록
③ increases 증가한다	cooperate 협력하도록
④ decreases 감소한다	participate 참여하도록
⑤ decreases 감소한다	argue 논쟁하도록

(A) 학생들의 의견이 다를 때 주제에 대한 학생들의 흥미가 올라간다고 했음
(B) 학생들 간에 서로 의견이 달라야 한다고 했음

왜 2등급? (A)와는 달리 다섯 개의 선택지가 다 다른 단어로 이루어진 (B)를 모두 넣어 확인해야 하는 2등급 대비 문제이다. (A)에 들어갈 수 있는 단어를 먼저 찾은 후 선택지의 폭을 줄여 확인해야 시간을 절약할 수 있다.

| 문제 풀이 순서 |

1st 요약문을 통해 글에서 무엇을 찾아야 하는지 확인한다.

요약문	위의 연구에 따르면, 주제에 대한 학생들의 흥미는 학생들이 의견을 '(B)_____ 하도록' 장려될 때 '(A)_____ 한다'.

➡ 글에서 찾아야 하는 것
(A): 주제에 대한 학생들의 흥미가 증가했는지, 감소했는지
(B): 학생들이 의견을 달리하도록, 승인하도록, 협력하도록, 참여하도록, 논쟁하도록 장려했는지

2nd 글의 내용을 파악하여 요약문을 완성한다.

· 쉽게 합의에 도달한 학생들은 주제에 흥미를 덜 보이고 부가적인 정보를 얻기 위해 도서관에 가는 경향이 더 적었다. **단서 1**
· 동의한 그룹의 18퍼센트만이 영화를 보기 위해 점심시간을 놓쳤으나 동의하지 않은 그룹의 45퍼센트는 그 영화를 보기 위해 남았다. **단서 2**

➡ 연구 결과, 학생들은 합의를 보지 못할수록 열정적으로 학습했고, 의견 불일치가 나타난 그룹에서 많은 비율의 학생들이 점심시간에도 주제와 관련된 영화를 보기 위해 남았다고 했으므로 흥미가 증가한 것이다.
▶ 따라서 (A)에는 ①, ②, ③의 increases가 들어가야 한다.

그룹 내에서 누가 옳았는지 알기 위해 지식 차이를 채우려는 열망은 미끄럼틀과 정글짐을 향한 열망보다 더 강했던 것이다. **단서 3**

➡ 결론을 도출하지 못한 학생들은 해답을 찾기 위해 자발적 노력을 했고, 앞에서 살펴본 것처럼 주제에 대해 서로 다른 의견을 가져야 학생들이 흥미를 갖고 보다 적극적인 태도를 갖게 된다고 했다.
▶ 따라서 (B)에는 ② differ가 적절하다.

| 선택지 분석 |

① 학생들의 의견이 달라야 주제에 대한 흥미가 올라간다는 실험 결과에 대한 내용이다.
② 서로에 대해 '승인하도록(approve)' 하는 것이 흥미에 미치는 영향은 언급되지 않았다.
③ 학생들이 서로 '협동한다고(cooperate)' 흥미가 올라간다는 내용은 없었다.
④ 두 그룹의 학생들 모두 토론에 참여했고 합의를 보지 못하면 더 열심히 노력했다고 했으므로 '참여하도록(participate)' 할수록 흥미가 '감소한다(decreases)'는 내용은 반대로 볼 수 있다.
⑤ 실험을 통해 학생들끼리 '논쟁하도록(argue)' 장려될 때 오히려 흥미가 높아졌다는 것을 알 수 있다.

Q 21 정답 ① 〈2등급 대비 [정답률 41%]〉

* 설득시키려는 의도에 방어적으로 대응하는 사람들의 경향

My colleagues and I / ran an experiment / [experiment를 수식하는 현재분사구] testing two different messages / meant to convince / thousands of resistant alumni / to make a donation. // **단서 1** 기부하도록 설득하는 것을 의도한 두 개의 다른 메시지들을 실험하는 연구를 진행했음
나의 동료들과 나는 / 한 연구를 진행했다 / 납득시키는 것을 의도한 두 개의 다른 메시지들을 실험하는 / 수천 명의 저항하는 졸업생이 / 기부하도록 //

[두 개 중 하나] One message emphasized the opportunity / [형용사적 용법] to do good: / donating would benefit students, faculty, and staff. //
하나의 메시지는 기회를 강조했다 / 좋은 일을 할 / 기부하는 것은 학생들, 교직원, 그리고 직원들에게 이익을 줄 것이다 //

[두 개 중 나머지 하나] The other emphasized the opportunity / [형용사적 용법] to feel good: / donors would enjoy / the warm glow of giving. //
나머지 하나는 기회를 강조했다 / 좋은 기분을 느끼는 / 기부자들은 즐길 것이다 / 기부의 따뜻한 온기를 //

The two messages were equally effective: / in both cases, / 6.5 percent of the unwilling alumni / [end up –ing: 결국 ~하다] ended up donating. //
그 두 개의 메시지들은 똑같이 효과적이었다 / 두 경우 모두에서 / 6.5퍼센트의 마음 내키지 않은 졸업생이 / 결국에는 기부했다 //

Then we combined them, / because two reasons are better / than one. //
그러고 나서 우리는 그것들을 결합했는데 / 왜냐하면 두 개의 이유가 더 낫기 때문이다 / 한 개보다 //

Except they weren't. //
그러나 그렇지 않았다 //

When we put the two reasons together, / the giving rate dropped / below 3 percent. // **단서 2** 두 개의 이유를 합치면 기부율이 떨어짐
우리가 그 두 개의 이유를 합쳤을 때 / 기부율은 떨어졌다 / 3퍼센트 아래로 //

Each reason alone / was more than [배수사+as+원급+as~: ~의 몇 배 만큼 …한] twice as effective / as the two combined. //
각각의 이유가 단독으로는 / 두 배 넘게 더 효과적이었다 / 그 두 개가 합쳐진 것보다 //

The audience was already skeptical. //
청중은 이미 회의적이었다 // **단서 3** 기부해야 할 두 개의 이유를 주면, 설득하려고 한다는 인식을 유발해서 사람들이 스스로를 보호하려고 함

When we gave them / different kinds of reasons / to donate, / we triggered their awareness / [동격절을 이끄는 접속사] that someone was trying / to persuade them / — and they shielded [재귀대명사] themselves / against it. //
우리가 그들에게 주었을 때 / 서로 다른 종류의 이유를 / 기부해야 할 / 우리는 그들의 인식을 유발했다 / 누군가가 하려고 한다는 / 그들을 설득하려고 / 그리고 그들은 스스로를 보호했다 / 그것에 맞서 //

→ In the experiment mentioned above, / when the two different reasons to donate / were given (A) **simultaneously**, / the audience was less likely to be (B) **convinced** / because they could recognize / the intention to persuade them. //
위에서 언급된 실험에서 / 기부하라는 두 개의 다른 이유가 / 동시에 주어졌을 때 / 청자는 납득될 가능성이 더 작았다 / 알아차릴 수 있었기 때문에 / 자신을 설득시키려는 의도를 //

· experiment ⓝ 실험   · convince ⓥ 납득시키다
· resistant ⓐ 저항하는   · alumni ⓝ 졸업생   · donation ⓝ 기부
· emphasize ⓥ 강조하다   · faculty ⓝ (특정 대학의) 모든 교수들, 교직원
· donor ⓝ 기부자   · glow ⓝ (기쁨·만족감을 동반한 은근한) 감정
· unwilling ⓐ 꺼리는, 내키지 않는   · combine ⓥ 결합하다
· trigger ⓥ 유발하다   · awareness ⓝ 인식
· persuade ⓥ 설득하다   · shield ⓥ 보호하다
· simultaneously ⓐⓓ 동시에   · intention ⓝ 의도

나의 동료들과 나는 수천 명의 저항하는 졸업생이 기부하도록 납득시키는 것을 의도한 두 개의 다른 메시지들을 실험하는 한 연구를 진행했다. 하나의 메시지는 좋은 일을 할 기회를 강조했다. 기부하는 것은 학생들, 교직원, 그리고 직원들에게 이익을 줄 것이다. 나머지 하나는 좋은 기분을 느끼는 기회를 강조했다. 기부자들은 기부의 따뜻한 온기를 즐길 것이다. 그 두 개의 메시지들은 똑같이 효과적이었다. 두 경우 모두에서, 6.5퍼센트의 마음 내키지 않은 졸업생이 결국에는 기부했다. 그러고 나서 우리는 그것들을 결합했는데, 왜냐하면 두 개의 이유가 한 개보다 더 낫기 때문이다. 그러나 그렇지 않았다. 우리가 그 두 개의 이유들을 합쳤을 때, 기부율은 3퍼센트 아래로 떨어졌다. 각각의 이유가 단독으로는 그 두 개가 합쳐진 것보다 두 배 넘게 더 효과적이었다. 청중은 이미 회의적이었다. 우리가 그들에게 기부해야 할 서로 다른 종류의 이유를 주었을 때, 우리는 누군가가 그들을 설득하려고 하는 중이라는 그들의 인식을 유발했고 — 그리고 그들은 그것에 맞서 스스로를 보호했다.
→ 위에서 언급된 실험에서, 기부하라는 두 개의 다른 이유가 (A) 동시에 주어졌을 때, 청자는 자신을 설득시키려는 의도를 알아차릴 수 있었기 때문에 (B) 납득될 가능성이 더 작았다.

다음 글의 내용을 한 문장으로 요약하고자 한다. 빈칸 (A), (B)에 들어갈 말로 가장 적절한 것은?

	(A)		(B)
①	simultaneously 동시에	—	convinced 납득될
②	separately 별개로	—	confused 혼동될
③	frequently 빈번히	—	annoyed 언짢을
④	separately 별개로	—	satisfied 만족될
⑤	simultaneously 동시에	—	offended 불쾌하게 여길

(A) 기부하라는 두 개의 이유가 '동시에' 제시됨
(B) 청자는 자신을 설득시키려는 의도를 알아차리면 '납득될' 가능성이 작아짐

왜 2등급? 기부를 장려하는 두 개의 메시지가 제시되어서 각 이유에 따라 기부율이 달라질 것이라고 생각하기 쉽다. 하지만 제시되는 메시지 개수에 따라 기부율이 달라진다는 예상과는 다른 내용이 이어지는 2등급 대비 문제이다.

| 문제 풀이 순서 |

1st 요약문을 통해 글에서 무엇을 찾아야 하는지 확인한다.

요약문	위에서 언급된 실험에서, 기부하라는 두 개의 다른 이유가 '(A) _____ 하게' 주어졌을 때, 청자는 자신을 설득시키려는 의도를 알아차릴 수 있었기 때문에 '(B) _____ 할' 가능성이 더 작았다.

⇒ 글에서 찾아야 하는 것
(A): 실험에서 기부하라는 두 개의 다른 이유가 동시에, 별개로, 빈번히 주어졌는지
(B): 설득시키려는 의도를 알아차린 청자가 납득될, 혼동될, 언짢을, 만족될, 불쾌하게 여길 가능성이 더 작았는지

2nd 글의 내용을 파악하여 요약문을 완성한다.

┌ • 수천 명의 저항하는 졸업생이 기부하도록 납득시키는 것을 의도한 두 개의 다른 메시지들을 실험하는 한 연구를 진행함 **단서 1**
└ • 두 개의 메시지들은 똑같이 효과적이었지만, 그 두 개의 메시지들을 합쳤을 때, 기부율은 3퍼센트 아래로 떨어짐 **단서 2**

⇒ 졸업생들이 기부하도록 납득시키는 것을 의도한 두 개의 메시지를 따로 들었을 때는 기부에 대해 똑같이 효과적인 결과를 보였지만, 두 개의 메시지를 '동시에' 제시하자 기부를 더 적게 하는 결과를 보였다.
▶ 따라서 빈칸 (A)에는 ①, ⑤의 simultaneously가 들어가야 한다.

┌ 기부해야 할 서로 다른 종류의 이유를 주었을 때, 누군가가 그들을 설득하려고 하는
└ 중이라는 인식을 유발해서 그들은 스스로를 보호함 **단서 3**

⇒ 연구에서 기부하라는 두 개의 이유가 동시에 주어졌을 때, 졸업생들은 자신이 설득당하고 있다고 느껴서 방어적인 자세로 스스로를 보호하고 잘 '납득되지' 않는 경향이 있다고 했다.
▶ (B) 앞에 less가 있으므로 (B)에는 ① convinced가 적절하다.

| 선택지 분석 |

① 기부하라는 두 개의 이유가 '동시에' 제시되면 자신을 설득시키려는 의도를 알아차리고 '납득될' 가능성이 작아진다고 했다.
② 두 개의 이유가 동시에 제시된다고 했는데 (A)에 '별개로(separately)'가 들어가면 반대의 의미가 되므로 적절하지 않다.
③ 청자들이 납득되지 않는다고 했는데 (B)에 '언짢을(annoyed)'이 들어가면 앞의 less 때문에 글의 내용과 반대가 된다.
④ 두 개의 이유가 동시에 제시된다고 했는데 (A)에 '별개로(separately)'가 들어가면 반대의 의미가 되므로 적절하지 않다.
⑤ 청자들이 납득되지 않는다고 했는데 (B)에 '불쾌하게 여길(offended)'이 들어가면 앞의 less 때문에 글의 내용과 반대가 된다.

Q 22 정답 ①   ☆ 1등급 대비 [정답률 38%]

*common blackberry가 식물에 미치는 영향

The common blackberry (*Rubus allegheniensis*) / has an amazing ability / to move manganese / from one layer of soil to another / using its roots. // **단서 1** common blackberry는 토양의 한 층에서 다른 층으로 망가니즈를 옮기는 능력이 있음
common blackberry(Rubus allegheniensis)는 / 놀라운 능력이 있다 / 망가니즈를 옮기는 / 토양의 한 층에서 다른 층으로 / 뿌리를 이용하여 //

This may seem like a funny talent / for a plant to have, / but it all becomes clear / when you realize the effect / it has on nearby plants. //
이것은 기이한 재능처럼 보일 수도 있다 / 식물이 가지기에는 / 그러나 전부 명확해진다 / 영향을 깨닫고 나면 / 그것이 근처의 식물에 미치는 //

Manganese can be very harmful to plants, / especially at high concentrations. // **단서 2** 망가니즈는 식물에게 해로울 수 있음
망가니즈는 식물에 매우 해로울 수 있으며 / 특히 고농도일 때 그렇다 //

Common blackberry is unaffected / by damaging effects of this metal / and has evolved / two different ways of using manganese / to its advantage. //
common blackberry는 영향을 받지 않는다 / 이 금속 원소의 해로운 효과에 / 그리고 발달시켰다 / 망가니즈를 사용하는 두 가지 다른 방법을 / 자신에게 유리하게 //

First, / it redistributes manganese / from deeper soil layers / to shallow soil layers / using its roots as a small pipe. //
첫째로 / 그것은 망가니즈를 재분배한다 / 깊은 토양층으로부터 / 얕은 토양층으로 / 뿌리를 작은 관으로 사용하여 //

Second, / it absorbs manganese / as it grows, / concentrating the metal in its leaves. //
둘째로 / 그것은 망가니즈를 흡수하여 / 성장하면서 / 그 금속 원소를 잎에 농축한다 //

When the leaves drop and decay, / their concentrated manganese deposits / further poison the soil / around the plant. //
잎이 떨어지고 부패할 때 / 그것의 농축된 망가니즈 축적물은 / 토양을 독성 물질로 더욱 오염시킨다 / 그 식물 주변의 // **단서 3** 망가니즈 축적물이 토양을 더욱 오염시킴

For plants / that are not immune / to the toxic effects of manganese, / this is very bad news. //
식물에게 / 면역이 없는 / 망가니즈의 유독한 영향에 / 이것은 매우 나쁜 소식이다 //

Essentially, / the common blackberry eliminates competition / by poisoning its neighbors / with heavy metals. //
본질적으로 / common blackberry는 경쟁자를 제거한다 / 그것의 이웃을 중독시켜 / 중금속으로 //

→ The common blackberry has an ability / to (A) **increase** the amount of manganese / in the surrounding upper soil, / which [계속적 용법의 관계대명사] makes the nearby soil quite (B) **deadly** / for other plants. //
common blackberry는 능력이 있다 / 망가니즈의 양을 증가시키는 / 주변의 위쪽 토양의 / 그런데 그것은 근처의 토양이 치명적이게 만든다 / 다른 식물에게 //

- layer ⓝ 층 · soil ⓝ 토양 · root ⓝ 뿌리
- concentration ⓝ 농도 · damaging ⓐ 해로운
- evolve ⓥ 발달시키다 · redistribute ⓥ 재분배하다
- shallow ⓐ 얕은 · absorb ⓥ 흡수하다 · decay ⓥ 부패하다
- poison ⓥ (독성 물질로) 오염시키다, 중독시키다
- immune ⓐ 면역이 있는 · toxic ⓐ 유독한
- essentially ⓐⓓ 본질적으로 · eliminate ⓥ 제거하다
- competition ⓝ 경쟁자 · surrounding ⓐ 주변의
- deadly ⓐ 치명적인 · nutritious ⓐ 영양이 풍부한

common blackberry(*Rubus allegheniensis*)는 뿌리를 이용하여 토양의 한 층에서 다른 층으로 망가니즈를 옮기는 놀라운 능력이 있다. 이것은 식물이 가지기에는 기이한 재능처럼 보일 수도 있지만, 그것이 근처의 식물에 미치는 영향을 깨닫고 나면 전부 명확해진다. 망가니즈는 식물에 매우 해로울 수 있으며, 특히 고농도일 때 그렇다. common blackberry는 이 금속 원소의 해로운 효과에 영향을 받지 않으며, 망가니즈를 자신에게 유리하게 사용하는 두 가지 다른 방법을 발달시켰다. 첫째로, 그것은 뿌리를 작은 관으로 사용하여 망가니즈를 깊은 토양층으로부터 얕은 토양층으로 재분배한다. 둘째로, 그것은 성장하면서 망가니즈를 흡수하여 그 금속 원소를 잎에 농축한다. 잎이 떨어지고 부패할 때, 그것의 농축된 망가니즈 축적물은 그 식물 주변의 토양을 독성 물질로 더욱 오염시킨다. 망가니즈의 유독한 영향에 면역이 없는 식물에게 이것은 매우 나쁜 소식이다. 본질적으로, common blackberry는 중금속으로 그것의 이웃을 중독시켜 경쟁자를 제거한다.
→ common blackberry는 주변의 위쪽 토양의 망가니즈의 양을 (A) **증가시키는** 능력이 있는데, 그것이 근처의 토양이 다른 식물에게 (B) **치명적이게** 만든다.

다음 글의 내용을 한 문장으로 요약하고자 한다. 빈칸 (A), (B)에 들어갈 말로 가장 적절한 것은?

(A)		(B)
① increase 증가시키다	—	deadly 치명적인
② increase 증가시키다	—	advantageous 이로운
③ indicate 나타내다	—	nutritious 영양이 풍부한
④ reduce 감소시키다	—	dry 건조한
⑤ reduce 감소시키다	—	warm 따뜻한

(A) common blackberry는 토양의 한 층에서 다른 층으로 망가니즈를 이동시켜 상부토양층의 망가니즈 양을 증가시킴
(B) 망가니즈는 축적물이 토양을 더욱 오염시켜 식물에게 해로울 수 있음

왜 1등급? common blackberry에게 놀라운 능력이 있다고 하면서 글을 시작하고 있지만, 끝까지 읽어보면 이 common blackberry가 다른 식물에게 미치는 악영향을 이야기하고 있다는 것을 알 수 있다. 놀라운 능력이 곧 좋은 영향일 것이라고 착각하면 정반대의 답을 고르게 되는 1등급 대비 문제이다.

| 문제 풀이 순서 |

1st 요약문을 통해 글에서 무엇을 찾아야 하는지 확인한다.

요약문	common blackberry는 주변의 위쪽 토양의 망가니즈의 양을 '(A)_____ 하는' 능력이 있는데, 그것이 근처의 토양이 다른 식물에게 '(B)_____ 하게' 만든다.

➡ 글에서 찾아야 하는 것
 (A): common blackberry가 주변 위쪽 토양의 망가니즈의 양과 관련해서 갖고 있는 능력이 증가시키는지, 나타내는지, 감소시키는지

(B): common blackberry의 능력은 근처의 토양이 다른 식물에게 치명적인지, 이로운지, 영양이 풍부한게 하는지, 건조하게 하는지, 따뜻하게 하는지

2nd 글의 내용을 파악하여 요약문을 완성한다.

- common blackberry는 토양의 한 층에서 다른 층으로 망가니즈를 옮기는 능력이 있음 **단서1**
- 또한 망가니즈를 흡수하여 잎에 농축시킴
➡ 뿌리를 이용해 토양의 한 층에서 다른 층으로 망가니즈를 이동시키거나 잎에 저장하여 주변 위쪽 토양의 망가니즈 양을 증가시킨다.
 ▶ 빈칸 (A)에는 ①, ②의 increase가 들어가야 한다.
- 이렇게 증가한 토양 속 망가니즈는 식물에게 해로울 수 있음 **단서2**
- 망가니즈가 농축된 잎이 떨어져 토양을 더욱 오염시킴 **단서3**
➡ 망가니즈의 양이 토양에서 증가하고 독성 물질을 만들어 식물에게 나쁜 영향을 끼친다.
 ▶ 따라서 (B)에는 ① deadly가 적절하다.

| 선택지 분석 |

① 망가니즈가 증가하여 치명적 영향을 미친다고 했다.
② 망가니즈는 common blackberry에게만 이롭다.
③ 늘어난 망가니즈의 양이 식물에게 유해한 영향을 끼친다는 내용이므로 (B)에 '영양이 풍부한(nutritious)'과 같은 긍정적인 말이 들어가는 것은 어색하다.
④ 망가니즈가 식물의 습도에 영향을 주는 것이 아니다.
⑤ 망가니즈가 식물에 온도에 영향을 주는 것이 아니다.

Q 23 정답 ② ⭐ 1등급 대비 [정답률 37%]

*미디어가 과학적 연구를 단순화하는 이유

단서1 과학에는 불확실성이 많아서 일반 대중은 그것을 불편하게 생각함
There is often a lot of uncertainty / in the realm of science, / which [계속적 용법의 관계대명사] the general public finds uncomfortable. //
종종 많은 불확실성이 존재한다 / 과학의 영역에는 / 그리고 일반 대중은 그것을 불편하다고 느낀다 //

단서2 일반 대중은 확실성을 원하지만 과학은 이러한 요구를 만족시키지 못함
They don't want "informed guesses," / they want certainties / that make their lives easier, [주격 관계대명사절] / and science is often unequipped / to meet these demands. [부사적 용법] //
그들은 '정보에 근거한 추측'을 원하지 않으며 / 그들은 확실성을 원한다 / 자신의 삶을 더 편하게 만들어 주는 / 그리고 과학이 종종 갖춰져 있지 않다 / 이러한 요구를 만족시키도록 //

In particular, / the human body is fantastically complex, / and some scientific answers can never be provided / in black-or-white terms. //
특히 / 인간의 신체는 굉장히 복잡하다 / 그리고 어떤 과학적인 답변은 절대 제공될 수 없다 / 흑백 양자택일의 말로는 //

단서3 미디어는 과학적 연구를 대중들에게 제시할 때 지나치게 단순화함
All this is / why the media tends to oversimplify scientific research / when presenting it to the public. [=when the media presents] //
이 모든 것이 ~이다 / 미디어가 과학적 연구를 지나치게 단순화하는 경향이 있는 이유 / 그것을 대중에게 제시할 때 //

In their eyes, / they're just "giving people what they want" [간접목적어] [직접목적어] / as opposed to offering / more accurate but complex information / that very few people will read or understand. [목적격 관계대명사] //
그들의 눈에는 / 그들은 단지 '사람들에게 그들이 원하는 것을 제공하고' 있는 것이다 / 제공하는 것과는 반대로 / 더 정확하지만 복잡한 정보를 / 극소수의 사람들만이 읽거나 이해할 //

A perfect example of this / is how people want definitive answers / as to which foods are "good" and "bad." [=about] [의문형용사] //
이것의 완벽한 하나의 예시는 / 사람들이 확정적인 답변을 원하는 방식이다 / 어떤 음식이 '좋은'지 그리고 '나쁜'지에 관해 //

Scientifically speaking, / there are no "good" and "bad" foods; / rather, food quality exists on a continuum, /
과학적으로 말하자면 / '좋고', '나쁜' 음식은 없으며 / 오히려 음식의 질은 연속성에 존재한다 /

meaning / <u>that</u> some foods are *better* than others / when it comes
to general health and well-being. //
목적어절을 이끄는 접속사
이는 의미한다 / 어떤 음식들이 다른 것들보다 '더 낫다'는 것을 / 일반 건강과 웰빙 면에서 //

> → With regard to general health, / science, by its nature, / does
> not (A) **satisfy** the public's demands for certainty, /
> 일반 건강과 관련하여 / 과학이 본질적으로 / 확실성에 대한 대중의 요구를 만족시키지
> 않는다 /
> 계속적 용법의 관계대명사
> <u>which</u> leads to the media giving less (B) **complicated** answers
> / to the public. // 이것은 미디어가 덜 복잡한 답변을 제공하도록 이끈다 / 대중에게 //

- uncertainty ⓝ 불확실성   • realm ⓝ 영역, 영토
- general public 일반 대중   • certainty ⓝ 확실성
- unequipped ⓐ 준비가 안 된   • demand ⓝ 요구
- complex ⓐ 복잡한   • black-or-white 흑백 양자택일의
- oversimplify ⓥ 지나치게 단순화하다   • present ⓥ 제시하다
- opposed to ~과 반대로   • accurate ⓐ 정확한
- definitive ⓐ 확정적인   • quality ⓝ 질   • exist ⓥ 존재하다

과학의 영역에는 종종 많은 불확실성이 존재하며 일반 대중은 그것을
불편하다고 느낀다. 그들은 '정보에 근거한 추측'을 원하지 않으며 그들은
자신의 삶을 더 편하게 만들어 주는 확실성을 원하는데, 과학이 종종
이러한 요구를 만족시키도록 갖춰져 있지 않다. 특히 인간의 신체는
굉장히 복잡하며 어떤 과학적인 답변은 흑백 양자택일의 말로는 절대
제공될 수 없다. 이 모든 것이 미디어가 과학적 연구를 대중에게 제시할
때 그것을 지나치게 단순화하는 경향이 있는 이유이다. 그들의 눈에는
극소수의 사람들만이 읽거나 이해할 더 정확하지만 복잡한 정보를
제공하는 것과는 반대로 그들은 단지 '사람들에게 그들이 원하는 것을
제공하고' 있는 것이다. 이것의 완벽한 하나의 예시는 어떤 음식이 '좋은'지
그리고 '나쁜'지에 관해 사람들이 확정적인 답변을 원하는 방식이다.
과학적으로 말하자면 '좋고', '나쁜' 음식은 없으며, 오히려 음식의 질은
연속체상에 존재하는데 이는 어떤 음식들이 다른 것들보다 일반 건강과
웰빙 면에서 '더 낫다'는 것을 의미한다.
→ 일반 건강과 관련하여 과학이 본질적으로 확실성에 대한 대중의 요구를
(A) **만족시키지** 않으며, 이것은 미디어가 대중에게 덜 (B) **복잡한** 답변을
제공하도록 이끈다.

다음 글의 내용을 한 문장으로 요약하고자 한다. 빈칸 (A), (B)에 들어갈
말로 가장 적절한 것은?

	(A)		(B)
①	satisfy 만족시키다	—	simple 단순한
②✓	satisfy 만족시키다	—	complicated 복잡한
③	ignore 무시하다	—	difficult 어려운
④	ignore 무시하다	—	simple 단순한
⑤	reject 거절하다	—	complicated 복잡한

(A) 과학은 확실성에 대한 대중의 요구를 '만족시키지' 못함
(B) 미디어는 대중에게 과학적 연구를 단순화해서(덜 '복잡하게') 제시함

왜 1등급? 도입부에서 과학의 불확실성에 대해 언급한 후, 이에 대해 미디어가
어떻게 하는지에 대한 내용이 이어진다. 과학과 미디어는 어려운 소재일 수 있으므로
글을 끝까지 꼼꼼하게 읽어야 오답을 고르지 않을 수 있다.

| 문제 풀이 순서 |

1st 요약문을 통해 글에서 무엇을 찾아야 하는지 확인한다.

요약문	일반 건강과 관련하여 과학이 본질적으로 확실성에 대한 대중의 요구를 '(A) _____ 하지' 않으며, 이것은 미디어가 대중에게 덜 '(B) _____ 한' 답변을 제공하도록 이끈다.

⇒ 글에서 찾아야 하는 것
(A): 과학이 건강과 관련해서 확실성에 대한 대중의 요구를 <u>만족시키는지</u>,
무시하는지, 거절하는지
(B): 과학의 대중에 대한 이 특징이 대중에게 답변을 제공하는데 그 답변이 덜
<u>단순한지</u>, 복잡한지, 어려운지

2nd 글의 내용을 파악하여 요약문을 완성한다.

- 과학에는 불확실성이 많아서 일반 대중은 그것을 불편하다고 느낌 단서 1
- 그들은 삶을 더 편하게 만들어주는 확실성을 원하지만 과학은 이러한 요구를
  만족시키지 못함 단서 2

⇒ 과학의 불확실성 때문에 과학은 확실성에 대한 일반 대중의 요구를 만족시키지
못한다고 했다.
▶ 따라서 빈칸 (A)에는 ①, ②의 satisfy가 들어가야 한다.

- 미디어는 과학적 연구를 대중들에게 제시할 때 지나치게 단순화하는 경향이
  있음 단서 3
- 예를 들어, 사람들은 어떤 음식이 '좋은'지, '나쁜'지에 관해 확실한 답변을 원하지만
  사실 과학적으로 좋고 나쁜 음식은 없음

⇒ 미디어는 일반 대중에게 과학적 연구를 단순화해서, 즉 덜 복잡하게 제시한다고
했다.
▶ (B) 앞에 less가 있으므로 (B)에는 ② complicated가 적절하다.

| 선택지 분석 |

① (B) 앞에 있는 less 때문에 오히려 반대의 의미를 나타낸다.
②✓ 불확실성이 많은 과학은 대중을 만족시키지 못하는데, 이로 인해 덜 복잡한 정보를
제공한다고 했다.
③ 과학이 대중의 요구를 무시하는 것은 아니다.
④ (B) 앞에 있는 less 때문에 오히려 반대의 의미를 나타낸다.
⑤ 과학이 대중의 요구를 만족시키지 못하는 것이지 거절하는 것은 아니다.

Q 어휘 Review 정답 ⸺⸺⸺⸺⸺ 문제편 p. 275

01 실시하다	11 be opposed to	21 statement
02 편향	12 converse with	22 revised
03 전망	13 exposed to	23 disabilities
04 판단	14 by definition	24 comparison
05 외과 의사	15 point out	25 concentrations
06 recreate	16 assumption	26 challenges
07 encounter	17 application	27 conception
08 miser	18 layers	28 strategy
09 reasoning	19 resistant	29 originate
10 neutral	20 empathy	30 Authoritative

 **R 장문의 이해** 문제편 p. 278~292

R 01~02 *신용카드 사용이 소비를 증가시키는 이유

Paying with plastic / fundamentally **changes** the way we spend money, / **altering the calculus** / of our financial decisions. //
신용카드로 지불하는 것은 / 우리가 돈을 소비하는 방식을 근본적으로 바꾸며 / 계산법을 변화시킨다 / 우리의 재정적 결정에 대한 //

When you buy something with cash, / the purchase involves an actual (a) loss — / your wallet is literally lighter. //
당신이 무언가를 현금으로 구매할 때 / 그 구매는 실제 손실을 수반한다 / 당신의 지갑이 말 그대로 더 가벼워진다 //

Credit cards, however, / make the purchase abstract, / **so that** you don't really feel / the downside of spending money. //
하지만, 신용카드는 / 구매를 추상화시켜 / 당신은 실제로 느끼지 못한다 / 돈을 소비하는 것의 부정적인 면을 //
01번 단서 1: 신용카드는 소비의 부정적인 면을 느끼지 못하게 함

Brain-imaging experiments suggest / that paying with credit cards / actually (b) **reduces** activity / in **the insula**, / **a brain region associated with negative feelings.** //
뇌 영상 실험은 보여준다 / 신용카드로 지불하는 것이 / 실제로 활동을 감소시킨다는 것을 / 뇌섬엽에서의 / 부정적인 감정과 관련된 뇌 영역인 //
01번 단서 2: 신용카드 지불은 부정적 감정과 관련된 뇌 영역의 활동을 감소시킴

As **George Loewenstein,** / **a neuroeconomist at Carnegie Mellon**, / says, /
George Loewenstein이 / Carnegie Mellon의 신경경제학자인 / 말하듯이 /

"The nature of credit cards / ensures / that your brain is anesthetized / against the pain of payment." //
신용카드의 본질은 / 확실하게 한다 / 당신의 뇌가 마비되는 것을 / 지불의 고통에 대해 //

Spending money / doesn't feel (c) bad, / so you spend more money. //
돈을 쓰는 것이 / 나쁘게 느껴지지 않는다 / 그래서 당신은 더 많은 돈을 쓴다 //
01번 단서 3, 02번 단서 1: 신용카드는 돈을 더 많이 쓰게 만듦

Consider this experiment: /
이 실험을 생각해 보자 /

Drazen Prelec and Duncan Simester, / two business professors at MIT, / organized a real-life, sealed-bid auction / for tickets to a Boston Celtics game. //
Drazen Prelec과 Duncan Simester / MIT의 두 경영학 교수인 / 실제 봉인 입찰 경매를 준비했다 / Boston Celtics 경기 티켓을 위한 //

Half the participants in the auction / **were** informed / that they had to pay with cash; / the other half / were told / they had to pay with credit cards. //
경매에 참여한 사람들 중 절반은 / 들었다 / 현금으로 지불해야 한다는 말을 / 나머지 절반은 / 들었다 / 신용카드로 지불해야 한다는 말을 //

Prelec and Simester / then averaged the bids / for the two different groups. //
Prelec과 Simester는 / 그리고 나서 입찰가의 평균을 냈다 / 다른 두 집단의 //

It turns out / **that** the average credit card bid / was *twice* as (d) high / as the average cash bid. //
나타났다 / 평균 신용카드 입찰 금액이 / '두 배'만큼 높은 것으로 / 평균 현금 입찰금액의 //
01번 단서 4: 평균 신용카드 입찰가가 현금 입찰가보다 두 배 높음

When people used their credit cards, / their bids / were much more (e) careful(→ reckless). //
사람들이 신용카드를 사용할 때 / 그들의 입찰은 / 훨씬 더 신중(→ 무모)했다 //

They no longer felt the need / **to limit** their expenses. //
그들은 더 이상 필요성을 느끼지 못했다 / 지출을 억제해야 할 //
02번 단서 2: 신용카드를 사용한 사람들은 지출을 억제해야 할 필요성을 느끼지 못함

- plastic ⓝ 신용카드 • fundamentally ⓐ⒟ 근본적으로
- alter ⓥ 바꾸다 • financial ⓐ 재정적인 • involve ⓥ 수반하다
- loss ⓝ 손실 • literally ⓐ⒟ 말 그대로 • abstract ⓐ 추상적인
- downside ⓝ 부정적인 면 • insula ⓝ 뇌섬엽 • region ⓝ 영역

- associated with ~와 관련된 • sealed-bid ⓝ 봉인 입찰
- auction ⓝ 경매 • inform ⓥ 알리다 • average ⓥ 평균을 내다
- expense ⓝ 지출

신용카드로 지불하는 것은 우리가 돈을 소비하는 방식을 근본적으로 바꾸며, 우리의 재정적 결정에 대한 계산법을 변화시킨다. 당신이 무언가를 현금으로 구매할 때, 그 구매는 실제 (a) 손실을 수반한다 — 당신의 지갑이 말 그대로 더 가벼워진다. 하지만, 신용카드는 구매를 추상화시켜, 당신은 돈을 소비하는 것의 부정적인 면을 실제로 느끼지 못한다. 뇌 영상 실험은 신용카드로 지불하는 것이 부정적인 감정과 관련된 뇌 영역인 뇌섬엽에서의 활동을 실제로 (b) 감소시킨다는 것을 보여준다. Carnegie Mellon의 신경경제학자 George Loewenstein이 말하듯이, "신용카드의 본질은 당신의 뇌가 지불의 고통에 대해 마비되는 것을 확실하게 한다." 돈을 쓰는 것이 (c) 나쁘게 느껴지지 않아서, 당신은 더 많은 돈을 쓴다.

이 실험을 생각해 보자: MIT의 두 경영학 교수인 Drazen Prelec과 Duncan Simester는 Boston Celtics 경기 티켓을 위한 실제 봉인 입찰 경매를 준비했다. 경매에 참여한 사람들 중 절반은 현금으로 지불해야 한다는 말을 들었고; 나머지 절반은 신용카드로 지불해야 한다는 말을 들었다. 그러고 나서 Prelec과 Simester는 다른 두 집단의 입찰가의 평균을 냈다. 평균 신용카드 입찰 금액은 평균 현금 입찰 금액의 '두 배'만큼 (d) 높은 것으로 나타났다. 사람들이 신용카드를 사용할 때, 그들의 입찰은 훨씬 더 (e) 신중(→ 무모)했다. 그들은 더 이상 지출을 억제해야 할 필요성을 느끼지 못했다.

R 01 정답 ②

윗글의 제목으로 가장 적절한 것은?
① Once Set, Spending Habits Seldom Change
한번 형성된 소비 습관은 좀처럼 변하지 않는다 소비 습관의 변화는 언급되지 않음
② Why Do We Spend More with Credit Cards? 신용카드를 사용할 때
왜 우리는 신용카드를 사용할 때 더 많이 지출하는가? 더 많이 지출하게 되는 이유를 설명함
③ Credit Cards: A Safer Way to Pay than Cash
신용카드: 현금보다 더 안전한 결제 수단 결제 수단의 안전성은 언급되지 않음
④ Paying with Plastic: The Secret to Saving Money
신용카드 결제: 돈을 절약하는 비결 신용카드는 돈을 절약하는 것이 아니라 더 쓰게 만듦
⑤ Using Cash Leads to Taking More Financial Risks
현금 사용은 더 많은 재정적 위험으로 이어진다 현금 사용의 위험성은 언급되지 않음

왜 정답? ✱✱✿ [정답률 77%]

- 신용카드는 소비의 부정적인 면을 느끼지 못하게 한다. 01번 단서 1
- 신용카드 지불은 부정적 감정과 관련된 뇌 영역의 활동을 감소시킨다. 01번 단서 2
- 신용카드는 돈을 더 많이 쓰게 만든다. 01번 단서 3
- 평균 신용카드 입찰가가 현금 입찰가보다 두 배 높았다. 01번 단서 4

➡ 신용카드로 지불하는 것은 돈을 소비하는 것의 부정적인 면을 느끼지 못하게 하여 현금으로 지불할 때보다 돈을 더 많이 쓰게 만든다고 했다.

▶ 따라서 제목으로 가장 적절한 것은 ② '왜 우리는 신용카드를 사용할 때 더 많이 지출할까?'이다.

왜 오답?

① 소비 습관의 변화는 언급되지 않았다.
③ 신용카드가 현금보다 더 안전한 결제 수단이라는 것은 언급되지 않았다.
④ 신용카드는 돈을 절약하게 하지 않고 더 많이 쓰게 만든다는 것이 글의 주제이다.
⑤ 현금 사용이 더 많은 재정적 위험으로 이어진다는 것은 언급되지 않았다.

R 02 정답 ⑤

밑줄 친 (a)~(e) 중에서 문맥상 낱말의 쓰임이 적절하지 않은 것은? [3점]
① (a) 지갑이 더 가벼워지는 실제적인 손실을 수반함
손실
② (b) 신용카드 결제는 부정적인 감정과 관련된 뇌 부위의 활동을 감소시킴
감소시키다
③ (c) 뇌가 지불의 고통에 대해 마비되어 소비가 나쁘게 느껴지지 않음
나쁜
④ (d) 신용카드 입찰가가 현금 입찰가보다 평균적으로 두 배 높음
높은
⑤ (e) 신용카드를 사용한 사람들은 더 무모하게 입찰했음
신중한

왜 정답? ✱✱✲ [정답률 72%]

⑤ (e) careful 신중한

[사람들이 신용카드를 사용할 때, 그들의 입찰은 훨씬 더 (e) ~~신중했다~~.]
무모했다

➡ 신용카드는 돈을 더 많이 쓰게 만들며 지출을 억제할 필요성을 느끼지 못하게 만든다고 했으므로, 신용카드를 쓸 때 사람들의 입찰은 신중하지 않고 훨씬 더 '무모했을' 것이다. ▶ careful을 reckless(무모한)와 같은 반의어로 바꿔야 함

왜 오답?

① (a) loss 손실

[당신이 무언가를 현금으로 구매할 때, 그 구매는 실제 (a) 손실을 수반한다.]

➡ 현금 지불은 지갑이 더 가벼워지는 실제적인 '손실'을 수반한다.
   ▶ loss는 문맥에 맞음

② (b) reduces 감소시키다

[뇌 영상 실험은 신용카드로 지불하는 것이 부정적인 감정과 관련된 뇌 영역인 뇌섬엽에서의 활동을 실제로 (b) 감소시킨다는 것을 보여준다.]

➡ 신용카드 지불은 돈을 쓰는 것의 단점을 느끼지 못하게 만든다고 했으므로, 부정적인 감정과 관련된 뇌 부위의 활동을 '감소시킬' 것이다. ▶ reduces는 문맥에 맞음

③ (c) bad 나쁜

[돈을 쓰는 것이 (c) 나쁘게 느껴지지 않아서, 당신은 더 많은 돈을 쓴다.]

➡ 뇌가 지불의 고통에 대해 마비되어 소비가 '나쁘게' 느껴지지 않는다.
   ▶ bad는 문맥에 맞음

④ (d) high 높은

[평균 신용카드 입찰 금액은 평균 현금 입찰 금액의 '두 배'만큼 (d) 높은 것으로 나타났다.]

➡ 신용카드는 더 많은 돈을 쓰게 만든다고 했으므로, 평균 신용카드 입찰가가 현금 입찰가보다 두 배 '높은' 것으로 나타났다는 것이 적절하다. ▶ high는 문맥에 맞음

R 03~04 ＊수량화의 문제점

view A as B: A를 B로 여기다
Some researchers __view__ spoken languages / __as__ incomplete devices / for capturing precise differences. //
일부 연구자는 발화된 언어를 여긴다 / 불완전한 도구로 / 정확한 차이를 포착하는 데에 //

They think / numbers represent / the most neutral language of description. //
그들은 생각한다 / 숫자가 나타낸다고 / 묘사의 가장 중립적인 언어를 //

However, / when our language of description is changed to numbers, / we do not move / toward greater (a) accuracy. //
그러나 / 우리의 묘사의 언어가 숫자로 바뀔 때 / 우리가 나아가지는 않는다 / 더 큰 정확성으로 //
03번 단서 1: 숫자로 묘사하는 것이 더 정확하지 않음

Numbers are no more appropriate 'pictures of the world' / than words, music, or painting. // **03번** 단서 2: 숫자가 세상을 묘사하는 최고의 방법은 아님
숫자가 더 적절한 '세상의 묘사'는 아니다 / 말, 음악, 또는 그림보다 //

부사절 접속사 (양보)
__While__ useful for specific purposes (e.g. census taking, income distribution), / they (b) include(→ exclude) information of enormous value. // **04번** 단서 1: 숫자에는 엄청난 가치(질적 및 심리적)를 지닌 정보가 없음
특정한 목적(예를 들어, 인구 조사, 소득 분포)에는 유용하지만 / 숫자는 엄청난 가치를 지닌 정보를 포함한다(→ 제외한다) //

For example, / the future lives of young students are tied / to their scores on national tests. //
예를 들어 / 어린 학생들의 미래의 삶은 매여 있다 / 그들의 전국 단위 시험 점수에 //

명사절 접속사 (~인지 아닌지)
In effect, / __whether__ they can continue with their education, /
단수 동사
where, / and at what cost / __depends__ importantly on a handful of numbers. //
사실상, / 그들이 교육을 지속할 수 있는지 / 어디에서일지 / 그리고 얼마의 비용일지가 / 한 줌의 숫자에 중대하게 달려 있다 // **03번** 단서 3, **04번** 단서 2: 질적인 측면처럼 숫자가 설명할 수 없는 부분이 존재함

These numbers do not account for / the (c) quality of schools they have attended, / whether they have been tutored, / have supportive parents, / have test anxiety, and so on. //
이들 숫자는 설명하지 않는다 / 그들이 다닌 학교의 질 / 그들이 개인 교습을 받아 오는지 / 지지적인 부모가 있는지 / 시험 불안이 있는지 등의 여부를 //

분사구문을 이끄는 현재분사
Finally, / __putting__ aside the many ways / __in which__ statistical
「전치사+관계대명사」 (ways 수식)
results can be manipulated, / there are ways / __in which__ turning people's lives into numbers / is (d) morally insulating. //
마지막으로 / 많은 방식을 제쳐 두더라도 / 통계 결과가 조작될 수 있는 / 측면이 있다 / 사람들의 삶을 숫자로 바꾸는 것이 / 도덕적으로 차단하는 // **03번** 단서 4: 삶을 수치화하면 도덕성이 차단됨

Statistics on crime, homelessness, or the spread of a disease say nothing / of people's suffering. //
범죄, 노숙자 문제, 질병의 확산에 관한 통계는 아무것도 말하지 않는다 / 사람들의 고통에 대해 //

전치사 (~처럼)
We read the statistics / __as__ reports on events at a distance, / thus
동명사의 수동태
allowing us to (e) escape / without __being disturbed__. //
우리는 그 통계를 읽는데 / 멀리 있는 사건에 대한 보고서처럼 / 그러므로 이것은 우리가 도망갈 수 있도록 해준다 / 동요되지 않고 //

「with + 명사 + 분사」: with 분사구문
Statistics are human beings / __with the tears wiped off__. //
통계는 인간이다 / 눈물이 닦인 //

Quantify with caution. //
수량화할 때는 신중해라 //

- -

- represent ⓥ 나타내다, 표현하다   • accuracy ⓝ 정확성
- census taking 인구 조사   • income distribution 소득 분포
- in effect 사실상   • test anxiety 시험 불안   • put aside 제쳐 두다
- way ⓝ 방식, 측면   • morally ⓐⓓ 도덕적으로
- homelessness ⓝ 노숙자 문제   • spread ⓝ 확산
- suffering ⓝ 고통   • disturb ⓥ 동요시키다   • wipe off 닦아 내다
- quantify ⓥ 수량화하다   • uncovered ⓐ 드러난, 밝혀진
- framework ⓝ 체계   • convey ⓥ 전달하다

일부 연구자는 발화된 언어를 정확한 차이를 포착하는 데에 불완전한 도구로 여긴다. 그들은 숫자가 묘사의 가장 중립적인 언어를 나타낸다고 생각한다. 그러나, 우리의 묘사의 언어가 숫자로 바뀔 때, 우리가 더 큰 (a) 정확성으로 나아가지는 않는다. 숫자가 말, 음악, 또는 그림보다 더 적절한 '세상의 묘사'는 아니다. 특정한 목적(예를 들어, 인구 조사, 소득 분포)에는 유용하지만, 숫자는 엄청난 가치를 지닌 정보를 (b) 포함한다(→ 배제한다). 예를 들어, 어린 학생들의 미래의 삶은 그들의 전국 단위 시험 점수에 매여 있다. 사실상, 그들이 교육을 지속할 수 있는지, 어디에서일지, 그리고 얼마의 비용일지가 한 줌의 숫자에 중대하게 달려 있다. 이들 숫자는 그들이 다닌 학교의 (c) 질, 그들이 개인 교습을 받아 오는지, 지지적인 부모가 있는지, 시험 불안이 있는지 등의 여부를 설명하지 않는다. 마지막으로, 통계 결과가 조작될 수 있는 많은 방식을 제쳐 두더라도, 사람들의 삶을 숫자로 바꾸는 것이 (d) 도덕적으로 차단하는 측면이 있다. 범죄, 노숙자 문제, 질병의 확산에 관한 통계는 사람들의 고통에 대해 아무것도 말하지 않는다. 우리는 그 통계를 멀리 있는 사건에 대한 보고서처럼 읽는데, 그러므로 이것은 우리가 동요되지 않고 (e) 도망갈 수 있도록 해준다. 통계는 눈물이 닦인 인간이다. 수량화할 때는 신중해라.

R 03 정답 ①

윗글의 제목으로 가장 적절한 것은?
① Numbers Don't Tell Us Everything 숫자로 묘사할 수 없는 삶의 부분도
숫자가 우리에게 모든 것을 말해주지는 않음 있음
② Human Stories Uncovered by the Numbers 인간의 삶의 모든 부분을
숫자로만 나타낼 수 없다는 것이 글의 내용임
③ Data: A Framework for Understanding Humans
데이터: 인간을 이해하기 위한 체계 데이터가 인간 이해의 체계로 작용하기에는 부족함
④ The Limitations of Language in Conveying Truth
진실을 전달하는 데 있어 언어의 한계 언어의 한계가 아니라 숫자의 한계에 관한 글임
⑤ The Advantages of Quantifying Human Experiences
인간의 경험을 수량화하는 것의 이점들 수량화의 이점은 언급되지 않음

➔왜 정답 ? ✶✶✶ [정답률 60%]

- 숫자로 묘사하는 것이 더 정확하지는 않다. 03번 단서 1
- 숫자가 세상을 묘사하는 최고의 방법은 아니다. 03번 단서 2
- 질적인 측면처럼 숫자로 설명할 수 없는 부분도 있다. 03번 단서 3
- 삶을 수치화하면 도덕성이 차단되고 심리적 측면을 파악할 수 없다. 03번 단서 4

➔ 일부 연구자들은 숫자가 가장 중립적인 묘사 도구라고 여기지만, 숫자는 질적 및 심리적 정보를 담아내지 못하므로 모든 것을 설명하지는 못한다.
▶ 따라서 제목으로 가장 적절한 것은 ① '숫자가 우리에게 모든 것을 말해주지는 않는다'이다.

➔왜 오답 ?

② 인간의 이야기, 즉 삶의 모든 부분을 숫자로 나타낼 수는 없다는 것이 글의 주제이다.
③ 데이터는 인간을 이해하기 위한 체계 중 하나지만 절대적인 도구는 아니다.
④ 언어의 한계가 아닌 숫자의 한계에 관한 내용이다.
⑤ 인간 경험을 수량화하는 것의 이점이 아닌 한계가 글의 주제이다.

R 04 정답 ②

밑줄 친 (a)~(e) 중에서 문맥상 낱말의 쓰임이 적절하지 <u>않은</u> 것은? [3점]
① (a) 숫자가 정확성의 향상을 보장하진 않음
정확성
② (b) 숫자는 질적 및 심리적 정보를 배제함
포함하다
③ (c) 질은 숫자로 표현할 수 없음
질
④ (d) 삶을 수치화하면 사회 문제에 대한 공감이 떨어지기에 도덕성과 멀어지게 함
도덕적으로
⑤ (e) 사회 문제에 관한 통계 결과에 감정적으로 동요되지 않고 멀어질 수 있게 함
도망가다

➔왜 정답 ? ✶✶✶ [정답률 29%]

② (b) include 포함하다

특정한 목적(예를 들어, 인구 조사, 소득 분포)에는 유용하지만, 숫자는 엄청난 가치를 지닌 정보를 (b) ~~포함한다~~.
배제한다.

➔ 숫자는 삶의 질적 및 심리적 측면을 묘사할 수 없으므로, 숫자가 엄청난 가치를 가진 정보를 '포함한다'가 아니라 '배제한다'가 더 자연스럽다.
▶ include를 exclude(배제한다)와 같은 반의어로 바꿔야 함

➔왜 오답 ?

① (a) accuracy 정확성

그러나, 우리의 묘사의 언어가 숫자로 바뀔 때, 우리가 더 큰 (a) 정확성으로 나아가지는 않는다.
➔ 설명을 제공할 때, 숫자가 도움이 될 경우도 있지만 꼭 더 정확한 정보를 주는 것은 아니므로 '정확성'은 적절하다. ▶ accuracy는 문맥에 맞음

③ (c) quality 질

이들 숫자는 그들이 다닌 학교의 (c) 질, 그들이 개인 교습을 받아 오는지, 지지적인 부모가 있는지, 시험 불안이 있는지 등의 여부를 설명하지 않는다.

➔ 숫자로 '양'을 나타낼 수는 있지만 '질'을 설명할 수는 없으므로 문맥상 자연스럽다.
▶ quality는 문맥에 맞음

④ (d) morally 도덕적으로

마지막으로, 통계 결과가 조작될 수 있는 많은 방식을 제쳐 두더라도, 사람들의 삶을 숫자로 바꾸는 것이 (d) 도덕적으로 차단하는 측면이 있다.
➔ 삶을 수치화하면 그 삶에 대한 인간의 '도덕적인' 판단을 차단할 것이다.
▶ morally는 문맥에 맞음

⑤ (e) escape 도망가다

우리는 그 통계를 멀리 있는 사건에 대한 보고서처럼 읽는데, 그러므로 이것은 우리가 동요되지 않고 (e) 도망갈 수 있도록 해준다.
➔ 사회 문제에 관한 통계는 결과 외에 어떤 정보도 말하지 않기 때문에, 우리가 그 문제에 공감할 수 없게 되므로 감정적으로 동요되지 않고 '도망갈' 수 있게 한다.
▶ escape는 문맥에 맞음

구문 서술형

정답 While과 useful 사이, numbers[they] are
해석 특정한 목적에는 유용하지만, 숫자는 엄청난 가치를 지닌 정보를 배제한다.
→ 부사절과 주절의 주어가 같을 때, 부사절의 「주어+be동사」를 생략할 수 있다. 주절의 주어가 numbers이므로 생략된 주어는 numbers[they]이고, 이는 복수형이므로 생략된 be동사는 are이다.

R 05~06 ✶소매 판매에 "도와드릴까요?"라는 표현이 잘못된 이유

"May I help you?" / are the worst four words / 목적격 관계대명사 that a retail salesperson can utter / 05번 단서 1: "도와드릴까요?"는 고객을 방어적으로 만드는 최악의 표현임
"도와드릴까요"는 / 최악의 네 단어이다 / 소매 판매원이 말할 수 있는
because they don't encourage encourage의 목적어와 목적격 보어 (to부정사) the customer to talk / and put them on the defensive. //
고객이 말을 하도록 하지 않고 / 그들이 방어적이게 하기 때문에 //

The four words usually draw out a negative response / that stops cold a sales transaction. //
그 네 단어는 부정적인 반응을 주로 끌어낸다 / 판매 거래를 완전히 막는 //
부사절에서 「주어+be동사」 생략
Examples of (a) <u>better</u> questions to use / when approaching customers / are "Is there anything in particular 목적격 관계대명사 (선행사: anything) that you are looking for?" / and "Are you shopping for a gift?" //
사용할 수 있는 더 나은 질문들의 예들로는 / 고객에게 다가갈 때 / "특별히 당신이 찾고 계신 어떤 것이 있나요"와 / "당신은 선물을 위한 쇼핑을 하고 있나요"가 있다 //

If a fashion salesperson approached you with / "May I help chances are (that): ~일 가능성이 있다 you?" / chances are you would feel / the salesperson didn't (b) care. //
만약 패션 판매원이 당신에게 다가온다면 / "도와드릴까요"로 / 당신은 느낄 가능성이 있다 / 그 판매원이 신경 쓰지 않는다고 //
= "May I help you?"
주격 관계대명사
This line is a rote approach / that is so overused / by untrained and uninterested salespeople. // 05번 단서 2: "도와드릴까요?"는 훈련되지 않고 무관심한 판매원의 기계적인 접근 방식임
이 문장은 기계적인 접근 방식이다 / 매우 지나치게 사용되는 / 훈련되지 않고 무관심한 판매원들에 의해 //

In fact, / most of us shudder in horror / on hearing these words. //
실제로 / 우리 대부분은 기겁하여 몸서리친다 / 이 단어들을 들을 때 //

The very meaning of the question "May I help you?" / (c) rejects(→ implies) that the customer is in trouble of some sort and needs rescuing. // 06번 단서: "도와드릴까요?"는 고객이 실제로 문제에 처했음을 암시함
"도와드릴까요?"라는 이 질문의 진짜 의미는 / 고객이 어떤 종류의 곤경에 처해 있고 구출될 필요가 있다는 것을 부인한다(→ 내포한다) //

This almost always puts the customer on the defense. //
이는 거의 항상 그 고객이 방어적이게 한다 //

"No, thank you" is usually the immediate response, / **even if** the customer is actually in need of assistance. //
부사절 접속사 (양보)
"아니요, 괜찮습니다"는 주로 즉각적인 반응이다 / 그 고객이 실제로 도움이 필요할지라도 //

The subconscious thought by the customer is often / "I'm **smart enough to figure** out what I want, / and I don't need your help!" //
형용사 + enough + to부정사: …할 만큼 충분히 ~한
고객의 잠재의식적인 생각은 종종 ~이다 / "나는 내가 원하는 것을 알 만큼 충분히 현명해 / 그래서 나는 당신의 도움이 필요하지 않아" //

If customers feel pressured or cornered, / then salespeople won't make any sales. // **05번 단서 3**: 고객이 압박감을 느끼면 판매로 이어지지 않음
만약 고객들이 압박과 궁지에 몰림을 느낀다면 / 그러면 판매원들은 어떤 판매도 못할 것이다 //

The approach has to promote / a (d) <u>comfortable</u> environment **that** makes customers feel / there is no rush. //
주격 관계대명사
그 접근 방식은 조장해야 한다 / 고객들이 느끼게 만드는 편안한 환경을 / 서두름이 없다고 //

Furthermore, / if customers just want to look around, / they should feel / that **it** is all right **to do so**. //
가주어 진주어 (do so = look around)
게다가 / 만약 고객들이 그저 둘러보길 원한다면 / 그들은 느껴야만 한다 / 그렇게 하는 것이 괜찮다는 것을 //

In situations **where** customers really **do** want / to look around on their own, /
관계부사 강조의 do
고객들이 정말로 원하는 상황들에서는 / 혼자 둘러보길 /

salespeople should give customers their business cards / and keep themselves (e) <u>accessible</u> / **in case** customers have questions or concerns. //
'~인 경우에 대비해서'
판매원들은 고객들에게 그들의 명함을 주고 / 그들 스스로를 접근할 수 있는 상태로 유지해야 한다 / 고객들이 질문이나 걱정이 있을 경우를 대비하여 //

- retail ⓝ 소매 • utter ⓥ (말을) 하다 • encourage ⓥ 장려하다
- defensive ⓐ 방어적인 • stop cold 갑자기 멈추다
- transaction ⓝ 거래 • approach ⓥ 접근하다 • rote ⓐ 기계적인
- overused ⓐ 남용되는 • immediate ⓐ 즉각적인
- assistance ⓝ 도움, 지원 • subconscious ⓐ 잠재의식의
- figure out 알아내다 • promote ⓥ 촉진하다, 조성하다
- furthermore ⓐⓓ 게다가 • accessible ⓐ 접근 가능한

"도와드릴까요?"는 고객이 말을 하도록 하지 않고, 그들이 방어적이게 하기 때문에 소매 판매원이 말할 수 있는 최악의 네 단어이다. 그 네 단어는 판매 거래를 완전히 막는 부정적인 반응을 주로 끌어낸다. 고객에게 다가갈 때 사용할 수 있는 (a) 더 나은 질문들의 예들로는 "특별히 당신이 찾고 계신 어떤 것이 있나요?"와 "당신은 선물을 위한 쇼핑을 하고 있나요?"가 있다. 만약 패션 판매원이 "도와드릴까요?"로 당신에게 다가온다면, 당신은 그 판매원이 (b) 신경 쓰지 않는다고 느낄 가능성이 있다. 이 문장은 훈련되지 않고 무관심한 판매원들에 의해 매우 지나치게 사용되는 기계적인 접근 방식이다. 실제로, 우리 대부분은 이 단어들을 들을 때 기겁하여 몸서리친다. "도와드릴까요?"라는 이 질문의 진짜 의미는 고객이 어떤 종류의 곤경에 처해 있고 구출될 필요가 있다는 것을 (c) 부인한다(→ 내포한다). 이는 거의 항상 그 고객이 방어적이게 한다. 그 고객이 실제로 도움이 필요할지라도 "아니요, 괜찮습니다"는 주로 즉각적인 반응이다. 고객의 잠재의식적인 생각은 종종 "나는 내가 원하는 것을 알 만큼 충분히 현명해, 그래서 나는 당신의 도움이 필요하지 않아!"이다. 만약 고객들이 압박과 궁지에 몰림을 느낀다면, 그러면 판매원들은 어떤 판매도 못할 것이다. 그 접근 방식은 고객들이 서두름이 없다고 느끼게 만드는 (d) 편안한 환경을 조장해야 한다. 게다가, 만약 고객들이 그저 둘러보길 원한다면, 그들은 그렇게 하는 것이 괜찮다는 것을 느껴야만 한다. 고객들이 정말로 혼자 둘러보길 원하는 상황들에서는, 고객들이 질문이나 걱정이 있을 경우를 대비하여, 판매원들은 고객들에게 그들의 명함을 주고 그들 스스로를 (e) 접근할 수 있는 상태로 유지해야 한다.

R 05 정답 ③

윗글의 제목으로 가장 적절한 것은?

① Breaking the Ice: Building Trust with Customers
어색함 깨기: 고객과의 신뢰 구축 신뢰 구축보다는 특정 표현의 문제점에 관한 내용임
② To Be a Smart Consumer or Not 판매원의 전략에 관한 내용임
현명한 소비자가 될 것인가 말 것인가
③ Why "May I Help You?" Fails
왜 "도와드릴까요?"가 실패하는가 '도와드릴까요?'라는 표현의 악영향과 대안을 설명함
④ How "Buy One Get One" Opens Your Wallet '하나 사면 하나 더'와
어떻게 '하나 사면 하나 더'가 당신의 지갑을 여는가 같은 마케팅 전략은 언급되지 않았음
⑤ The Closer to Customers, the More Money You Make
고객에게 더 가까이 다가갈수록, 더 많은 돈을 번다
고객이 판매원에게 접근할 수 있도록 하는 전략을 설명함

왜 정답 ? ✽✽❀ [정답률 81%]

- "도와드릴까요?(May I help you?)"는 고객을 방어적으로 만든다. **05번 단서 1**
- 이 표현은 훈련되지 않은 판매원들이 사용하는 기계적인 접근 방식이다. **05번 단서 2**
- 고객에게 압박감을 주어 결국 판매 실패로 이어진다. **05번 단서 3**

➡ "도와드릴까요?(May I help you?)"라는 표현이 고객에게 미치는 악영향을 설명하고 그 대안을 설명하는 내용이다.

▶ 따라서 글의 제목으로 가장 적절한 것은 ③ '왜 "도와드릴까요?"가 실패하는가'이다.

왜 오답 ?

① 고객과의 신뢰 구축이 아니라, 특정 표현의 문제점과 그 대안이 핵심 내용이다.
② 소비자의 선택이 아니라, 판매원의 전략에 관한 내용이다.
④ '하나 사면 하나 더'와 같은 구체적인 판매 전략은 언급되지 않았다.
⑤ 고객에게 접근하라는 것이 아니라, 고객을 막는 특정 표현을 삼가고 고객이 판매원에게 접근할 수 있는 전략을 취하라는 내용이다.

R 06 정답 ③

밑줄 친 (a)~(e) 중에서 문맥상 낱말의 쓰임이 적절하지 않은 것은? [3점]

① (a) May I help you? 대신 사용할 수 있는 더 나은 질문의 예시를 제시함
더 나은
② (b) 기계적인 질문은 판매원이 고객에게 신경 쓰지 않는다는 느낌을 줌
신경 쓰다
③ (c) 이 질문은 고객이 곤경에 처했다는 의미를 내포하므로 고객을 방어적으로 만듦
부인하다
④ (d) 고객을 압박하지 않는 편안한 환경을 만들어야 한다고 조언함
편안한
⑤ (e) 도움이 필요할 경우를 대비해 판매원이 접근 가능한 상태로 있어야 함
접근할 수 있는

왜 정답 ? ✽✽✽ [정답률 53%]

③ (c) rejects 부인한다

"도와드릴까요?"라는 이 질문의 진짜 의미는 고객이 어떤 종류의 곤경에 처해 있고 구출될 필요가 있다는 것을 (c) 부인한다.
내포한다

➡ 이 질문은 고객이 혼자서 해결할 수 없는 곤경에 처해 있고 도움이 필요하다는 의미를 '부인하는' 것이 아니라 '내포하기' 때문에, 고객이 방어적으로 변한다는 내용이 되어야 한다.

▶ rejects를 implies(내포한다)와 같은 어휘로 바꿔야 함

왜 오답 ?

① (a) better 더 나은

고객에게 다가갈 때 사용할 수 있는 (a) 더 나은 질문들의 예들로는 "특별히 당신이 찾고 계신 어떤 것이 있나요?"와 "당신은 선물을 위한 쇼핑을 하고 있나요?"가 있다.

➡ 앞에서 "도와드릴까요?"는 소매 판매원이 말할 수 있는 최악의 네 단어라고 했으므로 그것보다 '더 나은' 두 가지 질문을 제시하고 있다. ▶ better는 문맥에 맞음

② (b) care 신경 쓰다

만약 패션 판매원이 "도와드릴까요?"로 당신에게 다가온다면, 당신은 그 판매원이 (b) 신경 쓰지 않는다고 느낄 가능성이 있다.

➡ 이어지는 문장에서 훈련되지 않고 무관심한 판매원이 사용하는 기계적인 접근이라고 했으므로, 고객은 판매원이 '신경 쓰지' 않는다고 느낄 것이다.
　▶ care는 문맥에 맞음

④ (d) comfortable 편안한
그 접근 방식은 고객들이 서투름이 없다고 느끼게 만드는 (d) 편안한 환경을 조장해야 한다.

➡ 고객이 압박감을 느끼면 판매가 이뤄지지 않는다고 했으므로, 판매원은 '편안한' 환경을 조장해야 한다. ▶ comfortable은 문맥에 맞음

⑤ (e) accessible 접근할 수 있는
고객들이 정말로 혼자 둘러보길 원하는 상황들에서는, 고객들이 질문이나 걱정이 있을 경우를 대비하여, 판매원들은 고객들에게 그들의 명함을 주고 그들 스스로를 (e) 접근할 수 있는 상태로 유지해야 한다.

➡ 고객이 혼자 둘러보길 원하더라도, 도움이 필요할 때를 대비하여 고객들이 언제든지 판매원에게 '접근할 수 있도록' 해야 한다는 내용이다.
　▶ accessible은 문맥에 맞음

구문 서술형

정답 do want, 정말로 원하다

해석 고객들이 정말로 혼자 둘러보길 원하는 상황들에서는, 판매원들은 그들 스스로를 접근할 수 있는 상태로 유지해야 한다.
→ 조동사 do를 써서 「do[does]/did+ 동사원형」의 형태로 동사의 의미를 강조할 수 있다. 복수형으로 쓰인 현재시제 동사 want를 강조하므로, do want로 써야 한다.

R 07~08 *생존을 위한 행위 감지 메커니즘

From an early age, / we assign purpose to objects and events, /
분사구문을 이끄는 현재분사　　　prefer A to B: A를 B보다 선호하다
preferring this reasoning / to random chance. //
어릴 때부터 / 우리는 사물과 사건에 목적을 부여하며 / 이러한 논리를 선호한다 / 무작위적인 우연보다 //

Children assume, / for instance, / that pointy rocks are that way
　　　　　　　　　　　목적어절 접속사
/ because they don't want you to sit on them. //
　　　　　　　　　　want의 목적어와 목적격 보어
아이들은 가정한다 / 예를 들어 / 뾰족한 돌은 그렇게 생겼다고 / 아이들이 그 위에 앉기를 원치 않기 때문에 //

When we encounter something, / we first need to (a) determine
　　　　　　　간접의문문
/ what sort of thing it is. //
우리가 무언가를 마주칠 때 / 우리는 먼저 결정할 필요가 있다 / 그것이 어떤 종류의 것인지 //

Inanimate objects and plants / generally do not move / and can be evaluated from physics alone. //
무생물과 식물은 / 일반적으로 움직이지 않으며 / 물리적 현상만으로 평가될 수 있다 //
　　　　　　　　by -ing: ~함으로써
However, / by attributing intention to animals and even objects, / we are able to make fast decisions / about the (b) likely behaviour of that being. // 07번 단서 1: 동물 및 사물에 의도를 부여하여 그것의 예상 행동을 빨리 판단할 수 있음
그러나 / 동물과 심지어 사물도 의도가 있다고 생각함으로써 / 우리는 빠른 결정을 내릴 수 있다 / 그 존재가 할 것 같은 행동에 대해 //
　　　　　　　　　　　　　avoid의 목적어 (동명사의 수동태)
This was essential / in our hunter-gatherer days / to avoid being eaten by predators. //
이는 필수적이었다 / 우리의 수렵 채집 시절에 / 포식자에게 잡아먹히는 것을 피하기 위해 //
　　　　　　　　　　　　　　　　　　　　　동격절 접속사
The anthropologist Stewart Guthrie made the point / that survival in our evolutionary past meant / that we interpret ambiguous objects /
인류학자 Stewart Guthrie는 주장했다 / 우리의 진화상 과거에서 생존이 의미한다고 / 우리가 모호한 사물을 해석한다는 것을 /

전치사 (~로서)　　　　　　　　　　　　접속사 (이유)
as agents with human mental characteristics, / as those are the
　　　　　　　　　　　　목적격 관계대명사
mental processes which we understand. //
인간의 정신적 특성을 가진 행위자로 / 그것들(인간의 정신적 특성)이 우리가 이해하는 정신 과정이기 때문에 ┐ 07번 단서 2: 생존을 위해 모호한 대상을 의도를 가진 행위자로 해석하는 경향을 발전시킴

Ambiguous events are caused / by such agents. //
모호한 사건은 발생한다 / 이러한 행위자에 의해 // 08번 단서 1: 행위자(사물)에 의해 사건이 발생한다고 생각함
'그 결과 ~가 되다'
This results in a perceptual system / strongly (c) resistant(→ biased) towards anthropomorphism. // 앞에 주격 관계대명사와 be동사가 생략됨
이는 지각 체계로 귀결된다 / 의인화에 강하게 저항하는(→ 편향된) //

Therefore, / we tend to assume intention / even where there is none. // 07번 단서 3, 08번 단서 2: 인간은 모든 것에서 의도를 가정하려는 경향을 지님
그러므로 / 우리는 의도를 가정하는 경향이 있다 / 의도가 없는 곳에서도 //
　　　　　　　　　　would have p.p.: ~했을 것이다
This would have arisen as a survival mechanism. //
이는 발생해 왔을 것이다 / 생존 메커니즘으로 //
　　　be about to ~ : 막 ~하려 하다
If a lion is about to attack you, / you need to react (d) quickly, / given its probable intention to kill you. //
만약 사자가 당신을 막 공격하려 한다면 / 당신은 빠르게 반응할 필요가 있다 / 당신을 죽이려는 그것의 가능한 의도를 고려하여 //
'~ 할 즈음'
By the time you have realized / that the design of its teeth and
　　　　　　　　　　　　목적어절 접속사
claws / could kill you, / you are dead. //
당신이 깨달았을 즈음 / 그것의 이빨과 발톱의 구조가 / 당신을 죽일 수 있다는 것을 / 당신은 죽어 있다 //
　　　　　　동명사 (주어)
So, / assuming intent, / without detailed design analysis or
　　　　　　　　　　　　　　　단수 동사
understanding of the physics, / has (e) saved your life. //
따라서 / 의도를 부여하는 것이 / 상세한 구조 분석 또는 물리적 현상의 이해 없이 / 당신의 목숨을 구해 왔다 //

- • assign ⓥ 부여하다　• prefer ⓥ 선호하다
- • reasoning ⓝ 논리, 추론　• assume ⓥ 가정하다
- • pointy ⓐ 뾰족한　• encounter ⓥ 마주치다
- • determine ⓥ 결정하다　• inanimate ⓐ 무생물의
- • evaluate ⓥ 평가하다　• physics ⓝ 물리
- • attribute ~ to … ~을 …의 것으로 보다　• likely ⓐ ~할 것 같은
- • hunter-gatherer ⓝ 수렵 채집인　• predator ⓝ 포식자
- • anthropologist ⓝ 인류학자　• evolutionary ⓐ 진화상의
- • agent ⓝ 행위자　• perceptual ⓐ 지각의　• resistant ⓐ 저항하는
- • claw ⓝ 발톱　• intent ⓝ 의도

어릴 때부터 우리는 사물과 사건에 목적을 부여하며, 무작위적인 우연보다 이러한 논리를 선호한다. 예를 들어 뾰족한 돌은 아이들이 그 위에 앉기를 원치 않기 때문에 그것이 그렇게 생겼다고 그들(아이들)은 가정한다. 우리가 무언가를 마주칠 때 우리는 먼저 그것이 어떤 종류의 것인지 (a) 결정할 필요가 있다. 무생물과 식물은 일반적으로 움직이지 않으며 물리적 현상만으로 평가될 수 있다. 그러나 동물과 심지어 사물도 의도가 있다고 생각함으로써 우리는 그 존재가 (b) 할 것 같은 행동에 대해 빠른 결정을 내릴 수 있다. 이는 우리의 수렵 채집 시절에 포식자에게 잡아먹히는 것을 피하기 위해 필수적이었다.

인류학자 Stewart Guthrie는 인간의 정신적 특성이 우리가 이해하는 정신 과정이기 때문에, 우리의 진화상 과거에서 생존이란 우리가 모호한 사물을 인간의 정신적 특성을 가진 행위자로 해석하는 것을 의미한다고 주장했다. 모호한 사건은 이러한 행위자에 의해 발생한다. 이는 의인화에 강하게 (c) 저항하는(→편향된) 지각 체계로 귀결된다. 그러므로, 우리는 의도가 없는 곳에서도 의도를 가정하는 경향이 있다. 이는 생존 메커니즘으로 발생해 왔을 것이다. 만약 사자가 당신을 막 공격하려 한다면 당신을 죽이려는 그것의 가능한 의도를 고려하여 당신은 (d) 빠르게 반응할 필요가 있다. 당신이 그것의 이빨과 발톱의 구조가 당신을 죽일 수 있다는 것을 깨달았을 즈음 당신은 죽어 있다. 따라서 상세한 구조 분석 또는 물리적 현상의 이해 없이 의도를 부여하는 것이 당신의 목숨을 (e) 구해 왔다.

윗글의 제목으로 가장 적절한 것은? [3점]
인간은 생존을 위해 행위자에 의도를 부여하여 판단하는 경향을 발전시켰음
① Agency Detection: Inherited from Survival Mechanism
행위자 감지: 생존 메커니즘으로부터 물려받은 것
② How Humans' Perceptual System Is Operated for Hunting 사냥을 위한 인간의 지각 체계에 관한 내용이 아님
사냥을 위해 인간의 지각 체계가 어떻게 작동하는가
③ Hiding Intentions: The Unique Trait of Human Mentality
의도 숨기기: 인간 정신의 독특한 특성   의도를 숨기는 것이 인간의 특성이라는 내용이 아님
④ Our Ambiguous Intention Makes Understanding Confusing 모호한 의도로 인한 혼동은 언급되지 않았음
우리의 모호한 의도가 이해를 혼란스럽게 만든다
⑤ How We Interpret Animate and Inanimate Objects Differently 생물과 무생물을 구분하는 방법에 관한 내용이 아님
우리는 어떻게 생물과 무생물을 다르게 해석하는가

›왜 정답? ★★★ [정답률 46%]

- 동물 및 사물에 의도를 부여하여 그 존재의 예상 행동을 빨리 판단할 수 있음 07번 단서 1
- 진화상 과거에서 생존이란 모호한 사물을 인간의 정신적 특성을 가진 행위자로 해석하는 것 07번 단서 2
- 우리는 의도가 없는 곳에서도 의도를 가정하는 경향이 있음 07번 단서 3

➡ 인간은 동물 및 사물, 즉 의도가 없을 듯한 존재들도 의도를 가진 행위자로 해석하여 그들의 행동을 빠르게 예측했다. 이러한 경향이 생존에 유리했기 때문에 인간은 모든 것에 의도를 부여하여 판단하는 특성을 가지게 되었다는 내용이다.

▶ 따라서 정답은 ① '행위자 감지: 생존 메커니즘으로부터 물려받은 것'이다.

›왜 오답?

② 사냥을 위한 인간의 지각 체계를 설명하는 내용이 아니다.
③ 의도를 숨기는 것이 인간의 특성이라는 내용이 아니다.
④ 우리가 모호한 사물에 의도를 부여한다는 내용이지, 우리의 의도가 모호하다거나 그로 인해서 인간의 이해가 혼란스러워진다는 내용이 아니다.
⑤ 무생물과 식물의 경우 물리적 현상만으로 평가될 수 있다고 했지만, 글의 중심 내용은 무생물과 생물을 구분하는 방법이 아니라 생존을 위해 모호한 사물에 의도를 부여하여 행위자로 해석하는 경향을 발전시켰다는 것이다. 주의

밑줄 친 (a)~(e) 중에서 문맥상 낱말의 쓰임이 적절하지 않은 것은?
① (a) 우리가 무엇을 마주치면 그것의 종류를 결정해야 함
결정하다
② (b) 동물과 사물에게 의도를 부여하면서 그것들이 할 것 같은 행동을 예측함
할 것 같은
③ (c) 우리의 지각 체계는 의인화하는 데 편향되도록 발전해 왔음
저항하는
④ (d) 공격을 당할 때 그것의 의도를 고려하여 빠르게 반응해야 함
빠르게
⑤ (e) 의도를 부여하는 성향은 우리의 목숨을 구해왔음
구하다

›왜 정답? ★★★ [정답률 55%]

③ (c) resistant 저항하는

이는 의인화에 강하게 (c) ~~저항하는~~ 지각 체계로 귀결된다.
                      편향된

➡ 우리는 모호한 사물을 의도를 가진 행위자로 해석하는 성향, 즉 사물을 의인화하는 성향을 발전시켰다고 했다. 따라서 인간의 지각 체계는 의인화에 '저항하는' 것이 아니라 '편향된' 것이다.

▶ resistant를 biased(편향된)와 같은 반의어로 바꿔야 함

›왜 오답?

① (a) determine 결정하다

우리가 무언가를 마주칠 때 우리는 먼저 그것이 어떤 종류의 것인지 (a) 결정할 필요가 있다.

➡ 글의 앞부분에서 우리는 사물과 사건에 목적을 부여한다고 했으므로, 우리가 무언가를 마주칠 때 그것이 어떤 종류의 것인지 먼저 '결정하는' 것은 적절하다.

▶ determine은 문맥에 맞음

② (b) likely 할 것 같은

그러나 동물과 심지어 사물도 의도가 있다고 생각함으로써 우리는 그 존재가 (b) 할 것 같은 행동에 대해 빠른 결정을 내릴 수 있다.

➡ 어떤 존재에 의도가 있다고 생각하면 그 존재가 '할 것 같은' 행동에 대해 빠른 결정(예측)을 내릴 수 있다. ▶ likely는 문맥에 맞음

④ (d) quickly 빠르게

만약 사자가 당신을 막 공격하려 한다면 당신을 죽이려는 그것의 가능한 의도를 고려하여 당신은 (d) 빠르게 반응할 필요가 있다.

➡ 뒤 문장에서 사자가 공격하려 할 때 사자의 이빨과 발톱의 구조를 이해할 즈음이면 우리는 이미 죽었을 것이라고 했으므로, 우리는 사자를 만났을 때 그것의 의도를 고려하여 '빠르게' 반응해야 한다. ▶ quickly는 문맥에 맞음

⑤ (e) saved 구해 왔다

따라서 상세한 구조 분석 또는 물리적 현상의 이해 없이 의도를 부여하는 것이 당신의 목숨을 (e) 구해 왔다.

➡ 앞 문장에서 사자가 공격할 때 그것의 의도를 고려하여 빠르게 반응할 수 있다고 했으므로, 이해 없이 의도를 부여하는 것이 결국 우리의 목숨을 '구해 왔다'라는 것은 적절하다. ▶ saved는 문맥에 맞음

구문 서술형

정답 by attributing intention to animals, 바로 동물에게 의도를 부여함으로써 우리가 그 존재가 할 것 같은 행동에 대해 빠른 결정을 내릴 수 있는 것이다.

→ 「It is/was ~ that …」 구문에서 It is/was와 that 사이에 강조하고자 하는 어구를 둔다. 전치사구 by attributing intention to animals를 강조하므로, '바로 동물에게 의도를 부여함으로써'로 해석한다.

분사구문을 이끄는 현재분사
Norms are everywhere, / defining what is "normal" / and
병렬 구조
guiding our interpretations of social life / at every turn. //
규범은 어디에나 존재한다 / 무엇이 '정상적'인지를 규정하고 / 사회적 생활에 대한 우리의
해석을 안내해 주며 / 모든 순간 // 09번 단서 1: 규범은 무엇이 정상적인지 규정하고 사회생활에서 우리를 안내함

형용사적 용법(a norm 수식)
As a simple example, / there is a norm in Anglo society / to say
주격 관계대명사(선행사:strangers)   형용사적 용법(something 수식)
Thank you to strangers / who have just done something to (a) help, /
간단한 예로 / Anglo 사회에 규범이 있다 / 낯선 사람에게 '감사합니다'라고 말하는 / 도움을 줄 수 있는 무언가를 이제 막 해준 /

목적어절 접속사
such as open a door for you, / point out that you've just dropped something, / or give you directions. //
문을 열어 주거나 / 여러분이 물건을 방금 떨어뜨렸다는 것을 짚어 주거나 / 길을 알려주는 것과 같이 //

주격 관계대명사(선행사: law)
There is no law / that forces you to say Thank you. //
법은 없다 / 여러분이 '감사합니다'라고 말하도록 강요하는 //

But if people don't say Thank you / in these cases, / it is marked. //
하지만 사람들이 '감사합니다'라고 말하지 않으면 / 이런 상황에서 / 그것은 눈에 띄게 된다 //

목적어절 접속사
People expect / that you will say it. //
사람들은 기대한다 / 여러분이 그렇게 말하기를 //

You become responsible. //
여러분은 책임을 지게 되는 것이다 //

동명사구 주어   both A and B: A와 B 둘 다
(b) Failing to say it / will be both surprising and worthy of criticism. //
그렇게 말하지 못하는 것은 / (주변을) 놀라게 하기도 하고 비판을 받을 만하다 //

동명사 주어(단수 취급)　　　　　　　　　　　　　　　단수 동사
Not knowing the norms of another community / **is** the (c) central problem of cross-cultural communication. //
다른 집단의 규범을 모른다는 것은 / 문화 간 의사소통에서 중심적인 문제이다 //
09번 단서 2: 다른 집단의 규범을 모르는 것은 문화 간 의사소통의 중심 문제임

To continue the *Thank you* example, / **even though** another
　　　　　　　　　　　　　　　　　부사절 접속사(양보)
culture may have an expression / **that** appears translatable /
　　　　　　　　　　　　　　주격 관계대명사
= many cultures don't
(many don't), /
'감사합니다'의 예를 이어 보자면 / 비록 또 다른 문화권이 어떤 표현을 가지고 있다 할지라도 / 번역할 수 있는 것처럼 보이는 / (다수는 그렇지 못하지만) /

there may be (d) similar(→ different) norms for its usage, / for
10번 단서 1: 다른 문화권에서는 누군가 초래한 대가가 상당할 때만 '감사합니다'라고 말함
example, / such that you should say *Thank you* / only when the
앞에 목적격 관계대명사 생략
cost someone has caused is considerable. //
그것의 사용법에 대해 유사한(→ 다른) 규범이 있을 수 있다 / 예를 들어 '감사합니다'라고 말해야 한다는 것처럼 / 누군가가 초래한 대가가 상당할 때만 //

In such a case / **it would sound** ridiculous / (i.e., unexpected,
　　　　　　　　　주절이 앞에 온 가정법 미래 문장
surprising, and worthy of criticism) / **if you were** to thank
someone /
그 같은 상황에서 / 그것은 우스꽝스럽게 들릴 수 있을 것이다 / (즉, 예상치 못하게, 놀랍게, 비판을 받을 만하게) / 만약 여러분이 혹시라도 누군가에게 감사해한다면 /
-thing으로 끝나는 대명사는 뒤에서 수식함
for **something** so (e) minor / as holding a door open for you. //
아주 사소한 일에 대해 / 여러분을 위해 문을 잡아주는 것과 같이 //
10번 단서 2: 사소한 일에 감사해한다면 우스꽝스럽게 들릴 수 있음

- norm ⓝ 규범　　• define ⓥ 규정하다　　• interpretation ⓝ 해석
- point out ~을 짚어 주다　　• give directions 길을 알려주다
- force ⓥ 강요하다　　• marked ⓐ 눈에 띄는　　• expect ⓥ 기대하다
- responsible ⓐ 책임이 있는　　• worthy of ~을 받을 만한
- criticism ⓝ 비난　　• central ⓐ 중심적인
- cross-cultural ⓐ 문화 간의　　• translatable ⓐ 번역할 수 있는
- usage ⓝ 사용　　• cost ⓝ 대가, 비용　　• considerable ⓐ 상당한
- ridiculous ⓐ 우스꽝스러운　　• i.e.(id est) 즉
- unexpected ⓐ 예상치 못한　　• minor ⓐ 사소한

규범은 무엇이 '정상적'인지를 규정하고 모든 순간 사회적 생활에 대한 우리의 해석을 안내해 주며 어디에나 존재한다. 간단한 예로, 문을 열어 주거나, 여러분이 물건을 방금 떨어뜨렸다는 것을 짚어 주거나, 길을 알려주는 것과 같이 (a) 도움을 줄 수 있는 무언가를 이제 막 해준 낯선 사람에게 '감사합니다'라고 말하는 규범이 Anglo 사회에 있다. 여러분이 '감사합니다'라고 말하도록 강요하는 법은 없다. 하지만 이런 상황에서 사람들이 '감사합니다'라고 말하지 않으면 그것은 눈에 띄게 된다. 사람들은 여러분이 그렇게 말하기를 기대한다. 여러분은 책임을 지게 되는 것이다. 그렇게 말하지 (b) 못하는 것은 (주변을) 놀라게 하기도 하고 비판을 받을 만하다. 다른 집단의 규범을 모른다는 것은 문화 간 의사소통에서 (c) 중심적인 문제이다. '감사합니다'의 예를 이어 보자면, 비록 또 다른 문화권이 번역할 수 있는 것처럼 보이는 어떤 표현(다수는 그렇지 못하지만)을 가지고 있다 할지라도, 그것의 사용법에 대해, 예를 들어, 누군가가 초래한 대가가 상당할 때만 '감사합니다'라고 말해야 한다는 것처럼 (d) 유사한(→ 다른) 규범이 있을 수 있다. 그 같은 상황에서 만약 여러분이 혹시라도, 여러분을 위해 문을 잡아주는 것과 같이 아주 (e) 사소한 일에 대해 누군가에게 감사해한다면, 그것은 우스꽝스럽게(즉, 예상치 못하게, 놀랍게, 비판을 받을 만하게) 들릴 수 있을 것이다.

R 09 정답 ①

윗글의 제목으로 가장 적절한 것은?

① Norms: For Social Life and Cultural Communication 원활한
규범: 사회생활과 문화적 의사소통을 위한 것　　사회생활과 문화적 의사소통을 위해 규범이 존재함
② Don't Forget to Say "Thank you" at Any Time
언제든지 "감사합니다"라고 말하는 것을 잊지 마라
③ How to Be Responsible for Your Behaviors　글 전체 내용이 행동에
당신의 행동에 책임을 지는 방법　　　　　책임을 지는 방법에 관해 설명하고 있다고 볼 수 없음
④ Accept Criticism Without Hurting Yourself
스스로 상처받지 않으면서 비판을 수용해라　　　비판을 수용하라는 내용에 관한 글이 아님
⑤ How Did Diverse Languages Develop?
다양한 언어는 어떻게 발전했을까?　　　다양한 언어의 발견에 대해서는 전혀 언급하지 않음
"Thank you" 사용법에 관한 규범이 예시로 내용에 나온 것을 이용한 함정임

왜 정답? ★★❈ [정답률 80%]

- 규범은 무엇이 '정상적'인지를 규정하고 모든 순간 사회적 생활에 대한 우리의 해석을 안내해 주며 어디에나 존재한다. **09번 단서 1**
- 다른 집단의 규범을 모른다는 것은 문화 간 의사소통에서 중심적인 문제이다. **09번 단서 2**

→ 사회적 규범이 일상생활과 문화 간 소통에서 중요한 역할을 한다는 것을 설명하며, '감사합니다'라는 말의 사용법에 대해 문화마다 달라질 수 있는 규범을 예시로 제시하였다.

▶ 따라서 제목으로 적절한 것은 ① '규범: 사회생활과 문화적 의사소통을 위한 것'이다.

왜 오답?

② 언제든지 "Thank you"라고 말하라는 내용의 글이 아니다. (✕ 이유: 문화권에 따라 다른 "Thank you" 사용법이 예시로 나온 것으로 만든 오답이다.)
③ 행동에 책임을 지는 방법에 관해 설명하는 글이 아니다.
④ Anglo 사회에서 '감사합니다'를 말하지 못하면 비판을 받을 만하다는 내용이 나오지만, 글에서 비판을 수용하라는 생각을 중심적으로 전달하지는 않는다. 함정
⑤ 다양한 언어의 발전에 대해서는 전혀 언급하지 않았다.

R 10 정답 ④

밑줄 친 (a)~(e) 중에서 문맥상 낱말의 쓰임이 적절하지 <u>않은</u> 것은?

① (a) 낯선 사람이 도움이 되는 일을 해줌
도움을 주다
② (b) 감사의 말을 못하는 것은 주변을 놀라게 하기도 하고 비판을 받을 만함
못하는 것
③ (c) 다른 문화 규범을 모르는 것은 문화 간 의사소통에 중심적인 큰 문제가 될 수 있음
중심적인
④ (d) 유사한 규범이 아닌 다른 규범이 있음
유사한
⑤ (e) 문을 잡아주는 것은 사소한 작은 행동임
사소한

왜 정답? ★★❈ [정답률 74%]

④ (d) similar 유사한

- '감사합니다'의 예를 이어 보자면, 비록 또 다른 문화권이 번역할 수 있는 것처럼 보이는 어떤 표현(다수는 그렇지 못하지만)을 가지고 있다 할지라도, 그것의 사용법에 대해, 예를 들어, 누군가가 초래한 대가가 상당할 때만 '감사합니다'라고 말해야 한다는 것처럼 (d) ~~유사한~~ 규범이 있을 수 있다.
다른

→ Anglo 사회에서는 사소한 도움을 받을 때 '감사합니다'를 말하는 것이 규범이지만 다른 문화권에서는 누군가가 초래한 대가가 상당할 때만 '감사합니다'를 말하므로 규범이 다르다. ▶ 유사한 규범이 아니라 다른 규범이 있을 수 있다는 내용이어야 하므로 similar를 different(다른)와 같은 어휘로 바꾸어야 한다.

왜 오답?

① (a) help 도움을 주다

- 간단한 예로, 문을 열어 주거나, 여러분이 물건을 방금 떨어뜨렸다는 것을 짚어 주거나, 길을 알려주는 것과 같이 (a) 도움을 줄 수 있는 무언가를 이제 막 해준 낯선 사람에게 '감사합니다'라고 말하는 규범이 Anglo 사회에 있다.

→ 낯선 사람이 문을 열어주거나, 물건을 방금 떨어뜨렸다는 것을 짚어 주거나, 길을 알려주는 것은 '도움을 주는' 것이다. ▶ help는 문맥에 맞음

② (b) Failing 못하는 것

- 그렇게 말하지 (b) 못하는 것은 (주변을) 놀라게 하기도 하고 비판을 받을 만하다.

→ 주변을 놀라게 하고 비판을 받게 될 경우는 감사하다고 말하지 '못했을' 때이다.

▶ Failing은 문맥에 맞음

③ (c) central 중심적인

└ 다른 집단의 규범을 모른다는 것은 문화 간 의사소통에서 (c) 중심적인
  문제이다.

→ 다른 문화의 규범을 모르는 것은 문화 간 의사소통에서 '중심적인' 문제가 될 수
  있다. ▶ central은 문맥에 맞음

⑤ (e) minor 사소한

┌ 그 같은 상황에서 만약 여러분이 혹시라도, 여러분을 위해 문을 잡아주는
  것과 같이 아주 (e) 사소한 일에 대해 누군가에게 감사해한다면, 그것은
  우스꽝스럽게(즉, 예상치 못하게, 놀랍게, 비판을 받을 만하게) 들릴 수
└ 있을 것이다.

→ 문을 잡아주는 것은 누군가가 초래한 대가가 상당한 일이 아니라 '사소한' 일이므로
  감사해하면 우스꽝스럽게 들릴 수 있다. ▶ minor는 문맥에 맞음

R 11~12 *고통 속에서 쾌락을 느끼는 인간

All humans, to an extent, / seek activities **that** cause a degree of
pain / **in order to experience** pleasure, /
모든 인간은 어느 정도는 / 약간의 고통을 유발하는 활동을 추구한다 / 쾌락을 경험하기 위해 /
whether this is found in spicy food, strong massages, / **or**
stepping into a too-cold or too-hot bath. //
이것이 매운 음식 또는 강한 마사지에서 발견되든 / 너무 차갑거나 뜨거운 욕조에 들어가기 중
(어디에서 발견되든지 간에 말이다) //

The key is / that it is a 'safe threat'. //
핵심은 / 그것이 '안전한 위협'이라는 점이다 //

The brain perceives **the stimulus to be** painful / but ultimately
(a) non-threatening. // **11번** 단서 1: 뇌에게 '안전한 위협'은 고통스럽지만 위협적이지 않은 것으로 인식함
뇌는 자극을 고통스러운 것으로 인식한다 / 하지만 궁극적으로 위협적이지 않은 것으로 //

Interestingly, / this could be similar to the way **humor works**: a
'safe threat' **that** causes pleasure / by playfully violating norms. //
흥미롭게도 / 이것은 유머가 작동하는 방식과 유사할 수 있다 / 즉 쾌락을 유발하는 '안전한
위협'과 / 규범을 장난스럽게 위반함으로써 //

We feel uncomfortable, / but safe. //
우리는 불편하지만 / 안전하다고 느낀다 //

In this context, / **where** (b) survival is clearly not in danger, / the
desire for pain is actually the desire for a reward, / not suffering
or punishment. // **11번** 단서 2: 생존이 위협되지 않을 때 고통에 대한 욕구는 사실 보상에 대한 욕구임
이런 상황에서 / 생존이 위협되지 않은 / 고통에 대한 욕구는 실제로는 보상에 대한 욕구이다 /
고통이나 처벌이 아닌 //

This reward-like effect / comes from the feeling of mastery over
the pain. //
이러한 보상과 같은 효과는 / 고통에 대한 숙달된 느낌에서 비롯된다 //

The closer you look at your chilli-eating habit, / **the more**
remarkable it seems. //
칠리를 먹는 습관을 자세히 들여다볼수록 / 이는 더욱 분명하게 드러난다 //

When the active ingredient of chillies — capsaicin — touches
the tongue, / it stimulates exactly the same receptor / **that** is
activated / when any of these tissues are burned. //
칠리의 활성 성분인 캡사이신이 혀에 닿으면 / 똑같은 수용체를 자극한다 / 활성화되는 / 피부
조직이 화상을 입었을 때 //
Knowing that our body is firing off danger signals, / but that we
are actually completely safe, / (c) produces pleasure. //
우리 몸이 위험 신호를 보내고 있음을 아는 것 / 하지만 실제로는 완전히 안전하다는 것을
아는 것은 / 쾌감이 생긴다 // **11번** 단서 3, **12번** 단서: 위험 신호를 받지만 실제로는
안전한 상황 속에서 고통은 쾌감을 줌

All children start off hating chilli, / but many learn to derive
pleasure from it / through repeated exposure / and **knowing**
that they will never experience any real (d) joy(→ harm). //
모든 아이들은 처음에는 칠리를 싫어한다 / 하지만 그것에서 쾌락을 얻는 방법을 배우게 된다 /
반복적인 노출을 통해서 / 그리고 실질적인 기쁨을(→ 해를) 경험하지 않는다는 것을 통해서 //
Interestingly, / **seeking pain for the pain itself** / **appears** to be (e)
uniquely human. //
흥미롭게도 / 고통 그 자체를 위해 고통을 추구하는 것은 / 인간만이 할 수 있는 행동으로
보인다 //
The only way **scientists have trained animals** / **to have a**
preference for chilli or to self-harm / is to have **the pain** always
directly **associated** with a pleasurable reward. //
과학자들이 동물을 훈련시키는 유일한 방법은 / 칠리를 선호하게 하거나 스스로에게 해를
가하도록 / 고통을 항상 즐거운 보상과 직접적으로 연관시키는 것이다 //

• seek ⓥ 찾다 • pleasure ⓝ 쾌락 • perceive ⓥ 인식하다
• stimulus ⓝ 자극 • ultimately ⓐⓓ 궁극적으로
• violate ⓥ 침해하다 • norm ⓝ 표준 • suffering ⓝ 고통
• punishment ⓝ 처벌 • mastery ⓝ 숙달
• remarkable ⓐ 놀라운 • stimulate ⓥ 자극시키다
• receptor ⓝ 수용체 • activate ⓥ 활성화시키다
• tissue ⓝ (세포) 조직 • fire off 발사하다 • derive ⓥ 끌어내다
• exposure ⓝ 노출 • preference ⓝ 선호

모든 인간은 어느 정도는 쾌락을 경험하기 위해 약간의 고통을 유발하는 활동
을 추구한다. 이것이 매운 음식 또는 강한 마사지, 너무 차갑거나 뜨거운 욕조
에 들어가기 중 어디에서 발견되든지 간에 말이다. 핵심은 그것이 '안전한 위협'
이라는 점이다. 뇌는 자극이 고통스럽지만 궁극적으로 (a) 위협적이지 않은 것
으로 인식한다. 흥미롭게도 이것은 유머가 작동하는 방식, 즉 규범을 장난스럽
게 위반함으로써 쾌락을 유발하는 '안전한 위협'과 유사할 수 있다. 우리는 불편
하지만 안전하다고 느낀다. (b) 생존이 위협하지 않은 이런 상황에서 고통에 대
한 욕구는 실제로는 고통이나 처벌이 아닌 보상에 대한 욕구이다. 이러한 보상
과 같은 효과는 고통에 대한 숙달된 느낌에서 비롯된다. 칠리를 먹는 습관을 자
세히 들여다볼수록 이는 더욱 분명하게 드러난다. 칠리의 활성 성분인 캡사이
신이 혀에 닿으면 피부 조직이 화상을 입었을 때 활성화되는 것과 똑같은 수용
체를 자극한다. 우리 몸이 위험 신호를 보내고 있지만 실제로는 완전히 안전하
다는 것을 알면 쾌감이 (c) 생긴다. 모든 아이들은 처음에는 칠리를 싫어하지만,
반복적인 노출과 실질적인 (d) 기쁨을(→ 해를) 경험하지 않는다는 것을 알게 됨
을 통해 그것에서 쾌락을 얻는 방법을 배우게 된다. 흥미롭게도 고통 그 자체를
위해 고통을 추구하는 것은 인간만이 (e) 고유하게 할 수 있는 행동으로 보인다.
동물이 칠리를 선호하게 하거나 스스로에게 해를 가하도록 과학자들이 훈련시
키는 유일한 방법은 고통을 항상 즐거운 보상과 직접적으로 연관시키는 것이다.

R 11 정답 ①

윗글의 제목으로 가장 적절한 것은?

① The Secret Behind Painful Pleasures
  고통스러운 쾌락 뒤에 숨겨진 비밀   고통 속에서 쾌락을 느끼는 이유를 설명함
② How 'Safe Threat' Changes into Real Pain
  어떻게 '안전한 위협'이 실제 고통으로 바뀌는가   '안전한 위협'이 언급된 것으로 만든 오답
③ What Makes You Stronger, Pleasure or Pain?
  무엇이 당신을 더 강하게 만드는가, 쾌락인가, 고통인가?   쾌락과 고통을 비교하는 것이 아님
④ How Does Your Body Detect Danger Signals?
  당신의 몸은 어떻게 위험 신호를 감지할까?   몸이 위험 신호를 감지하는 방법에 대한 내용이 아님
⑤ Recipes to Change Picky Children's Eating Habits
  까다로운 아이들의 식습관을 바꾸는 요리법   요리법을 소개하는 글이 아님

왜 정답? ★★☆ [정답률 63%]

┌ • 뇌는 자극(안전한 위협)이 고통스럽지만 궁극적으로 위협적이지 않은 것으로
│   인식한다. **11번 단서 1**
│ • 생존이 위협하지 않은 이런 상황에서 고통에 대한 욕구는 실제로는 고통이나
│   처벌이 아닌 보상에 대한 욕구이다. **11번 단서 2**
│ • 우리 몸이 위험 신호를 보내고 있지만 실제로는 완전히 안전하다는 것을 알면
└   쾌감이 생긴다. **11번 단서 3**

➡ '안전한 위협' 속에서 느끼는 고통은 위협적이지 않은 것으로 뇌가 인식하기 때문에, 이러한 고통에 대한 욕구는 실제로는 보상에 대한 욕구이다. 그래서 몸이 위험 신호(고통)를 보내더라도 실제로는 완전히 안전하다는 것을 앎으로써 쾌감이 생긴다는 내용이다.

▶ 따라서 제목으로 적절한 것은 ① '고통스러운 쾌락 뒤에 숨겨진 비밀'이다.

왜 오답?

② 안전한 위협이 쾌감을 불러일으킨다는 글이다.
③ 인간을 더 강하게 만드는 것이 쾌락인지 고통인지를 비교하는 글이 아니다.
④ 우리의 몸이 위험 신호를 감지하는 방법이나 과정을 설명하는 글이 아니다.
⑤ 식습관이 까다로운 아이들이나 요리법에 관한 글이 아니다.

R 12 정답 ④

밑줄 친 (a)~(e) 중에서 문맥상 낱말의 쓰임이 적절하지 <u>않은</u> 것은?
① (a) 위협적이지 않은 안전한 위협임
　　위협적이지 않은
② (b) 안전한 상황은 생존에 위험이 되지 않는 것임
　　생존
③ (c) 고통을 느껴도 안전하다는 것을 알기 때문에 쾌감(보상)이 생김
　　생산하다
④ (d) 해를 경험하지 않는다는 안전함을 알기 때문에 쾌감이 생김
　　기쁨
⑤ (e) 인간만이 가질 수 있는 고유한 특성임
　　고유하게

왜 정답? ★★★ [정답률 50%]

④ (d) joy 기쁨

모든 아이들은 처음에는 칠리를 싫어하지만, 반복적인 노출과 실질적인 (d) ~~기쁨~~(피해)를 경험하지 않는다는 것을 알게 됨을 통해 그것에서 쾌락을 얻는 방법을 배우게 된다.

➡ 기쁨을 경험하지 않는 것이 아니라, 고통을 느껴도 실질적으로 피해를 경험하지 않는다는 안전함을 알기 때문에 쾌감이 생기는 것이므로 실질적인 '기쁨'을 경험하지 않는다는 것은 문맥에 맞지 않는다.

▶ joy를 harm(피해)과 같은 반의어로 바꾸어야 한다.

왜 오답?

① (a) non-threatening 위협적이지 않은

뇌는 자극이 고통스럽지만 궁극적으로 (a) 위협적이지 않은 것으로 인식한다. ~ 우리는 불편하지만 안전하다고 느낀다.

➡ 우리는 '안전한 위협'이 있을 때 불편하지만 안전하다고 느낀다고 했으므로 뇌가 '안전한 위협'을 고통스럽지만 '위협적이지 않은' 것으로 인식할 것이다.

▶ non-threatening은 문맥에 맞음

② (b) survival 생존

(b) 생존이 위험하지 않은 이런 상황에서(In this context) 고통에 대한 욕구는 실제로는 고통이나 처벌이 아닌 보상에 대한 욕구이다.

➡ this context란 안전한 위협을 느끼는 상황이므로 '생존'이 위험하지 않다.

▶ survival은 문맥에 맞음

③ (c) produce 생산하다

우리 몸이 위험 신호를 보내고 있지만 실제로는 완전히 안전하다는 것을 알면 쾌감이 (c) 생긴다.

➡ 매운 칠리를 먹으면 몸이 위험 신호를 보내지만 우리는 실제로 안전하다는 것을 알고 있으므로 쾌감이 '생긴다.' ▶ produce는 문맥에 맞음

⑤ (e) uniquely 고유하게

흥미롭게도 고통 그 자체를 위해 고통을 추구하는 것은 인간만이 (e) 고유하게 할 수 있는 행동으로 보인다.

➡ 동물이 스스로에게 고통을 가하게 하는 방법은 보상의 직접적인 연관밖에 없다고 바로 뒤 문장에서 언급하고 있으므로, 이러한 행동은 인간만이 '고유하게' 할 수 있는 행동이라고 볼 수 있다. ▶ uniquely는 문맥에 맞음

R 13~14 *고등 교육의 확대에 따른 평가 방식의 변화

Higher education **has grown** / **from** an elite **to** a mass system / 　　　　　　　　　현재완료(계속)　　from A to B: A에서 B로
across the world. // 13번 단서 1: 고등 교육이 엘리트에서 대중 체제로 변화함
고등 교육은 성장해 왔다 / 엘리트에서 대중 체제로 / 전 세계에 걸쳐 //

In Europe and the USA, / (a) increased rates of participation **occurred** / in the decades / after the Second World War. //
　　완전자동사
유럽과 미국에서는 / 증가된 참여율이 나타났다 / 수십 년 동안 / 2차 세계 대전 이후 //

Between 2000 and 2014, / rates of participation in higher education almost **doubled** / from 19% to 34% across the world /
　　　　　　　　　완전자동사
2000년과 2014년 사이에 / 고등 교육 참여율은 거의 두 배가 되었다 / 전 세계에 걸쳐 19%에서 34%로 /

among the members of the population / in the school-leaving age category (typically 18–23). //
집단 구성원 사이에서의 / 졸업 연령 범주 (대체로 18세에서 23세) 내 //

The dramatic expansion of higher education / **has been marked** / by a wider range of institutions of higher learning / and a more diverse demographic of students. //
　　　　　현재완료 수동태　　병렬 구조
고등 교육의 극적인 확대는 / 특징지어져 왔다 / 더 광범위한 고등 학습 기관과 / 더 다양한 학생 인구 집단으로 //
핵심 주어(복수)
Changes from an elite system to a mass higher education system / **are associated** with political needs / **to build** a (b) specialised
복수 동사(복수)　　　　　　　　　　　　　　　형용사적 용법(needs 수식)
workforce / for the economy. //
엘리트 체제에서 대중 고등 교육 체제로의 변화는 / 정치적 필요성과 관련이 있다 / 전문화된 노동력을 구축하려는 / 경제를 위한 //

In theory, / the expansion of higher education / **to develop** a highly skilled workforce / should diminish the role of examinations / in the selection and control of students, /
　　　　　　　　　　　　　부사적 용법(목적)
이론적으로 / 고등 교육의 확대는 / 고도로 숙련된 노동력을 개발하기 위한 / 시험의 역할을 감소시킬 것이다 / 학생의 선발과 통제에 있어 / 13번 단서 2: 이론적으로는 고등 교육 확대가 시험의 역할을 감소시킬 것임
　분사구문
initiating approaches to assessment / **which** (c) block(→ facilitate) lifelong learning: / assessment for learning and a focus
　　　　　　　　　　　　　　　주격 관계대명사
on feedback for development. // 14번 단서: 학습을 위한 평가와 발달을 위한 피드백은 평생학습을 가능하게 함
평가로의 접근 방법을 시작하면서 / 평생학습을 막는(→ 가능하게 하는) / 즉, 학습을 '위한' 평가와 발달을 위한 피드백에 집중을 (시작하면서) //
　　　　　　　　　　　형용사적 용법(changes 수식)
In reality, / socio-political changes / **to expand** higher education / have set up a 'field of contradictions' / for assessment in higher education. // 13번 단서 3: 실제로는 고등 교육의 평가에 모순이 있음
실제로는 / 사회 정치적 변화는 / 고등 교육을 확대하기 위한 / '모순의 장'을 조성해 왔다 / 고등 교육에서의 평가에 있어 //

Mass higher education requires / efficient approaches to assessment, / such as examinations and multiple-choice quizzes, / with minimalist, (d) impersonal, or standardised feedback, /
대중 고등 교육은 필요로 하며 / 평가로의 효율적인 접근 방법을 / 시험과 선다형 퀴즈와 같은 / 최소한이거나 비개인적이거나 표준화된 피드백을 갖춘 /
　　　分사구문을 이끄는 현재분사　　causing의 목적격 보어(to부정사)
often **causing** students **to focus** more on grades than feedback. //
이는 종종 학생이 피드백보다 성적에 더 집중하게 만든다 //
13번 단서 4: 대중 고등 교육은 학생들이 피드백보다 성적에 더 집중하게 함
In contrast, / the relatively small numbers of students / in elite systems in the past / (e) allowed for closer relationships / between students and their teachers, /
대조적으로 / 상대적으로 적은 학생의 수는 / 과거에 엘리트 체제의 / 더 긴밀한 관계를 허용했다 / 학생과 그들의 선생님 사이의 /

「with + 명사 + 현재분사」: ~이 …하면서

<mark>with formative feedback shaping</mark> / the minds, academic skills, and even the characters of students. //
형성적 피드백이 형성하면서 / 학생의 마음, 학업 기술, 그리고 심지어 학생의 성격을 //

- participation ⓝ 참여
- decade ⓝ 10년
- typically ⓐⓓ 일반적으로
- dramatic ⓐ 극적인
- expansion ⓝ 확대
- range ⓝ 범주
- institution ⓝ 기관
- specialised ⓐ 전문화된
- workforce ⓝ 노동력
- diminish ⓥ 줄어들다
- initiate ⓥ 시작하다
- approach ⓝ 접근법
- development ⓝ 발달
- socio-political ⓐ 사회 정치적인
- contradiction ⓝ 모순
- assessment ⓝ 평가
- minimalist ⓐ 최소한의
- impersonal ⓐ 비개인적인
- standardised ⓐ 표준화된
- relatively ⓐⓓ 비교적으로
- character ⓝ 성격
- class ⓝ 계급
- status ⓝ 지위

고등 교육은 전 세계에 걸쳐 엘리트에서 대중 체제로 성장해 왔다. 유럽과 미국에서는 2차 세계 대전 이후 수십 년 동안 (a) <u>증가된</u> 참여율이 나타났다. 2000년과 2014년 사이에 졸업 연령 범주 (대체로 18세에서 23세) 내 집단 구성원 사이에서의 고등 교육 참여율은 전 세계에 걸쳐 19%에서 34%로 거의 두 배가 되었다. 고등 교육의 극적인 확대는 더 광범위한 고등 학습 기관과 더 다양한 학생 인구 집단으로 특징지어져 왔다.

엘리트 체제에서 대중 고등 교육 체제로의 변화는 경제를 위한 (b) <u>전문화된</u> 노동력을 구축하려는 정치적 필요성과 관련이 있다. 이론적으로, 고도로 숙련된 노동력을 개발하기 위한 고등 교육의 확대는 평생학습을 (c) <u>막는(→ 가능하게 하는)</u> 평가로의 접근 방법, 즉, 학습을 '위한' 평가와 발달을 위한 피드백에 집중을 시작하면서, 학생의 선발과 통제에 있어 시험의 역할을 감소시킬 것이다. 실제로는 고등 교육을 확대하기 위한 사회 정치적 변화는 고등 교육에서의 평가에 있어 '모순의 장'을 조성해 왔다. 대중 고등 교육은 최소한이거나 (d) <u>비개인적</u>이거나 표준화된 피드백을 갖춘, 시험과 선다형 퀴즈와 같은, 평가로의 효율적인 접근 방법을 필요로 하며, 이는 종종 학생이 피드백보다 성적에 더 집중하게 만든다. 대조적으로, 과거에 엘리트 체제의 상대적으로 적은 학생의 수는 형성적 피드백이 학생의 마음, 학업 기술, 그리고 심지어 학생의 성격을 형성하면서, 학생과 그들의 선생님 사이의 더 긴밀한 관계를 (e) <u>허용했다</u>.

R 13 정답 ③

윗글의 제목으로 가장 적절한 것은?
① Is It Possible to Teach Without Assessment?
평가 없이 교육이 가능할까? 평가 없는 교육에 대한 언급은 없음
② Elite vs. Public: A History of Modern Class Society
엘리트 대 대중: 현대 계급 사회의 역사 계급 사회에 관한 내용이 아님
③ Mass Higher Education and Its Reality in Assessment
대중 고등 교육과 그 평가의 현실 고등 교육의 대중화에 따른 평가의 현실에 관한 내용임
④ Impacts of Mass Higher Education on Teachers' Status
대중 고등 교육이 교사의 지위에 미치는 영향 교사의 지위에 대한 언급은 없음
⑤ Mass Higher Education Leads to Economic Development
대중 고등 교육이 경제 발전으로 이어진다 경제 발전은 글의 핵심 내용이 아님

왜 정답? ✱✱❈ [정답률 64%]
- 고등 교육은 전 세계에 걸쳐 엘리트에서 대중 체제로 성장해 왔다. `13번 단서 1`
- 이론적으로, 고등 교육의 확대는 학생의 선발과 통제에 있어 시험의 역할을 감소시킬 것이다. `13번 단서 2`
- 실제로는 고등 교육을 확대하기 위한 사회 정치적 변화는 고등 교육에서의 평가에 있어 '모순의 장'을 조성해 왔다. `13번 단서 3`
- 대중 고등 교육은 학생들이 피드백보다 성적에 집중하게 한다. `13번 단서 4`

➡ 고등 교육은 대중 체제로 성장해 왔는데, 이론적으로는 대중 고등 교육의 확대가 평가를 위한 시험의 역할을 감소시켰어야 했다. 하지만 실제로는 고등 교육이 확대되면서 학생들이 피드백보다 성적에 집중하게 되는 모순이 발생했다.
▶ 따라서 제목으로 적절한 것은 ③ '대중 고등 교육과 그 평가의 현실'이다.

왜 오답?
① 평가 없는 교육은 언급되지 않았다.
② 고등 교육이 엘리트 중심에서 대중 체제로 성장해 왔다는 것일 뿐, 계급 사회의 역사에 관한 내용이 아니다.
④ 마지막 문장에서 학생과 교사의 관계가 언급되지만, 교사의 지위는 언급되지 않았다.
⑤ <mark>대중 고등 교육 체제로의 변화가 경제를 위한 것은 맞지만</mark>, 글의 핵심 내용은 대중 고등 교육 체제로 변화하면서 고등 교육의 평가에 모순이 발생했다는 것이다.

> 글의 내용과 일치하더라도 핵심 주제가 맞는지 다시 한번 확인하기! 🍯팁

R 14 정답 ③

밑줄 친 (a)~(e) 중에서 문맥상 낱말의 쓰임이 적절하지 <u>않은</u> 것은?
[3점]
① (a) 고등 교육이 점차 대중 체제로 확대됨 증가된
② (b) 대중 고등 교육 체제로의 변화는 전문화된 노동력을 구축하려는 것임 전문화된
③ (c) 발달을 위한 피드백과 배움을 위한 평가는 평생학습을 촉진함 막는
④ (d) 개별화되지 않고 최소한이고 표준화된 피드백은 비개인적이라 할 수 있음 비개인적인
⑤ (e) 학생의 마음, 학습 기술, 성격을 형성하는 형성적 피드백은 사제간에 더 가까운 관계를 가능하게 함 허용했다

왜 정답? ✱✱✱ [정답률 41%]
③ (c) block 막는
> 이론적으로, 고도로 숙련된 노동력을 개발하기 위한 고등 교육의 확대는 평생학습을 (c) <s>막는</s> (가능하게 하는) 평가로의 접근 방법, 즉, 학습을 '위한' 평가와 발달을 위한 피드백에 집중을 시작하면서, 학생의 선발과 통제에 있어 시험의 역할을 감소시킬 것이다.

➡ '학습을 위한 평가'와 '발달을 위한 피드백'을 평가로의 접근 방법이라고 언급했는데, 이들은 모두 평생학습을 '막는' 것이 아니라 '가능하게 하는' 방법이다.
▶ block을 facilitate(가능하게 하는)와 같은 반의어로 바꿔야 함

왜 오답?
① (a) increased 증가된
> 고등 교육은 전 세계에 걸쳐 엘리트에서 대중 체제로 성장해 왔다. 유럽과 미국에서는 2차 세계 대전 이후 수십 년 동안 (a) 증가된 참여율이 나타났다.

➡ 고등 교육이 엘리트에서 대중 체제로 성장해 왔다는 것은 더 많은 사람들이 고등 교육에 참여했다는 것이므로, (고등 교육의) '증가된' 참여율이 나타났다는 것은 적절하다.
▶ increased는 문맥에 맞음

② (b) specialised 전문화된
> 엘리트 체제에서 대중 고등 교육 체제로의 변화는 경제를 위한 (b) 전문화된 노동력을 구축하려는 정치적 필요성과 관련이 있다. 이론적으로, 고도로 숙련된 노동력을 개발하기 위한 고등 교육의 확대는 ~

➡ 바로 뒤 문장에 고도로 숙련된 인력을 개발하기 위한 고등 교육의 확대가 언급된다. 따라서 대중 고등 교육 체제로의 변화는 경제를 위해 '전문화된' 노동력을 구축하려는 것이다. ▶ specialised는 문맥에 맞음

④ (d) impersonal 비개인적인
> 대중 고등 교육은 최소한이거나 (d) 비개인적이거나 표준화된 피드백을 갖춘, 시험과 선다형 퀴즈와 같은, 평가로의 효율적인 접근 방법을 필요로 하며, 이는 종종 학생이 피드백보다 성적에 더 집중하게 만든다.

➡ 효율에 초점이 맞춰진 선다형 퀴즈, 즉, 최소한이고 표준화된 피드백을 제공하는 평가는 학생 개인에게 맞춰진 피드백을 제공하지 않으므로 '비개인적'이다.
▶ impersonal은 문맥에 맞음

⑤ (e) allowed 허용했다
[대조적으로, 과거에 엘리트 체제의 상대적으로 적은 학생의 수는 형성적 피드백이 학생의 마음, 학업 기술, 그리고 심지어 학생의 성격을 형성하면서, 학생과 그들의 선생님 사이의 더 긴밀한 관계를 (e) 허용했다.]
➡ 과거의 엘리트 체제에서는 학생의 수가 적어서 선생님이 학생들을 개별적으로 평가할 수 있었을 것이다. 그렇기에 형성적 피드백이 가능했으므로, 학생과 선생님 사이의 더 긴밀한 관계를 '허용했다'는 것은 적절하다. ▶ allowed는 문맥에 맞음

R 15~16 *농업의 발전이 불러온 변화

Early hunter-gatherer societies / had (a) minimal structure. //
초기 수렵 채집 사회는 / 최소한의 구조만 가지고 있었다 //

A chief or group of elders / usually led the camp or village. //
추장이나 장로 그룹이 / 주로 캠프나 마을을 이끌었다 //

Most of these leaders / had to hunt and gather / along with the other members /
대부분의 이러한 지도자들은 / 사냥과 채집을 해야 했다 / 다른 구성원들과 함께 /
부사절 접속사(이유)
because the surpluses of food and other vital resources / were
'거의 ~않는'
seldom (b) sufficient / to support a full-time chief or village
council. // 15번 단서 1: 초기 수렵 채집 사회에는 잉여 식량과 자원이 충분하지 않았음
왜냐하면 식량과 기타 필수 자원의 잉여분이 / 거의 충분하지 않았기 때문에 / 전임 추장이나 마을 의회를 지원할 만큼 //

The development of agriculture / changed work patterns. // 15번 단서 2: 농업의 발전으로 작업 패턴이 변화함
농업의 발전은 / 작업 패턴을 변화시켰다 //

Early farmers could reap 3–10 kg of grain / from each 1 kg of
앞에 주격 관계대명사와 be동사가 생략됨
seed planted. //
초기 농부들은 / 3kg에서 10kg의 곡물을 수확할 수 있었다 / 심은 씨앗 1kg마다 //
수동태 동사
Part of this food/energy surplus was returned to the community
/ and (c) limited(→ provided) support for nonfarmers /
이 식량/에너지 잉여분의 일부는 지역 사회에 환원되었고 / 비농민에 대한 지원을 제한했다
(→ 제공했다) /
주격 관계대명사
such as chieftains, village councils, men who practice medicine,
priests, and warriors. // 15번 단서 3: 농업의 발전으로 생긴 잉여분이 사회에 환원되어 비농민들에게 제공됨
족장, 마을 의회, 의술가, 사제, 전사와 같은 /
'~에 대한 반응으로'
In return, / the nonfarmers provided leadership and security /
분사구문을 이끄는 현재분사
for the farming population, / enabling it to continue to increase
food/energy yields / and provide ever larger surpluses. //
그 대가로 / 비농민들은 리더십과 안보를 제공하였다 / 농업 인구에게 / 그들이 식량/에너지
생산량을 지속적으로 늘릴 수 있게 하면서 / 그리고 항상 더 많은 잉여를 (제공할 수 있게
하면서) // 16번 단서: 비농민들은 농민들이 지속해서 잉여를 제공할 수 있도록 리더십과 안보를 제공함
전치사구
With improved technology and favorable conditions, /
agriculture produced consistent surpluses of the basic
완전자동사
necessities, / and population groups grew in size. //
개선된 기술과 유리한 조건으로 / 농업은 기본 생필품의 지속적인 흑자를 창출했고 / 인구
집단은 규모가 커졌다 //

These groups concentrated in towns and cities, / and human
tasks (d) specialized further. //
이러한 집단은 마을과 도시에 집중되었고 / 인간의 업무는 더욱 전문화되었다 //

Specialists such as carpenters, blacksmiths, merchants, traders,
and sailors / developed their skills / and became more efficient /
in their use of time and energy. // 15번 단서 4: 지원을 받은 비농민들은 여러 분야에서 전문가가 됨
목수, 대장장이, 상인, 무역업자, 선원과 같은 전문가들은 / 그들의 기술을 발전시키고 / 더
효율적으로 되었다 / 그들의 시간과 에너지 사용에 //

앞에 목적격 관계대명사가 생략됨
The goods and services they provided brought about / an (e)
improved quality of life, / a higher standard of living, / and, for
삽입구
most societies, increased stability. //
그들이 제공한 재화와 서비스는 가져왔다 / 향상된 삶의 질 / 더 높은 생활 수준 / 그리고
대부분의 사회에 향상된 안정성을 //

- -
• minimal ⓐ 최소한의   • structure ⓝ 구조
• chief ⓝ 우두머리, 족장   • elder ⓝ 원로, 어른
• surplus ⓝ 잉여, 흑자   • vital ⓐ 필수적인   • sufficient ⓐ 충분한
• council ⓝ 의회   • agriculture ⓝ 농업   • grain ⓝ 곡물
• priest ⓝ 성직자, 사제   • warrior ⓝ 전사   • favorable ⓐ 유리한
• consistent ⓐ 지속적인   • necessity ⓝ 필수품
• concentrate ⓥ 집중하다   • efficient ⓐ 효율적인
• standard ⓝ 기준, 수준   • stability ⓝ 안정성
• shadow ⓝ 그림자   • repetition ⓝ 반복

초기 수렵 채집 사회는 (a) 최소한의 구조만 가지고 있었다. 추장이나 장로 그룹이 주로 캠프나 마을을 이끌었다. 식량과 기타 필수 자원의 잉여분이 전임 추장이나 마을 의회를 지원할 만큼 거의 (b) 충분하지 않았기 때문에 대부분의 이러한 지도자들은 다른 구성원들과 함께 사냥과 채집을 해야 했다. 농업의 발전은 작업 패턴을 변화시켰다. 초기 농부들은 심은 씨앗 1kg마다 3kg에서 10kg의 곡물을 수확할 수 있었다. 이 식량/에너지 잉여분의 일부는 지역 사회에 환원되었고 족장, 마을 의회, 의술가, 사제, 전사와 같은 비농민에 대한 지원을 (c) 제한했다(→ 제공했다). 그 대가로, 비농민들은 농업 인구에게 리더십과 안보를 제공하여, 그들이 식량/에너지 생산량을 지속적으로 늘리고 항상 더 많은 잉여를 제공할 수 있게 하였다.
개선된 기술과 유리한 조건으로, 농업은 기본 생필품의 지속적인 흑자를 창출했고, 인구 집단은 규모가 커졌다. 이러한 집단은 마을과 도시에 집중되었고, 인간의 업무는 더욱 (d) 전문화되었다. 목수, 대장장이, 상인, 무역업자, 선원과 같은 전문가들은 기술을 발전시키고 자신의 시간과 에너지 사용을 더 효율적으로 하게 되었다. 그들이 제공한 재화와 서비스는 (e) 향상된 삶의 질, 더 높은 생활 수준, 그리고, 대부분의 사회에 향상된 안정성을 가져왔다.

R 15 정답 ①

윗글의 제목으로 가장 적절한 것은?
농업의 발달로 발생한 잉여 자원/에너지를 활용하여 비농민들은 다양한 분야에서 전문가가 됨
① How Agriculture Transformed Human Society
농업이 인간 사회를 변화시킨 방법
② The Dark Shadow of Agriculture: Repetition
농업의 어두운 그림자 반복   농업의 긍정적인 측면을 이야기함
③ How Can We Share Extra Food with the Poor?
어떻게 하면 우리는 남은 식량을 가난한 사람들과 나눌 수 있을까?
④ Why Were Early Societies Destroyed by Agriculture?
왜 초기 사회는 농업으로 인해 파괴되었는가?   언급되지 않음
⑤ The Advantages of Large Groups Over Small Groups
in Farming   농업의 규모를 비교한 글이 아님
농업에서 대규모 집단이 소규모 집단에 비해 갖는 이점들
잉여 식량을 가난한 사람들과 나누자고 하는 글이 아님

> 왜 정답? ★★☆ [정답률 67%]
[• 초기 수렵 사회에서는 식량과 기타 자원의 잉여분이 충분하지 않았기 때문에 대부분의 지도자들은 다른 구성원들과 함께 사냥과 채집을 해야 했다. 15번 단서 1
• 농업의 발전은 작업 패턴을 변화시켰다. 15번 단서 2
• 식량/에너지 잉여분은 지역 사회에 환원되어 비농민에게 제공되었다. 15번 단서 3
• 다양한 분야의 비농민 전문가들은 기술을 발전시키고 더 효율적으로 시간과 에너지를 사용하게 되었다. 15번 단서 4]
➡ 초기 수렵 사회에는 식량과 자원이 남지 않았음 → 농업으로 잉여분이 생김 → 남은 자원은 사회에 환원되어 비농민들에게 제공됨 → 비농민들은 다양한 기술을 발전시켜 여러 분야에서 전문가가 됨
▶ 따라서 글의 제목으로 가장 적절한 것은 ① '농업이 인간 사회를 변화시킨 방법'이다.

R

왜 오답?

② 농업의 부정적 측면이 아니라 긍정적인 영향을 이야기한 글이다.
③ 잉여 자원은 가난한 사람이 아니라 비농민에게 제공되었다고 했다.
(▶ 이유: 비농민이 가난한지는 글에 언급되지 않았다.)
④ 초기 사회가 파괴되었다거나 그 원인을 이야기한 글이 아니다.
⑤ 농업에 있어 집단의 규모가 클수록 유리하다고 주장한 글이 아니다.

R 16 정답 ③

밑줄 친 (a)~(e) 중에서 문맥상 낱말의 쓰임이 적절하지 않은 것은? [3점]
① (a) 이후 농업의 발전으로 사회의 규모가 증가함
최소한의
② (b) 지도자들도 사냥과 채집을 해야 했음
충분한
③ (c) 비농민들이 그 대가로 리더십과 안보를 제공함
제한된
④ (d) 전문가들이 생겨 기술을 발전시킬 수 있었음
전문화되었다
⑤ (e) 사회에 더 나은 안전성을 가져왔음
향상된

왜 정답? ★★※ [정답률 63%]

③(c) limited 제한했다
이 식량/에너지 잉여분의 일부는 지역 사회에 환원되었고 족장, 마을 의회, 의술가, 사제, 전사와 같은 비농민에 대한 지원을 (c) 제한했다.
그 대가로(In return), 비농민들은 농업 인구에게 리더십과 안보를 제공하여, 그들이 식량/에너지 생산량을 지속적으로 늘리고 항상 더 많은 잉여를 제공할 수 있게 하였다.

➡ 결과: 비농민들이 리더십과 안보를 제공하여, 농민들이 더 많은 잉여를 만들도록 함
원인: 자원의 잉여분을 비농민에게 '제공'한 것
▶ limited를 provided(제공했다)와 같은 반의어로 바꿔야 함

왜 오답?

①(a) minimal 최소한의
초기 수렵 채집 사회는 (a) 최소한의 구조만 가지고 있었다. 추장이나 장로 그룹이 주로 캠프나 마을을 이끌었다.
➡ 중간 지도자 없이 추장이나 장로가 마을을 이끌었다는 것은 사회가 '최소한의' 구조만 가졌기 때문일 것이다. ▶ minimal은 문맥에 맞음

②(b) sufficient 충분한
식량과 기타 필수 자원의 잉여분이 전임 추장이나 마을 의회를 지원할 만큼 거의 (b) 충분하지 않았기 때문에 대부분의 이러한 지도자들은 다른 구성원들과 함께 사냥과 채집을 해야 했다.
➡ 남는 자원이 '충분하지' 않았기 때문에 지도자들까지 사냥과 채집을 해야 했을 것이다. ▶ sufficient는 문맥에 맞음

④(d) specialized 전문화되었다
이러한 집단은 마을과 도시에 집중되었고, 인간의 업무는 더욱 (d) 전문화되었다. 목수, 대장장이, 상인, 무역업자, 선원과 같은 전문가들은 기술을 발전시키고 자신의 시간과 에너지 사용을 더 효율적으로 하게 되었다.
➡ 다양한 분야의 전문가들이 등장했으므로 인간의 업무는 더욱 '전문화된' 것이다.
▶ specialized는 문맥에 맞음

⑤(e) improved 향상된
그들이 제공한 재화와 서비스는 (e) 향상된 삶의 질, 더 높은 생활 수준, 그리고, 대부분의 사회에 향상된 안정성을 가져왔다.
➡ '향상된' 삶의 질 = 더 높은 생활 수준, 향상된 안정성
▶ improved는 문맥에 맞음

342 자이스토리 영어 독해 기본

R 17~18 *익숙함에 비례하는 기억의 범위

앞에 주격 관계대명사와 be동사가 생략됨
Chess masters / shown a chess board in the middle of a game / for 5 seconds / with 20 to 30 pieces still in play / can immediately reproduce the position of the pieces / from memory. //
체스의 달인들은 / 체스판을 게임 중간에 본 / 5초 동안 / 20개에서 30개의 말들이 아직 놓여 있는 상태로 / 그 말들의 위치를 즉시 재현할 수 있다 / 기억으로부터 //

Beginners, / of course, / are able to place only a few. //
초보자들은 / 물론 / 겨우 몇 개만 위치시킬 수 있다 //

Now take the same pieces / and place them on the board randomly / and the (a) difference is much reduced. //
이제 같은 말들을 가져다가 / 체스판에 무작위로 놓으면 / 그 차이는 크게 줄어든다 //

= patterns
The expert's advantage / is only for familiar patterns / — those previously stored in memory. // 17번 단서 1: 전문성은 익숙한 패턴에 대한 기억에서 나옴
전문가의 유리함은 / 익숙한 패턴에 대해서만 있다 / 즉 이전에 기억에 저장된 패턴 //

앞에 Being이 생략됨
Faced with unfamiliar patterns, / even when it involves the same familiar domain, / the expert's advantage (b) disappears. //
익숙하지 않은 패턴에 직면하면 / 같은 익숙한 분야와 관련 있는 경우라도 / 전문가의 유리함은 사라진다 //

핵심 주어(복수) 복수 동사
The beneficial effects / of familiar structure on memory / have been observed for many types of expertise, / including music. //
유익한 효과는 / 익숙한 구조가 기억에 미치는 / 많은 유형의 전문 지식에서 관찰되어 왔다 / 음악을 포함하여 // 18번 단서 1: 익숙한 구조를 접할 때 전문 지식이 발휘됨

비교 표현
People with musical training can reproduce / short sequences of musical notation / more accurately / than those with no musical training / when notes follow (c) unusual(→ usual) sequences, /
음악 훈련을 받은 사람은 재현할 수 있다 / 짧은 연속된 악보를 / 더 정확하게 / 음악 훈련을 받지 않은 사람보다 / 음표가 특이한(→ 전형적인) 순서를 따를 때는 /

수동태 동사
but the advantage is much reduced / when the notes are ordered randomly. // 18번 단서 2: 음표가 무작위면 전문성의 발휘가 덜 됨
하지만 그 유리함이 훨씬 줄어든다 / 음표가 무작위로 배열되면 //

Expertise also improves memory / for sequences of (d) movements. // 17번 단서 2: 전문성은 연속 동작에 대한 기억력을 향상시킴
전문 지식은 또한 기억을 향상시킨다 / 연속 동작에 대한 //

Experienced ballet dancers / are able to repeat longer sequences of steps / than less experienced dancers, /
숙련된 발레 무용수가 / 더 긴 연속 스텝을 반복할 수 있다 / 경험이 적은 무용수보다 /

and they can repeat a sequence of steps / making up a routine / better than steps ordered randomly. //
앞에 주격 관계대명사와 be동사가 생략됨
그리고 그들은 연속 스텝을 반복할 수 있다 / 정해진 춤 동작을 이루는 / 무작위로 배열된 스텝보다 더 잘 //

형용사적 용법(ability 수식)
In each case, / memory range is (e) increased / by the ability to recognize familiar sequences and patterns. //
각각의 경우 / 기억의 범위는 늘어난다 / 익숙한 순서와 패턴을 인식하는 능력에 의해 //

- master ⓝ 달인 · reproduce ⓥ 재현하다
- randomly ⓐⓓ 무작위로 · expert ⓝ 전문가
- advantage ⓝ 유리함 · familiar ⓐ 익숙한
- previously ⓐⓓ 이전에 · face ⓥ 직면하다 · domain ⓝ 분야
- beneficial ⓐ 유익한 · structure ⓝ 구조 · observe ⓥ 관찰하다
- accurately ⓐⓓ 정확하게 · note ⓝ 음표 · order ⓥ 배열하다
- guarantee ⓥ 보장하다 · experienced ⓐ 숙련된
- range ⓝ 범위 · recognize ⓥ 인식하다

체스판을 게임 중간에 20개에서 30개의 말들이 아직 놓여 있는 상태로 5초 동안 본 체스의 달인들은 그 말들의 위치를 기억으로부터 즉시 재현할 수 있다. 물론 초보자들은 겨우 몇 개만 위치시킬 수 있다. 이제 같은 말들을 가져다가 체스판에 무작위로 놓으면 그 (a) 차이는 크게 줄어든다. 전문가의 유리함은 익숙한 패턴, 즉 이전에 기억에 저장된 패턴에 대해서만 있다. 익숙하지 않은 패턴에 직면하면, 같은 익숙한 분야와 관련 있는 경우라도 전문가의 유리함은 (b) 사라진다.

익숙한 구조가 기억에 미치는 유익한 효과는 음악을 포함하여 많은 유형의 전문 지식에서 관찰되어 왔다. 음표가 (c) 특이한(→ 전형적인) 순서를 따를 때는 음악 훈련을 받은 사람이 음악 훈련을 받지 않은 사람보다 짧은 연속된 악보를 더 정확하게 재현할 수 있지만, 음표가 무작위로 배열되면 그 유리함이 훨씬 줄어든다. 전문 지식은 또한 연속 (d) 동작에 대한 기억을 향상시킨다. 숙련된 발레 무용수가 경험이 적은 무용수보다 더 긴 연속 스텝을 반복할 수 있고, 무작위로 배열된 스텝보다 정해진 춤 동작을 이루는 연속 스텝을 더 잘 반복할 수 있다. 각각의 경우, 기억의 범위는 익숙한 순서와 패턴을 인식하는 능력에 의해 (e) 늘어난다.

R 17 정답 ②

윗글의 제목으로 가장 적절한 것은?
① How Can We Build Good Routines? 루틴 형성에 초점을 두고 있지는 않음
어떻게 하면 좋은 루틴을 형성할 수 있는가?
②Familiar Structures Help Us Remember
익숙한 구조가 우리가 기억하는 것을 돕는다   자주 접하는 익숙한 구조를 잘 기억할 수 있다는 내용
③ Intelligence Does Not Guarantee Expertise
지능이 전문 지식을 보장하지 않는다   지능과는 관련이 없는 내용임
④ Does Playing Chess Improve Your Memory?
체스를 두는 것이 기억력을 향상시키는가?   체스는 중심 내용을 설명하기 위한 예시일 뿐임
⑤ Creative Art Performance Starts from Practice
창의적인 예술 작업은 연습으로부터 시작한다   창의성보다는 익숙함이 초점임

>왜 정답? ★★※ [정답률 69%]

• 전문가의 유리함은 익숙한 패턴, 즉 이전에 기억에 저장된 패턴에 대해서만 있다. 17번 단서 1
• 전문 지식은 또한 연속 동작에 대한 기억을 향상시킨다. 17번 단서 2
➡ 전문가들은 자신에게 익숙한 패턴은 잘 기억하지만, 익숙하지 않은 경우에는 전문성을 발휘하기 어렵다고 했고, 전문 지식 또한 연속 동작에 대한 기억을 향상시킨다고 했다.
▶ 따라서 제목으로는 ② '익숙한 구조가 우리가 기억하는 것을 돕는다'가 적절하다.

>왜 오답?
① 루틴을 형성하는 방법에 대해 초점을 둔 글이 아니라 익숙함이 갖는 영향력에 대한 글이다.
③ 지능보다는 반복적인 경험을 통한 패턴의 인식 능력이 전문성에 기여한다고 했다.
④ 체스는 전문가의 패턴 파악 능력에 대한 예시로 쓰였을 뿐 중심 내용은 아니다. 함정
⑤ 창의적인 예술 작업과는 관련이 없다.

R 18 정답 ③

밑줄 친 (a)~(e) 중에서 문맥상 낱말의 쓰임이 적절하지 않은 것은?
① (a) 익숙함이 사라지면 전문가와 일반인 간의 차이는 줄어들 것임
차이
② (b) 익숙함이라는 요인을 제거하면 전문가와 일반인 간의 격차는 사라짐
사라지다
③(c) 전문가에게 익숙한 전형적인 패턴에 대한 설명임
특이한, 일반적이지 않은
④ (d) 전문 지식을 가지고 있으면 패턴화된 움직임을 더 잘 기억할 수 있음
동작
⑤ (e) 익숙한 것을 접할 경우 기억할 수 있는 범주가 늘어남
늘어나다

>왜 정답? ★★★ [정답률 50%]

③(c) unusual 특이한
전형적인
음표가 (c) ~~특이한~~ 순서를 따를 때는 음악 훈련을 받은 사람이 음악 훈련을 받지 않은 사람보다 짧은 연속된 악보를 더 정확하게 재현할 수 있지만(but), 음표가 무작위로 배열되면 그 유리함이 훨씬 줄어든다.

음표가 무작위로 배열되는 것(= 익숙하지 않은 것)과 역접의 연결어 but으로 연결되고 있으므로 특이한 순서(= 익숙하지 않은 것)를 따르는 상황과 반대되는 상황이어야 자연스럽다.
▶ unusual을 usual(전형적인)과 같은 반의어로 바꿔야 함

>왜 오답?
①(a) difference 차이
이제 같은 말들을 가져다가 체스판에 무작위로 놓으면 그 (a) 차이는 크게 줄어든다. 전문가의 유리함은 익숙한 패턴, 즉 이전에 기억에 저장된 패턴에 대해서만 있다.
➡ 전문가의 유리함은 익숙한 패턴에 대해서만 있다는 설명이 이어진다. 앞에서 초보자들은 게임 중인 말의 위치를 겨우 몇 개만 기억해 낼 수 있다고 했으므로, 무작위로 놓으면 전문가와 초보자가 위치시키는 말들의 수 '차이'는 크게 줄어들 것이다.
▶ difference는 문맥에 맞음

②(b) disappears 사라지다
전문가의 유리함은 익숙한 패턴, 즉 이전에 기억에 저장된 패턴에 대해서만 있다. 익숙하지 않은 패턴에 직면하면, 같은 익숙한 분야와 관련 있는 경우라도 전문가의 유리함은 (b) 사라진다.
➡ 전문가는 익숙한 패턴에 대해서만 유리하다고 했으므로, 익숙하지 않은 패턴에 대해서는 이 유리함이 '사라질' 것이다.
▶ disappears는 문맥에 맞음

④(d) movements 동작
전문 지식은 또한 연속 (d) 동작에 대한 기억을 향상시킨다. 숙련된 발레 무용수가 경험이 적은 무용수보다 더 긴 연속 스텝을 반복할 수 있고, 무작위로 배열된 스텝보다 정해진 춤 동작을 이루는 연속 스텝을 더 잘 반복할 수 있다.
➡ 숙련된 발레 무용수가 더 긴 연속 스텝을 반복할 수 있다고 했으므로 전문 지식은 연속 '동작'에 대한 기억을 향상시킬 것이다.
▶ movements는 문맥에 맞음

⑤(e) increased 늘어나다
각각의 경우, 기억의 범위는 익숙한 순서와 패턴을 인식하는 능력에 의해 (e) 늘어난다.
➡ 앞에서 더 긴 연속 스텝을 반복할 수 있다고 했으므로 기억의 범위는 익숙한 패턴을 인식하는 능력에 의해 '늘어날 것이다.
▶ increased는 문맥에 맞음

R 19~20 *유전자를 넘어선 우리의 건강에 대한 소유권

전치사
Since the turn of the twentieth century / we've believed in genetic
앞에 주격 관계대명사와 be동사 생략
causes of diagnoses / — a theory called genetic determinism. //
20세기로 전환된 이래로 / 우리는 진단의 유전적인 원인을 믿어 왔다 / 유전자 결정론이라 불리는 이론을 //

Under this model, / our genes (and subsequent health) are determined / at birth. //
이 모델 하에서 / 우리의 유전자는 (그리고 차후의 건강은) 결정된다 / 태어날 때 //

~을 바탕으로
We are "destined" to inherit certain diseases / based on the misfortune of our DNA. //
우리는 특정 질병을 물려받을 '운명'이다 / 자신의 DNA의 불행을 바탕으로 //

Genetic determinism doesn't (a) consider / the role of family backgrounds, traumas, habits, / or anything else within the environment. //
유전자 결정론은 고려하지 않는다 / 가정 환경, 정신적 충격, 습관 / 또는 환경 내의 다른 어떤 것의 역할을 //

In this dynamic / we are not (b) <u>active</u> participants / in our own health and wellness. //

이 역학 관계에서 / 우리는 능동적인 참여자가 아니다 / 우리 자신의 건강과 안녕에 있어 //

Why would we be? //

우리는 왜 이러할까 //

If something is predetermined, / ^{가주어}it's not (c) <u>necessary</u> / ^{진주어}to look at anything / beyond our DNA. //

만약 무언가가 미리 결정되어 있다면 / 필요하지 않다 / 어떤 것을 보는 것이 / 우리의 DNA 를 넘어서 //

But <u>the more</u> science has learned / about the body and its interaction with the environment around it / (in its various forms, /

「the+비교급 ~, the+비교급 ...」: ~할수록 더 …하다

하지만 과학이 더 많이 알게 될수록 / 신체와 그것의 그 주변 환경과의 상호 작용에 대해 / (다양한 형태로 …

from our nutrition / to our relationships to our racially oppressive systems), / <u>the more</u> (d) <u>simplistic (→ complex)</u> the story becomes. // 20번 단서 1: 과학이 신체와 주변 환경의 상호 작용을 다양한 형태로 알게 됨

우리의 영양에서부터 / 우리의 관계 그리고 우리의 인종적으로 억압적인 시스템에 이르기까지 / 그 이야기는 더욱 단순해진다(→ 복잡해진다) //

^{not merely[only] A but (also) B: A뿐만 아니라 B도}
We are not merely expressions of coding / <u>but</u> products of a ^{주격 관계대명사} remarkable variety of interactions / <u>that</u> are both within and outside of our control. // 19번 단서 1, 20번 단서 2: 우리는 유전자의 영향을 받는 것만이 아니라 통제할 수 있는 부분도 있고 다양한 상호 작용의 산물임

우리는 단지 (유전)암호화의 표현이 아니라 / 놀랍도록 다양한 상호 작용의 산물이다 / 우리의 통제 내부와 외부 모두에 있는 //

^{동격절 접속사}
Once we see beyond the narrative / <u>that</u> genetics are (e) <u>destiny</u>, / we can take ownership of our health. //

일단 우리가 이야기를 넘어서 보게 된다면 / 유전자가 운명이라는 / 우리는 자신의 건강에 대한 소유권을 가질 수 있다 // 19번 단서 2: 유전자가 우리를 결정한다는 생각을 넘어서면 우리가 스스로의 건강에 영향을 미칠 수 있음

This <u>allows</u> us to see / how "choiceless" we once were / and ^{동사의 병렬 구조} <u>empowers</u> us with the ability / ^{형용사적 용법}to create real and lasting change. //

이것은 우리에게 알 수 있게 해 준다 / 자신이 한때 얼마나 '선택권이 없는' 상태였는지 / 그리고 우리에게 능력을 부여한다 / 실제적이고 지속적인 변화를 만들어 낼 수 있는 //

- genetic ⓐ 유전적인 · diagnosis ⓝ 진단
- determinism ⓝ 결정론 · gene ⓝ 유전자
- subsequent ⓐ 차후의 · destined to ~할 운명이다
- inherit ⓥ 물려받다 · misfortune ⓝ 불행
- dynamic ⓝ 역학 (관계) · wellness ⓝ 건강
- predetermine ⓥ 미리 결정하다 · racially ⓐⓓ 인종적으로
- simplistic ⓐ 단순한 · coding ⓝ 암호화 · narrative ⓝ 이야기
- ownership ⓝ 소유권 · choiceless ⓐ 선택권이 없는
- dominate ⓥ 지배하다 · innovation ⓝ 혁신

20세기로 전환된 이래로 우리는 진단의 유전적인 원인, 즉 유전자 결정론이라 불리는 이론을 믿어 왔다. 이 모델 하에서 우리의 유전자는 (그리고 차후의 건강은) 태어날 때 결정된다. 우리는 자신의 DNA의 불행을 바탕으로 특정 질병을 물려받을 '운명'이다. 유전자 결정론은 가정 환경, 정신적 충격, 습관 또는 환경 내의 다른 어떤 것의 역할을 (a) 고려하지 않는다. 이 역학 관계에서 우리는 우리 자신의 건강과 안녕에 있어 (b) 능동적인 참여자가 아니다. 우리는 왜 이러할까? 만약 무언가가 미리 결정되어 있다면 우리의 DNA를 넘어서 어떤 것을 보는 것이 (c) 필요하지 않다. 하지만 과학이 신체와 그것의 그 주변 환경 (우리의 영양에서부터, 우리의 관계 그리고 우리의 인종적으로 억압적인 시스템에 이르기까지의 다양한 형태로)과의 상호 작용에 대해 더 많이 알게 될수록, 그 이야기는 더욱 (d) 단순해진다(→ 복잡해진다). 우리는 단지 (유전) 암호화의 표현이 아니라 우리의 통제 내부와 외부 모두에 있는 놀랍도록 다양한 상호 작용의 산물이다. 일단 우리가 유전자가 (e) 운명이라는 이야기를 넘어서 보게 된다면 우리는 자신의 건강에 대한 소유권을 가질 수 있다. 이것은 우리에게 자신이 한때 얼마나 '선택권이 없는' 상태였는지 알 수 있게 해 주며 우리에게 실제적이고 지속적인 변화를 만들어 낼 수 있는 능력을 부여한다.

R 19 정답 ①

윗글의 제목으로 가장 적절한 것은?

건강은 유전자가 결정하기만 하는 것이 아니고 우리가 통제할 수 있는 부분이 있다는 내용
① Health Is in Our Hands, Not Only in Our Genes
건강은 우리의 유전자뿐만이 아니라 우리의 손에 있다
② Genetics: A Solution to Enhance Human Wellness 건강을 유전에
유전학: 인간의 건강을 증진시키는 해결책   의해서만 결정되는 것으로 보고 있으므로 부적절함
③ How Did DNA Dominate Over Environment in Biology?
DNA가 생물학에서 어떻게 환경을 지배했는가?   '환경과의 상호 작용'이라고 했으므로 오답임
④ Never Be Confident in Your Health, but Keep Checking!
당신의 건강을 결코 확신하지 말고 계속 점검하라!   건강에 대한 확신과 점검에 대한 내용이 아님
⑤ Why Scientific Innovation Affects Our Social Interactions
과학 혁신이 우리의 사회적 상호 작용에 영향을 주는 이유   핵심어인 건강과 관련된 제목이 아님

▶왜 정답? ★★★ [정답률 55%]

유전자만이 건강을 결정한다고 믿어 왔지만 과학이 더 많은 것을 알게 될수록 건강은 유전에 의해서만 결정되는 것이 아니라고 했다. 건강은 신체와 환경의 상호 작용에 의해 영향을 받기 때문에 우리가 통제할 수 있는 부분이 있다는 내용의 글이다. 따라서 건강이 유전에 의해서만 결정되는 것이 아니라 우리가 통제할 수 있다는 내용을 담고 있는 ① '건강은 우리의 유전자뿐만이 아니라 우리의 손에 있다'가 글의 제목으로 가장 적절하다.

▶왜 오답?

② 건강이 유전에만 영향을 받는 것이 아니라 우리가 통제할 수 있는 부분이 있다는 것인데, 이것은 유전의 영향만 강조하고 있으므로 답이 될 수 없다. 주의

③ '환경과 상호 작용한다'고 했는데 DNA 즉, 유전적인 요소만을 강조하고 있으므로 오답이다.

④ 건강에 대한 확신이나 점검에 대한 내용이 아니므로 제목이 될 수 없다.

⑤ 핵심어인 '건강'이 포함되지 않고 글의 내용과 관련 없는 '사회적' 상호 작용에 대한 제목이므로 부적절하다.

R 20 정답 ④

밑줄 친 (a)~(e) 중에서 문맥상 낱말의 쓰임이 적절하지 않은 것은? [3점]

① (a) 유전자 결정론은 주변 환경의 영향을 고려하지 않음
고려하다
② (b) 유전자 결정론에서는 유전자가 모든 것을 결정함
능동적인
③ (c) DNA가 건강을 결정한다고 가정하면, DNA 이상의 것을 고려할 필요가 없음
필요한
④ (d) 단순하게 유전자만으로 건강을 모두 설명할 수 없다고 했으므로 복잡한 것임
단순한
⑤ (e) 건강에 대한 소유권을 가지려면 유전이 운명이라는 생각을 넘어서야 함
운명

▶왜 정답? ★★✿ [정답률 61%]

과학이 신체와 주변 환경의 상호 작용을 다양한 형태로 더 많이 알게 된다고 했으므로 단순하게 유전자만으로 건강을 모두 설명할 수 없고, 우리는 다양한 상호 작용의 산물이라고 했으므로 더 '복잡해질' 것이다. 따라서 ④ simplistic(단순한)을 complex(복잡한)와 같은 낱말로 바꾸는 것이 문맥상 자연스럽다.

▶왜 오답?

① 유전자 결정론은 DNA가 건강을 결정하는 것이므로 주변 환경의 영향은 '고려하지' 않는다는 맥락은 자연스럽다.

② 유전자 결정론에서는 DNA가 건강을 결정하므로 우리는 건강에 대해 '능동적인' 참여자가 아니다.

③ 유전자 결정론에서는 DNA가 건강을 결정하므로 DNA 이상의 것을 보는 건 '필요하지' 않다는 흐름이 자연스럽게 연결된다.

⑤ 유전이 '운명'이라는 생각을 넘어서야 우리가 스스로의 건강에 대한 소유권을 갖는다는 것이 문맥상 자연스럽다.

R 21~22 *식품 생산 과정에서 환경을 보호하는 진정한 방법

핵심 주어(복수) 동격절 접속사
Claims / **that** local food production cut greenhouse gas emissions
by v-ing: ~함으로써   복수동사
/ **by reducing** the burning of transportation fuel / **are** usually not
well founded. // **21번** 단서 1: 지역 음식 생산이 온실가스 배출을 줄였음을 뒷받침하는 근거는 충분하지 않음

주장들은 / 지역 음식 생산이 온실가스 배출을 줄였다 / 운송 연료의 연소를 줄임으로써 / 대개 근거가 충분하지 않다. //

Transport is the source / of only 11 percent of greenhouse gas
emissions / within the food sector, /
운송은 원천이다 / 온실가스 배출의 11퍼센트만을 차지하는 / 식품 부문 내에서 /
동명사 주어(단수 취급)   목적격 관계대명사
so **reducing** the distance / **that** food travels / after it leaves the
단수동사   비교급 강조 부사
farm / **is far** (a) **less** important / than reducing wasteful energy
use / on the farm. // **21번** 단서 2: 음식의 이동 거리를 줄이는 것보다 생산자에서 낭비되는 에너지를 줄이는 것이 더 중요함
그래서 거리를 줄이는 것은 / 식품이 이동하는 / 그것이 농장을 떠난 후 / 훨씬 덜 중요하다 / 낭비되는 에너지 사용을 줄이는 것보다 / 농장에서 //

Food coming from a distance / can actually be better / for the (b)
'~에 따라'   전치사의 목적어 역할을 하는 간접의문문
climate, / **depending on how it was grown.** //
먼 곳에서 오는 식품은 / 실제로 더 좋을 수 있다 / 기후에 / 그것이 어떻게 재배되었느냐에 따라 //

For example, / field-grown tomatoes / **shipped** from Mexico in
the winter months / will have a smaller carbon footprint / than
앞에 주격 관계대명사와 be동사가 생략됨
(c) local winter tomatoes / **grown** in a greenhouse. //
예를 들어 / 밭에서 재배된 토마토는 / 겨울에 멕시코로부터 수송된 / 더 적은 탄소 발자국을 가질 것이다 / 현지의 겨울 토마토보다 / 온실에서 재배된 //
주격 관계대명사
In the United Kingdom, / lamb meat **that** travels 11,000 miles
from New Zealand / generates only one-quarter the carbon
emissions per pound / compared to British lamb /
영국에서 / 뉴질랜드에서 11,000마일을 이동하는 양고기는 / 파운드당 탄소 배출량의 4분의 1만 발생시킨다 / 영국의 양고기에 비해 /
부사절 접속사(이유)
because farmers in the United Kingdom raise their animals / on
조동사가 포함된 수동태
feed / (which **must be produced** using fossil fuels) / rather than
on clover pastureland. //
왜냐하면 영국의 농부들이 자신의 동물들을 기르기 때문에 / 사료로 / (화석 연료를 사용하여 생산되어야만 하는) / 클로버 목초지에서가 아닌 //
강조 용법의 do동사   선행사를 포함하는 관계대명사
When food **does** travel, / **what** matters most is **not** the (d)
not A but B: A가 아니라 B
distance traveled / **but** the travel mode (surface versus air), /
and most of all the load size. // **22번** 단서 1: 식품 이동에 가장 중요한 것은 이동 거리가 아니라 적재량의 규모임
식품이 정말 이동할 때 / 가장 중요한 것은 이동 거리가 아니라 / 이동 방식 (지상 대 공중) / 그리고 무엇보다 적재량의 규모이다 //

Bulk loads of food can travel / halfway around the world / by
ocean freight / with a smaller carbon footprint, / per pound
과거분사(pound 수식)
delivered, /
대량의 적재된 식품은 이동할 수 있다 / 세계의 절반을 / 해상 화물 운송으로 / 더 적은 탄소 발자국으로 / 배달된 파운드당 /
현재분사(foods 수식)
than foods / **traveling** just a short distance / but in much (e)
larger(→ smaller) loads. //
22번 단서 2: 대형트럭이 픽업트럭보다 더 많은 적재량을 운반해 연료 연소를 줄임
식품에 비해 / 단지 단거리를 이동하지만 / 훨씬 더 많은(→ 더 적은) 적재량인 //

For example, / 18-wheelers carry much larger loads / than pickup
trucks / so they can move food / 100 times as far / **while burning**
접속사가 생략되지 않은 분사구문
only one-third as much gas / per pound of food delivered. //
예를 들어 / 18륜 대형트럭은 훨씬 더 많은 적재량을 운반한다 / 픽업트럭보다 / 그래서 그것들은 식품을 이동시킬 수 있다 / 100배 멀리 / 오직 3분의 1의 가스만 연소하면서 / 배달된 식품의 파운드당 //

- claim ⓝ 주장   - production ⓝ 생산
- greenhouse gas 온실가스   - emission ⓝ 방출, 배출
- transportation ⓝ 운송, 수송   - found ⓥ 근거를 부여하다, 설립하다
- sector ⓝ 부문   - wasteful ⓐ 낭비하는   - climate ⓝ 기후
- carbon ⓝ 탄소   - footprint ⓝ 발자국   - lamb ⓝ ((동물)) 양
- fossil ⓝ 화석   - pastureland ⓝ 목초지   - bulk ⓝ 큰 규모
- route ⓝ 길, 경로   - mass ⓐ 대량의   - agriculture ⓝ 농업

지역 음식 생산이 운송 연료의 연소를 줄임으로써 온실가스 배출을 줄였다는 주장들은 대개 근거가 충분하지 않다. 운송은 식품 부문 내에서 온실가스 배출의 11퍼센트만을 차지하는 원천이라서, 식품이 농장을 떠난 후 이동하는 거리를 줄이는 것은 농장에서 낭비되는 에너지 사용을 줄이는 것보다 훨씬 (a) 덜 중요하다. 먼 곳에서 오는 식품은 그것이 어떻게 재배되었느냐에 따라 실제로 (b) 기후에 더 좋을 수 있다. 예를 들어, 겨울에 멕시코로부터 수송된 밭에서 재배된 토마토는 온실에서 재배된 (c) 현지의 겨울 토마토보다 탄소 발자국이 더 적을 것이다. 영국에서는, 영국의 농부들이 클로버 목초지에서가 아닌 (화석 연료를 사용하여 생산되어야 하는) 사료로 자신의 동물들을 기르기 때문에 뉴질랜드에서 11,000마일을 이동하는 양고기는 영국의 양고기에 비해 파운드당 탄소 배출량의 4분의 1만 발생시킨다.
식품이 이동할 때, 가장 중요한 것은 이동 (d) 거리가 아니라 이동 방식 (지상 대 공중), 그리고 무엇보다 적재량의 규모이다. 대량의 적재된 식품은 단지 단거리를 이동하지만 훨씬 (e) 더 많은(→ 더 적은) 적재량인 식품에 비해 배달된 파운드당 탄소 발자국이 더 적은 해상 화물 운송으로 세계의 절반을 이동할 수 있다. 예를 들어, 18륜 대형트럭은 픽업트럭보다 훨씬 더 많은 적재량을 운반하므로 배달된 식품 파운드당 오직 3분의 1의 가스만 연소하면서 100배 멀리 식품을 이동시킬 수 있다.

R 21 정답 ②

윗글의 제목으로 가장 적절한 것은?
① Shorten the Route, Cut the Cost 경로가 아니라 적재량이 중요하다는 내용임
경로를 줄이고 비용을 절감하라
② Is Local Food Always Better for the Earth?
지역 음식은 항상 지구에 더 좋을까?   지역 음식 생산이 환경에 좋지만은 않다는 내용임
③ Why Mass Production Ruins the Environment
대량 생산이 환경을 파괴하는 이유   대량 생산의 환경 파괴와는 관련 없는 내용임
④ New Technologies: What Matters in Agriculture
새로운 기술: 농업에서 중요한 것   농업에서 새로운 기술이 중요하다는 내용이 아님
⑤ Reduce Food Waste for a Smaller Carbon Footprint
더 적은 탄소 발자국을 위해 음식물 쓰레기를 줄여라   음식물 쓰레기는 언급되지 않음

왜 정답? ★★❀ [정답률 60%]

- 지역 음식 생산이 온실가스 배출을 줄였다는 근거는 충분하지 않음 **21번 단서 1**
- 음식의 이동 거리를 줄이는 것보다 생산지에서 낭비되는 에너지 사용을 줄이는 것이 더 중요함 **21번 단서 2**

➡ 탄소 발자국 배출량

예시 **1**: 멕시코 밭에서 재배되어 수송된 토마토 ＜ 온실에서 재배된 현지 토마토
예시 **2**: 11,000마일을 이동한 뉴질랜드 양
＜ 화석 연료를 사용하여 생산되는 사료로 기른 현지 양

▶ 현지에서 식품을 생산하는 것보다 멀리에서 이동한 식품이 환경에 더 좋을 수 있다는 것이므로 제목으로 가장 적절한 것은 ② '지역 음식은 항상 지구에 더 좋을까?'이다.

왜 오답?
① 이동 거리가 아니라 적재량이 중요하다는 글이며, 가격과 관련된 내용도 아니다. 함정
③ 대량 생산이 아니라 대량 적재가 환경에 더 좋다는 내용이다.
④ 새로운 기술이 중요하다는 언급은 없다.
⑤ 더 적은 탄소 배출을 위해 음식물 쓰레기를 줄이라는 글이 아니다.
(이유: 탄소 배출하면 떠오르는 쓰레기 배출로 만든 오답이다.)

R 22 정답 ⑤

밑줄 친 (a)~(e) 중에서 문맥상 낱말의 쓰임이 적절하지 <u>않은</u> 것은? [3점]

① (a) 이동 거리는 현지에서 낭비되는 에너지 줄이는 것보다 중요하지 않음
   덜
② (b) 먼 곳에도 온 식품이 오히려 환경에 좋을 수 있음
   기후
③ (c) 멕시코에서 온 토마토가 현지의 토마토보다 탄소 발자국이 더 적을 수 있음
   현지의
④ (d) 이동 거리가 아니라 이동 방식과 적재량이 중요함
   거리
⑤ (e) 대량으로 적재된 식품과 적재량이 적은 식품을 비교하고 있음
   더 많은

✓왜 정답? ★★★ [정답률 42%]

⑤(e) larger 더 많은

대량의 적재된 식품은 단지 단거리를 이동<u>하지만(but)</u> 훨씬 (e) ~~더 많은(larger)~~ 더 적은
적재량인 식품에 비해 배달된 파운드당 탄소 발자국이 더 적은 해상 화물
운송으로 세계의 절반을 이동할 수 있다.

➡ 식품을 이동할 때 이동 거리보다 이동 방식과 적재량이 중요하다는 것을 설명하는
부분이다.
따라서 세계의 절반을 이동하는 대량의 적재량을 배달하는 것이 탄소 발자국을 더
적게 남기는 것으로 비교되어야 하는 것은 단거리를 이동하는 '더 적은' 적재량을
배달하는 것이다.

▶ larger을 smaller(더 적은)와 같은 반의어로 바꿔야 함

✓왜 오답?

①(a) less 덜

운송은 식품 부문 내에서 온실가스 배출의 11퍼센트만을 차지하는
원천이라서, 식품이 농장을 떠난 후 이동하는 거리를 줄이는 것은 농장에서
낭비되는 에너지 사용을 줄이는 것보다 훨씬 (a) 덜 중요하다.

➡ 운송이 온실가스 배출에 미치는 영향력이 크지 않으므로, 식품의 이동 거리를
줄이는 것은 농장에서 낭비되는 에너지 사용을 줄이는 것보다 훨씬 '덜' 중요할
것이다.

▶ less는 문맥에 맞음

②(b) climate 기후

먼 곳에서 오는 식품은 그것이 어떻게 재배되었느냐에 따라 실제로
(b) 기후에 더 좋을 수 있다.

➡ 이동 거리가 온실가스 배출에 크게 중요하지 않다고 했으므로 먼 곳에서 오는
식품이라도 재배 방식에 따라 '기후'에, 즉 환경에 더 좋을 수도 있을 것이다.

▶ climate는 문맥에 맞음

③(c) local 현지의

예를 들어, 겨울에 멕시코로부터 수송된 밭에서 재배된 토마토는 온실에서
재배된 (c) 현지의 겨울 토마토보다 탄소 발자국이 더 적을 것이다.

➡ 먼 곳에서 오는 식품이라도 재배 방식에 따라 기후에 더 좋을 수 있는 예시가
언급되었다. 먼 멕시코에서 온 토마토가 '현지의' 토마토보다 탄소 발자국이 더 적을
수 있다는 흐름은 적절하다.

> 온실에서 재배된 경우 = 재배할 때 낭비되는 에너지가 많음 🍯팁

▶ local은 문맥에 맞음

④(d) distance 거리

식품이 이동할 때, 가장 중요한 것은 이동 (d) 거리가 아니라 이동 방식
(지상 대 공중), 그리고 무엇보다 적재량의 규모이다. ~ 예를 들어, 18륜
대형트럭은 픽업트럭보다 훨씬 더 많은 적재량을 운반하므로 배달된 식품
파운드당 오직 3분의 1의 가스만 연소하면서 100배 멀리 식품을 이동시킬
수 있다.

➡ 식품을 이동할 때 '거리'보다 적재량이 더 중요하다는 예시가 이어진다.

▶ distance는 문맥에 맞음

R 23~24 *언어 발달의 핵심인 대화

Like all humans, / the first *Homo* species / to begin / the long
difficult process / of constructing a language / from scratch /
almost certainly never said entirely / what was on their minds. //
모든 인간처럼 / 최초의 '호모' 종은 / 시작한 / 길고 힘든 과정을 / 언어를 구성하는 / 맨 처음
부터 / 거의 틀림없이 온전히 말하지 않았다 / 자신의 마음에 있는 것을 //

At the same time, / these primitive hominins / would not have
simply made / (a) random sounds or gestures. //
동시에 / 이 원시 호미닌(인간의 조상으로 분류되는 종족)들은 / 단순히 만들지는 않았을 것이
다 / 무작위적인 소리나 몸짓을 //

Instead, / they would have used means / to communicate / that
they believed / others would understand. //
대신 / 그들은 수단을 사용했을 것이다 / 의사소통할 / 그들이 믿는 것을 / 남들이 이해할 것
이라고 //

And they also thought / their hearers could "fill in the gaps", /
and connect their knowledge / of their culture and the world /
to interpret what was uttered. //
그리고 그들은 또한 생각했다 / 자신의 청자들이 '빈틈을 메울' 수 있다고 / 그리고 지식을 연
결할 수 있다고 / 그들의 문화와 세계에 대한 / 발화된 것을 해석하기 위해 //

These are some of the reasons / why the (b) origins of human
language / cannot be effectively discussed / unless conversation
is placed / at the top of the list / of things to understand. //
이러한 것들이 몇 가지 이유이다 / 인간 언어의 기원이 / 효과적으로 논의될 수 없는 / 대화가
놓이지 않는 한 / 목록 중 맨 위에 / 이해해야 할 것들의 //

Every aspect of human language has evolved, / as have
components of the human brain and body, / to (c) engage / in
conversation and social life. //
인간 언어의 모든 측면은 진화해 왔다 / 인간의 뇌와 신체의 구성 요소들이 그래왔듯이 / 관여
하도록 / 대화와 사회 생활에 //

Language did not fully begin / when the first hominid uttered /
the first word or sentence. // 23번 단서 1: 단어나 문장의 발화는 언어의 중심 요소가 아님
언어는 온전히 시작된 것은 아니었다 / 최초의 호미니드(사람과의 동물)가 발화했을 때 / 최초
의 단어나 문장을 //

It began / in earnest / only with the first conversation, / which is
both the source and the (d) goal / of language. //
그것은 시작되었다 / 본격적으로 / 최초의 대화와 함께 / 그리고 이것이 근원이자 목적이다 /
언어의 //

Indeed, / language changes lives. //
실제로 / 언어는 삶을 변화시킨다 //

It builds society / and expresses / our highest aspirations, our
basest thoughts, / our emotions and our philosophies of life. //
그것은 사회를 세운다 / 그리고 표현한다 / 우리의 가장 높은 열망, 가장 기본적인 생각 / 감정
그리고 삶의 철학을 //

But all language / is ultimately at the service of human
interaction. // 24번 단서: 언어의 궁극적인 목적은 상호 작용을 위한 것이므로 나머지 요소들은 부차적인 것이 됨
하지만 모든 언어는 / 궁극적으로 인간의 상호 작용을 위한 것이다 //

Other components of language / — things like grammar and
stories — / are (e) crucial(→ secondary) to conversation. //
언어의 다른 요소들 / 즉 문법과 이야기와 같은 것은 / 대화에 중요한(→ 부차적인) 것들이다 //

- species ⓝ 종(種)   · construct ⓥ 구성하다
- from scratch 처음부터   · mind ⓝ 마음   · primitive ⓐ 원시의
- means ⓝ 수단   · gap ⓝ 차이, 틈새   · connect ⓥ 연결하다
- interpret ⓥ 해석하다   · utter ⓥ 말하다   · origin ⓝ 기원
- effectively ⓐⓓ 효과적으로   · place ⓥ 두다   · evolve ⓥ 진화하다
- component ⓝ 구성 요소, 성분   · engage in ~에 관여하다
- in earnest 본격적으로   · aspiration ⓝ 열망   · emotion ⓝ 감정
- philosophy ⓝ 철학   · ultimately ⓐⓓ 궁극적으로
- interaction ⓝ 상호 작용   · crucial ⓐ 중대한
- various ⓐ 다양한   · strategy ⓝ 전략   · ancestor ⓝ 조상
- core ⓝ 핵심   · offend ⓥ 감정을 상하게 하다
- shape ⓥ 형성하다   · communicator ⓝ 의사 전달자

모든 인간처럼, 맨 처음부터 언어를 구성하는 길고 힘든 과정을 시작한 최초의 '호모' 좋은 거의 틀림없이 자신의 마음에 있는 것을 온전히 말하지 않았다. 동시에, 이 원시 호미닌(인간의 조상으로 분류되는 종족)들은 단순히 (a) 무작위적인 소리를 내거나 몸짓을 하지는 않았을 것이다. 대신, 그들은 남들이 이해할 것이라고 믿는 의사소통 수단을 사용했을 것이다. 그리고 그들은 또한 자신의 청자들이 '빈틈을 메울' 수 있고, 발화된 것을 해석하기 위해 그들의 문화와 세계에 대한 지식을 연결할 수 있다고 생각했다. 이러한 것들이 대화가 이해해야 할 것들의 목록 중 맨 위에 놓이지 않는 한, 인간 언어의 (b) 기원이 효과적으로 논의될 수 없는 몇 가지 이유이다. 인간의 뇌와 신체의 구성 요소들이 그래왔듯이, 인간 언어의 모든 측면은 대화와 사회생활에 (c) 관여하도록 진화해 왔다. 언어는 최초의 호미니드 (사람과의 동물)가 최초의 단어나 문장을 발화했을 때 온전히 시작된 것은 아니었다. 그것은 최초의 대화와 함께 본격적으로 시작되었는데, 이는 언어의 근원이자 (d) 목적이다. 실제로, 언어는 삶을 변화시킨다. 그것은 사회를 세우고, 우리의 가장 높은 열망, 가장 기본적인 생각, 감정 그리고 삶의 철학을 표현한다. 하지만 모든 언어는 궁극적으로 인간의 상호 작용을 위한 것이다. 언어의 다른 요소들, 즉 문법과 이야기와 같은 것은 대화에 (e) 중요한(→ 부차적인) 것들이다.

R 23 정답 ②

윗글의 제목으로 가장 적절한 것은?
① Various Communication Strategies of Our Ancestors
우리 조상들의 여러 가지 의사소통 전략들 · 조상의 의사소통 방법은 첫 단락에만 일부 언급됨
②Conversation: The Core of Language Development
대화: 언어 발달의 핵심 · 언어의 목적은 대화와 상호 작용임
③ Ending Conversation Without Offending Others
다른 사람의 기분을 상하게 하지 않고 대화를 끝내는 것 · 대화를 마치는 방법에 관한 글이 아님
④ How Language Shapes the Way You Think
언어가 당신이 생각하는 방식을 형성하는 법 · 언어는 인간의 상호 작용을 위한 것임
⑤ What Makes You a Good Communicator?
무엇이 당신을 훌륭한 의사 전달자로 만드는가? · 훌륭한 의사 전달자가 되는 조건은 알 수 없음

왜 정답? ★★☆ [정답률 68%]
전반부에서는 최초의 인간 조상들이 어떤 방식으로 언어를 사용했는지를 설명하고 있는데, 그들은 무작위적인 소리나 몸짓을 내는 것이 아니라 남들이 이해할 것이라고 믿는 의사소통 수단을 사용했다고 했다. 따라서 언어의 기원은 최초의 호미니드가 발화한 최초의 단어나 문장부터가 아니라 발화된 말을 해석하기 위해 그들의 문화나 세계에 대한 지식을 연결할 수 있는 대화와 함께 본격적으로 시작된 것이다. 즉 대화가 바로 언어의 근원이자 목적이라고 했으므로 이 글의 제목으로 가장 적절한 것은 ② '대화: 언어 발달의 핵심'이다.

왜 오답?
① 조상의 의사소통 방법은 첫 단락에만 일부 언급되었으며 전체 지문을 포괄할 수 있는 내용이 아니다.
③ 대화를 끝내는 방법에 관해서는 전혀 언급되지 않았다.
④ 글의 핵심 내용인 '언어가 인간의 상호 작용을 위한 것'이라는 주제를 포함하지 않는다.
⑤ 훌륭한 의사 전달자가 되는 방법에 대한 언급은 없다.

R 24 정답 ⑤

밑줄 친 (a)~(e) 중에서 문맥상 낱말의 쓰임이 적절하지 않은 것은? [3점]
① (a) 뒤 문장에 '대신에, 남들이 이해할 것을 말했다'는 내용이 있음
무작위의
② (b) 언어의 진화에 대해 언급하고 있음
기원
③ (c) 대화에 '관여한다'는 의미임
관여하다
④ (d) 언어의 핵심은 대화라는 주제가 여러 번 언급됨
목적
⑤(e) 인간의 상호 작용과 대화가 언어에 가장 중요함
중요한

왜 정답? ★★★ [정답률 48%]
(e)가 포함되어 있는 문장의 바로 앞 문장에서 all language is ultimately at the service of human interaction(모든 언어는 궁극적으로 인간의 상호 작용을 위한 것이다.)이라고 말하고 있으므로, 문법과 이야기 등 언어의 다른 요소들은 대화만큼 중요한 요소는 아니라는 것을 추측할 수 있다. 따라서 (e) crucial(중요한)을 secondary(부차적인)와 같은 낱말로 바꾸어야 문맥상 적절하다.

왜 오답?
① 뒤 문장에서 '대신에, 남들이 이해할 것을 말했다'는 내용이 있으므로 '무작위적인' 소리를 내지는 않았을 것임을 알 수 있다.
② 앞 문장에는 원시 조상들의 의사소통이 언급되었고 뒤 문장에는 언어의 진화에 대해 언급하고 있으므로 'origins(기원)'라는 단어는 자연스러운 맥락에서 사용되었다.
③ 대화가 언어의 목적이라는 주제를 가지고 있는 글이므로 대화에 '관여한다'는 의미의 engage는 어색하지 않다.
④ 언어의 핵심은 대화라는 주제가 여러 번 언급되었으므로 '목적'이라는 의미의 goal이 알맞게 사용되었다.   주의

R 25~26 ∗반복의 중요성

As kids, / we worked hard at learning to ride a bike; / when we fell off, / we got back on again, / until it became second nature to us. // 아이였을 때 / 우리는 열심히 자전거 타기를 배웠고 / 넘어지면 / 다시 올라탔는데 / 그것이 우리에게 제2의 천성이 될 때까지 그렇게 했다 //
-thing으로 끝나는 대명사는 뒤에서 수식함
But when we try something new / in our adult lives / we'll usually make just one attempt / before judging / whether it's (a) worked. //
그러나 새로운 것을 시도해 볼 때 / 어른으로 살면서 / 우리는 대체로 단 한 번만 시도해 보려고 한다 / 판단하기 전에 / 그것이 잘되었는지 안되었는지 //
조건의 부사절을 이끄는 접속사가 아닌 연결됨
If we don't succeed the first time, / or if it feels a little awkward, / we'll tell ourselves it wasn't a success / rather than giving it (b) another shot. // 만일 우리가 처음에 그것을 성공하지 못하거나 / 혹은 약간 어색한 느낌이 들면 / 그것이 성공이 아니었다고 스스로에게 말할 것이다 / 다시 시도해 보기보다는 //
That's a shame, / because repetition is central / to the process of rewiring our brains. // 25번 단서 1: 성공에 반복이 핵심적인 역할을 함
그것은 애석한 일인데 / 반복이 핵심적이기 때문이다 / 우리 뇌를 재연결하는 과정에서 //
동격의 that
Consider the idea / that your brain has a network of neurons. //
개념을 생각해 보라 / 여러분의 뇌가 뉴런의 연결망을 가지고 있다는 //
복합관계부사(= every time)
They will (c) connect with each other / whenever you remember to use / a brain-friendly feedback technique. //
그것들은 서로 연결되고는 한다 / 여러분이 잊지 않고 사용할 때마다 / 뇌 친화적인 피드백 기술을 // 26번 단서 1: 뇌는 뉴런 연결망을 가지고 있고, 피드백 기술을 사용할 때마다 연결됨
계속적 용법
Those connections / aren't very (d) reliable at first, / which may make your first efforts / a little hit-and-miss. // 그 연결은 / 처음에는 그리 신뢰할 만하지 않고 / 여러분의 첫 번째 시도를 만들 수도 있다 / 다소 마구잡이가 되도록 //
= 앞에 제시된 one을 제외한 모든 것
You might remember / one of the steps involved, / and not the others. // 여러분은 기억할 수도 있다 / 연관된 단계 중 하나를 / 그리고 다른 것들을 (기억하지) 못할 (수도 있다) //
But scientists have a saying: / "neurons that fire together, / wire together." // 26번 단서 2: 활성화되는 뉴런들은 서로 연결된다고 했음
그러나 과학자들은 말한다 / "함께 활성화되는 뉴런들은 / 함께 연결된다."라고 //
In other words, / repetition of an action / (e) blocks(→ reinforces) the connections / between the neurons involved in that action. //
앞에 주격 관계대명사와 be동사 생략
다시 말하자면 / 어떤 행동의 반복은 / 연결을 차단한다(→ 강화한다) / 그 행동에 연관된 뉴런들의 사이들을 //
That means / the more times you try using / that new feedback technique, / the more easily it will come to you / when you need it. // 25번 단서 2: 반복을 거듭할수록 새로운 기술을 보다 쉽게 구사할 수 있음
the+비교급 ~, the+비교급 ...: ~할수록 더 ...하다
그것은 의미한다 / 여러분이 더 여러 차례 사용해 볼수록 / 그 새로운 피드백 기술을 / 그것이 더 쉽게 여러분에게 다가올 것을 / 여러분에게 그것이 필요할 때 //

- nature ⓝ 천성 • give it another shot 다시 시도해 보다
- shame ⓝ 애석한 일, 수치 • repetition ⓝ 반복
- rewire ⓥ 재연결하다, 전선을 다시 배치하다
- consider ⓥ 생각하다, 고려하다 • neuron ⓝ 뉴런, 신경 세포
- technique ⓝ 기술 • reliable ⓐ 신뢰할 만한
- hit-and-miss ⓐ 마구잡이의, 되는대로 하는

아이였을 때, 우리는 열심히 자전거 타기를 배웠고, 넘어지면 다시 올라탔는데, 그것이 우리에게 제2의 천성이 될 때까지 그렇게 했다. 그러나 어른으로 살면서 새로운 것을 시도해 볼 때 우리는 대체로 단 한 번만 시도해 보고 나서 그것이 (a) 잘되었는지 안되었는지 판단하려 한다. 만일 우리가 처음에 그것을 성공하지 못하거나 혹은 약간 어색한 느낌이 들면, (b) 다시 시도해 보기보다는 그것이 성공이 아니었다고 스스로에게 말할 것이다. 그것은 애석한 일인데, 우리 뇌를 재연결하는 과정에서 반복이 핵심적이기 때문이다. 여러분의 뇌가 뉴런의 연결망을 가지고 있다는 개념을 생각해 보라. 여러분이 뇌 친화적인 피드백 기술을 잊지 않고 사용할 때마다 그것들은 서로 (c) 연결되고는 한다. 그 연결은 처음에는 그리 (d) 신뢰할 만하지 않고, 여러분의 첫 번째 시도를 다소 마구잡이가 되도록 할 수도 있다. 여러분은 연관된 단계 중 하나를 기억하고, 다른 것들을 기억하지 못할 수도 있다. 그러나 과학자들은 "함께 활성화되는 뉴런들은 함께 연결된다."라고 말한다. 다시 말하자면, 어떤 행동의 반복은 그 행동에 연관된 뉴런들 사이의 연결을 (e) 차단한다(→ 강화한다). 그것은 여러분이 그 새로운 피드백 기술을 더 여러 차례 사용해 볼수록, 여러분에게 그것이 필요할 때 그것이 더 쉽게 여러분에게 다가올 것을 의미한다.

R 25 정답 ①

윗글의 제목으로 가장 적절한 것은?
① Repeat and You Will Succeed
  반복하면 성공할 것이다
② Be More Curious, Be Smarter
  호기심을 더 갖고 더 똑똑해져라
③ Play Is What Makes Us Human
  놀이가 우리를 인간으로 만드는 것이다
④ Stop and Think Before You Act
  행동하기 전에 멈추고 생각하라
⑤ Growth Is All About Keeping Balance
  균형 유지의 핵심은 성장이다

- 반복이 성공에 핵심적이며, 새로운 기술을 습득하는 데 좋다는 내용
- 호기심은 새로운 기술 강화의 요소로 언급되지 않음
- 자전거 타기를 놀이와 관련시켜 만든 함정
- 섣부른 행동의 문제점에 대한 내용이 아님
- 성장의 핵심이 반복이라는 내용임

왜 정답? ❋❋❋ [정답률 76%]
핵심 소재가 '반복'임을 파악하기!! 꿀팁

아이였을 때 자전거를 타기 위해서 넘어져도 여러 번 반복해서 다시 올라탔다고 하면서, 성공에 반복이 핵심적인 역할을 한다고 말했다. 그리고 반복을 거듭할수록 뇌가 더 잘 기억해서 새로운 기술을 보다 쉽게 구사할 수 있다는 내용이다. 따라서 이 글의 제목으로 가장 적절한 것은 ① '반복하면 성공할 것이다'이다.

왜 오답?
② 호기심이 기술 강화에 있어서 갖는 역할이 언급되지 않았으므로 적절하지 않다.
③ 놀이를 통해서 인간이 발전한다는 것은 글의 흐름상 관련이 없다.
④ 섣부른 행동이 가져올 수 있는 문제에 대한 글이 아니다.
⑤ 균형 유지의 핵심이 성장이라는 것이 아니라 성장의 핵심이 반복이라는 내용이다.

R 26 정답 ⑤

밑줄 친 (a)~(e) 중에서 문맥상 낱말의 쓰임이 적절하지 않은 것은?
① (a) — 한 번의 시도 후에 성공인지 아닌지
  잘되다   성급히 결론을 내리려 함
② (b) 또 하나의
③ (c) 뇌 친화적 피드백 기술을 사용할수록
  연결하다   뉴런 간의 연결이 이루어짐
④ (d) 뉴런 간의 연결이 처음에는 어설프거나
  신뢰할 만한 덜 강력할 수 있음
⑤ (e) 반복을 통해 뉴런 간의 연결이 보다 공고해지고 그 결과 기술 습득이 가능하다고 했음
  차단하다

왜 정답? ❋❋❋ [정답률 64%]
뇌는 뉴런 연결망을 가지고 있고, 피드백 기술을 사용할 때마다 연결된다고 했다. 활성화되는 뉴런들은 서로 연결된다고 했으므로 어떤 일을 반복하면 뉴런들이 연결되는 것이 '강화되어' 그 결과 기술 습득을 용이하게 해 줄 것이다. 따라서 ⑤ (e) blocks(차단하다)를 reinforces(강화하다) 등의 낱말로 바꿔야 한다.

왜 오답?
① 어릴 때와 달리 성인이 되면 한 번 시도 후에 성공 여부를 성급히 결론을 내리려 한다는 내용이다.
② 재도전할 수도 있는데 실패로 결론을 내리는 경향이 있다고 했다.
③ 뇌 친화적 피드백 기술의 반복은 뉴런을 서로 연결시킨다는 내용이다.
④ 초반 시도에서는 뉴런 간의 연결이 어설프거나 덜 강력할 수 있다는 맥락이다.

R 27~28 *눈과 뇌의 협력의 결과인 시각

Mike May lost his sight / at the age of three. //
Mike May는 자신의 시력을 잃었다 / 세 살 때 //

Because he had spent the majority of his life / adapting to being blind / — and even cultivating a skiing career in this state — /
병렬 구조
그는 자신의 인생의 대부분을 보냈기 때문에 / 보이지 않는 것에 적응하는 데 / 그리고 심지어 이 상태에서 스키 경력을 쌓는 데 (보냈기 때문에) //

his other senses compensated / by growing (a) stronger. //
by v-ing: ~함으로써
그의 다른 감각들은 보충되었다 / 더 강해지는 것을 통해 //

28번 단서 1: 시력이 회복되었을 때 전반적 인식이 방해받았음
However, / when his sight was restored through a surgery / in his forties, / his entire perception of reality was (b) disrupted. //
그러나 / 그의 시력이 수술을 통해 회복되었을 때 / 40대에 / 그의 현실에 대한 전반적 인식은 방해받았다 //

27번 단서 1: 시력이 회복된 후 뇌에 과부하가 걸려서 세상은 두려운 장소가 되었음
Instead of being thrilled that he could see now, / as he'd expected, / his brain was so overloaded with new visual stimuli / that the world became a frightening and overwhelming place. //
동명사의 수동태
so ~ that...: 너무 ~해서 …하다
이제 볼 수 있다는 것에 감격하는 대신 / 그가 예상했던 것처럼 / 그의 뇌가 새로운 시각적 자극으로 너무 과부하가 걸려서 / 세상은 두렵고 압도적인 장소가 되었다 //

After he'd learned to know his family / through touch and smell, / he found that he couldn't recognize his children / with his eyes, / and this left him puzzled. //
목적어절 접속사
그가 자신의 가족을 아는 것을 배운 후 / 만지는 것과 냄새를 통해 / 그는 자신의 아이들을 알아볼 수 없다는 것을 알게 되었다 / 자신의 눈으로 / 그리고 이것은 그를 혼란스러운 상태로 남겨 두었다 //

Skiing also became a lot harder / as he struggled to adapt / to the visual stimulation. //
비교급 강조 부사
27번 **28번** 단서 2: 시력을 회복하고 오히려 스키가 어려워짐
스키 또한 훨씬 더 어려워졌다 / 그가 적응하려고 힘쓰면서 / 시각적인 자극에 //

This (c) confusion occurred / because his brain hadn't yet learned to see. //
이 혼란은 일어났다 / 그의 뇌가 아직 보는 것을 배우지 못했기 때문에 //

Though we often tend to assume / our eyes function as video cameras / which relay information to our brain, /
부사절 접속사(양보)
주격 관계대명사
비록 우리는 종종 가정하는 경향이 있지만 / 우리의 눈이 비디오카메라로서 기능한다고 / 우리의 뇌에 정보를 전달하는 /

advances in neuroscientific research have proven / that this is actually not the case. //
목적어절 접속사
27번 **28번** 단서 3: 시력은 우리의 눈과 뇌 사이의 협력적인 노력임
신경 과학 연구의 발전은 증명했다 / 이것이 실제로 그렇지 않다는 것을 //

Instead, / sight is a collaborative effort / between our eyes and our brains, / and the way we process (d) visual reality / depends on the way these two communicate. //
핵심 주어(단수)
단수 동사
대신 / 시력은 협력적인 노력이다 / 우리의 눈과 뇌 사이의 / 그리고 우리가 시각적 현실을 처리하는 방법은 / 이 두 가지가 소통하는 방식에 달려 있다 //

If communication between our eyes and our brains is disturbed, / our perception of reality is altered accordingly. //
만약 우리의 눈과 뇌 사이의 의사소통이 방해된다면 / 현실에 대한 우리의 인식은 그에 따라 바뀐다 //

And because other areas of May's brain had adapted / to process information / primarily through his other senses, /
그리고 May의 뇌의 다른 부분들은 적응했기 때문에 / 정보를 처리하는 것에 / 주로 그의 다른 감각을 통해 /

the process of learning **how to see**(how to-v: ~하는 방법) / was (e) easier(→ harder) / than he'd anticipated. //
보는 방법을 배우는 과정은 / 더 쉬웠다(→ 더 어려웠다) / 그가 예상했던 것보다 //

- majority ⓝ 대다수, 대부분   · adapt ⓥ 적응하다
- cultivate ⓥ 경작하다, (관계를) 쌓다   · state ⓝ 상태
- compensate ⓥ 보상하다, 보충되다   · entire ⓐ 전체의
- perception ⓝ 인식   · disrupt ⓥ 방해하다
- thrilled ⓐ 감격한, 짜릿한
- overload ⓥ (짐을) 너무 많이 싣다, 과부하가 걸리게 하다
- stimulus ⓝ 자극(pl. stimuli)   · overwhelming ⓐ 압도적인
- recognize ⓥ 알아보다, 인식하다   · puzzled ⓐ 혼란스러워하는
- stimulation ⓝ 자극   · confusion ⓝ 혼란, 혼동
- assume ⓥ 가정하다   · function ⓥ 기능하다
- relay ⓥ 전달하다   · neuroscientific ⓐ 신경 과학의
- collaborative ⓐ 협력적인, 공동 작업의   · alter ⓥ 바꾸다, 고치다
- accordingly ⓐd 그에 따라   · anticipate ⓥ 예상하다, 기대하다

Mike May는 세 살 때 자신의 시력을 잃었다. 그는 자신의 인생의 대부분을 보이지 않는 것에 적응하는 데, 그리고 심지어 이 상태에서 스키 경력을 쌓는 데도 보냈기 때문에, 자신의 다른 감각들은 (a) 더 강해지는 것을 통해 보충되었다. 그러나 그의 시력이 40대에 수술을 통해 회복되었을 때, 그의 현실에 대한 전반적 인식은 (b) 방해받았다. 그가 예상했던 것처럼 이제 볼 수 있다는 것에 감격하는 대신, 자신의 뇌가 새로운 시각적 자극으로 너무 과부하가 걸려 세상은 두렵고 압도적인 장소가 되었다. 그가 만지는 것과 냄새를 통해 자신의 가족을 아는 것을 배운 후, 그는 자신의 눈으로 자신의 아이들을 알아볼 수 없다는 것을 알게 되었고 이것은 그를 혼란스러운 상태로 남겨 두었다. 스키 또한 그가 시각적인 자극에 적응하려고 힘쓰면서 훨씬 더 어려워졌다.

이 (c) 혼란은 그의 뇌가 아직 보는 것을 배우지 못했기 때문에 일어났다. 비록 우리는 종종 우리의 눈이 우리의 뇌에 정보를 전달하는 비디오카메라로서 기능한다고 가정하는 경향이 있지만, 신경 과학 연구의 발전은 이것이 실제로 그렇지 않다는 것을 증명했다. 대신, 시력은 우리의 눈과 뇌 사이의 협력적인 노력이며, 우리가 (d) 시각적 현실을 처리하는 방법은 이 두 가지가 소통하는 방식에 달려 있다. 만약 우리의 눈과 뇌 사이의 의사소통이 방해된다면, 현실에 대한 우리의 인식은 그에 따라 바뀐다. 그리고 May의 뇌의 다른 부분들은 주로 그의 다른 감각을 통해 정보를 처리하는 것에 적응했기 때문에, 보는 방법을 배우는 과정은 그가 예상했던 것보다 (e) 더 쉬웠다(→ 더 어려웠다).

R 27 정답 ①

윗글의 제목으로 가장 적절한 것은?
① Eyes and Brain Working Together for Sight
시력을 위해 함께 일하는 눈과 뇌   시력은 눈과 뇌 사이의 협력적인 노력임
② Visualization: A Useful Tool for Learning
시각화: 학습을 위한 유용한 도구   학습을 위해 시각화하는 것에 대한 내용이 아님
③ Collaboration Between Vision and Sound
시각과 소리의 협업   시각과 소리가 아니라 눈과 뇌의 협업에 대한 내용임
④ How to Ignore New Visual Stimuli
새로운 시각적 자극을 무시하는 방법   시각적 자극을 무시하라는 내용이 아님
⑤ You See What You Believe
당신은 당신이 믿는 것을 본다   믿는 대로 보게 된다는 내용이 아님

| 문제 풀이 순서 | **✱✱❊** [정답률 75%]

1st 글의 앞부분을 읽으며 이어질 내용을 예상한다.

| 글의 앞부분 | Mike May는 세 살 때 자신의 시력을 잃었다. 그는 자신의 인생의 대부분을 보이지 않는 것에 적응하는 데, 그리고 심지어 이 상태에서 스키 경력을 쌓는 데도 보냈기 때문에, 자신의 다른 감각들은 (a) 더 강해지는 것을 통해 보충되었다. |

➡ 어렸을 때 시력을 잃은 Mike May는 보이지 않는 것에 적응하며 스키 경력을 쌓았는데, 이는 다른 감각들이 더 강해져 시각을 보충했기 때문이다. **단서**
따라서 시각을 보충하는 다른 감각들과 관련된 내용일 것이다. **발상**

2nd **1st** 에서 발상한 것을 토대로 글을 읽고, 내용을 파악한다.

- 시력이 회복됐을 때 현실에 대한 인식은 방해받았다. ➡ 세상은 두렵고 압도적인 장소가 되었다. **27번 단서 1**
- 시각적 자극에 적응하려 하자 스키도 어려워졌다. **27번 단서 2**

➡ 그의 시력은 회복되었지만, 뇌가 전에는 없던 새로운 시각적 자극으로 과부하가 걸려 세상은 두려워졌고 스키를 타는 것도 어려워졌다.
▶ 즉, 시각은 눈과 뇌가 함께 작용하는 것임

3rd 글의 주제에 알맞은 제목을 고른다.

시력은 눈과 뇌 사이의 협력적인 노력이며, 이들이 소통하는 방식에 시각적 현실 처리 방법이 달라진다. **27번 단서 3**
➡ 시력은 눈과 뇌 사이의 협력적인 노력이며, 그 소통을 통해 현실을 인식하게 된다고 말하는 글이다.
▶ 따라서 글의 제목으로 가장 적절한 것은 ① '시력을 위해 함께 일하는 눈과 뇌'이다.

| 선택지 분석 |
① 시력은 눈과 뇌 사이의 협력적인 노력이라고 했다.
② 학습을 위해 시각화를 활용하라고 말하는 글이 아니다.
③ 시각과 소리가 아니라 눈과 뇌의 협업에 관해 설명하는 글이다.
④ Mike May가 시각적 자극 때문에 과부하가 걸렸다고 했지, 이를 무시하라는 내용이 아니다.
⑤ 믿는 대로 보게 된다는 것은 언급되지 않았다.

R 28 정답 ⑤

밑줄 친 (a)~(e) 중에서 문맥상 낱말의 쓰임이 적절하지 않은 것은?
① (a) 시력을 잃은 상태로 스키를 타면 다른 감각들은 더 강해질 것임
더 강한
② (b) 시력이 회복된 후 뇌에 과부하가 생겼으므로 인식이 방해받은 것임
방해받다
③ (c) 시력을 회복하고 혼란스러워졌다고 했음
혼란
④ (d) 시각적인 인식을 위해 눈과 뇌가 협력해야 함
시각적인
⑤ (e) 시력을 되찾은 후 스키 타는 것이 더 어려워졌다고 했음
더 쉬운

왜 정답? **✱✱❊** [정답률 64%]

⑤ (e) easier 더 쉬운

그리고 May의 뇌의 다른 부분들은 주로 그의 다른 감각을 통해 정보를 처리하는 것에 적응했기 때문에, 보는 방법을 배우는 과정은 그가 예상했던 것보다 (e) ~~더 쉬웠다~~.
더 어려웠다

➡ May가 시력을 되찾은 후에도 시각이 아닌 감각들로 정보를 처리하는 것에 익숙했다고 했으므로 보는 방법을 배우는 과정이 '더 쉬웠다'고 하는 것은 문맥에 맞지 않는다.
▶ easier를 harder(더 어려운)와 같은 반의어로 바꿔야 함

① (a) stronger 더 강한

그는 자신의 인생의 대부분을 보이지 않는 것에 적응하는 데, 그리고 심지어 이 상태에서 스키 경력을 쌓는 데도 보냈기 때문에, 자신의 다른 감각들은 (a) 더 강해지는 것을 통해 보충되었다.

➜ 시력이 없는 상태로 스키 경력을 쌓는 데 인생의 대부분을 보냈다고 했으므로 다른 감각들은 '더 강해'졌을 것이다.

▶ stronger는 문맥에 맞음

② (b) disrupted 방해받다

그러나 그의 시력이 40대에 수술을 통해 회복되었을 때, 그의 현실에 대한 전반적 인식은 (b) 방해받았다.

그가 예상했던 것처럼 이제 볼 수 있다는 것에 감격하는 대신, 자신의 뇌가 새로운 시각적 자극으로 너무 과부하가 걸려 세상은 두렵고 압도적인 장소가 되었다.

➜ 시력이 회복된 후 뇌에 과부하가 생겼다고 했으므로 현실에 대한 인식은 '방해받은' 것이라고 할 수 있다.

▶ disrupted는 문맥에 맞음

③ (c) confusion 혼란

그가 만지는 것과 냄새를 통해 자신의 가족을 아는 것을 배운 후, 그는 자신의 눈으로 자신의 아이들을 알아볼 수 없다는 것을 알게 되었고 이것은 그를 혼란스러운 상태로 남겨 두었다. 스키 또한 그가 시각적인 자극에 적응하려고 힘쓰면서 훨씬 더 어려워졌다.

이 (c) 혼란은 그의 뇌가 아직 보는 것을 배우지 못했기 때문에 일어났다.

➜ 시력을 회복한 후 눈으로 아이들을 알아볼 수 없고 스키도 훨씬 더 어려워졌기 때문에 '혼란'이 생겼다고 했다.

▶ confusion은 문맥에 맞음

④ (d) visual 시각적인

대신, 시력은 우리의 눈과 뇌 사이의 협력적인 노력이며, 우리가 (d) 시각적 현실을 처리하는 방법은 이 두 가지가 소통하는 방식에 달려 있다.

➜ 시력은 눈과 뇌 사이의 협력적인 노력이라고 했으므로 '시각적' 현실을 처리하는 방법은 눈과 뇌의 소통 방식에 달려 있을 것이다.

▶ visual은 문맥에 맞음

R 29~30 *그룹 행동에서 드러나는 인간의 본성

A ball **thrown into the air** / is acted upon by the initial force
과거분사구
given it, / **persisting** as inertia of movement / and **tending** to
과거분사구 분사구문을 이끎   병렬 구조
carry it in the same straight line, /
공중으로 던져진 공은 / 초기에 그것에 주어진 힘에 의해 움직여지는데 / 운동의 관성으로 지속하며 / 같은 직선으로 나아가려는 경향을 보이고 /

and by the constant pull of gravity downward, / as well as by the resistance of the air. //
아래로 지속적으로 당기는 중력에 의해서도 움직여진다 / 공기의 저항뿐만 아니라 //

It moves, accordingly, / in a (a) **curved** path. //
그에 맞춰 공은 움직인다 / 곡선의 경로로 //

Now the path does not represent / the working of any particular force; /
이제 그 경로는 나타내지는 않는다 / 어떤 특정한 힘의 작동을 /

there is simply the (b) **combination** / of the three elementary forces **mentioned**; /
과거분사(forces 수식)
결합이 존재할 뿐이다 / 언급된 세 가지 기본적인 힘의 /

but in a real sense, / there is something in the total action / besides the isolated action of three forces, / namely, their joint action. // **29번** 단서 1: 공의 움직임은 세 가지 힘의 각각의 작용 외에도 공동 작용으로 일어남
30번 단서 1: 개별적인 힘에만 집중하면 볼 수 없는 공동 작용이 존재함
하지만 사실은 / 전체적인 작용에 무언가가 있는데 / 세 가지 힘의 고립된 작용 외에 / 이름하여 그들의 공동 작용이다 //

In the same way, / when two or more human individuals are together, / their mutual relationships and their arrangement into a group /
같은 방식으로 / 두 명 혹은 그 이상의 인간 개인이 같이 있을 때 / 그들의 상호 관계와 그들의 집단으로의 배치는 //

                  주격 관계대명사
are things **which** would not be (c) **concealed(→ revealed)** / if we confined our attention to each individual separately. //
감춰지지(→ 드러나지) 않을 것이다 / 만약 우리가 관심을 개별적으로 각각의 개인에게 국한시킨다면 //

The significance of group behavior / is greatly (d) **increased** in the case of human beings / by the fact /
그룹 행동의 중요성이 / 인간의 경우 크게 증가된다 / 사실로 인해 /

동격절 접속사
that some of the tendencies to action of the individual / are related definitely to other persons, / and could not be aroused /
                         현재분사(other persons 수식)
except by other persons **acting** as stimuli. //
개인 행동의 몇몇 경향은 / 명백하게 다른 사람들과 관련이 있고 / 유발되지 않을 수 있다는 / 자극으로 작동하는 다른 사람들 없이는 // **30번** 단서 2: 고립된 인간은 자신의 본성을 드러내지 않으며, 다른 사람들과의 관계 속에서만 본성이 드러남

An individual in complete (e) **isolation** / would not reveal / their competitive tendencies, / their tendencies towards the opposite sex, / their protective tendencies towards children. //
완전한 고립 속의 개인은 / 드러내지 않을 것이다 / 그들의 경쟁적인 성향 / 이성에 대한 그들의 성향 / 아이에 대한 그들의 보호적 성향을 //

                명사절 접속사
This shows / **that** the traits of human nature do not fully appear / until the individual is brought into relationships with other individuals. // **29번** 단서 2: 마찬가지로, 인간의 본성은 다른 개인과의 관계 속에서 완전히 드러남
이것은 보여 준다 / 인간 본성의 특성이 완전히 나타나지 않는다는 것을 / 개인이 다른 개인과의 관계에 관여될 때까지는 //

- **persist** ⓥ 지속하다
- **tend to** ~하는 경향이 있다
- **constant** ⓐ 지속적인
- **downward** ⓐ 아래로
- **resistance** ⓝ 저항
- **accordingly** ⓐ 그에 따라
- **represent** ⓥ 나타내다
- **combination** ⓝ 결합
- **elementary** ⓐ 기본적인
- **besides** prep ~ 외에
- **isolated** ⓐ 고립된
- **joint** ⓐ 공동의
- **mutual** ⓐ 상호의
- **arrangement** ⓝ 배치
- **conceal** ⓥ 감추다, 숨기다
- **confine** ⓥ 제한하다, 국한하다
- **attention** ⓝ 관심
- **separately** ⓐ 개별적으로
- **significance** ⓝ 중요성
- **tendency** ⓝ 경향
- **definitely** ⓐ 명백히
- **stimulus** ⓝ 자극 (pl. stimuli)
- **competitive** ⓐ 경쟁적인
- **human nature** 인간 본성

공중으로 던져진 공은 초기에 그것에 주어진 힘에 의해 움직여지는데, 운동의 관성으로 지속하며 같은 직선으로 나아가려는 경향을 보이고, 공기의 저항뿐만 아니라 아래로 지속적으로 당기는 중력에 의해서도 움직여진다. 그에 맞춰 공은 (a) 곡선의 경로로 움직인다. 이제 그 경로는 어떤 특정한 힘의 작동을 나타내지는 않는다. 언급된 세 가지 기본적인 힘의 (b) 결합이 존재할 뿐이다. 하지만 사실은 세 가지 힘의 고립된 작용 외에 전체적인 작용에 무언가가 있는데, 이름하여 그들의 공동 작용이다. 같은 방식으로, 두 명 혹은 그 이상의 인간 개인이 같이 있을 때 그들의 상호 관계와 그들의 집단으로의 배치는 만약 우리가 관심을 개별적으로 각각의 개인에게 국한시킨다면 (c) 감춰지지(→ 드러나지) 않을 것들이다. 개인 행동의 몇몇 경향은 명백하게 다른 사람들과 관련이 있고 자극으로 작동하는 다른 사람들 없이는 유발되지 않을 수 있다는 사실로 인해 그룹 행동의 중요성이 인간의 경우 크게 (d) 증가된다. 완전한 (e) 고립 속의 개인은 그들의 경쟁적인 성향, 이성에 대한 그들의 성향, 아이에 대한 그들의 보호적 성향을 드러내지 않을 것이다. 이것은 개인이 다른 개인과의 관계에 관여될 때까지는 인간 본성의 특성이 완전히 나타나지 않는다는 것을 보여 준다.

R 29 정답 ⑤

윗글의 제목으로 가장 적절한 것은?

① Common Misunderstandings in Physics
물리학의 흔한 오해들 / 물리학에 비유하여 인간의 그룹 행동을 설명한 글임
② Collaboration: A Key to Success in Relationships
협력: 관계에서의 성공의 열쇠 / 협력에 대한 언급은 없음
③ Interpersonal Traits and Their Impact on Science
대인관계의 특성과 그들이 과학에 미치는 영향 / 대인관계의 특성이 과학에 미치는 영향은 언급되지 않음
④ Unbalanced Forces Causing Objects to Accelerate
물체의 가속을 일으키는 불균형한 힘들 / 물체에 가해지는 힘은 인간의 그룹 행동을 설명하기 위한 비유일 뿐이었음
⑤ Human Traits Uncovered by Interpersonal Relationships
대인관계로 드러나는 인간의 특성들 / 인간이 다른 사람들과 관계를 맺으며 드러나는 특성들을 설명한 글임

왜 정답 ? ★★★ [정답률 53%]

- 공의 움직임은 세 가지 힘의 각각의 작용 외에도 공동 작용으로 일어남 **29번 단서 1**
- 마찬가지로, 인간의 본성은 다른 개인과의 관계 속에서 완전히 드러남 **29번 단서 2**
→ **그룹 행동에서 드러나는 인간의 본성**
  비유: 공을 하늘에 던졌을 때 개별적으로 작용하는 힘 외에도 그 힘들이 합쳐져서 공동 작용이 발생함
  주제: 인간의 본성도 이와 마찬가지로, 고립될 때는 드러나지 않던 본성들이 다른 사람들과의 관계 속에서 드러남
  ▶ 따라서 제목으로 가장 적절한 것은 ⑤ '대인관계로 드러나는 인간의 특성들'이다.

왜 오답 ?

① 물리학에 비유하여 그룹 속에서의 인간의 특성을 설명한 글이다.
② 협력에 대한 언급은 없다.
③ 대인관계의 특성이 과학에 미치는 영향에 대한 언급은 없다.
④ 물체의 가속을 일으키는 힘들에 관한 글이 아니다. (☞ 이유: 물체에 가해지는 힘은 그룹 속에서의 인간의 행동을 설명하기 위한 비유일 뿐이다.)

R 30 정답 ③

밑줄 친 (a)~(e) 중에서 문맥상 낱말의 쓰임이 적절하지 <u>않은</u> 것은?
[3점]

① (a) curved 곡선의 / 공중으로 던져진 공은 직선으로 나아가다가 아래로 떨어지므로 곡선으로 움직임
② (b) 운동의 관성, 공기의 저항, 중력이 결합하여 운동을 만들어냄 결합
③ (c) 감춰지다 / 개인에게만 초점을 맞추면 그 특성이 드러나지 않음
④ (d) 인간에게는 그룹 행동의 중요성이 증가됨 증가된다
⑤ (e) 인간은 고립 상태에서는 그들의 본성을 드러내지 않음 고립

왜 정답 ? ★★★ [정답률 45%]

③ (c) concealed 감춰지다

같은 방식으로(In the same way), 두 명 혹은 그 이상의 인간 개인이 같이 있을 때 그들의 상호 관계와 그들의 집단으로의 배치는 만약 우리가 관심을 개별적으로 각각의 개인에게 국한시킨다면 (c) ~~감춰지지~~ **드러나지** 않을 것들이다.

→ 앞서 공에 가해지는 힘의 비유에서 개별적인 힘들 외에도 공동 작용이 존재한다고 설명했으므로, 인간도 개인에게만 초점을 맞추면 그 특성이 '드러나지' 않을 것이라고 해야 흐름이 자연스럽다.
  ▶ concealed를 revealed(드러나다)와 같은 반의어로 바꿔야 함

왜 오답 ?

① (a) curved 곡선의
그에 맞춰 공은 (a) 곡선의 경로로 움직인다.
→ 공중으로 던져진 공은 운동의 관성에 의해 직선으로 나아가다가 공기의 저항, 아래로 당기는 중력 등이 작용하여 땅으로 떨어지게 되므로 '곡선의' 경로로 움직인다. ▶ curved는 문맥에 맞음

② (b) combination 결합
언급된 세 가지 기본적인 힘의 (b) 결합이 존재할 뿐이다.
→ 공이 곡선의 경로로 움직이는 것은 운동의 관성, 공기의 저항, 중력이 각각 작용한 것이 아니라 세 힘이 '결합'하여 운동을 만들어낸 것이다.
  ▶ combination은 문맥에 맞음

④ (d) increased 증가된다
개인 행동의 몇몇 경향은 명백하게 다른 사람들과 관련이 있고 자극으로 작동하는 다른 사람들 없이는 유발되지 않을 수 있다는 사실로 인해 그룹 행동의 중요성이 인간의 경우 크게 (d) 증가된다.
→ 인간도 그룹 속에서 다른 사람들과 관계를 맺을 때 개인의 행동 경향이 드러나게 되므로, 인간에게는 그룹 행동의 중요성이 '증가된다'는 내용이다.
  ▶ increased는 문맥에 맞음

⑤ (e) isolation 고립
완전한 (e) 고립 속의 개인은 그들의 경쟁적인 성향, 이성에 대한 그들의 성향, 아이에 대한 그들의 보호적 성향을 드러내지 않을 것이다.
→ 인간이 다른 사람들과 관계를 전혀 맺지 않고 있는 완전한 '고립' 상태에서는 그들의 본성을 드러내지 않을 것이라는 내용이다. ▶ isolation은 문맥에 맞음

[자이 쌤's Follow Me! – 홈페이지에서 제공]

R 31~32 *취침 시간이 심장 질환에 미치는 영향

뒤에 목적어절을 이끄는 접속사 that 생략
<u>U.K. researchers say</u> / a bedtime of between 10 p.m. and 11 p.m. / is best. //
영국 연구원들은 이야기한다 / 밤 10시와 밤 11시 사이의 취침 시간이 / 가장 좋다고 //

주격 관계대명사
They say / people <u>who</u> go to sleep between these times / have a (a) <u>lower</u> risk of heart disease. //
그들은 이야기한다 / 이 시간대 사이에 잠드는 사람들이 / 더 낮은 심장 질환의 위험성을 가지고 있다고 // **31번** 단서 1: 밤 10시와 11시 사이에 취침하는 사람들은 심장 질환의 위험성이 더 낮음

Six years ago, / the researchers collected data / on the sleep patterns of 80,000 volunteers. //
6년 전 / 그 연구원들은 데이터를 수집했다 / 8만 명의 자원자들의 수면 패턴에 대한 //

The volunteers had to wear a special watch / for seven days / so the researchers could collect data / on their sleeping and waking times. //
그 자원자들은 특별한 시계를 착용해야만 했다 / 7일간 / 그래서 그 연구원들은 데이터를 수집할 수 있었다 / 그들의 수면과 기상 시간에 대한 //

The scientists then monitored / the health of the volunteers. //
그리고 나서 연구원들은 관찰했다 / 그 자원자들의 건강에 대해 //

Around 3,000 volunteers / later showed heart problems. //
약 3천 명의 자원자들이 / 이후에 심장 문제를 보였다 //

비교급 표현
They went to bed <u>earlier</u> or <u>later</u> / <u>than</u> the (b) ideal 10 p.m. to 11 p.m. timeframe. // **31번** 단서 2, **32번** 단서 1: 심장 문제를 보인 사람들은 이상적인 시간대에 잠들지 않음
그들은 더 이른 혹은 더 늦은 시간에 잠자리에 들었다 / 밤 10시에서 밤 11시 사이의 이상적인 시간대보다 /

「one of+복수 명사: ~ 중 하나」
<u>One of the authors</u> of the study, / Dr. David Plans, / commented / on his research / and the (c) effects of bedtimes on the health of our heart. //
그 연구 저작자 중 한 명인 / Dr. David Plans는 / 언급했다 / 그의 연구에 대해 / 그리고 우리의 심장 건강에 취침 시간이 끼치는 영향(에 대해) //

He said / the study could not give a certain cause / for their results, /
그는 이야기했다 / 그 연구가 특정한 원인을 제시할 수는 없다고 / 그들의 결과에 / **32번** 단서 2: 이른 혹은 늦은 취침 시간은 체내 시계를 혼란케 할 가능성을 높임

목적어절을 이끄는 접속사
but it suggests / <u>that</u> early or late bedtimes / may be more likely to disrupt the body clock, / with (d) positive (→ negative) consequences for cardiovascular health. //
하지만 그 연구가 제시한다고 / 이른 혹은 늦은 취침 시간이 / 체내 시계를 혼란케 할 가능성이 더 높을 수 있다고 / 심장 혈관 건강에 긍정적인(→ 부정적인) 결과와 함께 //

R

He said / that **it** was important **for our body to wake up** / to the morning light, / and that the worst time **to go** to bed / was after midnight /

가주어 / to부정사의 의미상 주어 / 진주어 / 형용사적 용법

그는 이야기했다 / 우리의 몸이 일어나는 것이 중요하고 / 아침 빛에 맞추어 / 잠자리에 드는 가장 나쁜 시간이 / 자정 이후인데 /

because it may (e) reduce the likelihood / of seeing morning light / **which** resets the body clock. //

주격 관계대명사

그것은 가능성을 낮출 수도 있기 때문이다 / 아침 빛을 볼 / 우리의 체내 시계를 재설정하는 //

He added / that we risk cardiovascular disease / if our body clock **is not reset** properly. //

수동태

32번 단서 3: 체내 시계가 적절하게 재설정되지 않으면 심장 혈관 질환의 위험을 갖게 됨

그는 덧붙였다 / 우리가 심장 혈관 질환의 위험을 안게 된다고 / 만약 우리의 체내 시계가 적절하게 재설정되지 않으면 //

- risk ⓝ 위험
- disease ⓝ 질환, 질병
- monitor ⓥ 관찰하다
- ideal ⓐ 이상적인
- timeframe ⓝ 시간대
- author ⓝ 저자
- cause ⓝ 원인
- suggest ⓥ 제시하다
- be likely to-v ~할 가능성이 있다
- body clock ⓝ 체내 시계(하루 중 특정 시간에 잠을 자야 하는 등의 신체적 자연 현상을 관장하는 몸의 기능)
- consequence ⓝ 결과
- midnight ⓝ 자정
- likelihood ⓝ 가능성
- reset ⓥ 재설정하다
- properly ⓐⓓ 적절하게
- reflect ⓥ 반영하다
- personality ⓝ 성격

영국 연구원들은 밤 10시와 밤 11시 사이의 취침 시간이 가장 좋다고 이야기한다. 그들은 이 시간대 사이에 잠드는 사람들이 (a) 더 낮은 심장 질환의 위험성을 가지고 있다고 이야기한다. 6년 전, 그 연구원들은 8만 명의 자원자들의 수면 패턴 데이터를 수집했다. 그 자원자들은 7일간 특별한 시계를 착용해야만 했고 그래서 그 연구원들은 그들의 수면과 기상 시간에 대한 데이터를 수집할 수 있었다. 그리고 나서 연구원들은 그 자원자들의 건강에 대해 관찰했다. 약 3천 명의 자원자들이 이후에 심장 문제를 보였다. 그들은 밤 10시에서 밤 11시 사이의 (b) 이상적인 시간대보다 더 이른 혹은 더 늦은 시간에 잠자리에 들었다.

그 연구 저자 중 한 명인, Dr. David Plans는 그의 연구와 우리의 심장 건강에 취침 시간이 끼치는 (c) 영향에 대해 언급했다. 그는 그 연구가 그들의 결과에 특정한 원인을 제시할 수는 없지만, 이른 혹은 늦은 취침 시간이 심장 혈관 건강에 (d) 긍정적인(→ 부정적인) 결과와 함께 체내 시계를 혼란케 할 가능성이 더 높을 수 있다고 그 연구가 제시한다고 이야기했다. 그는 우리의 몸이 아침 빛에 맞추어 일어나는 것이 중요하고, 잠자리에 드는 가장 나쁜 시간이 자정 이후인데 그것은 우리의 체내 시계를 재설정하는 아침 빛을 볼 가능성을 (e) 낮출 수도 있기 때문이다. 그는 만약 우리의 체내 시계가 적절하게 재설정되지 않으면 우리가 심장 혈관 질환의 위험을 안게 된다고 덧붙였다.

R 31 정답 ①

윗글의 제목으로 가장 적절한 것은?

① **The Best Bedtime for Your Heart**
심장에 가장 좋은 취침 시간　　밤 10시와 밤 11시 사이에 잠들면 심장 질환의 위험성이 낮아짐
② Late Bedtimes Are a Matter of Age
늦은 취침 시간은 나이 문제이다　　나이와 취침 시간의 관련성을 설명하는 내용이 아님
③ For Sound Sleep: Turn Off the Light
숙면을 위하여: 불을 끄세요　　숙면을 위한 방법이 제시되어 있지 않음
④ Sleeping Patterns Reflect Personalities
수면 패턴은 성격을 반영한다　　연구에서 자원자들의 수면 패턴을 수집했다는 내용을 이용해 만든 함정
⑤ Regular Exercise: A Miracle for Good Sleep
규칙적인 운동: 숙면을 위한 기적　　운동이 잠에 미치는 영향은 언급되지 않음

>왜 정답? ★★☆ [정답률 85%]

밤 10시와 밤 11시 사이에 잠드는 사람들이 심장 질환의 위험성이 더 낮다고 이야기하는 영국 연구원들이 있다고 했다. 이 연구원들이 했던 연구에 참여한 자원자들 중에서 심장 문제를 가진 사람들은 이 시간대보다 이른 혹은 늦은 시간에 잠들었는데, 취침 시간에 따라 체내 시계가 영향을 받고 심장 혈관 질환의 위험을 높일 수 있다는 것을 보여줬다고 했다.

따라서 밤 10시와 밤 11시 사이에 취침하면 심장 질환의 위험성을 낮춘다는 것이 핵심 내용이므로 ① '심장에 가장 좋은 취침 시간'이 글의 제목으로 가장 적절하다.

>왜 오답?

② 나이와 취침 시간의 관련성을 설명하고 있는 내용이 아니다.
③ 불을 끄면 숙면을 할 수 있다는 내용을 말하는 글이 아니다.
④ 자원자들의 수면 패턴을 수집했다는 내용을 이용하여 만든 함정이다. ◀주의
⑤ 운동이 잠에 미치는 영향을 설명한 글이 아니다.

R 32 정답 ④

밑줄 친 (a)~(e) 중에서 문맥상 낱말의 쓰임이 적절하지 않은 것은?

① (a) 밤 10시에서 밤 11시 사이의 취침 시간이 가장 좋다고 했음 → 더 낮은
② (b) 밤 10시에서 밤 11시 사이가 취침 시간으로 가장 좋다고 했기 때문에 이 때가 이상적인 시간대임 → 이상적인
③ (c) Dr. David Plans는 취침 시간이 심장 질환에 미치는 영향을 설명함 → 영향
④ (d) 이른 혹은 늦은 취침 시간이 체내 시계를 혼란케 할 수 있고 심장 혈관 건강에 부정적인 영향을 줌 → 긍정적인
⑤ (e) 자정 이후에 잠들면 늦게 일어나게 되어 아침 빛을 볼 가능성을 낮출 수 있음 → 낮추다

>왜 정답? ★★☆ [정답률 73%]

Dr. David Plans는 이른 혹은 늦은 취침 시간이 체내 시계를 혼란케 할 가능성을 더 높일 수 있다는 것을 연구가 제시한다고 말했다. 글의 후반부에는 체내 시계가 적절하게 재설정되지 않으면 심장 혈관 질환의 위험을 갖게 된다는 내용이 이어진다.

따라서 이른 혹은 늦은 취침 시간이 심장 혈관 건강에 '부정적인' 결과와 함께 체내 시계를 혼란케 할 가능성이 더 높을 수 있다고 해야 한다. 따라서 ④ positive (긍정적인)를 negative(부정적인)와 같은 낱말로 바꾸는 것이 문맥상 적절하다.

>왜 오답?

① 앞에서 밤 10시와 밤 11시 사이의 취침 시간이 가장 좋다는 내용이 나오므로, 이 시간대에 잠드는 사람들이 더 '낮은' 심장 질환의 위험성을 가진다고 하는 것은 문맥상 적절하다.
② 영국의 연구원들이 밤 10시에서 밤 11시 사이에 취침하는 것이 가장 좋다고 말하기 때문에 이 시간대를 '이상적인' 시간대라고 할 것이다.
③ Dr. David Plans가 취침 시간이 체내 시계와 심장 혈관 질환에 미치는 영향을 설명했기 때문에 그는 우리의 심장 건강에 취침 시간이 끼치는 '영향'에 대해 언급했다고 볼 수 있다.
⑤ 자정 이후에 잠들면 늦게 일어날 가능성이 높기 때문에, 우리가 아침 빛을 볼 가능성을 '낮출' 수 있다고 한 것은 문맥상 자연스럽다.

✱ 수면과 수면 장애　　─ 배경 지식 ─

수면은 뇌의 활동에 의해 이뤄지지만 다른 신체 부위들의 생리학적 변화와도 많이 연관되어 있다. 수면은 비렘수면(non-rapid eye movement-sleep)과 렘수면 (rapid eye movement-sleep)으로 나뉘는데, 정상적인 성인이 밤에 잘 때 수면은 이 비렘수면과 렘수면이 돌아가며 4~6회의 주기가 반복된다. 수면이 시작되고 난 후에 80~100분에 첫 번째 렘수면이 나타나고, 그 후에는 비렘수면과 렘수면이 대략 90분을 주기로 반복된다.

인구의 약 20% 이상이 수면 장애를 앓은 적이 있거나 앓고 있다고 한다. 그만큼 수면 장애는 꽤 흔한 질환인데, 수면 장애는 크게는 교통사고나 안전사고를 일으킬 수 있고, 작게는 학습 장애를 일으키거나 일의 능률을 저하시킬 수 있다.

＊고객의 불평 수용을 통한 제품의 변화

The market's way / of telling a firm / about its failures / is harsh and brief. //
> 33번 단서 1: 고객의 불평을 잘 다루고 받아들이면 판매자가 향상되도록 만들 수도 있음

시장의 방식은 / 회사에 말해주는 / 실패에 대해 / 가혹하면서 간단하다 //

Not only are complaints less expensive / to handle / **but** they **also** can cause / the seller to (a) improve. //
> not only A but also B: A뿐만 아니라 B도

불평은 비용이 덜 들뿐 아니라 / 다루기에 / 만들 수도 있다 / 판매자가 향상되도록 //

The seller may learn something / as well. //

판매자는 어떤 교훈을 얻을지도 모른다 / 또한 //

I remember a cosmetics company / **that** received complaints / about sticky sunblock lotion. //
> 주격 관계대명사

나는 한 화장품 회사를 기억한다 / 불평을 받은 / 끈적거리는 선크림 로션에 대한 //

At the time, / all such lotions were more or less sticky, / so the **risk** / of having customers buy products / from a rival company / **was** not (b) great. //
> 핵심 주어 / 동사

그 당시에 / 그러한 로션은 모두 다소 끈적거렸고 / 그래서 위험은 / 고객들이 제품을 사게 하는 / 경쟁사의 / 크지 않았다 //

But / this was also an opportunity. //

하지만 / 이것은 또한 기회였다 //
> 33번 단서 2: 선크림 로션이 끈적거린다는 불평을 수용하고 새로운 제품을 개발해낸 회사는 시장의 20퍼센트를 점유했음

The company **managed** to develop a product / **that** was not sticky / and **captured** 20 percent of the market / in its first year. //
> 병렬 구조 / 주격 관계대명사

그 회사는 제품을 개발해냈다 / 끈적거리지 않는 / 그리고 시장의 20퍼센트를 점유했다 / 첫해에 //

Another company / had the (c) opposite problem. //

또 다른 회사는 / 반대의 문제를 가졌다 //

Its products were not sticky / enough. //

그 회사의 상품은 끈적거리지 않았다 / 충분히 //

The company was a Royal Post Office in Europe / and the product was a stamp. //

그 회사는 유럽에 있는 Royal Post Office였고 / 상품은 우표였다 //
> 주격 보어절을 이끄는 접속사

The problem was / **that** the stamp didn't stick to the envelope. //

문제는 / 우표가 편지 봉투에 붙지 않았다는 것이다 //
> 주격 관계대명사

Management contacted the stamp producer / **who** made it clear **that** / if people just moistened the stamps properly, / they would stick to any piece of paper. //
> 목적어절을 이끄는 접속사

경영진은 우표 제작자에게 연락했다 / 그는 명확히 밝혔다 / 만약 사람들이 우표를 적절히 적시기만 한다면 / 우표가 어떤 종이에도 달라붙을 것이라고 //

What to do? //

어떻게 할까 //
> 34번 단서 1: 풀을 더 첨가하는 것보다 우표를 적시도록 고객들을 교육하려고 하는 방식이 비용 면에서 어떤지 판단해야 함

Management didn't take long / to come to the conclusion / **that** it would be (d) less (→ more) costly / **to try** to educate its customers / to wet each stamp / **rather than** to add more glue. //
> 동격의 that / 가주어 / 진주어 / ~하기 보다

경영진은 오래 걸리지 않았다 / 결론에 도달하는 데에는 / 비용이 덜(→ 더) 들 것이라는 / 고객을 교육하려고 하는 것에 / 우표를 적시도록 / 더 많은 풀을 첨가하는 것보다 //
> 수동태

The stamp producer **was told** / to add more glue / and the problem didn't occur again. //
> 34번 단서 2: 더 많은 풀을 첨가하자 문제는 더 이상 일어나지 않았음

우표 제작자는 지시받았다 / 더 많은 풀을 첨가하라고 / 그리고 그 문제는 더는 일어나지 않았다 //
> 이유를 나타내는 접속사 / 33번 단서 3, 34번 단서 3: 고객이 불평하는 것을 더 쉽게 만드는 것이 고객이 다른 곳으로 가 제품을 사게 만드는 것보다 나은 일임

Since it is better for the firm / to have buyers complain / rather than go elsewhere, / **it** is important to **make** it (e) easier / for dissatisfied customers to complain. //
> 가주어 / 진주어 / 가주어 / 의미상의 주어 / 진주어

회사에는 더 나은 일이기 때문에 / 구매자가 불평하게 하는 것이 / 다른 곳으로 가게 하는 것보다 / 더 쉽게 만드는 것이 중요하다 / 불만족한 고객들이 불평하는 것을 //

- firm ⓝ 회사, 기업　　· failure ⓝ 실패　　· harsh ⓐ 가혹한
- handle ⓥ 다루다　　· sticky ⓐ 끈적거리는　　· envelope ⓝ 봉투
- management ⓝ 경영진　　· moisten ⓥ 적시다
- conclusion ⓝ 결론　　· dissatisfied ⓐ 불만족한

회사에 실패에 대해 말해주는 시장의 방식은 가혹하면서 간단하다. 불평은 다루기에 비용이 덜 들뿐 아니라 판매자가 (a) 향상되도록 만들 수도 있다. 판매자는 또한 어떤 교훈을 얻을지도 모른다. 나는 끈적거리는 선크림 로션에 대한 불평을 받은 한 화장품 회사를 기억한다. 그 당시에, 그러한 로션은 모두 다소 끈적거렸고, 그래서 고객들이 경쟁사의 제품을 사게 하는 위험은 (b) 크지 않았다. 하지만 이것은 또한 기회였다. 그 회사는 끈적거리지 않는 제품을 개발해냈고 첫해에 시장의 20퍼센트를 점유했다. 또 다른 회사는 (c) 반대의 문제를 가졌다. 그 회사의 상품은 충분히 끈적거리지 않았다. 그 회사는 유럽에 있는 Royal Post Office였고 상품은 우표였다. 문제는 우표가 편지 봉투에 붙지 않았다는 것이다. 경영진은 우표 제작자에게 연락했는데, 그는 만약 사람들이 우표를 적절히 적시기만 한다면, 우표가 어떤 종이에도 달라붙을 것이라는 점을 명확히 밝혔다. 어떻게 할까? (우표에) 더 많은 풀을 첨가하는 것보다 고객에게 우표를 적시도록 교육하려고 하는 것에 비용이 (d) 덜(→ 더) 들 것이라는 결론에 경영진이 도달하는 데에는 오래 걸리지 않았다. 우표 제작자는 더 많은 풀을 첨가하라고 지시받았고 그 문제는 더는 일어나지 않았다. 구매자가 다른 곳으로 가게 하는 것보다는 불평하게 하는 것이 회사에는 더 나은 일이기 때문에, 불만족한 고객들이 불평하는 것을 (e) 더 쉽게 만드는 것이 중요하다.

R 33 정답 ②

윗글의 제목으로 가장 적절한 것은?
① Designs That Matter the Most to Customers
> 고객에게 가장 중요한 디자인
> 고객의 선택에 디자인이 미치는 영향은 언급되지 않음

② Complaints: Why Firms Should Welcome Them
> 불만 사항: 회사들이 그것들을 환영해야 하는 이유
> 고객의 불평을 잘 받아들여 반영하면 회사가 제품을 개선할 수 있다는 내용

③ Cheap Prices Don't Necessarily Mean Low Quality
> 저렴한 가격이 반드시 낮은 품질을 의미하지는 않는다
> 가격과 품질의 관계에 대한 언급은 없음

④ More Sticky or Less Sticky: An Unsolved Problem
> 더 끈적거리는 것 혹은 덜 끈적거리는 것: 해결되지 않은 문제
> 끈적거리는 것과 관련된 문제가 언급되긴 했지만 무엇이 더 낫다는 내용은 아님

⑤ Treat Your Competitors Like Friends, Not Enemies
> 경쟁자를 적이 아닌 친구처럼 대하라
> 경쟁 업체와의 관계가 핵심 내용은 아님

2등급? 선크림 로션, 우표 등의 예시를 통해 제목을 추론해야 하는 2등급 대비 문제이다. 글의 마지막 문장에서 결론을 말하고 있는데, 그 앞에 제시된 선크림 로션과 우표의 사례를 글의 결론과 어떻게 연관 지어야 할지 생각하며 글을 읽어야 제목을 고를 수 있다.

| 문제 풀이 순서 | [정답률 59%]

1st 선택지와 앞부분을 통해 핵심 소재를 확인하고 글의 내용을 예상한다.

선택지	거의 모든 선택지에 '고객', '불만', '회사', '품질', '경쟁자'와 같은 어휘가 등장한다.
앞부분	회사에 실패에 대해 말해주는 시장의 방식은 가혹하면서 간단하다. 불평은 다루기에 비용이 덜 들뿐 아니라 판매자가 향상되도록 만들 수도 있다. **33번 단서 1**

➡ 고객의 불평을 잘 다루면 판매자가 향상되도록 만들 수도 있다고 했으므로 [단서] 고객의 불만에 대한 이런 시각이 반영된 내용이 이어질 것이다. [발상]

2nd **1st**에서 발상한 것을 토대로 글을 읽고, 내용을 파악하여 제목을 고른다.

- 그 회사는 끈적거리지 않는 제품을 개발해냈고 첫해에 시장의 20퍼센트를 점유함 **33번 단서 2**
- 구매자가 다른 곳으로 가게 하는 것보다는 불평하게 하는 것이 회사에는 더 나은 일이므로, 고객들이 불평하는 것을 더 쉽게 만드는 것이 중요함 **33번 단서 3**

➡ 고객들의 불평을 듣고 새로운 선크림 로션을 개발해낸 화장품 회사는 시장의 20퍼센트를 점유했다고 했다.
즉, 고객들의 불평을 적극적으로 반영해서 제품을 개선하면 고객들의 만족도가 오르고 경쟁사에 고객을 뺏기지 않아 고객을 유지할 수 있다는 내용이다.

▶ 따라서 이 글의 제목으로 가장 적절한 것은 ② '불만 사항: 회사들이 그것들을 환영해야 하는 이유'이다.

| 선택지 분석 |

① 디자인으로 인해 고객들의 선택이 바뀌었다는 것은 언급되지 않았다.
② 회사가 고객의 불평을 잘 받아들여서 제품에 반영하면 고객을 유지할 수 있다고 했다.
③ 가격과 품질의 관계에 대한 내용은 없다.
④ 더 끈적거리는 것과 덜 끈적거리는 것 중에 무엇이 더 나은지를 말하는 글이 아니다.
⑤ 경쟁사에 대한 언급은 있었지만, 그들과의 관계에 대한 것은 주제와 관련이 없다.

R 34 정답 ④

밑줄 친 (a)~(e) 중에서 문맥상 낱말의 쓰임이 적절하지 <u>않은</u> 것은? [3점]

① (a) 불평은 다루기에 비용이 덜 든다고 했고, 판매자가 '향상되는' 화장품 회사의 예가 나옴
　　향상되다
② (b) 다른 선크림 로션도 끈적거리는 비슷한 상황이므로 다른 경쟁사 상품을 살 위험도 크지 않음
　　크다
③ (c) 선크림 로션이 끈적거리는 앞 회사와는 반대되는 상황
　　반대의
④ (d) 고객 교육과 제품을 바꾸는 것 중 전자에 돈이 더 많이 든다고 했음
　　덜
⑤ (e) 경쟁사 제품을 사는 것보다 고객이 불평하게 하는 게 낫다고 했음
　　더 쉽게

2등급? 우표에 더 많은 풀을 첨가하는 것과 고객에게 우표를 적시도록 교육하는 것 중에 비용이 '덜' 들 것이 어느 것인지를 뒤에 이어지는 내용을 통해 확인해야 한다. 우표 제작자가 더 많은 풀을 첨가한 뒤 문제가 더 발생하지 않았다는 것이 비용이 많이 든 것인지, 적게 든 것인지 추론해야 하는 2등급 대비 문제이다.

왜 정답? [정답률 44%]

④ (d) less 덜

(우표에) 더 많은 풀을 첨가하는 것보다 고객에게 우표를 적시도록 교육하려고 하는 것에 비용이 (d) ~~덜~~(더) 들 것이라는 결론에 경영진이 도달하는 데에는 오래 걸리지 않았다. 우표 제작자는 더 많은 풀을 첨가하라고 지시받았고 그 문제는 더는 일어나지 않았다.

➡ 풀을 더 첨가하는 것보다 우표를 적시도록 고객들을 교육하려고 하는 방식이 비용 면에서 어땠을지 판단해야 한다. 뒤에서 더 많은 풀을 첨가하자 문제는 더 이상 일어나지 않았다고 했으므로 비용이 '덜' 들 것이라는 결론이 나올 수 없다.
▶ less를 more(더)와 같은 반의어로 바꿔야 함

왜 오답?

① (a) improve 향상되다

불평은 다루기에 비용이 덜 들뿐 아니라 판매자가 (a) 향상되도록 만들 수도 있다. 판매자는 또한 어떤 교훈을 얻을지도 모른다.

➡ 문장의 앞부분에서 불평은 다루기에 비용이 덜 든다고 했고, 다음 문장에서 판매자가 교훈을 얻을 수 있다고 했으므로 판매자가 '향상되도록' 만들 것이다.
▶ improve는 문맥에 맞음

② (b) great 큰

그 당시에, 그러한 로션은 모두 다소 끈적거렸고, 그래서 고객들이 경쟁사의 제품을 사게 하는 위험은 (b) 크지 않았다.

➡ 다른 회사에서 나오는 선크림 로션도 끈적거리는 비슷한 상황이었으므로 다른 경쟁사의 제품을 살 위험도 '크지' 않을 것이다. ▶ great는 문맥에 맞음

③ (c) opposite 반대의

그 회사는 끈적거리지 않는 제품을 개발해냈고 첫해에 시장의 20퍼센트를 점유했다. 또 다른 회사는 (c) 반대의 문제를 가졌다. 그 회사의 상품은 충분히 끈적거리지 않았다.

➡ 앞에 나온 화장품 회사는 선크림 로션이 끈적거려서 끈적거리지 않는 제품을 개발했고, 뒤에 나오는 회사의 상품은 충분히 끈적거리지 않아서 문제라고 했으므로 '반대의' 문제라는 표현은 적절하다. ▶ opposite는 문맥에 맞음

⑤ (e) easier 더 쉬운

구매자가 다른 곳으로 가게 하는 것보다는 불평하게 하는 것이 회사에는 더 나은 일이기 때문에, 불만족한 고객들이 불평하는 것을 (e) 더 쉽게 만드는 것이 중요하다.

➡ 경쟁사 제품을 사는 것보다 고객이 불평하게 하는 것이 더 낫다고 했으므로 고객이 '더 쉽게' 불평할 수 있게 하는 것이 중요할 것이라는 표현은 적절하다.
▶ easier는 문맥에 맞음

R 35~36　　　　　　　　　★ 2등급 대비

＊곤충 섭취에 대한 관점

In a society / that rejects the consumption of insects / there are some individuals / who overcome this rejection, / but most will continue with this attitude. //
사회에서는 / 곤충 섭취를 거부하는 / 몇몇 개인들이 있다 / 이러한 거부를 극복한 / 그러나 대부분은 이러한 태도를 지속할 것이다 //

It may be very (a) difficult / to convince an entire society / that insects are totally suitable / for consumption. //
매우 어려울지도 모른다 / 전체 사회에 납득시키는 것은 / 곤충이 완전히 적합하다는 것을 / 섭취에 //

However, / there are examples / in which this (b) reversal of attitudes about certain foods / has happened / to an entire society. // 35번 단서 1: 곤충에 대한 부정적 태도의 역전이 발생한 사례들이 있음
하지만 / 사례들이 있다 / 특정 음식에 대한 이러한 태도의 역전이 / 발생해 온 / 전체 사회에 //

Several examples / in the past 120 years / from European-American society / are: considering lobster a luxury food / instead of a food for servants and prisoners; /
몇몇 사례는 / 지난 120년 간 / 유럽-아메리카 사회로부터의 / ~이다 / 로브스터를 고급진 음식으로 여기는 것 / 하인과 죄수용 음식 대신에 /

considering sushi a safe and delicious food; / and considering pizza / not just a food for the rural poor of Sicily. //
초밥을 안전하고 맛있는 음식으로 여기는 것 / 그리고 피자를 여기는 것이다 / 단지 시칠리아 시골의 가난한 사람용 음식은 아닌 것으로 //

In Latin American countries, / where insects are already consumed, / a portion of the population hates their consumption / and (c) associates it with poverty. // 36번 단서 1: 곤충을 섭취하는 것을 싫어하고 빈곤과 연관 짓는다고 했음
라틴 아메리카 국가들에서는 / 곤충이 이미 섭취되는 / 인구의 일부는 그들의 섭취를 싫어하고 / 그것을 빈곤과 연관 짓는다 //

There are also examples of people / who have had the habit of consuming them / and (d) encouraged (→ abandoned) that habit /
사람들의 사례 또한 있다 / 그것을 섭취하는 습관이 있어 왔으나 / 그 습관을 장려한(→ 버린) /

due to shame, / and because they do not want to be categorized / as poor or uncivilized. // 36번 단서 2: 수치심을 느끼거나, 가난하거나 미개하다고 분류되고 싶지 않다고 했음
수치심 때문에 / 그리고 그들은 분류되고 싶지 않았기 때문에 / 가난하거나 미개하다고 //

According to Esther Katz, / an anthropologist, / if the consumption of insects / as a food luxury / is to be promoted, /
Esther Katz에 따르면 / 인류학자인 / 만약 곤충 섭취가 / 음식 호사로서의 / 장려된다면 /

there would be more chances / that some individuals / who do not present this habit / overcome ideas / under which they were educated. // 35번 단서 2: 곤충 섭취가 음식 호사로 장려되면 곤충 섭취에 대한 부정적 생각을 극복할 가능성이 더 많을 것임
가능성이 더 많을 것이다 / 몇몇 개인들이 / 이러한 습관을 보이지 않은 / 생각을 극복할 / 그들이 교육받았던 //

And this could also help / to (e) revalue the consumption of insects / by those people / who already eat them. // 35번 단서 3: 곤충의 섭취를 재평가하는 데 도움을 줄 수 있음
그리고 이것은 또한 도움을 줄 수 있다 / 곤충의 섭취를 재평가하는 데에도 / 그 사람들에 의한 / 이미 그것을 먹고 있는 //

- reject ⓥ 거부하다
- consumption ⓝ 섭취
- insect ⓝ 곤충
- overcome ⓥ 극복하다
- rejection ⓝ 거부
- convince ⓥ 납득시키다
- entire ⓐ 전체의
- suitable ⓐ 적합한
- reversal ⓝ 역전
- luxury ⓐ 고급진, 호사
- servant ⓝ 하인
- prisoner ⓝ 죄수
- rural ⓐ 시골의
- portion ⓝ 일부
- associate ⓥ 연관 짓다
- poverty ⓝ 빈곤
- categorize ⓥ 분류하다
- uncivilized ⓐ 미개한
- anthropologist ⓝ 인류학자
- promote ⓥ 장려하다
- revalue ⓥ 재평가하다
- edible ⓐ 먹을 수 있는
- perspective ⓝ 관점, 시각
- shortage ⓝ 부족
- uniqueness ⓝ 독특함
- disappear ⓥ 사라지다

곤충 섭취를 거부하는 사회에서는 이러한 거부를 극복한 몇몇 개인들이 있지만, 대부분은 이러한 태도를 지속할 것이다. 곤충이 섭취에 완전히 적합하다는 것을 전체 사회에 납득시키는 것은 매우 (a) 어려울지도 모른다. 하지만, 특정 음식에 대한 이러한 태도의 (b) 역전이 전체 사회에 발생해 온 사례들이 있다. 지난 120년 간 유럽-아메리카 사회로부터의 몇몇 사례는 로브스터를 하인과 죄수용 음식 대신에 고급진 음식으로 여기는 것, 초밥을 안전하고 맛있는 음식으로 여기는 것, 그리고 피자를 단지 시칠리아 시골의 가난한 사람용 음식으로 여기지 않는 것이다. 곤충이 이미 섭취되는 라틴 아메리카 국가들에서는 인구의 일부는 그들의 섭취를 싫어하고 그것을 빈곤과 (c) 연관 짓는다. 그것을 섭취하는 습관이 있어 왔으나 수치심 때문에 그리고 그들은 가난하거나 미개하다고 분류되고 싶지 않았기 때문에 그 습관을 (d) 장려한(→ 버린) 사람들의 사례들 또한 있다. 인류학자인 Esther Katz에 따르면, 만약 음식 호사로서의 곤충 섭취가 장려된다면, 이러한 습관을 보이지 않은 몇몇 개인들이 그들이 교육받았던 생각을 극복할 가능성이 더 많을 것이다. 그리고 이것은 또한 이미 그것을 먹고 있는 그 사람들에 의한 곤충의 섭취를 (e) 재평가하는 데에도 도움을 줄 수 있다.

R 35 정답 ②

윗글의 제목으로 가장 적절한 것은?
① The More Variety on the Table, The Healthier You Become 다양한 음식을 먹으면 건강해진다는 내용이 아님
② Edible or Not? Change Your Perspectives on Insects 먹을 수 있는가? 아닌가? 곤충에 대한 당신의 관점을 바꿔라 [곤충 섭취에 대한 부정적 생각을 바꿀 수 있다는 내용]
③ Insects: A Key to Solve the World Food Shortage 곤충: 세계 식량난을 해결할 열쇠 [곤충이 식량난에 대한 해결책이라는 내용은 없음]
④ Don't Let Uniqueness in Food Culture Disappear 음식 문화의 독특함이 사라지지 않도록 하라 [곤충을 섭취하는 것을 음식 문화의 독특함으로 연결시켜 고를 수 있는 오답]
⑤ Experiencing Various Cultures by Food 음식을 통해 다양한 문화 경험하기 [음식을 통해 다양한 문화를 경험하는 내용은 없음]

왜 2등급? 곤충 섭취를 향한 인식의 변화를 이야기하는 글이다. 다섯 개의 선택지가 모두 곤충이나 음식과 관련된 내용이라 오답을 가려내기가 까다로운 2등급 대비 문제이다. 곤충 섭취를 바라보는 인식을 어떻게 바꿀 수 있는지를 정확히 파악해야 알맞은 정답을 고를 수 있다.

| 문제 풀이 순서 | [정답률 58%]

1st 선택지와 앞부분을 통해 핵심 소재를 확인하고 글의 내용을 예상한다.

선택지	모든 선택지에 '다양성', '곤충', '음식', '독특함', '문화'와 같은 어휘가 등장한다.
앞부분	곤충 섭취를 거부하는 사회에서는 이러한 거부를 극복한 몇몇 개인들이 있지만, ~ 사회에 납득시키는 것은 매우 어려울지도 모른다.

→ 이 글은 곤충을 먹는 것과 같이 독특한 음식 문화와 관련된 내용이다. 곤충 섭취에 부정적인 사회에서는 개인도 대부분 곤충 섭취에 대해 부정적일 것이라고 하면서 곤충 섭취가 괜찮음을 납득시키는 것에 대해 언급했으므로 [단서] 이에 대한 어떤 시각이 제시될 것이다. [발상]

2nd **1st** 에서 발상한 것을 토대로 글을 읽고, 내용을 파악하여 제목을 고른다.

- 특정 음식에 대한 이러한 태도의 역전이 전체 사회에 발생해 온 사례들이 있음 [35번 단서 1]
- Esther Katz에 따르면, 음식 호사로서의 곤충 섭취가 장려된다면, 이러한 습관을 보이지 않은 몇몇 개인들이 그들이 교육받았던 생각을 극복할 가능성이 더 많을 것임 [35번 단서 2]
- 그리고 이것은 이미 그것을 먹고 있는 그 사람들에 의한 곤충의 섭취를 재평가하는 데에도 도움을 줄 수 있음 [35번 단서 3]

→ 곤충 섭취를 빈곤과 연결 짓거나 그 습관을 싫어하는 사람들이 있지만, 곤충 섭취를 빈곤이 아니라 음식 호사와 연결 짓도록 장려한다면 곤충 섭취에 대한 부정적 생각이 바뀔 수 있다고 했다. ▶ 따라서 ② '먹을 수 있는가 없는가? 곤충에 대한 당신의 관점을 바꿔라'가 이 글의 제목으로 가장 적절하다.

| 선택지 분석 |
① 다양한 음식을 섭취하면 더 건강해진다는 내용이 아니므로 이 글의 제목이 될 수 없다.
② 곤충 섭취를 빈곤과 연결 짓는 등 부정적인 생각을 가진 사회가 많지만, 긍정적인 것들과 연결 짓는다면 부정적인 생각을 바꿀 수도 있다는 내용이다.
③ 곤충이 세계 식량난의 해결책이라는 내용이 아니다.
④ 곤충을 섭취하는 것을 음식 문화의 독특함으로 연결시켜 고를 수 있는 오답일 뿐이다.
⑤ 음식을 통해 다양한 문화를 경험하는 내용이 아니므로 부적절하다.

R 36 정답 ④

밑줄 친 (a)~(e) 중에서 문맥상 낱말의 쓰임이 적절하지 않은 것은?
① (a) 어려운 곤충이 음식으로 적합하다는 것을 전체 사회에 납득시키기는 어려울 수 있음
② (b) 역전 곤충 섭취에 대한 태도 역전을 보여주는 사례들이 있음
③ (c) 연관 짓다 곤충 섭취를 빈곤과 연결 짓는 일이 있음
④ (d) 장려한 곤충 섭취를 하던 사람들이 가난하거나 미개하다고 분류되고 싶어 하지 않음
⑤ (e) 재평가하다 곤충 섭취 재평가가 가능할 수 있음

왜 2등급? 곤충을 섭취하는 습관을 이미 가진 사람들이 가난하거나 미개하다고 여겨지고 싶지 않았다면 그 습관을 '장려했을' 것인지 '버렸을' 것인지 판단해야 한다. 이 글은 곤충 섭취를 바라보는 두 가지 인식을 말하고 있으므로 각각의 입장을 구분해야 낱말의 쓰임이 적절한지 알 수 있다.

왜 정답? [정답률 50%]
④ (d) encouraged 장려하다

그것을 섭취하는 습관이 있어 왔으나 수치심 때문에 그리고 그들은 가난하거나 미개하다고 분류되고 싶지 않았기 때문에 그 습관을 (d) 장려한(→버린) 사람들의 사례들 또한 있다.

→ 곤충 섭취 습관을 가지고 있던 사람들이 수치심을 느끼고, 가난하거나 미개하다고 분류되고 싶어 하지 않는다고 했으므로 곤충 섭취 습관을 '장려한' 사람들의 사례를 이야기하고 있는 것이 아니다.

▶ encouraged를 abandoned(버린)와 같은 반의어로 바꿔야 함

왜 오답?
① (a) difficult 어려운

곤충 섭취를 거부하는 사회에서는 이러한 거부를 극복한 몇몇 개인들이 있지만, 대부분은 이러한 태도를 지속할 것이다. 곤충이 섭취에 완전히 적합하다는 것을 전체 사회에 납득시키는 것은 매우 (a) 어려울지도 모른다.

→ 앞에서 곤충 섭취를 거부하는 사회의 개인들은 그 태도를 지속할 것이라고 했으므로 곤충이 음식으로 적합하다는 것을 전체 사회에 납득시키기는 '어려울' 수 있다는 표현은 자연스럽다. ▶ difficult는 문맥에 맞음

R

② (b) reversal 역전

하지만, 특정 음식에 대한 이러한 태도의 (b) 역전이 전체 사회에 발생해 온 사례들이 있다.

→ However(하지만)로 연결되므로 앞의 내용과 반대로, 곤충 섭취에 대한 부정적인 태도의 '역전'을 보여주는 사례들이 있다는 흐름은 자연스럽다.

▶ reversal은 문맥에 맞음

③ (c) associates 연관 짓다

곤충이 이미 섭취되는 라틴 아메리카 국가들에서는 인구의 일부는 그들의 섭취를 싫어하고 그것을 빈곤과 (c) 연관 짓는다.

→ 곤충 섭취를 싫어한다고 했으므로 빈곤과 '연관 짓는다'는 것은 문맥상 적절하다.

▶ associates는 문맥에 맞음

⑤ (e) revalue 재평가하다

인류학자인 Esther Katz에 따르면, 만약 음식 호사로서의 곤충 섭취가 장려된다면, 이러한 습관을 보이지 않은 몇몇 개인들이 그들이 교육받았던 생각을 극복할 가능성이 더 많을 것이다. 그리고 이것은 또한 이미 그것을 먹고 있는 그 사람들에 의한 곤충의 섭취를 (e) 재평가하는 데에도 도움을 줄 수 있다.

→ 곤충 섭취를 음식 호사로서 장려하면 개인들이 갖고 있던 생각을 극복할 것이라고 했으므로 곤충 섭취에 대한 '재평가'가 가능할 수 있다는 표현은 자연스럽다.

▶ revalue는 문맥에 맞음

R 37~38 ★ 1등급 대비

＊불행함에서 벗어나기 위해 다른 사람 이해하기

The longest journey / we will make / is the eighteen inches / between our head and heart. //
앞에 목적격 관계대명사 생략

가장 긴 여정은 / 우리가 갈 / 18인치이다 / 우리의 머리에서 가슴까지의 //

If we take this journey, / it can shorten / our (a) misery in the world. // 37번 단서 1: 머리에서 가슴까지의 여행을 하면 비참함을 줄일 수 있음
우리가 이 여행을 한다면 / 그것은 줄일 수 있다 / 세상에서 우리의 비참함을 //

Impatience, judgment, frustration, and anger / reside / in our heads. //
조급함, 비난, 좌절, 그리고 분노가 / 있다 / 우리 머릿속에 //

When we live in that place / too long, / it makes us (b) unhappy. //
우리가 그 장소에서 살면 / 너무 오래 / 그것은 우리를 불행하게 만든다 //

But when we take the journey / from our heads to our hearts, / something shifts (c) inside. //
그러나 우리가 여행을 하면 / 머리부터 가슴까지의 / 내면에서 무엇인가 바뀐다 //

가정법 과거   주격 관계대명사
What if we were able to love / everything / that gets in our way? //
만일 우리가 사랑할 수 있다면 어떻게 될까 / 모든 것을 / 우리를 가로막는 //

가정법 과거   37번 단서 2, 38번 단서 1: 우리를 가로막는 것들을 사랑하는 것에 대해 말함
What if we tried loving / the shopper / who unknowingly steps / in front of us in line, / the driver / who cuts us off in traffic, /
주격 관계대명사
만일 우리가 사랑하려고 노력한다면 어떨까 / 그 쇼핑객을 / 무심코 들어온 / 줄을 서 있는 우리 앞에 / 그 운전자를 / 차량 흐름에서 우리 앞에 끼어든 /

주격 관계대명사
the swimmer / who splashes us with water / during a belly dive, / or the reader / who pens a bad online review / of our writing? //
수영하는 그 사람을 / 우리에게 물을 튀게 한 / 배 쪽으로 다이빙하면서 / 또는 그 독자를 / 나쁜 온라인 후기를 쓴 / 우리의 글에 대해 //

38번 단서 2: 우리를 비참하게 만드는 모든 사람들이 우리와 같은 인간이라고 했음
주격 관계대명사
Every person / who makes us miserable / is (d) like us — / a human being, / most likely doing the best they can, / deeply loved / by their parents, / a child, or a friend. //
모든 사람은 / 우리를 비참하게 만드는 / 우리와 같다 / 그들은 인간 / 아마도 분명히 최선을 다하고 있으며 / 깊이 사랑받는 / 부모로부터 / 자녀 혹은 친구일 것이다 //

And how many times / have we unknowingly stepped / in front of someone in line? //
그리고 몇 번이나 / 우리는 무심코 들어갔을까 / 줄을 서 있는 누군가의 앞에 //

Cut someone off in traffic? //
차량 흐름에서 누군가에게 끼어든 적은 //

Splashed someone in a pool? //
수영장에서 누군가에게 물을 튀게 한 적은 //

앞에 목적격 관계대명사 생략
Or made a negative statement / about something we've read? //
혹은 부정적인 진술을 한 적은 몇 번이었을까 / 우리가 읽은 것에 대해 //

가주어   진주어   목적절을 이끄는 접속사
It helps to (e) deny(→ admit) / that a piece of us resides / in every person we meet. // 37번 단서 3: 다른 사람도 우리와 같음을 기억하는 것이
도움이 됨
앞에 목적격 관계대명사 생략
부정하는(→ 인정하는) 것은 도움이 된다 / 우리의 일부가 있다는 것을 / 우리가 만나는 모든 사람 속에 //

- journey ⓝ 여정, 여행 ・ shorten ⓥ 줄이다 ・ misery ⓝ 비참함
- impatience ⓝ 조급함 ・ judgment ⓝ 비난
- frustration ⓝ 좌절 ・ anger ⓝ 분노 ・ shift ⓥ 바뀌다
- unknowingly ⓐⓓ 무심코 ・ cut off 끼어들다
- splash ⓥ (액체류를) 튀기다 ・ pen ⓥ (글을) 쓰다
- miserable ⓐ 비참한 ・ statement ⓝ 진술 ・ deny ⓥ 부정하다
- forgive ⓥ 용서하다

우리가 갈 가장 긴 여정은 우리의 머리에서 가슴까지의 18인치이다. 우리가 이 여행을 한다면, 그것은 세상에서 우리의 (a) 비참함을 줄일 수 있다. 조급함, 비난, 좌절, 그리고 분노가 우리 머릿속에 있다. 우리가 그 장소에서 너무 오래 살면, 그것은 우리를 (b) 불행하게 만든다. 그러나 우리가 머리부터 가슴까지의 여행을 하면, (c) 내면에서 무엇인가 바뀐다. 만일 우리를 가로막는 모든 것을 우리가 사랑할 수 있다면 어떻게 될까? 만일 줄을 서 있는 우리 앞에 무심코 들어온 그 쇼핑객을, 차량 흐름에서 우리 앞에 끼어든 그 운전자를, 배 쪽으로 다이빙하면서 우리에게 물을 튀게 한 수영하는 그 사람을, 우리의 글에 대해 나쁜 온라인 후기를 쓴 그 독자를 우리가 사랑하려고 노력한다면 어떨까?
우리를 비참하게 만드는 모든 사람은 우리와 (d) 같다. 그들은 아마도 분명히 최선을 다하고 있으며, 부모로부터 깊이 사랑받는 인간, 자녀 혹은 친구일 것이다. 그리고 우리는 몇 번이나 무심코 줄을 서 있는 누군가의 앞에 들어갔을까? 차량 흐름에서 누군가에게 끼어든 적은? 수영장에서 누군가에게 물을 튀게 한 적은? 혹은 우리가 읽은 것에 대해 부정적인 진술을 한 적은 몇 번이었을까? 우리가 만나는 모든 사람 속에 우리의 일부가 있다는 것을 (e) 부정하는(→ 인정하는) 것은 도움이 된다.

R 37 정답 ⑤

윗글의 제목으로 가장 적절한 것은?

① Why It Is So Difficult to Forgive Others
왜 다른 사람들을 용서하는 것이 그렇게 어려운가   다른 사람을 이해하는 것에 대해 이야기하는 글임

② Even Acts of Kindness Can Hurt Somebody
친절한 행동도 누군가에게 상처를 줄 수 있다   친절함이 상처를 줄 수 있다는 내용이 아님

③ Time Is the Best Healer for a Broken Heart
시간이 실연의 상처에 대한 최고의 치료이다   시간이 상처를 치료해 준다는 내용은 없음

④ Celebrate the Happy Moments in Your Everyday Life
일상 생활에서 가장 행복한 순간들을 기념해라   일상에서 행복한 순간들을 기념하라는 언급은 없음

⑤ Understand Others to Save Yourself from Unhappiness
불행으로부터 자신을 구하기 위해 다른 사람을 이해하라   불행에서 벗어나려면 다른 사람도 나와 같다는 생각으로 이해해야 한다는 내용

왜 1등급 ❓ 우리가 갈 가장 긴 여정이 머리에서 가슴까지의 18인치라는 모호한 문장으로 시작한 글이다. 이 '18인치의 여정'이 비유하는 바가 무엇인지 전체 글을 통해 파악해야만 글의 제목을 고를 수 있는 1등급 대비 문제이다.

| 문제 풀이 순서 | [정답률 55%]

1st 선택지와 앞부분을 통해 핵심 소재를 확인하고 글의 내용을 예상한다.

선택지	거의 모든 선택지에 '다른 사람', '용서', '친절한', '누군가', '행복한', '불행'과 같은 표현들이 등장한다.
앞부분	우리가 갈 가장 긴 여정은 우리의 머리에서 가슴까지의 18인치이다. 우리가 이 여행을 한다면, 그것은 세상에서 우리의 비참함을 줄일 수 있다. **37번 단서 1**

➡ 이 글은 다른 사람을 용서하는 것, 행복하고 불행한 것과 관련된 내용이다.

➡ 앞부분에서 머리에서 가슴까지의 거리가 아주 멀다고 하면서 이 여행을 하면 비참함을 줄일 수 있다고 했으므로 (단서) 이에 대한 설명이 나올 것이다. (발상)

2nd **1st** 에서 발상한 것을 토대로 글을 읽고, 내용을 파악한다.

· 우리를 가로막는 모든 것을 우리가 사랑할 수 있다면 어떻게 될까? **37번 단서 2**
· 우리를 비참하게 만드는 모든 사람은 우리와 같다.

➡ 줄을 서 있는 우리 앞에 무심코 들어온 쇼핑객과 같은 사람들을 예로 들면서, 우리를 가로막는 사람들을 사랑할 수 있다면 어떻게 될지에 대한 질문을 던졌다. 그러면서 우리도 마찬가지로 다른 사람에게 불편을 끼친 적이 있을 것이라는 점을 이해하는 것이 도움이 된다고 했다.

3rd 글의 주제에 알맞은 제목을 고른다.

➡ 결국 '우리 자신을 불행에서 구하기 위해서는 다른 사람을 이해하는 것이 필요하다'는 것이 이 글의 주제이다.
▶ 따라서 ⑤ '불행으로부터 자신을 구하기 위해 다른 사람을 이해하라'가 이 글의 제목으로 가장 적절하다.

| 선택지 분석 |

① 우리를 가로막고 비참하게 하는 사람들을 언급한 것으로 만든 함정으로, 다른 사람을 이해하라는 내용의 글이지 용서하는 것의 어려움에 대한 글이 아니다.
② 친절한 행동이 누군가에게는 상처가 될 수 있다는 내용이 아니다.
③ 시간이 실연의 상처를 치료해 주는 최고의 방법이라는 내용이 아니다.
④ 일상에서 가장 행복한 순간들을 기념하라는 내용이 아니므로 제목이 될 수 없다.
⑤ 불행에서 벗어나기 위해서는 다른 사람도 결국 우리와 같은 사람이라는 생각을 해야 한다는 내용이다.

R 38 정답 ⑤

밑줄 친 (a)~(e) 중에서 문맥상 낱말의 쓰임이 적절하지 <u>않은</u> 것은?

① (a) 머리에서 가슴까지의 여행이 비참함을 줄여줄 수 있음
  비참함
② (b) 조급함, 비난, 좌절, 분노가 머릿속에 너무 오래 머물면 불행해질 것임
  불행한
③ (c) 머리에서 가슴까지의 여행이 무엇인가를 바꾸어 주는 것은 내면에서일 것임
  내면에서
④ (d) 우리를 비참하게 만드는 다른 사람도 우리와 같은 사람임을 이야기했음
  같은
⑤ (e) 다른 사람이 우리와 같다는 것을 부정하는 게 아니라 기억하는 것이 도움이 된다는 내용
  부정하다

왜 1등급? 반의어가 확실하지 않은 선택지는 정답이 아닌 경우가 많은데, 모든 선택지의 반의어가 명확한 1등급 대비 문제이다. 이런 경우에는 선택지가 포함된 다섯 문장 모두 전체 흐름과 반대되는 내용은 아닌지 확인해야 해서 시간이 더 걸리므로 이 점을 염두에 두고 글을 읽어야 한다.

| 문제 풀이 순서 | [정답률 59%]

1st 각 낱말의 의미를 먼저 확인하고, 반의어를 미리 생각해 놓는다.

(a) misery: 비참함 ↔ happiness: 행복
(b) unhappy: 불행한 ↔ happy: 행복한
(c) inside: 내면에서 ↔ outside: 외면에서
(d) like: ~와 같은 ↔ unlike: ~와 같지 않은
(e) deny: 부정하다 ↔ admit: 인정하다

➡ 선택지에 제시된 낱말과 반대 의미를 나타내는 낱말을 넣었을 때 문맥이 성립되는 경우에 정답인 경우가 많은데 모든 선택지가 반의어를 떠올릴 수 있으므로 정답이 될 가능성이 있다.

2nd 선택지의 앞뒤 내용을 파악해서 문맥이 자연스러운지 확인한다.

① (a) misery 비참함
┌ 우리가 갈 가장 긴 여정은 우리의 머리에서 가슴까지의 18인치이다. 우리가 이 여행을 한다면, 그것은 세상에서 우리의 (a) 비참함을 줄일 수 있다.
└ 조급함, 비난, 좌절, 그리고 분노가 우리 머릿속에 있다.

➡ 앞 문장에서 머리에서 가슴까지의 거리가 아주 멀다고 했고, 뒤 문장에서 조급함이나 분노와 같은 부정적인 것들이 머릿속에 있다고 했다. 따라서 머리에서 가슴까지의 여행을 한다면 우리의 '비참함'을 줄일 수 있을 것이다.
▶ misery는 문맥에 맞음

② (b) unhappy 불행한
┌ 조급함, 비난, 좌절, 그리고 분노가 우리 머릿속에 있다. 우리가 그 장소에서 너무 오래 살면, 그것은 우리를 (b) 불행하게 만든다.

➡ 조급함, 비난과 같은 부정적인 감정이 있는 머릿속에 너무 오래 있으면 우리는 '불행하게' 될 것이라는 표현은 적절하다.
▶ unhappy는 문맥에 맞음

③ (c) inside 내면에서
┌ 그러나 우리가 머리부터 가슴까지의 여행을 하면, (c) 내면에서 무엇인가 바뀐다.

➡ 앞의 내용과 반대로 머릿속에 너무 오래 있지 않고 가슴까지의 여행을 하면 '내면에서' 바뀌는 것이 있을 것이다.
▶ inside는 문맥에 맞음

④ (d) like ~와 같은
┌ 우리를 비참하게 만드는 모든 사람은 우리와 (d) 같다. 그들은 아마도 분명히 최선을 다하고 있으며, 부모로부터 깊이 사랑받는 인간, 자녀 혹은 친구일 것이다.

➡ 뒤 문장에서 우리를 비참하게 만드는 사람들도 사랑받는 사람들이라고 했으므로 우리와 '같다'고 하는 것은 적절하다.
▶ like는 문맥에 맞음

⑤ (e) deny 부정하다
┌ 우리가 만나는 모든 사람 속에 우리의 일부가 있다는 것을 (e) ~~부정하는~~ 것은 도움이 된다.
                                           인정하는

➡ 앞에서 다른 사람이 우리와 같이 사랑받는 사람이라고 했으므로 다른 사람에게 우리의 일부가 있다는 것을 '부정하는' 것은 정반대이다.
▶ deny는 문맥에 맞지 않음 → 반의어로 바꿔 볼 것
➡ deny를 반의어인 admit으로 바꿔야 앞뒤 문맥이 자연스러워진다.
▶ 정답은 ⑤임

R 39~40 ───────── ⭐ 1등급 대비

*사회적 불안감을 극복하는 방법
         ┌──가정법 과거──┐
If you were afraid of standing on balconies, / you would start on some lower floors / and slowly work your way up to higher ones. // 발코니에 서 있는 것을 두려워한다면 / 당신은 더 낮은 층에서 시작해서 / 천천히 더 높은 층으로 올라갈 것이다 //
가주어   진주어
It would be easy / to face a fear of standing / on high balconies /
      생략 가능(주격 관계대명사+be동사)
in a way that's totally controlled. //
쉬울 것이다 / 서 있는 두려움을 직면하기가 / 높은 발코니에 / 완전히 통제된 방식으로 //
Socializing / is (a) trickier. // **39번** 단서 1: 사회적 불안감이 발생하는 이유에 대해 말함
사람을 사귀는 것은 / 더 까다롭다 //

People aren't <u>like</u> inanimate features of a building / that you just have to be around / to get used to. //
전치사(~같은) · 목적격 관계대명사
사람은 건물과 같은 무생물이 아니다 / 주변에 있어서 / 익숙해지는 //

You have to interact with them, / and their responses can be unpredictable. //
당신은 그들과 상호 작용을 해야 하며 / 그들의 반응을 예측하기가 힘들 수 있다 //

Your feelings toward them / are more complex too. //
그들에 대한 당신의 느낌도 / 역시 더 복잡하다 //

Most people's self-esteem / isn't going to be affected that much / if they don't like balconies, / but your confidence can (b) <u>suffer</u> / if you can't socialize effectively. // 대부분의 사람들의 자존감은 / 그렇게
양보의 부사절을 이끄는 접속사
많이 영향을 받지 않을 것이다 / 그들이 발코니를 좋아하지 않는다 할지라도 / 하지만 당신의 자신감은 상처받을 수 있다 / 당신이 효과적으로 사람들을 사귈 수 없다면 //

<u>It's also harder</u> / <u>to design</u> a tidy way / <u>to gradually face</u> many social fears. // **39번** 단서 2: 사회적 두려움에 맞서는 방법을 찾기는 어렵다고 말함
가주어 · 진주어 · 형용사적 용법
또한 더 어렵다 / 깔끔한 방법을 설계하는 것 / 수많은 사교적 두려움을 점진적으로 마주하게 할 //

The social situations / you need to expose yourself to / may not be (c) <u>available</u> / when you want them, / or they may not go well enough / for you to sense / that things are under control. //
뒤에 목적격 관계대명사 생략 · **40번** 단서 1: 사회적 관계 맺기와 관련된 부정적 내용에 대해 말함 · to sense의 의미상의 주어
사교적 상황이 / 당신을 드러낼 필요가 있는 / 형성되지 않을 수 있고 / 당신이 원할 때 / 또는 그것들은 잘 진행되지 않을지도 모른다 / 당신이 감지할 만큼 / 상황이 통제 가능하다고 //

The progression from one step to the next / may not be clear, / creating unavoidable large (d) <u>decreases(→ increases)</u> in difficulty / from one to the next. //
40번 단서 2: 사회적 관계 맺기와 관련된 부정적 내용이 추가로 나옴
한 단계에서 다음 단계로의 진행은 / 분명하지 않을 수 있으며 / 피할 수 없이 큰 어려움이 줄어들게(→ 늘어나게) 된다 / 한 단계에서 다음 단계로 진행할 때 //

People around you / aren't robots / that you can endlessly experiment with / for your own purposes. // 우리 주변의 사람들은 /
목적격 관계대명사
로봇이 아니다 / 당신이 끊임없이 실험해 볼 수 있는 / 당신 자신의 목적을 위해서 //

This is not to say / that facing your fears is pointless / when socializing. // **39번** 단서 3: 사회적 두려움에 점진적으로 노출하는 것의 유용함
목적어절 접속사
이것이 말하는 것은 아니다 / 당신의 두려움을 직면하는 것은 의미가 없다고 / 사람을 사귈 때 //

<u>The principles of gradual exposure</u> / <u>are</u> still very (e) <u>useful</u>. // **39번** 단서 4: 점진적 노출의 유용함을 재진술함
주어 · 동사
점진적인 노출의 원칙은 / 여전히 매우 유용하다 //

The <u>process of applying them</u> / <u>is</u> just messier, / and knowing that before you start / <u>is</u> helpful. //
주어(동명사구) · 동사
그것들을 적용하는 과정은 / 더 복잡하지만 / 시작하기 전에 그것을 아는 것은 / 도움이 된다 //

- face ⓥ 직면하다 · socialize ⓥ (사람을) 사귀다, 어울리다
- tricky ⓐ 까다로운 · inanimate ⓐ 무생물의
- get used to ~에 익숙해지다 · unpredictable ⓐ 예측할 수 없는
- self-esteem ⓝ 자존감 · tidy ⓐ 깔끔한
- expose ⓥ 노출시키다 · sense ⓥ 감지하다, 알아차리다
- progression ⓝ 진행 · unavoidable ⓐ 피할 수 없는
- endlessly ⓐ 끊임없이 · experiment ⓥ 실험하다
- pointless ⓐ 무의미한 · principle ⓝ 원칙, 원리

발코니에 서 있는 것을 두려워한다면, 당신은 더 낮은 층에서 시작해서 천천히 더 높은 층으로 올라갈 것이다. 완전히 통제된 방식으로 높은 발코니에 서 있는 두려움을 직면하기는 쉬울 것이다. 사람을 사귄다는 것은 (a) 더 까다롭다. 사람은 주변에 있어서 익숙해지는 건물과 같은 무생물이 아니다. 당신은 그들과 상호 작용을 해야 하며 그들의 반응을 예측하기가 힘들 수 있다. 그들에 대한 당신의 느낌도 역시 더 복잡하다. 대부분의 사람들의 자존감은 그들이 발코니를 좋아하지 않는다고 해도 그렇게 많이 영향을 받지 않을 것이지만, 당신이 효과적으로 사람들을 사귈 수 없다면 당신의 자신감은 (b) 상처받을 수 있다.
수많은 사교적 두려움을 점차적으로 마주하게 할 깔끔한 방법을 설계하는 것 또한 더 어렵다. 당신을 드러낼 필요가 있는 사교적 상황이 당신이 원할 때 (c) 형성되지 않을 수 있고, 또는 그것들은 상황이 통제 가능하다고 감

지할 만큼 잘 진행되지 않을지도 모른다. 한 단계에서 다음 단계로의 진행은 분명하지 않을 수 있으며, 한 단계에서 다음 단계로 진행할 때 피할 수 없이 큰 어려움이 (d) 줄어들게(→ 늘어나게) 된다. 우리 주변의 사람들은 당신 자신의 목적을 위해서 끊임없이 실험해 볼 수 있는 로봇이 아니다. 이것이 사람을 사귈 때 당신의 두려움을 직면하는 것은 의미가 없다고 말하는 것은 아니다. 점진적인 노출의 원칙은 여전히 매우 (e) 유용하다. 그것들을 적용하는 과정은 더 복잡하지만, 시작하기 전에 그것을 아는 것은 도움이 된다.

R 39 정답 ⑤

윗글의 제목으로 가장 적절한 것은?
① How to Improve Your Self-Esteem 글에 나온 self-esteem을 넣어 만든 함정
자존감을 향상시키는 방법
② Socializing with Someone You Fear: Good or Bad? 두려워하는
두려워하는 사람을 사귀는 것 긍정적인가 아니면 부정적인가? 사람을 사귀는 것에 대한 평가는 하지 않음
③ Relaxation May Lead to Getting Over Social Fears 사회적 두려
여유는 사회적 두려움을 극복하는 것으로 이끌 수 있다 움을 점진적으로 극복하는 것이 핵심 내용임
④ Are Social Exposures Related with Fear of Heights? 높은 층
사회적 노출이 고소공포증과 관련이 있는가? (higher ones')과 관련된 내용을 이용하여 만든 오답
⑤ Overcoming Social Anxiety Is Difficult; Try Gradually!
사회적 불안감을 극복하는 것은 어렵다; 점진적으로 시도하라! 사회적 불안감을 해결하는
방법을 찾는 것이 어렵지만, 사회적 관계에 점진적으로 자신을 노출시키는 것이 효과적이라는 내용

왜 1등급? 발코니의 낮은 층에서 높은 층으로 올라가는 방식을 인간관계에도 활용하라고 조언하는 글이다. 이 결론에 도출하는 과정에서 사람은 건물과 같지 않다면서 상반된 주장을 했다가, 그럼에도 도움이 된다는 결론에 도달하고 있으므로 내용이 뒤집히는 부분을 놓치면 정답을 고르기 어려운 1등급 대비 문제이다.

| 문제 풀이 순서 | [정답률 44%]

1st 선택지와 첫 문장을 통해 핵심 소재를 확인하고 글의 내용을 예상한다.

선택지	거의 모든 선택지에 '자존감', '사회적 두려움', '극복', '사회적 노출', '사회적 불안감'과 같은 표현들이 등장한다.
첫 문장	발코니에 서 있는 것을 두려워한다면, 당신은 더 낮은 층에서 시작해서 천천히 더 높은 층으로 올라갈 것이다.

→ 이 글은 사회적 두려움이나 사회적 불안감을 극복하는 것에 대한 내용이다.
→ 첫 문장에서 발코니에 서 있는 것이 무서우면 낮은 층부터 천천히 높은 층으로 올라갈 것이라고 했으므로 **단서**
사회적 두려움이나 사회적 불안감을 천천히 극복하는 것과 관련된 내용으로 예상할 수 있다. **발상**

2nd **1st** 에서 발상한 것을 토대로 글을 읽고, 내용을 파악한다.

- 사람을 사귄다는 것은 더 까다롭다. **39번 단서 1**
- 수많은 사교적 두려움을 점차적으로 마주하게 할 깔끔한 방법을 설계하는 것은 더 어렵다. **39번 단서 2**
- 이것이 사람을 사귈 때 당신의 두려움을 직면하는 것은 의미가 없다고 말하는 것은 아니며, 점진적인 노출의 원칙은 여전히 매우 유용하다. **39번 단서 3**

→ 사람을 사귀는 것은 까다롭고 이로 인해 생기는 사회적 불안감을 해결하는 방법을 찾는 것이 어렵다고 했다.
하지만 사회적 관계에 점진적으로 자신을 노출시키는 것이 이러한 사회적 불안감을 해결하는 데 매우 도움이 된다고 강조하고 있다.

3rd 글의 주제에 알맞은 제목을 고른다.

→ 낮은 층부터 천천히 높은 층으로 올라가면서 발코니에 서 있는 것의 두려움을 극복하는 것처럼, '사회적 관계에 점진적으로 노출시켜서 사회적 불안감을 극복할 수 있다'는 것이 이 글의 주제이다.
▶ 따라서 이 글의 제목으로 가장 적절한 것은 ⑤ '사회적 불안감을 극복하는 것은 어렵다; 점진적으로 시도하라!'이다.

| 선택지 분석 |

① 글에 나온 self-esteem을 넣어 만든 함정일 뿐, 자존감을 향상시키는 방법에 대한 내용은 아니다.
② 두려워하는 사람을 사귀는 것에 대한 평가를 하는 내용은 없다.
③ 사회적 두려움을 극복하는 것이 어려우므로 점진적으로 극복을 시도하라는 것이 글의 핵심 내용이므로 이 글의 제목으로 적절하지 않다.
④ 글 초반에 언급된 '높은 층(higher ones)'과 관련된 내용을 이용하여 만든 오답이다.
⑤ 사회적 불안감을 극복하는 방법을 찾는 것은 어렵지만 사회적 관계에 자신을 노출시키는 것이 효과적이라고 했다.

R 40 정답 ④

밑줄 친 (a)~(e) 중에서 문맥상 낱말의 쓰임이 적절하지 않은 것은?

① (a) 사람은 무생물이 아니고, 사람들의 반응은 예측 불가능함
  더 까다로운
② (b) 앞에 접속사 but이 있으므로 앞의 내용과 상반되는 내용이 나와야 함
  상처받다
③ (c) 사회적 두려움에 맞서는 방법을 찾는 것이 매우 어려움
  이용할 수 있는(형성되는)
④ (d) 사회적 관계 맺기와 관련된 부정적인 내용이 연속해서 언급됨
  줄어들다
⑤ (e) 점진적 노출의 원칙을 적용하는 과정을 인식하는 것은 도움이 됨
  유용한

🔴오예 **1등급?** 큰 어려움이 '줄어드는' 것과 '늘어나는' 것 모두 선택지가 포함된 문장 내에서는 자연스럽게 해석되기 때문에 글의 전체 흐름과 앞뒤 문장의 내용을 정확하게 이해하여 어느 것이 문맥상 적절한 낱말인지를 파악해야 하는 1등급 대비 문제이다.

| 문제 풀이 순서 | [정답률 58%]

1st 각 낱말의 의미를 먼저 확인하고, 반의어를 미리 생각해 놓는다.

(a) trickier: 더 까다로운 ↔ simpler 더 쉬운
(b) suffer: 상처받다 ↔ cure: 치유하다
(c) available: 이용할 수 있는 ↔ unavailable: 이용할 수 없는
(d) decreases: 줄어들다 → increases: 늘어나다
(e) useful: 유용한 ↔ unuseful: 쓸모 없는

→ 반의어를 확실히 떠올리기 힘든 (b)는 정답이 아닐 가능성이 높다.

2nd 선택지의 앞뒤 내용을 파악해서 문맥이 자연스러운지 확인한다.

① (a) trickier 더 까다로운

사람을 사귄다는 것은 (a) 더 까다롭다. 사람은 주변에 있어서 익숙해지는 건물과 같은 무생물이 아니다. 당신은 그들과 상호 작용을 해야 하며 그들의 반응을 예측하기가 힘들 수 있다.

→ 사람은 무생물이 아니고, 사람들의 반응은 예측 불가능하다고 했으므로 사람을 사귄다는 것은 '더 까다로운' 것이다.

▶ trickier는 문맥에 맞음

② (b) suffer 상처받다

대부분의 사람들의 자존감은 그들이 발코니를 좋아하지 않는다고 해도 그렇게 많이 영향을 받지 않을 것이지만, 당신이 효과적으로 사람들을 사귈 수 없다면 당신의 자신감은 (b) 상처받을 수 있다.

→ 문장의 앞부분에 접속사 but이 있으므로 발코니에는 영향을 받지 않겠지만, 사람을 효과적으로 사귈 수 없다면 자신감은 '상처받을' 것이라는 표현은 적절하다.

▶ suffer는 문맥에 맞음

③ (c) available 이용할 수 있는

수많은 사교적 두려움을 점차적으로 마주하게 할 깔끔한 방법을 설계하는 것 또한 더 어렵다. 당신을 드러낼 필요가 있는 사교적 상황이 당신이 원할 때 (c) 형성되지 않을 수 있고, 또는 그것들은 상황이 통제 가능하다고 감지할 만큼 잘 진행되지 않을지도 모른다.

→ 사교적 두려움을 마주할 방법을 설계하는 것이 더 어렵다고 했으므로, 적절한 사교적 상황이 원할 때 '형성되지' 않을 수 있다는 표현은 적절하다.

▶ available는 문맥에 맞음

④ (d) decreases 줄어들다

한 단계에서 다음 단계로의 진행은 분명하지 않을 수 있으며, 한 단계에서 다음 단계로 진행할 때 피할 수 없이 큰 어려움이 (d) ~~줄어들게~~ 된다.
  늘어나게

→ 앞에서 인간과의 사교적 두려움은 점차적으로 마주하게 할 깔끔한 방법을 설계하는 것이 어렵다고 했으므로 한 단계에서 다음 단계로 진행할 때 피할 수 없는 큰 어려움이 '줄어들게' 되는 것이 아니다.

▶ decreases는 문맥에 맞지 않음 → 반의어로 바꿔 볼 것

→ decreases를 반의어인 increases로 바꿔야 앞뒤 문맥이 자연스러워진다.

▶ 정답은 ④임

⑤ (e) useful 유용한

점진적인 노출의 원칙은 여전히 매우 (e) 유용하다. 그것들을 적용하는 과정은 더 복잡하지만, 시작하기 전에 그것을 아는 것은 도움이 된다.

→ 뒤에 점진적 노출의 원칙을 적용하는 과정을 인식하는 것은 도움이 된다는 내용이 이어졌으므로 '유용한'이라는 표현은 적절하다.

▶ useful은 문맥에 맞음

─── **어법 특강**

✱ 동명사의 역할
– 동명사는 문장에서 주어, 목적어, 보어의 역할을 한다. 동명사가 주어로 쓰일 때는 단수 취급한다.
• <u>Drawing</u> is my favorite hobby. (주어)
(그림 그리기는 내가 가장 좋아하는 취미이다.)
• What I like most about my job is <u>meeting</u> many people. (보어)
(내가 내 직업에서 가장 좋아하는 점은 많은 사람들을 만나는 것이다.)
• He enjoys <u>playing</u> basketball with his friends. (목적어)
(그는 친구들과 농구하는 것을 즐긴다.)

✱ 동명사의 부정
– 동명사의 부정은 동명사 앞에 not 또는 never를 써서 표현한다.
• I'm sorry for <u>not telling</u> you the truth.
(너에게 진실을 말하지 못해서 미안해.)
• I can't understand her <u>not inviting</u> me to her housewarming party.
(난 그녀가 그녀의 집들이에 나를 초대하지 않은 것을 이해할 수 없다.)

R 어휘 Review 정답 ──── 문제편 p. 293

01 효과적으로	11 in earnest	21 suffering
02 천성	12 put aside	22 Inanimate
03 구성하다	13 engage in	23 rewiring
04 말하다	14 in return	24 domain
05 개념	15 from scratch	25 minimal
06 core	16 majority	26 evolved
07 average	17 cosmetics	27 ultimately
08 region	18 species	28 predators
09 morally	19 aspirations	29 carbon
10 quantify	20 accuracy	30 fundamentally

S 01~03 *Iktomi의 교훈과 드림캐처

(A) Long ago, / when the world was young, / an old Native American spiritual leader Odawa / had a dream on a high mountain. // 03번 ① Odawa는 높은 산에서 꿈을 꿈

오래전 / 세상이 생겨난 지 오래지 않을 무렵 / 아메리카 원주민의 늙은 영적 지도자인 Odawa는 / 높은 산에서 꿈을 꾸었다 //

동격
In his dream, / Iktomi, the great spirit and searcher of wisdom, / = Odawa
appeared to (a) him in the form of a spider. //

자신의 꿈속에서 / 위대한 신령이자 지혜의 구도자인 Iktomi가 / 거미의 형태로 그에게 나타났다 //

01번 단서 1: Iktomi가 Odawa에게 성스러운 언어로 말함
Iktomi spoke to him / in a holy language. //

Iktomi는 그에게 말했다 / 성스러운 언어로 //

*(A) 문단 요약: Odawa가 산에서 꿈을 꾸었고 Iktomi가 나타나서 성스러운 언어로 말함

= Odawa's
(B) Odawa shared Iktomi's lesson / with (b) his people. //

Odawa는 Iktomi의 교훈을 나누었다 / 그의 마을 사람들과 //
01번 단서 2: Odawa가 마을 사람들과 Iktomi의 교훈을 나눔
Today, many Native Americans / have dream catchers hanging above their beds. // 03번 ② 오늘날 많은 미국 원주민은 침대 위에 드림캐처를 걸어놓음
현재분사(dream catchers 수식)
오늘날 많은 미국 원주민은 / 침대 위에 드림캐처를 건다 //

Dream catchers are believed / to filter out bad dreams. //

드림캐처는 믿어진다 / 나쁜 꿈을 걸러 준다고 //

병렬 구조
The good dreams are captured in the web of life / and carried with the people. //

좋은 꿈은 인생이라는 거미집에 걸리고 / 사람들과 동반하게 된다 //

병렬 구조
The bad dreams pass through the hole in the web / and are no longer a part of their lives. //

나쁜 꿈은 거미집의 구멍 사이로 빠져나가고 / 더 이상 그들의 삶의 한 부분이 되지 못한다 //

*(B) 문단 요약: Odawa는 Iktomi의 교훈을 부족에 전하였고, 오늘날 많은 미국 원주민들은 나쁜 꿈을 걸러내고 좋은 꿈을 담는 드림캐처를 침대 위에 걸어둠

동명사(finished의 목적어)
(C) When Iktomi finished speaking, / he spun a web / and gave it to Odawa. // 03번 ③ Iktomi는 Odawa에게 거미집을 짜서 줌

Iktomi가 말을 끝냈을 때 / 그는 거미집을 짜서 / Odawa에게 주었다 //

He said to Odawa, / "The web is a perfect circle / with a hole in the center. //

그가 Odawa에게 말했다 / "그 거미집은 완벽한 원이다 / 가운데 구멍이 뚫린 //

준사역동사 help의 목적격 보어(동사원형)
Use the web / to help your people reach their goals. //

거미집을 사용해라 / 너의 마을 사람들이 자신들의 목표에 도달할 수 있도록 //

Make good use of their ideas, dreams, and visions. //

그들의 생각, 꿈, 비전을 잘 활용해라 //

= Odawa
If (c) you believe in the great spirit, / the web will catch your
= ideas
good ideas / and the bad ones will go through the hole." //

만약 네가 위대한 신령을 믿는다면 / 그 거미집이 네 좋은 생각을 붙잡아 줄 것이고 / 나쁜 생각은 구멍을 통해 빠져 나갈 것이다"라고 //
01번 단서 3, 03번 ④ Odawa는 잠에서 깨자마자 자신의 마을로 돌아감
Right after Odawa woke up, / he went back to his village. //

Odawa는 잠에서 깨자마자 / 자기 마을로 되돌아갔다 //

*(C) 문단 요약: Iktomi가 말을 마친 후에 거미집을 짜서 Odawa에게 주었고 거미집의 용도를 설명함
03번 ⑤ Iktomi는 Odawa에게 삶의 순환에 대해 말함
(D) Iktomi told Odawa / about the cycles of life. //

Iktomi는 Odawa에게 말했다 / 삶의 순환에 관해서 //

= Iktomi
(d) He said, / "We all begin our lives as babies, / move on to childhood, and then to adulthood. //

그는 말했다 / "우리는 모두 아기로 삶을 출발하고 / 유년기를 거쳐 그다음 성년기에 이르게 된다 //

계속적 용법의 관계부사(선행사: old age)
Finally, we come to old age, / where we must be taken care of / as babies again." // 01번 단서 4: Iktomi가 Odawa에게 성스러운 언어로 말한 내용

결국 우리는 노년기에 도달하고 / 거기서 우리는 보살핌을 받아야 한다 / 다시 아기처럼" 이라고 //

= Odawa 목적어절 접속사
Iktomi also told (e) him / that there are good and bad forces / in each stage of life. // 01번 단서 5: Iktomi가 Odawa에게 성스러운 언어로 말한 내용

또한 Iktomi는 그에게 말했다 / 좋고 나쁜 힘이 있다고 / 삶의 각 단계에는 //

"If we listen to the good forces, / they will guide us in the right direction. //

"우리가 좋은 힘에 귀를 기울이면 / 그들은 우리를 올바른 방향으로 인도할 것이다 //

But if we listen to the bad forces, / they will lead us the wrong way / and may harm us," / Iktomi said. //

하지만 만약 나쁜 힘에 귀를 기울이면 / 그들은 우리를 잘못된 길로 이끌고 / 우리를 해칠 수도 있다"라고 / Iktomi는 말했다 //

*(D) 문단 요약: Iktomi가 Odawa에게 삶의 순환에 관해 설명하며 삶의 각 단계에는 좋은 힘과 나쁜 힘이 있고 좋은 힘에 귀를 기울여야 한다고 말함

- Native American 미국 원주민　　• spiritual ⓐ 영적인
- in the form of ~의 모양으로　　• holy ⓐ 성스러운　　• lesson ⓝ 교훈
- filter out ~을 걸러내다　　• pass through ~을 통과하다
- spin ⓥ 짜다 (과거형 spun)　　• reach ⓥ 도달하다　　• cycle ⓝ 순환
- guide ⓥ 인도하다　　• harm ⓥ 해치다

(A) 오래전, 세상이 생겨난 지 오래지 않을 무렵, 아메리카 원주민의 늙은 영적 지도자인 Odawa는 높은 산에서 꿈을 꾸었다. 자신의 꿈속에서 위대한 신령이자 지혜의 구도자인 Iktomi가 거미의 형태로 (a) 그에게 나타났다. Iktomi는 성스러운 언어로 그에게 말했다.

(D) Iktomi는 Odawa에게 삶의 순환에 관해서 말했다. (d) 그는 "우리는 모두 아기로 삶을 출발하고, 유년기를 거쳐 그다음 성년기에 이르게 된다. 결국 우리는 노년기에 도달하고, 거기서 우리는 다시 아기처럼 보살핌을 받아야 한다."라고 말했다. 또한 Iktomi는 삶의 각 단계에는 좋고 나쁜 힘이 있다고 (e) 그에게 말했다. "우리가 좋은 힘에 귀를 기울이면 그들은 우리를 올바른 방향으로 인도할 것이다. 하지만 만약 나쁜 힘에 귀를 기울이면 그들은 우리를 잘못된 길로 이끌고 우리를 해칠 수도 있다."라고 Iktomi는 말했다.

(C) Iktomi가 말을 끝냈을 때, 그는 거미집을 짜서 Odawa에게 주었다. 그가 Odawa에게 말하기를, "그 거미집은 가운데 구멍이 뚫린 완벽한 원이다. 너의 마을 사람들이 자신들의 목표에 도달할 수 있도록 거미집을 사용해라. 그들의 생각, 꿈, 비전을 잘 활용해라. 만약 (c) 네가 위대한 신령을 믿는다면 그 거미집이 네 좋은 생각을 붙잡아 줄 것이고 나쁜 생각은 구멍을 통해 빠져 나갈 것이다." Odawa는 잠에서 깨자마자 자기 마을로 되돌아갔다.

(B) Odawa는 Iktomi의 교훈을 (b) 그의 마을 사람들과 나누었다. 오늘날 많은 미국 원주민은 침대 위에 드림캐처를 건다. 드림캐처는 나쁜 꿈을 걸러 준다고 믿어진다. 좋은 꿈은 인생이라는 거미집에 걸리고 사람들과 동반하게 된다. 나쁜 꿈은 거미집의 구멍 사이로 빠져나가고 더 이상 그들의 삶의 한 부분이 되지 못한다.

S 01 정답 ⑤

주어진 글 (A)에 이어질 내용을 순서에 맞게 배열한 것으로 가장 적절한 것은?

① (B) — (D) — (C) 주어진 글에 Iktomi가 준 교훈이 나오지 않았기 때문에 (B)가 올 수 없음

② (C) — (B) — (D) 주어진 글에 Iktomi가 어떤 말을 했는지 나오지 않았기 때문에 (C)가 올 수 없음

③ (C) — (D) — (B)

④ (D) — (B) — (C) 마을 사람들과 Iktomi의 교훈을 나누는 (B) 앞에 Odawa가 잠에서 깨어 마을로 돌아가는 (C)가 와야 함

⑤ (D) — (C) — (B) (D) Iktomi가 Odawa에게 가르침을 줌 — (C) Iktomi가 Odawa에게 거미집을 주고 용도를 설명함 — (B) Odawa는 Iktomi의 교훈을 마을 사람들과 나누고 오늘날 많은 미국 원주민은 드림캐처를 침대에 걸어둠

(A): Odawa가 산에서 꿈을 꾸었고 Iktomi가 나타나서 성스러운 언어로 말했다.

➡ Iktomi가 Odawa에게 전한 이야기가 이어질 것이다.

(B): Odawa는 Iktomi의 교훈을 부족에 전하였고, 오늘날 많은 미국 원주민들은 나쁜 꿈을 걸러내고 좋은 꿈을 담는 드림캐처를 침대 위에 걸어둔다.

➡ Iktomi가 준 교훈이 오늘날에 미친 영향을 설명하므로 글의 마무리 부분에 해당한다. Iktomi가 준 교훈의 내용과 드림캐처를 왜 걸어두게 되었는지가 앞에 와야 한다.

(C): Iktomi가 말을 마친 후에 거미집을 짜서 Odawa에게 주었고 거미집의 용도를 설명하였다.

➡ Iktomi가 Odawa에게 어떤 말을 했는지가 앞에 와야 한다.

(D): Iktomi가 Odawa에게 삶의 순환에 관해 설명하며 삶의 각 단계에는 좋은 힘과 나쁜 힘이 있고 좋은 힘에 귀를 기울여야 한다고 말했다.

➡ Iktomi가 나타나서 성스러운 언어로 이야기한 내용이므로 (A)의 바로 뒤에 이어진다.

▶ (A) Odawa가 산에서 꿈을 꾸었고 Iktomi가 나타나서 성스러운 언어로 이야기함 → (D) Iktomi가 Odawa에게 삶의 순환과, 좋고 나쁜 힘에 대해 설명함 → (C) Iktomi가 말을 마친 후에 거미집을 짜서 Odawa에게 주었고 거미집의 용도를 설명함 → (B) Odawa는 Iktomi의 교훈을 부족에 전하였고, 오늘날 많은 미국 원주민들은 나쁜 꿈을 걸러내고 좋은 꿈을 담는 드림캐처를 침대 위에 걸어두게 됨

▶ 글의 순서는 ⑤ (D) - (C) - (B)임

S 02 정답 ④

밑줄 친 (a)~(e) 중에서 가리키는 대상이 나머지 넷과 **다른** 것은?

① (a) ② (b) ③ (c) ④ (d) ⑤ (e)
= Odawa = Odawa's = Odawa = Iktomi = Odawa

왜 정답? ✽❀❀ [정답률 87%]

④ (d) He: Odawa에게 삶의 순환에 관해 설명하고 있는 사람 ▶ Iktomi

왜 오답?

① (a) him: Iktomi가 거미의 형태로 찾아간 사람 ▶ Odawa
② (b) his: Iktomi의 교훈을 Odawa가 자신의 마을 사람들과 나눔 ▶ Odawa's
③ (c) you: Iktomi가 '너'라고 지칭하는 사람 ▶ Odawa
⑤ (e) him: Iktomi가 삶의 각 단계에는 좋고 나쁜 힘이 있다고 말한 대상 ▶ Odawa

S 03 정답 ②

윗글에 관한 내용으로 적절하지 **않은** 것은?

① Odawa는 높은 산에서 꿈을 꾸었다. Odawa had a dream on a high mountain
② 많은 미국 원주민은 드림캐처를 현관 위에 건다. Today, many Native Americans have dream catchers hanging above their beds.
③ Iktomi는 Odawa에게 거미집을 짜서 주었다. he spun a web and gave it to Odawa
④ Odawa는 잠에서 깨자마자 자신의 마을로 돌아갔다. Right after Odawa woke up, he went back to his village.
⑤ Iktomi는 Odawa에게 삶의 순환에 대해 알려주었다. Iktomi told Odawa about the cycles of life.

왜 정답? ✽✽❀ [정답률 89%]

오늘날 많은 미국 원주민은 침대 위에 드림캐처를 건다고 했으므로 (Today, many Native Americans have dream catchers hanging above their beds.) 현관 위에 드림캐처를 건다는 ②은 적절하지 않다.

왜 오답?

① Odawa는 높은 산에서 꿈을 꾸었다. (Odawa had a dream on a high mountain)
③ Iktomi는 Odawa에게 거미집을 짜서 주었다. (he spun a web and gave it to Odawa)
④ Odawa는 잠에서 깨자마자 자신의 마을로 돌아갔다. (Right after Odawa woke up, he went back to his village.)
⑤ Iktomi는 Odawa에게 삶의 순환에 대해 알려주었다. (Iktomi told Odawa about the cycles of life.)

S 04~06 ＊알면 보물, 모르면 돌덩이

(A) Jack, / an Arkansas farmer, / was unhappy / because he
   동격   06번 ① Jack은 자신의 농장에서 충분한 돈을 벌지 못했음
couldn't make enough money / from his farm. //
Jack은 / Arkansas주의 농부인 / 불행했다 / 충분한 돈을 벌지 못해 / 자신의 농장에서 //

He worked hard for many years, / but things didn't improve. //
여러 해 동안 열심히 일했지만 / 상황은 나아지지 않았다 //

He sold his farm / to his neighbor, Victor, / who was by no
means wealthy. // 06번 ② Jack은 자신의 이웃인 Victor에게 농장을 판매함
그는 자신의 농장을 팔았는데 / 자신의 이웃인 Victor에게 / 그는 결코 부유하지 않았다 //
   분사구문   부사적 용법(목적)
Hoping for a fresh start, / he left for the big city / to find better
opportunities. //
새로운 출발을 기대하며 / 그는 대도시로 떠났다 / 더 나은 기회를 찾아 //
                                            앞에 목적격 관계대명사가 생략됨
Years passed, / but Jack still couldn't find the fortune / he was
looking for. //
몇 년이 흘렀지만 / Jack은 여전히 부를 얻지 못했다 / 자신이 찾고 있던 //
   Being이 생략된 분사구문   = Jack   관계부사
Tired and broke, / (a) he returned to the area / where his old
farm was. // 04번 단서 1: 타지에서 실패 후 자신이 살던 곳으로 돌아옴
지치고 무일푼이 되어서 / 그는 그 지역으로 돌아왔다 / 자신의 옛 농장이 있던 //

＊ (A) 문단 요약: 농부인 Jack은 연속되는 실패 끝에 고향에 다시 돌아옴

(B) "How did you do all this?" / he asked. //
"어떻게 이 모든 걸 해냈어요"라고 / 그가 물었다 //

And he continued, / "When you bought the farm, / you barely
had any money. //
그리고 그는 계속해서 물었다 / "당신이 농장을 샀을 때 / 당신은 돈이 거의 없었잖아요 //

How did you get so rich?" //
어떻게 그렇게 부자가 되었죠"라고 //
                                       = Jack
Victor smiled and said, / "I owe it all to (b) you. //
Victor는 미소를 지으며 / "그 모든 것이 다 당신 덕분이에요 //

There were diamonds on this land / — acres and acres of
diamonds! //
이 땅에는 다이아몬드가 있었어요 / 대량의 다이아몬드가 //

I got rich / because I discovered those diamonds." //
저는 부자가 되었어요 / 그 다이아몬드를 발견했기 때문에 // 04번 단서 2, 06번 ③ Victor는 다이아몬드를 발견하여 부자가 되었음

"Diamonds?" / Jack said in disbelief. //
"다이아몬드요"라고 / Jack은 믿지 못하며 말했다 //

And he said, / "I knew every part of that land, / and there were
no diamonds!" //
그리고 그는 말했다 / "제가 그 땅에 대해 전부 아는데 / 다이아몬드는 없었어요"라고 //

＊ (B) 문단 요약: Victor는 Jack의 옛 농장에서 다이아몬드를 발견해 부자가 되었다고 말함

(C) Victor reached into his pocket / and carefully pulled out
something small and shiny. // 06번 ④ 주머니에서 작고 반짝이는 다이아몬드를 꺼냄
Victor는 자신의 주머니로 손을 뻗어 / 조심스럽게 작고 반짝이는 것을 꺼냈다 //
   분사구문을 이끄는 현재분사   = Victor's
Holding it between (c) his fingers, / he let it catch the light. //
그것을 자신의 손가락 사이에 잡고 / 그는 그것이 빛을 받도록 했다 //

He said, / "This is a diamond." //
그는 말했다 / "이것이 다이아몬드입니다"라고 //

Jack was amazed and said, / "I saw so many rocks like that / and
thought **they** were useless. //
= many rocks

Jack은 놀라서 말했다 / "저는 그런 돌을 많이 봤는데 / 그것들이 쓸모가 없다고 생각했어요 //

They made farming so hard!" //

그것들이 농사짓는 걸 너무 힘들게 만들었어요 //

Victor laughed and said, / "(d) **You** didn't know / what diamonds
= Jack

look like. // 04번 단서 3: Victor는 다이아몬드를 알아보고 부자가 되었고, Jack은 그러지 못함

Victor는 웃으며 말했다 / "당신은 몰랐군요 / 다이아몬드가 어떻게 생겼는지 //
수동태 동사

Sometimes, / treasures **are hidden** / right in front of us." //

때때로 / 보물은 숨겨져 있으니까요 / 바로 우리 앞에"라고 //

* (C) 문단 요약: Jack과 달리 Victor는 다이아몬드를 알아봄

(D) One day, / he drove past his old land / and was shocked by
what he saw. //

어느 날 / 그는 자신의 옛 땅을 운전해 지나가다가 / 그가 본 것에 깜짝 놀랐다 //
동격

Victor, / **the man who had bought the farm with very little**
money, / now seemed to be living a life of great success. //

Victor가, / 아주 적은 돈으로 농장을 샀던 / 이제는 대단한 성공을 거둔 삶을 살고 있는 것처럼 보였다 // 04번 단서 4: 농장을 팔고 나니 농장주는 부자가 되어 있었음

He had torn down the farmhouse / and built a massive house
in its place. // 06번 ⑤ 농가가 있던 자리에는 거대한 집이 생김

그는 농가를 허물었고 / 그것이 있던 자리에 거대한 집을 지었다 //

New buildings, trees, and flowers / adorned the well-kept
property. //

새 건물들, 나무들, 그리고 꽃들이 / 잘 관리된 소유지를 꾸몄다 //

Jack could hardly believe / that (e) **he** had ever worked on this
= Jack

same land. //

Jack은 도저히 믿을 수 없었다 / 자신이 예전에 이 똑같은 땅에서 일했던 것을 //
Being이 생략된 분사구문

Curious, / he stopped to talk to Victor. // 04번 단서 5: 부자가 된 비결을 알기 위해 질문함

궁금해서 / 그는 Victor에게 말을 걸기 위해 멈췄다 //

* (D) 문단 요약: Jack은 옛 농지가 크게 변한 것에 놀라서 Victor에게 말을 걺

- by no means 결코 ~이 아닌   - barely ad 거의 ~ 없이
- owe v 덕분이다   - disbelief n 믿지 않음, 불신   - treasure n 보물
- tear down 허물다   - massive a 거대한   - property n 소유지

(A) Arkansas주의 농부인 Jack은 자신의 농장에서 충분한 돈을 벌지 못해 불행했다. 여러 해 동안 열심히 일했지만, 상황은 나아지지 않았다. 그는 자신의 농장을 자신의 이웃인 Victor에게 팔았는데, 그는 결코 부유하지 않았다. 새로운 출발을 기대하며, 그는 더 나은 기회를 찾아 대도시로 떠났다. 몇 년이 흘렀지만, Jack은 여전히 자신이 찾고 있던 부를 얻지 못했다. 지치고 무일푼이 되어서, (a) 그는 자신의 옛 농장이 있던 지역으로 돌아왔다.

(D) 어느 날, 그는 자신의 옛 땅을 운전해 지나가다가 그가 본 것에 깜짝 놀랐다. 아주 적은 돈으로 농장을 샀던 Victor가 이제는 대단한 성공을 거둔 삶을 살고 있는 것처럼 보였다. 그는 농가를 허물었고 그것이 있던 자리에 거대한 집을 지었다. 새 건물들, 나무들, 그리고 꽃들이 잘 관리된 소유지를 꾸몄다. Jack은 (e) 자신이 예전에 이 똑같은 땅에서 일했던 것을 도저히 믿을 수 없었다. 궁금해서, 그는 Victor에게 말을 걸기 위해 멈췄다.

(B) "어떻게 이 모든 걸 해냈어요?"라고 그가 물었다. 그리고 그는 계속해서 "당신이 농장을 샀을 때, 당신은 돈이 거의 없었잖아요. 어떻게 그렇게 부자가 되었죠?"라고 물었다. Victor는 미소를 지으며, "그 모든 것이 다 (b) 당신 덕분이에요. 이 땅에는 다이아몬드가, 대량의 다이아몬드가 있었어요! 제가 부자가 된 것은 그 다이아몬드를 발견했기 때문이에요."라고 말했다. "다이아몬드요?"라고 Jack은 믿지 못하며 말했다. 그리고 그는 "제가 그 땅에 대해 전부 아는데, 다이아몬드는 없었어요!"라고 말했다.

(C) Victor는 자신의 주머니로 손을 뻗어 조심스럽게 작고 반짝이는 것을 꺼냈다. 그것을 (c) 자신의 손가락 사이에 잡고, 그는 그것이 빛을 받도록 했다. 그는 "이것이 다이아몬드입니다."라고 말했다. Jack은 놀라서 "저는 그런 돌을 많이 봤는데 그것들이 쓸모가 없다고 생각했어요. 그것들이 농사짓는 걸 너무 힘들게 만들었어요!"라고 말했다. Victor는 웃으며 "(d) 당신은 다이아몬드가 어떻게 생겼는지 몰랐군요. 때때로 보물은 바로 우리 앞에 숨겨져 있으니까요."라고 말했다.

S 04 정답 ④

주어진 글 (A)에 이어질 내용을 순서에 맞게 배열한 것으로 가장 적절한 것은?

① (B) — (D) — (C)
② (C) — (B) — (D)   Victor가 부자가 된 사실을 발견했다는 (D)가 (A) 바로 뒤에 이어짐
③ (C) — (D) — (B)   부자가 된 비결을 밝히는 (C)가 가장 마지막에 옴
④ (D) — (B) — (C)   (D) Jack이 자신이 팔았던 농장이 발전했음을 발견 — (B) Victor가 농장에서 다이아몬드를 발견하여 부자가 되었음을 밝힘 — (C) Jack은 눈앞의 보물을 발견하지 못했으나 Victor는 이를 발견하여 부자가 되었음
⑤ (D) — (C) — (B)   Jack이 농장에 다이아몬드가 없었다고 한 (B) 바로 뒤에 Victor가 다이아몬드를 직접 보여 주는 (C)가 와야 함

왜 정답·오답? ★★★ [정답률 79%]

[**(A):** Jack은 농장에서 충분한 수입을 얻지 못해 Victor에게 농장을 팔고 대도시로 떠났지만 결국 실패하고 고향으로 돌아왔다.

→ Jack이 고향으로 돌아온 후 어떤 일이 일어났는지에 주목한다.

[**(B):** Jack이 Victor에게 어떻게 성공했는지 묻자, Victor는 농장 땅에서 다이아몬드를 발견해 부자가 되었다고 답했고, Jack은 그럴 리가 없다고 했다.

→ Victor의 성공이 구체적으로 어떤 것인지 앞에 나와야 한다. 뒤에는 농장 땅에 다이아몬드가 있을 리 없다는 Jack의 말에 대한 Victor의 말이 이어져야 한다.

[**(C):** Victor는 Jack에게 실제 다이아몬드를 보여줬는데, Jack은 그것들이 보물임을 몰랐고 Victor는 때때로 보물이 우리 앞에 숨겨져 있다고 말했다.

→ Jack이 농장 땅에 다이아몬드가 있을 리 없다고 한 (B)에 이어지는 내용으로, 눈앞의 보물을 알아보는 사람이 부자가 될 수 있다고 하며 글이 마무리된다.

[**(D):** Jack은 자신이 팔았던 농장이 Victor에 의해 멋지게 바뀐 것을 보고 놀라 Victor에게 말을 걸었다.

→ Jack이 Victor에게 농장을 팔고 실패한 뒤에, 농장이 있던 지역으로 돌아왔다는 (A)에 이어지는 내용이다. Victor에게 어떻게 성공했는지 묻는 (B)가 뒤에 이어진다.

▶ 글의 순서는 ④ (D) — (B) — (C)임

S 05 정답 ③

밑줄 친 (a)~(e) 중에서 가리키는 대상이 나머지 넷과 다른 것은?

① (a)   ② (b)   ③(c)   ④ (d)   ⑤ (e)
= Jack   = Jack   = Victor's   = Jack   = Jack

왜 정답? ★★☆ [정답률 77%]

③ (c) his: 다이아몬드를 손가락 사이에 잡아 보여준 사람 ▶ Victor's

왜 오답?

① (a) he: 무일푼이 되어서 옛 농장이 있던 지역으로 돌아온 사람 ▶ Jack
② (b) you: Victor가 부자가 될 수 있도록 도와준 사람 ▶ Jack
④ (d) You: 다이아몬드가 어떻게 생겼는지 몰랐던 사람 ▶ Jack
⑤ (e) he: 자신이 이 똑같은 땅에서 일했던 것을 믿지 못하는 사람 ▶ Jack

S 06 정답 ②

윗글에 관한 내용으로 적절하지 않은 것은?

① Jack은 자신의 농장에서 충분한 돈을 벌지 못했다.
② Jack은 자신의 이웃인 Victor에게서 농장을 샀다.
   he couldn't make enough money from his farm
   He sold his farm to his neighbor, Victor
③ Victor는 다이아몬드를 발견해서 부자가 되었다.
④ Victor는 자신의 주머니에서 작고 반짝이는 것을 꺼냈다.
   I got rich because I discovered those diamonds
⑤ Victor는 농가가 있던 자리에 거대한 집을 지었다.
   Victor reached into his pocket ~ pulled out something small and shiny.
   He had torn down the farmhouse and built a massive house in its place.

>왜 정답? ✹✹❀ [정답률 82%]

Jack이 Victor에게 농장을 판 것이므로 (He sold his farm to his neighbor, Victor) Jack이 자신의 이웃 Victor에게서 농장을 샀다는 ②은 적절하지 않다.

>왜 오답?

① Jack은 자신의 농장에서 충분한 돈을 벌지 못했다. (he couldn't make enough money from his farm)

③ Victor는 다이아몬드를 발견해서 부자가 되었다. (I got rich because I discovered those diamonds)

④ Victor는 자신의 주머니에서 작고 반짝이는 것을 꺼냈다. (Victor reached into his pocket ~ pulled out something small and shiny.)

⑤ Victor는 농가가 있던 자리에 거대한 집을 지었다. (He had torn down the farmhouse and built a massive house in its place.)

구문 서술형

정답 Never was he happy because he couldn't make enough money from his farm.

해석 그는 자신의 농장에서 충분한 돈을 벌지 못했기 때문에 불행했다 (→ 결코 행복하지 않았다).

→ never와 같은 부정어가 강조를 위해 문장 맨 앞에 올 때 주어와 동사가 도치된다. 따라서 Never가 맨 앞에 온 뒤 주어(he)와 동사(was)가 도치된 Never was he ~로 쓴다.

S 07~09 ＊친절이 낳는 선한 영향력

(A) The sun shone / in the cloudless sky / **as** Becky, a retired teacher, walked to the fruit market. // 09번 ① Becky가 과일 시장으로 걸어갔음
부사절 접속사 (시간)
태양은 빛났다 / 구름 한 점 없는 하늘에서 / 퇴직한 교사인 Becky가 과일 시장으로 걸어갈 때 //

Across town, / Dana was riding a bus / towards the museum / for a job interview. //
도시를 가로질러 / Dana는 버스를 타고 가고 있었다 / 미술관으로 / 취업 면접을 위해 //

Just before reaching her stop, / Dana noticed / **the sky** had suddenly darkened. //
앞에 목적어절 접속사 that이 생략됨
그녀가 내릴 정류장에 다다르기 직전에 / Dana는 알아챘다 / 하늘이 갑자기 어두워진 것을 //

Her heart sank / — she had no umbrella. //
그녀는 가슴이 철렁했다 / 그녀는 우산이 없었다 //

As (a) <u>she</u> stepped off the bus / next to the market, / **where** Becky had just finished shopping, / raindrops began to fall. //
= Dana   계속적 용법의 관계부사
그녀가 버스에서 내렸을 때 / 시장 옆에서 / Becky가 장보기를 막 끝낸 / 빗방울이 떨어지기 시작했다 //
07번 단서 1: Dana가 버스에서 내렸을 때 비가 내리기 시작함

* (A) 문단 요약: Dana가 취업 면접을 보러 미술관에 가던 중 갑자기 비가 오기 시작했음
07번 단서 2: Dana는 Becky로부터 우산을 받고 고마워했음
병렬 구조
(B) Dana **thanked** her, / **took** the umbrella, / and **opened** it. //
Dana는 그녀에게 고마워했고 / 우산을 받아 / 그것을 펼쳤다 //

과거분사구 (a small card 수식)
She saw a small card / **tied to the handle**. // 09번 ② Dana가 받은 우산 손잡이에 작은 카드가 묶여 있었음
그녀는 작은 카드를 보았다 / 손잡이에 묶인 //
'~라고 적혀 있다'
It **read**: "Cover each other." //
그것에는 "서로를 감싸주세요"라고 적혀 있었다 //

She was touched by the message. // 그녀는 그 메시지에 감동받았다 //

She **hurried** to the museum, / arriving dry and comfortable, /
병렬 구조
and **performed** well in her interview. //
그녀는 미술관에 서둘러 갔다 / 마른 채로 편안하게 도착해서 / 인터뷰에서 잘 해냈다 //

= Dana
The Museum CEO was impressed by Dana / and offered (b) <u>her</u>
목적격
/ **the Event Manager position, her dream job**. //
미술관 CEO는 Dana에 의해 감명받았고 / 그녀에게 제시했다 / 그녀의 꿈의 직업인, 이벤트 매니저직을 //

Throughout the years ahead, / she often thought back / to Becky's kind gesture. // 09번 ③ Dana는 Becky의 친절한 행동을 종종 떠올렸음
향후 몇 년 동안 / 그녀는 종종 떠올렸다 / Becky의 친절한 행동을 //

* (B) 문단 요약: Dana는 인터뷰를 잘 해내고 이벤트 매니저직을 받은 뒤 종종 Becky의 친절한 행동을 떠올렸음
Being이 생략된 분사구문
(C) **Inspired by the memory**, / Dana created a museum event /
과거분사구 (a museum event 수식)   현재분사구 (people 수식)
called "Cover Each Other" / with paintings of people **supporting others**. // 07번 단서 3: Dana가 Becky의 친절한 행동에 영감을 받아 미술관 행사를 엶
그 기억에 영감을 받아서 / Dana는 미술관 행사를 만들었다 / "서로를 감싸주세요"라는 / 다른 사람을 돕는 사람들의 그림으로 //

주격 관계대명사 (families 수식)
She donated / half of the money from ticket sales / to families / **who** lost their homes to natural disasters. // 09번 ④ Dana는 티켓 판매금의 절반을 기부함
그녀는 기부했다 / 티켓 판매로 얻은 돈의 절반을 / 가족들에게 / 자연재해로 그들의 집을 잃은 //

kept의 목적어와 목적격 보어 (과거분사)   = Dana's
Dana kept **Becky's message framed** / in (c) <u>her</u> office / as a reminder / **that** one kind gesture could change someone's life. //
동격절 접속사
Dana는 Becky의 메시지를 액자로 넣어두었다 / 그녀의 사무실에 / 상기시키는 것으로서 / 하나의 친절한 행동이 누군가의 삶을 바꿀 수 있음을 //

The kindness of one stranger / had shaped her path, / and she made sure **it continued** to shape the world. //
앞에 목적어절 접속사 that이 생략됨
낯선 한 사람의 친절이 / 그녀의 길을 만들었고 / 그녀는 그것이 계속해서 세상을 만들어가도록 했다 //

* (C) 문단 요약: Becky로부터 영감을 받은 Dana는 미술관 행사를 열어 기부하고 Becky의 메시지를 상기함

(D) Dana felt panic. // Dana는 당황했다 // 07번 단서 4: 면접에 가야 하는 Dana는 비를 맞고 싶지 않았음
분사구문
She didn't want to show up / to her interview / **soaked**. //
그녀는 나타나고 싶지 않았다 / 면접에 / 흠뻑 젖어서 //
형용사적 용법 (stores 수식)
She looked around but couldn't find any stores nearby / **to buy** an umbrella, / and she didn't have time / **to search** around. //
형용사적 용법 (time 수식)
그녀는 주위를 둘러보았지만 어떤 가게도 / 근처에서 찾을 수 없었고 / 우산을 구매할 만한 / 시간도 없었다 / 주변을 찾아볼 // 09번 ⑤ Dana는 우산을 구매할 가게를 찾을 수 없었음
타동사(뒤에 전치사 없이 목적어를 이끄는 현재분사) = Dana
Just then, / Becky **approached** (d) <u>her</u>, / **holding** an open umbrella in one hand / and a closed **one** **in the other**. //
= umbrella   = the other hand
바로 그때 / Becky가 그녀에게 다가왔다 / 한 손에는 펼친 우산을 들고서 / 다른 손에는 접힌 것을 //
= Becky
"Take this," / (e) <u>she</u> said with a smile. //
"이거 받아요" / 그녀가 미소를 지으며 말했다 // 07번 단서 5: Becky가 Dana에게 우산을 건넴

Dana's eyes widened. // Dana의 눈이 커졌다 //

"Are you sure?" // "정말이세요" //

Becky nodded. // Becky는 고개를 끄덕였다 //

"I always carry an extra / on rainy days." //
"저는 항상 여분 하나를 가지고 다녀요 / 비 오는 날에" //

* (D) 문단 요약: 우산 없이 비를 만나 당황한 Dana에게 Becky가 여분의 우산을 건넴

• retired ⓐ 퇴직한   • notice ⓥ 알아채다   • step off 내리다
• tie ⓥ 묶다   • touched ⓐ 감동한   • impressed ⓐ 감명받은
• offer ⓥ 제안하다   • inspired ⓐ 영감을 받은   • donate ⓥ 기부하다
• natural disaster 자연재해   • frame ⓥ 액자에 넣다
• shape ⓥ 형성하다   • nod ⓥ (고개를) 끄덕이다

(A) 퇴직한 교사인 Becky가 과일 시장으로 걸어갈 때, 태양은 구름 한 점 없는 하늘에서 빛났다. 도시를 가로질러, Dana는 취업 면접을 위해 버스를 타고 미술관으로 가고 있었다. 그녀가 내릴 정류장에 다다르기 직전에, Dana는 하늘이 갑자기 어두워진 것을 알아챘다. 그녀는 가슴이 철렁했다 — 그녀는 우산이 없었다. Becky가 장보기를 막 끝낸 시장 옆에서 (a) 그녀가 버스에서 내렸을 때, 빗방울이 떨어지기 시작했다.

(D) Dana는 당황했다. 그녀는 흠뻑 젖어서 면접에 나타나고 싶지 않았다. 그녀는 주위를 둘러보았지만 우산을 구매할 만한 어떤 가게도 근처에서 찾을 수 없었고, 주변을 찾아볼 시간도 없었다. 바로 그때, Becky가 한 손에는 펼친 우산을 다른 손에는 접힌 것을 들고서, (d) 그녀에게 다가왔다. "이거 받아요," (e) 그녀가 미소를 지으며 말했다. Dana의 눈이 커졌다. "정말이세요?" Becky는 고개를 끄덕였다. "저는 비 오는 날에 항상 여분 하나를 가지고 다녀요."

(B) Dana는 그녀에게 고마워했고, 우산을 받아, 그것을 펼쳤다. 그녀는 손잡이에 묶인 작은 카드를 보았다. 그것에는 "서로를 감싸주세요."라고 적혀 있었다. 그녀는 그 메시지에 감동받았다. 그녀는 미술관에 서둘러 갔고, 마른 채로 편안하게 도착해서, 인터뷰에서 잘 해냈다. 미술관 CEO는 Dana에 의해 감명받았고, (b) 그녀에게 그녀의 꿈의 직업인, 이벤트 매니저직을 제시했다. 향후 몇 년 동안, 그녀는 종종 Becky의 친절한 행동을 떠올렸다.
(C) 그 기억에 영감을 받아서, Dana는 다른 사람을 돕는 사람들의 그림들로 "서로를 감싸주세요"라는 미술관 행사를 만들었다. 그녀는 티켓 판매로 얻은 돈의 절반을 자연재해로 그들의 집을 잃은 가족들에게 기부했다. Dana는 하나의 친절한 행동이 누군가의 삶을 바꿀 수 있음을 상기시키는 것으로서 Becky의 메시지를 (c) 그녀의 사무실에 액자로 넣어두었다. 낯선 한 사람의 친절이 그녀의 길을 만들었고, 그녀는 그것이 계속해서 세상을 만들어가도록 했다.

S 07 정답 ④

> 주어진 글 (A)에 이어질 내용을 순서에 맞게 배열한 것으로 가장 적절한 것은?

① (B) — (D) — (C)   갑자기 비가 내리기 시작했다는 (A) 뒤에 Dana가 당황했다는 (D)가 이어져야 함
② (C) — (B) — (D)   Becky의 친절한 행동에 영감을 받아 이를 실천했다는 (C)가 마지막에 와야 함
③ (C) — (D) — (B)
④ (D) — (B) — (C)   (D) 비가 내려 당황한 Dana에게 Becky가 여분의 우산을 건네줌 — (B) 인터뷰를 잘 해내고 미술관 이벤트 매니저직을 받은 Dana가 Becky의 친절한 행동을 종종 떠올렸음 — (C) Dana는 미술관 행사를 열어 기부하고 Becky의 메시지를 상기했음
⑤ (D) — (C) — (B)   Dana가 Becky로부터 우산을 받았다는 (D) 뒤에 Dana가 Becky에게 고마워했다는 (B)가 이어져야 함

> **왜** 정답·오답 **?** ✽✽✽ [정답률 89%]

[**(A):** Dana는 취업 면접을 위해 미술관에 가던 중 우산 없이 갑작스럽게 비를 만났다.

➡ 우산이 없는 Dana에게 어떤 일이 일어났는지 주목한다.

[**(B):** Dana는 Becky에게 고마워하며 우산을 받았고, 무사히 인터뷰를 마친 덕에 미술관 이벤트 매니저직을 맡게 된 Dana는 Becky의 친절한 행동을 종종 떠올린다.

➡ Dana가 고마워하는 내용 앞에 Becky가 Dana에게 우산을 건네주는 내용이 먼저 나와야 한다.

[**(C):** Dana는 미술관 행사를 열어 기부하고 Becky의 메시지를 상기한다.

➡ Becky의 친절에 영감을 받은 Dana가 행사를 열어 기부하고, 친절한 행동이 누군가의 삶을 바꿀 수 있다는 내용으로 글이 마무리된다.

[**(D):** 우산이 없어서 당황한 Dana에게 Becky가 여분의 우산을 건넸다.

➡ Dana가 우산 없이 갑자기 비를 만났다는 (A)에 이어지는 내용이다. 우산을 받고 고마워했다는 (B)가 뒤에 이어진다.
▶ 글의 순서는 ④ (D) — (B) — (C)임

S 08 정답 ⑤

> 밑줄 친 (a)~(e) 중에서 가리키는 대상이 나머지 넷과 <u>다른</u> 것은?

① (a)   ② (b)   ③ (c)   ④ (d)   ⑤ (e)
= Dana   = Dana   = Dana's   = Dana   = Becky

> **왜** 정답 **?** ✽✽✽ [정답률 83%]

⑤ (e) she: 미소를 지으며 Dana에게 우산을 준 사람 ▶ Becky

> **왜** 오답 **?**

① (a) she: 시장 옆에서 버스에서 내린 사람 ▶ Dana
② (b) her: 미술관 CEO에게 이벤트 매니저직을 제안받은 사람 ▶ Dana
③ (c) her: Becky의 메시지를 사무실 액자에 넣어둔 사람 ▶ Dana's
④ (d) her: Becky가 다가간 사람 ▶ Dana

S 09 정답 ④

> 윗글에 관한 내용으로 적절하지 <u>않은</u> 것은?

① Becky는 과일 시장으로 걸어갔다.   Becky ~ walked to the fruit market.
② 작은 카드는 Dana가 받은 우산 손잡이에 매여 있었다.   She saw a small card tied to the handle.
③ Dana는 Becky의 친절한 행동을 종종 떠올렸다.   she often thought back to Becky's kind gesture
④ Dana는 티켓 판매금 전액을 기부했다.   She donated half of the money from ticket sales
⑤ Dana는 우산을 구매할 가게를 찾을 수 없었다.   She ~ couldn't find any stores nearby to buy an umbrella

> **왜** 정답 **?** ✽✽✽ [정답률 89%]

Dana가 티켓 판매금의 절반을 기부했으므로 (She donated half of the money from ticket sales) 티켓 판매금 전액을 기부했다는 ④은 적절하지 않다.

> **왜** 오답 **?**

① Becky는 과일 시장으로 걸어갔다. (Becky ~ walked to the fruit market.)
② 작은 카드는 Dana가 받은 우산 손잡이에 매여 있었다. (She saw a small card tied to the handle.)
③ Dana는 Becky의 친절한 행동을 종종 떠올렸다. (she often thought back to Becky's kind gesture)
⑤ Dana는 우산을 구매할 가게를 찾을 수 없었다. (She ~ couldn't find any stores nearby to buy an umbrella)

구문 서술형

정답 was, did

→ 주어 뒤에 일반동사 want가 있으므로 Never 뒤의 조동사는 do/does/did로 써야 한다. 과거시제이므로 was를 did로 고쳐야 한다.

S 10~12 ✽예상치 못한 친절에서 비롯된 Dave에 대한 이해

(A) While the cafeteria was full of high school students on that afternoon, / Dave was thirsty. // 12번① 그날 오후 식당은 고등학생들로 가득 찼음
그날 오후 식당이 고등학생들로 가득 차 있었던 동안 / Dave는 목이 말랐다 //
We sat near yet away from him, / fixing our hair and worrying about the test next period / we hadn't studied for. //   분사구문 / 목적격 관계사절 (the test 수식)
우리는 가까이 앉아 있었지만 그와는 먼 곳에 앉아 있었고 / 머리를 매만지며 다음 교시에 있을 시험을 걱정했다 / 공부하지 않았던 //
  = Dave
(a) He was far away from our world, / yet forced to be a part of it. // 그는 우리 세계와는 동떨어져 있었지만 / 억지로 그 안의 일부가 되어야만 했다 //
* (A) 문단 요약: Dave는 목이 말랐고, 다른 학생들과 어울리지 못하고 있었음
  가주어   진주어절 접속사
(B) Although it was clear / that they were from very different worlds, / for one moment, / they'd shared a real understanding. //
비록 분명했지만 / 그들이 매우 다른 세상에서 온 것은 / 어느 한순간 / 그들은 진실한 이해를 나누었다 //
  10번 단서 1: 다른 세상에서 온 둘(Dave와 상급생)이서 진실한 이해를 나눔
As I walked away from my lunch table that day, / I looked at Dave. // 그날 점심 테이블에서 떠나며 / 나는 Dave를 바라보았다 //
I thought / he and the dollar were very much alike. //
나는 생각했다 / 그와 그 달러가 많이 비슷하다고 //   12번② I'는 Dave와 그 달러가 비슷하다고 생각함
  관계부사
They both weren't accepted / where the world said / they were supposed to be. //
그들 둘 다 받아들여지지 않았다 / 세상이 말한 곳에서 / 그들이 있어야 할 자리라고 //
But just as the dollar had found a place / in a warm-hearted senior's pocket, / I was sure (b) he would eventually find his, too. //   = Dave   = his place
하지만 그 달러가 자리를 찾았듯 / 마음씨 따뜻한 상급생의 주머니 속에서 / 나는 그 역시 결국 그의 자리를 찾을 거라고 확신했다 //
* (B) 문단 요약: 글쓴이는 결국 제자리를 찾은 달러처럼 Dave도 그럴 것이라고 확신함

(C) But for some reason, / he decided against it. // **10번** 단서 2: Dave는 포기하지 않기로 함

하지만 무슨 이유에서인지 / 그는 그렇게 하지 않기로 했다 //
부사절 접속사 (~까지)
He wasn't leaving / until he got a drink. //

그는 떠나지 않고 있었다 / 음료를 얻을 때까지 //
= Dave
With a determined expression, / (c) he kept aimlessly pushing

the dollar bill into the machine. //

단호한 표정을 지으며 / 그는 그 달러 지폐를 자판기에 계속 아무렇게나 밀어 넣었다 //

Just then / a popular senior boy stood up from his seat, / and

walked over to the boy. // **10번** 단서 3: 인기 많은 상급생이 자리에서 일어나 Dave에게 다가감

바로 그때 / 한 인기 많은 상급생이 자리에서 일어나더니 / 그 소년에게 다가갔다 //
= a popular senior boy
(d) He calmly explained / how the machine often had trouble

accepting dollar bills. // **10번** 단서 4: 상급생은 Dave에게 자판기가 지폐를 자주 인식하지 못함을 설명해 줌

그는 차분히 설명해 주었다 / 자판기가 얼마나 자주 지폐를 잘 인식하지 못하는지 //
병렬 구조 (동사)
After that, / he pulled some coins from his pocket / and put

them into the machine. // **12번 ③** 상급생은 주머니에서 동전을 꺼냈음

그 후 / 그는 자신의 주머니에서 동전을 꺼내 / 자판기에 넣었다 //
병렬 구조 (동사)
Dave gave him his dollar / and chose a flavor of fruit juice. //

Dave는 자신의 달러를 그에게 주었고 / 과일 주스 맛을 골랐다 //

Then the two walked off / in different directions. //

그러고 나서 그들은 떠났다 / 다른 방향으로 // **12번 ④** Dave와 상급생은 다른 방향으로 떠남

★ (C) 문단 요약: 포기하지 않던 Dave를 한 상급생이 동전으로 도와주고 각자 갈 길을 감
분사구문을 이끄는 현재분사
(D) He stood at the drink machine with purpose, / fumbling

through his fake leather wallet for some change. //

그는 목적을 가지고 음료 자판기 앞에 섰고 / 인조 가죽 지갑에서 잔돈을 더듬어 찾았다 //

He came up with a wrinkled dollar bill, / and nervously glanced
관계부사   = Dave's
back at his table / where other students in (e) his class were

sitting. //

그는 구겨진 1달러 지폐를 꺼내어 / 테이블을 불안하게 돌아보았다 / 그의 학급의 다른 학생들이 앉아 있는 //
make의 목적어와 목적격 보어 (원형부정사)
Dave tried to make the machine accept his money. //

Dave는 자판기에 돈이 들어가게 하려고 노력했다 // **10번** 단서 5: Dave는 자판기에 돈을 넣기 위해 애씀

After he failed a few times, / some students began to laugh at

him. //

그가 여러 번 실패한 후 / 몇몇 학생들은 그를 비웃기 시작했다 //

He started shaking, / and tears began to form in his eyes. //

그는 떨기 시작했고 / 눈에 눈물이 맺히기 시작했다 // **12번 ⑤** Dave의 눈에 눈물이 맺히기 시작함
지각동사 saw의 목적어와 목적격 보어 (원형부정사)
I saw him turn to sit down, / looking like he had given up. //

나는 그가 자리에 앉으려 돌아서는 모습을 보았는데 / 그는 포기했던 듯 보였다 //

★ (D) 문단 요약: Dave는 자판기 이용에 어려움을 겪고 다른 학생들이 비웃자 포기하는 듯 보였음

- period ⓝ 교시   · force ⓥ 강요하다   · understanding ⓝ 이해
- alike ⓐ 비슷한, 닮은   · accept ⓥ 받아들이다
- determined ⓐ 단호한, 결심이 굳은   · expression ⓝ 표정
- aimlessly ⓐⓓ 목적 없이, 아무렇게나   · direction ⓝ 방향
- wrinkled ⓐ 구겨진   · nervously ⓐⓓ 초조하게
- glance ⓥ 힐끗 보다   · give up 포기하다

(A) 그날 오후 식당이 고등학생들로 가득 차 있었던 동안, Dave는 목이 말랐다. 우리는 가까이 앉아 있었지만 그와는 먼 곳에 앉아 있었고, 머리를 매만지며 다음 교시에 있을 공부하지 않았던 시험을 걱정했다. (a) 그는 우리 세계와는 동떨어져 있었지만, 억지로 그 안의 일부가 되어야만 했다.

(D) 그는 목적을 가지고 음료 자판기 앞에 섰고, 인조 가죽 지갑에서 잔돈을 더듬어 찾았다. 그는 구겨진 1달러 지폐를 꺼내어, (e) 그의 학급의 다른 학생들이 앉아 있는 테이블을 불안하게 돌아보았다. Dave는 자판기에 돈이 들어가게 하려고 노력했다. 그가 여러 번 실패한 후, 몇몇 학생들은 그를 비웃기 시작했다. 그는 떨기 시작했고, 눈에 눈물이 맺히기 시작했다. 나는 그가 자리에 앉으려 돌아서는 모습을 보았는데, 그는 포기했던 듯 보였다.

(C) 하지만 무슨 이유에서인지 그는 그렇게 하지 않기로 했다. 그는 음료를 얻을 때까지 떠나지 않고 있었다. 단호한 표정을 지으며, (c) 그는 그 달러 지폐를 자판기에 계속 아무렇게나 밀어 넣었다. 바로 그때 한 인기 많은 상급생이 자리에서 일어나더니, 그 소년에게 다가갔다. (d) 그는 자판기가 얼마나 자주 지폐를 잘 인식하지 못하는지 차분히 설명해 주었다. 그 후 그는 자신의 주머니에서 동전을 꺼내 자판기에 넣었다. Dave는 자신의 달러를 그에게 주었고 과일 주스 맛을 골랐다. 그러고 나서 그들은 다른 방향으로 떠났다.

(B) 비록 그들이 매우 다른 세상에서 온 것은 분명했지만, 어느 한순간 그들은 진실한 이해를 나누었다. 그날 점심 테이블에서 떠나며 나는 Dave를 바라보았다. 나는 그와 그 달러가 많이 비슷하다고 생각했다. 세상이 그들이 있어야 할 자리라고 말한 곳에서 그들 둘 다 받아들여지지 않았다. 하지만 그 달러가 마음씨 따뜻한 상급생의 주머니 속에서 자리를 찾았듯, 나는 (b) 그 역시 결국 그의 자리를 찾을 거라고 확신했다.

S 10 정답 ⑤

주어진 글 (A)에 이어질 내용을 순서에 맞게 배열한 것으로 가장 적절한 것은?

① (B) — (D) — (C) 소감이 나온 (B)가 사건의 시작이 서술된 (D)보다 먼저 올 수 없음
② (C) — (B) — (D) 사건의 해결이 나온 (C)가 문제 상황인 (B)보다 먼저 나올 수 없음
③ (C) — (D) — (B)
④ (D) — (B) — (C) (D)의 문제 상황 바로 뒤에 사건의 해결인 (C)가 와야 함
⑤ (D) — (C) — (B) (A) Dave는 목이 말랐음 - (D) Dave는 자판기 이용에 어려움을 겪음 - (C) 상급생의 도움으로 자판기에서 음료를 뽑아 마심 - (B) 글쓴이는 Dave가 달러처럼 그의 자리를 찾을 것이라고 확신함

> **왜 정답·오답?** ✱✱✱ [정답률 69%]

[(A): Dave는 목이 말랐고, 다른 학생들과 어울리지 못하고 있었다.

➡ Dave가 목을 축이기 위해 취할 행동이 이어질 것이다.

[(B): 글쓴이는 일련의 사건을 보며, 처음에는 거부당했지만 결국 제자리를 찾은 달러처럼 Dave도 그럴 것이라고 확신했다.

➡ 모든 상황을 지켜본 뒤에 'I'가 느낀 점이기에 마지막에 올 것이다.

[(C): 포기하지 않던 Dave를 한 상급생이 동전으로 도와주고 각자 다른 방향으로 갔다.

➡ Dave가 자판기에서 음료를 뽑아서 마시기 위해 어떤 노력을 했는지가 앞에 설명되어야 하고, 문제 상황이 끝났으므로 (B)가 (C) 뒤에 올 것이다.

[(D): Dave는 자판기에 돈을 넣으려다 실패하고 다른 학생들이 비웃자, 포기하려 했다.

➡ 목을 축이기 위해 한 행동을 설명하는 첫 부분이기에 (A) 뒤에 이어져야 한다.
▶ 글의 순서는 ⑤ (D) — (C) — (B)임

S 11 정답 ④

밑줄 친 (a)~(e) 중에서 가리키는 대상이 나머지 넷과 다른 것은?
① (a)   ② (b)   ③ (c)   ④ (d)   ⑤ (e)
= Dave   = Dave   = Dave   = a popular senior boy   = Dave's

> **왜 정답?** ✱✱✱ [정답률 76%]

④ (d) He: 자판기가 지폐를 잘 인식하지 못한다고 Dave에게 차분히 설명해 준 사람
▶ a popular senior boy

> **왜 오답?**

① (a) He: 다른 학생들의 세계와 동떨어져 있던 사람 ▶ Dave
② (b) he: 결국 자신의 자리를 찾을 것이라고 'I'가 확신한 사람 ▶ Dave
③ (c) he: 단호한 표정으로 자판기에 지폐를 계속 밀어 넣던 사람 ▶ Dave
⑤ (e) his: 그의 반 학생들이 앉아 있던 테이블을 돌아본 사람 ▶ Dave's

S

S 12 정답 ④

윗글에 관한 내용으로 적절하지 <u>않은</u> 것은?

① 그날 오후 식당은 고등학생들로 가득 찼다.
the cafeteria was full of high school students on that afternoon
② 'I'는 Dave와 그 달러가 비슷하다고 생각했다.
I thought he and the dollar were very much alike.
③ 상급생은 주머니에서 동전을 꺼냈다. he pulled some coins from his pocket
④ Dave와 상급생은 같은 방향으로 떠났다.
Then the two walked off in different directions.
⑤ Dave의 눈에 눈물이 맺히기 시작했다. tears began to form in his eyes

✎왜 정답? ★★★※ [정답률 85%]

상급생이 Dave를 도와준 후, 그 둘은 각자 다른 방향으로 떠났으므로 (Then the two walked off in different directions.) 같은 방향으로 떠났다는 ④은 적절하지 않다.

✎왜 오답?

① 그날 오후 식당은 고등학생들로 가득 찼다. (the cafeteria was full of high school students on that afternoon)
② 'I'는 Dave와 그 달러가 비슷하다고 생각했다. (I thought he and the dollar were very much alike.)
③ 상급생은 주머니에서 동전을 꺼냈다. (he pulled some coins from his pocket)
⑤ Dave의 눈에 눈물이 맺히기 시작했다. (tears began to form in his eyes)

구문 서술형

정답 why the machine had trouble accepting dollar bills

→ 의문사가 이끄는 간접의문문의 어순은 「의문사 + 주어 + 동사」이므로 why the machine had ~로 쓴다.

S 13~15 *비행 중 비상 대처 훈련

(A) An airplane flew high / above the deep blue seas / far from any land. //
비행기가 높이 날고 있었다 / 깊고 푸른 바다 위를 / 육지에서 멀리 떨어진 //
보어인 현재분사가 문두로 오면서 주어와 동사가 도치됨 / 주격 관계대명사
Flying the small plane was a student pilot / who was sitting alongside an experienced flight instructor. // 15번 ① 교관과 교육생이 소형 비행기에 타고 있음
소형 비행기를 조종하고 있는 것은 한 파일럿 교육생이었다 / 노련한 비행 교관과 나란히 앉아 있는 //
부사절 접속사(시간) / = the student
As the student looked out the window, / (a) she was filled with wonder and appreciation / for the beauty of the world. //
교육생이 창문 밖을 바라볼 때 / 그녀는 경이로움과 감탄으로 가득 찼다 / 세상의 아름다움에 대한 //
형용사적 용법
Her instructor, / meanwhile, / waited patiently for the right time / to start a surprise flight emergency training exercise. //
비행 교관은 / 한편 / 적절한 때를 인내심을 가지고 기다리고 있었다 / 비행 중 돌발 비상 상황 대처 훈련을 시작할 // 13번 단서 1: 교관은 비상 상황 훈련을 시작할 적절한 때를 기다리고 있음
*(A) 문단 요약: 교관과 교육생이 평화롭게 비행하고 있는 상황
명사절 접속사
(B) Then, / the student carefully flew low enough / to see if she
find의 목적어와 목적격 보어(현재분사)
could find any ships / making their way across the surface of the ocean. // 13번 단서 2: 배가 보이는지 확인하기 위해 낮게 비행함
그런 다음 / 교육생은 충분히 낮게 조심히 비행하였다 / 배가 보이는지 확인할 수 있을 정도로 / 바다 표면을 가로지르는 //
Now the instructor and the student / could see some ships. //
이제 교관과 교육생은 / 배 몇 척을 볼 수 있었다 //
Although the ships were far apart, / they were all sailing in a line. // 15번 ② 배들은 서로 떨어져 있었지만 한 줄로 항해함
배들은 멀리 떨어져 있지만 / 모두 한 줄을 이루고 항해하고 있었다 //

With the line of ships in view, / the student could see the way to home and safety. // 13번 단서 3: 안전하게 복귀하는 방법을 알아냄
배들이 줄을 지어있는 것이 보이자 / 교육생은 안전하게 복귀하는 길을 알 수 있었다 //
= the instructor 계속적 용법의 주격 관계대명사
The student looked at (b) her in relief, / who smiled proudly back at her student. //
교육생은 안도하며 그녀를 바라봤다 / 그녀도 교육생을 향해 자랑스럽게 웃어보였다 //
*(B) 문단 요약: 교육생은 바다 위의 배를 확인함으로써 안전하게 복귀하는 길을 찾음
(C) When the student began to panic, / the instructor said, /
= the student
"Stay calm and steady. / (c) You can do it." // 13번 단서 4: 교육생이 당황하기 시작함
교육생이 당황하기 시작하자 / 교관은 말했다 / "침착하세요. / 당신은 할 수 있습니다" //
앞에 Being이 생략된 분사구문
Calm as ever, / the instructor told her student, / "Difficult times always happen during flight. // The most important thing is / to focus on your flight / in those situations." // 15번 ③ 교관이 어려운 상황에서는 집중이 가장 중요하다고 말함
여느 때처럼 침착하게 / 교관은 교육생에게 말했다 / "비행 중에는 항상 어려운 상황이 발생합니다 / 가장 중요한 것은 / 비행에 집중하는 것입니다 / 그런 상황에서" //
encouraged의 목적어와 목적격 보어(to부정사)
Those words encouraged / the student to focus on flying the aircraft first. //
그 말은 용기를 주었다 / 교육생이 먼저 비행에 집중할 수 있게끔 //
= the student
"Thank you, / I think (d) I can make it," / she said, / "As I've been trained, / I should search for visual markers." //
"감사합니다 / 제가 해낼 수 있을 것 같아요"라고 그녀는 말했다 / "훈련받은 대로 / 저는 시각 표식을 찾아야겠어요" // 13번 단서 5: 교육생은 훈련받은 대로 시각 표식을 찾아야겠다고 함
*(C) 문단 요약: 당황한 교육생에게 교육관이 용기를 주었고 교육생은 해결책을 찾아냄
(D) When the plane hit a bit of turbulence, / the instructor pushed a hidden button. // 13번 단서 6: 난기류를 만나 비상 상황 훈련이 시작됨
비행기가 약간의 난기류를 만났을 때 / 교관은 숨겨진 버튼을 눌렀다 //
병렬 구조
Suddenly, / all the monitors inside the plane flashed several times / then went out completely! // 15번 ④ 비행기 내부의 모니터가 깜박이다가 완전히 꺼짐
완전히 꺼짐
갑자기 / 비행기 안의 모든 모니터가 여러 번 깜박이다가 / 완전히 꺼졌다 //
주격 관계대명사
Now the student was in control of an airplane / that was flying
= the student
well, / but (e) she had no indication / of where she was or where she should go. //
이제 교육생은 비행기를 조종하고 있었다 / 잘 날고 있는 / 그러나 그녀는 알 수 없었다 / 자신이 어디에 있는지, 어디로 가야 하는지 // 15번 ⑤ 교육생은 지도 이외의 다른 도구는 가지고 있지 않음
She did have a map, / but no other instruments. //
교육생은 지도는 가지고 있었지만 / 다른 도구는 가지고 있지 않았다 //
She was at a loss / and then the plane shook again. //
그녀는 어쩔 줄 몰라 했고 / 그때 비행기가 다시 흔들렸다 //
*(D) 문단 요약: 교관이 비상 상황 훈련을 시작하였고 교육생은 당황하게 됨

• flight instructor 비행 교관 • appreciation ⓝ 감상
• patiently ㉮ 인내심 있게 • panic ⓥ 당황하다
• indication ⓝ 표시 • instrument ⓝ 도구

(A) 비행기가 육지에서 멀리 떨어진 깊고 푸른 바다 위를 높이 날고 있었다. 소형 비행기를 조종하고 있는 것은 노련한 비행 교관과 나란히 앉아 있는 한 파일럿 교육생이었다. 교육생이 창문 밖을 바라볼 때, (a) 그녀는 세상의 아름다움에 대한 경이로움과 감탄으로 가득 찼다. 한편, 비행 교관은 비행 중 돌발 비상 상황 대처 훈련을 시작할 적절한 때를 인내심을 가지고 기다리고 있었다.

(D) 비행기가 약간의 난기류를 만났을 때, 교관은 숨겨진 버튼을 눌렀다. 갑자기, 비행기 안의 모든 모니터가 여러 번 깜박이다가 완전히 꺼졌다! 이제 교육생은 잘 날고 있는 비행기를 조종하고 있었지만, (e) 그녀는 자신이 어디에 있는지, 어디로 가야 하는지 알 방도가 없었다. 교육생은 지도는 가지고 있었지만, 다른 도구는 가지고 있지 않았다. 그녀는 어쩔 줄 몰라 했고 그때 비행기가 다시 흔들렸다.

(C) 교육생이 당황하기 시작하자 교관은 "침착하세요. (c) 당신은 할 수 있습니다." 여느 때처럼 침착한 교관은 교육생에게 "비행 중에는 항상 어려운 상황이 발생합니다. 그러한 상황에서는 비행에 집중하는 것이 가장 중요합니다."라고 말했다. 그 말이 교육생이 먼저 비행에 집중할 수 있게끔 용기를 주었다. "감사합니다. (d) 제가 해낼 수 있을 것 같아요."라고 그녀는 말했다. "훈련받은 대로, 저는 시각 표식을 찾아야겠어요."

(B) 그런 다음 교육생은 바다 표면을 가로지르는 배가 보이는지 확인할 수 있을 정도로 충분히 낮게 조심히 비행하였다. 이제 교관과 교육생은 배 몇 척을 볼 수 있었다. 배들은 멀리 떨어져 있었지만 모두 한 줄을 이루고 항해하고 있었다. 배들이 줄을 지어있는 것이 보이자, 교육생은 안전하게 복귀하는 길을 알 수 있었다. 교육생은 안도하며 (b) 그녀를 바라봤고, 그녀도 교육생을 향해 자랑스럽게 웃어보였다.

S 13 정답 ⑤

주어진 글 (A)에 이어질 내용을 순서에 맞게 배열한 것으로 가장 적절한 것은?

① (B) — (D) — (C) 주어진 글에서 안전하게 복귀해야 하는 비상 상황이 나오지 않음
② (C) — (B) — (D)
③ (C) — (D) — (B) 주어진 글에서 아직 교육생이 당황할 상황이 시작하지 않음
④ (D) — (B) — (C) (B)의 안전한 복귀를 위해서 생각해 낸 방법이 (C)에서 먼저 나옴
⑤ (D) — (C) — (B) (D) 비상 훈련 시작 - (C) 당황했지만 훈련받은 대로 시각 표식을 찾으려함 - (B) 배를 확인함으로써 안전하게 복귀하는 길을 찾음

> **왜** 정답·오답? ✱✱✿ [정답률 76%]

(A): 비행 교관과 교육생이 소형 비행기를 운전하고 있는 중 교관이 곧 비행 중 돌발 비상 상황 대처 훈련을 시작할 적절한 때를 기다리고 있다.

➡ 교관과 교육생이 비행 중이며 교관이 훈련을 위해 앞으로 할 행동에 주목한다.

(B): 교육생이 바다의 배가 보이는지 확인하기 위해 낮게 비행하였고, 배들이 줄을 지어있는 것이 보이자, 교육생은 안전하게 복귀하는 길을 알 수 있었고 안도할 수 있었다.

➡ 바다의 배를 확인하게 된 이유와 안전하게 복귀하는 길을 찾아야 했던 상황이 앞에 나와야 한다. 안도할 수 있었다는 것으로 볼 때, 비상 상황이 끝나는 글의 마무리 부분임을 알 수 있다.

(C): 교육생이 당황하기 시작했지만 교관은 교육생이 비행에 집중할 수 있게끔 용기를 주자 교육생은 훈련받은 대로 시각 표식을 찾아야겠다는 생각을 하게 되었다.

➡ 교육생이 당황하기 시작한 이유가 앞에 나와야 한다. 시각 표식을 찾아야겠다고 생각하여 바다의 배가 보이는지 확인한 것으로, (B)가 뒤에 이어질 것이다.

(D): 난기류를 만나자 교관이 숨겨진 버튼을 눌렀고, 비행기 안의 모든 모니터가 꺼지자 교육생은 당황스러워했다.

➡ 비상 훈련을 시작할 때를 기다리는 (A)에 이어지는 내용으로, 교육생이 당황하기 시작했지만 교관이 용기를 주었다는 (C)가 뒤에 이어질 것이다.
▶ (D) 난기류를 만나 교관이 비상 상황 훈련을 시작하였고 교육생은 당황하게 됨
→ (C) 당황한 교육생에게 교관이 용기를 주었고 교육생은 해결책을 찾아냄 → (B) 교육생은 바다 위의 배를 확인함으로써 안전하게 복귀하는 길을 알아내고 안도감을 느낌
▶ 글의 순서는 ⑤ (D) — (C) — (B)임

S 14 정답 ②

밑줄 친 (a)~(e) 중에서 가리키는 대상이 나머지 넷과 다른 것은?

① (a) ②(b) ③ (c) ④ (d) ⑤ (e)
= the student = the instructor = The student = the student = the student

> **왜** 정답? ✱✱✿ [정답률 73%]

② (b) her: 교육생이 안도감을 느끼며 쳐다본 사람 ▶ the instructor

> **왜** 오답?

① (a) she: 비행 중 세상의 아름다움에 대한 경이로움과 감탄을 느낀 사람
▶ the student

③ (c) You: 교관이 용기를 주고 있는 대상 ▶ The student

④ (d) I: 스스로 비상 상황에 대처할 수 있다고 믿는 사람 ▶ The student

⑤ (e) she: 꺼진 모니터 속 자신이 어디에 있는지 모른 채 비행기를 조종하고 있는 사람 ▶ the student

S 15 정답 ④

윗글에 관한 내용으로 적절하지 <u>않은</u> 것은?
① 교관과 교육생이 소형 비행기에 타고 있었다. Flying the small plane was a student pilot who was sitting alongside an experienced flight instructor.
② 배들은 서로 떨어져 있었지만 한 줄을 이루고 있었다. Although the ships were far apart, they were all sailing in a line.
③ 교관은 어려운 상황에서는 집중이 가장 중요하다고 말했다. The most important thing is to focus on your flight in those situations.
④ 비행기 내부의 모니터가 깜박이다가 다시 정상 작동했다. Suddenly, all the monitors inside the plane flashed several times then went out completely!
⑤ 교육생은 지도 이외의 다른 도구는 가지고 있지 않았다. She did have a map, but no other instruments.

> **왜** 정답? ✱✱✿ [정답률 74%]

비행기 내부의 모니터가 깜박이다가 완전히 꺼졌다고(all the monitors ~ then went out completely!) 했다. 따라서 비행기 내부의 모니터가 깜박이다가 다시 정상 작동했다는 ④은 적절하지 않다.

> **왜** 오답?

① 교관과 교육생이 소형 비행기에 타고 있었다. (Flying the small plane was a student pilot ~ an experienced flight instructor.)
② 배들은 서로 떨어져 있었지만 한 줄을 이루고 있었다. (Although the ships were far apart, they were all sailing in a line.)
③ 교관은 어려운 상황에서는 집중이 가장 중요하다고 말했다. (The most important thing is to focus on your flight in those situations.)
⑤ 교육생은 지도 이외의 다른 도구는 가지고 있지 않았다. (She did have a map, but no other instruments.)

S 16~18 ✱부자의 결혼식에 초대받은 시인의 일침

(A) Once upon a time / in the Iranian city of Shiraz, / there lived the famous poet Sheikh Saadi. //
옛날 옛적에 / 이란의 도시 Shiraz에 / 유명한 시인 Sheikh Saadi가 살았다 //

lead a life: 생활을 하다
Like most other poets and philosophers, / he **led a** very simple **life**. //
대부분의 다른 시인들과 철학자들처럼 / 그는 매우 검소한 생활을 했다 //

A rich merchant of Shiraz / **was preparing** for his daughter's wedding / and **invited** (a) **him** / along with a lot of big businessmen of the town. //
병렬 구조(동사) = the poet
Shiraz의 부유한 상인은 / 그의 딸의 결혼식을 준비하고 있었고 / 그를 초대했다 / 그 마을의 많은 큰 사업가들과 함께 //

16번 단서 1, 18번 ① 시인은 상인의 결혼식 초대를 수락했음
The poet accepted the invitation / and decided to attend. //
그 시인은 초대를 수락했고 / 참석하기로 결정했다 //

✱(A) 문단 요약: 검소한 삶을 사는 유명한 시인 Sheikh Saadi는 부유한 상인의 딸의 결혼식에 초대받아 참석하기로 결정함

(B) The host personally led the poet to his seat / and served out chicken soup to him. //
혼주는 직접 시인을 그의 자리로 안내했고 / 그에게 닭고기 수프를 내주었다 //

After a moment, / the poet suddenly dipped the corner of his coat in the soup / **as if he fed it**. //
as if 가정법 과거 18번 ② 시인은 외투 자락을 수프에 담갔음
잠시 후에 / 시인은 갑자기 그의 외투 자락을 수프에 담갔다 / 마치 음식을 먹이듯 //

all + 복수 명사 + 복수 동사 = the poet
All the guests were now staring at (b) **him** in surprise. //
모든 손님이 바로 그를 놀라서 바라보고 있었다 //

The host said, / "Sir, what are you doing?" //
혼주가 말했다 / "선생님, 뭐 하는 겁니까" //

'~이므로'
The poet very calmly replied, / "**Now that** I have put on expensive clothes, / I see a world of difference here. //
주격 관계대명사
시인은 매우 침착하게 대답했다 / "내가 비싼 옷을 입으니 / 이곳에서 엄청난 차이를 봅니다 //

목적어절 접속사
All **that** I can say now / is **that** this feast is meant for my clothes, / not for me." //
내가 지금 할 수 있는 모든 말은 / 이 진수성찬이 내 옷을 위한 것이라는 것뿐입니다 / 나를 위한 것이 아니라" //

*(B) 문단 요약: 시인은 외투 자락을 수프에 담갔고, 왜 그러냐는 질문에 진수성찬이 옷을 위한 것일 뿐, 자신을 위한 것이 아니라고 했음

분사구문
(C) Seeing all this, / the poet quietly left the party / and went to a shop where he could rent clothes. // 16번 단서 2, 18번 ③ 시인은 파티를 떠나 옷을 빌릴 수 있는 가게로 감
이 모든 것을 보고 / 시인은 조용히 파티를 떠나 / 그가 옷을 빌릴 수 있는 가게로 갔다 //
There he chose a richly decorated coat, / which made him look
made의 목적격 보어(원형부정사)
like a new person. //
계속적 용법의 주격 관계대명사
그곳에서 그는 화려하게 장식된 외투를 골랐고 / 그것은 그를 새로운 사람처럼 보이게 만들었다 //
With this coat, / he entered the party / and this time was welcomed with open arms. // 16번 단서 3: 화려한 외투를 입고 파티에 가니 환영을 받음
이 외투를 입고 / 그는 파티에 들어갔고 / 이번에는 두 팔 벌려 환영을 받았다 //
= the host
The host embraced him / as (c) he would do to an old friend /
앞에 목적격 관계대명사가 생략됨
and complimented him / on the clothes he was wearing. //
혼주는 그를 껴안았고 / 그가 오랜 친구에게 하듯이 / 그에게 칭찬했다 / 그가 입고 있는 옷에 대해 //
allowed의 목적격 보어(to부정사)
The poet did not say a word / and allowed the host to lead (d)
= the poet
him to the dining room. //
시인은 한마디도 하지 않고 / 혼주가 그를 식당으로 안내하도록 허락했다 //

*(C) 문단 요약: 시인은 파티를 떠난 뒤에 화려한 옷을 빌려 입고 다시 파티에 갔는데, 이번에는 환영받았음
16번 단서 4, 18번 ④ 결혼식 날에 부유한 상인은 입구에서 손님을 맞이하고 있었음
동격
(D) On the day of the wedding, / the rich merchant, the host of the wedding, / was receiving the guests at the gate. //
결혼식 날 / 결혼식의 혼주인 부유한 상인은 / 입구에서 손님을 맞이하고 있었다 //
Many rich people of the town attended the wedding. //
마을의 많은 부유한 사람들이 결혼식에 참석했다 // 18번 ⑤ 마을의 많은 부유한 사람들이 결혼식에 참석함
= Many rich people
They had come out / in their best clothes. //
그들은 나왔다 / 자신의 가장 좋은 옷차림으로 //
「neither A nor B」: A도 B도 아닌
The poet wore simple clothes / which were neither grand nor expensive. //
주격 관계대명사
시인은 소박한 옷을 입었다 / 거창하지도 비싸지도 않은 //
He waited for someone to approach him / but no one gave (e)
= the poet
him as much as even a second glance. // 16번 단서 5: 소박한 옷을 입고 간 시인에게 아무도 눈길을 주지 않음
그는 누군가가 자신에게 다가오기를 기다렸지만 / 아무도 그에게 단 일 초의 눈길도 주지 않았다 //
Even the host did not greet him / and looked away. //
혼주조차 그에게 인사하지 않고 / 눈길을 돌렸다 //

*(D) 문단 요약: 결혼식 날에 시인은 소박한 옷을 입고 갔는데, 혼주를 포함하여 아무도 눈길을 주지 않았음

- philosopher ⓝ 철학자
- businessman ⓝ 사업가
- personally ⓐⓓ 직접
- a world of 막대한, 엄청난
- compliment ⓥ 칭찬하다
- approach ⓥ 접근하다
- merchant ⓝ 상인
- attend ⓥ 참석하다
- dip ⓥ 담그다
- rent ⓥ 대여하다
- grand ⓐ 거창한, 웅장한
- glance ⓝ 눈길
- stare at ~을 바라보다
- embrace ⓥ 껴안다
- greet ⓥ 맞이하다

(A) 옛날 옛적에 이란의 도시 Shiraz에 유명한 시인 Sheikh Saadi가 살았다. 대부분의 다른 시인들과 철학자들처럼 그는 매우 검소한 생활을 했다. Shiraz의 부유한 상인은 그의 딸의 결혼식을 준비하고 있었고 (a) 그를 그 마을의 많은 큰 사업가들과 함께 초대했다. 그 시인은 초대를 수락했고 참석하기로 결정했다.
(D) 결혼식 날, 결혼식의 혼주인 부유한 상인은 입구에서 손님을 맞이하고 있었다. 마을의 많은 부유한 사람들이 결혼식에 참석했다. 그들은 자신의 가장 좋은 옷차림으로 나왔다. 시인은 거창하지도 비싸지도 않은 소박한 옷을 입었다. 그는 누군가가 자신에게 다가오기를 기다렸지만 아무도 (e) 그에게 단 일 초의 눈길도 주지 않았다. 혼주조차도 그에게 인사하지 않고 눈길을 돌렸다.
(C) 이 모든 것을 보고 시인은 조용히 파티를 떠나 그가 옷을 빌릴 수 있는 가게로 갔다. 그곳에서 그는 화려하게 장식된 외투를 골랐고, 그것은 그를 새로운 사람처럼 보이게 만들었다. 이 외투를 입고, 그는 파티에 들어갔고 이번에는 두 팔 벌려 환영을 받았다. 혼주는 (c) 그가 오랜 친구에게 하듯이 그를 껴안았고, 그가 입고 있는 옷에 대해 그에게 칭찬했다. 시인은 한마디도 하지 않고 혼주가 (d) 그를 식당으로 안내하도록 허락했다.

(B) 혼주는 직접 시인을 그의 자리로 안내했고 그에게 닭고기 수프를 내주었다. 잠시 후에 시인은 마치 음식을 먹이듯 그의 외투 자락을 수프에 갑자기 담갔다. 모든 손님이 바로 (b) 그를 놀라서 바라보고 있었다. 혼주가 말했다. "선생님, 뭐 하는 겁니까?" 시인은 매우 침착하게 대답했다. "내가 비싼 옷을 입으니, 이곳에서 엄청난 차이를 봅니다. 내가 지금 할 수 있는 모든 말은 이 진수성찬이 내 옷을 위한 것이지, 나를 위한 것이 아니라는 것뿐입니다."

S 16 정답 ⑤

주어진 글 (A)에 이어질 내용을 순서에 맞게 배열한 것으로 가장 적절한 것은?
① (B) — (D) — (C)　혼주가 시인을 자리로 안내했다는 (B)보다 혼주가 결혼식장 입구에서 손님을 맞이했다는 (D)가 먼저 와야 함
② (C) — (B) — (D)　결혼식에 참석하기로 결정했다는 (A) 바로 뒤에 파티를 떠났다는 (C)가 오는 것은 어색함
③ (C) — (D) — (B)
④ (D) — (B) — (C)　혼주가 눈길조차 주지 않았다는 (D) 뒤에 혼주가 직접 시인을 자리로 안내했다는 (B)가 오는 것은 어색함
⑤ (D) — (C) — (B)　(D) 시인은 소박한 옷을 입고 갔더니 모두가 무시함 — (C) 화려한 옷을 입고 다시 파티에 갔더니 환영받음 — (B) 시인은 외투 자락을 수프에 담갔고, 진수성찬이 옷을 위한 것일 뿐이며 자신을 위한 것이 아니라고 말함

> 왜 정답·오답 ? ✱✱❀ [정답률 69%]

[(A): 검소한 삶을 사는 Sheikh Saadi라는 유명한 시인은 부유한 상인의 딸의 결혼식에 초대받아 참석하기로 결정했다.
⇒ 앞으로 결혼식에서 어떤 일이 생겼는지를 확인해야 한다.
[(B): 자리로 안내받고 치킨 수프를 대접받은 시인은 외투 자락을 수프에 담갔고, 왜 그러냐는 질문에 진수성찬이 옷을 위한 것일 뿐, 자신을 위한 것이 아니라고 했다.
⇒ 결혼식장에 들어갔다는 내용이 앞에 있어야 하고, 시인이 옷을 위한 것일 뿐인 결혼식에 일침을 가하며 글이 마무리된다.
[(C): 시인은 파티를 떠난 뒤에 화려한 옷을 빌려 입고 다시 파티에 갔는데, 이번에는 환영받았다.
⇒ 파티를 떠났다는 내용이 있으므로 파티(결혼식)에 참석했다는 내용이 앞에 있어야 한다.
[(D): 결혼식 날에 시인은 소박한 옷을 입고 갔는데, 혼주를 포함하여 아무도 눈길을 주지 않았다.
⇒ 결혼식 당일 시인이 소박한 옷을 입고 갔을 때 겪은 일이므로 (A) 다음에 오는 내용이고, 뒤에는 파티를 떠났다는 내용이 이어져야 한다.
▶ (A) Sheikh Saadi라는 유명한 시인이 부유한 상인의 딸의 결혼식에 초대받았고 그곳에 가기로 결정함 → (D) 결혼식에 소박한 옷을 입고 가자, 혼주를 포함한 모두가 무시함 → (C) 시인은 파티를 떠나 화려한 옷을 빌려 입고 다시 파티에 가는데, 이번에는 환영받음 → (B) 시인은 외투 자락을 수프에 담갔고, 왜 그러냐는 물음에 진수성찬이 옷을 위한 것이지, 나를 위한 것은 아니라고 말했음
▶ 글의 순서는 ⑤ (D) — (C) — (B)임

S 17 정답 ③

밑줄 친 (a)~(e) 중에서 가리키는 대상이 나머지 넷과 다른 것은?
① (a)　② (b)　③ (c)　④ (d)　⑤ (e)
= the poet　= the poet　= the host　= the poet　= the poet

> 왜 정답 ? ✱✱❀ [정답률 72%]
③ (c) he: 오랜 친구에게 하듯 시인을 껴안은 사람 ▶ the host

> 왜 오답 ?
① (a) him: 상인이 자신의 딸의 결혼식에 초대한 사람 ▶ the poet
② (b) him: 모든 손님이 놀라서 바라본 사람 ▶ the poet
④ (d) him: 혼주가 식당으로 안내한 사람 ▶ the poet
⑤ (e) him: 소박한 옷을 입고 가서 누구의 시선도 받지 못한 사람 ▶ the poet

윗글에 관한 내용으로 적절하지 <u>않은</u> 것은?
① 시인은 상인의 초대를 받아들였다. The poet accepted the invitation
② 상인은 시인의 외투 자락을 수프에 담갔다.
the poet suddenly dipped the corner of his coat in the soup
③ 시인은 옷을 빌릴 수 있는 가게로 갔다.
the poet quietly left the party and went to a shop where he could rent clothes
④ 결혼식 날 상인은 입구에서 손님을 맞이했다. On the day of the wedding,
the rich merchant, the host of the wedding, was receiving the guests at the gate.
⑤ 마을의 많은 부유한 사람들이 결혼식에 참석했다.
Many rich people of the town attended the wedding.

> **왜 정답?** ★★❀ [정답률 76%]

시인이 스스로 자신의 외투 자락을 수프에 담근 것이므로 (the poet suddenly dipped the corner of his coat in the soup) 상인이 시인의 외투 자락을 수프에 담갔다는 ②은 적절하지 않다.

> **왜 오답?**

① 시인은 상인의 초대를 받아들였다. (The poet accepted the invitation)
③ 시인은 옷을 빌릴 수 있는 가게로 갔다. (the poet quietly left the party and went to a shop where he could rent clothes)
④ 결혼식 날 상인은 입구에서 손님을 맞이했다. (On the day of the wedding, the rich merchant, the host of the wedding, was receiving the guests at the gate.)
⑤ 마을의 많은 부유한 사람들이 결혼식에 참석했다. (Many rich people of the town attended the wedding.)

S 19~21 *손자에게 최고의 학교를 찾아주려고 했던 노인

(A) A boy had a place / at the best school in town. //
한 소년이 한 자리를 얻었다 / 마을에 있는 가장 좋은 학교에 //

In the morning, / his granddad took him / to the school. //
아침에 / 그의 할아버지는 그를 데리고 갔다 / 학교에 //

When (a) <u>he</u> went onto the playground / with his grandson, / the
= the old man
children surrounded them. //
그가 운동장으로 들어갔을 때 / 그의 손자와 함께 / 아이들이 그들을 둘러쌌다 //

"What a funny old man," / one boy smirked. //
what 감탄문: What+a(n)+형용사+명사(+주어+동사)!
"진짜 우스꽝스러운 할아버지다" / 한 소년이 히죽히죽 웃었다 //

A girl with brown hair pointed / at the pair / and jumped up
and down. // 21번① 갈색 머리 소녀가 노인과 소년을 향해 손가락질했음
갈색 머리 소녀가 손가락질했다 / 그 둘(노인과 소년)을 향해 / 그리고 위아래로 뛰었다 //

Suddenly, / the bell rang / and the children ran off / to their first
lesson. // 19번 단서 1: 아이들이 두 사람을 놀리다가 첫 수업에 급히 들어감
갑자기 / 종이 울렸다 / 그리고 아이들이 급히 뛰어갔다 / 그들의 첫 수업에 //

*(A) 문단 요약: 노인이 한 학교에 손자를 데리고 갔다가 아이들에게 놀림을 당함

(B) In some schools / the children completely ignored the old
man / and in others, / they made fun of (b) <u>him</u>. //
= the old man
몇몇 학교에서는 / 아이들이 노인을 완전히 무시했다 / 그리고 다른 학교들에서는 / 아이들이
그를 놀렸다 // 19번 단서 2: 혼자 학교를 찾아 나간 (D)의 마지막에 이어짐

When this happened, / he would turn sadly / and go home. //
이런 일이 일어났을 때 / 그는 슬프게 돌아서서 / 집으로 가곤 했다 //

Finally, / he went onto the tiny playground / of a very small
school, / and leant against the fence, / exhausted. //
분사구문
마침내 / 그는 아주 작은 운동장으로 들어섰다 / 매우 작은 한 학교의 / 그리고 울타리에
기댔다 / 지쳐서 // 21번② 노인은 지쳐서 울타리에 기댔음

The bell rang, / and the crowd of children ran out onto the
playground. //
종이 울렸다 / 그리고 아이들의 무리가 운동장으로 달려 나왔다 //

"Sir, are you all right? // Shall I bring you a glass of water?" // a
voice said. //
"할아버지, 괜찮으세요 // 물 한 잔 가져다드릴까요" // 누군가가 말했다 //

"We've got a bench in the playground / — come and sit down,"
/ another voice said. //
"우리 운동장에 벤치가 있어요 / 오셔서 앉으세요" / 또 다른 누군가가 말했다 //

Soon a young teacher / came out onto the playground. //
곧 한 젊은 선생님이 / 운동장으로 나왔다 //

*(B) 문단 요약: 여러 학교에서 놀림을 당한 할아버지가 한 작은 학교에 들어가
아이들의 환대를 받음

(C) The old man greeted (c) <u>him</u> / and said: / "Finally, I've
= a young teacher
found my grandson / the best school in town." //
19번 단서 3: 노인은 마침내 마을 최고의 학교를 찾았음
노인은 그에게 인사하면서 / 말했다 / "마침내 / 제가 제 손자에게 찾아주었네요 / 마을 최고의
학교를" //

"You're mistaken, sir. // Our school is not the best / — it's small
and cramped." //
"잘못 아신 겁니다, 어르신 // 우리 학교는 최고가 아니에요 / 작고 비좁은걸요" //

The old man didn't argue with the teacher. //
노인은 선생님과 논쟁을 벌이지 않았다 // 21번③ 노인은 선생님과 논쟁을 벌이지 않았음

Instead, / he made arrangements / for his grandson to join the
school, / and then the old man left. //
대신 / 그는 준비했다 / 손자가 그 학교에 다닐 수 있도록 / 그런 다음에 노인은 떠났다 //

That evening, / the boy's mom said to (d) <u>him</u>: / "Dad, you can't
= the old man
뒤에 목적어절을 이끄는 접속사 that 생략
even read. // How do you <mark>know</mark> / you've found the best teacher
of all?" // 21번④ 노인은 글을 읽을 줄 몰랐음
그날 저녁 / 소년의 어머니는 그에게 말했다 / "아버지, 글을 읽을 줄도 모르시잖아요 //
어떻게 아세요 / 최고의 선생님을 찾았다는 것을" //

"Judge a teacher / by his pupils," / the old man replied. //
"선생님은 판단해야 해 / 그 제자를 보고" / 노인이 대답했다 //

*(C) 문단 요약: 노인은 작은 학교 학생들의 환대를 본 뒤, 선생님은 그 제자를 보고 알
수 있다며 그 학교에 손자를 보내기로 함

(D) The old man <mark>took</mark> his grandson / firmly by the hand, / and
병렬 구조
<mark>led</mark> him / out of the school gate. // 19번 단서 4: 아이들이 놀리고 수업에 들어간
후에 노인은 손자를 데리고 교문 밖으로 나감
노인은 손자를 잡았다 / 손을 꽉 / 그리고 그를 데리고 나갔다 / 교문 밖으로 //

"Brilliant, / I don't have to go to school!" / the boy exclaimed. //
"굉장한 걸 / 나 학교에 가지 않아도 되네" / 소년이 소리쳤다 // 21번⑤ 소년은 학교에 가지
않아도 된다고 소리쳤음

"You do, / but not this one," / his granddad replied. //
"가긴 가야지 / 그렇지만 이 학교는 아니야" / 할아버지가 대답했다 //

"I'll find you a school / myself." //
"내가 네게 학교를 찾아주마 / 직접" //

Granddad <mark>took</mark> his grandson / back to his own house, / <mark>asked</mark>
병렬 구조
grandma / to look after him, / and <mark>went</mark> off to look for a teacher
= the old man
/ (e) <u>himself</u>. //
할아버지는 손자를 데리고 갔다 / 집으로 / 할머니에게 부탁했다 / 그를 돌봐달라고 / 그리고
선생님을 찾아 나섰다 / 직접 //

<mark>Every time</mark> he spotted a school, / the old man went onto the
~할 때마다
playground, / and waited for the children to come out / at break
time. //
학교를 발견할 때마다 / 노인은 운동장으로 들어가서 / 아이들이 나오기를 기다렸다 / 쉬는
시간에 //

*(D) 문단 요약: 노인은 손자를 집에 두고 혼자서 손자를 위한 학교를 찾아 나섬

- surround ⓥ 둘러싸다
- completely [ad] 완전히
- make fun of ~을 놀리다
- exhaust ⓥ 지치게 하다
- judge ⓥ 판단하다
- exclaim ⓥ 소리치다
- run off 급히 뛰어가다
- ignore ⓥ 무시하다
- lean ⓥ 기대다
- make arrangements for ~의 준비를 하다
- pupil ⓝ 제자
- firmly [ad] 꽉
- reply ⓥ 대답하다

(A) 한 소년이 마을에 있는 가장 좋은 학교에 한 자리를 얻었다. 아침에
그의 할아버지는 그를 학교에 데리고 갔다. (a) 그가 그의 손자와 함께
운동장으로 들어갔을 때, 아이들이 그들을 둘러쌌다. "진짜 우스꽝스러운
할아버지다."라며 한 소년이 히죽히죽 웃었다. 갈색 머리 소녀가 그
둘(노인과 소년)을 향해 손가락질하며 위아래로 뛰었다. 갑자기 종이
울렸고, 아이들이 그들의 첫 수업에 급히 뛰어갔다.

(D) 노인은 손자의 손을 꽉 잡고, 그를 교문 밖으로 데리고 나갔다. "굉장한 걸, 나 학교에 가지 않아도 되네!"라고 소년이 소리쳤다. "가긴 가야지, 그렇지만 이 학교는 아니야."라고 할아버지가 대답했다. "내가 직접 네게 학교를 찾아주마." 할아버지는 손자를 집으로 데리고 돌아가 할머니에게 그를 돌봐달라고 하고 나서, (e) 그 자신이 선생님을 찾아 나섰다. 학교를 발견할 때마다, 노인은 운동장으로 들어가서 아이들이 쉬는 시간에 나오기를 기다렸다.

(B) 몇몇 학교에서는 아이들이 노인을 완전히 무시했고, 다른 학교들에서는 아이들이 (b) 그를 놀렸다. 이런 일이 일어났을 때, 그는 슬프게 돌아서서 집으로 가곤 했다. 마침내, 그는 매우 작은 한 학교의 아주 작은 운동장으로 들어섰고, 지쳐서 울타리에 기댔다. 종이 울렸고, 아이들의 무리가 운동장으로 달려 나왔다. "할아버지, 괜찮으세요? 물 한 잔 가져다드릴까요?" 누군가가 말했다. "우리 운동장에 벤치가 있어요 — 오셔서 앉으세요." 또 다른 누군가가 말했다. 곧 한 젊은 선생님이 운동장으로 나왔다.

(C) 노인은 (c) 그에게 인사하면서 이렇게 말했다. "마침내, 제가 제 손자에게 마을 최고의 학교를 찾아주었네요." "잘못 아신 겁니다, 어르신. 우리 학교는 최고가 아니에요 — 작고 비좁은걸요." 노인은 선생님과 논쟁을 벌이지 않았다. 대신, 그는 손자가 그 학교에 다닐 수 있도록 준비해주고, 그런 다음에 노인은 떠났다. 그날 저녁, 소년의 어머니는 (d) 그에게 말했다. "아버지, 글을 읽을 줄도 모르시잖아요. 최고의 선생님을 찾았다는 것을 어떻게 아세요?" "선생님은 그 제자를 보고 판단해야 해."라고 노인이 대답했다.

S 19 정답 ④

주어진 글 (A)에 이어질 내용을 순서에 맞게 배열한 것으로 가장 적절한 것은?

① (B) — (D) — (C)
노인이 첫 학교에서 손자를 데리고 나온 (D)가 좋은 학교를 찾아 다니는 (B)보다 먼저 나와야 함
② (C) — (B) — (D)
③ (C) — (D) — (B)
(C)는 글의 전체 내용을 마무리하는 문단이므로 맨 마지막에 와야 함
④ (D) — (B) — (C)
(D) 노인은 혼자서 손자를 위한 학교를 찾아 나섬 - (B) 여러 학교에서 놀림을 당한 노인이 작은 학교에 들어가 아이들의 환대를 받음 - (C) 노인이 작은 학교 학생들의 환대를 본 뒤, 그 학교에 손자를 보내기로 함
⑤ (D) — (C) — (B)
(B)에서 작은 학교 아이들의 환대를 받고 난 뒤에 그 학교에 보내기로 결정하는 (C)가 와야 함

>왜 정답? ✿✿✿ [정답률 72%]

노인이 손자를 데리고 처음 학교에 갔다가 아이들에게 놀림을 당한 (A) 뒤에는 그 학교에서 손자를 데리고 나온 뒤 혼자 좋은 학교를 찾아보겠다고 하는 내용의 (D)가 와야 한다. 여러 학교를 혼자 다니며 놀림을 받던 노인이 지친 채로 매우 작은 학교에 갔다가 아이들의 환대를 받는 내용의 (B)가 (D) 다음에 이어져야 한다. 아이들의 환대를 통해 선생님의 자질을 판단하고 작은 학교에 손자를 보내기로 한 (C)가 맨 마지막에 와야 글의 흐름이 자연스럽다. 따라서 ④ (D) – (B) – (C)가 가장 적절하다.

>왜 오답?

① 노인이 첫 학교에서 손자를 데리고 나온 (D)가 좋은 학교를 찾아 다니는 구체적인 내용의 (B)보다 먼저 나와야 글의 흐름이 자연스럽다. 함정
②, ③ (C)는 글의 전체 내용을 마무리하는 문단이므로 맨 마지막에 와야 한다.
⑤ (B)에서 작은 학교 아이들의 환대를 받고 난 뒤에 그 학교에 보내기로 결정하는 (C)가 와야 적절한 순서이다.

S 20 정답 ③

밑줄 친 (a)~(e) 중에서 가리키는 대상이 나머지 넷과 다른 것은?

① (a)　　② (b)　　③ (c)　　④ (d)　　⑤ (e)
 = the old man　 = the old man　= a young teacher　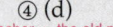 = the old man　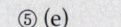 = the old man

>왜 정답? ✿✿✿ [정답률 71%]

(c)는 노인이 인사한 대상을 가리키므로 젊은 선생님이다. 나머지는 모두 노인을 가리키므로 정답은 ③이다.

>왜 오답?

① 손자와 함께 운동장에 들어간 사람은 노인이다.
② 아이들에게 놀림을 당한 사람은 노인이다.
④ 소년의 어머니가 말을 한 대상은 노인이다.
⑤ 직접 손자를 위한 선생님(학교)를 찾아 나선 사람은 노인이다.

S 21 정답 ③

윗글에 관한 내용으로 적절하지 않은 것은?

① 갈색 머리 소녀가 노인과 소년을 향해 손가락질했다.
A girl with brown hair pointed at the pair
② 노인은 지쳐서 울타리에 기댔다.
Finally, he went onto the tiny playground of a very small school, and leant against the fence, exhausted
③ 노인은 선생님과 논쟁을 벌였다.
The old man didn't argue with the teacher.
④ 노인은 글을 읽을 줄 몰랐다. Dad, you can't even read.
⑤ 소년은 학교에 가지 않아도 된다고 소리쳤다.
"Brilliant, I don't have to go to school!" the boy exclaimed.

>왜 정답? ✿✿✿ [정답률 75%]

(C)에서 노인은 선생님과 논쟁을 벌이지 않았다고(The old man didn't argue with the teacher.) 했으므로 ③이 윗글에 관한 내용으로 적절하지 않다.

>왜 오답?

① 갈색 머리 소녀가 노인과 소년을 향해 손가락질했다고 했다. (A girl with brown hair pointed at the pair)
② 노인은 지쳐서 울타리에 기댔다고 했다. (Finally, he went onto the tiny playground of a very small school, and leant against the fence, exhausted)
④ 소년의 어머니의 말을 통해 노인은 글을 읽을 줄 몰랐음을 알 수 있다. (Dad, you can't even read.)
⑤ 소년은 학교에 가지 않아도 된다고 소리쳤다. ("Brilliant, I don't have to go to school!" the boy exclaimed.)

S 22~24 *테디 베어를 양보한 Marie

(A) On my daughter Marie's 8th birthday, / she received a bunch of presents / from her friends at school. //
나의 딸 Marie의 8번째 생일에 / 그녀는 많은 선물을 받았다 / 학교에서 친구들로부터 //

That evening, / with her favorite present, a teddy bear, in her arms, / we went to a restaurant / to celebrate her birthday. //
부사적 용법(목적)
그날 저녁 / 그녀가 가장 좋아하는 선물인 테디 베어를 팔에 안고 / 우리는 식당에 갔다 / 그녀의 생일을 축하하기 위해 //
24번 ① 테디 베어를 팔에 안고 생일을 축하하기 위해 식당에 갔음

Our server, a friendly woman, / noticed my daughter holding the teddy bear / and said, / "My daughter loves teddy bears, too." //
동격
다정한 여성인 우리의 종업원은 / 나의 딸이 테디 베어를 안고 있다는 것을 알아차렸다 / 그리고 말했다 / "나의 딸도 테디 베어를 좋아해요"라고 //

Then, / we started chatting / about (a) her family. //
= our server's
그리고 나서 / 우리는 담소를 나누기 시작했다 / 그녀의 가족에 대해 //
22번 단서 1: Marie의 가족은 종업원의 가족에 대해 담소를 나누기 시작했음

*(A) 문단 요약: Marie의 생일에 간 식당에서 종업원이 자신의 딸도 테디 베어를 좋아한다고 말했음

(B) When Marie came back out, / I asked her / what she had been doing. //
부사절 접속사　　　　　　　　　　　　　　　　　　과거완료 진행형
22번 단서 2: 식당으로 다시 뛰어 들어갔다가 돌아온 Marie에게 무엇을 했는지 물었음
Marie가 돌아왔을 때 / 나는 그녀에게 물었다 / 무엇을 하고 있었느냐고 //

She said / **that** she gave her teddy bear to our server / **so that** she
<small>목적어절 접속사</small> <small>= our server's</small> <small>'(그래서) ~하도록'</small>
could give it to (b) her daughter. //

그녀는 말했다 / 자신의 테디 베어를 우리의 종업원에게 주었다고 / 그녀가 자신의 딸에게 그것을 줄 수 있도록 //

<small>24번 ② T는 Marie의 갑작스러운 행동에 놀랐음</small>
I was surprised at her sudden action / because I could see / how
much she loved that bear already. //

나는 그녀의 갑작스러운 행동에 놀랐다 / 알 수 있었기 때문에 / 이미 그녀가 그 테디 베어를 얼마나 좋아하는지 //

<small>= Marie must have p.p.: ~했음에 틀림없다</small>
(c) She **must have seen** the look on my face, / because she said, /

그녀는 내 얼굴의 표정을 봤음에 틀림없다 / 왜냐하면 그녀가 말했기 때문이다 /

"I can't imagine being stuck in a hospital bed. // I just want her
to get better soon." //

"저는 병원 침대에 갇혀 있는 것을 상상할 수 없어요 // 전 그저 그녀가 빨리 낫기를 바랄 뿐이에요"라고 //

*(B) 문단 요약: Marie는 자신이 정말 좋아하는 테디 베어를 종업원에게 주며 그녀의 딸에게 주라고 했음

<small>부사절 접속사(시간)</small>
(C) I felt moved by Marie's words / **as** we walked toward the
car. // <small>22번 단서 3: Marie가 종업원의 딸이 빨리 낫기를 바란다고 말한 것에 감동했음</small>

나는 Marie의 말에 감동받았다 / 우리가 차를 향해 걸어갈 때 //

<small>병렬 구조</small>
Then, / our server **ran** out to our car / and **thanked** Marie for her
generosity. // <small>24번 ③ 종업원은 Marie의 관대함에 고마워했음</small>

그때 / 우리의 종업원이 우리 차로 달려 나왔다 / 그리고 Marie의 관대함에 고마워했다 //

<small>목적어절 접속사</small> <small>= our server</small>
The server said / **that** (d) **she** had never had anyone / doing
anything like that / for her family before. //

종업원은 말했다 / 어떤 사람도 가진 적이 없었다고 / 그런 일을 해 준 / 이전에 자신의 가족을 위해 //

Later, Marie said / it was her best birthday ever. //

나중에 Marie는 말했다 / 그날이 그녀의 최고의 생일이었다고 //

I was so proud of her empathy and warmth, / and this was an
unforgettable experience / for our family. //

나는 그녀의 공감과 따뜻함이 너무 자랑스러웠다 / 그리고 이것은 잊을 수 없는 경험이었다 / 우리 가족에게 //

*(C) 문단 요약: 종업원이 Marie에게 고마워했고 Marie의 가족에게도 잊을 수 없는 경험이었음

<small>22번 단서 4, 24번 ④ 종업원은 자신의 딸이 다리가 부러져서 병원에 있다고 말했음</small>
(D) The server mentioned / during the conversation / **that** her
daughter was in the hospital / with a broken leg. // <small>목적어절 접속사</small>

그 종업원은 말했다 / 대화 중에 / 자신의 딸이 병원에 있다고 / 다리가 부러져 //

<small>= Our server</small> <small>목적어절 접속사</small>
(e) She also said / that Marie looked about the same age / as her
daughter. //

그녀는 또한 말했다 / Marie가 나이가 거의 똑같아 보인다고 / 자신의 딸과 //

She was so kind and attentive all evening, / and even gave
<small>간접목적어 직접목적어</small>
Marie cookies for free. // <small>24번 ⑥ 종업원은 Marie에게 쿠키를 무료로 주었음</small>

그녀는 저녁 내내 매우 친절하고 세심했다 / 그리고 심지어 Marie에게 쿠키를 무료로 주었다 //

After we finished our meal, / we paid the bill / and began to
walk to our car / when unexpectedly Marie **asked** me to wait /
and **ran** back into the restaurant. // <small>병렬 구조</small>

우리가 식사를 마친 후 / 우리는 요금을 지불하고 우리 차로 걸어가기 시작했다 / 그때 갑자기 Marie가 나에게 기다려 달라고 부탁했다 / 그리고 식당으로 다시 뛰어 들어갔다 //

*(D) 문단 요약: 종업원의 딸은 Marie와 나이가 비슷한데 지금 병원에 있다고 했고, 식사 후에 Marie가 식당으로 다시 들어갔음

- a bunch of 다수의, 많은
- notice ⓥ 알아차리다
- chat ⓥ 담소를 나누다
- sudden ⓐ 갑작스러운
- be stuck in ~에 갇히다
- generosity ⓝ 관대함, 너그러움
- empathy ⓝ 공감 (능력)
- unforgettable ⓐ 잊을 수 없는
- mention ⓥ 언급하다, 말하다
- conversation ⓝ 대화
- attentive ⓐ 주의를 기울이는, 세심한
- unexpectedly ⓐⓓ 예상치 못하게, 갑자기

(A) 나의 딸 Marie의 8번째 생일에, 그녀는 학교에서 친구들로부터 많은 선물을 받았다. 그날 저녁, 그녀가 가장 좋아하는 선물인 테디 베어를 팔에 안고 우리는 그녀의 생일을 축하하기 위해 식당에 갔다. 다정한 여성인 우리의 종업원은 나의 딸이 테디 베어를 안고 있다는 것을 알아차렸고, "나의 딸도 테디 베어를 좋아해요."라고 말했다. 그리고 나서, 우리는 (a) 그녀의 가족에 대해 담소를 나누기 시작했다.

(D) 그 종업원은 대화 중에 자신의 딸이 다리가 부러져 병원에 있다고 말했다. (e) 그녀는 또한 Marie가 자신의 딸과 나이가 거의 똑같아 보인다고 말했다. 그녀는 저녁 내내 매우 친절하고 세심했고, 심지어 Marie에게 쿠키를 무료로 주었다. 우리가 식사를 마친 후, 우리는 요금을 지불하고 우리 차로 걸어가기 시작했는데 그때 갑자기 Marie가 나에게 기다려 달라고 부탁하고 식당으로 다시 뛰어 들어갔다.

(B) Marie가 돌아왔을 때 나는 그녀에게 무엇을 하고 있었느냐고 물었다. 그녀는 자신의 테디 베어를 우리의 종업원에게 주어서 그녀가 (b) 자신의 딸에게 그것을 줄 수 있도록 했다고 말했다. 나는 이미 그녀가 그 테디 베어를 얼마나 좋아하는지 알 수 있었기 때문에 그녀의 갑작스러운 행동에 놀랐다. (c) 그녀는 내 얼굴의 표정을 분명히 봤을 것인데, 왜냐하면 그녀가 "저는 병원 침대에 갇혀 있는 것을 상상할 수 없어요. 전 그저 그녀가 빨리 낫기를 바랄 뿐이에요."라고 말했기 때문이다.

(C) 우리가 차를 향해 걸어갈 때 나는 Marie의 말에 감동했다. 그때 우리의 종업원이 우리 차로 달려 나와 Marie의 관대함에 고마워했다. (d) 그녀는 이전에 자신의 가족을 위해 그런 일을 해 준 어떤 사람도 가진 적이 없었다고 종업원은 말했다. 나중에 Marie는 그날이 그녀의 최고의 생일이었다고 말했다. 나는 그녀의 공감과 따뜻함이 너무 자랑스러웠고, 이것은 우리 가족에게 잊을 수 없는 경험이었다.

S 22 정답 ④

주어진 글 (A)에 이어질 내용을 순서에 맞게 배열한 것으로 가장 적절한 것은?

① (B) — (D) — (C)
<small>테디 베어를 종업원에게 주는 (B)보다 종업원의 딸이 병원에 있다고 하는 (D)가 먼저 와야 함</small>
② (C) — (B) — (D)
<small>(C)는 Marie의 행동에 감동하는 마무리 부분이므로 마지막에 와야 함</small>
③ (C) — (D) — (B)
④ (D) — (B) — (C)
<small>(D) 식사 후에 Marie가 식당으로 다시 들어감 — (B) Marie는 테디 베어를 종업원에게 주고 그녀의 딸에게 주라고 했음 — (C) Marie의 가족에게도 잊을 수 없는 경험이었음</small>
⑤ (D) — (C) — (B)
<small>(B)에서 한 Marie의 행동에 대해 (C)에서 감동하는 순서가 되어야 함</small>

왜 정답·오답? ❀❀❀ [정답률 82%]

[(A): 나의 딸 Marie는 생일 선물로 받은 테디 베어를 팔에 안고 식당에 갔는데, 이를 본 종업원이 자신의 딸도 테디 베어를 좋아한다고 말했고 우리는 대화를 하기 시작했다.

→ 어떤 대화를 나눴는지가 이어질 것이다.

[(B): 돌아온 Marie에게 무엇을 했는지 묻자, 자신의 테디 베어를 종업원의 딸에게 줄 수 있도록 그녀에게 주었다고 했다. 나는 Marie가 테디 베어를 얼마나 좋아하는지 알았기 때문에 놀랐다.

→ Marie가 돌아오기 전에 어딘가로 갔다는 내용이 앞에 있어야 하고, 뒤에는 테디 베어를 받은 종업원의 행동이 이어질 것이다.

[(C): 그때 종업원이 달려 나와 Marie에게 고마워했고, Marie의 가족에게도 잊을 수 없는 경험이었다.

→ Marie와 그녀의 가족에게 잊을 수 없는 경험이었다며 글을 마무리했다.

[(D): 종업원은 그녀의 딸이 Marie와 나이가 같아 보인다고 하며, 다리가 부러져 병원에 있다고 했다. 식사를 마친 후 차로 걸어가던 중 Marie가 갑자기 식당으로 뛰어 들어갔다.

→ 대화를 시작했다는 (A)에 이어지는 내용이고 뒤에는 Marie가 어딘가에서 돌아왔다는 (B)가 이어져야 한다.

▶ (D) 식사 후 Marie가 식당으로 다시 들어감 → (B) 돌아온 Marie는 테디 베어를 종업원에게 주며 그녀의 딸에게 주라고 했음 → (C) 종업원은 Marie에게 고마워했고, Marie의 가족에게도 잊을 수 없는 경험이었음

▶ 글의 순서는 ④ (D) → (B) → (C)임

S 23 정답 ③

밑줄 친 (a)~(e) 중에서 가리키는 대상이 나머지 넷과 다른 것은?

① (a)　② (b)　③(c)　④ (d)　⑤ (e)
= our server's　= our server's　= Marie　= our server　= Our server

왜 정답? ❋❋❋ [정답률 71%]

③ (c) She: 'I'의 표정을 보고 종업원의 딸이 빨리 낫기를 바란다는 말을 한 사람
▶ Marie

왜 오답?

① (a) her: Marie의 가족이 담소를 나누기 시작한 대상 ▶ our server's

② (b) her: Marie가 테디 베어를 준 대상 ▶ our server's

④ (d) she: 자신의 가족을 위해 관대함을 베풀어 준 사람이 없었다고 말한 사람
▶ our server

⑤ (e) She: 자신의 딸과 Marie의 나이가 비슷해 보인다고 말한 사람 ▶ Our server

S 24 정답 ④

윗글에 관한 내용으로 적절하지 않은 것은?

① Marie는 테디 베어를 팔에 안고 식당에 갔다.
with her favorite present, a teddy bear, in her arms, we went to a restaurant
② 'I'는 Marie의 갑작스러운 행동에 놀랐다.
I was surprised at her sudden action
③ 종업원은 Marie의 관대함에 고마워했다.
our server ~ thanked Marie for her generosity
④ 종업원은 자신의 딸이 팔이 부러져 병원에 있다고 말했다.
The server mentioned ~ that her daughter was in the hospital with a broken leg.
⑤ 종업원은 Marie에게 쿠키를 무료로 주었다.
even gave Marie cookies for free

왜 정답? ❋❋❋ [정답률 76%]

종업원은 자신의 딸이 다리가 부러져 병원에 있다고(The server mentioned during the conversation that her daughter was in the hospital with a broken leg.) 했다. 따라서 팔이 부러져서 병원에 있다고 한 ④은 적절하지 않다.

왜 오답?

① Marie는 테디 베어를 팔에 안고 생일을 축하하기 위해 식당에 갔다고 했다. (That evening, with her favorite present, a teddy bear, in her arms, we went to a restaurant to celebrate her birthday.)

② 'I'는 Marie의 갑작스러운 행동에 놀랐다고 했다. (I was surprised at her sudden action)

③ 종업원이 차로 달려와서 Marie의 관대함에 고마워했다고 했다. (Then, our server ran out to our car and thanked Marie for her generosity.)

⑤ 종업원은 Marie에게 쿠키를 무료로 주었다고 했다. (She was so kind and attentive all evening, and even gave Marie cookies for free.)

S 25~27 *노인 곁에 머물렀던 군인

(A) A nurse took a tired, anxious soldier / to the bedside. //
한 간호사가 피곤하고 불안해하는 군인을 데려갔다 / 침대 곁으로 //
앞에 주격 관계대명사와 be동사가 생략됨
"Jack, / your son is here," / the nurse said to an old man / lying on the bed. //
"Jack 씨 / 당신의 아들이 왔어요"라고 / 간호사가 한 노인에게 말했다 / 침대에 누워있는 //

She had to repeat the words several times / before the old man's eyes opened. //
그녀는 그 말을 여러 번 반복해야 했다 / 그 노인의 눈이 떠지기 전에 //
분사구문을 이끄는 현재분사
Suffering from the severe pain / because of heart disease, / he barely saw / the young uniformed soldier / standing next to him. // 27번① 노인은 심장병으로 극심한 고통을 겪고 있었음
극심한 고통을 겪고 있어 / 심장병 때문에 / 그는 간신히 보았다 / 제복을 입은 젊은 군인이 / 그의 옆에 서 있는 것을 //

= The old man
(a) He reached out his hand / to the soldier. //
그는 손을 뻗었다 / 그 군인에게 //　25번 단서 1: 노인은 군인에게 손을 뻗었음

　*(A) 문단 요약: 간호사가 젊은 군인을 심장병으로 병원 침대에 누워있는 노인에게 데려감
복합관계부사　　　　　25번 단서 2: 군인은 계속해서 노인의 손을 잡고 위로의 말을 건넴
(B) Whenever the nurse came into the room, / she heard / the soldier say a few gentle words. //
간호사가 병실에 들어올 때마다 / 그녀는 들었다 / 그 군인이 부드러운 몇 마디의 말을 하는 것을 //
앞에 being이 생략됨　　　= the soldier
The old man said nothing, / only held tightly to (b) him / all through the night. //
노인은 아무 말도 하지 않았다 / 그에게 손이 꼭 쥐어진 채로 / 밤새도록 //

Just before dawn, / the old man died. //
동트기 직전에 / 그 노인은 죽었다 //
병렬 구조　　　　　부사적 용법(목적)
The soldier released the old man's hand / and left the room / to find the nurse. // 27번② 군인은 간호사를 찾기 위해 병실을 나감
그 군인은 노인의 손을 놓고 / 병실을 나갔다 / 간호사를 찾기 위해 //
선행사를 포함하는 관계대명사
After she was told what happened, / she went back to the room with him. //
그녀는 무슨 일이 있었는지 들은 후 / 그녀는 그와 함께 병실로 돌아갔다 //
병렬 구조
The soldier hesitated for a while / and asked, "Who was this man?" // 25번 단서 3: 노인이 죽자, 군인은 간호사에게 노인이 누구였는지 물어봄
군인은 잠시 머뭇거리고는 / "그 남자는 누구였나요"라고 물었다 //

　*(B) 문단 요약: 군인은 말이 없는 노인의 곁을 지켰고, 노인이 죽은 뒤 간호사에게 그가 누구였는지 물어봄
　　　　　　　25번 단서 4: 간호사는 노인이 군인의 아버지가 아니었음을 듣고 놀람
(C) She was surprised and asked, / "Wasn't he your father?" //
그녀는 깜짝 놀라서 물었다 / "그가 당신의 아버지가 아니었나요" //
현재완료(경험)
"No, / he wasn't. // I've never met him before," / the soldier replied. // 27번③ 군인은 노인과 이전에 만난 적이 없다고 말함
"아니요 / 그는 아니었어요 / 저는 그를 이전에 만난 적이 없어요"라고 / 군인이 대답했다 //
부사절 접속사
She asked, / "Then why didn't you say something / when I took you to (c) him?"//
= the old man
그녀는 물었다 / "그러면 왜 아무 말도 하지 않았나요 / 내가 당신을 그에게 데리고 갔을 때"라고 //
뒤에 목적어절 접속사 that이 생략됨
He said, / "I knew there had been a mistake, / but when I
목적어절 접속사
realized / that he was too sick to tell whether or not I was his
= the old man
son, / I could see / how much (d) he needed me. // So, I stayed." //
그가 말했다 / "저는 실수가 있었다는 것을 알았습니다 / 하지만 제가 알게 되었을 때 / 그가 너무 위독해서 제가 그의 아들인지 아닌지 구별할 수 없다는 것을 / 저는 알 수 있었습니다 / 그가 얼마나 저를 필요로 하는지 // 그래서, 저는 머물렀습니다"라고 //

　*(C) 문단 요약: 놀란 간호사는 왜 진작 말하지 않았냐고 물었고, 군인은 노인이 자신을 필요로 하는 것을 느껴 머물렀다고 말함

(D) The soldier gently wrapped his fingers / around the weak hand of the old man. // 25번 단서 5: 노인이 뻗은 손을 군인이 부드럽게 감쌌음
그 군인은 손가락으로 부드럽게 감쌌다 / 노인의 병약한 손을 //
'~하도록'
The nurse brought a chair / so that the soldier could sit / beside the bed. // 27번④ 간호사는 군인이 앉을 수 있도록 의자를 가져옴
간호사는 의자를 가져왔다 / 군인이 앉을 수 있도록 / 침대 옆에 //

All through the night / the young soldier sat there, / holding
병렬 구조
the old man's hand / and offering (e) him words of support and
= the old man
comfort. //
밤새 / 젊은 군인은 거기에 앉아 있었다 / 노인의 손을 잡고 / 그에게 지지와 위로의 말을 건네면서 //
목적어절 접속사
Occasionally, / she suggested that the soldier take a rest for a while. //
가끔 / 그녀는 군인에게 잠시 쉬라고 제안했다 //

He politely said no. // 27번⑤ 군인은 잠시 쉬라는 간호사의 제안을 정중히 거절함
그는 정중하게 거절했다 //

　*(D) 문단 요약: 군인은 침대 옆 의자에 앉아 노인에게 쉬지 않고 밤새도록 지지와 위로의 말을 건넴

- anxious ⓐ 불안해하는　　· suffer ⓥ 고통받다　　· severe ⓐ 극심한
- barely ⓐⓓ 간신히, 겨우　　· gentle ⓐ 부드러운, 온화한
- tightly ⓐⓓ 꽉, 단단히　　· hesitate ⓥ 망설이다　　· wrap ⓥ 감싸다
- weak ⓐ (병)약한　　· support ⓝ 지지　　· comfort ⓝ 위로, 위안
- occasionally ⓐⓓ 가끔　　· politely ⓐⓓ 정중하게

(A) 한 간호사가 피곤하고 불안해하는 군인을 침대 곁으로 데려갔다. "Jack 씨, 당신 아들이 왔어요."라고 간호사가 침대에 누워있는 한 노인에게 말했다. 그 노인이 눈을 뜨기 전에 그녀는 그 말을 여러 번 반복해야 했다. 심장병 때문에 극심한 고통을 겪고 있어, 그는 제복을 입은 젊은 군인이 그의 옆에 서 있는 것을 간신히 보았다. (a) 그는 손을 그 군인에게 뻗었다.

(D) 그 군인은 노인의 병약한 손을 손가락으로 부드럽게 감쌌다. 간호사는 군인이 침대 옆에 앉을 수 있도록 의자를 가져왔다. 밤새 젊은 군인은 거기에 앉아, 노인의 손을 잡고 (e) 그에게 지지와 위로의 말을 건넸다. 가끔, 그녀는 군인에게 잠시 쉬라고 제안했다. 그는 정중하게 거절했다.

(B) 간호사가 병실에 들어올 때마다, 그녀는 그 군인이 부드러운 몇 마디의 말을 하는 것을 들었다. 밤새도록 (b) 그에게 손이 꼭 쥐어진 채로 노인은 아무 말도 하지 않았다. 동트기 직전에, 그 노인은 죽었다. 그 군인은 노인의 손을 놓고 간호사를 찾기 위해 병실을 나갔다. 그녀는 무슨 일이 있었는지 들은 후, 그와 함께 병실로 돌아갔다. 군인은 잠시 머뭇거리고는 "그 남자는 누구였나요?"라고 물었다.

(C) 그녀는 깜짝 놀라서 물었다. "그가 당신의 아버지가 아니었나요?" "아니요, 그는 아니었어요. 저는 그를 이전에 만난 적이 없어요."라고 군인이 대답했다. 그녀는 물었다. "그러면 내가 당신을 (c) 그에게 데리고 갔을 때 왜 아무 말도 하지 않았나요?" 그가 말했다. "저는 실수가 있었다는 것을 알았지만, 그가 너무 위독해서 제가 그의 아들인지 아닌지 구별할 수 없다는 걸 알게 되었을 때, 저는 (d) 그가 얼마나 저를 필요로 하는지 알 수 있었습니다. 그래서, 저는 머물렀습니다."

S 25 정답 ④

주어진 글 (A)에 이어질 내용을 순서에 맞게 배열한 것으로 가장 적절한 것은?

① (B) — (D) — (C)　　노인이 죽은 (B) 뒤에 노인에게 말은 건네는 (D)가 올 수 없음
② (C) — (B) — (D)
③ (C) — (D) — (B)
④ (D) — (B) — (C)　　(D) 군인은 노인 곁을 밤새 지킴 – (B) 노인이 죽고, 군인은 간호사에게
⑤ (D) — (C) — (B)　　그가 누구였는지 물어봄 – (C) 간호사는 그 사실에 놀람

노인이 죽은 (B) 뒤에 군인이 왜 그의 곁에 머물렀는지 설명하는 (C)가 와야 함

왜 정답 · 오답❓ ✽❊❊ [정답률 82%]

[A]: 한 간호사가 젊은 군인을 심장병 때문에 극심한 고통을 겪으며 침대에 누워있는 노인에게 데려갔고, 그를 본 노인은 손을 뻗었다.

➡ 노인을 본 군인이 어떤 행동을 하는지 이어질 것이다.

[B]: 밤새도록 군인은 말이 없는 노인의 곁을 지켰고, 노인이 죽은 뒤 군인은 간호사에게 그가 누구였는지 물었다.

➡ 뒤에 간호사의 대답이 이어질 것이다.

[C]: 놀란 간호사는 왜 진작 말하지 않았냐고 물었고, 군인은 노인이 자신을 필요로 하는 것을 느껴 머물렀다고 말했다.

➡ 군인의 물음에 대한 답이므로 (B)에 이어지는 내용이며, 글의 마무리 부분에 해당한다.

[D]: 군인은 노인의 손을 잡고 밤새 쉬지 않고 지지와 위로의 말을 건넸다.

➡ 노인이 군인에게 손을 뻗은 (A)에 이어지는 내용으로, 밤새 노인의 곁을 지켰다는 (B)가 뒤에 이어질 것이다.
　▶ (D) 군인은 침대 옆 의자에 앉아 노인 곁을 밤새 지킴
　→ (B) 동트기 전 노인이 죽고, 군인은 간호사를 찾아가 그가 누구였는지 물어봄
　→ (C) 간호사는 놀라 왜 그의 아들이 아님을 밝히지 않았는지 물었고,
　　군인은 그가 자신을 필요로 하는 것을 느껴 머물렀다고 말함
　▶ 글의 순서는 ④ (D) → (B) → (C)임

S 26 정답 ②

밑줄 친 (a)~(e) 중에서 가리키는 대상이 나머지 넷과 다른 것은?

① (a)　②(b)　③ (c)　④ (d)　⑤ (e)
= The old man　= the soldier　= the old man　= the old man　= the old man

왜 정답❓ ✽✽❊ [정답률 69%]

② (b) him: 노인의 손을 꼭 쥔 사람 ▶ the soldier

왜 오답❓

① (a) He: 군인에게 손을 뻗은 사람 ▶ The old man
③ (c) him: 간호사가 군인을 데리고 간 대상 ▶ the old man
④ (d) he: 군인을 필요로 했던 사람 ▶ the old man
⑤ (e) him: 군인이 지지와 위로의 말을 건넨 사람 ▶ the old man

S 27 정답 ③

윗글에 관한 내용으로 적절하지 않은 것은?

① 노인은 심장병으로 극심한 고통을 겪고 있었다.
　Suffering from the severe pain because of heart disease
② 군인은 간호사를 찾기 위해 병실을 나갔다.
　The soldier released the old man's hand and left the room to find the nurse.
③ 군인은 노인과 이전에 만난 적이 있다고 말했다.
　"I've never met him before."
④ 간호사는 군인이 앉을 수 있도록 의자를 가져왔다.
　The nurse brought a chair so that the soldier could sit beside the bed.
⑤ 군인은 잠시 쉬라는 간호사의 제안을 정중히 거절하였다.
　He politely said no.

왜 정답❓ ✽❊❊ [정답률 79%]

군인은 노인과 이전에 만난 적이 없다고("I've never met him before,") 했다. 따라서 군인은 노인과 이전에 만난 적이 있다고 한 ③은 적절하지 않다.

왜 오답❓

① 노인은 심장병으로 극심한 고통을 겪고 있었다.
　(Suffering from the severe pain because of heart disease)
② 노인이 죽자, 군인은 간호사를 찾기 위해 병실을 나갔다.
　(The soldier released the old man's hand and left the room to find the nurse.)
④ 간호사는 군인이 앉을 수 있도록 의자를 가져왔다.
　(The nurse brought a chair so that the soldier could sit beside the bed.)
⑤ 군인은 잠시 쉬라는 간호사의 제안을 정중히 거절하였다.
　(He politely said no.)

S 28~30 *성자가 준 깨달음

(A) There once lived a man in a village / who was not happy
　　　　　　　　　　　　　　　　　　주격 관계대명사
with his life. //
옛날 어느 마을에 한 남자가 살았다 / 자신의 삶이 행복하지 않은 //

He was always troubled / by one problem or another. //
그는 항상 어려움을 겪었다 / 하나 혹은 또 다른 문제로 //

One day, a saint with his guards / stopped by his village. //
어느 날 한 성자가 그의 경호인들과 함께 / 그의 마을에 들렀다 //

Many people heard the news / and started going to him / with
their problems. //　30번 ① 많은 사람들이 자신들의 문제를 가지고 성자에게 갔음
많은 사람들이 그 소식을 듣고 / 그에게 가기 시작했다 / 그들의 문제를 가지고 //

The man also decided to visit the saint. //
그 남자 역시 성자를 방문하기로 결정했다 //

Even after reaching the saint's place in the morning, / (a) he didn't get the opportunity / to meet him till evening. //
형용사적 용법(opportunity 수식) *= a man*
아침에 성자가 있는 곳에 도착하고 난 후에도 / 그는 기회를 얻지 못했다 / 저녁 때까지 그를 만날 //
28번 단서 1: 남자는 저녁까지 성자를 기다림

*(A) 문단 요약: 한 남자는 자신의 문제를 해결하기 위해 성자를 기다림

(B) But the saint also asked / if the man could do a small job for him. //
명사절 접속사
28번 단서 2, **30번** ② 성자는 남자에게 작은 일을 부탁함
그런데 성자는 또한 물었다 / 그 남자가 그를 위해 작은 일을 해 줄 수 있는지 //

He told the man / to take care of a hundred camels in his group that night, / saying "When all hundred camels sit down, / you can go to sleep." //
30번 ③ 성자는 남자가 낙타를 모두 재우는 것이 아니라 앉히면 잠을 자러 가도 좋다고 했음
성자는 그 남자에게 말했다 / 그날 밤에 그의 일행에 있는 백 마리 낙타를 돌봐 달라고 / "백 마리 낙타 모두가 자리에 앉으면 / 당신은 자러 가도 좋습니다"라고 말하면서 //

The man agreed. //
그 남자는 동의했다 //

The next morning when the saint met that man, / (b) he asked if the man had slept well. //
명사절 접속사 *과거완료(대과거)* *= a saint*
다음 날 아침에 성자가 그 남자를 만났을 때 / 그는 남자가 잠을 잘 잤는지 물어보았다 //
Being이 생략된 분사구문
Tired and sad, / the man replied / that he couldn't sleep even for a moment. //
피곤해하고 슬퍼하면서 / 남자는 대답했다 / 한순간도 잠을 자지 못했다고 //

*(B) 문단 요약: 성자는 낙타 백 마리가 모두 앉았을 때 잠에 들라고 부탁함

(C) In fact, the man tried very hard / but couldn't make all the camels sit at the same time / because every time (c) he made one camel sit, / another would stand up. //
사역동사 + 목적어 + 목적격 보어(원형부정사) *= a man*
사실 그 남자는 아주 열심히 노력했지만 / 모든 낙타를 동시에 앉게 할 수 없었다 / 그가 낙타 한 마리를 앉힐 때마다 / 다른 낙타 한 마리가 일어섰기 때문에 //

The saint told him, / "You realized / that no matter how hard you try, / you can't make all the camels sit down. //
'아무리 ~하더라도' *사역동사 + 목적어 + 목적격 보어(원형부정사)*
그 성자는 그에게 말했다 / "당신이 깨달았습니다 / 아무리 열심히 노력하더라도 / 모든 낙타를 앉게 만들 수는 없다는 것을 //

If one problem is solved, / for some reason, / another will arise / like the camels did. //
수동태 동사
28번 단서 3: 성자는 남자에게 문제들이 낙타와 같다는 깨달음을 전해줌
만약 한 가지 문제가 해결되면 / 어떤 이유로 / 또 다른 문제가 일어날 것입니다 / 낙타가 그런 것처럼 //

So, humans should enjoy life / despite these problems." //
30번 ④ 성자는 문제가 있어도 인생을 즐겨야 한다고 말했음
그래서 인간은 삶을 즐겨야 합니다 / 이러한 문제에도 불구하고"라고 //

*(C) 문단 요약: 한숨도 자지 못한 남자에게 성자는 문제들이 낙타와 같다는 깨달음을 전해줌

28번 단서 4: 남자가 마침내 성자를 만남 *= a man* *명사절 접속사*
(D) When the man got to meet the saint, / (d) he confessed / that he was very unhappy with life /
마침내 그가 성자를 만났을 때 / 그는 고백했다 / 삶이 매우 불행하다고 /

because problems always surrounded him, / like workplace tension or worries about his health. //
항상 문제가 자기를 둘러싸고 있어서 / 직장 내 긴장이나 건강에 대한 걱정과 같이 //
= A man
(e) He said, / "Please give me a solution / so that all the problems in my life will end / and I can live peacefully." //
그는 말했다 / "제발 해결책을 주세요 / 나의 삶의 모든 문제가 끝나고 / 제가 평화롭게 살 수 있도록"이라고 //
명사절 접속사
The saint smiled and said / that he would answer the request the next day. //
28번 단서 5, **30번** ⑤ 성자는 남자에게 다음 날 요청에 답을 주겠다고 함
성자는 미소 지으면서 말했다 / 그가 다음 날 그 요청에 답해 주겠다고 //

*(D) 문단 요약: 그 남자는 해결책을 요구했고, 성자는 다음 날에 답을 주기로 함

- **saint** ⓝ 성자　・**guard** ⓝ 경호인　・**opportunity** ⓝ 기회
- **camel** ⓝ 낙타　・**reply** ⓥ 답하다　・**in fact** 사실
- **arise** ⓥ 일어나다　・**despite** ⓟⓡⓔⓟ ~에도 불구하고
- **confess** ⓥ 고백하다　・**surround** ⓥ 둘러싸다　・**tension** ⓝ 긴장
- **solution** ⓝ 해결책　・**request** ⓝ 요청

(A) 옛날 어느 마을에 자신의 삶이 행복하지 않은 한 남자가 살았다. 그는 항상 하나 혹은 또 다른 문제로 어려움을 겪었다. 어느 날 한 성자가 그의 경호인들과 함께 그의 마을에 들렀다. 많은 사람들이 그 소식을 듣고 그들의 문제를 가지고 그에게 가기 시작했다. 그 남자 역시 성자를 방문하기로 결정했다. 아침에 성자가 있는 곳에 도착하고 난 후에도 (a) 그는 저녁 때까지 그를 만날 기회를 얻지 못했다.

(D) 마침내 그가 성자를 만났을 때 (d) 그는 직장 내 긴장이나 건강에 대한 걱정과 같이 항상 문제가 자기를 둘러싸고 있어서 삶이 매우 불행하다고 고백했다. (e) 그는 "나의 삶의 모든 문제가 끝나고 제가 평화롭게 살 수 있도록 제발 해결책을 주세요."라고 말했다. 성자는 미소 지으면서 그가 다음 날 그 요청에 답해 주겠다고 말했다.

(B) 그런데 성자는 또한 그 남자가 그를 위해 작은 일을 해 줄 수 있는지 물었다. 성자는 그 남자에게 "백 마리 낙타 모두가 자리에 앉으면 당신은 자러 가도 좋습니다."라고 말하면서 그날 밤에 그의 일행에 있는 백 마리 낙타를 돌봐 달라고 말했다. 그 남자는 동의했다. 다음 날 아침에 성자가 그 남자를 만났을 때 (b) 그는 남자가 잠을 잘 잤는지 물어보았다. 피곤해하고 슬퍼하면서 남자는 한순간도 잠을 자지 못했다고 대답했다.

(C) 사실 그 남자는 아주 열심히 노력했지만 (c) 그가 낙타 한 마리를 앉힐 때마다 다른 낙타 한 마리가 일어섰기 때문에 모든 낙타를 동시에 앉게 할 수 없었다. 그 성자는 그에게 "당신이 아무리 열심히 노력하더라도 모든 낙타를 앉게 만들 수는 없다는 것을 깨달았습니다. 만약 한 가지 문제가 해결되면 낙타가 그런 것처럼 어떤 이유로 또 다른 문제가 일어날 것입니다. 그래서 인간은 이러한 문제에도 불구하고 삶을 즐겨야 합니다."라고 말했다.

S 28 정답 ④

주어진 글 (A)에 이어질 내용을 순서에 맞게 배열한 것으로 가장 적절한 것은?

① (B) — (D) — (C) 　저녁까지 성자를 기다렸다는 (A)에 이어 마침내 남자가 성자를 만났다는 (D)가 가장 먼저 와야 함
② (C) — (B) — (D) 　성자가 부탁하는 (B) 뒤에 깨달음을 주는 (C)가 와야 함
③ (C) — (D) — (B) 　(D) 그 남자는 성자를 만나 문제의 해결책을 요구했고, 성자는 다음 날에 답을 주겠다고 함 - (B) 성자는 밤에 낙타 백 마리를 돌보면서
④ (D) — (B) — (C) 　모든 낙타가 앉았을 때 잠에 들라고 부탁함 - (C) 한숨도 자지 못한 남자에게 성자는 문제들이 낙타와 같다는 깨달음을 전해줌
⑤ (D) — (C) — (B) 　성자가 남자에게 낙타와 관련된 깨달음을 주는 (C)가 가장 마지막에 와야 함

왜? 정답 · 오답? ✱✱✱ [정답률 86%]

[(A): 한 남자는 성자가 마을을 방문한다는 소식을 듣고, 자신의 문제를 해결하기 위해 성자를 기다렸다.

➡ 남자가 성자를 만나 깨달음을 얻는 이야기가 이어질 것이다.

[(B): 성자는 밤에 낙타 백 마리를 돌보면서 모든 낙타가 앉았을 때 잠에 들라고 부탁했다.

➡ 남자가 성자와 만난 내용이 앞에 나와야 하고, 성자가 낙타를 부탁한 후 벌어지는 일이 뒤에 이어져야 한다.

[(C): 한숨도 자지 못한 남자에게 성자는 문제들이 낙타와 같다는 깨달음을 전해주었다.

➡ 성자가 밤새 남자에게 낙타를 부탁했던 (B)에 이어지는 내용이고, 이 부탁을 통해 문제들이 낙타와 같다는 깨달음을 전해주는 글의 마무리 부분이다.

[(D): 그 남자는 성자를 만나 문제의 해결책을 요구했고, 성자는 다음 날에 답을 주겠다고 했다.

➡ 남자가 성자를 기다렸다는 (A)에 이어지는 내용이고, 뒤에는 남자가 성자를 통해 문제의 해결책을 얻어가는 과정이 이어져야 한다.

▶ (A) 성자가 마을을 방문한다는 소식을 듣고 한 남자가 밤가지 그를 기다림 → (D) 그 남자는 성자를 만나 문제의 해결책을 요구했고, 성자는 다음 날에 답을 주겠다고 함 → (B) 성자는 밤에 낙타 백 마리를 돌보면서 모든 낙타가 앉았을 때 잠에 들 것을 부탁함 → (C) 한숨도 자지 못한 남자에게 성자는 문제들이 낙타와 같다는 깨달음을 전해줌 ▶ 글의 순서는 ④ (D) — (B) — (C)임

S 29 정답 ②

밑줄 친 (a)~(e) 중에서 가리키는 대상이 나머지 넷과 다른 것은?
① (a) = a man ②(b) = a saint ③ (c) = a man ④ (d) = a man ⑤ (e) = A man

> 왜 정답 ? ✱✱✲ [정답률 80%]

② (b) he: 남자에게 잘 잤는지 물어본 사람 ▶ a saint

> 왜 오답 ?

① (a) he: 저녁까지 성자를 만날 기회를 얻지 못한 사람 ▶ a man
③ (c) he: 밤새 낙타를 한 마리씩 앉히려고 노력했던 사람 ▶ a man
④ (d) he: 성자를 만나 삶이 여러 문제로 불행하다고 고백했던 사람 ▶ a man
⑤ (e) He: 성자에게 자신이 평화롭게 살도록 해결책을 요청했던 사람 ▶ A man

S 30 정답 ③

윗글에 관한 내용으로 적절하지 않은 것은?
① 많은 사람들이 자신들의 문제를 가지고 성자에게 갔다.
　Many people heard the news and started going to him with their problems.
② 성자는 자신을 위해 작은 일을 해 줄 수 있는지 남자에게 물었다.
　But the saint also asked if the man could do a small job for him.
③ 성자는 남자가 낙타를 모두 재우면 잠을 자러 가도 좋다고 했다.
　When all hundred camels sit down, you can go to sleep.
④ 성자는 문제가 있어도 인생을 즐겨야 한다고 말했다.
　So, humans should enjoy life despite these problems.
⑤ 성자는 남자의 요청에 대한 답을 다음 날 말해 주기로 했다.
　The saint smiled and said that he would answer the request the next day.

> 왜 정답 ? ✱✱✲ [정답률 70%]

성자는 남자에게 낙타를 앉히고 나면 잠을 자러 가도 좋다고(When all hundred camels sit down, you can go to sleep.) 했으므로, ③은 적절하지 않다.

> 왜 오답 ?

① 많은 사람들이 자신들의 문제를 가지고 성자에게 갔다. (Many people heard the news and started going to him with their problems.)
② 성자는 자신을 위해 작은 일을 해 줄 수 있는지 남자에게 물었다. (But the saint also asked if the man could do a small job for him.)
④ 성자는 문제가 있어도 인생을 즐겨야 한다고 말했다. (So, humans should enjoy life despite these problems.)
⑤ 성자는 남자의 요청에 대한 답을 다음 날 말해 주기로 했다. (The saint smiled and said that he would answer the request the next day.)

S 31~33 *보자기로 도둑을 잡은 상인

(A) A rich merchant lived alone / in his house. //
부유한 상인이 혼자 살았다 / 그의 집에 //
33번 ① 상인은 부유한 집에 혼자 살아서 항상 위험에 대비하고 있었음 앞에 who was 생략
分사구문
Knowing that he was the only person / living in the house, / he was always prepared / in case thieves came to his house. //
사람이 자기밖에 없다는 것을 알았기 때문에 / 그 집에 사는 / 그는 항상 대비하고 있었다 / 자신의 집에 도둑이 드는 상황에 //

So, / one day, / when a thief entered his home, / he remained calm and cool. //
그래서 / 어느 날 / 도둑이 집에 들어왔을 때 / 그는 차분하고 침착했다 //

Although he was awake, / the merchant pretended to be in a deep sleep. //
비록 상인은 깨어 있었지만 / 깊이 잠든 척했다 //

He lay in bed / and watched the thief in action. //
그는 침대에 누워 있었다 / 그리고 도둑이 움직이는 것을 지켜보았다 //

물건의 뜻으로 쓸 때 항상 복수형으로 씀　= the thief
The thief had brought a new white sheet / with (a) him / to carry away the stolen goods. // **31번** 단서 1: 도둑이 훔친 물건들을 가져가기 위해 흰 새 보자기를 가지고 침입함
도둑은 흰 새 보자기를 가지고 왔다 / 그와 함께 / 훔친 물건들을 운반하기 위해 //

*(A) 문단 요약: 어느날 도둑이 훔친 물건들을 운반하기 위해 흰 새 보자기를 가지고 부유한 상인의 집에 들어왔음
31번 단서 2: 보자기를 바꿔치기 해놓고 일부러 자는 척을 했음 = the merchant
(B) (b) He then lay down / and pretended to be asleep. //
그리고 나서 그는 누웠다 / 그리고 자는 척했다 //

as many ~ as one could: …가 가능한 많은 ~
When the thief had finished collecting / as many valuables as he could, / he hurriedly tied a knot in the white sheet / which he thought was his. //
도둑이 훔치는 것을 마쳤을 때 / 가능한 많은 귀중품들을 / 그는 흰 보자기의 매듭을 서둘러 묶었다 / 자신의 것이라고 생각했던 //

33번 ② 상인은 도둑을 놀라게 하려고 정원에서 크게 소리쳤음
The merchant / meanwhile / ran out into the garden and yelled / —"Thief! Thief!" / with all the air in his lungs. //
상인은 / 그 동안에 / 정원으로 뛰어나가 크게 소리쳤다 / — "도둑이야! 도둑!" / 그는 있는 힘껏 소리쳤다 //

The thief got nervous / and quickly lifted the sheet. //
도둑은 초조해졌다 / 그리고 서둘러서 보자기를 들어올렸다 //

앞에 주격 관계대명사와 be동사 생략
= the thief's
To (c) his surprise, / the thin white sheet, / filled with stolen goods, / was torn apart. //
그가 놀랍게도 / 얇은 흰 보자기가 / 훔친 물건들로 가득 찬 / 찢어졌다 //

*(B) 문단 요약: 상인은 도둑을 놀라게 하기 위해 정원에서 크게 소리쳤고 도둑이 급하게 보자기를 들어 올리자 보자기가 찢어졌음

分사구문
(C) All the stolen goods / fell down on the floor / creating a very loud and unpleasant noise. // **31번** 단서 3, **33번** ③ (B)의 마지막에 보자기가 찢어진 것에 이어지는 내용으로, 훔치려던 물건들이 바닥으로 떨어짐
훔친 모든 물건들이 / 바닥에 떨어졌다 / 아주 크고 불쾌한 소리를 내면서 //

分사구문
Seeing many people run towards him, / the thief had to give up on all of the stolen goods. //
많은 사람들이 그에게 달려드는 것을 보고 / 도둑은 훔친 모든 물건들을 포기해야만 했다 //

Leaving the goods behind in the house, / he ran away in a hurry / saying under his breath: / "This man is such a skillful merchant; / he is a businessman to the core. // **33번** ④ 도둑은 물건을 집 밖으로 가지고 나가지 못함
= and he said
그 물건들을 집에 남겨두고 떠나면서 / 그는 서둘러 도망치며 / 작은 목소리로 말했다 / "이 사람은 교활한 상인이다 / 그는 뼛속까지 장사꾼이다 //

not only A but also B: A 뿐만 아니라 B도
He has not only managed to save his valuables / but has also taken away (d) my new sheet. //
= the thief's
그는 그의 귀중품들을 지켜냈을 뿐만 아니라 / 나의 새 보자기도 빼앗았다 //

He has stolen from a thief!" //
그는 도둑한테서 훔쳤다!" //

As he said that to himself, / he ran away from the house. //
이렇게 말하면서 / 그는 그 집밖으로 뛰쳐나갔다 //

*(C) 문단 요약: 도둑은 도망치면서 상인이 자신의 귀중품도 지키고 도둑의 새 보자기도 빼앗았다고 말했음
31번 단서 4: 물건을 훔치기 위해 가지고 온 보자기를 사용해 물건을 담음
병렬 구조
(D) He spread it out on the floor / with the idea / of putting all the stolen valuables into it, / tying it, / and carrying it away. //
그는 그것을 바닥에 펼쳐놓았다 / 생각으로 / 훔친 귀중품들을 모두 넣어 / 묶은 뒤 / 운반한다는 //

= the thief
While (e) he was busy / gathering expensive-looking items / from the merchant's luxurious house, / the merchant quickly got out of the bed. //
그가 분주한 사이 / 비싸게 보이는 물건을 모으느라 / 상인의 호화로운 집에서 / 상인은 재빨리 침대에서 일어났다 //

계속적 용법의 관계대명사
Then / he replaced the new white sheet / with a similar looking white sheet, / which was much weaker and much cheaper / than the thief's one. // **33번** ⑤ 상인의 보자기는 도둑의 보자기보다 값싼 것이었음
그리고 나서 / 그는 도둑의 흰 새 보자기를 교체했다 / 비슷하게 생긴 (자신의) 흰 보자기로 / 이것은 훨씬 약하고 값싼 것이었다 / 도둑의 것보다 //

*(D) 문단 요약: 도둑이 분주한 사이 상인이 자신의 값싼 보자기와 바꿔치기 했음

- merchant ⓝ 상인　　• prepare ⓥ 준비하다, 대비하다
- pretend ⓥ ~인 척하다　　• valuable ⓝ 귀중품
- hurriedly ⓐⓓ 서둘러　　• knot ⓝ 매듭　　• lung ⓝ 폐
- tear apart 찢어지다　　• skillful ⓐ 교활한　　• unpleasant ⓐ 불쾌한
- luxurious ⓐ 호화로운　　• replace ⓥ 교체하다

S

(A) 부유한 상인이 그의 집에 혼자 살았다. 그 집에 사는 사람이 자기밖에 없다는 것을 알았기 때문에, 그는 자신의 집에 도둑이 드는 상황에 항상 대비하고 있었다. 그래서 어느 날, 도둑이 집에 들어왔을 때, 그는 차분하고 침착했다. 비록 상인은 깨어 있었지만, 깊이 잠든 척했다. 그는 침대에 누워서 도둑이 움직이는 것을 지켜보았다. 도둑은 훔친 물건들을 운반하기 위해 흰 새 보자기를 ((a) 그와 함께) 가지고 왔다.

(D) 그는 훔친 귀중품들을 모두 넣어 묶은 뒤 운반한다는 생각으로 그것을 바닥에 펼쳐놓았다. (e) 그가 상인의 호화로운 집에서 비싸게 보이는 물건을 모으느라 분주한 사이, 상인은 재빨리 침대에서 일어났다. 그리고 나서 그는 도둑의 흰 새 보자기를 비슷하게 생긴 (자신의) 흰 보자기로 교체했는데, 이것은 도둑의 것보다 훨씬 약하고 값싼 것이었다.

(B) 그리고 나서 (b) 그는 누워서 자는 척했다. 도둑이 가능한 많은 귀중품들을 훔치는 것을 마쳤을 때, 그는 자신의 것이라고 생각했던 흰 보자기의 매듭을 서둘러 묶었다. 그 동안에 상인은 정원으로 뛰어나가 크게 소리쳤다. ― "도둑이야! 도둑!" 그는 있는 힘껏 소리쳤다. 도둑은 초조해져서 서둘러서 보자기를 들어올렸다. ((c) 그가) 놀랍게도 훔친 물건들로 가득 찬 얇은 흰 보자기가 찢어졌다.

(C) 훔친 모든 물건들이 바닥에 떨어져 아주 크고 불쾌한 소리를 냈다. 많은 사람들이 그에게 달려드는 것을 보고 도둑은 훔친 모든 물건들을 포기해야만 했다. 그 물건들을 집에 남겨두고 떠나면서, 그는 서둘러 도망치며 작은 목소리로 말했다. "이 사람은 교묘한 상인이다. 그는 뼛속까지 장사꾼이다. 그는 그의 귀중품들을 지켜냈을 뿐만 아니라, (d) 나의 새 보자기도 빼앗았다. 그는 도둑한테서 훔쳤다!" 이렇게 말하면서 그는 그 집밖으로 뛰쳐나갔다.

S 31 정답 ④

주어진 글 (A)에 이어질 내용을 순서에 맞게 배열한 것으로 가장 적절한 것은?

① (B) — (D) — (C) 도둑이 들었는데 바로 자는 척하는 (B)가 나오는 것은 어색함
② (C) — (B) — (D) 적절한 글의 흐름과 정반대
③ (C) — (D) — (B) 주어진 글 다음에 상인이 보자기를 바꿔치기 하는 내용인 (D)가 이어져야 함
④ (D) — (B) — (C) (D) 상인이 자신의 값싼 보자기와 도둑의 보자기를 바꿔치기 했음-(B) 도둑이 급하게 보자기를 들어 올리자 보자기가 찢어졌음-(C) 도둑은 도망치면서 상인이 자신의 귀중품도 지키고 도둑의 새 보자기도 빼앗았다고 말했음
⑤ (D) — (C) — (B) 도둑이 도망치는 내용인 (C)는 결말임

> **왜 정답?** ✹✹✸ [정답률 71%]

> 하나의 이야기이므로 시간의 선후 관계를 잘 파악하기! **꿀팁**

(A)에는 혼자 살고 있던 부유한 상인이 도둑의 위험에 항상 대비하고 있었는데, 어느 날 도둑이 훔친 물건들을 운반하기 위해 가져온 흰 새 보자기를 가지고 상인의 집에 들어왔다는 내용이 나온다. 이 뒤에는 도둑이 가져온 보자기에 물건을 담고 있었는데, 도둑이 분주한 사이 상인이 자신의 값싼 보자기와 바꿔치기 했다는 (D)가 와야 한다. 그리고 (B)에서 도둑이 보자기의 매듭을 묶었을 때 상인이 도둑을 놀라게 하기 위해 정원에서 크게 소리쳤고 도둑이 급하게 보자기를 들어올리자 보자기가 찢어졌고, 마지막으로 (C)에서 사람들이 달려들자 도둑은 바닥에 떨어지는 훔친 물건들을 포기하고 도망치면서 상인이 자신의 귀중품도 지키고 도둑의 새 보자기도 빼앗았다고 말했다는 결말로 끝나는 것이 적절하다. 따라서 정답은 ④ (D)-(B)-(C)이다.

> **왜 오답?**
① 도둑이 들었는데 바로 자는 척하는 (B)가 나오는 것은 어색하다.
② 적절한 글의 흐름과 정반대이므로 오답이다.
③ 주어진 글에서 도둑이 들어온 후에 상인이 보자기를 바꿔치기 하는 내용인 (D)가 이어져야 적절하다.
⑤ 도둑이 도망치는 내용인 (C)는 결말이므로 마지막에 와야 한다.

S 32 정답 ②

밑줄 친 (a)~(e) 중에서 가리키는 대상이 나머지 넷과 다른 것은?
① (a) = the thief　② (b) = the merchant　③ (c) = the thief's　④ (d) = the thief's　⑤ (e) = the thief

> **왜 정답?** ✹✹✸ [정답률 71%]

도둑을 보고도 자는 척하는 것은 부유한 상인이고, 나머지는 모두 도둑을 가리키므로 ②이 정답이다.

> **왜 오답?**
① 상인의 물건을 훔쳐가기 위해서 보자기를 들고 침입한 사람은 도둑이다.
③ 물건을 보자기에 싸고 도망간 사람은 도둑이다.
④ 물건을 훔치기 위해 보자기를 갖고 간 사람은 도둑이다.
⑤ 훔치기 위해 물건을 싸는 사람은 도둑이다.

S 33 정답 ④

윗글에 관한 내용으로 적절하지 않은 것은?
① 상인은 도둑이 드는 상황에 항상 대비하고 있었다. Knowing that he was the only person ~ in case thieves came to his house.
② 상인은 정원으로 뛰어나가 크게 소리쳤다. The merchant meanwhile ~ with all the air in his lungs.
③ 도둑이 훔친 물건들이 바닥에 떨어졌다. All the stolen goods fell down on the floor creating a very loud and unpleasant noise.
④ 도둑은 상인의 물건들을 집밖으로 가지고 달아났다. Leaving the goods behind in the house; ~ "This man is such a skillful merchant; he is a businessman to the core.
⑤ 상인의 보자기는 도둑의 보자기보다 값싼 것이었다. Then he replaced the new white sheet ~ and much cheaper than the thief's one.

> **왜 정답?** ✹✹✸ [정답률 73%]

상인은 도둑이 물건을 집밖으로 가지고 나가기 전에 소리쳐서 집 안에 물건이 떨어지게 했으므로(Leaving the goods behind in the house, ~ he is a businessman to the core.) ④이 글의 내용과 일치하지 않는다.

> **왜 오답?**
① 상인은 혼자 살고 있기 때문에 도둑이 드는 상황에 항상 대비하고 있었다. (Knowing that he was the only person ~ came to his house.)
② 상인은 정원으로 뛰쳐나가 최대한 소리를 크게 질러 도둑을 놀라게 만들었다. (The merchant meanwhile ~ with all the air in his lungs.)
③ 도둑은 놀라서 보자기를 들어 올렸는데 찢어져서 모든 물건들이 집 안 바닥에 떨어졌다. (All the stolen goods ~ and unpleasant noise.)
⑤ 상인은 도둑의 튼튼한 새 보자기를 일부러 자신의 낡고 값싼 것으로 바꾸어 두었다. (Then he replaced the new white sheet ~ which was much weaker and much cheaper than the thief's one.)

S 34~36 *농부의 시계를 찾아준 어린 소년의 지혜

(A) Once, / a farmer lost his precious watch / while working in his barn. // 사이에 주어와 be동사(he was) 생략됨
어느 날 / 한 농부가 그의 귀중한 시계를 잃어버렸다 / 헛간에서 일하는 동안 //

It may have appeared / to be an ordinary watch to others, / but it brought a lot of happy childhood memories / to him. //
그것은 보였을 수도 있다 / 다른 이들에게는 평범한 시계로 / 하지만 그것은 어린 시절의 많은 행복한 기억을 불러왔다 / 그에게 // 36번 ① 농부의 시계는 어린 시절의 행복한 기억을 불러일으킴

It was one of the most important things / to (a) him. // 「one of+최상급+복수 명사」: 가장 ~한 것들 중 하나 = the farmer
그것은 가장 중요한 것들 중 하나였다 / 그에게 //

After searching for it / for a long time, / the old farmer became exhausted. // 34번 단서 1: 농부가 귀중한 시계를 잃어버려서 찾다가 지쳐버림
그것을 찾아본 뒤에 / 오랜 시간 동안 / 그 나이 든 농부는 지쳐버렸다 //

*(A) 문단 요약: 귀중한 시계를 잃어버린 농부가 시계를 찾다가 지침

34번 단서 2. 아이들이 시계를 찾다가 지쳤다고 한 (D)의 마지막에 이어지는 내용

(B) The number of children / looking for the watch / slowly decreased / and only a few tired children were left. //
(현재분사구(children 수식) / 수동태)

아이들의 숫자가 / 시계를 찾는 / 천천히 줄어들었다 / 그리고 지친 아이들 몇 명만이 남았다

The farmer gave up all hope / of finding it / and called off the search. //
(병렬 구조)

그 농부는 모든 희망을 포기했다 / 시계를 찾을 거라는 / 그리고 찾는 것을 멈추었다 //

Just when the farmer was closing the barn door, / a little boy came up to him / and asked the farmer / to give him another chance. //
(asked의 목적격보어(to부정사))

36번 ② 한 어린 소년이 농부에게 또 한 번의 기회를 달라고 요청함

농부가 막 헛간 문을 닫고 있었을 때 / 한 어린 소년이 그에게 다가왔다 / 그리고 농부에게 요청했다 / 자신에게 또 한 번의 기회를 달라고 //

The farmer did not want to lose out / on any chance of finding the watch / so let (b) him in the barn. //
(= the little boy)

농부는 놓치고 싶지 않아서 / 시계를 찾을 어떤 가능성도 / 그를 헛간 안으로 들어오게 해주었다 //

*(B) 문단 요약: 농부가 시계 찾기를 포기했을 때, 어린 소년이 다시 한번 기회를 달라고 함

(C) After a little while / the boy came out with the farmer's watch / in his hand. //

34번 단서 3. **36번 ③** (B)에서 시계를 더 찾아보겠다고 한 소년이 결국 한 손에 농부의 시계를 들고 나옴

잠시 후 / 그 소년이 농부의 시계를 들고 나왔다 / 한 손에

(c) He was happily surprised / and asked how he had succeeded / to find the watch / while everyone else had failed. //
(= the farmer / 반면)

그는 행복에 겨워 놀랐다 / 그리고 소년이 어떻게 성공했는지를 물었다 / 시계를 찾는 데 / 다른 모두가 실패했던 반면 //

He replied / "I just sat there / and tried listening for the sound of the watch. //

그는 답했다 / "저는 거기에 앉았어요 / 그리고 시계의 소리를 들으려고 했어요 //

In silence, / it was much easier / to hear it / and follow the direction of the sound." //
(비교급 강조 부사(much, far, even, still, a lot 등))

침묵 속에서 / 훨씬 쉬웠어요 / 그것을 듣는 것이 / 그리고 소리의 방향을 따라가는 것이" //

(d) He was delighted to get his watch back / and rewarded the little boy / as promised. //
(= the farmer)

그는 시계를 되찾아 기뻤다 / 그리고 그 어린 소년에게 보상해 주었다 / 약속했던 대로 //

*(C) 문단 요약: 어린 소년이 시계를 찾았고, 침묵 속에서 시계 소리의 방향을 따라갔기 때문에 찾을 수 있었다고 말함

(D) However, / the tired farmer did not want to give up / on the search for his watch / and asked a group of children playing outside / to help him. //
(현재분사구(a group of children 수식))

34번 단서 4. (A)에서 농부가 시계를 찾다가 지친 내용에 이어짐

그러나 / 그 지친 농부는 포기하고 싶지 않았기에 / 그의 시계를 찾는 것을 / 밖에서 놀던 한 무리의 아이들에게 요청했다 / 그를 도와 달라고 //

(e) He promised an attractive reward / for the person / who could find it. //
(= the farmer / 주격 관계대명사)

그는 매력적인 보상을 약속했다 / 사람에게 / 그것을 찾는 //

After hearing about the reward, / the children hurried inside the barn / and went through and round the entire pile of hay / looking for the watch. //
(분사구문)

36번 ④ 아이들은 시계를 찾기 위해 헛간 안으로 들어감

보상에 대해 듣고 난 뒤 / 그 아이들은 헛간 안으로 서둘러 들어갔다 / 그리고 전체 건초 더미 사이와 주변으로 걸어갔다 / 시계를 찾으러 //

After a long time searching for it, / some of the children / got tired and gave up. //

36번 ⑤ 아이들 중 일부는 지쳐서 시계 찾기를 포기함

시계를 찾느라 오랜 시간을 보낸 후 / 아이들 중 일부는 / 지쳐서 포기했다 //

*(D) 문단 요약: 지친 농부가 아이들에게 시계를 찾는 것을 도와달라고 요청했는데, 오랜 시간 후에 아이들도 찾지 못하고 일부 아이들은 지쳐서 포기함

- precious ⓐ 귀중한   · ordinary ⓐ 평범한   · memory ⓝ 기억
- search for ~을 찾다   · exhausted ⓐ 지친
- decrease ⓥ 줄다[감소하다]   · give up ~을 포기하다
- call off ~을 멈추다, 중지하다   · chance ⓝ 기회, 가능성
- succeed ⓥ 성공하다   · fail ⓥ 실패하다   · reply ⓥ 대답하다

- silence ⓝ 침묵   · direction ⓝ 방향   · delighted ⓐ 기쁜
- reward ⓥ 보상하다 ⓝ 보상   · promise ⓥ 약속하다
- attractive ⓐ 매력적인   · entire ⓐ 전체의   · pile ⓝ 더미
- hay ⓝ 건초

(A) 어느 날, 한 농부가 헛간에서 일하는 동안 그의 귀중한 시계를 잃어버렸다. 그것은 다른 이들에게는 평범한 시계로 보일 수도 있었지만 그것은 그에게 어린 시절의 많은 행복한 기억을 불러왔다. 그것은 (a) 그에게 가장 중요한 것들 중 하나였다. 오랜 시간 동안 그것을 찾아본 뒤에 그 나이 든 농부는 지쳐버렸다.

(D) 그러나, 그 지친 농부는 그의 시계를 찾는 것을 포기하고 싶지 않았기에 밖에서 놀던 한 무리의 아이들에게 도와 달라고 요청했다. (e) 그는 그의 시계를 찾는 사람에게 매력적인 보상을 약속했다. 보상에 대해 듣고 난 뒤, 그 아이들은 헛간 안으로 서둘러 들어갔고 시계를 찾으러 전체 건초 더미 사이와 주변으로 걸어갔다. 시계를 찾느라 오랜 시간을 보낸 후, 아이들 중 일부는 지쳐서 포기했다.

(B) 시계를 찾는 아이들의 숫자가 천천히 줄어들었고 지친 아이들 몇 명만이 남았다. 그 농부는 시계를 찾을 거라는 모든 희망을 포기하고 찾는 것을 멈추었다. 농부가 막 헛간 문을 닫고 있었을 때 한 어린 소년이 그에게 다가와서 자신에게 또 한 번의 기회를 달라고 요청했다. 농부는 시계를 찾을 어떤 가능성도 놓치고 싶지 않아서 (b) 그를 헛간 안으로 들어오게 해주었다.

(C) 잠시 후 그 소년이 한 손에 농부의 시계를 들고 나왔다. (c) 그는 행복에 겨워 놀랐고 다른 모두가 실패했던 반면 소년이 어떻게 시계를 찾는 데 성공했는지를 물었다. 그는 "저는 거기에 앉아서 시계의 소리를 들으려고 했어요. 침묵 속에서, 그것을 듣고 소리의 방향을 따라가는 것이 훨씬 쉬웠어요."라고 답했다. (d) 그는 시계를 되찾아 기뻤고 그 어린 소년에게 약속했던 대로 보상해 주었다.

S 34 정답 ④

주어진 글 (A)에 이어질 내용을 순서에 맞게 배열한 것으로 가장 적절한 것은?

① (B) — (D) — (C)
(B)에서 아이들이 왜 시계를 찾게 되었는지에 대한 내용이 나오는 (D)가 (B) 앞에 와야 함

② (C) — (B) — (D)
(C)는 소년이 농부의 시계를 찾은 결말이므로 마지막에 와야 함

③ (C) — (D) — (B)

④ (D) — (B) — (C)
(D) 농부가 아이들에게 시계를 찾는 것을 도와달라고 요청함 ~ (B) 아이들도 찾지 못하자 농부가 포기했을 때, 어린 소년이 다시 한번 기회를 달라고 함 ~ (C) 소년이 시계를 찾았고 농부가 기뻐하며 약속한 보상을 줌

⑤ (D) — (C) — (B)
(C)에 나오는 '그 소년(the boy)'이 처음 등장하는 (B)가 (C) 앞에 오는 것이 적절함

왜 정답? ★★❀ [정답률 81%]

귀중한 시계를 잃어버린 농부가 시계를 찾다가 지쳐버린 내용이 나오는 (A) 뒤에는 지친 농부가 아이들에게 도움을 요청하는 (D)가 와야 한다. 일부 아이들이 지쳐서 포기했다는 (D) 뒤에 시계를 찾는 아이들의 수가 줄고 몇 안 되는 아이들만 남았다는 내용으로 시작하는 (B)가 와야 한다.

(B)에 한 어린 소년이 한 번 더 기회를 달라고 요청했고 (C)에서 그 소년이 농부의 시계를 찾아서 들고 나오는 내용으로 이어지는 것이 자연스럽다.

따라서 가장 적절한 순서는 ④ (D)-(B)-(C)이다.

왜 오답?

① (B)에서 아이들이 왜 시계를 찾게 되었는지에 대한 내용인 (D)가 (B)보다 앞에 나와야 한다. **함정**

②, ③ (C)는 소년이 농부의 시계를 찾은 내용이 나오는 이야기의 결말이므로 마지막에 오는 것이 자연스럽다.

⑤ (C)에 나오는 '그 소년(the boy)'이 처음 등장하는 (B)가 (C) 앞에 오는 것이 적절하다.

S 35 정답 ②

밑줄 친 (a)~(e) 중에서 가리키는 대상이 나머지 넷과 <u>다른</u> 것은?

① (a)   ②(b)   ③ (c)   ④ (d)   ⑤ (e)
= the farmer   = the little boy   = the farmer   = the farmer   = the farmer

> **왜 정답 ?** ※※※ [정답률 76%]

(b)는 농부에게 한 번 더 기회를 달라고 요청하여 헛간으로 들어간 어린 소년을 가리킨다. 나머지는 모두 농부를 가리키므로 정답은 ②이다.

> **왜 오답 ?**

① 시계는 농부에게 가장 소중한 것들 중 하나이다.
🎀 소년이 시계를 들고 나오자 행복에 겨워 놀란 사람은 농부이다.
④ 시계를 되찾아 기뻐하며 어린 소년에게 보상을 해 준 사람은 농부이다.
⑤ 농부가 시계를 찾는 사람에게 매력적인 보상을 약속했다.

S 36 정답 ④

윗글에 관한 내용으로 적절하지 <u>않은</u> 것은?

① 농부의 시계는 어린 시절의 행복한 기억을 불러일으켰다.
　　　it brought a lot of happy childhood memories to him
② 한 어린 소년이 농부에게 또 한 번의 기회를 달라고 요청했다.
　　　a little boy came up to him and asked the farmer to give him another chance
③ 소년이 한 손에 농부의 시계를 들고 나왔다.
　　　the boy came out with the farmer's watch in his hand
④ 아이들은 시계를 찾기 위해 헛간을 뛰쳐나왔다. the children hurried inside the
　　　barn and went through and round the entire pile of hay looking for the watch
⑤ 아이들 중 일부는 지쳐서 시계 찾기를 포기했다
　　　some of the children got tired and gave up

> **왜 정답 ?** ※※※ [정답률 80%]

(D)에서 the children hurried inside the barn and went through and round the entire pile of hay looking for the watch (그 아이들은 헛간 안으로 서둘러 들어갔고 시계를 찾으러 전체 건초 더미 사이와 주변으로 걸어갔다)라고 했으므로 아이들은 시계를 찾기 위해 헛간을 뛰쳐나온 것이 아니다.
따라서 ④이 윗글에 관한 내용으로 적절하지 않다.

> **왜 오답 ?**

① 농부의 시계는 어린 시절의 많은 행복한 기억을 농부에게 가져다준다고 했다.
(it brought a lot of happy childhood memories to him)
② 한 어린 소년이 농부에게 와서 또 한 번의 기회를 달라고 요청했다고 했다. (a little boy came up to him and asked the farmer to give him another chance)
③ 소년이 한 손에 농부의 시계를 들고 나왔다고 했다. (the boy came out with the farmer's watch in his hand)
⑤ 아이들 중 일부는 지쳐서 포기했다고 했다. (some of the children got tired and gave up)

S 37~39 *사원 관리인이 될 자격

(A) Long ago, / an old man built a grand temple / at the center of his village. // 39번① 노인은 마을 중심부에 사원을 지음
옛날에 / 한 노인이 큰 사원을 지었다 / 마을 중심부에 //
　　　부사적 용법(목적)
People traveled / to worship at the temple. //
사람들이 멀리서 왔다 / 사원에서 예배를 드리기 위해 //

So the old man made arrangements / for food and accommodation / inside the temple itself. //
　　　　　　　　　　강조 용법의 재귀대명사
그래서 노인은 준비했다 / 음식과 숙소를 / 사원 그 안에 //
　　　주격 관계대명사
He needed someone / who could look after the temple, / so (a)
= the old man
he put up a notice: / Manager needed. //
그는 사람이 필요했다 / 사원을 관리할 수 있는 / 그래서 그는 공고를 붙였다 /
'관리자 구함'이라는 // 37번 단서 1: 노인은 사원 관리자를 구하는 공고를 붙임

*(A) 문단 요약: 사원을 지은 노인은 그것을 관리할 사람이 필요해 구인 공고를 붙임

　　　　지시형용사
(B) When that young man left the temple, / the old man called him and asked, / "Will you take care of this temple?" //
그 젊은이가 사원을 나섰을 때 / 노인이 그를 불러 질문했다 / "이 사원의 관리를 맡아 주겠소" // 37번 단서 2, 39번② 젊은이가 사원을 나설 때 노인이 그를 불러서 질문함
　　　　　　　　　　　　　　　　　　　병렬 구조
The young man was surprised / by the offer / and replied, / "I
　　　　　　　　　　　　　　　현재분사(experience 수식)
have no experience / caring for a temple. // 39번③ 젊은이는 노인의
젊은이는 놀랐다 / 그 제안에 / 그리고 대답했다 / "저는 경험이 없습니다 / 사원을 관리하는 // 제안에 놀람
I'm not even educated."//
저는 심지어 교육도 받지 못했습니다."//

The old man smiled and said, / "I don't want any educated man. //
노인은 미소를 지으며 말했다 / "나는 교육을 받은 사람이 필요한 게 아니오 //
I want a qualified person." //
나는 자격 있는 사람을 원하오"라고 //
앞에 Being이 생략됨　　　　　　　　　　　　　　　= the old man
Confused, / the young man asked, / "But why do (b) you
　　　consider A (as) B: A를 B라고 여기다
consider me / a qualified person?" // 37번 단서 3: 젊은이는 노인에게 질문을 함
당황하여 / 젊은이는 물었다 / "그런데 당신은 왜 저를 여기시나요 / 자격이 있는 사람이라고" 라고 //

*(B) 문단 요약: 노인이 젊은이에게 사원 관리를 부탁하자 젊은이는 놀라 왜 자신을 자격 있는 사람이라고 여기는지 물음

(C) The old man replied, / "I buried a brick / on the path to the temple. // 37번 단서 4: 노인이 대답함
노인은 대답했다 / "나는 벽돌 한 개를 묻었소 / 사원으로 통하는 길에 //
I watched for many days / as people tripped over / that brick. //
나는 여러 날 동안 지켜보았소 / 사람들이 발이 걸려 넘어지는 것을 / 그 벽돌에 //
　　　　　　　　　　명사적 용법(thought의 목적어)
No one thought / to remove it. //
아무도 생각을 하지 않았소 / 그것을 치울 //

But you dug up / that brick." // 39번④ 젊은이가 벽돌을 파냄
하지만 당신은 파냈소 / 그 벽돌을" //
　　　　　　　　　　　　　-thing으로 끝나는 대명사는 형용사가 뒤에서 수식함
The young man said, / "I haven't done anything great. //
젊은이는 말했다 / "저는 대단한 일을 한 것이 아닙니다 //
가주어
It's the duty of every human being / to think about others. //
　　　　　　　　　　　　　　　　　　진주어
~은 모든 인간의 의무입니다 / 타인을 생각하는 것은 //
= the young man
(c) I only did my duty." //
저는 제 의무를 다했을 뿐입니다" //
　　　　　　　　　　　　　　핵심 주어(복수)   주격 관계대명사
The old man smiled and said, / "Only people who know their
　　　　　　　　　　　　　　복수 동사
duty and perform it / are qualified people." //
노인은 미소를 지으며 말했다 / "자신의 의무를 알고 그것을 수행하는 사람만이 / 자격이 있는 사람이오"라고 //

*(C) 문단 요약: 노인이 길에 묻어둔 벽돌을 치운 사람이 젊은이뿐이었고, 노인은 타인을 생각하는 의무를 다하는 사람만이 자격 있는 사람이라고 함
　　　　　분사구문
(D) Seeing the notice, / many people went to the old man. //
공고를 보고 / 많은 사람들이 노인을 찾아갔다 // 37번 단서 5, 39번⑤ 공고를 보고
　　　　　　　　　　　　　　　　　　　　　　　많은 사람들이 노인을 찾아감
But he returned / all the applicants / after interviews, / telling
　　　　　　　　　　　　　　　　　　　　　　　　　분사구문
them, / "I need a qualified person for this work." //
그러나 그는 돌려보냈다 / 모든 지원자들을 / 면접 후에 / 그들에게 말하면서 / "나는 이 일에 자격을 갖춘 사람이 필요합니다"라고 //
　　　　　　　　　　　　　　　　　　　　= the old man's
The old man would sit / on the roof of (d) his house / every
분사구문을 이끄는 현재분사   목적격 보어(원형부정사)
morning, / watching people / go through the temple doors. //
노인은 앉아 있곤 했다 / 그의 집 지붕에 / 매일 아침 / 사람들을 지켜보면서 / 사원의 문을 통과하는 것을 // 37번 단서 6: 노인은 사원에 온 한 젊은이를 발견함
= the old man　　　　　　　　　　목적격 보어(원형부정사)
One day, / (e) he saw a young man / come to the temple. //
어느 날 / 그는 한 젊은이를 보았다 / 사원으로 오는 //

*(D) 문단 요약: 노인은 면접을 보러 온 사람들을 돌려보냈고, 매일 아침 사람들을 지켜보다가 한 젊은이가 오는 것을 보게 됨

- **grand** ⓐ 웅장한, 큰　• **temple** ⓝ 사원, 절　• **worship** ⓥ 예배하다
- **arrangement** ⓝ 준비　• **accommodation** ⓝ 숙소, 거처
- **look after** ~을 관리하다[돌보다]　• **offer** ⓝ 제안
- **qualified** ⓐ 자격이 있는　• **bury** ⓥ 묻다　• **brick** ⓝ 벽돌
- **path** ⓝ 길, 경로　• **trip over** ~에 발이 걸려 넘어지다
- **remove** ⓥ 제거하다　• **dig up** ~을 파내다　• **duty** ⓝ 의무

(A) 옛날에, 한 노인이 마을 중심부에 큰 사원을 지었다. 사람들이 사원에서 예배를 드리기 위해 멀리서 왔다. 그래서 노인은 사원 안에 음식과 숙소를 준비했다. 그는 사원을 관리할 수 있는 사람이 필요했고, 그래서 (a) 그는 '관리자 구함'이라는 공고를 붙였다.

(D) 공고를 보고 많은 사람들이 노인을 찾아갔다. 그러나 그는 면접 후에 그들에게 "나는 이 일에 자격을 갖춘 사람이 필요합니다."라고 말하며, 모든 지원자들을 돌려보냈다. 노인은 사람들이 사원의 문을 통과하는 것을 지켜보며 매일 아침 (d) 그의 집 지붕에 앉아 있곤 했다. 어느 날 (e) 그는 한 젊은이가 사원으로 오는 것을 보았다.

(B) 젊은이가 사원을 나설 때, 노인이 그를 불러 "이 사원의 관리를 맡아 주겠소?"라고 질문했다. 젊은이는 그 제안에 놀라서 "저는 사원을 관리한 경험이 없고, 심지어 교육도 받지 못했습니다."라고 대답했다. 노인은 미소 지으며 "나는 교육을 받은 사람이 필요한 게 아니오. 나는 자격 있는 사람을 원하오."라고 말했다. 당황하여, 젊은이는 "그런데 (b) 당신은 왜 저를 자격이 있는 사람이라고 여기시나요?"라고 물었다.

(C) 노인은 대답했다. "나는 사원으로 통하는 길에 벽돌 한 개를 묻었소. 나는 여러 날 동안 사람들이 그 벽돌에 발이 걸려 넘어지는 것을 지켜보았소. 아무도 그것을 치울 생각을 하지 않았소. 하지만 당신은 그 벽돌을 파냈소." 젊은이는 "저는 대단한 일을 한 것이 아닙니다. 타인을 생각하는 것은 모든 인간의 의무입니다. (c) 저는 제 의무를 다했을 뿐입니다."라고 말했다. 노인은 미소를 지으며 "자신의 의무를 알고 그 의무를 수행하는 사람만이 자격이 있는 사람이오."라고 말했다.

S 37 정답 ④

주어진 글 (A)에 이어질 내용을 순서에 맞게 배열한 것으로 가장 적절한 것은?

① (B) — (D) — (C)
② (C) — (B) — (D) ─ 공고를 보고 사람들이 왔다는 (D)가 가장 먼저 와야 함
③ (C) — (D) — (B)
④ (D) — (B) — (C) ─ (D) 공고를 보고 온 사람들을 돌려보낸 노인이 한 젊은이가 사원에 오는 걸 발견함 — (B) 노인은 젊은이에게 사원 관리를 제안했고, 젊은이는 이유를 물음 — (C) 노인은 그가 의무를 수행한 유일한 사람이라고 대답함
⑤ (D) — (C) — (B) ─ 젊은이가 질문한 (B)가 노인이 대답한 (C) 앞에 와야 함

왜 정답·오답? ✽✽✽ [정답률 87%]

[(A): 사원 관리자를 찾기 위해 노인이 구인 공고를 올렸다.

➡ 공고에 대한 사람들의 반응이 이어질 것이다.

[(B): 노인이 한 젊은이에게 자격 있는 사람이라며 사원 관리를 제안하자 젊은이는 놀라 그 이유를 물었다.

➡ 한 젊은이가 등장했다는 내용이 앞에 있어야 하고, 뒤에는 젊은이의 질문에 대한 노인의 답이 이어질 것이다.

[(C): 사원으로 오는 길에 묻은 벽돌을 파낸 사람은 젊은이뿐이며, 이처럼 타인을 생각하는 의무를 다하는 사람만이 사원 관리인으로서 자격 있는 사람이라고 노인이 대답했다.

➡ 젊은이가 질문한 (B)에 이어지는 내용이고, 어떤 사람이 자격 있는 사람인지를 설명하는 글의 마무리 부분이다.

[(D): 공고를 보고 온 사람들은 돌려보내고 사원에 오는 사람들을 지켜보던 노인이 한 젊은이가 사원에 오는 것을 보게 됐다.

➡ 공고를 붙였다는 (A)에 이어지는 내용이고, 뒤에는 노인이 젊은이에게 사원 관리직을 제안하는 (B)가 이어져야 한다.
   ▶ (D) 공고를 보고 온 사람들을 돌려보낸 노인은 한 젊은이가 사원에 오는 것을 발견함 → (B) 노인은 그 젊은이에게 사원 관리를 제안했고, 젊은이는 이유를 물음 → (C) 노인은 그가 의무를 수행한 유일한 사람이라고 대답함
   ▶ 글의 순서는 ④ (D) → (B) → (C)임

S 38 정답 ③

밑줄 친 (a)~(e) 중에서 가리키는 대상이 나머지 넷과 다른 것은?

① (a)   ② (b)   ③ (c)   ④ (d)   ⑤ (e)
= the old man   = the old man   = the young man   = the old man's   = the old man

왜 정답? ✽✽✽ [정답률 87%]

③ (c) I: 그저 의무를 다했을 뿐이라고 말한 사람 ▶ the young man

왜 오답?

① (a) he: 사원 관리자를 구하는 구인 공고를 붙인 사람 ▶ the old man
② (b) you: 젊은이를 자격 있는 사람이라고 여긴 사람 ▶ the old man
④ (d) his: 매일 아침 집 지붕에 앉아 있던 사람 ▶ the old man's
⑤ (e) he: 한 젊은이가 사원으로 오는 것을 본 사람 ▶ the old man

S 39 정답 ④

윗글에 관한 내용으로 적절하지 않은 것은?

① 노인은 마을 중심부에 사원을 지었다. an old man built a grand temple at the center of his village
② 젊은이가 사원을 나설 때 노인이 그를 불렀다. When that young man left the temple, the old man called him
③ 젊은이는 노인의 제안에 놀랐다. The young man was surprised by the offer
④ 노인은 사원으로 통하는 길에 묻혀있던 벽돌을 파냈다. But you dug up that brick.
⑤ 공고를 보고 많은 사람들이 노인을 찾아갔다. Seeing the notice, many people went to the old man.

왜 정답? ✽✽✽ [정답률 83%]

노인은 젊은이에게 '하지만 당신은 그 벽돌을 파냈소.(But you dug up that brick.)'라고 이야기했다. 따라서 벽돌을 파낸 것은 젊은이이므로 노인이 벽돌을 파냈다고 한 ④은 적절하지 않다.

왜 오답?

① 노인은 마을 중심부에 사원을 지었다. (an old man built a grand temple at the center of his village)
② 젊은이가 사원을 나설 때 노인이 그를 불렀다. (When that young man left the temple, the old man called him)
③ 젊은이는 노인의 제안에 놀랐다. (The young man was surprised by the offer)
⑤ 공고를 보고 많은 사람들이 노인을 찾아갔다. (Seeing the notice, many people went to the old man.)

S 40~42 ✽친절을 베풀어라

                                         주격 관계대명사
(A) Once upon a time, / there was a king / who lived in a beautiful palace. // 옛날 옛적에 / 한 왕이 있었다 / 아름다운 궁전에 사는 //

While the king was away, / a monster approached the gates of the palace. // 42번① 왕이 없는 동안 괴물이 궁전 문으로 접근함
왕이 없는 동안 / 한 괴물이 궁전 문으로 접근했다 //
                                                  so ~ that ...: 너무 ~해서 …하다
The monster was so ugly and smelly / that the guards froze in shock. // 그 괴물이 너무 추하고 냄새가 나서 / 경비병들은 충격으로 얼어붙었다 //

He passed the guards / and sat on the king's throne. //
그(괴물)는 경비병들을 지나 / 왕의 왕좌에 앉았다 // 40번 단서 1: 경비병들이 괴물에게 왕좌에서 내려올 것을 요구했음
                                                    '정신을 차리다'
The guards soon came to their senses, / went in, / and shouted at
                                              분사구문을 이끄는 현재분사 = the monster
the monster, / demanding that (a) he get off the throne. //
경비병들은 곧 정신을 차리고 / 안으로 들어가 / 그 괴물을 향해 소리쳤다 / 그에게 왕좌에서
내려올 것을 요구하며 //   앞에 should가 생략됨

*(A) 문단 요약: 왕이 궁전을 비운 동안에 추하고 냄새나는 괴물이 왕좌에 앉았고, 경비병들이 괴물에게 왕좌에서 내려올 것을 요구함

(B) Eventually / the king returned. // 40번 단서 2: 왕좌를 차지하고 경비병들과 대치 중인 상황에서 자리의 주인이 나타남
마침내 / 왕이 돌아왔다 //

병렬 구조
He was wise and kind / and saw what was happening. //
그는 현명하고 친절했으며 / 무슨 일이 일어나고 있는지 알아차렸다 //
knew의 목적어로 쓰인 「의문사+to부정사」
He knew what to do. //
그는 알았다 / 무엇을 해야 할지 //

42번 ② 왕이 미소를 지으며 괴물에게 환영한다고 말함
He smiled and said to the monster, / "Welcome to my palace!" //
그는 미소를 지으며 그 괴물에게 말했다 / "나의 궁전에 온 것을 환영하오"라고 //

= the monster
He asked the monster / if (b) he wanted a cup of coffee. //
왕은 그 괴물에게 물었다 / 그가 커피 한 잔을 원하는지 //

The monster began to grow smaller / as he drank the coffee. //
괴물은 더 작아지기 시작했다 / 그 커피를 마시면서 //

*(B) 문단 요약: 돌아온 왕이 괴물에게 커피를 권했고 괴물은 작아짐

= the monster
(C) The king offered (c) him / some take-out pizza and fries. //
왕은 그에게 제안했다 / 약간의 테이크아웃 피자와 감자튀김을 // 40번 단서 3: 현명한 왕은 괴물을 겁주어 쫓아내지 않고 친절을 베풀었음

The guards immediately called for pizza. //
경비병은 즉시 피자를 시켰다 //

The monster continued to get smaller / with the king's kind gestures. // 42번 ③ 왕의 친절한 행동에 괴물의 몸이 계속 더 작아짐
그 괴물은 몸이 계속 더 작아졌다 / 왕의 친절한 행동에 //

= the king   간접목적어   직접목적어
(d) He then offered the monster / a full body massage. //
그러고 나서 그는 그 괴물에게 제안했다 / 전신 마사지를 //

As the guards helped with the relaxing massage, / the monster became tiny. // 42번 ④ 경비병들이 편안한 마사지를 제공함
경비병들이 편안한 마사지를 도와주자 / 그 괴물은 매우 작아졌다 //

With another act of kindness to the monster, / he just disappeared. //
그 괴물에게 또 한 번의 친절한 행동을 베풀자 / 그는 바로 사라졌다 //

*(C) 문단 요약: 왕이 괴물에게 다양한 음식을 제공했고 마사지까지 해주며 친절을 베풀었더니 괴물이 사라짐

앞에 목적격 관계대명사가 생략됨
(D) With each bad word the guards used, / the monster grew more ugly and smelly. // 40번 단서 4: 경비들이 왕좌에 앉은 괴물을 몰아내려 함
경비병들이 나쁜 말을 사용할 때마다 / 그 괴물은 더 추해졌고, 더 냄새가 났다 //
비교급 강조 부사
The guards got even angrier / — they began to brandish their swords / to scare the monster away / from the palace. //
부사적 용법(목적)
경비병들은 한층 더 화가 났다 / 그들은 칼을 휘두르기 시작했다 / 그 괴물을 겁주어 쫓아내려고 / 궁전에서 // 42번 ⑤ 경비병들은 겁을 주어 괴물을 쫓아내려 함
= the monster   분사구문(결과)
But (e) he just grew bigger and bigger, / eventually taking up the whole room. //
하지만 그는 그저 점점 더 커져서 / 결국 방 전체를 차지했다 //

He grew more ugly and smelly / than ever. //
그는 더 추해졌고, 더 냄새가 났다 / 그 어느 때 보다 //

*(D) 문단 요약: 경비병들이 괴물을 겁주어 쫓아내려고 위협하자 괴물은 더욱 추하고 더 냄새가 나게 되었고 크기도 더 커짐

- approach ⓥ 접근하다   - smelly ⓐ 냄새가 나는
- guard ⓝ 경비병   - shock ⓝ 충격   - demand ⓥ 요구하다
- wise ⓐ 현명한   - offer ⓥ 제안하다   - immediately ⓐⓓ 즉시
- call for ~을 시키다   - gesture ⓝ 행동   - tiny ⓐ 매우 작은
- kindness ⓝ 친절(한 행위)   - sword ⓝ 칼
- eventually ⓐⓓ 결국, 마침내   - take up ~을 차지하다

(A) 옛날 옛적에, 아름다운 궁전에 사는 한 왕이 있었다. 왕이 없는 동안, 한 괴물이 궁전 문으로 접근했다. 그 괴물이 너무 추하고 냄새가 나서 경비병들은 충격으로 얼어붙었다. 그(괴물)는 경비병들을 지나 왕의 왕좌에 앉았다. 경비병들은 곧 정신을 차리고 안으로 들어가 그 괴물을 향해 소리치며 (a) 그에게 왕좌에서 내려올 것을 요구했다.
(D) 경비병들이 나쁜 말을 사용할 때마다, 그 괴물은 더 추해졌고, 더 냄새가 났다. 경비병들은 한층 더 화가 났다. 그들은 그 괴물을 겁주어 궁전에서 쫓아내려고 칼을 휘두르기 시작했다. 하지만 (e) 그는 그저 점점 더 커져서 결국 방 전체를 차지했다. 그는 그 어느 때보다 더 추해졌고, 더 냄새가 났다.

(B) 마침내 왕이 돌아왔다. 그는 현명하고 친절했으며 무슨 일이 일어나고 있는지 알아차렸다. 그는 무엇을 해야 할지 알았다. 그는 미소를 지으며 그 괴물에게 "나의 궁전에 온 것을 환영하오!"라고 말했다. 왕은 그 괴물에게 (b) 그가 커피 한 잔을 원하는지 물었다. 괴물은 그 커피를 마시면서 더 작아지기 시작했다.
(C) 왕은 (c) 그에게 약간의 테이크아웃 피자와 감자튀김을 제안했다. 경비병들은 즉시 피자를 시켰다. 그 괴물은 왕의 친절한 행동에 몸이 계속 더 작아졌다. 그러고 나서 (d) 그는 그 괴물에게 전신 마사지를 제안했다. 경비병들이 편안한 마사지를 도와주자 그 괴물은 매우 작아졌다. 그 괴물에게 또 한 번의 친절한 행동을 베풀자, 그는 바로 사라졌다.

S 40 정답 ④

주어진 글 (A)에 이어질 내용을 순서에 맞게 배열한 것으로 가장 적절한 것은?
① (B) — (D) — (C) 왕이 부재중일 때 괴물이 더 커졌다는 내용인 (D)가 먼저 나와야 함
② (C) — (B) — (D) 글의 순서와 정반대임
③ (C) — (D) — (B) 괴물이 사라진 (C)는 결말임
④ (D) — (B) — (C) [(D) 괴물은 더욱 추하고 크기도 더 커지게 됨 — (B) 왕이 괴물에게 커피를 권했고 괴물은 작아짐 — (C) 왕이 괴물에게 친절을 더 베풀었더니 괴물이 사라짐]
⑤ (D) — (C) — (B) (B)에서 왕이 돌아온 것이 친절을 베푸는 (C)보다 먼저 나와야 함

> 왜 정답·오답? ✿✿✿ [정답률 80%]

[(A): 왕이 궁전을 비운 동안 추하고 냄새나는 괴물이 왕좌에 앉았고, 경비병들은 괴물에게 왕좌에서 내려올 것을 요구했다.
➡ 경비병들이 괴물에게 왕좌에서 내려오라고 어떻게 요구했는지가 이어질 것이다.

[(B): 돌아온 왕이 권한 커피를 마시면서 괴물은 더 작아졌다.
➡ 왕이 돌아오기 전에, 왕이 없는 상태에서 진행되는 내용이 앞에 나와야 하고, 뒤에는 괴물이 작아진 후에 벌어진 일이 이어져야 한다.

[(C): 왕이 괴물에게 다양한 음식을 제공했고 마사지까지 해주며 친절을 베풀었더니 괴물이 사라졌다.
➡ 괴물이 사라졌다는 문장으로 끝나므로 이야기의 결말일 가능성이 크다.

[(D): 경비병들이 괴물을 겁주어서 쫓아내려고 공격하자 괴물은 더욱 추하고 더 냄새가 나게 되었고 크기도 더 커졌다.
➡ 경비병들이 괴물에게 왕좌에서 내려오라고 소리쳤다는 (A)에 이어지는 내용이다.
  ▶ (D) 경비병들이 괴물을 겁주어서 쫓아내려 하자 괴물은 더욱 추하고 냄새가 나며 크기도 더 커짐 ▶ (B) 돌아온 왕이 괴물에게 커피를 권하자 괴물이 작아짐
  → (C) 왕이 괴물에게 음식과 마사지 등 친절을 더 베풀었더니 괴물이 사라짐
  ▶ 글의 순서는 ④ (D) — (B) — (C)임

S 41 정답 ④

밑줄 친 (a)~(e) 중에서 가리키는 대상이 나머지 넷과 다른 것은?
① (a)   ② (b)   ③ (c)   ④ (d)   ⑤ (e)
= the monster   = the monster   = the monster   = the king   = the monster

> 왜 정답? ✿✿✿ [정답률 79%]
④ (d) He: 괴물에게 전신 마사지를 제안한 사람 ▶ the king

> 왜 오답?
① (a) he: 왕좌에 앉아서 내려올 것을 요구받는 것 ▶ the monster
② (b) he: 왕이 친절하게 커피를 원하는지 물은 대상 ▶ the monster
③ (c) him: 테이크아웃 피자와 감자튀김을 제안한 대상 ▶ the monster
⑤ (e) he: 경비병들의 자극으로 몸이 커진 것 ▶ the monster

윗글에 관한 내용으로 적절하지 <u>않은</u> 것은?
① 왕이 없는 동안 괴물이 궁전 문으로 접근했다.
　While the king was away, a monster approached the gates of the palace.
② 왕은 미소를 지으며 괴물에게 환영한다고 말했다.
　He smiled and said to the monster, "Welcome to my palace!"
③ 왕의 친절한 행동에 괴물의 몸이 계속 더 작아졌다.
　The monster continued to get smaller with the king's kind gestures.
④ 경비병들은 괴물을 마사지해 주기를 거부했다.
　As the guards helped with the relaxing massage, the monster became tiny.
⑤ 경비병들은 겁을 주어 괴물을 쫓아내려 했다.
　they began to brandish their swords to scare the monster away from the palace

왜 정답? ❀❀❀ [정답률 86%]
경비병들이 편안한 마사지를 제공하자 괴물은 더 작아졌다고(As the guards helped with the relaxing massage, the monster became tiny.) 했다. 따라서 괴물을 마사지해 줄 것을 거부했다는 ④이 글의 내용과 일치하지 않는다.

왜 오답?
① 왕이 없는 동안 괴물이 궁전 문으로 접근했다고 했다. (While the king was away, a monster approached the gates of the palace.)
② 왕은 미소를 지으며 괴물에게 환영한다고 말했다고 했다. (He smiled and said to the monster, "Welcome to my palace!")
③ 왕의 친절한 행동에 괴물의 몸이 계속 더 작아졌다고 했다. (The monster continued to get smaller with the king's kind gestures.)
⑤ 경비병들은 겁을 주어 괴물을 쫓아내려 했다고 했다. (they began to brandish their swords to scare the monster away from the palace)

S 43~45　★2등급 대비

★수도승의 조언

(A) One day / a young man was walking along a road / on his journey / from one village to another. //
어느 날 / 한 젊은이가 길을 따라 걷고 있었다 / 여행 중에 / 한 마을로부터 다른 마을로의 //
As he walked / he noticed a monk / working in the fields. //
그는 걷다가 / 한 수도승을 보게 되었다 / 들판에서 일하는 // <45번 ① 한 수도승이 들판에서 일하고 있었음>
The young man turned to the monk / and said, / "Excuse me. //
Do you mind / if I ask (a) you a question?" //
그 젊은이는 그 수도승을 향해 돌아보며 / 말했다 / "실례합니다 / 괜찮으십니까 / 제가 스님께 질문을 하나 드려도"라고 // <43번 단서 1: 뒤에 젊은이의 질문이 이어져야 함을 알 수 있음>
"Not at all," / replied the monk. //
"물론입니다"라고 / 그 수도승은 대답했다 //

*(A) 문단 요약: 들판에서 일하고 있던 한 수도승에게 젊은이가 질문을 하나 해도 되는지 물었음

<43번 단서 2: 젊은이의 일화가 마무리되고 중년 남자의 일화가 시작됨>

(B) A while later / a middle-aged man journeyed down the same road / and came upon the monk. //
잠시 후 / 한 중년 남자가 같은 길을 걸어왔다 / 그리고 그 수도승을 만났다 //
"I am going to the village in the valley," / said the man. / "Do you know / what it is like?" // <45번 ② 중년 남자는 골짜기에 있는 마을로 가고 있었음> <45번 ③ 수도승에게 골짜기에 있는 마을에 대해 질문함>
"저는 골짜기의 마을로 가고 있습니다" / 그 남자는 말했다 / "아십니까 / 그곳이 어떤지"라고 //
"I do," / replied the monk, / "but first tell (b) me / about the village / where you came from." //
"알고 있습니다" / 그 수도승은 대답했다 / "그러나 먼저 저에게 말해 주십시오 / 마을에 관해 / 선생님께서 떠나오신"라고 //
"I've come from the village / in the mountains," / said the man. //
"저는 마을로부터 왔습니다 / 산속의" / 그 남자는 말했다 //
"It was a wonderful experience. // I felt / as though I was a member / of the family in the village." //
"그것은 멋진 경험이었습니다 // 저는 느꼈습니다 / 마치 제가 일원인 것처럼 / 그 마을의 가족의" //

*(B) 문단 요약: 중년 남자는 산속 마을에서의 경험이 멋졌다고 했음

(C) "I am traveling / from the village in the mountains / to the village in the valley / and I was wondering / if (c) you knew / what it is like / in the village in the valley." // <43번 단서 3: (A)의 마지막에 해도 되냐고 한 질문이 이어짐>
"저는 가고 있습니다 / 산속의 마을로부터 / 골짜기의 마을로 / 그리고 궁금합니다 / 스님께서 아시는지 / 어떤지 / 골짜기의 마을은" //
"Tell me," / said the monk, / "what was your experience / of the village in the mountains?" //
"저에게 말해 보십시오" / 수도승은 말했다 / "경험은 어땠습니까 / 산속의 마을에서의"라고 //
"Terrible," / replied the young man. //
"끔찍했습니다"라고 / 그 젊은이는 대답했다 //
"I am glad / to be away from there. // I found / the people most unwelcoming. // So tell (d) me, / what can I expect / in the village in the valley? //
"저는 기쁩니다 / 그곳을 벗어나게 되어 / 저는 생각했습니다 / 그곳 사람들이 정말로 불친절하다고 // 그러니 저에게 말씀해 주십시오 / 제가 무엇을 기대할 수 있을까요 / 골짜기의 마을에서" //
"I am sorry to tell you," / said the monk, / "but I think / your experience will be much the same there." //
"말씀드리기에 유감입니다" / 수도승이 말했다 / "하지만 저는 생각합니다 / 선생님의 경험은 그곳에서도 거의 같을 것 같다"라고 //
The young man lowered his head / helplessly / and walked on. //
그 젊은이는 고개를 숙였다 / 힘없이 / 그리고 계속 걸어갔다 // <45번 ④ 수도승의 말을 듣고 젊은이는 고개를 숙였음>

*(C) 문단 요약: 젊은이가 골짜기의 마을이 어떤지 수도승에게 물었는데, 산속의 마을에서의 경험과 비슷할 것이라고 말해줌

(D) "Why did you feel like that?" / asked the monk. //
"왜 그렇게 느끼셨습니까"라고 / 그 수도승은 물었다 // <43번 단서 4: (B)의 마지막에 산속 마을에서의 경험이 왜 멋졌는지 물었음>
"The elders gave me much advice, / and people were kind and generous. // I am sad / to have left there. //
"어르신들은 저에게 많은 조언을 해 주셨습니다 / 그리고 사람들은 친절하고 너그러웠습니다 // 저는 슬픕니다 / 그곳을 떠나서 // <45번 ⑤ 중년 남자는 산속 마을을 떠나서 슬프다고 했음>
And what is the village in the valley like?" / he asked again. //
그런데 골짜기의 마을은 어떻습니까"라고 / 그는 다시 물었다 //
"(e) I think / you will find it much the same," / replied the monk. //
"저는 생각합니다 / 선생님은 그곳이 (산속 마을과) 거의 같다고 생각하실 것으로"라고 / 수도승은 대답했다 //
"I'm glad to hear that," / the middle-aged man said / smiling and journeyed on. //
"그 말씀을 들으니 기쁩니다"라고 / 그 중년 남자는 말했다 / 미소를 지으며 / 그리고 여행을 계속했다 //

*(D) 문단 요약: 수도승은 이번에도 산속 마을에서의 경험과 골짜기 마을에서의 경험이 비슷할 것이라고 대답함

- village ⓝ 마을　　• field ⓝ 들판　　• reply ⓥ 대답하다
- middle-aged 중년의　　• come upon ~을 만나다
- valley ⓝ 골짜기　　• wonderful ⓐ 멋진
- unwelcoming ⓐ 불친절한　　• helplessly ⓐⓓ 힘없이
- generous ⓐ 너그러운

(A) 어느 날 한 젊은이가 한 마을로부터 다른 마을로의 여행 중에 길을 따라 걷고 있었다. 그는 걷다가 들판에서 일하는 한 수도승을 보게 되었다. 그 젊은이는 그 수도승을 향해 돌아보며 "실례합니다. 제가 (a) 당신께 질문을 하나 드려도 되겠습니까?"라고 말했다. "물론입니다."라고 그 수도승은 대답했다.
(C) "저는 산속의 마을로부터 골짜기의 마을로 가고 있는데 (c) 당신이 골짜기의 마을은 어떤지 아시는지 궁금합니다." 수도승은 "저에게 말해 보십시오. 산속의 마을에서의 경험은 어땠습니까?"라고 말했다. 그 젊은이는 "끔찍했습니다."라고 대답했다. "그곳을 벗어나게 되어 기쁩니다. 그곳 사람들이 정말로 불친절하다고 생각했습니다. 그러니 (d) 저에게 말씀해 주십시오, 제가 골짜기의 마을에서 무엇을 기대할 수 있을까요?" "말씀드리기에 유감이지만, 제 생각에 선생님의 경험은 그곳에서도 거의 같을 것 같다고 생각합니다." 수도승이 말했다. 그 젊은이는 힘없이 고개를 숙이고 계속 걸어갔다.

(B) 잠시 후 한 중년 남자가 같은 길을 걸어와서 그 수도승을 만났다. 그 남자는 "저는 골짜기의 마을로 가고 있습니다. 그곳이 어떤지 아십니까?"라고 말했다. "알고 있습니다만, 먼저 (b) 저에게 선생님께서 떠나오신 마을에 관해 말해주십시오."라고 그 수도승은 대답했다. 그 남자는 "저는 산속의 마을로부터 왔습니다. 그것은 멋진 경험이었습니다. 저는 마치 그 마을의 가족의 일원인 것처럼 느꼈습니다."라고 말했다. (D) 그 수도승은 "왜 그렇게 느끼셨습니까?"라고 물었다. "어르신들은 저에게 많은 조언을 해 주셨고, 사람들은 친절하고 너그러웠습니다. 그곳을 떠나서 슬픕니다. 그런데 골짜기의 마을은 어떻습니까?"라고 그는 다시 물었다. "(e) 저는 선생님은 그곳이 (산속 마을과) 거의 같다고 생각하실 것으로 생각합니다."라고 수도승은 대답했다. "그 말씀을 들으니 기쁩니다."라고 그 중년 남자는 미소를 지으며 말하고서 여행을 계속했다.

★ 글이 수도승과 젊은이, 중년 남자가 등장하는 이야기로 이루어져 있으므로 사건의 전후 관계를 잘 파악하는 것이 핵심이다. 등장하는 인물들이 모두 남자라서 밑줄 친 부분이 가리키는 대상이 이 셋 중 누구인지 유심히 봐야 한다.

S 43 정답 ②

주어진 글 (A)에 이어질 내용을 순서에 맞게 배열한 것으로 가장 적절한 것은?

① (B) — (D) — (C)   (A)에서 언급한 젊은이의 질문이 무엇인지 그 내용이 이어지는 (C)가 앞에 와야 함
② (C) — (B) — (D)   (C) 젊은이의 질문과 그에 대한 수도승의 답 – (B) 중년 남자의 등장과 질문 – (D) 중년 남자의 질문에 대한 수도승의 답
③ (C) — (D) — (B)   (D)는 (B)에 대한 부연 설명이자 답이므로 (B) 뒤에 와야 함
④ (D) — (B) — (C)   (D)에서 수도승이 중년 남자에게 질문을 하는데 (A)에는 아직 중년 남자가 등장하지 않음
⑤ (D) — (C) — (B)

왜 정답?

여행 중이던 젊은이가 들판에서 일하고 있던 한 수도승에게 질문을 하나 해도 되는지 물었다는 내용의 (A) 뒤에는 이 질문이 무엇인지 나오는 (C)가 와야 한다. 젊은이가 골짜기의 마을이 어떤지 수도승에게 물었는데, 산속의 마을에서의 경험과 비슷할 것이라고 말해줬고, 이 다음에는 같은 길을 걸어온 중년 남자가 등장해 수도승에게 같은 질문을 하는 (B)가 나와야 한다.
마지막으로 중년 남자가 산속의 마을에서의 경험이 멋졌다고 말하고 그 이유를 설명하는 (D)가 이어지는 것이 자연스럽다. 따라서 ② (C) – (B) – (D)가 가장 적절하다.

왜 오답?

① (B)에서 중년 남자가 등장하기 전에 (A)에서 언급한 젊은이의 질문이 무엇인지 그 내용이 이어지는 (C)가 와야 한다.
③ (D)는 (B)에서 멋진 경험이었다고 언급한 중년 남자에게 수도승이 그 이유를 묻고, 중년 남자가 답을 하는 내용이 담겨 있으므로 (B) 뒤에 와야 자연스럽다.
④, ⑤ (D)에서 수도승이 그렇게 느낀 이유에 대해 중년 남자에게 질문을 하는데 (A)에는 아직 중년 남자가 등장하지 않았다.

S 44 정답 ④

밑줄 친 (a)~(e) 중에서 가리키는 대상이 나머지 넷과 <u>다른</u> 것은?

① (a)   ② (b)   ③ (c)   ④ (d)   ⑤ (e)
= the monk   = the monk   = the monk   =the young man   = the monk

왜 정답?

(d)는 젊은이가 수도승에게 산속 마을에 대해 '자신에게' 말해 달라고 이야기하는 부분이므로 젊은이를 가리킨다. 나머지는 모두 수도승을 가리키므로 정답은 ④이다.

왜 오답?

① 젊은이가 수도승에게 당신에게 질문해도 되겠냐고 묻고 있으므로 수도승이다.
② 중년 남자에게 떠나온 마을에 대해 말해 달라고 하는 사람은 수도승이다.
③ 수도승에게 골짜기 마을이 어떤지 아느냐고 젊은이가 묻고 있으므로 수도승을 가리킨다.
⑤ 자신의 생각을 중년 남자에게 말하는 사람은 수도승이다.

S 45 정답 ⑤

윗글에 관한 내용으로 적절하지 <u>않은</u> 것은?
① 한 수도승이 들판에서 일하고 있었다. he noticed a monk working in the fields
② 중년 남자는 골짜기에 있는 마을로 가는 중이었다.
  "I am going to the village in the valley," said the man.
③ 수도승은 골짜기에 있는 마을에 대해 질문 받았다.
  "Do you know what it is like?"
④ 수도승의 말을 듣고 젊은이는 고개를 숙였다.
  The young man lowered his head helplessly and walked on.
⑤ 중년 남자는 산속에 있는 마을을 떠나서 기뻤다고 말했다.
  I am sad to have left there.

왜 정답?

(D)에서 중년 남자는 산속 마을에서의 경험이 너무 좋고, 사람들도 너무 친절해 그곳을 떠나는 것이 슬프다고 말했으므로(I am sad to have left there.) ⑤이 윗글에 관한 내용으로 적절하지 않다.

왜 오답?

① 한 수도승이 들판에서 일하고 있었다고 했다. (he noticed a monk working in the fields)
② 중년 남자는 골짜기에 있는 마을로 가는 중이었다고 했다. ("I am going to the village in the valley," said the man.)
③ 수도승은 골짜기에 있는 마을에 대해 질문 받았다고 했다. ("Do you know what it is like?")
④ 수도승의 말을 듣고 젊은이는 고개를 숙였다고 했다. (The young man lowered his head helplessly and walked on.)

S 46~48   ★ 2등급 대비

*특별해지고 싶었던 판다의 깨달음

(A) Once long ago, / deep in the Himalayas, / there lived a little panda. //
옛날에 / 히말라야 산맥 깊숙한 곳에 / 작은 판다가 살았다 //

동급 비교: ~만큼 ~한
He was as ordinary as all the other pandas. //
그는 다른 모든 판다들만큼 평범했다 //

He was completely white / from head to toe. //
그는 전부 하얬다 / 머리부터 발끝까지 //

His two big ears, his four furry feet and his cute round nose /
분사구문을 이끄는 현재분사 = the little panda
were all frosty white, / leaving (a) him feeling ordinary and sad. //
leaving의 목적격 보어(현재분사)
그의 두 개의 큰 귀, 네 개의 털 많은 발, 그리고 귀여운 둥근 코는 / 모두 서리처럼 하얘서 / 그가 평범하고 슬프게 느끼게 하였다 //

Unlike the cheerful and contented pandas around him, / he desired to be distinctive, special, and unique. //
그의 주위에 있는 명랑하고 만족스러운 판다들과 달리 / 그는 특이하고 특별하며 독특해지기를 갈망했다 //
46번 단서 1, 48번 ① 작은 판다는 특별해지기를 갈망했음

* (A) 문단 요약: 평범한 작은 판다는 특별해지길 원했음

(B) The little panda changed his path / and hurried to the nearest berry bush, / greedily eating a mouthful of juicy red berries. //
분사구문
작은 판다는 경로를 바꾸어 / 가장 가까운 베리 덤불로 서둘러 가서 / 탐욕스럽게 한입 가득 즙이 많은 빨간 베리를 먹었다 //
46번 단서 2: 베리 덤불에서 빨간 베리를 먹음

so ~ (that) can't … : 너무 ~해서 …할 수 없다
However, / they were so bitter / he couldn't swallow even one. //
하지만 / 그것들은 너무 써서 / 그는 한 개도 삼킬 수 없었다 // 48번 ② 베리가 너무 써서 한 개도 삼킬 수 없었음

At dusk, / he finally got home / and slowly climbed his favorite bamboo tree. // 48번 ③ 집에 도착한 후 검고 붉은 꽃을 발견함
해질 무렵 / 그는 마침내 집에 도착했고 / 그가 가장 좋아하는 대나무에 천천히 올라갔다 //

There, / he discovered a strange black and red flower / with a
　　　　　　　　　　　　　　　　　주격 관계대명사　　　　　tempted의 목적격 보어 (to부정사)
sweet scent / that tempted (b) him to eat all its blossoms. //
그곳에서 / 그는 기묘한 검고 붉은 꽃을 발견하였다 / 달콤한 향기를 가진 / 그가 그것의 모든 꽃을 먹도록 유혹하는 //

* (B) 문단 요약: 베리를 먹는 것에 실패한 작은 판다는 집에 돌아와 검고 붉은 꽃을 발견함

46번 단서 3: 특별해지기를 원했던 작은 판다는 영감을 찾으려 함
　　　　　　분사구문
(C) Driven by the desire for uniqueness, / the little panda sought
　　　　　　　　　　　= the little panda's　　　　　동격
inspiration / from (c) his distant cousin, / a giant white panda
covered with heavenly black patches. //
독특함에 대한 열망에 사로잡혀 / 작은 판다는 영감을 찾으려 했다 / 그의 먼 사촌으로부터 / 멋진 검은 반점으로 뒤덮인 거대한 흰 판다인 //

But the cousin revealed / the patches were from an unintended
　　　　　　　　　　　　　　　　　　　　　　　　　　= the patches
encounter with mud, / and he disliked them. //
그러나 사촌은 밝혔다 / 그 반점이 진흙과 의도치 않게 접촉한 결과이며 / 그는 그것(반점)을 싫어한다고 //
　　　　　　　　　└ 48번 ④ 사촌은 검은 반점을 싫어함
　분사구문
Disappointed, / the little panda walked home. //
실망한 채로 / 작은 판다는 집으로 걸어갔다 //

On his way, / he met a red-feathered peacock, / who explained /
= the peacock　　　　　　　　　　　　　　　　　계속적 용법의 주격 관계대명사
(d) he turned red from eating wild berries. //
가는 길에 / 그는 붉은 깃털을 가진 공작새를 만났는데 / 그 공작새는 설명했다 / 그가 야생 베리를 먹어서 붉게 변했다고 //

* (C) 문단 요약: 독특함에 대한 열망에 사로잡힌 작은 판다는 야생 베리를 먹고 붉게 변했다는 공작새를 만남

(D) The following morning, / under sunny skies, / the little panda felt remarkably better. //
다음 날 아침 / 맑은 하늘 아래에서 / 작은 판다는 기분이 매우 좋아졌다 //
　　　　　　　　　　　　　　　　　　　　found의 목적격 보어 (현재분사)
During breakfast, / he found the other pandas chatting
enthusiastically / and asked why. // 48번 ⑤ 다른 판다들이 왜 신나게 수다를 떠는지 물어봄
아침 식사 중에 / 그는 다른 판다들이 신나게 수다를 떨고 있는 것을 발견하고 / 이유를 물어보았다 //
　'웃음을 터뜨리다'　　　　　　　분사구문
They burst into laughter, / exclaiming, "Look at yourself!" //
그들은 웃음을 터뜨리며 / "네 자신을 좀 봐"라고 외쳤다 //
　분사구문
Glancing down, / he discovered / his once white fur / was now stained jet black and glowing red. //
아래를 흘긋 보고 / 그는 발견했다 / 한때 하얗던 자신의 털이 / 이제 새까맣고 빛나는 붉은색으로 얼룩져 있다는 것을 //
　　　　　　　　　　　　　목적어절 접속사
He was overjoyed / and realized that, / rather than by imitating
others, / (e) his wishes can come true / from unexpected places
= the little panda's
and genuine experiences. // 46번 단서 4: 자신만의 특별한 얼룩을 갖게 되어 기뻐함
그는 매우 기뻐했고 / 깨달았다 / 남들을 모방하기보다는 / 그의 소원이 실현될 수 있음을 / 예상치 못한 곳과 진정한 경험으로부터 //

* (D) 문단 요약: 검고 붉게 변한 작은 판다는 진정한 특별함에 대해 깨달음

- ordinary ⓐ 평범한　　　· furry ⓐ 털이 많은　　　· frosty ⓐ 서리가 내리는
- cheerful ⓐ 명랑한　　　· contented ⓐ 만족하는
- distinctive ⓐ 특이한　　　· greedily 〔ad〕탐욕스럽게
- swallow ⓥ 삼키다　　　· dusk ⓝ 해질 무렵[황혼]
- bamboo ⓝ 대나무　　　· tempt ⓥ 유혹하다　　　· blossom ⓝ 꽃
- seek ⓥ 찾다, 추구하다　　　· distant ⓐ 먼　　　· reveal ⓥ 밝히다
- unintended ⓐ 의도치 않은　　　· encounter ⓝ 접촉, 만남
- remarkably 〔ad〕매우, 정말　　　· chat ⓥ 수다를 떨다
- enthusiastically 〔ad〕신나게, 열정적으로　　　· exclaim ⓥ 외치다
- glance ⓥ 흘긋 보다　　　· imitate ⓥ 모방하다　　　· genuine ⓐ 진정한

(A) 옛날에 히말라야 산맥 깊숙한 곳에 작은 판다가 살았다. 그는 다른 모든 판다들만큼 평범했다. 그는 머리부터 발끝까지 전부 하얬다. 그의 두 개의 큰 귀, 네 개의 털 많은 발, 그리고 귀여운 둥근 코는 모두 서리처럼 하얘서 (a) 그가 평범하고 슬프게 느끼게 하였다. 그의 주위에 있는 명랑하고 만족스러운 판다들과 달리 그는 특이하고 특별하며 독특해지기를 갈망했다.

(C) 독특함에 대한 열망에 사로잡혀 작은 판다는 (c) 그의 먼 사촌인 멋진 검은 반점으로 뒤덮인 거대한 흰 판다로부터 영감을 찾으려 했다. 그러나 사촌은 그 반점이 진흙과 의도치 않게 접촉한 결과이며, 그는 그것(반점)을 싫어한다고 밝혔다. 실망한 채로 작은 판다는 집으로 걸어갔다. 가는 길에 그는 붉은 깃털을 가진 공작새를 만났는데 그 공작새는 (d) 그가 야생 베리를 먹어서 붉게 변했다고 설명했다.

(B) 작은 판다는 경로를 바꾸어 가장 가까운 베리 덤불로 서둘러 가서, 탐욕스럽게 한입 가득 즙이 많은 빨간 베리를 먹었다. 하지만 그것들은 너무 써서 그는 한 개도 삼킬 수 없었다. 해질 무렵 그는 마침내 집에 도착했고 그가 가장 좋아하는 대나무에 천천히 올라갔다. 그곳에서 (b) 그가 그것의 모든 꽃을 먹도록 유혹하는 달콤한 향기를 가진 기묘한 검고 붉은 꽃을 발견하였다.

(D) 다음 날 아침 맑은 하늘 아래에서 작은 판다는 기분이 매우 좋아졌다. 아침 식사 중에 그는 다른 판다들이 신나게 수다를 떨고 있는 것을 발견하고 이유를 물어보았다. 그들은 웃음을 터뜨리며 "네 자신을 좀 봐!"라고 외쳤다. 아래를 흘긋 보고, 그는 한때 하얬던 자신의 털이 이제 새까맣고 빛나는 붉은색으로 얼룩져 있다는 것을 발견했다. 그는 매우 기뻤고 (e) 그의 소원이 남들을 모방하기보다는 예상치 못한 곳과 진정한 경험으로부터 실현될 수 있음을 깨달았다.

왜 2등급? 내용 일치 문제에서 사건의 순서와 구체적인 행동을 꼼꼼히 파악해야 정답과 오답을 가려낼 수 있는 2등급 대비 문제이다. 판다가 집에 돌아갈 때 만난 것과 집에 도착해서 발견한 것은 명확히 다르다.

S 46 정답 ②

주어진 글 (A)에 이어질 내용을 순서에 맞게 배열한 것으로 가장 적절한 것은?
① (B) — (D) — (C)　─ 베리를 먹고 붉게 변한 공작새를 만났다는 (C)가 판다가 붉은 베리를 먹었다는 (B)보다 먼저 와야 함
② (C) — (B) — (D)　─ (C) 특별해지기 위해 사촌을 찾아갔지만 실망하고 붉은 깃털의 공작새가 베리를 먹고 붉게 변했다는 것을 들음 - (B) 베리는 너무 써서 먹지 못했고 집에 돌아와 대나무에서 검고 붉은 꽃을 보고 먹음 - (D) 자신의 털이 검고 붉게 변한 것을 발견하고 기뻐하며 깨달음을 얻음
③ (C) — (D) — (B)　─ 검고 붉은 꽃을 먹은 (B)가 자신의 털이 검고 붉게 변한 것을 발견하여 기뻐한 (D)보다 먼저 와야 함
④ (D) — (B) — (C)
⑤ (D) — (C) — (B)　─ 깨달음을 얻는 끝부분에 해당하는 (D)는 (A) 바로 다음에 올 수 없음

왜 정답·오답? ★★★ [정답률 79%]

(A): 평범한 작은 판다가 살았는데 그는 온몸이 새하얘서 자신을 특별하지 않다고 느꼈고, 독특해지기를 갈망했다.
→ 독특해지기를 갈망했던 작은 판다가 겪는 일이 이어질 것이다.

(B): 그는 가까운 베리 덤불로 가서 빨간 베리를 먹었지만 너무 써서 삼킬 수 없었다. 집으로 돌아와 대나무에 올랐는데, 그곳에서 달콤한 향을 풍기는 검고 붉은 꽃을 발견했다.
→ 베리 덤불로 가서 베리를 먹은 이유가 앞에 나와야 하고, 검고 붉은 꽃을 발견하고 어떤 행동을 했는지가 뒤에 이어져야 한다.

(C): 그는 독특해지기 위해 검은 반점을 가진 사촌을 찾아갔으나, 정작 그는 자신의 반점을 싫어한다고 말하여 작은 판다는 실망했다. 집에 가던 길에 붉은 깃털의 공작새를 만나, 그가 야생 베리를 먹고 붉게 변했다는 이야기를 들었다.
→ 독특해지기를 갈망하여 사촌을 찾아간 것이므로 (A)에 이어지는 내용이다. 집에 가던 길에 붉은 깃털의 공작새를 만나 야생 베리에 대한 이야기를 들었으므로 (B)가 (C) 뒤에 이어진다.

(D): 다음 날 아침, 작은 판다는 자신의 털이 검고 붉게 변한 것을 발견하고는 기뻐했고 특별함은 남을 따라 하는 것이 아니라, 예상치 못한 경험에서 얻어진다는 깨달음을 얻었다.
→ 작은 판다의 털이 검고 붉게 변하게 된 이유가 나오는 (B)에 이어지는 내용이다. 작은 판다가 자신만의 특별한 색깔을 가지게 되어 기뻐하며 깨달음을 얻는 것으로 글이 마무리된다. ▶ 글의 순서는 ② (C) — (B) — (D)임

밑줄 친 (a)~(e) 중에서 가리키는 대상이 나머지 넷과 <u>다른</u> 것은?

① (a)   ② (b)   ③ (c)   ④(d)   ⑤ (e)
= the little panda   = the little panda   = the little panda's   = the peacock   = the little panda's

왜 정답? ★★※ [정답률 77%]

④ (d) he: 야생 베리를 먹고 붉게 변했다고 말하는 동물 ▶ the peacock

왜 오답?

① (a) him: 자신이 너무 하얘서 평범함과 슬픔을 느낀 동물 ▶ the little panda

② (b) him : 검고 붉은 꽃을 발견하고 그것을 먹도록 유혹당한 동물
▶ the little panda

③ (c) his : 검은 반점을 가진 거대한 흰 판다와 먼 사촌 관계인 동물
▶ the little panda's

⑤ (e) his : 소원이 예상치 못한 경험으로부터 실현될 수 있음을 깨달은 동물
▶ the little panda's

S **48** 정답 ③

윗글의 'little panda'에 관한 내용으로 적절하지 <u>않은</u> 것은?

① 다른 판다들과는 달리 특별해지기를 갈망했다.
　　Unlike ~ pandas around him, he desired to be distinctive ~.
② 베리가 너무 써서 한 개도 삼킬 수 없었다.
　　they were so bitter he couldn't swallow even one
③ 집에 돌아오는 길에 검고 붉은 꽃을 발견하였다.
　　he finally got home ~ discovered a strange black and red flower
④ 그의 사촌은 자신의 검은 반점을 싫어했다. he disliked them
⑤ 다른 판다들이 왜 신나게 수다를 떠는지 물어보았다.
　　he found the other pandas chatting enthusiastically and asked why

왜 정답? ★★※ [정답률 46%]

작은 판다가 집에 도착한 후 대나무에서 검고 붉은 꽃을 발견한 것이므로 집에 돌아오는 길에 검고 붉은 꽃을 발견했다는 ③은 적절하지 않다.

왜 오답?

① 다른 판다들과는 달리 특별해지기를 갈망했다. (Unlike ~ pandas around him, he desired to be distinctive, special, and unique.)
② 베리가 너무 써서 한 개도 삼킬 수 없었다. (they were so bitter he couldn't swallow even one)
④ 그의 사촌은 자신의 검은 반점을 싫어했다. (the cousin revealed the patches were from an unintended encounter with mud, and he disliked them)
⑤ 다른 판다들이 왜 신나게 수다를 떠는지 물어보았다. (he found the other pandas chatting enthusiastically and asked why)

S **49~51** ⭐ 2등급 대비

*가난한 남자의 감정을 배려한 왕자의 사려 깊음

(A) One day / a poor man brought a bunch of grapes / to a prince / as a gift. // 49번 ① 왕자는 가난한 남자에게 포도 한 송이를 선물로 받았음

어느 날 / 한 가난한 남자가 한 송이의 포도를 가져왔다 / 왕자에게 / 선물로 /

He was very excited / to be able to bring a gift for (a) him / = the prince
because he was **too** poor **to** afford more. // too ~ to … : 너무 ~해서 …할 수 없다

그는 매우 흥분했다 / 그를 위한 선물을 가져올 수 있어서 / 너무 가난해서 그 이상의 여유가 없었기 때문에 //

He placed the grapes beside the prince / and said, "Oh, Prince, please accept this small gift from me."

그는 그 왕자의 옆에 포도를 놓았다 / 그리고 "오, 왕자님, 저의 이 작은 선물을 부디 받아주세요"라고 말했다 // 완전자동사

His face **beamed** with happiness / as he offered his small gift. // 49번 단서 1: 가난한 남자가 포도를 왕자에게 선물하면서 행복해함

그의 얼굴은 행복으로 빛났다 / 그가 자신의 작은 선물을 바치면서 //

*(A) 문단 요약: 가난한 남자가 한 송이의 포도를 왕자에게 선물함

(B) 가정법 과거완료의 if절 If the prince had offered the grapes to them, / 가정법 과거완료의 주절 ① they might have made funny faces / and shown their distaste for the grapes. // 49번 단서 2: 왕자는 포도가 너무 시어서 일부러 혼자 다 먹었다는 (D)의 마지막 내용에 이어짐

만약 그 왕자가 그들에게 그 포도를 권했다면 / 그들은 우스꽝스러운 표정을 지었을 것이다 / 그리고 포도에 대한 불쾌감을 드러냈을 것이다 // 가정법 과거완료의 주절 ② (주절 ①: 원인, 주절 ②: 결과)
That **would have hurt** / the feelings of that poor man. //

그것은 상하게 했을 것이다 / 그 가난한 남자의 감정을 //
가주어 진주어
He thought to himself / that **it** would be better / **to eat** all of them cheerfully / and please (b) him. // = that poor man

그는 속으로 생각했다 / 더 낫다고 / 모든 포도를 기분 좋게 먹는 것이 / 그리고 그를 기쁘게 하는 것이 //

He did not want to hurt / the feelings of that poor man. // 51번 ② 가난한 남자의 감정 을 상하게 하고 싶지 않았음

그는 상하게 하고 싶지 않았다 / 그 가난한 남자의 감정을 //

Everyone around him was moved / by his thoughtfulness. //

그의 주위의 모든 사람들은 감동 받았다 / 그의 사려 깊음에 //

*(B) 문단 요약: 가난한 남자의 감정을 상하게 하고 싶지 않아서 포도를 다 먹은 왕자에게 사람들이 감동 받음

(C) The prince thanked him politely. //

그 왕자는 그에게 정중하게 감사를 표했다 // 49번 단서 3: 가난한 남자가 포도를 선물해서 감사를 표함

As the man looked at him expectantly, / the prince ate one grape. //

그 남자가 기대에 부풀어 그를 바라보았을 때 / 그 왕자는 포도 한 알을 먹었다 //
= the prince
Then (c) he ate another one. //

그러고 나서 그는 또 다른 하나를 먹었다 //

Slowly / the prince finished the whole bunch of grapes / by himself. //

천천히 / 그 왕자는 포도 한 송이 전부를 다 먹었다 / 혼자서 //

He did not offer grapes / to anyone near him. // 51번 ③ 곁에 있던 어떤 이에게도 포도를 권하지 않았음

그는 포도를 권하지 않았다 / 자신의 곁에 있는 어떤 이에게도 //
주격 관계대명사   = the prince
The man **who** brought those grapes to (d) **him** / **was** very pleased and **left**. // 동사의 병렬 구조

그 포도를 그에게 가져온 남자는 / 매우 기뻐하고 떠났다 //
주격 관계대명사
The close friends of the prince / **who** were around him / were very surprised. //

그 왕자의 가까운 친구들은 / 그의 주변에 있던 / 매우 놀랐다 //

*(C) 문단 요약: 왕자는 가난한 남자가 선물한 포도 한 송이를 다른 사람에게 권하지 않고 전부 혼자 다 먹었음   49번 단서 4, 51번 ④ (C)의 마지막에 이어지는 내용으로, 왕자는 가지고 있는 어떤 것이든 평소에 다른 사람들과 나눠 먹음

(D) Usually the prince shared / whatever he had / with others. //

평소에 그 왕자는 나눴다 / 자신이 가지고 있는 어떤 것이든 / 다른 사람들과 //

He would offer them / whatever he was given / and they would eat it together. //

그는 그들에게 권했다 / 자신이 받은 것은 무엇이든지 / 그리고 그들은 그것을 함께 먹곤 했다 //

This time was different. //

이번에는 달랐다 //
= the prince
Without offering it to anyone, / (e) he finished the bunch of grapes / by himself. //

아무에게도 그것을 권하지 않고 / 그는 포도 한 송이를 다 먹었다 / 혼자서 //
= Why
One of the friends asked, / "Prince! How come you ate all the grapes by yourself / and did not offer them to any one of us?" //

그 친구들 중 한 명이 물었다 / "왕자님! 어찌하여 혼자서 포도를 다 드시고 / 우리 중 그 누구에게도 그것을 권하지 않으셨나요"라고 // 51번 ⑤ 포도가 너무 시어서 혼자 다 먹었다고 했음
목적어절을 이끄는 접속사
He smiled and said / **that** he ate all the grapes by himself / because the grapes were too sour. //

그는 웃으며 말했다 / 혼자서 모든 포도를 다 먹었다고 / 그 포도가 너무 시어서 //

*(D) 문단 요약: 평소에는 다른 사람과 무엇이든 나누었던 왕자가 포도를 혼자 다 먹은 이유는 포도가 너무 시었기 때문임

- **bunch** ⓝ 다발, 송이   **place** ⓥ 놓다, 두다
- **beam** ⓥ 빛나다, 활짝 웃다   **distaste** ⓝ 불쾌감
- **cheerfully** ⓐⓓ 쾌활하게, 명랑하게   **thoughtfulness** ⓝ 사려 깊음
- **politely** ⓐⓓ 정중하게   **expectantly** ⓐⓓ 기대에 부풀어
- **pleased** ⓐ 기쁜   **sour** ⓐ (맛이) 신

(A) 어느 날 한 가난한 남자가 한 송이의 포도를 왕자에게 선물로 가져왔다. 그는 너무 가난해서 그 이상의 여유가 없었기 때문에 (a) 그를 위한 선물을 가져올 수 있어서 매우 흥분했다. 그는 그 왕자의 옆에 포도를 놓고 "오, 왕자님, 저의 이 작은 선물을 부디 받아주세요."라고 말했다. 그의 얼굴은 그가 자신의 작은 선물을 바치면서 행복으로 빛났다.
(C) 그 왕자는 그에게 정중하게 감사를 표했다. 그 남자가 기대에 부풀어 그를 바라보았을 때 그 왕자는 포도 한 알을 먹었다. 그러고 나서 (c) 그는 또 다른 하나를 먹었다. 천천히 그 왕자는 혼자서 포도 한 송이 전부를 다 먹었다. 그는 자신의 곁에 있는 어떤 이에게도 포도를 권하지 않았다. 그 포도를 (d) 그에게 가져온 남자는 매우 기뻐하고 떠났다. 그 왕자의 주변에 있던 그의 가까운 친구들은 매우 놀랐다.
(D) 평소에 그 왕자는 자신이 가지고 있는 어떤 것이든 다른 사람들과 나눴다. 그는 그들에게 자신이 받은 것은 무엇이든지 권하고 그들은 그것을 함께 먹곤 했다. 이번에는 달랐다. 아무에게도 그것을 권하지 않고 (e) 그는 포도 한 송이를 혼자 다 먹었다. 그 친구들 중 한 명이 "왕자님! 어찌하여 혼자서 포도를 다 드시고 우리 중 그 누구에게도 그것을 권하지 않으셨나요?"라고 물었다. 그는 웃으며 그 포도가 너무 시어서 혼자서 모든 포도를 다 먹었다고 말했다.
(B) 만약 그 왕자가 그들에게 그 포도를 권했다면 그들은 우스꽝스러운 표정을 지으며 포도에 대한 불쾌감을 드러냈을 것이다. 그것은 그 가난한 남자의 감정을 상하게 했을 것이다. 그는 모든 포도를 기분 좋게 먹고 (b) 그를 기쁘게 하는 것이 더 낫다고 속으로 생각했다. 그는 그 가난한 남자의 감정을 상하게 하고 싶지 않았다. 그의 주위의 모든 사람들은 그의 사려 깊음에 감동받았다.

⭐ 각 문단마다 직접적인 단서를 주는 연결어나 지시어가 있다기보다는, 왕자가 가난한 남자의 감정을 배려한 사려 깊음에 대한 이야기가 자연스럽게 이어지고 있으므로 내용의 흐름을 이해하는 것이 중요하다.

S 49 정답 ③

> 주어진 글 (A)에 이어질 내용을 순서에 맞게 배열한 것으로 가장 적절한 것은?
> ① (B) — (C) — (D) (B)는 전체 내용의 결론 부분으로 마지막에 와야 함
> ② (C) — (B) — (D) (D)에서 포도를 다 먹은 이유를 말한 후 (B)에서 사람들이 감동한 것으로 이어져야 함
> ③ (C) — (D) — (B) (C) 왕자는 가난한 남자가 선물한 포도를 혼자 다 먹었음 – (D) 왕자가 포도를 혼자 다 먹은 이유는 포도가 너무 시었기 때문임 – (B) 포도를 다 먹은 왕자에게 사람들이 감동 받았음
> ④ (D) — (B) — (C) (A)에서 왕자가 가난한 남자에게 포도를 받고 (C)에서 감사를 표하는 것으로 이어져야 함
> ⑤ (D) — (C) — (B)

> **왜 정답?**
가난한 남자가 왕자에게 포도 한 송이를 선물한 (A) 뒤에는 왕자가 감사를 표현한 후 포도를 혼자 전부 먹는 (C)가 와야 한다. 왕자가 포도를 혼자 다 먹어서 사람들이 놀란 (C)의 마지막에는 그 이유가 드러나는 (D)가 이어져야 한다. 포도가 너무 시어서 혼자 다 먹었다고 말한 뒤에는, 가난한 남자의 기분을 상하게 하고 싶지 않았던 왕자의 사려 깊음에 사람들이 감동했다는 (B)가 오는 것이 자연스럽다. 따라서 ③ (C)-(D)-(B)가 가장 적절하다.

> **왜 오답?**
① (B)는 전체 이야기의 결론에 해당하므로 마지막에 오는 것이 자연스럽다.
② (D)에서 왕자가 포도를 혼자서 다 먹은 이유를 말한 후, 그것을 듣고 사람들이 감동하는 (B)로 이어지는 것이 적절하다. (함정)
④, ⑤ (A)에서 가난한 남자가 왕자에게 포도를 선물로 주고 (C)에서 왕자가 감사를 표하는 것으로 이어지는 흐름이 알맞다.

S 50 정답 ②

> 밑줄 친 (a)~(e) 중에서 가리키는 대상이 나머지 넷과 다른 것은?
> ① (a)   ② (b)   ③ (c)   ④ (d)   ⑤ (e)
>   = the prince   = that poor man   = the prince   = the prince   = the prince

> **왜 정답?**
(b)는 왕자가 기쁘게 하려고 했던 가난한 남자를 가리킨다. 나머지는 모두 왕자를 가리키므로 정답은 ②이다.

> **왜 오답?**
① 가난한 남자가 가져온 포도는 왕자를 위한 선물이다.
③ 포도를 한 알 더 먹은 사람은 그것을 선물 받은 왕자이다.
④ 가난한 남자가 포도를 준 사람은 왕자이다.
⑤ 포도를 혼자 다 먹은 사람은 왕자이다.

S 51 정답 ⑤

> 윗글의 왕자에 관한 내용으로 적절하지 않은 것은?
> ① 가난한 남자에게 포도 한 송이를 선물로 받았다.
>   One day a poor man brought a bunch of grapes to a prince as a gift.
> ② 가난한 남자의 감정을 상하게 하고 싶지 않았다.
>   He did not want to hurt the feelings of that poor man.
> ③ 곁에 있던 어떤 이에게도 포도를 권하지 않았다.
>   He did not offer grapes to anyone near him.
> ④ 가지고 있는 어떤 것이든 평소에 다른 사람들과 나눴다.
>   Usually the prince shared whatever he had with others.
> ⑤ 포도가 너무 시어서 혼자 다 먹지 못했다.
>   He smiled and said that he ate all the grapes by himself because the grapes were too sour.

> **왜 정답?**
왕자는 오히려 포도가 너무 시어서 포도 한 송이를 다 먹었다고 했으므로 ⑤이 왕자에 대한 내용으로 적절하지 않다.

> **왜 오답?**
① 가난한 남자가 왕자에게 포도 한 송이를 선물로 주었다고 했다. (One day a poor man brought a bunch of grapes to a prince as a gift.)
② 왕자는 가난한 남자의 감정을 상하게 하고 싶지 않았다고 했다. (He did not want to hurt the feelings of that poor man.)
③ 왕자는 곁에 있던 어떤 이에게도 포도를 권하지 않았다고 했다. (He did not offer grapes to anyone near him.)
④ 왕자는 가지고 있는 어떤 것이든 평소에 다른 사람들과 나눴다고 했다. (Usually the prince shared whatever he had with others.)

S 어휘 Review 정답 ─── 문제편 p. 315

01 서리가 내리는	11 come upon	21 helplessly
02 상실	12 a world of	22 sudden
03 세심한	13 be stuck in	23 worship
04 자격이 있는	14 step off	24 barely
05 불친절한	15 tear down	25 precious
06 generous	16 unintended	26 wrinkled
07 entire	17 gesture	27 rewarded
08 stare	18 noticed	28 property
09 disaster	19 tension	29 ignored
10 merchant	20 village	30 grand

1회 01 정답 ④ *채소의 성장을 위한 불안정성

The concept of ecosystem states / should be familiar to anyone / with a home vegetable garden. //
생태계 상태라는 개념은 / 누구나 익숙할 것이다 / 가정용 텃밭이 있는 사람이라면 //

목적격 관계대명사
The garden is a small ecosystem / that the grower attempts to keep in a specific state, / namely the maximization of fruit and vegetable production. //
텃밭은 작은 생태계이다 / 재배자가 특정한 상태를 유지하려고 애쓰는 / 즉 과일과 채소 생산의 극대화를 //

부사적 용법 (목적)
단서 1 텃밭의 재배자는 과일과 채소 생산을 극대화하기 위해 텃밭의 생태계에 개입함
To achieve this, / the grower is almost always intervening / in the dynamics of the ecosystem; /
이를 달성하기 위해 / 재배자는 거의 항상 개입한다 / 생태계의 역학 관계에 /

주격 관계대명사
they remove unwanted plants / that begin to grow / and perhaps
병렬 구조 (동사)
spray insecticides / and fence off the patch / to stop insects and
stop A from B: A가 B하는 것을 막다
other animals from consuming the vegetables. //
즉, 그들은 원치 않는 식물을 제거하고 / 자라나기 시작하는 / 어쩌면 살충제를 뿌리고 / 밭에 울타리를 칠 수도 있다 / 곤충과 다른 동물들이 채소를 먹는 것을 막기 위해 //

단수 주어 (동명사구) 단수 동사
Since maximizing vegetable growth / is an inherently unstable state / for the ecosystem, / the grower is effectively keeping the ball on a slope. //
채소의 성장을 극대화하는 것은 / 본질적으로 불안정한 상태이기 때문에 / 생태계에게는 / 재배자는 사실상 경사면 위에 공을 잡아 두고 있는 것이다 //

동명사 (stops의 목적어)
If the grower stops intervening, / even for a day, / the ecosystem, that small patch of ground, / will naturally begin to
동격
단서 2 재배자의 개입이 없다면
shift / to a more stable state. // 텃밭은 더 안정된 상태로 변할 것임
만약 재배자가 개입을 멈춘다면 / 단 하루만이라도 / 그 생태계, 즉 그 땅의 작은 밭은 / 자연히 변화하기 시작할 것이다 / 더 안정된 상태로 //

부사절 접속사 (이유)
Vegetables may still grow, / but yield will almost certainly be lower / as other plants crowd out the vegetables / and wildlife consume the produce. // **단서 3** 안정된 상태의 텃밭에서는 채소 수확량이 더 적어질 것임
채소는 여전히 자라겠지만 / 수확량은 거의 틀림없이 더 적을 것이다 / 다른 식물이 채소를 밀어내고 / 야생 동물이 작물을 먹기 때문에 //

- ecosystem ⓝ 생태계
- maximization ⓝ 극대화
- intervene ⓥ 개입하다
- dynamics ⓝ 역학 관계
- spray ⓥ 뿌리다
- fence ⓥ 울타리를 치다
- patch ⓝ 좁은 땅
- inherently ⓐⓓ 본질적으로
- unstable ⓐ 불안정한
- effectively ⓐⓓ 사실상
- slope ⓝ 경사면
- yield ⓝ 수확량, 생산량
- crowd out ~을 밀어내다
- intervention ⓝ 개입
- alter ⓥ 바꾸다
- stability ⓝ 안정성
- diversity ⓝ 다양성
- boost ⓥ 촉진하다
- harmonious ⓐ 조화로운

생태계 상태라는 개념은 가정용 텃밭이 있는 사람이라면 누구나 익숙할 것이다. 텃밭은 재배자가 특정한 상태, 즉 과일과 채소 생산의 극대화를 유지하려고 애쓰는 작은 생태계이다. 이를 달성하기 위해, 재배자는 거의 항상 생태계의 역학 관계에 개입한다. 즉, 자라나기 시작하는 원치 않는 식물을 제거하고, 곤충과 다른 동물들이 채소를 먹는 것을 막기 위해 어쩌면 살충제를 뿌리고 밭에 울타리를 칠 수도 있다. 채소의 성장을 극대화하는 것은 생태계에게는 본질적으로 불안정한 상태이기 때문에, 재배자는 사실상 경사면 위에 공을 잡아 두고 있는 것이다. 만약, 단 하루만이라도, 재배자가 개입을 멈춘다면, 그 생태계, 즉 그 땅의 작은 밭은 자연히 더 안정된 상태로 변화하기 시작할 것이다. 채소는 여전히 자라겠지만, 다른 식물이 채소를 밀어내고 야생 동물이 작물을 먹기 때문에 수확량은 거의 틀림없이 더 적을 것이다.

밑줄 친 keeping the ball on a slope가 다음 글에서 의미하는 바로 가장 적절한 것은? [3점]

생태계 안정성을 추구하면 채소 생산량의 극대화라는 목표를 이룰 수 없음
① improving the garden's environment without human intervention
인간의 개입이 필수적이라고 했음
인간의 개입 없이 텃밭의 환경을 개선하는 것
② altering the ecosystem of the garden to maximize its stability
안정성을 극대화하기 위해 텃밭의 생태계를 바꾸는 것 채소 생산을 극대화하기 위함임
③ balancing increased plant diversity with ecosystem stability
생태계 안정성과 증가한 식물 다양성의 균형을 맞추는 것
④ maintaining an unstable ecosystem for high vegetable yield
높은 채소 생산량을 위해 불안정한 생태계를 유지하는 것
maximizing vegetable growth ~ for the ecosystem
⑤ boosting the harmonious growth of plants in the wild
야생 식물들의 조화로운 성장을 촉진하는 것 관련 없는 내용

> **왜 정답?** ★★★ [정답률 52%]

- 텃밭의 재배자는 채소 생산을 극대화하기 위해 텃밭의 생태계에 개입함 **단서 1**
- 재배자의 개입이 없다면 텃밭은 안정된 상태로 변할 것임 → 안정된 상태의 텃밭에서는 다른 식물이 채소를 밀어내고 야생 동물이 작물을 먹기 때문에 채소 수확량이 더 적어질 것임 **단서 2, 3**

→ 재배자의 개입이 없다면 텃밭 생태계는 안정되고 채소 수확량도 줄어들 것이므로 채소 생산성을 극대화하기 위해서는 텃밭 생태계의 불안정성을 유지해야 한다. 즉, 채소 생산을 극대화하기 위해 텃밭의 재배자가 '경사면 위에 공을 잡아 두고 있다'라는 표현은 생태계에서 채소 생산을 극대화하는 데 필요한 불안정성을 유지한다는 의미이다.

▶ 따라서 정답은 ④ '높은 채소 생산량을 위해 불안정한 생태계를 유지하는 것'이다.

> **왜 오답?**

① 텃밭에서 채소 생산의 극대화라는 목표를 이루려면 인간의 개입이 필수적이라고 했다.
② 텃밭의 생태계를 가꾸는 이유는 안정성을 위해서가 아니라 채소 생산을 극대화하기 위함이며, 안정성을 극대화하면 채소 생산을 극대화할 수 없다.
③ 식물 다양성과 생태계 안정성을 추구하면 채소 생산량의 극대화라는 목표를 이룰 수 없으며, 생태계 안정성의 균형을 맞추면 채소 생산을 극대화할 수 없다.
⑤ 야생 식물들의 조화로운 성장에 관한 언급은 없었다.

1회 02 정답 ⑤ *익숙한 것과 기억을 떠올리는 것의 차이

현재완료
If the brain has already stored / someone's face and name, / why
end up -ing: 결국 ~해버리다
do we still end up / remembering one and not the other? //
뇌가 이미 저장했다면 / 누군가의 얼굴과 이름을 / 왜 우리는 여전히 되는 것일까 / 하나는 기억하고 다른 하나는 기억하지 못하게 //

this is because + 원인 cf) this is why + 결과
This is because / the brain has something of a two-tier memory
'~하는 데 있어서'
system at work / when it comes to retrieving memories, / and this gives rise to a common yet infuriating sensation: /
이는 때문이며 / 뇌가 2단계의 기억 시스템을 가진 무언가를 작동하도록 만들기 / 기억을 생각해 내는 것에 있어서 / 이것이 흔하지만 짜증 나는 감정을 유발한다 /

병렬 구조
recognising someone, / but not being able to remember / how or
단서 1 우리의 뇌는 누군가를 알아볼 수는 있지만
why, or what their name is. // 기억하지 못하는 경우가 있음
누군가를 알아볼 수는 있지만 / 기억하지 못하는 / 어떻게, 왜 (아는지) 또는 그 사람의 이름이 무엇인지는 //

단서 2 이는 뇌가 친숙함과 회상을 구별하기 때문에 발생함
This happens / because the brain differentiates / between familiarity and recall. //
이는 발생한다 / 뇌가 구별하기 때문에 / 친숙함과 회상을 //

현재완료
To clarify, / familiarity (or recognition) is / when you encounter someone or something / and you know you've done so before. //
명확하게 하자면 / 친숙함(또는 인식)은 / 누군가 또는 무언가를 마주쳤고 / 이전에 그런 적이 있다는 것을 아는 경우이다 //

단서 3 친숙함은 누군가를 마주쳤을 때 이전에도 현재완료 마주친 경험이 있다는 것을 아는 것임
But beyond that, / you've got nothing; / all you can say / is this person/thing is already in your memories. //
하지만 그 이상으로는 / 당신이 아는 것이 없고 / 당신이 말할 수 있는 것은 / 이 사람/사물이 이미 기억 속에 있다는 것뿐이다 //

Recall is when you can access the original memory / of how and why you know this person; / recognition is just flagging up the fact / that the memory exists. // 단서4 회상은 단지 원래의 기억에 접근할 수 있는 것임
회상은 원래의 기억에 접근할 수 있는 경우이며 / 이 사람을 어떻게, 왜 알고 있는지에 대한 / 인식은 단지 사실만을 표시해 줄 뿐이다 / 기억이 존재한다는 //

- tier ⓝ 단계, 층위　　· give rise to ~을 유발하다　　· sensation ⓝ 감정
- differentiate ⓥ 구별하다　　· familiarity ⓝ 친숙함
- recall ⓝ 회상　　· clarify ⓥ 명확하게 하다　　· encounter ⓥ 마주치다
- flag up ~을 표시하다　　· partial ⓐ 부분적인　　· retrieval ⓝ 회복, 복구
- danger ⓝ 위험성　　· memory loss 기억 상실
- distinction ⓝ 구분

뇌가 이미 누군가의 얼굴과 이름을 저장했다면, 왜 우리는 여전히 하나를 기억하고 다른 하나는 기억하지 못하게 되는 것일까? 이는 기억을 생각해 내는 것에 있어서 뇌가 2단계의 기억 시스템을 가진 무언가를 작동하도록 만들기 때문이며, 이것이 누군가를 알아볼 수는 있지만 어떻게, 왜 (아는지) 또는 그 사람의 이름이 무엇인지는 기억하지 못하는, 흔하지만 짜증 나는 감정을 유발한다. 이는 뇌가 친숙함과 회상을 구별하기 때문에 발생한다. 명확하게 하자면, 친숙함(또는 인식)은 누군가 또는 무언가를 마주쳤고 이전에 그런 적이 있다는 것을 아는 경우이다. 하지만 그 이상으로는, 당신이 아는 것이 없고, 당신이 말할 수 있는 것은 이 사람/사물이 이미 기억 속에 있다는 것뿐이다. 회상은 이 사람을 어떻게, 왜 알고 있는지에 대한 원래의 기억에 접근할 수 있는 경우이며, 인식은 단지 기억이 존재한다는 사실만을 표시해 줄 뿐이다.

다음 글의 주제로 가장 적절한 것은?
① process of recalling details from partial memories
부분적인 기억들로부터 세부 사항을 떠올리는 과정　　과정을 설명한 것이 아님
② impact of emotional responses on memory retrieval patterns
감정적 반응이 기억 복구 패턴에 미치는 영향　　감정적 반응의 영향에 관한 언급은 없음
③ dangers of memory loss regarding face and name recognition
얼굴과 이름 인식과 관련해 기억 상실의 위험성　　기억 상실의 위험에 관한 언급은 없음
④ ways to manage the difficulty of recognising faces and names
얼굴과 이름을 인식하는 것의 어려움을 다루는 방법　　어려움을 다루는 내용이 아님
⑤ distinction between recall and familiarity in the memory system
기억 체계에서 회상과 친숙함 사이의 구분　　the brain differentiates between familiarity and recall

▷왜 정답? ✽✽❀ [정답률 73%]

문제: 우리의 뇌는 누군가를 알아볼 수는 있지만 기억하지 못하는 경우가 있음 단서1
원인: 이는 뇌가 친숙함과 회상을 구별하기 때문에 발생함 단서2
구체화1: 친숙함(또는 인식)은 누군가를 마주쳤을 때 이전에도 그와 마주친 경험이 있다는 것을 아는 것임 단서3
구체화2: 회상은 그를 어떻게, 왜 알고 있는지에 대한 원래의 기억에 접근할 수 있는 것임 단서4

➡ 뇌는 기억을 떠올릴 때 2단계의 기억 시스템을 작동하기 때문에 누군가를 알아보면서도 기억하지 못하는 경우가 있다고 했다. 그 두 단계는 친숙함과 회상으로, 친숙함은 누군가와 마주쳤던 경험을 아는 것이고, 회상은 그 상황에 대한 원래의 기억을 떠올리는 것이다. ▶ 친숙함은 회상과 달리 기억이 존재한다는 사실만 알려준다고 했으므로, 글의 주제는 ⑤ '기억 체계에서 회상과 친숙함 사이의 구분'이다.

▷왜 오답?

① 부분적인 기억들로부터 세부 사항을 떠올리는 과정을 설명한 것이 아니라, 친숙한 것과 회상의 차이를 설명한 글이다.
② 기억을 인출하는 것과 친숙함의 차이에 관한 내용이지, 감정적 반응의 영향에 관한 언급은 없었다.
③ 얼굴과 이름을 인식하는 것과 회상하는 것의 차이에 관한 내용이지, 기억 상실의 위험에 관한 언급은 없었다.
④ 얼굴과 이름을 인식하는 것과 회상하는 것의 차이에 관한 내용이지, 그 어려움을 다루는 내용이 아니다.

1회 03　정답 ⑤　✱진보적인 가치들을 수용하도록 돕는 시트콤

단서1 미국의 TV 시트콤은 미국 사회의 많은 사회 갈등을 보여줌
Since their start in the early 1950s / U.S. television sitcoms have charted / many of the social conflicts in U.S. society: / 현재완료
1950년대 초반에 시작된 이래로 / 미국의 텔레비전 시트콤은 보여주었는데 / 미국 사회의 많은 사회 갈등을 /

civil rights, women's rights in the home and in the workplace, / children's rights, immigration and multiculturalism, / as well as evolving conceptions of the family. 현재분사 (conceptions 수식)　A as well as B: B뿐만 아니라 A도
시민권, 가정과 직장에서의 여성 권리 / 아동권, 이민과 다문화주의와 같은 것들이다 / (점층) 진화하는 가족 개념뿐만 아니라 //

단수 주어　　단수 동사 (현재완료 수동태)
Each of these issues / has been addressed through humour / in a way that has helped / to make more progressive values more acceptable / than previously. // make의 목적어와 목적격 보어 (형용사)
단서2 시트콤은 각 쟁점을 유머로 다루면서 진보적인 가치가 수용되도록 만듦
이 각각의 쟁점은 / 유머를 통해 다루어져 왔다 / 도움을 주는 방식으로 / 보다 진보적인 가치들이 더 수용 가능하도록 하는 데 / 이전보다 //

과거분사구 (someone 수식)
Often a character, / usually someone marked as a bigot, / resisted one or more of these developments / and was then made to appear ridiculous. // appear의 주격 보어 (형용사)　수동태 동사
종종 등장인물 한 명 / 대개는 편견이 아주 심한 사람이라고 특징지어졌던 누군가가 / 이러한 발전 중 하나 이상에 저항하고 나서 / (그가) 어리석어 보이게 되었다 //

수동태 동사
They were cut down / either through their own stupidity, / a brief scolding from others, / or both. // = their own stupidity and a brief scolding from others
이들은 배제되었다 / 자신의 어리석음이나 / 다른 사람들의 짧은 비난 / 또는 이 두 가지 모두에 의해 //

단서3 시트콤의 유머는 더 다원적이고 관용적인 사회의 수용을 장려하는 수단으로 작용함
In this way, / the humour of sitcoms acted as a cost-effective means / to encourage acceptance / of a more pluralistic and tolerant society. // 형용사적 용법 (means 수식)
이러한 방식으로 / 시트콤의 유머는 비용 효율적인 수단으로 작용했다 / 수용을 장려하는 / 더 다원적이고 관용적인 사회의 //

- sitcom ⓝ 시트콤　　· chart ⓥ 기록하다, 보여주다　　· conflict ⓝ 갈등
- multiculturalism ⓝ 다문화주의　　· conception ⓝ 개념
- progressive ⓐ 진보적인　　· ridiculous ⓐ 어리석은
- stupidity ⓝ 어리석음　　· scolding ⓝ 비난, 꾸짖음
- tolerant ⓐ 관용적인　　· acceptability ⓝ 수용 가능성

1950년대 초반에 시작된 이래로, 미국의 텔레비전 시트콤은 미국 사회의 많은 사회 갈등을 보여주었는데, (점층) 진화하는 가족 개념뿐만 아니라 시민권, 가정과 직장에서의 여성 권리, 아동권, 이민과 다문화주의와 같은 것들이다. 이 각각의 쟁점은 유머를 통해 보다 진보적인 가치들이 이전보다 더 수용 가능하도록 하는 데 도움을 주는 방식으로 다루어져 왔다. 종종 등장인물 한 명, 대개는 편견이 아주 심한 사람이라고 특징지어졌던 누군가가 이러한 발전 중 하나 이상에 저항하고 나서 (그가) 어리석어 보이게 되었다. 이들은 자신의 어리석음이나 다른 사람들의 짧은 비난, 또는 이 두 가지 모두에 의해 배제되었다. 이러한 방식으로, 시트콤의 유머는 더 다원적이고 관용적인 사회의 수용을 장려하는 비용 효율적인 수단으로 작용했다.

다음 글의 제목으로 가장 적절한 것은?
the humour of sitcoms acted as a cost-effective means ~ tolerant society
① Why Do Sitcoms Criticize Progressive Ideas? 비판한다는 것은 반대임
왜 시트콤은 진보적인 생각을 비판하는가?
② Acceptability of Humour in Multicultural Society 유머를 통해 다문화
다문화 사회에서 유머의 수용 가능성　　사회와 같은 가치를 수용할 수 있도록 해준다는 내용임
③ The Decline of U.S. Sitcoms along with Social Change
사회 변화에 따른 미국 시트콤의 쇠퇴　　쇠퇴한다는 내용이 아님
④ Production Costs: Why TV Commercials Are Necessary
생산 비용: TV 광고가 필요한 이유　　언급되지 않음
⑤ Humour in Sitcoms Helps Acceptance of Progressive Values
시트콤의 유머가 진보적인 가치의 수용을 돕는다

▷왜 정답? ✽✽❀ [정답률 71%]

- 미국의 TV 시트콤은 미국 사회의 많은 사회 갈등을 보여줌 단서1
- 시트콤은 각 쟁점을 유머로 다루면서 진보적인 가치가 수용되도록 만듦 단서2
- 시트콤의 유머는 더 다원적이고 관용적인 사회의 수용을 장려하는 수단으로 작용함 단서3

➡ 미국의 TV 시트콤은 미국 사회에 나타난 많은 사회 갈등을 보여주었는데, 각각의 쟁점을 유머로 다룸으로써 사람들이 진보적인 가치를 수용할 수 있도록 해 주었다는 내용이다. ▶ 따라서 제목으로 가장 적절한 것은 ⑤ '시트콤의 유머가 진보적인 가치의 수용을 돕는다'이다.

> 왜 오답 ?

① 시트콤은 진보적인 생각의 수용을 돕는다는 내용이므로, 이를 비판한다는 것은 내용과 반대된다.

② 시트콤이 유머를 통해 다문화 사회와 같은 가치를 수용할 수 있도록 해준다는 내용이다. (▷ 이유: 흔한 주제인 다문화 사회에서 유머가 수용될 수 있는지에 관한 내용이 아니다.)

③ 시트콤이 쇠퇴한다는 내용은 언급되지 않았다.

④ 생산 비용과 광고에 관한 내용은 언급되지 않았다.

1회 04 정답 ④ *맛에 앞서는 음식의 사회적 기능 ———

다음 글의 밑줄 친 부분 중, 어법상 틀린 것은?

The prominence of the social dimension / in food writing /
목적어절 접속사
might suggest / that the flavor of food / is taking a back seat. //
현재진행
사회적 측면이 부각되는 것은 / 음식에 관한 글에서 / 시사할지도 모른다 / 음식의 맛이 /
뒷전으로 밀려나고 있음을 //

view A as B: A를 B로 여기다   of+형용사+명사 = 부사+형용사
(= secondarily important)
I suspect / ① that most people view flavor / as of secondary
목적어절 접속사   관계부사
importance / in social settings where food is served. //
나는 생각한다 / 대부분의 사람들이 맛을 여긴다고 / 부수적인 중요성을 띤 것으로 / 음식이
제공되는 사교적 상황에서 //
부사절 접속사 (양보)
Although our social gatherings / coalesce around food, / the
meaning of these gatherings / does not seem to depend on
flavor. //
우리의 사교 모임이 / 음식을 중심으로 모인다 하더라도 / 이러한 모임의 의의는 / 맛에 달려
있지 않은 듯하다 //
문장의 본동사
Flavor ② assists / with the narrow purpose of filling the belly,
부사절 접속사 (일단 ~하면)
/ and once that is accomplished / it provides the backdrop / for
복합관계형용사
whatever social dynamics characterize the gathering. //
맛은 도움이 되고 / 배를 채운다는 좁은 (의미의) 목적에 / 그 목적이 달성되면 / (맛은) 그
배경을 제공한다 / 모임을 특징짓는 사회적 역학 관계가 어떤 것이든지 간에 //
선행사
These can be understood / independently of the flavor of the
관계대명사
food on offer, / the appreciation of ③ which / is understood to
수동태 동사
be personal and subjective. //
이(사회적 역학 관계)는 이해될 수 있으며 / 제공되는 음식의 맛과는 별개로 / 그것(음식의 맛)
에 대한 감상은 / 개인적이고 주관적인 것으로 이해된다 //
단서 문장의 주어는 복수임
According to this conventional wisdom, / the ceremonies and
동격
rituals around food, / the social events that supply food with
주격 관계대명사
its meaning, / ④ does(→ do) not depend on the quality of
과거분사구 (sensations 수식)
sensations / provided by the food. //
이러한 통념에 따르면 / 음식을 중심으로 하는 예식과 의식 / 즉 음식에 의미를 부여하는 사교
행사는 / 감각의 질에 의존하지 않는다 / 음식이 제공하는 //
명사적 용법 (주어)   to부정사를 수식하는 부사
To focus ⑤ excessively on flavor / is to miss the larger
명사적 용법 (주격 보어)
significance / of these social relations. //
맛에 지나치게 집중하는 것은 / 더 큰 중요성을 놓치는 것이다 / 이러한 사회적 관계의 //

- prominence ⓝ 부각, 눈에 띔   • dimension ⓝ 측면, 차원
- back seat 뒷좌석, 뒷전   • secondary ⓐ 부수적인   • belly ⓝ 배
- dynamics ⓝ 역학   • characterize ⓥ 특징을 짓다
- independently of ~와는 독립적으로, 별개로
- appreciation ⓝ 감상, 소감   • ritual ⓝ 의식   • sensation ⓝ 감각
- excessively ⓐⓓ 지나치게   • significance ⓝ 중요성

음식에 관한 글에서 사회적 측면이 부각되는 것은 음식의 맛이 뒷전으로 밀려나고 있음을 시사할지도 모른다. 나는 대부분의 사람들이 음식이 제공되는 사교적 상황에서 맛을 부수적인 중요성을 띤 것으로 여긴다고 생각한다. 우리의 사교 모임이 음식을 중심으로 모인다 하더라도, 이러한 모임의 의의는 맛에 달려 있지 않은 듯하다. 맛은 배를 채운다는 좁은 (의미의) 목적에 도움이 되고, 그 목적이 달성되면 (맛은) 모임을 특징짓는 사회적 역학 관계가 어떤 것이든지 간에 그 배경을 제공한다. 이(사회적 역학 관계)는 제공되는 음식의 맛과는 별개로 이해될 수 있으며, 그것(음식의 맛)에 대한 감상은 개인적이고 주관적인 것으로 이해된다. 이러한 통념에 따르면, 음식을 중심으로 하는 예식과 의식, 즉 음식에 의미를 부여하는 사교 행사는, 음식이 제공하는 감각의 질에 의존하지 않는다. 맛에 지나치게 집중하는 것은 이러한 사회적 관계의 더 큰 중요성을 놓치는 것이다.

> 왜 정답 ? ★★★ [정답률 67%]

④ 문장의 동사는 주어와 수를 일치시켜야 한다!

⌜ According to this conventional wisdom, / the ceremonies and
복수 주어
rituals around food, / the social events that supply food with
its meaning, / ④ does(→ do) not depend on the quality of
주어가 복수이므로 복수 동사가 와야 함
⌞ sensations / provided by the food. //

수식어구와 동격의 명사구 등을 전부 제외하면 문장의 주어는 the ceremonies and rituals around food가 된다. 복수이므로 동사 또한 복수 동사인 do가 와야 한다.

> 왜 오답 ?

① 접속사 that은 명사절을 이끈다.

⌜ I suspect / ① that most people view flavor / as of secondary
목적어절 접속사   완전한 절 (주어+동사+목적어)
⌞ importance / in social settings where food is served. //

접속사 that은 문장에서 주어, 목적어, 보어의 역할을 하는 명사절을 이끌 수 있다.   개념

동사 suspect의 목적어절을 명사절 접속사 that이 알맞게 이끌고 있다.

② 절에는 하나의 주어와 하나의 동사가 있어야 한다.

⌜ Flavor ② assists / with the narrow purpose of filling the belly,
첫 번째 절의 주어와 동사
/ and once that is accomplished / it provides the backdrop / for
절과 절을 잇는 등위접속사   두 번째 절의 주어와 동사
⌞ whatever social dynamics characterize the gathering. //

등위접속사 and로 두 개의 절이 연결되고 있다. 첫 번째 절의 주어는 Flavor, 동사는 assists이고, 두 번째 절의 주어는 it, 동사는 provides이다.

첫 번째 절에서 assists 외에 다른 본동사 역할을 하는 성분이 없으므로, 동사의 형태로 쓰인 assists는 적절하다. 또한 3인칭 단수 주어 Flavor에 맞게 동사 또한 단수 형태로 온 것은 적절하다.

③ 관계대명사는 불완전한 절을 이끈다.

⌜ These can be understood / independently of the flavor of the
관계대명사   선행사
food on offer, / the appreciation of ③ which / is understood to
전치사 of의 목적어가 없는 불완전한 절
⌞ be personal and subjective. //

which는 의미상 the flavor of the food on offer(제공되는 음식의 맛)를 선행사로 한다. 관계대명사가 이끄는 절은 전치사 of에 대한 목적어가 없는 불완전한 절이므로, 관계대명사 which는 알맞게 쓰였다.

┌─────────────────────────────────┐
│ 관계대명사 자리에 선행사 the flavor of the food 꿀팁 │
│ on offer를 삽입하면 원래 문장으로 완전해진다. │
└─────────────────────────────────┘

⑤ 준동사는 부사의 수식을 받는다.

⌜ To focus ⑤ excessively on flavor / is to miss the larger
명사적 용법 (주어)   To focus를 수식하는 부사
⌞ significance / of these social relations. //

to부정사와 같은 준동사는 부사의 수식을 받을 수 있다. 따라서 주어 자리에 온 to부정사 To focus를 부사 excessively가 수식하는 것은 알맞다.

정답 ④ *자금 조달 출처 공개의 필요성

다음 글의 밑줄 친 부분 중, 문맥상 낱말의 쓰임이 적절하지 <u>않은</u> 것은?

There are reasons / why science is not fully trusted / and why
관계부사   수동태 동사   관계부사
healthy skepticism and critical thinking are essential. //
이유가 있다 / 왜 과학이 완전히 신뢰받지 못하는지 / 그리고 왜 건강한 회의주의와 비판적
사고가 필수적인지에는 //

In spite of / professional standards, / claims of objectivity, /
and the peer review process, / the conduct of science can be
                                문장의 주어   문장의 동사
① biased. //
~에도 불구하고 / 전문적인 기준 / 객관성에 대한 주장 / 동료 검토 과정 / 과학의 실행은
편향적일 수 있다 //
                    부정어가 문두로 오며 주어와 동사가 도치됨
All experts are not the same, / nor do they submit their work /
                                        submit A to B: A를 B에 따르게 하다
to the same scrutiny. //
모든 전문가가 동일하지 않으며 / 그들이 자신의 연구를 따르게(거치게) 하는 것도 아니다 /
동일한 심층 조사를
        명사구 (주어)
Knowing the source of funding / can be ② important / in
명사구 (전치사의 목적어)
evaluating scientific claims. //
자금 조달의 출처를 아는 것은 / 중요할 수 있다 / 과학 (분야)의 주장을 평가할 때 //
                    문장의 주어   주격 관계대명사
For example, / the Harvard researchers / who made claims in
the late 1960s / about the problems with dietary fat, /
예를 들어 / 하버드의 연구자들은 / 1960년대 후반에 주장한 / 식용 지방의 문제점에 관해 /
분사구문을 이끄는 현재분사   perceive A as B: A를 B로 인식하다
leading the nation away from perceiving / sugar as one of the
main causes in health problems, /
전 국민이 인식하지 못하게 만들었는데 / 설탕이 건강 문제의 주요 원인 중 하나라고 /
        문장의 동사
were funded in part / by the sugar industry. //
일부 자금을 지원받았다 / 설탕 업계로부터 // **단서 1** 하버드 연구원들이 설탕 업계 자금을 받고
                                              설탕의 해로움을 축소 주장함
The authors did not reveal / their funding source / to the *New*
                                        관계부사
England Journal of Medicine, / where their ③ influential article
appeared. //
그 저자들은 공개하지 않았는데 / 자금 출처를 / 'New England Journal of Medicine'에 /
거기에 그들의 영향력 있는 논문이 실렸다 // **단서 2** 하버드 연구원들의 논문은 설탕을
                                              많이 사용하는 식습관을 장려하게 됨
Their article shaped / a generation of changes in eating patterns
/ that appears to have ④ discouraged(→ fostered) higher use of
주격 관계대명사 (선행사: Their article)
sugar, /
그들의 논문은 만들어 냈는데 / 식습관 변화의 시대를 / 더 많은 설탕의 사용을
저지한(→ 조장한) 것으로 보이는 /

now widely implicated / as a source of the rise in obesity and
diabetes. //
지금은 널리 알려졌다 / (설탕이) 비만과 당뇨병 증가의 원인과 관련이 있음이 //
                                (not only) A but also B 구문
Stories such as this one / fuel suspicion / — but also lead to
further safeguards / in the scientific process. //
이와 같은 이야기는 / 의심을 부채질했을 뿐만 아니라 / 추가적인 안전장치를 이끌어 냈다 /
과학의 절차에 //
                    부사절에서 「주어+be동사」 생략
Funding ⑤ disclosures, / although not required five decades
        현재완료 수동태   능동태의 목적격 보어
ago, / have since been made compulsory. //
자금 조달의 출처 공개는 / 비록 50년 전에는 요구되지 않았지만 / 이후 의무화되었다 //

- critical ⓐ 비판적인
- objectivity ⓝ 객관성
- biased ⓐ 편향된, 편파적인
- dietary ⓐ 식용의, 식단의
- fund ⓥ 자금을 지원하다
- obesity ⓝ 비만
- diabetes ⓝ 당뇨병
- fuel ⓥ 부채질하다, 연료를 넣다
- suspicion ⓝ 의심
- safeguard ⓝ 안전장치
- disclosure ⓝ 공개
- compulsory ⓐ 의무의

왜 과학이 완전히 신뢰받지 못하는지, 그리고 왜 건강한 회의주의와 비판적 사고가 필수적인지에는 이유가 있다. 전문적인 기준, 객관성에 대한 주장, 동료 검토 과정에도 불구하고, 과학의 실행은 ① 편향적일 수 있다. 모든 전문가가 동일하지 않으며, 그들이 자신의 연구를 동일한 심층 조사를 따르게(거치게) 하는 것도 아니다. 자금 조달의 출처를 아는 것은 과학 (분야)의 주장을 평가할 때 ② 중요할 수 있다. 예를 들어, 1960년대 후반에 식용 지방의 문제점에 관해 주장하여 설탕이 건강 문제의 주요 원인 중 하나라고 전 국민이 인식하지 못하게 만든 하버드의 연구자들은 설탕 업계로부터 일부 자금을 지원받았다. 그 저자들은 'New England Journal of Medicine'에 자금 출처를 공개하지 않았는데, 거기에 그들의 ③ 영향력 있는 논문이 실렸다. 더 많은 설탕의 사용을 ④ 저지한(→ 조장한) 것으로 보이는 그들의 논문은 식습관 변화의 시대를 만들어 냈는데, 지금은 (설탕이) 비만과 당뇨병 증가의 원인과 관련이 있음이 널리 알려졌다. 이와 같은 이야기는 의심을 부채질했을 뿐만 아니라 과학의 절차에 추가적인 안전장치를 이끌어 냈다. 자금 조달의 출처 ⑤ 공개는, 비록 50년 전에는 요구되지 않았지만, 이후 의무화되었다.

왜 정답? ★★★ [정답률 59%]

④ discouraged 저지하다

[더 많은 설탕의 사용을 ④ ~~저지한~~ 것으로 보이는 그들의 논문은 식습관 변화
                    조장한
의 시대를 만들어 냈는데, 지금은 (설탕이) 비만과 당뇨병 증가의 원인과 관
련이 있음이 널리 알려졌다.]

➡ 하버드 연구원들은 설탕 업계에서 자금을 지원받고, 대중들로 하여금 설탕이 건강 문제의 주요 원인이라는 인식을 하지 못하도록 했음 ➡ 이 하버드 연구원들의 논문은 설탕을 많이 사용하는 식습관을 '조장하게' 됨 ▶ 대중의 설탕 사용을 저지했던 (discouraged) 것이 아니라 오히려 조장했다(fostered)고 해야 함

왜 오답?

① biased 편향인

[전문적인 기준, 객관성에 대한 주장, 동료 검토 과정에도 불구하고, 과학의
실행은 ① 편향적일 수 있다.]

➡ In spite of(~에도 불구하고)로 전문적인 기준, 객관성에 대한 주장, 동료 검토 과정이 연결되므로 과학을 전문적, 객관적으로 시행하려고 해도 '편향적'일 수 있다는 흐름은 적절함 ▶ biased는 문맥에 맞음

② important 중요한

[자금 조달의 출처를 아는 것은 과학 (분야)의 주장을 평가할 때 ② 중요할
수 있다.]

➡ 이어지는 예시에서 하버드 연구원들이 설탕 업계에서 자금을 지원받고 설탕의 위험성을 축소 주장한 논문을 소개함 ➡ 자금 조달의 출처를 아는 것이 '중요함' ▶ important는 문맥에 맞음

③ influential 영향력 있는

[그 저자들은 'New England Journal of Medicine'에 자금 출처를 공개
하지 않았는데, 거기에 그들의 ③ 영향력 있는 논문이 실렸다.]

➡ 하버드 연구원들은 설탕 업계의 자금을 지원받아 작성한 논문의 자금 출처를 공개하지 않았음 ➡ 해당 논문은 설탕의 사용을 조장하는 방향으로 대중의 식습관 변화를 끌어낼 정도로 '영향력 있는' 논문이었음 ▶ influential은 문맥에 맞음

⑤ disclosures 공개

[자금 조달의 출처 ⑤ 공개는, 비록 50년 전에는 요구되지 않았지만, 이후 의
무화되었다.]
〔50년 전에는 요구되지 않았다는 내용이 although로 연결됨〕 **꿀팁**

➡ 하버드 연구자들의 자금 출처가 공개되지 않았던 사례 이후, 자금 조달의 투명성을 확보하기 위해 출처 '공개'가 의무화된 것은 과학의 객관성을 지키기 위한 적절한 조치임 ▶ disclosures는 문맥에 맞음

모의고사 **1회**

06 정답 ① *대중음악 확산으로 촉진된 음악의 접근성

The explosion of popular music / in the second half of the
twentieth century / **as well as** the global circulation and
(A as well as B: B뿐만 아니라 A도)
dissemination of music / by the creative industries /
대중음악의 폭발적 증가는 / 20세기 후반의 / 전 세계적 음악 유통과 보급뿐만 아니라 / 창작
산업계의 /
문장의 본동사
propelled a new understanding / of **accessibility** in relation to
music. // 새로운 이해를 촉진했다 / 음악과 관련된 접근성에 대한 //

Suddenly, in the 1950s, / anyone could **pick up** spoons, a couple
of pans, a second-hand guitar / and **start** a band. /
병렬 구조 (could 뒤에 연결)
갑자기, 1950년대에 / 누구나 숟가락, 냄비 몇 개, 중고 기타를 집어 들고 / 밴드를 시작할 수
있었다 //

(not only) A but also B 구문
This **led** to specific genres / such as skiffle, / **but also**, more
└ 병렬 구조 (동사) ┐
generally, / **reflected** a **much** more relaxed and inclusive attitude
비교급 강조
/ to music making. //
이는 특정 장르로 이어졌을 뿐만 아니라 / 스키플(skiffle)과 같은 / 또한, 더 일반적으로는 /
훨씬 더 여유롭고 포용적인 태도를 반영했다 / 음악 제작에 대한 //

병렬 구조 (had 뒤에 연결)
While ordinary people had always **sung** / and **made** music, / the
과거시제 수동태
popular music movement / **was driven** by a spirit of rebellion
and freedom. // 평범한 사람들이 항상 노래를 부르고 / 음악을 만들어 왔지만 /
대중음악 운동은 / 저항과 자유의 정신에 의해 촉진되었다 //

소유격 관계대명사
This approach / led to the punk movement, / **whose** musicians
가목적어   to be의 의미상 주어 진목적어 (to부정사)
even made **it** a condition / **for their music to be** non-virtuosic /
and accessible to all / in the 1970s. [단서 1] 음악가들은 자신의 전문성이 높지 않고
누구나 접근할 수 있는 음악을 필수 조건으로 삼음
이러한 접근 방식은 / 펑크 운동으로 이어졌으며 / 이 음악가들은 심지어 필수 요건으로
삼았다 / 자신들의 음악이 전문성이 높지 않고 / 누구나 접근할 수 있는 것을 / 1970년대에 //
주격 관계대명사   과거완료 수동태
Groups **who had been entirely excluded** from music / revelled
형용사적 용법 (opportunities 수식) [단서 2] 음악에서 배제되었던 집단도
in opportunities **to create**.   음악을 창작할 수 있게 됨
음악에서 완전히 배제되었던 집단들이 / 창작의 기회를 만끽했다 //

This led to a sense of novelty and empowerment / in and beyond
the music sphere. //
이는 참신성과 자율성이라는 인식으로 이어졌다 / 음악계 안팎에서 //

- explosion ⓝ 폭발적인 증가   • circulation ⓝ 유통, 순환
- propel ⓥ 촉진하다   • second-hand 중고의
- inclusive ⓐ 포용적인   • rebellion ⓝ 저항
- punk ⓝ ((음악의 장르)) 펑크   • condition ⓝ 조건, 필수 요건
- novelty ⓝ 참신성   • empowerment ⓝ 자율성
- sphere ⓝ 계, 영역   • accessibility ⓝ 접근성
- responsibility ⓝ 책임감   • preservation ⓝ 보존
- profitability ⓝ 수익성

창작 산업계의 전 세계적 음악 유통과 보급뿐만 아니라 20세기 후반의 대
중음악의 폭발적 증가는 음악과 관련된 **접근성**에 대한 새로운 이해를 촉진
했다. 갑자기, 1950년대에, 누구나 숟가락, 냄비 몇 개, 중고 기타를 집어
들고 밴드를 시작할 수 있었다. 이는 스키플(skiffle)과 같은 특정 장르로
이어졌을 뿐만 아니라, 또한, 더 일반적으로는, 음악 제작에 대한 훨씬 더
여유롭고 포용적인 태도를 반영했다. 평범한 사람들이 항상 노래를 부르고
음악을 만들어 왔지만, 대중음악 운동은 저항과 자유의 정신에 의해 촉
진되었다. 이러한 접근 방식은 펑크 운동으로 이어졌으며, 1970년대에 이
음악가들은 심지어 자신들의 음악이 전문성이 높지 않고 누구나 접근할 수
있는 것을 필수 요건으로 삼았다. 음악에서 완전히 배제되었던 집단들이
창작의 기회를 만끽했다. 이는 음악계 안팎에서 참신성과 자율성이라는 인
식으로 이어졌다.

다음 빈칸에 들어갈 말로 가장 적절한 것을 고르시오.

① accessibility 포용성과 접근 가능성에 대한   ② responsibility 언급되지 않음
접근성 인식을 새롭게 촉진함   책임감
③ exchange 교환이나 맞바꿈에 관한 내용은   ④ preservation 언급되지 않음
교환 언급되지 않음   보존
⑤ profitability 언급되지 않음
수익성

왜 정답 ? ★★★ [정답률 67%]

빈칸은 '대중음악의 증가로 인해 음악과 관련하여 새로운 이해가 촉진된' 것으로, 대중
음악이 발달하면서 사람들이 새롭게 이해하게 된 개념이 무엇인지를 찾아야 한다.

➡ 음악가들은 자신의 전문성이 높지 않고 누구나 접근할 수 있는 음악을 필수 조건으
로 삼았다고 설명하고 있다. [단서 1]
이는 음악에서 배제되었던 집단도 음악을 창작할 수 있게 하였으며, [단서 2]
참신성과 자율성이라는 인식으로 이어졌다고 설명하고 있다. ▶ 따라서 대중음악은
포용적이면서도 누구나 접근할 수 있는 음악, 모두를 아우르면서도 자율적인 음악
이라는 인식을 불러일으켰으므로, 빈칸에 들어갈 말은 ① '접근성'이다.

왜 오답 ?

② 대중음악이 저항과 자유의 정신에 의해 촉진되었다는 언급은 있었지만, 책임감에
관한 내용은 언급되지 않았다.
③ 대중음악의 교환이나 맞바꿈에 관한 내용은 언급되지 않았다.
④ 대중음악의 보존에 관한 내용은 언급되지 않았다.
⑤ 대중음악의 수익성에 관한 내용은 언급되지 않았다.

07 정답 ⑤ *과학자들이 꾸준히 성과를 낼 수 있는 이유

부정어
Great scientists are / **seldom** one-hit wonders. //
위대한 과학자가 / 반짝 스타인 경우는 드물다 [단서 1] 위대한 과학자는 한 번의
성과로만 그치지 않음
Newton is a prime example: / beyond the Newtonian mechanics,
/ he developed / the theory of gravitation, calculus, laws of
motion, and optimization. //
뉴턴이 대표적인 예인데 / 뉴턴 역학을 넘어 / 그는 발전시켰다 / 중력 이론, 미적분학, 운동
법칙 및 최적화를 //

수동태 동사
In fact, / well-known scientists **are** often **involved** / in multiple
discoveries, / **a phenomenon potentially explained by the**
동격의 명사구
Matthew effect. 과거분사구 (phenomenon 수식)
사실 / 잘 알려진 과학자들은 종종 관여하는데 / 여러 발견에 / 이는 아마도 매튜 효과로
설명되는 현상일 것이다 //

Indeed, / an initial success **may offer** a scientist legitimacy, /
병렬 구조(may 뒤에 연결)
improve peer perception, / **provide** knowledge of **how to score**
and win, /   how to-v: ~하는 법
실제로 / 최초의 성공은 과학자에게 정당성을 부여하고 / 동료들의 인식을 향상시키며 /
어떻게 성과를 내고 성공하는지에 대한 지식을 제공하고 /

병렬 구조(may 뒤에 연결)
enhance social status, / and **attract** resources and quality
collaborators, / **each of these payoffs** further **increasing** / her
분사구문의 주어 분사구문
odds of scoring another win. // [단서 2] 최초의 성공 덕분에 이후에
다른 성공을 거둘 가능성이 높아짐
사회적 지위를 높이며 / 자원과 우수한 협력자를 끌어당기는데 / 이러한 각각의 보상들은 더욱
높여 준다 / 과학자가 또 다른 성공을 거둘 가능성을 //

Yet, there is an appealing alternative explanation: /
그러나, 매력적인 대안이 되는 설명이 있는데 / [단서 3] 매튜 효과의 대안으로, 그들이 유난히
재능이 있기 때문이라고 설명하기도 함
Great scientists have multiple hits / and consistently succeed /
in their scientific endeavors / simply because they're exceptionally
talented. //
위대한 과학자들이 여러 번의 성공을 거두고 / 지속적으로 성과를 이루는데 / 과학적 노력에서
/ 그 이유는 단지 그들이 유난히 재능이 있기 때문이라는 것이다 //

현재완료
Therefore, future success again goes / to **those who have had**
success earlier, /   those who: ~한 사람들
따라서, 미래의 성공이 다시 돌아가는데 / 이전에 성공한 적이 있는 사람에게 /
과거분사구 (advantages 수식)
not because of advantages / **offered by the previous success**,
not A but B 구문
/ **but** because the earlier success / was **indicative of a hidden**
talent. // [단서 4] 이 설명에 따르면, 여러 번 성공하는 이유는
이전의 성공으로 얻은 이점 때문이 아님
이는 이점 때문이 '아니라' / 이전의 성공으로 인해 제공된 / 이전의 성공이 / 숨겨진 재능을
나타내는 것이기 때문이다 //

The Matthew effect posits / **that** success *alone* increases / the
future probability of success, / **raising the question:** /
목적어절 접속사
분사구문
매튜 효과는 상정하며 / 성공은 '하나만으로' 높인다고 / 미래의 성공 확률을 / 다음과 같은
의문을 제기한다 /

Does status dictate outcomes, / or does it simply reflect / an
underlying talent or quality? //
지위가 결과를 좌우하는 것일까 / 아니면 그것은 단순히 반영하는 것일까 / 근본적인 재능이나
자질을 //

In other words, / is there really a Matthew effect after all? //
다시 말하면 / 결론적으로 매튜 효과가 정말로 존재하는 것일까 //

- one-hit wonder 반짝 스타 ・ prime ⓐ 주요한, 대표적인
- mechanics ⓝ 역학 ・ gravitation ⓝ 중력
- calculus ⓝ 미적분학 ・ optimization ⓝ 최적화
- legitimacy ⓝ 정당성 ・ quality ⓐ 고급의, 우수한
- collaborator ⓝ 협력자 ・ payoff ⓝ 보상 ・ odds ⓝ 가능성
- appealing ⓐ 매력적인 ・ alternative ⓐ 대안의
- endeavor ⓝ 노력 ・ exceptionally ⓐⓓ 유난히, 이례적으로
- probability ⓝ 확률 ・ dictate ⓥ 좌우하다, 결정하다
- inseparable ⓐ 분리될 수 없는 ・ indicative ⓐ 나타내는

위대한 과학자가 반짝 스타인 경우는 드물다. 뉴턴이 대표적인 예인데, 그
는 뉴턴 역학을 넘어 중력 이론, 미적분학, 운동 법칙 및 최적화를 발전시
켰다. 사실, 잘 알려진 과학자들은 종종 여러 발견에 관여하는데, 이는 아
마도 매튜 효과로 설명되는 현상일 것이다. 실제로, 최초의 성공은 과학자
에게 정당성을 부여하고, 동료들의 인식을 향상시키며, 어떻게 성과를 내
고 성공하는지에 대한 지식을 제공하고, 사회적 지위를 높이며, 자원과 우
수한 협력자를 끌어들이는데, 이러한 각각의 보상들은 과학자가 또 다른
성공을 거둘 가능성을 더욱 높여 준다. 그러나, 매력적인 대안이 되는 설명
이 있는데, 위대한 과학자들이 여러 번의 성공을 거두고 지속적으로 과학
적 노력에서 성과를 이루는 이유는 단지 그들이 유난히 재능이 있기 때문
이라는 것이다. 따라서, 미래의 성공이 이전에 성공한 적이 있는 사람에게
다시 돌아가는데, 이는 이전의 성공으로 인해 제공된 이점 때문이 '아니라',
이전의 성공이 **숨겨진 재능을 나타내는** (것이기) 때문이다. 매튜 효과는 성
공은 '(그) 하나만으로' 미래의 성공 확률을 높인다고 상정하며, 다음과 같
은 의문을 제기한다. 지위가 결과를 좌우하는 것일까, 아니면 그것은 근본
적인 재능이나 자질을 단순히 반영하는 것일까? 다시 말하면, 결론적으로
매튜 효과가 정말로 존재하는 것일까?

다음 빈칸에 들어갈 말로 가장 적절한 것을 고르시오. [3점]
① inseparable from consistent efforts 지속적인 노력에 관한 언급은 없음
지속적인 노력으로부터 분리될 수 없는
② attributed to talented collaborators
재능이 있는 협력자들 덕분인
③ dependent on financial resources ──매튜 효과에 관한 설명임
재정적 자원에 의존하는
④ driven by societal recognition
사회적 인식으로 촉진된
⑤ indicative of a hidden talent 그들이 유달리 재능이 있기 때문이라고 설명함
숨겨진 재능을 나타내는

| 문제 풀이 순서 | ★★★ [정답률 34%]

1st 빈칸이 포함된 문장을 읽고, 빈칸에 들어갈 말에 대한 단서를 얻는다.

빈칸 문장
따라서(Therefore), 미래의 성공이 이전에 성공한 적이 있는 사
람에게 다시 돌아가는데, 이는 이전의 성공으로 인해 제공된 이
점 때문이 '아니라', 이전의 성공이 (것이기) 때문이다.

➡ 이전에 성공했던 사람이 미래에도 다시 성공하게 되는데, 그 이유가 무엇인지에 관
한 부분이 빈칸임 ➡ 이전 성공으로 인해 얻은 이점 때문이 아니라, 이전 성공이 어
떠했기 때문인지를 묻고 있음 ➡ '따라서(Therefore)'라는 표현으로 빈칸 문장이 시
작되고 있으므로, 빈칸은 앞 문장의 내용과 연결되고 있을 것임

▶ 빈칸을 채우려면 미래의 성공이 이전에 성공했던 사람에게 다시 돌아가는 이유
를 앞 문장에서 무엇 때문이라고 설명하고 있는지를 살펴보아야 한다.

2nd 글을 마저 읽으며 반복적인 성공의 이유를 어떻게 설명하고 있는지 찾는다.

위대한 과학자는 여러 번 성공의 경험을 가짐
매튜 효과: 이는 첫 성공이 그들의 지위와 명성을 높여 이후의 성공으로 이어질 가능성
을 올려주기 때문임
매튜 효과의 대안: 위대한 과학자들이 유난히 재능이 있기 때문임
▶ 빈칸은 매튜 효과의 대안에 대해 설명하는 부분이므로, 저명한 과학자들이 여러 번
성공하는 이유는 이전의 성공으로 얻은 이점 때문이 아니라, 이전의 성공이 ⑤ '숨겨진
재능을 나타내는' 것임

| 선택지 분석 |

① 과학자들의 꾸준한 성공이 그들의 지속적인 노력이라는 언급은 없었다.
② 과학자들의 꾸준한 성공이 이전 성공 덕분에 협력자들을 끌어들인 덕분이라는 설명
은 매튜 효과에 관한 것이다.
③ 과학자들의 꾸준한 성공이 이전 성공 덕분에 재정적 자원을 끌어들인 덕분이라는
설명은 매튜 효과에 관한 것이다.
④ 과학자들의 꾸준한 성공이 이전 성공 덕분에 사회적 지위가 높아진 덕분이라는 설
명은 매튜 효과에 관한 것이다.
⑤ 과학자들의 꾸준한 성공에 대한 대안적인 설명으로 그들이 유달리 재능이 있기 때
문이라고 소개했다.

1회 08 정답 ② *식량 안보를 달성하기 위한 메커니즘

The governments / of virtually **every country** on the planet /
전치사 to every + 단수 명사
attach great importance / **to** achieving food security /
정부는 / 사실상 전 세계 모든 국가의 / 큰 중요성을 부여하며 / 식량 안보를 달성하는 것에 /
철과 절을 잇는 등위접속사 현재완료 수동태
and a wide variety of mechanisms / **have been developed** /
부사적 용법(목적)
to realize this goal. //
다양한 메커니즘이 / 개발되었다 / 이 목표를 실현하기 위해 //

단서 1 (B)의 식량 자급자족의 채택과 상반되는 내용이 이어짐
(A)However, food security does not require food self-sufficiency
/ because countries can import food items / **not easily produced**
과거분사구(items 수식)
within the country. // 그러나, 식량 안보는 식량 자급자족을 (반드시) 필요로 하지
않는데 / 이는 국가가 식품을 수입할 수 있기 때문이다 / 자국 내에서 쉽게 생산되지 않는 //

Agricultural products are, after all, / highly sensitive to climatic,
주격 관계대명사
soil and other conditions / **that** tend to vary around the world. //
어쨌든, 농산물은 / 기후, 토양, 그 외 다른 조건에 매우 민감하다 / 전 세계적으로 국가에 따라
달라지는 //
단서 2 주어진 글에서 언급한 식량 안보를
앞에 목적격 관계대명사 생략 달성하려는 정부가 직면하는 첫 번째 문제
(B) The first issue **governments face** / in achieving national food
목적어절 접속사
security / is the problem of insuring / **that** adequate amounts of
food are available / to the resident population. //
정부가 직면하는 첫 번째 문제는 / 국가 식량 안보를 달성하는 데 있어 / 보장하는 것이다 /
충분한 양의 식량이 제공되도록 / 거주민에게 // 단서 3 일부 정부는 식량 안보를 달성하기 위해
현재완료 자급자족이라는 목표를 설정함
Some governments **have set** goals / of food self-sufficiency, /
which means / most **if not all** of the food available in a country /
계속적 용법의 주격 관계대명사 '전부는 아니더라도' (삽입구)
comes from the domestic farming system. //
일부 정부는 목표를 설정했는데 / 식량 자급자족이라는 / 이는 의미한다 / 한 국가에서 구할 수
있는 식량의 전부는 아니더라도 대부분이 / 국내 농업 시스템에서 나온다는 것을 //

(C) Even countries / with extremely productive agricultural
sectors / are not fully self-sufficient / in all food items. //
국가도 / 매우 생산성이 높은 농경 지역을 보유한 / 완전히 자급자족할 수 있는 것은 아니다 /
모든 식품에서 //
단서 4 (A)의 자급자족이 필수 조건이 아니라는 내용에 대한 구체적인 예시임
The United States, for example, / depends on imports / for its
supply of coffee, tea, bananas and other tropical products. //
예를 들어, 미국은 / 수입품에 의존한다 / 커피, 차, 바나나 및 다른 열대 지역 (농)산물의
공급을 //
수동태 동사
In general, / the problem of assuring adequate food supplies / **is**
by -ing: ~함으로써 both A and B 구문
solved by relying on / **both** domestic production **and** imports. //
일반적으로 / 적절한 식량 공급을 보장하는 문제는 / 의존함으로써 해결된다 / 국내 생산과
수입에 모두 //

- virtually @ 사실상   • security ⓝ 안보
- self-sufficiency 자급자족   • agricultural ⓐ 농사의
- sensitive ⓐ 민감한   • climatic ⓐ 기후의   • soil ⓝ 토양
- vary ⓥ 다양하다, 달라지다   • issue ⓝ 문제, 이슈
- insure ⓥ 보장하다   • adequate ⓐ 적절한   • resident ⓐ 거주하는
- domestic ⓐ 국내의   • productive ⓐ 생산적인
- sector ⓝ 구역, 지역   • import ⓝ 수입   • supply ⓝ 공급
- tropical ⓐ 열대의   • assure ⓥ 보장하다

사실상 전 세계 모든 국가의 정부는 식량 안보를 달성하는 것에 큰 중요성을 부여하며, 이 목표를 실현하기 위해 다양한 메커니즘이 개발되었다. (B) 정부가 국가 식량 안보를 달성하는 데 있어 직면하는 첫 번째 문제는 거주민에게 충분한 양의 식량이 제공되도록 보장하는 것이다. 일부 정부는 식량 자급자족이라는 목표를 설정했는데, 이는 한 국가에서 구할 수 있는 식량의 전부는 아니더라도 대부분이 국내 농업 시스템에서 나온다는 것을 의미한다. (A) 그러나, 식량 안보는 식량 자급자족을 (반드시) 필요로 하지 않는데 이는 국가가 자국 내에서 쉽게 생산되지 않는 식품을 수입할 수 있기 때문이다. 어쨌든, 농산물은 전 세계적으로 국가에 따라 달라지는 기후, 토양, 그 외 다른 조건에 매우 민감하다. (C) 매우 생산성이 높은 농경 지역을 보유한 국가도 모든 식품에서 완전히 자급자족할 수 있는 것은 아니다. 예를 들어, 미국은, 커피, 차, 바나나 및 다른 열대 지역 (농)산물의 공급을 수입품에 의존한다. 일반적으로, 적절한 식량 공급을 보장하는 문제는 국내 생산과 수입에 모두 의존함으로써 해결된다.

주어진 글 다음에 이어질 글의 순서로 가장 적절한 것을 고르시오. [3점]

① (A) — (C) — (B) (A)의 자급자족에 관한 내용과 상반된 내용이 주어진 글에 없음
② (B) — (A) — (C) (B) 식량 안보를 위해 자급자족을 채택하기도 함 — (A) 하지만 자급자족이 식량 안보에 필수는 아님 — (C) 미국의 경우 수입과 국내 생산 모두에 의존하고 있음
③ (B) — (C) — (A)
④ (C) — (A) — (B) (C)는 (A)의 자급자족이 필수 조건이 아니라는 내용의 예시임
⑤ (C) — (B) — (A)

| **문제 풀이 순서** | ★★★ [정답률 61%]

1st 각 문단의 내용을 파악하고, 글의 논리적인 순서를 추론한다.

주어진 글: 사실상 전 세계 모든 국가의 정부는 식량 안보를 달성하는 것에 큰 중요성을 부여하며, 이 목표를 실현하기 위해 다양한 메커니즘이 개발되었다.

→ **주어진 글 뒤:** 여러 국가가 식량 안보를 달성하기 위해 내세운 메커니즘이 소개될 것이다.

(A): 그러나(However), 식량 안보는 식량 자급자족을 (반드시) 필요로 하지 않는데 이는 국가가 자국 내에서 쉽게 생산되지 않는 식품을 수입할 수 있기 때문이다. 어쨌든, 농산물은 전 세계적으로 국가에 따라 달라지는 기후, 토양, 그 외 다른 조건에 매우 민감하다.

→ **(A) 앞:** '그러나(However)'로 상반되는 내용을 설명하고 있으므로, 식량 자급자족을 목표로 한다는 내용이 제시되었을 것이다.

▶ 해당 내용이 없는 주어진 글 바로 뒤에 (A)가 올 수 없음

(A) 뒤: 식품은 자급자족뿐만 아니라 수입을 통해서도 해결될 수 있다고 설명하고 있으므로, 이와 관련된 구체적인 예시가 이어질 것이다.

(B): 정부가 국가 식량 안보를 달성하는 데 있어 직면하는 첫 번째 문제는 거주민에게 충분한 양의 식량이 제공되도록 보장하는 것이다. 일부 정부는 식량 자급자족이라는 목표를 설정했는데, 이는 한 국가에서 구할 수 있는 식량의 전부는 아니더라도 대부분이 국내 농업 시스템에서 나온다는 것을 의미한다.

→ **(B) 앞:** 국가가 식량 안보를 달성하고자 한다는 목표가 제시되었을 것이다.

▶ 주어진 글에서 말했던 식량 안보의 중요성에 대해 '식량 자급자족'이라는 메커니즘을 채택한 국가가 있음을 소개함 (순서: 주어진 글 → (B))

(B) 뒤: 식량 안보를 위한 메커니즘으로 식량 자급자족을 설명했으므로, However로 꼭 필요한 것은 아니라고 설명하는 (A)가 (B) 뒤에 이어질 것이다.

▶ 순서: 주어진 글 → (B) → (A)

(C): 매우 생산성이 높은 농경 지역을 보유한 국가도 모든 식품에서 완전히 자급자족할 수 있는 것은 아니다. 예를 들어(for example), 미국은, 커피, 차, 바나나 및 다른 열대 지역 (농)산물의 공급을 수입품에 의존한다. 일반적으로, 적절한 식량 공급을 보장하는 문제는 국내 생산과 수입에 모두 의존함으로써 해결된다.

→ **(C) 앞:** 미국의 예시를 들며 생산성이 높은 국가에서도 모든 식품을 완전히 자급자족할 수 없다고 설명하고 있으므로, 수입이라는 대체 수단을 설명했던 내용이 제시되었을 것이다.

▶ 식량 안보를 위해서는 수입이라는 경로도 있기 때문에 자급자족할 필요는 없다는 (A)의 내용에 이어, 수입과 국내 생산 모두에 의존함으로써 식량 공급을 보장하는 미국의 예시를 구체적으로 제시함 (순서: 주어진 글 → (B) → (A) → (C))

2nd 글이 한눈에 들어오도록 정리하여 정답을 확인한다.

주어진 글: 식량 안보를 달성하기 위한 각국의 다양한 메커니즘이 개발되었다.

→ **(B):** 일부 정부는 모든 국민에게 식량이 제공되도록 하는 식량 안보를 달성하기 위해 자급자족이라는 목표를 설정했다.

→ **(A):** 하지만 식량 안보는 반드시 자급자족이어야만 하는 것은 아닌데, 자국 내 생산이 불가능한 식품은 수입할 수도 있기 때문이다.

→ **(C):** 생산성이 높은 국가도 모든 식품을 자급자족할 수 있는 것은 아니며, 미국도 수입과 국내 생산 모두에 의존하며 식량 안보를 확보하고 있다.

▶ 주어진 글 다음에 이어질 글의 순서는 (B) → (A) → (C)이므로 정답은 ②임

⓵09 정답 ③ *과학 지식의 형성 과정과 베이즈 정리

글의 흐름으로 보아, 주어진 문장이 들어가기에 가장 적절한 곳을 고르시오. [3점]

Knowledge is information / that has demonstrated its usefulness. // **단서1** 지식은 유용성이 입증된 정보임
지식은 정보이다 / 자신의 유용성을 입증한 //

It is important to recognize / that although science is a rule-based procedure, / it is very much a creative process. //
인식하는 것이 중요하다 / 비록 과학은 규칙에 기반한 절차이지만 / 매우 창의적인 과정임을 //

(①) A conjecture is a philosophical invention, / cooked up rather mystically / by the mind through the mental computation / we call careful contemplation. //
추론은 철학적 발명으로 / 다소 신비롭게 만들어진 것이다 / 머릿속 계산을 거쳐 사고를 통해 / 우리가 신중한 숙고라 부르는 //

(②) However, / until the hypothesis is tested against reality, / it is not yet truly knowledge; / it is just information / that represents speculation. // **단서2** 가설이 검증될 때까지는 진정한 지식이 아니라 정보에 불과함
그러나 / 가설이 현실에 비추어 검증되기 전에는 / 그것은 아직 진정한 지식이 아니며 / 그것은 단지 정보에 불과하다 / 추측을 나타내는 // **단서3** 주어진 문장의 '지식'을 가리킴

(③) It is what is left over / after cycles of experimental testing have eliminated false theories. //
그것(지식)은 남은 것이다 / 수차례의 실험적 검증이 잘못된 이론들을 제거한 후 //

(④) As scientists continually test their hypotheses / and modify their models / to account for new and surprising data, /
과학자들이 끊임없이 가설을 검증하고 / 그들의 모델을 수정함에 따라 / 새롭고 놀라운 데이터를 설명하기 위해 /

a kind of "learning loop" emerges / that statisticians call Bayesian updating. //
일종의 '학습 루프'가 나타난다 / 통계학자들이 '베이지안 업데이팅'이라고 부르는 //

(⑤) Based on Bayes' Rule, / developed by eighteenth-century English statistician and philosopher Thomas Bayes, /
베이즈 정리에 기초하여 / 18세기 영국의 통계학자이자 철학자였던 Thomas Bayes가 개발한 /

Bayesian updating refers to a mathematical process / whereby an **accepted** theory or predictive model / gets increasingly accurate / through the repetitive testing / of competing variants of that theory. //
과거분사 (theory 수식)
베이지안 업데이팅은 수학적 과정을 일컫는다 / 수용된 이론이나 예측 모델이 / 점점 더 정확해지는 / 반복적으로 검증하는 과정을 통해 / 그 이론의 다양한 변형을 //

- demonstrate ⓥ 입증하다
- usefulness ⓝ 유용성
- rule-based 규칙에 기반한
- procedure ⓝ 절차, 과정
- cook up 만들어내다
- mystically 🔤 신비롭게
- computation ⓝ 계산
- hypothesis ⓝ 가설
- experimental ⓐ 실험의
- eliminate ⓥ 제거하다
- modify ⓥ 수정하다
- account for ~을 설명하다
- statistician ⓝ 통계학자
- whereby 🔤 (그것에 의하여) ~하는
- predictive ⓐ 예측의
- repetitive ⓐ 반복적인
- variant ⓝ 변형

비록 과학은 규칙에 기반한 절차이지만, 매우 창의적인 과정임을 인식하는 것이 중요하다. (①) 추론은 철학적 발명으로, 우리가 신중한 숙고라 부르는 머릿속 계산을 거쳐 사고를 통해 다소 신비롭게 만들어진 것이다. (②) 그러나, 가설이 현실에 비추어 검증되기 전에는, 그것은 아직 진정한 지식이 아니며, 그것은 단지 추측을 나타내는 정보에 불과하다. (③ 지식은 자신의 유용성을 입증한 정보이다.) 그것(지식)은 수차례의 실험적 검증이 잘못된 이론들을 제거한 후 남은 것이다. (④) 과학자들이 끊임없이 가설을 검증하고 새롭고 놀라운 데이터를 설명하기 위해 그들의 모델을 수정함에 따라, 통계학자들이 '베이지안 업데이팅'이라고 부르는 일종의 '학습 루프'가 나타난다. (⑤) 18세기 영국의 통계학자이자 철학자였던 Thomas Bayes가 개발한 베이즈 정리에 기초하여, 베이지안 업데이팅은 수용된 이론이나 예측 모델이 그 이론의 다양한 변형을 반복적으로 검증하는 과정을 통해 점점 더 정확해지는 수학적 과정을 일컫는다.

| 문제 풀이 순서 | ★★★ [정답률 50%]

1st 주어진 문장을 해석하고, 앞뒤에 어떤 내용이 올지 생각한다.
┌ Knowledge is information that has demonstrated its usefulness.
└ 지식은 자신의 유용성을 입증한 정보이다.
➡ 유용성을 입증한 정보만이 지식이 된다.
▶ 주어진 문장이 들어갈 곳: 정보가 지식이 되는 조건을 설명한 곳이자, 지식에 대한 설명이 이어지는 곳

2nd 각 선택지의 앞뒤 흐름이 매끄러운지 확인한다.

①의 앞 문장과 뒤 문장
┌ 앞 문장: 비록 과학은 규칙에 기반한 절차이지만, 매우 창의적인 과정이라는 것을 인식하는 것이 중요하다.
│ 뒤 문장: 추론은 철학적 발명으로, 우리가 신중한 숙고라 부르는 머릿속 계산
└ 을 거쳐 사고를 통해 다소 신비롭게 만들어진 것이다.
➡ 과학은 단순히 규칙만 따르는 것이 아니라, 창의력이 필요하다는 앞 문장에 이어 추론은 복잡한 사고 과정을 통해 만들어지는 창의적인 활동이라는 내용으로 자연스럽게 이어진다. ▶ 주어진 문장이 ①에 들어갈 수 없음

②의 앞 문장과 뒤 문장
┌ 앞 문장: ①의 뒤 문장과 같음
│ 뒤 문장: 그러나(However), 가설이 현실에 비추어 검증되기 전에는, 그것은 아직 진정한 지식이 아니며, 그것은 단지 추측을 나타내는 정보에 불과
└ 하다.
➡ 추론한 가설은 검증이 되어야 추측성 정보에서 진정한 지식이 된다는 내용이므로, 추론은 철학적으로 만들어졌다는 앞 문장에 '그러나'로 자연스럽게 이어진다.
▶ 주어진 문장이 ②에 들어갈 수 없음

③의 앞 문장과 뒤 문장
┌ 앞 문장: ②의 뒤 문장과 같음
│ 뒤 문장: 그것(지식)은 수차례의 실험적 검증이 잘못된 이론들을 제거한 후
└ 남은 것이다.
➡ '여러 검증을 통해 잘못된 이론들을 제거한 후 남은 것'은 문맥상 '지식'을 가리키므로, 앞 문장에서 설명하고 있는 '가설'을 가리키는 것이 아니다.
▶ 주어진 문장에서 '지식'은 여러 정보 중 유용성이 입증된 것이라고 정의하고 있으므로, 주어진 문장은 지식에 대한 설명이 이어지는 ③에 들어가야 함

④의 앞 문장과 뒤 문장
┌ 앞 문장: ③의 뒤 문장과 같음
│ 뒤 문장: 과학자들이 끊임없이 가설을 검증하고 새롭고 놀라운 데이터를 설명하기 위해 그들의 모델을 수정함에 따라, 통계학자들이 '베이지안 업데이팅'
└ 이라고 부르는 일종의 '학습 루프'가 나타난다.
➡ 과학자들은 실험 결과에 따라 계속 검증 모델을 바꾸는 '베이지안 업데이팅'을 한다는 내용이므로, 지식은 가설을 끊임없이 검증하여 다듬어진 것이라는 앞 문장에 대한 구체적인 절차를 설명하고 있다. ▶ 주어진 문장이 ④에 들어갈 수 없음

⑤의 앞 문장과 뒤 문장
┌ 앞 문장: ④의 뒤 문장과 같음
│ 뒤 문장: 18세기 영국의 통계학자이자 철학자였던 Thomas Bayes가 개발한 베이즈 정리에 기초하여, 베이지안 업데이팅은 수용된 이론이나 예측 모델이 그 이론의 다양한 변형을 반복적으로 검증하는 과정을 통해 점점 더 정
└ 확해지는 수학적 과정을 일컫는다.
➡ '베이지안 업데이팅'은 반복 검증을 통해 이론이 점점 정확해지는 수학적 과정이라는 내용이므로, 앞 문장의 베이즈의 학습 루프를 구체적으로 설명하고 있다.
▶ 주어진 문장이 ⑤에 들어갈 수 없음

1회 10 정답 ① *언어 차용의 일방향성

Quite often / the interaction between groups / is socially unequal, / 종종 / 집단 간의 상호 작용은 / 사회적으로 불평등하며 /
절과 절을 잇는 등위접속사 / 동격절 접속사
and this is reflected in the fact / that in many cases / borrowing of words or constructions / goes mostly or entirely in one direction, / 이는 사실에 반영된다 / 많은 경우에 / 단어 또는 구조의 차용이 / 대부분 혹은 완전히 한 방향으로 이동한다는 /
from A to B: A에서 B로
from the more powerful or prestigious group / to the less favored one. // **단서 1** 집단 간의 상호 작용이 불평등하다는 것은 언어가 지배 집단에서 종속 집단으로 차용된다는 사실로 나타남
= group
즉 더 강하거나 권력을 가진 집단에서 / 혜택을 덜 받는 집단 쪽 //
과거분사구 (groups 수식)
The languages of socially subordinated groups / may from quite an early period of contact provide / terminology for objects or practices / 사회적으로 종속된 집단의 언어가 / (집단 간) 접촉의 상당히 이른 시기부터 제공할 수도 있지만 / 물건이나 관습에 대한 용어를 /
「전치사+관계대명사」
with which speakers of the more powerful group were previously unfamiliar, / but the effects of contact in that direction / may not progress any further than this. // 더 강한 권력을 가진 집단의 화자들이 전에 잘 몰랐던 / 그런 방향으로의 접촉의 결과는 / 이것 이상 진전되지는 않을 수도 있다 //

In some cases, / as with the Dharug language of Sydney, Australia, / the source of some of the earliest loans / from Indigenous Australian languages into English, /
from A (in)to B: A에서 B(내)로
몇몇 경우에는 / 호주 시드니의 Dharug 언어와 같은 / 몇몇 최초의 차용 출처인 / 호주 토착 언어에서 영어로의 /

전치사
the fate of the language system / is extinction / after the obliteration of many of its speakers. // **단서 2** 종속 집단의 언어 체계는 화자의 소멸과 함께 멸종하는 운명을 맞이함
그러한 언어 체계(사회적으로 종속된 집단의 언어 체계)의 운명은 / 멸종하는 것이었다 / 화자들 중 다수가 소멸되고 나면 //

The remainder shifted to varieties of English, / the language of
／ 동격
the people / who had suppressed them. //
주격 관계대명사   과거완료
남은 사람들은 영어의 다양한 변종으로 전환했다 / 사람들의 언어인 / 그들을 억압했던 //

> → Language borrowing / from dominant to subordinate
> from A to B 구문
> groups / reflects social (A) inequality, /
> 언어 차용은 / 지배 집단으로부터 종속 집단으로의 / 사회적 불평등을 반영하는데 /
> 계속적 용법의 관계부사   = subordinate groups
> where the language systems of the latter / often (B) vanish
> 부사절 접속사 (양보)   may have p.p.: ~이었을지도 모른다
> / even though they may have provided some terms, / as
> 부사절에서
> exemplified by Dharug in Australia. //   「주어 + be동사」생략
> 후자의 언어 체계는 / 종종 사라진다 / 몇몇 용어를 제공하기도 했지만 / 호주의 Dharug
> 언어의 예시에서 보이듯이 //

- construction ⓝ 구조   - favored ⓐ 혜택을 받고 있는
- progress ⓥ 진전되다   - loan ⓝ 차용, 빌림
- indigenous ⓐ 토착의   - fate ⓝ 운명   - extinction ⓝ 멸종
- suppress ⓥ 억압하다   - vanish ⓥ 사라지다
- imbalance ⓝ 불균형   - prevail ⓥ 널리 퍼지다
- integration ⓝ 통합   - prosper ⓥ 번영하다

종종 집단 간의 상호 작용은 사회적으로 불평등하며, 이는 많은 경우에 단
어 또는 구조의 차용이 대부분 혹은 완전히 한 방향, 즉 더 강하거나 권력
을 가진 집단에서 혜택을 덜 받는 집단 쪽으로 이동한다는 사실에 반영된
다. (집단 간) 접촉의 상당히 이른 시기부터 사회적으로 종속된 집단의 언
어가 더 강한 권력을 가진 집단의 화자들이 전에 잘 몰랐던 물건이나 관습
에 대한 용어를 제공할 수도 있지만, 그런 방향으로의 접촉의 결과는 이것
이상 진전되지는 않을 수도 있다. 호주 토착 언어에서 영어로의 몇몇 최초
의 차용 출처인 호주 시드니의 Dharug 언어와 같은 몇몇 경우에는, 화자
들 중 다수가 소멸되고 나면 그러한 언어 체계(사회적으로 종속된 집단의
언어 체계)의 운명은 멸종하는 것이었다. 남은 사람들은 그들을 억압했던
사람들의 언어인 영어의 다양한 변종으로 (사용 언어를) 전환했다.
→ 지배 집단으로부터 종속 집단으로의 언어 차용은 사회적 (A) 불평등을
반영하는데, 호주의 Dharug 언어의 예시에서 보이듯이, 후자의 언어 체계
는 몇몇 용어를 제공하기도 했지만 종종 (B) 사라진다.

> 다음 글의 내용을 한 문장으로 요약하고자 한다. 빈칸 (A), (B)에 들어갈
> 말로 가장 적절한 것은?
>
> (A)   (B)
> ① inequality   —   vanish   지배 집단의 언어는 결국 사라짐
>   불평등   사라진다
> ② imbalance   —   prevail   종속 집단의 언어가 널리 퍼지게 되는 것이 아님
>   불균형   널리 퍼지다
> ③ integration   —   prosper   종속 집단의 언어가 번영하게 되는 것이 아님
>   통합   번영한다
> ④ variety   —   decline   사회의 다양성을 보여주는 것이 아님
>   다양성   감소한다
> ⑤ coordination —   disappear 조화를 보여주는 것이 아님
>   조화   사라진다

> ⟩왜 정답 ? ✭✭✭ [정답률 60%]

(A):
┌ 집단 간의 상호 작용이 불평등하다는 것은 언어가 지배 집단에서 종속 집단으로 차
└ 용된다는 사실로 나타난다. 단서 1
➡ 지배 집단에서 종속 집단으로 언어가 차용된다는 사실을 통해 집단 간의 상호 작용
  이 불평등하다는 것을 알 수 있다고 했으므로, 언어 차용의 방향은 사회의 '불평등
  (inequality)'을 반영한다는 표현이 알맞다.
(B):
┌ Dharug 언어의 예시에서처럼, 종속 집단의 언어 체계는 화자의 소멸과 함께 멸종
└ 하는 운명을 맞이한다. 단서 2
➡ 호주의 종속 집단의 언어였던 Dharug 언어는 호주 영어에 일부 차용되기도 했지
  만, 화자의 소멸과 함께 멸종되었다고 했으므로, 종속 집단의 언어 체계는 종종 '사
  라진다(vanish)'는 표현이 알맞다.
  ▶ 요약문의 빈칸에는 각각 ① '불평등'과 '사라진다'가 들어가야 함

⟩왜 오답 ?

② 사회 불평등의 예시로 언어 차용의 일방향성을 설명하고 있으며, 종속 집단의 언어
   가 널리 퍼지게 되는 것이 아니라 결국 소멸하게 된다는 내용이다.
③ 사회 불평등의 예시로 언어 차용의 일방향성을 설명하고 있으며, 종속 집단의 언어
   가 번영하게 되는 것이 아니라 결국 소멸하게 된다는 내용이다.
④ 언어의 차용은 사회의 다양성이 아니라 불평등을 보여주는 것이다.
⑤ 언어의 차용은 사회의 조화가 아니라 불평등을 보여주는 것이다.

* 글의 흐름

주제	집단 간의 상호 작용이 불평등하다는 것은 언어가 지배 집단에서 종속 집단으로 일방적으로 차용된다는 사실로 나타남
부연	종속 집단의 언어가 지배 집단의 언어에 일부 용어를 제공할 수는 있지만, 그 이상의 진전은 일어나지 않음
예시	호주의 Dharug 언어는 호주 영어에 일부 차용되기도 했지만, 대다수 사용자의 소멸과 함께 멸종되었고, 남은 이들도 영어로 전환함

⓵회 11~12 *전력 사용이 공장을 바꾼 점과 바꾸지 않은 점

In 1900, / at the close of the first decade / in which electric
「전치사+관계대명사」
systems had become a practical alternative / for manufacturers, /
과거완료
1900년에 / 첫 10년이 끝날 무렵인 / 전력 체계가 실용적인 대안으로 자리 잡은 / 제조업자를
위한 /
less than 5 percent of the power / used in factories / came from
과거분사구 (power 수식)
electricity. //
동력의 5% 미만이 / 공장에서 사용되는 / 전기에서 왔다 //

But the technological advances of suppliers / made electric
made의 목적어와 목적격 보어 (형용사)
systems and electric motors / ever more affordable and reliable, /
그러나 (전력) 공급자의 기술적인 진보가 / 전력 체계와 전기 모터를 만들었고 / 유례없이
저렴하면서도 신뢰할 만하도록 /
절과 절을 잇는 등위접속사
and the suppliers' intensive marketing programs / also (a) sped
the adoption / of the new technology. //
공급자의 집중적인 홍보 활동도 / 또한 수용을 촉진시켰다 / 이 새로운 기술의 //

Further accelerating the shift / was the rapid (b) expansion / in
the number of skilled electrical engineers, / who provided the
「~의 수」   계속적 용법의 주격 관계대명사
expertise / needed to install and run / the new systems. //
        과거분사 (expertise 수식)
변화를 더욱 가속화한 것은 / 급격한 증가였는데 / 숙련된 전기 기술자 수의 / 이들은 전문
지식을 제공했다 / 설치하고 운영하는 데 필요한 / 새로운 (전력) 체계를 //

In short order, / electric power had gone / from exotic to
과거완료   from A to B 구문
commonplace. // 11번 단서 1: 전력이 공장의 주요 동력으로
빠르게 자리매김하며 공장의 모습을 바꿈
순식간에 / 전력은 바뀌었다 / 생소한 것에서 일상적인 것으로 //
11번 단서 2: 하지만 변하지 않은 것도 있었음
But one thing didn't change. //   하지만 한 가지는 변하지 않았다 //

Factories continued to build / their own power-supply systems
/ on their own premises. // 12번 단서 1: 공장들은 자체 전력 공급 시스템을 구축함
공장들은 계속해서 구축했다 / 자체 전력 공급 시스템을 / 공장 부지에 //
부정어
(c) Few manufacturers considered / buying electricity / from the
동명사구 (목적어)
small central stations. //
고려하는 제조업자는 거의 없었다 / 전기를 구매하는 것을 / 소규모 중앙 발전소에서 //
과거분사 (분사구문)
Designed to supply lighting / to local homes and shops, / the
부사적 용법 (목적)
central stations had neither the size nor the skill / to serve the
neither A nor B: A도 B도 아닌   형용사적 용법 (the skill 수식)
needs of big factories. //
조명을 공급하기 위해 설계되었기 때문에 / 지역의 가정과 상점에 / 중앙 발전소는 규모도
기술도 갖추지 못했다 / 대규모 공장의 수요를 충족시킬 만한 //
분사구문의 완료형 (주절의 시제보다 앞섬)
And the factory owners, / having always supplied their own
power, / were (d) willing(→ reluctant) to assign / such a critical
「such a 형용사+명사」어순
function to an outsider. // 12번 단서 2: 공장 소유주들은 자체적으로 동력을 공급해 옴
그리고 공장 소유주들은 / 항상 자체적으로 동력을 공급해 왔기 때문에 / 맡기려고 했다
(→ 맡기는 것을 꺼렸다) / 그런 중요한 기능을 외부인에게 //

They knew / that a glitch in power supply / would bring their
operations to a (e) halt / — and that a lot of glitches / might well
mean bankruptcy. //
└ 병렬 구조 (목적어절 접속사) ┘   might well+동사원형: ~하는 것도 당연하다
그들은 알고 있었다 / 전력 공급에서의 결함 하나가 / 운영을 중지시킬 수 있으며 / 많은
결함은 / 반드시 파산을 초래한다는 것을 //

As the new century began, / a survey found / that there
                                          목적어절 접속사
were already 50,000 private electric plants in operation, / far
surpassing the 3,600 central stations. //
분사구문
새로운 세기가 시작될 때 / 한 조사는 밝혔다 / 이미 50,000개의 민간 발전소가 운영되고
있었으며 / (이는) 중앙 발전소 3,600개를 훨씬 초과한다는 것을 //

- alternative ⓝ 대안   - manufacturer ⓝ 제조업자
- electricity ⓝ 전기   - electric ⓐ 전기의   - affordable ⓐ 저렴한
- intensive ⓐ 집중적인   - speed ⓥ 촉진시키다
- accelerate ⓥ 가속화하다 - shift ⓝ 변화   - rapid ⓐ 빠른
- expertise ⓝ 전문 지식   - exotic ⓐ 이국적인, 생소한
- commonplace ⓐ 일상의   - halt ⓝ 중단   - bankruptcy ⓝ 파산
- plant ⓝ 공장   - surpass ⓥ 능가하다, 초과하다

전력 체계가 제조업자를 위한 실용적인 대안으로 자리 잡은 첫 10년이 끝
날 무렵인 1900년에, 공장에서 사용되는 동력의 5% 미만이 전기에서 왔
다. 그러나 (전력) 공급자의 기술적인 진보가 전력 체계와 전기 모터를 유
례없이 저렴하면서도 신뢰할 만하도록 만들었고, 공급자의 집중적인 홍보
활동 또한 이 새로운 기술의 수용을 (a) 촉진시켰다. 변화를 더욱 가속화한
것은 숙련된 전기 기술자 수의 급격한 (b) 증가였는데, 이들은 새로운 (전
력) 체계를 설치하고 운영하는 데 필요한 전문 지식을 제공했다. 순식간에,
전력은 생소한 것에서 일상적인 것으로 바뀌었다.
하지만 한 가지는 변하지 않았다. 공장들은 계속해서 공장 부지에 자체 전
력 공급 시스템을 구축했다. 소규모 중앙 발전소에서 전기를 구매하는 것
을 고려하는 제조업자는 (c) 거의 없었다. 지역의 가정과 상점에 조명을 공
급하기 위해 설계되었기 때문에, 중앙 발전소는 대규모 공장의 수요를 충
족시킬 만한 규모도 기술도 갖추지 못했다. 그리고 공장 소유주들은, 항상
자체적으로 동력을 공급해 왔기 때문에, 그런 중요한 기능을 외부인에게
(d) 맡기려고 했다(→ 맡기는 것을 꺼렸다). 그들은 전력 공급에서의 결함
하나가 운영을 (e) 중지시킬 수 있으며, 많은 결함은 반드시 파산을 초래한
다는 것을 알고 있었다. 새로운 세기가 시작될 때, 한 조사는 이미 50,000
개의 민간 발전소가 운영되고 있었으며, (이는) 중앙 발전소 3,600개를 훨
씬 초과한다는 것을 밝혔다.

1회 11 정답 ②

윗글의 제목으로 가장 적절한 것은?
공장의 운영 방식이 바뀌었으나, 공장 자체 동력을 선호한다는 점은 바뀌지 않았음
① How to Avoid Minor Errors in Factory Operation
  공장 운영에서 사소한 오류들을 피하는 방법   이를 피하는 방법을 설명한 글이 아님
②Power Use in Factories: What Changed and What Didn't
  공장에서의 전력 사용: 바뀐 것과 바뀌지 않은 것
③ Technical Advances in Power Supply by Central Stations
  중앙 발전소의 전력 공급의 기술적 발전들   대부분은 자체 민간 발전을 통해 동력을 얻고 있었음
④ Threats from the Increased Use of Electricity in Factories
  공장에서 전력 사용의 증가로부터 오는 위협들   언급되지 않음
⑤ From Private to Central Power Supply: A Revolutionary
  Change
  민간에서 중앙 전력 공급으로: 혁명적인 변화   이후에도 여전히 자체적으로 공급함

왜 정답? ★★★ [정답률 55%]

┌ • 전력이 공장의 주요 동력으로 빠르게 자리매김하며 공장의 모습을 바꿨음
│   11번 단서 1
└ • 하지만 변하지 않은 것도 있었음 11번 단서 2

➡ 전력이 빠르게 일상에 파고들면서 공장의 모습을 어떻게 바꾸었고, 그 와중에 바뀌
  지 않은 것은 무엇인지에 관한 글이다. 기술적 진보, 홍보, 기술자의 증가 등이 공장
  에서의 전력 사용을 일상적인 것으로 바꾸어 놓았으나, 공장이 중앙 전력 공급자에
  게 의존하기보다는 여전히 자체 동력 공급을 추구했다는 점은 바꾸지 않았다고 설
  명하고 있다. ▶ 따라서 제목으로 적절한 것은 ② '공장에서의 전력 사용: 바뀐 것과
  바뀌지 않은 것'이다.

왜 오답?
① 전력 공급에서의 사소한 오류들이 전체 운영을 중지시킬 수 있다는 내용은 언급되
   었으나, 이를 피하는 방법을 설명한 글이 아니다.   함정
③ 중앙 발전소의 전력 공급 기술이 발전했다는 내용은 언급되었으나, 대부분의 공장
   은 자체 민간 발전을 통해 동력을 얻고 있었다는 내용이다.
④ 전력 사용의 증가에서 오는 위협은 언급되지 않았다.
⑤ 중앙 전력 공급이 발달한 이후에도 여전히 공장들은 민간 발전소를 운영하며 자체
   적으로 전력을 공급하고 있었다는 내용이다.   주의

1회 12 정답 ④

밑줄 친 (a)~(e) 중에서 문맥상 낱말의 쓰임이 적절하지 않은 것은?
① (a) 홍보가 전력 기술의 수용을 '촉진시킴'   ② (b) 숙련된 전기 기술자의 '증가'가
    촉진시켰다   증가 전력으로의 변화를 가속화함
③ (c) 중앙 발전소에서 전력을 구매하려는
    거의 없는 공장주는 '거의 없었음'
④ (d) 공장주들은 외부인에게 맡기는 것을
    ~하려고 하는 '꺼림'
⑤ (e) 공장주들은 사소한 결함 하나가 전체
    중지 운영을 '중지시킨다'는 것을 알았음

왜 정답? ★★★ [정답률 46%]

④ (d) willing ~하려고 하는
┌ 그리고 공장 소유주들은, 항상 자체적으로 동력을 공급해 왔기 때문에, 그런
│   맡기는 것을 꺼렸다
└ 중요한 기능을 외부인에게 (d) 맡기려고 했다.

➡ 공장 소유주들은 중앙 발전소에서 전력을 구매할 수 있게 되었음에도, 그렇게 하지
  않았는데, 그 이유는 공장주들이 전력 공급과 같은 중요한 기능을 외부인에게 맡기
  려고 '하지 않았기' 때문이라는 내용이다.
  ▶ willing을 reluctant와 같은 어휘로 바꾸어야 한다.

왜 오답?
① (a) sped 촉진시켰다
┌ 그러나 (전력) 공급자의 기술적인 진보가 전력 체계와 전기 모터를 유례없이
│ 저렴하면서도 신뢰할 만하도록 만들었고, 공급자의 집중적인 홍보 활동 또
└ 한 이 새로운 기술의 수용을 (a) 촉진시켰다.

➡ 공장에 전력이 빠르게 자리 잡을 수 있었던 이유를 설명하는 부분이다. 전력의 기술
  적 진보뿐만 아니라, 공급자의 집중 홍보 또한 전력이 공장에 수용되는 과정을 '촉진
  시켰을' 것이다. ▶ sped는 문맥에 맞음

② (b) expansion 증가
┌ 변화를 더욱 가속화한 것은 숙련된 전기 기술자 수의 급격한 (b) 증가였는
│ 데, 이들은 새로운 (전력) 체계를 설치하고 운영하는 데 필요한 전문 지식
└ 을 제공했다.

➡ 전력이 빠르게 공장에 자리매김할 수 있었던 이유를 추가로 설명하는 부분이다. 공
  장에 전력 체계를 설치하고 운영할 수 있도록 전문 지식을 제공하는 숙련된 전기 기
  술자가 '증가'했기 때문에 전력으로의 변화가 가속화되었다.
  ▶ expansion은 문맥에 맞음

③ (c) Few 거의 없는
┌ 소규모 중앙 발전소에서 전기를 구매하는 것을 고려하는 제조업자는 (c) 거
└ 의 없었다.

➡ 전력이 바뀌지 못한 것을 설명하는 부분이다. 공장주들은 중앙 발전소에서 전력을
  구매할 수 있게 되었음에도 여전히 자체 동력을 추구했다는 내용으로 이어지고 있
  으므로, 중앙 발전소에서 전기 구매를 고려한 제조업자는 '거의 없었다'는 내용이다.
  ▶ Few는 문맥에 맞음

⑤ (e) halt 중지
┌ 그들은 전력 공급에서의 결함 하나가 운영을 (e) 중지시킬 수 있으며, 많은
└ 결함은 반드시 파산을 초래한다는 것을 알고 있었다.

➡ 공장주들이 중앙 발전소에서 전기 구매를 꺼린 이유는 전력 공급과 같은 중대한 일
  을 외부인에게 맡기기를 꺼렸기 때문인데, 전력 공급에서의 결함 하나가 운영을 '중
  지'시킬 정도로 중대한 사안이기 때문이다. ▶ halt는 문맥에 맞음

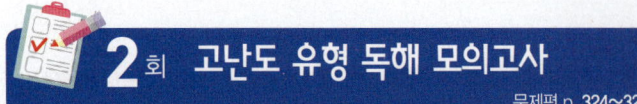

2회 01 정답 ④ *의학계의 기술 변화

If you **had wanted** to create a "self-driving" car / in the 1950s,
／가정법 과거완료
/ your best option **might have been** to strap a brick / to the
accelerator. // 만약 '자율 주행' 자동차를 만들고 싶었다면 / 1950년대에 / 가장 좋은
과거의 상황 가정 (~이었을 텐데)
선택은 벽돌을 끈으로 묶는 것이었을 것이다 / 가속 페달에 //

Yes, the vehicle **would have been** able to move forward on
its own, / but it could not slow down, stop, or turn **to avoid**
부사적 용법 (목적)
barriers. // 물론, 자동차가 스스로 앞으로 나아갈 수는 있었겠지만 / 속도를 줄이거나
멈추거나, 또는 장애물을 피하기 위해 방향을 전환할 수는 없었다 //

Obviously not ideal. // 분명히, 이상적이지는 않다 //
뒤에 목적어절 접속사 that 생략
But **does that mean** / the entire concept of the self-driving car /
is not worth pursuing? //
그러나 그것이 의미할까 / 자율 주행 자동차라는 전체 개념이 / 추구할 만한 가치가 없다는 //
목적어절 접속사
No, it only means / **that** at the time we did not yet have the
앞에 목적격 관계대명사 생략 형용사적 용법 (tools 수식)
tools / **we now possess** / **to help** enable vehicles to operate / both
단서 1 과거에는 도구가 없었기 때문에 자율 주행 자동차를
autonomously and safely. // 오늘날처럼 안전하게 만들지 못했음
아니다, 그것은 단지 의미할 뿐이다 / 그 당시에는 우리가 아직 도구를 갖고 있지 않았다는 것을
/ 우리가 지금은 갖고 있는 / 자동차를 작동할 수 있도록 해 주는 / 자율적이고도 안전하게 //

This once-distant dream now seems / within our reach. //
한때 멀게만 느껴졌던 이 꿈이 이제 보인다 / 우리의 손이 닿는 곳에 있는 것처럼 //

It is much the same story in medicine. // 단서 2 자율 주행 자동차의 이야기를
이는 의학에서도 마찬가지이다 // 의학계에 적용하고 있음
과거진행시제
Two decades ago, / we **were** still **taping** bricks to accelerators. //
20년 전에 / 우리는 여전히 가속 페달에 벽돌을 테이프로 묶어 두고 있었다 //
관계부사
Today, we are approaching the point / **where** we can begin to
형용사적 용법 (technology 수식)
bring some appropriate technology / **to bear** in ways /
오늘날, 우리는 지점에 접근하고 있다 / 적절한 기술을 도입하기 시작하는 / 방식에 맞는 /
주격 관계대명사
that advance our understanding / of patients as unique
individuals. // 단서 3 오늘날에는 환자 개인에게 맞는 방식을 이해할 수 있는 기술이 도입됨
이해하는 것을 증진하는 / 환자를 고유한 개인으로서 //
주격 관계대명사
In fact, / many patients are already wearing devices / **that**
monitor their conditions in real time, /
사실, 많은 환자들이 이미 장치를 착용하고 있는데 / 자신의 상태를 실시간으로 관찰하는 /
계속적 용법의 주격 관계대명사
which allows **doctors to talk** to their patients / in a specific,
allows의 목적어와 목적격 보어 (to부정사)
refined, and feedback-driven way / **that** was not even possible
주격 관계대명사
a decade ago. //
이는 의사가 환자에게 말할 수 있도록 해 주었다 / 구체적이고도 정제되었으며 피드백을
기반으로 하는 방식으로 / 십 년 전에는 전혀 가능하지 않았던 //

- **brick** ⓝ 벽돌   • **accelerator** ⓝ 가속 페달   • **barrier** ⓝ 장애물
- **be worth -ing** ~할 가치가 있다   • **pursue** ⓥ 추구하다
- **possess** ⓥ 소유하다   • **operate** ⓥ 작동하다   • **refined** ⓐ 정제된
- **pose a challenge** 어려움을 주다

만약 '자율 주행' 자동차를 1950년대에 만들고 싶었다면, 가장 좋은 선택은
가속 페달에 벽돌을 끈으로 묶는 것이었을 것이다. 물론, 자동차가 스스로
앞으로 나아갈 수는 있었겠지만, 속도를 줄이거나 멈추거나 또는 장애물을
피하기 위해 방향을 전환할 수는 없었다. 분명히, 이상적이지는 않다. 그
러나 그것이 자율 주행 자동차라는 전체 개념이 추구할 만한 가치가 없다
는 의미일까? 아니다, 그것은 단지 우리가 지금은 갖고 있는, 자동차를 자
율적이고도 안전하게 작동할 수 있도록 해 주는 도구를, 그 당시에는 우리
가 아직 갖고 있지 않았다는 것을 의미할 뿐이다. 한때 멀게만 느껴졌던 이
꿈이 이제 우리의 손이 닿는 곳에 있는 것처럼 보인다. 이는 의학에서도 마
찬가지이다. 20년 전에, 우리는 여전히 가속 페달에 벽돌을 테이프로 묶어

두고 있었다. 오늘날, 우리는 환자를 고유한 개인으로서 이해하는 것을 증
진하는 방식에 맞는 적절한 기술을 도입하기 시작하는 지점에 접근하고 있
다. 사실, 많은 환자들이 이미 자신의 상태를 실시간으로 관찰하는 장치를
착용하고 있는데, 이는 의사가 구체적이고도 정제되었으며 피드백을 기반
으로 하는, 십 년 전에는 전혀 가능하지 않았던 방식으로 환자에게 말할 수
있도록 해 주었다.

**밑줄 친 we were still taping bricks to accelerators가 다음 글에서 의
미하는 바로 가장 적절한 것은? [3점]**
안전 운행을 위한 장치가 없었다는 내용은 의학계가 아니라 자율 주행 자동차에서의 내용임
① the importance of medical education was overlooked
의학 교육의 중요성이 간과되었다   의학 교육의 중요성은 언급되지 않음
② self-driving cars enabled patients to move around freely
자율 주행 자동차들이 환자가 자유롭게 돌아다니도록 해주었다   의학계에 적용한 내용임
③ the devices for safe driving were unavailable at that time
안전 운전을 위한 장치들이 당시에는 없었음
④ lack of advanced tools posed a challenge in understanding
patients   It is much the same story in medicine.
발전된 도구의 결여가 환자를 이해하는 데 어려움을 주었다
⑤ appropriate technologies led to success in developing a new
medicine   신약 개발에 관한 언급은 없었음
알맞은 기술이 신약 개발의 성공으로 이끌었다

| 문제 풀이 순서 | ★★★ [정답률 55%]

1st 첫 문장과 밑줄 친 부분이 포함된 문장을 읽고, 글의 내용을 예상한다.

첫 문장	만약 '자율 주행' 자동차를 1950년대에 만들고 싶었다면, 가장 좋은 선택은 가속 페달에 벽돌을 끈으로 묶는 것이었을 것이다.
밑줄 친 부분이 포함된 문장	20년 전에, 우리는 여전히 가속 페달에 벽돌을 테이프로 묶어 두고 있었다.

➡ 첫 문장: 과거에 자율 주행 자동차를 만들기 위해서는 가속 페달에 벽돌을 끈으로
묶었을 것임
밑줄 친 부분이 포함된 문장: 과거에 우리는 여전히 가속 페달에 벽돌을 테이프로
묶어 두고 있었음
➡ 과거에는 기술이 부족했기 때문에 자율 주행 자동차를 가속 페달에 벽돌을 묶어서
눌러놓는 엉성한 방식을 사용해야만 했다는 내용이다. 밑줄 친 부분이 포함된 문장
앞을 보면 의학계에서도 마찬가지라고 했으므로, 이를 기술 부족으로 어려움을
겪었던 과거의 의학계에 적용한 내용일 것이다.

2nd 글의 나머지 부분을 읽고, 예상한 내용이 맞는지 확인한다.

- 과거에는 우리가 지금 보유한 도구가 없었으므로 자율 주행 자동차를 오늘날처럼
  안전하게 만들지 못했음 단서 1
- 자율 주행 자동차의 이야기는 의학계에서도 마찬가지임 ➡ 오늘날에는 환자
  개인에게 맞는 방식을 이해할 수 있는 기술이 도입됨 단서 2, 3
➡ 과거에는 발전된 기술이 없어서 진정한 의미의 자율적이고 안정적인 자율 주행
자동차를 만들 수 없었다면, 오늘날에는 기술의 발전으로 그 꿈이 실현 가능해지고
있다는 내용을 의학계에도 그대로 적용하여 설명하고 있다.

3rd 파악한 글의 내용을 종합하여 밑줄 친 부분의 의미를 파악한다.

의학계에서도 '여전히 가속 페달에 벽돌을 테이프로 묶어 두고 있었다'는 것은 과거
자율 주행 자동차의 경우처럼 발전된 도구가 없어서 그 기능(환자를 이해하는 것)을
다하지 못했다는 의미이므로, 정답은 ④ '발전된 도구의 결여가 환자를 이해하는 데
어려움을 주었다'이다.

| 선택지 분석 |

① 의학 교육의 중요성은 언급되지 않았다.
② 자율 주행 자동차의 기술 변화를 의학계에 적용한 내용으로, 두 개념을 묶어서
  언급하지 않았다.
③ 안전 운행을 위한 장치가 없었다는 내용은 의학계가 아니라 자율 주행
  자동차에서의 내용이다.
④ 과거에는 기술이 부족해 환자를 이해하기 어려웠지만, 오늘날에는 이를 극복하고
  있다는 내용이 이어지고 있다.
⑤ 신약 개발에 관한 언급은 없었다.

정답 ⑤ *공감의 의미에 대한 다양한 해석

Empathy is frequently listed / as one of the most desired skills / in an employer or employee, / 부사절의 주어와 동사가 생략됨 although without specifying 의문사절 (specifying의 목적어) exactly / **what is meant by** *empathy*. // 단서 1 공감은 사업에 중요한 덕목이지만, '공감'의 의미는 정확히 특정되지 않음
공감은 목록에 종종 오른다 / 가장 바라는 기술 중 하나로 / 고용주나 직원에게 / 정확히 밝히지는 않지만 / '공감'이 무엇을 의미하는지 //

단서 2 공감의 예시 ① Some businesses stress cognitive empathy, / 분사구문을 이끄는 현재분사 emphasizing the need **for leaders to understand** / the perspective of to understand의 의미상 주어 형용사적 용법 (the need 수식) employees and customers /
일부 기업은 인지적 공감을 강조하여 / 리더가 이해할 필요성에 중점을 둔다 / 직원과 고객의 관점을 /

부사절에서 「주어+be동사」 생략 when negotiating deals and making decisions. //
거래를 협상하고 결정을 내릴 때 //

단서 3 공감의 예시 ② Others stress affective empathy and empathic concern, / 분사구문을 이끄는 현재분사 emphasizing the ability of leaders to gain trust / from employees and customers /
다른 기업은 정서적 공감과 공감적 관심을 강조하여 / 신뢰를 얻는 리더의 능력에 중점을 둔다 / 직원과 고객의 /

by treating them with real concern and compassion. //
진정한 관심과 동정심으로 그들을 대함으로써 // 단서 4 공감의 예시 ③

When some consultants argue / that successful companies 목적어절 접속사 foster empathy, / what that translates to / is that companies 지시대명사 주격 보어절 접속사 should conduct good market research. //
일부 자문 위원이 주장할 때 / 성공하려는 기업은 공감 능력을 길러야 한다고 / 그것이 의미하는 바는 / 기업이 시장 조사를 잘 수행해야 한다는 것이다 //

In other words, / an "empathic" company understands the 병렬 구조 (동사) needs and wants of its customers / and seeks to fulfill those needs and wants. //
다시 말해 / '공감적인' 기업은 고객의 필요와 요구를 이해하고 / 그 필요와 요구를 충족시키기 위해 노력한다 // 단서 5 공감의 예시 ④

When some people speak of design with empathy, / what that 지시대명사 translates to / is that companies should take into account / the 주격 보어절 접속사 specific needs of different populations /
일부 사람들이 공감을 담은 디자인을 말할 때 / 그것이 의미하는 바는 / 회사가 고려해야 한다는 것이다 / 다양한 사람들의 구체적인 필요 사항을 /

— the blind, the deaf, the elderly, non-English speakers, the 부사절에서 「주어+be동사」 생략 color-blind, and so on — when designing products. //
시각 장애인, 청각 장애인, 노인, 비영어권 화자, 색맹 등 / 제품을 디자인할 때 //

- specify ⓥ 명시하다   - stress ⓥ 강조하다
- emphasize ⓥ 강조하다   - perspective ⓝ 관점
- negotiate ⓥ 협상하다   - affective ⓐ 정서적인
- empathic ⓐ 공감의   - consultant ⓝ 자문 위원
- foster ⓥ 기르다, 양육하다   - market research 시장 조사
- fulfill ⓥ 충족시키다   - color-blind 색맹의
- interpretation ⓝ 해석

'공감'이 무엇을 의미하는지 정확히 밝히지는 않지만, 공감은 고용주나 직원에게 가장 바라는 기술 중 하나로 목록에 종종 오른다. 일부 기업은 인지적 공감을 강조하여 리더가 거래를 협상하고 결정을 내릴 때 직원과 고객의 관점을 이해할 필요성에 중점을 둔다. 다른 기업은 정서적 공감과 공감적 관심을 강조하여 진정한 관심과 동정심으로 직원과 고객을 대함으로써 그들의 신뢰를 얻는 리더의 능력에 중점을 둔다. 일부 자문 위원이 성공하려는 기업은 공감 능력을 길러야 한다고 주장할 때, 그것이 의미하는 바는 기업이 시장 조사를 잘 수행해야 한다는 것이다. 다시 말해, '공감적인' 기업은 고객의 필요와 요구를 이해하고, 그 필요와 요구를 충족시키기 위해 노력한다. 일부 사람들이 공감을 담은 디자인을 말할 때, 그것이 의미하는 바는 회사가 제품을 디자인할 때 시각 장애인, 청각 장애인, 노인, 비영어권 화자, 색맹 등 다양한 사람들의 구체적인 필요 사항을 고려해야 한다는 것이다.

다음 글의 주제로 가장 적절한 것은?

① diverse benefits of good market research 훌륭한 시장 조사의 다양한 혜택들 시장 조사의 혜택에 관한 언급은 없었음
② negative factors in making business decisions 사업 결정을 내릴 때 부정적인 요소들 사업 결정을 내리는 내용이 아님
③ difficulties in designing products with empathic concern 공감적 관심으로 상품을 디자인하는 것의 어려움들 예시로 언급됐을 뿐임
④ efforts to build cognitive empathy among employees 직원들 간에 인지적 공감을 쌓으려는 노력들 공감을 쌓으려는 노력에 관한 언급은 없음
⑤different interpretations of empathy in business 사업에서 공감에 대한 다른 해석들 without specifying exactly what is meant by *empathy*

>왜 정답? ★★★ [정답률 46%]

'공감'이 무엇을 의미하는지 정확히 밝히지는 않지만, 공감은 고용주나 직원에게 가장 바라는 기술 중 하나로 목록에 종종 오른다. 단서 1
예시 1: 일부 기업은 인지적 공감을 강조함 단서 2
예시 2: 다른 기업은 정서적 공감을 강조함 단서 3
예시 3: 일부 자문 위원은 시장 조사를 잘 수행하는 것을 강조함 단서 4
예시 4: 일부 사람들은 다양한 사람들의 구체적인 필요를 고려하는 것을 강조함 단서 5
➡ 공감은 사업에서 중요한 덕목이지만, '공감'의 의미는 정확히 특정되지 않았다고 설명하며, 다양한 사업 측면에서 공감의 다른 의미와 해석을 소개하고 있다.
▶ 따라서 글의 주제는 ⑤ '사업에서 공감에 대한 다른 해석들'이다.

>왜 오답?

① 시장 조사에서의 공감의 의미를 설명하는 예시는 있었으나, 그 혜택에 관한 내용은 아니다.
② 사업 결정을 내리는 내용은 언급되지 않았다.
③ 디자인 측면에서의 공감의 의미를 설명하는 예시는 있었으나, 글의 주제는 아니다.
④ 직원들에게 공감은 필요한 기술이라는 언급은 있었으나, 공감을 쌓으려는 노력에 관한 언급은 없었다. (함정)

정답 ⑤ *항상 연락될 수 있어야 한다는 부담감

앞에 목적격 관계대명사 생략 The most prevalent problem / kids report / is that they feel like / 주격 보어절 접속사 they need to be accessible at all times. //
가장 일반적인 문제는 / 아이들이 이야기하는 / 그들이 느낀다는 것이다 / 항상 연락될 수 있어야 한다고 //

단서 1 디지털 기술의 발달로 아이들은 연락의 의무감을 느낌 Because technology allows for it, / they feel an obligation. //
기술이 그것을 허용하기 때문에 / 그들은 의무감을 느낀다 //
가주어 의미상 주어 진주어 It's easy for most of us to relate / — you probably feel the same pressure / in your own life! //
우리 대부분은 공감하기 쉬운데 / 아마 여러분도 같은 압박을 느낄 것이다 / 자신의 삶에서 //
가주어 진주어 동격절 접속사 It is really challenging / to deal with the fact / that we're human / and can't always respond instantly. // 단서 2 항상 즉각적으로 응답할 수는 없기 때문에 힘듦
매우 힘들다 / 사실에 대처하는 것은 / 우리가 인간이고 / 항상 즉각적으로 응답할 수 없다는 //
주격 관계대명사 For a teen or tween / who's still learning the ins and outs of 비교급 강조 social interactions, / it's even worse. //
십 대(13~19세)나 십 대 초반(10~12세)의 아동에게 / 아직 사회적 상호 작용의 세부적인 것들을 배우고 있는 / 상황은 훨씬 더 심각하다 //
= the way Here's how this behavior plays out sometimes: //
때때로 이 행동이 나타나는 방식은 다음과 같다 //

Your child texts one of his friends, / and the friend doesn't text back right away. //
여러분의 자녀가 친구 중 한 명에게 문자 메시지를 보내고 / 그 친구가 즉시 답장을 보내지 않는다 //
가주어 의미상 주어 진주어 Now it's easy for your child to think, / "This person doesn't want to be my friend anymore!" //
이제 여러분의 자녀는 생각하기 쉽다 / "얘는 더 이상 내 친구가 되기를 원하지 않는구나"라고 //

So he texts again, and again, and again / — "blowing up their phone." //
그래서 다시, 다시, 그리고 또 다시 문자 메시지를 보내다가 / '전화기를 폭파하는(과부하 상태로 만드는) 것'이다 //

This can be stress-inducing / and even read as aggressive. //
이것은 스트레스를 유발하고 / 심지어 공격적인 것으로 읽힐 수 있다 //

But you can see / how easily this could happen. //
의문사절
하지만 여러분은 알 수 있다 / 이것이 얼마나 쉽게 일어날 수 있는지 //

- prevalent ⓐ 만연한, 일반적인   - obligation ⓝ 의무감
- pressure ⓝ 압박   - instantly ⓐⓓ 즉각적으로
- ins and outs 세부 사항들   - blow up ~을 폭파시키다
- inducing ⓐ 유발하는   - aggressive ⓐ 공격적인
- within reach 손이 닿는 곳에

아이들이 이야기하는 가장 일반적인 문제는 그들이 항상 연락될 수 있어야 한다고 느낀다는 것이다. 기술이 그것을 허용하기 때문에, 그들은 의무감을 느낀다. 우리 대부분은 공감하기 쉬운데, 아마 여러분도 자신의 삶에서 같은 압박을 느낄 것이다! 우리가 인간이고 항상 즉각적으로 응답할 수 없다는 사실에 대처하는 것은 매우 힘들다. 아직 사회적 상호 작용의 세부적인 것들을 배우고 있는 십 대(13~19세)나 십 대 초반(10~12세)의 아동에게 상황은 훨씬 더 심각하다. 때때로 이 행동이 나타나는 방식은 다음과 같다. 예를 들어, 여러분의 자녀가 친구 중 한 명에게 문자 메시지를 보내고, 그 친구가 즉시 답장을 보내지 않는다. 이제 여러분의 자녀는 "얘는 더 이상 내 친구가 되기를 원하지 않는구나!"라고 생각하기 쉽다. 그래서 다시, 다시, 그리고 또 다시 문자 메시지를 보내다가, '전화기를 폭파하는(과부하 상태로 만드는)' 것'이다. 이것은 스트레스를 유발하고, 심지어 공격적인 것으로 읽힐 수 있다. 하지만 여러분은 이것이 얼마나 쉽게 일어날 수 있는지 알 수 있다.

다음 글의 제목으로 가장 적절한 것은?

① From Symbols to Bytes: History of Communication
기호에서 바이트로: 통신의 역사   통신의 역사를 설명한 내용은 아님
② Parents' Desire to Keep Their Children Within Reach 연락이 되어야
자식을 힘이 미치는 곳에 두고자 하는 부모의 욕구   한다는 압박감을 느끼는 건 십 대만이 아니라고 했음
③ Building Trust: The Key to Ideal Human Relationships
신뢰 형성하기: 이상적인 인간관계의 열쇠   인간관계의 중요한 부분으로 신뢰를 소개하는 것이 아님
④ The Positive Role of Digital Technology in Teen Friendships
십 대의 우정에서 디지털 기술의 긍정적인 역할   디지털 기술이 미치는 부정적인 영향력을 설명함
⑤ Connected but Stressed: Challenges for Kids in the Digital
Era   항상 연락되어야 한다는 압박감이 스트레스가 된다는 내용임
연결되어 있지만 스트레스가 되는: 디지털 시대 아이들의 어려움

왜 정답? ❋❋❋ [정답률 77%]

- 아이들은 디지털 기술의 발달로 항상 연락될 수 있게 되어 연락의 의무감을 느낌
단서1
- 항상 즉각적으로 응답할 수는 없기에 대처하기 힘듦 단서2
- 즉각적인 응답을 요구하는 상황은 스트레스를 유발함 단서3
➡ 기술의 발달로 모두와 즉각적인 연락이 가능한 시대가 되었지만, 이는 오히려 우리에게 압박감을 준다는 내용이다. 특히 십 대에게는 이것이 인간관계 형성에 스트레스를 준다고 설명하고 있다.
▶ 따라서 제목으로 가장 적절한 것은 ⑤ '연결되어 있지만 스트레스가 되는: 디지털 시대 아이들의 어려움'이다.

왜 오답?

① 디지털 시대의 통신의 문제점을 설명하고 있지, 통신의 역사를 설명한 글은 아니다.
② 십 대도 연락이 되어야 한다는 압박감을 느끼고 있으나, 이건 십 대만의 문제가 아니라고 했다.   주의
③ 신뢰를 형성한다는 내용은 언급되지 않았다.
④ 십 대의 우정에서 디지털 기술이 미치는 긍정적인 영향이 아니라 부정적인 영향력을 설명했다.

2회 04 정답 ④ *부정적인 건강 습관을 해결하기 위한 행동 바꾸기

다음 글의 밑줄 친 부분 중, 어법상 틀린 것은?

현재완료시제
For years, / many psychologists have held strongly to the belief
동격절 접속사
/ ① that the key to addressing negative health habits / is to
전치사   명사적 용법 (주격 보어)
change behavior. //
수년 동안 / 많은 심리학자들이 믿음을 굳게 갖고 있었다 / 부정적인 건강 습관을 해결하기 위한 열쇠는 / 행동을 바꾸는 것이라는 //
단수 주어   단수 동사
This, / more than values and attitudes, / ② is the part of
주격 관계대명사   부사적 용법 (~하기에)
personality / that is easiest to change. //
이것이 / 가치관이나 태도보다 / 성격의 한 부분이다 / 가장 바꾸기 쉬운 //
복수 주어
Ingestive habits such as smoking, drinking and various eating
복수 동사
behaviors / are the most common health concerns / targeted for
과거분사구 (concerns 수식)
behavioral changes. //
흡연, 음주, 그리고 다양한 섭식 행동과 같은 섭취 습관은 / 가장 일반적인 건강 문제이다 / 행동 변화의 대상이 되는 //

Process-addiction behaviors (workaholism, shopaholism, and
the like) / fall into this category as well. //
과정 중독 행동(일중독, 쇼핑 중독 등) / 또한 이 범주에 속한다 //
과거분사구 (imagery 수식)   수동태 동사
Mental imagery combined with power of suggestion / was
형용사적 용법 (medicine 수식)
taken up as the premise of behavioral medicine / to help people
= health behaviors
change negative health behaviors / into positive ③ ones. //
암시의 힘과 결합된 마음속 이미지는 / 행동 의학의 전제가 되었다 / 사람들이 부정적인 건강 행동을 바꾸는 데 도움을 주는 / 긍정적인 것으로   단서 when이 이끄는 부사절의 주어는
this technique이고, 기술이 '사용되는' 것임
Although this technique alone will not produce changes, /
이 기술만으로는 변화를 만들어 내지는 않지만 /

when ④ using(→ used) alongside other behavior modification
tactics and coping strategies, / behavioral changes have proved
현재완료시제
effective for some people. //
다른 행동 수정 기법 및 대응 전략과 함께 사용되면 / 행동 변화가 일부 사람들에게는 효과적인 것으로 입증되었다 //
명사절을 이끄는 관계대명사   단수 동사
⑤ What mental imagery does / is reinforce a new desired
앞에 to 생략
behavior. //
마음속 이미지가 하는 일은 / 새로운 바람직한 행동을 강화하는 것이다 //
과거분사 (use 수식)
Repeated use of images / reinforces the desired behavior more
strongly / over time. //
이미지의 반복적 사용은 / 그 바람직한 행동을 더욱 강력하게 강화한다 / 시간이 지남에 따라 //

- psychologist ⓝ 심리학자   - address ⓥ 해결하다
- personality ⓝ 성격   - workaholism ⓝ 일중독
- shopaholism ⓝ 쇼핑 중독   - and the like 기타 등등
- fall into ~에 속하다   - suggestion ⓝ 암시
- modification ⓝ 수정, 변경   - tactic ⓝ 전략
- reinforce ⓥ 강화하다

수년 동안 많은 심리학자들이 부정적인 건강 습관을 해결하기 위한 열쇠는 행동을 바꾸는 것이라는 믿음을 굳게 갖고 있었다. 가치관이나 태도보다, 이것이 가장 바꾸기 쉬운 성격의 한 부분이다. 흡연, 음주, 그리고 다양한 섭식 행동과 같은 섭취 습관은 행동 변화의 대상이 되는 가장 일반적인 건강 문제이다. 과정 중독 행동(일중독, 쇼핑 중독 등) 또한 이 범주에 속한다. 암시의 힘과 결합된 마음속 이미지는 사람들이 부정적인 건강 행동을 긍정적인 것으로 바꾸는 데 도움을 주는 행동 의학의 전제가 되었다. 이 기술만으로는 변화를 만들어 내지는 않지만, 다른 행동 수정 기법 및 대응 전략과 함께 사용되면, 행동 변화가 일부 사람들에게는 효과적인 것으로 입증되었다. 마음속 이미지가 하는 일은 새로운 바람직한 행동을 강화하는 것이다. 이미지의 반복적 사용은 시간이 지남에 따라 그 바람직한 행동을 더욱 강력하게 강화한다.

④ 수동의 관계인데 현재분사가 왔다!

부사절 ①
[Although this technique alone will not produce changes,] /
부사절 ②
[when ④ using(→ used) alongside other behavior modification
생략된 주어 this technique가 '사용되는' 것임
tactics and coping strategies.] /
주절의 주어   주절의 동사
behavioral changes have proved effective for some people. //

단서 부사절에서 「동사원형+-ing」의 형태에 밑줄이 있으므로

발상 현재분사가 능동의 의미로 알맞게 쓰였는지를 확인한다.

해결 when으로 시작되는 부사절에서 생략된 주어는 this technique이고, 그 기술이 다른 것들과 함께 '사용되었을' 때라는 의미의 수동태가 되어야 한다. 따라서 현재분사 using을 과거분사 used로 바꾸어야 어법상 알맞다.

개념 현재분사는 능동을, 과거분사는 수동의 관계를 나타낸다.

왜 오답?

① 접속사 that은 동격의 의미를 나타낼 수 있다.

For years, / many psychologists have held strongly to the
동격절 접속사   주어   동사
belief / ① that the key to addressing negative health habits / is
주격 보어
to change behavior. //

단서 완전한 절을 이끄는 that에 밑줄이 있으므로

발상 문장에서 주어, 목적어, 보어 등의 역할을 하는 명사절을 이끌고 있는지, 선행사와 함께 쓰여 동격을 나타내는지 등을 확인한다.

해결 선행사 the belief를 보충하는 동격절의 역할을 하고 있으므로 명사절 접속사 that은 알맞게 쓰였다.

개념 명사절 접속사 that은 선행사의 의미를 동격으로 보충할 수 있다.

② 문장의 본동사는 주어와 수 일치가 되어야 한다.

단수 주어   삽입구   단수 동사
This, [more than values and attitudes,] / ② is the part of
주격 관계대명사절
personality / that is easiest to change. //

단서 동사 is에 밑줄이 있으므로

발상 문장에서 본동사의 역할을 하고 있는지, 주어와 수 일치가 되는지 등을 확인한다.

해결 관계사절을 제외하면 문장에서 동사 역할을 할 수 있는 다른 성분이 없으므로, 문장에서 본동사의 역할을 하고 있고, 주어 This에 수를 맞춰 단수 동사로 알맞게 쓰였다.

개념 문장에서 본동사는 하나이며, 주어와 수 일치가 되어야 한다.

③ 부정대명사 ones는 복수 명사를 가리킨다.

Mental imagery combined with power of suggestion / was

taken up as the premise of behavioral medicine / to help

people change negative health behaviors / into positive
= health behaviors
③ ones. //

단서 부정대명사 ones에 밑줄이 있으므로

발상 부정대명사가 대신하는 것을 찾아 그 수가 일치하는지 확인한다.

해결 의미상 부정적인 건강 행동을 긍정적인 것으로 바꾸는 것이므로, ones는 health behaviors를 가리킨다. 따라서 복수형 ones를 쓰는 것은 알맞다.

개념 대명사는 앞에서 언급된 명사를 대신하며, 그 선행사와 수 일치가 되어야 한다.

⑤ 관계대명사 what은 명사절을 이끈다.

⑤ What mental imagery does / is reinforce a new desired
명사절을 이끄는 관계대명사   동사
behavior. //

단서 관계대명사 What에 밑줄이 있으므로

발상 선행사가 없고 불완전한 절을 이끌어 문장에서 명사절의 역할을 하는지 확인한다.

해결 What이 수식하고 있는 선행사가 없고, 주어가 빠진 불완전한 절을 이끌고 있다. 또한 What이 이끄는 절이 명사의 역할을 하며 전체 문장에서 주어의 역할을 하고 있으므로 관계대명사 What은 알맞게 쓰였다.

개념 관계대명사 what은 선행사가 없고, 불완전한 절을 이끌어 명사절의 역할을 한다.

2회 05 정답 ③ *청소년기 자녀의 감정 사회화를 돕는 방법

다음 글의 밑줄 친 부분 중, 문맥상 낱말의 쓰임이 적절하지 않은 것은? [3점]

단수 주어
Emotion socialization / — learning from other people about
~하는 방법
emotions and how to deal with them — /
감정 사회화는 / 다른 사람들로부터 감정과 감정을 다루는 방법을 배우는 /
병렬 구조 (단수 동사)
starts early in life / and plays a foundational role / for emotion
regulation development. //
어릴 때부터 시작되며 / 기초적인 역할을 한다 / 감정 조절 발달에 //

복수 주어
Although extra-familial influences, / such as peers or media, /
복수 동사
gain in importance / during adolescence, / parents remain the
① primary socialization agents. //
가족 이외의 영향이 / 또래나 미디어와 같은 / 중요해지지만 / 청소년기에는 / 부모는 여전히 주된 사회화 주체이다 //

For example, / their own responses to emotional situations /
serve as a role model for emotion regulation, /
예를 들어 / 감정적 상황에 대한 부모 자신의 반응이 / 감정 조절의 롤모델이 되어 /
분사구문   동격절 접속사
increasing the likelihood / that their children will show
② similar reactions / in comparable situations. //
가능성을 높인다 / 자녀가 유사한 반응을 보일 / 비슷한 상황에서 //

복수 주어   관계부사 (선행사 times)
Parental practices / at times when their children are faced
with emotional challenges / also impact emotion regulation
복수 동사
development. //
부모의 (습관적) 행동 / 자녀가 정서적 어려움에 직면했을 때 / 또한 감정 조절 발달에 영향을 미친다 //
단서 1 도움이 된다는 내용이 Whereas로 연결됨
Whereas direct soothing and directive guidance of what to do
/ are beneficial for younger children, / they may ③ cultivate(→
intrude on) / adolescents' autonomy striving. //
직접적인 위로와 어떻게 해야 하는지에 대한 지시적 안내가 ~이지만 / 어린 자녀에게는
도움이 되지만 / 장려할(→ 방해할) 수 있다 / 청소년의 자율성 추구를 //

In consequence, / adolescents might pull away from, / rather
병렬 구조 (might 뒤에 연결)
than turn toward, / their parents / in times of emotional crisis, /
단서 2 청소년은 오히려
unless parental practices are ④ adjusted. // 부모에게서 멀어질 수 있음
결과적으로 / 청소년은 오히려 멀어질 수 있다 / 의지하기보다 / 부모로부터 / 정서적 위기
상황에서 / 부모의 행동이 조정되지 않는다면 //
보어(형용사)가 문두로 오면서 주어와 동사가 도치됨   도치된 원래 주어(명사)
More suitable in adolescence / is ⑤ indirect support of
autonomous emotion regulation, /
청소년기에 더 적합한 것은 / 자율적 감정 조절을 간접적으로 지원하는 것이다 /

such as through interest in, / as well as awareness and
nonjudgmental acceptance / of, adolescents' emotional
병렬 구조
experiences, / and being available / when the adolescent wants
to talk. //
(그에 대한) 관심과 같은 방법으로 / 인식과 무비판적 수용뿐만 아니라 / 청소년의 정서적
경험에 대한 / 그리고 곁에 있어 주는 것과 (같은 방법으로) / 청소년이 대화하고 싶을 때 //

모의고사
2회

- socialization ⓝ 사회화 • foundational ⓐ 기초적인
- regulation ⓝ 조절 • extra-familial 가족 이외의 • agent ⓝ 주체
- comparable ⓐ 비슷한, 상응하는 • soothing ⓝ 위로, 위안
- directive ⓐ 지시적인 • cultivate ⓥ 기르다, 장려하다
- adolescent ⓝ 청소년 • autonomy ⓝ 자율성
- striving ⓝ 추구 • crisis ⓝ 위기 • autonomous ⓐ 자율적인
- nonjudgmental ⓐ 무비판적인 • acceptance ⓝ 수용

다른 사람들로부터 감정과 감정을 다루는 방법을 배우는 감정 사회화는 어릴 때부터 시작되며 감정 조절 발달에 기초적인 역할을 한다. 청소년기에는 또래나 미디어와 같은 가족 이외의 영향이 중요해지지만, 부모는 여전히 ① 주된 사회화 주체이다. 예를 들어, 감정적 상황에 대한 부모 자신의 반응이 감정 조절의 롤모델이 되어 자녀가 비슷한 상황에서 ② 유사한 반응을 보일 가능성을 높인다. 자녀가 정서적 어려움에 직면했을 때 부모의 (습관적) 행동 또한 감정 조절 발달에 영향을 미친다. 직접적인 위로와 어떻게 해야 하는지에 대한 지시적 안내가 어린 자녀에게는 도움이 되지만, 청소년의 자율성 추구를 ③ 장려할 (→ 방해할) 수 있다. 결과적으로 부모의 행동이 ④ 조정되지 않는다면, 청소년은 정서적 위기 상황에서 부모에게 의지하기보다 오히려 부모로부터 멀어질 수 있다. 청소년기에 더 적합한 것은 청소년의 정서적 경험에 대한 인식과 무비판적 수용뿐만 아니라 (그에 대한) 관심, 그리고 청소년이 대화하고 싶을 때 곁에 있어 주는 것과 같은 방법으로 자율적 감정 조절을 ⑤ 간접적으로 지원하는 것이다.

⟫왜 정답 ? ★★★ [정답률 29%]
③ cultivate 장려하다
┌ 직접적인 위로와 어떻게 해야 하는지에 대한 지시적 안내가 어린
│   방해할
└ 자녀에게는 도움이 되지만, 청소년의 자율성 추구를 ③ 장려할 수 있다.

→ 부모가 자녀에게 하는 직접적인 위로나 지시가 어린 자녀들에게는 도움이 되지만
  → 청소년 시기에는 도움이 되지 않는 부분도 있다는 상반된 내용이 이어져야 함 →
  이어지는 내용에서도 부모의 직접적인 지원이 자녀에게 미치는 부정적인 영향을
  소개함 → cultivate는 잘못된 표현임
  ▶ 부모의 직접적인 지원이 청소년의 자율성 추구를 '장려하는(cultivate)' 것이
  아니라 '방해할(intrude on)' 수도 있다고 해야 함

⟫왜 오답 ?
① primary 주된
┌ 청소년기에는 또래나 미디어와 같은 가족 이외의 영향이 |중요해지지만|
└ (Although), 부모는 여전히 ① 주된 사회화 주체이다.

→ 가족 이외의 영향도 중요하다는 내용이 Although로 연결됨 → 부모는 여전히
  '주된' 사회화 주체임 ▶ primary는 문맥에 맞음

② similar 유사한
┌ 예를 들어, 감정적 상황에 대한 부모 자신의 반응이 감정 조절의 롤모델이
└ 되어 자녀가 비슷한 상황에서 ② 유사한 반응을 보일 가능성을 높인다.

→ 부모는 자녀의 감정 조절의 롤모델이 됨 → 부모가 특정 상황에 어떻게 감정적으로
  반응하는지를 보고 자녀도 '유사한' 반응을 보일 가능성이 높아짐
  ▶ similar는 문맥에 맞음

④ adjusted 조정되다
┌ 결과적으로 부모의 행동이 ④ 조정되지 않는다면, 청소년은 정서적 위기
└ 상황에서 부모에게 의지하기보다 오히려 부모로부터 멀어질 수 있다.

→ 청소년의 자율성을 방해하는 부모의 행동이 지속된다면 청소년은 부모와 멀어질 수
  있음 → 부모의 행동이 '조정되어야 함 ▶ adjusted는 문맥에 맞음

⑤ indirect 간접적인
┌ 청소년기에 더 적합한 것은 청소년의 정서적 경험에 대한 인식과 무비판적
│ 수용뿐만 아니라 (그에 대한) 관심, 그리고 청소년이 대화하고 싶을 때 곁에
│ 있어 주는 것과 같은 방법으로 자율적 감정 조절을 ⑤ 간접적으로 지원하는
└ 것이다.

→ 부모의 직접적인 위로나 지시는 청소년의 자율성을 방해할 수 있음 → 청소년기에
  더 적합한 부모의 행동은 관심, 수용, 동행 등 '간접적인' 지원임
  ▶ indirect는 문맥에 맞음

2회 06 정답 ③ *신체적 제약을 이해하는 것의 중요성 ─

재귀적 용법의 재귀대명사
Dancers often push **themselves** / to the limits of their physical
capabilities. //   단서1 신체적으로 불가능한
무용수는 종종 자신을 밀어붙인다 / 자신의 신체 능력의 한계까지 //   것을 달성하려는 것은 잘못된
                                                              것임
But that push is misguided / if it is directed / toward
accomplishing something physically impossible. //
그러나 그렇게 밀어붙이는 것은 잘못 이해한 것이다 / 향하게 된다면 / 물리적으로 불가능한
것을 달성하는 쪽으로 //

For instance, / a tall dancer with long feet / may wish to perform
repetitive vertical jumps / to fast music, /
예를 들어 / 키가 크고 발이 긴 무용수가 / 반복적인 수직 점프를 수행하고 싶을 수 있다 / 빠른
음악에 맞춰 /
          ── 병렬 구조 (분사구문을 이끄는 현재분사) ──
pointing his feet while in the air / and **lowering** his heels to the
floor between jumps. //
공중에서 발끝을 뾰족하게 하고 / 점프 사이에 발뒤꿈치를 바닥에 내리면서 //
                           no matter+의문사=의문사+ever
That may be impossible / **no matter how** strong the dancer is. //
그것은 불가능할 수 있다 / 무용수가 아무리 힘이 좋을지라도 // 단서2 발이 긴 무용수에게는 힘과
                                              상관없이 불가능한 동작이 있음
But a short-footed dancer / may have no trouble! //
하지만 발이 짧은 무용수는 / 전혀 문제가 없을 것이다 // 단서3 하지만 같은 동작도 발이 짧은
                                              무용수에게는 문제가 되지 않음
Another dancer may be struggling / to complete a half-turn in
the air. //
또 다른 무용수는 애쓰고 있을 수 있다 / 공중에서 반 회전을 완성하려고 //
     동명사 주어   between A and B: A와 B 사이의
Understanding the connection / **between** a rapid turn rate / **and**
the alignment of the body close to the rotation axis / **tells** her
how to accomplish her turn successfully. //   단수 동사
연관성을 이해하는 것은 / 빠른 회전 속도와 / 회전축에 가깝게 몸을 정렬하는 것의 / 그
무용수에게 성공적으로 회전을 해내는 방법을 알려준다 //
                                                    동명사 주어
In both of these cases, / **understanding and working** within the
         ── 병렬 구조 (constraints 수식) ──
constraints / **imposed** by nature and **described** by physical laws /
이 두 경우 모두에서 / 제약을 이해하고 그 안에서 움직이는 것은 / 선천적으로 주어지고
물리적 법칙에 의해 설명되는 /
     단수 동사   분사구문
allows dancers to work efficiently, / **minimizing potential risk**
of injury. // 단서4 자신의 신체적 제약을 이해하는 것이 부상을 줄이고 효율적인 움직임을 가능케 함
무용수가 효율적으로 움직이게 해 준다 / 잠재적인 부상 위험을 최소화하면서 //

- capability ⓝ 능력 • misguided ⓐ 잘못 이해한
- repetitive ⓐ 반복적인 • vertical ⓐ 수직의 • rotation ⓝ 회전
- axis ⓝ 축 • minimize ⓥ 최소화하다 • constraint ⓝ 제약
- hostility ⓝ 적대감 • morality ⓝ 도덕성

무용수는 종종 자신의 신체 능력의 한계까지 자신을 밀어붙인다. 그러나 그렇게 밀어붙이는 것이 물리적으로 불가능한 것을 달성하는 쪽으로 향하게 된다면, 잘못 이해한 것이다.
예를 들어, 키가 크고 발이 긴 무용수가 공중에서 발끝을 뾰족하게 하고 점프 사이에 발뒤꿈치를 바닥에 내리면서 빠른 음악에 맞춰 반복적인 수직 점프를 수행하고 싶을 수 있다. 무용수가 아무리 힘이 좋을지라도 그것은 불가능할 수 있다. 하지만 발이 짧은 무용수는 전혀 문제가 없을 것이다! 또 다른 무용수는 공중에서 반 회전을 완성하려고 애쓰고 있을 수 있다. 빠른 회전 속도와 회전축에 가깝게 몸을 정렬하는 것의 연관성을 이해하는 것은 그 무용수에게 성공적으로 회전을 해내는 방법을 알려준다.
이 두 경우 모두에서, 선천적으로 주어지고 물리적 법칙에 의해 설명되는 제약을 이해하고 그 안에서 움직이는 것은 잠재적인 부상 위험을 최소화하면서 무용수가 효율적으로 움직이게 해 준다.

┌──────────────────────────────────────┐
다음 빈칸에 들어갈 말로 가장 적절한 것을 고르시오.
① habits   습관에 관한 내용이 아니라, 선천적인   ② cultures 문화를 이해하는 것과 관련된
   습관   신체적 한계를 설명하고 있음   문화   내용은 언급되지 않음
③ constraints 자신의 선천적인 신체적 제약을   ④ hostilities 적대감에 관한 내용은
   제약   이해하는 것이 중요하다고 설명함   적대감   언급되지 않음
⑤ moralities 도덕성에 관한 내용은 언급되지 않음
   도덕성
└──────────────────────────────────────┘

2회 07 정답 ② *모든 연령대에서 소비되는 어린이 영화

We must explore the relationship / between children's film
between A and B: A와 B 사이의
production and consumption habits. //
우리는 관계를 탐구해야 한다 / 어린이 영화 제작과 소비 습관 사이의 //

The term "children's film" / implies ownership by children / —
their cinema — / **단서1** 어린이 영화는 어린이들의 소유임을 암시하지만, 실제로는 반대임
'어린이 영화'라는 용어는 / 어린이에 의한 소유권을 암시하지만 / 즉 '그들의' 영화 /
but films supposedly made for children / have always been
과거분사구 (films 수식) **현재완료시제 수동태**
consumed by audiences of all ages, / particularly in commercial
cinemas. //
소위 어린이를 위해 만들어진 영화는 / 항상 모든 연령대의 관객들에게 소비되어 왔다 / 특히
상업 영화에서 //
단서2 어린이 영화의 관객 구성은 나이대를 넘나들고 있음이 증명됨

The considerable crossover / in audience composition for
children's films / can be shown by the fact /
상당한 (연령 간의) 넘나듦이 있다는 것은 / 어린이 영화의 관객 구성에서 / 사실에 의해
증명될 수 있다 /
동격절 접속사
that, in 2007, eleven Danish children's and youth films /
attracted 59 per cent of theatrical admissions, /
2007년에 11개의 덴마크의 어린이 및 청소년 영화가 / 극장 입장객의 59퍼센트를
끌어모았고 /

and in 2014, German children's films / comprised seven out of
the top twenty films / at the national box office. //
2014년에는 독일의 어린이 영화가 / 상위 20개 영화 중 7개를 차지했다 / 전국 극장 흥행
수익에서 //
단서3 어린이 영화가 다양한 연령의 관객에게서 광범위하고 국제적으로 수용되고 있음
This phenomenon corresponds with a broader, international
관계대명사 (명사절)
embrace / of what is seemingly children's culture / among
audiences of diverse ages. //
이 현상은 더 광범위하고 국제적으로 수용되는 것과 일치한다 / 겉으로는 어린이 문화처럼
보이는 것이 / 다양한 연령대의 관객들 사이에서 //
단수 주어 **동격절 접속사**
The old prejudice / that children's film is some other realm, /
separate from / (and forever subordinate to) / a more legitimate
cinema for adults /
오래된 편견은 / 어린이 영화가 다른 영역이라는 / 별개의 (그리고 영원히 하위의) / 성인을
위한 더 제대로 된 영화와는 / **단서4** 어린이 영화가 성인을 위한 영화와는 별개라는 편견은 사실이 아님
단수 동사
is not supported by the realities of consumption: /
소비의 실상에 의해 뒷받침되지 않는다 /

children's film is at the heart / of contemporary popular
culture. //
즉, 어린이 영화가 중심에 있다 / 현대 대중문화의 //

• consumption ⓝ 소비　　• imply ⓥ 암시하다
• supposedly ⓐ𝖽 소위　　• considerable ⓐ 상당한
• composition ⓝ 구성　　• Danish ⓐ 덴마크의
• theatrical ⓐ 극장의　　• comprise ⓥ ~으로 구성되다

• correspond with ~와 부합하다　　• embrace ⓝ 수용, 포용
• seemingly ⓐ𝖽 겉보기에는　　• prejudice ⓝ 편견　　• realm ⓝ 영역
• legitimate ⓐ 정통의　　• artistic ⓐ 예술적인
• inexperienced ⓐ 경험이 부족한

우리는 어린이 영화 제작과 소비 습관 사이의 관계를 탐구해야 한다. '어린이 영화'라는 용어는 어린이에 의한 소유권, 즉 '그들의' 영화를 암시하지만, 소위 어린이를 위해 만들어진 영화는 특히 상업 영화에서, 항상 **모든 연령대의 관객들에게 소비되어 왔다.** 어린이 영화의 관객 구성에서 상당한 (연령 간의) 넘나듦이 있다는 것은, 2007년에 11개의 덴마크의 어린이 및 청소년 영화가 극장 입장객의 59퍼센트를 끌어모았고 2014년에는 독일의 어린이 영화가 전국 극장 흥행 수익 상위 20개 영화 중 7개를 차지했다는 사실에 의해 증명될 수 있다. 이 현상은 다양한 연령대의 관객들 사이에서 겉으로는 어린이 문화처럼 보이는 것이 더 광범위하고 국제적으로 수용되는 것과 일치한다. 어린이 영화가 성인을 위한 더 제대로 된 영화와는 별개의 (그리고 영원히 하위의) 다른 영역이라는 오래된 편견은 소비의 실상에 의해 뒷받침되지 않는다. 즉, 어린이 영화가 현대 대중문화의 중심에 있다.

> **다음 빈칸에 들어갈 말로 가장 적절한 것을 고르시오.**
> ① centered on giving moral lessons 도덕적 교훈은 언급되지 않았음
> 　도덕적 교훈을 주는 것에 초점이 맞춰져 왔다
> ② consumed by audiences of all ages 실제로는 다양한 연령대의 관객들에게
> 　모든 연령대의 관객들에게 소비되어 왔다　소비되었음
> ③ appreciated through an artistic view 예술적 관점을 통한 감상은 언급되지
> 　예술적 관점을 통해 감상되어 왔다　않음
> ④ produced by inexperienced directors 언급되지 않음
> 　경험이 적은 감독들에 의해 제작되어 왔다
> ⑤ separated from the cinema for adults 빈칸의 내용과는 반대임
> 　성인을 위한 영화와 분리되어 왔다

| 문제 풀이 순서 | ★★★ [정답률 61%]

1st 빈칸이 포함된 문장을 읽고, 빈칸에 들어갈 말에 대한 단서를 얻는다.

빈칸 문장	'어린이 영화'라는 용어는 어린이에 의한 소유권, 즉 '그들의' 영화를 암시하지만, 소위 어린이를 위해 만들어진 영화는 특히 상업 영화에서, 항상 ＿＿＿＿＿＿.

➡ '어린이 영화'라는 용어는 어린이들의 소유임을 암시함 → 하지만(but), 빈칸은 이와 반대되는 내용이 이어질 것임
　▶ 빈칸을 채우려면 어린이 영화가 특히 상업 영화에서 어떤 특징을 지녔는지를 살펴보아야 한다.

2nd 글을 마저 읽으며 어린이 영화를 어떻게 설명하고 있는지를 찾는다.
・ 어린이 영화의 관객 구성은 나이대를 넘나들고 있음이 증명됨 **단서2**
・ 어린이 영화가 다양한 연령의 관객에게서 광범위하게 수용되고 있음 **단서3**
・ 어린이 영화가 성인을 위한 영화와는 별개라는 편견은 소비 실태를 살펴보면 뒷받침되지 않음 **단서4**

➡ 어린이 영화는 어린이의 소유라는 편견과는 달리, 실제로는 다양한 나이대의 관객들이 보고 있음 → 실제 소비 실태를 살펴보면 어린이 영화는 다양한 연령의 관객에게 수용됨
▶ 따라서 빈칸에 들어갈 말은 ② '모든 연령대의 관객들에게 소비되어 왔다'이다.

| 선택지 분석 |

① 어린이 영화가 도덕적 교훈을 준다는 내용은 언급되지 않았다.
② 어린이 영화라는 편견과는 달리 실제로는 다양한 연령대의 관객들에게 소비되었다.
③ 어린이 영화가 예술적 관점으로 감상되었다는 내용은 언급되지 않았다.
④ 어린이 영화가 경험이 적은 감독에 의해 제작되었다는 내용은 언급되지 않았다.
⑤ 어린이 영화는 성인을 위한 영화와는 분리된다는 오랜 편견이 있었으나, 소비 실태를 살펴보면 어린이 영화도 다양한 연령의 관객에게 소비된다는 내용이다.

2회 08 정답 ⑤ ＊무작위적인 변이와 비무작위적인 선택

단서 1 인체의 발달은 무작위적인 변이가 비무작위적인 선택과 결합하여 만들어짐

Development of the human body / from a single cell / provides many examples of the structural richness /
인체가 발달하는 것은 / 단일 세포로부터 / 구조적 풍부함의 많은 예를 제공한다 /

주격 관계대명사
that is possible / when the repeated production of random variation / is combined with nonrandom selection. //
가능해지는 / 무작위적인 변이의 반복적 생성이 / 비무작위적인 선택과 결합될 때 //

복수 주어
(A) Those in the right place that make the right connections
복수 동사   주격 관계대명사
are stimulated, / and those that don't are eliminated. //
제 자리에서 제대로 된 연결을 만들어 낸 것(세포)들은 활성화되고 / 그렇지 않은 것들은 제거된다 //

단서 2 (B)의 '위치에 의한 선택'이 먼저 나와야 함

This process is much like sculpting. //
이 과정은 마치 조각을 하는 것과 같다 //

A natural consequence of the strategy / is great variability from individual to individual / at the cell and molecular levels, / even though large-scale structures are quite similar. //
이 전략의 필연적 결과는 / 개인마다 큰 변이성이 있다는 것이다 / 세포와 분자 수준에서 / 전체 구조가 상당히 비슷하더라도 //

단서 3 (C) 뒤에 이어져서 살아남은 세포의 이야기를 이어감

(B) The survivors serve / to produce new cells / that undergo
주격 관계대명사
further rounds of selection. //
생존한 세포들은 역할을 한다 / 새로운 세포들을 만들어 내는 / 추가적인 선택의 과정을 거치는 //

Except in the immune system, / cells and extensions of cells / are not genetically selected during development, / but rather, are
not A but rather B 구문
positionally selected. //
면역계를 제외하면 / 세포와 세포의 확장은 / 발달 과정에서 유전적으로 선택되는 것이 아니라 / 위치에 의해 선택된다 //

'A부터 B까지'
(C) All phases of body development / from embryo to adult / exhibit random activities / at the cellular level, /
신체 발달의 모든 단계는 / 배아에서 성체에 이르기까지 / 무작위 활동을 보이고 / 세포 수준에서는 /

단서 4 주어진 글에서 말했던 인체의 발달 과정(세포의 무작위적인 변이+기준이 있는 선택)을 구체적으로 설명함

과거분사구 (possibilities 수식)   과거분사 (activities 수식)
and body formation depends on / the new possibilities / generated by these activities / coupled with selection of those
주격 관계대명사
outcomes / that satisfy previously built-in criteria. //
신체 형성은 달려 있다 / 새로운 가능성에 / 이러한 활동(무작위 활동)에 의해 만들어진 / 결과물의 선택과 더불어 / 이전에 확립된 기준을 만족시키는 //

병렬 구조 (동사)
Always new structure is based on old structure, / and at every stage / selection favors some cells and eliminates others. //
항상 새로운 구조는 오래된 구조를 기반으로 하며 / 모든 단계에서 / 선택은 일부 세포들을 선호하고 다른 세포들은 제거한다 //

- structural ⓐ 구조적인   • richness ⓝ 풍부함
- random ⓐ 무작위의   • nonrandom ⓐ 비무작위의
- stimulate ⓥ 자극하다, 활성화하다   • eliminate ⓥ 제거하다
- sculpt ⓥ 조각하다   • variability ⓝ 변이성
- undergo ⓥ 거치다, 겪다   • immune ⓐ 면역의
- extension ⓝ 확장   • genetically ⓐⓓ 유전적으로
- positionally ⓐⓓ 위치적으로   • phase ⓝ 단계   • cellular ⓐ 세포의
- built-in 확립된   • criterion ⓝ 기준 (pl. criteria)

단일 세포로부터 인체가 발달하는 것은 무작위적인 변이의 반복적 생성이 비무작위적인 선택과 결합될 때 가능해지는 구조적 풍부함의 많은 예를 제공한다. (C) 배아에서 성체에 이르기까지 신체 발달의 모든 단계는 세포 수준에서는 무작위 활동을 보이고, 신체 형성은 이전에 확립된 기준을 만족시키는 결과물의 선택과 더불어 이러한 활동(무작위 활동)에 의해 만들어진 새로운 가능성에 달려 있다. 항상 새로운 구조는 오래된 구조를 기반으로 하며, 모든 단계에서 선택은 일부 세포들을 선호하고 다른 세포들은 제거한다. (B) 생존한 세포들은 추가적인 선택의 과정을 거치는 새로운 세포들을 만들어 내는 역할을 한다. 면역계를 제외하면 세포와 세포의 확장은 발달 과정에서 유전적으로 선택되는 것이 아니라 위치에 의해 선택된다.

(A) 제 자리에서 제대로 된 연결을 만들어 낸 것(세포)들은 활성화되고, 그렇지 않은 것들은 제거된다. 이 과정은 마치 조각을 하는 것과 같다. 이 전략의 필연적 결과는 전체 구조가 상당히 비슷하더라도 세포와 분자 수준에서 개인마다 큰 변이성이 있다는 것이다.

주어진 글 다음에 이어질 글의 순서로 가장 적절한 것을 고르시오. [3점]

① (A) ─ (C) ─ (B) (A)의 '올바른 자리'에 관한 내용은 주어진 글에 없음
② (B) ─ (A) ─ (C)
③ (B) ─ (C) ─ (A) (B)의 '생존한 세포들'에 관한 내용은 주어진 글에 없음
④ (C) ─ (A) ─ (B) (A)의 '올바른 자리'에 관한 내용은 (B)에 제시됨
⑤ (C) ─ (B) ─ (A) (C) 인체는 세포의 임의 변이와 근거 있는 구조적 선택이 결합하여 발달함
─ (B) 선택에서 살아남은 세포는 확장하며 발달하는데, 이는 위치에 의해 선택됨 ─ (A) 올바른 자리에서 연결된 세포만이 살아남게 됨

| 문제 풀이 순서 | ★★★ [정답률 41%]

1st 각 문단의 내용을 파악하고, 글의 논리적인 순서를 추론한다.

주어진 글: 단일 세포로부터 인체가 발달하는 것은 무작위적인 변이의 반복적 생성이 비무작위적인 선택과 결합될 때 가능해지는 구조적 풍부함의 많은 예를 제공한다.

➡ **주어진 글 뒤:** 인체가 발달하는 과정에서 세포는 무작위적으로 변이하지만, 그 선택과 결합은 무작위가 아닌 규칙적으로 이뤄질 것이라는 내용이 이어질 것이다.

(A): 제 자리에서 제대로 된 연결을 만들어 낸 것(세포)들은 활성화되고, 그렇지 않은 것들은 제거된다. 이 과정은 마치 조각을 하는 것과 같다. 이 전략의 필연적 결과는 전체 구조가 상당히 비슷하더라도 세포와 분자 수준에서 개인마다 큰 변이성이 있다는 것이다.

➡ **(A) 앞:** '제 자리에서 제대로 된 연결'이 가리키는 내용이 제시되어야 한다.
(A) 뒤: 세포의 변이와 선택의 과정에 대한 설명을 마무리했고, 이에 따른 결과까지 제시하고 있으므로 (A)가 마지막임을 알 수 있다.

(B): 생존한 세포들은 추가적인 선택의 과정을 거치는 새로운 세포들을 만들어 내는 역할을 한다. 면역계를 제외하면 세포와 세포의 확장은 발달 과정에서 유전적으로 선택되는 것이 아니라 위치에 의해 선택된다.

➡ **(B) 앞:** '생존한 세포들'이 가리키는 내용이 제시되어야 한다.
▶ 주어진 글과 (A)에는 생존한 세포에 관한 내용이 없으므로 (C)에 있을 것이고, (C)가 (B)의 앞에 올 것이다. (순서: (C) ➡ (B))
(B) 뒤: 세포의 발달은 유전이 아니라 위치에 의해 선택된다고 했으므로, 위치와 관련된 내용인 (A)가 뒤에 올 것이다. ▶ 순서: (C) ➡ (B) ➡ (A)

(C): 배아에서 성체에 이르기까지 신체 발달의 모든 단계는 세포 수준에서는 무작위 활동을 보이고, 신체 형성은 이전에 확립된 기준을 만족시키는 결과물의 선택과 더불어 이러한 활동(무작위 활동)에 의해 만들어진 새로운 가능성에 달려 있다. 항상 새로운 구조는 오래된 구조를 기반으로 하며, 모든 단계에서 선택은 일부 세포들을 선호하고 다른 세포들은 제거한다.

➡ **(C) 앞:** 배아에서 성체에 이르기까지 인체가 발달하는 과정을 설명하고 있으므로, 관련된 내용이 있어야 한다.
▶ 주어진 글에서 말했던 인체의 발달 과정(세포의 무작위적인 변이+기준이 있는 선택)을 구체적으로 설명함 (순서: 주어진 글 ➡ (C) ➡ (B) ➡ (A))

2nd 글이 한눈에 들어오도록 정리하여 정답을 확인한다.

주어진 글: 인체의 발달은 무작위적인 변이가 비무작위적인 선택과 결합하여 만들어진다.
→ **(C):** 인체는 세포의 임의 변이와 근거 있는 구조적 선택이 결합하여 발달하며, 구조적 선택은 선호가 있다.
→ **(B):** 선택에서 살아남은 세포는 확장하며 발달하는데, 이는 위치에 의해 선택된다.
→ **(A):** 올바른 자리에서 연결된 세포만이 살아남게 되는데, 이 과정을 통해 세포 수준에서는 개인마다 변이가 있더라도, 전체 구조에서는 유사성이 생긴다.
▶ 주어진 글 다음에 이어질 글의 순서는 (C) ➡ (B) ➡ (A)이므로 정답은 ⑤임

2회 09 정답 ③ *새가 무리에서 떨어지는 것의 생태학적 의의*

글의 흐름으로 보아, 주어진 문장이 들어가기에 가장 적절한 곳을 고르시오. [3점]

단서 1 무리에서 떨어지는 것이 의미 없는 현상이라는 내용 뒤에 와야 함

형용사적 용법 (evidence 수식)

However, there are many lines of evidence / to suggest / that vagrancy can, / on rare occasions, / dramatically alter the fate / of populations, species or even whole ecosystems. //
하지만 많은 증거가 있다 / 시사하는 / 무리에서 떨어져 헤매는 것이 / 드문 경우에 / 운명을 극적으로 바꿀 수 있다는 것을 / 개체 수, 종, 심지어 생태계 전체의 //

가주어   진주어절 접속사
It is a common assumption / that most vagrant birds are ultimately doomed, /
일반적인 가정이다 / 무리에서 떨어져 헤매는 대부분의 새들은 궁극적으로 죽을 운명이라는 것이 /

관계부사
aside from the rare cases / where individuals are able to reorientate / and return to their normal ranges. //
드문 경우를 제외하고 / 개체들이 방향을 다시 잡고 / 그들의 일반적인 (서식) 범위로 돌아갈 수 있는 //

단서 2 무리에서 떨어지는 것은 그다지 중요하지 않은 생물학적 현상으로 여겨짐

가주어   진주어절 접속사   강조적 용법의 재귀대명사
(①) In turn, it is also commonly assumed / that vagrancy itself is / a relatively unimportant biological phenomenon. //
결국, 일반적으로 여겨지기도 한다 / 무리에서 떨어져 헤매는 것 자체가 / 비교적 중요하지 않은 생물학적 현상이라고 //

부사절 접속사 (이유)
(②) This is undoubtedly true for the majority of cases, / as the most likely outcome of any given vagrancy event is /
이것은 대부분의 경우에 의심할 여지 없이 사실인데 / 무리에서 떨어져 헤매는 어떤 경우든 가장 가능성 있는 결과는 /

주격 보어절 접속사
that the individual will fail to find enough resources, / and/or be exposed to inhospitable environmental conditions, / and perish.
병렬 구조 (will 뒤에 연결)
개체가 충분한 자원을 찾지 못한다 / 그리고/또는 살기 힘든 환경 조건에 노출되어 / 죽기 때문이다 /

단서 3 '이러한 경우'는 주어진 문장을 가리킴
(③) Despite being infrequent, / these events can be extremely important / when viewed at the timescales / over which
앞에 「주어+be동사」 생략   「전치사+관계대명사」
ecological and evolutionary processes unfold. //
드물기는 하지만 / 이러한 경우들은 매우 중요할 수 있다 / 시간의 관점에서 볼 때 / 생태학적이고 진화적인 과정이 진행되는 //

(④) The most profound consequences of vagrancy / relate to the establishment / of new breeding sites, / new migration routes and wintering locations. //
무리에서 떨어져 헤매는 것의 가장 중대한 결과는 / 확보와 관련이 있다 / 새로운 번식지 / 새로운 이동 경로 및 월동 장소의 //

(⑤) Each of these can occur / through different mechanisms, / and at different frequencies, / and they each have their own
절과 절을 잇는 등위접속사
unique importance. //
이들 각각은 발생할 수 있으며 / 서로 다른 메커니즘을 통해 / 서로 다른 빈도로 / 각각 고유한 중요성을 가지고 있다 //

- fate ⓝ 운명   · population ⓝ 개체 수
- vagrant ⓐ 부랑하는, 헤매는   · reorientate ⓥ 방향을 다시 잡다
- range ⓝ 범위   · phenomenon ⓝ 현상
- undoubtedly ⓐ 의심의 여지 없이   · perish ⓥ 죽다, 멸망하다
- infrequent ⓐ 드문   · unfold ⓥ 펼쳐지다
- profound ⓐ 중대한, 심오한   · breeding ⓝ 번식
- migration ⓝ 이동   · wintering ⓝ 월동, 겨울나기

무리에서 떨어져 헤매는 대부분의 새들은 방향을 다시 잡고 그들의 일반적인 (서식) 범위로 돌아갈 수 있는 드문 경우의 개체들을 제외하고, 궁극적으로 죽을 운명이라는 것이 일반적인 가정이다. (①) 결국, 무리에서 떨어져 헤매는 것 자체가 비교적 중요하지 않은 생물학적 현상이라고 일반적으로 여겨지기도 한다. (②) 이것은 대부분의 경우에 의심할 여지 없이 사실

인데, 무리에서 떨어져 헤매는 어떤 경우든 가장 가능성 있는 결과는 개체가 충분한 자원을 찾지 못하고/못하거나, 살기 힘든 환경 조건에 노출되어 죽기 때문이다. (③ 하지만, 드문 경우에, 무리에서 떨어져 헤매는 것이 개체 수, 종, 심지어 생태계 전체의 운명을 극적으로 바꿀 수 있다는 것을 시사하는 많은 증거가 있다.) 드물기는 하지만, 이러한 경우들은 생태학적이고 진화적인 과정이 진행되는 시간의 관점에서 볼 때 매우 중요할 수 있다. (④) 무리에서 떨어져 헤매는 것의 가장 중대한 결과는 새로운 번식지, 새로운 이동 경로 및 월동 장소의 확보와 관련이 있다. (⑤) 이들 각각은 서로 다른 메커니즘을 통해, 서로 다른 빈도로 발생할 수 있으며, 각각 고유한 중요성을 가지고 있다.

| 문제 풀이 순서 | ★★❀ [정답률 51%]

1st 주어진 문장을 해석하고, 앞뒤에 어떤 내용이 올지 생각한다.

However, there are many lines of evidence to suggest that vagrancy can, on rare occasions, dramatically alter the fate of populations, species or even whole ecosystems.
하지만, 드문 경우에, 무리에서 떨어져 헤매는 것이 개체 수, 종, 심지어 생태계 전체의 운명을 극적으로 바꿀 수 있다는 것을 시사하는 많은 증거가 있다.

➡ 무리에서 떨어지는 것이 생태계의 운명을 바꿀 수 있다는 점을 설명했다.
  ▶ 주어진 문장이 들어갈 곳: However로 이어지고 있으므로 무리에서 떨어지는 것이 생태계에 그다지 중요하지 않다고 여겨진다는 내용이 끝나는 곳

2nd 각 선택지의 앞뒤 흐름이 매끄러운지 확인한다.

- ①의 앞 문장과 뒤 문장
앞 문장: 무리에서 떨어져 헤매는 대부분의 새들은 방향을 다시 잡고 그들의 일반적인 (서식) 범위로 돌아갈 수 있는 드문 경우의 개체들을 제외하고, 궁극적으로 죽을 운명이라는 것이 일반적인 가정이다.
뒤 문장: 결국, 무리에서 떨어져 헤매는 것 자체가 비교적 중요하지 않은 생물학적 현상이라고 일반적으로 여겨지기도 한다.

➡ 무리에서 떨어지는 것 자체는 비교적 중요하지 않은 현상으로 여겨진다는 내용이 자연스럽게 이어진다. ▶ 주어진 문장이 ①에 들어갈 수 없음

- ②의 앞 문장과 뒤 문장
앞 문장: ①의 뒤 문장과 같음
뒤 문장: 이것은 대부분의 경우에 의심할 여지 없이 사실인데, 무리에서 떨어져 헤매는 어떤 경우든 가장 가능성 있는 결과는 개체가 충분한 자원을 찾지 못하고/못하거나, 살기 힘든 환경 조건에 노출되어 죽기 때문이다.

➡ 무리에서 떨어지는 경우 대부분 죽게 된다는 내용이므로, 무리에서 떨어지는 것이 그다지 중요하지 않은 현상이라는 점은 사실이라는 내용으로 자연스럽게 이어진다.
  ▶ 주어진 문장이 ②에 들어갈 수 없음

- ③의 앞 문장과 뒤 문장
앞 문장: ②의 뒤 문장과 같음
뒤 문장: 드물기는 하지만, 이러한 경우들은 생태학적이고 진화적인 과정이 진행되는 시간의 관점에서 볼 때 매우 중요할 수 있다.

➡ 이러한 경우들이 진화적인 관점에서 매우 중요할 수 있다고 했으므로, 무리에서 떨어지는 것이 그다지 중요하지 않다고 주장했던 앞의 내용과 상반된다.
  ▶ 주어진 문장은 무리에서 떨어지는 것이 생태계에 엄청난 영향을 미칠 수 있다는 내용이 시작되는 부분이므로, ③에 들어가야 함

- ④의 앞 문장과 뒤 문장
앞 문장: ③의 뒤 문장과 같음
뒤 문장: 무리에서 떨어져 헤매는 것의 가장 중대한 결과는 새로운 번식지, 새로운 이동 경로 및 월동 장소의 확보와 관련이 있다.

➡ 무리에서 떨어지는 것이 종에 미치는 영향을 설명하고 있다.
  ▶ 주어진 문장이 ④에 들어갈 수 없음

- ⑤의 앞 문장과 뒤 문장
앞 문장: ④의 뒤 문장과 같음
뒤 문장: 이들 각각은 서로 다른 메커니즘을 통해, 서로 다른 빈도로 발생할 수 있으며, 각각 고유한 중요성을 가지고 있다.

➡ 이러한 결과는 다른 메커니즘과 다른 빈도로 발생하며, 각각이 중요한 의미를 지닌다고 설명하고 있다. ▶ 주어진 문장이 ⑤에 들어갈 수 없음

무리에서 떨어져 헤매는 새들은 궁극적으로 죽을 운명이라는 것이 일반적인 가정이다.
(①) 무리에서 떨어져 헤매는 것 자체가 중요하지 않은 생물학적 현상으로 여겨진다.
(②) 무리에서 떨어져 헤매는 어떤 경우든 죽기 때문이다.
(③ 하지만, 드문 경우에, 무리에서 떨어져 헤매는 것이 개체 수, 종, 심지어 생태계 전체의 운명을 극적으로 바꿀 수 있다는 것을 시사하는 많은 증거가 있다.)
드물기는 하지만, 이러한 경우들은 생태학적이고 진화적인 과정이 진행되는 시간의 관점에서 볼 때 매우 중요할 수 있다.
(④) 무리에서 떨어져 헤매는 것의 가장 중대한 결과는 새로운 번식지, 새로운 이동 경로 및 월동 장소의 확보와 관련이 있다.
(⑤) 이들 각각은 서로 다른 메커니즘을 통해, 서로 다른 빈도로 발생할 수 있다.

2회 10 정답 ① *가치 있는 지식을 찾게 하는 도구의 필요성

과거분사구 (data 수식)
The fast-growing, tremendous amount of data, / collected and stored in large and numerous data repositories, /
빠르게 증가하는 엄청난 양의 데이터는 / 크고 많은 데이터 저장소에 수집되고 저장되어 /

has far exceeded our human ability / for understanding without powerful tools. // **단서 1** 데이터는 인간이 도구 없이 이해할 수 있는 능력을 훨씬 능가하여 압도하고 있음
우리 인간의 능력을 훨씬 뛰어넘었다 / 효과적인 도구 없이는 이해할 수 있는 //

과거분사구 (data 수식)
As a result, / data collected in large data repositories / become "data tombs" / — data archives that are hardly visited. //
주격 관계대명사
결과적으로 / 대규모 데이터 저장소에서 수집된 데이터는 / '데이터 무덤'이 된다 / 즉 찾는 사람이 거의 없는 데이터 보관소 //

Important decisions are often made / based not on the information-rich data stored in data repositories / but rather on a decision maker's instinct, /
not A but rather B 구문
중요한 의사 결정이 종종 내려지기도 하는데 / 데이터 저장소에 저장된 정보가 풍부한 데이터가 아닌 / 의사 결정자의 직관에 기반하여 /

형용사적 용법 (tools 수식)
simply because the decision maker does not have the tools / to extract the valuable knowledge / hidden in the vast amounts of data. //
과거분사구 (knowledge 수식)
이는 단지 의사 결정자가 도구를 가지고 있지 않기 때문이다 / 가치 있는 지식을 추출할 수 있는 / 방대한 양의 데이터에 숨겨진 //

현재완료의 수동태   형용사적 용법 (efforts 수식)
Efforts have been made / to develop expert system and knowledge-based technologies, /
노력이 있어 왔는데 / 전문가 시스템과 지식 기반 기술을 개발하려는 /

which typically rely on / users or domain experts / to manually input knowledge into knowledge bases. //
계속적 용법의 주격 관계대명사
이는 일반적으로 의존한다 / 사용자나 분야(별) 전문가가 / 지식을 '수동으로' 지식 기반에 입력하는 것에 //

'~하기 쉽다'
However, this procedure / is likely to cause biases and errors / and is extremely costly and time consuming. //
그러나 이 방법은 / 편견과 오류를 일으키기 쉽고 / 비용과 시간이 엄청나게 든다 //

The widening gap between data and information / calls for the systematic development of tools / that can turn data tombs / into "golden nuggets" of knowledge. //
주격 관계대명사   turn A into B: A를 B로 바꾸다
점점 더 벌어지는 데이터와 정보 간의 격차로 인해 / 도구의 체계적인 개발이 요구된다 / **단서 2** 데이터 무덤에서 가치 있는 지식을 얻을 수 있도록 도와주는 도구가 개발되어야 함
데이터 무덤을 바꿀 수 있는 / 지식의 '금괴'로 //

→ As the vast amounts of data / stored in repositories / (A) overwhelm human understanding, /
과거분사구 (data 수식)
방대한 양의 데이터는 / 저장소에 저장된 / 인간의 이해를 압도하기 때문에 /

형용사적 용법 (tools 수식)
effective tools to (B) obtain valuable knowledge / are required / for better decision-making. //
가치 있는 지식을 얻기 위한 효과적인 도구가 / 요구된다 / 더 나은 의사 결정을 위해 //

- fast-growing 빨리 성장하는 · tremendous ⓐ 엄청난
- numerous ⓐ 수많은 · exceed ⓥ 능가하다 · tomb ⓝ 무덤
- archive ⓝ 보관소 · extract ⓥ 추출하다 · manually ⓐⓓ 수동으로
- input ⓥ 입력하다 · costly ⓐ 비용이 드는
- time consuming 시간 소모가 큰 · call for ~을 요구하다

빠르게 증가하는 엄청난 양의 데이터는, 크고 많은 데이터 저장소에 수집되고 저장되어, 우리 인간이 효과적인 도구 없이는 이해할 수 있는 능력을 훨씬 뛰어넘었다. 결과적으로, 대규모 데이터 저장소에서 수집된 데이터는 '데이터 무덤', 즉 찾는 사람이 거의 없는 데이터 보관소가 된다. 중요한 의사 결정이 종종 데이터 저장소에 저장된 정보가 풍부한 데이터가 아닌 의사 결정자의 직관에 기반하여 내려지기도 하는데, 이는 단지 의사 결정자가 방대한 양의 데이터에 숨겨진 가치 있는 지식을 추출할 수 있는 도구를 가지고 있지 않기 때문이다. 전문가 시스템과 지식 기반 기술을 개발하려는 노력이 있어 왔는데, 이는 일반적으로 사용자나 분야(별) 전문가가 지식을 '수동으로' 지식 기반에 입력하는 것에 의존한다. 그러나 이 방법은 편견과 오류를 일으키기 쉽고 비용과 시간이 엄청나게 든다. 점점 더 벌어지는 데이터와 정보 간의 격차로 인해 데이터 무덤을 지식의 '금괴'로 바꿀 수 있는 도구의 체계적인 개발이 요구된다.
→ 저장소에 저장된 방대한 양의 데이터는 인간의 이해를 (A) 압도하기 때문에, 더 나은 의사 결정을 위해 가치 있는 지식을 (B) 얻기 위한 효과적인 도구가 요구된다.

다음 글의 내용을 한 문장으로 요약하고자 한다. 빈칸 (A), (B)에 들어갈 말로 가장 적절한 것은?

	(A)		(B)
①	overwhelm 압도하다	—	obtain 얻다
②	overwhelm	—	exchange 교환하다
③	enhance 향상하다	—	apply 적용하다
④	enhance	—	discover 발견하다
⑤	fulfill 달성하다	—	access 접근하다

① 엄청난 양의 데이터는 인간의 이해를 압도해, 가치 있는 지식을 얻기 위한 도구가 필요함
② 지식을 교환하는 것은 아님
③④ 인간의 이해를 향상한다는 것은 아님
⑤ 인간의 이해를 달성한다는 것은 아님

왜 정답? ★★❋ [정답률 52%]

(A):
┌ 빠르게 증가하는 엄청난 양의 데이터는, 크고 많은 데이터 저장소에 수집되고
│ 저장되어, 우리 인간이 효과적인 도구 없이는 이해할 수 있는 능력을 훨씬
└ 뛰어넘었다. **단서 1**
➡ 데이터 저장소에 수집된 방대한 양의 데이터는 인간이 도구 없이 이해할 수 있는 능력을 훨씬 능가했다고 했으므로, 인간의 이해를 '압도했다(overwhelm)'는 표현이 알맞다.

(B):
┌ 점점 더 벌어지는 데이터와 정보 간의 격차로 인해 데이터 무덤을 지식의 '금괴'로
└ 바꿀 수 있는 도구의 체계적인 개발이 요구된다. **단서 2**
➡ 데이터 무덤을 지식의 금괴로 바꿀 도구가 개발되어야 한다고 했으므로, 방대한 데이터에서 가치 있는 지식을 '얻는다(obtain)'는 표현이 알맞다.
▶ 요약문의 빈칸에는 각각 ① '압도하다'와 '얻다'가 들어가야 함

왜 오답?
② 가치 있는 지식을 얻기 위한 도구가 필요할 뿐, 지식을 교환하는 것은 아니다.
③ 인간의 이해를 압도할 정도의 방대한 데이터를 설명하고 있으므로, 인간의 이해를 향상한다는 것은 아니고, 가치 있는 지식을 얻기 위한 도구를 설명하고 있으므로, 지식을 적용한다는 것은 아니다.
④ 인간의 이해를 압도할 정도의 방대한 데이터를 설명하고 있으므로, 인간의 이해를 향상한다는 것은 아니다.
⑤ 인간의 이해를 압도할 정도의 방대한 데이터를 설명하고 있으므로, 인간의 이해를 달성한다는 것은 아니다.

도입	데이터 저장소에 수집된 방대한 양의 데이터는 인간이 도구 없이 이해할 수 있는 능력을 훨씬 능가함
문제	방대한 데이터에서 가치 있는 지식을 찾도록 도와주는 도구가 없어서 의사 결정은 데이터보다는 결정권자의 직관에 의존하게 됨
해결	더 나은 의사 결정을 위해서는 데이터의 무덤에서 중요한 지식을 얻을 수 있는 도구가 개발되어야 함

2회 11~12 ＊멀티태스킹을 하는 동안 뇌에서 일어나는 일들

It's untrue / that teens can focus on two things at once / — what they're doing is / shifting their attention / from one task to another. //
사실이 아니며 / 십 대들이 동시에 두 가지 일에 집중할 수 있다는 것은 / 그들이 하고 있는 것은 / 주의를 전환하는 것이다 / 한 작업에서 다른 작업으로 //

In this digital age, / teens wire their brains / to make these shifts very quickly, / but they are still, like everyone else, / paying attention to one thing at a time, sequentially. //
디지털 시대에 / 십 대의 뇌는 발달하지만 / 매우 빠르게 작업을 전환하도록 / 여전히 십 대들도 다른 모든 사람들과 마찬가지로 / 한 번에 한 가지씩 순차적으로 주의를 기울이고 있다 //

Common sense tells us / multitasking should (a) increase brain activity, / but Carnegie Mellon University scientists / using the latest brain imaging technology / find it doesn't. //
상식적으로 생각하지만 / 멀티태스킹이 뇌 활동을 증가시킬 것이라고 / Carnegie Mellon 대학의 과학자들은 / 최신 뇌 영상 기술을 사용하여 / 그렇지 않다는 것을 발견했다 //

As a matter of fact, / they discovered / that multitasking actually decreases brain activity. //
사실 / 그들은 발견했다 / 멀티태스킹이 실제로는 두뇌 활동을 감소시킨다는 것을 //

Neither task is done / as well as if each were performed (b) individually. //
어느 작업도 되지 못한다 / 각각 개별적으로 수행될 때만큼 잘 //

Fractions of a second are lost / every time we make a switch, / and a person's interrupted task / can take 50 percent (c) longer to finish, / with 50 percent more errors. //
시간이 아주 조금씩 낭비되며 / 우리가 (작업을) 전환할 때마다 / 중단된 작업은 완료하기까지 50퍼센트 더 오래 걸리고 / 50퍼센트 더 많은 오류가 발생할 수 있다 //

Turns out / the latest brain research (d) contradicts(→ supports) the old advice / "one thing at a time." //
드러났다 / 최신 뇌 연구가 오래된 조언을 반박하는(→ 뒷받침하는) 것으로 / '한 번에 한 가지 일만 하라'는 //

It's not / that kids can't do some tasks simultaneously. //
아니다 / 아이들이 동시에 여러 작업을 할 수 없다는 것은 //

But if two tasks are performed at once, / one of them has to be familiar. //
하지만 동시에 두 가지 작업이 수행된다면 / 그 중 하나는 익숙한 작업이어야 한다 //

Our brains perform a familiar task / on "automatic pilot" / while really paying attention to the other one. //
우리의 뇌는 익숙한 작업은 수행하고 / '자동 조종' 상태에서 / 실제로는 다른 작업에 주의를 기울인다 //

That's why insurance companies consider / talking on a cell phone and driving / to be as (e) dangerous as driving while drunk /
그것이 보험 회사가 간주하는 이유이다 / 휴대전화로 통화하면서 운전하는 것을 / 술에 취한 상태에서 운전하는 것만큼 위험한 것으로 /

— it's the driving / that goes on "automatic pilot" / while the conversation really holds our attention. //
운전이다 / '자동 조종' 상태에서 수행되는 것은 / 대화가 실제로 우리의 주의를 끌고 있는 동안 //

Our kids may be living in the Information Age / but our brains have not been redesigned yet. //
우리 아이들이 정보화 시대에 살고 있을지 모르지만 / 우리의 뇌는 아직 (정보화 시대에 맞게) 재설계되지 않았다 //

- shift ⓥ 전환하다, 이동하다 ・ wire ⓥ 회로를 연결하다, 발달시키다
- sequentially ⓐⓓ 순차적으로
- multitasking ⓝ 멀티태스킹 (동시에 여러 가지 일을 하는 것)
- fraction ⓝ 일부 ・ turn out 드러나다
- simultaneously ⓐⓓ 동시에 ・ insurance ⓝ 보험
- redesign ⓥ 재설계하다 ・ attention span 주의집중 시간
- automaticity ⓝ 자동성

십 대들이 동시에 두 가지 일에 집중할 수 있다는 것은 사실이 아니며, 그들이 하고 있는 것은 한 작업에서 다른 작업으로 주의를 전환하는 것이다. 디지털 시대에, 십 대의 뇌는 매우 빠르게 작업을 전환하도록 발달하지만, 여전히 다른 모든 사람들과 마찬가지로 십 대들도 한 번에 한 가지씩 순차적으로 주의를 기울이고 있다. 상식적으로 멀티태스킹이 뇌 활동을 (a) 증가시킬 것이라고 생각하지만, Carnegie Mellon 대학의 과학자들은 최신 뇌 영상 기술을 사용하여 그렇지 않다는 것을 발견했다. 사실, 그들은 멀티태스킹이 실제로는 두뇌 활동을 감소시킨다는 것을 발견했다. 어느 작업도 각각 (b) 개별적으로 수행될 때만큼 잘 되지 못한다. 우리가 (작업을) 전환할 때마다 시간이 아주 조금씩 낭비되며, 중단된 작업은 완료하기까지 50퍼센트 (c) 더 오래 걸리고, 50퍼센트 더 많은 오류가 발생할 수 있다. 최신 뇌 연구가 '한 번에 한 가지 일만 하라'는 오래된 조언을 (d) 반박하는(→ 뒷받침하는) 것으로 드러났다.

아이들이 동시에 여러 작업을 할 수 없다는 것은 아니다. 하지만 동시에 두 가지 작업이 수행된다면, 그 중 하나는 익숙한 작업이어야 한다. 우리의 뇌는 익숙한 작업은 '자동 조종' 상태에서 수행하고 실제로는 다른 작업에 주의를 기울인다. 그것이 보험 회사가 휴대전화로 통화하면서 운전하는 것을 술에 취한 상태에서 운전하는 것만큼 (e) 위험한 것으로 간주하는 이유이다. 대화가 실제로 우리의 주의를 끌고 있는 동안 '자동 조종' 상태에서 수행되는 것은 운전이다. 우리 아이들이 정보화 시대에 살고 있을지 모르지만, 우리의 뇌는 아직 (정보화 시대에 맞게) 재설계되지 않았다.

2회 11 정답 ①

윗글의 제목으로 가장 적절한 것은?

① Multitasking Unveiled: What Really Happens in Teens' Brains
멀티태스킹이 밝혀지다: 실제로 십 대들의 머리에서 일어나는 일
② Optimal Ways to Expand the Attention Span of Teens
십 대들의 주의집중 시간을 확대하는 최적의 방법 주의집중 시간을 늘리는 방법이 소개된 글이 아님
③ Unknown Approaches to Enhance Brain Development
뇌 발달을 강화하는 알려지지 않은 방법들 멀티태스킹은 뇌 활동을 감소시킨다는 내용의 글임
④ Multitasking for a Balanced Life in a Busy World
바쁜 세상에서 균형잡힌 삶을 위한 멀티태스킹 오히려 작업 시간과 오류를 더 늘린다고 했음
⑤ How to Build Automaticity in Performing Tasks
작업을 수행할 때 자동성을 기르는 방법 자동 조종 상태에서 수행된다는 부분을 이용한 오답

＞왜 정답? ✽✽✽ [정답률 78%]

- 상식적으로 멀티태스킹이 뇌 활동을 증가시킬 것이라고 생각하지만, 그렇지 않다는 것을 발견함 11번 단서 1
- 우리의 뇌는 익숙한 작업은 '자동 조종' 상태에서 수행하고 실제로는 다른 작업에 주의를 기울임 11번 단서 2

➡ 십 대들이 멀티태스킹을 할 때 뇌가 어떻게 작업을 수행하는지를 연구한 글이다. 우리의 상식과는 달리 멀티태스킹은 뇌 활동을 증가시키지 않으며, 익숙한 작업은 '자동 조종' 상태에서 수행하고, 실제로는 다른 작업에 주의를 기울인다는 점을 설명하고 있다.

▶ 따라서 제목으로 적절한 것은 ① '멀티태스킹이 밝혀지다: 실제로 십 대들의 머리에서 일어나는 일'이다.

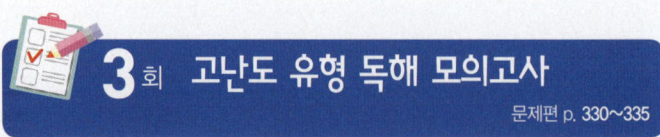
왜 오답?

② 멀티태스킹 중에는 하나의 작업에만 주의집중을 하게 된다는 부분을 이용한 오답이다.

③ 멀티태스킹은 오히려 뇌 활동을 감소시킨다고 했다. 뇌 발달 방법을 소개하는 글이 아니다.

④ 멀티태스킹이 오히려 작업 시간과 오류를 더 늘릴 수 있다고 했으므로 균형 잡힌 삶을 위한 방법으로 멀티태스킹을 소개하는 글이 아니다.

⑤ 멀티태스킹 중 익숙한 작업은 자동화된다는 언급만 있었을 뿐, 자동성을 기르는 방법을 소개한 글이 아니다. 주의

2회 12 정답 ④

밑줄 친 (a)~(e) 중에서 문맥상 낱말의 쓰임이 적절하지 않은 것은?

① (a) 상식적으로는 뇌 활동을 증가시킬 것이라 착각함
② (b) 멀티태스킹과 개별 작업의 수행력을 개별적으로 비교함
③ (c) 작업을 전환할 때마다 조금씩 시간 낭비를 더 오래 일으킴
④ (d) 멀티태스킹은 뇌 활동을 감소시킨다는 연구 결과는 '한 번에 한 가지 일만 하라'는 조언을 뒷받침함 반박하다
⑤ (e) 운전 중에 전화를 받는 행동은 음주운전만큼이나 위험함

왜 정답? ★★☆ [정답률 51%]

④ (d) contradicts 반박하다

┌ 최신 뇌 연구가 '한 번에 한 가지 일만 하라'는 오래된 조언을 (d) ~~반박하~~ 뒷받침하는
└ 것으로 드러났다.

➡ 멀티태스킹이 뇌 활동을 감소시킨다는 연구 결과는 '한 번에 한 가지 일만 하라'는 조언의 내용과 일맥상통하므로, 조언을 '반박하는' 것이 아니라 '뒷받침한다'는 내용이 와야 한다.

▶ contradicts를 supports(뒷받침하다)와 같은 어휘로 바꾸어야 한다.

왜 오답?

① (a) increase 증가시키다

┌ 상식적으로 멀티태스킹이 뇌 활동을 (a) 증가시킬 것이라고 생각하지만, Carnegie Mellon 대학의 과학자들은 최신 뇌 영상 기술을 사용하여 그렇지 않다는 것을 발견했다. 사실, 그들은 멀티태스킹이 실제로는 두뇌
└ 활동을 감소시킨다는 것을 발견했다.

➡ 이어지는 문장에서 멀티태스킹이 실제로는 두뇌 활동을 감소시킨다는 것을 발견했다고 했으므로 상식적으로는 멀티태스킹이 뇌 활동을 '증가시킬 것'이라고 생각했을 것이다. ▶ increase는 문맥에 맞음

② (b) individually 개별적으로

┌ 사실, 그들은 멀티태스킹이 실제로는 두뇌 활동을 감소시킨다는 것을
└ 발견했다. 어느 작업도 각각 (b) 개별적으로 수행될 때만큼 잘 되지 못한다.

➡ 멀티태스킹은 뇌 활동을 감소시키므로, 두 가지 일을 각각 '개별적으로' 수행할 때보다 수행력이 떨어진다. ▶ individually는 문맥에 맞음

③ (c) longer 더 오래

┌ 우리가 (작업을) 전환할 때마다 시간이 아주 조금씩 낭비되며, 중단된 작업은 완료하기까지 50퍼센트 (c) 더 오래 걸리고, 50퍼센트 더 많은
└ 오류가 발생할 수 있다.

➡ 멀티태스킹은 작업을 전환할 때마다 조금씩 시간 낭비를 일으켜 작업 완료까지 '더 오랜' 시간이 걸리는 등 뇌 활동을 감소시킨다. ▶ longer는 문맥에 맞음

⑤ (e) dangerous 위험한

┌ 그것이 보험 회사가 휴대전화로 통화하면서 운전하는 것을 술에 취한
└ 상태에서 운전하는 것만큼 (e) 위험한 것으로 간주하는 이유이다.

➡ 멀티태스킹은 한 가지 작업만 집중하고, 익숙한 작업은 자동으로 처리되도록 하므로, 운전 중에 전화를 받는 행동은 음주 운전만큼이나 '위험'하다.

▶ dangerous는 문맥에 맞음

3회 01 정답 ③ ⭐ 1등급 대비 [정답률 59%]

＊완벽함 추구 대신 조금씩 변화 일으키기

Everyone's heard the expression / don't let the perfect become the enemy of the good. //
현재완료시제 (경험)
누구나 표현을 들어 본 적이 있다 / '완벽함이 좋음의 적이 되게 두지 말라'는 //

If you want to get over an obstacle / so that your idea can
부사절 접속사 (목적)
become / the solution-based policy / you've long dreamed of, /
앞에 목적격 관계대명사 생략
여러분이 장애물을 극복하고 싶다면 / 자기 아이디어가 될 수 있도록 / 해결을 기반으로 한 방책이 / 자신이 오랫동안 꿈꿔 왔던 / 단서 1 전부 아니면 전무라는 사고방식을 가져서는 안 됨

you can't have / an all-or-nothing mentality. //
가져서는 안 된다 / 전부 아니면 전무라고 여기는 사고방식을 //

You have to be willing to alter your idea / and let others influence
let의 목적어와 목적격 보어 (원형부정사)
its outcome. //
여러분은 기꺼이 자기 아이디어를 바꾸고 / 다른 사람이 그것의 결과에 영향을 미치도록 해야 한다 //

You have to be okay / with the outcome being a little different, /
동명사 being의 의미상 주어
even a little less, / than you wanted. // 단서 2 원했던 결과를 얻지 못해도 괜찮다고 여겨야 함
여러분은 괜찮다고 여겨야 한다 / 결과가 조금 다르거나 / 심지어 조금 '못'하여도 / 여러분이 원했던 것보다 //

Say / you're pushing for a clean water act. //
가정해 보자 / 여러분이 수질 오염 방지법을 추진하고 있다고 //
주어절
Even if what emerges isn't as well-funded / as you wished, / or
병렬 구조
doesn't match / how you originally conceived the bill, /
비록 나타난 것이 자금이 충분하게 지원되지 않았거나 / 여러분이 원했던 만큼의 / 일치하지 않더라도 / 여러분이 처음에 이 법안을 고안한 방식과 /

you'll have still succeeded in ensuring / that kids in troubled
목적어절 접속사
areas / have access to clean water. //
여러분은 확실히 하는 데 여전히 성공하는 것이다 / 힘든 지역의 아이들이 / 깨끗한 물에 접근할 수 있도록 //

That's what counts, / that they will be safer / because of your
동격절 접속사
idea and your effort. //
중요한 것은 / 바로 '그들'이 더 안전하리라는 것이다 / 여러분의 아이디어와 노력 덕분에 //

Is it perfect? // No. //
완벽한가 // 아니다 //

Is there more work to be done? // Absolutely. //
형용사적 용법 (more work 수식)
더 해야 할 일이 있는가 // 당연하다 //

But in almost every case, / helping move the needle forward / is vastly better than not helping at all. //
하지만 거의 모든 경우에 / 바늘을 앞으로 이동시키는 것을 돕는 것이 / 전혀 돕지 않는 것보다 훨씬 더 낫다 //

- expression ⓝ 표현
- obstacle ⓝ 장애물
- all-or-nothing 양단의
- mentality ⓝ 사고방식
- alter ⓥ 변경하다
- outcome ⓝ 결과
- emerge ⓥ 나타나다
- conceive ⓥ 고안하다
- bill ⓝ 법안
- vastly ⓐⓓ 훨씬
- cost-saving 비용 절감
- donation ⓝ 기부(금)

'완벽함이 좋음의 적이 되게 두지 말라'는 표현은 누구나 들어 본 적이 있다. 여러분이 장애물을 극복해 자기 아이디어가 자신이 오랫동안 꿈꿔 왔던 해결을 기반으로 한 방책이 될 수 있도록 하고 싶다면, 전부 아니면 전무라고 여기는 사고방식을 가져서는 안 된다. 여러분은 기꺼이 자기 아이디어를 바꾸고 다른 사람이 그것의 결과에 영향을 미치도록 해야 한다. 결과가 조금 다르거나, 심지어 원했던 것보다 조금 '못'하여도 괜찮다고 여겨야 한다.

여러분이 수질 오염 방지법을 추진하고 있다고 가정해 보자. 비록 나타난 것이 여러분이 원했던 만큼의 자금이 충분하게 지원되지 않았거나, 여러분이 처음에 이 법안을 고안한 방식과 일치하지 않더라도, 여러분은 힘든 지역의 아이들이 깨끗한 물에 접근할 수 있도록 하는 데 여전히 성공하는 것이다. 중요한 것은 바로 여러분의 아이디어와 노력 덕분에 '그들'이 더 안전하리라는 것이다.
완벽한가? 아니다. 더 해야 할 일이 있는가? 당연하다. 하지만 거의 모든 경우에, 바늘을 앞으로 이동시키는 것을 돕는 것이 전혀 돕지 않는 것보다 훨씬 더 낫다.

밑줄 친 helping move the needle forward가 다음 글에서 의미하는 바로 가장 적절한 것은? [3점]

① spending time and money on celebrating perfection
완벽을 축하하는 데 시간과 돈을 쓰는 것   완벽을 추구하라는 내용이 아님
② suggesting cost-saving strategies for a good cause
좋은 목적을 위한 비용 절감 전략을 제안하는 것   비용 절감 전략에 대한 내용은 언급되지 않음
③ making a difference as best as the situation allows
상황이 허락하는 한 최선의 변화를 만드는 것   You have to be okay ~ than you wanted
④ checking your resources before altering the original goal
원래 목표를 변경하기 전에 자원을 확인하는 것   자원을 신경 쓰라는 글이 아님
⑤ collecting donations to help the education of poor children
가난한 아이들의 교육을 돕기 위해 기부금을 모으는 것   힘든 지역의 아이들은 예시일 뿐임

왜 1등급? move the needle이 '눈에 띌 정도로 바꾸다'를 의미하는 표현임을 알았다면 밑줄 친 부분의 표면적인 의미를 파악하는 데 도움이 되었겠지만, 그러지 못했다면 헤맬 수 있는 어려운 문제였다.

| 문제 풀이 순서 |

1st 첫 문장과 밑줄 친 부분이 포함된 문장을 읽고, 글의 내용을 예상한다.

첫 문장	'완벽함이 좋음의 적이 되게 두지 말라'는 표현은 누구나 들어 본 적이 있다.
밑줄 친 부분이 포함된 문장	하지만 거의 모든 경우에, 바늘을 앞으로 이동시키는 것을 돕는 것이 전혀 돕지 않는 것보다 훨씬 더 낫다.

→ 첫 문장: 완벽함을 추구하는 것은 오히려 좋지 않을 수 있음
밑줄 친 부분이 포함된 문장: 바늘을 앞으로 이동시키는 것만으로도 좋음 (단서)
→ 완벽함만을 추구하지 말라는 글일 것이므로, 전혀 돕지 않는 것보다 훨씬 더 낫다고 설명한 '바늘을 앞으로 이동시키는 것을 돕는 것'은 완벽한 것은 아니지만 최선의 것을 가리킬 것이다. (발상)

2nd 글의 나머지 부분을 읽고, 예상한 내용이 맞는지 확인한다.
- 전부 아니면 전무라고 여기는 사고방식을 가져서는 안 됨 → 기꺼이 자기 아이디어를 바꾸고 다른 사람이 결과에 영향을 미치도록 해야 함 (단서1)
- 결과가 원했던 것과 조금 다르거나, 심지어 원했던 것보다 조금 '못'하여도 괜찮다고 여겨야 함 (단서2)
→ 전부 아니면 전무라는 사고방식에서 벗어나 원했던 결과를 얻지 못하더라도 괜찮다는 태도를 지니면 점점 변화를 일으켜갈 수 있다는 것이 글의 중심 내용이다.

3rd 파악한 글의 내용을 종합하여 밑줄 친 부분의 의미를 파악한다.
밑줄 친 부분은 전혀 돕지 않는 것과 대조되어 조금씩이라도 변화를 만들어내는 것을 의미하기 때문에 ③ '상황이 허락하는 한 최선의 변화를 만드는 것'을 의미한다.

| 선택지 분석 |
① 밑줄 친 부분은 완벽을 추구한 것이 아닌 조금이라도 나아가는 것을 가리킨다.
② 비용을 절감할 수 있는 전략과 같은 내용에 대해서는 글에서 다루어지지 않았다.
③ 완벽하지 않더라도 조금씩 변화를 일으킬 수 있다는 내용의 글이다.
④ 전부 아니면 전무라고 여기는 사고방식을 바꾸어 원했던 결과를 얻지 못해도 괜찮다는 사고방식을 가지라는 내용이며, 자원을 신경 쓰는 것과는 무관하다.
⑤ 힘든 지역의 아이들은 예시일 뿐, 기부금을 모금하는 내용은 글에 제시되어 있지 않다.

---

02 정답 ⑤ * 고당도 과일의 과도한 섭취가 일으키는 문제

What consequences / of **eating** too many grapes and other sweet fruit / could there possibly be / for our brains? //
동명사 (전치사의 목적어)
어떤 영향이 / 포도와 그 외 달콤한 과일을 너무 많이 먹는 것의 / 과연 있을 수 있을까 / 우리의 뇌에 //

A few large studies / have helped to shed some light. //
몇 가지 대규모 연구가 / 새로운 견해를 밝히는 데 도움이 되었다 // 단서1 과일을 더 많이 섭취하면 해마 용적이 더 작아짐

In one, / **higher fruit intake** / in older, cognitively healthy adults / **was linked** with less volume in the hippocampus. //
단수 주어 / 단수 동사
한 연구에서는 / 더 많은 과일 섭취가 / 더 나이가 많고 인지적으로 건강한 성인에서 / 해마의 더 작은 용적과 연관되었다 //

This finding was unusual, / **since** people who eat more fruit / usually display the benefits / **associated with a healthy diet**. //
부사절 접속사 (이유)   과거분사구 (the benefits 수식)
이 발견은 특이했는데 / 그 이유는 과일을 더 많이 먹는 사람들은 / 보통 이점을 보여 주기 때문이었다 / 건강한 식단과 관련된 //

In this study, / however, / the researchers **isolated** various components of the subjects' diets / and **found** / that fruit didn't seem to be doing / their memory centers / any favors. //
병렬 구조 (동사)
이 연구에서 / 하지만 / 연구원들은 피실험자 식단의 다양한 요소들을 분리했고 / 발견했다 / 과일이 하지 않는 것처럼 보인다는 것을 / 그들의 기억 중추에 / 어떤 도움도 //

Another study from the Mayo Clinic / saw a similar inverse relationship / between fruit intake and **volume of the cortex**, **the large outer layer of the brain**. //
동격
Mayo Clinic의 또 다른 연구에서는 / 유사한 역관계를 확인했다 / 과일 섭취와 피질의 용적 사이의 / 뇌의 커다란 바깥층인 //

Researchers in the latter study noted / **that** excessive consumption of high-sugar fruit / (such as mangoes, bananas, and pineapples) /
목적어절 접속사
후자의 연구에서 연구원들은 주목했다 / 고당도 과일의 과도한 섭취가 / (망고, 바나나, 파인애플 같은) /
단서2 고당도 과일의 과도한 섭취가 신진대사와 인지 문제를 일으킬 수 있음

may cause metabolic and cognitive problems / as much as processed carbs do. //
신진대사 문제와 인지적 문제를 일으킬 수 있다는 점에 / 가공된 탄수화물 식품만큼이나 크게 //

- consequence ⓝ 결과, 영향
- shed ⓥ (빛을) 비추다
- intake ⓝ 섭취
- cognitively ⓐⓓ 인지적으로
- isolate ⓥ 분리하다
- component ⓝ 요소, 부품
- inverse ⓐ 역의, 반대의
- cortex ⓝ (대뇌의) 피질
- excessive ⓐ 지나친, 과도한
- consumption ⓝ 섭취
- metabolic ⓐ 신진대사의
- universal ⓐ 보편적인
- enhance ⓥ 향상시키다
- nutritional ⓐ 영양학적인

포도와 그 외 달콤한 과일을 너무 많이 먹는 것이 과연 우리의 뇌에 어떤 영향을 미칠 수 있을까? 몇 가지 대규모 연구가 (그것에 관한) 새로운 견해를 밝히는 데 도움이 되었다.
한 연구에서는, 더 나이가 많고 인지적으로 건강한 성인에서 더 많은 과일 섭취가 해마의 더 작은 용적과 연관되었다. 이 발견은 특이했는데, 그 이유는 과일을 더 많이 먹는 사람들은 보통 건강한 식단과 관련된 이점을 보여 주기 때문이었다. 하지만 이 연구에서, 연구원들은 피실험자 식단의 다양한 요소들을 분리했고 과일이 그들의 기억 중추에 어떤 도움도 주지 않는 것처럼 보인다는 것을 발견했다.
Mayo Clinic의 또 다른 연구에서는 과일 섭취와 뇌의 커다란 바깥층인 피질의 용적 사이의 유사한 역관계를 확인했다. 후자의 연구에서 연구원들은 (망고, 바나나, 파인애플 같은) 고당도 과일의 과도한 섭취가 가공된 탄수화물 식품만큼이나 크게 신진대사 문제와 인지적 문제를 일으킬 수 있다는 점에 주목했다.

모의고사 3회

다음 글의 주제로 가장 적절한 것은?

① benefits of eating whole fruit on the brain health
과일을 통째로 먹는 것이 뇌 건강에 미치는 이점　　　과일의 부정적인 측면에 관한 글임
② universal preference for sweet fruit among children
아이들 사이에서 달콤한 과일에 대한 보편적인 선호　　아이들에 관련된 내용이 아님
③ types of brain exercises enhancing long-term memory
장기 기억력을 향상시키는 뇌 운동의 종류들　　뇌 운동의 종류에 대해서는 언급되지 않음
④ nutritional differences between fruit and processed carbs
과일과 가공 탄수화물의 영양학적 차이　　과일과 가공 탄수화물의 영양을 비교하지 않았음
⑤ negative effect of fruit overconsumption on the cognitive brain
지나친 과일 섭취가 인지 뇌에 미치는 부정적인 영향　　may cause metabolic and cognitive problems

왜 정답? ✽✽✽ [정답률 74%]

• 더 나이가 많고 인지적으로 건강한 성인이 과일을 더 많이 섭취하면 해마 용적이 더 작아진다. 단서1
• 고당도 과일의 과도한 섭취가 신진대사 문제와 인지적 문제를 일으킬 수 있다. 단서2

→ 과일을 지나치게 많이 섭취함으로써 뇌, 인지와 관련된 문제가 발생할 수 있다고 했으므로, ⑤ '지나친 과일 섭취가 인지 뇌에 미치는 부정적인 영향'이 글의 주제이다.

왜 오답?
① 과일을 먹는 것의 이점이 아니라 부정적인 측면에 대한 글이다.
② 아이들을 대상으로 한 연구가 아니라 성인을 대상으로 한 연구를 소개했다.
③ 뇌 운동과 기억력의 관계에 대해서는 전혀 언급하지 않았다.
④ 둘의 영양학적 차이를 비교하지는 않았다. (이유: 과일이 가공된 탄수화물만큼 뇌 건강에 좋지 않다고만 언급했을 뿐이다.)

3회 03 정답 ④ ＊승리가 촉발하는 자의식적 인식의 영향

Winning turns on a self-conscious awareness / that others are watching. //
승리는 자의식적 인식을 촉발한다 / 다른 사람이 바라보고 있다는 //
It's a lot easier / to move under the radar / when no one knows you / and no one is paying attention. //
훨씬 더 쉽다 / 눈에 띄지 않게 움직이기가 / 아무도 여러분을 모르고 / 아무도 (여러분에게) 집중하고 있지 않으면 //
You can mess up and be rough and get dirty / because no one even knows / you're there. //
여러분은 일을 망치고, 난폭해지며, 비열해져도 되는데 / 왜냐하면 아무도 심지어 알지 못하기 때문이다 / 여러분이 그곳에 있다는 것을 // 단서1 승리하기 시작하면 관찰되고 있다는 것을 인식하게 됨
But as soon as you start to win, / and others start to notice, /
you're suddenly aware / that you're being observed. //
하지만 여러분이 승리하기 시작하고 / 다른 사람이 알아차리기 시작하는 순간부터 / 여러분은 갑자기 인식한다 / 여러분이 관찰되고 있다는 것을 //
You're being judged. //
여러분은 평가받고 있다 //
You worry / that others will discover your flaws and weaknesses, / and you start hiding your true personality, / 단서2 승리하면 본래의 성격을 숨기기 시작함
여러분은 걱정하고 / 다른 사람이 여러분의 실수와 약점을 발견할 것이라고 / 여러분 본래의 성격을 숨기기 시작한다 /
so you can be a good role model and good citizen and a leader / that others can respect. //
여러분이 좋은 본보기이자 훌륭한 시민이고 지도자가 될 수 있도록 / 다른 사람이 존경할 수 있는 //
There is nothing wrong with that. //
그것에 문제는 없다 //
But if you do it / at the expense of being who you really are, / making decisions / that please others / instead of pleasing yourself, /
하지만 만약 여러분이 그렇게 한다면 / 자신의 진정한 모습이 되는 것을 희생하면서까지 / 결정을 내리면서 / 타인을 기쁘게 하는 / 자기 자신을 기쁘게 하기보다 /

you're not going to be / in that position / very long. //
여러분은 머물지 못할 것이다 / 그 지위에 / 그리 오래 단서3 진정한 모습을 숨기는 것은 승리의 지위에 오래 머물지 못하게 함
When you start apologizing for who you are, / you stop growing / and you stop winning. //
여러분이 시작하는 순간 / 누구인지에 대해 사과하는 것을 / 여러분은 성장을 멈추고 / 승리를 멈추게 된다 //
Permanently. //
영원히 //

• awareness ⓝ 인식　　• mess up ~을 망치다
• discover ⓥ 발견하다　• weakness ⓝ 약점　• expense ⓝ 희생
• permanently ⓐⓓ 영원히　• disappointment ⓝ 실망
• criticism ⓝ 비판　• mislead ⓥ 잘못 인도하다
• mindset ⓝ 사고방식　• trap ⓝ 덫, 함정

승리는 다른 사람이 바라보고 있다는 자의식적 인식을 촉발한다. 아무도 여러분을 모르고 (여러분에게) 집중하고 있지 않으면 눈에 띄지 않게 움직이기가 훨씬 더 쉽다. 여러분은 일을 망치고, 난폭해지며, 비열해져도 되는데, 왜냐하면 여러분이 그곳에 있다는 것을 아무도 심지어 알지 못하기 때문이다.
하지만 여러분이 승리하기 시작하고, 다른 사람이 알아차리기 시작하는 순간부터, 여러분은 관찰되고 있다는 것을 갑자기 인식한다. 여러분은 평가받고 있다. 여러분은 다른 사람이 여러분의 실수와 약점을 발견할 것이라고 걱정하고, 여러분이 좋은 본보기이자 훌륭한 시민이고 다른 사람이 존경할 수 있는 지도자가 될 수 있도록 여러분 본래의 성격을 숨기기 시작한다.
그것에 문제는 없다. 하지만 자기 자신을 기쁘게 하기보다, 타인을 기쁘게 하는 결정을 내리면서 자신의 진정한 모습이 되는 것을 희생하면서까지 그렇게 한다면, 여러분은 그 지위에 그리 오래 머물지 못할 것이다. 여러분이 누구인지에 대해 사과하기 시작하는 순간, 여러분은 성장을 멈추고, 승리를 멈추게 된다. 영원히.

But as soon as ~ that you're being observed.
다음 글의 제목으로 가장 적절한 것은?
① Stop Judging Others to Win the Race of Life 경쟁에서 이기기 위한 방법은 언급되지 않음
인생의 경쟁에서 이기기 위해 다른 사람들을 판단하는 것을 멈춰라
② Why Disappointment Hurts More than Criticism
실망이 비판보다 더 많이 상처를 주는 이유　　비판과 실망에 대한 내용은 없음
③ Winning vs. Losing: A Dangerously Misleading Mindset
승리 대 패배: 위험할 정도로 잘못된 사고방식　　승리와 패배의 이분법적 사고방식에 관한 글은 아님
④ Winners in a Trap: Too Self-Conscious to Be Themselves
함정에 빠진 우승자: 너무 자의식이 강해서 그들 자신이 되지 못한다
⑤ Is Honesty the Best Policy to Turn Enemies into Friends?
정직이 적을 친구로 만드는 최선의 방책일까?　　정직이 최선의 방책이라는 방향의 글이 아님

왜 정답? ✽✽✽ [정답률 65%]

• 승리하기 시작하면 관찰되고 있다는 것을 인식하게 된다. 단서1
• 좋은 본보기이자 훌륭한 시민, 존경할 수 있는 지도자가 될 수 있도록 본래의 성격을 숨기기 시작한다. 단서2
• 자신의 진정한 모습이 되는 것을 희생하면서까지 타인을 기쁘게 하려고 한다면 승리의 지위에 그리 오래 머물지 못할 것이다. 단서3

→ 승리는 자의식적 인식을 촉발하여 승리한 사람은 자신의 본래 성격을 숨기기 시작하는데 그렇게 되면 승리의 지위에 오래 머물지 못할 것이라는 내용의 글이다.
▶ 따라서 제목으로 가장 적절한 것은 ④ '함정에 빠진 우승자: 너무 자의식이 강해서 그들 자신이 되지 못한다'이다.

왜 오답?
① 경쟁에서 이긴 사람들이 겪게 되는 자의식적 인식의 영향에 관한 글이지 경쟁에서 이기는 방법에 관한 글이 아니다.
② 승리하고 나서 다른 사람의 시선을 의식한다는 내용은 있으나 비판과 실망으로 인해 상처를 받는 내용의 글이 아니다.
③ 승리와 패배의 이분법적 사고방식이 잘못되었다는 글이 아니다.
⑤ 정직하게 이기라는 것을 말하는 글이 아니다.

3회 **04** 정답 ⑤ ━━━━━━━ ⭐ **1등급 대비** [정답률 63%]

*확실성을 통한 인간의 생존

다음 글의 밑줄 친 부분 중, 어법상 틀린 것은? [3점]

Human beings like certainty. //
인간은 확실성을 좋아한다 //

This liking stems from our ancient ancestors / ① who needed
to survive / alongside saber-toothed tigers and poisonous
berries. //
이 선호는 고대의 우리 선조들로부터 유래한다 / 살아남아야 했던 / 검치호와 독이 있는
딸기류 열매 곁에서 //

Our brains evolved to help / us attend to threats, / keep away
from ② them, / and remain alive afterward. //
우리의 뇌는 돕도록 진화했다 / 우리가 위협에 주의하고 / 그것들에서 벗어나 / 그 후에
살아남을 수 있게 //

In fact, / we learned / that the more ③ certain we were / about
something, / the better chance we had / of making the right
choice. //
사실 / 우리는 학습했다 / 우리 자신이 더 확신할수록 / 무언가에 대해 / 가능성이 더 크다는
것을 / 옳은 선택을 할 //

Is this berry the same shape / as last time? //
이 딸기류 열매는 모양이 같은가 / 지난번과 //

The same size? //
같은 크기인가 //

If I know for certain / it ④ is, / my brain will direct me to eat it /
because I know it's safe. //
내가 확실히 안다면 / 그것이 그렇다는 것을 / 나의 뇌는 내가 그것을 먹도록 안내한다 /
그것이 안전하다는 것을 내가 알기 때문에 //

And if I'm uncertain, / my brain will send out a danger alert /
to protect me. //
그리고 만약 내가 확실하지 않다면 / 나의 뇌는 위험 신호를 보낼 것이다 / 나를 보호하기 위해 //

The dependence on certainty / all those millennia ago / ensured
our survival to the present day, / and the danger-alert system /
continues to protect us. //
확실성에 대한 의존은 / 그 모든 수천 년 전의 / 현재까지 우리의 생존을 책임졌고 / 그 위험을
알리는 시스템은 / 계속하여 우리를 지키고 있다 //

This is achieved / by our brains labeling / new, vague, or
unpredictable everyday events and experiences / as uncertain. //
이것은 이루어진다 / 우리의 뇌가 명명함으로써 / 새롭거나 모호하거나 예측할 수 없는 매일의
사건과 경험을 / 불확실한 것으로 //

Our brains then ⑤ generating(→ generate) / sensations,
thoughts, and action plans / to keep us safe / from the uncertain
element, / and we live to see another day. //
그런 후 우리의 뇌는 만들어내고 / 감각, 사고, 그리고 행동 계획을 / 우리를 안전하게 지키기
위해 / 그 불확실한 요소로부터 / 우리는 살아서 또 다른 날을 보게 된다 //

- certainty Ⓝ 확실성 • alongside prep 옆에, 곁에서
- poisonous ⓐ 독이 있는 • threat Ⓝ 위협 • afterward ad 그 후에
- label ⓥ 꼬리표를 붙이다 • vague ⓐ 모호한
- unpredictable ⓐ 예측할 수 없는 • sensation Ⓝ 느낌, 감각

인간은 확실성을 좋아한다. 이 선호는 검치호와 독이 있는 딸기류 열매
곁에서 살아남아야 했던 고대의 우리 선조들로부터 유래한다. 우리의 뇌는
우리가 위협에 주의하고 그것들에서 벗어나 그 후에 살아남을 수 있게
돕도록 진화했다. 사실, 우리는 우리 자신이 무언가에 대해 더 확신할수록
옳은 선택을 할 가능성이 더 크다는 것을 학습했다. 이 딸기류 열매는
지난번과 모양이 같은가? 같은 크기인가? 그것이 그렇다는 것을 내가
확실히 안다면, 그것이 안전하다는 것을 내가 알기 때문에 나의 뇌는 내가

그것을 먹도록 안내한다. 그리고 만약 내가 확실하지 않다면, 나의 뇌는
나를 보호하기 위해 위험 신호를 보낼 것이다.
그 모든 수천 년 전의 확실성에 대한 의존은 현재까지 우리의 생존을
책임졌고, 그 위험을 알리는 시스템은 계속하여 우리를 지키고 있다.
이것은 우리의 뇌가 새롭거나 모호하거나 예측할 수 없는 매일의 사건과
경험을 불확실한 것으로 명명함으로써 이루어진다. 그런 후 우리의 뇌는
그 불확실한 요소로부터 우리를 안전하게 지키기 위해 감각, 사고, 그리고
행동 계획을 만들어내고, 우리는 살아서 또 다른 날을 보게 된다.

왜 1등급? 동사 자리에 is만 온 것이 완전하지 못하다고 판단하여 ④을 정답으로
고를 수 있는 1등급 대비 문제이다. is는 앞에 온 동사구 is the same shape and
the same size를 대신하는 대동사이고, be동사를 대신하는 대동사는 be동사이므로
is가 어법상 옳다는 것을 알아야 한다.

왜 정답?

⑤ 문장에 동사가 없다!

Our brains then ⑤ generating(→ generate) / sensations,
thoughts, and action plans / to keep us safe / from the uncertain
element, / and we live to see another day. //

(단서) 「동사원형+-ing」의 형태에 밑줄이 있으므로
(발상) 동명사로 쓰여 문장에서 주어, 목적어, 보어의 역할을 하는지, 현재분사로 쓰여
명사를 수식하거나 보어 역할을 하는지 등을 확인한다.
(해결) 등위접속사 and로 연결된 두 개의 절 중, 첫 번째 절에 밑줄이 있다. 첫 번째
절의 주어는 Our brains인데, 이에 대한 동사가 없다. 따라서 동사 역할을 할 수
없는 준동사 generating을 generate로 고쳐야 어법상 알맞다.
(개념) 주어와 동사는 문장의 필수 요소로서, 그중 하나라도 없으면 의미가 통하지
않으므로 문장이 될 수 없다.

왜 오답?

① 주격 관계대명사절에는 주어가 없다.

This liking stems from our ancient ancestors / ①[who needed
to survive / alongside saber-toothed tigers and poisonous
berries]. //

(단서) 밑줄 친 who 뒤에 동사 needed가 곧바로 이어지는 것으로 보아
(발상) who는 주격 관계대명사로 쓰였음을 알 수 있다.
(해결) who는 선행사가 사람인 주격 관계대명사로 쓰일 수 있다. 따라서 앞에 있는
our ancient ancestors를 선행사로 하는 주격 관계대명사 who는 알맞게
쓰였다.
(개념) 관계대명사는 주어나 목적어가 빠진 불완전한 절을 이끈다.

② 대명사 them은 복수 명사를 가리킨다.

Our brains evolved to help / us attend to threats, / keep away
from ② them, / and remain alive afterward. //

(단서) 대명사에 밑줄이 있으므로
(발상) 대명사가 대신하는 것을 찾아 그 수가 일치하는지 확인한다.
(해결) 의미상 앞에서 주의한 위협에서 벗어나는 것이므로, them은 threats를
가리킨다. 따라서 복수형 대명사 them을 쓰는 것은 알맞다.
(개념) 대명사는 사람이나 사물 등의 이름을 대신한다.

③ 보어로 쓰이는 것은 부사가 아닌 형용사이다.

In fact, / we learned / that the more ③ certain we were / about
something, / the better chance we had / of making the right
choice. //

정답 및 해설 **409**

단서 형용사 certain에 밑줄이 있으므로

발상 명사를 수식하고 있는지, 또는 문장의 필수 요소인지 확인한다.

해결 the 비교급 ~, the 비교급 ...(~할수록 더 …한) 구문에 형용사 certain이 왔다. 어지는 we were 뒤에 주격 보어가 없으므로 주격 보어 역할을 할 수 있는 형용사 certain이 온 것은 적절하다.

개념 형용사의 역할: 명사 수식, 보어로서 주어나 목적어 보충 설명
부사의 역할: 동사, 형용사, 부사, 문장 수식

④ 앞에 온 동사를 대동사로 대신할 수 있다.

Is this berry the same shape / as last time? // The same size? //

If I know for certain / it ④ is, / my brain will direct me to eat it
is the same shape and the same size를 받는 대동사
/ because I know it's safe. //

단서 동사 is에 밑줄이 있으므로

발상 주어와 수 일치하는지 먼저 확인하고, 대동사라면 be동사를 대신하고 있는 것이 맞는지 확인한다.

해결 주어는 it이고, 단수이므로 단수 동사 is가 온 것은 알맞다. 문맥상 앞의 두 문장의 is the same shape and the same size를 대신 받는 동사 자리이다. 따라서 be동사 is가 온 것은 적절하다.

개념 앞서 등장한 일반동사(구)를 대신할 때는 대동사로 do를 사용하고, be동사(구)를 대신할 때는 대동사로 be동사를 쓴다.

3 05 정답 ③ *변화를 감지하는 능력

다음 글의 밑줄 친 부분 중, 문맥상 낱말의 쓰임이 적절하지 않은 것은? [3점]

Robert Blattberg and Steven Hoch noted /
Robert Blattberg와 Steven Hoch는 주목했다 /
병렬 구조 (noted의 목적어절 접속사)   가주어   진주어절 접속사
that, in a changing environment, / it is not clear / that consistency

is always a virtue /
변화하는 환경에서 / 분명하지 않다는 것에 / 일관성이 항상 장점인지가 /

and that one of the advantages of human judgment / is the
형용사적 용법 (the ability 수식)
ability to detect change. //
그리고 인간이 판단하는 것의 이점 중 하나는 / 변화를 감지하는 능력이라는 것에 //
가주어
Thus, / in changing environments, / it might be ① advantageous
진주어
/ to combine human judgment and statistical models. //
따라서 / 변화하는 환경에서는 / 유리할 수 있다 / 인간의 판단과 통계 모델들을 결합하는 것이 //

Blattberg and Hoch examined this possibility / by having
having의 목적어와 목적격 보어 (원형부정사)   병렬 구조 (전치사 by의 목적어)
supermarket managers forecast / demand for certain products /
Blattberg와 Hoch는 이러한 가능성을 조사했다 / 슈퍼마켓 관리자들에게 예측하게 함으로써 / 특정한 제품에 대한 수요를 /

and then creating a composite forecast / by averaging these

judgments with the forecasts of statistical models / based on ②

past data. //
그리고 다음으로 종합적인 예측을 생성해 봄으로써 / 이 판단을 통계 모델의 예측과 평균을 내어 / 지난 데이터에 근거한 //
주격 보어절 접속사
The logic was / that statistical models ③ deny(→ assume) stable

conditions / and therefore cannot account for the effects / on
단서2 통계 모델은 새로운 사건이 수요에 미치는 영향을
demand of novel events / 설명할 수 없다는 논리
논리는 ~이었다 / 통계 모델들은 변동이 없는 조건을 부정하고(→ 가정하고) / 그렇기 때문에 영향을 설명할 수 없다는 것 / 새로운 사건이 수요에 미치는 /

such as actions taken by competitors / or the introduction of
과거분사구 (actions 수식)
new products. //
경쟁자들에 의해 취해진 행동이나 / 신제품의 도입과 같은 //

Humans, however, / can ④ incorporate these novel factors / in

their judgments. //
그러나 인간은 / 이러한 새로운 요인들을 통합할 수 있다 / 자신들의 판단에서 //

The composite / — or average of human judgments and
비교급 비교
statistical models — / proved to be more ⑤ accurate / than
either A or B: A나 B 둘 중 하나
either the statistical models / or the managers working alone. //
종합된 것 / 즉 인간의 판단과 통계 모델의 평균이 / 더 정확하다는 것이 증명되었다 / 통계 모델이나 / 관리자들이 단독으로 처리하는 것보다 //

- consistency ⓝ 일관성   • virtue ⓝ 장점   • detect ⓥ 감지하다
- combine ⓥ 결합하다   • statistical ⓐ 통계의
- forecast ⓥ 예측하다   • demand ⓝ 수요   • average ⓥ 평균을 내다
- competitor ⓝ 경쟁자   • introduction ⓝ 도입
- incorporate ⓥ 통합하다   • accurate ⓐ 정확한

Robert Blattberg와 Steven Hoch는 변화하는 환경에서 일관성이 항상 장점인지가 분명하지 않다는 것과 인간이 판단하는 것의 이점 중 하나는 변화를 감지하는 능력이라는 것에 주목했다. 따라서 변화하는 환경에서는 인간의 판단과 통계 모델들을 결합하는 것이 ① 유리할 수 있다. Blattberg와 Hoch는 슈퍼마켓 관리자들에게 특정한 제품에 대한 수요를 예측하게 한 다음, 이 판단을 ② 지난 데이터에 근거한 통계 모델의 예측과 평균을 내어 종합적인 예측을 생성해 봄으로써 이러한 가능성을 조사했다. (그들의) 논리는 통계 모델들은 변동이 없는 조건을 ③ 부정하기(→ 가정하기) 때문에 경쟁자들에 의해 취해진 행동이나 신제품의 도입과 같은 새로운 사건이 수요에 미치는 영향을 설명할 수 없다는 것이었다. 그러나 인간은 이러한 새로운 요인들을 자신들의 판단에서 ④ 통합할 수 있다. 종합된 것, 즉 인간의 판단과 통계 모델의 평균이 통계 모델이나 관리자들이 단독으로 처리하는 것보다 더 ⑤ 정확하다는 것이 증명되었다.

>왜 정답? ★★★ [정답률 45%]

③ deny 부정하다

(그들의) 논리는 통계 모델들은 변동이 없는 조건을 ③ 부정하기(가정하기) 때문에 경쟁자들에 의해 취해진 행동이나 신제품의 도입과 같은 새로운 사건이 수요에 미치는 영향을 설명할 수 없다는 것이었다.

→ 통계 모델은 새로운 사건이 수요에 미치는 영향을 설명할 수 없음 → 통계 모델은 변동이 없는 조건을 바탕으로 함을 추론할 수 있음 → deny는 잘못 사용된 표현임
▶ deny를 assume(가정하다)과 같은 단어로 바꾸어야 함

>왜 오답?

① advantageous 유리한

~ 변화하는 환경에서 일관성이 항상 장점인지가 분명하지 않다는 것과 인간이 판단하는 것의 이점 중 하나는 변화를 감지하는 능력이라는 것에 주목했다. 따라서 변화하는 환경에서는 인간의 판단과 통계 모델들을 결합하는 것이 ① 유리할 수 있다.

→ 변화하는 환경에서 일관성이 항상 장점은 아니고, 변화 감지 능력이 인간 판단 이점 중 하나이므로 통계 모델(일관성을 대표함)을 인간 판단(변화 감지 능력 있음)과 결합하는 것이 유리할 수 있음
▶ advantageous는 문맥에 맞음

② past 지난, 과거의

Blattberg와 Hoch는 슈퍼마켓 관리자들에게 특정한 제품에 대한 수요를 예측하게 한 다음, 이 판단을 ② 지난 데이터에 근거한 통계 모델의 예측과 평균을 내어 종합적인 예측을 생성해 봄으로써 이러한 가능성을 조사했다.

→ 통계 모델은 첫 문장에서 언급된 일관성을 대표하는 사례이고 변화하는 환경과 대치되는 대상이므로 예측과는 반대되는 개념임
▶ '지난(past)' 혹은 '과거의' 데이터는 문맥에 맞음

④ incorporate 통합하다

┌ 그러나 인간은 이러한 새로운 요인들을 자신들의 판단에서 ④ **통합**할 수
└ however는 앞의 통계 모델에 관련된 내용과 반대되는 내용이 이어짐을 나타냄
  있다.

➡ 인간이 판단하는 것의 이점 중 하나는 변화를 감지하는 능력임 → 새로운 요인들을
  감지하고 판단할 수 있음
  ▶ 새로운 요인을 자신의 것으로 만들 수 있다는 차원에서 incorporate는 문맥에
  맞음

⑤ accurate 정확한

┌ 종합된 것, 즉 인간의 판단과 통계 모델의 평균이 통계 모델이나
└ 관리자들이 단독으로 처리하는 것보다 더 ⑤ **정확하다는** 것이 증명되었다.

➡ 통계 모델은 새로운 요인의 영향을 고려할 수 없는 단점이 있음 → 인간의 판단은
  통계 모델의 한계를 보완할 수 있음 → 통계 모델과 인간의 판단이 결합될 때 더
  정확한 결과를 얻을 수 있음
  ▶ accurate는 문맥에 맞음

[3회] 06 정답 ④ ━━━━ ✪ **2등급 대비** [정답률 31%]

*자유 놀이가 아이들에게 미치는 긍정적 영향

Free play is nature's means of teaching <mark>children</mark> / <mark>that</mark> they are
                                   간접목적어   직접목적어절 접속사
not **helpless**. //
자유 놀이는 아이들에게 가르치는 자연의 수단이다 / 자신이 무력하지 않다는 것을 //

In play, / away from adults, / children really <mark>do</mark> have control /
                                  동사 have 강조
and can practice asserting it. // **[단서 1]** 통제력을 가지고 발휘하는 연습을 함
놀면서 / 어른과 떨어져 / 아이들은 통제력을 정말로 가지고 / 그것을 발휘하는 것을 연습할
수 있다 //

In free play, / children learn / <u>to make</u> their own decisions, /
병렬구조 (learn의 목적어)
<mark>solve</mark> their own problems, / <mark>create and follow</mark> rules, /
자유 놀이를 통해 / 아이들은 배운다 / 스스로 결정을 내리고 / 자신들만의 문제를 해결하고 /
규칙을 만들고 지키며 /

and <mark>get along with</mark> others / as equals / rather than as obedient or
rebellious subordinates. // **[단서 2]** 결정 내리기, 문제 해결하기 등을 배움
다른 사람과 어울리는 것을 / 동등한 사람으로서 / 복종적이거나 반항적인
아랫사람이라기보다는 //

In active outdoor play, / children deliberately dose themselves /
with moderate amounts of fear /
활동적인 야외 놀이를 통해 / 아이들은 의도적으로 자기 자신에게 주고 / 적절한 수준의
두려움을 / **[단서 3]** 신체와 두려움 통제하는 법도 배움
and they thereby learn / how to control / <mark>not only</mark> their bodies, /
<mark>but also</mark> their fear. //   not only A but also B: A뿐만 아니라 B도
그렇게 함으로써 배운다 / 통제하는 법을 / 그들의 신체뿐만 아니라 / 두려움 또한 //

In social play / children learn / how to negotiate with others, /
how to please others, / and how to manage and overcome the
                              주격 관계대명사
anger / <mark>that</mark> can arise from conflicts. // **[단서 4]** 다른 사람과 협상하기,
                                             분노 다스리기 등을 배움
사회적인 놀이를 통해 / 아이들은 배운다 / 어떻게 다른 사람과 협상하고 / 다른 사람을 기쁘게
하며 / 분노를 다스리고 극복할 수 있는지를 / 갈등으로부터 생길 수 있는 //
                              수동태 동사
None of these lessons <mark>can be taught</mark> / through verbal means; /
              수동태 동사
they <mark>can be learned</mark> / only through experience, / <mark>which</mark> free play
provides. //   계속적 용법의 목적격 관계대명사
이러한 교훈 중 어느 것도 배울 수 없다 / 언어적 수단을 통해서는 / 그것들은 배울 수 있는데 /
오로지 경험을 통해서만 / 그것은 자유 놀이가 제공하는 것이다 //

• assert ⓥ 발휘하다 • obedient ⓐ 복종적인
• subordinate ⓝ 부하, 하급자 • deliberately ⓐⅾ 의도적으로
• dose ⓥ 주다, 투여하다 • moderate ⓐ 적절한
• negotiate ⓥ 협상하다 • conflict ⓝ 갈등 • verbal ⓐ 언어의
• complicated ⓐ 복잡한 • selective ⓐ 선택력이 있는

자유 놀이는 아이들에게 자신이 **무력하지** 않다는 것을 가르치는 자연의
수단이다. 어른과 떨어져 놀면서, 아이들은 통제력을 정말로 가지고
그것을 발휘하는 것을 연습할 수 있다. 자유 놀이를 통해, 아이들은 스스로
결정을 내리고, 자신들만의 문제를 해결하고, 규칙을 만들고 지키며,
복종적이거나 반항적인 아랫사람이라기보다는 동등한 사람으로서 다른
사람과 어울리는 것을 배운다. 활동적인 야외 놀이를 통해, 아이들은
의도적으로 자기 자신에게 적절한 수준의 두려움을 주고, 그렇게 함으로써
그들의 신체뿐만 아니라 두려움 또한 통제하는 법을 배운다. 사회적인
놀이를 통해 아이들은 어떻게 다른 사람과 협상하고, 다른 사람을 기쁘게
하며, 갈등으로부터 생길 수 있는 분노를 다스리고 극복할 수 있는지를
배운다.
이러한 교훈 중 어느 것도 언어적 수단을 통해서는 배울 수 없다. 그것들은
오로지 경험을 통해서만 배울 수 있는데, 그것은 자유 놀이가 제공하는
것이다.

┌───┐
│ **다음 빈칸에 들어갈 말로 가장 적절한 것을 고르시오.** │
│ ① noisy 아이들이 소음을 만드는 것을 다룬 ② sociable 앞에 not이 있음 │
│   시끄러운 내용이 아님   사교적인 │
│ ③ complicated 아이들이 놀이를 통해 ④ helpless 앞의 not과 함께 무기력하지 │
│   복잡한   단순해진다는 내용이 아님   무기력한   않다는 것을 가르침을 의미함 │
│ ⑤ selective 앞에 not이 있음 │
│   선택력이 있는 │
└───┘

━━━━━━━━━━━━━━━━━━━━━━━━━━━━

2등급 ? 글에서 자유 놀이가 아이들에게 가르치는 것에 해당하는
sociable(사교적인), selective(선택력이 있는)가 선택지에 있다. 하지만 빈칸 앞에
not이 있기 때문에 반대의 것을 골라야 한다. 따라서 선택지만 보고 정답을 고른다면
틀릴 수 있어 정답률이 실제로 아주 낮은 문제였다.

| 문제 풀이 순서 |

1st 빈칸이 포함된 문장을 읽고, 빈칸에 들어갈 말에 대한 단서를 얻는다.

빈칸 문장	Free play is nature's means of teaching children that they are _____. 자유 놀이는 아이들에게 자신이 _____ 않다는 것을 가르치는 자연의 수단이다.

➡ 빈칸 앞에 부정어 not이 있다. 자유 놀이가 '~하지 않다는 것'을 아이들에게 가르칠
것이고, not과 결합했을 때 글에서 말하고자 하는 말과 통하는 선택지를 골라야
한다.

2nd 글을 마저 읽으며 빈칸에 들어갈 적절한 말을 찾는다.

자유 놀이를 통해 아이들이 얻을 수 있는 이점
1 통제력을 가지고 그것을 발휘하는 것을 연습함
2 스스로 결정을 내리고, 자신들만의 문제를 해결하고, 규칙을 만들고 지키며, 동등한
사람으로서 다른 사람과 어울리는 것을 배움
3 신체뿐만 아니라 두려움 또한 통제하는 법을 배움
4 다른 사람과 협상하는 법, 다른 사람을 기쁘게 하는 법, 갈등으로부터 생길 수 있는
분노를 다스리고 극복할 수 있는 법을 배움

3rd **2nd** 에서 이해한 내용을 선택지에서 고른다.

자유 놀이를 하면서 스스로를 통제할 수 있고 능동적인 문제 해결력을 키워가기
때문에 아이들은 무기력에서 벗어날 수 있다.
▶ 따라서 빈칸에 들어갈 말은 ④ '무기력한'이다.

| 선택지 분석 |

① 아이들이 시끄럽고 소란스럽다는 것을 부정적으로 바라보며, 놀이가 그것을
  해결한다는 내용이 아니다.
② 놀이를 통해 오히려 아이들은 사회성이 더 발달하게 되므로 not sociable, 즉
  사교적이지 않은 상태가 되는 것이 아니다.
③ 아이들은 놀이를 통해 더 복잡한 사회적 상황을 배워나갈 것이므로 not
  complicated, 즉 단순한 존재가 되는 것이 아니다.
④ 아이들은 놀이를 통해 스스로 결정하는 법 등을 배우기 때문에 '무기력하지' 않다는
  것을 배우게 된다.
⑤ 아이들은 놀이를 통해 스스로 결정을 내리고 문제를 해결해 나가는 법을 배우기
  때문에 not selective, 즉 선택력이 없는 상태가 되는 것이 아니다.

정답 ②   ⭐1등급 대비 [정답률 53%]

＊초기 닷컴 투자자들의 수익 증가 관행

Many early dot-com investors / focused almost entirely on revenue growth / instead of net income. //
초기의 많은 닷컴 투자자들은 / 거의 전적으로 수익 증가에만 집중했다 / 순이익보다 //

Many early dot-com companies earned / most of their revenue / from selling advertising space / on their Web sites. //
동명사 (전치사의 목적어)
초기의 많은 닷컴 회사들은 벌어들였다 / 그들의 수익 대부분을 / 광고를 게재하는 공간을 판매하는 것으로부터 / 자신들의 웹 사이트에 //

부사적 용법 (목적)
To boost reported revenue, / some sites began exchanging ad space. //
과거분사 (revenue 수식)
보고되는 수익을 끌어올리기 위해 / 몇몇 사이트는 광고 게재 공간을 서로 주고받기 시작했다 //

Company A would put an ad for its Web site / on company B's Web site, / and company B would put an ad for its Web site / on company A's Web site. //
A 회사는 자기 회사의 웹 사이트 광고를 게시하곤 했고 / B 회사의 웹 사이트에 / B 회사는 자기 회사의 웹 사이트 광고를 게시하곤 했다 / A 회사의 웹 사이트에 //

No money ever changed hands, / 단서 1 돈이 다른 회사로 넘어가지 않음, 즉 실제로 받은 돈은 없음
돈은 다른 회사에게로 전혀 넘어가지 않았지만 //

but each company recorded revenue / (for the value of the space / that it gave up on its site) / and expense / (for the value of its ad / that it placed on the other company's site). //
병렬 구조 (목적어)
목적격 관계대명사
각 회사는 수익을 보고했다 / (공간의 가치에 대한 / 자신의 사이트에서 내어 준) / 그리고 비용을 / (광고의 가치에 대한 / 타 회사의 사이트에 게재한) //

단서 2 순이익을 끌어올리지 못함, 즉 실제로 돈을 번 것은 아님
This practice did little / to boost net income / and **resulted in no additional cash inflow** — but it did boost *reported* revenue. //
동사 boost 강조
이러한 관행은 거의 효과가 없었고 / 순이익을 끌어올리는 데 / 부가적인 현금 유입을 초래하지는 않았다 / 하지만 '보고되는' 수익을 정말로 끌어올렸다 //

'종료되다'
This practice was quickly put to an end / because accountants felt / that it did not meet / the criteria of the revenue recognition principle. //
목적어절 접속사
이 관행은 빠르게 종식되었다 / 회계사들은 생각했기 때문에 / 이러한 관행이 충족시키지 못한다고 / 수익 인식의 원칙에 대한 기준을 //

- investor ⓝ 투자자
- entirely ㉿ 전적으로
- boost ⓥ 끌어올리다
- exchange ⓥ 교환하다
- expense ⓝ 비용
- accountant ⓝ 회계사
- recognition ⓝ 인식
- simplify ⓥ 간소화하다
- additional ⓐ 부가적인
- intensify ⓥ 강화하다
- trigger ⓥ 유발하다

초기의 많은 닷컴 투자자들은 거의 전적으로 순이익보다 수익 증가에만 집중했다. 초기의 많은 닷컴 회사들은 그들의 수익 대부분을 자신들의 웹 사이트에 광고를 게재하는 공간을 판매하는 것으로부터 벌어들였다. 보고되는 수익을 끌어올리기 위해, 몇몇 사이트는 광고 게재 공간을 서로 주고받기 시작했다. A 회사는 자기 회사의 웹 사이트 광고를 B 회사의 웹 사이트에 게시하곤 했고, B 회사는 자기 회사의 웹 사이트 광고를 A 회사의 웹 사이트에 게시하곤 했다. 돈은 다른 회사에게로 전혀 넘어가지 않았지만, 각 회사는 (자신의 사이트에서 내어 준 공간의 가치에 대한) 수익과 (타 회사의 사이트에 게재한 광고의 가치에 대한) 비용을 보고했다. 이러한 관행은 순이익을 끌어올리는 데 거의 효과가 없었고 **부가적인 현금 유입을 초래하지는 않았지만**, '보고되는' 수익을 정말로 끌어올렸다. 회계사들은 이러한 관행이 수익 인식의 원칙에 대한 기준을 충족시키지 못한다고 생각했기 때문에 이 관행은 빠르게 종식되었다.

다음 빈칸에 들어갈 말로 가장 적절한 것을 고르시오.
① simplified the Web design process 웹 사이트에 광고를 게재함
  웹 설계 프로세스를 간소화했다
② resulted in no additional cash inflow 보고되는 수익만 끌어올림
  부가적인 현금 유입을 초래하지는 않았다
③ decreased the salaries of the employees 알 수 없음
  직원의 급여를 감소시켰다
④ intensified competition among companies
  기업 간 경쟁을 강화했다 수익을 올리기 위해 서로 협력했음
⑤ triggered conflicts on the content of Web ads
  웹 광고의 콘텐츠에 갈등을 유발했다 몇몇 사이트는 광고 게재 공간을 서로 주고받음

왜 1등급? dot-com investors, revenue, net income 등 생소한 경제 관련 용어가 계속해서 제시되기 때문에 글이 어렵게 느껴진다. 또한 '보고되는 수익'과 대조되는 내용이 빈칸에 들어가야 하는데, 글에 나오지 않은 cash inflow라는 어구를 선택지에서 골라야 하기 때문에 정답을 고르는 것 또한 어려웠다.

| 문제 풀이 순서 |

1st 빈칸이 포함된 문장을 읽고, 빈칸에 들어갈 말에 대한 단서를 얻는다.

빈칸 문장	This practice did little to boost net income and _____ — but it did boost *reported* revenue. 이러한 관행은 순이익을 끌어올리는 데 거의 효과가 없었고 _____, '보고되는' 수익을 정말로 끌어올렸다.

➡ 순이익을 끌어올리는 데 거의 효과가 없었고 수익으로서 '보고만' 되었음 → 실제로 얻은 이익은 없었다는 의미임 단서
▶ 빈칸을 채우려면 닷컴 회사의 관행으로 실제 번 돈이 있는지 살펴보아야 한다. 발상

2nd 글의 나머지 부분을 읽고, 닷컴 회사들의 관행이 순이익 창출에 어떤 결과를 초래했는지를 찾는다.

- 초기의 많은 닷컴 투자자들은 거의 전적으로 순이익보다 수익 증가에만 집중했다.
- 보고되는 수익을 끌어올리기 위해, 몇몇 사이트는 광고 게재 공간을 서로 주고받기 시작했다.
- 돈은 다른 회사에게로 전혀 넘어가지 않았지만, 각 회사는 수익과 비용을 보고했다. 단서 1

➡ 순이익과는 다른 보고되는 수익 증가에 집중했음 → 실제 돈이 회사로 넘어가지 않았음

3rd 2nd 에서 이해한 내용을 선택지에서 고른다.

닷컴 회사의 입장에서는 실제로 벌어들인 돈이 없는 셈이므로 정답은 ② '부가적인 현금 유입을 초래하지는 않았다'이다.

| 선택지 분석 |

① 웹 설계 프로세스에 대한 내용은 제시되지 않았고, 수익 대부분을 자신들의 웹 사이트에 광고를 게재하는 공간을 판매하는 것으로부터 벌어들였다고 했다.
② 보고되는 수익만 증가했을 뿐 순이익은 증가하지 않았으며 실제 돈이 회사로 넘어가지 않았다.
③ 순이익을 끌어올리는 데 거의 효과가 없어 관행이 빠르게 종식됐다고 했을 뿐, 이를 직원의 연봉 감소와 관련짓지 않았다.
④ 보고되는 수익 증가에 집중하여 몇몇 사이트는 광고 게재 공간을 서로 주고받기 시작했다고 했기 때문에 경쟁 강화로 볼 수는 없다.
⑤ 몇몇 사이트는 광고 게재 공간을 서로 주고받기 시작했다고 했고 이로 인한 갈등에 대해서는 언급하지 않았다.

정답 ④ ＊나쁜 습관 없애기에 대한 오해

Like positive habits, / bad habits exist / on a continuum of easy-to-change and hard-to-change. // 단서 1 나쁜 습관은 바꾸기 쉬움과 바꾸기 어려움의 연속체에 존재
긍정적인 습관과 마찬가지로 / 나쁜 습관은 존재한다 / 바꾸기 쉬움과 바꾸기 어려움의 연속체에 //

앞에 목적격 관계대명사 생략
(A) But this kind of language / (and the approaches it spawns) / frames these challenges / in a way that isn't helpful or effective. //
주격 관계대명사
단서 2 이런 종류의 언어는 (C)에서 언급한 '깨기'와 '싸우기'를 말함
그러나 이러한 종류의 언어는 / (그리고 그것이 낳는 접근법) / 이러한 도전에 틀을 씌운다 / 도움이 되지 않거나 효과적이지 않은 방식으로 //

동명사구 (will stop의 목적어)
I specifically hope / we will stop using this phrase: / "break a habit." //
나는 특히 바란다 / 우리가 이런 문구를 그만 사용하기를 / '습관을 깨다'라는 //

This language misguides people. //
이 언어는 사람들을 잘못된 길로 이끈다 //

The word "break" sets the wrong expectation / for how you get rid of a bad habit. //
'깨다'라는 단어는 잘못된 기대를 형성한다 / 나쁜 습관을 없애는 방법에 대해 //

(B) This word implies / <mark>that</mark> if you input a lot of force in one moment, / the habit will be gone. // ^{목적어절 접속사} 단서 3 (A)에서 말한 '깨다'를 가리킴

이 단어는 암시한다 / 여러분이 한순간에 많은 힘을 가하면 / 그 습관이 없어질 것이라고 //

However, that rarely works, / because you usually cannot get rid of an unwanted habit / by <mark>applying force one time</mark>. // ^{동명사구 (전치사의 목적어)}

하지만 그것은 거의 효과가 없는데 / 왜냐하면 대체로 여러분이 바람직하지 못한 습관을 없앨 수 없기 때문이다 / 한 번 힘을 가함으로써 // 단서 4 주어진 글에서 말한 나쁜 습관이 존재하는 연속체를 가리킴

(C) When you get toward / the "hard" end of the spectrum, / note the language <mark>you hear</mark> — / *breaking* bad habits and *battling* addiction. // 앞에 목적격 관계대명사 생략

가까워질 때 / 그 연속체의 '어려운' 끝에 / 여러분이 듣는 언어에 주목하라 / 즉 나쁜 습관을 '깨기'와 중독과 '싸우기'에 //

It's <mark>as if</mark> an unwanted behavior is a nefarious villain / to be aggressively defeated. // '마치 ~인 것처럼'

바람직하지 못한 행동은 마치 사악한 악당인 것 같다 / 격렬하게 패배되어야 할 //

- continuum ⓝ 연속체 · misguide ⓥ 잘못 이끌다
- imply ⓥ 암시하다 · input ⓥ 가하다 · get rid of ~을 제거하다
- unwanted ⓐ 원치 않는 · addiction ⓝ 중독 · villain ⓝ 악당
- aggressively ⓐⓓ 격렬하게, 공격적으로 · defeat ⓥ 패배시키다

긍정적인 습관과 마찬가지로, 나쁜 습관은 바꾸기 쉬움과 바꾸기 어려움의 연속체에 존재한다. (C) 그 연속체의 '어려운' 끝에 가까워질 때, 여러분이 듣는 언어, 즉 나쁜 습관을 '깨기'와 중독과 '싸우기'에 주목하라. 바람직하지 못한 행동은 마치 격렬하게 패배되어야 할 사악한 악당인 것 같다.
(A) 그러나 이러한 종류의 언어(그리고 그것이 낳는 접근법)는 도움이 되지 않거나 효과적이지 않은 방식으로 이러한 도전에 틀을 씌운다. 나는 특히 우리가 '습관을 깨다'라는 문구를 그만 사용하기를 바란다. 이 언어는 사람들을 잘못된 길로 이끈다. '깨다'라는 단어는 나쁜 습관을 없애는 방법에 대해 잘못된 기대를 형성한다. (B) 이 단어는 여러분이 한순간에 많은 힘을 가하면, 그 습관이 없어질 것이라고 암시한다. 하지만 그것은 거의 효과가 없는데 왜냐하면 대체로 여러분이 한 번 힘을 가함으로써 바람직하지 못한 습관을 없앨 수 없기 때문이다.

주어진 글 다음에 이어질 글의 순서로 가장 적절한 것을 고르시오.
① (A) — (C) — (B) (A)의 '이러한 종류의 언어'는 주어진 글에 없음
② (B) — (A) — (C) ┐ (B)의 '이 단어'가 가리키는 것이 주어진 글에 없음
③ (B) — (C) — (A) ┘
④ (C) — (A) — (B) (C) 바꾸기 어려운 나쁜 습관은 '깨기'나 '싸우기'와 같은 언어에 주목해야 함 — (A) 그런 언어는 잘못된 길로 이끎 — (B) 습관을 없애는 잘못된 방법을 암시함
⑤ (C) — (B) — (A) (B)의 '이 단어'가 가리키는 것이 (A)에 제시됨

| 문제 풀이 순서 | ★★★ [정답률 56%]

1st 각 문단의 내용을 파악하고, 글의 논리적인 순서를 추론한다.

주어진 글: 긍정적인 습관과 마찬가지로, 나쁜 습관은 바꾸기 쉬움과 바꾸기 어려움의 연속체에 존재한다.

→ 주어진 글 뒤: 나쁜 습관이 바꾸기 쉽거나 어려운 경우 가지는 특징 등에 관한 내용이 이어질 것이다.

(A): 그러나 이러한 종류의 언어 (그리고 그것이 낳는 접근법)는 도움이 되지 않거나 효과적이지 않은 방식으로 이러한 도전에 틀을 씌운다. ~ '깨다'라는 단어는 나쁜 습관을 없애는 방법에 대해 잘못된 기대를 형성한다.

→ (A) 앞: '이러한 종류의 언어'가 가리키는 내용이 제시되어야 한다.
(A) 뒤: '깨다'라는 단어가 왜 나쁜 습관을 없애는 방법에 대해 잘못된 기대를 형성하는지 부연 설명이 이어질 것이다.

(B): 이 단어(This word)는 여러분이 한순간에 많은 힘을 가하면, 그 습관이 없어질 것이라고 암시한다. 하지만 그것은 거의 효과가 없는데 왜냐하면 대체로 여러분이 한 번 힘을 가함으로써 바람직하지 못한 습관을 없앨 수 없기 때문이다.

→ **(B)** 앞: This word(이 단어)가 가리키는 내용이 제시되어야 한다.
▶ 한순간에 많은 힘을 가하면 습관이 없어질 것을 암시하는 '이 단어(This word)'는 (A)의 '깨다'를 가리키므로 (B) 앞에 (A)가 와야 함 (순서: (A) → (B))
(B) 뒤: 제기한 문제에 대한 이유가 제시되었으므로 (B)가 마지막임을 알 수 있다.

(C): 그 연속체(the spectrum)의 '어려운' 끝에 가까워질 때, 여러분이 듣는 언어, 즉 나쁜 습관을 '깨기'와 중독과 '싸우기'에 주목하라. 바람직하지 못한 행동은 마치 격렬하게 패배시켜야 할 사악한 악당인 것 같다.

→ **(C)** 앞: the spectrum(그 연속체)에 관한 내용이 있어야 한다.
▶ the spectrum은 주어진 글에서 바꾸기 쉬움과 바꾸기 어려움의 연속체로 제시됨 (순서: 주어진 글 → (C))
(C) 뒤: 나쁜 습관 깨기, 즉 바람직하지 못한 행동 없애기에 대한 설명이 이어질 것으로 예측된다.
▶ (C)는 the spectrum이 가리키는 내용이 제시된 주어진 글과, 나쁜 습관을 깨는 것에 대한 설명이 제시된 (A) 사이에 들어가야 함 (순서: 주어진 글 → (C) → (A) → (B))

2nd 글이 한눈에 들어오도록 정리하여 정답을 확인한다.

주어진 글: 나쁜 습관은 바꾸기 쉬움과 바꾸기 어려움의 연속체에 존재한다.
→ **(C):** 그 연속체의 '어려운' 끝에 가까워질 때 듣는 언어인 나쁜 습관 '깨기'와 중독과 '싸우기'에 주목해야 한다.
→ **(A):** 이런 종류의 언어는 바람직하지 못한데, 특히 '습관을 깨다'는 사람들을 잘못된 길로 이끈다.
→ **(B):** 그 말은 한순간에 많은 힘을 가하면 그 습관이 없어질 것을 암시하지만 한 번 힘을 가함으로써 바람직하지 못한 습관을 없앨 수 없다.
▶ 주어진 글 다음에 이어질 글의 순서는 (C) → (A) → (B)이므로 정답은 ④임

3회 09 정답 ② *물고기들의 전기적 의사소통

글의 흐름으로 보아, 주어진 문장이 들어가기에 가장 적절한 곳을 고르시오.

In the electric organ / the muscle cells are connected / in larger chunks, / <mark>which</mark> makes the total current intensity larger / than in ordinary muscles. // ^{계속적 용법의 주격 관계대명사} 단서 1 전기 기관에서 만드는 전류의 강도가 일반 근육에서보다 더 크다는 내용임

전기 기관 안에서 / 근육 세포는 연결되어 있으며 / 더 큰 덩어리로 / 이는 총 전류 강도를 더 크게 만든다 / 일반 근육에서보다 //

Electric communication is mainly known / in fish. //
전기적 의사소통은 주로 알려져 있다 / 물고기에서 //

The electric signals <mark>are produced</mark> / in special electric organs. // ^{수동태 동사}
전기 신호는 생성된다 / 특수 전기 기관에서 // 단서 2 전기 신호는 특수 전기 기관에서 만들어짐

When the signal is discharged / the electric organ will be negatively loaded / compared to the head / <mark>and</mark> an electric field is created / around the fish. // 절과 절을 잇는 등위접속사

신호가 방출되면 / 전기 기관이 음전하를 띠고 / 머리에 비해 / 전기장이 생긴다 / 물고기 주위에 //

(①) A weak electric current is created / also in ordinary muscle cells / when they contract. // 단서 3 일반 근육 세포에서도 약한 전류가 만들어짐
약한 전류가 발생한다 / 일반 근육 세포 안에서도 / 그것이 수축할 때 //

(②) The fish varies the signals / <mark>by changing</mark> / the form of the electric field / or the frequency of discharging. // ^{by -ing: ~함으로써}
물고기는 신호를 다양하게 한다 / 변화시켜 / 전기장의 형태나 / 방출 주파수를 //

(③) The system is only working / over small distances, / about one to two meters. //
이 체계는 오직 작동한다 / 짧은 거리에서 / 약 1~2미터 정도의 //

(④) This is an advantage / <mark>since</mark> the species <mark>using the signal system</mark> often live in large groups / with several other species. // ^{부사절 접속사 (이유)} ^{현재분사구 (the species 수식)}
이것은 이점이다 / 신호 체계를 사용하는 종들은 흔히 큰 무리를 지어 살기 때문에 / 다른 여러 종과 함께 //

(⑤) If many fish send out signals / at the same time, / the short range decreases / the risk of interference. //
많은 물고기가 신호를 보내면 / 동시에 / 짧은 (도달 가능) 범위는 줄여 준다 / 간섭의 위험을 //

- connect ⓥ 연결하다   • chunk ⓝ 덩어리   • intensity ⓝ 강도, 세기
- ordinary ⓐ 보통의   • discharge ⓥ 해방시키다
- contract ⓥ 줄어들다, 수축하다   • vary ⓥ 변화를 주다
- range ⓝ 범위   • interference ⓝ 간섭

전기적 의사소통은 주로 물고기에서 알려져 있다. 전기 신호는 특수 전기 기관에서 생성된다. 신호가 방출되면 머리에 비해 전기 기관이 음전하를 띠고 물고기 주위에 전기장이 생긴다. (①) 일반 근육 세포가 수축할 때 약한 전류가 그 안에서도 발생한다. (② 전기 기관 안에서 근육 세포는 더 큰 덩어리로 연결되어 있으며, 이는 일반 근육에서보다 총 전류 강도를 더 크게 만든다.) 물고기는 전기장의 형태나 방출 주파수를 변화시켜 신호를 다양하게 한다. (③) 이 체계는 약 1~2미터 정도의 짧은 거리에서만 작동한다. (④) 신호 체계를 사용하는 종들은 흔히 큰 무리를 지어 다른 여러 종과 함께 살기 때문에 이것은 이점이다. (⑤) 많은 물고기가 동시에 신호를 보내면, 짧은 (도달 가능) 범위는 간섭의 위험을 줄여 준다.

| 문제 풀이 순서 | ★★★ [정답률 31%]

1st 주어진 문장을 해석하고, 앞뒤에 어떤 내용이 올지 생각한다.

In the electric organ the muscle cells are connected in larger chunks, which makes the total current intensity larger than in ordinary muscles.
전기 기관 안에서 근육 세포는 더 큰 덩어리로 연결되어 있으며, 이는 일반 근육에서보다 총 전류 강도를 더 크게 만든다.

➡ 전기 기관 안에서의 전류 강도를 일반 근육에서의 전류 강도와 비교하고 있다.
  ▶ 주어진 문장이 들어갈 곳: 일반 근육의 전류를 설명한 곳 다음에 들어갈 수 있다.

2nd 각 선택지의 앞뒤 흐름이 매끄러운지 확인한다.

- ①의 앞 문장과 뒤 문장
앞 문장: 신호가 방출되면 머리에 비해 전기 기관이 음전하를 띠고 물고기 주위에 전기장이 생긴다.
뒤 문장: 일반 근육 세포가 수축할 때 약한 전류가 그 안에서도 발생한다.
➡ 전기 기관에서 전기 신호가 생성되어 전기장이 생기고 일반 근육 세포에서도 전류가 발생한다는 내용이 자연스럽게 이어진다.
  ▶ 주어진 문장이 ①에 들어갈 수 없음

- ②의 앞 문장과 뒤 문장
앞 문장: ①의 뒤 문장과 같음
뒤 문장: 물고기는 전기장의 형태나 방출 주파수를 변화시켜 신호를 다양하게 한다.
➡ 전류 발생, 전기장 발생에 대한 내용에서 전기장의 형태나 방출 주파수의 내용으로 넘어갔다.
  ▶ 주어진 문장은 전기 기관 안에서의 전류 강도를 일반 근육에서의 전류 강도와 비교한 내용이므로 다른 내용으로 넘어가기 전인 ②에 들어가야 함

- ③의 앞 문장과 뒤 문장
앞 문장: ②의 뒤 문장과 같음
뒤 문장: 이 체계는 약 1~2미터 정도의 짧은 거리에서만 작동한다.
➡ '이 체계'는 전기장의 형태나 방출 주파수를 변화시켜 신호를 다양하게 하는 것을 가리킨다.
  ▶ 전기장의 형태나 방출 주파수의 변화를 다룬 앞의 내용과 긴밀하게 관련이 있으므로 주어진 문장은 ③에 들어갈 수 없음

- ④의 앞 문장과 뒤 문장
앞 문장: ③의 뒤 문장과 같음
뒤 문장: 신호 체계를 사용하는 종들은 흔히 큰 무리를 지어 다른 여러 종과 함께 살기 때문에 이것은 이점이다.

➡ 앞에서 제시된 신호 체계가 짧은 거리에서만 작동한다는 내용과, 무리 지어 살기 때문에 그 체계에 알맞다는, 이점이 있다는 내용이 자연스럽게 이어진다.
  ▶ 신호 체계에 대한 내용이 계속 이어지고 있으므로 주어진 문장은 ④에 들어갈 수 없음

- ⑤의 앞 문장과 뒤 문장
앞 문장: ④의 뒤 문장과 같음
뒤 문장: 많은 물고기가 동시에 신호를 보내면, 짧은 (도달 가능) 범위는 간섭의 위험을 줄여 준다.

➡ 무리를 지어 사는 종이 신호 체계를 사용하는 이점에 대한 앞 내용에 이어 무리의 많은 물고기가 동시에 신호를 보내는 경우에 일어나는 일에 대해 설명하고 있다.
  ▶ 주어진 문장이 ⑤에 들어갈 수 없음

3회 10 정답 ① ＊공간 지각의 진화 ─────────

A young child may be puzzled / 접속사가 생략되지 않은 분사구문 when asked to distinguish / between the directions of right and left. //
어린아이는 당황할 수 있다 / 구분하라고 요구받으면 / 오른쪽과 왼쪽의 방향을 //

But that same child may have no difficulty / in 동명사 (전치사의 목적어) determining the directions / of up and down or back and front. //
하지만 그 아이는 전혀 어려움이 없을 것이다 / 방향을 알아내는 데에는 / 위아래나 앞뒤의 //

Scientists propose / 목적어절 접속사 that this occurs 부사절 접속사 (이유) because, / 부사절 접속사 (양보) although we experience three dimensions, / only two had a strong influence on our evolution: /
과학자들은 주장한다 / 이것이 ~ 때문에 발생한다고 / 비록 우리가 세 가지 차원을 경험하지만 / 두 가지만이 우리의 진화에 강력한 영향을 미쳤기 (때문이라고) /

the vertical dimension / as defined by gravity / and, in mobile species, / the front/back dimension / as defined by the positioning of sensory and feeding mechanisms. // 단서 1 수직적 차원과 앞/뒤 차원만 진화에 영향을 미침
수직적 차원 / 중력에 의해 정의되는 / 그리고 이동하는 종의 / 앞/뒤 차원 / 감각과 먹이 섭취 메커니즘의 배치로 정의되는 //

These influence / our perception of vertical versus horizontal, 병렬 구조 (목적어) far versus close, / and the search for dangers / from above (such as an eagle) / or below (such as a snake). //
이것들은 영향을 미친다 / 수직 대 수평, 원거리 대 근거리에 대한 우리의 지각에 / 그리고 위험 탐색에 / (독수리와 같은) 위로부터의 / 또는 (뱀과 같은) 아래로부터의 //

However, / the left-right axis is not as relevant in nature. // 단서 2 자연에서 좌우 축은 중요하지 않음
그러나 / 좌-우 축은 자연에서는 그만큼 중요하지 않다 //

A bear is equally dangerous / from its left or the right side, / but = a bear is not equally dangerous not / if it is upside down. //
곰은 똑같이 위험하지만 / 그것의 왼쪽 편에서든 오른쪽 편에서든 / 그렇지 않다 / 거꾸로 뒤집혀 있다면 //

In fact, / 접속사가 생략되지 않은 분사구문 when observing a scene / 현재분사 (a scene 수식) containing plants, animals, and man-made objects / such as cars or street signs, /
사실 / 장면을 관찰할 때 / 식물, 동물, 그리고 인간이 만든 물체를 포함하는 / 자동차나 도로 표지판과 같은 /

we can only tell / when left and right 현재완료시제 수동태 have been inverted / if we observe those artificial items. //
우리는 겨우 구별할 수 있을 뿐이다 / 좌우가 뒤바뀐 것을 / 만약 그 인공적인 물체들을 관찰한다면 //

┌─────────────────────────────
→ Having affected / the evolution of our (A) **spatial**
  분사구문을 이끄는 현재분사 perception, / vertical and front/back dimensions are easily perceived, /
  영향을 미쳤기 때문에 / 우리의 공간 지각의 진화에 / 수직적 차원과 앞/뒤 차원은 쉽게 인식된다 /

but 단수 주어 the left-right axis, / which is not (B) **significant** in nature, / 단수 동사 doesn't come instantly to us. //
하지만 좌-우 축은 / 자연에서 유의미하지 않은 / 우리에게 즉각 이해되지 않는다 //
└─────────────────────────────

- **distinguish** ⓥ 구별하다, 식별하다
- **direction** ⓝ 방향
- **determine** ⓥ 알아내다
- **occur** ⓥ 발생하다
- **dimension** ⓝ 차원, 관점
- **influence** ⓝ 영향
- **evolution** ⓝ 진화
- **vertical** ⓐ 수직의
- **gravity** ⓝ 중력
- **mobile** ⓐ 이동하는
- **positioning** ⓝ 배치
- **perception** ⓝ 지각, 자각
- **horizontal** ⓐ 수평의
- **relevant** ⓐ 의미가 있는, 중요한
- **upside down** 거꾸로
- **observe** ⓥ 관찰하다
- **contain** ⓥ 포함하다
- **invert** ⓥ 바꾸다
- **artificial** ⓐ 인공적인
- **perceive** ⓥ 인식하다
- **instantly** ⓐd 즉각, 즉시
- **spatial** ⓐ 공간의
- **scarce** ⓐ 희소한
- **auditory** ⓐ 청각의
- **accessible** ⓐ 접근 가능한
- **desirable** ⓐ 바람직한

오른쪽과 왼쪽의 방향을 구분하라고 요구받으면 어린아이는 당황할 수 있다. 하지만 그 아이는 위아래나 앞뒤의 방향을 알아내는 데에는 전혀 어려움이 없을 것이다. 과학자들은 이것이 발생하는 이유는, 비록 우리가 세 가지 차원을 경험하지만, 두 가지만이 우리의 진화에 강력한 영향을 미쳤기 때문이라고 주장하는데, 그것들은 중력에 의해 정의되는 수직적 차원과 이동하는 종의 감각과 먹이 섭취 메커니즘의 배치로 정의되는 앞/뒤 차원이다. 이것들은 수직 대 수평, 원거리 대 근거리에 대한 우리의 지각과 (독수리와 같은) 위로부터의 또는 (뱀과 같은) 아래로부터의 위험 탐색에 영향을 미친다.

그러나 좌-우 축은 자연에서는 그만큼 중요하지 않다. 곰은 그것의 왼쪽 편에서든 오른쪽 편에서든 똑같이 위험하지만, 거꾸로 뒤집혀 있다면 그렇지 않다. 사실, 우리가 식물, 동물, 그리고 자동차나 도로 표지판과 같은 인간이 만든 물체가 포함된 장면을 관찰할 때, 만약 그 인공적인 물체들을 관찰한다면 좌우가 뒤바뀐 것을 겨우 구별할 수 있을 뿐이다.
→ 우리의 (A) 공간 지각의 진화에 영향을 미쳤기 때문에, 수직적 차원과 앞/뒤 차원은 쉽게 인식되지만, 자연에서 (B) 유의미하지 않은 좌-우 축은 우리에게 즉각 이해되지 않는다.

다음 글의 내용을 한 문장으로 요약하고자 한다. 빈칸 (A), (B)에 들어갈 말로 가장 적절한 것은?

	(A)		(B)
①	spatial 공간의	—	significant 유의미한 위아래, 앞뒤는 진화에 영향을 미친 공간적 개념이고 좌-우 축은 자연에서 중요하지 않음
②	spatial	—	scarce 희소한 좌-우 축이 희소하지 않은 것이 아님
③	auditory 청각의	—	different 서로 다른 위아래, 앞뒤는 청각이 아닌 공간적 개념임
④	cultural 문화적인	—	accessible 접근 가능한 좌-우 축이 접근 가능하지 않은지는 알 수 없음
⑤	cultural	—	desirable 바람직한 좌-우 축이 바람직하지 않은 것이 아니라 자연에서 중요하지 않은 것임

>왜 정답? ★★❀ [정답률 59%]

(A):
⌈ 중력에 의해 정의되는 수직적 차원과 이동하는 종의 감각과 먹이 섭취 메커니즘의
⌊ 배치로 정의되는 앞/뒤 차원만이 우리의 진화에 강력한 영향을 미쳤다. **단서 1**

➡ 원거리 대 근거리, 위와 아래는 공간에 관한 지각이므로 ①, ② 'spatial(공간의)'이 알맞다.

(B):
⌈ 그러나 좌-우 축은 자연에서는 그만큼 중요하지 않다. **단서 2**

➡ 좌우 축은 자연에서 그만큼 '중요하지 않다' = '유의미하지 않다'
▶ 요약문의 빈칸에는 각각 ① '공간의'와 '유의미한'이 들어가야 함

>왜 오답?

② 좌-우 축이 자연에서 희소하지 않은지는 이 글을 통해서는 알 수 없다.

③ 위아래, 앞뒤는 공간적 개념이지 청각적 개념이 아니다.

④ 좌-우 축이 자연에서 접근 가능하지 않은지는 이 글을 통해서는 알 수 없는 정보이다.

⑤ 위아래, 앞뒤는 공간적 개념이지 문화적인 개념이 아니며, 좌-우 축이 바람직하지 않은 것이 아니라 자연에서 중요하지 않은 것이다.

도입	어린이는 오른쪽과 왼쪽 방향 구분은 어려워하지만 위아래나 앞뒤의 방향을 알아내는 데 어려움이 없음
이유	인간이 경험하는 세 가지 차원 중 수직적 차원과 앞/뒤 차원만 진화에 강력한 영향을 미쳤기 때문임
부연	좌-우 축은 자연에서 중요하지 않음
예시	곰의 경우 왼쪽 편이든 오른쪽 편이든 똑같이 위험하고, 인공적인 물체를 관찰할 때 좌우가 바뀐 것은 구별하기 어려움

---

③회 11~12 *사람 관리에서 고려해야 할 점

Creative people aren't all / cut from the same cloth. // `같은 부류인`
창의적인 사람들이 모두 ~은 아니다 / 같은 부류인 것 //

They have / (a) varying levels of maturity and sensitivity. //
그들은 가진다 / 다양한 수준의 성숙도와 민감성을 //

They have / different approaches / to work. //
그들은 가진다 / 서로 다른 접근법을 / 일에 대한 //

And they're each motivated / by different things. //
그리고 그들은 각자 동기가 부여된다 / 서로 다른 것에 의해 //

Managing people is about being aware / of their unique `동명사구 주어 / 단수 동사`
personalities. // **11번** 단서 1: 사람 관리에서 중요한 것은 그들의 개성을 아는 것임
사람들의 관리에서 중요한 것은 아는 것이다 / 그들의 고유한 개성을 //

It's also about empathy and adaptability, and knowing / how `명사절을 이끄는 의문사`
the things you do and say will be interpreted / and adapting `앞에 목적격 관계대명사 생략`
accordingly. // **11번** 단서 2: 사람 관리에서 중요한 다른 요소들
또한 중요한 것은 공감과 적응성 그리고 아는 것이다 / 어떻게 여러분이 하는 일과 하는 말이 해석될지를 / 그에 따라 보조를 맞추는 것이다 //

Who you are and what you say / may not be the (b) same / from
one person to the next. // **12번** 단서 1: 사람마다 다를 수 있음
여러분이 누구인지와 무슨 말을 하는지는 / 같지 않을 수 있다 / 사람마다 //

For instance, / if you're asking someone / to work a second `asking의 목적어와 목적격 보어 (to부정사)`
weekend in a row, / or telling them / they aren't getting / that `병렬 구조 / 앞에 직접목적어절 접속사 생략 / 지시형용사`
deserved promotion / just yet, /
예를 들어 / 여러분이 누군가에게 요청하고 있다면 / 2주 연속 주말에 일하라고 / 또는 그들에게 말하고 있다면 / 그들이 받지 못할 것이라고 / 받아 마땅한 그 승진을 / 지금 당장은 //
12번 단서 2: 명심해야 하는 건 개인의 특성임
you need to bear in mind / the (c) group(→ individual). //
여러분은 명심해야 한다 / 그 집단(→ 개인)을 //

Vincent will have a very different reaction / to the news / than
Emily, / and they will each be more receptive to the news / if it's
bundled with different things. //
Vincent는 매우 다른 반응을 보일 것이고 / 그 소식에 대해 / Emily와 / 그들 각자는 그 소식을 더 잘 받아들일 것이다 / 그것이 서로 다른 것과 묶인다면 //

Perhaps that promotion news will land (d) easier / if Vincent `수동태 동사`
is given a few extra vacation days / for the holidays, /
아마 그 승진 소식은 더 쉽게 도달할 것이고 / Vincent에게 며칠간의 추가적인 휴무일이 주어진다면 / 명절에 //
`부사절 접속사 (대조)`
while you can promise Emily / a bigger promotion / a year from
now. //
한편 Emily에게는 약속할 수도 있을 것이다 / 더 큰 승진을 / 지금보다 1년 후에 //

12번 단서 3: 사람 각각의 특징을 고려해야 함
Consider / each person's complex positive and negative
personality traits, / their life circumstances, / and their mindset `접속사가 생략되지 않은 분사구문`
in the moment / when deciding what to say and how to say it. //
고려하라 / 사람 각각의 복잡한 긍정적 및 부정적인 개성의 특징 / 그들의 삶의 상황 / 그 순간의 그들의 사고방식을 / 무슨 말을 할지와 그 말을 어떻게 할지를 정할 때 //

Personal connection, compassion, / and an individualized
management style / are (e) key / to **drawing** consistent, rock
star-level work / out of everyone. // **11번** 단서 3: 개인적인 연관, 동감, 그리고
개별화된 관리 방식이 중요함
개인적인 연관, 동감 / 그리고 개별화된 관리 방식은 / 핵심이다 / 일관되고 록 스타와 같은
수준의 일을 끌어내는 / 모든 사람으로부터 //

- maturity Ⓝ 성숙도, 성숙함   • sensitivity Ⓝ 예민함, 민감성
- personality Ⓝ 개성, 특성   • empathy Ⓝ 공감
- adaptability Ⓝ 적응성, 융통성   • interpret Ⓥ 해석하다
- adapt Ⓥ 맞추다   • accordingly 🔟 부응해서, 그에 맞춰
- deserve Ⓥ ~을 받을 만하다   • bear in mind ~을 명심하다
- receptive ⓐ 수용적인   • bundle Ⓥ 묶다   • trait Ⓝ 특성
- circumstance Ⓝ 상황, 환경   • mindset Ⓝ 사고방식
- connection Ⓝ 관련성, 연관성   • compassion Ⓝ 동감
- individualize Ⓥ 개별화하다   • consistent ⓐ 일관된
- guarantee Ⓥ 보장하다   • flexible ⓐ 유연한
- appealing ⓐ 매력적인   • recognition Ⓝ 인식
- suffer Ⓥ 어려움을 겪다

창의적인 사람들이 모두 같은 부류인 것은 아니다. 그들은 (a) 다양한
수준의 성숙도와 민감성을 가진다. 그들은 일에 대한 서로 다른 접근법을
가진다. 그리고 그들은 각자 서로 다른 것에 의해 동기가 부여된다.
사람들의 관리에서 중요한 것은 그들의 고유한 개성을 아는 것이다. 또한
중요한 것은 공감과 적응성, 그리고 여러분이 하는 일과 하는 말이 어떻게
해석될지 알고 그에 따라 보조를 맞추는 것이다.
여러분이 누구인지와 무슨 말을 하는지는 사람마다 (b) 같지 않을
수 있다. 예를 들어, 여러분이 누군가에게 2주 연속 주말에 일하라고
요청하고 있다면, 또는 그들에게 받아 마땅한 그 승진을 지금 당장은 받지
못할 것이라고 말하고 있다면, 그 (c) 집단(→ 개인)을 명심해야 한다.
Vincent는 그 소식에 대해 Emily와 매우 다른 반응을 보일 것이고, 그
소식이 서로 다른 것과 묶인다면 그들 각자는 더 잘 받아들일 것이다. 아마
Vincent에게 명절에 며칠간의 추가적인 휴무일이 주어진다면 그 승진
소식은 (d) 더 쉽게 도달할 것이고, 한편 Emily에게는 지금보다 1년 후에
더 큰 승진을 약속할 수도 있을 것이다.
무슨 말을 할지와 그 말을 어떻게 할지를 정할 때 사람 각각의 복잡한
긍정적 및 부정적인 개성의 특징, 그들의 삶의 상황, 그 순간의 그들의
사고방식을 고려하라. 개인적인 연관, 동감, 그리고 개별화된 관리 방식은
모든 사람으로부터 일관되고 록 스타와 같은 수준의 일을 끌어내는
(e) 핵심이다.

---

③ 11   정답 ①

윗글의 제목으로 가장 적절한 것은?
① Know Each Person to Guarantee Best Performance
최고의 성과를 보장하기 위해 사람 각각을 알아라   사람 관리에서 고유한 개성을 아는 것이 중요함
② Flexible Hours: An Appealing Working Condition
유연한 근무 시간: 매력적인 근무 조건   예로 제시된 부분을 이용한 오답
③ Talk to Employees More Often in Hard Times
어려운 시기에 직원들과 더 자주 대화하라   말의 내용과 방식을
정할 때 사람들의 특징을 고려하라는 내용임
④ How Empathy and Recognition Are Different
공감과 인식이 어떻게 다른가   사람 관리에서 공감과 적응성이 중요하다는 내용만 있음
⑤ Why Creativity Suffers in Competition
창의성이 경쟁에서 어려움을 겪는 이유   창의적인 사람이 다 같은 부류가 아니라는 내용만 있음

❯왜 정답 ? ★★★ [정답률 46%]

- 사람들의 관리에서 중요한 것은 그들의 고유한 개성을 아는 것이다. **11번 단서 1**
- 사람 각각의 복잡한 긍정적 및 부정적인 개성의 특징, 그들의 삶의 상황, 그 순간의
  그들의 사고방식을 고려하라.
➡ 사람 관리에서 중요한 것은 그 사람의 고유한 개성을 아는 것이다. 그 사람에게 할
  말의 내용과 방식을 정할 때 그 사람의 특징, 상황, 사고방식 등을 고려한 개별화된
  관리 방식을 취해야 한다.
  ▶ 따라서 제목으로 적절한 것은 ① '최고의 성과를 보장하기 위해 사람 각각을
  알아라'이다.

❯왜 오답 ?
② 글의 주제를 뒷받침하기 위해 예로 든 내용일 뿐이다.
③ 어려운 시기를 이겨내는 방법을 설명하는 글이 아니다.
④ 공감과 인식의 차이점에 대해서는 전혀 언급되지 않았다.
⑤ 창의성과 경쟁에서 이기는 것의 관련성에 대한 글이 아니다.

---

③ 12   정답 ③

밑줄 친 (a)~(e) 중에서 문맥상 낱말의 쓰임이 적절하지 않은 것은?
① (a) 사람들이 모두 같은 부류인 것은 아님   ② (b) 무슨 말을 하는지는 사람마다 다름
다양한   같음
③ (c) 집단이 아닌 개인에 맞게 전달해야 함   ④ (d) 서로 다른 방식을 통해서 더 쉽게
집단   더 쉽게 전달할 수 있음
⑤ (e) 개별화된 관리 방식이 성과를 이끌어내는 핵심임
핵심

❯왜 정답 ? ★★★ [정답률 37%]

③ (c) group 집단
[예를 들어, 여러분이 누군가에게 2주 연속 주말에 일하라고 요청하고
있다면, 또는 그들에게 받아 마땅한 그 승진을 지금 당장은 받지 못할
것이라고 말하고 있다면, 그 (c) 집단개인을 명심해야 한다.
➡ 무슨 말을 하는지는 사람마다 같지 않을 수 있다고 했다. 같은 소식을 들은
  Vincent는 그 소식에 대해 Emily와 매우 다른 반응을 보일 것이라고 했다.
  ▶ 집단이 아니라 사람마다 다를 수 있으므로 group을 individual과 같은 어휘로
  바꾸어야 한다.

❯왜 오답 ?

① (a) varying 다양한
[창의적인 사람들이 모두 같은 부류인 것은 아니다. 그들은 (a) 다양한
  수준의 성숙도와 민감성을 가진다. 그들은 일에 대한 서로 다른 접근법을
  가진다.
➡ 창의적인 사람들이 모두 같은 부류인 것은 아니라고 했고 그들은 일에 대한 서로
  다른 접근법을 가진다고 했다. ▶ varying은 문맥에 맞음

② (b) same 같은
[여러분이 누구인지와 무슨 말을 하는지는 사람마다 (b) 같지 않을 수 있다.
➡ 뒤에 이어지는 예에서 같은 말에 대해 Vincent와 Emily가 매우 다른 반응을
  보인다고 했다.
  ▶ 부정어 not과 함께 '같지 않음'을 나타내므로 same은 문맥에 맞음

④ (d) easier 더 쉽게
[~ 그 소식이 서로 다른 것과 묶인다면 그들 각자는 더 잘 받아들일 것이다.
  아마 Vincent에게 명절에 며칠간의 추가적인 휴무일이 주어진다면 그
  승진 소식은 (d) 더 쉽게 도달할 것이고, 한편 Emily에게는 지금보다 1년
  후에 더 큰 승진을 약속할 수도 있을 것이다.
➡ 같은 소식이라도 그 소식이 서로 다른 것과 묶인다면 그들 각자는 더 잘 받아들일
  것이라고 했다. 서로 다른 것을 묶는 예시로 Emily에게는 1년 후에 더 큰 승진을,
  Vincent에게는 추가적인 휴무일을 승진 소식과 함께 전하는 것이 이어진다.
  ▶ easier는 문맥에 맞음

⑤ (e) key 핵심
[개인적인 연관, 동감, 그리고 개별화된 관리 방식은 모든 사람으로부터
  일관되고 록 스타와 같은 수준의 일을 끌어내는 (e) 핵심이다.
➡ Vincent와 Emily의 예로부터 개별화된 관리 방식을 활용하면 어려운 요청을 할
  때 도움이 된다는 것을 알 수 있었다. 따라서 개인적인 연관, 동감, 그리고 개별화된
  관리 방식이 사람들에게서 성과를 이끌어내는 데 중요한 요소임을 알 수 있다.
  ▶ key는 문맥에 맞음

자이스토리

Xi story

대한민국 No.1 수능 기출문제집

2026

휴대용

단어장

영어 **독해 기본**

- 최신 6개년 고1 학력평가 기출 어휘 총정리
- 문제편 문항 순서대로 어휘 수록
- 단어+품사+뜻 수록
- 내신 + 수능 필수 어휘 암기 학습 가능
- 핸드폰으로 휴대하면서 암기

단어장 전체 pdf ▶

수경출판사

휴대용 단어장 활용법 7단계

01 늘 주머니에 넣고 다니세요. 쉬는 시간 틈틈이 단어 공부를 하세요.

02 미리 아는 단어들을 체크하세요.

03 모르는 단어는 철자와 발음, 뜻을 익히세요.

04 단어마다 최소 다섯 번씩 소리 내어 읽고 뜻을 외우세요.
(가능하면 직접 써보며 외우는 것이 좋습니다.)

05 다음 날에 외운 단어를 보며 확실히 외웠는지 체크하세요.

06 일주일 단위로 모르는 단어들만 다시 체크하며 복습하세요.

07 위의 과정을 최소 2회 반복하세요.

차 례

고난도 유형 독해 모의고사

pdf 파일

A  목적 찾기

A01
□ coordinator ⓝ 코디네이터
□ community ⓝ 지역 사회
□ recently ⓐⓓ 최근에
□ grassy area 잔디밭
□ separate ⓐ 별도의
□ ensure ⓥ 보장하다
□ newly ⓐⓓ 새롭게

A02
□ appreciate ⓥ 감사하다
□ available ⓐ 이용 가능한
□ switch ⓥ 전환하다
□ subscription ⓝ 구독
□ access ⓥ 이용하다, 접근하다
□ via ⓟⓡⓔⓟ ~을 통해

A03
□ introduce ⓥ 소개하다
□ handmade ⓐ 수공예의
□ organize ⓥ 조직하다
□ exhibition plan 전시 배치도
□ inform ⓥ 알리다
□ requirement ⓝ 요구 사항
□ further ⓐ 추가적인
□ assistance ⓝ 도움

A04
□ reach out 연락하다
□ current ⓐ 현재의

□ operating hour 운영 시간
□ resource ⓝ 자원
□ entrance ⓝ 입학
□ academic ⓐ 학문의, 학업의
□ extend ⓥ 연장하다
□ proposal ⓝ 제안

A05
□ funding ⓝ 재정 지원
□ construction ⓝ 건축, 건설
□ additional ⓐ 추가적인
□ functional ⓐ 기능을 하는
□ submit ⓥ 제출하다
□ documentation ⓝ 서류
□ notification ⓝ 통지
□ considerable ⓐ 상당한
□ consequence ⓝ 결과
□ budgetary ⓐ 예산의
□ constraint ⓝ 제약
□ notify A of B A에게 B를 통지하다

A06
□ science ⓝ 과학
□ recently ⓐⓓ 최근에
□ impressed ⓐ 감명을 받은
□ environment ⓝ 환경
□ discussion ⓝ 토론
□ lecture ⓝ 강의
□ suit ⓥ 맞추다
□ experience ⓝ 경험
□ grateful ⓐ 감사한

A07
□ concern ⓝ 우려
□ traditional ⓐ 전통적인
□ vending machine 자동판매기
□ assistance ⓝ 도움
□ urge ⓥ 촉구하다
□ regain ⓥ 되찾다
□ prompt ⓐ 신속한
□ resolution ⓝ 해결

A08
□ appreciate ⓥ 감사하다
□ confident ⓐ 자신감 있는
□ in response to ~에 대한 응답으로
□ ad(= advertisement) ⓝ 광고
□ graduate ⓥ 졸업하다
□ at one's convenience 편한 때에

A09
□ director ⓝ 책임자, 관리자
□ chemistry ⓝ 화학
□ local ⓐ 지역의
□ goal ⓝ 목표
□ experiment ⓝ 실험
□ contact ⓥ 연락하다
□ recommend ⓥ 추천하다
□ department ⓝ (대학의) 학과
□ qualified ⓐ 자격이 있는
□ look forward to ~을 고대하다

A 10

- choir ⓝ 합창단
- announce ⓥ 알리다, 공고하다
- compete ⓥ 겨루다, 경쟁하다
- take place 열리다
- participate in ~에 참가하다
- necessary ⓐ 필요한
- support ⓥ 후원하다
- fundraising ⓝ 모금
- passion ⓝ 열정
- in advance 미리, 앞서

A 11

- guardian ⓝ 보호자
- crisp ⓝ 포테이토 칩
- request ⓥ 요청하다
- seal ⓥ 밀봉하다
- ingredient ⓝ 성분
- list ⓥ 목록으로 작성하다
- contain ⓥ 포함하다
- nut ⓝ 견과
- severe ⓐ 심각한
- cooperation ⓝ 협조

A 12

- include ⓥ 포함하다
- meditation ⓝ 명상
- instructor ⓝ 강사
- book ⓥ 예약하다
- reasonable ⓐ 합리적인
- unforgettable ⓐ 잊지 못할

A 13

- tour ⓝ 여행
- return ⓥ 돌아오다
- discover ⓥ 발견하다
- leave behind ~을 놓아 둔 채 잊고 오다
- lap ⓝ 무릎
- ask ⓥ 부탁하다, 요청하다
- appreciate ⓥ 감사히 여기다

A 14

- delighted ⓐ 아주 기뻐하는
- annual ⓐ 연례의
- dish ⓝ 요리
- showcase ⓥ 전시하다, 소개하다
- gifted ⓐ 재능이 있는
- recipe ⓝ 조리법
- grateful ⓐ 고마워하는
- occasion ⓝ 행사
- celebration ⓝ 축하 행사
- look forward to -ing ~을 학수고대하다

A 15

- successfully ⓐⓓ 성공적으로
- raise ⓥ (자금 등을) 모으다
- remodel ⓥ 리모델링하다, 개축하다
- local ⓐ 지역의
- builder ⓝ 건축업자
- volunteer ⓥ 자원하다
- assistance ⓝ 도움

- grab ⓥ 쥐다
- hammer ⓝ 망치
- donate ⓥ 기부하다
- construction ⓝ 공사

A 16

- librarian ⓝ 사서
- president ⓝ 회장
- aware ⓐ 알고[자각하고] 있는
- access ⓥ 접근하다, 이용하다
- humble ⓐ 겸허한, 겸손한
- request ⓝ 요청
- store ⓥ 저장[보관]하다
- grant ⓥ 주다, 수여하다
- permission ⓝ 허락

A 17

- PR director 홍보부 이사
- corporation ⓝ 기업, 회사
- redesign ⓥ 다시 설계하다
- identity ⓝ 정체성
- celebrate ⓥ 축하하다
- anniversary ⓝ 기념일
- request ⓥ 요청하다
- suit ⓥ 어울리다, 적합하다
- core ⓝ 핵심
- inspire ⓥ 영감을 주다
- humanity ⓝ 인류애
- convey ⓥ 전달하다
- capture ⓥ (사진이나 글로 감정·분위기 등을) 정확히 담아내다

A 18

- □ resident ⓝ 거주자
- □ recently ⓐⓓ 최근에
- □ observe ⓥ 알다, 목격하다
- □ repair ⓝ 수리
- □ attention ⓝ 주의
- □ condition ⓝ 상태
- □ playground ⓝ 놀이터
- □ equipment ⓝ 설비
- □ swing ⓝ 그네
- □ damage ⓥ 손상하다
- □ fall off 떨어져 나가다
- □ slide ⓝ 미끄럼틀
- □ facility ⓝ 시설
- □ terrible ⓐ 형편없는
- □ appreciate ⓥ 감사하다
- □ immediate ⓐ 즉각적인
- □ solve ⓥ (문제 등을) 해결하다

A 19

- □ loyal ⓐ 충성스러운, 충실한
- □ essential ⓐ 필수적인
- □ innovative ⓐ 혁신적인
- □ contribute ⓥ 기여하다
- □ voluntarily ⓐⓓ 자발적으로, 자원해서
- □ total ⓥ 합계가 ~이 되다
- □ request ⓥ 요청하다
- □ consideration ⓝ 고려
- □ reflect ⓥ 반영하다
- □ performance ⓝ 성과

B 심경의 이해

B 01

- □ damp ⓐ 습기 찬
- □ thick ⓐ (공기가) 짙은
- □ make out 알아보다, 식별하다
- □ shadow ⓝ 그림자
- □ shaking ⓐ 떨리는
- □ figure ⓝ 형체, 형상
- □ faint ⓐ 희미한
- □ beam ⓝ 빛줄기
- □ crack ⓝ 틈새
- □ escape ⓥ (웃음 등이) 새어 나오다
- □ stare at ~을 바라보다
- □ hop ⓥ 깡충 뛰다
- □ at ease 편안한

B 02

- □ immediately ⓐⓓ 즉시
- □ glance ⓝ 흘긋 보다
- □ swiftly ⓐⓓ 신속하게
- □ kneel ⓥ 무릎을 꿇다
- □ combined ⓐ 합쳐진
- □ effort ⓝ 노력
- □ revive ⓥ 소생시키다
- □ thrilled ⓐ 흥분한
- □ desperate ⓐ 간절한

B 03

- □ check in (비행기) 탑승 수속을 하다
- □ expectation ⓝ 기대
- □ look forward to ~을 기대하다
- □ approach ⓥ 다가가다
- □ passport ⓝ 여권
- □ ruin ⓥ 망치다
- □ heartbroken ⓐ 상심한
- □ board ⓥ 탑승하다
- □ indifferent ⓐ 무관심한

B 04

- □ glance ⓥ 흘긋 보다
- □ casting director 섭외 감독
- □ chew ⓥ 씹다
- □ jiggle ⓥ 가볍게 흔들다
- □ rush ⓝ 물결
- □ production ⓝ 작품

B 05

- □ hard-fought ⓐ 치열히 싸운
- □ figure ⓥ 생각하다
- □ race ⓥ 빠르게 뛰다
- □ anticipation ⓝ 기대감
- □ fall apart 무너지다

B 06

- □ sandcastle ⓝ 모래성
- □ enormous ⓐ 거대한
- □ destroy ⓥ 부수다
- □ stream ⓥ 흐르다
- □ respond ⓥ 반응하다
- □ enthusiasm ⓝ 열정
- □ regretful ⓐ 후회하는

B 07

- rapidly @ 빠르게
- application letter 지원서
- sleep a wink 한숨 자다
- envelope ⓝ 봉투
- emerge ⓥ 나타나다
- phrase ⓝ 문구
- faraway @ 거리가 먼

B 08

- thrilled @ 흥분한, 감격한
- draw ⓥ 그리다
- awe ⓝ 경외심
- reply ⓥ 대답하다
- at a loss 어쩔 줄을 모르는
- rooted @ ~에 뿌리를
  둔[정착한]

B 09

- awaken ⓥ 잠에서 깨다
- glance ⓥ 흘깃 보다
- for an instant 잠시 동안
- rub ⓥ 비비다
- assure ⓥ 안심시키다
- rhythmic @ 리드미컬한,
  규칙적으로 순환하는

B 10

- notice ⓥ 알아차리다
- park ⓥ 주차하다
- neighbor ⓝ 이웃
- joyfully @ 기쁘게
- playmate ⓝ 놀이 친구
- pray ⓥ 기도하다

B 11

- absolutely @ 절대적으로,
  완전히
- thrilled @ 들뜬
- daydream ⓥ 공상에 잠기다
- flip through 휙휙 넘기다, ~을
  훑어보다
- figure ⓥ 생각[판단]하다
- realize ⓥ 깨닫다, 실현하다
- furious @ 몹시 화가 난
- ashamed @ 부끄러운
- anticipating @ 기대하는
- satisfied @ 만족하는
- disappointed @ 실망한

B 12

- submission ⓝ 제출
- deadline ⓝ 마감 시간
- typewriter ⓝ 타자기
- tap ⓥ (가볍게) 두드리다
- strike ⓥ (세게) 치다, 두드리다
- desperately @ 필사적으로
- lap ⓝ 무릎
- room ⓝ 공간
- smoothly @ 매끄럽게
- frustrated @ 좌절한
- indifferent @ 무관심한
- disappointed @ 실망한

B 13

- swing set 스윙 세트(그네와
  미끄럼틀 등으로 이뤄진 아이들
  놀이 기구)
- available @ 이용할 수 있는

- sink ⓥ 가라앉다, 침몰하다
- embarrassed @ 난처한
- indifferent @ 무관심한
- ashamed @ 부끄러운
- touched @ 감동한

B 14

- principal ⓝ (학)교장
- present ⓥ 수여하다
- academic @ 학업의
- award ⓝ 상
- row ⓝ 열, 횡렬
- finalist ⓝ 최종 입상 후보자
- gather ⓥ 모이다
- sweaty @ 땀에 젖은
- handkerchief ⓝ 손수건
- glance ⓥ 힐끗 보다
- pale @ 창백한
- uneasy @ 불안한
- subject ⓝ 과목
- rank ⓥ 평가하다, 순위를 매기다
- confidence ⓝ 자신감
- declare ⓥ 공표하다
- thunder of applause
  우레와 같은 박수갈채
- disappointed @ 실망한
- guilty @ 죄책감을 느끼는
- confident @ 자신감 있는
- delighted @ 기쁜

B 15

- day off (근무를) 쉬는 날
- mute ⓥ (소리를) 작게 하다, 음
  소거하다

- disconnect ⓥ 단절하다
- calm ⓐ 침착한, 차분한
- immediately ⓐⓓ 즉시
- fall over ~에 걸려 넘어지다
- injured ⓐ 다친, 부상을 입은
- concerned ⓐ 걱정되는
- recover ⓥ 회복하다
- surgery ⓝ 수술
- indifferent ⓐ 무관심한
- annoyed ⓐ 화난

B 16
- grizzly bear 회색곰
- native ⓐ 자연의
- habitat ⓝ 서식지
- sniff ⓥ (코를) 킁킁거리다
- realize ⓥ 깨닫다
- giant ⓐ 거대한
- freeze ⓥ 얼어붙다
- issue ⓝ 문제
- survival ⓝ 생존
- motivation ⓝ 동기
- clearly ⓐⓓ 분명히

B 17
- risk ⓝ 위험
- definitely ⓐⓓ 분명히
- persuade ⓥ 설득하다
- pin ⓥ 꼼짝 못하게 하다
- deceptively ⓐⓓ 속을 정도로, 믿을 수 없게
- handhold ⓝ 손으로 잡을 곳
- clumsily ⓐⓓ 서투르게
- cliff ⓝ 절벽

- reach ⓝ (닿을 수 있는) 거리[범위]
- tremble ⓥ 떨(리)다
- exhaustion ⓝ 기진맥진
- fright ⓝ 공포, 놀람
- fearful ⓐ 두려운
- regretful ⓐ 후회하는

B 18
- shade ⓝ 색조
- honeymoon ⓥ 신혼여행을 하다
- exotic ⓐ 이국적인
- track ⓝ (이동하는) 길[방향]
- land ⓥ (땅에) 떨어지다
- fine ⓐ 고운

B 19
- midnight ⓝ 자정
- nowhere ⓐⓓ 아무 데도 (없다)
- crowd ⓝ 군중, 무리
- approach ⓥ 다가가다
- suddenly ⓐⓓ 갑자기
- familiar ⓐ 익숙한, 친숙한
- calm ⓐ 침착한
- disappear ⓥ 사라지다
- indifferent ⓐ 무관심한
- embarrassed ⓐ 당황한

C 주장 찾기

C 01
- gestural ⓐ 몸짓의
- nod ⓥ 고개를 끄덕이다
- complement ⓥ 보완하다
- layer ⓝ 겹
- indicate ⓥ 나타내다, 보여 주다
- honesty ⓝ 정직함
- atmosphere ⓝ 분위기
- collaboration ⓝ 협력
- palm ⓝ 손바닥
- willing to 기꺼이 ~ 하는
- engage in ~에 참여하다
- over-gesturing ⓝ 과도한 몸짓
- distract from ~에 집중이 안 되게 하다
- chaos ⓝ 혼돈
- overshadow ⓥ 가리다

C 02
- maintain ⓥ 유지하다
- constant ⓐ 일정한
- attention ⓝ 주의 (집중)
- characterise ⓥ 특징으로 하다
- peaks and valleys 정점과 저점
- achieve ⓥ 이루다
- confident ⓐ 자신감 있는
- benefit ⓝ 이익, 혜택

□ demanding ⓐ (일이) 힘든
□ task ⓝ 과업, 작업
□ cope with ~을 처리하다

C 03
□ astonish ⓥ 놀라게 하다
□ degree ⓝ 정도
□ convenience ⓝ 편리성
□ decision making 의사 결정
□ remarkable ⓐ 놀라운
□ extent ⓝ 정도
□ chore ⓝ 일, 잡일
□ stay in touch 연락을 유지하다

C 04
□ inefficient ⓐ 비효율적인
□ overlook ⓥ 간과하다
□ potential ⓐ 잠재적인
□ demand ⓝ 요구
□ disappear ⓥ 사라지다
□ get ~ off to a great start ~을 순조롭게 시작하다
□ set the tone 분위기를 잡다
□ brief ⓐ 짧은
□ transition ⓝ 변화
□ material ⓝ 자료
□ establish ⓥ 설립하다, 마련하다

C 05
□ commitment ⓝ 전념, 헌신
□ obligation ⓝ 의무
□ dedicated ⓐ 전념[헌신]하는

□ integrate ⓥ 통합하다
□ chore ⓝ 일
□ come into play 작동하다
□ realistic ⓐ 현실적인
□ inevitable ⓐ 피할 수 없는
□ seize ⓥ 잡다
□ engage in ~을 시작하다
□ incorporate ⓥ 포함하다

C 06
□ magic ⓝ 마법, 마술
□ challenge ⓝ 어려움, 도전
□ statement ⓝ 진술
□ positive ⓐ 긍정적인
□ struggle ⓥ 어려움을 겪다
□ witness ⓥ 목격하다
□ confidence ⓝ 자신감
□ surprise ⓥ 놀라게 하다
□ shift ⓝ 변화
□ powerful ⓐ 강력한

C 07
□ messy ⓐ 지저분한
□ destructive ⓐ 파괴적인
□ disorderly ⓐ 무질서한
□ indicate ⓥ 나타내다
□ disorganized ⓐ 체계적이지 못한
□ mental state 정신 상태
□ tidy ⓥ 정돈하다
□ gain ⓥ 얻다
□ surroundings ⓝ 주변 환경
□ atmosphere ⓝ 분위기
□ neatly ⓐⓓ 단정하게

C 08
□ be aware of ~을 알다[주의하다]
□ nonstop ⓐⓓ 연속적으로
□ remarkable ⓐ 놀라운
□ bragging ⓐ 자랑하는
□ expectation ⓝ 기대
□ incredible ⓐ 엄청난
□ achievement ⓝ 업적
□ end up with 결국 ~로 끝나다
□ driven ⓐ 지나친
□ perfectionist ⓝ 완벽주의자
□ drop-out ⓝ 학업 중단자, 중퇴자

C 09
□ remind ⓥ 상기시키다
□ argument ⓝ 논점, 주장
□ committed ⓐ 몰입된
□ insight ⓝ 통찰력
□ expose ⓥ 노출시키다
□ passivity ⓝ 수동성

C 10
□ avoid ⓥ 피하다
□ discomfort ⓝ 불편
□ shut out ~을 차단하다[가로막다]
□ overcome ⓥ 극복하다
□ instinct ⓝ 본능
□ essential ⓐ 필수적인
□ comfort zone 편안함을 주는 곳, 안락 지대
□ magical ⓐ 마법의
□ formula ⓝ 공식

C11

- ☐ **overhear** ⓥ 우연히 듣다
- ☐ **priority** ⓝ 우선순위
- ☐ **tempting** ⓐ 솔깃한
- ☐ **character** ⓝ 인격
- ☐ **uphold** ⓥ 유지하다
- ☐ **self-discipline** ⓝ 자제력
- ☐ **honesty** ⓝ 정직함

C12

- ☐ **launch** ⓥ (새로운 일을) 시작하다[개시하다]
- ☐ **promote** ⓥ 홍보하다
- ☐ **strictly** ⓐⓓ 엄격하게
- ☐ **shamelessly** ⓐⓓ 뻔뻔스럽게
- ☐ **give ~ away** ~을 나누어 주다
- ☐ **entertaining** ⓐ 재미있는, 즐거움을 주는
- ☐ **audience** ⓝ 청중, 독자

C13

- ☐ **personal** ⓐ 개인적인
- ☐ **sensible** ⓐ 실용적인
- ☐ **separate** ⓐ 별도의
- ☐ **distraction** ⓝ 주의산만
- ☐ **multiple** ⓐ 많은
- ☐ **organize** ⓥ 정리하다
- ☐ **media** ⓝ 매체, 수단
- ☐ **professional** ⓐ 직업의
- ☐ **divide** ⓥ 나누다
- ☐ **informed** ⓐ 정보에 입각한

C14

- ☐ **encourage** ⓥ 촉진하다, 장려하다
- ☐ **creative** ⓐ 창의적인
- ☐ **on one's own** 혼자서, 혼자 힘으로
- ☐ **on average** 평균적으로
- ☐ **unproductive** ⓐ 비생산적인
- ☐ **productive** ⓐ 생산적인
- ☐ **prepare** ⓥ 준비하다
- ☐ **in advance** 미리, 사전에
- ☐ **discuss** ⓥ 논의하다, 의논하다
- ☐ **share** ⓥ 공유하다
- ☐ **participant** ⓝ 참석자
- ☐ **participate** ⓥ 참여하다

C15

- ☐ **take responsibility for** ~에 책임을 지다
- ☐ **advance** ⓥ 발전하다
- ☐ **manage to** (간신히) 해내다
- ☐ **well-run** ⓐ 잘 운영되는
- ☐ **commit to** ~에 전념하다
- ☐ **devote ~ to …** ~을 …에 쏟다[바치다]
- ☐ **otherwise** ⓐⓓ 그렇지 않으면
- ☐ **career** ⓝ 경력

C16

- ☐ **expert** ⓝ 전문가
- ☐ **get rid of** ~을 삭제하다
- ☐ **adequately** ⓐⓓ 적절히
- ☐ **elaborate** ⓥ 부연 설명하다
- ☐ **equipped with** ~을 갖춘

- ☐ **distract** ⓥ 집중이 안 되게 하다
- ☐ **crucial** ⓐ 중요한

C17

- ☐ **army** ⓝ 군대
- ☐ **instructor** ⓝ 교관
- ☐ **inspect** ⓥ 검사하다, 점검하다
- ☐ **require** ⓥ 요구하다
- ☐ **make one's bed** 침대를 정돈하다
- ☐ **ridiculous** ⓐ 우스꽝스러운
- ☐ **prove** ⓥ 증명하다
- ☐ **encourage** ⓥ 용기를 주다
- ☐ **complete** ⓥ 완수하다
- ☐ **turn into** ~으로 변하다

C18

- ☐ **estimate** ⓥ 추정하다
- ☐ **pay attention to** ~에 주의를 기울이다
- ☐ **nonverbal** ⓐ 비언어적인
- ☐ **significant** ⓐ 중요한
- ☐ **make a difference** 차이를 만들다
- ☐ **closely** ⓐⓓ 면밀히, 밀접하게
- ☐ **tuned in (to)** (~에) 맞춰진, (~에 대해) 잘 아는
- ☐ **initial** ⓐ 처음의, 초기의
- ☐ **encouraging** ⓐ 격려의, 힘을 북돋아 주는
- ☐ **empower** ⓥ 힘을 주다
- ☐ **a great deal of** 많은
- ☐ **effort** ⓝ 노력
- ☐ **climate** ⓝ 분위기, 기후

D 밑줄 친 부분의 의미 찾기

D 01

- □ common sense 상식
- □ belief ⓝ 신념
- □ drive ⓥ 이끌다
- □ external ⓐ 외적인
- □ behavior ⓝ 행동
- □ socialize ⓥ 어울리다, 교류하다
- □ internal ⓐ 내적의, 내면의
- □ obviously ⓐⓓ 분명히
- □ reflect ⓥ 반영하다
- □ remarkable ⓐ 놀랄 만한, 놀라운
- □ likely ⓐ ~할 가능성이 있는
- □ reverse ⓐ 반대의
- □ direction ⓝ 방향
- □ entirely ⓐⓓ 완전히
- □ separate ⓐ 분리된
- □ be dependent on ~에 의존하다
- □ surroundings ⓝ (주변) 환경
- □ matter ⓥ 중요하다

D 02

- □ adopt ⓥ 받아들이다, 채택하다
- □ traditional ⓐ 전통적인
- □ livelihood ⓝ 생계 수단
- □ progress ⓝ 발전
- □ remove ⓥ 없애다
- □ physical ⓐ 육체의

- □ disability ⓝ 장애
- □ mass ⓐ 대중의
- □ avoid ⓥ 피하다
- □ divorce ⓝ 단절, 이혼
- □ indeed ⓐⓓ 실제로, 참으로
- □ risk ⓝ 위험 (요소)
- □ ignorance ⓝ 무지, 무식
- □ endless ⓐ 끝없는
- □ labor ⓝ 노동

D 03

- □ gene editing 유전자 편집
- □ logical ⓐ 합리적인
- □ preferable ⓐ 바람직한
- □ correct ⓥ 교정하다
- □ transform ⓥ 변형하다, 바꾸다
- □ temptation ⓝ 유혹
- □ superior ⓐ 우수한
- □ characteristics ⓝ 특징
- □ pursuit ⓝ 추구
- □ slippery ⓐ 미끄러운
- □ slope ⓝ 경사
- □ end up 결국 ~하게 되다
- □ alteration ⓝ 개조, 변경
- □ stick to ~을 고수하다
- □ belief ⓝ 믿음, 신념
- □ moral ⓐ 도덕적인

D 04

- □ atom ⓝ 원자
- □ inhale ⓥ 흡입하다
- □ exhale ⓥ 내뱉다

- □ means ⓝ 수단, 방법
- □ make up ~을 구성하다
- □ cycle ⓥ 순환하다
- □ sweat ⓝ 땀
- □ grand ⓐ 거대한
- □ scale ⓝ 규모
- □ limitless ⓐ 제한 없는
- □ caretaker ⓝ 관리인

D 05

- □ automatically ⓐⓓ 자동적으로
- □ break up 해체하다
- □ concept ⓝ 개념
- □ recode ⓥ 재부호화하다
- □ reconstruct ⓥ 재구성하다
- □ trait ⓝ 특성
- □ store ⓥ 저장하다
- □ optimal ⓐ 최적의
- □ compression ⓝ 압축
- □ raw ⓐ 날것의, 가공되지 않은
- □ generalize ⓥ 일반화하다
- □ make connections between ~ 사이를 연결하다
- □ represent ⓥ 재현하다
- □ abstract ⓐ 추상적인
- □ assumption ⓝ 가정
- □ undermine ⓥ 손상시키다
- □ legal ⓐ 법적인
- □ eyewitness ⓝ 목격자
- □ testimony ⓝ 증언
- □ relevant ⓐ 관련 있는
- □ fall short of ~이 부족하다

□ comprehension ⓝ 이해
□ precede ⓥ (~보다) 먼저 일어나다

D 06
□ seemingly ⓐⓓ 겉보기에
□ sense ⓝ 감각
□ sight ⓝ 시각
□ philosopher ⓝ 철학자
□ doubt ⓥ 의심하다
□ perception ⓝ 인식
□ balance ⓝ 균형
□ vision ⓝ 시각
□ categorize ⓥ 분류하다
□ detect ⓥ 감지하다
□ prey ⓝ 먹잇감
□ divide ⓥ 나누다
□ specific ⓐ 특정한
□ bucket ⓝ 양동이

D 07
□ technique ⓝ 기술
□ helplessness ⓝ 무력감
□ depression ⓝ 우울감
□ predominantly ⓐⓓ 현저히
□ resolve ⓥ 해결하다
□ self-help ⓝ 자조, 자립
□ energize ⓥ 활기를 북돋우다
□ be in one's presence ~의 자리에 (함께) 있다
□ psychic ⓐ 정신의
□ transfer ⓝ 이동
□ relight ⓥ 재점화하다

D 08
□ passive ⓐ 수동적인
□ browse ⓥ 훑어보다
□ effective ⓐ 효과적인
□ claim ⓥ 주장하다, 공언하다
□ direct ⓐ 직접적인
□ focused ⓐ 집중하는
□ rest ⓝ 나머지
□ herd ⓝ 무리
□ proactive ⓐ 진취적인
□ logically ⓐⓓ 논리적으로
□ occasional ⓐ 가끔의
□ resume ⓝ 이력서
□ sheep ⓝ 양, 어리석은 사람
□ job-seeker ⓝ 구직자
□ competition ⓝ 경쟁
□ employer ⓝ 고용주
□ stand out 돋보이다

D 09
□ tendency ⓝ 경향
□ interpret ⓥ 해석하다
□ selectively ⓐⓓ 선택적으로
□ stack ⓥ 쌓다
□ viewpoint ⓝ 관점
□ perception ⓝ 지각, 인식
□ stand out 두드러지다, 눈에 띄다
□ be related to ~와 관련이 있다
□ interest ⓝ 관심, 관심사
□ expectation ⓝ 기대
□ demand ⓝ 요구

□ hammer ⓝ 망치
□ nail ⓝ 못
□ quote ⓝ 인용문
□ highlight ⓥ 강조하다
□ phenomenon ⓝ 현상

D 10
□ react ⓥ 반응하다
□ behavior ⓝ 행동
□ influence ⓝ 영향
□ likelihood ⓝ 가능성
□ repurchase ⓥ 재구매하다
□ determine ⓥ 알아내다
□ encourage ⓥ 권장하다
□ satisfied ⓐ 만족한
□ ambassador ⓝ 대사
□ persuade ⓥ 설득하다
□ monitor ⓥ 추적 관찰하다
□ word-of-mouth ⓐ 구두의, 구전의

D 11
□ reveal ⓥ 드러내다
□ assumption ⓝ 추정, 전제
□ accomplish ⓥ 성취하다
□ achievement ⓝ 성취, 성과
□ imply ⓥ 암시하다, 넌지시 나타내다
□ obtain ⓥ 얻다
□ illegal ⓐ 불법적인
□ questionable ⓐ 의심스러운
□ means ⓝ 수단
□ criticism ⓝ 비판, 비평

- □ **automatically** (ad) 자동으로, 무의식적으로
- □ **inevitably** (ad) 반드시, 불가피하게
- □ **challenge** (v) 도전하다, 의문을 제기하다
- □ **sacred** (a) 신성한
- □ **pause** (v) 잠시 멈추다
- □ **valuable** (a) 가치 있는
- □ **matter** (v) 중요하다
- □ **false** (a) 잘못된
- □ **tendency** (n) 경향
- □ **hardship** (n) 고난
- □ **solid** (a) 확고한
- □ **abandon** (v) 버리다
- □ **notion** (n) 개념, 생각
- □ **superstition** (n) 미신

D 12

- □ **indeed** (ad) 정말로
- □ **hearer** (n) 듣는 사람
- □ **process** (n) 과정
- □ **signal** (n) 신호
- □ **useless** (a) 쓸모없는
- □ **perceive** (v) 감지하다
- □ **receive** (v) 수신하다, 받다
- □ **intended** (a) 의도된
- □ **audience** (n) 관객, 독자
- □ **restate** (v) 다시 말하다
- □ **experiment** (n) 실험
- □ **publication** (n) 출판
- □ **previous** (a) 이전의
- □ **demand** (n) 요구

D 13

- □ **trash** (n) 쓰레기
- □ **anthropologist** (n) 인류학자
- □ **bring back** 소환하다
- □ **analyze** (v) 분석하다
- □ **common** (a) 흔한, 일반적인
- □ **relative** (a) 상대적인
- □ **emphasize** (v) 강조하다
- □ **indoors** (ad) 실내에서
- □ **systematic** (a) 체계적인
- □ **classify** (v) 분류하다
- □ **eliminate** (v) 제거하다
- □ **process** (n) 과정

D 14

- □ **commonsense** (a) 상식적인
- □ **objective** (a) 객관적인
- □ **property** (n) 속성, 성질
- □ **bounce off** 튕겨 나오다
- □ **reflect** (v) 반사하다
- □ **inhabit** (v) ~에 살다[존재하다]
- □ **physical** (a) 물리적인
- □ **subjective** (a) 주관적인

D 15

- □ **psychology** (n) 심리학
- □ **professor** (n) 교수
- □ **management** (n) 관리
- □ **principle** (n) 원칙
- □ **reply** (v) 대답하다
- □ **absolute** (a) 절대적인
- □ **weight** (n) 무게

- □ **matter** (v) 중요하다
- □ **depend on** ~에 달려 있다
- □ **quite** (ad) 꽤
- □ **light** (a) 가벼운
- □ **straight** (ad) 계속해서
- □ **severe** (a) 심각한
- □ **nod** (v) (고개를) 끄덕이다
- □ **agreement** (n) 동의
- □ **continue** (v) (쉬지 않고) 계속되다
- □ **put down** ~을 내려놓다

D 16

- □ **return** (v) 반품하다
- □ **fixture** (n) 설비
- □ **replacement** (n) 대체품
- □ **warranty** (n) (상품 등의) 보증
- □ **undamaged** (a) 손상되지 않은, 멀쩡한
- □ **abuse** (v) 남용하다
- □ **entrepreneur** (n) 기업가
- □ **e-commerce** (n) 전자 상거래
- □ **resolve** (v) 해결하다
- □ **complaint** (n) 불평, 불만
- □ **dissatisfy** (v) 불만을 느끼게 하다
- □ **attention** (n) 주의
- □ **delete** (v) 삭제하다
- □ **reject** (v) 거절하다
- □ **unreasonable** (a) 불합리한
- □ **demand** (n) 요구
- □ **intention** (n) 의도
- □ **influential** (a) 영향력 있는

D

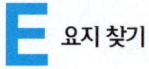

□meditative ⓐ 명상의

□anxiety ⓝ 불안감

□mindfulness ⓝ 마음 돌봄

□meditation ⓝ 명상

□elevate ⓥ 증진시키다

□cognition ⓝ 인지

□depression ⓝ 우울함

□accomplishment ⓝ 성취감

□thrive ⓥ 번성하다, 번영하다

□boost ⓥ 높이다

□self-esteem ⓝ 자아존중감

E 06

□conduct ⓥ 수행하다

□deliberation ⓝ 숙고

□feature ⓝ 특징

□inaccurate ⓐ 부정확한

□identification ⓝ 식별

□recognize ⓥ 알아채다

□accurate ⓐ 정확한

□immediate ⓐ 즉각적인

□automatic ⓐ 자동적인

□interpretation ⓝ 해석

□impression ⓝ 인상

□reasoned ⓐ 논리적인

□self-narrative ⓝ 자기 서사

□demonstrate ⓥ 보여 주다

□superior ⓐ 우수한

□relatively ⓐⓓ 상대적으로

□unconscious ⓐ 무의식의

□logical ⓐ 논리적인

□justification ⓝ 정당화

E 07

□care ⓥ 관심을 보이다

□social ⓐ 사교적인, 사회적인

□owe ⓥ 빚지다

□ignore ⓥ 무시하다

□pass by 지나가다

E 08

□contribute ⓥ 기여하다

□species ⓝ 종

□bond ⓥ 유대감을 형성하다

□evolutionary ⓐ 진화론적인

□direct ⓥ 지시하다

□attentive ⓐ 주의를 기울이는

□narrow ⓥ 좁히다

□stimuli ⓝ 자극

□acutely ⓐⓓ 강렬하게

E 09

□negotiate ⓥ 협상하다

□realise ⓥ 알아차리다

□traditional ⓐ 전통적인

□approach ⓝ 접근(법)

□agreement ⓝ 합의, 동의

□one-off ⓐ 단 한 번의

□transaction ⓝ 거래

□rare ⓐ 드문

□repeatedly ⓐⓓ 반복적으로

□spouse ⓝ 배우자

□essential ⓐ 매우 중요한

□maintain ⓥ 유지하다

□interdependent ⓐ 상호 의존적인

□acceptable ⓐ 받아들일 수 있는

E 10

□demand ⓥ 요구하다

□crime fiction 범죄 소설

□organize ⓥ 계획하다, 준비하다

□get it right 제대로 이해하다

□permission ⓝ 허가

□drive ~ to … ⓥ ~을 …하게 만들다

□boredom ⓝ 지루함

□reveal ⓥ 드러내다

□crucial ⓐ 중요한

□tension ⓝ 긴장

□conflict ⓝ 갈등

□blueprint ⓝ 청사진

E 11

□approach ⓥ 접근하다

□tuxedo ⓝ 턱시도

□funeral ⓝ 장례식

□bathing suit 수영복

□religious ⓐ 종교적인

□appropriate ⓐ 적합한, 알맞은

□occasion ⓝ 행사

□setting ⓝ 상황

□skillful ⓐ 숙련된, 능숙한

□flexible ⓐ 유연한

□strategy ⓝ 전략

□multiple-choice test 선다형 시험

E

E 12

□ **saying** ⓝ 속담, 격언

□ **threatening** ⓐ 위협적인

□ **opposite** ⓝ 반대

□ **frightening** ⓐ 두려움을 주는

□ **inner** ⓐ 내면의

□ **pessimistic** ⓐ 비관적인

□ **take a step** 조치를 취하다

□ **intend** ⓥ 의도하다

□ **rate** ⓝ 비율

□ **screen** ⓥ (특정 질병이 있는지) 검진하다

□ **terrified** ⓐ 두려워하는, 겁이 난

E 13

□ **emotion** ⓝ 감정

□ **deserve** ⓥ ~할 만하다, ~받을 가치가 있다

□ **information** ⓝ 정보

□ **unreliable** ⓐ 신뢰할 수 없는

□ **inaccurate** ⓐ 부정확한

□ **source** ⓝ 원천

□ **reflection** ⓝ 반영

□ **conclude** ⓥ 결론을 내리다

□ **behavior** ⓝ 행동

□ **reflect** ⓥ 반영하다, 나타내다

□ **mislead** ⓥ 속이다

E 14

□ **worthless** ⓐ 가치가 없는

□ **valuable** ⓐ 소중한, 귀중한

□ **end up** 결국 ~하다

□ **bury** ⓥ 묻다

□ **ensure** ⓥ 보장하다

□ **accessible** ⓐ 접근[이용] 가능한

□ **appropriate** ⓐ 적절한

□ **indication** ⓝ 표시, 암시

□ **recognize** ⓥ 인식하다, 알아보다

□ **store** ⓥ 저장하다

□ **prime** ⓐ 주된, 최고의

□ **utilize** ⓥ 활용[이용]하다

□ **loyalty** ⓝ 충성(도)

E 15

□ **indicate** ⓥ 보여주다

□ **distraction** ⓝ 주의 산만

□ **cognitive** ⓐ 인지적인

□ **performance** ⓝ 수행

□ **overstimulate** ⓥ 지나치게 자극시키다

□ **concentrate** ⓥ 집중하다

□ **excessive** ⓐ 지나친

□ **complete** ⓐ 완전한

□ **absence** ⓝ 없음, 부재

E 16

□ **view** ⓥ 보다, 여기다

□ **merely** ⓐ 그저

□ **down time** 가동되지 않는 시간

□ **shut off** 멈추다

□ **in a rush** 서둘러

□ **responsibility** ⓝ 책임

□ **cut back on** ~을 줄이다

□ **reveal** ⓥ 밝히다

□ **a number of** 많은

□ **carry out** ~을 수행하다

□ **at one's best** 최상의 수준으로

□ **form** ⓥ 형성하다

□ **pathway** ⓝ 경로

□ **memory** ⓝ 기억

□ **insight** ⓝ 통찰

□ **respond** ⓥ 반응하다

□ **lack** ⓝ 부족

□ **cause** ⓥ 일으키다

□ **evidence** ⓝ 증거

□ **risk** ⓝ 위험

□ **serious** ⓐ 심각한

□ **disease** ⓝ 질병

E 17

□ **independently** ⓐⓓ 독자적으로

□ **trustworthy** ⓐ 신뢰할 만한

□ **extremely** ⓐⓓ 극도로

□ **ultimately** ⓐⓓ 궁극적으로

□ **faith** ⓝ 믿음

□ **evidence** ⓝ 증거, 단서

□ **confident** ⓐ 자신감 있는

□ **incredibly** ⓐⓓ 놀랍게

□ **encounter** ⓥ 만나다, 마주치다

F 주제 찾기

F01
- □ a wealth of 수많은
- □ supervisor ⓝ 상사
- □ perceive ⓥ 여기다, 인식하다
- □ motivate ⓥ 동기를 부여하다
- □ value ⓥ 소중히 여기다
- □ peer ⓝ 또래, 동료
- □ relatedness ⓝ 관계성
- □ internalization ⓝ 내면화
- □ fuel ⓥ 자극하다, 연료를 공급하다
- □ competence ⓝ 유능함, 능숙함
- □ crucial ⓐ 중요한
- □ enhance ⓥ 강화하다, 향상시키다
- □ a sense of connectedness 유대감
- □ take on ~에 맞서다

F02
- □ possess ⓥ 지니다, 소유하다
- □ desirable ⓐ 바람직한
- □ characteristic ⓝ 특성, 특징
- □ majority ⓝ 다수
- □ general ⓐ 일반적인
- □ intelligent ⓐ 지적인
- □ fair-minded ⓐ 공정한
- □ prejudiced ⓐ 편견이 있는
- □ fictional ⓐ 허구적인

- □ senior ⓝ (고등학교의) 졸업반 학생
- □ self-image ⓝ 자아상
- □ tendency ⓝ 경향
- □ superior ⓐ (~보다) 우월한
- □ prejudice ⓝ 편견

F03
- □ observation ⓝ 관찰
- □ physical ⓐ 물리적인, 신체적인
- □ lower ⓥ 낮추다
- □ risk ⓝ 위험
- □ personal ⓐ 개인의
- □ act on ~을 행동으로 옮기다
- □ article ⓝ 기사
- □ humanity ⓝ 인류
- □ strategic ⓐ 전략적인
- □ act against ~을 거슬러 행동하다
- □ lack ⓝ 부족

F04
- □ translate ⓥ 바꾸다
- □ perception ⓝ 지각
- □ feed into ~에 들어가다
- □ sensory ⓐ 감각의
- □ telescope ⓝ 망원경
- □ ultraviolet ⓐ 자외(선)의
- □ property ⓝ 속성
- □ capacity ⓝ 수용
- □ difficulty ⓝ 어려움
- □ replace A with B A를 B로 대체하다

- □ inspire ⓥ 영감을 주다
- □ visual ⓐ 시각의
- □ auditory ⓐ 청각의
- □ imagination ⓝ 상상

F05
- □ quantitative ⓐ 양적인
- □ measure ⓥ 측정하다
- □ recall ⓥ 회상하다
- □ yield ⓥ 산출하다
- □ reliable ⓐ 신뢰할 만한
- □ recollection ⓝ 회상
- □ inaccurate ⓐ 부정확한
- □ vary ⓥ 다르다
- □ prompt ⓥ 유발[촉구]하다
- □ concrete ⓐ 구체적인
- □ rate ⓥ 평가하다
- □ utility bill 공과금 고지서
- □ afford to (~을 살) 여유가 있다
- □ seek ⓥ 요구하다, 찾다
- □ abstract ⓐ 추상적인
- □ ensure ⓥ 보장하다
- □ consistency ⓝ 일관성
- □ overgeneralize ⓥ 지나치게 일반화하다
- □ enhance ⓥ 높이다
- □ attain ⓥ 얻다

F06
- □ accessibility ⓝ 접근성
- □ disadvantage ⓝ 불리함
- □ labour ⓝ 노동
- □ inclusiveness ⓝ 포괄성

□assistive ⓐ 도움이 되는
□recognition ⓝ 인지
□caption ⓝ 자막
□facilitate ⓥ 촉진하다
□capability ⓝ 능력
□potentially ⓐⓓ 잠재적으로
□wage ⓝ 임금
□prospect ⓝ 전망
□domain ⓝ 영역
□ethical ⓐ 윤리적인
□necessity ⓝ 필요성
□support ⓥ 지원하다
□cure ⓥ 치료하다

F 07

□route ⓝ 경로, 길
□acquire ⓥ 획득하다
□compete ⓥ 경쟁하다
□mastery ⓝ 숙달
□prosperity ⓝ 번영
□equipment ⓝ 장비
□hardship ⓝ 고난
□mindset ⓝ 마음가짐
□struggle ⓝ 투쟁, 분투
□resistance ⓝ 저항
□confront ⓥ 직면하다

F 08

□evolution ⓝ 진화
□survival ⓝ 생존
□reproduction ⓝ 번식
□criteria ⓝ 기준
□natural selection 자연
  선택

□predator ⓝ 포식자
□efficiency ⓝ 효율성
□contribute ⓥ 기여하다
□individual ⓝ 개인
□prevail ⓥ 이기다
□competition ⓝ 경쟁
□belongingness
  ⓝ (단체에의) 귀속, 소속성
□promote ⓥ 촉진시키다
□potential ⓐ 잠재적인
□mate ⓝ 짝
□evolutionary ⓐ 진화의
□theory ⓝ 이론

F 09

□nearly ⓐⓓ 거의
□go through ~을 거쳐가다
□adequate ⓐ 적당한
□lung ⓝ 폐
□gum ⓝ 잇몸
□harmful ⓐ 해로운
□bloodstream ⓝ 혈류
□oral ⓐ 구강의
□affect ⓥ 영향을 미치다
□aspect ⓝ 측면
□tip of the iceberg 빙산의
  일각
□reflection ⓝ 반영, 반사
□entire ⓐ 전체의
□pose ⓥ ~을 초래하다,
  제기하다
□immune system 면역 체계

F 10

□vegetarian eating 채식
□mainstream ⓝ 주류
□dietetic ⓐ 식이(성)의
□approximately ⓐⓓ 거의, 대략
□nutritionally ⓐⓓ
  영양학적으로
□adequate ⓐ 적당한
□prevention ⓝ 예방
□treatment ⓝ 치료
□concern ⓝ 관심, 염려
□confinement ⓝ 갇힘
□vegetarianism ⓝ 채식주의
□vast ⓐ 거대한

F 11

□remarkable ⓐ 놀라운,
  주목할 만한
□unbelievable ⓐ 믿을 수 없는
□consequence ⓝ 결과
□alter ⓥ 바꾸다, 고치다
□duration ⓝ (지속되는) 기간
□glacier ⓝ 빙하
□gravity ⓝ 중력
□equator ⓝ (지구의) 적도
□rotation ⓝ 회전
□spread out (몸을) 뻗다
□barely ⓐⓓ 간신히, 거의 ~
  아니게
□noticeable ⓐ 알아차릴 수
  있는, 뚜렷한
□add up 누적되다, 쌓이다
□dinosaur ⓝ 공룡
□last ⓥ 지속하다

□**temperature** ⓝ 온도

□**principle** ⓝ 원리

□**maintain** ⓥ 유지하다

□**implication** ⓝ 영향, 결과

□**biodiversity** ⓝ (균형 잡힌 환경을 위한) 생물의 다양성

□**keep track of** ~을 기록하다

F 12

□**interaction** ⓝ 상호작용

□**productivity** ⓝ 생산성

□**spillover** ⓝ 여파, 파급

□**degree** ⓝ 정도

□**excessive** ⓐ 과도한

□**transaction** ⓝ 거래

□**diversity** ⓝ 다양성

□**labour** ⓝ 노동

□**tolerant** ⓐ 관대한

□**multicultural** ⓐ 다문화의

□**distortion** ⓝ 왜곡

□**discriminate** ⓥ 차별하다

□**ethnic** ⓐ 민족의

□**conflict** ⓝ 갈등

□**nationality** ⓝ 국적

□**import** ⓥ 수입하다, 유입하다

□**contrastive** ⓐ 대조하는

F 13

□**economic** ⓐ 경제의

□**wage** ⓝ 임금, 급료

□**condition** ⓝ 여건, 조건

□**gradually** ⓐd 점차

□**transport** ⓥ 운송, 수송

□**industrial** ⓐ 산업의

□**revolution** ⓝ 혁명

□**railway** ⓝ 철도

□**open up** ~을 가능하게 하다

□**seaside** ⓐ 해안가의

□**coast-to-coast** ⓐ 대륙 횡단의

□**arrival** ⓝ 출현

□**factor** ⓝ 요인

□**expansion** ⓝ 확장, 확대

□**discomfort** ⓝ 불편함

□**destination** ⓝ 목적지

□**impact** ⓝ 영향

F 14

□**crop rotation** 윤작

□**process** ⓝ 과정

□**field** ⓝ 밭

□**order** ⓝ 순서

□**rotate** ⓥ 순환하다

□**original** ⓐ 원래의

□**enrich** ⓥ 비옥하게 하다

□**soil** ⓝ 토양

□**type** ⓝ 유형

□**maintain** ⓥ 유지하다

□**organic** ⓐ 유기농의

□**impact** ⓝ 영향

F 15

□**explore** ⓥ 탐구하다

□**construct** ⓥ 구성하다

□**object** ⓝ 사물

□**frequently** ⓐd 빈번히

□**exist** ⓥ 존재하다

□**compare** ⓥ 비교하다

□**calculate** ⓥ 계산하다

□**fit** ⓥ 적합하다, 알맞다

□**develop** ⓥ 발달시키다

□**notion** ⓝ 개념

□**quantity** ⓝ 양

□**reveal** ⓥ 밝히다

□**investigate** ⓥ 조사하다, 연구하다

□**mathematical** ⓐ 수학적인

□**figure out** ~을 알아내다

□**sort** ⓥ 분류하다

□**shell** ⓝ 조개껍질

□**pile** ⓝ (수북이 쌓여 있는) 더미

□**count** ⓥ (수를) 세다

□**advantage** ⓝ 이점

F 16

□**neuroscientist** ⓝ 신경과학자

□**circuit** ⓝ 회로

□**fundamentally** ⓐd 기본적으로

□**grateful** ⓐ 고마워하는

□**relaxed** ⓐ 편안한

□**confident** ⓐ 자신감 있는

□**gratitude** ⓝ 감사

□**relaxation** ⓝ 휴식

□**confidence** ⓝ 자신감

□**shape** ⓥ 형성하다

□**neuron** ⓝ 뉴런, 신경 세포

□**premise** ⓝ 전제

□**fire** ⓥ 발화[점화]하다

□**activate** ⓥ 활성화시키다, 작동시키다

□**neural** ⓐ 신경의

□biased ⓐ 편파적인, 편향된
□interpret ⓥ 해석하다

G 05
□opponent ⓝ 반대자
□mortality ⓝ 사망률
□advance ⓝ 발전, 진보
□contribute ⓥ 기여하다
□defender ⓝ 옹호자
□correlation ⓝ 상관관계
□inference ⓝ 추론
□prescribe ⓥ 규정하다
□surgical ⓐ 외과의
□evidence ⓝ 증거
□biomedical ⓐ 생물 의학의
□substantial ⓐ 중요한
□unlock ⓥ 열다
□frontier ⓝ 경계, 지평
□refer to ~을 참고하다
□strict ⓐ 엄격한
□adoption ⓝ 입양
□extend ⓥ 연장하다
□life span 수명

G 06
□evolution ⓝ 진화
□singularity ⓝ 특이점
□exceed ⓥ 넘어서다, 능가하다
□intelligence ⓝ 지능
□predict ⓥ 예측하다
□accelerate ⓥ 가속하다
□pursue ⓥ 추구하다
□conscious ⓐ 의식이 있는

□insight ⓝ 통찰력
□significant ⓐ 상당한
□direction ⓝ 방향
□incorporate ⓥ 통합시키다
□mutual ⓐ 상호의
□coexistence ⓝ 공존
□recognize ⓥ 인식하다
□unsolvable ⓐ 해결할 수 없는
□resistance ⓝ 저항
□upcoming ⓐ 다가오는
□stare in the face 노려보다

G 07
□concentrate ⓥ 집중하다
□keep on v-ing 계속 ~하다
□from time to time 때때로
□assess ⓥ 평가하다
□progress ⓝ 진행 상황, 진전
□spoil ⓥ 망치다
□impact ⓝ 영향(력)
□overwork ⓥ 과하게 작업하다
□struggle ⓥ 어려움을 겪다, 분투하다
□benefit ⓥ 득을 보다
□inspiration ⓝ 영감
□incomplete ⓐ 미완성의, 불완전한
□interpretation ⓝ 해석, 이해

G 08
□storage ⓝ 저장
□atmosphere ⓝ 대기
□comparison ⓝ 비교

□absorb ⓥ 흡수하다
□marine ⓐ 해양의
□equivalent ⓝ (~에) 상응하는 것
□fertilize ⓥ 비옥하게 하다
□release ⓥ 내보내다
□estimate ⓥ 추정하다
□incentive ⓝ 장려책
□preindustrial ⓐ 산업화 이전의
□restoration ⓝ 복원
□extinct ⓐ 멸종된
□overpopulation ⓝ 과밀(과잉 밀집)
□industry ⓝ 산업
□habitat ⓝ 서식지

G 09
□chemicals ⓝ 화학 물질
□muscular ⓐ 근육의
□chemistry ⓝ 화학 작용
□genuine ⓐ 참된, 진정한
□participant ⓝ 참가자
□intensity ⓝ 강도
□response ⓝ 반응
□lower ⓥ 낮추다
□recover ⓥ 회복하다

G 10
□development ⓝ 발전
□critical ⓐ 중요한, 결정적인
□vertical ⓐ 수직의
□transportation ⓝ 운송, 수송

□ expand ⓥ 확장시키다

□ skyscraper ⓝ 고층 건물, 마천루

□ architecture ⓝ 건축

□ under construction 건설 중인

G 11

□ particle ⓝ 작은 조각

□ swallow ⓥ 삼키다

□ expose ⓥ 노출하다

□ digestive ⓐ 소화의

□ act on ~에 작용하다

□ extraction ⓝ 추출

□ raw material 원료

□ mouthful ⓝ 한 입

□ mammal ⓝ 포유류

□ sustain ⓥ 유지하다

□ predator ⓝ 포식자, 천적

□ capture ⓥ 포획하다

□ prey ⓝ 먹이

□ habitat ⓝ 서식지

□ Arctic ⓐ 북극의

□ Antarctic ⓐ 남극의

□ pack ice 총빙(叢氷), 유빙

□ high-altitude ⓐ 고도가 높은

□ mountaintop ⓝ 산꼭대기

□ in no small measure 어느 정도

□ ease ⓥ 완화시키다

□ indigestion ⓝ 소화불량

□ harsh ⓐ 가혹한

G 12

□ be good for ~에 좋다

□ enemy ⓝ 적

□ essential ⓐ 필수적인

□ take in ~을 들이마시다

□ drown ⓥ 물에 빠져 죽다, 익사하다

□ education ⓝ 교육

□ exception ⓝ 예외

□ knowledge ⓝ 지식

□ in one's lifetime 평생

□ be yet to-v 아직 ~하지 못하다

□ hurt ⓥ 피해를 보다

□ long-term ⓐ 장기적인

□ investment ⓝ 투자

G 13

□ end up -ing 결국 ~하다

□ electronic equipment 전자 기기

□ estimate ⓥ 추산하다

□ average ⓝ 평균

□ billion ⓝ 십 억

□ approximately ⓐⓓ 약, 대략

□ goods ⓝ 물건, 제품, 상품

□ household ⓝ 가구, 세대

□ gather ⓥ 모으다

□ dust ⓝ 먼지

□ waste ⓝ 낭비, 쓰레기

□ in the sense of ~이라는 의미에서

□ pure ⓐ 순전한, 순수한

□ rubbish ⓝ 쓸모없는 물건, 쓰레기

□ observe ⓥ (발언, 의견을) 말하다

G 14

□ partly ⓐⓓ 부분적으로

□ primary care doctor 일반 진료 의사, 1차 진료 의사

□ diagnose ⓥ 진단하다

□ treatment ⓝ 처방, 치료

□ be replaced by ~에 의해 대체되다

□ groundbreaking ⓐ 획기적인

□ surgical ⓐ 수술의, 외과의

□ procedure ⓝ 절차

□ drone ⓝ 드론

□ eliminate ⓥ 없애다, 제거하다

□ maintenance ⓝ 정비

□ analysis ⓝ 분석

□ security ⓝ 보안, 안보

G 15

□ lead ⓥ 이끌다

□ intend ⓥ 의도하다

□ path ⓝ 길

□ reward ⓥ 보상하다

□ realize ⓥ 깨닫다

□ breathe ⓥ 호흡하다

□ slippery ⓐ 미끄러운

□ superhuman ⓐ 초인적인

□ effectively ⓐⓓ 사실상, 실제로

□ employment ⓝ 고용

□ secure ⓐ 안정적인

□ ultimately ⓐⓓ 궁극적으로

□ unsatisfying ⓐ 만족스럽지 못한

□ trap ⓝ 함정, 덫

□ influential ⓐ 영향력 있는

G 16

□ tire of ~에 질리다[싫증이 나다]

□ get sick of ~에 싫증이 나다

□ cafeteria ⓝ 구내식당, 카페테리아

□ sooner or later 머지않아

□ the bottom line is ~ 요점은 ~이다

□ be designed to ~하도록 설계되다

□ initial ⓐ 초기의

□ response ⓝ 반응

□ stimulus ⓝ 자극(pl. stimuli)

□ occur ⓥ 발생하다

□ enhance ⓥ 강화하다

□ especially ⓐⓓ 특히

□ value ⓝ 가치

□ threat ⓝ 위협

□ firefly ⓝ 반딧불이

□ brilliant ⓐ 영특한

□ detect ⓥ 감지하다

□ destruction ⓝ 파괴

G 17

□ operate ⓥ 움직이다

□ process ⓝ 과정

□ path ⓝ 경로

□ return ⓝ 보상

□ derive ⓥ 끌어내다

□ satisfaction ⓝ 만족

□ courageous ⓐ 용감한

□ move ⓝ 행동

□ overcautious ⓐ 지나치게 조심하는

□ attain ⓥ 달성하다

□ flow ⓥ 흐르다, 나오다

□ bold ⓐ 용감한

□ courage ⓝ 용기

□ satisfying ⓐ 만족스러운

□ overcome ⓥ 극복하다

G 18

□ development ⓝ 개발

□ construction ⓝ 건축(물)

□ carve ⓥ 조각하다

□ ancestor ⓝ 조상

□ erect ⓥ (똑바로) 세우다

□ successive ⓐ 연속적인

□ innovator ⓝ 혁신가

□ settle down 정착하다

□ radically ⓐⓓ 근본적으로

□ transform ⓥ 바꾸다

G 19

□ diversity ⓝ 다양성

□ conflict ⓝ 갈등

□ maintain ⓥ 유지하다

□ assume ⓥ 단정하다

□ insurance ⓝ 보험

□ sufficient ⓐ 충분한

□ capability ⓝ 능력

□ navigate ⓥ 운전하다

□ landscape ⓝ 풍경, 지형

□ trial ⓝ 시련

□ occasional ⓐ 이따금씩의

G 20

□ dynamic ⓐ 역동적인

□ mobility ⓝ 유동성

□ exercise ⓥ 행사하다

□ profession ⓝ 직업

□ religion ⓝ 종교

□ pose ⓥ 제기하다

□ traditional ⓐ 전통적인

□ evident ⓐ 분명한

□ commit to ~에 전념[헌신]하다

□ alternative ⓝ 대안

□ identity ⓝ 정체성

□ ready-made 이미 주어진

□ at birth 태어날 때

□ discover ⓥ 발견하다

□ prescribe ⓥ 규정하다

□ underneath ⓐⓓ ~의 아래에

□ competitive ⓐ 경쟁적인

□ trustworthy ⓐ 신뢰할 수 있는

G 21

□ bring up (화제를) 꺼내다

□ suggestion ⓝ 제안

□ immediately ⓐⓓ 즉시

□ close off ~을 차단하다[막다]

□ possibility ⓝ 가능성

□viewpoint ⓝ 관점
□period ⓝ 마침표, 끝
□consider ⓥ 고려하다
□option ⓥ 선택(지)
□point of view 관점
□beneficial ⓐ 유익한, 이로운
□eliminate ⓥ 제거하다, 없애다
□invention ⓝ 발명
□honest ⓐ 정직한
□filter out (액체·빛 등에서) ~을 걸러내다
□block ⓥ 막다, 차단하다

G 22

□generation ⓝ 세대
□mention ⓥ 언급하다
□draw a blank 아무 반응을 얻지 못하다
□appear ⓥ 나타나다
□civilization ⓝ 문명
□connect ⓥ 연결하다
□laptop ⓝ 노트북
□appliances ⓝ 가전제품
□web ⓝ 망
□schedule ⓥ 일정을 잡다, 예정하다
□run ⓥ 운영하다
□trade ⓥ 거래하다
□goods ⓝ 상품
□transportation ⓝ 운송
□driving force 원동력, 추진력
□industry ⓝ 산업

G 23

□accurately ⓐⓓ 정확하게
□recognize ⓥ 인식하다
□granularity ⓝ 입자도
□psychologist ⓝ 심리학자
□absolutely ⓐⓓ 절대적으로
□transformative ⓐ (사람을) 변화시키는
□communicate ⓥ 전달하다
□support ⓝ 지지
□distinguish ⓥ 구별하다
□a range of 다양한
□manage ⓥ 관리하다
□ordinary ⓐ 평범한
□existence ⓝ 존재
□psychosocial ⓐ 심리 사회적인
□endure ⓥ 견디다
□categorize ⓥ 분류하다
□efficiency ⓝ 효율성

H 도표의 이해

H 01

□emission ⓝ 배출량
□rank ⓥ (순위를) 차지하다
□major ⓐ 주요한
□respectively ⓐⓓ 각각

H 02

□consume ⓥ 먹다
□sort ⓥ 분류하다
□frequency ⓝ 빈도
□frequently ⓐⓓ 자주
□account for ~을 차지하다
□percentage ⓝ 비율
□combine ⓥ 합치다
□share ⓝ 몫
□rarely ⓐⓓ 거의 ~ 않는

H 03

□share ⓝ 점유율, 몫
□retail ⓝ 소매
□trade ⓝ 거래
□record ⓥ 기록하다
□reach ⓥ 도달하다
□increase ⓝ 증가
□fall behind 뒤처지다

H 04

□consumption ⓝ 소비
□preference ⓝ 선호(도)

□ consume ⓥ 소비하다
□ least ⓐ 가장 적게

H 05

□ extent ⓝ 정도
□ youth ⓝ 청소년, 젊은 사람들
□ fear ⓝ 두려움
□ climate change 기후 변화
□ extremely ⓐ 극도로
□ generation ⓝ 세대

H 06

□ electronic waste 전자 폐기물
□ recycling ⓝ 재활용
□ region ⓝ 지역
□ respectively ⓐ 각각
□ gap ⓝ 격차

H 07

□ birth ⓝ 출생
□ decrease ⓥ 감소하다
□ period ⓝ 기간
□ gap ⓝ 차이
□ slightly ⓐ 약간
□ increase ⓥ 증가하다
□ steadily ⓐ 꾸준히
□ except 〔prep〕 ~을 제외하고

H 08

□ household ⓝ 가정
□ own ⓥ 보유하다
□ period ⓝ 기간

□ ownership ⓝ 보유
□ additional ⓐ 추가적인
□ rate ⓝ 비율

H 09

□ homeschool ⓥ 홈스쿨링을 하다
□ public school 공립 학교
□ exception ⓝ 예외
□ performance ⓝ 공연
□ account for ~을 차지하다
□ respectively ⓐ 각각

H 10

□ share ⓝ 점유율
□ urban ⓐ 도시의
□ population ⓝ 인구
□ còntinent ⓝ 대륙
□ reverse ⓝ 역전

H 11

□ share ⓝ 몫, 점유율
□ region ⓝ 지역
□ decline ⓥ 감소하다

H 12

□ survey ⓝ 설문조사
□ gap ⓝ 차이, 격차
□ outweigh ⓥ 능가하다
□ share ⓝ 부분, 몫

H 13

□ course ⓝ 강의

□ learning material 학습 자료
□ age group 연령 집단
□ among 〔prep〕 ~ 중에서

H 14

□ investment ⓝ 투자, 투자액
□ fossil fuel 화석 연료
□ gap ⓝ 차이

H 15

□ given ⓐ 주어진, 정해진
□ among 〔prep〕 ~ 중에서
□ decrease ⓝ 감소

H 16

□ generation ⓝ 생산
□ fossil ⓝ 화석
□ fuel ⓝ 연료
□ nuclear ⓐ 핵의
□ renewables ⓝ 재생 가능 에너지
□ combine ⓥ 합치다, 결합하다

H 17

□ motivator ⓝ 동기 (요인)
□ welfare ⓝ 복지
□ account for (부분·비율을) 차지하다
□ cite ⓥ 언급하다
□ consumption ⓝ 섭취, 소비
□ management ⓝ 관리
□ rank ⓥ (순위를) 차지하다

H

I 08

- coin ⓥ (새로운 낱말 · 어구를) 만들다
- advanced ⓐ 진보된
- emigrate ⓥ (타국으로) 이주하다
- numerous ⓐ 수많은
- profound ⓐ 심오한
- influence ⓝ 영향
- appoint ⓥ 임명하다
- astronomy ⓝ 천문학

I 09

- physicist ⓝ 물리학자
- submit ⓥ 제출하다
- sponsor ⓥ 후원하다
- publish ⓥ 출판하다
- relativity ⓝ 상대성
- significant ⓐ 주요한
- symbol ⓝ 상징
- enlightenment ⓝ 계몽주의
- struggle ⓝ 투쟁
- participation ⓝ 참여

I 10

- publish ⓥ 출판하다
- edit ⓥ 편집하다
- financially ⓐⓓ 재정적으로
- operator ⓝ 기사, 운전자
- expense ⓝ 지출, 비용
- recognition ⓝ 인정
- dialect ⓝ 방언
- outnumber ⓥ ~보다 많다
- term ⓥ 이름짓다, 칭하다

I 11

- social activist 사회 운동가
- orphan ⓥ 고아로 만들다
- mark ⓥ 특징짓다
- hardship ⓝ 고난
- washerwoman ⓝ 세탁부
- decade ⓝ 10년
- barely ⓐⓓ 겨우, 가까스로
- backbreaking ⓐ 대단히 힘든
- maid ⓝ 가정부, 하녀
- chemist ⓝ 화학자
- recruit ⓥ 모집하다
- sales agent 판매 대리인
- share ⓝ 몫, 할당
- self-made ⓐ 자수성가한
- female ⓐ 여성의
- financial ⓐ 재정적인
- independence ⓝ 독립

I 12

- on account of ~ 때문에
- rock-like ⓐ 바위 같은
- commonly ⓐⓓ 일반적으로
- garden center 식물원
- nursery ⓝ 종묘원
- compacted ⓐ 꽉 찬, 빡빡한
- extreme ⓐ 극단적인
- temperature ⓝ 온도
- surface ⓝ 표면
- stem ⓝ 줄기
- conserve ⓥ 보존하다
- moisture ⓝ 습기

I 13

- disallow ⓥ 거절하다, 허가하지 않다
- entrance ⓝ 입학, 입장
- master's degree 석사 학위
- fine arts 순수 미술
- represent ⓥ 대변하다, 나타내다
- injustice ⓝ 부당함, 부정

I 14

- graduate from ~을 졸업하다
- nursing ⓝ 간호(학)
- suggest ⓥ 제안하다
- passenger ⓝ 승객
- frightened ⓐ 무서워하는, 겁먹은
- female ⓐ 여성[여자]인
- flight attendant 비행기 승무원
- injury ⓝ 부상
- end one's career 일을 그만두다
- degree ⓝ 학위
- serve ⓥ 근무[복무]하다
- captain ⓝ 대위
- hometown ⓝ 고향
- name A after B A에게 B의 이름을 따서 붙이다

▎15

- □ graduate from ~을 졸업하다
- □ poetry ⓝ 시
- □ editor ⓝ 편집자
- □ encourage ⓥ 격려하다
- □ fiction writer 소설가
- □ critic ⓝ 비평가, 평론가
- □ ultimately ⓐⅾ 결국, 궁극적으로
- □ racial ⓐ 인종의
- □ identity ⓝ 정체성

▎16

- □ knowledge ⓝ 지식
- □ engineering ⓝ 기술
- □ good ⓐ 상당한
- □ literature ⓝ 문학
- □ unconcerned ⓐ 무관심한
- □ escape ⓥ 달아나다, 탈출하다
- □ occupation ⓝ 점령

▎17

- □ trousers ⓝ 바지
- □ adventurous ⓐ 모험적인
- □ activity ⓝ 활동
- □ wildlife ⓝ 야생 동물
- □ persuade ⓥ 설득하다
- □ slightly ⓐⅾ 약간
- □ dealer ⓝ 판매원
- □ nonetheless ⓐⅾ 그렇더라도

▎18

- □ exceptionally ⓐⅾ 유난히, 특출나게
- □ inventor ⓝ 발명가
- □ journalist ⓝ 기자, 언론인
- □ occasionally ⓐⅾ 가끔
- □ nickname ⓥ 별명을 붙이다
- □ textile ⓝ 직물
- □ witness ⓥ 목격하다
- □ faulty ⓐ 결함이 있는
- □ equipment ⓝ 장비, 설비
- □ device ⓝ 장치
- □ flat-bottomed ⓐ 바닥이 평평한
- □ eliminate ⓥ 제거하다, 없애다
- □ assemble ⓥ 조립하다

▎19

- □ financial ⓐ 금융의
- □ political ⓐ 정치의
- □ major in ~을 전공하다
- □ economics ⓝ 경제학
- □ dissatisfy ⓥ 불만을 느끼게 하다
- □ handle ⓥ 다루다
- □ earn ⓥ 얻다, 취득하다
- □ doctor's degree 박사 학위
- □ doctoral ⓐ 박사 학위의
- □ mention ⓥ 언급하다
- □ contribution ⓝ 기여
- □ regular ⓐ 정기적인, 규칙적인
- □ analysis ⓝ 분석

▎20

- □ soar ⓥ 날아오르다
- □ international ⓐ 국제적인
- □ pilot ⓝ 비행사
- □ license ⓝ 면허
- □ appearance ⓝ 출현
- □ female ⓐ 여성의
- □ pioneer ⓝ 개척자
- □ inspire ⓥ 영감을 주다
- □ generation ⓝ 세대
- □ pursue ⓥ 추구하다

▎21

- □ composer ⓝ 작곡가
- □ classical music 클래식 음악
- □ youth ⓝ 청년
- □ introduce ⓥ 소개하다
- □ schoolmate ⓝ 학교 친구
- □ successful ⓐ 성공한
- □ collaborate ⓥ 협업하다
- □ publish ⓥ 발매하다
- □ well-known ⓐ 잘 알려진

▎22

- □ known for ~로 알려진
- □ research ⓝ 연구
- □ Dutch ⓝ 네덜란드어
- □ unusual ⓐ 드문
- □ curiosity ⓝ 호기심
- □ endless ⓐ 끝없는
- □ come in handy 도움이 되다

□ microscope ⓝ 현미경

□ flow ⓥ 흐르다

□ pond ⓝ 연못

□ pay attention to ~에
주의를 기울이다

□ observation ⓝ 관찰

□ hire ⓥ 고용하다

□ describe ⓥ 설명하다

I 23

□ novelist ⓝ 소설가

□ specialise in ~을 전문으로
하다

□ journalist ⓝ 언론인

□ supportive ⓐ 지지하는

□ accountant ⓝ 회계사

□ rejection ⓝ 거절

□ publish ⓥ 출간[발행]하다

□ right ⓝ (작품·영화 등에 대한)
판권

□ worldwide ⓐⓓ 전 세계적으로

J 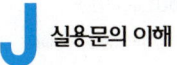 실용문의 이해

J 01

□ opportunity ⓝ 기회

□ prove ⓥ 증명하다

□ requirement ⓝ 필요 요건

□ award ⓥ 수여하다

□ participant ⓝ 참가자

□ souvenir ⓝ 기념품

J 02

□ explore ⓥ 탐험하다

□ amazing ⓐ 놀라운

□ walking path 보행로

□ operation ⓝ 운영

□ admission ⓝ 입장

□ seasonal ⓐ 계절에 따른

□ indoors ⓐⓓ 실내에

□ depart ⓥ 출발하다

J 03

□ stuffed toy 봉제 인형

□ transform ⓥ 변형하다,
바꾸다

□ decorative ⓐ 장식의

□ flowerpot ⓝ 화분

□ participation fee 참가비

□ material ⓝ 재료

□ detail ⓝ 세부 사항

J 04

□ houseplant ⓝ 실내 식물

□ explore ⓥ 구경하다, 둘러보다

□ available ⓐ 이용 가능한

□ purchase ⓝ 구매

□ unique ⓐ 독특한

□ eco-friendly ⓐ 친환경적인

□ recycle ⓥ 재활용하다

□ allow ⓥ 허용하다

J 05

□ annual ⓐ 연례의, 매년의

□ featured ⓐ 주요한

□ drawing ⓝ 그림 그리기

□ beginners ⓝ 초급자

□ costumed ⓐ 의상을 갖춰
입은

□ receive ⓥ 받다

□ detailed ⓐ 자세한

□ check out 확인하다

J 06

□ annual ⓐ 연례의, 매년의

□ participation ⓝ 참가, 참여

□ fee ⓝ 요금

□ additional ⓐ 추가의

□ refund ⓝ 환불

□ cancellation ⓝ 취소

□ participant ⓝ 참가자

□ registration ⓝ 등록

J 07

□ creativity ⓝ 창의성

□ slogan ⓝ 슬로건, 구호

□ commercialized
ⓐ 상업화된

□ submission ⓝ 제출
□ limit ⓥ 제한하다
□ entry ⓝ 출품작
□ submit ⓥ 제출하다

J 08
□ furry ⓐ 털이 많은
□ register ⓥ 등록하다
□ limit ⓥ 제한하다
□ participant ⓝ 참가자
□ payment ⓝ 지불
□ require ⓥ 요구하다
□ ingredient ⓝ 재료
□ additional ⓐ 추가적인
□ available ⓐ 이용 가능한
□ safety ⓝ 안전
□ refund ⓝ 환불

J 09
□ talent ⓝ 재능
□ contest ⓝ 대회
□ judge ⓥ 심사하다
□ criterion ⓝ 기준 (pl. criteria)
□ cooperation ⓝ 협동
□ costume ⓝ 의상
□ gift certificate 상품권
□ management agency
　매니지먼트 회사[기획사]
□ application ⓝ 신청
□ submit ⓥ 제출하다

J 10
□ delightful ⓐ 즐거운
□ experience ⓥ 경험하다

□ various ⓐ 다양한
□ host ⓥ (파티 등을) 주최하다
□ in advance 미리

J 11
□ passionate ⓐ 열정적인
□ environment ⓝ 환경
□ contest ⓝ 대회
□ upcycled ⓐ 업사이클된
□ winning prize 우승 상품
□ local ⓐ 지역의
□ announce ⓥ 발표하다

J 12
□ dust off 먼지를 털다; 방치했던
　것을 오랜만에 꺼내다
□ competition ⓝ 대회
□ souvenir ⓝ 기념품

J 13
□ provide ⓥ 제공하다
□ for free 무료로

J 14
□ competition ⓝ 대회
□ participant ⓝ 참가자
□ category ⓝ 분야
□ remote ⓐ 원격의
□ registration ⓝ 등록
□ honor ⓥ 수여하다

J 15
□ annual ⓐ 매년의
□ participate ⓥ 참가하다

□ exhibition ⓝ 전시

J 16
□ host ⓥ (행사를) 주최하다, 열다
□ registration ⓝ 등록
□ cancel ⓥ 취소하다
□ unfavorable ⓐ 좋지 않은

J 17
□ participant ⓝ 참가자
□ activity ⓝ 활동
□ self-defense ⓝ 자기 방어
□ develop ⓥ 발달시키다
□ fee ⓝ 요금
□ include ⓥ 포함하다

J 18
□ fascinating ⓐ 매력적인,
　대단히 흥미로운
□ witness ⓥ 목격하다
□ marine life 해양 생물
□ requirement ⓝ 요건,
　필요조건
□ insurance ⓝ 보험
□ experienced ⓐ 경험 있는,
　숙련된
□ accompany ⓥ 동반하다,
　동행하다
□ underwater ⓐ 수중의

J 19
□ available ⓐ 이용할 수 있는
□ material ⓝ 재료
□ registration ⓝ 등록

□limit ⓥ 제한하다
□participant ⓝ 참가자
□refund ⓝ 환불
□cancellation ⓝ 취소

J20
□popular ⓐ 인기 있는
□process ⓝ 과정
□taste ⓥ 맛보다
□notice ⓝ 알림
□require ⓥ 요구하다

J21
□palace ⓝ 궁궐
□book ⓥ 예약하다
□traditional ⓐ 전통적인
□charge ⓝ 비용

J22
□propose ⓥ 제안하다
□measure ⓝ 대책
□pollution ⓝ 오염
□submission ⓝ 제출
□submit ⓥ 제출하다
□proposal ⓝ 제안서
□gift certificate 상품권

J23
□awareness ⓝ 인식
□annual ⓐ 연례의
□knowledge ⓝ 지식
□marine ⓐ 해양의
□conservation ⓝ 보존

□pollution ⓝ 오염
□submission ⓝ 제출
□entry ⓝ 출품[응모]작

J24
□article ⓝ 기사
□publish ⓥ 출간하다
□look for ~을 찾다
□length ⓝ 길이
□include ⓥ 포함하다
□reward ⓝ 사례금

J25
□get set 준비하다
□competition ⓝ 대회, 경기
□doubles match 복식 경기
□participant ⓝ 참가자
□certificate ⓝ 증서
□award ⓥ (상을) 주다

J26
□flower arrangement
 꽃꽂이
□material ⓝ 재료
□refund ⓝ 환불
□cancellation ⓝ 취소

J27
□e-waste ⓝ 전자 폐기물
□annual ⓐ 해마다의, 연례의
□electronics ⓝ 전자 제품
□accept ⓥ 받아들이다,
 허용하다
□light bulb 전구

□microwave ⓝ 전자레인지
□wipe out ~을 완전히
 없애다[삭제하다]
□in advance 사전에, 미리
□resident ⓝ 거주자, 주민

J28
□fee ⓝ 요금
□session ⓝ 수업
□admission ⓝ 입장
□first-come, first-served
 basis 선착순
□reservation ⓝ 예약
□accompany ⓥ 동행하다
□lend ⓥ 빌려주다
□contact ⓥ 연락하다

J29
□underwater ⓐ 수중의
□explorer ⓝ 탐험가
□private ⓐ 개인을 위한
□rent ⓥ 대여하다
□equipment ⓝ 장비
□register ⓥ 등록하다

J30
□urban ⓐ 도시의
□clue ⓝ 단서
□registration ⓝ 등록
□sign up 등록하다
□save ⓥ ~을 절약하다[아끼다]
□discount ⓝ 할인

J

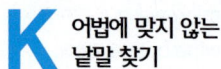

K 어법에 맞지 않는 낱말 찾기

K 01
- □ routine ⓝ 루틴, 일상의 과정
- □ enable ⓥ ~할 수 있게 하다
- □ athlete ⓝ 운동선수
- □ evaluate ⓥ 평가하다
- □ competition ⓝ 경기, 경쟁
- □ condition ⓝ 조건
- □ bounce ⓥ (공을) 튕기다
- □ supply ⓥ 제공하다
- □ properly ⓐⓓ 적절히
- □ adjust ⓥ 조절하다, 조정하다
- □ fine-tune ⓥ 미세하게 조정하다
- □ in pursuit of ~을 추구하여
- □ adaptation ⓝ 적응
- □ internal ⓐ 내적인
- □ influence ⓝ 영향
- □ affect ⓥ 영향을 미치다
- □ performance ⓝ 수행
- □ achieve ⓥ 해내다

K 02
- □ deny ⓥ 부정하다
- □ recently ⓐⓓ 최근에
- □ consume ⓥ 소비하다
- □ globally ⓐⓓ 전세계적으로
- □ resource ⓝ 자원
- □ advance ⓝ 발전
- □ promise ⓝ 가능성, 기대
- □ material ⓝ 재료

- □ cause ⓥ 야기하다, 일으키다
- □ industrial ⓐ 산업의

K 03
- □ insight ⓝ 통찰
- □ flexible ⓐ 유연한
- □ domain ⓝ 분야
- □ interconnected ⓐ 상호 연결된
- □ exceptionally ⓐⓓ 유난히
- □ generalist ⓝ 다방면의 지식을 가진 사람
- □ expertise ⓝ 전문성
- □ organize ⓥ 조직하다
- □ framework ⓝ 틀
- □ central ⓐ 핵심적인
- □ organized ⓐ 조직적인
- □ flexibility ⓝ 유연성
- □ application ⓝ 적용
- □ context ⓝ 맥락

K 04
- □ mammalian ⓐ 포유류의
- □ species ⓝ 종
- □ react ⓥ 반응하다
- □ predator ⓝ 포식자
- □ instant ⓐ 즉각적인
- □ perceive ⓥ 인지하다, 감지하다
- □ threat ⓝ 위협
- □ protection ⓝ 보호
- □ captivity ⓝ 사육, 감금
- □ enclosure ⓝ 우리, 울타리
- □ panic ⓥ 공황 상태에 빠지다

- □ repeatedly ⓐⓓ 반복적으로
- □ attempt ⓝ 시도
- □ frequently ⓐⓓ 빈번하게
- □ opportunity ⓝ 기회
- □ domesticate ⓥ 길들이다, 사육하다
- □ blindly ⓐⓓ 맹목적으로
- □ leap ⓥ 뛰어오르다

K 05
- □ essentially ⓐⓓ 근본적으로
- □ metaphor ⓝ 은유
- □ linguistic ⓐ 언어적인
- □ passive ⓐ 수동적인
- □ propose ⓥ 제시하다
- □ beggar ⓝ 구걸하는 사람
- □ cognitive ⓐ 인지적인
- □ engage ⓥ 사로잡다
- □ prose ⓝ 산문
- □ imposing ⓐ 강요[강압]적인
- □ artifact ⓝ 인공물
- □ forcefully ⓐⓓ 강력하게
- □ horizon ⓝ 지평선
- □ selling point 매력, 장점
- □ at first glance 첫눈에
- □ immediately ⓐⓓ 즉각적으로

K 06
- □ overstate ⓥ 과장해서 말하다
- □ meaningful ⓐ 의미 있는
- □ human being 인간
- □ provide ⓥ 제공하다
- □ fulfillment ⓝ 성취감
- □ empowerment ⓝ 권한

- □career ⓝ 직업, 경력
- □energizing ⓐ 활기찬
- □count ~ as ... ~을 ...라고 여기다
- □employment ⓝ 직업, 고용
- □psychology ⓝ 심리
- □workplace ⓝ 업무 현장, 직장
- □overall ⓐd 전반적으로
- □satisfaction ⓝ 만족

K 07

- □hunter-gatherer ⓝ 수렵 채집인
- □examination ⓝ 조사
- □abundant ⓐ 풍부한
- □obtainable ⓐ 획득할 수 있는
- □excessive ⓐ 지나친, 과도한
- □permanent ⓐ 영구적인
- □domesticate ⓥ 길들이다, 재배하다
- □cultivate ⓥ 경작하다
- □take root 뿌리를 내리다
- □immediate ⓐ 즉각적인
- □density ⓝ 밀도
- □civilization ⓝ 문명

K 08

- □organizational ⓐ 조직의
- □viewpoint ⓝ 관점
- □fascinating ⓐ 매력적인
- □functional ⓐ 기능상의
- □operation ⓝ 운영
- □varying ⓐ 가지각색의
- □division ⓝ (조직의) 분과

- □inevitably ⓐd 필연적으로
- □prejudiced ⓐ 편견이 있는
- □acquire ⓥ 습득하다
- □disallow ⓥ 허가하지 않다
- □conflict ⓝ 갈등
- □mechanistic ⓐ 기계적인
- □organic ⓐ 유기적인
- □profound ⓐ 깊은
- □management ⓝ 관리
- □vertical ⓐ 수직의
- □procedure ⓝ 절차
- □horizontal ⓐ 수평의

K 09

- □get along with ~와 잘 지내다
- □seek ~ out (특히 많은 노력을 기울여) ~을 찾아내다
- □exist ⓥ 존재하다
- □race ⓝ 인종
- □religion ⓝ 종교
- □value ⓝ 가치관
- □feather ⓝ 깃털
- □flock ⓥ (많은 수가) 모이다
- □tendency ⓝ 경향
- □be rooted in ~에 뿌리박고 있다
- □conditioned ⓐ 조건부의
- □unfamiliar ⓐ 친숙하지 않은
- □likelihood ⓝ 가능성
- □relate ⓥ 관련시키다, 마음이 통하다

K 10

- □praise ⓝ 칭찬
- □equally ⓐd 동등하게
- □self-esteem ⓝ 자존감
- □preschooler ⓝ 미취학 아동
- □cognitive ⓐ 인지적인
- □reason ⓥ 추론하다
- □analytically ⓐd 분석적으로
- □consistently ⓐd 지속적으로
- □incorporate ⓥ 통합하다
- □self-image ⓝ 자아상
- □endure ⓥ 지속하다, 견디다

K 11

- □noticeable ⓐ 눈에 띄는
- □characteristic ⓝ 특징, 특성
- □project ⓥ 투영하다
- □physically ⓐd 신체적으로
- □emotionally ⓐd 감정적으로
- □appealing ⓐ 매력적인
- □enlarge ⓥ 확대하다
- □childlike ⓐ 어린이 같은

K 12

- □propose ⓥ 제안하다
- □tough ⓐ 엄격한, 힘든
- □transplantation ⓝ 이식
- □transfer ⓥ 전달하다, 옮기다
- □legal requirement 법적 요건
- □specify ⓥ 명시하다
- □potential ⓐ 잠재적인
- □regulation ⓝ 규정, 규제

K

□ **no doubt** 의심할 바 없이, 틀림없는

□ **ease** ⓥ 완화하다

□ **premature** ⓐ 너무 이른

□ **obtain** ⓥ 확보하다

□ **suspicion** ⓝ 의심

□ **belief** ⓝ 믿음, 신념

□ **unreliable** ⓐ 믿을 수 없는

□ **precision** ⓝ 정확성

□ **consistency** ⓝ 일관성

□ **criterion** ⓝ 기준(pl. criteria)

□ **burial** ⓝ 매장

K 13

□ **artificial intelligence** 인공 지능(AI)

□ **task** ⓝ 과업, 작업

□ **perform** ⓥ 수행하다

□ **mind-blowing** ⓐ 놀라운, 감동적인

□ **feature** ⓝ 특징, 특색

□ **core** ⓐ 핵심적인

□ **virtual** ⓐ 가상의

□ **implication** ⓝ 영향, 결과

K 14

□ **shrink** ⓥ 줄어들다

□ **mass** ⓝ 부피

□ **peak** ⓥ 정점에 달하다

□ **predator** ⓝ 포식자

□ **domesticate** ⓥ 길들이다

□ **immediate** ⓐ 즉각적인

□ **shelter** ⓝ 은신처

□ **obtain** ⓥ 얻다

□ **outsource** ⓥ (회사가 작업·생산을) 외부에 위탁하다

□ **characteristic** ⓝ 특징

□ **domestic** ⓐ 가정의

□ **indicator** ⓝ 지표

□ **intelligence** ⓝ 지능

K 15

□ **exist** ⓥ 존재하다

□ **professional** ⓝ 전문가

□ **degree** ⓝ 학위

□ **expertise** ⓝ 전문 지식

□ **executive** ⓝ 경영진, 간부

□ **decade** ⓝ 10년

□ **respective** ⓐ 각자의

□ **criticism** ⓝ 비판, 비난

□ **surgery** ⓝ 수술

□ **accountant** ⓝ 회계사

□ **organization** ⓝ 조직

K 16

□ **reduction** ⓝ 감소

□ **mineral** ⓝ 미네랄

□ **fertilizer** ⓝ 비료

□ **beneficial** ⓐ 유익한

□ **earthworm** ⓝ 지렁이

□ **bug** ⓝ 벌레

□ **soil** ⓝ 토양

□ **essential** ⓐ 필수적인

□ **nutrient** ⓝ 영양소

□ **in the first place** 우선적으로

□ **uptake** ⓝ 흡수

□ **fertilize** ⓥ 비료를 주다

□ **nitrogen** ⓝ 질소

□ **potassium** ⓝ 칼륨

□ **zinc** ⓝ 아연

□ **iron** ⓝ 철

□ **on average** 평균적으로

□ **content** ⓝ 내용물, 함량

□ **wheat** ⓝ 밀

□ **blocker** ⓝ 방해물

□ **absorption** ⓝ 흡수

□ **acidic** ⓐ 산성의

□ **farmland** ⓝ 농지

□ **characteristic** ⓝ 특징, 특성

□ **determine** ⓥ 결정하다

□ **accumulation** ⓝ 축적

L 문맥에 맞지 않는 낱말 찾기

L01

□term ⓝ 용어

□impression ⓝ 인상

□sacrifice ⓥ 희생하다

□possession ⓝ 소유물

□insecurity ⓝ 불안

□stem from ~에서 비롯되다

□attachment ⓝ 애착

□distance … from ~ …을 ~로부터 멀리 두다

□hurt ⓥ 상하게 하다

□assumption ⓝ 가정

□fundamentally ⓐⓓ 근본적으로

□get rid of ~을 제거하다

□sooner than later 머지않아

□clarity ⓝ 명료함

□convenience ⓝ 편의

□modern era 현대

□be of the view that ~라는 견해를 갖다

□eliminate ⓥ 없애다

L02

□major ⓐ 주요한

□philosophical ⓐ 철학적인

□shift ⓝ 변화

□industrial ⓐ 산업의

□competitive ⓐ 경쟁적인

□geographically ⓐⓓ 지리적으로

□client ⓝ 고객

□quality ⓐ 질 좋은

□reasonable ⓐ 합리적인

□equally ⓐⓓ 마찬가지로

□essential ⓐ 매우 중요한

□modernization ⓝ 현대화

□revolution ⓝ 혁명

□desire ⓝ 욕망, 욕구

□diverse ⓐ 다양한

□complex ⓐ 복잡한

L03

□promotion ⓝ 프로모션, 홍보

□deal with ~을 다루다

□consumer ⓝ 소비자

□psychology ⓝ 심리

□one way or another 어떤 한 방식으로

□fashion ⓝ 방식, 방법

□possibility ⓝ 가능성

□sales ⓝ 매출, 판매

□fool ⓥ 속이다

□purchase ⓥ 구매하다

□long-term ⓐ 장기적인

□relate ⓥ 전하다

□experience ⓝ 경험

□identify ⓥ 확인하다

□appreciate ⓥ 진가를 인정하다

□reach ⓥ 도달하다

L04

□observe ⓥ 관찰하다

□happening ⓝ 사건

□explanation ⓝ 설명

□reasoning ⓝ 추론

□misconception ⓝ 오해

□ecological ⓐ 생태학적인

□fallacy ⓝ 오류

□argument ⓝ 논지, 주장

□causal ⓐ 인과적인

□merely ⓐⓓ 단지 ~만으로

□crime rate 범죄율

□numerous ⓐ 많은

□co-occurrence ⓝ 동시 발생

□reveal ⓥ 밝혀내다

□afford ⓥ ~할 여력[여유]이 있다

□commit ⓥ 저지르다

□misinterpret ⓥ 잘못 해석하다, 오해하다

□construct ⓥ 구성하다, 형성하다

□faulty ⓐ 잘못된

L05

□resource ⓝ 자원

□tendency ⓝ 경향

□cooperate ⓥ 협력하다

□complicated ⓐ 복잡한

□plenty ⓐ 풍부한

□interest ⓝ 이익

□survival ⓝ 생존

□depend on ~에 달려있다

□shelter ⓝ 안식처

□ironically ⓐⓓ 역설적으로

□sophisticated ⓐ 정교한

□desire ⓝ 욕망

□combine A with B A를 B와 결합하다

□interaction ⓝ 상호작용

□disconnection ⓝ 단절

L 06

□limitation ⓝ 한계

□cognitive ⓐ 인지적인

□capacity ⓝ 능력

□independently ⓐⓓ 독립적으로

□distribute ⓥ 분배하다

□computation ⓝ 계산

□generation ⓝ 세대

□flush ⓥ (변기의) 물을 내리다

□transmit ⓥ 전달하다

□essentially ⓐⓓ 근본적으로

□dedicate ⓥ 바치다, 헌신하다

□calculation ⓝ 계산

□benefit ⓥ 이득을 얻다

□contribute to ~에 기여하다

□collective ⓐ 집합적인

L 07

□rate ⓝ 빠르기

□travel ⓥ 이동하다

□determine ⓥ 결정하다

□ability ⓝ 능력

□process ⓥ 처리하다

□evolutionary ⓐ 진화의

□ideally ⓐⓓ 이상적으로

□suited ⓐ 맞추어진

□motorist ⓝ 운전자

□limited ⓐ 제한된

□appreciate ⓥ 감상하다

□allow for ~을 가능하게 하다[허락하다]

□polar ⓐ 극과 극의

□opposite ⓝ 반대의 것

□ordinarily ⓐⓓ 보통

□typical ⓐ 전형적인

L 08

□alternative ⓝ 대안

□reserve ⓥ 마련하다

□extensive ⓐ 광범위한

□lane ⓝ 길, 도로

□pedestrian ⓝ 보행자

□vehicle ⓝ 교통 수단

□occasional ⓐ 가끔의

□motivate ⓥ 동기를 부여하다

□automobile ⓝ 자동차

□accommodate ⓥ 수용하다

□frequently ⓐⓓ 자주

□distribute ⓥ 나누어주다

□neighborhood ⓝ 이웃

□vendor ⓝ 상점

□operate ⓥ 운영하다

□resident ⓝ 거주자

L 09

□particularly ⓐⓓ 특히

□security ⓝ 안도감, 안심

□disoriented ⓐ 혼란에 빠진

□disrupt ⓥ 파괴하다

□take away ~을 제거하다

□literal ⓐ 융통성이 없는, 문자 그대로의

□beforehand ⓐⓓ 미리

□establish ⓥ 확고히 하다, 설립하다

□validate ⓥ 인정하다

□contribute ⓥ 기여하다

□transition ⓝ 변화

L 10

□display ⓥ 보여주다, 전시하다

□considerable ⓐ 상당한

□facility ⓝ 재능, 시설

□adapt ⓥ 조절하다

□claim ⓝ 주장

□status ⓝ 지위

□promote ⓥ 홍보하다

□yeast ⓝ 효모

□ingredient ⓝ 재료

□demand ⓝ 수요, 요구

□hire ⓥ 고용하다

□strategy ⓝ 전략

□boost ⓥ 촉진하다

□significant ⓐ 상당한

□thereafter ⓐⓓ 그 후에

□transform ⓥ 바꾸다

□reposition ⓥ 이미지 전환을 꾀하다

L 11

□tip ⓝ 끝 (부분)

□stem ⓝ (식물의) 줄기

□accumulate ⓥ 축적하다

□shade ⓝ 그늘

□accordingly @ad 따라서, 그래서

□stimulate ⓥ 자극하다

□face ⓥ 직면하다, 마주하다

□phenomenon ⓝ 현상

□bend ⓥ 구부러지다, 휘어지다

□opposite @ 반대의

□limit ⓥ 제한하다

□horizontal @ 수평의

□soil ⓝ 토양

□interfere with ~을 방해하다

□development ⓝ 발달

□in turn 결국, 결과적으로

L 12

□rejection ⓝ 거절

□handle ⓥ 다루다

□painful @ 고통스러운

□risk ⓥ 위험을 무릅쓰다

□affect ⓥ 영향을 미치다

□aspect ⓝ 측면

□tough @ 강한

□therapy ⓝ 요법

□request ⓝ 요청

□discount ⓝ 할인

□unfavorable @ 호의적이지 않은

□circumstance ⓝ 상황

L 13

□magically @ad 마법처럼

□organ ⓝ 장기

□statement ⓝ 진술

□unscientific @ 비과학적인

□groundless @ 근거가 없는

□circulation ⓝ 순환

□aggressive @ 적극적인

□attempt ⓝ 시도

□eliminate ⓥ 제거하다

□temporary @ 일시적인

□intelligence ⓝ 지성

□regain ⓥ 되찾다

□direct ⓥ 인도하다

□intelligently @ad 영리하게

□fix ⓥ 해결하다

□intelligent @ 지적인

L 14

□species ⓝ 종

□extinction ⓝ 멸종

□survival ⓝ 생존

□recovery ⓝ 회복

□establish ⓥ 수립하다

□coordinate ⓥ 통합하다, 조정하다

□field ⓝ 현장

□conservationist ⓝ 환경 보호 활동가

□wildlife ⓝ 야생 동물

□authority ⓝ 당국

□population ⓝ 개체 수

□diminish ⓥ 감소하다

□individual ⓝ 개체

□release ⓥ 방생하다

□supplement ⓥ 보충하다

□adulthood ⓝ 성체

□crocodile ⓝ 악어

□hatchling ⓝ 갓 부화한 유생

□equip ⓥ 장비를 갖추다

L 15

□commodity ⓝ 상품

□consumption ⓝ 소비

□reveal ⓥ 드러내다

□preference ⓝ 선호

□delay ⓥ 지연하다

□reward ⓝ 보상

□agent ⓝ 행위자

□prematurely @ad 조기에

□set aside ~을 확보하다

□judge ⓥ 판단하다

□resolve ⓥ 결심하다

□temptation ⓝ 유혹

L 16

□missing @ (제자리나 집에 있지 않고) 없어진, 빠진

□meet ⓥ (필요, 요구 등을) 충족시키다

□expectation ⓝ 기대

□deceiving @ 속이는, 현혹시키는

□notice ⓥ 눈치채다, 알아채다

□ownership ⓝ 소유권

□ignore ⓥ 무시하다

□passion ⓝ 열정

□recover ⓥ 회복하다

□get rid of ~을 버리다

□treat ⓥ 대하다, 다루다

□accept ⓥ 받아들이다

□room ⓝ 여지

L

M 빈칸 완성하기

M01
- document ⓥ 기록하다
- literary ⓐ 문학적인
- coincidence ⓝ 우연
- untimely ⓐ 시기가 적절하지 않은
- particularly ⓐⅾ 특히
- inspiration ⓝ 영감
- sudden ⓐ 갑작스러운
- disruption ⓝ 방해
- significant ⓐ 상당한
- consequence ⓝ 결과
- critical ⓐ 중요한
- impact ⓥ 영향을 끼치다
- productivity ⓝ 생산성

M02
- be aware that ~을 인식하다
- have a clue 짐작하다
- on the tip of one's tongue 당장 떠오르지 않는, 혀 끝에서 맴도는
- argument ⓝ 말다툼, 논쟁
- overtired ⓐ 극도로 지친
- recital ⓝ 연주회
- justify ⓥ 정당화하다
- circumstances ⓝ 상황, 환경
- a series of 연속된
- frown ⓥ (얼굴을) 찡그리다
- mention ⓥ 얘기를 꺼내다

- push ~ for … ~에게 …을 요구하다
- observation ⓝ 관찰
- cool down 식히다, 진정시키다

M03
- predict ⓥ 예측하다
- environment ⓝ 환경
- illustrate ⓥ 설명하다
- describe ⓥ 묘사하다
- wander ⓥ 돌아다니다, 방랑하다
- relate ⓥ 말하다, 이야기하다
- task ⓝ 과업
- detect ⓥ 감지하다
- predator ⓝ 포식자
- tear down 철거하다, 허물다
- shelter ⓝ 피난처
- cooperation ⓝ 협력
- instinct ⓝ 본능

M04
- respect ⓝ 측면
- relatively ⓐⅾ 비교적
- a small number of 소수의
- species ⓝ 종
- evolve ⓥ 진화시키다
- strategy ⓝ 전략
- mature ⓥ 성숙하다
- leisurely ⓐ 느긋한, 여유 있는
- pace ⓝ 속도
- raise ⓥ 키우다
- pup ⓝ 새끼
- approximately ⓐⅾ 약, 대략

- majority ⓝ 대부분, 다수
- give birth to ~을 낳다
- make it to ~에 이르다
- make use of ~을 사용하다
- reproduce ⓥ 번식하다
- intention ⓝ 의도
- pass down ~을 물려주다

M05
- uncertainty ⓝ 불확실성
- appreciate ⓥ 이해하다, 진가를 알다
- relatively ⓐⅾ 상대적으로
- precise ⓐ 정확한, 정밀한
- digit ⓝ 자릿수
- accuracy ⓝ 정확도
- quoted ⓐ 인용된
- depend on ~에 달려 있다
- intend ⓥ 의도하다
- satellite ⓝ (인공)위성
- orbit ⓥ 궤도를 돌다
- accurately ⓐⅾ 정확하게
- significance ⓝ 중요성
- relative ⓐ 상대적인
- intention ⓝ 의도

M06
- suffer ⓥ 고통받다
- explode ⓥ 폭발하다
- deficit ⓝ 부족, 결핍
- psychologically ⓐⅾ 정신적으로
- boundary ⓝ 경계
- endurance ⓝ 인내력

□ distance ⓝ 거리

□ passive ⓐ 수동적인

□ therapy ⓝ 치료

□ practitioner ⓝ 의사

□ mobilise ⓥ 풀어주다, 움직이게 하다

□ pressure ⓝ 압박

□ treatment ⓝ 치료법

□ sore ⓐ 아픈

□ tissue ⓝ (근육) 조직

□ frame ⓥ 구성하다

□ expert ⓝ 전문가

M 07

□ evidence ⓝ 증거

□ demonstrate ⓥ 보여주다

□ attention ⓝ 주의 집중

□ auditory ⓐ 청각의

□ sharp ⓐ 예리한

□ eyesight ⓝ 시력

□ dramatic ⓐ 극적인

□ expansion ⓝ 확장

□ represent ⓥ 나타내다

□ precisely ⓐⓓ 정확하게

□ vital ⓐ 중요한

□ spatial ⓐ 공간의

□ enlarge ⓥ 확대하다

□ physical ⓐ 신체적인

□ architecture ⓝ 건축, 설계

□ direct ⓥ 지시하다

M 08

□ evolve ⓥ 진화하다

□ possibility ⓝ 가능성

□ tribe ⓝ 부족

□ out-think ⓥ ~보다 우수한 생각을 하다

□ slightly ⓐⓓ 약간

□ possess ⓥ 소유하다

□ vital ⓐ 중요한

□ predict ⓥ 예측하다

□ hostile ⓐ 적대적인

□ accordingly ⓐⓓ 그에 맞춰

□ decisive ⓐ 결정적인

□ succeeding ⓐ 다음의

□ opponent ⓝ 반대자

□ offspring ⓝ 자손

□ descendant ⓝ 후손

M 09

□ concept ⓝ 개념

□ vital ⓐ 필수적인

□ essentialism ⓝ 본질주의

□ proverb ⓝ 속담

□ statement ⓝ 진술

□ essence ⓝ 본질

□ fruitlessly ⓐⓓ 헛되이

□ hypothesis ⓝ 가설(pl. hypotheses)

□ luminiferous ⓐ 발광의, 빛을 내는

□ mysterious ⓐ 신비로운

□ substance ⓝ 물질

□ theorize ⓥ 이론을 세우다

□ simplify ⓥ 단순하게 만들다

□ philosophy ⓝ 철학

M 10

□ striking ⓐ 두드러진

□ characteristic ⓝ 특징

□ respond ⓥ 반응하다

□ environmental ⓐ 환경의

□ eyelid ⓝ 눈꺼풀

□ mammal ⓝ 포유류

□ visual ⓐ 시각의

□ apparently ⓐⓓ 분명히

□ process ⓥ 처리하다

□ shorten ⓥ 짧아지다

□ weaken ⓥ 약해지다

□ essential ⓐ 필수적인

□ nevertheless ⓐⓓ 그럼에도 불구하고

□ derive ⓥ 얻다

□ perceptual ⓐ 지각의

□ activate ⓥ 활성화하다

M 11

□ boost ⓥ 증가시키다, 촉진하다

□ investigate ⓥ 조사하다

□ effectiveness ⓝ 효과

□ persuade ⓥ 설득하다

□ condition ⓝ 조건

□ control ⓝ 통제 집단

□ volume ⓝ 용량, 양

□ on average 평균적으로

□ scarce ⓐ 부족한, 드문

□ scarcity ⓝ 희소성

□ particularly ⓐⓓ 특히

□ genuine ⓐ 진짜의

□ claimed ⓐ 주장된

M

□ laboratory ⓝ 실험실
□ restrict ⓥ 제한하다

M 12
□ differ ⓥ 다르다
□ reset ⓥ 재설정하다
□ biological ⓐ 생물체의
□ overcome ⓥ 극복하다
□ recovery ⓝ 회복
□ westward ⓐⒹ 서쪽으로
□ lengthen ⓥ 연장하다
□ eastward ⓐⒹ 동쪽으로
□ sizable ⓐ 큰
□ impact ⓝ 영향
□ significantly ⓐⒹ 상당히
□ additional ⓐ 추가의
□ evidence ⓝ 증거
□ tough ⓐ 힘든
□ purpose ⓝ 목적

M 13
□ set out ~에 착수하다
□ over-optimism ⓝ 지나친
  낙관주의
□ certain ⓐ 특정한
□ estimate ⓥ 추산하다,
  어림잡다
□ alongside ⓟⓡⓔⓟ ~와 함께
□ task ⓝ 과제
□ fit ⓥ 맞추다
□ available ⓐ 이용 가능한
□ significant ⓐ 상당한
□ spare ⓐ 남겨둔

□ practical ⓐ 실용적인
□ leisure ⓝ 여가

M 14
□ conclusively ⓐⒹ 결정적으로
□ teaching method 교수법
□ practice ⓥ 실천하다
□ lecture ⓥ (설명식) 강의를 하다
□ pull together 모으다
□ break off ~을 분리시키다,
  나누다
□ eventually ⓐⒹ 결국
□ concept ⓝ 개념

M 15
□ evolutionary ⓐ 진화의
□ biologist ⓝ 생물학자
□ establish ⓥ 확립하다
□ conduct ⓥ 거래하다
□ handy ⓐ 간편한
□ confusing ⓐ 혼란스러운
□ terms ⓝ (합의 · 계약 등의) 조항
□ bond ⓝ 결속

M 16
□ engagement ⓝ 참여
□ achievement ⓝ 성취
□ scholarly ⓐ 학문적인
□ physicist ⓝ 물리학자
□ biochemist ⓝ 생화학자
□ significant ⓐ 중요한, 상당한
□ bypass ⓥ 우회하다
□ compensate ⓥ 보완하다
□ strategy ⓝ 전략

□ enthusiastic ⓐ 열성적인
□ rarely ⓐⒹ 좀처럼 ~않는
□ seek ⓥ 찾다
  (seek-sought-sought)
□ subject ⓝ 실험대상자, 대상
□ passionate ⓐ 열정적인

M 17
□ competitive advantage
  비교우위
□ fixed-gear ⓐ 고정식 기어의
□ feature ⓝ 특징
□ overall ⓐ 전반적인
□ profitability ⓝ 수익성
□ complexity ⓝ 복잡성
□ competitor ⓝ 경쟁 업체
□ pressure ⓝ 압박

M 18
□ remarkable ⓐ 두드러진
□ characteristic ⓝ 특징
□ visual system 시각 체계
□ adapt ⓥ 적응하다
□ psychologist ⓝ 심리학자
□ self-experiment ⓝ 자가
  실험
□ literally ⓐⒹ 말 그대로
□ upside down 거꾸로
□ difficulty ⓝ 어려움
□ challenge ⓝ 도전
□ stimulus ⓝ 자극 (pl. stimuli)
□ concentrate ⓥ 집중하다
□ be confronted with ~에
  직면하다

□ fortunately (ad) 다행히
□ perception (n) 지각

M 19

□ underlie (v) 기반이 되다
□ preserve (v) 보존하다
□ heart failure 심장 부전
□ artificial heart 인공 심장
□ replace (v) 대체하다
□ essentially (ad) 본질적으로
□ advanced (a) (발달 단계상) 후기의
□ fade (v) 흐려지다, 점점 희미해지다
□ have to do with ~와 관련이 있다

M 20

□ tend to ~하는 경향이 있다
□ fur (n) 털
□ to the extent where ~할 정도까지
□ uniform (a) 동일한, 획일적인
□ object (n) 개체
□ unit (n) 단위
□ species (n) 종(種)
□ ecosystem (n) 생태계
□ perspective (n) 관점
□ additional (a) 추가적인
□ individual (a) 개별의
□ entire (a) 전체의
□ crucially (ad) 결정적으로
□ varied (a) 다양한
□ behavior (n) 행동

□ unite (v) 통합하다
□ ecological (a) 생태학적인
□ emphasize (v) 강조하다
□ aspect (n) 측면
□ ignore (v) 무시하다, 외면하다
□ framework (n) 틀

M 21

□ freshness (n) 신선함
□ environmental (a) 환경적인
□ produce (n) 생산물[품]
□ exotic (a) 외국산의
□ widespread (a) 광범위한
□ reliance (n) 의존성
□ quality (n) 품질
□ management (n) 관리
□ satellite (n) 위성
□ contribute (v) (~의) 원인이 되다
□ concern (n) 우려
□ wastage (n) 낭비
□ legally (ad) 법적으로
□ institutional (a) 제도적인
□ expose (v) 폭로하다
□ practice (n) 행태
□ retail (n) 소매 산업
□ sector (n) 분야
□ regularly (ad) 정기적으로
□ exceed (v) 초과하다
□ worsen (v) 악화시키다
□ technological (a) 기술적인
□ advance (n) 발전, 진전
□ diversify (v) 다양화하다

M 22

□ innovation (n) 혁신
□ theme (n) 주제
□ steadily (ad) 꾸준히
□ specialized (a) 전문화된
□ diversified (a) 다양화된, 여러 가지의
□ unstable (a) 불안정한
□ self-sufficiency (n) 자급자족
□ mutual (a) 서로의, 상호간의
□ interdependence (n) 상호 의존
□ concentrate (v) 집중하다
□ rely (v) 의존하다, 믿다
□ afford (v) (금전적·시간적) 여유[형편]가 되다
□ sesame oil 참기름
□ lamb (n) 어린 양
□ humanity (n) 인류
□ creatively (ad) 창의적으로
□ personalized (a) 개인화된
□ commercialize (v) 상품화하다

M 23

□ judgment (n) 판단력
□ warehouse (n) 창고
□ economy (n) 경제
□ picker (n) 집게
□ instruction (n) 지시 사항
□ minimise (v) 줄이다
□ maximise (v) 최대화하다
□ productivity (n) 생산성

M

- politely (ad) 정중하게
- instruct (v) 지시하다
- flesh (n) 살
- adapt (v) 적응하다
- process (n) (특정 결과를 달성하기 위한) 과정[절차] (v) 가공[처리]하다
- opposable (a) 마주 볼 수 있는
- reliability (n) 신뢰성
- endurance (n) 참을성
- sociability (n) 사회성

M 24

- conduct (v) 전도하다, 전달하다
- electricity (n) 전기
- more or less 꽤, 다소
- efficiently (ad) 효율적으로
- drop (n) 방울
- conscious mind 의식(적 마음)
- have much say in ~에 발언권이 많대[영향력이 크다]
- intense (a) 강렬한
- viewpoint (n) 관점
- objective (a) 객관적인
- subjective (a) 주관적인
- track (v) 추적하다
- subconscious (a) 잠재의식의
- intensity (n) 강도
- figure out 계산하다
- transfer (v) 전달하다
- electrical current 전류

M 25

- strike (v) 인상을 주다
- partial (a) 부분적인
- reflection (n) 반영
- capture (v) 포착하다, 담아내다
- idea (n) 관념
- physical (a) 물리적인, 구체적인
- each and every 각각의 모든
- somehow (ad) 어떻게든
- abstract (a) 추상적인
- practical (a) 실용적인
- imperfect (a) 불완전한
- visualized (a) 시각화된

M 26

- renewable energy 재생 가능 에너지
- infrastructure (n) 사회 기반 시설
- alternative (a) 대안의
- procedure (n) 절차
- transformation (n) 변화, 변혁
- fossil fuel 화석 연료
- steel (n) 강철
- element (n) 요소
- require (v) 필요로 하다
- scarce (a) 희귀한
- mineral (n) 광물
- undermining (a) 약화시키는
- effort (n) 노력
- emission (n) 배출(물)

- remark (v) 말하다, 언급하다
- transition (n) 전환
- supply (n) 공급
- take advantage of ~을 활용하다
- construction (n) 건설
- competitive (a) 경쟁력 있는

M 27

- defence (n) 방어
- species (n) (생물의) 종
- shallows (n) 얕은 곳
- fold (v) 접다
- stare (v) 응시하다
- eyesight (n) 시력
- asset (n) 이점, 자산
- creature (n) 생물체
- transform (v) 변신하다
- spectacle (n) 광경
- octopodian (a) 문어와 같은
- stick (v) 찔러 넣다
- grab (v) 움켜잡다
- broad (a) 넓은
- illusion (n) 착시[착각]
- territory (n) 영토, 지역

M 28

- disaster (n) 재난
- scope (n) 범위
- transformation (n) 변화
- indeed (ad) 실제로
- eliminate (v) 없애다
- obvious (a) 명백한
- marginal (a) 주변적인

- isolated ⓐ 고립된
- impact ⓝ 영향
- expand ⓥ 확장하다
- horizon ⓝ 지평선
- plainly ⓐⓓ 뚜렷하게
- escapist ⓐ 현실 도피(주의)의
- pretend ⓥ 가장하다
- suffering ⓝ 고통
- distant ⓐ 먼
- resolve ⓥ 해결하다
- cease ⓥ 멈추다, 중단하다
- reborn ⓐ 다시 태어난
- overestimated ⓐ 과대평가된
- plot ⓝ 줄거리
- complex ⓐ 복잡한

M 29
- climatic ⓐ 기후의
- requirement ⓝ 요건
- endure ⓥ 견디다
- satisfy ⓥ 충족시키다
- species ⓝ 종(種)
- force ⓥ 강요하다
- creature ⓝ 생명체
- be capable of ~을 할 수 있다
- immobile ⓐ 움직이지 않는
- larva ⓝ 유충
- occupy ⓥ 점유하다
- survive ⓥ 생존하다
- reproduce ⓥ 번식하다
- endurance ⓝ 인내
- transformation ⓝ 변형

M 30
- respectable ⓐ 존경할 만한
- make it a point 반드시 ~하도록 하다
- discourage ⓥ 못하게 하다
- speak up 자유롭게 의견을 내다
- maintain ⓥ 유지하다
- viewpoint ⓝ 관점
- get aired 공공연히 알려지다
- if anything 오히려
- boss ⓝ 상사
- conversation ⓝ 대담, 대화
- corporate ⓝ 기업
- nonprofit ⓐ 비영리인
- publish ⓥ 발행하다, 출판하다
- section ⓝ 구역, (신문의) ~란
- feature ⓥ (기사로) 다루다
- management ⓝ 경영
- techniques ⓝ 기법
- regularly ⓐⓓ 어김없이, 규칙적으로
- claim ⓥ 주장하다
- continually ⓐⓓ 계속해서
- remark ⓥ 말하다

M 31
- potential ⓝ 잠재력
- shift ⓥ 바꾸다
- initial ⓐ 초기의
- generate ⓥ 발생하다
- separately ⓐⓓ 따로, 별도로
- pool ⓥ 모으다
- preserve ⓥ 보존하다

- judgment ⓝ 판단
- evaluate ⓥ 평가하다
- refine ⓥ 다듬다
- promising ⓐ 유망한
- elaborate ⓥ 정교하게 말하다
- advance ⓥ 발전시키다
- struggle to ~ ~하기 위해 애쓰다
- collective ⓐ 집단적인
- intelligence ⓝ 지능

M 32
- potentially ⓐⓓ 잠재적으로
- instrument ⓝ 도구
- end ⓝ 목적
- celebrity ⓝ 유명인, 명성
- criticize ⓥ 비판하다
- highlight ⓥ 강조하다
- barrier ⓝ 장애물
- phenomenon ⓝ 현상
- symbolize ⓥ 상징하다
- metaphor ⓝ 은유
- characterize ⓥ 특징짓다
- hierarchical ⓐ 계층적인
- scale ⓝ 척도
- shift ⓥ 전환하다
- gradually ⓐⓓ 점차
- solely ⓐⓓ 오로지, 단지
- restrict ⓥ 제한하다

M 33
- coastal ⓐ 해안의
- prepare ⓥ 준비하다
- sea level 해수면

M

□ risk ⓝ 위험

□ assessment ⓝ 평가

□ rare ⓐ 드문

□ carry out ~을 실행하다

□ act on ~에 따라 행동하다[대처하다]

□ climate ⓝ 기후

□ decade ⓝ 10년

□ prediction ⓝ 예측

□ tense ⓝ 시제

□ crisis ⓝ 위기

□ ongoing ⓐ 계속 진행 중인

□ region ⓝ 지역

□ affect ⓥ 영향을 주다

□ Antarctic ⓐ 남극 지방의

□ physically ⓐⓓ 물리적으로

□ remote ⓐ 멀리 떨어진

□ efficiency ⓝ 효율(성)

M 34

□ assume ⓥ 가정하다, 추정하다

□ concern ⓥ 관련되다

□ primarily ⓐⓓ 주로

□ sociocultural ⓐ 사회 문화적인

□ standpoint ⓝ 관점

□ in the absence of ~의 부재 속에서, ~이 없는 상황에서

□ distantiation ⓝ 거리두기

□ interaction ⓝ 상호 작용

□ constantly ⓐⓓ 끊임없이

□ confront ⓥ 직면하다, 맞서다

□ blend into ~와 뒤섞이다

□ perspective ⓝ 관점

M 35

□ economy ⓝ 경제

□ emerge ⓥ 나타나다

□ interaction ⓝ 상호 작용

□ element ⓝ 요소

□ merchant ⓝ 상인

□ operation ⓝ 작용, 작동

□ resident ⓝ 거주자

□ scale ⓝ 정도, 규모

□ distantly ⓐⓓ 멀리에서

□ textile ⓝ 직물

□ raw ⓐ 가공되지 않은

□ sensory ⓐ 감각의

□ organ ⓝ (체내의) 장기

□ transport ⓥ 전하다, 이동하다

□ superhighway ⓝ 초고속도로

□ undergo ⓥ 겪다

□ conscious ⓐ 의식적인

□ isolation ⓝ 독립, 분리

□ resemble ⓥ 유사하다

□ systemic ⓐ 체계적인

M 36

□ organism ⓝ 유기체

□ prey ⓝ 먹이

□ glow ⓝ 빛 ⓥ 빛나다

□ firefly ⓝ 반딧불이

□ sexual ⓐ 성적인

□ attractant ⓝ 유인 물질

□ mate ⓝ 짝

□ evolutionary ⓐ 진화의

□ theory ⓝ 이론

□ cloak ⓝ 망토

□ invisibility ⓝ 눈에 보이지 않음

□ molecule ⓝ 분자

□ creature ⓝ 생물

□ cast a shadow 그림자를 드리우다

□ silhouette ⓝ 실루엣

□ blend into ~와 섞이다

□ sparkle ⓝ 반짝임

□ reflection ⓝ 반사

□ scattered ⓐ 분산된

□ threaten ⓥ 위협하다

M 37

□ downplay ⓥ 경시하다

□ offender ⓝ 범죄자

□ primate ⓝ 영장류

□ crow ⓝ 까마귀

□ qualitatively ⓐⓓ 질적으로

□ humanity ⓝ 인류

□ beat ⓥ 이기다

□ cognitive ⓐ 인지적인

□ precise ⓐ 정확한

□ instinct ⓝ 본능

□ intelligence ⓝ 지능

□ linguistic ⓐ 언어(학)의

□ castration ⓝ 거세

□ overestimate ⓥ 과대평가하다

□ misconception ⓝ 오해

M 38

□ generalization ⓝ 일반화

□ specific ⓐ 구체적인

□ humanize ⓥ 인간미 있게 하다

□ fine ⓐ 훌륭한

□ humanitarian ⓐ 인도주의적인

□ describe ⓥ 서술하다

□ heroic ⓐ 영웅적인

□ brave ⓐ 용감한

□ tragic ⓐ 비극적인

□ description ⓝ 묘사

□ particular ⓐ 세부 사항

□ boredom ⓝ 지루함

□ detailed ⓐ 세밀한

□ engaging ⓐ 마음을 끄는, 매력적인

M 39

□ telegraph ⓝ 전보

□ metaphor ⓝ 비유, 은유

□ advance notice 사전 통보

□ inform A of B A에게 B를 알리다

□ upcoming ⓐ 다가오는

□ convey ⓥ 전달하다

□ huge ⓐ 큰, 거대한

□ accept ⓥ 수용하다

□ empower ⓥ 권한을 부여하다

□ involve ⓥ 포함하다

□ circumstance ⓝ 상황

□ process ⓥ 처리하다

□ make the most of ~을 최대한으로 활용하다

□ adapt ⓥ 적응하다

□ object ⓥ 반대하다

□ compete ⓥ 경쟁하다

□ recover ⓥ 회복하다

M 40

□ echo ⓝ 메아리

□ accordingly ⓐⓓ 그에 따라

□ transmit ⓥ 전달하다

□ via ⓟⓡⓔⓟ ~을 통하여

□ theory ⓝ 이론

□ mood ⓝ 기분, 분위기

□ judge ⓥ 판단하다

□ disappear ⓥ 사라지다

M 41

□ maintain ⓥ 유지하다

□ be supposed to ~하기로 되어 있다

□ be related to ~와 관계가 있다

□ weight ⓝ 비중

□ consideration ⓝ 고려사항

□ unburden ⓥ 벗어나게 하다

□ sort out ~을 가려내다

□ negotiate ⓥ 협상하다

M 42

□ confirm ⓥ 확인하다

□ athlete ⓝ 운동선수

□ unacceptable ⓐ 받아들일 수 없는

□ moral ⓐ 도덕적인

□ decline ⓥ 감소하다

□ competitive ⓐ 경쟁하는, 경쟁의

□ emphasis ⓝ 강조

□ cheat ⓥ 속이다

□ undesirable ⓐ 바람직하지 않은

□ enhance ⓥ 강화하다, 향상시키다

□ resist ⓥ 저항하다

□ temptation ⓝ 유혹

□ systematically ⓐⓓ 체계적으로

M 43

□ construct ⓥ 구성하다

□ expectation ⓝ 기대

□ hypothesis ⓝ 가설 (pl. hypotheses)

□ calculate ⓥ 계산하다

□ statistics ⓝ 통계

□ systematic ⓐ 체계적인

□ interval ⓝ 간격

□ pitch ⓝ 음조

□ track ⓥ 추적하다

□ neural circuit 신경 회로

□ frequency ⓝ 빈도

□ prediction ⓝ 예측

□ preference ⓝ 선호

□ imitate ⓥ 모방하다

□ caregiver ⓝ (아이 등을) 돌보는 사람

M 44

□ countryside ⓝ 시골

□ biologist ⓝ 생물학자

□ evolutionary ⓐ 진화의

M

□ principle ⓝ 원리
□ evolve ⓥ 진화하다
□ generation ⓝ 세대
□ bunny ⓝ 토끼
□ pass on ~을 물려주다
□ gene ⓝ 유전자
□ run into ~와 마주치다
□ adapt ⓥ 적응하다

M 45
□ communicate ⓥ
의사소통을 하다
□ discontent ⓝ 불만
□ frequency ⓝ 주파수
□ researcher ⓝ 연구자
□ experiment ⓥ 실험하다
□ survival ⓐ 살아남기 위한
□ organism ⓝ 유기체
□ objective ⓝ 목표
□ defend ⓥ 지키다, 방어하다
□ neighboring ⓐ 인접한,
이웃한
□ dissatisfaction ⓝ 불만
□ nutrient ⓝ 영양소
□ genetic ⓐ 유전적인

M 46
□ launch ⓥ 출시하다
□ overprice ⓥ 과한 가격을
매기다
□ distort ⓥ 왜곡하다
□ perception ⓝ 인식
□ initial ⓐ 초기의
□ be willing to-v 기꺼이 ~하다

□ costly ⓐ 손해가 큰, 비용이
많이 드는
□ priority ⓝ 우선순위
□ sufficient ⓐ 충분한
□ volume ⓝ 양
□ maximize ⓥ 극대화하다
□ sacrifice ⓥ 희생하다
□ strategy ⓝ 전략
□ switch ⓥ 전환하다
□ brand-new ⓐ 새로운

M 47
□ experimentally
ⓐⓓ 실험적으로
□ hypothesis ⓝ 가설
□ in general 일반적으로
□ publish ⓥ 발표하다
□ inspection ⓝ 점검
□ construct ⓥ 세우다
□ assumption ⓝ 가정
□ end up -ing 결국 ~하게 되다
□ sense ⓝ 의미
□ pursue ⓥ 추구하다
□ stick to ~을 고수하다

M 48
□ content ⓐ 만족하는
□ discontent ⓐ 불만족하는
□ determined ⓐ 결정되는
□ merely ⓐⓓ 단지
□ successive ⓐ 연속적인
□ affect ⓥ 영향을 미치다
□ adjust ⓥ 적응하다
□ default ⓝ 기본값

□ well-being ⓝ 행복, 안녕
□ baseline ⓝ 기준선
□ fade ⓥ 사라지다, 희미해지다
□ despair ⓝ 절망
□ tendency ⓝ 경향
□ long for ~을 갈망하다
□ adapt ⓥ 적응하다
□ regret ⓥ 후회하다
□ struggle ⓥ 고군분투하다

M 49
□ put off 미루다, 연기하다
□ eventually ⓐⓓ 결국
□ overwhelming ⓐ 압도적인
□ drive ⓝ 욕구, 충동
□ chemical ⓝ 화학물질
□ build up 쌓이다
□ break down 분해하다
□ molecule ⓝ 분자
□ trigger ⓥ 유발하다
□ optimal ⓐ 최적의
□ debt ⓝ 빚
□ make up 보충하다
□ built-in ⓐ 내재된
□ lack ⓝ 부족, 결핍
□ take away 뺏다
□ swing ⓝ (기분의) 변화
□ catch up with ~을 따라잡다

M 50
□ research ⓝ 연구
□ expert ⓝ 전문가 ⓐ 능숙한
□ field ⓝ 분야, 영역
□ difficulty ⓝ 어려움

□newcomer ⓝ 초보
□genuine ⓐ 실제의
□remarkably ⓐⓓ 놀랍게도
□accurate ⓐ 정확한
□insensitive ⓐ 무감각한
□acquire ⓥ 습득하다
□underestimate
　ⓥ 과소평가하다
□session ⓝ 기간, 시간
□assumption ⓝ 추정, 가정

M 51

□medium ⓝ 매체
□invention ⓝ 발명
□absorb ⓥ 흡수하다
□communicate ⓥ 소통하다
□surface ⓝ 표면
□appearance ⓝ 겉모습
□code ⓝ 규칙, 방식
□interpret ⓥ 해석하다

M 52

□demonstrate ⓥ 보여주다,
　설명하다
□defeat ⓥ 패배시키다, 이기다
□delay ⓥ 미루다
□behavioral ⓐ 행동의, 행동에
　관한
□assign ⓥ 맡기다, 배정하다
□due date 마감일, 만기일
□for oneself 스스로
□submit ⓥ 제출하다
□conclude ⓥ 결론을 내리다
□restrict ⓥ 제한하다

□recognize ⓥ 인식하다
□tendency ⓝ 경향, 성향
□performance ⓝ 수행, 성과
□reward ⓝ 보상
□obstacle ⓝ 장애물
□assignment ⓝ 과제
□competition ⓝ 경쟁

M 53

□participant ⓝ 참가자
□be allowed to ~하도록
　허용되다
□be unrelated to ~와
　연관되지 않다
□absolutely ⓐⓓ 절대적으로
□equally ⓐⓓ 동등하게
□rate ⓥ 평가하다
□knowledgeable ⓐ 유식한
□suggest ⓥ 시사하다
□have access to ~에
　접근하다
□judgment ⓝ 판단
□pump up 부풀리다, 증대하다
□intellectual ⓐ 지능의
□confidence ⓝ 자신감
□endure ⓥ 견디다
□challenging ⓐ 힘든
□collaboration ⓝ 협동
□motivate ⓥ 동기를 부여하다
□pursue ⓥ 추구하다
□in-depth ⓐ 심도 있는, 면밀한

M 54

□creator ⓝ 창조자
□clothing ⓝ 의복
□nail ⓝ 못
□drive ⓥ (못 · 말뚝 등을) 박다
□physical ⓐ 물리적인
□harmony ⓝ 조화
□existence ⓝ 존재
□potential ⓝ 잠재력
□accomplish ⓥ 완성하다
□careless ⓐ 부주의한
□irresponsible ⓐ 무책임한
□observe ⓥ 탐색하다
□professional ⓝ 전문직
　(종사자)

M

M 55

□terrified ⓐ 두려워하는
□stem from ~에서 생겨나다
□passenger ⓝ 승객
□potential ⓐ 잠재적인
□destination ⓝ 목적지
□base ⓥ 근거하다
□solely ⓐⓓ 오로지
□logic ⓝ 논리
□statistically ⓐⓓ 통계적으로
□odds ⓝ (어떤 일이 있을) 가능성
□boredom ⓝ 지루함
□responsibility ⓝ 책임감

M 56

□refer to ~을 나타내다
□intellectual ⓐ 지적인

□competence ⓝ 능력, 능숙함

□brilliant ⓐ 훌륭한

□legal ⓐ 법률과 관련된

□brief ⓝ 업무 (보고서)

□elegant ⓐ 우아한, 정연한

□exceptionally ⓐⓓ 각별히

□witty ⓐ 재치 있는

□gadget ⓝ 기기, 장치

□measure ⓝ 척도, 기준

□take into account ~을 고려하다

□outstanding ⓐ 뛰어난

□sole ⓐ 유일한

□determinant ⓝ 결정 요인

□accompany ⓥ 동반하다

M 57

□foreign language 외국어

□translate ⓥ 통역하다

□dialogue ⓝ 대화

□viewer ⓝ 관객

□occasion ⓝ 경우

□mainly ⓐⓓ 주로

□viewpoint ⓝ 관점, 시각

□particular ⓐ 특정한

□absence ⓝ 부재

□incomprehension ⓝ 몰이해

□impress ⓥ 감명을 주다

□heated ⓐ 열띤

□debate ⓝ 토론

M 58

□face-to-face 대면의

□interaction ⓝ 상호 작용

□uniquely ⓐⓓ 유례없이

□knowledge ⓝ 지식

□complex ⓐ 복잡한

□stimulate ⓥ 자극하다

□shoelace ⓝ 신발 끈

□psychologist ⓝ 심리학자

□previous ⓐ 이전의

□access ⓝ 접근

□crucial ⓐ 결정적인, 매우 중요한

□factor ⓝ 요소

□professional ⓐ 전문적인

□talent ⓝ 재능

□complex ⓐ 복합적인

□motivation ⓝ 동기

M 59

□intellectually ⓐⓓ 지적으로

□superior ⓐ 우월한 ⓝ 상급자

□modify ⓥ 변형하다

□gene ⓝ 유전자

□receptor ⓝ 수용체

□chemical ⓝ 화학 물질

□necessary ⓐ 필수적인

□genetically ⓐⓓ 유전적으로

□inferior ⓐ 열등한

□raise ⓥ 기르다

□standard ⓐ 표준의

□social ⓐ 사회적인

□interaction ⓝ 상호 작용

□handicapped ⓐ 장애가 있는

□triumph ⓝ 승리

□nurture ⓝ 양육

□nature ⓝ 천성

□genetic ⓐ 유전의

□superiority ⓝ 우월성

M 60

□demand ⓝ 수요

□goods ⓝ 상품

□price ⓝ 가격

□traditional ⓐ 전통적인

□apply for ~에 적용하다

□instead of ~ 대신에

□switch ⓥ 바꾸다

□replacement ⓝ 대체품

□purchase ⓥ 구매하다

□dairy ⓝ 유제품

□consume ⓥ 소비하다

□savings ⓝ 저축한 돈, 저금

□invest ⓥ 투자하다

M 61

□face ⓥ 직면하다

□innovation ⓝ 혁신

□entirely ⓐⓓ 완전히

□virtual ⓐ 가상의

□constraint ⓝ 제약

□collaboration ⓝ 협업

□face-to-face ⓐ 대면의

□enforce ⓥ 강요하다

□at a time 한 번에

□nonverbal ⓐ 비언어적인
□diminish ⓥ 제한하다, 줄이다
□arrangement ⓝ 배정, 배치
□assign ⓥ 할당하다

M 62

□prevailing ⓐ 지배적인
□view ⓝ 견해
□developmental ⓐ 발달의
□contributor ⓝ 기여자
□development ⓝ 발달
□physical ⓐ 물리적인
□context ⓝ 환경
□interact ⓥ 상호 작용하다
□infant ⓝ 유아
□construct ⓥ 구성하다
□engage ⓥ (관심을) 끌다, 참여하다
□object ⓝ 사물
□individual ⓝ 개인
□manufacturer ⓝ 생산하는 사람, 제조자
□generation ⓝ 세대
□shield ⓝ 방패
□explorer ⓝ 탐험가

M 63

□institute ⓝ (특히 교육 전문 직종과 관련된) 기관[협회]
□contain ⓥ 포함하다
□shadow ⓥ 따라하다
□comprise ⓥ 구성하다
□process ⓥ 처리하다

M 64

□realism ⓝ 실재론
□geometrical ⓐ 기하학적인
□nature ⓝ 본성
□indicate ⓥ 가리키다
□carve ⓥ 조각하다, 새기다
□point out 지적하다
□indeed ⓐⓓ 진실로, 진정
□physical ⓐ 물리적인
□flaw ⓝ 결함
□be subject to ~에 영향을 받다
□decay ⓥ 부패하다, 쇠하다
□extraordinary ⓐ 비범한
□reflection ⓝ 반영, 반영물
□unseen ⓐ 보이지 않는
□exist ⓥ 존재하다
□observable ⓐ 관찰 가능한
□overlap ⓥ 겹치다
□sense ⓝ 감각
□stereotype ⓝ 고정관념
□generalization ⓝ 일반화

M 65

□trick ⓥ 속이다
□contract ⓝ 계약
□myth ⓝ 신화
□tribe ⓝ 부족
□victim ⓝ 희생자
□irresistible ⓐ 저항할 수 없는
□otherwise ⓐⓓ 그렇지 않으면
□resist ⓥ 저항하다
□instruct ⓥ 지시하다

□crew ⓝ (배 · 비행기의) 선원[승무원]
□stuff ⓥ 채워 넣다
□temptation ⓝ 유혹
□concentrate ⓥ 집중하다
□distract ⓥ 주의를 산만하게 하다
□mindset ⓝ 사고방식
□track ⓥ 추적하다
□progress ⓝ 과정

M 66

□individual ⓝ 개인
□profession ⓝ 직업
□instant ⓐ 즉각적인
□credibility ⓝ 신뢰
□admire ⓥ 존경하다
□advice ⓝ 조언
□knowledge ⓝ 지식
□certain ⓐ 특정한
□expertise ⓝ 전문 지식[기술]
□talent ⓝ 재능
□patience ⓝ 인내심, 참을성
□sacrifice ⓝ 희생

M 67

□ecosystem ⓝ 생태계
□adapt ⓥ 적응하다
□evolution ⓝ 진화
□microbe ⓝ 미생물
□evolve ⓥ 진화하다
□resistance ⓝ 저항(력), 내성
□antibacterial ⓝ 항균제

M

□insecticide ⓝ 살충제
□cockroach ⓝ 바퀴벌레
(= roach)

□distaste ⓝ 혐오감, 불쾌감
□counterpart ⓝ 상대(방)
□ecologist ⓝ 생태학자
□urban ⓐ 도시의
□trait ⓝ 특성, 속성
□thrive ⓥ 번성하다, 번창하다
□indoorsy ⓐ 실내 생활을 좋아하는

□humanity ⓝ 인류
□extinct ⓐ 멸종된
□habitat ⓝ 서식지
□organism ⓝ 유기체
□boundary ⓝ 경계

M 68

□manufacture
ⓥ 생산[제조]하다
□goods ⓝ 상품
□be willing to-v 기꺼이
~하려고 하다
□income ⓝ 수입
□feature ⓝ 기능
□fancy ⓐ 고급의
□unaware ⓐ 알지 못하는
□manipulate ⓥ 조종하다
□presence ⓝ 존재
□high-volume ⓐ 대량의
□low-margin ⓐ 가격이 싼,
수익이 적은
□trick ⓥ 속이다
□unnecessary ⓐ 불필요한

□fool ⓥ 속이다
□repeatedly ⓐⓓ 반복적으로

M 69

□audience ⓝ 관중
□in public 공공연히
□species ⓝ 종(種)
□reflect on ~을 되돌아보다
□individual ⓐ 개인의
□history ⓝ 역사
□trial and error 시행착오

M 70

□individual ⓝ 개인
□unheard-of ⓐ 전례가 없는
□confront ⓥ 맞서다, 직면하다
□orient oneself 적응하다,
순응하다
□restrict ⓥ 제한하다
□distributor ⓝ 분배업자
□be associated with ~와
관련이 있다
□considerable ⓐ 상당한

M 71

□misunderstand ⓥ 진가를
못 알아보다
□composition ⓝ 작품
□initial ⓐ 초기의
□lack ⓝ 부족
□acceptance ⓝ 수용
□unfamiliarity ⓝ 낯섦
□host ⓝ 주인공

□depict ⓥ 묘사하다
□composer ⓝ 작곡가
□overshadow ⓥ 가리다
□original ⓐ 독창적인
□conventional ⓐ 관습적인

M 72

□dynamic ⓝ 역학
□dramatically ⓐⓓ 극적으로
□concept ⓝ 개념
□home-field advantage
홈 이점
□circumstance ⓝ 상황
□play a role 역할을 하다
□provide ⓥ 제공하다
□point out ~을 지적하다
□competitive ⓐ 경쟁력이
있는
□struggling ⓐ 고전하는
□advertise ⓥ 광고하다
□upcoming ⓐ 다가오는

N 흐름에 맞지 않는 문장 찾기

N01

□psychologist ⓝ 심리학자
□severe ⓐ 심각한
□mental ⓐ 정신적인
□illness ⓝ 병, 질환
□compose ⓥ 작곡하다
□improve ⓥ 개선하다
□participant ⓝ 참가자
□session ⓝ 활동, 기간
□benefit ⓝ 이점
□review ⓥ 검토하다
□treatment ⓝ 치료
□setting ⓝ 환경
□finding ⓝ 결과
□choir ⓝ 합창단
□wellbeing ⓝ 행복
□significantly ⓐⓓ 상당히
□state ⓝ 상태
□enhance ⓥ 강화하다

N02

□sensory ⓐ 감각의
□nerve ⓝ 신경
□ending ⓝ 끝, 말단
□tissue ⓝ (세포로 이루어진) 조직
□sensation ⓝ 감각
□transmit ⓥ 전달하다
□protective ⓐ 보호하는
□mechanism ⓝ 방법, 메커니즘
□capacity ⓝ 능력, 용량

□polite ⓐ 공손한
□muscle ⓝ 근육
□contract ⓥ 수축하다
□function ⓝ 기능
□sweating ⓝ 발한

N03

□as opposed to ～와 대비되는
□essential ⓐ 필수적인
□establish ⓥ 수립하다
□positive ⓐ 긍정적인
□tragedy ⓝ 비극
□misfortune ⓝ 불행
□draw out 끌어내다
□recognizable ⓐ 알아볼 수 있는, 인식할 수 있는
□portrayal ⓝ 묘사
□fictional ⓐ 허구의, 가상의
□documentary ⓐ 사실을 기록한, 사실적인
□companion ⓝ 동료
□valued ⓐ 소중한, 가치 있는
□ally ⓝ 협력자
□dozens of 많은, 수십의
□incidental ⓐ 부수적인

N04

□psychologist ⓝ 심리학자
□recall ⓥ 기억해 내다
□random ⓐ 무작위의
□particularly ⓐⓓ 특히
□audience ⓝ 청중
□face ⓥ 직면하다
□draw upon ～을 활용하다
□minor ⓐ 사소한

□gap ⓝ 틈
□imaginative ⓐ 상상의

N05

□intelligent ⓐ 지능적인
□decision ⓝ 결정
□myth ⓝ 신화
□literature ⓝ 문학
□mathematician ⓝ 수학자
□reason ⓥ 추론하다
□measure ⓥ 측정하다
□intelligence ⓝ 지능
□autonomously ⓐⓓ 자율적으로
□coin ⓥ (신조어를) 만들다
□previously ⓐⓓ 이전에
□appearance ⓝ 등장
□practice ⓝ 실행, 실제
□reasoning ⓝ 추론

N06

□agency ⓝ 행위자
□genuine ⓐ 진정한
□authority ⓝ 권한
□examine ⓥ 살펴보다
□assembly ⓝ 조립
□empower ⓥ (권한을) 부여하다
□scale ⓝ 규모
□efficiency ⓝ 효율성
□uniform ⓐ 똑같은
□organizational ⓐ 조직의
□productivity ⓝ 생산성
□self-discipline ⓝ 자기 통제력

N 07

- illusion ⓝ 착각
- cram ⓥ 벼락치기를 하다
- strategy ⓝ 전략
- differentiate ⓥ 구분하다
- present ⓐ 존재하는
- conscious ⓐ 의식적인
- enormous ⓐ 엄청난
- vanish ⓥ 사라지다
- material ⓝ 자료
- academic ⓐ 학업적인
- performance ⓝ 성취
- essential ⓐ 필수적인

N 08

- effect ⓝ 효과, 영향
- phenomenon ⓝ 현상
- apply to ~에 적용되다
- statement ⓝ 진술, 서술
- on the surface 표면적으로
- psychology ⓝ 심리(학)
- identify ⓥ 동일시하다
- seek ⓥ 찾다, 구하다
- fill ⓥ 채우다
- rest ⓝ 나머지
- principle ⓝ 원리
- rely on ~에 의존하다
- offer ⓥ 제공하다
- make sense 타당하다, 말이 되다
- countless ⓐ 무수한, 셀 수 없이 많은
- beneficial ⓐ 유익한

N 09

- commonly ⓐ 보통
- refer to 나타내다
- tendency ⓝ 경향
- subconscious ⓐ 잠재의식의
- incomplete ⓐ 불완전한
- complicated ⓐ 복잡한
- interrupt ⓥ 방해하다
- cooperation ⓝ 협동

N 10

- engagement ⓝ 관계
- poetry ⓝ (집합적으로) 시
- benefit ⓝ 이점, 혜택
- professional ⓐ 전문적인
- capacity ⓝ 능력, 용량
- expressive ⓐ 표현의, 표현적인
- immune ⓐ 면역의
- lung ⓝ 폐, 허파
- function ⓝ 기능
- diminish ⓥ 줄이다, 약화하다
- psychological ⓐ 심리적인
- distress ⓝ 고통
- enhance ⓥ (질을) 높이다, 향상하다
- aid ⓥ 지원하다, 돕다
- empathy ⓝ 공감 (능력)
- incredibly ⓐ 믿을 수 없을 정도로
- target ⓥ 목표로 삼다, 겨냥하다
- productivity ⓝ 생산성
- frustration ⓝ 좌절감

N 11

- spread ⓝ 확산
- be linked to ~와 연관되다[관련이 있다]
- incredibly ⓐ 믿을 수 없을 정도로
- epidemic ⓝ 유행병, 전염병
- outbreak ⓝ 발발, 창궐
- typhoid ⓝ 장티푸스
- sanitation ⓝ 위생
- recognition ⓝ 인식
- decline ⓥ 하락하다, 감소하다
- pioneering ⓐ 선구적인
- as a result of ~의 결과로

N 12

- business ⓝ 사업
- gone ⓐ (특정한 상황이) 끝난
- gatekeeper ⓝ 문지기, 정보 관리[통제]자
- prevent ⓥ 막다
- let in ~을 들여 보내다
- label ⓝ 음반사
- spotlight ⓝ 주목
- ask for ~을 요청하다
- permission ⓝ 허락, 허가
- fanbase ⓝ 팬층
- rising ⓐ 증가하는
- concern ⓝ 우려, 염려
- deliver ⓥ 전달하다, 배달하다
- directly ⓐ 직접, 곧장
- exposure ⓝ 노출, 매스컴 출연

N 13

- interpret ⓥ 해석하다
- sympathy ⓝ 공감
- conflict ⓝ 갈등
- arise ⓥ 발생하다
- outcome ⓝ 결과
- tale ⓝ 이야기
- shift ⓥ 바꾸다
- viewpoint ⓝ 관점
- evil ⓐ 사악한
- stepsister ⓝ 의붓자매
- exist ⓥ 존재하다
- willingly ⓐⓓ 기꺼이

N 14

- mild ⓐ 가벼운
- attentive ⓐ 주의 깊은
- beneficial ⓐ 이로운
- improve ⓥ 향상하다
- performance ⓝ 수행
- ideal ⓐ 이상적인
- currently ⓐⓓ 현재
- unknown ⓐ 알려지지 않은
- stimulation ⓝ 자극
- further ⓐⓓ 더욱
- suffer ⓥ 저하되다

N 15

- potential ⓝ 잠재력
- productivity ⓝ 생산성
- access ⓝ 접근
- introduce ⓥ 도입하다
- factor ⓝ 요소, 요인
- decline ⓝ 감소

N 16

- statistics ⓝ 통계학
- law of large numbers 대수의 법칙
- describe ⓥ 설명하다
- prediction ⓝ 예측
- conduct ⓥ 수행하다
- average ⓝ 평균
- state ⓝ 상태
- encounter ⓝ 만남, 접함
- relative ⓐ 상대적인
- frequency ⓝ 빈도
- approach ⓥ 접근하다
- fade away 사라지다
- symbolic ⓐ 상징적인
- interpret ⓥ 해석하다
- unexpectedly ⓐⓓ 예상치 못하게
- insurer ⓝ 보험사
- figure out ~을 알아내다
- balance ⓥ 균형을 맞추다

N 17

- contribute to ~에 기여하다
- medium ⓝ 수단
- exhibit ⓥ 나타내다, 전시하다
- innovative ⓐ 혁신적인
- display ⓥ 드러내다, 전시하다
- creativity ⓝ 창의성
- taste ⓝ 취향
- represent ⓥ 보여주다, 상징하다
- self-respect ⓝ 자아 존중
- pleasure ⓝ 즐거움
- doubt ⓝ 의심

- link A to B A와 B를 연결하다
- sociable ⓐ 친교적인
- aspect ⓝ 관점
- opportunity ⓝ 기회
- identity ⓝ 정체성

N 18

- algorithm ⓝ 알고리즘
- grab hold of ~을 움켜잡다
- confirm ⓥ 확인하다
- belief ⓝ 신념, 믿음
- ignore ⓥ 무시하다
- match ⓥ 일치하다
- constantly ⓐⓓ 일관되게
- expose ⓥ (유해한 환경 등에) 노출시키다
- acknowledge ⓥ 인정하다
- existence ⓝ 존재
- diversity ⓝ 다양성
- sheltered ⓐ 보호받는
- extreme ⓐ 극단적인
- particular ⓐ 특정한
- disastrous ⓐ 참담한, 재앙의
- intellectual ⓐ 지적인
- isolation ⓝ 고립

N 19

- inevitable ⓐ 피할 수 없는
- capacity ⓝ 능력
- functionally ⓐⓓ 기능적으로
- distressing ⓐ 괴로움을 주는
- abundant ⓐ 풍족한
- scarce ⓐ 부족한
- neglect ⓝ 소홀함
- indifference ⓝ 무관심

N

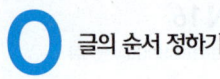

O 글의 순서 정하기

□ effort ⓝ 노력

□ end up -ing 결국 ~하게 되다

□ take on ~을 받아들이다, 맡다

□ tough ⓐ 힘든

□ emphasize ⓥ 강조하다

□ control ⓥ 통제하다

□ continue ⓥ 계속[지속]하다

□ improve ⓥ 발전하다

□ underperform ⓥ 기대에 못 미치는 성과를 내다

□ evidence ⓝ 증거

O 06

□ cope with ~에 대처하다

□ extreme ⓐ 극심한

□ avoid ⓥ 피하다

□ reptile ⓝ 파충류

□ rely on ~에 의존하다

□ sophisticated ⓐ 정교한

□ reabsorb ⓥ 재흡수하다

□ take in ~을 섭취하다

□ freshwater ⓝ 담수

□ creature ⓝ 생물

□ immobile ⓐ 움직이지 않는

□ surface ⓥ 표면으로 나오다

□ stock up on ~을 비축하다

□ survival ⓝ 생존

□ ranger ⓝ 경비대원, 순찰대원

□ reserves ⓝ 비축물

O 07

□ level ⓐ 평평한

□ force ⓝ 힘

□ act ⓥ 작용하다

□ friction ⓝ 마찰

□ rub ⓥ 문지르다

□ resistance ⓝ 저항

□ generate ⓥ 발생시키다

□ rotate ⓥ 회전하다

□ gradually ⓐd 점차적으로

□ exert ⓥ (힘을) 가하다

□ grip ⓥ 꽉 잡다

O 08

□ conventional ⓐ 전통적인

□ depression ⓝ 우울증

□ cause ⓥ 발생시키다

□ imbalance ⓝ 불균형

□ explanation ⓝ 설명

□ substance ⓝ 물질

□ consequence ⓝ 결과

□ decrease ⓝ 감소

□ root ⓝ 근본

□ distortion ⓝ 왜곡

□ revise ⓥ 수정하다

□ cause-and-effect ⓝ 인과 관계

□ reframe ⓥ 재구성하다

□ fundamental ⓐ 근본적인

□ entity ⓝ 실체

□ organ ⓝ (인체의) 기관[장기]

O 09

□ realize ⓥ 깨닫다

□ impossibility ⓝ 불가능

□ field ⓝ 경기장

□ competitive ⓐ 경쟁적인

□ structure ⓝ 구조

□ period ⓝ 기간

□ racket ⓝ 라켓

□ appropriate ⓐ 적절한

□ progressive ⓐ 점진적인

□ relate to ~와 관련되다

□ arena ⓝ 경기장

□ equipment ⓝ 장비

□ handle ⓥ 다루다

□ compete ⓥ 경쟁하다

□ common sense (일반인들의) 공통된 견해, 상식

□ adaptation ⓝ 조정

O 10

□ available ⓐ 구할 수 있는

□ empire ⓝ 제국

□ on foot 걸어서

□ near ⓥ 다가가다

□ relay ⓥ 이어가다

□ under good condition 좋은 상황에서, 사정이 좋으면

□ station ⓥ 배치하다

□ royal ⓐ 왕의, 왕실의

□ order ⓝ 명령

□ hut ⓝ 오두막

□ place ⓥ 배치하다

□ apart ⓐd 떨어져

□ along ⓟrep ~을 따라

□ especially ⓐd 특히

□ direction ⓝ 방향

□ catch sight of ~을 찾아내다

O

O 11

□ shift ⓥ 전환하다
□ archive ⓥ 보관하다
□ assume ⓥ 추정하다
□ store ⓥ 저장하다
□ carbon ⓝ 탄소
□ emission ⓝ 배출
□ footprint ⓝ 발자국
□ via ⓟⓡⓔⓟ ~을 통하여
□ attachment ⓝ 첨부
□ threaten ⓥ 위협하다
□ harm ⓝ 해
□ hazardous ⓐ 위험한
□ promising ⓐ 유망한
□ neglect ⓥ 소홀히 하다
□ declare ⓥ 선언하다
□ fossil fuel 화석 연료

O 12

□ discovery ⓝ 발견
□ profoundly ⓐⓓ 완전히
□ fundamental ⓐ 근본적인
□ capacity ⓝ 능력
□ observation ⓝ 관찰
□ newborn ⓝ 신생아
□ stick out ~을 내밀다
□ imitate ⓥ 모방하다
□ inborn ⓐ 선천적인
□ tendency ⓝ 성향
□ restrict ⓥ 제한하다
□ behavior ⓝ 행동
□ trial and error 시행착오

O 13

□ pathway ⓝ 경로
□ route ⓝ 경로
□ perceive ⓥ 인지하다
□ external ⓐ 외부의
□ travel ⓥ 이동하다
□ vibrate ⓥ 진동하다
□ internal ⓐ 내부의
□ conduct ⓥ 전하다
□ stimulate ⓥ 자극하다
□ emphasize ⓥ 강조하다
□ pronounced ⓐ 강조된
□ fairly ⓐⓓ 꽤

O 14

□ productivity ⓝ 생산성
□ output ⓝ 산출량
□ efficient ⓐ 효율적인
□ division ⓝ 분배
□ specialize in ~을 전문으로 하다
□ separate ⓐ 별개의
□ manufactured ⓐ 제작된
□ straighten ⓥ 펴다
□ polish ⓥ 다듬다

O 15

□ architectural ⓐ 건축학의
□ attitude ⓝ 사고방식
□ emerge ⓥ 나타나다
□ industrial ⓐ 산업의
□ argument ⓝ 주장
□ inhuman ⓐ 비인간적인

□ have to do with ~와 관련 있다
□ craftsman ⓝ 장인
□ rootedness ⓝ 뿌리박음
□ locality ⓝ 지역, 인근
□ approach ⓝ 접근
□ ordinary ⓐ 평범한
□ generation ⓝ 세대
□ demonstrate ⓥ 보여 주다
□ mastery ⓝ 숙달한 기술
□ simplicity ⓝ 단순함
□ plain ⓐ 평범한
□ whitewashed ⓐ 회반죽을 바른

O 16

□ beech tree 너도밤나무
□ vary ⓥ (상황에 따라) 달라지다
□ nutrient ⓝ 영양분
□ underground ⓐⓓ 지하에서
□ abundance ⓝ 풍부(함)
□ run short (~이) 부족하다
□ plenty of 풍부한, 많은
□ equalize ⓥ 균등하게 하다
□ transfer ⓥ 전달하다, 옮기다
□ accordingly ⓐⓓ 따라서, 그에 따라

O 17

□ livestock ⓝ 가축
□ priest ⓝ 성직자
□ religious ⓐ 종교적인
□ invent ⓥ 발명하다
□ device ⓝ 장치

□ gradually @ad 점점
□ settlement ⓝ 정착지
□ timetable ⓝ 시간표
□ aeroplane ⓝ 비행기

O 18
□ hexagon ⓝ 육각형
□ condition ⓝ 조건
□ twisted ⓐ 뒤틀린
□ atom ⓝ 원자
□ display ⓝ 배열
□ steady ⓐ 안정적인, 꾸준한
□ individual ⓐ 개별적인

O 19
□ string ⓝ 줄, 끈
□ vibration ⓝ 진동
□ pressure ⓝ 압력
□ eardrum ⓝ 고막
□ flex ⓥ 굽히다
□ blurred ⓐ 흐릿한
□ outline ⓝ 윤곽, 개요
□ hardly @ad 거의 ~ 않다
□ hollow ⓐ (속이) 빈
□ pass on ~을 전달하다
□ panel ⓝ 판

O 20
□ at risk 위험에 처한
□ advance ⓝ 발전, 진전
□ automation ⓝ 자동화
□ automate ⓥ 자동화하다
□ dependent ⓐ 의존하는

□ irreplaceable ⓐ 대체할 수 없는
□ crew ⓝ (한 팀으로 일하는) 직원
□ draw on ~을 이용하다

O 21
□ adolescent ⓐ 청소년기의
□ decision-making ⓝ 의사결정
□ circuit ⓝ 회로
□ process ⓥ 처리하다
□ put ~ at a disadvantage ~을 불리하게 만들다
□ on the other hand 반면에
□ mature ⓥ 성숙해지다 ⓐ 성숙한
□ influence ⓥ 영향을 미치다
□ factor ⓝ 요인
□ imbalance ⓝ 불균형
□ feeling-based ⓐ 감정에 기반한
□ rule ⓥ 지배하다
□ logical-based ⓐ 논리에 기반한
□ evaluate ⓥ 평가하다
□ initial ⓐ 초기의
□ modify ⓥ 수정하다

O 22
□ remarkable ⓐ 눈에 띄는, 두드러진
□ progress ⓝ 발전, 진전
□ facial ⓐ 얼굴의
□ recognition ⓝ 인식

□ identification ⓝ 식별
□ performance ⓝ 성능
□ limitation ⓝ 한계
□ relate to ~와 관련이 있다
□ counteract ⓥ 대응하다
□ compensate for ~을 보완하다
□ characteristic ⓝ 특징
□ instance ⓝ 사례, 예시
□ systematically @ad 체계적으로
□ enroll ⓥ 등록하다
□ factor ⓝ 요인
□ texture ⓝ 질감
□ particularly @ad 특히
□ appearance ⓝ 발현, 나타나는 것
□ wrinkle ⓝ 주름
□ highlight ⓥ 강조하다

O 23
□ natural ⓐ 자연의
□ mineral ⓝ 광물
□ melt ⓥ 녹이다, 녹다
□ material ⓝ 물질
□ surface ⓝ 표면
□ trap ⓥ 가두다
□ atom ⓝ 원자
□ crystal ⓝ 결정(체)
□ rapidly @ad 빨리
□ unaided ⓐ 도움 없는
□ arrange ⓥ 배열하다
□ orderly ⓐ 질서 있는
□ element ⓝ 원소

O

O 24

- legend ⓝ 전설
- bite ⓥ 물다
- seek ⓥ 갈구하다
- come up with ~을 제시하다[생각해내다]
- highly ⓐⓓ 매우
- creature ⓝ 존재
- exist ⓥ 존재하다
- original ⓐ 원래의
- take over ~을 정복하다
- existence ⓝ 존재
- and so on 등등
- myth ⓝ 사회적 통념, 미신
- suppose ⓥ 가정하다
- population ⓝ 인구

O 25

- turkey ⓝ 칠면조
- Thanksgiving ⓝ 추수감사절
- responsive ⓐ 호응하는
- alone ⓐⓓ 혼자서
- break ⓝ 휴식
- immediately ⓐⓓ 즉시
- attract ⓥ (마음을) 끌다
- rush ⓥ 서두르다, 급히 움직이다
- raise ⓥ 기르다

O 26

- band ⓝ 무리
- wander ⓥ 돌아다니다
- settle down 정착하다

- crop ⓝ 농작물
- toolmaker ⓝ 도구 제작자
- axe ⓝ 도끼
- community ⓝ 공동체
- organize ⓥ 조직하다
- efficiently ⓐⓓ 효율적으로
- divide ⓥ 나누다

O 27

- obviously ⓐⓓ 분명히
- local ⓐ 현지의
- citizen ⓝ 시민
- afford ⓥ (…을 살 · 할 · 금전적 · 시간적) 여유[형편]가 되다
- starve ⓥ 굶주리다
- far and away 단연, 훨씬
- poverty ⓝ 빈곤
- grand ⓐ 거대한
- trend ⓝ 추세
- lower ⓥ 낮추다

O 28

- alert ⓐ 기민한, 주의하는
- peak ⓐ 정점의
- muse ⓝ 영감
- awaken ⓥ 깨어나다
- mental ⓐ 정신의
- machinery ⓝ 기제, 시스템
- loose ⓥ 느슨하게 하다, 풀다
- attention ⓝ 집중, 주의력
- demand ⓥ 요구하다
- novel ⓐ 새로운
- tackle ⓥ (힘든 문제 · 상황과) 씨름하다

- early bird 일찍 일어나는 사람
- vice versa 반대로
- night owl 밤에 깨어 있는 사람
- organize ⓥ 계획하다
- divide ⓥ 분배하다

O 29

- literary ⓐ 문학의
- work ⓝ 작품
- imply ⓥ 암시하다
- state ⓥ 진술하다
- claim ⓝ 주장
- boldly ⓐⓓ 뚜렷하게
- directly ⓐⓓ 직접적으로
- figure out 이해하다
- implication ⓝ 함축
- analytical ⓐ 분석적인
- proportion ⓝ 비율
- interpret ⓥ 해석하다
- interpretation ⓝ 해석
- generalization ⓝ 일반화
- literature ⓝ 문학
- include ⓥ 포함하다
- statement ⓝ 진술
- contain ⓥ 포함하다
- suggestion ⓝ 암시

O 30

- moral ⓝ 도덕, 교훈
- performance ⓝ 연주
- necessarily ⓐⓓ 반드시
- accomplished ⓐ 숙달된
- tragic ⓐ 비극적인

□uplift ⓥ 향상시키다
□doubtful ⓐ 미덥지 못한
□character ⓝ 사람, 등장인물
□composer ⓝ 작곡가
□show off 뽐내다
□communicate ⓥ 전달하다
□honestly ⓐⓓ 정직하게

O31

□thrive ⓥ 성공하다
□navigate ⓥ 다루다, 길을 찾다
□value ⓥ 가치 있게 여기다
□count on ~을 기대하다
□mate ⓝ 짝
□crucially ⓐⓓ 결정적으로
□conscious ⓐ 의식적인
□cynical ⓐ 냉소적인
□persuasive ⓐ 설득력 있는
□merit ⓝ 이점
□physically ⓐⓓ 신체적으로
□genetically ⓐⓓ 유전적으로
□select for ~을 선택하다
□sensitive ⓐ 민감한
□skilled ⓐ 능숙한
□maximize ⓥ 최대화하다
□standing ⓝ 지위
□tendency ⓝ 경향
□unconsciously
　ⓐⓓ 무의식적으로
□perceive ⓥ 인식하다
□self-esteem ⓝ 자존감
□pride ⓝ 자존심

□shame ⓝ 수치심
□insecurity ⓝ 불안
□compel ⓥ 강요하다

O32

□roughly ⓐⓓ 대략
□give way to ~로 바뀌다
□electronic commerce
　전자 상거래
□shift ⓝ 이동, 변화
□perception ⓝ 인식
□expand ⓥ 확장하다
□category ⓝ 범주, 항목
□snowball ⓥ 눈덩이처럼
　불어나다
□enormous ⓐ 거대한
□obvious ⓐ 명백한
□physical ⓐ 물리적인
□virtual ⓐ 가상의
□variety ⓝ 다양성
□aggressive ⓐ 공격적인
□operating cost 운영비
□combination ⓝ 조합, 결합

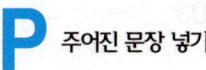

P 주어진 문장 넣기

P01

□argue ⓥ 주장하다
□morality ⓝ 도덕(성)
□amount ⓝ 양
□narrow ⓐ 좁은
□level ⓝ 수위, 높이
□volume ⓝ 부피
□self-constructed
　ⓐ 스스로 구성해 낸
□reach ⓥ ~에 이르다
□fairness ⓝ 공평함

P02

□integrate ⓥ 통합하다
□boundary ⓝ 경계(선)
□blur ⓥ 흐릿해지다
□portable ⓐ 휴대용의
□responsibility ⓝ 책임(감)
□separate ⓥ 분리하다
□segment ⓥ 분할하다
□minimize ⓥ 최소화하다
□conduct ⓥ 수행하다
□flexible ⓐ 유연한
□distinction ⓝ 구별, 차이
□constantly ⓐⓓ 거듭,
　지속적으로
□inbox ⓝ 받은 편지함

P 03

□ air-conditioning ⓝ 냉방 설비

□ accelerate ⓥ 가속화하다

□ box ⓝ 구조물

□ airflow ⓝ 공기 흐름

□ unit ⓝ 장치

□ architect ⓝ 건축가

□ breeze ⓝ 산들바람

□ comfort ⓝ 안락

P 04

□ obvious ⓐ 명확한

□ convenience ⓝ 편리함

□ surroundings ⓝ 주변

□ mark ⓥ 특징짓다

□ specific ⓐ 구체적인

□ emerge ⓥ 나타나다

□ passenger ⓝ 승객

□ behavior ⓝ 행동

□ examine ⓥ 조사하다

□ factor ⓝ 요인

□ shape ⓥ 형성하다

□ navigate ⓥ 탐색하다

□ findings ⓝ 연구 결과

□ involve ⓥ ~와 관련이 있다

□ abstract ⓐ 추상적인

□ sensation ⓝ 느낌

□ desire ⓝ 욕구

□ accidentally ⓐⓓ 우연히

□ influence ⓥ ~에 영향을 미치다

P 05

□ sink ⓥ 가라앉히다

□ marine ⓐ 해양의

□ mammal ⓝ 포유류

□ nerve ⓝ 신경

□ region ⓝ 부위, 지역

□ automatically ⓐⓓ 자동으로

□ airway ⓝ 기도

□ risk ⓝ 위험

□ swallow ⓥ 삼키다

□ narrow ⓥ 좁히다

□ passage ⓝ 통로

□ lung ⓝ 폐

□ heart rate 심박수

□ vital ⓐ 중요한

□ organ ⓝ 장기

□ brief ⓐ 짧은

□ below ⓟⓡⓔⓟ ~의 아래에

□ panic ⓥ 당황하다

□ drown ⓥ 익사하다

P 06

□ nonlinear ⓐ 비선형의

□ random ⓐ 임의의

□ scene ⓝ 장면

□ reverse ⓥ 되감다

□ highlight ⓝ 주요 특징

□ editor ⓝ 편집자

□ remove ⓥ 제거하다

□ adjust ⓥ 조정하다

□ automatically ⓐⓓ 자동적으로

□ compose ⓥ 작성하다, 구성하다

□ retype ⓥ 다시 타이핑하다

□ delete ⓥ 삭제하다

□ keystroke ⓝ 키 입력

P 07

□ prevent ⓥ 막다, 예방하다

□ harm ⓝ 해, 손해

□ morally ⓐⓓ 도덕적으로

□ significantly ⓐⓓ 상당히, 훨씬

□ judge ⓥ 판단하다

□ intention ⓝ 의도

□ motive ⓝ 동기

□ relevant ⓐ 관련된

□ intend ⓥ 의도하다

□ unintentionally ⓐⓓ 의도치 않게

□ occur ⓥ 발생하다

□ impression ⓝ 인상

□ actual ⓐ 실제의

□ consequence ⓝ 결과

□ count ⓥ 중요하다

□ contrary to ~와는 반대로

□ necessary ⓐ 필요한

□ regard ⓥ 여기다, 간주하다

P 08

□ evidence ⓝ 증거

□ firmly ⓐⓓ 확고하게

□ derive from ~로부터 도출하다

□ assumption ⓝ 가정

□ account ⓝ 설명

□ float ⓥ 떠돌다

□ plain ⓐ 순전한
□ silliness ⓝ 어리석음
□ branch ⓝ 분야
□ devote ⓥ 전념[헌신]하다
□ hearsay ⓝ 소문
□ fundamental ⓐ 근본적인
□ principle ⓝ 원리
□ generate ⓥ 만들어 내다
□ diversity ⓝ 다양성

P 09

□ demonstrate ⓥ 보여주다
□ explanation ⓝ 설명
□ map ⓥ (지도에) 구획하다
□ separate ⓐ 개별적인, 별개의
□ register ⓥ 등록하다
□ tip ⓝ 끝
□ sourness ⓝ 신맛
□ bitterness ⓝ 쓴맛
□ misinterpretation ⓝ 오해
□ mistranslation ⓝ 오역
□ conduct ⓥ 수행하다
□ turn ⓝ 전환기
□ leading ⓐ 선도적인
□ specialty ⓝ 특화된 분야
□ perceive ⓥ 지각하다
□ intensity ⓝ 강도
□ mechanism ⓝ 기제
□ at work 작동 중인

P 10

□ factor ⓝ 요인
□ determine ⓥ 결정하다
□ respond ⓥ 반응하다

□ treatment ⓝ 치료
□ alike ⓐ 비슷한, 같은
□ display ⓥ 보이다
□ feature ⓝ 특징
□ therefore ⓐⓓ 그런 까닭에
□ entirely ⓐⓓ 완전히
□ healing session 치료 활동
□ rescue center 구조 센터
□ domestic ⓐ 가정의
□ illness ⓝ 질병
□ react ⓥ 반응하다
□ confusion ⓝ 동요, 혼란
□ with ~ in mind ~을 염두에 두고
□ explore ⓥ 탐구하다
□ specific ⓐ 특정한, 구체적인
□ constant ⓐ 끊임없는
□ process ⓝ 과정

P 11

□ transport ⓥ 이동시키다
□ distance ⓝ 거리
□ crop ⓝ 농작물
□ typically ⓐⓓ 보통, 일반적으로
□ frequently ⓐⓓ 자주, 빈번하게
□ possession ⓝ 소유
□ space ⓥ 간격을 두다
□ birth ⓝ 출산
□ settle down 정착하다
□ shorten ⓥ 단축하다
□ interval ⓝ 간격
□ rapid ⓐ 빠른
□ labor ⓝ 노동력

P 12

□ trait ⓝ 형질
□ descend ⓥ 내려오다
□ ancestor ⓝ 조상
□ hence ⓐⓓ 이런 이유로
□ structure ⓝ 구조
□ indicate ⓥ 나타내다
□ organ ⓝ 기관
□ distinguish ⓥ 구별하다
□ similarity ⓝ 유사성
□ arise ⓥ 생겨나다
□ independently ⓐⓓ ~와 관계없이
□ modification ⓝ 수정
□ forelimb ⓝ 앞다리
□ mammal ⓝ 포유류
□ nonfunctional ⓐ 비기능적
□ architecture ⓝ 구성
□ property ⓝ 특성

P 13

□ marine ⓐ 해양의
□ self-evident ⓐ 자명한
□ abundance ⓝ 풍부함
□ breathe ⓥ 호흡하다
□ established ⓐ 확립된
□ polar ⓐ 극지의
□ tropical ⓐ 열대의
□ worrisome ⓐ 걱정스러운
□ potentially ⓐⓓ 잠재적으로
□ disastrous ⓐ 처참한
□ consequence ⓝ 결과
□ analyze ⓥ 분석하다
□ potential ⓝ 잠재력

P

□ organism ⓝ 생물(체)
□ displace ⓥ 쫓아내다

P 14
□ interact ⓥ 소통하다
□ commonly ⓐⓓ 흔히
□ assumption ⓝ 가정
□ automatically ⓐⓓ 자동적으로
□ description ⓝ 설명, 묘사
□ contain ⓥ 포함하다
□ discussion ⓝ 토론
□ impression ⓝ 인상
□ expectation ⓝ 기대
□ behaviour ⓝ 행동

P 15
□ stare ⓥ 쳐다보다, 응시하다
□ pace ⓝ 속도
□ reflect ⓥ 비추다
□ proof ⓝ 증거
□ interval ⓝ 간격
□ recognize ⓥ 알아보다

P 16
□ deal ⓝ 거래
□ reward ⓥ 보상하다
□ material ⓐ 물질적인
□ recognize ⓥ 인정하다
□ interrupt ⓥ 방해하다
□ unbelievably ⓐⓓ 믿을 수 없이
□ amazingly ⓐⓓ 놀랄 만큼

P 17
□ alertness ⓝ 깨어 있음
□ mental ⓐ 정신의
□ consistently ⓐⓓ 일관적으로
□ effective ⓐ 효과적인
□ pain reliever 진통제
□ correlation ⓝ 상관관계
□ intake ⓝ 섭취
□ establish ⓥ 확립하다
□ adequate ⓐ 적절한

P 18
□ rub ⓥ 비비다
□ friction ⓝ 마찰력
□ force ⓝ 힘
□ surface ⓝ 표면
□ slide ⓥ 미끄러지다
□ work ⓥ 작용하다
□ direction ⓝ 방향
□ opposite ⓐ 반대편의
□ object ⓝ 물체
□ amount ⓝ 양
□ depend on ~에 달려 있다[의존하다]
□ material ⓝ 물질
□ rough ⓐ 거친
□ produce ⓥ 발생시키다
□ slip ⓥ 미끄러지다
□ grip ⓥ 붙잡다

P 19
□ represent ⓥ 구현하다, 나타내다
□ sight ⓝ 시각, 시력

□ visual ⓐ 시각의
□ sense ⓝ 감각
□ entirely ⓐⓓ 전적으로
□ birth ⓝ 탄생, 출생
□ ability ⓝ 능력
□ memory ⓝ 기억
□ vivid ⓐ 생생한
□ imaginative ⓐ 상상력이 풍부한
□ normal ⓐ 정상적인
□ construct ⓥ 구성하다
□ overall ⓐ 전반적인

P 20
□ produce ⓥ 만들어 내다
□ sustainable ⓐ 지속적인
□ contribution ⓝ 기여
□ well-being ⓝ 행복
□ consume ⓥ 소비하다
□ tune out ~을 무시하다, 관심을 끄다
□ evidence ⓝ 증거
□ motivate ⓥ 동기를 부여하다
□ tune in to (TV 프로그램 등을) 보다, 시청하다
□ connection ⓝ 관계
□ satisfy ⓥ 만족시키다
□ extent ⓝ 정도

P 21
□ absorb ⓥ 흡수하다
□ possibility ⓝ 가능성
□ decline ⓝ 감소
□ trace ⓥ (원인을) 추적하다

□infant ⓐ 유아의
□neural ⓐ 신경의
□wiring ⓝ 연결, 배선
□mess ⓝ 엉망
□efficient ⓐ 효율적인
□perception ⓝ 인식
□consequently ⓐⓓ 결과적으로
□intensely ⓐⓓ 매우
□wildly ⓐⓓ 상당히, 극도로
□disordered ⓐ 무질서한

P 22

□assume ⓥ 가정하다
□complementary ⓐ (상호) 보완적인
□lock ⓥ 고정하다, 잠그다
□alongside ⓟⓡⓔⓟ ~와 함께
□pillow ⓝ 베개
□journey ⓝ 여행
□popularity ⓝ 인기
□complement ⓥ 보완하다
□ensure ⓥ 보장하다
□steady ⓐ 꾸준한
□stream ⓝ 흐름, 연속
□status ⓝ 상태
□motorist ⓝ 운전자
□gasoline ⓝ 휘발유

P 23

□substance ⓝ 물질
□ingredient ⓝ 재료, 성분
□label ⓝ 표시, 라벨
□nutrition ⓝ 영양
□absorb ⓥ 흡수하다

□whole food 자연식품
□pill ⓝ 알약
□powder ⓝ 분말
□obtain ⓥ 획득하다
□artificial ⓐ 인공적인
□completely ⓐⓓ 완전히
□recent ⓐ 최근의
□investigative ⓐ 조사의, 연구의
□heavy metal 중금속
□protein ⓝ 단백질
□regulation ⓝ 규제
□gamble ⓝ 도박
□costly ⓐ 대가가 큰

P 24

□complex ⓐ 복합의
□compound ⓝ 화합물
□nutrient ⓝ 영양소
□chain ⓝ 사슬
□release ⓥ 방출하다
□provide ⓥ 제공하다
□fuel ⓝ 연료
□structure ⓝ 구조

P 25

□approach ⓥ 다가가다, 접근하다
□compress ⓥ 압축하다
□wave ⓝ 파장
□pond ⓝ 연못
□disturbance ⓝ 방해, 교란
□bang ⓥ 쾅 하고 치다
□release ⓥ 방출하다
□experiment ⓝ 실험
□density ⓝ 밀도

□displace ⓥ 바꾸다
□atmosphere ⓝ 대기

P 26

□magically ⓐⓓ 마법처럼
□remove ⓥ 제거하다, 없애다
□essentially ⓐⓓ 본질적으로
□completely ⓐⓓ 완전히
□chemical ⓐ 화학적인
□makeup ⓝ 성질, 구성
□contain ⓥ ~이 들어 있다
□temperature ⓝ 온도
□separate ⓐ 분리된, 따로 떨어진
□float ⓥ (물이나 공기 위에) 떠 있다
□differ ⓥ 다르다
□salt content 염분

P 27

□brief ⓐ 짧은
□swing ⓥ 흔들리다
□form ⓝ 형태
□kinetic energy 운동 에너지
□associated with ~과 관련된
□potential energy 위치 에너지
□represent ⓥ 나타내다
□conserve ⓥ 보존하다
□back and forth 앞뒤로
□sweep out 쓸어내다
□constantly ⓐⓓ 끊임없이

P 28

□effect ⓝ 영향
□sudden ⓐ 갑작스러운

P

□ dramatic ⓐ 극적인
□ ecosystem ⓝ 생태계
□ wildlife ⓝ 야생 생물
□ opportunity ⓝ 기회
□ obtain ⓥ 얻다
□ shelter ⓝ 서식지
□ react ⓥ 작용하다
□ respond ⓥ 반응하다
□ entire ⓐ 전체의
□ prey (up)on 먹이로 삼다
□ drought ⓝ 가뭄
□ rely on ~ ~에 의존하다
□ at the death 종말에 처한

P 29
□ observe ⓥ 관찰하다
□ transfer ⓝ 이동 ⓥ 이동하다
□ proportion ⓝ 비율, 부분
□ food chain 먹이 사슬
□ a series of 일련의
□ organism ⓝ 유기체
□ in turn 차례로, 결국
□ imply ⓥ 의미하다
□ sequence ⓝ 연쇄, 사슬
□ consumer ⓝ 소비자
□ restrict ⓥ 제한하다
□ intake ⓝ 섭취량

P 30
□ leave A to one side A를 보류하다
□ contribution ⓝ 기여
□ strategy ⓝ 전략

□ be at risk 위험에 처하다
□ disaster ⓝ 재앙
□ decline ⓝ 감소
□ diversity ⓝ 다양성
□ entirely ⓐⓓ 전적으로
□ process ⓝ 과정
□ extreme ⓐ 극심한
□ hunger ⓝ 배고픔
□ grain ⓝ 곡물
□ enormous ⓐ 거대한
□ scale ⓝ 규모
□ traditional ⓐ 전통적인
□ variety ⓝ 품종
□ super-productive ⓐ 초생산적인
□ spectacularly ⓐⓓ 극적으로, 굉장히
□ specifically ⓐⓓ 특히
□ depend on ~ ~에 의존하다
□ climate extreme 기후 위기

P 31
□ alter ⓥ 바꾸다
□ modernize ⓥ 현대화하다
□ conform to ~ ~에 순응하다
□ interestingly ⓐⓓ 흥미롭게도
□ decline ⓥ 쇠퇴하다
□ rule ⓥ 지배하다
□ contrast ⓝ 대조
□ feature ⓥ ~을 특징으로 하다
□ athletic ⓐ 운동의
□ opposing team 상대 팀
□ tradition ⓝ 전통
□ adjust ⓥ 조정하다

□ keep up with ~에 따르다
□ abandon ⓥ 버리다
□ neglect ⓥ 무시하다
□ root ⓝ 뿌리, 기원
□ effect ⓝ 영향

P 32
□ enormously ⓐⓓ 엄청나게, 대단히
□ contribute ⓥ 기여하다
□ cooperate ⓥ 협력하다
□ deal with ~을 다루다
□ analytic philosophy 분석 철학
□ assume ⓥ 가정하다
□ cognitive science 인지 과학
□ rightly ⓐⓓ 당연히
□ fundamental ⓐ 근본적인, 기본적인
□ countless ⓐ 셀 수 없이 많은
□ navigate ⓥ 항해하다, 길을 찾다
□ preserve ⓥ 보존하다
□ operation ⓝ 작용, 작동
□ astonishingly ⓐⓓ 놀라운 정도로
□ contributor ⓝ 기여 요소, 원인 제공자
□ collaborative ⓐ 협력적인, 공동의
□ collective ⓐ 협력적인

P 33
□ reliable ⓐ 신뢰할 수 있는
□ reproducible ⓐ 재현 가능한

□transfer ⓥ 전달하다 ⓝ 전도
□qualitative ⓐ 정성적인
□indication ⓝ 지표
□unreliable ⓐ 신뢰할 수 없는
□mislead ⓥ 잘못 인도하다
□bare feet 맨발
□rate ⓝ 비율
□a variety of 다양한
□quantitative ⓐ 정량적인
□measurement ⓝ 측정

P34

□stable ⓐ 안정적인
□collective ⓐ 집합적인
□emerge ⓥ 나타나다
□dimensional ⓐ 차원적인
□cell ⓝ 세포
□molecule ⓝ 분자
□enormous ⓐ 거대한
□tissue ⓝ (근육) 조직
□drastic ⓐ 극적인
□outcome ⓝ 결과
□organism ⓝ 유기체
□switch ⓥ 바꾸다
□well-defined ⓐ 명확히 정의된
□state ⓝ 상태
□rough ⓐ 울퉁불퉁한
□landscape ⓝ 경관
□illness ⓝ 질병
□manifestation ⓝ 발현
□symptomatic ⓐ 증상적인
□strikingly ⓐⓓ 놀랍게도

P35

□civilization ⓝ 문명
□ancestor ⓝ 선조
□myth ⓝ 신화
□legendary ⓐ 전설의
□inspire ⓥ 영감을 주다
□wonder ⓥ 궁금해하다
□element ⓝ 요소
□narrative ⓝ 이야기
□identity ⓝ 정체성
□practical ⓐ 실용적인
□keep track of ~을 기록하다
□aid ⓝ 보조 도구
□seasonal ⓐ 계절에 따른
□gathering ⓝ 수확
□navigation ⓝ 항해
□vital ⓐ 필수적인
□explore ⓥ 탐험하다
□remote ⓐ 외딴
□observe ⓥ 관찰하다
□purpose ⓝ 목적

P36

□migrate ⓥ 이동하다
□route ⓝ 경로
□adapt ⓥ 적응하다
□breeding ⓝ 번식
□farther ⓐⓓ 더 멀리
□facilitate ⓥ 촉진하다
□passing on 전달, 대물림
□evolve ⓥ 진화하다
□gene ⓝ 유전자
□flexibility ⓝ 유연성

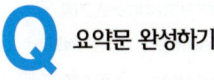

Q 요약문 완성하기

Q01

□conscious ⓐ 의식적인
□subconscious ⓐ 잠재의식적인
□recognition ⓝ 인식
□frequently ⓐⓓ 자주, 빈번히
□judgment ⓝ 판단(력)
□cloud ⓥ (기억력, 판단력 등을) 흐리게 하다
□bias ⓝ 편견
□negativity ⓝ 부정성
□fear ⓝ 두려움
□originate ⓥ 비롯되다
□controllable ⓐ 통제할 수 있는
□overcome ⓥ 극복하다

Q02

□scholar ⓝ 학자
□organize ⓥ 정리하다
□present ⓥ 제시하다
□preserve ⓥ 보존하다
□neglect ⓥ 소홀히 하다
□disability ⓝ 장애
□distinguish ⓥ 구별하다
□embrace ⓥ 포용하다
□ensure ⓥ 반드시 ~ 하게 하다

Q03

□invention ⓝ 발명품
□encounter ⓥ 맞닥뜨리다, 직면하다

□ resistance ⓝ 저항
□ logically ⓐⓓ 논리적으로
□ reasoning ⓝ 추론
□ viewpoint ⓝ 관점
□ by definition 정의상
□ application ⓝ 적용
□ conception ⓝ 구상
□ effective ⓐ 효과적인
□ nonlinear ⓐ 비선형적
□ manner ⓝ 방식
□ state ⓥ 말하다
□ innovative ⓐ 혁신적인
□ flexible ⓐ 유연한
□ instant ⓐ 즉각적인
□ proven ⓐ 증명된
□ superior ⓐ 우월한
□ collaborative ⓐ 협력하는

Q 04

□ assumption ⓝ 가정
□ bias ⓝ 편향
□ in other words 다시 말해
□ automatic ⓐ 자동적인
□ work out 잘 작동하다, 잘 풀리다
□ assume ⓥ 가정하다
□ response ⓝ 응답
□ converse with ~와 대화하다
□ indeed ⓐⓓ 정말로
□ statement ⓝ 진술
□ additional ⓐ 추가적인
□ cognitive ⓐ 인지적인
□ miser ⓝ 구두쇠
□ typically ⓐⓓ 전형적으로, 일반적으로

□ effort ⓝ 노력
□ make sense 일리가 있다
□ fake ⓐ 가짜의
□ at least 적어도
□ due to ~ 때문에
□ tendency ⓝ 경향

Q 05

□ preconception ⓝ 선입견
□ establish ⓥ 확립하다
□ unconscious ⓐ 무의식적인
□ hierarchy ⓝ 위계
□ reflect ⓥ 반영하다
□ functional ⓐ 기능적인
□ momentary ⓐ 순간적인
□ priority ⓝ 우선순위
□ visualize ⓥ 마음속에 그리다
□ tend to-v ~하는 경향이 있다
□ profile ⓝ 옆모습
□ interfere with ~을 방해하다
□ document ⓥ 기록하다
□ impartially ⓐⓓ 공정하게
□ interpret ⓥ 해석하다
□ mechanical ⓐ 기계적인
□ indifference ⓝ 무관심
□ unrecognizable ⓐ 알아볼 수 없는
□ perspective ⓝ 관점
□ enhance ⓥ 향상시키다
□ neutral ⓐ 중립적인

Q 06

□ punish ⓥ 벌주다, 처벌하다
□ trick ⓝ 트릭, 속임수

□ scolding ⓝ 꾸짖음
□ discourage ⓥ 단념[좌절]시키다
□ invisible ⓐ 눈에 띄지 않는
□ adopt ⓥ 채택하다
□ strategy ⓝ 전략
□ congratulate ⓥ 자랑스러워하다
□ constantly ⓐⓓ 계속, 지속적으로
□ point out 지적하다
□ reward ⓥ 보상하다
□ unwanted ⓐ 바람직하지 못한, 원치 않는
□ imply ⓥ 시사하다
□ reinforce ⓥ 강화하다
□ maximize ⓥ 최대화하다
□ lower ⓥ 낮추다

Q 07

□ captivity ⓝ 감금
□ trade ⓥ 거래하다
□ cucumber ⓝ 오이
□ universally ⓐⓓ 일반적으로
□ experimenter ⓝ 실험자
□ source ⓥ 모으다
□ comparison ⓝ 비교
□ abandon ⓥ 포기하다
□ communicate ⓥ 전달하다
□ displeasure ⓝ 불쾌함

Q 08

□ evolution ⓝ 진화
□ draw ⓥ 이끌어내다

□noticeable ⓐ 주목할 만한

□connection ⓝ 접점, 연결

□gene ⓝ 유전자

□concept ⓝ 개념

□theoretical population genetics 이론 집단 유전학

□apply ⓥ 적용하다

□transmission ⓝ 전파

□innovation ⓝ 혁신

□selection ⓝ 선택

□conceptually ⓐⅾ 개념적으로

□liken to ~와 유사하다

□mutation ⓝ 돌연변이

□modify ⓥ 수정하다

□account for ~을 설명하다

□strictly ⓐⅾ 엄격하게

□trait ⓝ 특성

□acquire ⓥ 습득하다

□further ⓐⅾ 더욱이

□nonparental ⓐ 부모가 아닌

□peer ⓝ 동료

□frequency ⓝ 빈도

□probability ⓝ 개연성, 확률

□revise ⓥ 수정하다, 개정하다

□credible ⓐ 믿을 만한

Q 09

□colleague ⓝ 동료

□tendency ⓝ 경향

□identify ⓥ 동일시하다

□in-group ⓝ 내(內)집단

□infancy ⓝ 유아기

□innate ⓐ 타고난

□psychology ⓝ 심리학

□measure ⓝ 척도, 기준

□interest ⓝ 관심

□apparently ⓐⅾ 명백하게

□stare ⓥ 응시하다

□infant ⓝ 유아

□routinely ⓐⅾ 일상적으로

□cite ⓥ 인용하다

□evolutionary ⓐ 진화의

□preference ⓝ 선호

□favorable ⓐ 호의적인

Q 10

□association ⓝ 연관, 관련

□minor key 단조

□note ⓝ 음, 음색

□funeral ⓝ 장례식

□interpret ⓥ 이해하다, 통역하다

□unfamiliar ⓐ 친숙하지 않은

□be opposed to ~에 반대하다

□resemblance ⓝ 유사, 유사성

□low-pitched ⓐ 낮은 음의

Q 11

□adolescent ⓝ 청소년

□factor ⓝ 요인

□academic ⓐ 학문적인

□challenge ⓝ 어려움

□face ⓥ 직면하다

□exposed to ~에 노출된

□authoritative ⓐ 권위적인

□passive ⓐ 수동적인

□helpless ⓐ 무기력한

□indicate ⓥ 밝히다, 나타내다

□effort ⓝ 노력

□involve ⓥ 관여시키다

□significantly ⓐⅾ 크게, 의미가 있게

□attend ⓥ 참여하다

□select ⓥ 선택하다

□be aware of ~을 인지하다

□perform ⓥ 수행하다

□praise ⓥ 칭찬하다

□involvement ⓝ 관여

Q 12

□pair ⓝ 짝

□stranger ⓝ 모르는 사람, 낯선 사람

□chat ⓥ 이야기하다

□place ⓥ 놓다, 두다

□nearby ⓐ 근처의

□present ⓐ 있는, 존재하는

□conversation ⓝ 대화

□participant ⓝ 참가자

□report ⓥ 말하다, 전하다

□quality ⓝ 질

□relationship ⓝ 관계

□connection ⓝ 관계, 연결

Q 13

□reflective ⓐ 성찰적인

□journaling ⓝ 일기 쓰기

□think back on ~을 돌이켜 보다

□undergraduate ⓝ (대학) 학부생

□value ⓝ 가치
□handle ⓥ 다루다
□reflect ⓥ 성찰하다, 숙고하다
□support ⓥ 뒷받침하다
□perspective ⓝ 관점
□demonstration ⓝ 입증, (분명히) 보여줌
□reframe ⓥ 재구성하다
□worthwhile ⓐ 가치 있는

Q 14

□judgment ⓝ 판단
□expectation ⓝ 예상, 기대
□surgeon ⓝ 외과 의사
□scrub ⓝ 수술복
□notable ⓐ 눈에 띄는
□exception ⓝ 예외
□explore ⓥ 탐구하다
□norm ⓝ 규범, 기준
□affair ⓝ (공식적인) 일
□competence ⓝ 능숙함, 능력
□deviation ⓝ 일탈

Q 15

□spoiled ⓐ 상한
□stew ⓝ 스튜(고기와 채소를 넣고 천천히 끓인 요리)
□poison ⓝ 독
□label ⓥ 분류하다
□combination ⓝ 조합
□boiled ⓐ 끓인, 삶은
□tofu ⓝ 두부
□nutrient ⓝ 영양소

□occasionally ⓐⓓ 가끔
□otherwise ⓐⓓ 그렇지 않으면
□load ⓥ 채우다, 싣다
□supersized ⓐ 초대형의
□soft drink (청량) 음료
□appropriate ⓐ 적절한

Q 16

□notice ⓥ 알아채다
□athlete ⓝ (운동) 선수
□happen ⓥ 일어나다
□drop ⓥ 떨어뜨리다
□recreate ⓥ 재현하다
□surprisingly ⓐⓓ 놀랍게도
□perform ⓥ 수행하다
□thought ⓝ 생각
□ineffective ⓐ 유능하지 않은
□successful ⓐ 성공적인

Q 17

□evolutionary ⓐ 진화적인
□cooperation ⓝ 협동, 협력
□means ⓝ 수단
□eye contact 시선의 마주침
□force ⓝ 힘
□traffic ⓝ (차량) 운행, 교통
□arguably ⓐⓓ 주장하건대
□noncooperative ⓐ 비협조적인

Q 18

□attend ⓥ 다니다, 참석하다
□toilet paper 화장실 휴지

□classic ⓐ 전형적인
□tragedy ⓝ 비극
□common ⓝ 공유지
□share ⓝ 몫
□remove ⓥ 없애다
□satisfaction ⓝ 만족
□reappear ⓥ 다시 나타나다
□note-free ⓐ 쪽지가 없는
□following ⓐ (시간상으로) 그다음의
□behavior ⓝ 행동

Q 19

□risky ⓐ 위험한
□trustworthy ⓐ 신뢰할 수 있는
□evidence ⓝ 증거
□evolutionary ⓐ 진화의
□prospect ⓝ 전망
□sensible ⓐ 분별 있는
□psychologist ⓝ 심리학자
□cue ⓝ 신호
□signal ⓥ 나타내다
□local ⓐ 지역의, 현지의
□tasty ⓐ 맛있는
□adopt ⓥ 따르다, 채택하다
□practice ⓝ 행동, 관행
□uncertain ⓐ 불확실한
□unrealistic ⓐ 비현실적인

Q 20

□conduct ⓥ 진행하다
□assign ⓥ 부여하다
□interact ⓥ 상호작용하다
□discussion ⓝ 토론

□ agreement ⓝ 합의
□ noticeable ⓐ 눈에 띄는
□ difference ⓝ 차이
□ thirst ⓝ 열망
□ knowledge ⓝ 지식
□ slide ⓝ 미끄럼틀

Q 21

□ experiment ⓝ 실험
□ convince ⓥ 납득시키다
□ resistant ⓐ 저항하는
□ alumni ⓝ 졸업생
□ donation ⓝ 기부
□ emphasize ⓥ 강조하다
□ faculty ⓝ (특정 대학의) 모든
   교수들, 교직원
□ donor ⓝ 기부자
□ glow ⓝ (기쁨·만족감을 동반한
   은근한) 감정
□ unwilling ⓐ 꺼리는, 내키지 않는
□ combine ⓥ 결합하다
□ trigger ⓥ 유발하다
□ awareness ⓝ 인식
□ persuade ⓥ 설득하다
□ shield ⓥ 보호하다
□ simultaneously ⓐ 동시에
□ intention ⓝ 의도

Q 22

□ layer ⓝ 층
□ soil ⓝ 토양
□ root ⓝ 뿌리
□ concentration ⓝ 농도
□ damaging ⓐ 해로운

□ evolve ⓥ 발달시키다
□ redistribute ⓥ 재분배하다
□ shallow ⓐ 얕은
□ absorb ⓥ 흡수하다
□ decay ⓥ 부패하다
□ poison ⓥ (독성 물질로)
   오염시키다, 중독시키다
□ immune ⓐ 면역이 있는
□ toxic ⓐ 유독한
□ essentially ⓐ 본질적으로
□ eliminate ⓥ 제거하다
□ competition ⓝ 경쟁자
□ surrounding ⓐ 주변의
□ deadly ⓐ 치명적인
□ nutritious ⓐ 영양이 풍부한

Q 23

□ uncertainty ⓝ 불확실성
□ realm ⓝ 영역, 영토
□ general public 일반 대중
□ certainty ⓝ 확실성
□ unequipped ⓐ 준비가 안 된
□ demand ⓝ 요구
□ complex ⓐ 복잡한
□ black-or-white 흑백
   양자택일의
□ oversimplify ⓥ 지나치게
   단순화하다
□ present ⓥ 제시하다
□ opposed to ~과 반대로
□ accurate ⓐ 정확한
□ definitive ⓐ 확정적인
□ quality ⓝ 질
□ exist ⓥ 존재하다

R 장문의 이해

R 01~02

□ plastic ⓝ 신용카드
□ fundamentally
   ⓐⓓ 근본적으로
□ alter ⓥ 바꾸다
□ financial ⓐ 재정적인
□ involve ⓥ 수반하다
□ loss ⓝ 손실
□ literally ⓐⓓ 말 그대로
□ abstract ⓐ 추상적인
□ downside ⓝ 부정적인 면
□ insula ⓝ 뇌섬엽
□ region ⓝ 영역
□ associated with ~와
   관련된
□ sealed-bid 봉인 입찰
□ auction ⓝ 경매
□ inform ⓥ 알리다
□ average ⓥ 평균을 내다
□ expense ⓝ 지출

R 03~04

□ represent ⓥ 나타내다,
   표현하다
□ accuracy ⓝ 정확성
□ census taking 인구 조사
□ income distribution 소득
   분포
□ in effect 사실상
□ test anxiety 시험 불안

R

□put aside 제쳐 두다

□way ⓝ 방식, 측면

□morally ⓐⓓ 도덕적으로

□homelessness ⓝ 노숙자 문제

□spread ⓝ 확산

□suffering ⓝ 고통

□disturb ⓥ 동요시키다

□wipe off 닦아 내다

□quantify ⓥ 수량화하다

□uncovered ⓐ 드러난, 밝혀진

□framework ⓝ 체계

□convey ⓥ 전달하다

R 05~06

□retail ⓝ 소매

□utter ⓥ (말을) 하다

□encourage ⓥ 장려하다

□defensive ⓐ 방어적인

□stop cold 갑자기 멈추다

□transaction ⓝ 거래

□approach ⓥ 접근하다

□rote ⓐ 기계적인

□overused ⓐ 남용되는

□immediate ⓐ 즉각적인

□assistance ⓝ 도움, 지원

□subconscious ⓐ 잠재의식의

□figure out 알아내다

□promote ⓥ 촉진하다, 조성하다

□furthermore ⓐⓓ 게다가

□accessible ⓐ 접근 가능한

R 07~08

□assign ⓥ 부여하다

□prefer ⓥ 선호하다

□reasoning ⓝ 논리, 추론

□assume ⓥ 가정하다

□pointy ⓐ 뾰족한

□encounter ⓥ 마주치다

□determine ⓥ 결정하다

□inanimate ⓐ 무생물의

□evaluate ⓥ 평가하다

□physics ⓝ 물리

□attribute ~ to … ~을 …의 것으로 보다

□likely ⓐ ~할 것 같은

□hunter-gatherer ⓝ 수렵 채집인

□predator ⓝ 포식자

□anthropologist ⓝ 인류학자

□evolutionary ⓐ 진화상의

□agent ⓝ 행위자

□perceptual ⓐ 지각의

□resistant ⓐ 저항하는

□claw ⓝ 발톱

□intent ⓝ 의도

R 09~10

□norm ⓝ 규범

□define ⓥ 규정하다

□interpretation ⓝ 해석

□point out ~을 짚어 주다

□give directions 길을 알려주다

□force ⓥ 강요하다

□marked ⓐ 눈에 띄는

□expect ⓥ 기대하다

□responsible ⓐ 책임이 있는

□worthy of ~을 받을 만한

□criticism ⓝ 비난

□central ⓐ 중심적인

□cross-cultural ⓐ 문화 간의

□translatable ⓐ 번역할 수 있는

□usage ⓝ 사용

□cost ⓝ 대가, 비용

□considerable ⓐ 상당한

□ridiculous ⓐ 우스꽝스러운

□i.e.(id est) 즉

□unexpected ⓐ 예상치 못한

□minor ⓐ 사소한

R 11~12

□seek ⓥ 찾다

□pleasure ⓝ 쾌락

□perceive ⓥ 인식하다

□stimulus ⓝ 자극

□ultimately ⓐⓓ 궁극적으로

□violate ⓥ 침해하다

□norm ⓝ 표준

□suffering ⓝ 고통

□punishment ⓝ 처벌

□mastery ⓝ 숙달

□remarkable ⓐ 놀라운

□stimulate ⓥ 자극시키다

□receptor ⓝ 수용체

□activate ⓥ 활성화시키다

□tissue ⓝ (세포) 조직

□fire off 발사하다

□derive ⓥ 끌어내다

□ exposure ⓝ 노출
□ preference ⓝ 선호

R 13~14

□ participation ⓝ 참여
□ decade ⓝ 10년
□ typically ㉿ 일반적으로
□ dramatic ⓐ 극적인
□ expansion ⓝ 확대
□ range ⓝ 범주
□ institution ⓝ 기관
□ specialised ⓐ 전문화된
□ workforce ⓝ 노동력
□ diminish ⓥ 줄어들다
□ initiate ⓥ 시작하다
□ approach ⓝ 접근법
□ development ⓝ 발달
□ socio-political ⓐ 사회
　정치적인
□ contradiction ⓝ 모순
□ assessment ⓝ 평가
□ minimalist ⓐ 최소한의
□ impersonal ⓐ 비개인적인
□ standardised ⓐ 표준화된
□ relatively ㉿ 비교적으로
□ character ⓝ 성격
□ class ⓝ 계급
□ status ⓝ 지위

R 15~16

□ minimal ⓐ 최소한의
□ structure ⓝ 구조
□ chief ⓝ 우두머리, 족장
□ elder ⓝ 원로, 어른

□ surplus ⓝ 잉여, 흑자
□ vital ⓐ 필수적인
□ sufficient ⓐ 충분한
□ council ⓝ 의회
□ agriculture ⓝ 농업
□ grain ⓝ 곡물
□ priest ⓝ 성직자, 사제
□ warrior ⓝ 전사
□ favorable ⓐ 유리한
□ consistent ⓐ 지속적인
□ necessity ⓝ 필수품
□ concentrate ⓥ 집중하다
□ efficient ⓐ 효율적인
□ standard ⓝ 기준, 수준
□ stability ⓝ 안정성
□ shadow ⓝ 그림자
□ repetition ⓝ 반복

R 17~18

□ master ⓝ 달인
□ reproduce ⓥ 재현하다
□ randomly ㉿ 무작위로
□ expert ⓝ 전문가
□ advantage ⓝ 유리함
□ familiar ⓐ 익숙한
□ previously ㉿ 이전에
□ face ⓥ 직면하다
□ domain ⓝ 분야
□ beneficial ⓐ 유익한
□ structure ⓝ 구조
□ observe ⓥ 관찰하다
□ accurately ㉿ 정확하게
□ note ⓝ 음표
□ order ⓥ 배열하다

□ guarantee ⓥ 보장하다
□ experienced ⓐ 숙련된
□ range ⓝ 범위
□ recognize ⓥ 인식하다

R 19~20

□ genetic ⓐ 유전적인
□ diagnosis ⓝ 진단
□ determinism ⓝ 결정론
□ gene ⓝ 유전자
□ subsequent ⓐ 차후의
□ destined to ~할 운명이다
□ inherit ⓥ 물려받다
□ misfortune ⓝ 불행
□ dynamic ⓝ 역학 (관계)
□ wellness ⓝ 건강
□ predetermine ⓥ 미리
　결정하다
□ racially ㉿ 인종적으로
□ simplistic ⓐ 단순한
□ coding ⓝ 암호화
□ narrative ⓝ 이야기
□ ownership ⓝ 소유권
□ choiceless ⓐ 선택권이 없는
□ dominate ⓥ 지배하다
□ innovation ⓝ 혁신

R 21~22

□ claim ⓝ 주장
□ production ⓝ 생산
□ greenhouse gas 온실가스
□ emission ⓝ 방출, 배출
□ transportation ⓝ 운송,
　수송

□ found ⓥ 근거를 부여하다, 설립하다

□ sector ⓝ 부문

□ wasteful ⓐ 낭비하는

□ climate ⓝ 기후

□ carbon ⓝ 탄소

□ footprint ⓝ 발자국

□ lamb ⓝ ((동물)) 양

□ fossil ⓝ 화석

□ pastureland ⓝ 목초지

□ bulk ⓝ 큰 규모

□ route ⓝ 길, 경로

□ mass ⓐ 대량의

□ agriculture ⓝ 농업

R 23~24

□ species ⓝ 종(種)

□ construct ⓥ 구성하다

□ from scratch 처음부터

□ mind ⓝ 마음

□ primitive ⓐ 원시의

□ means ⓝ 수단

□ gap ⓝ 차이, 틈새

□ connect ⓥ 연결하다

□ interpret ⓥ 해석하다

□ utter ⓥ 말하다

□ origin ⓝ 기원

□ effectively ⓐⓓ 효과적으로

□ place ⓥ 두다

□ evolve ⓥ 진화하다

□ component ⓝ 구성 요소, 성분

□ engage in ~에 관여하다

□ in earnest 본격적으로

□ aspiration ⓝ 열망

□ emotion ⓝ 감정

□ philosophy ⓝ 철학

□ ultimately ⓐⓓ 궁극적으로

□ interaction ⓝ 상호 작용

□ crucial ⓐ 중대한

□ various ⓐ 다양한

□ strategy ⓝ 전략

□ ancestor ⓝ 조상

□ core ⓝ 핵심

□ offend ⓥ 감정을 상하게 하다

□ shape ⓥ 형성하다

□ communicator ⓝ 의사 전달자

R 25~26

□ nature ⓝ 천성

□ give it another shot 다시 시도해 보다

□ shame ⓝ 애석한 일, 수치

□ repetition ⓝ 반복

□ rewire ⓥ 재연결하다, 전선을 다시 배치하다

□ consider ⓥ 생각하다, 고려하다

□ neuron ⓝ 뉴런, 신경 세포

□ technique ⓝ 기술

□ reliable ⓐ 신뢰할 만한

□ hit-and-miss ⓐ 마구잡이의, 되는대로 하는

R 27~28

□ majority ⓝ 대다수, 대부분

□ adapt ⓥ 적응하다

□ cultivate ⓥ 경작하다, (관계를) 쌓다

□ state ⓝ 상태

□ compensate ⓥ 보상하다, 보충되다

□ entire ⓐ 전체의

□ perception ⓝ 인식

□ disrupt ⓥ 방해하다

□ thrilled ⓐ 감격한, 짜릿한

□ overload ⓥ (짐을) 너무 많이 싣다, 과부하가 걸리게 하다

□ stimulus ⓝ 자극(pl. stimuli)

□ overwhelming ⓐ 압도적인

□ recognize ⓥ 알아보다, 인식하다

□ puzzled ⓐ 혼란스러워하는

□ stimulation ⓝ 자극

□ confusion ⓝ 혼란, 혼동

□ assume ⓥ 가정하다

□ function ⓥ 기능하다

□ relay ⓥ 전달하다

□ neuroscientific ⓐ 신경 과학의

□ collaborative ⓐ 협력적인, 공동 작업의

□ alter ⓥ 바꾸다, 고치다

□ accordingly ⓐⓓ 그에 따라

□ anticipate ⓥ 예상하다, 기대하다

R 29~30

□ persist ⓥ 지속하다

□ tend to ~하는 경향이 있다

□ constant ⓐ 지속적인

□ downward ad 아래로

□ resistance ⓝ 저항

□ accordingly ad 그에 따라

□ represent ⓥ 나타내다

□ combination ⓝ 결합

□ elementary ⓐ 기본적인

□ besides prep ~ 외에

□ isolated ⓐ 고립된

□ joint ⓐ 공동의

□ mutual ⓐ 상호의

□ arrangement ⓝ 배치

□ conceal ⓥ 감추다, 숨기다

□ confine ⓥ 제한하다, 국한하다

□ attention ⓝ 관심

□ separately ad 개별적으로

□ significance ⓝ 중요성

□ tendency ⓝ 경향

□ definitely ad 명백히

□ stimulus ⓝ 자극 (pl. stimuli)

□ competitive ⓐ 경쟁적인

□ human nature 인간 본성

R 31~32

□ risk ⓝ 위험

□ disease ⓝ 질환, 질병

□ monitor ⓥ 관찰하다

□ ideal ⓐ 이상적인

□ timeframe ⓝ 시간대

□ author ⓝ 저자

□ cause ⓝ 원인

□ suggest ⓥ 제시하다

□ be likely to-v ~할 가능성이 있다

□ body clock ⓝ 체내 시계(하루 중 특정 시간에 잠을 자야 하는 등의 신체적 자연 현상을 관장하는 몸의 기능)

□ consequence ⓝ 결과

□ midnight ⓝ 자정

□ likelihood ⓝ 가능성

□ reset ⓥ 재설정하다

□ properly ad 적절하게

□ reflect ⓥ 반영하다

□ personality ⓝ 성격

R 33~34

□ firm ⓝ 회사, 기업

□ failure ⓝ 실패

□ harsh ⓐ 가혹한

□ handle ⓥ 다루다

□ sticky ⓐ 끈적거리는

□ envelope ⓝ 봉투

□ management ⓝ 경영진

□ moisten ⓥ 적시다

□ conclusion ⓝ 결론

□ dissatisfied ⓐ 불만족한

R 35~36

□ reject ⓥ 거부하다

□ consumption ⓝ 섭취

□ insect ⓝ 곤충

□ overcome ⓥ 극복하다

□ rejection ⓝ 거부

□ convince ⓥ 납득시키다

□ entire ⓐ 전체의

□ suitable ⓐ 적합한

□ reversal ⓝ 역전

□ luxury ⓝ 고급진 ⓝ 호사

□ servant ⓝ 하인

□ prisoner ⓝ 죄수

□ rural ⓐ 시골의

□ portion ⓝ 일부

□ associate ⓥ 연관 짓다

□ poverty ⓝ 빈곤

□ categorize ⓥ 분류하다

□ uncivilized ⓐ 미개한

□ anthropologist ⓝ 인류학자

□ promote ⓥ 장려하다

□ revalue ⓥ 재평가하다

□ edible ⓐ 먹을 수 있는

□ perspective ⓝ 관점, 시각

□ shortage ⓝ 부족

□ uniqueness ⓝ 독특함

□ disappear ⓥ 사라지다

R 37~38

□ journey ⓝ 여정, 여행

□ shorten ⓥ 줄이다

□ misery ⓝ 비참함

□ impatience ⓝ 조급함

□ judgment ⓝ 비난

□ frustration ⓝ 좌절

□ anger ⓝ 분노

□ shift ⓥ 바꾸다

□ unknowingly ad 무심코

□ cut off 끼어들다

□ splash ⓥ (액체류를) 튀기다

□ pen ⓥ (글을) 쓰다

□ miserable ⓐ 비참한

□ statement ⓝ 진술

R

□ deny ⓥ 부정하다
□ forgive ⓥ 용서하다

R 39~40
□ face ⓥ 직면하다
□ socialize ⓥ (사람을) 사귀다, 어울리다
□ tricky ⓐ 까다로운
□ inanimate ⓐ 무생물의
□ get used to ~에 익숙해지다
□ unpredictable ⓐ 예측할 수 없는
□ self-esteem ⓝ 자존감
□ tidy ⓐ 깔끔한
□ expose ⓥ 노출시키다
□ sense ⓥ 감지하다, 알아차리다
□ progression ⓝ 진행
□ unavoidable ⓐ 피할 수 없는
□ endlessly ⓐⓓ 끊임없이
□ experiment ⓥ 실험하다
□ pointless ⓐ 무의미한
□ principle ⓝ 원칙, 원리

S 복합 문단의 이해

S 01~03
□ Native American 미국 원주민
□ spiritual ⓐ 영적인
□ in the form of ~의 모양으로
□ holy ⓐ 성스러운
□ lesson ⓝ 교훈
□ filter out ~을 걸러내다
□ pass through ~을 통과하다
□ spin ⓥ 짜다 (과거형 spun)
□ reach ⓥ 도달하다
□ cycle ⓝ 순환
□ guide ⓥ 인도하다
□ harm ⓥ 해치다

S 04~06
□ by no means 결코 ~이 아닌
□ barely ⓐⓓ 거의 ~ 없이
□ owe ⓥ 덕분이다
□ disbelief ⓝ 믿지 않음, 불신
□ treasure ⓝ 보물
□ tear down 허물다
□ massive ⓐ 거대한
□ property ⓝ 소유지

S 07~09
□ retired ⓐ 퇴직한
□ notice ⓥ 알아채다
□ step off 내리다
□ tie ⓥ 묶다

□ touched ⓐ 감동한
□ impressed ⓐ 감명받은
□ offer ⓥ 제안하다
□ inspired ⓐ 영감을 받은
□ donate ⓥ 기부하다
□ natural disaster 자연재해
□ frame ⓥ 액자에 넣다
□ shape ⓥ 형성하다
□ nod ⓥ (고개를) 끄덕이다

S 10~12
□ period ⓝ 교시
□ force ⓥ 강요하다
□ understanding ⓝ 이해
□ alike ⓐ 비슷한, 닮은
□ accept ⓥ 받아들이다
□ determined ⓐ 단호한, 결심이 굳은
□ expression ⓝ 표정
□ aimlessly ⓐⓓ 목적 없이, 아무렇게나
□ direction ⓝ 방향
□ wrinkled ⓐ 구겨진
□ nervously ⓐⓓ 초조하게
□ glance ⓥ 힐끗 보다
□ give up 포기하다

S 13~15
□ flight instructor 비행 교관
□ appreciation ⓝ 감상
□ patiently ⓐⓓ 인내심 있게
□ panic ⓥ 당황하다
□ indication ⓝ 표시
□ instrument ⓝ 도구

S 16~18

- philosopher ⓝ 철학자
- merchant ⓝ 상인
- businessman ⓝ 사업가
- attend ⓥ 참석하다
- personally ⓐⓓ 직접
- dip ⓥ 담그다
- stare at ~을 바라보다
- a world of 막대한, 엄청난
- rent ⓥ 대여하다
- embrace ⓥ 껴안다
- compliment ⓥ 칭찬하다
- grand ⓐ 거창한, 웅장한
- approach ⓥ 접근하다
- glance ⓝ 눈길
- greet ⓥ 맞이하다

S 19~21

- surround ⓥ 둘러싸다
- run off 급히 뛰어가다
- completely ⓐⓓ 완전히
- ignore ⓥ 무시하다
- make fun of ~을 놀리다
- lean ⓥ 기대다
- exhaust ⓥ 지치게 하다
- make arrangements for ~의 준비를 하다
- judge ⓥ 판단하다
- pupil ⓝ 제자
- firmly ⓐⓓ 꽉
- exclaim ⓥ 소리치다
- reply ⓥ 대답하다

S 22~24

- a bunch of 다수의, 많은
- notice ⓥ 알아차리다
- chat ⓥ 담소를 나누다
- sudden ⓐ 갑작스러운
- be stuck in ~에 갇히다
- generosity ⓝ 관대함, 너그러움
- empathy ⓝ 공감 (능력)
- unforgettable ⓐ 잊을 수 없는
- mention ⓥ 언급하다, 말하다
- conversation ⓝ 대화
- attentive ⓐ 주의를 기울이는, 세심한
- unexpectedly ⓐⓓ 예상치 못하게, 갑자기

S 25~27

- anxious ⓐ 불안해하는
- suffer ⓥ 고통받다
- severe ⓐ 극심한
- barely ⓐⓓ 간신히, 겨우
- gentle ⓐ 부드러운, 온화한
- tightly ⓐⓓ 꽉, 단단히
- hesitate ⓥ 망설이다
- wrap ⓥ 감싸다
- weak ⓐ (병)약한
- support ⓝ 지지
- comfort ⓝ 위로, 위안
- occasionally ⓐⓓ 가끔
- politely ⓐⓓ 정중하게

S 28~30

- saint ⓝ 성자
- guard ⓝ 경호인
- opportunity ⓝ 기회
- camel ⓝ 낙타
- reply ⓥ 답하다
- in fact 사실
- arise ⓥ 일어나다
- despite ⓟⓡⓔⓟ ~에도 불구하고
- confess ⓥ 고백하다
- surround ⓥ 둘러싸다
- tension ⓝ 긴장
- solution ⓝ 해결책
- request ⓝ 요청

S 31~33

- merchant ⓝ 상인
- prepare ⓥ 준비하다, 대비하다
- pretend ⓥ ~인 척하다
- valuable ⓝ 귀중품
- hurriedly ⓐⓓ 서둘러
- knot ⓝ 매듭
- lung ⓝ 폐
- tear apart 찢어지다
- skillful ⓐ 교묘한
- unpleasant ⓐ 불쾌한
- luxurious ⓐ 호화로운
- replace ⓥ 교체하다

S 34~36

- precious ⓐ 귀중한
- ordinary ⓐ 평범한
- memory ⓝ 기억
- search for ~을 찾다
- exhausted ⓐ 지친

S

□ decrease ⓥ 줄다[감소하다]

□ give up ~을 포기하다

□ call off ~을 멈추다, 중지하다

□ chance ⓝ 기회, 가능성

□ succeed ⓥ 성공하다

□ fail ⓥ 실패하다

□ reply ⓥ 대답하다

□ silence ⓝ 침묵

□ direction ⓝ 방향

□ delighted ⓐ 기쁜

□ reward ⓥ 보상하다 ⓝ 보상

□ promise ⓥ 약속하다

□ attractive ⓐ 매력적인

□ entire ⓐ 전체의

□ pile ⓝ 더미

□ hay ⓝ 건초

S 37~39

□ grand ⓐ 웅장한, 큰

□ temple ⓝ 사원, 절

□ worship ⓥ 예배하다

□ arrangement ⓝ 준비

□ accommodation ⓝ 숙소, 거처

□ look after ~을 관리하다[돌보다]

□ offer ⓝ 제안

□ qualified ⓐ 자격이 있는

□ bury ⓥ 묻다

□ brick ⓝ 벽돌

□ path ⓝ 길, 경로

□ trip over ~에 발이 걸려 넘어지다

□ remove ⓥ 제거하다

□ dig up ~을 파내다

□ duty ⓝ 의무

S 40~42

□ approach ⓥ 접근하다

□ smelly ⓐ 냄새가 나는

□ guard ⓝ 경비병

□ shock ⓝ 충격

□ demand ⓥ 요구하다

□ wise ⓐ 현명한

□ offer ⓥ 제안하다

□ immediately ⓐⓓ 즉시

□ call for ~을 시키다

□ gesture ⓝ 행동

□ tiny ⓐ 매우 작은

□ kindness ⓝ 친절(한 행위)

□ sword ⓝ 칼

□ eventually ⓐⓓ 결국, 마침내

□ take up ~을 차지하다

S 43~45

□ village ⓝ 마을

□ field ⓝ 들판

□ reply ⓥ 대답하다

□ middle-aged 중년의

□ come upon ~을 만나다

□ valley ⓝ 골짜기

□ wonderful ⓐ 멋진

□ unwelcoming ⓐ 불친절한

□ helplessly ⓐⓓ 힘없이

□ generous ⓐ 너그러운

S 46~48

□ ordinary ⓐ 평범한

□ furry ⓐ 털이 많은

□ frosty ⓐ 서리가 내리는

□ cheerful ⓐ 명랑한

□ contented ⓐ 만족하는

□ distinctive ⓐ 특이한

□ greedily ⓐⓓ 탐욕스럽게

□ swallow ⓥ 삼키다

□ dusk ⓝ 해질 무렵[황혼]

□ bamboo ⓝ 대나무

□ tempt ⓥ 유혹하다

□ blossom ⓝ 꽃

□ seek ⓥ 찾다, 추구하다

□ distant ⓐ 먼

□ reveal ⓥ 밝히다

□ unintended ⓐ 의도치 않은

□ encounter ⓝ 접촉, 만남

□ remarkably ⓐⓓ 매우, 정말

□ chat ⓥ 수다를 떨다

□ enthusiastically ⓐⓓ 신나게, 열정적으로

□ exclaim ⓥ 외치다

□ glance ⓥ 흘긋 보다

□ imitate ⓥ 모방하다

□ genuine ⓐ 진정한

S 49~51

□ bunch ⓝ 다발, 송이

□ place ⓥ 놓다, 두다

□ beam ⓥ 빛나다, 활짝 웃다

□ distaste ⓝ 불쾌감

□ cheerfully ⓐⓓ 쾌활하게, 명랑하게

□ thoughtfulness ⓝ 사려 깊음

□ politely ⓐⓓ 정중하게

□ expectantly ⓐⓓ 기대에 부풀어

□ pleased ⓐ 기쁜

□ sour ⓐ (맛이) 신

1회 모의고사

01
- ecosystem ⓝ 생태계
- maximization ⓝ 극대화
- intervene ⓥ 개입하다
- dynamics ⓝ 역학 관계
- spray ⓥ 뿌리다
- fence ⓥ 울타리를 치다
- patch ⓝ 좁은 땅
- inherently ⓐⓓ 본질적으로
- unstable ⓐ 불안정한
- effectively ⓐⓓ 사실상
- slope ⓝ 경사면
- yield ⓝ 수확량, 생산량
- crowd out ~을 밀어내다
- intervention ⓝ 개입
- alter ⓥ 바꾸다
- stability ⓝ 안정성
- diversity ⓝ 다양성
- boost ⓥ 촉진하다
- harmonious ⓐ 조화로운

02
- tier ⓝ 단계, 층위
- give rise to ~을 유발하다
- sensation ⓝ 감정
- differentiate ⓥ 구별하다
- familiarity ⓝ 친숙함
- recall ⓝ 회상
- clarify ⓥ 명확하게 하다
- encounter ⓥ 마주치다
- flag up ~을 표시하다
- partial ⓐ 부분적인
- retrieval ⓝ 회복, 복구
- danger ⓝ 위험성
- memory loss 기억 상실
- distinction ⓝ 구분

03
- sitcom ⓝ 시트콤
- chart ⓥ 기록하다, 보여주다
- conflict ⓝ 갈등
- multiculturalism ⓝ 다문화주의
- conception ⓝ 개념
- progressive ⓐ 진보적인
- ridiculous ⓐ 어리석은
- stupidity ⓝ 어리석음
- scolding ⓝ 비난, 꾸짖음
- tolerant ⓐ 관용적인
- acceptability ⓝ 수용 가능성

04
- prominence ⓝ 부각, 눈에 띔
- dimension ⓝ 측면, 차원
- back seat 뒷좌석, 뒷전
- secondary ⓐ 부수적인
- belly ⓝ 배
- dynamics ⓝ 역학
- characterize ⓥ 특징을 짓다
- independently of ~와는 독립적으로, 별개로
- appreciation ⓝ 감상, 소감
- ritual ⓝ 의식

- sensation ⓝ 감각
- excessively ⓐⓓ 지나치게
- significance ⓝ 중요성

05
- critical ⓐ 비판적인
- objectivity ⓝ 객관성
- biased ⓐ 편향된, 편파적인
- dietary ⓐ 식용의, 식단의
- fund ⓥ 자금을 지원하다
- obesity ⓝ 비만
- diabetes ⓝ 당뇨병
- fuel ⓥ 부채질하다, 연료를 넣다
- suspicion ⓝ 의심
- safeguard ⓝ 안전장치
- disclosure ⓝ 공개
- compulsory ⓐ 의무의

06
- explosion ⓝ 폭발적인 증가
- circulation ⓝ 유통, 순환
- propel ⓥ 촉진하다
- second-hand 중고의
- inclusive ⓐ 포용적인
- rebellion ⓝ 저항
- punk ⓝ ((음악의 장르)) 펑크
- condition ⓝ 조건, 필수 요건
- novelty ⓝ 참신성
- empowerment ⓝ 자율성
- sphere ⓝ 계, 영역
- accessibility ⓝ 접근성
- responsibility ⓝ 책임감
- preservation ⓝ 보존
- profitability ⓝ 수익성

07

□ one-hit wonder 반짝 스타
□ prime ⓐ 주요한, 대표적인
□ mechanics ⓝ 역학
□ gravitation ⓝ 중력
□ calculus ⓝ 미적분학
□ optimization ⓝ 최적화
□ legitimacy ⓝ 정당성
□ quality ⓐ 고급의, 우수한
□ collaborator ⓝ 협력자
□ payoff ⓝ 보상
□ odds ⓝ 가능성
□ appealing ⓐ 매력적인
□ alternative ⓐ 대안의
□ endeavor ⓝ 노력
□ exceptionally ⓐⓓ 유난히, 이례적으로
□ probability ⓝ 확률
□ dictate ⓥ 좌우하다, 결정하다
□ inseparable ⓐ 분리될 수 없는
□ indicative ⓐ 나타내는

08

□ virtually ⓐⓓ 사실상
□ security ⓝ 안보
□ self-sufficiency 자급자족
□ agricultural ⓐ 농사의
□ sensitive ⓐ 민감한
□ climatic ⓐ 기후의
□ soil ⓝ 토양
□ vary ⓥ 다양하다, 달라지다
□ issue ⓝ 문제, 이슈
□ insure ⓥ 보장하다

□ adequate ⓐ 적절한
□ resident ⓐ 거주하는
□ domestic ⓐ 국내의
□ productive ⓐ 생산적인
□ sector ⓝ 구역, 지역
□ import ⓝ 수입
□ supply ⓝ 공급
□ tropical ⓐ 열대의
□ assure ⓥ 보장하다

09

□ demonstrate ⓥ 입증하다
□ usefulness ⓝ 유용성
□ rule-based 규칙에 기반한
□ procedure ⓝ 절차, 과정
□ cook up 만들어내다
□ mystically ⓐⓓ 신비롭게
□ computation ⓝ 계산
□ hypothesis ⓝ 가설
□ experimental ⓐ 실험의
□ eliminate ⓥ 제거하다
□ modify ⓥ 수정하다
□ account for ~을 설명하다
□ statistician ⓝ 통계학자
□ whereby ⓐⓓ (그것에 의하여) ~하는
□ predictive ⓐ 예측의
□ repetitive ⓐ 반복적인
□ variant ⓝ 변형

10

□ construction ⓝ 구조
□ favored ⓐ 혜택을 받고 있는
□ progress ⓥ 진전되다

□ loan ⓝ 차용, 빌림
□ indigenous ⓐ 토착의
□ fate ⓝ 운명
□ extinction ⓝ 멸종
□ suppress ⓥ 억압하다
□ vanish ⓥ 사라지다
□ imbalance ⓝ 불균형
□ prevail ⓥ 널리 퍼지다
□ integration ⓝ 통합
□ prosper ⓥ 번영하다

11~12

□ alternative ⓝ 대안
□ manufacturer ⓝ 제조업자
□ electricity ⓝ 전기
□ electric ⓐ 전기의
□ affordable ⓐ 저렴한
□ intensive ⓐ 집중적인
□ speed ⓥ 촉진시키다
□ accelerate ⓥ 가속화하다
□ shift ⓝ 변화
□ rapid ⓐ 빠른
□ expertise ⓝ 전문 지식
□ exotic ⓐ 이국적인, 생소한
□ commonplace ⓐ 일상의
□ halt ⓝ 중단
□ bankruptcy ⓝ 파산
□ plant ⓝ 공장
□ surpass ⓥ 능가하다, 초과하다

2회 모의고사

01
- brick ⓝ 벽돌
- accelerator ⓝ 가속 페달
- barrier ⓝ 장애물
- be worth -ing ~할 가치가 있다
- pursue ⓥ 추구하다
- possess ⓥ 소유하다
- operate ⓥ 작동하다
- refined ⓐ 정제된
- pose a challenge 어려움을 주다

02
- specify ⓥ 명시하다
- stress ⓥ 강조하다
- emphasize ⓥ 강조하다
- perspective ⓝ 관점
- negotiate ⓥ 협상하다
- affective ⓐ 정서적인
- empathic ⓐ 공감의
- consultant ⓝ 자문 위원
- foster ⓥ 기르다, 양육하다
- market research 시장 조사
- fulfill ⓥ 충족시키다
- color-blind 색맹의
- interpretation ⓝ 해석

03
- prevalent ⓐ 만연한, 일반적인
- obligation ⓝ 의무감
- pressure ⓝ 압박
- instantly ⓐⓓ 즉각적으로
- ins and outs 세부 사항들
- blow up ~을 폭파시키다
- inducing ⓐ 유발하는
- aggressive ⓐ 공격적인
- within reach 손이 닿는 곳에

04
- psychologist ⓝ 심리학자
- address ⓥ 해결하다
- personality ⓝ 성격
- workaholism ⓝ 일중독
- shopaholism ⓝ 쇼핑 중독
- and the like 기타 등등
- fall into ~에 속하다
- suggestion ⓝ 암시
- modification ⓝ 수정, 변경
- tactic ⓝ 전략
- reinforce ⓥ 강화하다

05
- socialization ⓝ 사회화
- foundational ⓐ 기초적인
- regulation ⓝ 조절
- extra-familial 가족 이외의
- agent ⓝ 주체
- comparable ⓐ 비슷한, 상응하는
- soothing ⓝ 위로, 위안
- directive ⓐ 지시적인
- cultivate ⓥ 기르다, 장려하다
- adolescent ⓝ 청소년
- autonomy ⓝ 자율성
- striving ⓝ 추구
- crisis ⓝ 위기
- autonomous ⓐ 자율적인
- nonjudgmental ⓐ 무비판적인
- acceptance ⓝ 수용

06
- capability ⓝ 능력
- misguided ⓐ 잘못 이해한
- repetitive ⓐ 반복적인
- vertical ⓐ 수직의
- rotation ⓝ 회전
- axis ⓝ 축
- minimize ⓥ 최소화하다
- constraint ⓝ 제약
- hostility ⓝ 적대감
- morality ⓝ 도덕성

07
- consumption ⓝ 소비
- imply ⓥ 암시하다
- supposedly ⓐⓓ 소위
- considerable ⓐ 상당한
- composition ⓝ 구성
- Danish ⓐ 덴마크의
- theatrical ⓐ 극장의
- comprise ⓥ ~으로 구성되다
- correspond with ~와 부합하다

□ embrace ⓝ 수용, 포용
□ seemingly ⓐⓓ 겉보기에는
□ prejudice ⓝ 편견
□ realm ⓝ 영역
□ legitimate ⓐ 정통의
□ artistic ⓐ 예술적인
□ inexperienced ⓐ 경험이 부족한

08

□ structural ⓐ 구조적인
□ richness ⓝ 풍부함
□ random ⓐ 무작위의
□ nonrandom ⓐ 비무작위의
□ stimulate ⓥ 자극하다, 활성화하다
□ eliminate ⓥ 제거하다
□ sculpt ⓥ 조각하다
□ variability ⓝ 변이성
□ undergo ⓥ 거치다, 겪다
□ immune ⓐ 면역의
□ extension ⓝ 확장
□ genetically ⓐⓓ 유전적으로
□ positionally ⓐⓓ 위치적으로
□ phase ⓝ 단계
□ cellular ⓐ 세포의
□ built-in 확립된
□ criterion ⓝ 기준 (pl. criteria)

09

□ fate ⓝ 운명
□ population ⓝ 개체 수
□ vagrant ⓐ 부랑하는, 헤매는

□ reorientate ⓥ 방향을 다시 잡다
□ range ⓝ 범위
□ phenomenon ⓝ 현상
□ undoubtedly ⓐⓓ 의심의 여지 없이
□ perish ⓥ 죽다, 멸망하다
□ infrequent ⓐ 드문
□ unfold ⓥ 펼쳐지다
□ profound ⓐ 중대한, 심오한
□ breeding ⓝ 번식
□ migration ⓝ 이동
□ wintering ⓝ 월동, 겨울나기

10

□ fast-growing 빨리 성장하는
□ tremendous ⓐ 엄청난
□ numerous ⓐ 수많은
□ exceed ⓥ 능가하다
□ tomb ⓝ 무덤
□ archive ⓝ 보관소
□ extract ⓥ 추출하다
□ manually ⓐⓓ 수동으로
□ input ⓥ 입력하다
□ costly ⓐ 비용이 드는
□ time consuming 시간 소모가 큰
□ call for ~을 요구하다

11~12

□ shift ⓥ 전환하다, 이동하다
□ wire ⓥ 회로를 연결하다, 발달시키다
□ sequentially ⓐⓓ 순차적으로

□ multitasking ⓝ 멀티태스킹 (동시에 여러 가지 일을 하는 것)
□ fraction ⓝ 일부
□ turn out 드러나다
□ simultaneously ⓐⓓ 동시에
□ insurance ⓝ 보험
□ redesign ⓥ 재설계하다
□ attention span 주의집중 시간
□ automaticity ⓝ 자동성

3회 모의고사

01
□ expression ⓝ 표현
□ obstacle ⓝ 장애물
□ all-or-nothing 양단의
□ mentality ⓝ 사고방식
□ alter ⓥ 변경하다
□ outcome ⓝ 결과
□ emerge ⓥ 나타나다
□ conceive ⓥ 고안하다
□ bill ⓝ 법안
□ vastly ⓐⓓ 훨씬
□ cost-saving 비용 절감
□ donation ⓝ 기부(금)

02
□ consequence ⓝ 결과, 영향
□ shed ⓥ (빛을) 비추다
□ intake ⓝ 섭취
□ cognitively ⓐⓓ 인지적으로
□ isolate ⓥ 분리하다
□ component ⓝ 요소, 부품
□ inverse ⓐ 역의, 반대의
□ cortex ⓝ (대뇌의) 피질
□ excessive ⓐ 지나친, 과도한
□ consumption ⓝ 섭취
□ metabolic ⓐ 신진대사의
□ universal ⓐ 보편적인
□ enhance ⓥ 향상시키다
□ nutritional ⓐ 영양학적인

03
□ awareness ⓝ 인식
□ mess up ~을 망치다
□ discover ⓥ 발견하다
□ weakness ⓝ 약점
□ expense ⓝ 희생
□ permanently ⓐⓓ 영원히
□ disappointment ⓝ 실망
□ criticism ⓝ 비판
□ mislead ⓥ 잘못 인도하다
□ mindset ⓝ 사고방식
□ trap ⓝ 덫, 함정

04
□ certainty ⓝ 확실성
□ alongside ⓟⓡⓔⓟ 옆에, 곁에서
□ poisonous ⓐ 독이 있는
□ threat ⓝ 위협
□ afterward ⓐⓓ 그 후에
□ label ⓥ 꼬리표를 붙이다
□ vague ⓐ 모호한
□ unpredictable ⓐ 예측할 수 없는
□ sensation ⓝ 느낌, 감각

05
□ consistency ⓝ 일관성
□ virtue ⓝ 장점
□ detect ⓥ 감지하다
□ combine ⓥ 결합하다
□ statistical ⓐ 통계의
□ forecast ⓥ 예측하다
□ demand ⓝ 수요

06
□ average ⓥ 평균을 내다
□ competitor ⓝ 경쟁자
□ introduction ⓝ 도입
□ incorporate ⓥ 통합하다
□ accurate ⓐ 정확한

06
□ assert ⓥ 발휘하다
□ obedient ⓐ 복종적인
□ subordinate ⓝ 부하, 하급자
□ deliberately ⓐⓓ 의도적으로
□ dose ⓥ 주다, 투여하다
□ moderate ⓐ 적절한
□ negotiate ⓥ 협상하다
□ conflict ⓝ 갈등
□ verbal ⓐ 언어의
□ complicated ⓐ 복잡한
□ selective ⓐ 선택력이 있는

07
□ investor ⓝ 투자자
□ entirely ⓐⓓ 전적으로
□ boost ⓥ 끌어올리다
□ exchange ⓥ 교환하다
□ expense ⓝ 비용
□ accountant ⓝ 회계사
□ recognition ⓝ 인식
□ simplify ⓥ 간소화하다
□ additional ⓐ 부가적인
□ intensify ⓥ 강화하다
□ trigger ⓥ 유발하다

모의고사 **3회**

08

- continuum ⓝ 연속체
- misguide ⓥ 잘못 이끌다
- imply ⓥ 암시하다
- input ⓥ 가하다
- get rid of ~을 제거하다
- unwanted ⓐ 원치 않는
- addiction ⓝ 중독
- villain ⓝ 악당
- aggressively ⓐⓓ 격렬하게, 공격적으로
- defeat ⓥ 패배시키다

09

- connect ⓥ 연결하다
- chunk ⓝ 덩어리
- intensity ⓝ 강도, 세기
- ordinary ⓐ 보통의
- discharge ⓥ 해방시키다
- contract ⓥ 줄어들다, 수축하다
- vary ⓥ 변화를 주다
- range ⓝ 범위
- interference ⓝ 간섭

10

- distinguish ⓥ 구별하다, 식별하다
- direction ⓝ 방향
- determine ⓥ 알아내다
- occur ⓥ 발생하다
- dimension ⓝ 차원, 관점
- influence ⓝ 영향

- evolution ⓝ 진화
- vertical ⓐ 수직의
- gravity ⓝ 중력
- mobile ⓐ 이동하는
- positioning ⓝ 배치
- perception ⓝ 지각, 자각
- horizontal ⓐ 수평의
- relevant ⓐ 의미가 있는, 중요한
- upside down 거꾸로
- observe ⓥ 관찰하다
- contain ⓥ 포함하다
- invert ⓥ 바꾸다
- artificial ⓐ 인공적인
- perceive ⓥ 인식하다
- instantly ⓐⓓ 즉각, 즉시
- spatial ⓐ 공간의
- scarce ⓐ 희소한
- auditory ⓐ 청각의
- accessible ⓐ 접근 가능한
- desirable ⓐ 바람직한

11~12

- maturity ⓝ 성숙도, 성숙함
- sensitivity ⓝ 예민함, 민감성
- personality ⓝ 개성, 특성
- empathy ⓝ 공감
- adaptability ⓝ 적응성, 융통성
- interpret ⓥ 해석하다
- adapt ⓥ 맞추다
- accordingly ⓐⓓ 부응해서, 그에 맞춰

- deserve ⓥ ~을 받을 만하다
- bear in mind ~을 명심하다
- receptive ⓐ 수용적인
- bundle ⓥ 묶다
- trait ⓝ 특성
- circumstance ⓝ 상황, 환경
- mindset ⓝ 사고방식
- connection ⓝ 관련성, 연관성
- compassion ⓝ 동감
- individualize ⓥ 개별화하다
- consistent ⓐ 일관된
- guarantee ⓥ 보장하다
- flexible ⓐ 유연한
- appealing ⓐ 매력적인
- recognition ⓝ 인식
- suffer ⓥ 어려움을 겪다

수경출판사 교재를 풀면서 궁금한 점이 생기셨나요?

 NAVER [수경출판사 ▼] 🔍 www.book-sk.kr

★ 수경출판사 홈페이지에서 다음 서비스를 이용하실 수 있습니다.

• 공부할 때 꼭 필요한 [학습자료실]

해설지, 빠른 정답, 정오표, 듣기 MP3, 교재관련
자료와 같은 공부할 때 꼭 필요한 파일을 다운로드
받을 수 있습니다.

• 궁금하거나 이상한 것이 있으면 [회원 마당]

1:1문의, 오류신고, 도서제안 코너를 통하여 궁금한 부분을
언제든지 상담할 수 있고, 공부해 보거나 강의하고 싶은
교재의 기획을 제안할 수 있습니다.

• 선생님을 위한 강의 지원 서비스 [선생님방]

선생님 자료실 코너를 통하여 강의 파일을 다운로드 받을 수
있고, 수학문제은행 코너를 통하여 시험지를 만들 수 있고,
교사용 교재신청 코너를 통하여 원하는 교사용 교재를 받아
볼 수 있습니다.

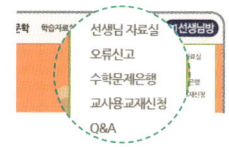

★수경출판사 공식 채널을 소개합니다! www.book-sk.kr

▶ [채널명: 자이스토리] 국어, 영어, 수학, 사회탐구, 과학탐구 과목의 문제별 온라인
   판서 강의를 시청할 수 있습니다.

🄾 [ID: xistory_insta] 각종 학습 관련 소식과 여러 이벤트를 접할 수 있습니다.

🄵 [검색: 자이스토리] 각종 학습 관련 소식과 여러 이벤트를 접할 수 있습니다.

🄱log [http://blog.naver.com/sookyungsto] 각종 학습 관련 소식과 여러 이벤트를
   접할 수 있습니다.

TALK [채널명: 수경출판사(자이스토리)] 궁금한 부분을 언제든지 실시간 상담
   (1:1 상담)할 수 있습니다.

DREAMS COME TRUE

물이 강줄기를 따라 흐르는 것은
그것이 물의 흐름을 가장 쉽게 하는 자연의 순리이기 때문입니다.
최소 저항의 길이라는 이 길을
우리는 세상을 살아가면서 끊임없이 부딪히고, 또 이쪽저쪽 재며 갈등합니다.
순리대로 힘들이지 않고 가면 되는 길인 것 같지만 꼭 그렇지만은 않은가 봅니다.
모두가 으레 밟고 지나가는 이 길이 때로는 버거운 짐이라 느껴져
어떻게든 거슬러 보려고 하지만 바로 이 길만이 최소 저항의 길인 것입니다.

가장 자유로워야 할, 그리고 무한한 가능성을 알맞게 빚어나가야 할 나이에
여러 가지 족쇄에 얽매여 날개를 움츠러뜨린
이 땅의 수많은 수험생들 여러분,
내 앞에 놓인 이 길을 어차피 지나가야 하는 거라면
저 멀고 높은 곳을 목표로 삼아 한 번 멋지게 이뤄보는 것은 어떤가요?
현재가 불안한 사람일수록 앞날을 알고 싶어합니다.
그러나 미래를 아는 사람은 이 세상에 단 한 사람도 없습니다.
그런데 100%는 아니지만 조금이나마
미래를 알 수 있는 방법이 하나 있습니다.

그것은 자신의 현재를 살펴보는 것입니다.
현재에 충실한 것이 곧 내가 꿈꾸는 미래를 만들어 가는 것입니다.
내일을 염려하지 말고 오늘에 충실하면 됩니다.
스스로를 신뢰하고 긍정적인 사고로 전환하면 꿈꾸던 미래가 현실이 됩니다.
더 나은 내일을 위해 고전 분투하는 수험생들을 위해
오늘날의 교육 환경 모두를 개선하는 것은 역부족이지만,
뜻을 모으고, 머리를 맞대고, 마음의 정성을 쏟아
오로지 공부만을 위한 공부가 아닌 편안한 마음으로 볼 수 있는 교재,
노력한 만큼 뿌듯한 결과를 안겨줄 수 있는 교재를
만들어 드리기 위해 꾸준히 노력하겠습니다.

이 땅의 수험생 여러분께 진심으로 경의를 표합니다!!

수경출판사 올림